A
B
C
D
E
F
G
H
I
J
K
L
M
N
O
P
Q
R
S
T
U
V
W
X
Y
Z

The University of Chicago Spanish Dictionary

Diccionario de la Universidad de Chicago Inglés-Español y Español-Inglés

Cuarta Edición

Un Diccionario Manual Nuevo y Conciso que
Contiene las Voces y Locuciones Básicas de
Ambos Idiomas y Además una Lista de 500
Modismos y Refranes Españoles con Variantes
y Traducción al Inglés

Recopilación de
Carlos Castillo y Otto F. Bond

Con la ayuda de
Barbara M. García

Revisada y Ampliada por
D. Lincoln Canfield

The University of Chicago Press
Chicago & London

The University of Chicago Spanish Dictionary

Fourth Edition

A New Concise Spanish-English and English-Spanish
Dictionary of Words and Phrases Basic to the Written
and Spoken Languages of Today, plus a List
of 500 Spanish Idioms and Sayings, with Variants
and English Equivalents

Compiled by
Carlos Castillo & Otto F. Bond

With the Assistance of
Barbara M. García

Revised and Enlarged by
D. Lincoln Canfield

The University of Chicago Press
Chicago & London

The University of Chicago Press, Chicago 60637
The University of Chicago Press, Ltd., London

03 02 01 00 99 98 97 96 95   11 12 13 14

Library of Congress Cataloging-in-Publication Data

The University of Chicago Spanish dictionary.

    Added t.p. in Spanish: Diccinario de la Universidad de Chicago, inglés-español
y español-inglés.
    1. Spanish language—Dictionaries—English.
    2. English language—Dictionaries—Spanish.
I. Castillo, Carlos, 1890–   . II. Bond,
Otto Ferdinand, 1885–   . III. García, Barbara M.
IV. Canfield, D. Lincoln (Delos Lincoln), 1903–

V. University of Chicago. IV. Title: Diccionario
inglés-español y español-inglés.
PC4640.US   1987   463′.21   86-24886
ISBN 0-226-10400-1
ISBN 0-226-10402-8 (pbk.)

Contents

Foreword to the Fourth Edition

The University of Chicago Spanish Dictionary has been compiled for the general use of the American learner of Spanish and the Spanish-speaking learner of English, with special reference to New World usages as found in the United States and Spanish America.

With this purpose in mind, the editors and the author of the revisions of this new fourth edition have gone far beyond the frequency-based vocabulary of the revised second edition of 1972, with its numerous new entries from such realms as aviation, energy, rocketry, and linguistics, and the augmented third edition of 1977, with its thorough syllabication and phonetic transcriptions and its highly useful section of idiomatic expressions, including many dialectal variants, of the Spanish-speaking world.

This edition incorporates hundreds of current terms from the basic vocabularies of the office worker, the welder, the machinist, the builder, and the automotive mechanic, as well as important entries relating to food preparation and serving, the environment, computer science, and telecommunications.

Indications of regional occurrence, used to show that a term is characteristic of the Spanish of Mexico or Chile, for instance, or that it is common to all of Central America, Colombia, and Venezuela, have been considerably refined.

One of the distinctive features of this dictionary, among the bilingual lexicons, has always been the parenthetical synonym that helps to distinguish meanings or shades of meaning. More than a thousand of these helpful expressions have been added in this fourth edition.

A short history of the Spanish language has been added in the form of descriptions of typical developments in the Vulgar Latin that eventually became Castilian or Spanish.

The much-used section on the Spanish of America in the introductory material for the first half of the dictionary has a short counterpart in the English-Spanish half in the form of a map with brief commentary on the dialectal manifestations of English in the United States.

Part One Spanish-English

List of Abbreviations

adj.	adjective	*math.*	mathematics
adv.	adverb	*neut.*	neuter
arith.	arithmetic	*num.*	numeral
conj.	conjunction	*p.p.*	past participle
contr.	contraction	*pers.*	personal
def.	definite	*pers. pron.*	personal pronoun
def. art.	definite article	*pl.*	plural
dem.	demonstrative	*poss.*	possessive
dem. adj.	demonstrative adjective	*prep.*	preposition
dem. pron.	demonstrative pronoun	*pron.*	pronoun
etc.	et cetera	*refl.*	reflexive
f.	feminine noun	*refl. pron.*	reflexive pronoun
fam.	familiar	*rel.*	relative
indef.	indefinite	*rel. adv.*	relative adverb
indef. art.	indefinite article	*rel. pron.*	relative pronoun
inf.	infinite	*sing.*	singular
interj.	interjection	*subj.*	subjunctive
interr.	interrogative	*v.*	verb
irr.	irregular	*v. irr.*	irregular verb
m.	masculine noun		

Special Words and Abbreviations Used to Indicate Regional Occurrence

Am.[1]	Spanish-American
Andalusia	
Andes	(Ecuador, Peru, Bolivia)
Arg.	Argentina
Bol.	Bolivia
Carib.	(Cuba, Puerto Rico, Dominican Republic)
C.A.	Central America (Guatemala, El Salvador, Honduras, Nicaragua, Costa Rica)
Ch.	Chile
Col.	Colombia
C.R.	Costa Rica
Cuba	
Ec.	Ecuador
Guat.	Guatemala
Hond.	Honduras
Mex.	Mexico
Nic.	Nicaragua
N.Sp.	Northern Spain
Pan.	Panama
Par.	Paraguay
Peru	
P.R.	Puerto Rico
Riopl.	Rio de la Plata region (Eastern Argentina, Uruguay)
S.A.	South America
Sal.	El Salvador
Spain	
Ur.	Uruguay
Ven.	Venezuela

Spanish Pronunciation

The Spanish of central and northern Spain has 24 phonemes, or minimum units of sound-meaning distinction. The Spanish of southwest Spain and most of Spanish America has 22 phonemes. These minimum units of sound are indicated in the

---

[1]This abbreviation is employed to indicate general Spanish-American usage, usually with the implication of obsolescence in Spain. It is also used to identify words that are currently little used but which may occur in literary works of bygone days.

Phonetic Manifestations of the Consonant Phonemes of Spanish

	Bilabial		Labiodental		Interdental		Dental		Alveolar		Palatal		Velar		Glottal	
Voice	vs	vd	vs	vd	vs	vd	vs	vd	vs	vd	vs	vd	vs	vd	vs	vd
Occlusive	p	b											k	g		
Fricative	ø	ƀ	f		θ	đ						y	x	ǥ	h	
Sibilant							s	z	S	Z	Š	Ž				
Affricate											č	ŷ				
Nasal										n		ñ		ŋ		
Lateral										l		ļ				
Vibrant										r rr						
Semiconsonant		w										j				

following charts and descriptions by slashes, /b/, /e/, /č/, and stand for an abstract representation of a group or class of sounds, the individual members of which are variants or allophones. The latter are indicated by brackets: [b̦], [e], [ȳ]. Some of the phonemes of Spanish have two or three variants, depending on position within the phrase.

The two principal characteristics of Spanish pronunciation as contrasted with English are tenseness of articulation and continuity in transition from word to word within the breath group. Thus all the vowels have a clear nondiphthongal character and sound "clipped" to the English-speaking person. The consonants, especially /p/, /t/, /k/, /l/, /r/, /rr/, have much less vocalic interference than in English, and the first three have no aspiration. The glottal stop, so common in the Germanic languages, including English, is very rare in Spanish. The transition between vowels of contiguous words is smooth. **El hado, helado, el lado** sound very much alike. **Para hacerlo** is [paraasérlo] or in rapid speech [parasérlo]. So marked is the continuity that following sounds influence the preceding ones: **los dos niños** [lozdozníños]; **un peso** [umpéso] **en que** [éŋke].

The Consonantal Phonemes of the Spanish of Northern Spain

$$/p/ \quad /b/ \quad /t/ \quad /d/ \quad /k/ \quad /g/$$
$$/f/ \quad /\theta/ \quad /S/ \quad /y/ \quad /x/$$
$$/\check{c}/$$
$$/m/ \qquad\qquad /n/ \quad /\tilde{n}/ \qquad\qquad 24$$
$$/l/ \quad /\underset{\smile}{l}/$$
$$/r/ \quad /rr/$$

The Vocalic Phonemes of Spanish

$$i \qquad\qquad\qquad u$$
$$e \qquad\qquad o$$
$$a$$

The Consonantal Phonemes of Andalusian and Latin American Spanish

$$/p/ \quad /b/ \quad /t/ \quad /d/ \quad /k/ \quad /g/$$
$$/f/ \qquad /s/ \quad /y/ \quad /x/$$
$$/\check{c}/$$
$$/m/ \qquad\qquad /n/ \quad /\tilde{n}/ \qquad\qquad 22 \text{ or } 23$$
$$/l/ \quad (/\underset{\smile}{l}/) \text{ [Bolivia, Paraguay, Peru]}$$
$$/r/ \quad /rr/$$

The Spanish Spelling System and the Sounds Represented

I. The Vowels

1. **i** as a single vowel always represents [i], similar to the second vowel of *police*. Examples: **hilo, camino, piso.** As a part of a diphthong, it represents [j], much like English **/y/** in *yes, year*. Examples: **bien** [bjen], **diablo** [djab̦lo], **ciudad, baile, reina, boina.** The first syllable of **baile** is much like *by* in English.

2. **e** represents [e], which has no exact equivalent in most English dialects. It is higher than the /e/ of *get* but without the diphthong of *they*. It is much more tense in articulation than either English sound. It varies slightly according to adjacent sounds. The vowel of **perro** is more open than that of **pero**. Generally it is more open in a closed syllable. Examples: **mesa, del, hablé, en, tres.**

3. **a** represents [a], which is similar to the first vowel of *mama,* stressed on the first syllable. Examples: **caso, cano, ¡ah!, América.** Even when not stressed, it has the same clear sound. English *America* has at least two neutral or *schwa* sounds [ə].

4. **o** represents [o], which is more like the first syllable of the American slang expression *gonna* ("going to") than the British or American *old.* It has no off-glide or diphthongal character such as is heard in the latter. It varies slightly according to adjacent sounds: the first syllable of **corro** is slightly more open than the first of **coro. Sol** is slightly more open than **no.** Examples: **boto, modo, señor, oso, amó.**

5. **u** represents [u], which always has the value of the sound indicated by English *oo* in *boot, fool,* never that of *book,* nor that of the *u* in *union.* Examples: **cura, agudo, uno.**

   a. Note that the spelling combinations **qui, que, gui, gue** represent [ki], [ke], [gi], [ge].

   b. **u** is used to represent the semiconsonant [w] in a diphthong: **cuida, cuento, cuadro, cuota** [kwída], [kwénto], [kwáđro], [kwóta].

   c. Likewise **u** is used to represent the semivocalic element of a diphthong: **bou, deuda, causa** [bow], [déwđa], [káwsa].

II. The Consonants

1. **p** represents [p], which never has the aspiration of English /p/ *(pill, papa),* but is like that of *spot.* Examples: **padre, capa, apuro, punto.**

2. **b** and **v** represent /b/, which has two variants, according to position in the phrase: [b], [ƀ]. These do not depend on spelling, which goes back centuries to the Latin. Either letter represents [b] at the beginning of a breath group or when preceded by [m] (spelled either **m** or **n**), and is much like English /b/. Examples: **bomba, burro, en vez de, vine, invierno.** In spite of spelling, the last three examples are [embézđe], [bíne], [imbjérno]. Either letter represents [ƀ] in all other situations. English has no equivalent. It is a /b/ with the lips slightly open. Examples: **haba, uva, Cuba, la vaca, habla, la barba.**

3. **m** represents [m], which is essentially the same as English /m/ *(much).* Examples: **madre, mano, cama.** [m] does not occur syllable final in Spanish. **Álbum** is pronounced [álƀun].

4. **f** represents [f], which is similar to the /f/ of English. In some areas and among certain strata of Hispanic society the articulation is bilabial [ɸ] rather than labiodental.

5. **t** represents [t], which never has the aspiration of English /t/ in prevocalic stressed position *(tea, two, ten).* It is more similar to the English /t/ of the

cluster [st] *(stop, step)*. Examples in Spanish: **tela, tino, tinta**. The point of articulation is dental.

6. **d** represents /d/, which has three variants according to position in the phrase: [d], [ɗ], [ɸ]. At the beginning of the breath group or after /n/ and /l/, **d** represents [d], which is similar to the English /d/ of *dame, did, darn*. Examples: **donde, falda, conde.** In all other situations the letter represents [ɗ], or even silence. There is a tendency in modern Spanish to move from the fricative [ɗ] (similar to the sound represented by the *th* in *mother, this, then*) to zero articulation [ɸ]. Examples: **hado, cuerda, es de, dos dados, cuadro, padre, abad, usted, Madrid.** The last two words are usually pronounced without final consonant, and the consonant tends to be very weak or even to disappear in the ending /-ado/: **hablado, estado, mercado.**

7. **s** in Spain, except the south, represents [S], an apicoalveolar sibilant, similar to the /s/ of southern Scotland and that of older speakers of the Midland dialect of the United States. Examples: **solo, casa, es.** Before a voiced consonant within the phrase it usually represents [Z]. Examples: **desde, mismo, es verde, los labios, las manos.**

   In southern Spain and in all of Spanish America except a small area of Colombia, this letter represents [s], a dental sibilant of high resonance similar to the usual "feminine" sibilant of much of the United States. In some areas it is actually lisped. Before a voiced consonant within the phrase it usually represents [z], a voiced sibilant similar to the /z/ of English *razor, ooze,* Examples: **desde, mismo, es verde, los labios, las manos.** In the Caribbean and in coastal Spanish generally, there is a strong tendency to aspirate or eliminate the /s/ syllable final, and the above voicing does not occur.

8. **z,** and **c** before **e** and **i** represent in Spain, except the southwest, [θ], an interdental fricative of tenser and more prolonged articulation than that represented by English *th* in *thin, cloth, ether*. Examples: **zagal, zorro, luz** [θagál], [θórro], [luθ]; or **luces, ciento, cerro** [lúθes], [θjento], [θerro]. In southern Spain and in Spanish America, these letters represent [s] (see paragraph 7). Examples: **zagal, zorro, luz, luces, ciento, cerro** [saǵál], [sórro], [lus], [lúses], [sjénto], [sérro]. Before a voiced consonant in the phrase, the **z** represents [z] (see paragraph 7). Examples: **en vez de, mayorazgo, la luz de.**

9. **l** always represents [l], a clear alveolar lateral that is rarely heard in English, except in Irish and Scottish dialects. It is never velar as in English *bell, full*. Examples: **lado, ala, el, al, sol.**

10. **n** represents /n/, which has variants according to the following consonants. It stands for [n] in all cases except before /b/, /p/, /m/, where it represents [m], and before /k/, /g/, /x/, where it represents [ŋ] (similar to the final consonant of *sing*). Examples of [n]: **no, nada, mano, aman;** of [m]: **en vez de, en Barcelona, un peso;** of [ŋ]: **anca, banco, en que, tengo, naranja.**

11. **ll** represents [ḷ] (a palatal lateral) in northern Spain and in Bolivia, parts of Ecuador, Paraguay, and most of Peru, as well as in the eastern cordillera of Colombia. This sound is similar to that heard in English *million*. In other parts of the Spanish-speaking world, *ll* represents [y]. Examples: **calle, llano, olla.**

12. **ñ** represents [ñ] among all speakers of Spanish. It is similar to the sound heard in English *canyon*, but is more one articulation than the English. Examples: **cañón, año, ñato.**

13. **ch** represents [č], which is similar to English /č/ *(church, cheek, reach).* Examples: **chato, chaleco, mucho.**

14. **y** represents [y], which varies regionally from [y] to [ž] (as in *azure*), and in most regions it represents [ŷ] (similar to *just* of English) in initial position in the phrase and after /l/ and /n/. Examples: **ayer, mayo** [ayér], [máyo]; ¡**yo! un yugo, el yerno** [ŷo], [unŷúǥo], [elŷérno]. In nearly all areas, Spanish /y/ has more palatal friction than English /y/.

15. a. **x** represents between vowels [ǥs] or simply [S] in Spain (see paragraph 7) and [ks] in Spanish America. Examples: **examen, próximo.**

    b. Before a consonant **x** represents [S] in Spain and [s] in Spanish America, except in affected speech, when one hears [ks]. Examples: **extranjero, experiencia.** Before *c* [s] it is [k]: [eksépto].

    c. In several Indian words of Mexico and Central America **x** represents [x] (see paragraph 20). **México** is one of these and is spelled **Méjico** in Spain.

16. a. **c** represents [k] before **a, o, u, l,** or **r.** The [k] of Spanish does not have the aspiration of English /k/ in the word-initial position *(can, quill, coal)* but is more like the sound in *scan.* Examples: **casa, cosa, cuna, quinto, queso, crudo, aclamar.** Note that **quinto** and **queso** are [kinto] and [késo]. The syllable final [k] in Spanish occurs only in "learned" terms and is dealt with in various ways by the people. In Spain generally it tends to voice to [ǥ]: **técnico, acto, doctor** [téǥnico], [áǥto], doǥtór], but today in Madrid and farther north, the latter becomes [doθtór]. In Central America, Cuba, Venezuela, and Colombia [kt] often becomes [pt] and vice versa; [ps] is [ks]: **Pepsi Cola** [péksi kóla].

    b. **c** before **e** and **i** represents [θ] in Spain, except the southwest, and [s] in Spanish America (see paragraph 8).

17. **k** represents [k] in certain words of foreign origin, mainly Greek, German, and English: **kilo, kilómetro, kermesse, kiosko.**

18. **q** combined with **u** represents [k]. Examples: **queso, aquí, quien** [késo], [akí], [kjen]. **qu** occurs only before **e** and **i.**

19. a. **g** represents [g] before **a, o, u** when initial in the breath group or after /n/. Examples: **ganga, goma, guarda, tengo. gue, gui** represents [ge], [gi], **güe, güi** represent [gwe], [gwi].
    Before **a, o, u** under other circumstances, **g** represents [ǥ], a voiced velar fricative. Examples: **la guerra** [laǥérra], **lago** [láǥo], **la goma** [laǥóma], **agrado** [aǥráđo].

    b. **g** before **e, i,** represents [x], a palatal or velar fricative, which is also represented by **j.** Examples: **gente, giro** [xénte], [xíro]. In the Caribbean and Central America, as well as in southern Spain, the /x/ is simply [h].

20. **j** always represents /x/. The usual manifestation of this phoneme is [x], but in some areas (see paragraph 19) it is [h]. Examples: **jamás, jugo, jota** [xamás], [xúǥo], [xóta].

21. **h** represents a former aspiration that is no longer present except in some rural areas of southern Spain and Spanish America. Examples: **hoja** [óxa], **humo** [úmo], **harto** [árto].

22. **r** represents [r], a single alveolar flap, similar to the sound represented by *tt* in American English *kitty* in rapid speech. However, at the beginning of a word or after **n, l, s,** it represents [rr], a multiple vibrant (trill). Examples of [r]: **caro, farol, mero, tren, comer.** Examples of [rr] written **r: rosa, rana, Enrique, Israel, alrededor.**
rr represents [rr] under all circumstances. Examples: **carro, correr, guerrero.**

The Noun

I. Gender[2]

A. *Masculine Gender*

1. Names of male beings are naturally masculine: **el hombre** the man; **el muchacho** the boy; **el tío** the uncle; **el rey** the king; **el buey** the ox.

2. Nouns ending in **-o** are masculine: **el libro** the book; **el banco** the bank. *Exception:* **la mano** the hand, **la radio** the radio.

3. Days of the week, months, rivers, oceans, and mountains are masculine: **el martes** Tuesday; **enero** January; **el Pacífico** the Pacific; **el Rin** the Rhine; **los Andes** the Andes.

4. Most nouns in **-l** or **-r,** and nouns of Greek origin ending in **-ma** are masculine: **el papel** the paper; **el azúcar** the sugar; **el favor** the favor; **el drama** the drama. *Common exceptions:* **la miel** the honey; **la sal** the salt; **la catedral** the cathedral; **la flor** the flower. Note that **mar** is both masculine and feminine.

B. *Feminine Gender*

1. Names of female beings are naturally feminine: **la mujer** the woman; **la muchacha** the girl; **la tía** the aunt; **la vaca** the cow.

2. Nouns ending in **-a** are feminine: **la pluma** the pen; **la carta** the letter; **la casa** the house. *Common exceptions:* **el día** the day; **el mapa** the map; nouns of Greek origin ending in **-ma: el dogma** the dogma; **el programa** the program.

3. Letters of the alphabet are feminine: **la e, la s, la t.**

4. Nouns ending in **-ión, -tad, -dad, -tud, -umbre** are feminine: **la canción** the song; **la facultad** the faculty; **la ciudad** the city; **la virtud** the virtue; **la muchedumbre** the crowd. *Exceptions:* **el gorrión** the sparrow; **el sarampión** the measles; **el camión** the truck; **el avión** the airplane.

Note that *(a)* some nouns have different genders according to their meanings: **el corte** the cut or the cutting edge; **la corte** the court; **el guía** the guide; **la guía** the guidebook; **el capital** the capital (money); **la capital** the capital (city); *(b)* some nouns have invariable endings which are used for both the masculine and the feminine: **arista** (and all nouns ending in **-ista**), **amante, mártir, testigo, reo, demócrata, aristócrata, intérprete, consorte, comensal, homicida, suicida, indígena, cómplice, cliente.**
2. There is no general gender rule for the type of nouns not treated in this section.

C. *Formation of the Feminine*

1. Nouns ending in **-o** change **-o** to **-a: tío** uncle, **tía** aunt; **niño** boy, **niña** girl.

2. Nouns ending in **-ón, -or,** and **-án** add **-a: patrón** patron, **patrona** patroness; **pastor** shepherd, **pastora** shepherdess; **holgazán** lazy man, **holgazana** lazy woman.

3. Certain nouns have a special form for the feminine: **el poeta, la poetisa; el cantante, la cantatriz; el sacerdote, la sacerdotisa; el emperador, la emperatriz; el abad, la abadesa; el conde, la condesa; el duque, la duquesa.**

II. Plural of Nouns[3]

1. Nouns ending in an unaccented vowel add **-s** to form the plural: **el libro, los libros; la casa, las casas.**

2. Nouns ending in a consonant, in **-y,** or in an accented vowel add **-es: el papel, los papeles; la canción, las canciones: la ley, las leyes; el rubí, los rubíes.** The accepted plural, however, of **papá** is **papás,** and of **mamá** is **mamás,** and of **café** is **cafés.**

3. Nouns ending in unaccented **-es** and **-is** do not change in the plural: **el lunes** Monday, **los lunes** Mondays; **la tesis** the thesis, **las tesis** the theses.

The Adjective and the Adverb

I. The Adjective

A. *Agreement.* The adjective in Spanish agrees in gender and number with the noun it modifies: **el lápiz rojo** the red pencil; **la casa blanca** the white house; **los libros interesantes** the interesting books; **las muchachas hermosas** the beautiful girls.

B. *Formation of the plural.* Adjectives follow the same rules as nouns for the formation of the plural: **pálido, pálidos** pale; **fácil, fáciles** easy; **cortés, corteses** courteous; **capaz, capaces** capable.

C. *Formation of the feminine.*

1. Adjectives ending in **-o** change **-o** to **-a: blanco, blanca.**

2. Adjectives ending in other vowels are invariable: **verde** green; **fuerte** strong; **indígena** indigenous, native; **pesimista** pessimistic; **baladí** trivial.

3. Adjectives ending in a consonant are invariable: **fácil** easy; **cortés** courteous. *Exceptions:* (a) adjectives ending in **-ón, -án, -or** (except comparatives) add **-a** to form the feminine: **holgazán, holgazana** lazy; **preguntón, preguntona** inquisitive; **hablador, habladora** talkative (Note that **mayor, mejor, menor, peor, superior, inferior, exterior, interior, anterior,** and **posterior** are invariable). **Superior** adds an **-a** when it is used as a noun meaning ("mother

---

3. The plurals of certain masculine nouns may include the masculine and feminine genders: **los padres** the father(s) and mother(s), the parents; **los tíos** the uncle(s) and aunt(s); **los reyes** the king(s) and queen(s). Note that (a) nouns ending in **-z** change **z** to **c** before **-es: lápiz, lápices;** (b) nouns ending in **-ión** lose the written accent in the plural: **canción, canciones.**

superior''). *(b)* adjectives of nationality ending in a consonant add **-a** to form the feminine: **francés, francesa** French; **español, española** Spanish; **alemán, alemana** German; **inglés, inglesa** English.

II. The Adverb

Many adverbs are formed by adding **-mente** to the feminine form of the adjective: **claro, claramente; lento, lentamente; fácil, fácilmente.**

III. Comparison of Adjectives and Adverbs

A. *Comparative of inequality.* The comparative of inequality is formed by placing **más** or **menos** before the positive form of the adjective or adverb: **más rico que** richer than; **menos rico que** less rich than; **más tarde** later; **menos tarde** less late. The superlative is formed by placing the definite article **el** before the comparative: **el más rico** the richest; **el menos rico** the least rich. Note the position of the article in the following examples: **la niña más linda** or **la más linda niña** the prettiest girl.

The following adjectives and adverbs have in addition irregular forms of comparison:

Positive	Comparative	Superlative
bueno	mejor	el (la) mejor
malo	peor	el (la) peor
grande	mayor	el (la) mayor
pequeño	menor	el (la) menor
alto	superior	supremo
bajo	inferior	ínfimo
mucho	más	
poco	menos	

B. *Comparative of equality.* With adjectives and adverbs the comparative of equality is formed with **tan . . . como: tan fácil como** as easy as; **tan bien como** as well as; with nouns the comparative of equality is formed with **tanto (tanta, tantos, tantas) . . . como: tanto dinero como** as much money as; **tantas personas como** as many people as.

C. *Absolute superlative of adjectives.* The absolute superlative of adjectives is formed by placing **muy** (very) before the adjective or by adding the suffix **-ísimo:**

Positive	Absolute Superlative
feliz	muy feliz, felicísimo
fácil	muy fácil, facilísimo
importante	muy importante, importantísimo
limpio	muy limpio, limpísimo
feo	muy feo, feísimo
rico	muy rico, riquísimo
largo	muy largo, larguísimo
notable	muy notable, notabilísimo

A few adjectives have, in addition, other forms derived from the Latin superlatives:

bueno	muy bueno, bonísimo[4], óptimo
malo	muy malo, malísimo, pésimo
grande	muy grande, grandísimo, máximo
pequeño	muy pequeño, pequeñísimo, mínimo

Some adjectives ending in **-ro** or **-re** revert to the corresponding Latin superlative:

acre	muy acre, acrérrimo
célebre	muy célebre, celebérrimo
mísero	muy mísero, misérrimo
salubre	muy salubre, salubérrimo

D. *Absolute superlative of adverbs.* The absolute superlative of adverbs not ending in **-mente** is formed in the same manner as that of adjectives:

tarde	muy tarde, tardísimo
pronto	muy pronto, prontísimo
mucho	muchísimo
poco	muy poco, poquísmo
cerca	muy cerca, cerquísima
lejos	muy lejos, lejísimos

Superlative adverbs ending in **-mente** are formed by adding the suffix **-ísima** to the corresponding feminine adjective:

claramente	muy claramente, clarísimamente
noblemente	muy noblemente, nobilísimamente

Common Spanish Suffixes

I. Diminutives

The most common diminutive endings in Spanish are:

-ito, -ita　　(**-cito, -cita, -ecito, -ecita**). Examples: **librito** (from **libro**), **casita** (from **casa**), **corazoncito** (from **corazón**), **mujercita** (from **mujer**), **cochecito** (from **coche**), **florecita** (from **flor**).

-illo, -illa　　(**-cillo, -cilla, -ecillo, -ecilla**). Examples: **corderillo** (from **cordero**), **dolorcillo** (from **dolor**), **viejecillo** (from **viejo**), **piedrecilla** (from **piedra**).

-ico, -ica　　(**-cico, -cica, -ecico, -ecica**). Examples: **niñico** (from **niño**), **hermanica** (from **hermana**), **corazoncico** (from **corazón**), **mujercica** (from **mujer**), **pobrecico** (from **pobre**).

-uelo, -uela　　(**-zuelo, -zuela, -ezuelo, -ezuela**). Examples: **arroyuelo** (from **arroyo**), **mozuela** (from **moza**), **mujerzuela** (from **mujer**), **reyezuelo** (from **rey**), **piedrezuela** (from **piedra**).

-ete, -eta　　Examples: **vejete** (from **viejo**), **vejeta** (from **vieja**).
-uco, -uca　　Example: **casuca** (from **casa**).

-ucho, -ucha　　Examples: **serrucho** (from **sierra**), **casucha** (from **casa**).

4. Also **buenísimo**.

II. Augmentatives

The most common augmentative endings in Spanish are:

-acho, -acha	Example: **ricacho** (from **rico**).
-azo, -aza	Examples: **gigantazo** (from **gigante**), **bribonazo** (from **bribón**), **manaza** (from **mano**), **bocaza** (from **boca**).
-on, -ona	Examples: **hombrón** (from **hombre**), **mujerona** (from **mujer**), **almohadón** (from **almohada**), **borrachón** (from **borracho**).
-ote, -ota	Examples: **grandote** (from **grande**), **muchachote** (from **muchacho**), **muchachota** (from **muchacha**).

III. Depreciatives

The most common depreciative endings in Spanish are:

-aco, -aca	Example: **pajarraco** ugly bird.
-ejo, -eja	Example: **librejo** old, worthless book.

Note that a depreciative or ironic connotation is often conveyed by many of the augmentatives and by the diminutive endings **-uelo, -ete, -uco, -ucho, -illo**.

IV. Other Suffixes

-ada	*a.* is sometimes equal to the English suffix *-ful:* **cucharada** spoonful; **palada** shovelful; *b.* often indicates a blow: **puñada** blow with the fist; **puñalada** stab or blow with a dagger; **topetada** butt, blow with the head; *c.* indicates a group or a crowd of: **peonada** a group or crowd of peons; **indiada** a group or crowd of Indians.
-al, -ar	denote a grove, field, plantation or orchard: **naranjal** orange grove; **cauchal** rubber plantation; **pinar** pine grove.
-azo	indicates a blow or explosion: **puñetazo** blow with the fist; **topetazo** butt, blow with the head; **escobazo** blow with a broom; **cañonazo** cannon shot; **cabezazo** header (soccer)
-dad, -tad	are suffixes forming many abstract nouns and are usually equivalent to the English suffix *-ty:* **fraternidad** fraternity; **facultad** faculty; **cantidad** quantity; **calidad** quality.
-dizo	is an adjective-forming suffix which means sometimes *tending to,* or *in the habit of:* **resbaladizo** slippery; **olvidadizo** forgetful; **enojadizo** irritable, easily angered; **asustadizo** easily frightened, scary, timid; **movedizo** movable, loose, changeable.
-ería	*a.* denotes a place where something is made or sold: **panadería** bakery; **librería** bookstore; **zapatería** shoestore; **pastelería** pastry shop;

b. indicates a profession, business or occupation: **carpintería** carpentry; **ingeniería** engineering.
c. means sometimes a collection: **pastelería** pastry, pastries;
d. is sometimes equivalent to English suffix *-ness;* it also suggests a single act or action: **tontería** foolishness; foolish act; **niñería** childishness; childish act.

-ero
a. indicates a person who makes, sells, or is in charge of: **panadero** baker; **librero** bookseller; **zapatero** shoemaker, **carcelero** jailer; **cajero** cashier;
b. is an adjective-forming suffix; **parlero** talkative; **guerrero** warlike; **extranjero** foreign.

-ez, -eza
are used to make abstract nouns: **vejez** old age; **niñez** childhood; **viudez** widowhood; **grandeza** greatness.

ía
a. is the ending of the names of many arts and sciences: **geología** geology; **geometría** geometry; **biología** biology;
b. see **-ería.**

-iento
indicates a *resemblance,* or a *tendency to:* **ceniciento** ashlike; **soñoliento** sleepy, drowsy; **amarillento** yellowish.

ísimo
is the ending of the absolute superlative: **hermosísimo** very beautiful.

-izo
is a suffix meaning *tending to* or *somewhat:* **rojizo** reddish. See **-dizo.**

-mente
is the adverbial ending attached to the feminine form of the adjective: **generosamente** generously; **claramente** clearly.

-ón
a. is an augmentative suffix;
b. is also a suffix without an augmentative force, meaning *in the habit of,* or *full of:* **juguetón** playful; **preguntón** full of questions, inquisitive; **llorón** tearful; crybaby;
c. indicates suddenness or violence of an action: **estirón** pull, tug, jerk; **apretón** squeeze.

-or, -dor
a. are equivalent to the English suffixes *-or, -er,* and indicate the agent or doer: **hablador** talker; **regulador** regulator;
b. may also be used as adjectives: **hablador** talkative; **regulador** regulating.

-oso
is an adjective-forming suffix which usually means *having, full of,* or *characterized by:* **rocoso** rocky; **tormentoso** stormy; **fangoso** muddy; **herboso** grassy; **lluvioso** rainy; **maravilloso** marvelous; **famoso** famous.

-udo
is an adjective-forming suffix meaning *having* or *characterized by:* **zancudo** long-legged; **peludo** hairy; **panzudo** big-bellied; **caprichudo** stubborn.

-ura
is a suffix forming many abstract nouns: **negrura** blackness; **blancura** whiteness; **altura** height; **lisura** smoothness.

-uzco

indicates *resemblance* or *a tendency to;* it is akin to the English suffix *-ish:* **blancuzco** whitish; **negruzco** blackish.

Spanish Regular Verbs

First Conjugation

Infinitive	hablar
Pres. Indic.	hablo, hablas, habla, hablamos, habláis, hablan
Pres. Subj.	hable, hables, hable, hablemos, habléis, hablen
Pret. Indic.	hablé, hablaste, habló, hablamos, hablasteis, hablaron
Imp. Indic.	hablaba, hablabas, hablaba, hablábamos, hablabais, hablaban
Imp. Subj.	hablara or hablase, hablaras or hablases, hablara or hablase, habláramos or hablásemos, hablarais or hablaseis, hablaran or hablasen
Fut. Indic.	hablaré, hablarás, hablará, hablaremos, hablaréis, hablarán
Cond.	hablaría, hablarías, hablaría, hablaríamos, hablaríais, hablarían
Imper.	habla tú, hable Vd., hablad vosotros, hablen Vds.
Pres. Part.	hablando
Past Part.	hablado

Second Conjugation

Infinitive	comer
Pres. Indic.	como, comes, come, comemos, coméis, comen
Pres. Subj.	coma, comas, coma, comamos, comáis, coman
Pret. Indic.	comí, comiste, comió, comimos, comisteis, comieron
Imp. Indic.	comía, comías, comía, comíamos, comíais, comían
Imp. Subj.	comiera or comiese, comieras or comieses, comiera or comiese, comiéramos or comiésemos, comierais or comieseis, comieran or comiesen
Fut. Indic.	comeré, comerás, comerá, comeremos, comeréis, comerán
Cond.	comería, comerías, comería, comeríamos, comeríais, comerían
Imper.	come tú, coma Vd., comed vosotros, coman Vds.
Pres. Part.	comiendo
Past Part.	comido

Third Conjugation

Infinitive	vivir
Pres. Indic.	vivo, vives, vive, vivimos, vivís, viven
Pres. Subj.	viva, vivas, viva, vivamos, viváis, vivan
Pret. Indic.	viví, viviste, vivió, vivimos, vivisteis, vivieron
Imp. Indic.	vivía, vivías, vivía, vivíamos, vivíais, vivían
Imp. Subj.	viviera or viviese, vivieras or vivieses, viviera or viviese, viviéramos or viviésemos, vivierais or vivieseis, vivieran or viviesen
Fut. Indic.	viviré, vivirás, vivirá, viviremos, viviréis, vivirán
Cond.	viviría, vivirías, viviría, viviríamos, viviríais, vivirían
Imper.	vive tú, viva Vd., vivid vosotros, vivan Vds.
Pres. Part.	viviendo
Past Part.	vivido

Spanish Irregular and Orthographic Changing Verbs

The superior number, or numbers, after a verb entry indicate that it is conjugated like the model verb in this section which has the corresponding number. Only the tenses which have irregular forms or spelling changes are given. The irregular forms and spelling changes are shown in bold-face type.

1. pensar (if stressed, the stem vowel **e** becomes **ie**)
   Pres. Indic. **pienso, piensas, piensa,** pensamos, pensáis, **piensan.**
   Pres. Subj. **piense, pienses, piense,** pensemos, penséis, **piensen.**
   Imper. **piensa** tú, **piense** Vd., pensad vosotros, **piensen** Vds.

2. contar (if stressed, the stem vowel **o** becomes **ue**)
   Pres. Indic. **cuento, cuentas, cuenta,** contamos, contáis, **cuentan.**
   Pres. Subj. **cuente, cuentes, cuente,** contemos, contéis, **cuenten.**
   Imper. **cuenta** tú, **cuente** Vd. contad vosotros, **cuenten** Vds.

3.*a.* sentir (if stressed, the stem vowel **e** becomes **ie**; if unstressed, the stem vowel **e** becomes **i** when the following syllable contains stressed **a, ie,** or **ió**)
   Pres. Indic. **siento, sientes, siente,** sentimos, sentís, **sienten.**
   Pres. Subj. **sienta, sientas, sienta, sintamos, sintáis, sientan.**
   Pret. Indic. **sentí, sentiste, sintió,** sentimos, sentisteis, **sintieron.**
   Imp. Subj. **sintiera** or **sintiese, sintieras** or **sintieses, sintiera** or **sintiese, sintiéramos** or **sintiésemos, sintierais** or **sintieseis, sintieran** or **sintiesen.**
   Imper. **siente** tú, **sienta** Vd., sentid vosotros, **sientan** Vds.
   Pres. Part. **sintiendo.**

   b. erguir (this verb has same vowel changes as *sentir,* but the initial **i** of the diphthong **ie** is changed to **y.** For regular spelling changes see No. 12,*a*)
   Pres. Indic. **yergo, yergues, yergue,** erguimos, erguís, **yerguen.**
   Pres. Subj. **yerga, yergas, yerga, irgamos, irgáis, yergan.**
   Pret. Indic. erguí, erguiste, **irguió,** erguimos, erguisteis, **irguieron.**
   Imp. Subj. **irguiera** or **irguiese, irguieras** or **irguieses, irguiera** or **irguieses, irguiéramos** or **irguiésemos, irguierais** or **irguieseis, irguieran** or **irguiesen.**
   Imper. **yergue** tú, **yerga** Vd., erguid vosotros, **yergan** Vds.
   Pres. Part. **irguiendo.**

4. dormir (if stressed, the stem vowel **o** becomes **ue**; if unstressed, the stem vowel **o** becomes **u** when the following syllable contains stressed **a, ie,** or **ió**)
   Pres. Indic. **duermo, duermes, duerme,** dormimos, dormís, **duermen.**
   Pres. Subj. **duerma, duermas, duerma, durmamos, durmáis, duerman.**
   Pret. Indic. dormí, dormiste, **durmió,** dormimos, dormisteis, **durmieron.**
   Imp. Subj. **durmiera** or **durmiese, durmieras** or **durmieses, durmiera** or **durmiese, durmiéramos** or **durmiésemos, durmierais** or **durmieseis, durmieran** or **durmiesen.**
   Imper. **duerme** tú, **duerma** Vd., dormid vosotros, **duerman** Vds.
   Pres. Part. **durmiendo.**

5. pedir (if stressed, the stem vowel **e** becomes **i**; if unstressed, the stem vowel **e** becomes **i** when the following syllable contains stressed **a, ie,** or **ió**)
   Pres. Indic. **pido, pides, pide,** pedimos, pedís, **piden.**
   Pres. Subj. **pida, pidas, pida, pidamos, pidáis, pidan.**

Pret. Indic.	pedí, pediste, **pidió**, pedimos, pedisteis, **pidieron.**
Imp. Subj.	**pidiera** or **pidiese, pidieras** or **pidieses, pidiera** or **pidiese, pidiéramos** or **pidiésemos, pidierais** or **pidieseis, pidieran** or **pidiesen.**
Imper.	**pide** tú, **pida** Vd., pedid vosotros, **pidan** Vds.
Pres. Part.	**pidiendo.**

6. buscar (verbs ending in **car** change **c** to **qu** before **e**)

Pres. Subj.	**busque, busques, busque, busquemos, busquéis, busquen.**
Pret. Indic.	**busqué,** buscaste, buscó, buscamos, buscasteis, buscaron.
Imper.	busca tú, **busque** Vd., buscad vosotros, **busquen** Vds.

7. llegar (verbs ending in **gar** change the **g** to **gu** before **e**)

Pres. Subj.	**llegue, llegues, llegue, lleguemos, lleguéis, lleguen.**
Pret. Indic.	**llegué,** llegaste, llegó, llegamos, llegasteis, llegaron.
Imper.	llega tú, **llegue** Vd., llegad vosotros, **lleguen** Vds.

8. averiguar (verbs ending in **guar** change the **gu** to **gü** before **e**)

Pres. Subj.	**averigüe, averigües, averigüe, averigüemos, averigüéis, averigüen.**
Pret. Indic.	**averigüé,** averiguaste, averiguó, averiguamos, averiguasteis, averiguaron.
Imper.	averigua tú, **averigüe** Vd., averiguad vosotros, **averigüen** Vds.

9. abrazar (verbs ending in **zar** change **z** to **c** before **e**)

Pres. Subj.	**abrace, abraces, abrace, abracemos, abracéis, abracen.**
Pret. Indic.	**abracé,** abrazaste, abrazó, abrazamos, abrazasteis, abrazaron.
Imper.	abraza tú, **abrace** Vd., abrazad vosotros, **abracen** Vds.

10.*a.* convencer (verbs ending in **cer** preceded by a consonant change **c** to **z** before **a** and **o**)

Pres. Indic.	**convenzo,** convences, convence, convencemos, convencéis, convencen.
Pres. Subj.	**convenza, convenzas, convenza, convenzamos, convenzáis, convenzan.**
Imper.	convence tú, **convenza** Vd., convenced vosotros, **convenzan** Vds.

b. esparcir (verbs ending in **cir** preceded by a consonant change **c** to **z** before **a** and **o**)

Pres. Indic.	**esparzo,** esparces, esparce, esparcimos, esparcís, esparcen.
Pres. Subj.	**esparza, esparzas, esparza, esparzamos, esparzáis, esparzan.**
Imper.	esparce tú, **esparza** Vd., esparcid vosotros, **esparzan** Vds.

c. mecer (two verbs ending in **cer** preceded by a vowel change **c** to **z** before **a** and **o**; see No. 13.*a*): mecer and cocer.

Pres. Indic.	**mezo,** meces, mece, mecemos, mecéis, mecen.
Pres. Subj.	**meza, mezas, meza, mezamos, mezáis, mezan.**
Imper.	mece tú, **meza** Vd., meced vosotros, **mezan** Vds.

11.*a.* dirigir (verbs ending in **gir** change **g** to **j** before **a** and **o**)

Pres. Indic.	**dirijo,** diriges, dirige, dirigimos, dirigís, dirigen.
Pres. Subj.	**dirija, dirijas, dirija, dirijamos, dirijáis, dirijan.**
Imper.	dirige tú, **dirija** Vd., dirigid vosotros, **dirijan** Vds.

b. coger (verbs ending in **ger** change **g** to **j** before **o** and **a**)
Pres. Indic. **cojo,** coges, coge, cogemos, cogéis, cogen.
Pres. Subj. **coja, cojas, coja, cojamos, cojáis, cojan.**
Imper. coge tú, **coja** Vd., coged vosotros, **cojan** Vds.

12.*a.* distinguir (verbs ending in **guir** drop the **u** before **o** and **a**)
Pres. Indic. **distingo,** distingues, distingue, distinguimos, distinguís, distinguen.
Pres. Subj. **distinga, distingas, distinga, distingamos, distingáis, distingan.**
Imper. distingue tú, **distinga** Vd., distinguid vosotros, **distingan** Vds.

b. delinquir (verbs ending in **quir** change **qu** to **c** before **o** and **a**)
Pres. Indic. **delinco,** delinques, delinque, delinquimos, delinquís, delinquen.
Pres. Subj. **delinca, delincas, delinca, delincamos, delincáis, delincan.**

13.*a.* conocer (verbs ending in **cer** when preceded by a vowel insert **z** before **c** when **c** is followed by **o** or **a**; see No. 10.*c*)
Pres. Indic. **conozco,** conoces, conoce, conocemos, conocéis, conocen.
Pres. Subj. **conozca, conozcas, conozca, conozcamos, conozcáis, conozcan.**
Imper. conoce tú, **conozca** Vd., conoced vosotros, **conozcan** Vds.

b. lucir (verbs ending in **cir** when preceded by a vowel insert **z** before **c** when **c** is followed by **o** or **a**; see No. 25)
Pres. Indic. **luzco,** luces, luce, lucimos, lucís, lucen.
Pres. Subj. **luzca, luzcas, luzca, luzcamos, luzcáis, luzcan.**
Imper. luce tú, **luzca** Vd., lucid vosotros, **luzcan** Vds.

14. creer (unstressed **i** between vowels is changed to **y**)
Pret. Indic. creí, creíste, **creyó,** creímos, creísteis, **creyeron.**
Imp. Subj. **creyera** or **creyese, creyeras** or **creyeses, creyera** or **creyese, creyéramos** or **creyésemos, creyerais** or **creyeseis, creyeran** or **creyesen.**
Pret. Part. **creyendo.**

15. reír (like No. 5, except that when the **i** of the stem would be followed by **ie** or **ió** the two **i**'s are reduced to one)
Pres. Indic. **río, ríes, ríe,** reimos, reís, **ríen.**
Pres. Subj. **ría, rías, ría, riamos, riáis, rían.**
Pret. Indic. rei, reíste, **rió,** reímos, reísteis, **rieron.**
Imp. Subj. **riera** or **riese, rieras** or **rieses, riera** or **riese, riéramos** or **riésemos, rierais** or **rieseis, rieran** or **riesen.**
Imper. **ríe** tú, **ría** Vd., reíd vosotros, **rían** Vds.
Pres. Part. **riendo.**

16. podrir or pudrir
Pres. Indic. **pudro, pudres, pudre,** podrimos or pudrimos, podris or pudrís, **pudren.**
Pres. Subj. **pudra, pudras, pudra, pudramos pudráis, pudran.**
Imp. Indic. pudría or podría, etc. (Seldom *podría* because of confusion with *poder*)
Pret. Indic. podrí or pudrí, podriste or pudriste, **pudrió,** podrimos or pudrimos, podristeis or pudristeis, **pudrieron.**
Imp. Subj. **pudriera** or **pudriese, pudrieras** or **pudrieses, pudriera** or

pudriese, pudriéramos or pudriésemos, pudrierais or
pudrieseis, pudrieran or pudriesen.

Fut. Indic.	pudriré or podriré, etc.
Cond.	pudriría or podriría, etc.
Pres. Part.	**pudriendo.**
Past Part.	podrido or pudrido.

17. enviar

Pres. Indic.	envío, envías, envía, enviamos, enviáis, envían.
Pres. Subj.	envíe, envíes, enviemos, enviéis, envíen.
Imper.	envía tú, envíe Vd., enviad vosotros, envíen Vds.

18. continuar

Pres. Indic.	continúo, continúas, continúa, continuamos, continuáis, continúan.
Pres. Subj.	continúe, continúes, continúe, continuemos, continuéis, continúen.
Imper.	continúa tú, continúe Vd., continuad vosotros, continúen Vds.

19. gruñir (i of the diphthong ie or ió is lost after ñ)

Pret. Indic.	gruñí, gruñiste, **gruñó,** gruñisteis, **gruñeron.**
Imp. Subj.	**gruñera** or **gruñese, gruñeras** or **gruñeses, gruñera** or **gruñese, gruñéramos** or **gruñésemos, gruñerais** or **gruñeseis, gruñeran** or **gruñesen.**
Pres. Part.	**gruñendo.**

20. bullir (i of the diphthong ie or ió is lost after ll)

Pret. Indic.	bullí, bulliste, **bulló,** bullimos, bullisteis, **bulleron.**
Imp. Subj.	**bullera** or **bullese, bulleras** or **bulleses, bullera** or **bullese, bulléramos** or **bullésemos, bullerais** or **bulleseis, bulleran** or **bullesen.**
Pres. Part.	**bullendo.**

21. andar

Pret. Indic.	**anduve, anduviste, anduvo, anduvimos, anduvisteis, anduvieron.**
Imp. Subj.	**anduviera** or **anduviese, anduvieras** or **anduvieses, anduviera** or **anduviese, anduviéramos** or **anduviésemos, anduvierais** or **anduvieseis, anduvieran** or **anduviesen.**

22. asir

Pres. Indic.	**asgo,** ases, ase, asimos, asis, asen.
Pres. Subj.	**asga, asgas, asga, asgamos, asgáis, asgan.**
Imper.	ase tú, **asga** Vd., asid vosotros, **asgan** Vds.

23. caber

Pres. Indic.	**quepo,** cabes, cabe, cabemos, cabéis, caben.
Pres. Subj.	**quepa, quepas, quepa, quepamos, quepáis, quepan.**
Pret. Indic.	**cupe, cupiste, cupo, cupimos, cupisteis, cupieron.**
Imp. Subj.	**cupiera** or **cupiese, cupieras** or **cupieses, cupiera** or **cupiese, cupiéramos** or **cupiésemos, cupierais** or **cupieseis, cupieran** or **cupiesen.**
Fut. Indic.	**cabré, cabrás, cabrá, cabremos, cabréis, cabrán.**

Cond.	**cabría, cabrías, cabría, cabríamos, cabríais, cabrían.**
Imper.	cabe tú, **quepa** Vd., cabed vosotros, **quepan** Vds.

24. **caer**

Pres. Indic.	**caigo,** caes, cae, caemos, caéis, caen.
Pres. Subj.	**caiga, caigas, caiga, caigamos, caigáis, caigan.**
Pret. Indic.	caí, caiste, **cayó,** caímos, caísteis, **cayeron.**
Imp. Subj.	**cayera** or **cayese, cayeras** or **cayases, cayera** or **cayese, cayéramos** or **cayésemos, cayerais** or **cayeseis, cayeran** or **cayesen.**
Imper.	cae tú, **caiga** Vd., caed vosotros, **caigan** Vds.
Pres. Part.	**cayendo.**

25. **conducir** (all verbs ending in **ducir** have the irregularities of conducir)

Pres. Indic.	**conduzco,** conduces, conduce, conducimos, conducís, conducen.
Pres. Subj.	**conduzca, conduzcas, conduzca, conduzcamos, conduzcáis, conduzcan.**
Pret. Indic.	**conduje, condujiste, condujo, condujimos, condujisteis, condujeron.**
Imp. Subj.	**condujera** or **condujese, condujeras** or **condujeses, condujera** or **condujese, condujéramos** or **condujésemos, condujerais** or **condujeseis, condujeran** or **condujesen.**
Imp.	conduce tú, **conduzca** Vd., conducid vosotros, **conduzcan** Vds.

26. **dar**

Pres. Indic.	**doy,** das, da, damos, dais, dan.
Pres. Subj.	dé, des, dé, demos, deis, den.
Pret. Indic.	**di, diste, dio, dimos, disteis, dieron.**
Imp. Subj.	**diera** or **diese, dieras** or **dieses, diera** or **diese, diéramos** or **diésemos, dierais** or **dieseis, dieran** or **diesen.**

27. **decir**[5]

Pres. Indic.	**digo, dices, dice,** decimos, decís, **dicen.**
Pres. Subj.	**diga, digas, diga, digamos, digáis, digan.**
Pret. Indic.	**dije, dijiste, dijo, dijimos, dijisteis, dijeron.**
Imp. Subj.	**dijera** or **dijese, dijeras** or **dijeses, dijera** or **dijese, dijéramos** or **dijésemos, dijerais** or **dijeseis, dijeran** or **dijesen.**
Fut. Indic.	**diré, dirás, dirá, diremos, diréis, dirán.**
Cond.	**diría, dirías, diría, diríamos, diríais, dirían.**
Imper.	**di** tú, **diga** Vd., decid vosotros, **digan** Vds.
Pres. Part.	**diciendo.**
Past Part.	**dicho.**

28. **errar** (like No. 1, except that the initial **ie** is spelled **ye**)

Pres. Indic.	**yerro, yerras, yerra,** erramos, erráis, **yerran.**

---

5. The compound verbs of *decir* have the same irregularities with the exception of the following:

   a. The future and conditional of the compound verbs *bendecir* and *maldecir* are regular: *bendeciré, maldeciré,* etc.; *bendeciría, maldeciría,* etc.

   b. The familiar imperative is regular: *bendice tu, maldice tu, contradice tu,* etc.

   c. The past participles of *bendecir* and *maldecir* are regular when used with *haber* or in the passive with *ser: bendecido, maldecido;* when used as an adjective with *estar* or with *ser* as a noun, the forms are: *bendito, maldito.*

Pres. Subj.	yerre, yerres, yerre, erremos, erréis, yerren.
Imper.	yerra tú, yerre Vd., errad vosotros, yerren Vds.

29. estar

Pres. Indic.	estoy, estás, está, estamos, estáis, están.
Pres. Subj.	esté, estés, esté, estemos, estéis, estén.
Pret. Indic.	estuve, estuviste, estuvo, estuvimos, estuvisteis, estuvieron.
Imp. Subj.	estuviera or estuviese, estuvieras or estuvieses, estuviera or estuviese, estuviéramos or estuviésemos, estuvierais or estuvieseis, estuvieran or estuviesen.
Imper.	está tú, esté Vd., estad vosotros, estén Vds.

30. haber

Pres. Indic.	he, has, ha, hemos, habéis, han.
Pres. Subj.	haya, hayas, haya, hayamos, hayáis, hayan.
Pret. Indic.	hube, hubiste, hubo, hubimos, hubisteis, hubieron.
Imp. Subj.	hubiera or hubiese, hubieras or hubieses, hubiera or hubiese, hubiéramos or hubiésemos, hubierais or hubieseis, hubieran or hubiesen.
Fut. Indic.	habré, habrás, habrá, habremos, habréis, habrán.
Cond.	habría, habrías, habría, habríamos, habríais, habrían.

31. hacer

Pres. Indic.	hago, haces, hace, hacemos, hacéis, hacen.
Pres. Subj.	haga, hagas, haga, hagamos, hagáis, hagan.
Pret. Indic.	hice, hiciste, hizo, hicimos, hicisteis, hicieron.
Imp. Subj.	hiciera or hiciese, hicieras or hicieses, hiciera or hiciese, hiciéramos or hiciésemos, hicierais or hicieseis, hicieran or hiciesen.
Fut. Indic.	haré, harás, hará, haremos, haréis, harán.
Cond.	haría, harías, haría, haríamos, haríais, harían.
Imper.	haz tú, haga Vd., haced vosotros, hagan Vds.
Past Part.	hecho.

32.*a.* huir

Pres. Indic.	huyo, huyes, huye, huimos, huís, huyen.
Pres. Subj.	huya, huyas, huya, huyamos, huyáis, huyan.
Pret. Indic.	huí, huiste, huyó, huimos, huisteis, huyeron.
Imp. Subj.	huyera or huyese, huyeras or huyeses, huyera or huyese, huyéramos or huyésemos, huyerais or huyeseis, huyeran or huyesen.
Imper.	huye tú, huya Vd., huid vosotros, huyan Vds.
Pres. Part.	huyendo.

b. argüir

Pres. Indic.	arguyo, arguyes, arguye, argüimos, argüís, arguyen.
Pres. Subj.	arguya, arguyas, arguya, arguyamos, arguyáis, arguyan.
Pret. Indic.	argüí, argüiste, arguyó, argüimos, argüisteis, arguyeron.
Imp. Subj.	arguyera or arguyese, arguyeras or arguyeses, arguyera or arguyese, arguyéramos or arguyésemos, arguyerais or arguyeseis, arguyeran or arguyesen.

	Imper.	**arguye** tú, **arguya** Vd., argüid vosotros, **arguyan** Vds.
	Pres. Part.	**arguyendo.**
33.	ir	
	Pres. Indic.	**voy, vas, va, vamos, vais, van.**
	Pres. Subj.	**vaya, vayas, vaya, vayamos, vayáis, vayan.**
	Imp. Indic.	**iba, ibas, iba, íbamos, ibais, iban.**
	Pret. Indic.	**fui, fuiste, fue, fuimos, fuisteis, fueron.**
	Imp. Subj.	**fuera** or **fuese, fueras** or **fueses, fuera** or **fuese, fuéramos** or **fuésemos, fuerais** or **fueseis, fueran** or **fuesen.**
	Imper.	**ve** tú, **vaya** Vd., id vosotros, **vayan** Vds.
	Pres. Part.	**yendo.**
34.	jugar (cf. Nos. 2 and 7)	
	Pres. Indic.	**juego, juegas, juega,** jugamos, jugáis, **juegan.**
	Pres. Subj.	**juegue, juegues, juegue,** juguemos, juguéis, **jueguen.**
	Pret. Indic.	**jugué,** jugaste, jugó, jugamos, jugasteis, jugaron.
	Imper.	**juega** tú, **juegue** Vd., jugad vosotros, **jueguen** Vds.
35.	adquirir	
	Pres. Indic.	**adquiero, adquieres, adquiere,** adquirimos, adquirís, **adquieren.**
	Pres. Subj.	**adquiera, adquieras, adquiera,** adquiramos, adquiráis, **adquieran.**
	Imper.	**adquiere** tú, **adquiera** Vd., adquirid vosotros, **adquieran** Vds.
36.	oír	
	Pres. Indic.	**oigo, oyes, oye,** oímos, oís, **oyen.**
	Pres. Subj.	**oiga, oigas, oiga, oigamos, oigáis, oigan.**
	Pret. Indic.	oí, oíste, **oyó,** oímos, oísteis, **oyeron.**
	Imp. Subj.	**oyera** or **oyese, oyeras** or **oyeses, oyera** or **oyese, oyéramos** or **oyésemos, oyerais** or **oyeseis, oyeran** or **oyesen.**
	Imper.	**oye** tú, **oiga** Vd., oíd vosotros, **oigan** Vds.
	Pres. Part.	**oyendo.**
37.	oler (like No. 2, except that initial **ue** is spelled **hue**)	
	Pres. Indic.	**huelo, hueles, huele,** olemos, oléis, **huelen.**
	Pres. Subj.	**huela, huelas, huela,** olamos, oláis, **huelan.**
	Imper.	**huele** tú, **huela** Vd., oled vosotros, **huelan** Vds.
38.	placer	
	Pres. Indic.	**plazco,** places, place, placemos, placéis, placen.
	Pres. Subj.	**plazca, plazcas, plazca, plazcamos, plazcáis, plazcan.** (There are also the antiquated forms, **plegue** and **plega,** used now only in the third person in poetic language.)
	Pret. Indic.	In addition to the regular forms, there is the antiquated form **plugo,** used now only in poetic language.
	Imp. Subj.	In addition to the regular forms, there are the antiquated forms, **pluguiera** and **pluguiese,** used now only in poetic language.
39.	poder	
	Pres. Indic.	**puedo, puedes, puede,** podemos, podéis, **pueden.**
	Pres. Subj.	**pueda, puedas, pueda,** podamos, podáis, **puedan.**

Pret. Indic.	**pude, pudiste, pudo, pudimos, pudisteis, pudieron.**
Imp. Subj.	**pudiera** or **pudiese, pudieras** or **pudieses, pudiera** or **pudiese, pudiéramos** or **pudiésemos, pudierais** or **pudieseis, pudieran** or **pudiesen.**
Fut. Indic.	**podré, podrás, podrá, podremos, podréis, podrán.**
Cond.	**podría, podrías, podría, podríamos, podríais, podrían.**
Pres. Part.	**pudiendo.**

40. poner

Pres. Indic.	**pongo,** pones, pone, ponemos, ponéis, ponen.
Pres. Subj.	**ponga, pongas, ponga, pongamos, pongáis, pongan.**
Pret. Indic.	**puse, pusiste, puso, pusimos, pusisteis, pusieron.**
Imp. Subj.	**pusiera** or **pusiese, pusieras** or **pusieses, pusiera** or **pusiese, pusiéramos** or **pusiésemos, pusierais** or **pusieseis, pusieran** or **pusiesen.**
Fut. Indic.	**pondré, pondrás, pondrá, pondremos, pondréis, pondrán.**
Cond.	**pondría, pondrías, pondría, pondríamos, pondríais, pondrían.**
Imper.	**pon** tú, **ponga** Vd., poned vosotros, **pongan** Vds.
Past Part.	**puesto.**

41. querer

Pres. Indic.	**quiero, quieres, quiere,** queremos, queréis, **quieren.**
Pres. Subj.	**quiera, quieras, quiera,** queramos, queráis, **quieran.**
Pret. Indic.	**quise, quisiste, quiso, quisimos, quisisteis, quisieron.**
Imp. Subj.	**quisiera** or **quisiese, quisieras** or **quisieses, quisiera** or **quisiese, quisiéramos** or **quisiémos, quisierais** or **quisieseis, quisieran** or **quisiesen.**
Fut. Indic.	**querré, querrás, querrá, querremos, querréis, querrán.**
Cond.	**querría, querrías, querría, querríamos, querríais, querrían.**
Imper.	**quiere** tú, **quiera** Vd., quered vosotros, **quieran** Vds.

42. saber

Pres. Indic.	**sé,** sabes, sabe, sabemos, sabéis, saben.
Pres. Subj.	**sepa, sepas, sepa, sepamos, sepáis, sepan.**
Pret. Indic.	**supe, supiste, supo, supimos, supisteis, supieron.**
Imp. Subj.	**supiera** or **supiese, supieras** or **supieses, supiera** or **supiese, supiéramos** or **supiésemos, supierais** or **supieseis, supieran** or **supiesen.**
Fut. Indic.	**sabré, sabrás, sabrá, sabremos, sabréis, sabrán.**
Cond.	**sabría, sabrías, sabría, sabríamos, sabríais, sabrían.**
Imper.	sabe tú, **sepa** Vd., sabed vosotros, **sepan** Vds.

43. salir

Pres. Indic.	**salgo,** sales, sale, salimos, salís, salen.
Pres. Subj.	**salga, salgas, salga, salgamos, salgáis, salgan.**
Fut. Indic.	**saldré, saldrás, saldrá, saldremos, saldréis, saldrán.**
Cond.	**saldría, saldrías, saldría, saldríamos, saldríais, saldrían.**
Imper.[6]	**sal** tú, **salga** Vd., salid vosotros, **salgan** Vds.

---

6. The compound *sobresalir* is regular in the familiar imperative: **sobresale tú.**

44. ser
Pres. Indic.	**soy, eres, es, somos, sois, son.**
Pres. Subj.	**sea, seas, sea, seamos, seáis, sean.**
Imp. Indic.	**era, eras, era, éramos, erais, eran.**
Pret. Indic.	**fui, fuiste, fue, fuimos, fuisteis, fueron.**
Imp. Subj.	**fuera** or **fuese, fueras** or **fueses, fuera** or **fuese, fuéramos** or **fuésemos, fuerais** or **fueseis, fueran** or **fuesen.**
Imper.	**sé** tú, **sea** Vd., sed vosotros, **sean** Vds.

45. tener
Pres. Indic.	**tengo, tienes, tiene,** tenemos, tenéis, **tienen.**
Pres. Subj.	**tenga, tengas, tenga, tengamos, tengáis, tengan.**
Pret. Indic.	**tuve, tuviste, tuvo, tuvimos, tuvisteis, tuvieron.**
Imp. Subj.	**tuviera** or **tuviese, tuvieras** or **tuvieses, tuviera** or **tuviese, tuviéramos** or **tuviésemos, tuvierais** or **tuvieseis, tuvieran** or **tuviesen.**
Fut. Indic.	**tendré, tendrás, tendrá, tendremos, tendréis, tendrán.**
Cond.	**tendría, tendrías, tendría, tendríamos, tendríais, tendrían.**
Imper.	**ten** tú, **tenga** Vd., tened vosotros, **tengan** Vds.

46. traer
Pres. Indic.	**traigo,** traes, trae, traemos, traéis, traen.
Pres. Subj.	**traiga, traigas, traiga, traigamos, traigáis, traigan.**
Pret. Indic.	**traje, trajiste, trajo, trajimos, trajisteis, trajeron.**
Imp. Subj.	**trajera** or **trajese, trajeras** or **trajeses, trajera** or **trajese, trajéramos** or **trajésemos, trajerais** or **trajeseis, trajeran** or **trajesen.**
Imper.	trae tú, **traiga** Vd., traed vosotros, **traigan** Vds.
Pres. Part.	**trayendo.**

47. valer
Pres. Indic.	**valgo,** vales, vale, valemos, valéis, valen.
Pres. Subj.	**valga, valgas, valga, valgamos, valgáis, valgan.**
Fut. Indic.	**valdré, valdrás, valdrá, valdremos, valdréis, valdrán.**
Cond.	**valdría, valdrías, valdría, valdríamos, valdríais, valdrían.**
Imper.	**val** or **vale** tú, **valga** Vd., valed vosotros, **valgan** Vds.

48. venir
Pres. Indic.	**vengo, vienes, viene,** venimos, venís, **vienen.**
Pres. Subj.	**venga, vengas, venga, vengamos, vangáis, vengan.**
Pret. Indic.	**vine, viniste, vino, vinimos, vinisteis, vinieron.**
Imp. Subj.	**viniera** or **viniese, vinieras** or **vinieses, viniera** or **viniese, viniéramos** or **viniésemos, vinierais** or **vinieseis, vinieran** or **viniesen.**
Fut. Indic.	**vendré, vendrás, vendrá, vendremos, vendréis, vendrán.**
Cond.	**vendría, vendrías, vendría, vendríamos, vendríais, vendrían.**
Imper.	**ven** tú, **venga** Vd., venid vostros, **vengan** Vds.
Pres. Part.	**viniendo.**

49. ver
Pres. Indic.	**veo,** ves, ve, vemos, veis, ven.
Pres. Subj.	**vea, veas, vea, veamos, veáis, vean.**

Imp. Indic.	veía, veías, veía, veíamos, veíais, veían.
Imper.	ve tú, vea Vd., ved vosotros, vean Vds.
Past Part.	visto.

50. yacer

Pres. Indic.	yazco or yazgo, yaces, yace, yacemos, yacéis, yacen.
Pres. Subj.	yazca or yazga, yazcas or yazgas, yazca or yazga, yazcamos or yazgamos, yazcáis or yazgáis, yazcan or yazgan.
Imper.	yace tú, yazca or yazga Vd., yaced vosotros, yazcan or yazgan Vds.

51. Defective Verbs

a. The following verbs are used only in the forms that have an **i** in the ending: abolir, agredir, aterirse, empedernir, transgredir.

b. atañer
This verb is used only in the third person. It is most frequently used in the present indicative: atañe, atañen.

c. concernir
This verb is used only in the third person of the following tenses:

Pres. Indic.	concierne, conciernen.
Pres. Subj.	concierna, conciernan.
Imp. Indic.	concernia, concernían.
Imp. Subj.	concerniera or concerniese, concernieran or concerniesen.
Pres. Part.	concerniendo.

d. soler
This verb is used most frequently in the present and imperfect indicative. It is less frequently used in the present subjunctive.

Pres. Indic.	suelo, sueles, suele, solemos, soléis, suelen.
Pres. Subj.	suela, suelas, suela, solamos, soláis, suelan.
Imp. Indic.	solía, solías, solía, solíamos, solíais, solían.

The preterit is seldom used. Of the compound tenses, only the present perfect is commonly used: he solido, etc. The other tenses are very rare.

e. roer
This verb has three forms in the first person of the present indicative: **roo, royo, roigo,** all of which are infrequently used. In the present subjunctive the preferable form is **roa, roas, roa,** etc., although the forms **roya** and **roiga** are found.

52. Irregular Past Participles

abrir—abierto	deshacer—deshecho
absorber—absorbido, absorto	devolver—devuelto
bendecir—bendecido, bendito	disolver—disuelto
componer—compuesto	encubrir—encubierto
cubrir—cubierto	entreabrir—entreabierto
decir—dicho	entrever—entrevisto
deponer—depuesto	envolver—envuelto
descomponer—descompuesto	escribir—escrito
describir—descrito	freir—frito, freído
descubrir—descubierto	hacer—hecho
desenvolver—desenvuelto	imprimir—impreso

inscribir—**inscrito**	resolver—**resuelto**
maldecir—maldecido, **maldito**	revolver—**revuelto**
morir—**muerto**	romper—rompido, **roto**
poner—**puesto**	satisfacer—**satisfecho**
prescribir—**prescrito**	subscribir—**subscrito**
proscribir—**proscrito**	ver—**visto**
proveer—proveído, **provisto**	volver—**vuelto**

A Short History of the Spanish Language

Introduction

In a sense, Latin is not dead. The speech of Roman soldiers, merchants, and colonists, the spoken Latin of another day, was taken bodily to Iberia, Gaul, Dacia, and many other regions that became parts of the Roman Empire. As this spoken Latin developed under the influence of the languages native to the areas, it became known eventually by several other names, according to the vast political entities that gradually took shape: Spanish, Portuguese, French, Italian, Romanian, and so forth.

The Latin of north central Spain (Iberia) came to be called Castilian, since its speakers were from the province of Castilla (Latin *Castella,* "castles"), and although later it was referred to as Spanish **(español),** to this day the people of many regions call it **castellano,** and the children of Argentina and Chile, for instance, study **composición castellana.**

Castilian became prominent among the other Latin dialects in the Iberian Peninsula during the late Middle Ages because of the hegemony of Christian north-central Iberia in the reconquest of the peninsula from the Arabs, Moors, and other Muslims who had conquered most of it between 711 and 718 and who had coexisted with their Christian enemy in most of the area for several centuries, even as these Christians gradually drove them southward toward Africa. After finally taking over the last stronghold, Granada, in early 1492, these same Christians, who were culturally Castilians, left by the thousands from the ports of southern Spain to take an active part in the discovery and settlement of America. Thus it is that the predominence of Castilian over the other manifestations of Latin *(gallego, leonés, aragonés)* is due not to its own nature but rather to nonlinguistic factors: political and military power and organization, church-state relations, and literary ascendance.

Today Spanish **(castellano** or **español)** is the most extensive manifestation of the former spoken Latin. Those who think and express themselves in this language number many more than 300,000,000 and live in some twenty countries, most of which have rapidly growing populations. It is estimated that by A.D. 2000, Spanish will be the language of nearly 500,000,000 people, most of whom will be **hispanoamericanos.** Spanish is one of the principal languages of the world and is to be found in such widely separated parts of the globe as Morocco, Equatorial Guinea, the Philippines (among older people), and in several parts of the United States where there are about twenty million Spanish speakers. Moreover, hundreds of thousands of Jews who were exiled from Spain in 1492 spoke only Spanish, and their descendants now live in Holland, Greece, Bulgaria, Yugoslavia, Turkey, Israel, Egypt, Libya, Syria, the United States, and many countries of Latin America. They are known as Sephardic Jews and are sometimes referred to as **ladinos.**

As the great essayist Ortega y Gasset reminds us, man has history, not nature, and the history of Spanish is a part of the continuum of those who spoke Latin. It is remarkable that Spanish is still so recognizably Latin after nearly two thousand years. About 85 percent of its present forms were brought to Iberia before the time of Christ! Since Spain has suffered many invasions and has also engaged in many conquests, vocabulary from other than Latin sources became a part of what was to be called Castilian or Spanish. Lexical adoptions, so to speak, were to be made from the language of the Visigothic invaders who overran the Iberian Peninsula in the fifth century; from Arabic over some seven centuries; and from several Indian languages of America after 1492, notably Caribbean dialects, Náhuatl (Aztec) of Mexico, and Quechua of the Andean cordillera. In modern times, first French and then English have provided important contributions to the vocabulary.

Of major importance in the evolution of Latin to Spanish over the centuries are changes in physical articulation, in function indicators, in order and arrangement of the various elements, and in lexical items (vocabulary), along with changes in the actual meaning of a given form. The pronunciation of syllables and hence words gradually changed through the principle of least effort and through the influence of such substratum languages as Basque, still spoken by the descendents of those who learned the Romance language that was to be Spanish.

Latin usually indicated grammatical function and situation by affixes (*ad-, pre-, -or, -i,* etc.), while the developing Castilian language tended in some cases to signal these circumstances by prepositions: *Catullus fīlĭō Caesarĭs lĭbrum dat* becomes **Catullus da al hijo el libro de César.** Of the six grammatical cases of Latin—nominative, genitive, dative, accusative, ablative, and vocative—Spanish generally kept only the accusative. The functions signaled by *ō* in *fīlĭō* and by *ĭs* in *Caesarĭs* are taken over by **al** and **de** respectively. Although word order in Latin was quite flexible, Spanish order became more fixed because of, among other things, the use of prepositions in the place of suffixes.

During the evolution of the language, some terms gradually took on new shades of meaning, while others were lost or replaced by vocabulary foreign to the Latin continuum. Latin *ĕquus* ("horse") was replaced by *căballus* (Spanish **caballo**), the original meaning of which was "nag." The Latin *cănis* ("dog") was replaced by **perro,** probably of Iberian origin. In many cases Castilian developed pairs from one Latin term, one learned and the other popular: *căthedra* ("chair") gave both **cátedra** ("class," "audience," "professorship"), and **cadera** ("hip"); *causam* ("cause") became both **causa** ("cause") and **cosa** ("thing"); for "cold," both **frígido** and **frío** exist, one poetic and one of everyday use.

Sound Changes in the Evolution of Latin to Spanish

All languages tend to change gradually through the centuries, some faster than others, and some more consistently than others. Since the Middle Ages, Spanish appears to have changed much more slowly than English and more consistently than French. In all languages, one can cite and describe certain trends in these changes, and on the basis of frequency of occurrence, one can establish "rules" of transformation: this particular sound or syllable tends to become that under these circumstances; e.g. the *ŏ* of Latin tends to change to *ue* when it is stressed. The Latin *pŏrta* becomes **puerta** in Spanish. The forces behind the changes can't always be identified, but one of them is analogy, whereby two distinctive features are leveled to one. One such change in

American English has been the leveling of *wh* and *w* to *w,* so that *which* and *witch* sound alike in the speech of millions, especially in the large cities of the Eastern United States.

One interesting case of leveling is that of the Spanish sibilants or "whistling sounds." Old Spanish (during the Middle Ages and up to 1492, let's say) had six sibilants (dental, alveolar, palatal):

/s/ spelled *ç* or *z* (syllable final): **çapato, luz, haces**
/z/ spelled *z:* **dezir, hazes, zero**
/S/ spelled *s* (*ss* between vowels): **seis, classe, osso**
/Z/ spelled *s* (between vowels or final): **cosa, casas, oso**
/š/ spelled *x:* **dixe, exe, relox**
/ž/ spelled *j* (*g* before *i* and *e*): **jardín, ojo, gente**

These basic sounds (phonemes) first began to "level" by losing the distinction between voiced and voiceless qualities (the /z/, /Z/, and /ž/ were voiced). Thus both **haces** and **hazes** leveled to **haces** [háseS] (the *h* represented an aspirate then). Likewise **osso** and **oso** leveled to [óSo] phonetically. To the listener, there was no longer any difference between **osso** (bear) and **oso** (I dare), nor between **haces** (bundles) and **hazes** (you do). The spelling wasn't changed until centuries later. Besides analogy, there is an element of less effort in all this.

In the late sixteenth century another loss of distinction began to be evident. The sibilant spelled *s* or *ss,* and today pronounced in all of northern and central Spain with an alveolar articulation (the point of the tongue turned up toward the upper gum ridge), gradually leveled to the same articulation as the [s] of **çapato,** first in the area of Sevilla and finally in nearly all of Andalucía and much of Extremadura, perhaps reinforced by the speech habits of those who had lived longer under Arabic domination. This change became especially important with the conquest and settlement of the Americas, because about 70 percent of those who settled the American colonies of Spain during the first two centuries of colonization were from southwestern Andalucía and Extremadura.

The final stage of this sibilant leveling has been going on since the seventeenth century in southwestern Spain and in regions of America accessible to influences from the mother country during the colonial period, that is, coastal areas on the trade routes, especially the Caribbean and coastal South America: the aspiration or complete elimination of the sound (**hasta dos o tres** [áhta doh o treh] or [áta do o tre]).

A process that is quite consistent in the evolution of Spanish is the tendency to voice the unvoiced consonants between vowels and to eliminate those that are already voiced. Good examples of the two developments in a single word are **dĭgĭtu** to **dedo** ("finger") and **cŭbĭtu** to **codo** ("elbow"). A case of three voiceless consonants changing to voiced is to be seen in **apothēca** to **bodega** ("wine cellar," "storeroom"). As in the case of **căthedra** some Latin terms were retained as learned forms but also evolved along popular lines.

Since both Spain and Portugal were exploring and colonizing distant lands after 1485, the spellings of these two languages were applied to the representation of languages spoken in the newly discovered territories and are still in evidence today. The letter *x,* for example, came to represent [š] (the *sh* of English) in the Indian languages of America and in several languages of Asia, because it represented this sound in Spanish and Portuguese at that time. The sound has since changed in Spanish but still prevails in Portuguese. The map of Mexico is filled with words that have an *x,* and **Mexico** itself was pronounced as if the *x* were English *sh.* An Englishman who was there in the sixteenth century wrote *Washaca* for what is today **Oaxaca.** Sephardic Jews pronounce **dixe** [díše].

Since Castilla is adjacent to the Basque Provinces, it is to be expected that Basque might have had some influence on those who learned the Latin that eventually became **castellano.** Basque had no labio-dentals (/f/ and /v/), and Spanish developed /h/ for the /f/ and /b/ for the /v/ of Latin. Although the /h/ has disappeared (**hierro** is actually [yérro]), Spanish /b/ today may be spelled either *v* or *b: va* and *bah* are [ba]. We now believe that the five vowels of Basque may account for the leveling of seven in popular Latin, and that the strong /rr/ of Spanish is that of Basque in contrast to a weaker general Romance /rr/.

While Basque must have contributed considerably to the phonology of Spanish, Arabic contributed a great deal to the vocabulary during the more than seven centuries that it was spoken in at least part of the peninsula. Hundreds of words from Arabic form part of the Castilian lexicon today, among them **ojalá** ("would that, I hope that"), in which we see the Arabic **Allah;** *alcalde* ("mayor"), and incidentally the English *mayor,* is from Spanish! **Alcohol, algebra, alfalfa, algodón** ("cotton") are all from Arabic, as are *arroz* ("rice"), **azúcar** ("sugar"), *naranja* ("orange"), **Gibraltar, Guadalquivir, Guadalupe, Guadalajara,** and even **cero** ("zero"), an Arabic concept.

The Spanish Language in America

The Spanish of Latin America, like most "colonial" speech, tends to be conservative in its structural changes compared with that of the mother country. In addition, it reflects regional traits of the southwestern part of Spain, notably Andalusia and adjacent areas, from where a large part of the sailors, conquistadores, and cólonists came. In other words, the Spanish of America would seem to be Andalusian Castilian of the sixteenth and seventeenth centuries, as far as pronunciation and grammar are concerned. But in vocabulary hundreds of Indian words have entered the language, especially in Mexico, Guatemala, the Andes (Ecuador, Peru, and Bolivia), and in the Río de la Plata region. The Indian words of the Caribbean islands were taken to other parts of Latin America by the original Spanish settlers and often form a part of the general Spanish lexicon. It should be noted that these Indian languages belong to distinct, unrelated families, so that an **ahuacate** (avocado) in Mexico and Central America becomes a **palta** in the Andes. Although Spanish Americans generally have little difficulty understanding each other, the following variants represent rather extreme divergences:

	Little boy	*bus*	*blond*
Mexico	**chamaco**	**camión**	**güero**
Guatemala	**patojo**	**camioneta**	**canche**
El Salvador	**cipote**	**camioneta**	**chele**
Panama	**chico**	**chiva**	**fulo**
Colombia	**pelado**	**autobús**	**mono**
Argentina	**pibe**	**colectivo**	**rubio**
Chile	**cabro**	**micro**	**rubio**
Cuba	**chico**	**guagua**	**rubio**

Although most of these words are actually Spanish (of Latin origin), several are from the Indian languages of the respective areas. The fact that there are differences of this sort is to be expected in a general culture that contains so many national boundaries.

The Pronunciation of Latin-American Spanish

The fundamental phonological traits of American Spanish are to be found in Castilla, but only changes that have taken place in the Andalusian dialect of Castilian have become established in America. Furthermore, these changes apparently took place between the fifteenth and the eighteenth centuries, during the settlement of Latin America. Evidence indicates that inaccessible areas of Spanish America (the mountainous regions of Mexico, Guatemala, Colombia, Ecuador, Peru, Bolivia, as well as Paraguay, inland Venezuela, and northern Argentina) received only the early changes of Andalusian Castilian, while the accessible coastal areas and port cities tend to reflect both early changes and those of the late colonial period. Thus it is that Cuban and Panamanian Spanish resemble that of present-day Sevilla more than does Mexican Spanish or that of Bogotá. In the meantime Madrid Spanish (called Castilian by many North Americans) developed one or two features that never reached America.

The outstanding common feature of American-Spanish pronunciation that goes back to the early colonial period is the so-called **seseo**. About the time of Columbus the people of southwestern Spain began to confuse the two sibilant sounds of **casa** [káSa] ("house") and **caza** [kása] ("hunt") (the capital [S] representing a "thick" alveolar sound and the [s] representing a "normal" dental sound), with the result that only the dental sound survived. Since most settlers of America were from the south, this became the general Spanish-American tendency. **Coser** and **cocer** are alike in southern Spain and in Latin America. The sibilant is a delicate dental one. In northern and central Spain a distinction between these two sounds is still maintained, and the second or dental one has become interdental [θ], similar to the voiceless *th* of English. The former [S] is still apicoaveolar, and to the foreigner approaches the sound represented by English *sh*.

In the seventeenth and eighteenth centuries other changes occurred in the pronunciation of southern Spanish. As has been indicated, these became part of the Spanish of the accessible areas of America, but most did not reach the high mountains and plateaus. The first of these was the aspiration or even the loss of /s/ syllable final. **Estos** becomes [ehtoh] or even [éto], the result of what might be termed a "relaxed" articulation. About the same time the /l/ (written *ll*) tended to be "relaxed" to the extent that it coincided with the /y/ (written *y*), so that **valla** and **vaya** were levelled to [báya] in Andalusia and parts of America. Today Bolivia, Paraguay, and much of Peru and Ecuador still maintain a distinction. One of the latest levelings of Andalusia was the confusion of /l/ and /r/ syllable final. This is heard today in Puerto Rico, Panama, and Venezuela, and to a certain extent in Cuba, the Dominican Republic, and central Chile. **Puerta** sounds like [pwelta], **mar** like [mal] and the infinitives seem to end in /l/. A final Andalusian trait is the velar /n/ [ŋ] as a sign of word boundaries. **Enamora** is [enamóra], but **en amor** is [eŋamór]. English-speakers think of *ng* when they hear **son** and **pan** pronounced [soŋ] and [paŋ].

Perhaps the only outstanding feature of American Spanish that is not traceable to Andalusia is the assibilation of /rr/ [r̃r̃] and /r/ [r̃] final and postconsonantal. This occurs in vast areas of America: Guatemala, Costa Rica, in the eastern cordillera of Colombia, highland Ecuador, Bolivia, Chile, western and northern Argentina, and Paraguay. The maps show the distribution of the distinguishing features of Spanish-American pronunciation.

Syntactic Features

The familiar form of address in Spanish, **tú,** is a direct descendant of the Latin *tu.* The Latin plural form *vos* also came down to Spanish, but by the late Middle Ages it had assumed the function of polite singular as well as familiar plural. To make the distinction, people began to say **vosotros** (you others) for the plural. In the sixteenth century there came into being a very polite form of address: **vuestra merced** (your mercy), used with the third person of the verb, as one might say, "Does his majesty wish to enter?" It has been shortened to **usted.** With this new polite form, **vos,** the former polite singular, lost prestige and became a familiar form. This was the state of affairs when the colonists came to America. As a result, vast sections of Latin America use **vos** instead of **tú** as the singular familiar form of address. All of Spanish America uses **ustedes** for the familiar plural as well as the polite plural. It will be noted in map 1 that the **vos** areas are generally far from the old Viceroyalties of Mexico and Lima. Only in Chile is there a social distinction.

The verb used with **vos** is the modified plural of Old Spanish: **hablás, comés, vivís;** the imperative is **hablá, comé, viví.** The object pronoun and the possessive are from the singular **te, tu,** the object of the preposition, **vos:** and **llevate tu perro con vos.** Since the imperative of **ir** would be simply **i,** the verb **andar** is used instead: **¡andate!** Another interesting syntactic trait is the general tendency to differentiate gender of nouns of occupation and status of people and to create feminine forms where they may not have existed in so-called standard Spanish. **Presidenta, ministra, dependienta, liberala, abogada,** and **arquitecta** have been heard. Equally general are the tendencies to use adjectives as adverbs **(corre ligero, toca el piano lindo)** and to make certain adverbs "agree" with adjectives they modify **(media muerta; medias locas)** as well as to use the impersonal **haber** in the plural **(habían dos; ¿cuántos habrán?).**

The Vocabulary of Spanish America

There are three main tendencies in the development of Hispanic-American lexical elements: (1) to use words that were popular at the time of the settlement of America, especially maritime terms or rural expressions, often out of popular etymology; (2) to adopt Indian words, especially those related to the domestic scene; and (3) to borrow directly from English and to develop cases of correlative analogy due to English influence.

Of the first category are such terms as **flota** for a bus line, **amarrar** for **atar; botar** for **echar; virar** for **volverse.** In the tropical zone of America (from Guatemala south

Map 1

 Vos used instead of tú in informal address.

 In Chile the distinction is one of class: vos is used in the lower economic levels.

Map 2

▦ Aspiration or loss of /s/ syllable final

Map 3

 Distinction between /l̬/ and /y/

 Assibilation of /rr/ and /tr/

through Peru), where there are no seasons of heat and cold, since these depend on altitude, the Spaniards began to call the wet periods **invierno** (winter) and the dry, **verano** (summer). The custom continues to this day in Guatemala, El Salvador, Honduras, Nicaragua, Costa Rica, Panama, Colombia, Venezuela, Ecuador, and Peru. One may ask, **¿qué tal el invierno?** ("How was the winter?") and receive the answer **¡copioso!** ("copious").

Indian words entered the Spanish of America by the hundreds. In the Caribbean the Spaniards learned **tabaco, canoa, huracán, maíz, ají;** in Mexico, from Náhuatl, **chocolate, tomate, coyote, chicle, cacao;** in the Andes, from Quechua, **pampa, quinina, cóndor, puma, poncho;** and in the Río de la Plata region, from Guaraní, **ananá, ñandú, ombú, yajá, tapioca.**

During the twentieth century the influence of English has been strong in Latin America, and the direct borrowings in some areas could be counted in the hundreds: **control, lonche, lonchería, sándwich, jáibol** ("highball"), **cóctel, ponche, bar, twist, chance, fútbol, béisbol, fildear** ("to field"), **jonrón** ("home run"), **noquear** ("to knock out"), **lobista,** and even such verbs as **taipear** ("to type") and **blofear** ("to bluff"). In the realm of correlative analogy or sense loans, English has tremendous influence, and **educación** ("upbringing") takes the place of **pedagogía, instrucción,** and **enseñanza; argumento** ("plot of a story") moves into the slot of **discusión; atender** ("to wait on") into that of **asistir; audiencia** into that of **concurrencia; acta** ("minutes") takes the place of **ley; complexión** ("physical constitution") takes the place of **tez.**

Regional Features: Mexico

Among speakers of Spanish, a Mexican is recognized by his intonation and by his tendency to lengthen the articulation of his /s/ and by his general preference for the consonant over the vowel. If intonation of Spanish is represented in a pattern of four levels, Mexicans, especially males in a "man-about-town" mood, tend to strike a terminal point between standard statement and emphatic statement, giving the utterance a "minor-key" effect. The tensely-grooved /s/ of Mexican Spanish leads to the virtual elimination of unstressed vowels, especially /e/, in rapid speech: **accidentes de coches** may tend to be [aksidénts de kočs].

Typical adjectives of Mexico are **mero** and **puro.** The first of these is so popular that it means not only "mere" but "very," "real," "just," "same," and many other things, and is even used adverbially: **ya merito** ("It won't be long now").

As has been noted, Mexico is the center of Aztec vocabulary that has entered Spanish and eventually many languages of the world; **tomate, chocolate, cacao, coyote, chicle,** and hundreds of less common terms.

Guatemala

The Spanish of Guatemala is characterized by a strong assibilated /rr/ [řř] and by [ř] for /r/ except in intervocalic position. The **jota** tends to be [h] rather than [x], and velar [ŋ] marks open transition. Along with those of other Central-American areas, Guatemalan speakers tend to weaken intervocalic /y/ to the extent that **silla** sounds like [sía] and **bella** like [bea]. Through a process of ultracorrection, **vea** may become [béya]. Guatemalans generally pronounce their /s/ syllable final with clarity and tension.

A fairly universal feature of the Spanish of Guatemala is the **voseo,** or use of **vos** as the subject form of familiar address in the singular. The verb used with this is the plural familiar, but the pronoun objects and possessives are always singular **Cuando te vayas, llévate tu perro contigo,** as one might say in Spain or in Mexico, would be **Cuando te vayás, llevate tu perro con vos** in Guatemala.

Little boys are **patojos** in Guatemala, and blonds are **canches.**

El Salvador, Honduras, Nicaragua

Perhaps more than any other group of independent countries, these three form a linguistic unity in most respects. They represent in phonology a middle point between the highland conservatism (Mexico and the Andes, for instance) and the later trends of the lowlands (Cuba and Panamá, for example). The inhabitants of these countries call each other **guanacos, catrachos,** and **nicas** respectively, and are always talking of Central-American union.

The phonological phenomenon of recent discovery—although it is probably an "archaic" trait—is the occlusive pronunciation of /b/, /d/, /g/ after another consonant, a situation in which they would be fricative in "standard" Spanish.

It is in this region of Central America that one hears a lisped /s/ that approaches [θ] among many residents, and especially among the working classes. As in northern Mexico, the intervocalic /y/ (representing orthographic **y** and **ll**) tends to be a semivowel or even disappears. The **jota** /x/ is [h] in all speakers, and there is a strong tendency to aspirate syllable final /s/.

The Salvador-Honduras-Nicaragua region is rich in forms of combinative analogy, especially noun formation on the basis of other nouns. The suffixes **-ada** and **-ón** are of extensive application: **babosada, pendejada, lambida, atolada, paisanada, perrada, barbón, narizón, pistón, quemazón;** and the longer diminutive form **-ecito** that might be used in Spain and in Mexico is simply **-ito: llavita, lucita, crucita, piedrita.** The place where things grow or are to be found is indicated by the suffix **-al: cañal, guacal, platanal, cafetal, piñal, pinal.**

Along with Guatemala and the other Central-American countries, except Panama, this region uses the **vos** form of familiar address, and in the way described for Guatemala: **Vení y decime, ¿son vos y tu padre carpinteros?**

Many indigenous words are used in everyday conversation, most of them from the Pipil, a sublanguage of the Náhuatl. A blond is a **chele,** a boy is a **cipote, pushco** is dirty, **peche** is slender, and there is the usual stock of Aztec terms that were imported after the conquest of Mexico.

Costa Rica

Like Guatemala, Costa Rica is noted for its assibilated /rr/, along with assibilated /r/ syllable final. It also shares with Guatemala a fairly conservative articulation of /s/ syllable final. As in all Central-American and Caribbean countries, the /n/ is velar when final, as a sign of open juncture: [eŋ amor] but [enamorár], and intervocalic /y/ weakens to the point of elimination through vocalization.

As a part of the syntactic structure of the dialect, **vos** and related forms operate where **tú** would prevail in Spain or Mexico today, and lexically, Costa Rica shows less Aztec influence than Guatemala, El Salvador, or Honduras.

Costa Ricans are known affectionately as **ticos.**

Panama

The Spanish of Panama might be termed "trade route Spanish," in that it has the phonological character of parts of America that were in constant communication with Spain at the grass-roots level and yet were removed from the courtly influences of the viceregal centers (Mexico and Lima). It resembles strongly the Spanish of Cuba, Puerto Rico, and Venezuela and the northern coast of Colombia.

Along with other Caribbean residents, the Panamanians tend to aspirate their /s/ at the end of a syllable, or to eliminate it entirely.

Colombia

The development of the language in Colombia, which has three high mountain ranges and several important ports, might serve as an example of how American Spanish grew in disparate ways from Peninsular models. The relative inaccessibility of the high sierras and valleys makes it possible to find at least five distinct linguistic zones in the former Nueva Granada. The "dialects" therefore represent stages in the historical development of southern Peninsular Spanish, the most inaccessible regions generally representing the earliest and the most accessible in general representing the latest in Andalusian vogues, before independence.

Strange as it may seem, Colombian Spanish has two general traits in common with that of El Salvador, Honduras, and Nicaragua: the /x/ is [h] in all regions, and the /b/, /d/, /g/ are occlusive after any consonant. Thus **pardo, barba, algo, desde, las vacas,** all have occlusives where a Spaniard or a Mexican would use fricatives.

The Spanish of older Bogotá residents has the conservative distinction of /l/ and /y/ and, like that of Costa Rica and Guatemala, tends to assibilate the /rr/, the /tr/, and the /r/ final.

Pastuso Spanish (or Nariño) is in many ways Ecuadorean, and like the Spanish of highland Mexico, slights the vowel in favor of the consonant, tends to pronounce the /d/ of **-ado,** and uses an apicodental /s/, strong and well defined.

Antioquia's Spanish is unique in America in one way. The /s/ is apicoalveolar [S], like that of Spain, and although no distinction is made between **casa** and **caza,** one Colombian ambassador to Spain, an **antioqueño,** gave the impression of "talking like a Spaniard." The second distinguishing feature of this region's Spanish is the /y/ of such tenseness that it even becomes affricate intervocalically [mayo, kabayo].

Colombia is unusually formal in most sections as far as direct address is concerned. Many speakers use **usted** almost exclusively—even to cats and dogs. Not only is this the case within the family, but some relatives speak to each other as **su merced.** The **voseo** prevails in Antioquia and in Santander and in the **Valle,** while Bogotá and the Coast always employ the **tuteo.**

Typical of Colombia are the idiomatic expressions ¡siga! and ¡a la orden! The first is said to invite one to enter, and the other to ask, "What can I do for you?" Black coffee, especially the demitasse, is a **tinto,** and to invite one to partake, one says: ¿**Le provoca un tinto?** This same sentence to a Spaniard might mean, "Does red wine make you fight?" Instead of sending regards with **saludos,** Colombians use **saludes** ("healths").

Venezuela

The speech pattern of Venezuela is for the most part that of the Caribbean, and therefore late Andalusian. One "eats" his final /s/; /l/ and /r/ are confused at syllable end; /n/ is velar [ŋ] as a sign of word finality; and as in El Salvador, Honduras, and Nicaragua, many people pronounce the /s/ as [θ].

As far as address is concerned most of Venezuela is **tuteo** country, but sections near the Colombian frontier are **vos** areas.

Ecuador

In a country where thousands speak Quechua (the language of the Incas) in preference to Spanish and where many are bilingual, the Spanish language of the upper inter-Andean region is very conservative in its phonological evolution. Ecuadoreans (except those of the coast) still distinguish /l/ and /y/ as [ž] and [y], still pronounce /s/ with deliberate tenseness and, like many Mexicans, slight the vowel in favor of the consonant. Because Quechua is so widely spoken, and because this language has a simple three-vowel system, the Spanish of the highlands tends to heighten /o/ to /u/ and /e/ to /i/. Unique in Latin America is the final /s/ as [z] before a vowel in the following word: [laz aǵwas].

Peru

About 19,000,000 **peruanos,** or as their neighbors may say, **peruleros** or **cholos,** occupy the territory of the central Inca Empire of preconquest days. Their money is counted in **soles** and their babies are **guaguas.** Along with Ecuador and Bolivia, Peru belongs to heavily populated Andean Spanish America, and besides having many Quechua-speaking inhabitants, the region boasts a clear Spanish that gives evidence of sixteenth-century origin and viceregal nurture.

Except in Lima and along the northern coast, Peruvians still distinguish the /l/ and /y/, and the general impression of Peruvian Spanish is similar to that of Mexico, Bolivia, and Ecuador.

Nearly all of Peru uses the **tú** form of familiar address, and as one might expect, hundreds of Quechua words have entered the Spanish of everyday life. In fact, several **quechuismos** have become universal terms: **pampa, cóndor, puma, puna, quinina, llama, alpaca, gaucho, china** (''sweetheart''), **poncho,** and many others.

Bolivia

This country, once Alto Peru, was settled by Spanish colonists from two directions, the high altiplano from Peru and the llanos from Paraguay and Argentina. As a result, Bolivia has two principal manifestations of Andalusian Spanish, a very early type in the highlands and a later form in the lowlands. The later includes changes brought from the Iberian Peninsula via the main trade route to Buenos Aires during the late colonial period.

Bolivia is one of two countries of Spanish America that still maintain a universal distinction between the phonemes /l/ and /y/: *valla* and *vaya* are different.

The highlands, especially La Paz and Potosí, tend to have the apico-alveolar /S/ of northern and central Spain, and the /rr/ tends to be a fricative [řř]. As in Mexico, vowel reduction in the unstressed syllable is common: *Potsí, ofsina, cochs.*

In the lowlands, /s/ syllable final tends to be aspirated or dropped.

Chile

Linguistically, Chile can be divided into three sections, north, middle, and south. The north and the south resemble each other more than they do the middle. The heavily populated central valley partakes of many of the traits of late Andalusian, through the port of Valparaíso and the city of Santiago. Final /s/ is aspirated, /l/ and /r/ are confused in the syllable final situation, and /l̦/ and /y/ are not distinguished. Chiloé still distinguishes these latter two, and in the north there are vowel-heightening influences of Quechua. Two features that seem to characterize all Chilean Spanish are the /č/ of alveolar articulation rather than palatal and the /x/ with a palatal element of semiconsonantal nature before /e/. One seems to hear **la gente de Chile** as [la xjénte de tSíle].

The **five o'clock** tea of Argentina may be **onces** in Chile.

Argentina, Uruguay, Paraguay

The Spanish of this vast territory is of two main types, according to the direction from which the settlers came. The western and northwestern sections were settled from Peru and Chile from about 1590. Although Buenos Aires and the humid Pampa were first settled about 1535, it was not until 1580 that a permanent settlement was established. The important factor producing the differences of today was the accessibility of Buenos Aires and surrounding country to constant influences from the ports of southern Spain in the colonial period. Thus the interior shows more conservative features: an /s/ of more tense articulation, a distinction between /l̦/ and /y/ in some areas, and the assibilated /rr/ of Costa Rica, Bogotá, and Guatemala.

The **porteño** of the Río de la Plata region is noted for his /y/ with strong [ž] articulation: **bayo, calle** [bážo], [káže] and sometimes even [š], especially among women.

Both Argentina and Uruguay are **voseo** territories, and the style has been recorded extensively in gaucho poetry. As a cattle region, the pampas have a lexicon that is rich in the terminology of the ranch and of horses. English and French are contributors to the vocabulary of the area, and one hears of **five o'clock tea a todas horas,** and the frequency of **chau** for "good-by" attests the influence of Italian, the original language of more than half of the inhabitants of Argentina. **Argentinos** are often called **che,** since they use this term to attract attention.

Paraguay, being more inaccessible, has two conservative features in its phonology: the distinction of /l̦/ and /y/, and the assibilation of /rr/. It is unique in that nearly all its inhabitants are bilingual. They speak the original Indian language, Guaraní, and Spanish. The occasion usually dictates which will be used, and speakers will often shift from one to the other in the same utterance.

Cuba, The Dominican Republic, and Puerto Rico

The Spanish of the Caribbean, like that of Panama, could be termed "trade route" Spanish, since it shows rather typically the American evolution of Andalusian trends of the seventeenth and eighteenth centuries, trends that do not seem to be present in the more inaccessible hinterland. Add to this the Afro-Cuban influences of slave days and the many American English loans of the twentieth century, and we have perhaps the least "conservative" Castilian.

Cubans tend to aspirate their syllable final /s/ or drop it altogether, and the tendency is as marked or more so in Puerto Rico and Santo Domingo. In all three, syllable final /l/ and /r/ are confused, most of all in Puerto Rico, where the /l/ is favored: **puerta, izquierdo** [pwélta], [ihkjéldo]. In contrast to Mexico, Ecuador, Peru, and Bolivia, where the vowel may be slighted, those of the Caribbean tend to slight the consonant in favor of the vowel. In Puerto Rico /rr/ is now velar in about half of the population. It resembles the **jota** of Spain: [x]. Thus **rota** sounds like **jota** to other Spanish speakers.

Cuba, Puerto Rico, and the Dominican Republic are **tuteo** countries.

This brief description of some of the features of the Castilian of America may help to show that distinctive features do not correspond to geographical or political entities to the extent that has been believed, and one might indicate as many as a hundred dialects—and yet it is all Spanish.

Numerals—Números

Cardinal Numbers	Números Cardinales	Ordinal Numbers	Números Ordinales[7]
1 ....one	uno, una	first	primero
2 ....two	dos	second	segundo
3 ....three	tres	third	tercero
4 ....four	cuatro	fourth	cuarto
5 ....five	cinco	fifth	quinto
6 ....six	seis	sixth	sexto
7 ....seven	siete	seventh	séptimo (sétimo)
8 ....eight	ocho	eighth	octavo
9 ....nine	nueve	ninth	noveno, nono
10 ....ten	diez	tenth	décimo
11 ....eleven	once	eleventh	undécimo
12 ....twelve	doce	twelfth	duodécimo
13 ....thirteen	trece	thirteenth	décimotercio
14 ....fourteen	catorce	fourteenth	décimocuarto
15 ....fifteen	quince	fifteenth	décimoquinto
16 ....sixteen	dieciséis, diez y seis	sixteenth	décimosexto
17 ....seventeen	diecisiete, diez y siete	seventeenth	décimoséptimo
18 ....eighteen	dieciocho, diez y ocho	eighteenth	décimoctavo
19 ....nineteen	diecinueve, diez y nueve	nineteenth	décimonono
20 ....twenty	veinte	twentieth	vigésimo
21 ....twenty-one	veintiuno, veinte y uno	twenty-first	vigésimo primero
30 ....thirty	treinta	thirtieth	trigésimo
40 ....forty	cuarenta	fortieth	cuadragésimo
50 ....fifty	cincuenta	fiftieth	quincuagésimo
60 ....sixty	sesenta	sixtieth	sexagésimo
70 ....seventy	setenta	seventieth	septuagésimo

7. The ordinals beyond the "tenth" are less used in Spanish than in English. They are often replaced by the cardinals: *Alfonso the Thirteenth* **Alfonso trece.**

80 ....eighty	ochenta	eightieth	octogésimo
90 ....ninety	noventa	ninetieth	nonagésimo
100 ....one hundred	ciento, cien	(one) hundredth	centésimo
101 ....one hundred and one	ciento (y) uno	(one) hundred and first	centésimo primo
200 ....two hundred	doscientos	two-hundredth	ducentésimo
300 ....three hundred	trescientos	three-hundredth	tricentésimo
400 ....four hundred	cuatrocientos	four-hundredth	cuadringentésimo
500 ....five hundred	quinientos	five-hundredth	quingentésimo
600 ....six hundred	seiscientos	six-hundredth	sexcentésimo
700 ....seven hundred	setecientos	seven-hundredth	septingentésimo
800 ....eight hundred	ochocientos	eight-hundredth	octingentésimo
900 ....nine hundred	novecientos	nine-hundredth	noningentésimo
1000 ....one thousand	mil	(one) thousandth	milésimo
100,000 ....one hundred thousand	cien mil	(one) hundred thousandth	cienmilésimo
1,000,000 ..one million	un millón	(one) millionth	millonésimo

Nations, Cities, and Adjectives of Nationality

Afganistán	afgano
Albania	albanés
Alto Volta	voltaico
Arabia Saudita	árabe saudita
Argelia	argelino
Argentina	argentino
Asunción	asunceño
Basutolandia	basutolandés
Bechuanalandia	bechuanalandés
Bélgica	belga
Birmania	birmano
Bogotá	bogotano
Bolivia	boliviano
Brasil	brasileño
Bruselas	bruselense
Buenos Aires	bonaerense or porteño
Bulgaria	búlgaro
Burundi	burundi
Camboya	camboyano
Camerún	camerunés
Canadá	canadiense
Caracas	caraqueño
Ceilán (Sri Lanka)	ceilanés
Colombia	colombiano
Congo (both)	congoleño
Costa de Marfil	marfileño
Costa Rica	costarricense

Cuba	cubano
Chad	chadiano
Checoslovaquia	checoslovaco
Chile	chileno
China	chino
Chipre	chipriota
Dahomey	dahomeyano
Dinamarca	dinamarqués or danés
Ecuador	ecuatoriano
El Salvador	salvadoreño
Escocia	escocés
España	español
Estados Unidos de América	estadounidense
Etiopía	etíope
Filipinas	filipino
Finlandia	finlandés or finés
Francia	francés
Gabón	gabonés
Gales	galés
Gambia	gambio
Ghana	ghanés
Ginebra	ginebrino
Grecia	griego
Guatemala	guatemalteco
Guayaquil	guayaquileño
Guinea	guineo
Haití	haitiano
Honduras	hondureño
Hungría	húngaro
Ifni	ifneño
India	indio
Indonesia	indonesio
Inglaterra	inglés
Irak	iraqués
Irán	iranio
Irlanda	irlandés
Islandia	islandés
Israel	israelí
Italia	italiano
Jamaica	jamaicano
Japón	japonés
Jordania	jordanio
Jerusalém	jerosolimitano
Kenia	kenio
Kuwait	kuwaiteño

Laos	laosiano
La Paz	paceño
Líbano	libanés
Liberia	liberiano
Libia	libio
Lima	limeño
Lisboa	lisboeta or lisbonense
Londres	londinense
Luxemburgo	luxemburgués
Madagascar	malache
Madrid	madrileño
Malasia	malayo
Malavi	malavio
Malí	maliense
Managua	managüense
Marruecos	marroquí
Mauritania	mauritano
México (Méjico)	mexicano (mejicano in Spain)
Mongolia	mongol
Montevideo	montevideño or montevideano
Nepal	nepalés
Nicaragua	nicaragüense
Níger	nigerino
Nigeria	nigeriano
Noruega	noruego
Nueva York	neoyorquino
Nueva Zelanda	neozelandés
Países Bajos	holandés
Pakistán	pakistano
Panamá	panameño
Paraguay	paraguayo
París	parisiense
Perú	peruano
Polonia	polaco
Portugal	portugués
Puerto Rico	puertorriqueño or portorriqueño
Reino Unido de Gran Bretaña e Irlanda del Norte	británico
República Arabe Unida	egipcio
República Centroafricana	centroafricano
República Dominicana	dominicano
República Socialista Soviética de Bielorrusia	bieloruso
República Socialista Soviética de Ucrania	ucranio
Río de Janeiro	carioca

Río Muni	ríomuniense
Rodesia	rodesio
Rumania	rumano
Rusia	ruso
Rwanda	rwandés
San José	josefino
San Pablo	paulista
Santa Cruz	cruceño
Santiago	santiagueño or santiaguino
Senegal	senegalés
Sierra Leona	leonense
Siria	sirio
Somalia	somalí
Suazilandia	suazilandés
Sudáfrica	sudafricano
Sudán	sudanés
Suecia	sueco
Suiza	suizo
Tailandia	tailandés
Tangañica	tangañicano
Tanzania	tanzanio
Tegucigalpa	tegucigalpense
Tenerife	tinerfeño
Tetuán	tetuaní
Togo	togolés
Trinidad y Tobago	trinitario
Túnez	tunecí
Turquía	turco
Uganda	ugandés
Unión de Repúblicas Socialistas Soviéticas	ruso
Uruguay	uruguayo
Venecia	veneciano or véneto
Venezuela	venezolano
Viena	vienés
Yemen	yemenita
Yugoslavia	yugoslavo
Wáshington	washingtoniano
Zambia	zambio
Zanzíbar	zanzibareño

Monetary Units

Exchange rates vary from day to day. Consult your bank.

Country	Basic Unit	Standard Subdivision	Symbol
Argentina	peso nuevo	100 centavos	$
Bolivia	peso	100 centavos	$b
Brazil	cruzeiro	100 centavos	Cr$
Chile	peso	100 centésimos	$
Colombia	peso	100 centavos	$
Costa Rica	colón	100 céntimos	¢
Cuba	peso	100 centavos	$
Dominican Republic	peso	100 centavos	$
Ecuador	sucre	100 centavos	S/
El Salvador	colón	100 centavos	¢
Guatemala	quetzal	100 centavos	Q
Haiti	gourde	100 centimes	G
Honduras	lempira	100 centavos	L
Mexico	peso	100 centavos	$
Nicaragua	córdoba	100 centavos	C$
Panama	balboa	100 centésimos	B
Paraguay	guaraní	100 céntimos	G
Peru	sol	100 centavos	S/
Spain	peseta	100 céntimos	Pts.
Uruguay	peso	100 centésimos	N$
Venezuela	bolívar	100 céntimos	Bs

A : a

a [a] *prep.* to; in, into; on; by.
abacería [a·ba·se·rí·a] *f.* grocery;
grocery store; **abacero**
[a·ba·sé·ro] *m.* grocer.
abad [a·bád] *m.* abbot; **abadía** [a·ba·dí·a] *f.* abbey.
abadejo [a·ba·dé·xo] *m.* *N.Sp.* codfish.
abadesa [a·ba·dé·sa] *f.* abbess.
abajarse [a·ba·xár·se] *v.* to lower oneself, humiliate
oneself.
abajeño [a·ba·xé·ño] *adj. Mex., C.A.* lowland; *n.*
lowlander.
abajo [a·bá·xo] *adv.* down, below; downstairs.
abalanzar[9] [a·ba·lan·sár] *v.* to balance; to hurl, impel;
-se to hurl oneself; to rush (upon), swoop down
(upon); *Am.* to rear, balk.
abalear [a·ba·le·ár] *v.* to "shoot up"; *Am.* to
winnow.
abanderado [a·ban·de·rá·do] *adj.* standard-bearing;
n. standard-bearer.
abandonamiento [a·ban·do·na·mjén·to] = **abandono**.
abandonar [a·ban·do·nár] *v.* to abandon, desert; to
give up.
abandono [a·ban·dó·no] *m.* abandon; desertion;
neglect.
abanicar[6] [a·ba·ni·kár] *v.* to fan.
abanico [a·ba·ní·ko] *m.* fan.
abaratar [a·ba·ra·tár] *v.* to cheapen, lower the price
of.
abarcar[6] [a·bar·kár] *v.* to embrace, contain, include;
Carib., Ríopl. to buy up, monopolize.
abarrancarse[6] [a·ba·rran·kár·se] *v.* to fall into an
opening; to get into a difficult situation.
abarrotería [a·ba·rro·te·rí·a] *f. Mex., C.A., Andes*
grocery, grocery store; **abarrotero** [a·ba·rro·té·ro]
m. Mex., C.A., Andes grocer.
abarrotes [a·ba·rró·tes] *m. pl.* small packages (*in hold
of a ship*); *Mex., C.A., Andes* groceries; **tienda de
— ** *Mex., C.A., Andes* grocery store.
abastecer[13] [a·bas·te·sér] *v. irr.* to supply.
abastecimiento [a·bas·te·si·mjén·to] *m.* supply;
provisions.
abasto [a·bás·to] *m.* supply; **no dar — a** to be unable
to cope with.
abatido [a·ba·tí·do] *adj.* dejected, depressed,
crestfallen, humbled; fallen; lowered.
abatimiento [a·ba·ti·mjén·to] *m.* discouragement,
dejection, depression; descent, swoop, drop.
abatir [a·ba·tir] *v.* to lower; to knock down; to
depress; to humble; **-se** to become discouraged; to
swoop down.
abdicar[6] [ab·di·kár] *v.* to abdicate.
abdomen [ab·dó·men] *m.* abdomen.
abecedario [a·be·se·dá·rjo] *m.* alphabet; primer.
abedul [a·be·dúl] *m.* birch.
abeja [a·bé·xa] *f.* bee; **abejera** [a·be·xé·ra] *f.* beehive;
abejón [a·be·xón] *m.* drone; bumblebee; **abejorro**
[a·be·xó·rro] *m.* bumblebee.
aberración [a·be·rra·sjón] *f.* aberration, mental or
moral deviation.
abertura [a·ber·tú·ra] *f.* aperture, opening, hole, slit.
abeto [a·bé·to] *m.* fir (*tree and wood*).
abierto [a·bjér·to] *p.p. of* **abrir** opened; *adj.* open;
frank; *Am.* proud, self-satisfied; *Am.* generous.
abigarrado [a·bi·ga·rrá·do] *adj.* motley; multicolored;
variegated.
abigeato [a·bi·xe·á·to] *m.* cattle stealing.
abismado [a·biz·má·do] *p.p.* absorbed, buried in
thought; overwhelmed.
abismal [a·biz·mál] *adj.* abysmal.
abismar [a·biz·már] *v.* to overwhelm; to depress; **-se**
to be plunged (into); to bury oneself (*in thought*,

grief, *etc.*).
abismo [a·bíz·mo] *m.* abyss, precipice, chasm.
abjurar [ab·xu·rár] *v.* to abjure; to renounce
solemnly.
ablandar [a·blan·dár] *v.* to soften.
ablativo [a·bla·tí·bo] *m.* ablative.
abnegación [ab·ne·ga·sjón] *f.* abnegation, self-denial,
self-sacrifice.
abnegado [ab·ne·gá·do] *adj.* self-sacrificing.
abnegarse[7] [ab·ne·gár·se] *v.* to deny oneself, sacrifice
oneself.
abobado [a·bo·bá·do] *adj.* stupid, silly.
abocar[6] [a·bo·kár] *v.* to bite; to bring near; to flow
into.
abocinador [a·bo·si·na·dór] *m.* flaring tool.
abocinar [a·bo·si·nár] *v.* to flare; to fall on one's
face.
abochornar [a·bo·čor·nár] *v.* to overheat; to
embarrass; **-se** to get overheated; to blush; to be
embarrassed.
abofetear [a·bo·fe·te·ár] *v.* to slap.
abogacía [a·bo·ga·sí·a] *f.* the legal profession; a law
career.
abogado [a·bo·gá·do] *m.* lawyer.
abogar[7] [a·bo·gár] *v.* to advocate, plead in favor of;
to intercede.
abolengo [a·bo·léŋ·go] *m.* lineage, ancestry;
inheritance, patrimony.
abolición [a·bo·li·sjón] *f.* abolition.
abolir[51] [a·bo·lír] *v.* to abolish; to repeal.
abolsarse [a·bol·sár·se] *v.* to bag.
abollado [a·bo·yá·do] *p.p. & adj.* dented; bumped;
bruised.
abolladura [a·bo·ya·dú·ra] *f.* dent, bump.
abollar [a·bo·yár] *v.* to dent; to bump, to crush,
crumple; to bruise.
abombar [a·bom·bár] *v.* to make bulge; **-se** *Ríopl.* to
get drunk.
abominable [a·bo·mi·ná·ble] *adj.* abominable,
detestable.
abominar [a·bo·mi·nár] *v.* to abominate, abhor,
detest.
abonado [a·bo·ná·do] *m.* subscriber; *p.p. of* **abonar.**
abonar [a·bo·nár] *v.* to credit with; to make a
payment; to endorse, back (*a person*); to fertilize
(*soil*); **-se** to subscribe.
abonaré [a·bo·na·ré] *m.* promissory note; I.O.U.
abono [a·bó·no] *m.* (*monetario*) payment; installment;
endorsement; guarantee; (*del suelo*) fertilizer;
(*suscripción*) subscription.
abordar [a·bor·dár] *v.* to board (*a ship*); to dock, put
into port; to approach; to undertake, take up (*a
matter, problem, etc.*).
aborigen [a·bo·rí·xen] *adj.* aboriginal, indigenous,
native; **aborígenes** [a·bo·rí·xe·nes] *m. pl.*
aborigines, primitive inhabitants.
aborrascarse[6] [a·bo·rras·kár·se] *v.* to become stormy.
aborrecer[13] [a·bo·rre·sér] *v. irr.* to abhor, hate,
detest.
aborrecible [a·bo·rre·sí·ble] *adj.* abominable, hateful.
aborrecimiento [a·bo·rre·si·mjén·to] *m.* abhorrence;
hatred.
abortar [a·bor·tár] *v.* to miscarry, have a miscarriage;
to give birth prematurely; to fail.
aborto [a·bór·to] *m.* abortion, miscarriage; monster.
abotagarse[7] [a·bo·ta·gár·se] *v.* to bloat; to swell.
abotonador [a·bo·to·na·dór] *m.* buttonhook.
abotonar [a·bo·to·nár] *v.* to button, button up; to bud;
-se to button up.
abovedar [a·bo·be·dár] *v.* to vault, cover with a vault;
to arch.

abozalar [a·bo·sa·lár] v. to muzzle.
abra [á·bra] f. cove; mountain gap or pass; dale; Am. breach (in the jungle); Am. leaf (of a door).
abrasador [a·bra·sa·dór] adj. burning, very hot.
abrasar [a·bra·sár] v. to burn; to parch; -se to burn up, be consumed.
abrasivo [a·bra·si·bo] adj. abrasive.
abrazar⁹ [a·bra·sár] v. to hug, embrace; to include.
abrazo [a·brá·so] m. hug, embrace.
abrebotellas [a·bre·bo·té·yas] m. bottle opener.
abrelatas [a·bre·lá·tas] m. can opener.
abrevadero [a·bre·ba·dé·ro] m. drinking trough; watering place for cattle.
abrevar [a·bre·bár] v. to water (livestock).
abreviación [a·bre·bja·sjón] f. abbreviation.
abreviar [a·bre·bjár] v. to abbreviate, shorten, condense.
abreviatura [a·bre·bja·tú·ra] f. abbreviation.
abrigar⁷ [a·bri·gár] v. to shelter, cover, protect; to wrap up; to harbor (fear), cherish (hope); -se to find shelter; to wrap oneself up.
abrigo [a·bri·go] m. shelter, cover, protection; wrap; overcoat.
abril [a·bríl] m. April.
abrillantar [a·bri·yan·tár] v. to polish, shine; to glaze.
abrir⁵² [a·brír] v. to open; to unlock.
abrochar [a·bro·čár] v. to button; to clasp; to fasten.
abrogación [a·bro·ga·sjón] f. repeal.
abrogar⁷ [a·bro·gár] v. to abrogate, repeal, annul.
abrojo [a·bró·xo] m. thistle, thorn; -s reef.
abrumador [a·bru·ma·dór] adj. crushing, overwhelming; oppressive; fatiguing.
abrumar [a·bru·már] v. to crush, overwhelm; to trouble, annoy; -se to become foggy.
abrupto [a·brúp·to] adj. abrupt, steep.
absceso [ab·sé·so] m. abscess.
absolución [ab·so·lu·sjón] f. absolution; acquittal.
absoluto [ab·so·lú·to] adj. absolute; unconditional.
absolver²,⁵² [ab·sol·bér] v. irr. to absolve, free from guilt; to pardon, acquit.
absorbente [ab·sor·bén·te] adj. & m. absorbent.
absorber⁵² [ab·sor·bér] v. to absorb.
absorción [ab·sor·sjón] f. absorption.
absorto [ab·sór·to] p.p. irr. of absorber & adj. absorbed, engrossed; amazed.
abstenerse⁴⁵ [abs·te·nér·se] v. irr. to abstain, refrain.
abstinencia [abs·ti·nén·sja] f. abstinence; fasting.
abstracción [abs·trak·sjón] f. abstraction, reverie.
abstracto [abs·trák·to] adj. abstract.
abstraer⁴⁶ [abs·tra·ér] v. irr. to abstract; to withdraw, remove; -se to be lost in thought.
abstraído [abs·tra·í·do] adj. lost in thought, absentminded; aloof.
absuelto [ab·swél·to] p.p. of absolver absolved, acquitted.
absurdo [ab·súr·do] adj. absurd, ridiculous, senseless; m. absurdity.
abuela [a·bwé·la] f. grandmother.
abuelo [a·bwé·lo] m. grandfather; -s grandparents; ancestors.
abulia [a·bú·lja] f. abulia, loss of will power.
abultado [a·bul·tá·do] adj. bulky, bulgy.
abultar [a·bul·tár] v. to bulge; to be bulky; to enlarge.
abundancia [a·bun·dán·sja] f. abundance, plenty.
abundante [a·bun·dán·te] adj. abundant, plentiful.
abundar [a·bun·dár] v. to abound, be plentiful.
aburrido [a·bu·rrí·do] p.p. & adj. bored; boring, tiresome; weary.
aburrimiento [a·bu·rri·mjén·to] m. weariness, dullness, boredom.

aburrir [a·bu·rrír] v. to bore, vex; -se to become bored or vexed.
abusar [a·bu·sár] v. to abuse, mistreat; to misuse; — de to take unfair advantage of; to impose upon.
abuso [a·bú·so] m. abuse; misuse.
abyecto [ab·yék·to] adj. abject.
acá [a·ká] adv. here, over here; this way, hither.
acabado [a·ka·bá·do] m. a finishing material; paint, varnish; acabado y compostura m. finish and repair.
acabamiento [a·ka·ba·mjén·to] m. finish, completion, end; death; Am. exhaustion, physical decline.
acabar [a·ka·bár] v. to end, finish, complete; — de (+ inf.) to have just; — por (+ inf.) to end by; — con to put an end to, make short work of; to destroy; -se to be over, finished; to be consumed; Am. to wear oneself out; Ríopl., Mex., C.A. to age or decline in health.
academia [a·ka·dé·mja] f. academy; a special school; a scientific, literary, or artistic society.
académico [a·ka·dé·mi·ko] adj. academic; m. academician, member of an academy.
acaecer¹³ [a·ka·e·sér] v. irr. to happen, occur.
acaecimiento [a·ka·e·si·mjén·to] m. event, happening.
acalorado [a·ka·lo·rá·do] adj. heated, excited, angry.
acaloramiento [a·ka·lo·ra·mjén·to] m. heat, ardor, excitement.
acalorar [a·ka·lo·rár] v. (calentar) to heat, warm; (emocionar) to excite.
acallar [a·ka·yár] v. to silence; to calm, quiet.
acampar [a·kam·pár] v. to encamp; to camp.
acanalar [a·ka·na·lár] v. to groove; to flute (as a column); to form a channel in.
acantilado [a·kan·ti·lá·do] adj. sheer, steep (cliff); m. bluff, cliff.
acantonar [a·kan·to·nár] v. to quarter (troops).
acaparar [a·ka·pa·rár] v. to corner (the market); to monopolize; to gather in.
acaramelarse [a·ka·ra·me·lár·se] v. to caramelize.
acarear [a·ka·re·ár] v. to bring face to face; to confront.
acariciar [a·ka·ri·sjár] v. to caress, pet; to cherish (a hope or illusion).
acarreador [a·ka·rre·a·dór] m. carter; carrier.
acarrear [a·ka·rre·ár] v. to cart, transport; to bring about (harm, disaster).
acarreo [a·ka·rré·o] m. cartage, carriage, transport, haul.
acaso [a·ká·so] adv. perhaps; by chance; por si — just in case; m. chance, accident.
acatamiento [a·ka·ta·mjén·to] m. homage, reverence, respect.
acatar [a·ka·tár] v. to revere, respect; to pay homage to; Mex., C.A. Ven. to realize; Mex., C.A., Ven. to notice, pay attention.
acatarrar [a·ka·ta·rrár] v. to chill; Mex. Ven. to bother, annoy; -se to get chilled, catch cold; Ríopl. to get tipsy.
acaudalado [a·kaw·da·lá·do] adj. wealthy.
acaudillar [a·kaw·di·yár] v. to lead, command.
acceder [ak·se·dér] v. to accede.
accesible [ak·se·sí·ble] adj. accessible; approachable.
acceso [ak·sé·so] m. access; entrance, admittance; attack; fit (of madness, anger, etc.).
accesorio [ak·se·só·rjo] adj. & m. accessory.
accidentado [ak·si·den·tá·do] adj. seized with a fit; in a swoon; rough, uneven (ground).
accidental [ak·si·den·tál] adj. accidental, casual.
accidentarse [ak·si·den·tár·se] v. to have a seizure or fit; to swoon, faint.
accidente [ak·si·den·te] m. accident, mishap; chance;

sudden fit, swoon.

acción [ak·sjón] *f.* (*física*) action; act; gesture; (*militar*) battle; (*de bolsa*) share of stock; — **de gracias** thanksgiving.

accionador [ak·sjo·na·ðór] *m.* switch; — **de corriente** power switch.

accionar [ak·sjo·nár] *v.* to gesticulate, make gestures; *Am.* to act, be active.

accionista [ak·sjo·nís·ta] *m. & f*, shareholder, stockholder.

acecinar [a·se·si·nár] *v.* to dry-cure; to salt down.

acecino [a·se·sí·no] *m.* corned beef.

acechanza [a·se·čán·sa] *f.* snare; ambush.

acechar [a·se·čár] *v.* to lurk; to spy.

acecho [a·sé·čo] *m.* ambush; spying; **al** (*or* **en**) — waiting in ambush, lying in wait.

acedo [a·sé·ðo] *adj.* rancid; acid; sour; harsh, disagreeable.

aceitar [a·sej·tár] *v.* to oil, grease.

aceite [a·séj·te] *m.* oil; — **alcanforado** camphorated oil; — **de hígado de bacalao** cod-liver oil; — **de oliva** olive oil; — **de ricino** castor oil.

aceitera [a·sej·té·ra] *f.* oil can; oil cruet (*bottle for the table*).

aceitoso [a·sej·tó·so] *adj.* oily.

aceituna [a·sej·tú·na] *f.* olive; **aceitunado** *adj.* olive green.

aceituno [a·sej·tú·no] *m.* olive tree.

aceleración [a·se·le·ra·sjón] *f.* acceleration.

acelerador [a·se·le·ra·ðór] *m.* accelerator.

acelerante [a·se·le·rán·te] *adj.* stimulator.

acelerar [a·se·le·rár] *v.* to accelerate, speed up; to quicken; to hurry, hasten.

acelga [a·sél·ǵa] *f.* chard.

acémila [a·sé·mi·la] *f.* pack mule.

acendrado [a·sen·drá·ðo] *adj.* pure, without blemish; purified.

acendrar [a·sen·drár] *v.* to refine (*metals*); to purify, cleanse.

acento [a·sén·to] *m.* accent; emphasis.

acentuar[18] [a·sen·twár] *v.* to accentuate, emphasize; to accent; **-se** to become worse (*as an illness*).

acepción [a·sep·sjón] *f.* acceptation, usual meaning.

acepillar [a·se·pi·yár] *v.* to brush; to plane.

aceptación [a·sep·ta·sjón] *f.* acceptance; approval.

aceptar [a·sep·tár] *v.* to accept; to approve; to admit.

acequia [a·sé·kja] *f.* irrigation canal or ditch; *Peru, Ch.* small stream; *Ven., Mex., Andes* sewer.

acera [a·sé·ra] *f.* sidewalk.

acerado [a·se·rá·ðo] *adj.* steely, made of steel; steel-like; sharp.

acerar [a·se·rár] *v.* to steel.

acerbo [a·sér·βo] *adj.* bitter; harsh, cruel.

acerca de [a·sér·ka·ðe] *prep.* about, concerning.

acercamiento [a·ser·ka·mjén·to] *m.* approach; approaching; rapprochement (*coming together*).

acercar[6] [a·ser·kár] *v.* to bring near, draw up; **-se** to get near, approach.

acero [a·sé·ro] *m.* steel; — **parco en carbono** mild steel.

acérrimo [a·sé·rri·mo] *adj.* very sour, very tart; very harsh; very strong, stanch, stalwart, steadfast.

acertado [a·ser·tá·ðo] *adj.* accurate; right; sure.

acertar[1] [a·ser·tár] *v. irr.* to hit (*the mark*); to hit upon; find by chance; to guess right; — **a** (+ *inf.*) to happen to.

acertijo [a·ser·tí·xo] *m.* riddle.

acetileno [a·se·ti·lé·no] *m.* acetylene.

acetona [a·se·tó·na] *f.* acetone.

aciago [a·sjá·ǵo] *adj.* ill-fated, unlucky.

acicalado [a·si·ka·lá·ðo] *p.p. & adj.* polished; dressed

up; adorned; trim, neat.

acicalar [a·si·ka·lár] *v.* to polish; to adorn; **-se** to dress up, doll up.

acicate [a·si·ká·te] *m.* spur; incentive.

acidez [a·si·ðés] *f.* acidity, sourness.

ácido [á·si·ðo] *m.* acid; *adj.* acid, sour.

acierto [a·sjér·to] *m.* right guess; lucky hit; good aim; good judgment; **con** — effectively, successfully.

aclamación [a·kla·ma·sjón] *f.* acclamation, applause.

aclamar [a·kla·már] *v.* to acclaim, cheer, hail, applaud.

aclaración [a·kla·ra·sjón] *f.* explanation.

aclarar [a·kla·rár] *v.* to clarify, explain; to clear up, (*enjuagar*) to rinse; (*amanecer*) to dawn.

aclimatar [a·kli·ma·tár] *v.* to acclimatize, accustom to a climate or new environment.

acné [ak·né] *m.* acne.

acobardar [a·ko·βar·ðár] *v.* to frighten, intimidate.

acogedor [a·ko·xe·ðór] *adj.* friendly; hospitable.

acoger[11] [a·ko·xér] *v.* to receive; to give shelter; **-se** to take refuge.

acogida [a·ko·xí·ða] *f.* reception, welcome; refuge.

acogimiento [a·ko·xi·mjén·to] *m.* reception, welcome.

acojinar [a·ko·xi·nár] *v.* to cushion; to quilt.

acolchar [a·kol·čár] *v.* to quilt.

acólito [a·kó·li·to] *m.* acolyte, altar boy.

acometer [a·ko·me·tér] *v.* to attack; (*emprender*) to undertake.

acometida [a·ko·me·tí·ða] *f.* **acometimiento** [a·ko·me·ti·mjén·to] *m.* attack, assault.

acomodadizo [a·ko·mo·ða·ðí·so] *adj.* obliging; accommodating.

acomodado [a·ko·mo·ðá·ðo] *adj.* well-off, wealthy; suitable, convenient; *p.p. of* **acomodar.**

acomodador [a·ko·mo·ða·ðór] *m.* usher (*in a theater*).

acomodar [a·ko·mo·ðár] *v.* (*cosa*) to arrange, adjust; (*a una persona*) to lodge; to give employment to; **-se** to make oneself comfortable; to adapt oneself.

acomodo [a·ko·mó·ðo] *m.* occupation, employment; arrangement.

acompañador [a·kom·pa·ña·ðór] *m.* companion; accompanist.

acompañamiento [a·kom·pa·ña·mjén·to] *m.* accompaniment; retinue, company.

acompañante [a·kom·pa·ñán·te] *m.* companion; escort; attendant; accompanist.

acompañar [a·kom·pa·ñár] *v.* to accompany; to escort; to be with; (*incluir*) to enclose (*in a letter*).

acompasado [a·kom·pa·sá·ðo] *adj.* rhythmical; measured; slow, deliberate.

acondicionado [a·kon·di·sjo·ná·ðo] *adj.* conditioned; comfortable; air-conditioned; *Am.* adequate, suitable.

acondicionar [a·kon·di·sjo·nár] *v.* to condition; to prepare; to arrange; **-se** to become conditioned or prepared.

acongojar [a·koŋ·go·xár] *v.* to grieve; **-se** to grieve; to be distressed.

aconsejar [a·kon·se·xár] *v.* to advise, counsel.

acontecer[13] [a·kon·te·sér] *v. irr.* to happen, occur.

acontecimiento [a·kon·te·si·mjén·to] *m.* event, happening.

acopiar [a·ko·pjár] *v.* to gather, accumulate, store up.

acopio [a·kó·pjo] *m.* storing; accumulation; stock, store, supply.

acoplamiento [a·ko·pla·mjén·to] *m.* coupling; joint, connection.

acoplador [a·ko·pla·ðór] *m.* coupler; — **acústico** acoustic coupler.

acoplar [a·ko·plár] *v.* to couple, connect; to fit or join together; (*enyugar*) to yoke; to pair, mate.

acorazado [a·ko·ra·sá·do] *m.* armored ship, battleship.

acorazar[9] [a·ko·ra·sár] *v.* to armor.

acordar [a·kor·dár] *v. irr* (*estar conforme*) to arrange, to decide; (*instrumento*) to tune, put in harmony (*stringed instrument*); *Peru, Ch., Ríopl., Mex., Cuba* to grant; **-se** to remember.

acorde [a·kór·de] *adj.* in harmony; in tune; *m.* chord.

acordelar [a·kor·de·lár] *v.* to measure with a cord; to rope off, put a cord around.

acordeón [a·kor·de·ón] *m.* accordion.

acordonar [a·kor·do·nár] *v.* to tie with a cord, string, or rope; to rope off, tie a rope around (*a place*); (*acuñar*) to mill (*a coin*).

acornear [a·kor·ne·ár] *v.* to gore, wound with a horn; (*topar*) to butt.

acorralar [a·ko·rra·lár] *v.* to corral; to surround.

acortamiento [a·kor·ta·mjén·to] *m.* shortening.

acortar [a·kor·tár] *v.* to shorten, diminish; **-se** to shrink; to be shy, bashful.

acosar [a·ko·sár] *v.* to pursue, harass.

acostado [a·kos·tá·do] *adj.* reclining, lying down, in bed; tilted.

acostar[2] [a·kos·tár] *v. irr.* to put to bed; to lay down; **-se** to lie down, go to bed; to tilt.

acostumbrado [a·kos·tum·brá·do] *adj.* accustomed, used, usual, habitual.

acostumbrar [a·kos·tum·brár] *v.* (*enseñar*) to accustom, train; (*soler*) to be used to, be accustomed to; **-se** to get accustomed.

acotación [a·ko·ta·sjón] *f.* marginal note; stage directions (*for a play*); (*límites*) boundary mark; mark on a map showing altitude.

acotar [a·ko·tár] *v.* to mark off (*with boundary marks*); to make marginal notes or citations; to put the elevation marks on (*maps*).

acre [á·kre] *adj.* sour, (*sabor*) tart, sharp; (*tosco*) rude, harsh; *m.* acre.

acrecentamiento [a·kre·sen·ta·mjén·to] *m.* growth, increase.

acrecentar[1] [a·kre·sen·tár] *v. irr.* to increase; to advance, promote.

acreditar [a·kre·di·tár] *v.* to credit; to bring fame or credit to; (*autorizar*) to accredit, authorize, **-se** to win credit or fame.

acreedor [a·kre·e·dór] *adj.* worthy, deserving; *m.* creditor.

acribillar [a·kri·bi·yár] *v.* to riddle; to perforate; to pierce.

acriollar [a·krjo·yár] *v.* to make Spanish American; **-se** to become Spanish American like; to take on Spanish-American customs.

acróbata [a·kró·ba·ta] *m. & f.* acrobat.

acta [ák·ta] *f.* minutes (*of a meeting*); document; **levantar** — to write the minutes.

actitud [ak·ti·túd] *f.* attitude; posture, pose.

activar [ak·ti·bár] *v.* to activate, make active; to speed up, hasten.

actividad [ak·ti·bi·dad] *f.* activity; energy.

activista [ak·ti·bís·ta] *m. & f.* activist.

activo [ak·tí·bo] *adj.* active, lively; *m.* assets.

acto [ák·to] *m.* act; action, deed; ceremony; — **continuo** (*or* **seguido**) immediately after; **en el** — immediately.

actor [ak·tór] *m.* actor; **actriz** *f.* actress.

actuación [ak·twa·sjón] *f.* action; intervention, participation, performance; **-es** legal proceedings.

actual [ak·twál] *adj* present (*time*); of the present month; **-mente** *adv.* at present, nowadays.

actualidad [ak·twa·li·dad] *f.* present time; **-es** latest news, fashions, or events; **de** — current, up-to-date.

actuar[18] [ak·twár] *v.* to act, perform a function or act; to set in motion, cause to act.

acuarela [a·kwa·ré·la] *f.* water color.

acuario [a·kwá·rjo] *m.* aquarium.

acuartelar [a·kwar·te·lár] *v.* to quarter (*troops*).

acuático [a·kwá·ti·ko] *adj.* aquatic; **deportes -s** water sports.

acuchillar [a·ku·či·yár] *v.* to knife; to stab; to slash.

acudir [a·ku·dír] *v.* to come up to; to respond to a call; (*asistir*) to attend, be present; to resort or turn to for help.

acueducto [a·kwe·dúk·to] *m.* aqueduct, water channel or pipe.

acuerdo [a·kwér·do] *m.* agreement; decision, resolution; opinion; (*recuerdo*) remembrance; **estar de** — to be in agreement; **ponerse de** — to come to an agreement; **tomar un** — to take a decision.

acullá [a·ku·yá] *adv.* yonder, over there.

acumulación [a·ku·mu·la·sjón] *f.* accumulation.

acumulador [a·ku·mu·la·dór] *m.* storage battery.

acumular [a·ku·mu·lár] *v.* to accumulate, gather, pile up.,

acuñación [a·ku·ña·sjón] *f.* coinage, minting; wedging.

acuñar [a·ku·ñár] *v.* to mint, coin, to wedge.

acuoso [a·kwó·so] *adj.* watery.

acurrucarse[6] [a·ku·rru·kár·se] *v.* to cuddle, nestle; to huddle.

acusación [a·ku·sa·sjón] *f.* accusation, charge.

acusado [a·ku·sá·do] *p.p. & adj.* accused; *m.* defendant.

acusar [a·ku·sár] *v.* to accuse, denounce; to acknowledge (*receipt*).

acusativo [a·ku·sa·tí·bo] *adj.* accusative.

acuse [a·kú·se] *m.* acknowledgment (*of receipt*).

acústica [a·kús·ti·ka] *f.* acoustics.

acústico [a·kús·ti·ko] *adj.* acoustic.

achacar[6] [a·ča·kár] *v.* to impute, attribute.

achacoso [a·ča·kó·so] *adj.* sickly.

achaparrado [a·ča·pa·rrá·do] *adj.* shrub, of shrub size; squat, squatty.

achaque [a·čá·ke] *m.* slight chronic illness; excuse; pretext; infirmity.

achicar[6] [a·či·kár] *v.* to shorten, to make small; (*vaciar*) to bail (*water*); (*humillar*) to humiliate; *Col.* to kill; *Ríopl.* to tie, fasten; **-se** to get smaller; to shrink.

achicoria [a·či·kó·rja] *f.* chicory.

adagio [a·dá·xjo] *m.* adage, proverb, wise saying.

adaptar [a·dap·tár] *v.* to adapt, fit, adjust.

adecuado [a·de·kwá·do] *adj.* adequate, fit, suitable.

adecuar [a·de·kwár] *v.* to fit, adapt.

adefesio [a·de·fé·sjo] *m.* absurdity, nonsense; ridiculous sight, dress, or person.

adelantado [a·de·lan·tá·do] *p.p. & adj.* anticipated; advanced; ahead; forward, bold; **por** — in advance; *m.* governor of a province (*in colonial Spanish America*).

adelantamiento [a·de·lan·ta·mjén·to] *m.* advancement, progress, betterment.

adelantar [a·de·lan·tár] *v.* to advance; to move forward; to progress; (*mejorar*) to better; **-se** to get ahead.

adelante [a·de·lán·te] *adv.* forward, ahead; **en** — from now on.

adelanto [a·de·lán·to] *m.* advance; advancement; progress; (*mejoramiento*) betterment.

adelfa [a·dél·fa] *f.* oleander.

adelgazar[9] [a·del·ga·sár] *v.* to thin out, taper; **-se** to get thin, slender.

ademán [a·de·mán] *m.* gesture, gesticulation; attitude.

además [a·de·más] *adv.* moreover, besides; — **de** *prep.* in addition to, besides.

adentro [a·dén·tro] *adv.* within, inside; **tierra** — inland; **mar** — out to sea; **hablar para sus -s** to talk to oneself.

aderezamiento [a·de·re·sa·mjén·to] *m.* dressing; (*adorno*) adornment, decoration.

aderezar [a·de·re·sár] *v.* (*embellecer*) to fix up, adorn, beautify, garnish; (*condimentar*) to season, prepare; (*almidonar*) to starch, stiffen.

aderezo [a·de·ré·so] *m.* (*adorno*) adornment, garnish, trappings, finery, set of jewels; (*alimento*) seasoning; (*almidón*) starch, stiffener, filler (*used in cloth*).

adestrado [a·des·trá·do] *adj.* trained, skilled.

adestrar[1] [a·des·trár] *v. irr.* to train; to guide.

adeudado [a·dew·dá·do] *adj.* indebted; in debt; *p.p.* of **adeudar.**

adeudar [a·dew·dár] *v.* to owe; to debit, charge; **-se** to run into debt.

adeudo [a·déw·do] *m.* debt, indebtedness; (*derechos*) duty (*on imports*); debit, charge.

adherencia [a·de·rén·sja] *f.* adherence; attachment.

adherir[3] [a·de·rír] *v. irr.* to adhere, stick.

adhesión [a·de·sjón] *f.* adhesion; attachment.

adicto [a·dík·to] *adj.* addicted; devoted; *m.* addict; follower.

adiestrado [a·djes·trá·do] = **adestrado.**

adiestramiento [a·djes·tra·mjén·to] *m.* training; drill.

adiestrar [a·djes·trár] = **adestrar.**

adinerado [a·di·ne·rá·do] *adj.* wealthy.

¡adiós! [a·djós] *interj.* good-bye!; farewell!; (*hola*) hello!; *Am.* you don't say!

aditamento [a·di·ta·mén·to] *m.* addition; annex.

aditivo [a·di·tí·bo] *m.* additive.

adivinación [a·di·bi·na·sjón] *f.* divination, prediction; guess.

adivinanza [a·di·bi·nán·sa] *f.* conundrum, riddle.

adivinar [a·di·bi·nár] *v.* to guess.

adivino [a·di·bí·no] *m.* fortuneteller; soothsayer.

adjetivo [ad·xe·tí·bo] *m. & adj.* adjective.

adjudicar[6] [ad·xu·di·kár] *v.* to adjudge, award, assign; **-se** to appropriate.

adjuntar [ad·xun·tár] *v.* to put with; to bring together; (*incluir*) to enclose (*in a letter*).

adjunto [ad·xún·to] *adj.* adjoining; attached, enclosed.

adminículo [ad·mi·ní·ku·lo] *m.* accessory; gadget.

administración [ad·mi·nis·tra·sjón] *f.* administration; management; headquarters; *Ven., Mex., Cuba* extreme unction, last sacrament; **administración y gerencia** *f.* public administration and management.

administrador [ad·mi·nis·tra·dór] *m.* administrator, manager.

administrar [ad·mi·nis·trár] *v.* to administer; to manage; **-se** *Ven., Mex., Cuba* to receive the extreme unction or last sacrament.

administrativo [ad·mi·nis·tra·tí·bo] *adj.* administrative.

admirable [ad·mi·rá·ble] *adj.* admirable, wonderful.

admiración [ad·mi·ra·sjón] *f.* admiration, wonder; **punto de** — exclamation point.

admirador [ad·mi·ra·dór] *m.* admirer.

admirar [ad·mi·rár] *v.* to admire; **-se** to be astonished or amazed; to wonder.

admisible [ad·mi·sí·ble] *adj.* admissible, allowable.

admisión [ad·mi·sjón] *f.* admission; acceptance; acknowledgment.

admitir [ad·mi·tír] *v.* (*dejar entrar*) to admit; to let in; (*aceptar*) to accept; (*permitir*) to allow, permit.

adobar [a·do·bár] *v.* to fix, cook, prepare (*food*), to

tan (*hides*); to pickle (*meats, fish*).

adobe [a·dó·be] *m.* adobe, sun-dried mud brick.

adobo [a·dó·bo] *m.* repairing; (*salsa*) sauce for seasoning or pickling; mixture for dressing skins or cloth; rouge.

adoctrinamiento [a·dok·tri·na·mjén·to] *m.* indoctrination, teaching, instruction.

adoctrinar [a·dok·tri·nár] *v.* to indoctrinate, teach, instruct.

adolecer[13] [a·do·le·sér] *v. irr.* to suffer (*from an illness, defect, etc.*).

adolescencia [a·do·le·sén·sja] *f.* adolescence.

adolescente [a·do·le·sén·te] *adj.* adolescent.

adonde [a·dón·de] *rel. adv.* where; **¿adónde?** *interr. adv.* where to?; where?

adoptar [a·dop·tár] *v.* to adopt; to accept (*an opinion*).

adoptivo [a·dop·ti·bo] *adj.* adoptive, related by adoption; adopted.

adoración [a·do·ra·sjón] *f.* adoration, worship.

adorar [a·do·rár] *v.* to adore, worship.

adormecer[13] [a·dor·me·sér] *v. irr.* to make sleepy or drowsy; to lull; **-se** to get sleepy; to get numb; to fall asleep.

adormilado [a·dor·mi·lá·do] *adj.* drowsy.

adornar [a·dor·nár] *v.* to adorn, decorate, ornament.

adorno [a·dór·no] *m.* adornment, ornament, decoration.

adquirir[35] [ad·ki·rír] *v. irr.* to acquire, gain, win, obtain.

adquisición [ad·ki·si·sjón] *f.* acquisition; attainment.

adrede [a·dré·de] *adv.* on purpose, intentionally.

aduana [a·dwá·na] *f.* customhouse.

aduanero [a·dwa·né·ro] *m.* customhouse officer; *adj.* customhouse.

aduar [a·dwár] *m.* gypsy camp; *Ríopl.* Indian camp or ranch.

aducir[25] [a·du·sír] *v. irr.* to cite, allege, offer as proof.

adueñarse [a·dwe·ñár·se] *v.* to take possession.

adulación [a·du·la·sjón] *f.* flattery.

adulador [a·du·la·dór] *m.* flatterer.

adular [a·du·lár] *v.* to flatter.

adulterar [a·dul·te·rár] *v.* to adulterate, corrupt, make impure.

adulterio [a·dul·té·rjo] *m.* adultery.

adúltero [a·dúl·te·ro] *m.* adulterer.

adulto [a·dúl·to] *m. & adj.* adult.

adusto [a·dús·to] *adj.* stern, severe, austere.

advenedizo [ad·be·ne·dí·so] *m.* newcomer, stranger; upstart; *Mex., Carib., Andes* novice, beginner; *adj.* newly arrived; upstart; *Mex., Carib., Andes* inexperienced.

advenimiento [ad·be·ni·mién·to] *m.* advent, arrival, coming.

adverbio [ad·bér·bjo] *m.* adverb.

adversario [ad·ber·sá·rjo] *m.* adversary, opponent, foe.

adversidad [ad·ber·si·dád] *f.* adversity; calamity.

adverso [ad·bér·so] *adj.* adverse; contrary; unfavorable.

advertencia [ad·ber·tén·sja] *f.* notice; warning; advice.

advertir[3] [ad·ber·tír] *v. irr.* to notice; to warn; to advise.

adyacente [ad·ya·sén·te] *adj.* adjacent.

aéreo [a·é·re·o] *adj.* aerial; airy; **correo** — air mail.

aerodinámico [a·e·ro·di·ná·mi·ko] *adj.* aerodynamic; *f.* aerodynamics.

aeródromo [a·e·ró·dro·mo] *m.* airport.

aerofluyente [a·e·ro·flu·yén·te] *adj.* streamlined.

aeronautica [a·e·ro·náw·ti·ka] *f.* aeronautics.
aeronave [a·e·ro·ná·ḇe] *f.* airship.
aeropista [a·e·ro·pís·ta] *f.* landing strip; runway.
aeroplano [a·e·ro·plá·no] *m.* airplane.
aeropuerto [a·e·ro·pwér·to] *m.* airport.
aerosol [a·e·ro·sól] *m.* aerosol.
afabilidad [a·fa·ḇi·li·dád] *f.* friendliness, pleasantness, courtesy; **afable** [a·fá·ḇle] *adj.* affable, pleasant, courteous.
afamado [a·fa·má·do] *adj.* famous.
afán [a·fán] *m.* eagerness, anxiety, ardor.
afanar [a·fa·nár] *v.* to urge, press; **-se** to hurry; to worry; to work eagerly; to toil.
afanoso [a·fa·nó·so] *adj.* laborious, hardworking.
afasia [a·fá·sja] *f.* aphasia.
afear [a·fe·ár] *v.* to make ugly; to disfigure; to blame, censure, condemn.
afección [a·fek·sjón] *f.* affection, fondness; disease.
afectado [a·fek·tá·do] *p.p. & adj.* affected; *Am.* hurt, harmed; *Am.* **estar — del corazón** to have heart trouble.
afectar [a·fek·tár] *v.* (*promover*) to affect, move; (*fingir*) to pretend to have or feel; *Am.* to hurt, to harm, to injure.
afecto [a·fék·to] *m.* affection; *adj.* fond; **— a** fond of; given to; prone to.
afectuoso [a·fek·twó·so] *adj.* affectionate, tender.
afeitada [a·fej·tá·da] *f. Am.* shave, shaving.
afeitar [a·fej·tár] *v.* to shave; **-se** to shave oneself; to put on make-up.
afeite [a·féj·te] *m.* make-up, cosmetics.
afelpado [a·fel·pá·do] *adj.* velvety.
afeminado [a·fe·mi·ná·do] *adj.* effeminate.
aferrado [a·fe·rrá·do] *adj.* stubborn, obstinate; *p.p. of* **aferrar.**
aferramiento [a·fe·rra·mjén·to] *m.* grasping, seizing; attachment; subbornness; tenacity.
aferrar [a·fe·rrár] *v.* to seize, grasp, grapple; **-se** to take or seize hold of; to cling; **-se a una opinión** to cling to an opinion.
afianzar [a·fjan·sár] *v.* to fasten, secure; to steady; to give bail or bond.
afición [a·fi·sjón] *f.* taste, inclination; fondness; affection.
aficionado [a·fi·sjo·ná·do] *adj.* fond; *m.* amateur, fan.
aficionar [a·fi·sjo·nár] *v.* to inspire a liking or fondness; **-se a** to become fond of.
afiche [a·fí·če] *m. Ríopl.,* poster.
afijo [a·fí·xo] *m.* affix.
afilador [a·fi·la·dór] *m.* grinder, sharpener.
afilar [a·fi·lár] *v.* to sharpen; to grind; *Am.* to make love to, woo; *Am.* to flatter; *Am.* **— con** to flirt with.
afín [a·fín] *adj.* kindred, related; **ideas afines** related ideas.
afinado [a·fi·ná·do] *m.* polishing.
afinador [a·fi·na·dór] *m.* piano tuner.
afinar [a·fi·nár] *v.* to refine, polish; (*instrumento*) to tune.
afinidad [a·fi·ni·dád] *f.* affinity; similarity; relationship.
afirmación [a·fir·ma·sjón] *f.* affirmation, assertion.
afirmado [a·fir·má·do] *m.* tamping.
afirmar [a·fir·már] *v.* to affirm, assert; to make firm; *Am.* **— un golpe** to deal a blow.
afirmativa [a·fir·ma·tí·ḇa] *f.* affirmative.
afirmativo [a·fir·ma·tí·ḇo] *adj.* affirmative.
aflicción [a·flik·sjón] *f.* affliction, trouble, (*dolor*) pain, grief.
afligir[11] [a·fli·xír] *v.* to afflict, trouble, grieve; *Ríopl., Ven.* to mistreat, harm, beat, strike; **-se** to worry,

grieve.
aflojar [a·flo·xár] *v.* to slacken; to loosen, unfasten; to let go; *Mex. Ríopl., Carib.* to let go of money, spend easily; *Mex. Ríopl., Carib.* **— un golpe** to hit.
afluente [a·flwén·te] *m.* tributary; *adj.* abundant.
afluir[32] [a·flwír] *v. irr.* to flow (into).
afortunado [a·for·tu·ná·do] *adj.* fortunate; lucky.
afrenta [a·frén·ta] *f.* affront, offense, insult.
afrentar [a·fren·tár] *v.* to insult, offend, dishonor.
afrentoso [a·fren·tó·so] *adj.* outrageous, shameful, disgraceful.
africado [a·fri·ká·do] *adj.* affricative; *f.* affricate.
africano [a·fri·ká·no] *adj & m.* African.
afrontar [a·fron·tár] *v.* to face; to confront.
afuera [a·fwé·ra] *adv.* out, outside; **-s** *f. pl.* outskirts.
agachar [a·ga·čár] *v.* to lower; to bend down; **-se** to stoop, bend down, duck; to crouch; *Am.* to give in, yield; *Col.* **-se con algo** to make away with or steal something.
agalla [a·gá·ya] *f.* gill; tonsil; *Col., Ven.* greed; **tener -s** to have guts, have courage; *Ríopl., Ch., Carib.* to be unscrupulous and bold in business deals; *Ríopl., Ch., Carib.* to be greedy or stingy; *C.A.* to be smart, astute, cunning.
agarrar [a·ga·rrár] *v.* to seize, grasp, grab; **-se** to cling, hold on.
agarro [a·gá·rro] *m.* clench, clutch, grasp, grip. grab; **agarrón** *m.* tight clench, sudden grasp, grab; *Mex., Col., Ven., C.A.* pull, tug.
agasajar [a·ga·sa·xár] *v.* to entertain; to flatter.
agasajo [a·ga·sá·xo] *m.* entertainment, kind reception; friendliness; (*adulación*) flattery.
agazapar [a·ga·sa·pár] *v.* to nab, seize (*a person*), **-se** to crouch; to squat.
agencia [a·xén·sja] *f.* agency; *Ch.* pawnshop.
agenciar [a·xen·sjár] *v.* to negotiate; to procure by negotiation; to promote.
agente [a·xén·te] *m.* agent; *Am.* police officer, official.
ágil [á·xil] *adj.* agile, nimble, limber.
agilidad [a·xi·li·dád] *f.* agility, nimbleness.
agitación [a·xi·ta·sjón] *f.* agitation; excitement.
agitador [a·xi·ta·dór] *m.* agitator; *adj.* agitating; stirring.
agitar [a·xi·tár] *v.* to agitate, excite; (*menear*) to stir; to wave; to shake.
aglomeración [a·glo·me·ra·sjón] *f.* conglomeration, heap, pile, mass.
aglomerar [a·glo·me·rár] *v.* to mass together; to cluster; **-se** to crowd together, pile up.
aglutinante [a·glu·ti·nán·te] *adj.* agglutinative.
agobiar [a·go·ḇjár] *v.* to oppress, weigh down; to overwhelm.
agolparse [a·gol·pár·se] *v.* to crowd together, jam.
agonía [a·go·ní·a] *f.* agony.
agonizante [a·go·ni·sán·te] *adj.* dying; *m.* dying person.
agonizar[9] [a·go·ni·sár] *v.* to be dying.
agorero [a·go·ré·ro] *adj.* ominous, of bad omen; prophetic; *m.* augur, prophet, fortune-teller.
agostar [a·gos·tár] *v.* to parch, dry up; to pasture; to plow (*in August*).
agosto [a·gós·to] *m.* August; harvest; **hacer su —** to make hay while the sun shines.
agotado [a·go·tá·do] *adj. & p.p.* exhausted; out-of-print.
agotamiento [a·go·ta·mjén·to] *m.* exhaustion; draining.
agotar [a·go·tár] *v.* to exhaust, use up; to drain off; **-se** (*acabarse*) to be exhausted, used up;

(*terminarse la edición*) to go out of print.
agraciado [a·gra·sjá·do] *adj*. graceful; *m*. winner (*of a favor, prize, etc.*).
agraciar [a·gra·sjár] *v*. to grace; to adorn.
agradable [a·gra·dá·ble] *adj*. agreeable, pleasant.
agradar [a·gra·dár] *v*. to please, be agreeable (to).
agradecer[13] [a·gra·de·sér] *v*. *irr*. to thank for; to be grateful for.
agradecido [a·gra·de·si·do] *adj*. thankful, grateful.
agradecimiento [a·gra·de·si·mjén·to] *m*. gratitude, thankfulness.
agrado [a·grá·do] *m*. agreeableness; liking, pleasure; **de su** — to his liking.
agrandar [a·gran·dár] *v*. to enlarge; to aggrandize, make greater.
agravar [a·gra·bár] *v*. to aggravate, make worse; to make heavier; (*oprimir*) to oppress; **-se** to get worse.
agraviar [a·gra·bjár] *v*. to offend, insult, affront.
agravio [a·grá·bjo] *m*. offense, insult, affront.
agredir[51] [a·gre·dír] *v*. to assail, assault, attack.
agregado [a·gre·gá·do] *m*. attaché, person attached to a staff; (*colección*) aggregate, collection.
agregar[7] [a·gre·gár] *v*. to add; to join; to attach.
agresivo [a·gre·sí·bo] *adj*. aggressive, offensive.
agresor [a·gre·sór] *m*. aggressor; assailant.
agreste [a·grés·te] *adj*. rustic; (*flora*) wild (*fruit, flower, etc.*).
agriar[17] [a·grjár] *v*. to sour, make sour; **-se** to sour, turn sour, become sour.
agrícola [a·grí·ko·la] *adj*. agricultural.
agricultor [a·gri·kul·tór] *m*. agriculturist, farmer.
agricultura [a·gri·kul·tú·ra] *f*. agriculture.
agridulce [a·gri·dúl·se] *adj*. bittersweet, tart.
agrietarse [a·grje·tár·se] *v*. to crack; to chap (*said of the skin*).
agrimensor [a·gri·men·sór] *m*. surveyor.
agrimensura [a·gri·men·sú·ra] *f*. survey, surveying (*of land*).
agrio [á·grjo] *adj*. sour; disagreeable.
agropecuario [a·gro·pe·kwá·rjo] *adj*. farming (*crops and cattle*).
agrupación [a·gru·pa·sjón] *f*. group; bunch; grouping; gathering.
agrupar [a·gru·pár] *v*. to group, bunch up.
agrura [a·grú·ra] *f*. sourness.
agua [á·gwa] *f*. water; rain; — **abajo** downstream; — **arriba** upstream; **aguas inmundas** *f*. sewage.
aguacate [a·gwa·ká·te] *m*. *Mex., C.A., Carib., Col., Ven*. avocado, alligator pear; *Am*. avocado tree; *Am*. phlegmatic person.
aguacero [a·gwa·sé·ro] *m*. shower. *C.A.*, party to honor.
aguada [a·gwá·da] *f*. watering place; supply of drinking water; flood; wall wash; water color.
aguadero [a·gwa·dé·ro] *m*. watering place.
aguado [a·gwá·do] *adj*. watery; watered; *Am*. soft, unstarched; *Am*. weak, limp; *Andes* insipid, uninteresting, dull; **sopa aguada** thin soup; *p.p. of* **aguar**.
aguaitar [a·gwaj·tár] *v*. *Col., Ven., Andes, Ch*. to spy; to watch; to wait for.
aguantar [a·gwan·tár] *v*. to endure, bear; to resist; **-se** to be silent, restrain oneself.
aguante [a·gwán·te] *m*. endurance, fortitude, resistance.
aguar[9] [a·gwár] *v*. to water, dilute with water; to spoil (*pleasure*); *Ríopl., Ven., C.A*. to water (*livestock*); **-se** to become diluted; to get watery; to fill up with water; **se aguó la fiesta** the party was spoiled.

aguardar [a·gwar·dár] *v*. to wait; to wait for.
aguardentoso [a·gwar·den·tó·so] *adj*. alcoholic; (*ronco*) hoarse, raucous.
aguardiente [a·gwar·djén·te] *m*. brandy, hard liquor; — **de caña** rum.
aguarrás [a·gwa·rrás] *m*. turpentine, oil of turpentine.
aguazal [a·gwa·sál] *m*. marsh, swamp.
agudeza [a·gu·dé·sa] *f*. sharpness; keenness; (*viveza*) wit; witty remark or saying.
agudo [a·gú·do] *adj*. sharp; sharp-pointed; (*listo*) keen, witty; acute; shrill.
agüero [a·gwé·ro] *m*. augury, prediction; sign, omen; *Ríopl., Mex., Carib*. fortune-teller.
aguijar [a·gi·xár] *v*. (*picar*) to prick, goad, spur; (*animar*) to encourage, excite.
aguijón [a·gi·xón] *m*. prick; sting; spur, goad.
aguijonear [a·gi·xo·ne·ár] *v*. to goad; to prick.
águila [á·gi·la] *f*. eagle; **es un** — he is sharp.
aguileño [a·gi·lé·ño] *adj*. aquiline; eaglelike.
aguinaldo [a·gi·nál·do] *m*. Christmas or New Year's gift; bonus.
aguja [a·gú·xa] *f*. needle; crochet hook; watch hand; church spire; railroad switch.
agujerear [a·gu·xe·re·ár] *v*. to pierce, perforate; to riddle.
agujero [a·gu·xé·ro] *m*. hole; (*vendedor*) needle peddler; (*caja*) needle box; pincushion; **agujeros de burbuja** *m*. blowholes.
aguzar[9] [a·gu·sár] *v*. to sharpen; to goad, stimulate; — **las orejas** to prick up one's ears.
ahí [a·í] *adv*. there; **por** — over there.
ahijado [a·i·xá·do] *m*. godchild.
ahijar [a·i·xár] *v*. to adopt.
ahínco [a·íŋ·ko] *m*. effort, eagerness, zeal.
ahogar[7] [a·o·gár] *v*. to drown; (*estrangular*) to choke, strangle; to smother; (*apagar*) to quench, extinguish.
ahogo [a·ó·go] *m*. suffocation; breathlessness; (*angustia*) anguish, grief.
ahondar [a·on·dár] *v*. to deepen, to dig; to penetrate, go deep into.
ahora [a·ó·ra] *adv*. now; — **mismo** right now; **por** — for the present; — **que** *Am*. as soon as; **ahorita** [a·o·rí·ta] instantly, this very minute; **ahoritica** [a·o·ri·tí·ka], **ahoritita** [a·o·ri·tí·ta] *Am*. this very second, in a jiffy.
ahorcar[6] [a·or·kár] *v*. to hang, kill by hanging.
ahorrar [a·o·rrár] *v*. to save; to spare; to avoid.
ahorro [a·ó·rro] *m*. saving, economy; **caja de -s** savings bank.
ahuecar[6] [a·we·kár] *v*. to make hollow; to hollow out; — **la voz** to speak in a hollow voice; *Am*. **¡ahueca!** get out of here!; **-se** to become puffed up, get conceited.
ahuehuete [a·we·wé·te] *m*. *Mex., C.A*. a Mexican cypress.
ahumado [a·u·má·do] *adj*. smoked; smoky.
ahumar [a·u·már] *v*. to smoke; to fume.
ahuyentar [a·u·yen·tár] *v*. to drive away; to scare away; **-se** to go away, flee; *Ven., Carib., Mex*. to stop frequenting a place.
aindiado [ajn·djá·do] *adj*. Indian-like.
airado [aj·rá·do] *adj*. irate; angry.
airar [aj·rár] *v*. to annoy, irritate; **-se** to get angry.
aire [áj·re] *m*. air; wind; (*melodía*) tune; (*aspecto*) appearance; conceit; **-cito** *m*. breeze; a little tune; a certain air or appearance.
airear [aj·re·ár] *v*. to air, ventilate.
airoso [aj·ró·so] *adj*. windy; airy; graceful, elegant; lively, spirited.
aislador [ajz·la·dór] *m*. insulator; isolator; *adj*.

insulating; isolating.
aislamiento [ajz·la·mjén·to] *m.* isolation; insulation.
aislar [ajz·lár] *v.* to isolate, place apart; to insulate.
¡ajá! [a·xá] *interj.* great! fine! so!
ajar [a·xár] *v.* to crumple, wither.
ajedrez [a·xe·drés] *m.* chess.
ajenjo [a·xéŋ·xo] *m.* absynthe.
ajeno [a·xé·no] *adj.* (*de otro*) another's; (*inconciente*) unaware; (*extranjero*) alien; — **a mi voluntad** beyond my control; — **de cuidados** free from cares.
ajetrearse [a·xe·tre·ár·se] *v.* to hustle and bustle, (*cansarse*) to get tired out.
ajetreo [a·xe·tré·o] *m.* bustle, hustle; hubbub; fuss; (*cansancio*) fatigue.
ají [a·xí] *m. S.A., Carib.* chili pepper, chili sauce.
ajo [á·xo] *m.* garlic; garlic clove; garlic sauce; (*maldición*) swear word.
ajuar [a·xwár] *m.* furniture set; trousseau, bride's outfit; bride's portion or dowry.
ajustado [a·xus·tá·do] *adj.* tight, fitting tight; (*acordado*) agreed upon (*as a price*); — **a la ley** in accordance with the law; *p.p. of* **ajustar.**
ajustamiento [a·xus·ta·mjén·to] *m.* adjustment.
ajustar [a·xus·tár] *v.* to adjust; to fit tight; to regulate; to tighten; to settle (*accounts*); (*nombrar*) to hire (*a person*); *Col.* to stint, scrimp, save; *C.A.* — **una bofetada** to give a good slap; *C.A., Mex.* **hoy ajusta quince años** he is just fifteen years old today; **-se** to come to an agreement.
ajuste [a·xús·te] *m.* adjustment, fit; agreement; settlement (*of accounts*); truing.
adjusticiar [a·xus·ti·sjár] *v.* to execute, put to death.
al [al] = **a** + **el** to the.
ala [á·la] *f.* wing; hat brim.
alabanza [a·la·bán·sa] *f.* praise.
alabar [a·la·bár] *v.* to praise.
alabastro [a·la·bás·tro] *m.* alabaster.
alacena [a·la·sé·na] *f.* cupboard; closet; *Am.* booth, stall, market stand.
alacrán [a·la·krán] *m.* scorpion.
alado [a·la·do] *adj.* winged.
alambicado [a·lam·bi·ka·do] *p.p. & adj.* distilled; over-refined, (*sutil*) over-subtle (*applied to style*).
alambique [a·lam·bí·ke] *m.* still.
alambrada [a·lam·brá·da] *f.* wire, entanglement.
alambrado [a·lam·brá·do] *m.* wire fence; wire screening; wiring.
alambre [a·lám·bre] *m.* wire.
alameda [a·la·mé·da] *f.* poplar grove; park.
álamo [á·la·mo] *m.* poplar.
alancear [a·lan·se·ár] *v.* to lance, spear.
alano [a·lá·no] *m.* mastiff.
alarde [a·lár·de] *m.* boast, bluff, brag.
alardear [a·lar·de·ár] *v.* to boast, brag.
alargar[7] [a·lar·gár] *v.* to lengthen; to prolong; to stretch out, extend.
alarido [a·la·rí·do] *m.* shout, scream, howl.
alarma [a·lár·ma] *f.* alarm.
alarmar [a·lar·már] *v.* to alarm.
alazán [a·la·sán] *adj.* chestnut-colored; sorrel.
alba [ál·ba] *f.* dawn; alb (*white robe worn by priest*).
albacea [al·ba·sé·a] *m.* executor.
albañal [al·ba·ñál] *m.* sewer.
albañil [al·ba·ñíl] *m.* mason, brickmason; **albañilería** [al·ba·ñi·le·rí·a] *f.* masonry.
albaricoque [al·ba·ri·kó·ke] *m.* apricot; **albaricoquero** [al·ba·ri·ko·ke·ro] *m.* apricot tree.
albayalde [al·ba·yál·de] *m.* white lead.
albazo [al·bá·so] *m. Mex.* early morning serenade; *Mex.* bad surprise, surprise attack at dawn.

albear [al·be·ár] *v.* to show white (*in the distance*); *Am.* to rise at dawn.
albedrío [al·be·drí·o] *m.* free will.
albéitar [al·béj·tar] *m.* veterinary.
alberca [al·bér·ka] *f.* water reservoir, tank; *Mex.* swimming pool.
albergar[7] [al·ber·gár] *v.* to house, shelter, lodge; **-se** to take shelter; to lodge.
albino [al·bí·no] *m. & f.* albino.
albo [ál·bo] *adj.* white; *Am.* white-footed (*horse*).
albóndiga [al·bón·di·ga] *f.* meat ball; fish ball.
albor [al·bór] *f.* dawn; whiteness.
alborada [al·bo·rá·da] *f.* dawn; reveille (*morning bugle call*).
alborear [al·bo·re·ár] *v.* to dawn.
alborotador [al·bo·ro·ta·dór] *m.* agitator, troublemaker.
alborotar [al·bo·ro·tár] *v.* to disturb, upset; *Am.* to excite, arouse enthusiasm; **-se** to get upset; to mutiny; to riot; *Am.* to get excited; *Am.* to rear, balk (*said of a horse*).
alboroto [al·bo·ró·to] *m.* uproar, disturbance; riot; *Am.* excitement, enthusiasm; *Col., C.A.* popcorn, candied popcorn ball.
alborozado [al·bo·ro·sá·do] *adj.* elated, excited.
alborozar[9] [al·bo·ro·sár] *v.* to gladden; **-se** to rejoice.
alborozo [al·bo·ró·so] *m.* joy, delight.
albricias [al·brí·sjas] *f. pl.* good news; reward (*for good news*).
alcachofa [al·ka·có·fa] *f.* artichoke; *Ch.* blow.
alcahuete [al·ka·wé·te] *m.* procurer, panderer; gobetween; **alcahueta** *f.* bawd, procuress, gobetween.
alcaide [al·káj·de] *m.* warden (*of a fortress, prison, etc.*).
alcalde [al·kál·de] *m.* mayor; justice of the peace; — **mayor** mayor.
alcance [al·kán·se] *m.* (*extensión*) reach, scope; (*capacidad*) talent, capacity; (*noticas*) last minute news, newspaper extra; **cortos -s** meagre intellect; **dar** — **a** to catch up with.
alcancía [al·kan·sí·a] *f.* money box (*with slit for coin*); savings bank.
alcanfor [al·kan·fór] *m.* camphor.
alcantarilla [al·kan·ta·rí·ya] *f.* conduit; drain.
alcantarillado [al·kan·ta·ri·yá·do] *m.* sewage system.
alcanzado [al·kan·sá·do] *adj.* needy; broke, short of funds.
alcanzar[9] [al·kan·sár] *v.* to reach; to overtake; (*obtener*) to obtain; (*suceder*) to befall; (*bastar*) to be enough; *Am.* to hand, pass, put within reach.
alcaravea [al·ka·ra·bé·a] *f.* caraway.
alcayata [al·ka·yá·ta] *f.* wall hook; meat hook.
alcázar [al·ká·sar] *m.* castle, fortress.
alcoba [al·kó·ba] *f.* alcove, bedroom.
alcohol [al·ko·ól] *m.* alcohol; **alcohólico** [al·ko·ó·li·ko] *adj.* alcoholic.
alcor [al·kór] *m.* hill.
alcornoque [al·kor·nó·ke] *m.* cork tree; cork wood; (*tonto*) blockhead, dunce.
alcuza [al·kú·sa] *f.* oil can; cruet, oil bottle.
aldaba [al·dá·ba] *f.* knocker (*of a door*); crossbar, bolt, latch; handle (*of a door, chest, etc.*); **tener buenas -s** to have "pull", influential connections.
aldabón [al·da·bón] *m.* large iron knocker; large handle; **aldabonazo** [al·da·bo·ná·so] *m.* knock, knocking.
aldea [al·dé·a] *f.* village; **aldehuela** [al·de·wé·la] *f.* little village, hamlet.
aldeano [al·de·á·no] *adj.* rustic, countrified; *m.* villager; peasant.

aleación [a·le·a·sjón] *f.* alloy; alloying.
alear [a·le·ár] *v.* to alloy, mix (*metals*); (*moverse*) to flutter; to flap (*wings, arms, etc.*).
aleccionar [a·lek·sjo·nár] *v.* to coach; to teach, instruct; to train; to drill.
aledaños [a·le·dá·ños] *m. pl.* borders, frontiers.
alegar[7] [a·le·gár] *v.* to allege, assert; *Am.* to argue, dispute.
alegato [a·le·gá·to] *m.* allegation; assertion.
alegrar [a·le·grár] *v.* to cheer up, gladden; to brighten; **-se** to be glad, rejoice; to get tipsy.
alegre [a·lé·gre] *adj.* merry, gay, joyful, cheerful, bright; tipsy.
alegría [a·le·grí·a] *f.* joy, mirth, gaiety, merriment.
alejamiento [a·le·xa·mjén·to] *m.* withdrawal; retirement, aloofness.
alejar [a·le·xár] *v.* to remove, move away from; **-se** to move away; to withdraw, be aloof.
alelado [a·le·lá·do] *adj.* stupefied, open-mouthed; silly.
alemán [a·le·mán] *adj. & m.* German.
alentar[1] [a·len·tár] *v. irr.* to breathe; (*animar*) to encourage, cheer, cheer up; **-se** to take heart; *Am.* to recover (*from illness*).
alergia [a·lér·xja] *f.* allergy.
alero [a·lé·ro] *m.* eaves; projecting edge.
alerón [a·le·rón] *m.* aileron; flap.
alerto [a·lér·to] *adj.* alert, watchful; ¡**alerta!** attention! look out!; **estar alerta** to be on the alert.
aleta [a·lé·ta] *f.* small wing; flap; fin.
aletargado [a·le·tar·gá·do] *adj.* drowsy, sluggish.
aletargarse[7] [a·le·tar·gár·se] *v.* to fall into a state of lethargy; to become drowsy.
aletazo [a·le·tá·so] *m.* flap, blow with a wing.
aletear [a·le·te·ár] *v.* to flap, flutter.
aleteo [a·le·té·o] *m.* flapping, flutter (*of wings*).
aleve [a·lé·be] *adj.* treacherous.
alevosía [a·le·bo·sí·a] *f.* treachery.
alevoso [a·le·bó·so] *adj.* treacherous.
alfabeto [al·fa·bé·to] *m.* alphabet.
alfalfa [al·fál·fa] *f.* alfalfa; **alfalfar** [al·fa·fár] *m.* alfalfa field.
alfarería [al·fa·re·rí·a] *f.* pottery; **alfarero** [al·fa·ré·ro] *m.* potter.
alfeñicar[6] [al·fe·ñi·kár] *v.* to frost with sugar (*a cake, cookie, etc.*); **-se** to get frail, delicate; to act affectedly.
alfeñique [al·fe·ñí·ke] *m.* sugar paste; delicate person; gingerbread.
alférez [al·fé·res] *m.* ensign; second lieutenant.
alfil [al·fíl] *m.* bishop (*in chess*).
alfiler [al·fi·lér] *m.* pin; brooch; **-es** pin money; **ponerse de veinticinco -es** to doll up, dress up.
alfombra [al·fóm·bra] *f.* carpet; **alfombrilla** [al·fom·brí·ya] *f.* (*tapete*) carpet, rug; (*enfermedad*) measles; *Mex.* plant of the vervain family; *Carib.* black smallpox; *Carib.* skin eruption.
alforja [al·fór·xa] *f.* saddlebag; knapsack; food provisions for a trip; *Am.* **pasarse a la otra —** to take undue liberties.
alforza [al·fór·sa] *f.* tuck, fold, pleat; (*cicatriz*) scar.
alga [ál·ga] *f.* seaweed; alga.
algarabía [al·ga·ra·bí·a] *f.* jargon; chatter; (*alboroto*) uproar.
algarrobo [al·ga·rró·bo] *m.* locust tree; carob tree.
algazara [al·ga·sá·ra] *f.* clamor; shouting; uproar.
álgebra [ál·xe·bra] *f.* algebra.
algo [ál·go] *pron.* something; *adv.* somewhat.
algodón [al·go·dón] *m.* cotton; **algodonal** [al·go·do·nál] *m.* cotton plantation.
algoritmo [al·go·rít·mo] *m.* algorithm.

alguacil [al·gwa·síl] *m.* constable.
alguien [ál·gjen] *pron.* somebody, someone.
algún(o) [al·gún(o)] *adj.* some; any; *pron.* someone.
alhaja [a·lá·xa] *f.* jewel.
alharaca [a·la·rá·ka] *f.* rumpus, clamor, racket.
aliado [a·ljá·do] *adj.* allied; *m.* ally.
alianza [a·lján·sa] *f.* alliance, union; *Andes* wedding ring; *Am.* mixture of liquors.
aliar[17] [a·ljár] *v.* to ally; to unite; **-se** to form an alliance; to unite.
alicaído [a·li·ka·í·do] *adj.* crestfallen, downcast, discouraged; drooping.
alicatado [a·li·ka·tá·do] *m.* tiling.
alicates [a·li·ká·tes] *m. pl.* pliers, small pincers; tongs.
aliciente [a·li·sjén·te] *m.* inducement, incentive, attraction.
alienista [a·lje·nís·ta] *m.* alienist (*doctor who treats mental diseases*).
aliento [a·ljén·to] *m.* (*de los pulmones*) breath; (*ánimo*) encouragement.
aligerar [a·li·xe·rár] *v.* to lighten; to hasten; **-se** to hurry.
alijar [a·li·xár] *v.* to smooth.
alimentación [a·li·men·ta·sjón] *f.* nourishment, food, nutrition; feeding; **— por fricción** friction-feed; **— por tracción** tractor-feed.
alimentar [a·li·men·tár] *v.* to feed, nourish.
alimenticio [a·li·men·tí·sjo] *adj.* nutritious, nourishing; related to food.
alimento [a·li·mén·to] *m.* food; **-s** meals.
alinear [a·li·ne·ár] *v.* to line up, put into line; to range; **-se** to fall in line; form into a line.
aliño [a·lí·ño] *m.* ornament, decoration; neatness; (*alimento*) condiment, dressing, seasoning.
alisar [a·li·sár] *v.* to smooth; to polish; to plane.
alistamiento [a·lis·ta·mjén·to] *m.* enlistment; enrollment.
alistar [a·lis·tár] *v.* to enlist; to enroll; to make ready; **-se** to enlist; to get ready; *Am.* to dress up.
aliviar [a·li·bjár] *v.* to lighten; to alleviate, relieve, remedy, soothe; **-se** to get better, recover.
alivio [a·lí·bjo] *m.* relief, remedy; aid, (*ayuda*) help; (*mejora*) improvement.
aljibe [al·xí·be] *m.* cistern, reservoir, tank; water tanker; *Ríopl.* well, artesian well, spring.
alma [ál·ma] *f.* soul, spirit; inhabitant.
almacén [al·ma·sén] *m.* warehouse; (*tienda*) department store; store.
almacenaje [al·ma·se·ná·xe] *m.* storage.
almacenamiento [al·ma·se·na·mjén·to] *m.* storage
almacenar [al·ma·se·nár] *v.* to store, store up; to put in storage.
almacenista [al·ma·se·nís·ta] *m. & f.* department store owner; warehouse owner or manager; wholesale merchant.
almanaque [al·ma·ná·ke] *m.* almanac, calendar.
almeja [al·mé·xa] *f.* clam.
almendra [al·mén·dra] *f.* almond; **almendrado** [al·men·drá·do] *m.* almond paste; **almendro** [al·mén·dro] *m.* almond tree.
almíbar [al·mí·bar] *m.* syrup.
almidón [al·mi·dón] *m.* starch; *Col., Ven.* paste (*for gluing*); **almidón de arrarruz** arrowroot starch; **almidón de maíz** corn starch; *Mex.* **maicena**.
almidonar [al·mi·do·nár] *v.* to starch.
alminar [al·mi·nár] *m.* turret.
almirante [al·mi·rán·te] *m.* admiral.
almirez [al·mi·rés] *m.* metal mortar.
almohada [al·mo·á·da] *f.* pillow; **almohadón** *m.* large cushion or pillow.

almohadillar [al·mo·a·di·yár] *m.* padding.
almohaza [al·mo·á·sa] *f.* currycomb (*for grooming horses*).
almoneda [al·mo·né·da] *f.* auction.
almorranas [al·mo·rrá·nas] *f.* hemorrhoids, piles.
almorzar[2, 9] [al·mor·sár] *v. irr.* to lunch, eat lunch.
almuerzo [al·mwér·so] *m.* lunch.
alojamiento [a·lo·xa·mjén·to] *m.* lodging.
alojar [a·lo·xár] *v.* to lodge; to house; to quarter (*troops*); **-se** to lodge, room.
alondra [a·lón·dra] *f.* lark.
alpaca [al·pá·ka] *f.* alpaca (*sheeplike animal of South America*); alpaca wool; alpaca cloth.
alpargata [al·par·gá·ta] *f.* sandal (*usually of canvas and with hemp sole*).
alpinismo [al·pi·níz·mo] *m.* mountain climbing.
alpinista [al·pi·nís·ta] *m. & f.* mountain climber.
alquería [al·ke·rí·a] *f.* farmhouse.
alquilar [al·ki·lár] *v.* to rent; to hire; **-se** to hire out.
alquiler [al·ki·lér] *m.* rent, rental; **de** — for rent, for hire.
alquitrán [al·ki·trán] *m.* tar.
alrededor [al·rre·de·dór] *adv.* about, around; — **de** *prep.* around; **-es** *m. pl.* environs, outskirts.
altanería [al·ta·ne·rí·a] *f.* haughtiness.
altanero [al·ta·né·ro] *adj.* haughty, proud.
altar [al·tár] *m.* altar; — **mayor** high altar.
altavoz [al·ta·bós] *m.* loud-speaker.
alteración [al·te·ra·sjón] *f.* alteration, change; disturbance.
alterar [al·te·rár] *v.* to alter, change; to disturb.
altercar[6] [al·ter·kár] *v.* to argue, dispute; to quarrel.
alternador [al·ter·na·dór] *m.* alternator.
alternar [al·ter·nár] *v.* to alternate; to take turns; — **con** to rub elbows with, be friendly with.
alternativa [al·ter·na·tí·ba] *f.* alternative, choice, option.
alternativo [al·ter·na·tí·bo] *adj.* alternating, alternative.
alterno [al·tér·no] *adj.* alternate.
alteza [al·té·sa] *f.* highness (*title*); lofty height.
altibajo [al·ti·bá·xo] *m.* (*esgrima*) downward thrust (*in fencing*); **-s** ups and downs; uneven ground.
altiplanicie [al·ti·pla·ní·sje] *f.* upland; high plateau.
altiplano [al·ti·plá·no] *m. Am.* high plateau.
altisonante [al·ti·so·nán·te] *adj.* high-sounding.
altitud [al·ti·túd] *f.* altitude.
altivez [al·ti·bés] *f.* haughtiness, arrogance.
altivo [al·tí·bo] *adj.* haughty, proud, arrogant.
alto [ál·to] *adj.* (*tamaño*) high; *m.* height; upper story (*of a building*); *Am.* heap, pile; **-s** *Am.* upper floors; *v.* **hacer** — to halt, stop; **pasar por** — to omit, overlook; **¡**—**!** halt!
altoparlante [al·to·par·lán·te] *m.* loud-speaker.
altura [al·tú·ra] *f.* height, altitude.
alud [a·lúd] *m.* avalanche.
aludir [a·lu·dír] *v.* to allude, refer indirectly.
alumbrado [a·lum·brá·do] *m.* lighting; *adj.* lit, lighted; (*borracho*) tipsy.
alumbramiento [a·lum·bra·mjén·to] *m.* childbirth; lighting.
alumbrar [a·lum·brár] *v.* to light, give light; to enlighten; to give birth; **-se** to get tipsy.
aluminio [a·lu·mí·njo] *m.* aluminum.
alumnado [a·lum·ná·do] *m.* student body.
alumno [a·lúm·no] *m.* student.
alusión [a·lu·sjón] *f.* allusion.
alveolar [al·be·o·lár] *adj.* alveolar.
alza [ál·sa] *f.* rise; lift (*for shoes*).
alzada [al·sá·da] *f.* height (*of a horse*).
alzamiento [al·sa·mjén·to] *m.* raising, lifting;

uprising, insurrection.
alzaprima [al·sa·prí·ma] *f.* crowbar, lever.
alzar[9] [al·sár] *v.* to lift, raise; (*la baraja*) to cut (*cards*); **-se** to rebel, rise up in arms; *Col., Ven., C.A., Mex., Andes* to puff up with pride; **-se con** algo to run off with something, steal something.
allá [a·yá] *adv.* there, over there; **más** — farther.
allanar [a·ya·nár] *v.* to level, even off; (*invadir*) to invade, break into (*a house*); to raid; — **una dificultad** to smooth out a difficulty.
allegado [a·ye·gá·do] *adj.* near; related; allied; *m.* relative; partisan, follower.
allegar[7] [a·ye·gár] *v.* to accumulate, heap up, gather.
allende [a·yén·de] *adv.* on the other side; beyond; — **el mar** across the sea, overseas.
allí [a·yí] *adv.* there; **por** — through that place, around there.
ama [á·ma] *f.* mistress, owner; — **de leche** wet nurse; — **de llaves** housekeeper.
amabilidad [a·ma·bi·li·dád] *f.* kindness, courtesy.
amable [a·má·ble] *adj.* kind, amiable.
amador [a·ma·dór] *m.* lover.
amaestrar [a·ma·es·trár] *v.* to teach, coach, train.
amagar[7] [a·ma·gár] *v.* (*amenazar*) to threaten; (*fingir*) to feint, make a threatening motion; (*golpear*) to strike at.
amago [a·má·go] *m.* threat; indication.
amalgamar [a·mal·ga·már] *v.* to amalgamate, combine, mix, blend.
amamantar [a·ma·man·tár] *v.* to nurse, suckle.
amanecer[13] [a·ma·ne·sér] *v. irr.* to dawn; — **malo** to wake up ill; *Mex.* to get up; *m.* dawn, sunrise.
amanecida [a·ma·ne·sí·da] *f.* dawn, sunrise.
amansar [a·man·sár] *v.* to tame; to subdue; to pacify.
amante [a·mán·te] *m.* lover; — **de** fond of.
amañarse [a·ma·ñár·se] *v. Ec., Col., Ven.* to be accustomed; to acclimate oneself.
amapola [a·ma·pó·la] *f.* poppy.
amar [a·már] *v.* to love.
amargar[7] [a·mar·gár] *v.* to embitter, make bitter.
amargo [a·már·go] *adj.* bitter; *m.* bitters; *Am.* mate (*Paraguayan tea*) without sugar.
amargor [a·mar·gór] *m.* bitterness.
amargura [a·mar·gú·ra] *f.* bitterness; grief.
amarillear [a·ma·ri·ye·ár] *v.* to show or have a yellowish tinge; to turn yellow.
amarillento [a·ma·ri·yén·to] *adj.* yellowish.
amarillo [a·ma·rí·yo] *adj.* yellow.
amarra [a·má·rra] *f.* cable; rope; strap.
amarrar [a·ma·rrár] *v.* to tie, fasten, rope; to moor (*a ship*); *Am.* **amarrárselas** [a·ma·rrár·se·las] to get "tight," drunk.
amasar [a·ma·sár] *v.* to knead, mix; to mash; *Am.* to amass, accumulate (*a fortune*).
amatista [a·ma·tís·ta] *f.* amethyst.
ambages [am·bá·xes] *m. pl.* circumlocutions; **hablar sin** — to go straight to the point, speak plainly, not to beat about the bush.
ámbar [ám·bar] *m.* amber; **ambarino** [am·ba·rí·no] *adj.* amber; like amber.
ambición [am·bi·sjón] *f.* ambition; aspiration.
ambicionar [am·bi·sjo·nár] *v.* to seek, aspire after; to covet.
ambicioso [am·bi·sjó·so] *adj.* ambitious, eager; (*codicioso*) greedy, grasping.
ambiente [am·bjén·te] *m.* atmosphere, environment.
ambigüedad [am·bi·gwe·dád] *f.* ambiguity.
ambiguo [am·bí·gwo] *adj.* ambiguous; uncertain, doubtful.
ámbito [ám·bi·to] *m.* precinct, enclosure.
ambos [ám·bos] *adj. & pron.* both.

ambulancia [am·bu·lán·sja] *f.* ambulance; field hospital.

ambulante [am·bu·lán·te] *adj.* walking; itinerant; (*movedizo*) moving; wandering.

amedrentar [a·me·dren·tár] *v.* to scare, frighten.

amenaza [a·me·ná·sa] *f.* menace, threat.

amenazador [a·me·na·sa·dór], **amenazante** [a·me·na·sán·te] *adj.* threatening.

amenazar[9] [a·me·na·sár] *v.* to menace, threaten.

amenguar[8] [a·men̦·gwár] *v.* to lessen, diminish; to defame, dishonor.

amenidad [a·me·ni·dád] *f.* pleasantness.

amenizar[9] [a·me·ni·sár] *v.* to make pleasant, cheer, brighten.

ameno [a·mé·no] *adj.* pleasant, agreeable.

americana [a·me·ri·ká·na] *f.* suit coat.

americanismo [a·me·ri·ka·níz·mo] *m.* Americanism; characteristic of any part of America.

americano [a·me·ri·ká·no] *adj. & m.* American.

ametrallador [a·me·tra·ya·dór] *m.* gunner; **ametralladora** [a·me·tra·ya·dó·ra] *f.* machine gun.

amigable [a·mi·gá·ble] *adj.* friendly; affable, pleasant.

amígdala [a·míg·da·la] *f.* tonsil; **amigdalitis** [a·mig·da·lí·tis] *f.* tonsilitis.

amigo [a·mí·go] *m.* friend; — **de** fond of.

aminorar [a·mi·no·rár] *v.* to lessen.

amistad [a·mis·tád] *f.* friendship; friendliness.

amistoso [a·mis·tó·so] *adj.* friendly.

amnistía [am·nis·tí·a] *f.* amnesty.

amo [á·mo] *m.* master, owner, boss.

amodorrado [a·mo·do·rrá·do] *adj.* drowsy.

amodorrar [a·mo·do·rrár] *v.* to make drowsy; **-se** to become drowsy.

amolador [a·mo·la·dór] *m.* grinder, sharpener; *adj.* grinding, sharpening.

amoladora [a·mo·la·dó·ra] *f.* grinding machine.

amolar [a·mo·lár] *v. irr.* to grind, hone, sharpen; (*molestar*) to annoy; *Col., Mex., C.A.* to ruin, harm; **-se** *Mex., C.A., Col.* to go to rack and ruin.

amoldar [a·mol·dár] *v.* to mold; to shape; (*ajustar*) to adjust; to adapt.

amonestación [a·mo·nes·ta·sjón] *f.* admonition, advice, warning; **-es** marriage banns.

amonestar [a·mo·nes·tár] *v.* to admonish, advise, warn.

amoníaco [a·mo·ní·a·ko] *m.* ammonia.

amontonamiento [a·mon·to·na·mjén·to] *m.* accumulation, pile, heap.

amontonar [a·mon·to·nár] *v.* to heap up, pile up, crowd up.

amor [a·mór] *m.* love; — **propio** self-esteem.

amoratado [a·mo·ra·tá·do] *adj.* livid, bluish, purplish.

amordazar[9] [a·mor·da·sár] *v.* to gag; to muzzle.

amorío [a·mo·rí·o] *m.* love affair; love-making.

amoroso [a·mo·ró·so] *adj.* loving, tender, affectionate.

amortajar [a·mor·ta·xár] *v.* to shroud.

amortiguador [a·mor·ti·gwa·dór] *m.* shock absorber; silencer, muffler.

amortiguar[8] [a·mor·ti·gwár] *v.* to muffle; to deafen (*a sound*); to deaden (*a blow or sound*); to soften, tone down (*a color or sound*).

amortizar[9] [a·mor·ti·sár] *v.* to pay on account; to liquidate, pay (*a debt*); to provide a sinking fund.

amoscarse[6] [a·mos·kár·se] *v.* to get peeved, annoyed; *Am.* to blush, be inhibited or embarrassed.

amostazar[9] [a·mos·ta·sár] *v.* to anger, irritate; **-se** to get angry or irritated.

amotinar [a·mo·ti·nár] *v.* to incite to rebellion; **-se** to mutiny; to riot.

amparar [am·pa·rár] *v.* to protect; to defend; *Am.* to

grant mining rights; **-se** to seek protection or refuge; to protect oneself.

amparo [am·pá·ro] *m.* protection; habeas corpus (*protection against imprisonment*); *Am.* mining rights.

AL

amperio [am·pé·rjo] *m.* ampere; **amperaje** *m.* amperage.

ampliación [am·plja·sjón] *f.* enlargement, widening.

ampliar[17] [am·pljár] *v.* to enlarge, widen.

amplificador [am·pli·fi·ka·dór] *m.* amplifier.

amplificar[6] [am·pli·fi·kár] *v.* to amplify, expand, extend, enlarge; to magnify.

amplio [ám·pljo] *adj.* ample; wide, large, roomy.

amplitud [am·pli·túd] *f.* breadth, extent, width.

ampolla [am·pó·ya] *f.* (*condición*) blister, water bubble; (*vasija*) narrow-necked bottle or vase, cruet.

ampollar [am·po·yár] *v.* to blister; **-se** to blister.

ampuloso [am·pu·ló·so] *adj.* inflated, wordy, bombastic, pompous.

amputar [am·pu·tár] *v.* to amputate, cut off.

amueblar [a·mwe·blár] *v.* to furnish (*with furniture*).

ánade [á·na·de] *m. & f.* duck; **anadeja** [a·na·dé·xa] *f.* duckling.

anadear [a·na·de·ár] *v.* to waddle.

anales [a·ná·les] *m. pl.* annals, historical records.

analfabeto [a·nal·fa·bé·to] *adj. & m.* illiterate; **analfabetismo** [a·nal·fa·be·tíz·mo] *m.* illiteracy.

analgésico [a·nal·xé·si·ko] *adj.* analgesic.

analisis [a·ná·li·sis] *m.* analysis.

analítico [a·na·lí·ti·ko] *adj.* analytical.

analizador [a·na·li·sa·dór] *m.* digital differential.

analizar[9] [a·na·li·sár] *v.* to analyze, examine.

analogía [a·na·lo·xí·a] *f.* analogy, similarity.

análogo [a·ná·lo·go] *adj.* analogous, similar, comparable.

ananá [a·na·ná], **ananás** [a·na·nás] *f.* pineapple. *See* **piña**.

anaquel [a·na·kél] *m.* shelf; bookshelf; **anaquelería** [a·na·ke·le·rí·a] *f.* shelves, bookshelves, library stacks.

anaranjado [a·na·ran̦·xá·do] *adj.* orange-colored; *m.* orange color.

anarquía [a·nar·kí·a] *f.* anarchy.

anatomía [a·na·to·mí·a] *f.* anatomy.

anatómico [a·na·tó·mi·ko] *adj.* anatomical.

anca [áŋ·ka] *f.* haunch, hind quarter, rump; *Andes* popcorn.

ancianidad [an·sja·ni·dád] *f.* old age.

anciano [an·sjá·no] *adj.* old, aged; *m.* old man.

ancla [áŋ·kla] *f.* anchor.

anclar [aŋ·klár] *v.* to anchor.

ancho [án·čo] *adj.* wide, broad; loose; roomy; *Col., Ven.* self-satisfied, conceited; **a sus anchas** at one's ease; comfortable; leisurely; *m.* width.

anchoa [an·čó·a], **anchova** [an·čó·ba] *f.* anchovy.

anchura [an·čú·ra] *f.* width, breadth; comfort, ease.

anchuroso [an·ču·ró·so] *adj.* vast, extensive; spacious.

andada [an·dá·da] *f. Mex., Ven.* walk, stroll; **-s** tracks, footprints; **volver a las -s** to fall back into one's old ways or habits.

andadura [an·da·dú·ra] *f.* gait, pace.

andaluz [an·da·lús] *adj.* Andalusian, of or pertaining to Andalusia, Spain; *m.* Andalusian, native or Andalusia.

andamiada [an·da·mjá·da] *f.* **andamiaje** [an·da·mjá·xe] *m.* scaffolding; framework.

andamio [an·dá·mjo] *m.* scaffold, scaffolding.

andanada [an·da·ná·da] *f.* (*localidad*) grandstand; (*descarga*) broadside; **soltar una** — to discharge a

broadside; (*regañar*) to reprimand.
andante [an·dán·te] *adj.* walking; errant, wandering; moderately slow (*music*); **caballero** — knight-errant.
andanzas [an·dán·sas] *f. pl.* rambles, wanderings.
andar²¹ [an·dár] *v. irr.* to walk; to go, go about; to run (*as a watch or machinery*); — **con cuidado** to be careful; **anda en quince años** he is about fifteen; **a todo** — at full (walking) speed; **a más** — walking briskly; **¡anda!** move on!; **¿qué andas haciendo?** what are you doing?; *Am.* — **andando** to be walking around; *Am.* **¡ándale!** hurry!; *Mex.* O.K., fine! now you're talking!
andariego [an·da·rjé·ǥo] *adj.* fond of walking; roving; *m.* walker.
andas [án·das] *f. pl.* portable platform; litter.
andén [an·dén] *m.* railway station platform; *C.A., Col., Ven.,* sidewalk.
andino [an·dí·no] *adj.* Andean, of or from the Andes.
andrajo [an·drá·xo] *m.* rag.
andrajoso [an·dra·xó·so] *adj.* ragged, in rags.
anécdota [a·nék·do·ta] *f.* anecdote, story.
anegar⁷ [a·ne·ǥár] *v.* to drown; to flood.
anejo [a·né·xo] *adj.* annexed, attached.
anestesia [a·nes·té·sja] *f.* anesthesia.
anestésico [a·nes·té·si·ko] *m. & adj.* anesthetic.
anexar [a·nek·sár] *v.* to annex.
anexo [a·nék·so] *m.* annex; *adj.* annexed, joined.
anfibio [an·fí·bjo] *adj.* amphibian.
anfiteatro [an·fi·te·á·tro] *m.* amphitheater.
anfitrión [an·fi·trjón] *m.* generous host.
ángel [áŋ·xel] *m.* angel.
angélico [aŋ·xé·li·ko] *adj.* angelic.
angina [aŋ·xí·na] *f.* angina, inflammation of the throat; *Mex., Ven.* tonsil; — **del pecho** angina pectoris.
anglosajón [aŋ·glo·sa·xón] *adj & m.* Anglo-Saxon.
angostar [aŋ·gos·tár] *v.* to narrow; **-se** to narrow, become narrow; (*contratar*) to contract.
angosto [aŋ·gós·to] *adj.* narrow.
angostura [aŋ·gos·tú·ra] *f.* narrowness; narrows.
anguila [aŋ·gí·la] *f.* eel.
angular [aŋ·gu·lár] *adj.* angular; **piedra** — cornerstone.
ángulo [áŋ·gu·lo] *m.* angle, corner.
anguloso [aŋ·gu·ló·so] *adj.* angular, sharp-cornered.
angustia [aŋ·gús·tja] *f.* anguish, sorrow, grief, (*preocupación*) worry.
angustiar [aŋ·gus·tjár] *v.* to distress, grieve, (*preocuparse*) worry.
angustioso [aŋ·gus·tjó·so] *adj.* anguished, worried, grievous; distressing.
anhelante [a·ne·lán·te] *adj.* anxious, desirous, longing; panting.
anhelar [a·ne·lár] *v.* to long for; (*desalentado*) to breathe hard; (*respirar*) to pant.
anhelo [a·né·lo] *m.* longing.
anheloso [a·ne·ló·so] *adj.* anxious; eager.
anidar [a·ni·dár] *v.* to nest; to nestle; to dwell; (*amparar*) to shelter.
anillo [a·ní·yo] *m.* ring; **anillos anuales** *m.* annual rings.
ánima [á·ni·ma] *f.* soul, spirit.
animación [a·ni·ma·sjón] *f.* animation, liveliness, life.
animal [a·ni·mál] *m.* animal; *adj.* animal; (*estúpido*) stupid; beastly; **animalejo** *m.* little animal; **animalucho** *m.* insignificant animal; hideous little beast.
animar [a·ni·már] *v.* to animate, give life to; to inspire, encourage.
ánimo [á·ni·mo] *f.* spirit, mind; courage, valor;

(*intención*) intention.
animosidad [a·ni·mo·si·dád] *f.* animosity, ill will; courage, energy.
animoso [a·ni·mó·so] *adj.* spirited; courageous.
aniñado [a·ni·ñá·do] *adj.* boyish; childish; **aniñada** girlish.
aniquilar [a·ni·ki·lár] *v.* to annihilate, wipe out, destroy completely.
anís [a·nís] *m.* anise.
aniversario [a·ni·ber·sá·rjo] *m.* anniversary.
anoche [a·nó·če] *adv.* last night.
anochecer³ [a·no·če·sér] *v. irr.* to grow dark; to be or arrive at nightfall; *m.* nightfall.
anochecida [a·no·če·sí·da] *f.* nightfall.
anonadar [a·no·na·dár] *v.* to annihilate; (*humillar*) to humiliate.
anónimo [a·nó·ni·mo] *adj.* anonymous; nameless; *m.* anonymous letter or note.
anormal [a·nor·mál] *adj.* abnormal.
anotación [a·no·ta·sjón] *f.* annotation; note.
anotar [a·no·tár] *v.* to annotate, provide with notes; to write down.
anquilosado [aŋ·ki·lo·sá·do] *adj.* stiff-jointed; gnarled.
anquilosarse [aŋ·ki·lo·sár·se] *v.* to become stiff in the joints; (*ponerse*) to become mentally stagnant.
ansia [án·sja] *f.* anxiety, anguish; longing, eagerness; **-s** anguish; *Col., Ven., P.R.* nausea.
ansiar¹⁷ [an·sjár] *v.* to long for, desire eagerly.
ansiedad [an·sje·dád] *f.* anxiety; (*preocupación*) worry.
ansioso [an·sjó·so] *adj.* anxious, troubled; eager.
antagonismo [an·ta·ǥo·niz·mo] *m.* antagonism.
antagonista [an·ta·ǥo·nís·ta] *m. & f.* antagonist, adversary, opponent.
antaño [an·tá·ño] *adv.* yesteryear, formerly; **días** — days of old.
ante [án·te] *prep.* before, in the presence of; — **todo** above all; *m.* elk; buckskin.
anteanoche [an·te·a·nó·če] *adv.* night before last.
anteayer [an·te·a·yér] *adv.* day before yesterday.
antebrazo [an·te·brá·so] *m.* forearm.
antecámara [an·te·ká·ma·ra] *f.* antechamber, waiting room.
antecedente [an·te·se·dén·te] *m.* antecedent; *adj.* antecedent, preceding.
antecesor [an·te·se·sór] *m.* ancestor; predecessor.
antedicho [an·te·dí·čo] *adj.* aforesaid.
antelación [an·te·la·sjón] *f.* precedence, priority (*in time*).
antemano [an·te·má·no]: **de** — beforehand.
antena [an·té·na] *f.* antenna (*of a radio or wireless*); lateen yard (*of a ship*); **-s** antennae, feelers; — **emisora** *f.* broadcasting antenna; — **receptora** *f.* receiving antenna; — **parabólica** *f.* parabolic (*TV*) antenna.
antenoche [an·te·nó·če] = **anteanoche.**
anteojera [an·te·o·xé·ra] *f.* blinder.
anteojo [an·te·ó·xo] *m.* spyglass; small telescope; eyeglass; **-s** spectacles; **-s de larga vista** field glasses; **-s de seguridad** safety glasses.
antepasado [an·te·pa·sá·do] *adj.* passed; **el año** — year before last; *m.* ancestor.
antepecho [an·te·pé·čo] *m.* sill, railing.
anteponer⁴⁰ [an·te·po·nér] *v. irr.* to place before; to prefer.
antepuesto [an·te·pwés·to] *p.p. of* **anteponer.**
anterior [an·te·rjór] *adj.* front, toward the front; earlier, previous; **el día** — the day before.
antes [án·tes] *adv.* before, formerly; — **de** *prep.* before; — (**de**) **que** *conj.* before.
antesala [an·te·sá·la] *f.* anteroom, waiting room.

antiaéreo [an·tja·é·re·o] *adj.* antiaircraft.
antibiótico [an·ti·bjó·ti·ko] *adj. & m.* antibiotic.
anticipación [an·ti·si·pa·sjón] *f.* anticipation, advance
  consideration; **con** — in advance.
anticipado [an·ti·si·pa·do] *adj.* early, ahead of time;
  advanced (*payment*); **por** — in advance; *p.p. of*
  anticipar anticipated.
anticipar [an·ti·si·pár] *v.* to anticipate; to advance,
  pay in advance; **-se** to get ahead (of).
anticipo [an·ti·sí·po] *m.* advance, advance payment.
anticlericalismo [an·ti·kle·ri·ka·líz·mo] *m.*
  anticlericalism.
anticoncepción [an·ti·kon·sep·sjón] contraconception;
  birth control.
anticuado [an·ti·kwá·do] *adj.* antiquated, out-of-date.
antídoto [an·tí·do·to] *m.* antidote.
antigualla [an·ti·gwá·ya] *f.* antique; anything old.
antigüedad [an·ti·gwe·dád] *f.* antiquity, ancient times;
  -es antique objects, antiques.
antiguo [an·tí·gwo] *adj.* ancient, old; antique.
antílope [an·tí·lo·pe] *m.* antelope.
antimonio [an·ti·mó·njo] *m.* antimony.
antiparras [an·ti·pá·rras] *f. pl.* goggles; spectacles.
antipatía [an·ti·pa·tí·a] *f.* antipathy, dislike; mutual
  antagonism.
antipático [an·ti·pá·ti·ko] *adj.* disagreeable;
  unlikeable, unpleasant.
antipoliomielítico [an·ti·po·lio·mje·lí·ti·ko] *adj.*
  antipolio
antiséptico [an·ti·sép·ti·ko] *adj. & m.* antiseptic.
antisocial [an·ti·so·sjál] *adj. & m.* antisocial;
  criminal.
antojadizo [an·to·xa·dí·so] *adj.* fanciful, whimsical.
antojarse [an·to·xár·se] *v.:* **antojársele a uno** to take
  a notion or fancy to; to strike one's fancy; to want,
  desire.
antojo [an·tó·xo] *m.* whim, notion, fancy.
antorcha [an·tór·ča] *f.* torch; **-de propano** propane
  torch.
antracita [an·tra·sí·ta] *f.* anthracite, hard coal.
antropología [an·tro·po·lo·xí·a] *f.* anthropology.
antropólogo [an·tro·pó·lo·go] *m.* anthropologist.
anual [a·nwál] *adj.* annual, yearly.
anuario [a·nwá·rjo] *m.* annual, yearbook.
anublar [a·nu·blár] *v.* to cloud; to dim, obscure; **-se**
  to become cloudy.
anudar [a·nu·dár] *v.* to knot; **anudársele a uno la
  garganta** to choke up with emotion.
anulación [a·nu·la·sjón] *f.* voiding, cancellation.
anular [a·nu·lár] *v.* to annul, void, cancel, abolish.
anunciador [a·nun·sja·dór] *m.* announcer; advertiser;
  adj. announcing; advertising.
anunciante [a·nun·sján·te] *m. & f.* announcer,
  advertiser.
anunciar [a·nun·sjár] *v.* to announce; to advertise.
anuncio [a·nún·sjo] *m.* announcement; advertisement.
anzuelo [an·swé·lo] *m.* fishhook; lure, attraction.
añadidura [a·ña·di·dú·ra] *f.* addition.
añadir [a·ña·dír] *v.* to add.
añejado [a·ñe·xá·do] *adj.* aged (*wine, cheese, etc.*).
añejo [a·ñé·xo] *adj.* old; of old vintage; stale.
añicos [a·ñí·kos] *m. pl.* bits, shatters, fragments;
  hacer(se) — to shatter, break into a thousand
  pieces.
añil [a·ñíl] *m.* indigo (*plant*); indigo blue.
año [á·ño] *m.* year; — **bisiesto** leap year; **¿cuántos -s
  tiene Vd?** how old are you?
añoranza [a·ño·rán·sa] *f.* nostalgia, longing.
añorar [a·ño·rár] *v.* to long for, yearn for, be
  homesick for; to make reminiscences.
añoso [a·ñó·so] *adj.* old, aged.

aojar [a·o·xár] *v.* to bewitch; to cast the evil eye.
apabullar [a·pa·bu·yár] *v.* to crush, crumple.
apacentar[1] [a·pa·sen·tár] *v. irr.* to graze, pasture; to
  feed (*the spirit, desires, passions, etc.*); **-se** to
  graze, pasture.
apacibilidad [a·pa·si·bi·li·dád] *f.* gentleness, mildness,
  pleasantness; **apacible** [a·pa·sí·ble] *adj.* pleasant,
  quiet, gentle.
apaciguamiento [a·pa·si·gwa·mjén·to] *m.*
  appeasement.
apaciguar[8] [a·pa·si·gwár] *v.* to pacify, calm, appease;
  -se to calm down.
apachurrar [a·pa·ču·rrár] *v. Mex., C.A., Carib.,
  Andes* to crush. *See* **despachurrar.**
apadrinar [a·pa·dri·nár] *v.* to sponsor; to act as a
  godfather; to act as a second in a duel.
apagamiento [a·pa·ga·mjén·to] *m.* quenching.
apagar[7] [a·pa·gár] *v.* to put out, extinguish; to deafen
  (*a sound*).
apagón [a·pa·gón] *m.* blackout.
apalabrar [a·pa·la·brár] *v.* to speak for, engage,
  reserve; **-se con** to make a verbal agreement with.
apalear [a·pa·le·ár] *v.* to beat up, thrash, to thresh.
aparador [a·pa·ra·dór] *m.* sideboard; cupboard;
  showcase; show window; workshop.
aparato [a·pa·rá·to] *m.* apparatus; pomp;
  -interuterino *m.* I.U.D (*interuterine device*).
aparatoso [a·pa·ra·tó·so] *adj.* pompous, ostentatious.
aparcero [a·par·sé·ro] *m.* co-owner of land; *Am.* pal,
  comrade.
aparear [a·pa·re·ár] *v.* to mate; to match; to pair; **-se**
  to mate; to match; to pair.
aparecer[13] [a·pa·re·sér] *v. irr.* to appear, show up.
aparecido [a·pa·re·sí·do] *m.* ghost, specter, phantom.
aparejar [a·pa·re·xár] *v.* to prepare; to harness; to rig;
  to equip.
aparejo [a·pa·ré·xo] *m.* harness; packsaddle; rigging
  (*of a boat*); preparation; fishing tackle; **-s**
  equipment, tools.
aparentar [a·pa·ren·tár] *v.* to appear, seem; to
  pretend, feign, affect.
aparente [a·pa·rén·te] *adj.* apparent.
aparición [a·pa·ri·sjón] *f.* apparition, ghost;
  appearance.
apariencia [a·pa·rjén·sja] *f.* appearance.
apartado [a·par·tá·do] *m.* compartment; — **postal**
  post office letter box; *p.p. oj* **apartar.**
apartamento [a·par·ta·mén·to] *m.* apartment.
apartamiento [a·par·ta·mjén·to] *m.* separation;
  retirement; aloofness; retreat, refuge; *Am.*
  apartment, flat.
apartar [a·par·tár] *v.* to set apart, separate; to
  remove; *Am.* — **las reses** to sort out cattle; **-se** to
  withdraw; to step aside; to go away.
aparte [a·pár·te] *adv.* apart; aside; *m.* aside (*in a
  play*); new paragraph; *Am.* sorting out of cattle.
apasionado [a·pa·sjo·ná·do] *adj.* passionate; very fond
  (of); impassioned, emotional.
apasionar [a·pa·sjo·nár] *v.* to arouse passion; to fill
  with passion; **-se** to become impassioned; to fall
  ardently in love.
apatía [a·pa·tí·a] *f.* apathy, indolence, indifference.
apático [a·pá·ti·ko] *adj.* apathetic, indifferent,
  indolent.
apear [a·pe·ár] *v.* (*de caballo*) dismount; (*bajar*) to
  lower, take down; to shackle (*a horse*); (*cortar*) to
  fell (*a tree*); *Ríopl.* to fire, dismiss from a position;
  — **el tratamiento** to omit the title (*in addressing a
  person*); **-se** to get off, alight; *Am.* **-se por la cola**
  (*or* **por las orejas**) to go off at a tangent, make an
  irrelevant remark.

apechugar[7] [a·pe·ču·ǧár] *v.* to push with the chest; to push ahead; — **con** to accept reluctantly; to go through with (*something*) courageously; *P.R.* to snatch, take possession of.

apedrear [a·pe·dre·ár] *v.* to stone, hit with stones.

apegado [a·pe·ǧá·do] *adj.* devoted, attached; *p.p. of* **apegarse**.

apegarse[7] [a·pe·ǧár·se] *v.* to become attached (to); to become fond (of).

apego [a·pé·ǧo] *m.* attachment, fondness.

apelación [a·pe·la·sjón] *f.* appeal.

apelar [a·pe·lár] *v.* to appeal.

apelotonar [a·pe·lo·to·nár] *v.* to form or roll into a ball; to pile up, bunch together.

apellidar [a·pe·yi·dár] *v.* to call, name; **-se** to be named; to have the surname of.

apellido [a·pe·yí·do] *m.* surname.

apenar [a·pe·nár] *v.* to grieve, afflict; **-se** to be grieved; *Col., Ven., C.A., Carib.* to feel embarrassed, feel ashamed.

apenas [a·pé·nas] *adv.* hardly, scarcely; *conj.* as soon as.

apéndice [a·pén·di·se] *m.* appendix.

apercibir [a·per·si·bír] *v.* to prepare beforehand; to supply; to warn, advise; to perceive; **-se a la pelea** to get ready to fight; *Am.* **-se de** to notice.

apergaminado [a·per·ǧa·mi·ná·do] *adj.* parchmentlike; dried up.

aperitivo [a·pe·ri·tí·bo] *m.* aperitif, appetizer; cocktail.

aperlado [a·per·lá·do] *adj.* pearly, pearl-colored.

apero [a·pé·ro] *m.* farm equipment; **-s** tools, implements; *Ríopl., Ch., Mex., Ven., Andes* saddle and trappings.

apertura [a·per·tú·ra] *f.* (*acto*) opening; (*crédito*) issue.

apestar [a·pes·tár] *v.* to infect; to corrupt; to sicken; to stink; **-se** to turn putrid, become corrupted; *Am.* to catch cold.

apestoso [a·pes·tó·so] *adj.* putrid, foul-smelling.

apetecer[13] [a·pe·te·sér] *v. irr.* to desire, crave.

apetecible [a·pe·te·sí·ble] *adj.* desirable, appetizing.

apetencia [a·pe·tén·sja] *f.* hunger, appetite; desire.

apetito [a·pe·tí·to] *m.* appetite; hunger.

apetitoso [a·pe·ti·tó·so] *adj.* appetizing; gluttonous.

apiadarse [a·pja·dár·se] *v.* to pity; — **de** to pity, take pity on.

ápice [á·pi·se] *m.* apex, top, summit.

apiladores [a·pi·la·dó·res] *m.* stackers.

apilar [a·pi·lár] *v.* to pile up, stack, heap.

apiñado [a·pi·ñá·do] *p.p. of* **apiñar** *& adj.* crowded, jammed, cone-shaped, shaped like a pine cone.

apiñamiento [a·pi·ña·mjén·to] *m.* crowd, jam (*of people or animals*); crowding together.

apiñar [a·pi·ñár] *v.* to cram together; to crowd; **-se** to pile up, crowd together.

apio [á·pjo] *m.* celery.

apisonadora [a·pi·so·na·dó·ra] *f.* road roller.

apisonar [a·pi·so·nár] *v.* to pack down, flatten by pounding.

aplacar[6] [a·pla·kár] *v.* to appease, pacify, soothe.

aplanamiento [a·pla·na·mjén·to] *m.* flattening, leveling; dejection, depression.

aplanar [a·pla·nár] *v.* to level; to flatten; to astonish; *Am.* — **las calles** to tramp the streets; **-se** to be flattened out; to be leveled to the ground; to lose one's strength; *Col.* to give in, yield.

aplastar [a·plas·tár] *v.* to squash, crush, flatten; *Am.* (*cansar*) to tire out, break (*a horse*); **-se** *Am.* to plump oneself down; *Col., Andes* to overstay a call (*remaining seated*).

aplaudir [a·plaw·dír] *v.* to applaud, clap, to approve,

praise.

aplauso [a·pláw·so] *m.* applause; praise, approval.

aplazamiento [a·pla·sa·mjén·to] *m.* postponement; adjournment.

aplazar[9] [a·pla·sár] *v.* to postpone; to adjourn.

aplicable [a·pli·ká·ble] *adj.* applicable, suitable, fitting.

aplicación [a·pli·ka·sjón] *f.* application; effort, diligence; **-es** applique.

aplicado [a·pli·ká·do] *adj.* industrious, diligent.

aplicar[6] [a·pli·kár] *v.* to apply; to put on, lay on; **-se** to apply oneself, work hard.

aplomado [a·plo·má·do] *adj.* gray, lead-colored; *p.p. of* **aplomar**.

aplomar [a·plo·már] *v.* to plumb (*a wall*); to make vertical; to make heavier; **-se** *Am.* to become ashamed or embarrassed; *Am.* to be slow.

aplomo [a·plo·mo] *m.* assurance, confidence, self-possession, serenity; **estar** — to be plumb, vertical.

apocado [a·po·ká·do] *adj.* cowardly; timid; *p.p. of* **apocar**.

apocamiento [a·po·ka·mjén·to] *m.* timidity; bashfulness; belittling.

apocar[6] [a·po·kár] *v.* to lessen; to belittle, give less importance to; **-se** to humble oneself.

apodar [a·po·dár] *v.* to nickname.

apoderado [a·po·de·rá·do] *m.* attorney; proxy, substitute.

apoderar [a·po·de·rár] *v.* to empower, give power of attorney, **-se de** to take possession of, seize.

apodo [a·pó·do] *m.* nickname.

apogeo [a·po·xé·o] *m.* apogee; highest point, height (*of glory, fame, etc.*).

apolillado [a·po·li·yá·do] *adj.* moth-eaten; worm-eaten.

apología [a·po·lo·xí·a] *f.* praise, apologia.

apoplejía [a·po·ple·xí·a] *f.* apoplexy, stroke.

aporrear [a·po·rre·ár] *v.* to beat; to maul; *Am.* to beat (*in a game*); defeat.

aportación [a·por·ta·sjón] *f.* contribution.

aportar [a·por·tár] *v.* to bring; to contribute; to arrive in port; to reach an unexpected place (*having gone astray*); **-se** *Am.* to appear, approach.

aporte [a·pór·te] *m.* contribution.

aposento [a·po·sén·to] *m.* room; lodging.

apostar[2] [a·pos·tár] *v. irr.* to bet; to post, station.

apóstol [a·pós·tol] *m.* apostle; religious leader.

apostólico [a·pos·tó·li·ko] *adj.* apostolic.

apostura [a·pos·tú·ra] *f.* elegant bearing, graceful carriage.

apoyar [a·po·yár] *v.* to lean, rest; to back, support; to aid, favor; to confirm; **-se** to lean (on).

apoyo [a·pó·yo] *m.* support; favor, protection.

apreciable [a·pre·sjá·ble] *adj.* estimable, esteemed; valuable; appraisable; noticeable.

apreciación [a·pre·sja·sjón] *f.* appreciation; valuation; estimation.

apreciar [a·pre·sjár] *v.* to appreciate, value, esteem; to price, fix the price of; to appraise.

aprecio [a·pré·sjo] *m.* esteem, high regard; appraisal, valuation, estimate; *Mex., Ven., Cuba* **hacer** — to notice, pay attention.

aprehender [a·pre·en·dér] *v.* to apprehend, seize, arrest.

aprehensión [a·pre·en·sjón], **aprensión** [a·pren·sjón] *f.* apprehension; fear, dread; seizure, arrest; *Am.* prejudice.

aprehensor [a·pre·en·sór], **aprensor** [a·pren·sór] *m.* captor.

apremiante [a·pre·mján·te] *adj.* pressing, urgent.

apremiar [a·pre·mjár] *v.* to press, urge onward, hurry.

apremio [a·pré·mjo] *m.* pressure; urgency.

aprender [a·pren·dér] *v.* to learn.

aprendiz [a·pren·dís] *m.* apprentice.

aprendizaje [a·pren·di·sá·xe] *m.* apprenticeship; learning (*act of learning*).

apresar [a·pre·sár] *v.* to seize, grab; to capture; to imprison.

aprestar [a·pres·tár] *v.* to prepare, make ready; **-se** to get ready.

apresto [a·prés·to] *m.* preparation; readiness.

apresurado [a·pre·su·rá·do] *adj.* hasty.

apresurar [a·pre·su·rár] *v.* to hurry, hasten; **-se** to hurry, hasten.

apretado [a·pre·tá·do] *adj.* tight; compact; (*tacaño*) stingy, miserly; (*difícil*) difficult, dangerous; *p.p. of* **apretar.**

apretar[1] [a·pre·tár] *v. irr.* to press, squeeze, tighten; to urge on; *Am.* to increase in strength or intensity (*as rain, wind, etc.*); *Am.* (*reforzarse*) to redouble one's effort; — **a correr** to start to run; **-se** *Col.* to gorge, overeat.

apretón [a·pre·tón] *m.* sudden pressure; squeeze; dash, short run; — **de manos** hand-shake.

apretura [a·pre·tú·ra] *f.* jam, crush; tight squeeze, narrow place; (*dificultad*) difficulty, predicament; (*pobreza*) dire poverty.

aprieto [a·prjé·to] *m.* tight spot, difficulty.

aprisa [a·prí·sa] *adv.* quickly, fast, speedily.

aprisco [a·prís·ko] *m.* sheepfold.

aprisionar [a·pri·sjo·nár] *v.* to imprison; to tie, fasten.

aprobación [a·pro·ba·sjón] *f.* approbation, approval; consent; pass, passing grade.

aprobar[2] [a·pro·bár] *v. irr.* to approve; to pass (*in an examination*).

aprontar [a·pron·tár] *v.* to make ready; to expedite; (*entregar*) to hand over without delay; *Am.* to pay in advance.

apropiación [a·pro·pja·sjón] *f.* appropriation; confiscation.

apropiado [a·pro·pjá·do] *adj.* appropriate, proper, fitting, suitable; *p.p. of* **apropiar.**

apropiar [a·pro·pjár] *v.* to fit; to adapt; **-se** to take possession (of); to confiscate.

aprovechable [a·pro·be·čá·ble] *adj.* (*disponible*) available; usable, (*útil*) fit to use.

aprovechado [a·pro·be·čá·do] *adj.* diligent, industrious; *p.p. of* **aprovechar.**

aprovechamiento [a·pro·be·ča·mjén·to] *m.* use, utilization; exploitation; profit, benefit; progress.

aprovechar [a·pro·be·čár] *v.* to profit, be profitable; to progress, get ahead; to utilize; **-se de** to take advantage of; **¡que aproveche!** may you enjoy it!

aproximado [a·prok·si·má·do] *adj.* approximate; near; nearly correct.

aproximar [a·prok·si·már] *v.* to place or bring near; to approximate; **-se** to get near, approach.

aproximativo [a·prok·si·ma·tí·bo] *adj.* approximate.

aptitud [ap·ti·túd] *f.* aptitude, capacity, ability.

apto [áp·to] *adj.* apt; competent.

apuesta [a·pwés·ta] *f.* bet, wager.

apuesto [a·pwés·to] *adj.* smart, stylish; goodlooking.

apuntación [a·pun·ta·sjón] *f.* note; memorandum; (*música*) musical notation, set of musical symbols or signs.

apuntalar [a·pun·ta·lár] *v.* to prop; to shore up.

apuntar [a·pun·tár] *v.* (*señalar*) to point; (*arma*) to aim; (*escribir*) to write down; (*a un actor*) to prompt; (*remendar*) to mend, to stitch; to sharpen; (*brotar*) to begin to show; — **el día** to begin to

dawn; **-se** to sprout.

apunte [a·pún·te] *m.* note, memorandum.

apuñalar [a·pu·ña·lár] *v.* to stab.

apuración [a·pu·ra·sjón] *f.* worry; trouble.

apurado [a·pu·rá·do] *adj.* worried; needy; difficult; dangerous; in a hurry.

apurar [a·pu·rár] *v.* (*acabar*) to exhaust, to drain to the last drop; (*preocupar*) to worry, annoy; (*acelerar*) to hurry, press; **-se** to be or get worried; to hurry up.

apuro [a·pú·ro] *m.* need; worry; predicament; *Am.* (*prisa*) rush, hurry.

aquejar [a·ke·xár] *v.* to grieve, afflict.

aquel [a·kél], **aquella** [a·ké·ya] *dem. adj.* that (*at a distance*); **aquellos** [a·ké·yos], **aquellas** [a·ké·yas] those; **aquél, aquélla** *m., f. dem. pron.* that one; the former; **aquello** [a·ké·yo] that, that thing; **aquéllos, aquéllas** *m., f. pl.* those; the former.

aquí [a·kí] *adv.* here; **por** — this way; through here; around here.

aquietar [a·kje·tár] *v.* to quiet, calm; to hush; **-se** to calm down, become calm.

aquilón [a·ki·lón] *m.* north wind.

ara [á·ra] *f.* altar.

árabe [á·ra·be] *m.* Arab; *adj.* Arabic.

arado [a·rá·do] *m.* plow; *Am.* (*tierra*) plowed land, piece of cultivated land.

aragonés [a·ra·go·nés] *adj.* Aragonese, of or from Aragón, Spain, *m.* Aragonese.

arancel [a·ran·sél] *m.* tariff; — **de aduanas** customs, duties.

arancelario [a·ran·ce·lá·rjo] *adj.* pertaining to tariffs.

arándano [a·rán·da·no] *m.* cranberry.

araña [a·rá·ña] *f.* spider; chandelier.

arañar [a·ra·ñár] *v.* to scratch; to claw.

araño [a·rá·ño] *m.* scratch; **arañazo** [a·ra·ñá·so] *m.* big scratch.

arar [a·rár] *v.* to plow.

arbitración [ar·bi·tra·sjón] *f.* arbitration.

arbitrador [ar·bi·tra·dór] *m.* arbitrator; referee; umpire.

arbitraje [ar·bi·trá·xe] *m.* arbitration.

arbitrar [ar·bi·trár] *v.* to arbitrate; to umpire.

arbitrario [ar·bi·trá·rjo] *adj.* arbitrary.

arbitrio [ar·bí·trjo] *m.* free will; (*plan*) scheme, means; compromise, arbitration; (*fallo*) sentence (*of a judge*); judgment.

árbitro [ár·bi·tro] *m.* arbitrator, sole judge, umpire.

árbol [ár·bol] *m.* tree; mast; **arbolado** [ar·bo·lá·do] *adj.* wooded; *m.* grove of trees.

arboleda [ar·bo·lé·da] *f.* grove.

arbusto [ar·bús·to] *m.* shrub.

arca [ár·ka] *f.* ark; chest, coffer; **arcón** [ar·kón] *m.* large coffer or chest; bin.

arcada [ar·ká·da] *f.* arcade; archway.

arcaico [ar·káj·ko] *adj.* archaic.

arcano [ar·ká·no] *adj.* hidden, secret; *m.* secret, mystery.

arce [ár·se] *m.* maple, maple tree.

arcilla [ar·sí·ya] *f.* clay.

arco [ár·ko] *m.* arc; arch; bow; violin bow; — **iris** rainbow.

archipiélago [ar·či·pjé·la·go] *m.* archipelago.

archisabido [ar·či·sa·bí·do] *adj.* very well-known.

archivo [ar·čí·bo] *m.* archives; file; public records; — **de cinta** tape archive; *Am.* (*despacho*) office, business office; **archivero** [ar·či·bé·ro] *m.* keeper of archives; city clerk.

arder [ar·dér] *v.* to burn; to be consumed (*with fever or passion*); *C.A. Mex., Col., Carib.* (*picar*) to smart, sting.

ardid [ar·díd] *m.* trick, scheme.
ardiente [ar·djén·te] *adj.* ardent, burning, fervent; (*apasionante*) passionate; fiery.
ardilla [ar·dí·ya] *f.* squirrel.
ardite [ar·dí·te] *m.* ancient coin of small value; bit, trifle; **no valer un** — not to be worth a penny.
ardor [ar·dór] *m.* ardor; heat; fervor, eagerness; *Ríopl., C. A., Mex.* smart.
ardoroso [ar·do·ró·so] *adj.* ardent, fiery.
arduo [ár·dwo] *adj.* arduous, hard, difficult.
área [á·re·a] *f.* area.
arena [a·ré·na] *f.* sand; arena; **-s** kidney stones; **arenal** [a·re·nál] *m.* sand pit.
arenga [a·réŋ·ga] *f.* address, speech.
arenisco [a·re·nís·ko] *adj.* sandy; gritty; **piedra arenisca** sandstone.
arenoso [a·re·nó·so] *adj.* sandy; gritty.
arenque [a·réŋ·ke] *m.* herring.
arepa [a·ré·pa] *f. Col., Ven., Carib.* a fried (*griddle*) cake made of corn meal that corresponds to the Mexican tortilla.
arete [a·ré·te] *m.* earring.
argamasa [ar·ga·má·sa] *f.* mortar.
argentar [ar·xen·tár] *v.* to plate (*with silver*); to polish.
argentino [ar·xen·tí·no] *adj.* silvery; Argentine; *m.* Argentine; Argentine gold coin worth 5 pesos.
argolla [ar·gó·ya] *f.* large iron ring; *Am.* (*anillo*) plain finger ring, engagement ring; *Am.* **tener** — to be lucky.
argón [ar·gón] *m.* argon (gas).
argucia [ar·gú·sja] *f.* cunning, astuteness; scheme; subtlety.
argüir[32] [ar·gwír] *v. irr.* to argue; to deduce, infer.
argumentación [ar·gu·men·ta·sjón] *f.* argumentation, argument, reasoning.
argumento [ar·gu·mén·to] *m.* reasoning; substance; subject matter, (*trama*) plot, resumé (*of a play or story*).
aridez [a·ri·dés] *f.* barrenness; dryness; drought.
árido [á·ri·do] *adj.* arid, dry, barren; **-s** *m. pl.* grains and dry vegetables; **medida para -s** dry measure.
ariete [a·rjé·te] *m.* ram, battering ram; — **hidráulico** hydraulic ram.
arisco [a·rís·ko] *adj.* gruff, harsh, unsociable; *Am.* (*tímido*) shy, distrustful.
arista [a·rís·ta] *f.* sharp edge; ridge.
aristocracia [a·ris·to·krá·sja] *f.* aristocracy.
aristócrata [a·ris·tó·kra·ta] *m. & f.* aristocrat.
aristocrático [a·ris·to·krá·ti·ko] *adj.* aristocratic.
aritmética [a·rit·mé·ti·ka] *f.* arithmetic.
arma [ár·ma] *f.* arm, weapon; (*ramo*) branch (*of the army*); **-s** armed forces; — **arrojadiza** missile weapon; — **blanca** sword or knife; **de -s tomar** ready for any emergency; ready to fight.
armada [ar·má·da] *f.* armada, fleet.
armador [ar·ma·dór] *m.* shipbuilder; assembler.
armadura [ar·ma·dú·ra] *f.* armor; armature (*of a generator or dynamo*); framework; mounting.
armamento [ar·ma·mén·to] *m.* armament; equipment.
armar [ar·már] *v.* to arm; (*componer*) to set up, assemble, rig up; — **una pendencia** to start a quarrel; *Col.* — **un trique** to lay a snare, set a trap; *Am.* **-se** to balk, to be stubborn; *Ven., Mex.* **-se con alguna cosa** to refuse to return something.
armario [ar·má·rjo] *m.* wardrobe, clothes closet; cabinet.
armatoste [ar·ma·tós·te] *m.* unwieldy object or machine; clumsy thing; heavy, clumsy fellow.
armazón [ar·ma·són] *f.* framework, skeleton; *m.* skeleton (*of an animal*); — **provisional** balloon

framing; *Am.* (*estante*) truss, shelf, set of shelves.
armella [ar·mé·ya] *f.* staple; screw eye.
armiño [ar·mí·ño] *m.* ermine.
armisticio [ar·mis·tí·sjo] *m.* armistice.
armonía [ar·mo·ní·a] *f.* harmony.
armónico [ar·mó·ni·ko] *adj.* harmonic; harmonious.
armonioso [ar·mo·njó·so] *adj.* harmonious, musical.
armonizar[9] [ar·mo·ni·sár] *v.* to harmonize.
arnés [ar·nés] *m.* harness; (*malla*) coat of mail; **-es** harness and trappings; equipment, outfit.
aro [á·ro] *m.* hoop; rim (*of a wheel*); *Am.* (*anillo*) finger ring; *Ch., Ríopl.* (*arete*) earring.
aroma [a·ró·ma] *f.* aroma, scent, perfume.
aromático [a·ro·má·ti·ko] *adj.* aromatic, fragrant, spicy; **sales aromáticas** smelling salts.
arpa [ár·pa] *f.* harp.
arpía [ar·pí·a] *f.* shrew.
arpón [ar·pón] *m.* harpoon, spear.
arqueado [ar·ke·á·do] *adj.* arched.
arquear [ar·ke·ár] *v.* to arch.
arquitecto [ar·ki·ték·to] *m.* architect.
arquitectónico [ar·ki·tek·tó·ni·ko] *adj.* architectural.
arquitectura [ar·ki·tek·tú·ra] *f.* architecture.
arrabal [a·rra·bál] *m.* outlying district; **-es** outskirts, suburbs.
arracada [a·rra·ká·da] *f.* earring.
arraigar[7] [a·rraj·gár] *v.* to root, take root; **-se** to become rooted, attached.
arrancado [a·rraŋ·ká·do] *adj. Mex., Carib., C.A., Andes* without money, broke.
arrancar[6] [a·rraŋ·kár] *v.* to uproot; to pull out; to start, start out; *Ch., Mex.* to flee, run away.
arranque [a·rráŋ·ke] *m.* start; pull; uprooting; automobile starter; — **de ira** fit or outburst of anger; **punto de** — starting point.
arras [á·rras] *f. pl.* earnest money; pledge; (*dote*) dowry.
arrasar [a·rra·sár] *v.* to level; to tear down, raze; to fill to the brim; **-se** to clear up (*said of the sky*); **-se de lágrimas** to fill up with tears.
arrastrado [a·rras·trá·do] *adj.* poor, destitute; (*vil*) mean, vile; wretched; rascally; **llevar una vida arrastrada** to lead a dog's life.
arrastrar [a·rras·trár] *v.* to drag, haul; *Ven.* (*rastrear*) to harrow (*land*); **-se** to drag along, crawl.
arrayán [a·rra·yán] *m.* myrtle.
¡arre! [á·rre] *interj.* gee! get up there!
arrear [a·rre·ár] *v.* to drive (*mules, cattle*); *Guat.* (*robar*) to rustle, steal cattle; *Am.* **-le a uno una bofetada** to give a person a slap.
arrebatamiento [a·rre·ba·ta·mjén·to] *m.* snatch; (*éxtasis*) ecstasy; rage.
arrebatar [a·rre·ba·tár] *v.* to snatch away; **-se de cólera** to have a fit of anger.
arrebatiña [a·rre·ba·tí·ña] *f.* grab, snatch; scramble; **arrebatón** [a·rre·ba·tón] *m.* quick or violent grab.
arrebato [a·rre·bá·to] *m.* rage; rapture, ecstasy; (*rabia*) fit; (*éxtasis*) anger.
arrebol [a·rre·ból] *m.* red color of the sky; rouge; **-es** red clouds.
arreciar [a·rre·sjár] *v.* to increase in intensity, get stronger.
arrecife [a·rre·sí·fe] *m.* reef.
arredrar [a·rre·drár] *v.* to frighten, intimidate; **-se** to be or get scared.
arreglar [a·rre·glár] *v.* to arrange, put in order; to regulate; to fix; to adjust, settle; *Am.* (*pagar*) to pay (*a debt*); *Am.* (*castigar*) to correct, punish; **-se** to doll up, fix oneself up; to settle differences, come to an agreement.
arreglo [a·rré·glo] *m.* arrangement; adjustment;

settlement; conformity, agreement; **con — a** according to.

arrellanarse [a·rre·ya·nár·se] *v.* to sprawl, lounge; (*estar satisfecho*) to be self-satisfied.

arremangado [a·rre·maŋ·gá·do] *adj. & p.p.* turned up; **nariz arremangada** turned up nose.

arremangar⁷ [a·rre·maŋ·gár] *v.* to tuck up, turn up, roll up (*the sleeves, trousers, etc.*); **-se** to roll up one's sleeves; **-se los pantalones** to roll up one's trousers.

arremeter [a·rre·me·tér] *v.* to attack, assail, assault.

arremetida [a·rre·me·tí·da] *f.* thrust, push, attack.

arremolinarse [a·rre·mo·li·nár·se] *v.* to whirl, swirl; to eddy; to mill around.

arrendamiento [a·rren·da·mjén·to] *m.* renting; lease; rental, rent.

arrendar [a·rren·dár] *v. irr.* to rent, lease, let; to hire; (*amarrar*) to tie (*a horse*); to bridle; *Am.* (*dirigirse*) to head for.

arrendatario [a·rren·da·tá·rjo] *m.* renter, tenant.

arreo [a·rré·o] *m.* raiment; ornament; *Am.* (*animales*) driving of horses or mules; *Ríopl., Ch., Mex., Ven.* (*grupo*) drove of horses or mules; **-s** trappings; equipment; finery; *adv.* uninterruptedly, without interruption.

arrepentido [a·rre·pen·tí·do] *adj.* repentant; *p.p. of* **arrepentirse.**

arrepentimiento [a·rre·pen·ti·mjén·to] *m.* repentance, regret.

arrepentirse³ [a·rre·pen·tír·se] *v. irr.* to repent, regret.

arrestado [a·rres·tá·do] *adj.* daring, rash; *p.p. of* **arrestar.**

arrestar [a·rres·tár] *v.* to arrest; *Am.* to return, strike back (*a ball*); *Peru* (*regañar*) to reprimand; **-se** to dare, venture.

arresto [a·rrés·to] *m.* arrest, imprisonment; detention; daring, rashness; rash act.

arriar¹⁷ [a·rrjár] *v.* to haul down, lower (*the flag*); to lower (*the sails*); (*aflojar*) to slacken (*a rope*).

arriba [a·rrí·ba] *adv.* above; upstairs; **de — abajo** from top to bottom; up and down; **río — upstream; ¡ — !** hurrah!

arribada [a·rri·bá·da] *f.* arrival; *Am.* back talk, impudent answer.

arribar [a·rri·bár] *v.* to arrive; to put into port; *Am.* (*prosperar*) to prosper, better one's lot.

arribo [a·rrí·bo] *m.* arrival.

arriendo [a·rrjén·do] = **arrendamiento.**

arriero [a·rrjé·ro] *m.* muleteer.

arriesgado [a·rrjez·gá·do] *adj.* risky, daring.

arriesgar⁷ [a·rrjez·gár] *v.* to risk; **-se** to dare, run a risk.

arrimar [a·rri·már] *v.* to bring or place near; (*apartar*) to lay aside; (*golpear*) to strike (*a blow*); **-se** to lean (on); to get near; to seek shelter.

arrinconar [a·rriŋ·ko·nár] *v.* to corner; to put in a corner; to lay aside; to slight, neglect; **-se** to retire; to live a secluded life.

arriscado [a·rris·ká·do] *adj.* bold; daring; brisk; spirited (*horse*); craggy, rugged; *Col.* **ser — to** have vigor.

arriscar⁶ [a·rris·kár] *v.* to risk, venture; *Mex.* (*arrollar*) to roll up, curl up, tuck up, fold back; *Col.* to have vim and vigor; *Am.* **— a** to reach, amount to; **-se** to get angry; *Peru., C.A.* to dress up, doll up.

arroba [a·rró·ba] *f.* weight of 25 pounds.

arrobamiento [a·rro·ba·mjén·to] *m.* trance, rapture.

arrobarse [a·rro·bár·se] *v.* to be entranced; to be in a trance; to be enraptured.

arrodillarse [a·rro·di·yár·se] *v.* to kneel.

arrogancia [a·rro·gán·sja] *f.* arrogance, pride.

arrogante [a·rro·gán·te] *adj.* arrogant, haughty, proud.

arrogarse⁷ [a·rro·gár·se] *v.* to appropriate, usurp, assume (*power or rights*).

arrojadizo [a·rro·xa·dí·so] *adj.* missile; **arma arrojadiza** missile weapon.

arrojado [a·rro·xá·do] *adj.* daring, rash, fearless; *p.p. of* **arrojar.**

arrojar [a·rro·xár] *v.* to throw, hurl, cast; to expel; *Am.* (*vomitar*) to throw up, vomit; **— un saldo de** to show a balance of; **-se a** to hurl oneself upon or at; (*osar*) to dare to.

arrojo [a·rró·xo] *m.* boldness, daring.

arrollador [a·rro·ya·dór] *adj.* sweeping, overwhelming, violent; (*que arrolla*) winding (*that serves to wind or roll up*).

arrollar [a·rro·yár] *v.* to roll up; to sweep away; (*pisar*) to trample upon; to destroy.

arropar [a·rro·pár] *v.* to wrap, cover; *Col.* (*aceptar*) to snap up, accept on the spot (*a deal*); **-se** to wrap up, cover up.

arrostrar [a·rros·trár] *v.* to face, defy; **-se** to dare, dare to fight face to face.

arroyada [a·rro·yá·da] *f.* gully, valley of a stream; bed (*formed by a stream*); (*inundación*) river flood.

arroyo [a·rró·yo] *m.* brook, small stream, rivulet; creek; gutter; **arroyuelo** [a·rro·ywé·lo] *m.* rivulet.

arroz [a·rrós] *m.* rice; **arrozal** [a·rro·sál] *m.* rice field.

arruga [a·rrú·ga] *f.* wrinkle.

arrugar⁷ [a·rru·gár] *v.* to wrinkle; *Carib.* (*fastidiar*) to bother, annoy; **-se** to get wrinkled; *Mex., Col.* (*agacharse*) to crouch with fear, be afraid.

arruinar [a·rrwi·nár] *v.* to ruin, destroy; **-se** to become ruined; *Am.* to go "broke", lose all one's fortune.

arrullar [a·rru·yár] *v.* to lull; to coo.

arrullo [a·rrú·yo] *m.* lullaby; cooing.

arrumbar [a·rrum·bár] *v.* to lay aside (*as useless*), put away in a corner, discard; (*despedir*) to dismiss, remove (*from office or a position of trust*); (*orientarse*) to take bearings, **— a su adversario** to corner one's opponent, overpower him.

arsenal [ar·se·nál] *m.* arsenal; navy yard.

arsénico [ar·sé·ni·ko] *m.* arsenic.

arte [ár·te] *m. & f.* art; skill, aoility; cunning; craft; **por — de** by way or means of; **bellas -s** fine arts.

artefacto [ar·te·fák·to] *m.* piece of workmanship, manufactured object; handiwork; contrivance.

arteria [ar·té·rja] *f.* artery.

artero [ar·té·ro] *adj.* crafty, astute.

artesa [ar·té·sa] *f.* trough.

artesano [ar·te·sá·no] *m.* artisan, craftsman; **artesanía** [ar·te·sa·ní·a] *f.* arts and crafts; workmanship, craftsmanship.

artesonado [ar·te·so·ná·do] *m.* ceiling decorated with carved panels.

ártico [ár·ti·ko] *adj.* arctic.

articulación [ar·ti·ku·la·sjón] *f.* articulation; pronunciation; (*juntura*) joint.

articular [ar·ti·ku·lár] *v.* to articulate; to join, unite.

artículo [ar·tí·ku·lo] *m.* article; **— de fondo** editorial.

artífice [ar·tí·fi·se] *m.* artisan, craftsman.

artificial [ar·ti·fi·sjál] *adj.* artificial.

artificio [ar·ti·fí·sjo] *m.* artifice, clever device; craft, skill; cunning, deceit.

artificioso [ar·ti·fi·sjó·so] *adj.* cunning, astute, deceitful; skilful.

artillería [ar·ti·ye·rí·a] *f.* artillery, gunnery; **— de plaza** (*or* **de sitio**) heavy artillery; **— de montaña**

light mountain artillery.

artillero [ar·ti·yé·ro] *m.* artilleryman, gunner.

artimaña [ar·ti·má·ña] *f.* trick.

artista [ar·tís·ta] *m. & f.* artist; actor.

artístico [ar·tís·ti·ko] *adj.* artistic.

arveja [ar·bé·xa] *f. C.A., Col., Ven.* pea. *Also referred to as* **alverja** [al·bér·xa].

arzobispo [ar·so·bís·po] *m.* archbishop.

arzon [ar·són] *m.* saddletree.

as [as] *m.* ace.

asa [á·sa] *f.* handle.

asado [a·sá·do] *m.* roast; *p.p. & adj.* roasted.

asador [a·sa·dór] *m.* spit (*for roasting*).

asaltador [a·sal·ta·dór] *m.* assailant; highway robber.

asaltar [a·sal·tár] *v.* to assault, attack; **-le a uno una idea** to be struck by an idea; *Ríopl., Carib.* — **la casa de un amigo** to give a surprise party.

asalto [a·sál·to] *m.* assault, attack; *Ríopl., Carib.* surprise party.

asamblea [a·sam·blé·a] *f.* assembly, legislature; meeting.

asar [a·sár] *v.* to roast; **-se** to roast; to feel hot.

asaz [a·sás] *adv.* enough, very.

ascendencia [a·sen·dén·sja] *f.* ancestry; origin.

ascendente [a·sen·dén·te] *adj.* ascendant, ascending, upward, rising.

ascender[1] [a·sen·dér] *v. irr.* to ascend, climb; (*de puesto*) to promote; (*sumar*) to amount (to).

ascendiente [a·sen·djén·te] *m.* ancestor; influence.

ascensión [a·sen·sjón] *f.* ascension; ascent.

ascenso [a·sén·so] *m.* ascent, rise; (*de puesto*) promotion.

ascensor [a·sen·sór] *m.* elevator.

asco [ás·ko] *m.* disgust, loathing; nausea; **me da** — it makes me sick; it disgusts me; *Mex., Ven.* **poner a uno del** — to call a person all kinds of bad names; to soil.

ascua [ás·kwa] *f.* ember.

aseado [a·se·á·do] *adj.* clean, neat; well-groomed; *p.p. of* **asear**.

asear [a·se·ár] *v.* to adorn; to make neat and clean; to groom; **-se** to clean oneself up.

asechanza [a·se·chán·sa] = **acechanza**.

asediar [a·se·djár] *v.* to besiege, attack.

asedio [a·sé·djo] *m.* siege.

asegurar [a·se·gu·rár] *v.* to assure; to secure; to affirm; to insure; **-se** to make sure; to hold on; to get insured.

asemejar [a·se·me·xár] *v.* to liken, compare; **-se a** to resemble.

asentaderas [a·sen·ta·dé·ras] *f. pl.* buttocks.

asentador [a·sen·ta·dór] *m.* razor strop.

asentar [a·sen·tár] *v.* (*poner*) to set; to put down in writing; (*afirmar*) to assert; to iron out; to establish; (*afilar*) to hone; strop; **-se** to settle.

asentimiento [a·sen·ti·mjén·to] *m.* assent, acquiescence, agreement.

asentir[3] [a·sen·tír] *v. irr.* to assent, agree.

aseo [a·sé·o] *m.* neatness, cleanliness.

asequible [a·se·kí·ble] *adj.* obtainable, available.

aserción [a·ser·sjón] *f.* assertion, affirmation.

aserradero [a·se·rra·dé·ro] *m.* sawmill.

aserrar[1] [a·se·rrár] *v. irr.* to saw.

aserrín [a·se·rrín] *m.* sawdust.

aserto [a·sér·to] *m.* assertion.

asesinar [a·se·si·nár] *v.* to assassinate, murder.

asesinato [a·se·si·ná·to] *m.* assassination, murder.

asesino [a·se·sí·no] *m.* assassin, murderer; *adj.* murderous.

asestar [a·ses·tár] *v.* to point, aim, direct; — **un golpe** to deal a blow; — **un tiro** to fire a shot.

aseveración [a·se·be·ra·sjón] *f.* assertion, affirmation, contention.

aseverar [a·se·be·rár] *v.* to assert, affirm.

asfalto [as·fál·to] *m.* asphalt.

asfixia [as·fík·sja] *f.* suffocation.

asfixiar [as·fik·sjár] *v.* to suffocate, smother.

así [a·sí] *adv.* so, thus, like this; therefore; — — so- so; — **que** so that; — **que** (*or* **como**) *conj.* as soon as; *Ríopl., Ch., Ven., Mex., Andes* — **no más** so-so; just so.

asiático [a·sjá·ti·ko] *adj. & m.* Asiatic.

asidero [a·si·dé·ro] *m.* handle; hold.

asiduo [a·si·dwo] *adj.* assiduous, diligent, persevering.

asiento [a·sjén·to] *m.* seat; site, location; bottom; entry (*in bookkeeping*); **-de abono** credit entry; **-de cargo** debit entry; **-s** dregs, sediment.

asignación [a·si·ǥ·na·sjón] *f.* assignment; allowance.

asignar [a·si·ǥ·nár] *v.* to assign; to allot; to attribute; to appoint.

asilado [a·si·lá·do] *m.* inmate (*of an asylum*).

asilar [a·si·lár] *v.* to house, shelter; to put in an asylum.

asilo [a·sí·lo] *m.* asylum, refuge, shelter.

asimilar [a·si·mi·lár] *v.* to assimilate, digest, absorb; (*asemejar*) to liken, compare.

asimismo [a·si·míz·mo] *adv.* likewise, also.

asir[22] [a·sír] *v. irr.* to seize, take hold of.

asistencia [a·sis·tén·sja] *f.* presence; attendance; assistance, help; *Mex.* sitting room; **-s** allowance; *Col., Ven., Mex.* **casa de** — boarding house.

asistente [a·sis·tén·te] *m.* assistant; helper; military orderly; *Col., Ven., P.R.* servant; **los -s** those present.

asistir [a·sis·tír] *v.* to attend, be present; (*ayudar*) to help; *Am.* to board, serve meals.

asno [áz·no] *m.* ass, donkey.

asociación [a·so·sja·sjón] *f.* association.

asociado [a·so·sjá·do] *m.* associate.

asociar [a·so·sjár] *v.* to associate; **-se** to join; to associate.

asolamiento [a·so·la·mjén·to] *m.* devastation, ravage, havoc, destruction.

asolar[2] [a·so·lár] *v. irr.* to raze; to lay waste; to parch; **-se** to dry up, become parched; (*depositar*) to settle (*as liquids*).

asoleado [a·so·le·á·do] *adj.* sunny; *p.p. of* **asolear**.

asolear [a·so·le·ár] *v.* to sun; **-se** to bask in the sun; to get sunburnt.

asomar [a·so·már] *v.* to show, appear; — **la cabeza** to stick one's head out; **-se** to look out (*of a window*); to peep out (*or* into); *Peru* (*acercarse*) to draw near, approach.

asombrar [a·som·brár] *v.* (*hacer sombra*) to cast a shadow, darken; (*asustar*) to astonish, amaze, frighten; **-se** to be astonished, amazed.

asombro [a·sóm·bro] *m.* astonishment, amazement; fright.

asombroso [a·som·bró·so] *adj.* astonishing, amazing.

asomo [a·só·mo] *m.* sign, indication; conjecture, suspicion; **ni por** — by no means.

aspa [ás·pa] *f.* wing of a windmill; blade (*of a propeller*); reel (*for winding yarn*).

aspecto [as·pék·to] *m.* aspect, look, appearance.

aspereza [as·pe·ré·sa] *f.* roughness, ruggedness; harshness; severity.

áspero [ás·pe·ro] *adj.* rough, uneven, harsh; gruff.

aspiración [as·pi·ra·sjón] *f.* aspiration, ambition, longing; (*inspiración*) inhalation, breathing in.

aspiradora [as·pi·ra·dó·ra] *f.* vacuum cleaner.

aspirante [as·pi·rán·te] *m. & f.* applicant; candidate.

aspirar [as·pi·rár] *v.* (*anhelar*) to aspire, long for
seek; (*inspirar*) to breathe in, to inhale; to aspirate
(*a sound*).

asquear [as·ke·ár] *v.* to disgust, nauseate, sicken.

asqueroso [as·ke·ró·so] *adj.* loathsome, disgusting,
sickening, filthy.

asta [ás·ta] *f.* horn; antler; (*poste*) mast, pole, staff,
flagstaff; (*lanza*) lance; **a media** — at half mast.

asterisco [as·te·rís·ko] *m.* asterisk, star (*used in
printing*).

astilla [as·tí·ya] *f.* chip; splinter; splint.

astillar [as·ti·yár] *v.* to chip; to splinter; **-se** to
splinter, break into splinters.

astillero [as·ti·yé·ro] *m.* dry dock; shipyard; lumber
yard; (*colgadero*) rack (*for lances or spears*).

astringente [as·triŋ·xén·te] *adj.* & *m.* astringent.

astro [ás·tro] *m.* star; planet.

astronauta [as·tro·náw·ta] *m.* & *f.* astronaut.

astronomía [as·tro·no·mí·a] *f.* astronomy; **astrónomo**
m. astronomer.

astucia [as·tú·sja] *f.* shrewdness, cunning; trick

asturiano [as·tu·rjá·no] *adj.* Asturian, of or from
Asturias, Spain; *m.* Asturian.

astuto [as·tú·to] *adj.* astute, shrewd, wily, crafty.

asueto [a·swé·to] *m.* recess, vacation; **dia de** —
holiday.

asumir [a·su·mír] *v.* to assume.

asunto [a·sún·to] *m.* topic, subject matter; business;
affair.

asustadizo [a·sus·ta·dí·so] *adj.* shy, scary, easily
frightened, jumpy.

asustar [a·sus·tár] *v.* to frighten, scare.

atacante [a·ta·kán·te] *m.* attacker; *adj.* attacking.

atacar[6] [a·ta·kár] *v.* to attack; (*apretar*) to tighten,
fasten; to ram; (*tapar*) to plug, wad (*a gun*).

atadura [a·ta·dú·ra] *f.* tie, knot; fastening.

atajar [a·ta·xár] *v.* to intercept; to interrupt, cut off;
to take a short cut; to cross out.

atajo [a·tá·xo] *m.* short cut; interception; *Col., Ven.*
(*rebaño*) drove. *See* **hatajo**.

atalaya [a·ta·lá·ya] *f.* lookout, watchtower; *m.*
lookout, watchman, guard.

atañer[19, 51] [a·ta·ñér] *v.* to concern.

ataque [a·tá·ke] *m.* attack; fit.

atar [a·tár] *v.* to tie, fasten; **-se** to get tied up; to be
puzzled or perplexed.

atardecer [a·tar·de·sér] *m.* late afternoon.

atareado [a·ta·re·á·do] *adj.* busy, over-worked.

atarear [a·ta·re·ár] *v.* to overwork, load with work;
-se to toil, work hard; to be very busy.

atascadero [a·tas·ka·dé·ro] *m.* muddy place;
obstruction.

atascar[6] [a·tas·kár] *v.* to stop up; to jam, obstruct; **-se**
to get stuck; to stick; to jam, get obstructed; to
stall.

ataúd [a·ta·úd] *m.* coffin.

ataviar[17] [a·ta·bjár] *v.* to attire, deck, adorn; **-se** to
dress up, doll up.

atavío [a·ta·bí·o] *m.* attire, costume; ornaments,
finery.

atemorizar[9] [a·te·mo·ri·sár] *v.* to frighten, scare.

atención [a·ten·sjón] *f.* attention, care, thought;
courtesy; **-es** business, affairs; **en — a** having in
mind, considering.

atender[1] [a·ten·dér] *v. irr.* to heed, pay attention; to
attend to, take care of; to take into account or
consideration.

atendido [a·ten·dí·do] *adj. Am.* attentive, courteous;
paid.

ateneo [a·te·né·o] *m.* literary forum.

atenerse[45] [a·te·nér·se] *v. irr.* to rely (on); (*aceptar*)

to accept, abide (by).

atenido [a·te·ní·do] *adj. Mex., Carib., C.A., Andes*
habitually dependent on another; *p.p. of* **atenerse.**

atentado [a·ten·tá·do] *m.* offense, violation; crime,
violence.

atentar[1] [a·ten·tár] *v. irr.* to attempt, try; — **contra
la vida de alguien** to attempt the life of someone.

atento [a·tén·to] *adj.* attentive; courteous, polite.

atenuar[18] [a·te·nwár] *v.* to attenuate, lessen; to tone
down; to dim; (*adelgazar*) to make thin or slender.

ateo [a·té·o] *m.* atheist; *adj.* atheistic.

aterciopelado [a·ter·sjo·pe·lá·do] *adj.* velvety.

aterido [a·te·rí·do] *adj.* stiff, numb from cold.

aterirse[3, 51] [a·te·rír·se] *v. irr.* to become numb with
cold.

aterrador [a·te·rra·dór] *adj.* terrifying, appalling.

aterrar [a·te·rrár] *v.* to terrify, frighten.

aterrizaje [a·te·rri·sá·xe] *m.* landing (*of a plane*);
pista de — landing strip.

aterrizar[9] [a·te·rri·sár] *v.* to land (*said of a plane*).

aterronar [a·te·rro·nár] *v.* to make lumpy, form into
lumps; **-se** to lump, form into lumps, become
lumpy.

aterrorizar[9] [a·te·rro·ri·sár] *v.* to terrify, frighten,
appal.

atesorar [a·te·so·rár] *v.* to treasure; to hoard, lay up,
accumulate.

atestado [a·tes·tá·do] *adj.* crowded, jammed, stuffed;
witnessed; *p.p. of* **atestar.**

atestar [a·tes·tár] *v.* (*legal*) to attest, testify, witness;
(*llenar*) to fill up, cram, stuff, crowd; **-se de** to
stuff oneself with, to get stuffed with.

atestiguar[8] [a·tes·ti·gwár] *v.* to testify, witness; to
attest.

atiborrar [a·ti·bo·rrár] *v.* to stuff; **-se** to stuff oneself.

atiesar [a·tje·sár] *v.* to stiffen.

atildado [a·til·dá·do] *adj.* spruce, trim; painstaking in
dress or style.

atinar [a·ti·nár] *v.* to hit the mark; to guess right.

atisbar [a·tiz·bár] *v.* to spy, look cautiously; to
watch, pry; to catch a glimpse of; to peek.

atisbo [a·tíz·bo] *m.* glimpse; insight; peek; spying.

atizar[9] [a·ti·sár] *v.* to poke, stir (*the fire*); to kindle,
rouse; to trim (*a wick*); — **un bofetón** to give a
wallop.

atlántico [ad·lán·ti·ko] *adj.* Atlantic; **el Atlántico** the
Atlantic.

atlas [ád·las] *m.* atlas.

atleta [ad·lé·ta] *m.* & *f.* athlete.

atlético [ad·lé·ti·ko] *adj.* athletic.

atletismo [ad·le·tíz·mo] *m.* athletics.

atmósfera [ad·mós·fe·ra] *f.* atmosphere, air.

atmosférico [ad·mos·fé·ri·ko] *adj.* atmospheric.

atole [a·tó·le] *m. Mex.* Mexican drink made of corn
meal; **atol** in C.A.

atolondrado [a·to·lon·drá·do] *p.p. & adj.* confused,
muddled; stunned; heedless, harebrained,
thoughtless.

atolondramiento [a·to·lon·dra·mjén·to] *m.*
thoughtlessness, recklessness; confusion,
perplexity.

atolondrar [a·to·lon·drár] *v.* to confuse, muddle;
perplex; to stun; **-se** to get muddled, confused; to
get stunned.

atómico [a·tó·mi·ko] *adj.* atomic.

atomizar [a·to·mi·sár] *v.* to atomize.

átomo [á·to·mo] *m.* atom; small particle, tiny bit.

atónito [a·tó·ni·to] *adj.* astonished, amazed.

átono [á·to·no] *adj.* unstressed.

atontado [a·ton·tá·do] *adj.* stupefied, stupid, stunned.

atontar [a·ton·tár] *v.* to stupefy, stun; to confuse.

atorar [a·to·rár] v. to jam; to stop up, clog; *Am.* to hold up, stop; **-se** to get stuck (*in the mud*); to get clogged; to get jammed; to choke (*with food*).

atormentar [a·tor·men·tár] v. to torment; to worry, afflict; to tease, bother, vex.

atornasolado [a·tor·na·so·lá·do] = **tornasolado**.

atornillar [a·tor·ni·yár] v. to screw; *Am.* (*molestar*) to bother, torment.

atorrante [a·to·rrán·te] m. & f. *Col., Ch. Ríopl., Bol.* vagabond, tramp.

atrabancar[6] [a·tra·baŋ·kár] v. to rush awkwardly; to run over; **-se** *Ríopl.* (*meterse*) to get involved in difficulties; *Ríopl.* to rush into things.

atrabiliario [a·tra·bi·ljá·rjo] adj. melancholy; bad-tempered.

atracar [a·tra·kár] v. (*llenar*) to cram, stuff; (*amarrar*) to moor, to approach land; (*atacar*) to hold up, assault; *Am.* to seize; *Col.* to pursue, harass; *Mex., C.A.* (*aporrear*) to thrash, beat; **— al muelle** to dock, moor to the wharf; **-se** to stuff oneself, overeat; *Ch.* to have a fist fight; *Ríopl.* (*vacilar*) to falter, stutter; **-se a** to come alongside of (*a ship*).

atracción [a·trak·sjón] f. attraction.

atraco [a·trá·ko] m. holdup, assault; *Am.* **darse un — de comida** to stuff oneself, gorge.

atracón [a·tra·kón] m. stuffing, gorging; *C.A.* (*riña*) violent quarrel; **darse un — de comida** to stuff oneself, gorge.

atractivo [a·trak·tí·bo] adj. attractive; m. attractiveness, charm.

atraer[46] [a·tra·ér] v. irr. to attract.

atragantarse [a·tra·gan·tár·se] v. to gobble up; to choke (*with food*).

atrancar[6] [a·traŋ·kár] v. to bolt, fasten with a bolt; *Am.* **-le a una cosa** (*encararse con*) to face something, stand up against something; **-se** to get crammed, obstructed; *Am.* to be stubborn, stick to one's opinion; *Col.* to stuff oneself, choke (*with food*).

atrapar [a·tra·pár] v. to trap, ensnare; to seize, grab; (*alcanzar*) to overtake.

atrás [a·trás] adv. back; behind; backward; *Am.* **echarse — (or para —)** to back out, go back on one's word.

atrasado [a·tra·sá·do] adj. late; behind time; backward; behind (*in one's work, payments, etc.*); slow (*said of a clock*); p.p. of **atrasar**.

atrasar [a·tra·sár] v. to delay; to be slow or behind time; **-se** to get behind, lose time; *Am.* to suffer a setback (*in one's health or fortune*).

atraso [a·trá·so] m. backwardness; delay; setback; **-s** arrears.

atravesar[1] [a·tra·be·sár] v. irr. to cross; to walk across; to go through; to pierce; *Am.* to buy wholesale.

atreverse [a·tre·bér·se] v. to dare, risk; (*ser respondón*) to be insolent, saucy.

atrevido [a·tre·bí·do] adj. bold, daring; insolent.

atrevimiento [a·tre·bi·mjén·to] m. boldness, daring; insolence.

atribuir[32] [a·tri·bwír] v. irr. to attribute, ascribe, impute.

atribular [a·tri·bu·lár] v. to grieve, distress; **-se** to grieve; to be distressed.

atributo [a·tri·bú·to] m. attribute, quality.

atril [a·tríl] m. lectern, reading desk; book stand; music stand.

atrincherar [a·trin·če·rár] v. to entrench, fortify with trenches; **-se** to entrench oneself.

atrio [á·trjo] m. court, patio in front of a church; entrance hall.

atrocidad [a·tro·si·dád] f. atrocity.

atronador [a·tro·na·dór] adj. thunderous, deafening.

atronar[2] [a·tro·nár] v. irr. to deafen; to stun.

atropellar [a·tro·pe·yár] v. to run over, run down, knock down; to trample upon; to insult; **— por** to knock down, overcome with violence; **-se** to rush.

atropello [a·tro·pé·yo] m. violent act; insult; outrage; trampling.

atroz [a·trós] adj. atrocious, awful; inhuman.

atún [a·tún] m. tunny fish, tuna fish.

aturdido [a·tur·dí·do] adj. & p.p. stupid, awkward; stunned, bewildered.

aturdimiento [a·tur·di·mjén·to] m. daze, bewilderment, confusion.

aturdir [a·tur·dír] v. to stun; to deafen; to bewilder.

atusar [a·tu·sár] v. to trim.

audacia [aw·dá·sja] f. daring, boldness.

audaz [aw·dás] adj. daring, bold.

audencia [aw·djén·sja] f. audience, hearing; court of justice.

audífono [aw·dí·fo·no] m. hearing aid; earphone.

auditor [aw·di·tór] m. judge advocate.

auditorio [aw·di·tó·rjo] m. audience.

auge [áw·xe] f. boom (*in the market*); (*alza*) boost (*in prices*); (*apogeo*) topmost height (*of fortune, fame, dignity, etc.*); **estar** (*or* **ir**) **en —** to be on the increase.

augurar [aw·gu·rár] v. to fortell, predict.

augusto [aw·gús·to] adj. venerable; majestic.

aula [áw·la] f. schoolroom, classroom; lecture hall.

aullar [aw·yár] v. to howl; to shriek; to bawl.

aullido [aw·yí·do] m. howl.

aumentar [aw·men·tár] v. to augment, increase.

aumento [aw·mén·to] m. increase, advance, rise.

aun [awn] (**aún**) adv. even, still, yet.

aunque [áwŋ·ke] conj. though, although.

aura [áw·ra] f. breeze; favor, applause; *Carib.* bird of prey, buzzard, vulture.

áureo [áw·re·o] adj. golden.

aureola [aw·re·ó·la] f. aureole, halo.

aureomicina [aw·re·o·mi·sí·na] f. Aureomycin (*trademark for chlortetracycline*).

aurora [aw·ró·ra] f. dawn; beginning; **— boreal** aurora borealis, northern lights.

auscultar [aws·kul·tár] v. to sound, examine by listening to (*the chest, lungs, heart, etc.*).

ausencia [aw·sén·sja] f. absence.

ausentarse [aw·sen·tár·se] v. to absent oneself; to be absent; to leave.

ausente [aw·sén·te] adj. absent.

auspicios [aws·pí·sjos] m. pl. auspices, patronage; omens.

austeridad [aws·te·ri·dád] f. austerity, severity, sternness, harshness.

austero [aws·té·ro] adj. austere, stern, strict; harsh.

austral [aws·trál] adj. southern.

austríaco [aws·trí·a·ko] adj. & m. Austrian.

austro [áws·tro] m. south wind.

auténtico [aw·tén·ti·ko] adj. authentic, true, genuine.

auto [áw·to] m. auto, automobile; one-act play; writ; order; **— sacramental** one-act religious play; **-s** proceedings.

autobús [aw·to·bús] m. bus, autobus.

autocarga [aw·to·kár·ga] f. (*computadora*) auto-boot.

autóctono [aw·tók·to·no] adj. indigenous, native.

autógena [aw·tó·ge·na] f. fusion welding.

autogiro [aw·to·xí·ro] m. autogiro.

automático [aw·to·má·ti·ko] adj. automatic.

automotriz [aw·to·mo·tríz] adj. automotive, self-moving.

automóvil [aw·to·mó·bil] *m.* automobile, auto.
automovilista [aw·to·mo·bi·lís·ta] *m. & f.* motorist, driver.
autonomía [aw·to·no·mí·a] *f.* autonomy.
autopista [aw·to·pís·ta] *f.* expressway, superhighway, freeway, throughway, turnpike.
autor [aw·tór] *m.* author.
autoridad [aw·to·ri·dád] *f.* authority.
autoritario [aw·to·ri·tá·rjo] *adj.* authoritative; authoritarian, domineering; bossy.
autorización [aw·to·ri·sa·sjón] *f.* authorization, sanction.
autorizar[9] [aw·to·ri·sár] *v.* to authorize, give power (to).
autoservicio [aw·to·ser·bí·sjo] *m.* self-service.
autoverificar [aw·to·be·ri·fi·kár] *v.* to selftest.
auxiliar [awk·si·ljár] *v.* to aid, help; *adj.* auxiliary, helping, assisting; *m.* assistant.
auxilio [awk·sí·ljo] *m.* aid, help.
avalar [a·ba·lár] *v.* to endorse; **avalista** *m. & f.* guarantor.
avaluación [a·ba·lwa·sjón] *f.* valuation, appraisal, assessment.
avaluar[18] [a·bal·wár] *v.* to value, appraise.
avalúo [a·ba·lú·o] *m.* valuation, appraisal.
avance [a·bán·se] *m.* advance, progress, headway; advanced payment; attack.
avanzada [a·ban·sá·da] *f.* advance guard; outpost; advanced unit, spearhead.
avanzar[9] [a·ban·sár] *v.* to advance.
avaricia [a·ba·rí·sja] *f.* avarice, greed.
avariento [a·ba·rjén·to] *adj.* avaricious, miserly; *m.* miser.
avaro [a·bá·ro] *adj.* miserly, greedy; *m.* miser.
avasallar [a·ba·sa·yár] *v.* to subject, dominate, subdue.
ave [á·be] *f.* bird; fowl; — **de corral** domestic fowl; — **de rapiña** bird of prey.
avecindarse [a·be·sin·dár·se] *v.* to settle, locate, establish oneself, take up residence (*in a community*).
avellana [a·be·yá·na] *f.* hazelnut; **avellano** [a·be·yá·no] *m.* hazel; hazelnut tree; **avellanado** [a·be·ya·ná·do] *adj.* hazel, light brown.
avellanar [a·be·ya·nár] *v.* to countersink.
avena [a·bé·na] *f.* oats.
avenencia [a·be·nén·sja] *f.* harmony, agreement; conformity.
avenida [a·be·ní·da] *f.* avenue; flood.
avenir[48] [a·be·nír] *v. irr.* to adjust; to reconcile; **-se a** to adapt oneself to; **-se con alguien** to get along with someone.
aventador [a·ben·ta·dór] *m.* fan (*for fanning a fire*); ventilator; winnower (*machine for separating wheat from chaff*).
aventajar [a·ben·ta·xár] *v.* to excel; to be ahead (of); **-se a** to get ahead of.
aventar[1] [a·ben·tár] *v. irr.* to fan; to winnow, blow chaff from grain; to throw out, expel; *Am.* (*tirar*) to pitch, throw; *Am.* to dry sugar (*in the open*); *Am.* to rouse (*game*); **-se** to be full of wind; to flee, run away; *Am.* (*atacar*) to attack, hurl oneself (*on someone*).
aventón [a·ben·tón] *m. Mex.* free ride, a "lift".
aventura [a·ben·tú·ra] *f.* adventure; risk, danger; chance.
aventurado [a·ben·tu·rá·do] *adj.* adventurous, risky; bold, daring.
aventurar [a·ben·tu·rár] *v.* to venture, risk; **-se a** to risk, run the risk of; to dare.
aventurero [a·ben·tu·ré·ro] *adj.* adventurous; *m.*

adventurer.
avergonzar[2, 9] [a·ber·gon·sár] *v. irr.* to shame; **-se** to feel ashamed.
avería [a·be·rí·a] *f.* damage; aviary, (*de pájaros*) birdhouse; *Am.* (*desgracia*) misfortune; *Mex.*, *Cuba* (*travesura*) mischief.
averiar[17] [a·be·rjár] *v.* to damage, spoil, hurt; **-se** to become damaged; to spoil.
averiguar[8] [a·be·ri·gwár] *v.* to find out; to investigate.
aversión [a·ber·sjón] *f.* aversion, dislike; reluctance.
avestruz [a·bes·trús] *m.* ostrich.
avezado [a·be·sá·do] *p.p. & adj.* accustomed; trained, practiced.
aviación [a·bja·sjón] *f.* aviation.
aviador [a·bja·dór] *m.* aviator, flyer; (*suplidor*) purveyor, provider; *Am.* moneylender (*to miners or laborers*), promoter.
aviar[17] [a·bjár] *v.* to equip; to supply; to prepare, make ready; *Am.* (*prestar*) to lend money or equipment; **estar aviado** to be surrounded by difficulties; to be in a fix.
ávido [á·bi·do] *adj.* eager; greedy.
avinagrado [a·bi·na·grá·do] *adj.* sour; acid; cross.
avinagrar [a·bi·na·grár] *v.* to sour, make sour or acid; **-se** to sour, become sour.
avío [a·bí·o] *m.* provision, supply; preparation; *Cuba, Mex.* (*préstamo*) loan of money or equipment; **-s** equipment; **-s de pescar** fishing tackle.
avión [a·bjón] *m.* airplane; martin (*a bird similar to a swallow*).
avisar [a·bi·sár] *v.* to inform, give notice, advise; to announce; to warn.
aviso [a·bí·so] *m.* notice, advice, announcement; warning.
avispa [a·bís·pa] *f.* wasp; **avispero** [a·bis·pé·ro] *m.* wasp's nest; **avispón** [a·bis·pón] *m.* hornet.
avispado [a·bis·pá·do] *adj.* lively, keen, clever, wide-awake; *Am.* (*asustado*) frightened, scared.
avispar [a·bis·pár] *v.* to spur, incite; **-se** to be on the alert; to be uneasy; *Am.* (*asustarse*) to become frightened, scared.
avistar [a·bis·tár] *v.* to glimpse, catch sight of; **-se** to see each other, meet.
avivar [a·bi·bár] *v.* to enliven, give life to; to revive; to brighten; to quicken.
avizor [a·bi·sór] *adj.* alert, watchful.
avizorar [a·bi·so·rár] *v.* to spy, watch closely.
aya [á·ya] *f.* child's nurse, governess; **ayo** [á·yo] *m.* tutor guardian.
ayer [a·yér] *adv.* yesterday.
ayuda [a·yú·da] *f.* aid, help.
ayudante [a·yu·dán·te] *m.* assistant.
ayudar [a·yu·dár] *v.* to aid, help.
ayunar [a·yu·nár] *v.* to fast.
ayunas [a·yú·nas]: **en** — fasting; **en** — **de** totally ignorant of.
ayuno [a·yú·no] *m.* fast; — **de** wholly ignorant of.
ayuntamiento [a·yun·ta·mjén·to] *m.* municipal government; town hall.
azabache [a·sa·bá·če] *m.* jet; **-s** jet ornaments.
azada [a·sá·da] *f.* spade; hoe; **azadón** [a·sa·dón] *m.* hoe.
azafata [a·sa·fá·ta] *f.* airline hostess.
azafrán [a·sa·frán] *m.* saffron.
azahar [a·sa·ár] *m.* orange or lemon blossom.
azar [a·sár] *m.* hazard; chance; accident; disaster.
azaroso [a·sa·ró·so] *adj.* risky; coincidental.
azogue [a·só·ge] *m.* quicksilver.
azolvar [a·sol·bár] *v.* to clog, obstruct; **-se** to clog, get clogged.
azorar [a·so·rár] *v.* to disturb, startle; to bewilder; **-se**

to be startled, astonished; to be bewildered, perplexed; to be uneasy.
azotaina [a·so·táj·na] *f.* flogging, lashing, beating.
azotar [a·so·tár] *v.* to whip, lash, beat; *Am.* (*trillar*) to thresh (*rice*), — **las calles** to ''beat the pavement'', walk the streets.
azote [a·só·te] *m.* whip; lash with a whip; (*aflicción*) scourge; affliction, calamity.
azotea [a·so·té·a] *f.* flat roof.
azteca [as·té·ka] *adj.*, *m.* & *f.* Aztec.
azúcar [a·sú·kar] *m.* & *f.* sugar.
azucarar [a·su·ka·rár] *v.* to sugar; to sweeten; **-se** to become sweet; *Am.* to crystallize, turn to sugar.
azucarera [a·su·ka·ré·ra] *f.* sugar bowl; sugar mill.
azucarero [a·su·ka·ré·ro] *adj.* sugar (*used as adj.*); *m.* sugar manufacturer, producer or dealer; sugar bowl.
azucena [a·su·sé·na] *f.* white lily.
azufre [a·sú·fre] *m.* sulphur.
azul [a·súl] *adj.* blue; — **celeste** sky-blue; — **marino** navy blue; — **turquí** indigo; *Am.* **tiempos -es** hard times.
azulado [a·su·lá·do] *adj.* bluish.
azular [a·su·lár] *v.* to dye or color blue.
azulejo [a·su·lé·xo] *m.* glazed tile; *Am.* (*pájaro*) bluebird; *adj.* bluish.
azuzar[9] [a·su·sár] *v.* to urge, egg on; to incite.

B:b

baba [bá·ba] *f.* drivel, slaver, saliva; slime, slimy secretion; *Am.* small alligator.
babear [ba·be·ár] *v.* to drivel; to slobber.
babero [ba·bé·ro] *m.* baby's bib.
babor [ba·bór] *m.* port, port side (*of a ship*).
babosear [ba·bo·se·ár] *v.* to slaver, drivel; to keep one's mouth open; to act like a fool.
baboso [ba·bó·so] *adj.* driveling, slobbering; slimy; foolishly sentimental; *Am.* silly, idiotic, foolish; **babosa** *f.* slug (*creature like a snail, but without a shell*).
babucha [ba·bú·ča] *f.* slipper; *Ríopl.* **a** — pickaback, on the back or shoulders.
bacalao [ba·ka·lá·o], **bacallao** *m.* Andalusia, *Am.* codfish.
bacía [ba·sí·a] *f.* basin.
bacilo [ba·sí·lo] *m.* bacillus.
bacín [ba·sín] *m.* pot, chamber pot; **bacinica** [ba·si·ní·ka] *f.* chamber pot.
bacteria [bak·té·rja] *f.* bacterium; **-s** bacteria.
bacteriología [bak·te·rjo·lo·xí·a] *f.* bacteriology.
bacteriológico [bak·te·rjo·ló·xi·ko] *adj.* bacteriological, pertaining to bacteriology.
báculo [bá·ku·lo] *m.* staff, cane; aid, support.
bache [bá·če] *m.* rut, hole in the road, pothole.
bachiller [ba·či·yér] *m.* bachelor (*one who holds degree*); talkative person; **bachillerato** [ba·či·ye·rá·to] *m.* bachelor's degree; studies for the bachelor's degree.
badajo [ba·dá·xo] *m.* clapper of a bell; foolish talker.
badana [ba·dá·na] *f.* sheepskin.
bagaje [ba·gá·xe] *m.* military baggage, army pack mule.
bagatela [ba·ga·té·la] *f.* trifle.
bagazo [ba·gá·so] *m.* waste pulp (*of sugarcane, olives, grapes, etc.*).
bagual [ba·gwál] *adj. Ríopl.* wild, untamed, unruly; *Ríopl.* rude, discourteous; *Ríopl.* (*flaco*) lanky,

awkward; *m. Ríopl.* wild horse.
bahía [ba·í·a] *f.* bay, harbor.
bailador [baj·la·dór] *m.* dancer; *adj.* dancing.
bailar [baj·lár] *v.* to dance; to spin around.
bailarín [baj·la·rín] *m.* dancer; **bailarina** [baj·la·rí·na] *f.* dancer.
baile [báj·le] *m.* dance; ball; ballet.
bailotear [baj·lo·te·ár] *v.* to jig, jiggle; to dance poorly; to dance around.
baivel [baj·bél] *m.* bevel.
baja [bá·xa] *f.* fall (*of prices*); war casualty; **dar de** — to discharge, muster out.
bajá [ba·xá] *m.* pasha.
bajada [ba·xá·da] *f.* descent; slope, dip (*on a road*); **de** — on the way down; — **vertical** *f.* waste stack; **subidas y -s** ups and downs.
bajar [ba·xár] *v.* to go down; to drop (*as price or value*); to lower; to take or carry down; to humble; **-se** to get down or off; to alight.
bajel [ba·xél] *m.* boat, ship.
bajeza [ba·xé·sa] *f.* vile act or remark; meanness; baseness; degradation.
bajío [ba·xí·o] *m.* shoal, sand bank; *Mex.*, *Bol.* lowland.
bajo [bá·xo] *adj.* low; short; soft, bass (*tone or voice*); shallow (*water*); subdued (*color*); (*humilde*) humble; (*vil*) base; **piso** — first floor, ground floor; *prep.* under, underneath; *m.* bass.
bala [bá·la] *f.* bullet, shot, ball; (*bulto*) bale (*of cotton*).
balada [ba·lá·da] *f.* ballad.
baladí [ba·la·dí] *adj.* trivial; flimsy.
balance [ba·lán·se] *m.* balance; equilibrium; balance sheet; (*vaivén*) rocking, rolling.
balancear [ba·lan·se·ár] *v.* to balance; to rock, roll; to swing, sway; to waver.
balanceo [ba·lan·séo] *m.* rocking, rolling, swinging; balancing; wavering; wobbling.
balanza [ba·lán·sa] *f.* balance, scale.
balar [ba·lár] *v.* to bleat.
balaustrada [ba·laws·trá·da] *f.* balustrade, banister; railing.
balaustre [ba·láws·tre] *m.* banister.
balazo [ba·lá·so] *m.* shot; (*herida*) bullet wound; *adj. Ch.* (*listo*) clever, cunning.
balbucear [bal·bu·se·ár] *v.* to stammer, stutter; to babble.
balbuceo [bal·bu·séo] *m.* babble.
balcón [bal·kón] *m.* balcony.
baldado [bal·dá·do] *m.* cripple; *adj.* & *p.p.* crippled.
baldar [bal·dár] *v.* to cripple; to trump (*a card*).
balde [bál·de] *m.* pail; bucket; **de** — free of charge; **en** — in vain.
baldío [bal·dí·o] *adj.* barren; fallow, uncultivated; *m.* fallow land; wasteland.
baldón [bal·dón] *m.* infamy, insult.
baldosa [bal·dó·sa] *f.* floor tile; paving stone.
balido [ba·lí·do] *m.* bleat, bleating.
balneario [bal·ne·á·rjo] *m.* bathing resort; *adj.* pertaining to bathing resorts or medicinal springs.
balompié [ba·lom·pjé] *m.* soccer.
balota [ba·ló·ta] *f.* ballot.
balotar [ba·lo·tár] *v.* to ballot, vote.
balsa [bál·sa] *f.* (*de agua*) pond, pool; (*embarcación*) raft; *Mex.* marsh; *Am.* (*árbol*) a species of ceiba (*a tropical tree*).
bálsamo [bál·sa·mo] *m.* balsam, balm.
baluarte [ba·lwár·te] *m.* bulwark.
ballena [ba·yé·na] *f.* whale; (*hueso*) whalebone.
bambolear [bam·bo·le·ár] *v.* to sway, swing, rock; **-se** to stagger; to sway.

bambú [bam·bú] *m.* bamboo.
banana [ba·ná·na] *f.* banana; **banano** [ba·ná·no] *m.* banana tree.
banasta [ba·nás·ta] *f.* large basket.
banca [báŋ·ka] *f.* bench; (*naipes*) card game; (*negocio*) banking; banking house.
bancada [baŋ·ká·da] *f.* work table.
bancario [baŋ·ká·rjo] *adj.* bank, pertaining to a bank.
bancarrota [baŋ·ka·rró·ta] *f.* bankruptcy; failure, collapse.
banco [báŋ·ko] *m.* bank; (*asiento*) bench, stool; (*de peces*) school (*of fish*); *Mex.* pile of grain; *Ven.* (*meseta*) small hill on a plain.
banda [bán·da] *f.* (*musical*) band; (*cinta*) ribbon, sash; (*grupo*) gang, group, party; flock; (*lindero*) side, edge, border.
bandada [ban·dá·da] *f.* flock of birds; *Am.* (*porra*) gang.
bandeja [ban·dé·xa] *f.* tray; *Mex., Ven., Col.* bowl.
bandera [ban·dé·ra] *f.* banner, flag; *Ríopl., Cuba, Mex.* **parar uno** — to take the lead, be a gangleader.
banderilla [ban·de·rí·ya] *f.* dart with a small flag or streamers (*used in bullfights*); **clavar a uno una** — to goad or taunt someone; **tercio de** — the **banderilla** phase of the bullfight; *Am.* **pegar una** — to touch for a loan.
banderillero [ban·de·ri·yé·ro] *m.* bullfighter who sticks the **banderillas** into the bull.
banderín [ban·de·rín] *m.* small flag; signal flag; pennant; (*oficina*) recruiting office.
banderola [ban·de·ró·la] *f.* streamer, small banner or flag; pennant.
bandidaje [ban·di·dá·xe] *m.* banditry, highway robbery; bandits.
bandido [ban·dí·do] *m.* bandit, gangster.
bando [bán·do] *m.* (*decreto*) decree, proclamation; (*partido*) party, faction.
bandolero [ban·do·lé·ro] *m.* bandit.
bandurria [ban·dú·rrja] *f.* bandore (*stringed instrument*); *Ríopl.* a species of wading bird.
banquero [baŋ·ké·ro] *m.* banker.
banqueta [baŋ·ké·ta] *f.* bench (*without a back*); stool; footstool; *Mex.* sidewalk.
banquete [baŋ·ké·te] *m* banquet.
banquetear [baŋ·ke·te·ár] *v.* to banquet, feast.
banquillo [baŋ·kí·yo] *m.* bench, stool.
bañada [ba·ñá·da] *f.* shower, spray; (*inmersión*) dip, bath.
bañar [ba·ñár] *v.* to bathe, wash; to dip; **-se** to take a bath.
bañera [ba·ñé·ra] *f.* bathtub.
bañista [ba·nís·ta] *m. & f.* bather.
baño [bá·ño] *m.* (*aseo*) bath; bathtub; (*acabado*) cover, coating; — **de María** double boiler; *Am.* — **ruso** steam bath.
baqueta [ba·ké·ta] *f.* rod; whip; **-s** (*muslo*) drumsticks; **tratar a la** — to treat scornfully, despotically.
baquiano [ba·kjá·no], **baqueano** [ba·ke·á·no] *m. Ríopl., Ven., Andes* native guide; *adj. Ríopl., Andes* having an instinctive sense of direction.
bar [bar] *m.* bar, taproom, tavern.
baraja [ba·rá·xa] *f.* pack of cards.
barajar [ba·ra·xár] *v.* to shuffle; to mix, jumble together; to scuffle, wrangle; *Am.* (*impedir*) to hinder, obstruct.
baranda [ba·rán·da] *f.* railing; **barandal** [ba·ran·dál] *m.* banister, railing.
barandilla [ba·ran·dí·ya] *f.* balustrade, rail, railing.
barata [ba·rá·ta] *f.* barter, exchange; *Mex., C.A.,*

Andes, Ven. bargain sale; *Peru, Ch.* cockroach.
baratear [ba·ra·te·ár] *v.* to sell cheap; to cheapen; to cut the price of.
baratija [ba·ra·tí·xa] *f.* trinket, trifle.
barato [ba·rá·to] *adj.* cheap; *m.* bargain sale; (*premio*) money given by the winning gambler.
baratura [ba·ra·tú·ra] *f.* cheapness.
baraúnda [ba·ra·ún·da] *f.* clamor, uproar, clatter.
barba [bár·ba] *f.* chin; beard; **-s** whiskers.
barbacoa [bar·ba·kó·a] *f. Mex., C.A., Col., Ríopl.* barbecue; barbecued meat.
barbado [bar·bá·do] *adj.* bearded.
barbaridad [bar·ba·ri·dád] *f.* cruelty, brutality; rudeness; **una** — **de** a lot of; **¡que** — **!** what nonsense!; what an atrocity!
barbarie [bar·bá·rje] *f.* barbarousness; savagery; lack of culture, ignorance; cruelty, brutality.
bárbaro [bár·ba·ro] *adj.* barbarous, cruel, savage; crude, coarse; *m.* barbarian.
barbechar [bar·be·čár] *v.* to plow; to fallow.
barbecho [bar·bé·čo] *m.* first plowing; plowed land; fallow, fallow land.
barbería [bar·be·rí·a] *f.* barbershop.
barbero [bar·bé·ro] *m.* barber; *Mex.* flatterer.
barbilla [bar·bí·ya] *f.* point of the chin.
barbón [bar·bón], **barbudo** [bar·bú·do] *adj.* bearded.
barca [bár·ka] *f.* boat, launch, barge.
barco [bár·ko] *m.* boat, ship.
bardo [bár·do] *m.* bard, minstrel, poet.
bario [bá·rjo] *m.* barium.
barítono [ba·rí·to·no] *m.* baritone.
barlovento [bar·lo·bén·to] *m.* windward.
barniz [bar·nís] *m.* varnish; glaze; (*de prensa*) printer's ink.
barnizar[9] [bar·ni·sár] *v.* to varnish; to glaze.
barómetro [ba·ró·me·tro] *m.* barometer.
barquero [bar·ké·ro] *m.* boatman; bargeman.
barquillo [bar·kí·yo] *m.* rolled wafer; ice-cream cone.
barquinazo [bar·ki·ná·so] *m.* tumble, bad fall, hard bump, somersault; *Am.* lurch (*of a vehicle or boat*).
barra [bá·rra] *f.* bar; rod; railing; (*de arena*) sand bar; claque, audience; — **de jabón** bar of soap; — **de tabulación** tabulator; — **espaciadora** space bar.
barrabasada [ba·rra·ba·sá·da] *f.* mischief, mean prank; rash, hasty act.
barraca [ba·rrá·ka] *f.* hut, cabin; *Andes* large shed, warehouse.
barranca [ba·rráŋ·ka] *f.*, **barranco** [ba·rráŋ·ko] *m.* ravine, gorge; *Am.* (*peña*) cliff.
barreminas [ba·rre·mí·nas] *m.* mine-sweeper.
barrena [ba·rré·na] *f.* auger, drill; gimlet (*small tool for boring holes*); (*avión*) spinning dive (*of a plane*).
barrenar [ba·rre·nár] *v.* to drill, bore; to scuttle (*a ship*); (*volar*) to blast (*a rock*).
barrendero [ba·rren·dé·ro] *m.* sweeper.
barrer [ba·rrér] *v.* to sweep; to sweep away; *Am.* to defeat; *Am.* **al** — altogether, as a whole.
barrera [ba·rré·ra] *f.* barrier; obstacle; — **arancelarias** tariff barriers.
barreta [ba·rré·ta] *f.* small iron bar; *Mex., Cuba, Col.* pick, pickaxe.
barrica [ba·rrí·ka] *f.* cask, keg.
barrida [ba·rrí·da] *f. Am.* sweep, sweeping.
barrido [ba·rrí·do] *m.* sweep, sweeping; sweepings; *p.p. of* **barrer.**
barriga [ba·rrí·ga] *f.* belly; (*bombeo*) bulge.
barrigón [ba·rri·gón], **barrigudo** [ba·rri·gú·do] *adj.* big-bellied.

barril [ba·rríl] *m.* barrel, keg.
barrilete [ba·rri·lé·te] *m.* clamp; *Arg.* kite.
barrio [bá·rrjo] *m.* district, neighborhood, quarter; **-s bajos** slums.
barro [bá·rro] *m.* (*tierra*) mud, clay; (*granillo*) pimple; *Am.* **hacer** (*or* **cometer**) **un** — to commit a blunder.
barroso [ba·rró·so] *adj.* muddy; pimply; reddish.
barrote [ba·rró·te] *m.* short, thick bar; brace; (*de silla*) rung (*of a ladder or chair*).
barruntar [ba·rrun·tár] *v.* to foresee; to have a presentiment; to conjecture.
barrunto [ba·rrún·to] *m.* foreboding, presentiment; guess; hint, indication, sign.
bártulos [bár·tu·los] *m. pl.* household goods; implements, tools.
barullo [ba·rú·yo] *m.* hubbub, racket, disorder.
basa [bá·sa] *f.* base, pedestal; basis, foundation.
basar [ba·sár] *v.* to base; to put on a base.
basca [bás·ka] *f.* nausea, sickness to one's stomach; **tener -s** to be nauseated, sick to one's stomach.
báscula [bás·ku·la] *f.* scale (*for weighing*), platform scale.
base [bá·se] *f.* base, basis, foundation; — **de datos** data base.
basic [bá·sik] *m.* (*computadora*) basic.
básico [bá·si·ko] *adj.* basic.
basquear [bas·ke·ár] *v.* to heave, try to vomit; to be nauseated, sick to one's stomach.
basquetbol [bas·ke·ból] *m.* basketball.
bastante [bas·tán·te] *adj.* enough, sufficient; *adv.* enough.
bastar [bas·tár] *v.* to be enough; to suffice.
bastardilla [bas·tar·dí·ya] *f.* italic type, italics.
bastardo [bas·tár·do] *adj.* bastard.
bastidor [bas·ti·dór] *m.* (*teatro*) wing (*of a stage*); (*marco*) frame; embroidery frame; (*ventana*) window sash; easel (*support for a picture, blackboard, etc.*); **entre -es** behind the scenes, off stage.
bastilla [bas·tí·ya] *f.* hem.
bastimento [bas·ti·mén·to] *m.* supply, provisions; vessel, ship.
basto [bás·to] *adj.* coarse; *m.* (*naipes*) club (*in cards*); *Am.* saddle pad.
bastón [bas·tón] *m.* cane, walking stick.
basura [ba·sú·ra] *f.* rubbish, scraps; garbage; refuse.
basurero [ba·su·ré·ro] *m.* garbage or rubbish dump; manure pile; garbage man, rubbish man; street cleaner.
bata [bá·ta] *f.* lounging robe; housecoat, wrapper, dressing gown; smock; **batín** [ba·tín] *m.* smock.
batahola [ba·ta·ó·la] *f.* hubbub, racket, uproar.
batalla [ba·tá·ya] *f.* battle; struggle.
batallar [ba·ta·yár] *v.* to battle, fight, struggle.
batallón [ba·ta·yón] *m.* battalion.
batata [ba·tá·ta] *f.* *Caribe, Sp.* sweet potato.
bate [bá·te] *m.* baseball bat.
batea [ba·té·a] *f.* tray; trough; bowl; *Mex., Ven., Col. C.A.* barge; *Am.* washtub.
bateador [ba·te·a·dór] *m.* batter (*in baseball*).
batear [ba·te·ár] *v. Mex., Carib., C.A., Ven.* to bat.
batería [ba·te·rí·a] *f.* battery (*military, naval, or electric*); — **de cocina** set of kitchen utensils; — **de jazz** a jazz combo; *Mex.* **dar** — to raise a rumpus; (*trabajar*) to plod, work hard.
batidor [ba·ti·dór] *m.* beater; scout; — **de alambre** wire beater.
batintín [ba·tin·tín] *m.* gong.
batir [ba·tír] *v.* (*combatir*) to beat, whip, defeat; (*reconocer*) reconnoiter, explore; (*mover*) to flap;

Ch. to rinse (*clothes*); *Ríopl.* to denounce; **-se** to fight; — **palmas** to clap, applaud.
batisfera [ba·tis·fé·ra] *f.* bathysphere.
baturrillo [ba·tu·rrí·yo] *m.* medley, mixture; hodgepodge.
batuta [ba·tú·ta] *f.* orchestra conductor's baton or wand; **llevar la** — to lead; to be the leader.
baudio [báw·djo] *m.* (*computadora*) baud.
baúl [ba·úl] *m.* trunk, chest; — **mundo** large trunk.
bautismo [baw·tíz·mo] *m.* baptism, christening; **nombre de** — Christian name.
bautista [baw·tís·ta] *m. & f.* Baptist; baptizer.
bautizar[9] [baw·ti·sár] *v.* to baptize, christen.
bautizo [baw·tí·so] *m.* christening, baptism.
bauxítica [baw·ksí·ti·ka] *f.* bauxite.
baya [bá·ya] *f.* berry.
bayeta [ba·yé·ta] *f.* flannel; flannelette; **bayetón** *m.* thick wool cloth; *Col.* long poncho lined with flannel.
bayo [bá·yo] *adj.* bay, reddish-brown.
baza [bá·sa] *f.* trick (*cards played in one round*); **meter** — to meddle; to butt into a conversation; **no dejar meter** — not to let a person put a word in edgewise.
bazar [ba·sár] *m.* bazaar; department store.
bazo [bá·so] *m.* spleen.
bazofia [ba·só·fja] *f.* scraps, refuse, garbage; dregs.
beatitud [be·a·ti·túd] *f.* bliss, blessedness.
beato [be·á·to] *adj.* blessed; beatified; devout; overpious; (*hipócrita*) hypocritical.
bebé [be·bé] *m.* baby.
bebedero [be·be·dé·ro] *m.* drinking trough; watering place; spout.
bebedor [be·be·dór] *m.* drinker; drunkard.
beber [be·bér] *v.* to drink; to drink in, (*absorber*) absorb.
bebida [be·bí·da] *f.* drink, beverage; **dado a la** — given to drink.
beca [bé·ka] *f.* scholarship, fellowship; (*faja*) sash worn over the academic gown.
becario [be·ká·rjo] *m.* scholar, fellow, holder of a scholarship.
becerro [be·sé·rro] *m.* young bull (*less than a year old*); calf; calfskin.
becuadro [be·kwá·dro] *m.* natural sign (*in music*).
bedel [be·dél] *m.* beadle.
befa [bé·fa] *f.* scoff, jeer.
befar [be·fár] *v.* to scoff, jeer at, mock.
bejuco [be·xú·ko] *m.* reed; **silla de** — cane chair.
beldad [bel·dád] *f.* beauty.
belga [bél·ga] *adj., m. & f.* Belgian.
bélico [bé·li·ko] *adj.* warlike.
beligerante [be·li·xe·rán·te] *adj., m. & f.* belligerent.
bellaco [be·yá·ko] *adj.* sly, deceitful; *m.* villain; rascal.
bellaquear [be·ya·ke·ár] *v.* to cheat; to play tricks; *Ríopl.* to rear, stand up on the hind legs; *Ríopl.* to balk; *Am.* to be touchy, oversensitive.
bellaquería [be·ya·ke·rí·a] *f.* cunning, trickery; sly act or remark.
belleza [be·yé·sa] *f.* beauty.
bello [bé·yo] *adj.* beautiful.
bellota [be·yó·ta] *f.* acorn.
bemol [be·mól] *adj.* flat (*in music*); **tener -es** to have difficulties.
bendecir[27, 52] [ben·de·sír] *v. irr.* to bless.
bendición [ben·di·sjón] *f.* benediction, blessing; *Mex., C.A., Col., Ven.* **echarle la** — **a una cosa** to give something up for lost.
bendito [ben·dí·to] *adj.* blessed; saintly; **es un** — he is a saint, he is a simple soul; *p.p. of* **bendecir.**

benefactor [be·ne·fak·tór] *m.* benefactor; patron.
beneficencia [be·ne·fi·sén·sja] *f.* beneficence, kindness, charity; — **pública** welfare.
beneficiar [be·ne·fi·sjár] *v.* to benefit, do good; to cultivate (*land*); to exploit (*a mine*); to treat (*metals*); *Col., Ven.* (*matar*) to slaughter (*cattle*) for marketing.
beneficio [be·ne·fí·sjo] *m.* (*provecho*) benefit, profit; exploitation of a mine; (*cultivo*) cultivation of land; *Ch.* fertilizer; *Am.* slaughtering (*of cattle*).
benéfico [be·né·fi·ko] *adj.* beneficent, good, kind.
benemérito [be·ne·mé·ri·to] *m.* worthy, notable; *adj.* worthy.
benevolencia [be·ne·bo·lén·sja] *f.* benevolence, kindness.
benévolo [be·né·bo·lo] *adj.* benevolent, good, kindly.
benigno [be·níg·no] *adj.* benign, gentle, mild, kind.
beodo [be·ó·do] *adj.* drunk; *m.* drunkard.
berbiquí [ber·bi·kí] *m.* carpenter's brace.
berenjena [be·reŋ·xé·na] *f.* eggplant; *Mex., C.A.* kind of squash; **berenjenal** *m.* egg-plant patch; **meterse uno en un** — to get into a mess.
bergantín [ber·ġan·tín] *m.* brigantine, brig (*square-rigged ship with two masts*).
beriberi [be·ri·bé·ri] *m.* beriberi.
berilio [be·rí·ljo] *m.* beryllium.
bermejo [ber·mé·xo] *adj.* crimson, bright red.
bermellón [ber·me·yón] *adj.* vermilion (*bright red*).
berrear [be·rre·ár] *v.* to bellow; to scream; to sing off key.
berrido [be·rrí·do] *m.* bellow, bellowing; scream.
berrinche [be·rrín·če] *m.* fit of anger; tantrum.
berro [bé·rro] *m.* water cress.
berza [bér·sa] *f.* cabbage.
besar [be·sár] *v.* to kiss.
beso [bé·so] *m.* kiss.
bestia [bés·tja] *f.* beast.
bestialidad [bes·tja·li·dád] *f.* bestiality, brutality.
besugo [be·sú·ġo] *m.* sea bream (*a fish*).
besuquear [be·su·ke·ár] *v.* to kiss repeatedly.
betabel [be·ta·bél] *f. Mex.* beet.
betún [be·tún] *m.* bitumen (*combustible mineral*); black pitch; (*de zapatos*) shoeblacking.
Biblia [bí·blja] *f.* Bible.
bíblico [bí·bli·ko] *adj.* Biblical.
biblioteca [bi·bljo·té·ka] *f.* library; set of volumes; bookcase.
bibliotecario [bi·bljo·te·ká·rjo] *m.* librarian.
bicarbonato [bi·kar·bo·ná·to] *m.* bicarbonate; — **de sosa** bicarbonate of soda.
bicicleta [bi·si·klé·ta] *f.* bicycle; **biciclista** [bi·si·klís·ta], **bicicletista** [bi·si·kle·tís·ta] *m. & f.* bicyclist, bicycle rider.
bicho [bí·čo] *m.* insect, bug; any small animal; an insignificant person; *C.A.* baby at creeping stage.
biela [bjé·la] *f.* connecting rod (*of an engine*).
bien [bjen] *adv.* well; — **que** although; **ahora** — now then; **más** — rather; **si** — although; *m.* good, benefit; **-es** property; **-es muebles** goods and chattels; **-es inmuebles** real estate; **-es raíces** real estate.
bienaventurado [bje·na·ben·tu·rá·do] *adj.* blessed, happy.
bienaventuranza [bje·na·ben·tu·rán·sa] *f.* blessedness; beatitude; bliss.
bienestar [bje·nes·tár] *m.* well-being, comfort, welfare.
bienhechor [bje·ne·čór] *m.* benefactor.
bienvenida [bjem·be·ní·da] *f.* welcome.
bienvenido [bjem·be·ní·do] *adj.* welcome.
biftec [bif·ték], **bistec** [bis·ték], **bisté** [bis·té] *m.*

beefsteak.
bifurcación [bi·fur·ka·sjón] *f.* fork, forking, branching out; (*empalme*) railway junction; branch, railroad.
bifurcarse[6] [bi·fur·kár·se] *v.* to fork, branch off, divide into two branches.
bigamía [bi·ġa·mí·a] *f.* bigamy.
bigote [bi·ġó·te] *m.* mustache.
bikini [bi·kí·ni] *m.* bikini.
bilabial [bi·la·bjál] *adj.* bilabial.
bilingüe [bi·líŋ·gwe] *adj.* bilingual.
bilingüismo [bi·liŋ·gwíz·mo] *m.* bilingualism.
bilis [bí·lis] *f.* bile.
billar [bi·yár] *m.* billiards; billiard room.
billete [bi·yé·te] *m.* ticket; note; bill, banknote.
billón [bi·yón] *m.* billion.
bimestre [bi·més·tre] *m.* two-month period; bi-monthly salary, rent, etc.; *adj.* bi-monthly; **bimestral** [bi·mes·trál] *adj.* bimonthly.
binario [bi·ná·rjo] *adj. & n.* (*computadora*) binary system.
biografía [bjo·ġra·fí·a] *f.* biography.
biología [bjo·lo·xí·a] *f.* biology.
biombo [bjóm·bo] *m.* folding screen.
biopsia [bjóp·sja] *f.* biopsy.
birlar [bir·lár] *v.* to snatch away; to steal; (*matar*) to kill or knock down with one blow.
birrete [bi·rré·te] *m.* academic cap; mortarboard.
bisabuelo [bi·sa·bwé·lo] *m.* great-grandfather; **bisabuela** *f.* great-grandmother.
bisagra [bi·sá·ġra] *f.* hinge.
bisel [bi·sél] *m.* bevel.
bisiesto [bi·sjés·to] *adj.* leap (*year*).
bismuto [biz·mú·to] *m.* bismuth.
bisnieto [biz·njé·to] *m.* great-grandson; **bisnieta** [biz·njé·ta] *f.* great-granddaughter.
bisojo [bi·só·xo] *adj.* squint-eyed.
bisonte [bi·són·te] *m.* bison; the American buffalo.
bisturí [bis·tu·rí] *m.* bistoury, surgical knife.
bitoque [bi·tó·ke] *m.* barrel plug, stopper; *Mex.,* faucet; *Col., Cuba, Mex.* injection point (*of a syringe*).
bizarría [bi·sa·rrí·a] *f.* gallantry, bravery; generosity.
bizarro [bi·sá·rro] *adj.* gallant, brave; generous.
bizco [bís·ko] *adj.* cross-eyed.
bizcocho [bis·kó·čo] *m.* hardtack, hard biscuit; cake; cookie; — **borracho** cake dipped in wine.
biznieto [biz·njé·to] *m.* great-grandson; **biznieta** *f.* great-granddaughter.
blanco [bláŋ·ko] *adj.* (*color*) white; *m.* white man; (*nada escrito*) blank, blank sheet; (*objeto de tiro*) target, goal.
blancura [blaŋ·kú·ra] *f.* whiteness.
blancuzco [blaŋ·kús·ko], **blanquecino** [blaŋ·ke·sí·no], **blanquizco** [blaŋ·kís·ko] *adj.* whitish.
blandir [blan·dír] *v.* to brandish, flourish, swing.
blando [blán·do] *adj.* bland, smooth; soft; **blanducho** *adj.* flabby; soft.
blandura [blan·dú·ra] *f.* softness; mildness, gentleness.
blanquear [blaŋ·ke·ár] *v.* to whiten, bleach; to whitewash; to show white; to begin to turn white; to blanch.
blanqueo [blaŋ·ké·o] *m.* whitening, bleach, bleaching.
blanquillo [blaŋ·kí·yo] *adj.* whitish; white (*flour*); *m. Mex., C.A.* egg; *Peru, Ch., Andes* white peach.
blasfemar [blas·fe·már] *v.* to blaspheme, curse, swear.
blasfemia [blas·fé·mja] *f.* blasphemy.
blasón [bla·són] *m.* coat of arms; honor, glory.
blasonar [bla·so·nár] *v.* to boast.

blindaje [blin·dá·xe] *m.* armor, armor plating.
blindar [blin·dár] *v.* armor.
bloc [blok] *m. Am.* tablet, pad of paper.
blocaje [blo·ká·xe] *m.* action of blocking.
blondo [blón·do] *adj.* blond.
bloque [bló·ke] *m.* block (*of stone, wood, etc.*); *Am.* tablet, pad of paper; *Cuba, Mex., Ríopl.* political bloc; **-s calibradores** gauge blocks.
bloquear [blo·ke·ár] *v.* to blockade.
bloqueo [blo·ké·o] *m.* blockade.
blusa [blú·sa] *f.* blouse.
boato [bo·á·to] *m.* pomp, ostentation.
bobada [bo·bá·da] *f.* foolishness, folly.
bobalicón [bo·ba·li·kón] *adj.* foolish, silly; *m.* simpleton, blockhead, dunce.
bobear [bo·be·ár] *v.* to act like a fool; to fool around; (*mirar*) to gawk, stare foolishly.
bobería [bo·be·rí·a] *f.* foolishness, folly; nonsense; foolish remark.
bobina [bo·bí·na] *f.* bobbin, reel; electric coil; — **distribuidora** feeding reel; — **receptora** rewind reel (*on a tape recorder*).
bobo [bó·bo] *adj.* simple, foolish, stupid; *m.* booby, fool, dunce.
boca [bó·ka] *f.* mouth; opening; — **abajo** face downward; — **arriba** face upward; **a — de jarro** at close range; **bocaza** *f.* large mouth.
bocacalle [bo·ka·ká·ye] *f.* street intersection.
bocado [bo·ká·do] *m.* mouthful, morsel, bite; bit (*of a bridle*); **bocadillo** [bo·ka·dí·yo], **bocadito** [bo·ka·dí·to] *m.* snack; sandwich; tidbit; *Mex.* piece of candy.
bocanada [bo·ka·ná·da] *f.* mouthful; puff (*of smoke*).
boceto [bo·sé·to] *m.* sketch; outline; skit.
bocina [bo·sí·na] *f.* horn; trumpet; automobile horn; speaking tube; megaphone; **bocinazo** *m.* honk.
bochorno [ba·čór·no] *m.* sultry weather; suffocating heat; (*vergüenza*) blush, flush; embarrassment.
bochornoso [bo·čor·nó·so] *adj.* sultry; embarrassing.
boda [bó·da] *f.* marriage, wedding; — **de negros** a noisy party; **-s de Camacho** lavish feast, banquet.
bodega [bo·dé·ga] *f.* cellar; wine cellar; storeroom; (*almacén*) warehouse; *Cuba, Ven., Col.* grocery store; **bodeguero** *m.* keeper of a wine cellar; liquor dealer; *Cuba, Ven., Col.* grocer.
bodoque [bo·dó·ke] *m.* wad; lump; dunce; *Mex.* bump, swelling.
bofe [bó·fe] *m.* lung; *P.R.* snap, easy job; **echar uno los -s** to throw oneself into a job; to work hard; *Am.* **ser un** ⇀ to be a bore; to be repulsive.
bofetada [bo·fe·tá·da] *f.* slap; **bofetón** *m.* big slap, blow, hard sock, wallop.
boga [bó·ga] *f.* vogue, fashion; rowing; *m.* rower.
bogar [bo·gár] *v.* to row.
bohemio [bo·é·mjo] *adj. & m.* Bohemian.
bohío [bo·í·o] *m. Carib., Ven.* cabin, shack, hut.
boina [bój·na] *f.* beret.
bola [bó·la] *f.* (*esfera*) ball, bowling; (*mentira*) fib, lie; (*betún*) shoe polish; *C.A.* disturbance, riot, false rumor; **no dar pie con** — not to do things right; not to hit the mark; to make mistakes; *Am.* **darle a la** — to hit the mark.
boleada [bo·le·á·da] *f. Ríopl.* lassoing with **boleadoras**; *Ríopl.* hunting expedition (*with* **boleadoras**); *Mex.* shoeshine; *Col.* affront, insult.
boleadoras [bo·le·a·dó·ras] *f. pl. Ríopl.* throwing weapon made of three united thongs with balls at the ends.
bolear [bo·le·ár] *v.* to play billiards; to bowl; to lie, fib; *Ríopl.,* to lasso with **boleadoras**; *Mex.* to entangle; *Am.* to polish (*shoes*); *Am.* to dismiss:

Am. to blackball, vote against; *Am.* to flunk; **-se** *Am.* to rear, balk (*said of a horse*); *Andes, Ríopl., Mex., Ch.* to blush, be ashamed.
boleta [bo·lé·ta] *f.* certificate; pass; pay order; *Mex., C.A.* ballot; *Ch.* first draft of a deed.
boletín [bo·le·tín] *m.* bulletin.
boleto [bo·lé·to] *m. Am.* ticket; **boletería** *f. Am.* ticket office.
boliche [bo·lí·če] *m.* bowling; bowling alley; *Ríopl.* cheap tavern; *Ch.* gambling joint; *Ríopl.* cheap store or shop, notions store, variety store.
bolígrafo [bo·lí·gra·fo] *m.* ball point pen.
bolillo [bo·lí·yo] *m. Mex., C.A.* hard roll.
bolita [bo·lí·ta] *f.* small ball; *Am.* ballot (*small ball used in voting*); *Col., Ven.* marble; *S.A.* armadillo.
bolo [bó·lo] *m.* one of the pins (*used in bowling*); dunce, stupid fellow; **-s** bowls, bowling; **jugar a los -s** to bowl.
bolsa [ból·sa] *f.* bag, purse; (*de acciones*) stock exchange; *Ríopl.* pocket.
bolsillo [bol·sí·yo] *m.* pocket; pocketbook.
bolsista [bol·sís·ta] *m.* stockbroker, market operator.
bollo [bó·yo] *m.* bun, muffin; (*chichón*) bump, lump; puff (*in a dress*); tuft (*on upholstery*); *Andes* loaf of bread; *Am.* a kind of tamale; **-s** *Am.* difficulties, troubles.
bomba [bóm·ba] *f.* pump; (*bombilla*) lamp bulb; bomb; — **atómica** atomic bomb; — **de hidrógeno** hydrogen bomb; *Carib.* false news; *Carib.* stanza improvised by a dancer; *Ríopl.* firecracker; skyrocket; *Mex., Col.* satirical remark; *P.R.* large drum; — **de líquido refrigerante** coolant pump; — **para incendios** fire engine; *Am.* **estar con una** — to be drunk; **bombita** *f.* soap bubble; *Col.* shame, embarrassment.
bombachas [bom·bá·čas] *f. pl. Ríopl.* loose-fitting breeches.
bombacho [bom·bá·čo] *adj.* loose-fitting (*trousers or breeches*).
bombardear [bom·bar·de·ár] *v.* to bomb.
bombardeo [bom·bar·dé·o] *m.* bombardment, bombing; **avión de** — bomber, bombing plane.
bombardero [bom·bar·dé·ro] *m.* bombardier; bomber.
bombear [bom·be·ár] *v.* (*echar bombas*) to bomb; (*alabar*) to praise, extol *Am.* to pump; *Col.* to fire, dismiss; *Mex.* to puff hard on a cigar or cigarette.
bombero [bom·bé·ro] *m.* fireman; pumper.
bombilla [bom·bí·ya] *f.* electric-light bulb; *Am.* kerosene lamp tube; *Ríopl.* small tube for drinking **mate.**
bombo [bóm·bo] *m.* large drum; bass drum; player on a bass drum; *Mex., Col., Ch.* pomp, ostentation; *Ríopl.* buttocks, rump; **dar** — to praise, extol (*in the press or newspapers*); *Col., Ríopl.* **darse** — to put on airs; *Am.* **irse uno al** — to fail; *adj.* stunned; *Am.* lukewarm; *Am.* slightly rotten; *Cuba* stupid, silly, simple; *Cuba* **fruta bomba** papaya (*tropical fruit*).
bombón [bom·bón] *m.* bonbon, candy; — **de altea** marshmallow.
bonachón [bo·na·čón] *adj.* good-natured, naïve, simple.
bonanza [bo·nán·sa] *f.* fair weather; (*riqueza*) prosperity; rich vein of ore.
bondad [bon·dád] *f.* goodness.
bondadoso [bon·da·dó·so] *adj.* good, kind.
boniato [bo·njá·to] *m. Carib., Ríopl.* sweet potato.
bonito [bo·ní·to] *adj.* pretty, *m.* striped tunny (*a fish*).
bono [bó·no] *m.* certificate; bond.
boñiga [bo·ñí·ga] *f.* dung, manure.
boqueada [bo·ke·á·da] *f.* gape, gasp.

boquear [bo·ke·ár] *v.* to open one's mouth; to gape, gasp; to be dying; *C.R.* break a horse.

boquete [bo·ké·te] *m.* breach, gap, hole, opening.

boquiabierto [bo·kja·bjér·to] *adj.* openmouthed.

boquilla [bo·kí·ya] *f. (abertura)* little mouth; small opening; *(de cigarro)* holder; tip; *(de instrumento)* mouthpiece; pastry tube.

borbollón [bor·bo·yón], **borbotón** [bor·bo·tón] *m.* spurt; spurting; big bubble; bubbling up; **a -es** in spurts; **boquillo cortador** *m.* cutting head.

borbotar [bor·bo·tár] *v.* to bubble up; to spurt, gush forth; to boil over.

bordado [bor·dá·do] *m.* embroidery.

bordadura [bor·da·dú·ra] *f.* embroidery.

bordar [bor·dár] *v.* to embroider.

borde [bór·de] *m.* border, edge.

bordear [bor·de·ár] *v.* to skirt, go along the edge of; *Am.* to trim with a border; *Am.* to make a **bordo** *(small, temporary dam);* **-se** *Ch., Mex., Ven.* to approach, get near.

bordo [bór·do] *m.* board, side of a ship; tack *(of a ship); Mex., Ven.* ridge *(of a furrow); Mex.,* small dam; **a** — on board.

borla [bór·la] *f. (indumentaria)* tassel; doctor's cap; *(título)* doctor's degree; *(cosmético)* powder puff; tuft; **tomar uno la** — to get a doctor's degree.

borlarse [bor·lár·se] *v. Am.* to get a doctor's degree.

boro [bó·ro] *m.* boron.

borrachera [bo·rra·čé·ra] *f.* drunkenness; drunken spree.

borrachín [bo·rra·čín] *m.* toper, drunk.

borracho [bo·rrá·čo] *adj.* drunk; *m.* drunkard; **borrachón** [bo·rra·čón] *m.* drunkard, heavy drinker.

borrador [bo·rra·dór] *m.* rough draft; *Am.* rubber eraser.

borrar [bo·rrár] *v.* to blot out; to erase.

borrasca [bo·rrás·ka] *f.* storm, tempest.

borrascoso [bo·rras·kó·so] *adj.* stormy.

borrego [bo·rré·go] *m.* lamb; *(tonto)* fool, simpleton; *Mex., C.A.* false news.

borrico [bo·rrí·ko] *m.* donkey, ass; fool; sawhorse.

borrón [bo·rrón] *m.* blotch *(of ink),* blot.

borronear [bo·rro·ne·ár] *v.* to blot, blotch; *(garrapatear)* to scribble; to blur; to make a rough sketch.

borroso [bo·rró·so] *adj.* blurry.

boruca [bo·rú·ka] *f.* racket, noise.

boscaje [bos·ká·xe] *m.* grove, thicket, woods; *(paisaje)* landscape.

bosque [bós·ke] *m.* forest, woods; **bosquecillo** *m.* small forest, grove.

bosquejar [bos·ke·xár] *v.* to sketch; to outline.

bosquejo [bos·ké·xo] *m.* sketch, plan, outline, rough draft.

bostezar[9] [bos·te·sár] *v.* to yawn.

bostezo [bos·té·so] *m.* yawn.

bota [bó·ta] *f. (calzado)* boot; *(bolsa)* leather wine bag; *adj. Am.* stupid, clumsy; *Mex.* drunk.

botar [bo·tár] *v. (echar)* to launch; to fling; to throw away; *(rebotar)* to bounce; *Ven.* to waste, squander; *Am.* to fire, dismiss; **-se** *Am.* to lie down.

botarate [bo·ta·rá·te] *m.* fool; braggart; *Mex., Carib.* spendthrift.

bote [bó·te] *m. (jarro)* small jar; *(embarcación)* boat; *(rebote)* bounce; *(golpe)* blow; jump; *Ríopl.* liquor bottle; *Mex., C.A.* jail; **estar de — en —** to be crowded, completely filled up.

botella [bo·té·ya] *f.* bottle.

botica [bo·tí·ka] *f.* drugstore.

boticario [bo·ti·ká·rjo] *m.* druggist.

botija [bo·tí·xa] *f.* earthen jug; fat person; *Am.* buried treasure; *Am.* belly; *Col.* **poner a uno como —** **verde** to dress down, scold, insult a person.

botijo [bo·tí·xo] *m.* earthen jar with spout and handle.

botín [bo·tín] *m.* booty, plunder; *(zapato)* high shoe; *Ch.* sock.

botiquín [bo·ti·kín] *m.* medicine cabinet; medicine kit; *Ven.* liquor store, wine shop.

botón [bo·tón] *m.* bud; button; knob; handle; **-es** bellboy.

bóveda [bó·be·da] *f.* arched roof; vault, underground cellar; burial place.

boxeador [bok·se·a·dór] *m.* boxer.

boxear [bok·se·ár] *v.* to box, fight with the fists.

boxeo [bok·sé·o] *m.* boxing.

boya [bó·ya] *f.* buoy; float net; *Am.* crease, dent; *Bol.* rich mineral vein; *Am.* **estar en la buena** — to be in a good humor.

bozal [bo·sál] *m. (de animal)* nuzzle; *(cascabel)* bells on a harness; *(novicio)* novice; *(negro)* Negro native of Africa; *Am.* headstall *(of a halter); Spain* person *(especially a Negro)* who speaks broken Spanish; *Am.* coarse, crude individual; *adj.* green, inexperienced; wild, untamed; stupid.

bozo [bó·so] *m.* down *(on the upper lip);* mustache; outside part of the mouth; headstall *(of a halter).*

bracear [bra·se·ár] *v.* to swing one's arms; to struggle; *(nadar)* to crawl, swim with a crawl.

bracero [bra·sé·ro] *m.* day laborer; **de** — arm in arm; **servir de** — **a una señora** to serve as an escort, give a lady one's arm.

bracete [bra·sé·te]: **de** — arm in arm.

bragueta [bra·gé·ta] *f.* fly *(pants).*

bramante [bra·mán·te] *m.* hemp cord, hemp string; Brabant linen; *adj.* roaring, bellowing.

bramar [bra·már] *v.* to bellow, roar, howl; to rage.

bramido [bra·mí·do] *m.* roar; howl; bellow.

brasa [brá·sa] *f.* red-hot coal.

brasero [bra·sé·ro] *m.* brazier *(pan for burning coal),* grate; hearth; *Ríopl.* brick cooking stove.

bravata [bra·bá·ta] *f.* bravado, boastfulness, defiance.

bravear [bra·be·ár] *v.* to bluster; to bully.

bravío [bra·bí·o] *adj.* savage, wild; rustic.

bravo [brá·bo] *adj. (agresivo)* wild, ferocious, harsh; ill-tempered; *(valiente)* brave; *Carib., C.A., Andes* angry; *Ch.* hot, highly seasoned.

bravura [bra·bú·ra] *f.* fierceness; courage; bravado, show of boldness.

braza [brá·sa] *f.* fathom; *(natación)* stroke.

brazada [bra·sá·da] *f.* armful; movement of the arms *(swimming stroke);* **a una** — at arm's length.

brazalete [bra·sa·lé·te] *f.* bracelet.

brazo [brá·so] *m.* arm; branch; **-s** day laborers; *Ríopl., Cuba* **de** — arm in arm; **luchar a** — **partido** to wrestle; to fight hand to hand.

brea [bré·a] *f.* pitch; tar; *(lona)* canvas.

brecha [bré·ča] *f.* breach, gap.

brega [bré·ga] *f.* fight, scrap.

bregar[7] [bre·gár] *v.* to struggle; to fight.

breña [bré·ña] *f.* rough, craggy ground covered with brambles; bramble; **breñal** *m.* brambles; bush country.

breve [bré·be] *adj.* brief, short; **en** — shortly.

brevedad [bre·be·dád] *f.* brevity, shortness.

bribón [bri·bón] *adj.* idle, indolent; *m.* rascal, rogue; **bribonazo** *m.* scoundrel, cheat.

brida [brí·da] *f.* bridle; rein.

brigada [bri·gá·da] *f.* brigade.

brillante [bri·yán·te] *adj.* brilliant, bright; *m.* diamond.

BL

brillantez [bri·yan·tés] *f.* brilliance, dazzle.
brillar [bri·yár] *v.* to shine.
brillo [brí·yo] *m.* luster, sparkle, shine.
brincar[6] [briŋ·kár] *v.* to hop, skip, jump, bounce.
brinco [bríŋ·ko] *m.* hop, skip, bounce, leap.
brindar [brin·dár] *v.* to toast, drink to the health of; (*ofrecer*) give, to offer.
brindis [brín·dis] *m.* toast (*to a person's health*).
brío [brí·o] *m.* vigor, liveliness; (*valor*) valor, courage.
brioso [brjó·so] *adj.* lively; brave.
brisa [brí·sa] *f.* breeze.
británico [bri·tá·ni·ko] *adj.* British.
brizna [bríz·na] *f.* particle, chip, fragment; blade of grass.
broca [bró·ka] *f.* drill.
brocal [bro·kál] *m.* curb, curbstone (*of a well*).
brocha [bró·ča] *f.* house painter's brush; (*dados*) loaded dice; **cuadro de** — **gorda** badly done painting; **pintor de** — **gorda** house painter
brochada *f.* stroke of the brush, brush stroke;
brochazo *m.* blow with a brush; brush stroke; — **de pastelero** pastry brush.
broche [bró·če] *m.* brooch; clasp, clip, fastener; hook and eye.
brocheta [bro·čé·ta] *f.* skewer.
broma [bró·ma] *f.* jest, joke; fun, merriment; *Am.* disappointment, irritation; **de** — in jest; **fuera de** — all joking aside.
bromear [bro·me·ár] *v.* to joke, jest.
bronca [bróŋ·ka] *f.* quarrel, dispute, wrangle; **armar una** — to cause a disturbance, raise a rumpus.
bronce [brón·se] *m.* bronze.
bronceado [bron·se·á·ðo] *adj.* bronzed; bronze-colored; *m.* bronze finish.
bronco [bróŋ·ko] *adj.* hoarse; raspy, harsh; (*burdo*) coarse, rough; uncouth; wild, untamed (*horse*).
bronquio [bróŋ·kjo] *m.* bronchus, bronchial tube.
broquel [bro·kél] *m.* buckler, shield (*worn on the arm*).
brotar [bro·tár] *v.* to shoot forth; to bud; to break out (*on the skin*); to gush, flow; to spring forth.
broza [bró·sa] *f.* brushwood, underbush; (*basura*) rubbish, refuse, trash; coarse, hard brush.
bruces [brú·ses]: **de** — face downward.
bruja [brú·xa] *f.* witch; hag; owl; *adj. Mex.* broke, poor; **brujo** *m.* sorcerer, magician, wizard.
brújula [brú·xu·la] *f.* (*compás*) compass; magnetic needle; (*mira*) peephole; gunsight.
bruma [brú·ma] *f.* mist, fog; **brumoso** *adj.* foggy, misty, hazy.
bruñido interior [bru·ñí·ðo in·te·rjór] *m.* honing.
bruñir[19] [bru·ñír] *v. irr.* to burnish, polish; to put on make-up.
brusco [brús·ko] *adj.* blunt, rude, abrupt.
brutal [bru·tál] *adj.* brutal, beastly, savage.
brutalidad [bru·ta·li·ðáð] *f.* brutality.
bruto [brú·to] *adj.* (*tonto*) stupid, brutal; (*burdo*) coarse, rough; **peso** — gross weight; **diamante en** — diamond in the rough, unpolished diamond; *m.* brute, beast.
bucal [bu·kál] *adj.* oral, pertaining to the mouth.
bucear [bu·se·ár] *v.* to dive; to dive into, plunge into; to explore thoroughly a subject.
bucle [bú·kle] *m.* curl, ringlet; (*computadora*) loop.
buche [bú·če] *m.* crop (*of a bird*); (*bocada*) mouthful (*of water*); wrinkle, bag (*in clothes*); *Ríopl., Mex., Ven.* goiter.
budín [bu·ðín] *m.* pudding.
buen(o) [bwé·n(o)] *adj.* good; kind; useful; well, in good health; **de buenas a primeras** all of a

sudden, unexpectedly, on the spur of the moment; **por la(s) buena(s) o por la(s) mala(s)** willingly or unwillingly, by hook or crook.
buey [bwej] *m.* ox.
búfalo [bú·fa·lo] *m.* buffalo.
bufanda [bu·fán·da] *f.* muffler, scarf.
bufar [bu·fár] *v.* to snort; to puff with anger; **-se** *Mex.* to swell, bulge (*as a wall*).
bufete [bu·fé·te] *m.* desk, writing table; lawyer's office.
bufido [bu·fí·ðo] *m.* snort.
bufón [bu·fón] *m.* buffoon, jester, clown; *adj.* comical, funny; **bufonada** [bu·fo·ná·ða] *f.* wisecrack; jest.
bufonear [bu·fo·ne·ár] *v.* to clown; to jest.
buhardilla [bu·ar·ðí·ya], [bwar·ðí·ya] *f.* garret, attic; skylight; dormer.
búho [bú·o] *m.* owl.
buhonero [bu·o·né·ro] *m.* peddler.
buitre [bwí·tre] *m.* vulture.
buje [bú·xe] *m.* bushing; axle box.
bujía [bu·xí·a] *f.* candle; candle power; candlestick; spark plug.
bula [bú·la] *f.* bull (*papal document*); papal seal.
buldózer [bul·dó·ser] *m.* bulldozer.
bulevar [bu·le·bár] *m.* boulevard.
bulto [búl·to] *m.* (*cuerpo*) body, bundle, shadow, lump, swelling; (*tamaño*) bulk, volume; **a** — haphazardly, by guess; **escurrir el** — to dodge; **imagen de** — statue, sculpture; **una verdad de** — an evident truth.
bulla [bú·ya] *f.* shouting, uproar; noisy crowd.
bullicio [bu·yí·sjo] *m.* noise, uproar.
bullicioso [bu·yi·sjó·so] *adj.* boisterous, noisy; (*alegre*) lively; turbulent, stormy.
bullir[20] [bu·yír] *v. irr.* to boil; to buzz about; to bustle; to stir, move; *Mex.* to deride.
buñuelo [bu·ñwé·lo] *m.* fritter; *P.R.* botch, poor piece of work.
buque [bú·ke] *m.* ship, boat.
burbuja [bur·bú·xa] *f.* bubble.
burdo [búr·ðo] *adj.* coarse.
burgués [bur·gés] *adj.* bourgeois, middle-class.
burla [búr·la] *f.* jest, mockery; **de** — in jest.
burlador [bur·la·ðór] *m.* practical joker; jester; scoffer; seducer.
burlar [bur·lár] *v.* to mock, ridicule, deceive; **-se de** to scoff at; to make fun of.
burlón [bur·lón] *m.* jester, teaser.
burocracia [bu·ro·krá·sja] *f.* bureaucracy.
burócrata [bu·ró·kra·ta] *m.* bureaucrat.
burro [bú·rro] *m.* ass, donkey; *Mex., Cuba, Ríopl.* stepladder; *adj.* stupid; **burrito** *m.* small donkey; *Am.* saddle rack.
busca [bús·ka] *f.* search; hunting party; *Mex.* **-s** profit on the side; graft.
buscar [bus·kár] *v.* to seek, search, look for; *Mex., Andes* to provoke.
búsqueda [bús·ke·ða] *f.* search.
busto [bús·to] *m.* bust (*upper part of body*).
butaca [bu·tá·ka] *f.* armchair; orchestra seat; **butacón** [bu·ta·kón] *m.* large armchair.
buzo [bú·so] *m.* diver; deep-sea or "skin" diver.
buzón [bu·són] *m.* mailbox; letter drop.

C:c **cabal** [ka·bál] *adj.* complete, entire; exact; **estar uno en sus -es** to be in one's right mind.
cabalgar[7] [ka·bal·gár] *v.* to ride, mount (*a horse*); to ride horseback.
caballa [ka·bá·ya] *f.* horse mackeral.
caballada [ka·ba·yá·da] *f.* herd of horses; *Am.* nonsense, stupidity, blunder.
caballejo [ka·ba·yé·xo] *m.* nag; poor horse.
caballeresco [ka·ba·ye·rés·ko] *adj.* gentlemanly; knightly; chivalrous, gallant.
caballería [ka·ba·ye·rí·a] *f.* calvary; horsemanship; mount, horse; knighthood; chivalry.
caballeriza [ka·ba·ye·rí·sa] *f.* stable; horses of a stable.
caballerizo [ka·ba·ye·rí·so] *m.* groom, stableman.
caballero [ka·ba·yé·ro] *m.* gentleman; knight; horseman; *adj.* gentlemanly.
caballerosidad [ka·ba·ye·ro·si·dád] *f.* chivalry, gentlemanly conduct.
caballeroso [ka·ba·ye·ró·so] *adj.* chivalrous, gentlemanly.
caballete [ka·ba·yé·te] *m.* (*de casa*) ridge of a roof, hip; (*madero*) sawhorse; (*de la cara*) bridge of the nose.
caballo [ka·bá·yo] *m.* horse; (*ajedrez*) knight (*in chess*); *Am.* stupid or brutal person; **a — on** horseback; **caballuco** [ka·ba·yú·ko] *m.* nag.
cabaña [ka·bá·ña] *f* hut, cabin; *Ríopl.* cattle ranch.
cabecear [ka·be·se·ár] *v.* to nod; to shake the head; to pitch (*as a boat*); *Ven.* to begin to rise or fall (*said of a river*).
cabeceo [ka·be·sé·o] *m.* nodding; pitching (*of a boat*).
cabecera [ka·be·sé·ra] *f.* head (*of bed or table*); seat, chief city (*of a district*).
cabecilla [ka·be·sí·ya] *f.* small head; *m.* ringleader.
cabellera [ka·be·yé·ra] *f.* head of hair, long hair; wig; tail of a comet.
cabello [ka·bé·yo] *m.* hair; **traer algo por los -s** to bring in a far-fetched fact or quotation; **-s de ángel** cotton candy.
cabelludo [ka·be·yú·do] *adj.* hairy; **cuero —** scalp.
caber[23] [ka·bér] *v. irr.* to fit into, go into; to have enough room for; to befall; **no cabe duda** there is no doubt; **no cabe más** there is no room for more; **no — uno en sí** to be puffed up with pride; **no cabe en lo posible** it is absolutely impossible.
cabestro [ka·bés·tro] *m.* halter; leading ox; *Carib., Mex.* rope, cord; *S.A.* advance payment; **cabestrillo** [ka·bes·trí·yo] *m.* sling (*for an arm*).
cabeza [ka·bé·sa] *f.* (*parte superior*) head; upper part; (*director*) chief, leader; capital (*of a district*); *Carib.* source (*of a river*); **— de playa** beachhead; **— de puente** bridgehead; **— sonora** recording head.
cabezada [ka·be·sá·da] *f.* butt (*with the head*); bump on the head; (*cabeceo*) nod; shake of the head; pitching (*of a ship*); headgear (*of a harness*).
cabezal [ka·be·sál] *m.* headstock (*lathe*).
cabezazo [ka·be·sá·so] *m.* butt (*with the head*), bump on the head.
cabezudo [ka·be·súdo] *adj.* big-headed; hard-headed, pig-headed, stubborn, headstrong.
cabezón [ka·be·són] *adj.* big-headed; pig-headed, stubborn; *Ch.* strong (*liquor*); *m.* large head; cavesson (*iron noseband used in breaking a horse*); *Col.* rapids or whirlpool in a river.
cabida [ka·bí·da] *f.* space, room, capacity; **tener — con alguien** to have influence with someone.
cabildo [ka·bíl·do] *m.* cathedral chapter; municipal council; council room; town hall.

cabina [ka·bí·na] *f.* cabin (*of an airplane*).
cabio [ká·bjo] *m.* joist; **cabio de cresta** hip rafter.
cabizbajo [ka·biz·bá·xo] *adj.* crestfallen, downcast; pensive.
cable [ká·ble] *m.* cable.
cablegrafiar[17] [ka·ble·gra·fjár] *v.* to cable.
cablegrama [ka·ble·grá·ma] *m.* cablegram.
cabo [ká·bo] *m.* (*cosa*) end, tip, handle; piece of rope; (*geográfico*) cape, headland; (*persona*) foreman, corporal; **al —** finally; **al fin y al —** anyway, in the long run; **de — a rabo** from beginning to end; **estar al — de** to be well informed about; **llevar a —** to carry out, finish.
cabotaje [ka·bo·tá·xe] *m.* coastal trade or traffic.
cabra [ká·bra] *f.* goat; *Col.* fraud, trick; *Col., Cuba, Ven.* loaded dice; *Am.* light two-wheeled carriage; **cabrillas** [ka·brí·yas] *f. pl.* whitecaps (*small waves with white crests*); Pleiades (*constellation*); game of skipping stones on the water.
cabrero [ka·bré·ro] *m.* goatherd.
cabrio [ká·brjo] *m.* rafter.
cabrío [ka·brí·o] *adj.* goatish; **macho —** he-goat; *m.* herd of goats.
cabriola [ka·brjó·la] *f.* caper, leap, hop, skip; somersault; **hacer -s** to cut capers; to prance.
cabriolar [ka·brjo·lár] *v.* to prance; to caper; to romp, frolic, frisk.
cabrito [ka·brí·to] *m.* kid; **cabritilla** [ka·bri·tí·ya] *f.* kid, kidskin.
cabrón [ka·brón] *m.* he-goat; cuckold (*man whose wife is unfaithful*).
caca [ká·ka] *f.* excrement (*popular children's expression*).
cacahuate [ka·ka·wá·te] *m. Mex., C.A.* peanut; *Spain* **cacahuete** [ka·ka·wé·te], **cacahuey** [ka·ka·wéj].
cacao [ka·ká·o] *m.* cocoa.
cacarear [ka·ka·re·ár] *v.* to cackle; to boast; *Am.* to run away from a fight.
cacareo [ka·ka·ré·o] *m.* cackle.
cacería [ka·se·rí·a] *f.* hunt, hunting.
cacerola [ka·se·ró·la] *f.* saucepan.
cacique [ka·sí·ke] *m.* chief; political boss; *Mex.* tyrant; *Ch., Ven.* one who leads an easy life.
caciquismo [ka·si·kíz·mo] *m.* political bossism (*rule by political bosses*).
cacofonía [ka·ko·fo·ní·a] *f.* cacophony.
cacto [kák·to] *m.* cactus.
cacumen [ka·kú·men] *m.* acumen, keen insight.
cacha [ká·ča] *f.* handle (*of a knife or pistol*); *Am.* the horns of a bull; *C.A.* **hacer la —** to complete a task, to get.
cacharro [ka·čá·rro] *m.* earthen pot or vase; broken piece of a pot; crude utensil; *Am.* cheap trinket; "jalopy".
cachaza [ka·čá·sa] *f.* slowness; calm; rum.
cachazudo [ka·ča·sú·do] *adj.* slow, easy going.
cachetada [ka·če·tá·da] *f. Am.* slap on the face.
cachete [ka·čé·te] *m.* cheek; slap on the cheek.
cachimbo [ka·čím·bo] *m. Am.* pipe (*for smoking*); *Cuba* small sugar mill; also **cachimba** [ka·čím·ba].
cachivache [ka·či·bá·če] *m.* piece of junk; (*persona*) worthless fellow; *Mex., Carib., Ven.* trinket.
cacho [ká·čo] *m. Am.* horn (of an animal); *adj.* bent, crooked.
cachorro [ka·čó·rro] *m.* (*oso*) cub; (*perro*) puppy; small pistol; *Carib.* rude, ill-bred person.
cachucha [ka·čú·ča] *f.* cap; rowboat; popular Andalusian dance, song and music; *Am.* slap.
cada [ká·da] *adj.* each, every; **— uno** each one; **— y cuando que** whenever; *Am.* **a — nada** every second.

cadalso [ka·dal·so] *m.* gallows; scaffold, platform.
cadáver [ka·dá·ber] *m.* corpse; **cadavérico** [ka·da·bé·ri·ko] *adj.* deadly, ghastly, pale, like a corpse.
cadena [ka·dé·na] *f.* chain.
cadencia [ka·dén·sja] *f.* cadence.
cadencioso [ka·den·sjó·so] *adj.* rhythmical.
cadera [ka·dé·ra] *f.* hip.
cadete [ka·dé·te] *m.* cadet.
cadmio [kad·mjo] *m.* cadmium.
caducar[6] [ka·du·kár] *v.* to dote, be in one's dotage; (*vencer*) to lapse, expire; to become extinct, fall into disuse.
caduco [ka·dú·ko] *adj.* decrepit, very old, feeble; perishable.
caer[24] [ka·ér] *v. irr.* to fall; to fall down; to fall off; **-se** to fall down, tumble; — **a** to face, overlook; — **bien** to fit, be becoming; — **en cama** to fall ill; — **en la cuenta** to catch on, get the point; — **en gracia** to please; **al** — **de la noche** at nightfall; **dejar** — to drop.
café [ka·fé] *m.* coffee, café; *Mex.* annoyance, bad time.
cafeína [ka·fe·í·na] *f.* caffein.
cafetal [ka·fe·tál] *m.* coffee plantation.
cafetera [ka·fe·té·ra] *f.* coffeepot; woman café owner, coffee vendor or merchant; coffee-bean picker.
cafetería [ka·fe·te·rí·a] *f.* café, bar, lunchroom.
cafetero [ka·fe·té·ro] *adj.* pertaining to coffee; *m.* coffee grower; coffee merchant; owner of a café or coffee-house; *Am.* coffee drinker.
cafeto [ka·fé·to] *m.* coffee bush.
cagar[7] [ka·gár] *v. irr.* to defecate (*popular term*).
caída [ka·í·da] *f.* fall, drop; descent; **a la** — **del sol** (*or* **de la tarde**) at sunset.
caimán [kaj·mán] *m.* cayman, alligator.
caja [ká·xa] *f.* case, box; — **de ahorros** savings bank; — **de cambios** transmission (*automobile*); — **de fusibles** fuse box; **-s de ingletes** mitre boxes; — **de píldora** pillbox; — **fuerte** safe; **echar a uno con -s destempladas** to give someone the gate.
cajero [ka·xé·ro] *m.* cashier; box maker.
cajetilla [ka·xe·tí·ya] *f.* small box; package of cigarettes.
cajón [ka·xón] *m.* large box, chest; drawer; vendor's booth or stand; *Ch., Mex.* narrow canyon; — **de muerto** coffin; *Mex.* — **de ropa** dry-goods and clothing store.
cal [kal] *f.* lime (*mineral*).
calabaza [ka·la·bá·sa] *f.* pumpkin, squash; gourd; an ignorant person; **dar -s** to jilt, turn down (*a suitor*); to flunk; fail.
calabozo [ka·la·bó·so] *m.* dungeon; prison cell.
calado [ka·lá·do] *m.* drawn work; openwork (*in wood, metal linen, etc.*), fretwork; draft (*of a ship*).
calafatear [ka·la·fa·te·ar] *v.* to caulk.
calamar [ka·la·már] *m.* squid, cuttlefish.
calambre [ka·lám·bre] *m.* body cramp.
calamidad [ka·la·mi·dád] *f.* calamity, misfortune.
calandria [ka·lán·drja] *f.* lark, skylark.
calar [ka·lár] *v.* (*penetrar*) to pierce, penetrate; to soak through; to make openwork (*in cloth, metal*); (*probar*) to probe, search into; **-se el sombrero** to put on one's hat; to pull down one's hat.
calavera [ka·la·bé·ra] *f.* skull; *m.* libertine, rounder, reckless fellow; *Mex.* taillight.
calcar[6] [kal·kár] *v.* to trace; to copy, imitate.
calceta [kal·sé·ta] *f.* hose, stocking; **hacer** — to knit; **calcetería** [kal·se·te·rí·a] *f.* hosiery shop; hosiery.
calcetín [kal·se·tín] *m.* sock.

calcinar [kal·si·nár] *v.* to burn, char, heat.
calcio [kál·sjo] *m.* calcium.
calco [kál·ko] *m.* tracing, traced copy; exact copy; imitation.
calculadora [kal·ku·la·dó·ra] *f.* calculator — **electrónica** computer; — **e integradora electrónica numérica** UNIVAC.
calcular [kal·ku·lár] *v.* to calculate, figure, estimate.
cálculo [kál·ku·lo] *m.* calculation, estimate; calculus; gravel (*in the gall bladder, kidney, etc.*).
caldear [kal·de·ár] *v.* to heat; to weld; **-se** *Mex.* to become overheated, excited; *Mex., Ríopl.* to get "lit up", get drunk.
caldera [kal·dé·ra] *f.* boiler; caldron, kettle; **calderilla** [kal·de·rí·ya] *f.* copper coin.
caldo [kál·do] *m.* broth; gravy.
calefacción [ka·le·fak·sjón] *f.* heat, heating.
calendario [ka·len·dá·rjo] *m.* calendar; almanac.
caléndula [ka·lén·du·la] *f.* marigold.
calentador [ka·len·ta·dór] *m.* heater.
calentar[1] [ka·len·tár] *v. irr.* to warm, heat; to spank; *Am.* to annoy, bother; **-se** to warm oneself; to become heated, excited; to be in heat; *Am.* to become angry.
calentura [ka·len·tú·ra] *f.* fever; *Col.* fit of temper; — **de pollo** feigned illness; **calenturón** [ka·len·tu·rón] *m.* high fever.
calenturiento [ka·len·tu·rjén·to] *adj.* feverish; *Ch.* tubercular.
caletre [ka·lé·tre] *m.* judgment, acumen, keen insight.
calibrar [ka·li·brár] *v.* to gauge, measure; to measure the caliber of.
calibre [ka·lí·bre] *m.* caliber; bore, gauge (*of a gun*); diameter (*of a pipe, tube, wire*).
calicanto [ka·li·kán·to] *m.* stone masonry.
calicó [ka·li·kó] *m.* calico, cotton cloth.
calidad [ka·li·dád] *f.* quality.
cálido [ká·li·do] *adj.* warm, hot.
caliente [ka·ljén·te] *adj.* warm, hot; heated; fiery; *Am.* angry; *Col.* bold brave; *m. Col.* brandy in hot water; **calientito** *adj.* nice and warm.
calificación [ka·li·fi·ka·sjón] *f.* qualification; (*nota*) grade, mark; (*juicio*) judgment.
calificar[6] [ka·li·fi·kár] *v.* to qualify; to rate, consider, judge; to grade; *Mex.* to compute (*election returns*); **-se** *Ch.* to qualify or register (*as a voter*).
caligrafía [ka·li·gra·fí·a] *f.* penmanship.
calina [ka·lí·na] *f.* haze, mist.
cáliz [ká·lis] *m.* chalice, communion cup; cup, goblet; calyx (*of a flower*).
calma [kál·ma] *f.* calm.
calmante [kal·mán·te] *adj.* soothing; *m.* sedative; tranquilizer.
calmar [kal·már] *v.* to calm, quiet, soothe.
calmo [kál·mo] *adj.* calm, quiet.
calmoso [kal·mó·so] *adj.* calm; soothing; (*torpe*) phlegmatic, slow.
caló [ka·ló] *m.* underworld jargon.
calor [ka·lór] *m.* heat, warmth; ardor; — **exotérmico** exothermic heat.
caloría [ka·lo·rí·a] *f.* calorie.
calorífero [ka·lo·rí·fe·ro] *m.* heater, radiator; furnace.
calosfrío [ka·los·frí·o], **calofrío** [ka·lo·frí·o] *m.* chill.
calumnia [ka·lúm·nja] *f.* slander.
calumniar [ka·lum·njár] *v.* to slander.
caluroso [ka·lu·ró·so] *adj.* (*literal*) hot; warm; (*figurado*) heated; excited; cordial, enthusiastic.
calva [kál·ba] *f.* bald head; bald spot; barren spot.
calvario [kal·bá·rjo] *m.* Calvary, place of the Cross; suffering, tribulation.
calvo [kál·bo] *adj.* bald; barren.

calza [kál·sa] *f.* wedge; shoehorn; *Col., Ven.* gold inlay, tooth filling; **-s** breeches.

calzada [kal·sá·da] *f.* paved road; highway; *Mex., Carib.* wide avenue.

calzado [kal·sá·do] *m.* footwear.

calzador [kal·sa·dór] *m.* shoehorn.

calzar⁹ [kal·sár] *v.* to put on (*shoes, gloves, spurs*); to put a wedge under a wheel; *Am.* to fill (*a tooth*).

calzón [kal·són] *m.* (*or* **calzones** [kal·só·nes]) breeches, short trousers; *Mex., Ven.* drawers; *Mex.* white cotton trousers; **calzoncillos** [kal·son·sí·yos] *m. pl.* drawers, men's shorts; **calzoneras** [kal·so·né·ras] *f. p. Mex.* trousers open down the sides.

callado [ka·yá·do] *adj.* silent, quiet.

callar [ka·yár] *v.* to be silent; to hush; **-se** to be or keep silent.

calle [ká·ye] *f.* street.

calleja [ka·yé·xa] *f.* small street, alley, lane; **callejuela** [ka·ye·xwé·la] *f.* small, narrow street; lane.

callejear [ka·ye·xe·ár] *v.* to walk the streets, ramble.

callejero [ka·ye·xé·ro] *m.* street-rambler, street-stroller; street-loiterer; *adj.* fond of walking the streets; rambling.

callejón [ka·ye·xón] *m.* alley; lane; narrow pass; — **sin salida** blind alley.

callo [ká·yo] *m.* callus, corn; *Spain* **-s** tripe (*food*).

calloso [ka·yó·so] *adj.* callous, hard.

cama [ká·ma] *f.* bed, couch, cot; litter **caer en** — to fall ill; **guardar** — to be confined to bed; *Am.* **tenderle uno la** — **a otro** to help one in his love affairs; to set a trap for someone; **camastro** [ka·más·tro] *m.* poor, uncomfortable bed.

camada [ka·má·da] *f.* litter; brood.

camaleón [ka·ma·le·ón] *m.* chameleon.

cámara [ká·ma·ra] *f.* chamber, hall, parlor; house (*of a legislative body*); cabin, stateroom; chamber (*of a gun*); — **de aire** inner tube; — **fotográfica** camera.

camarada [ka·ma·rá·da] *m.* comrade; **camaradería** [ka·ma·ra·de·rí·a] *f.* comradeship, companionship.

camarera [ka·ma·ré·ra] *f.* waitress; chambermaid; stewardess.

camarero [ka·ma·ré·ro] *m.* waiter; chamberlain; steward; valet.

camarilla [ka·ma·rí·ya] *f.* political lobby; small group of politicians, "kitchen cabinet", group of unofficial advisers; (*cuarto*) small room.

camarón [ka·ma·rón] *m.* shrimp.

camarote [ka·ma·ró·te] *m.* cabin, stateroom.

cambalache [kam·ba·lá·če] *m.* swap, barter, exchange.

cambalachear [kam·ba·la·če·ár] *v.* to swap, barter, exchange.

cambiador [kam·bja·dór] *m.* barterer; money changer; *Mex., Ch.* switchman.

cambiante [kam·bján·te] *adj.* changing; exchanging; **-s** *m. pl.* iridescent colors.

cambiar [kam·bjár] *v.* to change; to exchange; to shift; — **de marcha** to shift gears.

cambiavía [kam·bja·bí·a] *m. Carib., Mex., Andes* railway switchman. *See* **guardagujas** *and* **cambiador**.

cambio [kám·bjo] *m.* change; exchange; (*ferrocarril*) railway switch; **libre** — free trade; **en** — on the other hand; in exchange; **caja de** — *f.* transmission.

cambista [kam·bís·ta] *m.* exchange broker, banker; *Am.* railway switchman.

camello [ka·mé·yo] *m.* camel.

camilla [ka·mí·ya] *f.* stretcher; cot; **camillero** [ka·mi·yé·ro] *m.* stretcher bearer.

caminante [ka·mi·nán·te] *m. & f.* walker, traveler.

caminar [ka·mi·nár] *v.* to travel; to walk; *Am.* to progress, prosper.

caminata [ka·mi·ná·ta] *f.* long walk; hike; jaunt.

camino [ka·mí·no] *m.* road; course; *Ríopl.* table runner; *Am.* hall runner; — **de hierro** railroad; — **real** highway; **de** — on the way.

camión [ka·mjón] *m.* truck; wagon; *Mex.* bus; **camionero** [ka·mjo·né·ro] *m.* truck driver; **camioneta** [ka·mjo·né·ta] *f.* small truck; station wagon; *C.A.* bus.

camisa [ka·mí·sa] *f.* shirt; — **de fuerza** straitjacket; **meterse en** — **de once varas** to attempt more than one can manage, bite off more than one can chew; **camiseta** [ka·mi·sé·ta] *f.* undershirt.

camisón [ka·mi·són] *m.* long shirt; *Mex.* nightgown, *Am.* gown, dress.

camote [ka·mó·te] *m. Mex., C.A.* sweet potato.

campamento [kam·pa·mén·to] *m.* encampment; camp.

campana [kam·pá·na] *f.* bell; *Ríopl., Andes* spy, lookout (*for thieves*); **campanada** [kam·pa·ná·da] *f.* stroke of a bell; *Mex.* — **de vacante** once in a blue moon, very seldom.

campanario [kam·pa·ná·rjo] *m.* bell tower.

campanilla [kam·pa·ní·ya] *f.* small bell; (*burbuja*) bubble; uvula; tassel, bell-flower.

campanillazo [kam·pa·ni·yá·so] *m.* loud ring of a bell.

campanilleo [kam·pa·ni·yé·o] *m.* ringing; tinkling.

campaña [kam·pá·ña] *f.* (*paisaje*) level, open country; (*política*) campaign; period of active service.

campear [kam·pe·ár] *v.* to pasture; (*enverdecer*) to grow green (*said of the fields*); to excel; (*destacarse*) to be prominent, stand out; to be in the field; *Ríopl.* to search the plains for lost cattle; *Col., Ven.* (*hacer el guapo*) to act the bully.

campechano [kam·pe·čá·no] *adj.* frank, open.

campéon [kam·pe·ón] *m.* champion; defender.

campeonato [kam·pe·o·ná·to] *m.* championship.

campero [kam·pé·ro] *adj.* out in the open; related to the country; *m.* (*auto*) camper.

campesino [kam·pe·sí·no] *adj.* rural, rustic; *m.* peasant, countryman; farmer.

campestre [kam·pés·tre] *adj.* rural, rustic.

campiña [kam·pí·ña] *f.* large field; open country.

campo [kám·po] *m.* country; field; camp; **a** — **raso** in the open; **a** — **traviesa** (*or* **travieso**) cross-country.

camposanto [kam·po·sán·to] *m.* churchyard, cemetery.

camuesa [ka·mwé·sa] *f.* pippin (*a variety of apple*).

camuflaje [ka·mu·flá·xe] *m.* camouflage.

can [kan] *m.* dog; (*de arma*) trigger (*of a gun*).

cana [ká·na] *f.* white hair, grey hair; *Carib.* a kind of palm; **echar una** — **al aire** to go out for a good time; to go out on a fling.

canadiense [ka·na·djén·se] *adj., m. & f.* Canadian.

canal [ka·nál] *m.* canal, channel; (*telecomunicaciones*) channel; *f.* eaves trough.

canalla [ka·ná·ya] *f.* rabble, mob; *m.* mean fellow.

canana [ka·ná·na] *f.* cartridge belt; **-s** *Col., Ven.* (*esposas*) handcuffs.

canapé [ka·na·pé] *m.* couch, lounge, sofa; settee.

canario [ka·ná·rjo] *m.* canary; native of the Canary Islands; *interj.* gosh!

canasta [ka·nás·ta] *f.* basket; crate.

cancelación [kan·se·la·sjón] *f.* cancellation.

cancelar [kan·se·lár] *v.* to cancel.

canciller [kan·si·yér] *m.* chancellor.

canción [kan·sjón] *f.* song; a kind of lyric poem;

volver a la misma — to repeat, harp on the same thing.

cancha [kán·ča] *f.* court (*for tennis, etc.*); sports ground or field; cockpit, enclosure for cockfights; *Peru* roasted corn or beans; *Am.* ¡abran — ! gangway!; make room!; ¡cancha! down in front!

candado [kan·dá·do] *m.* padlock; *Col.* goatee.

candela [kan·dé·la] *f. Carib.* fire, forest fire; light.

candelabro [kan·de·lá·bro] *m.* candelabrum.

candelero [kan·de·lé·ro] *m.* candlestick.

candente [kan·dén·te] *adj.* incandescent, white-hot, red-hot.

candidato [kan·di·dá·to] *m.* candidate.

candidatura [kan·di·da·tú·ra] *f.* candidacy.

candidez [kan·di·dés] *f.* candor, simplicity.

cándido [kán·di·do] *adj.* candid, simple, innocent; white.

candil [kan·díl] *m.* lamp; *Ríopl., Mex.* chandelier; **candileja** [kan·di·lé·xa] *f.* small oil lamp; oil receptacle (*of a lamp*); **-s** footlights (*of a stage*).

candor [kan·dór] *m.* candor, simplicity, innocence; frankness, sincerity.

canela [ka·né·la] *f.* cinnamon; (*cosa*) an exquisite thing.

caney [ka·néj] *m. Caribe* hut; crude structure (*often without walls*).

cangrejo [kan·gré·xo] *m.* crab.

canguro [kan·gú·ro] *m.* kangaroo.

caníbal [ka·ní·bal] *m.* cannibal.

canica [ka·ní·ka] *f.* (game) marble (*small glass or marble ball*).

canilla [ka·ní·ya] *f.* long bone (*of the arm or leg*); cock (*of a barrel*), faucet; (*carrete*) spool (*for a sewing machine*); *C.A.* slender leg; *Ch., Col., Ríopl.* calf (*of the leg*); *Mex., Ven.* **tener** — to have physical strength; **canillita** [ka·ni·yí·ta] *m. Ríopl., Ch., C.A., Andes* newspaper boy.

canino [ka·ní·no] *adj.* canine; **tener un hambre canina** to be ravenous; to be hungry as a dog.

canje [kán·xe] *m.* interchange, exchange.

canjear [kaŋ·xe·ár] *v.* to exchange, interchange.

cano [ká·no] *adj.* grey-headed, grey-haired.

canoa [ka·nó·a] *f.* canoe.

canon [ká·non] *m.* canon; precept, rule, principle.

canónigo [ka·nó·ni·ḡo] *m.* canon (*churchman*).

canonizar[9] [ka·no·ni·sár] *v.* to canonize, saint.

canoso [ka·nó·so] *adj.* grey, grey-haired.

cansado [kan·sá·do] *adj.* tired; tiresome, boring.

cansancio [kan·sán·sjo] *m.* fatigue, weariness.

cansar [kan·sár] *v.* to tire, fatigue; **-se** to get tired.

cantar [kan·tár] *v.* to sing; (*confesar*) to squeal, confess; *Am.* — **alto** to ask a high price; — **claro** (*or* **-las claras**) to speak with brutal frankness; *m.* song, epic poem.

cántaro [kán·ta·ro] *m.* pitcher, jug.

cantatriz [kan·ta·trís] *f.* singer.

cantera [kan·té·ra] *f.* quarry; *Ríopl., Mex., Carib.* stone block.

cántico [kán·ti·ko] *m.* canticle, religious song.

cantidad [kan·ti·dád] *f.* quantity.

cantilena [kan·ti·lé·na] *f.* song, ballad; monotonous repetition.

cantimplora [kan·tim·pló·ra] *f.* canteen; metal vessel for cooling water; *Col.* flask for carrying gunpowder.

cantina [kan·tí·na] *f.* mess hall; wine cellar; wine shop; canteen; *Carib., Mex., Ríopl.* barroom, tavern; *Col.* saddlebag.

cantinela [kan·ti·né·la] = **cantilena.**

cantinero [kan·ti·né·ro] *m.* bartender; tavern keeper.

canto [kán·to] *m.* song; singing; canto (*division of a long poem*); (*piedra*) stone; edge; *Col.* lap; *P.R.* piece.

cantón [kan·tón] *m.* canton, region; corner; *Mex.* cotton cloth.

cantor [kan·tór] *m.* singer; song bird.

canturrear [kan·tu·rre·ár], **canturriar** [kan·tu·rrjár] *v.* to hum, sing softly.

canturreo [kan·tu·rré·o] *m.* hum, humming.

caña [ká·ña] *f.* cane, reed; tall, thin glass; stem; *Ríopl., Col., Ven.* sugar-cane brandy; *Col.* a kind of dance; *Am.* bluff, boast.

cañada [ka·ñá·da] *f.* narrow canyon, dale, dell, gully, ravine; *Carib.* brook.

cáñamo [ká·ña·mo] *m.* hemp; hemp cloth; *Am.* hemp cord, rope; **cañamazo** [ka·ña·má·so] *m.* (*lona*) canvas.

cañaveral [ka·ña·be·rál] *m.* cane field; reed patch; sugar-cane plantation.

cañería [ka·ñe·rí·a] *f.* conduit, pipe line; tubing, piping; gas or water main.

caño [ká·ño] *m.* pipe, tube; spout; sewer; narrow channel; *Ven.* branch of a river, stream.

cañón [ka·ñón] *m.* (*arma*) cannon, gun; barrel (*of a gun*); (*topográfico*) ravine, gorge, canyon; (*tubo*) pipe, tube; (*figurado*) beard stubble; pinfeather; quill (*of a feather*); chimney shaft; **cañonazo** [ka·ño·ná·so] *m.* cannon shot.

cañonear [ka·ño·ne·ár] *v.* to cannonade, bombard.

cañoneo [ka·ño·né·o] *m.* cannonade; bombardment.

cañonero [ka·ño·né·ro] *m.* gunboat; gunner; **lancha cañonera** gunboat.

caoba [ka·ó·ba] *f.* mahogany.

caos [ká·os] *m.* chaos, confusion.

capa [ká·pa] *f.* (*ropa*) cape, cloak; (*cubierta*) covering, coating; layer; scum; **so** — **de** under the guise of, under pretense of.

capacidad [ka·pa·si·dád] *f.* capacity; ability.

capacitador [ka·pa·si·ta·dór] *m.* capacitor (condenser).

capacitar [ka·pa·si·tár] *v.* to enable, prepare, fit, qualify; *Col.* to empower, authorize.

capataz [ka·pa·tás] *m.* boss, foreman, overseer.

capaz [ka·pás] *adj.* capable, able, competent; (*extenso*) spacious, roomy.

capellán [ka·pe·yán] *m.* chaplain, priest, clergyman.

caperuza [ka·pe·rú·sa] *f.* pointed hood.

capicúa [ka·pi·kú·a] *f.* a number which reads the same from right to left as from left to right.

capilla [ka·pí·ya] *f.* chapel; hood.

capirote [ka·pi·ró·te] *m.* hood; **tonto de** — dunce, plain fool.

capital [ka·pi·tál] *m.* capital, funds; *f.* capital, capital city; *adj.* capital; **capitalismo** [ka·pi·ta·líz·mo] *m.* capitalism; **capitalista** [ka·pi·ta·lís·ta] *m. & f.* capitalist; *adj.* capitalistic.

capitalino [ka·pi·ta·lí·no] *adj.* relative to the capital city; *m.* a resident of the capital.

capitalizar[9] [ka·pi·ta·li·sár] *v.* to capitalize.

capitán [ka·pi·tán] *m.* captain.

capitanear [ka·pi·ta·ne·ár] *v.* to command, lead.

capitolio [ka·pi·tó·ljo] *m.* capitol.

capitular [ka·pi·tu·lár] *v.* to surrender; to come to an agreement.

capítulo [ka·pí·tu·lo] *m.* chapter.

capó [ka·pó] *m.* hood (of a car).

caporal [ka·po·rál] *m.* boss, leader; *Am.* foreman in a cattle ranch.

capote [ka·pó·te] *m.* cloak (*with sleeves*); bullfighter's cloak; *Ch.* thrashing, beating; **decir para su** — to say to oneself; *Mex.* **de** — in an underhanded way; *Ven., Carib.* **dar** — to get ahead; to deceive.

capricho [ka·prí·čo] *m.* caprice, whim, notion.

caprichoso [ka·pri·čó·so] *adj.* capricious, whimsical; changeable, fickle.

caprichudo [ka·pri·čú·do] *adj.* whimsical; *(terco)* stubborn, willful.

cápsula [káp·su·la] *f.* capsule; percussion cap, cartridge shell; metal cap *(on bottles)*.

captar [kap·tár] *v.* to win, attract; to captivate; *Am.* to tune in.

captura [kap·tú·ra] *f.* capture.

capturar [kap·tu·rár] *v.* to capture, arrest.

capucha [ka·pú·ča] *f.* hood.

capullo [ka·pú·yo] *m.* cocoon; bud; acorn cup.

cara [ká·ra] *f.* face; *(gesto)* expression, countenance; front; **de —** opposite; **de dos -s** two-sided; **echar** *(or* **dar) en —** to reproach, blame; **sacar la — por alguien** to take someone's part, defend him.

carabina [ka·ra·ƀí·na] *f.* carbine, rifle.

caracol [ka·ra·kól] *m.* snail; *(escalera)* winding stairs; *Mex.* embroidered blouse; *Am.* curl; **¡caracoles!** gosh!

caracolear [ka·ra·ko·le·ár] *v.* to caper, prance around *(said of horses)*; *Col., Ven.* to muddle, entangle; *Col.* to sidestep an obligation.

caracoleo [ka·ra·ko·lé·o] *m.* prancing around; *(vuelta)* winding, turn.

carácter [ka·rák·ter] *m.* character; temper; **de — alfanumérico** *(computadora)* alphanumeric character.

característico [ka·rak·te·rís·ti·ko] *adj.* characteristic; **característica** [ka·rak·te·rís·ti·ka] *f.* characteristic, trait.

caracterizar[9] [ka·rak·te·ri·sár] *v.* to characterize.

¡caramba! [ka·rám·ba] *interj.* great guns! my goodness!

carámbano [ka·rám·ba·no] *m.* icicle.

caramelo [ka·ra·mé·lo] *m.* caramel; piece of candy.

caramillo [ka·ra·mí·yo] *m.* reed pipe, small flute; **armar un —** to raise a rumpus, create a disturbance.

carancho [ka·rán·čo] *m.* Ríopl. buzzard.

carátula [ka·rá·tu·la] *f.* mask; *Col., Ven., Ríopl., Carib., Andes* title page of a book; *C.A., Mex., Andes* dial, face of a watch.

caravana [ka·ra·ƀá·na] *f.* caravan.

caray [ka·ráj] *m.* tortoise shell; *interj.* gosh!

carbólico [kar·ƀó·li·ko] *adj.* carbolic.

carbón [kar·ƀón] *m.* carbon; coal; **— de leña** charcoal; **carbono** [kar·ƀó·no] *m.* carbon.

carbonera [kar·ƀo·né·ra] *f.* coal bin; coal cellar; woman coal or charcoal vendor; *Am.* coal mine; **carbonero** [kar·ƀo·né·ro] *m.* coal dealer; charcoal vendor; *adj.* coal, relating to coal or charcoal.

carburador [kar·ƀu·ra·dór] *m.* carburetor.

carburo de boro [kar·ƀú·ro·de·ƀó·ro] *m.* boron carbide; **— de silicio** silicon carbide.

carcajada [kar·ka·xá·da] *f.* loud laughter, peal of laughter.

cárcel [kár·sel] *f.* jail, prison.

carcelero [kar·se·lé·ro] *m.* jailer; *adj.* relating to a jail.

carcomido [kar·ko·mí·do] *adj.* worm-eaten; decayed.

cardán [kar·dán] *m.* universal joint.

cardar [kar·dár] *v.* to card, comb *(wool)*.

cardenal [kar·de·nál] *m.* cardinal; cardinal bird; bruise.

cárdeno [kár·de·no] *adj.* dark-purple.

cardíaco [kar·dí·a·ko] *adj.* cardiac; *m, f.* cardiac.

cardiólogo [kar·djó·lo· go] *m.* cardiologist.

cardo [kár·do] *m.* thistle; a kind of cactus.

carear [ka·re·ár] *v.* to confront, bring face to face; to compare; **-se** to meet face to face.

carecer[13] [ka·re·sér] *v. irr.* to lack, be in need of.

carencia [ka·rén·sja] *f.* lack, want.

carente [ka·rén·te] *adj.* lacking.

carero [ka·ré·ro] *adj.* overcharging; profiteering; *m.* profiteer.

carestía [ka·res·tí·a] *f.* dearth, scarcity; high price.

careta [ka·ré·ta] *f.* mask.

carga [kár·ga] *f.* load, burden; freight; cargo; charge or gunpowder; **volver a la —** to insist again and again.

cargado [kar·gá·do] *p.p. & adj.* loaded; *(fuerte)* strong *(as tea or coffee)*; *(nublado)* cloudy, sultry; **— de espaldas** round-shouldered, stoop-shouldered.

cargador [kar·ga·dór] *m.* loader; stevedore; *Mex.* baggage handler.

cargamento [kar·ga·mén·to] *m.* cargo.

cargar[6] [kar·gár] *v. (poner carga)* to load; to charge; *(atacar)* to charge; *(molestar)* to bother, annoy; *Am.* to carry, lug; *Cuba* to punish; **— con** to carry away; to assume *(responsibility)*; **— con el muerto** to get the blame *(unjustly)*.

cargas [kár·gas] *f.* fillers.

cargo [kár·go] *m.* charge, position, duty, burden; loading; accusation; **hacerse — de** to take charge of; to realize.

carguero [kar·gé·ro] *adj.* load-carrying; freight-carrying; *m. Col., Ríopl.* beast of burden; *Col., Ríopl.* skilled loader of pack animals; *Am.* patient, long-suffering person.

cari [ká·ri] *m.* curry.

caribe [ka·rí·ƀe] *adj.* Caribbean; *m.* Carib, Caribbean Indian; *(salvaje)* cannibal; savage.

caricatura [ka·ri·ka·tú·ra] *f.* caricature; cartoon.

caricia [ka·rí·sja] *f.* caress.

caridad [ka·ri·dád] *f.* charity; alms.

caries [ká·rjes] *f.* decay *(of a bone)*; tooth cavity.

cariño [ka·rí·ño] *m.* affection, love; *Am.* gift.

cariñoso [ka·ri·ñó·so] *adj.* affectionate, loving.

carioca [ka·rjó·ka] *adj. & m.f.* native of Rio de Janeiro.

caritativo [ka·ri·ta·tí·ƀo] *adj.* charitable.

cariz [ka·rís] *m.* aspect, appearance.

carmesí [kar·me·sí] *adj. & m.* crimson.

carmín [kar·mín] *m.* crimson.

carnal [kar·nál] *adj.* carnal, sensual; blood relative; *Mex.* buddy, pal.

carnaval [kar·na·ƀál] *m.* carnival.

carne [kár·ne] *f.* meat; flesh; **— de gallina** "goose flesh", "goose pimples"; **echar -s** to put on weight, get fat; *Am.* **— de res** beef.

carneada [kar·ne·á·da] *f. Ríopl.* butchering, slaughtering.

carnear [kar·ne·ár] *v. Ríopl.* to butcher; *Ríopl.* to kill.

carnero [kar·né·ro] *m. (animal)* ram, male sheep; *(carne)* mutton; *Am.* a weak-willed person; *Ch.* waste basket; *Am.* **— de la tierra** llama *(or any fleece-bearing animal)*; *Am.* **cantar uno el —** to die.

carnet [kar·né] *m.* identification card; notebook.

carnicería [kar·ni·se·rí·a] *f. (tienda)* meat market; *(matanza)* butchery, slaughter; *C.A., Ec.* slaughterhouse.

carnicero [kar·ni·sé·ro] *m.* butcher; *adj.* carnivorous, flesh-eating; cruel.

carnívoro [kar·ní·ƀo·ro] *adj.* carnivorous.

carnosidad [kar·no·si·dád] *f.* fleshiness, fatness; abnormal growth *(on animal or plant tissues)*.

carnoso [kar·nó·so] *adj.* fleshy; meaty; pulpy.

caro [ká·ro] *adj.* expensive; dear; *adv.* at a high

price.

carona [ka·ró·na] *f.* saddle pad.

carozo [ka·ró·so] *m.* cob, corncob; fruit pit, seed.

carpa [kár·pa] *f.* carp (*fresh-water fish*); *Mex.* canvas tent, circus tent; — **dorada** goldfish.

carpeta [kar·pé·ta] *f.* (*cubierta*) table cover; desk pad; (*cartera*) portfolio, letter case or file; *Andes* office desk; *Carib.* bookkeeping department; **carpetazo** [kar·pe·tá·so]: **dar** — to table (*a motion*); to set aside, pigeonhole or dismiss.

carpintería [kar·pin·te·rí·a] *f.* carpentry; carpenter's workshop.

carpintero [kar·pin·té·ro] *m.* carpenter; **pájaro** — woodpecker.

carraspear [ka·rras·pe·ár] *v.* to cough up; to clear one's throat; to be hoarse.

carraspera [ka·rras·pé·ra] *f.* hoarseness.

carrera [ka·rré·ra] *f.* career; race, run; course; (*de media*) stocking run.

carreta [ka·rré·ta] *f.* long narrow wagon; cart; *Col., Ven.* wheelbarrow.

carretaje [ka·rre·tá·xe] *m.* cartage (*transporting by cart, truck, etc.*); price paid for cartage.

carrete [ka·rré·te] *m.* spool; reel — **distribuidor** feeding reel; — **receptor** take-up reel (*tape recorder*).

carretel [ka·rre·tél] *m.* reel, spool, bobbin; fishing reel; log reel (*of a boat*).

carretera [ka·rre·té·ra] *f.* highway.

carretero [ka·rre·té·ro] *m.* carter, teamster; cart maker; **camino** — highway.

carretilla [ka·rre·tí·ya] *f.* wheelbarrow; small cart; baggage truck; *Ríopl.* wagon; *Ch.* jaw; *Col.* string, series; *Am.* firecracker; **repetir de** — to rattle off, repeat mechanically.

carretón [ka·rre·tón] *m.* truck; wagon, cart.

carril [ka·rríl] *m.* highway lane; — **prensatelas** work holder; rut; furrow.

carrillo [ka·rrí·yo] *m.* (*de la cara*) cheek; (*mecánico*) pulley; cart.

carrizo [ka·rrí·so] *m.* reed; reed grass.

carro [ká·rro] *m.* cart; cartload; *Am.* car, auto, streetcar, coach; *Am.* **pararle a uno el** — to restrain someone; *Am.* **pasarle a uno el** — to suffer an injury or misfortune; **carroza** [ka·rró·sa] *f.* large and luxurious carriage; chariot; *Am.* hearse; **carrito-guía** track torch; — **portaherramientas** apron (machine).

carrocería [ka·rro·se·rí·a] *f.* chassis; frame for a parade float.

carroña [ka·rró·ña] *f.* dead and decaying flesh; putrid, decaying carcass.

carruaje [ka·rrwá·xe] *m.* carriage, vehicle.

carta [kár·ta] *f.* (*misiva*) letter; (*naipe*) card; (*documento*) charter; map; — **blanca** full authority, freedom to act; — **de naturaleza** naturalization papers; — **de venta** bill of sale; *Ch.* **retirar** — to repent, back down; *Am.* **ser la última** — **de la baraja** to be the worst or most insignificant person or thing.

cartearse [kar·te·ár·se] *v.* to correspond, write to each other.

cartel [kar·tél] *m.* poster, handbill; cartel, written agreement; **cartela** [kar·té·la] *f.* tag, slip of paper, small card, piece of cardboard; **cartelera** [kar·te·lé·ra] *f.* billboard; **cartelón** [kar·te·lón] *m.* large poster.

cartera [kar·té·ra] *f.* (*objeto*) wallet; briefcase; desk pad; (*puesto*) portfolio, cabinet post; **carterista** [kar·te·rís·ta] *m. & f.* pickpocket.

cartero [kar·té·ro] *m.* mailman, letter carrier, postman.

cartilla [kar·tí·ya] *f.* primer; note, short letter; **leerle a uno la** — to scold, lecture someone concerning his duties.

cartografiar[17] [kar·to·ǵra·fjár] *v.* to chart; to make charts.

cartón [kar·tón] *m.* cardboard; pasteboard; **cartulina** [kar·tu·lí·na] *f.* fine cardboard.

cartuchera [kar·tu·čé·ra] *f.* cartridge belt.

cartucho [kar·tú·čo] *m.* cartridge; roll of coins; paper cone or bag.

casa [ká·sa] *f.* (*doméstica*) house, home; household; (*negocio*) business firm; square (*of a chessboard*); *Col.* bet, wager; — **de empeños** pawnshop; — **de huéspedes** boardinghouse; **echar la** — **por la ventana** to spend recklessly, squander everything; **poner** — to set up housekeeping; — **rodante** mobile home.

casabe [ka·sá·ḃe], **cazabe** *m. Am.* cassava; *Am.* cassava bread.

casaca [ka·sá·ka] *f.* long military coat; **volver** — to be a turncoat, change sides or parties.

casamiento [ka·sa·mjén·to] *m.* wedding; marriage.

casar [ka·sár] *v.* to marry; to match; *Ven.* to graft (*trees*); **-se** to get married.

cascabel [kas·ka·ḃél] *m.* jingle bell, tinkle bell; snake's rattle; *Am.* rattlesnake; **cascabela** [kas·ka·ḃé·la] *f. C.R.* rattlesnake.

cascada [kas·ká·ḋa] *f.* cascade, waterfall.

cascajo [kas·ká·xo] *m.* coarse gravel; crushed stone; pebble; fragment; (*basura*) rubbish.

cascanueces [kas·ka·nwé·ses] *m.* nutcracker.

cascar[6] [kas·kár] *v.* to crack, break; **-se** to crack or break open.

cáscara [kás·ka·ra] *f.* shell, husk, hull, rind; bark of a tree; *Ríopl.* **dar a uno** — **de novillo** to give someone a whipping; **cascarudo** [kas·ka·rú·ḋo] *adj.* having a thick husk; having a thick rind.

cascarrabias [kas·ka·rrá·ḃjas] *m. & f.* crab, grouch, ill-tempered person; *adj.* grouchy, cranky, irritable.

casco [kás·ko] *m.* (*yelmo*) helmet; (*uña*) hoof; (*calavera*) skull; broken piece of earthenware; cask; (*botella*) empty bottle; hull of a ship; *Mex., Ríopl.* compound, main buildings of a farm; **caliente de -s** hot-headed; **ligero de -s** light-headed, frivolous; **romperse los -s** to rack one's brain.

caserío [ka·se·rí·o] *m.* hamlet, small settlement.

casero [ka·sé·ro] *adj.* domestic; homemade; *m.* landlord; (*consierje*) janitor, caretaker; *Ch.* customer; *Col., Peru, Ven.* delivery boy; **casera** [ka·sé·ra] *f.* landlady; housekeeper.

caseta [ka·sé·ta] *f.* small house, cottage; booth, stall.

casi [ká·si] *adv.* almost.

casilla [ka·sí·ya] *f.* (*puesto*) stall, booth; (*apartado*) post office box; pigeonhole; **sacarle a uno de sus -s** to change someone's way of life or habits; to irritate, annoy, try someone's patience; **salirse de sus -s** to lose one's temper; to do something out of the way.

casino [ka·sí·no] *m.* club, society; clubhouse; recreation hall.

caso [ká·so] *m.* case; point; matter; event — **que** (*or* **en** — **de que**) in case that; **dado** — supposing; **hacer** — to pay attention to; **hacer** — **omiso de** to omit; **no viene al** — that is not to the point.

casorio [ka·só·rjo] *m.* wedding, marriage.

caspa [kás·pa] *f.* dandruff.

casquillo [kas·kí·yo] *m.* tail stock (machine).

casta [kás·ta] *f.* race, breed; caste, distinct class; quality, kind.

castaña [kas·tá·ña] *f.* chestnut; jug; knot or roll of hair; *Mex.* small barrel; *Mex.* trunk, large suitcase.

castañetear [kas·ta·ñe·te·ár] *v.* to rattle the castanets; to chatter (*said of the teeth*); to crackle (*said of the knees or joints*); — **con los dedos** to snap one's fingers.

castañeteo [kas·ta·ñe·té·o] *m.* rattle or sound of castanets; chatter, chattering (*of the teeth*).

castaño [kas·tá·ño] *m.* chestnut (*tree and wood*); *adj.* chestnut-colored.

castañuela [kas·ta·ñwé·la] *f.* castanet.

castellano [kas·te·yá·no] *adj. & m.* Castilian, Spanish.

castidad [kas·ti·dád] *f.* chastity.

castigar[7] [kas·ti·gár] *v.* to chastise, punish.

castigo [kas·tí·go] *m.* punishment; correction.

castillo [kas·tí·yo] *m.* castle.

castizo [kas·tí·so] *adj.* pure, correct (*language*); pure-blooded.

casto [kás·to] *adj.* chaste, pure.

castor [kas·tór] *m.* beaver; beaver cloth.

casual [ka·swál] *adj.* casual, accidental.

casualidad [ka·swa·li·dád] *f.* chance, accident.

casuca [ka·sú·ka] *f.* little house; hut, shanty.

casucha [ka·sú·ča] *f.* hut, hovel, shack.

catadura [ka·ta·dú·ra] *f.* aspect, appearance.

catalán [ka·ta·lán] *adj.* Catalan, Catalonian, of or from Catalonia, Spain; *m.* Catalan.

catalejo [ka·ta·lé·xo] *m.* telescope.

catalizador [ka·ta·li·sa·dór] *m.* catalyst.

catalogar[7] [ka·ta·lo·gár] *v.* to catalogue.

catálogo [ka·tá·lo·go] *m.* catalogue.

catar [ka·tár] *v.* to look at, examine; (*saber*) to taste, sample.

catarata [ka·ta·rá·ta] *f.* cataract; waterfall.

catarro [ka·tá·rro] *m.* catarrh, cold.

catástrofe [ka·tás·tro·fe] *f.* catastrophe, mishap.

catear [ka·te·ár] *v.* to explore, look around; *Ch., C.A., Mex.* to search or raid (*a home*); *Am.* to explore for ore; *Col., Ríopl.* to test, try.

catecismo [ka·te·síz·mo] *m.* catechism.

cátedra [ká·te·dra] *f.* class; subject; chair, professorship.

catedral [ka·te·drál] *f.* cathedral.

catedrático [ka·te·drá·ti·ko] *m.* professor.

categoría [ka·te·go·rí·a] *f.* category, rank; kind, class.

categórico [ka·te·gó·ri·ko] *adj.* categorical, positive.

catequizar[9] [ka·te·ki·sár] *v.* to catechize, give religious instruction to); (*inducir*) to induce, persuade.

católico [ka·tó·li·ko] *adj.* Catholic; universal; *m.* Catholic; **catolicismo** [ka·to·li·síz·mo] *m.* Catholicism.

catorce [ka·tór·se] *num.* fourteen.

catre [ká·tre] *m.* cot, small bed; *Ríopl.* raft, float; *C.A.*, camp stool, folding stool; — **de tijera** folding cot.

catrín [ka·trín] *m. Am.* dandy; *adj. Mex., C.A.* over-elegant, dressy.

cauce [káw·se] *m.* river bed.

caución [kaw·sjón] *f.* precaution; security, guarantee; bail.

cauchero [kaw·čé·ro] *m. Am.* rubber gatherer; *Am.* rubber producer; *adj. Am.* rubber, pertaining to rubber.

caucho [káw·čo] *m.* rubber; — **sintético** synthetic rubber; *Am.* rubber tree; *Col.* rubber raincoat or cloak; **cauchal** [kaw·čál] *m.* rubber grove or plantation.

caudal [kaw·dál] *m.* (*monetario*) wealth; (*torrente*) river current; volume of water.

caudaloso [kaw·da·ló·so] *adj.* wealthy; abundant.

caudillaje [kaw·di·yá·xe] *m.* military leadership; *Am.* political bossism; *Am.* tyranny.

caudillo [kaw·dí·yo] *m.* leader, chief; *Am.* political boss.

causa [káw·sa] *f.* cause; (*pleito*) case, lawsuit; *Ch., Perú* light lunch, snack; **a causa de** on account of.

causar [kaw·sár] *v.* to cause.

cautela [kaw·té·la] *f.* caution; cunning, craftiness; trick, deception.

cauteloso [kaw·te·ló·so] *adj.* cautious; crafty.

cautivar [kaw·ti·bár] *v.* to capture; to charm, fascinate.

cautiverio [kaw·ti·bé·rjo] *m.* captivity.

cautivo [kaw·tí·bo] *m.* captive, war prisoner.

cauto [káw·to] *adj.* cautious.

cavar [ka·bár] *v.* to dig, spade; to excavate.

caverna [ka·bér·na] *f.* cavern, cave.

cavernoso [ka·ber·nó·so] *adj.* cavernous, like a cavern; hollow; **voz cavernosa** deep, hollow voice.

cavidad [ka·bi·dád] *f.* cavity.

cayado [ka·yá·do] *m.* shepherd's crook, staff.

cayo [ká·yo] *m.* key, island reef.

caza [ká·sa] *f.* hunt, hunting; wild game; *m.* attack plane; **dar** — to pursue, track down.

cazador [ka·sa·dór] *adj.* hunting; *m.* hunter.

cazar[9] [ka·sár] *v.* to chase, hunt; to track down.

cazatorpedero [ka·sa·tor·pe·dé·ro] *m.* destroyer, torpedo-boat.

cazo [ká·so] *m.* dipper; (*cazuela*) pot, pan.

cazuela [ka·swé·la] *f.* stewing pan; earthenware cooking pan; — **para perdigar** braiser; — **plana** sheet pan; topmost theatre gallery; *Ven.* stewed hen; *P.R.* candied sweet potatoes with spices.

cebada [se·bá·da] *f.* barley; *Ríopl.* brewing of **mate; cebadal** [se·ba·dál] *m.* barley field.

cebar [se·bár] *v.* to feed, fatten (*animals*); to encourage, nourish (*a passion*); to prime (*a gun, pump, etc.*); to bait (*a fishhook*); *Ríopl.* to brew and serve **mate** or tea; **-se** to vent one's fury.

cebo [sé·bo] *m.* feed (*for animals*); bait; incentive.

cebolla [se·bó·ya] *f.* onion.

cebollanas [se·bo·yá·nas] *f.* chives; *Mex.* **cebollines.**

cebollar [se·bo·yár] *m.* onion patch.

cecear [se·se·ár] *v.* to lisp.

ceceo [se·sé·o] *m.* lisp, lisping; pronunciation of both /s/ and /θ/ as [θ].

cecina [se·sí·na] *f.* dried beef, jerked beef.

cedazo [se·dá·so] *m.* sieve.

ceder [se·dér] *v.* to cede, transfer; to yield, surrender, submit; to diminish, abate.

cedilla [se·dí·ya] *f.* cedilla.

cedro [sé·dro] *m.* cedar.

cédula [sé·du·la] *f.* slip of paper; certificate; — **de vecindad** (*or* — **personal**) official identification card.

céfiro [sé·fi·ro] *m.* zephyr, soft breeze; *Am.* fine muslin.

cegar[1, 7] [se·gár] *v. irr.* to blind; to become blind; to confuse; to fill up, stop up (*a hole*).

ceguedad [se·ge·dád], **ceguera** [se·gé·ra] *f.* blindness.

ceiba [séj·ba] *f. Am.* ceiba, silk-cotton tree.

ceja [sé·xa] *f.* eyebrow; brow of a hill.

cejar [se·xár] *v.* to go backward; to back; to back down, give in, yield; to slacken.

cejijunto [se·xi·xún·to] *adj.* frowning; with knitted eyebrows.

celada [se·lá·da] *f.* ambush, snare, trap.

celador [se·la·dór] *m.* guard.

celaje [se·lá·xe] *m.* colored clouds; skylight; presage, portent; *P.R.* shadow, ghost; *Am.* **como un** — like lightning.

celar [se·lár] v. to guard, watch; to watch over jealously; (*esconder*) to conceal.

celda [sél·da] f. cell.

celebración [se·le·bra·sjón] f. celebration.

celebrar [se·le·brár] v. to celebrate; to praise, honor; to be glad.

célebre [sé·le·bre] adj. famous; funny, witty; *Col.* graceful, pretty (*woman*).

celebridad [se·le·bri·dád] f. fame, renown; celebrity, famous person; celebration.

celeridad [se·le·ri·dád] f. swiftness, speed.

celeste [se·lés·te] adj. celestial, heavenly.

celestial [se·les·tjál] adj. celestial, heavenly, divine.

célibe [sé·li·be] adj. unmarried; m. & f. unmarried person.

celo [sé·lo] m. (*humano*) zeal, ardor; envy; (*animal*) heat (*sexual excitement in animals*); -s jealousy, suspicion; **tener -s** to be jealous.

celosía [se·lo·sí·a] f. window lattice; Venetian blind.

celoso [se·ló·so] adj. jealous; zealous, eager; suspicious.

célula [sé·lu·la] f. cell.

celuloide [se·lu·lój·de] m. celluloid.

cellisca [se·yís·ka] f. sleet; rain and snow.

cementación [se·men·ta·sjón] f. case hardening.

cementar [se·men·tár] v. to cement.

cementerio [se·men·té·rjo] m. cemetery.

cemento [se·mén·to] m. cement; — **armado** reinforced concrete.

cena [sé·na] f. supper.

cenagal [se·na·gál] m. quagmire, muddy ground, swamp.

cenagoso [se·na·gó·so] adj. muddy, miry.

cenar [se·nár] v. to eat supper.

cencerrada [sen·se·rrá·da] f. racket, noise (*with cowbells, tin cans, etc.*); tin pan serenade.

cencerrear [sen·se·rre·ár] v. to make a racket (*with cowbells, tin cans, etc.*); serenade with cowbells.

cencerro [sen·sé·rro] m. cowbell.

cendal [sen·dál] m. gauze; thin veil.

cenicero [se·ni·sé·ro] m. ash tray; ash pit; ash pan.

cenicienta [se·ni·sjén·ta] f. a Cinderella.

ceniciento [se·ni·sjén·to] adj. ashen, ash-colored.

cenit [sé·nit] m. zenith.

ceniza [se·ní·sa] f. ashes, cinders.

cenizo [se·ní·so] adj. ash-colored.

censo [sén·so] m. census.

censor [sen·sór] m. censor.

censura [sen·sú·ra] f. censure, criticism, disapproval; censorship.

censurador [sen·su·ra·dór] m. censor, critic; critical person; adj. critical.

censurar [sen·su·rár] v. to censure, criticize, reprove; to censor.

centavo [sen·tá·bo] m. cent.

centella [sen·té·ya] f. lightning, flash; spark.

centelleante [sen·te·ye·án·te] adj. sparkling, flashing.

centellear [sen·te·ye·ár] v. to twinkle; to sparkle, glitter; to flash.

centelleo [sen·te·yé·o] m. glitter, sparkle.

centenar [sen·te·nár] m. one hundred; (*campo*) field of rye.

centenario [sen·te·ná·rjo] m. centennial, one hundredth anniversary; adj. centennial; old, ancient.

centeno [sen·té·no] m. rye.

centésimo [sen·té·si·mo] adj. & m. hundredth.

centímetro [sen·tí·me·tro] m. centimeter.

céntimo [sén·ti·mo] m. *Sp.* one hundredth part of a **peseta.**

centinela [sen·ti·né·la] m. sentry, sentinel.

central [sen·trál] adj. central; f. main office; headquarters; *Carib.* main sugar mill or refinery.

centrar [sen·trár] v. to center.

céntrico [sén·tri·ko] adj. central.

centrífugo [sen·trí·fu·go] adj. centrifugal.

centrípeto [sen·trí·pe·to] adj. centripetal.

centro [sén·tro] m. center, middle.

ceñidor [se·ñi·dór] m. girdle, belt, sash.

ceñir[5, 19] [se·ñír] v. irr. (*rodear*) to gird, girdle; to tighten; to encircle; (*abreviar*) to diminish; to limit; **-se a** to limit oneself to.

ceño [sé·ño] m. frown; scowl; **fruncir el —** to frown; to scowl.

cepa [sé·pa] f. stump, stub (*of a tree or plant*); vinestock; (*ascendencia*) origin, stock (*of a family*); *Am.* mass of plants growing from a common root; *Am.* excavation (*for a building*), hole, pit (*for planting trees*); **de buena —** of good stock.

cepillo [se·pí·yo] m. brush; (*limosna*) alms box; carpenter's plane; *Am.* flatterer; **— de dientes** toothbrush.

cepo [sé·po] m. branch, stock.

cera [sé·ra] f. wax.

cerámica [se·rá·mi·ka] f. ceramics, pottery.

cerca [sér·ka] adv. near, near by; **— de** prep. near, nearly; f. fence, low wall.

cercado [ser·ká·do] m. enclosure; fenced-in garden; fence; *Am.* Peruvian political division; p.p. of **cercar.**

cercanía [ser·ka·ní·a] f. proximity; -s surroundings, vicinity.

cercano [ser·ká·no] adj. near; neighboring.

cercar[6] [ser·kár] v. to fence, enclose; to surround; (*sitiar*) to besiege.

cercenar [ser·se·nár] v. to clip off; to curtail, diminish, reduce.

cerciorar [ser·sjo·rár] v. to assure, affirm; **-se** to ascertain, find out.

cerco [sér·ko] m. fence enclosure; siege; circle; *Ch.* small farm or orchard.

cerda [sér·da] f. bristle; *Col.* **ir en -s** to go halves or share in a deal.

cerdo [sér·do] m. hog; pig; pork.

cerdoso [ser·dó·so] adj. bristly.

cereal [se·re·ál] m. cereal, grain.

cerebro [se·ré·bro] m. brain.

ceremonia [se·re·mó·nja] f. ceremony.

ceremonial [se·re·mo·njál] adj. & m. ceremonial.

ceremonioso [se·re·mo·njó·so] adj. ceremonious.

cereza [se·ré·sa] f. cherry; **cerezo** [se·ré·so] m. cherry tree; cherry wood.

cerilla [se·rí·ya] f. wax taper; *Sp.* wax match; earwax.

cerillo [se·rí·yo] m. *Mex., C.A., Ven., Andes* match.

cerner[1] [ser·nér] v. irr. to sift; to drizzle; *Am.* to strain through a sieve; **-se** to hover (*as a bird or plane*).

cero [sé·ro] m. zero; nothing.

cerquita [ser·kí·ta] adv. quite near, nice and near.

cerrado [se·rrá·do] adj. closed; (*nublado*) cloudy; (*espeso*) thick (*beard*); reserved (*person*); dull; *Am.* stubborn.

cerradura [se·rrá·du·ra] f. locking, closing; lock; **— de golpe** spring lock.

cerrajería [se·rra·xe·rí·a] f. locksmith's shop; locksmith's trade.

cerrajero [se·rra·xé·ro] m. locksmith.

cerrar[1] [se·rrár] v. irr. to close, shut, lock; **-se el cielo** to become overcast or cloudy.

cerrazón [se·rra·són] f. cloudiness, darkness.

cerro [sé·rro] m. hill.

cerrojo [se·rró·xo] *m.* latch, bolt.
certamen [ser·tá·men] *m.* contest, literary contest; debate; competition.
certero [ser·té·ro] *adj.* accurate, exact; well-aimed; **tirador** — good shot.
certeza [ser·té·sa] *f.* certainty.
certidumbre [ser·ti·dúm·bre] *f.* certainty.
certificado [ser·ti·fi·ká·do] *adj.* certified, registered; *m.* certificate.
certificar[6] [ser·ti·fi·kár] *v.* to certify; to register (*a letter*).
cervato [ser·bá·to] *m.* fawn, young deer.
cerveza [ser·bé·sa] *f.* beer; **cervecería** [ser·be·se·rí·a] *f.* beer tavern; brewery.
cervis [ser·bís] *f.* cervix.
cesante [se·sán·te] *adj.* unemployed.
cesar [se·sár] *v.* to cease, stop; to quit.
cesáreo [se·sá·re·o] *adj. & m.* Caesarean.
cesio [sé·sjo] *m.* cesium.
cesionario [se·sjo·ná·rjo] *m.* grantee, assignee; **cesionista** [se·sjo·nís·ta] *m., f.* grantor.
cesta [sés·ta] *f.* basket; for playing jai alai (*Basque ball game*).
cesto [sés·to] *m.* large basket, hamper.
cetrino [se·trí·no] *adj.* greenish-yellow, lemon-colored; citronlike; melancholy, gloomy.
cetro [sé·tro] *m.* scepter, staff.
cibernética [si·ber·né·ti·ka] *f.* cybernetics, computer science.
cicatero [si·ka·té·ro] *adj.* miserly, stingy.
cicatriz [si·ka·trís] *f.* scar.
cicatrizar[9] [si·ka·tri·sár] *v.* to heal, close (*a wound*).
ciclo [sí·klo] *m.* cycle; period of time; school term.
ciclón [si·klón] *m.* cyclone.
ciclotrón [si·klo·trón] *m.* cyclotron.
ciego [sjé·ǥo] *adj.* blind; **a ciegas** blindly; *m.* blindman.
cielo [sjé·lo] *m.* sky; heaven; — **de la boca** palate; **poner en el** — to praise, extol; **poner el grito en el** — to "hit the ceiling", **cielito** *m. Ríopl.* gaucho group dance and tune.
ciempiés [sjem·pjés], **cientopiés** [sjen·to·pjés] *m.* centipede.
cien(to) [sjén·to] *num.* hundred.
ciénaga [sjé·na·ǥa] *f.* swamp, bog, quagmire, marsh.
ciencia [sjén·sja] *f.* science; learning; skill; **a** (*or* **de**) — **cierta** with certainty.
cieno [sjé·no] *m.* mud, mire.
científico [sjen·tí·fi·ko] *adj.* scientific; *m.* scientist.
cierre [sjé·rre] *m.* clasp, fastener; zipper; closing, fastening, locking; method of closing.
cierto [sjér·to] *adj.* certain, true, sure; **por** — certainly; *Col., C.A.* **ciertas hierbas** so-and-so (*person not named*).
ciervo [sjér·bo] *m.* deer; **cierva** [sjér·ba] *f.* doe, hind, female deer.
cierzo [sjér·so] *m.* north wind.
cifra [sí·fra] *f.* cipher, number; figure; (*resumen*) abridgment, summary; (*código*) code; monogram; (*emblema*) emblem.
cifrar [si·frár] *v.* to write in code; to summarize; — **la esperanza en** to place one's hop in.
cigarra [si·ǥá·rra] *f.* cicada, locust.
cigarrera [si·ǥa·rré·ra] *f.* cigar or cigarette case; woman cigar maker or vendor.
cigarrillo [si·ǥa·rrí·yo] *m. Sp.* cigarette.
cigarro [si·ǥá·rro] *m.* cigarette.
cigüeña [si·ǥwé·ña] *f.* stork; (*mecánico*) crank, handle (*for turning*).
cigüeñal [si·ǥwe·ñál] *m.* crankshaft.
cilantro [si·lán·tro] *m.* coriander, also **culantro.**

cilíndrico [si·lín·dri·ko] *adj.* cylindrical.
cilindro [si·lín·dro] *m.* cylinder; *Mex.* hand organ.
cima [sí·ma] *f.* peak, summit, top; **dar** — to complete, carry out.
cimarrón [si·ma·rrón] *adj. Ríopl., Mex., Carib., Ven., Andes* wild, untamed; *Ríopl.* **mate** — black, bitter **mate.**
cimarronear [si·ma·rro·ne·ár] *v. Ríopl.* to drink **mate** without sugar.
cimbrar [sim·brár], **cimbrear** [sim·bre·ár] *v.* to brandish, flourish, swing; to shake; to bend; *Am.* to swing around, change suddenly one's direction, — **a uno de un golpe** to knock a person down with a blow; **-se** to swing, sway; to vibrate, shake.
cimiento [si·mjén·to] *m.* foundation, base; source, root; **abrir los -s** to break ground for a building.
cinc [siŋk] *m.* zinc.
cincel [sin·sél] *m.* chisel.
cincelar [sin·se·lár] *v.* to chisel; to engrave.
cinco [síŋ·ko] *num.* five.
cincuenta [siŋ·kwén·ta] *num.* fifty.
cincha [sín·ča] *f.* cinch, girth; *Mex., C.A.* blows with the flat of a sword; *Col., Ríopl.* **a revienta -s** unwillingly; hurriedly; at breakneck speed.
cinchar [sin·čár] *v.* to cinch, tighten the saddle girth; *Mex., C.A.* to hit with the flat of a sword.
cine [sí·ne], **cinema** [si·né·ma] *m.* cinema, motion picture, movie; **cinematógrafo** [si·ne·ma·tó·ǥra·fo] *m.* motion picture.
cinematografía [si·ne·ma·to·ǥra·fí·a] *f.* cinematography, the science of motion picture photography.
cíngulo [síŋ·ǥu·lo] *m.* girdle, cord, belt.
cínico [sí·ni·ko] *adj.* cynical, sarcastic, sneering; *m.* cynic.
cinta [sín·ta] *f.* ribbon, band; tape; strip; (*película*) movie film; (*red*) coarse fishing net; — **magnetofónica** recording tape; *Ríopl.* tin can.
cintarada [sin·ta·rá·da] *f.* beating, flogging; **cintarazo** *m.* blow with the flat of a sword.
cintilar [sin·ti·lár] *v.* to sparkle, twinkle; to glimmer.
cinto [sín·to] *m.* belt; girdle.
cintura [sin·tú·ra] *f.* waist; **meter en** — to subdue, subject.
cinturón [sin·tu·rón] *m.* belt; — **de seguridad** safety belt.
ciprés [si·prés] *m.* cypress.
circo [sír·ko] *m.* circus.
circonio [sir·kó·njo] *m.* zirconium.
circuitería física [sir·kwi·te·rí·a fí·si·ka] *f.* ⟨ (*computadora*) hardware.
circuito [sir·kwí·to] *m.* circuit.
circulación [sir·ku·la·sjón] *f.* circulation; traffic.
circular [sir·ku·lár] *v.* to circulate; to circle; *adj.* circular; *f.* circular letter, notice.
círculo [sír·ku·lo] *m.* circle; group; club; clubhouse.
circundante [sir·kun·dán·te] *adj.* surrounding.
circundar [sir·kun·dár] *v.* to surround.
circunferencia [sir·kun·fe·rén·sja] *f.* circumference.
circunlocución [sir·kun·lo·ku·sjón] *f.* circumlocution, roundabout expression.
circunspección [sir·kun·spek·sjón] *f.* circumspection, decorum, prudence, restraint.
circunspecto [sir·kuns·pék·to] *adj.* circumspect, prudent.
circunstancia [sir·kuns·tán·sja] *f.* circumstance.
circunstante [sir·kuns·tán·te] *adj.* surrounding; present; **-s** *m. pl.* bystanders, onlookers, audience.
circunvecino [sir·kum·be·sí·no] *adj.* neighboring, surrounding.
cirio [sí·rjo] *m.* wax candle; saguaro cactus.

CE

ciruela [si·rwé·la] *f.* plum; prune; — **pasa** prune, dried prune; **ciruelo** *m.* plum tree.

cirugía [si·ru·xí·a] *f.* surgery.

cirujano [si·ru·xá·no] *m.* surgeon.

cisne [síz·ne] *m. Ríopl., Ch.* powder puff.

cisterna [sis·tér·na] *f.* cistern.

cita [sí·ta] *f.* date, appointment; (*citación*) citation, summons; quotation.

citación [si·ta·sjón] *f.* (*de texto*) quotation; citation, summons.

citar [si·tár] *v.* (*convocar*) to make a date or appointment with; (*referir*) to cite, quote; (*incitar*) incite, provoke; to summon.

cítrico [sí·tri·ko] *adj.* citric.

ciudad [sju·dád] *f.* city.

ciudadano [sju·da·dá·no] *m.* citizen; resident of a city; *adj.* of or pertaining to a city; **ciudadanía** [sju·da·da·ní·a] *f.* citizenship.

ciudadela [sju·da·dé·la] *f.* citadel.

cívico [sí·bi·ko] *adj.* civic.

civil [si·bíl] *adj.* civil; polite, courteous.

civilidad [si·bi·li·dád] *f.* civility, courtesy.

civilización [si·bi·li·sa·sjón] *f.* civilization.

civilizador [si·bi·li·sa·dór] *adj.* civilizing; *m.* civilizer.

civilizar[9] [si·bi·li·sár] *v.* to civilize.

cizaña [si·sá·ña] *f.* weed; (*vicio*) vice; discord; **sembrar** — to sow discord.

clamar [kla·már] *v.* to clamor, shout; (*gimotear*) to whine.

clamor [kla·mór] *m.* clamor, shout; whine; knell.

clamoreo [kla·mo·ré·o] *m.* clamoring; shouting.

clamorear [kla·mo·re·ár] *v.* to clamor, shout; to toll, knell.

clandestino [klan·des·tí·no] *adj.* clandestine, underhanded, secret.

clara [klá·ra] *f.* white of egg; bald spot; (*calvicie*) thin spot (*in a fabric*); **a las -s** clearly, openly, frankly.

claraboya [kla·ra·bó·ya] *f.* skylight.

clarear [kla·re·ár] *v.* (*poner claro*), to clarify, make clear; (*haber más luz*) to grow light, begin to dawn; to clear up; *Mex.* to pierce through and through; **-se** to become transparent; to reveal oneself.

claridad [kla·ri·dád] *f.* clarity, clearness; (*franqueza*) blunt remark, slam; fame.

claridoso [kla·ri·dó·so] *adj. Mex., Ven., C.A.* (*franco*) blunt, outspoken, plainspoken.

clarificar[6] [kla·ri·fi·kár] *v.* to clarify, make clear.

clarín [kla·rín] *m.* bugle; (*persona*) bugler; organ stop; *Am.* song bird.

clarinete [kla·ri·né·te] *m.* clarinet; clarinet player.

clarito [kla·rí·to] *adj. & adv.* quite clear, nice and clear.

clarividencia [kla·ri·bi·dén·sja] *f.* clairvoyance; keen insight.

claro [klá·ro] *adj.* clear; light (*color*); illustrious; *adv.* clearly; *m.* skylight; space, gap; clearing (*in a forest*); **pasar la noche de — en** — not to sleep a wink; *Mex., Carib.* **en** — without eating or sleeping; *Am.* **poner en** — to copy (*a rough draft*).

clase [klá·se] *f.* class; classroom; kind, sort.

clásico [klá·si·ko] *adj.* classic, classical.

clasificación [kla·si·fi·ka·sjón] *f.* classification.

clasificar[6] [kla·si·fi·kár] *v.* to classify; (*computadora*) to sort.

claustro [kláws·tro] *m.* cloister; (*reunión*) meeting of a university faculty; — **de profesores** university faculty.

cláusula [kláw·su·la] *f.* clause.

clausura [klaw·sú·ra] *f.* closing; seclusion, (*vida*) monastic life.

clavado [kla·bá·do] *m. Mex.* a dive into water.

clavar [kla·bár] *v.* to nail; to fix; to deceive, cheat; **-se** to be deceived; *Mex.* to fall into a trap; *Mex.* to dive.

clave [klá·be] *f.* key, code; (*piedra angular*) keystone; clef; **puesta en** — set in code.

clavel [kla·bél] *m.* carnation, pink.

clavetear [kla·be·te·ár] *v.* to nail; to stud with nails.

clavícula [kla·bí·ku·la] *f.* collarbone.

clavija [kla·bí·xa] *f.* peg; electric plug; peg (*of a stringed instrument*).

clavijero [kla·bi·xé·ro] *m.* hat or clothes rack.

clavo [klá·bo] *m.* nail; (*clavero*) clove (*spice*); (*dolor*) sharp pain or grief; sick headache; *Mex.* rich mineral vein; *Mex., Ch.* bother, worry; *Col.* surprise, disappointment; *Ríopl.* drug on the market (*unsaleable article*); **dar en el** — to hit the nail on the head; *Mex.* **meter a uno en un** — to put a person in a predicament; *P.R.* **ser un** — to be punctual, exact.

clemencia [kle·mén·sja] *f.* mercy; **clemente** [kle·mén·te] *adj.* merciful.

clerical [kle·ri·kál] *adj.* clerical, of a clergyman or the clergy.

clérigo [klé·ri·go] *m.* clergyman.

clero [klé·ro] *m.* clergy.

cliché [kli·čé] *m.* photographic plate; also **clisé.**

cliente [kljén·te] *m. & f.* client; customer; **clientela** [kljen·té·la] *f.* clientele, clients; customers.

clima [klí·ma] *m.* climate.

climatización [kli·ma·ti·sa·sjón] *f.* air conditioning.

clímax [klí·maks] *m.* climax.

clínica [klí·ni·ka] *f.* clinic.

clíper [klí·per] *m.* clipper.

cloaca [klo·á·ka] *f.* sewer.

cloquear [klo·ke·ár] *v.* to cluck.

cloqueo [klo·ké·o] *m.* cluck, clucking.

cloro [kló·ro] *m.* chlorine.

clorofila [klo·ro·fí·la] *f.* chlorophyll.

cloruro [klo·rú·ro] *m.* chloride.

club [klub] *m.* club, society.

clueca [klwé·ka] *f.* brooding hen.

coacción [ko·ak·sjón] *f.* compulsion, force; enforcement.

coagular [ko·a·gu·lár] *v.* to coagulate, thicken, clot; to curd, curdle; **-se** to coagulate, clot; to curd, curdle.

coágulo [ko·á·gu·lo] *m.* coagulation, clot.

coartar [ko·ar·tár] *v.* to restrain, limit.

coba [kó·ba] *f.* flattery; fib; **dar** — to flatter; to tease.

cobalto [ko·bál·to] *m.* cobalt.

cobarde [ko·bár·de] *adj.* cowardly; timid; weak; *m.* coward.

cobardía [ko·bar·dí·a] *f.* cowardice.

cobertizo [ko·ber·tí·so] *m.* shed; shanty.

cobertor [ko·ber·tór] *m.* bedcover, quilt.

cobertura [ko·ber·tú·ra] *f.* cover, covering.

cobija [ko·bí·xa] *f.* cover; shelter; roof; *Mex., C.A., Col., Ríopl.* blanket; *Am.* shawl, serape, poncho; **-s** *Mex.* bedclothes.

cobijar [ko·bi·xár] *v.* to cover; to shelter.

cobrador [ko·bra·dór] *m.* collector; ticket collector.

cobranza [ko·brán·sa] *f.* collection (*of a sum of money*); cashing.

cobrar [ko·brár] *v.* to collect (*bills, debts*); (*cargar*) to charge; (*hacer efectivo*) to cash (*a draft, check, etc.*); to recover, regain; to gain, acquire; *Am.* to demand payment; — **cariño a** to take a liking to; — **a la entrega** C.O.D. (collect on delivery).

cobre [kó·bre] *m.* copper; copper kitchen utensils; *Am.* copper coin; **-s** brass musical instruments; **batir el** — to hustle, work with energy; *Am.* **mostrar el** — to show one's worse side.

cobrizo [ko·brí·so] *adj.* coppery, copper-colored.

cobro [kó·bro] *m.* collection (*of bills*); **poner en** — to put in a safe place; **ponerse en** — to take refuge, get to a safe place.

coca [kó·ka] *f. Andes* coca (*South American shrub and its leaves*); *Am.* cocaine; *Col.* coca tea; *Col.* eggshell; *Col.* fruit skin or rind; *Am.* **de** — free of charge; in vain.

cocaína [ko·ka·í·na] *f.* cocaine.

cocear [ko·se·ár] *v.* to kick.

cocer[2, 10] [ko·sér] *v. irr.* to cook; to boil; to bake.

cocido [ko·sí·do] *m.* Spanish stew; *p.p. of* **cocer**.

cociente [ko·sjén·te] *m.* quotient.

cocimiento [ko·si·mjén·to] *m.* cooking; baking; liquid concoction (*generally made of medicinal herbs*).

cocina [ko·sí·na] *f.* kitchen; cuisine, cooking; — **económica** stove, range.

cocinar [ko·si·nár] *v.* to cook.

cocinero [ko·si·né·ro] *m.* cook.

coco [kó·ko] *m.* coconut; coconut palm; bogeyman, goblin; *Col.* derby hat; *Mex., Carib., Ríopl.* head; *Am.* blow on the head; **hacer -s a** to make eyes at, flirt with; *Col., Ven., Andes* **pelar a** — to crop the hair; **cocotal** [ko·ko·tál] *m.* grove of coconut palms; coconut plantation; **cocotero** [ko·ko·té·ro] *m.* coconut palm.

cocodrilo [ko·ko·drí·lo] *m.* crocodile.

cocoliche [ko·ko·lí·če] *m. Ríopl.* jargon of Italians who are learning Spanish.

coche [kó·če] *m.* coach; car; taxi.

cochero [ko·čé·ro] *m.* coachman; cabman; taxi driver.

cochinada [ko·či·ná·da] *f.* filth, filthiness; filthy act or remark; dirty trick; herd of swine.

cochinilla [ko·či·ní·no] *m.* hog, pig; dirty person; *Ch.* stingy person; *Am.* — **de monte** wild boar; *adj.* filthy, dirty; *Ch.* miserly, stingy.

codazo [ko·dá·so] *m.* nudge; poke (*with the elbow*).

codear [ko·de·ár] *v.* to elbow; to nudge; **-se con alguien** to rub elbows with someone.

códice [kó·di·se] *m.* codex.

codicia [ko·dí·sja] *f.* greed; greediness.

codiciar [ko·di·sjár] *v.* to covet.

codicioso [ko·di·sjó·so] *adj.* covetous, greedy.

codificación [ko·di·fi·ka·sjón] *f.* coding.

código [kó·di·go] *m.* code of laws.

codo [kó·do] *m.* elbow; bend; — **doble** double elbow (plumbing); **alzar (empinar) el** — to drink too much; **hablar por los -s** to talk too much; **meterse** (*or* **estar metido**) **hasta los -s** to be up to the elbows, be very busy.

codorniz [ko·dor·nís] *f.* partridge.

coetáneo [ko·e·tá·ne·o] *adj.* contemporary.

cofrade [ko·frá·de] *m. & f.* fellow member (*of a brotherhood, club, society, etc.*).

cofradía [ko·fra·dí·a] *f.* brotherhood; sisterhood; guild; trade union.

cofre [kó·fre] *m.* coffer, jewel box; chest, truck.

coger[11] [ko·xér] *v.* to seize; to catch; to grasp; to gather; *Mex., Ch. Ven. Col. Ríopl.* to copulate; *Am.* **-se una cosa** to steal something.

cogollo [ko·gó·yo] *m.* heart (*of lettuce*), head (*of cabbage*).

cogote [ko·gó·te] *m.* nape, back of the neck.

cohechar [ko·e·čár] *v.* to bribe.

coheredero [ko·e·re·dé·ro] *m.* joint heir.

coherente [ko·e·rén·te] *adj.* coherent; connected.

cohete [ko·é·te] *m.* skyrocket; rocket; *Ríopl.* **al** — in vain, uselessly.

cohetería [ko·e·te·rí·a] *f.* rocketry; rocket weaponry; shop for making fireworks.

cohibición [koj·bi·sjón] *f.* repression, inhibition, restraint.

cohibido [koj·bí·do] *p.p. & adj.* inhibited; embarrassed, uneasy.

cohibir [koj·bír] *v.* to restrain, repress; to inhibit.

coincidencia [kojn·si·dén·sja] *f.* coincidence.

coincidir [kojn·si·dír] *v.* to coincide.

cojear [ko·xe·ár] *v.* to limp; **cojeamos del mismo pie** we both have the same weakness.

cojera [ko·xé·ra] *f.* limp, lameness.

cojín [ko·xín] *m.* cushion; pad; **cojincillo** *m.* pad.

cojinete [ko·xi·né·te] *m.* small pillow or cushion, pad; (*balero*) bearing, ball bearing; — **del cabezal** headstock bearing (machine).

cojo [kó·xo] *adj.* lame, crippled; one-legged.

col [kol] *f.* cabbage; — **de Bruselas** Brussels sprouts.

cola [kó·la] *f.* (*rabo*) tail; train of a dress; (*hilera de gente*) line of people; glue; **piano de** — grand piano; **piano de media** — baby grand; **hacer** — to stand in line; *Ríopl.* **comer** — to be the last one in a contest.

colaboración [ko·la·bo·ra·sjón] *f.* collaboration, mutual help.

colaborar [ko·la·bo·rár] *v.* to collaborate, work together.

coladera [ko·la·dé·ra] *f.* colander, strainer, sieve; *Mex., Ven.* drain.

colador [ko·la·dór] *m.* colander.

colar[2] [ko·lár] *v. irr.* to strain, filter; to bleach with lye; **-se** to slip in or out, sneak in.

colcha [kól·ča] *f.* quilt; bedspread; **-s** *Ríopl.* saddle and trappings; *Ch.* gaucho clothing.

colchón [kol·čón] *m.* mattress.

colear [ko·le·ár] *v.* to wag the tail; to grab a bull by the tail and throw him over; *Ch.* to flunk (*a student*); *Am.* to trail, tag behind (*a person*); *Col.* to bother, nag, harass; *Mex.* to smoke one cigarette after another.

colección [ko·lek·sjón] *f.* collection; set; gathering.

coleccionar [ko·lek·sjo·nár] *v.* to collect, make a collection.

coleccionista [ko·lek·sjo·nís·ta] *m. & f.* collector (*of stamps, curios, etc.*).

colecta [ko·lék·ta] *f.* collection of voluntary gifts; assessment; collect (*a short prayer of the mass*).

colectivo [ko·lek·tí·bo] *adj.* collective; *m. Ríopl.* small bus.

colector [ko·lek·tór] *m.* collector; water pipe, drain.

colega [ko·lé·ga] *m. & f.* colleague, fellow worker.

colegiatura [ko·le·xja·tú·ra] *f.* college fellowship or scholarship; *C.A.* tuition in a college.

colegio [ko·lé·xjo] *m.* boarding school; high school, academy; college, body of professional persons; *Col.* any private school.

colegir[5, 11] [ko·le·xír] *v.* to gather; to conclude, infer.

cólera [kó·le·ra] *f.* anger, rage; *m.* cholera (*disease*).

colérico [ko·lé·ri·ko] *adj.* irritable; angry.

coleto [ko·lé·to] *m.* leather jacket; one's inner self; *Am.* impudence, shamelessness; **decir para su** — to say to oneself; **echarse al** — to drink down; to devour.

colgadero [kol·ga·dé·ro] *m.* hanger; hook, peg; (*percha*) hat or clothes rack.

colgadura [kol·ga·dú·ra] *f.* drape, hanging; drapery; tapestry.

colgante [kol·gán·te] *adj.* hanging; dangling; **puente** — suspension bridge.

colgar[2, 7] [kol·gár] *v. irr. (suspender)* to hang, suspend; to dangle; to drape *(walls); (achacar)* to impute, attribute; *Cuba* to flunk, fail *(a student); Col.* -se to fall behind.

colibrí [ko·li·brí] *m.* hummingbird.

coliflor [ko·li·flór] *f.* cauliflower.

coligarse[7] [ko·li·gár·se] *v.* to league together, band together.

colilla [ko·lí·ya] *f.* small tail; butt *(of a cigarette),* stub *(of a cigar).*

colina [ko·lí·na] *f. N. Sp.* hill.

colindante [ko·lin·dán·te] *adj.* contiguous, neighboring, adjacent.

colindar [ko·lin·dár] *v.* to border (on); to be adjoining.

colisión [ko·li·sjón] *f.* collision, clash.

colmar [kol·már] *v.* to fill to the brim; — **de** to fill with; to shower with *(gifts, favors, etc.);* **-le a uno el plato** to exhaust one's patience.

colmena [kol·mé·na] *f.* beehive; *Mex.* bee.

colmillo [kol·mí·yo] *m.* eyetooth, canine tooth; *(animal)* tusk; fang.

colmo [kól·mo] *m.* overfullness; limit; — **de la locura** height of folly; ¡eso es el — ! that's the limit! *adj.* overfull, filled to the brim.

colocación [ko·lo·ka·sjón] *f.* placing, arrangement; *(puesto)* position, job.

colocar[6] [ko·lo·kár] *v.* to place; to put in place, arrange; *(emplear)* to give employment to.

colocho [ko·ló·čo] *m. C.A.* curly hair; wood shavings.

colombiano [ko·lom·bjá·no] *adj.* Colombian, of or pertaining to Colombia, South America.

colon [kó·lon] *m.* colon *(of the large intestine).*

colonia [ko·ló·nja] *f.* colony; silk ribbon; *Mex., Carib.* city district; *Am.* sugar plantation.

coloniaje [ko·lo·njá·xe] *m. Am.* colonial period.

colonial [ko·lo·njál] *adj.* colonial.

colonización [ko·lo·ni·sa·sjón] *f.* colonization.

colonizador [ko·lo·ni·sa·dór] *m.* colonizer, colonist; *adj.* colonizing.

colonizar[9] [ko·lo·ni·sár] *v.* to colonize.

colono [ko·ló·no] *m.* colonist, settler; tenant farmer; *Carib.* owner of a sugar plantation; *Am.* bootlicker, flatterer.

coloquio [ko·ló·kjo] *m.* conversation, talk; literary dialogue; *Col.* street comedy farce.

color [ko·lór] *m.* color; coloring; paint; rouge; **so — de** under the pretext of.

coloración [ko·lo·ra·sjón] *f.* coloring.

colorado [ko·lo·ra·do] *adj.* red, reddish; colored; **ponerse** — to blush.

colorante [ko·lo·rán·te] *adj. & m.* coloring.

colorar [ko·lo·rár] *v.* to color; to stain; to dye.

colorear [ko·lo·re·ár] *v.* to color; to redden; to give color to.

colorete [ko·lo·ré·te] *m.* rouge.

colorido [ko·lo·rí·do] *m.* coloring; color; *adj.* colored; colorful.

colosal [ko·lo·sál] *adj.* colossal, huge.

columbrar [ko·lum·brár] *v.* to see faintly; to glimpse.

columna [ko·lúm·na] *f.* column.

columpiar [ko·lum·pjár] *v.* to swing; -se to swing; to sway.

columpio [ko·lúm·pjo] *m.* swing.

collado [ko·yá·do] *m.* hillock, knoll.

collar [ko·yár] *m.* necklace; dog collar; *Am.* collar *(of a draft horse);* **collera** [ko·yé·ra] *f.* collar *(for draft animals).*

coma [kó·ma] *f.* comma; *m. (inconsciente)* coma, stupor, prolonged unconsciousness.

comadre [ko·má·dre] *f. (amiga)* woman friend; *(chismosa)* gossip; *(partera)* midwife; *(alcahueta)* go-between; *name used to express kinship between mother and godmother;* **comadrona** [ko·ma·dró·na] *f.* midwife.

comadreja [ko·ma·dré·xa] *f.* weasel.

comandancia [ko·man·dán·sja] *f.* command; position and headquarters of a commander.

comandante [ko·man·dán·te] *m.* major; commander.

comandar [ko·man·dár] *v.* to command *(troops).*

comandita [ko·man·dí·ta] *f.* silent partnership; **sociedad en** — limited company.

comando [ko·mán·do] *m.* military command; *(computadora)* command.

comarca [ko·már·ka] *f.* district, region.

comba [kóm·ba] *f.* bulge, warp.

combar [kom·bár] *v.* to warp, bend, twist; -se to warp; to sag; to bulge.

combate [kom·bá·te] *m.* combat, battle, fight.

combatiente [kom·ba·tjén·te] *m.* combatant, fighter.

combatir [kom·ba·tír] *v.* to combat; to fight.

combinación [kom·bi·na·sjón] *f.* combination.

combinar [kom·bi·nár] *v.* to combine, unite.

comburente [kom·bu·rén·te] *m.* the chemical agent that causes combustion, e.g., oxygen; *adj.* causing combustion.

combustible [kom·bus·tí·ble] *adj.* combustible; *m.* fuel.

combustión [kom·bus·tjón] *f.* combustion.

comedero [ko·me·dé·ro] *m.* trough *(for feeding animals); adj.* edible, eatable.

comedia [ko·mé·dja] *f.* comedy; farce.

comediante [ko·me·dján·te] *m.* actor, comedian.

comedido [ko·me·dí·do] *adj.* courteous, polite; obliging; *p.p. of* comedirse.

comedirse[5] [ko·me·dír·se] *v. irr.* to be civil, polite, obliging; *Ec.* to meddle; *Am.* — **a hacer algo** to volunteer to do something.

comedor [ko·me·dór] *m.* dining room; *(comilón)* great eater.

comején [ko·me·xén] *m.* termite.

comelón [ko·me·lón] *m. Am.* big eater. *See* comilón.

comendador [ko·men·da·dór] *m.* commander *(of certain military orders).*

comensal [ko·men·sál] *m. & f.* table companion; dinner guest.

comentador [ko·men·ta·dór] *m.* commentator.

comentar [ko·men·tár] *v.* to comment.

comentario [ko·men·tá·rjo] *m.* commentary, explanation.

comentarista [ko·men·ta·rís·ta] *m. & f.* commentator.

comenzar[1, 9] [ko·men·sár] *v. irr.* to begin.

comer [ko·mér] *v.* to eat; to dine; to take *(in chess or checkers);* **dar de** — to feed; **ganar de** — to earn a living, -se to eat; to eat up; to skip *(a letter, syllable, word, etc.); Ríopl., Col.* -se uno a otro to deceive each other.

comercial [ko·mer·sjál] *adj.* commercial.

comerciante [ko·mer·sján·te] *m.* merchant; storekeeper.

comerciar [ko·mer·sjár] *v.* to trade; to have dealings (with).

comercio [ko·mér·sjo] *m.* commerce, trade.

comestible [ko·mes·tí·ble] *adj.* edible, eatable; -s *m. pl.* food, groceries.

cometa [ko·mé·ta] *m.* comet; *Mex., Ch., C.A.* person seldom seen; *f.* kite.

cometer [ko·me·tér] *v.* to commit; to entrust; to use *(a figure of speech).*

cometido [ko·me·tí·do] *m.* commission, assignment, charge; task, duty.

comezón [ko·me·són] *f.* itch.

comicios [ko·mí·sjos] *m. pl.* primaries, elections.
cómico [kó·mi·ko] *adj.* comic, of comedy; comical, funny, amusing; *m.* comedian, actor.
comida [ko·mí·da] *f.* meal; dinner; good; **comidilla** *f.* small meal; gossip; **la comidilla de la vecindad** the talk of the town.
comienzo [ko·mjén·so] *m.* beginning; origin.
comilitona [ko·mi·li·tó·na] *f.* spread, big feast.
comilón [ko·mi·lón] *m.* big eater.
comillas [ko·mí·yas] *f. pl.* quotation marks.
comino [ko·mí·no] *m.* cuminseed.
comisar [ko·mi·sár] *v.* to confiscate.
comisario [ko·mi·sá·rjo] *m.* commissary, deputy, delegate; manager; *Mex., Arg.* police inspector.
comisión [ko·mi·sjón] *f.* commission; committee.
comisionado [ko·mi·sjo·ná·do] *adj.* commissioned, charged, delegated; *m.* commissioner; *Cuba* constable.
comisionar [ko·mi·sjo·nár] *v.* to commission.
comistrajo [ko·mis·trá·xo] *m.* mess, strange food concoction, mixture.
comité [ko·mi·té] *m.* committee, commission.
comitiva [ko·mi·tí·ba] *f.* retinue, group of attendants or followers.
como [kó·mo] *adv. & conj.* as, like, such as; if, provided that, since, when; *Mex., Ven.* about, approximately; **¿cómo?** [kó·mo] *interr. adv.* how?, what (did you say)?; *Am.* **¡cómo no!** yes, of course!
cómoda [kó·mo·da] *f.* bureau, chest of drawers.
comodidad [ko·mo·di·dád] *f.* comfort; convenience.
comodín [ko·mo·dín] *m.* joker, wild card.
cómodo [kó·mo·do] *adj.* comfortable; convenient; *m. Am.* bedpan.
compactar [kom·pak·tár] *v.* roll out (fiber glass).
compacto [kom·pák·to] *adj.* compact.
compadecer[13] [kom·pa·de·sér] *v. irr.* to pity, sympathize with; **-se con** to be in harmony with; **-se de** to take pity on.
compadrazgo [kom·pa·dráz·go] *m.* compaternity (*spiritual affinity between the godfather and the parents of a child*); friendship; relationship; clique, group of friends; cronyism.
compadre [kom·pá·dre] *m.* (*amigo*) pal, crony, comrade; (*padrino*) cosponsor; *name used to express kinship between father and godfather.*
compañero [kom·pa·ñé·ro] *m.* companion; partner; mate; **compañerismo** [kom·pa·ñe·ríz·mo] *m.* companionship.
compañía [kom·pa·ñí·a] *f.* company; *Mex.* — **del ahorcado** silent companion, poor company.
comparación [kom·pa·ra·sjón] *f.* comparison.
comparar [kom·pa·rár] *v.* to compare.
comparativo [kom·pa·ra·tí·bo] *adj.* comparative.
comparecer[13] [kom·pa·re·sér] *v. irr.* to appear (*before a judge or tribunal*).
compartimiento [kom·par·ti·mjén·to] *m.* compartment.
compartir [kom·par·tír] *v.* to share; to divide into shares.
compás [kom·pás] *m.* compass; measure; beat; **llevar el** — to beat time; — **de gruesas** calipers.
compasión [kom·pa·sjón] *f.* compassion, pity.
compasivo [kom·pa·sí·bo] *adj.* compassionate, sympathetic.
compatible [kom·pa·tí·ble] *adj.* compatible, in harmony.
compatriota [kom·pa·trjó·ta] *m. & f.* compatriot, fellow countryman.
compeler [kom·pe·lér] *v.* to compel, force.
compendiar [kom·pen·djár] *v.* to abstract,

summarize, condense.
compendio [kom·pén·djo] *m.* summary, condensation.
compensación [kom·pen·sa·sjón] *f.* compensation; recompense.
compensar [kom·pen·sár] *v.* to balance; to make equal; to compensate, recompense.
competencia [kom·pe·tén·sja] *f.* competition, rivalry; competence, ability.
competente [kom·pe·tén·te] *adj.* competent; capable; adequate.
competidor [kom·pe·ti·dór] *m.* competitor; rival; *adj.* competing.
competir[5] [kom·pe·tír] *v. irr.* to compete, vie.
compilador [kom·pi·la·dór] *m.* (*computadora*) compiler.
compilar [kom·pi·lár] *v.* to compile.
compinche [kom·pín·če] *m.* chum, pal, comrade.
complacencia [kom·pla·sén·sja] *f.* complacency, satisfaction, contentment.
complacer[38] [kom·pla·sér] *v. irr.* to please, humor; to comply, **-se** to take pleasure or satisfaction (in).
coplaciente [kom·pla·sjén·te] *adj.* obliging, agreeable, willing to please.
complejidad [kom·ple·xi·dád] *f.* complexity.
complejo [kom·plé·xo] *adj. & m.* complex.
complemento [kom·ple·mén·to] *m.* complement; (*gramática*) object (*of a verb*).
completamiento [kom·ple·ta·mjén·to] *m.* completion.
completar [kom·ple·tár] *v.* to complete; to finish.
completo [kom·plé·to] *adj.* complete, full, perfect.
complexión [kom·plek·sjón] *f.* constitution, make-up.
complicar[6] [kom·pli·kár] *v.* to complicate.
cómplice [kóm·pli·se] *m. & f.* accomplice, companion in crime.
complot [kom·plót], [kom·pló] *m.* plot, conspiracy; intrigue.
componenda [kom·po·nén·da] *f.* adjustment; compromise.
componente [kom·po·nén·te] *adj.* component, constituent; *m.* component, essential part.
componer[40] [kom·po·nér] *v. irr.* to fix, repair; to fix up; to adorn, trim; to compose; (*imprenta*) to set up (*type*); (*arreglar*) to settle (*a dispute*); *Col.* to set (*bones*).
comportamiento [kom·por·ta·mjén·to] *m.* conduct, behavior.
composición [kom·po·si·sjón] *f.* composition; settlement.
compositor [kom·po·si·tór] *m.* composer.
compostura [kom·pos·tú·ra] *f.* (*arreglo*) repair; settlement, adjustment; (*aseo*) neatness, composition; (*dignidad*) composure, dignity.
compota [kom·pó·ta] *f.* fruit preserves; — **de manzana** applesauce.
compra [kóm·pra] *f.* purchase; buying; **ir de -s** to go shopping.
comprador [kom·pra·dór] *m.* buyer, purchaser.
comprar [kom·prár] *v.* to buy, purchase.
comprender [kom·pren·dér] *v.* to understand, grasp, comprehend; to comprise, embrace.
comprensible [kom·pren·sí·ble] *adj.* comprehensible, understandable.
comprensión [kom·pren·sjón] *f.* understanding; comprehension; keenness.
comprensivo [kom·pren·sí·bo] *adj.* comprehensive; understanding.
compresión [kom·pre·sjón] *f.* compression.
compresor [kom·pre·sór] *m.* compressor.
comprimido [kom·pri·mí·do] *adj.* compressed; *m.* medicinal tablet.
comprimir [kom·pri·mír] *v.* to compress; to repress.

CO

comprobación [kom·pro·ba·sjón] *f.* confirmation, check, proof, test.

comprobante [kom·pro·bán·te] *adj.* proving, verifying; *m.* proof; evidence; certificate; voucher; warrant.

comprobar[2] [kom·pro·bár] *v. irr.* to verify; to check; to prove.

comprometer [kom·pro·me·tér] *v.* (*exponer*) to compromise; to endanger; to bind; to force; (*concordar*) to come to an agreement; **-se** to promise, bind oneself; to become engaged; to compromise oneself.

compromiso [kom·pro·mí·so] *m.* (*convenio*) compromise; (*obligación*) engagement; appointment; (*dificultad*) predicament, trouble.

compuerta [kom·pwér·ta] *f.* sluice, floodgate.

compuesto [kom·pwés·to] *p.p. of* **componer** & *adj.* repaired; fixed, adorned; composed; *m.* composite; compound.

compungirse[11] [kom·puŋ·xír·se] *v.* to feel regret or remorse.

computación [kom·pu·ta·sjón] *f.* (*computadora*) computing.

computadora electrónica [kom·pu·ta·dó·ra e·lek·tró·ni·ka] *f.* electronic computer; — **analógica** analogical computer; — **digital** digital computer; — **casera** home computer; — **personal** personal computer.

computar [kom·pu·tár] *v.* to compute, calculate.

cómputo [kóm·pu·to] *m.* computation, calculation.

comulgar[7] [ko·mul·gár] *v.* to commune, take communion.

común [ko·mún] *adj.* common; **por lo** — generally; *m.* toilet; **el** — **de las gentes** the majority of the people; the average person.

comunero [ko·mu·né·ro] *adj.* common, popular; *Am.* pertaining to a community; *m.* commoner (*one of the common people*); *Col., Ven., Andes* member of an Indian community.

comunicación [ko·mu·ni·ka·sjón] *f.* communication.

comunicar[6] [ko·mu·ni·kár] *v.* to communicate; to notify; **-se** to communicate; to correspond; to be in touch (with); to connect.

comunicativo [ko·mu·ni·ka·tí·bo] *adj.* communicative, talkative.

comunidad [ko·mu·ni·dád] *f.* community; commonwealth; the common people; commonness; guild.

comunión [ko·mu·njón] *f.* communion; political party.

comunismo [ko·mu·níz·mo] *m.* communism; **comunista** [ko·mu·nís·ta] *m. & f.* communist; *adj.* communistic, communist.

con [kon] *prep.* with; — **ser** in spite of being; — **tal que** provided that; — **todo** however.

conato [ko·ná·to] *m.* attempt, effort; (*asalto*) assault (*law*).

concavidad [koŋ·ka·bi·dád] *f.* hollow, cavity; hollowness.

cóncavo [kóŋ·ka·bo] *adj.* concave, hollow.

concebible [kon·se·bí·ble] *adj.* conceivable.

concebir[5] [kon·se·bír] *v. irr.* to conceive; to imagine; to understand, grasp.

conceder [kon·se·dér] *v.* to concede, grant; (*confesar*) to admit.

concejal [kon·se·xál] *m.* councilman, alderman.

concejo [kon·sé·xo] *m.* town council.

concentración [kon·sen·tra·sjón] *f.* concentration.

concentrar [kon·sen·trár] *v.* to concentrate.

concepción [kon·sep·sjón] *f.* conception.

concepto [kon·sép·to] *m.* concept, idea, thought.

concernir[51] [kon·ser·nír] *v. irr.* to concern.

concertar[1] [kon·ser·tár] *v. irr.* (*arreglar*) to arrange, plan, settle; (*llevar a cabo*) to conclude (*a treaty or business deal*); (*concordar*) to harmonize; to agree.

concesión [kon·se·sjón] *f.* concession, grant; granting; acknowledgment.

conciencia [kon·sjén·sja] *f.* conscience.

concienzudo [kon·sjen·sú·do] *adj.* conscientious.

concierto [kon·sjér·to] *m.* concert; harmony; agreement; **de** — by common agreement.

conciliar [kon·si·ljár] *v.* to conciliate, win over; to reconcile, bring into harmony; — **el sueño** to get to sleep.

concilio [kon·sí·ljo] *m.* council.

concision [kon·si·sjón] *f.* conciseness, brevity.

conciso [kon·sí·so] *adj.* concise, brief.

conciudadano [kon·sju·da·dá·no] *m.* fellow citizen, fellow countryman.

concluir[32] [koŋ·klwír] *v. irr.* to conclude, finish; to infer.

conclusión [koŋ·klu·sjón] *f.* conclusion.

concordancia [koŋ·kor·dán·sja] *f.* concord, agreement, harmony.

concordar[2] [koŋ·kor·dár] *v. irr.* to agree; to be in harmony; to put in harmony.

concordia [koŋ·kór·dja] *f.* concord, harmony, agreement.

concretar [koŋ·kre·tár] *v.* to summarize, condense; to limit; **-se a** to limit oneself to.

concreto [koŋ·kré·to] *adj.* concrete, real, specific; **en**— concretely; to sum up; *m. Mex.* concrete.

concupiscente [koŋ·ku·pi·sen·te] *adj.* sensual.

concurrencia [koŋ·ku·rrén·sja] *f.* gathering, audience; concurrence, simultaneous meeting or happening; competition.

concurrido [koŋ·ku·rrí·do] *adj.* well-patronized, well-attended, much frequented.

concurrir [koŋ·ku·rrír] *v.* to concur, (*reunirse*) meet together; to happen at the same time or place; (*asistir*) to attend; to agree.

concurso [koŋ·kúr·so] *m.* gathering; (*contienda*) contest; competitive examination; assistance.

concha [kón·ča] *f.* shell; shellfish; (*de teatro*) prompter's box; *Mex.* **tener** — to be indifferent, unruffled, tough.

conchabar [kon·ča·bár] *v.* to unite, join; *Mex., S.A.* to hire (*labor*); **-se** to join, gang together; to conspire; *Ríopl.* to hire oneself out, get a job.

conchabo [kon·čá·bo] *m. Am.* hiring of a laborer or servant; *Ríopl.* job, menial job.

conde [kón·de] *m.* count; condesa *f.* countess.

condecoración [kon·de·ko·ra·sjón] *f.* decoration; badge, medal.

condecorar [kon·de·ko·rár] *v.* to decorate (*with a badge or medal*).

condena [kon·dé·na] *f.* term in prison, sentence, penalty.

condenación [kon·de·na·sjón] *f.* condemnation; conviction; (*teología*) damnation.

condenar [kon·de·nár] *v.* to condemn; to sentence; *Ven.* to annoy, irritate; **-se** to be damned, go to hell.

condensación [kon·den·sa·sjón] *f.* condensation; "sweating" of containers.

condensar [kon·den·sár] *v.* to condense.

condescendencia [kon·de·sen·dén·sja] *f.* condescension, patronizing attitude.

condescender[1] [kon·de·sen·dér] *v. irr.* to condescend; to comply, yield.

condición [kon·di·sjón] *f.* condition.

condimentar [kon·di·men·tár] *v.* to season.
condimento [kon·di·mén·to] *m.* condiment, seasoning.
condiscípulo [kon·di·sí·pu·lo] *m.* schoolmate, classmate.
condolerse[2] [kon·do·lér·se] *v. irr.* to condole (with), sympathize (with), be sorry (for).
condón [kon·dón] *m.* condom.
cóndor [kón·dor] *m. Am.* condor, vulture; *Am.* gold coin of Ecuador, Chile and Colombia.
conducir[25] [kon·du·sír] *v. irr.* to conduct, lead; (*manejar*) to drive (*an auto*); **-se** to behave, act.
conducta [kon·dúk·ta] *f.* conduct; behavior; convoy, escort; management.
conducto [kon·dúk·to] *m.* conduit, pipe, channel; — **lacrimar** tear duct; **por — de** through.
conductor [kon·duk·tór] *adj.* conducting; *m.* leader; (*motorista*) chauffeur; guide; conductor (*electrical*); *Am.* conductor, ticket collector (*on trains, buses, streetcars*); *Ríopl.* teamster, driver.
conectar [ko·nek·tár] *v.* to connect.
conejera [ko·ne·xé·ra] *f.* burrow; rabbit warren (*piece of land for breeding rabbits*); (*tasca*) den, joint, dive (*of ill repute*).
conejo [ko·né·xo] *m.* rabbit; *Am.* guinea pig; **conejillo de Indias** [ko·ne·xí·yo·de ín·djas] guinea pig.
conexión [ko·nek·sjón] *f.* connection.
conexo [ko·nék·so] *adj.* connected; coherent.
confección [kon·fek·sjón] *f.* making; confection; manufactured article; workmanship; concoction, compound.
confeccionar [kon·fek·sjo·nár] *v.* to make; to manufacture; to mix, put up (*a prescription*).
confederación [kon·fe·de·ra·sjón] *f.* confederation, alliance, league.
confederar [kon·fe·de·rár] *v.* to confederate; **-se** to confederate, form into a confederacy.
conferencia [kon·fe·rén·sja] *f.* lecture; conference, meeting.
conferenciante [kon·fe·ren·sján·te] *m. & f.* lecturer.
conferencista [kon·fe·ren·sís·ta] *m. & f. Am.* lecturer.
conferir[3] [kon·fe·rír] *v. irr.* to confer; to give, bestow.
confesar[1] [kon·fe·sár] *v. irr.* to confess.
confesión [kon·fe·sjón] *f.* confession.
confesionario [kon·fe·sjo·ná·rjo] *m.* confessional, confessional box.
confesor [kon·fe·sór] *m.* confessor.
confiado [kon·fjá·do] *adj.* confident, trusting, credulous; (*presuntuoso*) presumptuous, self-confident.
confianza [kon·fján·sa] *f.* confidence, trust; familiarity; informality; **reunión de** — informal gathering or party.
confianzudo [kon·fjan·sú·do] *adj.* over-friendly, over-familiar; *Ven.* meddlesome.
confiar[17] [kon·fjár] *v.* to confide, entrust; to trust, hope firmly.
confidencia [kon·fi·dén·sja] *f.* confidence, trust; secret, confidential remark; **confidencial** [kon·fi·den·sjál] *adj.* confidential.
confidente [kon·fi·dén·te] *m.* confidant; spy, secret agent; (*sofá*) settee or sofa for two people, love seat; *adj.* faithful, trustworthy.
confín [kon·fín] *m.* limit, border, boundary; *adj.* bordering, limiting.
confinar [kon·fi·nár] *v.* to border (upon); to confine, (*desterrar*) exile to a specific place.
confirmación [kon·fir·ma·sjón] *f.* confirmation.
confirmar [kon·fir·már] *v.* to confirm.
confiscar[6] [kon·fis·kár] *v.* to confiscate.
confitar [kon·fi·tár] *v.* to candy; to make into candy or preserves; to sweeten.
confite [kon·fí·te] *m.* candy, bonbon; **confitería** [kon·fi·te·rí·a] *f.* confectionery; candy shop; **confitura** [kon·fi·tú·ra] *f.* confection.
conflicto [kon·flík·to] *m.* conflict.
confluencia [kon·flwén·sja] *f.* junction (*of two rivers*).
conformar [kon·for·már] *v.* to adapt, adjust; **-se** to conform, comply; to agree; to be resigned (to); to be satisfied.
conforme [kon·fór·me] *adj.* in agreement; resigned, satisfied; alike, similar; — **a** in accordance with.
conformidad [kon·for·mi·dád] *f.* conformity; agreement, harmony; compliance; — **con la voluntad de Dios** resignation to the will of God; **en — con** in compliance with; **estar de — con** to be in accordance or agreement with.
confortar [kon·for·tár] *v.* to comfort, console.
confraternidad [kon·fra·ter·ni·dád] *f.* brotherhood.
confrontar [kon·fron·tár] *v.* to confront; to face; to compare, check.
confundir [kon·fun·dír] *v.* to confound, confuse, mix up; to bewilder; (*avergonzar*) to shame.
confusión [kon·fu·sjón] *f.* confusion.
confuso [kon·fú·so] *adj.* confused, bewildered; blurred; (*vago*) vague.
congelado [koŋ·xe·lá·do] *p.p. & adj.* frozen; icy
congelador [koŋ·xe·la·dór] *m.* freezer.
congelar [koŋ·xe·lár] *v.* to congeal, freeze.
congenial [koŋ·xe·njál] *adj.* congenial.
congeniar [koŋ·xe·njár] *v.* to be congenial (with), to harmonize, be in harmony (with).
congoja [koŋ·gó·xa] *f.* anguish, grief, anxiety.
congratular [koŋ·gra·tu·lár] *v.* to congratulate.
congregación [koŋ·gre·ga·sjón] *f.* congregation; assembly; religious fraternity.
congregar[7] [koŋ·gre·gár] *v.* to congregate, call together; to assemble; **-se** to congregate, assemble.
congresista [koŋ·gre·sís·ta] *m.* congressman; conventionite; *f.* congresswoman.
congreso [koŋ·gré·so] *m.* congress, assembly; convention; — **de los Diputados** House of Representatives.
conjetura [koŋ·xe·tú·ra] *f.* conjecture, guess, surmise.
conjeturar [koŋ·xe·tu·rár] *v.* to conjecture, guess, surmise.
conjugación [koŋ·su·ga·sjón] *f.* conjugation; (*juntura*) coupling, joining together.
conjugar[7] [koŋ·xu·gár] *v.* to conjugate.
conjunción [koŋ·xun·sjón] *f.* conjunction; union, combination.
conjunto [koŋ·xún·to] *m.* total, whole, entirety; set aggregate; **en —** as a whole; *adj.* joined; related, allied; — **lógico** *m.* (*computadora*) software.
conjuración [koŋ·xu·ra·sjón] *f.* conspiracy, plot.
conjurado [koŋ·xu·rá·do] *m.* conspirator.
conjurar [koŋ·su·rár] *v.* to conspire, plot; to join a conspiracy; to entreat; to conjure; to ward off.
conjuro [koŋ·xú·ro] *m.* conspiracy; exorcism.
conmemorar [kom·me·mo·rár] *v.* to commemorate.
conmemorativo [kom·me·mo·ra·tí·bo] *adj.* memorial, serving to commemorate.
conmigo [kom·mí·go] with me.
conminación [kom·mi·na·sjón] *f.* threat.
conminatorio [kom·mi·na·tó·rjo] *adj.* threatening.
conmoción [kom·mo·sjón] *f.* commotion.
conmovedor [kom·mo·be·dór] *adj.* moving, touching; stirring.
conmover[2] [kom·mo·bér] *v. irr.* to move, touch, affect (*with emotion*); to stir (*emotions*).
conmutador [kom·mu·ta·dór] *m.* electric switch; **cuadro —** switchboard.

connatural [kon·na·tu·rál] *adj.* inborn.
cono [kó·no] *m.* cone; pine cone.
conocedor [ko·no·se·dór] *adj.* knowing, aware,
 expert; *m.* connoisseur, judge, expert; **ser — de** to
 be judge of.
conocer[13] [ko·no·sér] *v. irr.* (*tener idea de*) to know,
 be acquainted with; to recognize; (*llegar a
 conocer*) to meet; **se conoce que** it is clear or
 evident that.
conocido [ko·no·sí·do] *p.p. & adj.* known; well-
 known; *m.* acquaintance.
conocimiento [ko·no·si·mjén·to] *m.* (*inteligencia*)
 knowledge, understanding; acquaintance;
 (*documento*) bill of lading; **-s** knowledge, learning;
 poner en — to inform.
conque [kóŋ·ke] *conj.* so then, well then, and so.
conquista [koŋ·kís·ta] *f.* conquest.
conquistador [koŋ·kis·ta·dór] *m.* conqueror; *adj.*
 conquering, victorious.
conquistar [koŋ·kis·tár] *v.* to conquer, defeat; to win.
consabido [kon·sa·bí·do] *adj.* aforementioned,
 aforesaid.
consagración [kon·sa·gra·sjón] *f.* consecration.
consagrar [kon·sa·grár] *v.* to consecrate.
consciencia [kon·sjén·sja] *f.* consciousness.
consciente [kon·sjén·te] *adj.* conscious.
consecución [kon·se·ku·sjón] *f.* attainment.
consecuencia [kon·se·kwén·sja] *f.* consequence; result;
 a — de as a result of; **por** (*or* **en**) **—** therefore;
 consequently.
consecuente [kon·se·kwén·te] *adj.* consequent,
 logical; consistent; *m.* consequence, result.
consecutivo [kon·se·ku·tí·bo] *adj.* consecutive,
 successive.
conseguir[5, 12] [kon·se·gír] *v. irr.* to get, obtain; to
 reach, attain.
conseja [kon·sé·xa] *f.* old wives' tale, fable.
consejero [kon·se·xé·ro] *m.* adviser counselor.
consejo [kon·sé·xo] *m.* counsel, advice; council;
 (*lugar*) council hall.
consentimiento [kon·sen·ti·mjén·to] *m.* consent.
consentir[3] [kon·sen·tír] *v. irr.* to consent, permit; to
 pamper, spoil.
conserje [kon·sér·xe] *m.* janitor, caretaker.
conserva [kon·sér·ba] *f.* preserve; (*en escabeche*)
 pickled fruit or vegetables; *Ch.* filling (*for tarts or
 candy*).
conservación [kon·ser·ba·sjón] *f.* conservation.
conservador [kon·ser·ba·dór] *m.* conservative;
 preserver; guardian; *adj.* conservative.
conservar [kon·ser·bár] *v.* to conserve, keep; to
 preserve.
considerable [kon·si·de·rá·ble] *adj.* considerable.
consideración [kon·si·de·ra·sjón] *f.* consideration.
considerado [kon·si·de·rá·do] *adj.* considerate,
 thoughtful; respected; prudent.
considerar [kon·si·de·rár] *v.* to consider; to treat with
 consideration.
consigna [kon·síg·na] *f.* watchword, password; *Am.*
 checkroom.
consignar [kon·sig·nár] *v.* to consign; to deliver; to
 deposit; to assign; (*facturar*) to check (*baggage*).
consigo [kon·sí·go] with oneself; with himself
 (herself, themselves).
consiguiente [kon·si·gjén·te] *adj.* consequent; *m.*
 consequence; **por —** consequently.
consistente [kon·sis·tén·te] *adj.* firm, substantial.
consistir [kon·sis·tír] *v.* to consist; to be based on;
 ¿en qué consiste? of what does it consist?
consocio [kon·só·sjo] *m.* associate, partner.
consola [kon·só·la] *f.* console.

consolación [kon·so·la·sjón] *f.* consolation.
consolar[2] [kon·so·lár] *v. irr.* to console, cheer.
consolidar [kon·so·li·dár] *v.* to consolidate, make
 solid; to unite, combine.
consonante [kon·so·nán·te] *m.* perfect rhyme; *f.*
 consonant; *adj.* in harmony.
consorte [kon·sór·te] *m. & f.* consort; mate;
 companion.
conspicuo [kons·pí·kwo] *adj.* conspicuous.
conspiración [kons·pi·ra·sjón] *f.* conspiracy, plot.
conspirador [kons·pi·ra·dór] *m.* conspirator, plotter.
conspirar [kons·pi·rár] *v.* to conspire, plot.
constancia [kons·tán·sja] *f.* (*firmeza*) constancy;
 perseverance; (*certeza*) evidence, certainty; *Am.*
 documentary proof, record.
constante [kons·tán·te] *adj.* constant; continual; (*fiel*)
 firm, faithful.
constar [kons·tár] *v.* to be evident, clear; (*consistir
 en*) to consist (of), be composed (of); to be on
 record.
constatación [kons·ta·ta·sjón] *f. Am.* proof, check,
 evidence.
constelación [kons·te·la·sjón] *f.* constellation.
constipado [kons·ti·pá·do] *adj.* suffering from a cold;
 m. cold in the head.
constipar [kons·ti·pár] *v.* to stop up (*the nasal
 passages*); to cause a cold; **-se** to catch cold.
constitución [kons·ti·tu·sjón] *f.* constitution.
constitucional [kons·ti·tu·sjo·nál] *adj.* constitutional.
constituir[32] [kons·ti·twír] *v. irr.* to constitute, form;
 to set up, establish; **-se en** to set oneself up as.
constitutivo [kons·ti·tu·tí·bo] = **constituyente.**
constituyente [kons·ti·tu·yén·te] *adj.* constituent.
constreñir[5, 19] [kons·tre·ñír] *v. irr.* to constrain; to
 compel, oblige.
construcción [kons·truk·sjón] *f.* construction;
 structure; building.
construir[32] [kons·trwír] *v. irr.* to construct, build.
consuelo [kon·swé·lo] *m.* consolation, comfort; relief;
 cheer.
consuetudinario [kon·swe·tu·di·ná·rjo] *adj.* habitual,
 customary; **derecho —** common law.
consul [kón·sul] *m.* consul.
consulado [kon·su·lá·do] *m.* consulate.
consulta [kon·súl·ta] *f.* consultation; opinion.
consultar [kon·sul·tár] *v.* to consult.
consultoría [kon·sul·to·rí·a] *f.* consulting (services).
consultorio [kon·sul·tó·rjo] *m.* office for consultation;
 doctor's office or clinic.
consumado [kon·su·má·do] *p.p. of* **consumar;** *adj.*
 consummate, perfect, complete; accomplished.
consumar [kon·su·már] *v.* to consummate, complete.
consumidor [kon·su·mi·dór] *m.* consumer; *adj.*
 consuming.
consumir [kon·su·mír] *v.* to consume; to waste; **-se** to
 be consumed; to burn out; to be exhausted;
 (*acabarse*) to waste away.
consumo [kon·sú·mo] *m.* consumption (*of food,
 provisions, etc.*).
consunción [kon·sun·sjón] *f.* consumption (*illness*).
contabilidad [kon·ta·bi·li·dád] *f.* accounting;
 bookkeeping.
contacto [kon·ták·to] *m.* contact.
contado [kon·tá·do] **al —** in cash; **de —**
 immediately; **por de —** of course; **contados** *adj.*
 few, scarce, rare.
contador [kon·ta·dór] *m.* accountant; purser; cashier;
 counter; (*medidor*) meter (*for water, gas, or
 electricity*); **— geiger** Geiger counter; Geiger-
 Müller counter.
contaduría [kon·ta·du·rí·a] *f.* accounting; accountant's

or auditor's office; box office; cashier's office.

contagiar [kon·ta·xjár] *v.* to infect; to corrupt; to contaminate.

contagio [kon·tá·xjo] *m.* contagion; infection.

contagioso [kon·ta·xjó·so] *adj.* contagious; infectious.

contaminar [kon·ta·mi·nár] *v.* to contaminate, defile; to corrupt.

contar[2] [kon·tár] *v. irr.* to count; to tell, relate; — **con** to count on, rely on; **a** — **desde** starting from, beginning with.

contemplación [kon·tem·pla·sjón] *f.* contemplation; gazing; meditation.

contemplar [kon·tem·plár] *v.* to contemplate, gaze at; (*examinar*) to examine; to meditate.

contemporáneo [kon·tem·po·rá·ne·o] *adj.* contemporary.

contender[1] [kon·ten·dér] *v. irr.* to contend, fight; to compete.

contener[45] [kon·te·nér] *v. irr.* to contain; to restrain, check; **-se** to refrain; to restrain oneself.

contenido [kon·te·ní·đo] *m.* contents; *adj.* restrained, moderate.

contentamiento [kon·ten·ta·mjén·to] *m.* contentment, joy.

contentar [kon·ten·tár] *v.* to give pleasure, make happy; **-se** to be satisfied, pleased; *Am.* to make up, renew friendship.

contento [kon·tén·to] *adj.* content, contented, satisfied, glad; *m.* gladness, contentment.

conteo [kon·té·o] *m.* (blood) count.

contera [kon·té·ra] *f.* metal tip (*of a cane, umbrella, etc.*); tip, end; (*refrán*) refrain of a song; **por** — as a finishing touch.

contertulio [kon·ter·tú·ljo] *m.* fellow-member.

contestación [kon·tes·ta·sjón] *f.* answer, reply; argument.

contestar [kon·tes·tár] *v.* to answer, reply.

contextura [kon·tes·tú·ra] *f.* texture, composition; structure (*of animal or vegetable tissues*).

contienda [kon·tjén·da] *f.* fight; dispute; contest.

contigo [kon·tí·ɣo] with you (with thee).

contiguo [kon·tí·ɣwo] *adj.* contiguous, next, neighboring.

continental [kon·ti·nen·tál] *adj.* continental.

continente [kon·ti·nén·te] *m.* continent; countenance; *adj.* continent, moderate, sober.

contingencia [kon·tiŋ·xén·sja] *f.* contingency, possibility; risk.

contingente [kon·tiŋ·xén·te] *adj.* contingent.

continuación [kon·ti·nwa·sjón] *f.* continuation; continuance; **a** — below, as follows.

continuar[18] [kon·ti·nwár] *v.* to continue; to last.

continuidad [kon·ti·nwi·đáđ] *f.* continuity.

continuo [kon·tí·nwo] *adj.* continuous, connected; continual; steady, constant.

contonearse [kon·to·ne·ár·se] *v.* to strut, swagger; to waddle.

contoneo [kon·to·né·o] *m.* strut; waddle.

contorno [kon·tór·no] *m.* (*circuito*) environs, surrounding country (*usually used in plural*); (*línea*) contour, outline.

contra [kón·tra] *prep.* against; **el pro y el** — the pro and con; *f.* opposition; *Am.* antidote, remedy; **-s** *Am.* play-off, final game (*to determine the winner*); **llevar a uno la** — to contradict a person, take the opposite view.

contraalmirante [kon·tra·al·mi·rán·te] *m.* rear admiral.

contrabajo [kon·tra·bá·xo] *m.* bass fiddle, string bass.

contrabandear [kon·tra·ban·de·ár] *v.* to smuggle.

contrabandista [kon·tra·ban·dís·ta] *m.* smuggler.

contrabando [kon·tra·bán·do] *m.* contraband;

smuggled goods; smuggling.

contracción [kon·trak·sjón] *f.* contraction; *Ch., Peru* diligence, application, devotion.

contradecir[27] [kon·tra·đe·sír] *v. irr.* to contradict.

contradicción [kon·tra·đik·sjón] *f.* contradiction.

contradictorio [kon·tra·đik·tó·rjo] *adj.* contradictory, contrary, opposing.

contradicho [kon·tra·đí·čo] *p.p. of* **contradecir.**

contraer[46] [kon·tra·ér] *v. irr.* to contract; — **matrimonio** to get married; **-se** to shrink; to contract.

CO

contraflujo [kon·tra·flú·xo] *m.* counterflow.

contrafuerte [kon·tra·fwér·te] *m.* buttress; spur (*of a mountain*); **-s** secondary chain of mountains.

contrahacer[31] [kon·tra·a·sér] *v. irr.* to counterfeit; (*forjar*) to forge; to copy, imitate; to mimic.

contrahecho [kon·tra·é·čo] *p.p. of* **contrahacer** & *adj.* counterfeit; forged; deformed.

contralor [kon·tra·lór] *m. Ven., Col., C.A., Andes, Ríopl.* controller or comptroller (*of accounts or expenditures*). *See* **controlador.**

contraorden [kon·tra·ór·den] *f.* countermand; cancellation of an order.

contrapartida [kon·tra·par·tí·đa] *f.* balancing entry.

contrapelo [kon·tra·pé·lo]: **a** — against the grain.

contrapesar [kon·tra·pe·sár] *v.* to counterbalance, balance; to offset.

contrapeso [kon·tra·pé·so] *m.* counterpoise, counterweight, counterbalance; *Ch.* fear, uneasiness.

contrariar[17] [kon·tra·rjár] *v.* to oppose; to contradict; (*molestar*) to irritate, vex.

contrariedad [kon·tra·rje·đáđ] *f.* opposition; contradiction; bother, irritation; disappointment.

contrario [kon·trá·rjo] *adj.* contrary; opposite; *m.* opponent.

contrarrestar [kon·tra·rres·tár] *v.* to counteract; to resist, oppose; to strike back (*a ball*).

contrarrevolución [kon·tra·rre·bo·lu·sjón] *f.* counterrevolution.

contraseña [kon·tra·sé·ña] *f.* password, watchword mark; (*talón*) check (*for baggage*); — **de salida** theatre check.

contrastar [kon·tras·tár] *v.* (*contrapesar*) to contrast; to test (*scales, weights, measures, etc.*); to assay (*metals*); (*resistir*) to resist, oppose.

contraste [kon·trás·te] *m.* contrast; (*prueba*) assay, test; assayer, tester; assayer's office.

contrata [kon·trá·ta] *f.* contract, bargain, agreement.

contratar [kon·tra·tár] *v.* to contract for; to trade; to engage, hire (*someone*); **-se** to come to, or make, an agreement.

contratiempo [kon·tra·tjém·po] *m.* accident, mishap.

contratista [kon·tra·tís·ta] *m. & f.* contractor.

contrato [kon·trá·to] *m.* contract.

contraventana [kon·tra·ben·tá·na] *f.* shutter.

contribución [kon·tri·bu·sjón] *f.* contribution; (*impuesto*) tax.

contribuir[32] [kon·tri·bwír] *v. irr.* to contribute.

contribuyente [kon·tri·bu·yén·te] *m.* contributor; tax-payer; *adj.* contributing.

contrincante [kon·triŋ·kán·te] *m.* rival.

control [kon·tról] *m. Am.* control; — **de calidad** quality control.

controlador [kon·tro·la·đór] *Mex., Ch.* (*desacato*) controller.

controlar [kon·tro·lár] *v. Am.* to control.

controversia [kon·tro·bér·sja] *f.* controversy.

contumacia [kon·tu·má·sja] *f.* stubbornness, obstinacy; contempt of court, failure to appear in court; rebelliousness.

contumaz [kon·tu·más] *adj.* stubborn; rebellious.
contusión [kon·tu·sjón] *f.* bruise.
convalecer[13] [kom·ba·le·sér] *v. irr.* to convalesce, recover from an illness.
convecino [kom·be·sí·no] *adj.* near, neighboring; *m.* neighbor.
convencedor [kom·ben·se·dór] *adj.* convincing.
convencer[10] [kom·ben·sér] *v.* to convince.
convencimiento [kom·ben·si·mjén·to] *m.* conviction, belief; convincing.
convención [kom·ben·sjón] *f.* convention, assembly; pact, agreement; *Ríopl., Col., Ven., Mex., Carib.* political convention; **convencional** [kom·ben·sjo·nál] *adj.* conventional.
convenido [kom·be·ní·do] *adj.* agreed; O.K., all right; *p.p. of* **convenir.**
conveniencia [kom·be·njén·sja] *f.* convenience, comfort; (*utilidad*) utility, profit.
conveniente [kom·be·njén·te] *adj.* convenient, useful, profitable; (*propio*) fit, proper, suitable; opportune.
convenio [kom·bé·njo] *m.* pact, agreement.
convenir[48] [kom·be·nír] *v. irr.* to agree; to convene, assemble; (*cuadrar*) to be suitable, proper, advisable; to suit, fit; **-se** to agree.
conventillo [kom·ben·tí·yo] *m. Ríopl., Ch.* tenement house.
convento [kom·bén·to] *m.* convent.
convergente [kom·ber·xén·te] *adj.* convergent, coming together.
converger[11] [kom·ber·xér], **convergir**[11] [kom·ber·xír] *v.* to converge.
conversación [kom·ber·sa·sjón] *f.* conversation.
conversar [kom·ber·sár] *v.* to converse.
conversión [kom·ber·sjón] *f.* conversion.
convertidores [kom·ber·ti·dó·res] *m.* transformers.
convertir[3] [kom·ber·tír] *v. irr.* to convert.
convicción [kom·bik·sjón] *f.* conviction.
convicto [kom·bík·to] *p.p. irr. of* **convencer;** convicted, guilty.
convidado [kom·bi·dá·do] *m.* guest; *Am.* — **y con ollita** guest who abuses hospitality.
convidar [kom·bi·dár] *v.* to invite; **-se** to volunteer one's services; to invite oneself.
convincente [kom·bin·sén·te] *adj.* convincing.
convite [kom·bí·te] *m.* invitation; banquet.
convocación [kom·bo·ka·sjón] *f.* convocation.
convocar[6] [kom·bo·kár] *v.* to convoke, call together.
convoyar [kom·bo·yár] *v.* to convoy, escort.
convulsión [kom·bul·sjón] *f.* convulsion.
convulsivo [kom·bul·sí·bo] *adj.* convulsive; **tos convulsiva** whooping cough.
conyugal [kon·ŷu·gál] *adj.* conjugal, pertaining to marriage or a married couple; **vida** — married life.
cónyuge [kón·yu·xe] *m.* husband; *f.* wife.
cooperación [ko·o·pe·ra·sjón] *f.* cooperation.
cooperador [ko·o·pe·ra·dór] *adj.* cooperating, cooperative; *m.* cooperator, co-worker.
cooperar [ko·o·pe·rár] *v.* to cooperate.
cooperativo [ko·o·pe·ra·tí·bo] *adj.* cooperative; **cooperativa** *f.* cooperative, cooperative society.
coordinación [ko·or·di·na·sjón] *f.* coordination.
coordinar [ko·or·di·nár] *v.* to coordinate.
copa [kó·pa] *f.* (*vaso*) goblet; (*de árbol*) treetop; (*de sombrero*) crown; (*palo de la baraja*) card in the suit of copas (*Spanish deck of cards*); *Am.* **empinar la** — to drink, get drunk.
copartícipe [ko·par·tí·si·pe] *adj.* participant; *m. & f.* joint partner.
copete [ko·pé·te] *m.* tuft; crest; top, summit; ornamental top on furniture; **de** — of high rank, important; proud; **estar uno hasta el** — to be

stuffed; to be fed up; **tener mucho** — to be arrogant, haughty.
copia [kó·pja] *f.* copy, imitation; (*computadora*) — **de seguridad** backup copy, — **dura** hard copy, printout; (*cantidad*) abundance.
copiar [ko·pjár] *v.* to copy.
copioso [ko·pjó·so] *adj.* copious, abundant.
copita [ko·pí·ta] *f.* little glass; little drink.
copla [kó·pla] *f.* couplet; stanza (*of variable length and meter*); popular song.
copo [kó·po] *m.* (*de nieve*) snowflake; (*mechón*) wad, tuft (*of wool or cotton*).
copularse [ko·pu·lár·se] *v.* to have sexual relations.
coqueta [ko·ké·ta] *f.* coquette, flirt.
coquetería [ko·ke·te·rí·a] *f.* coquetry, flirting.
coraje [ko·rá·xe] *m.* courage, valor; anger.
coral [ko·rál] *m.* coral; *Am.* red poisonous snake; **-es** coral beads; *adj.* choral, pertaining to a choir; **coralino** [ko·ra·lí·no] *adj.* coral, like coral.
coraza [ko·rá·sa] *f.* cuirass, armor; armor plate or plating; (*concha*) shell (*of a turtle*).
corazón [ko·ra·són] *m.* heart; core, center.
corazonada [ko·ra·so·ná·da] *f.* presentiment, foreboding; hunch.
corbata [kor·bá·ta] *f.* necktie; cravat; *Ríopl.* colorful kerchief, scarf.
corcel [kor·sél] *m.* charger, steed.
corcova [kor·kó·ba] *f.* hump, hunch; **corcovado** [kor·ko·bá·do] *adj.* hunchbacked; *m.* hunchback.
corcovear [kor·ko·be·ár] *v.* to prance about, leap; *Ch.* to kick, protest against.
corchete [kor·čé·te] *m.* hook and eye.
corcho [kór·čo] *m.* cork; (*colmena*) beehive; *adj. Am.* cork-like, spongy.
cordel [kor·dél] *m.* cord, rope; — **entizado** chalk line.
cordero [kor·dé·ro] *m.* lamb; lambskin.
cordial [kor·djál] *adj.* cordial, friendly; **dedo** — middle finger.
cordialidad [kor·dja·li·dád] *f.* cordiality, friendliness, warmth.
cordillera [kor·di·yé·ra] *f.* mountain range.
cordobés [kor·do·bés] *adj.* Cordovan, of or pertaining to Cordova; *m.* native of Cordova.
cordón [kor·dón] *m.* cord; braid; cordon, line of soldiers; *Ríopl.* — **de la acera** curb, curbstone of the sidewalk — **de rizo** ripple beads; **cordonería** [kor·do·ne·rí·a] *f.* lace or cord maker's shop; collection of cords and laces; cordmaker's work; braiding.
cordoncillo [kor·don·sí·yo] *m.* small cord, drawstring, lace, lacing; braid; (*de moneda*) mill (*ridged edge of a coin*); ridge, rib (*of certain fabrics*).
cordura [kor·dú·ra] *f.* good judgment, wisdom; sanity.
corindón [ko·rin·dón] *m.* corundum.
cornada [kor·ná·da] *f.* goring; butt with the horns; **dar -s** to gore, horn, butt with the horns.
corneta [kor·né·ta] *f.* cornet; bugle; horn; *m.* (*persona*) bugler.
cornisa [kor·ní·sa] *f.* cornice.
coro [kó·ro] *m.* choir; chorus.
corona [ko·ró·na] *f.* crown; wreath.
coronar [ko·ro·nár] *v.* to crown; to top.
coronel [ko·ro·nél] *m.* colonel.
coronilla [ko·ro·ní·ya] *f.* small crown; crown of the head; **estar uno hasta la** — to be fed up, be satiated.
corpanchón [kor·pan·čón] *m.* large body; carcass.
corpiño [kor·pí·ño] *m.* bodice.
corporación [kor·po·ra·sjón] *f.* corporation.

corporal [kor·po·rál] *adj.* corporal, of the body; *m.* (*de iglesia*) corporal.

corpóreo [kor·pó·re·o] *adj.* corporeal, bodily; tangible, material.

corpulento [kor·pu·lén·to] *adj.* corpulent, fat, stout.

corral [ko·rrál] *m.* yard; corral, cattle yard; **corralón** [ko·rra·lón] *m.* large corral; *Am.* lumber warehouse.

correa [ko·rré·a] *f.* leather strap; (*resistencia*) resistance; *Ch.* **-s** leather blanket carrier; *Am.* **tener muchas -s** to be phlegmatic, calm.

corrección [ko·rrek·sjón] *f.* correction; correctness.

correcto [ko·rrék·to] *adj.* correct, proper.

corredizo [ko·rre·dí·so] *adj.* sliding, slipping; **nudo —** slip knot.

corredor [ko·rre·dór] *m.* (*que corre*) runner, racer; (*pasillo*) corridor; gallery around a patio; (*revendedor*) broker; *Carib., Andes* covered porch; *Am.* beater of wild game; *adj.* running; speedy.

corregidor [ko·rre·xi·dór] *m.* corrector; Spanish magistrate.

corregir[5, 11] [ko·rre·xír] *v. irr.* to correct; to reprove; to punish; **-se** to mend one's ways.

correligionario [ko·rre·li·xjo·ná·rjo] *adj.* of the same religion; of the same political party or sympathies; *m.* coreligionist.

correntada [ko·rren·tá·da] *f. Ch., Ríopl., C.A., Carib.* strong river current.

correo [ko·rré·o] *m.* mail; mail service; postman; post office; **— aéreo** air mail.

correón [ko·rre·ón] *m.* large strap.

correoso [ko·rre·ó·so] *adj.* flexible; leathery, tough; **correosidad** [ko·rre·o·si·dád] *f.* toughness; flexibility.

correr [ko·rrér] *v.* (*caminar*) to run; to blow (*said of the wind*); (*encarrera*) to race; to chase; (*pasar*) to pass, elapse (*time*); to draw (*a curtain*); *Mex.* to dismiss, throw out; **-se** to slip through; to slide; (*apenarse*) to be embarrassed.

correría [ko·rre·rí·a] *f.* foray, raid for plunder; (*viaje*) excursion, short trip; **-s** wanderings, travels; raids.

correspondencia [ko·rres·pon·dén·sja] *f.* correspondence; letters, mail; agreement; interchange.

corresponder [ko·rres·pon·dér] *v.* to reciprocate; return (*love, favors*); (*pertenecer*) to belong; (*tratarse de*) to concern; to correspond (*one thing with another*).

correspondiente [ko·rres·pon·djén·te] *adj.* corresponding, agreeing; respective; *m.* correspondent.

corresponsal [ko·rres·pon·sál] *m.* correspondent; agent; newspaper reporter.

corretaje [ko·rre·tá·xe] *m.* brokerage.

corretear [ko·rre·te·ár] *v.* to run around; to roam, rove; *Am.* to pursue, chase.

corretelas [ko·rre·té·las] *m.* puller (*drape*).

corrida [ko·rrí·da] *f.* race; *Ch.* row, file; *P.R.* night spree; *Am.* beating up of game; **— del tiempo** swiftness of time; **— de toros** bullfight; **de —** without stopping; **comida — a** the regular meal.

corrido [ko·rrí·do] *adj.* embarrassed, ashamed; worldly-wise; flowing, fluent; **de —** without stopping; *m. Mex., Col., Ven., Ríopl., Andes* popular ballad.

corriente [ko·rrjén·te] *adj.* (*que corre*) running; flowing, fluent; (*común*) usual, common, ordinary; *Am.* frank, open; **¡ — !** all right! O.K.!; **el ocho del —** the eighth of the current month; **estar al —** to be up-to-date; to be well-informed (*about current news*); **poner a uno al —** to keep someone posted or well informed; *f.* current; flow; course;

Am. **hay que llevarle la —** one must humor him; **— alternativa** A.C. (alternating current); **— continua** D.C. (direct current).

corrillo [ko·rrí·yo] *m.* circle or group of gossipers.

corro [kó·rro] *m.* group of talkers or spectators.

corroer[51] [ko·rro·ér] *v. irr.* to corrode.

corromper [ko·rrom·pér] *v.* to corrupt; to seduce; to bribe; **-se** to rot; to become corrupted.

corrompido [ko·rrom·pí·do] *adj.* corrupt; rotten, spoiled; degenerate; *p.p. of* **corromper.**

corrupción [ko·rrup·sjón] *f.* corruption.

corrupto [ko·rrúp·to] *adj.* corrupt, rotten.

corsé [kor·sé] *m.* corset.

corsetería [kor·se·te·rí·a] *f.* maker or seller of inner garments.

cortacircuito [kor·ta·sir·kwí·to] *m.* circuit breaker, cut-out.

cortada [kor·tá·da] *f. Col., Ven., Carib.* cut, slash.

cortador [kor·ta·dór] *m.* cutter.

cortadura [kor·ta·dú·ra] *m.* cut; gash; slash.

cortafrío [kor·ta·frí·o] *m.* cold chisel.

cortante [kor·tán·te] *adj.* cutting; sharp.

cortaplumas [kor·ta·plú·mas] *m.* penknife.

cortar [kor·tár] *v.* to cut; to cut off; to cut out; to cut down; to interrupt; *Ven.* to harvest, pick (*fruit*); to gossip, speak ill of someone; **-se** to be embarrassed, ashamed; to sour, curdle (*said of milk*); *Mex., Arg.* to become separated, cut off; *Mex., Cuba* to leave in a hurry; *Am.* to die.

corte [kór·te] *m.* cut; cutting; cutting edge; fit, style; *Carib., Mex., Ríopl.* cut (*in cards*); **— por arco y aire** arc-air cutting (*welding*); *Am.* harvest; *Mex., Carib.* weeding; *Arg.* gracefulness in dancing; *f.* royal court; retinue; *P.R., Ven.* court of justice; **-s** Spanish parliament; **hacer la —** to court, woo; *Am.* **darse uno —** to put on airs.

cortedad [kor·te·dád] *f.* smallness; timidity; bashfulness, shyness.

cortejar [kor·te·xár] *v.* to court, woo.

cortejo [kor·té·xo] *m.* cortege, procession; retinue; courtship; suitor.

cortés [kor·tés] *adj.* courteous, polite.

cortesana [kor·te·sá·na] *f.* courtesan, prostitute.

cortesano [kor·te·sá·no] *m.* courtier; *adj.* courtlike; courteous.

cortesía [kor·te·sí·a] *f.* courtesy, politeness.

corteza [kor·té·sa] *f.* bark; crust; peel.

cortijo [kor·tí·xo] *m.* farmhouse.

cortina [kor·tí·na] *m.* curtain.

corto [kór·to] *adj.* short; scanty; bashful.

cortocircuito [kor·to·sir·kwí·to] *m.* short circuit.

corveta [kor·bé·ta] *f.* buck, leap, bound (*of a horse*); **hacer -s** to prance.

corvo [kór·bo] *m. C.A.* machete.

cosa [kó·sa] *f.* thing; **— de** approximately, about; **no es —** it is not worth anything; **otra —** something else; **como si tal —** serene, as if nothing had happened; *Mex.* **ni por una de estas nueve -s** absolutely not, not for anything in the world.

cosecha [ko·sé·ča] *f.* crop; harvest.

cosechar [ko·se·čár] *v.* to reap; to harvest.

coser [ko·sér] *v.* to sew; to stitch.

cosmético [koz·mé·ti·ko] *m. & adj.* cosmetic.

cosquillas [kos·kí·yas] *f. pl.* ticklishness; tickling; **hacer —** to tickle; to excite (*one's desire or curiosity*); **tener —** to be ticklish.

cosquillear [kos·ki·ye·ár] *v.* to tickle; to excite (*one's curiosity or desire*).

cosquilleo [kos·ki·yé·o] *m.* tickle, tickling sensation.

cosquilloso [kos·ki·yó·so] *adj.* ticklish; touchy.

costa [kós·ta] *f.* coast; (*precio*) cost, expense, price; **a**

CO

toda — at all costs, by all means.
costado [kos·tá·ɖo] *m.* side; (*de animal*) flank.
costal [kos·tál] *m.* sack; **estar hecho un — de huesos** to be nothing but skin and bones; to be very thin.
costanero [kos·ta·né·ro] *adj.* coastal, relating to a coast; (*inclinado*) sloping.
costar[2] [kos·tár] *v. irr.* to cost; **— trabajo** to be difficult.
costarricense [kos·ta·rri·sén·se] *adj., m. & f.* Costa Rican.
coste [kós·te], **costo** [kós·to] *m.* cost; expense.
costear [kos·te·ár] *v.* (*pagar*) to defray or pay costs; to pay, (*valer*) be profitable; (*pasar junto a*) to navigate along the coast; to go along the edge of; **no costea** it does not pay.
costero [kos·té·ro] *adj.* coastal; **navegación costera** coastal navigation.
costilla [kos·tí·ya] *f.* rib; (*carne*) chop, cutlet.
costoso [kos·tó·so] *adj.* costly, expensive.
costra [kós·tra] *f.* crust; scab; **— de óxido** scale.
costroso [kos·tró·so] *adj.* crusty, scabby.
costumbre [kos·túm·bre] *f.* custom, habit.
costura [kos·tú·ra] *f.* sewing; stitching; seam; **— invisible** blind stitching; **— cruzada** cross stitching.
costurera [kos·tu·ré·ra] *f.* seamstress.
costurero [kos·tu·ré·ro] *m.* sewing table or cabinet; sewing box; sewing room.
costurón [kos·tu·rón] *m.* coarse stitching; large seam; (*remiendo*) patch, mend; (*cicatriz*) big scar.
cotejar [ko·te·xár] *v.* to confront, compare; collate.
cotejo [ko·té·xo] *m.* comparison; collation.
contense [kon·tén·se] *m. Ch., Mex.* burlap.
cotidiano [ko·ti·ɖjá·no] *adj.* daily.
cotizable [ko·ti·sá·ble] *adj.* quotable (*price*).
cotización [ko·ti·sa·sjón] *f.* quotation of prices; current price.
cotizar[9] [ko·ti·sár] *v.* to quote (*prices*); *Ch.* to contribute one's share or quota; *Am.* to prorate, distribute proportionally.
coto [kó·to] *m.* enclosure; (*mojón*) landmark; (*límite*) limitation; limit, boundary; **poner — a** to set a limit to; to put an end to.
cotón [ko·tón] *m. Mex., C.A.* shirt of cheap fabric (muslin).
cotorra [ko·tó·rra] *f.* small parrot; magpie; (*persona*) talkative person, chatterbox.
cotorrear [ko·to·rre·ár] *v.* to chatter; to gossip.
covacha [ko·bá·ča] *f.* small cave; grotto; *Mex., Cuba, Andes* hut, shanty; *Col.* cubbyhole, small dark room.
coyote [ko·yó·te] *m. Am.* coyote, prairie wolf; *Mex.* (*traficante*) shyster, tricky, lawyer; *Mex., C.A.* agent, broker (*often illegal*).
coyuntura [ko·yun·tú·ra] *f.* joint; articulation; occasion; precise moment.
coz [kos] *f.* kick; recoil of a gun; butt of a firearm; **dar** (*or* **tirar**) **coces** to kick.
cráneo [krá·ne·o] *m.* cranium, skull.
craso [krá·so] *adj.* fat; (*bruto*) thick, coarse, gross; **ignorancia crasa** gross ignorance.
cráter [krá·ter] *m.* crater of a volcano.
creación [kre·a·sjón] *f.* creation.
creador [kre·a·ɖór] *m.* creator; *adj.* creating, creative.
crear [kre·ár] *v.* to create.
crecer[13] [kre·sér] *v. irr.* to grow; to increase; **-se** to swell (*as a river*); to become or feel important.
crecida [kre·sí·ɖa] *f.* river flood.
crecido [kre·sí·ɖo] *adj.* grown, increased; large; swollen.

creciente [kre·sjén·te] *adj.* growing, increasing; crescent (*moon*); *f.* river flood; *m.* crescent.
crecimiento [kre·si·mjén·to] *m.* growth, increase.
credenciales [kre·den·sjá·les] *f. pl.* credentials.
crédito [kré·ɖi·to] *m.* credit; (*creencia*) credence, belief; (*fama*) fame, reputation; letter of credit; **dar a —** to loan on credit.
credo [kré·ɖo] *m.* creed; **en un —** in a jiffy, in a minute.
crédulo [kré·ɖu·lo] *adj.* credulous, too ready to believe.
creencia [kre·én·sja] *f.* belief, faith.
creer[14] [kre·ér] *v.* to believe; to think, suppose; **¡ya lo creo!** I should say so!; yes, of course!
creíble [kre·í·ble] *adj.* credible, believable.
crema [kré·ma] *f.* cream; custard; cold cream.
cremallera [kre·ma·yé·ra] *f.* rack (*rack and pinion*).
crémor tártaro [kre·mor·tár·ta·ro] *m.* cream of tartar.
crepitar [kre·pi·tár] *v.* to crackle, snap; to creak; to rattle.
crepuscular [kre·pús·ku·lár] *adj.* twilight.
crepúsculo [kre·pús·ku·lo] *m.* twilight.
crespo [krés·po] *adj.* curly; artificial (*style*); angry, crisp.
crespón [kres·pón] *m.* crepe.
cresta [krés·ta] *f.* crest; top, summit; tuft, comb (*of a bird*).
cretona [kre·tó·na] *f.* cretonne.
creyente [kre·yén·te] *m. & f.* believer; *adj.* believing.
creyón [kre·yón] *m. Am.* crayon.
cría [krí·a] *f.* brood; suckling; breeding.
criadero [krja·ɖé·ro] *m.* tree nursery; breeding place; (*semillero*) hotbed; rich mine.
criado [krjá·ɖo] *m.* servant; *adj.* bred; **mal —** ill-bred; **criada** *f.* maid, servant.
criador [krja·ɖór] *m.* breeder, raiser, rearer; creator; *adj.* creating, creative; breeding; nourishing.
crianza [krján·sa] *f.* breeding; nursing; (*modales*) manners.
criar[17] [krjar] *v.* to breed; to bring up, rear, educate; to nurse.
criatura [krja·tú·ra] *f.* creature; baby, child.
criba [krí·ba] *f.* sieve.
cribar [kri·bár] *v.* to sift.
crimen [krí·men] *m.* crime.
criminal [kri·mi·nál] *adj., m. & f.* criminal.
crin [krin] *f.* mane.
crinudo [kri·nú·ɖo] *adj. Am.* with a long or thick mane.
criollo [krjó·yo] *m. Am.* Creole; native of Spanish America; *adj.* national, domestic (*not foreign to Spanish America*).
criptón [krip·tón] *m.* krypton.
crisantema [kri·san·té·ma] *f.*, **crisantemo** [kri·san·té·mo] *m.* chrysanthemum.
crisis [krí·sis] *f.* crisis.
crisol [kri·sól] *m.* crucible, melting pot; (*hogar*) hearth of a blast furnace.
crispar [kris·pár] *v.* to contract (*muscles*); to clench (*fists*); to put (*nerves*) on edge.
cristal [kris·tál] *m.* crystal; glass; (*espejo*) mirror; (*lente*) lens; **— líquido** liquid glass.
cristalería [kris·ta·le·rí·a] *f.* glassware shop or factory; glassware.
cristalino [kris·ta·lí·no] *adj.* crystalline, transparent, clear; *m.* lens of the eye.
cristalizar[9] [kris·ta·li·sár] *v.* to crystallize.
cristiandad [kris·tjan·dáð] *f.* Christianity; Christendom.
cristianismo [kris·tja·níz·mo] *m.* Christianity.
cristiano [kris·tjá·no] *m.* Christian; person; **hablar en**

— to speak clearly; *adj.* Christian.

criterio [kri·té·rjo] *m.* criterion, rule, standard; judgment.

crítica [krí·ti·ka] *f.* criticism; censure; (*chisme*) gossip.

criticador [kri·ti·ka·ðór] *adj.* critical; *m.* critic, faultfinder.

criticar[6] [kri·ti·kár] *v.* to criticize; to censure; to find fault with.

crítico [krí·ti·ko] *adj.* critical; *m.* critic, judge; *Am.* faultfinder, slanderer; **criticón** [kri·ti·kón] *m.* critic, knocker, faultfinder; *adj.* critical, over-critical, faultfinding.

croar [kro·ár] *v.* to croak.

cromo [kró·mo] *m.* chromium.

cromosoma [kro·mo·só·ma] *m.* chromosome.

crónica [kró·ni·ka] *f.* chronicle, history; **cronista** [kro·nís·ta] *m.* & *f.* chronicler.

crónico [kró·ni·ko] *adj.* chronic.

cronómetro [kro·nó·me·tro] *m.* chronometer, timepiece.

croquis [kró·kis] *m.* rough sketch.

cruce [krú·se] *m.* crossing; crossroads; crossbreeding.

crucero [kru·sé·ro] *m.* (*cruciforme*) crossing; crossbearer; crossroads; transept (*of a church*); crossbeam; cross (*a constellation*); (*buque*) cruiser.

cruceta [kru·sé·ta] *f.* crosspiece; crosstree; universal joint (*automobile*).

crucificar[6] [kru·si·fi·kár] *v.* to crucify.

crucifijo [kru·si·fí·xo] *m.* crucifix.

crucigrama [kru·si·grá·ma] *m.* crossword puzzle.

crudo [krú·ðo] *adj.* raw; (*sin cocer*) uncooked; unripe; harsh; **agua cruda** hard water; **petróleo** — crude oil; *Mex.* **estar** — to have a hang-over; **cruda** *f. Mex.* hang-over.

cruel [krwel] *adj.* cruel.

crueldad [krwel·dáð] *f.* cruelty.

crujido [kru·xí·ðo] *m.* creak, crack, creaking; rustle.

crujir [kru·xír] *v.* to creak, crackle; to grate (*one's teeth*); to rustle; to crunch.

cruz [krus] *f.* cross.

cruzada [kru·sá·ða] *f.* crusade; holy war; campaign.

cruzado [kru·sá·ðo] *m.* crusader; *adj.* crossed; cross, crosswise, transverse.

cruzamiento [kru·sa·mjén·to] *m.* crossing; crossroads.

cruzar[9] [kru·sár] *v.* to cross; *Ch.* to fight, dispute; **-se con** to meet.

cuaco [kwá·ko] *m. Mex.* horse; *S.A.* cassava flour.

cuaderno [kwa·ðér·no] *m.* notebook; memorandum book; booklet; *Mex., Ven.* pamphlet.

cuadra [kwá·ðra] *f.* hall, large room; stable; hospital or prison ward; *Am.* city block; *Perú* reception room.

cuadrado [kwa·ðrá·ðo] *adj.* square; *m.* square; square ruler; die, metal block or plate.

cuadrante [kwa·ðrán·te] *m.* dial, face of a clock or watch; sundial; quadrant (*fourth part of circle; instrument used in astronomy*).

cuadrar [kwa·ðrár] *v.* (*cuadriforme*) to square; to form into a square; (*agradar*) to please; to conform; to harmonize; to set well; *Am.* to be becoming (*said of clothes*); *Ch.* to be ready; *Am.* to contribute a large sum; *P.R.* to come out well, succeed; **-se** to stand at attention.

cuadricular [kwa·ðri·ku·lár] *v.* to square off, divide into squares.

cuadrilla [kwa·ðrí·ya] *f.* group, troupe, gang; armed band; quadrille, (*baile*) square dance.

cuadro [kwá·ðro] *m.* square; picture; scene; frame; flower bed; *Col.* blackboard; *Ch.* slaughterhouse.

cuajada [kwa·xá·ða] *f.* curd.

cuajado [kwa·xá·ðo] *p.p.* & *adj.* coagulated, curdled; filled, covered; — **de** full or covered with (*flowers, dew, etc.*).

cuajar [kwa·xár] *v.* to coagulate, thicken, curd, curdle; to turn out well; to jell; to please; *Am.* to chatter, prattle; **-se** to coagulate, curd; to become crowded, be filled; **la cosa no cuajó** the thing did not work, did not jell.

cuajarón [kwa·xa·rón] *m.* clot.

cual [kwal] *rel. pron.* which; **cada** — each one; — **más** — **menos** some people more, others less; **el** —, **la** —, **los -es, las -es** which; who; **lo** — which; *adv.* as, like; **¿cuál?** *interr. pron.* which one? what?

cualidad [kwa·li·ðáð] *f.* quality; trait.

cualquier(a) [kwal·kjér(a)] *indef. adj.* & *pron.* any, anyone; whichever; **un hombre cualquiera** any man whatever.

cuando [kwán·do] *rel. adv.* & *conj.* when; **aun** — even though; **¿cuándo?** *interr. adv.* when?

cuantía [kwan·tí·a] *f.* quantity; rank, importance.

cuantioso [kwan·tjó·so] *adj.* plentiful, abundant; numerous.

cuanto [kwán·to] *rel. adj.* & *pron.* as much as, as many as; all that; — **antes** as soon as possible, immediately; **en** — *conj.* as soon as; **en** — **a** as for, with regard to; **unos -s** a few; **¿cuánto?** *interr. adj.* & *pron.* how much?; **¿cuántos?** how many?

cuaquerismo [kwa·ke·ríz·mo] *m.* the Quaker sect, or doctrine.

cuáquero [kwá·ke·ro] *m.* Quaker.

cuarenta [kwa·rén·ta] *num.* forty.

cuarentena [kwa·ren·té·na] *f.* quarantine; forty units of anything; period of forty days, months, or years.

cuarentón [kwa·ren·tón] *m.* man in his forties; **cuarentona** [kwa·ren·tó·na] *f.* woman in her forties.

cuaresma [kwa·réz·ma] *f.* Lent.

cuarta [kwár·ta] *f.* fourth, fourth part; span of a hand; *Mex.* horse whip; *P.R.* **echar** — to beat, flog.

cuartear [kwar·te·ár] *v.* to quarter, divide into quarters; *P.R.* to whip; **-se** to crack, split (*said of walls or ceilings*); *Mex.* to back down, go back on one's word.

cuartel [kwar·tél] *m.* quarter, one fourth; quarters, barracks; district; quarter, mercy; **no dar** — to give no quarter.

cuartelada [kwar·te·lá·ða] *f.* military coup d'état, uprising, insurrection.

cuartelazo [kwar·te·lá·so] *m. Am.* military coup d'état, insurrection.

cuarterón [kwar·te·rón] *m.* quarter, fourth part; fourth of a pound; panel (*of a door or window*); *adj.* & *m.* quarter-breed (*one fourth Indian and three fourths Spanish*); quadroon (*person of quarter negro blood*).

cuarteto [kwar·té·to] *m.* quartet; (*verso*) quatrain (*stanza of four lines*).

cuartilla [kwar·tí·ya] *f.* (*hoja*) sheet of paper; (*medida*) about 4 quarts; about 1½ pecks; fourth of an **arroba** (about 6 pounds); *Am.* three cents' worth; *Am.* **no valer uno** — not to be worth a penny.

cuartillo [kwar·tí·yo] *m.* fourth of a peck; about a pint; fourth of a **real.**

cuarto [kwár·to] *m.* room; (*cantidad*) quarter, one fourth; **tener -s** to have money; *adj.* fourth.

cuarzo [kwár·so] *m.* quartz.

cuate [kwá·te] *adj., m.* & *f. Mex.* twin; pal, buddy.

CO

cuatrero [kwa·tré·ro] *m.* horse thief, cattle thief; *Mex.* Indian who speaks "broken" Spanish.

cuatro [kwá·tro] *num.* four.

cuba [kú·ba] *f.* cask, barrel; tub, vat; (*panzón*) big-bellied person; drunkard.

cubano [ku·bá·no] *adj. & m.* Cuban.

cubeta [ku·bé·ta] *f.* small barrel or keg; bucket, pail.

cúbico [kú·bi·ko] *adj.* cubic.

cubierta [ku·bjér·ta] *f.* cover; covering; (*carta*) envelope; deck (*of a ship*); *Mex.* sheath.

cubierto [ku·bjér·to] *p.p. of* **cubrir**; *m.* cover; place setting for one person at a table.

cubismo [ku·bíz·mo] *m.* cubism.

cubo [kú·bo] *m.* cube; bucket, pail; hub of a wheel; mill pond; *Arg.* finger bowl.

cubremesa [ku·bre·mé·sa] *f.* table cover.

cubrir[52] [ku·brír] *v.* to cover; to hide; to coat; to settle, pay (*a bill*); **-se** to cover oneself; to put on one's hat.

cucaracha [ku·ka·rá·ča] *f.* cockroach.

cuclillas [ku·klí·yas] **en —** in a squatting position; **sentarse en —** to squat.

cuclillo [ku·klí·yo] *m.* cuckoo.

cuco [kú·ko] *adj.* dainty, cute; sly, shrewd; *m.* cuckoo; a kind of caterpillar; card game; *Ríopl.* peach, peach tree; *Mex.* **hacer — a** to make fun of; to fool.

cucurucho [ku·ku·rú·čo] *m.* paper cone; *Am.* peak, summit; *Peru, C.A., Mex.* cowl, cloak with a hood (*worn by penitents in Holy Week processions*).

cuchara [ku·čá·ra] *f.* spoon; trowel; *Am.* mason's trowel; **media —** mediocre person; *Am.* mason's helper; *Am.* **hacer —** to pout; *Am.* **meter uno su —** to butt into a conversation; to meddle;

cucharada [ku·ča·rá·da] *f.* spoonful; scoop;

cucharón [ku·ča·rón] *m.* large spoon; ladle; dipper; scoop.

cuchichear [ku·či·če·ár] *v.* to whisper.

cuchicheo [ku·či·čé·o] *m.* whispering, whisper.

cuchilla [ku·čí·ya] *f.* large knife, cleaver; *Mex., P.R.* mountain ridge; *Am.* gore (*in a garment*); *Am.* narrow tract of land.

cuchillada [ku·či·yá·da] *f.* thrust with a knife, stab, slash; cut, gash.

cuchillo [ku·čí·yo] *m.* knife; gore (*in a garment*); **— de monte** hunting knife; **cuchillería** [ku·či·ye·rí·a] *f.* cutlery; cutlery shop.

cueca [kwé·ka] *f. Ch., Arg.* a Chilean dance.

cuello [kwé·yo] *m.* neck; collar.

cuenca [kwéŋ·ka] *f.* river basin; narrow valley; wooden bowl; socket of the eye.

cuenco [kwéŋ·ko] *m.* earthen bowl.

cuenta [kwén·ta] *f.* (*cálculo*) count, calculation; bill; account; (*bolita*) bead (*of a rosary or necklace*); **a fin de -s** in the final analysis; **caer en la —** to see, get the point; **darse —** to realize; *Col.* **de toda —** anyway; **eso corre de mi —** that is my responsibility; I'll take charge of that; **eso no me tiene —** that does not pay me; it is of no profit to me; **en resumidas -s** in short; *P.R.* **hacerle — una cosa a uno** to be useful or profitable for one; **tomar en —** to take into account; **tomar una cosa por su —** to take charge of something, take the responsibility for it; **vamos a -s** let's understand or settle this.

cuentagotas [kwen·ta·gó·tas] *m.* dropper (*for counting drops*).

cuento [kwén·to] *m.* story, tale; **— de nunca acabar** never-ending tale; **déjese de -s** come to the point; **no viene a —** it is not opportune or to the point.

cuerda [kwér·da] *f.* cord, string, rope; chord; watch spring; **dar — a** to wind (*a watch*).

cuerdo [kwér·do] *adj.* sane; wise.

cuereada [kwe·re·á·da] *f. Mex., C.A., Col., Ven.* flogging, whipping; *Am.* skinning of an animal.

cuerear [kwe·re·ár] *v. Am.* to flog, whip; *Am.* to harm, dishonor; *Am.* to beat (*in a game*); *Arg.* to skin (*an animal*).

cuerno [kwér·no] *m.* horn; antenna, feeler; **poner -s a** to be unfaithful to, deceive (*a husband*); *Am.* **mandar al —** to send to the devil.

cuero [kwé·ro] *m.* hide, skin; leather; wineskin; *Col., Ven.* whip; **en -s** naked.

cuerpeada [kwer·pe·á·da] *f. Ríopl.* dodge; evasion.

cuerpo [kwér·po] *m.* body; bulk; corps; **en —** without hat or coat; **luchar — a —** to fight in single combat; *Am.* **sacar el —** to dodge; to escape, avoid doing something.

cuervo [kwér·bo] *m.* crow; raven; *Ven.* buzzard; *Ch.* dishonest priest; *Ríopl., Ch.* **hacer uno la del —** to leave abruptly and not return.

cuesta [kwés·ta] *f.* hill, slope; **a -s** on one's shoulders or back; in one's care; **— abajo** downhill; **— arriba** uphill.

cuestión [kwes·tjón] *f.* question; controversy, dispute; problem, matter.

cuestionario [kwes·tjo·ná·rjo] *m.* questionnaire, list of questions.

cueva [kwé·ba] *f.* cave, cavern; cellar.

cuico [kwí·ko] *m. Mex.* cop, policeman; *Am.* gossiper, tattletale, "squealer"; *Ch., Bol., Peru* half-breed; *Ríopl.* short, chubby person.

cuidado [kwi·dá·do] *m.* care, attention; worry, misgiving; **al — de** in care of; **tener —** to be careful; **¡ — !** look out!; be careful! **¡cuidadito!** be very careful!

cuidadoso [kwi·da·dó·so] *adj.* careful; attentive; anxious.

cuidar [kwi·dár] *v.* to take care of, look after, keep; to make or do carefully.

cuita [kwí·ta] *f.* grief, care, anxiety; misfortune; *C.A.* bird dung.

cuitado [kwi·tá·do] *adj.* unfortunate; timid, shy.

culata [ku·lá·ta] *f.* haunch, buttock; rear; butt (*of a firearm*).

culatazo [ku·la·tá·so] *m.* blow with the butt of a rifle; recoil, kick of a firearm.

culebra [ku·le·bra] *f.* snake; coil; *Mex.* money belt.

culebrear [ku·le·bre·ár] *v.* to zigzag; to twist; wriggle.

culminación [kul·mi·na·sjón] *f.* culmination, climax.

culminar [kul·mi·nár] *v.* to culminate; to come to a climax.

culo [kú·lo] *m.* anus, behind.

culpa [kúl·pa] *f.* fault; guilt; blame; **echar la — a** to blame; **tener la —** to be to blame.

culpabilidad [kul·pa·bi·li·dád] *f.* guilt; **culpable** [kul·pá·ble] *adj.* guilty.

culpar [kul·pár] *v.* to blame; to declare guilty.

cultivación [kul·ti·ba·sjón] *f.* cultivation.

cultivador [kul·ti·ba·dór] *m.* cultivator; **máquina cultivadora** cultivator.

cultivar [kul·ti·bár] *v.* to cultivate.

cultivo [kul·tí·bo] *m.* cultivation, culture.

culto [kúl·to] *adj.* cultured; *m.* cult, worship; religious sect; **rendir — a** to pay homage to; to worship.

cultura [kul·tú·ra] *f.* culture; cultivation.

cumbre [kúm·bre] *f.* summit; top.

cumpleaños [kum·ple·á·ños] *m.* birthday.

cumplido [kum·plí·do] *adj.* (*completo*) complete, full; perfect; (*cortés*) courteous; *p.p.* fulfilled; due, fallen due; **tiene tres años -s** he is just over three years old; *m.* courtesy, attention; compliment.

cumplimentar [kum·pli·men·tár] *v.* to compliment; to congratulate; to pay a courtesy visit.

cumplimiento [kum·pli·mjén·to] *m.* fulfilment; courtesy; completion; compliment; **de —** formal, ceremonious.

cumplir [kum·plír] *v.* to fulfill; to comply; to carry out; to fall due; **— año,** to have a birthday; to be (*so many*) years old.

cúmulo [kú·mu·lo] *m.* pile, heap; accumulation; cumulus (*mass of clouds*).

cuna [kú·na] *f.* cradle; origin; *Mex.* coffin for the poor; *Cuba* dive, den (*for gambling and dancing*).

cundir [kun·dír] *v.* to spread (*as news, disease, liquids*); to propagate, extend, multiply.

cuña [kú·ña] *f.* wedge; splinter; beadpan; *Ch., Ríopl.* influential person; *Arg.* spot commercial.

cuñado [ku·ñá·do] *m.* brother-in-law; **cuñada** [ku·ñá·da] *f.* sister-in-law.

cuota [kwó·ta] *f.* quota; dues, fee; **— de entrada** admission fee.

cuotidiano [kwo·ti·djá·no] *adj.* everyday, daily.

cupé [ku·pé] *m.* coupé.

cupo [kú·po] *m.* quota; *Col.* place, seat (*on a plane or train*).

cupón [ku·pón] *m.* coupon.

cúpula [kú·pu·la] *f.* dome.

cura [kú·ra] *f.* cure; *m.* curate, priest.

curación [ku·ra·sjón] *f.* cure.

curandero [ku·ran·dé·ro] *m.* healer (*not a doctor*); quack; medicine man (*among Indians*).

curar [ku·rár] *v.* to cure, heal; to treat; to cure (*meats, tobacco*); to tan (*skins*); *Arg.* to load (*dice*), fix (*cards*); **— de** to take care of; **-se** to cure oneself; to get well; *Ríopl.* to get drunk.

curiosear [ku·rjo·se·ár] *v.* to snoop, peek, peer, pry; to observe with curiosity.

curiosidad [ku·rjo·si·dád] *f.* curiosity; neatness, daintiness.

curioso [ku·rjó·so] *adj.* curious; neat, dainty; **libros raros y -s** rare books.

curita [ku·rí·ta] *f.* bandaid.

curro [kú·rro] *adj.* showy, gaudy, flashy; *m.* dandy.

currutaco [ku·rru·tá·ko] *m.* fop, dandy; *adj.* affected (*in one's dress*).

cursi [kúr·si] *adj.* common, in bad taste; cheap, ridiculous; **cursilería** [kur·si·le·rí·a] *f.* bad taste, cheapness, false elegance; group of cheap, ridiculous people.

curso [kúr·so] *m.* course, direction; scholastic year; course of study.

cursor [kur·sór] *m.* (*computadora*) cursor.

curtidor [kur·ti·dór] *m.* tanner.

curtiduría [kur·ti·du·rí·a] *f.* tannery.

curtir [kur·tír] *v.* to tan; to harden, accustom to hardships; *Col., Ven.* to dirty, soil; **-se** to get tanned or sunburned; to become accustomed to hardships.

curva [kúr·ba] *f.* curve.

curvo [kúr·bo] *adj.* curved; bent, crooked; arched.

cúspide [kús·pi·de] *f.* summit, peak, top; spire, steeple.

custodia [kus·tó·dja] *f.* custody; guard, guardian; monstrance (*vessel in which the consecrated Host is exposed*); **en —** in escrow.

custodiar [kus·to·djár] *v.* to guard, watch; to keep in custody.

custodio [kus·tó·djo] *m.* guardian, keeper.

cutícula [ku·tí·ku·la] *f.* cuticle.

cutis [kú·tis] *m.* skin; complexion.

cuyo [kú·yo] *rel. poss. adj.* whose, of whom, of which.

cuz! [kus] *interj.* come here! here! (*to a dog*).

CH:ch

chabacano [ča·ba·ká·no] *adj.* crude, unpolished; inartistic; cheap, in bad taste; *m. Mex.* a variety of apricot.

chacota [ča·kó·ta] *f.* fun; jest; **echar a —** to take as a joke; **hacer — de** to make fun of.

chacotear [ča·ko·te·ár] *v.* to frolic, joke, make merry; to be boisterous; to show off.

chacra [čá·kra] *f. Ec., Peru, Ch.* small farm; *Col., Ec.* cultivated field.

chaflán [ča·flán] *m.* chamfer (arch.).

chagra [čá·gra] *f. Col., Ec.* farm, piece of farm land; *m. & f. Ec.* peasant; *adj.* uncivilized, unrefined.

chal [čal] *m.* shawl.

chalán [ča·lán] *m.* horse trader; *Am.* broncobuster, horse breaker; *Mex.* ferry boat.

chaleco [ča·lé·ko] *m.* waistcoat, vest.

chalote [ča·ló·te] *m.* shallot.

chalupa [ča·lú·pa] *f.* sloop, sailboat; launch; *Mex., Col., Ven., Ríopl.* canoe; *P.R.* raft; *Mex.* Mexican tortilla with sauce.

chamaco [ča·má·ko] *m. Mex., C.A.* boy; **chamaquito** *m. Mex., C.A.* little boy.

chamarra [ča·má·rra] *f.* coarse wool jacket or sweater; *Mex.* sheepskin jacket, leather jacket; *Am.* heavy wool blanket.

chamarreta [ča·ma·rré·ta] *f.* short loose jacket; *Am.* square poncho.

chambergo [čam·bér·go] *m.* gaucho sombrero.

chambón [čam·bón] *adj.* clumsy, awkward, unskillful; *m.* bungler, clumsy performer, awkward workman; clumsy player.

champaña [čam·pá·ña] *f.* champagne.

champiñón [čam·pi·ñón] *m.* mushroom.

champú [čam·pú] *m.* shampoo.

champurrado [čam·pu·rrá·do] *m. Mex.* a mixed drink of chocolate and **atole**; *Col.* a mixed alcoholic beverage.

champurrar [čam·pu·rrár], *Am.* **champurrear** [čam·pu·rre·ár] *v.* to mix (*drinks*).

chamuescar [ča·mwes·kár] *v.* to frizzle.

chamuscada [ča·mus·ká·da], **chamuscadura** [ča·mus·ka·dú·ra] *f. Am.* singe, scorch.

chamuscar[6] [ča·mus·kár] *v.* to scorch; to singe; to sear; *Am.* to sell at a low cost; **-se** to get scorched, singed, or seared; *Col.* to get peeved, offended.

chamusquina [ča·mus·kí·na] *f.* singe, scorch.

chancear [čan·se·ár] *v.* to fool, joke, jest.

chancero [čan·sé·ro] *m.* jester, joker; *adj.* jolly.

chancla [čáŋ·kla] *f.* slipper; old shoe; **chancleta** *f.* slipper; *m. Am.* good-for-nothing.

chanclo [čáŋ·klo] *m.* galosh, overshoe; clog; rubber overshoe; **-s** rubbers.

chancho [čán·čo] *m. S.A.* pig, pork.

changador [čaŋ·ga·dór] *m. Ríopl.* carrier, porter; *Am.* handy man, person who does odd jobs.

chango [čáŋ·go] *m. Mex.* monkey; **ponerse —** to be alert, wary.

chantaje [čan·tá·xe] *m.* blackmail, blackmailing.

chanza [čán·sa] *f.* joke, jest.

chapa [čá·pa] *f.* metal plate; veneer (*thin leaf of wood*); rosy spot on the cheeks; *Mex., C.A., Andes* lock; *S.A.* Indian spy; **-s** game of tossing coins;

hombre de — serious, reliable man.

chapado [ča·pá·đo] *adj.* veneered (*covered with a thin layer of wood or other material*); — **a la antigua** old-fashioned.

chapalear [ča·pa·le·ár] = **chapotear.**

chapapote [ča·pa·pó·te] *m. Mex.* tar; asphalt.

chaparro [ča·pá·rro] *m.* scrub oak; short, chubby person; *Am.* a kind of tropical shrub with rough leaves; *Am.* short whip; *adj. Mex., C.A.* short, squatty person.

chaparrón [ča·pa·rrón] *m.* downpour, heavy shower.

chapetón [ča·pe·tón] *m.* red spot on the cheek; *Col.* nickname for a Spaniard.

chapitel [ča·pi·tél] *m.* spire, steeple; capital (*of a column*).

chapotear [ča·po·te·ár] *v.* to splash, paddle in the water.

chapoteo [ča·po·té·o] *m.* splash.

chapucear [ča·pu·se·ár] *v.* to fumble; to botch, bungle, do or make clumsily; *Am.* to deceive, trick.

chapulín [ča·pu·lín] *m. Mex., C.A.* grasshopper.

chapurrar [ča·pu·rrár] *v.* to speak (*a language*) brokenly; to mix (*drinks*).

chapuz [ča·pús] *m.* dive, duck, ducking.

chapuza [ča·pú·sa] *f.* botch, clumsy piece of work; *Am.* foul trick, fraud.

chapuzar[9] [ča·pu·sár] *v.* to duck; to dive.

chaqueta [ča·ké·ta] *f.* jacket; **chaquetón** [ča·ke·tón] *m.* long jacket, coat.

charamusca [ča·ra·mús·ka] *f. Mex.* twisted candy stick or cane; *Col., Ven.* brushwood, firewood; *C.A.* hubbub, uproar.

charamusquero [ča·ra·mus·ké·ro] *m. Am.* candystick maker or vendor.

charca [čár·ka] *f.* pond.

charco [čár·ko] *m.* puddle, pool; **pasar el** — to cross the pond, cross the ocean.

charla [čár·la] *f.* chat, chatter, prattle.

charladuría [čar·la·đu·rí·a] *f.* chatter, gossip.

charlar [čar·lár] *v.* to chat, chatter, prate.

charlatán [čar·la·tán] *m.* chatterer, prater; gossiper; charlatan, quack.

charol [ča·ról] *m.* varnish; patent leather; *Col.* tray; **charola** *f. Mex.* tray.

charolar [ča·ro·lár] *v.* to varnish, polish.

charqui [čár·ki] *m.* jerky, jerked beef.

charro [čá·rro] *m. Spain* a villager of Salamanca province; *Mex.* Mexican horseman of special costume and cultural status.

charrúa [ča·rrú·a] *m. & f. Am.* Charruan Indian (*Indian of Uruguay*).

chascarrillo [čas·ka·rrí·yo] *m.* joke, funny story.

chasco [čás·ko] *m.* joke, prank; surprise; disillusionment, disappointment; **llevarse** — to be disappointed, surprised or fooled; *adj. S.A.* thick, curly (*hair*); *Am.* ruffled (*plumage*).

chasquear [čas·ke·ár] *v.* to play a trick on; to disappoint; to crack (*a whip*); to smack (*the lips*); to click (*the tongue*); to crack, snap; *Col., Ven.* to chatter (*said of the teeth*); *Am.* to munch (*food*); **-se** to be disappointed or disillusioned; to be tricked or fooled.

chasqui [čás·ki] *m. Andes, Ríopl.* courier, messenger.

chasquido [čas·kí·đo] *m.* crack of a whip; crackle; smack (*of the lips*); click (*of the tongue*).

chata [čá·ta] *f.* bedpan; scow, barge, flat-bottomed boat; *Ríopl.* platform wagon, platform car, flatcar, **chatita** [ča·tí·ta] *f. Mex.* "honey", "cutie", "funny face".

chato [čá·to] *adj.* snub-nosed, flat-nosed; flat; flattened; squatty; *Mex.* **quedarse uno** — to be left flat or in the lurch; to be disappointed.

chaval [ča·bál] *m.* lad; young man.

chayote [ča·yó·te] *m. Mex.* vegetable pear (*a tropical fruit growing on a vine*); *Mex., Ven., C.A.* dunce, silly fool.

che [če] *interj. Ríopl.* word used to attract attention among intimates; say! listen! hey!; nickname for citizens of Argentina; *Bol.* buddy, pal.

cheque [čé·ke] *m.* check, bank check.

chequera [če·ké·ra] *f.* check book.

chica [čí·ka] *f.* little girl; girl, maid, servant.

chicle [čí·kle] *m. Am.* chicle; *Mex.* chewing gum.

chico [čí·ko] *adj.* small, little; *m.* child, boy; *Col.* each game of billiards; *Mex.* = **chicozapote** [či·ko·sa·pó·te] (*tropical fruit and tree from which chicle is extracted*).

chicote [či·kó·te] *m.* cigar; piece of rope; *Am.* whip; *Col., Ven.* cigar butt.

chicotear [či·ko·te·ár] *v. Ríopl., Col., Peru* to lash, whip, flog; *Ven.* to fight, quarrel, *Col.* to kill.

chicoteo [či·ko·té·o] *m. Ríopl.* whipping; *Am.* shooting, killing; *Am.* crackling, rattling (*as of machine guns*); *Am.* quarreling.

chicha [čí·ča] *f. Peru, Col., Ch., Ríopl., C.A.* chicha (*a popular alcoholic beverage*); *Peru* thick-soled shoe; **no ser ni** — **ni limonada** to be worth nothing, be neither fish nor fowl.

chícharo [čí·ča·rro] *m. Mex.* pea; *Col.* bad cigar; *Mex.* apprentice.

chicharra [či·čá·rra] *f.* cicada, locust; talkative person; *Mex.* person with a shrill voice; *Am.* rickety, squeaky car; *Ch.* harsh-sounding musical instrument or bell; *C.A., Mex., Cuba* piece of fried pork skin.

chicharrón [či·ča·rrón] *m.* crackling, crisp piece of fried pork skin; burned piece of meat; sunburnt person; *Am.* dried-up, wrinkled person; *Mex.* bootlicker, flatterer.

chiche [čí·če] *m. Mex., C.A.* breast, teat; wet nurse.

chichón [či·čón] *m.* bump, lump; *Am.* joker, jester; **chichona** [či·čó·na] *adj. Mex., C.A.* large-breasted; "stacked".

chiflado [či·flá·đo] *adj.* "cracked", nuts, crazy; *p.p. of* **chiflar.**

chifladura [či·fla·đú·ra] *f.* craziness, mania; mockery, jest.

chiflar [či·flár] *v.* to whistle; to hiss; *Mex.* to sing (*said of birds*); **-se** to lose one's head; to become unbalanced, crazy.

chiflido [či·flí·đo] *m.* whistle; hiss; *Am.* **en un** — in a jiffy, in a second.

chile [čí·le] *m.* chili, red pepper.

chileno [či·lé·no] *adj. & m.* Chilean.

chillante [či·yán·te] *adj.* flashy, bright, showy, loud; shrieking.

chillar [či·yár] *v.* to shriek, scream; to hiss; *Am.* to shout, protest, moan; *Mex.* to "squeal", turn informer; *Ríopl., Ven., C.A., P.R.* **no** — not to say a word; *Mex.* **-se** to be piqued, offended.

chillido [či·yí·đo] *m.* shriek, scream.

chillón [či·yón] *adj.* shrieking, screaming; shrill; loud, gaudy; *Col., Andes* whining, discontented; *Ríopl.* touchy.

chimenea [či·me·né·a] *f.* chimney; fireplace, hearth.

china [čí·na] *f.* (*de la China*) Chinese woman; China silk or cotton; porcelain; (*piedra*) pebble; marble; *Andes, Ch., Ríopl., Col.* girl, young woman (*usually half-breed or Indian*); *S.A.* servant girl; *P.R.* sweet orange; *Col.* spinning top; **chinita** [či·ní·ta] *f. Am.* little Indian girl; darling.

chinche [čin·če] *f.* bedbug; thumbtack; tiresome person, bore; *Col., Ven., Ríopl.* touchy or irritable person; *Am.* plump, squatty person.

chinchilla [čin·čí·ya] *f.* chinchilla.

chinchorro [čin·čó·rro] *m. Ven., Col.* hammock.

chingar [čiŋ·gár] *v. S.A.* to frustrate; to fail; *Mex.* to copulate.

chino [čí·no] *adj.* Chinese; *Mex.* curly; *m. Ríopl.* Chinese; Chinaman; *C.R.* pig; *Ríopl.* half-breed (*Negro and Indian, white and Indian*); *Am.* Indian, *Col.* house servant; *Am.* coarse, rough, ugly person, *Col.* straight, coarse hair.

chiquero [čí·ké·ro] *m.* pigsty, pigpen; pen for bulls; goat shelter.

chiquilín [čí·ki·lín] *m. Mex., C.A.* tot, little boy; **chiquilina** [čí·ki·lí·na] *f. Am.* little girl.

chiquito [čí·kí·to] *adj.* tiny, very small; *m.* tiny tot, tiny child; **chiquitico** [čí·ki·tí·ko] *adj.* tiny.

chiripa [čí·rí·pa] *f.* stroke of good luck.

chiripá [čí·rí·pá] *m. Ríopl.* loose riding trousers (*square of cloth draped from the waist and between the legs*).

chirola [čí·ró·la] *f. Mex., Ven., Ríopl.* ''jug'', jail; coin of low value.

chirona [čí·ró·na] *f.* ''jug'', jail.

chirriado [čí·rrjá·do] *adj. Col.* attractive; lively.

chirriar[17] [čí·rrjár] *v.* to squeak, creak; to sizzle; to chirp; to sing out of tune; *Col.* to go on a spree.

chirrido [čí·rrí·do] *m.* creak, squeak; chirp; squeaking, creaking; chirping.

chisguete [čiz·ǵé·te] *m.* squirt.

chisme [číz·me] *m.* gossip, piece of gossip; trifle, trinket, knickknack, gadget.

chismear [čiz·me·rí·a] *v.* to gossip; to tattle.

chismería [čiz·me·rí·a] *f.* gossiping, talebearing.

chismero [čiz·mé·ro] *adj.* gossiping; *m.* gossip.

chismoso [čiz·mó·so] *adj.* gossiping; *m.* gossip, talebearer, tattletale.

chispa [čís·pa] *f.* spark; small diamond; wit; *Col.* false rumor, lie; *Am.* two-wheeled cart; *Mex.* brazen, shameless woman; *Am.* **da** — it clicks, works, functions; *Am.* **ponerse** — to get drunk.

chispeante [čis·pe·án·te] *adj.* sparkling.

chispear [čis·pe·ár] *v.* to spark; to sparkle; to twinkle; to drizzle.

chisporrotear [čis·po·rro·te·ár] *v.* to sputter, throw off sparks.

chiste [čís·te] *m.* joke, jest; **dar en el** — to guess right, hit the nail on the head.

chistera [čis·té·ra] *f.* top hat; fish basket.

chistoso [čis·tó·so] *adj.* funny, amusing, humorous.

¡chito! [čí·to] **¡chitón!** [čí·tón] *interj.* hush!

chiva [čí·ba] *f.* female goat; *Am.* goatee; *Pan., Col.* flivver, small bus; **chivo** *m.* he-goat; *Am.* fit of anger; *Am.* insulting remark; *C.R.* **estar hecho un** — to be very angry; *adj. Am.* angry; **chivato** [čí·bá·to] *m. Cuba* informer, squealer.

chocante [čo·kán·te] *adj.* striking, surprising; shocking; disgusting; *Col., Andes* tiresome, annoying, impertinent.

chocar[6] [čo·kár] *v.* to bump, collide, clash; to fight; to shock, surprise, disgust; **me choca ese hombre** I loathe that man.

chocarrear [čo·ka·rre·ár] *v.* to tell coarse jokes; to clown.

chocarrería [čo·ka·rre·rí·a] *f.* coarse joke; **chocarrero** [čo·ka·rré·ro] *adj.* coarse, vulgar; clownish.

choclo [čó·klo] *m.* overshoe; clog; *Mex.* low shoe or slipper; *Andes, Col., Ch., Ríopl.* ear of corn; *Ven.* corn stew, *Ch.* spike, ear of wheat.

chocolate [čo·ko·lá·te] *m.* chocolate.

chochear [čo·če·ár] *v.* to be in one's dotage, act senile.

chochera [čo·čé·ra], **chochez** [čo·čés] *f.* senility, dotage; **chocheras** [čo·čé·ras], **chocheces** [čo·čé·ses] senile actions or habits.

chocho [čó·čo] *adj.* doting; *m.* childish old man.

chófer [čó·fer], [čo·fér] *m.* chauffeur.

cholo [čó·lo] *m. Andes, Ríopl., Ch.* half-breed; *Am.* half-civilized Indian; *adj. Mex., Perú* coarse, rude; *C.R.* dark-skinned; *Ch.* black (*dog*); member of U.S. Southwest anti-social, counter-prestige culture.

chopo [čó·po] *m.* black poplar; *adj. Am.* stupid.

choque [čó·ke] *m.* collision, bump; shock; clash, conflict; dispute.

chorizo [čo·rí·so] *m.* sausage; *Am.* string of things; *Am.* fool.

chorrazo [čo·rrá·so] *m.* spurt, large stream or jet.

chorrear [čo·rre·ár] *v.* to drip; to spout.

chorro [čó·rro] *m.* spurt, jet; stream, flow; *Arg.* strand of a whip; *Col.* river rapids.

choteador [čo·te·a·dór] *m. Carib.* joker, jester.

chotear [čo·te·ár] *v. Cuba* to make fun of, jeer, jest, mock, kid; *Mex., C.A.* to idle, fool around; *Col.* to pamper.

choteo [čo·té·o] *m. Cuba* joking, jeering, kidding.

choza [čó·sa] *f.* hut, cabin.

chubasco [ču·bás·ko] *m.* squall, sudden shower; **aguantar el** — to weather the storm.

chuchería [ču·če·rí·a] *f.* trifle, trinket; knick-knack; tidbit.

chueco [čwé·ko] *adj. Mex.* crooked, bent; *Col.* crook-legged, bow-legged, knock-kneed; *Am.* worn-out, dejected; *Mex.* disgusted, annoyed; *Mex.* **commerciar en** — to trade in stolen goods.

chuleta [ču·lé·ta] *f.* cutlet, chop; blow, slap.

chulo [čú·lo] *m.* elegant person; effeminate man; clownish fellow; bullfighter's assistant; *Col.* buzzard; *Mex.* coarse, thick brush; *adj. C.A., Col., Mex.* goodlooking, pretty.

chumpipe [čum·pí·pe] *m. C.A.* turkey; also **chompipe**.

chupada [ču·pá·da] *f.* sucking; suction; suck, sip; *Mex., C.A., Ven., Andes* puff from a cigarette; *Ríopl.* big swallow of liquor.

chupador [ču·pa·dór] *m.* sucker; teething ring; *Ríopl.* toper, heavy drinker; *Am.* smoker.

chupaflor [ču·pa·flór], **chuparrosa** [ču·pa·rró·sa] *m. Am.* hummingbird.

chupar [ču·pár] *v.* to suck; to sip; to absorb, take in; *Am.* to smoke; *C.A., Ríopl., Andes* to drink, get drunk; **-se** to shrivel up.

churrasco [ču·rrás·ko] *m. Ríopl., Andes* roasted meat; *Ríopl., Andes* barbecued meat; *Ríopl., Andes* large piece of meat for barbecuing.

churrasquear [ču·rras·ke·ár] *v. Ríopl., Andes* to barbecue, roast over coals; *Ríopl., Andes* to prepare (*meat*) for barbecuing; *Ríopl., Andes* to eat barbecued meat.

churrasquito [ču·rras·kí·to] *m.* small piece of roast.

churrigueresco [ču·rri·ge·rés·ko] *adj.* baroque, ornate (*architecture*).

churro [čú·rro] *adj.* coarse; *m. Spain* doughnut-like fritter.

chuscada [čus·ká·da] *f.* jest, joke.

chusco [čús·ko] *adj.* funny, witty; ridiculous; *Peru* **perro** — mongrel dog.

chusma [čúz·ma] *f.* rabble, mob.

chuzo [čú·so] *m.* pike or cane carried by the watchman (*sereno*).

D:d

dable [dá·ble] *adj.* feasible, possible.
daca [dá·ka] = **de acá**
dadiva [dá·di·ba] *f.* gift.
dadivoso [da·di·bó·so] *adj.* liberal, generous.
dado [dá·do] *m.* die; **-s** dice.
dador [da·dór] *m.* giver.
daga [dá·ga] *f.* dagger.
dama [dá·ma] *f.* lady; **jugar a las -s** to play checkers.
damajuana [da·ma·xwá·na] *f.* demijohn.
damasquinado [da·mas·ki·ná·do] *m.* damascene (*incrustation of gold in steel*).
damisela [da·mi·sé·la] *f.* damsel, girl.
danza [dán·sa] *f.* dance.
danzante [dan·sán·te] *m.* & *f.* dancer.
danzar[9] [dan·sár] *v.* to dance.
danzarina [dan·sa·rí·na] *f.* dancer.
dañar [da·ñár] *v.* to harm, hurt, damage; **-se** to spoil, rot; to get hurt; to get damaged.
dañino [da·ñí·no] *adj.* harmful; destructive.
daño [dá·ño] *m.* damage, harm, loss.
dañoso [da·ñó·so] *adj.* harmful.
dar[26] [dar] *v. irr.* (*hacer don*) to give, confer; (*golpear*) to strike, hit; (*emitir*) give off, emit; — **a luz** to give birth to; to publish; — **con** to encounter, find; — **de alta** to discharge, release from the hospital; — **de comer** to feed; — **de si** to give, stretch; — **en** to hit upon; to persist in; — **largas a un asunto** to prolong or postpone a matter; *C.A., Ven., Col.* — **cuero** (**guasca, puños**) to beat, thrash, lash; **lo misma da** it makes no difference; **-se** to give up; **dárselas de** to boast of.
dardo [dár·do] *m.* dart, arrow.
dares y tomares [dá·res·i·to·má·res] *m. pl.* give-and-take, dispute; dealings.
dársena [dár·se·na] *f.* dock, wharf.
datar [da·tár] *v.* to date; — **de** to date from.
dátil [dá·til] *m.* date (*fruit of the date palm*).
dato [dá·to] *m.* datum, fact; **-s** data.
de [de] *prep.* of, from; about, concerning; in (*after a superlative*); if (*before inf.*); — **no llegar** if he does not arrive; **el** — **la gorra azul** the one with the blue cap; **el mejor** — **América** the best in America; **más** — **lo que dice** more than he says.
debajo [de·bá·xo] *adv.* under, underneath; — **de** *prep.* under.
debate [de·bá·te] *m.* debate; dispute, quarrel.
debatir [de·ba·tír] *v.* to debate, argue, discuss; to fight; **-se** to struggle.
debe [dé·be] *m.* debit.
debelar [de·be·lár] *v.* to subdue, defeat.
deber [de·bér] *v.* to owe; to have to (must, should, ought); **debe de ser** it must be, probably is; **¡me la debes!** I have an account to settle with you!
deber [de·bér] *m.* duty, obligation; debt; debit, debit side (*in bookkeeping*).
debido [de·bí·do] *adj.* due, owing; just, appropriate.
débil [dé·bil] *adj.* weak, feeble.
debilidad [de·bi·li·dád] *f.* debility, weakness.
debilitación [de·bi·li·ta·sjón] *f.* **debilitamiento** [de·bi·li·ta·mjén·to] *m.* weakening; weakness.
debilitar [de·bi·li·tár] *v.* to weaken.
débito [dé·bi·to] *m.* debt; debit.
debutar [de·bu·tár] *v.* to make a debut, make a first public appearance.
década [dé·ka·da] *f.* decade, ten years; series of ten.
decadencia [de·ka·dén·sja] *f.* decadence, decline, falling off.
decaer[23] [de·ka·ér] *v. irr.* to decay, decline, wither,

fade; to fall to leeward.
dacaimiento [de·kaj·mjén·to] *m.* decline, decay; dejection; weakness.
decano [de·ká·no] *m.* dean; senior member of a group.
decantado [de·kan·tá·do] *p.p.* & *adj.* much talked about; overrated.
decapitar [de·ka·pi·tár] *v.* to behead.
decencia [de·sén·sja] *f.* decency; **decente** [de·sén·te] *adj.* decent; respectable; fair.
decenio [de·sé·njo] *m.* decade.
decepción [de·sep·sjón] *f.* disillusion, disappointment.
decepcionante [de·sep·sjo·nán·te] *adj.* disappointing.
decepcionar [de·sep·sjo·nár] *v.* to disillusion, disappoint.
decibel [de·si·bél] *m.* decibel (*unit for the measurement of the intensity of sound*).
decidir [de·si·dír] *v.* to decide, resolve; **-se a** to make up one's mind to; to decide to.
décima [dé·si·ma] *f.* tenth; tithe; stanza of ten octosyllabic lines.
décimo [dé·si·mo] *adj.* tenth.
decir[27] [de·sír] *v. irr.* to say; to tell; to speak; **es** — that is; **querer** — to mean, signify.
decisión [de·si·sjón] *f.* decision.
decisivo [de·si·sí·bo] *adj.* decisive, final.
declamar [de·kla·már] *v.* to declaim, recite.
declaración [de·kla·ra·sjón] *f.* declaration; statement; deposition, testimony.
declarar [de·kla·rár] *v.* to declare, state, affirm; to testify; **-se** to propose, declare one's love; to give one's views or opinion.
declinar [de·kli·nár] *v.* to decline; to go down; to lose vigor, decay; to bend down.
declive [de·klí·be] *m.* declivity, slope.
decoración [de·ko·ra·sjón] *f.* decoration, ornament; stage setting.
decorar [de·ko·rár] *v.* to decorate, adorn.
decorativo [de·ko·ra·tí·bo] *adj.* decorative, ornamental.
decoro [de·kó·ro] *m.* decorum, propriety, dignity; honor.
decoroso [de·ko·ró·so] *adj.* decorous, becoming, proper, decent.
decrépito [de·kré·pi·to] *adj.* decrepit, old, feeble.
decretar [de·kre·tár] *v.* to decree.
decreto [de·kré·to] *m.* decree; decision, order.
dechado [de·čá·do] *m.* model, pattern, example.
dedal [de·dál] *m.* thimble.
dedicar[6] [de·di·kár] *v.* to dedicate; to devote; **-se** to apply oneself.
dedicatoria [de·di·ka·tó·rja] *f.* dedication, inscription.
dedo [dé·do] *m.* (*de la mano*) finger; (*del pie*) toe; — **del corazón** middle finger; — **meñique** little finger; — **pulgar** thumb; **no mamarse el** — not to be easily fooled; **dedillo** *m.* small finger; **saber al dedillo** to know perfectly, know by heart.
deducción [de·duk·sjón] *f.* deduction; inference.
deducir[25] [de·du·sír] *v. irr.* to deduce, conclude; to deduct.
defecar[6] [de·fe·kár] *v. irr.* to defecate.
defecto [de·fék·to] *m.* defect, fault.
defectuoso [de·fek·twó·so] *adj.* defective, faulty.
defender[1] [de·fen·dér] *v. irr.* to defend.
defensa [de·fén·sa] *f.* defense; *Mex.* automobile bumper.
defensivo [de·fen·sí·bo] *adj.* defensive; *m.* defense, safeguard; **defensiva** [de·fen·si·ba] *f.* defensive.
defensor [de·fen·sór] *m.* defender.
deficiencia [de·fi·sjén·sja] *f.* deficiency; **deficiente** [de·fi·sjén·te] *adj.* deficient.

déficit [dé·fi·sit] *m.* deficit, shortage.
definición [de·fi·ni·sjón] *f.* definition.
definido [de·fi·ní·do] *adj.* definite; *p.p.* of **definir.**
definir [de·fi·nír] *v.* to define, explain; to determine.
definitivo [de·fi·ni·tí·bo] *adj.* definitive, conclusive, final; **en definitiva** in short, in conclusion; definitely.
deformación [de·for·ma·sjón] *f.* deformation, deformity.
deformar [de·for·már] *v.* to deform; **-se** to become deformed; to lose its shape or form.
deforme [de·fór·me] *adj.* deformed; ugly.
deformidad [de·for·mi·dád] *f.* deformity.
defraudar [de·fraw·dár] *v.* to defraud, cheat, rob of.
defunción [de·fun·sjón] *f.* death, decease.
degenerado [de·xe·ne·rá·do] *adj. & m.* degenerate.
degenerar [de·xe·ne·rár] *v.* to degenerate.
deglución [de·glu·sjón] *f.* swallowing.
deglutir [de·glu·tír] *v.* to swallow.
degollar[2] [de·go·yár] *v. irr* to behead; to slash the throat; to cut (*a dress*) low in the neck.
degradar [de·gra·dár] *v.* to degrade; to debase.
degüello [de·gwé·yo] *m.* beheading; throat-slashing.
dehesa [de·é·sa] *f.* pasture, grazing ground.
deidad [dej·dád] *f.* deity.
dejadez [de·xa·dés] *f.* lassitude, languor, listlessness; self-neglect, slovenliness.
dejado [de·xá·do] *adj.* indolent, listless; slovenly.
dejar [de·xár] *v.* (*abandonar*) to leave; to quit; to abandon; to omit; (*permitir*) to permit, let; (*soltar*) to let go; **— de** to stop, cease; **— caer** to drop; *Am.* **no -se** not to be an easy mark, not to let others pick on one.
dejo [dé·xo] *m.* (*sabor*) aftertaste; slight taste; (*acento*) slight accent, peculiar inflection.
del [del] = **de + el** of the.
delaminación [de·la·mi·na·sjón] *f.* delamination.
delantal [de·lan·tál] *m.* apron.
delante [de·lán·te] *adv.* before, in front; **— de** *prep.* in front of.
delantera [de·lan·té·ra] *f.* lead, forepart, front.
delantero [de·lan·té·ro] *adj.* front, foremost, first.
delatar [de·la·tár] *v.* to denounce, accuse, inform against.
delator [de·la·tór] *m.* accuser, informer.
delegación [de·le·ga·sjón] *f.* delegation.
delegado [de·le·gá·do] *m.* delegate.
delegar[7] [de·le·gár] *v.* to delegate.
deleitable [de·lej·tá·ble] *adj.* delightful, enjoyable.
deleitar [de·lej·tár] *v.* to delight, please.
deleite [de·léj·te] *m.* delight, joy, pleasure.
deleitoso [de·lej·tó·so] *adj.* delightful.
deletrear [de·le·tre·ár] *v.* to spell.
deleznable [de·lez·ná·ble] *adj.* perishable; brittle.
delfín [del·fín] *m.* dolphin; dauphin.
delgadez [del·ga·dés] *f.* thinness; slimness; fineness.
delgado [del·gá·do] *adj.* thin, slender, slim.
deliberado [de·li·be·rá·do] *adj.* deliberate; *p.p.* of **deliberar.**
deliberar [de·li·be·rár] *v.* to deliberate, consider, ponder.
delicadeza [de·li·ka·dé·sa] *f.* fineness; delicacy; softness, exquisiteness.
delicado [de·li·ká·do] *adj.* delicate; weak, frail; exquisite, dainty; tender.
delicia [de·lí·sja] *f.* delight.
delicioso [de·li·sjó·so] *adj.* delicious, delightful.
delincuente [de·liŋ·kwén·te] *adj., m. & f.* deliquent.
delineación [de·li·ne·a·sjón] *f.*, **delineamiento** [de·li·ne·a·mjén·to] *m.* delineation, design, outline, drawing; portrayal.

delinear [de·li·ne·ár] *v.* to delineate, sketch, outline.
delirante [de·li·rán·te] *adj.* delirious, raving.
delirar [de·li·rár] *v.* to be delirious; to rave, talk wildly or foolishly.
delirio [de·lí·rjo] *m.* delirium, temporary madness; wild excitement; foolishness.
delito [de·lí·to] *m.* crime; misdemeanor.
demacrado [de·ma·krá·do] *adj.* scrawny, emaciated, thin.
demanda [de·mán·da] *f.* demand; petition; question; claim; complaint; lawsuit.
demandado [de·man·dá·do] *m.* defendant; *p.p.* of **demandar.**
demandante [de·man·dán·te] *m. & f.* plaintiff.
demandar [de·man·dár] *v.* to demand; to petition; to sue, file a suit; to indict.
demás [de·más] *indef. adj. & pron.:* **los** — the rest; the others; **las** — **personas** the other people; **lo** — the rest; **por** — useless; uselessly; **por lo** — as to the rest; moreover.
demasía [de·ma·sí·a] *f.* excess; boldness, insolence; offense, outrage; **en** — excessively.
demasiado [de·ma·sjá·do] *adv.* too much, excessively; too; *adj.* too much, excessive.
demente [de·mén·te] *adj.* demented, insane, crazy.
democracia [de·mo·krá·sja] *f.* democracy; **demócrata** [de·mó·kra·ta] *m. & f.* democrat; **democrático** [de·mo·krá·ti·ko] *adj.* democratic.
demográfico [de·mo·grá·fi·ko] *adj.* demographic.
demoler[2] [de·mo·lér] *v. irr.* to demolish, tear down.
demonio [de·mó·njo] *m.* demon, devil; evil spirit.
demontre [de·món·tre] *m.* devil; **¡ — !** the deuce!
demora [de·mó·ra] *f.* delay.
demorar [de·mo·rár] *v.* to delay; to retard; **-se** to linger; to be delayed.
demostración [de·mos·tra·sjón] *f.* demonstration; proof, explanation.
demostrar[2] [de·mos·trár] *v. irr.* to demonstrate, show, prove, explain.
demostrativo [de·mos·tra·tí·bo] *adj.* demonstrative.
demovilizar[9] [de·mo·bi·li·sár] *v.* to demobilize.
demudar [de·mu·dár] *v.* to change, alter; to disguise; **-se** to change color or one's facial expression; to turn pale.
dengoso [deŋ·gó·so], **denguero** [deŋ·gé·ro] *adj.* affected; finicky.
dengue [déŋ·ge] *m.* primness; coyness, affectation; dengue, breakbone fever; *Arg.* marigold; *Ch.* zigzag; *Am.* swagger **hacer -s** to act coy, make grimaces.
denigrar [de·ni·grár] *v.* to blacken, defame, revile, insult.
denodado [de·no·dá·do] *adj.* dauntless, daring.
denominación [de·no·mi·na·sjón] *f.* denomination, name, title, designation.
denominar [de·no·mi·nár] *v.* to name, call, entitle.
denostar[2] *v. irr.* to insult, outrage, revile.
denotar [de·no·tár] *v.* to denote, indicate, mean.
densidad [den·si·dád] *f.* density; (*computadora*) — **doble** double density; — **simple** single density.
denso [dén·so] *adj.* dense, compact; thick.
dentado [den·tá·do] *adj.* toothed, notched; pinking (sewing).
dentadura [den·ta·dú·ra] *f.* set of teeth.
dentar[1] [den·tár] *v. irr.* to tooth, furnish (*a saw*) with teeth; to indent; to cut teeth, grow teeth (*referring to a child*).
dentellada [den·te·yá·da] *f.* bite; tooth mark; **a -s** with big bites.
dentición [den·ti·sjón] *f.* teething.
dentífrico [den·tí·fri·ko] *m.* dentrifice, tooth cleanser;

pasta dentífrica toothpaste; **polvos dentífricos** toothpowder.

dentista [den·tís·ta] *m.* dentist.

dentro [dén·tro] *adv.* inside, within; — **de** *prep.* inside of; **por** — on the inside.

denuedo [de·nwé·ďo] *m.* spirit, courage, daring.

denuesto [de·nwés·to] *m.* affront, insult.

denuncia [de·nún·sja] *f.* denunciation, condemnation, accusation; miner's claim.

denunciar [de·nun·sjár] *v.* to denounce, accuse; to proclaim, advise, give notice; to claim (*a mine*).

deparar [de·pa·rár] *v.* to furnish, offer, supply.

departamento [de·par·ta·mén·to] *m.* department; compartment; apartment.

departir [de·par·tír] *v.* to talk, converse.

dependencia [de·pen·dén·sja] *f.* dependence; dependency; branch office.

depender [de·pen·dér] *v.* to depend, rely (on).

dependiente [de·pen·djén·te] *m.* clerk; dependent, subordinate; *adj.* dependent.

depilar [de·pi·lár] *v.* to depilate.

depilatorio [de·pi·la·tó·rjo] *adj. & m.* depilatory.

deplorar [de·plo·rár] *v.* to deplore, lament, regret.

deponer[40] [de·po·nér] *v. irr.* to set aside; to depose, remove (*an official*); to testify, declare; to have a bowel movement; *Mex., C.A.* to vomit.

deportar [de·por·tár] *v.* to deport, banish.

deporte [de·pór·te] *m.* sport; pastime, recreation.

deportista [de·por·tís·ta] *m.* sportsman; *f.* sportswoman.

deportivo [de·por·ti·ḃo] *adj.* sport, sports (*used as an adj.*); **copa deportiva** loving cup.

deposición [de·po·si·sjón] *f.* declaration, assertion; testimony; dismissal, removal (*from office or power*); bowel movement.

depositar [de·po·si·tár] *v.* to deposit; to deliver, intrust.

depositario [de·po·si·tá·rjo] *m.* receiver, trustee.

depósito [de·pó·si·to] *m.* deposit; storage; warehouse; — **de agua** reservoir.

depravado [de·pra·ḃá·ďo] *adj.* depraved, corrupt, degenerate.

depravar [de·pra·ḃár] *v.* to corrupt, pervert, contaminate.

depreciar [de·pre·sjár] *v.* to depreciate, lessen the value of.

depresión [de·pre·sjón] *f.* depression; dip, sag.

deprimente [de·pri·mén·te] *adj.* depressing.

deprimir [de·pri·mír] *v.* to depress; to press down; to humiliate, belittle.

depuesto [de·pwés·to] *p.p. of* **deponer.**

depuración [de·pu·ra·sjón] *f.* (*computadora*) debugging.

depurar [de·pu·rár] *v.* to purify.

derecha [de·ré·ča] *f.* right hand; right side; right wing (*in politics*); **a la** — to the right; **derechazo** [de·re·čá·so] *m.* a blow with the right hand, a right (*boxing*).

derechista [de·re·čís·ta] *adj. & m. f.* rightist.

derecho [de·ré·čo] *adj.* right; straight; *m.* law; duty, tax; fee; — **mercantil** business law.

derechura [de·re·čú·ra] *f.* straightness.

deriva [de·rí·ḃa] *f.* drift (*of a boat or plane*); **irse** (*or* **andar**) **a la** — to drift, be drifting.

derivar [de·ri·ḃár] *v.* to derive; to come (from).

dermatólogo [der·ma·tó·lo·go] *m.* dermatologist.

derogar[7] [de·ro·gár] *v.* to revoke, repeal, abolish.

derramamiento [de·rra·ma·mjén·to] *m.* spill, spilling, shedding; overflow; scattering; — **de sangre** bloodshed.

derramar [de·rra·már] *v.* to spill; to spread, scatter;

to shed.

derrame [de·rrá·me] *m.* spill, spilling, shedding; overflow; discharge (*of secretion, blood, etc.*); slope; — **cerebral** stroke.

derredor [de·rre·ďór] *m.* circuit; contour; **al** — around; **en** — around.

derrengado [de·rreŋ·gá·ďo] *p.p. & adj.* lame, crippled; dislocated (*said of hip or spine*).

derrengar[1, 7] [de·rreŋ·gár] *v. irr.* to dislocate or sprain (*hip or spine*); to cripple; to bend.

derretimiento [de·rre·ti·mjén·to] *m.* thaw, thawing, melting.

derretir[5] [de·rre·tír] *v. irr.* to melt, dissolve; **-se** to be consumed; to melt.

derribar [de·rri·ḃár] *v.* to demolish, knock down, fell; to overthrow; **-se** to lie down, throw oneself down.

derrocamiento [de·rro·ka·mjén·to] *m.* overthrow.

derrocar[6] [de·rro·kár] *v.* to fling down; to fell; to overthrow.

derrochador [de·rro·ča·ďór] *m.* squanderer, spendthrift; *adj.* wasteful, extravagant.

derrochar [de·rro·čár] *v.* to waste; to squander.

derroche [de·rró·če] *m.* waste; dissipation, lavish spending.

derrota [de·rró·ta] *f.* rout, defeat; ship's route or course.

derrotar [de·rro·tár] *v.* to defeat; to squander; to destroy, ruin; to lose or shift its course (*said of a ship*).

derrotero [de·rro·té·ro] *m.* course, direction; ship's course; book of marine charts.

derrumbadero [de·rrum·ba·ďé·ro] *m.* precipice.

derrumbamiento [de·rrum·ba·mjén·to] *m.* landslide; collapse.

derrumbar [de·rrum·bár] *v.* to fling down, *Mex.* to knock down; *Mex.* to go down in a hurry; **-se** to crumble away; to topple over; *Col., Ven.* to dwindle (*as a business*).

derrumbe [de·rrúm·be] *m.* landslide; collapse.

desabotonar [de·sa·ḃo·to·nár] *v.* to unbutton.

desabrido [de·sa·ḃrí·ďo] *adj.* tasteless, insipid; harsh; sour.

desabrigar[7] [de·sa·ḃri·gár] *v.* to uncover; **-se** to uncover oneself.

desabrimiento [de·sa·ḃri·mjén·to] *m.* tastelessness; harshness; sourness.

desabrochar [de·sa·ḃro·čár] *v.* to unfasten, unbutton, unclasp; **-se** to unbutton oneself, unfasten one's clothes.

desacato [de·sa·ká·to] *m.* irreverence, disrespect; profanation.

desacierto [de·sa·sjér·to] *m.* mistake, error.

desacoplar [de·sa·ko·plár] *v.* to uncouple, disconnect.

desacostumbrado [de·sa·kos·tum·brá·ďo] *adj.* unaccustomed; unusual; *p.p. of* **desacostumbrar.**

desacostumbrar [de·sa·kos·tum·brár] *v.* to disaccustom, rid of a habit; **-se** to become unaccustomed; to lose a custom.

desacreditar [de·sa·kre·ďi·tár] *v.* to discredit; to disgrace.

desacuerdo [de·sa·kwér·ďo] *m.* disagreement; discord; blunder; forgetfulness.

desafiar[17] [de·sa·fjár] *v.* to challenge; to compete; to defy.

desafinado [de·sa·fi·ná·ďo] *adj.* out of tune.

desafinar [de·sa·fi·nár] *v.* to be discordant; to be out of tune; **-se** to get out of tune.

desafío [de·sa·fí·o] *m.* challenge, defiance; duel; contest.

desafortunado [de·sa·for·tu·ná·ďo] *adj.* unfortunate,

unlucky.

desafuero [de·sa·fwé·ro] *m.* violation; outrage, abuse.

desagradable [de·sa·gra·dá·ble] *adj.* disagreeable, unpleasant.

desagradar [de·sa·gra·dár] *v.* to displease.

desagradecido [de·sa·gra·de·sí·do] *adj.* ungrateful.

desagrado [de·sa·grá·do] *m.* displeasure; discontent.

desagraviar [de·sa·gra·bjár] *v.* to make amends; to compensate for a damage or injury; to right a wrong; to apologize; to vindicate.

desagravio [de·sa·grá·bjo] *m.* reparation; compensation for a wrong or injury; vindication; apology.

desaguadero [de·sa·gwa·dé·ro] *m.* drain, drain pipe, water outlet.

desaguar[8] [de·sa·gwár] *v.* to drain, draw off; to flow (into); *Ch.* to wash (*something*) two or more times; *Ch.* to extract the juice from; *Col., Ven., Mex.* to urinate; **-se** to drain.

desagüe [de·sá·gwe] *m.* drainage; drain.

desaguisado [de·sa·gi·sá·do] *m.* outrage, violence, wrong.

desahogado [de·sa·o·gá·do] *p.p. & adj.* (*aliviado*) relieved; (*espacioso*) roomy, spacious; **estar —** to be in easy or comfortable circumstances; to be well-off.

desahogar[7] [de·sa·o·gár] *v.* to relieve from pain or trouble; **-se** to find relief or release; to unbosom oneself, disclose one's feelings.

desahogo [de·sa·ó·go] *m.* relief from pain or trouble; release; ease, comfort, relaxation; freedom, unrestraint.

desairar [de·saj·rár] *v.* to slight, snub, disdain; to rebuff; to disappoint; to neglect.

desaire [de·sáj·re] *m.* rebuff, snub, slight, disdain.

desajustar [de·sa·xus·tár] *v.* to put out of order.

desalentar[1] [de·sa·len·tár] *v. irr.* to put out of breath; to discourage; **-se** to get discouraged.

desaliento [de·sa·ljén·to] *m.* discouragement, dejection.

desaliñado [de·sa·li·ñá·do] *adj.* disheveled, slovenly, unkempt, untidy; disorderly.

desaliño [de·sa·lí·ño] *m.* slovenliness, untidiness; neglect, carelessness; disorder.

desalmado [de·sal·má·do] *adj.* soulless, cruel, inhuman.

desalojar [de·sa·lo·xár] *v.* to dislodge; to evict, expel from a lodging; to vacate.

desamarrar [de·sa·ma·rrár] *v.* to untie, unfasten; to unmoor (*a ship*).

desamparar [de·sam·pa·rár] *v.* to abandon, forsake.

desamparo [de·sam·pá·ro] *m.* desertion, abandonment.

desamueblado [de·sa·mwe·blá·do] *adj.* unfurnished.

desangrar [de·saŋ·grár] *v.* to bleed, draw blood from; to drain; **-se** to bleed, lose blood.

desanimado [de·sa·ni·má·do] *adj.* discouraged; lifeless; dull.

desanimar [de·sa·ni·már] *v.* to dishearten, discourage.

desaparecer[13] [de·sa·pa·re·sér] *v. irr.* to disappear; to hide; **-se** to disappear, vanish.

desaparición [de·sa·pa·ri·sjón] *f.* disappearance.

desapasionado [de·sa·pa·sjo·ná·do] *adj.* dispassionate; free from passion; calm; impartial.

desapego [de·sa·pé·go] *m.* aloofness, indifference, detachment.

desapercibido [de·sa·per·si·bí·do] *adj.* unprepared; unprovided; unnoticed.

desaprobación [de·sa·pro·ba·sjón] *f.* disapproval.

desaprobar[2] [de·sa·pro·bár] *v. irr.* to disapprove.

desarmar [de·sar·már] *v.* to disarm; to dismount, take apart.

desarme [de·sár·me] *m.* disarmament.

desarraigar[7] [de·sa·rraj·gár] *v.* to root out, uproot.

desarreglado [de·sa·rre·glá·do] *p.p. & adj.* disordered; disorderly; slovenly.

desarreglar [de·sa·rre·glár] *v.* to disarrange, disorder, disturb, upset.

desarreglo [de·sa·rré·glo] *m.* disorder, confusion.

desarrollar [de·sa·rro·yár] *v.* to unroll, unfold; to ·develop, explain; **-se** to develop; to unfold.

desarrollo [de·sa·rró·yo] *m.* development.

desaseado [de·sa·se·á·do] *adj.* unkempt, untidy.

desaseo [de·sa·sé·o] *m.* slovenliness, untidiness.

desasir[22] [de·sa·sír] *v. irr.* to loosen, unfasten; **-se** to get loose (from); to let go (of).

desasosiego [de·sa·so·sjé·go] *m.* unrest, uneasiness, restlessness.

desastrado [de·sas·trá·do] *adj.* unfortunate, unhappy; ragged, dirty, untidy.

desastre [de·sás·tre] *m.* disaster.

desastroso [de·sas·tró·so] *adj.* disastrous, unfortunate.

desatar [de·sa·tár] *v.* to untie, loosen; to dissolve; to unravel, clear up; **-se** to let loose, let go; to break loose; **-se en improperios** to let out a string of insults.

desatascar[6] [de·sa·tas·kár] *v. irr.* to extricate, dislodge; to pull out of the mud.

desatención [de·sa·ten·sjón] *f.* inattention, lack of attention; discourtesy.

desatender[1] [de·sa·ten·dér] *v. irr.* to disregard, pay no attention (to); to slight, neglect.

desatento [de·sa·tén·to] *adj.* inattentive; discourteous.

desatinado [de·sa·ti·ná·do] *adj.* senseless; reckless.

desatinar [de·sa·ti·nár] *v.* to act foolishly; to talk nonsense; to blunder; to rave; to lose one's bearings.

desatino [de·sa·tí·no] *m.* blunder, error; folly, nonsense.

desatracar[6] [de·sa·tra·kár] *v.* to push off (*from shore or from another ship*); to cast off, unmoor.

desavenencia [de·sa·be·nén·sja] *f.* disagreement, discord; dispute, misunderstanding.

desayunarse [de·sa·yu·nár·se] *v.* to eat breakfast; **— con la noticia** to hear a piece of news for the first time.

desayuno [de·sa·yú·no] *m.* breakfast.

desazón [de·sa·són] *f.* uneasiness, anxiety; insipidity, flatness, tastelessness; displeasure.

desbandarse [dez·ban·dár·se] *v.* to disband, scatter, disperse; to desert the army or a party.

desbaratar [dez·ba·ra·tár] *v.* to destroy, ruin; to upset, disturb; to disperse, put to flight; to talk nonsense; **-se** to be upset, be in disorder; to fall to pieces.

desbocado [dez·bo·ká·do] *adj.* runaway (*horse*), dashing headlong; foul-mouthed, abusive; broken-mouthed (*jar, pitcher, etc.*).

desbordamiento [dez·bor·da·mjén·to] *m.* overflow, flood.

desbordante [dez·bor·dán·te] *adj.* overflowing; *Am.* frantic.

desbordar [dez·bor·dár] *v.* to overflow, flood; **-se** to spill over; to get overexcited.

desbravar [dez·bra·bár] *v.* to tame; **-se** to calm down.

descabalar [des·ka·ba·lár] *v.* to break (*a given amount, making it thereby incomplete*).

descabello [des·ka·bé·yo] *m.* the act of killing the bull by piercing the brain with the sword.

descabezado [des·ka·be·sá·do] *p.p.* beheaded; *adj.* headless; harebrained, thoughtless.

descabezar[9] [des·ka·be·sár] *v.* to behead; to chop off the head or tip of; — **el sueño** to take a nap; **-se** to break one's head; to rack one's brain.

descaecido [des·ka·e·sí·đo] *adj.* feeble, weak; — **de ánimo** depressed, dejected, despondent.

descaecimiento [des·ka·e·si·mjén·to] *m.* languor, weakness; depression, dejection.

descalabradura [des·ka·la·bra·đú·ra] *f.* blow or wound on the head; scar on the head.

descalabrar [des·ka·la·brár] *v.* to wound on the head; to hurt, injure; to damage; **-se** to suffer a head wound or skull fracture.

descalabro [des·ka·lá·bro] *m.* loss, misfortune.

descalzar[9] [des·kal·sár] *v.* to take off (*someone's*) shoes or (and) stockings; **-se** to take off one's shoes or (and) stockings; to lose a shoe (*said of horses*).

descalzo [des·kál·so] *adj.* barefoot; shoeless.

descaminar [des·ka·mi·nár] *v.* to mislead, lead astray; **-se** to go astray.

descamisado [des·ka·mi·sá·đo] *adj.* shirtless; in rags; *m.* ragamuffin, ragged fellow.

descansar [des·kan·sár] *v.* to rest.

descanso [des·kán·so] *m.* rest; staircase landing.

descarado [des·ka·rá·đo] *adj.* shameless, impudent, brazen.

descarga [des·kár·ga] *f.* discharge; unloading.

descargar[7] [des·kar·gár] *v.* to discharge; to unload.

descargo [des·kár·go] *m.* discharge (*of a duty or obligation*); unloading; relief.

descargue [des·kár·ge] *m.* unloading; discharge.

descarnado [des·kar·ná·đo] *adj.* fleshless, scrawny.

descarnar [des·kar·nár] *v.* to pull the flesh from the bone; to corrode, eat away; **-se** to become thin, emaciated.

descaro [des·ká·ro] *m.* effrontery, shamelessness, impudence, audacity.

descarriar[17] [des·ka·rrjár] *v.* to mislead, lead astray; to separate (*cattle*) from the herd; **-se** to stray; to go astray.

descarrilar [des·ka·rri·lár] *v.* to derail (*cause a train to run off the track*); to wreck (*a train*); **-se** to get or run off the track; to go astray.

descartar [des·kar·tár] *v.* to discard; to put aside.

descascarado [des·kas·ka·rá·đo] *p.p. & adj.* peeled off; chipped off.

descascarar [des·kas·ka·rár] *v.* to shell, hull, husk; to peel; to chip off (*plaster*); *Am.* to defame, discredit; *Col.* to flay; **-se** to chip off, peel off.

descendencia [de·sen·dén·sja] *f.* descent, lineage; descendants, offspring.

descendente [de·sen·dén·te] *adj.* descending, downward.

descender[1] [de·sen·dér] *v. irr.* to descend, go down; to get down; to come (from), originate.

descendiente [de·sen·djén·te] *m. & f.* descendant; *adj.* descending.

descendimiento [de·sen·di·mjén·to] *m.* descent.

descenso [de·sén·so] *m.* descent; fall.

descifrar [de·si·frár] *v.* to decipher, puzzle out, figure out.

descolgar[2, 7] [des·kol·gár] *v. irr.* to unhang, take down; to let down; **-se** to climb down (*a rope, tree, etc.*); to drop in, appear unexpectedly.

descolorar [des·ko·lo·rár] *v.* to discolor; to fade; **-se** to fade, lose its color; to discolor.

descolorido [des·ko·lo·rí·đo] *adj.* pale.

descollar[2] [des·ko·yár] *v. irr.* to excel; to stand out; tower (above).

descomedido [des·ko·me·đí·đo] *adj.* rude, discourteous, impolite; unobliging.

descompletar [des·kom·ple·tár] *v.* to make

incomplete, break (*a unit, sum, set, etc.*)

descomponer[40] [des·kom·po·nér] *v. irr.* (*estorbar*) to upset, disturb; (*echar a perder*) to put out of order; to decompose; **-se** to decompose, rot; to become upset, ill; to get out of order; *Col., Ven., C.A., Carib., Mex.* **se me descompuso el brazo** I dislocated my arm, my arm got out of joint.

descomposición [des·kom·po·si·sjón] *f.* decomposition; decay, corruption; disorder, confusion.

descompuesto [des·kom·pwés·to] *p.p. of* **descomponer**; *adj.* out of order; insolent; brazen; immodest.

descomunal [des·ko·mu·nál] *adj.* colossal, enormous, monstrous.

desconcertante [des·kon·ser·tán·te] *adj.* disconcerting, disturbing, confusing, baffling, embarrassing.

desconcertar[1] [des·kon·ser·tár] *v. irr.* to disconcert, bewilder, confuse; to disturb; **-se** to be confused, perplexed.

desconcierto [des·kon·sjér·to] *m.* disorder; confusion; disagreement; feeling of discomfort.

desconchadura [des·kon·ča·đú·ra] *f.* chip (*chipped off place*); chipping off, peeling off (*of plaster, varnish, etc.*).

desconchar [des·kon·čár] *v.* to scrape off (*plaster or stucco*); **-se** to peel off, chip off (*as plaster*).

desconectar [des·ko·nek·tár] *v.* to disconnect.

desconfiado [des·kon·fjá·đo] *adj.* distrustful, suspicious.

desconfianza [des·kon·fján·sa] *f.* mistrust, distrust.

desconfiar[17] [des·kon·fjár] *v.* to distrust; to lose confidence.

desconocer[13] [des·ko·no·sér] *v. irr.* to fail to recognize or remember; to disown; to disregard, slight; not to know.

desconocido [des·ko·no·sí·đo] *adj.* unknown; unrecognizable; *m.* stranger.

desconocimiento [des·ko·no·si·mjén·to] *m.* disregard; ignorance.

desconsolado [des·kon·so·lá·đo] *p.p. & adj.* disconsolate, forlorn; disheartened, grieved.

desconsolador [des·kon·so·la·đór] *adj.* disheartening, saddening.

desconsolar[2] [des·kon·so·lár] *v. irr.* to sadden, grieve; to discourage; **-se** to become disheartened, grieved.

desconsuelo [des·kon·swé·lo] *m.* dejection, sadness, distress.

descontar[2] [des·kon·tár] *v. irr.* to discount, deduct; to allow for.

descontentadizo [des·kon·ten·ta·đí·so] *adj.* discontented, fretful, hard to please.

descontentar [des·kon·ten·tár] *v.* to displease.

descontento [des·kon·tén·to] *adj.* discontent, displeased; *m.* discontent, displeasure.

descorazonado [des·ko·ra·so·ná·đo] *adj.* disheartened, discouraged, depressed.

descorchar [des·kor·čár] *v.* to uncork; to remove the bark from (*a cork tree*); to force or break open.

descortés [des·kor·tés] *adj.* discourteous, rude, impolite.

descortesía [des·kor·te·sí·a] *f.* discourtesy, rudeness, impoliteness.

descortezar[9] [des·kor·te·sár] *v.* to bark, strip the bark from (*trees*); to remove the crust or shell from; to peel; to civilize, remove the rough manners from.

descoser [des·ko·sér] *v.* to rip, unsew, unstitch; **-se** to rip, come unstitched; to talk too much or indiscreetly.

descosido [des·ko·sí·đo] *m.* rip; *adj.* too talkative, indiscreet; disorderly; *p.p. of* **descoser.**

descostrar [des·kos·trár] *v.* to flake; to scale off; to remove the crust from; **-se** to flake, scale off.

descoyuntado [des·ko·yun·tá·do] *p.p. & adj.* dislocated, out of joint.

descoyuntar [des·ko·yun·tár] *v.* to dislocate, put out of joint; **-se** to get out of joint.

descrédito [des·kré·di·to] *m.* discredit.

descreído [des·kre·í·do] *adj.* incredulous, unbelieving; *m.* unbeliever.

descreimiento [des·krej·mjén·to] *m.* unbelief, lack of faith.

describir[52] [des·kri·bír] *v.* to describe.

descripción [des·krip·sjón] *f.* description.

descriptivo [des·krip·ti·bo] *adj.* descriptive.

descrito [des·krí·to] *p.p. irr. of* **describir.**

descuartizar[9] [des·kwar·ti·sár] *v.* to quarter (*an animal*); to tear or cut into parts.

descubierto [des·ku·bjér·to] *p.p. of* **descubrir** *& adj.* (*sin cubierta*) uncovered; hatless, bareheaded; (*hallado*) discovered; *m.* deficit, shortage; **al —** openly, in the open; **en — uncovered**, unpaid; no funds.

descubridor [des·ku·bri·dór] *m.* discoverer.

descubrimiento [des·ku·bri·mjén·to] *m.* discovery; find; invention.

descubrir[52] [des·ku·brír] *v.* to discover; to uncover; **-se** to uncover; to take off one's hat.

descuento [des·kwén·to] *m.* discount; deduction.

descuidado [des·kwi·dá·do] *adj.* careless, negligent; untidy, slovenly; unaware; thoughtless.

descuidar [des·kwi·dár] *v.* to neglect; to overlook; to be careless or negligent; **-se** to be careless or negligent.

descuido [des·kwí·do] *m.* carelessness; neglect; oversight; disregard; inattention; slip, error.

desde [déz·de] *prep.* from; since; **— luego** of course; **— que** *conj.* since, ever since.

desdecir[27] [dez·de·sir] *v. irr.* to be out of harmony (with); to detract (from); **-se** to retract; to contradict oneself.

desdén [dez·dén] *m.* disdain, scorn.

desdentado [dez·den·tá·do] *adj.* toothless.

desdeñar [dez·de·ñár] *v.* to disdain, scorn.

desdeñoso [dez·de·ñó·so] *adj.* disdainful, scornful.

desdicha [dez·dí·ča] *f.* misfortune; misery; poverty.

desdichado [dez·di·čá·do] *adj.* unfortunate; unhappy, wretched; miserable; *m.* wretch.

desdoblamiento [dez·do·bla·mjén·to] *m.* unfolding.

desdoblar [dez·do·blár] *v.* to unfold; to spread out.

desdorar [dez·do·rár] *v.* to remove the gilt from; to tarnish; to dishonor.

desdoro [dez·dó·ro] *m.* tarnish, blemish; dishonor.

deseable [de·se·á·ble] *adj.* desirable.

desear [de·se·ár] *v.* to desire, want.

desecación [de·se·ka·sjón] *f.,* **desecamiento** [de·se·ka·mjén·to] *m.* drying; drainage.

desecar[6] [de·se·kár] *v.* to dry; to dry up; to drain (*land*).

desechar [de·se·čár] *v.* to discard; to reject; to refuse, decline; *Col.* to cut across, take a short cut.

desecho [de·sé·čo] *m.* remainder, residue; waste material; piece of junk; discard; **-s** refuse, scraps, junk; **hierro de —** scrap iron; **papel de —** wastepaper, scraps of paper.

desembalar [de·sem·ba·lár] *v.* to unpack.

desembarazar[9] [de·sem·ba·ra·sár] *v.* to rid, free, clear; *Ch.* to give birth; **-se** to get rid of.

desembarazo [de·sem·ba·rá·so] *m.* freedom, ease, naturalness; *Ch.* childbirth.

desembarcadero [de·sem·bar·ka·dé·ro] *m.* dock, wharf, pier.

desembarcar[6] [de·sem·bar·kár] *v.* to disembark, land; to unload; to go ashore.

desembarco [de·sem·bár·ko], **desembarque** [de·sem·bár·ke] *m.* landing; unloading.

desembocadura [de·sem·bo·ka·dú·ra] *f.* mouth (*of a river, canal, etc.*); outlet.

desembocar[6] [de·sem·bo·kár] *v.* to flow (into); to lead (to).

desembolsar [de·sem·bol·sár] *v.* to disburse, pay out.

desembolso [de·sem·ból·so] *m.* disbursement, outlay, expenditure.

desembragar[7] [de·sem·bra·gár] *v.* to throw out the clutch; to disconnect.

desemejante [de·se·me·xán·te] *adj.* unlike.

desempacar[6] [de·sem·pa·kár] *v.* to unpack.

desempañar [de·sem·pa·ñár] *v.* to wipe clean; to remove steam or smudge (*from glass*).

desempeñar [de·sem·pe·ñár] *v.* to recover, redeem, take out of pawn; **— un cargo** to perform the duties of a position; **— un papel** to play a part; **-se** to get out of debt.

desempeño [de·sem·pé·ño] *m.* fulfillment, carrying out, discharge; performance (*of a duty*); (*teatro*) acting (*of a role*); redeeming (*of a thing pawned*).

desempleado [de·sem·ple·á·do] *adj.* unemployed.

desempleo [de·sem·plé·o] *m.* unemployment.

desempolvar [de·sem·pol·bár] *v.* to dust, remove the dust from.

desencadenar [de·sen·ka·de·nár] *v.* to unchain, free from chains; to loosen, set free; **-se** to free oneself; to break loose.

desencajado [de·sen·ka·xá·do] *p.p. & adj.* disjointed; disfigured; sunken (*eyes*); emaciated.

desencajar [de·sen·ka·xár] *v.* to dislocate; **-se** to become dislocated.

desencantar [de·sen·kan·tár] *v.* to disillusion, disappoint.

desencanto [de·sen·kán·to] *m.* disillusion, disappointment.

desenfadar [de·sen·fa·dár] *v.* to free of anger; **-se** to calm down.

desenfado [de·sen·fá·do] *m.* ease, freedom; calmness.

desenfrenado [de·sen·fre·ná·do] *p.p. & adj.* unbridled; wanton, reckless; loose, immoral.

desenganchar [de·sen·gan·čár] *v.* to unhitch; to unhook; to unfasten.

desengañador [de·sen·ga·ña·dór] *adj.* disappointing, disillusioning.

desengañar [de·sen·ga·ñár] *v.* to undeceive, disillusion, disappoint.

desengaño [de·sen·gá·ño] *m.* disillusion, disappointment, blighted hope.

desengranar [de·sen·gra·nár] *v.* to throw out of gear.

desenmarañar [de·sem·ma·ra·ñár] *v.* to untangle; to unravel.

desenmascarar [de·sem·mas·ka·rár] *v.* to unmask.

desenredar [de·sen·rre·dár] *v.* to disentangle, unravel.

desenrollar [de·sen·rro·yár] *v.* to unroll.

desensartar [de·sen·sar·tár] *v.* to unstring; to unthread; to unfasten from a ring.

desensillar [de·sen·si·yár] *v.* to unsaddle.

desentenderse[1] [de·sen·ten·dér·se] *v. irr.* to neglect, ignore, pay no attention to; to pretend not to see, hear or understand.

desentendido [de·sen·ten·dí·do] *adj.* unmindful, heedless; *p.p. of* **desentenderse; hacerse el —** to pretend not to notice.

desenterrar[1] [de·sen·te·rrár] *v. irr.* to unearth, dig up.

desentonado [de·sen·to·ná·do] *adj.* inharmonious, out of tune.

desentonar [de·sen·to·nár] *v.* to be out of tune; to be out of harmony; to sing off key, play out of tune.

desenvoltura [de·sem·bol·tú·ra] *f.* freedom, ease, abandon; boldness, impudence.

desenvolver[2, 52] [de·sem·bol·bér] *v. irr.* to unroll, unfold; to unwrap; to develop.

desenvolvimiento [de·sem·bol·bi·mjén·to] *m.* development, unfolding.

desenvuelto [de·sem·bwél·to] *adj.* free, easy; forward, bold; shameless, brazen; *p.p. of* **desenvolver.**

deseo [de·sé·o] *m.* desire, wish.

deseoso [de·se·ó·so] *adj.* desirous, eager.

desequilibrado [de·se·ki·li·brá·do] *adj.* unbalanced; *p.p. of* **desequilibrar.**

desequilibrar [de·se·ki·li·brár] *v.* to unbalance; to derange.

desequilibrio [de·se·ki·lí·brjo] *m.* lack of balance; derangement, mental disorder.

deserción [de·ser·sjón] *f.* desertion.

desertar [de·ser·tár] *v.* to desert; to abandon; **-se de** to desert.

desertor [de·ser·tór] *m.* deserter; quitter.

desesperación [de·ses·pe·ra·sjón] *f.* despair; desperation; fury.

desesperado [de·ses·pe·rá·do] *adj.* desperate; despairing; hopeless; *p.p. of* **desesperar.**

desesperanzado [de·ses·pe·ran·sá·do] *p.p. & adj.* discouraged; hopeless; desperate, in despair.

desesperanzar[9] [de·ses·pe·ran·sár] *v.* to discourage, deprive of hope; **-se** to be discouraged; to despair, lose one's hope.

desesperar [de·ses·pe·rár] *v.* to despair, lose hope; to make (*someone*) despair; **-se** to despair, be desperate; to be furious.

desfachatez [des·fa·ča·tés] *f.* shamelessness, effrontery, impudence.

desfalcar[6] [des·fal·kár] *v.* to embezzle; to remove a part of.

desfalco [des·fál·ko] *m.* embezzlement; diminution, decrease.

desfallecer[13] [des·fa·ye·sér] *v. irr.* to grow weak; to faint.

desfallecimiento [des·fa·ye·si·mjén·to] *m.* faintness; weakness; languor; swoon, faint.

desfavorable [des·fa·bo·rá·ble] *adj.* unfavorable.

desfigurar [des·fi·gu·rár] *v.* to disfigure; to deface; to distort.

desfiladero [des·fi·la·dé·ro] *m.* narrow passage, narrow gorge; road on the edge of a precipice.

desfilar [des·fi·lár] *v.* to march, parade, pass by.

desfile [des·fí·le] *m.* parade.

desgana [dez·gá·na] *f.* lack of appetite; reluctance.

desgarrado [dez·ga·rrá·do] *p.p.* torn; *adj.* shameless; impudent.

desgarradura [dez·ga·rra·dú·ra] *f.* tear.

desgarrar [dez·ga·rrár] *v.* to tear, rend; to expectorate, cough up; **-se** to tear; to separate oneself (from).

desgastar [dez·gas·tár] *v.* to waste, consume, wear away; **-se** to waste away, lose one's strength or vigor; to wear off.

desgaste [dez·gás·te] *m.* waste; wear and tear.

desgracia [dez·grá·sja] *f.* misfortune, mishap; disgrace.

desgraciado [dez·gra·sjá·do] *adj.* unfortunate, wretched.

desgranar [dez·gra·nár] *v.* to thrash, thresh (*grain*); to remove the grain from; to shell (*peas, beans, etc.*).

desgreñado [dez·gre·ñá·do] *adj.* disheveled.

desgreñar [dez·gre·ñár] *v.* to dishevel; **-se** to muss up one's own hair.

deshabitado [de·sa·bi·tá·do] *adj.* uninhabited, deserted; empty, vacant.

deshacer[31] [de·sa·sér] *v. irr.* to undo; to dissolve; to destroy; to untie; **-se** to dissolve; to melt; to waste away; **-se de** to get rid of.

desharrapado, desarrapado [de·sa·rra·pá·do] *adj.* ragged, shabby, tattered.

deshecha [de·sé·ča] *f.* simulation, pretense; **hacer la —** to feign, pretend.

deshecho [de·sé·čo] *p.p. of* **deshacer** *& adj.* undone; ruined, destroyed, in pieces; violent (*said of rainstorms*); worn-out, fatigued; *Arg.* disorderly, untidy.

desheladora automática [de·se·la·dó·ra aw·to·má·ti·ka] *f.* automatic defroster.

deshelar[1] [de·se·lár] *v. irr.* to melt; to thaw; **-se** to melt; to thaw.

desherbar[1] [de·ser·bár] *v. irr.* to weed.

deshielo [dez·yé·lo] *m.* thaw.

deshierbe [dez·yér·be] *m.* weeding.

deshilachar [de·si·la·čár] *v.* to ravel, fray.

deshilar [de·si·lár] *v.* to unravel, **-se** to unravel; to fray.

deshojar [de·so·xár] *v.* to strip off the leaves, petals, or pages; **-se** to lose its leaves (*said of a plant or book*); to lose petals.

deshollejar [de·so·ye·xár] *v.* to husk, hull; to peel, pare, skin; to shell (*beans*).

deshonesto [de·so·nés·to] *adj.* immodest; unchaste, lewd.

deshonra [de·són·rra] *f.* dishonor; disgrace.

deshonrar [de·son·rrár] *v.* to dishonor, disgrace; to insult, offend; to seduce.

deshonroso [de·son·rró·so] *adj.* dishonorable; shameful.

deshora [de·só·ra] *f.* inopportune time; **a —** (*or* **a -s**) unexpectedly; **comer a —** to piece, eat between meals.

deshuesar [dez·we·sár] *v.* to stone, remove the pits or stones from (*fruits*); to bone, remove the bones from (*an animal*).

deshumanizar[9] [de·su·ma·ni·sár] *v. irr.* to dehumanize.

desidia [de·sí·dja] *f.* indolence, laziness.

desidioso [de·si·djó·so] *adj.* indolent, negligent, lazy; listless.

desierto [de·sjér·to] *adj.* deserted, uninhabited; alone; lonely; *m.* desert, wilderness.

designación [de·sig·na·sjón] *f.* designation; appointment.

designar [de·sig·nár] *v.* to designate, appoint, select; to design, plan, intend.

designio [de·síg·njo] *m.* design, plan, purpose.

desigual [de·si·gwál] *adj.* unequal; uneven; variable, changeable.

desigualdad [de·si·gwal·dád] *f.* inequality; unevenness; roughness (*of the ground*).

desilusión [de·si·lu·sjón] *f.* disillusion, disappointment.

desilusionar [de·si·lu·sjo·nár] *v.* to disillusion, disappoint; **-se** to become disillusioned; to lose one's illusions.

desinencia [de·si·nén·sja] *f.* termination, ending (*of a word*).

desinfectante [de·sin·fek·tán·te] *adj.* disinfecting; *m.* disinfectant.

desinfectar [de·sin·fek·tár] *v.* to disinfect.

desinflado [de·sin·flá·do] *adj.* deflated, not inflated, flat.

desinflar [de·sin·flár] *v.* to deflate.

desinterés [de·sin·te·rés] *m.* disinterestedness,

unselfishness, impartiality.

desinteresado [de·sin·te·re·sá·ðo] *adj.* disinterested, unselfish, fair, impartial.

desistir [de·sis·tír] *v.* to desist, stop, cease.

deslavado [dez·la·bá·ðo] *p.p. & adj.* half-washed; weakened; faded; pale; saucy.

deslavar [dez·la·bár] *v.* to wash away; to fade; to wash superficially.

desleal [dez·le·ál] *adj.* disloyal, faithless.

desleír[15] [dez·le·ír] *v. irr.* to dissolve; to dilute, make thin or weak; **-se** to become diluted.

deslindar [dez·lin·dár] *v.* to mark off, mark the boundaries of.

desliz [dez·lís] *m.* slip, slide; error.

deslizador [dez·li·sa·ðór] *m.* glider.

deslizamiento [dez·li·sa·mjén·to] *m.* slip, slipping; glide; sliding, skidding.

deslizar[9] [dez·li·sár] *v.* to slip, slide; **-se** to slip; to skid; to glide; to slip out.

deslucido [dez·lu·sí·ðo] *p.p. & adj.* tarnished; dull; discredited; dingy, shabby; awkward, ungraceful; inelegant.

deslucir[13] [dez·lu·sír] *v. irr.* to tarnish, dull the luster of; to discredit.

deslumbrador [dez·lum·bra·ðór] *adj.* dazzling, glaring.

deslumbramiento [dez·lum·bra·mjén·to] *m.* dazzle, glare; daze, confusion.

deslumbrar [dez·lum·brár] *v.* to dazzle.

deslustrado [dez·lus·trá·ðo] *adj. & p.p.* tarnished; dim, dull; opaque.

deslustrar [dez·lus·trár] *v.* to tarnish; to soil, stain (*one's honor or reputation*).

deslustre [dez·lús·tre] *m.* tarnish; disgrace.

desmadejado [dez·ma·ðe·xá·ðo] *p.p. & adj.* enervated, exhausted; depressed.

desmadejar [dez·ma·ðe·xár] *v.* to enervate, weaken.

desmán [dez·mán] *m.* misconduct, abuse, insult; calamity, disaster.

desmantelar [dez·man·te·lár] *v.* to dismantle, strip of furniture, equipment, etc.

desmañado [dez·ma·ñá·ðo] *adj.* unskillful, awkward, clumsy.

desmayar [dez·ma·yár] *v.* to dismay; to lose strength, courage; **-se** to faint.

desmayo [dez·má·yo] *m.* faint, swoon; dismay, discouragement.

desmazalado [dez·ma·sa·lá·ðo] *adj.* dejected, depressed.

desmedido [dez·me·ðí·ðo] *adj.* limitless; excessive.

desmejorar [dez·me·xo·rár] *v.* to impair; to make worse; **-se** to grow worse; to waste away, lose one's health.

desmentir[3] [dez·men·tír] *v. irr.* to contradict; to give the lie; **-se** to contradict oneself; to retract, take back one's word.

desmenuzar[9] [dez·me·nu·sár] *v.* to crumble, break into bits; to mince; to shred; **-se** to crumble, fall to pieces.

desmerecer[13] [dez·me·re·sér] *v. irr.* to become unworthy of; to deteriorate, lose merit or value; to be inferior to.

desmigajar [dez·mi·ga·xár] *v.* to crumb (*bread*); to crumble; **-se** to crumble.

desmochar [dez·mo·čár] *v.* to cut off, chop off (*the top or tip*).

desmolado [dez·mo·lá·ðo] *adj.* toothless, without molars.

desmontar [dez·mon·tár] *v.* to dismount; to cut down (*a forest*); to clear or level off (*ground*); to dismantle, take apart; to tear down; **-se** to

dismount, alight, get off.

desmoronar [dez·mo·ro·nár] *v.* to crumble; **-se** to crumble down, fall gradually to pieces.

desnatar [dez·na·tár] *v.* to skim, take the cream from (*milk*).

desnaturalizado [dez·na·tu·ra·li·sá·ðo] *adj.* unnatural, cruel; **alcohol** — denatured alcohol (*made unfit for drinking*); **madre desnaturalizada** unnatural mother (*one without motherly instincts*).

desnudar [dez·nu·ðár] *v.* to undress, uncover; **-se** to undress.

desnudez [dez·nu·ðés] *f.* nudity, nakedness.

desnudo [dez·nú·ðo] *adj.* nude, naked, bare.

desobedecer[13] [de·so·be·ðe·sér] *v. irr.* to disobey.

desobediencia [de·so·be·ðjén·sja] *f.* disobedience; **desobediente** [de·so·be·ðjén·te] *adj.* disobedient.

desocupación [de·so·ku·pa·sjón] *f.* unemployment; idleness; vacationing.

desocupado [de·so·ku·pá·ðo] *adj.* unoccupied; unemployed, idle; empty, vacant.

desocupar [de·so·ku·pár] *v.* to empty, vacate; **-se de un negocio** to get rid of, or not pay attention to, a business.

desoír[36] [de·so·ír] *v. irr.* to turn a deaf ear to, not to heed; to refuse (*a petition*).

desolación [de·so·la·sjón] *f.* desolation; ruin; loneliness; anguish, affliction, grief.

desolado [de·so·lá·ðo] *adj.* desolate; *p.p. of* **desolar.**

desolar[2] [de·so·lár] *v. irr.* to lay waste, ruin; **-se** to be in anguish; to grieve.

desollar[2] [de·so·yár] *v. irr.* to skin, flay; to fleece, extort money from.

desorbitado [de·sor·bi·tá·ðo] *adj.* out of its orbit; out of place or proportion; decentered; *Ch, Andes* popeyed; with bulging eyes; *Am.* crazy, eccentric.

desorden [de·sór·ðen] *m.* disorder, confusion.

desordenado [de·sor·ðe·ná·ðo] *adj.* disorderly; lawless; unsettled; *p.p. of* **desordenar.**

desordenar [de·sor·ðe·nár] *v.* to disturb, confuse, upset.

desorientar [de·so·rjen·tár] *v.* to throw off one's bearings; to lead astray; to misdirect, mislead; to confuse; **-se** to lose one's bearings; to go astray, get lost.

desoxidar [de·sok·si·ðár] *v.* to deoxidize.

despabilado [des·pa·bi·lá·ðo] *adj.* wakeful; wide-awake; bright, lively.

despabilar [des·pa·bi·lár] *v.* to snuff, trim the wick of (*a candle*); to enliven, awaken (*the mind*), sharpen (*the wits*); **-se** to wake up, rouse oneself, shake off drowsiness.

despacio [des·pá·sjo] *adv.* slowly.

despacioso [des·pa·sjó·so] *adj.* slow.

despachar [des·pa·čár] *v.* to dispatch; to send; to facilitate; to ship.

despacho [des·pá·čo] *m.* (*oficina*) office, bureau; salesroom; (*communicación*) dispatch; (*envío*) sending; shipment; (*sin demora*) promptness; *Ch.* country store, farm store.

despachurrar [des·pa·ču·rrár] *v.* to crush, squash.

desparejo [des·pa·ré·xo] *adj.* unequal, uneven.

desparpajar [des·par·pa·xár] *v.* to upset, disarrange; to rant, talk too much; *Mex.* to disperse, scatter.

desparpajo [des·par·pá·xo] *m.* ease, freedom of manner; freshness, pertness; *Col.* dispersion, scattering; *Am.* disorder, jumble.

desparramar [des·pa·rra·már] *v.* to scatter, spread; to spill; to squander; **-se** to "spread" oneself, spend lavishly; to scatter; to spill.

desparramo [des·pa·rrá·mo] *m. Ch., C.A.* scattering, spreading, spilling; *Ríopl., Carib.* disorder,

DE

commotion.

despatarrarse [des·pa·ta·rrár·se] *v.* to sprawl; to fall sprawling to the ground.

despecho [des·pé·čo] *m.* spite; grudge; despair; weaning; **a — de** in spite of.

despedazar[9] [des·pe·da·sár] *v.* to break, cut, tear into pieces.

despedida [des·pe·dí·da] *f.* farewell; departure; dismissal.

despedir[5] [des·pe·dír] *v. irr.* (*cesar*) to discharge, dismiss, (*emitir*) emit, throw off, give off; to see (*a person*) off (*at a station, airport, etc.*); **-se** to take leave, say good-bye.

despegar[7] [des·pe·gár] *v.* to detach; to unfasten; to take off (*said of a plane*); *Am.* to unhitch; **no — los labios** not to say a word, not to open one's mouth; **-se** to grow apart; to come loose or become detached.

despego [des·pé·go] = **desapego.**

despegue [des·pé·ge] *m.* takeoff (*of an airplane*).

despejado [des·pe·xá·do] *adj.* clear, cloudless; smart, bright; *p.p. of* **despejar.**

despejar [des·pe·xár] *v.* to clear; to remove obstacles from; **-se** to clear up (*as the sky*); to clear one's mind.

despellejar [des·pe·ye·xár] *v.* to skin, flay.

despensa [des·pén·sa] *f.* pantry; storeroom (*for food*); food provisions.

despensero [des·pen·sé·ro] *m.* butler; steward.

despeñadero [des·pe·ña·dé·ro] *m.* steep cliff, precipice.

despeñar [des·pe·ñár] *v.* to fling down a precipice; **-se** to fall down a precipice; to throw oneself down a cliff.

despepitar [des·pe·pi·tár] *v.* to seed, remove the seeds from; **-se** to talk or shout vehemently; to rave, talk wildly; **-se por una cosa** to long for something; to be crazy about something.

desperdiciado [des·per·di·sjá·do] *adj.* wasteful; *p.p. of* **desperdiciar.**

desperdiciar [des·per·di·sjár] *v.* to squander; to waste.

desperdicio [des·per·dí·sjo] *m.* waste; extravagance; **-s** leftovers, garbage; residue.

desperdigar [des·per·di·gár] *v.* to disperse; to scatter; to strew.

desperezarse[9] [des·pe·re·sár·se] *v.* to stretch oneself.

desperfecto [des·per·fék·to] *m.* damage; flaw, defect.

despertador [des·per·ta·dór] *m.* alarm clock.

despertar[1] [des·per·tár] *v. irr.* to awaken; to wake up; **-se** to wake up.

despiadado [des·pja·dá·do] *adj.* pitiless, heartless, cruel.

despido [des·pí·do] *m.* dismissal.

despierto [des·pjér·to] *adj.* awake; wide-awake.

despilfarrado [des·pil·fa·rrá·do] *adj.* wasteful, extravagant; ragged; *p.p. of* **despilfarrar.**

despilfarrar [des·pil·fa·rrár] *v.* to squander; to waste.

despilfarro [des·pil·fá·rro] *m.* extravagance, squandering; waste.

despistar [des·pis·tár] *v.* to throw off the track.

desplantador [des·plan·ta·dór] *m.* garden trowel.

desplante [des·plán·te] *m.* arrogance; impudent remark or act.

desplazar[9] [des·pla·sár] *v.* to displace.

desplegar[1, 7] [des·ple·gár] *v. irr.* to unfold; to unfurl; to show, manifest.

desplomar [des·plo·már] *v.* to cause (*a wall*) to lean; **-se** to slump; to topple over, tumble down, collapse.

desplome [des·pló·me] *m.* collapse; toppling over; landslide.

desplumar [des·plu·már] *v.* to pick, pluck (*a fowl*); to fleece, skin, rob, strip; **-se** to molt, shed the feathers.

despoblado [des·po·blá·do] *adj.* uninhabited, desolate; **— de árboles** treeless; *m.* open country; uninhabited place; wilderness.

despojar [des·po·xár] *v.* to despoil, rob; to strip (of), deprive (of); **-se** to undress; to deprive oneself.

despojo [des·pó·xo] *m.* plundering, robbery; spoil, booty; leftover, scrap; **-s** remains.

desportilladura [des·por·ti·ya·dú·ra] *f.* chip; nick.

desportillar [des·por·ti·yár] *v.* to chip; to nick.

desposar [des·po·sár] *v.* to marry; **-se** to become formally engaged; to get married.

déspota [dés·po·ta] *m. & f.* despot, tyrant.

despótico [des·pó·ti·ko] *adj.* despotic, tyrannical.

despotismo [des·po·tíz·mo] *m.* despotism, tyranny.

despreciable [des·pre·sjá·ble] *adj.* contemptible; worthless; insignificant, negligible.

despreciar [des·pre·sjár] *v.* to despise, scorn.

desprecio [des·pré·sjo] *m.* scorn, contempt.

desprender [des·pren·dér] *v.* to unfasten, loosen; to detach; **-se** to get loose, come unfastened; to climb down; to get rid (of); to be inferred, be deduced.

desprendimiento [des·pren·di·mjén·to] *m.* detachment; generosity; unfastening; landslide.

despreocupado [des·pre·o·ku·pá·do] *p.p. & adj.* unbiased; liberal, broadminded; unconventional, carefree; *Am.* careless, slovenly; *Am.* indifferent to criticism.

desprestigiar [des·pres·ti·xjár] *v.* to discredit, harm the reputation of; **-se** to lose one's prestige.

desprestigio [des·pres·tí·xjo] *m.* discredit, loss of prestige.

desprevenido [des·pre·be·ní·do] *adj.* unprepared; unaware.

despropósito [des·pro·pó·si·to] *m.* absurdity, nonsense.

desprovisto [des·pro·bís·to] *adj.* destitute; lacking; devoid.

después [des·pwés] *adv.* after, afterward; then, later; **— de** *prep.* after; **— (de) que** *conj.* after.

despuntado [des·pun·tá·do] *adj.* blunt, dull; *p.p. of* **despuntar.**

despuntar [des·pun·tár] *v.* (*quitar la punta*) to blunt; to cut off (*a point*); nip; (*brotar*) to bud or sprout; (*sobresalir*) to excel; to be clever, witty; **— el alba** to begin to dawn.

desquiciar [des·ki·sjár] *v.* to unhinge; to perturb.

desquitar [des·ki·tár] *v.* to retrieve, restore (*a loss*); **-se** to get even, take revenge; to win back one's money; to make up (for).

desquite [des·kí·te] *m.* retaliation, revenge; getting even; recovery of a loss; return game or match.

desrazonable [des·rra·so·ná·ble] *adj.* unreasonable.

destacado [des·ta·ká·do] *adj.* outstanding; *p.p. of* **destacar.**

destacamento [des·ta·ka·mjén·to] *m.* military detachment.

destacar[6] [des·ta·kár] *v.* to detach (*troops*); to make stand out; to stand out; **hacer —** to emphasize; to make stand out; **-se** to stand out.

destapar [des·ta·pár] *v.* to uncover; to uncork; *Mex.* to start running; **-se** to uncover, get uncovered; to get uncorked; *Am.* to burst out talking.

destartalado [des·tar·ta·la·do] *adj.* in disorder; in rack and ruin; dismantled, stripped of furniture.

destechado [des·te·čá·do] *adj.* roofless.

destellar [des·te·yár] *v.* to flash; to sparkle, twinkle; to gleam.

destello [des·té·yo] *m.* flash, sparkle, gleam.

destemplado [des·tem·plá·do] *adj.* out of tune, out of harmony; immoderate; **sentirse** — not to feel well; to feel feverish.

desteñir[5, 19] [des·te·ñír] *v. irr.* to discolor; to fade; to bleach; **-se** to become discolored; to fade.

desternillarse [des·ter·ni·yár·se] *v.* — **de risa** to split one's sides with laughter.

desterrado [des·te·rrá·do] *m.* exile; outcast; *p.p. & adj.* exiled, banished.

desterrar[1] [des·te·rrár] *v. irr.* to exile, banish; to remove earth (from).

destetar [des·te·tár] *v.* to wean.

destierro [des·tjé·rro] *m.* exile.

destilación [des·ti·la·sjón] *f.* distillation.

destiladera [des·ti·la·dé·ra] *f.* still; *Am.* filter.

destilar [des·ti·lár] *v.* to distill; to drip, trickle; to filter.

destilería [des·ti·le·rí·a] *f.* distillery.

destinación [des·ti·na·sjón] *f.* destination.

destinar [des·ti·nár] *v.* to destine; to employ.

destinatario [des·ti·na·tá·rjo] *m.* addressee.

destino [des·tí·no] *m.* destiny, fate; destination; employment, job.

destituido [des·ti·twí·do] *adj.* destitute; *p.p. of* **destituir.**

destituir[32] [des·ti·twír] *v. irr.* to deprive.

destorcer[10] [des·tor·sér] *v. irr.* to untwist.

destornillador [des·tor·ni·ya·dór] *m.* screwdriver.

destornillar [des·tor·ni·yár] *v.* to unscrew.

destrabar [des·tra·bár] *v.* to unlock, unfasten; to untie; to separate; to unfetter.

destreza [des·tré·sa] *f.* dexterity, skill, ability.

destronar [des·tro·nár] *v.* to dethrone, depose, overthrow.

destrozar[9] [des·tro·sár] *v.* to shatter, cut to pieces; to destroy; to squander.

destrozo [des·tró·so] *m.* destruction; ruin.

destrucción [des·truk·sjón] *f.* destruction.

destructivo [des·truk·tí·bo] *adj.* destructive.

destructor [des·truk·tór] *adj.* destructive; *m.* destroyer.

destruir[32] [des·trwír] *v. irr.* to destroy; to ruin.

desunir [de·su·nír] *v.* to divide, separate.

desusado [de·su·sá·do] *adj.* unusual, unaccustomed; obsolete, out of use.

desuso [de·sú·so] *m.* disuse; obsoleteness.

desvaído [dez·ba·í·do] *adj.* lanky, tall and awkward; gaunt; dull, faded.

desvainar [dez·baj·nár] *v.* to shell (*peas, beans, etc.*).

desvalido [dez·ba·lí·do] *adj.* abandoned; destitute; helpless.

desvalijar [dez·ba·li·xár] *v.* to ransack the contents of a valise; to rob.

desván [dez·bán] *m.* garret, attic.

desvanecer[13] [dez·ba·ne·sér] *v. irr.* to fade, dissolve; to make vain; to make dizzy; **-se** to evaporate; to vanish; to fade out, disappear; to get dizzy.

desvanecido [dez·ba·ne·sí·do] *adj.* (*desmayado*) dizzy, faint; (*orgulloso*) proud, haughty; *p.p. of* **desvanecer.**

desvanecimiento [dez·ba·ne·si·mjén·to] *m.* dizziness, faintness; vanity.

desvariar[17] [dez·ba·rjár] *v.* to rave, be delirious; to rant, talk excitedly; to talk nonsense.

desvarío [dez·ba·rí·o] *m.* raving; delirium; madness; inconstancy.

desvelado [dez·be·lá·do] *adj.* sleepless, awake; watchful; *p.p. of* **desvelar.**

desvelar [dez·be·lár] *v.* to keep (*another*) awake; **-se** to keep awake; to have insomnia, lose sleep; to be worried, anxious.

desvelo [dez·bé·lo] *m.* lack of sleep; restlessness; vigilance, watchfulness; worry, anxiety.

desvencijado [dez·ben·si·xá·do] *adj.* tottering, rickety, shaky, falling apart.

desventaja [dez·ben·tá·xa] *f.* disadvantage.

desventura [dez·ben·tú·ra] *f.* misfortune, unhappiness.

desventurado [dez·ben·tu·rá·do] *adj.* unfortunate, unhappy, miserable, wretched.

desvergonzado [dez·ber·gon·sá·do] *adj.* shameless, brazen.

desvergüenza [dez·ber·gwén·sa] *f.* shamelessness; disgrace; shame; insolence; impudent word.

desvestir[5] [dez·bes·tír] *v. irr.* to undress; **-se** to undress.

desviación [dez·bja·sjón] *f.* deviation, turning aside, shift; detour.

desviar[17] [dez·bjár] *v.* to deviate, turn aside; to swerve; **-se** to shift direction; to branch off, turn off the main road; to swerve.

desvío [dez·bí·o] *m.* deviation, turning aside; indifference, coldness; side track, railroad siding; detour.

desvirtuar[18] [dez·bir·twár] *v.* to impair, diminish the value or quality of.

desvivirse [dez·bi·bír·se] *v.* — **por** to long for; to be excessively fond of, be crazy about, make a fuss over; to do one's best for; **ella se desvive por complacerme** she does her utmost to please me.

desyerbar [dez·yer·bár] = **desherbar.**

detallar [de·ta·yár] *v.* to detail, report in detail; to retail.

detalle [de·tá·ye] *m.* detail; retail; **¡ahí está el** — **!** that's the point.

detallista [de·ta·yís·ta] *m. & f.* retailer; detailer, person fond of detail.

detective [de·tek·tí·be], **detectivo** [de·tek·tí·bo] *m.* detective.

detención [de·ten·sjón] *f.* detention, arrest; stop, halt; delay.

detener[45] [de·te·nér] *v. irr.* to detain, stop; to arrest; **-se** to halt; to delay oneself, stay.

detenimiento [de·te·ni·mjén·to] *m.* detention; delay; care, deliberation.

deteriorar [de·te·rjo·rár] *v.* to deteriorate, damage; **-se** to deteriorate, become impaired or damaged; to wear out.

deterioro [de·te·rjó·ro] *m.* deterioration, impairment.

determinación [de·ter·mi·na·sjón] *f.* determination; firmness.

determinar [de·ter·mi·nár] *v.* to determine; to decide; **-se** to resolve, decide.

detestable [de·tes·tá·ble] *adj.* detestable; hateful.

detestar [de·tes·tár] *v.* to detest.

detonación [de·to·na·sjón] *f.* detonation, report (*of a gun*), loud explosion; pop.

detonar [de·to·nár] *v.* to detonate, explode with a loud noise; to pop.

detrás [de·trás] *adv.* behind; — **de** *prep.* behind; **por** — from the rear, by the rear, from behind.

deuda [déw·da] *f.* debt; indebtedness.

deudo [déw·do] *m.* relative, kinsman.

deudor [dew·dór] *m.* debtor; *adj.* indebted, obligated.

devanar [de·ba·nár] *v.* to spool, wind on a spool; **-se los sesos** to rack one's brain.

devaneo [de·ba·né·o] *m.* frenzy; dissipation; wandering; idle pursuit; giddiness.

devastar [de·bas·tár] *v.* to devastate, lay waste, destroy.

devenir[48] [de·be·nír] *v. irr.* to befall; to become, be transformed into.

devoción [de·bo·sjón] *f.* devotion; piety; attachment.

DE

devocionario [de·bo·sjo·ná·rjo] *m.* prayer book.
devolución [de·bo·lu·sjón] *f.* return, giving back; replacement.
devolver[2, 52] [de·bol·bér] *v. irr.* to return, give back, pay back.
devorador [de·bo·ra·dór] *adj.* devouring; absorbing; ravenous; *m.* devourer.
devorar [de·bo·rár] *v.* to devour, gobble up.
devoto [de·bó·to] *adj.* devout, religious, pious; very fond (of).
devuelto [de·bwél·to] *p.p. of* devolver.
día [dí·a] *m.* day; **al otro** — on the next day; **hoy** — nowadays; **un** — **sí y otro no** every other day.
diablo [djá·blo] *m.* devil, demon.
diablura [dja·blú·ra] *f.* deviltry, mischief, devilish prank.
diabólico [dja·bó·li·ko] *adj.* diabolic, devilish, fiendish.
diácono [djá·ko·no] *m.* deacon.
diadema [dja·dé·ma] *f.* diadem, crown.
diáfano [djá·fa·no] *adj.* transparent, clear; sheer.
diagnosticar[6] [djag·nos·ti·kár] *v.* to diagnose.
diagrama [dja·grá·ma] *m.* diagram; graph; — **de flujo** (*computadora*) flow chart.
dialecto [dja·lék·to] *m.* dialect.
dialectología [dja·lek·to·lo·xí·a] *f.* dialectology.
dialogar[7] [dja·lo·gár] *v.* to dialogue.
diálogo [djá·lo·go] *m.* dialogue.
diamante [dja·mán·te] *m.* diamond.
diámetro [djá·me·tro] *m.* diameter.
diantre [dján·tre] *m.* devil.
diapasón [dja·pa·són] *m.* pitch (*of a sound*); tuning fork.
diapositiva [dja·po·si·tí·ba] *f. Spain* slide, lantern slide.
diario [djá·rjo] *adj.* daily; *m.* newspaper; daily expense; journal, diary.
diarrea [dja·rré·a] *f.* diarrhea.
dibujante [di·bu·xán·te] *m. & f.* draftsman; designer.
dibujar [di·bu·xár] *v.* (*diseñar*) to draw, make a drawing of; (*describir*) depict, portray; describe; **-se** to appear, show.
dibujo [di·bú·xo] *m.* drawing; delineation, protrayal, picture; — **natural** drawing of the human figure, drawing from life.
dicción [dik·sjón] *f.* diction; word; choice of words, style.
diciembre [di·sjém·bre] *m.* December.
dictado [dik·tá·do] *m.* dictation; title; dictate; **escribir al** — to take dictation.
dictador [dik·ta·dór] *m.* dictator.
dictadura [dik·ta·dú·ra] *f.* dictatorship.
dictamen [dik·tá·men] *m.* opinion, judgment.
dictaminar [dik·ta·mi·nár] *v.* to give an opinion or judgment.
dictar [dik·tár] *v.* to dictate.
dicha [dí·ča] *f.* happiness; good luck.
dicharachero [di·ča·ra·čé·ro] *adj.* fond of making wisecracks; witty.
dicharacho [di·ča·rá·čo] *m.* wisecrack, smart remark; malicious remark.
dicho [dí·čo] *p.p. of* decir said; — **y hecho** no sooner said than done; *m.* saying, popular proverb.
dichoso [di·čó·so] *adj.* happy, lucky.
diecinueve [dje·si·nwé·be] *num.* nineteen.
dieciocho [dje·sjó·čo] *num.* eighteen.
dieciséis [dje·si·séjs] *num.* sixteen.
diecisiete [dje·si·sjé·te] *num.* seventeen.
diente [djén·te] *m.* tooth; tusk; — **de león** dandelion, — **de leche** baby tooth; **de -s afuera** insincerely; *Am.* **pelar el** — to smile affectedly.

diéresis [djé·re·sis] *f.* diaeresis (*as in* **vergüenza**).
diesel [dí·sel] *m.* diesel; diesel motor.
diestra [djés·tra] *f.* right hand.
diestro [djés·tro] *adj.* skillful; right; *m.* matador; skillful swordsman; halter.
dieta [djé·ta] *f.* diet; assembly; salary, fee.
dietista [dje·tís·ta] *m. & f.* dietician.
diez [djes] *num.* ten.
diezmo [djéz·mo] *m.* tithe.
difamación [di·fa·ma·sjón] *f.* libel, slander.
difamador [di·fa·ma·dór] *m.* slanderer.
difamar [di·fa·már] *v.* to defame, libel, malign, slander.
difamatorio [di·fa·ma·tó·rjo] *adj.* scandalous, slandering.
diferencia [di·fe·rén·sja] *f.* difference.
diferencial [di·fe·ren·sjál] *m.* differential.
diferenciar [di·fe·ren·sjár] *v.* to differentiate, distinguish; to differ, disagree; **-se** to distinguish oneself; to become different.
diferente [di·fe·rén·te] *adj.* different.
diferir[3] [di·fe·rír] *v. irr.* to defer, put off, delay; to differ, disagree; to be different.
difícil [di·fí·sil] *adj.* difficult.
dificultad [di·fi·kul·tád] *f.* difficulty.
dificultar [di·fi·kul·tár] *v.* to make difficult; — **el paso** to impede or obstruct the passage; **-se** to become difficult.
dificultoso [di·fi·kul·tó·so] *adj.* difficult, hard.
difteria [dif·té·rja] *f.* diphtheria.
difundir [di·fun·dír] *v.* to diffuse, spread out, scatter; to broadcast by radio.
difunto [di·fún·to] *adj.* deceased, dead; *m.* corpse.
difusión [di·fu·sjón] *f.* diffusion, spreading, scattering; wordiness; broadcasting.
difuso [di·fú·so] *adj.* diffuse; diffused, widespread.
digerible [di·xe·rí·ble] *adj.* digestible.
digerir[3] [di·xe·rír] *v. irr.* to digest.
dígito [dí·xi·to] *m.* digit; (*computadora*) — **binario** binary (bit).
dignarse [dig·nár·se] *v.* to deign, condescend.
dignatario [dig·na·tá·rjo] *m.* dignitary (*person in a high office*).
dignidad [dig·ni·dád] *f.* dignity.
digno [díg·no] *adj.* worthy; dignified.
digresión [di·gre·sjón] *f.* digression.
dije [dí·xe] *m.* trinket, small piece of jewelry; locket; woman of fine qualities a "jewel"; *Am.* locket or charm.
dilación [di·la·sjón] *f.* delay.
dilatado [di·la·tá·do] *adj.* vast, spacious; extensive; *p.p. of* dilatar.
dilatar [di·la·tár] *v.* to dilate, widen, enlarge; to expand; to lengthen, extend; to spread out; to defer, put off, retard; **-se** to expand; to be diffuse, wordy; *Mex.* to delay oneself, take long.
diligencia [di·li·xén·sja] *f.* diligence, care, industry; speed; stagecoach; business, errand.
diligente [di·li·xén·te] *adj.* diligent; quick, speedy.
diluir[32] [di·lwír] *v. irr.* to dilute.
diluvio [di·lú·bjo] *m.* flood.
dimensión [di·men·sjón] *f.* dimension.
dimes: — **y diretes** [dí·mes·i·di·ré·tes] quibbling, arguing; **andar en** — **y diretes** to quibble, argue.
diminución [di·mi·nu·sjón] *f.* diminution, decrease; — **progresiva** tapering off.
diminutivo [di·mi·nu·tí·bo] *adj.* diminutive, tiny; diminishing; *m.* diminutive.
diminuto [di·mi·nú·to] *adj.* tiny, little.
dimisión [di·mi·sjón] *f.* resignation (*from an office*).
dimitir [di·mi·tír] *v.* to resign, give up (*a position,*

office, etc.).

dinámica [di·ná·mi·ka] *f.* dynamics; **dinámico** *adj.* dynamic.

dinamismo [di·na·míz·mo] *m.* vigor, forcefulness; dynamic force or energy.

dinamita [di·na·mí·ta] *f.* dynamite.

dínamo [dí·na·mo] *m.* dynamo.

dinastía [di·nas·tí·a] *f.* dynasty.

dineral [di·ne·rál] *m.* a lot of money.

dinero [di·né·ro] *m.* money; currency; *Peru* Peruvian silver coin equivalent to about ten cents; — **contante y sonante** ready cash, hard cash.

diodo electroluminiscente [djó·do e·lek·tro·lu·mi·ni·sén·te] *m.* (*computadora*) light emitting diode (LED).

dios [djos] *m.* god; **Dios** God; **a la buena de** — without malice; without plan, haphazard, at random.

diosa [djó·sa] *f.* goddess.

diplomacia [di·plo·má·sja] *f.* diplomacy; tact.

diplomático [di·plo·má·ti·ko] *adj.* diplomatic; tactful; *m.* diplomat.

diputación [di·pu·ta·sjón] *f.* deputation; committee.

diputado [di·pu·tá·do] *m.* deputy, representative.

diputar [di·pu·tár] *v.* to depute, delegate, commission.

dique [dí·ke] *m.* dike; barrier; — **de carena** dry dock.

dirección [di·rek·sjón] *f.* direction, course; advice, guidance; management; board of directors; office of the board of directors; address.

directivo [di·rek·tí·bo] *adj.* directive, directing, guiding; **mesa directiva** board of directors.

directo [di·rék·to] *adj.* direct, straight.

director [di·rek·tór] *m.* director, manager; *adj.* directing.

directorio [di·rek·tó·rjo] *adj.* directory, directive, directing; *m.* directory, book of instructions; directorate, board of directors.

directrices [di·rek·trí·ses] *f. pl.* directives.

dirigente [di·ri·xén·te] *adj.* directing, leading; *m.* leader, director.

dirigible [di·ri·xí·ble] *adj. & m.* dirigible.

dirigir[11] [di·ri·xír] *v.* to direct, manage, govern; to guide; to address (*letters, packages*); to dedicate; **-se a** to address (*a person*); to go to or toward.

discernimiento [di·ser·ni·mjén·to] *m.* discernment, keen judgment, insight, discrimination.

discernir[3] [di·ser·nír] *v. irr.* to discern; to distinguish; to discriminate.

disciplina [di·si·plí·na] *f.* discipline, training; rule of conduct; order; any art or science; scourge, whip.

disciplinar [di·si·pli·nár] *v.* to discipline; train; to drill; **-se** to discipline oneself; to scourge oneself.

discípulo [di·sí·pu·lo] *m.* pupil; disciple.

disco [dís·ko] *m.* disk; discus; phonograph record; — **flexible** (*computadora*) floppy disk, — **rígido** hard disk.

díscolo [dís·ko·lo] *adj.* unruly, disobedient; unfriendly.

discordancia [dis·kor·dán·sja] *f.* discord, disagreement.

discordia [dis·kór·dja] *f.* discord.

discreción [dis·kre·sjón] *f.* discretion; keenness; wit; **darse** (*or* **rendirse**) **a** — to surrender unconditionally; **discrecional** [dis·kre·sjo·nál] *adj.* optional.

discrepancia [dis·kre·pán·sja] *f.* discrepancy.

discreto [dis·kré·to] *adj.* discreet, prudent; clever.

disculpa [dis·kúl·pa] *f.* excuse; apology.

disculpable [dis·kul·pá·ble] *adj.* excusable.

disculpar [dis·kul·pár] *v.* to excuse, free from blame; **-se** to excuse oneself, apologize.

discurrir [dis·ku·rrír] *v.* (*charlar*) to discuss, (*recorrer*) to ramble about; (*imaginar*) to invent, think out.

discursear [dis·kur·se·ár] *v.* to make speeches.

discurso [dis·kúr·so] *m.* discourse; speech; reasoning; lapse of time.

discusión [dis·ku·sjón] *f.* discussion.

discutible [dis·ku·tí·ble] *adj.* debatable, questionable.

discutir [dis·ku·tír] *v.* to discuss.

disecar[6] [di·se·kár] *v.* to dissect; to stuff and mount (*the skins of animals*).

diseminación [di·se·mi·na·sjón] *f.* dissemination, spread, scattering.

diseminar [di·se·mi·nár] *v.* to disseminate, scatter, spread.

disensión [di·sen·sjón] *f.* dissension, dissent, disagreement.

disentería [di·sen·te·rí·a] *f.* dysentery.

disentir[3] [di·sen·tír] *v. irr.* to dissent, differ, disagree.

diseñador [di·se·ña·dór] *m.* designer.

diseñar [di·se·ñár] *v.* to design; to sketch, outline; — **la política** to outline policy.

diseño [di·sé·ño] *m.* design; sketch, outline; — **gráfico** graphic design.

disertar [di·ser·tár] *v.* to discourse, discuss.

disforme [dis·fór·me] *adj.* deformed; ugly, hideous; out of proportion.

disfraz [dis·frás] *m.* disguise, mask; masquerade costume.

disfrazar[9] [dis·fra·sár] *v.* to disguise, conceal; **-se** to disguise oneself; to masquerade.

disfrutar [dis·fru·tár] *v.* to enjoy; to reap benefit or advantage; to make use of.

disfrute [dis·frú·te] *m.* enjoyment, benefit, use.

disgustar [diz·gus·tár] *v.* to disgust, displease; **-se** to get angry; to get bored.

disgusto [diz·gús·to] *m.* displeasure; unpleasantness; annoyance; quarrel; grief; disgust.

disidente [di·si·dén·te] *m. & f.* dissident; protester.

disimulado [di·si·mu·lá·do] *adj.* underhanded, sly, cunning; *p.p. of* **disimular**.

disimular [di·si·mu·lár] *v.* to feign, hide, mask; to overlook, excuse.

disimulo [di·si·mú·lo] *m.* dissimulation, feigning, pretense; slyness; reserve.

disipación [di·si·pa·sjón] *f.* dissipation; waste, extravagance.

disipar [di·si·pár] *v.* to dissipate, scatter; to squander; **-se** to vanish.

dislocar[6] [diz·lo·kár] *v.* to dislocate, put out of joint; **-se** to become dislocated, get out of joint.

disminución [diz·mi·nu·sjón] = **diminución**.

disminuir[32] [di·mi·nwír] *v. irr.* to diminish, decrease, lessen.

disociación [di·so·sja·sjón] *f.* dissociation, separation.

disociar [di·so·sjár] *v.* to dissociate, separate.

disolución [di·so·lu·sjón] *f.* dissolution, breaking up; dissoluteness, lewdness.

disoluto [di·so·lú·to] *adj.* dissolute, loose, immoral, dissipated.

disolver[2, 52] [di·sol·bér] *v. irr.* to dissolve; to melt.

disonancia [di·so·nán·sja] *f.* discord.

disparada [dis·pa·rá·da] *f. C.A., Mex., Carib., Ríopl.* rush, run.

disparar [dis·pa·rár] *v.* to shoot, fire, discharge; to throw; **-se** to run away, dart out.

disparatado [dis·pa·ra·tá·do] *adj.* absurd, foolish, senseless.

disparatar [dis·pa·ra·tár] *v.* to talk nonsense; to

DE

blunder; to act foolishly.

disparate [dis·pa·rá·te] *m.* nonsense, blunder.

disparidad [dis·pa·ri·dád] *f.* inequality.

disparo [dis·pá·ro] *m.* shooting, discharge, explosion; shot; sudden dash, run.

dispensa [dis·pén·sa] *f.* dispensation; exemption.

dispensar [dis·pen·sár] *v.* to excuse, absolve, pardon; to grant, give.

dispensario [dis·pen·sá·rjo] *m.* dispensary; pharmaceutical laboratory; pharmacopoeia (*book containing list and description of drugs*).

dispersar [dis·per·sár] *v.* to disperse, scatter.

dispersión [dis·per·sjón] *f.* dispersion, dispersal.

displicencia [dis·pli·sén·sja] *f.* displeasure, discontent, dislike.

displicente [dis·pli·sén·te] *adj.* unpleasant, disagreeable, cross.

disponer[40] [dis·po·nér] *v. irr.* (*arreglar*) to dispose; to arrange, put in order; to prepare; (*mandar*) to order, command; **-se** to get ready; to make one's will and testament.

disponible [dis·po·ní·ble] *adj.* spare, available; on hand.

disposición [dis·po·si·sjón] *f.* disposition; arrangement; order, command; aptitude; disposal; — **legales** ordinances.

dispositivos [dis·po·si·tí·bos] *m. pl.* devices.

dispuesto [dis·pwés·to] *p.p. of* **disponer** & *adj.* disposed; ready; fit; smart, clever.

disputa [dis·pú·ta] *f.* dispute.

disputar [dis·pu·tár] *v.* to dispute.

distancia [dis·tán·sja] *f.* distance.

distante [dis·tán·te] *adj.* distant.

distar [dis·tár] *v.* to be distant, far (from).

distender[1] [dis·ten·dér] *v. irr.* to distend, stretch; to inflate; **-se** to distend, expand.

distinción [dis·tin·sjón] *f.* distinction.

distinguido [dis·tiŋ·gí·do] *adj. & p.p.* distinguished.

distinguir[12] [dis·tiŋ·gír] *v.* to distinguish; **-se** to distinguish oneself, excel; to differ, be different.

distintivo [dis·tin·tí·bo] *adj.* distinctive, distinguishing; *m.* distinguishing characteristic; mark, sign; badge.

distinto [dis·tín·to] *adj.* distinct, plain, clear; different.

distracción [dis·trak·sjón] *f.* distraction; diversion, amusement; lack of attention.

distraer[46] [dis·tra·ér] *v. irr.* to distract; to divert, amuse; to lead astray; to divert (*funds*); **-se** to have a good time; to be absentminded; to be inattentive.

distraído [dis·tra·í·do] *adj.* distracted; inattentive; absentminded; *Am.* slovenly, untidy.

distribución [dis·tri·bu·sjón] *f.* distribution, apportionment.

distribuidor [dis·tri·bwi·dór] *m.* distributor; *adj.* distributing.

distribuir[32] [dis·tri·bwír] *v. irr.* to distribute; to sort; classify.

distrito [dis·trí·to] *m.* district; region.

disturbio [dis·túr·bjo] *m.* disturbance.

disuadir [di·swa·dír] *v.* to dissuade.

disuelto [di·swél·to] *p.p. of* **disolver.**

diurno [djúr·no] *adj.* day, of the day.

divagación [di·ba·ga·sjón] *f.* rambling, digression.

divagar[7] [di·ba·gár] *v.* to ramble; to digress.

diván [di·bán] *m.* divan, sofa.

divergencia [di·ber·xén·sja] *f.* divergence; difference (*of opinion*).

divergir[11] [di·ber·xír] *v.* to diverge; to differ.

diversidad [di·ber·si·dád] *f.* diversity; variety.

diversión [di·ber·sjón] *f.* amusement.

diverso [di·bér·so] *adj.* diverse; different; **-s** several, various.

divertido [di·ber·tí·do] *adj.* amusing, funny.

divertir[3] [di·ber·tír] *v. irr.* to amuse, entertain; to divert, turn aside; **-se** to have a good time, amuse oneself.

dividendo [di·bi·dén·do] *m.* dividend.

dividir [di·bi·dír] *v.* to divide, split.

divinidad [di·bi·ni·dád] *f.* divinity, deity; ¡qué—! what a beauty!

divino [di·bí·no] *adj.* divine.

divisa [di·bí·sa] *f.* device, emblem; foreign exchange.

divisar [di·bi·sár] *v.* to sight; to make out, distinguish.

división [di·bi·sjón] *f.* division.

divisorio [di·bi·só·rjo] *adj.* dividing.

divorciar [di·bor·sjár] *v.* to divorce; to separate.

divorcio [di·bór·sjo] *m.* divorce.

divulgar[7] [di·bul·gár] *v.* to divulge, spread, make public, give out.

diz [dis] = **dice; dizque** [dís·ke] *they say that* ...

do [do] *m.* the first note of the diatonic scale in solfeggio.

dobladillar [do·bla·di·yár] *v.* to hem.

dobladillo [do·bla·dí·yo] *m.* hem; — **de ojo** hemstitch.

doblar [do·blár] *v.* to bend, fold; to double; to toll, knell; *Ríopl.* to knock down; — **la esquina** to turn the corner; **-se** to stoop; to bend down; to give in.

doble [dó·ble] *adj.* double, twofold; double-faced; hypocritical; *Ch., Perú, P.R.* broke, poor; *m.* fold, toll, tolling of bells, knell.

doblegar[7] [do·ble·gár] *v.* to bend; to fold; **-se** to bend over; to stoop; to submit, yield.

doblete [do·blé·te] *m.* doublet; a two-base hit.

doblez [do·blés] *m.* fold, crease; duplicity, hypocrisy.

doce [dó·se] *num.* twelve.

docena [do·sé·na] *f.* dozen.

docente [do·sén·te] *adj.* teaching; educational; **cuerpo** — faculty (*of a school*).

dócil [dó·sil] *adj.* docile, obedient, manageable, meek; flexible; **docilidad** [do·si·li·dád] *f.* obedience, meekness, gentleness; flexibility.

docto [dók·to] *adj.* learned; expert.

doctor [dok·tór] *m.* doctor.

doctorar [dok·to·rár] *v.* to grant a doctor's degree to; **-se** to get a doctor's degree.

doctrina [dok·trí·na] *f.* doctrine.

documentar [do·ku·men·tár] *v.* to document.

documento [do·ku·mén·to] *m.* document.

dogal [do·gál] *m.* halter; noose.

dogma [dóg·ma] *m.* dogma; **dogmático** [dog·má·ti·ko] *adj.* dogmatic, pertaining to dogma; positive.

dolencia [do·lén·sja] *f.* ailment; ache, aching.

doler[2] [do·lér] *v. irr.* to ache, hurt, cause pain; to cause grief; **-se de** to feel pity for, feel sorry for; to repent from.

doliente [do·ljén·te] *adj.* sorrowful; suffering; aching; *m.* sick person, patient; mourner.

dolor [do·lór] *m.* pain, ache; sorrow, grief.

dolorido [do·lo·rí·do] *adj.* aching, sore; afflicted; repentant; doleful.

doloroso [do·lo·ró·so] *adj.* painful; sorrowful.

doma [dó·ma] *f.* breaking of horses.

domador [do·ma·dór] *m.* horsebreaker, broncobuster.

domar [do·már] *v.* to tame, subdue.

domeñar [do·me·ñár] *v.* to tame; to subdue; to dominate.

domesticar[6] [do·mes·ti·kár] *v.* to domesticate, tame.

doméstico [do·més·ti·ko] *adj.* domestic; *m.* house servant.

domiciliar [do·mi·si·ljár] *v.* to house, lodge; *Ríopl.* to address (*a letter*); **-se** to take up residence; to settle down; to dwell, reside.

domicilio [do·mi·sí·ljo] *m.* home, dwelling.

dominación [do·mi·na·sjón] *f.* domination, rule, authority.

dominador [do·mi·na·dór] *adj.* dominant, dominating; domineering, bossy; *m.* ruler, boss.

dominante [do·mi·nán·te] *adj.* dominant; domineering; tyrannical; prevailing, predominant.

dominar [do·mi·nár] *v.* to dominate, rule, lead; to stand out, tower above; to master.

dómine [dó·mi·ne] *m.* teacher; pedagogue; pedant.

domingo [do·míŋ·go] *m.* Sunday; — **de ramos** Palm Sunday.

dominio [do·mí·njo] *m.* domain; dominion; authority; mastery (*of a science, art, language, etc.*).

dominó [do·mi·nó] *m.* domino.

don [don] *m.* gift; ability, knack; Don (*title used only before Christian names of men*).

donación [do·na·sjón] *f.* donation; grant.

donador [do·na·dór] *m.* donor, giver.

donaire [do·náj·re] *m.* grace, elegance; wit; humor; witty remark.

donairoso [do·naj·ró·so] *adj.* elegant, graceful; witty.

donar [do·nár] *v.* to donate.

doncella [don·sé·ya] *f.* virgin, maiden; maidservant; *Col.* felon (*sore or inflammation near a finger or toenail*).

donde [dón·de] *rel. adv.* where, in which; **a —** (**adonde**) where, to which; *C.A., Ríopl.* to the house of; **de —** from where, from which; **en —** where, in which; **por —** where, through which; wherefore; **— no** otherwise; if not; **¿donde?** *interr. adv.* where?; **¿por —?** which way?

dondequiera [don·de·kjé·ra] *adv.* wherever; anywhere.

donjuanismo [doŋ·xwa·níz·mo] *m.* Don Juanism, conduct reminiscent of Don Juan Tenorio.

donoso [do·nó·so] *adj.* witty, gay; graceful.

doña [dó·ña] *f.* Doña (*title used only before Christian names of women*).

dorada [do·rá·da] *f.* gilthead (fish).

dorado [do·rá·do] *p.p. & adj.* gilded, gilt; golden; *m.* gilding; *Am.* a kind of hummingbird; **doradillo** [do·ra·dí·yo] *adj.* C.R., Ríopl. honey-colored, golden (*applied to horses*).

dorar [do·rár] *v.* to gild.

dormir[4] [dor·mír] *v. irr.* to sleep; **-se** to go to sleep, fall asleep; to become numb.

dormitar [dor·mi·tár] *v.* to doze.

dormitorio [dor·mi·tó·rjo] *m.* dormitory; bedroom.

dorso [dór·so] *m.* back, reverse.

dos [dos] *num.* two.

DOS [dos] *m.* (*computadora*) disk operating system.

dosel [do·sél] *m.* canopy.

dosis [dó·sis] *f.* dose.

dotación [do·ta·sjón] *f.* endowment, endowing; donation, foundation; dowry; complement (*personnel of a warship*); office force.

dotar [do·tár] *v.* to endow; to provide with a dowry.

dote [dó·te] *m. & f.* dowry; *f.* natural gift, talent, or quality.

draga [drá·ga] *f.* dredge, dredging machine.

dragado [dra·gá·do] *m.* dredging.

dragaminas [dra·ga·mí·nas] *m.* mine sweeper.

dragar[7] [dra·gár] *v.* to dredge.

dragón [dra·gón] *m.* dragon.

drama [drá·ma] *m.* drama.

dramático [dra·má·ti·ko] *adj.* dramatic; *m.* dramatic actor; playwright, dramatist.

dramatizar[9] [dra·ma·ti·sár] *v.* to dramatize.

dramaturgo [dra·ma·túr·go] *m.* playwright, dramatist.

drenaje [dre·ná·xe] *m. Am.* drainage.

drenar [dre·nár] *v. Am.* to drain.

dril [dril] *m.* drill (*strong cotton or linen cloth*).

droga [dró·ga] *f.* (*medicina*) drug, medicine; (*mentira*) lie, fib; trick; (*molestia*) bother, nuisance; *Peru, Carib.* bad debt; *Ríopl.* drug on the market unsalable article.

drogadicto [dro·ga·dik·to] *m.* drug addict.

droguería [dro·ge·rí·a] *f.* drugstore; drug business.

droguero [dro·gé·ro] *m.* druggist; *Mex.* cheat, debt evader.

droguista [dro·gís·ta] *m. & f.* druggist; (*tramposo*) cheat, crook.

dúctil [dúk·til] *adj.* ductile.

ductilidad [duk·ti·li·dád] *f.* ductility.

ducha [dú·ča] *f.* shower bath; douche.

ducho [dú·čo] *adj.* expert, skillful.

duda [dú·da] *f.* doubt.

dudable [du·dá·ble] *adj.* doubtful.

dudar [du·dár] *v.* to doubt; to hesitate.

dudoso [du·dó·so] *adj.* doubtful; uncertain.

duela [dwé·la] *f.* stave (*of a barrel*); *Mex., Andes* long, narrow floor board.

duelo [dwé·lo] *m.* (*luto*) grief, sorrow; mourning; mourners (*pleito*) duel; **estar de —** to be in mourning; to mourn.

duende [dwén·de] *m.* goblin.

dueña [dwé·ña] *f.* owner, landlady; duenna, chaperon or governess.

dueño [dwé·ño] *m.* owner; master.

dueto [dwé·to], **dúo** [dú·o] *m.* duet.

dulce [dúl·se] *adj.* sweet; pleasant, agreeable; fresh (*water*); soft (*metal*); *m.* sweetmeat; candy; preserves; *Am.* sugar, honey; **dulcería** [dul·se·rí·a] *f.* candy shop.

dulcificar[6] [dul·si·fi·kár] *v.* to sweeten; to soften.

dulzón [dul·són] *adj.* over-sweet, sickeningly sweet.

dulzura [dul·sú·ra] *f.* sweetness; meekness.

duna [dú·na] *f.* dune, sand dune.

dúplex [dú·ples] *m.* (*computadora*) full duplex.

duplicado [du·pli·ká·do] *adj. & m.* duplicate; **por —** in duplicate; *p.p. of* **duplicar.**

duplicadora [du·pli·ka·dó·ra] *f.* duplicator (machine).

duplicar[6] [du·pli·kár] *v.* to duplicate, double; to repeat.

duplicidad [du·pli·si·dád] *f.* duplicity, deceit, deceitfulness, treachery.

duque [dú·ke] *m.* duke.

duquesa [du·ké·sa] *f.* duchess.

durabilidad [du·ra·bi·li·dád] *f.* durability, durable quality, wear.

durable [du·rá·ble] *adj.* durable.

duración [du·ra·sjón] *f.* duration.

duradero [du·ra·dé·ro] *adj.* durable, lasting.

durante [du·rán·te] *prep.* during, for.

durar [du·rár] *v.* to last, endure; to wear well.

durazno [du·ráz·no] *m.* peach; peach tree; **duraznero** [du·raz·né·ro] *m.* peach tree.

dureza [du·ré·sa] *f.* hardness; harshness.

durmiente [dur·mjén·te] *adj.* sleeping; *m.* sleeper; crossbeam; *Col., Ven., Mex., Ch.* railroad tie.

duro [dú·ro] *adj.* (*sólido*) hard; firm, solid; untiring; (*cruel*) cruel; harsh; rigid; (*tacaño*) stubborn; stingy; **a duras penas** with difficulty; *Mex., Ch., Arg.* **— y parejo** eagerly, tenaciously; *Am.* **hacer —** to resist stubbornly; *m.* **duro** (*Spanish dollar*).

DI

E:e

e[e] *conj.* and (*before words beginning with* i *or* hi).
ebanista [e·ba·nís·ta] *m.* cabinetmaker.
ébano [é·ba·no] *m.* ebony.
ebrio [é·brjo] *adj.* drunk
ebullición [e·bu·yi·sjón] *f.* boiling, bubbling up.
eclesiástico [e·kle·sjás·ti·ko] *adj.* ecclesiastic, belonging to the church; *m.* clergyman.
eclipsar [e·klip·sár] *v.* to eclipse; to outshine, surpass.
eclipse [e·klíp·se] *m.* eclipse.
écloga [é·klo·ǥa] *f.* eclogue, pastoral poem, idyll.
eco [é·ko] *m.* echo.
economía [e·ko·no·mí·a] *f.* economy; —**política** economics, political economy.
económico [e·ko·nó·mi·ko] *adj.* economic; economical, saving; **economista** [e·ko·no·mís·ta] *m.* economist.
economizar[9] [e·ko·no·mi·sár] *v.* to economize, save.
ecuación [e·kwa·sjón] *f.* equation.
ecuador [e·kwa·ǥór] *m.* equator.
echar [e·čár] *v.* (*tirar*) to throw, cast; to expel; to throw out; (*emitir*) to give off; to sprout; —**a correr** to run away; -**(se) a perder** to spoil; —**a pique** to sink; -**(se) a reír** to burst out laughing; —**carnes** to get fat; —**de menos** to miss; —**de ver** to notice; to make out; —**mano** to seize; —**papas** to fib; —**raíces** to take root; —**suertes** to draw lots; -**se** to lie down; *Am.* **echársela** [e·čár·se·la] to boast.
edad [e·ǥáǥ] *f.* age.
edecán [e·ǥe·kán] *m.* aide-de-camp.
edén [e·ǥén] *m.* Eden; paradise.
edición [e·ǥi·sjón] *f.* edition; publication; —**en pantalla** (*computadora*) screen editing.
edificación [e·ǥi·fi·ka·sjón] *f.* edification (*moral or spiritual uplift*); construction.
edificar[6] [e·ǥi·fi·kár] *v.* to construct, build; to edify, uplift.
edificio [e·ǥi·fí·sjo] *m.* edifice, building.
editar [e·ǥi·tár] *v.* to publish.
editor [e·ǥi·tór] *m.* publisher; *adj.* publishing.
editorial [e·ǥi·to·rjál] *adj.* publishing, editorial; *m.* editorial; *f.* publishing house.
edredón [e·ǥre·ǥón] *m.* down quilt, comforter, quilted blanket.
educación [e·ǥu·ka·sjón] *f.* education, training; breeding, manners.
educador [e·ǥu·ka·ǥór] *m.* educator; *adj.* educating.
educando [e·ǥu·kán·do] *m.* pupil; inmate (*of an orphanage, boarding school, etc.*).
educar[6] [e·ǥu·kár] *v.* to educate, teach, train, raise, bring up.
educativo [e·ǥu·ka·tí·bo] *adj.* — educational.
efectivo [e·fek·tí·bo] *adj.* effective; real; in operation, active; *m.* cash; -**s por cobrar** accounts receivable.
efecto [e·fék·to] *m.* (*resultado*) effect, result; (*fin*) end, purpose, -**s** goods, personal property; **en** — in fact, actually; **llevar a** — to carry out; **surtir** — to come out as expected; to give good results.
efectuar[18] [e·fek·twár] *v.* to effect, bring about.
eficacia [e·fi·ká·sja] *f.* efficacy; efficiency; effectiveness.
eficaz [e·fi·kás] *adj.* effective; active; efficient.
eficiencia [e·fi·sjén·sja] *f.* efficiency; **eficiente** [e·fi·sjén·te] *adj.* efficient.
efímero [e·fí·me·ro] *adj.* ephemeral, short-lived, brief.
efluvio [e·flú·bjo] *m.* emanation, exhalation, vapors.
efusión [e·fu·sjón] *f.* effusion, unrestrained expression of feeling, gushy manner; —**de sangre** bloodshed.

efusivo [e·fu·sí·bo] *adj.* effusive, too demonstrative, over-emotional.
egipcio [e·xíp·sjo] *adj. & m.* Egyptian.
egocéntrico [e·ǥo·sén·tri·ko] *adj.* egocentric, self-centered.
egoísmo [e·ǥo·íz·mo] *m.* selfishness.
egoísta [e·ǥo·ís·ta] *adj.* selfish; *m. & f.* selfish person.
egolatría [e·ǥo·la·trí·a] *f.* self-worship.
egreso [e·ǥré·so] *m.* outlay, expenses; graduation.
eje [é·xe] *m.* axis; axle; arbor (*machine*).
ejecución [e·xe·ku·sjón] *f.* execution; carrying out; (*computadora*) execution, running.
ejecutar [e·xe·ku·tár] *v.* to execute; to carry out; to perform, do.
ejecutivo [e·xe·ku·tí·bo] *adj.* executive; active; *m.* executive.
ejecutor [e·xe·ku·tór] *m.* executor; — **de la justicia** executioner.
ejemplar [e·xem·plár] *adj.* exemplary, model; *m.* copy; specimen.
ejemplo [e·xém·plo] *m.* example; model, pattern.
ejercer[10] [e·xer·sér] *v.* to practice (*a profession*); to exert.
ejercicio [e·xer·sí·sjo] *m.* exercise; practice; tenure; military drill; exercise (*of authority*); **hacer** — to take exercise; — **contable** accounting period.
ejercitar [e·xer·si·tár] *v.* to practice, exercise; to drill, train; -**se** to train oneself; to practice.
ejército [e·xér·si·to] *m.* army.
ejido [e·xí·do] *m.* public land, common.
ejote [e·jó·te] *m. Mex., Guat.* string bean.
el [el] *def. art. m.* the; — **de** the one with, that one with; — **que** *rel. pron.* he who, the one that; **él** *pers. pron.* he; him, it (*after a prep.*).
elaboración [e·la·bo·ra·sjón] *f.* manufacture, making; development.
elaborar [e·la·bo·rár] *v.* to elaborate.
elasticidad [e·las·ti·si·ǥáǥ] *f.* elasticity.
elástico [e·lás·ti·ko] *adj.* elastic; flexible; *m.* elastic; elastic tape; wire spring; -**s** *Am.* suspenders.
elección [e·lek·sjón] *f.* election; choice.
electo [e·lék·to] *adj.* elect, chosen; *m.* elect, person chosen.
elector [e·lek·tór] *m.* elector, voter; *adj.* electoral, electing.
electoral [e·lek·to·rál] *adj.* electoral.
electricidad [e·lek·tri·si·ǥáǥ] *f.* electricity.
electricista [e·lek·tri·sís·ta] *m.* electrician; electrical engineer.
eléctrico [e·lék·tri·ko] *adj.* electric, electrical.
electrizar[9] [e·lek·tri·sár] *v.* to electrify; to thrill, excite; *Am.* to anger, irritate.
electrocardiógrafo [e·lek·tro·kar·ǥjó·ǥra·fo] *m.* electrocardiograph.
electroimán [e·lek·troj·mán] *m.* electromagnet.
electrólisis [e·lek·tró·li·sis] *f.* electrolysis.
electromagnético [e·lek·tro·maǥ·né·ti·ko] *adj.* electromagnetic.
electrón [e·lek·trón] *m.* electron.
electrónico [e·lek·tró·ni·ko] *adj.* electronic; **electrónica** [e·lek·tró·ni·ka] *f.* electronics.
elefante [e·le·fán·te] *m.* elephant.
elegancia [e·le·ǥán·sja] *f.* elegance, grace, distinguished manner.
elegante [e·le·ǥán·te] *adj.* elegant, graceful, polished; stylish.
elegir[5, 11] [e·le·xír] *v. irr.* to elect, choose.
elemental [e·le·men·tál] *adj.* elementary; elemental, fundamental.
elemento [e·le·mén·to] *m.* element; -**s** elements, fundamentals; personnel; — **químicos** chemical

elements, simple substances; — **físico**
(*computadora*) hardware; *Am.* **ser** (*or* **estar**) **hecho
un** — to be an idiot, a fool.
elevación [e·le·ba·sjón] *f.* elevation; height; rise;
rapture.
elevador [e·le·ba·dór] *m. Am.* elevator, hoist.
elevar [e·le·bár] *v.* to elevate, raise, lift; **-se** to go up;
to soar.
eliminación [e·li·mi·na·sjón] *f.* elimination, removal.
eliminar [e·li·mi·nár] *v.* to eliminate.
elocuencia [e·lo·kwén·sja] *f.* eloquence.
elocuente [e·lo·kwén·te] *adj.* eloquent.
elogiar [e·lo·xjár] *v.* to praise.
elogio [e·ló·xjo] *m.* praise.
elote [e·ló·te] *m. Mex., C.A.* ear of corn, corn on the
cob.
elucidación [e·lu·si·da·sjón] *f.* elucidation,
explanation.
elucidar [e·lu·si·dár] *v.* to elucidate, illustrate,
explain.
eludir [e·lu·dír] *v.* to elude, avoid, dodge.
ella [é·ya] *pers. pron.* she; her, it (*after a prep.*).
ello [é·yo] *pron.* it; — **es que** the fact is that.
emanación [e·ma·na·sjón] *f.* emanation, flow; fumes,
vapor, odor; manifestation.
emanar [e·ma·nár] *v.* to emanate, spring, issue.
emancipación [e·man·si·pa·sjón] *f.* emancipation.
emancipar [e·man·si·pár] *v.* to emancipate, set free;
-se to become free.
embajada [em·ba·xá·da] *f.* embassy; errand, mission.
embajador [em·ba·xa·dór] *m.* ambassador.
embalador [em·ba·la·dór] *m.* packer.
embalaje [em·ba·lá·xe] *m.* packing.
embalar [em·ba·lár] *v.* to pack; to bale, crate.
embaldosar [em·bal·do·sár] *v.* to pave with flagstones
or tiles.
embalsamar [em·bal·sa·már] *v.* to embalm; to scent,
perfume.
embarazar[9] [em·ba·ra·sár] *v.* (*impedir*) to hinder, to
obstruct; (*preñar*) to make pregnant; **-se** to become
pregnant; to become embarrassed.
embarazo [em·ba·rá·so] *m.* (*obstáculo*) impediment,
obstacle; (*preñez*) pregnancy; (*timidez*) bashfulness,
awkwardness.
embarazoso [em·ba·ra·só·so] *adj.* embarrassing;
cumbersome, unwieldly.
embarcación [em·bar·ka·sjón] *f.* ship, boat;
embarkation.
embarcadero [em·bar·ka·dé·ro] *m.* wharf pier.
embarcador [em·bar·ka·dór] *m.* shipper.
embarcar[6] [em·bar·kár] *v.* to embark; to ship; *Am.* to
ship by train or any vehicle; **-se** to embark, sail; to
engage (in); *Am.* to board, get on a train.
embarco [em·bár·ko] *m.* embarkation.
embargar[7] [em·bar·gár] *v.* to impede; to restrain; to
attach, confiscate; to lay an embargo on; **estar
embargado de emoción** to be overcome with
emotion.
embargo [em·bár·go] *m.* embargo, restriction on
commerce; attachment, confiscation; **sin** —
nevertheless.
embarque [em·bár·ke] *m.* shipment.
embarrado [em·ba·rrá·do] *p.p. & adj.* smeared;
plastered; muddy.
embarrar [em·ba·rrár] *v.* to smear, daub.
embaucador [em·baw·ka·dór] *m.* cheat, impostor.
embaucar[6] [em·baw·kár] *v.* to fool, trick, swindle,
deceive.
embebecido [em·be·be·sí·do] *p.p. & adj.* absorbed;
amazed.
embebecimiento [em·be·be·si·mjén·to] *m.* absorption;

rapture.
embeber [em·be·bér] *v.* to imbibe, absorb; to soak;
take up; to shrink; **-se** to be fascinated; to be
absorbed.
embelesar [em·be·le·sár] *v.* to enrapture, delight,
charm.
embeleso [em·be·lé·so] *m.* delight, ectasy.
embellecer[13] [em·be·ye·sér] *v. irr.* to embellish,
beautify, adorn.
embestida [em·bes·tí·da] *f.* sudden attack, onset,
assault.
embestir[5] [em·bes·tír] *v. irr.* to attack, assail.
embetunar [em·be·tu·nár] *v.* to cover with pitch; to
black.
emblanquecer[13] [em·blaŋ·ke·sér] *v. irr.* to whiten; to
bleach; to become white; **-se** to whiten, become
white.
emblema [em·blé·ma] *m.* emblem.
embobar [em·bo·bár] *v.* to fool; to amuse; to
fascinate; to amaze; **-se** to be amazed; to be
fascinated.
embobinado [em·bo·bi·ná·do] *m.* reel assembly (*of a
tape recorder or computer*).
embocadura [em·bo·ka·dú·ra] *f.* mouth (*of a river*);
entrance (*through a narrow passage*); mouthpiece
(*of a wind instrument*); bit (*of a bridle*); taste,
flavor (*said of wines*).
embolado [em·bo·lá·do] *m.* bull whose horns have
been tipped with balls; impotent, ineffectual
person; *p.p. of* **embolar.**
embolar [em·bo·lár] *v.* (*al toro*) to tip a bull's horns
with balls; (*dar lustre*) to polish, to black; **-se** *C.A.*
to get drunk.
embolia [em·bó·lja] *f.* clot.
émbolo [ém·bo·lo] *m.* piston; plunger (*of a pump*);
embolus (*clot in a blood vessel*).
embolsar [em·bol·sár] *v.* to put into a pocket or
purse; **-se** to pocket, put into one's pocket.
emborrachar [em·bo·rra·čár] *v.* to intoxicate; **-se** to
get drunk.
emborronar [em·bo·rro·nár] *v.* to blot; to scribble.
emboscada [em·bos·ká·da] *f.* ambush.
emboscar[6] [em·bos·kár] *v.* to ambush; **-se** to lie in
ambush; to go into a forest.
embotado [em·bo·tá·do] *adj.* dull, blunt; *p.p. of*
embotar.
embotamiento [em·bo·ta·mjén·to] *m.* dullness,
bluntness; dulling, blunting; glazing.
embotar [em·bo·tár] *v.* to dull, blunt; to enervate,
weaken.
embotellador [em·bo·te·ya·dór] *m.* bottling machine;
embotelladora [em·bo·te·ya·dó·ra] bottling works.
embotellar [em·bo·te·yár] *v.* to bottle; to bottle up;
Mex. to jail; *Cuba* to learn by heart.
embozado [em·bo·sá·do] *adj.* cloaked; muffled,
covered up to the face.
embozar[7] [em·bo·sár] *v.* to muffle; to cloak, conceal,
disguise; to muzzle; **-se** to muffle oneself, wrap
oneself.
embragar[7] [em·bra·gár] *v.* to engage or throw in the
clutch.
embrague [em·brá·ge] *m.* clutch (*of a machine*);
coupling.
embriagar[7] [em·brja·gár] *v.* to intoxicate; **-se** to get
drunk, intoxicated.
embriaguez [em·brja·gés] *f.* intoxication;
drunkenness.
embrión [em·brjón] *m.* embryo.
embrollar [em·bro·yár] *v.* to involve, ensnare,
entangle; to confuse.
embrollo [em·bró·yo] *m.* confusion, tangle; trickery,

lie, deception.

embromar [em·bro·már] *v.* to chaff, make fun of, "kid"; *Am.* to bother, molest; *Mex., Ch.* to delay unnecessarily; *Col., Ven.* to ruin, harm; **-se** *Am.* to be bothered, disgusted; *Mex.* to get delayed.

embrujar [em·bru·xár] *v.* to bewitch, enchant.

embrujo [em·brú·xo] *m.* charm, enchantment; glamour.

embrutecer[13] [em·bru·te·sér] *v. irr.* to stupefy, render brutish; to dull the mind, make insensible.

embudo [em·bú·do] *m.* funnel; trick.

embuste [em·bús·te] *m.* lie, fraud; trinket.

embustero [em·bus·té·ro] *m.* liar; *adj.* deceitful, tricky.

embutido [em·bu·tí·do] *m.* sausage; inlaid work; *Am.* insertion of embroidery or lace; *p.p. of* **embutir.**

embutir [em·bu·tír] *v.* to insert, inlay; to stuff.

emerger[11] [e·mer·xér] *v.* to emerge, come out.

emigración [e·mi·ǧra·sjón] *f.* emigration.

emigrante [e·mi·ǧrán·te] *m. & f.* emigrant.

emigrar [e·mi·ǧrár] *v.* to emigrate; to migrate.

eminencia [e·mi·nén·sja] *f.* eminence; height.

eminente [e·mi·nén·te] *adj.* eminent, high, lofty.

emisión [e·mi·sjón] *f.* issue (*of bonds, money, etc.*); radio broadcast.

emisor [e·mi·sór] *adj.* emitting; broadcasting; *m.* radio transmitter; **emisora** [e·mi·só·ra] *f.* broadcasting station.

emitir [e·mi·tír] *v.* to emit, give off; to utter; to send forth; to issue; to broadcast.

emoción [e·mo·sjón] *f.* emotion.

emocional [e·mo·sjo·nál] *adj.* emotional.

emocionante [e·mo·sjo·nán·te] *adj.* moving, touching, thrilling.

emocionar [e·mo·sjo·nár] *v.* to cause emotion, touch, move; **-se** to be touched, moved, stirred.

emotivo [e·mo·tí·bo] *adj.* emotional.

empacador [em·pa·ka·dór] *m.* packer.

empacar[6] [em·pa·kár] *v.* to pack up, wrap up, bale, crate; *Ríopl.* to goad, irritate (*an animal*); **-se** to be stubborn; to get angry; *Ríopl.* to balk; *Ríopl.* to put on airs.

empachado [em·pa·čá·do] *p.p. & adj.* (*relleno*) clogged; stuffed; upset from indigestion; (*tímido*) embarrassed; bashful.

empachar [em·pa·čár] *v.* to stuff, cram; to cause indigestion; **-se** to get upset; to get clogged; to be stuffed; to suffer indigestion; to get embarrassed.

empacho [em·pá·čo] *m.* indigestion; bashfulness; **no tener — en** to have no objection to; to feel free to.

empalagar[7] [em·pa·la·ǧár] *v.* to cloy; to pall on, become distasteful; to disgust.

empalagoso [em·pa·la·ǧó·so] *adj.* cloying; sickeningly sweet; boring, wearisome.

empalizada [em·pa·li·sá·da] *f.* stockade, palisade.

empalmar [em·pal·már] *v.* to splice; to join; **— con** to join (*as railroads or highways*).

empalme [em·pál·me] *m.* junction; joint, connection; splice.

empanada [em·pa·ná·da] *f.* pie, meat pie; swindle, fraud.

empanar [em·pa·nár] *v.* to bread.

empanizar[9] [em·pa·ni·sár] *v. Carib., C.A., Mex.* to bread.

empañado [em·pa·ñá·do] *adj. & p.p.* tarnished; dim, blurred.

empañar [em·pa·ñár] *v.* to blur, dim, tarnish.

empapada [em·pa·pá·da] *f. Am.* drenching, soaking.

empapar [em·pa·pár] *v.* to soak, drench, saturate.

empapelador [em·pa·pe·la·dór] *m.* paper hanger.

empapelar [em·pa·pe·lár] *v.* to paper; to wrap in paper.

empaque [em·pá·ke] *m.* (*bulto*) packing; (*parecer*) looks, appearance, air; airs, importance; *Am., Peru* impudence.

empaquetadura [em·pa·ke·ta·dú·ra] *f.* gasket.

empaquetar [em·pa·ke·tár] *v.* to pack; to pack in; to make a package; **-se** to dress up, doll up.

emparedado [em·pa·re·dá·do] *adj.* shut up, confined between walls; *m.* sandwich; prisoner confined in a narrow cell.

emparejar [em·pa·re·xár] *v.* to even up; level off; to match; to pair off; to overtake, catch up with.

emparentado [em·pa·ren·tá·do] *adj. & p.p.* related by marriage.

emparentar [em·pa·ren·tár] *v.* to become related by marriage.

emparrado [em·pa·rrá·do] *m.* vine, arbor.

empastar [em·pas·tár] *v.* to paste; to fill (*a tooth*) to bind (*books*); **-se** *Ch.* to get lost in the pasture; *Mex.* to become overgrown with grass.

empaste [em·pás·te] *m.* tooth filling; binding (*of a book*).

empatar [em·pa·tár] *v.* (*igualar*) to tie (*in a game*), have an equal score; to have an equal number of votes; (*impedir*) to hinder, obstruct; *Col., Ven., Carib.* to tie, join.

empate [em·pá·te] *m.* tie, draw, equal score, equal number of votes; hindrance, obstruction; *Am.* joint, junction.

empecinado [em·pe·si·ná·do] *adj. Am.* stubborn.

empedernido [em·pe·der·ní·do] *adj.* hardened, hardhearted.

empedernir[51] [em·pe·der·nír] *v.* to harden, toughen; **-se** to become hardened.

empedrado [em·pe·drá·do] *m.* cobblestone pavement; *p.p. & adj.* paved with stones.

empedrar[1] [em·pe·drár] *v. irr.* to pave with stones.

empeine [em·péj·ne] *m.* instep; groin (*hollow between lower part of abdomen and thigh*).

empellón [em·pe·yón] *m.* push, shove; **a -es** by pushing.

empeñar [em·pe·ñár] *v.* (*dar en prenda*) to pawn; (*obligar*) to oblige, compel; **-se** to persist, insist; to apply oneself; to go into debt; **-se por** to plead for, intercede for; **se empeñaron en una lucha** they engaged in a fight.

empeño [em·pé·ño] *m.* (*fianza*) pledge, pawn; (*deseo*) persistence, insistence; eagerness; perseverance; *Mex.* pawnshop; **tener — en** to be eager to.

empeorar [em·pe·o·rár] *v.* to impair; to make worse; to grow worse; **-se** to grow worse.

empequeñecer[13] [em·pe·ke·ñe·sér] *v. irr.* to diminish, make smaller; to belittle.

emperador [em·pe·ra·dór] *m.* emperor; **emperatriz** [em·pe·ra·trís] *f.* empress.

emperifollar [em·pe·ri·fo·yár] *v.* to decorate, adorn; **-se** to dress up, deck out, doll up.

empero [em·pé·ro] *conj.* however, nevertheless.

empezar[1, 9] [em·pe·sár] *v. irr.* to begin.

empiezo [em·pjé·so] *m. Carib., Mex., C.A.* beginning.

empinado [em·pi·ná·do] *adj.* steep; lofty.

empinar [em·pi·nár] *v.* to raise, lift; to incline, bend; **— el codo** to drink; **-se** to stand on tiptoes; to rear (*said of horses*); to rise high; *Am.* to overeat.

empiojado [em·pjo·xá·do] *adj.* lousy, full of lice.

emplasto [em·plás·to] *m.* plaster, poultice.

empleado [em·ple·á·do] *m.* employee; *p.p. of* emplear.

emplear [em·ple·ár] *v.* to employ; to invest, spend;

-se en to be employed in.

empleo [em·plé·o] *m*. employment, position, job; employ; occupation; aim; investment.

emplumar [em·plu·már] *v*. to feather; to adorn with feathers; to tar and feather; *C.A.* to deceive; *Ec.* to send away to a house of correction or prison; *Am.* — **con algo** to run away with something, steal it; *Ch., Col., Ven.* **-las** (*or* **emplumárselas** [em·plu·már·se·las]) to take to one's heels, flee, escape.

empobrecer[13] [em·po·bre·sér] *v. irr.* to impoverish; **-se** to become poor.

empobrecimiento [em·po·bre·si·mjén·to] *m*. impoverishment.

empolvado [em·pol·bá·do] *adj*. dusty, covered with dust or powder.

empolvar [em·pol·bár] *v*. to sprinkle powder; to cover with dust; **-se** to get dusty; to powder one's face.

empollar [em·po·yár] *v*. to hatch, brood.

emponzoñar [em·pon·so·ñár] *v*. to poison.

empotrado [em·po·trá·do] *adj*. built-in, set in.

emprendedor [em·pren·de·dór] *adj*. enterprising.

emprender [em·pren·dér] *v*. to undertake.

empreñar [em·pre·ñár] *v*. to impregnate, make pregnant.

empresa [em·pré·sa] *f*. enterprise, undertaking; symbol; company, management; **empresarial** managerial.

empresario [em·pre·sá·rjo] *m*. manager; impresario, promoter.

empréstito [em·prés·ti·to] *m*. loan.

empujar [em·pu·xár] *v*. to push, shove.

empuje [em·pú·xe] *m*. push; shove; impulse; energy.

empujón [em·pu·xón] *m*. shove, push.

empuñar [em·pu·ñár] *v*. to grasp, grab, clutch, seize.

émulo [é·mu·lo] *m*. rival, competitor.

en [en] *prep*. in, on, upon.

enaguas [e·ná·ǥwas] *f. pl*. underskirt, petticoat; short skirt.

enajenamiento [e·na·xe·na·mjén·to] *m*. trance; abstraction, absence of mind; transfer (*of property*); — **mental** mental disorder; — **de los sentidos** loss of consciousness.

enajenar [e·na·xe·nár] *v*. (*distraer*) to enrapture, charm; to deprive (*of one's sense*); (*trasladar*) to transfer property; to dispossess; — **el afecto de** to alienate the affection of; **-se** to be enraptured, be in a trance.

enaltecer[13] [e·nal·te·sér] *v*. to extol, exalt.

enamorado [e·na·mo·rá·do] *adj*. in love; *m*. lover.

enamorar [e·na·mo·rár] *v*. to make love, woo, court; to enamor; **-se** to fall in love.

enano [e·ná·no] *m*. dwarf; *adj*. dwarfish, tiny, little.

enarbolar [e·nar·bo·lár] *v*. to hoist, lift, raise on high; to brandish (*a sword, cane, etc*.); **-se** to rear, balk.

enarcado [e·nar·ká·do] *p.p.* arched.

enarcar[6] [e·nar·kár] *v*. to arch; to hoop (*barrels, kegs, etc*.); — **las cejas** to arch one's eyebrows.

enardecer[13] [e·nar·de·sér] *v. irr.* to excite, kindle, fire with passion; **-se** to become excited; to become passionate; to get angry.

enardecimiento [e·nar·de·si·mjén·to] *m*. ardor, passion, unbridled enthusiasm; inflaming.

encabezado [eŋ·ka·be·sá·do] *m*. headline; heading.

encabezamiento [eŋ·ka·be·sa·mjén·to] *m*. heading; list or roll of taxpayers; registration of taxpayers.

encabezar[9] [eŋ·ka·be·sár] *v*. to give a heading or title to; to head; to lead; to make up (*a list or tax roll*); to strengthen (*wine*).

encabritarse [eŋ·ka·bri·tár·se] *v*. to rear, rise up on the hind legs.

encadenar [eŋ·ka·de·nár] *v*. to chain; to link together.

encajar [eŋ·ka·xár] *v*. to thrust in, fit into, insert; **-se** to squeeze into; to intrude, meddle.

encaje [eŋ·ká·xe] *m*. lace; adjustment; fitting together; (*enchufe*) socket, groove, hole; inlaid work; — **de electrodo** electrode holder (stinger).

encajonar [eŋ·ka·xo·nár] *v*. to box (*put or pack in a box*).

encallar [eŋ·ka·yár] *v*. to strand, run aground; to get stuck.

encamado [eŋ·ka·má·do] *p.p.* confined in bed.

encaminar [eŋ·ka·mi·nár] *v*. to direct, guide; **-se** to betake oneself, go (*forward*); to start out on a road.

encanecer[13] [eŋ·ka·ne·sér] *v. irr.* to get grey, get grey-haired.

encanijado [eŋ·ka·ni·xá·do] *adj*. emaciated, thin, sickly.

encanijarse [eŋ·ka·ni·xár·se] *v*. to get thin, emaciated.

encantado [eŋ·kan·tá·do] *p.p. & adj*. delighted, charmed; enchanted.

encantador [eŋ·kan·ta·dór] *adj*. charming; *m*. charmer, enchanter.

encantamiento [eŋ·kan·ta·mjén·to] *m*. enchantment.

encantar [eŋ·kan·tár] *v*. to charm, enchant.

encanto [eŋ·kán·to] *m*. charm, enchantment, delight.

encapillar [eŋ·ka·pi·yár] *v*. *P.R.* to confine in the death cell.

encapotado [eŋ·ka·po·tá·do] *p.p. & adj*. cloaked; overcast, cloudy; in a bad humor.

encapotarse [eŋ·ka·po·tár·se] *v*. to become overcast, cloudy; to cover up, put on a cloak or raincoat; to frown.

encapricharse [eŋ·ka·pri·čár·se] *v*. to persist in one's whims; to get stubborn.

encaramar [eŋ·ka·ra·már] *v*. to raise; to elevate; to extol; **-se** to climb; to climb upon, get upon, perch upon; *Ch*. to be ashamed; *Carib*. to go to one's head (*said of liquor*).

encarar [eŋ·ka·rár] *v*. to face; to aim; **-se con** to face; to confront.

encarcelación [eŋ·kar·se·la·sjón] *f*. imprisonment.

encarcelamiento [eŋ·kar·se·la·mjén·to] = **encarcelación**.

encarcelar [eŋ·kar·se·lár] *v*. to imprison, jail.

encarecer[13] [eŋ·ka·re·sér] *v. irr.* (*alzar precio*) to go up in value; to make dear, raise the price of; (*ponderar*) to exaggerate; to extol; to recommend highly, to enhance.

encarecidamente [eŋ·ka·re·si·da·mén·te] *adv*. earnestly.

encargar[7] [eŋ·kar·ǥár] *v*. (*dar cargo*) to put in charge; to entrust; to commission; (*aconsejar*) to recommend, advise; (*pedir*), to order; to beg; **-se de** to take charge of.

encargo [eŋ·kár·ǥo] *m*. recommendation, advice; charge; order; commission; errand.

encariñado [eŋ·ka·ri·ñá·do] *adj. & p.p* attached, fond, enamored.

encariñamiento [eŋ·ka·ri·ña·mjén·to] *m*. affection, fondness, attachment.

encariñar [eŋ·ka·ri·ñár] *v*. to awaken love or affection; **-se** to become fond (of), attached (to).

encarnado [eŋ·kar·ná·do] *adj*. flesh-colored; red; *p.p. of* **encarnar**.

encarnar [eŋ·kar·nár] *v*. to incarnate, embody; to bait (*a fishhook*).

encarnizado [eŋ·kar·ni·sá·do] *adj*. bloody; hard-fought, fierce.

encarnizar[9] [eŋ·kar·ni·sár] *v*. to infuriate, enrage; **-se** to get furious, enraged; to fight with fury.

EM

encasillar [eŋ·ka·si·yár] v. to pigeonhole, put in a pigeonhole or compartment; to put in a stall; to classify, sort out.

encauzamiento [eŋ·kaw·sa·mjén·to] m. channeling.

encender[1] [en·sen·dér] v. irr. to light, kindle; to set on fire; **-se** to take fire, be on fire; to get red.

encendido [en·sen·dí·ðo] adj. red; p.p. of **encender**; m. ignition (of a motor).

encerado [en·se·rá·ðo] m. blackboard; oilcloth; wax coating; p.p. & adj. waxed; wax-colored; **papel —** wax paper.

encerar [en·se·rár] v. to wax; to thicken (lime).

encerramiento [en·se·rra·mjén·to] m. enclosure, confinement; locking up; retreat; prison.

encerrar[1] [en·se·rrár] v. irr. to enclose; to lock up; to contain; **-se** to lock oneself up, go into seclusion.

encía [en·sí·a] f. gum (of the teeth).

enciclopedia [en·si·klo·pé·ðja] f. encyclopedia.

encierro [en·sjé·rro] m. confinement; retreat; prison.

encima [en·sí·ma] adv. above, overhead, over, on top; besides, in addition; **— de** on top of; **por — de** over; Col., Perú **de —** besides, in addition; Col., C.A., Ríopl., Carib. **echárselo todo —** to spend everything on clothes.

encina [en·sí·na] f. live oak.

encinta [en·sín·ta] adj. pregnant.

encintado [en·sin·tá·ðo] m. curb (of a sidewalk).

enclaustrar [eŋ·klaws·trár] v. to cloister.

enclavar [eŋ·kla·ßár] v. to nail, fix, fasten.

enclenque [eŋ·klén·ke] adj. sickly, wan; weak, feeble.

enclítico [eŋ·klí·ti·ko] adj. enclitic.

encobar [eŋ·ko·ßár] v. to brood.

encoger[11] [eŋ·ko·xér] v. to shrink, shrivel, shorten, contract; **-se** to shrink; to shrivel; **-se de hombros** to shrug one's shoulders.

encogido [eŋ·ko·xí·ðo] p.p. & adj. shrunk, shrivelled; timid, shy.

encogimiento [eŋ·ko·xi·mjén·to] m. shrinking; timidity; **— de hombros** shrug.

encolerizar[9] [eŋ·ko·le·ri·sár] v. to anger; **-se** to get angry.

encomendar[1] [eŋ·ko·men·dár] v. irr. (encargar) to charge, advise; to entrust (recomendar) to recommend, commend; **-se** to put oneself in the hands (of); to send regards; to pray (to).

encomiar [eŋ·ko·mjár] v. to extol, praise.

encomienda [eŋ·ko·mjén·da] f. charge, commission; recommendation; royal land grant (including Indian inhabitants); Mex. warehouse (for agricultural products); Col. parcel-post package.

encomio [eŋ·kó·mjo] m. encomium, high praise.

enconado [eŋ·ko·ná·ðo] p.p. & adj. inflamed; infected; sore; angry.

enconar [eŋ·ko·nár] v. to inflame; to infect; to irritate; **-se** to become inflamed, infected; to get irritated.

encono [eŋ·kó·no] m. rancor, animosity, ill will; Cuba, Mex. inflammation, swelling.

encontrado [eŋ·kon·trá·ðo] adj. opposite; opposing; contrary; p.p. of **encontrar**.

encontrar[2] [eŋ·kon·trár] v. irr. to encounter, meet; to find; **-se** to meet; to coincide; to be; to be found, be situated; to collide; to conflict; **-se con** to come across, meet up with.

encontrón [eŋ·kon·trón], **encontronazo** [eŋ·kon·tro·ná·so] m. bump, collision; **darse un —** to collide (with) bump (into); to bump into each other.

encordelar [eŋ·kor·ðe·lár] v. to string; to tie with strings.

encorvar [eŋ·kor·ßár] v. to curve, bend; **-se** to bend down; to stoop.

encrespar [eŋ·kres·pár] v. (rizar) to curl; to ruffle; (agitar) to irritate; **-se** to curl; to get ruffled; to become involved or entangled (a matter or affair); to become rough (said of the sea).

encrucijada [eŋ·kru·si·xá·ða] f. crossroads, street intersection; ambush.

encuadernación [eŋ·kwa·ðer·na·sjón] f. binding (of books).

encuadernar [eŋ·kwa·ðer·nár] v. to bind (books).

encuadrar [eŋ·kwa·ðrár] v. to enclose in a frame; to encompass; to fit (into); Arg. to suit; Ven. to summarize briefly, give a synthesis of.

encubierto [eŋ·ku·ßjér·to] p.p. of **encubrir**.

encubrir[52] [eŋ·ku·ßrír] v. to cover, hide.

encuentro [eŋ·kwén·tro] m. (hallazgo) encounter, meeting; find, finding; (conflicto) conflict, clash; collision; **salir al — de** to go out to meet; to make a stand against, oppose; Am. **llevarse de —** to run over, knock down; to drag along.

encuerado [eŋ·kwe·rá·ðo] adj. Am. naked.

encuerar [eŋ·kwe·rár] v. Am. to strip off clothes; Am. to skin, fleece, strip of money; **-se** Am. to strip, get undressed.

encuesta [eŋ·kwés·ta] f. search, inquiry, investigation; survey.

encumbrado [eŋ·kum·brá·ðo] p.p. & adj. elevated; exalted; high, lofty.

encumbramiento [eŋ·kum·bra·mjén·to] m. elevation; exaltation; height; eminence.

encumbrar [eŋ·kum·brár] v. to elevate; to exalt, extol; **-se** to climb to the top; to rise up; to hold oneself high; to soar.

encurtido [eŋ·kur·tí·ðo] m. pickle; p.p. of **encurtir**.

encurtir [eŋ·kur·tír] v. to pickle.

enchapar [en·ča·pár] v. to plate, to overlay.

enchilada [en·či·lá·ða] f. Mex., C.A. rolled **tortilla** served with chili.

enchuecar[6] [en·čwe·kár] v. to bend, twist; **-se** Col., Ven., Mex., Ríopl. to get bent or twisted.

enchufar [en·ču·fár] v. to plug in; to telescope; to fit (a tube or pipe) into another.

enchufe [en·čú·fe] m. socket; plug; electric outlet; Spain influence; position obtained through influence.

ende [én·de]: **por —** hence, therefore.

endeble [en·dé·ßle] adj. weak, feeble; flimsy.

endemoniado [en·de·mo·njá·ðo] adj. possessed by the devil; devilish; fiendish; mischievous.

endentar[1] [en·den·tár] v. irr. to indent, form notches in; to furnish (a saw, wheel, etc.) with teeth; to mesh.

enderezar[9] [en·de·re·sár] v. to straighten; to set upright; to right, correct; to direct; to address; **-se** to go straight (to); to straighten up.

endeudado [en·dew·ðá·ðo] p.p. & adj. indebted; in debt.

endeudarse [en·dew·ðár·se] v. to get into debt, become indebted.

endiablado [en·dja·ßlá·ðo] adj. devilish; possessed by the devil; ugly; mean, wicked; Col., Ven., Mex., Ríopl. dangerous, risky.

endibia [en·dí·ßja] f. endive.

endomingado [en·do·miŋ·gá·ðo] p.p. & adj. dressed up in one's Sunday, or best, clothes.

endosante [en·do·sán·te] m. endorser.

endosar [en·do·sár] v. to endorse (a check, draft, etc.).

endose [en·dó·se], **endoso** [en·dó·so] m. endorsement.

endulzar[9] [en·dul·sár] v. to sweeten; to soften.

endurecer[13] [en·du·re·sér] v. irr. to harden; **-se** to get hardened; to get cruel.

enebro [e·né·bro] m. juniper.

enemigo [e·ne·mí·ǵo] m. enemy; devil; adj. hostile; unfriendly; **ser — de una cosa** to dislike a thing.

enemistad [e·ne·mis·tád] f. enmity, hatred.

enemistar [e·ne·mis·tár] v. to cause enmity between; **-se con** to become an enemy of.

energía [e·ner·xí·a] f. energy; **— nuclear** nuclear energy.

enérgico [e·nér·xi·ko] adj. energetic.

enero [e·né·ro] m. January.

enervar [e·ner·bár] v. to enervate, weaken.

enfadar [en·fa·dár] v. to anger; **-se** to get angry.

enfado [en·fá·do] m. anger, disgust.

enfadoso [en·fa·dó·so] adj. annoying.

enfardar [en·far·dár] v. to bale, pack.

énfasis [én·fa·sis] m. emphasis; **enfático** [en·fá·ti·ko] adj. emphatic.

enfermar [en·fer·már] v. to become ill; to make ill; to weaken; **-se** to become ill.

enfermedad [en·fer·me·dád] f. sickness, illness.

enfermería [en·fer·me·rí·a] f. infirmary.

enfermero [en·fer·mé·ro] m. male nurse; **enfermera** [en·fer·mé·ra] f. nurse (for the sick).

enfermizo [en·fer·mí·so] adj. sickly; unhealthy.

enfermo [en·fer·mo] adj. sick, ill; feeble; m. patient.

enflaquecer [en·fla·ke·sér] v. irr. to become thin; to make thin; to weaken.

enfocar[6] [en·fo·kár] v. to focus.

enfoque [en·fó·ke] approach.

enfrenar [en·fre·nár] v. to bridle; to brake, put the brake on; to check, curb.

enfrentar [en·fren·tár] v. to put face to face; **-se con** to confront, face, meet face to face.

enfrente [en·frén·te] adv. in front, opposite; **— de** in front of, opposite.

enfriamiento [en·frja·mjén·to] m. cooling; chill; refrigeration.

enfriar[17] [en·frjár] v. to cool, chill; Carib. to kill; **-se** to cool, cool off; to get chilled.

enfurecer[13] [en·fu·re·sér] v. irr. to infuriate, enrage; **-se** to rage; to get furious; to get rough, stormy (said of the sea).

enfurruñarse [en·fu·rru·ñár·se] v. to get angry; to grumble.

engalanar [en·ga·la·nár] v. to adorn, decorate; **-se** to dress up, primp.

enganchamiento [en·gan·ča·mjén·to] = **enganche.**

enganchar [en·gan·čár] v. to hitch; to hook; to ensnare; to draft; to attract into the army; Col., Ven., Mex., Ríopl. to hire (labor with false promises); **-se** to engage, interlock; to get hooked; to enlist in the army.

enganche [en·gán·če] m. hooking; coupling; draft (into the army); Col., Ven., Mex., Ríopl. enrolling of laborers (for a rubber plantation or other risky business under false promises); Mex. down payment.

engañador [en·ga·ña·dór] adj. deceitful, deceiving; m. deceiver.

engañar [en·ga·ñár] v. to deceive; to while away (time); to ward off (hunger or sleep); **-se** to deceive oneself; to be mistaken.

engaño [en·gá·ño] m. deceit, trick, fraud; mistake, misunderstanding; Ch., C.A. bribe.

engañoso [en·ga·ñó·so] adj. deceitful; tricky; misleading.

engastar [en·gas·tár] v. to mount, set (jewels).

engaste [en·gás·te] m. setting (for a gem or stone).

engatusar [en·ga·tu·sár] v. to coax, entice; to fool.

engendrar [en·xen·drár] v. to engender, beget; produce; to cause.

engolfarse [en·gol·fár·se] v. to get deep (into); to go deeply (into); to become absorbed, lost in thought.

engomar [en·go·már] v. to gum; to glue.

engordar [en·gor·dár] v. to fatten; to get fat; to get rich.

engorroso [en·go·rró·so] adj. cumbersome; bothersome.

engranaje [en·gra·ná·xe] m. gear, gears, gearing.

engranar [en·gra·nár] v. to gear, throw in gear; to mesh gears.

engrandecer[13] [en·gran·de·sér] v. irr. to aggrandize, make greater; to magnify; to exalt.

engrane [en·grá·ne] m. engagement (of gears); gear.

engrasar [en·gra·sár] v. to lubricate, grease; to stain with grease; to fertilize, manure; to dress (cloth).

engrase [en·grá·se] m. grease job.

engreído [en·gre·í·do] adj. & p.p. conceited, vain; Col. attached, fond.

engreír[15] [en·gre·ír] v. irr. to make vain, conceited; **-se** to puff up, get conceited; Col. to become fond (of), become attached (to).

engrosar[2] [en·gro·sár] v. irr. to enlarge; to thicken; to fatten; to get fat.

engrudo [en·grú·do] m. paste (for gluing).

engullir[20] [en·gu·yír] v. to gobble, devour; to gorge.

enhebrar [en·e·brár] v. to thread (a needle); to string (beads).

enhiesto [en·jés·to] adj. straight, upright, erect.

enhorabuena [en·o·ra·bwé·na] f. congratulation; adv. safely; well and good; all right; with much pleasure.

enigma [e·níǵ·ma] m. enigma, riddle, puzzle.

enjabonar [en·xa·bo·nár] v. to soap; to soft-soap, flatter.

enjaezar[9] [en·xa·e·sár] v. to harness.

enjalbegar[7] [en·xal·be·ǵar] v. to whitewash; **-se** to paint (one's face).

enjambre [en·xám·bre] m. swarm of bees; crowd.

enjaular [en·xaw·lár] v. to cage; to confine; to jail.

enjuagar[7] [en·xwa·ǵár] v. to rinse, rinse out.

enjuague [en·xwá·ǵe] m. mouth wash; rinse; rinsing; scheme, plot.

enjugar[7] [en·xu·ǵár] v. to dry; to wipe; **-se** to dry oneself.

enjuiciar [en·xwi·sjár] v. to indict; to prosecute, bring suit against; to try (a case); to judge.

enjundia [en·xún·dja] f. substance, essence; fat; force, strength.

enjuto [en·xú·to] adj. dried; thin, skinny; **-s** m. pl. dry kindling.

enlace [en·lá·se] m. link; tie, bond; marriage.

enladrillado [en·la·dri·yá·do] m. brick pavement or floor.

enladrillar [en·la·dri·yár] v. to pave with bricks.

enlatar [en·la·tár] v. to can; Col. to roof with tin.

enlazar[9] [en·la·sár] v. to join, bind, tie; to rope; Ven., Mex. to lasso; **-se** to join; to marry; to become related through marriage.

enlodar [en·lo·dár] v. to cover with mud; to smear, sully, soil, dirty; **-se** to get in the mud; to get muddy.

enloquecer[13] [en·lo·ke·sér] v. irr. to make crazy; to drive mad; to lose one's mind; **-se** to go crazy.

enlosado [en·lo·sá·do] m. flagstone pavement; p.p. of **enlosar.**

enlosar [en·lo·sár] v. to pave with flagstones.

enmantecado [em·man·te·ká·do] m. Am. ice cream. See **mantecado.**

enmantecar[6] [em·man·te·kár] v. to butter; to grease

(with lard or butter).

enmarañar [emma·ra·ñár] *v.* to entangle; to snarl; to confuse, mix up.

enmascarar [em·mas·ka·rár] *v.* to mask; **-se** to put on a mask; to masquerade.

enmendar[1] [em·men·dár] *v. irr.* to amend, correct; to indemnify, compensate; **-se** to reform, mend one's ways.

enmienda [em·mjén·da] *f.* correction; amendment; reform; indemnity, compensation.

enmohecer[13] [em·mo·e·sér] *v.* to rust; to mold; **-se** to rust, become rusty; to mold.

enmudecer[13] [em·mu·de·sér] *v. irr.* to silence; to remain silent; to lose one's voice; to become dumb.

ennegrecer[13] [en·ne·ǥre·sér] *v. irr.* to blacken; to darken; **-se** to become dark; to get cloudy.

ennoblecer[13] [en·no·ble·sér] *v. irr.* to ennoble, dignify.

enojadizo [e·no·xa·dí·so] *adj.* irritable, ill-tempered.

enojado [e·no·xá·do] *adj.* angry.

enojar [e·no·xár] *v.* to make angry, vex, annoy; **-se** to get angry.

enojo [e·nó·xo] *m.* anger; annoyance.

enojoso [e·no·xó·so] *adj.* annoying, bothersome.

enorgullecer[13] [e·nor·ǥu·ye·sér] *v. irr.* to fill with pride; **-se** to swell up with pride; to be proud.

enorme [e·nór·me] *adj.* enormous.

enramada [en·rra·má·da] *f.* arbor, bower; shady grove.

enrarecer[13] [en·rra·re·sér] *v. irr.* to rarefy, thin, make less dense (*as air*); **-se** to become rarefied; to become scarce.

enrarecimiento [en·rra·re·si·mjén·to] *m.* rarity, thinness (*of the air*); rarefaction (*act of making thin, rare or less dense*).

enredadera [en·rre·da·dé·ra] *f.* climbing vine.

enredar [en·rre·dár] *v.* (*enmarañar*) to entangle, snare; to snarl; to mix up; to wind (*on a spool*); (*enemistar*) to raise a rumpus; **-se** to get tangled up, mixed up; to get trapped; **-se con** to have an affair with.

enredista [en·rre·dís·ta] *m. Am.* liar; gossip; *Am.* talebearer.

enredo [en·rré·do] *m.* tangle; confusion; lie; plot.

enredoso [en·rre·dó·so] *adj.* tangled up; *Am.* tattler.

enrejado [en·rre·xá·do] *m.* trellis; grating.

enrevesado [en·rre·be·sá·do] *adj.* turned around; intricate, complicated; unruly.

enriquecer[13] [en·rri·ke·sér] *v. irr.* to enrich; to become rich; **-se** to become rich.

enrojecer[13] [en·rro·xe·sér] *v. irr.* to redden; **-se** to get red, blush.

enrollar [en·rro·yár] *v.* to roll, roll up; to coil.

enronquecer[13] [en·rroŋ·ke·sér] *v. irr.* to make hoarse; to become hoarse; **-se** to become hoarse.

enroscar[6] [en·rros·kár] *v.* to coil; to twist, twine; **-se** to coil; to curl up.

ensacar[6] [en·sa·kár] *v.* to sack, bag, put in a bag or sack.

ensalada [en·sa·lá·da] *f.* salad; hodgepodge, mixture.

ensalmo [en·sál·mo] *m.* incantation.

ensalzar[9] [en·sal·sár] *v.* to exalt, praise.

ensanchar [en·san·čár] *v.* to widen, enlarge; **-se** to expand; to puff up.

ensanche [en·sán·če] *m.* widening, expansion, extension.

ensangrentado [en·saŋ·gren·tá·do] *adj.* gory, bloody; *p.p. of* **ensangrentar.**

ensangrentar [en·saŋ·gren·tár] *v.* to stain with blood; **-se** to be covered with blood; to get red with anger.

ensartar [en·sar·tár] *v.* to string; to thread; to link; to rattle off (*tales, stories, etc.*); *Ch.* to tie to a ring; *Mex.* to swindle, trick; **-se** *Andes* to fall into a trap.

ensayar [en·sa·yár] *v.* to try; to attempt; to test; to rehearse; **-se** to practice, train oneself.

ensayo [en·sá·yo] *m.* trial, attempt; rehearsal; test; experiment; essay.

ensenada [en·se·ná·da] *f.* small bay, cove.

enseñanza [en·se·ñán·sa] *f.* teaching; education, training.

enseñar [en·se·ñár] *v.* to show; to teach; to train; to point out.

enseres [en·sé·res] *m. pl.* household goods; utensils; implements; equipment.

ensillar [en·si·yár] *v.* to saddle; *Ch.* to abuse, mistreat, domineer; *Ríopl.* — **el picazo** to get angry.

ensimismarse [en·si·miz·már·se] *v.* to become absorbed in thought; *Col., Ven., Ch.* to become conceited or vain.

ensoberbecer[13] [en·so·ber·be·sér] *v. irr.* to make proud or haughty; **-se** to puff up with pride; to become haughty; to get rough, choppy (*said of the sea*).

ensordecer[13] [en·sor·de·sér] *v. irr.* to deafen; to become deaf.

ensortijar [en·sor·ti·xár] *v.* to curl; to ring the nose of (*an animal*); **-se** to curl.

ensuciar [en·su·sjár] *v.* to dirty, soil; to stain; **-se** to get dirty; to soil oneself.

ensueño [en·swé·ño] *m.* illusion, dream.

entablar [en·ta·blár] *v.* to board up; to plank; to splint; — **una conversación** to start a conversation; — **un pleito** to bring a lawsuit.

entablillar [en·ta·bli·yár] *v.* to splint; *Mex.* to cut (*chocolate*) into tablets or squares.

entallar [en·ta·yár] *v.* to fit closely (*a dress*); to carve.

entapizar[9] [en·ta·pi·sár] *v.* to cover with tapestry; to drape with tapestries; to upholster.

entarimar [en·ta·ri·már] *v.* to floor (*with boards*).

ente [én·te] *m.* entity, being; queer fellow.

enteco [en·té·ko] *adj.* sickly, skinny.

entender[1] [en·ten·dér] *v. irr.* to understand; — **de** to know, be an expert in; — **en** to take care of; to deal with; **-se con** to have dealings or relations with; to have an understanding with.

entendido [en·ten·dí·do] *p.p.* understood; *adj.* wise, prudent; well-informed; able, skillful; **no darse por** — to pretend not to hear or understand; not to take the hint.

entendimiento [en·ten·di·mjén·to] *m.* understanding; intellect; mind.

enterado [en·te·rá·do] *p.p. & adj.* informed; aware.

enterar [en·te·rár] *v.* to inform, acquaint; **-se** to know, learn, find out; to understand, get the idea.

entereza [en·te·ré·sa] *f.* entirety; integrity; fortitude; serenity; firmness; perfection.

enternecedor [en·ter·ne·se·dór] *adj.* touching, moving, pitiful.

enternecer[13] [en·ter·ne·sér] *v. irr.* to soften, touch, stir, move; **-se** to become tender; to be touched, stirred.

entero [en·té·ro] *adj.* (*completo*) entire, whole; (*justo*) just, right; firm; *m.* integer, whole number; *Col.* payment, reimbursement; *Ch.* balance of an account; **caballo** — stallion.

enterramiento [en·te·rra·mjén·to] *m.* burial.

enterrar[1] [en·te·rrár] *v. irr.* to bury; *Am.* to sink, stick into.

entibiar [en·ti·bjár] *v.* to make lukewarm; **-se** to become lukewarm.

entidad [en·ti·dáđ] *f.* entity; unit, group, organization; **de —** of value or importance.

entierro [en·tjé·rro] *m.* burial; funeral; grave; *Am.* hidden treasure.

entintar [en·tin·tár] *v.* to ink; to stain with ink; to dye.

entoldar [en·tol·dár] *v.* to cover with an awning; **-se** to puff up with pride; to become overcast, cloudy.

entonación [en·to·na·sjón] *f.* intonation.

entonar [en·to·nár] *v.* to sing in tune; to start a song (*for others to follow*); to be in tune; to harmonize; **-se** to put on airs.

entonces [en·tón·ses] *adv.* then, at that time; **pues —** well then.

entornado [en·tor·ná·đo] *adj.* half-open; half-closed, ajar.

entornar [en·tor·nár] *v.* to half-open.

entorpecer[13] [en·tor·pe·sér] *v. irr.* to stupefy; to be numb, make numb; to delay, obstruct; to thwart, frustrate.

entorpecimiento [en·tor·pe·si·mjén·to] *m.* numbness; dullness; delay, obstruction.

entrada [en·trá·đa] *f.* (*apertura*) entrance; entry; gate; opening; (*acción o privilegio*) entering, admission; entrée (*dish or dinner course*); ticket; (*computadora*) entry; *Mex., Cuba* attack, assault, goring; *Mex.* beating; **-s** cash receipts; **mecanismos de —** input.

entrambos [en·trám·bos] *adj. & pron.* both.

entrampar [en·tram·pár] *v.* to trap, ensnare; to trick; to burden with debts; **-se** to get trapped or entangled; to run into debt.

entrante [en·trán·te] *adj.* entering; incoming; **el año — next** year.

entraña [en·trá·ña] *f.* entrail; innermost recess; heart; disposition, temper; **-s** entrails, "innards", insides; **hijo de mis -s** child of my heart; **no tener -s** to be cruel.

entrar [en·trár] *v.* to enter, go in, come in; to attack; **me entró miedo** I became afraid; **-se** to slip in, get in, sneak in; to enter.

entre [én·tre] *prep.* between; among; **dijo — sí** he said to himself; **— tanto** meanwhile; *Am.* **— más habla menos dice** the more he talks the less he says.

entreabierto [en·tre·a·bjér·to] *p.p. of* **entreabrir;** *adj.* ajar, half-open, partly open.

entreabrir[52] [en·tre·a·brír] *v.* to half-open.

entreacto [en·tre·ák·to] *m.* intermission; intermezzo (*entertainment between the acts*); small cigar.

entrecano [en·tre·ká·no] *adj.* greyish.

entrecejo [en·tre·sé·xo] *m.* space between the eyebrows; **fruncir el —** to wrinkle one's brow.

entrecortado [en·tre·kor·tá·đo] *adj.* hesitating, faltering (*speech*); breathless, choking; *p.p.* interrupted.

entrecortar [en·tre·kor·tár] *v.* to cut halfway through or in between; to interrupt at intervals.

entrecruzar[9] [en·tre·kru·sár] *v.* to intercross, cross; to interlace; **-se** to cross.

entredicho [en·tre·đí·čo] *m.* prohibition, injunction.

entrega [en·tré·ga] *f.* (*acto de ceder*) delivery; surrender; (*parte suelta*) installment (*of a book*); **novela por -s** serial novel.

entregar[7] [en·tre·gár] *v.* to deliver, hand over; **-se** to surrender, submit, give up; to devote oneself (to); to abandon oneself (to).

entrelace [en·tre·lá·se] *m.* bridging.

entrelazar[9] [en·tre·la·sár] *v.* to interlace; to weave together.

entremés [en·tre·més] *m.* relish, side dish (*of olives, pickles, etc.*); one-act farce (*formerly presented between the acts of a play*).

entremeter [en·tre·me·tér] *v.* to insert; to place between; **-se** to meddle; to intrude.

entremetido [en·tre·me·tí·đo] *adj.* meddlesome; *m.* meddler; intruder.

entremetimiento [en·tre·me·ti·mjén·to] *m.* intrusion, meddling.

entremezclar [en·tre·mes·klár] *v.* to intermix, intermingle.

entrenador [en·tre·na·đór] *m. Am.* trainer.

entrenamiento [en·tre·na·mjén·to] *m. Am.* training, drill.

entrenar [en·tre·nár] *v. Am.* to train, drill; **-se** *Am.* to train.

entresacar[6] [en·tre·sa·kár] *v.* to pick out, select.

entresuelo [en·tre·swé·lo] *m.* mezzanine; second floor.

entretanto [en·tre·tán·to] *adv.* meanwhile.

entretejer [en·tre·te·xér] *v.* to weave together; to intertwine.

entretener[45] [en·tre·te·nér] *v. irr.* to delay, detain; to amuse, entertain; **-se** to amuse oneself; to delay oneself; **— el tiempo** to while away the time.

entretenido [en·tre·te·ní·đo] *adj.* entertaining, amusing; *p.p. of* **entretener.**

entretenimiento [en·tre·te·ni·mjén·to] *m.* entertainment; pastime; delay.

entrever[49] [entre·bér] *v.* to glimpse, catch a glimpse of; to half-see, see vaguely.

entreverar [en·tre·be·rár] *v.* to intermingle, intermix.

entrevista [en·tre·bís·ta] *f.* interview; date, appointment.

entrevistar [en·tre·bis·tár] *v.* to interview; **-se con** to have an interview with.

entrevisto [en·tre·bís·to] *p.p. of* **entrever.**

entristecer[13] [en·tris·te·sér] *v. irr.* to sadden, make sad; **-se** to become sad.

entrometer [en·tro·me·tér] = **entremeter.**

entrometido [en·tro·me·tí·đo] = **entremetido.**

entumecer[13] [en·tu·me·sér] *v. irr.* to make numb; **-se** to get numb; to surge; to swell.

entumido [en·tu·mí·đo] *adj.* numb, stiff; *Am.* timid, shy, awkward.

entumirse [en·tu·mír·se] *v.* to get numb.

enturbiar [en·tur·bjár] *v.* to make muddy; to muddle; to disturb; to obscure; **-se** to get muddy; to get muddled.

entusiasmar [en·tu·sjaz·már] *v.* to excite, fill with enthusiasm; **-se** to get enthusiastic, excited.

entusiasmo [en·tu·sjáz·mo] *m.* enthusiasm.

entusiasta [en·tu·sjás·ta] *m. & f.* enthusiast; **entusiástico** *adj.* enthusiastic.

enumeración [e·nu·me·ra·sjón] *f.* enumeration, counting.

enumerar [e·nu·me·rár] *v.* to enumerate.

enunciar [e·nun·sjár] *v.* to express, state, declare.

envainar [em·baj·nár] *v.* to sheathe.

envalentonar [em·ba·len·to·nár] *v.* to make bold or haughty; **-se** to get bold; to brag, swagger.

envanecer[13] [em·ba·ne·sér] *v. irr.* to make vain; **-se** to become vain.

envasar [em·ba·sár] *v.* to pack, put up in any container; to bottle; to can.

envase [em·bá·se] *m.* packing; container, jar, bottle, can (*for packing*).

envejecer[13] [em·be·xe·sér] *v. irr.* to make old; to grow old, get old; **-se** to grow old, get old.

envenenamiento [em·be·ne·na·mjén·to] *m.* poisoning.

envenenar [em·be·ne·nár] *v.* to poison; to infect.
envergadura [em·ber·ga·dú·ra] *f.* span (*of an airplane*); spread (*of a bird's wings*); breadth (*of sails*).
envés [em·bés] *m.* back or wrong side.
enviado [em·bjá·do] *m.* envoy.
enviar[17] [em·bjár] *v.* to send; — **a uno a paseo** to give someone his walking papers.
enviciar [em·bi·sjár] *v.* to vitiate, corrupt; **-se** to become addicted (to), overly fond (of).
envidar [em·bi·djár] *v.* to bid (*in cards*); to bet.
envidia [em·bi·dja] *f.* envy.
envidiable [em·bi·djá·ble] *adj.* enviable, desirable.
envidiar [em·bi·djár] *v.* to envy.
envidioso [em·bi·djó·so] *adj.* envious.
envilecer[13] [em·bi·le·sér] *v. irr.* to revile, malign, degrade; **-se** to degrade or lower oneself.
envilecimiento [em·bi·le·si·mjén·to] *m.* degradation, humiliation, shame.
envío [em·bí·o] *m.* remittance, sending; shipment.
envite [em·bí·te] *m.* bid; stake (*in cards*); offer; push.
envoltorio [em·bol·tó·rjo] *m.* bundle, package.
envoltura [em·bol·tú·ra] *f.* wrapping, cover; wrapper.
envolver[2, 52] [em·bol·bér] *v. irr.* to involve, entangle; to wrap; to wind (*a thread, rope, etc.*); to surround; **-se** to become involved, entangled; to cover up, wrap up.
envuelto [em·bwél·to] *p.p.* of **envolver.**
enyesar [en·ŷe·sár] *v.* to plaster; to chalk; to put a cast on.
enzolvar [en·sol·bár] *v. Mex.* to clog, obstruct; *Am.* **-se** to clog, get clogged. *See* **azolvar.**
¡epa! [é·pa] *interj. Ríopl., Ven., Col., Mex.* hey! listen! stop! look out!
épico [é·pi·ko] *adj.* epic.
epidemia [e·pi·de·mja] *f.* epidemic.
episodio [e·pi·só·djo] *m.* episode.
epístola [e·pís·to·la] *f.* epistle; letter.
epitafio [e·pi·tá·fjo] *m.* epitaph.
época [é·po·ka] *f.* epoch.
epopeya [e·po·pé·ya] *f.* epic poem.
equidad [e·ki·dád] *f.* equity, justice, fairness.
equidistante [e·ki·dis·tán·te] *adj.* equidistant, equally distant, halfway, midway.
equilibrar [e·ki·li·brár] *v.* to balance, poise.
equilibrio [e·ki·lí·brjo] *m.* equilibrium, balance; poise.
equilibrista [e·ki·li·brís·ta] *m. & f.* acrobat.
equipaje [e·ki·pá·xe] *m.* baggage, luggage; equipment, outfit; crew.
equipar [e·ki·pár] *v.* to equip, fit out; to man, equip and provision (*a ship*).
equipo [e·kí·po] *m.* (*materiales*) equipment, equipping; outfit; (*grupo*) work crew; sport team; — **de novia** trousseau.
equitación [e·ki·ta·sjón] *f.* horsemanship; horseback riding.
equitativo [e·ki·ta·tí·bo] *adj.* fair, just.
equivalente [e·ki·ba·lén·te] *adj.* equivalent.
equivaler[47] [e·ki·ba·lér] *v. irr.* to be equivalent.
equivocación [e·ki·bo·ka·sjón] *f.* error, mistake.
equivocado [e·ki·bo·ká·do] *p.p. & adj.* mistaken.
equivocar[6] [e·ki·bo·kár] *v.* to mistake; **-se** to be mistaken; to make a mistake.
equívoco [e·kí·bo·ko] *adj.* equivocal, ambiguous, vague; *Am.* mistaken; *m.* pun, play on words; *Am.* mistake, error.
era [é·ra] *f.* era, age; threshing floor.
erario [e·rá·rjo] *m.* public treasury.
erguido [er·gí·do] *adj.* erect; *p.p.* of **erguir.**
erguir[3] [er·gír] *v. irr.* to erect, set upright; to lift (*the head*) **-se** to sit up or stand erect; to become proud and haughty.
erial [e·rjál] *m.* uncultivated land; *adj.* unplowed, untilled.
erigir[11] [e·ri·xír] *v.* to erect, build; to found.
erizado [e·ri·sá·do] *adj.* bristly, prickly; — **de** bristling with.
erizar[9] [e·ri·sár] *v.* to set on end, make bristle; **-se** to bristle; to stand on end (*hair*).
erizo [e·rí·so] *m.* hedgehog, porcupine; thistle; — **de mar** sea urchin; **ser un** — to be irritable, harsh.
ermitaño [er·mi·tá·ño] *m.* hermit.
erosion [e·ro·sjón] *f.* erosion.
errabundo [e·rra·bún·do] *adj.* wandering.
errado [e·rrá·do] *adj.* mistaken, wrong, in error; *p.p.* of **errar.**
errante [e·rrán·te] *adj.* errant, roving, wandering.
errar[28] [e·rrár] *v. irr.* to err, make mistakes; to miss (*target, road*); to rove, wander.
errata [e·rrá·ta] *f.* misprint, printer's error.
erróneo [e·rró·ne·o] *adj.* erroneous, mistaken, wrong, incorrect.
error [e·rrór] *m.* error, fault, mistake.
eructar [e·ruk·tár] *v.* to belch, to burp.
eructo [e·rúk·to] *m.* belch.
erudición [e·ru·di·sjón] *f.* erudition, learning.
erudito [e·ru·dí·to] *adj.* erudite, scholarly, learned; *m.* scholar.
erupción [e·rup·sjón] *f.* eruption; outburst; rash.
esbelto [ez·bél·to] *adj.* slender.
esbozar[9] [ez·bo·sár] *v.* to sketch, outline.
esbozo [ez·bó·so] *m.* sketch, outline.
escabechar [es·ka·be·čár] *v.* to pickle.
escabeche [es·ka·be·če] *m.* pickled fish; pickle (*solution for pickling*).
escabel [es·ka·bél] *m.* stool; footstool.
escabrosidad [es·ka·bro·si·dád] *f.* roughness, unevenness; harshness; improper word or phrase.
escabroso [es·ka·bró·so] *adj.* rough; rugged; scabrous, rather indecent.
escabullirse[20] [es·ka·bu·yír·se] *v. irr.* to slip away; to slip through; to scoot, scamper, scurry.
escala [es·ká·la] *f.* ladder; scale; port of call; stopover; **hacer** — **en** to stop over at; **escalafón** [es·ka·la·fón] *m.* army register.
escalar [es·ka·lár] *v.* to scale; to climb.
escaldar [es·kal·dár] *v.* to scald; to make red-hot; **-se** to get scalded.
escalera [es·ka·lé·ra] *f.* stairs, staircase; ladder; — **mecánica** escalator.
escalfar [es·kal·fár] *v.* to poach (*eggs*).
escalinata [es·ka·li·ná·ta] *f.* flight of stairs (*usually on the outside*).
escalofriarse[17] [es·ka·lo·frjár·se] *v.* to become chilled.
escalofrío [es·ka·lo·frí·o] *m.* chill; **-s** chills and fever.
escalón [es·ka·lón] *m.* step (*of a ladder or staircase*); stepping stone; *Arg.* **-es** tribe of **quichua** Indians.
escalonar [es·ka·lo·nár] *v.* to echelon (*arrange in step-like formation*); to terrace; **-se** to rise in terraces.
escaloñas [es·ka·ló·ñas] *f. pl.* scallions.
escama [es·ká·ma] *f.* scale, fish scale; flake.
escamoso [es·ka·mó·so] *adj.* scaly.
escamotear [es·ka·mo·te·ár] *v.* to whisk out of sight; to steal or snatch away with cunning; to conceal by a trick of sleight of hand.
escampar [es·kam·pár] *v.* to clear (*weather*).
escandalizar[9] [es·kan·da·li·sár] *v.* scandalize, shock; **-se** to be shocked.
escándalo [es·kán·da·lo] *m.* scandal; bad example.
escandaloso [es·kan·da·ló·so] *adj.* scandalous,

shocking; *Mex., C.A., Col., Andes* showy, loud (*color*).

escandio [es·kán·djo] *m.* scandium.

escapada [es·ka·pá·da] *f.* escape, flight.

escapar [es·ka·pár] *v.* to escape, flee, avoid; **-se** to run away, escape.

escaparate [es·ka·pa·rá·te] *m.* show window; glass case, glass cabinet or cupboard.

escapatoria [es·ka·pa·tó·rja] *f.* escape, loophole, excuse.

escape [es·ká·pe] *m.* escape; vent, outlet; exhaust; **a** — rapidly, at full speed.

escarabajo [es·ka·ra·bá·xo] *m.* black beetle.

escaramuza [es·ka·ra·mú·sa] *f.* skirmish; quarrel.

escarbar [es·kar·bár] *v.* to scrape, scratch; to dig out; to pry into, investigate.

escarcear [es·kar·se·ár] *v. Ch., Ríopl.* to prance.

escarcha [es·kár·ča] *f.* frost; frosting.

escarchar [es·kar·čár] *v.* to frost; to freeze.

escardar [es·kar·dár] *v.* to weed; to weed out.

escarlata [es·kar·lá·ta] *f.* scarlet; scarlet fever; scarlet cloth; **escarlatina** [es·kar·la·tí·na] *f.* scarlet fever.

escarmentar[1] [es·kar·men·tár] *v. irr.* to punish (*as an example or warning*); to profit by one's misfortunes, punishment, etc.; — **en cabeza ajena** to profit by another's mistake or misfortune.

escarmiento [es·kar·mjén·to] *m.* lesson, example, warning; punishment.

escarnecer[13] [es·kar·ne·sér] *v. irr.* to jeer, insult, mock.

escarnio [es·kár·njo] *m.* scoff, jeer.

escarpa [es·kár·pa] *f.* steep slope, bluff, cliff; scarp (*of a fortification*).

escarpado [es·kar·pá·do] *adj.* steep; rugged.

escarpia [es·kár·pja] *f.* hook (*for hanging something*).

escasear [es·ka·se·ár] *v.* to be scarce; to grow less, become scarce; to stint.

escasez [es·ka·sés] *f.* scarcity, lack, scantiness.

escaso [es·ká·so] *adj.* scarce, limited; scant; scanty; stingy.

escatimar [es·ka·ti·már] *v.* to stint, skimp; to curtail.

escena [e·sé·na] *f.* scene; scenery, theatre, stage.

escenario [e·se·ná·rjo] *m.* stage.

escenificación [e·se·ni·fi·ka·sjón] *f.* dramatization, stage adaptation.

escepticismo [e·sep·ti·síz·mo] *m.* scepticism; doubt, unbelief.

escéptico [e·sép·ti·ko] *m. & adj.* sceptic.

esclarecer[13] [es·kla·re·sér] *v. irr.* to lighten, illuminate; to elucidate, make clear, explain.

esclarecimiento [es·kla·re·si·mjén·to] *m.* clarification, illumination, illustration; worth, nobility.

esclavitud [es·kla·bi·túd] *f.* slavery.

esclavizar[9] [es·kla·bi·sár] *v.* to enslave.

esclavo [es·klá·bo] *m.* slave.

esclusa [es·klú·sa] *f.* lock (*of a canal*); sluice, floodgate.

escoba [es·kó·ba] *f.* broom.

escobazo [es·ko·bá·so] *m.* blow with a broom.

escobilla [es·ko·bí·ya] *f.* whisk broom; small broom.

escobillón [es·ko·bi·yón] *m.* swab; push broom.

escocer[2, 10] [es·ko·sér] *v. irr.* to sting, smart.

escocés [es·ko·sés] *adj.* Scottish; Scotch; *m.* Scot; Scotchman.

escoger[11] [es·ko·xér] *v.* to choose, select, pick out.

escolar [es·ko·lár] *adj.* scholastic, academic; *m.* scholar, student.

escolástico [es·ko·lás·ti·ko] *adj. & m.* scholastic.

escolta [es·kól·ta] *f.* escort; convoy.

escollo [es·kó·yo] *m.* reef; danger; obstacle.

escombro [es·kóm·bro] *m.* debris, rubbish; mackerel.

esconder [es·kon·dér] *v.* to hide, conceal; **-se** to hide, go into hiding.

escondidas [es·kon·dí·das]: **a** — on the sly, under cover; *Am.* **jugar a las** — to play hide-and-seek.

escondite [es·kon·dí·te] *m.* hiding place; *Spain* **jugar al** — to play hide-and-seek.

escondrijo [es·kon·drí·xo] *m.* hiding place.

escopeta [es·ko·pé·ta] *f.* shotgun.

escopetazo [es·ko·pe·tá·so] *m.* gunshot; gunshot wound; (*malas noticias*) sudden bad news; *Am.* offensive or ironic remark.

escoplo [es·kó·plo] *m.* chisel.

escoria [es·kó·rja] *f.* slag; scum; **escorial** [es·ko·rjál] *m.* dump, dumping place; pile of slag.

escorpión [es·kor·pjón] *m.* scorpion.

escote [es·kó·te] *m.* low neck; **convite a** — Dutch treat (*where everyone pays his share*).

escotilla [es·ko·tí·ya] *f.* hatchway; **escotillón** *m.* hatch, hatchway; trap door.

escozor [es·ko·zór] *m.* smarting sensation, sting.

escribano [es·kri·bá·no] *m.* court clerk; lawyer's clerk; notary.

escribiente [es·kri·bjén·te] *m.* clerk, office clerk.

escribir[52] [es·kri·bír] *v.* to write.

escrito [es·krí·to] *p.p. of* **escribir** written; *m* — writing; manuscript.

escritor [es·kri·tór] *m.* writer.

escritorio [es·kri·tó·rjo] *m.* desk; office.

escritura [es·kri·tú·ra] *f.* writing, handwriting; deed, document; **Sagrada Escritura** Holy Scripture.

escrúpulo [es·krú·pu·lo] *m.* scruple, doubt.

escrupuloso [es·kru·pu·ló·so] *adj.* scrupulous; particular, exact.

escrutador [es·kru·ta·dór] *adj.* scrutinizing, examining; peering; penetrating; *m.* scrutinizer, examiner; inspector of election returns.

escrutar [es·kru·tár] *v.* to scrutinize.

escrutinio [es·kru·tí·njo] *m.* scrutiny, careful inspection.

escuadra [es·kwá·dra] *f.* squadron; fleet; square (*instrument for drawing or testing right angles*); — **de ángulo** angle plate; — **de hierro** steel square.

escuadrón [es·kwa·drón] *m.* squadron.

escualidez [es·kwa·li·dés] *f.* squalor.

escuálido [es·kwá·li·do] *adj.* squalid, filthy; thin, emaciated.

escuchar [es·ku·čár] *v.* to listen; to heed.

escudar [es·ku·dár] *v.* to shield.

escudero [es·ku·dé·ro] *m.* squire.

escudo [es·kú·do] *m.* shield; escutcheon, coat of arms; gold crown (*ancient coin*); *Am.* Chilean gold coin; — **protector** hood (*machine*).

escudriñar [es·ku·dri·ñár] *v.* to scrutinize, search, pry into.

escuela [es·kwé·la] *f.* school.

escuelante [es·kwe·lán·te] *m. & f. Col.* schoolboy; schoolgirl.

escueto [es·kwé·to] *adj.* plain, unadorned, bare.

esculcar[6] [es·kul·kár] *v. Am.* to search; *Carib., Col., Ven.* to frisk (*a person's pockets*).

esculpir [es·kul·pír] *v.* to sculpture; to engrave.

escultor [es·kul·tór] *m.* sculptor.

escultura [es·kul·tú·ra] *f.* sculpture.

escupidera [es·ku·pi·dé·ra] *f.* cuspidor.

escupir [es·ku·pír] *v.* to spit.

escurridero [es·ku·rri·dé·ro] *m.* drain pipe; drainboard.

escurrir [es·ku·rrír] *v.* to drip; to drain; to trickle; **-se** to ooze out, trickle; to slip out, sneak out.

ese [é·se], **esa** [é·sa] *dem. adj.* that; **esos** [é·sos], **esas** [é·sas] those; **ése, ésa** *m., f. dem. pron.* that one;

ésos, ésas *m., f. pl.* those.
esencia [e·sén·sja] *f.* essence.
esencial [e·sen·sjál] *adj.* essential.
esfera [es·fé·ra] *f.* sphere; clock dial.
esférico [es·fé·ri·ko] *adj.* spherical.
esforzado [es·for·sá·do] *adj.* strong; valiant; courageous.
esforzar[2, 9] [es·for·sár] *v. irr.* to give or inspire strength; to encourage; **-se** to make an effort; to strive, try hard.
esfuerzo [es·fwér·so] *m.* effort; spirit, courage, vigor; stress.
esfumar [es·fu·már] *v.* to shade, tone down; **-se** to vanish, disappear.
esgrima [ez·grí·ma] *f.* fencing.
esgrimir [ez·gri·mír] *v.* to fence; to brandish; to wield (*the sword or pen*).
eslabón [ez·la·bón] *m.* link of a chain; steel knife sharpener; black scorpion.
eslabonar [ez·la·bo·nár] *v.* to link; to join; to connect.
esmaltar [ez·mal·tár] *v.* to enamel; to beautify; adorn.
esmalte [ez·mál·te] *m.* enamel; enamel work; smalt (*a blue pigment*).
esmerado [ez·me·rá·do] *adj.* painstaking, careful, conscientious; *p.p. of* **esmerar.**
esmeralda [ez·me·rál·da] *f.* emerald; *Am.* an eel-like fish; *Col.* hummingbird; *Mex.* variety of pineapple.
esmerar [ez·me·rár] *v.* to polish, clean; **-se** to strive, take special pains, use great care.
esmeril [ez·me·ríl] *m.* emery.
esmeriladora [ez·me·ri·la·dó·ra] *f.* emery wheel.
esmero [ez·mé·ro] *m.* care, precision.
esmoquin [ez·mó·kin] *m.* tuxedo, dinner coat.
eso [é·so] *dem. pron.* that, that thing, that fact; — **es** that is it; **a** — **de** at about (*referring to time*); *Am.* **¡eso!** that's right!
espaciado [es·pa·sjá·do] *m.* pitch.
espaciar[17] [es·pa·sjár] *v.* to space; to spread; to expand; **-se** to enlarge (*upon a subject*); to relax, amuse oneself.
espacio [es·pá·sjo] *m.* space; interval; slowness, delay; (*imprenta*) pitch; *adv. Mex.* slowly.
espacioso [es·pa·sjó·so] *adj.* spacious; slow.
espada [es·pá·da] *f.* sword; skilled swordsman; matador (*bull-fighter who kills the bull*); **-s** swords (*Spanish card suit*).
espalda [es·pál·da] *f.* back, shoulders; **-s** back, back part; **a -s** behind one's back; **de -s** on one's back; **dar la** — **a** to turn one's back on; **espaldilla** [es·pal·dí·ya] *f.* shoulder blade.
espaldar [es·pal·dár] *m.* back (*of a chair*); trellis (*for plants*); backplate of a cuirass (*armor*).
espantadizo [es·pan·ta·dí·so] *adj.* scary, shy, timid.
espantajo [es·pan·tá·xo] *m.* scarecrow.
espantapájaros [es·pan·ta·pá·xa·ros] *m.* scarecrow.
espantar [es·pan·tár] *v.* to frighten, scare; to scare away; *Col.* to haunt; **-se** to be scared; to be astonished; *Mex.* **espantárselas** [es·pan·tár·se·las] to be wide-awake, catch on quickly.
espanto [es·pán·to] *m.* fright, terror; astonishment; *Col., Ven., Mex.* ghost.
espantoso [es·pan·tó·so] *adj.* frightful, terrifying; wonderful.
español [es·pa·ñól] *adj.* Spanish; *m.* Spaniard; Spanish language.
esparadrapo [es·pa·ra·drá·po] *m.* court plaster, adhesive tape. *See* **tela adhesiva.**
esparcir[10] [es·par·sír] *v.* to scatter, spread; **-se** to relax, amuse oneself.
espárrago [es·pá·rra·go] *m.* asparagus.
esparto [es·pár·to] *m.* esparto grass (*used for making*

ropes, mats, etc.).
espasmo [es·páz·mo] *m.* spasm; horror.
espátula [es·pá·tu·la] *f.* spatula.
especia [es·pé·sja] *f.* spice.
especial [es·pe·sjál] *adj.* special; **en** — in particular, specially.
especialidad [es·pe·sja·li·dád] *f.* specialty.
especialista [es·pe·sja·lís·ta] *m. & f.* specialist.
especializar[9] [es·pe·sja·li·sár] *v.* to specialize; **-se en** to specialize in.
especie [es·pé·sje] *f.* species; kind, sort; pretext; idea.
especificar[6] [es·pe·si·fi·kár] *v.* to specify; to name.
específico [es·pe·sí·fi·ko] *adj.* specific; *m.* specific (*medicine*).
espécimen [es·pé·si·men] *m.* specimen, sample.
espectacular [es·pek·ta·ku·lár] *adj.* spectacular.
espectáculo [es·pek·tá·ku·lo] *m.* spectacle.
espectador [es·pek·ta·dór] *m.* spectator.
espectro [es·pék·tro] *m.* spectre, ghost; spectrum.
espectrógrafo [es·pek·tró·gra·fo] *m.* spectrograph.
especulación [es·pe·ku·la·sjón] *f.* speculation.
especulador [es·pe·ku·la·dór] *m.* speculator.
especular [es·pe·ku·lár] *v.* to speculate.
especulativo [es·pe·ku·la·tí·bo] *adj.* speculative.
espejismo [es·pe·xíz·mo] *m.* mirage; illusion.
espejo [es·pé·xo] *m.* mirror; model; — **de cuerpo entero** full-length mirror.
espejuelos [es·pe·xwé·los] *m. pl.* glasses, goggles.
espeluznante [es·pe·luz·nán·te] *adj.* hair-raising, terrifying.
espeluznarse [es·pe·luz·nár·se] *v.* to be terrified; to bristle with fear.
espera [es·pé·ra] *f.* wait; stay (*granted by judge*), delay; extension of time (*for payment*); **sala de** — waiting room; **estar en** — **de** to be waiting for; to be expecting.
esperanza [es·pe·rán·sa] *f.* hope; expectation.
esperanzado [es·pe·ran·sá·do] *adj.* hopeful.
esperanzar[9] [es·pe·ran·sár] *v.* to give hope to.
esperar [es·pe·rár] *v.* (*tener esperanza*) to hope; to expect; to trust; (*permanecer*) to wait, wait for; — **en alguien** to place hope or confidence in someone.
esperezarse [es·pe·re·sár·se] = **desperezarse.**
esperma [es·pér·ma] *f.* sperm.
esperpento [es·per·pén·to] *m.* ugly thing; nonsense.
espesar [es·pe·sár] *v.* to thicken; to make dense; **-se** to thicken; to become thick or dense.
espeso [es·pé·so] *adj.* thick, dense; compact; slovenly; *Ríopl.* bothersome, boring.
espesor [es·pe·sór] *m.* thickness.
espesura [es·pe·sú·ra] *f.* density, thickness; thicket; thickest part (*of a forest*).
espetar [es·pe·tár] *v.* to spring (*a joke, story, etc.*) on (*a person*), surprise with (*a joke, speech, story, etc.*); to pop (*a question*); to run a spit through (*meat, fish, etc. for roasting*); to pierce; **-se** to be stiff, pompous.
espía [es·pí·a] *m. & f.* spy.
espiar[17] [es·pjár] *v.* to spy; *Col., Mex.* **-se** to bruise the hoofs, get lame (*said of horses*).
espiga [es·pí·ga] *f.* ear of wheat; peg; spike.
espigar[7] [es·pi·gár] *v.* to glean; to grow spikes (*said of corn or grain*); **-se** to grow tall and slender.
espina [es·pí·na] *f.* thorn; sharp splinter; fish bone; spine; fear, suspicion; **darle a uno mala** — to arouse one's suspicion.
espinaca [es·pi·ná·ka] *f.* spinach.
espinazo [es·pi·ná·so] *m.* spine, backbone.
espinilla [es·pi·ní·ya] *f.* shin (*front part of leg*); blackhead (*on the skin*).

espino [es·pí·no] *m.* hawthorn; thorny shrub; thorny branch.

espinoso [es·pi·nó·so] *adj.* thorny; difficult, dangerous.

espionaje [es·pjo·ná·xe] *m.* espionage, spying.

espiral [es·pi·rál] *adj. & f.* spiral.

espirar [es·pi·rár] *v.* to exhale; to emit, give off; to die. *See* **expirar.**

espíritu [es·pí·ri·tu] *m.* spirit; soul; courage; vigor; essence; ghost.

espiritual [es·pi·ri·tuál] *adj.* spiritual.

espita [es·pí·ta] *f.* spigot, faucet, tap; toper, drunkard.

esplendidez [es·plen·di·dés] *f.* splendor.

espléndido [es·plén·di·do] *adj.* splendid.

esplendor [es·plen·dór] *m.* splendor.

esplendoroso [es·plen·do·ró·so] *adj.* resplendent, shining.

espliego [es·pljé·ǥo] *m.* lavender (*plant*).

espolear [es·po·le·ár] *v.* to spur; to incite.

espoleta [es·po·lé·ta] *f.* bomb fuse.

espolón [es·po·lón] *m.* spur (*on a cock's leg*); ram (*of a boat*); spur; buttress.

espolvorear [es·pol·ɓo·re·ár] *v.* to powder, sprinkle with powder.

esponja [es·pón·xa] *f.* sponge; sponger, parasite; *Col., Peru, Ch., Ríopl.* souse, habitual drunkard.

esponjado [es·poŋ·xá·do] *adj.* fluffy; spongy; puffed up; *p.p. of* **esponjar.**

esponjar [es·poŋ·jár] *v.* to fluff; to make spongy or porous; **-se** to fluff up; to become spongy or porous; to swell, puff up; to puff up wjth pride.

esponjoso [es·poŋ·xó·so] *adj.* spongy.

esponsales [es·pon·sá·les] *m. pl.* betrothal.

espontaneidad [es·pon·ta·nej·dád] *f.* spontaneity, ease, naturalness.

espontáneo [es·pon·tá·ne·o] *adj.* spontaneous.

esposa [es·pó·sa] *f.* wife; **-s** handcuffs.

esposo [es·pó·so] *m.* husband.

espuela [es·pwé·la] *f.* spur.

espulgar[7] [es·pul·ǥár] *v.* to delouse, remove lice or fleas from; to scrutinize.

espuma [es·pú·ma] *f.* foam, froth; scum; — **de jabón** suds.

espumar [es·pu·már] *v.* to skim; to froth, foam.

espumarajo [es·pu·ma·rá·xo] *m.* froth, foam (*from the mouth*); **echar -s** to froth at the mouth; to be very angry.

espumoso [es·pu·mó·so] *adj.* foamy.

esputo [es·pú·to] *m.* sputum, spit, saliva.

esquela [es·ké·la] *f.* note, letter; announcement.

esqueleto [es·ke·lé·to] *m.* skeleton; carcass; framework; *Mex., C.A., Col., Ven.* blank (*to fill out*); *Am.* outline.

esquema [es·ké·ma] *f.* scheme, outline.

esquí[17] [es·kí] *m.* ski, skiing; — **náutico,** — **acuático** water ski.

esquiar[17] [es·kjár] *v.* to ski.

esquila [es·kí·la] *f.* small bell; cow bell; sheep-shearing.

esquilar [es·ki·lár] *v.* to shear; to clip; to crop.

esquina [es·kí·na] *f.* corner, angle; **esquinazo** [es·ki·ná·so] *m.* corner; *Am.* serenade; **dar esquinazo** to avoid meeting someone; to "ditch" someone.

esquivar [es·ki·ɓár] *v.* to avoid, dodge; to shun; **-se** to withdraw, shy away.

esquivez [es·ki·ɓés] *f.* shyness; aloofness; disdain.

esquivo [es·kí·ɓo] *adv.* reserved, unsociable; shy; disdainful, aloof.

estabilidad [es·ta·ɓi·li·dád] *f.* stability.

estable [es·tá·ɓle] *adj.* stable, firm, steady.

establecer[13] [es·ta·ɓle·sér] *v. irr.* to establish; to found; to decree, ordain.

establecimiento [es·ta·ɓle·si·mjén·to] *m.* establishment; foundation; statute, law.

establo [es·tá·ɓlo] *m.* stable; **establero** [es·ta·ɓlé·ro] *m.* groom.

estaca [es·tá·ka] *f.* stake, club; stick; picket.

estacada [es·ta·ká·da] *f.* stockade; picket fence; *Am.* predicament.

estacar[6] [es·ta·kár] *v.* to stake; to tie on a stake; to stake off, mark with stakes; *Am.* to fasten down with stakes; **-se** to remain stiff or rigid.

estación [es·ta·sjón] *f.* station; season; railway station.

estacionar [es·ta·sjo·nár] *v.* to station; to place; to park (*a car*); **-se** to remain stationary; to park.

estacionario [es·ta·sjo·ná·rjo] *adj.* stationary; motionless.

estada [es·tá·da] *f.* sojourn, stay.

estadía [es·ta·dí·a] *f.* detention, stay; stay in port (*beyond time allowed for loading and unloading*); *C.A., Carib.* sojourn, stay (*in any sense*).

estadio [es·tá·djo] *m.* stadium.

estadista [es·ta·dís·ta] *m.* statesman.

estadística [es·ta·dís·ti·ka] *f.* statistics.

estado [es·tá·do] *m.* state, condition; station, rank; estate; — **mayor** army staff; **hombre de** — statesman; *Am.* **en** — **interesante** pregnant.

estadounidense [es·ta·dow·ni·dén·se] *adj.* from the United States, American.

estafa [es·tá·fa] *f.* swindle, fraud, trick.

estafador [es·ta·fa·dór] *m.* swindler, crook.

estafar [es·ta·fár] *v.* to swindle, defraud, cheat.

estalactita [es·ta·lak·tí·ta] *f.* stalactite.

estalagmita [es·ta·laǥ·mí·ta] *f.* stalagmite.

estallar [es·ta·yár] *v.* to explode, burst; to creak, crackle.

estallido [es·ta·yí·do] *m.* explosion, outburst; crash; creaking; crack (*of a gun*), report (*of a gun or cannon*).

estambre [es·tám·bre] *m.* woolen yarn; stamen (*of a flower*).

estampa [es·tám·pa] *f.* image; print; stamp; cut, picture; footprint; figure, appearance.

estampado [es·tam·pá·do] *m.* print, printed fabric; printing.

estampar [es·tam·pár] *v.* to stamp, print.

estampida [es·tam·pí·da] *f.* crack, sharp sound; *Col., Ven., C.A.* stampede (*sudden scattering of a herd of cattle or horses*).

estampido [es·tam·pí·do] *m.* crack, sharp sound; report of a gun.

estampilla [es·tam·pí·ya] *f.* stamp, seal; *Mex., C.A., Andes* postage stamp.

estancar[6] [es·taŋ·kár] *v.* to stem; to stanch; to stop the flow of; to corner (*a market*); **-se** to stagnate, become stagnant.

estancia [es·tán·sja] *f.* (*permanencia*) stay; (*lugar*) hall, room; mansion; *Ríopl.* farm, cattle ranch; *Carib.* main building of a farm or ranch.

estanciero [es·tan·sjé·ro] *m. Ríopl.* rancher, ranch-owner, cattle raiser; *adj.* pertaining to an **estancia.**

estanco [es·táŋ·ko] *m.* monopoly; government store (*for sale of monopolized goods such as tobacco, stamps and matches*); tank, reservoir; *Ec., C.A.* liquor store.

estandar [es·tán·dar] *m. Am.* standard, norm.

estandardizar [es·tan·dar·di·sár], **estandarizar**[9] [es·tan·da·ri·sár] *v. Am.* standardize.

estandarte [es·tan·dár·te] *m.* standard, flag, banner.

estanque [es·táŋ·ke] *m.* pond, pool, reservoir.

estanquillo [es·táŋ·kí·yo] *m.* tobacco store; *Am.* small store; *C.A.*, *Mex.* small liquor store, tavern.

estante [es·tán·te] *m.* shelf; bookshelf; *Am.* prop, support; **estantería** [es·tan·te·rí·a] *f.* shelves; bookcases.

estaño [es·tá·ño] *m.* tin.

estaquilla [es·ta·kí·ya] *f.* peg; spike.

estar[29] [es·tár] *v. irr.* to be; **-le bien a uno** to be becoming to one; — **de prisa** to be in a hurry; **¿a cuántos estamos?** what day of the month is it today?; **-se** to keep, remain.

estático [es·tá·ti·ko] *adj.* static; **estática** [es·tá·ti·ka] *f.* statics; radio static.

estatua [es·tá·twa] *f.* statue.

estatura [es·ta·tú·ra] *f.* stature, height.

estatuto [es·ta·tú·to] *m.* statute.

este [és·te], **esta** [és·ta] *dem. adj.* this; **estos** [és·tos], **estas** [és·tas] these; **éste, ésta** *m., f. dem. pron.* this one, this thing; the latter; **esto** [és·to] this, this thing; **éstos, éstas** *m., f. pl.* these; the latter.

este [és·te] *m.* east; east wind.

estela [es·té·la] *f.* wake of a ship.

estenógrafo [es·te·nó·ǥra·fo] *m.* stenographer.

estentóreo [es·ten·tó·re·o] *adj.* loud, thundering (*voice*).

estepa [es·té·pa] *f.* steppe, treeless plain.

estera [es·té·ra] *f.* matting; mat; conveyor belt.

estercolar [es·ter·ko·lár] *v.* to manure, fertilize with manure.

estercolero [es·ter·ko·lé·ro] *m.* manure pile, manure dump; manure collector.

estereoscopio [es·te·re·os·kó·pjo] *m.* stereoscope.

estereotipo [es·te·re·o·tí·po] *m.* stereotype.

estéril [es·té·ril] *adj.* sterile, barren.

esterilidad [es·te·ri·li·ðáđ] *f.* sterility, barrenness.

esterilizar[9] [es·te·ri·li·sár] *v.* to sterilize.

esterlina [es·ter·li·í·na] *adj.* sterling; **libra** — pound sterling.

esternón [es·ter·nón] *m.* sternum.

estero [es·té·ro] *m.* estuary.

estertor [es·ter·tór] *m.* death-rattle; snort.

estético [es·té·ti·ko] *adj.* aesthetic; **estética** [es·té·ti·ka] *f.* aesthetics.

estetoscopio [es·te·tos·kó·pjo] *m.* stethoscope.

estibador [es·ti·ba·đór] *m.* stevedore, longshoreman.

estibar [es·ti·bár] *v.* to stow (*in a boat*); to pack down, compress.

estiércol [es·tjér·kol] *m.* manure; fertilizer.

estigma [es·tíǥ·ma] *m.* stigma; brand, mark of disgrace; birthmark.

estilar [es·ti·lár] *v.* to use, be accustomed to using; **-se** to be in style (*said of clothes*).

estilete [es·ti·lé·te] *m.* stiletto, narrow-bladed dagger; stylet (*instrument for probing wounds*); long, narrow sword.

estilo [es·tí·lo] *m.* style; fashion.

estima [es·tí·ma] *f.* esteem.

estimación [es·ti·ma·sjón] *f.* esteem, regard; valuation.

estimado al azar *n* a "guesstimate."

estimar [es·ti·már] *v.* to esteem, regard highly; to estimate, appraise; to judge, think.

estimulante [es·ti·mu·lán·te] *adj.* stimulant, stimulating; *m.* stimulant.

estimular [es·ti·mu·lár] *v.* to stimulate, excite, goad.

estímulo [es·tí·mu·lo] *m.* stimulation, incitement; stimulus.

estío [es·tí·o] *m.* summer.

estipulación [es·ti·pu·la·sjón] *f.* stipulation, specification, provision, proviso.

estipular [es·ti·pu·lár] *v.* to stipulate, specify.

estirado [es·ti·rá·đo] *p.p. & adj.* stretched; extended;

drawn out; stuck-up, conceited.

estirar [es·ti·rár] *v.* to stretch, extend; — **la pata** to die; **-se** to stretch out; *Mex.* to die.

estirón [es·ti·rón] *m.* hard pull, tug; stretch; **dar un** — to grow suddenly (*said of a child*).

estirpe [es·tír·pe] *f.* lineage, family, race.

estival [es·ti·bál] *adj.* summer, relating to summer.

estocada [es·to·ká·đa] *f.* thrust, stab; stab wound.

estofa [es·tó·fa] *f.* stuff, cloth; class, quality; **gente de baja** — low class people, rabble.

estofado [es·to·fá·đo] *m.* stew, stewed meat; *p.p. of* **estofar.**

estofar [es·to·fár] *v.* to quilt; to stew.

estoico [es·tój·ko] *adj. & m.* stoic.

estola [es·tó·la] *f.* stole; — **de visón** mink wrap.

estómago [es·tó·ma·ǥo] *m.* stomach.

estopa [es·tó·pa] *f.* burlap; oakum (*loose fiber of old ropes*).

estoque [es·tó·ke] *m.* long, narrow sword.

estorbar [es·tor·bár] *v.* to hinder; to obstruct.

estorbo [es·tór·bo] *m.* hindrance; nuisance, bother.

estornudar [es·tor·nu·đár] *v.* to sneeze.

estornudo [es·tor·nú·đo] *m.* sneeze.

estrado [es·trá·đo] *m.* dais (*platform for a throne, seats of honor, etc.*); main part of a parlor or drawing room.

estragado [es·tra·ǥá·đo] *p.p. & adj.* corrupted; spoiled; ruined; tired, worn out.

estragar[7] [es·tra·ǥár] *v.* to corrupt, contaminate; to spoil; to ruin.

estrago [es·trá·ǥo] *m.* havoc, ruin; massacre.

estragón [es·tra·gón] *m.* tarragon.

estrangulador [es·traŋ·gu·la·đór] *m.* strangler, choke (*of an automobile*); *adj.* strangling.

estrangular [es·traŋ·gu·lár] *v.* to strangle; to choke, throttle.

estratagema [es·tra·ta·xé·ma] *f.* stratagem, scheme.

estrategia [es·tra·té·xja] *f.* strategy.

estratégico [es·tra·té·xi·ko] *adj.* strategic; *m.* strategist, person trained or skilled in strategy.

estrato [es·trá·to] *m.* stratum, layer (*of mineral*).

estratorreactor [es·tra·to·rre·ak·tór] *m.* supersonic jet plane.

estratosfera [es·tra·tos·fé·ra] *f.* stratosphere.

estrechar [es·tre·čár] *v.* to tighten; to narrow down; to embrace, hug; — **la mano** to squeeze, grasp another's hand; to shake hands.

estrechez [es·tre·čés], **estrechura** [es·tre·čú·ra] *f.* narrowness; tightness; austerity; dire straits; poverty; closeness.

estrecho [es·tré·čo] *adj.* narrow; tight; *m.* strait, narrow passage.

estrella [es·tré·ya] *f.* star; — **de mar** starfish.

estrellado [es·tre·yá·đo] *adj.* starry; spangled with stars; **huevos -s** fried eggs.

estrellar [es·tre·yár] *v.* to shatter; to dash to pieces; to star, spangle with stars; **-se** to shatter, break into pieces; to fail.

estremecer[13] [es·tre·me·sér] *v. irr.* to shake; **-se** to shiver, shudder; to vibrate.

estremecimiento [es·tre·me·si·mjén·to] *m.* shiver, shudder; vibration; shaking.

estrenar [es·tre·nár] *v.* to wear for the first time; to perform (*a play*) for the first time; to inaugurate; to begin.

estreno [es·tré·no] *m.* début, first appearance or performance.

estreñimiento [es·tre·ñi·mjén·to] *m.* constipation.

estreñir[5, 19] [es·tre·ñír] *v. irr.* to constipate; **-se** to become constipated.

estrépito [es·tré·pi·to] *m.* racket, noise, crash.
estrepitoso [es·tre·pi·tó·so] *adj.* noisy; boisterous.
estriaciones [es·trja·sjó·nes] *f.* scratches, streaks.
estriado [es·trjá·do] *p.p. & adj.* fluted, grooved; streaked.
estriar[17] [es·trjár] *v.* to groove; to flute (*as a column*).
estribación [es·tri·ba·sjón] *f.* spur (*of a mountain or mountain range*).
estribar [es·tri·bár] *v.* to rest (upon); **eso estriba en que . . .** the basis or reason for it is that . . .
estribillo [es·tri·bí·yo] *m.* refrain.
estribo [es·trí·bo] *m.* (*de caballo o vehículo*) stirrup; footboard, running board; (*apoyo*) support; brace; spur (*of a mountain*); **perder los -s** to lose one's balance; to lose control of oneself.
estribor [es·tri·bór] *m.* starboard.
estricto [es·trík·to] *adj.* strict.
estrofa [es·tró·fa] *f.* strophe, stanza.
estroncio [es·trón·sjo] *m.* strontium.
estropajo [es·tro·pá·xo] *m.* fibrous mass (*for scrubbing*); **tratar a uno como un —** to treat someone scornfully.
estropear [es·tro·pe·ár] *v.* to spoil, ruin, damage; to cripple.
estructura [es·truk·tú·ra] *f.* structure.
estructural [es·truk·tu·rál] *adj.* structural.
estruendo [es·trwén·do] *m.* clatter; clamor, din, racket.
estruendoso [es·trwen·dó·so] *adj.* thunderous, uproarious, deafening.
estrujamiento [es·tru·xa·mjén·to] *m.* crushing, squeezing.
estrujar [es·tru·xár] *v.* to squeeze, press, crush.
estrujón [es·tru·xón] *m.* squeeze, crush; smashing.
estuario [es·twá·rjo] *m.* estuary.
estuco [es·tú·ko] *m.* stucco.
estuche [es·tú·če] *m.* jewel box; instrument case, kit; small casket; sheath; **— de primer auxilio** first aid kit.
estudiantado [es·tu·djan·tá·do] *m.* the student body (*of a school or college*).
estudiante [es·tu·dján·te] *m. & f.* student.
estudiantil [es·tu·djan·tíl] *adj.* pertaining to students.
estudiar [es·tu·djár] *v.* to study.
estudio [es·tú·djo] *m.* study; studio.
estudioso [es·tu·djó·so] *adj.* studious; *m.* learner.
estufa [es·tú·fa] *f.* heater; stove; hothouse; steam room; steam cabinet.
estupefacto [es·tu·pe·fák·to] *adj.* stunned; speechless.
estupendo [es·tu·pén·do] *adj.* stupendous, marvelous.
estupidez [es·tu·pi·dés] *f.* stupidity.
estúpido [es·tú·pi·do] *adj.* stupid.
esturión [es·tu·rjón] *m.* sturgeon.
etapa [e·tá·pa] *f.* stage, lap (*of a journey or race*); army food rations; epoch, period.
éter [é·ter] *m.* ether.
etéreo [e·té·re·o] *adj.* ethereal; heavenly.
eternidad [e·ter·ni·dád] *f.* eternity.
eternizar[9] [e·ter·ni·sár] *v.* to prolong excessively; to perpetuate, make eternal.
eterno [e·tér·no] *adj.* eternal, everlasting.
ética [é·ti·ka] *f.* ethics; **ético** *adj.* ethical, moral.
etimología [e·ti·mo·lo·xí·a] *f.* etymology.
etiqueta [e·ti·ké·ta] *f.* etiquette; formality; tag; **de —** formal (*dress, function, etc.*).
étnico [ét·ni·ko] *adj.* ethnic.
eucalipto [ew·ka·líp·to] *m.* eucalyptus.
Eucaristía [ew·ka·ris·tí·a] *f.* Eucharist.
euforia [ew·fó·rja] *f.* euphoria.
europeo [ew·ro·pé·o] *adj. & m.* European.

evacuación [e·ba·kwa·sjón] *f.* evacuation; bowel movement.
evacuar[18] [e·ba·kwár] *v.* to evacuate, empty; to vacate.
evadir [e·ba·dír] *v.* to evade, elude; **-se** to slip away, escape.
evaluar[18] [e·ba·lwár] *v.* to evaluate, appraise.
evangelio [e·baŋ·xé·ljo] *m.* gospel.
evaporar [e·ba·po·rár] *v.* to evaporate; **-se** to evaporate; to vanish, disappear.
evasión [e·ba·sjón] *f.* evasion, dodge, escape.
evasiva [e·ba·sí·ba] *f.* evasion, dodge, escape.
evasivo [e·ba·sí·bo] *adj.* evasive.
evasor [e·ba·sór] *m.* evader, dodger.
evento [e·bén·to] *m.* event.
evidencia [e·bi·dén·sja] *f.* evidence.
evidenciar [e·bi·den·sjár] *v.* to prove, show, make evident.
evidente [e·bi·dén·te] *adj.* evident.
evitable [e·bi·tá·ble] *adj.* avoidable.
evitar [e·bi·tár] *v.* to avoid, shun.
evocar[6] [e·bo·kár] *v.* to evoke, call forth.
evolución [e·bo·lu·sjón] *f.* evolution.
evolucionar [e·bo·lu·sjo·nár] *v.* to evolve; to perform maneuvers; to go through changes.
exacerbar [ek·sa·ser·bár] *v.* to exasperate, irritate; to aggravate, make worse.
exactitud [ek·sak·ti·túd] *f.* exactness, precision; punctuality.
exacto [ek·sák·to] *adj.* exact, precise; punctual.
exagerar [ek·sa·xe·rár] *v.* to exaggerate.
exaltación [ek·sal·ta·sjón] *f.* exaltation; excitement.
exaltado [ek·sal·tá·do] *adj.* elated; excited; hotheaded.
exaltar [ek·sal·tár] *v.* to exalt, elevate, glorify; to praise; **-se** to get excited; to become upset emotionally.
examen [ek·sá·men] *m.* examination; inspection.
examinar [ek·sa·mi·nár] *v.* to examine; to inspect.
exangüe [ek·sáŋ·gwe] *adj.* lacking blood; anemic; exhausted.
exánime [ek·sá·ni·me] *adj.* lifeless, motionless; weak, faint.
exasperar [ek·sas·pe·rár] *v.* to exasperate, irritate, annoy.
excavar [es·ka·bár] *v.* to excavate, dig, dig out.
excedente [ek·se·dén·te] *m.* surplus; *adj.* exceeding, extra.
exceder [ek·se·dér] *v.* to exceed, surpass; to overdo; **-se** to go beyond the proper limit; to misbehave.
excelencia [ek·se·lén·sja] *f.* excellence, superiority; excellency (*title*).
excelente [ek·se·lén·te] *adj.* excellent.
excelso [ek·sél·so] *adj.* lofty, elevated; sublime; **El Excelso** the Most High.
excéntrico [ek·sén·tri·ko] *adj.* eccentric; queer, odd.
excepción [ek·sep·sjón] *f.* exception.
excepcional [ek·sep·sjo·nál] *adj.* exceptional, unusual.
excepto [ek·sép·to] *adv.* except, with the exception of.
exceptuar[18] [ek·sep·twár] *v.* to except.
excesivo [ek·se·sí·bo] *adj.* excessive.
exceso [ek·sé·so] *m.* excess; crime; **— de equipaje** excess baggage; **en —** in excess, excessively.
excitación [ek·si·ta·sjón] *f.* excitement.
excitante [ek·si·tán·te] *adj.* exciting; stimulating.
excitar [ek·si·tár] *v.* to excite, stir; **-se** to get excited.
exclamación [es·kla·ma·sjón] *f.* exclamation.
exclamar [es·kla·már] *v.* to exclaim.
excluir[32] [es·klwír] *v. irr.* to exclude.
exclusivo [es·klu·sí·bo] *adj.* exclusive.
excomunicar[6] [es·ko·mu·ni·kár] *v.* to excommunicate.
excomunión [es·ko·mu·njón] *f.* excommunication.

ES

excrecencia [es·kre·sén·sja], **excrescencia** [es·kre·sén·sja] *f.* excrescence (*abnormal growth or tumor*).

excremento [es·kre·mén·to] *m.* excrement.

excursión [es·kur·sjón] *f.* excursion, tour, outing.

excusa [es·kú·sa] *f.* excuse.

excusado [es·ku·sá·ðo] *p.p. & adj.* excused; exempt; superfluous; unnecessary; reserved, private; *m.* toilet.

excusar [es·ku·sár] *v.* (*disculpar*) to excuse; to exempt; (*evitar*) to avoid, shun; **-se** to excuse oneself, apologize; to decline.

exención [ek·sen·sjón] *f.* exemption.

exentar [ek·sen·tár] *v.* to exempt. *See* **eximir.**

exento [ek·sén·to] *adj.* exempt, freed; free, unobstructed.

exequias [ek·sé·kjas] *f. pl.* obsequies, funeral rites.

exhalar [ek·sa·lár] *v.* to exhale; to emit, give off; to breathe forth; **-se** to evaporate; to run away.

exhibición [ek·si·ßi·sjón] *f.* exhibition; exposition; *Mex.* payment of an installment.

exhibir [ek·si·ßír] *v.* to exhibit; *Mex.* to pay for in installments (*stocks, policies, etc.*); **-se** to exhibit oneself, show off.

exhortar [ek·sor·tár] *v.* to exhort, admonish.

exigencia [ek·si·xén·sja] *f.* demand; urgent want; emergency.

exigente [ek·si·xén·te] *adj.* demanding, exacting; urgent.

exigir[11] [ek·si·xír] *v.* to require; to demand; to exact.

exiguo [ek·sí·ǥwo] *adj.* scanty, meager.

eximio [ek·sí·mjo] *adj.* very distinguished.

eximir [ek·si·mír] *v.* to exempt, except, excuse; **-se dé** to avoid, shun.

existencia [ek·sis·tén·sja] *f.* existence; **-s** stock on hand, goods; **en** — in stock, on hand.

existente [ek·sis·tén·te] *adj.* existent, existing; in stock.

existir [ek·sis·tír] *v.* to exist.

éxito [ék·si·to] *m.* outcome, result; success; **tener buen (mal)** — to be successful (unsuccessful).

éxodo [ék·so·ðo] *m.* exodus, emigration.

exonerar [ek·so·ne·rár] *v.* to exonerate, free from blame; to relieve of a burden or position; to dismiss.

exorbitante [ek·sor·ßi·tán·te] *adj.* exorbitant, excessive, extravagant.

exótico [ek·só·ti·ko] *adj.* exotic, foreign, strange; quaint.

expansión [es·pan·sjón] *f.* expansion; relaxation; recreation.

expansivo [es·pan·sí·ßo] *adj.* expansive; demonstrative, effusive.

expatriar [es·pa·trjár] *v.* to expatriate, exile; **-se** to expatriate oneself, renounce one's citizenship; to emigrate.

expectación [es·pek·ta·sjón] *f.* expectation.

expectativa [es·pek·ta·tí·ßa] *f.* expectation; hope, prospect; **estar en** — **de algo** to be expecting, or on the lookout for, something.

expectorar [es·pek·to·rár] *v.* to expectorate, cough up.

expedición [es·pe·ði·sjón] *f.* expedition; dispatch, promptness; papal dispatch or bull.

expedicionario [es·pe·ði·sjo·ná·rjo] *adj.* expeditionary; *m.* member of an expedition; explorer.

expediente [es·pe·ðjén·te] *m.* certificate; papers pertaining to a business matter; expedient, means; dispatch, promptness; — **personal** curriculum vitae.

expedir[5] [es·pe·ðír] *v. irr.* to dispatch; to issue

officially; to remit, send.

expeler [es·pe·lér] *v.* to expel, eject.

experiencia [es·pe·rjén·sja] *f.* experience; experiment.

experimentado [es·pe·ri·men·tá·ðo] *adj. & p.p.* experienced.

experimental [es·pe·ri·men·tál] *adj.* experimental.

experimentar [es·pe·ri·men·tár] *v.* to experiment, try, test; to experience, feel.

experimento [es·pe·ri·mén·to] *m.* experiment, trial.

experto [es·pér·to] *adj.* expert, skillful; *m.* expert.

expiación [es·pja·sjón] *f.* expiation, atonement.

expiar[17] [es·pjár] *v.* to atone for; to make amends for; to purify.

expirar [es·pi·rár] *v.* to die; to expire, come to an end.

explayar [es·pla·yár] *v.* to extend; **-se** to become extended; to relax in the open air; to enlarge upon a subject; **-se con un amigo** to unbosom oneself, speak with utmost frankness with a friend.

explicable [es·pli·ká·ßle] *adj.* explainable.

explicación [es·pli·ka·sjón] *f.* explanation.

explicar[6] [es·pli·kár] *v.* to explain; — **una cátedra** to teach a course; **-se** to explain oneself; to account for one's conduct.

explicativo [es·pli·ka·tí·ßo] *adj.* explanatory, explaining.

explícito [es·plí·si·to] *adj.* explicit, express, clear, definite.

exploración [es·plo·ra·sjón] *f.* exploration.

explorador [es·plo·ra·ðór] *m.* explorer, scout; *adj.* exploring.

explorar [es·plo·rár] *v.* to explore.

explosión [es·plo·sjón] *f.* explosion.

explosivo [es·plo·sí·ßo] *adj. & m.* explosive.

explotación [es·plo·ta·sjón] *f.* exploitation; operation of a mine; development of a business; plant.

explotar [es·plo·tár] *v.* to exploit, operate, develop; to utilize, profit by; to make unfair use of; *Am.* to explode.

exponer[40] [es·po·nér] *v. irr.* (*dejar ver*) to expose, reveal; to show, exhibit; to display; (*sin protección*) to leave unprotected, to expose (*film*); (*explicar*) to expound; to explain; **-se a** to expose oneself to; to run the risk of.

exportación [es·por·ta·sjón] *f.* exportation; export.

exportar [es·por·tár] *v.* to export.

exposición [es·po·si·sjón] *f.* exposition; exhibition; explanation; exposure.

exprés [es·prés] *m. Am.* express; *Am.* express company.

expresar [es·pre·sár] *v.* to express; **-se** to express oneself, speak.

expresión [es·pre·sjón] *f.* expression; utterance; **-es** regards.

expresivo [es·pre·sí·ßo] *adj.* expressive; affectionate.

expreso [es·pré·so] *adj.* expressed; express, clear, exact; fast; *m.* express train.

exprimir [es·pri·mír] *v.* to squeeze, extract (*juice*); to wring out; to express, utter.

expuesto [es·pwés·to] *p.p. of* **exponer** *& adj.* exposed; expressed; displayed; risky, dangerous; **lo** — what has been said.

expulsar [es·pul·sár] *v.* to expel, eject.

expulsión [es·pul·sjón] *f.* expulsion, expelling.

exquisitez [es·ki·si·tés] *f.* exquisiteness.

exquisito [es·ki·sí·to] *adj.* exquisite.

extasiado [es·ta·sjá·ðo] *adj.* rapt, in ecstasy; *p.p. of* **extasiar.**

extasiar[17] [es·ta·sjár] *v.* to delight; **-se** to be in ecstasy; to be entranced.

éxtasis [és·ta·sis] *m.* ecstasy.

extender[1] [es·ten·dér] *v. irr.* to extend; to spread; to unfold; to draw up (*a document*); **-se** to extend, spread; to expatiate, be too wordy.

extensión [es·ten·sjón] *f.* extension; extent; expanse; expansion.

extensivo [es·ten·sí·ƀo] *adj.* extensive.

extenso [es·tén·so] *p.p. irr of* **extender** extended; *adj.* extensive, vast, spacious; **por** — extensively, in detail.

extenuado [es·te·nwá·ðo] *adj.* wasted, weak, emaciated.

exterior [es·te·rjór] *adj.* exterior, outer; *m.* exterior; outside; outward appearance.

exterminar [es·ter·mi·nár] *v.* to exterminate.

exterminio [es·ter·mí·njo] *m.* extermination, destruction.

externo [es·tér·no] *adj.* external, outward.

extinción [es·tin·sjón] *f.* extinction; — **de derecho** foreclosure.

extinguir[12] [es·tiŋ·gír] *v.* to extinguish, put out; to destroy.

extinto [es·tín·to] *adj.* extinct.

extintor [es·tin·tór] *m.* extinguisher; — **de espuma** fire extinguisher.

extirpar [es·tir·pár] *v.* to eradicate, pull out by the roots, root out, remove completely; to destroy completely.

extorsión [es·tor·sjón] *f.* extortion.

extorsionar [es·tor·sjo·nár] *v. Am.* to extort, extract money, blackmail.

extorsionista [es·tor·sjo·nís·ta] *m. Am.* extortioner, profiteer, racketeer.

extracto [es·trák·to] *m.* extract; abstract; summary.

extraer[46] [es·tra·ér] *v. irr.* to extract.

extranjero [es·traŋ·xé·ro] *adj.* foreign; *m.* foreigner.

extrañamiento [es·tra·ña·mjén·to] *m.* wonder, surprise, amazement.

extrañar [es·tra·ñár] *v.* to wonder at; to banish; *Am.* to miss (*a person or thing*); **-se** to marvel, be astonished.

extrañeza [es·tra·ñé·sa] *f.* strangeness; surprise; astonishment; oddity, odd thing.

extraño [es·trá·ño] *adj.* strange; rare; odd; *m.* stranger.

extraordinario [es·tra·or·di·ná·rjo] *adj.* extraordinary.

extravagancia [es·tra·ƀa·ǵán·sja] *f.* extravagance; folly.

extravagante [es·tra·ƀa·ǵán·te] *adj.* extravagant, fantastic; queer, odd.

extraviar[17] [es·tra·ƀjár] *v.* to lead astray; to strand; to misplace; **-se** to lose one's way; to get stranded; to get lost; to miss the road.

extravío [es·tra·ƀí·o] *m.* deviation, straying; error; misconduct; damage.

extremado [es·tre·má·ðo] *adj.* extreme; extremely good or extremely bad; *p.p. of* **extremar.**

extremar [es·tre·már] *v.* to carry to an extreme; **-se** to take great pains, exert great effort.

extremidad [es·tre·mi·ðáđ] *f.* extremity; extreme degree; remotest part; **-es** extremities, hands and feet.

extremo [es·tré·mo] *adj.* extreme, last; farthest; excessive; utmost; *m.* extreme, highest degree or point; end, extremity; extreme care; **con (en** or **por)** — very much, extremely.

exuberante [ek·su·ƀe·rán·te] *adj.* exuberant; luxuriant.

F: f

fa [fa] *m.* fourth note of the musical scale.

fabada [fa·ƀá·ða] *f.* a bean and bacon soup popular in Spain.

fábrica [fá·ƀri·ka] *f.* manufacture; factory, mill; structure.

fabricación [fa·ƀri·ka·sjón] *f.* manufacture.

fabricante [fa·ƀri·kán·te] *m.* manufacturer, maker.

fabricar[6] [fa·ƀri·kár] *v.* to manufacture, make; to construct, build; to fabricate, make up, invent.

fabril [fa·ƀríl] *adj.* manufacturing.

fábula [fá·ƀu·la] *f.* fable, tale; falsehood.

fabuloso [fa·ƀu·ló·so] *adj.* fabulous; false, imaginary.

facción [fak·sjón] *f.* faction, band, party; battle; **-es** features; **estar de** — to be on duty.

faceta [fa·sé·ta] *f.* facet.

faceto [fa·sé·to] *adj. Mex.* cute, funny; *Am.* affected.

fácil [fá·sil] *adj.* easy; docile, yielding, manageable; likely; probable.

facilidad [fa·si·li·ðáđ] *f.* facility, ease; opportunity.

facilitar [fa·si·li·tár] *v.* to facilitate, make easy; to furnish; give; — **todos los datos** to furnish all the data.

facón [fa·kón] *m. Ríopl., Bol.* dagger, large knife; **faconazo** [fa·ko·ná·so] *m. Ríopl., Bol.* stab.

factible [fak·tí·ƀle] *adj.* feasible.

factor [fak·tór] *m.* factor; element, joint cause; commercial agent; baggage man.

factoría [fak·to·rí·a] *f.* trading post; *Mex.* factory.

factura [fak·tú·ra] *f.* (*cuenta*) invoice, itemized bill; (*hechura*) make; workmanship, form; *Am.* roll, biscuit, muffin; — **simulada** temporary invoice, memorandum.

facturar [fak·tu·rár] *v.* to invoice, bill; to check (*baggage*).

facultad [fa·kul·táđ] *f.* faculty; ability, aptitude; power, right; permission; branch of learning; school or college of a university.

facultativo [fa·kul·ta·tí·ƀo] *m.* doctor, physician.

facundia [fa·kún·dja] *f.* eloquence, fluency, facility in speaking, gift of expression.

facha [fá·ča] *f.* appearance, figure, aspect, looks.

fachada [fa·čá·ða] *f.* façade, front (*of a building*); title page.

fachenda [fa·čén·da] *f.* ostentation, vanity.

fachendoso [fa·čen·dó·so] *adj.* vain, boastful, ostentatious.

faena [fa·é·na] *f.* task, job, duty; *Carib., Mex., C.A.* extra job; *Ch.* work crew, labor gang.

faja [fá·xa] *f.* sash; girdle; band; *Am.* belt, waist band.

fajar [fa·xár] *v.* to girdle; to bind, wrap, or bandage with a strip of cloth; *Am.* to beat, strike, thrash; *Am.* — **un latigazo a uno** to whip, thrash someone; **-se** to put on a sash or belt; to tighten one's sash or belt; *Am.* **-se con** to have a fight with, come to blows with.

fajo [fá·xo] *m.* bundle; sheaf.

falaz [fa·lás] *adj.* illusive, illustory; deceitful, deceiving.

falda [fál·da] *f.* skirt; lap; hat brim; foothill, slope; **faldón** [fal·dón] *m.* coattail; shirttail.

faldear [fal·de·ár] *v.* to skirt (*a hill*).

falsario [fal·sá·rjo] *m.* crook, forger; liar.

falsear [fal·se·ár] *v.* to falsify, misrepresent; to counterfeit; to forge; to pick (*a lock*); to flag, grow weak; to hit a wrong note.

falsedad [fal·se·ðáđ] *f.* falsehood, lie; deceit.

falsificación [fal·si·fi·ka·sjón] *f.* falsification, forgery; counterfeit.

falsificar[6] [fal·si·fi·kár] *v.* to falsify, make false; to counterfeit; to forge.

falso [fál·so] *adj.* false; untrue, unreal; deceitful; counterfeit; sham; *C.A.* cowardly; *m.* inside facing of a dress; lining; *Mex.* false testimony, slander; **en** — upon a false foundation; without proper security; *Am.* **coger a uno en** — to catch one lying.

falta [fál·ta] *f.* (*defecto*) lack, want; fault, mistake; defect; absence; (*infracción*) misdemeanor, offense; **a** — **de** for want of; **hacer** — to be necessary; to be missing; **me hace** — I need it; **sin** — without fail.

faltar [fal·tár] *v.* to be lacking, wanting; to be absent or missing; to fail, be of no use or help; to fail to fulfill (*a promise or duty*); to die; *Mex., C.A.* to insult; — **poco para las cinco** to be almost five o'clock; **¡no fáltaba más!** that's the last straw!; why, the very idea!

falto [fál·to] *adj.* lacking; deficient, short; *Am.* foolish, stupid.

faltriquera [fal·tri·ké·ra] *f.* pocket.

falla [fá·ya] *f.* fault, defect; failure; fault (*fracture in the earth's crust*); *Ríopl.* baby's bonnet; **-s** popular *fiestas* of Valencia, Spain.

fallar [fa·yár] *v.* (*juzgar*) to render a verdict; (*fracasar*) to fail, be deficient; to default; to miss; to fail to hit; to give way, break; to trump.

fallecer[13] [fa·ye·sér] *v. irr.* to die.

fallecimiento [fa·ye·si·mjén·to] *m.* decease, death.

fallido [fa·yí·do] *adj.* frustrated; bankrupt.

fallo [fá·yo] *m.* verdict, judgment; decision; *adj.* lacking (*a card, or suit, in card games*); *Ch.* silly, foolish.

fama [fá·ma] *f.* fame, reputation; rumor, report; *Ch.* bull's-eye, center of a target.

famélico [fa·mé·li·ko] *adj.* ravenous, hungry, starved.

familia [fa·mí·lja] *f.* family.

familiar [fa·mi·ljár] *adj.* domestic, homelike; familiar, well-known; friendly, informal; colloquial (*phrase or expression*); *m.* intimate friend; member of a household; domestic servant; familiar spirit, demon; *Am.* relative.

familiaridad [fa·mi·lja·ri·dád] *f.* familiarity, informality.

familiarizar[9] [fa·mi·lja·ri·sár] *v.* to familiarize, acquaint; **-se** to acquaint oneself, become familiar (with).

famoso [fa·mó·so] *adj.* famous; excellent.

fanal [fa·nál] *m.* beacon, lighthouse; lantern; headlight; bell jar, glass cover.

fanático [fa·ná·ti·ko] *adj. & m.* fanatic.

fanatismo [fa·na·tíz·mo] *m.* fanaticism.

fanega [fa·né·ga] *f.* Spanish bushel (1.58 bushels); — **de tierra** land measure (1.59 acres).

fanfarrón [fan·fa·rrón] *m.* braggart, boaster; bluffer.

fanfarronada [fan·fa·rro·ná·da] *f.* boast, brag, swagger, bluff.

fanfarronear [fan·fa·rro·ne·ár] *v.* to bluff, brag; to swagger.

fango [fáŋ·go] *m.* mud, mire.

fangoso [faŋ·gó·so] *adj.* muddy, miry.

fantasear [fan·ta·se·ár] *v.* to fancy; to imagine.

fantasía [fan·ta·sí·a] *f.* fantasy, imagination, fancy, whim; **-s** string of pearls; *Ven.* **tocar por** — to play by ear.

fantasma [fan·táz·ma] *m.* phantom, image; vision, ghost; *f.* scarecrow.

fantasmagórico [fan·taz·ma·gó·ri·ko] *adj.* fantastic, unreal, illusory.

fantástico [fan·tás·ti·ko] *adj.* fantastic.

fardel [far·dél] *m.* knapsack, bag; bundle.

fardo [fár·do] *m.* bundle; bale, *Ríopl., Andes* **pasar el** — **to** "pass the buck", shift the responsibility to someone else.

faringe [fa·ríŋ·xe] *f.* pharynx.

faríngeo [fa·ríŋ·xe·o] *adj.* pharyngeal.

farmacéutico [far·ma·séw·ti·ko] *m.* pharmacist, druggist; *adj.* pharmaceutical.

farmacia [far·má·sja] *f.* pharmacy; drugstore.

faro [fá·ro] *m.* lighthouse; beacon; *Am.* headlight.

farol [fa·ról] *m.* (*linterna*) lantern; street lamp; (*fachendoso*) conceit, self-importance; *Ríopl.* balcony; *Am.* presumptuous man; *Am.* bluff; **darse** — to show off; to put on airs.

farola [fa·ró·la] *f.* street light; lamppost.

farolero [fa·ro·lé·ro] *adj.* vain, ostentatious; *m.* lamp maker or vendor; lamplighter (*person*).

farra [fá·rra] *f. Ríopl., Ch., Col., Ven., Andes* spree, revelry, wild party, noisy merrymaking; *Ríopl., Ch., Col., Ven., Andes* **ir de** — to go on a spree.

farsa [fár·sa] *f.* farce; company of actors; sham, fraud.

farsante [far·sán·te] *m.* charlatan, bluffer; quack; comedian; wag.

fascinación [fa·si·na·sjón] *f.* fascination; glamour.

fascinador [fa·si·na·dór] *adj.* fascinating, glamorous; charming.

fascinar [fa·si·nár] *v.* to fascinate, bewitch, charm; to allure.

fascismo [fa·síz·mo] *m.* fascism.

fascista [fa·sís·ta] *m. & f.* fascist.

fase [fá·se] *f.* phase, aspect.

fastidiar [fas·ti·djár] *v.* to annoy, bother; to bore; *Col., P.R.* to hurt, harm, ruin.

fastidio [fas·tí·djo] *m.* boredom; disgust; nuisance, annoyance.

fastidioso [fas·ti·djó·so] *adj.* annoying, bothersome; boring, tiresome.

fatal [fa·tál] *adj.* fatal; mortal, deadly; unfortunate.

fatalidad [fa·ta·li·dád] *f.* fatality, destiny; calamity, misfortune.

fatalismo [fa·ta·líz·mo] *m.* fatalism.

fatiga [fa·tí·ga] *f.* fatigue, weariness; toil; **-s** hardships.

fatigar[7] [fa·ti·gár] *v.* to fatigue, weary; to bother.

fatigoso [fa·ti·gó·so] *adj.* fatiguing, tiring.

fatuo [fá·two] *adj.* foolish, stupid; vain; **fuego** — will-o'-the-wisp.

favor [fa·bór] *m.* favor; kindness; help, aid; protection; *Col.* ribbon bow; **a** — **de** in favor of; **hágame el** — please.

favorable [fa·bo·rá·ble] *adj.* favorable.

favorecer[13] [fa·bo·re·sér] *v. irr.* to favor, help; protect.

favoritismo [fa·bo·ri·tíz·mo] *m.* favoritism.

favorito [fa·bo·rí·to] *adj. & m.* favorite.

faz [fas] *f.* face.

fe [fe] *f.* faith; — **de bautismo** baptismal certificate.

fealdad [fe·al·dád] *f.* ugliness, homeliness; foulness, foul or immoral action.

febrero [fe·bré·ro] *m.* February.

febril [fe·bríl] *adj.* feverish.

fécula [fé·ku·la] *f.* starch.

fecundar [fe·kun·dár] *v.* to fertilize.

fecundo [fe·kún·do] *adj.* fruitful, fertile, productive.

fecha [fé·ča] *f.* date.

fechar [fe·čár] *v.* to date.

fechoría [fe·čo·rí·a] *f.* misdeed, misdemeanor.

federación [fe·de·ra·sjón] *f.* federation, union.

federal [fe·de·rál] *adj.* federal.

felicidad [fe·li·si·dád] *f.* happiness; **¡-es!** congratulations.

felicitación [fe·li·si·ta·sjón] *f.* congratulation.
felicitar [fe·li·si·tár] *v.* to congratulate.
feligrés [fe·li·grés] *m.* parishioner.
feliz [fe·lís] *adj.* happy; lucky.
felpa [fél·pa] *f.* plush.
felpudo [fel·pú·do] *adj.* plushy, like plush; *m.* small plushlike mat; door mat.
femenil [fe·me·níl] *adj.* womanly, feminine.
femenino [fe·me·ní·no] *adj.* feminine.
fementido [fe·men·tí·do] *adj.* false; treacherous.
fenecer[13] [fe·ne·sér] *v. irr.* to die; to finish, end.
fénico [fé·ni·ko] *adj.* carbolic; **acido** — carbolic acid.
fénix [fé·nis] *m.* phoenix *(mythical bird)*.
fenómeno [fe·nó·me·no] *m.* phenomenon.
feo [fé·o] *adj.* ugly, homely; *Am., Col. (referring to taste or odor);* **feote** [fe·ó·te] *adj.* hideous, very ugly.
féretro [fé·re·tro] *m.* bier; coffin.
feria [fé·rja] *f.* fair; market; *Mex.* change *(money); C.A.* tip; **-s** *Am.* present given to servants or the poor during holidays.
feriante [fe·rján·te] *m. & f.* trader at fairs; trader; peddler.
feriar [fe·rjár] *v.* to trade.
fermentar [fer·men·tár] *v.* to ferment.
fermento [fer·mén·to] *m.* ferment; yeast, leaven.
ferocidad [fe·ro·si·dád] *f.* ferocity, fierceness.
feroz [fe·rós] *adj.* ferocious, wild, fierce.
férreo [fé·rre·o] *adj.* ferrous *(pertaining to or derived from iron);* ironlike; harsh; **vía férrea** railroad.
ferretería [fe·rre·te·rí·a] *f.* hardware shop; hardware.
ferrocarril [fe·rro·ka·rríl] *m.* railroad.
ferroso [fe·rró·so] *adj.* iron-like.
ferroviario [fe·rro·bjá·rjo] *adj.* railway, railroad *(used as adj.); m.* railroad man; railroad employee.
fértil [fér·til] *adj.* fertile, productive; **fertilidad** [fer·ti·li·dad] *f.* fertility.
fertilizar[9] [fer·ti·li·sár] *v.* to fertilize.
ferviente [fer·bjén·te] *adj.* fervent, ardent.
fervor [fer·bór] *m.* fervor, zeal, devotion.
fervoroso [fer·bo·ró·so] *adj.* fervent, ardent; pious, devout; zealous.
festejar [fes·te·xár] *v.* to feast, entertain; to celebrate; to woo; *Mex.* to thrash, beat.
festejo [fes·té·xo] *m.* entertainment, festival, celebration; courtship; *Ch.* revelry.
festín [fes·tín] *m.* feast; banquet.
festividad [fes·ti·bi·dád] *f.* festival; holiday; holy day; festivity, gaiety, rejoicing.
festivo [fes·tí·bo] *adj.* festive, gay; **día** — holiday.
fétido [fé·ti·do] *adj.* foul, foul-smelling.
fiado [fjá·do] *p.p. of* **fiar; al** — on credit.
fiador [fja·dór] *m.* guarantor, backer, bondsman; *Ec., Ch.* chin strap, hat guard.
fiambre [fjám·bre] *m.* cold meat; cold or late news; *Ríopl., Mex., Col., Ven.* cold meat salad; *Am.* flop, failure *(referring to a party).*
fianza [fján·sa] *f.* bond, security, surety, guarantee; bail.
fiar[17] [fjar] to trust; to guarantee, back; *Am.* to borrow on credit; **-se de** to place confidence in.
fibra [fí·bra] *f.* fiber; wood grain; — **de vidrio** fiber glass; **-s de vidrio trituradas** milled fibers; **fibroso** *adj.* fibrous.
ficción [fik·sjón] *f.* fiction.
ficticio [fik·tí·sjo] *adj.* fictitious.
ficha [fí·ča] *f. (pieza)* chip; token; domino; *(tarjeta)* file card; *Am.* check *(used in barbershops and stores); Am.* rascal, scamp; **fichero** [fi·čé·ro] *m.* file, card index, filing cabinet.
fidedigno [fi·de·díg·no] *adj.* trustworthy, reliable.

fidelidad [fi·de·li·dád] *f.* fidelity, faithfulness.
fideo [fi·dé·o] *m.* vermicelli, thin noodle; thin person.
fiebre [fjé·bre] *f.* fever; excitement, agitation; *Ch.* astute person.
fiel [fjel] *adj.* faithful; true, accurate; *m.* public inspector; pointer of a balance or scale; pin of the scissors; **los -es** the worshipers, the congregation.
fieltro [fjél·tro] *m.* felt; felt hat; felt rug.
fiera [fjé·ra] *f.* wild beast; *Cuba, Mex.* go-getter, hustler; **ser una** — **para el trabajo** to be a demon for work.
fiereza [fje·ré·sa] *f.* ferocity, fierceness; cruelty; ugliness.
fiero [fjé·ro] *adj.* fierce, ferocious, wild; cruel; ugly, horrible; huge; *m.* threat; **echar** *(or* **hacer)** **-s** to threaten; to boast.
fierro [fjé·rro] *m. Am.* iron; *Am.* iron bar; *Am.* cattle brand; — **fundido** cast iron; **-s** *Mex.* tools, implements. *See* **hierro.**
fiesta [fjés·ta] *f.* festivity, celebration, entertainment; holiday; **estar de** — to be in a holiday mood; **hacer -s a uno** to fawn on a person.
fiestero [fjes·té·ro] *adj.* fond of parties, fond of entertaining; gay, festive; playful; *m.* merrymaker.
figón [fi·gón] *m.* cheap eating house; "joint."
figura [fi·gú·ra] *f.* figure; shape, form; countenance; face card.
figurado [fi·gu·rá·do] *adj.* figurative.
figurar [fi·gu·rár] *v.* to figure; to form; to represent, symbolize; **-se** to imagine; **se me figura** I think, guess, or imagine.
figurín [fi·gu·rín] *m.* fashion plate; dandy.
fijar [fi·xár] *v.* to fix, fasten; to establish; **-se** to settle; **-se en** to notice, pay attention to.
fijeza [fi·xé·sa] *f.* firmness, solidity, steadiness.
fijo [fí·xo] *adj.* fixed; firm; secure.
fila [fí·la] *f.* row, tier; rank.
filamento [fi·la·mén·to] *m.* filament.
filatelia [fi·la·té·lja] *f.* philately.
filete [fi·lé·te] *m. (moldura)* edge, rim; *(carne)* fillet, tenderloin; *(freno)* snaffle bit *(for horses);* hem; screw thread; **en** — fillet welding.
filial [fi·ljál] *adj.* filial.
filigrana [fi·li·grá·na] *f.* filigree.
filmar [fil·már] *v.* to film, screen *(a play or novel).*
filo [fí·lo] *m.* cutting edge; *Andes* hunger; **por** — exactly; *Am.* **de** — resolutely.
filología [fi·lo·lo·xí·a] *f.* philology.
filólogo [fi·ló·lo·go] *m.* philologist.
filón [fi·lón] *m.* seam, layer *(of metallic ore).*
filoso [fi·ló·so] *adj. Am.* sharp, sharp-edged.
filosofía [fi·lo·so·fí·a] *f.* philosophy.
filosófico [fi·lo·só·fi·ko] *adj.* philosophic, philosophical.
filósofo [fi·ló·so·fo] *m.* philosopher.
filtrar [fil·trár] *v.* to filter; **-se** to leak through, leak out; to filter.
filtro [fíl·tro] *m.* filter; — **de aire** air filter.
filudo [fi·lú·do] *adj. Am.* sharp, sharp-edged.
fin [fin] *m.* end, ending; purpose; **al** — at last; **al** — **y al cabo** at last; anyway; in the end; **a** — **de que** so that; **a -es del mes** toward the end of the month; **en** — in conclusion; well; in short.
finado [fi·ná·do] *m.* the deceased.
final [fi·nál] *adj.* final.
finalizar[9] [fi·na·li·sár] *v.* to finish; to end.
financiamiento [fi·nan·sja·mjén·to] *m. Am.* financing.
financiar [fi·nan·sjár] *v. Am.* to finance.
financiero [fi·nan·sjé·ro] *adj. Am.* financial; *m.* financier.
financista [fi·nan·sís·ta] *m. Am.* financier.
finanza [fi·nán·sa] *f. Am.* finance; **-s** *Col.* public

treasury, government funds.

finca [fíŋ·ka] *f.* real estate; property; country house; *Mex., C.A., Col., Ven.* ranch, farm.

fincar [fiŋ·kár] *v.* to buy real estate; *Am.* to rest (on), be based (on); *Am.* to build a farmhouse or country house.

fineza [fi·né·sa] *f.* fineness; nicety; courtesy; favor, kindness; present.

fingimiento [fiŋ·xi·mjén·to] *m.* pretense, sham.

fingir[11] [fiŋ·xír] *v.* to feign, pretend, fake; to imagine.

finiquito [fi·ni·kí·to] *m.* settlement (*of an account*); quittance, final receipt; **dar —** to finish up.

fino [fí·no] *adj.* fine; nice; delicate; sharp; subtle; refined.

finura [fi·nú·ra] *f.* fineness; nicety; subtlety; courtesy, good manners.

fiordo [fjór·do] *m.* fjord.

firma [fír·ma] *f.* signature; firm, firm name.

firmamento [fir·ma·mén·to] *m.* firmament, sky.

firmante [fir·mán·te] *m. & f.* signer.

firmar [fir·már] *v.* to sign.

firme [fír·me] *adj.* firm; solid, hard; **de —** without stopping, hard, steadily.

firmeza [fir·mé·sa] *f.* firmness.

fiscal [fis·kál] *m.* public prosecutor, district attorney; *adj.* fiscal.

fisgar[7] [fiz·gár] *v.* to pry; to snoop; to spy on.

fisgón [fiz·góŋ] *m.* snoop, snooper; *adj.* snooping, curious.

fisgonear [fiz·go·ne·ár] *v.* to pry about; to snoop.

física [fí·si·ka] *f.* physics.

físico [fí·si·ko] *adj.* physical; *Ven., Cuba* vain, prudish, affected; *Arg.* real; *m.* physicist.

fisiología [fi·sjo·lo·xí·a] *f.* physiology.

fisiológico [fi·sjo·ló·xi·ko] *adj.* physiological.

fisionomía [fi·sjo·no·mí·a] *f.* face, features.

flaco [flá·ko] *adj.* lean, skinny; frail, weak; **su lado —** his weak side, his weakness.

flacura [fla·kú·ra] *f.* thinness.

flama [flá·ma] *f.* flame.

flamante [fla·mán·te] *adj.* bright, shiny; brand-new.

flameante [fla·me·án·te] *adj.* flaming, flashing.

flamear [fla·me·ár] *v.* to flame; to flap, flutter (*in the wind*).

flamenco [fla·méŋ·ko] *adj.* Flemish; *C.A., P.R.* skinny; *m.* Flemish, Flemish language; flamingo; Andalusian dance.

flan [flan] *m.* custard.

flanco [fláŋ·ko] *m.* flank, side.

flanquear [flaŋ·ke·ár] *v.* to flank.

flaps [flaps] *m. pl.* flaps (*of an airplane*).

flaquear [fla·ke·ár] *v.* to weaken, flag.

flaqueza [fla·ké·sa] *f.* thinness, leanness; weakness, frailty.

flauta [fláw·ta] *f.* flute; **flautista** [flaw·tís·ta] *m. & f.* flute player; flutist.

fleco [flé·ko] *m.* fringe; bangs, fringe of hair.

flecha [flé·ča] *f.* arrow, dart.

flechar [fle·čár] *v.* to dart, shoot (*an arrow*); to strike, wound or kill with an arrow; to cast an amorous or ardent glance; *Ven.* to prick, sting; *Am.* to burn (*said of the sun*).

flechazo [fle·čá·so] *m.* arrow shot; wound from an arrow.

flema [flé·ma] *f.* phlegm.

flequillos [fle·kí·yos] *m. pl.* bangs.

fletamento [fle·ta·mén·to] *m.* charter, charter party (*of a ship*).

fletar [fle·tár] *v.* to charter (*a ship*); to freight; *Ch.* to hire (*pack animals*); *Peru* to let loose (*strong words*); *Am.* to scatter (*false rumors*); **-se** *Col., Mex., Carib., Ch.* to run away, slip away; *Am.* to slip in uninvited; *Am.* **salir fletado** to leave on the run.

flete [flé·te] *m.* freight, freightage; cargo; load; *Col., Ríopl.* fine horse, race horse; *Arg.* bother, nuisance; *Col., Ven.* **salir sin -s** to leave in a hurry.

flexibilidad [flek·si·βi·li·dád] *f.* flexibility; **flexible** [flek·sí·βle] *adj.* flexible.

flexión [flek·sjón] *f.* bending, bend; sag.

flojear [flo·xe·ár] *v.* to slacken; to weaken; to idle, to be lazy.

flojedad [flo·xe·dád] *f.* laxity, looseness; slackness; laziness; slack.

flojera [flo·xé·ra] = **flojedad.**

flojo [fló·xo] *adj.* (*mal atado*) lax; loose, slack; (*sin fuerza*) lazy; weak.

flor [flor] *f.* flower, blossom; compliment; **— de la edad** prime; **— de lis** iris (*flower*); **— y nata** the best, the cream, the chosen few; **a — de** flush with; **echar -es** to throw a bouquet; to compliment, flatter.

floreado [flo·re·á·do] *p.p. & adj.* flowered; made of the finest wheat.

florear [flo·re·ár] *v.* to decorate with flowers; to brandish, flourish; to make a flourish on the guitar; to flatter, compliment; to bolt, sift out (*the finest flour*); *Am.* to flower, bloom; *Ch.* to choose the best; **-se** *C.A.* to shine, excel; *Am.* to burst open like a flower.

florecer[13] [flo·re·sér] *v. irr.* to flower, bloom; to flourish, thrive.

floreciente [flo·re·sjén·te] *adj.* flourishing, thriving, prosperous.

florecimiento [flo·re·si·mjén·to] *m.* flourishing, flowering, bloom.

floreo [flo·ré·o] *m.* flourish; idle talk; flattery, compliment.

florería [flo·re·rí·a] *f.* florist's shop.

florero [flo·ré·ro] *m.* florist; flower vase; flatterer; *adj.* flattering.

floresta [flo·rés·ta] *f.* wooded place, grove; arbor.

florete [flo·ré·te] *m.* fencing foil.

florido [flo·rí·do] *adj.* flowery.

flota [fló·ta] *f.* fleet; *Col.,* **echar -s** to brag, boast.

flotador [flo·ta·dór] *m.* floater; float; pontoon (*of a hydroplane*); *adj.* floating.

flotante [flo·tán·te] *adj.* floating; *m. Col., Ven.* bluffer, braggart.

flotar [flo·tár] *v.* to float.

flote [fló·te]: **a —** afloat.

fluctuación [fluk·twa·sjón] *f.* fluctuation; wavering, hesitation.

fluctuar[18] [fluk·twár] *v.* to fluctuate; to waver; to hesitate.

fluente [flwén·te] *adj.* fluent, flowing.

fluidez [flwi·dés] *f.* fluidity, easy flow, fluency; **temperatura crítica de —** pour point.

fluido [flú·i·do] *adj.* fluid, flowing, fluent; *m.* fluid.

fluir[32] [flwir] *v. irr.* to flow.

flujo [flú·xo] *m.* flux; flow; flood tide.

flúor [flú·or] *m.* fluorin.

fluorescente [flwo·re·sén·te] *adj.* fluorescent.

fluoroscopio [flwo·ros·kó·pjo] *m.* fluoroscope.

flux [flus] *f.* flush (*in cards*); *P.R., Col., Ven.* suit of clothes; **hacer —** to use up one's funds, lose everything; *Am.* **tener uno —** to be lucky.

foca [fó·ka] *f.* seal, sea lion.

foco [fó·ko] *m.* focus, center; *Mex., C.A., Andes* electric-light bulb.

fofo [fó·fo] *adj.* spongy, porous; light (*in weight*); soft.

fogata [fo·gá·ta] *f.* fire, blaze, bonfire.

fogón [fo·gón] *m.* hearth, fireplace; grill (*for cooking*); vent of a gun; *C.A., Mex.* fire, bonfire; **fogonazo** [fo·go·ná·so] *m.* flash (*of gunpowder*).

fogoso [fo·gó·so] *adj.* fiery, ardent; lively, spirited.

follaje [fo·yá·xe] *m.* foliage.

folletín [fo·ye·tín] *m.* small pamphlet; serial story.

folleto [fo·yé·to] *m.* pamphlet.

fomentar [fo·men·tár] *v.* to foment, encourage, promote, foster.

fomento [fo·mén·to] *m.* promotion, encouragement; development; aid.

fonda [fón·da] *f.* inn; restaurant.

fondear [fon·de·ár] *v.* to cast anchor; to sound, make soundings; to search (*a ship*); to sound out; **-se** *Cuba* to save up for the future.

fondero [fon·dé·ro] *m. Am.* innkeeper.

fondillos [fon·dí·yos] *m. pl.* seat of trousers.

fondista [fon·dís·ta] *m. & f.* innkeeper.

fondo [fón·do] *m.* (*hondura*) bottom; depth; background; back, rear end; (*esencia*) nature, heart, inner self; fund; *Cuba, Ven.* underskirt; **-s** funds; **a** — thoroughly; **echar a** — to sink.

fonducho [fon·dú·čo] *m.* cheap eating place.

fonema [fo·né·ma] *m.* phoneme.

fonética [fo·né·ti·ka] *f.* phonetics, study of pronunciation.

fonógrafo [fo·nó·gra·fo] *m.* phonograph.

fonología [fo·no·lo·xí·a] *f.* phonology.

foque [fó·ke] *m.* jib (sail).

forajido [fo·ra·xí·do] *m.* outlaw, fugitive; highwayman, bandit.

foráneo [fo·rá·ne·o] *adj.* foreign; *m.* outsider, stranger.

forastero [fo·ras·té·ro] *m.* stranger; foreigner; outsider; *adj.* foreign.

forcejear [for·se·xe·ár], **forcejar** [for·se·xar] *v.* to struggle; to strive; to oppose, resist.

fórceps [fór·seps] *m.* forceps.

forja [fór·xa] *f.* forge, forging; blacksmith's shop.

forjador [for·xa·dór] *m.* forger (*of metals*); smith, blacksmith; inventor (*of lies, stories, tricks, etc.*).

forjar [for·xár] *v.* to forge; to form, shape; to invent, feign, fake.

forma [fór·ma] *f.* form, shape, figure; manner; format (*size and shape of a book*); (*hostia*) host (*unleavened bread for communion*).

formación [for·ma·sjón] *f.* formation.

formal [for·mál] *adj.* formal; serious, trustworthy, punctual; reliable.

formalidad [for·ma·li·dád] *f.* formality; seriousness, reliability; gravity, dignity; punctuality; red tape.

formalismo [for·ma·líz·mo] *m.* formality, red tape (*excess of formalities*); **formalista** [for·ma·lís·ta] *adj.* fond of excessive formalities, fond of red tape.

formalizar[9] [for·ma·li·sár] *v.* to give proper form to; to legalize; to make official; **-se** to settle down, become serious.

formar [for·már] *v.* to form; to shape, mold; **-se** to get into line; to be molded, educated; to take form.

formatear [for·ma·te·ár] *v.* (*computadora*) to format; **formato** *m.* format; **formateo** *m.* formatting.

fórmico [fór·mi·ko] *adj.* formic.

formidable [for·mi·dá·ble] *adj.* formidable; fearful.

formón [for·món] *m.* wide chisel; wood chisel.

fórmula [fór·mu·la] *f.* formula.

formular [for·mu·lár] *v.* to formulate, word.

fornido [for·ní·do] *adj.* stout, strong, sturdy.

foro [fó·ro] *m.* stage; back, rear (*of a stage*); forum, court; bar (*profession of law*).

forraje [fo·rrá·xe] *m.* forage, green grass, fodder, feed.

forrajear [fo·rra·xe·ár] *v.* to forage, gather forage.

forrar [fo·rrár] *v.* to line; to cover, put a sheath, case, or covering on; **-se** *Ríopl., C.A.* to eat well; *Am.* to supply oneself with provisions; *Ríopl., Mex., Cuba* to save money.

forro [fó·rro] *m.* lining; sheathing, casing; covering; book cover.

fortalecer[13] [for·ta·le·sér] *v. irr.* to fortify; to strengthen.

fortaleza [for·ta·lé·sa] *f.* fortress; fortitude; strength, vigor; *Ch.* stench, stink.

fortificación [for·ti·fi·ka·sjón] *f.* fortification; fort.

fortificar[6] [for·ti·fi·kár] *v.* to fortify.

fortuito [for·twí·to] *adj.* fortuitous, accidental, unexpected.

fortuna [for·tú·na] *f.* fortune; fate, chance; wealth; **por** — fortunately.

forzar[9] [for·sár] *v. irr.* to force; to compel; to take (*a fort*); to rape; — **la entrada en** to break into.

forzoso [for·só·so] *adj.* compulsory; necessary.

fosa [fó·sa] *f.* grave; cavity.

fosco [fós·ko] *adj.* dark; cross, irritable, frowning; *see* **hosco.**

fosfato [fos·fá·to] *m.* phosphate.

fosforecer[13] [fos·fo·re·sér], **fosforescer** [fos·fo·re·sér] *v.* to glow.

fósforo [fós·fo·ro] *m.* phosphorus; match.

fósil [fó·sil] *adj. & m.* fossil.

foso [fó·so] *m.* hole, pit; stage pit; ditch.

fotingo [fo·tíŋ·go] *m.* ''jalopy''.

foto [fó·to] *f.* snapshot.

fotocopia [fo·to·có·pja] *f.* photocopy.

fotoeléctrico [fo·to·e·lék·tri·ko] *adj.* photoelectric.

fotograbado [fo·to·gra·bá·do] *m.* photoengraving.

fotografía [fo·to·gra·fí·a] *f.* photograph; photography.

fotografiar[17] [fo·to·gra·fjár] *v.* to photograph.

fotógrafo [fo·tó·gra·fo] *m.* photographer.

fotosíntesis [fo·to·sín·te·sis] *f.* photosynthesis.

fracasado [fra·ka·sá·do] *adj.* failed; *m.* failure.

fracasar [fra·ka·sár] *v.* to fail; to come to ruin; to crumble to pieces.

fracaso [fra·ká·so] *m.* failure, ruin; calamity; crash.

fracción [frak·sjón] *f.* fraction.

fractura [frak·tú·ra] *f.* fracture; break, crack.

fracturar [frak·tu·rár] *v.* to fracture, break.

fragancia [fra·gán·sja] *f.* fragrance, scent, perfume.

fragante [fra·gán·te] *adj.* fragrant; **en** — in the act.

fragata [fra·gá·ta] *f.* frigate.

frágil [frá·xil] *adj.* fragile, breakable; frail, weak.

fragilidad [fra·xi·li·dád] *f.* brittleness.

fragmento [frag·mén·to] *m.* fragment.

fragor [fra·gór] *m.* clang, din; crash.

fragoroso [fra·go·ró·so] *adj.* deafening, thunderous.

fragoso [fra·gó·so] *adj.* rugged, craggy, rough, uneven; noisy.

fragua [frá·gwa] *f.* forge; blacksmith's shop.

fraguar [fra·gwár] *v.* to forge; to scheme, hatch (*a plot*).

fraile [fráj·le] *m.* friar; priest; **frailuco** [fraj·lú·ko] *m.* little old friar.

frambuesa [fram·bwé·sa] *f.* raspberry; **frambueso** [fram·bwé·so] *m.* raspberry bush.

francés [fran·sés] *adj.* French; *m.* Frenchman; French language.

franco [fráŋ·ko] *adj.* (*sincero*) frank, open, candid, sincere; (*exento*) free; *m.* franc; **francote** [fraŋ·kó·te] *adj.* very frank, blunt, outspoken.

franela [fra·né·la] *f.* flannel.

franja [frán·xa] *f.* fringe, border; stripe; braid.

franquear [fraŋ·ke·ár] *v.* to exempt; to free; to frank (*a letter*); to dispatch, send; to make grants; — **el paso** to permit the passage (of); **-se** to unbosom oneself, disclose one's innermost thoughts and feelings.

franqueo [fraŋ·ké·o] *m.* postage; franking (*of a letter*); freeing (*of slaves or prisoners*).

franqueza [fraŋ·ké·sa] *f.* frankness; freedom.

franquicia [fraŋ·kí·sja] *f.* franchise, grant, privilege; freedom or exemption (*from fees*).

frasco [frás·ko] *m.* flask, vial, small bottle.

frase [frá·se] *f.* phrase; sentence.

fraternal [fra·ter·nál] *adj.* fraternal, brotherly.

fraternidad [fra·ter·ni·dád] *f.* fraternity; brotherhood.

fraude [fráw·de] *m.* fraud.

fraudulento [fraw·đu·lén·to] *adj.* fraudulent, tricky, deceitful, dishonest.

fray [fraj] *m.* (*contr. of* **fraile** [fráj·le], *used before Christian name*) friar.

frazada [fra·sá·da] *f.* blanket.

frecuencia [fre·kwén·sja] *f.* frequency; **con** — frequently.

frecuentar [fre·kwen·tár] *v.* to frequent.

frecuente [fre·kwén·te] *adj.* frequent.

fregadero [fre·ga·dé·ro] *m.* sink.

fregado [fre·gá·đo] *m.* scrub, scrubbing; *p.p. of* **fregar**; *adj.* *Ch., Andes, Mex.* bothersome, annoying; *Col.* stubborn; *Mex., C.A.* brazen.

fregar[7] [fre·gár] *v. irr.* to scour; to scrub; to rub; to wash (*dishes*); *Am.* to molest, annoy.

fregona [fre·gó·na] *f.* scrub woman; dishwasher, kitchen maid.

freír[15] [fre·ír] *v. irr.* to fry; to tease; to bother.

frenar [fre·nár] *v.* to apply the brakes; to restrain.

frenesí [fre·ne·sí] *m.* frenzy, madness.

frenético [fre·né·ti·ko] *adj.* frantic; furious; in a frenzy.

freno [fré·no] *m.* bridle; brake; control; bit (*for horses*).

frente [frén·te] *f.* forehead; countenance; *m.* front; **en** — **de** in front of; — **a** in front of, facing; **hacer** — to face.

freón [fre·ón] *m.* freon.

fresa [fré·sa] *f.* strawberry.

fresado [fre·sá·đo] *m.* milling; — **de refrentar** face milling; — **en superficie plana** slab milling.

fresca [frés·ka] *f.* fresh air; fresh remark.

fresco [frés·ko] *adj.* (*bastante frío*) fresh; cool, (*sereno*) calm, serene; (*descarado*) forward, bold; *m.* coolness; cool air; fresco (*painting*); *C.A., Col.* refreshment; **al** — in the open air; **pintura al** — painting in fresco.

frescor [fres·kór] *m.* freshness, coolness.

frescura [fres·kú·ra] *f.* (*temperatura baja*) freshness; coolness; (*serenidad*) calm; freedom; ease; (*insolencia*) boldness, impudence; impudent remark.

fresno [fréz·no] *m.* ash, ash tree.

fresquecillo [fres·ke·sí·yo] *adj.* nice and cool; *m.* cool air, fresh breeze; **fresquecito** [fres·ke·sí·to], **fresquito** [fres·kí·to] *adj.* nice and cool.

frialdad [frjal·dád] *f.* coldness; coolness, indifference.

fricativo [fri·ka·tí·bo] *adj.* fricative.

fricción [frik·sjón] *f.* friction, rub, rubbing.

friccionar [frik·sjo·nár] *v.* to rub; to massage.

friega [frjé·ga] *f.* rub, rubbing; *Am.* bother, nuisance, irritation; *Am.* flogging, beating.

frigorífico [fri·go·rí·fi·ko] *adj.* freezing; *m. Spain*

refrigerator, icebox; *Ríopl.* meatpacking house.

frijol [fri·xól] *m.* bean; kidney bean, navy bean.

frío [frí·o] *adj.* cold; frigid; cool, indifferent; *m.* cold; **-s** *Mex.* chills and fever; *Col., C.A., Ven.* malaria.

friolento [frjo·lén·to] *adj.* cold-blooded, sensitive to cold; chilly.

friolera [frjo·lé·ra] *f.* trifle.

fritada [fri·tá·da] *f.* dish of fried food.

frito [frí·to] *p.p. irr. of* **freír** fried; *m.* fry, dish of fried food.

fritura [fri·tú·ra] *f.* fry, dish of fried food; fritter.

frivolidad [fri·bo·li·dád] *f.* frivolity; **frívolo** [frí·bo·lo] *adj.* frivolous.

fronda [frón·da] *f.* leaf; fern leaf; foliage.

frondoso [fron·dó·so] *adj.* leafy.

frontera [fron·té·ra] *f.* frontier, border; **fronterizo** [fron·te·rí·so] *adj.* frontier (*used as an adj.*); opposite, facing.

frontero [fron·té·ro] *adj.* facing, opposite.

frontis [frón·tis] *m.* façade, front (*of a building*).

frontispicio [fron·tis·pí·sjo] *m.* front, façade (*front of a building*); title page.

frontón [fron·tón] *m.* main wall of a handball court; handball court; jai alai court; game of *pelota*.

frotación [fro·ta·sjón] *f.* friction, rubbing.

frotar [fro·tár] *v.* to rub; to scour.

frote [fró·te] *m.* rubbing; friction.

fructificar[6] [fruk·ti·fi·kár] *v.* to fruit, bear or produce fruit; to yield profit.

fructuoso [fruk·twó·so] *adj.* fruitful.

frugal [fru·gál] *adj.* frugal, economical, saving, thrifty; **frugalidad** [fru·ga·li·dád] *f.* frugality, thrift.

fruncir[10] [frun·sír] *v.* to wrinkle; to gather in pleats; to contract, shrivel; to shir; — **las cejas** to frown; to knit the eyebrows; — **los labios** to purse or curl the lips.

fruslería [fruz·le·rí·a] *f.* trifle, trinket.

frustración [frus·tra·sjón] *f.* frustration; failure.

frustrar [frus·trár] *v.* to frustrate, thwart, foil; **-se** to fail, be thwarted.

fruta [frú·ta] *f.* fruit; **frutería** [fru·te·rí·a] *f.* fruit store.

frutero [fru·té·ro] *m.* fruit vendor; fruit dish; *adj.* fruit (*used as adj.*); **buque** — fruit boat; **plato** — fruit dish.

fruto [frú·to] *m.* fruit (*any organic product of the earth*); result; benefit, profit.

¡fuche! [fú·če] *interj. Mex.* phew! ugh! pew! phooey!

fuego [fwé·go] *m.* (*incendio*) fire; (*pasión*) passion; (*erupción*) skin eruption; *Am.* cold sore; **-s artificiales** fireworks; **hacer** — to fire, shoot; **estar hecho un** — to be very angry; **romper** — to begin to fire, start shooting.

fuelle [fwé·ye] *m.* (*instrumento*) bellows; (*arruga*) pucker, wrinkle, fold; (*hablador*) tattletale, windbag, gossiper.

fuente [fwén·te] *f.* fountain; source, origin; spring; platter, serving dish; — **de alimentación** (*computadora*) power supply (source).

fuera [fwé·ra] *adv.* outside, out; — **de** *prep.* outside of; in addition to.

fuereño [fwe·ré·ño] *m. Mex., Ven., Andes* outsider, stranger.

fuero [fwé·ro] *m.* law, statute; power, jurisdiction; code of laws; exemption, privilege.

fuerte [fwér·te] *adj.* (*robusto*) strong; loud; secure, fortified; (*grave*) grave, serious; (*áspero*) excessive; *Ch.* stinking; *m.* fort; forte, strong point; forte (*music*); *Mex.* alcohol, liquor; *adv.* strongly; excessively; loud; hard.

fuerza [fwér·sa] *f.* force; power, strength; violence;

compulsion; **a — de** by dint of; **a la — (por —, por la —, de por —,** *Am.* **de —)** by force, forcibly; necessarily; **ser —** to be necessary.
fuete [fwé·te] *m. Col., Cuba, Ríopl., Mex., Ven., Andes* whip; **fuetazo** [fwe·tá·so] *m. Am.* lash.
fuga [fú·ga] *f.* flight, escape; leak, leakage; fugue (*musical composition*).
fugarse[7] [fu·gár·se] *v.* to flee, escape.
fugaz [fu·gás] *adj.* fleeing; fleeting, brief, passing.
fugitivo [fu·xi·tí·bo] *adj.* fugitive; fleeting, passing; perishable; *m.* fugitive.
fulano [fu·lá·no] *m.* so-and-so (*referring to person*).
fulgor [ful·gór] *m.* radiance, brilliance.
fulgurar [ful·gu·rár] *v.* to gleam, flash, shine.
fulminar [ful·mi·nár] *v.* to thunder, thunder forth; to utter (*threats*).
fulo [fú·lo] *m. Pan.* blond.
fullero [fu·yé·ro] *m.* cardsharp; crooked gambler; cheat.
fumada [fu·má·da] *f.* puff, whiff (*of smoke*).
fumadero [fu·ma·dé·ro] *m.* smoking room.
fumador [fu·ma·dór] *m.* smoker, habitual smoker.
fumar [fu·már] *v.* to smoke (*tobacco*); *Am.* **-se a uno** to swindle or cheat someone.
fumigar[7] [fu·mi·gár] *v.* to fumigate.
función [fun·sjón] *f.* (*actividad*) function; functioning; (*empleo*) office; occupation; (*espectáculo*) show, performance; religious festival.
funcionamiento [fun·sjo·na·mjén·to] *m.* functioning, action, working, operation.
funcionar [fun·sjo·nár] *v.* to function; to work, run (*said of machines*).
funcionario [fun·sjo·ná·rjo] *m.* public employee, officer or official.
funda [fún·da] *f.* cover, case; *Col.* skirt; **— de almohada** pillowcase.
fundación [fun·da·sjón] *f.* foundation.
fundador [fun·da·dór] *m.* founder.
fundamental [fun·da·men·tál] *adj.* fundamental.
fundamento [fun·da·mén·to] *m.* foundation, groundwork; basis; *Col.* skirt.
fundar [fun·dár] *v.* to found, establish; to erect; to base, ground.
fundición [fun·di·sjón] *f.* foundry; smelting.
fundido [fun·dí·do] *adj.* molten.
fundir [fun·dír] *v.* to smelt, fuse, melt; to cast, mold; *Am.* to ruin; **-se** to fuse, melt together; to unite; *Ríopl., Mex.* to be ruined.
fundo [fún·do] *m. Ch.* farm, country estate; property, land.
fúnebre [fú·ne·bre] *adj.* funeral; funereal, gloomy, dismal.
funeral [fu·ne·rál] *adj. & m.* funeral.
funeraria [fu·ne·rá·rja] *f.* undertaking establishment, funeral parlor.
funesto [fu·nés·to] *adj.* ill-fated, unlucky; sad, unfortunate.
fungosidad [fuŋ·go·si·dád] *f.* fungus, fungous growth.
funicular [fu·ni·ku·lár] *adj. & m.* funicular.
furgón [fur·gón] *m.* freight car, boxcar; baggage car; **furgonada** [fur·go·ná·da] *f.* carload.
furia [fú·rja] *f.* fury, rage; speed.
furibundo [fu·ri·bún·do] *adj.* furious.
furioso [fu·rjó·so] *adj.* furious.
furor [fu·rór] *m.* fury, rage, anger; frenzy.
furtivo [fur·tí·bo] *adj.* furtive, sly, secret.
fuselaje [fu·se·lá·xe] *m.* fuselage (*of an airplane*).
fusible [fu·sí·ble] *adj.* fusible; *m.* electric fuse.
fusil [fu·síl] *m.* gun, rifle.
fusilar [fu·si·lár] *v.* to shoot, execute.
fusión [fu·sjón] *f.* fusion; melting; **— nuclear** nuclear

fusion; **punto de —** melting point.
fustigar[7] [fus·ti·gár] *v.* to lash, whip; to censure severely, scold sharply.
fútbol [fú·bol] *m.* soccer.
fútil [fú·til] *adj.* futile, useless; trivial; **futilidad** [fu·ti·li·dád] *f.* futility, uselessness.
futuro [fu·tú·ro] *adj.* future; *m.* fiancé, future husband; future.

G:g

gabacho [ga·bá·čo] *adj.* from or of the Pyrenees; Frenchlike; foreigner; *m.* Frenchman (*used depreciatively*); *Am.* **me salió — it** turned out wrong.
gabán [ga·bán] *m.* overcoat.
gabeta [ga·bé·ta] = **gaveta.**
gabinete [ga·bi·né·te] *m.* cabinet (*of a government*); studio; study, library room; dressing room; sitting room; private room; dentist's office; laboratory; *Am.* glassed-in **mirador.**
gablete [ga·blé·te] *m.* (*techo de dos aguas*) gable.
gaceta [ga·sé·ta] *f.* gazette, official newspaper; professional periodical; *Col.* any newspaper.
gacetilla [ga·se·tí·ya] *f.* short newspaper article; column of short news items; gossip column; *m. & f.* newsmonger, tattletale; **gacetillero** [ga·se·ti·yé·ro] *m.* newspaper reporter; newsmonger.
gacha [gá·ča] *f.* watery mass or mush; *Col.* china or earthenware bowl; **-s** porridge, mush; caresses; **-s de avena** oatmeal.
gacho [gá·čo] *adj.* drooping; bent downward; turned down; stooping; slouching; with horns curved downward; **sombrero —** slouch hat; **a gachas** on all fours; **con las orejas gachas** with drooping ears; crestfallen, discouraged.
gachupín [ga·ču·pín] *m. Mex.* Spaniard (generally derogatory).
gafas [gá·fas] *f. pl.* spectacles; grappling hooks.
gaita [gáj·ta] *f.* flageolet, a kind of flute; *Mex.* good-for-nothing, lazy bum; **— gallega** bagpipe; **sacar la —** to stick out one's neck; **gaitero** [gaj·té·ro] *m.* piper, bagpipe player.
gaje [gá·xe] *m.* fee; **-s** wages, salary; fees.
gajo [gá·xo] *m.* broken branch; bunch.
gala [gá·la] *f.* elegance; full dress or uniform; ostentation; *Am.* award, prize, tip; **-s** finery, regalia, best clothes; **-s de novia** trousseau; **hacer — de** to boast of.
galán [ga·lán] *m.* gallant, lover; leading man (*in a play*).
galante [ga·lán·te] *adj.* gallant, attentive to ladies; polite.
galanteador [ga·lan·te·a·dór] *m.* gallant, lady's man; flatterer.
galantear [ga·lan·te·ár] *v.* to court, woo; to make love.
galanteo [ga·lan·té·o] *m.* wooing, courtship.
galantería [ga·lan·te·rí·a] *f.* gallantry, compliment, attention to ladies; courtesy; gracefulness; generosity.
galardón [ga·lar·dón] *m.* recompense, reward.
galeote [ga·le·ó·te] *m.* galley slave.
galera [ga·lé·ra] *f.* galley; large wagon; women's jail; printer's galley; *Mex.* jail; *Ch., Ríopl.* tall hat.
galerada [ga·le·rá·da] *f.* galley, galley proof; wagon load, van load.
galería [ga·le·rí·a] *f.* gallery; corridor.
galgo [gál·go] *m.* greyhound; *adj. Col.* gluttonous,

always hungry.

galicismo [ga·li·síz·mo] *m.* gallicism.

galillo [ga·lí·yo] *m.* uvula.

galio [gá·ljo] *m.* gallium.

galón [ga·lón] *m.* galloon, braid, trimming; gallon.

galoneado [ga·lo·ne·á·do] *adj.* gallooned, trimmed with braid.

galopada [ga·lo·pá·da] *f.* gallop; **pegar una —** to break into a gallop.

galopar [ga·lo·pár] *v.* to gallop.

galope [ga·ló·pe] *m.* gallop; **a (al** *or* **de) —** at a gallop; speedily.

galopear [ga·lo·pe·ár] = **galopar.**

galpón [gal·pón] *m. Ríopl., Andes* large open shed.

galvanómetro [gal·ba·nó·me·tro] *m.* galvanometer.

gallardete [ga·yar·dé·te] *m.* streamer.

gallardía [ga·yar·dí·a] *f.* elegance; gracefulness; bravery.

gallardo [ga·yár·do] *adj.* elegant, graceful; brave.

gallego [ga·yé·go] *adj.* Galician, from or of Galicia, Spain; *m.* Galician; *Carib., Ríopl.* Spaniard (*used as a nickname*).

galleta [ga·yé·ta] *f.* cracker; hardtack, hard biscuit; hard cookie; blow, slap; small pot; *Ríopl.* bread of coarse meal or bran; *Ch.* reproof; *Mex., Arg.* **colgarle la — a uno** to fire, dismiss someone; *Am.* **tener —** to have strength, muscle.

gallina [ga·yí·na] *f.* hen; *m. & f.* chickenhearted person.

gallinero [ga·yi·né·ro] *m.* chicken coop, house, or yard; flock of chickens; basket for carrying chickens; poultryman; noisy gathering; top gallery of a theater.

gallo [gá·yo] *m.* cock, rooster; (*agresivo*) aggressive, bossy, person; cork float; false note (*in singing*); frog (*in one's throat*); *Am.* secondhand clothing; *Am.* fire wagon; *Mex., Ríopl.* serenade.

gama [gá·ma] *f.* gamut.

gamba [gám·ba] *f. Spain* large shrimp.

gamo [gá·mo] *m.* buck, male deer.

gamonal [ga·mo·nál] *m. Am.* boss; overseer.

gamuza [ga·mú·sa] *f.* chamois, chamois skin.

gana [gá·na] *f.* desire, appetite; **de buena (mala) —** willingly (unwillingly); **tener —** (*or* **-s**) to feel like, want to; **no me da la —** I don't want to.

ganadero [ga·na·dé·ro] *m.* cattleman; cattle dealer; *adj.* cattle, pertaining to cattle.

ganado [ga·ná·do] *m.* cattle; herd; livestock; **— mayor** cattle; horses; mules; **— menor** sheep; **— de cerda** swine.

ganador [ga·na·dór] *m.* winner; *adj.* winning.

ganancia [ga·nán·sja] *f.* profit, gain; *Am.* something to boot, something extra.

ganancioso [ga·nan·sjó·so] *adj.* winning; profitable; *m.* winner.

ganar [ga·nár] *v.* to win; to profit, gain; to earn; to get ahead of.

gancho [gán·čo] *m.* hook; hooked staff; *Mex., Cuba, Ríopl., Col., C.A.* hairpin; *Am.* bait, lure, trick; *Arg.* bonus; **aguja de —** crochet hook; **echar a uno el —** to hook someone; **tener —** to be attractive, alluring.

gandul [gan·dúl] *m.* bum, loafer.

ganga [gáŋ·ga] *f.* bargain; snap, easy job; kind of prairie hen.

gangoso [gaŋ·gó·so] *adj.* twangy, nasal (*voice*).

gangrena [gaŋ·gré·na] *f.* gangrene.

gangrenar [gaŋ·gre·nár] *v.* to gangrene, cause gangrene; **-se** to gangrene.

ganguear [gaŋ·ge·ár] *v.* to talk "through the nose."

ganoso [ga·nó·so] *adj.* desirous; *Am.* lively, spirited

ganso [gán·so] *m.* goose, gander; lazy, slovenly person; dunce.

ganzúa [gan·sú·a] *f.* hook; picklock (*tool for picking locks*); *m. & f.* burglar.

garabato [ga·ra·bá·to] *m.* hook; scrawl, scribble; **hacer -s** to scribble, write poorly.

garaje [ga·rá·xe] *m.* garage.

garantía [ga·ran·tí·a] *f.* guarantee; security; bail, bond.

garantizar[9] [ga·ran·ti·sár] *v.* to guarantee, vouch for.

garañón [ga·ra·ñón] *m.* jackass, male ass; male camel (*for breeding*); *Ríopl., Mex., C.A.* stallion.

garapiñar [ga·ra·pi·ñár] *v.* to candy (*almonds, fruits, etc.*); to decorate (cake).

garbanzo [gar·bán·so] *m.* chickpea.

garbo [gár·bo] *m.* elegance, graceful air, good carriage.

garboso [gar·bó·so] *adj.* graceful; elegant; sprightly.

garduña [gar·dú·ña] *f.* marten.

garfio [gár·fjo] *m.* hook.

garganta [gar·gán·ta] *f.* throat, neck; gorge, ravine; **gargantilla** [gar·gan·tí·ya] *f.* necklace.

gárgara [gár·ga·ra] *f.* gargling; **-s** *Am.* gargle, gargling solution; **hacer -s** to gargle.

gargarear [gar·ga·re·ár] *v. Am.* to gargle.

gargarismo [gar·ga·ríz·mo] *m.* gargling; gargle, gargling solution.

gargarizar[9] [gar·ga·ri·sár] *v.* to gargle.

garita [ga·rí·ta] *f.* sentry box; watchman's booth; *Col.* vendor's booth.

garito [ga·rí·to] *m.* gambling house, gambling joint; gambler's winnings.

garra [gá·rra] *f.* claw, paw; hook; *Mex.* strength; *Col.* leather or cloth remnant; *Col.* skinny person or animal; *Am.* margin of profit in a business deal; **echar la —** to arrest; to grab; *Mex., C.A., Ven., Andes* **hacer -s** to tear to pieces.

garrafa [ga·rrá·fa] *f.* decanter; **garrafón** [ga·rra·fón] *m.* large decanter; demijohn.

garrapata [ga·rra·pá·ta] *f.* tick (*an insect*).

garrapatear [ga·rra·pa·te·ár] *v.* to scribble, scrawl, write poorly.

garrocha [ga·rró·ča] *f.* pole; iron-pointed staff; **salto de —** pole vault; *Mex.* goad (*for goading oxen*).

garrote [ga·rró·te] *m.* club, cudgel, heavy stick; *Mex., Ríopl., C.A.* brake; **dar —** to strangle; *Mex.* to brake, set the brakes; **garrotazo** [ga·rro·tá·so] *m.* blow with a club; huge stick.

garrotero [ga·rro·té·ro] *m. Mex., Ven.* brakeman; *Am.* beater (*one who beats with a club*); *adj. Am.* stingy.

garrucha [ga·rrú·ča] *f.* pulley.

garúa [ga·rú·a] *f. C.A., Ríopl., Ven., Andes* drizzle.

garza [gár·sa] *f.* heron; egret.

garzo [gár·so] *adj.* blue, bluish; blue-eyed.

gas [gas] *m.* gas, vapor; *Col., Ríopl., Ven.* gasoline; **— lacrimógeno** tear gas.

gasa [gá·sa] *f.* gauze.

gaseosa [ga·se·ó·sa] *f.* soda water; soda pop.

gaseoso [ga·se·ó·so] *adj.* gaseous.

gasolina [ga·so·lí·na] *f.* gasoline.

gastador [gas·ta·dór] *adj.* lavish, extravagant, wasteful; *m.* spendthrift, lavish spender.

gastar [gas·tár] *v.* to spend; to wear; to use; to waste; **-se** to wear out; to get old.

gasto [gás·to] *m.* expense, expenditure; wear.

gatas [gá·tas] **a —** on all fours; **andar a —** to creep, crawl; **salir a —** to crawl out of a difficulty.

gateado [ga·te·á·do] *adj.* catlike; veined, streaked; *Am.* light-colored horse with black streaks.

gatear [ga·te·ár] *v.* to creep, crawl; to walk on all fours; to claw, scratch; to steal.

gatillo [ga·tí·yo] *m.* kitten; trigger; forceps (*for extracting teeth*); petty thief.

gato [gá·to] *m.* cat; moneybag; jack (*for lifting weights*); sneak thief; sly fellow; *Am.* trigger; *Perú* outdoor market; *Ch.* hot-water bottle; *Ríopl.* a gaucho song and tap dance (*by extension,* the dancer); *Arg.* blunder.

gatuperio [ga·tu·pé·rjo] *m.* fraud, intrigue.

gauchada [gaw·čá·da] *f. Ríopl.* gaucho deed or exploit.

gauchaje [gaw·čá·xe] *m. Ríopl.* band of Gauchos, Gaucho folk.

gauchesco [gaw·čés·ko] *adj. Am.* relating to Gauchos.

gaucho [gáw·čo] *m. Am.* Gaucho, Argentine and Uruguayan cowboy; *Ríopl., Ven.* good horseman; *adj. Am.* relating to Gauchos, Gaucho-like; *Ríopl.* sly, crafty.

gaveta [ga·bé·ta] *f.* drawer.

gavilla [ga·bí·ya] *f.* sheaf; gang, band (*of rogues, thieves, etc.*).

gaviota [ga·bjó·ta] *f.* sea gull.

gaza [gá·sa] *f.* loop; *Carib.* noose of a lasso.

gazmoñería [gaz·mo·ñe·rí·a] *f.* prudery, affected modesty; **gazmoño** [gaz·mó·ño] *adj.* prudish, affected, coy.

gaznate [gaz·ná·te] *m.* windpipe; a kind of fritter; *Andes* a sweetmeat made a pineapple or coconut.

gazpacho [gas·pá·čo] *m. Spain* cold vegetable soup.

gela (*resina coloide coagulada*) [xé·la] *f.* gel (*fiber glass*); **gela-capa** gel-coat.

gelatina [xe·la·tí·na] *f.* gelatin; jelly; — **de caldo de tomate** aspic.

gema [xé·ma] *f.* gem, jewel; bud.

gemelo [xe·mé·lo] *m.* twin; **-s** twins; binoculars, opera glasses, field glasses; cuff links.

gemido [xe·mí·do] *m.* moan; wail, cry.

gemir[5] [xe·mír] *v. irr.* to moan; to wail, cry.

gendarme [xen·dár·me] *m. Mex., Ven., Ríopl., C.A.* policeman; (now less used than *policía, agente*).

genealogía [xe·ne·a·lo·xí·a] *f.* genealogy.

generación [xe·ne·ra·sjón] *f.* generation.

generador [xe·ne·ra·dór] *m.* generator; — **molecular** atom smasher.

general [xe·ne·rál] *adj. & m.* general; **por lo** — generally.

generalidad [xe·ne·ra·li·dád] *f.* generality; majority.

generalizar[9] [xe·ne·ra·li·sár] *v.* to generalize; **-se** to spread, become general.

genérico [xe·né·ri·ko] *adj.* generic.

género [xé·ne·ro] *m.* (*clase*) kind, sort, class; gender; (*tela*) goods, material, cloth; — **humano** human race.

generosidad [xe·ne·ro·si·dád] *f.* generosity.

generoso [xe·ne·ró·so] *adj.* generous; best (*wine*).

genial [xe·njál] *adj.* genial, jovial, pleasant.

genio [xé·njo] *m.* genius; temperament, disposition, spirit.

gente [xén·te] *f.* (*personas*) people; crowd; (*pueblo*) race, nation; clan; *Am.* — **bien** upper-class or important person; *Am.* **ser** — to be a somebody; to be cultured; to be socially important.

gentil [xen·tíl] *adj.* graceful; genteel; courteous; gentile; *m.* pagan; gentile.

gentileza [xen·ti·lé·sa] *f.* grace, courtesy; nobility; gavor.

gentilicio [xen·ti·lí·sjo] *adj.* national; *m.* name used to identify national or local origin.

gentío [xen·tí·o] *m.* crowd, throng.

gentuza [xen·tú·sa] *f.* rabble.

genuino [xe·nwí·no] *adj.* genuine.

geofísica [xe·o·fí·si·ka] *f.* geophysics.

geografía [xe·o·gra·fí·a] *f.* geography; **geográfico** [xe·o·grá·fi·ko] *adj.* geographical.

geología [xe·o·lo·xí·a] *f.* geology; **geológico** [xe·o·ló·xi·ko] *adj.* geological.

geometría [xe·o·me·trí·a] *f.* geometry; **geométrico** [xe·o·mé·tri·ko] *adj.* geometric.

geranio [xe·rá·njo] *m.* geranium.

gerencia [xe·rén·sja] *f.* management, administration.

gerente [xe·rén·te] *m.* manager.

germen [xér·men] *m.* germ; origin, source.

germinar [xer·mi·nár] *v.* to germinate.

gerundio [xe·rún·djo] *m.* gerund; present participle.

gesticular [xes·ti·ku·lár] *v.* to gesticulate.

gestión [xes·tjón] *f.* action, step, maneuver; intervention; **-es** negotiations.

gestionar [xes·tjo·nár] *v.* to manage; to take steps; to negotiate or carry out (*a deal, transaction, etc.*); (*computadora*) to control.

gesto [xés·to] *m.* face, expression; grimace; gesture; **estar de buen** (*or* **mal**) — to be in a good (*or* bad) humor; **hacer -s a** to make faces at.

giba [xí·ba] *f.* hump, hunch.

gigante [xi·gán·te] *adj.* gigantic; *m.* giant.

gigantesco [xi·gan·tés·ko] *adj.* gigantic.

gimnasia [xim·ná·sja] *f.* gymnastics; **gimnasio** [xim·ná·sjo] *m.* gymnasium; German institute (*for secondary instruction*).

gimotear [xi·mo·te·ár] *v.* to whimper, whine.

gimoteo [xi·mo·té·o] *m.* whimper, whining.

ginebra [xi·né·bra] *f.* gin (*liquor*).

ginecología [xi·ne·ko·lo·xí·a] *f.* gynecology.

gira [xí·ra] *f.* excursion, tour; outing, picnic.

girador [xi·ra·dór] *m.* drawer (*of a check or draft*).

girar [xi·rár] *v.* to revolve, rotate, whirl; to send, issue, or draw (*checks, drafts, etc.*); to manage (*a business*).

girasol [xi·ra·sól] *m.* sunflower.

giratorio [xi·ra·tó·rjo] *adj.* rotary, revolving.

giro [xí·ro] *m.* (*movimiento circular*) rotation; bend, turn; (*dirección*) direction, trend; (*estructura*) turn of phrase; (*monetario*) draft; — **postal** money order; *adj.* yellowish (*rooster*); *Am.* black and white (*rooster*); *Am.* cocky.

gitano [xi·tá·no] *adj.* gypsy; gypsylike; sly, clever; *m.* gypsy.

gitomate [xi·to·má·te] *Mex.* = **jitomate.**

glacial [gla·sjál] *adj.* glacial, icy, very cold.

glaciar [gla·sjár] *m.* glacier.

glándula [glán·du·la] *f.* gland.

glasear [gla·se·ár] *v.* to glaze (*paper, fruits, etc.*), make glossy.

glaucoma [glaw·kó·ma] *m.* glaucoma.

globo [gló·bo] *m.* globe, sphere; world; balloon.

glóbulo [gló·bu·lo] *m.* globule; corpuscle.

gloria [gló·rja] *f.* glory; gloria (*song of praise to God*).

gloriarse[17] [glo·rjár·se] *v.* to glory (in), delight (in), be proud (of); to boast (of).

glorieta [glo·rjé·ta] *f.* arbor, bower; secluded nook in a park (*with benches*); traffic circle.

glorificar[6] [glo·ri·fi·kár] *v.* to glorify; **-se** to glory (in), take great pride (in).

glorioso [glo·rjó·so] *m.* glorious.

glosa [gló·sa] *f.* gloss.

glosar [glo·sár] *v.* to gloss, comment upon, explain (*a text*).

glosario [glo·sá·rjo] *m.* glossary.

glotal [glo·tál] *adj.* glottal.

glotis [gló·tis] *f.* glottis.

GA

glotón [glo·tón] *adj.* gluttonous; *m.* glutton.
glotonería [glo·to·ne·rí·a] *f.* gluttony.
gobernador [go·ber·na·dór] *adj.* governing; *m.* governor, ruler.
gobernante [go·ber·nán·te] *adj.* governing, ruling; *m.* governor, ruler.
gobernar[1] [go·ber·nár] *v. irr.* to govern, rule; to lead, direct; to steer (*a boat*).
gobierno [go·bjér·no] *m.* government; management; control; helm, rudder.
goce [gó·se] *m.* enjoyment; joy.
goleta [go·lé·ta] *f.* schooner, sailing vessel.
golfo [gól·fo] *m.* gulf; open sea; faro (*gambling game*); vagabond, bum, ragamuffin.
golondrina [go·lon·drí·na] *f.* swallow; swallow fish.
golosina [go·lo·sí·na] *f.* sweet, dainty, tidbit; trifle; appetite, desire.
goloso [go·ló·so] *adj.* sweet-toothed, fond of sweets; gluttonous.
golpazo [gol·pá·so] *m.* bang, whack, heavy blow, hard knock.
golpe [gól·pe] *m.* blow, hit, stroke; knock; beat; *Col.* facing (*of a garment*); *Mex.* sledge hammer; — **de fortuna** stroke of good luck; — **de gente** crowd, throng; — **de gracia** death blow; finishing stroke; **de** — suddenly; **de un** — all at once; **pestillo de** — spring latch; *Am.* **al** — instantly, at once; *Am.* **al** — **de vista** at one glance.
golpear [gol·pe·ár] *v.* to strike, hit; to knock; to beat; *Mex.* to knock at a door.
golpetear [gol·pe·te·ár] *v.* to tap, knock or pound continuously; to flap; to rattle.
golpeteo [gol·pe·té·o] *m.* tapping, pounding, knocking; flapping; rattling.
gollería [go·ye·rí·a] *f.* dainty, delicacy; superfluous thing.
goma [gó·ma] *f.* gum; rubber; elastic; eraser; tire; — **de repuesto** spare tire; *Am.* **estar de** — to have a hang-over (*after excessive drinking*).
gomero [go·mé·ro] *adj.* rubber, pertaining to rubber; *m. Ríopl.* gum or rubber tree; *S.A.* rubber producer; *S.A.* rubber-plantation worker; *Mex., Ch., Ven.* glue container or bottle.
gomífero [go·mí·fe·ro] *adj.* rubber-bearing, rubber-producing.
gomoso [go·mó·so] *adj.* gummy, sticky; *m.* dandy.
gordiflón [gor·di·flón] *adj.* fat; chubby.
gordo [gór·do] *adj.* fat; plump; *m.* suet, fat; **gorda** [gór·da] *f. Mex.* thick tortilla or cornmeal cake; **se armo la gorda** all hell broke loose; there was a big rumpus.
gordura [gor·dú·ra] *f.* fatness; stoutness; fat.
gorgojo [gor·gó·xo] *m.* weevil; (*persona*) puny person; *Am.* wood borer, wood louse; **gorgojoso** *adj.* infested with weevils.
gorila [go·rí·la] *m.* gorilla.
gorjeador [gor·xe·a·dór] *m.* warbler; *adj.* warbling; **pájaro** — warbler.
gorjear [gor·xe·ár] *v.* to warble; to chirp.
gorjeo [gor·xé·o] *m.* warble; warbling.
gorra [gó·rra] *f.* cap; bonnet; **de** — at another's expense; **vivir de** — to sponge, live at another's expense.
gorrino [go·rrí·no] *m.* sucking pig.
gorrión [go·rrjón] *m.* sparrow.
gorro [gó·rro] *m.* cap; bonnet.
gorrón [go·rrón] *m.* sponge, parasite; bum; rake (*dissolute fellow*).
gota [gó·ta] *f.* (*líquido*) drop; (*enfermedad*) gout; **sudar la** — **gorda** to sweat profusely, toil, work hard.

gotear [go·te·ár] *v.* to drip; to leak; to dribble, trickle; to sprinkle, begin to rain; **-se** to leak.
goteo [go·té·o] *m.* trickle, drip.
gotera [go·té·ra] *f.* leak, hole (*in the roof*); eaves, trough; **-s** *Mex.* surroundings, outskirts.
gotero [go·té·ro] *m. Carib., Mex.* dropper (*for counting drops*).
gótico [gó·ti·ko] *adj.* Gothic; *m.* Goth; Gothic language.
gozar[9] [go·sár] *v.* to enjoy; to possess, have; **-se** to rejoice.
gozne [góz·ne] *m.* hinge.
gozo [gó·so] *m.* pleasure, joy.
gozoso [go·só·so] *adj.* joyful, glad, merry.
gozque [gós·ke] **gozquejo,** [gos·ké·xo] **gozquecillo** [gos·ke·sí·yo] *m.* a small dog.
grabación [gra·ba·sjón] *f.* recording (*tape*).
grabado [gra·bá·do] *adj.* engraved; recorded; *m.* engraving; woodcut, print; — **al agua fuerte** etching.
grabadora [gra·ba·dó·ra] *f.* tape recorder; *Spain* **grabadora magnetofónica.**
grabar [gra·bár] *v.* to engrave; to carve; to fix, impress; to record on tape; — **al agua fuerte** to etch.
gracejada [gra·se·xá·da] *f. C.A.* clownish act or expression.
gracejo [gra·sé·xo] *m.* grace; cuteness; humor, wit.
gracia [grá·sja] *f.* (*humorismo*) witty remark; joke; humor; (*garbo*) grace; gracious act; (*favor*) favor; pardon; **caer en** — to please; **hacer** — to amuse, make (*someone*) laugh; **¡-s!** thanks!; **dar -s** to thank.
gracioso [gra·sjó·so] *adj.* (*chistoso*) amusing; funny; witty; (*con garbo*) graceful, attractive; *m.* comedian, clown.
grada [grá·da] *f.* step of a staircase; harrow; **-s** steps; seats of an amphitheater; bleachers.
gradación [gra·da·sjón] *f.* gradation.
gradería [gra·de·rí·a] *f.* series of steps; rows of seats (*in an amphitheater or stadium*); — **cubierta** grandstand; **-s** bleachers.
grado [grá·do] *m.* (*medida*) degree; step; (*título*) degree; **de (buen)** — willingly, with pleasure; **de mal** — unwillingly; **de** — **en** — by degrees, gradually.
graduación [gra·dwa·sjón] *f.* graduation; military rank.
gradual [gra·dwál] *adj.* gradual; *m.* response sung at mass.
graduar[18] [gra·dwár] *v.* to graduate, give a diploma, rank or degree to; to gauge; to classify, grade; **-se** to graduate, take a degree.
gráfico [grá·fi·ko] *adj.* graphic; vivid, lifelike; **gráfica** *f.* graph, diagram, chart.
grafito [gra·fí·to] *m.* graphite.
grajo [grá·xo] *m.* rook; crow.
grama [grá·ma] *f.* grama grass.
gramática [gra·má·ti·ka] *f.* grammar; **gramatical** [gra·ma·ti·kál] *adj.* grammatical; **gramático** [gra·má·ti·ko] *adj.* grammatical; *m.* grammarian.
gramo [grá·mo] *m.* gram.
gran [gran] *contr. of* **grande.**
grana [grá·na] *f.* cochineal, kermes (*insects used for producing a red dye*); scarlet color; scarlet cloth; any small seed.
granada [gra·ná·da] *f.* pomegranate; grenade, shell, small bomb; — **de mano** hand grenade.
granado [gra·ná·do] *m.* pomegranate tree; *adj.* notable; illustrious; select.
grande [grán·de] *adj.* large, big; great, grand; *Mex.,*

C.A., Ven., Andes **mamá (papá)** — grandmother (grandfather); *m.* grandee (*Spanish or Portuguese nobleman*); **en** — on a large scale.
grandeza [gran·dé·sa] *f.* greatness; grandeur, splendor; bigness; size; grandeeship; body of grandees.
grandiosidad [gran·djo·si·dáḍ] *f.* grandeur, grandness; greatness; **grandioso** [gran·djó·so] *adj.* grandiose, great, grand, magnificent.
granero [gra·né·ro] *m.* granary; grain bin; country or region rich in grain.
granito [gra·ní·to] *m.* granite; small grain; small pimple.
granizada [gra·ni·sá·ḍa] *f.* hailstorm; shower, volley.
granizar[9] [gra·ni·sár] *v.* to hail.
granizo [gra·ní·so] *m.* hail; hailstorm; web or film in the eye; *adj. Mex.* spotted (*horse*).
granja [gráŋ·xa] *f.* grange, farm; country house.
granjear [graŋ·xe·ár] *v.* to earn, gain; to acquire, obtain; *Ch., C.A.* to steal; **-se** to win for oneself (*favor, goodwill, esteem, etc.*).
granjería [graŋ·xe·rí·a] *f.* farming; business profit.
granjero [graŋ·xé·ro] *m.* farmer.
grano [grá·no] *m.* (*cereal*) grain; seed; grain (*unit of measure*); **ir al** — to come to the point.
granuja [gra·nú·xa] *m.* ragamuffin, urchin; scamp.
granular [gra·nu·lár] *v.* to granulate; **-se** to become granulated; to break out with pimples.
grapa [grá·pa] *f.* clamp; staple; (*carbunclo*) pimple.
grasa [grá·sa] *f.* grease; fat; tallow; *Mex., Ríopl., Ven.* shoe polish; *Am.* **dar** — to polish (*shoes*).
grasiento [gra·sjén·to] *adj.* greasy, oily.
grasoso [gra·só·so] *adj.* greasy, oily.
gratificación [gra·ti·fi·ka·sjón] *f.* gratuity, bonus, tip; recompense, reward.
gratis [grá·tis] *adv.* gratis, for nothing, free of charge.
gratitud [gra·ti·túḍ] *f.* gratitude.
grato [grá·to] *adj.* pleasing, pleasant; gratuitous; **su grata** your favor, your letter.
gratuito [gra·twí·to] *adj.* gratuitous, free, free of charge.
grava [grá·ba] *f.* gravel.
gravamen [gra·bá·men] *m.* burden; mortgage; assessment, levy.
grave [grá·be] *adj.* grave; serious; weighty, heavy; grievous; deep, low (*in pitch*).
gravedad [gra·be·dáḍ] *f.* (*fuerza*) gravity; (*seriedad*) seriousness, gravity; (*tono*) depth (*of a sound*); — **específica** specific gravity.
gravoso [gra·bó·so] *adj.* burdensome; **serle a uno** — to be burdensome; to weigh on one's conscience.
graznar [graz·nár] *v.* to caw, croak, squawk, cackle, quack.
graznido [graz·ní·ḍo] *m.* caw, croak, squawk, cackle, quack.
greca [gré·ka] *f.* fret; ornamental design.
greda [gré·ḍa] *f.* clay, chalk; chalk cleaner.
gremial [gre·mjál] *adj.* pertaining to a labor union; *m.* member of a union.
gremio [gré·mjo] *m.* guild, society, brotherhood, trade union; fold (*referring to the Church*).
greña [gré·ña] *f.* shock of hair, tangled mop of hair (*usually* **greñas**): **greñudo** [gre·ñú·ḍo] *adj.* shaggy, with long, unkempt hair.
grey [grej] *f.* flock; congregation (*of a church*).
griego [grjé·ɡo] *adj.* Greek, Grecian; *m.* Greek.
grieta [grjé·ta] *f.* crevice; crack; fissure.
grifo [grí·fo] *m.* faucet; *Andes* cheap tavern (*where* **chicha** *is sold*); *Peru* gas station; *Cuba, P.R.* colored person; *Col.* drug addict; *Mex.* drunkard;

adj. curly, kinky, woolly (*hair*); *Col.* vain, conceited; **letra grifa** script; **ponerse** — to bristle, stand on end (*said of hair*); **grifería** faucets.
grillo [grí·yo] *m.* cricket; sprout, shoot; **-s** fetters; obstacle, hindrance.
grima [grí·ma] *f.* uneasiness; displeasure, disgust; *Ríopl., Carib.* sadness, compassion, pity; *Ch.* bit, small particle; **dar** — to disgust; to make uneasy; *Am.* to make sad, inspire pity.
gringo [gríŋ·go] *adj. Ch., Ríopl.* (*Italian*) foreign (*not Spanish*); *m. Ch., Ríopl.* (*Italian*) foreigner (*not Spanish*); *Mex., C.A., Andes, Col., Ven.* Yankee or English-speaking person.
griñones [gri·ñó·nes] *m. pl.* nectarines.
gripe [grí·pe] *f.* grippe, flu, influenza.
gris [gris] *adj.* grey; **grisáceo** *adj.* greyish.
grita [grí·ta] *f.* shouting, hooting; clamor, uproar.
gritar [gri·tár] *v.* to shout, cry.
gritería [gri·te·rí·a] *f.* shouting, clamor, uproar.
grito [grí·to] *m.* shout, cry; **poner el** — **en el cielo** to complain loudly, "hit the ceiling". **GL**
grosella [gro·sé·ya] *f.* currant; — **blanca** gooseberry; **grosellero** [gro·se·yé·ro] *m.* currant bush.
grosería [gro·se·rí·a] *f.* rudeness; coarseness; crudeness; insult.
grosero [gro·sé·ro] *adj.* rough, coarse; rude, impolite.
grosor [gro·sór] *m.* thickness.
grotesco [gro·tés·ko] *adj.* grotesque, fantastic; absurd.
grúa [grú·a] *f.* crane, derrick.
gruesa [grwé·sa] *f.* gross, twelve dozen.
grueso [grwé·so] *adj.* (*voluminoso*) fat, stout; thick; bulky, big, heavy; (*burdo*) dense; coarse; *m.* thickness; bulk; density; main part; **en** — in gross, in bulk, by wholesale.
grulla [grú·ya] *f.* crane (*bird*).
gruñido [gru·ñí·ḍo] *m.* growl, grumble; grunt.
gruñir[19] [gru·ñír] *v. irr.* to grunt; to growl; to snarl; to grumble.
gruñón [gru·ñón] *adj.* growling; grunting; grumbly; *m.* growler; grumbler.
grupa [grú·pa] *f.* rump; **volver -s** to turn around (*usually on horseback*).
grupo [grú·po] *m.* group; set.
gruta [grú·ta] *f.* grotto, cavern.
guacal [gwa·kál] *m. Col., Mex., C.A.* crate (*for transporting fruit, vegetables, etc., carried on the back*). *Also* **huacal**.
guacamayo [gwa·ka·má·yo] *m. Am.* macaw (*large parrot*); *Am.* flashily dressed person.
guacamole [gwa·ka·mó·le] *m. Mex., C.A., Cuba* avocado salad; also **guacamol**.
guacho [gwá·čo] *m.* birdling, chick; young animal; *Andes, Ríopl.* orphan; *Andes, Ríopl.* foundling; abandoned child; *adj. Am.* odd, not paired; *Andes, Ríopl.* forlorn, alone, abandoned.
guadal [gwa·dál] *m. Am.* small dune, sand hill; *Ven.* quagmire, bog, swamp; *Am.* growth of bamboo grass.
guadaña [gwa·ḍá·ña] *f.* scythe.
guagua [gwá·ɡwa] *f. Carib., Ven.* bus; trifle, insignificant thing; *m. & f. Andes, Ch., Ríopl.* baby; **de** — for nothing, gratis, free.
guaje [gwá·xe] *m. Am.* a species of gourd; *Mex.* vessel or bowl made of a gourd; *Mex.* simpleton, fool; *Am.* trifle, trinket, piece of junk; *adj. Mex.* foolish; *Am.* **hacerse uno** — to play the fool; *Am.* **hacer a uno** — to fool, deceive someone.
guajiro [gwa·xí·ro] *m.* Indian of the Guajira peninsula (*in Venezuela and Colombia*); *Cuba* rustic, peasant.
guajolote [gwa·xo·ló·te] *m. Mex.* turkey; *Mex.* fool.

guanaco [gwa·ná·ko] *m. Andes, Ch., Ríopl.* guanaco (*a kind of llama*); *Ch., Arg.* tall, lanky, gawky person; *Mex., C.A.* fool, simpleton; nickname for Salvadoreans.

guanajo [gwa·ná·xo] *m. Carib.* turkey, dunce.

guano [gwá·no] *m. Carib.* palm tree; *Carib.* palm leaves (*used for thatching*); *Am.* guano, bird dung, fertilizer.

guantada [gwan·tá·da] *f.* wallop, blow, slap.

guante [gwán·te] *m.* glove; *Andes* whip, scourge; **echar el — a uno** to seize or grab a person; **guantelete** [gwan·te·lé·te] *m.* gauntlet.

guapo [gwá·po] *adj.* handsome, good-looking; ostentatious, showy; daring, brave; *Ch., Andes* harsh, severe; *Carib., Mex.* angry; *m.* brawler, quarreler, bully.

guarache [gwa·rá·če] *m. Mex.* Mexican leather sandal; *Mex.* tire patch. *Also* **huarache** [wa·rá·če].

guaraní [gwa·ra·ní] *adj.* pertaining to the Guarani Indians of Paraguay; *m. & f.* Guarani Indian.

guarapo [gwa·rá·po] *m. Col., C.A., Andes* juice of the sugar cane; *Col., C.A., Andes* sugar-cane liquor; *Col., C.A., Andes* low-grade brandy.

guarda [gwár·da] *m. & f.* guard; keeper; *Ríopl.* ticket collector on a streetcar; *f.* custody, care, keeping; observance of a law; **-s** outside ribs of a fan; flyleaves.

guardabarros [gwar·da·bá·rros], **guardafango** [gwar·da·fáŋ·go] *m.* fender.

guardabosques [gwar·da·bós·kes] *m.* forest ranger, forester, forest keeper.

guardabrisa [gwar·da·brí·sa] *f.* windshield.

guardacostas [gwar·da·kós·tas] *m.* coast guard.

guardafrenos [gwar·da·fré·nos] *m.* brakeman.

guardagujas [gwar·da·gú·xas] *m.* switchman.

guardalmacén [gwar·dal·ma·sén] *m.* warehouse keeper, storekeeper.

guardamonte [gwar·da·món·te] *m.* trigger guard; forest keeper.

guardapapeles [gwar·da·pa·pé·les] *m.* file, filing cabinet or box.

guardapelo [gwar·da·pé·lo] *m.* locket.

guardar [gwar·dár] *v.* to guard, watch over; to keep; to store; to observe (*laws, customs*); **-se de** to guard against, keep from, avoid.

guardarropa [gwar·da·rró·pa] *m.* wardrobe; cloakroom; keeper of a cloakroom.

guardia [gwár·dja] *f.* guard, body of guards; defense, protection; *m.* guard, guardsman.

guardiamarina [gwar·dja·ma·rí·na] *f.* midshipman.

guardián [gwar·djan] *m.* guardian, keeper; superior of a Franciscan monastery.

guarecer[13] [gwa·re·sér] *v. irr.* to protect, shelter; **-se** to take shelter.

guarida [gwa·rí·da] *f.* den, cave, lair.

guarismo [gwa·ríz·mo] *m.* number.

guarnecer[13] [gwar·ne·sér] *v. irr.* to garnish, decorate; to adorn; to trim; to harness; to garrison; to set (*jewels*).

guarnición [gwar·ni·sjón] *f.* adornment; trimming; setting of a jewel; guard of a sword; garrison; **-es** trappings, harness.

guaro [gwá·ro] *m. C.A.* rum.

guasa [gwá·sa] *f.* joking; foolishness.

guasca [gwás·ka] *f. Andes, Ch., Ríopl.* leather thong; *Andes, Ch., Ríopl.* rope, cord; *Andes, Ch.* whip; *Andes, Ch., Ríopl.* **dar —** to whip, beat, thrash.

guaso [gwá·so] *m. Am.* stag, male deer; *Ch., Andes, Ríopl.* peasant; *Cuba* half-breed; *Am.* lasso; *adj.* rustic, peasant-like.

guasón [gwa·són] *adj.* funny, comical; *m.* joker,

jester.

guata [gwá·ta] *f. Am.* padding; *Ven.* fib; *Col.* a species of potato; *Ch., Andes* paunch, belly; *Am.* **echar —** to get fat.

guatemalteco [gwa·te·mal·té·ko] *m. & adj.* Guatemalan.

guayaba [gwa·yá·ba] *f.* guava (*pear-shaped tropical fruit*); **guayabo** *m.* guava tree; *Am.* lie, fraud, trick.

guayabera [gwa·ya·bé·ra] *f.* tropical pleated jacket.

gubernativo [gu·ber·na·tí·bo] *adj.* governmental, administrative.

gubia [gú·bja] *f.* gouge (chisel).

guedeja [ge·dé·xa] *f.* forelock; lock of hair; lion's mane.

güero [gwé·ro] *adj. Mex.* blond; *m. Ven.* cassava liquor. *See* **huero.**

guerra [gé·rra] *f.* war; **— a muerte** war to the finish; **dar —** to bother, trouble.

guerrear [ge·rre·ár] *v.* to war; *Am.* to do mischief or to bother (*said of children*).

guerrero [ge·rré·ro] *adj.* warlike, martial; *m.* warrior, soldier.

guerrilla [ge·rrí·ya] *f.* small war; skirmish; body of soldiers; band of fighters.

guerrillero [ge·rri·yé·ro] *m.* guerrilla fighter.

guía [gí·a] *m. & f.* guide, leader; *f.* guidebook, directory; signpost; shoot, sprout; *Ríopl.* garland of flowers.

guiar[17] [gjar] *v.* to guide; to drive (*a car*).

guija [gí·xa] *f.* pebble; **guijarro** [gi·xá·rro] *m.* cobblestone.

guijo [gí·xo] *m.* gravel.

guinda [gín·da] *f.* sour cherry.

guindilla [gin·dí·ya] *f. Spain* small hot pepper.

guineo [gi·né·o] *m. C.A.* banana.

guiñada [gi·ñá·da] *f.* wink.

guiñapo [gi·ñá·po] *m.* tag, tatter, rag; ragamuffin, ragged person.

guiñar [gi·ñár] *v.* to wink.

guiño [gi·ño] *m.* wink.

guión [gjón] *m.* hyphen; repeat sign (*in music*); cross (*carried before a prelate in a procession*); guide, leader (*among birds and animals*); leader in a dance.

guirnalda [gir·nál·da] *f.* garland, wreath.

guisa [gí·sa] *f.* way, manner; **a — de** like, in the manner of.

guisado [gi·sá·do] *m.* stew.

guisante [gi·sán·te] *m. Sp.* pea; **— de olor** sweet pea.

guisar [gi·sár] *v.* to cook; to prepare, arrange.

guiso [gí·so] *m.* dish, dish of food.

güisquil [gwis·kíl] *m. C.A.* chayote (*a pear-shaped fruit*).

guitarra [gi·tá·rra] *f.* guitar.

gula [gú·la] *f.* gluttony.

gusano [gu·sá·no] *m.* worm; caterpillar; **— de la conciencia** remorse; **— de luz** glowworm; *Col., Mex.* **matar el —** to satisfy a need or desire (*particularly hunger or thirst*).

gustar [gus·tár] *v.* (*agradar*) to please, be pleasing; (*saborear*) to taste; to experience; **-le a uno una cosa** to like something; **— de** to have a liking for, be fond of.

gusto [gús·to] *m.* (*agrado*) pleasure; whim; fancy; (*sabor*) taste; flavor; **dar —** to please; **estar a —** to be comfortable, contented; **tener — en** to be glad to; **tomar el — a una cosa** to become fond of something.

gustoso [gus·tó·so] *adj.* (*con agrado*) glad; pleasant; willing; merry; (*sabroso*) tasty; *adv.* willingly.

H:h

haba [á·ba] *f.* large bean; Lima bean.
habano [a·bá·no] *m.* Havana cigar.
haber[30] [a·bér] *v. irr.* to have (*auxiliary verb*); **habérselas con** to have it out with; **ha de llegar mañana** he is to arrive tomorrow; **ha de ser verdad** it must be true; **hay (había, hubo,** *etc.*) there is, there are (there was, there were, *etc.*); **hay que** (+ *inf.*) it is necessary; **no hay de qué** you are welcome? **¿qué hay?** what's the matter?
haber [a·bér] *m.* credit, credit side (*in book-keeping*); **-es** property, goods, cash, assets.
habichuela [a·bi·čwé·la] *f.* bean; — **verde** string bean.
hábil [á·bil] *adj.* skilful, capable, able.
habilidad [a·bi·li·dád] *f.* ability, skill.
habilitar [a·bi·li·tár] *v.* to enable; to equip; to qualify.
habitación [a·bi·ta·sjón] *f.* apartment; room; lodging.
habitante [a·bi·tán·te] *m.* inhabitant; resident.
habitar [a·bi·tár] *v.* to inhabit; to live, reside.
hábito [á·bi·to] *m.* habit; custom.
habitual [a·bi·twál] *adj.* habitual, customary.
habituar[18] [a·bi·twár] *v.* to accustom; **-se** to get used, accustomed.
habla [á·bla] *f.* speech; language, dialect; **al** — within speaking distance; in communication (with).
hablador [a·bla·dór] *m.* talker; gossip; *adj.* talkative.
habladuría [a·bla·du·rí·a] *f.* gossip, rumor; empty talk; impertinent remark.
hablar [a·blár] *v.* to speak; to talk; — **alto** (*or* **en voz alta**) to speak loudly; — **bajo (quedo** *or* **en voz baja)** to speak softly; — **por los codos** to chatter constantly.
hablilla [a·blí·ya] *f.* gossip, rumor, malicious tale.
hacedero [a·se·dé·ro] *adj.* feasible.
hacedor [a·se·dór] *m.* maker; **el Supremo Hacedor** the Maker.
hacendado [a·sen·dá·do] *m.* landholder; *Ríopl., Ch., Ven.* owner of a farm, plantation, or ranch.
hacendoso [a·sen·dó·so] *adj.* industrious, diligent.
hacer[31] [a·sér] *v. irr.* (*crear*) to do; to make; (*formar*) to form; to accustom; (*causar*) to cause, order (*followed by inf.*); — **caso** to mind, pay attention; — **frío (calor)** to be cold (warm); — **la maleta** to pack one's suitcase; — **la mortecina** play possum; — **un papel** to play a part; *Am.* — **aprecio** to pay attention; *Ríopl., Mex.* — **caras** (*or* **caritas**) to flirt; **no le hace** it makes no difference; **-se** to become, grow, get to be; **-se a** to get used to; **-se de rogar** to want to be coaxed.
hacia [á·sja] *prep.* toward; about; — **adelante** forward; — **atrás** backward.
hacienda [a·sjén·da] *f.* estate; property; finance; large farm; *Ríopl.* cattle, livestock.
hacina [a·sí·na] *f.* shock (*of grain*), stack, pile.
hacinar [a·si·nár] *v.* to shock (*grain*); to stack, pile up; to accumulate.
hacha [á·ča] *f.* ax; hatchet; torch.
hachero [a·čé·ro] *m.* axman, woodcutter.
hachuela de uña [a·čwé·la de ú·ña] claw (tool).
hada [á·da] *f.* fairy.
hado [á·do] *m.* fate, fortune, destiny.
halagar[7] [a·la·gár] *v.* to coax; to flatter; to allure, attract.
halago [a·lá·go] *m.* flattery; caress; allurement.
halagüeño [a·la·gwé·ño] *adj.* alluring, attractive; flattering; promising.
halar [a·lár] = **jalar.**
halcón [al·kón] *m.* falcon.
hálito [á·li·to] *m.* breath; vapor.

hallar [a·yár] *v.* to find; to discover, find out; **-se** to be; to fare, get along.
hallazgo [a·yáz·go] *m.* find; discovery; reward (*for finding something*).
hamaca [a·má·ka] *f.* hammock.
hambre [ám·bre] *f.* hunger; famine; appetite; **tener** — to be hungry; **hambruna** [am·brú·na] *f. Am.* great hunger, starvation.
hambrear [am·bre·ár] *v.* to starve; to be hungry.
hambriento [am·brjén·to] *adj.* hungry; greedy; *C.A., Mex., Andes* stingy.
hampa [ám·pa] *f. Spain* underworld.
hangar [aŋ·gár] *m.* hangar.
haragán [a·ra·gán] *adj.* lazy, indolent; *m.* loafer, idler.
haraganear [a·ra·ga·ne·ár] *v.* to lounge, loaf, be lazy.
haraganería [a·ra·ga·ne·rí·a] *f.* laziness.
harapiento [a·ra·pjén·to] *adj.* tattered, ragged.
harapo [a·rá·po] *m.* rag, tatter; **andar hecho un** — to be in tatters.
haraposo [a·ra·pó·so] *adj.* tattered, ragged.
harina [a·rí·na] *f.* flour; — **de utilidad general** all-purpose flour; **eso es** — **de otro costal** that is something entirely different; **harinoso** [a·ri·nó·so] *adj.* floury; flourlike.
harmonía [ar·mo·ní·a] *f.* harmony.
hartar [ar·tár] *v.* to fill up, gorge; to sate, satiate; **-se** to have one's fill; to overeat, eat too much.
harto [ár·to] *adj.* full; sated, satiated; fed up; too much; *adv.* too much; *Mex., C.A., Col., Ven., Ríopl., Andes* much, very much.
hasta [ás·ta] *prep.* till, until; up to; — **luego** goodbye, see you later; *conj.* even; — **que** until.
hastiar[17] [as·tjár] *v.* to surfeit; to cloy; to disgust.
hastío [as·tí·o] *m.* surfeit, excess; boredom; loathing, disgust.
hato [á·to] *m.* herd; flock; sheepfold; shepherd's hut; gang, crowd; pile; *Col., Ven.* cattle ranch.
haya [á·ya] *f.* beech; **hayuco** *m.* beechnut.
haz [as] *f.* face; surface; *m.* fagot, bundle, bunch.
hazaña [a·sá·ña] *f.* deed, exploit, feat.
hazmerreír [az·me·rre·ír] *m.* laughing stock.
he [e] (*used with* **aquí** *or* **allí**) behold, here is, here you have; **heme aquí** here I am; **helo aquí** here it is.
hebilla [e·bí·ya] *f.* buckle.
hebra [é·bra] *f.* thread; fiber; fine string; *Am.* **de una** — all at once, at one stroke, *Col.* **ni** — absolutely nothing; — **de vidrio troceadas** chopped strand (fiber glass); **hebroso** *adj.* fibrous, stringy.
hecatombe [e·ka·tóm·be] *m.* massacre, great slaughter; hecatomb (*sacrifice of 100 oxen*).
hectárea [ek·tá·re·a] *f.* hectare.
hechicera [e·či·sé·ra] *f.* witch, enchantress; hag.
hechicería [e·či·se·rí·a] *f.* witchcraft; magic; charm; enchantment.
hechicero [e·či·sé·ro] *adj.* bewitching, charming; *m.* magician; charmer; sorcerer.
hechizar[9] [e·či·sár] *v.* to bewitch; to charm.
hechizo [e·čí·so] *m.* charm; enchantment.
hecho [é·čo] *m.* fact; act, deed; **de** — in fact; *p.p. of* **hacer** done, made.
hechura [e·čú·ra] *f.* make; shape, cut; workmanship.
heder[1] [e·dér] *v. irr.* to stink; to reek.
hediondez [e·djon·dés] *f.* stink, stench.
hediondo [e·djón·do] *adj.* foul-smelling, stinking; filthy; *m. Ríopl.* skunk.
hedor [e·dór] *m.* stink, stench.
helada [e·lá·da] *f.* frost.
helado [e·lá·do] *adj.* frozen; freezing; frosty; icy; *m.* ice cream; ice, sherbet; **heladería** [e·la·de·rí·a] *f.*

GU

Am. ice-cream parlor.
heladora [e·la·đó·ra] *f.* freezer.
helar[1] [e·lár] *v. irr.* to freeze.
helecho [e·lé·čo] *m.* fern.
hélice [é·li·se] *f.* screw propeller; helix, spiral.
helicóptero [e·li·kóp·te·ro] *m.* helicopter.
helio [e·ljo] *m.* helium.
heliógrafo [e·ljó·gra·fo] *m.* blueprint.
helipuerto [e·li·pwér·to] *m.* heliport.
hembra [ém·bra] *f.* female; staple; nut (*of a screw*), **macho y —** hook and eye.
hemisferio [e·mis·fé·rjo] *m.* hemisphere.
hemofilia [e·mo·fí·lja] *f.* hemophilia.
hemoglobina [e·mo·glo·bí·na] *f.* hemoglobin.
hemorragia [e·mo·rrá·xja] *f.* hemorrhage.
henchir[5] [en·čír] *v. irr.* to swell, stuff, fill.
hendedura [en·de·đú·ra], **hendidura** [en·di·đú·ra] *f.* crack, crevice, fissure.
hender[1] [en·dér] *v. irr.* to split, crack, cleave.
henequén [e·ne·kén] *m. Mex., Ven., C.A., Col.* sisal, sisal hemp.
heno [é·no] *m.* hay.
henil [e·níl] *m.* hayloft.
hepatitis [e·pa·tí·tis] *f.* hepatitis.
heráldico [e·rál·di·ko] *adj.* heraldic; **heráldica** heraldry.
heraldo [e·rál·do] *m.* herald.
herbazal [er·ba·sál] *m.* field of grass.
herboso [er·bó·so] *adj.* grassy; weedy.
heredad [e·re·đáđ] *f.* parcel of land; rural property; estate.
heredar [e·re·đár] *v.* to inherit; to bequeath, leave in a will.
heredero [e·re·đé·ro] *m.* heir; successor; **heredera** [e·re·đé·ra] *f.* heiress.
hereditario [e·re·đi·tá·rjo] *adj.* hereditary.
hereje [e·ré·xe] *m.* heretic; **cara de —** hideous face.
herejía [e·re·xí·a] *f.* heresy; offensive remark.
herencia [e·rén·sja] *f.* inheritance; heritage; heredity.
herida [e·rí·da] *f.* wound; injury.
herido [e·rí·do] *adj.* wounded; *m.* wounded man; *Am.* small drainage channel.
herir[3] [e·rír] *v. irr.* to wound; to hurt; to strike; to offend.
hermana [er·má·na] *f.* sister.
hermanastro [er·ma·nás·tro] *m.* stepbrother, half brother; **hermanastra** [er·ma·nás·tra] *f.* stepsister, half sister.
hermandad [er·man·dáđ] *f.* brotherhood, fraternity.
hermano [er·má·no] *m.* brother.
hermético [er·mé·ti·ko] *adj.* hermetic; airtight; tight-lipped; close-mouthed; **hermetismo** [er·me·tíz·mo] *m.* complete silence.
hermosear [er·mo·se·ár] *v.* to beautify, adorn.
hermoso [er·mó·so] *adj.* beautiful, handsome.
hermosura [er·mo·sú·ra] *f.* beauty.
hernia [ér·nja] *f.* hernia.
héroe [é·ro·e] *m.* hero; **heroína** [e·ro·í·na] *f.* heroine; heroin (*drug*).
heroico [e·rój·ko] *adj.* heroic.
heroísmo [e·ro·íz·mo] *adj.* heroism.
herradura [e·rra·đú·ra] *f.* horseshoe.
herraje [e·rrá·xe] *m.* ironwork; iron trimmings; horseshoes and nails; *Am.* silver saddle trimmings; *Arg.* horseshoe.
herramienta [e·rra·mjén·ta] *f.* tool; **— con punta de diamante** diamond tool; *pl.* set of tools.
herrar[1] [e·rrár] *v. irr.* to shoe (*a horse*); to brand; to trim with iron.
herrería [e·rre·rí·a] *f.* blacksmith's shop or trade; forge; ironworks.

herrero [e·rré·ro] *m.* blacksmith.
herrete [e·rré·te] *m.* metal tip (*for a shoelace, for instance*); *Am.* branding iron.
herrumbre [e·rrúm·bre] *f.* rust; plant rot.
hervidero [er·bi·đé·ro] *m.* bubbling sound (*of boiling water*); bubbling spring; swarm, crowd; **un — de gente** a swarm of people.
hervir[3] [er·bír] *v. irr.* to boil; **— de gente** to swarm with people.
hervor [er·bór] *m.* boiling; boiling point; **soltar el —** to come to a boil.
heterodoxia [e·te·ro·đók·sja] *f.* heterodoxy.
heterogéneo [e·te·ro·xé·ne·o] *adj.* heterogeneous.
hez [es] *f.* scum; **la — del pueblo** the scum of society; **heces** [é·ses] dregs, sediment.
hiato [já·to] *m.* hiatus.
híbrido [í·bri·do] *adj. & m.* hybrid.
hidalgo [i·đál·go] *m.* hidalgo (*Spanish nobleman*); *adj.* noble, courteous.
hidalguía [i·đal·gí·a] *f.* nobility; generosity; courtesy.
hidrato [i·đrá·to] *m.* hydrate.
hidráulico [i·đráw·li·ko] *adj.* hydraulic; **fuerza hidráulica** water power; **ingeniero —** hydraulic engineer.
hidroavión [i·đro·a·bjón] *m.* hydroplane, seaplane.
hidroeléctrico [i·đro·e·lék·tri·ko] *adj.* hydroelectric.
hidrógeno [i·đró·xe·no] *m.* hydrogen.
hidropesía [i·đro·pe·sí·a] *f.* dropsy.
hidroplano [i·đro·plá·no] *m.* hydroplane.
hiedra [jé·đra] *f.* ivy.
hiel [jel] *f.* gall, bile; bitterness.
hielo [jé·lo] *m.* ice; frost.
hierba [jér·ba] *f.* grass; herb; weed; *Ríopl., Andes* mate (*Paraguayan tea*); *Mex., Ven., Cuba* marihuana (*a narcotic*); *C.A.* **ciertas -s** so-and-so (*person not named*).
hierbabuena [jer·ba·bwé·na] *f.* mint. *Also* **yerbabuena** [ŷer·ba·bwé·na].
hierro [jé·rro] *m.* iron; brand; iron tool, instrument, or weapon; **-s** irons, chains, handcuffs; **-s para soldar** soldering iron.
hígado [í·ga·đo] *m.* (*órgano*) liver; (*valentía*) courage; valor; **malos -s** ill will.
higiene [i·xjé·ne] *f.* hygiene; **higiénico** [i·xjé·ni·ko] *adj.* hygienic, sanitary.
higo [í·go] *m.* fig; **higuera** [i·gé·ra] *f.* fig tree; **higuerilla** [i·ge·rí·ya] *f. Am.* castor-oil plant.
higrómetro [i·gró·me·tro] *m.* hygrometer.
hija [í·xa] *f.* daughter; native daughter.
hijo [í·xo] *m.* son; native son; offspring, fruit, result.
hilachas [i·lá·čas] *f. pl.* lint; **mostrar uno la hilacha** to show one's worst side or nature; **hilachos** [i·lá·čos] *m. pl. Am.* rags, tatters.
hilado [i·lá·đo] *m.* yarn; *p.p. of* **hilar.**
hilandera [i·lan·đé·ra] *f.* spinner.
hilandería [i·lan·đe·rí·a] *f.* spinning mill; art of spinning; spinning.
hilandero [i·lan·đé·ro] *m.* spinner; spinning room.
hilar [i·lár] *v.* to spin, make into thread; **— muy delgado** to be very subtle.
hilas [í·las] *f. pl.* lint, fine ravelings (*for dressing wounds*).
hilaza [i·lá·sa] *f.* coarse thread; yarn.
hilera [i·lé·ra] *f.* file, row, line; **— de perlas** strand or string of pearls.
hilo [í·lo] *m.* (*hebra*) thread; fine yarn; string; (*alambre*) filament; thin wire; (*tela*) linen; **a —** without interruption; **al —** along the thread; *Am.* very well, all right; **de —** straight, without stopping; *Am.* **de un —** constantly, without stopping; **tener el alma en un —** to be frightened

to death; to be in great anxiety or suspense.

hilván [il·bán] *m.* basting stitch; basting; *Am.* hem.

hilvanar [il·ba·nár] *v.* to baste; to put together, connect; to do hastily; *Ven.* to hem.

himno [ím·no] *m.* hymn.

hincapié [iŋ·ka·pjé]: **hacer** — to emphasize, stress; to insist (upon).

hincar[6] [iŋ·kár] *v.* to drive, thrust (into); **-se** (*or* **-se de rodillas**) to kneel down.

hinchado [in·čá·do] *adj. & p.p.* swollen; inflated; presumptuous.

hinchar [in·čár] *v.* to swell; **-se** to swell; to swell up, puff up.

hinchazón [in·ča·són] *f.* swelling; inflation; conceit; bombast, inflated style.

hinojo [i·nó·xo] *m.* fennel.

hinojos [i·nó·xos]: **de** — on one's knees.

hipérbole [i·pér·bo·le] *f.* hyperbole.

hiperbólico [i·per·bó·li·ko] *adj.* hyperbolic.

hipo [í·po] *m.* hiccough; sob; longing; grudge, ill will.

hipocresía [i·po·kre·sía] *f.* hypocrisy.

hipócrita [i·pó·kri·ta] *adj.* hypocritical, insincere; *m. & f.* hypocrite.

hipódromo [i·pó·dro·mo] *m.* race track.

hipoteca [i·po·té·ka] *f.* mortgage.

hipotecar[6] [i·po·te·kár] *v.* to mortgage.

hipótesis [i·pó·te·sis] *f.* hypothesis, theory.

hipotético [i·po·té·ti·ko] *adj.* hypothetic(al).

hirviente [ir·bjén·te] *adj.* boiling.

hispanidad [is·pa·ni·dád] *f.* Hispanic solidarity.

hispanista [is·pa·nís·ta] *m. & f.* Hispanist; one who is interested in Hispanic studies.

hispano [is·pá·no] *adj.* Hispanic, Spanish; *m.* Spanish-speaking person.

hispanoamericano [is·pa·no·a·me·ri·ká·no] *adj.* Spanish-American.

histamina [is·ta·mí·na] *f.* histamine.

histerectomía [is·te·rek·to·mí·a] *f.* hysterectomy.

histérico [is·té·ri·ko] *adj.* hysterical.

historia [is·tó·rja] *f.* history; story; tale, fable; **dejarse de -s** to stop fooling and come to the point; **historieta** [is·to·rjé·ta] *f.* story, anecdote.

historiador [is·to·rja·dór] *m.* historian.

historial [is·to·rjál] *m.* record, data (*concerning a person or firm*); *adj.* historic.

histórico [is·tó·ri·ko] *adj.* historic, historical.

hito [í·to] *adj.* firm, fixed; **de hito en hito** fixedly.

hocico [o·sí·ko] *m.* snout; **caer de -s** to fall on one's face; **meter el — en todo** to meddle, stick one's nose in everything.

hogaño [o·gá·ño] *adv.* nowadays.

hogar [o·gár] *m.* hearth, fireplace; home.

hogareño [o·ga·ré·ño] *adj.* home-loving, domestic; homelike.

hogaza [o·gá·sa] *f.* loaf of bread.

hoguera [o·gé·ra] *f.* bonfire.

hoja [ó·xa] *f.* leaf; petal; sheet of paper or metal; blade; — **de lata** tin plate; — **electrónica** (*computadora*) spread sheet.

hojalata [o·xa·lá·ta] *f.* tin plate.

hojaldre [o·xál·dre] *m. & f.* puff pastry.

hojarasca [o·xa·rás·ka] *f.* fallen leaves; dry foliage; superfluous ornament; trash; useless words.

hojear [o·xe·ár] *v.* to leaf, turn the pages of; to browse.

hojuela [o·xwé·la] *f.* leaflet, small leaf; thin leaf (*of metal*); flake; thin pancake; — **de estaño** tin foil.

¡hola! [ó·la] *interj.* hello!; ho!; ah!

holandés [o·lan·dés] *adj.* Dutch; *m.* Dutchman; Dutch language.

holgado [ol·gá·do] *adj.* (*libre*) free, at leisure; comfortable; (*ancho*) wide, loose; roomy, spacious; *p.p. of* **holgar**.

holganza [ol·gán·sa] *f.* idleness.

holgar[2] [ol·gár] *v. irr.* to rest; to loaf; **-se** to be glad; to relax, have a good time; **huelga decir** needless to say.

holgazán [ol·ga·sán] *m.* idler, loafer; *adj.* lazy, idle.

holgazanear [ol·ga·sa·ne·ár] *v.* to loiter, lounge, idle, bum around.

holgazanería [ol·ga·sa·ne·rí·a] *f.* idleness, laziness.

holgorio [ol·gó·rjo] *m.* spree.

holgura [ol·gú·ra] *f.* (*descanso*) ease; rest, comfort; (*lugar*) roominess, plenty of room.

holocausto [o·lo·káws·to] *m.* holocaust, burnt offering, sacrifice.

hollar [o·yár] *v.* to tread, trample upon.

hollejo [o·yé·xo] *m.* skin, peel; husk.

hollín [o·yín] *m.* soot.

hombrada [om·brá·da] *f.* manly act; show of bravery.

hombre [óm·bre] *m.* man; **hombría** [om·brí·a] *f.* manliness, manly strength; — **de bien** honesty.

hombro [óm·bro] *m.* shoulder; **arrimar** (*or* **meter**) **el** — to help.

hombruno [om·brú·no] *adj.* mannish, masculine.

homenaje [o·me·ná·xe] *m.* homage, honor.

homeópata [o·me·ó·pa·ta] *adj.* homeopathic.

homicida [o·mi·sí·da] *m.* murderer; *f.* murderess; *adj.* homicidal, murderous.

homicidio [o·mi·sí·djo] *m.* homicide, murder.

homófono [o·mó·fo·no] *adj.* homophonous.

homogeneidad [o·mo·xe·nej·dád] *f.* homogeneity.

homogéneo [o·mo·xé·ne·o] *adj.* homogeneous, of the same kind or nature.

honda [ón·da] *f.* sling, slingshot.

hondo [ón·do] *adj.* deep; low; *m.* bottom, depth.

hondonada [on·do·ná·da] *f.* hollow, dip, gully, ravine.

hondura [on·dú·ra] *f.* depth; **meterse en -s** to go beyond one's depth; to get into trouble.

honestidad [o·nes·ti·dád] *f.* chastity, modesty, decency; decorum, propriety.

honesto [o·nés·to] *adj.* chaste, modest, decent; just; honest.

hongo [óŋ·go] *m.* mushroom; fungus; derby hat.

honor [o·nór] *m.* honor; glory; dignity.

honorario [o·no·rá·rjo] *m.* fee (*for professional services*); *adj.* honorary.

honorífico [o·no·rí·fi·ko] *adj.* honorary; **mención honorífica** honorable mention.

honra [ón·rra] *f.* honor; reputation; **-s** obsequies, funeral rites.

honradez [on·rra·dés] *f.* honesty, honor, integrity.

honrado [on·rrá·do] *adj.* honest, honorable; honored.

honrar [on·rrár] *v.* to honor; **-se** to be honored; to consider it an honor.

honroso [on·rró·so] *adj.* honorable; honoring.

hora [ó·ra] *f.* hour; time; **-s** canonical hours, office (*required daily prayers for priests and nuns*); **es — de** it is time to; **no ver la — de** (+ *inf.*) to be anxious to; **¿qué — es?** what time is it?

horadar [o·ra·dár] *v.* to pierce, bore, perforate.

horario [o·rá·rjo] *m.* schedule, timetable; hour hand.

horca [ór·ka] *f.* (*cadalso*) gallows; (*horcón*) pitchfork; *P.R.* birthday present; — **de ajos** string of garlic.

horcajadas [or·ka·xá·das]: **a** — astride (*with one leg on each side*); **ponerse a** — to straddle.

horcón [or·kón] *m.* forked pole, forked prop; *Mex., Cuba, Ven.* post, roof support; *Am.* roof.

horda [ór·da] *f.* horde.

horizontal [o·ri·son·tál] *adj.* horizontal.
horizonte [o·ri·són·te] *m.* horizon.
horma [ór·ma] *f.* form, mold; block (*for shaping a hat*); shoe last; shoe tree.
hormiga [or·mí·ga] *f.* ant.
hormigón [or·mi·gón] *m.* concrete.
hormigonera [or·mi·go·né·ra] *f.* concrete mixer.
hormiguear [or·mi·ge·ár] *v.* to swarm; to be crawling with ants; **me hormiguea el cuerpo** I itch all over.
hormigueo [or·mi·gé·o] *m.* itching, creeping sensation; tingle, tingling sensation.
hormiguero [or·mi·gé·ro] *m.* ant hill; ant nest; swarm; **oso** — anteater.
hormona [or·mó·na] *f.* hormone.
hornada [or·ná·da] *f.* batch of bread, baking.
hornear [or·ne·ár] *v.* to bake (*in an oven*).
hornilla [or·ní·ya] *f.* burner; grate (*of a stove*).
hornillo [or·ní·yo] *m.* kitchen stove; hot plate.
horno [ór·no] *m.* furnace; oven; kiln (*for baking bricks*); **alto** — blast furnace; — **de convección** convection oven; — **microhonda** microwave oven.
horquilla [or·kí·ya] *f.* hairpin; forked pole; small pitchfork.
horrendo [o·rrén·do] *adj.* horrible, hideous.
horrible [o·rrí·ble] *adj.* horrible.
horripilante [o·rri·pi·lán·te] *adj.* horrifying.
horror [o·rrór] *m.* horror; atrocity; **dar** — to cause fright; to horrify; **tenerle** — **a uno** to feel a strong dislike for one.
horrorizar[9] [o·rro·ri·sár] *v.* to horrify, shock, terrify.
horroroso [o·rro·ró·so] *adj.* horrid; frightful, hideous.
hortaliza [or·ta·lí·sa] *f.* vegetables; vegetable garden.
hortelano [or·te·lá·no] *m.* gardener.
hosco [ós·ko] *adj.* sullen; frowning; dark.
hospedaje [os·pe·dá·xe] *m.* board and lodging; lodging.
hospedar [os·pe·dár] *v.* to lodge, give lodging; **-se** to take lodging; to room, to stop (*at a hotel*).
hospedero [os·pe·dé·ro] *m.* innkeeper.
hospicio [os·pí·sjo] *m.* asylum; orphanage, orphan asylum; poorhouse; **hospiciano** [os·pi·sjá·no] *m.* inmate of a poorhouse or asylum.
hospital [os·pi·tál] *m.* hospital; — **de primera sangre** first-aid station.
hospitalidad [os·pi·ta·li·dád] *f.* hospitality.
hostería [os·te·rí·a] *f.* hostelry, inn.
hostia [ós·tja] *f.* host (*consecrated wafer*).
hostigar[7] [os·ti·gár] *v.* to harass, vex; to beat, lash; *C.A., Col.* to cloy.
hostil [os·tíl] *adj.* hostile; **hostilidad** [os·ti·li·dád] *f.* hostility.
hotel [o·tél] *m.* hotel; villa; **hotelero** [o·te·lé·ro] *m.* hotel-keeper; *adj.* pertaining to hotels.
hoy [oj] *adv.* today; — **día** nowadays; **de** — **en adelante** from now on; — **por** — at present; **de** — **más** henceforth.
hoya [ó·ya] *f.* pit, hole; grave; valley; *Col., Ch.* river basin.
hoyo [ó·yo] *m.* hole; pit; grave; *Ríopl., Carib* dimple.
hoyuelo [o·ywé·lo] *m.* dimple; tiny hole.
hoz [os] *f.* sickle; narrow ravine.
hozar[9] [o·sár] *v.* to root, turn up the earth with the snout (*as hogs*).
huacal [wa·kál] = **guacal.**
huarache [wa·rá·če] = **guarache.**
huaso [wá·so] = **guaso.**
hueco [wé·ko] *adj.* (*vacío*) hollow, empty; (*vano*) vain, affected; puffed up; high-sounding; *m.* gap, space, hole.
huelga [wél·ga] *f.* labor strike; rest; leisure; **declararse en** — to strike.

huelguista [wel·gís·ta] *m.* striker.
huella [wé·ya] *f.* trace; footprint.
huérfano [wér·fa·no] *adj. & m.* orphan.
huero [wé·ro] *adj.* empty; rotten, spoiled (*egg*). See **güero.**
huerta [wér·ta] *f.* orchard and vegetable garden; irrigated land.
huerto [wér·to] *m.* small orchard and vegetable garden; garden patch.
hueso [wé·so] *m.* bone; stone, pit; big seed; **la sin** — the tongue; **soltar la sin** — to talk too much; **no dejarle un** — **sano** to pick him to pieces.
huésped [wés·ped] *m.* (*convidado*) guest; (*anfitrión*) host; **ser** — **en su casa** to be seldom at home.
hueste [wés·te] *f.* host, army, multitude.
huesudo [we·sú·do] *adj.* bony.
huevo [wé·bo] *m.* egg; — **duro** hard-boiled egg; — **estrellado** fried egg; — **pasado por agua** soft-boiled egg; **-s revueltos** scrambled eggs; *Mex., C.A., Col., Ven.* **-s tibios** soft-boiled eggs; *Col., Ven.* **-s pericos** scrambled eggs; *Ven., Andes* **costar un** — to be very expensive.
huída [wí·da] *f.* flight; escape.
huir[32] [wir] *v. irr.* to flee, excape; to avoid, shun.
huizache [wi·sá·če] *m. Mex., C.A.* huisache (*a species of acacia*).
hule [ú·le] *m.* rubber; oilcloth; *Col., Ven.* rubber tree.
hulla [ú·ya] *f.* soft coal.
humanidad [u·ma·ni·dád] *f.* humanity, mankind; humaneness; **-es** humanities, letters.
humanitario [u·ma·ni·tá·rjo] *adj.* humanitarian, humane, kind, charitable.
humano [u·má·no] *adj.* human; humane; *m.* man, human being.
humareda [u·ma·ré·da] *f.* cloud of smoke.
humeante [u·me·án·te] *adj.* smoking, smoky; steaming.
humear [u·me·ár] *v.* to smoke, give off smoke; to steam; *Am.* to fumigate.
humedad [u·me·dád] *f.* humidity, moisture, dampness.
humedecer[13] [u·me·de·sér] *v. irr.* to moisten, wet, dampen.
húmedo [ú·me·do] *adj.* humid, moist, wet, damp.
humero [u·mé·ro] *m.* flue.
humildad [u·mil·dád] *f.* humility; humbleness; meekness.
humilde [u·míl·de] *adj.* humble, lowly, meek.
humillación [u·mi·ya·sjón] *f.* humiliation; submission.
humillar [u·mi·yár] *v.* to humiliate, humble, lower, crush; **-se** to humiliate oneself; to bow humbly.
humillos [u·mí·yos] *m. pl.* airs, conceit, vanity.
humo [ú·mo] *m.* smoke, fume, vapor; **-s** conceit, vanity.
humor [u·mór] *m.* substance; mood, disposition.
humorada [u·mo·rá·da] *f.* pleasantry, witty remark; caprice, notion.
humorismo [u·mo·ríz·mo] *m.* humor, humorous style.
humorístico [u·mo·rís·ti·ko] *adj.* humorous.
humoso [u·mó·so] *adj.* smoky.
hundimiento [un·di·mjén·to] *m.* sinking, collapse, cave-in.
hundir [un·dír] *v.* (*sumir*) to sink, submerge; (*batir*) to crush, oppress; to destroy; **-se** to sink; to collapse, cave in.
huracán [u·ra·kán] *m.* hurricane.
huraño [u·rá·ño] *adj.* diffident, shy, bashful; unsociable.
¡hurra! [ú·rra] *interj.* hurrah!
hurtadillas [ur·ta·dí·yas]·; **a** — on the sly, secretly,

stealthily.

hurtar [ur·tár] *v.* to steal, rob; **-se** to withdraw, slip away; to hide; — **el cuerpo** to dodge; to flee.

hurto [úr·to] *m.* robbery, theft; stolen article; **a** — stealthily, on the sly.

husillo [u·sí·yo] *m.* lead screw, spindle.

husmear [uz·me·ár] *v.* to scent, smell, follow the track of; to nose, pry (into).

husmeo [uz·mé·o] *m.* sniff, sniffing, smelling; prying.

huso [ú·so] *m.* spindle.

I:i **ibérico** [i·bé·ri·ko], **ibero** [i·bé·ro] *adj.* Iberian; **iberoamericano** [i·be·ro·a·me·ri·ká·no] *adj.* Ibero-American (*Spanish or Portuguese American*).

iconoclasta [i·ko·no·klás·ta] *m. & f.* iconoclast.

ida [í·da] *f.* departure; sally; **billete de** — **y vuelta** round-trip ticket; **-s y venidas** goings and comings.

idea [i·dé·a] *f.* idea; notion.

ideal [i·de·ál] *m. & adj.* ideal.

idealismo [i·de·a·líz·mo] *m.* idealism.

idealista [i·de·a·lís·ta] *adj.* idealistic; *m. & f.* idealist; dreamer.

idear [i·de·ár] *v.* to form an idea of; to devise, think out, plan.

ídem [í·den] idem (*abbreviation*, id.), ditto, the same.

idéntico [i·dén·ti·ko] *adj.* identical.

identidad [i·den·ti·dád] *f.* identity.

identificar[6] [i·den·ti·fi·kár] *v.* to identify.

idilio [i·dí·ljo] *m.* idyl.

idioma [i·djó·ma] *m.* language, tongue.

idiosincrasia [i·djo·siŋ·krá·sja] *f.* idiosyncrasy.

idiota [i·djó·ta] *m. & f.* idiot; *adj.* idiotic, foolish.

idiotez [i·djo·tés] *f.* idiocy.

idiotismo [i·djo·tíz·mo] *m.* idiom; idiocy.

idolatrar [i·do·la·trár] *v.* to idolize, worship.

ídolo [í·do·lo] *m.* idol.

idóneo [i·dó·ne·o] *adj.* fit, suitable; qualified.

iglesia [i·glé·sja] *f.* church.

ignición [ig·ni·sjón] *f.* ignition.

ignominia [ig·no·mí·nja] *f.* infamy, shame, disgrace.

ignominioso [ig·no·mi·njó·so] *adj.* ignominious; infamous, shameful, disgraceful.

ignorancia [ig·no·rán·sja] *f.* ignorance.

ignorante [ig·no·rán·te] *adj.* ignorant.

ignorar [ig·no·rár] *v.* to be ignorant of, not to know.

ignoto [ig·nó·to] *adj.* unknown, undiscovered.

igual [i·gwál] *adj.* (*semejante*) equal; (*liso*) even, smooth; uniform; (*siempre*) constant; **serle** — **a uno** to be all the same to one, make no difference to one; *m.* equal; **al** — equally.

igualar [i·gwa·lár] *v.* to equal; to equalize; to match; to level, smooth; to adjust; to be equal.

igualdad [i·gwal·dád] *f.* equality.

igualitario [i·gwa·li·tá·rjo] *adj.* equalitarian (*promoting the doctrine of equality*).

iguana [i·gwá·na] *f.* iguana.

ijada [i·xá·da] *f.* loin; flank (*of an animal*); pain in the side; **ijar** *m.* flank (*of an animal*).

ilegal [i·le·gál] *adj.* illegal, unlawful.

ilegítimo [i·le·xí·ti·mo] *adj.* illegitimate; illegal.

ileso [i·lé·so] *adj.* unharmed, uninjured, unhurt, safe and sound.

ilícito [i·lí·si·to] *adj.* illicit, unlawful.

ilimitado [i·li·mi·tá·do] *adj.* unlimited.

iluminación [i·lu·mi·na·sjón] *f.* illumination.

iluminar [i·lu·mi·nár] *v.* to illuminate; to light; to enlighten.

ilusión [i·lu·sjón] *f.* illusion.

ilusivo [i·lu·sí·bo] *adj.* illusive.

iluso [i·lú·so] *adj.* deluded; *m.* visionary, dreamer.

ilusorio [i·lu·só·rjo] *adj.* illusive; deceptive; worthless.

ilustración [i·lus·tra·sjón] *f.* illustration; elucidation; explanation.

ilustrado [i·lus·trá·do] *adj.* learned; enlightened.

ilustrador [i·lus·tra·dór] *m.* illustrator.

ilustrar [i·lus·trár] *v.* to illustrate.

ilustre [i·lús·tre] *adj.* illustrious, distinguished.

imagen [i·má·xen] *f.* image.

imaginable [i·ma·xi·ná·ble] *adj.* imaginable, conceivable.

imaginación [i·ma·xi·na·sjón] *f.* imagination.

imaginar [i·ma·xi·nár] *v.* to imagine.

imaginario [i·ma·xi·ná·rjo] *adj.* imaginary.

imaginativo [i·ma·xi·na·tí·bo] *adj.* imaginative; **imaginativa** [i·ma·xi·na·tí·ba] *f.* imagination.

imán [i·mán] *m.* magnet; attraction.

imantar [i·man·tár] *v.* to magnetize.

imbécil [im·bé·sil] *adj.* imbecile, stupid.

imborrable [im·bo·rrá·ble] *adj.* indelible, not erasable; unforgettable.

imbuir[32] [im·bwír] *v. irr.* to imbue; to instill, infuse, inspire (with).

imitación [i·mi·ta·sjón] *f.* imitation.

imitador [i·mi·ta·dor] *m.* imitator; follower; *adj.* imitative, imitating.

imitar [i·mi·tár] *v.* to imitate.

impaciencia [im·pa·sjén·sja] *f.* impatience.

impaciente [im·pa·sjén·te] *adj.* impatient.

impar [im·pár] *adj.* odd; **número** — odd number.

imparcial [im·par·sjál] *adj.* impartial; **imparcialidad** [im·par·sja·li·dád] *f.* impartiality, fairness, justice.

impasible [im·pa·sí·ble] *adj.* impassive, insensitive, insensible, unfeeling, unmoved.

impávido [im·pá·bi·do] *adj.* fearless; calm; *Am.* impudent, brazen.

impedimento [im·pe·di·mén·to] *m.* impediment, hindrance, obstacle.

impedir[5] [im·pe·dír] *v. irr.* to impede, prevent, hinder.

impeler [im·pe·lér] *v.* to impel, push; to incite, spur.

impenetrable [im·pe·ne·trá·ble] *adj.* impenetrable; impervious; incomprehensible.

impensado [im·pen·sá·do] *adj.* unforeseen, unexpected; offhand, done without thinking; **impensadamente** [im·pen·sa·da·mén·te] *adv.* offhand, without thinking; unexpectedly.

imperar [im·pe·rár] *v.* to rule, command, dominate; prevail.

imperativo [im·pe·ra·tí·bo] *adj.* imperative; urgent, compelling; *m.* imperative mood.

imperceptible [im·per·sep·tí·ble] *adj.* imperceptible.

imperdible [im·per·dí·ble] *m.* safety pin; *adj.* safe, that cannot be lost.

imperecedero [im·pe·re·se·dé·ro] *adj.* imperishable, enduring, everlasting.

imperfecto [im·per·fék·to] *adj.* imperfect; *m.* imperfect tense.

imperial [im·pe·rjál] *adj.* imperial; *f.* coach top; top seats on a coach or bus.

impericia [im·pe·rí·sja] *f.* inexperience.

imperio [im·pé·rjo] *m.* empire; command, rule; sway, influence.

imperioso [im·pe·rjó·so] *adj.* imperious, arrogant, domineering; urgent.

impermeable [im·per·me·á·ble] *adj.* waterproof,

HO

impervious, rainproof; *m.* raincoat.

impersonal [im·per·so·nál] *adj.* impersonal.

impertinencia [im·per·ti·nén·sja] *f.* impertinence; impudence; insolent remark or act; **decir -s** to talk nonsense; to make insolent remarks.

impertinente [im·per·ti·nén·te] *adj.* impertinent, impudent; meddlesome; irrelevant, not to the point; **-s** *m. pl.* lorgnette (*eyeglasses mounted on a handle*).

ímpetu [ím·pe·tu] *m.* impetus; violent force; impulse; *C.A., Ríopl.* vehement desire; — **de ira** fit of anger.

impetuoso [im·pe·twó·so] *adj.* impetuous, violent.

impío [im·pí·o] *adj.* impious, irreligious; profane.

implacable [im·pla·ká·ble] *adj.* implacable, relentless.

implantación [im·plan·ta·sjón] *f.* implantation, establishment, introduction (*of a system*).

implantar [im·plan·tár] *v.* to implant, establish, introduce.

implicar[6] [im·pli·kár] *v.* to imply; to implicate, involve.

implorar [im·plo·rár] *v.* to implore, entreat, beg.

imponente [im·po·nén·te] *adj.* imposing.

imponer[40] [im·po·nér] *v. irr.* to impose; to invest (*money*); — **miedo** to inspire fear; — **respeto** to inspire or command respect; **-se** to inspire fear or respect; to dominate; *Mex.* **-se a** to become accustomed to.

importancia [im·por·tán·sja] *f.* importance.

importante [im·por·tán·te] *adj.* important.

importar [im·por·tár] *v.* to be important; to matter; to amount to; to be necessary; to concern; to import.

importe [im·pór·te] *m.* amount, price, value; — **global** over-all costs.

importunar [im·por·tu·nár] *v.* to importune, nag, tease, pester.

importuno [im·por·tú·no] *adj.* annoying, persistent.

imposibilidad [im·po·si·bi·li·dád] *f.* impossibility.

imposibilitado [im·po·si·bi·li·tá·do] *p.p. & adj.* disabled, unfit; helpless.

imposibilitar [im·po·si·bi·li·tár] *v.* to make impossible; to disable.

imposible [im·po·sí·ble] *adj.* impossible; intolerable, unbearable; *Col., Ven.* disabled (*because of illness*); *Am.* slovenly, untidy.

imposición [im·po·si·sjón] *f.* imposition; burden; tax.

impostor [im·pos·tór] *m.* impostor, cheat; **impostura** [im·pos·tú·ra] *f.* imposture, fraud, deceit.

impotencia [im·po·tén·sja] *f.* impotence.

impotente [im·po·tén·te] *adj.* impotent, powerless.

impreciso [im·pre·sí·so] *adj.* vague, indefinite; inaccurate.

impregnar [im·preg·nár] *v.* to impregnate, saturate.

imprenta [im·prén·ta] *f.* press; printing shop; printing.

imprescindible [im·pre·sin·dí·ble] *adj.* essential, indispensable.

impresión [im·pre·sjón] *f.* impression; printing; mark; footprint.

impresionante [im·pre·sjo·nán·te] *adj.* impressive.

impresionar [im·pre·sjo·nár] *v.* to impress; to move, affect, stir; **-se** to be stirred, moved.

impreso [im·pré·so] *p.p. irr.* of **imprimir** printed; impressed, imprinted; *m.* printed matter.

impresor [im·pre·sór] *m.* printer (*person*).

impresora [im·pre·só·ra] *f.* printer (*device*); — **de margarita** daisy wheel printer; — **de matriz de puntos** dot-matrix printer; — **de cilindro** barrel printer; — **de bola** ball printer; — **gráfica** plotter.

imprevisión [im·pre·bi·sjón] *f.* carelessness, lack of foresight.

imprevisto [im·pre·bís·to] *adj.* unforeseen, unexpected.

imprimir [im·pri·mír] *v.* to print; to imprint, impress.

improbable [im·pro·bá·ble] *adj.* improbable, unlikely.

improperio [im·pro·pé·rjo] *m.* affront, insult.

impropio [im·pró·pjo] *adj.* improper; unsuitable.

improvisar [im·pro·bi·sár] *v.* to improvise.

improviso [im·pro·bí·so] *adj.* unforeseen; **de —** suddenly; *Col., Ven., Mex.* **en un —** in a moment, in the twinkling of an eye.

imprudencia [im·pru·dén·sja] *f.* imprudence, indiscretion, rash act.

imprudente [im·pru·dén·te] *adj.* imprudent; unwise; indiscreet.

impuesto [im·pwés·to] *p.p.* of **imponer** imposed; informed; *Am.* **estar — a** to be used or accustomed to; *m.* tax, duty.

impulsar [im·pul·sár] *v.* to impel, push, move; to force.

impulso [im·púl·so] *m.* impulse; push.

impulsor [im·pul·sór] *m.* (*computadora*) driving mechanism; — **de discos** disk drive.

impureza [im·pu·ré·sa] *f.* impurity.

impuro [im·pú·ro] *adj.* impure.

imputar [im·pu·tár] *v.* to impute, attribute.

inacabable [i·na·ka·bá·ble] *adj.* unending, endless.

inacabado [i·na·ka·bá·do] *adj.* unfinished.

inaccesible [i·nak·se·sí·ble] *adj.* inaccessible, unobtainable.

inacción [i·nak·sjón] *f.* inaction, inactivity, idleness.

inaceptable [i·na·sep·tá·ble] *adj.* unacceptable, unsatisfactory.

inactividad [i·nak·ti·bi·dád] *f.* inactivity.

inactivo [i·nak·tí·bo] *adj.* inactive.

inadecuado [i·na·de·kwá·do] *adj.* inadequate.

inadvertencia [i·nad·ber·tén·sja] *f.* oversight; inattention, heedlessness.

inadvertido [i·nad·ber·tí·do] *adj.* careless, heedless; unnoticed.

inafectado [i·na·fek·tá·do] *adj.* unaffected.

inagotable [i·na·go·tá·ble] *adj.* inexhaustible.

inaguantable [i·na·gwan·tá·ble] *adj.* insufferable, unbearable.

inalámbrico [i·na·lám·bri·ko] *adj.* wireless.

inalterable [i·nal·te·rá·ble] *adj.* unalterable, unchangeable.

inalterado [i·nal·te·rá·do] *adj.* unchanged.

inamovible [i·na·mo·bí·ble] = **inmovible**.

inanición [i·na·ni·sjón] *f.* starvation.

inanimado [i·na·ni·má·do] *adj.* inanimate, lifeless.

inapelable [i·na·pe·lá·ble] *adj.* unappealable; unavoidable.

inapetencia [i·na·pe·tén·sja] *f.* lack of appetite.

inaplicable [i·na·pli·ká·ble] *adj.* inapplicable, unsuitable; — **al caso** irrelevant.

inapreciable [i·na·pre·sjá·ble] *adj.* invaluable; inappreciable, too small to be perceived, very slight.

inasequible [i·na·se·kí·ble] *adj.* inaccessible, not obtainable; hard to attain or obtain.

inaudito [i·naw·dí·to] *adj.* unheard-of; unprecedented.

inauguración [i·naw·gu·ra·sjón] *f.* inauguration.

inaugurar [i·naw·gu·rár] *v.* to inaugurate, begin, open.

incaico [iŋ·káj·ko], **incásico** [in·ká·si·ko] *adj.* Incan (*of or pertaining to the Incas*).

incalculable [iŋ·kal·ku·lá·ble] *adj.* incalculable; innumerable, untold.

incandescente [iŋ·kan·de·sén·te] *adj.* incandescent.

incansable [iŋ·kan·sá·ble] *adj.* untiring, tireless.

incapacidad [iŋ·ka·pa·si·dád] *f.* incompetence,

inability, unfitness.

incapacitar [iŋ·ka·pa·si·tár] *v.* to cripple, disable, handicap, unfit, make unfit.

incapaz [iŋ·ka·pás] *adj.* incapable, unable.

incauto [iŋ·káw·to] *adj.* unwary, heedless, reckless.

incendiar [iŋ·sen·djár] *v.* to set fire to; **-se** to catch fire.

incendio [iŋ·sén·djo] *m.* conflagration, fire.

incentivo [in·sén·ti·ƀo] *m.* incentive, inducement.

incertidumbre [in·ser·ti·ðúm·bre] *f.* uncertainty, doubt.

incesante [in·se·sán·te] *adj.* incessant.

incidental [in·si·ðen·tál] *adj.* incidental.

incidente [in·si·ðén·te] *adj.* incidental; *m.* incident.

incienso [in·sjén·so] *m.* incense.

incierto [in·sjér·to] *adj.* uncertain, doubtful; unstable; unknown; untrue.

incisión [in·si·sjón] *f.* incision, cut, slit, gash.

incisivo [in·si·sí·ƀo] *adj.* incisive; *m.* incisor.

incitamiento [in·si·ta·mjén·to] *m.* incitement, inducement, incentive.

incitar [in·si·tár] *v.* to incite, rouse, stir up.

incivil [in·si·ƀíl] *adj.* uncivil, rude, impolite.

inclemencia [iŋ·kle·mén·sja] *f.* inclemency, severity, harshness; **inclemente** [iŋ·kle·mén·te] *adj.* unmerciful, merciless.

inclinación [iŋ·kli·na·sjón] *f.* inclination, affection; tendency, bent; bow; incline, slope.

inclinar [iŋ·kli·nár] *v.* (*bajar*) to incline; (*persuadir*) to persuade; **-se** to bow; to stoop; to incline, slope, slant; to lean, bend.

incluir[32] [iŋ·klwír] *v. irr.* to include; to inclose.

inclusive [iŋ·klu·sí·ƀe] *adv.* inclusive, including; even; **inclusivo** [in·klu·sí·ƀo] *adj.* inclusive; comprehensive.

incluso [iŋ·klú·so] *adj.* inclosed; included; including; even.

incógnito [iŋ·kóǵ·ni·to] *adj.* unknown; **de —** incognito (*with one's name or rank unknown*); **incógnita** *f.* unknown quantity (*in mathematics*).

incoherente [iŋ·ko·e·rén·te] *adj.* incoherent, disconnected, rambling.

incoloro [iŋ·ko·ló·ro] *adj.* colorless.

incombustible [iŋ·kom·bus·tí·ƀle] *adj.* incombustible; fireproof.

incomestible [iŋ·ko·mes·tí·ƀle] *adj.* inedible.

incomodar [iŋ·ko·mo·ðár] *v.* to inconvenience, disturb, trouble, annoy.

incomodidad [iŋ·ko·mo·ði·ðáð] *f.* inconvenience, discomfort; bother, annoyance.

incómodo [iŋ·kó·mo·ðo] *adj.* inconvenient, bothersome; uncomfortable.

incomparable [iŋ·kom·pa·rá·ƀle] *adj.* incomparable.

incompasivo [iŋ·kom·pa·sí·ƀo] *adj.* merciless, pitiless.

incompatible [iŋ·kom·pa·tí·ƀle] *adj.* incompatible; unsuitable, uncongenial.

incompetencia [iŋ·kom·pe·tén·sja] *f.* incompetence, inability, unfitness; **incompentente** [in·kom·pe·tén·te] *adj.* incompetent, unfit.

incompleto [iŋ·kom·plé·to] *adj.* incomplete.

incomprensible [iŋ·kom·pren·sí·ƀle] *adj.* incomprehensible.

inconcebible [iŋ·kon·se·ƀí·ƀle] *adj.* inconceivable.

inconcluso [iŋ·koŋ·klú·so] *adj.* unfinished.

incondicional [iŋ·kon·di·sjo·nál] *adj.* unconditional.

inconexo [iŋ·ko·nék·so] *adj.* unconnected; incoherent, disconnected.

inconfundible [iŋ·kon·fun·dí·ƀle] *adj.* unmistakable.

incongruente [iŋ·koŋ·grwén·te] *adj.* unsuitable, not appropriate; not harmonious.

inconquistable [iŋ·koŋ·kis·tá·ƀle] *adj.* unconquerable.

inconsciencia [iŋ·kon·sjén·sja] *f.* unconsciousness; unawareness.

inconsciente [iŋ·kon·sjén·te] *adj.* unconscious; unaware.

inconsecuente [iŋ·kon·se·kwén·te] *adj.* inconsistent; illogical.

inconsiderado [iŋ·kon·si·ðe·rá·ðo] *adj.* inconsiderate, thoughtless.

inconstancia [iŋ·kons·tán·sja] *f.* inconstancy, changeableness, fickleness.

inconstante [iŋ·kons·tán·te] *adj.* inconstant, fickle, changeable, variable.

incontable [iŋ·kon·tá·ƀle] *adj.* countless, innumerable.

inconveniencia [iŋ·kom·be·njén·sja] *f.* inconvenience; trouble.

inconveniente [iŋ·kom·be·njén·te] *adj.* inconvenient; improper; *m.* obstacle; objection.

incorporar [iŋ·kor·po·rár] *v.* to incorporate, unite; to embody; to include; **-se** to sit up; **-se a** to join.

incorrecto [iŋ·ko·rrék·to] *adj.* incorrect.

incredulidad [iŋ·kre·ðu·li·ðáð] *f.* incredulity, unbelief.

incrédulo [iŋ·kré·ðu·lo] *adj.* incredulous, unbelieving; *m.* unbeliever.

increíble [iŋ·kre·í·ƀle] *adj.* incredible, unbelievable.

incremento [iŋ·kre·mén·to] *m.* increment, increase.

incrustar [iŋ·krus·tár] *v.* to inlay; to encrust (*cover with a crust or hard coating*); **-se en** to penetrate impress itself deeply into.

incubadora [iŋ·ku·ƀa·ðó·ra] *f.* incubator.

inculcar[6] [iŋ·kul·kár] *v.* to inculcate, instill, impress.

inculto [iŋ·kúl·to] *adj.* uncultured; uncultivated; unrefined.

incumbencia [iŋ·kum·bén·sja] *f.* concern, duty, obligation; **no es de mi —** it does not concern me, it is not within my province.

incurable [iŋ·ku·rá·ƀle] *adj.* incurable.

incurrir [iŋ·ku·rrír] *v.* to incur, fall (into); **— en un error** to fall into or commit an error; **— en el odio de** to incur the hatred of.

incursión [iŋ·kur·sjón] *f.* raid, invasion.

indagación [in·da·ǵa·sjón] *f.* investigation, inquiry.

indagador [in·da·ǵa·ðór] *m.* investigator; inquirer; *adj.* investigating; inquiring.

indagar[7] [in·da·ǵár] *v.* to find out, investigate; to inquire.

indebido [in·de·ƀí·ðo] *adj.* undue, improper; illegal; **indebidamente** [in·de·ƀi·ða·mén·te] *adv.* unduly; illegally.

indecencia [in·de·sén·sja] *f.* indecency, obscenity, indecent act or remark.

indecente [in·de·sén·te] *adj.* indecent, improper.

indecible [in·de·sí·ƀle] *adj.* inexpressible, untold.

indeciso [in·de·sí·so] *adj.* undecided; doubtful, uncertain.

indefectible [in·de·fek·tí·ƀle] *adj.* unfailing; **-mente** unfailingly.

indefenso [in·de·fén·so] *adj.* defenseless, unprotected.

indefinible [in·de·fi·ní·ƀle] *adj.* indefinable.

indefinido [in·de·fi·ní·ðo] *adj.* indefinite.

indeleble [in·de·lé·ƀle] *adj.* indelible.

indemnización [in·dem·ni·sa·sjón] *f.* indemnity, compensation.

indemnizar[9] [in·dem·ni·sár] *v.* to indemnify, compensate.

independencia [in·de·pen·dén·sja] *f.* independence.

independiente [in·de·pen·djén·te] *adj.* independent.

indescriptible [in·des·krip·tí·ƀle] *adj.* indescribable.

indeseable [in·de·se·á·ƀle] *adj.* undesirable, unwelcome.

indiada [in·djá·ða] *f.* *Ríopl., C.A., Col.* community, group, or crowd of Indians; *Col., Ven., Carib., Andes* an Indian-like remark or act; *Am.* an uncontrollable fit of anger.

indianista [in·dja·nís·ta] *m. & f.* student of Indian culture; *adj.* pertaining to Indian culture.

indiano [in·djá·no] *adj.* of or pertaining to the West or East Indies; *m.* Spaniard who goes back to settle in his country after having lived for some time in Spanish America.

indicación [in·di·ka·sjón] *f.* indication.

indicar[6] [in·di·kár] *v.* to indicate, show, point out.

indicativo [in·di·ka·tí·bo] *adj.* indicative; *m.* indicative, indicative mood.

índice [ín·di·se] *m.* index; catalogue; sign; pointer; forefinger.

indicio [in·dí·sjo] *m.* indication, sign.

indiferencia [in·di·fe·rén·sja] *f.* indifference.

indiferente [in·di·fe·rén·te] *adj.* indifferent.

indígena [in·dí·xe·na] *adj.* indigenous, native; *m. & f.* native inhabitant; *Am.* Indian.

indigestión [in·di·xes·tjón] *f.* indigestion.

indignación [in·dig·na·sjón] *f.* indignation.

indignado [in·dig·ná·do] *p.p. & adj.* indignant, irritated, angry.

indignar [in·dig·nár] *v.* to irritate, anger; **-se** to become indignant, angry.

indignidad [in·dig·ni·dád] *f.* indignity, affront, insult; unworthy or disgraceful act.

indigno [in·dig·no] *adj.* unworthy; low, contemptible.

indio [ín·djo] *adj. & m.* Indian; Hindu; indium (*element*).

indirecta [in·di·rék·ta] *f.* hint, indirect remark, innuendo, insinuation.

indirecto [in·di·rék·to] *adj.* indirect.

indisciplinado [in·di·si·pli·ná·do] *adj.* undisciplined, untrained.

indiscreto [in·dis·kré·to] *adj.* indiscreet, imprudent, unwise, rash.

indiscutible [in·dis·ku·tí·ble] *adj.* indisputable, unquestionable.

indispensable [in·dis·pen·sá·ble] *adj.* indispensable.

indisponer[40] [in·dis·po·nér] *v. irr.* to indispose; to make ill; — **a uno con otro** to prejudice someone against another; **-se** to become ill; **-se con** to fall out with, quarrel with.

indisposición [in·dis·po·si·sjón] *f.* indisposition, upset, slight illness; reluctance, unwillingness.

indispuesto [in·dis·pwés·to] *p.p. of* **indisponer** *& adj.* indisposed, unwilling; ill.

indisputable [in·dis·pu·tá·ble] *adj.* unquestionable.

indistinto [in·dis·tín·to] *adj.* indistinct, dim, vague, not clear.

individual [in·di·bi·dwál] *adj.* individual.

individualidad [in·di·bi·dwa·li·dád] *f.* individuality.

individualismo [in·di·bi·dwa·líz·mo] *m.* individualism.

individuo [in·di·bí·dwo] *adj.* individual; indivisible; *m.* individual; person; member.

indócil [in·dó·sil] *adj.* unruly, disobedient, headstrong.

indocto [in·dók·to] *adj.* uneducated, ignorant.

índole [ín·do·le] *f.* disposition, temper; kind, class.

indolencia [in·do·lén·sja] *f.* indolence, laziness; insensitiveness, indifference.

indolente [in·do·lén·te] *adj.* indolent, lazy; insensitive, indifferent.

indomable [in·do·má·ble] *adj.* indomitable, unconquerable; unmanageable; untamable.

indómito [in·dó·mi·to] *adj.* untamed; uncontrollable, unruly.

inducir[25] [in·du·sír] *v. irr.* to induce; to persuade.

indudable [in·du·dá·ble] *adj.* unquestionable, certain.

indulgencia [in·dul·xén·sja] *f.* indulgence, tolerance, forgiveness; remission of sins.

indulgente [in·dul·xén·te] *adj.* indulgent, lenient.

indultar [in·dul·tár] *v.* to pardon, set free; to exempt.

indulto [in·dúl·to] *m.* pardon, forgiveness; exemption; privilege.

indumentaria [in·du·men·tá·rja] *f.* costume, dress; manner of dressing.

industria [in·dús·trja] *f.* industry; cleverness, skill; **de** — intentionally, on purpose.

industrial [in·dus·trjál] *adj.* industrial; *m.* industrialist; manufacturer.

industrioso [in·dus·trjó·so] *adj.* industrious.

inédito [i·né·di·to] *adj.* unpublished.

inefable [i·ne·fá·ble] *adj.* ineffable, inexpressible.

ineficaz [i·ne·fi·kás] *adj.* ineffective; inefficient.

inepto [i·nép·to] *adj.* incompetent; unsuitable.

inequívoco [i·ne·kí·bo·ko] *adj.* unmistakable.

inercia [i·nér·sja] *f.* inertia, lifelessness; inactivity.

inerme [i·nér·me] *adj.* unarmed, defenseless.

inerte [i·nér·te] *adj.* inert; inactive, sluggish, slow.

inesperado [i·nes·pe·rá·do] *adj.* unexpected.

inestable [i·nes·tá·ble] *adj.* unstable; unsettled; unsteady.

inestimable [i·nes·ti·má·ble] *adj.* inestimable, invaluable.

inevitable [i·ne·bi·tá·ble] *adj.* inevitable, unavoidable.

inexacto [i·nek·sák·to] *adj.* inexact, inaccurate.

inexorable [i·nek·so·rá·ble] *adj.* inexorable.

inexperiencia [i·nes·pe·rjén·sja] *f.* inexperience.

inexperto [i·nes·pér·to] *adj.* unskillful, unskilled, inexperienced.

inexplicable [i·nes·pli·ká·ble] *adj.* inexplicable.

inextinguible [i·nes·tiŋ·gí·ble] *adj.* inextinguishable, unquenchable.

infalible [in·fa·lí·ble] *adj.* infallible.

infame [in·fá·me] *adj.* infamous; *m.* scoundrel.

infamia [in·fá·mja] *f.* infamy, dishonor; wickedness.

infancia [in·fán·sja] *f.* infancy.

infante [in·fán·te] *m.* infant; infante (*royal prince of Spain, except the heir to the throne*); infantryman.

infantería [in·fan·te·rí·a] *f.* infantry.

infantil [in·fan·tíl] *adj.* infantile, childlike, childish.

infatigable [in·fa·ti·gá·ble] *adj.* tireless, untiring.

infausto [in·fáws·to] *adj.* unfortunate; unhappy.

infección [in·fek·sjón] *f.* infection; **infeccioso** *adj.* infectious.

infectar [in·fek·tár] *v.* to infect; to corrupt; **-se** to become infected.

infeliz [in·fe·lís] *adj.* unhappy, unfortunate; *m.* poor wretch.

inferior [in·fe·rjór] *adj.* inferior; lower; *m.* inferior.

inferioridad [in·fe·rjo·ri·dád] *f.* inferiority.

inferir[3] [in·fe·rír] *v. irr.* (*concluir*) to infer; to imply; (*causar*) to inflict.

infernal [in·fer·nál] *adj.* infernal.

infestar [in·fes·tár] *v.* to infest, invade, overrun, plague; to corrupt, infect.

inficionar [in·fi·sjo·nár] *v.* to infect; to contaminate.

infiel [in·fjél] *adj.* unfaithful, faithless; infidel; inaccurate.

infiernillo [in·fjer·ní·yo] *m.* chafing dish.

infierno [in·fjér·no] *m.* hell; **en el quinto** — very far away, at the end of nowhere.

infiltrar [in·fil·trár] *v.* to filter through; **-se** to leak (into), filter (through), infiltrate.

infinidad [in·fi·ni·dád] *f.* infinity; **una** — **de** a large number of.

infinito [in·fi·ní·to] *adj.* infinite; *adv.* infinitely; *m.* infinity.

inflamación [in·fla·ma·sjón] *f.* inflammation.

inflamado [in·fla·má·do] *p.p. & adj.* inflamed; sore.
inflamar [in·fla·már] *v.* to inflame, excite; to kindle, set on fire; **-se** to become inflamed.
inflar [in·flár] *v.* to inflate; to exaggerate; **-se** to become inflated; to swell up with pride.
inflexible [in·flek·sí·ble] *adj.* inflexible, stiff, rigid; unbending.
inflexión [in·flek·sjón] *f.* inflection.
infligir[11] [in·fli·xír] *v.* to inflict.
influencia [in·flwén·sja] *f.* influence.
influenza [in·flwén·sa] *f.* influenza, grippe, flu.
influir[32] [in·flwír] *v. irr.* to influence.
influjo [in·flú·xo] *m.* influence; influx, inward flow.
influyente [in·flu·yén·te] *adj.* influential.
información [in·for·ma·sjón] *f.* information.
informal [in·for·mál] *adj.* informal; unconventional; unreliable, not dependable, not punctual.
informar [in·for·már] *v.* to inform; to give form to; to give a report; to present a case; **-se** to find out.
informática [in·for·má·ti·ka] *f.* (*computadora*) computer science.
informatizar [in·for·ma·ti·sár] *v.* to computerize.
informe [in·fór·me] *m.* report, account; information; brief; *adj.* formless, shapeless.
infortunio [in·for·tú·njo] *m.* misfortune, mishap; misery.
infracción [in·frak·sjón] *f.* infraction, breach, violation (*of a law, treaty, etc.*).
infractor [in·frak·tór] *m.* transgressor, lawbreaker, violator (*of a law*).
infrascrito [in·fras·krí·to] *m.* undersigned, subscriber, signer (*of a letter, document, etc.*); **el — secretario** the secretary whose signature appears below.
infringir[11] [in·friŋ·xír] *v.* to infringe, break, violate.
infructuoso [in·fruk·twó·so] *adj.* fruitless.
ínfulas [ín·fu·las] *f. pl.* airs, false importance; **darse — to** put on airs.
infundado [in·fun·dá·do] *adj.* groundless, without foundation.
infundir [in·fun·dír] *v.* to infuse, inspire; to instill.
infusión [in·fu·sjón] *f.* infusion (*liquid extract obtained by steeping*); infusion, inspiration; **poner en — to** steep (*as tea leaves*).
ingeniería [iŋ·xe·nje·rí·a] *f.* engineering.
ingeniero [iŋ·xe·njé·ro] *m.* engineer.
ingenio [iŋ·xé·njo] *m.* genius; talent; ingenuity; mentality, mental power, mind; wit; **— de azúcar** sugar refinery; sugar plantation.
ingeniosidad [iŋ·xe·njo·si·dád] *f.* ingenuity, cleverness.
ingenioso [iŋ·xe·njó·so] *adj.* ingenious, clever.
ingenuidad [iŋ·xe·nwi·dád] *f.* candor, frankness; unaffected simplicity.
ingenuo [iŋ·xé·nwo] *adj.* frank, sincere; simple, unaffected; naive.
ingerir [iŋ·xe·rír] = **injerir.**
ingestion [iŋ·xes·tjón] *f.* ingestion.
ingle [íŋ·gle] *f.* groin.
inglés [iŋ·glés] *adj.* English; **a la inglesa** in the English fashion; *Am.* **ir a la inglesa** to go Dutch treat; *m.* Englishman; the English language.
inglete [iŋ·glé·te] *m.* miter.
ingobernable [iŋ·go·ber·ná·ble] *adj.* ungovernable, unruly, uncontrollable.
ingratitud [iŋ·gra·ti·túd] *f.* ingratitude.
ingrato [iŋ·grá·to] *adj.* ungrateful, thankless; harsh; cruel; disdainful.
ingrediente [iŋ·gre·djén·te] *m.* ingredient.
ingresar [iŋ·gre·sár] *v.* to enter; (*computadora*) to input; **— en** to join (*a society, club, etc.*).

ingreso [iŋ·gré·so] *m.* entrance; entry; **-s** receipts., profits; revenue.
inhábil [i·ná·bil] *adj.* unskilled; unskilful; unfit.
inhabilidad [i·na·bi·li·dád] *f.* inability; unfitness.
inhabilitar [i·na·bi·li·tár] *v.* to disqualify; to unfit, disable.
inherente [i·ne·rén·te] *adj.* inherent.
inhibir [i·ni·bír] *v.* to inhibit.
inhospitalario [i·nos·pi·ta·lá·rjo] *adj.* inhospitable.
inhumano [i·nu·má·no] *adj.* inhuman, cruel.
iniciador [i·ni·sja·dór] *m.* initiator; pioneer; *adj.* initiating.
inicial [i·ni·sjál] *adj. & f.* initial.
iniciar [i·ni·sjár] *v.* to initiate; to begin.
iniciativa [i·ni·sja·tí·ba] *f.* initiative.
inicuo [i·ní·kwo] *adj.* wicked.
iniquidad [i·ni·ki·dád] *f.* iniquity, wickedness; sin.
injerir[3] [iŋ·xe·rír] *v. irr.* to inject, insert; **-se** to interfere, meddle.
injertar [iŋ·xer·tár] *v.* to graft.
injerto [iŋ·xér·to] *m.* graft.
injuria [iŋ·xú·rja] *f.* affront, insult; harm, damage.
injuriar [iŋ·xu·rjár] *v.* to insult, offend; to harm, damage.
injurioso [iŋ·xu·rjó·so] *adj.* insulting, offensive; harmful.
injusticia [iŋ·xus·tí·sja] *f.* injustice.
injustificado [iŋ·xus·ti·fi·ká·do] *adj.* unjustified; unjustifiable.
injusto [iŋ·xús·to] *adj.* unjust, unfair.
inmaculado [im·ma·ku·lá·do] *adj.* immaculate, clean; pure.
inmediación [im·me·dja·sjón] *f.* vicinity; nearness; **-es** environs, outskirts.
inmediato [im·me·djá·to] *adj.* near, close; *Am.* **de —** immediately; suddenly; **inmediatamente** *adv.* immediately, at once.
inmejorable [im·me·xo·rá·ble] *adj.* unsurpassable.
inmensidad [im·men·si·dád] *f.* immensity, vastness; vast number.
inmenso [im·mén·so] *adj.* immense, vast, huge; boundless.
inmersión [im·mer·sjón] *f.* immersion, dip.
inmigración [im·mi·gra·sjón] *f.* immigration.
inmigrante [im·mi·grán·te] *adj., m. & f.* immigrant.
inmigrar [im·mi·grár] *v.* to immigrate.
inminente [im·mi·nén·te] *adj.* imminent.
inmiscuir[32] [im·mis·kwír] *v. irr.* to mix; **-se** to meddle, interfere.
inmoble [im·mó·ble] *adj.* motionless; unshaken.
inmoral [im·mo·rál] *adj.* immoral; **inmoralidad** [im·mo·ra·li·dád] *f.* immorality.
inmortal [im·mor·tál] *adj.* immortal; **inmortalidad** *f.* immortality.
inmovible [im·mo·bí·ble] *adj.* immovable, fixed; steadfast.
inmóvil [im·mó·bil] *adj.* motionless, still; immovable.
inmuebles [im·mwé·bles] *m. pl.* real estate.
inmundicia [im·mun·dí·sja] *f.* filth, dirt; nastiness.
inmundo [im·mún·do] *adj.* filthy, dirty; impure; nasty.
inmune [im·mú·ne] *adj.* immune; exempt.
inmunidad [im·mu·ni·dád] *f.* immunity.
inmutable [im·mu·tá·ble] *adj.* unchangeable, invariable.
inmutar [im·mu·tár] *v.* to alter, change; **-se** to show emotion (*either by turning pale or blushing*).
innato [in·ná·to] *adj.* innate, natural inborn.
innecesario [in·ne·se·sá·rjo] *adj.* unnecessary.
innegable [in·ne·gá·ble] *adj.* undeniable, not to be denied.

IN

innocuo [in·nó·kwo] *adj.* innocuous, harmless; **innocuidad** *f.* harmlessness.

innovación [in·no·ba·sjón] *f.* innovation; novelty.

innumerable [in·nu·me·rá·ble] *adj.* innumerable.

inobservancia [i·nob·ser·bán·sja] *f.* nonobservance, violation (*of a law*), lack of observance (*of a law, rule, or custom*).

inocencia [i·no·sén·sja] *f.* innocence.

inocente [i·no·sén·te] *adj.* innocent; *m.* innocent person; **inocentón** *adj.* quite foolish or simple; easily fooled; *m.* dupe, unsuspecting victim.

inocular [i·no·ku·lár] *v.* to inoculate.

inodoro [i·no·dó·ro] *adj.* odorless; *m. C.A., Ven., Col.* toilet, water closet.

inofensivo [i·no·fen·sí·bo] *adj.* inoffensive; harmless.

inolvidable [i·nol·bi·dá·ble] *adj.* unforgettable.

inopinado [i·no·pi·ná·do] *adj.* unexpected.

inoportuno [i·no·por·tú·no] *adj.* inopportune, untimely, unsuitable.

inoxidable [i·nok·si·dá·ble] *adj.* rust proof.

inquietar [iŋ·kje·tár] *v.* to worry, disturb, make uneasy; **-se** to become disturbed, uneasy.

inquieto [iŋ·kjé·to] *adj.* restless; uneasy, anxious.

inquietud [iŋ·kje·túd] *f.* restlessness; anxiety, uneasiness; fear.

inquilino [iŋ·ki·lí·no] *m.* tenant, renter; lodger.

inquina [iŋ·kí·na] *f.* aversion, grudge, dislike.

inquirir[35] [iŋ·ki·rír] *v. irr.* to inquire, investigate; to find out.

inquisición [iŋ·ki·si·sjón] *f.* inquisition, inquiry, investigation.

insaciable [in·sa·sjá·ble] *adj.* insatiable, never satisfied, greedy.

insalubre [in·sa·lú·bre] *adj.* unhealthy, unhealthful, unwholesome.

insano [in·sá·no] *adj.* insane, crazy; unhealthy.

inscribir[52] [ins·kri·bír] *v.* to inscribe; to register, enroll; to record; **-se** to register.

inscripción [ins·krip·sjón] *f.* inscription; registration.

inscripto [ins·kríp·to], **inscrito** [ins·krí·to] *p.p. of* inscribir.

insecto [in·sék·to] *m.* insect.

inseguro [in·se·gú·ro] *adj.* insecure; unsafe; doubtful; uncertain.

insensato [in·sen·sá·to] *adj.* senseless; foolish.

insensibilidad [in·sen·si·bi·li·dád] *f.* insensibility, unconsciousness; lack of feeling.

insensible [in·sen·sí·ble] *adj.* insensible; unfeeling; imperceptible.

inseparable [in·se·pa·rá·ble] *adj.* inseparable.

inserción [in·ser·sjón] *f.* insertion; insert.

insertar [in·ser·tár] *v.* to insert.

inserto *adj.* inserted.

inservible [in·ser·bí·ble] *adj.* useless.

insidioso [in·si·djó·so] *adj.* insidious; sly, crafty.

insigne [in·síg·ne] *adj.* famous.

insignia [in·síg·nja] *f.* badge, medal, decoration; flag, pennant; **-s** insignia.

insignificante [in·sig·ni·fi·kán·te] *adj.* insignificant.

insinuación [in·si·nwa·sjón] *f.* insinuation; intimation, hint.

insinuar[18] [in·si·nwár] *v.* to insinuate, hint; **-se** to insinuate oneself (*into another's friendship*); to creep (into) gradually.

insipidez [in·si·pi·dés] *f.* flatness, tastelessness, dullness; **insípido** [in·sí·pi·do] *adj.* insipid; tasteless.

insistencia [in·sis·tén·sja] *f.* insistence, persistence, obstinacy; **insistente** [in·sis·tén·te] *adj.* insistent, persistent.

insistir [in·sis·tír] *v.* to insist; to persist.

insociable [in·so·sjá·ble] *adj.* unsociable.

insolación [in·so·la·sjón] *f.* sunstroke.

insolencia [in·so·lén·sja] *f.* insolence.

insolentarse [in·so·len·tár·se] *v.* to sauce, become insolent, act with insolence.

insolente [in·so·lén·te] *adj.* insolent.

insólito [in·só·li·to] *adj.* unusual; uncommon.

insolvente [in·sol·bén·te] *adj.* insolvent, bankrupt.

insomne [in·sóm·ne] *adj.* sleepless.

insondable [in·son·dá·ble] *adj.* fathomless, deep; impenetrable.

insoportable [in·so·por·tá·ble] *adj.* unbearable.

insospechado [in·sos·pe·čá·do] *adj.* unsuspected.

inspección [ins·pek·sjón] *f.* inspection.

inspeccionar [ins·pek·sjo·nár] *v.* to inspect.

inspector [ins·pek·tór] *m.* inspector; overseer.

inspiración [ins·pi·ra·sjón] *f.* inspiration; inhalation, breathing in.

inspirar [ins·pi·rár] *v.* to inspire; to inhale.

instalación [ins·ta·la·sjón] *f.* installation.

instalar [ins·ta·lar] *v.* to install.

instancia [ins·tán·sja] *f.* instance, urgent request; petition; **a -s de** at the request of.

instantánea [ins·tan·tá·ne·a] *f.* snapshot.

instantáneo [ins·tan·tá·ne·o] *adj.* instantaneous; sudden.

instante [ins·tán·te] *m.* instant, moment; **al —** at once, immediately; **por -s** continually; from one moment to another; *adj.* instant, urgent.

instar [ins·tár] *v.* to urge, press; to be urgent.

instigar[7] [ins·ti·gár] *v.* to instigate, urge on, incite.

instintivo [ins·tin·tí·bo] *adj.* instinctive.

instinto [ins·tín·to] *m.* instinct.

institución [ins·ti·tu·sjón] *f.* institution; establishment, foundation; **-se** institutes, collection of precepts and principles.

instituir[32] [ins·ti·twír] *v. irr.* to institute; **— por heredero** to appoint as heir.

instituto [ins·ti·tú·to] *m.* institute; established principle, law, or custom; **— de segunda enseñanza** high school.

institutriz [ins·ti·tu·trís] *f.* governess.

instrucción [ins·truk·sjón] *f.* instruction; education.

instructivo [ins·truk·tí·bo] *adj.* instructive.

instruir[32] [ins·trwír] *v. irr.* to instruct, teach; to inform.

instrumento [ins·tru·mén·to] *m.* instrument.

insuficiencia [in·su·fi·sjén·sja] *f.* insufficiency, deficiency; incompetence; dearth, scarcity, lack.

insuficiente [in·su·fi·sjén·te] *adj.* insufficient.

insufrible [in·su·frí·ble] *adj.* insufferable, unbearable.

insula [ín·su·la] *f.* island.

insulina [in·su·lí·na] *f.* insulin.

insultante [in·sul·tán·te] *adj.* insulting, abusive.

insultar [in·sul·tár] *v.* to insult; **-se** to be seized with a fit.

insulto [in·súl·to] *m.* insult; sudden fit or attack.

insuperable [in·su·pe·rá·ble] *adj.* insuperable; insurmountable.

insurgente [in·sur·xén·te] *adj., m. & f.* insurgent.

insurrección [in·su·rrek·sjón] *f.* insurrection, uprising, revolt.

insurrecto [in·su·rrék·to] *m.* insurgent, rebel; *adj.* rebellious.

intacto [in·ták·to] *adj.* intact.

intachable [in·ta·čá·ble] *adj.* faultless, irreproachable.

integrador [in·te·gra·dór] *m.* integrator; *m.* **-s** members.

integral [in·te·grál] *adj.* integral; *f.* integral (*math*).

integrante [in·te·grán·te] *adj.* integral; integrating.

integrar [in·te·grár] *v.* to form; to integrate.

integridad [in·te·gri·dád] *f.* integrity; wholeness;

honesty; purity.

íntegro [ín·te·ǵro] *adj.* whole, complete; honest, upright.

intelecto [in·te·lék·to] *m.* intellect.

intelectual [in·te·lek·twál] *adj.* intellectual.

inteligencia [in·te·li·xén·sja] *f.* intelligence.

inteligente [in·te·li·xén·te] *adj.* intelligent.

intemperancia [in·tem·pe·rán·sja] *f.* intemperance, excess.

intemperie [in·tem·pé·rje] *f.* open air; bad weather; **a la —** unsheltered, outdoors, in the open air; exposed to the weather.

intención [in·ten·sjón] *f.* intention; **intencional** [in·ten·sjo·nál] *adj.* intentional.

intendente [in·ten·dén·te] *m.* manager, superintendent, supervisor; *Ríopl.* governor of a province; *Am.* police commissioner.

intensidad [in·ten·si·dáđ] *f.* intensity; stress.

intenso [in·tén·so] *adj.* intense; intensive; ardent, vehement.

intentar [in·ten·tár] *v.* to attempt, try; to intend.

intento [in·tén·to] *m.* intent, purpose, intention; **de —** on purpose.

intercalar [in·ter·ka·lár] *v.* to insert, place between.

intercambio [in·ter·kám·bjo] *m.* interchange; exchange.

interceder [in·ter·se·đér] *v.* to intercede.

interceptar [in·ter·sep·tár] *v.* to intercept.

intercesión [in·ter·se·sjón] *f.* intercession, mediation.

interdental [in·ter·den·tál] *adj.* interdental.

interdicción [in·ter·đik·sjón] *f.* interdiction; prevention.

interés [in·te·rés] *m.* interest; **— compuesto** compound interest.

interesante [in·te·re·sán·te] *adj.* interesting.

interesar [in·te·re·sár] *v.* to interest; to give an interest or share; **-se** to be or become interested.

interfaz [in·ter·fás] *f.* (*computadora*) interface.

interferencia [in·ter·fe·rén·sja] *f.* interference.

ínterin [ín·te·rin] *m.* interim, meantime; **en al —** in the meantime.

interino [in·te·rí·no] *adj.* acting, temporary.

interior [in·te·rjór] *adj.* interior; inner; internal; *m.* interior, inside.

interjección [in·ter·xek·sjón] *f.* interjection, exclamation.

interlineal [in·ter·li·ne·ál] *adj.* interlinear.

interlocutor [in·ter·lo·ku·tór] *m.* participant in a dialogue.

intermedio [in·ter·mé·đjo] *adj.* intermediate; intervening; *m.* intermission; interval; **por — de** by means of, through the intervention of.

interminable [in·ter·mi·ná·ble] *adj.* interminable, unending, endless.

intermisión [in·ter·mi·sjón] *f.* intermission, interruption, pause, interval.

intermitente [in·ter·mi·tén·te] *adj.* intermittent, occurring at intervals; **calentura** (*or* **fiebre**) **—** intermittent fever.

internacional [in·ter·na·sjo·nál] *adj.* international.

internado [in·ter·ná·đo] *m.* a boarding student.

internar [in·ter·nár] *v.* to intern, confine; **-se** to penetrate, go into the interior.

interno [in·tér·no] *adj.* internal; interior; *m.* boarding-school student.

interoceánico [in·te·ro·se·á·ni·ko] *adj.* interoceanic; transcontinental.

interpelar [in·ter·pe·lár] *v.* to interrogate, question, demand explanations; to ask the aid of.

interponer[40] [in·ter·po·nér] *v. irr.* to interpose, put between, insert; to place as a mediator; **-se** to

intervene, mediate.

interpretación [in·ter·pre·ta·sjón] *f.* interpretation.

interpretar [in·ter·pre·tár] *v.* to interpret.

intérprete [in·tér·pre·te] *m. & f.* interpreter.

interpuesto [in·ter·pwés·to] *p.p. of* **interponer.**

interrogación [in·te·rro·ǵa·sjón] *f.* interrogation, question; **signo de —** question mark.

interrogador [in·te·rro·ǵa·đór] *m.* questioner; *adj.* questioning.

interrogar[7] [in·te·rro·ǵár] *v.* to interrogate, question.

interrogativo [in·te·rro·ǵa·tí·ƀo] *adj.* interrogative.

interrogatorio [in·te·rro·ǵa·tó·rjo] *m.* interrogation, questioning.

interrumpir [in·te·rrum·pír] *v.* to interrupt.

interrupción [in·te·rrup·sjón] *f.* interruption.

interruptor [in·te·rrup·tór] *m.* interrupter; (*rilai fusible*) electric switch; **— de circuitos** circuit breaker.

intersección [in·ter·sek·sjón] *f.* intersection.

intersticio [in·ters·tí·sjo] *m.* interval.

intervalo [in·ter·ƀá·lo] *m.* interval.

intervención [in·ter·ƀen·sjón] *f.* intervention; mediation; participation; auditing of accounts.

intervenir[48] [in·ter·ƀe·nír] *v. irr.* to intervene; to mediate; to audit (*accounts*).

interventor [in·ter·ƀen·tór] *m.* inspector; controller, comptroller; auditor.

intestino [in·tes·tí·no] *m.* intestine; *adj.* intestine, internal.

intimación [in·ti·ma·sjón] *f.* intimation; hint, insinuation, suggestion.

intimar [in·ti·már] *v.* to announce, notify; to intimate, hint; to become intimate, become friendly.

intimidad [in·ti·mi·đáđ] *f.* intimacy.

intimidar [in·ti·mi·đár] *v.* to intimidate.

íntimo [ín·ti·mo] *adj.* intimate.

intitular [in·ti·tu·lár] *v.* to entitle; to give a title to (*a person or a thing*); **-se** to be entitled, be called; to call oneself (*by a certain name*).

intolerable [in·to·le·rá·ƀle] *adj.* intolerable.

intolerancia [in·to·le·rán·sja] *f.* intolerance; **intolerante** [in·to·le·rán·te] *adj.* intolerant, narrow-minded.

intoxicante [in·tok·si·kán·te] *m.* poison.

intoxicar[6] [in·tok·si·kár] *v.* to poison.

intranquilo [in·tran·kí·lo] *adj.* disturbed, uneasy.

intranquilidad [in·tran·ki·li·đáđ] *f.* uneasiness, restlessness.

intransigencia [in·tran·si·xén·sja] *f.* uncompromising act or attitude; intolerance.

intransigente [in·tran·si·xén·te] *adj.* uncompromising, unwilling to compromise or yield; intolerant.

intratable [in·tra·tá·ƀle] *adj.* unsociable; rude; unruly.

intravenoso [in·tra·ƀe·nó·so] *adj.* intravenous (*within a vein or the veins; into a vein*).

intrepidez [in·tre·pi·đés] *f.* fearlessness, courage.

intrépido [in·tré·pi·đo] *adj.* intrepid, fearless.

intriga [in·trí·ǵa] *f.* intrigue; scheme; plot.

intrigante [in·tri·ǵán·te] *m. & f.* intriguer, plotter; *adj.* intriguing.

intrigar[7] [in·tri·ǵár] *v.* to intrigue.

intrincado [in·triŋ·ká·đo] *adj.* intricate, complicated, entangled.

introducción [in·tro·đuk·sjón] *f.* introduction.

introducir[25] [in·tro·đu·sír] *v. irr.* to introduce; (*computadora*) to input; **-se** to introduce oneself; to get in; to penetrate.

intromisión [in·tro·mi·sjón] *f.* meddling; insertion.

introvertido [in·tro·ƀer·tí·đo] *m. & f.* introvert.

intruso [in·trú·so] *adj.* intrusive, intruding; *m.* intruder.

intuición [in·twi·sjón] *f.* intuition.
intuir[32] [in·twír] *v. irr.* to sense, feel by intuition.
inundación [i·nun·da·sjón] *f.* inundation, flood.
inundar [i·nun·dár] *v.* to inundate, flood.
inusitado [i·nu·si·tá·đo] *adj.* unusual, rare.
inútil [i·nú·til] *adj.* useless.
inutilidad [i·nu·ti·li·đáđ] *f.* uselessness.
inutilizar[9] [i·nu·ti·li·sár] *v.* to make useless, put out of commission; to disable; to ruin, spoil.
invadir [im·ba·đír] *v.* to invade.
invalidar [im·ba·li·dár] *v.* to render invalid; to void, annul.
inválido [im·bá·li·đo] *adj.* invalid; void, null; sickly, weak; *m.* invalid.
invariable [im·ba·rjá·ble] *adj.* invariable.
invasión [im·ba·sjón] *f.* invasion.
invasor [im·ba·sór] *m.* invader; *adj.* invading; **ejército —** invading army.
invencible [im·ben·sí·ble] *adj.* invincible, unconquerable.
invención [im·ben·sjón] *f.* invention.
invendible [im·ben·dí·ble] *adj.* unsaleable.
inventar [im·ben·tár] *v.* to invent.
inventariar[17] [im·ben·ta·rjár] *v.* to inventory, take an inventory of.
inventario [im·ben·tá·rjo] *m.* inventory.
inventiva [im·ben·tí·ba] *f.* inventiveness, power of inventing, ingenuity.
inventivo [im·ben·tí·bo] *adj.* inventive.
invento [im·ben·to] *m.* invention.
inventor [im·ben·tór] *m.* inventor; storyteller, fibber.
invernáculo [im·ber·ná·ku·lo] *m.* greenhouse, hothouse.
invernada [im·ber·ná·đa] *f.* wintering; *Am.* pasturing.
invernadero [im·ber·na·đé·ro] *m.* winter quarters; winter resort; winter pasture; greenhouse, hothouse.
invernal [im·ber·nál] *adj.* wintry, winter.
invernar[1] [im·ber·nár] *v. irr.* to winter, spend the winter.
inverosímil [im·be·ro·sí·mil] **inverisímil** [im·be·ri·sí·mil] *adj.* unlikely, improbable.
inversión [im·bér·sjón] *f.* inversion; investment.
inverso [im·bér·so] *adj.* inverse, inverted; reverse; **a** (*or* **por**) **la inversa** on the contrary.
invertir[3] [im·ber·tír] *v. irr.* to invert; to reverse; to invest; to employ, spend (*time*).
investigación [im·bes·ti·ga·sjón] *f.* investigation.
investigador [im·bes·ti·ga·đór] *m.* investigator; *adj.* investigating.
investigar[7] [im·bes·ti·gár] *v.* to investigate.
invicto [im·bík·to] *adj.* unconquered; always victorious.
invierno [im·bjér·no] *m.* winter; *C.A., Col., Ven., Ec., Peru* the rainy season.
invisible [im·bi·sí·ble] *adj.* invisible.
invitación [im·bi·ta·sjón] *f.* invitation.
invitar [im·bi·tár] *v.* to invite.
invocación [im·bo·ka·sjón] *f.* invocation.
invocar[6] [im·bo·kár] *v.* to invoke.
involuntario [im·bo·lun·tá·rjo] *adj.* involuntary.
inyección [in·ŷek·sjón] *f.* injection.
inyectado [in·ŷek·tá·đo] *p.p.* injected; *adj.* bloodshot, inflamed.
inyectar [in·ŷek·tár] *v.* to inject.
ion [jon] *m.* ion.
ionizar[9] [jo·ni·sár] *v. irr.* to ionize.
ir[33] [ír] *v. irr.* to go; to walk; **— corriendo** to be running; **— entendiendo** to understand gradually; to begin to understand; **— a caballo** to ride horseback; **— a pie** to walk; **— en automóvil** to drive, ride in an automobile; **no irle ni venirle a uno** to make no difference to one; **¿cómo le va?** how are you? **no me va nada en eso** that doesn't concern me; **¡vamos!** let's go! come on! **¡vaya!** well now!, **¡vaya un hómbre!** what a man!; **-se** to go, go away; to escape; **-se abajo** to fall down, topple over; to collapse; **-se a pique** to founder, sink.
ira [í·ra] *f.* ire, anger.
iracundo [i·ra·kún·do] *adj.* irritable; angry.
iridio [i·rí·djo] *m.* iridium.
iris [í·ris] *m.* iris (*of the eye*); **arco —** rainbow.
irisado [i·ri·sá·đo] *adj.* iridescent, rainbow-hued.
ironía [i·ro·ní·a] *f.* irony.
irónico [i·ró·ni·ko] *adj.* ironic, ironical.
irracional [i·rra·sjo·nál] *adj.* irrational, unreasonable.
irradiar [i·rra·djár] *v.* to radiate.
irreal [i·rre·ál] *adj.* unreal.
irreflexión [i·rre·flek·sjón] *f.* thoughtlessness.
irreflexivo [i·rre·flek·sí·bo] *adj.* thoughtless.
irrefrenable [i·rre·fre·ná·ble] *adj.* uncontrollable.
irrefutable [i·rre·fu·tá·ble] *adj.* irrefutable.
irregular [i·rre·gu·lár] *adj.* irregular.
irreligioso [i·rre·li·xjó·so] *adj.* irreligious.
irremediable [i·rre·me·djá·ble] *adj.* irremediable; hopeless, incurable.
irreprochable [i·rre·pro·čá·ble] *adj.* irreproachable, flawless.
irresistible [i·rre·sis·tí·ble] *adj.* irresistible.
irresoluto [i·rre·so·lú·to] *adj.* irresolute, undecided, hesitating.
irrespetuoso [i·rres·pe·twó·so] *adj.* disrespectful.
irreverencia [i·rre·be·rén·sja] *f.* irreverence.
irreverente [i·rre·be·rén·te] *adj.* irreverent.
irrigación [i·rri·ga·sjón] *f.* irrigation.
irrigar[7] [i·rri·gár] *v.* to irrigate.
irrisión [i·rri·sjón] *f.* mockery, ridicule, derision.
irritación [i·rri·ta·sjón] *f.* irritation.
irritante [i·rri·tán·te] *adj.* irritating.
irritar [i·rri·tár] *v.* to irritate.
irrumpir [i·rrum·pír] *v.* to enter violently; to invade.
irrupción [i·rrup·sjón] *f.* sudden attack, raid, invasion.
isla [iz·la] *f.* island.
islamismo [iz·la·míz·mo] *m.* islamism.
islandés [iz·lan·dés] *adj.* Icelandic.
isleño [iz·lé·ño] *m.* islander.
isobara [i·so·bá·ra] *f.* isobar.
islote [iz·ló·te] *m.* islet, small rocky island.
istmo [iz·mo] *m.* isthmus.
italiano [i·ta·ljá·no] *adj. & m.* Italian.
itinerario [i·ti·ne·rá·rjo] *m.* itinerary; timetable; schedule; railroad guide.
itrio [í·trjo] *m.* yttrium.
izar[9] [i·sár] *v.* to hoist; to heave.
izquierda [is·kjér·đa] *f.* left hand; left side; left wing (*in politics*); **a la —** to the left; **izquierdista** [is·kjer·đís·ta] *m. & f.* leftist, radical.
izquierdo [is·kjér·đo] *adj.* left; left-handed.

J : j

jabalí [xa·ba·lí] *m.* wild boar.
jabalina [xa·ba·lí·na] *f.* javelin; wild sow.
jabón [xa·bón] *m.* soap; *Ríopl.* fright, fear; **dar —** to soft-soap, flatter; **dar un —** to give a good scolding; to beat, thrash.
jabonadura [xa·bo·na·đú·ra] *f.* washing, soaping; **-s** suds, lather; **dar a uno una —** to reprimand or

scold someone.

jabonar [xa·bo·nár] *v.* (*lavar*) to lather, soap; (*reprender*) to scold; reprimand.

jabonera [xa·bo·né·ra] *f.* soap dish; woman soap vendor or maker.

jaca [xá·ka] *f.* pony, small horse; **jaco** [xa·ko] *m.* small nag; poor horse.

jacal [xa·kál] *m. Mex.* shack, adobe hut; **jacalucho** [xa·ka·lú·čo] *m. Am.* poor, ugly shack.

jacinto [xa·sín·to] *m.* hyacinth.

jactancia [xak·tán·sja] *f.* boast, brag; boasting.

jactancioso [xak·tan·sjó·so] *adj.* braggart, boastful.

jactarse [xak·tár·se] *v.* to brag, boast.

jaculatoria [xa·ku·la·tó·rja] *f.* short, fervent prayer.

jadeante [xa·de·án·te] *adj.* breathless, panting, out of breath.

jadear [xa·de·ár] *v.* to pant.

jadeo [xa·dé·o] *m.* pant, panting.

jaez [xa·és] *m.* harness; kind, sort; **jaeces** [xa·é·ses] trappings.

jaguar [xa·gwár] *m.* jaguar.

jagüey [xa·gwéj] *m.* puddle, pool.

jai alai [xaj·a·láj] *m.* Basque game played with basket and *pelota*.

jalar [xa·lár] *v. Am.* to pull; to haul; to jerk; *C.A.* to court, make love; *Ven., Andes* to flunk (*a student*); *Mex.* ¡**jala!** [xá·la] (*or* ¡**jálale!** [xá·la·le]) get going! get a move on there!; **-se** *Mex.* to get drunk; *Mex.* to go away, move away.

jalea [xa·lé·a] *f.* jelly.

jalear [xa·le·ár] *v.* to shout (*to hunting dogs*); to rouse, beat up (*game*); to shout and clap (*to encourage dancers*).

jaleo [xa·lé·o] *m.* shouting and clapping (*to encourage dancers*); an Andalusian dance; revelry, merrymaking, jesting; gracefulness.

jaletina [xa·le·tí·na] *f.* gelatin.

jalón [xa·lón] *m.* marker (*for boundaries*); *Am.* pull, jerk, tug; *Mex., C.A.* swallow of liquor; *Bol., C.A.* stretch, distance.

jalonear [xa·lo·ne·ár] *v. C.A., Mex.* to pull, jerk.

jamás [xa·más] *adv.* never.

jamón [xa·món] *m.* ham; *P.R.* fix, difficulty.

jamona [xa·mó·na] *f.* popular term for a fat middle-aged woman.

japonés [xa·po·nés] *adj. & m.* Japanese.

jaque [xá·ke] *m.* check (*in chess*); braggart, bully; — **mate** checkmate (*in chess*); **tener a uno en** — to hold someone under a threat.

jaqueca [xa·ké·ka] *f.* headache; sick headache.

jara [xá·ra] *f.* rockrose (*shrub*); *Ven., Col.* reed; **jaral** [xa·rál] *m.* bramble of rockroses; *Am.* reeds, clump of reeds.

jarabe [xa·rá·be] *m.* syrup; sweet beverage; *Mex., C.A.* a kind of tap dance; *Mex.* song and musical accompaniment of the **jarabe.**

jarana [xa·rá·na] *f.* merrymaking, revelry; trick; fib; jest; *Col., Ec., Carib.* a dance; *Mex.* small guitar; **ir de** — to go on a spree.

jarcia [xár·sja] *f.* rigging (*ropes, chains, etc. for the masts, yards and sails of a ship*); fishing tackle; pile, heap; jumble of things.

jardín [xar·dín] *m.* flower garden.

jardinero [xar·di·né·ro] *m.* gardener.

jarra [xá·rra] *f.* jar, vase, pitcher; **de** (*or* **en**) **-s** akimbo (*with hands on the hips*).

jarro [xá·rro] *m.* jar, jug, pitcher.

jarrón *m.* large vase or jar.

jaspe [xás·pe] *m.* jasper; veined marble; **jaspeado** *adj.* veined, streaked, mottled.

jaula [xáw·la] *f.* cage; cagelike cell or prison; *Am.*

roofless cattle car or freight car.

jauría [xaw·rí·a] *f.* pack of hounds.

jazmín [xaz·mín] *m.* jasmine.

jefatura [xe·fa·tú·ra] *f.* position of chief; headquarters of a chief.

jefe [xé·fe] *m.* chief, leader, head.

jengibre [xeŋ·xí·bre] *m.* ginger.

jerez [xe·rés] *m.* sherry wine.

jerga [xér·ga] *f.* (*tela*) thick coarse cloth; straw mattress; (*dialecto*) jargon; slang; *Am.* saddle pad; *Col.* poncho made of coarse cloth.

jergón [xer·gón] *m.* (*material*) straw mattress; ill-fitting suit or dress; (*persona*) big clumsy fellow; *Ríopl., Mex., Ven.* cheap coarse rug.

jerigonza [xe·ri·gón·sa] *f.* jargon; slang.

jeringa [xe·ríŋ·ga] *f.* syringe; **jeringazo** [xe·riŋ·gá·so] *m.* injection; squirt.

jeringar[7] [xe·riŋ·gár] *v.* to inject; to squirt; to bother, molest, vex, annoy.

jeroglífico [xe·ro·glí·fi·ko] *m.* hieroglyphic.

jesuita [xe·swi·ta] *m.* Jesuit.

jeta [xé·ta] *f.* snout; thick lips.

jiba [xí·ba] = **giba.**

jíbaro [xí·ba·ro] *adj. P.R.* rustic, rural, rude, uncultured; *m. P.R.* bumpkin, peasant.

jibia [xí·bja] *f.* cuttlefish.

jícara [xí·ka·ra] *f.* chocolate cup; *Am.* small bowl made out of a gourd; *Mex.* any small bowl; *Mex.* bald head.

jilguero [xil·gé·ro] *m.* linnet.

jinete [xi·né·te] *m.* horseman, rider.

jineteada [xi·ne·te·á·da] *f. Ríopl., C.A.* roughriding, horse-breaking.

jinetear [xi·ne·te·ár] *v.* to ride horseback; to perform on horseback; *Mex., C.A.* to break in (*a horse*); *Mex.* to ride a bronco or bull.

jira [xí·ra] *f.* excursion, tour; outing, picnic; strip of cloth.

jirafa [xi·rá·fa] *f.* giraffe; boom mike (*broadcasting*).

jitomate [xi·to·má·te] *m. Mex.* tomato. *Also* gitomate.

jocoso [xo·kó·so] *adj.* jocular.

jofaina [xo·fáj·na] *f.* basin, washbowl.

jolgorio [xol·gó·rjo] = **holgorio.**

jornada [xor·ná·da] *f.* day's journey; military expedition; working day; act (*of a Spanish play*).

jornal [xor·nál] *m.* day's wages; bookkeeping journal; **a** — by the day.

jornalero [xor·na·lé·ro] *m.* day laborer.

joroba [xo·ró·ba] *f.* hump; nuisance, annoyance.

jorobado [xo·ro·bá·do] *adj.* hunchbacked; annoyed, bothered, in a bad fix; *m.* hunchback.

jorobar [xo·ro·bár] *v.* to bother, pester, annoy.

jorongo [xo·róŋ·go] *m. Mex.* Mexican poncho.

jota [xó·ta] *f.* name of the letter *j*; iota (*anything insignificant*); Aragonese and Valencian dance and music; *Andes* (= **ojota**) leather sandal; **no saber una** — not to know anything.

joven [xó·ben] *adj.* young; *m. & f.* youth; young man; young woman.

jovial [xo·bjál] *adj.* jovial, jolly, merry; **jovialidad** [xo·bja·li·dád] *f.* gaiety, merriment, fun.

joya [xó·ya] *f.* jewel; piece of jewelry; **-s** jewels; trousseau.

joyería [xo·ye·rí·a] *f.* jeweler's shop.

joyero [xo·yé·ro] *m.* jeweler; jewel box.

juanete [xwa·né·te] *m.* bunion.

jubilación [xu·bi·la·sjón] *f.* retirement (*from a position or office*); pension.

jubilar [xu·bi·lár] *v.* to pension; to retire; **-se** to be pensioned or retired; to rejoice; *Col.* to decline, fall into decline; *Ven., Guat.* to play hooky or truant.

jubileo [xu·bi·lé·o] *m.* jubilee; time of rejoicing; concession by the Pope of plenary (*complete*) indulgence.

júbilo [xú·bi·lo] *m.* joy, glee.

jubiloso [xu·bi·ló·so] *adj.* jubilant, joyful.

jubón [xu·bón] *m.* jacket; bodice.

judía [xu·dí·a] *f. Spain* bean; string bean; Jewess; **-s tiernas** (*or* **verdes**) string beans.

judicial [xu·di·sjál] *adj.* judicial; **-mente** *adv.* judicially.

judío [xu·dí·o] *adj.* Jewish; *m.* Jew.

judo [xú·do] *m.* judo.

juego [xwé·ǥo] *m.* game; play; sport; gambling; pack of cards; set; **— de palabras** pun, play on words; **— de te** tea set; **hacer —** to match; **poner en —** to coordinate; to set in motion.

juerga [xwér·ǥa] *f.* spree, revelry, wild festivity; **irse de —** to go out on a spree; **juerguista** *m. & f.* merrymaker.

jueves [xwé·bes] *m.* Thursday.

juez [xwes] *m.* judge; juror, member of a jury; **— arbitrador** (*or* **árbitro**) arbitrator, umpire.

jugada [xu·ǥá·da] *f.* play, move; stroke; trick.

jugador [xu·ǥa·dór] *m.* player; gambler; **— de manos** juggler.

jugar[34] [xu·ǥár] *v. irr.* to play; to gamble; to toy; **— a la pelota** to play ball; *Mex.* **— a dos cartas** to be double-faced.

jugarreta [xu·ǥa·rré·ta] *f.* bad play, wrong play; mean trick; tricky deal; *Am.* noisy game.

jugo [xú·ǥo] *m.* juice; sap.

jugosidad [xu·ǥo·si·dád] *f.* juiciness; **jugoso** *adj.* juicy.

juguete [xu·ǥé·te] *m.* plaything, toy; jest, joke; **— cómico** skit; **por** (*or* **de**) **—** jokingly.

juguetear [xu·ǥe·te·ár] *v.* to play around, romp, frolic; to toy; to tamper (with), fool (with).

juguetón [xu·ǥe·tón] *adj.* playful.

juicio [xwí·sjo] *m.* judgment; sense, wisdom; opinion; trial; **perder el —** to lose one's mind, go crazy.

juicioso [xwi·sjó·so] *adj.* judicious, wise; sensible.

julio [xú·ljo] *m.* July.

jumento [xu·mén·to] *m.* ass, donkey.

juncal [xun·kál] *m.* growth of rushes.

junco [xúŋ·ko] *m.* rush, reed; junk (*Chinese sailboat*).

jungla [xúŋ·gla] *f. Am.* jungle.

junio [xú·njo] *m.* June.

junquillo [xuŋ·kí·yo] *m.* reed; jonquil (*yellow flower similar to the daffodil*), species of narcissus.

junta [xún·ta] *f.* (*reunión*) meeting, conference; (*funcionarios*) board, council; **-s** joints (plumbing); **— a inglete** miter joint; **— a traslapo** lap joint; **-s en tope** butt joints; **— en V** vee-butt; **— por puntas** tack weld; (*cepillo mecánico*) **juntera** jointer.

juntar [xun·tár] *v.* to join, unite; to connect; to assemble; to collect; **-se** to assemble, gather; to be closely united; to associate (with).

junto [xún·to] *adj.* joined, united; **-s** together; *adv.* near; **— a** neat to, close to; **en —** all together, in all; **por —** all together, in a lump; wholesale.

juntura [xun·tú·ra] *f.* juncture; junction; joint, seam.

jurado [xu·rá·do] *m.* jury; juror, juryman; *adj. & p.p.* sworn.

juramentar [xu·ra·men·tár] *v.* to swear in; **-se** to take an oath, be sworn in.

juramento [xu·ra·mén·to] *m.* oath; vow; curse.

jurar [xu·rár] *v.* to swear, vow; to take oath; to

curse.

jurisconsulto [xu·ris·kon·súl·to] *m.* jurist, expert in law; lawyer.

jurisdicción [xu·riz·dik·sjón] *f.* jurisdiction.

jurisprudencia [xu·ris·pru·dén·sja] *f.* jurisprudence, law.

juro; de — [xú·ro] *adv.* certainly, of course.

justa [xús·ta] *f.* joust, tournament, combat (*between horsemen with lances*); contest.

justicia [xus·tí·sja] *f.* justice; court of justice; judge; police.

justiciero [xus·ti·sjé·ro] *adj.* strictly just, austere (*in matters of justice*).

justificación [xus·ti·fi·ka·sjón] *f.* justification.

justificante [xus·ti·fi·kán·te] *adj.* justifying; *m.* voucher; written excuse; proof.

justificar[6] [xus·ti·fi·kár] *v.* to justify; to vindicate, clear of blame.

justo [xús·to] *adj.* just; pious; exact, correct; tight; *adv.* duly; exactly; tightly; *m.* just man; **los -s** the just.

juvenil [xu·be·níl] *adj.* juvenile, young, youthful.

juventud [xu·ben·túd] *f.* youth; young people.

juzgado [xuz·ǥá·do] *m.* court, tribunal.

juzgar[7] [xuz·ǥár] *v.* to judge.

K:k

kermesse [ker·mé·se] *f.* country fair; bazaar for charity.

keroseno [ke·ro·sé·no] *f.* kerosene, coal oil.

kilo [kí·lo] *m.* kilo, kilogram.

kilo-byte (KB) [ki·lo·bájt] *m.* (*computadora*) kilobyte (KBYTE).

kilociclo [ki·lo·sí·klo] *m.* kilocycle.

kilogramo [ki·lo·ǥrá·mo] *m.* kilogram.

kilometraje [ki·lo·me·trá·xe] *m.* number of kilometers.

kilómetro [ki·ló·me·tro] *m.* kilometer.

kilovatio [ki·lo·bá·tjo] *m.* kilowatt.

L:l

la [la] *def. art. f.* the; **— de** the one with, that one with; *obj. pron.* her; it; **— que** *rel. pron.* she who, the one that; which.

la [la] *m.* sixth note on the musical scale.

laberinto [la·be·rín·to] *m.* labyrinth, maze; labyrinth, internal ear.

labia [la·bja] *f.* fluency, talkativeness, gift of gab; **tener mucha —** to be a good talker.

labial [la·bjál] *adj.* labial.

labio [lá·bjo] *m.* lip.

labiodental [la·bjo·den·tál] *adj.* labiodental.

labor [la·bór] *f.* (*trabajo*) labor, work; (*cosido*) embroidery; needlework; (*agrícola*) tillage; **— de punto** knitting; **laborable** [la·bo·rá·ble] *adj.* workable; tillable; **día laborable** work day; **laboral** [la·bo·rál] *adj.* pertaining to labor.

laboratorio [la·bo·ra·tó·rjo] *m.* laboratory.

laboriosidad [la·bo·rjo·si·dád] *f.* laboriousness, industry.

laborioso [la·bo·rjó·so] *adj.* laborious; industrious.

laborista [la·bo·rís·ta] *m. & f.* laborite.

labrado [la·brá·do] *p.p. & adj.* (*agrícola*) tilled, cultivated; (*hecho*) wrought; manufactured; carved; *m.* carving; **— en madera** woodwork, carving; **-s**

cultivated lands.

labrador [la·bra·dór] *m.* farmer; peasant.

labranza [la·brán·sa] *f.* farming, tillage, plowing; cultivated land, farm.

labrar [la·brár] *v.* (*la tierra*) to till, cultivate, farm; to plow; (*crear*) to carve; to embroider; to work (*metals*); to build (*a monument*).

labriego [la·brjé·ɣo] *m.* peasant.

laca [lá·ka] *f.* lacquer; shellac.

lacayo [la·ká·yo] *m.* lackey, footman, flunky.

lacio [lá·sjo] *adj.* withered; languid; limp; straight (*hair*).

lacra [lá·kra] *f.* trace of an illness; blemish, defect; *Mex., Ven., C.A.* sore, ulcer, scab, scar.

lacre [lá·kre] *m.* red sealing wax; *adj. Am.* red.

lacrimógeno [la·kri·mó·xe·no] *adj.* tear-producing.

lactar [lak·tár] *v.* to nurse, suckle; to feed with milk.

lácteo [lák·te·o] *adj.* milky; **fiebre láctea** milk fever; **régimen** — milk diet; **Vía láctea** milk Way; **productor -s** milk products.

ladear [la·de·ár] *v.* to tilt, tip; to go along the slope or side of; to turn aside (*from a way or course*); **-se** to tilt; to sway; to incline or lean (towards); to move to one side; *Ch.* to fall in love.

ladeo [la·dé·o] *m.* inclination, tilt.

ladera [la·dé·ra] *f.* slope.

ladino [la·dí·no] *adj.* crafty, sly, shrewd; conversant with two or three languages; *m.* Sephardic Jew (*Spanish-speaking*); Romansch (*a Romance language of Switzerland*); *Guat.* Spanish-speaking person (*as opposed to one who speaks an Indian language*); *C.A.*, mestizo, half-breed; *Mex., Col., Ven.* talker, talkative person.

lado [lá·do] *m.* side; **al** — near, at hand, at one's side; **de** — tilted, obliquely; sideways; — **a** — side by side; **¡a un** — **!** gangway! **hacerse a un** — to move over, step aside, move to one side; *Mex., Ven.* **echársela de** — to boast.

ladrar [la·drár] *v.* to bark.

ladrido [la·drí·do] *m.* bark, barking.

ladrillo [la·drí·yo] *m.* brick.

ladrón [la·drón] *m.* thief, robber; **ladronzuelo** [la·dron·swé·lo] *m.* petty thief.

lagartija [la·ɣar·tí·xa] *f.* small lizard.

lagarto [la·ɣár·to] *m.* lizard; rascal, sly fellow.

lago [lá·ɣo] *m.* lake.

lágrima [lá·ɣri·ma] *f.* tear; **llorar a** — **viva** to weep abundantly.

lagrimear [la·ɣri·me·ár] *v.* to weep, shed tears.

laguna [la·ɣú·na] *f.* lagoon; gap, blank space.

laico [lái·ko] *adj.* lay; *m.* layman.

laísta [la·ís·ta] *m. & f.* one who uses *la* for indirect object.

laja [lá·xa] *f.* slab; flat stone.

lamedero [la·me·dé·ro] *m.* salt lick (*for cattle*).

lamentable [la·men·tá·ble] *adj.* lamentable, pitiful.

lamentación [la·men·ta·sjón] *f.* lamentation.

lamentar [la·men·tár] *v.* to lament, deplore; **-se** to moan, complain, wail.

lamento [la·mén·to] *m.* lament, moan, cry.

lamer [la·mér] *v.* to lick; to lap.

lamida [la·mí·da] *f. Mex., C.A.* lick; also **lambida.**

lámina [lá·mi·na] *f.* metal plate; sheet of metal; engraving; book illustration.

laminar [la·mi·nár] *v.* to laminate; **laminación a mano** hand lay-up; **con pistola de aire** spray-up.

lámpara [lám·pa·ra] *f.* lamp.

lampiño [lam·pí·ño] *adj.* hairless; beardless.

lana [lá·na] *f.* wool; *C.A.* tramp, vagabond.

lanar [la·nár] *adj.* wool-bearing; of wool.

lance [lán·se] *m.* occurrence, event; cast, throw,

move, turn; accident; quarrel; predicament.

lancear [lan·se·ár] *v.* to lance, spear.

lancha [lán·ča] *f.* launch; boat; slab; **lanchón** [lan·čón] *m.* barge.

langosta [laŋ·gós·ta] *f.* lobster; locust.

languidecer[13] [laŋ·gi·de·sér] *v. irr.* to languish.

languidez [laŋ·gi·dés] *f.* languor, faintness, weakness.

lánguido [láŋ·gi·do] *adj.* languid.

lanilla [la·ní·ya] *f.* nap (*of cloth*).

lanudo [la·nú·do] *adj.* woolly; *Ven.* coarse, crude, ill-bred; *Am.* dull, slow, weak-willed; *Ch., C.A., Col.* wealthy.

lanza [lán·sa] *f.* lance, spear; *Col.* swindler, cheat; *m.* **lanzabombas** [lan·sa·bóm·bas] bomb launcher; *m.* **lanzacohetes** [lan·sa·ko·é·tes] rocket launcher; *m.* **lanzallamas** [lan·sa·yá·mas] flame thrower.

lanzada [lan·sá·da] *f.* thrust (*with a spear*).

lanzadera [lan·sa·dé·ra] *f.* shuttle.

lanzamiento [lan·sa·mjén·to] *m.* launching (*boat or rocket*).

lanzar[9] [lan·sár] *v.* to fling, throw; to eject; to launch; **-se** to rush, fling oneself; to dart out.

lanzazo [lan·sá·so] *m.* thrust with a lance.

lapicero [la·pi·sé·ro] *m.* pencil (*a mechanical pencil, one with an adjustable lead*).

lápida [lá·pi·da] *f.* slab, tombstone; stone tablet.

lapidar [la·pi·dár] *v.* to stone; *Col., Ch.* to cut precious stones; **lapidado** lapping.

lapidario [la·pi·dá·rjo] *m.* lapidary.

lápiz [lá·pis] *m.* pencil; crayon; — **para los labios** lipstick; — **óptico** (*computadora*) light pen.

lapso [láp·so] *m.* lapse.

lardo [lár·do] *m.* lard; **lardear** to baste.

lares [lá·res] *m. pl.* home.

largar[7] [lar·gár] *v.* to loosen; to let go; to set free; to unfold (*a flag or sails*); *Am.* to hurl, throw; *Col.* to strike (*a blow*); *Ríopl.* to give, hand over; **-se** to go away, slip away; to leave.

largo [lár·go] *adj.* long; generous; *m.* length; largo (*music*); — **de arco** arc length; — **del encaje** length of engagement (machine) **a la larga** in the long run; slowly; **a lo** — along; lengthwise; **¡ — de aquí!** get out of here!

largor [lar·gór] *m.* length.

largucho [lar·gú·čo] *adj.* lanky.

larguero [lar·gé·ro] *m.* stud (machine).

largueza [lar·gé·sa] *f.* generosity, liberality; length.

larguísimo [lar·gí·si·mo] *adj.* very long.

largura [lar·gú·ra] *f.* length.

laringe [la·ríŋ·xe] *f.* larynx.

laríngeo [la·ríŋ·xe·o] *adj.* laryngeal.

laringitis [la·riŋ·xí·tis] *f.* laryngitis.

larva [lár·ba] *f.* larva.

las [las] *def. art. f. pl.* the; *obj. pron.* them; — **que** *rel. pron.* those which; which.

lascivia [la·sí·bja] *f.* lewdness.

lascivo [la·sí·bo] *adj.* lascivious, lewd.

lástima [lás·ti·ma] *f.* pity; compassion, grief.

lastimadura [las·ti·ma·dú·ra] *f.* sore, hurt.

lastimar [las·ti·már] *v.* to hurt; to offend; **-se** to get hurt; **-se de** to feel pity for.

lastimero [las·ti·mé·ro] *adj.* pitiful; mournful.

lastimoso [las·ti·mó·so] *adj.* pitiful.

lastre [lás·tre] *m.* ballast, weight.

lata [lá·ta] *f.* (*metal*) tin plate; tin can, can; (*madero*) small log; thin board; (*pesadez*) annoyance; embarrassment; boring speech; *Arg.* gaucho saber; *Arg.* prop.

latente [la·tén·te] *adj.* latent.

lateral [la·te·rál] *adj.* lateral, side; [1] (*phonetically*).

latido [la·tí·do] *m.* palpitation, throb, beat; bark,

howl.

latifundio [la·ti·fún·djo] *m.* large landed estate.

latigazo [la·ti·gá·so] *m.* lash, stroke with a whip; crack of a whip; harsh reprimand; unexpected blow or offense.

látigo [lá·ti·g̣o] *m.* whip; *Am.* whipping, beating; *Ch.* end or goal of a horse race; (*encaje de electrodo y su cable*) whip.

latín [la·tín] *m.* Latin language.

latinismo [la·ti·níz·mo] *m.* Latinism; imitating Latin.

latino [la·tí·no] *adj.* Latin; *m.* Latinist, Latin scholar; Latin.

latir [la·tír] *v.* to throb, beat, palpitate; to bark.

latitud [la·ti·túd] *f.* latitude; extent, breadth.

latón [la·tón] *m.* brass.

latrocinio [la·tro·sí·njo] *m.* larceny, theft, robbery.

laúd [la·úd] *m.* lute; catboat (*long, narrow boat with a lateen sail*).

laudable [law·dá·ble] *adj.* laudable, praiseworthy.

laurel [law·rél] *m.* laurel; laurel wreath.

lauro [láw·ro] *m.* laurel; glory, fame.

lava [lá·ba] *f.* lava; washing of minerals.

lavable [la·bá·ble] *adj.* washable.

lavabo [la·bá·bo] *m.* lavatory, washroom; washstand; washbowl.

lavadero [la·ba·dé·ro] *m.* washing place.

lavado [la·bá·do] *m.* wash, washing; laundry, laundry work; — **de cerebro** brain washing.

lavador [la·ba·dór] *m.* washer; cleaner; *adj.* washing; cleaning; **lavadora** [la·ba·dó·ra] *f.* washer, washing machine.

lavadura [la·ba·dú·ra] *f.* washing; slops, dirty water.

lavamanos [la·ba·má·nos] *m.* lavatory, washbowl, washstand.

lavandera [la·ban·dé·ra] *f.* laundress, washerwoman.

lavandería [la·ban·de·rí·a] *f.* laundry.

lavar [la·bár] *v.* to wash; to launder; to whitewash.

lavativa [la·ba·tí·ba] *f.* enema; syringe; bother, nuisance.

lavatorio [la·ba·tó·rjo] *m.* washing (*act of washing*); wash (*liquid or solution for washing*); lavatory (*ceremonial act of washing*); washbowl, washstand; *Am.* washroom.

lavazas [la·bá·sas] *f. pl.* slops, dirty water.

laxante [lak·sán·te] *m.* laxative.

lazada [la·sá·da] *f.* bow, bowknot; *Am.* throwing of the lasso, lassoing.

lazar [la·sár] *v.* to rope, lasso; to noose.

lazarillo [la·sa·rí·yo] *m.* blindman's guide.

lazo [lá·so] *m.* (*nudo*) bow, knot; slipknot; lasso, lariat; (*vínculo*) tie, bond; (*trampa*) snare, trap; trick.

le [le] *obj. pron.* him; you (*formal*); to him; to her; to you (*formal*).

leal [le·ál] *adj.* loyal.

lealtad [le·al·tád] *f.* loyalty.

lebrel [le·brél] *m.* greyhound.

lebrillo [le·brí·yo] *m.* earthenware basin or tub.

lección [lek·sjón] *f.* lesson; reading; **dar la** — to recite the lesson; **dar** — to teach; **tomarle a uno la** — to have someone recite his lesson.

lector [lek·tór] *m.* reader; lecturer.

lectura [lek·tú·ra] *f.* reading; **libro de** — reader.

lechada [le·čá·da] *f.* whitewash; *Am.* milking.

leche [lé·če] *f.* milk; *Col., Ven., C.A., Andes, Ríopl.* luck (*in games*); — **homogeneizada** homogenized milk; — **desnatada** skim milk; — **en polvo** powdered milk.

lechería [le·če·rí·a] *f.* dairy, creamery; **lechero** [le·čé·ro] *adj.* milk; milch; giving milk (*applied to animals*); *Am.* lucky (*in games of chance*); *m.*

milkman; **lechera** [le·čé·ra] *f.* milkmaid; milk can; milk pitcher.

lecho [lé·čo] *m.* bed; river bed.

lechón [le·čón] *m.* suckling pig; pig.

lechoso [le·čó·so] *adj.* milky; *m.* papaya tree; **lechosa** [le·čó·sa] *f. P.R.* papaya (*tropical fruit*).

lechuga [le·čú·g̣a] *f.* lettuce; — **romana** romaine lettuce.

lechuza [le·čú·sa] *f.* screech owl, barn owl.

leer[14] [le·ér] *v.* to read.

legación [le·g̣a·sjón] *f.* legation.

legado [le·g̣á·do] *m.* (*donación*) legacy; legato; (*representante*) representative, ambassador.

legajo [le·g̣á·xo] *m.* bundle of papers; dossier.

legal [le·g̣ál] *adj.* legal, lawful; truthful; reliable; *Col., Ven., Andes* excellent, best; *Mex.* just, honest.

legalizar[9] [le·g̣a·li·sár] *v.* to legalize.

legar[7] [le·g̣ár] *v.* to will, bequeath; to send as a delegate.

legendario [le·xen·dá·rjo] *adj.* legendary.

legión [le·xjón] *f.* legion.

legislación [le·xiz·la·sjón] *f.* legislation.

legislador [le·xiz·la·dór] *m.* legislator; *adj.* legislating, legislative.

legislar [le·xiz·lár] *v.* to legislate.

legislativo [le·xiz·la·tí·bo] *adj.* legislative.

legislatura [le·xiz·la·tú·ra] *f.* legislature, legislative assembly.

legítimo [le·xí·ti·mo] *adj.* legitimate; real, genuine.

lego [lé·g̣o] *adj.* lay; ignorant; *m.* layman.

legua [lé·g̣wa] *f.* league (*about 3 miles*).

leguleyo [le·g̣u·lé·yo] *m.* shyster.

legumbre [le·g̣úm·bre] *f.* vegetable.

leída [le·í·da] *f. Am.* reading. *See* **lectura.**

leísta [le·ís·ta] *m. & f.* one who uses the pronoun *le* for masculine direct object (*le conozco*).

lejanía [le·xa·ní·a] *f.* distance; distant place.

lejano [le·xá·no] *adj.* distant; remote.

lejía [le·xí·a] *f.* lye; harsh reprimand; *Am.* bleach.

lejos [lé·xos] *adv.* far, far away; **a lo** — in the distance; *Am.* **a un** — in the distance; **de** (*or* **desde**) — from afar; *m.* view, perspective; background.

lelo [lé·lo] *adj.* silly, stupid, foolish.

lema [lé·ma] *m.* motto; theme; slogan.

lencería [len·se·rí·a] *f.* dry goods, dry-goods store; linen room or closet.

lengua [lén·gwa] *f.* tongue; language; interpreter; — **de tierra** point, neck of land.

lenguado [len·gwá·do] *m.* sole (*a fish*).

lenguaje [len·gwá·xe] *m.* language (*manner of expression*); — **de alto nivel** (*computadora*) high level language; — **de ensamble** assembly language; — **de máquina** machine language.

lenguaraz [len·gwa·rás] *adj.* talkative, loose-tongued.

lengüeta [len·gwé·ta] *f.* small tongue; **lengüetada** [len·gwe·ta·da] *f.* lick.

leninismo [le·ni·níz·mo] *m.* Leninism.

lente [lén·te] *m. & f.* lens; — **filtrador** filter lens; **-s** *m. pl.* eyeglasses.

lenteja [len·té·xa] *f.* lentil; lentil seed; **lentejuela** [len·te·xwé·la] *f.* spangle.

lentitud [len·ti·túd] *f.* slowness.

lento [lén·to] *adj.* slow; dull.

leña [lé·ña] *f.* firewood, kindling; beating; **leñera** [le·ñé·ra] *f.* woodshed, woodbox.

leñador [le·ña·dór] *m.* woodcutter, woodman.

leño [lé·ño] *m.* log, timber, piece of firewood.

león [le·ón] *m.* lion; **leona** [le·ó·na] *f.* lioness; **leonera** [le·o·né·ra] *f.* lion's den or cage; dive, gambling

joint; disorderly room.
leontina [le·on·tí·na] *f. Mex., Carib., Col.* watch chain.
leopardo [le·o·pár·do] *m.* leopard.
leopoldina [le·o·pol·dí·na] *f. Mex., Ven.* watch chain.
lerdo [lér·do] *adj.* dull, heavy, stupid, slow.
les [les] *obj. pron.* to them; to you (*formal*).
lesión [le·sjón] *f.* wound, injury.
lesionar [le·sjo·nár] *v.* to injure, to wound, to hurt, to damage.
lesna [léz·na] = **lezna.**
letargo [le·tár·ǥo] *m.* lethargy, stupor, drowsiness.
letra [lé·tra] *f.* letter (*of the alphabet*); printing type; hand; handwriting; letter (*exact wording or meaning*); words of a song; — **abierta** letter of credit; — **de cambio** draft, bill of exchange; — **mayúscula** capital letter; — **minúscula** small letter; **al pie de la** — literally; **-s** letters, learning.
letrado [le·trá·do] *adj.* learned; *m.* lawyer.
letrero [le·tré·ro] *m.* notice, poster, sign; legend (*under an illustration*).
leva [lé·ba] *f.* levy, draft; weighing anchor, setting sail; **echar** — to draft, conscript; *Col.* **echar -s** to boast.
levadizo [le·ba·dí·so] *adj.* lift (*bridge*).
levadura [le·ba·dú·ra] *f.* leaven, yeast; — **en polvo** baking powder. — **instante** instant yeast.
levantamiento [le·ban·ta·mjén·to] *m.* (*revuelta*) uprising, revolt, insurrection; (*altura*) elevation; (*alzar*) lifting, raising; (*reunión*) adjournment (*of a meeting*); — **de un plano** surveying.
levantar [le·ban·tár] *v.* to raise, lift; to set up; to erect; to rouse, stir up; to recruit; *Ch.* to break land, plow; — **el campo** to break camp; — **la mesa** to clear the table; — **la sesión** to adjourn the meeting; — **un plano** to survey, map out; — **falso testimonio** to bear false witness; **-se** to stand up, get up, rise; to rebel.
levante [le·bán·te] *m.* east; east wind.
levantisco [le·ban·tís·ko] *adj.* turbulent; rebellious.
levar [le·bár] *v.* to weigh (*anchor*); — **el ancla** to weigh anchor; **-se** to weigh anchor, set sail.
leve [lé·be] *adj.* light; slight; unimportant.
levita [le·bí·ta] *f.* frock coat; *m.* Levite, member of the tribe of Levi.
léxico [lék·si·ko] *m.* lexicon, dictionary; vocabulary; glossary.
lexicografía [lek·si·ko·gra·fí·a] *f.* lexicography.
lexicología [lek·si·ko·lo·xí·a] *f.* lexicology.
ley [lej] *f.* law; rule; loyalty; standard quality; **de buena** — of good quality; **plata de** — sterling silver; **-es** jurisprudence, law; system of laws.
leyenda [le·yén·da] *f.* legend; reading; inscription.
lezna [léz·na] *f.* awl.
liar[17] [ljar] *v.* to tie, bind; to roll up; to deceive; — **el petate** *Mex.* to kick the bucket; **-se** to bind oneself; to get tangled up.
libelo [li·bé·lo] *m.* libel.
libélula [li·bé·lu·la] *f.* dragon fly.
liberación [li·be·ra·sjón] *f.* liberation; deliverance.
liberal [li·be·rál] *adj.* liberal; generous; **liberalidad** [li·be·ra·li·dád] *f.* liberality; generosity.
liberalismo [li·be·ra·líz·mo] *m.* liberalism.
libertad [li·ber·tád] *f.* liberty.
libertador [li·ber·ta·dór] *m.* liberator, deliverer.
libertar [li·ber·tár] *v.* to liberate, free, set free; **-se** to get free; to escape.
libertinaje [li·ber·ti·ná·xe] *m.* license, licentiousness, lack of moral restraint.
libertino [li·ber·tí·no] *m.* libertine.
libido [li·bí·do] *m.* libido.

libra [lí·bra] *f.* pound; Libra (*sign of the Zodiac*).
librado [li·brá·do] *m.* drawee.
librador [li·bra·dór] *m.* drawer (*of a bill, draft, etc.*); deliverer, liberator; measuring scoop.
libranza [li·brán·sa] *f.* bill of exchange, draft.
librar [li·brár] *v.* to free, set free; to issue; to draw (*a draft*); — **guerra** to wage war; **-se** to save oneself; to escape; **-se de** to get rid of, escape from.
libre [lí·bre] *adj.* free; unmarried; loose; vacant.
librea [li·bré·a] *f.* livery (*uniform*).
librecambista [li·bre·kam·bís·ta] *m., f.* free trader.
librería [li·bre·rí·a] *f.* bookstore.
librero [li·bré·ro] *m.* bookseller; *Am.* bookcase, bookshelves.
libreta [li·bré·ta] *f.* notebook, memorandum book; bankbook; — **de ahorros** savings book.
libreto [li·bré·to] *m.* libretto.
libro [lí·bro] *m.* book; — **de caja** cashbook; — **mayor** ledger.
licencia [li·sén·sja] *f.* license; permission; furlough, leave; looseness; license to practice.
licenciado [li·sen·sjá·do] *m.* licenciate (*person having a degree approximately equivalent to a master's degree*); *Ríopl., Mex., C.A.* lawyer.
licenciar [li·sen·sjár] *v.* to license; to give a license or permit; to dismiss, discharge (*from the army*); to confer the degree of **licenciado; -se** to get the degree of **licenciado.**
licenciatura [li·sen·sja·tú·ra] *f.* degree of **licenciado.**
licencioso [li·sen·sjó·so] *adj.* licentious, lewd.
liceo [li·sé·o] *m.* lyceum; high school; *Col.* private primary school or high school.
lícito [lí·si·to] *adj.* lawful; permissible, allowable.
licor [li·kór] *m.* liquid; liquor.
licuadora [li·kwa·dó·ra] *f.* blender.
lid [lid] *f.* fight; contest.
líder [lí·der] *m. Am.* (labor or political) leader.
lidiar [li·djár] *v.* to fight; to combat; to contend.
liebre [ljé·bre] *f.* hare; coward.
lienzo [ljén·so] *m.* cotton or linen cloth; canvas; painting.
liga [lí·ǥa] *f.* (*alianza*) league; alliance; (*cinta*) garter; allow; birdlime.
ligador [li·ǥa·dór] *m.* binder.
ligadura [li·ǥa·dú·ra] *f.* binding; tie, bond; — **de laca** shellac bond.
ligar[7] [li·ǥár] *v.* to bind, tie, unite; to alloy (*combine metals*); **-se** to unite, combine, form an alliance.
legereza [li·xe·ré·sa] *f.* lightness; swiftness; flippancy; frivolity.
ligero [li·xé·ro] *adj.* (*leve*) light; (*rápido*) swift; nimble; flippant; *adv. C.A., Col., Ven.* quickly; **a la ligera** quickly, superficially.
lija [lí·xa] *f.* sandpaper.
lijar [li·xár] *v.* to sandpaper; **lijadora** sander.
lila [lí·la] *f.* lilac; pinkish-purple.
lima [lí·ma] *f.* file; lime (*fruit*); finishing, polishing.
limar [li·már] *v.* to file; to file down; to smooth, polish.
limeño [li·mé·ño] *adj.* of or from Lima, Peru.
limero [li·mé·ro] *m.* lime tree.
limitación [li·mi·ta·sjón] *f.* limitation; district.
limitar [li·mi·tár] *v.* to limit; to restrict; to bound.
límite [lí·mi·te] *m.* limit; boundary.
limítrofe [li·mí·tro·fe] *adj.* limiting; bordering.
limo [lí·mo] *m.* slime.
limón [li·món] *m.* lemon; lemon tree; *Am.* lime; — **italiano** lemon; **limonada** *f.* lemonade; **limonero** *m.* lemon tree lemon dealer or vendor.
limosna [li·móz·na] *f.* alms, charity.
limosnero [li·moz·né·ro] *m.* beggar.

limpiabotas [lim·pja·bó·tas] *m.* bootblack; *Ch.* bootlicker, flatterer.

limpiadientes [lim·pja·djén·tes] *m.* toothpick.

limpiaparabrisas [lim·pja·pa·ra·brí·sas] *m.* windshield wiper.

limpiar [lim·pjár] *v.* to clean; to wipe; to cleanse, purify; *Am.* to beat up, whip, lash.

limpias [lím·pjas] *f.* cleanouts.

límpido [lím·pi·do] *adj.* limpid, clear.

limpieza [lim·pjé·sa] *f.* cleanliness, neatness; purity; honesty.

limpio [lím·pjo] *adj.* clean; neat; pure; **poner en —** to make a clean copy; *Col.* **— y soplado** absolutely broke, cleaned out.

linaje [li·ná·xe] *m.* lineage, family, race.

linajudo [li·na·xú·do] *adj.* highborn.

linaza [li·ná·sa] *f.* linseed.

lince [lín·se] *m.* lynx; sharp-sighted person.

linchar [lin·čár] *v.* to lynch.

lindar [lin·dár] *v.* to border, adjoin.

linde [lín·de] *m. & f.* limit, border, boundary; landmark.

lindero [lin·dé·ro] *adj.* bordering upon; *m. Carib., C.A.* landmark; boundary.

lindeza [lin·dé·sa] *f.* prettiness; exquisiteness; neatness; witty act or remark.

lindo [lín·do] *adj.* pretty; **de lo —** wonderfully; very much; to the utmost.

línea [lí·ne·a] *f.* line; limit.

lineal [li·ne·ál] *adj.* lineal, linear.

lingüista [lin·gwís·ta] *m. & f.* linguist.

lingüística [lin·gwís·ti·ka] *f.* linguistics.

lingüístico [lin·gwís·ti·ko] *adj.* linguistic.

lino [lí·no] *m.* linen; flax; **linón** *m.* lawn, thin linen or cotton.

linotipia [li·no·tí·pja] *f.* linotype.

linterna [lin·tér·na] *f.* lantern.

lío [lí·o] *m.* (*bulto*) bundle; (*enredo*) fib; mess, confusion; **armar un —** to raise a rumpus; to cause confusion; **hacerse un —** to be confused, get tangled up; **meterse en un —** to get oneself into a mess.

liquidación [li·ki·da·sjón] *f.* liquidation; settlement (*of an account*).

liquidar [li·ki·dár] *v.* to liquidate; to settle (*an account*).

líquido [lí·ki·do] *m.* liquid; **— refrigerador** coolant.

lira [lí·ra] *f.* lyre, small harp; a type of metrical composition; lira (*Italian coin*).

lírico [lí·ri·ko] *adj.* lyric, lyrical; *Am.* fantastic; *m. Ríopl.* visionary, dreamer.

lirio [lí·rjo] *m.* lily.

lirismo [li·ríz·mo] *m.* lyricism (*lyric quality*); *Am.* idle dream, fantasy.

lisiado [li·sjá·do] *adj.* lame, hurt, injured.

liso [lí·so] *adj.* smooth, even; flat; evident, clear; *Am.* crafty, sly; *Col., Ven., C.A., Andes* fresh, impudent.

lisonja [li·són·xa] *f.* flattery.

lisonjear [li·son·xe·ár] *v.* to flatter; to fawn on; to please.

lisonjero [li·son·xé·ro] *adj.* flattering, pleasing; *m.* flatterer.

lista [lís·ta] *f.* list; strip; stripe; **pasar —** to call the roll; **— de correos** general delivery.

listado [lis·tá·do] *adj.* striped.

listar [lis·tár] *v.* to register, enter in a list; *Ríopl., Mex., Ven.* to stripe, streak.

listo [lís·to] *adj.* ready, prompt; clever; *Ríopl., Ch.* mischievous.

listón [lis·tón] *m.* ribbon, tape; strip; **-s de enrasar**

furring (carpentry).

lisura [li·sú·ra] *f.* smoothness; sincerity, frankness; *Am.* freshness, impudence; *Andes* insulting or filthy remark.

litera [li·té·ra] *f.* berth (*on a boat or train*); litter (*for carrying a person*).

literario [li·te·rá·rjo] *adj.* literary.

literato [li·te·rá·to] *adj.* literary, learned; *m.* literary man, writer.

literatura [li·te·ra·tú·ra] *f.* literature.

litigio [li·tí·xjo] *m.* litigation, lawsuit.

litio [lí·tjo] *m.* lithium.

litoral [li·to·rál] *adj.* seaboard, coastal; *m.* coast, shore.

litro [lí·tro] *m.* liter (*about 1.05 quarts*).

liviandad [li·bja·ni·dád] *f.* lightness; frivolity; lewdness.

liviano [li·bjá·no] *adj.* (*leve*) light; slight, unimportant; (*lascivo*) frivolous, fickle; lewd; unchaste.

lívido [lí·bi·do] *adj.* livid, having a dull-bluish color; pale.

lo [lo] *obj. pron.* him; you (*formal*); it; so; *dem. pron.* **— de** that of, that affair of, that matter of; **— bueno** the good, what is good; **sé — bueno que Vd. es** I know how good you are; **— que** that which, what.

loable [lo·á·ble] *adj.* laudable, worthy of praise.

loar [lo·ár] *v.* to praise.

lobanillo [lo·ba·ní·yo] *m.* growth, tumor.

lobo [ló·bo] *m.* wolf.

lóbrego [ló·bre·go] *adj.* dark, gloomy.

lobreguez [lo·bre·gés] *f.* darkness, gloominess.

lóbulo [ló·bu·lo] *m.* lobe.

lobuno [lo·bú·no] *adj.* related to the wolf.

local [lo·kál] *adj.* local; *m.* place, quarters; site; premises.

localidad [lo·ka·li·dád] *f.* location; locality, town; place; seat (*in a theater*).

localización [lo·ka·li·sa·sjón] *f.* localization, localizing.

localizar[9] [lo·ka·li·sár] *v.* to localize.

loco [ló·ko] *adj.* insane, mad, crazy; **— de remate** stark mad; *m.* lunatic, insane person.

locomotor [lo·ko·mo·tór] *adj.* locomotive.

locomotora [lo·ko·mo·tó·ra] *f.* locomotive; **— diesel** diesel locomotive.

locuaz [lo·kwás] *adj.* loquacious, talkative.

locución [lo·ku·sjón] *f.* phrase; diction.

locura [lo·kú·ra] *f.* madness, insanity.

locutor [lo·ku·tór] *m.* radio announcer.

lodazal [lo·da·sál] *m.* muddy place; mire.

lodo [ló·do] *m.* mud; **lodoso** [lo·dó·so] *adj.* muddy, miry.

logaritmo [lo·ga·rím·mo] *m.* logarithm.

logia [ló·xja] *f.* lodge (*secret society*).

lógica [ló·xi·ka] *f.* logic; reasoning.

logical [lo·xi·kál] *m.*, (*computadora*) software.

lógico [ló·xi·ko] *adj.* logical.

lograr [lo·grár] *v.* to gain, obtain, accomplish; **— (+ *inf.*)** to succeed in; **-se** to succeed; to turn out well.

logrero [lo·gré·ro] *m.* usurer; profiteer.

logro [ló·gro] *m.* profit, gain; usury; attainment; realization.

loísta [lo·ís·ta] *m. & f.* one who uses the pronoun *lo* for the masculine direct object (*lo conozco*).

loma [ló·ma] *f.* small hill; **lomerío** [lo·me·rí·o] *m. Am.* group of hills.

lombriz [lom·brís] *f.* earthworm.

lomillo [lo·mí·yo] *m.* cross-stitch.

lomo [ló·mo] *m.* back (*of an animal, book, knife, etc.*); loin; ridge between two furrows; *Mex., Ven.* **hacer —** to bear with patience, resign oneself.

lona [ló·na] *f.* canvas.

lonche [lón·če] *m. Col., Ven., Mex.* lunch; **lonchería** [lon·če·rí·a] *f. Col., Ven., Mex.* lunchroom.

londinense [lon·di·nén·se] *m. & f.* of or from London.

longaniza [loŋ·ga·ní·sa] *f.* pork sausage.

longevidad [loŋ·xe·bi·dád] *f.* longevity, long life; span of life, length of life.

longitud [loŋ·xi·túd] *f.* longitude; length.

longitudinal [loŋ·xi·tu·di·nál] *adj.* longitudinal, lengthwise; **-mente** *adv.* longitudinally, lengthwise.

lonja [lóŋ·xa] *f.* (*mercado*) exchange; market; (*carne*) slice of meat; (*correa*) leather strap; *Ríopl.* rawhide.

lontananza [lon·ta·nán·sa] *f.* background; **en —** in the distance, in the background.

loro [ló·ro] *m.* parrot.

los [los] *def. art. m. pl.* the; *obj. pron.* them; **— que** *rel. pron.* those which; which.

losa [ló·sa] *f.* flagstone; slab; gravestone.

lote [ló·te] *m.* lot, share, part; *Am.* remnant lot; *Col.* swallow of liquor; *Am.* blockhead, dunce.

lotear [lo·te·ár] *v. Am.* to subdivide into lots; *Am.* to divide into portions.

lotería [lo·te·rí·a] *f.* lottery; raffle.

loza [ló·sa] *f.* fine earthenware; crockery; **— fina** chinaware.

lozanía [lo·sa·ní·a] *f.* luxuriance (*rich foliage or growth*); vigor.

lozano [lo·sá·no] *adj.* luxuriant; exuberant, vigorous, lusty.

lubricar[6] [lu·bri·kár] *v.* to lubricate, or grease; **lubricante** lubricant.

lucero [lu·sé·ro] *m.* morning star; any bright star; star on the forehead of certain animals; splendor, brightness.

lúcido [lú·si·do] *adj.* lucid, clear; shining, bright.

luciente [lu·sjén·te] *adj.* shining, bright.

luciérnaga [lu·sjér·na·ga] *f.* firefly; glowworm.

lucimiento [lu·si·mjén·to] *m.* splendor; brilliance; success.

lucir[13] [lu·sír] *v. irr.* (*brillar*) to shine, to illuminate, to brighten; (*superar*) to excel; (*alardear*) to show off; **-se** to shine, be brilliant; show off; to be successful.

lucrativo [lu·kra·tí·bo] *adj.* lucrative, profitable.

lucro [lú·kro] *m.* profit, gain.

luctuoso [luk·twó·so] *adj.* sad, mournful, dismal.

lucha [lú·ča] *f.* fight, struggle; dispute; wrestling match.

luchador [lu·ča·dór] *m.* fighter; wrestler.

luchar [lu·čár] *v.* to fight, to wrestle, to struggle, to dispute.

luego [lwé·go] *adv.* soon, presently; afterwards, then, next; **desde —** immediately, at once; naturally; of course; **— que** as soon as; **hasta —** good-bye, so long; **— —** right away.

luengo [lwéŋ·go] *adj.* long; **-s años** many years.

lugar [lu·gár] *m.* (*sitio*) place; site; town; space; (*empleo*) position, employment; (*ocasión*) time, occasion, opportunity; **dar — a** to give cause or occasion for; **hacer** (*or* **dar**) **—** to make room; **en — de** instead of.

lugareño [lu·ga·ré·ño] *m.* villager.

lúgubre [lú·gu·bre] *adj.* mournful, gloomy.

lujo [lú·xo] *m.* luxury, extravagance.

lujoso [lu·xó·so] *adj.* luxurious; elegant; showy.

lujuria [lu·xú·rja] *f.* lust, lewdness, sensuality.

lujurioso [lu·xu·rjó·so] *adj.* lustful, lewd, sensual.

lumbre [lúm·bre] *f.* fire; brightness.

luminoso [lu·mi·nó·so] *adj.* luminous, bright, shining.

luna [lú·na] *f.* moon; mirror, glass for mirrors.

lunar [lu·nár] *adj.* lunar; *m.* mole; blemish, spot.

lunático [lu·ná·ti·ko] *adj. & m.* lunatic.

lunes [lú·nes] *m.* Monday; *Ch.* **hacer San Lunes** to lay off on Monday.

lunfardo [lun·fár·do] *m.* social dialect of the Buenos Aires underworld.

lustre [lús·tre] *m.* luster, shine; glory.

lustroso [lus·tró·so] *adj.* lustrous, glossy, shining.

luto [lú·to] *m.* mourning; sorrow, grief.

luz [lus] *f.* light; clarity; hint, guidance; **dar a —** to give birth; to publish; **entre dos luces** at twilight.

LL:ll

llaga [ŷá·ga] *f.* wound; ulcer, sore.

llama [ŷá·ma] *f.* flame; (*animal*) llama.

llamada [ŷa·má·da] *f.* call; beckon, sign; knock; reference mark (*as an asterisk*).

llamador [ŷa·ma·dór] *m.* knocker (*of a door*); caller.

llamamiento [ŷa·ma·mjén·to] *m.* call, calling; calling together; appeal.

llamar [ŷa·már] *v.* to call; to summon; to name; to invoke; **— a la puerta** to knock at the door; **-se** to be called, named; *Mex.* to break one's word or promise.

llamarada [ŷa·ma·rá·da] *f.* flash; sudden flame or blaze; sudden flush, blush.

llamativo [ŷa·ma·tí·bo] *adj.* showy, loud, gaudy, flashy; thirst-exciting.

llameante [ŷa·me·án·te] *adj.* flaming.

llana [ŷá·na] *f.* mason's trowel.

llanero [ŷa·né·ro] *m. Ven., Col.* plainsman.

llaneza [ŷa·né·sa] *f.* simplicity, frankness, sincerity, plainness.

llano [ŷá·no] *adj.* plain, simple; even, smooth, level; frank; *m.* plain, flat ground.

llanta [ŷán·ta] *f. Spain* rim of a wheel; *Am.* tire; tire casing; *Peru* large sunshade (*used in Peruvian markets*).

llanto [ŷán·to] *m.* crying, weeping; tears.

llanura [ŷa·nú·ra] *f.* extensive plain; prairie; evenness, flatness.

llapa [ŷá·pa] *f. Andes, Ríopl.* a small gift from the vendor to the purchaser; also **yapa, ñapa.**

llave [ŷá·be] *f.* key; faucet; clef; **— de tuercas** wrench; **— inglesa** monkey wrench; **— maestra** master key.

llavera [ŷa·bé·ra] *f. Ch.* housekeeper.

llavero [ŷa·bé·ro] *m.* key ring; key maker; keeper of the keys.

llavín [ŷa·bín] *m.* small key.

llegada [ŷe·gá·da] *f.* arrival.

llegar[7] [ŷe·gár] *v.* to arrive; to reach; to amount; **— a ser** to get or come to be; **— a las manos** to come to blows; **-se** to approach, get near.

llenar [ŷe·nár] *v.* to fill; to stuff; **-se** to fill up; to overeat; **-se de** to get filled with; to get covered with, spattered with.

lleno [ŷé·no] *adj.* full; *m.* fullness, completeness; **de — totally, completely; un — completo** a full house (*said of a theater*).

llenura [ŷe·nú·ra] *f.* fullness; abundance.

llevadero [ŷe·ba·dé·ro] *adj.* bearable, tolerable.

llevar [ŷe·bár] *v.* (*transportar*) to carry; to bear; to transport; to wear; (*conducir*) to take; to lead; (*cobrar*) to charge; to ask a certain price; to keep (*accounts*); — **ventaja** to be ahead, have the advantage; — **un año a** to be one year older than; — **un mes aquí** to have been here one month; — **un castigo** to suffer punishment; **-se** to carry away; **-se bien con** to get along with.

llorar [ẏo·rár] *v.* to cry, weep.

lloriquear [ẏo·ri·ke·ár] *v.* to whimper, whine, weep.

lloriqueo [ẏo·ri·ké·o] *m.* whimper, whining.

lloro [ẏó·ro] *m.* weeping.

llorón [ẏo·rón] *adj.* weeping; **sauce** — weeping willow; *m.* weeper, crybaby, whiner.

llorona [ẏo·ró·na] *f.* weeping woman; **-s** *Arg., Bol.* large spurs.

lloroso [ẏo·ró·so] *adj.* tearful; weeping.

llovedizo [ẏo·be·dí·so] *adj.* rain (*used as adj.*); **agua llovediza** rain water.

llover[2] [ẏo·bér] *v. irr.* to rain, shower.

llovizna [ẏo·bíz·na] *f.* drizzle.

lloviznar [ẏo·biz·nár] *v.* to drizzle, sprinkle.

lluvia [ẏú·bja] *f.* rain; shower.

lluvioso [ẏu·bjó·so] *adj.* rainy.

M:m

macana [ma·ká·na] *f. Am.* club, cudgel, stick; *Ríopl., Ch., Bol.* lie, absurdity, nonsense.

macanudo [ma·ka·nú·do] *adj. Ríopl.* tremendous! great!

macarrón [ma·ka·rrón] *m.* macaroon; **-es** macaroni.

maceta [ma·sé·ta] *f.* (*tiesto*) flowerpot; (*martillo*) small mallet; stonecutter's hammer; handle of tools; *Am.* head; *adj. Am.* slow.

macilento [ma·si·lén·to] *adj.* thin, emaciated; pale.

macizo [ma·sí·so] *adj.* solid, firm; massive; *m.* massiveness; firmness; thicket; clump.

machacar[6] [ma·ča·kár] *v.* to pound, crush; to insist, harp on.

machacón [ma·ča·kón] *adj.* persistent; tenacious.

machete [ma·čé·te] *m.* machete, large heavy knife; **machetazo** *m.* large machete; blow with a machete.

machismo [ma·číz·mo] *m.* the quality of being a male; proven virility; male chauvinism.

macho [má·čo] *m.* male; he-mule; hook (*of a hook and eye*); abutment; pillar; stupid fellow; sledgehammer; *C.R.* a blond; North American; *Am.* **pararle a uno el** — to halt or repress a person; *adj.* masculine, male; strong.

machucar[6] [ma·ču·kár] *v.* to pound, beat, bruise; *Am.* to crush; *Am.* to break (*a horse*).

machucón [ma·ču·kón] *m.* smash; bruise.

madeja [ma·dé·xa] *f.* skein; mass of hair; limp, listless person.

madera [ma·dé·ra] *f.* wood; timber; lumber; — **contrachapada** (*triplay*) plywood; **maderero** *m.* lumberman, lumber dealer.

maderaje [ma·de·rá·xe] *m.* timber, lumber; timber work; woodwork.

maderamen [ma·de·rá·men] *m.* timber; timber work; woodwork.

madero [ma·dé·ro] *m.* beam; plank; piece of lumber; blockhead, dunce.

madrastra [ma·drás·tra] *f.* stepmother.

madre [má·dre] *f.* mother; womb; root, origin; river bed; **salirse de** — to overflow (*said of rivers*).

madrepeña [ma·dre·pé·ña] *f. Am.* moss.

madreperla [ma·dre·pér·la] *f.* mother-of-pearl.

madreselva [ma·dre·sél·ba] *f.* honeysuckle.

madriguera [ma·dri·gé·ra] *f.* burrow; den, lair.

madrileño [ma·dri·lé·ño] *adj.* Madrilenian, from or pertaining to Madrid; *m.* Madrilenian.

madrina [ma·drí·na] *f.* (*patrocinadora*) godmother; bridesmaid; sponsor; (*correa*) strap for yoking two horses; (*ganado*) leading mare; prop; *Am.* small herd of tame cattle (*used for leading wild cattle*).

madrugada [ma·dru·gá·da] *f.* dawn; early morning; **de** — at daybreak.

madrugador [ma·dru·ga·dór] *m.* early riser.

madrugar[7] [ma·dru·gár] *v.* to rise early; to be ahead of others; to "get the jump" on someone.

madurar [ma·du·rár] *v.* to mature; to ripen.

madurez [ma·du·rés] *f.* maturity; ripeness.

maduro [ma·dú·ro] *adj.* ripe; mature; prudent, wise; *Am.* bruised, sore.

maestría [ma·es·trí·a] *f.* mastery; great skill; advanced teaching degree.

maestro [ma·és·tro] *m.* master, teacher; chief craftsman; *adj.* master; masterly, skillful; **llave maestra** master key; **obra maestra** masterpiece.

MAGI (soldura) *s.* **en atmósfera de gas inerte** MIG welding.

magia [má·xja] *f.* magic; charm.

mágico [má·xi·ko] *adj.* magic; *m.* magician.

magín [ma·xín] *m.* imagination, fancy.

magisterio [ma·xis·té·rjo] *m.* teaching profession.

magistrado [ma·xis·trá·do] *m.* magistrate, judge.

magistral [ma·xis·trál] *adj.* masterly; masterful; authoritative.

magnánimo [mag·ná·ni·mo] *adj.* magnanimous, noble, generous.

magnesia [mag·né·sja] *f.* magnesia.

magnesio [mag·né·sjo] *m.* magnesium.

magnético [mag·né·ti·ko] *adj.* magnetic; attractive.

magnetofónico [mag·ne·to·fó·ni·ko] *adj.* recording (*tape or wire*).

magnetófono [mag·ne·tó·fo·no] *m.* tape recorder.

magnificencia [mag·ni·fi·sén·sja] *f.* magnificence, splendor.

magnífico [mag·ní·fi·ko] *adj.* magnificent, splendid.

magnitud [mag·ni·túd] *f.* magnitude, greatness.

magno [mág·no] *adj.* great.

magnolia [mag·nó·lja] *f.* magnolia.

mago [má·go] *m.* magician, wizard; **los tres Reyes Magos** the Three Wise Men.

magra [mág·ra] *f.* slice of ham.

magro [mág·ro] *adj.* lean.

maguey [ma·géj] *m.* maguey, century plant.

magullar [ma·gu·yár] *v.* to bruise; to maul; to mangle; *Ríopl., Ch., Col., Andes, P.R.* to crumple.

magullón [ma·gu·yón] *m.* a bruise.

mahometano [ma·o·me·tá·no] *adj. & m.* Mohammedan.

maicillo [maj·sí·yo] *m. Am.* gravel.

maíz [ma·ís] *m.* corn; **maizal** [maj·sál] *m.* cornfield.

majada [ma·xá·da] *f.* sheepfold; dung, manure; *Ríopl., Ch.* flock of sheep or goats.

majadería [ma·xa·de·rí·a] *f.* foolishness, nonsense.

majadero [ma·xa·dé·ro] *adj.* foolish; bothersome.

majar [ma·xár] *v.* to pound; to crush; to bruise; to crumple; to mash; to annoy, bother.

majestad [ma·xes·tád] *f.* majesty; dignity.

majestuoso [ma·xes·twó·so] *adj.* majestic, stately.

majo [má·xo] *adj.* gaudy, showy; gaily attired; pretty; *m.* dandy; **maja** [má·xa] *f.* belle.

mal [mal] *m.* evil; illness; harm; wrong. *See* **malo.**

malabarista [ma·la·brís·ta] *m. & f.* juggler; *Ch.* sly

thief.

malacate [ma·la·ká·te] *m.* hoist, hoisting machine; winch; *Am.* spindle (*for cotton*); *Am.* **parecer uno un —** to be constantly on the go, be in constant motion.

malagueña [ma·la·ǵé·ña] *f.* song and dance of Málaga; native (*f.*) of Málaga.

malandanza [ma·lan·dán·sa] *f.* misfortune.

malaquita [ma·la·kí·ta] *f.* malachite.

malaventura [ma·la·ben·tú·ra] *f.* misfortune, disaster.

malazo [ma·lá·so] *adj.* perverse, evil, wicked; vicious.

malbaratar [mal·ba·ra·tár] *v.* to undersell, sell at a loss; to squander.

malcontento [mal·kon·tén·to] *adj.* discontented; *m.* malcontent, troublemaker.

malcriado [mal·krjá·do] *adj.* ill-bred, rude.

maldad [mal·dád] *f.* badness, evil, wickedness.

maldecir[27, 52] [mal·de·sír] *v. irr.* to curse; to damn.

maldiciente [mal·di·sjén·te] *adj.* cursing.

maldición [mal·di·sjón] *f.* curse.

maldispuesto [mal·dis·pwés·to] *adj.* unwilling, not inclined.

maldito [mal·dí·to] *p.p. of* **maldecir** & *adj.* cursed; wicked; damned; *Ch.* tricky; *Mex.* bold, boastful.

maleable [ma·le·á·ble] *adj.* malleable; easily spoiled.

maleante [ma·le·án·te] *m.* crook, rogue, rascal, villain.

malecón [ma·le·kón] *m.* mole; dike.

maledicencia [ma·le·di·sén·sja] *f.* slander.

maleficio [ma·le·fí·sjo] *m.* spell, charm, witchery.

maléfico [ma·lé·fi·ko] *adj.* evil, harmful.

malestar [ma·les·tár] *m.* indisposition; slight illness; discomfort.

maleta [ma·lé·ta] *f.* travelling bag; suitcase; *Col., Ven., C.A.* bundle of clothes; *Col.* hump (*on the back*); *Ch.* saddlebag; *C.A.* rogue, rascal; *Ch.* lazy fellow.

maletín [ma·le·tín] *m.* small valise, satchel.

malevo [ma·lé·bo] *adj. Bol., Ríopl.* bad, wicked.

malévolo [ma·lé·bo·lo] *adj.* bad, evil, wicked.

maleza [ma·lé·sa] *f.* underbrush; thicket; weeds.

malgastar [mal·ǵas·tár] *v.* to squander, waste.

¡malhaya! [ma·lá·ya] *interj.* cursed; *Ríopl.* were it so!

malhechor [ma·le·čór] *m.* malefactor, evildoer, criminal.

malhora [ma·ló·ra] *f. Ríopl., C.A., Ven.* trouble, misfortune.

malhumorado [ma·lu·mo·rá·do] *adj.* ill-humored.

malicia [ma·lí·sja] *f.* malice; wickedness; shrewdness; suspicion; *Ch.* bit of brandy or cognac added to another drink.

maliciar [ma·li·sjár] *v.* to suspect.

malicioso [ma·li·sjó·so] *adj.* malicious; wicked; shrewd; suspicious.

maligno [ma·líǵ·no] *adj.* malign, malignant; pernicious, harmful.

malmandado [mal·man·dá·do] *adj.* disobedient; stubborn.

mal(o) [mál(o)] *adj.* bad, evil; wicked; ill; difficult; *Am.* **a la mala** treacherously; *Ríopl.* **de malas** by force; **estar de malas** to be out of luck; **por la mala** unwillingly, by force; **venir de malas** to come with evil intentions; **mal** *adv.* badly; poorly; wrongly.

malograr [ma·lo·ǵrár] *v.* to waste, lose; **-se** to turn out badly; to fail.

malón [ma·lón] *m.* mean trick; *Ríopl.* surprise Indian raid; *Ven.* tin-pan serenade, boisterous surprise party.

malpagar[7] [mal·pa·ǵár] *v.* to underpay, pay poorly.

malparto [mal·pár·to] *m.* miscarriage, abortion.

malquerencia [mal·ke·rén·sja] *f.* aversion, dislike, ill will.

malsano [mal·sá·no] *adj.* unhealthy; sickly.

malta [mál·ta] *f.* malt.

maltratar [mal·tra·tár] *v.* to treat badly; to misuse, abuse.

maltrato [mal·trá·to] *m.* mistreatment, abuse.

maltrecho [mal·tré·čo] *adj.* battered, bruised, injured.

malvado [mal·bá·do] *adj.* wicked; malicious.

malversación [mal·ber·sa·sjón] *f.* graft, corruption, misuse of public funds.

malversar [mal·ber·sár] *v.* to misuse (*funds in one's trust*); to embezzle.

malla [má·ya] *f.* mesh; coat of mail; *Ch.* species of potato; **hacer —** to knit.

mamá [ma·má] *f.* mamma.

mamada [ma·má·da] *f.* suck, sucking.

mamado [ma·má·do] *adj. Am.* drunk.

mamar [ma·már] *v.* to suckle; to suck; to gorge; **-se** *Ríopl., C.A.* to get drunk; *Col.* to go back on one's promise; *Col.* to fold up, crack up; **-se a uno** to get the best of someone, deceive someone; *Col., C.A.* to kill someone.

mamarracho [ma·ma·rrá·čo] *m.* a mess; a worthless guy.

mamífero [ma·mí·fe·ro] *m.* mammal; *adj.* mammalian, of mammals.

mamón [ma·món] *adj.* suckling; *m.* suckling (*very young animal or child*); shoot, sucker (*of a tree*); a tropical tree and its fruit; *Mex.* a kind of cake; *C.A.* public employee.

mampara [mam·pá·ra] *f.* screen.

mampostería [mam·pos·te·rí·a] *f.* masonry, stone masonry.

manada [ma·ná·da] *f.* herd, drove, pack, flock.

manantial [ma·nan·tjál] *m.* spring; source, origin.

manar [ma·nár] *v.* to spring, flow (from); to abound.

manaza [ma·ná·sa] *f.* large hand.

manazo [ma·ná·so] *m. Ríopl.* slap. *See* **manotazo.**

mancarrón [maŋ·ka·rrón] *m.* one-armed or one-handed man; cripple; old nag; *Ríopl., Andes* crude, clumsy fellow; *S.A.* disabled workman; *S.A.* dike, small dam.

mancebo [man·sé·bo] *m.* youth, young man; bachelor.

mancera [man·sé·ra] *f.* handle of a plough.

mancilla [man·sí·ya] *f.* stain, spot; dishonor.

manco [máŋ·ko] *adj.* one-armed; one-handed; maimed; lame (*referring to an arm* or *the front leg of an animal*); faulty, defective; *m. Ch.* nag.

mancuerna [maŋ·kwér·na] *f.* pair of animals tied together; *Mex., C.A. f. pl.* cuff links.

mancha [mán·ča] *f.* spot, stain, blemish; *Am.* cloud, swarm; *Ven., Cuba, Col.* roving herd of cattle.

manchar [man·čár] *v.* to stain, soil, spot; to tarnish.

manchego [man·čé·ǵo] *adj.* of or belonging to La Mancha (*region of Spain*); *m.* inhabitant of La Mancha.

manchón [man·čón] *m.* large stain; large patch.

mandadero [man·da·dé·ro] *m.* messenger, errand boy.

mandado [man·dá·do] *m.* (*orden*) command, order; (*recado*) errand; *p.p. of* **mandar; bien —** well-behaved; **mal —** ill-behaved.

mandamiento [man·da·mjén·to] *m.* command, order; writ; commandment.

mandar [man·dár] *v.* (*pedir*) to command, order; rule; (*enviar*) to send; to bequeath; will; *Col., Ven.* to throw, hurl; **— hacer** to have made, order; *Col., Ven., Mex., Carib., Andes* **— una bofetada** to give a slap; *Col., Ven., Mex., Carib., Andes* **—**

LL

una pedrada to throw a stone; **-se** *Am.* to be impudent; **-se mudar** *Ríopl., Carib.* to go away.

mandatario [man·da·tá·rjo] *m.* attorney, representative; *Am.* magistrate, chief.

mandato [man·dá·to] *m.* mandate; order, command; term of office; (*computadora*) command.

mandíbula [man·dí·ƀu·la] *f.* jaw, jawbone.

mandioca [man·djó·ka] *f.* manioc.

mando [mán·do] *m.* command, authority, power; (*computadora*) joystick.

mandolina [man·do·lí·na] *f.* mandolin.

mandón [man·dón] *adj.* bossy, domineering; *m.* bossy person; *Arg.* boss or foreman of a mine; *Ch.* race starter.

mandril [man·dríl] *m.* chuck, reamer; **— de la barra taladradora** boring bar holder.

maneador [ma·ne·a·dór] *m. Ríopl., Ven., Col.* hobble, leather lasso (*for the legs of an animal*); *Arg.* whip; *Ven., Andes* halter.

manear [ma·ne·ár] *v.* to hobble, lasso, tie the legs of (*an animal*); **-se** *Col., Ven.* to get tangled up.

manecilla [ma·ne·sí·ya] *f.* small hand; hand of a watch or clock.

manejable [ma·ne·xá·ƀle] *adj.* manageable.

manejar [ma·ne·xár] *v.* to manage, handle; to drive (*a car*); (*computadora*) to control; **-se** to move about, get around (*after an illness or accident*); *Carib., Ven.* to behave oneself.

manejo [ma·né·xo] *m.* handling; management; trick, intrigue.

manera [ma·né·ra] *f.* manner, way, mode; side opening in a shirt; front opening in breeches; **-s** customs; manners, behavior; **a — de** (*or* **a la — de**) like, in the style of; **de — que** so that; **sobre —** exceedingly; extremely.

manga [máŋ·ga] *f.* sleeve; bag; hose (*for watering*); body of troops; *Am.* multitude, herd, swarm; *Am.* cattle chute (*narrow passageway*); *Col., Ec.* corral; **— de agua** waterspout, whirlwind over the ocean; *Mex.* **— de hule** raincape; **por angas o por -s** by hook or crook, in one way or another.

mangana [man·gá·na] *f.* lariat, lasso.

manganeso [man·ga·né·so] *m.* manganese.

mangle [máŋ·gle] *m.* mangrove.

mango [máŋ·go] *m.* handle; *Am.* mango (*tropical tree and its fruit*).

manguera [maŋ·gé·ra] *f.* hose (*for water*); waterspout; *Ríopl.* large corral (*for livestock*).

manguito [maŋ·gí·to] *m.* muff; knitted half-sleeve (*worn on the forearm*); oversleeve; bushing.

maní [ma·ní] *m. Carib., C.A., Ch., Andes, Ven., Col.* peanut; **manicero** [ma·ni·sé·ro] *m. Carib., C.A., Ch., Andes, Ven., Col.* peanut vendor.

manía [ma·ní·a] *f.* mania, frenzy; craze, whim.

maniatar [ma·nja·tár] *v.* to tie the hands; to handcuff; to hobble (*an animal*).

maniático [ma·njá·ti·ko] *m.* crank, queer fellow; *adj.* cranky, queer, odd.

manicomio [ma·ni·kó·mjo] *m.* insane asylum.

manicura [ma·ni·kú·ra] *f.* manicure; manicurist.

manicurar [ma·ni·ku·rár] *v.* to manicure.

manido [ma·ní·đo] *adj.* rotting; *Ríopl., Carib., Col., Andes* trite, commonplace.

manifestación [ma·ni·fes·ta·sjón] *f.* manifestation; demonstration.

manifestar[1] [ma·ni·fes·tár] *v. irr.* to manifest; to show.

manifiesto [ma·ni·fjés·to] *adj.* manifest, clear, plain; *m.* manifesto, public declaration; customhouse manifest.

manigua [ma·ní·ǥwa] *f. Col., Ríopl., Cuba, P.R.*

Cuban jungle or thicket; *Carib.* **coger —** to get feverish; *Ríopl., Carib.* **irse a la —** to rise up in rebellion.

manija [ma·ni·xa] *f.* handle; crank; fetter.

manilla [ma·ní·ya] *f.* small hand; bracelet; **-s de hierro** handcuffs.

maniobra [ma·njó·ƀra] *f.* maneuver; operation.

maniobrar [ma·njo·ƀrár] *v.* to maneuver.

manipulación [ma·ni·pu·la·sjón] *f.* manipulation.

manipular [ma·ni·pu·lár] *v.* to manipulate, handle.

maniquí [ma·ni·kí] *m.* manikin, model, dummy, figure of a person; puppet.

manivela [ma·ni·ƀé·la] *f.* crank.

manjar [maŋ·xár] *m.* dish, food; choice bit of food.

mano [má·no] *f.* (*del cuerpo*) hand; forefoot; (*reloj*) clock hand; (*acabado*) coat of paint or varnish; quire (*25 sheets*) of paper; *Am.* adventure, mishap; *Am.* handful; **— de obra** workmanship; labor; **a —** at hand; by hand; *Am.* **estamos a —** we are even, we are quits; *Am.* **doblar las -s** to give up; **ser —** to be first (*in a game*); to lead (*in a game*); **venir a las -s** to come to blows.

manojo [ma·nó·xo] *m.* handful; bunch.

manopla [ma·nó·pla] *f.* gauntlet; heavy glove; huge hand.

manosear [ma·no·se·ár] *v.* to handle, touch, feel with the hand; *Am.* to fondle, pet, caress.

manotada [ma·no·tá·đa] *f.* slap, blow; sweep of the hand; *Col.* handful, fistful; **manotazo** [ma·no·tá·so] *m.* slap.

manotear [ma·no·te·ár] *v.* to gesticulate; to strike with the hands; *Ríopl.* to embezzle, steal; *Arg.* to snatch away.

mansalva [man·sál·ƀa]: **a —** without danger or risk; treacherously; **matar a —** to kill without warning or without giving a person a chance to defend himself.

mansedumbre [man·se·đúm·bre] *f.* meekness; gentleness.

mansión [man·sjón] *f.* sojourn, stay; abode, dwelling.

manso [mán·so] *adj.* meek; mild, gentle; tame; *Ríopl., Ch.* cultivated (*plant*), civilized (*Indian*); *m.* leading sheep, goat, or ox.

manta [mán·ta] *f.* blanket; large shawl; tossing in a blanket; *Mex., C.A., Ven., Ríopl.* coarse cotton cloth; *Arg.* poncho; *Am.* **— mojada** dull person, dunce; **darle a uno una —** to toss someone in a blanket.

mantear [man·te·ár] *v.* to toss (*someone*) in a blanket.

manteca [man·té·ka] *f.* fat; lard; butter; **— de hojaldre** pastry lard; *Am.* **— de cacao** cocoa butter; *Am.* **— de coco** coconut oil; **mantequera** [man·te·ké·ra] *f.* churn; butter dish; woman who makes or sells butter.

mantecado [man·te·ká·đo] *m.* ice cream.

mantel [man·tél] *m.* tablecloth; altar cloth; *C.A., Mex.* **estar de -es largos** to dine in style.

mantener[45] [man·te·nér] *v. irr.* to maintain; to support; to sustain; to defend; **-se** to continue, remain; to support oneself; **-se firme** to remain firm; **-se quieto** to stay or keep quiet.

mantenimiento [man·te·ni·mjén·to] *m.* maintenance, support; sustenance; livelihood.

mantequilla [man·te·kí·ya] *f.* butter; **mantequillería** [man·te·ki·ye·rí·a] *f. Am.* creamery, dairy (*for making butter*).

mantilla [man·tí·ya] *f.* mantilla (*Spanish veil or scarf for the head*); saddlecloth.

manto [mán·to] *m.* mantle, cloak; cape: large mantilla; mantel, mantelpiece.

mantón [man·tón] *m.* large shawl; — **de Manila** embroidered silk shawl.

manuable [ma·nwá·ble] *adj.* handy, easy to handle.

manual [ma·nwál] *adj.* manual; handy; *m.* manual, handbook.

manubrio [ma·nú·brjo] *m.* crank; handle.

manufacturar [ma·nu·fak·tu·rár] *v.* to manufacture.

manufacturero [ma·nu·fak·tu·ré·ro] *adj.* manufacturing; *m.* manufacturer.

manuscrito [ma·nus·krí·to] *adj.* written by hand; *m.* manuscript.

manutención [ma·nu·ten·sjón] *f.* maintenance; support; conservation.

manzana [man·sá·na] *f.* apple; block of houses; *Ríopl., Ch., Col., Ven.* Adam's apple; **manzano** [man·sá·no] *m.* apple tree.

manzanar [man·sa·nár] *m.* apple orchard.

maña [má·ña] *f.* skill, knack; cunning; **malas -s** bad tricks or habits.

mañana [ma·ñá·na] *f.* morning; *Ríopl.* **media** — mid-morning snack; *adv.* tomorrow, in the near future; **pasado** — day after tomorrow; **muy de** — very early in the morning; *m.* morrow; **mañanitas** [ma·ña·ní·tas] *f. pl. Mex., C.A.* popular song sung early in the morning to celebrate a birthday, saint's day, etc.

mañanero [ma·ña·né·ro] *m.* early riser; *adj.* early rising; **mañanista** [ma·ña·nís·ta] *m. & f. Am.* procrastinator, one who puts things off until tomorrow.

mañero [ma·ñe·ro] *adj.* astute, artful, clever; *Arg., P.R., C.A.* tricky; *Ch.* shy (*animal*); *Ríopl.* indolent, lazy (*child*).

mañoso [ma·ñó·so] *adj.* skillful; clever; (*tramposo*) sly; tricky; deceitful; *Am.* slow, lazy; *Am.* greedy; gluttonous (*child*).

mapa [má·pa] *m.* map, chart.

mapache [ma·pá·če] *m. Ch.* raccoon.

mapurite [ma·pu·rí·te], **mapurito** [ma·pu·rí·to] *m. Col., Ven.* skunk. *See* zorrino, zorrillo.

maqueta [ma·ké·ta] *f.* mock-up.

máquina [má·ki·na] *f.* machine; engine; — **de coser** sewing machine; — **de escribir** typewriter; — **amoladora** grinder; — **de rebanar** slicer.

maquinación [ma·ki·na·sjón] *f.* machination, scheming, plotting; plot, scheme.

maquinador [ma·ki·na·dór] *m.* schemer, plotter.

maquinal [ma·ki·nál] *adj.* mechanical, automatic; **-mente** *adv.* mechanically, automatically, in a mechanical manner.

maquinar [ma·ki·nár] *v.* to plot, scheme.

maquinaria [ma·ki·ná·rja] *f.* machinery; mechanism; mechanics.

maquinista [ma·ki·nís·ta] *m.* engineer, locomotive engineer; machinist; mechanic.

mar [mar] *m. & f.* sea; — **alta** rough sea; — **llena** high tide (*see* pleamar); — **de fondo** swell; **a -es** abundantly; **baja** — low tide; **en alta** — on the high seas; **la** — **de cosas** a lot of things.

maraca [ma·rá·ka] *f. Carib., Col., Ven.* maraca (*rhythm instrument made of a dried gourd filled with seeds or pebbles*).

maraña [ma·rá·ña] *f.* tangle; snarl; thicket; maze; plot, intrigue.

marañón [ma·ra·ñón] *m.* cashew.

maravedí [ma·ra·be·dí] *m.* maravedi (*an old Spanish coin*).

maravilla [ma·ra·bí·ya] *f.* wonder, marvel; marigold; **a las mil -s** wonderfully, perfectly.

maravillar [ma·ra·bi·yár] *v.* to astonish, dazzle; **-se** to wonder, marvel.

maravilloso [ma·ra·bi·yó·so] *adj.* marvellous, wonderful.

marbete [mar·bé·te] *m.* label, stamp; baggage tag or check.

marca [már·ka] *f.* mark, stamp; sign; brand, make; gauge, rule; march, frontier, province; — **de fábrica** trademark; **de** — of excellent quality.

marcapasos [mar·ka·pá·sos] *m.* pacemaker.

marcar[6] [mar·kár] *v.* to mark, stamp, brand; to note, observe.

marcial [mar·sjál] *adj.* martial, warlike; frank, abrupt.

marco [már·ko] *m.* frame; mark (*German coin*); mark (*unit of weight, equal to 8 ounces*).

marcha [már·ča] *f.* march; course, progress; speed; gait; running, functioning; movement of a watch.

marchamo [mar·čá·mo] *m.* customhouse mark; *Am.* tax on each slaughtered animal.

marchante [mar·čán·te] *m.* (*vendedor*) merchant, dealer; (*cliente*) customer, regular client.

marchar [mar·čár] *v.* to march, mark step; to walk; to parade; to run (*said of machinery*); **-se** to go away.

marchitar [mar·či·tár] *v.* to wither; **-se** to wither; to fade; to shrivel up.

marchito [mar·čí·to] *adj.* withered; faded; shriveled up.

marea [ma·ré·a] *f.* tide; *Ríopl., Ch.* sea fog.

mareado [ma·re·á·do] *adj.* seasick; dizzy.

marear [ma·re·ár] *v.* (*navegar*) to navigate, sail; (*fastidiar*) to annoy, upset (*a person*); to make dizzy; **-se** to get seasick, nauseated; dizzy.

mareo [ma·ré·o] *m.* seasickness; nausea; vexation, annoyance.

marfil [mar·fíl] *m.* ivory; *Ven.* fine-toothed comb.

margarita [mar·ga·rí·ta] *f.* marguerite, daisy; pearl.

margen [már·xen] *m.& f.* margin, border; river bank; **dar** — **a** to give an occasion to.

mariachi [ma·rjá·či] *m. Mex.* band and music typical of Guadalajara; *pl.* members of the band.

maricón [ma·ri·kón] *adj.* sissy, effeminate; *m.* sissy.

marido [ma·rí·do] *m.* husband.

marimacho [ma·ri·má·čo] *m.* mannish woman.

marimba [ma·rím·ba] *f.* marimba.

marina [ma·rí·na] *f.* (*costa*) seacoast, shore; (*fuerza naval*) fleet; navy; (*arte u oficio*) seascape; seamanship; — **de guerra** navy; — **mercante** merchant marine.

marinar [ma·ri·nár] *v.* to marinate.

marinero [ma·ri·né·ro] *m.* mariner, seaman, sailor.

marino [ma·rí·no] *adj.* marine; *m.* mariner, seaman, sailor.

mariposa [ma·ri·pó·sa] *f.* butterfly; moth, *Col.* blindman's bluff (*a game*).

mariquita [ma·ri·kí·ta] *f.* sissy; (*cap.*) Molly.

mariscal [ma·ris·kál] *m.* marshal; blacksmith; — **de campo** field marshal.

marisco [ma·rís·ko] *m.* shellfish.

marítimo [ma·rí·ti·mo] *adj.* maritime, marine.

marmita [mar·mí·ta] *f.* kettle, boiler, teakettle; — **doble** double boiler.

mármol [már·mol] *m.* marble.

marmóreo [mar·mó·re·o] *adj.* marble, of marble, like marble.

maroma [ma·ró·ma] *f.* rope; *Am.* somersault; *Am.* acrobatic performance; *Col.* sudden change of political views; **andar en la** — to walk the tightrope; **maromero** [ma·ro·mé·ro] *m. Carib.* acrobat.

marqués [mar·kés] *m.* marquis.

marquesa [mar·ké·sa] *f.* marquise; *Ch.* couch.

MA

marrano [ma·rrá·no] *m.* pig, hog; filthy person.
marrazo [ma·rrá·so] *m. Am.* bayonet, dagger.
marrón [ma·rrón] *adj.* reddish brown; *Spain* brown.
marroquí [ma·rro·kí] *adj.* from Morocco; *pl.*
  marroquíes [ma·rro·kí·es].
marrullero [ma·rru·yé·ro] *adj.* sly, wily.
martes [már·tes] *m.* Tuesday; — **de carnestolendas**
  Shove Tuesday (*Tuesday before Lent*).
martillar [mar·ti·yár] *v.* to hammer, pound.
martillo [mar·tí·yo] *m.* hammer; — **de orejas** claw
  hammer; — **de desbastar** chipping hammer.
martinete [mar·ti·né·te] *m.* pile driver; drop hammer;
  hammer of a piano.
mártir [már·tir] *m. & f.* martyr.
martirio [mar·tí·rjo] *m.* martyrdom; torture, torment.
martirizar[9] [mar·ti·ri·sár] *v.* to martyr; to torture,
  torment.
marxismo [mark·síz·mo] *m.* Marxism.
marzo [már·so] *m.* March.
mas [mas] *conj.* but.
más [mas] *adj.* more; most; *adv.* more; most; plus;
  — **bien** rather; — **de** more than, over; — **que**
  more than, **no . . .** — **que** only; **a** — **de** in
  addition to; **a lo** — at the most; **está de** — it is
  superfluous, unnecessary; *am.* **no** — only; *Am.* **no**
  quiero — **nada** (*instead of* **no quiero nada** —) I
  don't want anything more.
masa [má·sa] *f.* (*volumen*) mass; volume; (*pueblo*)
  crowd, the masses; (*pasta*) dough, paste; mortar;
  — **coral** glee club, choral society; **agarrarle a**
  uno con las manos en la — to catch someone in
  the act; **masilla** *f.* putty.
masaje [ma·sá·xe] *m.* massage.
mascada [mas·ká·da] *f.* chewing; *Am.* mouthful;
  Ríopl. chew or quid of tobacco; *Am.* reprimand,
  scolding; *Mex.* silk handkerchief, scarf.
mascar[6] [mas·kár] *v.* to chew.
máscara [más·ka·ra] *f.* mask; **-s** masquerade; *m. & f.*
  masquerader; **mascarada** [mas·ka·rá·da] *f.*
  masquerade.
masculino [mas·ku·lí·no] *adj.* masculine.
mascullar [mas·ku·yár] *v.* to mumble; to munch.
masón [ma·són] *m.* mason, freemason; **masonería**
  [ma·so·ne·rí·a] *f.* masonry, freemasonry.
masticar[6] [mas·ti·kár] *v.* to chew.
mástico [más·ti·ko] *m.* mastic; — **para tubos** pipe
  "dope".
mástil [más·til] *m.* mast; post.
mastín [mas·tín] *m.* mastiff.
mastuerzo [mas·twér·so] *m.* (*flor*) nasturtium; (*tonto*)
  simpleton, fool.
mata [má·ta] *f.* shrub, plant, bush; grove; clump of
  trees; *Ven., Col.* thicket, jungle; — **de pelo** head
  of hair.
matadero [ma·ta·dé·ro] *m.* slaughterhouse; hard work.
matador [ma·ta·dór] *m.* killer, murderer; bullfighter
  who kills the bull.
matamoros [ma·ta·mó·ros] *m.* bully; boastful person.
matamoscas [ma·ta·mós·kas] *m.* fly swatter.
matanza [ma·tán·sa] *f.* massacre, butchery; slaughter
  of livestock; *Mex.* slaughterhouse.
matar [ma·tár] *v.* to kill; to murder; **-se** to commit
  suicide; to overwork; **-se con alguien** to fight with
  somebody.
matasanos [ma·ta·sá·nos] *m.* quack, quack doctor.
matasellos [ma·ta·sé·yos] *m.* canceller (*of stamps*).
mate [má·te] *m.* checkmate (*winning move in chess*);
  Ríopl., Ch. Paraguayan tea (*used also in Argentina*
  and Uruguay); *Andes, Col.* teapot (*for* **mate**), any
  small pot; *Am.* bald head; *adj.* unpolished, dull
  (*surface*).

matear [ma·te·ár] *v.* to plant seeds or shoots; to hunt
  among the bushes; *Ríopl., Ch.* to drink **mate;** *Am.*
  to checkmate (*make the winning move in chess*).
matemática [ma·te·má·ti·ka] *f. pl.* mathematics.
matemático [ma·te·má·ti·ko] *adj.* mathematical; *m.*
  mathematician.
materia [ma·té·rja] *f.* matter; material; school subject;
  pus; — **prima** (*or* **primera** —) raw material.
material [ma·te·rjál] *adj.* material; rude, coarse; *m.*
  ingredient; material; equipment; *Ven.* **de** — made
  of adobe; — **que se trabaja** work at hand.
maternal [ma·ter·nál] *adj.* maternal.
maternidad [ma·ter·ni·dád] *f.* maternity, motherhood.
materno [ma·tér·no] *adj.* maternal.
matinal [ma·ti·nál] *adj.* morning, of the morning.
matiné [ma·ti·né] *m. Am.* matinée.
matiz [ma·tís] *m.* tint, shade, color, hue; shading.
matizar[9] [ma·ti·sár] *v.* to blend (*colors*); to tint; to
  shade, tone down.
matón [ma·tón] *m.* bully.
matorral [ma·to·rrál] *m.* thicket.
matoso [ma·tó·so] *adj.* bushy; weedy; full of weeds.
matrero [ma·tré·ro] *adj.* astute, shrewd; cunning, sly;
  m. Col. trickster, swindler; *Ríopl.* bandit, outlaw,
  cattle thief.
matrícula [ma·trí·ku·la] *f.* register, list; matriculation;
  registration; certificate of registration.
matricular [ma·tri·ku·lár] *v.* to matriculate, enroll,
  register.
matrimonio [ma·tri·mó·njo] *m.* matrimony, marriage;
  married couple.
matriz [ma·trís] *f.* matrix, mold, form; womb; screw
  nut; *adj.* main, principal, first; **casa** — main office
  (*of a company*); — **estencil** stencil master.
matungo [ma·tún·go] *m. Ríopl.* nag, old worn-out
  horse.
matutino [ma·tu·tí·no] *adj.* morning, of the morning.
maula [máw·la] *m.* a good-for-nothing.
maullar [maw·yár] *v.* to mew.
maullido, [maw·yí·do] **maúllo** [ma·ú·yo] *m.* mew.
máxima [mák·si·ma] *f.* maxim, rule; proverb.
máxime [mák·si·me] *adj.* principally, especially.
máximo [mák·si·mo] *adj. & m.* maximum.
maya [má·ya] *f.* daisy; May queen; *m. & f.* Maya,
  Mayan Indian; *m.* Mayan language.
mayo [má·yo] *m.* May; Maypole; *Am.* Mayo Indian
  (*from Sonora, Mexico*); *Am.* language of the Mayo
  Indian.
mayonesa [ma·yo·né·sa] *f.* mayonnaise; dish served
  with mayonnaise.
mayor [ma·yór] *adj.* greater; larger; older; greatest;
  largest; oldest; main; major; high (*altar, mass*); *m.*
  major; chief; **-es** elders; ancestors; — **de edad** of
  age; **por** — (*or* **al por** —) wholesale; *f.* major
  premise (*of a syllogism*).
mayoral [ma·yo·rál] *m.* head shepherd; stagecoach
  driver; foreman; overseer; boss.
mayorazgo [ma·yo·ráz·go] *m.* primogeniture (*right of*
  inheritance by the first-born); first-born son and
  heir; family estate left to the eldest son.
mayordomo [ma·yor·dó·mo] *m.* majordomo, steward,
  butler; manager of an estate.
mayorear [ma·yo·re·ár] *v. Mex., Arg., Ch.* to
  wholesale, sell at wholesale.
mayoreo [ma·yo·ré·o] *m. Mex., Arg., Ch.* wholesale.
mayoría [ma·yo·rí·a] *f.* majority.
mayorista [ma·yo·rís·ta] *m. Am.* wholesale dealer.
maza [má·sa] *f.* mace (*weapon, staff*); — **química**
  chemical mace.
mazmorra [maz·mó·rra] *f.* dungeon.
mazo [má·so] *m.* mallet; sledgehammer; bunch,

handful.

mazorca [ma·sór·ka] *f.* ear of corn; *Ríopl.* tyrannical government; *Ch., Arg.* cruel torture (*imposed by tyrants*).

me [me] *obj. pron.* me; to me; for me; myself.

mear [me·ár] *v.* to urinate.

mecánico [me·ká·ni·ko] *adj.* mechanical; *m.* mechanic, machinist, repairman; driver, chauffeur.

mecanismo [me·ka·níz·mo] *m.* mechanism.

mecanografía [me·ka·no·ǥra·fí·a] *f.* stenography, typewriting.

mecanógrafo [me·ka·nó·ǥra·fo] *m.* stenographer, typist.

mecate [me·ká·te] *m. Mex., C.A., Col., Ven.* rope, cord.

mecedor [me·se·dór] *m.* swing; *adj.* swinging, rocking.

mecedora [me·se·dó·ra] *f.* rocking chair.

mecer[10] [me·sér] *v.* to swing, rock, sway; to shake.

mecha [mé·ča] *f.* wick; lock of hair; fuse; strip of salt pork or bacon (*for larding meat*); *Ven.* tip of a whip; *Am.* scare, fright; *Andes, Col.* fib; *Andes, Col.* jest, joke; *Col.* trifle, worthless thing.

mechar [me·čár] *v.* to lard (*meat or fowl*).

mechero [me·čé·ro] *m.* (*canutillo*) lamp burner; gas jet; candlestick socket; (*encendedor*) pocket lighter; large wick; *Col.* disheveled hair; *Am.* joker, jester.

mechón [me·čón] *m.* large wick; large lock of hair.

medalla [me·ða·ya] *f.* medal.

médano [mé·ða·no] *m.* dune, sand hill, sand bank; *Ríopl., Carib.* sandy marshland.

media [mé·ðja] *f.* stocking; *Col., Ríopl., Ven.* — **corta** (*or* — —) sock.

mediación [me·ðja·sjón] *f.* mediation.

mediador [me·ðja·dór] *m.* mediator.

mediados: [me·ðjá·ðos] **a** — **de** about the middle of.

medianero [me·ðja·né·ro] *m.* mediator; go-between; *adj.* mediating; intermediate; **pared medianera** partition wall.

medianía [me·ðja·ní·a] *f.* mediocrity; average; middle ground; moderate circumstances; moderation; *Col.* partition wall.

mediano [me·ðjá·no] *adj.* medium; moderate; middle-sized; average; mediocre.

medianoche [me·ðja·nó·če] *f.* midnight.

mediante [me·ðján·te] *adj.* intervening; **Dios** — God willing; *prep.* by means of, through, with the help of.

mediar [me·ðjár] *v.* to mediate, intervene; to intercede; to arrive at, or be in, the middle.

medible [me·ðí·ble] *adj.* measurable.

medicamento [me·ði·ka·mén·to] *m.* medicament, medicine.

medicastro [me·ði·kás·tro] *m.* quack, quack doctor.

medicina [me·ði·sí·na] *f.* medicine.

medicinar [me·ði·si·nár] *v.* to doctor, treat, prescribe medicine for; **-se** to take medicine.

medición [me·ði·sjón] *f.* measurement; measuring.

médico [mé·ði·ko] *m.* doctor, physician; *adj.* medical.

medida [me·ðí·ða] *f.* measure; measurement; gauge, rule; — **para áridos** dry measure; **a** — **del deseo** according to one's desire; **a** — **que** as, in proportion as; at the same time as.

medidor [me·ði·dór] *m. Am.* meter gauge; — **de la humedad** wet tube.

medio [mé·ðjo] *adj.* half; middle; intermediate; medium, average; **media noche** midnight; **hacer una cosa a medias** to do something halfway; **ir a medias** to go halves; *adv.* half, not completely; *m.* middle; means, way; medium; environment; **-s** means, resources; **meterse de por** — to intervene,

meddle in a dispute.

mediocre [me·ðjó·kre] *adj.* mediocre; **mediocridad** [me·ðjo·kri·ðáð] *f.* mediocrity.

mediodía [me·ðjo·ðí·a] *m.* midday, noon; south.

medioeval [me·ðjo·e·bál], **medieval** [me·ðje·bál] *adj.* medieval.

medir[5] [me·ðír] *v. irr.* to measure; to scan (*verses*); *Col., Ven., Mex.* — **las calles** to walk the streets, be out of a job; **-se** to measure one's words or actions; *Mex., C.A., Ven., Col., Ríopl.* **-se con otro** to try one's strength or ability against another; to fight with another.

meditación [me·ði·ta·sjón] *f.* meditation.

meditar [me·ði·tár] *v.* to meditate; to muse.

medrar [me·ðrár] *v.* to flourish, thrive; to prosper.

medroso [me·ðró·so] *adj.* timid, faint-hearted; fearful, dreadful.

médula [mé·ðu·la] *f.* marrow; pith; — **oblongada** medulla oblongata (*the posterior part of the brain tapering off into the spinal cord*).

megáfono [me·ǥá·fo·no] *m.* megaphone.

megatón [me·ǥa·tón] *m.* megaton.

mejicano [me·xi·ká·no] *adj.* Mexican; *m.* Mexican; the Aztec language; inhabitant of Mexico City. *Also* **mexicano.**

mejilla [me·xí·ya] *f.* cheek.

mejor [me·xór] *adj.* better; **el** — the best; *adv.* better; **a lo** — suddenly, unexpectedly; **tanto** — so much the better.

mejora [me·xó·ra] *f.* betterment; improvement.

mejoramiento [me·xo·ra·mjén·to] *m.* improvement.

mejorana [me·xo·rá·na] *f.* sweet marjoram.

mejorar [me·xo·rár] *v.* to better, improve; to get better, recover; **-se** to get better, recover.

mejoría [me·xo·rí·a] *f.* betterment, improvement; superiority.

melado [me·lá·ðo] *adj.* honey-colored; *m.* sugar-cane syrup; honey cake.

melancolía [me·laŋ·ko·lí·a] *f.* melancholy, gloom.

melancólico [me·laŋ·kó·li·ko] *adj.* melancholy, gloomy.

melaza [me·lá·sa] *f.* molasses.

melena [me·lé·na] *f.* mane.

melindre [me·lín·dre] *m.* (*acto*) affectation; affected act or gesture; whim; (*comestible*) fritter, marzipan (*sweetmeat made of almond paste*).

melindroso [me·lin·dró·so] *adj.* affected; too particular, finicky, fussy.

melocotón [me·lo·ko·tón] *m.* peach; **melocotonero** [me·lo·ko·to·ne·ro] *m.* peach tree.

melodía [me·lo·ðí·a] *f.* melody; **melodioso** [me·lo·ðjó·so] *adj.* melodious.

melón [me·lón] *m.* melon; cantaloupe; musk-melon; melon vine.

melosidad [me·lo·si·ðáð] *f.* sweetness; softness; gentleness.

meloso [me·ló·so] *adj.* honeyed; soft, sweet; *m. Am.* honey-voiced person; *Ch.* over-affectionate person.

mella [mé·ya] *f.* nick; dent; **hacer** — to make a dent or impression; to cause pain, worry, or suffering.

mellar [me·yár] *v.* to notch, to nick, to dent; to impair, damage.

mellizo [me·yí·so] *adj. & m.* twin.

membrete [mem·bré·te] *m.* heading; letterhead; memorandum.

membrillo [mem·brí·yo] *m.* quince (*tree and its fruit*).

membrudo [mem·brú·ðo] *adj.* sinewy, robust, strong, muscular.

memorable [me·mo·rá·ble] *adj.* memorable, notable.

memorándum [me·mo·rán·dun] *m.* memorandum,

MA

note; memorandum book, notebook.

memoria [me·mó·rja] *f.* memory; remembrance; reminiscence; memoir, note, account; memorandum; (*computadora*) memory; — **residente** internal memory; — **de acceso aleatorio** random access memory (RAM); — **de sólo lectura** read only memory (ROM); **de** — by heart; **hacer** — to remember, recollect; — **de gallo** poor memory; **-s** regards; memoirs.

memorial [me·mo·rjál] *m.* memorandum book; memorial, brief, petition.

mención [men·sjón] *f.* mention.

mencionar [men·sjo·nár] *v.* to mention.

mendigar[7] [men·di·gár] *v.* to beg; to ask alms.

mendigo [men·dí·go] *m.* beggar.

mendrugo [men·drú·go] *m.* crumb of bread.

menear [me·ne·ár] *v.* to move, shake, stir; to wiggle, to wag; **-se** to hustle about; to wag; to wiggle.

meneo [me·né·o] *m.* shaking, swaying, wagging, wiggle, wiggling.

menester [me·nes·tér] *m.* need; job, occupation; **-es** bodily needs; implements, tools; tasks, chores; **ser** — to be necessary.

menesteroso [me·nes·te·ró·so] *adj.* needy, in want.

mengua [méŋ·gwa] *f.* diminution, decrease; waning; poverty, want; discredit.

menguante [meŋ·gwán·te] *adj.* waning, diminishing, declining.

menguar[8] [meŋ·gwár] *v.* to diminish, decrease; to wane.

menjurje [meŋ·xúr·xe] *m.* stuff, mixture.

menor [me·nór] *adj.* smaller, lesser, younger; smallest, least, youngest; minor; *m. & f.* — **de edad** minor; *m.* minor (*music*); Minorite, Franciscan; *f.* minor premise (*of a syllogism*); **por** — (**al por** —) at retail; in small quantities.

menoría [me·no·rí·a] = **minoría.**

menos [mé·nos] *adv.* less; least; except; *adj. & pron.* less, least; *m.* minus; — **de** (*or* — **que**) less than; **a lo** — (**al** —, *or* **por lo** —) at least; **a** — **que** unless; **echar de** — to miss, feel or notice the absence of; **no puede** — **de hacerlo** he cannot help doing it; **venir a** — to decline; to become weak or poor.

menoscabar [me·nos·ka·bár] *v.* to diminish, lessen; to impair, damage; — **la honra de** to undermine the reputation of.

menoscabo [me·nos·ká·bo] *m.* impairment; damage; diminution, lessening.

menospreciar [me·nos·pre·sjár] *v.* to despise, scorn; to underestimate.

menosprecio [me·nos·pré·sjo] *m.* scorn, contempt; underestimation.

mensaje [men·sá·xe] *m.* message.

mensajero [men·sa·xé·ro] *m.* messenger.

menstruo [méns·trwo] *m.* menstruation.

mensual [men·swál] *adj.* monthly.

mensualidad [men·swa·li·dád] *f.* monthly allowance; monthly payment.

mensurable [men·su·rá·ble] *adj.* measurable.

menta [mén·ta] *f.* mint; peppermint; *Ríopl.* rumor, hearsay; *Ríopl., Andes* **por -s** by hearsay; *Ríopl.* **persona de** — famous person.

mentado [men·tá·do] *adj.* famous; *p.p.* mentioned.

mental [men·tál] *adj.* mental.

mentalidad [men·ta·li·dád] *f.* mentality.

mentar[1] [men·tár] *v. irr.* to mention; to call, name.

mente [mén·te] *f.* mind; intellect.

mentecato [men·te·ká·to] *adj.* foolish, simple; *m.* fool.

mentir[3] [men·tír] *v. irr.* to lie, tell lies.

mentira [men·tí·ra] *f.* lie, falsehood, fib; white spot on the fingernails.

mentiroso [men·ti·ró·so] *adj.* lying; deceptive, false; *m.* liar, fibber; **mentirosillo** *m.* little fibber.

mentís [men·tís]: **dar un** — to give the lie (to).

mentón [men·tón] *m.* chin.

menú [me·nú] *m.* menu; (*computadora*) menu.

menudear [me·nu·de·ár] *v.* to occur frequently; to repeat over and over; to fall incessantly (*as rain, stones, projectiles, etc.*); to tell in detail; *Mex., C.A., Col., Ven.* to retail, sell at retail; *Arg.* to meet together often.

menudeo [me·nu·dé·o] *m.* retail; **vender al** — to retail, sell at retail.

menudo [me·nú·do] *adj.* minute, small; insignificant; exact, detailed; **dinero** — change; **a** — often; **por** — in detail; retail; *m.* entrails, "innards"; (*cambio*) change, small coins.

meñique [me·ñí·ke] *adj.* tiny, wee; **dedo** — little finger.

meollo [me·ó·yo] *m.* marrow; pith; kernel; substance; brain; brains.

meple [mé·ple] *m.* *Ríopl.* maple.

merca [mér·ka] *f.* purchase.

mercachifle [mer·ka·čí·fle] *m.* peddler, vendor; cheap merchant; cheap fellow.

mercadear [mer·ka·de·ár] *v.* to trade.

mercader [mer·ka·dér] *m.* trader, merchant.

mercadería [mer·ka·de·rí·a] *f.* merchandise; trade.

mercado [mer·ká·do] *m.* market; mart.

mercadotecnia [mer·ka·do·ték·nja] *f.* marketing management.

mercancía [mer·kan·sí·a] *f.* merchandise; goods.

mercantil [mer·kan·tíl] *adj.* mercantile, commercial.

mercar[6] [mer·kár] *v.* to purchase, buy.

merced [mer·séd] *f.* favor; present, gift; mercy; **Vuestra Merced** Your Honor; **a** — **de** at the mercy of; at the expense of.

mercería [mer·se·rí·a] *f.* notions (*pins, buttons, etc.*); notions store; *Ríopl., P.R.* drygoods store.

mercurio [mer·kú·rjo] *m.* mercury; quicksilver.

merecedor [me·re·se·dór] *adj.* worthy, deserving.

merecer[13] [me·re·sér] *v. irr.* to deserve.

merecido [me·re·sí·do] *adj. & p.p.* deserved; *m.* deserved punishment.

merecimiento [me·re·si·mjén·to] *m.* merit.

merendar[1] [me·ren·dár] *v. irr.* to have an afternoon snack or refreshment; *Carib., Ven.* **-se uno a alguien** to fleece or skin someone (*in a game or business deal*); to kill someone.

merendero [me·ren·dé·ro] *m.* lunchroom.

meridiano [me·ri·djá·no] *adj. & m.* meridian.

meridional [me·ri·djo·nál] *adj.* southern; *m.* southerner.

merienda [me·rjén·da] *f.* light afternoon meal; afternoon refreshments.

mérito [mé·ri·to] *m.* merit; **de** — notable.

merito [me·rí·to] *dim. of* **mero.**

meritorio [me·ri·tó·rjo] *adj.* meritorious, worthy, deserving; *m.* employee without salary (*learning trade or profession*).

merluza [mer·lú·sa] *f.* hake (*species of codfish*); drunken state.

merma [mér·ma] *f.* reduction, decrease.

mermar [mer·már] *v.* to dwindle; to decrease, reduce.

mermelada [mer·me·lá·da] *f.* marmalade.

mero [mé·ro] *adj.* mere, pure; *Mex., C.A.* exact, real; **la mera verdad** the real truth; *adv. Mex., C.A.* very, very same, exactly; *Mex., C.A.* soon; *Col.* only; *Mex., C.A.* **una mera de las tres** only

one of the three; *Mex., C.A.* **ya** — (*or* **merito**) very soon; *Mex., C.A.* **allí** — (*or* **merito**) right there; *m.* species of perch; *Ch.* species of thrush.
merodear [me·ro·de·ár] *v.* to rove in search of plunder.
mes [mes] *m.* month.
mesa [mé·sa] *f.* table; executive board; staircase landing; mesa, plateau; **levantar la** — to clear the table; **poner la** — to set the table; *Col., Carib., C.A., Mex.* **quitar la** — to clear the table.
mesada [me·sá·da] *f.* monthly salary or allowance.
mesarse [me·sár·se] *v.* to tear (*one's hair or beard*).
mesero [me·sé·ro] *m. Mex., C.A., Ven., Col.* waiter.
meseta [me·sé·ta] *f.* plateau; staircase landing.
mesón [me·són] *m.* inn.
mesonero [me·so·né·ro] *m.* innkeeper.
mestizo [mes·tí·so] *adj.* half-breed; hybrid; **perro** — mongrel dog; *m.* mestizo, half-breed.
mesura [me·sú·ra] *f.* moderation; composure; dignity; politeness.
mesurado [me·su·rá·do] *adj.* moderate, temperate; dignified.
meta [mé·ta] *f.* goal; objective.
metabolismo [me·ta·bo·líz·mo] *m.* metabolism.
metafísica [me·ta·fí·si·ka] *f.* metaphysics.
metáfora [me·tá·fo·ra] *f.* metaphor.
metafórico [me·ta·fó·ri·ko] *adj.* metaphorical.
metal [me·tál] *m.* metal; — **base** base metal; — **no ferroso** non-ferrous metal.
metálico [me·tá·li·ko] *adj.* metallic, metal; *m.* specie, coined money; cash in coin.
metalurgia [me·ta·lúr·xja] *f.* metallurgy.
metamorfosis [me·ta·mor·fó·sis] *f.* metamorphosis.
metate [me·tá·te] *m. Mex.* flat stone (*used for grinding corn, etc.*).
metátesis [me·tá·te·sis] *f.* metathesis.
meteorito [me·te·o·rí·to] *m.* meteorite.
meteoro [me·te·ó·ro] *m.* meteor.
meteorología [me·te·o·ro·lo·xí·a] *f.* meteorology; **meteorológico** [me·te·o·ro·ló·xi·ko] *adj.* meteorological; **oficina meteorológica** weather bureau.
meter [me·tér] *v.* to put (in); to get (in); to insert; to smuggle; to make (*noise, trouble, etc.*); to cause (*fear*); *Carib.* to strike (*a blow*); *Ríopl., Carib.* **-le** to hurry up; **-se** to meddle, interfere; to plunge (into); **-se monja** (*Am.* **-se de monja**) to become a nun; also **-se a monja; -se con** to pick a quarrel with.
metódico [me·tó·di·ko] *adj.* methodical.
método [mé·to·do] *m.* method.
metralleta [me·tra·yé·ta] *f.* hand machine gun.
métrico [mé·tri·ko] *adj.* metric.
metro [mé·tro] *m.* meter; subway; — **plegadizo** folding rule.
metrópoli [me·tró·po·li] *f.* metropolis.
metropolitano [me·tro·po·li·tá·no] *adj.* metropolitan; *m.* (*metro*) the subway.
mexicano [me·xi·ká·no] = **mejicano** (*pronounced identically*).
mezcal [mes·kál] *m. Mex.* mescal (*a species of maguey and an alcoholic beverage made from it*).
mezcla [més·kla] *f.* mixture; mortar; mixed cloth; **mezclilla** [mes·klí·ya] *f.* mixed cloth (*generally black and white*); tweed.
mezclar [mes·klár] *v.* to mix, blend; **-se** to mix, mingle; to meddle.
mezcolanza [mes·ko·lán·sa] *f.* jumble, mess, mixture.
mezquindad [mes·ki·ni·dád] *f.* meanness; stinginess; dire poverty.
mezquino [mes·kí·no] *adj.* poor, needy; mean, stingy;

meager; small, tiny; *m. Col., Mex.* wart (*usually on a finger*).
mezquita [mes·kí·ta] *f.* mosque.
mi [mi] *adj.* my.
mí [mi] *pers. pron* (*used after prep.*) me, myself.
miaja [mjá·xa] = **migaja.**
miau [mjáw] *m.* mew.
mico [mí·ko] *m.* long-tailed monkey; *C.A.* jack (*for lifting heavy objects*).
micro [mí·kro] *m. Peru, Ch.* bus.
microbio [mi·kró·bjo] *m.* microbe.
microbús [mi·kro·bús] *m.* microbus.
microfilm [mi·kro·fíln] *m.* microfilm.
micrófono [mi·kró·fo·no] *m.* microphone.
microprocesador [mi·kro·pro·se·sa·dór] *m.* (*computadora*) microprocessor.
microscopio [mi·kros·kó·pjo] *m.* microscope; — **electrónico** electron microscope; **microscópico** [mi·kro·skó·pi·ko] *adj.* microscopic.
miedo [mjé·do] *m.* fear; dread; **tener** — to be afraid.
miedoso [mje·dó·so] *adj.* afraid, fearful, timid.
miel [mjel] *f.* honey; molasses.
mielga [mjél·ga] *f.* plot of ground for planting.
miembro [mjém·bro] *m.* member; limb.
mientes [mjén·tes] *f. pl.* thought, mind; **parar — en** to consider, reflect on; **traer a las** — to recall; **venírsele a uno a las** — to occur to one, come to one's mind.
mientras [mjén·tras] *conj.* while; — **que** while; — **tanto** in the meantime, meanwhile; — **más . . . — menos . . .** the more . . . the less . . .
miércoles [mjér·ko·les] *m.* Wednesday.
mies [mjes] *f.* ripe grain; harvest; **-es** fields of grain.
miga [mí·ga] *f.* crumb; soft part of bread; substance; **-s** crumbs; fried crumbs of bread; **hacer buenas -s** (*or* **malas -s**) **con** to get along well (*or* badly) with.
migaja [mi·gá·xa] *f.* crumb; bit, fragment, small particle.
migración [mi·gra·sjón] *f.* migration.
mil [mil] *num.* thousand.
milagro [mi·lá·gro] *m.* miracle; wonder.
milagroso [mi·la·gró·so] *adj.* miraculous.
milicia [mi·lí·sja] *f.* militia; military science; military profession.
miligramo [mi·li·grá·mo] *m.* milligram.
milímetro [mi·lí·me·tro] *m.* millimeter.
militar [mi·li·tár] *adj.* military; *m.* soldier, military man; *v.* to serve in the army; to militate, fight (against).
milpa [míl·pa] *f. Mex., C.A.* cornfield.
milla [mí·ya] *f.* mile.
millar [mi·yár] *m.* thousand; **-es** thousands, a great number.
millón [mi·yón] *m.* million; **millonario** [mi·yo·ná·rjo] *adj. & m.* millionaire; **millonésimo** [mi·yo·né·si·mo] *adj. & m.* millionth.
mimar [mi·már] *v.* to pamper, spoil, humor; to pet.
mimbre [mím·bre] *m.* wicker; **mimbrera** [mim·bré·ra] *f.* willow.
mímico [mí·mi·ko] *adj.* mimic.
mimo [mí·mo] *m.* pampering; caress; coaxing.
mimoso [mi·mó·so] *adj.* tender, sensitive; delicate; finicky, fussy.
mina [mí·na] *f.* mine; source; fortune.
minar [mi·nár] *v.* to mine; to undermine; to sow with explosive mines.
mineral [mi·ne·rál] *m.* mineral; mine; ore; wealth, fortune; *adj.* mineral.
minería [mi·ne·rí·a] *f.* mining; miners.
minero [mi·né·ro] *m.* miner; wealth, fortune; source;

adj. mining; **compañía minera** mining company.

miniatura [mi·nja·tú·ra] *f.* miniature.

minifalda [mi·ni·fál·da] *f.* miniskirt.

minifundio [mi·ni·fún·djo] *m.* small farm (*privately owned*).

mínimo [mí·ni·mo] *adj.* least, smallest; *m.* minimum.

minino [mi·ní·no] *m.* kitten, kitty, pussy.

ministerio [mi·nis·té·rjo] *m.* ministry; administration, ministering; portfolio (*office of a cabinet member*); minister's office.

ministrar [mi·nis·trár] *v.* to minister; to give (*money, aid, etc.*).

ministro [mi·nís·tro] *m.* minister; cabinet member; office of justice.

minoría [mi·no·rí·a] *f.* minority.

minoridad [mi·no·ri·dáđ] *f.* minority (*in age*).

minucioso [mi·nu·sjó·so] *adj.* minute, detailed; scrupulous.

minúsculo [mi·nús·ku·lo] *adj.* small; **letra minúscula** small letter.

minuta [mi·nú·ta] *f.* minutes; memorandum; first draft (*of a contract, deed, etc.*); memorandum list; lawyer's bill; *Carib.* **a la —** breaded and fried (*said of meat or fish*).

minuto [mi·nú·to] *m.* minute; **minutero** [mi·nu·té·ro] *m.* minute hand.

mío [mí·o] *poss. adj.* my, of mine; *poss. pron.* mine; *Ríopl., Ch.* **detrás —** behind me.

miope [mjó·pe] *adj.* shortsighted, nearsighted; *m. & f.* nearsighted person.

miopía [mjo·pí·a] *f.* near-sightedness.

mira [mí·ra] *f.* (*de puntería*) gun sight; guiding point; (*intención*) intention, design; outlook; **estar a la — de** to be on the lookout for; to be on the alert for; **poner la — en** to fix one's eyes on; to aim at.

mirada [mi·rá·đa] *f.* glance, gaze, look.

mirador [mi·ra·đór] *m.* mirador, enclosed balcony (*commanding an extensive view*); watchtower; lookout site; onlooker, spectator; *Ríopl.* penthouse.

miramiento [mi·ra·mjén·to] *m.* consideration, respect, regard; reverence; circumspection, prudence.

mirar [mi·rár] *v.* to look; to glance; to behold; to see; **— por alguien** to take care of someone; **¡mira (tú)!** look!

miríada [mi·rjá·đa] *f.* myriad, multitude, great number.

miriñaque [mi·ri·ñá·ke] *m.* crinoline.

mirlo [mír·lo] *m.* blackbird.

mirón [mi·rón] *m.* bystander, onlooker, spectator; *adj.* curious.

mirra [mí·rra] *f.* myrrh.

mirto [mír·to] *m.* myrtle.

misa [mí·sa] *f.* mass; **— del gallo** midnight mass.

misántropo [mi·sán·tro·po] *m.* misanthrope.

misceláneo [mi·se·lá·ne·o] *adj.* miscellaneous.

miserable [mi·se·rá·ble] *adj.* miserable, unhappy; forlorn; miserly, stingy; mean.

miseria [mi·sé·rja] *f.* misery; poverty; stinginess; bit, trifle.

misericordia [mi·se·ri·kór·đja] *f.* mercy, compassion, pity.

misericordioso [mi·se·ri·kor·đjó·so] *adj.* merciful, compassionate.

mísero [mí·se·ro] *adj.* miserable, unhappy; forlorn; stingy.

misi [mí·si] *interj.* word used to call cats.

misión [mi·sjón] *f.* mission.

misionero [mi·sjo·né·ro] *m.* missionary.

mismo [míz·mo] *adj.* same; self, very; **ahora —** right away.

misterio [mis·té·rjo] *m.* mystery; secret.

misterioso [mis·te·rjó·so] *adj.* mysterious.

místico [mís·ti·ko] *adj.* mystical, mystic; *m.* mystic.

mitad [mi·táđ] *f.* half; middle.

mitigar[7] [mi·ti· gár] *v.* to mitigate, soften, soothe.

mitin [mí·tin] *m.* meeting.

mito [mí·to] *m.* myth; **mitología** [mi·to·lo·xí·a] *f.* mythology.

mitra [mí·tra] *f.* bishop's miter.

mixto [mís·to] *adj.* mixed; half-breed; *m.* composite; match; explosive compound.

mobiliario [mo·bi·ljá·rjo] *m.* furniture.

moblaje [mo·blá·xe] = **mueblaje.**

mocasín [mo·ka·sín] *m.* (*zapatilla y culebra*) moccasin.

mocedad [mo·se·đáđ] *f.* youth; youthfulness; youthful prank.

mocetón [mo·se·tón] *m.* tall, robust lad.

moción [mo·sjón] *f.* motion.

moco [mó·ko] *m.* mucus; snot.

mocoso [mo·kó·so] *adj.* sniffling; *m.* brat, scamp; sniffling boy.

mochar [mo·čár] *v. Am.* to cut off, chop off, cut, trim (*see* **desmochar**); *Arg.* to snitch, pilfer; *Col.* to depose, dismiss, put out of a job.

mochila [mo·čí·la] *f.* knapsack; soldier's kit.

mocho [mó·čo] *adj.* cut off; cropped, shorn; *Am.* maimed, mutilated; *Mex.* reactionary, conservative; *m.* butt of a firearm; *Col., Ven.* nag; *Carib.* cigar butt.

moda [mó·đa] *f.* mode, custom, style, fashion; **de —** fashionable.

modelar [mo·đe·lár] *v.* to model.

modelo [mo·đé·lo] *m.* model, copy, pattern; *m. & f.* life model.

modem m. (*computadora*) modem.

moderación [mo·đe·ra·sjón] *f.* moderation.

moderado [mo·đe·rá·đo] *adj.* moderate; conservative.

moderar [mo·đe·rár] *v.* to moderate, temper; to regulate; to restrain.

moderno [mo·đér·no] *adj.* modern.

modestia [mo·đés·tja] *f.* modesty.

modesto [mo·đés·to] *adj.* modest.

módico [mó·đi·ko] *adj.* moderate, reasonable (*price*).

modificación [mo·đi·fi·ka·sjón] *f.* modification.

modificar[6] [mo·đi·fi·kár] *v.* to modify.

modismo [mo·đíz·mo] *m.* idiom.

modista [mo·đís·ta] *f.* dressmaker; milliner.

modo [mó·đo] *m.* mode, manner, way; mood (*grammar*); (*computadora*) mode; **— directo** direct mode; **— indirecto** indirect mode; **a** (*or* **al**) **— de** like, in the manner of; **de — que** so that; and so; **de todos -s** at any rate, anyway.

modorra [mo·đó·rra] *f.* drowsiness; gid (*a disease of sheep*).

modular [mo·đu·lár] *v.* to modulate, tone down.

mofa [mó·fa] *f.* scoff, jeer, taunt; mockery.

mofar [mo·fár] *v.* to mock, scoff, jeer; **-se de** to make fun of, scoff at.

mofeta [mo·fé·ta] *f. S.A.* skunk.

moflete [mo·flé·te] *m.* fat cheek; **mofletudo** [mo·fle·tú·đo] *adj.* fat-cheeked.

mohín [mo·ín] *m.* grimace; wry face.

mohíno [mo·í·no] *adj.* moody, discontented, sad, melancholy; black (*referring to a horse, cow, or bull*).

moho [mó·o] *m.* rust; mold.

mohoso [mo·ó·so] *adj.* musty, moldy; rusty.

mojada [mo·xá·đa] *f.* drench, drenching, wetting.

mojado [mo·xá·đo] *adj.* wet, damp, moist; *p.p. of* **mojar.**

mojadura [mo·xa·đú·ra] *f.* wetting, dampening,

drenching.

mojar [mo·xár] *v.* to dampen, wet, moisten; *Ríopl., Ch.* to accompany (*a song*); *P.R.* to bribe; *Ríopl., Carib., Mex.* to celebrate by drinking; *Am.* **mojársele a uno los papeles** to get things mixed up.

mojicón [mo·xi·kón] *m.* punch, blow; muffin, bun.

mojigatería [mo·xi·ga·te·rí·a] *f.* prudery; false humility; affected piety.

mojigato [mo·xi·gá·to] *adj.* prudish; affectedly pious, overzealous (*in matters of religion*); hypocritical; *m.* prude; hypocrite.

mojón [mo·xón] *m.* landmark; milestone; heap, pile.

molde [mól·de] *m.* mold, cast; form; pattern, model; **venir de** — to come pat, be to the point; **letras de** — printed letters; print.

moldear [mol·de·ár] *v.* to mold; to cast; to decorate with moldings.

moldura [mol·dú·ra] *f.* molding.

mole [mó·le] *f.* mass, bulk; *adj.* soft, mild; *m. Mex.* — **de guajolote** a Mexican dish of turkey served with a chili gravy.

molécula [mo·lé·ku·la] *f.* molecule.

moler[2] [mo·lér] *v. irr.* to mill; to grind; to tire, fatigue; to wear out, destroy; to bother; — **a palos** to give a thorough beating.

molestar [mo·les·tár] *v.* to molest, disturb; to bother, annoy.

molestia [mo·lés·tja] *f.* bother, annoyance; discomfort.

molesto [mo·lés·to] *adj.* bothersome, annoying; uncomfortable.

molibdeno [mo·lib·dé·no] *m.* molybdenum.

molicie [mo·lí·sje] *f.* softness; fondness for luxury.

molienda [mo·ljén·da] *f.* grind, grinding, milling; portion to be, or that has been, ground; grinding season (*for sugar cane or olives*); fatigue, weariness; bother.

molinero [mo·li·né·ro] *m.* miller.

molinete [mo·li·né·te] *m.* small mill; ventilating fan; pin wheel; twirl, whirl, flourish.

molinillo [mo·li·ní·yo] *m.* small mill or grinder; chocolate beater; restless person.

molino [mo·lí·no] *m.* mill; restless person; — **de viento** windmill.

molusco [mo·lús·ko] *m.* mollusk.

mollejas [mo·yé·xas] *f. pl.* sweetbreads.

mollera [mo·yé·ra] *f.* crown of the head; judgment, good sense; **ser duro de** — to be stubborn; **no tener sal en la** — to be dull, stupid.

momentáneo [mo·men·tá·ne·o] *adj.* momentary; sudden, quick.

momento [mo·mén·to] *m.* moment; importance; momentum; **al** — immediately, without delay; **a cada** — continually; frequently.

momia [mó·mja] *f.* mummy.

mona [mó·na] *f.* female monkey; mimic; drunkenness; **dormir la** — to sleep it off; **pillar una** — to get drunk.

monada [mo·ná·da] *f.* (*típico de mono*) monkeyshine; monkey face; (*cosa graciosa*) cute little thing; cute gesture; nonsense; flattery.

monarca [mo·nár·ka] *m.* monarch.

monarquía [mo·nar·kí·a] *f.* monarchy.

monasterio [mo·nas·té·rjo] *m.* monastery.

mondadientes [mon·da·djen·tes] *m.* toothpick.

mondadura [mon·da·dú·ra] *f.* trimming; peeling.

mondar [mon·dár] *v.* to pare; to peel; to prune; to clean out; *Am.* to beat, thrash; *Am.* to beat, defeat; **-se los dientes** to pick one's teeth.

moneda [mo·né·da] *f.* coin; money; — **corriente**

currency; — **menuda** (*or* **suelta**) change, small coins; **casa de** — mint.

monería [mo·ne·rí·a] *f.* monkeyshine, antic; trifle, trinket; cute little thing.

monetario [mo·ne·tá·rjo] *adj.* monetary, pertaining to money; financial.

monigote [mo·ni·gó·te] *m.* puppet, ridiculous figure; dunce.

monitor [mo·ni·tór] *m.* (*computadora*) monitor.

monitorear [mo·ni·to·re·ár] *v.* to monitor (*a radio or TV program*).

monja [món·xa] *f.* nun.

monje [món·xe] *m.* monk.

mono [mó·no] *m.* monkey; silly fool; mimic; coveralls; *Ch.* pile of fruit or vegetables (*in a market*); **-s** *Ch.* worthless household utensils and furniture; *Am.* **meterle a uno los -s en el cuerpo** to frighten, terrify someone; *adj.* pretty, neat, cute; *Am.* sorrel, reddish-brown; *Col.* blond.

monóculo [mo·nó·ku·lo] *m.* monocle.

monologar[7] [mo·no·lo·gár] *v.* to soliloquize, talk to oneself; to recite monologues; to monopolize the conversation.

monólogo [mo·nó·lo·go] *m.* monologue.

monopolio [mo·no·pó·ljo] *m.* monopoly.

monopolizar[9] [mo·no·po·li·sár] *v.* to monopolize; to corner (*a market*).

monosílabo [mo·no·sí·la·bo] *adj.* monosyllabic, of one syllable; *m.* monosyllable.

monotonía [mo·no·to·ní·a] *f.* monotony; **monótono** [mo·nó·to·no] *adj.* monotonous.

monousuario [mo·now·swá·rjo] *adj.* used by a single person.

monserga [mon·sér·ga] *f.* gabble.

monstruo [móns·trwo] *m.* monster.

monstruosidad [mons·trwo·si·dád] *f.* monstrosity; monster, freak.

monstruoso [mons·trwó·so] *adj.* monstrous.

monta [món·ta] *f.* amount, sum; value, importance; **de poca** — of little value or importance.

montaje [mon·tá·xe] *m.* assembly, assembling (*of machinery*); mount, support for a cannon.

montante [mon·tán·te] *m.* broadsword; transom; upright; post; *Carib., Ven.* sum, amount, cost; *f.* high tide.

montaña [mon·tá·ña] *f.* mountain; — **rusa** roller coaster.

montañés [mon·ta·ñés] *adj.* mountain (*used as adj.*) of, from or pertaining to the mountains; *m.* mountaineer; native of the province of Santander, Spain.

montañismo [mon·ta·ñíz·mo] *m.* mountaineering.

montañoso [mon·ta·ñó·so] *adj.* mountainous.

montar [mon·tár] *v.* to mount; to ride horseback; to amount (to); to set (*jewels*); to cock (*a gun*); to assemble, set up (*machinery*); *Carib., C.A.* to organize, establish.

montaraz [mon·ta·rás] *adj.* wild, primitive, uncivilized; *m.* forester.

monte [món·te] *m.* mount, mountain; forest; thicket; monte (*a card game*); *C.A., Mex.* grass, pasture; *Am.* country, outskirts; **montecillo** [mon·te·sí·yo] *m.* mound, small hill; **montepío** [mon·te·pí·o] *m.* pawnshop.

montera [mon·té·ra] *f.* cap; *Andes* Bolivian cone-shaped hat (*worn by Indians*).

montés [mon·tés] *adj.* wild, mountain (*used as adj.*); *f.* **cabra** — mountain goat; *m.* **gato** — wildcat.

montículo [mon·tí·ku·lo] *m.* mound.

montón [mon·tón] *m.* pile, heap; mass, great number; **a -es** in abundance, in heaps, by heaps.

montonera [mon·to·né·ra] *f. Col., Ven., Ríopl.* band of mounted rebels or guerrilla fighters; *Col.* pile of wheat, hay, straw, etc.; *P.R.* pile, heap (*of anything*).

montuoso [mon·twó·so] *adj.* hilly; mountainous.

montura [mon·tú·ra] *f.* mount, horse; saddle and trappings.

monumento [mo·nu·mén·to] *m.* monument; **monumental** [mo·nu·men·tál] *adj.* monumental.

moña [mó·ña] *f.* doll; hair ribbon.

moño [mó·ño] *m.* knot or roll of hair; bow of ribbon; crest, tuft of feathers; *Mex.* forelock (*lock of hair on the fore part of the head*); *Am.* crest, peak (*of anything*); *Col.* whim; *Col.* a Colombian popular dance; **-s** frippery, gaudy ornaments; *Col.* **estar con el — torcido** to be in an ugly humor.

mora [mó·ra] *f.* blackberry; mulberry; brambleberry; *Ch.* blood pudding, sausage.

morada [mo·rá·da] *f.* dwelling, residence; stay.

morado [mo·rá·do] *adj.* purple; *m.* (*moretón*) bruise.

morador [mo·ra·dór] *m.* dweller, resident.

moral [mo·rál] *adj.* moral; *f.* ethics, moral philosophy; morale; *m.* mulberry tree; blackberry bush.

moraleja [mo·ra·lé·xa] *f.* moral, lesson, maxim.

moralidad [mo·ra·li·dád] *f.* morality.

moralista [mo·ra·lís·ta] *m. & f.* moralist.

morar [mo·rár] *v.* to live, dwell, reside.

morbidez [mor·bi·dés] *f.* softness; mellowness.

mórbido [mór·bi·do] *adj.* morbid; soft.

morboso [mor·bó·so] *adj.* morbid, unhealthy, diseased.

morcilla [mor·sí·ya] *f.* blood pudding, blood sausage; gag (*an amusing remark by a comedian*).

mordacidad [mor·da·si·dád] *f.* sharpness (*of tongue*).

mordaz [mor·dás] *adj.* biting, cutting, sarcastic.

mordaza [mor·dá·sa] *f.* gag (*for the mouth*); clamp; **— de tierra** ground clamp.

mordedor [mor·de·dór] *adj.* biting; snappy; *m.* biter; slanderer.

mordedura [mor·de·dú·ra] *f.* bite; sting.

mordelón [mor·de·lón] *adj. Col., Ven.* biting, snappy; *m. Am.* biter; *Mex.* public official who accepts a bribe.

morder[2] [mor·dér] *v. irr.* to bite; to nip; to gnaw; to corrode; to backbite, slander; *Ven.* to swindle; *Mex., C.A.* to "shake down", exact a bribe.

mordida [mor·dí·da] *f. Am.* bite; *Mex., C.A., Carib., Ven.* graft, money obtained by graft; bribe.

mordiscar[6] [mor·dis·kár], **mordisquear** [mor·dis·ke·ár] *v.* to nibble; to gnaw.

mordisco [mor·dís·ko] *m.* bite; nibble.

moreno [mo·ré·no] *adj.* brown; dark, brunette; *m. Ríopl., Carib., Mex., Ven., Andes* colored person.

moretón [mo·re·tón] *m.* bruise, black-and-blue mark.

morfema [mor·fé·ma] *m.* morpheme.

morfina [mor·fí·na] *f.* morphine; **morfinómano** [mor·fi·nó·ma·no] *m.* morphine addict, drug fiend.

morfología [mor·fo·lo·xí·a] *f.* morphology.

moribundo [mo·ri·bún·do] *adj.* dying.

morir[4, 52] [mo·rír] *v. irr.* to die; **-se** to die; to die out, be extinguished.

morisco [mo·rís·ko] *adj.* Moorish; Moresque, in the Moorish style; *m.* Morisco (*Christianized Moor*); language of the Moriscos.

mormonismo [mor·mo·níz·mo] *m.* Mormonism.

moro [mó·ro] *adj.* Moorish; *Mex., Ven., Ríopl., Cuba* dappled, spotted (*horse*); *Col., Ch., Andes* unbaptized; *m.* Moor; *Col.* frosted cookie.

morocho [mo·ró·čo] *adj. Am.* robust, strong; *Ríopl.* of dark complexion; *Ch.* rough, tough; *Andes* of

low social condition.

moroso [mo·ró·so] *adj.* delinquent.

morral [mo·rrál] *m.* nose bag; knapsack; hunter's bag.

morrillo [mo·rrí·yo] *m.* fat of the neck (*especially the bull*).

morriña [mo·rrí·ña] *f.* melancholy, blues, sadness.

morro [mó·rro] *m.* knoll.

morsa [mór·sa] *f.* walrus.

mortaja [mor·tá·xa] *f.* shroud; *Am.* cigarette paper; mortise (carpentry).

mortal [mor·tál] *adj.* mortal, fatal, deadly; *m.* mortal; **mortalidad** [mor·ta·li·dád] *f.* mortality; death rate.

mortandad [mor·tan·dád] *f.* mortality, death rate; massacre, slaughter.

mortecino [mor·te·sí·no] *adj.* deathly pale; dying; **hacer la mortecina** to pretend to be dead.

morterete [mor·te·ré·te] *m.* small mortar, small canon.

mortero [mor·té·ro] *m.* mortar (*for grinding*).

mortífero [mor·tí·fe·ro] *adj.* deadly, fatal.

mortificar[6] [mor·ti·fi·kár] *v.* to mortify; to torment; to vex, annoy; **-se** to do penance; to be grieved; *Mex., C.A., Ven.* to be embarrassed.

mortuorio [mor·twó·rjo] *adj.* funeral; funereal, mournful; *m.* funeral, burial.

mosaico [mo·sáj·ko] *adj. & m.* mosaic.

mosca [mós·ka] *f.* fly; bore; bother; *Am.* sponger, parasite; *Mex., C.A., Ven.* bull's-eye, center of a target; **moscón** *m.* large fly; *Am.* **ir de moscón** to go along as a chaperone.

mosquear [mos·ke·ár] *v.* to brush off or drive away flies; to whip, beat; *Ríopl.* to rage, be furious; **-se** to show pique or resentment; *Ch.* to go away.

mosquito [mos·kí·to] *m.* mosquito; gnat; *Am.* Mosquito Indian of Nicaragua; **mosquitero** *m.* mosquito net.

mostacho [mos·tá·čo] *m.* mustache.

mostaza [mos·tá·sa] *f.* mustard; mustard seed; bird shot.

mostrador [mos·tra·dór] *m.* demonstrator; store counter; clock dial.

mostrar[2] [mos·trár] *v. irr.* to show; to demonstrate; to exhibit.

mostrenco [mos·trén·ko] *adj.* (*sin dueño*) ownerless; homeless; stray (*animal*); (*torpe*) slow, dull; fat, heavy; *m.* dunce; *C.A.* worthless animal.

mota [mó·ta] *f.* mote, speck; knot in cloth; slight defect; mound, knoll; *Col., Ven., Carib.* powder puff; *Am.* tuft.

mote [mó·te] *m.* motto; slogan; nickname; *Andes, Ch., Col.* stewed corn; *Andes* grammatical error; *Ch.* **— pelado** hominy.

motear [mo·te·ár] *v.* to speck, speckle; to spot; *Am.* to mispronounce, enunciate badly.

motejar [mo·te·xár] *v.* to jeer at; to call bad names; to insult; to censure; **— de** to brand as.

motín [mo·tín] *m.* mutiny; riot.

motivar [mo·ti·bár] *v.* to cause; to give a cause for.

motivo [mo·tí·bo] *m.* motive, reason; motif, theme; *m.* **con — de** because of; on the occasion of; *adj.* motive.

motocicleta [mo·to·si·klé·ta] *f.* motorcycle; **motociclista** [mo·to·si·kle·tís·ta] *m. & f.* motorcyclist, motorcycle rider.

motociclismo [mo·to·si·klíz·mo] *m.* motorcycling.

motor [mo·tór] *m.* motor; **— de reacción** jet engine; **— de avance** feed motor; *adj.* motor, causing motion.

motorista [mo·to·rís·ta] *m. & f.* motorist; motorman, motorwoman.

motorreactor [mo·to·rre·ak·tór] *m.* jet engine.
motriz [mo·trís] *adj.* motive, impelling, driving;
  fuerza — power, driving force.
movedizo [mo·be·di·so] *adj.* movable; shaky; shifting;
  arena movediza quicksand.
mover[2] [mo·bér] *v. irr.* (*físicamente*) to move;
  (*persuadir*) to persuade; to stir, excite; to touch,
  affect; **-se** to move.
movible [mo·bí·ble] *adj.* movable; mobile; fickle.
móvil [mó·bil] *m.* motive, inducement, incentive;
  adj. mobile, movable.
movilización [mo·bi·li·sa·sjón] *f.* mobilization.
movilizar[9] [mo·bi·li·sár] *v.* to mobilize.
movimiento [mo·bi·mjén·to] *m.* movement; motion;
  commotion, disturbance; (*computadora*) —
  vertical scrolling.
moza [mó·sa] *f.* maid; girl; last hand of a game; *Ch.*
  last song or dance of a fiesta.
mozalbete [mo·sal·bé·te] *m.* youth, lad.
mozárabe [mo·sá·ra·be] *adj.* Mozarabic (*Christian in
  Moslem Spain*).
mozo [mó·so] *adj.* young; unmarried; *m.* youth;
  manservant; waiter; porter; errand boy; **buen** —
  handsome man.
mozuela [mo·swé·la] *f.* lass, young girl.
mozuelo [mo·swé·lo] *m.* lad, young boy.
mucama [mu·ká·ma] *f. Andes, Ríopl.* servant girl;
  mucamo [mu·ká·mo] *m. Andes, Ríopl.* servant.
mucoso [mu·kó·so] *adj.* mucous; slimy; **membrana
  mucosa** mucous membrane.
muchacha [mu·čá·ča] *f.* child; girl; servant, maid.
muchacho [mu·čá·čo] *m.* child; boy, lad.
muchedumbre [mu·če·dúm·bre] *f.* multitude; crowd.
mucho [mú·čo] *adj.* much, a lot of; long (*referring to
  time*); **-s** many; *adv.* much; a great deal; **ni con** —
  not by far, not by a long shot; **ni** — **menos** not by
  any means, nor anything like it; **por** — **que** no
  matter how much; **no es** — **que** it is no wonder
  that.
muda [mú·da] *f.* change; change of clothes; molt (*act
  or time of shedding feathers*); *Ríopl.* relay of draft
  animals.
mudable [mu·dá·ble] *adj.* changeable; fickle.
mudanza [mu·dán·sa] *f.* change; removal;
  inconstancy.
mudar [mu·dár] *v.* to change; to remove; to molt; —
  de casa to move; — **de traje** to change one's suit
  or costume; **-se** to change one's clothes; to change
  one's habits; to move, change one's abode.
mudez [mu·dés] *f.* muteness, dumbness.
mudo [mú·do] *adj.* mute, dumb; silent; *m.* dumb
  person.
mueblaje [mwe·blá·xe] *m.* furniture.
mueble [mwé·ble] *m.* piece of furniture; **-s** furniture,
  household goods; *adj.* movable; **bienes
  -s** chattels, movable possessions.
mueblería [mwe·ble·rí·a] *f.* furniture store.
mueca [mwé·ka] *f.* grimace; wry face.
muela [mwé·la] *f.* (*diente*) molar tooth; (*piedra*)
  millstone; grindstone; — **ahuecada** recessed
  wheel; — **cordal** (*or* — **del juicio**) wisdom tooth.
muelle [mwé·ye] *adj.* soft; voluptuous; *m.* spring;
  wharf; loading platform; — **real** main spring of a
  watch.
muerte [mwér·te] *f.* death.
muerto [mwér·to] *p.p. of* **morir** & *adj.* dead;
  withered; faded; **naturaleza muerta** still life; *m.*
  corpse.
muesca [mwés·ka] *f.* notch; groove.
muestra [mwés·tra] *f.* sample; pattern, model; shop
  sign; sign, indication; presence, bearing; face, dial

(*of a clock or watch*); **muestrario** [mwes·trá·rjo] *m.*
  book or collection of samples.
mugido [mu·xí·do] *m.* moo; mooing, lowing of cattle.
mugir[11] [mu·xír] *v.* to moo, low.
mugre [mú·gre] *f.* dirt, grime.
mugriento [mu·grjén·to] *adj.* grimy, dirty.
mujer [mu·xér] *f.* woman; wife.
mujeriego [mu·xe·rjé·go] *adj.* fond of women;
  womanly.
mujeril [mu·xe·ríl] *adj.* womanly, feminine;
  womanish, like a woman.
mula [mú·la] *f.* mule; *Mex.* cushion for carrying
  loads; *Am.* worthless merchandise; *Ríopl.* cruel,
  treacherous person; *Mex.* **echar a uno la** — to
  give someone the dickens, scold someone.
muladar [mu·la·dár] *m.* rubbish pile or dump;
  dunghill, pile of manure.
mulato [mu·lá·to] *adj.* & *m.* mulatto.
muleta [mu·lé·ta] *f.* crutch; red cloth draped over a
  rod (*used by bullfighters*).
muletilla [mu·le·tí·ya] *f.* cane with a crutchlike
  handle; red cloth draped over a rod (*used by
  bullfighters*); cliché (*hackneyed or trite phrase*);
  refrain; repetitious word or phrase; braid frog
  (*fastener for a coat*).
mulo [mú·lo] *m.* mule.
multa [múl·ta] *f.* fine.
multicolor [mul·ti·ko·lór] *adj.* many-colored, motley.
múltiple [múl·ti·ple] *adj.* multiple.
multiplicación [mul·ti·pli·ka·sjón] *f.* multiplication.
multiplicar[6] [mul·ti·pli·kár] *v.* to multiply.
multiplicidad [mul·ti·pli·si·dád] *f.* multiplicity,
  manifold variety.
múltiplo [múl·ti·plo] *m.* multiple number.
multitud [mul·ti·túd] *f.* multitude; crowd.
mullido [mu·yí·do] *adj.* soft; fluffy; *m.* stuffing for
  mattresses or pillows; soft cushion or mattress.
mullir[20] [mu·yír] *v.* to fluff; to soften.
mundanal [mun·da·nál] *adj.* worldly.
mundano [mun·dá·no] *adj.* mundane, worldly.
mundial [mun·djál] *adj.* universal; **la guerra** — the
  World War.
mundo [mún·do] *m.* world; trunk; **todo el** —
  everybody.
munición [mu·ni·sjón] *f.* ammunition; buckshot; —
  de guerra war supplies.
municipal [mu·ni·si·pál] *adj.* municipal;
  municipalidad [mu·ni·si·pa·li·dád] *f.* municipality;
  town hall; city government.
municipio [mu·ni·sí·pjo] *m.* municipality; *Arg.* city
  hall.
muñeca [mu·ñé·ka] *f.* doll; wrist; manikin (*figure for
  displaying clothes*); **muñeco** *m.* boy doll; dummy,
  puppet.
muñón [mu·ñón] *m.* stump (*of an arm or leg*).
muralla [mu·rá·ya] *f.* surrounding wall; rampart.
murciano [mur·sjá·no] *adj.* of or from Murcia, Spain;
  m. native of Murcia.
murciélago [mur·sjé·la·go] *m.* bat.
murga [múr·ga] *f.* brass band.
murmullo [mur·mú·yo] *m.* murmur, rumor; whisper;
  muttering.
murmuración [mur·mu·ra·sjón] *f.* slander, gossip;
  grumbling.
murmurar [mur·mu·rár] *v.* to murmur; to slander,
  gossip; to whisper; to grumble.
muro [mú·ro] *m.* wall.
murria [mú·rrja] *f.* sulkiness, sullenness,
  melancholy, blues; **tener** — to be sulky; to have
  the blues.
musa [mú·sa] *f.* Muse; muse, poetic inspiration;

MO

poetry; **-s** fine arts.
muscular [mus·ku·lár] *adj.* muscular.
musculatura [mus·ku·la·tú·ra] *f.* muscles; muscular system.
músculo [mús·ku·lo] *m.* muscle.
musculoso [mus·ku·ló·so] *adj.* muscular; sinewy.
muselina [mu·se·lí·na] *f.* muslin.
museo [mu·sé·o] *m.* museum.
musgo [múz·ǵo] *m.* moss.
musgoso [muz·ǵó·so] *adj.* mossy.
música [mú·si·ka] *f.* music.
musical [mu·si·kál] *adj.* musical.
músico [mú·si·ko] *adj.* musical; *m.* musician.
musitar [mu·si·tár] *v.* to mutter, mumble; to whisper.
muslo [múz·lo] *m.* thigh.
mustio [mús·tjo] *adj.* sad; withered; humble.
mutación [mu·ta·sjón] *f.* mutation; unsettled weather.
mutilar [mu·ti·lár] *v.* to mutilate; to butcher; to mar.
mutismo [mu·tíz·mo] *m.* muteness, silence.
mutuo [mú·two] *adj.* mutual; reciprocal.
muy [mwi(múj)] *adv.* very; greatly; most.

N:n

nabo [ná·ƀo] *m.* turnip.
nácar [ná·kar] *m.* mother-of-pearl; pearl color.
nacarado [na·ka·rá·ƀo] *adj.* pearly.
nacer[13] [na·sér] *v. irr.* (*salir del vientre*) to be born; (*brotar*) to spring, originate; to bud; to sprout, grow (*said of plants*) — **de pie** (*or* — **de pies**) to be born lucky.
naciente [na·sjén·te] *adj.* rising (*sun*); *m.* orient, east.
nacimiento [na·si·mjén·to] *m.* birth; origin; beginning; descent; source; crèche (*representation of the Nativity*).
nación [na·sjón] *f.* nation.
nacional [na·sjo·nál] *adj.* national; *m.* national, citizen.
nacionalidad [na·sjo·na·li·ƀáƀ] *f.* nationality.
nada [ná·ƀa] *f.* nothingness; *indef. pron.* nothing, not . . . anything; *adv.* not at all; **de** — you are welcome, don't mention it (*as a reply to* «gracias»); *Am.* **a cada** — constantly; **una nadita** [na·ƀí·ta] a trifle, just a little.
nadada [na·ƀá·ƀa] *f.* swim.
nadador [na·ƀa·ƀór] *m.* swimmer; *Ven.* fish-net float.
nadar [na·ƀár] *v.* to swim; to float.
nadería [na·ƀe·rí·a] *f.* a mere nothing, trifle, worthless thing.
nadie [ná·ƀje] *indef. pron.* nobody, no one, not . . . anyone.
nafta [náf·ta] *f.* naphtha.
naguas [ná·ǵwas] = **enaguas.**
náhuatl [ná·watl] *adj.* the language of the Aztec Indians.
naipe [náj·pe] *m.* playing card.
nalgas [nál·ǵas] *f. pl.* buttocks; rump; **nalgada** [nal·ǵá·ƀa] *f.* spank; **-s** spanking.
nana [ná·na] *f.* grandma; (*canción*) lullaby; *Mex.*, *Ríopl.*, *Ven.* child's nurse; *Spain* nice old lady.
naranja [na·rán·xa] *f.* orange; — **tangerina** [taŋ·xe·rí·na] tangerine; **naranjada** [na·raŋ·xá·ƀa] *f.* orangeade; orange juice; orange marmalade; **naranjal** [na·raŋ·xál] *m.* orange grove; **naranjo** [na·ráŋ·xo] *m.* orange tree.
narciso [nar·sí·so] *m.* narcissus; daffodil; fop, dandy.
narcótico [nar·kó·ti·ko] *adj. & m.* narcotic.
narcotizar[9] [nar·ko·ti·sár] *v.* to dope, drug with narcotics.
nariz [na·rís] *f.* nose; nostril; **narices** [na·rí·ses] nostrils.
narración [na·rra·sjón] *f.* narration, account, story.
narrar [na·rrár] *v.* to narrate, tell, relate.
narrativo [na·rra·ti·ƀo] *adj.* narrative; **narrativa** [na·rra·tí·ƀa] *f.* narrative.
nata [ná·ta] *f.* cream; best part; scum; **-s** whipped cream with sugar; custard; **natoso** [na·tó·so] *adj.* creamy.
natación [na·ta·sjón] *f.* swimming.
natal [na·tál] *adj.* natal; native; **natalicio** [na·ta·lí·sjo] *m.* birthday; **natalidad** [na·ta·li·ƀáƀ] *f.* birth rate.
natillas [na·tí·yas] *f. pl.* custard.
nativo [na·tí·ƀo] *adj.* native.
natural [na·tu·rál] *adj.* natural; native; simple, unaffected; *m. & f.* native; *m.* nature, disposition; **al** — without affectation; **del** — from nature, from life.
naturaleza [na·tu·ra·lé·sa] *f.* nature; disposition; nationality; naturalization; — **muerta** still life.
naturalidad [na·tu·ra·li·ƀáƀ] *f.* naturalness; simplicity; birthright.
naturalista [na·tu·ra·lís·ta] *adj.* naturalistic; *m. & f.* naturalist.
naturalización [na·tu·ra·li·sa·sjón] *f.* naturalization.
naturalizar[9] [na·tu·ra·li·sár] *v.* to naturalize; to acclimatize, accustom to a new climate; **-se** to become naturalized.
naufragar[7] [naw·fra·ǵár] *v.* to be shipwrecked; to fail.
naufragio [naw·frá·xjo] *m.* shipwreck; failure, ruin.
náufrago [náw·fra·ǵo] *m.* shipwrecked person.
náusea [náw·se·a] *f.* nausea; **dar -s** to nauseate, sicken; to disgust; **tener -s** to be nauseated, be sick to one's stomach.
nauseabundo [naw·se·a·ƀún·do] *adj.* nauseating, sickening.
nauseado [naw·se·á·ƀo] *adj.* nauseated, sick to one's stomach.
náutica [náw·ti·ka] *f.* navigation (*science of navigation*).
navaja [na·ƀá·xa] *f.* jackknife, pocketknife; penknife; razor.
navajazo [na·ƀa·xá·so] *m.* stab with a jackknife or razor; stab wound.
naval [na·ƀál] *adj.* naval.
navarro [na·ƀá·rro] *adj.* Navarrese, of or pertaining to Navarre, Spain; *m.* Navarrese.
nave [ná·ƀe] *f.* ship, boat; nave; — **cósmica** spaceship; — **cósmica pilotada** manned space vehicle.
navegable [na·ƀe·ǵá·ƀle] *adj.* navigable.
navegación [na·ƀe·ǵa·sjón] *f.* navigation; sea voyage; — **aérea** aviation.
navegador [na·ƀe·ǵa·ƀór] **navegante** [na·ƀe·ǵán·te] *m.* navigator; *adj.* navigating.
navegar[7] [na·ƀe·ǵár] *v.* to navigate; to sail.
navidad [na·ƀi·ƀáƀ] *f.* Nativity; Christmas; **-es** Christmas season.
navideño [na·ƀi·ƀé·ño] *adj.* pertaining to Christmas.
navío [na·ƀí·o] *m.* vessel, ship — **de guerra** warship.
neblina [ne·ƀlí·na] *f.* fog, mist.
nebulosidad [ne·ƀu·lo·si·ƀáƀ] *f.* cloudiness; nebulousness.
necedad [ne·se·ƀáƀ] *f.* foolishness, nonsense.
necesario [ne·se·sá·rjo] *adj.* necessary.
neceser [ne·se·sér] *m.* toilet case; sewing kit.
necesidad [ne·se·si·ƀáƀ] *f.* necessity, need, want.
necesitado [ne·se·si·tá·ƀo] *adj.* needy; in need, destitute, poor; *p.p. of* **necesitar**; *m.* needy person.

necesitar [ne·se·si·tár] *v.* to need; to necessitate.
necio [né·sjo] *adj.* stupid, ignorant; foolish; stubborn; *Col.* touchy.
necrología [ne·kro·lo·xí·a] *f.* necrology.
nefando [ne·fán·do] *adj.* abominable; wicked.
nefasto [ne·fás·to] *adj.* ominous; tragic.
nefritis [ne·frí·tis] *f.* nephritis.
negación [ne·ɡa·sjón] *f.* negation, denial; negative (*negative particle*).
negar[1, 7] [ne·ɡár] *v. irr.* to deny; to refuse; to prohibit; to disown; **-se** to refuse, decline.
negativa [ne·ɡa·tí·ba] *f.* negative; denial, refusal.
negativo [ne·ɡa·tí·bo] *adj.* negative.
negligencia [ne·ɡli·xén·sja] *f.* negligence, neglect, carelessness.
negligente [ne·ɡli·xén·te] *adj.* negligent, neglectful, careless.
negociación [ne·ɡo·sja·sjón] *f.* negotiation; business; business house; management; transaction, deal.
negociante [ne·ɡo·sján·te] *m.* merchant, trader, dealer; businessman; *adj.* negotiating.
negociar [ne·ɡo·sjár] *v.* to negotiate; to trade; to transact.
negocio [ne·ɡó·sjo] *m.* business; business deal; negotiation, transaction; *Ríopl., Carib., C.A., Ven., Andes* store; **hombre de -s** businessman.
negrear [ne·ɡre·ár] *v.* to become black; to appear black, look black (*in the distance*).
negrero [ne·ɡré·ro] *m.* slave trader.
negro [né·ɡro] *adj.* black; dark; sad, gloomy; unfortunate; *m.* black color; negro; *Ríopl., C.A., Ven., Col.* dear, darling; **negra** [né·ɡra] *f.* negress; *Ríopl., C.A., Ven., Col.* dear, darling.
negrura [ne·ɡrú·ra] *f.* blackness.
negruzco [ne·ɡrús·ko] *adj.* blackish.
nena [né·na] *f.* baby girl; **nene** [né·ne] *m.* baby boy.
neón [ne·ón] *m.* neon.
neófito [ne·ó·fi·to] *m. & f.* neophyte.
neologismo [ne·o·lo·xíz·mo] *m.* neologism.
neoplasma [ne·o·pláz·ma] *m.* neoplasm.
nepotismo [ne·po·tíz·mo] *m.* nepotism.
nervio [ner·bjo] *m.* nerve.
nervioso [ner·bjó·so], **nervoso** [ner·bó·so] *adj.* nervous, sinewy, strong.
nerviosidad [ner·bjo·si·dád], **nervosidad** [ner·bo·si·dád] *f.* nervousness; flexibility; vigor.
nervudo [ner·bú·do] *adj.* sinewy, tough, powerful.
neto [né·to] *adj.* clear, pure; net (*profit, price, etc.*); **netamente** [ne·ta·mén·te] *adv.* clearly, distinctly.
neumático [new·má·ti·ko] *m.* tire; *adj.* pneumatic.
neuralgia [new·rál·xja] *f.* neuralgia.
neurastenia [new·ras·té·nja] *f.* neurasthenia.
neutralidad [new·tra·li·dád] *f.* neutrality.
neutralizar[9] [new·tra·li·sár] *v.* to neutralize, counteract.
neutro [néw·tro] *adj.* neutral; neuter; sexless.
neutrón [new·trón] *m.* neutron.
nevada [ne·bá·da] *f.* snowfall.
nevado [ne·bá·do] *adj.* snowy, white as snow; covered with snow.
nevar[1] [ne·bár] *v. irr.* to snow.
nevasca [ne·bás·ka] *f.* snowstorm.
nevera [ne·be·ra] *f.* icebox; refrigerator; ice storehouse; ice or ice-cream vendor (*woman*).
nevería [ne·be·rí·a] *f.* ice cream parlor.
ni [ni] *conj. & adv.* not; not even; neither; — **siquiera** not even.
nicotina [ni·ko·tí·na] *f.* nicotine.
nicho [ní·čo] *m.* niche; recess, hollow in a wall.
nidada [ni·dá·da] *f.* nestful of eggs; brood of chicks; hatch, brood.

nido [ní·do] *m.* nest; abode; *Am.* **patearle el — a alguien** to ''upset the applecart'', upset someone's plans.
niebla [njé·bla] *f.* fog, mist; confusion.
nieto [njé·to] *m.* grandson, grandchild; **nieta** [njé·ta] *f.* granddaughter.
nieve [njé·be] *f.* snow; *Mex., Ríopl., Ven.* sherbet, ice cream; **tiempo de -s** snowy season.
nigua [ní·ɡwa] *f.* chigger, chigoe, ''sand flea,'' ''red bug.''
nihilismo [ni·i·líz·mo] *m.* nihilism.
nilon [náj·lon] *m.* nylon.
nimio [ní·mjo] *adj.* miserly, stingy; *Am.* very small, insignificant.
ninfa [nín·fa] *f.* nymph.
ningun(o) [niŋ·gún(o)] *indef. adj. & pron.* no one, none, not . . . any; nobody.
niña [ní·ña] *f.* girl; baby girl; *Andes, Ríopl., Mex., Carib.* lady, mistress (*title of respect and endearment given to adults*); **— del ojo** pupil of the eye.
niñada [ni·ñá·da] *f.* childishness, childish act or remark.
niñera [ni·ñé·ra] *f.* child's nurse.
niñería [ni·ñe·rí·a] *f.* childish act; child's play; trifle; foolishness.
niñez [ni·ñés] *f.* infancy; childhood.
niño [ní·ño] *m.* child, boy; infant; *C.A.* master (*title of respect given to a young man by his servants*); *adj.* childlike, childish; very young, immature.
niple [ní·ple] *m.* nipple (machine).
níquel [ní·kel] *m.* nickel.
niquelado [ni·ke·lá·do] *adj.* nickel-plated; *m.* nickel plating; nickel plate.
níspero [nís·pe·ro] *m.* loquat; medlar tree.
nitidez [ni·ti·dés] *f.* clarity, clearness.
nítido [ní·ti·do] *adj.* clear.
nitrato [ni·trá·to] *m.* nitrate; saltpeter.
nítrico [ní·tri·ko] *adj.*
nitro [ní·tro] *m.* niter, saltpeter.
nitrógeno [ni·tró·xe·no] *m.* nitrogen.
nitroglicerina [ni·tro·ɡli·se·rí·na] *f.* nitroglycerine.
nivel [ni·bél] *m.* level.
nivelar [ni·be·lár] *v.* to level; to grade; to equalize.
no [no] *adv.* no; not; nay; — **bien** as soon as; **un — sé qué** something indefinable; **por sí o por** — just in case, anyway.
noble [nó·ble] *adj.* noble; *m.* nobleman.
nobleza [no·blé·sa] *f.* nobility; nobleness.
noción [no·sjón] *f.* notion, idea.
nocivo [no·sí·bo] *adj.* noxious, harmful, injurious.
nocturno [nok·túr·no] *adj.* nocturnal, night, nightly; *m.* nocturne (*musical or lyrical composition*).
noche [nó·če] *f.* night; darkness; **a la —** tonight; **de — by** (at) night; **por (en) la —** at night, in the evening; **dejar a uno a buenas -s** to leave a person in the lurch.
Nochebuena [no·če·bwé·na] *f.* Christmas Eve.
nocherniego [no·čer·njé·ɡo] *m.* night owl (*person*).
nodriza [no·drí·sa] *f.* child's nurse; wet nurse.
nogal [no·ɡál] *m.* walnut (*tree and wood*).
nomás [no·más] *Am.* = **no más** just; only.
nombradía [nom·bra·dí·a] *f.* renown, fame.
nombramiento [nom·bra·mjén·to] *m.* nomination; appointment; naming.
nombrar [nom·brár] *v.* to nominate; to name; to appoint.
nombre [nóm·bre] *m.* name; fame; noun; watchword; **— de pila** (*or* **— de bautismo**) Christian name.
nomenclatura [no·men·kla·tú·ra] *f.* nomenclature.
nomeolvides [no·me·ol·bí·des] *f.* forget-me-not

MU

(flower).

nómina [nó·mi·na] *f.* list (*of names*); pay roll.

nominación [no·mi·na·sjón] *f.* nomination; appointment.

nominal [no·mi·nál] *adj.* nominal; **valor —** small, insignificant value.

nominar [no·mi·nár] *v.* to nominate.

non [non] *adj.* odd, uneven; *m.* odd number, uneven number; **estar** (*or* **quedar**) **de —** to be left alone, be left without a partner or companion.

nonada [no·ná·da] *f.* trifle, mere nothing.

nopal [no·pál] *m.* nopal, prickly pear tree (*species of cactus*).

nordeste [nor·dés·te] *adj. & m.* northeast.

nórdico [nór·di·ko] *adj.* Nordic.

noria [nó·rja] *f.* draw well; chain pump.

norma [nór·ma] *f.* norm, standard, model.

normal [nor·mál] *adj.* normal, standard; *f.* perpendicular line; normal school.

normalizar[9] [nor·ma·li·sár] *v.* to normalize, make normal; to standardize.

noroeste [nor·o·és·te] *adj. & m.* northwest.

nortada [nor·tá·da] *f.* strong north wind.

nortazo [nor·tá·so] *m. Mex., Ven.* sudden gust of wind, strong north wind.

norte [nór·te] *m.* north; north wind; guide; North Star; direction; *C.A.* wind.

norteamericano [nor·te·a·me·ri·ká·no] *adj.* North American; American (*from or of the United States*).

nortear [nor·te·ár] *v.* to blow from the north; *Sal.* to blow from any direction.

norteño [nor·té·ño] *adj.* northern; *m.* northerner.

noruego [no·rwé·ǥo] *adj. & m.* Norwegian.

nostalgia [nos·tál·xja] *f.* nostalgia, longing, homesickness.

nostálgico [nos·tál·xi·ko] *adj.* homesick; lonesome; longing.

nota [nó·ta] *f.* note; mark; fame.

notable [no·tá·ble] *adj.* notable; noticeable.

notar [no·tár] *v.* to note, observe; to mark; to write down.

notario [no·tá·rjo] *m.* notary.

noticia [no·tí·sja] *f.* notice, information; news; **recibir -s** to receive word, hear (from).

noticiario [no·ti·sjá·rjo] *m.* news sheet, news column, news bulletin or film; **noticiero** [no·ti·sjé·ro] *m.* = **noticiario;** *adj.* news (*used as adj.*); newsy, full of news.

noticioso [no·ti·sjó·so] *adj.* newsy, full of news; well-informed.

notificación [no·ti·fi·ka·sjón] *f.* notification, notifying; notice; summons.

notificar[6] [no·ti·fi·kár] *v.* to notify.

notorio [no·tó·rjo] *adj.* well-known; obvious, evident.

novato [no·bá·to] *m.* novice, beginner.

novedad [no·be·dád] *f.* novelty; latest news, event, or fashion; change; newness; **hacerle a uno —** to seem strange or new to one; to excite one's curiosity or interest; **sin —** as usual; well.

novel [no·bél] *adj.* new, inexperienced.

novela [no·bé·la] *f.* novel; fiction.

novelesco [no·be·lés·ko] *adj.* novelistic, fictional; fantastic.

novelista [no·be·lís·ta] *m. & f.* novelist.

novena [no·bé·na] *f.* novena of the Church.

noventa [no·bén·ta] *num.* ninety.

novia [nó·bja] *f.* fiancée; sweetheart; bride.

noviazgo [no·bjáz·ǥo] *m.* betrothal, engagement; courtship.

novicio [no·bí·sjo] *m.* novice; beginner; apprentice;

adj. inexperienced.

noviembre [no·bjém·bre] *m.* November.

novilla [no·bí·ya] *f.* heifer, young cow.

novillada [no·bi·yá·da] *f.* herd of young bulls; bullfight (*using young bulls*).

novillero [no·bi·yé·ro] *m.* a novice bullfighter; a fighter of 3-year-old bulls.

novillo [no·bí·yo] *m.* young bull; steer; **-s** bullfight (*using young bulls*); **hacer -s** to play hooky, cut classes; to play truant.

novio [nó·bjo] *m.* fiancé; sweetheart; bridegroom.

novocaína [no·bo·ka·í·na] *f.* novocaine.

nubarrón [nu·ba·rrón] *m.* large storm cloud.

nube [nú·be] *f.* cloud; film on the eyeball; **poner por las -s** to praise to the skies.

nublado [nu·blá·do] *m.* storm cloud; imminent danger; *adj.* cloudy.

nublar [nu·blar] *v.* to cloud; to darken, obscure; **-se** to grow cloudy.

nubloso [nu·bló·so] *adj.* cloudy; gloomy.

nuboso [nu·bó·so] *adj. Spain* cloudy.

nuca [nú·ka] *f.* nape.

nuclear [nu·kle·ár] *adj.* nuclear.

núcleo [nú·kle·o] *m.* nucleus; kernel.

nudillo [nu·dí·yo] *m.* small knot; knuckle; loop, knitted stitch.

nudo [nú·do] *m.* (*vinculo*) knot; joint; union, bond, tie; (*crisis*) crisis, turning point (*of a play*); knot, nautical mile; **— ciego** hard knot; **— corredizo** slip knot.

nudoso [nu·dó·so] *adj.* knotty, gnarled, knotted.

nuera [nwé·ra] *f.* daughter-in-law.

nueva [nwé·ba] *f.* news.

nueve [nwe·be] *num.* nine.

nuevecito [nwe·be·sí·to] *adj.* nice and new, brandnew.

nuevo [nwé·bo] *adj.* new; newly arrived; **de —** again; **¿qué hay de — ?** what's new? what's the news?

nuez [nwes] *f.* walnut; nut; **— (or — de Adán)** Adam's apple; **— moscada** (*or* **— de especia**) nutmeg.

nulidad [nu·li·dád] *f.* nullity (*state or quality of being null*); incompetence; nonentity, a nobody.

nulo [nú·lo] *adj.* null, void; useless.

numeral [nu·me·rál] *adj. & m.* numeral.

numerar [nu·me·rár] *v.* to number; to calculate; to enumerate.

numérico [nu·mé·ri·ko] *adj.* numerical.

número [nú·me·ro] *m.* number; numeral.

numeroso [nu·me·ró·so] *adj.* numerous.

numismática [nu·miz·má·ti·ka] *f.* numismatics.

nunca [nún·ka] *adv.* never; **no . . . —** not . . . ever; **más que —** more than ever.

nuncio [nún·sjo] *m.* herald, messenger; nuncio, Papal envoy.

nupcial [nup·sjál] *adj.* nuptial, relating to marriage or weddings.

nupcias [núp·sjas] *f. pl.* nuptials, wedding.

nutria [nú·trja] *f.* otter.

nutrición [nu·tri·sjón] *f.* nutrition; nourishment.

nutrido [nu·trí·do] *adj.* full, abundant; substantial; *p.p. of* **nutrir.**

nutrimento [nu·tri·mén·to], **nutrimiento** [nu·tri·mjén·to] *m.* nutrition; nourishment, food.

nutrir [nu·trír] *v.* nourish, feed.

nutritivo [nu·tri·tí·bo] *adj.* nutritious, nourishing.

Ñ:ñ

ñandú [ñan·dú] *m.* nandu; American ostrich.

ñapa [ñá·pa] *f. Andes, Ríopl., Cuba, Ven., Col.* additional amount, something extra; *Am.* **de** — to boot, in addition, besides.

ñato [ñá·to] *adj. C.A., Col., Ven., Andes* flat-nosed, pug-nosed, snub-nosed; *Am.* ugly, deformed; *Am.* insignificant.

ñoñería [ño·ñe·rí·a] *f.* silly remark or action; *Am.* dotage.

ñoño [ñó·ño] *adj.* feeble-minded; silly; *Am.* old, decrepit, feeble; *Col., Ec.* old-fashioned, out of style.

ñu [ñu] *m.* gnu.

O:o

o [o] *conj.* or, either.

oasis [o·á·sis] *m.* oasis.

obedecer[13] [o·be·de·sér] *v. irr.* to obey; — **a cierta causa** to arise from, be due to, a certain cause; **esto obedece a que . . .** this is due to the fact that . . .

obediencia [o·be·djén·sja] *f.* obedience.

obediente [o·be·djén·te] *adj.* obedient.

obelisco [o·be·lís·ko] *m.* obelisk.

obertura [o·ber·tú·ra] *f.* musical overture.

obispado [o·bis·pá·do] *m.* bishopric.

obispo [o·bís·po] *m.* bishop; *Cuba, Andes* **a cada muerte de** (*or* **por la muerte de un**) — once in a blue moon.

objeción [ob·xe·sjón] *f.* objection.

objetar [ob·xe·tár] *v.* to object.

objetivo [ob·xe·tí·bo] *adj.* objective; *m.* objective (*lens of any optical instrument*); objective.

objeto [ob·xé·to] *m.* object, purpose, aim; thing.

oblea [o·blé·a] *f.* wafer.

oblicuo [o·blí·kwo] *adj.* oblique, slanting, bias.

obligación [o·bli·ga·sjón] *f.* obligation; duty; bond, security; engagement.

obligar[7] [o·bli·gár] *v.* to oblige; to obligate, bind, compel, put under obligation; **-se** to bind oneself, obligate oneself.

obligatorio [o·bli·ga·tó·rjo] *adj.* obligatory; compulsory; binding.

oboe [o·bó·e] *m.* oboe.

óbolo [ó·bo·lo] *m.* mite, small contribution.

obra [ó·bra] *f.* (*resultado de acción*) work; act; labor, toil; (*creación artística*) book; building (*under construction*); masterpiece of art; repair; — **de** approximately; **por** — **de** through, by virtue of power of; **hacer mala** — to interfere, hinder; **poner por** — to undertake, begin; to put into practice.

obrar [o·brár] *v.* to work; to act; to operate; to function; to perform; to make; to do; to have a bowel movement; **obra en nuestro poder** we are in receipt of; **la carta que obra en su poder** the letter that is in his possession.

obrero [o·bré·ro] *m.* workman, laborer.

obscenidad [ob·se·ni·dád] *f.* obscenity.

obsceno [ob·sé·no] *adj.* obscene.

obscurecer[13] [obs·ku·re·sèr] *v. irr.* to obscure, darken; to tarnish; to grow dark; **-se** to get dark or cloudy.

obscuridad [obs·ku·ri·dád] *f.* obscurity; darkness; dimness.

obscuro [obs·kú·ro] *adj.* obscure; dark; dim; **a obscuras** (= **a oscuras**) in the dark; *m.* shade (*in painting*).

obsequiar [ob·se·kjár] *v.* to regale, entertain; to court; *Am.* to give, make a present of.

obsequio [ob·sé·kjo] *m.* attention, courtesy; gift; **en** — **de** for the sake of, in honor of.

obsequioso [ob·se·kjó·so] *adj.* attentive, courteous, obliging; obsequious, servile.

observación [ob·ser·ba·sjón] *f.* observation; remark.

observador [ob·ser·ba·dór] *m.* observer; *adj.* observing.

observancia [ob·ser·bán·sja] *f.* observance (*of a law, rule, custom, etc.*).

observante [ob·ser·bán·te] *adj.* observant (*of a law, custom, or rule*).

observar [ob·ser·bár] *v.* to observe; to watch; to remark.

observatorio [ob·ser·ba·tó·rjo] *m.* observatory.

obsesión [ob·se·sjón] *f.* obsession.

obsesionar [ob·se·sjo·nár] *v.* to obsess.

obstáculo [obs·tá·ku·lo] *m.* obstacle.

obstante: [obs·tán·te] **no** — notwithstanding; nevertheless.

obstar [obs·tár] *v.* to hinder, impede, obstruct.

obstétrica [obs·té·tri·ka] *f.* obstetrics.

obstinación [obs·ti·na·sjón] *f.* obstinacy, stubbornness.

obstinado [obs·ti·ná·do] *adj.* obstinate, stubborn.

obstinarse [obs·ti·nár·se] *v.* to persist (in); to be obstinate, stubborn (about).

obstrucción [obs·truk·sjón] *f.* obstruction.

obstruir[32] [obs·trwír] *v.* to obstruct, block.

obtener[45] [ob·te·nér] *v. irr.* to obtain, get; to attain.

obtenible [ob·te·ní·ble] *adj.* obtainable, available.

obturador [ob·tu·ra·dór] *m.* choke (*of an automobile*); throttle; plug, stopper; shutter (*of a camera*).

obviar [ob·bjár] *v.* to obviate, clear away, remove.

obvio [ób·bjo] *adj.* obvious.

ocasión [o·ka·sjón] *f.* occasion, opportunity; cause; danger, risk; **de** — reduced, bargain; **avisos de** — want ''ads'' (*advertisements*); *Am.* **esta** — this time.

ocasional [o·ka·sjo·nál] *adj.* occasional.

ocasionar [o·ka·sjo·nár] *v.* to occasion, cause.

ocaso [o·ká·so] *m.* sunset; setting (*of any star or planet*); west; decadence, decline, end.

occidental [ok·si·den·tál] *adj.* occidental, western.

occidente [ok·si·dén·te] *m.* occident, west.

océano [o·sé·a·no] *m.* ocean.

oceanografía [o·se·a·no·gra·fí·a] *f.* oceanography.

ocelote [o·se·ló·te] *m.* ocelot.

ocio [ó·sjo] *m.* leisure, idleness; recreation, pastime.

ociosidad [o·sjo·si·dád] *f.* idleness, leisure.

ocioso [o·sjó·so] *adj.* idle; useless.

ocre [ó·kre] *m.* ocher.

octava [ok·tá·ba] *f.* octave.

octubre [ok·tú·bre] *m.* October.

ocular [o·ku·lár] *adj.* ocular; **testigo** — eye witness; *m.* eyepiece, lens (*for the eye in a microscope or telescope*).

oculista [o·ku·lís·ta] *m. & f.* oculist; *Am.* flatterer.

ocultar [o·kul·tár] *v.* to hide, conceal.

oculto [o·kúl·to] *adj.* hidden, concealed; *m. Am.* species of mole (*small animal*).

ocupación [o·ku·pa·sjón] *f.* occupation; employment.

ocupante [o·ku·pán·te] *m. & f.* occupant.

ocupar [o·ku·pár] *v.* to occupy; to employ; **-se en** (*Am.* **-se de**) to be engaged in; to pay attention to, be interested in.

ocurrencia [o·ku·rrén·sja] *f.* occurrence, event; witticism, joke; bright or funny idea.

ocurrente [o·ku·rrén·te] *adj.* witty, funny, humorous;

occurring.

ocurrir [o·ku·rrír] *v.* to occur.

ocurso [o·kúr·so] *m. Ríopl.* petition, application.

ochavo [o·čá·bo] *m.* an ancient coin; **no tener** — not to have a red cent.

ochenta [o·čén·ta] *num.* eighty.

ochentón [o·čen·tón] *m.* octogenarian.

ocho [ó·čo] *num.* eight.

oda [ó·da] *f.* ode.

odiar [o·djár] *v.* to hate.

odio [ó·djo] *m.* hatred.

odioso [o·djó·so] *adj.* odious, hateful.

odontología [o·don·to·lo·xí·a] *f.* odontology.

odre [ó·dre] *m.* wine bag; drunk.

oeste [o·és·te] *m.* west; west wind.

ofender [o·fen·dér] *v.* to offend; to displease; **-se** to get offended; to become angry, take offense.

ofensa [o·fén·sa] *f.* offense.

ofensivo [o·fen·sí·bo] *adj.* offensive; obnoxious; attacking; **ofensiva** [o·fen·sí·ba] *f.* offensive.

ofensor [o·fen·sór] *m.* offender; *adj.* offending.

oferta [o·fér·ta] *f.* offer; promise.

oficial [o·fi·sjál] *m.* official, officer, skilled workman; *adj.* official.

oficiar [o·fi·sjár] *v.* to officiate, serve, minister; perform the duties of a priest or minister; to communicate officially; — **de** to serve as, act as.

oficina [o·fi·sí·na] *f.* office; shop; **oficinesco** *adj.* clerical, pertaining to an office.

oficio [o·fí·sjo] *m.* trade; function; official communication; religious office (*prayers*).

oficioso [o·fi·sjó·so] *adj.* officious, meddlesome.

ofrecer[13] [o·fre·sér] *v. irr.* to offer; to promise; **-se** to offer, occur, present itself; to offer oneself, volunteer; **¿qué se le ofrece a Vd.?** what do you wish?

ofrecimiento [o·fre·si·mjén·to] *m.* offer; offering.

ofrenda [o·frén·da] *f.* offering, gift.

ofuscamiento [o·fus·ka·mjén·to] *m.* clouded vision, blindness; cloudiness of the mind, bewilderment, mental confusion.

ofuscar[6] [o·fus·kár] *v.* to darken, cast a shadow on; to blind; to cloud; to bewilder, confuse.

ogro [ó·gro] *m.* ogre.

ohm, ohmio [on, ó·mjo] *m.* ohm; **ohmiómetro** ohmmeter.

oído [o·í·do] *m.* hearing; ear; **al** — confidentially; **de** (*or* **al**) — by ear; **de -s** (*or* **de oídas**) by hearsay or rumor.

oidor [oj·dór] *m.* hearer, listener; judge.

oír[36] [o·ír] *v. irr.* to hear; to listen; to understand; — **misa** to attend mass; — **decir que** to hear that; — **hablar de** to hear about.

ojal [o·xál] *m.* buttonhole; hole.

¡ojalá! [o·xa·lá] *interj.* God grant!; I hope so!; — **que** would that, I hope that.

ojazo [o·xá·so] *m.* large eye.

ojeada [o·xe·á·da] *f.* glimpse, quick glance.

ojear [o·xe·ár] *v.* to eye, stare; to bewitch; to beat up, rouse (*wild game*).

ojera [o·xé·ra] *f.* dark circle under the eye; eyecup.

ojeriza [o·xe·rí·sa] *f.* grudge, spite.

ojeroso [o·xe·ró·so] *adj.* with dark circles under the eyes.

ojete [o·xé·te] *m.* eyelet.

ojiva [o·xí·ba] *f.* pointed arch; **ojival** [o·xi·bál] *adj.* pointed (*arch*); **ventana ojival** window with a pointed arch.

ojo [ó·xo] *m.* (*órgano*) eye; (*agujero*) keyhole; hole; **¡—!** careful! look out!; **a** — by sight, by guess; **a -s vistas** visibly, clearly; — **de agua** spring (*of*

water); — **de buey** porthole; **mal** (*or* **mal de**) — evil eye; *Am.* **hacer** — to cast the evil eye; *Am.* **pelar el** — to be alert, keep one's eye peeled; *Mex., Ven.* **poner a uno los -s verdes** to deceive someone; **tener entre -s a** to have ill will toward, have a grudge against.

ojoso [o·xó·so] *adj.* full of holes.

ojota [o·xó·ta] *f. Andes, Ch., Ríopl.* leather sandal.

ola [ó·la] *f.* wave.

¡ole! [ó·le] *interj.* bravo! good!

oleada [o·le·á·da] *f.* big wave; swell; surge; abundant yield of oil.

oleaje [o·le·á·xe], **olaje** [o·lá·xe] *m.* swell, surge, succession of waves.

óleo [ó·le·o] *m.* oil, holy oil; **pintura al** — oil painting.

oleoducto [o·le·o·dúk·to] *m.* pipe line.

oleoso [o·le·ó·so] *adj.* oily.

oler[37] [o·lér] *v. irr.* to smell; to scent; — **a** to smack of; to smell like; *Am.* **olérselas** to suspect it, "smell a rat".

olfatear [ol·fa·te·ár] *v.* to scent, sniff, smell.

olfateo [ol·fa·té·o] *m.* sniff, sniffing.

olfato [ol·fá·to] *m.* sense of smell.

olfatorio [ol·fa·tó·rjo] *adj.* olfactory.

oligarquía [o·li·gar·kí·a] *f.* oligarchy.

olimpiada [o·lim·pjá·da] *f.* Olympiad; Olympic games.

olímpico [o·lím·pi·ko] *adj.* Olympian.

oliva [o·lí·ba] *f.* olive; olive tree; **olivar** *m.* olive grove; **olivo** *m.* olive tree.

olmo [ól·mo] *m.* elm.

olor [o·lór] *m.* (*en el olfato*) smell, odor, fragrance; (*fama*) smack, trace, suspicion; *Ch.* spice; **olorcillo** [o·lor·sí·yo] *m.* faint odor.

oloroso [o·lo·ró·so] *adj.* fragrant.

olote [o·ló·te] *m. Mex., C.A.* cob, corncob.

olvidadizo [ol·bi·da·dí·so] *adj.* forgetful.

olvidar [ol·bi·dár] *v.* to forget; to neglect; **-se de** to forget; **olvidársele a uno algo** to forget something.

olvido [ol·bí·do] *m.* forgetfulness; oblivion; neglect; **echar al** — to cast into oblivion; to forget on purpose.

olla [ó·ya] *f.* pot, kettle; — **profunda para freír** deep fat fryer; olla (*vegetable and meat stew*); — **podrida** Spanish stew of mixed vegetables and meat.

ombligo [om·blí·go] *m.* navel; middle center.

ombú [om·bú] *m.* umbra tree.

omisión [o·mi·sjón] *f.* omission; oversight, neglect.

omiso [o·mí·so] *adj.* careless, neglectful; *N. Arg.* guilty; **hacer caso** — to omit.

omitir [o·mi·tír] *v.* to omit; to overlook.

ómnibus [óm·ni·bus] *m.* omnibus, bus.

omnipotente [om·ni·po·tén·te] *adj.* omnipotent, almighty.

once [ón·se] *num.* eleven.

onda [ón·da] *f.* wave; ripple; sound wave; scallop.

ondear [on·de·ár] *v.* to wave; to waver; to ripple; to sway, swing.

ondulación [on·du·la·sjón] *f.* undulation, waving motion; wave; — **permanente** permanent wave.

ondulado [on·du·lá·do] *p.p. & adj.* wavy; scalloped (*edge*); — **permanente** permanent wave.

ondulante [on·du·lán·te] *adj.* wavy, waving.

ondular [on·du·lár] *v.* to undulate, wave.

oneroso [o·ne·ró·so] *adj.* onerous.

onomástico [o·no·más·ti·ko] *adj.* onomastic; *m.* saint's day.

onomatopeya [o·no·ma·to·pé·ya] *f.* onomatopoeia.

ontología [on·to·lo·xí·a] *f.* ontology.

onza [ón·sa] *f.* ounce; ounce, wildcat; *Ríopl., Bol.* small tiger.

opacidad [o·pa·si·dád] *f.* opacity; sadness.

opaco [o·pá·ko] *adj.* opaque, dim, dull.

ópalo [ó·pa·lo] *m.* opal.

ópera [ó·pe·ra] *f.* opera.

operación [o·pe·ra·sjón] *f.* operation; business transaction.

operador [o·pe·ra·dór] *m.* operator, surgeon.

operante [o·pe·rán·te] *adj.* operant (*behavior*).

operar [o·pe·rár] *v.* to operate; to take effect, work; to speculate (*in business*); to manipulate, handle.

operario [o·pe·rá·rjo] *m.* operator, workman, worker.

opereta [o·pe·ré·ta] *f.* operetta.

opinar [o·pi·nár] *v.* to express an opinion; to think; to judge; to argue.

opinión [o·pi·njón] *f.* opinion; reputation.

opio [ó·pjo] *m.* opium.

oponer[40] [o·po·nér] *v. irr.* to oppose; **-se** to disapprove; **-se a** to oppose, be against.

oporto [o·pór·to] *m.* port wine.

oportunidad [o·por·tu·ni·dád] *f.* opportunity.

oportuno [o·por·tú·no] *adj.* opportune; convenient, timely.

oposición [o·po·si·sjón] *f.* opposition; competition; **-es** competitive examinations.

opositor [o·po·si·tór] *m.* opponent; competitor.

opresión [o·pre·sjón] *f.* oppression.

opresivo [o·pre·sí·bo] *adj.* oppressive.

opresor [o·pre·sór] *m.* oppressor.

oprimir [o·pri·mír] *v.* to oppress; to crush; to press down; to press a button.

oprobio [o·pró·bjo] *m.* infamy; insult; shame; dishonor.

optar [op·tár] *v.* to choose, select; — **por** to decide upon; to choose.

óptica [óp·ti·ka] *f.* optics.

óptico [óp·ti·ko] *adj.* optical, optic; *m.* optician.

optimismo [op·ti·míz·mo] *m.* optimism; **optimista** *m. & f.* optimist; *adj.* optimistic.

óptimo [óp·ti·mo] *adj.* very good, very best.

opuesto [o·pwés·to] *p.p. of* **oponer** opposed; *adj.* opposite; contrary.

opulencia [o·pu·lén·sja] *f.* opulence, abundance, wealth.

opulento [o·pu·lén·to] *adj.* opulant, wealthy.

oquedad [o·ke·dád] *f.* cavity, hollow; chasm.

ora [ó·ra] *conj.* now, then; whether; either.

oración [o·ra·sjón] *f.* oration; prayer; sentence.

oráculo [o·rá·ku·lo] *m.* oracle.

orador [o·ra·dór] *m.* orator, speaker.

oral [o·rál] *adj.* oral.

orar [o·rár] *v.* to pray.

oratoria [o·ra·tó·rja] *f.* oratory, eloquence.

oratorio [o·ra·tó·rjo] *m.* oratory, private chapel; oratorio (*a religious musical composition*); *adj.* oratorical, pertaining to oratory.

orbe [ór·be] *m.* orb, sphere, globe; the earth; world, universe.

órbita [ór·bi·ta] *f.* orbit; eye socket.

orden [ór·den] *m.* (*colocación*) order; succession, series; class, group; relation; proportion; *f.* (*mando*) order, command; (*sociedad*) honorary or religious order; *m. & f.* sacrament of ordination; **a sus órdenes** at your service.

ordenado [or·de·ná·do] *p.p. & adj.* ordered; ordained; orderly; neat.

ordenanza [or·de·nán·sa] *f.* ordinance, decree, law; command, order; *m.* orderly (*military*).

ordenar [or·de·nár] *v.* to arrange, put in order; to order, command; to ordain; **-se** to become

ordained.

ordeño [or·dé·ña] *m.* milking.

ordeñar [or·de·ñár] *v.* to milk.

ordinariez [or·di·na·rjés] *f.* commonness, lack of manners.

ordinario [or·di·ná·rjo] *adj.* ordinary; usual; common, coarse; *m.* ordinary (*a bishop or judge*); ordinary mail; daily household expense; **de** — usually, ordinarily.

orear [o·re·ár] *v.* to air; **-se** to be exposed to the air; to dry in the air.

orégano [o·ré·ga·no] *m.* wild marjoram, oregano.

oreja [o·ré·xa] *f.* ear; hearing; loop; small flap; *Am.* handle (*shaped like an ear*); **orejano** [o·re·xá·no] *adj.* unbranded (*cattle*); *Ven., Col.* cautious; *m. Cuba* aloof, unsociable person; **orejera** [o·re·xé·ra] *f.* ear muff, ear flap; **orejón** [o·re·xón] *m.* a pull by the ear; *Col.* rancher or inhabitant of the *sabana*; *adj. Col.* long-eared, long-horned; *Col.* unbranded (*cattle*); *Col.* coarse, crude, uncouth.

orfandad [or·fan·dád] *f.* orphanage (*state of being an orphan*).

orfanato [or·fa·ná·to] *m.* orphanage, orphan asylum.

orfanatorio [or·fa·na·tó·rjo] *Mex., C.A., Andes =* **orfanato.**

orfebre [or·fé·bre] *m.* goldsmith; silversmith.

orfebrería [or·fe·bre·rí·a] *f.* silver or gold work.

orfeón [or·fe·ón] *m.* glee club, choir.

orgánico [or·gá·ni·ko] *adj.* organic.

organigrama [or·ga·ni·grá·ma] *m.* organization chart.

organillo [or·ga·ní·yo] *m.* hand organ, hurdy-gurdy.

organismo [or·ga·níz·mo] *m.* organism.

organización [or·ga·ni·sa·sjón] *f.* organization.

organizador [or·ga·ni·sa·dór] *m.* organizer.

organizar[9] [or·ga·ni·sár] *v.* to organize; to arrange.

órgano [ór·ga·no] *m.* organ; **organillo** [or·ga·ní·yo] *m.* hand organ.

orgía [or·xí·a] *f.* orgy, wild revel.

orgullo [or·gú·yo] *m.* pride; haughtiness, arrogance.

orgulloso [or·gu·yó·so] *adj.* proud; haughty, arrogant.

oriental [o·rjen·tál] *adj.* oriental, eastern.

orientar [o·rjen·tár] *v.* to orientate, orient; **-se** to orient oneself, find one's bearings.

oriente [o·rjén·te] *m.* orient, east; east wind; source, origin.

orificación [o·ri·fi·ka·sjón] *f.* gold filling.

orificio [o·ri·fí·sjo] *m.* orifice, small hole, aperture, outlet.

origen [o·rí·xen] *m.* origin; source.

original [o·ri·xi·nál] *adj.* original; strange, quaint; *m.* original; manuscript, copy; queer person; **originalidad** [o·ri·xi·na·li·dád] *f.* originality.

originar [o·ri·xi·nár] *v.* to originate, cause to be; **-se** originate, arise.

orilla [o·rí·ya] *f.* shore, bank; beach; edge, border; **-s** *Am.* outskirts, environs.

orillar [o·ri·yár] *v.* border, trim the edge of; to skirt, go along the edge of; to reach the edge or shore.

orín [o·rín] *m.* rust; **orines** *m. pl.* urine.

orina [o·rí·na] *f.* urine.

orinar [o·ri·nár] *v.* to urinate.

oriol [o·rjól] *m.* oriole.

oriundo [o·rjún·do] *adj.* native; **ser** — **de** to hail from, come from.

orla [ór·la] *f.* border; trimming, fringe.

orlar [or·lár] *v.* to border, edge, trim with a border or fringe.

orlón [or·lón] *m.* orlon.

ornado [or·ná·do] *adj.* ornate; *p.p.* adorned, ornamented.

ornamentar [or·na·men·tár] *v.* to ornament, adorn.

OC

ornamento [or·na·mén·to] *m.* ornament; decoration; **-s** sacred vestments.

ornar [or·nár] *v.* to adorn.

oro [ó·ro] *m.* gold; gold ornament; **-s** "gold coins" (*Spanish card suit*).

orondo [o·rón·do] *adj.* self-satisfied, puffed up, vain; *Am.* serene, calm.

oropel [o·ro·pél] *m.* tinsel.

orquesta [or·kés·ta] *f.* orchestra.

orquestar [or·kés·tár] *v.* to orchestrate.

orquídea [or·kí·de·a] *f.* orchid.

ortiga [or·tí·ga] *f.* nettle.

ortodoxo [or·to·dók·so] *adj.* orthodox.

ortografía [or·to·gra·fí·a] *f.* orthography, spelling.

ortográfico [or·to·grá·fi·ko] *adj.* orthographic (*pertaining to orthography or spelling*).

oruga [o·rú·ga] *f.* caterpillar.

orzuelo [or·swé·lo] *m.* sty (*on the eyelid*).

osadía [o·sa·dí·a] *f.* boldness, daring.

osado [o·sá·do] *adj.* bold, daring.

osamenta [o·sa·mén·ta] *f.* bones; skeleton.

osar [o·sár] *v.* to dare, venture.

oscilación [o·si·la·sjón] *f.* oscillation, sway; fluctuation, wavering.

oscilar [o·si·lár] *v.* to oscillate, swing, sway; to waver.

oscilatorio [o·si·la·tó·rjo] *adj.* oscillatory.

oscurecer [os·ku·re·sér] = **obscurecer.**

oscuridad [os·ku·ri·dád] = **obscuridad.**

oscuro [os·kú·ro] = **obscuro.**

oso [ó·so] *m.* bear; — **blanco** polar bear; — **hormiguero** anteater; — **marino** seal.

ostentación [os·ten·ta·sjón] *f.* ostentation, show, display.

ostentar [os·ten·tár] *v.* to display, show; (*jactarse*) to show off; to boast.

ostentoso [os·ten·tó·so] *adj.* ostentatious, showy.

ostión [os·tjón] *m.* large oyster.

ostra [ós·tra] *f.* oyster.

otate [o·tá·te] *m. Mex., C.A.* species of bamboo; *Mex., C.A.* bamboo stick or cane.

otero [o·té·ro] *m.* hillock, small hill, knoll.

otoñal [o·to·ñál] *adj.* autumnal, of autumn.

otoño [o·tó·ño] *m.* autumn, fall.

otorgante [o·tor·gán·te] *m.* grantor; maker of a deed.

otorgar[7] [o·tor·gár] *v.* to grant; to promise; to consent to.

otro [ó·tro] *adj.* another; **otra vez** again; *Am.* **como dijo el** — as someone said.

otrora [o·tró·ra] *adv.* formerly, in other times.

ovación [o·ba·sjón] *f.* ovation, enthusiastic applause.

oval [o·bál], **ovalado** [o·ba·lá·do] *adj.* oval; **óvalo** [ó·ba·lo] *m.* oval.

oveja [o·bé·xa] *f.* sheep.

ovejero [o·be·xé·ro] *m.* shepherd; sheep dog.

ovejuno [o·be·xú·no] *adj.* sheep, pertaining or relating to sheep.

overo [o·bé·ro] *adj.* peach-colored (*applied to horses and cattle*); *Ríopl.* mottled, spotted; *Ríopl.* multicolored; *Ríopl.* **ponerle a uno** — to insult someone.

overol [o·be·ról], **overoles** [o·be·ró·les] *m. Ch., Col.* overalls.

ovillar [o·bi·yár] *v.* to ball, wind or form into a ball; **-se** to curl up into a ball.

ovillo [o·bí·yo] *m.* ball of yarn or thread; tangle; prewinder; **hacerse uno un** — to curl up into a ball; to become entangled, confused.

oxidado [ok·si·dá·do] *p.p.* rusted; *adj.* rusty.

oxidar [ok·si·dár] *v.* to oxidize; to rust; **-se** to become oxidized; to rust.

óxido [ók·si·do] *m.* oxide.

oxígeno [ok·sí·xeno] *m.* oxygen.

oyente [o·yén·te] *m. & f.* listener, auditor, hearer; *adj.* listening.

ozono [o·só·no] *m.* ozone.

P:p

pabellón [pa·be·yón] *m.* pavilion; canopy; banner, flag; shelter; covering; external ear.

pabilo [pa·bí·lo] *m.* wick; snuff (*of a candle*).

pacer[13] [pa·sér] *v. irr.* to pasture; to graze.

paciencia [pa·sjén·sja] *f.* patience.

paciente [pa·sjén·te] *adj.* patient; *m. & f.* patient.

pacienzudo [pa·sjen·sú·do] *adj.* patient, long-suffering.

pacificar[6] [pa·si·fi·kár] *v.* to pacify; to appease.

pacífico [pa·sí·fi·ko] *adj.* pacific, peaceful, calm.

pacifismo [pa·si·fíz·mo] *m.* pacifism.

pacto [pák·to] *m.* pact, agreement.

padecer[13] [pa·de·sér] *v. irr.* to suffer.

padecimiento [pa·de·si·mjén·to] *m.* suffering.

padrastro [pa·drás·tro] *m.* stepfather; hangnail.

padre [pá·dre] *m.* father; **-s** parents; ancestors; *adj. Am.* very great, stupendous.

padrenuestro [pa·dre·nwés·tro] *m.* paternoster, the Lord's Prayer.

padrino [pa·drí·no] *m.* godfather; sponsor, patron; second in a duel; best man (*at a wedding*).

paella [pa·é·ya] *f.* a popular rice dish with chicken, vegetables, etc.

paga [pá·ga] *f.* payment; pay, salary.

pagadero [pa·ga·dé·ro] *adj.* payable.

pagado [pa·gá·do] *p.p. & adj.* paid; self-satisfied, conceited; — **de sí mismo** pleased with oneself.

pagador [pa·ga·dór] *m.* payer; paymaster; paying teller (*in a bank*).

paganismo [pa·ga·níz·mo] *m.* paganism, heathenism.

pagano [pa·gá·no] *adj.* pagan; *m.* pagan; payer; dupe, sucker.

pagar[7] [pa·gár] *v.* to pay; to pay for; to requite, return (*love*); **-se** to be proud of; to boast of; to be pleased with; *Ríopl.* **-se de palabras** to let oneself be tricked; *Ch.* — **a nueve** to pay in excess.

pagaré [pa·ga·ré] *m.* promissory note; I.O.U.

página [pá·xi·na] *f.* page.

paginar [pa·xi·nár] *v.* to page.

pago [pá·go] *m.* (*premio*) payment; prize, reward; (*distrito*) country district; *Ríopl.* one's native farm land or district; *adj.* paid; *Am.* **estar -s** to be quits; to be even.

paila [páj·la] *f.* large pan; *C.A.* saucer.

país [pa·ís] *m.* nation, country; region.

paisaje [paj·sá·xe] *m.* landscape.

paisanaje [paj·sa·ná·xe] *m.* peasantry, country people; civilians; *Andes* gang of farm laborers.

paisano [paj·sá·no] *m.* countryman; peasant; fellow countryman; civilian.

paja [pá·xa] *f.* straw; chaff; rubbish; *Andes* grass for pasture; **echar -s** to draw lots; **por quítame allá esas -s** for an insignificant reason or pretext; **en un quítame allá esas -s** in a jiffy, in a second; **a humo de -s** thoughtlessly; lightly; **no lo hizo a humo de -s** he did not do it without a special reason or intention.

pajar [pa·xár] *m.* straw loft, barn.

pájaro [pá·xa·ro] *m.* bird; shrewd, cautious person;

Ch. absent-minded person; *Ch., Ríopl.* person of suspicious conduct; — **carpintero** woodpecker; — **mosca** hummingbird.

paje [pá·xe] *m.* page, valet, attendant.

pajizo [pa·xí·so] *adj.* made of straw; covered with straw; straw colored.

pajonal [pa·xo·nál] *m.* plain or field of tall coarse grass.

pala [pá·la] *f.* shovel; trowel; scoop; paddle; blade of an oar; racket; upper (*of a shoe*); cunning, craftiness; **meter la** — to deceive with cunning; *Am.* **hacer la** — to deceive with cunning; to stall, pretend to work; to flatter; **palada** [pa·lá·da] *f.* scoop, shovelful; stroke of an oar.

palabra [pa·lá·bra] *f.* word; promise; — **clave** (*computadora*) reserved word, key word; **de** — by word of mouth; **cuatro -s** a few words; **empeñar la** — to promise, pledge; **tener la** — to have the floor; *Am.* ¡—! I mean it, it is true!

palabrero [pa·la·bré·ro] *adj.* wordy, talkative.

palabrita [pa·la·brí·ta] *f.* a little word, a few words, a word of advice.

palacio [pa·lá·sjo] *m.* palace; **palaciego** [pa·la·sjé·go] *m.* courtier; *adj.* relating to a palace or court; court (*used as an adj.*).

paladar [pa·la·dár] *m.* palate; taste, relish.

paladear [pa·la·de·ár] *v.* to relish, taste with relish.

paladín [pa·la·dín] *m.* knight; champion, defender.

paladio [pa·lá·djo] *m.* palladium.

palanca [pa·láŋ·ka] *f.* lever; crowbar; bar used for carrying a load; joystick; — **de arranque y detención** start-stop lever; — **del engranaje** gear lever; — **del embrague** clutch lever; influence, a "pipe line".

palangana [pa·laŋ·gá·na] *f.* washbowl, basin; *S.A.* platter; *Ch.* large wooden bowl; *m. Andes* bluffer, charlatan.

palatal [pa·la·tál] *adj.* palatal.

palco [pál·ko] *m.* theater box; — **escénico** stage.

palenque [pa·léŋ·ke] *m.* palisade, fence; enclosure; *Ríopl.* hitching post or plank.

paleta [pa·lé·ta] *f.* small flat shovel; mason's trowel; shoulder blade; blade (*of a rudder, of a ventilating fan*); paddle (*of a paddle wheel*); painter's palette; *Am.* candy, sweetmeat or ice cream attached to a stick; *Am.* a wooden paddle to stir with, or for beating clothes; **en dos -s** in a jiffy, in a second; **paletilla** [pa·le·tí·ya] *f.* shoulder blade.

palidecer[13] [pa·li·de·sér] *v. irr.* to turn pale.

palidez [pa·li·dés] *f.* pallor, paleness.

pálido [pá·li·do] *adj.* pallid, pale.

palillo [pa·lí·yo] *m.* small stick; toothpick; **tocar todos los -s** (*Ch.* **menear uno los -s**) to try every possible means.

paliza [pa·lí·sa] *f.* beating (*with a stick*), thrashing.

palizada [pa·li·sá·da] *f.* palisade; stockade.

palma [pál·ma] *f.* palm tree; palm leaf; palm of the hand; **batir -s** to clap, applaud; **llevarse la** — to triumph, win, carry off the honors; to be the best.

palmada [pal·má·da] *f.* slap; clap.

palmario [pal·má·rjo] *adj.* clear, evident.

palmatoria [pal·ma·tó·rja] *f.* small candlestick with handle.

palmear [pal·me·ár] *v.* to clap, applaud; *Am.* to pat, slap on the back; *Ríopl.* to flatter.

palmera [pal·mé·ra] *f.* palm tree.

palmo [pál·mo] *m.* span (*about 9 inches*); — **a** — slowly, foot by foot.

palmotear [pal·mo·te·ár] *v.* to clap, applaud.

palo [pá·lo] *m.* stick; pole; log; mast; wood; blow with a stick; suit (*in a deck of cards*); *Am.* tree;

Ríopl. reprimand, reproof; *P.R., Ven.* large swallow of liquor; — **del Brasil** Brazil wood; *Ven.* — **a pique** rail fence, barbed wire fence; *Mex., C.A.* **a medio** — half-done; half-drunk; *Am.* **a** — **entero** drunk.

paloma [pa·ló·ma] *f.* dove, pigeon; pleasant, mild person; **-s** whitecaps.

palomar [pa·lo·már] *m.* dovecot (*shelter for doves or pigeons*).

palomilla [pa·lo·mí·ya] *f.* little dove; moth; small butterfly; **-s** small whitecaps.

palomita [pa·lo·mí·ta] *f.* little dove; **-s** *Am.* popcorn.

palpable [pal·pá·ble] *adj.* palpable (*that can be felt or touched*); clear, obvious, evident.

palpar [pal·pár] *v.* to feel; to touch; to grope.

palpitación [pal·pi·ta·sjón] *f.* palpitation; beat, throb.

palpitante [pal·pi·tán·te] *adj.* palpitating, throbbing, trembling; exciting; **la cuestión** — the burning question.

palpitar [pal·pi·tár] *v.* to palpitate; to throb, beat.

palta [pál·ta] *f. Col., Ven., Andes, Ríopl., Ch.* avocado, alligator pear; **palto** [pál·to] *m. Col., Ven., Andes, Ríopl., Ch.* avocado tree. *See* **aguacate.**

palúdico [pa·lú·di·ko] *adj.* marshy; **fiebre palúdica** malarial, or marsh fever; malaria; **paludismo** *m.* malaria.

pampa [pám·pa] *f. Am.* (*vast treeless plain of South America*); *Am.* prairie; *Ch.* drill field (*military*); *m. & f.* pampa Indian of Argentina; *m. Ríopl.* language of the pampa Indian; *adj. Ríopl.* pertaining to the pampa Indian; *Ríopl.* **caballo** — horse with head and body of different colors; *Ríopl.* **trato** — dubious or dishonest deal; *Col., Arg.* **estar a la** — to be in the open; *Ríopl.* **tener todo a la** — to be ragged or to be indecently exposed; *Ch.* **quedar en** — to be left without clothes; to be left in the lurch.

pampeano [pam·pe·á·no] *adj. Ríopl.* of, or pertaining to the pampa.

pampero [pam·pé·ro] *adj. Ríopl.* of, or pertaining to, the pampas; *m. Ríopl.* inhabitant of the pampas; *Ríopl.* violent wind of the pampa.

pan [pan] *m.* bread; loaf of bread; wheat; — **rallado** crumbs; **-es** fields of grain; breadstuffs; *Arg.* **echar -es** to brag, boast.

pana [pá·na] *f.* corduroy.

panadería [pa·na·de·rí·a] *f.* bakery.

panadero [pa·na·dé·ro] *m.* baker; *Ch.* flatterer.

panal [pa·nál] *m.* honeycomb; sweetmeat (*made of sugar, egg white, and lemon*).

panamericano [pa·na·me·ri·ká·no] *adj.* Pan-American.

pandearse [pan·de·ár·se] *v.* to bulge, warp; to sag.

pandeo [pan·dé·o] *m.* sag; bulge.

pandilla [pan·dí·ya] *f.* gang, band.

panela [pa·né·la] *f. Col., C.A.* unrefined sugar.

panfleto [pan·flé·to] *m. Am.* pamphlet.

pánico [pá·ni·ko] *m.* panic; *adj.* panic, panicky.

panne [pán·ne] *f.* accident, car trouble.

panocha [pa·nó·ča] *f.* ear of corn; *Mex.* Mexican raw sugar; *Col., C.R.* a kind of tamale.

panqué [paŋ·ké] *m. Col., C.A., Mex.* small cake, cup cake; *Am.* pancake.

pantalón [pan·ta·lón] *m.* trousers; pants; **un par de -es** a pair of trousers.

pantalla [pan·tá·ya] *f.* light shade; screen; fireplace screen; motion-picture screen; — **de cabeza** helmet (welding); *C.R.* fan, palm leaf fan; *P.R.* earring.

pantano [pan·tá·no] *m.* swamp; dam; difficulty.

pantanoso [pan·ta·nó·so] *adj.* swampy, marshy; muddy.

OR

panteón [pan·te·ón] *m.* cemetery.

pantera [pan·té·ra] *f.* panther.

pantorrilla [pan·to·rrí·ya] *f.* calf (*of the leg*).

pantufla [pan·tú·fla] *f.* bedroom slipper.

panza [pán·sa] *f.* paunch, belly.

panzón [pan·són], panzudo [pan·sú·ðo] *adj.* big-bellied.

pañal [pa·ñál] *m.* diaper; estar en -es to be in one's infancy; to have little or no knowledge of a thing.

paño [pá·ño] *m.* cloth (*any cloth, especially woolen*); blotch or spot on the skin; film on the eyeball; *Mex., Cuba* parcel of tillable land; *Mex.* kerchief; shawl; — de manos towel; — de mesa tablecloth; al — off-stage; -s clothes, garments; -s menores underwear; pañero *m.* clothier.

pañolón [pa·ño·lón] *m.* scarf, large kerchief; shawl.

pañuelo [pa·ñwé·lo] *m.* handkerchief.

papa [pá·pa] *m.* pope; *f.* potato; fib, lie; *Am.* snap, easy job; -s pap (*soft food for babies*); -s horneadas baked potatoes; soup; *Ríopl., Ch.* cosa — something good to eat; excellent thing; echar -s to fib, lie; *Am.* importarle a uno una — not to matter to one a bit; *Am.* no saber ni — not to know a thing; to be completely ignorant.

papá [pa·pá] *m.* papa; *Mex., C.A., Andes* — grande grandfather.

papagayo [pa·pa·ǵá·yo] *m.* parrot; talker, chatterer.

papal [pa·pál] *adj.* papal.

papalote [pa·pa·ló·te], papelote [pa·pe·ló·te] *m. Carib., Mex.* kite.

papamoscas [pa·pa·mós·kas] *m.* flycatcher (*a bird*); simpleton, half-wit, dunce.

papanatas [pa·pa·ná·tas] *m.* simpleton, fool, dunce.

paparrucha [pa·pa·rrú·ča] *f.* fib, lie; paparruchero [pa·pa·rru·čé·ro] *m.* fibber.

papaya [pa·pá·ya] *f.* papaya.

papel [pa·pél] *m.* (*hoja*) paper; sheet of paper; document; (*parte dramática*) role; — de estraza brown wrapping paper; — de lija sandpaper; — de seda tissue paper; — continuo (*computadora*) fan-fold paper; — moneda paper money; — secante blotting paper; hacer el — de to play the role of; hacer buen (*or* mal) — to cut a good (*or* bad) figure.

papelera [pa·pe·lé·ra] *f.* folder, file, case or device for keeping papers; *Am.* wastepaper basket; papelero [pa·pe·lé·ro] *m.* paper manufacturer; *adj.* pertaining to paper; vain, ostentatious.

papelería [pa·pe·le·rí·a] *f.* stationery store; stationery; lot of papers.

papeleta [pa·pe·lé·ta] *f.* card, file card, slip of paper.

papelucho [pa·pe·lú·čo] *m.* worthless piece of paper.

papera [pa·pé·ra] *f.* goiter; -s mumps.

paquete [pa·ké·te] *m.* package; bundle; (*buque*) packet boat (*mail boat*); *adj. S.A.* dolled up, dressed up; *Ríopl., Col.* important, pompous; *Ríopl., Col.* insincere.

par [par] *adj.* even; *m.* pair, couple; peer; a la — at par; jointly; at the same time; al — de on a par with; bajo — below par; sin — peerless, without an equal, having no equal; sobre — above par; de — en — wide-open.

para [pá·ra] *prep.* for; to; toward; in order to; ¿— qué? what for?; — que so that; — siempre forever; — mis adentros to myself; sin qué ni — qué without rhyme or reason; *m. Ríopl.* Paraguayan tobacco; *Ríopl.* Paraguayan (*used as nickname*).

parabién [pa·ra·bjén] *m.* congratulations; dar el — to congratulate.

parabrisas [pa·ra·brí·sas] *m.* windshield.

paracaídas [pa·ra·ka·í·ðas] *m.* parachute; paracaidista [pa·ra·kaj·dís·ta] *m. & f.* parachutist.

parachoques [pa·ra·čó·kes] *m.* bumper.

parada [pa·rá·ða] *f.* stop; stopping place; bet, stake; military review; *P.R.* parade; *Ríopl.* boastfulness; *Ríopl.* tener mucha — to dress very well.

paradero [pa·ra·ðé·ro] *m.* stopping place; whereabouts; end.

parado [pa·rá·ðo] *p.p. & adj.* stopped; unoccupied, unemployed; fixed, motionless; *Am.* standing, erect, straight up; *Ch., P.R.* stiff, proud; *Ríopl.* cold, unenthusiastic; *P.R., Ch., Andes* caer uno — to land on one's feet; to be lucky; *Mex.* estar bien — to be well-fixed, well-established; to be lucky; *m. Mex.* air, appearance.

paradoja [pa·ra·ðó·xa] *f.* paradox.

paradójico [pa·ra·ðó·xi·ko] *adj.* paradoxical.

parafina [pa·ra·fí·na] *f.* paraffin.

paráfrasis [pa·rá·fra·sis] *f.* paraphrase.

paraguas [pa·rá·ǵwas] *m.* umbrella; paragüero [pa·ra·ǵwé·ro] *m.* umbrella stand; umbrella maker or seller.

paraguayo [pa·ra·ǵwá·yo] *adj. & m.* Paraguayan.

paraíso [pa·ra·í·so] *m.* paradise, heaven; upper gallery (*in a theater*).

paraje [pa·rá·xe] *m.* place; spot; situation.

paralelo [pa·ra·lé·lo] *adj.* parallel; similar; *m.* parallel; similarity; paralela [pa·ra·lé·la] *f.* parallel line; paralelismo [pa·ra·le·líz·mo] *m.* parallelism.

parálisis [pa·rá·li·sis] *f.* paralysis.

paralítico [pa·ra·lí·ti·ko] *adj.* paralytic.

paralizar[9] [pa·ra·li·sár] *v.* to paralyze; to stop.

parámetro [pa·rá·me·tro] *m.* parameter.

páramo [pá·ra·mo] *m.* high, bleak plain; cold region; *Andes* blizzard or a cold drizzle.

parangón [pa·raŋ·gón] *m.* comparison.

parangonar [pa·raŋ·go·nár] *v.* to compare.

paraninfo [pa·ra·nín·fo] *m.* assembly hall, lecture hall, auditorium.

parapeto [pa·ra·pé·to] *m.* parapet.

parar [pa·rár] *v.* to stop; to end, end up, come to an end; to parry (*in fencing*); to set up (*type*); *Am.* to stand, place in upright position; — atención to notice; — mientes en to observe; notice; *Ríopl.* — las orejas to prick up one's ears; to pay close attention; -se to stop; *Am.* to stand up, get up.

pararrayos [pa·ra·rrá·yos] *m.* lightning rod.

parásito [pa·rá·si·to] *m.* parasite; *adj.* parasitic.

parasol [pa·ra·sól] *m.* parasol.

parcela [par·sé·la] *f.* parcel of land; particle, small piece.

parcial [par·sjál] *adj.* partial; *m.* follower, partisan; parcialidad [par·sja·li·ðáð] *f.* partiality; faction, party.

parche [pár·če] *m.* mending patch; sticking plaster; medicated plaster; drum.

pardal [par·ðál] *m.* sparrow; linnet; sly fellow.

pardear [par·ðe·ár] *v.* to grow dusky; to appear brownish-grey.

pardo [pár·ðo] *adj.* dark-grey; brown; dark; cloudy; *m.* leopard; *Carib., Ríopl.* mulatto; pardusco [par·ðús·ko] *adj.* greyish; brownish.

parear [pa·re·ár] *v.* to pair, couple, match, mate.

parecer[13] [pa·re·sér] *v. irr.* to seem; to appear, show up; -se to resemble each other, look alike; *m.* opinion; appearance, looks; al — apparently, seemingly.

parecido [pa·re·sí·ðo] *adj.* alike, similar; bien — good-looking; *p.p. of* parecer; *m.* similarity, likeness, resemblance.

pared [pa·réð] *f.* wall; — maestra main wall; —

medianera partition wall.

paredón [pa·re·ðón] *m.* execution wall; thick wall.

pareja [pa·ré·xa] *f.* pair, couple; match; partner; *Am.* team of two horses; *Ríopl.* horse race.

parejero [pa·re·xé·ro] *m. Ríopl.* race horse; *Ríopl.* over-familar person, backslapper, hail-fellow-well-met.

parejo [pa·ré·xo] *adj.* even; smooth; equal; *adv. Ríopl.* hard.

parentela [pa·ren·té·la] *f.* relatives, kin.

parentesco [pa·ren·tés·ko] *m.* kinship, relationship.

paréntesis [pa·rén·te·sis] *m.* parenthesis; digression; **entre —** by the way.

pargo [pár·ɣo] *m.* red snapper.

paria [pá·rja] *m. & f.* outcast.

paridad [pa·ri·ðáð] *f.* par, equality, parity.

pariente [pa·rjén·te] *m. & f.* relative, relation.

parir [pa·rír] *v.* to give birth; to bear (*children*).

parlamentar [par·la·men·tár] *v.* to converse; to parley, discuss terms with an enemy.

parlamentario [par·la·men·tá·rjo] *adj.* parliamentary; *m.* member of parliament; envoy to a parley.

parlamento [par·la·mén·to] *m.* speech (*of a character in a play*); parley; parliament, legislative assembly.

parlanchín [par·lan·čín] *adj.* talkative; *m.* talker, chatterer.

parlero [par·lé·ro] *adj.* talkative; gossipy; chattering, chirping.

parlotear [par·lo·te·ár] *v.* to prate, prattle, chatter, chat.

parloteo [par·lo·té·o] *m.* chatter, prattle, idle talk.

paro [pá·ro] *m.* work, stoppage; lockout; *Am.* throw (*in the game of dice*); *Am.* **— y pinta** game of dice.

parodia [pa·ró·ðja] *f.* parody, take-off, humorous imitation.

parodiar [pa·ro·ðjár] *v.* to parody, take off, imitate.

parótidas [pa·ró·ti·ðas] *f. pl.* mumps.

parpadear [par·pa·de·ár] *v.* to wink; to blink; to flutter the eyelids; to twinkle.

parpadeo [par·pa·ðé·o] *m.* winking; blinking; fluttering of the eyelids; twinkling.

párpado [pár·pa·ðo] *m.* eyelid.

parque [pár·ke] *m.* park; *Am.* ammunition.

parra [pá·rra] *f.* grapevine; earthenware jug.

parrafada [pa·rra·fá·ða] *f.* chat.

párrafo [pá·rra·fo] *m.* paragraph; **echar un — con** to have a chat with.

parral [pa·rrál] *m.* grape arbor.

parranda [pa·rrán·da] *f.* revel, orgy, spree; *Col.* gang, band; **andar** (*or* **ir**) **de —** to go on a spree.

parrandear [pa·rran·de·ár] *v.* to revel, make merry, go on a spree.

parrilla [pa·rrí·ya] *f.* grill, gridiron, broiler; grate.

párroco [pá·rro·ko] *m.* parish priest.

parroquia [pa·rró·kja] *f.* parish; parish church; clientele, customers.

parroquiano [pa·rro·kjá·no] *m.* client, customer; parishioner; *adj.* parochial, of a parish.

parsimonia [par·si·mó·nja] *f.* thrift, economy; moderation; prudence.

parsimonioso [par·si·mo·njó·so] *adj.* thrifty; stingy; cautious; slow.

parte [pár·te] *f.* part; share; place; party (*legal term*); **-s** qualities; **parte** *m.* notice, announcement; *Am.* unnecessary excuses or explanations; **de algún tiempo a esta —** for some time past; **de — de** on behalf of; in favor of; **de — a —** through, from one side to the other; **dar —** to inform; **echar a mala —** to take amiss; **en —** partly; **por todas -s** everywhere; *m.* telegram; message.

partera [par·té·ra] *f.* midwife.

partición [par·ti·sjón] *f.* partition, division.

participación [par·ti·si·pa·sjón] *f.* participation, share; notice.

participante [par·ti·si·pán·te] *m. & f.* participant; *adj.* participating, sharing.

participar [par·ti·si·pár] *v.* to participate, share; to inform, notify.

partícipe [par·tí·si·pe] *m. & f.* participant; *adj.* participating.

participio [par·ti·sí·pjo] *m.* participle.

partícula [par·tí·ku·la] *f.* particle.

particular [par·ti·ku·lár] *adj.* particular, special; peculiar; private; personal; odd, strange; **en —** specially; **lecciones -es** private lessons; *m.* private citizen; individual; point, detail; matter.

partida [par·tí·ða] *f.* (*salida*) departure, leave; (*entidad*) item, entry; record; band, group; squad; shipment; game; set (*in tennis*); *Am.* part in the hair; **— de bautismo** (**de matrimonio** *or* **de defunción**) birth (marriage, *or* death) certificate; **— de campo** picnic; **— de caza** hunting party; **— doble** double-entry bookkeeping; *Mex., Ríopl.* **confesar la —** to tell the truth, speak plainly; **jugar una mala —** to play a mean trick.

partidario [par·ti·ðá·rjo] *m.* partisan, follower, supporter.

partido [par·tí·ðo] *m.* party, faction, group; contest; game; profit; district; *Bol.* **a** (*or* **al**) **—** in equal shares; *Am.* **dar —** to give a handicap or advantage (*in certain games*); **darse a —** to yield, give up; **sacar — de** to derive advantage from, make the best of; **tomar un —** to decide, make a decision.

partir [par·tír] *v.* (*dividir*) to split, divide; to crack, break; (*salir*) to depart, leave; **a — de hoy** starting today; from this day on; *Am.* **a** (*or* **al**) **—** in equal parts; *Am.* **— a uno por el eje** to ruin someone.

partitura [par·ti·tú·ra] *f.* musical score.

parto [pár·to] *m.* childbirth, delivery; product, offspring; **estar de —** to be in labor.

parvada [par·βá·ða] *f.* pile of unthreshed grain; brood; *Andes* flock (*of birds or children*).

parvedad [par·βe·ðáð] *f.* smallness; trifle; snack, bit of food.

párvulo [pár·βu·lo] *m.* child; *adj.* small; innocent.

pasa [pá·sa] *f.* raisin; woolly hair of negros.

pasada [pa·sá·ða] *f.* passing, passage; *Am.* stay; *Col.* embarrassment, shame; **una mala —** a mean trick; **de —** on the way; incidentally, by the way; **dar una — por** to pass by, walk by.

pasadizo [pa·sa·ðí·so] *m.* aisle; narrow hall; narrow passageway.

pasado [pa·sá·ðo] *m.* past; *p.p.* past, gone; *adj.* overripe, spoiled; *Mex.* dried (*fruits*); *Col.* thin, bony (*animal*); **— mañana** day after tomorrow; **el año —** last year; **en días -s** in days gone by.

pasaje [pa·sá·xe] *m.* passage; fare, ticket; total number of passengers; *Carib., Mex., Col.* private alley; *Col., Ven.* anecdote.

pasajero [pa·sa·xé·ro] *adj.* passing, temporary, fleeting, transitory; *m.* passenger; guest (*of a hotel*).

pasamano [pa·sa·má·no] *m.* railing, hand rail; gangplank; gangway (*of a ship*).

pasaporte [pa·sa·pór·te] *m.* passport.

pasar [pa·sár] *v.* to pass; to cross; to surpass, exceed; to pierce; to go forward; to go over (in, by, to); to enter; to carry over, take across; to happen; to get along; to swallow; to overlook; to tolerate; to suffer; **— a la computadora** to feed to the computer; **— las de Caín** to have a hard time; **— por alto** to omit, overlook; **— por las armas** to execute; **-se** to transfer, change over; to get overripe, spoiled; to exceed, go beyond; **se me pasó decirte** I forgot to tell you; *Ch.* **pasársela a uno** to deceive someone, break someone's confidence; **un buen —** enough to live on.

pasarela [pa·sa·ré·la] *f.* gangplank.

pasatiempo [pa·sa·tjém·po] *m.* pastime; *Am.* cookie.

pascua [pás·kwa] *f.* Easter; Jewish Passover; **— florida** (*or* **de resurrección**) Easter Sunday; **— de Navidad** Christmas.

pase [pá·se] *m.* pass, permit; thrust (*in fencing*); pass (*with the cape in bullfighting*).

pasear [pa·se·ár] *v.* to walk; to take a walk; to ride; **-se** to take a walk; to parade; **-se en automóvil** to take an automobile ride; **-se a caballo** to go horseback riding.

paseo [pa·sé·o] *m.* walk, ride; parade; public park; boulevard; **— en automóvil** automobile ride; **dar un —** to take a walk.

pasillo [pa·sí·yo] *m.* aisle; hallway, corridor; short step; short skit; *Col., Ec.* a type of dance music; *Mex.* runner, hall carpet.

pasión [pa·sjón] *f.* passion; suffering.

pasivo [pa·sí·βo] *adj.* passive; inactive; *m.* liabilities, debts; debit, debit side (*in bookkeeping*).

pasmar [paz·már] *v.* to astound, stun; **-se** to be amazed, stunned; to marvel; to get a sudden chill; to get frostbitten; *P.R.* to become dried up, shriveled up; *P.R., Mex.* to get bruised by the saddle or pack (*said of horses and mules*).

pasmo [páz·mo] *m.* amazement, astonishment; .wonder, awe.

pasmoso [paz·mó·so] *adj.* astonishing, astounding; marvellous.

paso [pá·so] *m.* pass; step; pace; gait; passage; passing; skit; incident; *P.R., Ch., Andes* ford; *Mex.* ferry, ferryboat wharf; *adv.* slowly; **de —** by the way, in passing; **al — que** while; **salir del —** to get out of a difficulty; *Am.* **marcar el —** to mark step, obey humbly; *adj.* dried (*figs, grapes, prunes, etc.*); **paso a nivel** grade crossing.

pasta [pás·ta] *f.* paste; dough; noodles; book cover, binding; *Am.* cookie, cracker; **de buena —** of good temper or disposition.

pastal [pas·tál] *m. Am.* range, grazing land, large pasture.

pastar [pas·tár] *v.* to pasture, graze.

pastear [pas·te·ár] *v. Mex., Ríopl.* to graze, pasture.

pastel [pas·tél] *m.* pie; pastry roll; filled pastry; trick, fraud; secret pact, plot; pastel crayon; **pintura al — pastel** painting.

pastelería [pas·te·le·rí·a] *f.* pastry shop, bakery; pastry.

pastelero [pas·te·lé·ro] *m.* pastry cook; *Cuba* turncoat (*person who changes easily from one political party to another*); *Ríopl.* political intriguer.

pasterizar[9] [pas·te·ri·sár], **pasteurizar**[9] [pas·tew·ri·sár] *v.* to pasteurize.

pastilla [pas·tí·ya] *f.* tablet (*of medicine, candy, etc.*); bar (*of chocolate*); cake (*of soap*); (*computadora*) chip.

pastinaca [pas·ti·ná·ka] *f.* parsnip.

pastizal [pas·ti·sál] *m.* pasture, grassland.

pasto [pás·to] *m.* pasture; grassland; grazing; nourishment; *Am.* grass; *Ch.* **a todo —** without restraint.

pastor [pas·tór] *m.* shepherd; pastor.

pastoral [pas·to·rál] *adj.* pastoral; *f.* pastoral play; idyll; pastoral letter; **pastorela** [pas·to·ré·la] *f.* pastoral, pastoral play; **pastoril** [pas·to·ríl] *adj.*

pastoral.

pastoso [pas·tó·so] *adj.* pasty, soft; mellow (*said of the voice*); *Am.* grassy.

pastura [pas·tú·ra] *f.* pasture; fodder, feed.

pata [pá·ta] *f.* foot, leg (*of an animal, table, chair, etc.*); female duck; (*computadora*) pin; **— de gallo** crow's-foot (*wrinkle at the corner of the eye*); *Ch., Andes* **— de perro** wanderer; *Ríopl.* **hacer — ancha** to stand firm, face a danger; **meter la —** to put one's foot in it, make an embarrassing blunder; **-s arriba** upside down, head over heels.

patacón [pa·ta·kón] *m. Ríopl.* silver coin worth about one peso.

patada [pa·tá·da] *f.* kick; stamp (*with the foot*); footprint; "kick", intoxicating effect; **a -s** with kicks; in great abundance; *Andes* **en dos -s** in a jiffy, in a second.

patalear [pa·ta·le·ár] *v.* to kick around; to stamp.

pataleo [pa·ta·lé·o] *m.* kicking; stamping.

pataleta [pa·ta·lé·ta] *f.* convulsion; fainting fit.

patán [pa·tán] *m.* boor, ill-mannered person; rustic; *adj.* rude, boorish, ill-mannered.

patata [pa·tá·ta] *f.* potato.

patear [pa·te·ár] *v.* to kick; to stamp the foot; to tramp about; to trample on; to humiliate; *Am.* to kick, spring back (*as a gun*); *Ch.* to have a kick or intoxicating effect.

patentar [pa·ten·tár] *v.* to patent.

patente [pa·tén·te] *adj.* patent, evident, clear; *f.* patent; grant; privilege; *Carib.* **de —** excellent, of best quality.

patentizar[9] [pa·ten·ti·sár] *v.* to evidence, reveal, show.

paternal [pa·ter·nál] *adj.* paternal; fatherly.

paternidad [pa·ter·ni·dád] *f.* paternity, fatherhood; authorship.

paterno [pa·tér·no] *adj.* paternal, fatherly.

patético [pa·té·ti·ko] *adj.* pathetic.

patibulario [pa·ti·bu·lá·rjo] *adj.* harrowing, frightful, hair-raising; criminal.

patíbulo [pa·tí·bu·lo] *m.* scaffold, gallows.

patilla [pa·tí·ya] *f.* small foot or paw; *Col., Ven.* watermelon; *Ríopl.* stone or brick bench (*near a wall*); *Ríopl.* railing of a balcony; *Ch.* slip from a plant; **-s** side whiskers; sideburns; **Patillas** [pa·tí·yas] the Devil.

patín [pa·tín] *m.* skate; a small patio; goosander (*a kind of duck*); **— de ruedas** roller skate; **patinadero** [pa·ti·na·dé·ro] *m.* skating rink.

patinar [pa·ti·nár] *v.* to skate; to skid.

patio [pá·tjo] *m.* patio, open court, courtyard; *Am.* railway switchyard; *Am.* **pasarse uno al —** to take undue liberties.

patitieso [pa·ti·tjé·so] *adj.* dumbfounded.

patituerto [pa·ti·twér·to] *adj.* crook-legged; knock-kneed; bow-legged.

patizambo [pa·ti·sám·bo] *adj.* knock-kneed.

pato [pá·to] *m.* duck; **pagar el —** to be the goat; to get the blame; *Ríopl.* **andar —** to be flat broke, penniless; *Am.* **hacerse —** to play the fool; *Mex., Ríopl.* **pasarse de — a ganso** to take undue liberties; *Am.* **ser el — de la boda** to be the life of the party; **patito** *m.* duckling.

patochada [pa·to·čá·da] *f.* stupidity, blunder, nonsense.

patojo [pa·tó·xo] *adj.* crooked-legged; bowlegged; *m. & f. Guat.* child; young person.

patología [pa·to·lo·xí·a] *f.* pathology.

patológico [pa·to·ló·xi·ko] *adj.* pathological.

patraña [pa·trá·ña] *f.* fabulous tale; lie, falsehood.

patria [pá·trja] *f.* fatherland, native country.

patriarca [pa·trjár·ka] *m.* patriarch; **patriarcal** [pa·trjar·kál] *adj.* patriarchal.

patrimonio [pa·tri·mó·njo] *m.* patrimony; inheritance.

patrio [pá·trjo] *adj.* native, of one's native country; paternal, belonging to the father.

patriota [pa·trjó·ta] *m. & f.* patriot.

patriótico [pa·trjó·ti·ko] *adj.* patriotic.

patriotismo [pa·trjo·tíz·mo] *m.* patriotism.

patrocinar [pa·tro·si·nár] *v.* to patronize, favor, sponsor.

patrocinio [pa·tro·sí·njo] *m.* patronage, protection.

patrón [pa·trón] *m.* (*protector*) patron; patron saint; sponsor; (*amo*) master, boss; proprietor, landlord; host; skipper; (*dechado*) pattern, standard, model; **patrona** [pa·tró·na] *f.* landlady; patroness; hostess.

patronato [pa·tro·ná·to] *m.* board of trustees; foundation (*for educational, cultural, or charitable purposes*).

patrono [pa·tró·no] *m.* patron, protector; trustee; patron saint.

patrulla [pa·trú·ya] *f.* patrol; squad, gang.

patrullar [pa·tru·yár] *v.* to patrol.

pausa [páw·sa] *f.* pause, stop, rest.

pausar [paw·sár] *v.* to pause.

pauta [páw·ta] *f.* norm, rule, standard; guide lines (*for writing*).

pava [pá·ba] *f.* turkey hen; *Ríopl.* kettle, teapot, teakettle; *Andes, Ch.* jest, coarse joke; **pelar la —** to talk by night at the window (*said of lovers*).

pavear [pa·be·ár] *v.* to talk nonsense.

pavesa [pa·bé·sa] *f.* cinder; small firebrand; burnt wick or snuff of a candle; **-s** cinders.

pavimentar [pa·bi·men·tár] *v.* to pave.

pavimento [pa·bi·mén·to] *m.* pavement.

pavo [pá·bo] *m.* turkey; *Ch.* sponger, parasite; — **real** peacock; **comer —** to be a wallflower at a dance; *adj.* silly, foolish; vain.

pavón [pa·bón] *m.* peacock.

pavonearse [pa·bo·ne·ár·se] *v.* to strut, swagger.

pavoneo [pa·bo·né·o] *m.* strut, swagger.

pavor [pa·bór] *m.* awe, dread, terror.

pavoroso [pa·bo·ró·so] *adj.* frightful, dreadful.

payador [pa·ya·dór] *m. Ríopl.* one who sings an improvised song accompanied on the guitar.

payasada [pa·ya·sá·da] *f.* clownish act or remark.

payasear [pa·ya·se·ár] *v.* to clown, play the fool.

payaso [pa·yá·so] *m.* clown.

paz [pas] *f.* peace.

pazguato [paz·ǵwá·to] *adj.* simple, dumb, stupid; *m.* simpleton.

peaje [pe·á·xe] *m.* toll (*for crossing a bridge or ferry*).

peal [pe·ál] = **pial.**

pealar [pe·a·lár] = **pialar.**

peatón [pe·a·tón] *m.* pedestrian.

peca [pé·ka] *f.* freckle.

pecado [pe·ká·do] *m.* sin.

pecador [pe·ka·dór] *m.* sinner; *adj.* sinful.

pecaminoso [pe·ka·mi·nó·so] *adj.* sinful.

pecar[6] [pe·kár] *v.* to sin; — **de bueno** to be too good; — **de oscuro** to be exceedingly unclear, too complicated.

pecera [pe·sé·ra] *f.* fish bowl.

pécora [pé·ko·ra] *f.* head of sheep.

pecoso [pe·kó·so] *adj.* freckly, freckled.

peculado [pe·ku·lá·do] *m.* embezzlement.

peculiar [pe·ku·ljár] *adj.* peculiar; **peculiaridad** [pe·ku·lja·ri·dád] *f.* peculiarity.

pechada [pe·čá·da] *f. Ríopl.* bump, push, shove with the chest; *Arg.* bumping contest between two riders; *Ríopl., Ch.* overthrowing an animal (*by*

bumping it with the chest of a horse).

pechar [pe·čár] *v. Ríopl., Ch., Bol.* to bump, push, shove with the chest; *Ríopl., Ch., Bol.* to drive one's horse against; *Ch., Ríopl.* to borrow, strike (*someone*) for a loan.

pechera [pe·čé·ra] *f.* shirtfront; chest protector; bib (*of an apron*).

pecho [pé·čo] *m.* chest; breast; bosom; heart; courage; **dar el —** to nurse; **tomar a -s** to take to heart; *P.R., Col.* **a todo —** shouting; *Am.* **en -s de camisa** in shirt sleeves.

pechuga [pe·čú·ǵa] *f.* breast, breast meat of a fowl; bosom; *C.A., Col., Ch., Andes* courage, nerve, audacity, impudence.

pedagogía [pe·da·ǵo·xí·a] *f.* pedagogy, science of education.

pedagógico [pe·da·ǵó·xi·ko] *adj.* pedagogic, relating to education or teaching.

pedagogo [pe·da·ǵó·ǵo] *m.* pedagogue, teacher, educator.

pedal [pe·dál] *m.* pedal.

pedalear [pe·da·le·ár] *v.* to pedal.

pedante [pe·dán·te] *adj.* pedantic, affected, vain, superficial; *m.* pedant; **pedantesco** [pe·dan·tés·ko] *adj.* pedantic.

pedazo [pe·dá·so] *m.* piece, portion, bit; **hacer -s** to tear or break into pieces; **caerse a -s** fall into pieces.

pedernal [pe·der·nál] *m.* flint.

pedestal [pe·des·tál] *m.* pedestal, base.

pedestre [pe·dés·tre] *adj.* pedestrian, walking, going on foot; commonplace, vulgar, low.

pediatra [pe·djá·tra] *m., f.* pediatrician; **pediatría** [pe·] pediatrics.

pedido [pe·dí·do] *m.* commercial order; request petition; *p.p.* of **pedir.**

pedigüeño [pe·di·ǵwé·ño] *adj.* begging, demanding.

pedir[5] [pe·dír] *v. irr.* to ask, beg, petition; to ask for; to demand; to require; to order (*merchandise*); **a — de boca** exactly as desired.

pedo [pé·do] *m.* wind, flatulence; *Mex.* **andar —** to be drunk.

pedrada [pe·drá·da] *f.* hit or blow with a stone; throw with a stone; mark or bruise made by a stone (*thrown*); **a -s** by stoning; with stones; **dar una —** to hit with a stone; **echar a alguien a -s** to stone someone out; **matar a -s** to stone to death.

pedregal [pe·dre·ǵál] *m.* rocky ground, ground strewn with rocks.

pedregoso [pe·dre·ǵó·so] *adj.* rocky, stony, pebbly.

pedrería [pe·dre·rí·a] *f.* precious stones; precious stone ornament; jewelry.

pedrusco [pe·drús·ko] *m.* boulder.

pedúnculo [pe·dúŋ·ku·lo] *m.* stem (*of a leaf, flower or fruit*), stalk.

pegajoso [pe·ga·xó·so] *adj.* sticky; contagious.

pegar[7] [pe·ǵár] *v.* (*golpear*) to hit, strike, slap, beat; (*adherir*) to stick, paste, glue; to sew on (*a button*); to infect; to be becoming; to be fitting, opportune, to the point; *Am.* to tie, fasten; *Am.* to yoke; — **fuego** to set on fire; — **un chasco** to play a trick; to surprise; disappoint; — **un susto** to give a scare; — **un salto** (**una carrera**) to take a jump (a run); **-se** to stick, cling; **pegársela a uno** to fool somebody.

pegote [pe·ǵó·te] *m.* sticky thing; sticking plaster; clumsy patch; sponger; thick, sticky concoction; clumsy addition or insertion (*in a literary or artistic work*).

peinado [pej·ná·do] *m.* coiffure, hairdo; hairdressing; *p.p.* combed; groomed; *adj.* effeminate; **bien —**

spruce, trim.

peinador [pej·na·dór] *m.* hairdresser; short wrapper or dressing gown; **peinadora** [pej·na·dó·ra] *f.* woman hairdresser.

peinar [pej·nár] *v.* to comb; *Ríopl.* to flatter.

peine [péj·ne] *m.* comb.

peineta [pej·né·ta] *f.* large ornamental comb.

peje [pé·xe] *m. C.A.* fish.

peladilla [pe·la·dí·ya] *f.* small pebble; sugar-coated almond.

pelado [pe·lá·do] *p.p. & adj.* peeled; plucked; skinned; hairless; featherless; barren, treeless, bare; penniless, broke; *m. Mex.* ragged fellow (*generally a peon*); *Mex.* ill-bred person; *Col.* child.

pelafustán [pe·la·fus·tán] *m.* tramp, vagabond.

pelagatos [pe·la·gá·tos] *m.* ragged fellow, tramp.

pelaje [pe·lá·xe] *m.* animal's coat, fur; external appearance.

pelar [pe·lár] *v.* to cut the hair of; to pluck the feathers or hair from; to peel, shell, skin, husk; to fleece, rob; *Am.* to beat, thrash; *Am.* to slander; *C.R.* — **los dientes** to show one's teeth; to smile affectedly; *C.A., Mex., Carib., Col., Andes* — **los ojos** to keep one's eyes peeled; to open one's eyes wide; **-se** to peel off; to lose one's hair; *Col., Ven.* to be confused; *Col., Ven.* to be careless, unaware; *Col., Ven.* to slip away; *Col., Ven.* to die; **pelárselas por algo** to be dying for something, want something very much; **peladora** peeler.

peldaño [pel·dá·ño] *m.* step (*of a staircase*).

pelea [pe·lé·a] *f.* fight, quarrel.

pelear [pe·le·ár] *v.* to fight; to quarrel.

peletería [pe·le·te·rí·a] *f.* fur store; fur trade; furs; *Am.* leather goods, leather shop; *Cuba* shoe store.

pelicano [pe·li·ká·no] *adj.* gray-haired.

pelícano [pe·lí·ka·no] *m.* pelican.

película [pe·lí·ku·la] *f.* thin skin; membrane; film; motion-picture film.

peligrar [pe·li·grár] *v.* to be in danger.

peligro [pe·lí·gro] *m.* danger.

peligroso [pe·li·gró·so] *adj.* dangerous.

pelillo [pe·lí·yo] *m.* short, fine hair; **-s** trouble, nuisance; **echar -s a la mar** to "bury the hatchet", become reconciled; **no pararse en -s** not to stop at small details, not to bother about trifles; **no tener -s en la lengua** to speak frankly.

pelirrojo [pe·li·rró·xo] *adj.* redheaded, red-haired.

pelo [pé·lo] *m.* (*cabello*) hair; (*haz*) nap (*of cloth*); (*fibra*) grain (*in wood*); **al** — perfectly; agreed; apropos, to the point; along the grain; **eso me viene al** — that suits me perfectly; **con todos sus -s y señales** with every possible detail; *Am.* **por** (*or* **en**) **un** — on the point of, almost, by a hair's breadth; **montar en** — to ride bareback; **tomar el** — **a** to kid, make fun of; *Ríopl., Carib., Mex., Andes* **no aflojar un** — not to yield an inch.

pelón [pe·lón] *adj.* bald.

pelota [pe·ló·ta] *f.* ball; ball game; *Ríopl.* boat made of cowhide; **en** — (*or* **en -s**) naked; *Am.* **darle a la** — to hit upon by chance; **pelotilla** [pe·lo·tí·ya] *f.* pellet, little ball.

pelotari [pe·lo·tá·ri] *m.* pelota (*jai-alai*) player.

pelotera [pe·lo·té·ra] *f.* brawl, row, riot; *C.A., Ven.* crowd.

pelotón [pe·lo·tón] *m.* large ball; crowd, gang; heap, pile; platoon of soldiers; firing squad.

peluca [pe·lú·ka] *f.* wig.

pelucón [pe·lu·kón] *adj.* wig-wearing; *Ch.* conservative.

peludo [pe·lú·do] *adj.* hairy; shaggy; *m.* plush carpet with shaggy pile; *Am.* a species of armadillo;

Ríopl. **agarrar un** — to get drunk.

peluquería [pe·lu·ke·rí·a] *f.* barbershop, hairdresser's shop.

peluquero [pe·lu·ké·ro] *m.* hairdresser, barber.

pelusa [pe·lú·sa] *f.* down; fuzz; nap (*of cloth*).

pellejo [pe·yé·xo] *m.* hide; skin; peel; **salvar el** — to save one's skin, escape punishment; *Am.* **jugarse el** — to gamble one's life.

pellizcar[6] [pe·yis·kár] *v.* to pinch, nip.

pellizco [pe·yís·ko] *m.* pinching, nipping; pinch, nip.

pena [pé·na] *f.* penalty; grief, worry; hardship; toil; *Mex., Carib., C.A., Col., Ven.* embarrassment; **a duras -s** with great difficulty; hardly; **me da** — it grieves me; *C.A., Ven., Col., Carib.* it embarrasses me; **valer la** — to be worthwhile; **tener** (*or* **estar con**) **mucha** — to be terribly sorry; *Am.* to be greatly embarrassed.

penacho [pe·ná·čo] *m.* tuft, crest; plume.

penado [pe·ná·do] *adj.* afflicted.

penal [pe·nál] *adj.* penal; **código** — penal code.

penalidad [pe·na·li·dád] *f.* hardship; trouble; penalty.

penar [pe·nár] *v.* to suffer; to worry, fret; to impose a penalty; — **por** to long for; to suffer because of.

penca [pén·ka] *f.* leaf of a cactus plant; *Arg.* sweetheart; *Ven.* **coger una** — to get drunk.

penco [pén·ko] *m.* nag, horse; *Am.* boor.

pendencia [pen·dén·sja] *f.* quarrel; scuffle, fight.

pendenciero [pen·den·sjé·ro] *adj.* quarrelsome.

pender [pen·dér] *v.* to hang; to dangle; to depend.

pendiente [pen·djén·te] *f.* slope; *m.* earring; pendant; *Am.* watch chain; *adj.* hanging, dangling; pending.

pendón [pen·dón] *m.* banner.

péndulo [pén·du·lo] *m.* pendulum.

pene [pé·ne] *m.* penis.

penetración [pe·ne·tra·sjón] *f.* penetration; acuteness; keen judgment.

penetrante [pe·ne·trán·te] *adj.* penetrating; acute; keen.

penetrar [pe·ne·trár] *v.* to penetrate; to pierce; to fathom, comprehend.

penicilina [pe·ni·si·lí·na] *f.* penicillin.

península [pe·nín·su·la] *f.* peninsula.

peninsular [pe·nin·su·lár] *adj.* peninsular.

penitencia [pe·ni·tén·sja] *f.* penance.

penitenciaría [pe·ni·ten·sja·rí·a] *f.* penitentiary.

penitente [pe·ni·tén·te] *adj.* repentant, penitent; *m. & f.* penitent.

penoso [pe·nó·so] *adj.* painful; hard, difficult; embarrassing; fatiguing; *Mex., Carib., C.A., Ven., Col.* timid, shy.

pensador [pen·sa·dór] *m.* thinker; *adj.* thinking.

pensamiento [pen·sa·mjén·to] *m.* thought; mind; pansy.

pensar[1] [pen·sár] *v. irr.* to think; to think over; to intend.

pensativo [pen·sa·tí·bo] *adj.* pensive.

pensión [pen·sjón] *f.* pension; board; scholarship for study; boardinghouse; *Col.* apprehension, anxiety; — **completa** room and board.

pensionado [pen·sjo·ná·do] *m.* pensioner (*person receiving a pension*); *adj. & p.p.* pensioned.

pensionar [pen·sjo·nár] *v.* to pension.

pensionista [pen·sjo·nís·ta] *m. & f.* boarder; pensioner (*person receiving a pension*).

pentagrama [pen·ta·grá·ma] *m.* musical staff.

penúltimo [pe·núl·ti·mo] *adj.* next to the last.

penumbra [pe·núm·bra] *f.* partial shadow, dimness.

penumbroso [pe·num·bró·so] *adj.* dim.

peña [pé·ña] *f.* rock, large stone.

peñasco [pe·ñás·ko] *m.* large rock; crag.

peñascoso [pe·ñas·kó·so] *adj.* rocky.

peón [pe·ón] *m.* unskilled laborer; foot soldier; spinning top; pawn (*in chess*); *Ch., Ríopl., C.A., Carib., Mex.* farm hand; *Am.* apprentice; *Mex.* — **de albañil** mason's helper.

peonada [peo·ná·da] *f.* gang of laborers or peons.

peonaje [pe·o·ná·xe] *m.* gang of laborers.

peonza [pe·on·sa] *f.* top (*toy*).

peor [pe·ór] *adj. & adv.* worse; worst; — **que** worse than; — **que** — that is even worse; **tanto** — so much the worse.

pepa [pé·pa] *f. Andes, Col., Ven., Ch., Mex., Ríopl.* seed (*of an apple, melon, etc.*); *Am.* marble (*to play with*); **Pepa** nickname for **Josefa.**

pepenar [pe·pe·nár] *v. Mex.* to pick up; *Am.* to seize, grab.

pepino [pe·pí·no] *m.* cucumber.

pepita [pe·pí·ta] *f.* seed (*of an apple, melon, etc.*); pip (*a disease of birds*); nugget (*lump of gold or other minerals*); *Am.* fruit stone, pit; **Pepita** = **Josefita** *dim. of* **Josefa.**

pequeñez [pe·ke·ñés] *f.* smallness; childhood; trifle; meanness.

pequeño [pe·ké·ño] *adj.* small, little; young; low, humble; *m.* child.

pera [pé·ra] *f.* pear; goatee; sinecure, easy job; *Am.* Peruvian alligator pear (*see* **aguacate**); *Am.* **hacerle a uno la** — to play a trick on someone; **peral** *m.* pear tree; pear orchard.

perca [pér·ka] *f.* perch (*fish*)

percal [per·kál] *m.* percale (*fine cotton cloth*).

percance [per·kán·se] *m.* misfortune, accident; occurrence.

percepción [per·sep·sjón] *f.* perception; idea.

perceptible [per·sep·tí·ble] *adj.* perceptible, noticeable.

percibir [per·si·bír] *v.* to perceive; to collect, receive.

percudido [per·ku·dí·do] *adj.* dirty, grimy.

percudir [per·ku·dír] *v.* to soil, make dirty or grimy; **-se** to get grimy.

percusión [per·ku·sjón] *f.* percussion.

percusor [per·ku·sór] *m.* firing pin.

percha [pér·ča] *f.* clothes or hat rack; pole; perch, roost; perch (*a fish*); **perchero** [per·čé·ro] *m.* clothes or hat rack.

perder[1] [per·dér] *v. irr.* to lose; to squander; to ruin, harm; to miss (*a train*); — **de vista** to lose sight of; **-se** to lose one's way; to get lost; to go astray; to get spoiled; to become ruined.

perdición [per·di·sjón] *f.* perdition, damnation, hell, ruin.

pérdida [pér·di·da] *f.* loss; damage.

perdidamente [per·di·da·mén·te] *adv.* excessively.

perdido [per·dí·do] *p.p. & adj.* lost; strayed; mislaid; ruined; **estar** — **por alguien** to be crazy about, or very fond of, someone; *m.* rake, dissolute fellow; bum, vagabond.

perdigar [per·di·gár] *v.* to braise.

perdigón [per·di·gón] *m.* young partridge; bird shot, buckshot; losing gambler.

perdiz [per·dís] *f.* partridge.

perdón [per·dón] *m.* pardon; forgiveness; remission.

perdonar [per·do·nár] *v.* to pardon; to forgive.

perdulario [per·du·lá·rjo] *m.* rake, dissolute person; reckless fellow; good-for-nothing; tramp.

perdurable [per·du·rá·ble] *adj.* lasting, everlasting.

perdurar [per·du·rár] *v.* to last, endure.

perecedero [pe·re·se·dé·ro] *adj.* perishable.

perecer[13] [pe·re·sér] *v. irr.* to perish; to die; **-se** to long (for); pine (for).

peregrinación [pe·re·gri·na·sjón] *f.* pilgrimage; long journey.

peregrinar [pe·re·gri·nár] *v.* to journey; to go through life.

peregrino [pe·re·grí·no] *m.* pilgrim; *adj.* foreign, strange; rare; beautiful, perfect; travelling, wandering; **ave peregrina** migratory bird, bird of passage.

perejil [pe·re·xíl] *m.* parsley; **-es** frippery, showy clothes or ornaments.

perenne [pe·rén·ne] *adj.* perennial, enduring, perpetual.

pereza [pe·ré·sa] *f.* laziness; idleness.

perezoso [pe·re·só·so] *adj.* lazy; *m. Am.* sloth (*an animal*); *Am.* safety pin; *Ch.* bed cushion.

perfección [per·fek·sjón] *f.* perfection; **a la** — to perfection, perfectly.

perfeccionamiento [per·fek·sjo·na·mjén·to] *m.* perfecting, perfection; completion.

perfeccionar [per·fek·sjo·nár] *v.* to perfect, finish, complete.

perfecto [per·fék·to] *adj.* perfect.

perfidia [per·fí·dja] *f.* perfidy, treachery.

pérfido [pér·fi·do] *adj.* perfidious, treacherous, faithless.

perfil [per·fíl] *m.* profile; outline; *Col., Ec.* pen or pen point.

perfilar [per·fi·lár] *v.* to silhouette; to outline; **-se** to show one's profile; to be silhouetted.

perforación [per·fo·ra·sjón] *f.* perforation, hole; puncture; perforating, boring, drilling; — **aumentadora** counter bore.

perforar [per·fo·rár] *v.* to perforate, pierce; to drill, bore.

perfumar [per·fu·már] *v.* to perfume, scent.

perfume [per·fú·me] *m.* perfume; fragrance.

perfumería [per·fu·me·rí·a] *f.* perfumery; perfume shop.

pergamino [per·ga·mí·no] *m.* parchment.

pericia [pe·rí·sja] *f.* expertness, skill.

perico [pe·rí·ko] *m.* parakeet, small parrot; *Col.* **huevos -s** scrambled eggs.

periferia [pe·ri·fé·rja] *f.* periphery; **periférico** belt-line highway; *adj.* peripheral.

perifollos [pe·ri·fó·yos] *m. pl.* frippery, finery, showy ornaments.

perifrasear [pe·ri·fra·se·ár] *v.* to periphrase.

perífrasis [pe·rí·fra·sis] *f.* periphrase.

perigeo [pe·ri·xé·o] *m.* perigee.

perilla [pe·rí·ya] *f.* small pear; pear-shaped ornament; knob; pommel of a saddle; goatee; **de** — apropos, to the point.

perímetro [pe·rí·me·tro] *m.* perimeter.

periódico [pe·rjó·di·ko] *m.* newspaper; periodical; *adj.* periodic, periodical.

periodismo [pe·rjo·díz·mo] *m.* journalism; **periodista** [pe·rjo·dís·ta] *m. & f.* journalist; newspaper editor or publisher; **periodístico** [pe·rjo·dís·ti·ko] *adj.* journalistic.

período [pe·rí·o·do] [pe·rjó·do] *m.* period; cycle; sentence.

peripecia [pe·ri·pé·sja] *f.* vicissitude, change in fortune; unforeseen incident.

peripuesto [pe·ri·pwés·to] *adj.* dressed up, dolled up, decked out.

perito [pe·rí·to] *adj.* learned; experienced; skillful; skilled; *m.* expert.

peritoneo [pe·ri·to·né·o] *m.* peritoneum.

peritonitis [pe·ri·to·ní·tis] *f.* peritonitis.

perjudicar[6] [per·xu·di·kár] *v.* to damage, impair, harm.

perjudicial [per·xu·di·sjál] *adj.* harmful, injurious.

perjuicio [per·xwí·sjo] *m.* damage, ruin, mischief;

PE

harm.

perjurar [per·xu·rár] v. to perjure oneself; to commit perjury; to curse, swear.

perjurio [per·xú·rjo] m. perjury.

perla [pér·la] f. pearl; **de -s** perfectly, just right, to the point.

perlino [per·lí·no] adj. pearly, pearl-colored.

permanecer[13] [per·ma·ne·sér] v. irr. to remain, stay.

permanencia [per·ma·nén·sja] f. permanence, duration; stability; stay, sojourn.

permanente [per·ma·nén·te] adj. permanent.

permiso [per·mí·so] m. permission; permit; **con —** with your permission; excuse me.

permitir [per·mi·tír] v. to permit, let; to grant.

permuta [per·mú·ta] f. exchange, barter.

permutar [per·mu·tár] v. to exchange; to barter; to change around.

pernetas [per·né·tas] **en —** barelegged, with bare legs.

pernicioso [per·ni·sjó·so] adj. pernicious, harmful.

perno [pér·no] m. bolt; spike; **-s** *Ch.* (*trampa*) tricks, frauds.

pero [pé·ro] *conj* but, except, yet; m. objection, exception; defect; a variety of apple tree; a variety of apple; **perón** [pe·rón] m. *Am.* a variety of apple.

perogrullada [pe·ro·ǵru·yá·ɖa] f. platitude, trite or commonplace remark.

peroración [pe·ro·ra·sjón] f. peroration, speech, harangue.

perorar [pe·ro·rár] v. to make an impassioned speech; to declaim, harangue; to plea, make a plea.

perorata [pe·ro·rá·ta] f. harangue, speech.

peróxido [pe·rók·si·ɖo] m. peroxide; **— benzoico** benzoyl peroxide.

perpendicular [per·pen·di·ku·lár] adj., m. & f. perpendicular.

perpetuar[18] [per·pe·twár] v. to perpetuate.

perpetuo [per·pé·two] adj. perpetual; **perpetua** [per·pé·twa] f. everlasting (*plant*).

perplejidad [per·ple·xi·ɖáɖ] f. perplexity.

perplejo [per·plé·xo] adj. perplexed, bewildered.

perra [pé·rra] f. bitch, female dog; drunkenness; **— chica** five-centime copper coin; **— grande** (*or* **gorda**) ten-centime copper coin.

perrada [pe·rrá·ɖa] f. pack of dogs; **hacer una —** to play a mean trick.

perrera [pe·rré·ra] f. kennel; toil, hard work, hard job; tantrum; *Carib.*, *Mex.*, *Ven.* brawl, dispute.

perrilla [pe·rrí·ya] f. *Am.* sty (*on the eyelid*). See **orzuelo.**

perro [pé·rro] m. dog; **— de arrastre** dog, pawl (machine); **— de busca** hunting dog; **— dogo** bulldog; **— de lanas** poodle; adj. dogged, tenacious; *Mex.*, *C.A.* hard, selfish, mean, stingy; *Ven.* vagabond.

perruno [pe·rrú·no] adj. canine, doglike.

persecución [per·se·ku·sjón] f. persecution; pursuit.

perseguidor [per·se·ǵi·ɖór] m. pursuer; persecutor.

perseguimiento [per·se·ǵi·mjén·to] m. pursuit; persecution.

perseguir[5, 12] [per·se·ǵír] v. irr. to pursue; to persecute; to harass, annoy.

perseverancia [per·se·ȼe·ran·sja] f. perseverance.

perseverar [per·se·ȼe·rár] v. to persevere.

persiana [per·sjá·na] f. Venetian blind; window shade.

persistencia [per·sis·tén·sja] f. persistence; **persistente** [per·sis·tén·te] adj. persistent.

persistir [per·sis·tír] v. to persist.

persona [per·só·na] f. person; personage.

personaje [per·so·ná·xe] m. personage; character (*in a book or play*).

personal [per·so·nál] adj. personal; m. personnel.

personalidad [per·so·na·li·ɖáɖ] f. personality; individuality; person, personage.

personalismo [per·so·na·líz·mo] m. personalism; individualism.

perspectiva [per·spek·tí·ȼa] f. perspective; view; appearance; outlook; prospect.

perspicacia [pers·pi·ká·sja] f. keenness of mind, penetration, keen insight.

perspicaz [pers·pi·kás] adj. keen, shrewd.

persuadir [per·swa·ɖír] v. to persuade.

persuasión [per·swa·sjón] f. persuasion.

persuasivo [per·swa·sí·ȼo] adj. persuasive.

pertenecer[13] [per·te·ne·sér] v. irr. to belong; to pertain; to concern.

perteneciente [per·te·ne·sjén·te] adj. pertaining, belonging, concerning.

pértiga [pér·ti·ǵa] f. pole, bar, rod; **salto con —** pole vault.

pertinente [per·ti·nén·te] adj. pertinent, to the point, apt, fitting.

pertrechos [per·tré·čos] m. pl. military supplies; tools, implements.

perturbación [per·tur·ȼa·sjón] f. uneasiness, agitation, disturbance.

perturbar [per·tur·ȼár] v. to perturb, disturb.

peruano [pe·rwá·no] adj. & m. Peruvian.

perulero [pe·ru·lé·ro] adj., m & f. Peruvian (*slang expression*).

perversidad [per·ȼer·si·ɖáɖ] f. perversity, wickedness.

perverso [per·ȼér·so] adj. perverse, wicked; m. pervert.

pervertir[3] [per·ȼer·tír] v. irr. to pervert; to corrupt; to distort; **-se** to become perverted; to go wrong.

pesa [pé·sa] f. weight (*for scales*); **— de reloj** clock weight; **-s y medidas** weights and measures.

pesadez [pe·sa·dés] f. heaviness; dullness, drowsiness; slowness; bother; stubbornness.

pesadilla [pe·sa·ɖí·ya] f. nightmare.

pesado [pe·sá·ɖo] adj. heavy; sound (*sleep*); tiresome, boring; annoying; slow; dull.

pesadumbre [pe·sa·ɖúm·bre] f. grief, sorrow; weight, heaviness.

pésame [pé·sa·me] m. condolence, expression of sympathy.

pesantez [pe·san·tés] f. gravity; heaviness.

pesar [pe·sár] v. (*penar*) to cause grief, sorrow, or regret; (*tener gravedad*) to weigh; to consider, to have weight, value, or importance; m. grief, sorrow; **a — de** in spite of.

pesaroso [pe·sa·ró·so] adj. grieved, sad; repentant.

pesca [pés·ka] f. fishing; catch, fish caught.

pescadería [pes·ka·ɖe·rí·a] f. fish market; **pescadero** [pes·ka·ɖé·ro] m. fishmonger, dealer in fish.

pescado [pes·ká·ɖo] m. fish (*especially after being caught*); salted codfish.

pescador [pes·ka·ɖór] m. fisherman.

pescar[6] [pes·kár] v. to fish; to catch; to catch unaware, catch in the act.

pescozón [pes·ko·són] m. blow on the back of the head or neck.

pescuezo [pes·kwé·so] m. neck.

pesebre [pe·sé·ȼre] m. manger.

peseta [pe·sé·ta] f. peseta (*monetary unit of Spain*).

pesimismo [pe·si·míz·mo] m. pessimism; **pesimista** [pe·si·mís·ta] m. & f. pessimist; adj. pessimistic.

pésimo [pé·si·mo] adj. very bad.

peso [pé·so] m. weight; weighing; burden; importance; *Am.* peso (*monetary unit of several Spanish American countries*).

pespunte [pes·pún·te] *m.* backstitching.
pesquera [pes·ké·ra] *f.* fishery (*place for catching fish*); **pesquería** [pes·ke·rí·a] *f.* fishery; fishing.
pesquero [pes·ké·ro] *adj.* fishing; **buque —** fishing boat; **industria pesquera** fishing industry.
pesquisa [pes·kí·sa] *f.* investigation, inquiry; *m. Am.* police investigator.
pestaña [pes·tá·ña] *f.* eyelash; edging, fringe; **quemarse las -s** to burn the midnight oil, study hard at night.
pestañear [pes·ta·ñe·ár] *v.* to blink; to wink; to flicker.
peste [pés·te] *f.* pest, pestilence, plague; epidemic; stench, stink, foul odor; overabundance, excess; *Arg., Ch.* smallpox; *Col.* head cold; **echar -s** to utter insults.
pestillo [pes·tí·yo] *m.* bolt; latch; lock.
pesuña [pe·sú·ña] *f.* hoof (*cloven*).
pesuño [pe·sú·ño] *m.* half of the cloven hoof.
petaca [pe·tá·ka] *f.* tobacco pouch; cigar case; leather covered hamper (*used as a pack*); *Mex.,* trunk; *adj. Andes* heavy, clumsy.
pétalo [pé·ta·lo] *m.* petal.
petate [pe·tá·te] *m.* bundle; impostor; *Mex., C.A., Ven., Col.* mat (*of straw or palm leaves*); *Am.* dunce; *Andes* coward; **liar el —** to pack up and go; *Mex.* to die; *Col., Ven.* **dejar a uno en un —** to ruin a person, leave him penniless.
petición [pe·ti·sjón] *f.* petition, request.
petirrojo [pe·ti·rró·xo] *m.* robin, robin redbreast.
petiso [pe·tí·so] *adj. Ríopl., Ch., Andes* small, short, dwarfish; *m. Am.* small horse, pony.
pétreo [pé·tre·o] *adj.* stone, stony.
petróleo [pe·tró·le·o] *m.* petroleum.
petrolero [pe·tro·lé·ro] *m.* oil man; dealer in petroleum; **compañía petrolera** oil company.
petulancia [pe·tu·lán·sja] *f.* flippancy; insolence; **petulante** [pe·tu·lán·te] *adj.* impertinent, flippant.
petunia [pe·tú·nja] *f.* petunia.
pez [pes] *m.* fish; *f.* pitch, tar.
pezón [pe·són] *m.* nipple; stem, stalk (*of a fruit, leaf or flower*); small point of land.
pezuña [pe·sú·ña] *f.* hoof.
piadoso [pja·dó·so] *adj.* pious; kind, merciful.
pial [pjal] *m. Mex.* lasso, lariat (*thrown in order to trip an animal*); *Ríopl.* snare, trap.
pialar [pja·lár] *v.* to lasso by tripping with a **pial.**
piano [pjá·no] *m.* piano; **— de cola** grand piano; **— vertical** upright piano.
piar[17] [pjar] *v.* to peep, chirp; to cry, whine.
pibe [pí·be] *m. Ríopl.* urchin, boy.
pica [pí·ka] *f.* pike, spear; picador's goad or lance; stonecutter's hammer; *Ven.* tapping of rubber trees; *Col.* trail; *Col., Ch.* pique, resentment; *Am.* cockfight.
picada [pi·ká·da] *f.* prick; bite (*as of an insect or fish*); puncture; sharp pain; dive (*of a plane*); *Cuba, Ríopl.* path, trail (*cut through a forest*); *Am.* narrow ford; *Col., Ven., Mex.* peck.
picadillo [pi·ka·dí·yo] *m.* meat and vegetable hash; minced meat, mincemeat.
picador [pi·ka·dór] *m.* picador (*mounted bullfighter armed with a goad*); horse-breaker; chopping block; *Ven.* tree tapper.
picadura [pi·ka·dú·ra] *f.* biting; pricking; bite; prick; sting; puncture; cut tobacco.
picante [pi·kán·te] *adj.* (*acerbo*) pricking, biting stinging; (*con chile o ají*) spicy; highly seasoned; *m.* strong seasoning; *Am.* highly seasoned sauce (*usually containing chili pepper*).
picapleitos [pi·ka·pléj·tos] *m.* quarrelsome person

(*one who likes to pick a fight*); shyster.
picaporte [pi·ka·pór·te] *m.* latch; latchkey; door knocker.
picar[6] [pi·kár] *v.* to prick; to pierce; to bite (*said of fish or insects*); to sting; to peck; to nibble; to mince, chop up; to goad; to stick, poke; to hew, chisel; to pique, vex; to itch, smart, burn; *Am.* to chop (*wood*); *Mex., Carib.* to open a trail; *Am.* to tap (*a tree*); *Am.* to slaughter (*cattle*); **— muy alto** to aim very high; **— en** to border on, be somewhat of; *Mex., Ven.* **¡pícale!** [pí·ka·le] hurry! **-se** to be piqued, angry; to be motheaten; to begin to sour; to begin to rot; *C.A., Ven.* to get tipsy; **-se de** to boast of.
picardía [pi·kar·dí·a] *f.* roguishness; offensive act or remark; roguish trick; mischief.
picaresco [pi·ka·rés·ko] *adj.* picaresque, roguish.
pícaro [pí·ka·ro] *m.* rogue, rascal; *adj.* roguish; mischievous; crafty, sly; low, vile; **picarón** [pa·ka·rón] *m.* big rascal.
picazo [pi·ká·so] *adj.* piebald; *m.* piebald horse.
picazón [pi·ka·són] *f.* itch, itching.
pico [pí·ko] *m.* beak, bill; sharp point; peak, pickaxe, pick, spout; mouth; additional amount, a little over; *C.A., Carib., Ríopl., Ven.* a small balance; *Mex.* a goodly sum; **tener el — de oro** to be very eloquent; **tener mucho —** to be very talkative.
picotada [pi·ko·tá·da] *f.,* **picotazo** [pi·ko·tá·so] *m.* peck.
picotear [pi·ko·te·ár] *v.* to peck; to chatter; *Am.* to mince, cut into small pieces.
pichel [pi·čél] *m.* pitcher; mug.
pichón [pi·čón] *m.* young pigeon; *C.A.* any male bird (*except a rooster*); *Mex.* dupe, easy mark; *Am.* novice, inexperienced person, apprentice; *adj.* timid, shy.
pie [pje] *m.* foot; leg; stand; stem; base; *Am.* down payment; *Mex.* strophe, stanza; *Am.* **— de amigo** wedge; prop; **— de banco** silly remark; **a — juntillas** steadfastly, firmly; **al — de la letra** to the letter, literally, exactly; **de — (or en —)** standing; **a cuatro -s** on all fours; **dar —** to give an opportunity or occasion; *Am.* **estar a — en** to be ignorant of; **ir a —** to walk.
piececito [pje·se·sí·to], **piecito** [pje·sí·to] *m.* little foot.
piedad [pje·dád] *f.* piety; pity; mercy; **monte de —** pawnshop.
piedra [pjé·dra] *f.* stone; gravel; hailstone; *Ven.* piece of a domino set; **— angular** (*or* **fundamental**) cornerstone; **— caliza** limestone; **— de aceite;** oil stone; **— de amolar** hone; **— pómez** pumice, pumice stone; **a — y lodo** shut tight; **ser — de escándalo** to be an object of scandal.
piel [pjel] *f.* skin; hide; leather; fur.
piélago [pjé·la·go] *m.* high sea; sea; great abundance, great plenty.
pienso [pjén·so] *m.* feed; thought; **ni por —** not even in thought.
pierna [pjér·na] *f.* leg; **dormir a — suelta** to sleep like a log, sleep soundly; *Am.* **ser una buena —** to be a good fellow, be always in a good mood.
pieza [pjé·sa] *f.* (*pedazo*) piece; part; (*cuarto*) room; (*comedia*) play; **de una —** solid, in one piece; *Am.* **ser de una —** to be an honest, upright man.
pífano [pí·fa·no] *m.* fife.
pifia [pí·fja] *f.* a miss, miscue.
pigmento [pig·mén·to] *m.* pigment.
pijama [pi·yá·ma] [pi·xá·ma] *m.* pajamas.
pila [pí·la] *f.* (*pieza cóncava*) basin; baptismal font; trough; (*cúmulo*) pile; heap; electric battery; **— atómica** atomic pile; *Am.* fountain; *Andes* hairless

PE

dog; *N. Arg.* bald head; **nombre de** — Christian name; *Andes* **andar** — to go naked; *Mex.* **tener las -s** (*or* **tener por -s**) to have a lot, have heaps.

pilar [pi·lár] *m.* pillar, column; basin of a fountain.

pilcha [píl·ča] *f. Ríopl.* any article of clothing; *Ríopl., Ch.* mistress; **-s** *Ríopl.* belongings.

píldora [píl·do·ra] *f.* pill.

pilmama [pil·má·ma] *f. Mex.* child's nurse, wet nurse.

pilón [pi·lón] *m.* basin (*of a fountain*); watering trough; sugar loaf; large wooden or metal mortar (*for grinding grain*); counterpoise; *Mex.* an additional amount, premium (*given to a buyer*); *Mex.* **de** — to boot, in addition, besides; **piloncillo** [pi·lon·sí·yo] *m. Mex.* unrefined sugar loaf.

pilotar [pi·lo·tár], **pilotear** [pi·lo·te·ár] *v.* to pilot.

pilote [pi·ló·te] *m.* pile (*for building*).

piloto [pi·ló·to] *m.* pilot; *Mex.* generous entertainer or host.

pillaje [pi·yá·xe] *m.* pillage, plunder.

pillar [pi·yár] *v.* to pillage, plunder; to pilfer; to seize, snatch, grasp; to catch; *Mex., P.R., Arg.* to surprise, catch in the act.

pillo [pí·yo] *adj.* roguish; sly, crafty; *m.* rogue, rascal; *Ch.* a species of heron; *Ch.* long-legged person; **pilluelo** [pi·ywé·lo] *m.* little rascal, scamp.

pimentero [pi·men·té·ro] *m.* pepper plant; pepperbox, pepper shaker.

pimentón [pi·men·tón] *m.* large pepper; cayenne, red pepper; paprika.

pimienta [pi·mjén·ta] *f.* black pepper.

pimiento [pi·mjén·to] *m.* green pepper; red pepper.

pimpollo [pim·pó·yo] *m.* rosebud; bud; shoot, sprout; attractive youth.

pináculo [pi·ná·ku·lo] *m.* pinnacle, top, summit.

pinar [pi·nár] *m.* pine grove.

pincel [pin·sél] *m.* artist's brush; **pincelada** [pin·se·lá·da] *f.* stroke of the brush.

pinchar [pin·čár] *v.* to prick; to puncture.

pinchazo [pin·čá·so] *m.* prick; puncture; stab.

pingajo [piŋ·gá·xo] *m.* tag, tatter, rag.

pingo [píŋ·go] *m. Ríopl., Andes* saddle horse; *Mex.* devil.

pingüe [píŋ·gwe] *adj.* abundant, copious; fat, greasy.

pingüino [piŋ·gwí·no] *m.* penguin.

pino [pí·no] *m.* pine; *Ch.* filling for a meat pie; **hacer -s** (*or* **hacer pinitos**) to begin to walk (*said of a baby*); to begin to do things (*said of a novice*).

pinta [pín·ta] *f.* spot, mark; outward sign, aspect; pint; *Mex.* **hacer** — to play hooky, cut class.

pintar [pin·tár] *v.* to paint; to describe, depict; to feign; to begin to turn red, begin to ripen (*said of fruit*); to fancy, imagine; *Mex.* to play hooky, play truant; *S.A.* to fawn, flatter; **no** — **nada** to be worth nothing, count for nothing; **las cosas no pintaban bien** things did not look well; *Mex.* — **venados** to play hooky; **-se** to put on make-up; *Arg.* to excel (in); to praise oneself; *Ven.* to go away.

pintarrajear [pin·ta·rra·xe·ár] *v.* to daub; to smear with paint or rouge.

pinto [pín·to] *adj. Am.* spotted, speckled.

pintor [pin·tór] *m.* painter, artist; — **de brocha gorda** house painter; poor artist; *adj. Am.* boastful, conceited.

pintoresco [pin·to·rés·ko] *adj.* picturesque.

pintura [pin·tú·ra] *f.* painting; picture; paint, color; description.

pinzas [pín·sas] *f. pl.* pincers; tweezers; claws (*of lobsters, crabs, etc.*); *Ríopl., Mex., Carib.* pliers, tongs.

piña [pí·ña] pineapple; pine cone; piña cloth; cluster; *Cuba* pool (*a billiard game*).

piñata [pi·ñá·ta] *f.* pot; hanging pot or other container (*filled with candies, fruit, etc.*).

piñón [pi·ñón] *m.* pine nut; nut pine; pinion.

pío [pí·o] *adj.* pious, devout; kind; merciful; dappled, spotted (*horse*); **obras pías** pious works, charitable deeds.

piocha [pjó·ča] *adj. Mex.* great! excellent.

piojo [pjó·xo] *m.* louse.

piojoso [pjo·xó·so] *adj.* lousy; mean, stingy.

pionero [pjo·né·ro] *m.* pioneer; boy scout.

pip (piip) [pip, piíp] *m.* beep.

pipa [pí·pa] *f.* tobacco pipe; (*barril*) keg, barrel; reed pipe (*musical instrument*); fruit seed (*of a lemon, orange, melon*); *Col.* green coconut; *Am.* potato; *Ven.* **estar** — to be drunk; *m. Ch.* species of green frog.

pipiar[17] [pi·pjár] *v.* to peep, chirp.

pipiolo [pi·pjó·lo] *m.* novice, beginner; *Am.* child, youngster.

pique [pí·ke] *m.* pique, resentment; chigger (*insect*); flea; *Am.* small chili pepper; *Arg.* trail; **a** — **de** in danger of, on the point of; **echar a** — to sink (*a ship*); to destroy; **irse a** — to capsize; to sink.

piquete [pi·ké·te] *m.* prick; bite, sting (*of insects*); small hole; picket, stake; picket (*military*); *Cuba* small band of musicians; *Arg., Col.* small corral; *Am.* cutting edge of scissors.

piragua [pi·rá·ǵwa] *f. Ríopl., Carib., Ven., Col., Andes* Indian canoe; dugout.

pirámide [pi·rá·mi·de] *f.* pyramid.

pirata [pi·rá·ta] *m.* pirate.

piratear [pi·ra·te·ár] *v.* to pirate.

piropo [pi·ró·po] *m.* flattery, compliment; a variety of garnet (*a semiprecious stone*); **echar un** — to "throw a bouquet"; to compliment.

pirotecnia [pi·ro·ték·nja] *f.* pyrotechnics; fireworks.

pirueta [pi·rwé·ta] *f.* whirl; somersault; caper; **hacer -s** to cut capers; to turn somersaults; to do stunts.

pisada [pi·sá·da] *f.* footstep; footprint; **dar una** — to step on, stamp on; **seguir las -s de** to follow in the footsteps of; to imitate.

pisapapeles [pi·sa·pa·pé·les] *m.* paperweight.

pisar [pi·sár] *v.* to step on, tread upon; to trample under foot; to pound; to cover (*said of a male bird*).

piscina [pi·sí·na] *f.* swimming pool, swimming tank; fish pond.

pisco [pís·ko] *m. Peru, Col.* fine anisette made in Pisco, Peru.

pise [pí·se] *m. Ven.* rut; *Ch.* tread (*of a wheel*). See **rodadura.**

piso [pí·so] *m.* floor; story; pavement; apartment, flat; tread; *Ríopl., Mex., Carib., Ven.* fee for pasturage rights; *Mex., Ch.* table scarf; *Am.* stool, footstool; *Am.* small rug.

pisón [pi·són] *m.* heavy mallet (*for pounding, flattening, crushing*).

pisotear [pi·so·te·ár] *v.* to tramp, tramp on, trample; to tread.

pisotón [pi·so·tón] *m.* hard step, stamp (*of the foot*); **dar un** — to step hard, stamp (upon).

pista [pís·ta] *f.* track, trace, trail; clew; race track; — **de aterrizaje** landing field.

pistola [pis·tó·la] *f.* pistol; **pistolera** [pis·to·lé·ra] *f.* holster.

pistolero [pis·to·lé·ro] *m.* gangster; body guard.

pistón [pis·tón] *m.* piston; *Col.* cornet.

pita [pí·ta] *f. Am.* agave or century plant; *Am.* fiber, or thread made from the fiber, of the agave or maguey.

pitar [pi·tár] v. to toot; to whistle; *Ríopl., Andes* to smoke; *Ven.* to hiss; *Carib., Mex.* to slip away, escape; *Am.* **-se una cosa** to steal something; *Ch., Col., Ven., C.A.* (*pitado*) **salir pitando** to leave on the run.

pitazo [pi·tá·so] m. toot, whistle, blast.

pitillo [pi·tí·yo] m. *Spain* cigarette; **pitillera** [pi·ti·yé·ra] f. cigarette case.

pito [pí·to] m. whistle; cigarette; *Am.* tick (*an insect*); **no vale un** — it is not worth a straw; *Am.* **no saber ni** — **de una cosa** not to know anything about a subject.

pitón [pi·tón] m. lump; horn of an animal.

pizarra [pi·sá·rra] f. slate; blackboard; **pizarrín** [pi·sa·rrín] m. slate pencil; **pizarrón** [pi·sa·rrón] m. blackboard.

pizca [pís·ka] f. pinch, small bit; *Mex.* harvest.

placa [plá·ka] f. badge, insignia; plaque, tablet; metal plate; photographic plate; license plate; (*computadora*) board, card; *Ven.* scab or skin blemish.

placentero [pla·sen·té·ro] adj. pleasant, agreeable.

placer[38] [pla·sér] v. *irr.* to please, content; m. pleasure; sand bank, shoal; placer (*place where gold is obtained by washing*); *Am.* pearl fishing.

placero [pla·sé·ro] m., **placera** f. market vendor.

plácido [plá·si·do] adj. placid, calm.

plaga [plá·ga] f. plague; calamity.

plagar [pla·gár] v. to plague, infest; **-se de** to become plagued or infested with.

plagiar [pla·xjár] v. to plagiarize, steal and use as one's own (*the writings, ideas, etc. of another*); to kidnap, abduct.

plan [plan] m. plan; design; project; drawing; mine floor; *C.A., Cuba, Ch.* clearing; *Am.* building grounds of a ranch.

plana [plá·na] f. page (*of a newspaper*); plain, flat country; mason's trowel; tally sheet; **enmendar la** — **a uno** to correct a person's mistakes.

plancton [plánk·ton] m. plankton.

plancha [plán·ča] f. flatiron; metal plate; gangplank; blunder; *Cuba* railway flatcar; *Ven., Col.* dental plate; — **de blindaje** armor plate; **hacer una** — to make a ridiculous blunder; **tirarse una** — to place oneself in a ridiculous situation.

planchado [plan·čá·do] m. ironing; clothes ironed or to be ironed; adj. *Am.* smart, clever; *Mex.* brave; *Ven.* dolled up, dressed up; *Peru, Ch.* broke, penniless.

planchar [plan·čár] v. to iron; to smooth out; *Mex.* to leave (*someone*) waiting; *Ven., Arg.* to strike with the flat of a blade; *P.R.* to flatter; *Mex., Ven.* — **el asiento** to be a wallflower at a dance.

planeador [pla·ne·a·dór] m. glider airplane.

planear [pla·ne·ár] v. to plan; to glide (*said of an airplane or bird*).

planeo [pla·né·o] m. planning; glide, gliding (*of an airplane*).

planeta [pla·né·ta] m. planet.

planetario [pla·ne·tá·rjo] m. planetary.

plano [plá·no] adj. plane, flat, level; m. plane; plan; map; **de** — flatly, clearly, openly; **dar de** — to hit with the flat of anything.

planta [plán·ta] f. (*ser orgánico*) plant; plantation; (*proyecto*) plan; ground plan, ground floor; (*del pie*) sole of the foot; — **baja** ground floor; **buena** — good looks; **echar -s** to brag.

plantación [plan·ta·sjón] f. plantation; planting.

plantar [plan·tár] v. plant; to strike (*a blow*); **-se** to stand firm; to balk; *C.A.* to doll up, dress up;

dejar a uno plantado to "stand someone up", keep someone waiting indefinitely.

plantear [plan·te·ár] v. to plan; to establish; to carry out; to state, present (*a problem*); to try.

plantel [plan·tél] m. establishment; firm; plant; nursery.

plantío [plan·tí·o] m. planting; plantation; recently planted garden; tree nursery.

plañidero [pla·ñi·dé·ro] m. professional mourner.

plasma [pláz·ma] m. plasma.

plástico [plás·ti·ko] adj. plastic; **-s reforzados con fibra de vidrio** fiber glass.

plata [plá·ta] f. silver; silver money; **hablar en** — to speak in plain language; *Carib., C.A., Ven., Col.* money.

plataforma [pla·ta·fór·ma] f. platform; — **de lanzamiento** launching pad.

platanal [pla·ta·nál], **platanar** [pla·ta·nár] m. grove of banana trees; banana plantation.

plátano [plá·ta·no] m. banana; banana tree; plane tree.

platea [pla·té·a] f. main floor of a theatre; a lower box seat.

plateado [pla·te·á·do] adj. silver-plated; silvery.

platear [pla·te·ár] v. to silver, plate, cover with silver.

platel [pla·tél] m. platter; tray.

platero [pla·té·ro] m. silversmith; jeweler.

plática [plá·ti·ka] f. conversation, talk, chat; informal lecture.

platicador [pla·ti·ka·dór] m. talker; adj. talkative.

platicar[6] [pla·ti·kár] v. to converse, talk, chat.

platillo [pla·tí·yo] m. saucer; pan (*of a pair of scales*); cymbal; stew.

platino [pla·tí·no] m. platinum.

plato [plá·to] m. plate; dish; dinner course; — **de tocadiscos** turntable; — **de sujeción** chuck (machine).

platón [pla·tón] m. large plate; platter.

platudo [pla·tú·do] adj. *Am.* wealthy, rich.

playa [plá·ya] f. beach, shore; *Ven.* wide, open space in front of a ranch house; *Ríopl., Andes* — **de estacionamiento** parking lot.

plaza [plá·sa] f. (*pública*) plaza, public square; public market; (*empleo*) job; employment; *Ríopl., Ch., Cuba, Ven.* park, promenade; — **de armas** parade ground; public square, fortress; — **fuerte** fortress; — **de gallos** cockpit (*for cockfights*); — **de toros** bull ring; **sacar a** — to bring out into the open, make public; **sentar** — to enlist; **plazoleta** [pla·so·lé·ta], **plazuela** [pla·swé·la] f. small square, court.

plazo [plá·so] m. term, time; **a** — on credit; in installments.

pleamar [ple·a·már] m. flood tide, high tide.

plebe [plé·be] f. rabble; masses.

plebeyo [ple·bé·yo] adj. plebeian.

plebiscito [ple·bi·sí·to] m. plebiscite, direct vote.

plegadizo [ple·ga·dí·so] adj. folding; pliable, easily bent.

plegar[1, 7] [ple·gár] v. to fold; to pleat; to crease; **-se** to bend, yield, submit.

plegaria [ple·gá·rja] f. supplication, prayer, prayer hour.

pleito [pléj·to] m. litigation, lawsuit; dispute; debate; duel; — **de acreedores** bankruptcy proceedings; **pleitista** m. & f. quarrelsome person.

plenario [ple·ná·rjo] adj. plenary (*session*).

plenipotenciario [ple·ni·po·ten·sjá·rjo] m. plenipotentiary (*diplomatic agent having full power or authority*); adj. plenipotentiary, having full

PI

power.

plenitud [ple·ni·túd] *f*. plenitude, fullness, completeness; abundance.

pleno [plé·no] *adj*. full, complete; **sesión plena** joint session; **en — día** in broad daylight, openly; **en — rostro** (*or* **en plena cara**) right on the face; *m*. joint session (*of a legislative body*).

pleuresía [plew·re·sí·a] *f*. pleurisy.

pliego [plié·go] *m*. sheet of paper; sealed letter or document.

pliegue [plié·ge] *m*. fold, crease, pleat.

plomada [plo·má·da] *f*. plumb, lead weight, plumb bob.

plomazo [plo·má·so] *m*. *Col., Ven., Mex*. shot, bullet.

plomería [plo·me·rí·a] *f*. plumbing; plumber's shop; lead roof.

plomero [plo·mé·ro] *m*. plumber.

plomizo [plo·mí·so] *adj*. leaden, lead-colored.

plomo [pló·mo] *m*. lead; plumb, lead weight; bullet; boring person; **a —** vertical; vertically; *adj*. *Carib., Mex*. lead-colored.

pluma [plú·ma] *f*. (*de ave*) feather; plume; (*instrumento*) pen; quill; — **estilográfica** (*or* — **fuente**) fountain pen; **plumada** [plu·má·da] *f*. dash, stroke of the pen, flourish; **plumaje** [plu·má·xe] *m*. plumage; plume, **plumero** [plu·mé·ro] *m*. feather duster; box for feathers; feather ornament (*on hats, helmets, etc*.); **plumón** [plu·món] *m*. down; feather mattress; **plumoso** [plu·mó·so] *adj*. downy, feathery.

plural [plu·rál] *adj*. plural.

plutonio [plu·tó·njo] *m*. plutonium.

pluralidad [plu·ra·li·dád] *f*. plurality.

pluvial [plu·bjál] *adj*. rain (*used as adj*.); **capa —** cope (*long cape used by priests during certain religious ceremonies*).

pluviómetro [plu·bjó·me·tro] *m*. rain gauge.

población [po·bla·sjón] *f*. (*acto*) populating; settlement; (*número*) population; (*lugar*) town, city.

poblado [po·blá·do] *m*. inhabited place; village; *p.p.* populated; covered with growth.

poblador [po·bla·dór] *m*. settler (*of a colony*).

poblar[2] [po·blár] *v. irr*. to populate, people; to colonize, settle; to stock (*a farm*); to breed; **-se** to become covered (*with leaves or buds*).

pobre [pó·bre] *adj*. poor; *m*. poor man; beggar; **pobrete** [po·bré·te] *m*. poor devil, poor wretch; **pobretón** [po·bre·tón] *m*. poor old fellow, poor wretch.

pobreza [po·bré·sa] *f*. poverty; need; lack; scarcity; barrenness.

pocilga [po·síl·ga] *f*. pigsty, pigpen.

pocillo [po·sí·yo] *m*. cup.

poco [pó·ko] *adj*. little, scanty; small; short (*time*); **-s** few, some; *m*. a little, a bit; *adv*. little; **a —** presently, after a short time; **a — rato** (*or* **al — rato**) after a short while; **— a —** slowly, little by little; **a los -s meses** after a few months; **por — me caigo** I almost fell; **tener en — a** to hold in low esteem.

podadera [po·da·dé·ra] *f*. pruning hook or knife.

podar [po·dár] *v*. to prune, trim, cut off.

podenco [po·dén·ko] *m*. hound.

poder[39] [po·dér] *v. irr*. to be able; can; may; **él puede mucho** (*or* **poco**) he has much (*or* little) power; **puede que** it is possible that, it may be that, perhaps; **hasta más no —** to the utmost, to the limit; **no — más** not to be able to do more; to be exhausted; **no puede menos de hacerlo** he

cannot help doing it; **no — con la carga** not to be equal to the burden, not to be able to lift the load; *Col., Ven*. **-le a uno algo** to be worried or affected by something, *m*. power, authority.

poderío [po·de·rí·o] *m*. power, dominion; might; wealth.

poderoso [po·de·ró·so] *adj*. powerful; wealthy.

podre [pó·dre] *f*. pus; decayed matter; **podredumbre** [po·dre·dúm·bre] *f*. corruption, decay; pus; rotten matter.

podrido [po·drí·do] *adj*. rotten; *p.p. of* **podrir.**

podrir[16] [po·drír] = **pudrir**[16]

poema [po·é·ma] *m*. poem.

poesía [po·e·sí·a] *f*. poetry; poem.

poeta [po·é·ta] *m*. poet; **poetastro** [po·e·tás·tro] *m*. bad poet.

poético [po·é·ti·ko] *adj*. poetic; **poética** [po·é·ti·ka] *f*. poetics.

poetisa [po·e·tí·sa] *f*. poetess.

polaco [po·lá·ko] *adj*. Polish; *m*. Polish, Polish language; Pole.

polaina [po·láj·na] *f*. legging.

polar [po·lár] *adj*. polar.

polea [po·lé·a] *f*. pulley; — **cono** cone pulley.

polémica [po·lé·mi·ka] *f*. controversy; polemics.

polen [pó·len] *m*. pollen.

policía [po·li·sí·a] *f*. police; *m*. policeman.

policial [po·li·sjál] *m*. *Col., Ven*. policeman.

policíaco [po·li·sjá·ko] [po·li·sí·a·ko] *adj*. police, detective (*story*).

poligamia [po·li·gá·mja] *f*. polygamy.

políglota [po·lí·glo·ta] *m. & f*. polyglot; one who speaks several languages.

polilla [po·lí·ya] *f*. moth; larva of the moth.

poliomielitis [po·ljo·mje·lí·tis] *f*. poliomyelitis, polio.

política [po·lí·ti·ka] *f*. politics; policy; *Am*. — **de campanario** politics of a clique.

politicastro [po·lí·ti·kás·tro] *m*. bad or incapable politician.

político [po·lí·ti·ko] *adj*. political; politic; polite; **madre política** mother-in-law; *m*. politician.

polivalente [po·li·ba·lén·te] *adj*. multiple.

póliza [pó·li·sa] *f*. policy, written contract; draft; customhouse certificate; — **de seguros** insurance policy.

polizonte [po·li·són·te] *m*. policeman.

polo [pó·lo] *m*. pole (*of a magnet or of an axis*); polo (*a game*); — **acuático** water polo.

polonio [po·ló·njo] *m*. polonium.

poltrón [pol·trón] *adj*. lazy, idel; **silla poltrona** easy chair.

polvareda [pol·ba·ré·da] *f*. cloud of dust; **armar** (*or* **levantar**) **una —** to kick up the dust; to raise a rumpus.

polvera [pol·bé·ra] *f*. powder box; compact; powder puff.

polvo [pól·bo] *m*. dust; powder; pinch of snuff or powder; — **férrico** iron oxide filings (*coating for recording tape*); **-s** toilet powder; **-s para dientes** tooth powder; **limpio de — y paja** entirely free; net; *Am*. cleaned out, without a penny; *Am*. innocent, ignorant, unaware; *Mex., Col., Ven*. **tomar el —** to escape, "beat it".

pólvora [pól·bo·ra] *f*. gunpowder; fireworks.

polvorear [pol·bo·re·ár] *v*. to powder, sprinkle with powder.

polvoriento [pol·bo·rjén·to] *adj*. dusty.

polvorín [pol·bo·rín] *m*. powder magazine; priming powder; powder flask; *Am*. tick (*parasitic insect*); *Ríopl*. spitfire, quick-tempered person.

polla [pó·ya] *f*. pullet (*young hen*); young lass; pool *(in cards).*

pollada [po·yá·da] *f.* hatch, brood; flock of chicks.

pollera [po·yé·ra] *f.* woman who raises and sells chickens; chicken coop; a bell-shaped basket for chickens; petticoat; *Ríopl., Ch., Col., Andes* skirt.

pollino [po·yí·no] *m.* young donkey, ass.

pollo [pó·yo] *m.* young chicken; nestling, young bird; *Spain* young man; **polluelo** [po·ywé·lo] *m.* chick.

pomelo [po·mé·lo] *m. Spain* grapefruit.

pómez [pó·mes] *m.* pumice.

pompa [póm·pa] *f.* pomp; pageant, procession; bubble; pump.

pomposo [pom·pó·so] *adj.* pompous.

pómulo [pó·mu·lo] *m.* cheek bone.

ponche [pón·če] *m.* punch (*a beverage*); **ponchera** [pon·čé·ra] *f.* punch bowl.

poncho [pón·čo] *m. Andes, Ch., Ríopl.* poncho; cape.

ponderación [pon·de·ra·sjón] *f.* pondering, careful consideration, weighing; exaggeration.

ponderar [pon·de·rár] *v.* (*pensar*) to ponder, consider, weigh; (*exagerar*) to exaggerate; to extol.

ponderativo [pon·de·ra·tí·ƀo] *adj.* exaggerating.

ponderoso [pon·de·ró·so] *adj.* ponderous, heavy.

poner[40] [po·nér] *v. irr.* to put; to place; to set; to lay; to suppose; **— como nuevo a alguien** to cover someone with insults; **— en claro** to clarify; **— en limpio** to recopy, make a clean copy; **— en tela de juicio** to doubt; **— todo de su parte** to do one's best; **pongamos que . . .** let us suppose that . . .; **-se** to place oneself; to become; **-se a** to begin to; **-se al corriente** to become informed; **-se de pie** to stand up; *Carib., Mex., Ch., Andes* **-se bien con alguien** to ingratiate oneself with someone, get on his good side; **-se en la sábana** strike it rich; *Am.* **ponérsela** to get drunk.

poniente [po·njén·te] *m.* west; west wind; **el sol —** the setting sun.

pontón [pon·tón] *m.* pontoon; scow, flat-bottomed boat; log bridge; pontoon bridge.

ponzoña [pon·só·ña] *f.* venom, poison.

ponzoñoso [pon·so·ñó·so] *adj.* venomous, poisonous.

popa [pó·pa] *f.* poop, stern; **viento en —** speedily; going well.

popote [po·pó·te] *m. Mex.* straw for brooms; *Mex.* drinking straw or tube.

populacho [po·pu·lá·čo] *m.* populace, rabble.

popular [po·pu·lár] *adj.* popular.

popularidad [po·pu·la·ri·dád] *f.* popularity.

populoso [po·pu·ló·so] *adj.* populous, densely populated.

popurrí [po·pu·rrí] *m.* potpourri.

poquito [po·kí·to] *adj.* very little; *Cuba, Ven., Col.* timid, shy; *m.* a small bit; **a -s** in small quantities.

por [por] *prep.* by; for; for the sake of, on account of, on behalf of; because of; through; along; on exchange for; in the place of; during; about, around; to, with the idea of; **— ciento** percent; **— consiguiente** consequently; **— entre** among, between; **— escrito** in writing; **— poco se muere** he almost died; **está —** **hacer** it is yet to be done; **él está — hacerlo** he is in favor of doing it; **recibir — esposa** to receive as a wife; **tener — to** consider, think of as; **¿— qué?** *interr. adv.* why? for what reason?

porcelana [por·se·lá·na] *f.* porcelain, china; enamel.

porcentaje [por·sen·tá·xe] *m.* percentage.

porcino [por·sí·no] *adj.* porcine; related to the pig.

porción [por·sjón] *f.* portion; part, share; **una — de gente** a lot of people.

porche [pór·če] *m.* porch.

pordiosear [por·djo·se·ár] *v.* to beg.

pordiosero [por·djo·sé·ro] *m.* beggar.

porfía [por·fí·a] *f.* stubbornness, obstinacy; persistence, insistence; **a —** in competition; with great insistence.

porfiado [por·fjá·do] *adj.* stubborn, obstinate, persistent.

porfiar[17] [por·fjár] *v.* to persist, to insist; to dispute obstinately; to argue.

pormenor [por·me·nór] *m.* detail.

pormenorizar[9] [por·me·no·ri·sár] *v.* to detail, tell in detail; to itemize.

pornografía [por·no·gra·fí·a] *f.* pornography.

pornográfico [por·no·grá·fi·ko] *adj.* pornographic.

poro [pó·ro] *m.* pore.

porosidad [po·ro·si·dád] *f.* porosity.

poroso [po·ró·so] *adj.* porous.

poroto [po·ró·to] *m. Ch., Ríopl., Andes* bean; *Ch., Ríopl., Andes* runt; urchin.

porque [pór·ke] *conj.* because; so that.

porqué [por·ké] *m.* cause, reason, motive.

porquería [por·ke·rí·a] *f.* filth; filthy act or word; nasty piece of food; trifle, worthless object.

porra [pó·rra] *f.* club, stick; mob; *Am.* **mandar a uno a la —** to send someone to the devil; **porrazo** *m.* blow; knock; bump; **porrón** *m.* wine vessel with long snout.

porta [pór·ta] *f.* porthole; cover for a porthole; goal (*in football*).

portaaviones [por·ta·a·ƀjó·nes] *m.* airplane carrier.

portabroca [por·ta·ƀró·ka] *m.* chuck.

portada [por·tá·da] *f.* façade, front (*of a building*); title page.

portador [por·ta·dór] *m.* carrier; bearer; tray.

portaherramientas [por·ta·e·rra·mjén·tas] *m.* tool post.

portal [por·tál] *m.* portal; entrance, vestibule; portico, porch; *C.A.* Christmas crèche; **-es** arcades, galleries; **portalón** [por·ta·lón] *m.* large portal; gangway (*of a ship*).

portamonedas [por·ta·mo·né·das] *m.* pocketbook, coin purse.

portapapeles [por·ta·pa·pé·les] *m.* briefcase.

portaplumas [por·ta·plú·mas] *m.* penholder.

portar [por·tár] *v. Am.* to carry; **-se** to behave.

portátil [por·tá·til] *adj.* portable.

portaviones [por·ta·ƀjó·nes] *m.* aircraft carrier; also **portaaviones.**

portavoz [por·ta·ƀós] *m.* megaphone; mouthpiece; spokesman.

portazgo [por·táz· go] *m.* toll.

portazo [por·tá·so] *m.* bang or slam of a door; **dar un —** to bang or slam the door.

porte [pór·te] *m.* portage, cost of carriage; freight; postage; manner, bearing; size, capacity; *Ch.* birthday present; *C.A.* size.

portear [por·te·ár] *v.* to carry on one's back; *Am.* to get out in a hurry; **porteador** carrier.

portento [por·tén·to] *m.* portent; wonder, marvel.

portentoso [por·ten·tó·so] *adj.* marvelous, extraordinary, amazing, terrifying.

porteño [por·té·ño] *adj.* from a port; *Ríopl.* from Buenos Aires.

portería [por·te·rí·a] *f.* porter's quarters; main door of a building.

portero [por·té·ro] *m.* doorkeeper, doorman; janitor.

pórtico [pór·ti·ko] *m.* portico, porch.

portilla [por·tí·ya] *f.* porthole; small gate or passageway.

portón [por·tón] *m.* gate.

portugués [por·tu·gés] *adj.* Portuguese; *m.*

PL

Portuguese; Portuguese language.

porvenir [por·be·nír] *m.* future.

pos [pos]: **en — de** after; in pursuit of.

posada [po·sá·da] *f.* lodging; inn; boardinghouse; dwelling, home; *Mex.* **las -s** a Christmas festivity lasting nine days; **posadero** [po·sa·dé·ro] *m.* innkeeper.

posaderas [po·sa·dé·ras] *f. pl.* posterior, buttocks, rump.

posar [po·sár] *v.* to lodge; to rest; to sit down; to pose (*as a model*); to perch (*said of birds*); **-se** to settle (*said of sediment*).

posdata [poz·dá·ta] *f.* postscript.

poseedor [po·se·e·dór] *m.* possessor, owner.

poseer[14] [po·se·ér] *v.* to possess, own; to master, know well; **-se** to have control of oneself.

posesión [po·se·sjón] *f.* possession.

posesivo [po·se·sí·bo] *adj. & m.* possessive.

posesor [po·se·sór] *m.* possessor, owner.

posibilidad [po·si·bi·li·dád] *p.* possibility.

posible [po·sí·ble] *adj.* possible; **hacer lo — to do** one's best; **-s** *m. pl.* goods, property, means.

posición [po·si·sjón] *f.* position; posture; status, rank, standing; placing.

positivo [po·si·tí·bo] *adj.* positive; effective; true; practical.

posponer[40] [pos·po·nér] *v. irr.* to postpone, put off; to put after; to subordinate.

pospuesto [pos·pwés·to] *p.p. of* **posponer.**

posta [pós·ta] *f.* (*bala*) small bullet; (*apuesta*) bet, wager; (*relevo*) relay (*of post horses*); post station; **-s** buckshot; **por la — posthaste;** fast, speedily; *m.* postboy, courier, messenger.

postal [pos·tál] *adj.* postal; **tarjeta — postcard.**

postdata [poz·dá·ta] = **posdata.**

poste [pós·te] *m.* post, pillar; **— de soporte** bearing post.

postergar[7] [pos·ter·gár] *v.* to delay; to postpone; to disregard someone's right.

posteridad [pos·te·ri·dád] *f.* posterity.

posterior [pos·te·rjór] *adj.* posterior, back, rear; later.

postigo [pos·tí·go] *m.* wicket, small door or gate; shutter; peep window.

postizo [pos·tí·so] *adj.* false, artificial; *m.* switch, false hair.

postración [pos·tra·sjón] *f.* prostration, collapse, exhaustion; dejection, lowness of spirits.

postrar [pos·trár] *v.* to prostrate; to humiliate; to throw down; to weaken, exhaust; to kneel to the ground; to be weakened, exhausted; to collapse.

postre [pós·tre] *m.* dessert; **a la — at last.**

postrer(o) [pos·tré·r(o)] *adj.* last; hindmost, nearest the rear.

postulante [pos·tu·lán·te] *m. & f.* petitioner; applicant, candidate.

póstumo [pós·tu·mo] *adj.* posthumous, after one's death.

postura [pos·tú·ra] *f.* posture, position; bid; wager; pact, agreement; egg-laying.

potable [po·tá·ble] *adj.* drinkable; **agua — drinking** water.

potaje [po·tá·xe] *m.* pottage, thick soup; porridge; mixed drink.

potasio [po·tá·sjo] *m.* potassium.

pote [pó·te] *m.* pot; jar; jug; *Carib., Ven., Mex., Ríopl.* flask; *Ch.* buzzard.

potencia [po·tén·sja] *f.* potency; power; faculty, ability; powerful nation.

potenciómetro [po·ten·sjó·me·tro] *m.* (*computadora*) paddle.

potentado [po·ten·tá·do] *m.* potentate.

potente [po·tén·te] *adj.* potent, powerful, strong.

potestad [po·tes·tád] *f.* power; dominion, authority.

potranca [po·tráŋ·ka] *f.* filly, young mare.

potrero [po·tré·ro] *m.* herdsman of colts; fenced-in pasture land; *Carib., Mex., C.A., Ven., Col., Ch.* cattle ranch, stock farm.

potro [pó·tro] *m.* colt; rack, torture; *Col., Ven., Mex., Ch., Ríopl.* wild horse.

poyo [pó·yo] *m.* stone or brick bench (*usually built against a wall*).

pozo [pó·so] *m.* well; hole, pit; mine shaft; hold of a ship; *Hond.* pool, puddle; *Ríopl., Ch., Ven., Col., Mex.* spring, fountain.

pozole [po·só·le] *m. Mex.* stew made of hominy and pig's head.

práctica [prák·ti·ka] *f.* practice; exercise; custom, habit; method.

practicante [prak·ti·kán·te] *m. & f.* doctor's assistant; hospital intern.

practicar[6] [prak·ti·kár] *v.* to practice; to put into practice.

práctico [prák·ti·ko] *adj.* practical; experienced, skilful; *m.* **— de puerto** harbor pilot.

pradera [pra·dé·ra] *f.* prairie; meadow.

prado [prá·do] *m.* meadow, field; lawn.

preámbulo [pre·ám·bu·lo] *m.* preamble, introduction; prologue.

precario [pre·ká·rjo] *adj.* precarious.

precaución [pre·kaw·sjón] *f.* precaution.

precaver [pre·ka·bér] *v.* to guard (against), keep (from); to warn, caution; **-se** to guard oneself (against); to take precautions.

precavido [pre·ka·bí·do] *adj.* cautious, on guard.

precedencia [pre·se·dén·sja] *f.* precedence; priority.

precedente [pre·se·dén·te] *adj.* preceding; *m.* precedent.

preceder [pre·se·dér] *v.* to precede; to have precedence.

precepto [pre·sép·to] *m.* precept; rule; order.

preceptor [pre·sep·tór] *m.* teacher, tutor.

preciado [pre·sjá·do] *adj.* prized, esteemed; precious, valuable.

preciar [pre·sjár] *v.* to appraise; to value; **-se de** to boast of, be proud of.

precio [pré·sjo] *m.* price; value, worth; esteem.

precioso [pre·sjó·so] *adj.* precious, valuable; fine, exquisite; beautiful.

precipicio [pre·si·pí·sjo] *m.* precipice; ruin.

precipitación [pre·si·pi·ta·sjón] *f.* precipitation; rush, haste, hurry.

precipitado [pre·si·pi·tá·do] *adj.* precipitate, hasty, rash; *m.* precipitate (*chemical term*).

precipitar [pre·si·pi·tár] *v.* to precipitate; to hasten, rush; to hurl, throw headlong; **-se** to throw oneself headlong; to rush (into).

precipitoso [pre·si·pi·tó·so] *adj.* precipitous, steep; rash.

precisar [pre·si·sár] *v.* to determine precisely; to force, compel, make necessary; *Ríopl., Col., Ven., Mex., Andes;* to be necessary or urgent; *Am.* to need.

precisión [pre·si·sjón] *f.* precision, exactness; accuracy; compulsion, force, necessity; *Am.* haste.

preciso [pre·sí·so] *adj.* necessary; precise, exact; clear; *m. Am.* small travelling bag.

precoz [pre·kós] *adj.* precocious.

precursor [pre·kur·sór] *m.* precursor, forerunner.

predecir[27] [pre·de·sír] *v. irr.* to predict, prophesy, forecast, foretell.

predestinar [pre·des·ti·nár] *v.* to predestine.

predicación [pre·di·ka·sjón] *f.* preaching.
predicado [pre·di·ká·do] *adj. & m.* predicate; *p.p. of*
  predicar.
predicador [pre·di·ka·dór] *m.* preacher.
predicar[6] [pre·di·kár] *v.* to preach.
predicción [pre·dik·sjón] *f.* prediction.
predilección [pre·di·lek·sjón] *f.* predilection,
  preference, liking.
predilecto [pre·di·lek·to] *adj.* favorite, preferred.
predisponer[40] [pre·dis·po·nér] *v. irr.* to predispose,
  bias, prejudice.
predispuesto [pre·dis·pwés·to] *p.p. of* **predisponer** *&*
  adj. predisposed, prejudiced, biased.
predominante [pre·do·mi·nán·te] *adj.* predominant;
  prevailing, ruling.
predominar [pre·do·mi·nár] *v.* to predominate,
  prevail.
predominio [pre·do·mí·njo] *m.* predominance; sway,
  influence.
prefacio [pre·fá·sjo] *m.* preface.
prefecto [pre·fék·to] *m.* prefect (*military or civil*
  chief; sometimes a mayor, sometimes governor of a
  province, as in Peru).
preferencia [pre·fe·rén·sja] *f.* preference; **de** — with
  preference; preferably.
preferente [pre·fe·rén·te] *adj.* preferable; preferred;
  preferential; **acciones -s** preferred shares.
preferible [pre·fe·rí·ble] *adj.* preferable.
preferir[3] [pre·fe·rír] *v. irr.* to prefer.
prefijar [pre·fi·xár] *v.* to prefix; to set beforehand (*as*
  a date).
prefijo [pre·fí·xo] *m.* prefix.
pregonar [pre·go·nár] *v.* to proclaim, cry out; to
  make known.
pregunta [pre·gún·ta] *f.* question; **hacer una** — to
  ask a question.
preguntar [pre·gun·tár] *v.* to ask, inquire.
preguntón [pre·gun·tón] *adj.* inquisitive.
prejuicio [pre·xwí·sjo] *m.* prejudice.
prejuzgar[7] [pre·xuz·gár] *v. irr.* to prejudge.
prelado [pre·lá·do] *m.* prelate.
preliminar [pre·li·mi·nár] *adj. & m.* preliminary.
preludiar [pre·lu·djár] *v.* to be the prelude or
  beginning of; to initiate, introduce; to try out (*a*
  musical instrument).
preludio [pre·lú·djo] *m.* prelude; introduction.
prematuro [pre·ma·tú·ro] *adj.* premature, untimely.
premeditado [pre·me·di·tá·do] *adj.* premeditated,
  deliberate.
premiar [pre·mjár] *v.* to reward.
premio [pré·mjo] *m.* prize; reward; recompense;
  premium; **a** — with interest, at interest.
premisa [pre·mí·sa] *f.* premise (*either of the first two*
  propositions of a syllogism).
premura [pre·mú·ra] *f.* pressure, urgency, haste.
prenda [prén·da] *f.* (*fianza*) pawn, pledge, security;
  token; (*partes del vestido*) article of clothing;
  anything valuable; loved person; jewel; **-s** good
  qualities, gifts, talents; — **de vestir** garment;
  juego de -s game of forfeits; **en** — **de** as a proof
  of, as a pledge of.
prendar [pren·dár] *v.* to pawn, pledge; to charm,
  please; **-se de** to get attached to; to fall in love
  with.
prendedor [pren·de·dór] *m.* clasp; stickpin; tie pin;
  brooch; *Am.* light.
prender [pren·dér] *v.* (*asir*) to seize, catch, grab; to
  bite (*said of an insect*); to fasten, clasp; to arrest,
  imprison; (*empezar*) to take root; to begin to burn;
  catch fire; *Ríopl., Carib., C.A., Mex.* to light (*a*
  lamp); *Am.* to start, begin, undertake; — **el fuego**

to start the fire; *Col.* **-las** to take to one's heels; **-se**
  to dress up.
prendero [pren·dé·ro] *m.* pawnbroker; second-hand
  dealer.
prensa [prén·sa] *f.* press; printing press; — **de**
  tornillo vise.
prensar [pren·sár] *v.* to press.
prensil [pren·síl] *adj.* prehensile.
preñado [pre·ñá·do] *adj.* pregnant; full.
preñez [pre·ñés] *f.* pregnancy.
preocupación [pre·o·ku·pa·sjón] *f.* preoccupation;
  worry; bias, prejudice.
preocupar [pre·o·ku·pár] *v.* to preoccupy; to worry;
  to prejudice; **-se** to be preoccupied; to worry; to be
  prejudiced.
preparación [pre·pa·ra·sjón] *f.* preparation.
preparar [pre·pa·rár] *v.* to prepare; **-se** to get ready;
  to be prepared.
preparativo [pre·pa·ra·tí·bo] *adj.* preparatory; *m.*
  preparation.
preparatorio [pre·pa·ra·tó·rjo] *adj.* preparatory.
preponderancia [pre·pon·de·rán·sja] *f.* preponderance.
preposición [pre·po·si·sjón] *f.* preposition.
prerrogativa [pre·rro·ga·tí·ba] *f.* prerogative, right,
  privilege.
presa [pré·sa] *f.* prey; dam; fang, tusk; claw; **hacer**
  — to seize.
presagiar [pre·sa·xjár] *v.* to foretell.
presagio [pre·sá·xjo] *m.* presage, omen, sign.
presbítero [prez·bí·te·ro] *m.* priest.
prescindir [pre·sin·dír] *v.* to disregard, set aside,
  leave aside; to omit; to dispense (with).
prescribir[52] [pres·kri·bír] *v.* to prescribe.
prescrito [pres·krí·to] *p.p. of* **prescribir.**
presencia [pre·sén·sja] *f.* presence; figure, bearing; —
  de ánimo presence of mind, serenity.
presenciar [pre·sen·sjár] *v.* to see, witness; to be
  present at.
presentación [pre·sen·ta·sjón] *f.* presentation; personal
  introduction; *Ven.* petition.
presentar [pre·sen·tár] *v.* to present; to introduce; **-se**
  to appear, present oneself; to introduce oneself; to
  offer one's services; *Ch., Arg.* to have recourse to
  justice, file suit.
presente [pre·sén·te] *adj.* present; *m.* present, gift; **al**
  — now, at the present time; **por el (la,** *or* **lo)** —
  for the present; **mejorando lo** — present company
  excepted; **tener** — to bear in mind.
presentimiento [pre·sen·ti·mjén·to] *m.* presentiment,
  foreboding.
presentir[3] [pre·sen·tír] *v. irr.* to have a presentiment,
  foreboding or hunch.
preservación [pre·ser·ba·sjón] *f.* preservation.
preservar [pre·ser·bár] *v.* to preserve, guard, protect,
  keep.
presidencia [pre·si·dén·sja] *f.* presidency; office of
  president; presidential term; chairmanship.
presidencial [pre·si·den·sjál] *adj.* presidential.
presidente [pre·si·dén·te] *m.* president; chairman;
  presiding judge.
presidiario [pre·si·djá·rjo] *m.* prisoner, convict.
presidio [pre·sí·djo] *m.* garrison; fortress;
  penitentiary, prison; **diez años de** — ten years at
  hard labor (*in a prison*).
presidir [pre·si·dír] *v.* to preside; to direct.
presilla [pre·sí·ya] *f.* loop, fastener; clip.
presión [pre·sjón] *f.* pressure.
preso [pré·so] *m.* prisoner; *p.p. irr. of* **prender**
  imprisoned.
prestado [pres·tá·do] *adj. & p.p.* loaned, lent; **dar** —
  to lend; **pedir** — to borrow.

PO

prestamista [pres·ta·mís·ta] *m. & f.* moneylender.
préstamo [prés·ta·mo] *m.* loan.
prestar [pres·tár] *v.* to loan, lend; *Col., Ven., C.A., Andes* to borrow; — **ayuda** to give help; — **atención** to pay attention; *Andes* **presta acá** give it here, give it to me; **-se** to lend oneself or itself.
presteza [pres·té·sa] *f.* promptness, speed.
prestidigitación [pres·ti·di·xi·ta·sjón] *f.* juggling, sleight of hand.
prestidigitador [pres·ti·di·xi·ta·dór] *m.* juggler.
prestigio [pres·tí·xjo] *m.* prestige; influence, authority; good reputation.
presto [prés·to] *adj.* quick; nimble; prompt; ready; *adv.* soon, at once; **de** — quickly, promptly.
presumido [pre·su·mí·do] *adj.* conceited, presumptuous; *p.p. of* **presumir.**
presumir [pre·su·mír] *v.* to presume; to boast; to show off; *Am.* to court, woo; — **de valiente** to boast of one's valor.
presunción [pre·sun·sjón] *f.* presumption, assumption; conceit, arrogance.
presunto [pre·sún·to] *adj.* presumed; supposed; prospective; **heredero** — heir apparent.
presuntuoso [pre·sun·twó·so] *adj.* presumptuous; conceited.
presuponer[40] [pre·su·po·nér] *v. irr.* to presuppose, take for granted, imply; to estimate.
presupuesto [pre·su·pwés·to] *p.p. of* **presuponer** presupposed; estimated; *m.* budget, estimate.
presuroso [pre·su·ró·so] *adj.* quick, prompt; hasty.
pretencioso [pre·ten·sjó·so] *adj.* presumptuous; conceited.
pretender [pre·ten·dér] *v.* to pretend; to solicit; seek; to claim; to try; to court.
pretendiente [pre·ten·djén·te] *m.* pretender, claimant; suitor; office seeker.
pretensión [pre·ten·sjón] *f.* pretension; claim; presumption; pretense.
pretérito [pre·té·ri·to] *adj.* preterite, past; *m.* preterite, the past tense.
pretexto [pre·tés·to] *m.* pretext, pretense, excuse.
pretil [pre·tíl] *m.* stone or brick railing; *Am.* ledge; *Mex., Ven.* stone or brick bench (*built against a wall*).
pretina [pre·tí·na] *f.* belt, girdle; waistband.
prevalecer[13] [pre·ba·le·sér] *v. irr.* to prevail.
prevaleciente [pre·ba·le·sjén·te] *adj.* prevalent, current.
prevención [pre·ben·sjón] *f.* prevention; foresight, preparedness; bias, prejudice; provision, supply; admonition, warning; police station; guardhouse.
prevenido [pre·be·ní·do] *adj. & p.p.* prepared, ready; forewarned; cautious; supplied.
prevenir[48] [pre·be·nír] *v. irr.* to prevent, avoid; to prepare beforehand; to foresee; to warn; to predispose; **-se** to get prepared, get ready.
prever[49] [pre·bér] *v. irr.* to foresee.
previo [pré·bjo] *adj.* previous; *m. Am.* preliminary examination.
previsión [pre·bi·sjón] *f.* foresight.
previsto [pre·bís·to] *p.p. of* **prever.**
prieto [prjé·to] *adj.* dark, black; tight; compact; *Ríopl., Ven., Col., Mex., C.A., Andes* dark-complexioned, swarthy.
prima [prí·ma] *f.* female cousin; premium; prime (*first of the canonical hours*).
primacía [pri·má·sja] *f.* priority, precedence; superiority.
primario [pri·má·rjo] *adj.* primary, principal.
primavera [pri·ma·bé·ra] *f.* spring; primrose; print, flowered silk cloth.

primaveral [pri·ma·be·rál] *adj.* spring, pertaining to spring.
primer(o) [pri·mér(o)] *adj.* first; former; leading, principal; **primera enseñanza** primary education; **primera materia** raw material; **de buenas a primeras** all of a sudden, unexpectedly; **a primera luz** at dawn; *adv.* first; rather.
primicia [pri·mí·sja] *f.* first fruit; first profit; **-s** first fruits.
primitivo [pri·mi·tí·bo] *adj.* primitive; primary; original.
primo [prí·mo] *m.* cousin; simpleton, sucker, dupe; — **hermano** (*or* — **carnal**) first cousin; *Carib.* **coger a uno de** — to deceive someone easily; *adj.* first; **número** — prime number.
primogénito [pri·mo·xé·ni·to] *adj. & m.* first-born; **primogenitura** [pri·mo·xe·ni·tú·ra] *f.* birthright; rights of the first-born.
primor [pri·mór] *m.* beauty; excellence; exquisiteness; skill, ability.
primordial [pri·mor·djál] *adj.* primordial.
primoroso [pri·mo·ró·so] *adj.* excellent, fine, exquisite; skillful.
prímula [prí·mu·la] *f.* primrose.
princesa [prin·sé·sa] *f.* princess.
principal [prin·si·pál] *adj.* principal; renowned, famous; **piso** — main floor (*usually, the second floor*); *m.* principal, capital sum; chief, head.
príncipe [prín·si·pe] *m.* prince; *adj.* princeps, first (*edition*).
principiante [prin·si·pján·te] *m.* beginner.
principiar [prin·si·pjár] *v.* to begin.
principio [prin·sí·pjo] *m.* principle; beginning; origin, source; entrée (*main dinner course*); **a -s de** towards the beginning of.
pringar[7] [prin·gár] *v. irr.* to dip (*in grease*).
pringoso [prin·gó·so] *adj.* greasy.
pringue [prín·ge] *m. & f.* grease drippings (*from bacon, ham, etc.*).
prioridad [prjó·ri·dád] *f.* priority; precedence.
prisa [prí·sa] *f.* speed, haste; **de** (*or* **a**) — quickly, speedily; **a toda** — with the greatest speed; **eso corre** — that is urgent; **dar** — **a** to hurry; **darse** — to hurry; **tener** (*or* **estar de**) — to be in a hurry.
prisión [pri·sjón] *f.* prison; imprisonment; seizure; shackle; **-es** shackles, fetters, chains.
prisionero [pri·sjo·né·ro] *m.* prisoner.
prisma [príz·ma] *f.* prism.
pristino [pris·tí·no] *adj.* first, early, former; primitive.
privación [pri·ba·sjón] *f.* privation; want, lack; loss.
privado [pri·bá·do] *adj.* private; personal; unconscious; *p.p.* deprived; *m.* favorite.
privar [pri·bár] *v.* (*destituir*) to deprive; to prohibit; (*tener aceptación*) to enjoy the favor of someone; to be in vogue; **-le a uno del sentido** to stun, daze; **ya no privan esas costumbres** those customs are no longer in vogue or in existence; **-se** to lose consciousness; **-se de** to deprive oneself of.
privativo [pri·ba·tí·bo] *adj.* exclusive; particular; distinctive.
privilegiado [pri·bi·le·xjá·do] *adj.* privileged.
privilegiar [pri·bi·le·xjár] *v.* to favor; to give a privilege to.
privilegio [pri·bi·lé·xjo] *m.* privilege; exemption; patent; copyright; — **de invención** patent on an invention.
pro [pro] *m. & f.* profit, advantage; **en** — **de** on behalf of; **en** — **y en contra** pro and con, for and against; **hombre de** — man of worth.

proa [pró·a] *f.* prow.
probabilidad [pro·ba·bi·li·dád] *f.* probability.
probable [pro·bá·ble] *adj.* probable.
probar[2] [pro·bár] *v. irr.* (*examinar*) to test; to taste; to prove; to try; to try on; (*gustar*) to suit, agree with; **no me prueba el clima** the climate does not agree with me.
probeta [pro·bé·ta] *f.* test tube; pressure gauge.
probidad [pro·bi·dád] *f.* integrity, uprightness, honesty.
problema [pro·blé·ma] *m.* problem.
problemático [pro·ble·má·ti·ko] *adj.* problematic.
procedente [pro·se·dén·te] *adj.* proceeding (from), originating; according to law.
proceder [pro·se·dér] *v.* to proceed; to originate; to behave; to take action (against); *m.* behavior, conduct.
procedimiento [pro·se·di·mjén·to] *m.* procedure; method; process; conduct.
prócer [pró·ser] *m.* distinguished person; hero; great statesman.
procesado [pro·se·sá·do] *p.p. & adj.* relating to, or included in, a lawsuit; accused, prosecuted; *m.* defendant.
procesar [pro·se·sár] *v.* to prosecute; to accuse; to indict; to sue; **procesamiento de datos** data processing.
procesión [pro·se·sjón] *f.* procession; parade.
proceso [pro·sé·so] *m.* process; lawsuit, legal proceedings; lapse of time; — **fundacional** chartering; — **verbal** minutes, record.
proclama [pro·klá·ma] *f.* proclamation, ban; marriage banns.
proclamación [pro·kla·ma·sjón] *f.* proclamation.
proclamar [pro·kla·már] *v.* to proclaim.
proclítico [pro·klí·ti·ko] *adj.* proclitic.
procurador [por·ku·ra·dór] *m.* attorney.
procurar [pro·ku·rár] *v.* (*pretender*) to try, endeavor; (*obtener*) to procure, obtain, get.
prodigar[7] [pro·di·gár] *v.* to lavish; to bestow upon; to squander, waste.
prodigio [pro·dí·xjo] *m.* prodigy, wonder, marvel; miracle.
prodigioso [pro·di·xjóso] *adj.* prodigious, marvelous; fine, exquisite.
pródigo [pró·di·go] *adj.* prodigal, wasteful; lavish; generous; *m.* spendthrift.
producción [pro·duk·sjón] *f.* production; produce; — **masiva** mass production.
producir[25] [pro·du·sír] *v. irr.* to produce; to bring about; to yield; **-se** to express oneself, explain oneself; *Col., Ven.* to occur, happen.
productivo [pro·duk·tí·bo] *adj.* productive; fruitful; profitable.
producto [pro·dúk·to] *m.* product; yield; result.
productor [pro·duk·tór] *m.* producer; *adj.* producing, productive.
proeza [pro·é·sa] *f.* prowess; *Col.* boast, exaggeration.
profanación [pro·fa·na·sjón] *f.* profanation.
profanar [pro·fa·nár] *v.* to profane; to defile.
profano [pro·fá·no] *adj.* profane, not sacred; irreverent; lay, uninformed (*about a branch of learning*).
profecía [pro·fe·sí·a] *f.* prophecy; prediction.
proferir[3] [pro·fe·rír] *v. irr.* to utter, express, speak.
profesar [pro·fe·sár] *v.* to profess; to avow, confess.
profesión [pro·fe·sjón] *f.* profession; avowal, declaration.
profesional [pro·fe·sjo·nál] *adj., m. & f.* professional.
profesionista [pro·fe·sjo·nís·ta] *m. & f. Am.*

professional.
profesor [pro·fe·sór] *m.* professor, teacher; **profesorado** [pro·fe·so·rá·do] *m.* faculty; body of teachers; teaching profession; professorship.
profeta [pro·fé·ta] *m.* prophet.
profético [pro·fé·ti·ko] *adj.* prophetic.
profetizar[9] [pro·fe·ti·sár] *v.* to prophesy.
proficiente [pro·fi·sjén·te] *adj.* proficient, skilled.
profilaxis [pro·fi·lák·sis] *f.* prophylaxis (*disease prevention*).
prófugo [pró·fu·go] *adj. & m.* fugitive.
profundidad [pro·fun·di·dád] *f.* profundity, depth.
profundizar[9] [pro·fun·di·sár] *v.* to deepen; to go deep into.
profundo [pro·fún·do] *adj.* profound; deep; low.
profuso [pro·fú·so] *adj.* profuse; lavish.
progenitor [pro·xe·ni·tór] *m.* progenitor.
programa [pro·grá·ma] *m.* program; plan.
programación [pro·gra·ma·sjón] *f.* programming.
programador [pro·gra·ma·dór] *m.* programmer.
programar [pro·gra·már] *v.* to plan; to program.
progresar [pro·gre·sár] *v.* to progress.
progresista [pro·gre·sís·ta] *m., f. & adj.* progressive.
progresivo [pro·gre·sí·bo] *adj.* progressive.
progreso [pro·gré·so] *m.* progress.
prohibición [proj·bi·sjón] *f.* prohibition; ban.
prohibir [proj·bír] *v.* to prohibit, forbid.
prohijar [pro·i·xár] *v.* to adopt.
prójimo [pró·xi·mo] *m.* neighbor, fellow being; *Ríopl., Carib., C.A.* ese — that fellow.
prole [pró·le] *f.* progeny, offspring.
proletariado [pro·le·ta·rjá·do] *m.* proletariat, working class.
proletario [pro·le·tá·rjo] *adj.* proletarian, belonging to the working class; plebeian; *m.* proletarian.
prolijo [pro·lí·xo] *adj.* prolix, too long, drawn out; too detailed; boring, tedious.
prologar[7] [pro·lo·gár] *v.* to preface, write a preface for.
prólogo [pró·lo·go] *m.* prologue.
prolongación [pro·loŋ·ga·sjón] *f.* prolongation; extension; lengthening.
prolongar[7] [pro·loŋ·gár] *v.* to prolong, lengthen, extend.
promediar [pro·me·djár] *v.* to average; to divide or distribute into two equal parts; to mediate; **antes de** — **el mes** before the middle of the month.
promedio [pro·mé·djo] *m.* middle; average.
promesa [pro·mé·sa] *f.* promise.
prometedor [pro·me·te·dór] *adj.* promising, hopeful.
prometer [pro·me·tér] *v.* to promise; to show promise; *Ríopl., C.A.* to affirm, assure; **-se** to become engaged, betrothed.
prometido [pro·me·tí·do] *adj. & p.p.* betrothed; *m.* fiancé, betrothed; promise.
prominente [pro·mi·nén·te] *adj.* prominent.
promiscuo [pro·mís·kwo] *adj.* promiscuous.
promisorio [pro·mi·só·rjo] *adj.* promissory.
promoción [pro·mo·sjón] *f.* promotion; advancement.
promontorio [pro·mon·tó·rjo] *m.* promontory, headland, cape; anything bulky; bulge.
promotor [pro·mo·tór] *m.* promoter.
promovedor [pro·mo·be·dór] *m.* promoter.
promover[2] [pro·mo·bér] *v. irr.* to promote; to advance.
promulgación [pro·mul·ga·sjón] *f.* promulgation, publication, proclamation (*of a law*).
promulgar[7] [pro·mul·gár] *v.* to promulgate, proclaim, announce publicly.
pronombre [pro·nóm·bre] *m.* pronoun.
pronominal [pro·no·mi·nál] *adj.* pronominal.

PR

pronosticar[6] [pro·nos·ti·kár] *v.* to prophesy, predict.
pronóstico [pro·nós·ti·ko] *m.* forecast; prediction; omen.
prontitud [pron·ti·túd] *f.* promptness; quickness.
pronto [prón·to] *adj.* quick, speedy; ready; prompt; *adv.* soon; quickly; **de** — suddenly; **al** — at first; **por de** (*or* **por lo**) — for the present; *m.* sudden impulse.
pronunciación [pro·nun·sja·sjón] *f.* pronunciation.
pronunciar [pro·nun·sjár] *v.* to pronounce; to utter; **-se** to rise up in rebellion.
propagación [pro·pa·ga·sjón] *f.* propagation, spread, spreading.
propaganda [pro·pa·gán·da] *f.* propaganda; advertising.
propagar[7] [pro·pa·gár] *v.* to propagate, reproduce; to spread.
propalar [pro·pa·lár] *v.* to spread (*news*).
propasarse [pro·pa·sár·se] *v.* to overstep one's bounds; to exceed one's authority, go too far.
propensión [pro·pen·sjón] *f.* tendency, inclination; bent, natural tendency or ability.
propenso [pro·pén·so] *adj.* prone, susceptible, inclined.
propiciar [pro·pi·sjár] *v.* to calm one's anger; *Am.* to propose.
propicio [pro·pí·sjo] *adj.* propitious, favorable.
propiedad [pro·pje·dád] *f.* property; ownership; attribute, quality; propriety, appropriateness.
propietario [pro·pje·tá·rjo] *m.* proprietor, owner.
propina [pro·pí·na] *f.* tip (*voluntary gift of money for service*).
propinar [pro·pi·nár] *v.* to give (*something to drink*); to give (*a beating, kick, slap*); *Am.* to tip, give a tip to; — **una paliza** to give a beating.
propio [pró·pjo] *adj.* proper; suitable; own; same; **amor** — vanity, pride, self-esteem; *m.* messenger.
proponer[40] [pro·po·nér] *v. irr.* to propose; to resolve; to present; **-se** to resolve, make a resolution.
proporción [pro·por·sjón] *f.* proportion; dimension; ratio; opportunity, chance.
proporcionar [pro·por·sjo·nár] *v.* to proportion; to adapt, adjust; to furnish, supply, give.
proposición [pro·po·si·sjón] *f.* proposition; proposal; assertion.
propósito [pro·pó·si·to] *m.* purpose, aim, design; **a** — apropos, suitable, fitting; by the way; **de** — on purpose; **fuera de** — irrelevant, beside the point.
propuesta [pro·pwés·to] *f.* proposal, offer; proposition.
propuesto [pro·pwés·to] *p.p. of* **proponer.**
propulsar [pro·pul·sár] *v.* to propel.
propulsión [pro·pul·sjón] *f.* propulsion; — **a chorro** (*por reacción*) jet propulsion; — **a cohete** rocket propulsion.
propulsor [pro·pul·sór] *m.* propeller; *adj.* propelling; *m.* propelling force.
prorratear [pro·rra·te·ár] *v.* to prorate, distribute or assess proportionally; to average.
prorrateo [pro·rra·té·o] *m.* apportionment, proportional distribution.
prórroga [pró·rro·ga] *f.* renewal, extension of time.
prorrogar[7] [pro·rro·gár] *v.* to put off, postpone; to adjourn; to extend (*time limit*).
prorrumpir [pro·rrum·pír] *v.* to break forth; — **en llanto** to burst into tears; — **en una carcajada** to let out a big laugh.
prosa [pró·sa] *f.* prose.
prosaico [pro·sáj·ko] *adj.* prosaic; dull; tedious.
proscribir[52] [pros·kri·bír] *v.* to proscribe, banish; to outlaw.

proscripción [pros·krip·sjón] *f.* banishment.
proscripto [pros·kríp·to], **proscrito** [pros·krí·to] *p.p. of* **proscribir; ** *m.* exile, outlaw.
proseguir[5, 12] [pro·se·gír] *v. irr.* to continue; to follow.
prosélito [pro·sé·li·to] *m.* proselyte.
prosódico [pro·só·di·ko] *adj.* prosodic.
prosperar [pros·pe·rár] *v.* to prosper.
prosperidad [pros·pe·ri·dád] *f.* prosperity; success.
próspero [prós·pe·ro] *adj.* prosperous; successful.
próstata [prós·ta·ta] *f.* prostate.
prostituir[32] [pros·ti·twír] *v.* to prostitute, corrupt.
prostituta [pros·ti·tú·ta] prostitute.
protagonista [pro·ta·go·nís·ta] *m. & f.* protagonist (*main character or actor*).
protección [pro·tek·sjón] *f.* protection; support.
proteccionista [pro·tek·sjo·nís·ta] *adj.* protective; **tarifa** — protective tariff; *m. & f.* protectionist (*follower of the economic principles of protection*).
protector [pro·tek·tór] *m.* protector, guardian; *adj.* protecting, protective.
protectorado [pro·tek·to·rá·do] *m.* protectorate.
proteger[11] [pro·te·xér] *v.* to protect; to shelter; to defend.
protegido [pro·te·xí·do] *m.* protege.
proteína [pro·te·í·na] *f.* protein.
proteínico [pro·te·í·ni·ko] *adj.* related to the proteins.
protesta [pro·tés·ta] *f.* protest; protestation.
protestación [pro·tes·ta·sjón] *f.* protestation, solemn declaration; protest.
protestante [pro·tes·tán·te] *m.* Protestant; one who protests.
protestar [pro·tes·tár] *v.* (*confesar*) to assert, assure; to avow publicly; (*negar*) to protest; — **una letra** to protest a draft.
protocolo [pro·to·kó·lo] *m.* protocol.
protón [pro·tón] *m.* proton.
protoplasma [pro·to·pláz·ma] *m.* protoplasm.
protuberancia [pro·tu·be·rán·sja] *f.* protuberance, bulge.
protuberante [pro·tu·be·rán·te] *adj.* protuberant, prominent, bulging.
provecho [pro·bé·čo] *m.* profit; benefit; utility; advantage; **hombre de** — worthy, useful man.
provechoso [pro·be·čó·so] *adj.* profitable; useful; beneficial; advantageous.
proveedor [pro·be·e·dór] *m.* provisioner, provider; supply man.
proveer[14, 52] [pro·be·ér] *v. irr.* to provide; to supply; to confer, bestow; to decide; **-se de** to supply oneself with.
provenir[48] [pro·be·nír] *v. irr.* to originate, arise, come (from).
proverbio [pro·ber·bjo] *m.* proverb.
providencia [pro·bi·dén·sja] *f.* providence; foresight; Providence, God; legal decision, sentence; provision, measure; **tomar una** — to take a step or measure.
providencial [pro·bi·den·sjál] *adj.* providential.
provincia [pro·bín·sja] *f.* province.
provincial [pro·bin·sjál] *adj.* provincial.
provinciano [pro·bin·sjá·no] *adj. & m.* provincial.
provisión [pro·bi·sjón] *f.* provision; supply, stock.
provisional [pro·bi·sjo·nál] *adj.* temporary; provisional.
provisorio [pro·bi·só·rjo] *adj.* provisional, temporary.
provisto [pro·bís·to] *p.p. of* **proveer.**
provocación [pro·bo·ka·sjón] *f.* provocation; dare, defiance.
provocador [pro·bo·ka·dór] *adj.* provoking; *m.* provoker.

provocar[6] [pro·ƀo·kár] v. to provoke; to excite, rouse; to stimulate.

provocativo [pro·ƀo·ka·tí·ƀo] adj. provocative.

proximidad [prok·si·mi·ðáð] f. proximity, nearness.

próximo [prók·si·mo] adj. next; neighboring; near; **del — pasado** of last month.

proyección [pro·yek·sjón] f. projection; jut.

proyectar [pro·yek·tár] v. to project; to plan; to throw; to cast; **-se** to be cast (as a shadow).

proyectil [pro·yek·tíl] m. projectile.

proyectista [pro·yek·tís·ta] m. & f. designer; schemer, planner.

proyecto [pro·yék·to] m. project; plan; **— de ley** bill (in a legislature).

prudencia [pru·ðén·sja] f. prudence, practical wisdom, discretion.

prudente [pru·ðén·te] adj. prudent, wise, discreet.

prueba [prwé·ƀa] f. proof; trial; test; fitting; sample; evidence; Andes, Ríopl., Col., C.A. acrobatic performance, stunt, trick, sleight of hand; **a — de incendio** fireproof; **— de doblaje** bend test.

prurito [pru·rí·to] m. itch; keen desire.

psicología [si·ko·lo·xí·a] f. see **sicología.**

psicosis [si·kó·sis] f. see **sicosis.**

psiquiatría [si·kja·trí·a] f. see **siquiatría.**

psitacosis [si·ta·kó·sis] f. see **sitacosis.**

ptomaína [toma·í·na] f. ptomaine.

púa [pú·a] f. prick; barb; prong; thorn; quill (of a porcupine, etc.); sharp, cunning person; Ríopl. cock's spur; **alambre de -s** barbed wire.

publicación [pu·ƀli·ka·sjón] f. publication.

publicar[6] [pu·ƀli·kár] v. to publish; to reveal; to announce.

publicidad [pu·ƀli·si·ðáð] f. publicity.

público [pú·ƀli·ko] adj. & m. public.

puchero [pu·čé·ro] m. pot, kettle; meat and vegetable stew; pout; **hacer -s** to pout.

pucho [pú·čo] m. cigar or cigarette butt; C.A. something of little value.

pudiente [pu·ðjén·te] adj. powerful; rich, wealthy; m. man of means.

pudín [pu·ðín] m. pudding.

pudor [pu·ðór] m. modesty; shyness.

pudrir[16] [pu·ðrír] v. to rot; to vex, annoy; **-se** to rot.

pueblero [pwe·ƀlé·ro] m. Ríopl. townsman (as opposed to countryman).

pueblo [pwé·ƀlo] m. town, village; people, race, nation; populace; common people.

puente [pwén·te] m. bridge; Carib., Mex., Ríopl. dental bridge; Am. knife and fork rest; **— colgante** suspension bridge; **— levadizo** drawbridge.

puerca [pwér·ka] f. sow.

puerco [pwér·ko] m. pig, hog; **— espín** porcupine; adj. filthy, dirty; coarse, ill-bred.

pueril [pwe·ríl] adj. puerile, childish.

puerro [pwé·rro] m. scallion.

puerta [pwér·ta] f. door; gate; entrance; **— accessoria (excusada,** or **falsa)** side door; **— de golpe** spring door; trap door; **— franca** back door; free entrance or entry; **— trasera** back door; **a — cerrada** secretly, behind closed doors; Am. **en —** in view, in sight, very near.

puerto [pwér·to] m. port; harbor; refuge; mountain pass; **— franco** free port.

puertorriqueño [pwer·to·rri·ké·ño] adj. & m. Puerto Rican.

pues [pwes] conj. since, because, for, inasmuch as; then; adv. then; well; **— bien** well then, well; **— que** since.

puesta [pwés·ta] f. set, setting (of a star or planet); stake at cards; **— de sol** sunset.

puestero [pwes·té·ro] m. Carib., Mex., Ríopl. vendor, seller (at a stand or stall); Ríopl. man in charge of livestock on Argentine ranches.

puesto [pwés·to] p.p. of **poner** placed, put, set; **mal** (or **bien**) — badly (or well) dressed; m. place; vendor's booth or stand; post, position, office; military post; Andes, Ríopl. station for watching and taking care of cattle on a ranch; **— de socorros** first-aid station; **— que** conj. since.

pugilato [pu·xi·lá·to] m. boxing.

pugilista [pu·xi·lís·ta] m. boxer, prize fighter.

pugna [púg·na] f. struggle; conflict; **estar en — con** to be in conflict with; to be opposed to.

pugnar [pug·nár] v. to fight; to struggle; to strive; to persist.

pujanza [pu·xán·sa] f. push, force, power.

pujar [pu·xár] v. to make a strenuous effort; to grope for words; to falter; to outbid (offer a higher bid than); C.A. to grunt; Peru to reject; Ven. to dismiss; Mex. **— para adentro** to forbear, keep silent; Peru **andar pujado** to go around crestfallen; to be in disgrace.

pujido [pu·xí·ðo] m. Am. grunt.

pulcritud [pul·kri·túð] f. neatness, trimness; excellence, perfection.

pulcro [púl·kro] adj. neat, trim; beautiful.

pulga [púl·ga] f. flea; Ríopl. small and insignificant person; **tener malas -s** to be illtempered; Col., Andes **ser de pocas -s** to be touchy, oversensitive; **pulgón** m. blight, plant louse.

pulgada [pul·gá·ða] f. inch.

pulgar [pul·gár] m. thumb.

pulguero [pul·gé·ro] m. jail (slang).

pulido [pu·lí·ðo] adj. polished, refined; polite; neat; exquisite.

pulidor [pu·li·ðór] adj. polishing; m. polisher.

pulimentar [pu·li·men·tár] v. to polish.

pulimento [pu·li·mén·to] m. polish; gloss.

pulir [pu·lír] v. to polish.

pulmón [pul·món] m. lung.

pulmonar [pul·mo·nár] adj. pulmonary, pertaining to the lungs.

pulmonía [pul·mo·ní·a] f. pneumonia.

pulpa [púl·pa] f. pulp; boneless meat.

pulpería [pul·pe·rí·a] f. Ríopl., C.A., Ch., Ven., Andes country general store; Am. tavern.

pulpero [pul·pé·ro] m. Ríopl., C.A., Ch., Ven., Andes owner of a country store or tavern.

púlpito [púl·pi·to] m. pulpit.

pulpo [púl·po] m. octopus.

pulque [púl·ke] m. Mex. pulque (fermented juice of the maguey).

pulquería [pul·ke·rí·a] f. Mex. pulque bar or cantina.

pulsación [pul·sa·sjón] f. pulsation, beat, throb; pulse, beating.

pulsar [pul·sár] v. to pulsate, throb, beat; to feel the pulse of; to sound out; examine; to play (the harp); Mex., C.A. to judge or try the weight of (by lifting).

pulsera [pul·sé·ra] f. bracelet; wrist bandage; **reloj de —** wrist watch.

pulso [púl·so] m. pulse; steadiness; tract; Ríopl., Carib., Col. bracelet, wrist watch; **un hombre de —** a prudent, steady man; Cuba, Mex. **beber a —** to drink straight down, gulp down; **levantar a —** to lift with the strength of the wrist or hand; **sacar a — un negocio** to carry out a deal by sheer perseverance.

pulsorreactor [pul·so·rre·ak·tór] m. jet engine of movable intake valves.

pulular [pu·lu·lár] v. to swarm; to multiply rapidly; to

PR

sprout, bud.

pulverizar[9] [pul·ƀe·ri·sár] *v*. to pulverize.

pulla [pú·ya] *f*. taunt; mean dig, quip, cutting remark; filthy word or remark.

puma [pú·ma] *f*. puma, mountain lion.

puna [pú·na] *f*. *Andes* cold, arid tableland of the Andes; *Ríopl.* desert; *Andes* sickness caused by high altitude.

pundonor [pun·do·nór] *m*. point of honor.

púnico [pú·ni·ko] *adj*. Punic.

punta [pún·ta] *f*. point, tip; bull's horn; cigar or cigarette butt; *Ven.* gang, band, herd, a lot (*of things, people, etc.*); *Am.* small leaf of fine tobacco; *Am.* jeer, cutting remark; **-s** point lace; scallops; **de** — on end; **de -s** (*or* **de puntillas**) on tiptoe; *Am.* **a** — **de** by dint of, by means of; **estar de** — **con** to be on bad terms with; **sacar** — **a un lápiz** to sharpen a pencil; **tener sus -s de poeta** to be something of a poet.

puntada [pun·ta·ða] *f*. stitch; hint; *Andes* prick, pricking, sting, sharp pain; **no he dado** — **en este asunto** I have left this matter completely untouched.

puntal [pun·tál] *m*. prop; support, basis; bull's horn; *Col.* snack (*between meals*).

puntapié [pun·ta·pjé] *m*. kick (*with the toe of the shoe*).

puntazo [pun·tá·so] *m. Col., Ven., Mex., Cuba* stab, jab.

puntear [pun·te·ár] *v*. to pluck (*the strings of a guitar*); to play (*a guitar*); to make dots; to engrave, draw or paint by means of dots; to stitch; to tack (*said of a boat*).

puntería [pun·te·rí·a] *f*. aim.

puntero [pun·té·ro] *m*. pointer; chisel; blacksmith's punch; *C.A., Col., Ch.* clock or watch hand; *Col., Ch.* leader of a parade; *Cuba, Mex., Ven., Col.* leading ox (*or other animal*); *Arg.* guide.

puntiagudo [pun·tja·ǥú·ðo] *adj*. sharp, sharp-pointed.

puntilla [pun·tí·ya] *f*. small point; tip; small dagger; tracing point; point lace; *Ven.* penknife; *Mex., Ch.* toe rubber; *Ch.* ridge (*of a hill*); **de -s** on tiptoe; **puntillazo** *m*. stab (*with a dagger*).

punto [pún·to] *m*. (*parada*) period; stop; point; dot; (*puntada*) stitch; mesh; (*sitio*) place; moment; (*mira*) gun sight; (*computadora*) pixel; — **de admiración** exclamation mark; — **de interrogación** question mark; — **y coma** semicolon; **dos -s** colon; **al** — at once, immediately; **a** — **de** on the point of; **de** — knitted, porous knit, stockinet or jersey weave; **en** — exactly, on the dot; **a** — **fijo** with certainty; **subir de** — to increase or get worse.

puntuación [pun·twa·sjón] *f*. punctuation.

puntual [pun·twál] *adj*. punctual, prompt; exact.

puntualidad [pun·twa·li·ðáð] *f*. punctuality, promptness; certainty.

puntualizar [pun·twa·li·sár] *v*. to point out.

puntuar[18] [pun·twár] *v*. to punctuate.

punzada [pun·sá·ða] *f*. puncture; prick; sharp pain.

punzante [pun·sán·te] *adj*. sharp; pricking; piercing, penetrating.

punzar[9] [pun·sár] *v*. to puncture; to sting; to prick; to punch, perforate.

punzón [pun·són] *m*. punch, puncher; pick; awl; — **de marcar** center punches (machine).

puñada [pu·ñá·ða] *f*. punch, box, blow with the fist.

puñado [pu·ñá·ðo] *m*. fistful, handful; **a -s** abundantly; by handfuls.

puñal [pu·ñál] *m*. dagger.

puñalada [pu·ña·la·ða] *f*. stab; sharp pain; **coser a -s**

to stab to death.

puñetazo [pu·ñe·tá·so] *m*. punch, blow with the fist.

puño [pú·ño] *m*. fist; fistful, handful; cuff; hilt, handle; *Ven., Col.* blow with the fist; **a** — **cerrado** firmly; **ser como un** — to be stingy; **tener -s** to be strong, courageous.

pupila [pu·pí·la] *f*. pupil (*of the eye*).

pupilo [pu·pí·lo] *m*. ward; boarding-school pupil; boarder.

pupitre [pu·pí·tre] *m*. desk, school desk.

puré [pu·ré] *m*. purée; thick soup.

pureza [pu·ré·sa] *f*. purity; chastity.

purga [púr·ga] *f*. purge, laxative, physic.

purgante [pur·gán·te] *adj*. purgative, laxative; *m*. purgative, physic, laxative.

purgar[7] [pur·gár] *v*. to purge; to purify; to atone for; **-se** to purge oneself; to take a laxative.

purgatorio [pur·ga·tó·rjo] *m*. purgatory.

purificar[6] [pu·ri·fi·kár] *v*. to purify.

purista [pu·rís·ta] *m. & f*. purist.

puro [pú·ro] *adj*. (*limpio*) pure; clean; chaste; (*sólo*) mere, only, sheer; **a pura fuerza** by sheer force; **a puros gritos** by just shouting; *m*. cigar.

púrpura [púr·pu·ra] *f*. purple; purple cloth.

purpúreo [pur·pú·re·o] *adj*. purple.

pus [pus] *m*. pus.

pusilánime [pu·si·lá·ni·me] *adj*. pusillanimous.

puta [pú·ta] *f*. whore, prostitute.

putativo [pu·ta·tí·ƀo] *adj*. reputed, supposed; **padre** — foster father.

putrefacción [pu·tre·fak·sjón] *f*. putrefaction, decay, rotting.

putrefacto [pu·tre·fák·to] *adj*. putrid, rotten, decayed.

puya [pú·ya] *f*. goad; lance head.

Q:q

que [ke] *rel. pron*. that; which; who; whom; **el** — who; which; the one who; the one which; *conj* that; for, because; **más** (**menos**) — more (less) than; **el mismo** — the same as; — (= *subj*.) let, may you, I hope that; **por mucho** — no matter how much; **quieras** — no whether you wish or not.

qué [ke] *interr. adj. & pron*. what?; what a!; *interr. adv*. how; ¡— **bonito!** how beautiful!; **¿a** —? what for?; **¿para** —? what for?; **¿por** —? why?; **¿— tal?** how?; hello!; ¡— **más da!** what's the difference!; **¡a mí** —! so what! and what's that to me!

quebracho [ke·ƀrá·čo] *m*. quebracho, breakax wood.

quebrada [ke·ƀrá·ða] *f*. ravine; gorge; failure, bankruptcy; *Ríopl., Col., Ven., C.A., Mex.* brook.

quebradizo [ke·ƀra·ðí·so] *adj*. breakable; brittle; fragile; delicate.

quebrado [ke·ƀrá·ðo] *adj*. broken; weakened; ruptured; bankrupt; rough or rugged (*ground*); *m*. common fraction; *Ven.* navigable waters between reefs.

quebrantar [ke·ƀran·tár] *v*. to break; to break open; to pound, crush; to violate (*a law*); to weaken; to vex; *Mex., Col.* to tame, break in (*a colt*); — **el agua** to take the chill off the water.

quebranto [ke·ƀrán·to] *m*. breaking; grief, affliction; discouragement; damage, loss.

quebrar[1] [ke·ƀrár] *v. irr*. to break; to crush; to interrupt; to wither (*said of the complexion*); to become bankrupt; **-se** to break; to get broken; to be ruptured; **-se uno la cabeza** to rack one's brain.

quebrazón [ke·bra·són] *m. Ven., Col.* breakage, breaking.

quechua [ké·čwa] *adj. Am.* Quechua; *m. & f.* Quechua, Quechua Indian; *m.* Quechua language.

queda [ké·da] *f.* curfew.

quedar [ke·dár] to stay; to remain; to be left over; to be left (*in a state or condition*); — **en** to agree to; *Am.* — **de** to agree to; — **bien** to acquit oneself well; to come out well; *Am.* to suit, become (*said of a dress, hat, etc.*); *Am.* — **bien con alguien** to please someone; **-se** to remain; **-se con una cosa** to keep something; to take something (*buy it*); *Am.* **-se como si tal cosa** to act as if nothing had happened.

quedo [ké·do] *adj.* quiet, still; gentle; *adv.* softly; in a low voice; **quedito** [ke·dí·to] *adj.* nice and quiet; *adv.* very softly.

quehacer [ke·a·sér] *m.* work, occupation; task, duty, chore.

queja [ké·xa] *f.* complaint; groan, moan; grudge.

quejarse [ke·xár·se] *v.* to complain; to grumble; to moan; to lament.

quejido [ke·xí·do] *m.* moan; groan.

quejoso [ke·xó·so] *adj.* complaining, whining.

quejumbre [ke·xúm·bre] *f.* whine, moan; murmur, complaint; **-s** *m. Cuba, Ven.* grumbler, whiner; **quejumbroso** [ke·xum·bró·so] *adj.* whining, complaining.

quemada [ke·má·da] *f.* burned forest; *Am.* burn.

quemado [ke·má·do] *m.* burned portion of a forest; *Col.* burned field; *Ec.* hot alcoholic drink; *adj.* dark, tan; *Am.* peeved, piqued; *Col., Ven., Cuba, Mex.* ruined; *p.p. of* **quemar**.

quemadura [ke·ma·dú·ra] *f.* burn; burning; scald; smut (*plant disease*).

quemar [ke·már] *v.* to burn; to scald; to scorch; to sell at a loss; to annoy; *Am.* to deceive, swindle; **-se** to burn; to be hot.

quemazón [ke·ma·són] *f.* (*calor*) burn, burning; great heat; fire, conflagration; (*desazón*) pique, anger; bargain sale; *Am.* mirage on the pampas.

quena [ké·na] *f. Andes* flute of the Quechua Indians.

querella [ke·ré·ya] *f.* quarrel; complaint; controversy.

querellante [ke·re·yán·te] *m.* plaintiff.

querellarse [ke·re·yár·se] *v.* to complain.

querencia [ke·rén·sja] *f.* affection; longing; favorite spot; haunt; stable.

querer[41] [ke·rér] *v. irr.* to want, wish, desire; to will; to be willing; to love; — **decir** to mean; **sin** — unwillingly; **no quiso hacerlo** he refused to do it; **quiere llover** it is trying to rain, it is about to rain; **como quiera** in any way; **como quiera que** since; no matter how; **cuando quiera** whenever; **donde quiera** wherever; anywhere; **-se** to love each other; *Ríopl., Ven., Col.* to be on the point of, be about to; **se quiere caer esa pared** that wall is about to fall.

querido [ke·rí·do] *p.p.* wanted, desired; *adj.* beloved, dear; *m.* lover; **querida** *f.* darling; mistress.

queroseno [ke·ro·sé·no] *m. variant of* **keroseno.**

querubín [ke·ru·bín] *m.* cherub.

quesería [ke·se·rí·a] *f.* dairy, creamery, cheese factory; **quesera** [ke·sé·ra] *f.* dairy, cheese factory; cheese dish; dairymaid, woman cheese vendor or cheesemaker; **quesero** [ke·sé·ro] *adj.* pertaining to cheese; *m.* cheesemaker.

queso [ké·so] *m.* cheese; *Ven.* — **de higos** fig paste; — **crema (de natas)** cream cheese.

quetzal [ket·sál] *m.* bird of paradise; quetzal (*monetary unit of Guatemala*).

quicio [kí·sjo] *m.* hinge of a door; **sacar a uno de** —

to exasperate someone.

quichua [kí·čwa] = **quechua.**

quiebra [kjé·bra] *f.* (*rotura*) break; crack; fissure; fracture; (*pérdida*) loss, damage; bankruptcy.

quien [kjen] *rel. pron.* who, whom; he who, she who; **¿quién?** *interr. pron.* who? whom?

quienquiera [kjen·kjé·ra] *pron.* whoever, whosoever, whomsoever.

quieto [kjé·to] *adj.* quiet, still; calm.

quietud [kje·túd] *f.* quiet, stillness, calmness.

quijada [ki·xá·da] *f.* jaw; jawbone.

quijotada [ki·xo·tá·da] *f.* quixotic deed.

quilate [ki·lá·te] *m.* carat (*twenty-fourth part in weight and value of gold*); unit of weight for precious stones and pearls; **-s** qualities; degree of perfection or purity.

quilla [kí·ya] *f.* keel.

quimbombó [kim·bom·bó] *m.* okra.

quimera [ki·mé·ra] *f.* absurd idea, wild fancy.

química [kí·mi·ka] *f.* chemistry.

químico [kí·mi·ko] *adj.* chemical; *m.* chemist.

quina [kí·na], **quinina** [ki·ní·na] *f.* quinine.

quincalla [kin·ká·ya] *f.* hardware.

quincallería [kin·ka·ye·rí·a] *f.* hardware; hardware store; hardware trade.

quince [kín·se] *num.* fifteen.

quincena [kin·sé·na] *f.* fortnight; semimonthly pay.

quinqué [kin·ké] *m.* oil lamp.

quinta [kín·ta] *f.* (*casa*) villa, country house; (*militar*) draft, military conscription; (*cartas*) sequence of five cards.

quintaesencia [kin·ta·e·sén·sja] *f.* quintessence, pure essence, purest form.

quiosco [kjós·ko] *m.* kiosk, small pavilion.

quiropráctico [ki·ro·prák·ti·ko] *m.* chiropractor.

quirúrgico [ki·rúr·xi·ko] *adj.* surgical.

quisquilloso [kis·ki·yó·so] *adj.* touchy, oversensitive.

quisto [kís·to]: **bien** — well-liked, well received; welcome; **mal** — disliked; unwelcome.

quitamanchas [ki·ta·mán·čas] *m.* cleaner, stain remover.

quitar [ki·tár] *v.* to remove; to take away (off, *or* from); to rob of; to deprive of; to subtract; to parry (*in fencing*); **-se** to take off (*clothing*); to remove oneself, withdraw; **-se de una cosa** to give up something, get rid of something; **-se a alguien de encima** to get rid of someone; **¡quita allá!** don't tell me that!; **¡quítese de aquí!** get out of here!

quitasol [ki·ta·sól] *m.* large sunshade, parasol.

quite [kí·te] *m.* parry (*in fencing*); revenge; dodge, dodging; *Ven., Col., Mex.* **andar a los -s** to be on the defensive; to take offense easily; to be afraid of one's own shadow; **eso no tiene** — that can't be helped.

quizá [ki·sá], **quizás** [ki·sás] *adv.* perhaps, maybe.

R:r   **rabadilla** [rra·ba·dí·ya] *f.* end of the spinal column; coccyx; tail of a fowl; rump.

rábano [rrá·ba·no] *m.* radish; **tomar el** — **por las hojas** to take one thing for another; to misinterpret something.

rabia [rrá·bja] *f.* rabies; rage; **tener** — **a alguien** to hate someone; *Ríopl., Carib., Mex.* **volarse de** — to get furious, angry.

rabiar [rra·bjár] *v.* to have rabies; to rage; to rave; to suffer a severe pain; — **por** to be dying to or for, be very eager to; **quema que rabia** it burns terribly.

rabieta [rra·bjé·ta] *f.* tantrum, fit of temper.

rabino [rra·bí·no] *m.* rabbi.

rabioso [rra·bjó·so] *adj.* rabid (*having rabies*), mad; furious, angry, violent.

rabo [rrá·bo] *m.* tail; **de cabo a** — from beginning to end; **mirar con el** — **del ojo** to look out of the corner of one's eye.

rabón [rra·bón] *m.* bobtail.

racimo [rra·sí·mo] *m.* bunch; cluster.

raciocinio [rra·sjo·sí·njo] *m.* reasoning.

ración [rra·sjón] *f.* ration; allowance; supply.

racional [rra·sjo·nál] *adj.* rational; reasonable.

racionamiento [rra·sjo·na·mjén·to] *m.* rationing.

racionar [rra·sjo·nár] *v.* to ration.

racismo [rra·síz·mo] *m.* racism.

racista [rra·sís·ta] *m. & f.* racist.

radar [rra·dár] *m.* radar.

radaroscopio [rra·da·ros·kó·pjo] *m.* radarscope.

radiación [rra·dja·sjón] *f.* radiation; — **cósmica** cosmic radiation.

radiatividad [rra·djak·ti·bi·dád] *f.* radioactivity.

radiactivo [rra·djak·tí·bo] *adj.* radioactive.

radiador [rra·dja·dór] *m.* radiator.

radiante [rra·dján·te] *adj.* radiant; shining; beaming.

radiar [rra·djár] *v.* to radiate; to radio; to broadcast.

radical [rra·di·kál] *adj.* (*básico*) fundamental, basic; radical; (*extremista*) extreme; *m.* radical; root of a word.

radicalismo [rra·di·ka·líz·mo] *m.* radicalism.

radicar[6] [rra·di·kár] *v.* to take root; to be, be found (*in a certain place*); **-se** to take root; to locate, settle.

radio [rrá·djo] *m.* radius; radium; *m. & f.* radio.

radiodifundir [rra·djo·di·fun·dír] *v.* to broadcast by radio. See **difundir.**

radiodifusión [rra·djo·di·fu·sjón] *f.* broadcasting. See **difusión.**

radiodifusora [rra·djo·di·fu·só·ra], **radioemisora** [rra·djo·e·mi·só·ra] *f.* broadcasting station.

radioeléctrico [rra·djo·e·lék·tri·ko] *adj.* radioelectric.

radioescucha [rra·djo·es·kú·ča] *m. & f.* radio listener.

radiofónico [rra·djo·fó·ni·ko] *adj.* radio (*used as adj.*); **estación radiofónica** radio station.

radiografía [rra·djo·gra·fí·a] *f.* radiography, X-ray photography; X-ray picture.

radiografiar[17] [rra·djo·gra·fjár] *v.* to take X-ray pictures.

radiolocutor [rra·djo·lo·ku·tór] *m.* radio announcer. See **locutor.**

radiotelefonía [rra·djo·te·le·fo·ní·a] *f.* radiotelephony, radio, wireless.

radiotelegrafía [rra·djo·te·le·gra·fí·a] *f.* radiotelegraphy, radio, wireless telegraphy.

radiotransmisor [rra·djo·trans·mi·sór] *m.* radio transmitter.

radón [rra·dón] *m.* radon.

radioyente [rra·djo·yén·te] = **radioescucha.**

raer[24] [rra·ér] *v. irr.* to scrape off; to rub off; to scratch off; to fray; to erase.

ráfaga [rrá·fa·ga] *f.* gust of wind; flash of light.

raído [rra·í·do] *p.p. & adj.* scraped off; rubbed off; frayed; worn, threadbare.

raigón [rraj·gón] *m.* large root; root of a tooth.

raíz [rra·ís] *f.* root; origin; foundation; — **cuadrada** square root; **a** — **de** close to, right after; **de** — by the roots, completely; **echar raíces** to take root, become firmly fixed.

raja [rrá·xa] *f.* slice; splinter; crack; split, crevice; **hacer -s** to slice; to tear into strips; to cut into splinters; **hacerse uno -s** to wear oneself out (*by dancing, jumping or any violent exercise*).

rajá [rra·xá] *m.* rajah.

rajadura [rra·xa·dú·ra] *f.* crack, crevice.

rajar [rra·xár] *v.* to split; to crack; to cleave; to slice; to chatter; to brag; *Col., Cuba, Mex., Andes* to defame, insult; *Col.* to flunk, fail (*a student*); **-se** to split open; to crack; *Mex.* to get afraid, back down.

rajatablas [rra·xa·tá·blas] *m. Col.* reprimand, scolding; **a** — in great haste.

ralea [rra·lé·a] *f.* breed, race, stock; species, kind.

ralear [rra·le·ár] *v.* to thin out, make less dense; to become less dense.

ralo [rrá·lo] *adj.* sparse, thin, thinly scattered.

rallador [rra·ya·dór] *m.* grater.

rallar [rra·yár] *v.* to grate; to grate on, annoy; *Am.* to goad, spur.

rama [rrá·ma] *f.* branch, limb; **en** — crude, raw; **andarse por las -s** to beat about the bush, not to stick to the point.

ramada [rra·má·da] *f.* branches, foliage; arbor; *Am.* shed, tent.

ramaje [rra·má·xe] *m.* foliage; branches.

ramal [rra·mál] *m.* strand (*of a rope, etc.*); branch; branch railway line; halter.

rambla [rrám·bla] *f.* avenue (*especially in Barcelona*).

ramera [rra·mé·ra] *f.* harlot, prostitute.

ramificación [rra·mi·fi·ka·sjón] *f.* (*computadora*) branching.

ramificarse[6] [rra·mi·fi·kár·se] *v.* to branch off, divide into branches.

ramillete [rra·mi·yé·te] *m.* bouquet; flower cluster.

ramo [rrá·mo] *m.* bunch (*of flowers*), bouquet; line, branch (*of art, science, industry, etc.*); branch, bough; **domingo de -s** Palm Sunday.

ramonear [rra·mo·ne·ár] *v.* to cut off twigs or tips of branches; to nibble grass, twigs, or leaves; *Am.* to eat scraps or leftovers.

rampa [rrám·pa] *f.* ramp; apron (*airport*); — **de cohetes**, — **de lanzamiento** launching ramp.

ramplón [rram·plón] *adj.* coarse; crude, uncouth; slovenly.

ramplonería [rram·plo·ne·rí·a] *f.* coarse act or remark; crudeness, coarseness; slovenliness.

rana [rrá·na] *f.* frog.

rancio [rrán·sjo] *adj.* rancid, stale; old (*wine*); **linaje** — old, noble lineage.

ranchero [rran·čé·ro] *m. Mex.* rancher, farmer; **ranchería** [rran·če·rí·a] *f.* group of huts; *Col.* inn (*for arrieros*).

rancho [rrán·čo] *m.* camp; hamlet; mess (*meal for a group and the group itself*); *Carib., Ven., Col., Andes, Ríopl.* hut; *Carib., Ven., Col., Andes, Ríopl.* country house; *Mex.* ranch, small farm (*usually for cattle raising*).

rango [rráŋ·go] *m.* rank, position.

ranura [rra·nú·ra] *f.* groove; slot; — **de acceso** (*computadora*) head slot, — **de protección** protect tab.

rapar [rra·pár] *v.* to shave off; to crop (*hair*); to strip bare, rob of everything.

rapaz [rra·pás] *adj.* rapacious, grasping, greedy; *m.* lad; **rapaza** *f.* lass, young girl.

rape [rrá·pe] *m.* quick or close haircut.

rapé [rra·pé] *m.* snuff (*pulverized tobacco*).

rapidez [rra·pi·dés] *f.* rapidity, speed.

rápido [rrá·pi·do] *adj.* rapid, swift; *m.* rapids.

rapiña [rra·pí·ña] *f.* plunder; **ave de** — bird of prey.

rapiñar [rra·pi·ñár] *v.* to plunder; to steal.

raposa [rra·pó·sa] *f.* fox.

raptar [rrap·tár] *v.* to kidnap, abduct.
rapto [rráp·to] *m.* (*delito*) abduction, kidnapping; (*sentimiento*) ecstasy, rapture; outburst.
raqueta [rra·ké·ta] *f.* racket (*used in games*); tennis.
raquítico [rra·kí·ti·ko] *adj.* rickety, feeble, weak, skinny, sickly.
rareza [rra·ré·sa] *f.* rarity; oddity; strangeness; freak; curiosity; queer act or remark; peculiarity; **por —** seldom.
raro [rrá·ro] *adj.* rare; thin, not dense; scarce; strange, odd; ridiculous; **rara vez** (*or* **raras veces**) rarely, seldom.
ras [rras]: **a — de** flush with, even with; **al — con** flush with; **estar — con —** to be flush, perfectly even.
rascacielos [rras·ka·sjé·los] *m.* skyscraper.
rascar[6] [rras·kár] *v.* to scratch; to scrape; *Andes, Mex.* to dig up potatoes; *Am.* **— uno para adentro** to seek one's own advantage, look out for oneself.
rasete [rra·sé·te] *m.* sateen.
rasgado [rraz·gá·do] *adj.* torn; open; *Col.* generous; *Carib.* outspoken; **ojos -s** large, wideopen eyes.
rasgadura [rraz·ga·dú·ra] *f.* tear, rip, rent.
rasgar[7] [rraz·gár] *v.* to tear; to rip.
rasgo [ráz·go] *m.* (*propiedad*) trait, characteristic; (*rúbrica*) stroke of the pen, flourish; (*hazaña*) feat; *Am.* irrigation ditch; *Ven.* **un — de terreno** a parcel of land; **-s** features; traits.
rasgón [rraz·gón] *m.* large tear, rent, rip.
rasguñar [rraz·gu·ñár] *v.* to scratch; to claw.
rasguño [rraz·gú·ño] *m.* scratch.
raso [rrá·so] *adj.* (*llano*) plain; flat, smooth; (*despejado*) clear, cloudless; *Ríopl., Mex.* even, level (*when measuring wheat, corn, etc.*); *Am.* scarce, scanty; **soldado —** private; **al —** in the open air; *m.* satin.
raspadura [rras·pa·dú·ra] *f.* scrape; scraping; erasure; shaving (*of wood or metal*).
raspar [rras·pár] *v.* to scrape, scrape off; to steal; *Andes* to scold, upbraid; *Col.* to leave.
rastra [rrás·tra] *f.* drag; sled; large rake; harrow; **a -s** dragging; unwillingly.
rastreador [rras·tre·a·dór] *m.* trailer, tracker, tracer.
rastrear [rras·tre·ár] *v.* to trail, track, trace; to rake, harrow; to drag (*a dragnet*); to skim, scrape the ground.
rastrero [rras·tré·ro] *adj.* low, vile.
rastrillar [rras·tri·yár] *v.* to rake; to comb (*flax or hemp*); *Ven.* to scrape; *Col.* to shoot; *Am.* to barter, exchange; *Ch.* to pilfer, steal (*in stores*).
rastrillo [rras·trí·yo] *m.* rake; *Col.* barter, exchange; *Am.* business deal.
rastro [rrás·tro] *m.* track, trail, scent; trace, sign; rake, harrow; slaughterhouse.
rastrojo [rras·tró·xo] *m.* stubble.
rasura [rra·sú·ra] *f.* shave, shaving.
rasurar [rra·su·rár] *v.* to shave.
rata [rrá·ta] *f.* rat; *m.* pickpocket.
ratear [rra·te·ár] *v.* to pilfer; to pick pockets; to creep, crawl.
ratería [rra·te·rí·a] *f.* petty larceny; meanness.
ratero [rra·té·ro] *m.* pickpocket; *adj.* comtemptible, mean.
ratificar[6] [rra·ti·fi·kár] *v.* to ratify.
rato [rrá·to] *m.* short time, little while; **buen —** pleasant time; long time; **-s perdidos** leisure hours; **a -s** at intervals, from time to time; **pasar el —** to while away the time, kill time; *Am.* ¡**hasta cada —** ! so long!; see you later!
ratón [rra·tón] *m.* mouse; *Am.* **tener un —** to have a

hangover; **ratonera** [rra·to·né·ra] *f.* mousetrap.
raudal [rraw·dál] *m.* torrent, downpour, flood; *Ríopl., Ch., Col., Ven., Andes* rapids.
raudo [rraw·do] *adj.* rapid, swift.
raya [rrá·ya] *f.* line; dash; stripe; boundary line; part in the hair; *Mex.* pay, wage; *Mex.* **día de —** payday; **tener a —** to keep within bounds; to hold in check; **pasar de la —** to overstep one's bounds, take undue liberties; *m.* sting ray (*a species of fish*).
rayador [rra·ya·dór] *m. Mex.* paymaster; *Ch.* umpire in a game.
rayar [rra·yár] *v.* to line, make lines on; to streak; to scratch, mark; to cross out; score; *Mex.* to pay or collect wages; *Am.* to stop a horse all of a sudden; *S.A.* to spur a horse to run at top speed; **— el alba** to dawn; **— en** to border on; *Am.* **-se uno** to help oneself; to get rich.
rayo [rrá·yo] *m.* ray, beam; lightning, thunderbolt; spoke; **-s X** X-rays; **-s infrarrojos** infrared rays.
rayón [rra·yón] *m.* rayon.
raza [rrá·sa] *f.* race; clan; breed; fissure, crevice; **caballo de —** thoroughbred horse.
razón [rra·són] *f.* (*facultad*) reason; (*justicia*) right, justice; (*cuenta*) ratio; account, information, word, message; **— social** firm, firm name; **a — de** at the rate of; ¡**con —** ! no wonder!; **dar —** to inform; **dar la — a una persona** to admit that a person is right; **perder la —** to lose one's mind; **poner en —** to pacify; **tener —** to be right.
razonable [rra·so·ná·ble] *adj.* reasonable.
razonamiento [rra·so·na·mjén·to] *m.* reasoning.
razonar [rra·so·nár] *v.* to reason; to discourse, talk; to argue.
re [rre] *m.* second note of the musical scale (*solfeggio*).
reabierto [rre·a·bjér·to] *p.p. of* **reabrir**.
reabrir[52] [rre·a·brír] *v.* to reopen.
reacción [rre·ak·sjón] *f.* reaction; **— nuclear** nuclear reaction; **— en cadena** chain reaction.
reaccionar [rre·ak·sjo·nár] *v.* to react.
reaccionario [rre·ak·sjo·ná·rjo] *adj.* & *m.* reactionary.
reacio [rre·á·sjo] *adj.* stubborn, obstinate.
reactor [rre·ak·tór] *m.* reactor; **— atómico** atomic reactor; **— nuclear** nuclear reactor.
reajustar [rre·a·xus·tár] *v.* to readjust.
reajuste [rre·a·xús·te] *m.* readjustment.
real [rre·ál] *adj.* real; royal; *m.* army camp; fairground; real (*Spanish coin worth one fourth of a peseta*); **-es** *Andes* money (*in general*); **levantar el —** (*or* **los -es**) to break camp.
realce [rre·ál·se] *m.* (*adorno*) embossment, raised work, relief; (*lustre*) prestige; lustre, splendor; **dar —** to enhance; to emphasize.
realeza [rre·a·lé·sa] *f.* royalty (*royal dignity*).
realidad [rre·a·li·dád] *f.* reality; truth; fact; **en —** really, truly, in fact.
realismo [rre·a·líz·mo] *m.* realism; royalism.
realista [rre·a·lís·ta] *adj.* realistic; royalist; *m.* realist; royalist.
realización [rre·a·li·sa·sjón] *f.* realization, fulfillment; conversion into money, sale.
realizar[9] [rre·a·li·sár] *v.* to realize, fulfill, make real; to convert into money; to sell out.
realzar[9] [rre·al·sár] *v.* to emboss; to raise; to enhance; to make stand out; to emphasize.
reanimar [rre·a·ni·már] *v.* to revive; to comfort; to cheer; to encourage.
reanudación [rre·a·nu·da·sjón] *f.* renewal.
reanudar [rre·a·nu·dár] *v.* to renew, resume, begin again.

reaparecer[13] [rre·a·pa·re·sér] *v. irr.* to reappear.
reasumir [rre·a·su·mír] *v.* to resume.
reata [rre·á·ta] *f.* lariat, rope, lasso.
reavivar [rre·a·bi·bár] *v.* to revive.
rebaba [rre·bá·ba] *f.* fin, flange.
rebaja [rre·bá·xa] *f.* deduction; reduction; discount.
rebajar [rre·ba·xár] *v.* to diminish; to lower, reduce; to tone down (*a painting*); to humiliate; — **una superficie** to grind; **-se** to lower or humble oneself.
rebajo [rre·bá·xo] *m.* rabbet; groove, offset.
rebanada [rre·ba·ná·da] *f.* slice.
rebanar [rre·ba·nár] *v.* to slice.
rebaño [rre·bá·ño] *m.* flock; herd.
rebatir [rre·ba·tír] *v.* to beat over and over; to repel, resist; to refute; to rebut (*come back with an argument*); to argue; to parry (*in fencing*).
rebato [rre·bá·to] *m.* alarm, call to arms; surprise attack.
rebelarse [rre·be·lár·se] *v.* to rebel.
rebelde [rre·bél·de] *adj.* rebellious; *m.* rebel; defaulter (*one who fails to appear in court*).
rebeldía [rre·bel·dí·a] *f.* rebelliousness; defiance; default, failure to appear in court; **en** — in revolt.
rebelión [rre·be·ljón] *f.* rebellion, revolt.
rebencazo [rre·beŋ·ká·so] *m. Ríopl., Ch., Andes* crack of a whip; *Am.* lash, stroke with a whip.
rebenque [rre·béŋ·ke] *m.* rawhide whip.
reborde [rre·bór·de] *m.* edge, border.
rebosante [rre·bo·sán·te] *adj.* brimming, overflowing.
rebosar [rre·bo·sár] *v.* to overflow, brim over; to abound.
rebotar [rre·bo·tár] *v.* to rebound, bounce back or again; to make rebound; to repel, reject; to annoy, vex; **-se** to become vexed, upset; *Col., Mex.* to become cloudy or muddy (*said of water*); *Am.* **rebotársele a uno la bilis** to get angry, become upset.
rebote [rre·bó·te] *m.* rebound, bounce; **de** — on the rebound; indirectly.
rebozar[9] [rre·bo·sár] *v.* to muffle up; **-se** to muffle oneself up; to wrap oneself up.
rebozo [rre·bó·so] *m.* shawl; **sin** — frankly, openly.
rebullir[20] [rre·bu·yír] *v. irr.* to stir, move; to boil up.
rebusca [rre·bús·ka] *f.* research; search; searching; gleaning; residue.
rebuscar[6] [rre·bus·kár] *v.* to search thoroughly; to pry into; to glean.
rebuznar [rre·buz·nár] *v.* to bray.
rebuzno [rre·búz·no] *m.* bray.
recabar [rre·ka·bár] *v.* to obtain, gain by entreaty.
recado [rre·ká·do] *m.* message; errand; gift; daily food supply, daily marketing; precaution; equipment; *Ríopl., Andes* saddle and trappings; — **de escribir** writing materials; **-s a** regards to.
recaer[24] [rre·ka·ér] *v. irr.* to fall (upon); to fall again; to relapse; to have a relapse.
recaída [rre·ka·í·da] *f.* relapse; falling again.
recalar [rre·ka·lár] *v.* to saturate, soak through; to reach port; to come within sight of land; to land, end up, stop at; *Am.* — **con alguien** to "land" on somebody, take it out on somebody.
recalcar[6] [rre·kal·kár] *v.* to emphasize; to harp on; to press down.
recalcitrante [rre·kal·si·trán·te] *adj.* obstinate, disobedient, stubborn.
recalentar[1] [rre·ka·len·tár] *v. irr.* to reheat, warm over; to overheat, heat too much.
recamar [rre·ka·már] *v.* to embroider (*usually with gold or silver*).
recámara [rre·ká·ma·ra] *f.* dressing room; *Mex., C.A., Col.* bedroom; *Ríopl., Col.* chamber for an

explosive charge.
recapitular [rre·ka·pi·tu·lár] *v.* to recapitulate, sum up, tell briefly.
recargar[7] [rre·kar·gár] *v.* to overload; to emphasize.
recargo [rre·kár·go] *m.* overload; extra load; extra charge; increase (*of fever*); new charge, new accusation.
recatado [rre·ka·tá·do] *adj.* cautious, prudent; modest; *p.p.* concealed.
recatar [rre·ka·tár] *v.* to cover, conceal; **-se** to show timidity; to be cautious; to hide (from), shun.
recato [rre·ká·to] *m.* caution, prudence; reserve, restraint, secrecy; modesty.
recaudación [rre·kaw·da·sjón] *f.* collection, collecting; office of tax collector.
recaudador [rre·kaw·da·dór] *m.* tax collector.
recaudar [rre·kaw·dár] *v.* to collect (*money, taxes, rents, etc.*).
recaudo [rre·kaw·do] *m.* collection, collecting; precaution; bond, security; *Mex.* spices, seasonings; *Ch., Guate.* daily supply of vegetables; **estar a buen** — to be safe; **poner a buen** — to place in safety.
recelar [rre·se·lár] *v.* to suspect, fear; **-se de** to be suspicious or afraid of.
recelo [rre·sé·lo] *m.* suspicion, fear.
receloso [rre·se·ló·so] *adj.* suspicious, distrustful, fearful.
recepción [rre·sep·sjón] *f.* reception; admission.
receptáculo [rre·sep·tá·ku·lo] *m.* receptacle.
receptivo [rre·sep·tí·bo] *adj.* receptive, capable of receiving, quick to receive.
receptor [rre·sep·tór] *m.* receiver; *adj.* receiving.
receta [rre·sé·ta] *f.* recipe; prescription.
recetar [rre·se·tár] *v.* to prescribe (*a medicine*).
recibidor [rre·si·bi·dór] *m.* receiver; reception room.
recibimiento [rre·si·bi·mjén·to] *m.* reception; welcome; reception room; parlor.
recibir [rre·si·bír] *v.* to receive; to admit, accept; to go out to meet; — **noticias de** to hear from; **-se de** to receive a title or degree of.
recibo [rre·sí·bo] *m.* (*monetario*) receipt; (*acción*) reception; (*sala*) reception room; parlor; **sala de** — reception room; **estar de** — to be at home for receiving callers; **ser de** — to be acceptable, be fit for use.
reciedumbre [rre·sje·dúm·bre] *f.* strength, force, vigor.
recién [rre·sjén] *adv.* recently, lately, newly (*used before a past participle*); *Ríopl., Ch., Andes* just now; *Ríopl., Ch., Andes* a short time ago; *Ríopl., Ch., Andes* — **entonces** just then.
reciente [rre·sjén·te] *adj.* recent, new.
recinto [rre·sín·to] *m.* enclosure; precinct; campus.
recio [rré·sjo] *adj.* strong, robust; harsh; hard, severe; fast; *adv.* strongly; harshly; rapidly; hard; loud.
recipiente [rre·si·pjén·te] *m.* receptacle, container; recipient, receiver (*he who receives*).
recíproco [rre·sí·pro·ko] *adj.* reciprocal, mutual.
recitación [rre·si·ta·sjón] *f.* recitation, recital.
recital [rre·si·tál] *m.* musical recital.
recitar [rre·si·tár] *v.* to recite.
reclamación [rre·kla·ma·sjón] *f.* protest, complaint; claim, demand.
reclamador [rre·kla·ma·dór] *m.* claimant; complainer.
reclamante [rre·kla·mán·te] *m. & f.* claimant; complainer; *adj.* complaining; claiming.
reclamar [rre·kla·már] *v.* (*protestar*) to complain, protest (*against*); (*exigir*) to claim, demand; to lure, call back (*a bird*).
reclamo [rre·klá·mo] *m.* (*protesta*) protest; claim;

advertisement; (*llamada*) call; bird call; decoy bird; lure.

reclinar [rre·kli·nár] *v.* to recline, lean; **-se** to recline, lean back.

recluir[32] [rre·klwír] *v. irr.* to seclude, shut up; **-se** to isolate oneself.

recluso [rre·klú·so] *m.* recluse, hermit; *adj.* shut in, shut up.

recluta [rre·klú·ta] *f.* recruiting; *Am.* roundup of cattle; *m.* recruit.

reclutamiento [rre·klu·ta·mjén·to] *m.* recruiting; levy, draft.

reclutar [rre·klu·tár] *v.* to recruit, enlist; *Am.* to round up (*cattle*).

recobrar [rre·ko·brár] *v.* to recover, regain; **-se** to recover; to recuperate.

recobro [rre·kó·bro] *m.* recovery.

recocido [rre·ko·sí·do] *m.* annealing.

recodo [rre·kó·do] *m.* bend, turn; elbow (*of a road*).

recoger[11] [rre·ko·xér] *v.* (*juntar*) to gather; to collect; to pick up; (*ceñir*) to take in, tighten; (*abrigar*) to shelter; **-se** to retire, go home; to withdraw; to seclude oneself; to take shelter.

recogida [rre·ko·xí·da] *f.* harvest.

recogimiento [rre·ko·xi·mjén·to] *m.* seclusion; concentration of thought, composure; retreat; collecting, gathering.

recolección [rre·ko·lek·sjón] *f.* collecting, gathering; harvest, crop; summary.

recolectar [rre·ko·lek·tár] *v.* to harvest; to gather.

recomendable [rre·ko·men·dá·ble] *adj.* praiseworthy, laudable; advisable.

recomendación [rre·ko·men·da·sjón] *f.* recommendation; request.

recomendar[1] [rre·ko·men·dár] *v. irr.* to recommend; to commend, praise; to enjoin, urge; to advise.

recompensa [rre·kom·pén·sa] *f.* recompense; compensation.

recompensar [rre·kom·pen·sár] *v.* to recompense, reward; to compensate.

reconcentrar [rre·kon·sen·trár] *v.* to concentrate, bring together; to hide in the depth of one's heart; **-se** to concentrate, become absorbed in thought, collect one's thoughts.

reconciliación [rre·kon·si·lja·sjón] *f.* reconciliation.

reconciliar [rre·kon·si·ljár] *v.* to reconcile; **-se** to become reconciled.

recóndito [rre·kón·di·to] *adj.* hidden, concealed; profound.

reconocer[13] [rre·ko·no·sér] *v. irr.* to recognize; to admit, acknowledge; to examine carefully; to reconnoiter, scout, explore.

reconocimiento [rre·ko·no·si·mjén·to] *m.* recognition; acknowledgment; gratitude; examination; scouting, exploring.

reconstruir[32] [rre·kons·trwír] *v. irr.* to reconstruct, rebuild.

recontar[2] [rre·kon·tár] *v. irr.* to recount; to tell, relate.

recopilar [rre·ko·pi·lár] *v.* to compile; to digest, make a digest of.

record [rré·kor] *m.* record.

recordación [rre·kor·da·sjón] *f.* recollection; remembrance.

recordar[2] [rre·kor·dár] *v. irr.* to remember; to recall; to remind; *Ríopl., C.A., Ven.* to rouse, awaken; **-se** to remember; to wake up.

recordativo [rre·kor·da·tí·bo] *m.* reminder; *adj.* reminding.

recordatorio [rre·kor·da·tó·rjo] *m.* reminder.

recorrer [rre·ko·rrér] *v.* to go over; to travel over; to

read over; to look over; to overhaul.

recorrido [rre·ko·rrí·do] *m.* trip, run; mileage, distance traveled.

recortar [rre·kor·tár] *v.* to trim, clip; to shorten; to cut out (*figures*); to pare off; **-se** to project itself (*as a shadow*); to outline itself.

recorte [rre·kór·te] *m.* clipping; cutting; outline; *Mex.* gossip, slander.

recostar [rre·kos·tár] *v.* to recline, lean; **-se** to recline, lean back.

recoveco [rre·ko·bé·ko] *m.* turn, bend; nook; sly or underhanded manner.

recreación [rre·kre·a·sjón] *f.* recreation.

recrear [rre·kre·ár] *v.* to entertain, amuse; to gratify, please; **-se** to amuse oneself; to take delight (in).

recreo [rre·kré·o] *m.* recreation, entertainment; place of amusement.

recrudecer[13] [rre·kru·de·sér] *v.* to recur, break out again, flare up, become worse (*said of an illness or evil*).

rectángulo [rrek·tán·gu·lo] *m.* rectangle; *adj.* rectangular, right-angled.

rectificar[6] [rrek·ti·fi·kár] *v.* to rectify, correct, amend; to refine (*liquors*); **rectificado cilíndrico** cylindrical grinding.

rectitud [rrek·ti·túd] *f.* rectitude, uprightness, righteousness; straightness; accuracy.

recto [rrék·to] *adj.* straight; right; just, honest; **ángulo —** right angle; *m.* rectum; *adv. C.A.* straight ahead.

rector [rrek·tór] *m.* college or university president; principal; rector, curate, priest.

recua [rré·kwa] *f.* drove of pack animals; drove, crowd.

recuento [rre·kwén·to] *m.* recount.

recuerdo [rre·kwér·do] *m.* remembrance; recollection; souvenir, keepsake; memory; **-s** regards; *adj. Ríopl., Col., Ven.* awake.

reculada [rre·ku·lá·da] *f.* recoil.

recular [rre·ku·lár] *v.* to recoil, spring back; to fall back, go back, retreat; to yield, back down.

recuperación [rre·ku·pe·ra·sjón] *f.* recovery.

recuperar [rre·ku·pe·rár] *v.* to recuperate, recover, regain; **-se** to recuperate, recover one's health.

recurrir [rre·ku ·rír] *v.* to resort (to); to have recourse (to).

recurso [rre·kúr·so] *m.* recourse, resort; petition, appeal; **-s** means, resources; **sin —** without remedy; without appeal.

recusar [rre·ku·sár] *v.* to reject; decline.

rechazar[9] [rre·ča·sár] *v.* to reject; to repel, drive back; to rebuff.

rechifla [rre·čí·fla] *f.* hooting; hissing; ridicule.

rechiflar [rre·či·flár] *v.* to hoot; to hiss; to ridicule.

rechinamiento [rre·či·na·mjén·to] *m.* creak; squeak; squeaking; gnashing.

rechinar [rre·či·nár] *v.* to squeak; to creak; *Mex.* to be furious, angry; *Ven.* to grumble, growl; **— los dientes** to gnash one's teeth.

rechino [rre·čí·no] = **rechinamiento.**

rechoncho [rre·čon·čo] *adj.* plump; chubby; squat.

rechuparse [rre·ču·pár·se] *v.* to smack one's lips.

red [rred] *f.* net; netting; network; snare; **redecilla** [rre·de·sí·ya] *f.* small net; mesh; hair net.

redacción [rre·dak·sjón] *f.* (*acto*) wording; editing; (*lugar*) newspaper offices; editorial department; (*cuerpo*) editorial staff.

redactar [rre·dak·tár] *v.* to word, compose; to edit.

redactor [rre·dak·tór] *m.* editor.

redada [rre·dá·da] *f.* catch; haul (*of criminals*).

redargüir[32] [rre·dar·gwír] *v. irr.* to retort, answer

RE

back; to contradict, call in question; to reargue.

rededor [rre·de·dór] *m.* surroundings; **al** (*or* **en**) — around, about.

redención [rre·den·sjón] *f.* redemption.

redentor [rre·den·tór] *m.* redeemer, savior; **el Redentor** the Savior.

redil [rre·díl] *m.* sheepfold.

redimir [rre·di·mír] *v.* to redeem; to ransom; to set free.

rédito [rré·di·to] *m.* interest, revenue, yield.

redituar[18] [rre·di·twár] *v.* to produce, yield (*interest*).

redoblar [rre·do·blár] *v.* to double; to clinch (*a nail*); to reiterate, repeat; to roll (*a drum*).

redoble [rre·dó·ble] *m.* roll (*of a drum*).

redoma [rre·dó·ma] *f.* flask, vial.

redomón [rre·do·món] *m. Ríopl.* half-tame horse or bull; *adj. Ríopl.* half-civilized, rustic.

redonda [rre·dón·da] *f.* surrounding district, neighborhood; whole note (*music*); **a la** — all around, round-about.

redondear [rre·don·de·ár] *v.* to round, make round; to round off; to round out.

redondel [rre·don·dél] *m.* arena, bull ring; circle.

redondez [rre·don·dés] *f.* roundness.

redondo [rre·dón·do] *adj.* round; whole, entire; clear, evident; *Andes* stupid; *Mex.* honest; **en** — all around.

redopelo [rre·do·pé·lo]: **a** — against the grain.

redor [rre·dór] *m.* round mat; **en** — around.

reducción [rre·duk·sjón] *f.* reduction; cut, discount; decrease.

reducido [rre·du·sí·do] *p.p. & adj.* reduced; compact, small.

reducir[25] [rre·du·sír] *v. irr.* to reduce; to diminish; to convert (into); to reset (*a bone*); **-se** to adapt oneself, adjust oneself; to be constrained, forced.

redundante [rre·dun·dán·te] *adj.* redundant.

reedificar[6] [rre·e·di·fi·kár] *v.* to rebuild, reconstruct.

reelección [rre·e·lek·sjón] *f.* re-election.

reelegir[11] [rre·e·le·xír] *v.* to re-elect.

reembolsar [rre·em·bol·sár] *v.* to reimburse, refund, repay, pay back.

reembolso [rre·em·ból·so] *m.* reimbursement, refund.

reemitir [rre·mi·tír] *v.* to emit again; to issue again; to rebroadcast; to relay (*a broadcast*).

reemplazable [rre·em·pla·sá·ble] *adj.* replaceable.

reemplazar[9] [rre·em·pla·sár] *v.* to replace; to substitute.

reemplazo [rre·em·plá·so] *m.* replacement; substitute, substitution.

reexpedir[5] [rre·es·pe·dír] *v. irr.* to forward (*mail*).

refacción [rre·fak·sjón] *f.* (*alimento*) light lunch, refreshment; (*compostura*) repair, reparation; *Mex., Col.* spare part; *Carib.* help, aid, loan.

refajo [rre·fá·xo] *m.* underskirt; short skirt.

referencia [rre·fe·rén·sja] *f.* reference; narration, account.

referente [rre·fe·rén·te] *adj.* referring.

referir[3] [rre·fe·rír] *v. irr.* to refer; to narrate; to relate; **-se** to refer (to), relate (to).

refinamiento [rre·fi·na·mjén·to] *m.* refinement.

refinar [rre·fi·nár] *v.* to refine; to purify.

refinería [rre·fi·ne·rí·a] *f.* refinery.

reflector [rre·flek·tór] *m.* reflector; floodlight.

reflejar [rre·fle·xár] *v.* to reflect; to think over; **-se** to be reflected.

reflejo [rre·flé·xo] *m.* reflection, image; reflex; *adj.* reflected; reflex.

reflexión [rre·flek·sjón] *f.* reflection; meditation, consideration.

reflexionar [rre·flek·sjo·nár] *v.* to reflect, meditate,

think over.

reflexivo [rre·flek·sí·bo] *adj.* reflexive; reflective, thoughtful.

reflujo [rre·flú·xo] *m.* ebb; ebb tide.

refocilar [rre·fo·si·lár] *v.* to cheer.

reforma [rre·fór·ma] *f.* reform; reformation; improvement.

reformador [rre·for·ma·dór] *m.* reformer.

reformar [rre·for·már] *v.* to reform; to correct, amend; to improve; **-se** to reform.

reformista [rre·for·mís·ta] *m. & f.* reformer.

reforzar[2,9] [rre·for·sár] *v. irr.* to reinforce; to strengthen.

refracción [rre·frak·sjón] *f.* refraction.

refractario [rre·frak·tó·rjo] *adj.* refractory; impervious; rebellious, unruly; stubborn.

refrán [rre·frán] *m.* popular proverb or saying.

refrenar [rre·fre·nár] *v.* to restrain, keep in check; to curb; to rein.

refrendar [rre·fren·dár] *v.* to legalize by signing; to countersign (*confirm by another signature*); — **un pasaporte** to visé a passport.

refrescante [rre·fres·kán·te] *adj.* refreshing.

refrescar[6] [rre·fres·kár] *v.* to refresh, renew; to cool; to get cool (*said of the weather*); **-se** to cool off; to take the fresh air; to take a cooling drink or refreshment; *Cuba, C.A.* to take an afternoon refreshment.

refresco [rre·frés·ko] *m.* refreshment.

refresquería [rre·fres·ke·rí·a] *f. Mex., C.A., Ven.* refreshment shop, outdoor refreshment stand.

refriega [rre·frjé·ga] *f.* strife, fray, scuffle.

refrigeración [rre·fri·xe·ra·sjón] *f.* refrigeration; light meal or refreshment.

refrigerador [rre·fri·xe·ra·dór] *m. Am.* refrigerator, freezer; *adj.* refrigerating, freezing; refreshing.

refrigerar [rre·fri·xe·rár] *v.* to cool.

refrigerio [rre·fri·xé·rjo] *m.* refreshment; relief; comfort; coolness.

refrito [rre·frí·to] *adj.* refried; **frijoles refritos** (*Mexican fried beans*).

refuerzo [rre·fwér·so] *m.* reinforcement.

refugiado [rre·fu·xjá·do] *m.* refugee; *p.p. of* **refugiar.**

refugiar [rre·fu·xjár] *v.* to shelter; **-se** to take shelter or refuge.

refugio [rre·fú·xjo] *m.* refuge, shelter.

refulgente [rre·ful·xén·te] *adj.* refulgent, radiant, shining.

refundir [rre·fun·dír] *v.* to remelt, refound, recast (*metals*); to recast, rewrite, reconstruct.

refunfuñar [rre·fun·fu·ñár] *v.* to grumble, mumble, growl, mutter.

refunfuño [rre·fun·fú·ño] *m.* grumble, growl; **refunfuñón** [rre·fun·fu·ñón] *adj.* grouchy; grumbly, grumbling.

refutar [rre·fu·tár] *v.* to refute.

regadera [rre·ga·dé·ra] *f.* sprinkler; *Mex.* shower bath.

regadío [rre·ga·dí·o] *adj.* irrigable, that can be irrigated; irrigated; *m.* irrigated land; **tierras de** — irrigable lands.

regalar [rre·ga·lár] *v.* (*dar*) to give, present as a gift; to regale; (*recrear*) to entertain; to delight, please; **-se** to treat oneself well, live a life of ease.

regalo [rre·gá·lo] *m.* present, gift; pleasure, delight; dainty, delicacy; luxury, comfort.

regañadientes [rre·ga·ña·djén·tes]: **a** — much against one's wishes; unwillingly.

regañar [rre·ga·ñár] *v.* to growl; to grumble; to quarrel; to scold.

regaño [rre·gá·ño] *m.* scolding, reprimand.

regañón [rre·ga·ñón] *adj.* grumbling; scolding; quarrelsome; *m.* growler, grumbler, scolder.

regar[1, 7] [rre·gár] *v. irr.* to irrigate; to water; to sprinkle, scatter; *Col.* to spill, throw off (*said of a horse*); **-se** *Am.* to scatter, disperse (*said of a group, herd, etc.*).

regatear [rre·ga·te·ár] *v.* to haggle, bargain; to dispute; to sell at retail; to race (*in a regatta or boat race*).

regateo [rre·ga·té·o] *m.* bargaining.

regazo [rre·gá·so] *m.* lap.

regencia [rre·xén·sja] *f.* regency.

regentar [rre·xen·tár] *v.* to direct, conduct, manage; **— una cátedra** to teach a course (*at a university*).

regente [rre·xén·te] *m.* regent; manager; *adj.* ruling.

regidor [rre·xi·dór] *m.* councilman, alderman; *adj.* governing, ruling.

régimen [rré·xi·men] *m.* regime; government, rule, management; **— lácteo** milk diet.

regimiento [rre·xi·mjén·to] *m.* regiment; (*administrativo*) administration; municipal council; position of alderman.

regio [rré·xjo] *adj.* regal, royal; splendid, magnificient.

región [rre·xjón] *f.* region.

regir[5, 11] [rre·xír] *v. irr.* to rule, govern; to direct, manage; to be in force (*said of a law*); to move (*said of the bowels*).

registrador [rre·xis·tra·dór] *m.* registrar, recorder; city clerk, official in charge of records; inspector (*in a customhouse*); searcher; *adj.* registering; **caja registradora** cash register.

registrar [rre·xis·trár] *v.* to examine, inspect, scrutinize; to register, record; **-se** to register, enroll.

registro [rre·xís·tro] *m.* search, inspection; registration; census; registration office; register; record; registration certificate; watch regulator; bookmark; organ stop; (*computadora*) record; *Ven.* wholesale textile store.

regla [rré·gla] *f.* (*precepto*) rule; ruler; order; precept, principle; (*medida*) measure, moderation; menstruation; **en —** in order, in due form; **por — general** as a general rule; usually.

reglamento [rre·gla·mén·to] *m.* regulations, rules; rule, bylaw.

regocijado [rre·go·si·xá·do] *adj.* joyful, merry, gay; *p.p.* of **regocijar.**

regocijar [rre·go·si·xár] *v.* to gladden, delight; **-se** to be glad; to rejoice.

regocijo [rre·go·sí·xo] *m.* joy; rejoicing.

regordete [rre·gor·dé·te] *adj.* plump.

regresar [rre·gre·sár] *v.* to return.

regreso [rre·gré·so] *m.* return; **estar de —** to be back.

reguero [rre·gé·ro] *m.* stream, rivulet; trickle; irrigation ditch.

regulación [rre·gu·la·sjón] *f.* regulation; adjustment.

regulador [rre·gu·la·dór] *m.* regulator; controller, governor (*of a machine*); **— de tiro** damper; *adj.* regulating.

regular [rre·gu·lár] *v.* to regulate; to adjust; *adj.* regular; ordinary; moderate; fair, medium; **por lo —** as a rule, usually; *adv.* fairly well.

regularidad [rre·gu·la·ri·dád] *f.* regularity.

regularizar[9] [rre·gu·la·ri·sár] *v.* to regulate, make regular.

rehacer[31] [rre·a·sér] *v. irr.* to remake; to make over; to repair; **-se** to recover one's strength; to rally.

rehen [rre·én] *m.* hostage; **en rehenes** as a hostage.

rehuir[32] [rre·wír] *v. irr.* to shun, avoid; to shrink (from).

rehusar [rre·u·sár] *v.* to refuse; **-se a** to refuse to.

reina [réj·na] *f.* queen.

reinado [rrej·ná·do] *m.* reign.

reinante [rrej·nán·te] *adj.* reigning; prevailing.

reinar [rrej·nár] *v.* to reign; to rule; to prevail.

reincidir [rrej·si·dír] *v.* to relapse, slide back (into).

reino [rréj·no] *m.* kingdom.

reintegro [rrejn·té·gro] *m.* reimbursement, refund.

reir[15] [rre·ír] *v. irr.* to laugh; **-se de** to laugh at; *Ríopl., Andes, Col., Ven., Carib.* **— de dientes para afuera** to laugh outwardly, laugh hypocritically.

reiterar [rrej·te·rár] *v.* to reiterate, repeat.

reivindicación [rrej·bin·di·ka·sjón] *f.* recovery.

reja [rré·xa] *f.* grate, grating; plowshare (*blade of the plow*); plowing; *Carib., C.A.* jail.

rejilla [rre·xí·ya] *f.* small grating, lattice; small latticed window; fireplace grate; cane upholstery; *Ch.* wire dish-cover.

rejo [rré·xo] *m.* point; plow share.

rejonear [rre·xo·ne·ár] *v.* to fight a bull from horseback (*Portuguese style*).

rejuvenecer[13] [rre·xu·be·ne·sér] *v. irr.* to rejuvenate, make young; **-se** to become rejuvenated.

relación [rre·la·sjón] *f.* relation; story, account; long speech in a play; *Ríopl.* verse recited alternately by a couple in a folk dance; **-es** personal relations, connections; acquaintances.

relacionar [rre·la·sjo·nár] *v.* to relate, connect; **-se** to be related, connected; to become acquainted, establish friendly connections.

relajación [rre·la·xa·sjón] *f.*, **relajamiento** [rre·la·xa·mjén·to] *m.* relaxation; laxity; slackening; hernia.

relajar [rre·la·xár] *v.* to relax; to slacken; to release from a vow or oath; **-se** to get a hernia or rupture; to become weakened; to become lax (*said of laws, customs, etc.*).

relajo [rre·lá·xo] *m. Carib., Mex.* disorderly conduct; lewdness; scandal.

relamerse [rre·la·mér·se] *v.* to lick one's lips; to gloat; to boast; to slick oneself up.

relámpago [rre·lám·pa·go] *m.* lightning; flash.

relampaguear [rre·lam·pa·ge·ár] *v.* to lighten; to flash; to sparkle, blink.

relampagueo [rre·lam·pa·gé·o] *m.* flashing; sheet lightning.

relatar [rre·la·tár] *v.* to relate, narrate.

relativo [rre·la·tí·bo] *adj.* relative; **— a** relative to, regarding.

relato [rre·lá·to] *m.* narration, account, story.

relé [rre·lé] *m.* relay; **— de televisión** television relay system.

relegar[7] [rre·le·gár] *v.* to relegate, banish; to postpone; to set aside, put away.

relente [rre·lén·te] *m.* night dampness; *Am.* fresh night breeze.

relevar [rre·le·bár] *v.* to relieve; to release; to absolve; to replace, substitute; to emboss; to make stand out in relief.

relevo [rre·lé·bo] *m.* relief (*from a post or military duty; person who relieves another from the performance of a duty*).

relicario [rre·li·ká·rjo] *m.* reliquary (*small box or casket for keeping relics*); *Col., Ven., Cuba, Mex., Andes* locket.

relieve [rre·ljé·be] *m.* relief, embossment, raised work; **-s** scraps, leftovers; **de —** in relief; prominent, outstanding; **poner de —** to make stand out; to emphasize.

RE

religión [rre·li·xjón] *f.* religion.
religiosidad [rre·li·xjo·si·dáđ] *f.* religiousness, piety; faithfulness.
religioso [rre·li·xjó·so] *adj.* religious; faithful; punctual; *m.* friar, monk.
relinchar [rre·lin·čár] *v.* to neigh.
relincho [rre·lín·čo] *m.* neigh.
reliquia [rre·lí·kja] *f.* relic; vestige; **-s** relics, remains.
reloj [rre·ló] *m.* clock; watch; — **de pulsera** wristwatch; — **de sol** (*or* — **solar**) sundial; — **despertador** alarm clock.
relojería [rre·lo·xe·rí·a] *f.* watch shop; jewelry store.
reluciente [rre·lu·sjén·te] *adj.* shining; sparkling.
relucir[13] [rre·lu·sír] *v. irr.* to glitter, sparkle; to shine.
relumbrante [rre·lum·brán·te] *adj.* brilliant, flashing, resplendent.
relumbrar [rre·lum·brár] *v.* to glare; to glitter.
relumbre [rre·lúm·bre] *m.* glare, glitter.
rellenar [rre·ye·nár] *v.* to refill; to fill up; to pad; to stuff.
relleno [rre·yé·no] *adj.* stuffed; *m.* meat stuffing; filling.
remachar [rre·ma·čár] *v.* to clinch; to hammer down; to flatten; to rivet; to fix firmly; **-se** *Am.* to be tight-lipped, stubbornly silent.
remache [rre·má·če] *m.* clinching; fastening; securing; riveting; rivet.
remanente [rre·ma·nén·te] *m.* remainder, balance; remnant; residue.
remar [rre·már] *v.* to row; to struggle.
rematado [rre·ma·tá·đo] *adj. & p.p.* (*acabado*) finished; (*vendido en subasta*) sold at auction; **loco** — completely crazy.
rematar [rre·ma·tár] *v.* (*acabar*) to finish; to end; to give the final or finishing stroke; (*vender*) to auction; (*afianzar*) to fasten (*a stitch*); *Ch.* to stop (*a horse*) suddenly; *Am.* to buy or sell at auction; **-se** to be finished, be completely destroyed or ruined.
remate [rre·má·te] *m.* (*fin*) finish, end; (*postura*) highest bid at an auction; sale at auction; (*punta*) pinnacle, spire; *Mex.* selvage, edge of a fabric; **de** — absolutely, without remedy; **loco de** — completely crazy, stark mad.
remedar [rre·me·đár] *v.* to imitate; to mimic.
remediar [rre·me·đjár] *v.* to remedy; to help; to avoid.
remedio [rre·mé·đjo] *m.* remedy; help; amendment; recourse, resort; **sin** — without help, unavoidable; **no tiene** — it can't be helped.
remedo [rre·mé·đo] *m.* imitation; mockery.
remembranza [rre·mem·brán·sa] *f.* remembrance, memory.
rememorar [rre·me·mo·rár] *v.* to remember, call to mind.
remendar[1] [rre·men·dár] *v. irr.* to mend, patch; to darn; to repair.
remendón [rre·men·dón] *m.* cobbler, shoe repairman; mender, patcher.
remero [rre·mé·ro] *m.* rower.
remesa [rre·mé·sa] *f.* shipment; remittance, payment.
remesar [rre·me·sár] *v.* to remit; to ship.
remiendo [rre·mjén·đo] *m.* mend; mending; patch; darn; repair; **a -s** piecemeal, piece by piece.
remilgado [rre·mil·gá·đo] *adj.* prudish, prim, affected.
remilgo [rre·míl·go] *m.* prudery, primness, affection.
reminiscencia [rre·mi·ni·sén·sja] *f.* reminiscence.
remisión [rre·mi·sjón] *f.* (*disculpa*) remission; forgiveness; (*remesa*) remittance, remitting; (*disminución*) abatement, slackening; *Mex., Ven.*

anything shipped or sent.
remitente [rre·mi·tén·te] *m. & f.* sender; shipper.
remitir [rre·mi·tír] *v.* (*enviar*) to remit; to send; (*diferir*) to defer; to pardon; to refer; to abate; **-se** to defer, yield (*to another's judgment*).
remo [rré·mo] *m.* oar; hard and long work; leg of a horse; **al** — at the oar; at hard labor.
remojar [rre·mo·xár] *v.* to soak; to steep; *Am.* to tip, bribe.
remojo [rre·mó·xo] *m.* soaking; steeping; *Am.* tip, bribe.
remolacha [rre·mo·lá·ča] *f.* beet.
remolcador [rre·mol·ka·đór] *m.* towboat, tug, tugboat; **lancha remolcadora** tugboat.
remolcar[6] [rre·mol·kár] *v.* to tow, tug; to take (*a person*) in tow.
remolino [rre·mo·lí·no] *m.* swirl, whirl; whirlwind; whirlpool; commotion; *Ríopl.* pin wheel; *Am.* ventilating wheel (*fan*); — **de gente** throng, crowd.
remolón [rre·mo·lón] *adj.* indolent, lazy.
remolque [rre·mól·ke] *m.* tow; towrope; **llevar a** — to tow; to take in tow.
remontar [rre·mon·tár] *v.* (*alzar*) to elevate, raise; (*reparar*) to repair, patch up; to resole; to revamp; *Am.* to go up; *Ríopl., Carib., C.A., Ven., Col.* to go upstream; **-se** to rise; to soar, fly upward; to date (from), go back (to); *Ríopl.* to take to the woods or hills.
rémora [rré·mo·ra] *f.* impediment, obstacle, hindrance.
remorder[4] [rre·mor·đér] *v. irr.* to sting.
remordimiento [rre·mor·đi·mjén·to] *m.* remorse.
remoto [rre·mó·to] *adj.* remote, distant; improbable.
remover[2] [rre·mo·ḃér] *v. irr.* to remove; to dismiss; to stir.
rempujar [rrem·pu·xár] *v.* to jostle, push.
rempujón [rrem·pu·xón] *m.* jostle, push.
remuda [rre·mú·đa] *f.* change; substitution; replacement; change of clothes; spare tire; relay of horses; *Am.* spare horse, spare pack animal.
remudar [rre·mu·đár] *v.* to change; to replace.
remuneración [rre·mu·ne·ra·sjón] *f.* remuneration, compensation, pay, reward.
remunerar [rre·mu·ne·rár] *v.* to remunerate, compensate, pay, reward (*for services*).
renacer[13] [rre·na·sér] *v. irr.* to be reborn; to spring up, grow up again.
renacimiento [rre·na·si·mjén·to] *m.* renascence, renaissance; revival; rebirth.
rencilla [rren·sí·ya] *f.* quarrel.
renco [rréŋ·ko] *adj.* lame.
rencor [rreŋ·kór] *m.* rancor, resentment, hatred, grudge.
rencoroso [rreŋ·ko·ró·so] *adj.* resentful, spiteful.
rendición [rren·di·sjón] *f.* (*comportamiento*) surrender; submission; yield, profit.
rendido [rren·dí·đo] *p.p. & adj.* tired out, fatigued; devoted; obsequious, servile.
rendija [rren·dí·xa] *f.* crack, crevice.
rendimiento [rren·di·mjén·to] *m.* yield, output, profit; surrender, submission; (*cansancio*) fatigue; performance.
rendir[5] [rren·dír] *v. irr.* to subdue; to surrender, hand over; to yield, produce; to fatigue; to render, do (*homage*); *Cuba, Ven.* — **la jornada** to end or suspend the day's work; **-se** to surrender, give up; to become fatigued, worn out.
renegado [rre·ne·gá·đo] *m.* renegade, traitor; *adj.* renegade, disloyal; wicked.
renegar[1, 7] [rre·ne·gárd] *v. irr.* to deny insistently; to

detest; to blaspheme, curse; — **de** to deny,
renounce (*one's faith*); *Am.* to hate, protest against.
renglón [rreŋ·glón] *m.* line (*written or printed*); item;
Ríopl., Col., Ven., Mex., Carib., Andes line of
business, specialty.
renio [rré·njo] *m.* rhenium.
reno [rré·no] *m.* reindeer.
renombrado [rre·nom·brá·ḏo] *adj.* renowned, famous.
renombre [rre·nóm·bre] *m.* renown, fame.
renovación [rre·no·ḇa·sjón] *f.* renovation, restoration;
renewal.
renovar[2] [rre·no·ḇár] *v. irr.* to renovate; to renew; to
replace.
renquear [rreŋ·ke·ár] *v.* to limp.
renta [rrén·ta] *f.* rent, rental; income; revenue.
renuencia [rre·nwén·sja] *f.* reluctance, unwillingness.
renuente [rre·nwén·te] *adj.* reluctant, unwilling.
renuevo [rre·nwé·ḇo] *m.* (*vástago*) sprout, shoot;
(*acto*) renovation, restoration.
renunciar [rre·nun·sjár] *v.* to renounce; to resign; to
refuse; to renege (*fail to follow suit in cards*).
reñidor [rre·ñi·ḏór] *adj.* quarrelsome.
reñir[5, 19] [rre·ñír] *v. irr.* to quarrel; to fight; to scold.
reo [rré·o] *adj.* guilty; *m.* culprit, criminal;
defendant.
reojo [rre·ó·xo] **mirar** — to look out of the corner
of one's eye; to look scornfully.
repantigarse[7] [rre·pan·ti·ǵár·se] *v.* to lounge, stretch
out (*in a chair*).
reparación [rre·pa·ra·sjón] *f.* reparation; repair;
indemnity.
reparar [rre·pa·rár] *v.* (*renovar*) to repair; to regain;
to recover; (*corregir*) to make amends for, atone
for; to remedy; to ward off (*a blow*); *Am.* to rear,
buck (*said of horses*); — **en** to observe, notice.
reparo [rre·pá·ro] *m.* (*arreglo*) repair; restoration;
(*observación*) notice; observation; (*duda*) doubt,
objection; (*abrigo*) shelter; parry (*fencing*); *Mex.*
sudden bound or leap of a horse.
repartimiento [rre·par·ti·mjén·to] *m.* distribution,
division; assessment.
repartir [rre·par·tír] *v.* to distribute; to allot.
reparto [rre·pár·to] *m.* distribution; mail delivery; cast
of characters.
repasar [rre·pa·sár] *v.* to review, look over, go over
again; to mend (*clothes*); to pass by again.
repaso [rre·pá·so] *m.* review; revision.
repelente [rre·pe·lén·te] *adj.* repellent, repulsive,
repugnant.
repeler [rre·pe·lér] *v.* to repel; to reject.
repelón [rre·pe·lón] *m.* pull; kink.
repente [rre·pén·te] *m.* sudden movement; *Am.*
attack, fit; **de** — suddenly.
repentino [rre·pen·tí·no] *adj.* sudden.
repercutir [rre·per·ku·tír] *v.* to resound, echo back; to
rebound; to reflect back (*as light*).
repetición [rre·pe·ti·sjón] *f.* repetition.
repetido [rre·pe·tí·ḏo] *p.p.* repeated; **repetidas veces**
repeatedly, often.
repetir[5] [rre·pe·tír] *v. irr.* to repeat; to belch.
repicar[6] [rre·pi·kár] *v.* (*tañer*) to chime, ring; (*hacer
menudo*) to mince, chop fine; *Carib., Ven.* to
drum, tap (*with the fingers or heels*); **-se** to boast;
to be conceited.
repique [rre·pí·ke] *m.* (*tañido*) chime, ringing, peal;
(*acción de picar*) mincing, chopping.
repiquetear [rre·pi·ke·te·ár] *v.* to chime, ring; to
jingle; *Am.* to tap (*with fingers or heels*).
repiqueteo [rre·pi·ke·té·o] *m.* chiming, ringing;
jingling, tinkling; *Ríopl., Carib., Ven.* clicking
sound of heels.

repisa [rre·pí·sa] *f.* shelf, ledge; sill; wall bracket; —
de ventana window sill.
replegar[1, 7] [rre·ple·ǵár] *v. irr.* to fold, pleat; **-se** to
retreat, fall back.
réplica [rré·pli·ka] *f.* reply, answer, retort; replica,
copy; *Am. m.* examiner.
replicar[6] [rre·pli·kár] *v.* to reply, answer back; to
retort.
repliegue [rre·pljé·ǵe] *m.* fold, crease; retreat (*of
troops*).
repollo [rre·pó·yo] *m.* cabbage.
reponer[40] [rre·po·nér] *v. irr* (*devolver*) to replace, put
back; to restore; (*contestar*) to reply, retort; **-se** to
recover one's health or fortune; to collect oneself,
become calm.
reportaje [rre·por·tá·xe] *m.* newspaper report;
reporting.
reportar [rre·por·tár] *v.* to check, control, restrain; to
attain, obtain; to bring; to carry; *Am.* to report; **-se**
to control oneself.
reporte [rre·pór·te] *m.* report, news.
repórter [rre·pór·ter], **reportero** *m.* reporter.
reposado [rre·po·sá·ḏo] *p.p. & adj.* reposed; quiet,
calm; restful.
reposar [rre·po·sár] *v.* to repose; to rest; to lie buried;
-se to settle (*said of sediment*).
reposición [rre·po·si·sjón] *f.* replacement; recovery (*of
one's health*).
reposo [rre·pó·so] *m.* repose, rest; calm.
repostada [rre·pos·tá·ḏa] *f.* sharp answer, back talk.
repostería [rre·pos·te·rí·a] *f.* pastry shop.
reprender [rre·pren·dér] *v.* to reprimand, scold.
reprensible [rre·pren·sí·ḇle] *adj.* reprehensible,
deserving reproof.
reprensión [rre·pren·sjón] *f.* reproof, rebuke.
represa [rre·pré·sa] *f.* dam; damming, stopping; *Col.,
Ven.* reservoir.
represalia [rre·pre·sá·lja] *f.* reprisal.
represar [rre·pre·sár] *v.* to bank, dam; to recapture (*a
ship*) from the enemy; to repress, check.
representación [rre·pre·sen·ta·sjón] *f.* representation;
play, performance; authority, dignity; petition,
plea.
representante [rre·pre·sen·tán·te] *adj.* representing; *m.
& f.* representative; actor.
representar [rre·pre·sen·tár] *v.* (*declarar*) to
represent; to declare, state; to express, show;
(*actuar*) to act, play, perform; **-se** to imagine,
picture to oneself.
representativo [rre·pre·sen·ta·tí·ḇo] *adj.*
representative.
represión [rre·pre·sjón] *f.* repression, control,
restraint.
reprimenda [rre·pri·mén·da] *f.* reprimand, rebuke.
reprimir [rre·pri·mír] *v.* to repress, check, curb; **-se**
to repress oneself; to refrain.
reprobar[2] [rre·pro·ḇár] *v. irr.* to reprove, blame; to
condemn; to flunk, fail.
reprochar [rre·pro·čár] *v.* to reproach.
reproche [rre·pró·če] *m.* reproach.
reproducción [rre·pro·ḏuk·sjón] *f.* reproduction.
reproducir[25] [rre·pro·ḏu·sír] *v. irr.* to reproduce.
reptil [rrep·tíl] *m.* reptile.
república [rre·pú·ḇli·ka] *f.* republic.
republicano [rre·pu·ḇli·ká·no] *adj. & m.* republican.
repudiar [rre·pu·ḏjár] *v.* to repudiate; to disown.
repuesto [rre·pwés·to] *m.* stock, supply, provisions;
sideboard; **de** — spare, extra; *p.p. of* **reponer** &
adj. recovered (*from an illness, loss, fright, etc.*);
replaced; restored.
repugnancia [rre·puǵ·nán·sja] *f.* repugnance, disgust;

RE

aversion; dislike, reluctance.

repugnante [rre·puǵ·nán·te] *adj.* repugnant, disgusting, loathsome.

repugnar [rre·puǵ·nár] *v.* to be repugnant; to disgust; to oppose, contradict.

repulido [rre·pu·lí·ǥo] *adj.* polished up, slick; shiny; spruce.

repulsa [rre·púl·sa] *f.* repulse; rebuff; rebuke.

repulsar [rre·pil·sár] *v.* to repulse, repel, reject.

repulsivo [rre·pul·sí·ƀo] *adj.* repulsive, repugnant.

repuntar [rre·pun·tár] *v. Am.* to round up (*cattle*).

reputación [rre·pu·ta·sjón] *f.* reputation.

reputar [rre·pu·tár] *v.* to repute.

requebrar[1] [rre·ke·ƀrár] *v. irr.* to compliment; to flatter; to flirt with; to court, woo; to break again.

requemado [rre·ke·má·ǥo] *p.p. & adj.* burned; parched; tanned, sunburned.

requemar [rre·ke·már] *v.* to parch, dry up; to·burn; to overcook; **-se** to become overheated; to burn inwardly; to get tanned, sunburned.

requerimiento [rre·ke·ri·mjén·to] *m.* requisition; requirement; summons; **-s** amorous advances, insinuations.

requerir[3] [rre·ke·rír] *v. irr.* (*exigir*) to require; to need; to summon; (*indagar*) to examine, investigate; (*avisar*) to notify; — **de amores** to court, woo.

requesón [rre·ke·són] *m.* cottage cheese.

requiebro [rre·kjé·ƀro] *m.* flattery; compliment.

requisito [rre·ki·sí·to] *m.* requirement, requisite; — **previo** prerequisite.

res [rres] *f.* head of cattle; any large animal.

resabio [rre·sá·ƀjo] *m.* disagreeable aftertaste; bad habit.

resaca [rre·sá·ka] *f.* undertow; surge, surf; redraft (*of a bill of exchange*); *Carib.* beating, thrashing; *Mex., Ríopl.* mud and slime (*left by a flood*).

resaltar [rre·sal·tár] *v.* to stand out; to project, jut out; to rebound, bounce or spring back; to be evident, obvious.

resarcir[10] [rre·sar·sír] *v.* to indemnify, compensate, repay; to make amends for; **-se** to make up for.

resbaladero [rrez·ƀa·la·ǥé·ro] *m.* slide, slippery place.

resbaladizo [rrez·ƀa·la·ǥí·so] *adj.* slippery.

resbalar [rrez·ƀa·lár] *v.* to slide; **-se** to slip; to slide; to skid; **resbalársele a uno una cosa** to let a thing slide off one's back, be impervious to a thing.

resbalón [rre·ƀa·lón] *m.* sudden or violent slip; slide; error; **darse un** — to slip.

resbaloso [rrez·ƀa·ló·so] *adj.* slippery.

rescatar [rres·ka·tár] *v.* to ransom; to redeem; to barter, exchange, trade; *Mex.* to resell.

rescate [rres·ká·te] *m.* ransom; redemption; barter, exchange.

rescoldo [rres·kól·do] *m.* embers, hot cinders, hot ashes; doubt, scruple.

resecar[6] [rre·sé·kár] *v.* to dry up; to parch.

reseco [rre·sé·ko] *adj.* very dry; dried up, parched; thin, skinny.

resentimiento [rre·sen·ti·mjén·to] *m.* resentment; impairment, damage (*to one's health*).

resentirse[3] [rre·sen·tír·se] *v. irr* (*tener pesar*) to show resentment, hurt, or grief; to resent; (*empoerar*) to weaken; to become worse.

reseña [rre·sé·ña] *f.* military review; book review; brief account; sign, signal.

reseñar [rre·se·ñár] *v.* to review (*a book*); to review (*troops*); to outline briefly, give a short account of.

resero [rre·sé·ro] *m. Ríopl.* cowboy, herdsman; *Ríopl.* dealer in livestock.

reserva [rre·ser·ƀa] *f.* reserve; reservation; exception;

caution; **a** — **de** reserving the right to, intending to; **sin** — without reserve, frankly.

reservación [rre·ser·ƀa·sjón] *f.* reservation.

reservar [rre·ser·ƀár] *v.* to reserve; to put aside; to postpone; to exempt; to keep secret; **-se** to conserve one's strength, spare oneself (*for another time*).

resfriado [rres·frjá·ǥo] *m.* cold (*illness*); *p.p.* of **resfriar**; *adj. Ríopl.* indiscreet.

resfriar[17] [rres·frjár] *v.* to cool; to chill; **-se** to catch cold; to cool.

resfrío [rres·frí·o] *m.* chill; cold.

resguardar [rrez·ǥwar·dár] *v.* to guard, defend; to shield; **-se de** to guard oneself against; to seek shelter from.

resguardo [rrez·ǥwár·do] *m.* defense; security; guarantee; guard.

residencia [rre·si·dén·sja] *f.* residence; office or post of a resident foreign minister; *Am.* luxurious dwelling.

residente [rre·si·dén·te] *adj.* resident, residing; *m. & f.* resident, dweller; resident foreign minister; *Col., C.A., Ríopl.* alien resident.

residir [rre·si·dír] *v.* to reside; to live, dwell; to be inherent, belong (to).

residuo [rre·sí·ǥwo] *m.* residue; remainder.

resignación [rre·siǵ·na·sjón] *f.* resignation; strength.

resignar [rre·siǵ·nár] *v.* to resign; to hand over; **-se** to resign oneself.

resiliencia [rre·si·ljén·sja] *f.* resilience; — **al choque o al desgaste** toughness (machine).

resina [rre·sí·na] *f.* resin.

resistencia [rre·sis·tén·sja] *f.* resistance.

resistente [rre·sis·tén·te] *adj.* resistant; resisting.

resistir [rre·sis·tír] *v.* to resist; to tolerate, endure; **-se** to resist, struggle.

resolución [rre·so·lu·sjón] *f.* (*ánimo*) resolution; courage, determination; (*resultado*) solution; **en** — in brief.

resolver[2, 52] [rre·sol·ƀér] *v. irr.* to resolve, decide; to solve; to dissolve; **-se** to resolve, decide; to be reduced (to), dissolve (into).

resollar[2] [rre·so·yár] *v. irr.* to breathe hard; to pant.

resonar[2] [rre·so·nár] *v. irr.* to resound.

resoplar [rre·so·plár] *v.* to puff, breathe hard; to snort.

resoplido [rre·so·plí·do] *m.* puff, pant; snort.

resorte [rre·sór·te] *m.* spring; elasticity; means (*to attain an object*); *Col.* elastic, rubber band; *Ven.* **no es de mi** — it doesn't concern me.

respaldar [rres·pal·dár] *v.* to endorse; to guarantee; *Am.* to back, support; **-se** to lean back; *Ch.* to protect one's rear.

respaldo [rres·pál·do] *m.* back (*of a chair or sheet of paper*); protecting wall; endorsement; *Am.* protection, security, guarantee.

respectivo [rres·pek·tí·ƀo] *adj.* respective.

respecto [rres·pék·to] *m.* respect, relation, reference; point, matter; (**con**) — **a** (*or* — **de**) with respect to, with regard to.

respetable [rres·pe·tá·ƀle] *adj.* respectable.

respetar [rres·pe·tár] *v.* to respect.

respeto [rres·pé·to] *m.* respect; reverence, regard; consideration.

respetuoso [rres·pe·twó·so] *adj.* respectful; respectable.

respingar[7] [rres·piŋ·gár] *v.* to buck; to balk (*said of a horse*); to grumble; to curl up (*said of the edge of a garment*).

respingo [rres·píŋ·go] *m.* buck, balking; muttering, grumbling.

respiración [rres·pi·ra·sjón] *f.* respiration, breathing.
respirar [rres·pi·rár] *v.* to breathe.
respiro [rres·pí·ro] *m.* breathing; breath; respite, pause, moment of rest; extension of time (*for payment*).
resplandecer[13] [rres·plan·de·sér] *v. irr.* to shine; to glitter.
resplandeciente [rres·plan·de·sjén·te] *adj.* resplendent, shining.
resplandor [rres·plan·dór] *m.* splendor, brilliance, brightness; *Am.* sun's glare.
responder [rres·pon·dér] *v.* to respond; to answer; to correspond, harmonize; to answer (for), be responsible (for).
respondón [rres·pon·dón] *adj.* saucy, pert, insolent (*in answering*).
responsabilidad [rres·pon·sa·bi·li·dád] *f.* responsibility.
responsable [rres·pon·sá·ble] *adj.* responsible.
respuesta [rres·pwés·ta] *f.* response; answer, reply.
resquebradura [rres·ke·bra·dú·ra], **resquebrajadura** [rres·ke·bra·xa·dú·ra] *f.* fissure, crevice, crack.
resquebrajar [rres·ke·brá·xár] = **resquebrar.**
resquebrar[1] [rres·ke·brár] *v. irr.* to crack; to split.
resquicio [rres·kí·sjo] *m.* crack, slit, crevice; opening; *Col., Ven., Mex.* vestige, sign, trace.
resta [rrés·ta] *f.* subtraction (*as an arithmetical operation*); remainder.
restablecer[13] [rres·ta·ble·sér] *v. irr.* to re-establish; to restore; **-se** to recover.
restante [rres·tán·te] *adj.* remaining; *m.* residue, remainder.
restañar [rres·ta·ñár] *v.* to staunch (*a wound*); to check the flow of.
restar [rres·tár] *v.* to deduct; to subtract; to remain, be left over; to strike back (*a ball*).
restauración [rres·taw·ra·sjón] *f.* restoration.
restaurante [rres·taw·rán·te] *m.* restaurant.
restaurantismo [rres·taw·ran·tíz·mo] *m.* food service; restaurant business.
restaurar [rres·taw·rár] *v.* to restore; to recover; to re-establish; to repair.
restitución [rres·ti·tu·sjón] *f.* restitution, restoration, return.
restituir[32] [rres·ti·twír] *v. irr.* to return, give back; to restore.
resto [rrés·to] *m.* rest, remainder; stakes at cards; return (*of a tennis ball*); player who returns the ball; **-s** remains.
restorán [rres·to·rán] *m. Am.* restaurant.
restregar[1, 7] [rres·tre·gár] *v. irr.* to rub hard; to scrub.
restricción [rres·trik·sjón] *f.* restriction; restraint; curb; limitation.
restringir[11] [rres·triŋ·xír] *v.* to restrict; to restrain; to limit.
resucitar [rre·su·si·tár] *v.* to resuscitate, bring to life; to come to life; to revive.
resuelto [rre·swél·to] *p.p. of* **resolver** resolved, determined; *adj.* resolute, bold; quick.
resuello [rre·swé·yo] *m.* breath; breathing, panting.
resulta [rre·súl·ta] *f.* result; effect, consequence; **de -s** as a result, in consequence.
resultado [rre·sul·tá·do] *m.* result, effect, consequence.
resultante [rre·sul·tán·te] *adj.* resulting; *f.* resultant (*force*).
resultar [rre·sul·tár] *v.* to result; to spring, arise as a consequence; to turn out ot be; **resulta que** it turns out that.
resumen [rre·sú·men] *m.* résumé, summary; **en —**

summing up, in brief.
resumidero [rre·su·mi·dé·ro] *m. Am.* = **sumidero.**
resumir [rre·su·mír] *v.* to summarize, sum up; **-se** to be reduced or condensed.
resurgir[11] [rre·sur·xír] *v.* to arise again; to reappear.
retablo [rre·tá·blo] *m.* altarpiece; religious picture hung as a votive offering; series of pictures that tell a story.
retaguardia [rre·ta·gwár·dja] *f.* rear guard.
retal [rre·tál] *m.* remnant.
retar [rre·tár] *v.* to challenge, defy; to reprimand, scold; *Ch., Andes* to insult; **retable** challenging; **poco —** unprofitable.
retardar [rre·tar·dár] *v.* to retard, delay.
retazo [rre·tá·so] *m.* remnant; piece; fragment.
retener[45] [rre·te·nér] *v. irr.* to retain; to keep; to withhold; to detain.
retintín [rre·tin·tín] *m.* jingle, tinkle; sarcastic tone of ring.
retirada [rre·ti·rá·da] *f.* retreat; withdrawal.
retirado [rre·ti·rá·do] *p.p. & adj.* retired; distant, remote; isolated; pensioned.
retirar [rre·ti·rár] *v.* to withdraw; to take away; **-se** to retire, withdraw; to retreat.
retiro [rre·tí·ro] *m.* retreat; retirement; withdrawal; place of refuge; pension of a retired officer.
reto [rré·to] *m.* challenge; defiance; *Ríopl.* scolding; *Andes* insult.
retobado [rre·to·bá·do] *adj. Col., Ríopl.* saucy; *Andes* stubborn, unruly; *Andes* peevish; *Am.* sly, astute.
retobar [rre·to·bár] *v. Col., Andes* to cover with leather; *Ch., Peru* to wrap with leather, oilcloth, or burlap; *Am.* to tan (*leather*); **-se** *Ríopl.* to revel, talk back, act saucy; *Andes, Col.* to become disagreeable and aloof.
retocar[6] [rre·to·kár] *v.* to retouch, touch up; to finish, perfect.
retoñar [rre·to·ñár] *v.* to sprout; to bud; to sprout again; to reappear.
retoño [rre·tó·ño] *m.* sprout, shoot; bud.
retoque [rre·tó·ke] *m.* retouching; finishing touch.
retorcer[2, 10] [rre·tor·sér] *v. irr.* to twist; to retort; to distort; **-se** to wriggle; to squirm.
retorcimiento [rre·tor·si·mjén·to] *m.* twisting; squirming.
retórica [rre·tó·ri·ka] *f.* rhetoric.
retornar [rre·tor·nár] *v.* to return; to give back.
retorno [rre·tór·no] *m.* return; repayment; barter.
retozar[9] [rre·to·sár] *v.* to gambol, frisk about, frolic, romp; to stir within (*said of passions*).
retozo [rre·tó·so] *m.* frolic; **retozón** [rre·to·són] *adj.* frisky, playful.
retractarse [rre·trak·tár·se] *v.* to retract, take back one's word.
retraer[46] [rre·tra·ér] *v. irr.* to withdraw, draw back, take back; **-se de** to withdraw from; to keep aloof or away from; to shun.
retraído [rre·tra·í·do] *adj.* shy, reserved.
retraimiento [rre·traj·mjén·to] *m.* retirement; reserve, aloofness, shyness.
retranca [rre·tráŋ·ka] *f. Cuba* brake; **retranquero** [rre·traŋ·ké·ro] *m. Am.* brakeman.
retrancar[6] [rre·traŋ·kár] *v. Cuba* to brake, put the brake on; *Cuba* **se ha retrancado el asunto** the affair has come to a standstill.
retrasado [rre·tra·sá·do] *p.p. & adj.* behind, behind time; backward; postponed, delayed.
retrasar [rre·tra·sár] *v.* to delay, retard; to set back; to go backward; **-se** to fall behind; to be late, behind time.
retraso [rre·trá·so] *m.* delay.

RE

retratar [rre·tra·tár] *v.* to portray; to photograph; to copy, imitate; **-se** to be portrayed; to be photographed; to be reflected.

retrato [rre·trá·to] *m.* portrait; photograph; copy, imitation; reflection.

retrete [rre·tré·te] *m.* toilet, water closet; place of retreat.

retroactivo [rre·tro·ak·tí·ƀo] *adj.* retroactive.

retroceder [rre·tro·se·đér] *v.* to turn back; to fall back, draw back; to recede.

retroceso [rre·tro·sé·so] *m.* retrogression, backward step; retreat; setback, relapse.

retrocohete [rre·tro·ko·é·te] *m.* retrorocket.

retropropulsión [rre·tro·pro·pul·sjon] *f.* retropropulsion.

retruécano [rre·trwé·ka·no] *m.* pun.

retumbar [rre·tum·bár] *v.* to resound; to rumble.

retumbo [rre·túm·ƀo] *m.* loud echo or sound; rumble (*of thunder, cannon, etc.*).

reubicar [rre·u·ƀi·kár] *v.* relocate.

reuma [rréw·ma] *m.* rheumatism.

reumatismo [rrew·ma·tíz·mo] *m.* rheumatism.

reunión [rrew·njón] *f.* reunion; meeting.

reunir [rrew·nír] *v.* to reunite; to unite; to group; to gather; to assemble; to collect; **-se** to meet, assemble; to reunite.

revancha [rre·ƀán·ča] *f.* revenge; return game or match.

revelación [rre·ƀe·la·sjón] *f.* revelation.

revelador [rre·ƀe·la·đór] *adj.* revealing; *m.* developer (*in photography*).

revelar [rre·ƀe·lár] *v.* to reveal; to develop (*a film*).

revendedor [rre·ƀen·de·đór] *m.* retailer; reseller; ticket scalper.

reventa [rre·ƀén·ta] *f.* resale.

reventar[1] [rre·ƀen·tár] *v. irr.* (*estallar*) to burst; to burst forth; to explode; to smash; (*fatigar*) to fatigue, exhaust; to bother; **-se** to burst; to blow out, explode.

reventón [rre·ƀen·tón] *m.* burst, bursting; blowout; steep hill; hard work, toil; *adj.* bursting.

reverdecer[13] [rre·ƀer·de·sér] *v. irr.* to grow fresh and green again; to gain new strength and vigor.

reverencia [rre·ƀe·rén·sja] *f.* reverence; bow.

reverenciar [rre·ƀe·ren·sjár] *v.* to revere, venerate.

reverendo [rre·ƀe·rén·do] *adj.* reverend; *Cuba, Ríopl., Mex., Andes* large, big (*ironically*).

reverente [rre·ƀe·rén·te] *adj.* reverent.

reverso [rre·ƀér·so] *m.* reverse; back side.

revertir[3] [rre·ƀer·tír] *v. irr.* to revert.

revés [rre·ƀés] *m.* reverse; back, wrong side; setback; backstroke or slap; backhanded thrust (*in fencing*); (*desgracia*) misfortune; **al** — backwards; wrong side out; in the opposite way; from left to right.

revestir[5] [rre·ƀes·tír] *v. irr.* to dress, clothe; to coat, cover with a coating; **-se** to dress, put on an outer garment or vestment; to be invested (*with power, authority, etc.*); **-se de paciencia** to arm oneself with patience; **revestimiento duro** hard surfacing.

revisar [rre·ƀi·sár] *v.* to revise; to review; to examine, inspect.

revisión [rre·ƀi·sjón] *m.* revision; review (*of a case*), new trial; inspection (*of baggage*).

revisor [rre·ƀi·sór] *m.* corrector; inspector, overseer.

revista [rre·ƀís·ta] *f.* (*inspección*) review; inspection; (*publicación*) magazine, journal; (*proceso*) second trial or hearing; **pasar** — to pass in review; to examine carefully; to review (*troops*).

revistar [rre·ƀis·tár] *v.* to review, inspect (*troops*).

revivir [rre·ƀi·ƀír] *v.* to revive.

revocación [rre·ƀo·ka·sjón] *f.* repeal, cancellation.

revocar[6] [rre·ƀo·kár] *v.* to revoke, repeal.

revolcar[6] [rre·ƀol·kár] *v.* (*derribar*) to knock down; to turn over and over; to floor, defeat; (*suspender*) to fail, flunk; **-se** to wallow; to roll over and over; to flounder.

revolotear [rre·ƀo·lo·te·ár] *v.* to fly about, flutter around; to hover; to circle around.

revoltijo [rre·ƀol·tí·xo], **revoltillo** [rre·ƀol·tí·yo] *m.* jumble, mixture, mess; tangle, muddle; **revoltillo de huevos** scrambled eggs.

revoltoso [rre·ƀol·tó·so] *adj.* turbulent, unruly, rebellious; mischievous; intricate; *m.* agitator, troublemaker; rebel.

revolución [rre·ƀo·lu·sjón] *f.* revolution; **-es por minuto** RPM.

revolucionario [rre·ƀo·lu·sjo·ná·rjo] *adj.* revolutionary; *m.* revolutionist, revolutionary.

revolver[2] [rre·ƀol·ƀér] *v. irr.* to revolve; to turn over; to stir up; to mix up; to turn around swiftly (*a horse*); **-se** to move back and forth; to roll over and over; to change (*said of the weather*).

revólver [rre·ƀól·ƀer] *m.* revolver, pistol.

revuelo [rre·ƀwé·lo] *m.* whirl; stir, commotion; flying around.

revuelta [rre·ƀwél·ta] *f.* revolt, revolution; second turn; turn, bend; quarrel, fight; *Ch.* sudden turning of a horse.

revuelto [rre·ƀwél·to] *p.p. of* **revolver** & *adj.* confused; mixed up; intricate, complicated; choppy (*sea*); changeable (*weather*); **huevos -s** scrambled eggs.

rey [rrej] *m.* king.

reyerta [rre·yér·ta] *f.* quarrel, dispute.

rezagado [rre·sa·gá·đo] *adj.* back, behind; *m.* straggler, slowpoke, latecomer.

rezagar[7] [rre·sa·gár] *v.* to leave behind; to separate (*the weak cattle*) from the herd; *Am.* to reserve, set aside; **-se** to lag behind.

rezar[9] [rre·sár] *v.* to pray; to say or recite (*a prayer*); to mutter, grumble; **así lo reza el libro** so the book says; **eso no reza conmigo** that has nothing to do with me.

rezo [rré·so] *m.* prayer.

rezongar[7] [rre·son·gár] *v.* to grumble, growl, mutter.

rezongón [rre·son·gón] *adj.* growling, grumbling; *m.* grumbler, growler; scolder.

rezumar [rre·su·már] *v.* to ooze; to leak; **se rezuma** it oozes, it seeps through.

ría [rrí·a] *f.* mouth of a river, estuary.

riachuelo [rrja·čwé·lo] *m.* rivulet, brook.

ribazo [rri·bá·so] *m.* bank, ridge.

ribera [rri·ƀé·ra] *f.* shore, bank, beach.

ribereño [rri·ƀe·ré·ño] *adj.* of, pertaining to, or living on, a river bank.

ribete [rri·ƀé·te] *m.* trimming, border, edge, binding; addition; **tiene sus -s de poeta** he is something of a poet.

ribetear [rri·ƀe·te·ár] *v.* to bind, put a binding on; to border, trim the edge or border of.

ricacho [rri·ká·čo] *adj.* quite rich (*often said sarcastically*); **ricachón** [rri·ka·čón] *adj.* extremely rich, disgustingly rich.

rico [rrí·ko] *adj.* rich, wealthy; delicious; exquisite; **ricote** [rri·kó·te] = **ricacho.**

ridiculizar[9] [rri·di·ku·li·sár] *v.* to ridicule, deride.

ridículo [rri·dí·ku·lo] *adj.* ridiculous; queer, strange; *m.* ridicule; ridiculous situation; **hacer el** — to be ridiculous; to act the fool.

riego [rrjé·go] *m.* irrigation; watering.

riel [rrjel] *m.* rail; **-es** track, railroad track.

rienda [rrjén·da] *f.* rein, bridle; moderation, restraint;

a — **suelta** with free rein, without restraint; violently, swiftly; **soltar la** — to let loose, act without restraint; **tirar las -s** to draw rein, tighten the reins; to restrain.

riente [rrjén·te] *adj.* laughing, smiling.

riesgo [rrjez·ǥo] *m.* risk.

rifa [rrí·fa] *f.* raffle; scuffle, quarrel.

rifar [rri·fár] *v.* to raffle; to scuffle, quarrel.

rifeño [rri·fé·ño] *m.* riff.

rifle [rrí·fle] *m.* rifle.

rigidez [rri·xi·dés] *f.* rigidity, stiffness; severity, strictness.

rígido [rrí·xi·do] *adj.* rigid, stiff; severe, strict.

rigor [rri·ǥór] *m.* rigor; severity; harshness; rigidity, stiffness; **en** — in reality; strictly; **ser de** — to be absolutely indispensable, be required by custom.

rigoroso [rri·ǥo·ró·so], **riguroso** [rri·ǥu·ró·so] *adj.* rigorous; harsh; severe; strict.

rima [rrí·ma] *f.* rhyme; **-s** poems.

rimar [rri·már] *v.* to rhyme.

rimbombante [rrim·bom·bán·te] *adj.* high-sounding; resounding.

rimero [rri·mé·ro] *m.* pile, heap.

rincón [rriŋ·kón] *m.* corner; nook; *Am.* narrow valley.

rinconada [rriŋ·ko·ná·da] *f.* corner; nook.

rinconera [rriŋ·ko·né·ra] *f.* corner cupboard, corner table, corner bracket.

ringlera [rriŋ·glé·ra] *f.* tier, row, line.

rinoceronte [rri·no·se·rón·te] *m.* rhinoceros.

riña [rri·ña] *f.* quarrel, dispute, fight.

riñón [rri·ñón] *m.* kidney; center, interior.

río [rrí·o] *m.* river.

ripio [rrí·pjo] *m.* rubble, stone or brick fragments; padding (*in a verse, speech, etc.*), useless word.

riqueza [rri·ké·sa] *f.* riches; wealth.

risa [rrí·sa] *f.* laugh; laughter; **reventar de** — to burst with laughter; **tomar a** — to take lightly; to laugh off.

risada [rri·sá·da] *f.* gale of laughter, loud laugh.

risco [rrís·ko] *m.* rocky cliff, crag; honey fritter.

risible [rri·sí·ble] *adj.* laughable, ridiculous.

risotada [rri·so·tá·da] *f.* guffaw, big laugh.

ristra [rrís·tra] *f.* string (*of onions, garlic, etc.*); series, row.

risueño [rri·swé·ño] *adj.* smiling; pleasant; delightful.

rítmico [rríd·mi·ko] *adj.* rhythmical.

ritmo [rríd·mo] *m.* rhythm.

rito [rrí·to] *m.* rite, ceremony.

rival [rri·bál] *m. & f.* rival, competitor; enemy.

rivalidad [rri·ba·li·dád] *f.* rivalry, competition; enmity.

rivalizar⁹ [rri·ba·li·sár] *v.* to rival, compete.

rizado [rri·sá·do] *p.p.* curled; *adj.* wavy, curly; *m.* curling; curls.

rizar⁹ [rri·sár] *v.* to curl; to ripple; to ruffle, gather into ruffles; **-se** to curl one's hair; to curl.

rizo [rrí·so] *m.* curl; ripple; *adj.* curly; **rizoso** [rri·só·so] *adj.* curly.

roano [rro·á·no] *adj.* roan (*red, bay, or chestnut-colored, mixed with white; applied to a horse*).

robalo [rro·bá·lo] *m.* bass.

robar [rro·bár] *v.* to rob, steal; to abduct, kidnap.

roble [rró·ble] *m.* oak tree; oak wood; **robledal** [rro·ble·dál], **robledo** [rro·blé·do] *m.* oak grove.

robo [rró·bo] *m.* robbery, theft; loot, plunder.

robusto [rró·bús·to] *adj.* robust, vigorous.

roca [rró·ka] *f.* rock, boulder; rocky cliff, crag.

rocalloso [rro·ka·yó·so] *adj.* rocky.

roce [rró·se] *m.* graze; friction; contact; **no tener** — **con** to have no contact with (*a person*).

rociada [rro·sjá·da] *f.* sprinkling; spray; dew; sprinkle, shower; volley of harsh words.

rociar¹⁷ [rro·sjár] *v.* to sprinkle; to spray; to fall (*said of dew*).

rocín [rro·sín] *m.* nag, hack; draft horse; coarse, ill-bred man; *Ríopl., Mex., Andes* riding horse.

rocío [rro·sí·o] *m.* dew; sprinkle; shower; spray; *adj. Am.* reddish, roan (*horse*).

rocoso [rro·kó·so] *adj.* rocky.

rodada [rro·dá·da] *f.* rut, wheel track; *Ríopl.* tumble, fall.

rodado [rro·dá·do] *adj.* dapple (*horse*); *p.p.* of **rodar.**

rodadura [rro·da·dú·ra] *f.* rolling; rut; — **del neumático** tire tread.

rodaja [rro·dá·xa] *f.* disk; small wheel; round slice.

rodaje [rro·dá·xe] *m.* works (*of a watch*); — **de película** the filming of a movie.

rodar² [rro·dár] *v. irr.* to roll; to revolve; to roam, wander about; to fall down (*rolling*) *Mex.* — **a patadas** to kick down.

rodear [rro·de·ár] *v.* to go around; to go by a roundabout way; to surround, encircle; *Ríopl., Cuba, Ven.* to round up (*cattle*).

rodela [rro·dé·la] *f.* round shield; *Mex., Ch.* padded ring for carrying loads on the head; *Am.* round slice; *Ch.* kettle lid; *Ch.* hoop; *Ch.* game of rolling a hoop.

rodeo [rro·dé·o] *m.* detour, roundabout way; circumlocution, roundabout expression; dodge, evasion; corral, stockyard; rodeo, roundup.

rodilla [rro·dí·ya] *f.* knee; **de -s** on one's knees; **hincarse de -s** to kneel down.

rodillo [rro·dí·yo] *m.* roller; rolling pin; road roller; (*computadora*) platen.

rodio [rró·djo] *m.* rhodium.

rododendro [rro·do·dén·dro] *m.* rhododendron.

roedor [rro·e·dór] *m.* rodent.

roer⁵¹ [rro·er] *v. irr.* to gnaw; to corrode, eat away; to torment, harass.

rogar²'⁷ [rro·ǥár] *v. irr.* to pray, beg, beseech; **hacerse** — to let oneself be coaxed.

rojez [rro·xés] *f.* redness.

rojizo [rro·xí·so] *adj.* reddish.

rojo [rró·xo] *adj.* red; red, radical.

rojura [rro·xú·ra] *f.* redness.

rollizo [rro·yí·so] *adj.* plump; *m.* log.

rollo [rró·yo] *m.* roll; bundle; rolling pin; log.

romadizo [rro·ma·dí·so] *m.* nasal catarrh, head cold.

romance [rro·mán·se] *adj.* Romance, Romanic (*language*); *m.* Romance language; Spanish language; romance, chivalric novel; ballad; eight-syllable meter with even verses rhyming in assonance; **en buen** — in plain language.

románico [rro·má·ni·ko] *adj.* Romanesque (*architecture*); Romance (*language*).

romano [rro·má·no] *adj. & m.* Roman.

romanticismo [rro·man·ti·síz·mo] *m.* romanticism.

romántico [rro·mán·ti·ko] *adj.* romantic; sentimental; *m.* romantic; sentimentalist.

rombo [rróm·bo] *m.* rhombus.

romería [rro·me·rí·a] *f.* pilgrimage.

romero [rro·mé·ro] *m.* pilgrim; rosemary (*shrub*).

romo [rró·mo] *adj.* blunt; snub-nosed.

rompe [rróm·pe]: **de — y rasga** resolute, bold; **al** — *Am.* suddenly.

rompecabezas [rrom·pe·ka·bé·sas] *m.* puzzle, riddle.

rompenueces [rrom·pe·nwé·ses] *m.* nutcracker.

rompeolas [rrom·pe·ó·las] *m.* breakwater, mole.

romper⁵² [rrom·pér] *v.* to break; to shatter; to tear; to wear through; *Ven.* to leave suddenly or on the run; — **el alba** to dawn; — **a** to start to; **-se** to

RE

break.

rompiente [rrom·pjén·te] *m.* shoal, sand bank, reef; -s breakers, surf.

rompimiento [rrom·pi·mjén·to] *m.* rupture, break; crack; breach; quarrel.

rompopo [rrom·pó·po] *m.* eggnog.

ron [rron] *m.* rum.

roncar[6] [rron·kár] *v.* to snore; to roar; to brag.

ronco [rrón·ko] *adj.* hoarse; harsh-sounding.

roncha [rrón·ča] *f.* hive; welt.

ronda [rrón·da] *f.* patrol; night serenaders; round (*of a game, of drinks, etc.*); *Ríopl., C.A., Andes* ring-around-a-rosy (*a children's* game); **hacer la — a** to court; *Ch.* to surround, trap (*an animal*).

rondar [rron·dár] *v.* to go around, hover around; to patrol; to make the rounds; to serenade.

ronquera [rron·ké·ra] *f.* hoarseness.

ronquido [rron·kí·do] *m.* snore; snort.

ronronear [rron·rro·ne·ár] *v.* to purr.

ronroneo [rron·rro·né·o] *m.* purr.

ronzal [rron·sál] *m.* halter.

roña [rró·ña] *f.* scab, mange; (*suciedad*) filth; (*infección*) infection; (*avaricia*) stinginess; trickery; *Ríopl., Col., Ven., Cuba* ill will, grudge, *Am., Col.* **hacer —** to fake an illness.

roñoso [rro·ñó·so] *adj.* scabby, mangy; dirty; stingy; *Carib., Mex.* spiteful; *Arg.* fainthearted, cowardly.

ropa [rró·pa] *f.* clothing, clothes; **— blanca** linen; **— vieja** old clothes; stew made from leftover meat; **a quema —** at close range (*when shooting*); suddenly, without warning.

ropaje [rro·pá·xe] *m.* clothes, clothing apparel; robe.

ropería [rro·pe·rí·a] *f.* clothing store.

ropero [rro·pé·ro] *m.* clothier; wardrobe, clothespress; wardrobe keeper; *Ven.* clothes rack.

roqueño [rro·ké·ño] *adj.* rocky; hard, like rock.

rorro [rró·rro] *m.* popular term for a baby.

rosa [rró·sa] *f.* rose; red spot on the skin; rose color; *Ch., Mex.* rosebush; **— de los vientos** (*or —* **náutica**) mariner's compass.

rosado [rro·sá·do] *adj.* rosy, rose-colored; frosted (*drink*); *Am.* roan, reddish-brown (*horse*).

rosal [rro·sál] *m.* rosebush.

rosario [rro·sá·rjo] *m.* rosary; **— de desdichas** chain of misfortunes.

rosbif [rroz·bíf] *m.* roast beef.

rosca [rrós·ka] *f.* screw and nut; screw thread; spiral, twist; ring-shaped roll; *Mex., Ven., Col.* ring-shaped cushion (*for carrying loads on the head*); *Am.* circle of card players; **roscada de tornillo** screw thread.

roseta [rro·sé·ta] *f.* rosette; small rose; -s popcorn; **rosetón** [rro·se·tón] *m.* large rosette; rose window.

rosillo [rro·sí·yo] *adj.* light red; roan (*horse*).

rostro [rrós·tro] *m.* face; **hacer —** to face.

rota [rró·ta] *f.* rout, defeat; ship's course; Rota (*ecclesiastical court*); rattan palm tree.

rotación [rro·ta·sjón] *f.* rotation.

rotario [rro·tá·rjo] *m.* member of the Rotary Club.

rotativo [rro·ta·tí·bo] *adj.* rotary; *f.* printing press.

rotatorio [rro·ta·tó·rjo] *adj.* rotary.

roto [rró·to] *p.p. irr.* of **romper** & *adj.* broken; shattered; torn; worn out, ragged; *m. Ch.* person of the poorer class.

rotular [rro·tu·lár] *v.* to label; to letter.

rótulo [rró·tu·lo] *m.* title, inscription; label.

rotundo [rro·tún·do] *adj.* round; sonorous; **una negativa rotunda** a flat denial.

rotura [rro·tú·ra] *f.* breach, opening; break; tear, rip; rupture; fracture.

roturar [rro·tu·rár] *v.* to break ground; to plow (*new*

ground).

rozadura [rro·sa·dú·ra] *f.* friction; chafe; chafing.

rozamiento [rro·sa·mjén·to] *m.* friction; rubbing.

rozar[9] [rro·sár] *v.* to graze; to scrape; to chafe; to clear of underbush; **-se con alguien** to have connections, contact, or dealings with someone.

rozón [rro·són] *m.* graze, sudden or violent scrape; short, broad scythe.

ruana [rrwá·na] *f. Col., Ven.* a woolen poncho.

ruano [rrwá·no] = **roano.**

rubí [rru·bí] *m.* ruby.

rubicundo [rru·bi·kún·do] *adj.* reddish; ruddy, healthy red; reddish-blond.

rubidio [rru·bí·djo] *m.* rubidium.

rubio [rrú·bjo] *adj.* blond, blonde.

rubor [rru·bór] *m.* blush; bashfulness, shyness.

ruborizarse[9] [rru·bo·ri·sár·se] *v.* to blush; to feel ashamed.

rúbrica [rrú·bri·ka] *f.* scroll, flourish (*added to a signature*); title, heading; **de —** according to ritual, rule, or custom.

rucio [rrú·sjo] *adj.* grey (*horse or donkey*); **— rodado** dapple-grey.

rudeza [rru·dé·sa] *f.* rudeness; coarseness; roughness.

rudo [rrú·do] *adj.* rude; coarse; rough; stupid.

rueca [rrwé·ka] *f.* distaff (*used for spinning*).

rueda [rrwé·da] *f.* (*máquina*) wheel; circle; spread of a peacock's tail; round object; (*grupo*) circle; group; **en —** in turn; in a circle; **hacer la — a** to court; to flatter; **— manivela** handwheel.

ruedo [rrwé·do] *m.* circuit, tour; border, rim; circumference.

ruego [rrwé·go] *m.* prayer, supplication, request.

rufián [rru·fján] *m.* ruffian; bully.

rugido [rru·xí·do] *m.* roar; rumbling.

rugir[11] [rru·xír] *v.* to roar; to bellow.

rugoso [rru·gó·so] *adj.* wrinkled; furrowed.

ruibarbo [rrwi·bár·bo] *m.* rhubarb.

ruidazo [rrwi·dá·so] *m.* big noise.

ruido [rrwí·do] *m.* noise; din; dispute; talk, rumor; **hacer** (*or* **meter**) **—** to make a noise; to create a sensation; to cause a disturbance.

ruidoso [rrwi·dó·so] *adj.* noisy; loud; sensational.

ruin [rrwin] *adj.* (*vicioso*) vile, base, mean; vicious (*animal*); (*mezquino*) small; petty; puny; stingy.

ruina [rrwí·na] *f.* ruin; destruction; downfall.

ruindad [rrwin·dád] *f.* baseness; meanness; stinginess; mean or vile act.

ruinoso [rrwi·nó·so] *adj.* ruinous; in a state of ruin or decay.

ruiseñor [rrwi·se·ñór] *m.* nightingale.

rumba [rrúm·ba] *f. Ven., Col., Carib., Mex., Ríopl.* rumba (*dance and music*); *Carib., Ven., Andes* spree; *Carib., Ven., Andes* **irse de —** to go on a spree.

rumbear [rrum·be·ár] *v. Ríopl., Andes* to head (towards), take a certain direction; *Am.* to cut a path through a forest; *S.A., Cuba* to go on a spree.

rumbo [rrúm·bo] *m.* (*ruta*) direction, course; route; (*pompa*) pomp; ostentation; *Arg.* cut on the head; *C.A.* revel, noisy spree; **hacer — a** to head or sail towards; *Am.* **ir al —** to be going in the right direction, be on the right track.

rumboso [rrum·bó·so] *adj.* pompous, ostentatious; generous.

rumiante [rru·mján·te] *m.* ruminant.

rumiar [rru·mjár] *v.* to ruminate; to chew the cud; to ponder, meditate.

rumor [rru·mór] *m.* rumor, report; murmur; rumble.

runfla [rrún·fla] *f.* series (*of things of the same kind*); sequence (*in cards*).

runrún [rrun·rrún] *m.* rumor; murmur.

ruptura [rrup·tú·ra] *f.* rupture; break; fracture.

rural [rru·rál] *adj.* rural.

ruso [rrú·so] *adj.* Russian; *m.* Russian; Russian language.

rústico [rrús·ti·ko] *adj.* rustic, rural; crude, coarse; *m.* peasant; **en** (*or* **a la**) **rústica** unbound, paperbound.

ruta [rrú·ta] *f.* route, course, way.

rutenio [rru·té·njo] *m.* ruthenium.

rutina [rru·tí·na] *f.* routine.

S:s

sábado [sá·ba·do] *m.* Saturday.

sábalo [sá·ba·lo] *m.* shad; *Am.* tarpon.

sábana [sá·ba·na] *f.* bed sheet; altar cloth.

sabana [sa·bá·na] *f. Col.* savanna, treeless plain; *Col.* **ponerse en la** — to become suddenly rich.

sabandija [sa·ban·dí·xa] *f.* small reptile; small lizard.

sabañón [sa·ba·ñón] *m.* chilblain.

sabedor [sa·be·dór] *adj.* knowing; aware, informed.

saber[42] [sa·bér] *v. irr.* to know; to know how to, be able to; to learn, find out; *Ríopl., Ven., Col.* to be in the habit of; — **a** to taste of, taste like; **sabe bien** it tastes good; **a** — namely; that is; *Am.* **¡a — si venga!** who knows whether he will come!; **un no sé qué** an indefinable something; **¿sabe Vd. a la plaza?** do you know the way to the square?; *m.* knowledge, learning.

sabiduría [sa·bi·du·rí·a] *f.* wisdom; knowledge.

sabiendas [sa·bjén·das]: **a** — consciously, knowingly.

sabino [sa·bí·no] *adj.* roan.

sabio [sá·bjo] *adj.* wise; judicious; learned; *m.* savant, scholar; sage, wise man.

sable [sá·ble] *m.* saber; **sablazo** [sa·blá·so] *m.* blow with a saber; saber wound; **dar un sablazo** to strike for a loan.

sabor [sa·bór] *m.* savor, taste, flavor.

saborear [sa·bo·re·ár] *v.* to savor, flavor, season; to relish, taste with pleasure; to enjoy; **-se** to eat or drink with relish; to smack one's lips.

sabotaje [sa·bo·tá·xe] *m.* sabotage.

sabotear [sa·bo·te·ár] *v.* to sabotage.

sabroso [sa·bró·so] *adj.* savory, tasty; delicious; delightful.

sabueso [sa·bwé·so] *m.* hound.

sacabocados [sa·ka·bo·ká·dos] *m.* punch (*tool*).

sacacorchos [sa·ka·cór·čos] *m.* corkscrew.

sacamuelas [sa·ka·mwé·las] *m. & f.* tooth puller; quack dentist.

sacapuntas [sa·ka·pún·tas] *m.* pencil sharpener.

sacar[6] [sa·kár] *v.* to draw, draw out, pull out, get out, or take out; to get, obtain; to infer; to make (*a copy*); to take (*a snapshot or picture*); to stick out (*one's tongue*); to serve (*a ball*); — **a bailar** to ask to dance, lead on to the dance floor; — **a luz** to publish; — **el cuerpo** to dodge; — **en claro** (*or* — **en limpio**) to deduce, conclude; *Am.* — **el sombrero** to take off one's hat; *Am.* **¡sáquese de allí!** get out of there!

sacarina [sa·ka·rí·na] *f.* saccharine.

sacerdocio [sa·ser·dó·sjo] *m.* priesthood.

sacerdote [sa·ser·dó·te] *m.* priest.

saciar [sa·sjár] *v.* to satiate, satisfy; **-se** to be satiated, satisfied completely.

saco [sá·ko] *m.* sack, bag; sackful, bagful; loose-fitting coat; sack, plundering; *Am.* suit coat; — **de**

noche overnight bag, satchel.

sacramento [sa·kra·mén·to] *m.* sacrament.

sacrificar[6] [sa·kri·fi·kár] *v.* to sacrifice.

sacrificio [sa·kri·fí·sjo] *m.* sacrifice.

sacrilegio [sa·kri·lé·xjo] *m.* sacrilege.

sacrílego [sa·krí·le·ɡo] *adj.* sacrilegious.

sacristán [sa·kris·tán] *m.* sacristan, sexton; *Am.* busybody, meddler.

sacro [sá·kro] *adj.* sacred.

sacrosanto [sa·kro·sán·to] *adj.* sacrosanct, holy and sacred.

sacudida [sa·ku·dí·da] *f.* shake, jolt, jerk.

sacudimiento [sa·ku·di·mjén·to] *m.* shaking; shake, jerk; shock, jolt.

sacudir [sa·ku·dír] *v.* to shake; to jerk; to beat; to beat the dust from; to shake off; **-se** to shake oneself; to brush oneself off; **-se de alguien** to shake someone off, get rid of someone.

sádico [sá·di·ko] *adj.* sadistic, cruel.

sadismo [sa·díz·mo] *m.* sadism.

saeta [sa·é·ta] *f.* arrow, dart.

sagacidad [sa·ɡa·si·dád] *f.* sagacity.

sagaz [sa·ɡás] *adj.* sagacious, shrewd.

sagrado [sa·ɡrá·do] *adj.* sacred; consecrated; *m.* asylum, refuge.

sahumar [sa·u·már] *v.* to perfume with incense; to fumigate.

sahumerio [sa·u·mé·rjo] *m.* vapor, fume; incense; burning of incense; fumigation.

sainete [sáj·né·te] *m.* one-act comedy or farce; delicacy, tasty tidbit; flavor, relish; sauce.

sajón [sa·xón] *adj. & m.* Saxon.

sal [sal] *f.* salt; wit, humor; grace; *Mex., Cuba, C.A., Col., Andes* misfortune, bad luck.

sala [sá·la] *f.* parlor; hall, large room; — **de justicia** courtroom.

salado [sa·lá·do] *adj.* salty; salted; witty; (*gracioso*) charming; *Ch., Arg.* costly; *Mex., Cuba, C.A., Col., Andes* **estar** — to be unlucky; *m. Col.* salt pit, salt mine.

salar [sa·lár] *v.* to salt; to cure or preserve with salt; *Mex., Cuba, C.A., Col., Andes* to bring bad luck (to); *Am.* to dishonor; *Am.* to ruin, spoil; *Am.* to bribe; *Am.* to feed salt to cattle; *m. Am.* salt pit.

salario [sa·lá·rjo] *m.* salary, wages.

salchicha [sal·čí·ča] *f.* sausage; **salchichón** [sal·či·čón] *m.* large sausage.

saldar [sal·dár] *v.* to balance, settle (*an account*).

saldo [sál·do] *m.* balance, settlement (*of an account*); bargain sale.

saledizo [sa·le·dí·so] = **salidizo.**

salero [sa·lé·ro] *m.* (*vaso*) saltcellar, saltshaker; place for storing salts; salt lick; (*gracia*) wit, grace, charm; *Col.* salt dealer.

saleroso [sa·le·ró·so] *adj.* charming; witty; attractive (*more common in feminine*).

salida [sa·lí·da] *f.* departure; exit; sally; outlet; way out; loophole; outskirts; outcome; jut, projection; outlay, expenditure; witty remark; (*computadora*) output; — **de pie de banco** silly remark, nonsense; — **de fácil** — best-seller; — **doble** loop vent; — **del sol** sunrise; *Cuba* — **de teatro** evening wrap.

salidizo [sa·li·dí·so] *m.* jut, ledge, projection; *adj.* salient, jutting, projecting.

saliente [sa·ljén·te] *adj.* salient, standing out; projecting; *m.* salient, salient angle; jut, projection; — **de la rosca** depth of thread (screw).

salina [sa·lí·na] *f.* salt mine or pit; salt works.

salir[43] [sa·lír] *v. irr.* (*partir*) to go out; to leave, depart; to get out (*of*); to come out; to sprout; to come (*from*); (*resultar*) to turn out to be; — **bien**

RO

to turn out well; to come out well; — **a su padre**
to turn out to be or look like his father; *Am.* — **a
mano** to come out even; **-se** to get out, slip out; to
leak out; **-se con la suya** to get one's own way.
salitral [sa·li·trál] *m.* saltpeter bed or mine.
salitre [sa·lí·tre] *m.* saltpeter; **salitrera** [sa·li·tré·ra] *f.*
saltpeter mine or bed; **salitroso** [sa·li·tró·so] *adj.*
nitrous, abounding in saltpeter.
saliva [sa·lí·ba] *f.* saliva.
salmo [sál·mo] *m.* psalm.
salmodiar [sal·mo·djár] *v.* to chant; to talk in a
monotone or singsong.
salmón [sal·món] *m.* salmon.
salmuera [sal·mwé·ra] *f.* brine.
salobre [sa·ló·bre] *adj.* briny, salty.
salón [sa·lón] *m.* salon, hall, large room; salted meat
or fish.
salpicadero [sal·pi·ka·dé·ro] *m.* dashboard.
salpicadura [sal·pi·ka·dú·ra] *f.* spatter, splash.
salpicar[6] [sal·pi·kár] *v.* to sprinkle, spray, spatter.
salpicón [sal·pi·kón] *m.* hash; hodgepodge; *Ec.* fruit
drink.
salpimentar[1] [sal·pi·men·tár] *v. irr.* to salt and
pepper.
salpimienta [sal·pi·mjén·ta] *f.* salt and pepper.
salpullido [sal·pu·yí·do] *m.* rash, skin eruption.
salsa [sál·sa] *f.* sauce; gravy; *Ch.* sound whipping or
beating; **salsera** [sal·sé·ra] *f.* sauce dish.
saltamontes [sal·ta·món·tes] *m.* grasshopper.
saltar [sal·tár] *v.* (*brincar*) to jump; to jump over; to
leap; to bounce; to skip; (*estallar*) to burst, break
into pieces; to come off; — **a la vista** to be
obvious, evident; — **a tierra** to disembark, land;
Mex. — **las trancas** to lose one's patience; to lose
one's head.
salteador [sal·te·a·dór] *m.* bandit, highway robber.
saltear [sal·te·ár] *v.* to assault, attack; to hold up,
rob; to take by surprise; to jump or skip around; to
sautee.
salto [sál·to] *m.* jump; leap; precipice; gap; — **de
agua** waterfall; **a -s** by jumps; **en un** (*or* **de un)**
— in a jiffy; quickly; **dar un** — to jump, leap.
saltón [sal·tón] *adj.* jumping, skipping, hopping;
jumpy; protruding; *Col.* half-cooked; **ojos -es**
popeyes, bulging eyes; *m.* grasshopper.
salubre [sa·lú·bre] *adj.* healthy, healthful.
salubridad [sa·lu·bri·dád] *f.* healthfulness, health;
sanitation.
salud [sa·lúd] *f.* health; welfare; salvation; ¡ — !
greetings!; your health!
saludable [sa·lu·dá·ble] *adj.* wholesome, healthful
beneficial.
saludador [sa·lu·da·dór] *m.* greeter; healer, quack.
saludar [sa·lu·dár] *v.* to salute, greet; to fire a salute.
saludo [sa·lú·do] *m.* salute, nod, greeting.
salutación [sa·lu·ta·sjón] *f.* salutation; greeting.
salva [sál·ba] *f.* salvo, salute with guns; greeting,
·welcome.
salvación [sal·ba·sjón] *f.* salvation.
salvado [sal·bá·do] *m.* bran.
salvador [sal·ba·dór] *m.* savior, rescuer; Savior
(Saviour); *adj.* saving.
salvaguardar [sal·ba·gwar·dár] *v.* to safeguard,
defend, protect.
salvaguardia [sal·ba·gwár·dja] *m.* safeguard,
protection; guard; *f.* safe-conduct paper, passport;
password.
salvajada [sal·ba·xá·da] *f.* savage act or remark.
salvaje [sal·bá·xe] *adj.* savage, wild; *m.* savage.
salvajez [sal·ba·xés] *f.* wildness, savagery.
salvajismo [sal·ba·xíz·mo] *m.* savagery; *Am.* savage

act or remark. *See* **salvajada.**
salvamento [sal·ba·mén·to] *m.* salvation, rescue; place
of safety; salvage (*rescur of property*); **bote de** —
lifeboat.
salvar [sal·bár] *v.* (*librar*) to save; to except; to
exclude; (*vencer*) to clear, jump over; **-se** to be
saved; to save oneself, escape.
salvavidas [sal·ba·bí·das] *m.* life preserver; **lancha** —
lifeboat.
¡salve! [sál·be] *interj.* hail!; **Salve** [sál·be] *f.* Salve
Regina, prayer to the Virgin Mary.
salvia [sal·bja] *f.* sage (*a plant*).
salvo [sál·bo] *adj.* saved; safe; *prep.* save, except
but; **a** — safe, without injury; **en** — in safety; out
of danger.
salvoconducto [sal·bo·kon·dúk·to] *m.* safe-conduct,
pass.
san [san] *adj.* (*contr. of santo*) saint.
sanalotodo [sa·na·lo·tó·do] *m.* cure-all.
sanar [sa·nár] *v.* to heal, cure; to recover, get well.
sanatorio [sa·na·tó·rjo] *m.* sanitarium.
sanción [san·sjón] *f.* sanction.
sancionar [san·sjo·nár] *v.* to sanction; to authorize,
ratify.
sancochar [saŋ·ko·čár] *v.* to parboil.
sancocho [saŋ·kó·čo] *m.* parboiled meat.
sandalia [san·dá·lja] *f.* sandal.
sandez [san·dés] *f.* stupidity; folly; foolish remark.
sandía [san·dí·a] *f.* watermelon.
sandio [san·dí·o] *adj.* silly, foolish.
saneamiento [sa·ne·a·mjén·to] *m.* sanitation; drainage
of land.
sanear [sa·ne·ár] *v.* to make sanitary (*land, property,
etc.*); to drain, dry up (*land*).
sangrar [saŋ·gár] *v.* to bleed; to drain; to tap (*a
tree*); to pilfer; to exploit (*someone*); to indent (*a
line*).
sangre [sáŋ·gre] *f.* blood; — **fría** calmness, coolness
of mind; **a** — **fría** in cold blood.
sangría [saŋ·grí·a] *f.* a refreshing Spanish drink made
of red wine, fruit juice, and sugar.
sangriento [saŋ·grjén·to] *adj.* bleeding; bloody;
bloodstained; bloodthirsty, cruel.
sanguijuela [saŋ·gi·xwé·la] *f.* leech.
sanguinario [saŋ·gi·ná·rjo] *adj.* bloody, cruel;
bloodthirsty, murderous.
sanidad [sa·ni·dád] *f.* health; soundness;
healthfulness; sanitation; — **pública** health
department.
sanitario [sa·ni·tá·rjo] *adj.* sanitary.
sano [sá·no] *adj.* (*de salud*) sound, healthy; healthful;
sane, sensible; (*íntegro*) whole; unbroken;
undamaged; — **y salvo** safe and sound.
sanseacabó [san·se·a·ka·bó] that's all; that's the end.
santiamén [san·tja·mén]: **en un** — in a jiffy.
santidad [san·ti·dád] *f.* sanctity, holiness, saintliness;
su Santidad his Holiness.
santificar[6] [san·ti·fi·kár] *v.* to sanctify; to consecrate.
santiguar[8] [san·ti·gwár] *v.* to bless; to make the sign
of the cross; to beat, hit, punish; **-se** to cross
oneself; to show astonishment (*by crossing
oneself*).
santísimo [san·tí·si·mo] *adj.* most holy; *m.* the Holy
Sacrament.
santo [sán·to] *adj.* saintly, holy; sacred; **esperar todo
el** — **día** to wait the whole blessed day; — **y
bueno** well and good; *Ríopl., Col., Ven., Mex.,
Carib., Andes* **¡santa palabra!** that's my final and
last word! *m.* saint; saint's day; *Mex., Ven.* **tener
el** — **de espaldas** to have a streak of bad luck;
santurrón *m.* religious hypocrite, affectedly pious

person.

santuario [san·twá·rjo] *m.* sanctuary; *Col.* buried treasure; *Am.* Indian idol.

saña [sá·ña] *f.* fury, rage.

sañudo [sa·ñú·do] *adj.* furious, enraged.

sapo [sá·po] *m.* toad; *Col.* despicable little man; *Col.* chubby person; *Mex., Ch.* sly person; **echar -s y culebras** to swear, curse.

saque [sá·ke] *m.* serve, service (*in tennis*); server.

saquear [sa·ke·ár] *v.* to sack, plunder, pillage, loot.

saqueo [sa·ké·o] *m.* sacking, pillaging, plunder; loot, booty.

saquillo [sa·kí·yo] *m.* small bag, handbag, satchel.

sarampión [sa·ram·pjón] *m.* measles.

sarao [sa·rá·o] *m.* soirée, evening party.

sarape [sa·rá·pe] *m. Mex.* serape, blanket.

sarcasmo [sar·káz·mo] *m.* sarcasm.

sarcástico [sar·kás·ti·ko] *adj.* sarcastic.

sarcófago [sar·kó·fa·ġo] *m.* sarcophagus.

sardina [sar·đí·na] *f.* sardine.

sardo [sár·đo] *adj.* Sardinian.

sargento [sar·xén·to] *m.* sergeant.

sarmentoso [sar·men·tó·so] *adj.* vinelike; full of vine shoots; gnarled, knotty.

sarmiento [sar·mjén·to] *m.* shoot or branch of a vine.

sarna [sár·na] *f.* itch; mange.

sarnoso [sar·nó·so] *adj.* itchy, scabby, mangy.

sarpullido [sar·pu·yí·đo] = **salpullido.**

sarro [sá·rro] *m.* tartar (*on teeth*); crust, sediment (*in utensils*).

sarta [sár·ta] *f.* string (*of beads*); series.

sartén [sar·tén] *f.* frying pan; **sartencillo** skillet.

sastre [sás·tre] *m.* tailor.

sastrería [sas·tre·rí·a] *f.* tailor shop.

satánico [sa·tá·ni·ko] *adj.* satanic, devilish.

satélite [sa·té·li·te] *m.* satellite; suburban development; **— artificial** artificial satellite.

satén [sa·tén] *m.* sateen.

sátira [sá·ti·ra] *f.* satire.

satírico [sa·tí·ri·ko] *adj.* satirical.

satirizar[9] [sa·ti·ri·sár] *v.* to satirize.

satisfacción [sa·tis·fak·sjón] *f.* satisfaction; apology, excuse; **tomar —** to vindicate oneself; to take revenge; **dar una —** to offer an apology; to apologize.

satisfacer[31] [sa·tis·fa·sér] *v. irr.* to satisfy; to pay (*a debt*); **— una letra** to honor a draft; **-se** to be satisfied; to take satisfaction.

satisfactorio [sa·tis·fak·tó·rjo] *adj.* satisfactory.

satisfecho [sa·tis·fé·čo] *p.p. of* **satisfacer** satisfied, gratified; *adj.* content, contented.

saturar [sa·tu·rár] *v.* to saturate; to satiate.

sauce [sáw·se] *m.* willow.

savia [sá·bja] *f.* sap.

saxófono [sak·só·fo·no] *m.* saxophone; also **saxofón** [sak·so·fón], *adj. f.* (*época*) season, opportune time; (*sabor*) taste, flavor; ripeness; **a la —** then, at that time; **en —** in season; ripe; opportunely; *adj. Ríopl., Mex., Cuba* ripe.

sazonado [sa·so·ná·đo] *adj. & p.p.* seasoned; mellow, ripe; expressive (*said of a phrase*).

sazonar [sa·so·nár] *v.* to season; to flavor; **-se** to become seasoned; to ripen, mature.

se [se] *obj. pron.* (*before* **le, la, lo, las,** *and* **los**) to him, to her; to you (*formal*); to them; *refl. pron.* himself, herself, yourself (*formal*), yourselves (*formal*) themselves; *reciprocal pron.* each other, one another.

sebo [sé·bo] *m.* tallow, fat; suet.

seboso [se·bó·so] *adj.* fatty; tallowy.

secador [se·ka·đór] *m. Am.* dryer (*clothes, hair*); *Arg.*

towel.

secante [se·kán·te] *adj.* drying, blotting; **papel —** blotter; *f.* secant (*math.*).

secar[6] [se·kár] *v.* to dry; to wipe dry; **-se** to dry or wipe oneself; to dry up; to wither; to get thin.

sección [sek·sjón] *f.* section; division; cutting.

seccionar [sek·sjo·nár] *v.* to section.

seco [sé·ko] *adj.* (*sin humedad*) dry; dried; withered; (*áspero*) harsh; abrupt; plain, unadorned; **en —** on dry land, out of the water; **parar en —** to stop short, stop suddenly; **a secas** plain; alone, without anything else; *Mex., Carib., Ríopl., Andes* simply, straight to the point; **comer pan a secas** to eat just bread; *Mex., Ven.* **bailar a secas** to dance without musical accompaniment.

secreción [se·kre·sjón] *f.* secretion.

secretar [se·kre·tár] *v.* to secrete.

secretaría [se·kre·ta·rí·a] *f.* secretary's office; position of secretary.

secretariado [se·kre·ta·rjá·đo] *m.* secretariat.

secretario [se·kre·tá·rjo] *m.* secretary; confidant; **secretaria** [se·kre·ta·rja] *f.* woman secretary; secretary's wife.

secretear [se·kre·te·ár] *v.* to whisper; **-se** to whisper to each other.

secreto [se·kré·to] *adj.* secret, hidden; secretive; *m.* secret; secrecy; secret place; **— a voces** open secret; **en —** secretly; **hablar en —** to whisper.

secta [sék·ta] *f.* sect.

sector [sek·tór] *m.* sector.

secuaz [se·kwás] *m.* partisan, follower.

secuela [se·kwé·la] *f.* sequel, outcome, consequence.

secuencia [se·kwén·sja] *f.* sequence.

secuestrador [se·kwes·tra·đór] *m.* kidnapper; confiscator.

secuestrar [se·kwes·trár] *v.* to seize; to kidnap; to confiscate.

secuestro [se·kwés·tro] *m.* kidnapping; seizure.

secular [se·ku·lár] *adj.* secular; lay, worldly; centennial; *m.* secular, secular priest.

secundar [se·kun·dár] *v.* to second, favor, back up.

secundario [se·kun·dá·rjo] *adj.* secondary.

sed [sed] *f.* thirst; craving, desire; **tener —** to be thirsty.

seda [sé·đa] *f.* silk; **como una —** soft as silk; sweet-tempered; smoothly, easily.

sedal [se·đál] *m.* fishing line.

sedán [se·đán] *m.* sedan.

sedativo [se·đa·tí·bo] *adj. & m.* sedative.

sede [sé·đe] *f.* seat, see; **Santa Sede** Holy See.

sedentario [se·đen·tá·rjo] *adj.* sedentary.

sedeño [se·đé·ño] *adj.* silky, silken.

sedería [se·đe·rí·a] *f.* silk goods; silk shop.

sedero [se·đé·ro] *m.* silk dealer or weaver; *adj.* silk, pertaining to silk; **industria sedera** silk industry.

sedición [se·đi·sjón] *f.* sedition.

sedicioso [se·đi·sjó·so] *adj.* seditious, turbulent.

sediento [se·đjén·to] *adj.* thirsty; dry, parched; anxious, desirous.

sedimento [se·đi·mén·to] *m.* sediment; dregs, grounds.

sedoso [se·đó·so] *adj.* silken, silky.

seducción [se·đuk·sjón] *f.* seduction.

seducir[25] [se·đu·sír] *v. irr.* to seduce; to entice; to charm.

seductivo [se·đuk·tí·bo] *adj.* seductive, alluring; inviting, enticing.

seductor [se·đuk·tór] *adj.* tempting, fascinating; *m.* seducer; tempter; charming person.

sefardí [se·far·đí] *adj.* Sephardic; *m.* Spanish-speaking Jew.

SA

segador [se·ga·dór] *m.* harvester, reaper; **segadora** [se·ga·dó·ra] *f.* harvester, mowing machine; woman reaper.

segar[1, 7] [se·gár] *v. irr.* to mow, reap; to cut off.

seglar [se·glár] *adj.* secular, lay; *m.* layman.

segmento [seg·mén·to] *m.* segment.

segregar[7] [se·gre·gár] *v. irr.* to segregate.

seguida [se·gí·da] *f.* succession; series, continuation; **de** — without interruption, continuously; **en** — at once, immediately.

seguido [se·gí·do] *p.p.* followed; continued; *adj.* continuous; straight, direct; *adv.* without interruption; *Am.* often; *Col., Ven.* **de** — at once, immediately.

seguidor [se·gi·dór] *m.* follower.

seguimiento [se·gi·mjén·to] *m.* pursuit.

seguir[5, 12] [se·gír] *v. irr.* to follow; to continue; to pursue; **-se** to follow as a consequence.

según [se·gún] *prep.* according to; *conj.* as; according to; — **y conforme** (*or* — **y como**) exactly as, just as; that depends.

segundar [se·gun·dár] *v.* to repeat a second time; to second.

segundero [se·gun·dé·ro] *m.* second hand (*of a watch or clock*).

segundo [se·gún·do] *adj. & m.* second.

segundón [se·gun·dón] *m.* second child.

seguridad [se·gu·ri·dád] *f.* security; safety; certainty; **alfiler de** — safety pin.

seguro [se·gú·ro] *adj.* secure; sure, certain; safe; *Ríopl., Mex., Carib., Andes* honest, trustworthy; *m.* assurance; insurance; safety device; **a buen** — (**al** —, *or* **de** —) truly, certainly; **en** — in safety; **sobre** — without risk; without taking a chance; *Am.* **irse uno del** — to lose one's temper; *Ch., Mex., Cuba, Andes* **a la segura** without risk.

seibó [sej·bó] *m. Cuba, Ven.* sideboard, hutch.

seis [sejs] *num.* six.

selección [se·lek·sjón] *f.* selection choice.

seleccionar [se·lek·sjo·nár] *v.* to select, choose.

selecto [se·lék·to] *adj.* select, choice.

selenio [se·lé·njo] *m.* selenium.

selectivo [se·lek·tí·bo] *adj.* selective.

selva [sél·ba] *f.* forest; jungle.

sellar [se·yár] *v.* (*imprimir*) to stamp; to seal; (*cerrar*) to close tightly, seal; (*concluir*) to conclude.

sello [sé·yo] *m.* seal; stamp; *Arg.* official stamped paper.

semáforo [se·má·fo·ro] *m.* traffic light.

semana [se·má·na] *f.* week; week's wages; **días de** — week days; **entre** — during the week.

semanal [se·ma·nál] *adj.* weekly; **-mente** *adv.* weekly, every week.

semanario [se·ma·ná·rjo] *m.* weekly publication; *adj.* weekly.

semblante [sem·blán·te] *m.* countenance; facial expression; appearance.

semblanza [sem·blán·sa] *f.* portrait, literary sketch.

sembrado [sem·brá·do] *m.* sown ground; cultivated field.

sembradora [sem·bra·dó·ra] *f.* seeder, sowing machine.

sembrar[1] [sem·brár] *v. irr.* to sow; to scatter.

semejante [se·me·xán·te] *adj.* similar, like; such a; *m.* fellow man; **nuestros -s** our fellow men.

semejanza [se·me·xán·sa] *f.* resemblance, similarity; simile; **a** — **de** in the manner of.

semejar [se·me·xár] *v.* to resemble; **-se** to resemble.

semental [se·men·tál] *adj.* sowing (*crops*); breeding (*animals*); used as stud.

semestre [se·més·tre] *m.* semester.

semiconsonante [se·mi·kon·so·nán·te] *f.* semiconsonant.

semiduplex [se·mi·du·plés] *m.* (*computadora*) half duplex.

semilla [se·mí·ya] *f.* seed.

semillero [se·mi·yé·ro] *m.* seed bed; plant nursery; — **de vicios** hotbed of vice.

seminario [se·mi·ná·rjo] *m.* seminary; plant nursery, seed plot.

semítico [se·mí·ti·ko] *adj.* Semitic.

semivocal [se·mi·bo·kál] *f.* semivowel.

sempiterno [sem·pi·tér·no] *adj.* everlasting; evergreen.

senado [se·ná·do] *m.* senate.

senador [se·na·dór] *m.* senator.

sencillez [sen·si·yés] *f.* simplicity; plainness.

sencillo [sen·sí·yo] *adj.* simple; easy; plain; unadorned; unaffected; *m.* loose change, small coins.

senda [sén·da] *f.* path; way, course.

sendero [sen·dé·ro] *m.* path.

sendos [sén·dos] *adj. pl.* one for each of two or more persons or things.

senectud [se·nek·túd] *f.* senility, old age.

senil [se·níl] *adj.* senile.

seno [sé·no] *m.* (*pecho*) breast, bosom; (*hueco*) cavity, hollow; womb; lap; cove, bay; innermost recess; sinus (*cavity in a bone*); sine (*math.*); *C.A.* armpit.

sensación [sen·sa·sjón] *f.* sensation.

sensacional [sen·sa·sjo·nál] *adj.* sensational.

sensatez [sen·sa·tés] *f.* prudence, common sense.

sensato [sen·sá·to] *adj.* sensible, wise, prudent.

sensibilidad [sen·si·bi·li·dád] *f.* sensibility; sensitiveness.

sensible [sen·sí·ble] *adj.* sensitive; perceptible; regrettable.

sensitivo [sen·si·tí·bo] *adj.* sensitive.

sensual [sen·swál] *adj.* sensual; sensuous.

sensualidad [sen·swa·li·dád] *f.* sensuality; lewdness.

sentada [sen·tá·da] *f.* sitting; **de una** — at one sitting.

sentado [sen·tá·do] *adj.* seated, sitting; **dar por** — to take for granted.

sentar[1] [sen·tár] *v. irr.* to seat; to set; to establish; to become, suit, fit; to agree with one (*as food or climate*); **-se** to sit down; to settle down; *Col.* **-se en la palabra** to do all the talking, monopolize the conversation.

sentencia [sen·tén·sja] *f.* sentence; verdict; judgment, maxim, proverb; statement.

sentenciar [sen·ten·sjár] *v.* to sentence; to pass judgment on; to decide.

sentido [sen·tí·do] *p.p.* felt; experienced; *adj.* heartfelt, filled with feeling; sensitive; touchy; **darse por** — to take offense; to have one's feelings hurt; **estar** — **con alguien** to be offended or peeved at someone; *m.* sense; meaning; judgment; **aguzar el** — to prick up one's ears; **perder el** — to faint.

sentimental [sen·ti·men·tál] *adj.* sentimental.

sentimentalismo [sen·ti·men·ta·líz·mo] *m.* sentimentalism, sentimentality.

sentimiento [sen·ti·mjén·to] *m.* sentiment; sensation, feeling; grief, regret.

sentir[3] [sen·tír] *v. irr.* to feel; to sense; to hear; to regret; **-se** to feel (*well, strong, sad, etc.*); to feel oneself, consider oneself; to feel resentment; to feel a pain; **sin** — without being realized or felt; inadvertently; unnoticed; *m.* feeling; judgment, opinion.

señá [se·ñá] *C.A., Ven., Col. familiar contraction of* **señora.**

seña [sé·ña] *f.* sign, mark; signal; password; **-s** address (*name and place of residence*); **por mas -s** as an additional proof.

señal [se·ñál] *f.* (*marca*) sign, mark; signal; trace, vestige; scar; (*indicio*) reminder; indication; token, pledge; *Riopl., Andes* earmark, brand (*on the ear of livestock*); **en — de** in proof of, in token of.

señalar [se·ña·lár] *v.* to mark; to point out; to indicate; to determine, fix; to appoint; to signal; to assign; *Am.* to earmark, brand (*cattle*); **-se** to distinguish oneself.

señero [se·ñé·ro] *adj.* unique.

señor [se·ñór] *m.* mister; sir; owner; master, lord; gentleman; **el Señor** the Lord.

señora [se·ñó·ra] *f.* lady; madam; mistress; Mrs.

señorear [se·ño·re·ár] *v.* to lord it over, domineer; to dominate; to master, control.

señoría [se·ño·rí·a] *f.* lordship.

señoril [se·no·ríl] *adj.* lordly.

señorío [se·ño·rí·o] *m.* dominion, rule; domain of a lord; lordship; dignity; mastery, control; body of noblemen.

señorita [se·ño·rí·ta] *f.* miss; young lady.

señorito [se·ño·rí·to] *m.* master, young gentleman.

señuelo [se·ñwé·lo] *m.* decoy; lure, bait; *Ven.* leading or guiding oxen.

separación [se·pa·ra·sjón] *f.* separation.

separado [se·pa·rá·do] *p.p. & adj.* separate; separated; **por —** separately.

separar [se·pa·rár] *v.* to separate; to set aside; to remove (*from*); to dismiss (*from*); **-se** to separate; to retire, resign; to withdraw, leave.

separata [se·pa·rá·ta] *f.* reprint; offprint.

septentrional [sep·ten·trjo·nál] *adj.* northern.

septiembre [sep·tjém·bre] *m.* September.

sepulcral [se·pul·král] *adj.* sepulchral (*pertaining to sepulchers or tombs*); **lápida —** tombstone.

sepulcro [se·púl·kro] *m.* sepulcher, tomb, grave.

sepultar [se·pul·tár] *v.* to bury; to hide.

sepultura [se·pul·tú·ra] *f.* burial; grave; **dar —** to bury.

sepulturero [se·pul·tu·ré·ro] *m.* gravedigger.

sequedad [se·ke·dád] *f.* dryness; gruffness.

sequía [se·kí·a] *f.* drought.

séquito [sé·ki·to] *m.* retinue, following.

ser[44] [ser] *v. irr.* to be; to exist; to happen, occur; **— de** (*or* **para**) **ver** to be worth seeing; *m.* being; essence, nature; existence; *Am.* **estar en un —** to be always in the same condition.

serafín [se·ra·fín] *m.* seraph.

serenar [se·re·nár] *v.* to pacify; to calm down; *Col.* to drizzle, rain gently; **-se** to become serene, calm down; to clear up (*said of the weather*).

serenata [se·re·ná·ta] *f.* serenade.

serenidad [se·re·ni·dád] *f.* serenity, calm.

sereno [se·ré·no] *adj.* serene, calm; clear, cloudless; *m.* night humidity, dew; night watchman; **al —** in the night air.

serie [sé·rje] *f.* series.

seriedad [se·rje·dád] *f.* seriousness; gravity; earnestness; dignity.

serio [sé·rjo] *adj.* serious; grave; earnest; dignified; formal; **en —** seriously.

sermón [ser·món] *m.* sermon; reproof.

sermonear [ser·mo·ne·ár] *v.* to preach; to admonish, reprimand.

serpentear [ser·pen·te·ár] *v.* to wind, twist, turn, zigzag.

serpentín [ser·pen·tín] *m.* coil.

serpentino [ser·pen·tí·no] *adj.* serpentine.

serpiente [ser·pjén·te] *f.* serpent, snake.

serrado [se·rrá·do] *adj.* toothed, notched (*like a saw*); jagged.

serrana [se·rrá·na] *f.* mountain girl; **serranilla** [se·rra·ní·ya] *f.* lyric poem with a rustic theme.

serranía [se·rra·ní·a] *f.* mountainous region; chain of mountains.

serrano [se·rrá·no] *m.* mountaineer; *adj.* of, pertaining to, or from the mountains.

serrar [se·rrár] = **aserrar.**

serrín [se·rrín] *m.* sawdust.

serrucho [se·rrú·čo] *m.* handsaw.

servible [ser·bí·ble] *adj.* serviceable, useful.

servicial [ser·bi·sjál] *adj.* helpful, obliging.

servicio [ser·bí·sjo] *m.* service; table service; tea or coffee set; chamber pot; *Am.* toilet, water closet.

servidor [ser·bi·dór] *m.* servant; waiter; **— de Vd.** at your service; **su seguro —** yours truly.

servidumbre [ser·bi·dúm·bre] *f.* domestic help, servants; servitude, slavery; service.

servil [ser·bíl] *adj.* servile; **servilón** [ser·bi·lón] *adj.* very servile; *m.* bootlicker, great flatterer.

servilismo [ser·bi·líz·mo] *m.* servility, servile behavior or attitude, servile submission.

servilleta [ser·bi·yé·ta] *f.* napkin.

servir[5] [ser·bír] *v. irr.* to serve; to be of use; **— de** to serve as, act as; to be used as; **— para** to be good for; to be used for; **-se** to serve or help oneself; to be pleased to; **-se de** to make use of; **sírvase Vd. hacerlo** please do it.

sésamo [sé·sa·mo] *m.* sesame.

sesenta [se·sén·ta] *num.* sixty.

seseo [se·sé·o] *m.* pronunciation of all sibilants as /s/.

sesgado [sez·gá·do] *adj.* slanting, oblique, bias.

sesgar[7] [sez·gár] *v.* to slant; to cut on the bias; to follow an oblique line.

sesgo [séz·go] *m.* bias; slant; diagonal cut; turn; **al —** on the bias; diagonally, obliquely.

sesión [se·sjón] *f.* session; meeting, conference.

seso [sé·so] *m.* brain; wisdom, intelligence; **devanarse los -s** to rack one's brain.

sestear [ses·te·ár] *v.* to snooze, take a nap.

sesudo [se·sú·do] *adj.* sensible, wise, prudent; *Mex., C.A.* stubborn.

seta [sé·ta] *f.* mushroom.

setenta [se·tén·ta] *num.* seventy.

setiembre [se·tjém·bre] *m. Spain* preferred form for **septiembre.**

sétimo [sé·ti·mo] *adj. Spain* preferred form for **séptimo.**

seto [sé·to] *m.* fence; hedge.

seudónimo [sew·dó·ni·mo] *m.* pseudonym, pen name.

severidad [se·be·ri·dád] *f.* severity; strictness; seriousness.

severo [se·bé·ro] *adj.* severe; strict; stern.

sevillano [se·bi·yá·no] *adj.* of, from, or pertaining to Seville, Spain.

sexo [sék·so] *m.* sex.

sexual [sek·swál] *adj.* sexual.

si [si] *conj.* if; whether; **¡ — ya te lo dije!** but I already told you!; **— bien** although; **por — acaso** just in case.

sí [si] *adv.* yes; **— que** certainly, really; **un — es no es a** trifle, somewhat; **¡si, fuí!** I did go!; *m.* assent, consent; *refl. pron.* (*used after a prep.*) himself, herself, yourself (*formal*), themselves; **de por —** separately, by itself; **estar sobre —** to be on the alert.

sibilante [si·bi·lán·te] *adj.* sibilant, whistling.

sicología [si·ko·lo·xí·a] *f.* psychology.

sicológico [si·ko·ló·xi·ko] *adj.* psychological.

SE

sicólogo [si·kó·lo·ǥo] *m*. psychologist.

sicosis [si·kó·sis] *f*. psychosis.

siderurgia [si·de·rúr·xja] *f*. iron and steel industry.

sidra [sí·dra] *f*. cider.

siega [sjé·ǥa] *f*. reaping, mowing; harvesting; harvest, harvest season.

siembra [sjém·bra] *f*. sowing; seedtime, sowing time; sown field.

siempre [sjém·pre] *adv*. always; *Mex., C.A., Col., Andes* in any case, anyway; **para** (*or* **por**) — forever, for always; **por — jamás** forever and ever; **— que** whenever; provided that; *Am*. **— sí me voy** I've decided to go anyway.

siempreviva [sjem·pre·bí·ba] *f*. evergreen; everlasting.

sien [sjen] *f*. temple (*of the forehead*).

sierpe [sjér·pe] *f*. serpent, snake.

sierra [sjé·rra] *f*. saw; **— caladora** jigsaw; **— para metales** hacksaw; **— sin fin** bandsaw; (*cordillera*) mountain range.

siervo [sjér·bo] *m*. serf; slave; servant.

siesta [sjés·ta] *f*. siesta, afternoon nap; early afternoon; **dormir la —** to take an afternoon nap.

siete [sjé·te] *num*. seven.

sifón [si·fón] *m*. siphon; siphon bottle; trap (*in plumbing fixtures*).

sigilo [si·xí·lo] *m*. secret; secrecy.

sigla [sí·ǥla] *f*. initial abbreviation.

siglo [sí·ǥlo] *m*. century; period, epoch; the world; worldly matters.

significación [siǥ·ni·fi·ka·sjón] *f*. meaning; significance.

significado [siǥ·ni·fi·ká·do] *m*. significance, meaning.

significar[6] [siǥ·ni·fi·kár] *v*. to signify; to mean; to make known, show; to matter, have importance.

significativo [siǥ·ni·fi·ka·tí·bo] *adj*. significant.

signo [síǥ·no] *m*. sign; mark; symbol.

siguiente [si·ǥjén·te] *adj*. following.

sílaba [sí·la·ba] *f*. syllable.

silabario [si·la·bá·rjo] *m*. speller, spelling book.

silabear [si·la·be·ár] *v*. to syllabicate.

silbar [sil·bár] *v*. to whistle; to hiss.

silbato [sil·bá·to] *m*. whistle.

silbido [sil·bí·do] *m*. whistle; hiss.

silenciador [si·len·sja·dór] *m*. silencer; muffler (*of an automobile*).

silencio [si·lén·sjo] *m*. silence; pause; *adj*. *Am*. silent, quiet, motionless.

silencioso [si·len·sjó·so] *adj*. silent, quiet.

silicio [si·lí·sjo] *m*. silicon.

silo [sí·lo] *m*. silo; cave.

silogismo [si·lo·xíz·mo] *m*. syllogism.

silueta [si·lwé·ta] *f*. silhouette.

silvestre [sil·bés·tre] *adj*. wild, uncultivated.

silvicultor [sil·bi·kul·tór] *m*. forester; **silvicultura** [sil·bi·kul·tú·ra] *f*. forestry.

silla [sí·ya] *f*. chair; saddle; **— de montar** saddle; *Ven*. **— de balanza** rocking chair. *See* **mecedora.**

sillón [si·yón] *m*. large chair; easy chair; *Am*. **— de hamaca** rocking chair.

sima [sí·ma] *f*. chasm, abyss.

simbólico [sim·bó·li·ko] *adj*. symbolic.

simbolismo [sim·bo·líz·mo] *m*. symbolism.

símbolo [sím·bo·lo] *m*. symbol; **— de la fe** (*or* **de los Apóstoles**) the Apostle's creed; **— de status** status symbol.

simetría [si·me·trí·a] *f*. symmetry.

simétrico [si·mé·tri·ko] *adj*. symmetrical.

simiente [si·mjén·te] *f*. seed.

símil [sí·mil] *m*. simile; similarity; *adj*. similar.

similar [si·mi·lár] *adj*. similar.

simpatía [sim·pa·tí·a] *f*. attraction, attractiveness;

accord, harmony; liking.

simpático [sim·pá·ti·ko] *adj*. sympathetic, congenial; pleasant, agreeable, nice.

simpatizar[9] [sim·pa·ti·sár] *v*. to be attractive to; to get on well with; to be congenial; **no me simpatiza** I don't like him or her.

simple [sím·ple] *adj*. simple; mere; plain; pure, unmixed; naïve, innocent; silly, foolish; *m*. simpleton.

simpleza [sim·plé·sa] *f*. simplicity; simpleness, stupidity, foolishness.

simplicidad [sim·pli·si·dád] *f*. simplicity; candor.

simplificar[6] [sim·pli·fi·kár] *v*. to simplify.

simplista [sim·plís·ta] *adj*. simplistic; *m. & f*. a person who is inclined to oversimplify.

simplón [sim·plón] *m*. simpleton.

simposio [sim·pó·sjo] *m*. symposium.

simulacro [si·mu·lá·kro] *m*. mimic battle, sham or mock battle; image, vision.

simular [si·mu·lár] *v*. to simulate, feign.

simultáneo [si·mul·tá·ne·o] *adj*. simultaneous.

sin [sin] *prep*. without; besides, not counting; **— que** *conj*. without; **— embargo** nevertheless, still, yet; **— qué ni para qué** without rhyme or reason.

sinagoga [si·na·ǥó·ǥa] *f*. synagogue.

sinapismo [si·na·píz·mo] *m*. mustard plaster; irritating person, nuisance, pest, bore.

sincerar [sin·se·rár] *v*. to square, justify, excuse; **-se** to square oneself (with), justify oneself (with).

sinceridad [sin·se·ri·dád] *f*. sincerity.

sincero [sin·sé·ro] *adj*. sincere.

síncopa [sín·ko·pa] *f*. syncopation; syncope.

sincronizar[9] [sin·kro·ni·sár] *v*. *irr*. to synchronize.

sindicar[6] [sin·di·kár] *v*. to syndicate; **-se** to syndicate, form a syndicate.

sindicato [sin·di·ká·to] *m*. syndicate; labor union.

síndico [sín·di·ko] *m*. receiver (*person appointed to take charge of property under litigation or to liquidate a bankrupt business*); trustee.

sinecura [si·ne·kú·ra] *f*. sinecure (*easy and well paid position*).

sinfonía [sin·fo·ní·a] *f*. symphony.

singular [sin·gu·lár] *adj*. singular; unique; striking; odd, strange.

singularizar[9] [sin·gu·la·ri·sár] *v*. to single out, choose; to distinguish; **-se** to distinguish oneself; to be singled out.

siniestro [si·njés·tro] *adj*. sinister; left (*side*); *m*. unforeseen loss, damage; **siniestra** [si·njés·tra] *f*. left hand; left-hand side.

sinnúmero [sin·nú·me·ro] *m*. great number, endless number.

sino [sí·no] *conj*. but; *prep*. except; **no hace — lo que le mandan** he only does what he is told; **— que** *conj*. but; *m*. fate, destiny.

sinónimo [si·nó·ni·mo] *m*. synonym; *adj*. synonymous.

sinrazón [sin·rra·són] *f*. injustice, wrong.

sinsabor [sin·sa·bór] *m*. displeasure; trouble, grief, distress.

sintaxis [sin·ták·sis] *f*. syntax.

síntesis [sín·te·sis] *f*. synthesis; summary.

sintético [sin·té·ti·ko] *adj*. synthetic.

sintetizar[9] [sin·te·ti·sár] *v*. to synthesize.

síntoma [sín·to·ma] *m*. sympton; indication, sign.

sintonizar[9] [sin·to·ni·sár] *v*. to tune in (on).

sinuoso [si·nwó·so] *adj*. sinuous, winding; wavy.

sinvergüenza [sim·ber·ǥwén·sa] *m. & f*. shameless person; scoundrel.

siquiatra [si·kjá·tra] *m. & f*. psychiatrist, alienist.

siquiatría [si·kja·trí·a] *f*. psychiatry.

siquiera [si·kjé·ra] *adv.* at least; even; **ni** — not even; *conj.* even though.

sirena [si·ré·na] *f.* siren; whistle, foghorn.

sirviente [sir·bjén·te] *m.* servant; waiter; **sirvienta** [sir·bjén·ta] *f.* housemaid; waitress.

sisa [sí·sa] *f.* petty theft; dart (*made in a garment*).

sisal [si·sál] *m. Am.* sisal or sisal hemp.

sisar [si·sár] *v.* to take in (*a garment*); to pilfer; to cheat out of, defraud.

sisear [si·se·ár] *v.* to hiss.

siseo [si·sé·o] *m.* hiss, hissing.

sistema [sis·té·ma] *m.* system; — **operativo** (*computadora*) operating sustem; — **binario** (*computadora*) binary system.

sistemático [sis·te·má·ti·ko] *adj.* systematic.

sitial [si·tjál] *m.* chair of a presiding officer; place of honor.

sitiar [si·tjár] *v.* to besiege; to surround.

sitio [sí·tjo] *m.* site, location; place, spot, space; siege; *Am.* cattle ranch; *Mex.* taxicab station; **poner** — **a** to lay siege to.

sito [sí·to] *adj.* situated, located.

situación [si·twa·sjón] *f.* situation; position; location; state, condition; *Mex., Carib., Ven., Col.* **hombre de la** — man of the hour, man of influence.

situado [si·twá·do] *p.p.* situated; placed.

situar[18] [si·twár] *v.* to locate; to place; **-se** to station oneself, place oneself; to be located, placed, situated.

snobismo [ez·no·bíz·mo] *m.* snobism (*in the European sense*); the tendency to try to do whatever seems to be in style.

so [so] *prep.* — **capa de** under the guise of; — **pena de** under penalty of; — **pretexto de** under the pretext of.

sobaco [so·bá·ko] *m.* armpit.

sobar [so·bár] *v.* (*ablandar*) to rub; to knead; to massage; to touch, handle; to fondle, pet; (*fastidiar*) to bother; to beat, slap; *Col., Ven., Mex.* to set bones; *Col.* to flay, skin; *Am.* to win (*in a fight*); *Am.* to tire out (*a horse*).

soberanía [so·be·ra·ní·a] *f.* sovereignty.

soberano [so·be·rá·no] *adj. & m.* sovereign.

soberbia [so·bér·bja] *f.* pride, arrogance; ostentation, pomp.

soberbio [so·ber·bjo] *adj.* proud, haughty, arrogant; pompous; (*excelente*) superb, magnificent; spirited (*horse*).

sobornar [so·bor·nár] *v.* to bribe.

soborno [so·bór·no] *m.* bribery; bribe; *Andes* overload (*on a pack animal*), extra load.

sobra [só·bra] *f.* surplus, excess; **-s** leftovers, leavings; **de** — more than enough; superfluous, unnecessary.

sobrado [so·brá·do] *m.* attic; loft; *Am.* pantry shelf; **-s** *Col., Ven.* leftovers, leavings; *adj.* leftover; excessive; superfluous; forward, brazen; **sobradas veces** many times, repeatedly.

sobrante [so·brán·te] *adj.* leftover, surplus, excess, spare; *m.* surplus, excess, remainder.

sobrar [so·brár] *v.* to exceed; to remain, be left over; to be more than enough.

sobre [só·bre] *prep.* (*encima de*) over; above; on, upon; (*acerca de*) about; approximately; besides; — **manera** excessively; **estar** — **sí** to be cautious, on the alert; — **que** besides, in addition to the fact that; *m.* envelope; address (*on an envelope*).

sobrecama [so·bre·ká·ma] *f.* bedspread.

sobrecarga [so·bre·kár·ga] *f.* overload; overburden.

sobrecargar[7] [so·bre·kar·gár] *v.* to overload; to overburden.

sobrecargo [so·bre·kár·go] *m.* purser (*on a ship*); *f.* airline hostess.

sobrecoger[11] [so·bre·ko·xér] *v.* to surprise, catch unaware; to startle; **-se** to be startled; **-se de miedo** to be seized with fear.

sobreentender[1] [so·bre·en·ten·dér] *v. irr.* to assume, understand; **-se** to be assumed, be obvious, be understood.

sobreescrito [so·bre·es·krí·to] *m.* address (*on an envelope*).

sobreesdrújulo [so·bre·ez·drú·xu·lo] *adj.* accented on syllable before antepenult.

sobreexcitación [so·bre·ek·si·ta·sjón] *f.* overexcitement; thrill.

sobreexcitar [so·bre·ek·si·tár] *v.* to overexcite.

sobregirar [so·bre·xi·rár] *v.* to overdraw.

sobrehumano [so·bre·u·má·no] *adj.* superhuman.

sobrellevar [so·bre·ye·bár] *v.* to endure, bear; to tolerate; to lighten (*another's burden*).

sobremesa [so·bre·mé·sa] *f.* table runner; after dinner conversation at the table; **de** — during the after dinner conversation.

sobrenadar [so·bre·na·dár] *v.* to float.

sobrenatural [so·bre·na·tu·rál] *adj.* supernatural.

sobrenombre [so·bre·nóm·bre] *m.* surname; nickname.

sobrepasar [so·bre·pa·sár] *v.* to exceed; to excel; **-se** to overstep, go too far.

sobreponer[40] [so·bre·po·nér] *v. irr.* to lay on top; **-se** to dominate oneself; **-se a** to overcome; to dominate.

sobrepuesto [so·bre·pwés·to] *p.p. of* **sobreponer**; *m.* appliqué (*trimming laid on a dress*); *C.A.* mend, patch.

sobrepujar [so·bre·pu·xár] *v.* to exceed, excel, surpass; to outweigh.

sobresaliente [so·bre·sa·ljén·te] *adj.* outstanding; projecting; excellent; *m. & f.* substitute (*a person*); understudy.

sobresalir[43] [so·bre·sa·lír] *v. irr.* to stand out; to project, jut out; to excel.

sobresaltar [so·bre·sal·tár] *v.* to startle, frighten; to assail; to stand out clearly **-se** to be startled, frightened.

sobresalto [so·bre·sál·to] *m.* start, scare, fright, shock; **de** — suddenly.

sobrestante [so·bres·tán·te] *m.* overseer; boss, foreman.

sobresueldo [so·bre·swél·do] *m.* overtime pay, extra pay or wages.

sobretodo [so·bre·tó·do] *m.* overcoat.

sobrevencer [so·bre·ben·sér] *v.* to be overdue.

sobrevenir[48] [so·bre·be·nír] *v. irr.* to happen, occur, come unexpectedly; to follow, happen after.

sobreviviente [so·bre·bi·bjén·te] *m. & f.* survivor; *adj.* surviving.

sobrevivir [so·bre·bi·bír] *v.* to survive.

sobriedad [so·brje·dád] *f.* sobriety, soberness, temperance, moderation.

sobrina [so·brí·na] *f.* niece.

sobrino [so·brí·no] *m.* nephew.

sobrio [só·brjo] *adj.* sober, temperate, moderate.

socarrar [so·ka·rrár] *v.* to sear, singe.

socarrón [so·ka·rrón] *adj.* cunning, sly, crafty.

socarronería [so·ka·rro·ne·rí·a] *f.* craftiness, slyness, cunning.

socavar [so·ka·bár] *v.* to dig under; to undermine.

socavón [so·ka·bón] *m.* tunnel; cave, cavern; underground passageway.

social [so·sjál] *adj.* social; sociable, friendly.

socialismo [so·sja·líz·mo] *m.* socialism.

SI

socialista [so·sja·lís·ta] *adj.* socialist, socialistic; *m. & f.* socialist.

sociedad [so·sje·ðáð] *f.* society; partnership; company, firm, corporation; — **anónima** (*or* — **por acciones**) stock company.

socio [só·sjo] *m.* associate, partner; member.

sociología [so·sjo·lo·xí·a] *f.* sociology.

socorrer [so·ko·rrér] *v.* to help, aid, assist.

socorro [so·kó·rro] *m.* help, aid, assistance, relief; *Am.* partial advance payment on a workman's wages.

sodio [só·ðjo] *m.* sodium.

sodomía [so·ðo·mí·a] *f.* sodomy.

soez [so·és] *adj.* low, vile, vulgar; coarse, ill-mannered.

sofá [so·fá] *m.* sofa, davenport.

sofocante [so·fo·kán·te] *adj.* suffocating, stifling.

sofocar[6] [so·fo·kár] *v.* to suffocate, choke; to smother; to bother; to embarrass.

sofoco [so·fó·ko] *m.* suffocation, choking; upset, annoyance; embarrassment.

sofrenar [so·fre·nár] *v.* to check; to control; to reprimand.

sofrito [so·frí·to] *m.* a preparation of lightly fried ingredients.

soga [só·ǥa] *f.* rope; *Ven., Col., Andes, Ch.* leather lasso or rope.

soja [só·xa] *f.* soy.

sojuzgamiento [so·xuz·ǥa·mjén·to] *m.* subjugation, subjection.

sojuzgar[7] [so·xuz·ǥár] *v.* to subjugate, subdue, subject.

sol [sol] *m.* sun; sunshine; sol (*fifth note of the scale*); sol (*monetary unit of Peru*); **de** — **a** — from sunrise to sunset; **hace** — it is sunny; **tomar el** — to bask in the sun; to enjoy the sunshine.

solana [so·lá·na] *f.* sunny place; sunroom; sun porch; intense sunlight; **solanera** [so·la·né·ra] *f.* sunburn; sunny place.

solapa [so·lá·pa] *f.* lapel.

solapado [so·la·pá·ðo] *adj.* sly, crafty, cunning, deceitful, underhanded.

solapo [so·lá·po] *m.* overlap.

solar [so·lár] *m.* lot, plot of ground; ancestral mansion, manor; *Carib., Mex.* tenement house; *Mex., Ven.* back yard; *Col.* town lot, field (*for growing alfalfa, corn, etc.*); *adj.* solar, of the sun.

solar[2] [so·lár] *v. irr.* to sole (*shoes*); to pave, floor.

solariego [so·la·rjé·ǥo] *adj.* manorial, pertaining to a manor; **casa solariega** ancestral manor or mansion.

solaz [so·lás] *m.* solace, comfort; relaxation, recreation.

solazar[9] [so·la·sár] *v.* to console, cheer, comfort; **-se** to seek relaxation or pleasure; to enjoy oneself.

soldado [sol·dá·ðo] *m.* soldier; — **raso** private; — **de línea** regular soldier.

soldadura [sol·da·ðú·ra] *f.* soldering; welding; — **autógena** arc welding; — **oxiacetilénica** oxyacetylene welding; solder.

soldar[2] [sol·dár] *v. irr.* to solder; to weld.

soleado [so·le·á·ðo] *adj.* sunny; *p.p.* sunned.

solear [so·le·ár] = **asolear.**

soledad [so·le·ðáð] *f.* solitude; loneliness; homesickness; lonely retreat.

solemne [so·lém·ne] *adj.* solemn; imposing; — **disparate** downright foolishness, huge blunder.

solemnidad [so·lem·ni·ðáð] *f.* solemnity; solemn ceremony.

soler[2, 51] [so·lér] *v. irr.* to have the custom of, be in the habit of.

solera [so·lé·ra] *f.* sill.

solfeo [sol·fé·o] *m.* sol-faing, solfeggio style.

solferino [sol·fe·rí·no] *adj.* reddish-purple.

solicitante [so·li·si·tán·te] *m. & f.* solicitor; applicant.

solicitar [so·li·si·tár] *v.* to solicit; to apply for; to beg, ask for; to court, woo.

solícito [so·lí·si·to] *adj.* solicitous, careful; anxious, concerned, diligent.

solicitud [so·li·si·túð] *f.* solicitude; care, concern, anxiety.

solidaridad [so·li·da·ri·ðáð] *f.* solidarity; union; bond, community of interests.

solidez [so·li·ðés] *f.* solidity; compactness.

solidificar[6] [so·li·ði·fi·kár] *v.* to solidify.

sólido [só·li·ðo] *adj.* solid; firm; strong; *m.* solid.

soliloquio [so·li·ló·kjo] *m.* soliloquy, monologue.

solista [so·lís·ta] *m. & f.* soloist.

solitario [so·li·tá·rjo] *adj.* solitary; lonely; *m.* recluse; hermit; solitaire (*card game*); solitaire (*gem set by itself*).

sólito [só·li·to] *adj.* customary.

sólito [só·li·to] *adj.* customary.

solo [só·lo] *adj.* sole, only; single; alone; lonely **a solas** alone; *m.* solo; **sólo** [só·lo] *adv.* only.

solomillo [so·lo·mí·yo], **solomo** [so·ló·mo] *m.* sirloin; loin; loin of pork (**lomo**).

solsticio [sols·tí·sjo] *m.* solstice.

soltar[2] [sol·tár] *v. irr.* to loosen, untie, unfasten; to let loose; to set free; to let go; to let out; to utter; **-se** to set oneself free; to come loose; to lose restraint; to loosen up; **-se a** to begin to, start to.

soltero [sol·té·ro] *adj.* single, unmarried; *m.* bachelor; **soltera** [sol·té·ra] *f.* spinster; **solterón** [sol·te·rón] *m.* old bachelor; **solterona** [sol·te·ró·na] *f.* old maid.

soltura [sol·tú·ra] *f.* looseness; freedom; facility; ease, agility, nimbleness; release (*of a prisoner*).

solución [so·lu·sjón] *f.* solution; loosening, untying.

solucionar [so·lu·sjo·nár] *v.* to solve, to resolve.

solventar [sol·ben·tár] *v.* to pay (*a bill*), settle (*an account*); to solve (*a problem or difficulty*).

sollozar[9] [so·yo·sár] *v.* to sob.

sollozo [so·yó·so] *m.* sob.

sombra [sóm·bra] *f.* (*oscuridad*) shadow; shade; darkness; (*abrigo*) shelter, protection; (*imagen*) image, reflection (*in the water*); *Am.* guide lines (*under writing paper*); *Ven.* awning, sunshade; **hacer** — to shade; to cast a shadow (on).

sombreado [som·bre·á·ðo] *adj.* shady; shaded.

sombrear [som·bre·ár] *v.* to shade; **-se** *Mex., Ven., Col.* to seek the shade, stand in the shade.

sombrerería [som·bre·re·rí·a] *f.* hat shop.

sombrero [som·bré·ro] *m.* hat; — **de copa** top hat, high hat; — **hongo** derby; — **de jipijapa** Panama hat; *C.A., Col., Ven.* — **de pelo** top hat.

sombrilla [som·brí·ya] *f.* parasol, sunshade.

sombrío [som·brí·o] *adj.* somber, gloomy; shady.

somero [so·mé·ro] *adj.* superficial, shallow; summary, concise.

someter [so·me·tér] *v.* to submit; to subject; **-se** to submit.

sometimiento [so·me·ti·mjén·to] *m.* submission; subjection.

somnolencia [som·no·lén·sja] *f.* drowsiness, sleepiness; **con** — sleepily.

son [son] *m.* sound; tune; rumor; **en** — **de guerra** in a warlike manner; **sin ton ni** — without rhyme or reason.

sonaja [so·ná·xa] *f.* jingles, tambourine (*to accompany certain dances*); rattle; **sonajero** [so·na·xé·ro] *m.* child's rattle.

sonámbulo [so·nám·bu·lo] *m.* sleepwalker.

sonante [so·nán·te] *adj.* sounding; ringing; sonorous; **en dinero — y contante** in hard cash.

sonar[2] [so·nár] *v. irr.* to sound; to ring; to sound familiar; **— a** to sound like; seem like; **-se** to blow one's nose; **suena que** it is rumored that.

sonda [són·da] *f.* plumb, string with lead weight (*for sounding the depth of water*); sounding; surgeon's probe.

sondar [son·dár] = **sondear.**

sondear [son·de·ár] *v.* to sound, fathom; to sound out; to probe; to examine into.

sondeo [son·dé·o] *m.* sounding, fathoming.

soneto [so·né·to] *m.* sonnet.

sonido [so·ní·do] *m.* sound.

sonoro [so·nó·ro] *adj.* sonorous; **consonante sonora** voiced consonant.

sonreír[15] [son·rre·ír] *v. irr.* to smile; **-se** to smile.

sonriente [son·rrjén·te] *adj.* smiling, beaming, radiant.

sonrisa [son·rrí·sa] *f.* smile.

sonrojarse [son·rro·xár·se] *v.* to blush.

sonrojo [son·rró·xo] *m.* blush.

sonrosado [son·rro·sá·do] *adj.* rosy.

sonsacar[6] [son·sa·kár] *v.* to lure away; to draw (*someone*) out; to extract (*a secret*); to take on the sly.

sonsonete [son·so·né·te] *m.* singsong; rhythmical tapping sound.

soñador [so·ña·dór] *m.* dreamer.

soñar[2] [so·ñár] *v. irr.* to dream; **— con** (*or* **— en**) to dream of; **— despierto** to daydream.

soñoliento [so·ño·ljén·to] *adj.* sleepy, drowsy.

sopa [só·pa] *f.* soup; **— juliana** julienne soup; sop; **estar hecho una —** to be sopping wet; *Am.* **es un -s** he is a fool.

sopapo [so·pá·po] *m.* chuck, tap, pat (*under the chin*); slap.

sopera [so·pé·ra] *f.* soup tureen.

sopero [so·pé·ro] *m.* soup dish.

sopesar [so·pe·sár] *v.* to weigh, consider.

sopetón [so·pe·tón] *m.* box, slap; **de —** all of a sudden, unexpectedly.

soplar [so·plár] *v.* (*despedir aire*) to blow; to blow away; to blow up, inflate; (*robar*) to swipe, steal; (*informar*) to prompt; to "squeal" on, inform against; *Col., Ven., Mex., Cuba, Andes* **— una bofetada** to strike a blow; **-se** to swell up, puff up; to eat up, gobble up; to gulp down; **se sopló el pastel** he gobbled up the pie; *Am.* **-se a uno** to deceive someone, get the best of someone.

soplete [so·plé·te] *m.* blow torch; blowpipe.

soplo [só·plo] *m.* (*de aire*) blowing; puff, gust of wind; breath; (*aviso*) whispered warning or advice; "squealing", informing; **en un —** in a jiffy, in a second.

soplón [so·plón] *m.* informer, "squealer" (*one who tells on someone*), tattletale.

sopor [so·pór] *m.* stupor; lethargy.

soportal [so·por·tál] *m.* arcade.

soportar [so·por·tár] *v.* to support, hold up, bear; to stand, endure, tolerate.

soporte [so·pór·te] *m.* support; (*computadora*) storage medium; **-s para el cabezal** arm braces (*machine*).

sorber [sor·bér] *v.* to sip; to suck; to swallow; to absorb; to snuff up one's nose.

sorbete [sor·bé·te] *m.* sherbet; fruit ice; *C.A., Mex., Ven.* cone, ice-cream cone; *Mex.* silk top hat.

sorbo [sór·bo] *m.* sip, swallow, gulp; sniff.

sordera [sor·dé·ra], **sordez** [sor·dés] *f.* deafness.

sórdido [sór·di·do] *adj.* sordid.

sordina [sor·dí·na] *f.* mute (*of a musical instrument*).

sordo [sór·do] *adj.* deaf; silent, noiseless; dull; muffled; **consonante sorda** voiceless consonant; *m.* deaf person; **hacerse el —** to pretend not to hear; to turn a deaf ear.

sordomudo [sor·do·mú·do] *adj.* deaf and dumb; *m.* deaf-mute.

sorna [sór·na] *f.* slyness, cunning; sneer.

soroche [so·ró·če] *m. Andes* shortness of breath, sickness caused by high altitude; *Am.* blush, flush.

sorprendente [sor·pren·dén·te] *adj.* surprising.

sorprender [sor·pren·dér] *v.* to surprise; **-se** to be surprised.

sorpresa [sor·pré·sa] *f.* surprise.

sortear [sor·te·ár] *v.* to draw lots; to raffle; to dodge; to shun; to fight (*bulls*) skillfully.

sorteo [sor·té·o] *m.* drawing or casting of lots; raffle.

sortija [sor·tí·xa] *f.* ring; finger ring; ringlet, curl.

sosa [só·sa] *f.* soda.

sosegado [so·se·gá·do] *adj.* calm, quiet, peaceful.

sosegar[1, 7] [so·se·gár] *v.* to calm, quiet; to be quiet; **-se** to quiet down.

sosiego [so·sjé·go] *m.* calm, peace, quiet.

soslayo [soz·lá·yo] **: al —** obliquely; slanting; on the bias; **de —** oblique, slanting; at a slant; sideways; **mirada de —** side glance; **pegar de —** to glance, hit at a slant.

soso [só·so] *adj.* flat, tasteless, insipid; dull, silly; awkward.

sospecha [sos·pé·ča] *f.* suspicion; mistrust.

sospechar [sos·pe·čár] *v.* to suspect; to mistrust.

sospechoso [sos·pe·čó·so] *adj.* suspicious; *m.* suspect.

sostén [sos·tén] *m.* support; prop; supporter; brassière.

sostener[45] [sos·te·nér] *v. irr.* to sustain; to hold; to support, maintain; to defend, uphold; to endure.

sostenido [sos·te·ní·do] *p.p. & adj.* sustained; supported, held up; *m.* sharp (*in music*).

sota [só·ta] *f.* jack (*at cards*); *m. Am.* foreman, boss, overseer.

sotana [so·tá·na] *f.* cassock (*black outer robe of a priest*).

sótano [só·ta·no] *m.* cellar, basement.

sotavento [so·ta·bén·to] *m.* leeward.

soterrar [so·te·rrár] *v.* to bury.

soto [só·to] *m.* grove; thicket.

sotreta [so·tré·ta] *m. Andes, Ríopl.* nag, old horse.

soviet [so·bjét] *m.* soviet; **soviético** [so·bjé·ti·ko] *adj.* soviet, of, or pertaining to, soviets.

sténcil [es·tén·sil] *m.* stencil.

suave [swá·be] *adj.* soft; smooth; mild; bland; gentle.

suavidad [swa·bi·dád] *f.* softness; smoothness; mildness; gentleness.

suavizar[9] [swa·bi·sár] *v.* to smooth; to soften.

subalterno [su·bal·tér·no] *adj. & m.* subordinate.

subarrendar [su·ba·rren·dár] *v.* to sublet.

subasta [su·bás·ta] *f.* public auction.

subastar [su·bás·tar] *v.* to sell at auction.

subconsciente [sub·kon·sjén·te] *adj.* subconscious.

subdesarrollado [sub·de·sa·rro·yá·do] *adj.* underdeveloped.

súbdito [súb·di·to] *m.* subject.

subida [su·bí·da] *f.* rise; ascent; carrying up; **de —** on the way up; **muchas -s y bajadas** many ups and downs; much going up and down.

subir [su·bír] *v.* to ascend, go up, climb; to raise, lift; to carry up; to mount; **— al tren** to board the train, get on the train.

súbito [sú·bi·to] *adj.* sudden; **de —** suddenly.

sublevación [su·ble·ba·sjón] *f.* revolt, uprising, insurrection.

sublevar [sub·le·bár] *v.* to excite to rebellion; **-se** to

SO

revolt.

sublimado [sub·li·má·do] *adj.* sublimated.

sublime [su·blí·me] *adj.* sublime.

submarino [sub·ma·rí·no] *m. & adj.* submarine; *m.* — **atómico** atomic submarine.

subordinado [su·bor·di·ná·do] *adj. & m.* subordinate.

subordinar [su·bor·di·nár] *v.* to subordinate; to subdue.

subrayar [sub·rra·yár] *v.* to underline; to emphasize.

subrutina [sub·rru·tí·na] *f.* (*computadora*) subroutine.

subsanar [sub·sa·nár] *v.* to mend, remedy, repair (*a damage, error, defect, etc.*); to make up for (*an error, fault, etc.*); to excuse (*a fault or error*).

subscribir [subs·kri·bír] = **suscribir.**

subscripción [subs·krip·sjón] = **suscripción.**

subscriptor [subs·krip·tór] = **suscritor.**

subsecretario [sub·se·kre·tá·rjo] *m.* undersecretary.

subsecuente [sub·se·kwén·te] *adj.* subsequent.

subsiguiente [sub·si·gjén·te] *adj.* subsequent.

subsistencia [sub·sis·tén·sja] *f.* living, livelihood; sustenance; permanence.

subsistir [sub·sis·tír] *v.* to subsist; to exist; to last.

substancia [subs·tán·sja] = **sustancia.**

substancial [subs·tan·sjál] = **sustancial.**

substancioso [subs·tan·sjó·so] = **sustancioso.**

substituíble [subs·ti·twí·ble] = **sustituíble.**

substantivo [subs·tan·tí·bo] = **sustantivo.**

substitución [subs·ti·tu·sjón] = **sustitución.**

substituir [subs·ti·twír] = **sustituir.**

substituto [subs·ti·tú·to] = **sustituto.**

substracción [subs·trak·sjón] = **sustracción.**

substraer [subs·tra·ér] = **sustraer.**

subsuelo [sub·swé·lo] *m.* subsoil.

subteniente [sub·te·njén·te] *m.* second lieutenant.

subterfugio [sub·ter·fú·xjo] *m.* subterfuge.

subterráneo [sub·te·rrá·ne·o] *adj.* subterranean, underground; *m.* underground; cave, tunnel, vault.

suburbano [su·bur·bá·no] *adj.* suburban; *m.* suburban resident.

suburbio [su·bur·bjo] *m.* suburb.

subvención [sub·ben·sjón] *f.* subsidy.

subvencionar [sub·ben·sjo·nár] *v.* to subsidize.

subyugar [sub·yu·gár] *v.* to subdue.

succión [suk·sjón] *f.* suction.

suceder [su·se·dér] *v.* to happen, occur; to succeed, follow.

sucesión [su·se·sjón] *f.* succession; heirs, offspring.

sucesivo [su·se·sí·bo] *adj.* successive; **en lo —** hereafter, in the future.

suceso [su·sé·so] *m.* event; outcome, result.

sucesor [su·se·sór] *m.* successor.

suciedad [su·sje·dád] *f.* dirt, filth; filthiness; filthy act or remark.

sucinto [su·sín·to] *adj.* compact, concise, brief.

sucio [sú·sjo] *adj.* dirty; foul, filthy.

suculento [su·ku·lén·to] *adj.* juicy.

sucumbir [su·kum·bír] *v.* to succumb; to yield.

sucursal [su·kur·sál] *f.* branch, branch office (*of a post office, bank, etc.*); *adj.* branch.

suche [sú·če] *adj.* *Ven.* sour, unripe; *m. Andes* pimple; *Ch.* office boy, insignificant employee; *Andes* suche (*a tree*).

sud [sud] *m.* south; south wind; **sudeste** [su·dés·te] *m. & adj.* southeast; **sudoeste** [su·do·és·te] *m. & adj.* southwest.

sudamericano [su·da·me·ri·ká·no] *adj. & m.* South American.

sudar [su·dár] *v.* to sweat, perspire; to ooze, to toil.

sudario [su·dá·rjo] *m.* shroud.

sudor [su·dór] *m.* sweat, perspiration; toil.

sudoroso [su·do·ró·so] *adj.* sweaty, sweating, perspiring.

sueco [swé·ko] *adj.* Swedish; *m.* Swede; Swedish language; **hacerse el —** to pretend not to see or understand.

suegra [swé·gra] *f.* mother-in-law.

suegro [swé·gro] *m.* father-in-law.

suela [swé·la] *f.* sole of a shoe; shoe leather.

sueldo [swél·do] *m.* salary.

suelo [swé·lo] *m.* soil, ground; floor; pavement; bottom.

suelto [swél·to] *adj.* (*no atado*) loose; free, easy; (*ágil*) agile, nimble; blank (*verse*); *m.* small change; short newspaper article, news item.

sueño [swé·ño] *m.* sleep; dream; sleepiness, drowsiness; **en -s** in one's sleep; **conciliar el —** to get to sleep; **tener —** to be sleepy.

suero [swé·ro] *m.* serum.

suerte [swér·te] *f.* (*fortuna*) fate; fortune; chance; luck; (*clase*) sort, kind; way, manner; (*truco*) trick; **de — que** so that, in such a way that; and so; **echar -s** to cast lots; **tener —** to be lucky; **tocarle a uno la —** to fall to one's lot; to be lucky.

suéter [swé·ter] *m.* *Am.* sweater.

suficiente [su·fi·sjén·te] *adj.* sufficient; competent, able.

sufijo [su·fí·xo] *m.* suffix; *adj.* suffixed.

sufragar[7] [su·fra·gár] *v.* to defray, pay; to help, aid; *Am.* — **por** to vote for.

sufragio [su·frá·xjo] *m.* suffrage; vote; help, aid.

sufrido [su·frí·do] *adj.* suffering, long-suffering, patient; **mal —** impatient.

sufridor [su·fri·dór] *m.* sufferer; *adj.* suffering.

sufrimiento [su·fri·mjén·to] *m.* suffering; patience; endurance.

sufrir [su·frír] *v.* to suffer; to endure; to allow, permit; to sustain; to undergo; — **un examen** to take an examination.

sugerencia [su·xe·rén·sja] *f.* *Am.* suggestion, hint.

sugerir[3] [su·xe·rír] *v. irr.* to suggest; to hint.

sugestión [su·xes·tjón] *f.* suggestion; hint.

sugestivo [su·xes·tí·bo] *adj.* suggestive.

suicida [swi·sí·da] *m. & f.* suicide (*person who commits suicide*).

suicidarse [swi·si·dár·se] *v.* to commit suicide.

suicidio [swi·sí·djo] *m.* suicide (*act of suicide*).

suizo [swí·so] *adj. & m.* Swiss.

sujeción [su·xe·sjón] *f.* subjection; control; submission.

sujetapapeles [su·xe·ta·pa·pé·les] *m.* paper clip.

sujetar [su·xe·tár] *v.* to subject; to control; to subdue; to fasten; to grasp, hold; **-se** to subject oneself; to submit; to adhere (to).

sujeto [su·xé·to] *adj.* subject; liable; fastened; under control; *m.* subject matter; subject; fellow, individual.

sulfamida [sul·fa·mí·da] *f.* common name for the sulfa drugs.

sulfato [sul·fá·to] *m.* sulphate.

sulfurarse [sul·fu·rár·se] *v.* to get angry.

sulfúrico [sul·fú·ri·ko] *adj.* sulphuric.

sulfuro [sul·fú·ro] *m.* sulphide.

sultán [sul·tán] *m.* sultan.

suma [sú·ma] *f.* sum; addition; substance; summary; **en —** in short.

sumador [su·ma·dór] *adj.* adding; **máquina sumadora** adding machine.

sumar [su·már] *v.* to add; to add up (to), amount (to); to sum up; **-se a** to join.

sumario [su·má·rjo] *m.* summary; indictment; *adj.* summary, brief, concise; swift (*punishment*).

sumergible [su·mer·xí·ble] *adj.* submergible; *m.*

submarine.

sumergir[11] [su·mer·xír] *v.* to submerge, plunge, sink; to immerse; **-se** to submerge; to sink.

sumidero [su·mi·dé·ro] *m.* sink; sewer, drain.

suministrar [su·mi·nis·trár] *v.* to give, supply with, provide with.

sumir [su·mír] *v.* to sink; to submerge; to immerse; *Ríopl., Mex., Carib.* to dent; **-se** to sink; *Andes* to shrink, shrivel; *Andes* to cower, crouch in fear; *Am.* **-se el sombrero hasta las cejas** to pull one's hat over one's eyes.

sumisión [su·mi·sjón] *f.* submission; obedience.

sumiso [su·mí·so] *adj.* submissive; obedient; meek.

sumo [sú·mo] *adj.* supreme, highest; high; greatest; **— pontífice** Sovereign Pontiff (*the Pope*); **a lo —** at the most.

suntuoso [sun·twó·so] *adj.* sumptuous, magnificent, luxurious.

superable [su·pe·rá·ble] *adj.* superable.

superabundancia [su·pe·ra·bun·dán·sja] *f.* superabundance, great abundance, overflow.

superar [su·pe·rár] *v.* to surpass; to exceed; to overcome.

superávit [su·pe·rá·bit] *m.* surplus.

superficial [su·per·fi·sjál] *adj.* superficial; shallow; frivolous; **superficialidad** [su·per·fi·sja·li·dád] *f.* superficiality, shallowness, frivolity.

superficie [su·per·fí·sje] *f.* surface; area.

superfluo [su·pér·flwo] *adj.* superfluous.

superintendente [su·pe·rin·ten·dén·te] *m.* superintendent; supervisor; overseer.

superior [su·pe·rjór] *adj.* superior; higher; better; upper; *m.* superior; father superior; **superiora** [su·pe·rjó·ra] *f.* superior, mother superior.

superioridad [su·pe·rjo·ri·dád] *f.* superiority; excellence.

superlativo [su·per·la·tí·bo] *adj. & m.* superlative.

supersónico [su·per·só·ni·ko] *adj.* supersonic.

superstición [su·pers·ti·sjón] *f.* superstition.

supersticioso [su·pers·ti·sjó·so] *adj.* superstitious.

supervivencia [su·per·bi·bén·sja] *f.* survival.

superviviente [su·per·bi·bjén·te] = **subreviviente.**

suplantar [su·plan·tár] *v.* to supplant; to forge (*a document or check*).

suplementar [su·ple·men·tár] *v.* supplement.

suplementario [su·ple·men·tá·rjo] *adj.* supplementary, extra.

suplemento [su·ple·mén·to] *m.* supplement; supply, supplying.

suplente [su·plén·te] *adj., m. & f.* substitute.

súplica [sú·pli·ka] *f.* entreaty; request; petition; prayer.

suplicante [su·pli·kán·te] *adj.* suppliant, beseeching; *m. & f.* suppliant; petitioner.

suplicar[6] [su·pli·kár] *v.* to beg, entreat, implore; to pray humbly; to appeal, petition.

suplicio [su·plí·sjo] *m.* torture; torment; anguish; execution; instrument of torture; scaffold, gallows.

suplir [su·plír] *v.* to supply; to make up for; to substitute, take the place of (*temporarily*).

suponer[40] [su·po·nér] *v. irr.* to suppose; to assume; to be important.

suposición [su·po·si·sjón] *f.* supposition; assumption.

supremacía [su·pre·ma·sía] *f.* supremacy.

supremo [su·pré·mo] *adj.* supreme; final, last.

supresión [su·pre·sjón] *f.* suppression; omission; elimination.

suprimir [su·pri·mír] *v.* to suppress; to abolish; to omit.

supuesto [su·pwés·to] *p.p. of* **suponer** supposed, assumed; **— que** supposing that; since; **por —** of

course; naturally; *m.* supposition; assumption.

supuración [su·pu·ra·sjón] *f.* formation or discharge of pus.

supurar [su·pu·rár] *v.* to fester, form or discharge pus.

sur [sur] *m.* south; south wind; **sureste** [su·rés·te] *m.* southeast; **suroeste** [su·ro·és·te] *m.* southwest.

suramericano [su·ra·me·ri·ká·no] = **sudamericano.**

surcar[6] [sur·kár] *v.* to furrow; to plow; to plow through; to cut through.

surco [súr·ko] *m.* furrow; rut; groove; wrinkle.

sureño [su·ré·ño] *adj.* southern, from the south; *m.* a southerner.

surgir[11] [sur·xír] *v.* to surge, rise; to spurt; spout; to appear.

surrealismo [su·rre·a·líz·mo] *m.* surrealism.

surtido [sur·tí·do] *m.* stock, supply, assortment; *adj.* assorted.

surtidor [sur·ti·dór] *m.* supplier; spout, jet.

surtir [sur·tír] *v.* to provide, supply, stock (with); to spout, spurt; **— efecto** to produce the desired result; **— un pedido** to fill an order.

susceptible [su·sep·tí·ble] *adj.* susceptible; sensitive; touchy.

suscitar [su·si·tár] *v.* to raise, stir up, provoke.

suscribir[52] [sus·kri·bír] *v.* to subscribe; to endorse; to agree (to); **-se** to subscribe.

suscripción [sus·krip·sjón] *f.* subscription.

suscrito [sus·krí·to] *p.p. of* **suscribir.**

suscritor [sus·kri·tór] *m.* subscriber.

susodicho [su·so·dí·čo] *adj.* aforesaid, above-mentioned.

suspender [sus·pen·dér] *v.* (*colgar*) to suspend; to hang; (*detener*) to stop; to defer; (*no aprobar*) to fail, flunk; to dismiss temporarily; to astonish.

suspensión [sus·pen·sjón] *f.* suspension; postponement, delay; uncertainty; cessation; a system of supporting devices (*automobile*).

suspenso [sus·pén·so] *adj.* suspended; hanging; pending; perplexed, astonished; **en —** in suspense; *m.* failure (*in an examination*).

suspicaz [sus·pi·kás] *adj.* suspicious.

suspirar [sus·pi·rár] *v.* to sigh; to sigh (for), long (for).

suspiro [sus·pí·ro] *m.* sigh; brief pause (*in music*).

sustancia [sus·tán·sja] *f.* substance; essence; *Andes* broth.

sustancial [sus·tan·sjál] *adj.* substantial; nourishing.

sustancioso [sus·tan·sjó·so] *adj.* substantial; nourishing.

sustantivo [sus·tan·tí·bo] *m.* noun; *adj.* substantive; real; independent.

sustentar [sus·ten·tár] *v.* to sustain; to support; to feed, nourish; to maintain; uphold.

sustento [sus·tén·to] *m.* sustenance; food; support.

sustitución [sus·ti·tu·sjón] *f.* substitution.

sustituíble [sus·ti·twí·ble] *adj.* replaceable.

sustituir[32] [sus·ti·twír] *v. irr.* to substitute.

sustituto [sus·ti·tú·to] *m.* substitute.

susto [sús·to] *m.* scare, fright.

sustracción [sus·trak·sjón] *f.* subtraction.

sustraer[46] [sus·tra·ér] *v. irr.* to subtract; to remove, withdraw; **-se a** to evade, avoid, slip away from.

susurrar [su·su·rrár] *v.* to whisper; to murmur; to rustle; **-se** to be whispered or rumored about.

susurro [su·sú·rro] *m.* whisper; murmur; rustle.

sutil [su·tíl] *adj.* subtle; keen; clever; crafty; thin, fine, delicate.

sutileza [su·ti·lé·sa] , **sutilidad** [su·ti·li·dád] *f.* subtlety; keenness, cleverness; cunning; thinness, fineness.

suyo [sú·yo] *adj.* his, of his; her, of hers; your, of

SU

yours (*formal*); their, of theirs; *pron.* his, hers, yours (*formal*), theirs; **de —** naturally, by nature; **salirse con la suya** to get one's own way; **hacer de las suyas** to be up to one's tricks; **los -s** his (hers, theirs); his (her, their) own people.

T:t **tabaco** [ta·bá·ko] *m.* tobacco; *Carib., Ven., Col.* cigar; snuff; *Col.* blow with the fist; **tabaquería** [ta·ba·ke·rí·a] *f.* tobacco store, cigar store.

tábano [tá·ba·no] *m.* horsefly, gadfly.

taberna [ta·bér·na] *f.* tavern, bar, liquor store.

tabernáculo [ta·ber·ná·ku·lo] *m.* tabernacle.

tabique [ta·bí·ke] *m.* partition, partition wall.

tabla [tá·bla] *f.* board, plank; plate of metal; slab; table, list; strip of ground; *Col.* chocolate tablet; **-s** draw, tie (*in games*); stage boards, the stage; **a raja —** cost what it may; *Am.* in great haste; **hacer — rasa de algo** to disregard, omit, or ignore something; *Am.* to clear away all obstacles in the way of something.

tablado [ta·blá·do] *m.* platform, stage; scaffold; floor boards.

tablero [ta·blé·ro] *m.* board; panel; timber, piece of lumber; chessboard, checkerboard; store counter; large work table; gambling table; dashboard; instrument panel; (*computadora*) keyboard; *Col., Ven., Mex.* blackboard; **poner al —** to risk, endanger; **— de mando** control panel.

tableta [ta·blé·ta] *f.* tablet; small thin board; memorandum pad.

tabletear [ta·ble·te·ár] *v.* to rattle; to make a continuous rattling or tapping sound.

tableteo [ta·ble·té·o] *m.* rattling sound; tapping.

tablilla [ta·blí·ya] *f.* tablet; slat, small thin board; splint; small bulletin board; **-s** wooden clappers.

tablón [ta·blón] *m.* plank; large, thick board.

taburete [ta·bu·ré·te] *m.* stool; footstool; *Sal.* chair.

tacañería [ta·ka·ñe·rí·a] *f.* stinginess, tightness, miserliness.

tacaño [ta·ka·ño] *adj.* stingy, tight, miserly; sly.

tácito [tá·si·to] *adj.* tacit, implied; silent.

taciturno [ta·si·túr·no] *adj.* taciturn, silent, sullen; sad.

taco [tá·ko] *m.* wad; roll; plug, stopper; billiard cue; bite, snack; swear word; *Mex., C.A.* Mexican folded tortilla sandwich; *Am.* leather legging; *Ch., Andes* short, fat person; *Mex.* heel of a shoe; *Am.* pile, heap; **echar -s** to curse, swear; *Mex.* **darse uno —** to strut, put on airs.

tacón [ta·kón] *m.* heel of a shoe.

taconear [ta·ko·ne·ár] *v.* to click the heels, walk hard on one's heels.

taconeo [ta·ko·né·o] *m.* click, clicking (*of the heels*).

táctica [ták·ti·ka] *f.* tactics.

tacto [ták·to] *m.* tact; touch, sense of touch.

tacha [tá·ča] *f.* flaw, defect, blemish.

tachar [ta·čár] *v.* (*borrar*) to cross out; to scratch out; to blot out; (*culpar*) to blame; to find fault with; to censure.

tachón [ta·čón] *m.* stud; trimming, braid; blot.

tachonar [ta·čo·nár] *v.* to stud, ornament with studs; to adorn with trimming.

tachuela [ta·čwé·la] *f.* tack, small nail; *Am.* metal dipper; *Am.* runt, "shorty".

tafetán [ta·fe·tán] *m.* taffeta; **— inglés** court plaster; **— adhesivo** "Band-Aid".

tahúr [ta·úr] *m.* gambler; cardsharp.

taimado [taj·má·do] *adj.* sly, crafty; *Am.* sullen, gloomy, gruff.

taita [táj·ta] = **tatita**. *See* **tata**.

tajada [ta·xá·da] *f.* slice; cut.

tajalápiz [ta·xa·lá·pis] *m.* pencil sharpener.

tajante [ta·xán·te] *adj.* cutting, sharp.

tajar [ta·xár] *v.* to slice; to cut; to sharpen (*a pencil*).

tajo [tá·xo] *m.* cut; gash; cutting edge; sheer cliff; chopping block.

tal [tal] *adj.* such; such a; **— cual** such as; so-so, fair; **— vez** perhaps; **el — Pedro** that fellow Peter; **un — García** a certain García; **— para cual** two of a kind; **un — por cual** a nobody; *adv.* just as, in such a way; **estaba — como le dejé** he was just as I left him; **con — (de) que** provided that; **¿qué —?** how are you?; hello!

talabarte [ta·la·bár·te] *m.* sword belt.

taladrar [ta·la·drár] *v.* to bore, drill; to pierce; to penetrate.

taladro [ta·lá·dro] *m.* auger, drill; bore, drill hole; *Am.* mine tunnel.

tálamo [tá·la·mo] *m.* bridal bed or chamber.

talante [ta·lán·te] *m.* disposition; mood; appearance, manner.

talar [ta·lár] *v.* to cut down; *Am.* to prune.

talco [tál·ko] *m.* talc (*a soft mineral*); **— en polvo** talcum powder.

talega [ta·lé·ga] *f.* money bag, sack.

talento [ta·lén·to] *m.* talent; ability, natural gift.

talentoso [ta·len·tó·so] *adj.* talented, gifted.

talio [tá·ljo] *m.* thallium.

talismán [ta·liz·mán] *m.* talisman, charm.

talón [ta·lón] *m.* heel; stub, check, coupon.

talonario [ta·lo·ná·rjo] *m.* stub book; **libro —** stub book.

talonear [ta·lo·ne·ár] *v.* to tap with one's heel; to walk briskly.

taloneo [ta·lo·né·o] *m.* tapping with the heel; loud footsteps.

talla [tá·ya] *f.* (*altura*) stature, height; size; (*labrado*) carving; (*lance entero*) round of a card game; (*rescate*) ransom; *Col.* chat; *Arg.* thrashing, beating.

tallar [ta·yár] *v.* to carve; to cut (*stone*); to appraise; to deal (*cards*); *Ch.* to court, make love; *Andes, Col.* to bother, disturb.

tallarín [ta·ya·rín] *m.* noodle.

talle [tá·ye] *m.* figure, form; waist; fit (*of a dress*); looks, appearance; *Ven.* bodice.

taller [ta·yér] *m.* workshop; laboratory; studio; factory.

tallo [tá·yo] *m.* stalk; stem; shoot, sprout.

tamal [ta·mál] *m.* *Mex., C.A.* tamale; *Cuba, Mex.* vile trick, intrigue; *Am.* clumsy bundle.

tamaño [ta·má·ño] *m.* size; *adj.* such a; of the size of; **— disparate** such a (big) mistake; **— como un elefante** big as an elephant; **tamañito** [ta·ma·ñí·to] *adj.* very small; **tamañito así** about this little; **se quedó tamañito** he was (left) astonished, amazed.

tamarindo [ta·ma·rín·do] *m.* tamarind; *Mex.* traffic cop (*because of color of uniform*).

tambalearse [tam·ba·le·ár·se] *v.* to totter, stagger, sway, reel.

también [tam·bjén] *adv.* also, too; likewise.

tambor [tam·bór] *m.* drum; drum-like object; drummer; pair of embroidery hoops; *Mex.* bedspring, spring mattress; **— de freno** brake drum; **tambora** [tam·bó·ra] *f.* bass drum; **tamboril** [tam·bo·ríl] *m.* small drum; **tamborilero** [tam·bo·ri·lé·ro] *m.* drummer.

tamborilear [tam·bo·ri·le·ár] *v.* to drum; to extol.

tamiz [ta·mís] *m.* fine sieve.

tamizar [ta·mi·sár] *v.* to sift; to blend.

tampoco [tam·pó·ko] *conj.* either (*after a negative*); **no lo hizo** — he did not do it either; **ni yo** — nor I either.

tan [tan] *adv.* (*contr. of* **tanto**) so, as; such a.

tanda [tán·da] *f.* turn; round, bout; task; gang, group; shift, relay; *Col., Ven., Mex., Carib.* section of a theatrical performance.

tangente [taŋ·xén·te] *adj. & f.* tangent; **salirse por la** — to go off at a tangent; to avoid the issue.

tangible [taŋ·xí·ble] *adj.* tangible.

tango [táŋ·go] *m.* tango.

tanque [táŋ·ke] *m.* tank; reservoir; *Col., Ven.* pond; *Mex.* swimming pool.

tantán [tan·tán] *m.* clang; knock! knock!; sound of a bell, drum, etc.

tantear [tan·te·ár] *v.* to probe, test; to sound out, feel out; to estimate, calculate approximately; *Cuba, Ven., Ríopl.* to grope, feel one's way; *Am.* to lie in wait; *Mex.* to fool, make a fool of; *Ven., Mex., C.A.* **¡tantee Vd.!** just imagine!

tanteo [tan·té·o] *m.* trial, test; calculation, estimate; score; **al** — by guess; hit or miss.

tanto [tán·to] *adj., pron. & adv.* so much, as much; so; **-s** so many, as many; *m.* certain amount; counter, chip (*to keep score*); **cuarenta y -s** forty odd; **el** — **por ciento** percentage, rate; **un** — (*or* **algún** —) somewhat; — **como** as well as; as much as; — . . . **como** both . . . and; — **en la ciudad como en el campo** both in the city and in the country; **entre** (*or* **mientras**) — meanwhile; **por lo** — therefore.

tañer [ta·ñér] *v.* to play (*an instrument*); to ring.

tañido [ta·ñí·do] *m.* sound, tune; ring; twang (*of a guitar*).

tapa [tá·pa] *f.* cover; cap; lid; book cover; heel lift.

tapacubos [ta·pa·kú·bos] *m.* hubcap.

tapadera [ta·pa·dé·ra] *f.* cover, lid; one who shields another.

tapar [ta·pár] *v.* to cover; to plug, stop up; to veil; to hide; *Am.* to fill (*a tooth*); *Col.* to crush, crumple; *Ch.* to cover with insults; **-se** to cover up; to wrap oneself up.

taparrabo [ta·pa·rrá·bo] *m.* loincloth; trunks.

tapera [ta·pé·ra] *f. Ríopl.* ruins; *Ríopl., Andes* abandoned room or house.

tapete [ta·pé·te] *m.* rug; table scarf.

tapia [tá·pja] *f.* abode wall; wall fence.

tapiar [ta·pjár] *v.* to wall up; to block up (*a door or window*).

tapicería [ta·pi·se·rí·a] *f.* tapestry; upholstery; tapestry shop; tapestry making.

tapioca [ta·pjó·ka] *f.* tapioca.

tapiz [ta·pís] *m.* tapestry.

tapizar[9] [ta·pi·sár] *v. irr.* to carpet; to cover.

tapón [ta·pón] *m.* plug, stopper, cork; bottle cap.

taquigrafía [ta·ki·gra·fí·a] *f.* shorthand.

taquígrafo [ta·kí·gra·fo] *m.* stenographer.

taquilla [ta·kí·ya] *f.* ticket office; box office; file (*for letters, papers, etc.*); *C.R.* tavern, liquor store.

tarántula [ta·rán·tu·la] *f.* tarantula.

tararear [ta·ra·re·ár] *v.* to hum.

tararero [ta·ra·ré·o] *m.* hum, humming.

tarascada [ta·ras·ká·da] *f.* snap, bite; snappy or harsh answer.

tardanza [tar·dán·sa] *f.* delay; slowness.

tardar [tar·dár] *v.* to delay; to be late; to be long (in); to take long (in); **-se** to delay oneself; to be delayed; **a más** — at the very latest.

tarde [tár·de] *f.* afternoon; *adv.* late; **de** — **en** — from time to time, now and then.

tardío [tar·dí·o] *adj.* late; slow.

tardo [tár·do] *adj.* slow, lazy; tardy, late; stupid, dull; **tardón** [tar·dón] *adj.* very slow; *m.* slowpoke, slow person.

tarea [ta·ré·a] *f.* task, job; anxiety, care.

tarifa [ta·rí·fa] *f.* tariff; list of duties, taxes, or prices; fare.

tarima [ta·rí·ma] *f.* wooden platform; low bench.

tarjeta [tar·xé·ta] *f.* card; (*computadora*) board, card; — **postal** postcard; — **de perforadora** key punchcard; — **registradora** time card.

tarro [tá·rro] *m.* earthen jar; glass jar; *Mex.* horn (*of an animal*); *Ch., Cuba, Andes* can; *Andes* top hat.

tarta [tár·ta] *f.* tart.

tartamudear [tar·ta·mu·de·ár] *v.* to stutter, stammer.

tartamudeo [tar·ta·mu·dé·o] *m.* stammer, stammering.

tartamudo [tar·ta·mú·do] *m.* stutterer, stammerer; *adj.* stuttering, stammering.

tártaro [tár·ta·ro] *m.* tartar.

tartera [tar·té·ra] *f.* griddle; baking pan.

tarugo [ta·rú·go] *m.* wooden block; wooden peg; blockhead, dunce; *adj. Andes* mischievous, devilish.

tasa [tá·sa] *f.* measure; standard; rate; appraisal; valuation.

tasación [ta·sa·sjón] *f.* assessment, valuation, appraisal.

tasajo [ta·sá·xo] *m.* piece of jerked beef.

tasar [ta·sár] *m.* to measure; to appraise; to rate.

tata [tá·ta] *f.* daddy, dad; *Mex., Andes* chief (*said by Indians to a superior*); **tatita** [ta·tí·ta] *m.* daddy; *Mex., Andes* dear chief or daddy (*said by Indians*).

tataranieto [ta·ta·ra·njé·to] *m.* great-great-grandson.

tatuar[18] [ta·twár] *v.* to tattoo.

taurino [taw·rí·no] *adj.* related to bullfighting.

tauromaquia [taw·ro·má·kja] *f.* bullfighting.

taxear [tak·se·ár] *v.* to taxi (*said of a plane*).

taxi [ták·si], **taxímetro** [tak·sí·me·tro] *m.* taxi, taxicab.

taxista [tak·sís·ta] *m. & f.* taxi driver.

taxonomía [tak·so·no·mí·a] *f.* taxonomy.

taza [tá·sa] *f.* cup; bowl; basin of a fountain.

tazón [ta·són] *m.* large cup; bowl; basin of a fountain.

té [te] *m.* tea; *f.* T-square, T-shaped ruler.

te [te] *obj. pron.* you (*fam. sing.*); to you; for you; yourself.

teatral [te·a·trál] *adj.* theatrical.

teatro [te·á·tro] *m.* theater; stage; scene, setting; **hacer** — to put on airs, show off.

tecla [té·kla] *f.* key (*of a piano, typewriter, computer, etc.*); — **para mayúsculas** capital letter key; — **de cambio** shift key; — **funcional** (*computadora*) function key; — **de retroceso** backspace key; **dar uno en la** — to hit the nail on the head, find the right way to do something.

teclado [te·klá·do] *m.* keyboard; — **numérico** (*computadora*) keypad.

teclear [te·kle·ár] *v.* to finger the keys; to play the piano; to type.

tecleo [te·klé·o] *m.* fingering; movement of the keys (*typewriter, piano*).

técnica [ték·ni·ka] *f.* technique.

técnico [ték·ni·ko] *adj.* technical; *m.* technical expert, technician.

tecnología [tek·no·lo·xí·a] *f.* technology.

tecolote [te·ko·ló·te] *m. Mex.* owl.

techado [te·čá·do] *m.* roof; shed; *p.p. of* **techar.**

techar [te·čár] *v.* to roof.

techo [té·čo] *m.* roof; ceiling; — **a cuatro vertientes** hip roof; — **a la holandesa** gabled roof.

techumbre [te·čúm·bre] *f.* roof; ceiling.

tedio [te·djo] *m.* tediousness; boredom; bother.

tedioso [te·djó·so] *adj.* tedious, boring, tiresome.

teja [té·xa] *f.* tile; linden tree; *Am.* rear part of a saddle; **de -s abajo** here below, in this world.

tejado [te·xá·do] *m.* roof; shed; roofing.

tejamanil [te·xa·ma·níl] *m.* shingle; small thin board; shake.

tejar [te·xár] *m.* tile factory; *v.* to cover with tiles.

tejedor [te·xe·dór] *m.* weaver.

tejer [te·xér] *v.* to weave; to interlace; to braid; to knit.

tejido [te·xí·do] *m.* textile, fabric; texture; weave; weaving; tissue.

tejo [té·xo] *m.* disk; quoit; weight.

tejón [te·xón] *m.* badger; bar of gold.

tela [té·la] *f.* cloth; membrane; web; film (*on the surface of liquids*); — **adhesiva** adhesive tape; — **de cebolla** onion skin; flimsy fabric; *Am.* — **emplástica** court plaster; — **metálica** wire screen; **poner en** — **de juicio** to call in question.

telar [te·lár] *m.* loom.

telaraña [te·la·rá·ña] *f.* cobweb, spider's web.

telecomunicación [te·le·co·mu·ni·ka·sjón] *f.* telecommunication

teleférico [te·le·fé·ri·ko] *m.* telpher; car suspended on aerial cables.

telefonear [te·le·fo·ne·ár] *v.* to telephone.

telefónico [te·le·fó·ni·ko] *adj.* telephonic, telephone (*used as adj.*); **receptor** — telephone receiver.

teléfono [te·lé·fo·no] *m.* telephone; **telefonista** [te·le·fo·nísta] *m. & f.* telephone operator.

telegrafía [te·le·gra·fí·a] *f.* telegraphy.

telegrafiar[17] [te·le·gra·fjár] *v.* to telegraph.

telegráfico [te·le·grá·fi·ko] *adj.* telegraphic.

telégrafo [te·lé·gra·fo] *m.* telegraph; — **sin hilos** (*or* — **inalámbrico**) wireless telegraph; **telegrafista** [te·le·gra·fís·ta] *m. & f.* telegraph operator.

telegrama [te·le·gra·ma] *m.* telegram.

telémetro [te·lé·me·tro] *m.* telemeter; range finder.

telepatía [te·le·pa·tí·a] *f.* telepathy.

telescopio [te·les·kó·pjo] *m.* telescope.

telesquí [te·les·kí] *m.* ski lift.

teletipo [te·le·tí·po] *m.* teletype.

televidente [te·le·bi·dén·te] *m. & f.* televiewer; one who watches television.

televisión [te·le·bi·sjón] *f.* television.

televisor [te·le·bi·sór] *m.* TV set.

telón [te·lón] *m.* theater curtain; — **de boca** drop curtain; — **de foro** drop scene.

telurio [te·lú·rjo] *m.* tellurium.

tema [té·ma] *m.* theme; subject; *f.* fixed idea, mania; **temario** agenda.

temático [te·má·ti·ko] *adj.* thematic; persistent.

temblar[1] [tem·blár] *v. irr.* to tremble; to shake; to quiver.

temblón [tem·blón] *adj.* tremulous, trembling, shaking, quivering.

temblor [tem·blór] *m.* tremor, trembling; shiver; quake; — **de tierra** earthquake.

tembloroso [tem·blo·ró·so] *adj.* trembling, shaking.

temer [te·mér] *v.* to fear; to dread; to suspect.

temerario [te·me·rá·rjo] *adj.* rash, reckless.

temeridad [te·me·ri·dád] *f.* temerity, recklessness; folly.

temeroso [te·me·ró·so] *adj.* fearful; suspicious; timid.

temible [te·mí·ble] *adj.* terrible, dreadful.

temor [te·mór] *m.* fear; dread, suspicion.

témpano [tém·pa·no] *m.* thick slice or chunk (*of anything*); kettledrum; drumhead (*parchment stretched over the end of a drum*); — **de hielo** block of ice; iceberg.

temperamento [tem·pe·ra·mén·to] *m.* temperament; climate.

temperatura [tem·pe·ra·tú·ra] *f.* temperature.

tempestad [tem·pes·tád] *f.* tempest, storm.

tempestuoso [tem·pes·twó·so] *adj.* tempestuous, stormy.

templado [tem·plá·do] *p.p. & adj.* (*moderado*) tempered; tuned; moderate; temperate; lukewarm; (*valiente*) brave; *Andes* in love; *Col., P.R.* half-drunk; *Col., Ven.* hard, severe; **estar mal** — to be in a bad humor.

templanza [tem·plán·sa] *f.* temperance; moderation; mildness.

templar [tem·plár] *v.* to temper; to moderate; to calm; to soften; to tune; **-se** to be tempered, moderate; to control oneself; *Andes* to fall in love; *Col.* to take to one's heels; *Mex., Ch.* to stuff oneself.

temple [tém·ple] *m.* temper; temperament; valor, courage; harmony (*of musical instruments*); *Arg.* sweetheart; **de mal** — in a bad humor.

templo [tém·plo] *m.* temple; church.

temporada [tem·po·rá·da] *f.* period of time, season; — **de ópera** opera season.

temporal [tem·po·rál] *adj.* temporal; secular, worldly; temporary; *m.* weather; storm; spell of rainy weather.

tempranero [tem·pra·né·ro] *adj.* habitually early or ahead of time; **ser** — to be an early riser.

temprano [tem·prá·no] *adj.* early; premature; *adv.* early.

tenacidad [te·na·si·dád] *f.* tenacity; tenaciousness; perseverance.

tenacillas [te·na·sí·yas] *f. pl.* small tongs; pincers, tweezers; sugar tongs; curling iron.

tenaz [te·nás] *adj.* tenacious; firm; strong, resistant; stubborn.

tenazas [te·ná·sas] *f. pl.* pincers; pliers; tongs; — **de agarre al tornillo** vise grip pliers; forceps (*for pulling teeth*); **tenazuelas** [te·na·swé·las] *f. pl.* tweezers, small pincers.

tendedero [ten·de·dé·ro] *m.* place to hang or spread clothes; clothesline.

tendencia [ten·dén·sja] *f.* tendency, inclination.

tender[1] [ten·dér] *v. irr.* (*extender*) to spread out; to hang to dry; to stretch out; to lay out; (*propender*) to tend, have a tendency, move (*toward*); *Carib., Mex., C.A., Ríopl., Andes* to make (*a bed*); **-se** to stretch oneself out; to lay all one's cards on the table; to run at full gallop; **tendedor** spreader.

ténder [tén·der] *m.* tender (*of a train*).

tendero [ten·dé·ro] *m.* storekeeper; tentmaker.

tendido [ten·dí·do] *m.* laying; a wash hung up to dry.

tendón [ten·dón] *m.* tendon, sinew.

tenducho [ten·dú·čo] *m.* wretched little shop.

tenebroso [te·ne·bró·so] *adj.* dark, shadowy; gloomy.

tenedor [te·ne·dór] *m.* table fork; holder, possessor, keeper; — **de libros** bookkeeper.

teneduría [te·ne·du·rí·a] *f.* office and position of bookkeeper; — **de libros** bookkeeping.

tener[45] [te·nér] *v. irr.* to have; to possess; to hold; — **en mucho** to esteem highly; — **por** to consider, judge; — **que** (+ *inf.*) to have to; — **gana** (*or* — **ganas**) **de** to desire, feel like; — **miedo** (**sueño, frío, hambre,** *etc.*) to be afraid (sleepy, cold, hungry, *etc.*); — . . . **años** to be . . . years old; **-se** to stand firm; to hold on.

tenería [te·ne·rí·a] *f.* tannery.

tenia [té·nja] *f.* tapeworm.
teniente [te·njén·te] *m.* first lieutenant; substitute, deputy.
tenis [té·nis] *m.* tennis.
tenista [te·nís·ta] *m. & f.* tennis player.
tenor [te·nór] *m.* tenor; text, literal meaning; kind, sort, nature.
tensión [ten·sjón] *f.* tension; strain.
tenso [tén·so] *adj.* tense; tight, taut.
tentación [ten·ta·sjón] *f.* temptation.
tentáculo [ten·tá·ku·lo] *m.* tentacle, feeler.
tentador [ten·ta·dór] *adj.* tempting; *m.* tempter; the devil.
tentalear [ten·ta·le·ár] *v.* to grope, feel around; to finger, touch; to fumble (*for something*).
tentar[1] [ten·tár] *v. irr.* to tempt; to touch, feel with the fingers; to grope; to attempt, try; to test; to probe, examine with a probe.
tentativa [ten·ta·tí·ba] *f.* attempt, trial.
tentativo [ten·ta·tí·bo] *adj.* tentative.
tenue [té·nwe] *adj.* delicate, thin; flimsy; worthless.
teñir[5, 19] [te·ñír] *v. irr.* to dye; to tinge; to darken (*the color of a painting*).
teologal [te·o·lo·gál], **teológico** *adj.* theological.
teología [te·o·lo·xí·a] *f.* theology.
teólogo [te·ó·lo·go] *m.* theologian.
teoría [te·o·rí·a] *f.* theory.
teórico [te·ó·ri·ko] *adj.* theoretical.
tequila [te·kí·la] *m. Mex.* tequila (*liquor made from the maguey plant*).
terapéutico [te·ra·péw·ti·ko] *adj.* therapeutic.
tercería [ter·se·rí·a] *f.* arbitration.
tercero [ter·sé·ro] *adj.* third; *m.* third person; mediator; go-between; tertiary (*member of the third order of St. Francis*).
terciar [ter·sjár] *v.* (*atravesar*) to sling across one's shoulders; (*dividir*) to divide into three parts; (*intervenir*) to intervene, mediate; to meddle, join (*in*); (*equilibrar*) to balance the load on a pack animal; *Mex., Col.* to load or carry on the back; *Am.* to adulterate, add water to; *Am.* to mix.
tercio [tér·sjo] *adj.* third; *m.* one third; half of a mule load; military regiment or division; *Col., Carib., Mex.* bale, bundle; **hacer uno mal** — to hinder, interfere; — **de varas** the banderilla part of the bullfight.
terciopelo [ter·sjo·pé·lo] *m.* velvet.
terco [tér·ko] *adj.* obstinate, stubborn; hard; *Ch., Ec.* harsh, severe.
tergiversar [ter·xi·ber·sár] *v.* to distort, twist.
terminación [ter·mi·na·sjón] *f.* termination, end; ending.
terminal [ter·mi·nál] *adj.* terminal, final.
terminante [ter·mi·nán·te] *adj.* closing, ending; decisive, final.
terminar [ter·mi·nár] *v.* to terminate, end; to finish; **-se** to end.
término [tér·mi·no] *m.* end; completion; goal, object; boundary, limit; terminal; term; word, phrase; **en otros -s** in other words; **por — medio** on an average; as a rule; **primer —** foreground.
termo [tér·mo] *m.* thermos bottle.
termómetro [ter·mó·me·tro] *m.* thermometer.
termonuclear [ter·mo·nu·kle·ár] *adj.* thermonuclear.
termoplástico [ter·mo·plás·ti·co] *adj.* thermoplastic.
Termos [tér·mos] *f.* Thermos bottle (*trademark*).
termóstato [ter·mós·ta·to] *m.* thermostat.
ternera [ter·né·ra] *f.* calf; veal.
terneza [ter·né·sa] *f.* tenderness; softness; affection; affectionate word; caress.
terno [tér·no] *m.* group or combination of three; suit

of clothes; *Carib., Mex.* set of jewels (*earrings, necklace, and brooch*); *Col., Mex.* cup and saucer; **echar** (*or* **soltar**) **un —** to utter a bad word; to curse, swear.
ternura [ter·nú·ra] *f.* tenderness.
terquedad [ter·ke·dád] *f.* obstinacy, stubbornness.
terrado [te·rrá·do] *m.* terrace; flat roof.
terraja [te·rrá·xa] diestock; **-s para tubos** pipe laps.
terramicina [te·rra·mi·sí·na] *f.* Terramycin.
terraplén [te·rra·plén] *m.* railroad embankment.
terrateniente [te·rra·te·njén·te] *m. & f.* landholder.
terraza [te·rrá·sa] *f.* terrace, veranda; flat roof.
terremoto [te·rre·mó·to] *m.* earthquake.
terrenal [te·rre·nál] *adj.* earthly, worldly.
terreno [te·rré·no] *m.* land; ground; field; *adj.* earthly, worldly.
terrestre [te·rrés·tre] *adj.* terrestrial; earthly.
terrible [te·rrí·ble] *adj.* terrible.
terrífico [te·rrí·fi·ko] *adj.* terrific.
territorial [te·rri·to·rjál] *adj.* territorial.
territorio [te·rri·tó·rjo] *m.* territory.
terrón [te·rrón] *m.* clod; lump (*of sugar*).
terror [te·rrór] *m.* terror.
terrorista [te·rro·rís·ta] *m. & f.* terrorist.
terruño [te·rrú·ño] *m.* native soil.
terso [tér·so] *adj.* polished, smooth.
tertulia [ter·tú·lja] *f.* evening party; social gathering; club; conversation; *Ríopl., Cuba, Ven.* theater gallery.
tertuliano [ter·tu·ljá·no], **tertulio** [ter·tú·ljo] *m.* member of a **tertulia.**
tesis [té·sis] *f.* thesis.
tesón [te·són] *m.* grit, endurance, pluck, persistence.
tesonero [te·so·né·ro] *adj. Mex., Cuba, Andes* tenacious, stubborn, persevering, persistent.
tesorería [te·so·re·rí·a] *f.* treasury; **tesorero** [te·so·ré·ro] *m.* treasurer.
tesoro [te·só·ro] *m.* treasure; treasury.
testa [tés·ta] *f.* head; crown of the head; front.
testamento [tes·ta·mén·to] *m.* testament; will.
testarudez [tes·ta·ru·dés] *f.* stubbornness, obstinacy.
testarudo [tes·ta·rú·do] *adj.* stubborn.
testigo [tes·tí·go] *m. & f.* witness; *m.* testimony, proof, evidence; — **de cargo** witness for the prosecution; — **de vista** eyewitness.
testimoniar [tes·ti·mo·njár] *v.* to give testimony of; to serve as a witness.
testimonio [tes·ti·mó·njo] *m.* testimony; proof, evidence; **levantar falso —** to bear false witness.
testuz [tes·tús] *m.* nape; crown of the head (*of certain animals*).
teta [té·ta] *f.* teat, nipple; breast; udder.
tétano [té·ta·no] *m.* tetanus.
tetera [te·té·ra] *f.* teapot; teakettle; *Mex., Cuba, Col.* **tetero** [te·té·ro] nursing bottle.
tétrico [té·tri·ko] *adj.* sad, melancholy, gloomy.
teutónico [tew·tó·ni·ko] *adj.* teutonic.
textil [tes·tíl] *adj.* textile.
texto [tés·to] *m.* text; quotation; textbook; **textual** textual; **textualmente** literally.
tez [tes] *f.* complexion, skin.
ti [ti] *pers. pron.* (*used after prep.*) you; yourself (*fam. sing.*).
tía [tí·a] *f.* aunt, older woman; *Ven.* **— rica** pawnshop; **no hay tu —** there is no use or hope; there is no way out of it; **quedarse una para —** to remain an old maid.
tibio [tí·bjo] *adj.* tepid, lukewarm; indifferent; *Col.* annoyed, angry.
tiburón [ti·bu·rón] *m.* shark.
tico [tí·ko] *adj. & m. Am.* Costa Rican (*humorous*

TE

nickname).

tictac [tik·ták] *m.* tick-tock.

tiempo [tjém·po] *m.* time; weather; tense; **a** — in time, on time; **a su** — in due time, at the proper time; **a un** — at one and the same time; **andando el** — in time, as time goes on; — **extra** overtime; — **y medio** time and a half.

tienda [tjén·da] *f.* store; tent; — **de campaña** camping tent, army tent.

tienta [tjén·ta] *f.* probe (*surgical instrument*); **a -s** gropingly, feeling one's way; **andar a -s** to grope, feel one's way.

tiento [tjén·to] *m.* touch; tact; blind man's stick; steady hand; blow; tentacle, feeler (*of an insect*); *Andes, Ríopl.* saddle strap, leather strap, thong; *Am.* snack; *Arg.* swallow of liquor; **dar un** — to make a trial or attempt; **hacer algo con mucho** — to do something with great care or caution; **perder el** — to lose one's skill; *Andes* **tener a uno a los -s** to keep someone within sight; *Ven.* **tener la vida en un** — to be in great danger.

tierno [tjér·no] *adj.* tender; soft; young; recent, new; sensitive; affectionate; *Am.* green, unripe.

tierra [tjé·rra] *f.* earth; land; ground; soil; native land; — **adentro** inland; — **firme** mainland; solid ground; **dar en** — **con alguien** to overthrow someone; **echar por** — to knock down; to demolish; **tomar** — to land.

tieso [tjé·so] *adj.* stiff, rigid; stuck-up; firm; stubborn.

tiesto [tjés·to] *m. Spain* flowerpot; broken piece of earthenware; *Ch.* pot.

tiesura [tje·sú·ra] *f.* stiffness.

tifo [tí·fo] *m.* typhus; **tifoidea** [ti·foj·de·a] *f.* typhoid fever.

tifón [ti·fón] *m.* typhoon; waterspout.

tifus [tí·fus] *m.* typhus.

tigre [tí·gre] *m.* tiger.

tijera [ti·xé·ra] *f.* (*usually* **tijeras**) scissors; sawhorse; **silla de** — folding chair; **tener buena** — (*or* **tener buenas -s**) to have a sharp tongue; to be a gossip.

tijeretada [ti·xe·re·tá·da] *f.,* **tijeretazo** [ti·xe·re·tá·so] *m.* snip, cut, clip (*with the scissors*).

tijeretear [ti·xe·re·te·ár] *v.* to snip, cut, clip (*with scissors*); to criticize others, gossip.

tila [tí·la] *f.* linden; linden blossom tea.

tildar [til·dár] *v.* to accent (*a word*); to put a tilde over the **n**; to stigmatize.

tilde [tíl·de] *f.* tilde (*mark over an* **n**); blemish; jot, bit, speck; *Col.* accent mark.

timbrar [tim·brár] *v.* to stamp, mark with a seal.

timbrazo [tim·brá·so] *m.* ring of an electric bell.

timbre [tim·bre] *m.* revenue stamp; seal; crest (*on a coat of arms*); call bell; timbre (*quality of tone, tone color*); merit, fame; glorious deed; *Am.* postage stamp.

timidez [ti·mi·dés] *f.* timidity, shyness.

tímido [tí·mi·do] *adj.* timid; shy.

timón [ti·món] *m.* helm; rudder; beam of a plow; *Col.* steering wheel.

timonear [ti·mo·ne·ár] *v.* to steer (*a ship*).

timorato [ti·mo·rá·to] *adj.* timorous, timid.

tímpano [tím·pa·no] *m.* eardrum; kettledrum.

tina [tí·na] *f.* large earthen jar; vat, tank, tub; bathtub.

tinaco [ti·ná·ko] *m.* tank, vat, tub.

tinaja [ti·ná·xa] *f.* large earthen jar.

tinglado [tiŋ·glá·do] *m.* shed.

tinieblas [ti·njé·blas] *f. pl.* darkness; obscurity; ignorance, confusion; Tenebrae (*Holy Week religious service*).

tino [tí·no] *m.* acumen, keen insight, good judgment;

tact; accurate aim; good sense of touch; tank, vat.

tinta [tín·ta] *f.* ink; dye; tint, hue; **-s** paints; — **simpática** invisible ink; **saber de buena** — to know on good authority.

tinte [tín·te] *m.* tint, hue; tinge; color; dye; dyeing.

tinterillo [tin·te·rí·yo] *m.* shyster. *See* **picapleitos.**

tintero [tin·té·ro] *m.* inkwell, inkstand; ink roller (*printing*); *Am.* writing materials, desk set.

tintinear [tin·ti·ne·ár] *v.* to tinkle.

tintineo [tin·ti·né·o] *m.* tinkle, tinkling.

tinto [tín·to] *adj.* tinged; red (*wine*); *m. Col.* black coffee; *Am.* dark-red; *p.p. irr. of* **teñir.**

tintorería [tin·to·re·rí·a] *f.* cleaner's and dyer's shop.

tintorero [tin·to·ré·ro] *m.* dyer.

tintura [tin·tú·ra] *f.* tincture; tint; color; dye.

tinturar [tin·tu·rár] *v.* to tincture; to tinge; to dye.

tiñoso [ti·ñó·so] *adj.* scabby, mangy; stingy.

tío [tí·o] *m.* uncle; old man; good old man; fellow, guy; *Ríopl., Mex., Ven., Andes* **el cuento del** — deceitful story (*told to extract money*).

tiovivo [tí·o·bí·bo] *m.* merry-go-round.

típico [tí·pi·ko] *adj.* typical; *Am.* corrected (*edition*).

tiple [tí·ple] *m. & f.* high soprano singer; *m.* treble; soprano voice; treble guitar.

tipo [tí·po] *m.* type; class; model, standard; fellow, guy; *Am.* rate of interest; *Am.* — **de cambio** rate of exchange; **buen** — good-looking fellow.

tipografía [ti·po·gra·fí·a] *f.* typography, printing; press, printing shop.

tira [tí·ra] *f.* strip; stripe; *Mex.* **estar hecho -s** to be in rags; *Ven.* **sacar a uno las -s** to tan one's hide, beat one to pieces; — **bimetálica** bimetallic strip.

tirabuzón [ti·ra·bu·són] *m.* corkscrew.

tirada [ti·rá·da] *f.* throw; issue, edition, printing; *Am.* tirade, long speech; *P.R.* sly trick; *Ch.* dash (*on horseback*); **de una** — all at once, at one fell swoop.

tirador [ti·ra·dór] *m.* shooter; thrower; slingshot; bell cord; handle; printer; *Am.* leather belt with pockets; — **de goma** slingshot.

tiranía [ti·ra·ní·a] *f.* tyranny.

tiránico [ti·rá·ni·ko] *adj.* tyrannical.

tirano [ti·rá·no] *adj.* tyrannical; *m.* tyrant.

tirante [ti·rán·te] *adj.* pulling; stretched, taut; strained; *m.* trace (*of a harness*); brace; **-s** suspenders; supporters (*for stockings*).

tirantez [ti·ran·tés] *f.* tension, tightness; strain; pull.

tirar [ti·rár] *v.* (*lanzar*) to throw; to throw away; to shoot, fire; (*imprimir*) to draw; to print; (*atraer*) to pull; to attract; *Cuba, Col., Ch.* to cart; — **a** to tend toward; to resemble; to aim at; — **de** to pull, tug; — **bien a la espada** to handle a sword well; **ir tirando** to get along; **a todo** (*or* **a más**) — at the most; *Ch.* **al** — haphazardly; **-se** to throw oneself; to lie down; *Mex., C.A., Col., Ven., Ríopl., Andes* **tirársela de** to boast of.

tiritar [ti·ri·tár] *v.* to shiver.

tiro [tí·ro] *m.* (*disparo*) throw; shot; (*pieza*) piece of artillery; (*alcance*) range of a gun; shooting range; (*carga*) charge of a gun; team (*of horses*); chimney draft; mine shaft; *Am.* issue, printing; *Am.* cartage, transport; — **al blanco** target practice; *Ch., Andes* **al** — at once; *Ven.* **de a** (*or* **de al**) — all at once; completely; **caballo de** — draft horse; **ni a -s** absolutely not (*not even if you shoot me*).

tirón [ti·rón] *m.* jerk, sudden pull; **de un** — all at once, with one big pull.

tironear [ti·ro·ne·ár] *v. C.A., Mex., Ríopl.* to pull, jerk; *Col.* to attract.

tirotear [ti·ro·te·ár] *v.* to shoot around; to shoot at random; **-se** to exchange shots.

tiroteo [ti·ro·té·o] *m.* shooting; exchange of shots; skirmish.

tirria [tí·rrja] *f.* aversion, grudge; **tenerle — a una persona** to have a strong dislike for someone; to hold a grudge against someone.

tísico [tí·si·ko] *adj.* tubercular, consumptive.

tisis [tí·sis] *f.* tuberculosis, consumption.

titanio [ti·tá·njo] *m.* titanium.

títere [tí·te·re] *m.* puppet; ridiculous little fellow; **-s** puppet show.

titilación [ti·ti·la·sjón] *f.* flicker; twinkle; **titileo** *m.* flickering; twinkling; glimmer.

titilar [ti·ti·lár] *v.* to flicker; to twinkle; (*computadora*) to blink.

titubear [ti·tu·be·ár] *v* to hesitate; to totter, stagger; to grope; to stutter, stammer.

titubeo [ti·tu·bé·o] *m.* hesitation, wavering.

titular [ti·tu·lár] *v.* to entitle; to name; **-se** to be called or named; to call oneself; to receive a title; *adj.* titular, in name only; *m.* officer; holder of a title.

título [tí·tu·lo] *m.* (*letrero*) title; heading; sign; inscription; (*derecho*) claim, legal right; (*grado*) degree, diploma; credential; titled person; merit; bond, certificate; **a — de** under the pretext of; in the capacity of.

tiza [tí·sa] *f.* chalk.

tiznado [tiz·ná·do] *adj.* sooty, covered with soot; smutty; dirty; *Ven.* drunk; *p.p.* **of tiznar.**

tiznar [tiz·nár] *v.* to smudge, smut; to smear with soot.

tizne [tíz·ne] *m.* soot; smut; **tiznón** [tiz·nón] *m.* smudge.

tizón [ti·són] *m.* firebrand (*piece of burning wood*); rust, blight (*on plants*); stain (*on one's honor*).

toalla [to·á·ya] *f.* towel.

tobillo [to·bí·yo] *m.* ankle.

tocadiscos [to·ka·dís·kos] *m.* record player; phonograph.

tocado [to·ká·do] *m.* headdress; hairdo, coiffure; *adj.* "touched", half-crazy; *p.p.* **of tocar.**

tocador [to·ka·dór] *m.* dressing table; boudoir, dressing room; dressing case; player (*of a musical instrument*).

tocar[6] [to·kár] *v.* to touch; to play (*an instrument*); to toll, ring; to knock, rap; **— en** to stop over in; **-le a uno** to fall to one's lot; to be one's share; to be one's turn; to concern one; **-se** to fix one's hair; to become "touched," go slightly crazy.

tocayo [to·ká·yo] *m.* namesake; one who has the same name.

tocino [to·sí·no] *m.* bacon; salt pork; lard.

tocón [to·kón] *m.* stub, stump (*of a tree, arm or leg*).

todavía [to·da·bí·a] *adv.* still; yet; even.

todo [tó·do] *adj.* all, whole; every, each; **— hombre** every man; **-s los días** every day; **a — correr** at full or top speed; *m.* whole; all; everything; **-s** everybody; **ante —** first of all; **así y —** in spite of that; **con —** in spite of that; **del —** wholly.

todopoderoso [to·do·po·de·ró·so] *adj.* almighty.

toga [tó·ga] *f.* gown, robe (*worn by a judge, professor, etc.*); Roman toga.

toldería [tol·de·rí·a] *f. Ríopl.* Indian camp, Indian village.

toldo [tól·do] *m.* awning; pomp, vanity; *Ríopl.* Indian hut.

tolerancia [to·le·rán·sja] *f.* tolerance, toleration; **tolerante** [to·le·rán·te] *adj.* tolerant.

tolerar [to·le·rár] *v.* to tolerate; to allow; to overlook, let pass.

tolete [to·lé·te] *m. Col., Mex., Cuba* stick, club, cudgel; *Col.* raft.

toma [tó·ma] *f.* taking; seizure, capture; dose; tap (*of a water main*); *Col.* irrigation ditch; **— de corriente** plug, electric outlet; *m.* **tomacorrientes** socket.

tomar [to·már] *v.* (*asir*) to take; to grasp, catch; to capture; (*beber*) to drink; **— a pechos** to take to heart, take seriously; **-lo a mal** to take it amiss; **— el pelo a** to make fun of, make a fool of; **— por la derecha** to turn to the right; **-se con** to quarrel with.

tomate [to·má·te] *m.* tomato.

tómbola [tóm·bo·la] *f.* raffle for charity.

tomillo [to·mí·yo] *m.* thyme.

tomo [tó·mo] *m.* tome, volume; *Am.* heavy person; *Ch.* dull, silent person; *Ch.* **buen —** a heavy drinker; **de — y lomo** bulky; important.

ton [ton]: **sin — ni son** without rhyme or reason.

tonada [to·ná·da] *f.* tune, song; *Andes* singsong; *Andes, Mex., Carib., Ríopl.* local accent; **tonadilla** [to·na·dí·ya] *f.* little tune; short popular song.

tonel [to·nél] *m.* keg, cask, barrel.

tonelada [to·ne·lá·da] *f.* ton.

tonelaje [to·ne·lá·xe] *m.* tonnage.

tónico [tó·ni·ko] *adj. & m.* tonic.

tono [tó·no] *m.* tone; tune; key, pitch; accent; manner; vigor, strength; **de buen —** of good taste, stylish; **subirse de —** to put on airs.

tonsura [ton·sú·ra] *f.* shearing.

tontera [ton·té·ra] = **tontería.**

tontería [ton·te·rí·a] *f.* foolishness; stupidity.

tonto [tón·to] *adj.* foolish; stupid; **a tontas y a locas** recklessly, without thought; *m.* fool; dunce; *Col., Ch.* a game of cards.

topar [to·pár] *v.* to collide with, run into, bump into; to encounter; to find; to run across; to butt; *Am.* to gamble; *Col.* to fight with the fists; *Carib.; Mex., Ríopl., Andes, Col.* to meet, greet.

tope [tó·pe] *m.* butt, bump, collision; encounter; bumper; dead-end; **hasta el —** up to the top; **estar hasta los -s** to be filled up; *Mex.* speed checks (on road); **-s marginales** margin regulators (stops) (typewriter).

topetada [to·pe·tá·da] *f.,* **topetazo** [to·pe·tá·so] *m.* butt; bump, bump on the head; **topetón** [to·pe·tón] *m.* hard bump, collision; butt.

topetear [to·pe·te·ár] *v.* to butt; to bump.

tópico [tó·pi·ko] *m.* topic, subject.

topo [tó·po] *m.* mole (*small animal*); dunce; awkward person.

topografía [to·po·gra·fí·a] *f.* topography.

toque [tó·ke] *m.* touch; ringing; beat (*of a drum*); tap, sound (*of a trumpet, clarinet, etc.*); assay; **piedra de —** touchstone; **¡allí está el —!** there is the difficulty!; there is the real test!

toquilla [to·kí·ya] *f.* triangular handkerchief; ribbon; hatband.

tórax [tó·raks] *m.* thorax.

torbellino [tor·be·yí·no] *m.* whirlwind; rush, bustle, confusion.

torcedura [tor·se·dú·ra] *f.* twist; sprain, strain.

torcer[2, 10] [tor·sér] *v. irr.* to twist; to turn; to bend; to sprain; to distort; **-se** to become twisted, bent, or sprained; to get crooked; to go astray; to turn sour (*said of wine*); *Am.* to get offended, angry.

torcido [tor·sí·do] *p.p. & adj.* twisted, turned, bent; crooked; angry, resentful; *Am.* unfortunate, unlucky; **estar — con** to be on unfriendly terms with; *m.* twisted roll of candied fruit; coarse silk twist; *Mex., Carib.* gesture or look of disdain; *Andes* lasso made of twisted leather.

tordillo [tor·dí·yo] *adj.* greyish, dapple-grey.
tordo [tór·do] *adj.* dapple-grey; *m.* thrush; dapple-grey horse.
torear [to·re·ár] *v.* to perform in a bullfight; to incite, provoke (*a bull*); to tease.
torero [to·ré·ro] *m.* bullfighter; *adj.* relating to bullfighting.
tormenta [tor·mén·ta] *f.* storm, tempest; misfortune.
tormento [tor·mén·to] *m.* torment; torture; rack (*instrument of torture*); anguish; pain.
tornar [tor·nár] *v.* to return; to turn; to change, alter; — **a hacerlo** to do it again.
tornasol [tor·na·sól] *m.* sunflower.
tornadizo [tor·na·dí·so] *adj.* changeable; fickle.
tornasolado [tor·na·so·lá·do] *adj.* iridescent, rainbow-colored; changeable (*silk*).
tornear [tor·ne·ár] *v.* to turn in a lathe; to do lathe work; to fight in a tournament.
torneo [tor·né·o] *m.* tournament.
tornillo [tor·ní·yo] *m.* screw; clamp, vise; **faltarle a uno un** — to have little sense, "have a screw loose"; — **sin fin** worm gear; — **de banco para tubos** pipe vise; — **de cabeza ranurada** slotted screw; — **de cabeza phillips (en cruz)** Phillips head.
torniquete [tor·ni·ké·te] *m.* turnbuckle; tourniquet.
torno [tór·no] *m.* turn; lathe; turnstile; revolving server; winch or windlass (*machine for lifting or pulling, turned by a crank*); — **de hilar** spinning wheel; **en** — around.
toro [tó·ro] *m.* bull; *Mex., Col.* difficult question; **-s** bullfight; *Am.* **estar en las astas del** — to be in a predicament.
toronja [to·rón·xa] *f. Am.* grapefruit.
torpe [tór·pe] *adj.* stupid, dull; clumsy; slow; lewd.
torpedo [tor·pé·do] *m.* torpedo; **torpedero** [tor·pe·dé·ro] *m.* torpedo boat.
torpeza [tor·pé·sa] *f.* stupidity, dullness; clumsiness; slowness; moral turpitude, lewdness.
torrar [to·rrár] *v.* to parch.
torre [tó·rre] *f.* tower; turret; castle (*in chess*).
torrencial [to·rren·sjál] *adj.* torrential.
torrente [to·rrén·te] *m.* torrent; flood; — **de voz** powerful voice.
torreón [to·rre·ón] *m.* large tower (*of a fortress, castle, etc.*).
tórrido [tó·rri·do] *adj.* torrid.
torsión [tor·sjón] *f.* twist; sprain.
torta [tór·ta] *f.* torte, round cake; round loaf.
tortilla [tor·tí·ya] *f.* omelet; *Mex., C.A.* tortilla (*flat, thin cornmeal cake*).
tórtola [tór·to·la] *f.* turtledove.
tortuga [tor·tú·ga] *f.* tortoise; turtle.
tortuoso [tor·twó·so] *adj.* tortuous, twisting, winding; sly.
tortura [tor·tú·ra] *f.* torture; grief, affliction.
torturar [tor·tu·rár] *v.* to torture.
torvo [tór·bo] *adj.* grim, stern, severe.
tos [tos] *f.* cough; — **ferina** whooping cough.
tosco [tós·ko] *adj.* coarse, harsh, rough.
toser [to·sér] *v.* to cough; *Am.* to brag, boast.
tosquedad [tos·ke·dád] *f.* coarseness, crudeness, roughness; rudeness.
tostada [tos·tá·da] *f.* toast, toasted bread; *Am.* boring visit or conversation; *Ven.* toasted **tortilla; dar** (*or* **pegar**) **una** — **a uno** to play a mean trick on someone; *Mex.* to make someone very angry.
tostado [tos·tá·do] *p.p. & adj.* toasted; roasted; tanned; *Am.* worn out, tired out; *m.* toasting; *Am.* roasted corn.
tostador [tos·ta·dór] *m.* toaster.

tostar[2] [tos·tár] *v. irr.* to toast; to tan; to overheat; to roast (*coffee*).
tostón [tos·tón] *m.* toast dipped in oil; small roasted pig; *Mex., C.A.* coin worth half a Mexican peso.
total [to·tál] *adj. & m.* total.
totalidad [to·ta·li·dád] *f.* entirety, whole.
totalitario [to·ta·li·tá·rjo] *adj.* totalitarian.
totuma [to·tú·ma] *f.* calabash.
tóxico [tók·si·ko] *adj.* toxic.
toxina [tok·sí·na] *f.* toxin (*poison produced within animals and plants*).
toza [tó·sa] *f.* wooden block; stump; log; piece of bark.
traba [trá·ba] *f.* bond, tie; binding or locking device; fastener, fetter, shackle; hindrance, obstacle.
trabado [tra·bá·do] *adj. Col., Ríopl., Mex.* tongue-tied; *p.p. of* **trabar**.
trabajador [tra·ba·xa·dor] *adj.* industrious; *m.* worker, laborer.
trabajar [tra·ba·xár] *v.* to work; to labor; to strive.
trabajo [tra·bá·xo] *m.* work; labor; difficulty, obstacle; trouble; hardship.
trabajoso [tra·ba·xó·so] *adj.* laborious, difficult; troublesome; *Am.* unobliging; *Am.* demanding.
trabalenguas [tra·ba·lén·gwas] *m.* tongue twister.
trabar [tra·bár] *v.* to join, fasten; to clasp; to shackle; to brace; to impede; — **amistad con alguien** to become friends with someone; — **batalla** to join in battle; — **conversación** to be engaged in conversation; to engage in conversation; **-se** *Ríopl., Mex., Ven.* to stammer; **-se de palabras** to get into an argument.
tracción [trak·sjón] *f.* traction; **resistencia a la** — tensile strength.
tractor [trak·tór] *m.* tractor.
tradición [tra·di·sjón] *f.* tradition.
tradicional [tra·di·sjo·nál] *adj.* traditional.
traducción [tra·duk·sjón] *f.* translation.
traducir[25] [tra·du·sír] *v. irr.* to translate; to interpret.
traductor [tra·duk·tór] *m.* translator.
traer[46] [tra·ér] *v. irr.* to bring; to carry; to lead, conduct; to have; to bring about; to wear; — **a uno inquieto** to keep one disturbed; — **a uno a mal** to mistreat someone; to bother someone; **-se bien** to dress well; to carry oneself well.
trafagar[7] [tra·fa·gár] *v.* to traffic, trade; to roam about; to bustle, hustle; to toil.
tráfago [trá·fa·go] *m.* trade, commerce; bustle, hustle; toil.
traficante [tra·fi·kán·te] *m.* trader; dealer; tradesman.
traficar[6] [tra·fi·kár] *v.* to traffic, trade; *Ven.* to pass or move back and forth (*as traffic*). See **transitar**.
tráfico [trá·fi·ko] *m.* traffic; trade, commerce.
tragaluz [tra·ga·lús] *f.* skylight.
tragar[7] [tra·gár] *v.* to swallow; to gulp; to engulf, swallow up.
tragedia [tra·xé·dja] *f.* tragedy.
trágico [trá·xi·ko] *adj.* tragic.
trago [trá·go] *m.* swallow, gulp; misfortune; *Am.* brandy, hard liquor; **a -s** slowly, by degrees; **echar un** — to take a drink; **tragón** *m.* glutton; *adj.* gluttonous.
traición [traj·sjón] *f.* treason; treachery; **a** — treacherously; deceitfully.
traicionar [traj·sjo·nár] *v.* to betray.
traicionero [traj·sjo·né·ro] *adj.* treacherous; deceitful; *m.* traitor.
traído [tra·í·do] *adj.* used, old, worn out; **muy** — **y llevado** very worn out; *p.p. of* **traer**.
traidor [traj·dór] *adj.* treacherous; *m.* traitor; betrayer.

traje [trá·xe] *m.* dress; suit; gown; — **de etiqueta** (— **de ceremonia,** *or Am.* — **de parada)** formal gown; formal suit; dress uniform; — **de luces** bullfighter's costume; *Col., C.A., Mex., Ríopl.* — **sastre** woman's tailor-made suit.

trajeado [tra·xe·á·do] *p.p. & adj.* dressed, clothed.

trajín [tra·xín] *m.* traffic, going and coming; hustle, bustle, commotion.

trajinar [tra·xi·nár] *v.* to carry, cart back and forth; to go back and forth; to bustle, hustle.

trama [trá·ma] *f.* plot; scheme; conspiracy; woof (*horizontal threads of a fabric*).

tramar [tra·már] *v.* to weave; to plot; to scheme.

tramitar [tra·mi·tár] *v.* to transact; to take legal steps; to negotiate.

trámite [trá·mi·te] *m.* transaction, procedure, step, formality.

tramo [trá·mo] *m.* stretch, lap, span; short distance; regular interval; flight of stairs.

tramoya [tra·mó·ya] *f.* stage devices and machinery.

trampa [trám·pa] *f.* trap; snare; hatch, trap door; hinged section of a counter; spring door; fraud; trick.

trampear [tram·pe·ár] *v.* to trick, cheat, swindle.

trampista [tram·pís·ta] *m. & f.* cheat, crook, swindler.

trampolín [tram·po·lín] *m.* springboard.

tramposo [tram·pó·so] *adj.* deceitful, tricky; *m.* swindler, cheat.

tranca [tráŋ·ka] *f.* crossbar, bolt; pole, prop; club, stick; *Ven., Ríopl.* rustic gate; *Ríopl.* fence with gates; *Mex., Ven.* **saltar las -s** to jump over the fence; to lose one's patience, rebel, get angry; *Ch., Ríopl., Andes, Mex.* **tener una** — to be drunk.

trance [trán·se] *m.* critical moment; dangerous situation; **el último** — the last moment of life; **a todo** — at any cost, cost what it may.

tranco [tráŋ·ko] *m.* stride, long step; threshold; **a -s** hurriedly; **en dos -s** in a jiffy; *Ríopl.* **al** — striding, with long steps.

tranquear [traŋ·ke·ár] *v.* to stride along.

tranquera [traŋ·ké·ra] *f.* stockade, wooden fence; *Ríopl., Cuba, Ven.* large gate (*made with* **trancas**).

tranquilidad [traŋ·ki·li·dád] *f.* tranquility, peacefulness.

tranquilizar[9] [traŋ·ki·li·sár] *v.* to quiet, calm down; to pacify; **-se** to become tranquil, calm down.

tranquilo [traŋ·kí·lo] *adj.* tranquil, peaceful.

transacción [tran·sak·sjón] *f.* transaction, negotiation; compromise.

transar [tran·sár] *v. Am.* to compromise, yield, give in.

transatlántico [tran·sa·tlán·ti·ko] *adj.* transatlantic; *m.* transatlantic steamer.

transbordar [trans·bor·dár] = **trasbordar.**

transbordo [trans·bór·do] = **trasbordo.**

transcendencia [trans·sen·dén·sja] *f.* consequence, importance; penetration.

transcendental [tran·sen·den·tál] *adj.* consequential, important, far-reaching.

transcribir [trans·kri·bír] *v.* to transcribe.

transcurrir [trans·ku·rrír] *v.* to pass, elapse.

transcurso [trans·kúr·so] *m.* passing, lapse (*of time*).

transeúnte [tran·se·ún·te] *m.* passer-by; pedestrian; transient; *adj.* transient.

transferencia [trans·fe·rén·sja] *f.* transference, transfer.

transferible [trans·fe·rí·ble] *f.* transference, transfer.

transferible [trans·fe·rí·ble] *adj.* transferable.

transferir[3] [trans·fe·rír] *v. irr.* to transfer.

transformación [trans·for·ma·sjón] *f.* transformation.

transformador [trans·for·ma·dór] *m.* transformer.

transformar [trans·for·már] *v.* to transform.

transfusión [trans·fu·sjón] *f.* transfusion.

transgredir[51] [trans·gre·dír] *v.* to transgress.

transgresión [trans·gre·sjón] *f.* transgression.

transgresor [trans·gre·sór] *m.* transgressor, offender.

transición [tran·si·sjón] *f.* transition.

transigente [tran·si·xén·te] *adj.* compromising, yielding, pliable.

transigir[11] [tran·si·xír] *v.* to compromise, yield, make concessions; to settle by compromise.

transistor [tran·sis·tór] *m.* transistor.

transitable [tran·si·tá·ble] *adj.* passable (*road*).

transitar [tran·si·tár] *v.* to pass or move back and forth (*as traffic*).

tránsito [trán·si·to] *m.* transit; traffic; passing; passage; transition; **de** — on the way, in transit, passing through.

transitorio [tran·si·tó·rjo] *adj.* transitory.

transmisión [trans·mi·sjón] *f.* transmission; — **automática** automatic transmission.

transmisor [trans·mi·sór] *m.* transmitter; *adj.* transmitting.

transmitir [trans·mi·tír] *v.* to transmit.

transparencia [trans·pa·rén·sja] *f.* transparency.

transparente [trans·pa·rén·te] *adj.* transparent; lucid, clear; *m.* window shade; stained-glass window.

transpirar [trans·pi·rár] *v.* to transpire; to leak out.

transponer[40] [trans·po·nér] *v. irr.* to transpose; to transfer; to transplant; to go beyond, go over to the other side; **-se** to hide from view, go behind; to set, go below the horizon.

transportación [trans·por·ta·sjón] *f.* transportation, transport.

transportar [trans·por·tár] *v.* to transport; to transpose (*music*); **-se** to be transported, carried away by strong feeling; to be in ecstasy.

transporte [trans·pór·te] *m.* transport; transportation; transport vessel; ecstasy; — **de locura** fit of madness.

transpuesto [trans·pwés·to] *p.p. of* **transponer.**

transversal [trans·ber·sál] *adj.* transversal, transverse; **sección** — cross section.

transverso [trans·bér·so] *adj.* transverse, cross.

tranvía [tram·bí·a] *m.* streetcar; streetcar track.

trapacear [tra·pa·se·ár] *v.* to swindle, cheat; to racketeer.

trapacería [tra·pa·se·rí·a] *f.* racket, fraud, swindle.

trapacero [tra·pa·sé·ro] *m.* racketeer; cheat, swindler; *adj.* cheating, deceiving.

trapacista [tra·pa·sís·ta] *m. & f.* racketeer; swindler, cheat.

trapeador [tra·pe·a·dór] *m. Am.* mopper; *Andes, Ven., Col., C.A., Mex., Cuba* mop.

trapear [tra·pe·ár] *v. Am.* to mop; *C.A.* to beat up, give (*someone*) a licking.

trapecio [tra·pé·sjo] *m.* trapeze.

trapiche [tra·pí·če] *m.* sugar mill; press (*for extracting juices*); *Andes* grinding machine (*for pulverizing minerals*).

trapisonda [tra·pi·són·da] *f.* escapade, prank; brawl; noisy spree.

trapo [trá·po] *m.* rag; *C.A., Ven., Ur.* cloth; **-s** clothes; **a todo** — at full sail; speedily; **poner a uno como un** — to make one feel like a rag; **sacarle a uno los -s al sol** to exhibit somebody's dirty linen; **soltar el** — to burst out laughing or crying.

traposo [tra·pó·so] *adj. Ch., P.R.* ragged, tattered, in rags.

tráquea [trá·ke·a] *f.* trachea, windpipe.

traquetear [tra·ke·te·ár] *v.* to rattle; to shake; to jolt; to crack, crackle.

traqueteo [tra·ke·té·o] *m.* rattling; shaking; jolting; cracking, crackling; *Ríopl., Col., Ven., C.A., Mex., Carib., Andes* uproar, din; *Am.* noisy, disorderly traffic.

tras [tras] *prep.* after; in search of; behind, in back of; — **de** behind, after; besides, in addition to; *interj.* ¡—! bang!

trasbordar [traz·bor·dár] *v.* to transfer.

trasbordo [traz·bór·do] *m.* transfer.

trascendencia [tra·sen·dén·sja] = **transcendencia.**

trascendental [tra·sen·den·tál] = **transcendental.**

trasegar[1, 7] [tra·se·gár] *v. irr.* to upset, overturn; to change from one place to another; to pour from one container to another.

trasero [tra·sé·ro] *adj.* rear, hind, back; *m.* rump.

trasladar [traz·la·dár] *v.* to move, remove; to transfer; to postpone; to translate; to transcribe, copy.

traslado [traz·lá·do] *m.* transfer; transcript, written copy.

traslapo [traz·lá·po] *m.* overlap.

traslucirse[13] [traz·lu·sír·se] *v. irr.* to be translucent; to be transparent, clear, evident.

trasnochar [traz·no·čár] *v.* to sit up all night; to stay awake all night; to spend the night out.

traspalar [tras·pa·lár] *v.* to shovel.

traspapelar [tras·pa·pe·lár] *v.* to mislay, misplace (*a paper, letter, document, etc.*); -**se** to become mislaid among other papers.

traspasar [tras·pa·sár] *v.* to pass over, cross over; to go beyond; to pass through; to pierce; to transfer (*property*); to trespass.

traspaso [tras·pá·so] *m.* transfer; transgression, trespass.

traspié [tras·pjé] *m.* stumble, slip; **dar un** — to stumble or trip.

trasplantar [tras·plan·tár] *v.* to transplant.

trasponer[40] [tras·po·nér] = **transponer.**

trasquila [tras·kí·la], **trasquiladura** [tras·ki·la·dú·ra] *f.* shearing, clip, clipping; bad haircut.

trasquilar [tras·ki·lár] *v.* to shear; to clip; to crop; to cut badly (*hair*).

trastazo [tras·tá·so] *m.* thump, blow.

traste [trás·te] *m.* fret, stop (*of a guitar*); buttocks; *C.A.* utensil, implement; **dar al** — **con** to destroy, ruin.

trasto [trás·to] *m.* household utensil; piece of junk; rubbish, trash; -**s** utensils; implements; -**s de pescar** fishing tackle.

trastornar [tras·tor·nár] *v.* to overturn; to upset; to disturb.

trastorno [tras·tór·no] *m.* upset; disorder; disturbance.

trastrocar[2, 6] [tras·tro·kár] *v. irr.* to invert, change; to upset.

trasudar [tra·su·dár] *v.* to perspire, sweat slightly.

trasudor [tra·su·dór] *m.* slight perspiration or sweat.

tratable [tra·tá·ble] *adj.* friendly, sociable; manageable.

tratado [tra·tá·do] *m.* treaty; treatise.

tratamiento [tra·ta·mjén·to] *m.* treatment; title of courtesy; form of address; — **de texto** word processing.

tratante [tra·tán·te] *m. & f.* dealer, tradesman, trader.

tratar [tra·tár] *v.* to treat; to handle; to discuss; to have social relations with; — **con** to have dealings with; — **de** to try to; to treat of, deal with; -**le a uno de** to address someone as; to treat someone as; — **en** to deal in; -**se bien** to treat oneself well; to behave well; -**se de** to be a question of; **no se**

trata de eso that isn't the question, that isn't the point.

trato [trá·to] *m.* (*acuerdo*) treatment; deal, pact; trade; (*manera*) manner, behavior; social relations; dealings; *Am.* — **pampa** unfair deal; ¡— **hecho!** it's a deal!; **tener buen** — to be affable, sociable.

traumático [traw·má·ti·ko] *adj.* traumatic.

través [tra·bés] *m.* crossbeam; reverse, misfortune; **a** (*or* **al**) — **de** through, across; **de** — across; **dar al** — **con** to ruin, destroy; to squander; **mirar de** — to squint in a sinister manner.

travesaño [tra·be·sá·ño] *m.* crosspiece, crossbar; bolster, long bedpillow; *Ven., Andes* railway tie.

travesear [tra·be·se·ár] *v.* to romp, frisk, frolic; to fool around; to misbehave.

travesía [tra·be·sí·a] *f.* crossing; sea voyage; wind blowing towards a coast; *Col.* wasteland, desert land; *Arg.* partition wall or fence.

travesura [tra·be·sú·ra] *f.* mischief; prank; lively wit.

traviesa [tra·bjé·sa] *f.* railway tie; rafter, crossbeam; *Col.* midyear crop.

travieso [tra·bjé·so] *adv.* mischievous; lively; restless; **a campo** (*or* **a campo traviesa**) cross-country.

trayecto [tra·yék·to] *m.* run, stretch, lap, distance (*traveled over*).

trayectoria [tra·yek·tó·rja] *f.* path (*of a bullet, missile, etc.*).

traza [trá·sa] *f.* (*plan*) plan; design; plot; invention; (*apariencia*) appearance; semblance; aspect; indication, sign; **darse -s** to use one's wits or ingenuity; **tener -s de** to have the appearance or signs of; **tiene** (*or* **lleva**) **-s de no acabar nunca** it looks as if he would never end.

trazado [tra·sá·do] *m.* draft, plan, sketch, outline; drawing; *p.p. & adj.* traced, sketched, outlined.

trazador [tra·sa·dór] *m.* tracer; — **gráfico** (*computadora*) touch tablet.

trazar[9] [tra·sár] *v.* to trace, sketch; to draw, mark out; to plan.

trébol [tré·bol] *m.* clover.

trece [tré·se] *num.* thirteen.

trecho [tré·čo] *m.* space, distance; lap (*in a race*); **a -s** by or at intervals; **de** — **en** — at certain points or intervals; from time to time.

tregua [tré·gwa] *f.* truce; rest, respite.

treinta [trejn·ta] *num.* thirty.

tremedal [tre·me·dál] *m.* quagmire, bog.

tremendo [tre·mén·do] *adj.* tremendous, huge; terrible.

trementina [tre·men·tí·na] *f.* turpentine.

tremolar [tre·mo·lár] *v.* to flutter, wave (*as a flag*).

trémolo [tré·mo·lo] *m.* tremolo (*of the voice*), quaver.

trémulo [tré·mu·lo] *adj.* tremulous, trembling, quivering; flickering.

tren [tren] *m.* train; *Mex., Guate.* traffic; — **correo** mail train; — **de aterrizaje** landing gear; *Ven., Carib.* — **de lavado** laundry; *Cuba, Ven.* — **de mudadas** moving company; — **de recreo** excursion train; — **mixto** freight and passenger train.

trenza [trén·sa] *f.* tress; braid; *Mex., Cuba, Ven.* string (*of garlic, onions, etc.*); **trencilla** *f.* braid.

trenzar[9] [tren·sár] *v.* to braid; -**se** to braid one's hair; *Ríopl., Andes, Col.* to fight hand to hand.

trepador [tre·pa·dór] *adj.* climbing.

trepar [tre·pár] *v.* to climb; to clamber; -**se** to climb; to clamber; to perch.

trepidación [tre·pi·da·sjón] *f.* jar, vibration; trembling, shaking.

trepidar [tre·pi·dár] *v.* to shake, vibrate, tremble, jar.

tres [tres] *num.* three.

treta [tré·ta] *f.* trick, wile; **malas -s** bad tricks, bad habits.

triaca [trjá·ka] *f.* treacle.

triangular [trjaŋ·gu·lár] *adj.* triangular.

triángulo [trjáŋ·gu·lo] *m.* triangle; **— de refuerzo** gusset.

tribu [trí·ƀu] *f.* tribe.

tribulación [tri·ƀu·la·sjón] *f.* tribulation, trouble.

tribuna [tri·ƀú·na] *f.* rostrum (*speaker's platform*).

tribunal [tri·ƀu·nál] *m.* tribunal; court of justice; body of judges.

tributar [tri·ƀu·tár] *v.* to pay tribute, pay homage.

tributario [tri·ƀu·tá·rjo] *adj.* & *m.* tributary.

tributo [tri·ƀú·to] *m.* tribute; contribution, tax.

triciclo [tri·sí·klo] *m.* tricycle.

trifulca [tri·fúl·ka] *f.* fight, quarrel, wrangle, row.

trigo [trí·ǥo] *m.* wheat.

trigueño [tri·ǥé·ño] *adj.* swarthy; brunet; dark.

trilogía [tri·lo·xí·a] *f.* trilogy.

trillado [tri·yá·ðo] *p.p.* beaten; *adj.* trite, hackneyed, commonplace; **camino —** beaten path.

trilladora [tri·ya·ðó·ra] *f.* threshing machine.

trillar [tri·yár] *v.* to thresh; to beat, mistreat; *Cuba* to cut a path.

trimestre [tri·més·tre] *m.* quarter, period of three months; quarterly payment, income, or salary; **trimestral** [tri·mes·trál] *adj.* quarterly.

trinar [tri·nár] *v.* to trill (*in singing*); to warble; to quaver (*said of the voice*); to get furious.

trinchante [trin·čán·te] *m.* carving fork; carving knife; carver.

trinchar [trin·čár] *v.* to carve (*meat*).

trinche [trín·če] *m. Col., Ven., C.A., Mex.* fork; *Ch., Ec.* carving table; *Am.* **plato —** carving platter.

trinchera [trin·čé·ra] *f.* trench; ditch; *C.A., Ven., Andes* stockade, fence; *Mex.* curved knife.

trinchero [trin·čé·ro] *m.* carving table; **plato —** carving platter.

trineo [tri·né·a] *m.* sleigh; sled.

trino [trí·no] *m.* trill (*in singing*).

tripa [trí·pa] *f.* intestine, bowel; paunch, belly; **-s** entrails, insides.

triple [trí·ple] *adj.* & *m.* triple.

triplicar[6] [tri·pli·kár] *v.* to triplicate, triple, treble.

tripode [trí·po·ðe] *m.* tripod.

tripulación [tri·pu·la·sjón] *f.* crew, ship's company.

tripular [tri·pu·lár] *v.* to man (*a ship*).

trique [trí·ke] *m.* crack, snap; *Mex.* utensil, trinket; *Col.* clever trick in a game; *Am.* drink made from barley; **-s** *Mex.* poor household utensils, goods, etc.

triquinosis [tri·ki·nó·sis] *f.* trichinosis.

triscar[6] [tris·kár] *v.* to romp, frisk, frolic; to stamp or shuffle the feet; *Col., Cuba* to tease, make fun of.

triste [trís·te] *adj.* sad; sorrowful; *Mex.* bashful, backward; *m. Ríopl.* melancholy love song.

tristeza [tris·té·sa] *f.* sadness; sorrow; *Arg.* tick fever.

tristón [tris·tón] *adj.* wistful, quite sad, melancholy.

triunfal [trjun·fál] *adj.* triumphal.

triunfante [trjun·fán·te] *adj.* triumphant.

triunfar [trjun·fár] *v.* to triumph; to trump (*at cards*).

triunfo [trjún·fo] *m.* triumph; trump card; trophy.

trivial [tri·ƀjál] *adj.* trivial, commonplace, trite.

triza [trí·sa] *f.* shred, fragment, small piece; cord, rope (*for sails*); **hacer -s** to tear into shreds; to tear to pieces.

trocar[2, 6] [tro·kár] *v. irr.* to change; to barter, exchange; to do one thing instead of another; **-se** to change; to be transformed; to exchange.

trocear [tro·se·ár] *v.* to divide into pieces.

troceadores [tro·se·a·ðó·res] *m. pl.* choppers.

trocha [tró·ča] *f.* path, trail; *Ríopl.* gauge (*of a railway*); *Col.* trot; *Am.* slice or serving of meat.

trofeo [tro·fé·o] *m.* trophy; booty, spoils.

troj [tro], troje [tró·xe] *m.* barn, granary.

trole [tró·le] *m.* trolley.

trolebús [tro·le·ƀús] *m.* trolleybus.

tromba [tróm·ba] *f.* waterspout.

trombón [trom·bón] *m.* trombone.

trompa [tróm·pa] *f.* trumpet; trunk of an elephant; large spinning top; *Am.* snout; *Col.* cowcatcher (*of a locomotive*).

trompada [trom·pá·ða] *f.* blow with the fist; bump.

trompeta [trom·pé·ta] *f.* trumpet; *m.* trumpeter; useless individual; *Andes* drunk, drunkard; *Andes* bold, shameless fellow.

trompetear [trom·pe·te·ár] *v.* to trumpet, blow the trumpet.

trompo [tróm·po] *m.* spinning top; stupid fellow, dunce.

tronada [tro·ná·ða] *f.* thunderstorm.

tronar[2] [tro·nár] *v. irr.* to thunder; to explode, burst; *Mex., C.A.* to execute by shooting; **— los dedos** to snap one's fingers; **por lo que pueda —** just in case.

tronco [tróŋ·ko] *m.* tree trunk; log; stem; trunk (*of the human body*); team (*of horses*).

tronchar [tron·čár] *v.* to bend or break (*a stalk or trunk*); to chop off; to break off; **-se** to break off or get bent (*said of a stalk or trunk*); *Col.* to get twisted or bent.

tronera [tro·né·ra] *f.* opening; porthole (*through which to shoot*); small, narrow window; pocket of a billiard table; *m.* madcap, reckless fellow.

tronido [tro·ní·ðo] *m.* thunder; detonation; sharp, sudden sound.

trono [tró·no] *m.* throne.

tropa [tró·pa] *f.* troop; crowd; *Ríopl.* herd of cattle, drove of horses (*often* **tropilla**).

tropel [tro·pél] *m.* throng; bustle; rush; jumble, confusion.

tropezar[1, 9] [tro·pe·sár] *v. irr.* to stumble; to blunder; **— con** to meet, come across, encounter.

tropezón [tro·pe·són] *m.* stumbling; stumble; slip; **a -es** falteringly, stumbling along clumsily; **darse un —** to stumble, trip.

tropical [tro·pi·kál] *adj.* tropical.

trópico [tró·pi·ko] *m.* tropic.

tropiezo [tro·pjé·so] *m.* stumble; stumbling block; slip, fault; dispute.

tropilla [tro·pí·ya] *f.* small troop; *Ríopl.* drove of horses guided by the **madrina;** *Mex.* pack of dogs; *Am.* group of spare saddle horses.

tropillero [tro·pi·yé·ro] *m. Am.* horse wrangler, herdsman.

troquel [tro·kél] *m.* die (machine); **troqueladora** clicker; **troqueles roscados** pipe-threading dies.

trotar [tro·tár] *v.* to trot; to hurry.

trote [tró·te] *m.* trot; **al —** quickly.

trovador [tro·ƀa·ðór] *m.* troubadour, minstrel.

troza [tró·sa] *f.* log.

trozar[9] [tro·sár] *v.* to cut off, break off (*a piece*); to break or cut into pieces.

trozo [tró·so] *m.* piece, bit, fragment; passage, selection.

truco [trú·ko] *m.* clever trick; pocketing of a ball (*in the game of pool*); *Am.* blow with the fist; *Andes, Ríopl.* a card game; **-s** game of pool (*game similar to billiards*); **-s devices.**

truculencia [tru·ku·lén·sja] *f.* cruelty, ferocity, ruthlessness.

TR

truculento [tru·ku·lén·to] *adj.* cruel, fierce, ruthless.

trucha [trú·ča] *f.* trout; *C.A.* vendor's portable stand.

trueno [trwé·no] *m.* thunder; explosion, report of a gun; wild youth, troublemaker; *Col., Ven.* firecracker, rocket.

trueque [trwé·ke], **trueco** [trwé·ko] *m.* exchange; barter; *Col., Ven., Andes* change, small money; **a** (*or* **en**) **— de** in exchange for.

truhán [tru·án] *m.* scoundrel; swindler; cheat; buffoon, jester.

truncar[6] [truŋ·kár] *v. irr.* to truncate.

tu [tu] *adj.* thy; your (*fam. sing.*).

tú [tu] *pers. pron.* thou; you (*fam. sing.*).

tuba [tú·ba] *f.* tuba (*instrument*).

tubérculo [tu·bér·ku·lo] *m.* tuber.

tuberculosis [tu·ber·ku·ló·sis] *f.* tuberculosis; **tuberculoso** [tu·ber·ku·ló·so] *adj.* tuberculous, tubercular.

tubería [tu·be·rí·a] *f.* tubing, piping; pipe line; **— principal** (water) main; **— vertical** riser; **— de fundición** cast iron pipe.

tubo [tú·bo] *m.* tube; pipe; lamp chimney; **— de ensayo** test tube; **— de escape** tail pipe; **-s de paso** yoke vents; **— en T** tee.

tuerca [twér·ka] *f.* nut (*of a screw*); **llave de -s** wrench.

tuerto [twér·to] *adj.* one-eyed; blind in one eye; *m.* wrong, injustice; **a — o a derecho** (*or* **a tuertas o a derechas**) rightly or wrongly; thoughtlessly.

tuétano [twé·ta·no] *m.* marrow; pith; innermost part; **mojado hasta los -s** soaked through and through.

tufo [tú·fo] *m.* vapor, fume; disagreeable odor; airs, conceit; **tufillo** [tu·fí·yo] *m.* whiff, pungent odor.

tul [tul] *m.* tulle (*a thin, fine net for veils*); **tul** [tul], **tule** [tú·le] *m. Mex.* a kind of reed or bulrush (*used in the manufacture of seats and backs of chairs*).

tulipán [tu·li·pán] *m.* tulip; *Mex.* hibiscus.

tullido [tu·yí·do] *p.p.* crippled; paralyzed; numb.

tullirse[20] [tu·yír·se] *v. irr.* to become crippled; to become numb or paralyzed.

tumba [túm·ba] *f.* tomb; grave; *Col., Cuba, Mex.* felling of timber; *Ven.* forest clearing.

tumbar [tum·bár] *v.* to knock down; *Col., Mex., Cuba* to fell timber; **-se** to lie down.

tumbo [túm·bo] *m.* tumble; somersault; **dar -s** to jump, bump along.

tumor [tu·mór] *m.* tumor; **tumorcillo** [tu·mor·sí·yo] *m.* boil; small tumor.

tumulto [tu·múl·to] *m.* tumult, uproar; mob, throng.

tumultuoso [tu·mul·twó·so] *adj.* tumultuous.

tuna [tú·na] *f.* prickly pear; *Spain* singing group.

tunante [tu·nán·te] *m. & f.* rascal, rogue, scamp; loafer; *Andes, Ch., C.A.* libertine, licentious or lewd person.

tunco [túŋ·ko] *m. C.A.* pig.

tunda [tún·da] *f.* whipping, thrashing; shearing (*the nap of cloth*).

tundir [tun·dír] *v.* to lash, beat, whip; to shear (*the nap of cloth*).

túnel [tú·nel] *m.* tunnel.

túnica [tú·ni·ka] *f.* tunic; gown, robe.

tungsteno [tuns·té·no] *m.* tungsten; **— en atmósfera de gas inerte** tungsten in inert gas.

tupido [tu·pí·do] *adj.* dense; compact, thick; blocked, obstructed; constipated.

tupir [tu·pír] *v.* to press, pack, squeeze together; to stop up, clog; **-se** to get stopped up; to stuff oneself; to become dense (*as a forest*); *Am.* to get astonished or confused.

turba [túr·ba] *f.* mob, throng.

turbación [tur·ba·sjón] *f.* disturbance, confusion; embarrassment.

turbamulta [tur·ba·múl·ta] *f.* throng, mob, crowd.

turbar [tur·bár] *v.* to perturb; to disturb; to trouble; **-se** to get disturbed, confused, embarrassed.

turbina [tur·bí·na] *f.* turbine.

turbio [túr·bjo] *adj.* muddy; muddled, confused.

turbión [tur·bjón] *m.* thunderstorm; heavy shower.

turbogenerador [tur·bo·xe·ne·ra·dór] *m.*, turbogenerator.

turbopropulsor [tur·bo·pro·pul·sór] *m.* turboprop.

turborreactor [tur·bo·rre·ak·tór] *m.* turbojet.

turbulento [tur·bu·lén·to] *adj.* turbulent; restless; disorderly.

turco [túr·ko] *adj.* Turkish; *m.* Turk; Turkish, Turkish language; *Am.* peddler.

turismo [tu·ríz·mo] *m.* tourist travel; touring, sightseeing; **oficina de —** travel bureau; **turista** [tu·rís·ta] *m. & f.* tourist; **turístico** [tu·rís·ti·ko] *adj.* tourist; related to tourism.

turnar [tur·nár] *v.* to alternate; **-se** to alternate; to take turns.

turno [túr·no] *m.* turn, alternate order.

turquesa [tur·ké·sa] *f.* turquoise.

turrón [tu·rrón] *m.* nougat, nut confection; almond cake; *Mex.* **romper el —** to decide to use the **tú** form of address (*as a mark of close friendship*).

tusa [tú·sa] *f. Am.* corn, corncob; *Cuba, Mex.* corn husk; *Am.* corn silk, tassel of an ear of corn.

tusar [tu·sár] *v. Cuba, Mex., Ríopl., Andes* to shear; *Ríopl.* to crop, cut badly (*hair*).

tutear [tu·te·ár] *v.* to address familiarly (*using the tú form*).

tutela [tu·té·la] *f.* guardianship; guidance, protection.

tutelar [tu·te·lár] *v.* to guide, coach, direct; *adj.* guiding, guardian (*used as adj.*).

tutor [tu·tór] *m.* tutor; guardian.

tuyo [tú·yo] *poss. adj.* your, of yours (*fam. sing.*); *poss. pron.* yours.

U:u

u [u] *conj.* (*before words beginning with o or ho*) or.

ubicar[6] [u·bi·kár] *v.* to be located; **-se** *am.* to situate.

ubre [ú·bre] *f.* udder.

ufanarse [u·fa·nár·se] *v.* to glory (in); to be proud (of).

ufano [u·fá·no] *adj.* proud; gay; self-satisfied.

ujier [u·xjér] *m.* usher, doorman.

úlcera [úl·se·ra] *f.* ulcer; sore.

ulterior [ul·te·rjór] *adj.* ulterior; further; later.

ultimar [ul·ti·már] *v.* to put an end to; *Am.* to give the finishing blow, kill.

último [úl·ti·mo] *adj.* last, final; ultimate; latest; **estar en las últimas** to be on one's last legs; to be at the end of one's rope, be at the end of one's resources.

ultrajar [ul·tra·xár] *v.* to outrage, insult; to scorn.

ultraje [ul·trá·xe] *m.* outrage, insult.

ultramar [ul·tra·már] *m.* country or place across the sea; **de —** overseas, from across the sea; **en** (*or* **a) — overseas.

ultramarinos [ul·tra·ma·rí·nos] *m. pl.* delicatessen; imported foods.

ultratumba [ul·tra·túm·ba] *adv.* beyond the grave.

ultravioleta [ul·tra·bjo·lé·ta] *adj.* ultraviolet.

ulular [u·lu·lár] *v.* to howl, shriek, hoot.

umbral [um·brál] *m.* threshold.

umbrío [um·brí·o] *adj.* shady.

un(o) [ú·no] *indef. art.* a, an; **-s** some, a few; **-s cuantos** a few; **uno** *pron. & num.* one.

unánime [u·ná·ni·me] *adj.* unanimous.

unanimidad [u·na·ni·mi·dád] *f.* unanimity, complete accord.

unción [un·sjón] *f.* unction (*anointing with oil*); religious fervor; spiritual grace; **Extremaunción** [es·tre·mawn·sjón] Extreme Unction (*the Last Sacrament of the Church*).

uncir[10] [un·sír] *v.* to yoke.

ungir[11] [uŋ·xír] *v.* to anoint; to consecrate.

ungüento [uŋ·gwén·to] *m.* ointment; salve.

único [ú·ni·ko] *adj.* only, sole; unique, singular, rare.

unicornio [u·ni·kór·njo] *m.* unicorn.

unidad [u·ni·dád] *f.* unity; unit; (*computadora*) unit, housing; — **de discos** disk drive; — **central de proceso** (UCP) control processing unit (CPU).

unificar[6] [u·ni·fi·kár] *v.* to unify; to unite.

uniformar [u·ni·for·már] *v.* to standardize; to make uniform; to furnish with uniforms.

uniforme [u·ni·fór·me] *adj. & m.* uniform.

uniformidad [u·ni·for·mi·dád] *f.* uniformity.

unilateral [u·ni·la·te·rál] *adj.* unilateral, one-sided.

unión [u·njón] *f.* union.

unir [u·nír] *v.* to unite; to join; to bring together; **-se** to unite, join together; to wed.

unísono [u·ní·so·no] *adj.* unison.

universal [u·ni·ber·sál] *adj.* universal.

universidad [u·ni·ber·si·dád] *f.* university.

universitario [u·ni·ber·si·tá·rjo] *adj.* pertaining to the university; *m. Am.* a university student.

universo [u·ni·bér·so] *m.* universe.

uno(a) [ú·no] *num.* one.

untar [un·tár] *v.* to anoint; to smear; to oil, grease; to bribe; to corrupt; **-se** to smear oneself; to get smeared.

unto [ún·to] *m.* grease, fat; ointment.

untuosidad [un·two·si·dád] *f.* greasiness; **untuoso** *adj.* unctuous; oily, greasy.

uña [ú·ña] *f.* fingernail; toenail; claw; hoof; hook (*on a tool*); **a — de caballo** at full gallop, at full speed; **largo de -s** prone to stealing; *Mex., C.A. Ven., Col., Andes* **largas -s** thief; **vivir de sus -s** to live by stealing; *Mex., C.A., Ven., Col., Andes* **echar la —** to steal; **ser — y carne** to be inseparable friends.

uñir [u·ñír] *v.* to yoke.

uranio [u·rá·njo] *m.* uranium.

urbanidad [ur·ba·ni·dád] *f.* courtesy, politeness; refinement.

urbanizar[9] [ur·ba·ni·sár] *v. irr.* to urbanize.

urbano [ur·bá·no] *adj.* urban; courteous, polite.

urbe [úr·be] *f.* metropolis, large city.

urdimbre [ur·dím·bre] *f.* warp (*of a fabric*); scheme.

urdir [ur·dír] *v.* to warp (*in weaving*); to plot, scheme; to invent (*a lie, story, etc.*).

uremia [u·ré·mja] *f.* uremia.

uretra [u·ré·tra] *f.* urethra.

urgencia [ur·xén·sja] *f.* urgency; pressing need.

urgente [ur·xén·te] *adj.* urgent, pressing.

urgir[11] [ur·xír] *v.* to urge; to be urgent.

úrico [ú·ri·ko] *adj.* uric.

urna [úr·na] *f.* urn; — **electoral** ballot box.

urólogo [u·ró·lo·ɡo] *m.* urologist.

urraca [u·rrá·ka] *f.* magpie.

usado [u·sá·do] *p.p. & adj.* used; accustomed; worn; threadbare.

usanza [u·sán·sa] *f.* usage, custom, habit.

usar [u·sár] *v.* to use; to wear; to wear out; to be accustomed; **-se** to be in use, be in vogue.

uso [ú·so] *m.* (*empleo*) use; usage; wear; (*costumbre*) usage; practice; habit; custom; **al — de la época** according to the custom or usage of the period; **estar en buen —** to be in good condition (*said of a thing*).

usted [us·té(d)] *pers. pron.* (*abbreviated as* **Vd., V.,** *or* **Ud.**) you.

usual [u·swál] *adj.* usual; ordinary, customary.

usuario [u·swá·rjo] *m.* user.

usufructo [u·su·frúk·to] *m.* use, enjoyment; profit.

usufructuar[18] [u·su·fruk·twár] *v.* to enjoy the use of; to make use of.

usura [u·sú·ra] *f.* usury.

usurero [u·su·ré·ro] *m.* usurer, loan shark.

usurpar [u·sur·pár] *v.* to usurp.

utensilio [u·ten·sí·ljo] *m.* utensil; implement, tool.

útero [ú·te·ro] *m.* uterus, womb.

útil [ú·til] *adj.* useful; profitable; **-es** *m. pl.* tools, instruments.

utilidad [u·ti·li·dád] *f.* utility; profit; usefulness.

utilitario [u·ti·li·tá·rjo] *adj.* utilitarian.

utilizar[9] [u·ti·li·zár] *v.* to utilize; to use.

utopía [u·to·pí·a] *f.* utopia.

uva [ú·ba] *f.* grape; — **espina** gooseberry; — **pasa** raisin; **estar hecho una —** to be tipsy, drunk.

úvula [ú·bu·la] *f.* uvula.

uvular [u·bu·lár] *adj.* uvular.

¡uy! [uj] *interj.* ouch! oh!

V : v

vaca [bá·ka] *f.* cow; **carne de —** beef; **cuero de —** cowhide; *Am.* **hacer —** to play hooky, play truant, cut class; to join in a quick business deal.

vacación [ba·ka·sjón] *f.* vacation (*usually* **vacaciones**).

vacada [ba·ká·da] *f.* herd of cows.

vacancia [ba·kán·sja] *f.* vacancy.

vacante [ba·kán·te] *adj.* vacant, unfilled, unoccupied; *f.* vacancy.

vaciar[17] [ba·sjár] (*dejar vacío*) to empty; to drain; to flow; (*amoldar*) to cast into a mold; (*ahuecar*) to hollow out; **-se** to spill; to empty; to become empty; to flow (into).

vaciedad [ba·sje·dád] *f.* emptiness; nonsense, silliness.

vacilación [ba·si·la·sjón] *f.* hesitation; wavering; doubt.

vacilante [ba·si·lán·te] *adj.* vacillating, hesitating, wavering; unsteady.

vacilar [ba·si·lár] *v.* to vacillate, waver, hesitate; to sway.

vacío [ba·sí·o] *adj.* empty; vacant; unoccupied; hollow; *m.* void; hollow; vacuum; vacancy; gap, blank.

vacuna [ba·kú·na] *f.* vaccine; vaccination; cowpox (*eruptive disease of the cow*); **vacunación** [ba·ku·na·sjón] *f.* vaccination; — **antipoliomelítica** antipolio inoculation.

vacunar [ba·ku·nár] *v.* to vaccinate.

vadear [ba·de·ár] *v.* to ford; to wade; to avoid (*a difficulty*).

vado [bá·do] *m.* ford; **no hallar —** to find no way out.

vagabundear [ba·ga·bun·de·ár] *v.* to tramp around, wander, rove; to loiter.

vagabundo [ba·ga·bún·do] *adj.* vagabond, wandering; *m.* vagabond, tramp; vagrant; wanderer.

vagar[7] [ba·gár] *v.* to wander, roam; to loiter; to loaf;

m. leisure; loitering.

vagina [ba·xí·na] *f.* vagina.

vago [bá·ġo] *adj.* vague; roaming; idle;.vagrant; *m.* vagrant, tramp.

vagón [ba·ġón] *m.* railway car or coach; **vagoneta** [ba·ġo·né·ta] *f.* small railway car or tram (*used in mines*); **vagonada** [ba·ġo·ná·da] *f.* carload.

vaguear [ba·ġe·ár] = **vagar.**

vahido [ba·í·do] *m.* dizziness, dizzy spell.

vaho [bá·o] *m.* vapor, steam, fume, mist; odor.

vaina [bái·na] *f.* sheath, scabbard; case; pod, husk; *Ven., Col., C.A., Mex.* bother, nuisance; *Ven., Col.* luck.

vainilla [baj·ní·ya] *f.* vanilla.

vaivén [baj·bén] *m.* sway; fluctuation, wavering; traffic, coming and going; **-es** comings and goings; ups and downs; inconstancy.

vajilla [ba·xí·ya] *f.* tableware; set of dishes; — **de plata** silverware; — **de porcelana** chinaware.

vale [bá·le] *m.* bond, promissory note; voucher; adieu, farewell; *m. & f. Col., Ven., Mex.* comrade, pal, chum.

valedero [ba·le·dé·ro] *adj.* valid, binding, effective.

valedor [ba·le·dór] *m.* defender, protector; *Am.* pal, comrade.

valenciano [ba·len·sjá·no] *adj.* Valencian, of or from Valencia, Spain; *m.* Valencian.

valentía [ba·len·tí·a] *f.* courage, valor; exploit; boast.

valentón [ba·len·tón] *adj.* blustering, boastful; *m.* bully, braggart.

valer[47] [ba·lér] *v. irr.* to favor, protect; to cost; to be worth; to be worthy; to be equivalent to; to be valid; to prevail; to be useful; *Spain* ¡**vale**! O.K.; now you're talking; — **la pena** to be worth while; — **por** to be worth; **-se de** to avail oneself of, make use of; **más vale** it is better; ¡**válgame Dios!** heaven help me! good heavens!

valeroso [ba·le·ró·so] *adj.* valiant, brave; valuable.

valía [ba·lí·a] *f.* worth, value; influence.

validez [ba·li·dés] *f.* validity; stability, soundness.

válido [bá·li·do] *adj.* valid.

valiente [ba·ljén·te] *adj.* valiant, brave; powerful; *m.* brave man; bully.

valija [ba·lí·xa] *f.* valise, satchel; mailbag.

valimiento [ba·li·mjén·to] *m.* favor, protection; **gozar de** — to enjoy protection or favor.

valioso [ba·ljó·so] *adj.* valuable; worthy; wealthy.

valor [ba·lór] *m.* value; worth; price; significance; valor, courage; boldness; efficacy, power; **-es** stocks, bonds.

valoración [ba·lo·ra·sjón] *f.* valuation, appraisal.

valorar [ba·lo·rár] *v.* to evaluate, value, appraise.

valorizar[9] [ba·lo·ri·sár] *v. Cuba, Ven., Ríopl., Andes* to value, appraise; *Am.* to realize, convert into money.

vals [bals] *m.* waltz.

valsar [bal·sár] *v.* to waltz.

valuación [ba·lwa·sjón] *f.* valuation, appraisal.

valuar[18] [ba·lwár] *v.* to value, price, appraise; to rate.

válvula [bál·bu·la] *f.* valve; — **de retención** check valve.

valla [bá·ya] *f.* stockade, fence; barrier; obstacle; *Cuba, Col.* cockpit (*for cockfights*).

vallado [ba·yá·do] *m.* stockade, fenced-in place; fence.

valle [bá·ye] *m.* valley; vale.

vampiro [bam·pí·ro] *m.* vampire.

vanadio [ba·ná·djo] *m.* vanadium.

vanagloria [ba·na·ġló·rja] *f.* vainglory, boastful vanity.

vanagloriarse[17] [ba·na·ġlo·rjár·se] *v.* to glory, take

great pride (in), boast (of).

vanaglorioso [ba·na·ġlo·rjó·so] *adj.* vain, boastful, conceited.

vándalo [bán·da·lo] *m.* vandal.

vanguardia [baŋ·gwár·dja] *f.* vanguard.

vanidad [ba·ni·dád] *f.* vanity; conceit; emptiness.

vanidoso [ba·ni·dó·so] *adj.* vain, conceited.

vano [bá·no] *adj.* vain; empty; hollow; *m.* opening in a wall (*for a door or window*).

vapor [ba·pór] *m.* vapor, steam, mist; steamer, steamship.

vaporoso [ba·po·ró·so] *adj.* vaporous, steamy, misty; vaporlike.

vapulear [ba·pu·le·ár] *v.* to beat, whip, thrash.

vapuleo [ba·pu·lé·o] *m.* beating, whipping, thrashing.

vaquería [ba·ke·rí·a] *f.* herd of cows; stable for cows; dairy.

vaquerizo [ba·ke·rí·so] *m.* herdsman; *adj.* pertaining to cows; **vaqueriza** [ba·ke·rí·sa] *f.* stable for cows.

vaquero [ba·ké·ro] *m.* cowherd, herdsman; cowboy; *Cuba* milkman; *adj.* relating to cowherds, cowboys, or cattle.

vaqueta [ba·ké·ta] *f.* sole leather; cowhide; *Mex.* **zurrar a uno la** — to tan someone's hide, beat someone up.

vara [bá·ra] *f.* twig; stick; rod; wand; staff; yard; yardstick; thrust with a picador's lance.

varadero [ba·ra·dé·ro] *m.* shipyard.

varar [ba·rár] *v.* to beach (*a boat*), run aground; to stop, come to a standstill (*said of business*).

varear [ba·re·ár] *v.* to beat; to whip; to sell by the yard; to measure with a **vara**; *Ríopl.* to exercise (*a horse before a race*).

variable [ba·rjá·ble] *adj.* variable, unstable, changeable; *f.* variable.

variación [ba·rja·sjón] *f.* variation.

variado [ba·rjá·do] *p.p. & adj.* varied; variegated.

variar[17] [ba·rjár] *v.* to vary; to change; to shift; to differ.

várices [bá·ri·ses] *f. pl.* varicose veins.

variedad [ba·rje·dád] *f.* variety; variation, change.

varilla [ba·rí·ya] *f.* small rod; wand; long, flexible twig; rib (*of an umbrella or fan*); corset stay; — **de aporte** filler rod. *Mex.* peddler's wares.

varillero [ba·ri·yé·ro] *m. Mex.* peddler.

vario [bá·rjo] *adj.* various; different; changeable; varied; **-s** various, several.

varón [ba·rón] *m.* male, man; *Am.* long beam, timber.

varonil [ba·ro·níl] *adj.* manly; strong; brave.

vasallo [ba·sá·yo] *adj. & m.* vassal, subject.

vasco [bás·ko], **vascongado** [bas·koŋ·gá·do] *adj. & m.* Basque.

vascuence [bas·kwén·se] *m.* the Basque language.

vasectomía [ba·sek·to·mí·a] *f.* vasectomy.

vaselina [ba·se·lí·na] *f.* vaseline.

vasija [ba·sí·xa] *f.* vessel, container, receptacle.

vaso [bá·so] *m.* drinking glass; glassful; vase; vessel; hull of a ship; horse's hoof; — **de elección** person chosen by God.

vástago [bás·ta·ġo] *m.* (*de planta*) shoot, sprout; stem; (*persona*) scion, offspring; *Mex., Col., Ven.* stem, trunk of a banana tree.

vasto [bás·to] *adj.* vast, extensive, large.

vate [bá·te] *m.* bard, poet.

vaticinar [ba·ti·si·nár] *v.* to prophesy, predict, foretell.

vaticinio [ba·ti·sí·njo] *m.* prophecy, prediction.

vecindad [be·sin·dád] *f.* vicinity; neighborhood; neighborliness; **casa de** — tenement.

vecindario [be·sin·dá·rjo] *m.* neighborhood;

neighbors; vicinity.

vecino [be·sí·no] *m.* neighbor; resident; citizen; *adj.* neighboring; next, near.

vedar [be·dár] *v.* to prohibit; to impede.

vega [bé·ga] *f.* fertile lowland or plain; *Cuba, Ven.* tobacco plantation.

vegetación [be·xe·ta·sjón] *f.* vegetation.

vegetal [be·xe·tál] *adj.* vegetable; *m.* vegetable, plant.

vegetar [be·xe·tár] *v.* to vegetate.

vegetariano [be·xe·ta·rjá·no] *m.* vegetarian.

vehemente [be·e·mén·te] *adj.* vehement, passionate, impetuous; violet.

vehículo [be·í·ku·lo] *m.* vehicle.

veinte [béjn·te] *num.* twenty.

veintena [bejn·té·na] *f.* score, twenty.

veintiuno [bejn·tjú·no] *num.* twenty-one.

vejamen [be·xá·men] annoyance, vexation.

vejar [be·xár] *v.* to annoy; to criticize.

vejestorio [be·xes·tó·rjo] *m.* wrinkled old person.

vejete [be·xé·te] *m.* little old man.

vejez [be·xés] *f.* old age.

vejiga [be·xí·ga] *f.* bladder; blister; smallpox sore; — **de la bilis** (*or* — **de la hiel**) gall bladder.

vela [bé·la] *f.* vigil, watch; night watch; candle; sail; **a toda** — under full sail; at full speed; **en** — on watch, without sleep; **hacerse a la** — to set sail.

velada [be·lá·da] *f.* watch, vigil; evening party; evening function or meeting.

velador [be·la·dór] *m.* night watchman; keeper, guard; lamp table; bedside table; candlestick; *Ríopl., Mex., Cuba, Col.* lamp shade.

velar [be·lár] *v.* to keep vigil; to stay up at night; to be vigilant; to watch over; to veil; to cover, hide.

velatorio [be·la·tó·rjo] *m.* wake (*vigil over a corpse*). *See* **velorio.**

veleidoso [be·lej·dó·so] *adj.* inconstant, fickle, changeable.

velero [be·lé·ro] *m.* sailboat; sailmaker; candlemaker; *adj.* swift-sailing; **buque** — sailboat.

veleta [be·lé·ta] *f.* weathervane, weathercock; *m. & f.* fickle person.

velís [be·lís] *m. Mex.* valise.

velo [bé·lo] *m.* veil; curtain, covering; — **del paladar** velum, soft palate.

velocidad [be·lo·si·dád] *f.* velocity.

velocímetro [be·lo·sí·me·tro] *m.* speedometer.

velorio [be·ló·rjo] *m. Am.* wake (*vigil over a corpse*); *Mex., C.A., Ven., Col., Ch., Andes* dull party.

veloz [be·lós] *adj.* swift, quick, fast.

vello [bé·yo] *m.* hair (*on the body*); down, fuzz; nap (*of cloth*).

vellón [be·yón] *m.* fleece; tuft of wool; sheepskin with fleece; silver and copper alloy; an ancient copper coin.

velloso [be·yó·so] *adj.* hairy; downy, fuzzy.

velludo [be·yú·do] *adj.* hairy; downy; fuzzy; *m.* plush, velvet.

vena [bé·na] *f.* vein; lode, vein of metal ore; mood, disposition; **estar en** — to be in the mood; to be inspired.

venado [be·ná·do] *m.* deer; venison, deer meat; *Mex.* **pintar** — to play hooky.

vencedor [ben·se·dór] *adj.* conquering, winning, victorious; *m.* conqueror, winner, victor.

vencer[10] [ben·sér] *v.* to conquer; vanquish; to defeat; to overcome; to surpass; to win; **-se** to control oneself; to mature, fall due; **se venció el plazo** the time limit expired.

vencido [ben·sí·do] *p.p. & adj.* conquered; defeated; due, fallen due.

vencimiento [ben·si·mjén·to] *m.* conquering, defeat;

maturity (*of a debt*), falling due; expiration (*of a period of time*).

venda [bén·da] *f.* bandage.

vendaje [ben·dá·xe] *m.* bandage.

vendar [ben·dár] *v.* to bandage; to blindfold.

vendaval [ben·da·bál] *m.* strong wind, gale.

vendedor [ben·de·dór] *m.* vendor, seller, peddler.

vender [ben·dér] *v.* to sell; to betray; **-se** to be sold; **se vende** for sale; to sell oneself; accept a bribe.

vendimia [ben·dí·mja] *f.* vintage; profit.

venduta [ben·dú·ta] *f. Col.* auction; *Cuba* small fruit and vegetable store.

veneno [be·né·no] *m.* venom, poison.

venenoso [be·ne·nó·so] *adj.* poisonous.

venerable [be·ne·rá·ble] *adj.* venerable.

veneración [be·ne·ra·sjón] *f.* veneration, reverence.

venerando [be·ne·rán·do] *adj.* venerable, worthy of respect.

venerar [be·ne·rár] *v.* to venerate, revere; to worship.

venéreo [be·né·re·o] *adj.* venereal.

venero [be·né·ro] *m.* water spring; source, origin; lode, layer, seam (*of mineral*).

venezolano [be·ne·so·lá·no] *adj.* Venezuelan; *m.* Venezuelan; *Ven.* Venezuelan silver coin.

vengador [beŋ·ga·dór] *adj.* avenging, revenging; *m.* avenger.

venganza [beŋ·gán·sa] *f.* vengeance, revenge.

vengar[7] [beŋ·gár] to avenge, revenge; **-se de** to take revenge on.

vengativo [beŋ·ga·tí·bo] *adj.* vindictive, revengeful.

venia [bé·nja] *f.* pardon; permission, leave; bow, nod; *C.A., Ven., Ríopl.* military salute.

venida [be·ní·da] *f.* arrival; return; river flood, onrush of water; attack (*in fencing*).

venidero [be·ni·dé·ro] *adj.* coming, future; **en lo** — in the future; **-s** *m. pl.* successors.

venir[48] [be·nír] *v. irr.* to come; to arrive; to fit; **-le a uno bien** (*or* **mal**) to be becoming (*or* unbecoming); — **a menos** to decline, decay; — **a pelo** to come just at the right moment; to suit perfectly; to be pat, opportune, to the point; — **en** to agree to; — **sobre** to fall upon; **¿a qué viene eso?** what is the point of that? **-se abajo** to fall down; to collapse; to fail.

venoso [be·nó·so] *adj.* veined; venous (*of or pertaining to the veins; with veins*).

venta [bén·ta] *f.* sale; roadside inn; *Ur.* store, vendor's stand; — **pública** auction.

ventaja [ben·tá·xa] *f.* advantage; gain, profit; bonus; odds.

ventajoso [ben·ta·xó·so] *adj.* advantageous, beneficial, profitable; *Mex.* self-seeking, profiteering.

ventana [ben·tá·na] *f.* window; window shutter; *Col.* clearing (*in a forest*); — (*or* **ventanilla** [ben·ta·ní·ya]) **de la nariz** nostril.

ventarrón [ben·ta·rrón] *m.* gale, strong wind.

ventear [ben·te·ár] *v.* (*oler*) to scent, sniff; (*soplar*) to blow, be windy; (*poner al aire*) to air; (*indagar*) to nose around; *Ven.* to toss in the wind; *Arg.* to flee; *Am.* to outrun; **-se** to expel air, break wind; *Col.* to stay outdoors.

ventero [ben·té·ro] *m.* innkeeper.

ventilación [ben·ti·la·sjón] *f.* ventilation.

ventilador [ben·ti·la·dór] *m.* ventilator; fan (*for ventilation*); — **de taller** blower.

ventilar [ben·ti·lár] *v.* to ventilate; to air.

ventisca [ben·tís·ka] *f.* blizzard, snowstorm; snowdrift.

ventiscar[6] [ben·tis·kár] *v.* to snow hard and blow (*as in a blizzard*); to drift (*as snow in a blizzard*).

ventisquero [ben·tis·ké·ro] *m.* blizzard, snowstorm; glacier; snowdrift; snow-capped mountain peak.

ventolera [ben·to·lé·ra] *f.* gust of wind; pride, vanity; whim; pin wheel; **darle a uno la — de** to take the notion to.

ventoso [ben·tó·so] *adj.* windy.

ventura [ben·tú·ra] *f.* happiness; fortune, chance; risk, danger; **a la —** at random; **buena —** fortune; **por —** perchance.

venturoso [ben·tu·ró·so] *adj.* fortunate, lucky; happy.

ver[49] [ver] *v. irr.* to see; to look; to look at; to look into, examine; **— de** to try to, see to it that; **a más** (*or* **hasta más — good-bye; no — la hora de** to be anxious to; **no tener nada que — con** not to have anything to do with; **-se** to be seen; to be; **-se obligado a** to be obliged to, be forced to; **a mi modo de —** in my opinion; **de buen —** good-looking; **ser de —** to be worth seeing.

vera [bé·ra] *f.* edge; **a la — del camino** at the edge of the road.

veracidad [ve·ra·si·dád] *f.* truthfulness.

veraneante [be·ra·ne·án·te] *m. & f.* summer resorter, vacationist, or tourist.

veranear [be·ra·ne·ár] *v.* to spend the summer.

veraneo [be·ra·né·o] *m.* summering, summer vacation.

veraniego [be·ra·njé·go] *adj.* summer, of summer.

verano [be·rá·no] *m.* summer.

veras [bé·ras] *f. pl.* reality, truth; **de —** in truth; truly; in earnest.

veraz [be·rás] *adj.* truthful.

verbal [ber·bál] *adj.* verbal; oral.

verbena [ber·bé·na] *f.* verbena (*a plant*); festival or carnival (*on eve of a religious holiday*).

verbigracia [ber·bi·grá·sja] *adv.* for instance, for example.

verbo [bér·bo] *m.* verb; **el Verbo** the Word (*second person of the Trinity*).

verboso [ber·bó·so] *adj.* verbose, wordy.

verdad [ber·dád] *f.* truth; **¿—?** really?; is that so?; isn't that so?; **— de Perogrullo** truism, evident truth; **de —** (*or* **a la —**) in truth, in earnest; **en —** really, truly.

verdadero [ber·da·dé·ro] *adj.* real; true; truthful; sincere; **verdadero/falso** true/false.

verde [bér·de] *adj.* green; unripe; young; offcolor, indecent; *m.* green; verdure; *Ur., Ven.* country, countryside.

verdear [ber·de·ár] *v.* to grow green; to look green.

verdinegro [ber·di·né·gro] *adj.* dark-green.

verdor [ber·dór] *m.* verdure, greenness.

verdoso [ber·dó·so] *adj.* greenish.

verdugo [ber·dú·go] *m.* executioner; cruel person; torment; rapier (*light sword*); lash, whip; welt; shoot of a tree; **verdugón** [ber·du·gón] *m.* large welt.

verdulera [ber·du·lé·ra] *f.* woman vendor of green vegetables; **verdulería** [ber·du·le·rí·a] *f.* green vegetable store or stand.

verdura [ber·dú·ra] *f.* verdure; greenness; green vegetables.

vereda [be·ré·da] *f.* path; *Ch., Ríopl., Andes* sidewalk; *Col.* small village; *C.R.* bank of a stream.

veredicto [be·re·dík·to] *m.* verdict.

vergonzoso [ber·gon·só·so] *adj.* shameful, disgraceful; shy, bashful; *m.* species of armadillo.

vergüenza [ber·gwén·sa] *f.* shame; disgrace; shyness, bashfulness; **tener —** to have shame; to be ashamed.

vericueto [be·ri·kwé·to] *m.* rugged, wild place (*often rocky*).

verídico [be·rí·di·ko] *adj.* truthful; true.

verificar[6] [be·ri·fi·kár] *v.* to verify; to confirm; to test, check; to carry out, fulfill; **-se** to be verified; to take place; **verificador** checking device.

verijas [be·rí·xas] *f. pl. Ríopl., Mex.* groin (*hollow between lower part of abdomen and thigh*); *Am.* flanks of a horse.

verja [bér·xa] *f.* grate, grating.

verónica [be·ró·ni·ka] *f.* veronica; a bullfighting pass executed with the cape held behind the body with both hands.

verruga [be·rrú·ga] *f.* wart; nuisance.

versado [ber·sá·do] *adj.* versed, skilled, expert.

versar [ber·sár] *v.* to deal (with), treat (of); **-se en** to become versed in.

versátil [ber·sá·til] *adj.* versatile.

versificar[6] [ber·si·fi·kár] *v. irr.* to versify.

versión [ber·sjón] *f.* version; translation.

verso [bér·so] *m.* verse; meter; **— suelto** (*or* **— libre**) free or blank verse.

vertebrado [ber·te·brá·do] *adj. & m.* vertebrate.

verter[1] [ber·tér] *v. irr.* to pour; to empty; to spill; to translate; to flow down.

vertical [ber·ti·kál] *adj.* vertical.

vértice [bér·ti·se] *m.* top, apex, summit.

vertiente [ber·tjén·te] *f.* slope; watershed; *adj.* flowing.

vertiginoso [ber·ti·xi·nó·so] *adj.* whirling, dizzy, giddy.

vértigo [bér·ti·go] *m.* dizziness, giddiness; fit of madness.

vesícula [be·sí·ku·la] *f.* gall bladder.

vestíbulo [bes·tí·bu·lo] *m.* vestibule; lobby.

vestido [bes·tí·do] *m.* clothing, apparel; dress; garment; suit.

vestidura [bes·ti·dú·ra] *f.* vestment; attire, apparel; raiment.

vestigio [bes·tí·xjo] *m.* vestige, sign, trace.

vestir[5] [bes·tír] *v. irr.* (*cubrir*) to dress; to clothe; to put on; to adorn; to cover; (*llevar*) to wear; **-se** to dress, get dressed; to be clothed; to be covered.

vestuario [bes·twá·rjo] *m.* wardrobe, apparel; theatrical costumes; cloakroom; dressing room; vestry (*room for church vestments*).

veta [bé·ta] *f.* vein, seam (*of mineral*); streak, grain (*in wood*); stripe; *Cuba* rope.

vetar [be·tár] *v.* to veto.

veteado [be·te·á·do] *adj.* veined; striped; streaked.

veterano [be·te·rá·no] *adj. & m.* veteran.

veterinario [be·te·ri·ná·rjo] *m.* veterinary.

veto [bé·to] *m.* veto.

vetusto [be·tús·to] *adj.* old, ancient.

vez [bes] *f.* time, occasion; turn; **a la —** at the same time; **cada — más** more and more; **cada — que** whenever; **de — en cuando** from time to time; **de una —** all at once; **en — de** instead of; **otra —** again; **una que otra —** rarely, once in a while; **tal — perhaps; a veces** sometimes; **raras veces** seldom; **hacer las veces de** to take the place of.

vía [bí·a] *f.* way; road; track; railroad track; conduit; **Vía Crucis** the Way of the Cross; **Vía Láctea** the Milky Way.

viaducto [bja·dúk·to] *m.* viaduct.

viajante [bja·xán·te] *m.* traveler; **— de comercio** traveling salesman.

viajar [bja·xár] *v.* to travel.

viaje [bjá·xe] *m.* voyage; trip; travel; **— de ida y vuelta** (*or* **— redondo**) round trip.

viajero [bja·xé·ro] *m.* traveler; *adj.* traveling.

vianda [bján·da] *f.* viands, food; meal.

viandante [bjan·dán·te] *m. & f.* wayfarer, walker, pedestrian; passer-by; vagabond.
viático [bjá·ti·ko] *m.* provisions for a journey; viaticum (*communion given to dying persons*).
víbora [bí·βo·ra] *f.* viper.
vibración [bi·βra·sjón] *f.* vibration.
vibrante [bi·βrán·te] *adj.* vibrant, vibrating.
vibrar [bi·βrár] *v.* to vibrate.
vicecónsul [bi·se·kón·sul] *m.* vice consul.
vicepresidente [bi·se·pre·si·dén·te] *m.* vice-president.
viceversa [bi·se·βér·sa] *adv.* vice versa, conversely.
viciado [bi·sjá·do] *adj.* contaminated, foul; corrupt; *p.p. of* **viciar.**
viciar [bi·sjár] *v.* to vitiate, corrupt; to adulterate; to falsify; **-se** to become corrupt.
vicio [bí·sjo] *m.* vice; bad habit; fault; craving; **de —** as a habit; **hablar de —** to talk too much; **-s** *Am.* articles and ingredients used for serving **mate.**
vicioso [bi·sjó·so] *adj.* vicious, evil, wicked; having bad habits; licentious; faulty, incorrect (*grammatical construction, reasoning, etc.*).
vicisitud [bi·si·si·túd] *f.* vicissitude; **-es** vicissitudes, ups and downs, changes of fortune or condition.
víctima [bík·ti·ma] *f.* victim.
victoria [bik·tó·rja] *f.* victory, triumph; victoria (*carriage*).
victorioso [bik·to·rjó·so] *adj.* victorious.
vicuña [bi·kú·ña] *f.* vicuña (*an Andean animal allied to the alpaca and llama*); vicuña wool; vicuña cloth.
vid [bid] *f.* vine, grapevine.
vida [bí·da] *f.* life; living; livelihood; **— mía** dearest; **hacer —** to live together; **pasar a mejor —** to die; **tener la — en un hilo** to be in great danger.
vidalita [bi·da·lí·ta] *f. Ríopl., Ch.* melancholy song of Argentina and Chile.
vidente [bi·dén·te] *m.* seer, prophet; *adj.* seeing.
video [bi·dé·o] *m.* video; **video inverso** inverse video.
vidriado [bi·drjá·do] *m.* glaze; glazed earthenware; *p.p. & adj.* glazed.
vidriar [bi·drjár] *v.* to glaze (*earthenware*).
vidriera [bi·drjé·ra] *f.* glass window; glass door; *Am.* show case, show window; **— de colores** stained-glass window.
vidriero [bi·drjé·ro] *m.* glazier (*one who installs windowpanes*); glass blower; glass maker; glass dealer.
vidrio [bí·drjo] *m.* glass; any glass article.
vidrioso [bi·drjó·so] *adj.* glassy; brittle; slippery, icy; touchy; irritable.
viejo [bjé·xo] *adj.* old; ancient; worn-out; *m.* old man; **— verde** old man who boasts of his youth and vigor; "dirty" old man; *Am.* **los -s** the old folks (*applied to one's parents*); **viejota** *f.* old hag.
viento [bjén·to] *m.* wind; scent; **hace —** it is windy; **a los cuatro -s** in all directions; **vientecito** *m.* gentle breeze.
vientre [bjén·tre] *m.* abdomen; belly; bowels; entrails; womb.
viernes [bjér·nes] *m.* Friday.
vierteaguas [bjer·te·a·gwas] *m.* flashing (roof).
viga [bí·ga] *f.* beam, rafter; **— central** collar beam.
vigencia [bi·xén·sja] *f.* operation (*of a law*); **entrar en —** to take effect (*said of a law*); **estar en —** to be in force (*said of a law*).
vigente [bi·xén·te] *adj.* effective, in force (*as a law*).
vigía [bi·xí·a] *f.* lookout, watchtower; watch (*act of watching*); reef; *m.* lookout, watchman.
vigilancia [bi·xi·lán·sja] *f.* vigilance.
vigilante [bi·xi·lán·te] *adj.* vigilant, watchful; *m.* watchman.

vigilar [bi·xi·lár] *v.* to keep guard; to watch over.
vigilia [bi·xí·lja] *f.* vigil, watch; wakefulness, sleeplessness; night hours (*spent in study*); eve before certain church festivals; vesper service; **día de —** day of abstinence; **comer de —** to abstain from meat.
vigor [bi·gór] *m.* vigor; **en —** in force (*said of a law*); **entrar en —** to become effective (*as a law, statute, etc.*).
vigorizar [bi·go·ri·sár] *v.* to invigorate, tone up, give vigor to, strengthen.
vigoroso [bi·go·ró·so] *adj.* vigorous.
viguería [bi·ge·rí·a] *f.* beams.
vihuela [bi·wé·la] *f.* guitar.
vil [bil] *adj.* vile, base, low, mean.
vileza [bi·lé·sa] *f.* villainy; baseness; vile act.
vilipendiar [bi·li·pen·djár] *v.* to revile.
vilo [bí·lo]: **en —** in the air; suspended; undecided; in suspense; **llevar en —** to waft.
villa [bí·ya] *f.* village; villa, country house.
villancico [bi·yan·sí·ko] *n.* carol; Christmas carol.
villanía [bi·ya·ní·a] *f.* villainy; lowliness.
villano [bi·yá·no] *adj.* rustic; uncouth; villainous, mean, base; *m.* villain; rustic, peasant.
villorrio [bi·yó·rrjo] *m.* small village, hamlet.
vinagre [bi·ná·gre] *m.* vinegar; **vinagrera** [bi·na·gré·ra] *f.* vinegar cruet.
vincular [biŋ·ku·lár] *v.* to tie, bond, unite; to entail (*limit the inheritance of property*); to found, base (on).
vínculo [bíŋ·ku·lo] *m.* bond, tie, chain; entailed inheritance.
vindicar [bin·di·kár] *v.* to vindicate; to avenge; to defend, assert (*one's rights*); **-se** to avenge oneself; to defend oneself.
vino [bí·no] *m.* wine; **— amontillado** good grade of pale sherry (*originally from Montilla*); **— tinto** dark-red wine; **vinería** [bi·ne·rí·a] *f. Ríopl., Andes* wineshop; **vinero** [bi·né·ro] *adj. Am.* pertaining to wine; **vinoso** [bi·nó·so] *adj.* winy.
viña [bí·ña] *f.* vineyard.
viñedo [bi·ñé·do] *m.* vineyard.
viola [bjó·la] *f.* viola.
violación [bjo·la·sjón] *f.* violation.
violado [bjo·lá·do] *adj.* violet; *m.* violet, violet color; *p.p.* violated.
violar [bjo·lár] *v.* to violate; to rape.
violencia [bjo·lén·sja] *f.* violence.
violentar [bjo·len·tár] *v.* to force; to break into (*a house*); **-se** to force oneself; to get angry.
violento [bjo·lén·to] *adj.* violent; impetuous; forced; strained; unnatural.
violeta [bjo·lé·ta] *f.* violet.
violín [bjo·lín] *m.* violin; *m. & f.* violinist; *Ven.* **estar hecho un —** to be very thin.
violinista [bjo·li·nís·ta] *m. & f.* violinist.
violonchelo [bjo·lon·čé·lo] *m.* violincello, cello.
virada [bi·rá·da] *f.* tack, change of direction, turn.
viraje [bi·rá·xe] *m.* change of direction; turn.
virar [bi·rár] *v.* to turn, turn around, change direction; to tack (*said of a ship*).
virgen [bír·xen] *adj. & f.* virgin.
virginal [bir·xi·nál] *adj.* virginal, virgin, pure.
viril [bi·ríl] *adj.* virile, manly.
virilidad [bi·ri·li·dád] *f.* virility, manhood, manly strength, vigor.
virreinal [bi·rrej·nál] *adj.* viceregal.
virreinato [bi·rrej·ná·to] *m.* viceroyalty (*office or jurisdiction of a viceroy*).
virrey [bi·rréj] *m.* viceroy.
virtud [bir·túd] *f.* virtue.

VE

virtuoso [bir·twó·so] *adj.* virtuous; *m.* virtuoso (*person skilled in an art*).

viruela [bir·wé·la] *f.* smallpox; pock (*mark left by smallpox*); **-s locas** (*or* **-s bastardas**) chicken pox.

viruta [bi·rú·ta] *f.* wood shaving.

visado [bi·sá·do] *m.* visa.

visaje [bi·sá·xe] *m.* grimace; wry face; **hacer -s** to make faces.

visar [bi·sár] *v.* to visé; to approve; to O.K.

viscoso [bis·kó·so] *adj.* slimy, sticky; **viscosidad** viscosity; **viscosímetro** viscometer.

visera [bi·sé·ra] *f.* visor; eye shade; *Cuba, Mex.* blinder (*on a horse's bridle*).

visible [bi·sí·ble] *adj.* visible; evident; conspicuous, notable.

visigodo [bi·si·gó·do] *adj.* visigothic; *m.* visigoth.

visillo [bi·sí·yo] *m.* window curtain.

visión [bi·sjón] *f.* vision; sight; fantasy; apparition; sight (*ridiculous-looking person or thing*).

visionario [bi·sjo·ná·rjo] *adj. & m.* visionary.

visita [bi·sí·ta] *f.* visit, call; visitor; callers, company; **— de confianza** informal call; **— de cumplimiento** (*or* **— de cumplido**) formal courtesy call; **— domiciliaria** police inspection of a house; home call (*of a social worker, doctor, etc.*).

visitación [bi·si·ta·sjón] *f.* visitation, visit.

visitador [bi·si·ta·dór] *m.* visitor, caller; inspector.

visitante [bi·si·tán·te] *m. & f.* caller, visitor; *adj.* visiting.

visitar [bi·si·tár] *v.* to visit; in inspect.

vislumbrar [biz·lum·brár] *v.* to catch a glimpse of; to guess, surmise; **-se** to be faintly visible.

vislumbre [biz·lúm·bre] *f.* glimmer; glimpse; vague idea; faint appearance.

viso [bí·so] *m.* appearance; semblance; pretense; pretext; luster, brilliance, glitter; glass curtain; **a dos -s** with a double view; with a double purpose.

visón [bi·són] *m.* mink.

víspera [bís·pe·ra] *f.* eve, evening or day before; time just before; **-s vespers; en -s de** on the eve of; about to.

vista [bís·ta] *f.* (*panorama*) view; landscape; sight; (*sentido*) sight; vision; (*acción*) look, glance; **a — de** in the presence of; in front of, within view of; **pagadero a la —** payable at sight or upon presentation; **¡hasta la —!** good-bye!; **bajar la —** to lower one's eyes; **conocer de —** to know by sight; **hacer la — gorda** to pretend not to see; **pasar la — por** to glance over; **perder de —** to lose sight of; **tener a la —** to have before one; to have received (*a letter*).

vistazo [bis·tá·so] *m.* glance; **dar un — a** to glance over.

visto [bís·to] *p.p.* of **ver** seen; *adj.* evident, clear; **bien —** well thought of, proper; **mal —** looked down upon, improper; **— bueno** (V°.B°.) approved (O.K.); **dar el — bueno** to approve, O.K.; **— que** whereas, considering that.

vistoso [bis·tó·so] *adj.* showy; colorful.

visualizar [bi·swa·li·sár] *v.* (*computadora*) to display; **visualización** *f.* display.

vital [bi·tál] *adj.* vital; important, necessary.

vitalicio [bi·ta·lí·sjo] *adj.* for life; *m.* life-insurance policy; lifetime pension.

vitalidad [bi·ta·li·dád] *f.* vitality.

vitamina [bi·ta·mí·na] *f.* vitamin.

vitaminado [bi·ta·mi·ná·do] *adj.* containing vitamins.

vítor [bí·tor] *m.* cheer, applause; **¡ — !** hurrah!

vitorear [bi·to·re·ár] *v.* to cheer, applaud.

vitrina [bi·trí·na] *f.* glass case; show case; show window.

vituallas [bi·twá·yas] *f. pl.* victuals, food, provisions.

vituperar [bi·tu·pe·rár] *v.* to revile, insult, call bad names.

vituperio [bi·tu·pé·rjo] *m.* affront, insult; reproach; censure.

viuda [bjú·da] *f.* widow.

viudez [bju·dés] *f.* widowhood.

viudo [bjú·do] *m.* widower.

¡viva! [bí·ba] *interj.* hurrah for; long live!

vivac [bi·bák], **vivaque** [bi·bá·ke] *m.* bivouac, military encampment; *Am.* police headquarters.

vivacidad [bi·ba·si·dád] *f.* vivacity; brightness; liveliness.

vivaracho [bi·ba·rá·čo] *adj.* lively; vivacious, gay.

vivaz [bi·bás] *adj.* vivacious, lively; bright, keen, witty.

víveres [bí·be·res] *m. pl.* food supplies, provisions.

vivero [bi·bé·ro] *m.* fish pond, fish hatchery, tree nursery.

viveza [bi·bé·sa] *f.* vivacity; animation, liveliness; quickness; brilliance, cleverness.

vívido [bí·bi·do] *adj.* vivid; colorful.

vivienda [bi·bjén·da] *f.* dwelling; apartment.

viviente [bi·bjén·te] *adj.* living.

vivir [bi·bír] *v.* to live; to endure, last; **¡viva!** hurrah! long live!; **¿quién vive?** who goes there?; *m.* existence, living.

vivisección [bi·bi·sek·sjón] *f.* vivisection.

vivo [bí·bo] *adj.* (*no muerto*) alive; living; (*ágil*) lively; quick; (*vistoso*) vivid; bright; (*listo*) clever, wide-awake; **tío —** merry-go-round; **al —** vividly; **de viva voz** by word of mouth; **tocar en lo —** to hurt to the quick, touch the most sensitive spot.

vizcacha [bis·ká·ča] *f. Andes, Ríopl.* viscacha (*South American rodent about the size of a hare*).

vizcachera [bis·ka·čé·ra] *f. Andes, Ríopl.* viscacha burrow or hole; *Arg.* room filled with junk; **vizcacheral** [bis·ka·če·rál] *m. Andes, Ríopl.* ground full of viscacha burrows.

vizcaíno [bis·ka·í·no] *adj.* Biscayan, of or from Biscay, Spain.

vocablo [bo·ká·blo] *m.* word, term.

vocabulario [bo·ka·bu·lá·rjo] *m.* vocabulary.

vocación [bo·ka·sjón] *f.* vocation; aptness, talent.

vocal [bo·kál] *adj.* vocal; oral; vowel; *f.* vowel; *m.* voter (*in an assembly or council*).

vocear [bo·se·ár] *v.* to shout; to cry out; to hail.

vocecita [bo·se·sí·ta] *f.* sweet little voice.

vocería [bo·se·rí·a] *f.* clamor, shouting.

vocerío [bo·se·rí·o] *m. Am.* clamor, shouting.

vocero *m.* spokesman.

vociferar [bo·si·fe·rár] *v.* to shout, clamor; to yell; to boast loudly of.

vodevil [bo·de·bíl] *m.* vaudeville.

volado [bo·lá·do] *m.* superior letter in printing; *Col.* angry person.

volante [bo·lán·te] *adj.* flying; floating; **papel** (*or* **hoja**) **—** handbill, circular; *m.* ruffle, frill; steering wheel; balance wheel; flywheel.

volar[2] [bo·lár] *v. irr.* to fly; to fly away; to explode; to irritate, pique; to rouse (*bird game*); **-se** *Carib., Col.* to fly off the handle, lose one's temper.

volátil [bo·lá·til] *adj.* volatile; fickle, changeable; flying.

volcán [bol·kán] *m.* volcano; *Col.* precipice; *S.A.* swift torrent; *C.A.* **un — de** many; lots of; a pile of.

volcánico [bol·ká·ni·ko] *adj.* volcanic.

volcar[2, 6] [bol·kár] *v. irr.* to overturn; to capsize; to upset; to make dizzy; **-se** to upset, get upset.

volear [bo·le·ár] *v.* to volley, hit (*a ball*) in the air.
volición [bo·li·sjón] *f.* volition.
voltaje [bol·tá·xe] *m.* voltage.
voltear [bol·te·ár] *v.* to turn, turn around; to revolve; to turn inside out; to overturn; to tumble or roll over; to turn a somersault; *Am.* to go prying around; *Col., Ven., C.A., Mex., Andes* — **la espalda** to turn one's back; **-se** to turn over; to change sides.
voltereta [bol·te·ré·ta] *f.* somersault, tumble.
voltio [ból·tjo], **volt** *m.* volt; **voltímetro** voltmeter.
voluble [bo·lú·ble] *adj.* fickle; moody; changeable; twining (*as a climbing vine*).
volumen [bo·lú·men] *m.* volume.
voluminoso [bo·lu·mi·nó·so] *adj.* voluminous, bulky, very large.
voluntad [bo·lun·tád] *f.* will; desire; determination; benevolence, good will; consent; **última** — last will, testament; **de** (*or* **de buena**) — willingly, with pleasure.
voluntario [bo·lun·tá·rjo] *adj.* voluntary; willful; *m.* volunteer.
voluntarioso [bo·lun·ta·rjó·so] *adj.* willful.
voluptuoso [bo·lup·twó·so] *adj.* voluptuous; sensual.
voluta [bo·lú·ta] *f.* scroll, spiral-like ornament; **-s de humo** spirals of smoke.
volver[2, 52] [bol·bér] *v. irr.* (*regresar*) to return; (*dar vuelta*) to turn; to turn up, over, or inside out; to restore; — **loco** to drive crazy; — **a** (+ *inf.*) to do again; — **en sí** to come to, recover one's senses; — **por** to return for; to defend; **-se** to become; to turn; to turn around; to change one's ideas; **-se atrás** to go back; to back out, go back on one's word; **-se loco** to go crazy.
vomitar [bo·mi·tár] *v.* to vomit.
vómito [bó·mi·to] *m.* vomit; vomiting.
voracidad [bo·ra·si·dád] *f.* voraciousness, greediness.
vorágine [bo·rá·xi·ne] *f.* vortex, whirlpool.
voraz [bo·rás] *adj.* voracious, ravenous, greedy.
vórtice [bór·ti·se] *m.* vortex, whirlpool; whirlwind, tornado; center of a cyclone.
votación [bo·ta·sjón] *f.* voting; vote, total number of votes.
votante [bo·tán·te] *m. & f.* voter.
votar [bo·tár] *v.* to vote; to vow; to curse; **¡voto a tal!** by Jove!
voto [bó·to] *m.* vote; vow; prayer; votive offering; oath; wish; — **de confianza** vote of confidence.
voz [bos] *f.* (*capacidad*) voice; (*sonido*) shout, outcry; (*palabra*) word; rumor; — **común** common rumor or gossip; **a** — **en cuello** (*or* **a** — **en grito**) shouting; at the top of one's lungs; **en** — **alta** aloud; **a voces** shouting, with shouts; **secreto a voces** open secret; **dar voces** to shout, yell.
vozarrón [bo·sa·rrón] *m.* loud, strong voice.
vuelco [bwél·ko] *m.* upset; overturning; capsizing; tumble.
vuelo [bwé·lo] *m.* flight; width, fullness (*of a dress or cloak*); frill, ruffle; jut, projection (*of a building*); **al** (*or* **a**) — on the fly; quickly; **levantar** (*or* **alzar**) **el** — to fly away; to soar.
vuelta [bwél·ta] *f.* (*giro*) turn; return; repetition; (*parte opuesta*) reverse side; cuff, facing of a sleeve; cloak lining; (*cambio*) change (*money returned*); **a la** — around the corner; on returning; **a la** — **de los años** within a few years; *Am.* **otra** — again; **dar** **-s** to turn over and over; to wander about; **dar una** — to take a walk; **estar de** — to be back; **no tiene** — **de hoja** there are no two ways about it.
vuelto [bwél·to] *p.p. of* **volver;** *m. Am.* change

(*money returned*).
vuestro [bwés·tro] *poss. adj.* your, of yours (*fam. pl.*); *poss. pron.* yours.
vulgar [bul·ǵár] *adj.* common, ordinary; in common use; low, vile, base.
vulgaridad [bul·ǵa·ri·dád] *f.* vulgarity, coarseness, commonness.
vulgarismo [bul·ǵa·ríz·mo] *m.* slang, slang expression, vulgar or ungrammatical expression.
vulgo [búl·ǵo] *m.* populace, the common people; *adv.* commonly, popularly.
vulva [búl·ba] *f.* external female genitalia.

W:w

water [gwá·ter] *m. Spain* toilet.

X:x

xilófono [si·ló·fo·no] *m.* xylophone.

Y:y

y [i] *conj.* and.
ya [ɏa] *adv.* already; now; finally; soon, presently; in time; **¡—!** now I see!; I understand; enough!; **¡** — **lo creo!** I should say so!; yes, of course!; — **no** no longer; — **que** since; although; — **se ve** of course; it is clear; — **voy** I am coming.
yacer[50] [ɏa·sér] *v. irr.* to lie (*in the grave*); to be lying down; to lie, be situated.
yacimiento [ɏa·si·mjén·to] *m.* bed, layer (*of ore*); — **de petróleo** oil field.
yanqui [ɏáŋ·ki] *m. & f.* North American, native of the United States; Yankee.
yantar [ɏan·tár] *v.* to eat; *m.* food, meal.
yapa [ɏá·pa] *f. Ríopl., Andes* a small gift from the vendor to the purchaser; also **llapa, ñapa; pilón** in Mexico.
yararᮁ [ɏa·ra·rá] *f. Ríopl.* Argentine poisonous snake.
yarda [ɏár·da] *f.* yard (*unit of measure*).
yate [ɏá·te] *m.* yacht.
yedra [ɏé·dra] = **hiedra.**
yegua [ɏé·ǵwa] *f.* mare; *C.A., Bol.* cigar butt; *adj. Am.* big, large; **yeguada** [ɏe·ǵwá·da] *f.* herd of mares.
yelmo [ɏél·mo] *m.* helmet.
yema [ɏé·ma] *f.* egg yolk; bud, shoot; candied egg yolk; — **del dedo** finger tip.
yerba [ɏér·ba] = **hierba.**
yerbabuena [ɏer·ba·bwé·na] *f.* mint; peppermint.
yerbero [ɏer·bé·ro] *m. Mex., Cuba, Ven., Col., Andes* herb vendor.
yermo [ɏér·mo] *m.* desert, wilderness; *adj.* desert uninhabited; uncultivated; sterile.
yerno [ɏér·no] *m.* son-in-law.
yerro [ɏé·rro] *m.* error, fault, mistake.
yerto [ɏér·to] *adj.* stiff, motionless, rigid.
yesca [ɏés·ka] *f.* tinder; anything highly inflammable; incentive (*to passion*); *Ríopl., Mex.* **estar hecho una** — to be in great anger.

yeso [ŷé·so] *m.* gypsum, chalk; plaster; chalk (*for blackboard*); — **blanco** whitewash; — **mate** plaster of Paris; **yesoso** [ŷe·só·so] *adj.* chalky.

yo [ŷo] *pers. pron.* I.

yod [ŷod] *f.* yod (linguistic symbol).

yodo [ŷó·do] *m.* iodine.

yoduro [ŷo·dú·ro] *m.* iodide.

yogi [ŷó·xi] *m.* yogi.

yuca [ŷú·ka] *f.* yucca; cassava.

yugo [ŷú·ɡo] *m.* yoke; marriage tie; burden.

yogur [ŷo·ɡúr] *m.* yogurt.

yoyo [ŷó·yo] *m.* yo-yo.

yunga [ŷuɳ·ɡa] *f.* valley of Peru and Bolivia.

yunque [ŷúɳ·ke] *f.* anvil.

yunta [ŷún·ta] *f.* yoke of oxen; pair of draft animals.

yuyo [ŷú·yo] *m. Cuba, Mex., Ríopl., Andes* wild grass, weeds; *C.A., Col.* an herb sauce; *Ec., Peru* garden stuff; *Andes, Ch.* **estar** — to be lifeless insipid; *Col.* **volverse uno** — to faint.

Z:z

zacate [sa·ká·te] *m. Mex., C.A.* grass, forage; hay.

zafado [sa·fá·do] *adj.* impudent, brazen, shameless; *Ven.* smart, wide-awake, keen; *Col., Mex., Andes* "touched", half-crazy; *p.p.* of **zafar**.

zafar [sa·fár] *v.* to release, set free; to dislodge; *Am.* to exclude; **-se** to slip away; to dodge; to get rid (of); to get loose; *Col., Ven., Andes* to get dislocated (*said of a bone*); *Col., Mex., Andes* to go crazy; *Col.* to use foul language.

zafio [sá·fjo] *adj.* coarse, uncouth, rude.

zafir [sa·fír], **zafiro** [sa·fí·ro] *m.* sapphire.

zafra [sá·fra] *f.* sugar-making season; sugar making; sugar crop.

zaga [sá·ɡa] *f.* rear; **a la** — (**a** *or* **en** —) behind.

zagal [sa·ɡál] *m.* young shepherd; lad; **zagala** [sa·ɡá·la] *f.* young shepherdess; lass, maiden; **zagalejo** [sa·ɡa·lé·xo] *m.* young shepherd; short skirt; petticoat.

zaguán [sa·ɡwán] *m.* vestibule.

zaherir[3] [sa·e·rír] *v. irr.* to hurt (*feelings*); to censure, reprove; to reproach.

zaino [sáj·no] *adj.* treacherous; vicious; chestnut-colored (*horse*).

zalamero [sa·la·mé·ro] *m.* fawner, flatterer, servile person; **zalamería** [sa·la·me·rí·a] *f.* flattery, scraping and bowing.

zalea [sa·lé·a] *f.* pelt, undressed sheepskin.

zamacueca [sa·ma·kwé·ka] *f.* popular dance of Peru and Chile.

zambo [sám·bo] *adj.* knock-kneed; *m. Col.* a species of South American monkey.

zambra [sám·bra] *f. Spain* uproar; lively *fiesta*.

zambullida [sam·bu·ýí·da] *f.* dive, dip, plunge.

zambullir[20] [sam·bu·ýír] *v.* to plunge, dip, duck; **-se** to dive; to plunge.

zambullón [sam·bu·yón] *m.* quick, sudden dip or dive.

zanahoria [sa·na·ó·rja] *f.* carrot.

zanca [sáɳ·ka] *f.* long leg of any fowl; long leg; long prop; **zancada** [saɳ·ká·da] *f.* stride, long step.

zanco [sáɳ·ko] *m.* stilt; **andar en -s** to walk on stilts.

zancón [saɳ·kón] *adj.* lanky, long-legged; *Col., Guat., Mex.* too short (*skirt or dress*).

zancudo [saɳ·kú·do] *adj.* long-legged; *m. Mex., C.A., Ven., Col., Andes* mosquito.

zángano [sáɳ·ɡa·no] *m.* drone; loafer, sponger; *Am.* rogue, rascal.

zangolotear [saɳ·ɡo·lo·te·ár] *v.* to shake, jiggle; **-se** to shake; to waddle; to sway from side to side.

zangoloteo [saɳ·ɡo·lo·té·o] *m.* jiggle, jiggling; shaking; waddling.

zanguanga [saɳ·ɡwáɳ·ɡa] *f.* feigned illness; **hacer la** — to pretend to be ill; **zanguango** [saɳ·ɡwáɳ·ɡo] *adj.* lazy; silly; *m.* fool.

zanja [sáɳ·xa] *f.* ditch; trench; *Am.* irrigation ditch.

zanjar [sa·xár] *v.* to excavate; to dig ditches in; to settle (*disputes*).

zapallo [sa·pá·yo] *m. Pan., Col., Ven., Andes* pumpkin; squash.

zapapico [sa·pa·pí·ko] *m.* pickaxe.

zapata [sa·pá·ta] *f.* half-boot; — **de freno** brake shoe.

zapateado [sa·pa·te·á·do] *m.* a Spanish tap dance.

zapatear [sa·pa·te·ár] *v.* to tap with the feet; to tap-dance.

zapateo [sa·pa·té·o] *m.* tapping with the feet; *Am.* a popular tap dance.

zapatería [sa·pa·te·rí·a] *f.* shoe store; shoemaker's shop.

zapatero [sa·pa·té·ro] *m.* shoemaker; shoe dealer.

zapatilla [sa·pa·tí·ya] *f.* slipper, pump.

zapato [sa·pá·to] *m.* shoe.

zapote [sa·pó·te] *m.* sapodilla.

zaragüeya [sa·ra·ɡwe·ya] *f.* opossum.

zarandajas [sa·ran·dá·xas] *f. pl.* trifles, trinkets, worthless things.

zarandear [sa·ran·de·ár] *v.* to winnow (*separate the chaff from grain*); to sift; to sift out; to move (*something*) quickly, wiggle, jiggle; *C.A., Ríopl.* to whip, lash, mistreat, abuse; **-se** to wiggle, jiggle; to bump along; to waddle; to strut, swagger.

zarandeo [sa·ran·dé·o] *m.* jiggle, jiggling; sifting; waddling; strutting.

zarcillo [sar·sí·yo] *m.* earring; tendril (*coil of a climbing vine*); *Andes, Mex.* earmark (*on the ear of an animal*).

zarco [sár·ko] *adj.* light-blue (*eyes*).

zarpa [sár·pa] *f.* paw, claw; weighting anchor; **echar la** — to grasp, seize; **zarpada** [sar·pá·da] *f.* pounce; blow with a paw; **zarpazo** [sar·pá·so] *m.* blow with the paw; big blow, thud; hard fall.

zarpar [sar·pár] *v.* to weigh anchor; to set sail.

zarpazo [sar·pá·so] *m.* blow with a claw or paw.

zarza [sár·sa] *f.* bramble; blackberry bush.

zarzamora [sar·sa·mó·ra] *f.* blackberry.

zarzuela [sar·swé·la] *f.* Spanish musical comedy.

¡zas! *interj.* [sas] *interj.* bang!

zigzag [siɡ·sáɡ] *m.* zigzag.

zigzaguear [siɡ·sa·ɡe·ár] *v.* to zigzag, weave.

zinc [siŋk] = **cinc.**

zócalo [só·ka·lo] *m.* base (*of a pedestal*); *Mex.* public square.

zodíaco [so·dí·a·ko] *m.* zodiac.

zona [só·na] *f.* zone; band, girdle; shingles (*a disease*); **zonificación** zoning.

zonzo [són·so] *adj.* dull, stupid, silly, foolish.

zoología [so·o·lo·xí·a] *f.* zoology.

zoológico [so·o·ló·xi·ko] *adj.* zoological; **jardín** — zoo.

zopenco [so·péɳ·ko] *adj.* stupid, dull, thick-headed *m.* blockhead, dunce.

zopilote [so·pi·ló·te] *m. Mex., C.A.* buzzard.

zoquete [so·ké·te] *m.* (*cosa*) block, chunk of wood; hunk of bread; (*persona*) blockhead, dunce, fool; ugly fat person; *Am.* grease, dirt, filth; *Am.* slap.

zorra [só·rra] *f.* fox; foxy person; drunkenness;

prostitute; **pillar una** — to get drunk.
zorro [só·rro] *m.* fox; foxy person; **-s** fox skins;
duster made of cloth or leather strips; **estar hecho
un** — to be drowsy; **hacerse uno el** — to pretend
to be stupid or not to hear; *adj.* foxy; zorrillo
[so·rrí·yo], **zorrino** [so·rrí·no] *m. Ríopl.* **skunk;
zorruno** [so·rrú·no] *adj.* foxy.
zorzal [sor·sál] *m.* thrush; (*persona*) crafty fellow;
Am. fool, scapegoat, dupe.
zozobra [so·só·bra] *f.* foundering; sinking; anxiety,
worry.
zozobrar [so·so·brár] *v.* to founder; to capsize; to
sink; to be in great danger; to fret, to worry.
zumbar [sum·bár] *v.* to buzz; to hum; to ring (*said of
the ears*); to scoff at; to strike, hit; *Ven., Col.* to
throw out or away; *Andes* to punish; — **una
bofetada** to give a slap; **-se** *Am.* to slip away,
disappear.

zumbido [sum·bí·do] *m.* buzzing, humming; ringing
(*in one's ears*); hit, blow, whack.
zumbón [sum·bón] *adj.* funny, playful; sarcastic; *m.*
jester.
zumo [sú·mo] *f. Spain* juice; (*ganancias*) profit;
zumoso [su·mó·so] *adj.* juicy.
zurcir[10] [sur·sír] *v.* to darn; to invent, make up (*lies*).
zurcido [sur·sí·do] *m.* darn; darning; *p.p. of* **zurcir.**
zurdo [súr·do] *adj.* left-handed; left; **a zurdas** with
the left hand; clumsily.
zuro [sú·ro] *m.* cob, corncob.
zurra [sú·rra] *f.* beating, flogging; tanning (*of
leather*).
zurrar [su·rrár] *v.* to flog, thrash; to tan (*leather*).
zurrón [su·rrón] *m.* pouch; bag; leather bag; *Ven.,
Col.* coward.
Zutano [su·tá·no] *m.* so-and-so; a certain person.
(*Used often with* **Fulano** *and* **Mengano**).

YE

A Spanish–English List of Five Hundred Common Idioms and Proverbs, with Dialectal Variants

The Spanish idioms, proverbs, and sayings are listed alphabetically, followed by American Spanish variants, then English equivalents, some of which are also idiomatic. American Spanish locutions that seem to be fairly common to most of Latin America are listed without regional designation, while local variations are indicated by country or region with the abbreviations employed in the text of the Dictionary. An English index follows the chart of idioms to facilitate the use of the compilation. It is to be noted that the basic element is the Spanish expression and also that the Spanish variants are intentionally more numerous than the English. This is because of the many political entities represented in the Spanish-speaking world, in contrast to American English idiomatic expression which tends to level to a general American form.

Quinientos Modismos, Refranes, y Dichos Españoles con Variantes Dialectales y Tradducción al Inglés

El cuadro de modismos, refranes, y dichos españoles tiene orden alfabético según la letra inicial de la primera palabra. Siguen variantes hispanoamericanas y luego equivalentes o semejantes del inglés, con ciertas variantes. Los modismos hispanoamericanos que son bastante generales no llevan indicación regional, y se señalan con abreviaturas del texto del Diccionario los que son típicos de ciertos países o regiones. Sigue al cuadro un índice inglés con los números de las locuciones castellanas correspondientes. Se nota que lo básico es la locución española y también que se dan más variantes dialectales en español, con motivo de las numerosas entidades políticas de América. El inglés, por lo visto, ha sufrido más nivelación en este siglo.

	Academy Spanish	American Spanish Variants	English Equivalents
1.	A aquél loar debemos cuyo pan comemos	No hay que darle patadas al pesebre	Don't bite the hand that feeds you
2.	¡A buenas horas!	¡Qué horitas! (*Mex.*)	Better late than never. It's about time!
3.	A buen hambre no hay pan duro	A buen hambre no hay gordas duras (*Mex.*)	Hunger is the best sauce
4.	A caballo regalado no hay que mirarle el diente	A caballo dado no se le mira el colmillo	Don't look a gift horse in the mouth
5.	A carta cabal		Through and through
6.	A continuación	Como sigue	Following; as follows
7.	¿A cuántos estamos?	¿Cuál es la fecha?	What is the date?
8.	A duras penas	Con gran dificultad	With great difficulty
9.	A empujones (empellones)	A codazos	By pushing; by shoving; by elbowing
10.	A fines de		Toward (around) the end of (month, week)
11.	A fondo		Thoroughly
12.	A grandes rasgos		Briefly; in outline form; in a sketchy way
13.	A la americana; a escote	Al aleluya, cada quien paga la suya; Americanamente (*Col.*)	Dutch treat; go Dutch

243

	Academy Spanish	American Spanish Variants	English Equivalents
14.	A la buena de Dios		Casually; as luck would have it
15.	A la carrera	Fletado (*Ven., Col.*)	On the run
16.	A la corta o a la larga	Tarde o temprano	Sooner or later
17.	A la larga	Al fin	In the long run; when all is said and done
18.	A la vez		At the same time
19.	A lo largo de		Along; bordering
20.	A lo más	Cuando más	At (the) most
21.	A lo mejor	Puede que; a la mejor (*Mex.*)	Like as not; it could be that
22.	A mano		By hand; at hand; tied (even)
23.	A más no poder	Hasta sacarse los zapatos (*Ch.*)	To the utmost
24.	A mediados de		About (around) the middle of (month)
25.	A menos que	A no ser que	Unless
26.	A menudo		Often
27.	A mi ver	En mi opinión	In my opinion; to my way of thinking
28.	A palabras necias, oídos sordos	A boca de borracho, oídos de cantinero	For foolish talk, deaf ears
29.	A pedir de boca		Exactly as desired; just as you want it
30.	A pesar de		In spite of
31.	A principios de		The early part of; around the first of (month)
32.	A propósito		By the way; on purpose
33.	A prueba de		Proof against (fire, etc.)
34.	A quemarropa	A boca de jarro	Point blank; at very close range
35.	A quien corresponda		To whom it may concern
36.	A quien madruga, Dios le ayuda		The early bird catches the worm
37.	A razón de		At the rate of
38.	A rienda suelta		Without restraint
39.	A saber	Es decir; o sea	Namely; that is
40.	A ver si como repican doblan	A ver si como roncan duermen	His bark is worse than his bite; all talk and no cider
41.	Abierto de par en par		Wide open
42.	Abundar como la mala hierba	Ser ajonjolí de todos los moles (*Mex.*)	To be as common as dirt; to be a dime a dozen
43.	Acabar de	Venir de (*Col.*); recién (*plus verb*) (*Riopl., Ch.*)	To have just
44.	Acusar recibo de		To acknowledge receipt of
45.	Aguzar los oídos	Parar la oreja	To prick up one's ears
46.	Al fin y al cabo	Al fin y al fallo (*Ch.*)	In the very end; when all is said and done
47.	Al fin se canta la gloria	Nadie diga ¡zape! hasta que no escape; el que quiera huevos, que aguante los cacareos (*Riopl.*)	Don't count your chickens before they're hatched
48.	Al mejor cazador se le escapa la liebre	Al mejor mono se le cae el zapote (*C.A.*); A la mejor cocinera se le queman los frijoles	Everyone makes mistakes; it's a good horse that never stumbles
49.	Al pie de la letra		To the letter; thoroughly
50.	Al por mayor	Al mayoreo	Wholesale
51.	Al por menor		Retail; in detail
52.	Algo por el estilo		Something like that; something on that order
53.	Amigo del buen tiempo, múdase con el viento	Al nopal lo van a ver sólo cuando tiene tunas (*Mex.*)	Fair-weather friend
54.	Andarse por las ramas	Andarse con medias tazas; emborrachar la perdiz (*Ch.*)	To beat around the bush
55.	Antes doblar que quebrar	Más vale rodear que rodar	Better bend than break; if you can't lick 'em, join 'em
56.	Aprovecha gaviota, que no hay otra	Atáscate ahora que hay lodo	Gather ye rosebuds while ye may; here's your chance

	Academy Spanish	*American Spanish Variants*	*English Equivalents*
57.	Armar un San Quintín	Armar una bronca; revolver el gallinero (*Ch.*)	To start a fight; to raise Cain
58.	¡Arriba los corazones!	¡No le afloje!	Courage! Cheer up! Chin up!
59.	A sus órdenes	Para servirle	At your service
60.	Aunque la mona se vista de seda, mona se queda		Clothes don't make the man
61.	Bajo cuerda	Por debajo del agua	In an underhanded manner; under the table
62.	Barrer para adentro	Rascarse para adentro es gran contento; antes mis dientes que mis parientes	To look after oneself first; to take care of number one
63.	Borracho como una cuba	Borracho perdido	Dead drunk; plastered; tight
64.	¡Buen provecho!	¡Que aproveche!	Good appetite!
65.	Buscarle tres pies al gato	Buscarle mangas al chaleco; buscarle cuatro pies al gato (*Ec.*)	To look for knots in a bulrush; to complicate things
66.	Buscar pelos en la sopa		To be given to fault finding; to look for an excuse to gripe
67.	Cada muerte de obispo	Como visita de obispo	In a month of Sundays; once in a blue moon
68.	Caer atravesado	Caer gordo; caer mal; caer gacho (*Col.*)	To rub (one) the wrong way; to be a pain in the neck
69.	Caer de bruces	Dar el azotón; caer de ancho; echarse de boca (*Andes*)	To fall flat; to bite the dust
70.	Caer en la cuenta		To realize; to take note of
71.	Caerse de su propio peso		To be self-evident (obvious)
72.	Calentarse los cascos		To rack one's brains
73.	Cara o cruz	Águila o sol (*Mex.*); cara o sello	Heads or tails
74.	Carne de gallina		Goose flesh; goose pimples; burr(brrr) bumps (South)
75.	Colgarle a uno el milagro	Colgarle a uno el muerto	To shift responsibility; to pass the buck
76.	Como perros y gatos	Como dos gatos en un costal	Like cats and dogs
77.	¿Cómo te (le) va?	¿Qué tal?	How are you? How's it going? What gives?
78.	Comprar a ciegas	Comprar potrillo en panza de yegua	To buy blindly; to buy a pig in a poke
79.	Con el ojo y con la fe jamás me burlaré	Aunque te digan que sí, espérate a que lo veas	Seeing is believing; (to say one is) from Missouri
80.	Con guante blanco	Con mucha mano izquierda	With kid gloves
81.	Con la cuchara que elijas, con ésa comerás	Cada quien se pone la corona que se labra	As you make your bed, so you must lie in it
82.	Con las bocas cosidas	¡Chitón!	To keep to oneself; mum's the word; button the lip
83.	Con las manos en la masa		To be caught in the act; to be caught red-handed
84.	Estar con los pelos de la dehesa	Estar con el pelo del potrero	To be a country bumpkin; (hayseed, hick)
85.	Con razón		No wonder! Small wonder!
86.	Con tal que	A condición de que	Provided that; if
87.	Contigo pan y cebolla	Más vale atole con risas que chocolate con lágrimas	Whither thou goest . . .; love in a cottage
88.	Con todas las de ley	Como Dios manda	According to Cocker (Hoyle)
89.	Consultar con la almohada		To think something over; to sleep on something
90.	Contra viento y marea		Come what may; come hell or high water
91.	Correr la voz	Correr la bola (*C.A.*); dizque (*Col. Andes*)	To be rumored; to be noised about; they say; people say
92.	Cortar el hilo	Cortar la hebra	To interrupt; to cut off
93.	Cosa de		About; more or less; a matter of
94.	Cosido a faldas de		To be tied to the apron strings of
95.	Costar un ojo de la cara	Costar un huevo (*Ven., Col., Andes*)	To cost a mint; to cost plenty; to bring a stiff price

Academy Spanish	American Spanish Variants	English Equivalents
96. Cruzarse de brazos		To remain indifferent; to be not interested
97. Cuanto antes	Tan pronto como posible	As soon as possible; the sooner the better
98. Cuanto más . . . más	Mientras más . . . más; entre más . . . más (*C.A., Col., Andes*)	The more . . . the more
99. Cuatro letras		
100. Dar a luz		To give birth
101. Dar al borracho las llaves de la bodega		To set the fox to keep the geese; to put the cat among the pigeons
102. Dar calabazas	Cortar: dar ayotes (*C.A.*); dar opio (*Andes*)	To break off relations; to give (one) the brush-off; to give (one) the mitten (N.E.)
103. Dar cuerda a		To wind (clock, etc.)
104. Dar de baja		To discharge; to drop (from a team, list, etc.)
105. Dar el pésame por		To present one's condolences for; to extend one's sympathy for
106. Dar en		To hit; to take a notion to
107. Dar gato por liebre	Hacerle guaje a uno (*Mex.*); pasársela a uno (*Ch.*)	To deceive; to cheat
108. Dar guerra		To make trouble
109. Dar (la) lata	Poner gorro (*Mex.*); poner pereque (*Col.*)	To bother; to annoy; to be a nuisance; to bug
110. Dar la razón a alguien		To acknowledge (a person) to be right; give credit for being right
111. Dar la vuelta a algo		To go around something; to rotate something
112. Dar parte	Avisar	To inform; to report
113. Dar por hecho	Suponer	To assume; to take for granted
114. Dar rienda suelta a	Dar curso libre	To give free rein to; to let go
115. Dar salida a	Disponer de	To dispose of; to clear out; to get rid of
116. Dar un paso en falso	Dar una metida de pata	To make a false move; to pull a boner
117. Dar una mano		To apply (a coat of paint, etc.)
118. Darle a uno coraje	Darle rabia a uno (*Carib.*);	To make one angry (mad)
119. Darle a uno en la matadura	Darle a uno en la mera matada (*Mex.*)	To touch to the quick; to strike home
120. Darle a uno la gana; apetecer	Provocarle a uno (*Col.*)	To feel like; to want to
121. Darle a uno lo mismo	Serle a uno igual	To be all the same to one; to make no difference to one
122. Darle a uno una soberana paliza	Darle a uno hasta por debajo de la lengua; aplanchar a uno (*Col.*)	To give one a trouncing; to knock the spots off one
123. Darse aires; darse tono; ¡cuántos humos!	Darse mucho taco (*Mex.*); Botarse el pucho (*Ch.*); Darse corte; darse paquete (*Ec.*)	To put on airs; to put on the dog; to be stuck up
124. Darse cuenta de		To realize; to be aware of
125. De bote en bote	Hasta el tope (*Mex.*)	Full to the brim; full up
126. De buena gana		Willingly
127. De buenas a primeras	En un improviso (*Ven., Col.*)	Without warning; suddenly
128. De cabo a rabo	De punta a punta	From beginning to end; from head to tail
129. De categoria	De número (*Ríopl.*); de oro (*Col.*); de mentas (*Arg.*)	Of importance; of class
130. De cuando en cuando	De vez en cuando; de pronto (*C.A.; Ríopl.*)	From time to time
131. De golpe	En un improviso (*Ven., Col.*)	Suddenly; all of a sudden

Academy Spanish	American Spanish Variants	English Equivalents
132. De gran subida, gran caida	De la subida más alta es la caida más lastimosa	The bigger they are, the harder they fall
133. De la noche a la mañana		Overnight; all at once
134. De lado		Sideways
135. De lleno		Fully; adequately
136. De lo contrario		Otherwise
137. De mala gana		Unwillingly
138. De mala muerte	Chafa (*Mex.*)	Worthless; crumby
139. De nuevo	Otra vez	Again; anew; once more
140. De paso		In passing; on the way
141. De pura casualidad		Purely by chance
142. De repente	De golpe; en un improviso (*Ven., Col.*)	All of a sudden
143. De tal palo, tal astilla	Cual el cuervo, tal su huevo; de tal jarro, tal tepalcate (*Mex.*)	Like father, like son; a chip off the old block
144. Descubrir el pastel	Hacer aparecer el peine	To let the cat out of the bag; to spill the beans
145. De una vez y para siempre	De una vez	Once and for all
146. De un solo sentido		One-way
147. De vuelta a las andadas	Otra vez la burra en el trigo	Back to the old tricks
148. Decidirse a		To make up one's mind to; to decide to
149. Decir a todo amén		To be a yes man
150. Decir entre dientes		To mumble; to mutter
151. Decir para sí	Decir para sus adentros	To say to oneself
152. Dejar de		To cease; to stop
153. Dejar a uno en la calle	Dejar a uno en la tendida; dejar a uno en un petate (*Col.; Ven.*)	To bleed (one) white; to take (one) to the cleaners
154. Dejar a uno plantado	Dejar a uno en la ecstacada; dejar a uno embarcado (*Mex.*)	To stand someone up
155. Dejarse de cuentos	Dejarse de historias; dejarse de rodeos	To come to the point; to stop beating around the bush
156. Del dicho al hecho hay gran trecho		Saying and doing are two different things; there's many a slip twixt the cup and the lip
157. Desde luego		Of course; naturally
158. Despedirse a la francesa	Irse como burro sin mecate; Pintarse (*Ven.*); emplumárselas (*Col., Ven.*)	To take French leave
159. Dia hábil		Workday
160. Dicho y hecho		No sooner said than done
161. Dijo la sartén a la caldera, quítate de allá, que me tiznas	El comal le dijo a la olla, qué tiznada estás (*Mex.*)	The pot called the kettle black
162. Dime con quien andas y te diré quién eres	Dime quien es tu junta y te diré si haces yunta	A man is known by the company he keeps; birds of a feather flock together
163. Dios mediante	Si Dios nos da vida; primero Dios (*C.A.*)	God willing; I hope so
164. Dirigir la palabra		To address; to speak to; to talk to
165. Doblar la hoja	Cambiar el disco	To change the subject
166. Don de gentes		Winning manners; a way with people
167. Donde hubo fuego hay cenizas	Donde camotes quemaron, cenizas quedaron (*Andes*)	Where there's smoke, there's fire
168. Donde menos se piensa salta la liebre	De cualquier maya salta un ratón (*Ríopl.*)	The unexpected always happens; it happens when least expected
169. Echar de ver	Catar de ver (*Col., Ven.*)	To notice; to observe
170. Echar indirectas		To make insinuations
171. Echar la casa por la ventana		To go all out; to kill the fatted calf; to blow the works

Academy Spanish	American Spanish Variants	English Equivalents
172. Echar la llave		To lock the door
173. Echar sapos y culebras	Echar tacos (*Mex.*) Echar ajos y cebollas; subir la prima (*Arg.*)	To swear a blue streak; to turn the air blue
174. Echar todo a rodar	Patearle el nido a alguien	To spoil things; to upset everything; to make a mess of everything
175. Echar un sueño (una siesta)	Tomar una siestita; tomar una pestañita (*Mex.*)	To take a nap; to catch a little shut-eye
176. Echar una mano		To lend a hand; to help out
177. Echar un párrafo	Echar guáguara (*Mex.*)	To pass the time of day; to chew the rag (fat)
178. Echarse un trago	Echarse un fogonazo (*Mex.*); empinar el codo; empinar el cacho (*Ch.*); pegarse un palo (*Carib., Col.*)	To take a drink (swig); to wet the whistle
179. El gallito del lugar	El mero mero (*Mex.*)	The cock of the walk; the top banana; the top dog
180. El hombre propone y Dios dispone	El hombre propone, Dios dispone y la mujer descompone	Man proposes, God disposes
181. El que no se arriesga no pasa la mar	El que no arriesga no gana	Nothing ventured, nothing gained
182. Empleo de cuello y levita	Empleo de camisa blanca y corbata	White-collar job
183. En calidad de		In the capacity of
184. En cuanto	Tan pronto como	As soon as
185. En cuanto a		Regarding; as for
186. En cueros	En traje de Adán; en pelota; pila (*Andes*)	Naked; in one's birthday suit; naked as a jay bird
187. En efectivo	En dinero contante y sonante; al chaz-chaz (*Mex.*)	In hard cash; in cold cash; cash on the barrel-head
188. En el extranjero		Abroad
189. En el peligro se conoce al amigo	En la cárcel se conocen los amigos	A friend in need is a friend indeed
190. En firme	A la segura (*Ch., Andes*); a la fija (*Col.*)	Definite; binding
191. En gustos no hay disputa	Sobre gustos se rompen géneros	Every man to his taste; some like it hot; some like it cold
192. En hora buena		Safely; luckily; o.k.
193. En la actualidad	Hoy; estos dias	At the present time; nowadays
194. En mi perra vida	En mi cochina vida	Never in all my life; never in all my born days
195. En principio		In principle; basically
196. En rueda	Entre pura raza (*Mex.*)	A friendly gathering; among friends
197. En un abrir y cerrar de ojos		In the twinkling of an eye
198. En un dos por tres	En menos que canta un gallo	When least expected; quick as a wink; in the shake of a lamb's tail
199. En vez de		Instead of
200. En voz alta		Out loud
201. En voz baja	Despacio	In a soft (low) voice
202. Entrado en años	Ya veterano	Well along in years; to be no spring chicken
203. Entrar en materia	Llegar al caso	To come to the point; get down to business
204. Entre azul y buenas noches	Entre dos aguas; ni un sí ni un no	To be undecided; to be on the fence
205. Entre bastidores		To be behind the scenes
206. Entre la espada y la pared	Entre dos fuegos	To be between the devil and the deep blue sea
207. Es decir	O sea	That is to say; in other words
208. Es fama que	Dizque (*Col.*); corre la bola que (*C.A.*)	It is rumored that; they say that

Academy Spanish	*American Spanish Variants*	*English Equivalents*
209. Es harina de otro costal	Es otro cantar; no viene al cuento	That's a horse of a different color
210. Es más bravo que un león	Es un perro; es una fiera	He is a tiger (wildcat)
211. ¡Esto es Jauja!	¡Esta es la tierra de Dios y María Santísima!	This is Seventh Heaven! This is Never-Never Land!
212. Escurrir el bulto	Emplumárselas (*Col., Ven.*); pelarse	To sneak away; to slip away
213. Está hasta en la sopa	Le dicen el diosito	There's no getting away from him; I'm sick of the sight of him
214. Está que pela	Está como para desplumar pollos	It's piping hot; It's as hot as blue blazes
215. Estar a disgusto		To be ill at ease; to feel awkward
216. Estar a gusto		To be contented; to be comfortable
217. Estar a la expectativa	Catiar la laucha (*Ch.*)	To be on the lookout for
218. Estar con ánimo de		To have a notion to
219. Estar chiflado	Le patina el embrague a uno; tener los alambres pelados (*Ch.*)	To have a screw loose; not to have all one's marbles
220. Estar de malas	Tener la de malas; tener el santo a espaldas (*Ven., Mex.*); estar salado (*Col., Andes*)	To be out of luck
221. Estar de moda	Estar en boga	To be fashionable; to be popular; to be the ''in'' thing
222. Estar de sobra		To be superfluous; to be too much
223. Estar de turno		To be on duty; to be on one's shift
224. Estar de viaje		To be traveling; to be on the road
225. Estar en buen uso	Estar en buenas condiciones	To be in good condition; to be in good shape
226. Estar en la luna		To be up in the clouds
227. Estar en las nubes		To daydream; to be high (prices)
228. Estar en los huesos	Estar hecho un violín (*Ven.*); no quedarle a uno más que hueso y cuero	To be nothing but skin and bone
229. Estar en plan de		To be in the mood for; to be out for
230. Estar en vigor		To be in effect; to be in force
231. Estar en vísperas de		To be on the eve of; to be about to
232. Estar hecho una furia	Estar como agua para chocolate; estar hecho un chivo; estar hecho un quique (*Ch.*)	To be beside oneself; to be hot under the collar
233. Estar muy metido en		To be deeply involved in
234. Estar para	Estar por	To be about to
235. Estar por	Estar a favor de	To be in favor of; to be for
236. Estar quebrado	Estar arrancado; estar bruja (*Mex.*); estar pato (*Ch.*)	To be broke (flat broke)
237. Estar rendido	Estar reventado	To be exhausted; to be all tired out; to be pooped
238. Estar sentido	Estar resentido	To be offended; to be hurt
239. Estar todo patas arriba	Ser todo un verdadero relajo	To be topsy-turvy; to be helter-skelter
240. Fuera de sí		Unconscious; beside oneself
241. Función corrida	Permanencia voluntaria	All-day program; come-and-go function
242. Fulano	Ciertas hierbas (*Col., C.A.*)	Mr. So-and-so; what's-his-name
243. Ganar a uno la mano	Coger a uno la delantera; madrugarle a uno	To get up too early for one; to beat one to it
244. Genio y figura hasta la sepultura	Al que nace barrigón, es al ñudo que lo fajen (*Ríopl.*)	You can't make a silk purse out of a sow's ear; the leopard doesn't change its spots

	Academy Spanish	American Spanish Variants	English Equivalents
245.	Gente menuda	La chiquilleria	Small fry
246.	Guiñar un ojo	Hacer ojos (Col.); hacer ojitos (Mex.); hacer caras (Ríopl.)	To make eyes at; to flirt; to give the glad eye to
247.	Haber de		To be expected to; to be scheduled to
248.	Haber de todo como en botica		There's a little of everything
249.	Haber moros en la costa		The coast is not clear; something's up
250.	Hablar como una cotorra	No pararle la boca a uno (Mex.)	To be a chatterbox; to be a windbag
251.	Hablar entre dientes		To mumble; to mutter
252.	Hablar hasta por los codos	Ser lengualarga	To chatter; to talk idly; to talk too much
253.	Hacer buenas migas		To get along well together
254.	Hacer caso a uno	Dar boleto a uno	To pay attention to one
255.	Hacer cola		To queue up; to stand in line; to line up
256.	Hacer comedia	Hacer tango	To put on a show; to make a scene
257.	Hacer la vista gorda		To pretend not to see; to wink at
258.	Hacer escala		To make a scheduled stop; to stopover
259.	Hacer falta		To be necessary; to have need of
260.	Hacer frente a		To confront; to face up to
261.	Hacer gracia	Parecer chistoso	To strike one as funny
262.	Hacer hincapié	Poner énfasis; porfiar	To emphasize; to insist upon
263.	Hacer juego		To match; to go well with
264.	Hacer novillos	Pintar venado (Mex.)	To cut classes; to play hooky
265.	Hacer presente		To notify; to remind
266.	Hacer puente		To take the intervening day off
267.	Hacer su agosto		To feather one's nest; to make a killing
268.	Hacer un mandado	Hacer un recado	To run an errand
269.	Hacerle a uno un flaco servicio	Hacerle a uno la pera; jugar sucio (Ch.)	To do someone a bad turn; to play a dirty trick on someone
270.	Hacerse tarde		To become (get) late
271.	Hallarse en el pellejo de otro		To be in somebody else's shoes
272.	Harto da quien da lo que tiene	El que da lo suyo, harto hace	You can't get blood from a turnip (stone)
273.	Hasta el tuétano	Hasta las cachas (Mex.)	To the core; to the very center
274.	Hay que	Es necesario	It is necessary; you have to
275.	Hecho a la medida		Custom-made; made to order
276.	Hecho y derecho		Mature; grown-up
277.	Historias de cuartel	Cuentos colorados; chistes verdes (Mex.)	Off-color jokes; pool-room talk
278.	Ida y vuelta		Round-trip
279.	Ir a medias	Ir mitad mitad	To go fifty-fifty
280.	Ir al grano	Ir a lo que truje	To get down to brass tacks; to get to the point
281.	Irle a úno bien (mal)		To be becoming (unbecoming); to be well
282.	Irse de juerga	Irse de parranda; irse de tuna (Col.); irse de farras (Ríopl.); irse de jarana (Ven.); irse de rumba (Carib.)	To go on a spree; to paint the town red
283.	Irsele a uno el santo al cielo	Irsele a uno la onda	One's mind goes blank; one clean forgets; to be spacy
284.	Jugar con dos barajas	Mamar a dos tetas	To double-cross; to play both ends against the middle
285.	Jugarle una mala pasada a uno	Hacerle a uno la cama (Ch.)	To play foul with one; to play a dirty trick on one
286.	La mar de	Cantidad de; un montón de; un volcán de (C.A.); a patadas (Ec.); a ponchadas (Andes)	Lots of; loads of; oodles of; right smart of

	Academy Spanish	*American Spanish Variants*	*English Equivalents*
287.	La madeja se enreda	Se enreda la pita	The plot thickens
288.	La letra con sangre entra		There's no royal road to learning
289.	La niña de mis (tus, etc.) ojos		The apple of one's eye
290.	La piedra quieta cría malva	Piedra que rueda no cría moho	A rolling stone gathers no moss
291.	Levantar la mesa	Quitar la mesa	To clear the table
292.	Levantarse del pie izquierdo	Levantarse de malas	To get up on the wrong side of the bed
293.	Lo de menos		The least of it
294.	Los estadistas de café		Arm-chair strategists; sidewalk superintendents
295.	Los niños y los locos dicen las verdades	Los niños y los borrachos siempre dicen la verdad	Out of the mouths of babes and sucklings
296.	Llegar a las manos	Irse a los moquetes; irse al moño (entre mujeres) (Ch.)	To come to blows; to get into a fight
297.	Llevar a cabo		To accomplish; to carry out
298.	Llevar la contra		To oppose; to contradict
299.	Llevar la delantera		To be ahead
300.	Llevar uno su merecido		To get what's coming (to one)
301.	Llevarse un chasco	Pegarse palo	To be disappointed; to have a setback
302.	Llorar a lágrima viva	Llorar como becerro en llano; soltar puchero (Ch.)	To cry like a baby
303.	Llover a cántaros	Llover con rabia (Carib.); caer burros aparejados (Carib.)	To rain bucketfuls; to pour; to rain cats and dogs
304.	Mal que le pese a uno		Whether one likes it or not
305.	Más allá (de)		Farther on; beyond
306.	Más bien		Rather
307.	Más falso que Judas		As false as a counterfeit penny; worthless as a plugged nickel
308.	Más vale pájaro en mano que buitre volando	Más vale pájaro en mano que cien(to) volando; más vale guajito tengo que acocote tendré (Mex.)	A bird in the hand is worth two in the bush
309.	Más vale prevenir que lamentar	Un gramo de previsión vale más que una tonelada de curación	An ounce of prevention is worth a pound of cure
310.	Matar dos pájaros de un tiro	Matar dos pájaros de una pedrada	To kill two birds with one stone
311.	Media naranja		Better half; spouse
312.	Mejor dicho		Or rather; better yet
313.	Menos mal	Date de santos que no fue peor	So much the better; it could have been worse
314.	Meter en un puño a uno	Tener a uno agarrado de las greñas	To have someone by the neck; to have someone over a barrel
315.	Meterlo en el bolsillo	Echarse a uno a la bolsa	To wrap someone around one's little finger
316.	Meterse con		To pick a fight with
317.	Mientras más . . . más	Entre más . . . más (C.A., Col.)	The more . . . the more
318.	Mientras menos . . . menos	Entre menos . . . menos (C.A., Col.)	The less . . . the less
319.	Mirar de hito en hito	Mirar fijamente	To stare at; to eye up and down
320.	¡Mucho ojo!	Un ojo al gato y otro al garabato	Look out! Watch your step!
321.	Mucho ruido, pocas nueces	Tanto cacarear para no poner huevo; más la bulla que la cabuya (Ven.); es más la bulla que las mazorcas (Col.)	Much ado about nothing; his bark is worse than his bite
322.	Muy campante	Como si nada; da muchas correas	Cool as a cucumber
323.	Nacer con estrella	Nacer de pie	To be born lucky; to be born with a silver spoon in one's mouth
324.	Nadar en la abundancia	Estar muy pesudo; estar bien parado	To be rolling in money (dough)

Academy Spanish	American Spanish Variants	English Equivalents
325. Negocio redondo		Good sound bargain
326. ¡Ni a tiros!	¡En absoluto! ¡ni de vainas! *(Col.);* ¡ni bamba! *(Col.)*	Not for anything; not for love or money
327. ¡Ni en sueños!	¡Qué esperanza! *(Ríopl.; Andes);* ¡cuando! *(Ec.);* ¡frijoles! *(Carib.)*	By no means! Not on your life!
328. ¡Ni mucho menos!		Far from it! Not by a long shot!
329. No cabe duda		There is no doubt; beyond a shadow of a doubt; have (has) got to be *(Jones has got to be the best pitcher)*
330. No caber en si de gozo	No caber en el pellejo de gozo	To be beside oneself with joy; to be overcome with joy
331. No caer en la cuenta	No encontrarle el chiste	Not to see the point; not to get it
332. No dar el brazo a torcer	No aflojar un pelo *(Ríopl.)* Andes; hacer pata ancha *(Ríopl.)*	To be stubborn; to be not easily deceived; to be unyielding; to stick to one's guns
333. No darse por entendido		To pretend not to understand
334. No dejarle a uno ni a sol ni a sombra	Seguirlo hasta que se eche	To breathe down someone's neck; to dog someone's footsteps; to bug someone
335. No hay de qué	De nada; por nada *(Mex.)*	Don't mention it; you're welcome
336. No hay mal que por bien no venga	Una afortunada desgracia	It's an ill wind that blows no good; it's a blessing in disguise
337. No hay que darle vueltas		There's no getting around it
338. No me importa un comino	No me importa un pito; no me importa un cacahuate *(Mex.);* no me importa un cacao *(C.A.)*	I don't care a bit
339. No le suena a uno		It doesn't mean a thing; It doesn't ring a bell
340. No morderse la lengua	Cantar claro; ser claridoso *(Ven., C.A.)*	Not to mince words; to speak straight from the shoulder
341. No poder con	No ser un hueso fácil de roer	Not to be able to stand something (someone); to be too much for one
342. No saber ni jota	No saber ni papa	Not to know a blessed thing; not to know enough to come in out of the rain
343. No se ganó Zamora en una hora	No se ganó Toledo en un credo	Rome wasn't built in a day
344. No tener ni en qué caerse muerto	No tener ni segunda camisa; estar arrancado; andar pato *(Ch., Ríopl.)*	Not to have a penny to call one's own; not to have a red cent
345. No tener pelos en la lengua	Ser claridoso *(Ven., C.A.);* hablar a calzón quitado *(Ch., Col.)*	To be outspoken; to speak one's mind
346. No tener remedio		To be beyond repair (help, recourse); (to say something) can't be helped
347. No valer un comino	No valer un cacahuate *(Mex.);* no valer un cacao; *(C.A.);* no valer un palo de tabaco *(Col.);* no valer un taco *(Col.);* estar para el gato *(Ch.)*	Not to be worth a brass farthing (cent)
348. Obras son amores, que no buenas razones	Acciones son amores, no besos ni apachurrones	Actions speak louder than words
349. Oír hablar de	Oír mentar	To hear about
350. Ojos que no ven, corazón que no siente	Ojos que no ven tienen menos que sentir	Ignorance is bliss; out of sight, out of mind
351. Padre mercader, hijo caballero, nieto limosnero	Padre pulpero, hijo caballero, nieto limosnero *(Perú)*	Three generations from shirt sleeve to shirt sleeve

Academy Spanish	American Spanish Variants	English Equivalents
352. ¡Palabra!	¡Palabra de honor! ¡En serio!	Word of honor! On the level! No fooling! Sure enough!
353. ¡Pamplinas!	¡Pura guasa! ¡Frijoles! (*Carib.*)	Nonsense! Horsefeathers! Baloney!
354. Para colmo de males	¡No faltaba más!	That's the last straw! That does it! That's the straw that broke the camel's back
355. Parar (la) oreja		To prick up one's ears; to sit up and take notice
356. Pararle los pies a uno	Pararle el carro a uno; pararle el macho a uno	To put an end to something; to put one's foot down
357. Parece mentira		It hardly seems possible; it seems impossible
358. Pasar estrecheces	Pasar hambres; andar torcido	To feel the pinch
359. Pasar la mano por el lomo	Darle la suave a uno; ser barbero (*Mex.*)	To butter someone up; to soft-soap someone; to polish the apple; to brown-nose
360. Pasársele a uno		To get over; to forget
361. Pasársele a uno la mano		To overdo; to go too far
362. Pedir prestado	Prestar (*C.A., Col.*)	To ask (someone) to lend (one something); to borrow
363. Pedirle peras al olmo	Andar buscando guayabas en los magueyes	To try to get blood from a turnip (stone)
364. Perder el hilo de	Perder la hebra de	To lose the thread of
365. Perder los estribos		To lose one's mind; to flip one's lid
366. Perro ladrador nunca buen mordedor	Perro que ladra no muerde	Barking dogs seldom bite
367. Poner a uno al corriente	Ponerle al tanto a uno	To inform one; to bring one up to date
368. Poner el grito en el cielo		To make a great fuss; to hit the ceiling
369. Poner en marcha		To start; to put in motion
370. Poner la mesa		To set the table
371. Poner mucho ojo		To pay close attention
372. Poner pies en polvorosa	Tomar el polvo (*Mex., Col.*); Emplumárselas (*Col.*); salir fletado (*Ven.*)	To run away; to beat it; to take a powder; to hightail it
373. Poner reparo(s)		To raise objections
374. Ponerse a la obra		To get to work
375. Ponerse disgustado	Ponerse bravo; picarse (*Col.*)	To get angry
376. Ponérsele a uno carne de gallina		To get gooseflesh; to get goose pimples; to get burr (brrr) bumps
377. Por adelantado	Con anticipación	In advance; beforehand
378. Por casualidad		By chance; by the way
379. Por consiguiente	Por lo tanto	Therefore; so
380. Por extenso		At length; in detail
381. Por el hilo se saca el olvillo	Por la hebra se saca el olvillo; En el modo de cortar el queso se conoce al tendero	By their fruits shall ye know them; a fool is known by his laughing
382. Por las buenas o por las malas	De mangas o de faldas (*Ec.*)	Whether one likes it or not; by hook or by crook
383. Por las nubes		Sky-high; up in the clouds
384. Por lo demás		As for the rest; moreover
385. Por lo menos	Cuando menos; al menos	At least
386. Por lo pronto	Por el momento	For the time being
387. Por lo visto		Apparently; evidently
388. Por más que		However much
389. Por poco	Por un pelito de rana; casi, casi	Almost; like(d) to
390. Por sabido se calla	¡Clarinete!	It goes without saying
391. Por si acaso		Just in case; if by chance
392. Por supuesto	Claro que sí; ¿cómo no?	Of course; certainly
393. Por sus puños		On one's own
394. Por término medio		On the average

Academy Spanish	American Spanish Variants	English Equivalents
395. Preguntarse si, cuándo, cómo, etc.		To wonder (if, when, how, etc.)
396. Prender fuego a	Prender candela (*Col., Andes*)	To set fire to; to set on fire
397. Presumir de		To consider oneself to be
398. Prometer el oro y el moro	Prometer las perlas de la Virgen	To promise wonders (the moon)
399. Puesto que	Ya que	Because of the fact that; since
400. Puro jarabe de pico	Pura guasa; pura parada (*Mex.*)	Just talk; lip service; eyewash
401. Que Dios le tenga en la gloria	Que en paz descanse	God rest his soul; may he rest in peace
402. ¿Qué más da?		What's the difference? So what?
403. ¿Qué mosca te picó?		What's the matter with you? What's bugging you?
404. ¿Qué hay de nuevo?	¿Quiubo? (qué hubo) (*Mex., Col.*)	What's up? What's the good word? How goes it?
405. Quedar en		To agree (on)
406. Quedar en (de)		To promise to
407. Quedar en los huesos	No quedar más que hueso y cuero	To be a mere skeleton; to be nothing but skin and bones
408. Quedar en paz	Quedar a mano	To be even; to be square
409. Quedar mal con		Not to be on good terms with; not to make a hit with
410. Quedarse a la luna de Valencia	Dejarle a uno de a pie; quedarse a la luna de Paita (*Andes*)	To be left holding the bag
411. Quedarse con		To agree to buy (take)
412. Quedarse para vestir santos	Quedarse para vender estampas y milagros	To be left on the shelf
413. Quemarse las cejas	Quemarse las pestañas; ponerse barbero (*Col.*); machetear (*Mex.*)	To burn the midnight oil; to cram for an exam
414. Querer decir		To mean
415. Quien bien te quiere, te hará llorar	Porque te quiero, te aporreo	Spare the rod and spoil the child
416. Quien fue a Sevilla perdió su silla	El que se fue para la villa perdió su silla	Finders keepers, losers weepers
417. Quien porfía mata venado	Quien mucho porfía logra algún día; hay que hacer collera (*Ch.*)	If at first you don't succeed, try, try again; never say die
418. Quitarse de en medio	Hacerse a un lado; borrarse	To get out of the way
419. Rezar con	Tener que ver con	To have to do with
420. Risa de conejo	Reír de dientes afuera (*Col., Mex.*); reír a diente pelado (*Ven.*)	Half-hearted laugh
421. Ropa blanca	Ropa interior; ropa intima (feminine)	Underclothes; underwear
422. Saber a (la) gloria		To be delicious
423. Saber al dedillo		To know perfectly; to know in detail
424. Saber de sobra		To be fully aware; to know only too well
425. Saber llevar el compás		To be able to beat time
426. Sacar en limpio		To deduce; to understand
427. Sacar jugo de		To get a lot out of
428. Sacar partido de		To profit (gain) by
429. Salir a pedir de boca	Salir al pelo	To be all one could wish for; to suit to a T
430. Salir de Málaga y entrar en Malagón	Salir de Guatemala y entrar en Guatepeor	Out of the frying pan and into the fire
431. Salir del paso		To manage; to get by
432. Saltar a la vista		To be obvious; not to be able to miss
433. Según el caso		According to the situation; it all depends
434. Sentir en el alma		To be terribly sorry
435. Sentir crecer la hierba	Tener oídos de tísico	To have ears like a fox; to have a sharp ear

	Academy Spanish	American Spanish Variants	English Equivalents
436.	Ser cabeza de turco		To be the scapegoat; to be the whipping boy; to be a patsy
437.	Ser correcto		To be well-mannered
438.	Ser de fiar		To be trustworthy; to be dependable
439.	Ser de rigor		To be proper; to be indispensable
440.	Ser mala pieza	Ser una mala ficha (*Col.*)	To be a misfit (bad penny)
441.	Ser mano	Llevar la punta	To lead; to be first
442.	Ser un éxito de taquilla		To be a box-office success (hit)
443.	Sin embargo		Nevertheless
444.	Sin faltar una jota		In minutest detail
445.	Sin fin de		Numberless; endless amount
446.	Sin ton ni son		Without rhyme or reason
447.	Sudar la gota gorda	Sudar petróleo	To have a hard time; to sweat blood; to be in a sweat
448.	Tal vez	A saber (*C.A.*); ¡quién quita! (*Col.*)	Perhaps; maybe
449.	Tanto peor		So much the worse
450.	Tener al corriente		To keep someone posted; to keep someone up to date
451.	Tener buenas aldabas	Tener buenas agarraderas; tener palanca; tener enchufe (*Spain*)	To know the right people; to know influential people; to have a pipeline; to have pull
452.	Tener el riñón bien cubierto	Estar bien parado; tener la canasta baja y el riñón bien cubierto (*Mex.*)	To be well-off; to be well-heeled
453.	Tener en cuenta		To consider; to keep in mind
454.	Tener en poco		To hold in low esteem; not to think much of
455.	Tener ganas de	Apetecer (*Spain*); provocarle a uno (*Col.*)	To feel like; to desire
456.	Tener gracia	Ser chistoso	To be funny
457.	Tener la palabra		To have permission to speak; to have the floor
458.	Tener lugar		To take place; to be held
459.	Tener mucho mundo		To be sophisticated
460.	Tener pesar por	Darle a uno pena	To be sorry about
461.	Tener presente		To realize; to bear in mind
462.	Tener sin cuidado		Not to be concerned; to care less
463.	Tener trazas		To show signs
464.	Tocar de oído		To play by ear
465.	Tocar en lo vivo		To hurt deeply; to cut to the quick
466.	Tocarle a uno		To concern one; to be one's turn
467.	Todo bicho viviente		Every living soul
468.	Todo lo contrario		Just the opposite
469.	Toma y daca	Dando y dando, pajarito volando	Cash and carry; put your money where your mouth is
470.	Tomar a pecho		To take to heart
471.	Tomar cuerpo		To take shape
472.	Tomar el rábano por las hojas		To put the cart before the horse
473.	Tomarla con		To pick on; to have a grudge against
474.	Tomarle el pelo a uno	Hacerle guaje a uno (*Mex.*)	To pull someone's leg; to kid someone
475.	Trabajar como una fiera	Trabajar como burro; trabajar como negro	To work like a dog
476.	Trabar amistad		To strike up a friendship
477.	Traer retraso		To be behind schedule; to be late
478.	¡Trato hecho!	¡Chóquela! ¡Echeme esos cinco!	It's a deal! Shake on it! Put 'er there!

Academy Spanish	American Spanish Variants	English Equivalents
479. ¡Tres hurras por fulano!	¡Una porra!	Three cheers for
480. Un bribón de siete suelas	Uno capaz de empeñar la sábana sagrada	An errant rogue; a dirty rat
481. Un no sé qué		A certain something
482. Una comilona	Un banquetazo	A feast fit for a king; quite a spread
483. Uno que otro		An occasional one; some; a few
484. Unos cuantos		Some; a few
485. Valerse de		To avail oneself of; to make use of
486. Variar de opinión		To hold a different opinion; to change one's mind
487. Venir a parar		To turn out; to end up
488. Venirse a tierra		To collapse; to fail
489. ¡Vete a freír espárragos!	¡Vete a freír chongos! (*Mex.*); ¡vete a freír monos! (*Col.*); ¡vete a freír mocos! (*Andes*)	Go peddle your papers! Get lost!
490. Vísteme despacio que tengo prisa	Más vale paso que dure y no que apresure	Haste makes waste; easy does it
491. Volver el estómago	Huacarear (*Mex.*); echar las migas; dársele vuelta la vianda a uno (*Ch.*)	To vomit; to have the heaves; to upchuck; to toss one's cookies
492. Voy y vengo	No me tardo un minuto; oritita vengo (*Mex.*)	I'll be right back; it won't be a minute
493. Y así sucesivamente		And so on
494. Y pico		And some odd; and something
495. Y sanseacabó	Ahí muere	That's final. It's all over with
496. Ya cayó el chivo en el lazo	Este arroz ya se coció	It's in the bag
497. Ya lo creo	A la fija (*Ríopl.*) ¿Cómo no?	Of course; certainly
498. Ya ni llorar es bueno	Nada logras con llorar delante del bien perdido	Don't cry over spilt milk
499. Zapatero a tus zapatos		Mind your own business
500. ¡Zas!		Bang!

English Index to Spanish Idioms and Proverbs

257

Parte Segunda Inglés-Español

Al Lector

El auge que desde el principio de la Segunda Guerra Mundial viene cobrando en la América española el aprendizaje del inglés, nos ha movido a recopilar en este breve Diccionario las voces y locuciones más indispensables de esta lengua tal como se habla y escribe en los Estados Unidos de América.

Al igual que en la Sección española-inglesa hemos antepuesto la abreviatura *Am.* y otras de señalados países o regiones a aquellos vocablos o modismos que son de uso exclusivo en alguna región de la América española, o bien de uso frecuentísimo en ésta, aunque ya hayan caído en desuso en la Península. Todo lo cual no excluye la posibilidad de que alguna acepción así designada se oiga en labios de un español o sea de uso esporádico en España.

Lo que sí hemos procurado con gran ahínco y anhelamos lograr, presentando al estudioso este caudal indispensable de palabras, es el acercamiento lingüístico de las Américas, como base para nuestra mutua comprensión y como instrumento poderosísimo para nuestra solidaridad.

LOS EDITORES

Lista de Abreviaturas

adj.	adjetivo	*irr.*	irregular
adv.	adverbio	*p.p.*	participio pasado o pasivo
art.	artículo	*pers.*	personal
art. indef.	artículo indefinido	*pl.*	plural
aux.	auxiliar	*pos.*	posesivo
comp.	comparativo	*prep.*	preposición
conj.	conjunción	*pron.*	pronombre
contr.	contracción	*pron. pers.*	pronombre personal
defect.	defectivo	*pron. pos.*	pronombre posesivo
etc.	etcétera	*s.*	sustantivo
ger.	gerundio	*sing.*	singular
gram.	gramatical, gramática	*subj.*	subjuntivo
imperf.	imperfecto	*v.*	verbo
indic.	indicativo	*v. defect.*	verbo defectivo
interj.	interjección	*v. irr.*	verbo irregular
interr.	interrogativo		

Abreviaturas Especiales de Indicación Regional

Am.[1]	Americanismo
Andalucía	
Andes	(Ecuador, Perú, Bolivia)
Arg.	Argentina
Bol.	Bolivia
Carib.	(Cuba, Puerto Rico, República Dominicana)

---

1. Esta abreviatura se emplea para indicar uso general hispanoamericano; se implica a la vez carácter arcaizante en cuanto a España. Se usa también para señalar los vocablos ya poco usados que puedan encontrarse en obras literarias del siglo pasado.

C.A.	Centroamérica (Guatemala, El Salvador, Honduras, Nicaragua, Costa Rica)
Ch.	Chile
Col.	Colombia
C.R.	Costa Rica
Cuba	
Ec.	El Ecuador
Esp.	España
Guat.	Guatemala
Hond.	Honduras
Méx.	México
N. Esp.	Norte de España
Nic.	Nicaragua
Pan.	Panamá
Par.	Paraguay
Perú	
P.R.	Puerto Rico
Ríopl.	Río de la Plata (La Argentina oriental, el Uruguay)
S.A.	Sudamérica
Sal.	El Salvador
Ur.	El Uruguay
Ven.	Venezuela

Pronunciación Inglesa[2]

I. Vocales

Símbolo fonético	Ortografía inglesa	Ortografía fonética	Explicación de los sonidos
i	see pea	si pi	Equivale a la *i* en *hilo*.
ɪ	bit	bɪt	El sonido más aproximado es la *i* en *virtud,* pero la [ɪ] inglesa es una *i* más abierta tirando a *e* cerrada
e	late they	let ðe	Equivale aproximadamente a *ei;* la *i* de este diptongo es muy relajada y más abierta que en español.
ɛ	bet	bɛt	El sonido más aproximado en español es la *e* abierta de *perro*.
æ	sat	sæt	Es una vocal intermedia entre la *a* y la *e*.
ɑ	car	kɑr	Equivale aproximadamente a la *a* en *cargo*.
ɔ	forge	fɔrdʒ	Equivale aproximadamente a la *o* en *corto, corre*.
o	mode	mod	Equivale aproximadamente a *ou;* la *u* de este diptongo es muy relajada y más abierta que en español.
ʊ	pull	pʊl	El sonido más aproximado en español es la *u* en *turrón,* pero la [ʊ] inglesa es todavía más abierta.
u	June moon	dʒun mun	Equivale aproximadamente a la *u* en *uno*.
ə	cudgel apply	kʌdʒəl əplaɪ	Es una *e* muy relajada. No tiene equivalente en español.
ɚ	teacher	títʃɚ	Es una *e* muy relajada, articulada simultáneamente con la *r*. No tiene equivalente en español.

2. El estudioso puede consultar el importante diccionario de pronunciación norteamericana: Kenyon and Knott, *A Pronouncing Dictionary of American English* (Springfield, Massachusetts: G & C. Merriam Company, Publishers, 1944).

Símbolo fonético	Ortografía inglesa	Ortografía fonética	Explicación de los sonidos
ɝ	earth fur	ɝθ fɝ	Es un sonido intermedio entre la *e* y la *o* articulado simultáneamente con la *r*. Se acerca más a la *e* que a la *o*. No tiene equivalente en español.
ʌ	duck	dʌk	Es una vocal intermedia entre la *e* muy abierta y la *o*. Se acerca más a la *o* que a la *e*. No tiene equivalente en español.

II. Diptongos

aɪ	aisle nice	aɪl naɪs	Equivale aproximadamente a *ai* en *aire*.
aʊ	now	naʊ	Equivale aproximadamente a *au* en *causa*.
ɔɪ	coy	kɔɪ	Equivale aproximadamente a *oy* en *hoy*. El segundo elemento del diptongo es más abierto y débil, tirando a *e*.
ju	used	juzd	Equivale aproximadamente a *iu* en *ciudad*.
jʊ	cure	kjʊr	Equivale aproximadamente al diptongo *iu*, pero la *u* es más abierta.

III. Consonantes

p	paper	pépɚ	Equivale aproximadamente a la *p* española, pero es aspirada.
b	bat	bæt	La *b* inglesa es semejante a la *b* inicial española, pero se pronuncia más explosivamente.
t	tea	ti	Es bastante diferente de la *t* española. Se articula colocando flojamente la lengua arriba de los dientes incisivos superiores y es aspirada.
d	day	de	Equivale a la *d* inicial española pronunciada con mayor énfasis y se articula arriba de los dientes.
k	cat kill	kæt kɪl	Equivale aproximadamente a la *c* española delante de *a, o, u* pronunciada con aspiracion.
g	go gum ago	go gʌm əgó	Equivale aproximadamente, a la *g* inicial delante de *a, o, u: goma, guerra, gana;* sólo que la *g* inglesa se pronuncia con mayor explosión.
f	fun affair	fʌn əfáɛr	Equivale aproximadamente a la *f* española.
v	very	vɛrɪ	De vez en cuando se oye en español como ultracorrección. Es una labiodental que se articula con el labio inferior y los dientes incisivos superiores.
θ	thin	θɪn	Equivale aproximadamente a la *z* en el castellano *cazar*.
ð	then other	ðɛn ʌðɚ	Equivale aproximadamente a la *d* española en *nada*.
s	send case cent	sɛnd kes sɛnt	Equivale aproximadamente a la *s* inicial española de Hispanoamérica; *santo*.
z	rose these zero	roz ðiz zíro	Equivale aproximadamente a la *s* sonora en *mismo*, pero se pronuncia con más sonoridad en inglés.
ʃ	sheet machine nation	ʃit maʃín néʃən	Es una *s* palatal que no tiene equivalente en español. Suena como la *ch* francesa; *chapeau*.
ʒ	vision	viʒən	Es una palatal fricativa sonora, semejante a la *y* argentina y uruguaya o la *j* de *jouer* en francés.
tʃ	chase	tʃes	Equivale aproximadamente a la *ch* en *charla*.
dʒ	judge gentle	dʒʌdʒ dʒɛntl	No tiene equivalente exacto en español. Se parece a la *y* de *inyectar* en la pronunciación de muchos hispanoamericanos.

Símbolo fonético	Ortografía inglesa	Ortografía fonética	Explicación de los sonidos
m	much	mʌtʃ	Equivale aproximadamente a la *m* española.
n	none	nʌn	Equivale aproximadamente a la *n* española en *nada*.
	any	ɛnɪ	
ṇ	eaten	itṇ	No tiene equivalente en español. Representa la *n* sin la articulación de la vocal anterior.
	button	bʌtṇ	
	lesson	lésṇ	
ŋ	ankle	ǽŋkl̥	Equivale a la *n* española en *mango, banco*.
	angle	ǽŋgl̥	
	ring	rɪŋ	
l	late	let	La *l* inicial equivale aproximadamente a la *l* española en *lado*. La *l* final de sílaba es más débil que la inicial y semejante a la portuguesa o a la catalana.
	altar	ɔ́ltɚ	
	fall	fɔl	
	folly	fálɪ	
l̥	able	ébl̥	No tiene equivalente en español. Se pronuncia como la *l* final de sílaba, omitiendo la vocal precedente.
	ankle	ǽŋkl̥	
w	weed	wid	Equivale a la *u* de los diptongos; *ui, ue, ua, uo*.
	well	wɛl	
	wall	wɔl	
h	hat	hæt	No tiene equivalente exacto en español. Equivale aproximadamente a una *j* suave que se reduce a una simple aspiración.
	whole	hol	
hw	where	hwɛr	Equivale a una *j* suave seguida de una *w* arriba explicada, y se usa en la mayoría de los dialectos norteamericanos.
j	year	jɪr	Equivale a la *i* española en los diptongos *ie, ia, io, iu*: *hiena*.
	yawn	jɔn	
	yet	jɛt	
r	rose	roz	No tiene equivalente en español. La punta de la lengua se arrolla hacia atrás sin tocar el paladar. A veces se pierde al grado de vocalizarse.
	bear	bɛr	

Pronunciación de la S del Plural[3]

I. La **-s** del plural es sorda cuando la palabra termina en las consonantes sordas representadas por los símbolos fonéticos [p], [t], [k], [f], [θ]. Pronúnciase como la *s* de *santo*: **caps** [kæps], **gates** [gets], **cats** [kæts], **books** [bʊks], **cliffs** [klɪfs], **lengths** [leŋkθs].

Las excepciones más comunes son: **oath** [oθ], **oaths** [oðz]; **leaf** [lif], **leaves** [livz], **wife** [waɪf], **wives** [waɪvz]; **knife** [naɪf], **knives** [naɪvz]; **calf** [kæf], **calves** [kævz]; **half** [hæf], **halves** [hævz].

II. La **-s** del plural es sonora cuando la palabra termina en vocal (incluyendo la **-y** que se cambia en **-ies**), o en las consonantes sonoras representadas por los símbolos fonéticos [b], [d], [g], [v], [ð], [m], [n], [ŋ], [l]: **cries** [kraɪz], **robes** [robz], **beds** [bɛdz], **logs** [lɔgz], **stoves** [stovz], **lathes** [leðz], **farms** [farmz], **bins** [bɪnz], **kings** [kɪŋz], **falls** [fɔlz], **furs** [fɝz], **papers** [pépɚz], **plows** [plaʊz].

III. Cuando la palabra termina **-en** las consonantes representadas por los símbolos [s], [ʃ], [tʃ], [z], [ʒ], [dʒ], se añade **-es** [ɪz], o **s** [ɪz], si la palabra termina en **-ce, -se, -dge, -ge**: **face** [fes], **faces** [fésɪz]; **kiss** [kɪs], **kisses** [kísɪz]; **ash** [æʃ], **ashes** [ǽʃɪz]; **lunch** [lʌntʃ], **lunches** [lʌntʃɪz]; **rose** [roz], **roses** [rózɪz]; **judge** [dʒʌdʒ], **judges** [dʒʌdʒɪz].

3. Las mismas reglas se aplican a la pronunciación del genitivo y de la tercera persona del presente de indicativo, singular: **keeps** [kips]; **Kate's** [kets]; **saves** [sevz]; **John's** [dʒanz]; **judges** [dʒʌdʒɪz]; **Alice's** [ǽlɪsɪz].

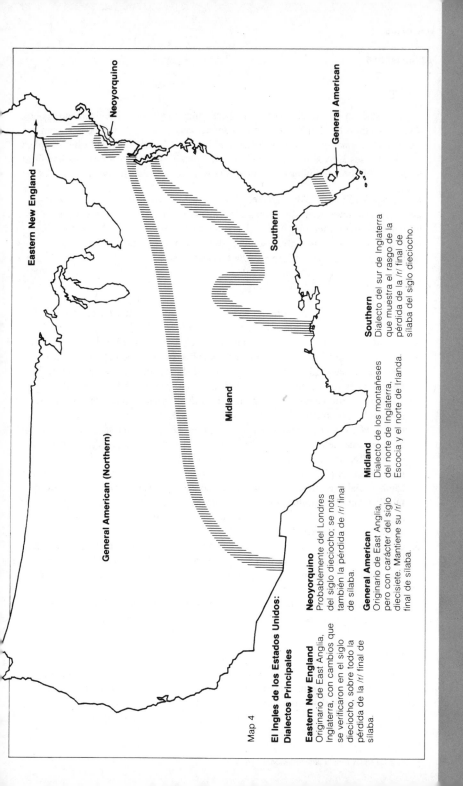

Map 4

El Ingles de los Estados Unidos: Dialectos Principales

Eastern New England
Originario de East Anglia, Inglaterra, con cambios que se verificaron en el siglo dieciocho, sobre todo la pérdida de la /r/ final de sílaba.

Neoyorquino
Probablemente del Londres del siglo dieciocho; se nota también la pérdida de /r/ final de sílaba.

General American
Originario de East Anglia, pero con carácter del siglo diecisiete. Mantiene su /r/ final de sílaba.

Midland
Dialecto de los montañeses del norte de Inglaterra, Escocia y el norte de Irlanda.

Southern
Dialecto del sur de Inglaterra que muestra el rasgo de la pérdida de la /r/ final de sílaba del siglo dieciocho.

Eastern New England

Neoyorquino

General American

General American (Northern)

Midland

Southern

El Sustantivo

I. Género

En la gramática inglesa el género tiene papel mínimo y resulta ser fenómeno léxico. Son masculinos los nombres de varón o animal macho, y son femeninos los nombres de mujer o animal hembra. Los demás son neutros. El artículo definido **the** se aplica a todos los sustantivos, singular y plural: **the man** el hombre; **the men** los hombres; **the book** el libro; **the books** los libros; **the woman** la mujer; **the women** las mujeres.

En ciertos sustantivos se distingue el género femenino por medio del sufijo **-ess:** **actor** actor; **actress** actriz. A veces es indispensable indicar el género por medio de las palabras **male** o **female, boy** o **girl, man** o **woman, she** o **he: baby boy** niño; **baby girl** niña; **woman writer** escritora; **she-bear** osa. En otros casos hay una palabra distinta para cada género; **uncle** tío; **aunt** tía.

II. Plural de los Sustantivos[4]

1. Generalmente se forma el plural añadiendo **-s** al singular: **paper, papers** papel, papeles; **book, books** libro, libros; **chief, chiefs** jefe, jefes.
2. Los sustantivos que terminan en **-ch** (pronunciada como la *ch* española), **-ss, -x, -sh, -z,** y **-o** añaden **-es** para formar el plural: **arch, arches** arco, arcos; **kiss, kisses** beso, besos; **box, boxes** caja, cajas; **dish, dishes** plato, platos; **buzz, buzzes** zumbido, zumbidos; **hero, heroes** héroe, héroes. Nótese que los sustantivos terminados en **-ch** (pronunciada [**k**]) forman el plural añadiendo **-s: monarch, monarchs** monarca, monarcas.
3. Los sustantivos que terminan en **-fe,** y ciertos sustantivos que terminan en **-f,** cambian estas letras en **v** y añaden **-es: leaf, leaves** hoja, hojas; **life, lives** vida, vidas; **wife, wives** esposa, esposas; **knife, knives** cuchillo, cuchillos.
4. Para formar el plural de los sustantivos terminados en **-y** precedida de consonante cámbiase la **-y** en **-ies: fly, flies** mosca, moscas; **cry, cries** grito, gritos; **family, families** familia, familias; **quantity, quantities** cantidad, cantidades. Nótese que los sustantivos terminados en **-y** precedida de vocal forman el plural añadiendo **-s** al singular: **day, days** día, días.
5. Ciertos sustantivos forman el plural de una manera irregular: **man, men** hombre, hombres; **woman, women** mujer, mujeres; **mouse, mice** ratón, ratones; **louse, lice** piojo, piojos; **goose, geese** ganso, gansos; **tooth, teeth** diente, dientes; **foot, feet** pie, pies; **ox, oxen** buey, bueyes.
6. Ciertos sustantivos que terminan en **-is** forman el plural cambiando la **i** de la terminación en **e: axis, axes** eje, ejes; **the crisis, the crises** la crisis, las crisis.

El Adjetivo

El adjetivo inglés es invariable en cuanto a género y número. Normalmente se coloca delante del sustantivo: **an interesting book** un libro interesante; **a large table** una mesa grande; **beautiful women** mujeres hermosas.

---

4. Véase las reglas para la pronunciación del plural.

Los comparativos y superlativos. Aunque no hay una regla general, por lo común los adjetivos monosílabos, los adjetivos acentuados en la última sílaba y algunos bisílabos fácilmente pronunciados forman *el comparativo de aumento y el superlativo* añadiendo **-er** y **-est**. Los demás adjetivos van precedidos de **more** y **most**. Nótese que (1) sólo se añaden **-r** y **-st** a los que terminan en **-e** muda; (2) los adjetivos terminados en **-y** cambian esta letra en **i**; (3) los adjetivos terminados en consonante precedida de vocal doblan la consonante:

Positivo	*Comparativo*	*Superlativo*
tall alto	**taller** más alto	**the tallest** el más alto
wise sabio	**wiser** más sabio	**the wisest** el más sabio
polite cortés	**politer** más cortés	**the politest** el más cortés
happy feliz	**happier** más feliz	**the happiest** el más feliz
fat gordo	**fatter** más gordo	**the fattest** el más gordo
careful cuidadoso	**more careful** maś cuidadoso	**the most careful** el más cuidadoso

El superlativo absoluto se forma anteponiendo **very** y a veces **most: very intelligent** muy inteligente; **she is a most beautiful woman** es una mujer hermosísima.

El comparativo y el superlativo de inferioridad se forman con los adverbios **less** y **least: less important** menos importante; **the least important** el menos importante.

El comparativo de igualdad se forma con el adverbio **as: as poor as** tan pobre como; **as much as** tanto como; **as much money as** tanto dinero como.

Los adjetivos siguientes forman el comparativo y el superlativo de una manera irregular:

good, well	**better**	**best**
bad, ill	**worse**	**worst**
little	**less, lesser**	**least**
far	**farther, further**	**farthest, furthest**
much, many	**more**	**most**
old	**older, elder**	**oldest, eldest**

El Adverbio

Fórmanse muchos adverbios, añadiendo **-ly** al adjetivo: **courteous** cortés, **courteously** cortésmente; **bold** atrevido, **boldly** atrevidamente. Existen las irregularidades siguientes en la formación de los adverbios que terminan en **-ly**: (1) los adjetivos terminados en **-ble** cambian la **-e** en **-y: possible, possibly**; (2) los terminados en **ic** añaden **-ally: poetic, poetically**; (3) los terminados en **-ll** añaden sólo la **-y: full, fully**; (4) los terminados en **-ue** pierden la **-e** final: **true, truly**; (5) los terminados en **-y** cambian la **-y** en **i: happy, happily**.

Como los adjetivos, la mayor parte de los adverbios forman el *comparativo* y el *superlativo* con los adverbios **more** (más), **most** (más), y **very** (muy). Asimismo los adverbios monosílabos añaden **-er** y **-est**:

Positivo	*Comparative*	*Superlativo*	*Superlativo Absoluto*
boldly	**more boldly**	**most boldly**	**very boldly**
generously	**more generously**	**most generously**	**very generously**
soon	**sooner**	**soonest**	**very soon**
early	**earlier**	**earliest**	**very early**

late	later	latest	very late
near	nearer	nearest	very near
fast	faster	fastest	very fast

Los adverbios siguientes forman el comparativo y el superlativo de una manera irregular:

well	better	best	very well
badly, ill	worse	worst	very badly
little	less	least	very little
much	more	most	very much
far	farther, further	farthest, furthest	very far

Sufijos Comunes en Inglés

-dom   denota dominio, jurisdicción, estado, condición, etc.: **kingdom** reino; **martyrdom** martirio; **boredom** aburrimiento; **freedom** libertad.

-ed, -d   es la terminación del pretérito y del participio pasivo o pasado de los verbos regulares: **I called** llamé; **called** llamado.

-ee   indica la persona que recibe la acción: **addressee** destinatario; **employee** empleado.

-eer   denota oficio u ocupación: **engineer** ingeniero; **auctioneer** subastador.

-en   *a)* terminación del participio de muchos verbos irregulares: **fallen, broken, shaken;**
b) sufijo que significa *hecho de:* **golden** dorado, de oro; **wooden** de madera; **leaden** de plomo;
c) terminación verbal equivalente a *hacer:* **whiten** hacer blanco, emblanquecer; **darken** hacer obscuro, obscurecer.

-er   *a)* indica la persona que hace o el agente de la acción del verbo: **player** jugador; **speaker** orador;
b) indica el residente de un lugar: **New Yorker** habitante o residente de Nueva York; **islander** isleño;
c) denota ocupación: **carpenter** carpintero; **baker** panadero.
d) es la terminación del comparativo de adjetivos y adverbios; **taller** más alto; **faster** más aprisa.

-ess   úsase para formar el género femenino de ciertos sustantivos: **actress** actriz; **princess** princesa; **countess** condesa.

-est   terminación del superlativo: **tallest** el más alto.

-fold   sufijo que significa *veces:* **twofold** dos veces; **hundredfold** cien veces.

-ful   *a)* equivale a *lleno,* y tratándose de adjetivos es igual a *-oso:* **hopeful** lleno de esperanzas; **careful** cuidadoso; **willful** voluntarioso; **merciful** misericordioso; **glassful** un vaso *(lleno);*
b) indica a veces hábito o inclinación: **forgetful** olvidadizo;
c) es a veces equivalente a los sufijos españoles *-ado, -ada:* **handful** puñado; **spoonful** cucharada.

-hood   indica estado, condición, carácter, grupo: a menudo equivale a *-dad:* **motherhood** maternidad; **brotherhood** fraternidad; **childhood** niñez; **likelihood** probabilidad.

-ician	denota especialidad en cierto ramo: **musician** músico; **technician** técnico; **electrician** electricista.
-ie	sufijo diminutivo: **birdie** pajarito; **Annie** Anita.
-ing	*a)* sufijo del gerundio: **speaking** hablando;
	b) sufijo del participio activo: **threatening** amenazante; **surprising** sorprendente;
	c) úsase a menudo para formar adjetivos: **running water** agua corriente; **drinking water** agua potable; **waiting room** sala de espera; **washing machine** máquina lavadora;
	d) úsase para formar sustantivos: **understanding** entendimiento; **supplying** abastecimiento; **clothing** ropa; **covering** cobertura; equivale al infinitivo castellano: **swimming is good exercise** el nadar es buen ejercicio.
-ish	*a)* úsase para formar ciertos adjetivos de nacionalidad: **Spanish** español; **English** inglés; **Turkish** turco;
	b) indica semejanza: **boyish** como niño, aniñado; **womanish** como mujer, mujeril, afeminado; **whitish** blancuzco, medio blanco, que tira a blanco.
-less	equivale a *sin, falto de:* **childless** sin hijos; **penniless** sin dinero; en ciertos casos el sufijo inglés se traduce por medio de un prefijo: **countless** innumerable, sin número; **endless** interminable, sin fin.
-like	significa *semejanza,* y equivale a *como, a manera de:* **lifelike** que parece vivo; **childlike** como niño, infantil; **tigerlike** como tigre.
-ly	*a)* sufijo adverbial: **slowly** lentamente; **happily** felizmente; **possibly** posiblemente;
	b) añadido a ciertos sustantivos equivale a *como, a la manera de:* **motherly** como madre, materno; **gentlemanly** como caballero, caballeroso; **friendly** amigable; **manly** varonil;
	c) equivale a *cada* en estos ejemplos: **daily** cada día; diario; **weekly** cada semana, semanal; **monthly** cada mes, mensual; **yearly** cada año, anual.
-ness	úsase para formar sustantivos abstractos: **goodness** bondad; **darkness** obscuridad; **foolishness** tontería; **shamelessness** desvergüenza.
-ship	*a)* úsase para formar sustantivos abstractos: **friendship** amistad; **relationship** relación, parentesco;
	b) denota arte o destreza: **horsemanship** equitación;
	c) expresa dignidad, oficio, cargo, o título: **professorship** profesorado o cátedra; **chairmanship** presidencia (*de un comité, asamblea, etc.*); **lordship** señoría;
	d) a veces expresa tan sólo un estado y su duración: **courtship** galanteo, cortejo, noviazgo.
-some	expresa en alto grado la cualidad representada por el vocablo al cual se añade: **tiresome** que cansa, cansado; **quarrelsome** dado a riñas, pendenciero; **loathsome** que repugna, asqueroso; **burdensome** gravoso.
-th	úsase para formar números ordinales: **fifth** quinto; **tenth** décimo.
-ty	*a)* terminación de los múltiples de diez: **twenty** veinte; **thirty** treinta; **forty** cuarenta;

b) terminación de muchos sustantivos abstractos; equivale frecuentemente al sufijo español *-tad* o *-dad:* **beauty** beldad; **paternity** paternidad; **falsity** falsedad.

-ward, -wards denotan *hacia:* **homeward** hacia casa; **downward** hacia abajo.

-ways, -wise expresan manera, dirección, posición, etc.: **edgewise** de lado; **sideways** de lado; **lengthwise** a lo largo.

-y *a)* terminación equivalente a los sufijos españoles *-ia, -ía:* **victory** victoria; **glory** gloria; **courtesy** cortesía; **biology** biología; **astronomy** astronomía;

b) sufijo diminutivo: **doggy** perrito; **Johnny** Juanito;

c) denota abundancia, y es a menudo equivalente a *-udo, -oso, -ado:* **rocky** lleno de rocas, rocoso, pedregoso; **rainy** lluvioso; **hairy** lleno de pelo, peludo; **bulky** abultado; **wavy** ondulado; **angry** enojado;

d) expresa semejanza: **rosy** rosado, como una rosa, color de rosa.

Números

Consúltese la tabla de la página 38 de la Sección Española-Inglesa para el aprendizaje de los números cardinales y ordinales desde uno hasta un millón.

Verbos Irregulares de la Lengua Inglesa

Se denominan verbos irregulares los que no forman el pretérito o el participio pasivo con la adición de **-d** o **-ed** al presente. Obsérvese que en ciertos verbos coexiste la forma regular al lado de la irregular. En otros coexisten dos formas irregulares juntamente con la regular.

Presente	*Pretérito*	*Participio pasivo o pasado*
abide	abode	abode
am, is, are	was, were	been
arise	arose	arisen
awake	awoke, awaked	awaked, awoke
bear	bore	born, borne
beat	beat	beat, beaten
become	became	become
befall	befell	befallen
beget	begat	begotten
begin	began	begun
behold	beheld	beheld
bend	bent	bent
bereave	bereft, bereaved	bereft, bereaved
beseech	besought, beseeched	besought, beseeched
beset	beset	beset
bet	bet	bet
bid	bid, bade	bidden, bid
bind	bound	bound
bite	bit	bitten, bit
bleed	bled	bled
blow	blew	blown
break	broke	broken
breed	bred	bred
bring	brought	brought
build	built	built
burn	burnt, burned	burnt, burned
burst	burst	burst
buy	bought	bought
can *(verbo defectivo)*	could	—

Presente	*Pretérito*	*Participio pasivo o pasado*
cast	cast	cast
catch	caught	caught
chide	chided, chid	chided, chidden
choose	chose	chosen
cleave	cleft, clove, cleaved	cleft, cleaved, cloven
cling	clung	clung
clothe	clad, clothed	clad, clothed
come	came	come
cost	cost	cost
creep	crept	crept
crow	crew, crowed	crowed
cut	cut	cut
deal	dealt	dealt
dig	dug, digged	dug, digged
dive	dived, dove	dived, dove
do	did	done
draw	drew	drawn
dream	dreamt, dreamed	dreamt, dreamed
drink	drank	drunk
drive	drove	driven
dwell	dwelled	dwelt, dwelled
eat	ate	eaten
fall	fell	fallen
feed	fed	fed
feel	felt	felt
fight	fought	fought
find	found	found
flee	fled	fled
fling	flung	flung
fly	flew	flown
forbear	forbore	forborne
forbid	forbade	forbidden
foresee	foresaw	foreseen
foretell	foretold	foretold
forget	forgot	forgotten, forgot
forgive	forgave	forgiven
forsake	forsook	forsaken
freeze	froze	frozen
get	got	got, gotten
gild	gilded	gilt, gilded
gird	girded	girt, girded
give	gave	given
go	went	gone
grind	ground	ground
grow	grew	grown
hang[5]	hung	hung
have, has	had	had
hear	heard	heard
heave	hove, heaved	hove, heaved
hew	hewed	hewn, hewed
hide	hid	hidden, hid
hit	hit	hit
hold	held	held
hurt	hurt	hurt
inlay	inlaid	inlaid
keep	kept	kept
kneel	knelt	knelt
knit	knit, knitted	knit, knitted
know	knew	known
lay	laid	laid
lead	led	led
lean	leaned	leaned, leant
leap	leapt, leaped	leapt, leaped
learn	learned	learned, learnt

5. Es regular cuando significa «ahorcar.»

Presente	*Pretérito*	*Participio pasivo o pasado*
leave	left	left
lend	lent	lent
let	let	let
lie[6] **(yacer; echarse)**	lay	lain
light	lit, lighted	lit, lighted
load	loaded	loaded, laden
lose	lost	lost
make	made	made
may *(verbo defectivo)*	might	—
mean	meant	meant
meet	met	met
melt	melted	melted, molten
mistake	mistook	mistaken
mow	mowed	mown, mowed
must *(verbo defectivo)*	—	—
ought *(verbo defectivo)*	ought	—
pay	paid	paid
plead	pled, pleaded	pled, pleaded
put	put	put
quit	quit, quitted	quit, quitted
read [rid]	read [rɛd]	read [rɛd]
rend	rent	rent
rid	rid, ridded	rid, ridded
ride	rode	ridden
ring	rang, rung	rung
rise	rose	risen
run	ran	run
saw	sawed	sawn, sawed
say	said	said
see	saw	seen
seek	sought	sought
sell	sold	sold
send	sent	sent
set	set	set
sew	sewed	sewn, sewed
shake	shook	shaken
shall	should	—
shave	shaved	shaved, shaven
shear	sheared	shorn, sheared
shed	shed	shed
shine[7]	shone	shone
shoe	shod	shod
shoot	shot	shot
show	showed	shown, showed
shred	shred, shredded	shred, shredded
shrink	shrank, shrunk	shrunk, shrunken
shut	shut	shut
sing	sang, sung	sung
sink	sank	sunk
sit	sat	sat
slay	slew	slain
sleep	slept	slept
slide	slid	slid, slidden
sling	slung	slung
slink	slunk	slunk
slit	slit	slit
smell	smelled	smelt, smelled
smite	smote	smitten
sow	sowed	sown, sowed
speak	spoke	spoken
speed	sped, speeded	sped, speeded
spell	spelled, spelt	spelled, spelt
spend	spent	spent

6. Es regular cuando significa «mentir.»
7. Es por lo común regular cuando significa «pulir, dar brillo.»

Presente	*Pretérito*	*Participio pasivo o pasado*
spill	spilled, spilt	spilled, spilt
spin	spun	spun
spit	spit, spat	spit, spat
split	split	split
spread	spread	spread
spring	sprang, sprung	sprung
stand	stood	stood
stave	staved, stove	staved, stove
steal	stole	stolen
stick	stuck	stuck
sting	stung	stung
stink	stank, stunk	stunk
strew	strewed	strewn, strewed
stride	strode	stridden
strike	struck	struck, striken
string	strung	strung
strive	strove, strived	striven, strived
swear	swore	sworn
sweep	swept	swept
swell	swelled	swollen, swelled
swim	swam	swum
swing	swung	swung
take	took	taken
teach	taught	taught
tear	tore	torn
tell	told	told
think	thought	thought
thrive	throve, thrived	thriven, thrived
throw	threw	thrown
thrust	thrust	thrust
tread	trod	trod, trodden
understand	understood	understood
undertake	undertook	undertaken
undo	undid	undone
uphold	upheld	upheld
upset	upset	upset
wake	woke, waked	waked
wear	wore	worn
weave	wove	woven
wed	wedded	wedded, wed
weep	wept	wept
wet	wet, wetted	wet, wetted
will *(verbo auxiliar)*	would	—
win	won	won
wind	wound	wound
withdraw	withdrew	withdrawn
withhold	withheld	withheld
withstand	withstood	withstood
work	worked, wrought	worked, wrought
wring	wrung	wrung
write	wrote	written

A : a

a [ə, e] *art. indef.* un, una; **what — ...! ¡qué ...!; such —** tal; tan.

a·ban·don [əbǽndən] *v.* abandonar; dejar; *s.* abandono, desahogo, desenvoltura; entrega.

a·ban·doned [əbǽndənd] *adj.* abandonado; dejado; perverso; inmoral.

a·ban·don·ment [əbǽndənmənt] *s.* abandono, abandonamiento; desamparo; desenvoltura, desembarazo.

a·bashed [əbǽʃt] *adj.* humillado, avergonzado.

a·bate [əbét] *v.* bajar, rebajar; disminuir; acabar con; mitigar(se); calmarse.

a·bate·ment [əbétmənt] *s.* diminución, merma; rebaja, descuento; mitigación.

ab·bess [ǽbəs] *s.* abadesa.

ab·bey [ǽbɪ] *s.* abadía, monasterio.

ab·bot [ǽbət] *s.* abad.

ab·bre·vi·ate [əbrívɪet] *v.* abreviar, acortar, reducir.

ab·bre·vi·a·tion [əbrivɪéʃən] *s.* abreviación, abreviatura; **initial —** sigla.

ab·di·cate [ǽbdəket] *v.* abdicar, renunciar.

ab·do·men [ǽbdəmən] *s.* abdomen; vientre.

ab·duct [ǽbdʌkt] *v.* secuestrar, raptar, *Am.* plagiar (*a alguien*).

ab·duc·tion [ǽbdʌkʃən] *s.* rapto, robo, secuestro (*de una persona*).

ab·er·ra·tion [ǽbəréʃən] *s.* aberración, extravío (*de la mente*).

a·bet [əbét] *v.* incitar; fomentar.

a·bey·ance [əbéəns] *s.* suspensión; **in —** pendiente.

ab·hor [əbhór] *v.* aborrecer, odiar, abominar.

ab·hor·rence [əbhórəns] *s.* aborrecimiento, aversión.

a·bide [əbáɪd] *v.* quedar, permanecer; morar, habitar; aguardar; soportar, tolerar; **to — by** conformarse a; atenerse a.

a·bil·i·ty [əbflətɪ] *s.* habilidad, capacidad.

ab·ject [ǽbdʒɛkt] *adj.* abatido; vil.

ab·jure [æbdʒúr] *v.* abjurar.

ab·la·tive [ǽblətɪv] *adj.* ablativo.

a·ble [ébl] *adj.* hábil, capaz; competente; **a·ble-bod·ied** de cuerpo sano; **to be — to** poder; saber.

a·bly [éblɪ] *adv.* hábilmente.

ab·nor·mal [æbnórml] *adj.* anormal.

a·board [əbórd] *adv.* a bordo; en el tren; **to go —** embarcarse; **all — !** *Sp.* ¡viajeros al tren!; *Méx., C.A.* ¡vámonos!

a·bode [əbód] *s.* morada, domicilio, casa; *pret. & p.p. de* **to abide.**

a·bol·ish [əbálɪʃ] *v.* abolir; anular.

ab·o·li·tion [æbəlfʃən] *s.* abolición.

a·bom·i·na·ble [əbámnəbl] *adj.* abominable, aborrecible.

a·bort [əbórt] *v.* abortar.

a·bor·tion [əbórʃən] *s.* aborto.

a·bound [əbáund] *v.* abundar; **to — with** abundar en.

a·bout [əbáut] *prep.* (*concerning*) acerca de, tocante a, respecto de; (*near, surrounding*) alrededor de, por; *adv.* (*almost*) casi, poco más o menos; **at — ten o'clock** a eso de las diez; **to be — one's business** atender a su negocio; **to be — to** estar para, estar a punto de; **to face —** dar media vuelta; **to have no money — one's person** no llevar dinero consigo.

a·bove [əbʌ́v] *prep.* por encima de; sobre; *adv.* arriba; **— all** sobre todo; **a·bove-men·tioned** susodicho, ya mencionado; **from —** de arriba; del cielo, de Dios; *adj.* **— -the -line** presupuesto corriente.

ab·ra·sive [əbrésɪv] *adj.* abrasivo; tosco.

a·breast [əbrést] *adj. adv.* al lado; **to keep abreast** ponerse al corriente.

a·bridge [əbrídʒ] *v.* abreviar; compendiar; condensar; privar (*a uno de sus derechos*).

a·broad [əbród] *adv.* en el extranjero; fuera de casa; **to go —** ir al extranjero; **to spread —** divulgar o publicar por todas partes.

a·brupt [əbrʌ́pt] *adj.* repentino; precipitado; (*steep*) áspero, brusco; escarpado; **-ly** *adv.* de repente; bruscamente.

ab·scess [ǽbsɛs] *s.* absceso.

ab·sence [ǽbsns] *s.* ausencia; falta; **— of mind** distracción; **leave of —** licencia (*para ausentarse*).

ab·sent [ǽbsnt] *adj.* ausente; abstraído, distraído; **ab·sent-mind·ed** absorto, abstraído; [ǽbsɛnt] *v.* **to — oneself** ausentarse.

ab·sinthe [ǽbsɪnθ] *s.* ajenjo.

ab·so·lute [ǽbsəlut] *adj.* absoluto; **the —** lo absoluto; **-ly** *adv.* absolutamente; en absoluto.

ab·so·lu·tion [æbsəlúʃən] *s.* absolución.

ab·solve [æbsálv] *v.* absolver, remitir; perdonar; alzar la pena o el castigo.

ab·sorb [əbsórb] *v.* absorber.

ab·sorb·ent [əbsórbənt] *adj. & s.* absorbente.

ab·sorp·tion [əbsórpʃən] *s.* absorción; abstracción, embebecimiento.

ab·stain [əbstén] *v.* abstenerse, privarse.

ab·sti·nence [ǽbstənəns] *s.* abstinencia.

ab·stract [ǽbstrækt] *adj.* abstracto; *s.* sumario; resúmen; **in the —** en abstracto; **— of account current** resúmen de cuenta corriente; **— of title** certificado de tradición [æbstrǽkt] *v.* abstraer; considerar aisladamente; separar, retirar; resumir, compendiar.

ab·strac·tion [æbstrǽkʃən] *s.* abstracción; idea abstracta.

ab·surd [əbsɛ́d] *adj.* absurdo; insensato; ridículo, disparatado.

ab·sur·di·ty [əbsɛ́dətɪ] *s.* absurdo, disparate.

a·bun·dance [əbʌ́ndəns] *s.* abundancia, copia.

a·bun·dant [əbʌ́ndənt] *adj.* abundante, copioso.

a·buse [əbjús] *s.* abuso; maltrato; ultraje; [əbjúz] *v.* abusar de; maltratar; injuriar; ultrajar.

a·bu·sive [əbjúsɪv] *adj.* abusivo; insultante, injurioso.

a·byss [əbfs] *s.* abismo; sima.

ac·a·dem·ic [ækədémɪk] *adj.* académico; escolar.

a·cad·e·my [əkǽdəmɪ] *s.* academia; colegio, instituto; escuela preparatoria.

ac·cede [æksíd] *v.* acceder, consentir.

ac·cel·er·ate [æksɛ́ləret] *v.* acelerar(se).

ac·cel·er·a·tion [ækseləréʃən] *s.* aceleración.

ac·cel·er·a·tor [æksɛ́ləretɚ] *s.* acelerador.

ac·cent [ǽksɛnt] *s.* acento; [æksɛ́nt] *v.* acentuar; recalcar.

ac·cen·tu·ate [æksɛ́ntʃuet] *v.* acentuar; recalcar; realzar.

ac·cept [əksɛ́pt] *v.* aceptar; admitir; acoger; aprobar.

ac·cept·a·ble [əksɛ́ptəbl] *adj.* aceptable; grato; acepto.

ac·cep·tance [əksɛ́ptəns] *s.* aceptación; aprobación; buena acogida; recibimiento.

ac·cess [ǽksɛs] *s.* acceso; (*attack*) ataque (*de una enfermedad*); arrebato (*de furia*).

ac·ces·si·ble [æksɛ́səbl] *adj.* accesible; asequible; obtenible.

ac·ces·so·ry [æksɛ́sərɪ] *adj.* accesorio; adjunto; *s.* accesorio; cómplice; **ac·ces·so·ries** cosas accesorias, adornos, adminículos.

ac·ci·dent [ǽksədənt] *s.* accidente; percance, contratiempo; **by —** por casualidad.

acc-act 282

ac·ci·den·tal [æksədéntl] *adj.* accidental; casual; **-ly** *adv.* accidentalmente; por casualidad.

ac·claim [əklém] *v.* aclamar, aplaudir; *s.* aclamación, aplauso.

ac·cla·ma·tion [ækləméʃən] *s.* aclamación, aplauso.

ac·cli·mate [əkláɪmət], [ǽkləmet] *v.* aclimatar(se); acostumbrar(se).

ac·cli·ma·tize [əkláɪmətaɪz] *v.* aclimatar(se).

ac·com·mo·date [əkamədét] *v.* (*adjust*) acomodar, ajustar, ayudar, hacer un favor; (*lodge*) hospedar, alojar, tener cabida para; **to — oneself** conformarse, adaptarse.

ac·com·mo·da·tion [əkamədéʃən] *s.* (*help*) favor, (*help*) ayuda; conveniencia; (*lodging*) alojamiento (*en un* hotel, casa, *etc.*); cabida; (*adjustment*) adaptación; ajuste.

ac·com·pa·ni·ment [əkʌ́mpənɪmənt] *s.* acompañamiento.

ac·com·pa·nist [əkʌ́mpənɪst] *s.* acompañador, acompañante.

ac·com·pa·ny [əkʌ́mpənɪ] *v.* acompañar.

ac·com·plice [əkɑ́mplɪs] *s.* cómplice.

ac·com·plish [əkɑ́mplɪʃ] *v.* cumplir; completar; lograr, conseguir; realizar, efectuar.

ac·com·plished [əkɑ́mplɪʃt] *adj.* cumplido; realizado; consumado; establecido; diestro; perfecto.

ac·com·plish·ment [əkɑ́mplɪʃmənt] *s.* cumplimiento; logro, realización; (*skill*) habilidad; perfección; mérito, proeza.

ac·cord [əkɔ́rd] *s.* acuerdo, convenio; armonía, concierto; **of one's own — voluntariamente;** espontáneamente; **in — with** de acuerdo con; **with one — unánimemente;** *v.* otorgar, conceder, dar; concordar.

ac·cord·ance [əkɔ́rdns] *s.* conformidad, acuerdo; **in — with** de acuerdo con, de conformidad con.

ac·cord·ing [əkɔ́rdɪŋ]: **— to** según; conforme a; de acuerdo con; **— as** según (que), a medida que.

ac·cord·ing·ly [əkɔ́rdɪŋlɪ] *adv.* en conformidad; así; como tal; por lo tanto; pro consiguiente.

ac·cor·di·on [əkɔ́rdɪən] *s.* acordeón.

ac·cost [əkɔ́st] *v.* abordar (*a alguien*) en la calle, acosar; molestar, perseguir.

ac·count [əkáʊnt] *s.* (*bill*) cuenta, computación; **-s payable (receivable)** cuentas por pagar, (*story*) relato; **on — of** a causa de; con motivo de; por; **on my — por mí; on my own** por mi propia cuenta; **on no — de ninguna manera; of no — de** ningún valor o importancia; **to turn to — aprovechar, hacer útil o provechoso;** *v.* dar cuenta (a); considerar, tener por; **to — for** dar cuenta o razón de; explicar; **how do you — for that?** ¿cómo se explica eso?

ac·count·a·ble [əkáʊntəbl] *adj.* responsable; explicable.

ac·count·ant [əkáʊntənt] *s.* contador, tenedor de libros; **certified public — (CPA)** contador público nacional; Ch. registrado.

ac·count·ing [əkáʊntɪŋ] *s.* contabilidad, contaduría; **-firm** empresa de contadores públicos; **— period** ejercicio contable; *Col.* período fiscal; **— system** sistema de contabilidad.

ac·cred·it [əkrédɪt] *v.* acreditar.

ac·crue [əkrú] *v.* acumular(se); **-d assets** activo acumulado; **-d interest** interés acumulado.

ac·cul·tur·ate [əkʌ́ltʃɚet] *v.* aculturar(se).

ac·cu·mu·late [əkjúmjəlet] *v.* acumular(se), juntar(se), amontonar(se).

ac·cu·mu·la·tion [əkjumjəléʃən] *s.* acumulación, amontonamiento.

ac·cu·ra·cy [ǽkjərəsɪ] *s.* precisión, exactitud, esmero.

ac·cu·rate [ǽkjərɪt] *adj.* preciso, exacto; correcto; esmerado; cierto; certero; acertado; **-ly** *adv.* con exactitud; correctamente; con esmero.

ac·cursed [əkɝ́st] *adj.* maldito; infame.

ac·cu·sa·tion [ækjəzéʃən] *s.* acusación.

ac·cu·sa·tive [əkjúzətɪv] *adj.* acusativo.

ac·cuse [əkjúz] *v.* acusar; denunciar.

ac·cus·er [əkjúzɚ] *s.* acusador; delator, denunciador.

ac·cus·tom [əkʌ́stəm] *v.* acostumbrar; **to — oneself** acostumbrarse; **to be -ed to** tener la costumbre de, acostumbrar, soler; estar acostumbrado a, estar hecho a.

ace [es] *s.* as; as, el mejor de su clase (*como un aviador excelente*); **within an — of** a punto de; muy cerca de.

ac·e·tate [ǽsətet] *s.* acetato.

a·cet·y·lene [əsétəlin] *s.* acetileno.

ache [ek] *s.* dolor; **tooth — dolor de muelas;** *v.* doler.

a·chieve [ətʃív] *v.* acabar, llevar a cabo; realizar; conseguir, lograr; alcanzar.

a·chieve·ment [ətʃívmənt] *s.* logro, realización; proeza, hazaña.

ac·id [ǽsɪd] *adj.* ácido; agrio; *s.* ácido; **— test** prueba de ácido.

a·cid·i·ty [əsídətɪ] *s.* acidez.

ac·knowl·edge [əknɑ́lɪdʒ] *v.* reconocer, admitir; confesar; **to — receipt** acusar recibo.

ac·knowl·edg·ment [əknɑ́lɪdʒmənt] *s.* reconocimiento, expresión de gratitud; confesión, admisión; **— of receipt** acuse de recibo.

a·corn [ékɔrn] *s.* bellota.

a·cous·tics [əkústɪks] *s.* acústica; **a·cous·tic coup·ler** [kʌplɚ] acoplador acustico.

ac·quaint [əkwént] *v.* enterar, informar; dar a conocer; familiarizar; **to — oneself with** ponerse al corriente de; enterarse de; **to be -ed with** conocer a (*una persona*); estar enterado de (*algo*); conocer (*una ciudad, un pais, etc.*).

ac·quain·tance [əkwéntəns] *s.* conocimiento; conocido; **-s** amistades.

ac·qui·esce [ækwɪɛ́s] *v.* asentir; consentir, quedar conforme.

ac·qui·es·cence [ækwɪɛ́sns] *s.* asentimiento, consentimiento; conformidad.

ac·quire [əkwáɪr] *v.* adquirir; obtener, conseguir; contraer (*costumbres, vicios*).

ac·qui·si·tion [ækwəzíʃən] *s.* adquisición.

ac·quit [əkwít] *v.* absolver, exonerar; pagar, redimir; librar de (*una obligación*); **to — oneself well** quedar bien; portarse bien; **acquittance** descarga de una deuda.

ac·quit·tal [əkwítl] *s.* absolución.

a·cre [ékɚ] *s.* acre (*medida de superficie*).

ac·ro·bat [ǽkrəbæt] *s.* acróbata.

ac·ro·nym [ǽkrənɪm] *s.* acrónimo.

a·cross [əkrɔ́s] *prep.* a través de; al otro lado de; por; por medio de; *adv.* a través, de través; **to go — atravesar; to come — , run — encontrarse con;** tropezar con.

a·cryl·ic [əkrílɪk] *adj.* acrílico.

act [ækt] *s.* acto; acción, hecho; (*law*) ley, decreto *v.* (*play the part*) hacer, desempeñar (*un papel*); representar (*en el teatro*); (*function*) obrar; actuar; portarse; funcionar; **to — as** servir de, estar de.

act·ing [ǽktɪŋ] *s.* representación, desempeño (*de un papel dramático*); acción, actuación; *adj.* interino, suplente.

ac·tion [ǽkʃən] *s.* acción; acto; actuación; funcionamiento.

ac·ti·vate [ǽktɪvet] *v.* activar.

ac·tive [ǽktɪv] *adj.* activo; — **capital** capital disponible; — **trade balance** balanza comercial favorable.

ac·tiv·ism [ǽktəvɪzm] *s.* activismo.

ac·tiv·ist [ǽktəvɪst] *s.* activista.

ac·tiv·i·ty [ætkívətɪ] *s.* actividad.

ac·tor [ǽktɚ] *s.* actor.

ac·tress [ǽktrɪs] *s.* actriz.

ac·tu·al [ǽktʃʊəl] *adj.* (*legitimate*) verdadero, real; (*current*) actual, existente; — **cost** costo efectivo; — **output** rendimiento efectivo; — **sales** ventas efectivas; **-ly** *adv.* realmente, en realidad; de hecho, electivamente.

ac·tu·ar·ial [æktuérɪəl] *adj.* actuarial.

a·cu·men [əkjúmɪn] *s.* caletre, tino, perspicacia.

a·cute [əkjút] *adj.* agudo; perspicaz; penetrante.

ad·a·mant [ǽdəmænt] *adj.* duro; firme, inflexible.

a·dapt [ədǽpt] *v.* adaptar; **to** — **oneself** adaptarse, acomodarse.

ad·ap·ta·tion [ædæptéʃən] *s.* adaptación.

add [æd] *v.* sumar; añadir, agregar; **adding machine** máquina sumadora; — **sign** signo de suma.

ad·dict [ǽdɪkt] *s.* adicto (*persona adicta al uso de narcóticos*); **drug** — morfinómano, drogadicto.

ad·dict·ed [ədíktɪd] *adj.* adicto, dado, (*keen*) entregado, habituado.

ad·di·tion [ədíʃən] *s.* adición; suma; añadidura, aditamento; **in** — **to** además de.

ad·di·tion·al [ədíʃənl] *adj.* adicional.

ad·di·tive [ǽdətɪv] *s. & adj.* aditivo.

ad·dress [ədrés] *s.* (*street*) dirección, domicilio, señas; sobrescrito; (*speech*) discurso, arenga, conferencia; **form of** — tratamiento; *v.* dirigir, poner la dirección, señas o sobrescrito a; hablar, dirigir la palabra a; dirigirse a; **to** — **oneself to a task** aplicarse a una tarea; **addressing machine** máquina rotuladora.

ad·dress·ee [ədresí] *s.* destinatario.

ad·duce [ədús] *v.* aducir.

a·dept [ədépt] *adj.* hábil; perito.

ad·e·quate [ǽdəkwɪt] *adj.* adecuado; proporcionado; suficiente.

ad·here [ədhír] *v.* adherirse; pegarse.

ad·her·ence [ədhírəns] *s.* adherencia.

ad·he·sion [ədhíʒən] *s.* adhesión.

ad·he·sive [ədhísɪv] *adj.* adhesivo; pegajoso; — **tape** tela adhesiva, esparadrapo.

ad·ja·cent [ədʒésn̩t] *adj.* adyacente, contiguo.

ad·jec·tive [ǽdʒɪktɪv] *s.* adjetivo.

ad·join [ədʒɔ́ɪn] *v.* estar contiguo o adyacente a, lindar con.

ad·journ [ədʒɝn] *v.* aplazar, diferir; **to** — **the meeting** suspender o levantar la sesión; **meeting -ed** se levanta la sesión.

ad·journ·ment [ədʒɝnmənt] *s.* aplazamiento, levantamiento (*de una sesión*).

ad·junct [ǽdʒʌŋkt] *s.* adjunto, aditamento, añadidura; asociado, acompañante; *adj.* adjunto, unido, subordinado.

ad·just [ədʒʌ́st] *v.* (*fix*) ajustar; (*adapt*) acomodar; arreglar; graduar; **to** — **oneself** adaptarse, conformarse; **adjuster** asesor.

ad·just·ment [ədʒʌ́stmənt] *s.* ajuste; ajustamiento; arreglo; regulación.

ad·lib [ǽdlíb] *v.* improvisar; expresarse espontáneamente.

ad·min·is·ter [ədmínəstɚ] *v.* (*control*) administrar; dirigir, regir, gobernar; (*apply*) aplicar (*remedio, castigo, etc.*); **to** — **an oath** tomar juramento.

ad·min·is·tra·tion [ədmɪnəstréʃən] *s.* administración; dirección, gobierno; gerencia; manejo.

ad·min·is·tra·tive [ədmínəstretɪv] *adj.* administrativo; ejecutive; gubernativo; — **agencies** órganos (agencias) administrativas.

ad·min·is·tra·tor [ədmínəstretɚ] *s.* administrador.

ad·mi·ra·ble [ǽdmərəbl] *adj.* admirable.

ad·mi·ra·bly [ǽdmərəblɪ] *adv.* admirablemente.

ad·mi·ral [ǽdmərəl] *s.* almirante.

ad·mi·ra·tion [ædməréʃən] *s.* admiración.

ad·mire [ədmáɪr] *v.* admirar; estimar.

ad·mir·er [ədmáɪrɚ] *s.* admirador; pretendiente.

ad·mis·si·ble [ædmísəbl] *adj.* admisible.

ad·mis·sion [ədmíʃən] *s.* (*entrance*) entrada, precio de entrada o de ingreso; (*confession*) confesión, admisión.

ad·mit [ədmít] *v.* admitir; aceptar; confesar, reconocer; conceder; dar entrada.

ad·mit·tance [ədmítns] *s.* entrada; derecho de entrar; admisión.

ad·mon·ish [ədmánɪʃ] *v.* amonestar.

ad·mo·ni·tion [ædmənɪ́ʃən] *s.* amonestación, consejo.

a·do [ədú] *s.* actividad; bulla; disturbio.

a·do·be [ədóbɪ] *s.* adobe; casa de adobe.

ad·o·les·cence [ædəlésn̩s] *s.* adolescencia.

ad·o·les·cent [ædəlésn̩t] *adj. & s.* adolescente.

a·dopt [ədápt] *v.* adoptar; ahijar, prohijar.

a·dop·tion [ədápʃən] *s.* adopción.

a·dor·a·ble [ədórəbl] *adj.* adorable; encantador.

ad·o·ra·tion [ædəréʃən] *s.* adoración.

a·dore [ədór] *v.* adorar.

a·dorn [ədɔ́rn] *v.* adornar; ornar; embellecer.

a·dorn·ment [ədɔ́rnmənt] *s.* adorno.

ad·re·nal [ədrínl] *adj.* suprarrenal.

ad·ren·a·lin [ædrénəlɪn] *s.* adrenalina.

a·drift [ədríft] *adj. & adv.* a la deriva, flotando, flotante.

a·droit [ədrɔ́ɪt] *adj.* hábil, diestro.

a·dult [ədʌ́lt] *adj. & s.* adulto.

a·dul·ter·ate [ədʌ́ltəret] *v.* adulterar.

a·dul·ter·er [ədʌ́ltərɚ] *s.* adúltero.

a·dul·ter·y [ədʌ́ltərɪ] *s.* adulterio.

ad·vance [ədvǽns] *v.* (*progress*) avanzar, adelantar; progresar; acelerar; (*promote*) promover; proponer; (*pay beforehand*) pagar por adelantado (anticipado); *s.* avance; progreso; adelanto, anticipo; alza aumento de precio; **-s** requerimientos, pretensiones, insinuaciones; **in** — por adelantado, con anticipación.

ad·vanced [ədvǽnst] *adj.* avanzado; adelantado; — **in years** entrado en años, viejo, anciano.

ad·vance·ment [ədvǽnsmənt] *s.* adelantamiento, mejora, progreso; promoción.

ad·van·tage [ədvǽntɪdʒ] *s.* ventaja; beneficio; provecho; **to have the** — **over** llevar ventaja a; **to take** — **of** aprovecharse de; **to take** — **of a person** abusar de la confianza o paciencia de alguien.

ad·van·ta·geous [ædvəntédʒəs] *adj.* ventajoso; provechoso.

ad·vent [ǽdvɛnt] *s.* advenimiento; venida.

ad·ven·ture [ədvéntʃɚ] *s.* aventura; riesgo.

ad·ven·tur·er [ədvéntʃərɚ] *s.* aventurero.

ad·ven·tur·ous [ədvéntʃərəs] *adj.* aventurero; atrevido; aventurado; arriesgado.

ad·verb [ǽdvɝb] *m.* adverbio.

ad·ver·sar·y [ǽdvɚserɪ] *s.* adversario, antagonista, contrario.

ad·verse [ədvɝ́s] *adj.* adverso; opuesto, contrario; hostil; desfavorable.

ad·ver·si·ty [ədvɝ́səti] *s.* adversidad; infortunio.

ad·ver·tise [ǽdvɚtaɪz] *v.* anunciar; avisar, dar aviso; hacer propaganda (publicidad) *Arg.* reclame.

ad·ver·tise·ment [ædvɚtáɪzmənt] *s.* anuncio, aviso.

ad·ver·tis·er [ǽdvɚtaɪzɚ] *s.* anunciador, anunciante.

ad·ver·tis·ing [ǽdvɚtaɪzɪŋ] *s.* anuncios; arte o negocio de anunciar.

ad·vice [ədváɪs] *s.* aviso, advertencia; consejo; noticia.

ad·vis·a·ble [ədváɪzəbl] *adj.* conveniente; prudente; recomendable.

ad·vise [ədváɪz] *v.* (*counsel*) aconsejar; (*inform*) avisar, informar, advertir; **to — with** consultar con; aconsejarse con.

ad·vis·er, ad·vi·sor [ədváɪzɚ] *s.* consejero, aconsejador.

ad·vo·cate [ǽdvəkɪt] *s.* abogado; defensor, intercesor; partidario; [ǽdvəket] *v.* abogar por; defender.

aer·i·al [ɛ́rɪəl] *adj.* aéreo; *s.* antena.

aer·o·dy·nam·ic [ɛrodaɪnǽmɪk] *adj.* aerodinámico

aer·o·dy·nam·ics [ɛrodaɪnǽmɪks] *s.* aerodinámica.

aer·o·plane [ɛ́rəplen] = **airplane.**

aer·o·sol [ɛ́rosol] *s.* aerosol.

aes·thet·ic [ɛsθɛ́tɪk] *adj.* estético; **-s** *s.* estética.

a·far [əfár] *adv.* lejos; **from —** desde lejos.

af·fa·ble [ǽfəbl] *adj.* afable, amable.

af·fair [əfɛ́r] *s.* (*social*) función, tertulia, fiesta, convite; (*venture*) asunto; negocio; lance; cosa; **love —** amorío.

af·fect [əfɛ́kt] *v.* afectar; conmover; fingir; hacer ostentación de.

af·fec·ta·tion [æfɛktéʃən] *s.* afectación.

af·fect·ed [əfɛ́ktɪd] *adj.* (*emotion*) afectado, conmovido, enternecido; (*feigned*) fingido, artificioso.

af·fec·tion [əfɛ́kʃən] *s.* afecto, cariño; inclinación; afección, dolencia.

af·fec·tion·ate [əfɛ́kʃənɪt] *adj.* afectuoso, cariñoso.

af·fi·da·vit [æfədévɪt] *s.* declaración jurada.

af·fil·i·ate [əfílɪet] *v.* afiliar; afiliarse, unirse, asociarse.

af·fin·i·ty [əfínətɪ] *s.* afinidad.

af·firm [əfɝm] *v.* afirmar, asegurar, aseverar.

af·firm·a·tive [əfɝmətɪv] *adj.* afirmativo; *s.* afirmativa.

af·fix [əfíks] *v.* fijar, pegar; **to — one's signature** poner su firma, firmar.

af·flict [əflíkt] *v.* afligir; **to be -ed with** padecer de sufrir de, adolecer de.

af·flic·tion [əflíkʃən] *s.* aflicción; pena, dolor; achaque; angustia; infortunio.

af·flu·ent [ǽfluənt] *adj.* acaudalado; abundante.

af·ford [əfórd] *v.* proveer, proporcionar; **I cannot — that expense** no puedo hacer ese gasto; **he cannot — to waste time** no le conviene perder el tiempo; no tiene tiempo que perder; **I cannot — that risk** no puedo (*o* no quiero) exponerme a ese riesgo.

af·fri·cate [ǽfrɪkət] *adj. & s.* africado.

af·front [əfrʌ́nt] *s.* afrenta, agravio, ultraje; *v.* afrentar, agraviar, ultrajar.

a·fire [əfáɪr] *adj.* ardiendo, quemándose.

a·float [əflót] *adj. & adv.* flotante; flotando; a flote; a flor de agua; a bordo; inundado; (*flooded*) a la deriva, sin rumbo; **the rumor is —** corre la voz.

a·foot [əfút] *adv.* a pie; en marcha, en movimiento.

a·fore·said [əfórsɛd] *adj.* susodicho, ya dicho.

a·fraid [əfréd] *adj.* miedoso, medroso; atemorizado, amedrentado; **to be —** temer, tener miedo.

a·fresh [əfrɛ́ʃ] *adv.* de nuevo, desde el principio.

Af·ri·can [ǽfrɪkən] *adj. & s.* africano; negro.

af·ter [ǽftɚ] *prep.* (*temporal*) después de, tras, tras de; (*position*) detrás de; (*following*) en busca de; *adv.* después; detrás; *conj.* después (de) que; *adj.* subsiguiente; siguiente; **— all** después de todo; de

todos modos; **day — tomorrow** pasado mañana; **after-dinner** de sobremesa; **— effect** consecuencia, resultado; **— math** consecuencias, resultados (*usualmente desastrosos*); **— thought** idea tardía.

af·ter·noon [æftɚnún] *s.* tarde.

af·ter·taste [ǽftɚtest] *s.* dejo, dejillo (*sabor que queda en la boca*).

af·ter·wards [ǽftɚwɚdz] *adv.* después.

a·gain [əgɛ́n] *adv.* otra vez, de nuevo; además; por otra parte; **— and —** repetidas veces; **never —** nunca jamás; **to come —** volver; **to do it —** volver a hacerlo.

a·gainst [əgɛ́nst] *prep.* contra; frente a; en contraste con; **— the grain** a contrapelo, a redopelo; **— a rainy day** para cuando llueva.

age [edʒ] *s.* edad; época; siglo; generación; **of —** mayor de edad; **old —** vejez, ancianidad; **to become of —** llegar a mayor edad; **under —** menor de edad; *v.* envejecer(se).

a·ged [édʒɪd, édʒd] *adj.* viejo, anciano, añejo; envejecido; **— forty years** de cuarenta años; **— in wood** añejado en toneles o barriles (*dícese del vino*).

a·gen·cy [édʒənsɪ] *s.* agencia; (*means*) medio, intermedio.

a·gen·da [ədʒɛ́ndə] *s.* temario; asuntos que han de tratarse en una reunión.

a·gent [édʒənt] *s.* agente; intermediario, representante; apoderado.

ag·glu·ti·na·tive [əglútɪnətɪv] *adj.* aglutinante.

ag·gran·dize [əgrǽndaɪz] *v.* engrandecer; agrandar.

ag·gra·vate [ǽgrəvet] *v.* agravar, empeorar; irritar, exasperar.

ag·gre·gate [ǽgrɪgɪt] *s.* agregado, conjunto, colección; suma global; *adj.* agregado, unido; **in the —** en conjunto.

ag·gres·sion [əgrɛ́ʃən] *s.* agresión.

ag·gres·sive [əgrɛ́sɪv] *adj.* agresivo; emprendedor.

ag·gres·sor [əgrɛ́sɚ] *s.* agresor.

a·ghast [əgǽst] *adj.* espantado, pasmado.

ag·ile [ǽdʒəl] *adj.* ágil.

a·gil·i·ty [ədʒílətɪ] *s.* agilidad.

ag·i·tate [ǽdʒətet] *v.* agitar; turbar, perturbar; alborotar; discutir acaloradamente; maquinar, tramar.

ag·i·ta·tion [ædʒətéʃən] *s.* agitación; alboroto.

ag·i·ta·tor [ǽdʒətetɚ] *s.* agitador, alborotador, revoltoso.

ag·nos·tic [ægnástɪk] *adj. s.* agnóstico.

a·go [əgó] *adj. & adv.* pasado; en el pasado; **many years —** hace muchos años; muchos años ha, mucho tiempo ha; **long —** hace mucho tiempo; ha mucho.

ag·o·nize [ǽgonaɪz] *v.* agonizar; sufrir angustiosamente; retorcerse de dolor; (*fight*) luchar.

ag·o·ny [ǽgənɪ] *s.* agonía; angustia; tormento; dolor; lucha.

a·gree [əgrí] *v.* (*accede*) acordar, concordar, consentir, estar de acuerdo, ponerse de acuerdo; (*suit*) sentarle bien a uno (*dícese del clima, del alimento, etc.*).

a·gree·a·ble [əgríəbl] *adj.* agradable, afable; complaciente; conveniente; satisfactorio.

a·gree·ment [əgrímənt] *s.* (*concord*) acuerdo, convenio, conformidad; (*grammatical*) concordancia; **to be in —** estar de acuerdo; **to come to an —** ponerse de acuerdo.

ag·ri·cul·tur·al [ægrɪkʌ́ltʃɚəl] *adj.* agrícola.

ag·ri·cul·ture [ǽgrɪkʌltʃɚ] *s.* agricultura.

ag·ri·cul·tur·ist [ægrɪkʌ́ltʃərɪst] *s.* agricultor.

a·ground [əgráund] *adj.* & *adv.* encallado.

a·head [əhéd] *adv.* delante, al frente; adelante; — **of time** adelantado; antes de tiempo; **to go** — ir adelante; **to get** — adelantar(se).

aid [ed] *s.* ayuda, auxilio, socorro; (*assistant*) ayudante, auxiliar; *v.* ayudar, auxiliar, socorrer.

aide-de-camp [édəkæmp] *s.* edecán.

ail [el] *v.* adolecer, padecer; **what -s you?** ¿qué tienes? ¿qué te aflige?

ai·le·ron [éləran] *s.* alerón.

ail·ment [élmənt] *s.* achaque, dolencia.

aim [em] *s.* (*pointing*) puntería; tino; (*objective*) fin, objeto; proposición; *v.* apuntar (*un arma*); dirigir, asestar; dirigir la puntería; aspirar (a); **to** — **to please** proponerse (*o* tratar de agradar).

aim·less [émlɪs] *adj.* sin propósito, sin objeto.

air [ɛr] *s.* (*atmosphere*) aire, brisa; (*music*) tonada; **in the** — en el aire; indeciso; incierto; **in the open** — al raso, al aire libre; **to be on the** — emitir, radiodifundir; **to put on -s** darse tono; *adj.* de aire; aéreo; — **brake** freno neumático; — **line** línea aérea; ruta aérea; **air traffic control** control de tránsito aéreo; — **pocket** bache aéreo; bolsa de aire; **by** — **mail** por correo aéreo, por avión; **air-conditioned** de aire acondicionado; *v.* airear; orear; ventilar; publicar, pregonar; ostentar.

air·borne [ɛ́rborn] *aéreo;* aerotransportado.

air·craft [ɛ́rkræft] *s.* avión, aeroplano; aeronave; aviones; — **carrier** portaaviones.

air·foil [ɛ́rfɔɪl] *s.* superficie de control en los aviones.

air·line [ɛ́rlaɪn] *s.* aerovía; línea aérea; compañía de transporte aéreo.

air·plane [ɛ́rplen] *s.* aeroplano, avión; — **carrier** portaaviones.

air·port [ɛ́rport] *s.* aeropuerto, aerodromo.

air·ship [ɛ́rʃɪp] *s.* aeronave.

air·tight [ɛ́rtaɪt] *adj.* hermético.

air·y [ɛ́rɪ] *adj.* airoso; aireado, ventilado; ligero; tenue.

aisle [aɪl] *s.* pasillo, pasadizo; nave (*de una iglesia*).

a·jar [ədʒár] *adj.* entreabierto, entornado.

al·a·bas·ter [ǽləbæstɚ] *s.* alabastro.

a·larm [əlárm] *s.* alarma; arrebato; inquietud; — **clock** despertador; *v.* alarmar; inquietar.

al·bi·no [ælbáɪno] *s.* albino.

al·bum [ǽlbəm] *s.* álbum.

al·che·my [ǽlkəmɪ] *s.* alquimia.

al·co·hol [ǽlkəhɔl] *s.* alcohol.

al·co·hol·ic [ælkəhɔ́lɪk] *adj.* alcohólico.

al·cove [ǽlkov] *s.* alcoba.

al·der·man [ɔ́ldɚmən] *s.* concejal, regidor.

ale [el] *s.* cerveza de tipo espeso y amargo.

a·lert [əlɚ́t] *adj.* alerto, vigilante; despierto; vivo; listo; *s.* alarma, rebato; **to be on the** — estar alerta.

al·fal·fa [ælfǽlfə] *s.* alfalfa.

algae [ǽldʒɪ] *s. pl.* algas.

al·ge·bra [ǽldʒəbrə] *s.* álgebra.

al·go·rithm [ǽlgərɪəm] *s.* algoritmo.

al·i·bi [ǽləbaɪ] *s.* coartado; excusa.

a·li·en [éljən] *s.* extranjero; residente extranjero; *adj.* extraño, ajeno.

al·ien·ate [éljənet] *v.* enajenar; apartar, alejar (*a una persona de otra*).

al·ien·ist [éljənɪst] *s.* alienista, psiquiatra.

a·light [əláɪt] *v.* apearse, desmontarse, bajar(de); posarse (*dícese de pájaros, mariposas, etc.*).

a·lign [əláɪn] *v.* alinear(se).

a·like [əláɪk] *adj.* semejante; parecido; **to be** — parecerse, asemejarse; ser iguales; *adv.* del mismo modo.

al·i·mo·ny [ǽləmonɪ] *s.* asistencia de divorcio; alimento.

a·live [əláɪv] *adj.* vivo; con vida; viviente; activo; — **with** lleno de.

al·ka·li [ǽlkəlaɪ] *s.* álcali.

all [ɔl] *adj.* todo (el); todos (los); *s.* todo; todo el mundo, todos; *adv.* enteramente; — **at once** de una vez; de un tirón; de repente; — **right** bueno; bien; — **the worse** tanto peor; — **around** en (por) todas partes; — **-round** global; **not at** — de ninguna manera; no hay de qué; **nothing at** — nada en absoluto; — **told** (*o* **in** —) en conjunto; **once (and) for** — por última vez; una vez por todas; **to be** — **in** estar agotado, estar rendido de fatiga; **it is** — **over** se acabó, ha terminado todo.

al·lay [əlé] *v.* aliviar; calmar.

al·le·ga·tion [æləgéʃən] *s.* alegación, alegato; aseveración.

al·lege [əlédʒ] *v.* alegar; declarar; sostener, asegurar.

al·le·giance [əlídʒəns] *s.* lealtad, fidelidad; homenaje.

al·le·go·ry [ǽləgorɪ] *s.* alegoría.

al·ler·gy [ǽlɚdʒɪ] *s.* alergia (*sensibilidad anormal a ciertos alimentos o sustancias*).

al·le·vi·ate [əlívɪet] *v.* aliviar.

al·ley [ǽlɪ] *c.* callejón; callejuela; **blind** — callejón sin salida; **bowling** — boliche, *Am.* bolera.

al·li·ance [əláɪəns] *s.* alianza.

al·lied [əláɪd] *adj.* aliado; relacionado.

al·li·ga·tor [ǽləgetɚ] *s.* lagarto; caimán; — **pear** aguacate.

al·lot [əlát] *v.* asignar; repartir; **allotment** asignación, cuota

al·low [əláu] *v.* permitir, dejar; conceder; admitir; asignar; abonar; **to** — **for certain errors** tener en cuenta ciertos errores.

al·low·a·ble [əláuəbl] *adj.* permisible, admisible, lícito.

al·low·ance [əláuəns] *s.* asignación; abono, pensión; ración; (*discount*) rebaja, descuento; (*permission*) permiso; concesión; **monthly** — mesada, mensualidad; **to make** — for tener en cuenta.

al·loy [ǽlɔɪ] *s.* aleación, liga, mezcla (*de dos o más metales*); [əlɔ́ɪ] *v.* alear, ligar, mezclar (*metales*).

al·lude [əlúd] *v.* aludir.

al·lure [əlúr] *v.* seducir, cautivar; atraer, halagar.

al·lure·ment [əlúrmənt] *s.* seducción, tentación; atractivo, halago.

al·lur·ing [əlúrɪŋ] *adj.* seductivo, halagüeño, encantador.

al·lu·sion [əlúʒən] *s.* alusión; indirecta, insinuación.

al·lu·vi·um [əlúvɪəm] *s.* aluvión.

al·ly [əláɪ] *v.* unir; aliarse; **to** — **oneself (itself) with** aliarse con, unirse con; [ǽlaɪ] *s.* aliado.

al·ma·nac [ɔ́lmənæk] *s.* almanaque, calendario.

al·might·y [ɔlmáɪtɪ] *adj.* todopoderoso, omnipotente.

al·mond [ámənd] *s.* almendra; — **tree** almendro.

al·most [ɔ́lmost] *adv.* casi; **I** — **fell down** por poco me caigo.

alms [amz] *s.* limosna; — **box** cepo o cepillo, alcancía (*para limosnas*).

a·lone [əlón] *adj.* solo; solitario; único; *adv.* sólo, solamente; **all** — a solas; completamente solo; solito; **to let** — no tocar; no molestar; dejar en paz; no hacer caso de.

a·long [əlɔ́ŋ] *prep.* a lo largo de; por; al lado de; — **with** junto con; en compañía de; **all** — todo el tiempo; de un extremo a otro; **all** — **the coast** por toda la costa; **to carry** — with one llevar consigo; **to go** — **with** acompañar; **to get** — ir bien; **to get** — **with** llevarse bien con; **get** — ! ¡vete! ¡váyase!

¡largo de aquí!

a·long·side [əlɔ́ŋsaɪd] *prep. & adv.* al lado (de); al costado (de); lado a lado.

a·loof [əlúf] *adj.* aislado, apartado, retirado; huraño; reservado; *adv.* aparte; lejos.

a·loof·ness [əlúfnɪs] *s.* alejamiento, desapego, aislamiento.

a·loud [əláud] *adv.* alto, recio, fuerte, en voz alta.

al·pha·bet [ǽlfəbɛt] *s.* alfabeto.

al·pha·num·er·ic [æfənumérɪk] *adj. (computer)* alfanumérico.

al·read·y [ɔlrédɪ] *adv.* ya.

al·so [ɔ́lso] *adv.* también, además, igualmente.

al·tar [ɔ́ltɚ] *s.* altar; **high** — altar mayor; — **piece** retablo.

al·ter [ɔ́ltɚ] *v.* alterar; cambiar; variar.

al·ter·a·tion [ɔltəréʃən] *s.* alteración, cambio; mudanza; modificación.

al·ter·nate [ɔ́ltɚnɪt] *adj.* alternativo; alterno; alternado; *s.* suplente; **-ly** *adv.* alternativamente, por turno; [ɔ́ltɚnet] *v.* alternar; variar; turnar.

al·ter·na·tive [ɔltɝ́nətiv] *adj.* alternativo; *s.* alternativa.

al·ter·na·tor [ɔ́ltɝ́nétɚ] *s.* alternador.

al·though [ɔlðó] *conj.* aunque, si bien, bien que.

al·tim·e·ter [ǽltímətɚ] *s.* altímetro.

al·ti·tude [ǽltətjud] *s.* altitud, altura, elevación; — **sickness** *Am.* soroche.

al·to [ǽlto] *s. & adj.* contralto.

al·to·geth·er [ɔltəgéðɚ] *adv.* del todo, completamente; en conjunto.

a·lu·mi·num [əlúmɪnəm] *s.* aluminio.

a·lum·nus [əlámnəs] *s.* graduado, exalumno.

al·ways [ɔ́lwɪz] *adv.* siempre.

am [æm] *1ᵃ persona del presente de indic. del verbo* **to be**: soy, estoy.

a·mal·ga·mate [əmǽlgəmet] *v.* amalgamar; combinar; unir.

a·mass [əmǽs] *v.* amontonar, acumular, apilar, *Am.* amasar.

am·a·teur [ǽmətʃur] *s.* aficionado; novicio, principiante.

a·maze [əméz] *v.* pasmar, maravillar, asombrar.

a·maze·ment [əmézmənt] *s.* pasmo, admiración, asombro.

a·maz·ing [əmézɪŋ] *adj.* pasmoso, asombroso, maravilloso.

am·bas·sa·dor [æmbǽsədɚ] *s.* embajador.

am·ber [ǽmbɚ] *s.* ámbar; color de ámbar; *adj.* ambarino; de ámbar.

am·bi·ance [ǽmbiəns] *s.* ambiente.

am·bi·gu·i·ty [æmbɪgjúətɪ] *s.* ambigüedad.

am·big·u·ous [æmbígjuəs] *adj.* ambiguo.

am·bi·tion [æmbíʃən] *s.* ambición, aspiración.

am·bi·tious [æmbíʃəs] *adj.* ambicioso.

am·biv·a·lent [æmbívələnt] *adj.* ambivalente.

am·ble [ǽmbl] *v.* andar, vagar.

am·bu·lance [ǽmbjələns] *s.* ambulancia.

am·bush [ǽmbuʃ] *s.* emboscada; celada; acecho; *Ven.* aguaite **to lie in** — estar emboscado, estar al acecho; *Ven.* estar al aguaite; *v.* emboscar; poner celada a.

a·me·na·ble [əmínəbl] *adj.* dócil; tratable.

a·mend [əménd] *v.* enmendar; rectificar; **-s** *s. pl.* satisfacción, compensación; **to make** — **for** resarcir, dar satisfacción por, compensar por.

a·mend·ment [əméndmənt] *s.* enmienda.

A·mer·i·can [əmɛ́rəkən] *adj. & s. (continental)* americano; *(U.S.A.)* norteamericano.

A·mer·i·can·ism [əmɛ́rɪkənɪzəm] *s.* americanismo.

am·e·thyst [ǽməθɪst] *s.* amatista.

a·mi·a·ble [émɪəbl] *adj.* amable, afable, amistoso.

am·i·ca·ble [ǽmɪkəbl] *adj.* amigable, amistoso.

a·mid [əmíd] *prep.* en medio de; entre; **amidst** [əmídst] = **amid**.

a·miss [əmís] *adj.* errado, equivocado; *(improper)* impropio; *adv.* mal, fuera de lugar, impropiamente; **to take** — llevar a mal.

am·mo·nia [əmónjə] *s.* amoníaco.

am·mu·ni·tion [æmjəníʃən] *s.* munición.

am·ne·sia [æmníʒjə] *s.* amnesia.

am·nes·ty [ǽmnɛstɪ] *s.* amnestía.

a·mong [əmáŋ] *prep.* entre, en medio de; **amongst** [əmáŋst] = **among**.

am·o·rous [ǽmərəs] *adj.* amoroso.

a·mor·phous [əmɔ́rfəs] *adj.* amorfo.

am·or·tize [ǽmɝ́taɪz] *v.* amortizar.

a·mount [əmáunt] *s.* suma; cantidad; total; importe; valor; *v.* montar, subir, importar, ascender (a); valer; **that -s to stealing** eso equivale a robar.

am·pere [ǽmpɪr] *s.* amperio; **amperage** amperaje.

am·per·sand [ǽmpɚsænd] *s.* signo &.

am·phib·i·ous [æmfíbɪəs] *adj.* anfibio.

am·phi·the·a·ter [ǽmfəθiətɚ] *s.* anfiteatro.

am·ple [ǽmpl] *adj.* amplio; abundante; bastante; suficiente.

am·pli·fy [ǽmpləfaɪ] *v.* ampliar; amplificar.

am·pu·tate [ǽmpjətet] *v.* amputar.

a·muck [əmák] *adv.* con frenesí; **to run** — atacar a ciegas.

a·muse [əmjúz] *v.* divertir, entretener, distraer; **to** — **oneself** divertirse.

a·muse·ment [əmjúzmənt] *s.* diversión, entretenimiento, pasatiempo, recreo, distracción.

a·mus·ing [əmjúzɪŋ] *adj.* divertido, entretenido; gracioso, chistoso.

an [ən, æn] *art. indef.* un, una.

a·nach·ro·nism [ənǽkrənɪzm] *s.* anacronismo.

an·al·ge·sic [ænəldʒízɪk] *s.* analgésico.

a·nal·o·gous [ənǽləgəs] *adj.* análogo.

a·nal·o·gy [ənǽlədʒɪ] *s.* analogía, semejanza.

a·nal·y·sis [ənǽləsɪs] *s.* análisis.

an·a·lyt·ic [ænəlítɪk] *adj.* analítico.

an·a·lyze [ǽnəlaɪz] *v.* analizar.

an·ar·chist [ǽnɚkɪst] *s.* anarquista.

an·ar·chy [ǽnɚkɪ] *s.* anarquía.

a·nath·e·ma [ənǽθəmə] *s.* anatema.

an·a·tom·i·cal [ænətámɪkl] *adj.* anatómico.

a·nat·o·my [ənǽtəmɪ] *s.* anatomía.

an·ces·tor [ǽnsɛstɚ] *s.* antepasado; **-s** abuelos, antepasados.

an·ces·tral [ænsɛ́strəl] *adj.* solariego, de los antepasados; hereditario.

an·ces·try [ǽnsɛstrɪ] *s.* linaje, abolengo, ascendencia.

an·chor [ǽŋkɚ] *s.* ancla; **anchorage** anclaje; — **man** ancla; **to drop** — anclar, echar anclas, dar fondo, fondear; **to weigh** — levar el ancla; *v.* anclar; echar anclas; fijar, asegurar.

an·cho·vy [ǽntʃovɪ] *s.* anchoa, anchova.

an·cient [énʃənt] *adj.* antiguo; vetusto; **the -s** los antiguos; la antigüedad.

and [ənd, ænd] *conj.* y; e *(delante de i o hi)*; — **so forth** etcétera; y así sucesivamente; **let us try** — **do it** tratemos de hacerlo; **let us go** — **see him** vamos a verle.

An·da·lu·sian [ændəlúʒən] *adj.* andaluz.

an·ec·dote [ǽnɪkdot] *s.* anécdota.

a·ne·mi·a [əními] *s.* anemia.

an·es·the·sia [ænɪsθíʒə] *s.* anestesia.

an·es·thet·ic [ænəsθétɪk] *adj. & s.* anestésico.

a·new [ənjú] *adv.* otra vez, de nuevo; nuevamente.

an·gel [éndʒəl] *s.* ángel.

an·gel·ic [ænʤélɪk] *adj.* angélico.

an·ger [ǽŋgɚ] *s.* enojo, enfado, ira, cólera; *v.* enojar, enfadar, encolerizar.

an·gi·na [ændʒáɪnə] *s.* angina; — **pectoris** angina de pecho.

an·gle [ǽŋgl] *s.* ángulo; (*interior*) rincón; (*exterior*) esquina; punto de vista, aspecto; *v.* pescar.

An·glo-Sax·on [ǽŋglosǽksṇ] *adj.* & *s.* anglosajón.

an·gry [ǽŋgrɪ] *adj.* enojado; colérico; airado.

an·guish [ǽŋgwɪʃ] *s.* angustia, ansia, pena, dolor.

an·gu·lar [ǽŋgjəlɚ] *adj.* angular; anguloso.

an·i·mal [ǽnəml] *s.* & *adj.* animal.

an·i·mate [ǽnəmɪt] *adj.* animado, viviente; **animated cartoon** dibujo animado; [ǽnəmet] *v.* animar; alentar.

an·i·ma·tion [ænəméʃən] *s.* animación; viveza.

an·i·mos·i·ty [ænəmásətɪ] *s.* animosidad, ojeriza, inquina, rencor.

an·ise [ǽnɪs] *s.* anís.

an·kle [ǽŋkl] *s.* tobillo.

an·nals [ǽnlz] *s. pl.* anales.

an·nex [ǽnɛks] *s.* (*building*) pabellón, ala; (*dependent addition*) anexo; añadidura; [ənɛks] *v.* anexar.

an·nex·a·tion [ænɛkséʃən] *s.* anexión.

an·ni·hi·late [ənáɪəlet] *v.* aniquilar; anonadar.

an·ni·ver·sa·ry [ænəvɝ́sərɪ] *s.* & *adj.* aniversario.

an·no·tate [ǽnotet] *v.* anotar.

an·no·ta·tion [ænotéʃən] *s.* anotación, acotación, nota.

an·nounce [ənáʊns] *v.* anunciar; proclamar.

an·nounce·ment [ənáʊnsmənt] *s.* anuncio; aviso; noticia.

an·nounc·er [ənáʊnsɚ] *s.* anunciador; **radio** — locutor.

an·noy [ənɔ́ɪ] *v.* molestar; fastidiar; incomodar; enfadar.

an·noy·ance [ənɔ́ɪəns] *s.* molestia; fastidio; enfado; vejamen.

an·nu·al [ǽnjʊəl] *adj.* anual; *s.* anuario; planta anual; **-ly** *adv.* anualmente, cada año, todos los años.

an·nu·i·ty [ənúətɪ] *s.* anualidad, renta anual; **annuitant** beneficiario de anualidad.

an·nul [ənʌ́l] *v.* anular; abolir.

an·nul·ment [ənʌ́lmənt] *s.* revocación; anulación.

a·noint [ənɔ́ɪnt] *v.* ungir; untar; administrar la Extremaunción.

a·non [ənán] *adv.* pronto, luego; otra vez.

a·non·y·mous [ənánəməs] *adj.* anónimo.

an·oth·er [ənʌ́ðɚ] *adj.* & *pron.* otro; **one** — uno a otro, unos a otros.

an·swer [ǽnsɚ] *s.* respuesta, contestación; réplica; (*solution*) solución; *v.* responder; contestar; replicar; **to** — **for** ser responsable de (*o* por); responder de; ser (salir) fiador de; **to** — **the purpose** ser adecuado, servir para el objeto; **answering service** servicio telefónico contratado.

ant [ænt] *s.* hormiga; — **eater** oso hormiguero; — **hill** hormiguero.

ant·ac·id [æntǽsɪd] *s.* & *adj.* antiácido.

an·tag·o·nism [æntǽgənɪzəm] *s.* antagonismo, oposición, antipatía.

an·tag·o·nist [æntǽgənɪst] *s.* antagonista, adversario.

an·tag·o·nize [æntǽgənaɪz] *v.* contrariar, oponerse a, hostilizar.

an·te·ce·dent [æntəsídṇt] *adj.* & *s.* antecedente.

an·te·lope [ǽntlop] *s.* antílope.

an·ten·na [ænténə] (*pl.* **antennae** [ænténi]) *s.* antena.

an·te·ri·or [æntírɪɚ] *adj.* anterior; delantero.

an·te·room [ǽntɪrum] *s.* antecámara; sala de espera.

an·them [ǽnθəm] *s.* himno.

an·thol·o·gy [ænθáLədʒɪ] *s.* antología.

an·thra·cite [ǽnθrəsaɪt] *s.* antracita.

an·thro·pol·o·gist [ænθrəpáLədʒɪst] *s.* antropólogo.

an·thro·pol·o·gy [ænθrəpáLədʒɪ] *s.* antropología.

an·ti·air·craft [æntiɛ́rkræft] *adj.* antiaéreo.

an·ti·bi·ot·ic [æntɪbaɪátɪk] *s.* & *adj.* antibiótico.

an·ti·bod·y [ǽntɪbadɪ] *s.* anticuerpo.

an·tic·i·pate [æntísəpet] *v.* anticipar(se); prever; esperar.

an·tic·i·pa·tion [æntɪsəpéʃən] *s.* anticipación; expectación; previsión.

an·tics [ǽntɪks] *s. pl.* travesuras, cabriolas.

an·ti·dote [ǽntɪdot] *s.* antídoto.

an·ti·freeze [ǽntɪfriz] *s.* anticongelante.

an·ti·mo·ny [ǽntəmóni] *s.* antimonio.

an·tip·a·thy [æntípəθɪ] *s.* antipatía, repugnancia.

an·ti·quat·ed [ǽntəkwetɪd] *adj.* anticuado; desusado.

an·tique [æntík] *adj.* antiguo; anticuado; *s.* antigualla.

an·tiq·ui·ty [æntíkwətɪ] *s.* antigüedad; vejez, ancianidad.

an·ti·sep·tic [æntəséptɪk] *adj.* & *s.* antiséptico.

an·ti·so·cial [æntɪsóʃel] *adj.* antisocial; *s. Am.* criminal.

an·tith·e·sis [æntíθəsɪs] *s.* antítesis.

an·ti·trust [ǽntɪtrʌst] *adj.* antimonopolio.

ant·ler [ǽntlɚ] *s.* asta, cuerno (*del venado, ciervo, etc.*).

an·vil [ǽnvɪl] *s.* yunque.

anx·i·e·ty [æŋzáɪətɪ] *s.* ansiedad, zozobra; ansia, anhelo, afán.

anx·ious [ǽŋkʃəs] *adj.* ansioso; inquieto, preocupado; (*desirous*) anheloso, deseoso; **-ly** *adv.* con ansiedad, con ansia, ansiosamente.

an·y [ɛ́nɪ] *adj.* & *pron.* cualquier(a), cualesquier (a); alguno, algunos; **in** — **case** de todos modos, en todo caso; **I have not** — **bread** no tengo pan; **she does not sing** — **more** ya no canta; **he does not want to work** — **more** no quiere trabajar más.

an·y·bod·y [ɛ́nɪbadɪ] *pron.* alguien, alguno; cualquiera; **not . . .** — **no . . .** nadie, no . . . ; ninguno; **he does not know** — no conoce a nadie.

an·y·how [ɛ́nɪhaʊ] *adv.* de todos modos; de cualquier modo.

an·y·one [ɛ́nɪwʌn] *pron.* = **anybody.**

an·y·thing [ɛ́nɪθɪŋ] *pron.* alguna cosa; cualquier cosa; algo; **not . . .** — **no . . .** nada; **not to know** — no saber nada; **you wish** todo lo que quiera Vd.

an·y·way [ɛ́nɪwe] *adv.* de todos modos; en cualquier caso.

an·y·where [ɛ́nɪhwɛr] *adv.* dondequiera; en cualquier parte o lugar; en todas partes; **not . . .** — no . . . en (*o* a) ninguna parte; **not to go** — no ir a ninguna parte.

a·part [əpárt] *adj.* aparte; *adv.* separadamente; (*aside*) a un lado; *adj.* aislado, separado; **to take** — desarmar, desmontar; **to tear** — despedazar, hacer pedazos.

a·part·ment [əpártmənt] *s.* departamento, piso, apartamento; vivienda; habitación.

ap·a·thet·ic [æpəθétɪk] *adj.* apático.

ap·a·thy [ǽpəθɪ] *s.* apatía, indiferencia, indolencia.

ape [ep] *s.* mono; **ape-like** símico; *v.* remedar, imitar.

ap·er·ture [ǽpɚtʃɚ] *s.* abertura.

a·pex [épɛks] *s.* ápice, cumbre.

a·pha·sia [əfézɪə] *s.* afasia.

a·piece [əpís] *adv.* cada uno, a cada uno, por persona.

a·poc·o·pe [əpákəpɪ] *s.* apócope.

ap·o·gee [ǽpədʒɪ] *s.* apogeo.

a·pol·o·get·ic [əpalədʒétɪk] *adj.* que se excusa o disculpa.

a·pol·o·gize [əpálədʒaɪz] *v.* disculparse, excusarse.

a·pol·o·gy [əpálədʒɪ] *s.* apología; excusa, disculpa, (*reason*) justificación, satisfacción.

ap·o·plex·y [ǽpəplɛksɪ] *s.* apoplejía.

a·pos·tle [əpásl] *s.* apóstol.

ap·os·tol·ic [æpəstálɪk] *adj.* apostólico.

a·pos·tro·phe [əpástrəfɪ] *s.* apóstrofe; (*punctuation*) apóstrofo.

ap·pall [əpɔ́l] *v.* aterrorizar, aterrar; asombrar, espantar.

ap·pall·ing [əpɔ́lɪŋ] *adj.* aterrador; espantoso, asombroso.

ap·pa·ra·tus [æpərétəs] *s.* aparato; aparejo.

ap·par·el [əpǽrəl] *s.* ropa; ropaje; vestidos; indumentaria.

ap·par·ent [əpǽrənt] *adj.* aparente; visible; claro, evidente; patente; **heir** — heredero presunto; **-ly** *adv.* aparentemente, al parecer, por lo visto.

ap·pa·ri·tion [æpərɪ́ʃən] *s.* aparición; aparecido, espectro, fantasma.

ap·peal [əpíl] *s.* (*legal*) apelación, recurso; (*request*) súplica; (*attraction*) atracción, atractivo, llamamiento; *v.* apelar; recurrir, acudir; atraer, despertar interés o simpatía; llamar la atención.

ap·pear [əpír] *v.* aparecer(se); parecer; comparecer.

ap·pear·ance [əpírəns] *s.* apariencia, semblante; facha; aparición; cariz.

ap·pease [əpíz] *v.* apaciguar, aplacar; pacificar; conciliar; sosegar.

ap·pease·ment [əpízmənt] *s.* apaciguamiento; conciliación.

ap·pel·late court [æpélətkort] *s.* tribunal de apelaciones.

ap·pen·dix [əpéndɪks] *s.* apéndice.

ap·per·tain [æpɚtén] *v.* pertenecer.

ap·pe·tite [ǽpətaɪt] *s.* apetito; gana, deseo.

ap·pe·tiz·er [ǽpətaɪzɚ] *s.* aperitivo.

ap·pe·tiz·ing [ǽpətaɪzɪŋ] *adj.* apetecible; apetitoso.

ap·plaud [əplɔ́d] *v.* aplaudir.

ap·plause [əplɔ́z] *s.* aplauso.

ap·ple [ǽpl̩] *s.* manzana; — **tree** manzano; — **grove** manzanar; **Adam's** — nuez (*del cuello*); *Ven., C.A., Col* manzana; — **of my eye** niña de mis ojos; **apple-pie order** orden (estado) perfecto.

ap·ple·sauce [ǽplsɔs] *s.* compota de manzana.

ap·pli·ance [əpláɪəns] *s.* utensilio, instrumento; herramienta; mueble utilitario.

ap·pli·ca·ble [ǽplɪkəbl̩] *adj.* aplicable.

ap·pli·cant [ǽpləkənt] *s.* solicitante, aspirante, candidato.

ap·pli·ca·tion [æpləkéʃən] *s.* (*dedication*) aplicación; (*petition*) solicitud, petición; *Méx., Carib., Ven.* aplicación; — **blank** formulario de solicitud.

ap·plied [əpláɪd] *adj. & p.p.* aplicado; — **for** pedido, solicitado.

ap·ply [əpláɪ] *v.* aplicar(se); **to** — **to** dirigirse a, acudir a, recurrir a; **to** — **for** solicitar, pedir; **to** — **oneself** aplicarse, dedicarse; **to** — **on account** acreditar en cuenta.

ap·point [əpɔ́ɪnt] *v.* (*designate*) nombrar, designar, señalar; (*furnish*) amueblar, equipar; **a well -ed house** una casa bien amueblada.

ap·point·ee [əpɔɪntí] *s.* electo.

ap·point·ment [əpɔ́ɪntmənt] *s.* (*designation*) nombramiento, designación; (*engagement*) cita, compromiso; **-s** mobiliario, mueblaje; accesorios.

ap·por·tion [əpɔ́rʃən] *v.* repartir proporcionadamente, prorratear.

ap·por·tion·ment [əpɔ́rʃənmənt] *s.* prorrateo, distribución, repartimiento.

ap·prais·al [əprézl] *s.* tasa, valuación.

ap·praise [əpréz] *v.* avaluar, valuar, tasar.

ap·pre·cia·ble [əpríʃəbl] *adj.* (*prized*) apreciable; (*perceived*) perceptible; (*quantity*) bastante.

ap·pre·ci·ate [əpríʃɪet] *v.* apreciar; estimar; agradecer; **to** — **in value** subir de valor.

ap·pre·ci·a·tion [əpriʃɪéʃən] *s.* apreciación; aprecio; valuación; agradecimiento; aumento, alza, subida (*de precio*).

ap·pre·hend [æprɪhénd] *v.* aprehender, asir, prender; comprender; percibir.

ap·pre·hen·sion [æprɪhénʃən] *s.* aprehensión, aprensión, recelo, desconfianza, presentimiento; captura.

ap·pre·hen·sive [æprɪhénsɪv] *adj.* aprensivo.

ap·pren·tice [əpréntɪs] *s.* aprendiz; novicio, principiante; *v.* poner de aprendiz.

ap·pren·tice·ship [əpréntɪsʃɪp] *s.* aprendizaje.

ap·prise [əpráɪz] *v.* enterar, informar; apreciar; dar parte.

ap·proach [əprótʃ] *s.* acercamiento; aproximación; acceso, entrada; **method of** — técnica o modo de plantear (*un problema*); enfoque; *v.* acercarse, aproximarse; abordar (*a alguien*).

ap·pro·ba·tion [æprəbéʃən] *s.* aprobación.

ap·pro·pri·ate [əprópriɪt] *adj.* apropiado, propio, apto, conveniente, a propósito; [əprópriet] *v.* apropiarse, apoderarse de; asignar (*una suma de dinero*).

ap·pro·pri·a·tion [əpropriéʃən] *s.* apropiación; asignación, suma asignada.

ap·prov·al [əprúvl] *s.* aprobación, asentimiento.

ap·prove [əprúv] *v.* aprobar; asentir a; **approved** visto bueno (V. B.).

ap·prox·i·mate [əpráksəmɪt] *adj.* aproximado; aproximativo; **-ly** *adv.* aproximadamente, casi, poco más o menos; [əpráksəmet] *v.* aproximar; aproximarse, acercarse.

a·pri·cot [éprɪkat] *s.* albaricoque; *Am.* chabacano.

A·pril [éprəl] *s.* abril.

a·pron [éprən] *s.* delantal.

ap·ro·pos [æprəpó] *adv.* a propósito; *adj.* oportuno; pertinente; — **of** a propósito de.

apt [æpt] *adj.* apto, capaz; pertinente, a propósito; — **to** propenso a.

ap·ti·tude [ǽptətjud] *s.* aptitud, capacidad; habilidad.

aq·ua·ma·rine [ækwəmərín] *s.* aguamarina.

a·quar·i·um [əkwérɪəm] *s.* acuario; pecera.

a·quat·ic [əkwǽtɪk] *adj.* acuático.

aq·ue·duct [ǽkwɪdʌkt] *s.* acueducto.

Ar·ab [ǽrəb] *adj. & s.* árabe.

Ar·a·go·nese [ærəgəniz] *adj. & s.* aragonés.

ar·bi·ter [árbɪtɚ] *s.* árbitro, arbitrador, juez árbitro.

ar·bi·trar·y [árbətrɛrɪ] *adj.* arbitrario; despótico.

ar·bi·trate [árbətret] *v.* arbitrar; decidir; someter al arbitraje; terciar.

ar·bi·tra·tion [arbətréʃən] *s.* arbitraje, arbitración.

ar·bi·tra·tor [árbətretɚ] *s.* arbitrador, árbitro; medianero.

ar·bor [árbɚ] *s.* emparrado, enramada, glorieta.

arc [ark] *s.* arco; — **lamp** lámpara de arco.

ar·cade [arkéd] *s.* arcada; galería; soportal.

arch [artʃ] *s.* arco; bóveda; **semicircular** — arco de medio punto; — **enemy** enemigo acérrimo; *v.* arquear(se); enarcar(se).

ar·chae·ol·o·gy [arkiálədʒɪ] *s.* arqueología.

ar·cha·ic [arkéɪk] *adj.* arcaico, desusado, anticuado.

arch·bish·op [ártʃbíʃəp] *s.* arzobispo.

arch·bish·op·ric [artʃbíʃəprɪk] *s.* arzobispado.

arch·er·y [ártʃərɪ] *s.* tiro de flechas.
ar·chi·pel·a·go [arkəpέləgo] *s.* archipiélago.
ar·chi·tect [arkətɛkt] *s.* arquitecto.
ar·chi·tec·tur·al [arkətέktʃərəl] *adj.* arquitectónico.
ar·chi·tec·ture [árkətɛktʃɚ] *s.* arquitectura.
ar·chives [árkaɪvz] *s.* archivo.
arch·way [ártʃwe] *s.* pasadiz (*bajo un arco*); arcada, galería abovedada.
arc·tic [árktɪk] *adj.* ártico.
ar·dent [árdṇt] *adj.* ardiente, apasionado.
ar·dor [árdɚ] *s.* ardor; enardecimiento; fervor.
ar·du·ous [árdʒʊəs] *adj.* arduo, trabajoso.
are [ar] *2ª persona y pl. del presente de indic. del verbo* to be: eres, estás; somos, estamos; sois, estáis; son, están.
ar·e·a [ɛ́rɪə] *s.* área, superficie; espacio; región.
a·re·na [ərínə] *s.* arena, redondel, plaza.
Ar·gen·ti·ne [árdʒəntin] *adj. & s.* argentino.
ar·gon [árgan] *s.* argón.
ar·gue [árgjʊ] *v.* argüir; debatir; altercar; **to — into** persuadir a.
ar·gu·ment [árgjəmənt] *s.* disputa; polémica; razonamiento; sumario, resumen.
ar·id [ǽrɪd] *adj.* árido.
a·rise [əráɪz] *v.* levantarse; elevarse; surgir; provenir.
a·ris·en [ərízṇ] *p.p. de* to arise.
ar·is·toc·ra·cy [ærəstákrəsɪ] *s.* aristocracia.
a·ris·to·crat [ərístəkræt] *s.* aristócrata.
a·ris·to·crat·ic [ərɪstəkrǽtɪk] *adj.* aristocrático.
a·rith·me·tic [əríθmətɪk] *s.* aritmética; *adj.* aritmético — **data processing** sistematizacion de datos aritméticos.
ark [ark] *s.* arca; **— of the covenant** arca del testamento; **Noah's —** arca de Noé.
arm [arm] *s.* (*anatomy*) brazo; (*weapon*) arma; **— in —** de bracete, de bracero; *Ríopl.*, *Cuba* de brazo, de brazos; **at -'s length** a una brazada; **with open -s** con los brazos abiertos; *v.* armar(se).
ar·ma·da [armádə] *s.* armada, flota.
ar·ma·ment [árməmənt] *s.* armamento.
ar·ma·ture [ármətʃɚ] *s.* armadura.
arm·chair [ármtʃɛr] *s.* silla de brazos, sillón, butaca.
armed for·ces [ármd fórsəz] *s.* fuerzas armadas.
arm·ful [ármfʊl] *s.* brazada.
ar·mi·stice [árməstɪs] *s.* armisticio.
ar·mor [ármɚ] *s.* armadura; blindaje, coraza; arnés; *v.* blindar, acorazar.
ar·mor·ed [ármɚd] *p.p.* blindado, acorazado.
ar·mor·y [ármərɪ] *s.* armería; arsenal.
arm·pit [ármpɪt] *s.* sobaco.
ar·my [ármɪ] *s.* ejército; muchedumbre; **— doctor** médico militar; **regular —** tropa de línea.
a·ro·ma [ərómə] *s.* aroma; fragancia.
ar·o·mat·ic [ærəmǽtɪk] *adj.* aromático.
a·rose [əróz] *pret. de* to arise.
a·round [əráʊnd] *adv.* alrededor; en redor; a la redonda; en torno; en derredor; cerca; **all —** por todos lados; *prep.* alrededor de; cerca de; **— here** por aquí; **to go — in circles** dar vueltas; **to go — the world** dar la vuelta al mundo.
a·rouse [əráʊz] *v.* despertar, *Ríopl.*, *C.A.*, *Ven.* recordar (*al dormido*); excitar; promover, animar.
ar·raign [ərén] *v.* acusar; procesar (*a un criminal*).
ar·range [əréndʒ] *v.* arreglar; disponer; colocar; acomodar; hacer arreglos (para), hacer planes (para).
ar·range·ment [əréndʒmənt] *s.* arreglo; disposición; colocación, orden; convenio.
ar·ray [əré] *s.* (*order*) arreglo, formación, orden; orden (*de batalla*); (*pomp*) pompa; gala, atavío; *v.* formar (*tropas*); poner en orden; ataviar, adornar.

ar·rears [ərírz] *s. pl.* atrasos, pagos o rentas vencidos y no cobrados; **in —** atrasado (*en el pago de una cuenta*).
ar·rest [ərέst] *s.* arresto, captura, aprehensión, detención; *v.* aprehender o prender, arrestar; detener; llamar, atraer (*la atención*).
ar·ri·val [əráɪvl] *s.* llegada; arribo; venida; **the new -s** los recién llegados.
ar·rive [əráɪv] *v.* llegar; arribar; **to — at a result** lograr (*o conseguir*) un resultado.
ar·ro·gance [ǽrəgəns] *s.* arrogancia.
ar·ro·gant [ǽrəgənt] *adj.* arrogante.
ar·row [ǽro] *s.* saeta, flecha.
ar·se·nal [ársṇəl] *s.* arsenal.
ar·se·nic [ársṇɪk] *s.* arsénico.
ar·son [ársən] *s.* delito de incendio.
art [art] *s.* arte; destreza; astucia; **fine -s** bellas artes; **master of -s** licenciado en letras, maestro en artes.
ar·ter·y [ártərɪ] *s.* arteria; **arterial** arterial; **— highway** carretera troncal.
art·ful [ártfʊl] *adj.* artero, mañero, ladino.
ar·ti·choke [ártɪtʃok] *s.* alcachofa.
ar·ti·cle [ártɪkl] *s.* artículo; **— of clothing** prenda de vestir; **— of merchandise** mercancía, mercadería; **— of agreement** convenio, contrato.
ar·tic·u·late [artíkjəlɪt] *adj.* articulado; claro, inteligible; capaz de hablar; [artíkjəlet] *v.* articular; enunciar; enlazar.
ar·tic·u·la·tion [artɪkjəléʃən] *s.* articulación; coyuntura.
ar·ti·fact [ártəfækt] *s.* artefacto.
ar·ti·fice [ártəfɪs] *s.* artificio; ardid.
ar·ti·fi·cial [artəfíʃəl] *adj.* artificial; postizo; afectado; artificioso.
ar·til·ler·y [artíləri] *s.* artillería; **— man** artillero.
ar·ti·san [ártəzṇ] *s.* artesano; artífice.
art·ist [ártɪst] *s.* artista.
ar·tis·tic [artístɪk] *adj.* artístico; **-ally** *adv.* artísticamente.
as [æz] *adv., conj., prep.* como; mientras; a medida que, según; en el momento en que; **— far —** hasta, hasta donde; **— for (— to)** en cuanto a; **— if** como si; **— it were** por decirlo así; **— large —** tan grande como; **— much —** tanto como; **— well —** tan bien; también; **— yet** hasta ahora, todavía; **— long — you wish** todo el tiempo que Vd. quiera; **— strong — he is** aunque es tan fuerte; **the same —** lo mismo que; **— of** con fecha de; **— per** según.
as·bes·tos [æsbέstəs] *s.* asbesto.
as·cend [əsɛ́nd] *v.* ascender; subir, elevarse.
as·cen·sion [əsɛ́nʃən] *s.* ascensión; subida.
as·cent [əsɛ́nt] *s.* ascenso; subida; ascensión.
as·cer·tain [æsɚtén] *v.* averiguar, indagar.
as·cet·ic [əsɛ́tɪk] *adj.* ascético; *s.* asceta.
as·cribe [əskráɪb] *v.* atribuir, imputar, achacar.
ash [æʃ] *s.* ceniza; **— tray** cenicero; **— tree** fresno; **Ash Wednesday** miércoles de ceniza; **ash-colored** *adj.* ceniciento, cenizo.
a·shamed [əʃémd] *adj.* avergonzado, corrido; **to be — tener** vergüenza; avergonzarse.
a·shore [əʃór] *adv.* a tierra; en tierra; **to go —** desembarcar.
A·si·at·ic [əʒɪǽtɪk] *adj. & s.* asiático.
a·side [əsáɪd] *adv.* aparte; a un lado; al lado; *s.* aparte (*en un drama*).
ask [æsk] *v.* (*request*) pedir, rogar, solicitar; (*inquire*) preguntar; (*invite*) invitar; **to — for** pedir; **to — for (about, after)** preguntar por; **to — a question** hacer una pregunta; **asking price** precio de oferta.
a·skance [əskǽns] *adv.* de soslayo; con recelo,

recelosamente; **to look** — mirar con recelo; no aprobar.

a·sleep [əslíp] *adj.* dormido; **to fall** — dormirse; **my arm is** — se me ha dormido (entumecido *o* entumido) el brazo.

as·par·a·gus [əspǽrəgəs] *s.* espárrago.

as·pect [ǽspɛkt] *s.* aspecto; cariz.

as·phalt [ǽsfɔlt] *s.* asfalto; chapapote.

as·pi·ra·tion [æspəréʃən] *s.* aspiración; anhelo.

as·pire [əspáɪr] *v.* aspirar; anhelar, ambicionar.

as·pi·rin [ǽspɚɪn] *s.* aspirina.

ass [æs] *s.* asno, burro; pollino.

as·sail [əsél] *v.* asaltar, acometer, agredir.

as·sail·ant [əsélənt] *s.* asaltador, agresor.

as·sas·sin [əsǽsɪn] *s.* asesino.

as·sas·si·nate [əsǽsṇet] *v.* asesinar.

as·sas·si·na·tion [əsæsṇéʃən] *s.* asesinato.

as·sault [əsɔ́lt] *s.* asalto, acometida; conato; ataque; *v.* asaltar, acometer, atacar; violar.

as·say [əsé] *v.* ensayar (*metales*); analizar, examinar; contrastar (*pesas, moneda*); *s.* ensaye (*de metales*); contraste (*de pesas, moneda*).

as·sem·ble [əsɛ́mbḷ] *v.* reunir(se), congregar(se), juntar(se); convocar; armar, montar (*maquinaria*).

as·sem·bly [əsɛ́mblɪ] *s.* asamblea; reunión; montaje (*de maquinaria*); — **hall** salón de sesiones; paraninfo; — **line** cadena de producción, tren de ensamblaje, línea de montaje; — **language** *s.* (*computer*) lenguaje de ensamble.

as·sent [əsɛ́nt] *s.* asentimiento; consentimiento; *v.* asentir; consentir.

as·sert [əsɝt] *v.* aseverar, asegurar, afirmar; **to — oneself** hacerse valer; obrar con firmeza; vindicarse.

as·ser·tion [əsɝʃən] *s.* aserción, aserto, afirmación.

as·sess [əsɛ́s] *v.* avaluar; tasar; asignar, imponer (*impuestos, multas, contribuciones, etc.*).

as·sess·ment [əsɛ́smənt] *s.* avaluación, tasación; imposición (*de contribuciones, multas, etc.*); contribución, (*tax*) impuesto.

as·set [ǽsɛt] *s.* cualidad, ventaja; **-s** capital, fondos, caudal; haber, activo; **personal -s** bienes muebles; **-s in hand** bienes disponibles; **capital -s** activo fijo; *Arg.* valores patrimoniales.

as·sid·u·ous [əsídʒʊəs] *adj.* asiduo, diligente.

as·sign [əsáɪn] *v.* asignar; señalar, designar; traspasar, ceder a favor de.

as·sign·ment [əsáɪnmənt] *s.* asignación; encargo; traspaso de bienes, designación; cesión (*de bienes*); tarea (*asignada*); lección (*señalada*).

as·sim·i·late [əsímlet] *v.* asimilar(se), absorber(se).

as·sist [əsíst] *v.* asistir, ayudar.

as·sis·tance [əsístəns] *s.* asistencia, ayuda.

as·sis·tant [əsístənt] *s.* asistente; ayudante; auxiliar; *adj.* subordinado, auxiliar.

as·so·ci·ate [əsóʃɪɪt] *adj.* asociado; *s.* asociado; socio; compañero; colega; [əsóʃɪet] *v.* asociar(se); relacionar.

as·so·ci·a·tion [əsosɪéʃən] *s.* asociación; sociedad; conexión, relación.

as·sort [əsɔ́rt] *v.* ordenar, clasificar.

as·sort·ed [əsɔ́rtɪd] *adj.* surtido, mezclado, variado, de todas clases.

as·sort·ment [əsɔ́rtmənt] *s.* variedad; clasificación; surtido; colección, grupo.

as·sume [əsúm] *v.* asumir; tomar; dar por sentado, dar por supuesto; arrogarse, apropiarse.

as·sump·tion [əsámpʃən] *d.* suposición; toma, apropiación; presunción; asunción (*de la Virgen*).

as·sur·ance [əʃúrəns] *s.* seguridad, certeza; convicción; confianza; **life** — seguro de vida.

Véase **insurance.**

as·sure [əʃúr] *v.* asegurar; afirmar; infundir confianza; **assured** asegurado.

as·sur·ed·ly [əʃúrɪdlɪ] *adv.* seguramente; sin duda, con seguridad.

as·ta·tine [ǽstətɪn] *s.* astato.

as·ter·isk [ǽstərɪsk] *s.* asterisco.

a·stig·ma·tism [əstígmətɪzəm] *s.* astigmatismo.

as·ton·ish [əstánɪʃ] *v.* asombrar, pasmar, espantar.

as·ton·ish·ing [əstánɪʃɪŋ] *adj.* asombroso, pasmoso, maravilloso.

as·ton·ish·ment [əstánɪʃmənt] *s.* asombro, pasmo, sorpresa.

as·tound [əstáʊnd] *v.* pasmar; aterrar, aturdir.

a·stray [əstré] *adv.* fuera de camino; *adj.* desviado, extraviado, descaminado; **to go** — perderse; errar el camino; extraviarse; **to lead** — desviar, extraviar; llevar por mal camino; seducir.

a·stride [əstráɪd] *adv.* a horcajadas.

as·trin·gent [æstríndʒənt] *adj., s.* astringente.

as·tro·dome [ǽstrədom] *s.* astródomo.

as·trol·o·gy [əstrálədʒɪ] *s.* astrología.

as·tro·naut [ǽstrənɔt] *s.* astronauta.

as·tron·o·mer [əstránəmɚ] *s.* astrónomo.

as·tron·o·my [əstránəmɪ] *s.* astronomía.

as·tro·phys·ics [ǽstrofízɪks] *s.* astrofísica.

As·tu·ri·an [æstjúrɪən] *adj. & s.* asturiano.

as·tute [əstjút] *adj.* astuto, sagaz.

a·sun·der [əsándɚ] *adj.* separado; **to cut** — separar, apartar; dividir en dos.

a·sy·lum [əsáɪləm] *s.* asilo; hospicio; **orphan** — orfanato, casa de huérfanos, *Méx., C.A., Andes* orfanatorio.

at [æt] *prep.* a; en; en (la) casa de; — **last** por fin, al fin; — **once** al punto; **to be** — **work** estar trabajando; **to enter** — **that door** entrar por aquella puerta.

at·a·vism [ǽtəvɪzəm] *s.* atavismo.

ate [et] *pret. de* **to eat.**

a·the·ist [éθɪɪst] *s.* ateo.

ath·lete [ǽθlɪt] *s.* atleta.

ath·let·ic [æθlétɪk] *adj.* atlético.

ath·let·ics [æθlétɪks] *s.* gimnasia; atletismo; deportes.

At·lan·tic [ətlǽntɪk] *adj.* atlántico; *s.* el Atlántico.

at·las [ǽtləs] *s.* atlas.

at·mos·phere [ǽtməsfɪr] *s.* atmósfera; ambiente.

at·mos·pher·ic [ætməsférɪk] *adj.* atmosférico.

at·om [ǽtəm] *s.* átomo; — **bomb** bomba atómica.

a·tom·ic [ətámɪk] *adj.* atómico; — **age** edad atómica; — **energy** fuerza atómica; — **pile** pila atómica; — **weight** peso atómico.

a·tone [ətón] *v.* expiar, purgar; reparar.

a·tone·ment [ətónmənt] *s.* expiación; reparación.

a·tro·cious [ətróʃəs] *adj.* atroz.

a·troc·i·ty [ətrásətɪ] *s.* atrocidad; maldad.

at·ro·phy [ǽtrəfɪ] *s.* atrofia.

at·tach [ətǽtʃ] *v.* unir, juntar; sujetar, pegar, adherir; poner (*sello o firma*); embargar (*bienes*); asignar; atribuir.

at·ta·ché [ǽtəʃe] *s.* agregado.

at·tach·ment [ətǽtʃmənt] *s.* adhesión; apego; vinculación; afición, cariño; embargo (*de bienes*); (*accessory*) accesorio.

at·tack [ətǽk] *s.* ataque, asalto; acceso; *v.* atacar; acometer, embestir.

at·tain [ətén] *v.* lograr, conseguir, alcanzar; llegar a.

at·tain·ment [əténmənt] *s.* logro, consecución; adquisición; dote; habilidad.

at·tempt [ətɛ́mpt] *s.* tentativa; prueba, ensayo; esfuerzo; atentado; *v.* tentar, intentar, procurar, tratar (de), probar; **to — the life of** atentar contra la vida de.

at·tend [ətɛ́nd] *v.* atender, cuidar, mirar por; asistir a; acompañar.

at·ten·dance [ətɛ́ndəns] *s.* asistencia; presencia; concurrencia.

at·ten·dant [ətɛ́ndənt] *s.* acompañante; sirviente, servidor; asistente; *adj.* acompañante.

at·ten·tion [ətɛ́nʃən] *s.* (*care*) cuidado; (*courtesy*) fineza, urbanidad, atención; **to pay —** hacer caso; prestar atención.

at·ten·tive [ətɛ́ntɪv] *adj.* atento; cortés.

at·test [ətɛ́st] *v.* atestiguar, atestar; certificar; dar fe.

at·tic [ǽtɪk] *s.* desván.

at·tire [ətáɪr] *s.* atavío; vestidura; vestido, traje; *v.* ataviar, adornar.

at·ti·tude [ǽtətjud] *s.* actitud; postura.

at·tor·ney [ətɝ́nɪ] *s.* abogado; procurador; apoderado; **— general** fiscal (*de una nación o estado*); **district —** fiscal de distrito; **power of —** procuración, poder.

at·tract [ətrǽkt] *v.* atraer; cautivar; **to — attention** llamar la atención.

at·trac·tion [ətrǽkʃən] *s.* atracción; atractivo; **-s** diversiones; lugares o sitios de interés.

at·trac·tive [ətrǽktɪv] *adj.* atractivo; seductor; simpático.

at·trac·tive·ness [ətrǽktɪvnɪs] *s.* atracción; atractivo.

at·trib·ute [ǽtrəbjut] *s.* atributo; propiedad; [ətrɪ́bjut] *v.* atribuir, achacar.

at·tri·tion [ətrɪ́ʃən] *s.* agotamiento; atrición.

auc·tion [ɔ́kʃən] *s.* subasta, almoneda, remate, *Am.* venduta; *v.* subastar; rematar; **auctioneer** subastador, *Arg.* martillo.

au·da·cious [ɔdéʃəs] *adj.* audaz, atrevido, osado.

au·dac·i·ty [ɔdǽsətɪ] *s.* audacia, osadía; descaro.

au·di·ble [ɔ́dəbl] *adj.* audible.

au·di·ence [ɔ́dɪəns] *s.* auditorio, concurrencia, público; audiencia.

au·di·o fre·quen·cy [ɔdɪofríkwɛnsɪ] *s.* audiofrecuencia.

au·di·o·vis·u·al [ɔdɪovíʒuəl] *adj.* audiovisual.

au·dit [ɔ́dɪt] *v.* intervenir (*cuentas*); glosar, revisar; asistir a (*una clase*) de oyente; *s.* intervención, comprobación de cuentas.

au·di·tion [ɔdíʃən] *s.* audición.

au·di·tor [ɔ́dɪtɚ] *s.* interventor; censor de cuentas; oyente.

au·di·to·ri·um [ɔdətɔ́rɪəm] *s.* salón de conferencias o conciertos; paraninfo.

au·di·to·ry [ɔ́dətorɪ] *adj.* auditivo.

au·ger [ɔ́gɚ] *s.* taladro, barrena.

aught [ɔt] *s.* algo.

aug·ment [ɔgmɛ́nt] *v.* aumentar.

au·gur [ɔ́gɚ] *s.* agorero; *v.* augurar, pronosticar; **to — well** (*o* **ill**) ser de buen (*o* mal) agüero.

Au·gust [ɔ́gəst] *s.* agosto.

aunt [ænt] *s.* tía.

aus·pic·es [ɔ́spɪsɪz] *s. pl.* auspicios; protección.

aus·pi·cious [ɔspíʃəs] *adj.* propicio; favorable.

aus·tere [ɔstír] *adj.* austero, adustro, severo.

aus·ter·i·ty [ɔstérətɪ] *s.* austeridad, severidad.

Aus·tri·an [ɔ́strɪən] *adj. & s.* austríaco.

au·then·tic [ɔθɛ́ntɪk] *adj.* auténtico.

au·thor [ɔ́θɚ] *s.* autor; escritor.

au·thor·i·ta·tive [əθɔ́rətetɪv] *adj.* autorizado, que tiene autoridad; autoritario.

au·thor·i·ty [əθɔ́rətɪ] *s.* autoridad; facultad; **to have on good —** saber de buena tinta.

au·thor·ize [ɔ́θəraɪz] *v.* autorizar.

au·to [ɔ́to] *s.* auto, automóvil.

au·to·boot [ɔ́tobut] *s.* (*computer*) autocarga.

au·to·crat [ɔ́təkræt] *s.* autócrata.

au·to·graph [ɔ́təgræf] *s.* autógrafo.

au·to·mat·ic [ɔtəmǽtɪk] *adj.* automático; **-ally** *adv.* automáticamente; **automation** automatización.

au·to·mo·bile [ɔ́təməbil] *s.* automóvil; **automotive** automovilístico.

au·ton·o·my [ɔtánəmɪ] *s.* autonomía.

au·top·sy [ɔ́tapsɪ] *s.* autopsia.

au·tumn [ɔ́təm] *s.* otoño.

au·tum·nal [ɔtʌ́mnl] *adj.* otoñal.

aux·il·ia·ry [ɔgzíljərɪ] *adj. & s.* auxiliar.

a·vail [əvél] *v.* aprovechar; beneficiar; **to — oneself of** aprovecharse de; *s.* provecho; ventaja; **of no —** de ninguna utilidad o ventaja.

a·vail·a·ble [əvéləbl] *adj.* disponible; aprovechable; obtenible.

av·a·lanche [ǽvlæntʃ] *s.* alud; torrente.

av·a·rice [ǽvərɪs] *s.* avaricia.

av·a·ri·cious [ævərɪ́ʃəs] *adj.* avaro, avariento.

a·venge [əvɛ́ndʒ] *v.* vengar; vindicar.

a·veng·er [əvɛ́ndʒɚ] *s.* vengador.

av·e·nue [ǽvənu] *s.* avenida.

a·ver [əvɝ́] *v.* afirmar, asegurar.

av·er·age [ǽvrɪdʒ] *s.* promedio, término medio; **on an —** por término medio; *adj.* medio, mediano; ordinario; *v.* promediar, calcular o sacar el promedio; **to — a loss** prorratear una pérdida; **he -s 20 miles an hour** avanza o recorre un promedio de 20 millas por hora.

a·verse [əvɝ́s] *adj.* adverso, renuente.

a·ver·sion [əvɝ́ʒən] *s.* aversión; malquerencia, inquina.

a·vert [əvɝ́t] *v.* apartar, desviar; evitar; impedir.

a·vi·a·tion [evɪéʃən] *s.* aviación.

a·vi·a·tor [évɪetɚ] *s.* aviador.

av·o·ca·do [ɑvəkɑ́do] *s.* aguacate, *Andes* palta.

av·o·ca·tion [ævəkéʃən] *s.* distracción; ocupación de distracción o diversión.

a·void [əvɔ́ɪd] *v.* evitar; eludir.

a·vow [əváʊ] *v.* confesar, reconocer, admitir.

a·vow·al [əváʊəl] *s.* confesión, admisión.

a·wait [əwét] *v.* esperar, aguardar.

a·wake [əwék] *adj.* despierto; alerto; **wide-awake** muy despierto; avispado; *v.* despertar(se).

a·wak·en [əwékən] *v.* despertar(se).

a·ward [əwɔ́rd] *s.* premio; decisión, sentencia; *v.* asignar; otorgar; conferir; adjudicar (*un premio, medalla, etc.*).

a·ware [əwɛ́r] *adj.* consciente; enterado, sabedor; cauto; sobre aviso.

a·way [əwé] *adv.* lejos; fuera; *adj.* ausente; **right —** ahora mismo, ahorita; **ten miles —** a diez millas de aquí; **to give —** regalar; **to go —** irse; **to take — quitar.**

awe [ɔ] *s.* pavor; pasmo; **to stand in —** quedarse, o estar, pasmado; pasmarse; *v.* atemorizar; infundir avor; maravillar.

aw·ful [ɔ́fʊl] *adj.* terrible; horroroso; tremendo; impresionante; **-ly** *adv.* terriblemente; horrorosamente; muy.

a·while [əhwáɪl] *adv.* (por) un rato; (por) algún tiempo.

awk·ward [ɔ́kwɚd] *adj.* torpe, desmañado; molesto, embarazoso; incómodo; inconveniente.

awl [ɔl] *s.* lezna, punzón.

aw·ning [ɔ́nɪŋ] *s.* toldo.

a·woke [əwók] *pret. & p.p. de* **to awake.**

ax, axe [æks] *s.* hacha.

ax·is [ǽksɪs] *pl.* **ax·es** [ǽksiz] *s.* eje.

ax·le [ǽksl] *s.* eje (*de una rueda*); **front —** eje delantero; **rear —** eje trasero.

aye [aɪ] *adv.* si; *s.* voto afirmativo.
Az·tec [ǽztɛk] *adj. & s.* azteca.
az·ure [ǽʒɚ] *adj.* azul; *s.* azur, azul celeste.

B:b

bab·ble [bǽbl] *s.* balbuceo; parloteo, charla; *v.* balbucear; parlotear, charlar.
babe [beb] = **baby.**
ba·boon [bæbún] *s.* mandril (*especie de mono*).
ba·by [bébɪ] *s.* nene, bebé, criatura; *Andes, Ch.* guagua; *C.A.* tierno; *adj.* infantil; de niño; — **girl** nena; — **sitter** [bébɪsftɚ] *s.* cuidaniños, niñera por horas; *v.* mimar.
bach·e·lor [bǽtʃələ·] *s.* bachiller; soltero.
ba·cil·lus [bəsíləs] *s.* bacilo.
back [bæk] *s.* (*anatomy*) espalda; lomo (de animal); (*opposite side*) revés; respaldo (*de silla*), espaldar; **behind one's** — a espaldas de uno, a espaldas vueltas; **in** — **of** detrás de, tras; **to fall on one's** — caer de espaldas, caer boca arriba; **to turn one's** — volver las espaldas; *adj.* posterior; trasero; retrasado, atrasado, rezagado; — **pay** sueldo atrasado; — **talk** respuesta insolente;— **yard** patio interior; corral; *adv.* atrás, detrás; — **and forth** de aquí para allá; **to come** — volver, regresar; **to give** — devolver; *v.* respaldar, endosar; sostener, apoyar, retroceder; hacer retroceder; **to** — **down** hacerse (para) atrás; retractarse.
back·bone [bǽkbón] *s.* espinazo, espina dorsal; firmeza, apoyo, sostén.
back·er [bǽkɚ] *s.* fiador; sostenedor, defensor; (*politics*) partidario.
back·fire [bǽkfaɪr] *s.* petardeo; *v.* fracasar, ser contraproducente.
back·ground [bǽkgraʊnd] *s.* fondo; educación; experiencia; **to keep in the** — dejar en último término; quedarse en último término; mantenerse retirado.
back·hand [bǽkhænd] *s.* revés; escritura inclinada a la izquierda; **-ed stroke** revés; **a -ed remark** una ironía; una indirecta.
back·ing [bǽkɪŋ] *s.* apoyo, garantía; endose, endoso; respaldo.
back·lash [bǽklæʃ] *s.* contragolpe; culateo.
back·log [bǽklɔg] *s.* reserva pendiente.
back·space [bǽksp es] *v.* espaciar hacia atrás.
back·stage [bǽkstédʒ] *adv.* detrás del telón.
back·up [bǽkəp] *adj.* de reserva.
back·ward [bǽkwɚd] *adj.* atrasado; retrasado; retrógrado; lerdo, tardo; huraño, tímido, esquivo; *adv.* = **backwards.**
back·ward·ness [bǽkwɚdnɪs] *s.* torpeza; atraso; timidez.
back·wards [bǽkwɚdz] *adv.* hacia (o para) atrás; de espaldas; **to go** — retroceder, andar hacia (o para) atrás.
ba·con [békən] *s.* tocino.
bac·te·ri·a [bæktírɪə] *s. pl.* bacterias.
bac·te·ri·ol·o·gy [bæktɪrɪúlədʒɪ] *s.* bacteriología.
bad [bæd] *adj.* malo; perverso; dañoso; podrido; **to go from** — **to worse** ir de mal en peor; **to look** — tener mal cariz, tener mala cara o mal aspecto; **-ly** *adv.* mal, malamente.
bade [bæd] *pret. de* **to bid.**
badge [bædʒ] *s.* insignia, divisa; distintivo; *Méx.* chapa.
bad·ger [bǽdʒɚ] *s.* tejón; *v.* atormentar, acosar,

molestar.
bad·ness [bǽdnɪs] *s.* maldad.
baf·fle [bǽfl] *v.* desconcertar, confundir; frustrar, impedir.
bag [bæg] *s.* (*sack*) saco, bolsa, talega; costal; (*baggage*) maleta; zurrón, morral; *v.* ensacar; cazar; agarrar; adueñarse de; inflarse; abolsarse.
bag·gage [bǽgɪdʒ] *s.* equipaje; bagaje; — **car** furgón, vagón de equipajes; — **check** talón, contraseña de equipajes; — **tag** marbete, etiqueta; — **inspection** revisión de equipaje.
bag·pipe [bǽgpaɪp] *s.* gaita.
bail [bel] *s.* fianza, caución; **to let out on** — poner en libertad bajo fianza; *v.* dar fianza; salir fiador; (*empty*) achicar (*agua*), vaciar; **to** — **out of a plane** tirarse (*con paracaídas*) de un aeroplano; **bailee** depositario.
bait [bet] *s.* cebo; atractivo, aliciente; *v.* tentar, atraer; cebar; acosar, perseguir.
bake [bek] *v.* hornear, cocer al horno; calcinar.
bak·er [békɚ] *s.* panadero, pastelero, hornero; — **'s dozen** la docena del fraile.
bak·ery [békɔrɪ] *s.* panadería, pastelería, tahona.
bak·ing [békɪŋ] *s.* hornado; cocimiento; — **powder** polvo de hornear.
bal·ance [bǽləns] *s.* (*instrument*) balanza; (*equilibrium*) contrapeso, equilibrio, balance; (*debit, credit*) saldo; — **of payments** balanza de pagos; — **wheel** volante del reloj; — **of trade** balanza comercial; — **due** saldo pagadero; — **sheet** estado de contabilidad, *Arg.* hoja de balance; — **of power** equilibrio político; **to lose one's** — perder el equilibrio; *v.* contrapesar; pesar; balancear(se); equilibrar; saldar (*una cuenta*).
bal·co·ny [bǽlkənɪ] *s.* balcón; galería (*de teatro*).
bald [bɔld] *adj.* calvo; pelado; pelón; sin vegetación; escueto, sin adornos; — **spot** calva.
bale [bel] *s.* bala, fardo (*de mercancías*); *v.* embalar, enfardar, empacar.
balk [bɔk] *v.* oponerse, rebelarse, resistirse; pararse de repente; negarse a seguir; encabritarse; **to** — **someone's plans** frustrar los planes de alguien.
ball [bɔl] *s.* (*plaything*) pelota, bola; (*string, thread*) ovillo; (*weapon*) bala; (*dance*) baile; — **bearing** cojinete de bolas; — **game** juego de pelota; béisbol; — **printer** (*computer*) impresora de bola; *v.* ovillar; **to** — **up** enredar, confundir.
bal·lad [bǽləd] *s.* romance; copla, canción; balada.
bal·last [bǽləst] *s.* lastre; grava (*usada en terraplenes, caminos, etc.*); *v.* lastrar, poner el lastre a (*una embarcación*).
bal·let [bǽlé] *s.* ballet.
bal·lis·tics [bælfstɪks] *s.* balística.
bal·loon [bəlún] *s.* globo (*aerostático*); **ballooning of prices** alza artificial de precios.
bal·lot [bǽlət] *s.* balota, *Méx., C.A.* boleta, cédula para votar; voto; — **box** urna electoral; *v.* balotar, votar.
ball point [bɔ́lpɔɪnt] *s.* bolígrafo.
balm [bam] *s.* bálsamo.
bal·my [bámɪ] *adj.* balsámico; fragante; refrescante; suave; algo loco, chiflado.
bal·sam [bɔ́lsəm] *s.* bálsamo; especie de abeto.
bam·boo [bæmbú] *s.* bambú.
ban [bæn] *s.* bando, proclama; excomunión; prohibición; **marriage -s** amonestaciones; *v.* proscribir, prohibir; condenar.
ba·nan·a [bənǽnə] *s.* plátano; banana; *C.A.* guineo; — **tree** banano; plátano.
band [bænd] *s.* (*group*) banda, partida, pandilla, cuadrilla; (*musicians*) banda; (*strip*) faja, lista,

cinta, tira; partida, pandilla, cuadrilla; **rubber** — liga de goma; *v.* unir, juntar; atar, ligar; **to** — **together** confederarse, juntarse.

ban·dage [bǽndɪdʒ] *s.* venda, vendaje; *v.* vendar.

bandanna [bændǽnə] *s.* pañuelo de hierbas.

ban·dit [bǽndɪt] *s.* bandido, bandolero.

bang [bæŋ] *s.* golpe, golpazo; estallido; fleco (*de pelo*); **with a** — de golpe, de golpazo; de repente; con estrépito; —! ¡pum!; *v.* golpear; hacer estrépito; cortar (*el pelo*) en fleco; **to** — **the door** dar un portazo.

ban·ish [bǽnɪʃ] *v.* proscribir, desterrar; **to** — **fear** desechar el temor.

ban·ish·ment [bǽnɪʃmənt] *s.* proscripción; destierro.

ban·is·ter [bǽnɪstɚ] *s.* balaustre; barandilla, barandal, pasamano.

ban·jo [bǽndʒo] *s.* banjo.

bank [bæŋk] *s.* (*institution*) banco; (*in card game*) banca; (*of a river*) orilla, ribera, banda; escarpa; (*pile*) montón; **savings** — caja de ahorros; — **statement** estado de cuenta; — **vault** bóveda, deposito de seguridad; *adj.* bancario; de banco; *v.* depositar en un banco; amontonar (*tierra o arena*); cubrir con cenizas, tapar (*el fuego*); ladear (*un aeroplano*); **to** — **upon** (*o* **on**) contar con.

bank·book [bǽŋkbʊk] *s.* libreta de banco.

bank·er [bǽŋkɚ] *s.* banquero.

bank·ing [bǽŋkɪŋ] *s.* transacciones bancarias banca; *adj.* bancario, de banca; — **house** banca, casa de banca.

bank·note [bǽŋknot] *s.* billete de banco.

bank·rupt [bǽŋkrʌpt] *adj.* en quiebra, arruinado, insolvente; *v.* quebrar; arruinar.

bank·rupt·cy [bǽŋkrʌptsɪ] *s.* bancarrota, quiebra; *Arg.*, *Ch.*, *Perú*, *Bol.* falencia; **to go into** — declararse insolvente; quebrar, hacer bancarrota.

ban·ner [bǽnɚ] *s.* bandera, estandarte, pendón; *adj.* primero, principal, sobresaliente.

ban·quet [bǽŋkwɪt] *s.* banquete; *v.* banquetear.

bap·tism [bǽptɪzəm] *s.* bautismo; bautizo.

Bap·tist [bǽptɪst] *s.* bautista.

bap·tize [bæptáɪz] *v.* bautizar.

bar [bɑr] *s.* (*of iron*) barra; barrote; tranca; (*obstacle*) barrera, obstáculo; (*of justice*) tribunal; foro; (*saloon*) cantina, taberna; (*counter*) mostrador; (*piece*) barra (*de jabón*); pastilla (*de chocolate*); **sand** — banco de arena; **-s** reja; **to be admitted to the** — recibirse de abogado; *v.* atrancar (*la puerta*); estorbar; prohibir; excluir; **barring error or omission** salvo error u omisión.

barb [bɑrb] *s.* púa.

bar·bar·i·an [bɑrbérɪən] *s.* & *adj.* bárbaro; salvaje.

bar·ba·rous [bɑrbərəs] *adj.* bárbaro; salvaje; inculto.

bar·be·cue [bɑrbɪkju] *s.* *Méx.*, *C.A.*, *Col.* barbacoa; *Ríopl.* churrasco; *v.* hacer barbacoa; *Ríopl.* churrasquear.

barbed [bɑrbd] *adj.* con púas; — **wire** alambre de púas.

bar·ber [bɑrbɚ] *s.* barbero; peluquero.

bar·ber·shop [bɑrbɚʃɑp] *s.* barbería; peluquería.

bard [bɑrd] *s.* bardo, vate, poeta.

bare [bɛr] *adj.* (*naked*) desnudo; descubierto; pelado; (*evident*) manifiesto, patente; (*unfurnished*) desamueblado, vacío; — **majority** mayoría escasa; **to lay** — poner de manifiesto, hacer patente, revelar; **to ride** — **back** montar en pelo.

bare·foot [bérfʊt] *adj.* descalzo, con los pies desnudos; **-ed** [bérfʊtɪd] = **barefoot.**

bare·head·ed [bérhédɪd] *adj.* descubierto, sin sombrero.

bare·leg·ged [bérlégɪd] *adj.* con las piernas desnudas;

sin medias.

bare·ly [bérlɪ] *adv.* apenas; escasamente; — **three pounds** tres libras escasas.

bare·ness [bérnɪs] *s.* desnudez.

bar·gain [bárgɪn] *s.* (*agreement*) convenio, pacto; negocio, trato; (*cheap*) ganga; — **sale** ganga, *Méx.*, *C.A.*, *Ven.*, *Andes* barata; **into the** — por añadidura; de ganancia; **to make a** — cerrar un convenio; *v.* regatear; negociar; **to** — **for** regatear; contar con, esperar.

barge [bardʒ] *s.* lanchón; barca.

bar·i·tone [bǽrətɑn] *s.* & *adj.* barítono.

bar·i·um [bérɪəm] *s.* bario.

bark [bɑrk] *s.* ladrido; corteza (*de árbol*); barco velero; *v.* ladrar; descortezar, quitar la corteza.

bar·ley [bárlɪ] *s.* cebada.

barn [bɑrn] *s.* establo, cuadra; granero, troje; pajar; **streetcar** — cobertizo para tranvías.

bar·na·cle [bárnəkəl] *s.* cirrópodo.

barn·yard [bárnjard] *s.* corral; — **fowl** aves de corral.

ba·rom·e·ter [bərámətɚ] *s.* barómetro.

bar·on [bǽrən] *s.* barón.

ba·roque [bərók] *adj.* & *s.* barroco.

bar·rage [bərádʒ] *s.* fuego de barrera; presa.

bar·rel [bǽrəl] *s.* barril, barrica, tonel, cuba; (*gun*) cañón (*de fusil, pistola, etc.*); *v.* embarrilar (*meter en barril*).

bar·ren [bǽrən] *adj.* árido; estéril.

bar·ren·ness [bǽrənnɪs] *s.* aridez; esterilidad.

bar·rette [bərét] *s.* broche, prendedor (*para sujetar el pelo*).

bar·ri·cade [bærəkéd] *s.* barricada, barrera; *v.* poner barricadas; obstruir el paso con barricadas.

bar·ri·er [bǽrɪɚ] *s.* barrera, valla; obstáculo.

bar·room [bárum] *s.* cantina; bar.

bar·ter [bártɚ] *v.* permutar, trocar, cambiar; *s.* permuta, trueque, cambio.

base [bes] *s.* base; basa; fundamento; *adj.* bajo, vil, ruin; inferior; *v.* basar, fundar; establecer.

base·ball [bésbɔl] *s.* baseball o béisbol.

base·ment [bésmənt] *s.* sótano.

base·ness [bésnɪs] *s.* bajeza, ruindad, vileza.

bash·ful [bǽʃfəl] *adj.* tímido, encogido, vergonzoso.

bash·ful·ness [bǽʃfəlnɪs] *s.* timidez, vergüenza, cortedad, apocamiento.

ba·sic [bésɪk] *adj.* básico; fundamental.

ba·sin [bésn̩] *s.* palangana, jofaina; lebrillo; tazón (*de fuente*); (*pond*) estanque, depósito de agua; **river** — cuenca de río.

ba·sis [bésɪs] (*pl.* **bases** [bésiz]) *s.* base, fundamento.

bask [bæsk] *v.* calentarse (*al sol*); asolearse, tomar el sol.

bas·ket [bǽskɪt] *s.* cesta, cesto, canasta.

bas·ket·ball [bǽskɪtbɔl] *s.* basquetbol.

Basque [bæsk] *adj.* & *s.* (*person*) vasco; (*language*) vascuence, vasco; (*territory*) vascongado, vasco.

bass [bes] *s.* bajo (*en música*); *adj.* bajo, grave; — **drum** tambora, bombo; — **horn** tuba.

bas·tard [bǽstɚd] *s.* & *adj.* bastardo.

baste [best] *v.* hilvanar; pringar (*empapar la carne con grasa*); apalear.

bat [bæt] *s.* palo, *Méx.*, *Carib.*, *Ven.*, *C.A.* bate (*de béisbol*); garrote; golpe, garrotazo; (*animal*) murciélago; *v.* apalear; dar palos; *Méx.*, *Carib.*, *Ven.*, *C.A.* batear; **not to** — **an eye** no pestañear.

batch [bætʃ] *s.* hornada; colección, grupo; partida, conjunto.

bath [bæθ] *s.* baño.

bathe [beð] *v.* bañar(se).

bath·er [béðɚ] *s.* bañista.

bath·house [bǽθhaʊs] *s.* casa de baños; bañadero.
bath·robe [bǽθrob] *s.* bata de baño.
bath·room [bǽθrum] *s.* baño, cuarto de baño.
bath·tub [bǽθtʌb] *s.* bañera, tina.
bath·y·sphere [bǽθɪsfɪr] *s.* batisfera.
bat·tal·ion [bətǽljən] *s.* batallón.
bat·ter [bǽtɚ] *s.* batido, masa; *Am.* bateador (*de béisbol*); *v.* golpear; **to — down** demoler.
bat·ter·y [bǽtərɪ] *s.* batería; acumulador; pila; (*assault*) asalto.
bat·tle [bǽtl] *s.* batalla, lucha, combate; *v.* batallar, luchar, combatir.
bat·tle·field [bǽtlfild] *s.* campo de batalla
bat·tle·ship [bǽtlʃɪp] *s.* buque de guerra, acorazado.
baud [bɔd] *s.* (*computer*) baudio.
bawl [bɔl] *s.* aullido; grito; *v.* aullar; gritar; pregonar; **to — out** regañar, reprender.
bay [be] *s.* bahía; ladrido, balido, aullido; **— rum** ron de laurel; **— tree** laurel; **— window** ventana saliente, mirador; **to hold at —** tener a raya; *adj.* bayo; *v.* dar aullidos, ladridos o balidos.
bay·o·net [béənɪt] *s.* bayoneta; *v.* traspasar; herir con bayoneta.
ba·zaar [bəzár] *s.* bazar; feria.
ba·zoo·ka [bəzúka] *s.* bazuca.
be [bi] *v.* (*innately*) ser; (*state or condition*) estar, verse, hallarse, encontrarse; **— that as it may** sea como sea; **to — cold (warm, hungry, right,** *etc.*) tener frío (calor, hambre, razón, *etc.*); **to — in a hurry** tener prisa; **he is to —** ha de ser; va a ser; **it is cold (hot, windy,** *etc.*) hace frío (calor, viento, *etc.*).
beach [bitʃ] *s.* playa, ribera; *v.* varar, poner en seco (*una embarcación*), encallar.
beach·head [bítʃhed] *s.* cabeza de playa.
bea·con [bíkən] *s.* faro, fanal; boya luminosa; señal; **aviation —** radiofaro.
bead [bid] *s.* cuenta (*de rosario, collar,* etc.); abalorio, glóbulo; gota (*de sudor*); **-s** rosario; collar de cuentas; *v.* adornar con abalorios o cuentecitas.
beak [bik] *s.* (*bird*) pico (*de ave*); (*ship*) espolón (*de nave*).
beak·er [bíkɚ] *s.* tazón.
beam [bim] *s.* rayo (*de luz o de calor*); (*smile*) sonrisa; viga, vigueta; (*scale*) brazo (*de balanza*); **radio —** línea de radiación, radiofaro; *v.* (*light*) emitir (*luz, rayos*); brillar; sonreír, estar radiante de alegría; radiar, transmitir por radio.
beam·ing [bímɪŋ] *adj.* radiante, resplandeciente; sonriente.
bean [bin] *s.* judía, habichuela; *Méx., C.A., Ven., Col.* frijol; *Ch., Ríopl.* poroto; **coffee —** grano de café; **Lima —** haba; **string —** judía o habichuela verde; *Méx., C.A.* ejote; *Ch., Ríopl.* chaucha.
bear [bɛr] *s.* oso, osa; (*market*) bajista; *v.* (*stand*) soportar; llevar; sobrellevar; tolerar, aguantar; (*give birth*) parir, dar a luz; producir; **to — down** deprimir; apretar; **to — a grudge** guardar rencor; **to — in mind** tener en cuenta; **to — on a subject** tener relación con un asunto; **to — oneself with dignity** portarse con dignidad; **to — out** confirmar; **to — testimony** dar testimonio; **to — interest** devengar interés.
beard [bɪrd] *s.* barba, barbas; aristas (*de trigo o maíz*); **-ed** *adj.* barbado, barbudo.
bearer [bérɚ] *s.* portador; mensajero; **bearing** [bérɪŋ] *s.* (*posture*) porte, presencia; (*relation*) relación, conexión; (*direction*) rumbo, orientación; (*mechanical*) cojinete; **ball —** cojinete de bolas; **beyond —** inaguantable, insufrible; **to lose one's -s** perder el rumbo, desorientarse; **fruit-bearing**

adj. fructífero.
beast [bist] *s.* bestia, animal.
beat [bit] *s.* golpe; toque (*de tambor*); latido, palpitación; compás; ronda (*que hace el policía*); *v.* batir; golpear; azotar; vencer, ganar; marcar (*el compás*); pulsar, latir; sonar (*tambores*); **to — around the bush** andarse por las ramas; valerse de rodeos; *pret. & p.p.* de **to beat**.
beat·en [bítn] *p.p.* de **to beat** & *adj.* batido; vencido; fatigado; **— path** camino trillado.
beat·er [bítɚ] *s.* batidor; molinillo; golpeador; **egg —** batidor de huevos.
be·a·tif·ic [beətífɪk] *adj.* beatífico.
beat·ing [bítɪŋ] *s.* paliza, tunda, zurra; latido, pulsación.
be·at·i·tude [bɪǽtətjud] *s.* beatitud, bienaventuranza; **the Beatitudes** las bienaventuranzas.
beau [bo] *s.* galán, pretendiente.
beau·te·ous [bjútɪəs] *adj.* bello, hermoso.
beau·ti·ful [bjútəfəl] *adj.* bello, hermoso.
beau·ti·fy [bjútəfaɪ] *v.* hermosear, embellecer.
beau·ty [bjútɪ] *s.* belleza, hermosura; beldad; **parlor —** salón de belleza.
bea·ver [bívɚ] *s.* castor; **— board** cartón para tabiques.
be·came [bɪkém] *pret.* de **to become**.
be·cause [bɪkɔ́z] *conj.* porque; **— of** *prep.* por, a causa de.
beck·on [békən] *s.* seña, llamada; *v.* llamar a señas.
be·come [bɪkʌ́m] *v.* (*suit*) sentar bien a, quedar bien a; convenir a; (*turn out to be*) hacerse; ponerse; llegar a ser; convertirse en; **to — crazy** volverse loco; enloquecer; **to — angry** enojarse; **to — frightened** asustarse; **to — old** envejecer(se); **what has — of him?** ¿qué ha sido de él?; ¿qué se ha hecho él?; *p.p.* de **to become**.
be·com·ing [bɪkʌ́mɪŋ] *adj.* propio, conveniente; decente, decoroso; **that dress is — to you** le sienta bien ese traje.
bed [bɛd] *s.* cama, lecho; cauce (*de un río*); fondo (*de lago o mar*); cuadro (*de jardín*); yacimiento (*mineral*); **to go to —** acostarse; **to put to —** acostar.
bed·bug [bédbʌg] *s.* chinche.
bed·clothes [bédklodz] *s. pl.* ropa de cama.
bed·ding [bédɪŋ] *s.* **= bedclothes.**
bed·pan [bédpæn] *s.* silleta; cómoda.
bed·rid·den [bédrɪdən] *adj.* en cama; postrado.
bed·rock [bédrák] *s.* roca sólida; lecho de roca.
bed·room [bédrum] *s.* cuarto de dormir, alcoba, dormitorio, *Méx., C.A.* recámara.
bed·side [bédsaɪd] *s.* **at the —** al lado de la cama; **— table** velador, mesilla de noche.
bed·spread [bédspred] *s.* colcha, sobrecama.
bed·time [bédtaɪm] *s.* hora de acostarse, hora de dormir.
bee [bi] *s.* abeja; reunión (*para trabajar o competir*); **to have a — in one's bonnet** tener una idea metida en la cabeza.
beech [bitʃ] *s.* haya; **— nut** nuez de haya, hayuco.
beef [bif] *s.* carne de vaca o toro; vaca, toro (*engordados para matar*); **roast —** rosbif.
beef·steak [bífstek] *s.* bistec, biftec o bisté.
bee·hive [bíhaɪv] *s.* colmena; abejera.
been [bɪn, bɛn] *p.p.* de **to be**.
beep [bip] *s.* pip, piip, piiip.
beer [bɪr] *s.* cerveza; **— tavern** cervecería.
beet [bit] *s.* remolacha, *Mex.* betabel.
bee·tle [bítl] *s.* escarabajo.
be·fall [bɪfɔ́l] *v.* sobrevenir, acaecer, suceder.
be·fall·en [bɪfɔ́lən] *p.p.* de **to befall**.

be·fell [bɪfɛ́l] *pret. de* **to befall.**
be·fit [bɪfɪ́t] *v.* convenir.
be·fore [bɪfór] *adv. (temporal)* antes; *(spatial)* delante; al frente; *prep.* antes de; delante de; enfrente de; ante; *conj.* antes (de) que.
be·fore·hand [bɪfórhænd] *adv.* de antemano, por adelantado, con antelación, con anticipación.
be·friend [bɪfrɛ́nd] *v.* ofrecer o brindar amistad a; favorecer; amparar.
beg [bɛg] *v.* rogar, suplicar, pedir; mendigar, pordiosear; **to — the question** dar por sentado lo mismo que se arguye.
be·gan [bɪgǽn] *pret. de* **to begin.**
be·get [bɪgɛ́t] *v.* engendrar; causar, producir.
beg·gar [bɛ́gɚ] *s.* mendigo, pordiosero; pobre; infeliz, miserable.
be·gin [bɪgín] *v.* comenzar, empezar, principiar.
be·gin·ner [bɪgínɚ] *s.* principiante; novicio.
be·gin·ning [bɪgínɪŋ] *s.* principio; comienzo; empiezo; origen; **— with** comenzando con (*o* por); **at the —** al principio.
be·got [bɪgát] *pret. & p.p. de* **to beget.**
be·got·ten [bɪgátn̩] *p.p. de* **to beget.**
be·grudge [bɪgrʌ́dʒ] *v.* envidiar; ceder de mala gana.
be·guile [bɪgáɪl] *v.* engañar; defraudar; seducir.
be·gun [bɪgʌ́n] *p.p. de* **to begin.**
be·half [bɪhǽf]: **in (on) — of** por; en nombre de; a favor de; en defensa de; **in my —** en mi nombre; a mi favor; por mí.
be·have [bɪhév] *v.* portarse, conducirse, obrar, proceder (*bien o mal*); **— yourself!** ¡pórtate bien!
be·hav·ior [bɪhévjɚ] *s.* comportamiento, proceder, conducta; funcionamiento; reacción.
be·head [bɪhɛ́d] *v.* decapitar, degollar, descabezar.
be·held [bɪhɛ́ld] *pret. & p.p de* **to behold.**
be·hind [bɪháɪnd] *adv.* detrás; atrás; a la zaga, en zaga; *prep.* detrás de, tras; **— one's back** a espaldas de uno; **— time** atrasado, retrasado **from — por** detrás; **to arrive ten minutes — time** llegar con diez minutos de retraso; **to fall —** atrasarse; retrasarse.
be·hold [bɪhóld] *v.* contemplar, mirar; **—!** ¡he aquí!
be·hoove [bɪhúv] *v.* serle necesario a uno; corresponderle a uno; atañerle a uno.
be·ing [bíɪŋ] *s.* ser; ente; esencia; existencia; *ger. de* **to be** siendo; **for the time —** por ahora; por el momento.
be·lat·ed [bɪlétɪd] *adj.* tardío; atrasado.
belch [bɛltʃ] *v.* eructar; **to — forth** echar, arrojar, vomitar; *s.* eructo.
bel·fry [bɛ́lfrɪ] *s.* campanario.
Bel·gian [bɛ́ldʒən] *adj. & s.* belga.
be·lief [bəlíf] *s.* creencia; fe; convicción; opinión.
be·liev·a·ble [bəlívəbl] *adj.* creíble.
be·lieve [bəlív] *v.* creer; pensar; **to — in** creer en, tener fe en; confiar en.
be·liev·er [bəlívɚ] *s.* creyente, fiel.
be·lit·tle [bɪlɪ́tl] *v.* menospreciar, apocar, empequeñecer; dar poca importancia a.
bell [bɛl] *s.* campana; campanilla; **cow —** cencerro, esquila; **call —** timbre; **jingle —** cascabel; **— flower** campanilla, campánula; **— jar** campana de cristal.
bell·boy [bɛ́lbɔɪ] *s.* mozo de hotel, botones.
belle [bɛl] *s.* beldad, mujer bella.
bel·lig·er·ent [bəlídʒɚənt] *adj. & s.* beligerante.
bel·low [bɛ́lo] *s.* bramido, rugido; *v.* rugir, bramar, berrear; gritar.
bel·lows [bɛ́loz] *s. (sing. & pl.)* fuelle.
bel·ly [bɛ́lɪ] *s.* barriga; panza; vientre; estómago.
bel·ly·ache [bɛ́liek] *s.* dolor de barriga (*estómago*).

be·long [bəlɔ́ŋ] *v.* pertenecer, corresponder; **it does not — here** está fuera de su sitio; está mal colocado.
be·long·ings [bəlɔ́ŋɪŋz] *s. pl.* posesiones, bienes, efectos, cosas.
be·lov·ed [bɪlʌ́vɪd] *adj.* querido, amado.
be·low [bəló] *adv.* abajo; bajo; debajo; **here —** aquí abajo; en este mundo, de tejas abajo; *prep.* bajo, debajo de.
belt [bɛlt] *s.* cinturón, cinto; correa; zona; **sword —** talabarte; **— conveyor** cinta (banda) transportadora; *v.* ceñir, fajar.
belt line [bɛ́ltlaɪn] *s.* vía de circunvalación.
be·moan [bɪmón] *v.* lamentarse de, quejarse de.
bench [bɛntʃ] *s.* banco, banca; tribunal.
bend [bɛnd] *s.* curva; vuelta, recodo; *v.* encorvar(se), doblar(se), *Col., Ven., Ríopl., Méx.* enchuecar(se); inclinar(se); someter(se), ceder; **to — one's efforts** esforzarse (por), dirigir sus esfuerzos.
be·neath [bɪníθ] *prep.* debajo de, bajo; indigno de; inferior a.
ben·e·dic·tion [bɛnədíkʃən] *s.* bendición.
ben·e·fac·tor [bɛ́nəfæktɚ] *s.* benefactor, bienhechor; patrón.
be·nef·i·cent [bənɛ́fəsn̩t] *adj.* benéfico.
ben·e·fi·cial [bɛnəfíʃəl] *adj.* benéfico; ventajoso, provechoso.
ben·e·fi·ci·ar·y [bɛnɪfíʃɪɛrɪ] *s.* beneficiario.
ben·e·fit [bɛ́nəfɪt] *s.* beneficio; provecho, ventaja; **— performance** función de beneficio; **— payments** beneficios; *v.* beneficiar; hacer bien; **to — by the advice** aprovecharse del consejo; **he -ed by the medicine** le hizo bien la medicina.
be·nev·o·lence [bənɛ́vələns] *s.* benevolencia.
be·nev·o·lent [bənɛ́vələnt] *adj.* benévolo.
be·nign [bɪnáɪn] *adj.* benigno; afable.
bent [bɛnt] *s.* inclinación; tendencia; propensión; *pret. & p.p. de* **to bend;** *adj.* encorvado; inclinado, doblado; corvo; *(stooped)* gacho; **to be — on** estar resuelto a.
ben·zene [bɛ́nzin] *s.* benceno.
be·queath [bɪkwíð] *v.* heredar, legar, dejar en testamento.
be·quest [bɪkwɛ́st] *s.* legado, donación.
be·rate [bɪrét] *v.* regañar, reñir, reprender.
be·ret [bəré] *s.* boina.
ber·ry [bɛ́rɪ] *s.* baya (*como mora, fresa, etc.*); grano (*de café*).
berth [bɝθ] *s.* litera (*de un camarote*); **to give a wide — de** sacarle el cuerpo a, hacerse a un lado para dejar pasar.
be·ryl·li·um [bərflɪəm] *s.* berilio.
be·seech [bɪsítʃ] *v.* suplicar, rogar.
be·set [bɪsɛ́t] *v.* atacar; rodear; acosar; *pret. & p.p. de* **to beset.**
be·side [bɪsáɪd] *prep. (spatial)* al lado de; cerca de; *(in addition)* además de; fuera de; **to be — oneself** estar fuera de sí, estar loco; **that is — the question** eso no hace al caso; no se trata de eso; no viene al caso; *adv.* además.
be·sides [bɪsáɪdz] *adv.* además; *prep.* además de.
be·siege [bɪsídʒ] *v.* sitiar, cercar; acosar, importunar.
be·sought [bɪsɔ́t] *pret. & p.p. de* **to beseech.**
best [bɛst] *adj.* mejor; *adv.* mejor; más; **the —** el mejor; lo mejor; **— girl** novia; querida; **— man** padrino de boda; **— seller** éxito de venta; de mayor venta; **at —** a lo más, cuando más; **to do one's —** hacer todo lo posible; **to get the — of a person** vencer o ganarle a una persona; **to make the — of** sacar el mejor partido de.
be·stow [bɪstó] *v.* otorgar, conferir; **to — gifts upon**

hacer regalos (*o* dádivas) a; **time well -ed** tiempo bien empleado.

bet [bet] *s.* apuesta; *v.* apostar; *pret. & p.p. de* **to bet.**

be·take [bɪték] *v.* **to — oneself** encaminarse, dirigirse.

be·tak·en [bɪtékən] *p.p. de* **to betake.**

be·took [bɪtúk] *pret. de* **to betake.**

be·tray [bɪtré] *v.* traicionar, vender, hacer traición; revelar, no guardar (*un secreto*); **to one's ignorance** hacer patente su ignorancia.

be·tray·er [bɪtréɚ] *s.* traidor, traicionera.

be·troth·al [bɪtróθəl] *s.* esponsales, compromiso, mutua promesa de matrimonio.

be·trothed [bɪtróθt] *s.* prometido, desposado; novio, novia.

bet·ter [bétɚ] *adj.* mejor; *adv.* mejor; más; **— half** cara mitad; **so much the —** tanto mejor; **to be — off** estar mejor así; estar en mejores condiciones; **to change for the —** mejorar(se); **to get —** (mejorar(se), restablecerse, aliviarse; *v.* mejorar; **to — oneself** mejorarse, mejorar de situación.

bet·ter·ment [bétɚmənt] *s.* mejoramiento, mejora, mejoría.

be·tween [bətwín] *prep.* entre, en medio de; *adv.* en medio.

bev·el [bévəl] *s.* bisel; *adj.* biselado; *v.* biselar.

bev·er·age [bévrɪdʒ] *s.* bebida.

bev·y [bévɪ] *s.* bandada, manada.

be·wail [bɪwél] *v.* lamentar; quejarse de.

be·ware [bɪwɛ́r] *v.* guardarse (de), cuidarse (de); **—!** ¡cuidado! ¡guárdese!

be·wil·der [bɪwfldɚ] *v.* confundir, turbar, perturbar, dejar perplejo; **to be -ed** estar turbado o perplejo; estar desorientado.

be·wil·der·ment [bɪwfldɚmənt] *s.* perplejidad, aturdimiento.

be·witch [bɪwítʃ] *v.* hechizar; encantar, cautivar.

be·yond [bɪjánd] *adv.* más allá, más lejos; *prep.* allende; más allá de; fuera de; **— my reach** fuera de mi alcance; **— the grave** ultratumba.

bi·as [báɪəs] *s.* (*tendency*) prejuicio; inclinación, tendencia; (*diagonal*) sesgo, oblicuidad; **on the —** sesgado, al sesgo, de lado; *adj.* sesgado, oblicuo; *v.* predisponer, inclinar, influir en.

bib [bɪb] *s.* babero; pechera (*de delantal*).

Bi·ble [báɪbl] *s.* Biblia.

bib·li·cal [bíblɪkl] *adj.* bíblico.

bib·li·og·ra·pher [bɪblɪágrəfɚ] *s.* bibliógrafo.

bib·li·og·ra·phy [bɪblɪágrəfɪ] *s.* bibliografía.

bi·car·bon·ate [baɪkárbənet] *s.* bicarbonato.

bick·er [bíkɚ] *v.* disputar, reñir.

bi·cy·cle [báɪsɪkl] *s.* bicicleta; *v.* andar en bicicleta.

bid [bɪd] *s.* postura, oferta; licitación, puja; envite (*en naipes*); turno (*para enviar*); invitación; *v.* ofrecer (*precio*); mandar; invitar, convidar; rogar; envidar (*en naipes*); **to — fair** parecer muy probable; **to — good-bye** decir adiós; despedirse; **to — up** alzar, pujar (*la oferta en una subasta*); *pret. & p.p. de* **to bid.**

bid·den [bídn̩] *p.p. de* **to bid & to bide.**

bide [baɪd] *v.* aguardar; **to — one's time** esperar una buena oportunidad.

bi·en·ni·um [baɪénɪəm] *s.* bienio.

bier [bɪr] *s.* féretro.

big [bɪg] *adj.* grande; importante; imponente; **— Dipper** Osa Mayor; **— game** caza mayor; **— sister** hermana mayor; **— with child** encinta; **to talk —** darse bombo, *Am.* darse corte; **big-bellied** panzudo, panzón, barrigón; **big-hearted** magnánimo.

big·a·my [bígəmɪ] *s.* bigamia.

big·ot [bígət] *s.* fanático.

big·ot·ry [bígətrɪ] *s.* fanatismo; intolerancia.

bi·ki·ni [bɪkínɪ] *s.* traje bikini.

bi·la·bi·al [baɪlébɪəl] *adj.* bilabial.

bile [baɪl] *s.* bilís, hiel, cólera, mal humor.

bi·lin·gual [baɪlíŋgwəl] *adj. & s.* bilingüe.

bill [bɪl] *s.* (*statement*) cuenta; factura; (*poster*) cartel, anuncio; (*bank note*) billete de banco; programa de teatro; (*bird*) pico; (*legislative*) proyecto de ley; **— of exchange** libranza, letra de cambio; **— of fare** menú; **— of lading** conocimiento de embarque; **— of rights** declaración de derechos; **— of sale** escritura o acta de venta; **-s payable** efectos a pagar; **— of credit** carta de crédito; *v.* cargar en cuenta; enviar una cuenta a; **to — and coo** acariciarse y arrullar (*como las palomas*).

bill·board [bílbord] *s.* cartelera.

bill·fold [bílfold] *s.* cartera; billetera.

bil·liards [bíljɚdz] *s.* billar.

bill·ing [bílɪŋ] *s.* importancia relativa de los anuncios de artistas de teatro.

bil·lion [bíljən] *s.* billón, millón de millones; mil millones (*en los Estados Unidos y Francia*).

bil·low [bílo] *s.* oleada; ola grande; *v.* alzarse en olas.

bin [bɪn] *s.* arcón, depósito; **coal —** carbonera; **grain — ** granero.

bi·nar·y [báɪnərɪ] *adj.* (*computer*) binario.

bind [baɪnd] *v.* (*unite*) unir, juntar; (*tie*) ligar; amarrar; vendar; ceñir; (*compel*) restringir, obligar, compeler; (*enclose*) encuadernar, empastar; rivetear; **binder** garantía.

bind·ing [báɪndɪŋ] *s.* encuadernación; ribete, cinta; **cloth —** encuadernación en tela; **paper —** encuadernación en rústica; *adj.* obligatorio.

binge [bɪndʒ] *s.* jarana; parranda; borrachera.

bi·og·ra·phy [baɪágrəfɪ] *s.* biografía.

bi·ol·o·gy [baɪálədʒɪ] *s.* biología.

bi·par·ti·san [baɪpártəzən] *adj.* de dos partidos; bipartito.

birch [bɝtʃ] *s.* abedul.

bird [bɝd] *s.* ave; pájaro; persona extraña o mal vista; **— of prey** ave de rapiña; **— seed** alpiste; **— shot** perdigones.

birth [bɝθ] *s.* nacimiento; parto; linaje; origen, principio; **— certificate** certificado (*o* fe) de nacimiento; **— control** control de la natalidad; anticoncepcionismo; limitación de partos; **— rate** natalidad; **to give —** dar a luz, parir.

birth·day [bɝθde] *s.* cumpleaños, natalicio.

birth·place [bɝθples] *s.* lugar de nacimiento, suelo natal.

birth·right [bɝθraɪt] *s.* derechos naturales o de nacimiento; naturalidad; primogenitura.

bis·cuit [bískɪt] *s.* bizcocho; galleta; panecillo.

bish·op [bíʃəp] *s.* obispo; alfil (*en ajedrez*).

bish·op·ric [bíʃəprɪk] *s.* obispado.

bis·muth [bízməθ] *s.* bismuto.

bi·son [báɪsn̩] *s.* bisonte, búfalo.

bit [bɪt] *s.* pedacito, trocito; pizca, miaja, migaja; poquito; bocado (*del freno*); taladro; (*computer*) dígito binario; bit; **I don't care a —** no me importa un ardite; *pret. & p.p. de* **to bite.**

bitch [bɪtʃ] *s.* perra; ramera, prostituta.

bite [baɪt] *s.* (*act*) mordedura, mordisco; (*morsel*) bocado, bocadito; picadura (*de insecto*); *v.* morder; mordiscar; picar.

bit·ten [bítn̩] *p.p. de* **to bite.**

bit·ter [bítɚ] *adj.* amargo; agrio; acre; (*harsh*)

áspero; mordaz; **to fight to the — end** luchar hasta morir; **-s** *s. pl.* amargo; **-ly** *adv.* amargamente; con amargura.

bit·ter·ness [bítəˑnɪs] *s.* amargura, amargor; (*anger*) rencor; aspereza.

black [blæk] *adj.* negro; obscuro; (*somber*) sombrío; **black-and-blue** amoratado, lleno de moretones; — **mark** mancha, estigma, marca de deshonra; *s.* negro; luto; — **out** obscurecimiento; **to put down in — and white** poner por escrito *v.* teñir de negro; embetunar, dar bola o betún a (*los zapatos*).

black·ber·ry [blǽkberɪ] *s.* zarzamora; mora.

black·bird [blǽkbɝd] *s.* mirlo.

black·board [blǽkbord] *s.* encerado; pizarrón; pizarra.

black·en [blǽkən] *v.* ennegrecer; (*weather*) obscurecer; teñir de negro; (*lower*) denigrar.

black·head [blǽkhɛd] *s.* espinilla.

black·ish [blǽkɪʃ] *adj.* negruzco.

black·jack [blǽkdʒæk] *s.* (*weapon*) cachiporra flexible; (*card game*) veintiuna.

black·mail [blǽkmel] *s.* chantaje, extorsión; *v.* ejercer el chantaje, extorsionar.

black·ness [blǽknɪs] *s.* negrura; obscuridad.

black·smith [blǽksmɪθ] *s.* herrero; **-'s shop** herrería.

black·top [blǽktap] *s.* camino de superficie bituminosa.

blad·der [blǽdɚ] *s.* vejiga.

blade [bled] *s.* hoja (*de navaja, cuchillo, etc.*); hoja (*de hierba*); espada; pala (*de remo*); aspa (*de hélice*); **shoulder —** espaldilla o paletilla.

blame [blem] *s.* culpa; *v.* culpar, echar la culpa a; **to be to —** tener la culpa.

blame·less [blémlɪs] *adj.* inculpable.

blanch [blæntʃ] *v.* blanquear; palidecer; escaldar (*almendras*).

bland [blænd] *adj.* blando, suave.

blank [blæŋk] *adj.* (*no writing*) en blanco; (*void*) vacío; (*confused*) aturdido; **— cartridge** cartucho vacío; **— face** cara sin expresión; **— form** blanco, forma en blanco, *Méx., C.A., Ven.* esqueleto; **— verse** verso suelto o libre; *s.* blanco; vacío; hueco, intermedio; papel en blanco; forma en blanco; **application —** forma (*o* blanco) para memorial o solicitud.

blan·ket [blǽŋkɪt] *s.* manta, frazada, cobertor; *Ríopl., C.A., Méx., Ven., Col.* cobija; *Méx.* sarape, poncho; *adj.* general, inclusivo, que abarca un grupo o clase.

blare [blɛr] *s.* fragor, son de trompetas, clarinada; *v.* trompetear, proclamar; sonar (*las trompetas*); hacer estruendo.

blas·pheme [blæsfím] *v.* blasfemar.

blas·phe·my [blǽsfɪmɪ] *s.* blasfemia.

blast [blæst] *s.* (*wind*) ráfaga de viento, golpe de viento; soplo repentino; (*trumpet*) trompetazo; (*whistle*) silbido; (*explosion*) explosión; estallido; carga de dinamita; **— furnace** alto horno; *v.* volar (*con dinamita, etc.*); destruir.

blaze [blez] *s.* llama, llamarada, incendio; resplandor; **— of anger** arranque de ira; *v.* arder; resplandecer; **to — a trail** abrir (*o* marcar) una senda.

bleach [blitʃ] *s.* blanqueador; blanqueo; *v.* blanquear(se); desteñir(se).

bleach·ers [blítʃɚz] *s. pl.* graderías.

bleak [blik] *adj.* yermo, desierto; helado.

blear [blɪr] *v.* nublar (*los ojos*).

blear·y [blɪrɪ] *adj.* nublado, inflamado, lagrimoso, lagañoso.

bleat [blit] *s.* balido; *v.* balar.

bled [blɛd] *pret. & p.p. de* **to bleed.**

bleed [blid] *v.* sangrar; desangrar; extorsionar.

blem·ish [blɛmɪʃ] *s.* mancha, tacha, defecto; *v.* manchar; empañar.

blend [blɛnd] *s.* mezcla, entremezcla; gradación (*de colores, sonidos, etc.*); *v.* mezclar, entremezclar; graduar (*colores o sonidos*); entremezclarse, fundirse; armonizar.

bless [blɛs] *v.* bendecir; **God — you!** ¡que Dios te bendiga!

bless·ed [blɛsɪd] *adj.* bendito; santo, beato; bienaventurado; **the whole — day** todo el santo día; [blɛst] *pret. & p.p. de* **to bless.**

bless·ing [blɛsɪŋ] *s.* bendición; gracia, don, beneficio.

blest [blɛst] *adj.* = **blessed.**

blew [blu] *pret. de* **to blow.**

blight [blaɪt] *s.* pulgón (*parásito*); tizón (*honguillo parásito*); quemadura (*enfermedad de las plantas*); roña (*de las plantas*); (*failure*) malogro, ruina; *v.* destruir, arruinar; frustrar (*esperanzas*).

blimp [blɪmp] *s.* dirigible pequeño.

blind [blaɪnd] *adj.* ciego; tapado, oculto; hecho a ciegas; **— alley** callejón sin salida; **— choice** selección hecha a ciegas; **— flying** vuelo ciego, vuelo a ciegas; **— man** ciego; **— man's buff** juego de la gallina ciega; **— date** [blaɪnddet] *s.* cita a ciegas; persiana, cortinilla; biombo; venda (*para los ojos*); anteojera (*para resguardar los ojos del caballo*); **to be a — for someone** ser tapadera de alguien; *v.* cegar; ofuscar; encubrir, tapar.

blind·er [bláɪndɚ] *s.* anteojera, *Méx., Cuba* visera (*para caballos de tiro*).

blind·fold [bláɪndfold] *v.* vendar (*los ojos*); *adj.* vendado (*de ojos*); *s.* venda (*para los ojos*).

blind·ly [bláɪndlɪ] *adv.* ciegamente; a ciegas.

blind·ness [bláɪndnɪs] *s.* ceguera, ceguedad.

blink [blɪŋk] *s.* pestañeo; parpadeo; guiño; guiñada; *v.* pestañear; parpadear; guiñar; (*computer*) parpadear, titilar.

blip [blɪp] *s.* bache de radar.

bliss [blɪs] *s.* beatitud, bienaventuranza, gloria; felicidad.

blis·ter [blístɚ] *s.* ampolla, vejiga (*en la piel o en cualquier superficie*); *v.* ampollar, levantar ampollas; ampollarse.

blitz [blɪts] *s.* ataque relámpago.

bliz·zard [blízɚd] *s.* nevasca; *v.* ventiscar.

bloat [blot] *v.* inflar(se); abotagarse.

blob [blab] *s.* burbuja.

block [blak] *s.* (*piece*) bloque, trozo de piedra; zoquete; (*city section*) manzana (*de casas*); *Am.* cuadra; (*obstacle*) estorbo, obstáculo; (*group*) grupo, sección (*hat*) horma; **— pulley** polea; **— chopping —** tajo; *v.* estorbar; tapar; bloquear; planchar (*sobre horma*); parar (*una pelota, una jugada*); **to — out** esbozar, bosquejar; **to — the door** impedir el paso; **to — up a door** tapiar una puerta.

block·ade [blakéd] *s.* bloqueo, obstrucción; *v.* bloquear.

block·head [blákhɛd] *s.* zoquete, tonto, zopenco.

blond(e) [bland] *adj. & s.* rubio, blondo; *Méx.* huero güero; *Guat.* canche; *Sal., Hond.,* chele; *C.R.* macho; *Col.* mono; *Ven.* catire.

blood [blʌd] *s.* sangre; **— count** análisis cuantitativo de la sangre; **— pudding** (*o* **— sausage**) morcilla; **— relative** pariente consanguíneo; **— vessel** vena; arteria; **in cold —** en sangre fría; **— bank** banco de sangre; **— poisoning** septicemia.

blood·shed [blʌ́dʃɛd] *s.* matanza; derrame, derramiento o efusión de sangre.

blood·shot [blʌ́dʃat] *adj.* inyectado de sangre.

blood·thirst·y [blʌ́dθɜ˞stɪ] *adj.* sanguinario.

blood·y [blʌ́dɪ] *adj.* sangriento; ensangrentado; sanguinario, feroz.

bloom [blum] *s.* flor; florecimiento, floración; lozanía; color rosado (*en las mejillas*) *v.* florecer, *Am.* florear.

bloom·ing [blúmɪŋ] *adj.* floreciente; fresco, lozano, vigoroso.

blos·som [blásəm] *s.* flor; floración, florecimiento; *v.* florecer.

blot [blat] *s.* mancha, borrón; tacha; *v.* manchar; borrar; secar (*con papel secante*); emborronar, echar manchas o borrones; **to — out** borrar, tachar; destruir; **this pen -s** esta pluma echa borrones; **blotting paper** papel secante.

blotch [blatʃ] *v.* emborronar o borronear, manchar, cubrir con manchas; *s.* mancha, borrón.

blot·ter [blátɚ] *s.* papel secante; libro borrador.

blouse [blaus] *s.* blusa.

blow [blo] *s.* (*stroke*) golpe; porrazo; (*shock*) choque, sorpresa, desastre; (*wind*) soplo, soplido; **to come to -s** venir a las manos; *v.* soplar; (*wind*) ventear; *C.A.* nortear; resoplar; sonar (*una trompeta*); fanfarronear; **to — a fuse** quemar un fusible; **to — one's nose** sonarse; **to — one's brains out** levantarse la tapa de los sesos; **to — open** abrirse; **to — out** apagar(se); estallar, reventar(se) (*un neumático*); **to — over** pasar; disiparse; **to — up** inflar, hinchar; volar (*con dinamita*); estallar, reventar.

blow·er [blóɚ] *s.* soplador; fuelle; ventilador, aventador.

blown [blon] *p.p.* de **to blow** & *adj.* soplado; inflado; **full-blown rose** rosa abierta.

blow·out [blóaut] *s.* reventón (*de neumático*); escape violento de gas, aire, etc.

blow·pipe [blópaɪp] *s.* soplete.

blow·torch [blótɔrtʃ] *s.* soplete.

blow·up [blóəp] *s.* ampliación.

blue [blu] *adj.* azul; (*sad*) triste, melancólico; **— chip** de primera línea; *s.* azul; **light —** (*ojos*) zarco; **the -s** melancolía, morriña, murria; *v.* azular, teñir de azul; **blue-pencil** tachar, vedar.

blue·bell [blúbɛl] *s.* campanilla azul (*flor*).

blue·bird [blúbɜ˞d] *s.* pájaro azul, *Am.* azulejo.

blue·jay [blúdʒe] *s.* gayo, especie de azulejo (*pájaro*).

blue·print [blúprɪnt] *s.* heliografía.

bluff [blʌf] *s.* acantilado, escarpa, risco; fanfarronada; fanfarrón, farsante; *v.* fanfarronear; alardear, hacer alarde; echar bravatas; embaucar.

bluff·er [blʌ́fɚ] *s.* farsante, fanfarrón.

blu·ing [blúɪŋ] *s.* añil (*para ropa blanca*).

blu·ish [blúɪʃ] *adj.* azulado, azulejo.

blun·der [blʌ́ndɚ] *s.* disparate, desatino; despropósito; *v.* disparatar, desatinar; equivocarse.

blunt [blʌnt] *adj.* despuntado, embotado; brusco, grosero, *Méx.* claridoso; *v.* despuntar, embotar.

blur [blɜ˞] *s.* mancha, tacha; nube, cosa obscura o confusa; *v.* empañar, borronear, manchar; nublar, ofuscar; empañarse, nublarse.

blush [blʌʃ] *s.* sonrojo; rubor; *v.* sonrojarse, ruborizarse, ponerse colorado.

blus·ter [blʌ́stɚ] *v.* ventear o soplar recio (*el viento*); fanfarronear; *s.* ventolera, ventarrón, fuerte golpe de viento; jactancia, fanfarronada.

blus·ter·ing [blʌ́stərɪŋ] *adj.* fanfarrón, jactancioso; **— wind** ventarrón.

boar [bor] *s.* jabalí.

board [bord] *s.* (*wood*) tabla, tablero; mesa; (*meals*) comidas; (*directors*) junta, consejo; (*pasteboard*) en pasta; cartón; (*computer*) tarjeta, placa; **the -s** las tablas, el teatro; **room and —** cuarto y comida, pensión completa; asistencia; **— of directors** junta directiva; **bulletin —** tablilla para anuncios; **free on — (f.o.b.)** franco a bordo; **on —** a bordo; en el tren; **to go by the —** caer en el mar; perderse; ser descartado; *v.* ir a bordo; subir (*al tren*); entablar, cubrir con tablas; tomar a pupilaje, dar asistencia, pensión o pupilaje; residir o comer (*en casa de huéspedes*).

board·er [bórdɚ] *s.* huésped, pupilo, pensionista.

board·ing·house [bórdɪŋhaus] *s.* casa de huéspedes, pensión.

boast [bost] *s.* jactancia; alarde; bravata; gloria, orgullo; *v.* jactarse, alardear; hacer alarde de; ostentar.

boast·ful [bóstfəl] *adj.* jactancioso.

boast·ful·ness [bóstfəlnɪs] *s.* jactancia; ostentación.

boat [bot] *s.* bote; barco, buque; lancha, chalupa.

boat·house [bóthaus] *s.* casilla o cobertizo para botes.

boat·ing [bótɪŋ] *s.* paseo en lancha o bote; **to go —** pasear en bote.

boat·man [bótmən] (*pl.* **boatmen** [bótmɛn]) *s.* barquero.

bob [bab] *s.* meneo, sacudida; pesa (*de metal*); **to wear a —** llevar el pelo corto (*o en melena*); *v.* menearse; **to — one's hair** cortarse el pelo en melena; **to — up** aparecer de repente; **to — up and down** saltar, brincar; cabecear (*dícese de una embarcación*).

bob·bin [bábɪn] *s.* carrete; bobina.

bob·tail [bábtel] *s.* rabón.

bob·white [bábhwait] *s.* codorniz.

bode [bod] *pret.* & *p.p.* de **to bide.**

bod·ice [bádɪs] *s.* corpiño, jubón.

bod·i·ly [bádli] *adj.* corpóreo; corporal; *adv.* todos juntos, colectivamente; **they rose —** se levantaron todos a una, se levantaron-todos juntos.

bod·y [bádɪ] *s.* cuerpo; agregado, conjunto; gremio; carrocería (*de automóvil*); fuselaje (*de aeroplano*); **— of water** extensión de agua; **— politic** grupo político; estado.

bod·y·guard [bádɪgard] *s.* guardaespaldas; *Am.* pistolero.

bog [bag] *s.* pantano; tremedal; *v.* hundir(se); atascarse.

Bo·he·mi·an [bohímɪən] *adj.* & *s.* bohemio.

boil [bɔɪl] *s.* hervor; (*skin*) tumorcillo; **to come to a —** soltar el hervor, hervir; *v.* hervir; cocer; bullir; **to — down** hervir hasta evaporar; abreviar.

boil·er [bɔ́ɪlɚ] *s.* caldera, marmita; caldera de vapor; calorífero central.

boil·ing point [bɔ́ɪlɪŋpɔɪnt] *s.* punto de ebullición.

bois·ter·ous [bɔ́ɪstərəs] *adj.* bullicioso; estrepitoso, ruidoso; tumultuoso.

bold [bold] *adj.* atrevido, osado; arriesgado; audaz; insolente; (*clear*) claro, bien delineado; **— cliff** risco escarpado; **bold-faced** descarado; **bold-faced type** negritas.

bold·ness [bóldnɪs] *s.* atrevimiento; osadía; audacia; descaro, insolencia.

bo·log·na [bəlóni] *s.* especie de embutido.

Bol·she·vik [bólʃəvik] *adj.* & *s.* bolchevique.

bol·ster [bólstɚ] *s.* travesaño, almohada larga (*para la cabecera de la cama*); refuerzo, sostén, soporte; *v.* sostener, apoyar; apuntalar; **to — someone's courage** infundirle ánimo a alguien.

bolt [bolt] *s.* (*door lock*) pestillo, cerrojo; (*pin*) perno, tornillo grande; (*movement*) salida de repente; (*cloth*) rollo; **thunder** — rayo; *v.* cerrar con cerrojo; tragar, engullir; romper con (*un partido político*); echarse a correr, lanzarse de repente; caer como rayo; **to** — **out** salir de golpe.

bomb [bɑm] *s.* bomba; *v.* bombardear; — **shelter** [bámʃɛləˑ] *s.* refugio antiaéreo.

bom·bard [bɑmbárd] *v.* bombardear, cañonear.

bom·bar·dier [bɑmbɚdír] *s.* bombardero.

bom·bard·ment [bɑmbárdmənt] *s.* bombardeo, cañoneo.

bom·bas·tic [bɑmbǽstɪk] *adj.* ampuloso, altisonante.

bom·ber [bámɚˑ] *s.* bombardero, avión de bombardeo.

bo·na fide [bónəfaɪd] *adj.* de buena fe.

bon·bon [bánbɑn] *s.* bombón, confite.

bond [bɑnd] *s.* (*tie*) lazo, vínculo; ligadura; (*obligation*) fianza, vale; obligación, bono; — **issue** emisión de bonos; **bonded debt** deuda consolidada.

bond·age [bándɪdʒ] *s.* servidumbre, esclavitud.

bonds·man [bándzmən] *s.* fiador.

bone [bon] *s.* hueso; espina (*de pez*); **-s** restos; osamenta; — **of contention** materia de discordia; **to make no -s about it** no pararse en pelillos; obrar francamente; *v.* deshuesar, quitar los huesos o espinas.

bon·fire [bánfaɪr] *s.* hoguera, fogata.

bon·net [bánɪt] *s.* gorra; sombrero (*de mujer*).

bo·nus [bónəs] *s.* prima, premio, gratificación; sobresueldo.

bon·y [bóni] *adj.* huesudo.

boo [bu] *v.* mofarse, burlarse (*a gritos*); — ! *interj.* ¡bu!; **-s** *s. pl.* rechifla, gritos de mofa.

boo·by [búbi] *s.* bobo, bobalicón.

book [bʊk] *s.* libro; **The book** la Biblia; **cash** — libro de caja; **memorandum** — libreta; **on the -s** cargado en cuenta; **to keep -s** llevar los libros o la contabilidad *v.* inscribir, asentar (*en un libro*); **to** — **passage** reservar pasaje.

book·case [bʊ́kkes] *s.* estante, estantería, armario para libros.

book·end [bʊ́kɛnd] *s.* apoyalibros, sujetalibros.

book·keep·er [bʊ́kkipɚˑ] *s.* tenedor de libros, contador.

book·keep·ing [bʊ́kkipɪŋ] *s.* teneduría de libros, contabilidad; **double entry** — partida doble.

book·let [bʊ́klɛt] *s.* librillo, librito, cuaderno, folleto.

book·sel·ler [bʊ́ksɛlɚˑ] *s.* librero.

book·shelf [bʊ́kʃɛlf] *s.* estante, repisa para libros.

book·shop [bʊ́kʃɑp] *s.* librería.

book·store [bʊ́kstor] *s.* librería.

boom [bum] *s.* (*noise*) estampido; (*increase*) alza, auge (*en el mercado o bolsa*); bonanza, prosperidad momentánea; *v.* rugir, resonar, hacer estampido; prosperar, medrar, florecer, estar en bonanza; fomentar.

boon [bun] *s.* don; bendición, gracia, favor; *adj.* jovial, congenial.

boon·dog·gle [búndagl] *s.* proyecto inútil y costoso.

boor [bʊr] *s.* patán, hombre zafio o grosero.

boor·ish [búrɪʃ] *adj.* grosero, zafio.

boost [bust] *s.* empuje, empujón (*de abajo arriba*); — **in prices** alza o auge de precios; *v.* empujar, alzar, levantar; hacer subir; (*advocate*) fomentar, promover.

boost·er [bústɚˑ] *s.* aumentador; (*rocket*) cohete de lanzamiento; (*electronics*) amplificador.

boot [but] *s.* bota, calzado; **to** — por añadidura, de ganancia, *Méx.* de pilón, *Ven.* de ñapa; *Ríopl.*,

Andes de yapa (*llapa*); *v.* dar un puntapié; **to** — **out** echar a puntapiés, echar a patadas.

boot·black [bútblæk] *s.* limpiabotas.

booth [buθ] *s.* casilla, puesto.

boot·leg·ger [bútlegɚˑ] *s.* contrabandista (*de licores*).

boot·lick·er [bútlɪkɚˑ] *s.* servilón, zalamero.

boo·ty [búti] *s.* botín, saqueo.

bo·rax [bóræks] *s.* bórax.

bor·der [bórdɚˑ] *s.* borde, margen, orilla; orla, franja; ribete; frontera; *v.* ribetear, guarnecer (*el borde*); orlar; **to** — **on** (*o* **upon**) lindar con, confinar con; rayar en; **it -s on madness** raya en locura.

bor·der·ing [bórdɚ·ɪŋ] *adj.* limítrofe.

bor·der·line [bórdɚ·laɪn] *adj.* fronterizo; indefinido.

bore [bor] *s.* taladro, barreno; agujero (*hecho con taladro*); calibre (*de un cañón, cilindro, etc.*); persona o cosa aburrida; *v.* taladrar, horadar, barrenar; aburrir, fastidiar; *pert. de* to bear.

bored [bord] *adj.* cansado, aburrido; *p.p. de* to bore.

bore·dom [bórdəm] *s.* aburrimiento, tedio, hastío fastidio.

bo·ric ac·id [bórɪk ǽsəd] *a.* ácido bórico.

bor·ing [bórɪŋ] *adj.* aburrido, fastidioso, tedioso.

born [bɔrn] *p.p. de* to bear & *adj.* nacido; innato; **to be** — nacer.

borne [bɔrn] *p.p.* to bear.

bo·ron [bóran] *s.* boro.

bor·ough [bɝ·o] *s.* villa; distrito de municipio.

bor·row [bɔ́ro] *v.* pedir prestado; tomar prestado; tomar fiado.

bor·row·er [bɔ́rəwɚˑ] *s.* el que pide prestado; prestatario.

bos·om [búzəm] *s.* seno, pecho, corazón; (*shirt*) pechera (*de camisa*); **in the** — **of the family** en el seno de la familia; *adj.* querido; — **friend** amigo íntimo.

boss [bɔs] *s.* jefe; patrón; mayoral, capataz; *Am.* gamonal; **political** — cacique político; *v.* mandar, dominar, dirigir.

boss·y [bɔ́si] *adj.* mandón, autoritario.

bo·tan·i·cal [bətǽnɪkl] *adj.* botánico.

bot·a·ny [bátn̩i] *s.* botánica.

botch [bátʃ] *s.* chapucería.

both [boθ] *adj. & pron.* ambos, entrambos, los dos; — **this and that** tanto esto como aquello; — **of them** ambos, ellos dos, los dos; — (**of**) **his friends** sus dos amigos, ambos amigos; — **-to- blame-clause** cláusula de responsabilidad mútua.

both·er [báðɚˑ] *s.* molestia; fastidio; incomodidad, enfado; *v.* molestar(se); fastidiar, enfadar; incomodar; estorbar.

both·er·some [báðɚ·səm] *adj.* molesto.

bot·tle [bátl] *s.* botella; *v.* embotellar.

bot·tle·neck [bátlnɛk] *s.* embotellamiento; gollete; cuello de botella; factor que impide.

bot·tom [bátəm] *s.* fondo; base; fundamento; (*naval*) casco, barco; asiento (*de silla*); **to be at the** — **of the class** ser el último de la clase; **what is at the** — **of all this?** ¿qué hay en el fondo de todo esto?

bou·doir [budwár] *s.* tocador.

bough [baʊ] *s.* rama.

bought [bɔt] *pret. & p.p. de* to buy.

bouil·lon [búljɑn] *s.* caldo.

boul·der [bóldɚˑ] *s.* peña, roca, guijarro grande, pedrusco.

boul·e·vard [búləvard] *s.* bulevar.

bounce [baʊns] *s.* bote, rebote (*de una pelota*); salto, brinco; *v.* hacer saltar; saltar, brincar; botar; echar, arrojar (*a alguien*); echar, despedir de un empleo.

bounc·er [baʊnsɚˑ] *s.* apagabroncas.

bound [baʊnd] *s.* (*jump*) salto, brinco; (*bounce*)

bote, rebote; (*limit*) límite, confín; *adj.* ligado; confinado; obligado; ceñido; encuadernado; **to be — for** ir para, ir con rumbo a; **to be — up in one's work** estar absorto en su trabajo; **it is — to happen** es seguro que sucederá; **I am — to do it** estoy resuelto a hacerlo; *v.* botar, resaltar; saltar, brincar; (*limit*) limitar; ceñir, cercar; *pret. & p.p.* **de to bind.**

bound·a·ry [báundərɪ] *s.* límite, linde; confín; frontera.

bound·less [báundlɪs] *adj.* ilimitado, sin límite, sin término.

boun·ti·ful [báʊntəfəl] *adj.* generoso, liberal; abundante.

boun·ty [báʊntɪ] *s.* larguez, generosidad; don, favor, gracia; premio, recompensa; subvención, prima.

bou·quet [buké] *s.* ramillete, ramo de flores; aroma, fragancia.

bour·geois [burʒwá.] *adj. & s.* burgués.

bout [baʊt] *s.* combate, lucha, contienda, asalto; **a — of pneumonia** un ataque de pulmonía.

bow [baʊ] *s.* (*inclination*) reverencia; inclinación, saludo; (*of a ship*) proa; *v.* hacer una reverencia, inclinarse (*para saludar*); someterse; **to — one's head** inclinar la cabeza **-ed down** agobiado.

bow [bo] *s.* arco (*para tirar flechas*); arco (*de violín*); curva; lazo, moño (*de cintas*); **bow-legged** *adj.* patizambo, patituerto; *v.* arquear; tocar (*un instrumento*) con arco.

bow·els [báʊəlz] *s. pl.* intestinos; entrañas; tripas.

bow·er [báʊɚ] *s.* enramada, ramada, glorieta.

bowl [bol] *s.* cuenco; tazón; jícara; (*game*) boliche, bola; **wash —** palangana, lavamanos; **-s** juego de bolos; *v.* bolear, jugar a los bolos, jugar al boliche.

box [bɑks] *s.* caja; estuche; palco de teatro; casilla; compartimiento; bofetada; **— car** furgón; **— office** taquilla; **— seat** asiento de palco; *v.* encajonar; meter en una caja; abofetear; boxear.

box·er [bɑ́ksɚ] *s.* boxeador, pugilista.

box·ing [bɑ́ksɪŋ] *s.* boxeo, pugilato.

boy [bɔɪ] *s.* niño; muchacho; mozo.

boy·cott [bɔ́ɪka.t] *v.* boicotear; *s.* boicoteo.

boy·hood [bɔ́ɪhʊd] *s.* niñez; mocedad, juventud.

boy·ish [bɔ́ɪɪʃ] *adj.* pueril; juvenil; aniñado.

brace [bres] *s.* traba; tirante; apoyo, refuerzo; corchete ({}); **carpenter's —** berbiquí; *v.* trabar, apoyar, reforzar; (*support*) asegurar; estimular, fortalecer; **to — up** animarse, cobrar ánimo.

brace·let [bréslɪt] *s.* brazalete, pulsera.

brack·et [brǽkɪt] *s.* ménsula, soporte, sostén; categoría; repisa; **-s** paréntesis cuadrados; *v.* colocar entre paréntesis; unir; agrupar.

brag [bræg] *s.* jactancia; *v.* jactarse (de); hacer alarde de.

brag·gart [brǽgɚt] *ajd. & s.* jactancioso, fanfarrón; matamoros, matamoscas.

braid [bred] *s.* trenza; galón, trencilla; *v.* trenzar; galonear, guarnecer con galones.

brain [bren] *s.* cerebro; seso; **to rack one's -s** devanarse los sesos, romperse la cabeza; *v.* saltar la tapa de los sesos; **— trust** [bréntrʌst] *s.* grupo de consejeros expertos; **— washing** [brénwɔʃɪŋ] *s.* lavado cerebral.

brake [brek] *s.* freno; *Ven., Col., Cuba* retranca; *Méx., Ríopl., C.A., Carib.* garrote; **— lining** forro de freno; **— shoe** zapata de freno; **— drum** tambor de freno; **— fluid** flúido de freno; **to apply the -s** frenar; *v.* frenar, enfrenar; *Ven., Col.* retrancar; *Méx., Ríopl., C.A., Carib.* dar garrote.

brake·man [brékmən] *s.* guardafrenos, *Ven., Col.*

retranquero, *Méx., Ríopl., C.A., Carib.* garrotero.

bram·ble [brǽmbl] *s.* zarza, breña.

bran [bræn] *s.* salvado.

branch [bræntʃ] *s.* rama (*de árbol*); gajo; ramo (*de la ciencia*); sucursal; bifurcación; sección; dependencia; tributario (*de un río*); ramificación; **— railway** ramal; *v.* ramificarse; bifurcarse.

brand [brænd] *s.* (*make*) marca; marca de fábrica; marca registrada; hechura; (*cattle mark*) hierro; *Ríopl., Méx.* fierro (*de marcar*); estigma; **brand-new** nuevecito, flamante, acabado de hacer o comprar; *v.* marcar; herrar, marcar (*con hierro candente*); difamar; **to — as** motejar de.

bran·dish [brǽndɪʃ] *v.* blandir; *s.* floreo, molinete.

bran·dy [brǽndɪ] *s.* aguardiente; coñac.

brash [bræʃ] *adj.* insolente; impetuoso; temerario.

brass [bræs] *s.* (*metal*) latón, bronce; (*actitud*) desfachatez, descaro; **-es** utensilios de latón; instrumentos músicos de metal; **— band** murga.

bras·siere [brəzír] *s.* corpiño, sostén (*para ceñir los pechos*).

brat [bræt] *s.* mocoso.

bra·va·do [brəvádo] *s.* bravata; jactancia.

brave [brev] *adj.* bravo, valiente, valeroso; *v.* arrostrar; desafiar, hacer frente a.

brav·er·y [brévərɪ] *s.* valor, valentía.

brawl [brɔl] *v.* reyerta, pendencia, riña; alboroto; *v.* armar una pendencia, alborotar, reñir.

bray [bre] *s.* rebuzno; *v.* rebuznar.

bra·zen [brézn] *adj.* bronceado; de bronce; de latón; descarado, desvergonzado.

bra·zier [brezjɚ] *s.* brasero; cazuela para perdigar.

breach [britʃ] *s.* (*opening*) brecha, abertura; (*infraction*) infracción; rompimiento; **— of contract** incumplimiento de contrato; **— of faith** abuso de confianza; **— of promise** violación de un compromiso; **— of peace** perturbación del orden público; *v.* abrir brecha.

bread [brɛd] *s.* pan; **— box** caja para pan; **— line** cola del pan; *v. Méx., C.A., Carib.* empanizar; *Ríopl., Ch.* empanar.

breadth [brɛdθ] *s.* anchura, ancho; extensión; amplitud.

break [brek] *s.* rompimiento; rotura; (*pause*) interrupción, pausa; bajón (*en la bolsa o mercado*); **to have a bad (good) —** tener mala (buena) suerte; **to make a bad —** cometer un disparate; *v.* romper(se), quebrantar(se), quebrar(se); amansar; domar; arruinar; **to — away** fugarse, escaparse; **— even** salir a mano; **to — into** forzar la entrada en, allanar (*una morada*); **to — loose** escaparse, desprenderse, soltarse; **to — out** estallar (*una guerra*); **to — out of prison** escaparse de la cárcel; **to — a promise** faltar a la palabra; **to — up** desmenuzar, despedazar; disolver; perturbar.

break·a·ble [brékəbl] *adj.* quebradizo.

break·down [brékdaʊn] *s.* parado imprevista; análisis, (*automobile*) avería, pane; *v.* descomponerse.

break·er [brékɚ] *s.* rompiente (*ola*); **law —** infractor.

break·fast [brékfəst] *s.* desayuno; **to eat —** tomar el desayuno; *v.* desayunarse.

break·through [brékθru] *s.* adelanto repentino; brecha.

break·wa·ter [brékwɔtɚ] *s.* rompeolas, malecón.

breast [brɛst] *s.* pecho; seno; teta; pechuga (*de ave*); **to make a clean — of it** confesarlo todo.

breath [brɛθ] *s.* aliento; resuello; respiro; soplo, hálito; **in the same —** al mismo instante, con el mismo aliento; **out of —** sin aliento, jadeante;

under one's — en voz baja, entre dientes.

breathe [bri ð] *v.* respirar; resollar; tomar aliento; exhalar; **to — into** infundir; **he -ed his last** exhaló el último suspiro; **he did not — a word** no dijo palabra.

breath·less [bɛθlɪs] *adj.* jadeante; sin aliento.

breath·tak·ing [brɛθtekɪŋ] *adj.* conmovedor; emocionante.

bred [brɛd] *pret. & p.p. de* **to breed.**

breech·es [brítʃɪz] *s. pl.* bragas, calzones; **riding —** pantalones de montar.

breed [brid] *s.* casta, raza; ralea, especie; *v.* criar; procrear, engendrar; educar; producirse; multiplicarse.

breed·er [brídɚ] *s.* criador; animal de cría.

breed·ing [brídɪŋ] *s.* cría, crianza; educación, modales.

breeze [briz] *s.* brisa, vientecillo.

breez·y [brízɪ] *adj.* airoso, ventilado; refrescado (*por la brisa*); animado, vivaz; **it is —** hace brisa.

breth·ren [brɛðrɪn] *s. pl.* hermanos (*los fieles de una iglesia o los miembros de una sociedad*).

brev·i·ty [brɛvətɪ] *s.* brevedad.

brew [bru] *s.* cerveza; mezcla; *v.* fermentar, hacer (*licores*); preparar (*té*); fomentar, tramar; fabricar cerveza; amenazar (*una tormenta, calamidad etc.*).

brew·er·y [brúərɪ] *s.* cervecería, fábrica de cerveza.

bri·ar, bri·er [bráɪɚ] *s.* zarza; rosal silvestre.

bribe [braɪb] *s.* soborno, cohecho; *Méx.* mordida; *v.* sobornar, cohechar.

brib·er·y [bráɪbərɪ] *s.* soborno, choecho.

brick [brɪk] *s.* ladrillo; ladrillos; *v.* enladrillar.

brick·bat [bríkbæt] *s.* pedazo de ladrillo; insulto.

bri·dal [bráɪdl] *adj.* nupcial; de bodas; de novia; **— dress** vestido de novia.

bride [braɪd] *s.* novia, desposada.

bride·groom [bráɪdgrum] *s.* novio, desposado.

brides·maid [bráɪdzmed] *s.* madrina de boda.

bridge [brɪdʒ] *a.* puente; caballete de la nariz; **draw —** puente levadizo; **suspension —** puente colgante; *v.* tender un puente; **to — a gap** llenar un vacío; salvar un obstáculo.

bri·dle [bráɪdl] *s.* brida, freno de caballo; freno, restricción; **— path** camino de harradura; *v.* embridar, enfrenar; reprimir, subyugar; erguirse, erguir la cabeza.

brief [brif] *adj.* breve, corto, conciso; *s.* sumario, resumen; (*report*) informe, memorial; breve apostólico; **to hold a — for** abogar por; **-ly** *adv.* brevemente; en resumen, en breve; *v.* dar instrucciones, aleccionar.

brief·case [brífkes] *s.* portapapeles, cartera grande.

brief·ing [brifɪŋ] *s.* reunión preparatoria.

bri·gade [brɪgéd] *s.* brigada.

bright [braɪt] *adj.* (*light*) brillante, claro, luciente; radiante; (*smart*) inteligente; (*cheerful*) alegre; listo, vivo; **— color** color subido.

bright·en [bráɪtn] *v.* abrillantar, pulir, dar lustre; avivar(se), alegrar(se); animar(se); aclararse, despejarse (*el cielo*).

bright·ness [bráɪtnɪs] *s.* brillo, lustre, esplendor; claridad; viveza, agudeza, inteligencia.

bril·liance [brɪljəns] *s.* brillantez, brillo; lustre; resplandor.

bril·liant [brɪljənt] *adj.* brillante; resplandeciente; espléndido; (*smart*) talentoso; *s.* brillante; diamante.

brim [brɪm] *s.* borde, margen, orilla; (*hat*) ala; **to fill to the —** llenar o arrasar hasta el borde; **to be filled to the —** estar hasta los topes; estar de bote en bote; *v.* **to — over** rebosar.

brine [braɪn] *s.* salmuera.

bring [brɪŋ] *v.* traer; llevar; ocasionar, causar; **to — about** producir, efectuar, ocasionar; **to — down** bajar; **to — forth** dar a luz; producir; **— back** devolver; **to — to** resucitar; **to — up** criar, educar; **to — up a subject** traer a discusión un asunto.

brink [brɪŋk] *s.* borde, orilla, margen; **on the — of** al borde de.

brisk [brɪsk] *adj.* vivo, animado; fuerte; rápido; **-ly** *adv.* aprisa; fuerte.

bris·tle [brɪsl] *s.* creda; *v.* erizar(se); **to — with** estar erizado (*o* lleno) de.

bris·tly [brɪstɪ] *adj.* serdoso; erizado.

Brit·ish [brítɪʃ] *adj.* británico; **the —** los ingleses.

brit·tle [brítl] *adj.* quebradizo; frágil.

broach [brotʃ] *v.* tracer a colación, comenzar a hablar de (*un asunto*).

broad [brɔd] *adj.* ancho; amplio, vasto, extenso; tolerante; **— hint** insinuación clara; **in — daylight** en pleno día; **broad-minded** tolerante; de amplias miras.

broad·cast [brɔdkæst] *s.* radiodifusión, difusión, emisión; transmisión; **broadcasting** radiodifusión; **— station** emisora, radiodifusora; *v.* difundir; radiodifundir, radiar, emitir; propalar, perifonear.

broad·cloth [brɔdklɔθ] *s.* paño fino de algodón o de lana.

broad jump [brɔddʒəmp] *s.* salto de longitud.

broad·side [brɔdsaɪd] *s.* (*guns*) andanada; (*announcement*) hoja suelta de propaganda.

bro·cade [brokéd] *s.* brocado.

brochure [broʃúr] *s.* folleto.

broil [brɔil] *v.* asar(se).

broke [brok] *pret. de* **to break;** *adj.* quebrado, arruinado; pelado, sin dinero; **to go —** quebrar, arruinarse.

bro·ken [brókən] *p.p. de* **to break** *& adj.* roto; rompido; quebrado; quebrantado; arruinado; abatido; **— English** inglés champurrado o champurreado; inglés mal pronunciado.

bro·ker [brókɚ] *s.* corredor, agente; bolsista; comisionista; **money —** cambista, corredor de cambio; **brokerage** corretaje.

bro·mide [brómaɪd] *s.* bromuro.

bro·mine [brómin] *s.* bromo.

bron·chi·tis [brɑŋkáɪtɪs] *s.* bronquitis.

bron·co, bron·cho [brɑŋko] *s.* potro o caballo bronco, *Ríopl.* redomón; **— buster** domador.

bronze [brɑnz] *s.* bronce; color de bronce; *v.* broncear.

brooch [brutʃ] *s.* broche (*alfiler de pecho*).

brood [brud] *s.* pollada; nidada; cría; casta; *v.* empollar; encobar; **to — over** cavilar.

brook [bruk] *s.* arroyuelo, riachuelo, *C.A., Col., Ven.* quebrada; caño; *Méx., Ríopl.* arroyo, *Col., Cuba* cañada; *v.* tolerar, aguantar.

broom [brum] *s.* escoba; retama (*arbusto*); **— stick** palo o mango de escoba.

broth [brɔθ] *s.* caldo.

broth·er [brʌðɚ] *s.* hermano; cofrade.

broth·er·hood [brʌðɚhud] *s.* hermandad; fraternidad; cofradía.

broth·er-in-law [brʌðɚrɪnlɔ] *s.* cuñado.

broth·er·ly [brʌðɚlɪ] *adj.* fraternal.

brought [brɔt] *pret. & p.p. de* **to bring.**

brow [braʊ] *s.* ceja; frente.

brown [braʊn] *adj.* moreno; café; castaño; pardo oscuro; tostado; *v.* tostar(se).

browse [braʊz] *v.* hojear; ramonear; pacer, pastar (*el ganado*).

bruise [bruz] *s.* magulladura, cardenal, magullón, contusión; *v.* magullar(se); estropear(se).

bru·net, bru·nette [brunέt] *adj.* moreno, trigueño.

brunt [brʌnt] *s.* fuerza (*de un golpe o ataque*); **the — of the battle** lo más reñido del combate.

brush [brʌʃ] *s.* (*tooth, clothes*) cepillo; (*paint, shaving*) brocha; (*artist's*) pincel; (*vegetation*) matorral; (*contact*) roce; encuentro; *v.* cepillar, acepillar; rozar; **to — aside** desechar, echar a un lado; **to — up** cepillarse; repasar (*una materia, una técnica, etc.*).

brush·wood [brʌʃwʊd] *s.* broza; maleza, matorral, zarzal.

brusque [brʌsk] *adj.* brusco.

Brus·sels sprouts [brʌsls sprauts] *s.* coles de Bruselas.

bru·tal [brútl] *adj.* brutal, bruto.

bru·tal·i·ty [brutǽlətɪ] *s.* brutalidad.

brute [brut] *s.* bruto, bestia; *adj.* bruto, brutal; bestial.

bub·ble [bʌbl] *s.* burbuja; borbollón; ampolla; *v.* borbotar; hacer espuma; bullir; **to — over with joy** rebosar de gozo.

bub·ble gum [bʌbl gʌm] *s.* chicle hinchable; chicle de globo.

buck [bʌk] *s.* (*goat*) macho cabrío, cabrón; (*deer*) gamo; macho (*del ciervo, antílope, etc.*); (*act*) corveta, respingo (*de un caballo*); embestida; — **private** soldado raso; **to pass the —** *Ríopl., Andes* pasar el fardo; *v.* cabriolear, respingar; embestir; encabritarse; bregar con (*el viento*); **to — up** cobrar ánimo; **the horse -ed the rider** el caballo tiró al jinete.

buck·et [bʌkɪt] *s.* cubo, cubeta, balde.

buck·le [bʌkl] *s.* hebilla; *v.* abrochar con hebilla; doblarse; abollarse; **to — down** aplicarse con empeño a; **to — with** luchar con.

buck·shot [bʌkʃɑt] *s.* posta, perdigón.

buck·skin [bʌkskɪn] *s.* badana; ante.

buck·wheat [bʌkhwit] *s.* trigo sarraceno.

bud [bʌd] *s.* botón, yema; capullo, pimpollo; retoño; *v.* echar botones o retoños; florecer.

bud·dy [bʌdɪ] *s.* camarada, compañero.

budge [bʌdʒ] *v.* mover(se), menear(se), bullir.

bud·get [bʌdʒɪt] *s.* presupuesto.

buff [bʌf] *s.* piel de ante o búfalo; color de ante; pulidor; **blindman's —** juego de la gallina ciega; *v.* pulir, pulimentar.

buf·fa·lo [bʌflo] *s.* búfalo.

buff·er [bʌfɚ] *s.* (*computer*) buffer, amortiguador, almacén temporal.

buf·fet [bʌfé] *s.* aparador; repostería; mostrador para refrescos; fonda de estación.

buf·fet·ing [bʌfɑtɪŋ] *s.* golpeteo, bataneo.

buf·foon [bʌfún] *s.* bufón; payaso.

bug [bʌg] *s.* insecto; bicho; microbio.

bug·gy [bʌgɪ] *s.* cochecillo.

bu·gle [bjúgl] *s.* clarín; corneta; trompeta.

build [bɪld] *s.* estructura; talle, forma, hechura; *v.* edificar, construir; fabricar; **to — up one's health** reconstituir su salud.

build·er [bɪldɚ] *s.* constructor.

build·ing [bɪldɪŋ] *s.* edificio; construcción; — **and loan association** sociedad de préstamos.

build-up [bɪldʌp] *s.* refuerzo paulatino.

built [bɪlt] *pret. & p.p. de* **to build.**

bulb [bʌlb] *s.* (*plant*) bulbo; planta bulbosa; **electric light —** bombilla, bujía eléctrica, ampolla, *Méx., C.A., Andes* foco; *Ríopl.* bombita.

bulge [bʌldʒ] *s.* bulto; protuberancia; panza; *v.* abultar; combarse.

bulg·y [bʌldʒɪ] *adj.* abultado.

bulk [bʌlk] *s.* bulto, volumen; masa; **the — of the army** el grueso del ejército; **in —** suelto, en grueso.

bulk·y [bʌlkɪ] *adj.* abultado, voluminoso, grueso.

bull [bʊl] *s.* toro; — **market** mercado alcista; **Papal —** bula; — **fight** corrida de toros; *adj.* taurino; — **fighter** torero; **bull's-eye** centro del blanco; tiro perfecto; **bullish** en alza.

bull·dog [bʊldɔg] *s.* perro dogo, perro de presa.

bull·doz·er [bʊldozɚ] *s.* topadora; buldózer.

bul·let [bʊlɪt] *s.* bala.

bul·le·tin [bʊlətɪn] *s.* boletín; — **board** tablilla para fijar anuncios o avisos.

bull·frog [bʊlfrɔg] *s.* rana grande.

bull·head·ed [bʊlhέdɪd] *adj.* terco, obstinado.

bul·lion [bʊljən] *s.* oro (*o* plata) en barras; metálico; lingotes de oro o plata.

bul·ly [bʊlɪ] *s.* pendenciero, valentón, fanfarrón, matón; *adj.* excelente, magnífico; *v.* intimidar; echar bravatas.

bul·wark [bʊlwɚk] *s.* baluarte; defensa.

bum [bʌm] *s.* holgazán, vagabundo; gorrón; borracho; **to go on a —** irse de juerga; *adj.* malo, mal hecho, de ínfima calidad; inútil, inservible; **to feel —** estar indispuesto; *v.* holgazanear; vivir de gorra.

bum·ble·bee [bʌmblbi] *s.* abejorro, abejón.

bump [bʌmp] *s.* (*blow*) tope, choque; golpe; (*lump*) chichón; abolladura; hinchazón, protuberancia; *v.* topar, topetear; chocar; abollar; **to — along** zarandearse, ir zarandeándose; **to — off** derribar; matar.

bump·er [bʌmpɚ] *s.* parachoques, defensa; tope; *adj.* grande, excelente; — **crop** cosecha abundante.

bun [bʌn] *s.* bollo (*de pan*).

bunch [bʌntʃ] *s.* manojo, puñado; racimo (*de uvas, plátanos, etc.*); grupo; — **of flowers** ramillete de flores; *v.* juntar(se), agrupar(se).

bun·dle [bʌndl] *s.* lío, bulto, fardo, hato; haz; paquete; *v.* liar, atar; envolver; **to — up** abrigarse, taparse bien.

bun·ga·low [bʌŋgəlo] *s.* casita de un piso.

bun·gle [bʌŋgl] *v.* chapucear; estropear; echar a perder.

bun·ion [bʌnjən] *s.* juanete.

bunk [bʌŋk] *s.* litera, camilla (*fija en la pared*); embuste, tontería, paparrucha, papa.

bun·ny [bʌnɪ] *s.* conejito.

buoy [bɔɪ] *s.* boya; *v.* boyar, mantener a flote; **to — up** sostener, apoyar.

buoy·ant [bɔɪənt] *adj.* boyante, flotante; vivaz, animado, alegre.

bur·den [bɝdn] *s.* carga, peso; cuidado; gravamen; *v.* cargar; agobiar.

bur·den·some [bɝdnsəm] *adj.* gravoso; pesado.

bu·reau [bjúro] *s.* oficina; despacho; división, ramo; cómoda; **travel —** oficina de turismo; **weather —** oficina de meteorología, observatorio meteorológico.

bu·reauc·ra·cy [bjurákrəsɪ] *s.* burocracia.

bu·reau·crat [bjúrəkræt] *s.* burócrata.

bur·glar [bɝglɚ] *s.* ladrón; — **alarm** alarma contra ladrones; — **proof** a prueba de ladrones; — **deterrent** disuadeladrones.

bur·gla·ry [bɝglərɪ] *s.* robo.

bur·i·al [bέrɪəl] *s.* entierro; — **place** cementerio.

bur·lap [bɝlæp] *s.* arpillera, tela burda de cáñamo.

bur·ly [bɝlɪ] *adj.* corpulento, voluminoso, grandote.

burn [bɝn] *s.* quemadura; *v.* quemar(se); incendiar;

arder; abrasar(se).

burn·er [bɝnɚ] *s.* (*heat*) quemador; (*lamp*) mechero; (*stove*) hornilla.

bur·nish [bɝnɪʃ] *v.* bruñir; pulir; *s.* bruñido, pulimento.

burn·out [bɝnaʊt] *s.* fundición, apagón.

burnt [bɝnt] *pret. & p.p. de* **to burn.**

bur·row [bɝo] *s.* madriguera, conejera; *v.* hacer madrigueras en; escarbar; socavar, minar; esconderse.

burst [bɝst] *s.* reventón, explosión; estallido; — **of laughter** carcajada; *v.* reventar(se); abrirse; estallar; **to — into** entrar de repente; **to — into tears** prorrumpir en lágrimas; **to — with laughter** estallar o reventar de risa; *pret. & p.p. de* **to burst.**

bur·y [bɛrɪ] *v.* enterrar; sepultar; soterrar; **to be buried in thought** estar absorto, meditabundo o pensativo.

bus [bʌs] *s.* autobús, ómnibus, *Méx.* camión; *C.A.* camioneta; *Ríopl.* colectivo; *Ch.* micro; *Carib.* guagua; (*computer*) bus, conjunto de líneas.

bus·boy [bʌsbɔi] *s.* ayudante de camarero.

bush [bʊʃ] *s.* arbusto; mata; matorral; breñal; **rose — rosal; to beat around the —** andarse por las ramas.

bush·el [bʊʃəl] *s.* fanega (*medida de áridos*).

bush·ing [bʊʃɪŋ] *s.* buje.

bush·y [bʊʃɪ] *adj.* matoso, espeso; lleno de arbustos.

bus·i·ly [bɪzlɪ] *adv.* diligentemente.

busi·ness [bɪznɪs] *s.* negocio; ocupación; comercio; asunto; — **house** casa de comercio, establecimiento mercantil; — **transaction** negocio, transacción comercial; — **cycles** ciclos económicos; — **day** día hábil; — **hours** horas habiles; **to do — with** negociar con, comerciar con; **he has no — doing it** no tiene derecho a hacerlo; **not to be one's —** no concernirle a uno, no importarle a uno; **to make a — deal** hacer un trato.

busi·ness·like [bɪznɪslaɪk] *adj.* eficaz, eficiente, práctico; formal.

busi·ness·man [bɪznɪsmæn] *s.* hombre de negocios, comerciante.

bust [bʌst] *s.* busto; pecho (*de mujer*); **to go out on a —** salir o ir de parranda; *v.* reventar; quebrar; domar (*un potro*).

bus·tle [bʌsl] *s.* bulla, bullicio, trajín, alboroto; polisón (*para abultar las caderas*); *v.* bullir(se); menearse; trajinar.

bus·y [bɪzɪ] *adj.* ocupado; activo; — **body** entremetido; — **street** calle de mucho tráfico; *v.* **to — oneself** ocuparse.

but [bʌt] *conj., prep. & adv.* pero, mas; sino; menos, excepto; sólo, no . . . más que; — **for you** a no ser por Vd.; **not only . . . — also** no sólo . . . sino (que) también; **I cannot help —** no puedo menos de; **she is — a child** no es más que una niña.

bu·tane [bjutén] *s.* butano.

butch·er [bʊtʃɚ] *s.* carnicero; **-'s shop** carnicería; *v.* matar (*reses*); hacer una matanza o carnicería; destrozar.

butch·er·y [bʊtʃɚɪ] *s.* carnicería, matanza.

but·ler [bʌtlɚ] *s.* despensero, mayordomo; **-'s pantry** despensa.

butt [bʌt] *s.* culata (*de rifle*); colilla (*de cigarro*); tope; topetazo; (*animal*) cabezada; **the — of ridicule** el blanco de las burlas; *v.* topetear, embestir; **to — in** entremeterse; **to — into a conversation** meter baza, *Am.* meter su cuchara.

but·ter [bʌtɚ] *s.* manteca, mantequilla; *v.* enmantecar, untar con manteca o mantequilla.

but·ter·cup [bʌtɚkʌp] *s.* botón de oro (*flor*).

but·ter·fly [bʌtɚflaɪ] *s.* mariposa; — **stroke** brazada mariposa.

but·ter·milk [bʌtɚmɪlk] *s.* suero de mantequilla.

but·ter·scotch [bʌtɚskátʃ] *s.* confite o jarabe de azúcar y mantequilla.

but·tocks [bʌtəks] *s. pl.* nalgas, asentaderas.

but·ton [bʌtn̩] *s.* botón; — **hook** abotonador; *v.* abotonar(se).

but·ton·hole [bʌtn̩hol] *s.* ojal; *v.* hacer ojales; **to — someone** detener, demorar a uno (*charlando*).

but·tress [bʌtrɪs] *s.* contrafuerte; refuerzo, sostén; *v.* sostener, reforzar, poner contrafuerte.

buy [baɪ] *v.* comprar; **to — off** sobornar; **to — up** acaparar; **to — a pig in a poke** carrar un trato a ciegas; **to — on credit** comprar al fiado; **to — on time** comprar a plazos; **buying power** poder adquisitivo.

buy·er [baɪɚ] *s.* comprador.

buzz [bʌz] *s.* zumbido; murmullo; *v.* zumbar; murmurar; **to — the bell** tocar el timbre.

buz·zard [bʌzɚd] *s.* buitre, *Carib.* aura, *Méx., C.A.* zopilote, *Ríopl.* carancho; *Col., Andes* gallinazo.

by [baɪ] *prep.* por; cerca de; al lado de; junto a; según; — **and —** luego, pronto; — **dint of** a fuerza de; — **far** con mucho; — **night** de noche; — **the way** de paso; a propósito; entre paréntesis; — **this time** ya; a la hora de ésta; — **two o'clock** para las dos; **days gone —** días pasados.

by·gone [báɪgɔn] *adj.* pasado; let **-s be -s** lo pasado pasado, lo pasado pisado.

by·law [báɪlɔ] *s.* estatuto; reglamento.

by·line [báɪlaɪn] *s.* renglón del autor con título.

by·pass [báɪpæs] *s.* desviación.

by·path [báɪpæθ] *s.* atajo, vereda.

by·prod·uct [báɪprɑdʌkt] *s.* producto secundario o accessorio; derivado, subproducto.

by·stand·ers [báɪstændɚz] *s.* circunstantes, presentes; mirones.

byte [baɪt] (*computer*) *s.* octeto, byte.

C:c

cab [kæb] *s.* coche de alquiler; taxímetro, taxi; casilla (*de una locomotra*); — **driver** cochero; chófer.

cab·bage [kǽbɪdʒ] *s.* col, repollo, berza.

cab·in [kǽbɪn] *s.* cabaña, choza; bohío, *Méx.* jacal; *Carib.* barraca; camarote (*de buque*); **airplane —** cabina de aeroplano.

cab·i·net [kǽbənɪt] *s.* gabinete; armario; escaparate, vitrina; (*dept. heads*) gabinete.

cab·i·net·ma·ker [kǽbənɪtmékɚ] *s.* ebanista.

ca·ble [kébl] *s.* cable, amarra; cablegrama; — **address** dirección cablegráfica; — **code** clave para cablegramas; *v.* cablegrafiar.

ca·ble·gram [kéblgræm] *s.* cablegrama.

cab·man [kǽbmən] *s.* cochero; chófer.

ca·boose [kəbús] *s.* vagón de cola.

cack·le [kǽkl] *s.* cacareo; (*talk*) charla; (*laughter*) risotada; *v.* cacarear; parlotear, charlar.

cac·tus [kǽktəs] (*pl.* **cacti** [kǽktaɪ]) *s.* cacto, cactos.

cad [kæd] *s.* canalla (*m.*); malcriado.

cad·die [kǽdɪ] *s.* muchacho que lleva los palos de golf; caddy.

ca·dence [kédns] *s.* cadencia.

ca·det [kədét] *s.* cadete.

cad·mi·um [kǽdmɪəm] *s.* cadmio.

ca·fé [kəfé] *s.* café, restaurante.

caf·e·te·ri·a [kæfətírɪə] *s.* restaurante (*en donde se sirve uno mismo*).

caf·fein [kǽfɪn] *s.* cafeína.

cage [kedʒ] *s.* jaula; *v.* enjaular.

ca·jole [kədʒól] *v.* halagar para conseguir algo.

cake [kek] *s.* pastel; bizcocho; bollo; torta; *Ven., C.A., Col.* panqué (*soap*) pastilla (*de jabón*); — **of ice** témpano de hielo; *v.* apelmazarse, formar masa compacta.

cal·a·bash [kǽləbæʃ] *s.* calabaza.

ca·lam·i·ty [kəlǽmətɪ] *s.* calamidad.

cal·ci·um [kǽlsɪəm] *s.* calcio.

cal·cu·late [kǽlkjəlet] *v.* calcular; **to — on** contar con.

cal·cu·la·tion [kælkjəléʃən] *s.* cálculo; cómputo, cuenta.

cal·cu·lus [kǽlkjələs] *s.* cálculo.

cal·en·dar [kǽləndɚ] *s.* calendario, almanaque; — **year** año corriente, año civil.

calf [kæf] (*pl.* **calves** [kævz]) *s.* ternero, ternera, becerro, becerra; pantorrilla (*de la pierna*); — **skin** piel de becerro o becerrillo.

cal·i·ber [kǽləbɚ] *s.* calibre.

cal·i·co [kǽləko] *s.* calico (*tela de algodón*).

call [kɔl] *s.* (*summons*) llamada; llamamiento; (*visit*) visita; (*demand*) demanda, pedido; **within —** al alcance de la voz; *v.* llamar; gritar; hacer una visita; pasar (*lista*); **to — at a port** hacer escala en un purerto; **to — for** ir por; demandar, exigir, pedir; **to — on** visitar a; acudir a (*en busca de auxilio*); **to — to order a meeting** abrir la sesión; **to — together** convocar; **to — up on the phone** llamar por teléfono.

cal·ler [kɔ́lɚ] *s.* visita, visitante; llamador (*el que llama*).

cal·lous [kǽləs] *adj.* calloso; duro.

cal·lus [kǽləs] *s.* callo.

calm [kɑm] *s.* calma; sosiego; *adj.* calmo, tranquilo, quieto, sosegado; *v.* calmar, tranquilizar, sosegar; desenfadar; **to — down** calmarse; **-ly** *adv.* tranquilamente, con calma.

calm·ness [kámnɪs] *s.* calma, sosiego, tranquilidad.

cal·o·rie [kǽlərɪ] *s.* caloría.

cal·um·ny [kǽləmnɪ] *s.* calumnia.

cam [kæm] *s.* leva.

cam·bist [kǽmbɪst] *s.* cambista.

came [kem] *pret. de* **to come.**

cam·el [kǽml] *s.* camello.

cam·e·o [kǽmɪo] *s.* camafeo.

cam·er·a [kǽmərə] *s.* cámara fotográfica.

cam·ou·flage [kǽməflɑʒ] *s.* camuflaje; disfraz; *v.* encubrir, disfrazar.

camp [kæmp] *s.* campo, campamento; — **chair** silla de tijera; **political —** partido político; *v.* acampar.

cam·paign [kæmpén] *s.* campaña; *v.* hacer campaña; hacer propaganda.

cam·phor [kǽmfɚ] *s.* alcanfor.

cam·pus [kǽmpəs] *s.* campo (*de una universidad*).

can [kæn] *s.* lata, bote, envase; — **opener** abrelatas; *v.* envasar, enlatar; *v. defect. y aux.* (*usado sólo en las formas* **can** *y* **could**) poder, saber.

Ca·na·di·an [kənédɪən] *adj. & s.* canadiense.

ca·nal [kənǽl] *s.* canal; **irrigation —** acequia.

ca·nar·y [kənérɪ] *s.* canario.

can·cel [kǽnsl] *v.* cancelar; anular; revocar; techar.

can·cel·er [kǽnsəlɚ] *s.* matasellos.

can·cel·la·tion [kænsléʃən] *s.* cancelación; anulación; revocación.

can·cer [kǽnsɚ] *s.* cáncer.

can·de·la·brum [kændəlǽbrəm] *s.* candelabro.

can·did [kǽndɪd] *adj.* cándido, franco, sincero.

can·di·da·cy [kǽndədəsɪ] *s.* candidatura.

can·di·date [kǽndədet] *s.* candidato; aspirante.

can·dle [kǽndl] *s.* candela, vela; bujía; cirio; — **power** potencia lumínica (*en bujías*).

can·dle·stick [kǽndlstɪk] *s.* candelero; palmatoria.

can·dor [kǽndɚ] *s.* candor, sinceridad.

can·dy [kǽndɪ] *s.* dulce, confite, bombón; — **shop** confitería, dulcería; *v.* confitar, azucarar; almibarar, garapiñar; cristalizarse (*el almíbar*); **candied almonds** almendras garapiñadas.

cane [ken] *s.* caña; — **plantation** (*o* — **field**) cañaveral; *C.A.* cañal; — **chair** silla de bejuco; **sugar —** caña de azúcar; **walking —** bastón; chuzo (*de sereno*); **to beat with a —** bastonear, apalear.

ca·nine [kénaɪn] *adj.* canino, perruno.

can·ker [kǽnkɚ] *s.* úlcera, llaga (*de la boca*).

canned [kænd] *adj.* enlatado, envasado, conservado (*en lato o en vidrio*); — **goods** conservas alimenticias.

can·ner·y [kǽnərɪ] *s.* fábrica de conservas alimenticias.

can·ni·bal [kǽnəbl] *s.* caníbal.

can·non [kǽnən] *s.* cañón.

can·non·ade [kænənéd] *s.* cañoneo; *v.* cañonear.

can·not [kǽnɑt] = **can not** no puedo, no puede, no podemos, etc.

can·ny [kǽnɪ] *adj.* sagaz; astuto.

ca·noe [kənú] *s.* canoa, *Ríopl.* piragua, *Méx.* chalupa.

can·on [kǽnən] *s.* canon; ley, regla; criterio, norma; canónigo.

can·o·py [kǽnəpɪ] *s.* dosel, pabellón; (*airplane*) capota, cúpula.

can·ta·loupe [kǽntlop] *s.* melón.

can·teen [kæntín] *s.* cantina; cantimplora.

can·ton [kǽntən] *s.* cantón, región, distrito.

can·vas [kǽnvəs] *s.* lona; lienzo; toldo; cañamazo.

can·vass [kǽnvəs] *s.* inspección; escrutinio; indagación, encuesta, pesquisa; solicitación (*de votos*); *v.* examinar, escudriñar; recorrer (*un distrito solicitando algo*); hacer una encuesta; solicitar votos o pedidos comerciales.

can·yon [kǽnjən] *s.* cañón, garganta.

cap [kæp] *s.* (*head covering*) gorro, gorra, boina; *Méx.* cachucha; (*academic*) birrete; (*bottle, wheel*) tapa, tapón; (*mountain*) cima, cumbre; **percussion —** cápsula fulminante; *v.* tapar, poner tapón a; **that -s the climax** eso es el colmo.

ca·pa·bil·i·ty [kepəbíləti] *s.* capacidad, aptitud.

ca·pa·ble [képəbl] *adj.* capaz; hábil; competente.

ca·pa·cious [kəpéʃəs] *adj.* capaz, amplio, espacioso.

ca·pac·i·ty [kəpǽsətɪ] *s.* capacidad; cabida; habilidad; aptitud; **in the — of a teacher** en calidad de maestro.

cape [kep] *s.* capa; capote; cabo, promontorio.

ca·per [képɚ] *s.* cabriola; voltereta, brinco; (*food*) alcaparra; **to cut -s** cabriolar, retozar, hacer travesuras; *v.* cabriolar, retozar, juguetear, brincar.

cap·il·lar·y [kǽpɪlerɪ] *s. & adj.* capilar.

cap·i·tal [kǽpətl] *s.* capital (*f.*), ciudad principal; capital (*m.*), caudal; capitel (*de una columna*); letra mayúscula; **to make — of** sacar partido de, aprovecharse de; *adj.* capital; principal; — **investment** inversión de capital; — **gains** ganancias en bienes de capital; excelente; — **punishment** pena capital, pena de muerte.

cap·i·tal·ism [kǽpətlɪzəm] *s.* capitalismo.

cap·i·tal·ist [kǽpətlɪst] *s.* capitalista; **-ic** *adj.*

capitalista.

cap·i·tal·i·za·tion [kǽpətləzéʃən] *s.* capitalización.

cap·i·tal·ize [kǽpətlaɪz] *v.* capitalizar; sacar provecho (de); escribir con mayúscula.

cap·i·tol [kǽpətl] *s.* capitolio.

ca·pit·u·late [kəpítʃəlet] *v.* capitular.

ca·price [kəprís] *s.* capricho.

ca·pri·cious [kəpríʃəs] *adj.* caprichoso.

cap·size [kǽpsáɪz] *v.* zozobrar, volcar(se).

cap·sule [kǽpsl] *s.* cápsula.

cap·tain [kǽptɪn] *s.* capitán; *v.* capitanear, mandar; servir de capitán.

cap·ti·vate [kǽptəvet] *v.* cautivar.

cap·tive [kǽptɪv] *s.* & *adj.* cautivo, prisionero.

cap·tiv·i·ty [kæptívətɪ] *s.* cautiverio, prisión.

cap·tor [kǽptɚ] *s.* aprehensor o aprensor.

cap·ture [kǽptʃɚ] *s.* captura; aprensión; presa; toma; *v.* capturar; prender; tomar (*una ciudad*).

car [kɑr] *s.* coche, automóvil, auto, *Am.* carro; (*de ferrocarril*); camarín (*de ascensor*), ascensor, *Am.* elevador; **dining** — coche comedor; **freight** — furgón, vagón de carga.

car·a·mel [kǽrəml] *s.* caramelo.

car·at [kǽrət] *s.* quilate.

car·a·van [kǽrəvæn] *s.* caravana.

car·bol·ic [kɑrbálɪk] *adj.* carbólico.

car·bon [kárbən] *s.* carbono; — **copy** copia en papel carbón; — **paper** papel carbón; — **monoxide** monóxido de carbono; — **dioxide** dióxido de carbono.

car·bu·re·tor [kárbəretɚ] *s.* carburador.

car·cass [kárkəs] *s.* esqueleto; cuerpo descarnado, despojo; res (*muerta*); casco (*de un buque*).

card [kɑrd] *s.* (*missive*) tarjeta; (*playing*) naipe, carta; carda (*para cardar lana*); — **index** índice de fichas; **fichero**; — **sharp** fullero; **file** — ficha, papeleta; **post** — tarjeta postal; (*computer*) tarjeta, placa; **pack of -s** baraja, naipes; **to play -s** jugar a la baraja, jugar a los naipes; *v.* cardar (*lana*).

card·board [kárdbord] *s.* cartón; **fine** — cartulina.

car·di·ac [kárdɪæk] *adj.* cardiaco, cardíaco.

car·di·nal [kárdnəl] *adj.* principal, fundamental; rojo, bermellón; — **number** número cardinal; *s.* cardenal (*dignatario eclesiástico*); — **bird** cardenal.

care [kɛr] *s.* (*worry*) cuidado; aflicción; ansiedad; (*caution*) cuidado, cautela, esmero; (*responsibility*) cargo, custodia; **to take** — **of** cuidar de; *v.* tener interés (por); **to** — **about** tener interés en (*o* por); preocuparse de; importarle a uno; **to** — **for** cuidar de; estimar, tenerle cariño a; gustarle a uno; simpatizarle a uno (*una persona*); **to** — **to** querer, desear, tener ganas de; **what does he** —? ¿a él qué le importa?

ca·reen [kərín] *v.* moverse con rapidez y sin control; volcar (*un buque*).

ca·reer [kərír] *s.* carrera, profesión.

care·free [kérfri] *adj.* libre de cuidado, sin cuidados, despreocupado.

care·ful [kérfəl] *adj.* cuidadoso; esmerado; cauteloso; **to be** — tener cuidado; **-ly** *adv.* cuidadosamente, con cuidado; con esmero.

care·ful·ness [kérfəlnɪs] *s.* cuidado; esmero; cautela.

care·less [kérlɪs] *adj.* descuido; falta de esmero; desaliño; negligencia.

ca·ress [kərɛ́s] *s.* caricia; *v.* acariciar.

care·tak·er [kértekɚ] *s.* cuidador, guardián, vigilante, celador.

car·fare [kárfɛr] *s.* pasaje de tranvía.

car·go [kárgo] *s.* carga, cargamento; flete.

car·i·ca·ture [kǽrɪkətʃɚ] *s.* caricatura; *v.* caricaturar

o caricaturizar.

car·load [kárlod] *s.* furgonada, vagonada, carga de un furgón o vagón.

car·nal [kárnl] *adj.* carnal.

car·na·tion [kɑrnéʃən] *s.* clavel; color encarnado o rosado.

car·ni·val [kárnəvl] *s.* carnaval; fiesta, holgorio; feria, verbena

car·niv·o·rous [kɑrnívərəs] *adj.* carnívoro, carnicero.

car·ol [kǽrəl] *s.* villancico; **Christmas** — villancico de Navidad; *v.* cantar villancicos; celebrar con villancicos.

car·om [kǽrəm] *s.* carambola; rebote.

ca·rouse [kəráuz] *v.* andar de parranda, *Ríopl.*, *Ch.* andar de farra; embriagarse.

car·pen·ter [kárpəntɚ] *s.* carpintero.

car·pen·try [kárpəntrɪ] *s.* carpintería.

car·pet [kárpɪt] *s.* alfombra; **small** — tapete; *v.* tapizar.

car·pet·bag·ger [kárpətbægɚ] explotador oportunista.

car·port [kárport] *s.* cobertizo.

car·riage [kǽrɪdʒ] *s.* carruaje, coche; acarreo, transporte; porte; — **paid** porte pagado; **good** — buen porte, garbo, manera airosa.

car·ri·er [kǽrɪɚ] *s.* portador; mensajero; carretero, trajinante; transportador; *Méx.* cargador; **airplane** — portaaviones; **disease** — transmisor de gérmenes contagiosos; **mail** — cartero.

car·rot [kǽrət] *s.* zanahoria.

car·ry [kǽrɪ] *v.* llevar; (*cart*) acarrear, transportar; *Am.* cargar; sostener (*una carga*); traer consigo; ganar, lograr (*una elección, un premio, etc.*); **to** — **away** llevarse; cargar con; entusiasmar, encantar; **to** — **on** continuar; no parar; **to** — **oneself well** andar derecho, airoso, garboso; **to** — **out** llevar a cabo, realizar; sacar; **carried forward** suma y sigue; **carry-over** sobrante, saldo anterior; **carrying charges** cargo mensual, gastos afines.

cart [kɑrt] *s.* carro, carreta, vagoncillo; *v.* acarrear.

cart·age [kártɪdʒ] *s.* carretaje, acarreo.

cart·er [kártɚ] *s.* carretero; acarreador.

car·ton [kártn] *s.* caja de cartón.

car·toon [kartún] *s.* caricatura.

car·toon·ist [kartúnɪst] *s.* caricaturista.

car·tridge [kártrɪdʒ] *s.* cartucho; — **belt** cartuchera, canana; — **box** cartuchera; — **shell** cápsula.

carve [kɑrv] *v.* tallar; labrar; cincelar; esculpir; trinchar, tajar (*carne*).

carv·er [kárvɚ] *s.* trinchador; trinchante (*cuchillo*); entallador, escultor.

carv·ing [kárvɪŋ] *s.* talla, obra de escultura, entalladura; — **knife** trinchante.

cas·cade [kæskéd] *s.* cascada, salto de agua.

case [kes] *s.* (*instance*) caso; (*box*) caja; (*pillow*) funda, cubierta; (*scabbard*) vaina; **window** — marco de ventana; **in** — **that** caso que, en caso que, dado que; **in any** — en todo caso; **just in** — por si acaso; — **work** trabajo con casos.

case·ment [késmənt] *s.* puerta ventana.

cash [kæʃ] *s.* dinero contante; en efectivo; — **advance** anticipo en efectivo; — **and carry** al contado y transporte cuenta del comprador; — **box** cofre; — **payment** pago al contado; — **on delivery (c.o.d.)** contra reembolso, cóbrese al entregar; — **register** caja registradora (*de dinero*); **to pay** — pagar al contado; — **assets** activo en efectivo, *Arg.* activos disponibles; — **voucher** comprobante; *v.* cambiar, cobrar (*un cheque*).

ca·shew [kǽʃju] *s.* anacardo, marañón.

cash·ier [kæʃír] *s.* cajero; **'s check** cheque de caja, de gerencia.

cask [kæsk] s. tonel, barril, cuba.
cas·ket [kǽskɪt] s. ataúd; **jewel** — joyero, cofrecillo.
cas·se·role [kǽsərol] s. cacerola.
cas·sette [kəsɛ́t] s. carrete pequeña de cinta magnetofónica; pequeña grabadora.
cas·sock [kǽsək] s. sotana.
cast [kæst] s. (throw) tirada (al pescar); (form) molde; matiz; apariencia; defecto (del ojo); (theater) reparto (de papeles dramáticos); actores; — **iron** hierro fundido o colado; v. echar; tirar; arrojar; lanzar; moldear; repartir (papeles dramáticos); escoger (para un papel dramático); **to** — **a ballot** votar; **to** — **a statue in bronze** vaciar una estatua en bronce; **to** — **about** buscar; hacer planes; **to** — **aside** desechar; **to** — **lots** echar suertes; **to be** — **down** estar abatido; pret. & p.p. de **to cast.**
cas·ta·nets [kæstənɛts] s. pl. castañuelas.
caste [kæst] s. casta; **to lose** — perder el prestigio social.
Cas·til·ian [kæstíljən] s. & adj. castellano.
cas·tle [kǽsl] s. castillo; alcázar; fortaleza; torre, roque (en ajedrez).
cas·tor oil [kǽstɚɔil] s. aceite de ricino.
cas·trate [kǽstret] v. capar, castrar.
cas·u·al [kǽʒuəl] adj. casual; accidental.
cas·u·al·ty [kǽʒuəltɪ] s. baja o pérdida (en el ejército); accidente.
cat [kæt] s. gato; gata.
cat·a·log [kǽtlɔg] s. catálogo; v. catalogar.
cat·a·lyst [kǽtəlist] s. catalizador.
cat·a·ract [kǽtərækt] s. catarata.
ca·tarrh [kətár] s. catarro.
ca·tas·tro·phe [kətǽstrəfɪ] s. catástrofe.
catch [kætʃ] s. presa, botin; presa; pestillo (de la puerta); trampa; cogida (de la pelota); — **phrase** frase llamativa; — **question** pregunta tramposa; **he is a good** — es un buen partido; **to play** — jugar a la pelota; v. coger; prender; asir; alcanzar; enganchar; comprender; ser contagioso, pegarse; **to** — **a glimpse of** vislumbrar; **to** — **cold** coger un resfriado, resfriarse; **to** — **on** comprender, caer en la cuenta; **to** — **one's eye** llamarle a uno la atención; **to** — **sight of** avistar; **to** — **unaware** sorprender, coger desprevenido; **to** — **up with** alcanzar a, emparejarse con.
catch·er [kǽtʃɚ] s. cogedor, agarrador; parador, (baseball) cácher o receptor (en béisbol).
catch·ing [kǽtʃɪŋ] adj. pegajoso, contagioso; (attractive) atractivo.
cat·e·chism [kǽtəkɪzəm] s. catecismo.
cat·e·go·ry [kǽtəgorɪ] s. categoría.
ca·ter [kétɚ] v.— surtir, abastecer, proveer los alimentos (para banquetes, fiestas, etc.) **to** — **to** proveer a las necesidades o al gusto de; **to** — **to the taste of** halagar el gusto de.
cat·er·pil·lar [kǽtəpilɚ] s. oruga; — **tractor** tractor.
ca·the·dral [kəθídrəl] s. catedral.
cath·ode [kǽθod] s. cátodo; — **rays** rayos catódicos.
Cath·o·lic [kǽθəlɪk] s. & adj. católico.
Ca·thol·i·cism [kəθáləsizəm] s. catolicismo.
cat·sup [kǽtsəp] s. salsa de tomate.
cat·tle [kǽtl] s. ganado, ganado vacuno; — **range** potrero; — **raiser** ganadero, Ríopl. estanciero; — **raising** ganadería; — **ranch** hacienda de ganado, Méx., C.A. rancho, Ríopl. estancia; Ven., Col. hato.
caught [kɔt] pret. & p.p. de **to catch.**
cau·li·flow·er [kɔ́ləflauɚ] s. coliflor.
cause [kɔz] s. causa; v. causar; originar; **to** — **to** hacer; inducir a.

caus·tic [kɔ́stɪk] adj. cáustico.
cau·ter·ize [kɔ́tɚraɪz] v. cauterizar.
cau·tion [kɔ́ʃən] s. precaución, cautela; aviso, advertencia; — ! ¡cuidado! ¡atención!, v. prevenir, avisar, advertir.
cau·tious [kɔ́ʃəs] adj. cauto; cauteloso, cuidadoso; precavido.
cav·a·lier [kævəlfr] s. caballero; galán; adj. orgulloso, altivo, desdeñoso.
cav·al·ry [kǽvlrɪ] s. caballería.
cave [kev] s. cueva; caverna; v. **to** — **in** hundirse; desplomarse.
cav·ern [kǽvɚn] s. caverna.
cav·i·ty [kǽvətɪ] s. cavidad, hueco; (tooth) carie.
ca·vort [kəvɔ́rt] v. cabriolar.
caw [kɔ] s. graznido; v. graznar.
cease [sis] v. cesar; parar, desistir; dejar de.
cease·less [síslɪs] adj. incesante.
ce·dar [sídɚ] s. cedro.
cede [sid] v. ceder.
ce·dil·la [sɪdɪlə] s. cedilla.
ceil·ing [sílɪŋ] s. techo (interior); cielo máximo (en aviación); altura máxima (en aviación); — **price** precio máximo.
cel·e·brate [sɛ́ləbret] v. celebrar.
cel·e·brat·ed [sɛ́ləbretɪd] adj. célebre, renombrado.
cel·e·bra·tion [sɛləbréʃən] s. celebración; fiesta.
ce·leb·ri·ty [səlɛ́brɪtɪ] s. celebridad; renombre.
cel·er·y [sɛ́lərɪ] s. apio.
ce·les·tial [səlɛ́stʃəl] adj. celestial, celeste.
cell [sɛl] s. (enclosure) celda; (structural) célula; (battery) pila eléctrica.
cel·lar [sɛ́lɚ] s. bodega, sótano.
cel·lu·loid [sɛ́ljəlɔɪd] s. celuloide.
cel·o·tex [sɛ́loteks] s. cartón de bagazo.
ce·ment [səmɛ́nt] s. cemento; hormigón; **reinforced** —cemento armado; — **mixer** hormigonera; v. unir, cementar, pegar con cemento; cubrir con cemento.
cem·e·ter·y [sɛ́mətɛrɪ] s. cementerio.
cen·sor [sɛ́nsɚ] s. censor; censurador, crítico; v. censurar (cartas, periódicos, etc.).
cen·sor·ship [sɛ́nsɚʃɪp] s. censura
cen·sure [sɛ́nʃɚ] s. censura, crítica, reprobación; v. censurar, criticar, reprobar.
cen·sus [sɛ́nsəs] s. censo; — **taker** empadronador.
cent [sɛnt] s. centavo (de peso o dólar); **per** — por ciento.
cen·ten·ni·al [sɛntɛ́nɪəl] adj. & s. centenario.
cen·ter [sɛ́ntɚ] s. centro; — **spread** doble página central; v. centrar; colocar en el centro; concentrar(se).
cen·ti·grade [sɛ́ntəgred] adj. centígrado.
cen·ti·pede [sɛ́ntəpid] s. ciempiés, cientopiés.
cen·tral [sɛ́ntrəl] adj. central; céntrico; s. (la) central de teléfonos.
cen·tral·ize [sɛ́ntrəlaɪz] v. centralizar.
cen·trif·u·gal [sɛntrɪfjʊgl] adj. centrífugo.
cen·tri·pe·tal [sɛntrípətl] adj. centrípeto.
cen·tu·ry [sɛ́ntʃərɪ] s. siglo.
ce·ram·ic [sərǽmɪk] adj. cerámico; **ceramics** s. cerámica.
ce·re·al [sɪríəl] adj. cereal; s. cereal; grano.
cer·e·mo·ni·al [sɛrəmónɪəl] adj. ceremonial; s. ceremonial; rito.
cer·e·mo·ni·ous [sɛrəmónɪəs] adj. ceremonioso.
cer·e·mo·ny [sɛ́rəmonɪ] s. ceremonia; ceremonial.
cer·tain [sɝ́tn] adj. cierto, seguro; **ly** adv. ciertamente; por cierto; de cierto; seguramente; de seguro.
cer·tain·ty [sɝ́tntɪ] s. certeza; certidumbre; seguridad.

cer·tif·i·cate [sɚtíffəkɪt] *s.* certificado; documento; testimonio; — **of baptism** fe de bautismo; — **of stock** bono, obligación; **birth** — partida de nacimiento; **death** — partida (*o* certificado) de defunción.

cer·ti·fi·ca·tion [sɚtɪfɪkéʃən] *s.* certificación.

cer·ti·fy [sɚ́təfaɪ] *v.* certificar; dar fe, atestiguar; **Certified Public Accountant (CPA)** contador público nacional (registrado, juramentado, titulado).

cer·vix [sɚ́vɪks] *s.* cerviz.

ces·sa·tion [sɛséʃən] *s.* suspensión, paro.

cess·pool [sɛ́spul] *s.* cloaca, rezumadero.

chafe [tʃef] *s.* rozadura; irritación, molestia; *v.* rozar(se); frotar; irritar(se).

chaff [tʃæf] *s.* hollejo, cáscara; *v.* embromar, bromear.

cha·grin [ʃəgrín] *s.* mortificación, desazón, pesar; **-ed** *p.p.* mortificado, afligido.

chain [ʃen] *s.* cadena; — **of mountains** cordillera; — **store** tiendas en serie (cadena); — **reaction** reacción en cadena; reacción eslabonada; — **saw** aserradora de cadena; — **smoker** el que fuma cigarro tras cigarro; *v.* encadenar.

chair [tʃɛr] *s.* silla; cátedra; presidencia; **arm** — sillón (de brazos); **easy** — butaca, poltrona; **folding** — silla de tijera; **rocking** — mecedora

chair·man [tʃɛ́rmən] *s.* presidente, director (*de una junta o de departamento*).

chair·man·ship [tʃɛ́rmənʃɪp] *s.* presidencia (*de una junta*).

chal·ice [tʃǽlɪs] *s.* cáliz (*vaso sagrado*).

chalk [tʃɔk] *s.* tiza, yeso; greda; *Méx.* gis; *v.* enyesar; marcar con tiza o yeso; **to — down** apuntar con tiza o yeso (*en el pizarrón*); **to — out** bosquejar, esbozar con tiza.

chalk·y [tʃɔ́kɪ] *adj.* yesoso; blanco.

chal·lenge [tʃǽlɪndʒ] *s.* desafío; reto; demanda; *v.* desafiar, retar; disputar; poner a prueba; dar el quienvive.

cham·ber [tʃémbɚ] *s.* cámara; aposento; — **of commerce** cámara de comercio.

cham·ber·maid [tʃémbɚmed] *s.* camarera, sirvienta.

cham·ois [ʃǽmɪ] *s.* gamuza.

cham·pi·on [tʃǽmpɪən] *s.* campeón; defensor; *v.* defender.

cham·pi·on·ship [tʃǽmpɪənʃɪp] *s.* campeonato.

chance [tʃæns] *s.* (*opportunity*) oportunidad ocasión; (*possibility*) posibilidad, probabilidad; (*fortune*) suerte, fortuna; casualidad, azar; (*risk*) riesgo; billete de rifa o lotería; **by** — por casualidad; **game of** — juego de azar; **to run a** — correr riesgo; *adj.* casual, accidental; *v.* arriesgar; **to — to** acertar a, hacer (*algo*) por casualidad.

chan·cel·lor [tʃǽnsəlɚ] *s.* canciller; primer ministro; magistrado; rector de universidad.

chan·de·lier [ʃændlír] *s.* araña de luces, *Ríopl.*, *Méx.* candil.

change [tʃendʒ] *s.* (*money*) cambio; vuelta, *Am.* vuelto; suelto; *Méx.* feria; (*fresh clothes*) muda de ropa; (*switch*) mudanza; **the — of life** la menopausia; *v.* cambiar; mudar; alterar; **to — clothes** mudar de ropa; **to — trains** transbordar(se), cambiar de tren.

change·a·ble [tʃéndʒəbl̩] *adj.* mudable, variable; inconstante; tornadizo; — **silk** seda tornasolada.

chan·nel [tʃǽnl̩] *s.* canal; cauce; canal (*de televisión*).

chant [tʃænt] *s.* canto llano o gregoriano; sonsonete; *v.* cantar (*salmos, himnos, etc.*).

cha·os [kéɑs] *s.* caos; desorden.

cha·ot·ic [keɑ́tɪk] *adj.* caótico.

chap [tʃæp] *s.* grieta, raja, rajadura (*en la piel*); chico; **what a fine — he is!** ¡qué buen tipo (*o* sujeto) es!; *v.* agrietarse, rajarse (*la piel*).

chap·el [tʃǽpl̩] *s.* capilla.

chap·er·on(e) [ʃǽpəron] *s.* acompañante, persona de respeto; **to go along as a** — *Am.* ir de moscón; *v.* acompañar, servir de acompañante.

chap·lain [tʃǽplɪn] *s.* capellán; **army** — capellán castrense.

chap·ter [tʃǽptɚ] *s.* capítulo; cabildo (*de una catedral*).

char [tʃɑr] *v.* requemar, carbonizar.

char·ac·ter [kǽrɪktɚ] *s.* carácter; personaje.

char·ac·ter·is·tic [kæriktərístɪk] *adj.* característico; típico; *s.* característica, rasgo característico; distintivo; peculiaridad.

char·ac·ter·ize [kǽrɪktəraɪz] *adj.* caracterizar.

cha·rade [ʃəréd] *s.* charada.

char·coal [tʃɑ́rkol] *s.* carbón; carboncillo (*para dibujar*); — **drawing** dibujo al carbón.

charge [tʃɑrdʒ] *s.* (*custody*) cargo; custodia; cuidado; (*order*) mandato, encargo; (*accusation*) cargo, acusación; (*load*) carga; peso; (*cost*) precio, coste; (*attack*) embestida, asalto, ataque; **chargé d'affaires** agregado; — **account** cuenta abierta; — **prepaid** porte pagado; **under my** — a mi cargo; **to be in** — **of** estar encargado de; *v.* cargar; cargar en cuenta; cobrar (*precio*); mandar; exhortar; atacar, embestir, asaltar; **to** — **with murder** acusar de homicidio; **to** — **off a loss** restar una pérdida.

charg·er [tʃɑ́rdʒɚ] *s.* cargador (*de batería*); caballo de guerra, corcel.

char·i·ot [tʃǽrɪət] *s.* carroza; carruaje.

cha·ris·ma [kərízmə] *s.* carisma.

char·i·ta·ble [tʃǽrətəbl̩] *adj.* caritativo.

char·i·ty [tʃǽrətɪ] *s.* caridad; limosna; beneficencia.

char·la·tan [ʃɑ́rlətn̩] *s.* charlatán; farsante.

charm [tʃɑrm] *s.* encanto; atractivo; hechizo; talismán; **watch** — dije; *v.* encantar; cautivar; hechizar.

charm·ing [tʃɑ́mɪŋ] *adj.* encantador, atractivo.

chart [tʃɑrt] *s.* carta (*hidrográfica o de navegar*); mapa; gráfica, representación gráfica; **flow—** (*computer*) diagrama de flujo; *v.* cartografiar, delinear mapas o cartas; **to** — **a course** trazar o planear una ruta o derrotero.

char·ter [tʃɑ́rtɚ] *s.* carta constitucional, constitución, código; título; carta de privilegio; — **member** socio fundador; *v.* fletar (*un barco*); alquilar (*un ómnibus*).

chase [tʃes] *s.* caza, persecución; *v.* cazar; perseguir; **to** — **away** ahuyentar.

chasm [kǽzəm] *s.* abismo; vacío.

chaste [tʃest] *adj.* casto; honesto; puro.

chas·tise [tʃæstáɪz] *v.* castigar.

chas·tise·ment [tʃæstáɪzmənt] *s.* castigo, escarmiento.

chas·ti·ty [tʃǽstətɪ] *s.* castidad; honestidad; pureza.

chat [tʃæt] *s.* charla, *Méx.* plática; *v.* charlar, *Méx.* platicar.

chat·tels [tʃǽtlz] *s. pl.* enseres, bienes muebles.

chat·ter [tʃǽtɚ] *s.* charla, parloteo; (*teeth*) castañeteo (*birds*) chirrido (*de aves*); *v.* charlar, parlotear, cotorrear; castañetear (*los dientes*).

chauf·feur [ʃófɚ] *s.* chófer, cochero de automóvil.

cheap [tʃip] *adj.* barato; cursi, de mal gusto; **to feel** — sentir vergüenza; **-ly** *adv.* barato, a poco precio.

cheap·en [tʃípən] *v.* abaratar.

cheap·ness [tʃípnɪs] *s.* baratura; cursilería.

cheat [tʃit] s. fraude, engaño; (*trick*) trampa; (*person*) trampista, tramposo; estafador; embaucador; v. engañar; trampear; embaucar; estafar.

check [tʃɛk] s. cheque (*de banco*); talón, marbete, contraseña (*de equipajes, etc.*); marca, señal; cuenta (*de restaurante*); restricción, represión; cuadro (*de un tejido o tela*); comprobación; jaque (*en ajedrez*); — **room** vestuario; — **stub** talón; — **tally** recuento; — **test** contraprueba; guardarropa; consigna (equipajes); — **point** punto de inspección; — **list** lista comprobante; v. refrenar, reprimir, restringir; facturar, depositar (*equipajes*); (verify) inspeccionar; confrontar, **to** — *Cuba, Col., P.R.* chequear, *Méx.* checar, comprobar; marcar (*con una señal*); dar jaque (*en ajedrez*); **to** — **out of a hotel** desocupar el cuarto o alojamiento de un hotel.

check·book [tʃɛkbʊk] s. libreta de cheques; talonario.

check·er [tʃɛkɚ] s. cuadro; casilla (*de un tablero de ajedrez, etc.*); pieza (*del juego de damas*); comprobador; inspector; **-s** juego de damas; — **board** tablero; v. cuadricular, marcar con cuadritos; **-ed career** vida azarosa, vida llena de variedad; **-ed cloth** paño o tela a cuadros.

check·mate [tʃɛkmet] s. jaque mate.

cheek [tʃik] s. mejilla, carrillo; cachete; descaro, desfachatez; **fat** — mejilla gorda, moflete; — **bone** pómulo; **red** — chapetón.

cheer [tʃɪr] s. alegría; buen ánimo, jovialidad; (*consolation*) consuelo; **-s** aplausos, vivas; v. alegrar, alentar, animar; refocilar; aplaudir, vitorear; **to** — **up** alentar, dar ánimo; cobrar ánimo, animarse.

cheer·ful [tʃɪrfəl] adj. animado, alegre, jovial; **-ly** adv. alegremente, con alegría, con júbilo; de buena gana, de buen grado.

cheer·ful·ness [tʃɪrfəlnɪs] s. jovialidad, alegría; buen humor.

cheer·i·ly [tʃɪrəlɪ] = **cheerfully.**

cheer·less [tʃɪrlɪs] adj. abatido, desalentado, desanimado; triste, sombrío.

cheer·y [tʃɪrɪ] = **cheerful.**

cheese [tʃiz] s. queso; **cottage** — requesón.

chef [ʃɛf] s. cocinero.

chem·i·cal [kɛmɪkl] adj. químico; s. producto químico.

chem·ist [kɛmɪst] s. químico.

chem·is·try [kɛmɪstrɪ] s. química.

cher·ish [tʃɛrɪʃ] v. acariciar, abrigar (*una esperanza, un ideal, etc.*); apreciar.

cher·ry [tʃɛrɪ] s. cereza; — **tree** cerezo.

cher·ub [tʃɛrəb] s. querubín.

chess [tʃɛs] s. ajedrez; — **board** tablero de ajedrez.

chest [tʃɛst] s. cofre, arca; caja; pecho; — **of drawers** cómoda.

chest·nut [tʃɛsnət] s. castaña; — **tree** castaño; adj. castaño; — **horse** caballo zaino.

chev·ron [ʃɛvrən] s. galón.

chew [tʃu] s. mascada, mordisco, bocado; v. mascar, masticar.

chew·ing gum [tʃúɪŋ gʌm] s. goma de mascar; *Am.* chicle.

chick [tʃɪk] s. polluelo, pollito; pajarito; **chick-pea** garbanzo.

chick·en [tʃɪkɪn] s. pollo; polluelo; — **pox** viruelas locas; **chicken-hearted** cobarde, gallina.

chic·o·ry [tʃɪkərɪ] s. achicoria.

chide [tʃaɪd] v. regañar, reprender, reprobar.

chief [tʃif] s. jefe, caudillo; cacique (*de una tribu*); **commander in** — comandante en jefe; adj.

principal; — **clerk** oficial mayor; — **justice** presidente de la corte suprema; **-ly** adv. principalmente, mayormente; sobre todo.

chief·tain [tʃíftən] s. cacique.

chif·fon [ʃífɑn] s. gasa.

chig·ger [tʃígɚ] s. nigua.

chil·blain [tʃɪ́blen] s. sabañón.

child [tʃaɪld] s. niño, niña; hijo, hija; **-'s play** cosa de niños; **to be with** — estar encinta.

child·birth [tʃáɪldbɚθ] s. parto, alumbramiento.

child·hood [tʃáɪldhʊd] s. niñez, infancia.

child·ish [tʃáɪdɪʃ] adj. pueril; infantil; — **action** niñería, niñada.

child·less [tʃáɪdlɪs] adj. sin hijos.

child·like [tʃáɪldlaɪk] adj. como niño, aniñado, pueril.

chil·dren [tʃɪ́ldrən] pl. de **child.**

Chil·e·an [tʃɪ́liən] adj. & s. chileno.

chil·i [tʃɪ́lɪ] s. *Méx., C.A.* chile, *Carib., S.A.* ají.

chill [tʃɪl] s. frío, (*illness*) resfrío; enfriamiento; (*sensation*) escalofrío; calofrío; **-s and fever** escalofríos; adj. frío; v. resfriar(se); enfriar(se); **to become -ed** resfriarse, escalofriarse.

chill·y [tʃɪlɪ] adj. frío; friolento.

chime [tʃaɪm] s. repique, campaneo; **-s** órgano de campanas, juego de campanas; v. repicar, campanear; tocar, sonar, tañer (*las campanas*); **to** — **with** estar en armonía con.

chim·ney [tʃɪ́mnɪ] s. chimenea; **lamp** — tubo de lámpara, *Am.* bombilla.

chin [tʃɪn] s. barba, mentón.

chi·na [tʃáɪnə] s. loza de china, procelana, loza fina; vajilla de porcelana; — **closet** chinero.

chi·na·ware [tʃáɪnəwɛr] = **china.**

Chi·nese [tʃaɪníz] adj. chino; s. chino; idioma chino.

chink [tʃɪŋk] s. grieta, hendidura.

chip [tʃɪp] s. astilla, brizna; fragmento; desconchadura; desportilladura; (*poker*) ficha (*de pócar*); (computer) ficha de silicón; v. astillar; desconchar(se); descascarar(se); desportillar(se); picar, tajar (*con cincel o hacha*); **to** — **in** contribuir con su cuota.

chip·munk [tʃɪ́pmʌŋk] s. especie de ardilla.

chi·ro·prac·tic [kaɪrəprǽktɪk] adj. quiropráctico.

chirp [tʃɝp] s. chirrido; pío; gorjeo; v. chirriar; piar; pipiar; gorjear.

chis·el [tʃɪ́zl] s. cincel, v. cincelar; sisar, estafar.

chiseler [tʃɪ́zlɚ] s. tramposo.

chiv·al·rous [ʃɪ́vlrəs] adj. caballeresco, caballeroso, galante, cortés.

chiv·al·ry [ʃɪ́vlrɪ] s. caballería; caballerosidad.

chlo·ride [klóraɪd] s. cloruro.

chlo·rine [klórin] s. cloro.

chlo·ro·form [klórəfɔrm] s. cloroformo.

chlo·ro·phyll [klórəfɪl] s. clorofila.

choc·o·late [tʃɔ́klɪt] s. chocolate; — **pot** chocolatera.

choice [tʃɔɪs] s. selección; preferencia; escogimiento; cosa elegida; favorito, preferido; alternativa; **to have no other** — no tener otra alternativa; adj. selecto; bien escogido; excelente.

choir [kwaɪr] s. coro.

choke [tʃok] s. sofoco, ahogo; (*cough*) tos ahogada; estrangulación; estrangulador, (*auto*) obturador (*de automóvil*); v. sofocar(se), ahogar(se); estrangular(se); obstruir, tapar; regularizar (*el motor*).

chol·er·a [kálərə] s. cólera (*m.*).

cho·les·ter·ol [kəlɛ́stɚol] s. colesterol.

choose [tʃuz] v. escoger; elegir; seleccionar; **to** — **to** optar por; preferir; **I do not** — **to do it** no se me antoja (*o* no es mi gusto) hacerlo.

chop [tʃɑp] s. chuleta, costilla, (*slice*) tajada (*de* *carne*); **-s** quijadas; *v.* tajar, cortar; picar, desmenuzar (*carne*).

chop·py [tʃápɪ] *adj.* picado, agitado.

cho·ral [kórəl] *adj.* coral.

chord [kɔrd] *s.* cuerda; acorde.

chore [tʃor] *s.* tarea; quehacer.

cho·re·og·ra·phy [korɪógrəfɪ] *s.* coreografía.

cho·rus [kórəs] *s.* coro; *v.* cantar o hablar en coro; contestar a una vos.

chose [tʃoz] *pret. de* **to choose.**

cho·sen [tʃózn̩] *p.p. de* **to choose.**

chris·ten [krísn̩] *v.* bautizar.

chris·ten·ing [krínɪŋ] *s.* bautizo, bautismo.

Chris·tian [krístʃən] *s. & adj.* cristiano; — **name** nombre de pila o bautismo.

Chris·ti·an·i·ty [krɪstʃiǽnətɪ] *s.* cristiandad, cristianismo.

Christ·mas [krísməs] *s.* Navidad, Pascua de Navidad; *adj.* navideño; — **Eve** Nochebuena; — **gift** regalo de Navidad; aguinaldo; **Merry —!** ¡Felices Navidades! ¡Felices Pascuas!

chrome [krom] *s.* cromo; *adj.* cromado.

chro·mi·um [krómɪəm] *s.* cromo.

chro·mo·some [króməsom] *s.* cromosoma.

chron·ic [kránɪk] *adj.* crónico.

chron·i·cle [kránɪkl̩] *s.* crónica; *v.* relatar; escribir la crónica de.

chron·i·cler [kránɪklɚ] *s.* cronista.

chron·o·log·i·cal [kranəládʒɪkl̩] *adj.* cronológico.

chro·nom·e·ter [krənámətɚ] *s.* cronómetro.

chry·san·the·mum [krɪsǽθəməm] *s.* crisantema, crisantemo.

chub·by [tʃábɪ] *adj.* rechoncho; gordiflón.

chuck [tʃʌk] *s.* mamola, golpecito, (*caress*) caricia (*debajo de la barba*); *v.* echar, tirar (*lo que no sirve*); **to — under the chin** hacer la mamola.

chuck·le [tʃʌkl̩] *s.* risita; *v.* reír entre dientes.

chum [tʃʌm] *s.* compañero, camarada, compinche.

chunk [tʃʌŋk] *s.* trozo; zoquete.

church [tʃɝt] *s.* iglesia.

church·man [tʃɝtʃmən] *s.* clérigo, eclesiástico, sacerdote; (*parishoner*) feligrés.

church·yard [tʃɝtʃjard] *s.* patio de iglesia; camposanto, cementerio.

churn [tʃɝn] *s.* mantequera (*para hacer manteca*); *v.* batir (*en una mantequera*); agitar, revolver.

ci·der [sáɪdɚ] *s.* sidra.

ci·gar [sɪgár] *s.* puro; *Carib., Col., Ven.* tabaco; — **store** tabaquería, estanquillo.

cig·a·rette [sɪgərét] *s.* cigarrillo, pitillo, *Méx., C.A., Ven., Col.* cigarro; — **case** cigarrera, pitillera; — **holder** boquilla; — **lighter** encendedor.

cinch [sɪntʃ] *s.* cincha; ganga, cosa fácil; *v.* cinchar; apretar.

cin·der [síndɚ] *s.* ceniza; carbón, brasa, ascua; cisco; **-s** cenizas; rescoldo.

cin·na·mon [sínəmən] *s.* canela; — **tree** canelo.

ci·pher [sáɪfɚ] *s.* cifra; número; cero.

cir·cle [sɝkl̩] *s.* círculo; cerco, rueda; *v.* cercar, circundar; circular, dar vueltas.

cir·cuit [sɝkɪt] *s.* circuito; rode o, vuelta.

cir·cu·lar [sɝkjələr] *adj.* circular; redondo; *s.* circular; hoja volante.

cir·cu·late [sɝkjəlet] *v.* circular; poner en circulación.

cir·cu·la·tion [sɝkjəléʃən] *s.* circulación.

cir·cum·fer·ence [sɚkámfərəns] *s.* circunferencia.

cir·cum·flex [sɝkəmflɛks] *adj.* circunflejo.

cir·cum·lo·cu·tion [sɝkəmlokjúʃən] *s.* circunlocución, redeo.

cir·cum·scribe [sɝkəmskráɪb] *v.* circunscribir, limitar.

cir·cum·spect [sɝkəmspɝkt] *adj.* circunspecto; prudente.

cir·cum·spec·tion [sɝkəmspɝkʃən] *s.* circunspección, miramiento, prudencia.

cir·cum·stance [sɝkəmstæns] *s.* circunstancia; incidente; ceremonia, pompa.

cir·cum·vent [sɝkəmvɛnt] *v.* evitar, embaucar.

cir·cus [sɝkəs] *s.* circo.

cir·rho·sis [sɪrósɪs] *s.* cirrosis.

cis·tern [sístɚn] *s.* cisterna.

cit·a·del [sftədl̩] *s.* ciudadela.

ci·ta·tion [saɪtéʃən] *s.* citación; cita; mención.

cite [saɪt] *v.* citar; citar a juicio; mencionar.

cit·i·zen [sftəzn̩] *s.* ciudadano, paisano.

cit·i·zen·ship [sftəzn̩ʃɪp] *s.* ciudadanía.

cit·ron [sftrən] *s.* acitrón.

cit·rus [sftrəs] *s.* cidro.

cit·y [sftɪ] *s.* ciudad, población; municipio; *adj.* municipal, urbano; — **council** ayuntamiento; — **hall** ayuntamiento, casa municipal; — **planning** urbanismo, urbanización.

civ·ic [sfvɪk] *adj.* cívico.

civ·ics [sfvɪks] *s.* derecho político.

civ·il [sfvl̩] *adj.* civil; cortés; — **engineer** ingeniero civil; — **rights** derechos civiles; — **disobedience** desobediencia civil.

ci·vil·ian [səvíjən] *s.* civil; paisano (*persona no militar*).

ci·vil·i·ty [səvílətɪ] *s.* civilidad, cortesía, urbanidad.

civ·i·li·za·tion [sɪvləzéʃən] *s.* civilización.

civ·i·lize [sfvlaɪz] *v.* civilizar.

civ·i·lized [sfvlaɪzd] *adj.* civilizado.

clad [klæd] *pret. & p.p. de* **to clothe.**

claim [klem] *s.* demanda; reclamación, reclamo; derecho, título; pretensión; **miner's** — denuncia; *v.* reclamar; demandar; pedir, exigir; afirmar, sostener; **to — a mine** denunciar una mina; **to — to be** pretender ser.

claim·ant [klémənt] *s.* reclamante o reclamador; pretendiente (*a un trono*).

clair·voy·ant [klɛrvɔɪənt] *adj.* clarividente.

clam [klæm] *s.* almeja.

clam·ber [klǽmbɚ] *v.* trepar, encaramarse, subir a gatas, subir gateando.

clam·my [klǽmɪ] *adj.* frío y húmedo.

clam·or [klǽmɚ] *s.* clamor; clamoreo; gritería, vocería; *v.* clamar; vociferar, gritar.

clam·or·ous [klǽmərəs] *adj.* clamoroso.

clamp [klæmp] *s.* grapa; tornillo de banco; *v.* afianzar, sujetar; pisar recio.

clan [klæn] *s.* clan; tribu.

clan·des·tine [klændéstɪn] *adj.* clandestino.

clang [klæŋ] *s.* tantán, retintín; campanada; campanillazo; **—! —!** ¡tan! ¡tan!; *v.* sonar, repicar (*una campana o timbre*); hacer sonar, tocar fuerte.

clap [klæp] *s.* palmada; golpe seco; — **of thunder** trueno; *v.* palmear, palmotear, aplaudir, dar palmadas; cerrar de golpe (*un libro*); dar una palmada, *Am.* palmear (*sobre la espalda*); **to — in jail** meter (*o* encajar) en la cárcel.

clap·per [klǽpɚ] *s.* badajo.

clar·i·fy [klǽrəfaɪ] *v.* aclarar.

clar·i·net [klærənét] *s.* clarinete.

clar·i·ty [klǽrətɪ] *s.* claridad, luz.

clash [klæʃ] *s.* choque, encontrón, colisión; (*fight*) riña, conflicto; estruendo; *v.* chocar; darse un encontrón; hacer crujir; oponerse, estar en conflicto.

clasp [klæsp] *s.* (*fastener*) broche; hebilla; cierre; traba; (*grip*) apretón, apretón de manos; *v.* abrochar; asir; agarrar, sujetar, asegurar; abrazar;

apretar (*la mano*).

class [klæs] *s.* clase; *v.* clasificar.

clas·sic [klǽsɪk] *adj. & s.* clásico; — **scholar** humanista, erudito clásico.

clas·si·cal [klǽsɪkl] *adj.* clásico.

clas·si·cism [klǽsɪsɪzm] *s.* clasicismo.

clas·si·fi·ca·tion [klæsəfəkéʃən] *s.* clasificación.

clas·si·fy [klǽsəfaɪ] *v.* clasificar.

class·mate [klǽsmet] *s.* compañero de clase, condiscípulo.

class·room [klǽsrum] *s.* clase, aula.

clat·ter [klǽtɚ] *s.* estrépito, boruca; traqueteo; bullicio; alboroto; *v.* hacer estrépito o boruca; traquetear; meter bulla o alboroto.

clause [klɔz] *s.* cláusula.

claw [klɔ] *s.* garra; zarpa; uña; (*crab*) pinza (*de langosta, cangrejo, etc.*); (*hammer*) orejas (*de un martillo*); (*scratch*) arañazo; *v.* desgarrar; aranar; rasgar.

claw·ing [klɔ́ɪŋ] *s.* zarpazo.

clay [kle] *s.* barro; arcilla, greda.

clean [klin] *adj.* limpio; puro; *adv.* limpiamente; **clean-cut** bien tallado, de buen talle, de buen parecer; *v.* limpiar; asear; desempañar; **to — up** limpiar(se), asear(se).

clean·er [klínɚ] *s.* limpiador; quitamanchas.

clean·li·ness [klénlɪnɪs] *s.* limpieza; aseo.

clean·ly [klénlɪ] *adj.* limpio; aseado; [klínlɪ] *adv.* limpiamente.

clean·ness [klínnɪs] *s.* limpieza; aseo.

cleanse [klɛnz] *v.* limpiar; asear; purificar, depurar.

cleans·er [klénzɚ] *s.* limpiador.

clear [klɪr] *adj.* (*evident*) claro; patente, manifiesto; (*clean*) límpido; despejado; (*free*) libre (*de culpa, estorbos, deudas, etc.*); — **profit** ganancia neta; **clear-cut** *adj.* bien delineado; clarividente; **to pass — through** atravesar, traspasar de lado a lado; **to be in the** — estar sin deudas; estar libre de culpa; *v.* aclarar(se); despejar(se); escampar; clarificar; quitar (*estorbos*); desmontar (*un terreno*); salvar, saltar por encima de; librar (*de culpa, deudas, etc.*); sacar (*una ganancia neta*); pasar (*un cheque*) por un banco de liquidación; liquidar (*una cuenta*); **to — the table** levantar la mesa; **to — up** aclarar(se).

clear·ance [klɪfrəns] *s.* espacio (*libre entre dos objetos*); despacho de aduana; — **sale** saldo, venta (*de liquidación*), *Méx., C.A., Andes* barata.

clear·ing [klɪfrɪŋ] *s.* aclaramiento; claro; terreno desmontado o desarbolado; liquidación de balances; — **house** banco de liquidación.

clear·ness [klɪfrnɪs] *s.* claridad.

cleav·age [klívɪdʒ] *s.* hendedura.

cleave [kliv] *v.* hender(se); tajar; rajar; partir.

cleav·er [klívɚ] *s.* cuchilla o hacha (*de carnicero*).

clef [klef] *s.* clave (*en música*).

cleft [klɛft] *s.* grieta, hendedura; *adj.* hendido, partido, rajado; *pret. & p.p.* de **to cleave.**

clem·en·cy [klémənsɪ] *s.* clemencia.

clem·ent [klémənt] *adj.* clemente.

clench [klɛntʃ] *s.* agarro, agarrada, agarrón; apretón; *v.* agarrar, asir; apretar (*los dientes, el puño*).

cler·gy [klɝdʒɪ] *s.* clero.

cler·gy·man [klɝdʒɪmən] *s.* clérigo, eclesiástico, pastor, sacerdote.

cler·i·cal [klérɪkl] *adj.* (*clergy*) clerical, eclesiástico; (*office*) oficinesco, de oficina; de dependientes; — **error** error de pluma (*de copista*); — **work** trabajo de escritorio.

clerk [klɝk] *s.* dependiente; empleado (*de oficina*); escribiente; archivero (*de municipio*); **law —**

escribano; *v.* estar de dependiente.

clev·er [klévɚ] *adj.* diestro, hábil; listo; talentoso; mañoso; **-ly** *adv.* hábilmente; con destreza; con maña.

clev·er·ness [klévɚnɪs] *s.* destreza, habilidad, maña; talento.

clew [klu] *s.* indicio (*que indica el camino para resolver un misterio o problema*).

cli·ché [kliʃé] *s.* (*plate*) clisé; *Am.* cliché; (*phrase*) cliché.

click [klɪk] *s.* golpecito; (*tongue*) chasquido (*de la lengua*); gatillazo (*sonido del gatillo de una pistola*); taconeo (*sonido de tacones*); *v.* sonar (*un pestillo, un broche, un gatillo, etc.*); chasquear (*la lengua*); **to — the heels** cuadrarse (*militarmente*); taconear.

cli·ent [kláɪənt] *s.* cliente.

cli·en·tele [klaɪəntél] *s.* clientela.

cliff [klɪf] *s.* risco, precipicio, peñasco, escarpa.

cli·mate [kláɪmɪt] *s.* clima.

cli·max [kláɪmæks] *s.* clímax, culminación; *v.* culminar; llegar al clímax.

climb [klaɪm] *s.* subida, ascenso; *v.* subir; trepar; encaramarse; **to — down** bajar a gatas; desprenderse (*de un árbol*).

climb·er [kláɪmɚ] *s.* trepador; enredadera, planta trepadora.

clime [klaɪm] *s.* clima.

clinch [klɪntʃ] *v.* remachar, redoblar (*un clavo*); (*assure*) afianzar, sujetar, asegurar bien; cerrar (*un trato*); abrazarse fuertemente; *s.* remache; abrazo; agarrón; **to be in a —** estar agarrados o abrazados.

cling [klɪŋ] *v.* pegarse, adherirse.

clin·ic [klɪnɪk] *s.* clínica.

clink [klɪŋk] *s.* tintín.

clip [klɪp] *s.* (*fastener*) broche, presilla; (*cutting*) tijeretada (*corte con tijeras*); trasquila, trasquiladura; **paper —** sujetapapeles; **to go at a good —** ir a paso rápido; andar de prisa; *v.* recortar; cortar; trasquilar (*el pelo o lana de los animales*); **to — together** sujetar.

clip·per [klɪpɚ] *s.* clíper (*velero o avión de gran velocidad*); trasquilador; recortador; **-s** tijeras; maquinilla (*para recortar el pelo*).

clip·ping [klɪpɪŋ] *s.* recorte.

cloak [klok] *s.* capa; manto; *v.* tapar, embozar, encubrir.

cloak·room [klókrum] *s.* guardarropa, vestuario.

clock [klak] *s.* reloj; **alarm —** despertador; *v.* marcar; cronometrar.

clock·wise [klákwaɪz] *adv.* en el sentido de las manecillas de reloj.

clock·work [klákwɝk] *s.* maquinaria de reloj; **like —** con precisión, puntualmente; sin dificultad.

clod [klad] *s.* terrón; tonto, necio.

clog [klag] *s.* estorbo, obstáculo; (*shoe*) zueco (*zapato de suela gruesa o de madera*); — **dance** zapateado; *v.* estorbar, embarazar; obstruir, atorar, tapar; obstruirse, atascarse, azolvarse (*Am.* enzolvarse), atorarse (*un caño, acequia, etc.*).

clois·ter [klɔ́ɪstɚ] *s.* claustro; monasterio; convento; *v.* enclaustrar.

close [kloz] *s.* fin, terminación, conclusión; cierre; *v.* cerrar(se); concluir; **to — an account** saldar una cuenta; **to — a meeting** levantar una sesión; **to — in upon** cercar, rodear; **to — out** liquidar, vender en liquidación.

close [klos] *adj.* (*near*) cercano, próximo; aproximado; íntimo; (*tight*) estrecho, ajustado; (*stingy*) cerrado; tacaño, mezquino; (*suffocating*) opresivo; sofocante; (*fought*) reñido; — **attention**

suma atención; — **questioning** interrogatorio detallado o minucioso; — **translation** traducción fiel; **at** — **range** de cerca; *adv.* cerca; **-ly** *adv.* aproximadamente; estrechamente; apretadamente; con sumo cuidado a atención; **closed shop** con sólo obreros sindicados.

closed cir·cuit [klozd sə́ˑkət] *s. & adj.* circuito cerrado.

close·ness [klósnɪs] *s.* cercanía, proximidad; aproximación; (*confinement*) estrechez; (*friendship*) intimidad; (*stingyness*) tacañería, avaricia; mala ventilación, falta de aire; fidelidad (*de una traducción*).

clos·et [klázɪt] *s.* ropero; alacena, armario; (*toilet*) gabinete, retrete, excusado; *v.* encerrar en un cuarto (*para una entrevista secreta*); **to** — **oneself** (**themselves**) encerrarse.

clot [klɑt] *v.* coagular(se), cuajar(se); *s.* coágulo, cuajarón.

cloth [klɔθ] *s.* tela, paño, género; (*rag*) trapo; *adj.* de paño; — **binding** encuadernación en tela.

clothe [kloð] *v.* vestir; cubrir; revestir; investir.

clothes [kloz] *s. pl.* ropa; ropaje, vestidos; **suit of** — terno, traje, *Carib., Ven.* flux; — **line** tendedero; — **pin** pinzas, gancho (*para tender la ropa*).

cloth·ier [klóðjɚ] *s.* comerciante en ropa o paño; ropero, pañero.

cloth·ing [klóðɪŋ] *s.* ropa; ropaje, vestidos.

cloud [klaʊd] *s.* nube; **storm** — nubarrón; *v.* nublar(se), anublar(se); obscurecer; manchar.

cloud·burst [kláʊdbɚst] *s.* chaparrón, aguacero; chubasco.

cloud·less [kláʊdlɪs] *adj.* claro, despejado; sin nubes.

cloud·y [kláʊdɪ] *adj.* nublado; *Esp.* nuboso; sombrío.

clove [klov] *s.* clavo (*especia*); — **of garlic** diente de ajo.

clo·ven [klóvən] *adj.* hendido; *S. & adj.* — **hoof** patihendido, pie hendido.

clo·ver [klóvɚ] *s.* trébol; **to be in** — estar o vivir en la abundancia; sentirse próspero.

clo·ver·leaf [klóvɚlɪf] *s.* (*highway*) cruce en trébol.

clown [klaʊn] *s.* payaso, bufón; *v.* payasear, bufonear, hacer el payaso.

cloy [klɔɪ] *v.* empalagar; hastiar.

club [klʌb] *s.* club, círculo; casino; (*stick*) garrote, porra; palo; (*cards*) basto (*de la baraja*); *v.* golpear, aporrear, apalear; **to** — **together** formar club; escotar, pagar la cuota que le toca a cada uno, *Am.* cotizar.

club·house [klʌ́bhaʊs] *s.* club, casino.

cluck [klʌk] *s.* cloqueo; *v.* cloquear.

clue = **clew.**

clump [klʌmp] *s.* terrón; pisada fuerte; — **of bushes** matorral; — **of trees** grupo de árboles, arboleda; *v.* apiñar, amontonar; **to** — **along** andar pesadamente.

clum·sy [klʌ́mzɪ] *adj.* torpe, desmañado; incómodo; difícil de manejar; mal hecho.

clung [klʌŋ] *pret. & p.p. de* **to cling.**

clus·ter [klʌ́stɚ] *s.* racimo; grupo; *v.* agrupar(se); arracimarse (*formar racimo*).

clutch [klʌtʃ] *s.* apretón fuerte; agarro, agarrón; (*auto*) embrague (*de automóvil*); **-es** garras; uñas; — **pedal** pedal del embrague; **to step on the** — pisar el embrague; desembragar, soltar el embrague; **to throw in the** — embragar; *v.* agarrar, asir; apretar.

clut·ter [klʌ́tɚ] *v.* obstruir; atestar (*de cosas*); poner en desorden; *s.* desorden, confusión.

coach [kotʃ] *s.* coche; (*sports*) entrenador (*en deportes*); maestro particular; *v.* aleccionar; guiar,

adiestrar, *Am.* entrenar; **to** — **with** ser instruido o entrenado por.

coach·man [kótʃmən] *s.* cochero.

co·ag·u·late [koǽgjəlet] *v.* coagular(se), cuajar(se).

coal [kol] *s.* carbón; ascua, brasa; **hard**— carbón de piedra, antracita; **soft** — hulla; — **barge** lanchón carbonero; — **bin** carbonera; — **dealer** carbonero; — **oil** kerosina; — **tar** alquitrán de carbón; *v.* cargar de carbón, echar carbón; proveer(se) de carbón.

co·a·li·tion [koəlɪ́ʃən] *s.* coalición.

coarse [kors] *adj.* (*crude*) burdo, basto; tosco; áspero; (*rude*) rudo; grosero; vulgar; tosco; — **sand** arena gruesa.

coarse·ness [kórsnɪs] *s.* tosquedad; vulgaridad, grosería, rudeza.

coast [kost] *s.* costa, litoral; — **guard** guardacostas, guarda de costas; *v.* costear, navegar por la costa; deslizar(se), resbalar(se) cuesta abajo.

coast·al [kóstl] *adj.* costero, costanero, de la costa; — **traffic** cabotaje.

coast·line [kóstlaɪn] *s.* costa, litoral.

coat [kot] *s.* chaqueta, americana; *Am.* saco; (*animals*) lana, pelo (*de un animal*); **lady's** — abrigo de senora; — **hanger** colgador; — **of arms** escudo de armas; — **of paint** capa de pintura; *v.* cubrir; revestir, dar una mano (*de pintura*); **to** — **with sugar** azucarar, bañar en azúcar.

coat·ing [kótɪŋ] *s.* capa.

coat·tail [kóttel] *s.* faldón.

coax [koks] *v.* rogar o persuadir con halagos, halagar, tentar.

cob [kɑb] *s.* (*corn*) carozo, zuro (*de la mazorca del maíz*), *Ven., Col., Carib.* tusa, *Méx., C.A.* elote; *Andes* marlo.

co·balt [kóbɔlt] *s.* cobalto.

cob·bler [kɑ́blɚ] *s.* remendón (*zapatero*); budin de bizcocho y fruta.

cob·ble·stone [kɑ́blston] *s.* guijarro; *adj.* empedrado.

cob·web [kɑ́bwɛb] *s.* telaraña.

co·caine [kokén] *s.* cocaína.

cock [kɑk] *s.* gallo; macho de ave; (*faucet*) espita, grifo; *Méx.* bidoque; martillo (*de armas de fuego*); — **sure** muy seguro de sí mismo; *v.* amartillar (*un arma de fuego*); ladear (*la cabeza*), ladearse (*el sombrero*).

cock·fight [kɑ́kfaɪt] *s.* pelea de gallos, riña de gallos.

cock·pit [kɑ́kpɪt] *s.* galera; (*airplane*) cabina.

cock·roach [kɑ́krotʃ] *s.* cucaracha.

cock·tail [kɑ́ktel] *s.* coctel; aperitivo (*de ostras, almejas, frutas, etc.*),

cock·y [kɑ́kɪ] *adj.* arrogante, *Ríopl.* retobado.

co·coa [kóko] *s.* cacao; bebida de cacao, chocolate.

co·co·nut [kókənət] *s.* coco (*fruta*).

co·coon [kəkún] *s.* capullo (*del gusano de seda, etc.*).

cod [kɑd] *s. N. Esp.* abadejo; *Andalucía, Am.* bacalao; **cod-liver oil** aceite de hígado de bacalao.

cod·dle [kɑ́dl] *v.* mimar, consentir.

code [kod] *s.* código; clave; — **message** comunicación en clave; **signal** — código de señales.

co·dex [kódɛks] *s.* codice.

cod·fish [kɑ́dfɪʃ] = **cod.**

co·erce [koɚ́s] *v.* forzar, obligar.

co·er·cion [koɚ́ʃən] *s.* coacción.

co·ex·is·tence [koɛgzístəns] *s.* coexistencia.

cof·fee [kɔ́fɪ] *s.* café; — **shop** café; — **tree** cafeto — **bean** grano de café; **black** — café solo; *Col.* tinto.

cof·fee·pot [kɔ́fɪpɑt] *s.* cafetera.

cof·fer [kɔ́fɚ] *s.* cofre, arca.

cof·fin [kɔ́fɪn] *s*. ataúd, féretro.
cog [kɑg] *s*. diente; — **wheel** rueda dentada.
cog·nate [kɑ́gnet] *s*. cognato.
co·her·ent [kohífrənt] *adj*. coherente; conexo.
co·he·sion [kohíʒən] *s*. cohesión.
coif·fure [kwɑfjúr] *s*. tocado, peinado.
coil [kɔɪl] *s*. rollo; rosca; espiral de alambre; **electric** — bobina; *v*. arrollar(se), enrollar(se); enroscar(se).
coin [kɔɪn] *s*. moneda; *v*. acuñar; (*make up*) inventar, forjar (*una frase o palabra*).
coin·age [kɔ́ɪnɪdʒ] *s*. acuñación; sistema monetario; moneda, monedas; invención (*de una palabra o frase*).
co·in·cide [koɪnsáɪd] *v*. coincidir.
co·in·ci·dence [koʃnsədəns] *s*. coincidencia; casualidad.
coke [kok] *s*. cok, coque (*combustible*).
cold [kold] *adj*. frío; — **cream** crema cosmética; — **meat** fiambre; — **storage almacenaje refrigerado, frigorífico**; — **wave** ola de frío; — **war** guerra fría; **to be** — tener frío; **it is** — **today** hace frío hoy; *s*. frío; catarro, resfriado; **to catch a** — resfriarse, acatarrarse.
cold·ness [kóldnɪs] *s*. frialdad; indiferencia, despego.
col·ic [kálɪk] *s*. cólico.
col·lab·o·rate [kəlǽbəret] *v*. colaborar.
col·lab·o·ra·tion [kəlǽbəréʃən] *s*. colaboración.
col·lapse [kəlǽps] *s*. desplome, derrumbe, derrumbamiento; hundimiento; (*person*) postración; *v*. doblar(se), plegar(se); contraer (*el volumen*); hundirse, derrumbarse, desplomarse; sufrir una postración.
col·lar [kálɚ] *s*. collar; cuello (*de vestido, camisa, etc*.); collera (*para mulas o caballos de tiro*); *v*. acollarar, poner collar a; coger o agarrar por el cuello; prender.
col·late [kəlét, kólet] *v*. cotejar; colacionar.
col·lat·er·al [kəlǽtərəl] *adj*. colateral; auxiliar, subsidiario, accesorio; *s*. garantía (*para un préstamo bancario*).
col·league [kálig] *s*. colega.
col·lect [kəlɛ́kt] *v*. recoger; coleccionar; (*money*) cobrar; (*taxes*) recaudar (*impuestos*); reunir(se); congregarse; **to** — **oneself** calmarse; sosegarse, reportarse; — **on delivery** (C.O.D.) contra reembolso; **collectable** cobradero.
col·lec·tion [kəlɛ́kʃən] *s*. colección; agrupación (*de gente*); recolección, cobranza, cobro, recaudación, colecta.
col·lec·tive [kəlɛ́ktɪv] *adj*. colectivo; — **bargaining** contrato (convenio) colectivo.
col·lec·tiv·ism [kəlɛ́ktəvɪzm] *s*. colectivismo.
col·lec·tor [kəlɛ́ktɚ] *s*. colector; coleccionista (*de sellos, objetos artísticos, etc*.); cobrador (*de billetes, deudas, etc*.) recaudador (*de impuestos*).
col·lege [kálɪdʒ] *s*. universidad; — **of engineering** facultad de ingeniería; — **of medicine** escuela (*facultad*) de medicina.
col·lide [kəláɪd] *v*. chocar; estar en conflicto, oponerse.
col·lie [kálɪ] *s*. perro de pastor.
col·li·sion [kəlíʒən] *s*. choque, colisión; oposición; pugna (*de intereses, ideas, etc*.).
col·lo·qui·al [kəlókwɪəl] *adj*. familiar; — **expression** locución o frase familiar.
col·lu·sion [kəlúʒɪən] *s*. confabulación.
co·lon [kólən] *s*. colon (*del intestino*); dos puntos (*signo de puntuación*).
colo·nel [ʒ́nl] *s*. coronel.
co·lo·ni·al [kəlónɪəl] *adj*. colonial.

col·o·nist [kálənɪst] *s*. colono, colonizador.
col·o·ni·za·tion [kɑlənəzéʃən] *s*. colonización.
col·o·nize [kálənaɪz] *v*. colonizar; establecerse en colonia.
col·o·ny [kálənɪ] *s*. colonia.
col·or [kʌ́ɚ] *s*. color; colorido; **the -s** la bandera; *v*. colorar; colorear; dar colorido; pintar; teñir; iluminar (*una fotografía, grabado, etc*.); ruborizarse.
col·ored [kʌ́lɚd] *adj*. colorado, teñido, colorido, pintado; de color; coloreado; — **person** persona de color.
col·or·ful [kʌ́lɚfəl] *adj*. lleno de color; colorido; vistoso; vívido; pintoresco.
col·or·ing [kʌ́lərɪŋ] *s*. colorido; coloración; colorante.
col·or·less [kʌ́lɚlɪs] *adj*. incoloro; descolorido.
co·los·sal [kəlásl] *adj*. colosal.
colt [kolt] *s*. potro.
Co·lum·bi·an [kəlʌ́mbɪən] *adj*. colombiano, de Colombia; colombino, referente a Cristóbal Colón.
col·umn [kálən] *s*. columna; — **inch** pulgada de columna.
co·ma [kómə] *s*. coma.
comb [kom] *s*. peine; peineta (*de mujer*); cresta (*de gallo*); rastrillo, carda (*para lana*); almohaza (*para caballos*); panal (*de miel*); *v*. peinar; rastrillar; cardar (*lana*); escudriñar; **to** — **one's hair** peinarse.
com·bat [kámbæt] *s*. combate, pelea; *v*. combatir.
com·bat·ant [kámbətənt] *adj*. & *s*. combatiente.
com·bi·na·tion [kɑmbənéʃən] *s*. combinación.
com·bine [kəmbáɪn] *v*. combinar(se), unir(se).
com·bo [kámbo] *s*. batería de jazz.
com·bus·ti·ble [kəmbʌ́stəbl] *adj*. & *s*. combustible.
com·bus·tion [kəmbʌ́stʃən] *s*. combustión.
come [kʌm] *v*. venir; llegar; provenir; **to** — **about** suceder; efectuarse, verificarse; **to** — **again** volver, volver a venir; **to** — **back** volver, regresar; **to** — **downstairs** bajar; **to** — **in** entrar; **to** — **out** salir; **to** — **of age** llegar a mayor edad; **to** — **off** soltarse, zafarse; **to** — **to** volver en sí; **to** — **up** subir; surgir (*una cuestión*); *p.p*. de **to come**.
co·me·di·an [kəmídɪən] *s*. cómico, comediante.
com·e·dy [kámədɪ] *s*. comedia.
come·ly [kámlɪ] *adj*. agradable a la vista, gentil, bien parecido.
com·et [kámɪt] *s*. cometa.
com·fort [kámfɚt] *s*. comodidad; bienestar, alivio, consuelo; *v*. consolar, confortar, aliviar.
com·fort·a·ble [kámfɚtəbl] *adj*. cómodo; confortable; — **life** vida holgada; — **income** un buen pasar, renta suficiente; **comfortably** *adv*. cómodamente; con comodidad; holgadamente.
com·fort·er [kámfɚtɚ] *s*. consolador; edredón, cobertor acolchado.
com·fort·less [kámfɚtlɪs] *adj*. incómodo; desconsolado.
com·ic [kámɪk] *adj*. cómico; chistoso, gracioso; **-s** *pl*. caricaturas, historietas cómicas.
com·i·cal [kámɪkl] *adj*. cómico, gracioso.
com·ing [kámɪŋ] *adj*. que viene, que llega; próximo; venidero; *s*. venida, llegada; — **of Christ** advenimiento de Cristo.
com·ma [kámə] *s*. coma.
com·mand [kəmǽnd] *s*. (*order*) mando; mandato, orden; mandamiento; (*post*) comandancia; (*dominance*) dominio; (*computer*) comando, mandato; **at your** — a la orden de Vd., a la disposición de Vd.; **he has a good** — **of English** domina bien el inglés; *v*. mandar; ordenar;

dominar; comandar; **to — respect** inspirar respeto, imponerse.

com·mand·er [kəmǽndɚ] *s.* jefe; comandante; teniente de navío; comendador *(de ciertas órdenes)*; **— in chief** comandante en jefe; general en jefe.

com·mand·ment [kəmǽndmənt] *s.* mandamiento; mandato, orden.

com·man·do [kəmǽndo] *s.* comando.

com·mem·o·rate [kəméməret] *v.* conmemorar.

com·mence [kəméns] *v.* comenzar.

com·mence·ment [kəménsmənt] *s.* comienzo, principio; acto de distribución de diplomas.

com·mend [kəménd] *v.* alabar, elogiar; encomendar, encargar; recomendar.

com·men·da·tion [kaməndéʃən] *s.* encomio, alabanza.

com·ment [kámɛnt] *s.* comentario, observación, nota; *v.* comentar; hacer observaciones; hacer comentarios.

com·men·tar·y [káməntɛrɪ] *s.* comentario.

com·men·ta·tor [káməntetɚ] *s.* comentador; comentarista; **radio —** comentarista radial.

com·merce [kámɚs] *s.* comercio.

com·mer·cial [kəmɝ́ʃəl] *adj.* comercial; *(advertising)* anuncio en radio o televisión; **commercialize** comercializar ocasiones no comerciales.

com·mis·er·a·tion [kəmɪzəréʃən] *s.* compasión.

com·mis·sar [kámɪsar] *s.* comisario.

com·mis·sar·y [káməsɛrɪ] *s.* comisario.

com·mis·sion [kəmíʃən] *s.* comisión; *(charge)* encargo; junta; *(title)* nombramiento; **to put out of — inutilizar; descomponer, quebrar; retirar del servicio *(un navío)*; *v.* comisionar; encargar; nombrar; poner en servicio *(un navío)*; **-ed officer** oficial comisionado *(alférez u oficial superior a éste)*.

com·mis·sion·er [kəmíʃənɚ] *s.* comisionado; comisario; **police —** comisario de policía.

com·mit [kəmít] *v.* *(perpetrate)* cometer; *(entrust)* encargar; **to — to memory** aprender de memoria; **to — to prison** encarcelar; **to — oneself** dar o expresar su opinión, expresarse abiertamente, comprometerse.

com·mit·tee [kəmítɪ] *s.* comité; comisión, junta; **— of one** comisionado o delegado único.

com·mod·i·ty [kəmádətɪ] *s.* mercancía; género, mercadería, artículo de consumo, producto.

com·mon [kámən] *adj.* común; general; corriente; vulgar, ordinario; público; **— law** derecho consuetudinario; **— sense** sentido común; **— soldier** soldado raso; **— mercado común; -s** *s. pl.* refectorio *(de un colegio o universidad)*; ejido, campo común; **-ly** *adv.* comúnmente, por lo común.

com·mon·ness [kámənnɪs] *s.* vulgaridad, ordinariez; frecuencia.

com·mon·place [kámənples] *adj.* común, trivial; *s.* lugar común.

com·mon·wealth [kámənwɛlθ] *s.* estado; república; pueblo, colectividad.

com·mo·tion [kəmóʃən] *s.* conmoción; tumulto; bullicio; levantamiento.

com·mune [kəmjún] *v.* comunicarse (con); comulgar.

com·mu·ni·cate [kəmjúnəket] *v.* comunicar(se); transmitir.

com·mu·ni·ca·tion [kəmjunəkéʃən] *s.* comunicación.

com·mu·ni·ca·tive [kəmjúnəketɪv] *adj.* comunicativo.

com·mun·ion [kəmjúnjən] *s.* comunión.

com·mu·nism [kámjʊnɪzəm] *s.* comunismo.

com·mu·nist [kámjʊnɪst] *s. & adj.* comunista.

com·mu·ni·ty [kəmjúnətɪ] *s.* comunidad; sociedad; vecindario, barrio; **— chest** caja de beneficencia, fondos de beneficencia.

com·mute [kəmjút] *v.* conmutar; viajar diario de una población a otra.

com·pact [kəmpǽkt] *adj.* compacto; denso; apretado; conciso; sucinto; [kámpǽkt] *s.* pacto, trato, convenio; polvera.

com·pact·ness [kəmpǽktnɪs] *s.* solidez; densidad; concisión.

com·pan·ion [kəmpǽnjən] *s.* compañero; acompañante.

com·pan·ion·ship [kəmpǽnjənʃɪp] *s.* compañerismo, camaradería; compañía.

com·pany [kámpənɪ] *s.* compañía; sociedad; visita; **ship's —** tripulación; **to keep — with** acompañar a; cortejar a; tener relaciones con, frecuentar la compañía de.

com·pa·ra·ble [kámpərəbl] *adj.* comparable.

com·par·a·tive [kəmpǽrətɪv] *adj.* comparativo.

com·pare [kəmpɛ́r] *v.* comparar; cotejar; confrontar; contrastar; **beyond —** incomparable, sin par, sin igual, sin comparación.

com·par·i·son [kəmpǽrəsn̩] *s.* comparación; símil; **beyond —** incomparable, sin comparación; **in — with** comparado con.

com·part·ment [kəmpártmənt] *s.* compartimiento, sección, división; departamento.

com·pass [kámpəs] *s.* compás *(para dibujar)*; brújula; área, ámbito; alcance.

com·pas·sion [kəmpǽʃən] *s.* compasión, lástima.

com·pas·sion·ate [kəmpǽʃənɪt] *adj.* compasivo, misericordioso.

com·pa·tri·ot [kəmpétrɪət] *s.* compatriota.

com·pel [kəmpɛ́l] *v.* compeler, obligar; exigir.

com·pen·sate [kámpənset] *v.* compensar; recompensar; remunerar.

com·pen·sa·tion [kampənséʃən] *s.* compensación; recompensa; remuneración.

com·pete [kəmpít] *v.* competir.

com·pe·tence [kámpətəns] *s.* competencia, aptitud, capacidad.

com·pe·tent [kámpətənt] *adj.* competente; calificado; capaz.

com·pe·ti·tion [kampətíʃən] *s.* competencia; concurso, certamen; contienda; **cutthroat —** competencia asesina (implacable).

com·pet·i·tive [kəmpétɪtɪv] *adj.* en competencia, **— examination** oposición, concurso.

com·pet·i·tor [kəmpétətɚ] *s.* competidor; rival; opositor.

com·pile [kəmpáɪl] *v.* compilar, recopilar.

com·pil·er [kəmpáɪlɚ] *s.* *(computer)* compilador.

com·pla·cen·cy [kəmplésn̩sɪ] *s.* complacencia, contentamiento.

com·pla·cent [kəmplésn̩t] *adj.* complaciente, satisfecho.

com·plain [kəmplén] *v.* quejarse; querellarse.

com·plain·ant [kəmplénənt] *s.* querellante.

com·plaint [kəmplént] *s.* queja; quejido, lamento; dolencia, enfermedad; **to lodge a —** hacer una reclamación.

com·ple·ment [kámpləmənt] *s.* complemento; [kámpləmənt] *v.* complementar, completar.

com·plete [kəmplít] *adj.* completo; *v.* completar; terminar; **-ly** *adv.* completamente, por completo.

com·plete·ness [kəmplítnɪs] *s.* perfección; minuciosidad; lo completo; lo cabal; lo acabado.

com·ple·tion [kəmplíʃən] *s.* completamiento; terminación, conclusión; cumplimiento.

com·plex [kámplɛks] *s.* complejo; [kəmplɛ́ks] *adj.*

complejo; compuesto; complicado.

com·plex·ion [kəmplέkʃən] *s.* (*skin*) cutis, tez; (*make-up*) aspecto.

com·plex·i·ty [kəmplέksətɪ] *s.* complejidad.

com·pli·ance [kəmpláɪəns] *s.* complacencia; condescendencia; conformidad; cumplimiento; **in — with** en conformidad con; de acuerdo con, conforme a.

com·pli·cate [kámpləkət] *v.* complicar.

com·pli·cat·ed [kámpləketɪd] *adj.* complicado.

com·pli·ca·tion [kampləkéʃən] *s.* complicación.

com·plic·i·ty [kəmplísətɪ] *s.* complicidad.

com·pli·ment [kámpləmənt] *s.* cumplido, cumplimiento; (*flattery*) requiebro, lisonja, galantería; **to send one's -s** enviar saludos; [kámpləmɛnt] *v.* cumplimentar; requebrar; lisonjear; alabar.

com·ply [kəmpláɪ] *v.* consentir, conformarse (con), obrar de acuerdo (con); cumplir (con).

com·po·nent [kəmpónənt] *adj. & s.* componente.

com·pose [kəmpóz] *v.* componer; **to — oneself** sosegarse, serenarse, calmarse.

com·posed [kəmpózd] *adj.* compuesto; tranquilo, sereno, sosegado; **to be — of** estar compuesto de, componerse de, constar de.

com·pos·er [kəmpózɚ] *s.* compositor; autor.

com·pos·ite [kəmpázɪt] *adj.* compuesto; *s.* compuesto; mezcla.

com·po·si·tion [kampəzíʃən] *s.* composición; arreglo; compuesto.

com·po·sure [kəmpóʒɚ] *s.* compostura, calma, serenidad.

com·pound [kámpaʊnd] *adj. & s.* compuesto; [kampáʊnd] *v.* componer; mezclar, combinar; **to — interest** calcular el interés compuesto.

com·pre·hend [kamprɪhέnd] *v.* comprender; abarcar, abrazar, incluir.

com·pre·hen·si·ble [kamprɪhέnsəbl̩] *adj.* comprensible, inteligible.

com·pre·hen·sion [kamprɪhέnʃən] *s.* comprensión.

com·pre·hen·sive [kamprɪhέnsɪv] *adj.* comprensivo; inclusivo.

com·press [kámprɛs] *s.* compresa; [kəmprέs] *v.* comprimir, apretar, condensar.

com·pres·sion [kəmprέʃən] *s.* compresión.

com·prise [kəmpráɪz] *v.* comprender, abarcar, incluir, abrazar; constar de.

com·pro·mise [kámprəmaɪz] *s.* compromiso; arreglo; avenencia; término medio; *v.* comprometer; avenirse, transigir; *Am.* transar.

comp·trol·ler [kəntrólɚ] *s.* interventor, *Am.* contralor.

com·pul·sion [kəmpʌ́læən] *s.* compulsión, coacción.

com·pul·so·ry [kəmpʌ́lsərɪ] *adj.* obligatorio.

com·pu·ta·tion [kampjətéʃən] *s.* cómputo, cálculo.

com·pute [kəmpjút] *v.* computar.

com·put·er [kəmpjútɚ] *s.* computadora; *Esp.* ordenador; **— science** informática.

com·put·er·ize [kəmpjútɚaɪz] *v.* informatizar, computarizar; suplir con sistema computador.

com·rade [kámræd] *s.* camarada, compañero.

con·cave [kankév] *adj.* cóncavo.

con·ceal [kənsíl] *v.* encubrir, ocultar, esconder.

con·ceal·ment [kənsílmənt] *s.* encubrimiento.

con·cede [kənsíd] *v.* conceder; otorgar; admitir, reconocer.

con·ceit [kənsít] *s.* presunción, amor propio, vanagloria; concepto, agudeza.

con·ceit·ed [kənsítɪd] *adj.* presuntuoso, presumido, vanidoso, engreído.

con·ceiv·a·ble [kənsívəbl̩] *adj.* concebible,

imaginable, comprensible.

con·ceive [kənsív] *v.* concebir; imaginar.

con·cen·trate [kánsn̩tret] *v.* concentrar(se), reconcentrar(se).

con·cen·tra·tion [kansn̩tréʃən] *s.* concentración; reconcentración; **— camp** reconcentración de presos.

con·cept [kánsɛpt] *s.* concepto, idea; opinión.

con·cep·tion [kənsέpʃən] *s.* concepción; concepto, idea

con·cern [kənsɝ́n] *s.* (*business*) compañía, negociación; negocio; establecimiento mercantil; (*interest*) cuidado; interés; preocupación; **to be of no —** no ser de consecuencia; *v.* concernir, importar, interesar; preocupar; **in all that -s him** en cuanto le atañe, en cuanto le concierne; **to whom it may —** a quien corresponda.

con·cerned [kənsɝ́nd] *adj.* interesado; preocupado, (*restless*) intranquilo, inquieto, ansioso; **to be — about** interesarse por, preocuparse por; **as far as I am —** por lo que me concierne, por lo que me toca, en cuanto a mí me atañe.

con·cern·ing [kənsɝ́nɪŋ] *prep.* tocante a, respecto a, acerca de.

con·cert [kánsɝt] *s.* concierto; [kənsɝ́t] *v.* concertar, arreglar (*un plan*).

con·ces·sion [kənsɝ́ʃən] *s.* concesión.

con·cil·i·ate [kənsílɪet] *v.* conciliar, poner en armonía; ganar la voluntad de.

con·cise [kənsáɪs] *adj.* conciso, sucinto.

con·cise·ness [kənsáɪsnɪs] *s.* concisión, brevedad.

con·clude [kənklúd] *v.* concluir; acabar, terminar; deducir; decidir.

con·clu·sion [kənklúʒən] *s.* conclusión.

con·clu·sive [kənklúsɪv] *adj.* conclusivo, concluyente.

con·coct [kankákt] *v.* confeccionar; preparar (*combinando diversos ingredientes*); inventar, urdir.

con·coc·tion [kankákʃən] *s.* cocimiento, menjurje; mezcla.

con·cord [kánkɔrd] *s.* concordia, conformidad; acuerdo; convenio, pacto.

con·crete [kankrít] *adj.* concreto; de hormigón, de cemento; *s.* hormigón, cemento, *Am.* concreto.

con·cu·bine [káŋkjubaɪn] *s.* concubina.

con·cur [kənkɝ́] *v.* estar de acuerdo, ser del mismo parecer; unirse.

con·cus·sion [kənkʌ́ʃən] *s.* concusión.

con·demn [kəndέm] *v.* condenar; **to — a building** condenar un edificio.

con·dem·na·tion [kandɛmnéʃən] *s.* condenación.

con·den·sa·tion [kandɛnséʃən] *s.* condensación; resumen, compendio.

con·dense [kəndέns] *v.* condensar(se).

con·de·scend [kandɪsέnd] *v.* condescender.

con·de·scen·sion [kandɪsέnʃən] *s.* condescendencia.

con·di·ment [kándəmənt] *s.* condimento.

con·di·tion [kəndíʃən] *s.* condición; estado; nota o calificación provisional; **on — that** a condición de que, con tal que; *v.* acondicionar; poner en buena condición; estipular; reprobar provisionalmente (*a un estudiante*).

con·di·tion·al [kəndíʃənl̩] *adj.* condicional.

con·dole [kəndól] *v.* condolerse; **to — with** dar el pésame a; consolar a.

con·do·lence [kəndóləns] *s.* pésame.

con·do·min·i·um [kandəmínɪəm] *s.* condominio.

con·done [kəndón] *v.* dispensar; perdonar; condonar.

con·duce [kəndjús] *v.* conducir.

con·du·cive [kəndjúsɪv] *adj.* conducente.

con·duct [kándʌkt] *s.* (*behavior*) conducta;

comportamiento, proceder; (*handling*) dirección, manejo; [kəndʌ́kt] *v.* conducir; dirigir; manejar; **to — oneself well** portarse bien.

con·duc·tor [kəndʌ́ktə·] *s.* conductor; guía; **orchestra — director de orquesta; train —** revisor; cobrador, *Am.* conductor.

con·duit [kándʊɪt] *s.* conducto; caño; cañería, tubería.

cone [kon] *s.* cono; **paper —** cucurucho; **pine —** piña.

con·fec·tion [kənfɛ́kʃən] *s.* confección; confitura; confite, dulce.

con·fec·tion·er·y [kənfɛ́kʃənɛrɪ] *s.* confitería; dulcería; confites, dulces.

con·fed·er·a·cy [kənfɛ́dərəsɪ] *s.* confederación.

con·fed·er·ate [kənfɛ́dərɪt] *adj. & s.* confederado; [kənfɛ́dəret] *v.* confederar(se).

con·fed·er·a·tion [kənfɛdəréʃən] *s.* confederación.

con·fer [kənfɝ·] *v.* conferir; conceder; conferenciar; consultar.

con·fer·ence [kánfərəns] *s.* convención; congreso; (*meeting*) consulta, junta, sesión.

con·fess [kənfɛ́s] *v.* confesar(se); reconocer, admitir.

con·fes·sion [kənfɛ́ʃən] *s.* confesión.

con·fes·sion·al [kənfɛ́ʃənl] *s.* confesionario.

con·fes·sor [kənfɛ́sə·] *s.* confesor.

con·fi·dant [kánfədænt] *s.* confidente.

con·fide [kənfáɪd] *v.* confiar; fiar.

con·fi·dence [kánfədəns] *s.* confianza; confidencia; **— game** estafa; **— man** estafador.

con·fi·dent [kánfədənt] *adj.* confiado; seguro, cierto; **-ly** *adv.* confiadamente, con toda seguridad.

con·fi·den·tial [kɑnfədɛ́nʃəl] *adj.* confidencial; íntimo; secreto; **-ly** *adv.* en confianza.

con·fine [kánfaɪn] *s.* confín; [kənfáɪn] *v.* confinar; encerrar; **to — oneself to** limitarse a; **to be -ed in bed** estar encamado, guardar cama.

con·fine·ment [kənfáɪnmənt] *s.* encerramiento; encierro; prisión, encarcelación.

con·firm [kənfɝ́m] *v.* confirmar.

con·fir·ma·tion [kɑnfə·méʃən] *s.* confirmación.

con·fis·cate [kánfɪsket] *v.* confiscar.

con·fla·gra·tion [kɑnfləgréʃən] *s.* conflagración, incendio.

con·flict [kánflɪkt] *s.* conflicto, oposición, choque; (*fight*) lucha, combate; [kənflɪ́kt] *v.* chocar, oponerse, estar en conflicto.

con·form [kənfɔ́rm] *v.* conformar(se).

con·form·i·ty [kənfɔ́rmətɪ] *s.* conformidad.

con·found [kɑnfáʊnd] *v.* confundir, perturbar; desconcertar, aturdir; **— it!** ¡caramba!

con·front [kənfrʌ́nt] *v.* confrontar; carear, poner cara a cara (*a dos reos*); encararse con, afrontar, hacer frente a, arrostrar.

con·fuse [kənfjúz] *v.* confundir; trastornar; embrollar; desconcertar.

con·fused [kənfjúzd] *adj.* confuso; revuelto; desconcertado, perplejo; **to become —** confundirse; desconcertarse.

con·fus·ing [kənfjúzɪŋ] *adj.* confuso, revuelto; desconcertante.

con·fu·sion [kənfjúʒən] *s.* confusión; desorden; tumulto; perplejidad.

con·geal [kəndʒíl] *v.* congelar(se), helar(se), cuajar(se).

con·gen·ial [kəndʒínjəl] *adj.* congenial; simpático; **to be — with** congeniar con, simpatizar con.

con·ges·tion [kəndʒɛ́stʃən] *s.* congestión; aglomeración.

con·glom·er·a·tion [kənɡlɑməréʃən] *s.* aglomeración.

con·grat·u·late [kənɡrǽtʃəlet] *v.* congratular,

felicitar, dar el parabién

con·grat·u·la·tion [kənɡrætʃəléʃən] *s.* congratulación, felicitación, parabién, enhorabuena.

con·gre·gate [kánɡrɪget] *v.* congregar(se), juntar(se), reunir(se).

con·gre·ga·tion [kɑŋɡrɪgéʃən] *s.* congregación; asamblea, reunión; colección, agregado; fieles, feligreses (*de una iglesia*).

con·gress [kánɡrəs] *s.* congreso; asamblea.

con·gres·sion·al [kənɡrɛ́ʃənl] *adj.* perteneciente al congreso.

con·gress·man [kánɡrəsmən] *s.* congresista, diputado, representante.

con·ic [kánɪk] *adj.* cónico.

con·jec·ture [kəndʒɛ́ktʃə·] *s.* conjetura, suposición; *v.* conjeturar, suponer.

con·ju·gate [kándʒəget] *v.* conjugar.

con·ju·ga·tion [kɑndʒəgéʃən] *s.* conjugación.

con·junc·tion [kəndʒʌ́ŋkʃən] *s.* conjunción.

con·jure [kándʒə·] *v.* conjurar; **to — up** evocar; [kəndʒúr] rogar, implorar.

con·nect [kənɛ́kt] *v.* conectar; unir(se), juntar(se); enlazar(se); relacionar(se); acoplar.

con·nect·ing rod [kənɛ́ktɪŋ rad] *s.* biela.

con·nec·tion [kənɛ́kʃən] *s.* conexión; enlace; vínculo; unión; relación; **-s** parientes; amigos, amistades.

con·nip·tion [kənɪ́pʃən] *s.* pataleta; **to have a —** darle a uno una pataleta.

con·nive [kənáɪv] *v.* conspirar; disimular; hacerse cómplice.

con·nois·seur [kɑnəsɝ·] *s.* conocedor, perito.

con·quer [kɑ́ŋkə·] *v.* conquistar; vencer.

con·quer·or [kɑ́ŋkərə·] *s.* conquistador; vencedor.

con·quest [kɑ́ŋkwɛst] *s.* conquista.

con·science [kɑ́nʃəns] *s.* conciencia.

con·sci·en·tious [kɑnʃɪɛ́nʃəs] *adj.* concienzudo.

con·scious [kɑ́nʃəs] *adj.* consciente; sabedor; **-ly** *adv.* conscientemente, a sabiendas.

con·scious·ness [kɑ́nʃəsnɪs] *s.* conciencia, estado conciente; **to lose —** perder el sentido o conocimiento.

con·script [kənskrɪ́pt] *v.* reclutar; [kánskrɪpt] *s.* recluta.

con·se·crate [kánsɪkret] *v.* consagrar; dedicar.

con·se·cra·tion [kɑnsɪkréʃən] *s.* consagración; dedicación.

con·sec·u·tive [kənsɛ́kjətɪv] *adj.* consecutivo.

con·sen·sus [kənsɛ́nsəs] *s.* consenso.

con·sent [kənsɛ́nt] *s.* consentimiento; permiso, asentimiento; autorización; *v.* consentir; permitir; asentir.

con·se·quence [kánsəkwɛns] *s.* consecuencia.

con·se·quent [kánsəkwɛnt] *adj.* consecuente; consiguiente; *s.* consecuente, consiguiente, consecuencia; **-ly** *adv.* por consiguiente, por consecuencia.

con·se·quen·tial [kɑnsəkwɛ́ntʃl] *adj.* de consecuencia.

con·ser·va·tion [kɑnsə·véʃən] *s.* conservación; preservación.

con·ser·va·tive [kənsɝ́vətɪv] *adj.* conservador; conservativo; *s.* conservador.

con·ser·va·to·ry [kənsɝ́vətorɪ] *s.* conservatorio; invernadero.

con·serve [kɑ́nsɝv] *s.* conserva, dulce; *v.* [kənsɝ́v] conservar; preservar.

con·sid·er [kənsɪ́də·] *v.* considerar.

con·sid·er·a·ble [kənsɪ́dərəbl] *adj.* considerable; cuantioso; **considerably** *adv.* considerablemente; **considerable older** bastante más viejo.

con·sid·er·ate [kənsɪ́dərɪt] *adj.* considerado.

con·sid·er·a·tion [kənsɪdəréʃən] *s.* (*respect*) respeto; consideración; importancia; (*pay*) remuneración; **in — of** en atención a, teniendo en cuenta, en razón de, en vista de.

con·sid·er·ing [kənsídərɪŋ] *prep.* en razón de, en vista de; en atención a, en consideración de.

con·sign [kənsáɪn] *v.* consignar; enviar; entregar.

con·sign·ee [kənsaɪní] *s.* consignatario.

con·sign·ment [kənsáɪnmənt] *s.* consignación.

con·sist [kənsíst] *v.* consistir (en); constar (de).

con·sis·ten·cy [kənsístənsɪ] *s.* consecuencia; consistencia, firmeza, solidez.

con·sis·tent [kənsístənt] *adj.* consecuente, lógico; compatible; consistente, coherente.

con·so·la·tion [kansəléʃən] *s.* consolación; consuelo.

con·sole [kənsól] *v.* consolar.

con·sol·i·date [kənsáledət] *v.* consolidar(se); unir(se), combinar(se).

con·so·nant [kánsənənt] *adj.* consonante; conforme; *s.* consonante.

con·sort [kánsɔrt] *s.* consorte; [kənsɔ́rt] *v.* **to — with** asociarse con.

con·spic·u·ous [kənspíkjuəs] *adj.* conspicuo, notorio; manifiesto, sobresaliente.

con·spir·a·cy [kənspírəsɪ] *s.* conspiración, conjuración.

con·spir·a·tor [kənspírətɚ] *s.* conspirador, conjurado.

con·spire [kənspáɪr] *v.* conspirar; tramar, maquinar.

con·sta·ble [kánstəbl̩] *s.* alguacil, policía; condestable (*titulo*).

con·stan·cy [kánstənsɪ] *s.* constancia.

con·stant [kánstənt] *adj.* constante; *s.* constante, cantidad constante; **-ly** *adv.* constantemente, contínuamente, siempre; a menudo.

con·stel·la·tion [kanstəleʃən] *s.* constelación.

con·ster·na·tion [kanstɚnéʃən] *s.* consternación.

con·sti·pate [kánstəpet] *v.* estreñir.

con·sti·pa·tion [kanstəpéʃən] *s.* estreñimiento.

con·stit·u·ent [kənstítʃuənt] *adj.* constituyente; constitutivo; componente; *s.* componente, elemento; elector, votante.

con·sti·tute [kánstətjut] *v.* constituir; componer; establecer.

con·sti·tu·tion [kanstətjúʃən] *s.* constitución.

con·sti·tu·tion·al [kastətjúʃənl̩] *adj.* constitucional; *s.* paseo a pie, caminata (*para hacer ejercicio*).

con·strain [kənstrén] *v.* constreñir; obligar, forzar; apretar, comprimir.

con·strict [kənstríkt] *v.* apretar; estrechar.

con·struct [kənstrÁkt] *v.* construir, fabricar.

con·struc·tion [kənstrÁktʃən] *s.* construcción; estructura; interpretación.

con·struc·tive [kənstrÁktɪv] *adj.* constructivo; de utilidad positiva; provechoso.

con·strue [kənstrú] *v.* interpretar, explicar.

con·sul [kánsl̩] *s.* cónsul.

con·su·late [kánslɪt] *s.* consulado.

con·sult [kənsÁlt] *v.* consultar.

con·sult·ant [kənsÁltənt] *s.* consultante.

con·sul·ta·tion [kansl+téʃən] *s.* consulta.

con·sume [kənsúm] *v.* consumir; gastar; perder (*el tiempo*).

con·sum·er [kənsúmɚ] *s.* consumidor; **— market** mercado de consumo.

con·sum·mate [kánsəmet] *v.* consumar, completar; llevar a cabo; [kənsÁmɪt] *adj.* consumado, perfecto, completo.

con·sump·tion [kənsÁmpʃən] *s.* consumo, gasto; consunción; tisis, tuberculosis.

con·sump·tive [kənsÁmptɪv] *adj.* tísico.

con·tact [kántækt] *s.* contacto; *v.* tocar; poner(se) en contacto con; estar en contacto con.

con·ta·gion [kəntédʒən] *s.* contagio.

con·ta·gious [kəntédʒəs] *adj.* contagioso.

con·tain [kəntén] *v.* contener; encerrar; tener cabida para; reprimir, refrenar; **to — oneself** contenerse, refrenarse.

con·tain·er [kənténɚ] *s.* envase, caja, recipiente.

con·tam·i·nate [kəntǽmənet] *v.* contaminar, viciar, inficionar, infectar.

con·tam·i·na·tion [kəntæmənéʃən] *s.* contaminación; cruce.

con·tem·plate [kántəmplet] *v.* contemplar; meditar; tener la intención de; proyectar.

con·tem·pla·tion [kantəmpléʃən] *s.* contemplación; meditación; intención, propósito.

con·tem·po·rar·y [kəntémpərɛrɪ] *adj.* contemporáneo; coetáneo.

con·tempt [kəntémpt] *s.* desdén, menosprecio; desprecio; **— of court** contumacia.

con·tempt·i·ble [kəntémptəbl̩] *adj.* despreciable, vil.

con·temp·tu·ous [kəntémptʃuəs] *adj.* desdeñoso.

con·tend [kənténd] *v.* contender; competir; argüir; altercar; sostener, afirmar.

con·tent [kántɛnt] *s.* contenido; sustancia; capacidad; volumen; **-s** contenido; **table of -s** tabla de materias, índice general.

con·tent [kəntént] *adj.* contento; satisfecho; *s.* contento; satisfacción; **to one's heart's —** a pedir de boca; hasta saciarse; a su entera satisfacción; *v.* contentar; satisfacer.

con·tent·ed [kənténtɪd] *adj.* contento, satisfecho.

con·ten·tion [kənténʃən] *s.* contención, contienda, disputa, controversia; tema, argumento; aseveración.

con·tent·ment [kənténtmənt] *s.* contentamiento, contento.

con·test [kántɛst] *s.* concurso, certamen; debate; contienda; torneo; [kəntést] *v.* contender; disputar; luchar por; **to — with** competir con.

con·text [kántɛkst] *s.* contexto.

con·tig·u·ous [kəntígjuəs] *adj.* contiguo; adyacente.

con·ti·nent [kántənənt] *s.* continente; *adj.* continente, casto, moderado.

con·ti·nen·tal [kantənɛ́ntl̩] *adj. & s.* continental.

con·tin·gen·cy [kəntíndʒənsɪ] *s.* contingencia, eventualidad.

con·tin·gent [kəntíndʒənt] *adj. & s.* contingente.

con·tin·u·al [kəntínjuəl] *adj.* contínuo; frecuente; **-ly** *adv.* de continuo, continuamente, frecuentemente.

con·tin·u·ance [kəntínjuəns] *s.* continuación; aplazamiento.

con·tin·u·a·tion [kəntɪnjuéʃən] *s.* continuación.

con·tin·ue [kəntínju] *v.* continuar.

con·ti·nu·i·ty [kantənúətɪ] *s.* continuidad.

con·tin·u·ous [kəntínjuəs] *adj.* continuo, sin parar, sin cesar.

con·tor·tion [kəntɔ́rʃən] *s.* contorsión.

con·tour [kántUr] *s.* contorno; perímetro.

con·tra·band [kántrəbænd] *s.* contrabando.

con·tract [kántrækt] *s.* contrato, pacto, convenio; contrata; **marriage —** esponsales; [kəntrǽkt] *v.* contratar; contraer(se), encoger(se); **to — an illness** contraer una enfermedad; **to — the brows** fruncir las cejas.

con·trac·tion [kəntrǽkʃən] *s.* contracción.

con·trac·tor [kántrǽktɚ] *s.* contratista.

con·tra·dict [katrədíkt] *v.* contradecir; contrariar.

con·tra·dic·tion [kantrədíkʃən] *s.* contradicción; contrariedad.

con·tra·dic·to·ry [kantrədíktərɪ] *adj.* contradictorio; opuesto, contrario.

con·tra·ry [kántrɛrɪ] *adj.* contrario; opuesto; testarudo, obstinado; *s.* contrario; **on the —** al contrario.

con·trast [kántræst] *s.* contraste; [kəntræst] *v.* contrastar.

con·tra·vene [kɑntrəvín] *v.* contravenir a; oponerse a.

con·tri·bute [kəntríbjut] *v.* contribuir.

con·tri·bu·tion [kɑntrəbjúʃən] *s.* contribución; aportación; cuota; dádiva.

con·trib·u·tor [kəntríbjətɚ] *s.* contribuidor; colaborador.

con·trib·u·to·ry [kəntríbjutorɪ] *adj.* contribuidor.

con·trite [kántraɪt] *adj.* contrito.

con·tri·vance [kəntráɪvəns] *s.* (*plan*) traza, maquinación; artificio, invención; designio; artefacto, aparato, máquina.

con·trive [kəntráɪv] *v.* tramar, maquinar; inventar, idear; proyectar; **to — to** buscar el medio de, tratar de, procurar.

con·trol [kəntról] *s.* (*authority*) mando, manejo; dirección; (*instrument*) freno, regulador; restricción; *Am.* control; **-s** mandos, controles; **— stick** palanca (*de un aeroplano*); **— tower** torre de mando; **— experiment** experimento controlado; **— key** tecla de control; **to lose — of one's temper** perder la paciencia; *v.* gobernar, manejar; (*computer*) gestionar; *Am.* controlar; regular, regularizar; restringir; contener, reprimir; tener a raya; **to — oneself** contenerse dominarse.

con·trol·ler [kəntrólɚ] *s.* interventor, registrador, *Ríopl., C.A., Andes, Ven., Col.* contralor, *Ch., Méx.* controlador; regulador; aparato de manejo y control.

con·tro·ver·sy [kántrəvɚsɪ] *s.* controversia, debate, disputa; polémica.

co·nun·drum [kənándrəm] *s.* adivinanza, acertijo.

con·va·lesce [kɑnvəlés] *v.* convalescer.

con·vene [kənvín] *v.* juntar, convocar; reunirse.

con·ven·ience [kənvínjəns] *s.* conveniencia, comodidad; **at one's —** cuando le convenga a uno, cuando tenga oportunidad, cuando buenamente pueda.

con·ven·ient [kənvínjənt] *adj.* conveniente; oportuno; cómodo; a propósito; **-ly** *adv.* convenientemente, cómodamente.

con·vent [kánvɛnt] *s.* convento.

con·ven·tion [kənvɛnʃən] *s.* convención; congreso, asamblea; convenio; costumbre, regla.

con·ven·tion·al [kənvɛnʃənl] *adj.* convencional; tradicional.

con·ven·tion·eer [kənvɛnʃənír] *s.* congresista.

con·verge [kənvɚdʒ] *v.* converger o convergir.

con·ver·sant [kánvɚsnt] *adj.:* **— with** versado en.

con·ver·sa·tion [kɑnvɚséʃən] *s.* conversación.

con·verse [kənvɚs] *v.* conversar, hablar, platicar.

con·ver·sion [kənvɚʒən] *s.* conversión.

con·vert [kánvɚt] *s.* converso, persona convertida; catecúmeno (*converso reciente*); [kənvɚt] *v.* convertir(se).

con·vex [kɑnvéks] *adj.* convexo.

con·vey [kənvé] *v.* llevar; transportar; transferir, traspasar; transmitir; comunicar; **to — thanks** expresar agradecimiento, dar las gracias.

con·vey·ance [kənvéəns] *s.* vehículo; transporte; (*transfer*) transmisión; entrega; comunicación; traspaso; escritura de propiedad o traspaso.

con·vey·er [kənvéɚ] *s.* correa de transmisión.

con·vict [kánvɪkt] *s.* presidiario; reo; [kənvíkt] *v.* convencer (*de un delito*), declarar culpable; probar la culpabilidad de.

con·vic·tion [kənvíkʃən] *s.* convicción;

convencimiento; prueba de culpabilidad.

con·vince [kənvíns] *v.* convencer.

con·vinc·ing [kənvínsɪŋ] *adj.* convincente.

con·vo·ca·tion [kɑnvəkéʃən] *s.* convocación; asamblea

con·voke [kənvók] *v.* convocar.

con·voy [kánvɔɪ] *s.* convoy, escolta, guardia; [kənvɔ́ɪ] *v.* convoyar.

con·vulse [kənvɔ́ls] *v.* crispar; agitar; convulsionar.

con·vul·sion [kənvʌ́lʃən] *s.* convulsión, agitación.

coo [ku] *s.* arrullo; *v.* arrullar.

cook [kʊk] *s.* cocinero, cocinera; *v.* cocinar, guisar; cocer; **to — up a plan** urdir un plan.

cook·er·y [kʊ́kərɪ] *s.* cocina, arte de cocinar.

cook·ie, cook·y [kʊ́kɪ] *s.* bizcochito, bollito.

cook·ing [kʊ́kɪŋ] *s.* cocina, arte culinaria; **— stove** cocina de gas, cocina eléctrica, estufa; **— utensils** batería de cocina, trastos de cocina.

cool [kul] *adj.* (*weather*) fresco; (*indifferent*) frío, indiferente; (*calm*) calmo, sereno; *s.* fresco, frescura; *v.* refrescar; enfriar; templar, calmar; **to — off** enfriarse; calmarse; **cooling-off period** tregua para evitar huelga.

cool·ant [kúlənt] *s.* líquido refrigerador.

cool·ness [kúlnɪs] *s.* fresco, frescura; frialdad, indiferencia.

coon [kun] *s.* coatí (*cuadrúpedo carnívoro*); **a -'s age** una eternidad, mucho tiempo.

coop [kup] *s.* jaula; **chicken —** gallinero; *v.* enjaular; **to — up** encerrar.

co·op·er·ate [koápəret] *v.* cooperar.

co·op·er·a·tion [koɑpəréʃən] *s.* cooperación.

co·op·er·a·tive [koápəretɪv] *adj.* cooperativo; *s.* cooperativa, sociedad cooperativa.

co·or·di·nate [koɔ́rdṇet] *v.* coordinar; [koɔ́rdṇɪt] *adj.* coordinado.

co·or·di·na·tion [koordṇéʃən] *s.* coordinación.

cop [kɑp] *s.* polizonte, policía.

cope [kop] *v.* **to — with** tener suficiente fuerza para; **I cannot — with this** no puedo con esto, no puedo dar abasto a esto.

co·pi·ous [kópɪəs] *adj.* copioso, abundante.

cop·per [kápɚ] *s.* cobre; (*cop*) polizonte, policía; **— coin** moneda de cobre, centavo; **— kettle** marmita o caldera de cobre; *adj.* cobrizo.

cop·y [kápɪ] *s.* copia; ejemplar (*de un libro*); manuscrito (*para el impresor*); *v.* copiar; imitar; remedar; **make fair copy** poner en limpio.

cop·y·right [kápɪraɪt] *s.* derecho de propiedad literaria; derechos de autor; *v.* registrar, obtener patente de propiedad literaria.

co·quette [kokét] *s.* coqueta.

cor·al [kɔ́rəl] *s.* coral; *adj.* coralino, de coral; **— reef** arrecife de coral.

cord [kɔrd] *s.* cuerda; cordón, cordel; cuerda (*medida de leña*); tendón; **-s** pantalones de pana; **spinal —** espinazo, espina dorsal.

cor·dial [kɔ́rdʒəl] *adj.* & *s.* cordial.

cor·du·roy [kɔrdərɔ́ɪ] *s.* pana; **-s** pantalones de pana; **— road** camino de troncos o maderos.

core [kor] *s.* corazón, centro; núcleo; esencia; *v.* cortar el centro o corazón de; despepitar (*una manzana*).

cork [kɔrk] *s.* corcho; tapón; **— tree** alcornoque; *v.* tapar con corcho.

cork·screw [kɔ́rkskru] *s.* tirabuzón, sacacorchos; *adj.* espiral, de forma espiral.

corn [kɔrn] *s.* maíz; grano, cereal; callo (*de los pies o manos*); **— bread** pan de maíz; **— meal** harina de maíz; **— cob** *Esp.* zuro; *Ven., Col. C.A. Méx.* elote; tusa; *v.* salar, curar, acecinar.

corned beef [kɔ́rnd bif] *s.* carne de vaca curada;

acecino.

cor·ner [kɔ́rnɚ] s. (*interior*) rincón; rinconada; ángulo; (*exterior*) esquina; ángulo; (*monopoly*) monopolio; — **stone** piedra angular; — **table** (— **shelf**, — **bracket**) rinconera; v. arrinconar; acorralar; acaparar, monopolizar.

cor·net [kɔrnét] s. corneta.

corn·field [kɔ́rnfild] s. maizal, *Méx., C.A.* milpa.

cor·nice [kɔ́rnɪs] s. cornisa.

cor·ol·lar·y [kɔ́rəlɛrɪ] s. corolario; consecuencia natural.

cor·o·na·tion [kɔrənéʃən] s. coronación.

cor·o·ner [kɔ́rənɚ] s. juez de guardia.

cor·o·net [kɔ́rənɪt] s. coronilla, guirnalda.

cor·po·ral [kɔ́rpərəl] adj. corporal; corpóreo; s. cabo (*militar*).

cor·po·ra·tion [kɔrpəréʃən] s. corporación; sociedad mercantil.

corps [kor] s. cuerpo (*grupo organizado*); **air** — cuerpo de aviación; **army** — cuerpo de ejército.

corpse [kɔrps] s. cadáver.

cor·pu·lent [kɔ́rpjələnt] adj. corpulento.

cor·pus·cle [kɔ́rpəsl] s. corpúsculo; glóbulo.

cor·ral [kəræl] s. corral; v. acorralar.

cor·rect [kərɛ́kt] v. corregir; adj. correcto; **it is** — está bien; **-ly** adv. correctamente; **-ly done** bien hecho.

cor·rec·tion [kərɛ́kʃən] s. corrección.

cor·rect·ness [kərɛ́ktnɪs] s. corrección.

cor·rec·tor [kərɛ́ktɚ] s. corregidor, corrector.

cor·re·late [kɔ́rəlet] v. correlacionar.

cor·re·spond [kɔrəspánd] v. corresponder; corresponderse, cartearse, escribirse.

cor·re·spon·dence [kɔrəspándəns] s. correspondencia.

cor·re·spon·dent [kɔrəspándənt] adj. correspondiente; s. correspondiente; corresponsal.

cor·re·spond·ing [kɔrəspándɪŋ] adj. correspondiente; conforme.

cor·ri·dor [kɔ́rədɚ] s. corredor, pasillo, pasadizo.

cor·rob·o·rate [kərábəret] v. corroborar.

cor·rode [kəród] v. corroer(se).

cor·ru·gat·ed i·ron [kɔ́rəgetəd aɪɚn] s. hierro acanalado.

cor·rupt [kərʌ́pt] adj. corrupto; perverso, depravado; **to become** — corromperse; v. corromper; pervertir; sobornar.

cor·rup·tion [kərʌ́pʃən] s. corrupción; soborno; descomposición.

cor·set [kɔ́rsɪt] s. corsé.

cor·ti·sone [kɔ́rtəzon] s. cortisona.

cos·met·ic [kazmétɪk] adj. & s. cosmético.

cos·mic [kázmɪk] adj. cósmico.

cos·mo·naut [kázmənɔt] s. cosmonauta.

cos·mo·pol·i·tan [kazməpálətn̩] adj. cosmopolita.

cost [kɔst] s. coste, costa o costo; **at all -s** a toda costa; **to sell at** — vender al costo; v. costar; pret. & p.p. de **to cost.**

cost·ly [kɔ́stlɪ] adj. costoso.

cos·tume [kástjum] s. vestuario, traje, vestido; atavío; indumentaria.

cot [kat] s. catre; **folding** — catre de tijera.

cot·tage [kátɪdʒ] s. casita, caseta; casa de campo; — **cheese** requesón.

cot·ter pin [kátɚ pɪn] s. chaveta.

cot·ton [katn̩] s. algodón; — **seed** semilla de algodón; — **wool** algodón en rama; — **yarn** hilaza.

couch [kautʃ] s. canapé, diván; v. expresar; estar escondido o en acecho; **-ed in difficult language** expresado en lenguaje difícil.

cough [kɔf] s. tos; — **drop** pastilla para la tos;

whooping — tos ferina; v. toser; **to** — **up** expectorar.

could [kʊd] pret. del. v. defect. **can.**

coun·cil [káʊnsl̩] s. concilio; concejo; **city** — concejo muncipal.

coun·cil·man [káʊnslmən] s. concejal.

coun·cil·or [káʊnslɚ] s. concejal.

coun·sel [káʊnsl̩] s. (*advice*) consejo; parecer; dictamen; (*lawyer*) abogado consultor; v. aconsejar; recomendar.

coun·sel·or [káʊnslɚ] s. consejero; abogado consultor.

count [kaʊnt] s. (*reckoning*) cuenta, cálculo; cómputo; (*charge*) cargo, acusación; (*noble*) conde; v. contar; valer, tener importancia; **to** — **on** contar con, confiar en.

count·down [káʊntdaʊn] s. recuento descendiente hasta cero.

coun·te·nance [káʊntənəns] s. semblante, aspecto; **to give** — **to** favorecer, apoyar; aprobar; v. aprobar; favorecer, apoyar; tolerar.

count·er [káʊntɚ] s. contador; mostrador; tablero; (*chip*) ficha; adj. contrario, opuesto; adv. al contrario; **to run** — **to** ser contrario a, oponerse a; v. oponerse; contradecir; **to** — **a blow** devolver un golpe.

coun·ter·act [kaʊntɚǽkt] v. contrarrestar, neutralizar.

coun·ter·at·tack [káʊntɚətæk] s. contraataque.

coun·ter·bal·ance [kaʊntɚbǽləns] v. contrapesar; equilibrar; [káʊntɚbæləns] s. contrapeso.

coun·ter·feit [káʊntɚfɪt] s. falsificación; adj. falso; falsificado, falseado; contrahecho; — **money** moneda falsa; v. contrahacer, falsificar, falsear.

coun·ter·mand [káʊntɚmænd] s. contraorden; contramando, revocación, cancelación; [káʊntɚmǽnd] v. contramandar, revocar, cancelar.

coun·ter·part [káʊntɚpɑrt] s. contraparte.

coun·ter·poise [káʊntɚpɔɪz] s. contrapeso; v. contrapesar.

coun·ter·rev·o·lu·tion [kaʊntɚˌrɛvəlúʃən] s. contrarrevolución.

coun·ter·sign [káʊntɚsaɪn] v. contraseña; v. visar, refrendar.

count·ess [káʊntɪs] s. condesa.

count·less [káʊntlɪs] adj. incontable, innumerable.

coun·try [kántrɪ] s. (*nation*) país; (*land*) tierra; (*homeland*) patria; (*field*) campo; adj. campestre; rural; rústico; campesino.

coun·try·man [kántrɪmən] s. compatriota, paisano; (*rural type*) campesino, *Méx., C.A.* ranchero, *P.R.* jíbaro; *Cuba* guajiro; *Ch.* huaso; *Arg.* gaucho; *Ec., Col.* paisa.

coun·try·side [kántrɪsaɪd] s. campiña, campo.

coun·ty [káʊntɪ] s. condado (*división de un estado*).

coup d'é·tat [ku detá] s. golpe de estado; cuartelazo.

cou·pé [kupé, kup] s. cupé.

cou·ple [kʌ́pl̩] s. par; pareja; v. parear; unir, acoplar.

coup·let [kʌ́plɪt] s. copla, versos pareados.

coup·ling [kʌ́plɪŋ] s. unión, conexión; acoplamiento; enganche.

cou·pon [kúpan] s. cupón; talón.

cour·age [kɝ·ɪdʒ] s. coraje, ánimo, valor.

cou·ra·geous [kɝédʒəs] adj. valeroso, valiente, animoso.

cou·ri·er [kúrɪɚ] s. mensajero.

course [kors] s. (*way*) curso; rumbo, trayecto; (*advance*) marcha, progreso; (*mode*) método; (*study*) asignatura; (*dish*) plato (*de una comida*); — **of conduct** conducta, proceder; **golf** — campo o cancha de golf; **race** — hipódromo, pista; **in the** — **of a year** en el transcurso de un año; **of** —

claro, por supuesto; **to follow a straight** — seguir una línea recta.

court [kort] *s.* (*house*) patio; (*city*) plazuela, plazoleta; (*justice*) juzgado, tribunal de justicia; corte; **tennis** — cancha para tenis; — **plaster** tela adhesiva, tafetán inglés, esparadrapo; **to pay** — **to** hacer la corte a, cortejar, galantear; *v.* cortejar; galantear; buscar; **to** — **danger** exponerse al peligro.

cour·te·ous [kɝ́tɪəs] *adj.* cortés.

cour·te·sy [kɝ́təsɪ] *s.* cortesía; fineza, atención; reverencia.

court·i·er [kórtɪɚ] *s.* cortesano, palaciego.

court·mar·tial [kórtmɑrʃəl] *s.* consejo de guerra; *v.* someter a consejo de guerra.

court·ship [kórtʃɪp] *s.* cortejo, galanteo.

court·yard [kórtjɑrd] *s.* patio.

cous·in [kʌ́zn̩] *s.* primo; prima; **first** — primo hermano, primo carnal.

cove [kov] *s.* cala, ensenada

cov·e·nant [kʌ́ənənt] *s.* convenio, pacto; contrato.

cov·er [kʌ́vɚ] *s.* (*lid*) cubierta, tapa, tapadera; (*blanket*) cobija; cobertor; (*binding*) encuadernación; envoltura; (*pillow*) funda; (*shelter*) albergue, abrido; **table** — tapete; — **charge** precio fijo que se agrega a la cuenta por servicios; **to send under separate** — enviar por separado; *v.* cubrir; tapar; encubrir; abrigar, proteger; abarcar; **to** — **a distance** recorrer una distancia.

cov·er·age [kʌ́vərɪdʒ] *s.* alcance; amplitud; (*journalism*) reportaje.

cov·er·ing [kʌ́vrɪŋ] *s.* cubierta; cobertura; envoltura; cobija, abrigo.

cov·et [kʌ́vɪt] *v.* codiciar; ambicionar.

cov·et·ous [kʌ́ɪtəs] *adj.* codicioso.

cow [kaʊ] *s.* vaca; hembra (*de elefante y otros cuadrúpedos*); *v.* atemorizar, acobardar.

cow·ard [káʊɚd] *adj. & s.* cobarde.

cow·ard·ice [káʊɚdɪs] *s.* cobardía.

cow·ard·li·ness [káʊɚdlɪnɪs] *s.* cobardía.

cow·ard·ly [káʊɚdlɪ] *adj.* cobarde; *adv.* cobardemente.

cow·boy [káʊbɔɪ] *s.* vaquero, *Ríopl.* resero, gaucho; *Ven., Col.* llanero.

cow·er [káʊɚ] *v.* agacharse (*de miedo o vergüenza*), achicarse, encogerse (*de miedo*), acobardarse.

cow·hide [káʊhaɪd] *s.* cuero de vaca, vaqueta.

cowl [kaʊl] *s.* capucha.

cox·swain [kɑ́ksən] *s.* timonel.

coy [kɔɪ] *adj.* recatado, esquivo, modesto; timido; gazmoño.

coy·o·te [káɪot, kaɪótɪ] *s.* coyote.

co·zy [kózɪ] *adj.* cómodo y abrigado; cómodo y agradable.

CPU (Central Processing Unit) *s.* (*computer*) UCP (unidad central de proceso).

crab [kræb] *s.* cangrejo; (*person*) cascarrabias; — **apple** manzana silvestre.

crack [kræk] *s.* (*space*) raja, grieta, rendija; (*sound*) crujido; estallido; trueno, estampido; (*blow*) golpe; (*joke*) pulla, chanza; **at the** — **of dawn** al romper el alba; *adj.* excelente; *v.* rajar(se), hender(se), agrietrase; crujir; estallar; **to** — **a joke** soltar un chiste; **to** — **nuts** cascar nueces.

crack·down [krǽkdaʊn] *s.* represión severa.

cracked [krækt] *adj.* agrietado, rajado; quebrado; chiflado, loco.

crack·er [krǽkɚ] *s.* galleta.

crack·le [krǽkl] *s.* crujido; crepitación; chasquido; *v.* crujir, crepitar.

crack·pot [krǽkpat] *s.* eccéntrico.

cra·dle [krédl] *s.* cuna.

craft [kræft] *s.* (*skill*) maña, destreza; astucia, artificio, cautela; (*occupation*) arte, oficio; (*boat*) embarcación; embarcaciones.

crafts·man [krǽftsmən] *s.* artesano, artífice.

craft·y [krǽftɪ] *adj.* mañoso, astuto, cauteloso, taimado.

crag [kræg] *s.* risco, peñasco.

cram [kræm] *v.* rellenar; atestar; atracar(se), hartar(se); engullir.

cramp [kræmp] *s.* calambre; grapa; *v.* comprimir, apretar, estrechar; afianzar, sujetar (*con grapa*).

cran·ber·ry [krǽnbɛrɪ] *s.* arándano.

crane [kren] *s.* grulla (*ave*); grúa (*máquina para levantar pesos*); *v.* **to** — **one's neck** estirar el cuello.

cra·ni·um [krénɪəm] *s.* cráneo.

crank [kræŋk] *s.* cigüeña, manubrio, manija, manivela; **he is a** — es un maniático; *v.* voltear el manubrio o la cigüeña.

crank·case [krǽŋkes] *s.* cárter del motor.

crank·shaft [krǽŋkʃæft] *s.* cigüeñal.

crank·y [krǽŋkɪ] *adj.* cascarrabias; maniático; enojadizo.

cran·ny [krǽnɪ] *s.* grieta, rendija.

crape [krep] *s.* crespón; crespón negro.

crash [kræʃ] *s.* (*noise*) estallido, golpazo, estruendo; (*collision*) choque; (*failure*) fracaso; quiebra; bancarrota; — **landing** aterrizaje violento; aterrizaje de barriga; — **program** programa de urgencia; *v.* estrellar(se); estallar; chocar; **to** — **an airplane** aterrizar de golpe un aeroplano; **to** — **into** chocar con, estrellarse contra.

crate [kret] *s.* canasto, cesta, jaula (*para el transporte de mercancías, etc.*); *Am.* huacal; *v.* embalar en jaula.

cra·ter [krétɚ] *s.* cráter.

cra·vat [krəvǽt] *s.* corbata.

crave [krev] *v.* ansiar, anhelar, apetecer; **to** — **mercy (pardon)** pedir misericordia (perdón).

crawl [krɔl] *s.* marcha lenta; natación a la marinera; *v.* arrastrarse; gatear, andar a gatas; marchar lentamente; **to be -ing with ants** hormiguear, estar lleno de hormigas.

cray·on [kréən] *s.* lápiz de color, *Am.* creyón; pastel; tiza, yeso.

craze [krez] *s.* manía, locura; (*vogue*) moda; antojo; *v.* enloquecer.

cra·zy [krézɪ] *adj.* loco; trastornado; **to go** — volverse loco, perder el juicio.

creak [krik] *s.* crujido, rechino, rechinamiento; *v.* crujir, rechinar.

cream [krim] *s.* crema; nata; — **of tomato soup** sopa de tomate; **cold** — crema cosmética; **ice** — helado; *v.* desnatar; batir, mezclar (*azúcar y mantequilla*); preparar (*legumbres*) con salsa blanca.

cream·er·y [krímərɪ] *s.* lechería, quesería, *Am.* mantequillería.

cream·y [krímɪ] *adj.* natoso; cremoso.

crease [kris] *s.* pliegue, arruga; *v.* plegar, hacer pliegues; arrugar.

cre·ate [krɪét] *v.* crear.

cre·a·tion [krɪéʃ;ən] *s.* creación; obra.

cre·a·tive [krɪétɪv] *adj.* creativo, creador.

cre·a·tor [krɪétɚ] *s.* creador.

crea·ture [krítʃɚ] *s.* criatura; ser viviente; animalejo.

cre·dence [krídn̩s] *s.* creencia, crédito.

cre·den·tials [krɪdɛ́nʃ;əlz] *s. pl.* credenciales.

cred·i·ble [krɛ́dəbl] *adj.* creíble.

cred·it [krɛ́dɪt] *s.* crédito; buena fama; — **and debit**

haber y deber; activo y pasivo; — **card** tarjeta de crédito; **on** — a crédito, al fiado, a plazo; **to give** — dar crédito, creer; acreditar, abonar; **that does him** — eso le acredita; — **line** línea de crédito; — **underwriters** aseguradores de crédito; *v.*, acreditar; abonar en cuenta; creer, dar credito atribuir.

cred·it·a·ble [krɛ́dɪtəbl] *adj.* loable.

cred·i·tor [krɛ́dɪtɚ] *s.* acreedor.

cred·u·lous [krɛ́dʒələs] *adj.* crédulo.

creed [krid] *s.* credo; creencia.

creek [krik, krɪk] *s.* riachuelo, arroyo; *Col.* quebrada; *Ven.* caño; *Cuba* cañada.

creep [krip] *v.* arrastrarse; gatear, andar a gatas; trepar (*las plantas*); andar lentamente; deslizarse; sentir hormigueo (*en el cuerpo*); *s. pl.* hormigueo; aprensión, horror.

creep·er [krípɚ] *s.* enredadera, planta trepadora.

cre·mate [krímet] *v.* incinerar.

Cre·ole [kríol] *s.* criollo; descendiente de los franceses de Luisiana; persona de sangre mestiza.

cre·o·sote [kriəsot] *s.* creosota.

crepe [krep] = **crape.**

crept [krɛpt] *pret. & p.p.* de **to creep.**

cres·cent [krɛ́sn̩t] *adj.* creciente; *s.* luna creciente; media luna (*emblema de turcos y mahometanos*).

crest [krɛst] *s.* cresta; penacho; copete; cima, cumbre; timbre (*de un escudo de armas*).

crest·fall·en [krɛ́stfɔlən] *adj.* cabizbajo, alicaído, abatido.

cre·tonne [krɪtán] *s.* cretona.

crev·ice [krɛ́vɪs] *s.* grieta, hendedura.

crew [kru] *s.* tripulación; cuadrilla (*de obreros*); *pret.* de **to crow.**

crib [krɪb] *s.* camita de niño; pesebre; (*grain*) granero, arcón; (*construction*) armazón (*usado en la construcción de edificios*); traducción o clave fraudulenta (*en un examen*); *v.* enjaular; usar traducción o clave fraudulenta (*en un examen*).

crick·et [krɪ́kɪt] *s.* grillo; viloria (*juego*).

crime [kraɪm] *s.* crimen.

crim·i·nal [krɪ́mənl] *adj. & s.* criminal.

crimp [krɪmp] *v.* rizar; *s.* rizo.

crim·son [krɪ́mzn̩] *adj. & s.* carmesí.

cringe [krɪndʒ] *v.* encogerse; arrastrarse.

crip·ple [krɪ́pl] *s.* cojo, manco; tullido, baldado, inválido; *v.* estropear; mutilar, derrengar; baldar; incapacitar.

cri·sis [kráɪsɪs] *s.* crisis.

crisp [krɪsp] *adj.* (*brittle*) quebradizo; tieso; bien tostado; (*curly*) crespo, encrespado; — **answer** contestación aguda; — **wind** brisa refrescante; *v.* encrespar.

cri·te·ri·on [kraɪtírɪən] *s.* criterio.

crit·ic [krɪ́tɪk] *s.* crítico; criticón.

crit·i·cal [krɪ́tɪkl] *adj.* crítico; criticador, criticón.

crit·i·cism [krɪ́təsɪzəm] *s.* crítica; criticismo.

crit·i·cize [krɪ́təsaɪz] *v.* criticar; censurar.

croak [krok] *v.* croar; graznar; *s.* canto de ranas; graznido.

cro·chet [kroʃé] *s.* labor de gancho; — **hook** aguja de gancho; *v.* hacer labor de gancho.

crock [krɑk] *s.* vasija de loza, jarra.

crock·er·y [krɑ́kərɪ] *s.* loza.

croc·o·dile [krɑ́kədaɪl] *s.* cocodrilo; *Am.* caimán.

cro·ny [króni] *s.* compadre, compinche, camarada, compañero.

crook [kruk] *s.* (*thief*) falsario; estafador, maleante, pícaro; (*curve*) curva, vuelta; recodo; gancho; **shepherd's** — cayado; *v.* torcer(se); **to** — **one's arm** doblar el brazo o codo.

crook·ed [krókɪd] *adj.* torcido; curvo, encorvado; *Méx.* chueco; *Ríopl.* chingado; falso, fraudulento.

croon [krun] *v.* cantar «tristes» (*con exagerado patetismo y exagerando los sonidos nasales*).

crop [krɑp] *s.* cosecha; (*bird*) buche (*de ave*); (*whip*) látigo, *Méx.* cuarta; — **of hair** cabellera; *v.* segar; recortar; rapar; **to** — **out** aparecer, asomar; **to** — **up** brotar, manifestarse inesperadamente.

cross [krɔs] *s.* cruz; (*roads*) cruce; cruzamiento (*de razas*); mezcla; *v.* cruzar(se); atravesar(se); santiguar(se); encontrarse; contrariar; *adj.* en cruz, cruzado, transversal; malhumorado; **cross-country** a campo traviesa; **cross-examine** *v.* interrogar, repreguntar; **cross-eyed** bizco; — **word puzzle** crucigrama; — **walk** cruce para transeúntes.

cross·bar [krɔ́sbɑr] *s.* travesaño.

cross·ing [krɔ́sɪŋ] *s.* cruce; cruzamiento; encrucijada, crucero, travesía; **railroad** — cruce; **river** — vado.

cross·road [krɔ́srod] *s.* vía transversal, encrucijada, crucero.

cross sec·tion [krɛs sɛ́kʃən] *s.* corte transversal; sección transversal.

crouch [krautʃ] *v.* agacharse, agazaparse.

crow [kro] *s.* cuervo; canto del gallo; **crow's-foot** pata de gallo (*arrugas en el rabo del ojo*); *v.* cantar (*el gallo*); cacarear; jactarse, hacer alarde.

crow·bar [króbɑr] *s.* barra, palanca de hierro.

crowd [kraud] *s.* muchedumbre; gentío, gente; cuadrilla, pandilla; grupo; *v.* agolparse, apiñar(se); estrujar, empujar.

crowd·ed [kráudɪd] *adj.* atestado, lleno, apiñado.

crown [kraun] *s.* corona; copa (*de sombrero*); cima; *v.* coronar.

cru·ci·ble [krúsəbl] *s.* crisol.

cru·ci·fix [krúsəfɪks] *s.* crucifijo.

cru·ci·fy [krúsəfaɪ] *v.* crucificar.

crude [krud] *adj.* basto, tosco, rudo; inculto; — **oil** petróleo crudo; — **sugar** azúcar bruto, asúcar crudo.

cru·el [krúəl] *adj.* cruel.

cru·el·ty [krúəltɪ] *s.* crueldad.

cru·et [krúɪt] *s.* ampolla (*pequeña vasija de cristal*); vinajera (*para servir vino en la misa*); **oil** — aceitera; **vinegar** — vinagrera.

cruise [kruz] *s.* travesía, viaje por mar; excursión; *v.* navegar.

cruis·er [krúzɚ] *s.* crucero (*buque*).

crumb [krʌm] *s.* migaja, miga; mendrugo; *v.* desmenuzar, desmigajar.

crum·ble [krʌ́mbl] *v.* desmenuzar(se); desmoronarse.

crum·ple [krʌ́mpl] *v.* arrugar(se); ajar, apabullar.

crunch [krʌntʃ] *v.* crujir; mascullar.

cru·sade [krúséd] *s.* cruzada; *v.* hacer una campaña; hacer una cruzada.

cru·sad·er [krúsédɚ] *s.* cruzado.

crush [krʌʃ] *s.* compresión, presión; estrujamiento, apiñamiento de gente; *v.* estrujar; aplastar; majar; subyugar; **to** — **stone** moler piedra.

crust [krʌst] *s.* corteza (*de pan, queso, etc.*); costra; mendrugo; *v.* encostrarse, cubrir(se) de costra.

crust·y [krʌ́stɪ] *adj.* costroso.

crutch [krʌtʃ] *s.* muleta.

cry [kraɪ] *s.* grito, lloro, lamento; **a far** — **from** muy distante de, muy lejos de; *v.* gritar; llorar; clamar; exclamar; vocear; **to** — **for help** pedir socorro.

crys·tal [krɪ́stl] *s.* cristal; — **clear** cristalino.

crys·tal·line [krɪ́stlɪn] *adj.* cristalino. **crys·tal·lize** [krɪ́stlaɪz] *v.* cristalizar(se).

cub [kʌb] *s.* cachorro (*de oso, tigre, lobo, león*);

—**reporter** reportero novato.
Cu·ban [kjúbən] *adj. & s.* cubano.
cub·by·hole [kʌ́bihol] *s.* chiribitil.
cube [kjúb] *s.* cubo; — **root** raíz cúbica.
cu·bic [kjúbɪk] *adj.* cúbico.
cu·bism [kúbɪzm] *s.* cubismo.
cuck·old [kʌ́kold] *s.* cornudo.
cuck·oo [kúku] *s.* cuco, cuclillo; *adj.* tocado, chiflado, medio loco.
cu·cum·ber [kjúkʌmbəˑ] *s.* pepino.
cud [kʌd] *s.* rumia; **to chew the** — rumiar.
cud·dle [kʌ́dl] *v.* abrazar, tener en brazos; estar abrazados.
cudg·el [kʌ́dʒəl] *s.* garrote; porra; *v.* aporrear, apalear.
cue [kju] *s.* señal, indicación; (theater) pie. **billiard** — taco de billar.
cuff [kʌf] *s.* puño (*de camisa o de vestido*); doblez (*del pantalón*); bofetada; *v.* bofetear, dar de bofetadas.
cull [kʌl] *v.* entresacar; extraer.
cul·mi·nate [kʌ́lmənet] *v.* culminar.
cul·prit [kʌ́lprɪt] *s.* reo, delincuente, culpable.
cult [kʌlt] *s.* culto; secta religiosa.
cul·ti·vate [kʌ́ltəvet] *v.* cultivar; labrar, barbechar.
cul·ti·vat·ed [kʌ́ltəvetɪd] *adj.* cultivado; culto.
cul·ti·va·tion [kʌltəvéʃən] *s.* cultivación, cultivo; cultura.
cul·ti·va·tor [kʌ́ltəvetəˑ] *s.* cultivador; máquina cultivadora.
cul·ture [kʌ́ltʃəˑ] *s.* (*societal*) cultura; (*tillage*) cultivo.
cul·tured [kʌ́ltʃəˑd] *adj.* culto; cultivado.
cum·ber·some [kʌ́mbəˑsəm] *adj.* engorroso, embarazoso, incómodo.
cu·mu·la·tive [kjúmjələtɪv] *adj.* acumulativo.
cun·ning [kʌ́nɪŋ] *adj.* astuto, socarrón, sagaz, taimado; diestro; cuco, mono, gracioso; *s.* astucia, maña, sagacidad.
cup [kʌp] *s.* taza, pocillo; copa (*trofeo*).
cup·board [kʌ́bəˑd] *s.* armario, aparador; alacena.
cur [kɜˑ] *s.* perro mestizo, *Perú* perro chusco; villano, vil, cobarde.
cu·rate [kjúrɪt] *s.* cura.
cu·ra·tor [kjúretəˑ] *s.* conservador.
curb [kɜˑb] *s.* reborde, encintado (*de la acera*); *Ríopl.* cordón de la acera; freno, restricción; barbada (*del freno de un caballo*); brocal de pozo; — **market** bolsa fuera de rueda; *v.* refrenar, reprimir.
curd [kɜˑd] *s.* cuajada; *v.* cuajar(se), coagular(se).
cur·dle [kɜˑdl] *v.* cuajar(se), coagular(se).
cure [kjʊr] *s.* cura, curación; remedio; *v.* curar(se); sanar.
cur·few [kɜˑfju] *s.* queda.
cu·ri·o [kjúrɪo] *s.* curiosidad, objeto raro y curioso.
cu·ri·os·i·ty [kjʊrɪɑ́səti] *s.* curiosidad; rareza.
cu·ri·ous [kjúrɪəs] *adj.* curioso; extraño, raro.
curl [kɜˑl] *s.* rizo, bucle; espiral (*de humo*); *v.* rizar(se); ensortijar(se); enroscar(se); retorcerse, alzarse en espirales (*el humo*).
curl·y [kɜˑli] *adj.* rizo, rizoso, rizado, crespo, *Méx.* chino.
cur·rant [kɜˑənt] *s.* grosella; — **bush** grosellero.
cur·ren·cy [kɜˑənsɪ] *s.* moneda corriente; circulación; **paper** — papel moneda.
cur·rent [kɜˑənt] *adj.* corriente; común, prevaleciente, en boga; *s.* corriente.
cur·ric·u·lum [kərɪ́kjələm] *s.* programa de estudios.
curse [kɜˑs] *s.* maldición; calamidad; *v.* maldecir.
cursed [kɜˑst] *adj.* maldito.

curs·ing [kɜˑsɪŋ] *adj.* maldiciente.
cur·sive [kɜˑsɪv] *adj.* cursivo.
cur·sor [kɜˑsəˑ] *s.* (*computer*) cursor.
curt [kɜˑt] *adj.* corto; brusco.
cur·tail [kɜˑtél] *v.* cercenar; acortar; restringir, reducir.
cur·tain [kɜˑtn̩] *s.* cortina; telón (*de teatro*); *v.* poner cortinas.
cur·va·ture [kɜˑvətʃəˑ] *s.* curvatura.
curve [kɜˑv] *s.* curva; *v.* encorvar(se); torcer(se); doblar(se).
curved [kɜˑvd] *adj.* encorvado; torcido; curvo, corvo, *Méx., C.A.* chueco.
cush·ion [kúʃən] *s.* cojín; almohadilla; almohadón; amortiguador (*para amortiguar un sonido o golpe*); *v.* acojinar; amortiguar (*un choque*).
cus·tard [kʌ́stəˑd] *s.* flan, natillas.
cus·to·dy [kʌ́stədɪ] *s.* custodia, cargo, cuidado; **to hold in** — custodiar.
cus·tom [kʌ́stəm] *s.* costumbre, hábito, uso, usanza; **-s** derechos de aduana; — **made** hecho a la medida; — **tailor** maestro sastre; — **built** construido según pedido; — **quota** cupo arancelario.
cus·tom·ar·y [kʌ́stəmɛrɪ] *adj.* acostumbrado, habitual, usual, de costumbre.
cus·tom·er [kʌ́stəməˑ] *s.* parroquiano, cliente, marchante.
cus·tom·house [kʌ́stəmhaʊs] *s.* aduana; — **official** aduanero; — **mark** marchamo.
cut [kʌt] *s.* corte (*m.*); cortadura, *Am.* cortada; rebanada, tajada; (*reduction*) rebaja, reducción (*de precios, sueldos*); hechura (*de un traje*); ausencia (*de la clase*); grabado; **short** — atajo, camino corto; *v.* cortar; tajar; truncar; talar (*árboles*); labrar, tallar; segar; rebajar, reducir (*precios, sueldos*); negar el saludo a; alzar (*los naipes*); **to** — **across** cruzar, atravesar; **to** — **capers** hacer cabriolas, cabriolar; **to** — **class** faltar a la clase; **to** — **out** recortar; excluir; **to be** — **out for** estar hecho para, tener vocación para; *pret. & p.p. de* **to cut.**
cut-and-dried [kʌ́tænddráɪd] *adj.* ya determinado; ordinario.
cut·back [kʌ́tbæk] *s.* reducción.
cute [kjut] *adj.* mono, cuco; astuto.
cu·ti·cle [kjútɪkl] *s.* cutícula.
cut·ler·y [kʌ́tləɾɪ] *s.* cuchillería, cuchillos.
cut·let [kʌ́tlɪt] *s.* chuleta.
cut·off [kʌ́tɔf] *s.* límite ya indicado.
cut·ter [kʌ́təˑ] *s.* cortador; máquina para cortar; trineo; **wood** — leñador; **coast guard** — barco guardacostas.
cut·ting [kʌ́tɪŋ] *adj.* cortante; penetrante; mordaz, sarcástico.
cy·ber·net·ics [saɪbəˑnétɪks] *s.* cibernética.
cy·cle [sáɪkl] *s.* ciclo.
cy·clone [sáɪklon] *s.* ciclón; huracán.
cy·clo·tron [sáɪklɑtran] *s.* ciclotrón.
cyl·in·der [sɪ́lɪndəˑ] *s.* cilindro; — **head** émbolo.
cy·lin·dri·cal [sɪlɪ́ndrɪkl] *adj.* cilíndrico.
cym·bal [sɪ́mbl] *s.* címbalo, platillo; **to play the -s** tocar los platillos.
cyn·ic [sɪ́nɪk] *s.* cínico.
cyn·i·cal [sɪ́nɪkl] *adj.* cínico.
cyn·i·cism [sɪ́nəsɪzəm] *s.* cinismo.
cy·press [sáɪprəs] *s.* ciprés.
cyst [sɪst] *s.* quiste.

CR

D:d

dab·ble [dǽbl] v. chapotear; trabajar superficialmente.

dad [dæd] s. papá, tata; **daddy** s. papaíto o papacito, tata, tatita, *Am.* taita.

daf·fo·dil [dǽfǝdɪl] s. narciso.

dag·ger [dǽgɚ] s. daga; puñal; **to look -s at** traspasar con la mirada.

dahl·ia [dǽljǝ] s. dalia.

dai·ly [délɪ] adj. diario; — **wage** jornal; adv. diariamente; s. diario, periódico.

dain·ty [déntɪ] adj. delicado, fino, primoroso, exquisito; s. golosina, manjar exquisito.

dair·y [dérɪ] s. lechería, vaquería; quesería, quesera; *Arg.* tambo.

dai·sy [dézɪ] s. margarita, maya; (*computer*) — **wheel** margarita, disco impresor; — **wheel printer** impresora de margarita.

dale [del] s. cañada.

dal·ly [dǽlɪ] v. juguetear; holgazanear; entretenerse, tardar; malgastar el tiempo.

dam [dæm] s. presa, represa; v. represar, estancar.

dam·age [dǽmɪdʒ] s. daño; perjuicio; avería; **to pay for -s** indemnizar, pagar los daños y perjuicios; v. dañar(se); averiar(se).

Dam·a·scene [dǽmǝsin] adj. s. damasquinado.

dame [dem] s. dama, señora; **old** — vieja.

damn [dæm] v. maldecir; condenar; blasfemar; — **it** ¡maldito sea!

dam·na·tion [dæmnéʃǝn] s. condenación, perdición.

damp [dæmp] adj. húmedo; mojado; s. humedad; v. humedecer, mojar.

damp·en [dǽmpǝn] v. mojar, humedecer; desalentar; amortiguar.

damp·ness [dǽmpnɪs] s. humedad.

dam·sel [dǽmzl] s. damisela.

dance [dæns] s. baile; danza; — **music** música de baile; v. bailar; danzar.

danc·er [dǽnsɚ] s. bailador; bailarín, bailarina; danzante.

dan·de·li·on [dǽndlaɪǝn] s. diente de león.

dan·druff [dǽndrǝf] s. caspa.

dan·dy [dǽndɪ] s. currutaco, majo, afectado; chulo; adj. elegante, excelente.

dan·ger [déndʒɚ] s. peligro, riesgo.

dan·ger·ous [déndʒǝrǝs] adj. peligroso; arriesgado; **-ly** adv. peligrosamente; **-ly ill** gravemente enfermo.

dan·gle [dǽŋgl] v. pender, colgar, bambolear(se) (*en el aire*).

dap·ple(d) [dǽpl(d)] adj. rodado, con manchas (*dícese de los caballos*); **dapple-grey** rucio, moteado, rodado, tordo, tordillo.

dare [dɛr] s. desafío, reto, provocación; — **devil** atrevido, osado; v. atreverse, osar; desafiar.

dar·ing [dérɪŋ] s. atrevimiento, osadía; adj. osado, atrevido, arrojado.

dark [dɑrk] adj. obscuro; sombrío; — **horse** caballo desconocido (*que gana inesperadamente la carrera*); (*politics*) candidato nombrado inesperadamente; — **secret** secreto profundo; enigma; **darkskinned** moreno, trigueño; s. obscuridad; sombra.

dark·en [dɑ́rkǝn] v. obscurecer(se); nublarse.

dark·ness [dɑ́rknɪs] s. obscuridad; tinieblas; sombra.

dar·ling [dɑ́rlɪŋ] adj. & s. amado, querido; **my** — vida mía (o mi vida), amor mío.

darn [dɑrn] s. zurcido; **it is not worth a** — no vale un comino, no vale un pito; v. zurcir; — ! ¡caramba! ¡canastos!; **-ing needle** aguja de zurcir.•

dart [dɑrt] s. dardo, flecha; (*tuck*) sisa (*en un vestido*); movimiento rápido; v. lanzar(se); flechar; **to** — **out** salir como una flecha; **to** — **in and out** entrar y salir precipitadamente.

dash [dæʃ] s. (*line*) raya; (*run*) carrera corta; (*vigor*) ímpetu; (*grace*) garbo; pizca (*de sal, azúcar, etc.*); rociada (*de agua*); — **board** tablero de instrumentos; **with a** — **of the pen** de una plumada; v. lanzar(se); echar(se); estrellar(se); salpicar; frustrar (*esperanzas*); **to** — **by** pasar corriendo; **to** — **out** salir a la carrera; **to** — **off a letter** escribir de prisa una carta.

da·ta [détǝ] s. pl. datos; — **collection** recopilación de datos; — **display** despliegue (presentación) de datos; — **processing** procesamiento de datos; — **base** base de datos.

date [det] s. (*time*) fecha; (*statement*) data; (*appointment*) cita, compromiso; (*fruit*) dátil; **out of** — anticuado, desusado; fuera de moda; **up to** — al día, moderno; **up to this** — hasta ahora, hasta la fecha; v. fechar; **to** — **from** datar de; remontarse a.

daub [dɔb] v. embarrar, untar; pintarrajear.

daugh·ter [dɔ́tɚ] s. hija; **daughter-in-law** nuera.

daunt [dɔnt] v. intimidar, asustar, espantar; desanimar.

daunt·less [dɔ́ntlɪs] adj. denodado, intrépido.

dav·en·port [dǽvǝnport] s. sofá.

dawn [dɔn] s. alba; amanecer, madrugada; v. amanecer; alborear, rayar (*el día*); **it just -ed upon me** acabo de darme cuenta.

day [de] s. día; — **after tomorrow** pasado mañana; — **before yesterday** anteayer o antier; — **laborer** jornalero; **by** — de día; **by the** — por día; **eight-hour** — jornada de ocho horas; **to win the** — ganar la jornada, triunfar; adj. diurno.

day·break [débrek] s. amanecer, alba; **at** — al amanecer, al romper el día, al rayar el día.

day·light [délaɪt] s. luz del día.

day·time [détaɪm] s. día (*tiempo de luz natural*); **in the** — durante el día; de día.

daze [dez] s. aturdimiento; deslumbramiento; **to be in a** — estar aturdido; v. aturdir; ofuscar; deslumbrar.

daz·zle [dǽzl] s. brillantez; v. deslumbrar; ofuscar.

dea·con [dikǝn] s. diácono.

dead [dɛd] adj. muerto; — **air** aire viciado o estancado; — **bolt** cerrojo dormido; — **letter** carta no reclamada; — **loss** pérdida absoluta; adv. completamente, absolutamente; sumamente, muy; — **sure** completamente seguro; — **tired** muerto de cansancio; s. **the** — los muertos; **in the** — **of the night** en el sigilo de la noche; **in the** — **of winter** en lo más crudo del invierno.

dead·en [dɛ́dṇ] v. amortiguar.

dead·head [dɛ́dhɛd] s. persona que no paga la entrada; colado.

dead·line [dɛ́dlaɪn] s. fin de plazo, vencimiento.

dead·lock [dɛ́dlak] s. desacuerdo insuperable.

dead·ly [dɛ́dlɪ] adj. mortal; fatal; como la muerte, cadavérico; adv. mortalmente; — **dull** sumamente aburrido.

deaf [dɛf] adj. sordo; **deaf-mute** s. & adj. sordomudo.

deaf·en [dɛ́fǝn] v. ensordecer; amortiguar, apagar, (*un sonido*).

deaf·en·ing [dɛ́fǝnɪŋ] adj. ensordecedor, estruendoso.

deaf·ness [dɛ́fnɪs] s. sordera.

deal [dil] s. trato, negocio; (*cards*) mano; distribución, reparto (*de los naipes*); **a great** — **of** una gran cantidad de, mucho; **to give a square** —

tratar con equidad; *v.* tallar (*en juegos de naipes*); distribuir, repartir; dar (*un golpe*); **to — in** comerciar en; **to — with** tratar de (*un asunto*); tratar con; negociar con.

deal·er [díla] *s.* negociante, comerciante, tratante; tallador (*en el juego de naipes*).

deal·ings [dílɪŋz] *s. pl.* relaciones (*comerciales o amistosas*); comercio, tratos; negocios.

dealt [dɛlt] *pret. & p.p. de* **to deal.**

dean [din] *s.* deán (*dignidad eclesiástica*); decano (*de universidad*).

dear [dɪr] *adj.* (*beloved*) querido, amado; (*expensive*) caro; costoso; *adv.* caro; **— me!** ¡Dios mío!; **oh —** ! ¡ay!; **my —** querido mío; **Dear Sir** Muy señor mío; **-ly** *adv.* cariñosamente; a precio alto; **my -ly beloved** muy amado mío; muy amados míos.

dearth [dɝθ] *s.* escasez, carestía, insuficiencia.

death [dɛθ] *s.* muerte; mortandad; **— rate** mortalidad; **— certificate** fe de óbito, partida de difunción.

death·bed [dɛθbɛd] *s.* lecho de muerte.

de·base [dɪbés] *v.* rebajar el valor de; degradar, humillar, envilecer.

de·bat·a·ble [dɪbétəbl] *adj.* discutible, disputable.

de·bate [dɪbét] *s.* debate, discusión; *v.* debatir, discutir; considerar; deliberar.

de·ben·ture [dɪbɛ́ntʃa] *s.* certificado de reintegro.

de·bil·i·tate [dəbɪlətet] *v.* debilitar.

deb·it [dɛ́bɪt] *s.* débito, adeudo, cargo; debe (*de una cuenta*); pasivo (*en contabilidad*); *v.* adeudar, cargar en cuenta.

de·brief·ing [dibrifɪŋ] *s.* informe de vuelo bajo, interrogación; informe.

de·bris [dəbrí] *s.* escombros; ruinas.

debt [dɛt] *s.* deuda; adeudo; débito; **bad —** cuenta incobrable; **to run into —** adeudarse, entramparse, cargarse de deudas.

debt·or [dɛ́ta] *s.* deudor.

de·bug·ging [dibʌ́gɪŋ] *s.* depuración.

de·bunk [dibʌ́ŋk] *s.* desbaratar; desenmascarar.

de·but [dɪbjú] *s.* estreno; **to make a —** debutar, estrenarse.

de·cade [dɛ́ked] *s.* década, decenio.

de·ca·dence [dɪkédns] *s.* decadencia.

de·cant·er [dɪkǽnta] *s.* garrafa; **large —** garrafón.

de·cay [dɪké] *s.* decaimiento; decadencia, ruina; podredumbre; caries (*de la dentadura*); *v.* decaer; venir a menos; pudrir(se) o podrir(se).

de·cease [dɪsís] *s.* muerte, fallecimiento; *v.* morir, fallecer.

de·ceased [dɪsíst] *adj. & s.* muerto, difunto.

de·ceit [dɪsít] *s.* engaño; fraude; trampa.

de·ceit·ful [dɪsítfəl] *adj.* engañador; tramposo; engañoso.

de·ceive [dɪsív] *v.* engañar.

De·cem·ber [dɪsɛmba] *s.* diciembre.

de·cen·cy [dísnsɪ] *s.* decencia.

de·cent [dísnt] *adj.* decente; decoroso.

de·ci·bel [dɛ́sɪbel] *s.* decibelio; decibel.

de·cide [dɪsáɪd] *v.* decidir, resolver, determinar; **to — to** resolverse a, decidirse a.

de·cid·ed [dɪsáɪdɪd] *adj.* decidido, resuelto.

dec·i·mal [dɛ́səml] *adj.* decimal; *s.* decimal, fracción decimal.

dec·i·mate [dɛ́sɪmet] *v.* diezmar.

de·ci·pher [dɪsáɪfa] *v.* descifrar.

de·ci·sion [dɪsɪ́ʒən] *s.* decisión, resolución.

de·ci·sive [dɪsáɪsɪv] *adj.* decisivo; terminante.

deck [dɛk] *s.* cubierta (*de un buque*); baraja; *v.* cubrir; ataviar; **to — oneself out** emperifollarse.

dec·la·ra·tion [dɛkləréʃən] *s.* declaración.

de·clare [dɪklǽr] *v.* declarar; afirmar.

de·cline [dɪkláɪn] *s.* declinación; decadencia; mengua; baja (*de precios*); *v.* declinar; decaer; rehusar; **to — to do something** negarse a hacer algo.

de·cliv·i·ty [dɪklɪ́vətɪ] *s.* declive.

de·col·le·te [dekɑltɛ] *adj.* escotado.

de·com·pose [dikəmpóz] *v.* descomponer(se); corromper(se), pudrir(se).

dec·o·rate [dɛ́kəret] *v.* decorar, adornar; condecorar.

dec·o·ra·tion [dɛkəréʃən] *s.* decoración; adorno; insignia, condecoración.

dec·o·ra·tive [dɛ́kəretɪv] *adj.* decorativo; ornamental.

de·co·rum [dɪkórəm] *s.* decoro; circunspección.

de·coy [dɪkɔ́ɪ] *s.* reclamo, señuelo, figura de ave (*que sirve para atraer aves*); cebo (*artificio para atraer con engaño*); (*trap*) trampa, lazo; *v.* atraer con señuelo o engaño.

de·crease [díkris] *s.* disminución o diminución; merma; mengua; [dɪkrís] *v.* disminuir(se); mermar; menguar.

de·cree [dɪkrí] *s.* decreto; *v.* decretar; mandar.

de·crep·it [dɪkrépɪt] *adj.* decrépito.

ded·i·cate [dɛ́dəket] *v.* dedicar.

ded·i·ca·tion [dɛdəkéʃən] *s.* dedicación; dedicatoria.

de·duce [dɪdjús] *v.* deducir, inferir.

de·duct [dɪdʌ́kt] *v.* deducir, descontar, rebajar.

de·duc·tion [dɪdʌ́kʃən] *s.* deducción; rebaja, descuento.

deed [did] *s.* hecho, acción, acto; hazaña; título de propiedad, escritura de traspaso.

deem [dim] *v.* juzgar, creer, considerar.

deep [dip] *adj.* (*down*) hondo, profundo; (*obscure*) oscuro; (*tone*) grave, bajo; **— in debt** cargado de deudas; **— in thought** absorto; **— mourning** luto riguroso; **to go off the — end** echarse a pique; caer en el abismo; **— into the night** en las tinieblas de la noche; *s.* **the —** el mar; **-ly** *adv.* profundamente, hondamente; intensamente.

deep·en [dípən] *v.* ahondar, profundizar.

deer [dɪr] *s.* ciervo, venado; **— skin** piel o cuero de venado.

de·face [dɪfés] *v.* desfigurar, estropear, mutilar.

de·fame [dɪfém] *v.* difamar, calumniar, denigrar.

de·fault [dɪfɔ́lt] *s.* falla, falta, negligencia (*de un deber, pago, obligación*); deficiencia; **in —** en mora, moroso; *v.* fallar, faltar (*en el cumplimiento de un deber, pago, obligación*); no comparecer a la cita de un tribunal.

de·feat [dɪfít] *s.* derrota, vencimiento; frustración (*de un plan*); *v.* vencer, derrotar; frustrar.

def·e·cate [dɛ́fəket] *v.* defecar.

de·fect [dɪfɛ́kt] *s.* defecto.

de·fec·tive [dɪfɛ́ktɪv] *adj.* defectuoso; incompleto; subnormal, falto de inteligencia; **— verb** verbo defectivo.

de·fend [dɪfɛ́nd] *v.* defender.

de·fen·dant [dɪfɛ́ndənt] *s.* acusado, demandado, procesado.

de·fend·er [dɪfɛ́nda] *s.* defensor; abogado defensor.

de·fense [dɪfɛ́ns] *s.* defensa.

de·fense·less [dɪfɛ́nslɪs] *adj.* indefenso, inerme.

de·fen·sive [dɪfɛ́nsɪv] *adj.* defensivo; . defensiva.

de·fer [dɪfɝ] *v.* diferir, posponer, aplazar; **to — another's opinion** remitirse o ceder al dictamen de otro; **deferred assets** activo diferido; **— payment** pago aplazado.

de·fi·ance [dɪfáɪəns] *s.* reto, desafío, provocación; oposición; **in — of** en abierta oposición con, a despecho de.

de·fi·cien·cy [dɪfíʃənsɪ] *s.* deficiencia; defecto; déficit.

de·fi·cient [dɪfíʃənt] *adj.* deficiente; defectuoso.

def·i·cit [défəsɪt] *s.* déficit; — **spending** gastos deficitarios.
de·file [dɪfáɪl] *v.* viciar, corromper; profanar; (*dirty*) manchar, ensuciar.
de·fine [dɪfáɪn] *v.* definir.
def·i·nite [défənɪt] *adj.* definido; claro, preciso; fijo; — **article** artículo determinado o definido; **-ly** *adv.* definidamente; claramente; **-ly not** terminantemente no.
def·i·ni·tion [dɛfənɪʃən] *s.* definición.
de·fin·i·tive [dɪfínətɪv] *adj.* definitivo.
de·flate [dɪflét] *v.* desinflar.
de·flect [dɪflékt] *v.* desviar(se).
de·form [dɪfɔ́rm] *v.* deformar; desfigurar, afear.
de·formed [dɪfɔ́rmd] *adj.* deforme, disforme; deformado; desfigurado.
de·form·i·ty [dɪfɔ́rmətɪ] *s.* deformidad; deformación.
de·fraud [dɪfrɔ́d] *v.* defraudar.
de·fray [dɪfré] *v.* sufragar, costear, pagar (*gastos*).
deft [dɛft] *adj.* diestro, ágil.
de·funct [dɪfʌ́ŋkt] *adj.* difunto.
de·fy [dɪfáɪ] *v.* desafiar; retar; oponerse a, resistirse a.
de·gen·er·ate [dɪdʒénərɪt] *adj. & s.* degenerado; [dɪdʒénərɪt] *v.* degenerar.
deg·ra·da·tion [dɛgrədéʃən] *s.* degradación; envilecimiento.
de·grade [dɪgréd] *v.* degradar; envilecer, rebajar.
de·gree [dɪgrí] *s.* grado; rango; **by -s** gradualmente; **to get a** — graduarse.
de·hu·man·ize [dihjúmənaɪz] *v.* deshumanizar.
de·hy·drate [dɪháɪdret] *v.* deshidratar(se).
deign [den] *v.* dignarse, condescender.
de·i·ty [díətɪ] *s.* deidad.
de·ject·ed [dɪdʒéktɪd] *adj.* abatido.
de·jec·tion [dɪdʒékʃən] *s.* abatimiento, melancolía, depresión.
de·lay [dɪlé] *s.* demora, tardanza, dilación, retraso; *v.* demorar; retardar, dilatar; deferir; tardarse.
de·layed ac·tion [dɪléd ǽkʃən] *adj.* atrasado; retardado.
del·e·gate [déləget] *s.* delegado, representante; *v.* delegar, diputar.
del·e·ga·tion [déləgéʃən] *s.* delegación, diputación.
de·le·tion [dɪlíʃən] *s.* suspensión.
de·lib·er·ate [dɪlíbərɪt] *adj.* deliberado, premeditado; cauto, prudente; lento; **-ly** *adv.* deliberadamente; con premeditación; [dɪlíbəret] *v.* deliberar.
de·lib·er·a·tion [dɪlíbəréʃən] *s.* deliberación.
del·i·ca·cy [déləkəsɪ] *s.* delicadeza; sensibilidad; finura; golosina.
del·i·cate [déləkət] *adj.* delicado; frágil; exquisito.
del·i·ca·tes·sen [dɛləkətésṇ] *s.* tienda de fiambres, queso, ensaladas, ultramarinos, etc.
de·li·cious [dɪlíʃəs] *adj.* delicioso.
de·light [dɪláɪt] *s.* deleite; delicia; *v.* deleitar(se); encantar; agradar; **to** — **in** gozarse en, deleitarse en.
de·light·ed [dɪláɪtɪd] *adj.* encantado; **to be** — **to** alegrarse de, tener mucho gusto en (de).
de·light·ful [dɪláɪtfəl] *adj.* deleitoso; delicioso; ameno, agradable.
de·lin·e·ate [dɪlíniet] *v.* delinear, trazar.
de·lin·quent [dɪlíŋkwənt] *adj. & s.* delincuente.
de·lir·i·ous [dɪlíriəs] *adj.* delirante; **to be** — delirar, desvariar.
de·lir·i·um [dɪlíriəm] *s.* delirio, desvarío.
de·liv·er [dɪlívɚ] *v.* entregar; librar, libertar; pronunciar (*un discurso*); dar (*un golpe*); — **the goods** cumplir.
de·liv·er·ance [dɪlívərəns] *s.* liberación, rescate.

de·liv·er·er [dɪlívərɚ] *s.* libertador; portador, mansajero.
de·liv·er·y [dɪlívərɪ] *s.* (*giving*) entrega; (*saving*) liberación; (*birth*) parto; (*speaking*) elocuencia, manera de hacer una conferencia; — **service** servicio de entrega; — **truck** camión (camioneta) de reparto; **mail** — reparto de correo.
dell [dɛl] *s.* cañada, hondonada.
del·ta wing [déltə wɪŋ] *s.* ala en delta.
de·lude [dɪlúd] *v.* engañar.
del·uge [déljudʒ] *s.* diluvio; *v.* inundar; abrumar.
de·lu·sion [dɪlúʒən] *s.* ilusión; engaño, error.
de·mand [dɪmǽnd] *s.* demanda; exigencia; solicitud; **on** — a solicitud; — **and supply** demanda y oferta; — **note** pagaré a la vista; *v.* demandar, reclamar; exigir.
de·mand·ing [dɪmǽndɪŋ] *adj.* exigente.
de·mean·or [dɪmínɚ] *s.* conducta, comportamiento, proceder.
de·ment·ed [dɪméntɪd] *adj.* demente.
dem·i·john [démidʒan] *s.* damajuana.
de·mise [dɪmáɪz] *s.* fallecimiento.
de·mo·bil·ize [dimóblaɪz] *v.* demovilizar.
de·moc·ra·cy [dəmákrəsɪ] *s.* democracia.
dem·o·crat [déməkræt] *s.* demócrata.
dem·o·crat·ic [dɛməkrǽtɪk] *adj.* democrático.
de·mol·ish [dɪmálɪʃ] *v.* demoler.
de·mon [dímən] *s.* demonio.
dem·on·strate [démənstret] *v.* demostrar.
dem·on·stra·tion [démənstréʃən] *s.* demostración; prueba; (*protest*) manifestación.
de·mon·stra·tive [dɪmánstrətɪv] *adj.* demostrativo; efusivo.
den [dɛn] *s.* guarida; escondrijo; cueva, lugar de retiro.
de·ni·al [dɪnáɪəl] *s.* negación; negativa; **self-denial** abnegación.
den·i·grate [dénɪgret] *v.* calumniar; ennegrecer.
de·nom·i·na·tion [dɪnamənéʃən] *s.* (*name*) denominación; nombre; título, designación; (*sect*) secta religiosa.
de·note [dɪnót] *v.* denotar.
de·nounce [dɪnáuns] *v.* denunciar; delatar, acusar.
dense [dɛns] *adj.* denso; espeso, apretado; estúpido.
den·si·ty [dénsətɪ] *s.* densidad; estupidez.
dent [dɛnt] *s.* abolladura; mella; *v.* abollar; mellar.
den·tal [déntḷ] *adj.* dental; *s.* dental, consonante dental.
den·ti·frice [déntɪfrɪs] *s.* pasta dentífrica; dentífrico.
den·tist [déntɪst] *s.* dentista.
de·nun·ci·a·tion [dɪnʌnsiéʃən] *s.* denuncia, acusación.
de·ny [dɪnáɪ] *v.* negar; rehusar; **to** — **oneself** sacrificarse, abnegarse; **to** — **oneself to callers** negarse a recibir visitas.
de·o·dor·ant [diódərənt] *s.* desodorante.
de·ox·i·dize [diáksədaɪz] *v.* desoxidar.
de·part [dɪpárt] *v.* partir, salir, irse; desviarse, apartarse.
de·part·ed [dɪpártɪd] *adj.* ido; ausente; difunto.
de·part·ment [dɪpártmənt] *s.* departamento; distrito; ramo, división; — **store** almacén.
de·par·ture [dɪpártʃɚ] *s.* salida, partida; desviación.
de·pend [dɪpénd] *v.* depender; **to** — **on** depender de; contar con, confiar en.
de·pend·a·ble [dɪpéndəbḷ] *adj.* seguro, fidedigno, digno de confianza; serio, formal.
de·pen·dence [dɪpéndəns] *s.* dependencia; confianza.
de·pen·den·cy [dɪpéndənsɪ] *s.* dependencia; sucursal.
de·pen·dent [dɪpéndənt] *adj.* dependiente; subordinado; *s.* dependiente, familiar.
de·pict [dɪpíkt] *v.* pintar, describir; representar.

dep·i·late [dépəlet] v. depilar.
de·pil·a·to·ry [dɪpílətorɪ] s. depilatorio.
de·plete [dɪplít] v. agotar; vaciar; **depletion** agotamiento.
de·plor·a·ble [dɪplórəbl] adj. deplorable, lamentable.
de·plore [dɪplór] v. deplorar.
de·port [dɪpórt] v. deportar; **to — oneself well** portarse bien.
de·port·ment [dɪpórtmənt] s. comportamiento, conducta.
de·pose [dɪpóz] v. deponer; declarar, (testify) atestiguar.
de·pos·it [dɪpázɪt] s. depósito; (mineral) yacimiento; (ernest money) prenda, anticipo; v. depositar.
dep·o·si·tion [dɛpəzíʃən] s. deposición; declaración.
de·pos·i·tor [dɪpázɪtɚ] s. depositador.
de·pot [dípo] s. depósito; almacén; estación de ferrocarril.
dep·re·cate [déprɪket] v. desaprobar.
de·pre·ci·ate [dɪpríʃɪet] v. depreciar; bajar de precio; abaratar(se); menospreciar.
de·press [dɪprés] v. deprimir; abatir; desanimar; depreciar, rebajar el valor de.
de·pressed [dɪprést] adj. abatido, decaído.
de·press·ing [dɪprésɪŋ] adj. deprimente.
de·pres·sion [dɪpréʃən] s. depresión; decaimiento, abatimiento; rebaja (de precios).
de·prive [dɪpráɪv] v. privar.
depth [dɛpθ] s. profundidad; hondura; fondo; (length) longitud (de un solar); gravedad (de los sonidos); viveza (de los colores); **in the — of the night** en las tinieblas de la noche; **in the — of winter** en lo más crudo del invierno.
dep·u·ta·tion [dɛpjətéʃən] s. diputación, delegación; comisión.
de·pute [dɪpjút] v. diputar, delegar.
dep·u·ty [dépjətɪ] s. diputado; agente; delegado.
de·range [dɪréndʒ] v. trastornar, desordenar.
der·by [dɝbɪ] s. sombrero hongo, Méx., Ven., Col. sombrero de bola.
der·e·lict [dérɪlɪkt] adj. abandonado; negligente.
de·ride [dɪráɪd] v. escarnecer, ridiculizar, mofarse de, burlarse de.
de·ri·sion [dɪríʒən] s. mofa, escarnio.
de·rive [dəráɪv] v. derivar(se); provenir; sacar (provecho); recibir (placer).
der·ma·tol·o·gy [dɚmətáledʒɪ] s. dermatología.
der·rick [dérɪk] s. grúa; armazón (para la explotación del petróleo).
de·scend [dɪsénd] v. descender; bajar; **to — upon** caer sobre, acometer.
de·scen·dant [dɪséndənt] adj. & s. descendiente.
de·scent [dɪsént] s. descenso; bajada; (lineage) descendencia, linaje; descendimiento; declive.
de·scribe [dɪskráɪb] v. describir; trazar.
de·scrip·tion [dɪskrípʃən] s. descripción; **of all -s** de todas clases.
de·scrip·tive [dɪskrítɪv] adj. descriptivo; — **linguistics** lingüística descriptiva.
des·ert [dézɚt] adj. desierto, despoblado; estéril; s. desierto, yermo; páramo; [dɪzɚt] v. abandonar, desamparar; desertar.
de·sert·er [dɪzɝtɚ] s. desertor.
de·ser·tion [dɪzpɝʃən] s. deserción, abandono, desamparo.
de·serve [dɪzɝv] v. merecer.
de·serv·ing [dɪzɝvɪŋ] adj. meritorio; merecedor.
de·sign [dɪzáɪn] s. (sketch) dibujo, diseño; (plan) designio, propósito, intención; plan, proyecto; v. diseñar, trazar; proyectar; idear.
des·ig·nate [dézɪgnet] v. designar; señalar, indicar,

nombrar.
de·sign·er [dɪzáɪnɚ] s. diseñador; dibujante; proyectista; intrigante.
de·sir·a·bil·i·ty [dɪzaɪrəbílətɪ] s. conveniencia, utilidad.
de·sir·a·ble [dɪzáɪrəbl] adj. deseable; agradable; conveniente.
de·sire [dɪzáɪr] s. deseo; anhelo, ansia; v. desear; anhelar, ansiar.
de·sir·ous [dɪzáɪrəs] adj. deseoso.
de·sist [dɪzíst] v. desistir.
desk [dɛsk] s. escritorio, bufete, (school) pupitre, mesa de escribir.
des·o·late [déslɪt] adj. desolado; despoblado, desierto; solitario [déslet] v. desolar; asolar, arrasar; despoblar.
des·o·la·tion [desléʃən] s. desolación; soledad.
de·spair [dɪspér] s. desesperación; desesperanza; v. desesperarse, perder la esperanza.
de·spair·ing [dɪspérɪŋ] adj. desesperado, sin esperanza.
des·patch [dɪspǽtʃ] = **dispatch.**
des·per·ate [désprɪt] adj. desesperado; arriesgado, temerario; — **illness** enfermedad gravísima; **-ly** adv. desesperadamente; **-ly ill** gravísimamente enfermo.
des·per·a·tion [despəréʃən] s. desesperación; temeridad.
des·pi·ca·ble [déspɪkəbl] adj. despreciable; desdeñable.
de·spise [dɪspáɪz] v. despreciar; desdeñar; menospreciar.
de·spite [dɪspáɪt] s. despecho; prep. a despecho de, a pesar de.
de·spoil [dɪspóɪl] v. despojar.
de·spon·den·cy [dɪspándənsɪ] s. abatimiento desaliento, descaecimiento o decaimiento del ánimo.
de·spon·dent [dɪspándənt] adj. abatido, descaecido o decaído de ánimo, desalentado, desesperanzado.
des·pot [déspət] s. déspota.
des·pot·ic [dɪspátɪk] adj. despótico.
des·pot·ism [déspətɪzəm] s. despotismo.
des·sert [dɪzɝt] s. postre.
des·ti·na·tion [destənéʃən] s. destinación, destino; paradero.
des·tine [déstɪn] v. destinar; **-ed for** con rumbo a, con destinación a; destinado a.
des·ti·ny [déstənɪ] s. destino, sino, hado.
des·ti·tute [déstətjut] adj. destituido, necesitado; falto, desprovisto.
de·stroy [dɪstróɪ] v. destruir.
de·stroy·er [dɪstróɪɚ] s. destruidor; destructor; cazatorpedero, destroyer.
de·struc·ti·ble [dɪstrʌ́ktəbl] adj. destructible.
de·struc·tion [dɪstrʌ́kʃən] s. destrucción; ruina.
de·struc·tive [dɪstrʌ́ktɪv] adj. destructivo.
de·tach [dɪtǽtʃ] v. separar, despegar, desprender; destacar (una porción de tropa).
de·tach·ment [dɪtǽtʃmənt] s. separación; desprendimiento; desapego, despego, alejamiento; destacamento (militar).
de·tail [dítel] s. detalle; pormenor; destacamento (militar); **to go into —** detallar, pormenorizar; [dɪtél] v. detallar; pormenorizar; destacar, asignar.
de·tain [dɪtén] v. detener; entretener, demorar, retardar.
de·tect [dɪtékt] v. descubrir.
de·tec·tive [dɪtéktɪv] s. detective, detectivo, policía secreto.
de·ten·tion [dɪténʃən] s. detención.

DE

de·ter [dɪtɚ] *v.* disuadir.

de·ter·gent [dɪtɚdʒənt] *s.* detergente.

de·te·ri·o·rate [dɪtírɪəret] *v.* deteriorar(se).

de·te·ri·o·ra·tion [dɪtɪrɪəréʃən] *s.* deterioro.

de·ter·mi·na·tion [dɪtɜmənéʃən] *s.* determinación; decisión; resolución, firmeza.

de·ter·mine [dɪtɜmɪn] *v.* determinar; decidir; **to —** determinarse a, decidirse a, resolverse a.

de·ter·mined [dɪtɜmɪnd] *adj.* determinado, decidido, resuelto.

de·test [dɪtést] *v.* detestar, aborrecer.

de·tour [dítUr] *s.* rodeo, desvío, desviación, vuelta; *v.* dar o hacer un rodeo.

devaluation [divæljuéʃən] *s.* devaluación.

dev·as·tate [dévəstet] *v.* devastar, arruinar, asolar.

de·vel·op [dɪvéləp] *v.* desarrollar(se); desenvolver(se); revelar (*una película o placa fotográfica*); explotar (*una mina*); **developing countries** países en desarrollo.

de·vel·op·ment [dɪvéləpmənt] *s.* (*evolution*) desarrollo; desenvolvimiento; evolución; crecimiento; (*generation*) fomento; explotación, (*photo*) revelado.

de·vi·ate [dívɪet] *v.* desviar(se).

de·vi·a·tion [divɪéʃən] *s.* desviación; desvío, extravío.

de·vice [dɪváɪs] *s.* artificio; mecanismo, aparato; ardid, recurso; divisa; dispositivo, plan; **left to one's own -s** abandonado a sus propios recursos.

dev·il [dévl] *s.* diablo; demonio.

dev·il·ish [dévlɪʃ] *adj.* diabólico; endiablado; travieso.

devilry [dévlrɪ] *s.* diablura.

de·vi·ous [dívɪəs] *adj.* desviado; tortuoso; indirecto.

de·vise [dɪváɪz] *v.* idear, trazar, urdir.

de·void [dɪvɔ́ɪd] *adj.* exento, libre, falto, privado, desprovisto.

de·vote [dɪvót] *v.* dedicar; consagrar; **to — oneself to** dedicarse a, consagrarse a, aplicarse a.

de·vot·ed [dɪvótɪd] *adj.* dedicado, consagrado; apegado; **— friend** amigo fiel o leal.

de·vo·tion [dɪvóʃən] *s.* devoción; piedad; afecto; lealtad.

de·vour [dɪváUr] *v.* devorar.

de·vout [dɪváUt] *adj.* devoto, piadoso; sincero.

dew [dju] *s.* rocío, sereno; *v.* rociar; caer (*el rocío*).

dew·drop [djúdrɑp] *s.* gota de rocío.

dew·y [djúɪ] *adj.* rociado, húmedo de rocío.

dex·ter·i·ty [dɛkstérətɪ] *s.* destreza.

dex·ter·ous [dékstrəs] *adj.* diestro.

dex·trose [dékstros] *s.* dextrosa.

di·a·dem [dáɪədɛm] *s.* diadema.

di·ag·nose [daɪəgnós] *v.* diagnosticar.

di·ag·o·nal [daɪǽgənl] *adj.* diagonal, oblicuo; *s.* diagonal.

di·a·gram [dáɪəgræm] *s.* diagrama.

di·al [dáɪəl] *s.* esfera; muestra (*del reloj*), *Méx.*, *C.A.* carátula; **— telephone** teléfono automático; (*clock*) cuadrante **— tone** señal para marcar (*girar*); *v.* sintonizar o captar (*una estación radiotelefónica*); (*telephone*) marcar, girar.

di·a·lect [dáɪəlɛkt] *s.* dialecto.

di·a·lec·tol·o·gy [daɪəlɛktáləðʒɪ] dialectología.

di·a·logue [dáɪəlɔg] *s.* diálogo; *v.* dialogar.

di·am·e·ter [daɪǽmətɚ] *s.* diámetro.

dia·mond [dáɪmənd] *s.* diamante; rombo (*figura geométrica*).

di·a·per [dáɪəpɚ] *s.* pañal.

di·ar·rhe·a [daɪəríə] *s.* diarrea.

di·a·ry [dáɪərɪ] *s.* diario.

dice [daɪs] *s.* *pl. de* **die** dados; *v.* cuadricular, cortar en cuarterones o cubos.

di·chot·o·my [daɪkátəmɪ] *s.* dicotomía.

dick·er [dɪkɚ] *v.* regatear.

dic·tate [dɪktet] *s.* dictado, precepto; *v.* dictar.

dic·ta·tion [dɪktéʃən] *s.* dictado; mando absoluto; **to take —** escribir al dictado.

dic·ta·tor [dɪktetɚ] *s.* dictador.

dic·ta·tor·ship [dɪktétɚʃɪp] *s.* dictadura.

dic·tion [dɪkʃən] *s.* dicción.

dic·tion·ar·y [dɪkʃənɛrɪ] *s.* diccionario.

did [dɪd] *pret. de* **to do.**

die [daɪ] *s.* (*pl.* **dice**) dado (*para jugar*); (*pl.* **dies**) matriz, molde; cuño (*sello para acuñar moneda*).

die [daɪ] *v.* morir(se); marchitarse; secarse (*las flores, plantas, etc.*); **to — out** morirse, extinguirse, apagarse.

di·er·e·sis [daɪɛrəsɪs] *s.* diéresis.

di·et [dáɪət] *s.* dieta; régimen; **to be on a —** estar a dieta; **to put on a —** adietar, poner a dieta; *v.* ponerse a dieta; estar a dieta.

dif·fer [dɪfɚ] *v.* diferir, diferenciarse, distinguirse; disentir; **to — with** no convenir con, no estar de acuerdo con.

dif·fer·ence [dɪfrəns] *s.* diferencia; distinción; discordia, controversia; **it makes no —** no importa, es igual, da lo mismo.

dif·fer·ent [dɪfrənt] *adj.* diferente; distinto.

dif·fer·en·tial [dɪfɚénʃəl] *s.* diferencial.

dif·fer·en·ti·ate [dɪfərénʃɪet] *v.* diferenciar(se); distinguir(se).

dif·fi·cult [dɪfəkʌlt] *adj.* difícil; dificultoso, trabajoso, penoso.

dif·fi·cul·ty [dɪfəkʌltɪ] *s.* dificultad; apuro, aprieto.

dif·fi·dence [dɪfədəns] *s.* timidez; desconfianza de sí propio.

dif·fi·dent [dɪfədənt] *adj.* huraño; tímido.

dif·fuse [dɪfjús] *adj.* difuso; prolijo; [dɪfjúz] *v.* difundir.

dif·fu·sion [dɪfjúʒən] *s.* difusión; diseminación.

dig [dɪg] *v.* cavar; excavar; ahondar; escarbar; trabajar duro; **to — under** socavar; **to — up** desenterrar; *s.* piquete; pulla, sarcasmo.

di·gest [dáɪdʒɛst] *s.* sumario, compendio; recopilación; código; [dədʒɛst] *v.* digerir; recopilar.

di·gest·i·ble [dədʒɛ́stəbl] *adj.* digestible, digerible.

di·ges·tion [dədʒɛ́stʃən] *s.* digestión.

di·ges·tive [dədʒɛ́stɪv] *adj.* digestivo.

dig·ni·fied [dígnəfaɪd] *adj.* digno, mesurado; serio, grave.

dig·ni·tar·y [dígnətɛrɪ] *s.* dignatario.

dig·ni·ty [dígnətɪ] *s.* dignidad.

di·graph [dáɪgræf] *s.* dígrafo.

di·gress [dəgrés] *v.* divagar.

di·gres·sion [dəgréʃən] *s.* digresión, divagación.

dike [daɪk] *s.* dique, represa; zanja.

di·late [daɪlét] *v.* dilatar(se), extender(se), ensanchar(se).

dil·i·gence [dɪlədʒəns] *s.* diligencia; aplicación, esmero.

dil·i·gent [dɪlədʒənt] *adj.* diligente, activo, aplicado.

di·lute [dɪlút] *v.* diluir, desleír; aguar; *adj.* diluido.

dim [dɪm] *adj.* penumbroso, obscuro; nublado; confuso; indistinto; deslustrado, sin brillo; *v.* obscurecer; anublar, ofuscar; atenuar.

dime [daɪm] *s.* moneda de diez centavos; **a — a dozen** una baratura.

di·men·sion [dəmɛ́nʃən] *s.* dimensión.

di·min·ish [dəmínɪʃ] *v.* disminuir; rebajar; **diminishing return** rendimiento decreciente.

dim·i·nu·tion [dɪmənjúʃən] *s.* diminución, mengua.

di·min·u·tive [dəmínjətɪv] *adj.* diminutivo; diminuto;

s. diminutivo.

dim·ness [dímnɪs] *s.* semi-obscuridad, penumbra; ofuscamiento.

dim·ple [dímpl] *s.* hoyuelo.

din [dɪn] *s.* estruendo, fragor, estrépito.

dine [daɪn] *v.* comer; festejar u obsequiar con una comida.

din·er [dáɪnə‑] *s.* coche-comedor; comensal (*persona que come a la mesa*).

din·gy [díndʒɪ] *adj.* negruzco; manchado, sucio.

din·ing [dáɪnɪŋ] *ger. de* **to dine**; — **car** coche-comedor; — **room** comedor.

din·ner [dínə‑] *s.* comida; — **coat** smoking o esmoquin.

dint [dɪnt]: **by** — **of** a fuerza de.

di·o·ram·a [daɪərǽmə] *s.* diorama.

dip [dɪp] *s.* zambullida; inmersión; (lower level) bajada; declive, depresión; *v.* meter(se); zambullirse; (*wet*) mojar (*la pluma en el tintero*); teñir; agachar (*la cabeza*); saludar (*con la bandera*); inclinarse (*un camino*); dar un bajón (*un avión*); hundirse (*el sol en el horizonte*); **to** — **out** vaciar (*con cucharón o cazo*).

diph·the·ri·a [dɪθfɪrɪə] *s.* difteria.

diph·thong [dífθɔŋ] *s.* diptongo.

di·plo·ma [dɪplómə] *s.* diploma.

di·plo·ma·cy [dɪplóməsɪ] *s.* diplomacia.

dip·lo·mat [dípləmæt] *s.* diplomático.

dip·lo·mat·ic [dɪpləmǽtɪk] *adj.* diplomático.

dip·per [dípə‑] *s.* cucharón, cazo; **the Big Dipper** la Osa Mayor.

dire [daɪr] *adj.* extremo; horrendo; fatal, de mal agüero.

di·rect [dərɛ́kt] *adj.* (*straight*) directo; derecho, en línea recta; *C.A.* recto; (*immediate*) inmediato; — **current** corriente continua; — **examination** primer interrogatorio; — **object** acusativo; — **mode** (*computer*) modo directo *adv.* directamente; **-ly** *adv.* directamente; inmediatamente; en seguida; *v.* dirigir; guiar; encaminar; dar direcciones u órdenes.

di·rec·tion [dərɛ́kʃən] *s.* dirección; administración; gerencia; rumbo.

di·rec·tion·al an·ten·na [dərɛ́kʃənl æntɛ́nə] *s.* antena direccional.

di·rec·tion·al sig·nal [dərɛ́kʃənl sígnl] *s.* señal direccional.

di·rec·tive [dərɛ́ktɪv] *adj.* directivo; *s.* orden, mandato.

di·rect·ness [dərɛ́ktnɪs] *s.* derechura; franqueza; lo directo; **with** — sin rodeos.

di·rec·tor [dərɛ́ktə‑] *s.* director; gerente.

di·rec·to·ry [dərɛ́ktərɪ] *s.* directorio; junta directiva; (*computer*) directorio; **telephone** — guía telefónica.

dir·i·gi·ble [dírədʒəbl] *adj. & s.* dirigible.

dirt [dɝt] *s.* suciedad; mugre; tierra, polvo, lodo; — **cheap** baratísimo.

dirt·y [dɝtɪ] *adj.* sucio; mugriento; cochino; enlodado; manchado; *v.* ensuciar; manchar; enlodar.

dis·a·bil·i·ty [dɪsəbílətɪ] incapacidad; — **clause** cláusula de incapacidad; — **claim** reclamación por incapacidad.

dis·a·ble [dɪsébl] *v.* incapacitar.

dis·ad·van·tage [dɪsədvǽntɪdʒ] *s.* desventaja; **to be at a** — estar en una situación desventajosa.

dis·a·gree [dɪsəgrí] *v.* (*dissent*) diferir, disentir; no convenir, no estar de acuerdo; (*bad effect*) no sentarle bien a uno (*el clima, la comida, etc.*).

dis·a·gree·a·ble [dɪsəgríəbl] *adj.* desagradable; áspero,

de mal genio.

dis·a·gree·ment [dɪsəgrímənt] *s.* desavenencia, desacuerdo; disensión; discordia; discordancia.

dis·al·low [dɪsəlaʊ] *v.* desaprobar; rechazar.

dis·ap·pear [dɪsəpfɪr] *v.* desaparecer.

dis·ap·pear·ance [dɪsəpfrəns] *s.* desaparición.

dis·ap·point [dɪsəpɔ́ɪnt] *v.* chasquear; contrariar; decepcionar; faltar a lo prometido; desilusionar **to be -ed** estar desilusionado o decepcionado; estar desengañado; quedar contrariado.

dis·ap·point·ing [dɪsəpɔ́ɪntɪŋ] *adj.* desilusionante, desengañador, decepcionante.

dis·ap·point·ment [dɪsəpɔ́ɪntmənt] *s.* desilusión; desengaño, decepción; chasco; contrariedad.

dis·ap·prov·al [dɪsəprúvl] *s.* desaprobación.

dis·ap·prove [dɪsəprúv] *v.* desaprobar.

dis·arm [dɪsárm] *v.* desarmar(se).

dis·ar·ma·ment [dɪsárməmənt] *s.* desarme.

dis·ar·ray [dɪsəré] *s.* desarreglo, confusión, desorden; *v.* desarreglar, desordenar.

dis·as·ter [dɪzǽstə‑] *s.* desastre.

dis·as·trous [dɪzǽstrəs] *adj.* desastroso.

dis·band [dɪsbǽnd] *v.* dispersar; licenciar (*las tropas*); desbandarse.

dis·be·lieve [dɪsbəlív] *v.* descreer, no creer.

dis·burse [dɪsbɝs] *v.* desembolsar.

dis·burse·ment [dɪsbɝsmənt] *s.* desembolso; gasto.

disc [dɪsk] = **disk.**

dis·card [dɪskard] *s.* descarte; desecho, cosa desechada; [dɪskárd] *v.* descartar; desechar.

dis·cern [dɪsɝn] *v.* discernir, distinguir; percibir.

dis·cern·ment [dɪsɝnmənt] *s.* discernimiento.

dis·charge [dɪstʃárdʒ] *s.* descarga (*de artillería*); (*obligation*) descargo; (*duty*) desempeño (*de un deber*); (*freedom*) exoneración; despedida; licencia (*militar*); pago (*de una deuda*); derrame, desagüe; supuración; *v.* descargar; exonerar; poner en libertad; despedir; echar, deponer; dar de baja (*a un soldado*); (*hospital*) dar de alta; pagar (*una deuda*); arrojar, supurar; desaguar.

dis·ci·ple [dɪsáɪpl] *s.* discípulo.

dis·ci·pline [dɪsəplɪn] *s.* disciplina; *v.* disciplinar.

dis·close [dɪsklóz] *v.* descubrir; revelar.

dis·col·or [dɪskʌ́lə‑] *v.* descolorar(se), desteñir(se).

dis·com·fort [dɪskʌ́mfə‑t] *s.* incomodidad; malestar.

dis·con·cert [dɪskənsɝt] *v.* desconcertar.

dis·con·nect [dɪskənɛ́kt] *v.* desconectar; desacoplar; desunir, separar.

dis·con·nect·ed [dɪskənɛ́ktɪd] *p.p. & adj.* desconectado; desunido; inconexo, incoherente.

dis·con·so·late [dɪskánslɪt] *adj.* desconsolado.

dis·con·tent [dɪskəntɛ́nt] *s.* descontento; *v.* descontentar.

dis·con·tent·ed [dɪskəntɛ́ntɪd] *adj.* descontento; descontentadizo.

dis·con·tin·ue [dɪskəntínju] *v.* descontinuar; parar; suspender, interrumpir; abandonar.

dis·cord [dískɔrd] *s.* discordia; disonancia, discordancia; desavenencia.

dis·count [dískaʊnt] *s.* descuento; rebaja; — **rate** tipo de descuento (tasa); *v.* descontar; rebajar.

dis·cour·age [dɪskɝɪdʒ] *v.* desanimar, desalentar, abatir; **to** — **from** disuadir de.

dis·cour·age·ment [dɪskɝɪdʒmənt] *s.* desaliento, abatimiento.

dis·course [dískors] *s.* discurso; conversación; [dɪskórs] *v.* disertar; discurrir, hablar.

dis·cour·te·ous [dɪskɝtɪəs] *adj.* descortés, desatento.

dis·cour·te·sy [dɪskɝtəsɪ] *s.* descortesía, desatención.

dis·cov·er [dɪskʌ́və‑] *v.* descubrir.

dis·cov·er·er [dɪskʌ́vərə‑] *s.* descubridor.

dis·cov·er·y [dɪskʌ́vrɪ] *s.* descubrimiento.
dis·cred·it [dɪskrédɪt] *s.* descrédito; deshonra; *v.* desacreditar; deshonrar; no creer.
dis·creet [dɪskrít] *adj.* discreto, prudente.
dis·crep·an·cy [dɪskrépənsɪ] *s.* discrepancia, diferencia, variación.
dis·cre·tion [dɪskréʃən] *s.* discreción; prudencia; **at one's own** — a discreción.
dis·crim·i·nate [dɪskrímənet] *v.* discernir; distinguir; hacer distinciones, hacer favoritismos; dar trato de inferioridad con motivos de perjuicio; **to** — **against** hacer favoritismos en perjuicio de.
dis·cuss [dɪskʌ́s] *v.* discutir.
dis·cus·sion [dɪskʌ́ʃən] *s.* discusión.
dis·dain [dɪsdén] *s.* desdén, menosprecio; *v.* desdeñar, menospreciar; desdeñarse de.
dis·dain·ful [dɪsdénfəl] *adj.* desdeñoso.
dis·ease [dɪzíz] *s.* enfermedad.
dis·eased [dɪzízd] *adj.* enfermo.
dis·em·bark [dɪsɪmbárk] *v.* desembarcar.
dis·en·tan·gle [dɪsɪntǽŋgl] *v.* desenredar, desenmarañar, deshacer (*una maraña o enredo*).
dis·fig·ure [dɪsfígjɚ] *v.* desfigurar; afear; desencajar.
dis·fran·chise [dɪsfrǽntʃaɪz] *v.* privar de derecho de voto o de ciudadanía.
dis·grace [dɪsgrés] *s.* ignominia, deshonra; vergüenza; **to be in** — estar desacreditado, haber perdido la gracia o el favor; *v.* deshonrar; degradar; desacreditar; avergonzar.
dis·grace·ful [dɪsgrésfəl] *adj.* vergonzoso.
dis·guise [dɪsgáɪz] *s.* disfraz; *v.* disfrazar.
dis·gust [dɪsgʌ́st] *s.* asco; repugnancia; disgusto; *v.* disgustar, dar asco; repugnar.
dis·gust·ed [dɪsgʌ́stɪd] *adj.* disgustado; descontento; asqueado.
dis·gust·ing [dɪsgʌ́stɪŋ] *adj.* asqueroso, repugnante.
dish [dɪʃ] *s.* plato; manjar, vianda; **-es** vajilla; *v.* servir.
dis·heart·en [dɪshártn̩] *v.* desalentar, desanimar, descorazonar.
di·shev·el [dɪʃévl] *v.* desgreñar.
di·shev·eled [dɪʃévld] *adj.* desgreñado, desaliñado, desaseado; revuelto.
dis·hon·est [dɪsánɪst] *adj.* engañoso, falso, tramposo, falto de honradez, fraudulento.
dis·hon·es·ty [dɪsánɪstɪ] *s.* fraude, falta de honradez.
dis·hon·or [dɪsánɚ] *s.* deshonra; afrenta; *v.* deshonrar; recusar (*un giro o cheque*).
dis·hon·or·a·ble [dɪsánərəbl] *adj.* deshonroso; infame.
dish·wash·er [dɪʃwɔʃɚ] *s.* (*person*) lavaplatos; (*machine*) máquina de lavar platos.
dis·il·lu·sion [dɪsɪlúʒən] *s.* desilusión, decepción, desengaño; *v.* desilusionar, decepcionar, desengañar.
dis·in·fect [dɪsɪnfékt] *v.* desinfectar.
dis·in·fec·tant [dɪsɪnféktənt] *s.* desinfectante.
dis·in·ter·est·ed [dɪsíntərəstɪd] *adj.* desinteresado.
disk [dɪsk] *s.* disco; (*computer*) disco, disquette; — **drive** impulsor de discos, unidad de discos; **floppy** — disco flexible; **hard** — disco rígido (duro); — **brake** freno de disco.
dis·like [dɪsláɪk] *s.* antipatía, aversión; *v.* sentir o tener aversión por; **I** — **it** me repugna, no me gusta, me desagrada.
dis·lo·cate [dísloket] *v.* dislocar, descoyuntar; desencajar.
dis·lodge [dɪsládʒ] *v.* desalojar.
dis·loy·al [dɪslɔ́ɪəl] *adj.* desleal.
dis·mal [dízml̩] *adj.* lúgubre, sombrío, tétrico.
dis·man·tle [dɪsmǽntl̩] *v.* desmantelar; desmontar, desarmar.

dis·may [dɪsmé] *s.* desmayo, desaliento, pavor; *v.* desalentar, desanimar; atemorizar.
dis·miss [dɪsmɪ́s] *v.* (*discharge*) despedir, expulsar, destituir; (*dispel*) desechar; (*allow to leave*) licenciar, dar de baja; (*close*) dar por terminado (*un pleito o caso jurídico*); **to** — **the meeting** disolver la junta, levantar la sesión.
dis·miss·al [dɪsmɪ́sl̩] *s.* despedida, expulsión, destitución (*de un cargo*).
dis·mount [dɪsmáʊnt] *v.* desmontar; apear(se); desarmar (*un cañón, una máquina*); desengastar (*joyas*).
dis·o·be·di·ence [dɪsəbídɪəns] *s.* desobediencia.
dis·o·be·di·ent [dɪsəbídɪənt] *adj.* desobediente.
dis·o·bey [dɪsəbé] *v.* desobedecer.
dis·or·der [dɪsɔ́rdɚ] *s.* (*confusion*) desorden; trastorno; confusión; (*illness*) enfermedad; *v.* desordenar; trastornar; desarreglar.
dis·or·der·ly [dɪsɔ́rdɚlɪ] *adj.* desordenado; desarreglado; revoltoso; escandaloso; *adv.* desordenadamente.
dis·own [dɪsón] *v.* repudiar; desconocer, negar.
dis·par·age [dɪspǽrɪdʒ] *v.* desacreditar; desdorar.
dis·pas·sion·ate [dɪspǽʃənɪt] *adj.* desapasionado.
dis·patch [dɪspǽtʃ] *s.* despacho; envío; parte (*m.*), comunicación, mensaje; prontitud, expedición; *v.* despachar; enviar, expedir; matar.
dis·pel [dɪspél] *v.* disipar; dispersar.
dis·pen·sa·ry [dɪspénsərɪ] *s.* dispensario.
dis·pen·sa·tion [dɪspənséʃən] *s.* dispensa, exención; dispensación; distribución.
dis·pense [dɪspéns] *v.* (*give*) dispensar, dar; repartir, distribuir; administrar (*la justicia*); despachar (*recetas, medicamentos*); **to** — **from** eximir de, dispensar de; **to** — **with** omitir; pasarse sin, prescindir de.
dis·per·sal [dɪspɝsl̩] *s.* dispersión; desbandada.
dis·perse [dɪspɝs] *v.* dispersar(se), disipar(se), esparcir(se).
dis·place [dɪsplés] *v.* desalojar; desplazar; poner fuera de su lugar; suplantar.
dis·placed per·son [dɪsplést pɝsən] *s.* persona desplazada.
dis·play [dɪsplé] *s.* manifestación, exhibición; — **poster** cartel de publicidad; ostentación; (*computer*) visualización; *v.* exhibir; mostrar, manifestar; desplegar; (*computer*) visualizar.
dis·please [dɪsplíz] *v.* desagradar; disgustar, fastidiar.
dis·pleas·ure [dɪsplɛ́ʒɚ] *s.* desagrado, disgusto, descontento.
dis·pos·al [dɪspózl̩] *s.* disposición; arreglo; venta (*de bienes*).
dis·pose [dɪspóz] *v.* disponer; arreglar; influir; **to** — **of** deshacerse de.
dis·po·si·tion [dɪspəzíʃən] *s.* disposición; arreglo; aptitud, inclinación; venta; **good (bad)** — buen (mal) genio.
dis·pos·ses [dɪspozɛ́s] *v.* desposeer; despojar.
dis·prove [dɪsprúv] *v.* refutar.
dis·pute [dɪspjút] *s.* disputa; *v.* disputar.
dis·qual·i·fy [dɪskwɑləfaɪ] *v.* inhabilitar, incapacitar, descalificar.
dis·re·gard [dɪsrɪgárd] *s.* desatención, falta de atención, negligencia, descuido; falta de respeto o consideración; *v.* desatender, no hacer caso de, desentenderse de.
dis·re·spect [dɪsrɪspékt] *s.* desacato, falta de respeto.
dis·re·spect·ful [dɪsrɪspéktfəl] *adj.* irrespetuoso.
dis·rupt [dɪsrʌ́pt] *v.* desbaratar; romper.
dis·sat·is·fied [dɪssǽtɪsfaɪd] *adj.* descontento, malcontento, mal satisfecho.

dis·sat·is·fy [dɪssǽtɪsfaɪ] v. descontentar, no
satisfacer.

dis·sect [dɪsɛ́kt] v. disecar, hacer una disección;
analizar.

dis·sem·ble [dɪsɛ́mbl] v. disimular, fingir.

dis·sen·sion [dɪsɛ́nʃən] s. disensión, discordia.

dis·sent [dɪsɛ́nt] v. disentir; s. desacuerdo; disensión,
desavenencia.

dis·ser·ta·tion [dɪsɝtéʃən] s. disertación; tratado;
tesis.

dis·sim·u·la·tion [dɪsɪmjəléʃən] s. disimulo.

dis·si·pate [dɪ́səpet] v. disipar(se).

dis·si·pa·tion [dɪsəpéʃən] s. disipación.

dis·so·lute [dɪ́səlut] adj. disoluto.

dis·so·lu·tion [dɪsəlúʃən] s. disolución.

dis·solve [dɪzálv] v. disolver(se); anular; derogar,
liquidar.

dis·suade [dɪswéd] v. disuadir.

dis·taff [dɪ́stæf] s. rueca.

dis·tance [dɪ́stəns] s. distancia; lejanía; alejamiento;
**in the — ** a lo lejos, en lontananza.

dis·tant [dɪ́stənt] adj. (far) distante; apartado, lejano,
remoto; (aloof) esquivo; **to be — from** distar de;
-ly adv. de lejos; remotamente; a distancia; en
lontananza.

dis·taste [dɪstést] s. disgusto, aversión, repugnancia.

dis·taste·ful [dɪstéstfəl] adj. desagradable,
repugnante.

dis·tem·per [dɪstɛ́mpɚ] s. moquillo; pepita (de las
gallinas).

dis·tend [dɪstɛ́nd] v. dilatar; ensanchar.

dis·til [dɪstɪ́l] v. destilar.

dis·til·la·tion [dɪstléʃən] s. destilación.

dis·till·er·y [dɪstɪ́lərɪ] s. destilería.

dis·tinct [dɪstɪ́ŋkt] adj. distinto, claro; diferente; **-ly**
adv. distintamente, claramente, con claridad.

dis·tinc·tion [dɪstɪ́ŋkʃən] s. distinción.

dis·tinc·tive [dɪstɪ́ŋktɪv] adj. distintivo.

dis·tin·guish [dɪstɪ́ŋgwɪʃ] v. distinguir; discernir.

dis·tin·guished [dɪstɪ́ŋgwɪʃt] adj. distinguido.

dis·tin·guish·ing [dɪstɪ́ŋgwɪʃɪŋ] adj. distintivo,
característico.

dis·tort [dɪstɔ́rt] v. desfigurar, deformar, torcer,
falsear; tergivesar.

dis·tract [dɪstrǽkt] v. distraer; perturbar.

dis·trac·tion [dɪstrǽkʃən] s. distracción, diversión;
perturbación; **to drive to — ** volver loco.

dis·tress [dɪstrɛ́s] s. angustia, aflicción, congoja;
dolor; **to be in — ** tener una aflicción; estar
apurado; estar en zozobra (un navío); v. angustiar,
acongojar, afligir; **to be -ed** estar afligido o
apurado.

dis·trib·ute [dɪstrɪ́bjut] v. distribuir, repartir.

dis·tri·bu·tion [dɪstrəbjúʃən] s. distribución;
repartimiento.

dis·trib·u·tor [dɪstrɪ́bjətɚ] s. distribuidor.

dis·trict [dɪ́strɪkt] s. distrito; **— attorney** fiscal de
distrito.

dis·trust [dɪstrʌ́st] s. deconfianza; recelo; v.
desconfiar; recelar.

dis·trust·ful [dɪstrʌ́stfəl] adj. desconfiado,
sospechoso, receloso.

dis·turb [dɪstɝ́b] v. turbar, perturbar, inquietar;
desarreglar; incomodar, molestar; **don't —
yourself!** ¡no se moleste Vd.!

dis·tur·bance [dɪstɝ́bəns] s. disturbio; perturbación;
desorden; alboroto; molestia.

dis·use [dɪsjús] s. desuso; **to fall into — ** caer en
desuso; caducar.

ditch [dɪtʃ] s. zanja; foso; **irrigation — ** acequia; v.
zanjar, abrir zanjas; meter en la zanja; **to —**

someone deshacerse de alguien.

dit·to [dɪ́to] s. idem, lo mismo.

di·u·ret·ic [daɪjʊrɛ́tɪk] adj. & s. diurético.

di·van [dáɪvæn] s. diván.

dive [daɪv] s. zambullida (echándose de cabeza),
buceada, chapuz; picada (descenso rápido de un
avión); Méx. clavado; (place) garito, leonera; v.
echarse de cabeza; zambullirse (de cabeza); bucear;
sumergirse (un submarino); **to — into someone**
abalanzarse sobre alguien.

div·er [dáɪvɚ] s. buzo; zambullidor.

di·verge [dəvɝ́dʒ] v. divergir, irse apartando,
separarse; diferir.

di·ver·gence [dəvɝ́dʒəns] s. divergencia; diferencia
(de opiniones).

di·vers [dáɪvɚz] adj. diversos, varios.

di·verse [dəvɝ́s] adj. diverso; diferente.

di·ver·sion [dəvɝ́ʒən] s. diversión, recreo;
desviación.

di·ver·si·ty [dəvɝ́sətɪ] s. diversidad, diferencia,
variedad.

di·vert [dəvɝ́t] v. divertir, entretener; distraer;
desviar, apartar.

di·vide [dəváɪd] v. dividir(se); partir.

div·i·dend [dɪ́vədɛnd] s. dividendo.

di·vid·ing [dɪváɪdɪŋ] adj. divisorio.

di·vine [dəváɪn] adj. divino; v. adivinar.

di·vin·i·ty [dəvínətɪ] s. divinidad; deidad; teología.

di·vi·sion [dəvíʒən] s. división.

di·vorce [dəvórs] s. divorcio; v. divorciar(se).

di·vulge [dəvʌ́ldʒ] v. divulgar.

diz·zi·ness [dɪ́zɪnɪs] s. vahido o vaguido,
desvanecimiento, mareo, vértigo.

diz·zy [dɪ́zɪ] adj. desvanecido, mareado; (confused)
confuse; aturdido; — **speed** velocidad vertiginosa.

do [du] v. hacer; **to — away with** deshacerse de;
prescindir de; **to — a lesson** estudiar una lección;
to — one's hair peinarse, arreglarse el pelo; **to —
the dishes** lavar los platos; **to — up** envolver;
limpiar, arreglar; lavar o planchar; **to — well in
business** prosperar en los negocios; **to — without**
pasarse sin; **to have nothing to — with** no tener
nada que ver con; **that will — ** basta, bastará; **that
won't — ** eso no sirve; eso no resultará bien; **this
will have to — ** habrá que conformarse con esto;
how — you — ? ¿cómo está Vd.?; **— you hear
me?** ¿me oye Vd.?; **yes, I — ** sí, le oigo; **I — say
it** sí lo digo.

doc·ile [dásl] adj. dócil.

dock [dɑk] s. muelle, desembarcadero; dársena;
dique; **dry — ** carenero, dique de carena; v. entrar
en el muelle; atracar, meter (una embarcación) en
el muelle o dique; **to — the wages** rebajar la paga.

doc·tor [dáktɚ] s. doctor; médico, facultativo; v.
medicinar, curar; **to — oneself** medicinarse, tomar
medicinas.

doc·trine [dáktrɪn] s. doctrina.

doc·u·ment [dákjəmənt] s. documento; [dákjəmɛnt]
v. documentar.

dod·der [dádɚ] v. tambalear; temblar.

dodge [dɑdʒ] s. evasión, evasiva; v. evadir(se);
escabullirse; hurtar el cuerpo; **to — around a
corner** dar un esquinazo.

doe [do] s. cierva; hembra (del antílope, del gamo,
de la liebre).

dog [dɔg] s. perro, perra; can; **hot — ** salchicha
caliente, Ch., C.A. perro caliente; Ríopl. pancho;
**to put on a lot of — ** emperifollarse; darse mucho
tono; Am. darse mucho corte; v. seguir la pista de,
perseguir, acosar; adv. sumamente, completamente;
dog-tired cansadísimo.

DI

dog·ma [dɔ́gmə] *s.* dogma.
dog·mat·ic [dɔgmǽtɪk] *adj.* dogmático.
doi·ly [dɔ́ɪlɪ] *s.* mantelito (*para platos, vasos, lámparas, etc.*).
do·ings [dúɪŋz] *s. pl.* hechos, acciones, acontecimientos; **great —** mucha actividad, fiesta, función.
do-it-your·self [duɪtjʊrsɛ́lf] *adj.* proyectado para que uno pueda hacer sus propios trabajos manuales en casa; autodidáctico.
dole [dol] *s.* reparto gratuito (*de dinero o alimento*); ración, limosna; *v.* repartir gratuitamente.
dole·ful [dólfəl] *adj.* lúgubre, triste, lastimoso.
doll [dɑl] *s.* muñeca, muñeco; *v.* **to — up** emperifollarse, ataviarse; **dolly** *s.* muñequita.
dol·lar [dɑ́lɚ] *s.* dólar; **— diplomacy** diplomacia mercantilista; **— exchange** divisa en dólares.
dol·phin [dɔ́lfɪn] *s.* delfín.
do·main [domén] *s.* dominio; heredad.
dome [dom] *s.* cúpula; media naranja (*de iglesia*).
do·mes·tic [dəmɛ́stɪk] *adj.* doméstico; hogareño; nacional, del país, *Am.* criollo; *s.* criado, sirviente.
do·mi·cile [dɑ́məsaɪl] *s.* domicilio.
dom·i·nant [dɑ́mənənt] *adj.* dominante.
dom·i·nate [dɑ́mənet] *v.* dominar.
dom·i·na·tion [dɑmənéʃən] *s.* dominación, dominio.
dom·i·neer [dɑmənír] *v.* dominar, señorear.
dom·i·neer·ing [dɑmənírɪŋ] *adj.* dominador, mandón, imperioso, tiránico.
do·min·ion [dəmínjən] *s.* dominio.
dom·i·no [dɑ́məno] *s.* dominó, traje de máscara; disfraz; (*game*) ficha (*de dominó*); **dominoes** dominó (*juego*).
don [dɑn] *s.* don (*título*); caballero; *v.* ponerse, vestirse.
do·nate [dónet] *v.* donar, regalar, hacer donación.
do·na·tion [donéʃən] *s.* donación; regalo, dádiva.
done [dʌn] *p.p. de* **to do** hecho; terminado, acabado; **to be — in** estar rendido de cansancio; **the meat is well —** está bien asada la carne.
don·key [dɑ́ŋkɪ] *s.* burro, asno.
doo·dad [dúdæd] *s.* chuchería, chisme.
doom [dum] *s.* hado, sino, destino; mala suerte, perdición, ruina; **the day of —** el día del juicio final; *v.* condenar, sentenciar; predestinar; **to be -ed to failure** estar predestinado al fracaso.
door [dor] *s.* puerta; entrada.
door·bell [dórbɛl] *s.* campanilla o timbre (*de llamada*).
door·knob [dórnɑb] *s.* tirador de puerta, perilla, manija.
door·man [dórmæn] *s.* portero.
door·step [dórstɛp] *s.* escalón de la puerta; umbral.
door·way [dórwe] *s.* puerta, entrada; vano (*de la puerta*).
dope [dop] *s.* (*narcotic*) narcótico; opio; droga; menjurje, medicamento; **— addict** drogadicto; **— racket** tráfico ilícito de narcóticos; (*information*) información; **— fiend** morfinómano; **he is a —** es un zoquete; *v.* narcotizar; **to — out** adivinar, conjeturar; **to — oneself up** medicinarse demasiado.
dor·mi·to·ry [dɔ́rmətorɪ] *s.* dormitorio.
DOS (Disk Operating System) *s.* (*computer*) SOD (Sistema operativo de disquettes)
dose [dos] *s.* dosis; *v.* medicinar; **to — oneself** medicinarse.
dos·si·er [dásie] *s.* expediente; legajo.
dot [dɑt] *s.* punto; **on the —** en punto; **dot-matrix printer** *s.* (*computer*) impresora de matriz de puntos; *v.* marcar con puntos; poner el punto

(*sobre la* i).
do·tage [dótɪdʒ] *s.* chochez; **to be in one's —** chochear.
dote [dot] *v.* chochear; **to — on** estar loco por.
dou·ble [dʌ́bl] *adj.* doble; doblado; **— boiler** baño de María; **— check** verificar, revisar; **— deal** trato doble; **— entry** partida doble; **— standard** norma de conducta sexual más restringida para la mujer; **— shift** turno doble; *s.* doble; **-s** juego de dobles (*en tenis*); *adv.* doblemente; **double-breasted** cruzado; **double-faced** de dos caras; **— density** (*computer*) doble densidad; **— sided** (de dos) caras; *v.* doblar(se); duplicar(se); **to — up** doblarse; duplicar; indudablemente; **doubly** *adv.* doblemente; por duplicado.
doubt [daʊt] *s.* duda; *v.* dudar.
doubt·ful [dáʊtfəl] *adj.* dudoso; dudable.
doubt·less [dáʊtlɪs] *adj.* indudable, cierto, seguro; *adv.* sin duda; indudablemente; probablemente.
douche [duʃ] *s.* ducha vaginal.
dough [do] *s.* pasta, masa; dinero.
dough·nut [dónət] *s.* bollito o buñuelo en rosca.
dove [dʌv] *s.* paloma.
dove [dov] *pret. de* **to dive.**
down [daʊn] *adv.* abajo, hacia abajo; **— to** hasta; **— East** en el este; **— the street** calle abajo; **to cut — prices** reducir o rebajar precios; **to get — to work** aplicarse; **to go (come) —** bajar; **to pay —** pagar al contado; **to put —** poner; anotar, apuntar, poner por escrito; *adj.* abatido, descorazonado; **— grade** declive, pendiente; **— payment** pago inicial; *Col.* cuota inicial; *Méx.* enganche; **prices are —** han bajado los precios; **to be — on someone** tenerle ojeriza a alguien; *s.* plumón; vello; pelusa; *v.* echar por tierra, derribar; rebajar (*precios*).
down·cast [dáʊnkæst] *adj.* cabizbajo, abatido; **with — eyes** con los ojos bajos.
down·fall [dáʊnfɔl] *s.* caída; ruina.
down·pour [dáʊnpor] *s.* aguacero, chaparrón.
down·right [dáʊnraɪt] *adj.* claro, positivo, categórico, absoluto; **— foolishness** solemne disparate; *adv.* enteramente; absolutamente.
down·stairs [dáʊnstɛrz] *adv.* abajo; en el piso bajo; *adj.* del piso bajo; *s.* piso bajo, piso inferior.
down·stream [dáʊnstrím] *adv.* río abajo, aguas abajo; con la corriente.
down-to-earth [daʊntəɝθ] *adj.* sensato; práctico.
down·town [dáʊntáʊn] *adv.* al centro, en el centro (*de una población*); *adj.* del centro; *s.* centro.
down·turn [dáʊntɚn] *s.* tendencia a la baja.
down·ward [dáʊnwɚd] *adj.* descendente; inclinado; *adv.* (= **downwards**) hacia abajo.
dow·ny [dáʊnɪ] *adj.* suave, blando; velloso; plumoso.
dow·ry [dáʊrɪ] *s.* dote.
doze [doz] *v.* siestecita, sueño ligero; *v.* dormitar.
doz·en [dʌ́zn̩] *s.* docena.
drab [dræb] *adj.* pardo, pardusco; monótono.
draft [dræft] *s.* corriente de aire; (*drink*) trago; (*bank*) libranza, letra de cambio, giro bancario; (*tracing*) trazado; plan, leva (*militar*), conscripción; (*stove*) tiro (*de estufa, hogar, etc.*); calado (*de un barco*); **— beer** cerveza de barril; **— horse** caballo de tiro; **— rough** croquis, borrador; *v.* trazar, dibujar, delinear, reclutar, echar leva; redactar (*un documento*).
drafts·man [dræftsmən] *s.* dibujante.
drag [dræg] *s.* rastra; traba, obstáculo; **to have a — with someone** tener buenas aldabas con alguien; *v.* arrastrar(se); rastrear; moverse despacio; **to — on and on** prolongarse demasiado, prolongarse hasta el fastidio.

drag·on [drǽgən] *s.* dragón.
drain [dren] *s.* (*channel*) desagüe; desaguadero, conducto; (*exhaust*) agotamiento; consumo; *v.* desaguar(se); apurar (*un vaso*); agotar, consumir; escurrir(se), secar(se); desecar (*un terreno*), *Am.* drenar.
drain·age [drénɪdʒ] *s.* desagüe, *Am.* drenaje; desaguadero; sistema de desaguaderos; desecamiento, desecación (*de un terreno, laguna, etc.*).
drake [drek] *s.* pato.
dra·ma [drámə] *s.* drama.
dra·mat·ic [drəmǽtɪk] *adj.* dramático.
dra·ma·tist [drámətɪst] *s.* dramaturgo, dramático.
dra·ma·tize [drǽmətaɪz] *v.* dramatizar.
drank [dræŋk] *pret. de* **to drink.**
drape [drep] *s.* colgadura, cortina, tapiz; *v.* colgar, entapizar, adornar con tapices; cubrir, revestir.
drap·er·y [drépərɪ] *s.* tapicería, colgaduras, cortinas; pañería, paños, géneros.
dras·tic [drǽstɪk] *adj.* extremo, fuerte, violento; **to take — steps** tomar medidas enérgicas.
draught [dræft] *véase* **draft.**
draw [drɔ] *v.* (*pull*) tirar, estirar; jalar; (*attract*) atraer, sacar; (*design*) dibujar, trazar; (*withdraw*) girar, librar (*una libranza*); hacer (*una comparación*); correr (*la cortina*); **to — aside** apartar(se); **to — a breath** aspirar, tomar aliento; **to — a blank** fracasar; **to — lots** echar suertes, sortear; **to — near** acercarse; **to — out** sacar; sonsacar (*a una persona*); alargar, prolongar; **to — up** acercar(se); redactar (*un documento*); *s.* empate (*en deportes o juegos*); número sacado (*en una rifa*); atracción; **— bridge** puente levadizo.
draw·back [drɔ́bæk] *s.* desventaja; obstáculo, inconveniente.
draw·ee [drɔ́f] *s.* girado, librado.
drawer [drɔr] *s.* cajón, gaveta; **-s** calzoncillos.
draw·er [drɔ́ɚ] *s.* librador, girador; dibujante.
draw·ing [drɔ́ɪŋ] *s.* (*design*) dibujo; delineación, trazado; (*raffle*) sorteo; **— paper** papel de dibujo; **— room** sala de recibo, recibidor, recibimiento.
drawn [drɔn] *p.p. de* **to draw.**
dread [drɛd] *s.* pavor, temor, aprensión; *adj.* terrible; temido; *v.* temer; sentir aprensión de.
dread·ful [drɛ́dfəl] *adj.* horrendo; espantoso.
dream [drim] *s.* sueño; ensueño; *v.* soñar; **to — of** soñar con, soñar en.
dream·er [drímɚ] *s.* soñador.
dream·land [drímlænd] *s.* tierra del ensueño; región de los sueños.
dreamt [drɛmpt] = **dreamed.**
drea·my [drímɪ] *adj.* soñoliento; soñador; melancólico; como un sueño; **a — recollection** un vago recuerdo.
drea·ry [drírɪ] *adj.* sombrío; melancólico.
dredge [drɛdʒ] *s.* draga; *v.* dragar.
dregs [drɛgz] *s. pl.* heces, sedimento.
drench [drɛnʃ] *s.* mojada, mojadura, empapada; *v.* empapar; mojar; remojar.
dress [drɛs] *s.* vestido, traje; (*apparel*) vestidura, ropaje, atavío; **— rehearsal** ensayo general y último (*antes de una función*); **— suit** traje de etiqueta; *v.* vestir(se); arreglarse, componerse; aderezar; adobar (*carne o pieles*); curar (*heridas*); alinear, formar (*las tropas*); **to — down** reprender, regañar; **to — up** emperifollarse, acicalarse, ataviarse.
dress·er [drɛ́sɚ] *s.* tocador, cómoda (*con espejo*); **she is a good —** viste con elegancia o buen gusto.
dress·ing [drɛ́sɪŋ] *s.* aderezo; salsa (*para ensaladas*);

relleno (*para carne, pollo, etc.*); medicamento, vendajes (*para heridas*); **a — down** regaño; **— gown** bata; **— room** tocador; **— table** tocador.
dress·mak·er [drɛ́smekɚ] *s.* modista.
drew [dru] *pret. de* **to draw.**
drib·ble [drɪbl] *v.* gotear; dejar caer en gotas; babear; *s.* goteo; chorrito.
drib·let [drɪblɪt] *s.* gota, gotita; **in -s** gota a gota; en pequeñas cantidades.
dried [draɪd] *pret. & p.p. de* **to dry;** *adj.* seco; paso; **— fig** higo paso.
drift [drɪft] *s.* (*direction*) rumbo dirección, tendencia, deriva; (*pile*) montón, amontonamiento (*de arena, nieve, etc.*); (*off course*) desvío (*de un barco o avión*); **to get the — of a conversation** enterarse a medias de una conversación; *v.* flotar; ir(se) a la deriva; dejarse llevar por la corriente; amontonarse (*la nieve, la arena*); esparcirse (*la arena, la nieve, las nubes*).
drift·wood [drɪ́ftwʊd] *s.* madera o leña flotante; madera de playa.
drill [drɪl] *s.* (*tool*) taladro; barrena; (*training*) ejercicio; adiestramiento; *Am.* entrenamiento; (*cloth*) dril (*tela*); *v.* taladrar, barrenar, perforar; hacer ejercicio; aleccionar; disciplinar (*un ejército*); adiestrar(se), *Am.* entrenar(se).
dri·ly [dráɪlɪ] *adv.* secamente.
drink [drɪŋk] *v.* beber; trago; *v.* beber; **to — a toast to** beber a la salud de, brindar por; **— it down!** ¡bébaselo! ¡trágueselo!
drink·a·ble [drɪ́ŋkəbl] *adj.* potable.
drip [drɪp] *s.* goteo; *v.* gotear, caer gota a gota; dejar caer gota a gota.
drive [draɪv] *s.* (*ride*) paseo en coche; (*road*) calzada, carretera, paseo; (*campaign*) campaña; (*impulse*) empuje; tiro, tirada (*de una pelota*); *v.* impulsar, impeler, empujar; arrear (*animales*); conducir, guiar o manejar (*un auto*); clavar; encajar, clavar (*una estaca, cuña, o clavo*); tirar, lanzar (*una pelota*); dar un paseo en auto; llevar (*a alguien*) en auto; cavar (*un pozo, túnel, etc.*); **to — away** ahuyentar; **to — a good bargain** hacer un buen trato; **to — a hard bargain** regatear mucho; **to — mad** volver loco; **what are you driving at?** ¿qué quieres decir con eso?
drive-in [dráɪvɪn] *s. adj.* establecimiento como tienda, banco, teatro que tiene pista automovilística que permite al cliente permanecer en su coche; automovilístico.
driv·el [drɪ́vl] *s.* baba; ñoñería, tontería; *v.* babear; chochear, decir ñoñerías.
driv·el·ing [drɪ́vlɪŋ] *adj.* baboso.
driv·en [drɪ́vən] *p.p. de* **to drive.**
driv·er [dráɪvɚ] *s.* cochero, chófer, mecánico, conductor (*de automóvil*); *C.A.* motorista; arriero (*de animales*); uno de los palos de golf; **pile —** martinete (*para clavar pilotes*); **slave —** mandón, tirano; **truck —** carretero, camionero.
drive·way [dráɪvwe] *s.* calzada de entrada, carretera de entrada.
driz·zle [drɪ́zl] *v.* lloviznar; *s.* llovizna.
drone [dron] *s.* zángano; holgazán; (*sound*) zumbido; *v.* zumbar; hablar con monotonía; (*be lazy*) holgazanear, perder el tiempo.
droop [drup] *v.* doblarse, andar o estar alicaído, estar abatido; languidecer; marchitarse; bajar (*los hombros, los párpados*); **his shoulders —** tiene los hombros caídos; **-ing eyelids** párpados caídos.
drop [drɑp] *s.* (*liquid*) gota; (*descent*) baja; caída; (*incline*) declive; **cough —** pastilla para la tos; **letter —** buzón; **— curtain** telón (*de teatro*); **—**

hammer martinete; — **out** dimitente; v. dejar caer, soltar; gotear; caer; dejar (un asunto, una amistad); **to — a line** poner unos renglones; **to — asleep** quedarse dormido, dormirse; **to — behind** dejar atrás; quedarse atrás; **to — in** hacer una visita inesperada, Am. descolgarse; **to — in a mailbox** echar al buzón; **to — out** retirarse; desaparecer; **to — the curtain** bajar el telón.

drought [draʊt] s. sequía.

drove [drov] s. manada, recua, rebaño; tropel; pret. de **to drive.**

drown [draʊn] v. ahogar(se), anegar(se); apagar, ahogar (un sonido).

drowse [draʊz] v. dormitar; estar amodorrado.

drows·i·ness [dráʊzɪnɪs] s. modorra, somnolencia.

drow·sy [dráʊzɪ] adj. soñoliento; adormilado, amodorrado; **to become —** amodorrarse.

drudge [drʌdʒ] v. afanarse, atarearse; s. trabajador, esclavo del trabajo.

drug [drʌg] s. droga; narcótico; **to be a — on the market** ser invendible (una mercancía); **— addict** drogadicto; v. jaropar (administrar drogas en demasía); narcotizar.

drug·gist [drʌ́gɪst] s. boticario, droguista, droguero, farmacéutico.

drug·store [drʌ́gstor] s. botica, droguería, farmacia.

drum [drʌm] s. tambor; tímpano (del oído); barril, tonel; **bass —** tambora, bombo; **— stick** bolillo de tambor; **— major** tambor mayor; v. tocar el tambor; tamborilear; **to — a lesson into someone** meterle a uno la lección en la cabeza; **to — up trade** solicitar o fomentar ventas.

drum·mer [drʌ́mɚ] s. tambor, tamborilero; viajante de comercio, agente.

drunk [drʌŋk] p.p. de **to drink;** adj. borracho, ebrio, emborrachado, bebido; Ríopl. mamado; C.A. bolo; Ch. cufifo; Méx. pedo; **to get —** emborracharse, embriagarse.

drunk·ard [drʌ́ŋkɚd] s. borracho, borrachón, beodo, bebedor.

drunk·en [drʌ́ŋjən] adj. borracho, ebrio.

drunk·en·ness [drʌ́ŋkənnɪs] s. borrachera, embriaguez.

dry [draɪ] adj. seco; árido; **a — book** un libro aburrido; **— cleaner** quitamanchas; tintorero; **— cleaning** lavado o limpieza al seco; **— goods** lencería, géneros, tejidos, telas; **— measure** medida para áridos, **— run** ejercicio de ensayo; ensayo; **— wash** ropa lavada pero no planchada; **— dock** dique seco, carenero; v. secar(se); enjugar; **to — up** secarse, resecarse.

dry·ness [dráɪnɪs] s. sequedad; aridez.

dub [dʌb] v. doblar (una película).

du·bi·ous [djúbɪəs] adj. dudoso.

duch·ess [dʌ́tjɪs] s. duquesa.

duck [dʌk] s. pato, pata; ánade; dril (género); zambullida, chapuz; agachada rápida (para evitar un golpe); v. zambullir(se), chapuzar(se); agachar(se); agachar (la cabeza).

duck·ling [dʌ́klɪŋ] s. patito, anadeja.

duc·tile [dʌ́ktɪl] adj. dúctil.

dud [dʌd] s. bomba que no estalla.

dude [dud] s. caballerete; novato.

due [dju] adj. debido; vencido, pagadero; **in — time** a su debido tiempo; **the bill is —** se ha vencido la cuenta; **the train is — at two o'clock** el tren debe llegar a las dos; adv. directamente; **— east** hacia el este, rumbo al oriente; s. derecho, privilegio; **-s** cuota.

du·el [djúəl] s. duelo, desafío, combate; v. batirse en duelo.

du·et [djuét] s. duo, dueto.

dug [dʌg] pret. & p.p. de **to dig.**

dug·out [dʌ́gaʊt] s. piragua.

duke [djuk] s. duque.

duke·dom [djúkdəm] s. ducado.

dull [dʌl] adj. (dim) opaco, empañado, mate; sin brillo; (boring) aburrido; (blunt) embotado, sin punta, sin filo; (stupid) torpe; tardo; **— pain** dolor sordo; **— sound** sonido sordo o apagado; **— spell** período de poco movimiento; v. embotar(se); empañar(se); ofuscar; amortiguar (un dolor o sonido).

dull·ness [dʌ́lnɪs] s. (dimness) falta de brillo; (sluggishness) estupidez, torpeza; (bluntness) falta de punta o filo; (monotony) aburrimiento; (heaviness) pesadez.

du·ly [djúlɪ] adv. debidamente.

dumb [dʌm] adj. (silent) mudo; silencioso, callado; (dull) estúpido, torpe; **— creature** animal.

dumb·found·ed [dʌmfáʊndəd] adj. patitieso.

dumb·ness [dʌ́mnɪs] s. mudez; mutismo; estupidez.

dum·my [dʌ́mɪ] s. (figure) maniquí, figurón, muñeco; (fool) zoquete, tonto; adj. falso, fingido.

dump [dʌmp] s. montón (de tierra, carbón, etc.); terrero, vaciadero, escorial; **garbage —** muladar; basurero; **to be in the -s** estar abatido; v. echar, vaciar, descargar; echar a la basura; **dumping** inundación del mercado con artículos baratos.

dunce [dʌns] s. zopenco, zoquete, tonto.

dune [djun] s. duna o médano.

dung [dʌŋ] s. boñiga, estiércol.

dun·geon [dʌ́ndʒən] s. mazmorra, calabozo.

dung·hill [dʌ́ŋhɪl] s. muladar, estercolero.

dupe [djup] s. inocentón, incauto, víctima (de un engaño); v. embaucar.

du·pli·cate [djúpləkɪt] adj. & s. doble, duplicado; [djúpləket] v. duplicar, copiar.

du·plic·i·ty [djuplísətɪ] s. duplicidad, doblez.

du·ra·ble [djúrəbl] adj. durable, duradero.

du·ra·tion [djuréʃən] s. duración.

dur·ing [dúrɪŋ] prep. durante.

dusk [dʌsk] s. crepúsculo (vespertino), anochecida; caída de la tarde; sombra, oscuridad; **at —** al atardecer.

dusk·y [dʌ́skɪ] adj. obscuro, negruzco; sombrío.

dust [dʌst] s. polvo; tierra; **cloud of —** polvareda; v. sacudir el polvo, desempolvar, quitar el polvo; empolvar, llenar de polvo; espolvorear.

dust·er [dʌ́stɚ] s. limpiador; quitapolvo; **feather —** plumero.

dust·y [dʌ́stɪ] adj. polvoriento; empolvado, lleno de polvo.

Dutch [dʌtʃ] adj. & s. holandés; **— treat** convite a escote.

Dutch·man [dʌ́tʃmən] s. holandés.

du·ty [djútɪ] s. deber, obligación; derechos aduaneales; impuesto; **— free** libre de derechos aduaneales.

dwarf [dwɔrf] s. & adj. enano; v. achicar, empequeñecer; impedir el desarrollo o crecimiento de.

dwell [dwel] v. residir, morar, habitar, vivir; **to — on a subject** espaciarse o dilatarse en un asunto.

dwell·er [dwélɚ] s. habitante, morador.

dwell·ing [dwélɪŋ] s. morada, habitación, domicilio.

dwelt [dwelt] pret. & p.p. de **to dwell.**

dwin·dle [dwɪndl] v. menguar, mermar; disminuir(se); gastarse.

dye [daɪ] s. tinte, tintura; v. teñir, tinturar.

dy·er [dáɪɚ] s. tintorero; **-'s shop** tintorería.

dy·ing [dáɪɪŋ] adj. moribundo; agonizante.

dy·nam·ic [daɪnǽmɪk] adj. dinámico; enérgico; **-s** s.

dinámica.

dy·na·mite [dáfnəmaɪt] *s.* dinamita; *v.* dinamitar, volar con dinamita.

dy·na·mo [dáɪnəmo] *s.* dínamo.

dy·nas·ty [dáɪnəstɪ] *s.* dinastía.

dys·en·ter·y [dínntɛrɪ] *s.* disentería.

E:e

each [itʃ] *adj.* cada; *pron.* cada uno; — **other** el uno al otro, uno(s) a otro(s).

ea·ger [ígɚ] *adj.* anhelante, ansioso, deseoso; **-ly** *adv.* con anhelo; con ahinco; ansiosamente.

ea·ger·ness [ígɚnɪs] *s.* anhelo, ansia, deseo vehemente; ahinco; ardor.

ea·gle [ígl] *s.* águila.

ear [ɪr] *s.* (*outer*) oreja; (*hearing*) oído; — **drum** tímpano; — **muff** orejera; — **of corn** mazorca; — **of wheat** espiga; **by** — de oído; **within** — **shot** al alcance del oído.

earl [ɝl] *s.* conde.

ear·ly [ɝlɪ] *adv.* temprano; *adj.* temprano; primitivo, remoto; — **riser** madrugador, tempranero, mañanero; **at an** — **date** en fecha a próxima.

earn [ɝn] *v.* ganar; merecer; *s.* **earned income** ingreso devengado.

ear·nest [ɝnɪst] *adj.* serio, formal; ardiente; **in** — en serio, con toda formalidad; de buena fe; — **money** dinero en prenda; **-ly** *adv.* seriamente; con ahinco; encarecidamente, ansiosamente.

ear·nest·ness [ɝnɪstnɪs] *s.* seriedad; celo; solicitud; sinceridad; **in all** — con todo ahinco; con toda formalidad; con toda sinceridad.

earn·ings [ɝnɪŋz] *s.* ganancias; sueldo, salario, paga.

ear·ring [írrɪŋ] *s.* arete, zarcillo, pendiente, arracada; *C.A.* arito; *P.R.* pantalla.

earth [ɝθ] *s.* tierra; suelo.

earth·en [ɝθən] *adj.* de tierra; de barro.

earth·en·ware [ɝθənwɛr] *s.* loza de barro; trastos, cacharros.

earth·ly [ɝθlɪ] *adj.* terrenal, terrestre, mundano; terreno; **to be of no** — **use** no servir para nada.

earth·quake [ɝθkwek] *s.* terremoto, temblor de tierra.

earth·shak·ing [ɝθʃekɪŋ] *adj.* desmedido.

earth·worm [ɝθwɝm] *s.* lombriz.

ease [iz] *s.* (*facility*) facilidad; naturalidad; soltura; (*comfort*) comodidad; tranquilidad; **at** — tranquilo; cómodo; (*military*) a discreción; *v.* facilitar; aliviar; mitigar; tranquilizar; aligerar (*el peso*); aflojar.

ea·sel [ízl] *s.* caballete (*de pintor*).

eas·i·ly [ízəlɪ] *adv.* fácilmente; sin dificultad; cómodamente.

east [ist] *s.* este; oriente, levante; *adj.* del este, oriental; *adv.* (*eastbound*) al este, hacia el este; en el este.

East·er [ístɚ] *s.* Pascuas, Pascua Florida; — **Sunday** Domingo de Resurrección o de Pascuas.

east·ern [ístɚn] *adj.* oriental; del este.

east·ward [ístwɚd] *adv. & adj.* hacia el este u oriente.

eas·y [ízɪ] *adj.* (*simple*) fácil; (*comfortable*) cómodo; tranquilo; — **chair** silla cómoda, poltrona, butaca; **easy-going man** hombre cachazudo o calmo; **at an** — **pace** a paso moderado; **within** — **reach** al alcance; a la mano.

eat [it] *v.* comer; **to** — **away** corroer, destruir; **to** — **breakfast** desayunarse, tomar el desayuno; **to** —

dinner tomar la comida, comer; **to** — **supper** tomar la cena, cenar; **to** — **one's heart out** sufrir en silencio; **to** — **one's words** retractarse.

eat·en [ítn] *p.p. de* **to eat**.

eaves [ivz] *s. pl.* alero (*de un tejado*).

ebb [ɛb] *s.* reflujo; decadencia; — **tide** marea menguante; **to be at a low** — estar decaído; *v.* menguar, decaer.

eb·on·y [ɛbənɪ] *s.* ébano.

ec·cen·tric [ɪksɛntrɪk] *adj. & s.* excéntrico.

ec·cle·si·as·tic [ɪklizɪǽstɪk] *adj. & s.* eclesiástico.

ech·e·lon [ɛʃəlɑn] *s.* escalón.

ech·o [ɛko] *s.* eco; *v.* hacer eco, repetir; resonar, repercutir.

ec·lec·tic [ɪklɛktɪk] *adj.* ecléctico.

e·clipse [ɪklíps] *s.* eclipse; *v.* eclipsar.

ec·o·nom·ic [ɪkənámɪk] *adj.* económico.

ec·o·nom·i·cal [ɪkənámɪkl] *adj.* económico.

ec·o·nom·ics [ɪkənámɪks] *s.* economía política.

e·con·o·mist [ɪkánəmɪst] *s.* economista.

e·con·o·mize [ɪkánəmaɪz] *v.* economizar.

e·con·o·my [ɪkánəmɪ] *s.* economía; parsimonia; **planned** — economía dirigida.

e·con·o·my class [ɪkánəmi klæs] *s.* segunda clase en las líneas aéreas.

ec·sta·sy [ɛkstəsɪ] *s.* éxtasis.

ec·u·men·i·cal [ɛkjumɛnəkl] *adj.* ecuménico.

ed·dy [ɛdɪ] *s.* remolino; *v.* arremolinarse.

E·den [ídn] *s.* Edén; paraíso.

edge [ɛdʒ] *s.* orilla, borde; filo; **to be on** — estar nervioso.

edge·wise [ɛdʒwaɪz] *adv.* de lado; de filo.

ed·i·ble [ɛdəbl] *adj. & s.* comestible.

ed·i·fice [ɛdəfɪs] *s.* edificio.

ed·i·fy [ɛdəfaɪ] *v.* edificar (*moral, espiritualmente*).

ed·it [ɛdɪt] *v.* redactar; preparar o corregir (*un manuscrito*) para la imprenta; cuidar (*una edición*).

e·di·tion [ɪdíʃən] *s.* edición.

ed·i·tor [ɛdɪtɚ] *s.* redactor; director de un periódico; revisor (*de manuscritos*).

ed·i·to·ri·al [ɛdətórɪəl] *adj.* editorial; *s.* editorial (*m.*), artículo de fondo.

ed·i·to·ri·al·ize [ɛdɪtórɪəlaɪz] *v.* expresar opiniones como en artículo de fondo; editorializar.

ed·u·cate [ɛdʒəket] *v.* educar; instruir.

ed·u·ca·tion [ɛdʒəkéʃən] *s.* (*up-bringing*) educación; crianza; (*instruction*) instrucción, enseñanza; pedagogía.

ed·u·ca·tion·al [ɛdʒəkéʃənl] *adj.* educativo, docente; pedagógico.

ed·u·ca·tor [ɛdʒəketɚ] *s.* educador.

eel [il] *s.* anguila.

ef·fect [əfɛkt] *s.* efecto; **-s** bienes, efectos; **to go into** — hacerse vigente, ponerse en operación (*una ley*); *v.* efectuar; ejecutar; realizar.

ef·fec·tive [əfɛktɪv] *adj.* efectivo, eficaz; vigente (*una ley*); — **date** fecha de vigencia; **-ly** *adv.* eficazmente.

ef·fec·tu·al [əfɛktʃuəl] *adj.* eficaz.

ef·fem·i·nate [əfɛmənɪt] *adj.* afeminado.

ef·fete [ɪfít] *adj.* gastado; estéril; decadente.

ef·fi·ca·cy [ɛfəkəsɪ] *s.* eficacia.

ef·fi·cien·cy [əfíʃənsɪ] *s.* eficiencia; eficacia.

ef·fi·cient [əfíʃənt] *adj.* eficiente; eficaz.

ef·fi·gy [ɛfɪdʒɪ] *s.* efigie; **to burn in** — quemar en efigie.

ef·fort [ɛfɚt] *s.* esfuerzo; empeño; conato.

ef·fron·ter·y [əfrʌ́ntərɪ] *s.* descaro, desvergüenza, desfachatez.

ef·fu·sive [ɛfúsɪv] *adj.* efusivo, demostrativo, expansivo.

egg [ɛg] *s.* huevo; **fried** — huevo frito o estrellado; **hard-boiled** — huevo cocido, huevo duro; **scrambled -s** huevos revueltos; **soft-boiled** — huevo pasado por agua; *Méx.* huevo tibio; *v.* **to — on** incitar.

egg·nog [ɛ́gnag] *s.* rompopo.

egg·plant [ɛ́gplænt] *s.* berenjena.

e·go·cen·tric [igosɛ́ntrɪk] *adj.* egocéntrico.

e·go·tism [íɡotɪzəm] *s.* egotismo; egoísmo.

E·gyp·tian [ɪdʒ̍ípʃən] *adj.* & *s.* egipcio.

eight [et] *num.* ocho.

eight·een [etín] *num.* dieciocho.

eight·y [étɪ] *num.* ochenta.

ei·ther [íðɚ] *adj.* & *pron.* uno u otro; — **of the two** cualquiera de los dos; **in — case** en ambos casos; *adv.* tampoco; **nor I** — ni yo tampoco; *conj.* o.

ejac·u·late [ɪdʒǽkjulet] *v.* eyacular.

e·ject [ɪdʒɛ́kt] *v.* echar, arrojar, expulsar.

e·jec·tion [ɪdʒɛ́kʃən] *s.* expulsión; — **seat** asiento lanzable.

e·lab·o·rate [ɪlǽbərɪt] *adj.* elaborado, primoroso; esmerado; [ɪlǽbəret] *v.* elaborar.

e·lapse [ɪlǽps] *v.* transcurrir, pasar.

e·las·tic [ɪlǽstɪk] *adj.* elástico; *s.* elástico; goma elástica; cordón elástico; liga elástica.

e·las·tic·i·ty [ɪlæstísətɪ] *s.* elasticidad.

e·lat·ed [ɪlétɪd] *adj.* exaltado, gozoso, alborozado.

el·bow [ɛ́lbo] *s.* codo; recodo, ángulo; **to be within — reach** estar a la mano; *v.* codear, dar codazos; **to — one's way through** abrirse paso a codazos.

eld·er [ɛ́ldɚ] *adj.* mayor, más grande, más viejo, de más edad; *s.* mayor; anciano; dignatario *(en ciertas iglesias)*; **our -s** nuestros mayores; nuestros antepasados.

el·der·ly [ɛ́ldɚlɪ] *adj.* viejo, anciano.

el·dest [ɛ́ldɪst] *adj.* mayor.

e·lect [ɪlɛ́kt] *adj.* & *s.* electo; elegido; *v.* elegir.

e·lec·tion [ɪlɛ́kʃən] *s.* elección.

e·lec·tor [ɪlɛ́ktɚ] *s.* elector.

e·lec·tor·al [ɪlɛ́ktərəl] *adj.* electoral.

e·lec·tric [ɪlɛ́ktrɪk] *adj.* eléctrico; — **meter** electrómetro, contador eléctrico; — **storm** tronada, tempestad; — **eye** ojo eléctrico; — **sign** anuncio luminoso; — **power plant** central generadora; *s.* tranvía o ferrocarril eléctrico.

e·lec·tri·cal [ɪlɛ́ktrɪkl̩] *adj.* eléctrico; — **engineering** electrotecnia, ingeniería eléctrica; — **engineer** ingeniero electricista; electrotécnico.

e·lec·tri·cian [ɪlɛktríʃən] *s.* electricista.

e·lec·tric·i·ty [ɪlɛktrísətɪ] *s.* electricidad.

e·lec·tri·fy [ɪlɛ́ktrəfaɪ] *v.* electrizar; electrificar.

e·lec·tro·car·di·o·graph [ɪlɛktrokárdɪəɡræf] *s.* electrocardiógrafo.

e·lec·tro·cute [ɪlɛ́ktrəkjut] *v.* electrocutar.

e·lec·trol·y·sis [ɪlɛktrálɪsɪs] *s.* electrólisis.

e·lec·tro·mag·net [ɪlɛktromǽɡnət] *s.* electroimán.

e·lec·tron [ɪlɛ́ktrɑn] *s.* electrón; — **microscope** microscopio electrónico.

e·lec·tron·ics [ɪlɛktrániks] *s.* electrónica.

el·e·gance [ɛ́ləgəns] *s.* elegancia.

el·e·gant [ɛ́ləgənt] *adj.* elegante.

el·e·ment [ɛ́ləmənt] *s.* elemento.

el·e·men·tal [ɛləmɛ́ntl̩] *adj.* elemental.

el·e·men·ta·ry [ɛləmɛ́ntərɪ] *adj.* elemental.

el·e·phant [ɛ́ləfənt] *s.* elefante.

el·e·vate [ɛ́ləvet] *v.* elevar; alzar, levantar.

el·e·va·tion [ɛləvéʃən] *s.* elevación; altura; exaltación.

el·e·va·tor [ɛ́ləvetɚ] *s.* ascensor, *Am.* elevador; **grain —** almacén de granos.

el·ev·en [əlɛ́vən] *num.* once.

e·lic·it [ɪlísɪt] *v.* extraer, sonsacar; **to — admiration** despertar admiración; **to — applause** suscitar el aplauso o los aplausos.

el·i·gi·ble [ɛ́lɪdʒəbl̩] *adj.* elegible.

e·lim·i·nate [ɪlímənet] *v.* eliminar.

e·lim·i·na·tion [ɪlɪmənéʃən] *s.* eliminación.

e·lite [ɛlít] *s.* lo selecto; los selectos; los escogidos.

elk [ɛlk] *s.* ante.

el·lip·tic [ɪlíptɪk] *adj.* elíptico.

elm [ɛlm] *s.* olmo.

e·lope [ɪlóp] *v.* fugarse *(con su novio)*.

el·o·quence [ɛ́ləkwəns] *s.* elocuencia.

el·o·quent [ɛ́ləkwənt] *adj.* elocuente.

else [ɛls] *adj.* & *adv.* otro *(úsase sólo en ciertas combinaciones)*; más, además; **or** — de otro modo; si no; **nobody** — ningún otro; **nothing** — nada más; **somebody** — algún otro, otra persona; **what** —? ¿qué más?

else·where [ɛ́lshwɛr] *adv.* en otra parte, a otra parte.

e·lu·ci·date [ɪlúsədet] *v.* elucidar, esclarecer, aclarar, clarificar.

e·lu·ci·da·tion [ɪlusədéʃən] *s.* elucidación, esclarecimiento, explicación.

e·lude [ɪlúd] *v.* eludir, evadir.

e·lu·sive [ɪlúsɪv] *adj.* evasivo; que elude.

e·ma·ci·at·ed [ɪméʃietɪd] *adj.* demacrado, escuálido, macilento.

em·a·nate [ɛ́mənet] *v.* emanar, brotar.

em·a·na·tion [ɛmənéʃən] *s.* emanación; efluvio.

e·man·ci·pate [ɪmǽnsəpet] *v.* emancipar.

e·man·ci·pa·tion [ɪmænsəpéʃən] *s.* emancipación.

em·balm [ɪmbám] *v.* embalsamar.

em·bank·ment [ɪmbǽŋkmənt] *s.* terraplén; dique.

em·bar·go [ɪmbárgo] *s.* embargo; prohibición; **to put an — on** embargar.

em·bark [ɪmbárk] *v.* embarcar(se).

em·bar·rass [ɪmbǽrəs] *v.* turbar, desconcertar; apenar; avergonzar; embarazar; **to be financially -ed** encontrarse escaso de fondos.

em·bar·rass·ing [ɪmbǽrəsɪŋ] *adj.* embarazoso, penoso; desconcertante; angustioso.

em·bar·rass·ment [ɪmbǽrəsmənt] *s.* turbación, vergüenza, desconcierto; aprieto, apuro, dificultad; estorbo, embarazo.

em·bas·sy [ɛ́mbəsɪ] *s.* embajada.

em·bel·lish [ɪmbɛ́lɪʃ] *v.* embellecer, hermosear.

em·ber [ɛ́mbɚ] *s.* ascua; **-s** ascuas, rescoldo.

em·bez·zle [ɪmbɛ́zl̩] *v.* desfalcar.

em·bez·zle·ment [ɪmbɛ́zlmənt] *s.* desfalco, peculado.

em·bit·ter [ɪmbítɚ] *v.* amargar.

em·blem [ɛ́mbləm] *s.* emblema.

em·bod·y [ɪmbádɪ] *v.* encarnar, dar cuerpo a; incorporar, abarcar.

em·boss [ɪmbɔ́s] *v.* realzar, grabar en relieve.

em·brace [ɪmbrés] *s.* abrazo; *v.* abrazar(se); abarcar.

em·broi·der [ɪmbrɔ́ɪdɚ] *v.* bordar; recamar; ornar, embellecer.

em·broi·der·y [ɪmbrɔ́ɪdərɪ] *s.* bordado; bordadura; recamo.

em·bry·o [ɛ́mbrɪo] *s.* embrión.

em·er·ald [ɛ́mərəld] *s.* esmeralda.

e·merge [ɪmɝ́dʒ] *v.* emerger; surtir.

e·mer·gen·cy [ɪmɝ́dʒənsɪ] *s.* caso fortuito; aprieto; urgencia; emergencia.

em·i·grant [ɛ́məɡrənt] *adj.* & *s.* emigrante.

em·i·grate [ɛ́məɡret] *v.* emigrar.

em·i·gra·tion [ɛməɡréʃən] *s.* emigración.

em·i·nence [ɛ́mənəns] *s.* eminencia.

em·i·nent [ɛ́mənənt] *adj.* eminente.

e·mit [ɪmít] *v.* emitir; exhalar, arrojar; despedir *(olor, humo, etc.)*.

e·mo·tion [ɪmóʃən] *s.* emoción.

e·mo·tion·al [ɪmóʃənl] *adj.* emocional; emotivo; sentimental; sensible.

em·pa·thy [émpəθɪ] *s.* empatía.

em·per·or [émpərɚ] *s.* emperador.

em·pha·sis [émfəsɪs] *s.* énfasis.

em·pha·size [émfəsaɪz] *v.* dar énfasis; hacer hincapié en; subrayar, recalcar; acentuar.

em·phat·ic [ɪmfǽtɪk] *adj.* enfático; recalcado; **-ally** *adv.* enfáticamente.

em·phy·se·ma [εmfəsímə] *s.* enfisema.

em·pire [émpaɪr] *s.* imperio.

em·pir·i·cal [εmpírəkl] *adj.* empírico.

em·ploy [ɪmplɔ́ɪ] *v.* emplear; dar empleo a; ocupar; **to be in his —** ser su empleado; trabajar a sus órdenes.

em·ploy·ee [ɪmplɔ́ɪí] *s.* empleado.

em·ploy·er [ɪmplɔ́ɪɚ] *s.* patrón, amo, principal.

em·ploy·ment [ɪmplɔ́ɪmənt] *s.* empleo; ocupación; **— legislation** legislación laboral.

em·pow·er [ɪmpáʊɚ] *v.* autorizar; apoderar (*dar poder a un abogado*).

em·press [émprɪs] *s.* emperatriz.

emp·ti·ness [émptɪnɪs] *s.* vaciedad, futilidad, vanidad.

emp·ty [émptɪ] *adj.* vacío; vacante, desocupado; vano; *v.* vaciar; desaguar, desembocar.

emp·ty-hand·ed [εmptɪhǽndɪd] *adj.* sin posesión.

em·u·late [émjulet] *v.* emular.

en·a·ble [ɪnébl] *v.* capacitar, hacer capaz; habilitar; dar poder; facilitar; hacer posible.

en·act [ɪnǽkt] *v.* decretar, promulgar; hacer el papel de.

en·am·el [ɪnǽml] *s.* esmalte; *v.* esmaltar.

en·am·or [ɪnǽmɚ] *v.* enamorar, mover a amar; encantar; **to be -ed of** estar enamorado de.

en·camp [ɪnkǽmp] *v.* acampar.

en·chant [ɪntʃǽnt] *v.* encantar, embelesar, hechizar.

en·chant·er [ɪntʃǽntɚ] *s.* encantador, hechicero, mago, brujo.

en·chant·ment [ɪntʃǽntmənt] *s.* encanto, encantamiento, hechicería.

en·chant·ress [ɪntʃǽntrɪs] *s.* encantadora, hechicera, bruja.

en·cir·cle [ɪnsɚ́kl] *v.* cercar, rodear, ceñir.

en·clit·ic [εnklítɪk] *adj.* enclítico.

en·close [ɪnklóz] *v.* encerrar; cercar, rodear, circundar; incluir.

en·clo·sure [ɪnklóʒɚ] *s.* recinto, cercado, vallado; remesa, lo remitido (*dentro de una carta*), lo adjunto; encerramiento.

en·com·pass [ɪnkʌ́mpəs] *v.* abarcar; encuadrar; rodear, ceñir, circundar.

en·coun·ter [ɪnkáʊntɚ] *s.* encuentro; combate; *v.* encontrar(se); encontrarse con; tropezar con.

en·cour·age [ɪnkɚ́ɪdʒ] *v.* alentar, animar, fomentar.

en·cour·age·ment [ɪnkɚ́ɪdʒmənt] *s.* aliento, ánimo; estímulo; fomento.

en·croach [ɪnkrótʃ] *v.* **to — upon** usurpar, invadir, meterse en; quitar (*el tiempo*).

en·cum·ber [εnkʌ́mbɚ] *v.* impedir; estorbar.

en·cy·clo·pe·di·a [ɪnsaɪkləpídɪə] *s.* enciclopedia.

end [εnd] *s.* (*temporal*) fin; cabo; término; (*spatial*) término; extremo; **no — of things** un sin fin de cosas; **odds and -s** retazos; **on —** de punta; **to put an —** to acabar con, poner fin a; *v.* acabar; terminar; concluir, dar fin.

en·dan·ger [ɪndéndʒɚ] *v.* poner en peligro, arriesgar.

en·dear [ɪndír] *v.* hacer amar, hacer querer; **to — oneself** hacerse querer.

en·deav·or [ɪndévɚ] *s.* esfuerzo, empeño; tentativa; tarea; *v.* procurar, tratar de, intentar; esforzarse por

o en.

en·dem·ic [εndέmɪk] *adj.* endémico.

end·ing [éndɪŋ] *s.* final; terminación; conclusión.

end·less [éndlɪs] *adj.* sin fin, interminable, inacabable; eterno.

en·dorse [εndɔ́rs] *v.* endosar; respaldar; apoyar, garantizar.

en·dorse·ment [εndɔ́rsmənt] *s.* (*signature*) endose, endoso; (*backing*) respaldo; garantía, apoyo.

en·dors·er [εndɔ́rsɚ] *s.* endosante.

en·dow [ɪndáʊ] *v.* dotar.

en·dow·ment [ɪndáʊmənt] *s.* dotación; dote, don; **— annuity** anualidad dotal; **— fund** fondo dotal; **— policy** póliza dotal.

en·dur·ance [ɪndjúrəns] *s.* resistencia, aguante; paciencia; duración.

en·dure [ɪndjúr] *v.* aguantar, soportar, sufrir; durar, perdurar.

en·e·ma [énəmə] *s.* lavativa.

en·e·my [énəmɪ] *s.* enemigo.

en·er·get·ic [εnɚdʒέtɪk] *adj.* enérgico.

en·er·gy [énɚdʒɪ] *s.* energía.

en·er·vate [énɚvet] *v.* enervar, debilitar.

en·fold = **infold.**

en·force [ɪnfórs] *v.* dar fuerza a; hacer cumplir (*una ley*); **to — obedience** hacer obedecer, imponer obediencia.

en·force·ment [ɪnfórsmənt] *s.* coacción; cumplimiento forzoso (*de una ley*).

en·gage [ɪngédʒ] *v.* (*employ*) ocupar; emplear, contratar; (*reserve*) alquilar; (*attract*) atraer; (*mesh*) engranar, acoplar; **to — in battle** trabar batalla; **to — (oneself) to do it** comprometerse a hacerlo; **to be -ed in something** estar ocupado en algo; **to be -ed to be married** estar comprometido para casarse.

en·gage·ment [ɪngédʒmənt] *s.* compromiso; cita; noviazgo; convenio, contrato; pelea; traba, engrane, acoplamiento (*de maquinaria*).

en·gen·der [ɪndʒéndɚ] *v.* engendrar, producir.

en·gine [éndʒən] *s.* máquina; motor; (*locomotive*) locomotora.

en·gi·neer [εndʒənír] *s.* ingeniero; (*of locomotive*) maquinista; *v.* dirigir, planear.

en·gi·neer·ing [εndʒənírɪŋ] *s.* ingeniería; manejo, planeo.

Eng·lish [íŋglɪʃ] *adj.* inglés; *s.* inglés, idioma inglés; **the —** los ingleses.

Eng·lish·man [íŋglɪʃmən] *s.* inglés.

en·grave [ɪngrév] *v.* grabar, esculpir.

en·grav·ing [ɪngrévɪŋ] *s.* grabado; estampa, lámina; **wood —** grabado en madera.

en·gross [εngrós] *v.* absorber; (*edit*) redactar en limpio.

en·grossed [ɪngróst] *adj.* absorto, ensimismado.

en·gulf [ɪngʌ́lf] *v.* engolfar, absorber, tragar.

en·hance [ɪnhǽns] *v.* realzar; engrandecer.

e·nig·ma [ɪnígmə] *s.* enigma.

en·join [ɪndʒɔ́ɪn] *v.* mandar, ordenar; **to — from** prohibir, vedar.

en·joy [ɪndʒɔ́ɪ] *v.* gozar de; disfrutar de; **to — oneself** divertirse, gozar, deleitarse; **to — the use of** usufructuar.

en·joy·a·ble [ɪndʒɔ́ɪəbl] *adj.* agradable, deleitable.

en·joy·ment [ɪndʒɔ́ɪmənt] *s.* placer, goce; disfrute; usufructo.

en·large [ɪnlárdʒ] *v.* agrandar(se); ensanchar; ampliar; **to — upon** explayarse en, extenderse en; comentar.

en·large·ment [ɪnlárdʒmənt] *s.* (*photo*) ampliación; ensachamiento.

en·light·en [ɪnláɪtn̩] *v.* alumbrar; iluminar; ilustrar, instruir.

en·list [ɪnlíst] *v.* alistar(se); sentar plaza (*de soldado*); reclutar.

en·list·ment [ɪnlístmənt] *s.* reclutamiento; alistamiento.

en·li·ven [ɪnláɪvən] *v.* avivar, animar, alegrar.

en·mi·ty [énmətɪ] *s.* enemistad.

en·no·ble [ɪnóbl̩] *v.* ennoblecer.

e·nor·mous [ɪnɔ́rməs] *adj.* enorme.

e·nough [ənʌ́f] *adj. & adv.* bastante; *s.* lo bastante, lo suficiente; **that is** — eso basta, con eso basta; — **!** ¡basta!

en·quire = **inquire.**

en·rage [ɪnréʤ] *v.* enrabiar, hacer rabiar; enfurecer.

en·rap·ture [ɪnrǽptʃɚ] *v.* extasiar, embelesar, enajenar.

en·rich [ɪnrítʃ] *v.* enriquecer.

en·roll [ɪnról] *v.* alistar(se); matricular(se); inscribir(se); hacerse miembro.

en·roll·ment [ɪnrólmənt] *s.* alistamiento; registro, matrícula.

en·sem·ble [ɑnsámbl̩] *s.* (*music*) conjunto musical; (*dress*) traje armonioso.

en·sign [énsn̩] *s.* alférez (*de la marina*); [énsaɪn] bandera; insignia.

en·slave [ɪnslév] *v.* esclavizar.

en·snare [ɛnsnɛ́r] *v.* enredar, entrampar, embaucar.

en·sue [ɛnsú] *v.* sobrevenir, seguir(se), resultar.

en·tail [ɪntél] *v.* envolver, ocasionar; vincular (*una herencia*).

en·tan·gle [ɪntǽŋgl̩] *v.* enredar, enmarañar, embrollar.

en·tente [ɑntánt] *s.* pacto no formal.

en·ter [éntɚ] *v.* entrar en; ingresar en; asentar (*una partida, cantidad, etc.*); registrar; salir (*al escenario*).

en·ter·prise [éntɚpraɪz] *s.* empresa.

en·ter·pris·ing [éntɚpraɪzɪŋ] *adj.* emprendedor.

en·ter·tain [ɛntɚtén] *v.* divertir; agasajar; obsequiar; banquetear; acariciar (*una idea*); abrigar (*una esperanza, un rencor*); **she -s a great deal** es muy fiestera u obsequiosa.

en·ter·tain·ing [ɛntɚténɪŋ] *adj.* entretenido, divertido, chistoso.

en·ter·tain·ment [ɛntɚténmənt] *s.* entretenimiento; pasatiempo; diversión; fiesta; convite.

en·thu·si·asm [ɪnθjúziæzəm] *s.* entusiasmo.

en·thu·si·ast [ɪnθjúziæstɪk] *adj.* entusiasta, entusiástico; **to be** — estar entusiasmado.

en·tice [ɪntáɪs] *v.* atraer, tentar, seducir, halagar.

en·tire [ɪntáɪr] *adj.* entero, cabal; **the** — **world** todo el mundo; **-ly** *adv.* enteramente, por entero.

en·tire·ty [ɪntáɪrtɪ] *s.* totalidad, entereza; conjunto; todo.

en·ti·tle [ɪntáɪtl̩] *v.* titular, intitular; autorizar, dar derecho.

en·ti·ty [éntətɪ] *s.* entidad; ente, ser.

en·trails [éntrəlz] *s. pl.* entrañas; tripas.

en·trance [éntrəns] *s.* entrada; ingreso.

en·treat [ɪntrít] *v.* suplicar, rogar; instar.

en·treat·y [ɪntrítɪ] *s.* súplica, ruego; instancia.

en·trench = **intrench.**

en·trust [ɪntrʌ́st] *v.* confiar; depositar, (*deliver*) entregar.

en·try [éntrɪ] *s.* entrada; ingreso; partida, registro, anotación; (*computer*) entrada; **make an** — asentar una partida; **double** — partida doble (*en teneduría*).

e·nu·mer·ate [ɪnjúməret] *v.* enumerar.

e·nun·ci·ate [ɪnʌ́snɪet] *v.* articular; enunciar, declarar.

en·vel·op [ɪnvéləp] *v.* envolver.

en·ve·lope [énvəlop] *s.* sobre, cubierta (*de una carta*).

en·vi·a·ble [énvɪəbl̩] *adj.* envidiable.

en·vi·ous [énvɪəs] *adj.* envidioso.

en·vi·ron·ment [ɪnváɪrənmənt] *s.* ambiente, medio ambiente; *adj.* **environmental** ambiental.

en·vi·rons [ɛnváɪrənz] *s. pl.* cercanías, contornos, alrededores.

en·vis·age [ɛnvízɪʤ] *v.* prever; encararse con.

en·voy [énvɔɪ] *s.* enviado.

en·vy [énvɪ] *s.* envidia; *v.* envidiar.

e·phem·er·al [ɪfémɚl̩] *adj.* efímero.

ep·ic [épɪk] *s.* epopeya, poema, épico; *adj.* épico.

ep·i·dem·ic [epədémɪk] *s.* epidemia; peste; *adj.* epidémico.

ep·i·logue [épəlɔg] *s.* epílogo.

E·piph·a·ny [ɪpífənɪ] *s.* Epifanía.

ep·i·sode [épəsod] *s.* episodio.

e·pis·tle [ɪpísl̩] *s.* epístola, carta.

ep·i·taph [épətæf] *s.* epitafio.

e·pit·o·me [ɪpítəmɪ] *s.* epítome.

ep·och [épək] *s.* época; — **making** transcendental.

EPROM (*computer*) erasable, programmable, read only memory *adj.* borrable, capaz de programarse, léase sólo memoria.

e·qual [íkwəl] *adj.* igual; **to be** — **to a task** ser competente (*o* tener suficientes fuerzas) para una tarea; — **rights** igualdad de derechos; *s.* igual; cantidad igual; *v.* igualar; ser igual a; **-ly** *adv.* igualmente; por igual.

e·qual·i·ty [íkwálətɪ] *s.* igualdad.

e·qual·ize [íkwəlaɪz] *v.* igualar; emparejar; equilibrar; nivelar.

e·qua·tion [ɪkwéʒən] *s.* ecuación.

e·qua·tor [ɪkwétɚ] *s.* ecuador.

e·qui·lib·ri·um [ikwəlfbrɪəm] *s.* equilibrio.

e·quip [ɪkwíp] *v.* equipar; proveer; habilitar.

e·quip·ment [ɪkwípmənt] *s.* equipo; aparatos; avíos; havilitación; **railroad** — material rodante.

eq·ui·ta·ble [ékwɪtəbl̩] *adj.* equitativo.

eq·ui·ty [ékwətɪ] *s.* equidad; justicia; **-s** derechos sobre el activo, valor libre de la hipoteca.

e·quiv·a·lent [ɪkwívələnt] *adj. & s.* equivalente.

e·quiv·o·cal [ɪkwívəkl̩] *adj.* equívoco, ambiguo.

e·ra [írə] *s.* era, época.

e·rad·i·cate [ɪrǽdɪket] *v.* desarraigar, extirpar.

e·rase [ɪrés] *v.* borrar; tachar.

e·ras·er [ɪrésɚ] *s.* goma, Am. borrador; **blackboard** — cepillo.

e·ra·sure [ɪréʃɚ] *s.* borradura, raspadura.

ere [ɛr] *prep.* antes de; *conj.* antes (de) que.

e·rect [ɪrékt] *adj.* erguido; derecho; levantado; Am. parado; *v.* erigir; levantar, alzar.

er·mine [ʒ́mɪn] *s.* armiño.

e·rode [ɪród] *v.* erosionar.

e·ro·sion [ɪróʒən] *s.* erosión; desgaste.

e·rot·ic [ɪrátɪk] *adj.* erótico.

err [ʒ] *v.* errar; equivocarse; descarriarse.

er·rand [érənd] *s.* mandado, recado, encargo; — **boy** mandadero.

er·rant [érənt] *adj.* errante; **knight-errant** caballero andante.

er·rat·ic [ɛrǽtɪk] *adj.* inconstante, errático; vagabundo.

er·ro·ne·ous [ərónɪəs] *adj.* erróneo, errado.

er·ror [érɚ] *s.* error; (*printing*) errata; **-s and omissions excepted** salvo error u omisión.

er·u·di·tion [ɛrudíʃən] *s.* erudición.

e·rupt [ɪrʌ́pt] *v.* arrojar.

e·rup·tion [ɪrʌ́pʃən] *s.* erupción.

es·ca·late [éskəlet] v. aumentar; intensificar.

es·ca·pade [éskəped] s. trapisonda, travesura.

es·cape [əskép] s. escape; fuga, huída; escapada; escapatoria; — **clause** cláusula que permite ajuste a las condiciones; v. escapar(se); fugarse; huir(se); eludir, evadir; **it -s me** se me escapa.

es·cort [éskɔrt] s. escolta; acompañante; convoy; [ɪskɔ́rt] v. escoltar; convoyar; acompañar.

es·crow [éskro] s. plica; **in** — en custodia.

es·cutch·eon [ɪskátʃ ən] s. escudo de armas, blasón.

Es·ki·mo [éskəmo] s. esquimal.

es·pe·cial [əspéʃ əl] adj. especial; **-ly** adv. especialmente.

es·pi·o·nage [éspɪənɪdʒ] s. espionaje.

es·pouse [ɛspáʊs] v. patrocinar; casarse.

es·say [ɛ́se] s. ensayo; [ɛsé] v. ensayar.

es·sence [ɛ́sn̩s] s. esencia.

es·sen·tial [əsénʃ əl] adj. esencial.

es·tab·lish [əstǽblɪʃ] v. establecer.

es·tab·lish·ment [əstǽblɪʃ mənt] s. establecimiento.

es·tate [əstét] s. hacienda, heredad; bienes, propiedades; — **tax** impuesto de sucesión; estado, condición; **country** — finca rural.

es·teem [əstím] s. estima, estimación, aprecio; v. estimar, apreciar; considerar, juzgar.

es·ti·ma·ble [éstəməbl̩] adj. estimable.

es·ti·mate [éstəmɪt] s. (calculation) tasa, cálculo aproximado; presupuesto; (judgment) opinión; [éstəmet] v. estimar, tasar, calcular aproximadamente; hacer un presupuesto; juzgar, opinar.

es·ti·ma·tion [ɛstəméʃ ən] s. juicio, opinión; estima; estimación.

es·trange [ɛstréndʒ] v. enajenar; apartar.

es·tu·ar·y [éstʃ ʊɛrɪ] s. estuario o estero, desembocadura de un río.

etch [ɛtʃ] v. grabar al agua fuerte.

etch·ing [étʃ ɪŋ] s. agua fuerte, grabado al agua fuerte.

e·ter·nal [ɪtɚ·nl̩] adj. eterno.

e·ter·ni·ty [ɪtɚ́·nətɪ] s. eternidad.

e·ther [íθɚ] s. éter.

e·the·re·al [ɪθírɪəl] adj. etéreo.

eth·i·cal [ɛ́θɪkl] adj. ético, moral.

eth·ics [ɛ́θɪks] s. ética, moral.

eth·nic [ɛ́θnɪk] adj. étnico.

eth·nol·o·gy [ɛθnáləd31] s. etnología.

et·i·quette [étɪkɛt] s. etiqueta (regla de conducta social).

et·y·mol·o·gy [ɛtəmáləd31] s. etimología.

eu·ca·lyp·tus [jukəlíptəs] s. eucalipto.

Eu·cha·rist [júkərɪst] s. Eucaristía.

eu·phe·mism [júfəmɪzm] s. eufemismo.

eu·pho·ri·a [jufórɪə] s. euforia.

Eu·ro·pe·an [jurəpíən] adj. & s. europeo.

e·vac·u·ate [ɪvǽkjʊet] v. evacuar; desocupar.

e·vade [ɪvéd] v. evadir.

e·val·u·ate [ɪvǽljʊet] v. valorar, avaluar.

e·vap·o·rate [ɪvǽpəret] v. evaporar(se).

e·vap·o·ra·tion [ɪvæpəréʃ ən] s. evaporación.

e·va·sion [ɪvéʒən] s. evasión, evasiva.

e·va·sive [ɪvésɪv] adj. evasivo.

eve [iv] s. víspera, vigilia; **Christmas Eve** Nochebuena; **New Year's Eve** víspera del Año Nuevo; **on the** — **of** en vísperas de.

e·ven [ívən] adj. (level) liso, plano, llano, a nivel; (same) parejo; uniforme; igual; — **dozen** docena cabal; — **number** número par; — **temper** genio apacible; **to be** — **with someone** estar mano a mano (o estar a mano) con alguien; **to get** — **with someone** desquitarse de alguien; adv. aun, hasta;

— **if** (o — **though**) aun cuando; — **so** aun así; **not** — ni siquiera, ni aun; v. allanar; nivelar(se); igualar(se); emparejar; **-ly** adv. igualmente; de un modo igual; con uniformidad; con suavidad.

eve·ning [ívnɪŋ] s. tarde; atardecer; noche (las primeras horas); — **gown** vestido de etiqueta; — **star** estrella vespertina, lucero de la tarde.

e·ven·ness [ívənnɪs] s. lisura; igualdad; — **of temper** apacibilidad o suavidad de genio.

e·vent [ɪvɛ́nt] s. suceso, acontecimiento; incidente, evento; resultado, coneecuencia; **in any** — en todo caso; **in the** — **of** en caso de.

e·vent·ful [ɪvɛ́ntfəl] adj. lleno de sucesos; importante, memorable.

e·ven·tu·al [ɪvɛ́ntʃ ʊəl] adj. eventual; último, final, terminal; **-ly** adv. finalmente, por fin, con el tiempo; eventualmente.

ev·er [ɛ́vɚ] adv. siempre; jamás; alguna vez; — **so much** muchísimo; **for** — **and** — por (o para) siempre jamás; **hardly** — casi nunca, apenas; **if** — si alguna vez; **more than** — más que nunca; **the best friend I** — **had** el mejor amigo que en mi vida he tenido.

ev·er·green [ɛ́vɚgrin] s. siempreviva, sempiterna; adj. siempre verde.

ev·er·last·ing [ɛvɚlǽstɪŋ] adj. sempiterno, eterno, perpetuo; duradero; s. eternidad; sempiterna (planta); siempreviva; perpetua, flor perpetua.

ev·er·more [ɛvɚmór] adv. para siempre; **for** — para siempre jamás.

eve·ry [ɛ́vrɪ] adj. cada; todo; todos los, todas las; — **bit of it** todo, todito; — **day** todos los días; — **once in a while** de vez en cuando; — **one of them** todos ellos; — **other day** cada dos días, un día sí y otro no.

eve·ry·bod·y [ɛ́vrɪbadɪ] pron. todos, todo el mundo.

eve·ry·day [ɛ́vrɪdé] adj. diario, cuotidiano, de todos los días; ordinario.

eve·ry·one [ɛ́vrɪwʌn] pron. todos; todo el mundo; cada uno.

eve·ry·thing [ɛ́vrɪθɪŋ] pron. todo.

eve·ry·where [ɛ́vrɪhwɛr] adv. por (o en) todas partes; a todas partes.

e·vict [ɪvíkt] v. desalojar; expulsar.

ev·i·dence [ɛ́vədəns] s. evidencia; prueba; demostración, señal; testimonio; **to be in** — mostrarse; v. hacer evidente, evidenciar; patentizar, revelar, mostrar.

ev·i·dent [ɛ́vədənt] adj. evidente, patente.

e·vil [ívl] adj. malo, malvado, maligno; aciago, de mal agüero; **to cast the** — **eye** aojar; **the Evil One** el Diablo; s. mal, maldad; adv. mal.

e·vil·do·er [ívldúɚ] s. malhechor.

e·voke [ɪvók] v. evocar; **to** — **laughter** provocar a risa.

ev·o·lu·tion [ɛvəlúʃ ən] s. evolución.

e·volve [ɪválv] v. desarrollar(se), desenvolver(se); urdir; evolucionar.

ewe [ju] s. oveja.

ex·act [ɪgzǽkt] adj. exacto; v. exigir; **-ly** adv. exactamente; en punto.

ex·act·ing [ɪgzǽktɪŋ] adj. exigente.

ex·ag·ger·ate [ɪgzǽdʒəret] v. exagerar.

ex·alt [ɪgzɔ́lt] v. exaltar, ensalzar.

ex·al·ta·tion [ɛgzɔltéʃ ən] s. exaltación.

ex·am·i·na·tion [ɪgzæmənéʃ ən] s. examen; reconocimiento (médico); (trial) interrogatorio.

ex·am·ine [ɪgzǽmɪn] v. examinar; reconocer (dícese del médico).

ex·am·ple [ɪgzǽmpl] s. ejemplo.

ex·as·per·ate [ɪgzǽspəret] v. exasperar, irritar.

EN

ex·ca·vate [ékskəvet] v. excavar.
ex·ca·va·tor [ékskəvetɚ] s. excavadora.
ex·ceed [ıksíd] v. exceder; sobrepasar; propasarse.
ex·ceed·ing·ly [ıksídıŋlı] adv. sumamente, extremamente; — well extremamente bien.
ex·cel [ıksέl] v. sobresalir en (entre); sobrepujar (a).
ex·cel·lence [éksləns] s. excelencia.
ex·cel·len·cy [ékslənsı] s. excelencia.
ex·cel·lent [ékslənt] adj. excelente.
ex·cept [ıksέpt] prep. excepto, menos; v. exceptuar.
ex·cept·ing [ıksέptıŋ] prep. excepto, salvo, menos, exceptuando.
ex·cep·tion [ıksέpʃən] s. (exclusion) excepción; (opposition) objeción; with the — of a excepción de, con excepción de; to take — objetar; ofenderse.
ex·cep·tion·al [ıksέpʃənl] adj. excepcional.
ex·cess [ıksέs] s. exceso; sobrante; — baggage exceso de equipaje; — weight exceso de peso; to drink to — beber en exceso; — profits tax impuesto sobre ganancias excesivas.
ex·ces·sive [ıksέsıv] adj. excesivo; desmedido; -ly adv. excesivamente, en exceso, demasiado.
ex·change [ıkstʃéndʒ] s. (money) cambio; (interchange) trueque; intercambio, canje (de publicaciones, prisioneros); (stock) lonja, bolsa; rate of — cambio, Am. tipo de cambio; telephone — central de teléfonos; foreign — divisa, v. cambiar; trocar; canjear (publicaciones, prisioneros); to — greetings saludarse; mandarse felicitaciones.
ex·cise tax [έksaız tǽks] s. alcabala, sisa.
ex·cite [ıksáıt] v. excitar; acalorar; agitar.
ex·cit·ed [ıksáıtıd] adj. excitado, acalorado; animado; to get — entusiasmarse; sobreexcitarse; acalorarse; -ly adv. acaloradamente, agitadamente.
ex·cite·ment [ıksáıtmənt] s. excitación; acaloramiento; agitación; alboroto; animación.
ex·cit·ing [ıksáıtıŋ] adj. excitante, excitador; estimulante.
ex·claim [ıksklém] v. exclamar.
ex·cla·ma·tion [ɛkskləméʃən] s. exclamación; — point punto de admiración.
ex·clude [ıksklúd] v. excluir.
ex·clu·sion [ıksklúʒən] s. exclusión.
ex·clu·sive [ıksklúsıv] adj. exclusivo; privativo; — of sin contar.
ex·com·mu·ni·cate [ɛkskəmjúnəket] v. excomunicar.
ex·com·mu·ni·ca·tion [ɛkskəmjunəkéʃən] s. excomunión.
ex·cre·ment [ékskrımənt] s. excremento; caca.
ex·cur·sion [ıkskɚ́ʒən] s. excursión; correría; expedición.
ex·cus·a·ble [ıkskjúzebl] adj. excusable, disculpable.
ex·cuse [ıkskjús] s. excusa; disculpa; [ıkskjúz] v. excusar; disculpar; perdonar, dispensar; eximir; — me! ¡dispense Vd.! ¡perdone Vd.!
ex·e·cute [éksıkjut] v. ejecutar; fusilar; ajusticiar; llevar a cabo; (computer) ejecutar.
ex·e·cu·tion [ɛksıkjúʃən] s. ejecución; desempeño; (computer) ejecución; — wall paredón.
ex·e·cu·tion·er [ɛksıkjúʃənɚ] s. verdugo.
ex·ec·u·tive [ıgzέkjutıv] adj. ejecutivo; s. ejecutivo, poder ejecutivo; gerente, administrador.
ex·ec·u·tor [ıgzέkjətɚ] s. albacea, ejecutor testamentario; [éksıkjutɚ] ejecutor.
ex·em·pla·ry [ıgzémplərı] adj. ejemplar.
ex·empt [ıgzémpt] adj. exento, libre; v. eximir, exentar.
ex·emp·tion [ıgzémpʃən] s. exención.
ex·er·cise [éksɚsaız] s. ejercicio; v. ejercitar(se);

ejercer (poder o autoridad); hacer ejercicio, hacer gimnasia; to be -d about something estar preocupado o sobreexcitado por algo.
ex·ert [ıgzɚ́t] v. ejercer; to — oneself esforzarse, hacer esfuerzos, empeñarse.
ex·er·tion [ıgzɚ́ʃən] s. ejercicio; esfuerzo, empeño.
ex·hale [ɛkshél] v. exhalar, emitir; espirar, soplar.
ex·haust [ıgzɔ́st] s. escape (de gas o vapor); v. agotar; consumir; debilitar, fatigar; I am -ed no puedo más; estoy agotado.
ex·haus·tion [ıgzɔ́stʃən] s. agotamiento; fatiga, postración.
ex·haus·tive [ɛgɔ́stıv] adj. comprensivo; detallado.
ex·hib·it [ıgzíbıt] v. exhibir; mostrar, exponer.
ex·hi·bi·tion [ɛksəbíʃən] s. exhibición; exposición; manifestación.
ex·hil·a·rate [ıgzíləret] v. alborozar, excitar, animar; entusiasmar; refocilar.
ex·hort [ıgzɔ́rt] v. exhortar.
ex·ile [égzaıl] s. destierro, exilio; desterrado; v. desterrar; expatriar.
ex·ist [ıgzíst] v. existir.
ex·is·tence [ıgzístəns] s. existencia.
ex·is·tent [ıgzístənt] adj. existente.
ex·it [égzıt] s. salida; salida (del foro); v. vase o vanse (un personaje o personajes al fin de una escena).
ex·o·dus [éksədəs] s. éxodo.
ex·on·er·ate [ıgzɑ́nəret] v. exonerar.
ex·or·bi·tant [ıgzɔ́rbətənt] adj. exorbitante.
ex·or·cism [éksɔrsızəm] s. exorcismo; conjuro.
ex·ot·ic [ıgzɑ́tık] adj. exótico; raro, extraño.
ex·pand [ıkspǽnd] v. ensanchar(se); dilatar(se); extender(se); agrandar(se); desarrollar (una ecuación).
ex·panse [ıkspǽns] s. espacio, extensión.
ex·pan·sion [ıkspǽnʃən] s. expansión; ensanche; desarrollo (de una ecuación).
ex·pan·sive [ıkspǽnsıv] adj. expansivo; efusivo.
ex·pect [ıkspέkt] v. esperar; contar con; I — so supongo que sí.
ex·pec·ta·tion [ɛkspɛktéʃən] s. expectación; expectativa; esperanza.
ex·pec·to·rate [ıkspέktəret] v. expectorar, desgarrar.
ex·pe·di·ent [ıkspídıənt] adj. conveniente, oportuno; ventajoso; prudente; s. expediente, medio.
ex·pe·dite [ékspədaıt] v. facilitar; despachar.
ex·pe·di·tion [ɛkspıdíʃən] s. expedición.
ex·pe·di·tion·ar·y [ɛkspıdíʃənɛrı] adj. expedicionario.
ex·pel [ıkspέl] v. expeler; expulsar.
ex·pend [ıkspénd] v. gastar; consumir.
ex·pen·di·ture [ıkspéndıtʃɚ] s. gasto; desembolso.
ex·pense [ıkspέns] s. gasto; coste, costa o costo.
ex·pen·sive [ıkspénsıv] adj. costoso.
ex·pen·sive·ness [ıkspénsıvnıs] s. precio subido, coste elevado.
ex·pe·ri·ence [ıkspírıəns] s. experiencia; aventura, lance; v. experimentar; pasar (penas, sufrimientos); sentir.
ex·pe·ri·enced [ıkspírıənst] adj. experimentado; ducho, perito, experto.
ex·per·i·ment [ıkspérəmənt] s. experimento, prueba; v. experimentar, hacer un experimento.
ex·per·i·men·tal [ıkspɛrəmɛ́ntl] adj. experimental.
ex·pert [ékspɚt] s. experto, perito; [ıkspɚ́t] adj. experto, perito, experimentado.
ex·pi·ra·tion [ɛkspəréʃən] s. terminación; vencimiento (de un plazo); espiración (del aire).
ex·pire [ıkspáır] v. expirar, morir; acabar; vencerse (un plazo); expeler (el aire aspirado).
ex·plain [ıksplén] v. explicar.

ex·plain·a·ble [ɪksplénəbl] *adj.* explicable.
ex·pla·na·tion [ɛksplənéʃən] *s.* explicación.
ex·plan·a·to·ry [ɪksplǽnətorɪ] *adj.* explicativo.
ex·plic·it [ɛksplísɪt] *adj.* explícito.
ex·plode [ɪksplód] *v.* estallar, hacer explosión, *Am.*
   explotar; reventar; volar (*con dinamita*);
   desacreditar (*una teoría*).
ex·ploit [ɛksplɔɪt] *s.* hazaña, proeza; [ɪksplɔ́ɪt] *v.*
   explotar; sacar partido de, abusar de.
ex·ploi·ta·tion [ɛksplɔɪtéʃən] *s.* explotación.
ex·plo·ra·tion [ɛksplɔréʃən] *s.* exploración.
ex·plore [ɪksplór] *v.* explorar.
ex·plor·er [ɪksplórɚ] *s.* explorador.
ex·plo·sion [ɪksplóʒən] *s.* explosión, estallido.
ex·plo·sive [ɪksplósɪv] *adj. & s.* explosivo.
ex·port [ɛ́ksport] *s.* exportación; artículo exportado,
   mercancía exportada; [ɪkspórt] *v.* exportar.
ex·por·ta·tion [ɛksportéʃən] *s.* exportación.
ex·pose [ɪkspóz] *v.* exponer; exhibir, mostrar, poner a
   la vista; revelar; desenmascarar.
ex·po·si·tion [ɛkspəzíʃn] *s.* exposición; exhibición.
ex·po·sure [ɪkspóʒɚ] *s.* exposición; revelación; **to die**
   of — morir a efecto de la intemperie.
ex·pound [ɪkspáʊnd] *v.* exponer, explicar.
ex·press [ɪksprɛ́s] *adj.* (*rapid*) expreso; (*explicit*)
   explícito, claro; — **company** compañía de expreso;
   expreso, *Am.* exprés; — **train** tren expreso; *adv.*
   por expreso, por exprés; *s.* expreso; tren expreso,
   Am. exprés; *v.* expresar; enviar por expreso (*o por*
   exprés).
ex·pres·sion [ɪksprɛ́ʃən] *s.* expresión.
ex·pres·sive [ɪksprɛ́sɪv] *adj.* expresivo.
ex·pul·sion [ɪkspʌ́lʃən] *s.* expulsión.
ex·qui·site [ɛkskwízɪt] *adj.* exquisito.
ex·qui·site·ness [ɪkskwízɪtnɪs] *s.* exquisitez; primor.
ex·tant [ɪkstǽnt] *adj.* existente.
ex·tem·po·ra·ne·ous [ɛkstɛmpərénɪəs] *adj.*
   improvisado.
ex·tend [ɪkstɛ́nd] *v.* extender(se); tender;
   prolongar(se); alargar(se); agrandar; dilatar,
   prorrogar (*un plazo*); dar (*el pésame, el parabién,*
   ayuda, etc.).
ex·tend·ed [ɪkstɛ́ndɪd] *adj.* extenso; prolongado;
   extendido.
ex·ten·sion [ɪkstɛ́nʃən] *s.* extensión; prolongación;
   prórroga (*de un plazo*); añadidura, anexo.
ex·ten·sive [ɪkstɛ́nsɪv] *adj.* extenso, ancho, dilatado;
   extensivo; **-ly** *adv.* extensamente, por extenso;
   extensivamente; **-ly used** de uso general o común.
ex·tent [ɪkstɛ́nt] *s.* extensión; grado; **to a great** — en
   gran parte, generalmente; **to such an** — **that** a tal
   grado que; **to the** — **of one's ability** en
   proporción a su habilidad; **up to a certain** — hasta
   cierto punto.
ex·ten·u·ate [ɪkstɛ́njʊet] *v.* atenuar, mitigar.
ex·te·ri·or [ɪkstírɪɚ] *adj.* exterior; externo; *s.*
   exterioridad; exterior, porte, aspecto.
ex·ter·mi·nate [ɪkstɚ́mənet] *v.* exterminar, destruir
   por completo, extirpar.
ex·ter·mi·na·tion [ɪkstɚmənéʃən] *s.* exterminio.
ex·ter·nal [ɪkstɚ́nl] *adj.* externo; exterior; *s.*
   exterioridad; lo externo.
ex·tinct [ɪkstíŋkt] *adj.* extinto; extinguido, apagado.
ex·tin·guish [ɪkstíŋgwɪʃ] *v.* extinguir; apagar.
ex·tol [ɪkstól] *v.* enaltecer; ensalzar.
ex·tort [ɪkstɔ́rt] *v.* obtener por fuerza o amenaza,
   exigir (*dinero, promesa, etc.*), *Am.* extorsionar.
ex·tor·tion [ɪkstɔ́rʃən] *s.* extorsión.
ex·tra [ɛ́kstrə] *adj.* extraordinario; de sobra, de más,
   adicional; suplementario; — **tire** neumático de
   repuesto o de recambio; — **workman** obrero

supernumerario; *adv.* extraordinariamente; *s.* extra;
extraordinario (*de un periódico*); suplemento; gasto
extraordinario; recargo (*cargo adicional*); actor
suplente o supernumerario.
ex·tract [ɛ́kstrækt] *s.* extracto; cita, trozo
   (*entresacado de un libro*); resumen; [ɪkstrǽkt] *v.*
   extraer; seleccionar; citar.
ex·traor·di·nar·y [ɪkstrɔ́rdnɛrɪ] *adj.* extraordinario;
   extraordinarily *adv.* extraordinariamente; de
   manera extraordinaria.
ex·trav·a·gance [ɪkstrǽvəgəns] *s.* despilfarro,
   derroche, gasto excesivo; lujo excesivo;
   extravagancia, capricho.
ex·trav·a·gant [ɪkstrǽvəgənt] *adj.* gastador,
   despilfarrado; extravagante, disparatado; — **praise**
   elogios excesivos; — **prices** precios exorbitantes.
ex·treme [ɪkstrím] *adj.* (*last*) último; extremo; más
   remoto; (*excessive*) excesivo; riguroso; radical; —
   opinions opiniones extremadas; *s.* extremo; cabo;
   to go to -s extremar, exagerar; hacer extremos;
   tomar las medidas más extremas; **-ly** *adv.*
   extremamente, en extremo.
ex·trem·i·ty [ɪkstrɛ́mətɪ] *s.* extremidad, extremo;
   medida extrema; **in** — en gran peligro; en un
   apuro.
ex·u·ber·ant [ɪgzjúbərənt] *adj.* exuberante.
ex·ult [ɪgzʌ́lt] *v.* alborozarse, regocijarse.
eye [aɪ] *s.*. ojo; — **shade** visera; **in a twinkling of an**
   — en un abrir y cerrar de ojos; **hook and** —
   macho y hembra; **to catch one's** — llamar la
   atención; **to have good -s** tener buena vista; **to**
   have before one's -s tener a (*o* tener ante) la vista;
   to keep an — **on** cuidar, vigilar; **to see** — **to** —
   estar completamente de acuerdo; *v.* mirar,
   observar.
eye·ball [áɪbɔl] *s.* globo del ojo.
eye·bolt [áɪbolt] *s.* perno de argolla.
eye·brow [áɪbraʊ] *s.* ceja.
eye·glass [áɪglæs] *s.* lente, cristal (*de anteojo*); ocular
   (*de microscopio o telescopio*); **-es** lentes, anteojos.
eye·lash [áɪlæʃ] *s.* pestaña.
eye·lid [áɪlɪd] *s.* párpado.
eye·sight [áɪsaɪt] *s.* vista; **poor** — mala vista.

F: f

fa·ble [fébl] *s.* fábula.
fab·ric [fǽbrɪk] *s.* género, tela;
   tejido; textura; estructura.
fab·u·lous [fǽbjələs] *adj.* fabuloso.
fa·çade [fəsád] *s.* fachada.
face [fes] *s.* (*human*) cara, rostro; (*building*) fachada,
   frente; (*surface*) haz, superficie; (*watch*) muestra;
   Ríopl. esfera; *Méx., C.A., Ven., Col.* carátula; —
   value valor nominal; **in the** — **of** en presencia de,
   ante, frente a; **to lose** — perder prestigio; **to make**
   -s hacer muecas o gestos; **to save one's** — salvar
   el amor propio; *v.* encararse con; enfrentarse con;
   hacer frente a; mirar hacia; forrar; **to** — **about**
   volverse, *Méx., C.A., Ven., Col., Andes* voltearse;
   to — **danger** afrontar o arrostrar el peligro; **to** —
   with marble revestir de mármol; **it -s the street** da
   a la calle.
fac·et [fǽsɪt] *s.* faceta.
fa·cil·i·tate [fəsílətet] *v.* facilitar.
fa·cil·i·ty [fəsílətɪ] *s.* facilidad.
fact [fækt] *s.* hecho; dato; verdad, realidad; **in** — de
   hecho; en realidad.
fac·tion [fǽkʃən] *s.* facción, bando, partido,
   pandilla.

EX

fac·tor [fǽktɚ] s. factor; elemento; agente; v. descomponer en factores.
fac·to·ry [fǽktrɪ] s. fábrica; — **automation** automatización fabril.
fac·ul·ty [fǽkltɪ] s. facultad; (college) profesorado; cuerpo docente.
fad [fæd] s. novedad; manía; moda.
fade [fed] v. descolorar(se), desteñir(se); marchitar(se); apagarse (un sonido); desvanecerse.
fagged [fægd] adj. agotado, rendido de cansancio.
fail [fel] v. (not effect) faltar; fallar; fracasar; no tener éxito; (wane) decaer; debilitarse; (go broke) quebrar, hacer bancarrota; **to — in an examination** fallar en un examen, salir mal en un examen; **to — a student** reprobar o suspender a un estudiante; **to — to do it** dejar de hacerlo, no hacerlo; **don't — to come** no deje Vd. de venir; **without** — sin falta.
fail·ure [féljɚ] s. fracaso; malogro; falta; descuido, negligencia; quiebra, bancarrota; debilitamiento.
faint [fent] adj. (weak) débil, lánguido; (indistinct) imperceptible, tenue, vago, indistinto; **to feel** — sentirse desvanecido; — **hearted** tímido, cobarde; s. desmayo; v. desmayarse; languidecer; **-ly** adv. débilmente; lánguidamente; indistintamente, vagamente, tenuemente; apenas.
faint·ness [féntnɪs] s. languidez, debilidad, desfallecimiento; falta de claridad; vaguedad.
fair [fɛr] adj. (just) justo, recto, honrado; imparcial; equitativo; — **market value** valor justo; — **trade** comercio legítimo; (mediocre) regular, mediano; (complexion) rubio, blondo; Méx. huero; Guat. canche; C.R. macho; Pan. fulo; Col. mono; Ven. catire; Sal. chele; (weather) claro, despejado; — **chance of success** buena probabilidad de éxito; — **complexion** tez blanca; — **hair** pelo rubio; — **name** reputación sin mancilla; — **play** juego limpio; — **sex** sexo bello; — **weather** buen tiempo, tiempo bonancible; **to act** — obrar con imparcialidad (o con equidad); **to play** — jugar limpio; s. feria; mercado; exposición; Valencia falla; **-ly** adv. justamente; imparcialmente; medianamente; **-ly difficult** medianamente difícil; **-ly well** regular, bastante bien.
fair·ness [fɛ́rnɪs] s. justicia, equidad, imparcialidad; blancura (de la tez); belleza.
fair·y [fɛ́rɪ] s. hada; — **godmother** hada madrina; — **tale** cuento de hadas.
fair·y·land [fɛ́rɪlænd] s. tierra de las hadas.
faith [feθ] s. fe; fidelidad; **in good** — de buena fe; **to have** — **in** tener fe o confianza en; **to keep** — cumplir con la palabra.
faith·ful [féθfəl] adj. fiel; leal; **-ly** adv. fielmente; con fidelidad; puntualmente; **-ly yours** suyo afectísimo; siempre suyo.
faith·ful·ness [féθfəlnɪs] s. fidelidad; lealtad; exactitud.
faith·less [féθlɪs] adj. infiel; sin fe; desleal; falso.
fake [fek] s. fraude, trampa; falsedad; embustero; adj. falso, fingido; v. falsear; fingir; simular.
fal·con [fólkən] s. halcón.
fall [fɔl] s. (drop) caída; bajada; (collapse) ruina; baja (de precios); (season) otoño; **-s** cascada, catarata, salto de agua; v. caer(se); decaer; bajar; **to — asleep** dormirse, quedarse dormido; **to — back** retroceder; **to — behind** atrasarse, rezagarse, quedarse atrás; **to — in love** enamorarse; **to — out with** reñir con, enemistarse con; **to — to one** tocarle a uno, corresponderle a uno; **his plans fell through** fracasaron (o se malograron) sus planes; — **guy** cabeza de turco.

fal·la·cy [fǽləsɪ] s. falsedad; error.
fall·en [fólən] p.p. de to fall.
fall·out [fólaʊt] s. precipitación radiactiva.
fal·low [fǽlo] adj. baldío; s. barbecho; v. barbechar.
false [fɔls] adj. falso; postizo (dientes, barba, etc.); fingido, simulado; — **pretense** dolo, estafa.
false·hood [fólshʊd] s. falsedad, mentira.
false·ness [fólsnɪs] s. falsedad.
fal·si·fy [fólsəfaɪ] v. falsificar, falsear; mentir.
fal·si·ty [fólsətɪ] s. falsedad; mentira.
fal·ter [fóltɚ] v. vacilar; titubear; tambalearse; bambolearse; **to — an excuse** balbucear una excusa; s. temblor, vacilación.
fame [fem] s. fama.
famed [femd] adj. afamado, famoso, renombrado.
fa·mil·iar [fəmíljɚ] adj. familiar, íntimo; confianzudo; **to be — with a subject** conocer bien, estar versado en o ser conocedor de una materia; s. familiar.
fa·mil·i·ar·i·ty [fəmɪlɪǽrətɪ] s. familiaridad; confianza, franqueza.
fam·i·ly [fǽmlɪ] s. familia; — **name** apellido; — **tree** árbol genealógico; **to be in the — way** estar encinta.
fam·ine [fǽmɪn] s. hambre; escasez, carestía.
fam·ished [fǽmɪʃt] adj. hambriento, muerto de hambre; **to be** — morirse de hambre.
fa·mous [fémos] adj. famoso.
fan [fæn] s. abanico; aventador; ventilador; aficionado (a deportes); admirador; v. abanicar; ventilar.
fa·nat·ic [fənǽtɪk] adj. & s. fanático.
fa·nat·i·cism [fənǽtəsɪzəm] s. fanatismo.
fan·ci·ful [fǽnsɪfəl] adj. fantástico; caprichoso; imaginario.
fan·cy [fǽnsɪ] s. fantasía, antojo, capricho; imaginación; afición, gusto; **to have a — for** tener afición a; **to strike one's** — antojársele a uno; **to take a — to a person** caerle a uno bien (o simpatizarle a uno) una persona; adj. fantástico, de fantasía; de adorno; elegante; — **ball** baile de fantasía o disfraces; — **free** libre de cuidados; — **work** labor; bordado fino; v. imaginar(se); fantasear; forjar, concebir (una idea); **to — oneself** imaginarse; **just — the idea!** ¡figúrate qué idea! **I don't — the idea of** no me gusta la idea de.
fan·fare [fǽnfɛr] s. toque de trompeta.
Fan-fold pa·per [fǽnfold pepɚ] s. papel continuo.
fang [fæŋ] s. colmillo (de ciertos animales).
fan·tas·tic [fæntǽstɪk] adj. fantástico; extravagante.
fan·ta·sy [fǽntəsɪ] s. fantasía.
far [fɑr] adv. lejos; — **away** muy lejos; — **and wide** por todas partes; — **better** mucho mejor; — **off** muy lejos; a lo lejos; **by** — con mucho; **as — as** hasta; en cuanto a; **as — as I know** según parece; a lo que parece; que yo sepa; **so** — hasta ahora; hasta aquí; hasta entonces; **how** — ? ¿hasta dónde?; adj. lejano, distante, remoto; — **journey** largo viaje; **it is a — cry from** dista mucho de.
far·a·way [fɑrəwé] adj. muy lejano, distante, remoto; abstraído.
farce [fɑrs] s. farsa.
fare [fɛr] s. pasaje, tarifa de pasajes; pasajero; comida, alimento; v. pasarla (vien o mal); irle a uno (bien o mal); **to — forth** salir.
fare·well [fɛrwél] s. despedida, adiós; **to bid — to** despedirse de; —! ¡adiós!
far·fetched [fɑrfétʃt] adj. traído de muy lejos; forzado; traído por los cabellos; que no hace al caso; improbable, poco creíble.
far·flung [fɑrflʌ́ŋ] adj. extenso, de gran alcance.

farm [fɑrm] *s.* hacienda, granja, finca; *Ríopl.*
estancia, *Méx.* rancho; — **hand** peón; — **produce**
productos agrícolas; — **loan bank** caja de crédito
agrario campesino; *v.* cultivar, labrar (*la tierra*); **to**
— **out** dar en arriendo; repartir.
farm·er [fɑrmɚ] *s.* labrador; granjero; agricultor,
Méx. ranchero, *Ríopl.* estanciero, *Am.* hacendado.
farm·house [fɑrmhaʊs] *s.* alquería, finca.
farm·ing [fɑrmɪŋ] *s.* labranza, agricultura, cultivo de
los campos; *adj.* agrícola.
farm·yard [fɑrmjɑrd] *s.* corral (*de una alquería*).
far·off [fɑrɔf] *adj.* distance, remoto.
far·sighted [fɑrsáɪtəd] *adj.* (*sight*) présbite.
far·ther [fɑrðɚ] *adv.* más lejos; más; — **on** más
adelante; *adj.* más remoto, más lejano.
far·thest [fɑrðɪst] *adj.* más lejano; más remoto; *adv.*
más lejos.
fas·ci·nate [fǽsɳet] *v.* fascinar.
fas·ci·na·tion [fæsɳéʃən] *s.* fascinación.
fas·cism [fǽʃɪzm] *s.* fascismo.
fas·cist [fǽʃɪst] *s.* fascista.
fash·ion [fǽʃən] *s.* (*style*) moda, boga, estilo; (*way*)
manera, modo; — **plate** figurín; **the latest** — la
última moda (*o* novedad); **after a** —
medianamente, no muy bien; **to be in** — estar de
moda; estilarse; *v.* forjar, hacer, formar; idear.
fash·ion·a·ble [fǽʃnəbl] *adj.* de moda; de buen tono;
elegante.
fast [fæst] *adj.* rápido, veloz; (*watch*) adelantado
(*dícese del reloj*); (*firm*) firme; fiel (*amigo*); fijo;
(*dissolute*) disipado, disoluto; *adv.* aprisa, de prisa;
firmemente, fijamente; — **asleep** profundamente
dormido; *s.* ayuno; *v.* ayunar.
fas·ten [fæsɳ] *v.* fijar(se); sujetar(se), asegurar(se);
atar, unir, abrochar(se).
fas·ten·er [fæsɳɚ] *s.* broche; abrochador.
fas·tid·i·ous [fæstídɪəs] *adj.* melindroso.
fat [fæt] *adj.* (*large*) gordo; (*greasy*) grasiento;
mantecoso; — **profits** ganancias pingües; *s.* grasa,
manteca; gordura; **the** — **of the land** lo mejor y
más rico de la tierra.
fa·tal [fétl] *adj.* fatal.
fa·tal·i·ty [fətǽlətɪ] *s.* fatalidad; muerte.
fate [fet] *s.* hado, sino, destino; fortuna, suerte.
fa·ther [fɑ́ðɚ] *s.* padre.
fa·ther·hood [fɑ́ðɚhʊd] *s.* paternidad.
fa·ther-in-law [fɑ́ðɚrɪnlɔ] *s.* suegro.
fa·ther·land [fɑ́ðɚlænd] *s.* patria.
fa·ther·ly [fɑ́ðɚlɪ] *adv.* paternal.
fath·om [fǽðəm] *v.* sondar, sondear; penetrar; *s.*
braza (*medida de profundidad*).
fath·om·less [fǽðəmlɪs] *adj.* insondable.
fa·tigue [fətíg] *s.* fatiga, cansancio; *v.* fatigar(se),
cansar(se).
fat·ness [fǽtnɪs] *s.* gordura.
fat·ten [fǽtɳ] *v.* engordar.
fat·ty [fǽtɪ] *adj.* grasiento; seboso.
fau·cet [fɔ́sɪt] *s.* grifo, llave, espita, canilla, *Méx.*
bitoque.
fault [fɔlt] *s.* (*defect*) falta; defecto; tacha; (*blame*)
culpa; (*geological*) falla; **to a** — excesivamente; **to
be at** — ser, culpable; **to find** — **with** criticar a.
fault·find·er [fɔ́ltfaɪndɚ] *s.* criticón, criticador.
fault·less [fɔ́ltlɪs] *adj.* intachable, sin tacha, perfecto.
fault·y [fɔ́ltɪ] *adj.* defectuoso, imperfecto.
fa·vor [févɚ] *s.* favor; — **your** — **of the ...** su grata
(carta) del ...; *v.* favorecer.
fa·vor·a·ble [févrəbl] *adj.* favorable; **favorably** *adv.*
favorablemente.
fa·vor·ite [févrɪt] *adj.* & *s.* favorito.
fa·vor·it·ism [févrɪtɪzəm] *s.* favoritismo.

fawn [fɔn] *s.* cervato; color de cervato; *v.* adular;
halagar.
fear [fɪr] *s.* temor, miedo; pavor; *v.* temer.
fear·ful [fírfəl] *adj.* terrible, espantoso; temible,
temeroso; miedoso.
fear·less [fírlɪs] *adj.* sin temor, intrépido, atrevido,
arrojado.
fear·less·ness [fírlɪsnɪs] *s.* intrepidez, arrojo, osadía,
atrevimiento.
fea·si·ble [fízəbl] *adj.* factible, hacedero, dable.
feast [fist] *s.* fiesta; festín, banquete; *v.* festejar,
obsequiar; banquetear; **to** — **one's eyes on** deleitar
la vista en.
feat [fit] *s.* (*heroics*) proeza, hazaña; (*trick*) acto de
destreza; suerte (*en el circo*).
feath·er [féðɚ] *s.* pluma; **-s** plumaje; **a** — **in one's
cap** un triunfo para uno; — **weight** de peso
mínimo; — **bedding** empleo de trabajadores
innecesarios; *v.* emplumar.
feath·er·y [féðərɪ] *adj.* plumoso; ligero, como una
pluma.
fea·ture [fítʃɚ] *s.* facción, rasgo distintivo; película
principal (*en el cine*); **-s** facciones (*de la cara*); —
article artículo sobresaliente o principal; *v.*
destacar, hacer sobresalir; dar realce a; mostrar,
exhibir (*como parte principal*), hacer resaltar.
Feb·ru·ar·y [fébrʊɛrɪ] *s.* febrero.
fed [fɛd] *pret.* & *p.p.* de **to feed**; **to be** — **up** estar
harto, estar hasta la coronilla, estar hasta el copete.
fed·er·al [fédərəl] *adj.* federal.
fed·er·a·tion [fɛdəréʃən] *s.* federación,
confederación, liga.
fee [fi] *s.* honorario (honorarios); derechos; cuota;
admission — derechos de entrada; precio de
entrada.
fee·ble [fibl] *adj.* débil, endeble; **feebly** *adv.*
débilmente.
feed [fid] *s.* forraje, pasto, pienso (*para los
caballos*); comida; *v.* alimentar(se); dar de comer;
pacer, pastar; **to** — **coal** echar carbón.
feed·back [fídbæk] *s.* regeneración; reacciones
informativas.
feel [fil] *v.* sentir; tocar, tentar; palpar; **to** — **better**
(sad, happy, *etc.*) sentirse mejor (triste, feliz, *etc.*);
to — **one's way** tantear el camino; **to** — **for
someone** compadecer a alguien; **it -s soft** está
suave; **it -s hot in here** se siente calor aquí; *s.*
tacto, sentido del tacto; **this cloth has a nice** —
esta tela es suave al tacto.
feel·er [filɚ] *s.* tentáculo, antena (*de los insectos*);
tiento; propuesta (*para averiguar la inclinación o
pensamiento de alguien*).
feel·ing [filɪŋ] *s.* (*touch*) tacto; sensación (*emotion*)
sentimiento; emoción; pasión; (*pity*) compasión;
ternura; **to hurt someone's -s** ofender la
sensibilidad de alguien; *adj.* sensible, compasivo.
feet [fit] *pl.* de **foot.**
feign [fen] *v.* fingir.
fell [fɛl] *v.* derribar, echar abajo; talar (*un árbol*);
pret. de **to fall.**
fel·low [félo] *s.* socio, miembro (*de una sociedad,
colegio, etc.*); (*scholar*) becario (*estudiante que
disfruta una beca*); (*companion*) camarada,
compañero; individuo, tipo, sujeto, hombre; —
citizen conciudadano; — **man** prójimo; —
member consocio; colega; — **student**
condiscípulo.
fel·low·ship [féloʃɪp] *s.* compañerismo; unión;
confraternidad; sociedad; beca; **to get a** — obtener
una beca.
fel·o·ny [félənɪ] *s.* crimen.

felt [fɛlt] *s.* fieltro; *adj.* de fieltro; *pret. & p.p. de* **to feel.**

fe·male [fímel] *s.* hembra; *adj.* hembra; femenino, mujeril, de la mujer; — **cat** (**dog**, *etc.*) gata (perra, *etc.*); — **screw** tuerca, hembra de tornillo.

fem·i·nine [fɛ́mənɪn] *adj.* femenino, femenil.

fem·i·nin·i·ty [fɛmɪnínɪtɪ] *s.* feminidad.

fe·mur [fímɚ] *s.* fémur.

fence [fɛns] *s.* cerca, valla, vallado; receptor de cosas robadas; **to be on the** — estar indeciso; *v.* esgrimir; **to** — **in** cercar, rodear con cerca.

fenc·ing [fɛ́nsɪŋ] *s.* esgrima; cercado.

fend·er [fɛ́ndɚ] *s.* guardabarros, guardafango; *Col.* trompa (*de locomotora*); *Ríopl.* parrilla.

fer·ment [fɝmɛnt] *s.* fermento; fermentación; [fɚmɛ́nt] *v.* fermentar; hacer fermentar.

fer·men·ta·tion [fɝməntéʃən] *s.* fermentación.

fern [fɝn] *s.* helecho.

fe·ro·cious [fəróʃəs] *adj.* feroz, fiero.

fe·roc·i·ty [fərásətɪ] *s.* ferocidad, fiereza.

fer·ret [fɛ́rɪt] *v.* **to** — **out** buscar, cazar; (*investigate*) escudriñar, indagar.

fer·ry [fɛ́rɪ] *s.* barca de pasaje (*a través de un río o bahía*); embarcadero; *Méx.* chalán, pango; *v.* transportar de una orilla a otra; atravesar (*un río*) en barca de pasaje.

fer·tile [fɝtl] *adj.* fértil; fecundo.

fer·til·i·ty [fɝtílɪtɪ] *s.* fertilidad.

fer·til·ize [fɝtlaɪz] *v.* fertilizar; abonar; fecundar.

fer·til·iz·er [fɝtlaɪzɚ] *s.* abono (*para la tierra*).

fer·vent [fɝvənt] *adj.* ferviente; fervoroso.

fer·vor [fɝvɚ] *s.* fervor; ardor.

fes·ter [fɛ́stɚ] *v.* supurar; enconarse (*una llaga*); *s.* llaga, úlcera.

fes·ti·val [fɛ́stəvl] *s.* fiesta.

fes·tive [fɛ́stɪv] *adj.* festivo; alegre.

fes·tiv·i·ty [fɛstívətɪ] *s.* júbilo, regocijo; festividad.

fetch [fɛtʃ] *v.* ir a buscar; coger; traer.

fete [fet] *s.* fiesta; *v.* festejar; agasajar.

fet·ish [fɛ́tɪʃ] *s.* fetiche.

fet·ter [fɛ́tɚ] *v.* engrillar, meter en grillos encadenar; **-s'** *pl.* grillos, cadenas, trabas.

fe·tus [fítəs] *s.* feto.

feud [fjud] *s.* riña, pelea, contienda; **old** — enemistad antigua (*entre dos personas o familias*).

feu·dal [fjúdl] *adj.* feudal.

fe·ver [fívɚ] *s.* fiebre, calentura.

fe·ver·ish [fívərɪʃ] *adj.* calenturiento, febril.

fe·ver·ish·ness [fívərɪʃnɪs] *s.* calentura; agitación febril.

few [fju] *adj. & pron.* pocos; **a** — unos pocos, unos cuantos.

fi·an·cé [fiɑnsé] *s.* novio; **fiancée** *f.* novia.

fi·as·co [fɪǽsko] *s.* fiasco.

fib [fɪb] *s.* bola, mentirilla, paparrucha, papa; *v.* echar papas, decir o contar paparruchas.

fib·ber [fɪ́bɚ] *s.* paparruchero, cuentero, mentirosillo.

fi·ber [fáɪbɚ] *s.* fibra.

fi·brous [fáɪbrəs] *adj.* fibroso.

fick·le [fɪkl] *adj.* inconstante, voluble, veleidoso; mudable; tornadizo.

fic·tion [fɪkʃən] *s.* ficción.

fic·tion·al [fɪkʃənl] *adj.* novelesco; ficticio.

fic·ti·tious [fɪktíʃəs] *adj.* ficticio.

fid·dle [fɪdl] *s.* violín; *v.* tocar el violín; **to** — **around** malgastar el tiempo; juguetear.

fi·del·i·ty [faɪdélətɪ] *s.* fidelidad.

fid·get [fɪ́dʒɪt] *v.* estar inquieto; agitarse, menearse nerviosamente.

fi·du·ci·ar·y [fɪdúʃɛrɪ] *adj.* fiduciario, fideicomisario.

field [fild] *s.* campo; campo o cancha (*de deportes*);

(*computer*) campo; — **artillery** artillería de campaña; — **glasses** anteojos de larga vista; — **work** trabajo de investigación en el campo.

fiend [find] *s.* demonio, diablo; **dope** — morfinómano.

fiend·ish [fíndɪʃ] *adj.* diabólico.

fierce [firs] *adj.* feroz, fiero; furioso, espantoso.

fierce·ness [fírsnɪs] *s.* ferocidad; fiereza; vehemencia.

fier·y [fáɪrɪ] *adj.* fogoso; ardiente; vehemente.

fife [faɪf] *s.* pífano.

fif·teen [fɪftín] *num.* quince.

fif·ty [fɪ́ftɪ] *num.* cincuenta.

fig [fɪg] *s.* higo; — **tree** higuera.

fight [faɪt] *s.* lucha; pelea; riña, pleito; **he has a lot of** — **left** le sobra fuerza para luchar; *v.* luchar (con) pelear; combatir; reñir; batirse; **to** — **it out** decidirlo a golpes o con argumentos; **to** — **one's way through** abrirse camino a la fuerza.

fight·er [fáɪtɚ] *s.* luchador; combatiente; guerrero; — **airplane** avión de caza.

fight·ing [fáɪtɪŋ] *s.* lucha, combate pelea; *adj.* combatiente; luchador.

fig·ure [fɪ́gjɚ] *s.* (*form*) figura; forma; talle (*de una persona*); (*numerical*) cifra, número; valor; precio; **-s** cuentas, cálculos; — **of speech** figura de dicción; **to be good at -s** sabe hacer bien las cuentas; ser listo en aritmética; **to cut a poor** — tener mala facha, hacer el ridículo; *v.* figurar; imaginarse, figurarse; adornar con dibujos; calcular; **to** — **on** contar con, confiar en; tener la intención de; proponerse; tomar en cuenta; **to** — **out** descifrar, resolver.

fil·a·ment [fɪləmənt] *s.* filamento.

file [faɪl] *s.* (*records*) fichero; archivo; registro, lista; (*computer*) archivo, fichero; legajo; (*cabinet*) guardapapeles; (*line*) fila; (*tool*) lima; — **card** ficha, papeleta; *v.* archivar; guardar en el fichero; registrar, asentar en el registro; limar; desfilar, marchar en fila; — **a claim** establecer reclamación; — **a suit** entablar un pleito.

fil·i·al [fɪ́lɪəl] *adj.* filial.

fil·i·bus·ter [fɪləbʌstɚ] *v.* emplear táctica parlamentaria dilatoria.

fil·i·gree [fɪ́lɪgri] *s.* filigrana.

fill [fɪl] *v.* llenar(se); ocupar (*un puesto*); empastar (*un diente*); servir, atender, despachar (*un pedido*); inflar (*un neumático*); tapar (*un agujero*); **to** — **out a blank** llenar un formulario (*forma o esqueleto*); **to** — **in** suministrar informes específicos; **her eyes -ed with tears** se le arrasaron los ojos de lágrimas.

fil·let [fɪlé] *s.* filete; [fɪlɪt] *cinta, lista de adorno*.

fill·ing [fɪlɪŋ] *s.* relleno; empaste (*dental*); **gold** — orificación.

fil·ly [fɪlɪ] *s.* potranca.

film [fɪlm] *s.* (*photographic*) película; (*membrane*) membrana; (*on liquid*) tela; (*in eye*) nube (*en el ojo*); *v.* filmar, cinematografiar.

fil·ter [fɪltɚ] *s.* filtro; *v.* filtrar(se).

filth [fɪlθ] *s.* suciedad; porquería; mugre.

filth·i·ness [fɪlθɪnɪs] *s.* suciedad, porquería.

filth·y [fɪlθɪ] *adj.* sucio, puerco, cochino; mugriento.

fin [fɪn] *s.* aleta (*de pez*).

fi·nal [fáɪnl] *adj.* final; terminante; definitivo; **-ly** *adv.* finalmente; en fin, por fin.

fi·nance [fənǽns] *s.* teoría bancaria, *Am.* finanza; **-s** fondos, recursos monetarios; negocios bancarios, *Am.* finanzas; *v.* hacer operaciones bancarias; fomentar (*un negocio o empresa*), *Am.* financiar.

fi·nan·cial [fənǽnʃəl] *adj.* financiero; monetario; — **backing** respaldo económico, apoyo financiero.

fin·an·cier [fɪnənsfr] *s.* financiero, *Am.* financista.

fi·nanc·ing [fənǽnsɪŋ] s. *Am.* financiamiento.

find [faɪnd] v. hallar; encontrar; declarar; **to — fault with** criticar a, censurar a; **to — guilty** declarar o encontrar culpable; **to — out** descubrir; averiguar; s. hallazgo.

find·ing [fáɪndɪŋ] s. descubrimiento; hallazgo; fallo, decisión; **-s** resultados, datos (*de una investigación*).

fine [faɪn] adj. (*delicate*) fino; (*good*) perfecto, excelente; superior; primoroso; **— arts** bellas artes; **— sand** arena fina o menuda; **— weather** tiempo claro o despejado; **to feel —** sentirse muy bien de salud; **to have a — time** pasar un rato muy divertido; **fine-looking** bien parecido, guapo; s. multa; **in —** en fin, en resumen; v. multar; **-ly** adv. finamente; con primor; excelentemente; muy bien, perfectamente.

fine·ness [fáɪnnɪs] s. finura; fineza; primor; excelencia, perfección.

fin·er·y [fáɪnərɪ] s. galas; atavíos, adornos.

fi·nesse [fɪnɛ́s] s. sutileza; artificio; soltura.

fin·ger [fíŋgɚ] s. dedo (*de la mano*); **—print** impresión digital; **the little —** el dedo meñique; **middle —** dedo del corazón, dedo de enmedio; **ring —** dedo anular; v. tocar; manosear.

fin·ger·nail [fíŋgɚnel] s. uña.

fin·ick·y [fínɪkɪ] adj. melindroso.

fin·ish [fínɪʃ] s. fin, término, conclusión; (*varnish*) acabado; pulimiento; **to have a rough —** estar sin pulir, sin pulimento o al natural; v. acabar, acabar con, terminar, finalizar; pulir, pulimentar.

fin·ished [fínɪʃt] adj. acabado; pulido, pulimentado; (*good*) excelente.

fir [fɝ] s. abeto.

fire [faɪr] s. (*flame*) fuego; lumbre; (*destructive*) quemazón; incendio; **— alarm** alarma de incendios; **— department** cuerpo o servicio de bomberos; servicio de incendios; **— engine** bomba (*para incendios*); **— escape** escalera de salvamento; **— insurance** seguro contra incendios; **— trap** edificio sin medios de escape en caso de incendio; **to be on —** estar ardiendo, estar quemándose; **to catch —** incendiarse, quemarse; **to set on —** pegar fuego, incendiar; **to be under enemy —** estar expuesto al fuego del enemigo; v. incendiar; pegar fuego; inflamar; disparar; **to — an employee** despedir (*o* expulsar) a un empleado.

fire·arm [fáɪrɑrm] s. arma de fuego.

fire·brand [fáɪrbrænd] s. tizón; pavesa.

fire·crack·er [fáɪrkrǽkɚ] s. triquitraque.

fire·fly [fáɪrflaɪ] s. luciérnaga.

fire·man [fáɪrmən] s. (*who extinguishes*) bombero; (*who makes*) fogonero.

fire·place [fáɪrples] s. chimenea, hogar.

fire·proof [fáɪrpruf] adj. incombustible; a prueba de incendio; v. hacer incombustible.

fire·side [fáɪrsaɪd] s. hogar.

fire·wood [fáɪrwʊd] s. leña.

fire·works [fáɪrwɝks] s. fuegos artificiales; pirotecnia.

fir·ing pin [fáɪrɪŋ pɪn] s. percusor.

firm [fɝm] adj. firme; fijo; estable; s. firma, razón social (*nombre de una casa comercial*); compañía (*comercial o industrial*); **-ly** adv. firmemente, con firmeza.

fir·ma·ment [fɝməmənt] s. firmamento.

firm·ness [fɝmnɪs] s. firmeza; estabilidad.

first [fɝst] adj. primero; adv. primero, en primer lugar, al principio, the — al principio; **from the —** desde el principio; **first-born** primogénito; **first-class** de primera clase; **first-cousin** primo hermano; **first-rate** de

primera clase; muy bien; **— hand** de primera mano; **— of exchange** primera de cambio.

first aid [fɝst éd] s. primeros auxilios.

fis·cal [fískl] adj. monetario, económico; **— period** período económico, *Méx.* año natural.

fish [fɪʃ] s. pez; *C.A.* peje; (*for market*) pescado; **— market** pescadería; (*for market*) pescado; **— story** patraña, cuento extravagante o increíble; **neither — nor fowl** ni chicha ni limonada; v. pescar.

fish·er [fíʃɚ] s. pescador.

fish·er·man [fíʃɚmən] s. pescador.

fish·er·y [fíʃɚrɪ] s. pesquera; pesquería, pesca.

fish·hook [fíʃhʊk] s. anzuelo.

fish·ing [fíʃɪŋ] s. pesca, pesquería; **— rod** caña de pescar; **— tackle** avíos o enseres de pescar; **to go — ir de pesca.

fis·sure [fíʃɚ] s. grieta, hendedura, *Am.* rajadura.

fist [fɪst] s. puño; **to shake one's — at** amenazar con el puño.

fit [fɪt] adj. (*proper*) apto; a propósito, propio, conveniente; (*healthy*) sano, de buena salud, en buen estado; capaz; **— to be tied** frenético; **not to see — to do it** no tener a bien hacerlo; s. talle (*de un traje*); ajuste; encaje (*de una pieza en otra*); ataque, convulsión; **— of anger** acceso, arrebato o arranque de cólera; **by -s and starts** espasmódicamente; **that suit is a good —** ese traje le entalla (*o* le viene) bien; v. ajustar(se); adaptar; encajar(se), caber (en); acomodar; entallar (*un vestido*); venir bien (*un vestido, zapatos, sombrero, etc.*); ser a propósito para, ser propio para; capacitar, preparar; **to — in with** armonizar con; llevarse bien con; **to — out** equipar, proveer; **it does not — the facts** no está de acuerdo con los hechos; no hace al caso.

fit·ness [fítnɪs] s. aptitud; capacidad; conveniencia; propiedad (*de una idea, de una palabra, etc.*); **physical —** buena salud.

fit·ting [fítɪŋ] adj. propio, apropiado; a propósito, conveniente; s. ajuste; **dress —** prueba de un traje o vestido; **-s** avíos, guarniciones, accesorios.

five [faɪv] num. cinco.

fix [fɪks] v. (*repair*) remendar; componer; reparar; ajustar; arreglar; (*prearrange*) fijar; asegurar; **to — up** arreglar(se); componer(se); s. apuro, aprieto.

fixed [fɪkst] adj. fijo, firme.

fix·ed·ly [fíksɪdlɪ] adv. de hito en hito; fijamente.

fix·ture [fíksʃɚ] s. (*thing*) accesorio fijo; (*person*) persona firmemente establecida (*en un sitio o empleo*); muebles y enseres; **electric light -s** instalaciones eléctricas (*como brazos de lámparas, arañas*).

fiz·zle out [fízl aʊt] v. hacer fiasco, fracasar.

flab·by [flǽbɪ] adj. blanducho.

flag [flæg] s. bandera, banderola; **— lily** flor de lis; v. hacer señas con banderola; adornar con banderas; decaer, debilitarse, menguar, flaquear.

fla·grant [flǽgrənt] adv. flagrante, notorio, escandaloso.

flag·staff [flǽgstæf] s. asta de bandera.

flag·stone [flǽgston] s. losa.

flair [fler] s. instinto, penetración, cacumen; disposición o aptitud natural.

flak [flæk] s. fuego antiaéreo; crítica abusiva.

flake [flek] s. copo (*de nieve*); escama; hojuela; **corn -s** hojuelas de maíz; v. descostrarse, descascararse.

flam·boy·ant [flæmbɔ́jənt] adj. rimbombante; flameante.

flame [flem] s. llama; flama; **— thrower** lanzallamas; v. llamear, flamear, echar llamas; inflamar(se); enardecer(se).

flam·ing [flémɪŋ] *adj.* llameante; flameante; encendido; ardiente, apasionado; — **red** rojo encendido.

flank [flæŋk] *s.* flanco; costado; lado; (*animal*) ijar (*de un animal*); *v.* flanquear; rodear.

flan·nel [flǽnl] *s.* franela.

flap [flæp] *s.* (*thing*) aleta; cubierta (*del bolsillo*); (*action*) golpeteo; aleteo; *v.* golpetear; aletear, batir (*las alas*); hojear con violencia (*las páginas*).

flare [flɛr] *s.* llamarada; llama; arranque (*de ira*); vuelo (*de una falda*); *v.* llamear, echar llamaradas; tener vuelo (*una falda*); **to** — **up** enfurecerse; encenderse; **the illness -ed up** recrudeció la enfermedad.

flash [flæʃ] *s.* rayo; destello, llamarada; fogonazo; — **of hope** rayo de esperanza; — **of lightning** relámpago; — **of wit** agudeza; — **bulb** bombilla de destello; bombilla flash; **in a** — en un instante; **news** — última noticia (*enviada por radio o telégrafo*); *v.* relampaguear; destellar; brillar; centellear; radiar o telegrafiar (*noticias*); **to** — **by** pasar como un relámpago.

flash·ing [flǽʃɪŋ] *s.* relampagueo, centello; *adj.* relumbrante; flameante.

flash·light [flǽʃlaɪt] *s.* linterna eléctrica.

flash·y [flǽʃɪ] *adj.* relumbrante; llamativo, de relumbrón, ostentoso; chillante, chillón (*dícese de los colores*).

flask [flæsk] *s.* frasco.

flat [flæt] *adj.* (*no curves*) plano, llano, chato; (*smashed*) aplastado; (*tasteless*) insípido; monótono; (*without air*) desinflado; — **denial** negativa terminante; — **note** nota desentonada; — **rate** precio o número redondo; **D** — re bemol (*nota musical*); — **car** vagón de plataforma; **to be** — **broke** estar completamente pelado, estar sin dinero; **to fall** — caer de plano; caer mal (*un discurso, chiste, etc.*); **to sing** — desafinarse, cantar desentonadamente; **to refuse -ly** negarse absolutamente; *s.* plano; palma (*de la mano*); apartamento, departamento, piso; bemol (*en música*).

flat·iron [flǽtaɪən] *s.* plancha.

flat·ness [flǽtnɪs] *s.* llanura; lisura; insipidez; desafinamiento (*en música*).

flat·ten [flǽtn] *v.* aplastar(se); aplanar(se); allanar(se).

flat·ter [flǽtər] *v.* lisonjear; adular.

flat·ter·er [flǽtərər] *s.* lisonjero, adulador.

flat·ter·ing [flǽtərɪŋ] *adj.* lisonjero, halagüeño, adulador.

flat·ter·y [flǽtərɪ] *s.* lisonja, halago; adulación.

flat·u·lence [flǽtjuləns] *s.* hinchazón, flatulencia.

flaunt [flɔnt] *v.* ostentar; hacer gala de.

fla·vor [flévər] *s.* sabor; gusto; (*seasoning*) condimento; *v.* sazonar; dar sabor a; condimentar.

fla·vor·less [flévərlɪs] *adj.* insípido, sin sabor.

flaw [flɔ] *s.* defecto; falta; tacha; imperfección.

flaw·less [flɔ́lɪs] *adj.* sin tacha, intachable, irreprochable; perfecto.

flax [flæks] *s.* lino.

flay [fle] *s.* desollar.

flea [fli] *s.* pulga.

fled [flɛd] *pret. & p.p. de* **flee.**

flee [fli] *v.* huir; huir de.

fleece [flis] *s.* vellón, lana; *v.* trasquilar, esquilar; despojar, estafar, defraudar.

fleet [flit] *s.* flota; (*navy*) armada; *adj.* veloz.

fleet·ing [flítɪŋ] *adj.* fugaz, transitorio, pasajero, efímero.

Flem·ish [flémɪʃ] *adj.* flamenco; *s.* flamenco, idioma

flamenco; **the** — los flamencos.

flesh [flɛʃ] *s.* carne; — **and blood** carne y hueso; — **color** color encarnado; **in the** — en persona.

flesh·y [flɛ́ʃɪ] *adj.* carnoso; gordo, gordiflón.

flew [flu] *pret. de* **fly.**

flex·i·bil·i·ty [flɛksəbflətɪ] *s.* flexibilidad.

flex·i·ble [flɛ́ksəbl] *adj.* flexible.

flick·er [flfkər] *s.* titilación, parpadeo, luz trémula; temblor momentáneo (*de emoción*); aleteo; especie de pájaro carpintero; *v.* titilar; temblar; parpadear; vacilar; aletear; **to** — **one's eyelash** pestañear.

fli·er [fláɪər] *s.* volador; aviador; (*train*) tren rápido.

flight [flaɪt] *s.* vuelo; bandada (*de pájaros*); escuadrilla (*de aviones*); fuga, huída; — **of stairs** tramo de escalera; **to put to** — poner en fuga.

flim·sy [flfmzɪ] *adj.* endeble, débil; tenue; quebradizo; frágil; baladí; **a** — **excuse** una excusa baladí.

fling [flɪŋ] *v.* arrojar(se), lanzar(se); tirar; echar; **to** — **open (shut)** abrir (cerrar) de golpe; *s.* tiro; tirada, lanzamiento; tentativa; **to go out on a** — irse a echar una cana al aire.

flint [flɪnt] *s.* pedernal.

flip [flɪp] *v.* arrojar, lanzar al aire; sacudir; dar un dedazo.

flip·pan·cy [flfpənsɪ] *s.* ligereza; frivolidad; impertinencia; petulancia.

flip·pant [flfpənt] *adj.* ligero (*en sus acciones y modales*), ligero de cascos; frívolo; impertinente; petulante.

flirt [flɝt] *s.* coqueta; coquetón, coquetona; *v.* coquetear, flirtear.

flir·ta·tion [flɝtéʃən] *s.* coquetería; **to carry on a** — coquetear.

flit [flɪt] *v.* pasar velozmente; volar; revolotear.

float [flot] *s.* boya; cosa flotante, flotador; (*fishing*) corcho (*de una caña de pescar*); balsa; (*parade*) carro o carroza (*de procesiones, fiestas, etc.*); *v.* flotar; sobrenadar; boyar; poner a flote; lanzar al mercado (*una nueva emisión de valores, bonos, etc.*).

flock [flak] *s.* bandada (*de pájaros, niños, etc.*); rebaño, grey; manada (*de animales*); grupo; — **of people** gentío, muchedumbre; *v.* agruparse; congregarse; **to** — **to** acudir juntos (*o* en bandadas) a; **to** — **together** andar juntos, volar en bandadas, ir en grupo.

flog [flag] *v.* azotar.

flood [flʌd] *s.* inundación; diluvio; avenida (*de agua*), crecida, creciente; torrente; — **gate** compuerta (*de una presa*); esclusa (*de un canal*); — **light** reflector; proyector de luz; — **tide** flujo (*o* marea ascendiente); *v.* inundar.

floor [flor] *s.* (*surface*) suelo; piso; (*story*) piso; (*bottom*) fondo; **to have the** — tener la palabra; *v.* solar; entarimar, enladrillar, enlosar; echar al suelo, derribar; asombrar.

flop [flap] *v.* (*flap*) caer o colgar flojamente; aletear; menearse; (*throw*) lanzar; dejar caer; (*fail*) fracasar; fallar; **to** — **down** dejarse caer; desplomarse, tumbarse; **to** — **over** voltear(se); dar vueltas; *s.* fracaso.

flop·py disk [flápɪ dɪsk] *s.* (*computer*) disco flexible.

flo·rist [flórɪst] *s.* florero, florera; **-'s shop** florería.

floss [flɔs] *s.* seda floja; pelusa; fibra sedosa; **dental** — seda dental.

floun·der [fláundər] *v.* patalear (*en el lodo, nieve, etc.*); forcejear (*por salir del lodo, nieve, o cualquier aprieto*); revolcarse; tropezar, cometer errores; *s.* lenguado (*pez*).

flour [flaʊr] *s.* harina.

flour·ish [flɔ́ːrɪʃ] v. (prosper) florecer, prosperar, medrar; (blandish) blandir; agitar en el aire; s. floreo; adorno o rasgo caprichoso; ostentación; (with the signature) rúbrica.

flour·y [fláʊrɪ] adj. harinoso.

flow [flo] s. flujo; corriente;—**chart** (computer) diagrama de flujo; — **of words** torrente de palabras; v. fluir; correr; flotar, ondear; **to — into** desembocar en; **to be -ing with riches** nadar en la abundancia.

flow·er [fláʊɚ] s. flor; — **bed** cuadro de jardín; — **vase** florero; v. florecer, Am. florear.

flow·er·pot [fláʊrpɑt] s. N. Esp. tiesto, And. Am. maceta.

flow·er·y [fláʊrɪ] adj. florido.

flow·ing [flóɪŋ] adj. (liquid) fluído, corriente, fluente; (clothing) suelto, ondeante.

flown [flon] p.p. de **to fly.**

flu [flu] s. influenza, gripe.

fluc·tu·ate [flʌ́ktʃʊet] s. fluctuar.

fluc·tu·a·tion [flʌ̀ktʃʊéʃən] s. fluctuación.

flue [flu] s. cañón (de chimenea); tubo de escape.

flu·en·cy [flúənsɪ] s. fluidez; labia.

flu·ent [flúənt] adj. fluente, fluído; **to speak -ly** hablar con facilidad.

fluff [flʌf] v. mullir; esponjar.

fluff·y [flʌ́fɪ] adj. mullido, suave, blando; cubierto de vello o plumón; — **hair** pelo esponjado o esponjoso.

flu·id [flúɪd] adj. & s. flúido.

flung [flʌŋ] pret. & p.p. de **to fling.**

flunk [flʌŋk] s. reprobación (en un examen o asignatura); v. reprobar, suspender (en un examen); salir mal, fracasar o fallar (en un examen).

flun·ky [flʌ́ŋkɪ] s. lacayo; ayudante servil; zalamero, persona servil.

flu·o·rine [flúərin] s. fluor.

flur·ry [flɚ́ɪ] s. (weather) ráfaga; nevisca; (action) agitación.

flush [flʌʃ] s. (face) sonrojo, rubor, bochorno; (liquid) flujo rápido; (cards) flux (de naipes); adj. lleno; rico; parejo, al mismo nivel; — **with** a flor de, a ras de; v. sonrojar(se), ruborizar(se), poner(se) colorado; hacer rebosar (de agua); **to — out** vaciar (un depósito), enjuagar.

flute [flut] s. flauta; (column) estría (de una columna); v. acanalar, estriar (una columna).

flut·ter [flʌ́tɚ] s. aleteo; agitación; alboroto; (heart) vuelco (del corazón); v. aletear; revolotear; agitar(se); palpitar; menear(se); tremolar (una bandera).

flux [flʌks] s. flujo.

fly [flaɪ] s. mosca; (pants) pliegue (para cubrir botones); bragueta (abertura de los pantalones); **on the** — al vuelo; **to hit a** — pegar una planchita o elevar una palomita (en béisbol); — **swatter** matamoscas; v. volar; pasar velozmente; huir; ondear; enarbolar (una bandera); **to — at** lanzarse sobre; **to — away** volar, irse, escaparse; **to — off the handle** perder los estribos (o la paciencia); **to — open (shut)** abrirse (cerrarse) de repente; **to — up in anger** montar en cólera.

fly·er = **flier.**

fly·leaf [fláɪlif] s. guarda (hoja en blanco al principio y al fin de un libro).

foam [fom] s. espuma; v. espumar, hacer espuma.

fo·cus [fókəs] s. foco; distancia focal; v. enfocar(se).

fod·der [fɑ́dɚ] s. forraje.

foe [fo] s. enemigo.

fog [fɑg] s. niebla, neblina, bruma; velo, nube (en una película o fotografía); — **horn** sirena; v. anublar, ofuscar, obscurecer; ponerse brumoso; velar(se) (una película).

fog·gy [fɑ́gɪ] adj. brumoso, nublado; obscuro, confuso.

foil [fɔɪl] s. oropel, hojuela, laminita de metal; (sword) florete (de esgrima); realce, contraste; **tin** — hojuela de estaño; v. frustrar.

fold [fold] s. (double over) pliegue, doblez; (enclosure) redil; grey; **three** — tres veces; **hundred** — cien veces; v. doblar(se); plegar(se); envolver; **to — one's arms** cruzarse de brazos.

fold·er [fóldɚ] s. (pamphlet) folleto, circular; (holder) papelera; pliego, carpeta, plegadera (máquina para plegar).

fold·ing [fóldɪŋ] adj. plegadizo; — **chair** silla plegadiza, silla de tijera; — **machine** plegadora, máquina plegadora; — **screen** biombo.

fo·li·age [fólɪɪdʒ] s. follaje, fronda.

fo·li·o [fólɪo] s. folio; infolio, libro en folio; pliego; — **edition** edición en folio.

folk [fok] s. gente; pueblo; **-s** parientes, allegados; familia; personas; amigos (vocativo familiar); adj. popular, del pueblo; — **dance** danza o baile tradicional; (regional) — **lore** folklore; cuentos, leyendas y tradiciones populares; — **song** canción popular, canción típica o tradicional; — **music** música del pueblo; música tradicional.

fol·low [fálo] v. seguir; ejercer (un oficio o profesión); seguir el hilo de (un argumento); seguirse (como consecuencia); **to — suit** jugar el mismo palo (en naipes); seguir el ejemplo, imitar.

fol·low·er [fálowɚ] s. seguidor; imitador; partidario.

fol·low·ing [fálowɪŋ] s. séquito, comitiva, partidarios; adj. siguiente; subsiguiente.

fol·ly [fálɪ] s. locura; necedad, tontería; desatino.

fo·ment [fomént] v. fomentar.

fond [fɑnd] adj. aficionado (a); amigo (de); amante (de), encariñado (con); cariñoso, afectuoso; tierno; **to be — of** querer a (una persona); estar encariñado con, ser aficionado a; gustar de (algo); **-ly** adv. cariñosamente, afectuosamente.

fon·dle [fándl] v. acariciar.

fond·ness [fándnɪs] s. cariño, afecto; afición.

font [fɑnt] s. pila bautismal; fuente.

food [fud] s. alimento, sustento; comida.

food·stuff [fúdstʌf] s. alimento; producto alimenticio; comestibles.

fool [ful] s. tonto, necio, zonzo; (clown) payaso; **to play the** — payasear, hacer el payaso; v. chasquear, chancear(se); bromear, embromar; engañar; **to — away the time** malgastar el tiempo.

fool·ish [fúlɪʃ] adj. tonto; necio, bobo, zonzo.

fool·ish·ness [fúlɪʃnɪs] s. tontería, necedad, bobería.

foot [fut] s. pie; pata (de animal); **on** — a pie; — **soldier** soldado de infantería; **to put one's** — **in it** meter la pata; v. andar a pie; **to** — **it** andar a pie; **to** — **the bill** pagar la cuenta; sufragar los gastos.

foot·ball [fútbɔl] s. fútbol, football.

foot·hold [fúthold] s. arraigo; puesto establecido.

foot·ing [fútɪŋ] s. base; posición firme; **to be on a friendly** — **with** tener relaciones amistosas con; **to lose one's** — perder pie.

foot·lights [fútlaɪts] s. pl. candilejas (del teatro); tablas, teatro.

foot·man [fútmən] s. lacayo.

foot·note [fútnot] s. nota al pie de una página.

foot·path [fútpæθ] s. vereda, senda, trocha (para gente de a pie).

foot·print [fútprɪnt] s. huella, pisada.

foot·step [fútstɛp] s. (action) pisada, paso; (trace)

huella; **to follow in the -s of** seguir las pisadas o huellas de.
foot·stool [fútstul] *s.* banquillo, taburete, escabel.
fop [fɑp] *s.* currutaco.
for [fɔr] *prep.* por; para; — **all of her intelligence** a pesar de su inteligencia; — **feat that** por miedo (de) que; — **the present** por el presente, por ahora; **as** — **him** en cuanto a él; **to know** — **a fact** saber de cierto, saber de hecho; **to pay him** — **it** pagárselo; **to thank him** — **it** agradecérselo; *conj.* porque, pues.
for·age [fɔ́rɪdʒ] *s.* forraje; *v.* forrajear; dar forraje a.
for·ay [fɔ́re] *s.* correría, incursión; saqueo; *v.* pillar, saquear.
for·bade [fɚbǽd] *pret. de* **to forbid.**
for·bear [fɔ́rbɛr] *s.* antepasado; [fɔrbɛ́r] *v.* abstenerse de; tener paciencia.
for·bid [fɚbíd] *v.* prohibir; vedar.
for·bid·den [fɚbídn̩] *adj.* prohibido; vedado; *p.p. de* **to forbid.**
for·bid·ding [fɚbídɪŋ] *adj.* austero, reservado; pavoroso; impenetrable.
for·bore [fɔrbór] *pret. de* **to forbear.**
for·borne [fɔrbórn] *p.p. de* **to forbear.**
force [fors] *s.* fuerza; (group) cuerpo (*de policía, de empleados, etc.*); **in** — en vigor, vigente; **armed -s** fuerzas armadas; *v.* forzar, obligar; **to** — **one's way** abrirse paso por fuerza; **to** — **out** echar por fuerza, echar a la fuerza.
forced [forst] *adj.* forzado.
force·ful [fórsfəl] *adj.* vigoroso; enérgico.
for·ceps [fɔ́rsəps] *s.* gatillo (*tenazas para sacar muelas*); pinzas.
for·ci·ble [fɔ́rsəbl̩] *adj.* (*strong*) fuerte, enérgico; potente; eficaz; (*by force*) violento; hecho a la fuerza; **forcibly** *adv.* fuertemente; con energía; forzosamente; por fuerza.
ford [ford] *s.* vado; *v.* vadear.
fore [for] *adj.* anterior, delantero; (*ship*) de proa; *s.* frente; puesto delantero; *adv.* delante, hacia adelante; *interj.* ¡cuidado! (*dícese en el campo de golf*).
fore·arm [fórɑrm] *s.* antebrazo.
fore·bode [forbód] *v.* presagiar; presentir.
fore·bod·ing [forbódɪŋ] *s.* presentimiento; presagio.
fore·cast [fórkæst] *s.* pronóstico; [forkǽst] *v.* pronosticar; predecir; *pret. & p.p. de* **to forecast.**
fore·clo·sure [forklóʒjur] *s.* juicio hipotecario.
fore·fa·ther [fórfɑðɚ] *s.* antepasado.
fore·fin·ger [fórfɪŋgɚ] *s.* (dedo) índice.
fore·foot [fórfʊt] *s.* pata delantera, mano (*de cuadrúpedo*).
fore·go [forgó] *v.* abstenerse de.
fore·gone [forgɔ́n] *p.p. de* **to forego; a** — **conclusion** una conclusión inevitable.
fore·ground [fórgraʊnd] *s.* frente, primer plano, primer término.
fore·head [fɔ́rɪd] *s.* frente (*f.*).
for·eign [fɔ́rɪn] *adj.* extranjero; (*not local*) foráneo; (*strange*) extraño; — **to his nature** ajeno a su índole; — **office** ministerio de relaciones exteriores; departamento de negocios extranjeros; — **trade** comercio exterior; **foreign-born** extranjero de nacimiento; — **exchange** divisas, cambio extranjero.
for·eign·er [fɔ́rɪnɚ] *s.* extranjero; forastero.
fore·lock [fórlɑk] *s.* guedeja.
fore·man [fórmən] *s.* capataz; (*jury*) presidente (*de un jurado*); *Méx., C.A., Ven., Col.* caporal (*de un rancho o hacienda*); *Ríopl.* capataz.
fore·most [fórmost] *adj.* (*first*) primero; delantero;

(*most important*) principal, más notable, más distinguido.
fore·noon [fornún] *s.* (la) mañana.
fore·run·ner [forrʌ́nɚ] *s.* precursor; presagio.
fore·saw [forsɔ́] *pret. de* **to foresee.**
fore·see [forsí] *s.* prever.
fore·seen [forsín] *p.p. de* **to foresee** previsto.
fore·sight [fórsaɪt] *s.* previsión; **-ed** precavido.
for·est [fɔ́rɪst] *s.* bosque, selva; — **ranger** guardabosques; *v.* arbolar, plantar de árboles.
for·stall [forstɔ́l] *v.* prevenir; madrugar.
for·est·er [fɔ́rɪstɚ] *s.* guardabosques; silvicultor; habitante de un bosque.
for·est·ry [fɔ́rɪstrɪ] *s.* silvicultura.
fore·tell [fortɛ́l] *v.* predecir, pronosticar, presagiar.
fore·told [fortóld] *pret. & p.p. de* **to foretell.**
for·ev·er [fɚɛ́vɚ] *adv.* por (*o* para) siempre.
for·feit [fɔ́rfɪt] *s.* multa; pena; prenda perdida; **game of -s** juego de prendas; *v.* perder, perder el derecho a.
for·gave [fɚgév] *pret. de* **to forgive.**
forge [fɔrdʒ] *s.* fragua; forja; *v.* fraguar; forjar; falsear, falsificar; **to** — **ahead** abrirse paso; avanzar.
for·ger·y [fɔ́rdʒɚrɪ] *s.* falsificación.
for·get [fɚgɛ́t] *v.* olvidar; olvidarse de; **to** — **oneself** cometer un desmán impensadamente; perder el tino o la paciencia.
for·get·ful [fɚgɛ́tfəl] *adj.* olvidadizo; negligente.
for·get·ful·ness [fɚgɛ́tfəlnɪs] *s.* olvido; negligencia.
for·get-me-not [fɚgɛ́tmɪnat] *s.* nomeolvides.
for·give [fɚgív] *v.* perdonar.
for·giv·en [fɚgívən] *p.p. de* **to forgive.**
for·give·ness [fɚgívnɪs] *s.* perdón.
for·giv·ing [fɚgívɪŋ] *adj.* perdonador, misericordioso, de buen corazón.
for·got [fɚgát] *pret. & p.p. de* **to forget.**
for·got·ten [fɚgátn̩] *p.p. de* **to forget.**
fork [fɔrk] *s.* tenedor, *Méx., Col., Ven., Andes* trinche; (*hay*) horquilla (*para heno*); horcón; bifurcación; *v.* bifurcarse; levantar o arrojar (*heno*) con horquilla.
for·lorn [fɚlɔ́rn] *adj.* desamparado, desdichado.
form [fɔrm] *s.* forma; (*state*) condición, estado; **blank** — blanco, forma en blanco, *Méx., Ven., Col., S.A.* esqueleto; *v.* formar(se).
for·mal [fɔ́rml̩] *adj.* formal, perteneciente a la forma; convencional, ceremonioso; — **party** reunión de etiqueta; **-ly** *adv.* formalmente, con ceremonia, solemnemente.
for·mal·i·ty [fɔrmǽlətɪ] *s.* formalidad, ceremonia; formalismo.
for·mat [fɔ́rmæt] *s.* (*computer*) formato; **formatting** formateo; *v.* formatear.
for·ma·tion [fɔrméʃən] *s.* formación.
for·ma·tive [fɔ́rmətɪv] *formativo.*
for·mer [fɔ́rmɚ] *adj.* primero, precedente, anterior; antiguo; **in** — **times** en otro tiempo, en días de antaño, antiguamente, anteriormente; **the** — aquél (aquélla, aquéllos, aquéllas); **-ly** *adv.* anteriormente; antes, en tiempos pasados.
for·mi·da·ble [fɔ́rmɪdəbl̩] *adj.* formidable.
for·mu·la [fɔ́rmjələ] *s.* fórmula.
for·mu·late [fɔ́rmjəlet] *v.* formular.
for·sake [fɚsék] *v.* desamparar; abandonar.
for·sak·en [fɚsékən] *p.p. de* **to forsake &** *adj.* desamparado, abandonado.
for·sook [fɔrsúk] *pret. de* **to forsake.**
for·swear [fɔrswɛ́r] *v.* abjurar.
fort [fort] *s.* fuerte, fortín, fortaleza.
forth [forθ] *adv.* adelante; hacia adelante; **to go** —

347

for-fre

salir; **and so** — etcétera, y así succesivamente.
forth·com·ing [fórθkʌ́mɪŋ] *adj.* venidero, próximo;
funds will not be — **until** no habrá fondos
disponibles hasta.
forth·with [forθwíθ] *adv.* en seguida, pronto, al
punto.
for·ti·fi·ca·tion [fɔrtəfəkéʃən] *s.* fortificación.
for·ti·fy [fɔ́rtəfaɪ] *v.* fortificar; fortalecer.
for·ti·tude [fɔ́rtətjud] *s.* fortaleza.
fort·night [fɔ́rtnaɪt] quincena, quince días, dos
semanas.
for·tress [fɔ́rtrɪs] *s.* fortaleza, fuerte.
for·tu·i·tous [fɔrtjúətəs] *adj.* fortuito; inopinado,
inesperado.
for·tu·nate [fɔ́rtʃənɪt] *adj.* afortunado. **-ly** *adv.*
afortunadamente, por fortuna.
for·tune [fɔ́rtʃən] *s.* fortuna; — **teller** agorero,
adivino.
for·ty [fɔ́rtɪ] *num.* cuarenta.
fo·rum [fórəm] *s.* foro; tribunal; ateneo.
for·ward [fɔ́rwɚd] *adj.* (*leading*) delantero;
(*progressive*) precoz; progresista; (*daring*) atrevido;
descarado; *adv.* adelante, hacia adelante; *v.*
transmitir; despachar; reenviar; reexpedir, **to** — **a**
plan fomentar un plan.
fos·sil [fɑ́sl] *adj.* fósil; anticuado; *s.* fósil.
fos·ter [fɔ́stɚ] *v.* criar, nutrir; fomentar; promover;
adj. putativo; adoptivo.
fought [fɔt] *pret.* & *p.p. de* **to fight.**
foul [faʊl] *adj.* sucio; asqueroso; puerco, cochino;
fétido; vil; injusto; — **air** aire viciado; — **ball**
pelota foul (*en béisbol*); — **mouthed** mal hablado,
obsceno; — **play** juego sucio; fraude; violencia; —
weather mal tiempo; *s.* mala jugada (*contraria a
las reglas del juego*), trampa, *Méx.* chapuza, foul;
v. ensuciar; violar (*las reglas de un juego*); *Am.*
pegar un foul (*en béisbol*).
found [faʊnd] *v.* fundar, establecer; *pret.* & *p.p de*
to find.
foun·da·tion [faʊndéʃən] *s.* fundación; base,
fundamento; dotación.
foun·der [fáʊndɚ] *s.* fundador; fundidor (*de
metales*); *v.* zozobrar, irse a pique; fracasar;
tropezar; hacer zozobrar.
foun·dry [fáʊndrɪ] *s.* fundición.
foun·tain [fáʊntn̩] *s.* fuente; manantial; — **pen** pluma
(de) fuente, pluma estilográfica.
four [for] *num.* cuatro.
four·score [fórskór] *adj.* cuatro veintenas, ochenta.
four·teen [fortín] *num.* catorce.
fourth [forθ] *adj.* cuarto; *s.* cuarto, cuarta parte; **the
Fourth of July** el cuarto de julio.
fowl [faʊl] *s.* ave; gallo, gallina; pollo.
fox [fɑks] *s.* zorra; zorro; persona astuta.
fox·y [fɑ́ksɪ] *adj.* zorro, zorruno, astuto.
frac·tion [frǽkʃən] *s.* fracción; quebrado.
frac·ture [frǽktʃɚ] *s.* fractura; quiebra; rotura; *v.*
fracturar; quebrar, romper.
frag·ile [frǽdʒəl] *adj.* frágil.
frag·ment [frǽgmənt] *s.* fragmento.
fra·grance [frégrəns] *s.* fragancia.
fra·grant [frégrənt] *adj.* fragante, oloroso.
frail [frel] *adj.* frágil; endeble, débil.
frail·ty [frélti] *s.* debilidad, flaqueza.
frame [frem] *s.* armazón, armadura, esqueleto;
estructura; (*picture*) marco; (*of mind*) disposición
(*de ánimo*); **embroidery** — bastidor para bordar;
— **house** casa con armazón de madera; *v.* formar,
forjar; fabricar; enmarcar (*poner en marco*);
inventar; **to** — **someone** conspirar contra una
persona; **to** — **up a charge** forjar un cargo o

acusación.
frame·work [frémwɚk] *s.* armazón, esqueleto;
estructura.
franc [fræŋk] *s.* franco (*moneda francesa*).
fran·chise [frǽntʃaɪz] *s.* (*privilege*) franquicia;
derecho o privilegio político; (*vote*) sufragio, voto.
fran·ci·um [frǽnsiəm] *s.* francio.
frank [fræŋk] *adj.* franco, sincero; **very** — francote;
s. sello de franqueo; franquicia de correos; *v.*
franquear, despachar, enviar (*carta*) exenta de
franqueo; **franking machine** máquina
franqueadora.
frank·furt·er [frǽŋkfɚtɚ] *s.* salchicha.
frank·ness [frǽŋknɪs] *s.* franqueza, sinceridad.
fran·tic [frǽntɪk] *adj.* frenético; **-ally** *adv.*
frenéticamente.
fra·ter·nal [frətɚnl] *adj.* fraternal.
fra·ter·ni·ty [frətɚnatɪ] *s.* fraternidad; confraternidad.
frat·er·nize [frǽtɚnaɪz] *v.* fraternizar.
fraud [frɔd] *s.* fraude, engaño; trampa, *Méx.*
chapuza; (*person*) trampista, tramposo.
fraud·u·lent [frɔ́dʒələnt] *adj.* fraudulento.
fray [fre] *s.* reyerta, riña, pelea, alboroto; raedura; *v.*
raer(se); deshilacharse.
frayed [fred] *adj.* raído, deshilachado.
freak [frik] *s.* (*whim*) capricho; (*rarity*) rareza,
hombre o cosa rara; (*monstrosity*) monstruosidad,
fenómeno.
freck·le [frékl] *s.* peca; *v.* ponerse pecoso.
freck·led [frékld] *adj.* pecoso.
freck·ly [frékli] *adj.* pecoso.
free [fri] *adj.* (*not bound*) libre; suelto; (*gratis*)
gratuito; exento; (*generous*) liberal, generoso; —
of charge gratis; — **on board (f.o.b.)** libre a
bordo; — **port** puerto franco; **postage** — franco
de porte; **to give someone a** — **hand** dar rienda
suelta o libertad de acción a una persona; — **hand
drawing** dibujo a pulso, dibujo a mano; —
thinker libre pensador; — **lance** a destajo; *adv.*
libremente; gratis, de balde; *v.* librar; libertar;
soltar; eximir; **-ly** *adv.* libremente; con soltura.
free·dom [frídəm] *s.* libertad; libre uso; exención.
freeze [friz] *v.* helar(se); congelar(se); (*stop*) bloquear
s. bloqueo.
freez·ing [frizɪŋ] *adj.* helado, glacial; — **point** punto
de congelación.
freight [fret] *s.* flete; carga; — **train** tren de carga,
tren de mercancías; — **yard** patio de carga; **by** —
por carga; *v.* fletar, cargar; enviar por carga.
French [frɛntʃ] *adj.* francés; **to take** — **leave**
marcharse a la francesa, irse sin despedirse; *s.*
francés, idioma francés; **the** — los franceses.
French·man [frɛ́ntʃmən] *s.* francés.
fren·zy [frɛ́nzɪ] *s.* frenesí.
fre·quen·cy [fríkwənsɪ] *s.* frecuencia.
fre·quent [fríkwənt] *adj.* frecuente; *v.* frecuentar; **-ly**
adv. frecuentemente, a menudo.
fresh [frɛʃ] *adj.* (*not stale*) fresco; (*new*) reciente;
nuevo; (*bold*) impertinente, entremetido; — **water**
agua dulce; **-ly** *adv.* frescamente; con frescura;
nuevamente, recientemente; **-ly painted** recién
pintado, acabado de pintar.
fresh·en [frɛ́ʃən] *v.* refrescar(se).
fresh·man [frɛ́ʃmən] *s.* novato, novicio, estudiante
del primer año.
fresh·ness [frɛ́ʃnɪs] *s.* frescura; frescor, fresco;
descaro.
fret [frɛt] *v.* irritar(se); apurarse; estar nervioso;
agitarse; *s.* agitación, apuro, preocupación; traste
(*de guitarra, mandolina, etc.*); — **work** calado.
fret·ful [frɛ́tfəl] *adj.* descontentadizo; malhumorado,

enojadizo; nervioso.

fri·ar [fráɪɚ] s. fraile.

fric·tion [fríkʃən] s. fricción; rozamiento; frotación; desavenencia; — **feed** (*computer*) alimentación por fricción.

Fri·day [fráɪdɪ] s. viernes.

fried [fraɪd] adj. frito; freído; *p.p. de* **to fry.**

friend [frɛnd] s. amigo, amiga.

friend·less [fréndlɪs] adj. sin amigos, solo.

friend·li·ness [fréndlɪnɪs] s. afabilidad; amistad.

friend·ly [fréndlɪ] adj. amistoso, afable, amigable; propicio, favorable; adv. amistosamente.

friend·ship [frénʃɪp] s. amistad.

frig·ate [frígət] s. fragata.

fright [fraɪt] s. espanto, susto; terror; espantajo, **she is a** — es un adefesio.

fright·en [fráɪtn] v. espantar, asustar, atemorizar; **to** — **away** espantar, ahuyentar; **to get -ed** espantarse, asustarse.

fright·ened [fráɪtnd] adj. espantado, asustado.

fright·ful [fráɪtfəl] adj. espantoso, terrible, horroroso.

frig·id [fríd͡ʒɪd] adj. frígido, frío.

fringe [frɪnd͡ʒ] s. fleco; flequillo; orla; — **benefits** beneficios laborales; *Col.* prestaciones sociales; v. adornar con fleco; orlar.

frip·per·y [frípərɪ] s. perifollos, moños, perejiles; cursilería.

frisk [frɪsk] v. retozar, cabriolar, saltar, brincar; (*search*) registrar (*los bolsillos*), *Ven., Méx.* exculcar.

frisk·y [frískɪ] adj. retozón, juguetón.

frit·ter [frítɚ] s. fritura, fruta de sartén; v. **to** — **away** malgastar, desperdiciar poco a poco.

fri·vol·i·ty [frɪvɑ́lətɪ] s. frivolidad.

friv·o·lous [frívələs] adj. frívolo.

fro [fro]: **to and** — de una parte a otra; de aquí para allá.

frock [frɑk] s. vestido (*de mujer*); — **coat** levita.

frog [frɑg] s. rana; broche (*de cordoncillos o galones*); — **in the throat** gallo en la garganta.

frol·ic [frɑ́lɪk] s. retozo, juego; holgorio, diversión; v. retozar, travesear, juguetear.

from [frɑm, frʌm] prep. de; desde; **to take something away** — **a person** quitarle algo a una persona.

front [frʌnt] s. frente (*m.*); (*building*) fachada; frontispicio; **in** — **of** enfrente de; delante de; **shirt** — pechera; adj. delantero; frontal; frontero; **front-wheel drive** tracción delantera; v. hacer frente a; **to** — **towards** mirar hacia; dar a, caer a.

fron·tier [frʌntír] s. frontera; adj. fronterizo.

frost [frɔst] s. escarcha; helada; v. escarchar; helar; cubrir de escarcha.

frost·ing [frɔ́stɪŋ] s. escarcha, (*cooking*) confitura (*para cubrir un pastel*).

frost·y [frɔ́stɪ] adj. escarchado, cubierto de escarcha; helado.

froth [frɔθ] s. espuma; v. espumar, hacer espuma; echar espuma o espumarajos; **to** — **at the mouth** echar espumarajos por la boca; enfurecerse.

frown [fraʊn] s. ceño; entrecejo; v. fruncir el ceño o las cejas; **to** — **at** mirar con ceño; desaprobar (*algo*).

froze [froz] pret. de **to freeze.**

fro·zen [frózn] p.p. de **to freeze;** — **assets** recursos inactivos, *Méx.* activo congelado.

fru·gal [frúgl] adj. frugal.

fruit [frut] s. fruto (*en general*); fruta (*comestible*); **to eat** — comer fruta; — **tree** árbol frutal; v. fructificar, producir frutas.

fruit·ful [frútfəl] adj. fructuoso; productivo; provechoso.

fruit·less [frútlɪs] adj. infructuoso, improductivo, estéril.

frus·trate [frʌ́stret] v. frustrar.

frus·tra·tion [frʌstréʃən] s. frustración.

fry [fraɪ] v. freír(se); s. fritada; **small** — pececillos; gente menuda; **French fries** patatas fritas a la francesa; **-ing pan** sartén.

fudge [fʌd͡ʒ] s. dulce.

fu·el [fjúəl] s. combustible; incentivo.

fu·gi·tive [fjúd͡ʒətɪv] adj. fugitivo; transitorio; s. fugitivo, prófugo.

ful·fill [fʊlfíl] v. cumplir; cumplir con; (*bring about*) realizar; llevar a cabo; llenar (*un requisito*).

ful·fill·ment [fʊlfílmənt] s. cumplimiento.

full [fʊl] adj. lleno; completo; harto; pleno; — **dress** traje de etiqueta; — **moon** plenilunio, luna llena; — **skirt** falda de vuelo entero; — **of fun** muy divertido, muy chistoso; **at** — **speed** a toda velocidad; **in** — completamente; por completo; **to the** — por completo, por entero, totalmente; — **time** tiempo completo, jornada completa; adv. completamente, enteramente; **to know** — **well** saber perfectamente, saber a ciencia cierta; **full-blooded** de raza pura; **full-fledged** hecho y derecho; maduro; completo; **-y** adv. completamente, enteramente, por completo.

full·ness [fʊ́lnɪs] s. plenitud; llenura.

fum·ble [fʌ́mbl] v. tentalear, buscar a tientas; chapucear, no coger la pelota o soltarla al correr.

fume [fjum] v. exhalar vapor o gas; (*rage*) rabiar; **-s** s. pl. vapores, emanaciones, gases.

fu·mi·gate [fjúməget] v. fumigar, sahumar, *Ríopl.* humear.

fun [fʌn] s. diversión; (*joke*) burla, broma, chanza, *Carib., Méx., C.A.* choteo; **for** — en (*o de*) broma; de chanza; de chiste; **full of** — muy divertido; **to have** — divertirse; **to make** — **of** burlarse de, chancearse con, *Carib., Méx., C.A.* chotear, chotearse con; *Ríopl.* jorobar.

func·tion [fʌ́ŋkʃən] s. función; — **key** (*computer*) tecla funcional; v. funcionar.

fund [fʌnd] s. fondo, caudal; **-s** fondos, recursos; **funded debt** deuda consolidada; v. consolidar (*una deuda*); prorrogar el plazo de (*una deuda*).

fun·da·men·tal [fʌndəméntl] adj. fundamental; s. fundamento, principio.

fu·ner·al [fjúnərəl] adj. funeral, fúnebre; s. funeral, exequias, funerales.

fun·gus [fʌ́ŋgəs] s. hongo; fungosidad.

fun·nel [fʌ́nl] s. embudo; humero (*cañón de chimenea*).

fun·ny [fʌ́nɪ] adj. (*comical*) chistoso, cómico, gracioso, divertido; (*odd*) extraño, raro; **the funnies** la sección cómica (*de un periódico*).

fur [fɝ] s. piel (*de animales peludos o lanudos*); sarro (*en la lengua*); — **coat** abrigo de pieles; v. forrar, cubrir o adornar con pieles.

fur·bish [fɝbɪʃ] v. acicalar, pulir.

fu·ri·ous [fjúrɪəs] adj. furioso.

furl [fɝl] v. arrollar, enrollar; plegar.

fur·lough [fɝlo] s. licencia militar; s. dar licencia militar.

fur·nace [fɝnɪs] s. calorífero; **blast** — alto horno.

fur·nish [fɝnɪʃ] v. (*equip*) equipar; amueblar; (*provide*) proveer, suministrar, surtir; **to** — **a room** amueblar un cuarto.

fur·ni·ture [fɝnɪtʃɚ] s. muebles, mobiliario, moblaje, mueblaje.

fur·row [fɝo] s. surco; arruga; v. surcar; arar.

fur·ther [fɝ́ðɚ] *adj.* adicional; más lejano, más remoto; *adv.* además; más; más lejos; *v.* promover, fomentar, adelantar.

fur·ther·more [fɝ́ðɚmor] *adv.* además.

fur·thest [fɝ́ðɪst] *adj.* (el) más lejano, (el) más remoto; *adv.* más lejos.

fur·tive [fɝ́tɪv] *adj.* furtivo.

fu·ry [fjúrɪ] *s.* furia; frenesí.

fuse [fjuz] *s.* fusible; mecha; *v.* fundir(se).

fu·se·lage [fjúzlɪdʒ] *s.* fuselaje.

fu·sion [fjúʒən] *s.* fusión; **nuclear** — fusión nuclear.

fuss [fʌs] *s.* melindre, preocupación inútil; bulla innecesaria; **to make a** — **over someone** darle a alguien demasiada importancia, desvivirse por alguien; *v.* hacer melindres, inquietarse (*por bagatelas*).

fuss·y [fʌ́sɪ] *adj.* melindroso; minucioso (*en demasía*); inquieto, nervioso; — **dress** vestido con demasiados adornos.

fu·tile [fjútl] *adj.* fútil; vano; **futility** *s.* futilidad.

fu·ture [fjútʃɚ] *adj.* futuro; **-s market** mercado de futuros; *s.* futuro; porvenir.

fuzz [fʌz] *s.* vello; pelusa.

fuzz·y [fʌ́zɪ] *adj.* velloso; cubierto de plumón fino; cubierto de pelusa.

G:g

gab [gæb] *v.* charlar, parlotear; *s.* charla; **gift of** — labia, facundia.

gab·ar·dine [gǽbɚdin] *s.* gabardina (*paño*).

gab·ble [gǽbl] *s.* charla, cotorreo; *v.* charlar, cotorrear.

ga·ble [gébl] *s.* gablete (*de un tejado*); — **roof** tejado de caballete o de dos aguas, — **window** ventana con gablete.

gad [gæd] *v.* vagar, callejear; andar de aquí para allá.

gadg·et [gǽdʒɪt] *s.* adminículo, artefacto, chisme, dispositivo.

gag [gæg] *s.* (*obstacle*) mordaza; — **law** ley de la mordaza; (*joke*) broma, burla; morcilla, chiste (*improvisado por un actor*); *v.* amordazar; dar náuseas, hacer vomitar, basquear; interpolar chistes (*en la escena*).

gage *véase* **gauge.**

gai·e·ty [géətɪ] *s.* alegría, viveza, alborozo.

gai·ly [gélɪ] *adv.* alegremente; vistosamente.

gain [gen] *s.* ganancia, provecho; *v.* ganar.

gain·ful [génfl] *adj.* ganancioso.

gait [get] *s.* paso, andadura, marcha.

gale [gel] *s.* ventarrón; — **of laughter** risotada, carcajada, risada.

gall [gɔl] *s.* (*bile*) bilis, hiel; (*bitterness*) amargura; odio; descaro; — **bladder** vesícula; *v.* irritar.

gal·lant [gǽlənt] *adj.* valiente; noble; vistoso; [gəlǽnt] *adj.* galante, atento, cortés; galanteador; *s.* galán.

gal·lant·ry [gǽləntrɪ] *s.* galantería; gallardía, valor.

gal·ler·y [gǽlərɪ] *s.* galería; paraíso, gallinero *del* (*teatro*).

gal·ley [gǽlɪ] *s.* galera; cocina (*de un buque*); — **proof** galerada; — **slave** galeote.

gal·lium [gǽlɪəm] *s.* galio.

gal·lon [gǽlən] *s.* galón (*aproximadamente cuatro litros*).

gal·lop [gǽləp] *s.* galope; *v.* galopar, galopear; ir a galope.

gal·lows [gǽloz] *s.* horca.

gal·osh·es [gəláʃɪz] *s. pl.* chanclos, zapatos fuertes, zapatones.

gal·va·nom·e·ter [gælvənámətɚ] *s.* galvanómetro.

gam·ble [gǽmbl] *v.* jugar, apostar, aventurar (*algo*) en el juego; **to** — **away** perder en el juego; **to** — **everything** jugar el todo por el todo; arriesgarlo todo; *s.* jugada (*en juegos de azar*), apuesta; riesgo.

gam·bol [gǽmbəl] *v.* retozar; cabriolar; juguetear; *s.* retozo, cabriola.

game [gem] *s.* juego; deporte; caza (*animales de caza y su carne*); **to make** — **of** mofarse de, burlarse de; *adj.* valiente, atrevido; resuelto; — **bird** ave de caza.

gam·ut [gǽmət] *s.* gama.

gan·der [gǽndɚ] *s.* ánsar, ganso.

gang [gæŋ] *s.* cuadrilla; pandilla; juego (*de herramientas o máquinas*); *v.* agrupar(se); **to** — **up against** conspirar contra.

gang·plank [gǽŋplæŋk] *s.* plancha, pasamano (*de un buque*), pasarela.

gan·grene [gǽŋgrin] *s.* gangrena; *v.* gangrenar(se).

gang·ster [gǽŋstɚ] *s.* bandolero, bandido, maleante, atracador.

gang·way [gǽŋwe] *s.* paso, pasadizo; plancha; pasamano; portalón (*de un barco*); — ! ¡a un lado! ¡ábranse!

gant·let = **gauntlet.**

gap [gæp] *s.* brecha, abertura; boquete; hueco; intervalo.

gape [gep] *s.* (*breach*) brecha, abertura; (*open jaws*) bostezo; boqueada; *v.* boquear, abrir la boca; estar boquiabierto (*mirando*); estar embobado; bostezar.

ga·rage [gərádʒ] *s.* garaje.

garb [garb] *s.* vestido; vestidura; aspecto, apariencia; *v.* vestir, ataviar.

gar·bage [gárbɪdʒ] *s.* desperdicios, basura.

gar·den [gárdn̩] *s.* jardín; huerta; huerto; *v.* cultivar un jardín.

gar·den·er [gárdnɚ] *s.* jardinero, hortelano, horticultor.

gar·gle [gárgl] *s.* gargarismo, *Am.* gárgaras; *v.* gargarizar, hacer gárgaras, *Am.* gargarear.

gar·land [gárlənd] *s.* guirnalda.

gar·lic [gárlɪk] *s.* ajo.

gar·ment [gármənt] *s.* prenda (*de vestir*).

gar·net [gárnɪt] *s.* granate.

gar·nish [gárnɪʃ] *s.* aderezo; adorno; *v.* aderezar; adornar; guarnecer; (*attach*) embargar; **garnishment** embargo.

gar·ret [gǽrɪt] *s.* desván, buhardilla.

gar·ri·son [gǽrəsn̩] *s.* guarnición; *v.* guarnecer o guarnicionar (*una fortaleza*).

gar·ru·lous [gǽrjələs] *adj.* locuaz, lenguaz, gárrulo.

gar·ter [gártɚ] *s.* liga (*para sujetar las medias*); *v.* sujetar con liga.

gas [gæs] *s.* (*gaseous*) gas; (*petroleum*) gasolina; — **burner** mechero; — **stove** estufa o cocina de gas; — **tear** — gas lacrimante o lacrimógeno; *v.* asfixiar con gas; envenenar con gas.

gas·e·ous [gǽsɪəs] *adj.* gaseoso.

gash [gæʃ] *s.* cuchillada, herida, incisión; *v.* dar una cuchillada, acuchillar.

gas·o·line [gǽslin] *s.* gasolina.

gasp [gæsp] *s.* boqueada; grito sofocado; *v.* boquear; jadear; sofocarse; abrir la boca (*de asombro*).

gas·tric [gǽstrɪk] *adj.* gástrico.

gas·tro·in·tes·ti·nal [gæstrointéstɪnl] *adj.* gastrointestinal.

gate [get] *s.* portón, entrada; puerta; *Ven., Col.*

tranquera (*puerta de trancas*).

gate·way [gétwe] *s.* paso, entrada.

gath·er [gǽðɚ] *v.* recoger; coger; (*unite*) reunir(se), juntar(se); (*deduce*) deducir, colegir; fruncir (*en pliegues*); cobrar (fuerzas); **to — dust** llenarse de polvo, empolvarse; *s.* pliegue.

gath·er·ing [gǽðrɪŋ] *s.* asamblea, reunión; muchedumbre; pliegue.

gaud·y [gɔ́dɪ] *adj.* vistoso, llamativo, chillón, chillante.

gauge [gedʒ] *s.* calibrador; indicador; medidor; instrumento para medir; medida; **manifold —** manómetro; **vacuum —** vacuómetro; calibre (*de un cañón, pistola, etc.*); (*track*) ancho (*del ferrocarril*), *Ven.* trocha; *v.* medir; calibrar; estimar, calcular.

gaunt [gɔnt] *adj.* macilento, demacrado, flaco.

gaunt·let [gɔ́ntlɪt] *s.* guantelete; manopla; **to throw down the —** retar, desafiar.

gauze [gɔz] *s.* gasa; cendal.

gave [gev] *pret. de* **to give.**

gav·el [gǽvl] *s.* mazo del que preside.

gawk [gɔk] *v.* bobear, mirar embobado; *s.* simplón, bobo.

gawk·y [gɔ́kɪ] *adj.* torpe, desmañado; bobo.

gay [ge] *adj.* alegre; vivo; vistoso; festivo; (*homosexual*) homosexual.

gay·e·ty *véase* **gaiety.**

gaze [gez] *s.*mirada (fija); *v.* contemplar, mirar con fijeza, clavar la mirada.

ga·zette [gɔzɛ́t] *s.* gaceta.

gear [gɪr] *s.* (*equipment*) aperos; herramientas; aparejo; equipo; (*wheel*) rueda dentada; (*assembly*) engranaje (*de ruedas dentadas*); **foot —** calzado; **low —** primera velocidad; **steering —** mecanismo de dirección; **to be in —** estar engranado; **to shift —** cambiar de engrane o velocidad; **to throw in —** engranar; **to throw out of —** desengranar; **— shift lever** palanca de engrane, palanca de cambios; *v.* engranar.

geese [gis] *pl. de* **goose.**

Gei·ger count·er [gáɪgɚkáʊntɚ] *s.* contador (de) Geiger.

gel·a·tin [dʒɛ́lɔtn̩] *s.* gelatina, jaletina.

gem [dʒɛm] *s.* gema, piedra preciosa; joya, alhaja, panecillo, bollo.

gem·i·nate [dʒɛ́mɔnet] *v.* geminar(se).

gen·der [dʒɛ́ndɚ] *s.* género.

gene [dʒin] *s.* gen.

ge·ne·al·o·gy [dʒiniǽlɔdʒɪ] *s.* genealogía.

gen·er·al [dʒɛ́nɔrɔl] *adj. & s.* general; **in —** en general, por lo común, por lo general; **— delivery** lista de correo.

gen·er·al·i·ty [dʒɛnɔrǽlɔtɪ] *s.* generalidad.

gen·er·al·ize [dʒɛ́nɔrɔlaɪz] *v.* generalizar.

gen·er·ate [dʒɛ́nɔret] *v.* engendrar; producir; originar.

gen·er·a·tion [dʒɛnɔréʃɔn] *s.* generación; producción.

gen·er·a·tor [dʒɛ́nɚetɚ] *s.* generador.

ge·ner·ic [dʒɔnɛ́rɪk] *adj.* genérico.

gen·er·os·i·ty [dʒɛnɔrásɔtɪ] *s.* generosidad.

gen·er·ous [dʒɛ́nɔrɔs] *adj.* generoso; magnánimo, liberal; amplio; abundante.

ge·net·ics [dʒɔnɛ́tɪks] *s.* genética.

gen·ial [dʒínjɔl] *adj.* genial, afable.

gen·i·tive [dʒɛ́nɔtɪv] *adj. & s.* genitivo.

gen·ius [dʒínjɔs] *s.* genio, ingenio, talento.

gen·teel [dʒɛntíl] *adj.* gentil, cortés; elegante; gallardo.

gen·tile [dʒɛ́ntaɪ] *adj. & s.* gentil.

gen·tle [dʒɛ́ntl̩] *adj.* suave; afable; apacible; manso, gentil.

gen·tle·man [dʒɛ́ntlmɔn] *s.* caballero; **gentlemen** *pl.* caballeros; señores.

gen·tle·man·ly [dʒɛ́ntlmɔnlɪ] *adj.* caballeroso, caballero, cortés.

gen·tle·ness [dʒɛ́ntlnɪs] *s.* suavidad, dulzura, apacibilidad; mansedumbre.

gen·tly [dʒɛ́ntlɪ] *adv.* suavemente; despacio; dulcemente; con ternura; mansamente.

gen·u·ine [dʒɛ́njʊɪn] *adj.* genuino; sincero.

ge·o·graph·i·cal [dʒiɔɡrǽfɪkl̩] *adj.* geográfico.

ge·og·ra·phy [dʒiɑ́ɡrɔfɪ] *s.* geografía.

ge·o·log·i·cal [dʒiɔlɑ́dʒɪkl̩] *adj.* geológico.

ge·ol·o·gy [dʒiɑ́lɔdʒɪ] *s.* geología.

ge·o·met·ric [dʒiɔmɛ́trɪk] *adj.* geométrico.

ge·om·e·try [dʒiɑ́mɔtrɪ] *s.* geometría.

ge·o·phys·ics [dʒiofízɪks] *s.* geofísica.

ge·ra·ni·um [dʒɔéniɔm] *s.* geranio.

germ [dʒɝm] *s.* germen; microbio.

Ger·man [dʒɝmɔn] *adj. & s.* alemán.

ger·mane [dʒɚmén] *adj.* pertinente, relacionado.

ger·ma·ni·um [dʒɝméniɔm] *s.* germanio.

ger·mi·nate [dʒɝmɔnet] *v.* germinar.

ger·und [dʒɛ́rɔnd] *s.* gerundio.

ges·ta·tion [dʒɛstéʃɔn] *s.* gestación.

ges·tic·u·late [dʒɛstíkjɔlet] *v.* gesticular, hacer gestos o ademanes, accionar, manotear.

ges·ture [dʒɛ́stʃɚ] *s.* gesto; ademán; **a mere —** una pura formalidad; *v.* gesticular, hacer gestos.

get [gɛt] *v.* (*obtain*) obtener, adquirir, lograr, conseguir; (*earn*) recibir, ganar; (*reach*) llegar (a); traer; (*catch*) coger, atrapar; preparar (*la lección, la comida, etc.*); **to — long** llevarse bien (*con alguien*); ir pasándolo (*o* ir pasándola); **to — angry** ponerse enojado, enojarse; **to — away** escaparse; irse; **to — down** bajar; **to — ill** ponerse enfermo, enfermar(se); **to — in** entrar; meter(se); llegar; **to — married** casarse; **to — off the train** bajar del tren; apearse del tren; **to — old** envejecer(se); **to — on** subir a; montar; **to — out** salir; irse; sacar; divulgarse (*un secreto*); **to — over** pasar por encima de; recuperarse de (*una enfermedad*); olvidar (*una ofensa*); pasársele a uno (*el susto*); **to — ready** preparar(se); alistar(se); **to — rich** enriquecerse, hacerse rico; **to — rid of** deshacerse de, desprenderse de; **to — through** pasar; terminar; **to — together** reunir(se); ponerse de acuerdo; **to — up** levantarse; **I got him to do it** le persuadí a que lo hiciese; **I (have) got to do it** tengo que hacerlo; **I don't — it** no lo comprendo; **that's what -s me** (*or* **-s my goat**) eso es lo que me irrita.

ghast·ly [gǽstlɪ] *adj.* horrible; pálido, lívido, cadavérico.

ghost [gost] *s.* espectro, fantasma; **the Holy Ghost** el Espíritu Santo; **not to have the — of a notion of** no tener la más remota idea de; **— writer** colaborador anónimo.

ghost·ly [góstlɪ] *adj.* como un espectro; de espectros, de aparecidos.

gi·ant [dʒáɪɔnt] *s.* gigante; *adj.* gigantesco; enorme.

gid·dy [gídɪ] *adj.* ligero de cascos, frívolo; voluble, inconstante; desvanecido; **— speed** velocidad vertiginosa.

gift [gɪft] *s.* regalo, dádiva; don; dote, talento, prenda; donación.

gift·ed [gíftɪd] *adj.* talentoso, de talento.

gi·gan·tic [dʒaɪgǽntɪk] *adj.* gigantesco.

gig·gle [gígl̩] *s.* risita, risilla; risa falsa; *v.* reírse falsamente; reírse sofocando la voz; reír con una risilla afectada.

gild [gɪld] *v.* dorar.

gill [gɪl] s. agalla (*de pez*).

gilt [gɪlt] adj. & s. dorado; *pret. & p.p. de* **to gild.**

gim·mick [gímɪk] s. adminículo.

gin [dʒɪn] s. ginebra (*licor*).

gin·ger [dʒíndʒɚ] s. jengibre; — **ale** cerveza de jengibre.

gin·ger·bread [dʒíndʒɚbrɛd] s. pan de jengibre; ornato de mal gusto.

ging·ham [gíŋəm] s. guinga (*tela de algodón*).

gip·sy *véase* **gypsy.**

gi·raffe [dʒəræf] s. jirafa.

gird [gɝd] v. ceñir; rodear; **to — oneself for** prepararse para.

gir·dle [gɝdl] s. ceñidor; cinto; faja; v. ceñir; fajar; cercar.

girl [gɝl] s. niña; muchacha; joven; chica, moza; criada.

girl·hood [gɝlhʊd] s. niñez; mocedad, juventud.

girl·ish [gɝlɪʃ] adj. pueril; de niña, de muchacha; juvenil.

girt [gɝt] *pret. & p.p. de* **to gird;** v. *véase* **gird.**

girth [gɝθ] s. circunferencia; cincha (*para caballos*); faja; v. cinchar; ceñir.

gist [dʒɪst] s. substancia, esencia.

give [gɪv] v. dar; regalar; (*give in*) ceder; dar de sí; **to — away** regalar; entregar; revelar (*un secreto*); **to — back** devolver; **to — birth** dar a luz, parir; **to — in** ceder; darse por vencido; **to — off** emitir; **to — out** divulgar; repartir; agotarse; **to — up** abandonar; desistir; renunciar a; perder la esperanza; rendir(se); ceder, darse por vencido; — **and take** toma y daca; s. elasticidad.

giv·en [gívən] p.p. de **to give;** adj. (*presented*) (dado); regalado; (*inclined*) adicto, entregado; dispuesto, inclinado; — **name** nombre de pila, nombre de bautismo; — **time** hora determinada; — **that** dada que, supuesto que.

giv·er [gívɚ] s. dador, donador.

gla·cial [gléʃəl] adj. glacial.

gla·cier [gléʃɚ] s. glaciar, helero.

glad [glæd] adj. contento; alegre; **to be — to** alegrarse de, tener mucho gusto en (*o* de); **-ly** adv. alegremente; con mucho gusto; de buena gana.

glad·den [glædn] v. regocijar, alegrar.

glade [gled] s. claro herboso (*en un bosque*).

glad·ness [glædnɪs] s. alegría, gozo.

glam·our [glæmɚ] s. encanto, hechizo; fascinación, embrujo; — **girl** niña hechicera.

glam·or·ous [glæmərəs] adj. fascinador, hechicero.

glance [glæns] s. mirada, vistazo, ojeada; vislumbre; v. echar (*o* dar) un vistazo; vislumbrar; pegar de soslayo; **to — off** rebotar de soslayo (*o* de lado).

gland [glænd] s. glándula.

glare [glɛr] s. (*light*) resplandor, relumbre; (*stare*) mirada furiosa; v. resplandecer, relumbrar; **to — at** mirar enfurecido a.

glass [glæs] s. (*substance*) vidrio; cristal; (*receptacle*) vaso; copa (*de cristal*); (*eye*) lente; **looking —** espejo; **-es** anteojos, lentes, gafas; adj. de vidrio; — **blower** vidriero, soplador de vidrio; — **case** escaparate; vitrina.

glass·ware [glæswɛr] s. vajilla de cristal, cristalería; — **shop** cristalería.

glass·y [glæsɪ] adj. vidrioso.

glau·co·ma [glɔkómə] s. glaucoma.

glaze [glez] s. vidriado; lustre; superficie lustrosa o glaseada; v. vidriar; glasear; lustrar; poner vidrios a.

gla·zier [gléʒɚ] s. vidriero.

gleam [glim] s. destello, rayo, fulgor, viso; v. destellar, fulgurar, centellear.

glean [glin] v. recoger; espigar.

glee [gli] s. regocijo; júbilo; — **club** orfeón, masa coral.

glib [glɪb] adj. locuaz; de mucha labia; — **excuse** excusa fácil.

glide [glaɪd] s. deslizamiento; ligadura (*en música*); planeo (*de un aeroplano*); v. deslizarse; resbalarse; planear (*un aeroplano*).

glid·er [gláɪdɚ] s. deslizador, planeador (*aeroplano*).

glam·mer [glfmɚ] s. vislumbre; viso; titileo; — **of hope** rayo de esperanza; v. titilar, centellear.

glimpse [glɪmps] s. vislumbre; vistazo, ojeada; **to catch a — of** vislumbrar; v. vislumbrar.

glint [glɪnt] s. fulgor, rayo, destello.

glis·ten [glísn] v. relucir, brillar.

glit·ter [glítɚ] s. lustre, brillo, resplandor; v. relumbrar, relucir, brillar.

gloat [glot] v. gozarse (en), deleitarse (en); relamerse (*de gusto*).

globe [glob] s. globo; esfera.

glob·ule [glábjul] s. glóbulo.

gloom [glum] s. lobreguez, sombra; abatimiento, tristeza, melancolía.

gloom·y [glúmɪ] adj. lóbrego, sombrío; triste, melancólico; abatido.

glo·ri·fy [glórəfaɪ] v. glorificar.

glo·ri·ous [glórɪəs] adj. glorioso; espléndido.

glo·ry [glórɪ] s. gloria; v. gloriarse; vanagloriarse.

gloss [glɔs] s. (*shine*) lustre, brillo; pulimento; (*note*) glosa, comentario; v. lustrar, dar brillo a; pulir; glosar, comentar; **to — over** encubrir, dar colorido de bueno (*a algo que no lo es*).

glos·sa·ry [glásərɪ] s. glosario.

gloss·y [glásɪ] adj. lustroso; pulido.

glove [glʌv] s. guante; v. enguantar, poner guantes.

glow [glo] s. incandescencia; brillo (*de un ascua*); calor vivo; fosforescencia; v. lucir, brillar (*como un ascua*); fosforecer; estar encendido o enardecido.

glow·ing [glóɪŋ] adj. encendido, ardiente.

glow·worm [glówɚm] s. luciérnaga.

glue [glu] s. cola (*para pegar*); v. encolar, pegar (*con cola*).

glum [glʌm] adj. hosco.

glut [glʌt] s. exceso, saturación; v. saturar.

glut·ton [glʌtn] s. glotón.

glut·ton·ous [glʌtnəs] adj. gloton; goloso.

glut·ton·y [glʌtnɪ] s. gula, glotonería.

glyc·er·in [glísɚɪn] s. glicerina.

gnarled [nɑrld] adj. nudoso, torcido.

gnash [næʃ] v. crujir, rechinar (*los dientes*).

gnat [næt] s. jején (*insecto*).

gnaw [nɔ] v. roer.

gnu [ñu] s. nu.

go [go] v. (*move*) ir(se); andar; (*function*) marchar, funcionar, servir; **to — around** andar alrededor de; dar vueltas; **to — away** irse; **to — back on one's word** faltar a la palabra; **to — by** pasar por; guiarse por (*una regla*); **to — down** bajar; **to — insane** volverse loco; **to — into** entrar en; investigar; caber en; **to — off** hacer explosión; dispararse; irse, salir disparado; **to — on** proseguir, continuar; **to — out** salir; apagarse; **to — over** pasar por encima de; examinar con cuidado; releer; repasar; recorrer; **to — to pot** arruinarse; **to — to sleep** dormirse; **to — under** ir o pasar por debajo de; hundirse; **to — up** subir; **to let — soltar; there is not enough to — around** no hay (bastante) para todos; s. empuje, energía; **it is a —** trato hecho; **to be on the — estar en continuo movimiento.

GA

goad [god] *s.* aguijón; puya; *v.* aguijonear; aguijar, incitar.

goal [gol] *s.* meta; fin, objetivo.

goat [got] *s.* cabra; **male** — macho cabrío; **to be the** — ser la víctima, pagar el pato.

goat·ee [gotí] *s.* perilla.

goat·herd [góthɚd] *s.* cabrero.

gob·ble [gabl] *v.* tragar, engullir; **to** — **up** engullirse.

gob·bler [gáblɚ] *s.* pavo.

go-be·tween [góbətwin] *s.* medianero.

gob·let [gáblɪt] *s.* copa grande.

gob·lin [gáblɪn] *s.* duende.

god [gad] *s.* dios; **God** Dios.

god·child [gádtʃaɪld] *s.* ahijado, ahijada.

god·dess [gádɪs] *s.* diosa.

god·fa·ther [gádfɑðɚ] *s.* padrino.

god·less [gádlɪs] *adj.* impío, ateo.

god·like [gádlaɪk] *adj.* como Dios; divino.

god·ly [gádlɪ] *adj.* pío, devoto; divino.

god·moth·er [gádmʌðɚ] *s.* madrina.

gog·gles [gáglz] *s. pl.* antiparras, gafas.

go·ing [góɪŋ] *ger. & adj.* que anda, marcha o funciona bien; **to be** — ir, irse; *s.* ida, partida; **comings and -s** idas y venidas.

goi·ter [góɪtɚ] *s.* papera; bocio; *Ríopl., Méx., C.A.* buche; *C.A.* güecho.

gold [gold] *s.* oro; — **standard** patrón de oro.

gold·en [góldn] *adj.* de oro; áureo; dorado.

gold·finch [góldfɪntʃ] *s.* jilguero amarillo.

gold·fish [góldfɪʃ] *s.* carpa dorada.

gold·smith [góldsmɪθ] *s.* orfebre; — **shop** orfebrería.

golf [galf] *s.* golf.

gon·do·la [gándələ] *s.* góndola; cabina (*de una aeronave*); — **car** vagón de mercancías (*sin techo*), *Am.* jaula.

gone [gɔn] *p.p. de* **to go** *& adj.* ido; perdido; **he is** — se fué; **it is all** — se acabó; ya no hay más.

gong [gɔŋ] *s.* gong, batintín.

good [gʊd] *adj.* bueno; (*valid*) válido; valedero; — **afternoon** buenas tardes; — **day** buenos días; adiós; — **evening** buenas noches; — **morning** buenos días; — **night** buenas noches; **Good Friday** Viernes Santo; **for** — para siempre, permanentemente; **to have a** — **time** pasar un buen rato; divertirse; **to make** — pagar, compensar; cumplir (*una promesa*); salir bien, tener buen éxito; *s.* bien; beneficio, provecho, ventaja; **-s** bienes, efectos; mercancías; — **and services** bienes y servicios.

good-bye [gʊdbáɪ] *s. & interj.* adiós.

good-looking [gúdlúkɪŋ] *adj.* bien parecido, guapo.

good·ly [gúdlɪ] *adj.* grande, considerable; de buena apariencia.

good-na·tured [gúdnétʃɚd] *adj.* de buen genio, bonachón, afable.

good·ness [gúdnɪs] *s.* bondad; — ! ¡Dios mío! ¡cielos!

good·y [gʊdɪ] *s.* golosina, bombón, dulce; *interj.* ¡qué gusto!; **goody-goody** beatuco (*el que afecta virtud*), papanatas.

goof [guf] *v.* chapucear.

goose [gus] *s.* ganso; bobo, tonto; — **flesh** carne de gallina.

goose·ber·ry [glúsbɛrɪ] *s.* grosella; grosellero (*arbusto*).

go·pher [gófɚ] *s.* roedor semejante a la ardilla.

gore [gor] *s.* (*blood*) cuajarón de sangre; sangre; (*cloth*) cuchillo (*Am.* cuchilla), sesga (*tira de lienzo en figura de cuchilla*); *v.* acornear, herir con los cuernos; hacer una sesga en (*un traje*).

gorge [gɔrdʒ] *s.* cañada, barranco, barranca; *v.* engullir(se), atracarse.

gor·geous [gɔ́rdʒəs] *adj.* primoroso, vistoso, hermosísimo.

go·ril·la [gərílə] *s.* gorila.

go·ry [góri] *adj.* sangriento, ensangrentado.

gos·pel [gáspl] *s.* evangelio; **it is the** — **truth** es la pura verdad.

gos·sip [gásɪp] *s.* (*rumors*) chisme, chismería; murmuración, hablilla; (*person*) murmurador, chismero, chismoso; *v.* chismear, murmurar.

gos·sip·y [gásəpɪ] *adj.* chismero, chismoso.

got [gat] *pret. & p.p. de* **to get.**

Goth·ic [gáθɪk] *adj.* gótico; *s.* gótico (*idioma de los godos*); estilo gótico.

got·ten [gátn] *p.p. de* **to get.**

gouge [gaʊdʒ] *s.* gubia (*especie de formón o escoplo curvo*); *v.* excavar con gubia, formón o escoplo; **to** — **someone's eyes out** sacarle los ojos a alguien.

gourd [gord] *s.* calabaza.

gour·met [gʊrmé] *s.* gastrónomo.

gout [gaʊt] *s.* gota (*enfermedad*).

gov·ern [gÁvɚn] *v.* gobernar; regir.

gov·ern·ess [gÁvɚnɪs] *s.* institutriz.

gov·ern·ment [gÁvɚmənt] *s.* gobierno.

gov·ern·ment·al [gʌvɚméntl] *adj.* gubernativo.

gov·er·nor [gÁɚnɚ] *s.* gobernador; regulador (*de una máquina*).

gown [gaʊn] *s.* vestido (*de mujer*); toga (*de un juez, profesor, etc.*); **dressing** — bata.

grab [græb] *v.* agarrar, asir; arrebatar; *s.* arrebatiña; agarro, agarrón; presa.

grace [gres] *s.* gracia; favor; donaire, garbo; **to say** — bendecir la mesa, dar gracias; **to be in the good -s of someone** gozar del favor de uno; *v.* agraciar, adornar.

grace·ful [grésfəl] *adj.* gracioso, agraciado, garboso; **-ly** *adv.* graciosamente, con gracia, con garbo.

grace·ful·ness [grésfəlnɪs] *s.* gracia, donaire, gallardía, garbo.

gra·cious [gréʃəs] *adj.* afable; cortés; — ! ¡válgame Dios!

gra·da·tion [gredéʃən] *s.* graduación; gradación; grado.

grade [gred] *s.* (*degree*) grado; (*mark*) nota, calificación; (*slope*) cuesta, declive, pendiente; *Am.* gradiente; — **crossing** cruce a nivel (*de un ferrocarril con una carretera*); **the -s** la escuela primaria; *v.* graduar, clasificar; calificar, dar una calificación; (*level*) nivelar, explanar.

grad·u·al [grǽdʒʊəl] *adj.* gradual; **-ly** *adv.* gradualmente, poco a poco.

grad·u·ate [grǽdʒʊɪt] *adj.* graduado, que ha recibido un grado académico; **to do** — **work** cursar asignaturas superiores (*al bachillerato*); *s.* estudiante graduado (*que estudia para licenciado o doctor*); [grǽdʒʊet] *v.* graduar(se).

grad·u·a·tion [grǽdʒʊéʃən] *s.* graduación.

graft [græft] *s.* (*insertion*) injerto; tejido injertado; (*extortion*) sisa, malversación (*de caudales públicos*); peculado, chanchullo; ganancia ilegal, *Méx.* mordida; *v.* injertar; malversar fondos ajenos; sisar, exigir gago ilegal, *Méx.* morder.

graft·er [grǽftɚ] *s.* malversador (*de fondos públicos*), estafador, *C.A.* coyote, *Méx.* mordelón.

grain [gren] *s.* (*cereal*) grano; (*markings*) fibra (*de la madera*), veta (*del mármol o madera*); **against the** — **a** (*o* al) redopelo, a contrapelo.

gram [græm] *s.* gramo.

gram·mar [grǽmɚ] *s.* gramática; — **school** escuela primaria.

gram·mat·i·cal [grəmǽtɪkl] *adj.* gramatical,

gramático.

gran·a·ry [grǽnərɪ] *s*. granero.

grand [grænd] *adj*. grande; grandioso, admirable; magnífico.

grand·child [grǽntʃaɪld] *s*. nieto.

grand·chil·dren [grǽntʃɪdrən] *s. pl*. nietos.

grand·daugh·ter [grǽndɔtɚ] *s*. nieta.

gran·deur [grǽndʒɚ] *s*. grandeza, grandiosidad; majestad.

grand·father [grǽnfɑðɚ] *s*. abuelo.

gran·di·ose [grǽndɪos] *adj*. grandioso, magnífico.

grand·ma [grǽnmɑ] *s*. abuela, abuelita, *Am*. mamá grande.

grand·moth·er [grǽnmʌðɚ] *s*. abuela.

grand·ness [grǽndnɪs] *s*. grandeza; grandiosidad; magnificencia.

grand·pa [grǽnpɑ] *s*. abuelo, abuelito, *Am*. papá grande.

grand·par·ent [grǽnpɛrənt] *s*. abuelo, abuela; **-s** abuelos.

grand·son [grǽnsʌn] *s*. nieto.

grand·stand [grǽnstænd] *s*. andanada, gradería cubierta.

grange [grendʒ] *s*. granja; asociación de agricultores.

gran·ite [grǽnɪt] *s*. granito (*roca*).

gran·ny [grǽnɪ] *s*. abuelita; viejecita, viejita.

grant [grænt] *s*. concesión; subvención; donación; dádiva; transferencia de propiedad (*mediante escritura*); *v*. conceder; otorgar; ceder, transferir (*derechos, propiedad, etc.*); **to take for -ed** dar por supuesto, dar por sentado.

gran·u·late [grǽnjələt] *v*. granular(se).

grape [grep] *s*. uva.

grape·fruit [grépfrut] *s*. toronja; *Esp*. pomelo.

grape·vine [grépvaɪn] *s*. vid; parra.

graph [græf] *s*. diagrama, gráfica; *v*. hacer una gráfica o diagrama; *paper* papel cuadriculado.

graph·ic [grǽfɪk] *adj*. gráfico; — **design** (*computer*) diseño gráfico.

graph·ite [grǽfaɪt] *s*. grafito.

grap·ple [grǽpl] *v*. luchar, pelear cuerpo a cuerpo; aferrar, agarrar.

grasp [græsp] *v*. (*seize*) agarrar; asir; apretar; (*understand*) comprender; abarcar; *s*. agarro, asimiento; apretón de manos; **to be within one's** — estar al alcance de uno; **to have a good** — **of a subject** estar fuerte en una materia, saber a fondo una materia.

grass [græs] *s*. hierba; césped; pasto; *Méx*. zacate; *Méx., Ven., Col*. grama.

grass·hop·per [grǽshɑpɚ] *s*. saltamontes, saltón, *Méx, C.C*. chapulín.

grass·roots [grǽsruts] *adj*. del pueblo; de la gente.

grass·y [grǽsɪ] *adj*. herboso, *Am*. pastoso.

grate [gret] *s*. (*window*) reja, verja, enrejado; (*grill*) parrilla, brasero; *v*. enrejar, poner enrejado; crujir, rechinar (*los dientes*); rallar (*queso*); **to** — **on** molestar, irritar.

grate·ful [grétfəl] *adj*. agradecido; grato, agradable.

grat·er [grétɚ] *s*. rallador.

grat·i·fy [grǽtəfaɪ] *v*. complacer, dar gusto, agradar; satisfacer.

grat·ing [grétɪŋ] *s*. reja, enrejado, verja; *adj*. rechinante; molesto, áspero.

gra·tis [grétɪs] *adv*. gratis, de balde.

grat·i·tude [grǽtətjud] *s*. gratitud.

gra·tu·i·tous [grətjúətəs] *adj*. gratuito; sin fundamento; — **statement** afirmación arbitraria.

grave [grev] *adj*. grave; serio; *s*. tumba, sepulcro, sepultura; acento grave; —**stone** losa o lápida sepulcral.

grave·dig·ger [grévdɪgɚ] *s*. sepulturero.

grav·el [grǽvl] *s*. grava, guijo, cascajo, *Am*. maicillo; cálculos (*en los riñones, la vejiga, etc.*); mal de piedra; *v*. cubrir con grava.

grave·yard [grévjɑrd] *s*. cementerio.

grav·i·ta·tion [grævɪtéʃən] *s*. atracción; gravitación.

grav·i·ty [grǽvətɪ] *s*. gravedad; seriedad.

gra·vy [grévɪ] *s*. salsa; jugo (*de carne*).

gray [gre] *adj*. gris; (*hair*) cano; pelicano; entrecano (*que empieza a encanecer*); — **horse** rucio, tordo, tordillo; — **matter** seso; **gray-headed** canoso; *s*. gris. color gris; *v*. encanecer; poner(se) gris.

gray·ish [gréɪʃ] *adj*. grisáceo, pardusco; — **hair** pelo entrecano.

gray·ness [grénɪs] *s*. grisura, gris, calidad de gris; encanecimiento.

graze [grez] *v*. (*feed*) pacer; apacentar, *Am*. pastear, pastar; (*brush*) rozar; raspar; *s*. roce, rozón, raspadura.

grease [gris] *s*. grasa; *v*. engrasar; (*anoint*) untar; lubricar; **to** — **the palm** untar la mano, sobornar.

greas·y [grísɪ] *adj*. grasiento, grasoso; pringoso.

great [gret] *adj*. gran(de); eminente; magnífico, excelente; **a** — **deal** una gran cantidad; muchos; mucho; **a** — **many** muchos; **a** — **while** un largo rato o tiempo; **-ly** *adv*. grandemente; mucho; muy; en gran parte; sobremanera.

great-grand·child [grétgrǽntʃaɪld] *s*. bisnieto.

great-grand·fa·ther [grétgrǽnfɑðɚ] *s*. bisabuelo.

great-grand·moth·er [grétgrǽnmʌðɚ] *s*. bisabuela.

great·ness [grétnɪs] *s*. grandeza.

Gre·cian [gríʃən] *adj. & s*. griego.

greed [grid] *s*. codicia; avaricia; gula.

greed·i·ly [grídɪlɪ] *adv*. vorazmente; con avaricia; con gula.

greed·i·ness [grídɪnɪs] *s*. codicia; avaricia; gula; voracidad.

greed·y [grídɪ] *adj*. codicioso; avaro; goloso; voraz.

Greek [grik] *adj. & s*. griego.

green [grin] *adj*. (*color*) verde; (*novice*) novato, inexperto; **to grow** — verdear; **the fields look** — verdean los campos; *s*. verde, verdor; césped, prado; campo de golf; **-s** verduras, hortalizas.

green·horn [grínhɔrn] *s*. novato, pipiolo.

green·house [grínhaʊs] *s*. invernáculo, invernadero.

green·ish [grínɪʃ] *adj*. verdoso.

green·ness [grínnɪs] *s*. (*color*) verdor, verdura; (*experience*) inmadurez; impericia.

greet [grit] *v*. saludar; **to** — **each other** saludarse.

greet·ing [grítɪŋ] *s*. saludo; salutación; **-s!** ¡salud! ¡saludos!

gre·nade [grɪnéd] *s*. granada, bomba pequeña.

grew [gru] *pret. de* **to grow**.

grey [gre] = **gray**.

grey·ish = **gray**.

grey·ness = **grayness**.

grey·hound [gréhaʊnd] *s*. lebrel, galgo.

grid·dle [grídl] *s*. tartera; plancha (*para tapar el hornillo*).

grief [grif] *s*. dolor, pesar; **to come to** — sobrevenirle a uno una desgracia; fracasar.

griev·ance [grívəns] *s*. queja; resentimiento; (*injustice*) motivo de queja, injusticia, ofensa.

grieve [griv] *v*. afligir(se); lamentar(se), acongojar(se).

grieved [grivd] *adj*. penado.

griev·ous [grívəs] *adj*. doloroso, penoso, grave, altroz.

grill [grɪl] *s*. parrilla; **men's** — restaurante para hombres; *v*. asar en parrillas; interrogar (*a un sospechoso*).

grim [grɪm] *adj.* austero, áspero; fiero; torvo, siniestro.

gri·mace [grɪmés] *s.* mueca, gesto; *v.* hacer muecas o gestos.

grime [graɪm] *s.* mugre; *v.* ensuciar.

grim·y [gráɪmɪ] *adj.* mugriento.

grin [grɪn] *s.* sonrisa abierta; sonrisa maliciosa; sonrisa canina; *v.* sonreír (*mostrando mucho los dientes*).

grind [graɪnd] *v.* (*crush*) moler; machacar; (*sharpen*) afilar, amolar; (*study hard*) afanarse demasiado; estudiar con empeño; **to — a hand organ** tocar el organillo; **to — one's teeth** rechinar los dientes; *s.* molienda; faena, trabajo penoso; estudiante tesonero; **the daily —** la rutina diaria.

grind·er [gráɪndɚ] *s.* moledor; molinillo (*para moler café*); amolador, afilador; muela (*piedra para afilar*); muela (*diente molar*).

grind·stone [gráɪndston] *s.* piedra de amolar.

grip [grɪp] *v.* (*seize*) agarrar; asir; apretar; empuñar; (*impress*) impresionar; conmover; *s.* agarro; asimiento; apretón; asidero, asa; (*suitcase*) valija, maletín; *Méx.*, velís; **to have a — on someone** tener agarrado a alguien.

grippe [grɪp] *s.* gripe, influenza.

grit [grɪt] *s.* (*gravel*) arenilla, arena; piedra arenisca; (*pluck*) firmeza, tesón; **-s** maíz, avena, o trigo a medio moler; *v.* rechinar, crujir.

grit·ty [grítɪ] *adj.* arenoso; valeroso, firme.

griz·zly [grízlɪ] *adj.* grisáceo, pardusco; **— bear** oso pardo.

groan [gron] *s.* gemido, quejido; *v.* gemir; quejarse; crujir (*por exceso de peso*).

gro·cer [grósɚ] *s.* abacero, *Méx.* abarrotero, *Carib.*, *C.A.* bodeguero; *Ríopl.* almacenero.

gro·cer·y [grósərɪ] *s.* abacería, tienda de comestibles, *Méx.*, abarrotería, *Méx.* tienda de abarrotes; *Ríopl.* almacén; *Carib.*, *C.A.* bodega; **groceries** comestibles, *Méx.* abarrotes.

groom [grum] *s.* (*bridegroom*) novio; (*stable groom*) caballerizo, mozo de caballeriza; establero; *v.* almohazar, limpiar con la almohaza (*a los caballos*), cuidar (*a los caballos*); **to — oneself** asearse, peinarse, componerse; **well-groomed** bien vestido, aseado, limpio.

groove [gruv] *s.* estría, ranura, acanaladura; surco (*en un camino*); muesca, encaje; *v.* acanalar, estriar.

grope [grop] *v.* tentalear, tentar, andar a tientas; **to — for** buscar tentando, buscar a tientas.

gross [gros] *adj.* grueso; burdo; tosco; grosero; *s.* **— earnings** ganancias totales; renta bruta, ingreso bruto; **— ignorance** ignorancia crasa; **— weight** peso bruto; *s.* grueso, totalidad; gruesa (*doce docenas*).

gro·tesque [grotésk] *adj.* & *s.* grotesco.

grot·to [gráto] *s.* gruta.

grouch [grautʃ] *s.* mal humor; gruñón, refunfuñón, cascarrabias; **to have a — against someone** tenerle ojeriza (*o* mala voluntad) a una persona; guardarle rencor a alguien; *v.* gruñir, refunfuñar; estar de mal humor.

grouch·y [gráutʃɪ] *adj.* gruñón, refunfuñón, malhumorado, cascarrabias.

ground [graund] *s.* (*earth*) suelo, tierra; terreno; (*motive*) motivo, razón; base, fundamento; **— crew** personal de tierra; **-s** heces, desperdicios, sedimento; **— floor** piso bajo, planta baja, **to break —** roturar, arar, cavar; **to give —** retroceder, ceder; **to hold one's —** mantenerse firme; *v.* conectar (*un alambre*) con la tierra;

encallar (*una embarcación*); aterrizar (*un aeroplano*); **to be well -ed** poseer las bases o principios fundamentales; *pret.* & *p.p. de* **to grind.**

ground·less [gráundlɪs] *adj.* infundado.

group [grup] *s.* grupo; **— insurance** seguros sociales; *v.* agrupar.

grove [grov] *s.* arboleda, bosquecillo.

grow [gro] *v.* crecer; brotar; cultivar; criar; producir; **to — angry** ponerse enojado o enfadado, enfadarse, enojarse; **to — better** ponerse mejor, mejorar; **to — difficult** dificultarse, hacerse difícil; **to — late** hacerse tarde; **to — old** ponerse viejo, envejecer; **to — out of a habit** perder la costumbre; **to — pale** ponerse pálido, palidecer; **to — tired** cansarse.

growl [graul] *s.* gruñido; *v.* gruñir.

growl·er [gráulɚ] *s.* gruñón; regañón.

grown [gron] *p.p. de* **to grow** & *adj.* crecido; desarrollado; **— man** hombre maduro, hombre hecho; **— with trees** poblado de árboles.

grown-up [grónʌp] *adj.* crecido, adulto; *s.* adulto.

growth [groθ] *s.* (*increase*) crecimiento, acrecentamiento; aumento; (*development*) desarrollo; (*vegetation*) vegetación; (*tissue*) tumor, lobanillo, excrecencia.

grub·by [grÁbɪ] *adj.* roñoso; sucio.

grudge [grʌdʒ] *s.* inquina, rencor, resentimiento, mala voluntad; *v.* tener inquina, envidia o mala voluntad; dar de mala gana.

gruff [graf] *adj.* áspero, rudo; grosero.

grum·ble [grÁmbl] *s.* refunfuño, gruñido, queja; *v.* refunfuñar, gruñir, quejarse.

grum·bler [grÁmblɚ] *s.* gruñón; regañón.

grump·y [grÁmpɪ] *adj.* malhumorado; gruñón.

grunt [grʌnt] *s.* gruñido, *Méx.*, *C.A.*, *Col.*, *Ven.* pujido; *v.* gruñir, *Ríopl.*, *Méx.*, *Ven.*, *Andes* pujar.

guar·an·tee [gærəntí] *s.* garantía; fianza; fiador; *v.* garantizar; dar fianza; salir fiador de.

guar·an·tor [gærəntɚ] *s.* fiador.

guar·an·ty [gǽrəntɪ] *s.* garantía; fianza; fiador; *v. véase* **guarantee.**

guard [gɑrd] *s.* guarda; guardia; resguardo; **to be on —** estar alerta; estar en guardia; **to keep —** vigilar; *v.* guardar; resguardar; vigilar; **to — (oneself) against** guardarse de.

guard·i·an [gárdɪən] *s.* guardián, custodio; tutor; **— angel** ángel custodio, ángel de la guarda.

guard·i·an·ship [gárdɪənʃɪp] *s.* tutela; guarda, custodia.

guard·rail [gárdrel] *s.* baranda.

Gua·te·ma·lan [gwɑtəmɑ́lən] *adj.* & *s.* guatemalteco.

guess [gɛs] *s.* conjetura, suposición; adivinación; *v.* adivinar; suponer, creer.

guest [gɛst] *s.* convidado; visita; huésped, pensionista, inquilino.

guf·faw [gʌfɔ́] *s.* risotada, carcajada.

gui·dance [gáɪdn̩s] *s.* guía, dirección.

guide [gaɪd] *s.* guía.

guide·book [gáɪdbʊk] *s.* guía del viajero; **railway —** guía de ferrocarriles.

guide·line [gáɪdlaɪn] *s.* norma; precepto.

guild [gɪld] *s.* gremio; cofradía; asociación.

guile [gaɪl] *s.* engaño, astucia.

guilt [gɪlt] *s.* culpa, delito; culpabilidad.

guilt·less [gɪ́ltlɪs] *adj.* libre de culpa; inocente.

guilt·y [gɪ́ltɪ] *adj.* culpable; reo, delincuente.

guise [gaɪz] *s.* aspecto, apariencia; modo; **under the — of** so capa de; disfrazado de.

gui·tar [gɪtár] *s.* guitarra.

gulf [gʌlf] *s.* golfo; abismo.

gull [gʌl] *s.* gaviota.
gul·let [gʌlɪt] *s.* gaznate.
gul·ly [gʌlɪ] *s.* barranco, barranca; hondonada.
gulp [gʌlp] *s.* trago; *v.* tragar; engullir; **to — it down** tragárselo.
gum [gʌm] *s.* (*product*) goma; (*of mouth*) encía; **chewing —** goma de mascar, *Am.* chicle; **— tree** arbol gomífero, *Col.* gomero; *v.* engomar, pegar con goma.
gun [gʌn] *s.* (*cannon*) cañón; (*rifle*) fusil, rifle; (*shotgun*) escopeta; pistola, revólver; **a 21 — salute** una salva de 21 cañonazos.
gun·boat [gʌnbot] *s.* cañonero, lancha cañonera.
gun·ner [gʌnɚ] *s.* artillero, cañonero; ametrallador.
gun·pow·der [gʌnpaʊdɚ] *s.* pólvora.
gur·gle [gɝgl] *v.* borbotar, hacer borbollones; *s.* borbollón, borbotón.
gush [gʌʃ] *s.* chorro; borbollón, borbotón; efusión (*de cariño o entusiasmo*); *v.* chorrear, borbotar, borbollar, borbollonear; brotar; ser demasiado efusivo.
gust [gʌst] *s.* ráfaga, ventolera.
gut [gʌt] *s.* tripa, intestino; cuerda de tripa; **to have -s** tener agallas (*ánimo*).
gut·ter [gʌtɚ] *s.* arroyo (*de la calle o de un camino*); gotera (*del techo*); zanja.
guy [gaɪ] *s.* (*person*) sujeto, tipo, individuo; (*wire*) tirante, alambre, cadena (*para sostener algo*); *v.* sostener (*algo*) con tirantes; burlarse de, mofarse de.
gym·na·si·um [dʒɪmnéziəm] *s.* gimnasio.
gym·nas·tics [dʒɪmnǽtɪks] *s.* gimnasia.
gy·ne·col·o·gy [gaɪnəkálədʒɪ] *s.* ginecología.
gyp·sy [dʒɪ́psɪ] *s. & adj.* gitano.
gy·rate [dʒáɪret] *v.* girar.
gy·ro·scope [dʒáɪrəskop] *s.* giroscopio.

H:h

hab·it [hǽbɪt] *s.* hábito, costumbre; **drinking —** vicio de la bebida; **riding —** traje de montar.
ha·bit·u·al [həbítʃuəl] *adj.* habitual; acostumbrado.
hack [hæk] *s.* (*cut*) tajo; (*cough*) tos seca; (*horse*) caballo de alquiler; rocín; (*writer*) escritor mercenario; *v.* tajar, picar; toser con tos seca.
hack·neyed [hǽknɪd] *adj.* trillado, muy común.
had [hæd] *pret. & p.p. de* **to have; you — better do it** es bueno que Vd. lo haga; sería bueno que Vd. lo hiciese; **I — rather go than stay** preferiría irme a quedarme.
haf·ni·um [hǽfnɪəm] *s.* hafnio.
hag [hæg] *s.* hechicera, bruja; viejota.
hag·gard [hǽgɚd] *adj.* macilento, flaco.
hag·gle [hǽgl] *v.* regatear.
hail [hel] *s.* (*storm*) granizo; (*greeting*) saludo; llamada, grito; **Hail Mary** Ave María; *interj.* ¡salud!; ¡salve!; *v.* granizar; saludar; llamar; aclamar; **to — from** proceder de, ser oriundo de.
hail·storm [hélstɔrm] *s.* granizada.
hair [hɛr] *s.* pelo; cabello; vello; filamento (*de las plantas*); **— net** red para el cabello.
hair·brush [hɛ́rbrʌʃ] *s.* cepillo para el cabello.
hair·cut [hɛ́rkʌt] *s.* corte de pelo; **close — rape; to have a —** hacerse cortar el pelo.
hair·do [hɛ́rdu] *s.* peinado.
hair·dress·er [hɛ́rdrɛsɚ] *s.* peluquero; peinadora.
hair·less [hɛ́rlɪs] *adj.* sin pelo, pelado; lampiño.
hair·pin [hɛ́rpɪn] *s.* horquilla, *Am.* gancho (*para el*

pelo).
hair·y [hɛ́rɪ] *adj.* peludo, cabelludo; hirsuto, velloso, velludo.
hale [hel] *adj.* sano, fuerte, robusto; *v.* llevar (*a una persona*) por fuerza.
half [hæf] *s.* mitad; **— an apple** media manzana; *adj.* medio; **— brother** hermanastro; **— cooked** a medio cocer, medio cocido; **— duplex** (*computer*) semiduplex; **half-past one** la una y media; **half-baked** a medio cocer; a medio planear.
half-breed [hǽfbrid] *adj. & s.* mestizo.
half-hour [hǽfáʊr] *s.* media hora; *adj.* de media hora.
half-mast [hǽfmǽst] *s.* media asta; *v.* poner a media asta (*la bandera*).
half-o·pen [hǽfópən] *adj.* entreabierto; medio abierto, entornado.
half·way [hǽfwe] *adj. & adv.* a medio camino; parcial, incompleto; **— between** equidistante de; **— finished** a medio acabar; **to do something —** hacer algo a medias.
half-wit·ted [hǽfwɪtɪd] *adj.* imbécil, zonzo.
hal·i·but [hǽləbət] *s.* mero, hipogloso (*pez*).
hall [hɔl] *s.* salón (*para asambleas, funciones, etc.*); edificio (*de un colegio o universidad*); vestíbulo; corredor, pasillo; **town —** ayuntamiento.
hall·mark [hɔ́lmɑrk] *s.* distintivo.
hal·lo = **hello.**
hal·low [hǽlo] *v.* santificar; consagrar.
Hal·low·een [hælóín] *s.* víspera de Todos los Santos.
hall·way [hɔ́lwe] *s.* corredor, pasillo; zaguán.
ha·lo [hélo] *s.* halo; aureola.
halt [hɔlt] *s.* alto, parada; *v.* parar(se), detener(se); hacer alto; vacilar.
hal·ter [hɔ́ltɚ] *s.* ronzal, cabestro.
halt·ing [hɔ́ltɪŋ] *adj.* vacilante; **-ly** *adv.* con vacilación.
halve [hæv] *v.* partir por la mitad; partir en dos.
halves [hævz] *pl. de* **half; to go — ir a medias.**
ham [hæm] *s.* jamón.
ham·burg·er [hǽmbɝgɚ] *s.* carne picada de vaca; bocadillo o emparedado de carne picada, *Am.* hamburguesa.
ham·let [hǽmlɪt] *s.* caserío, aldehuela.
ham·mer [hǽmɚ] *s.* martillo; martinete (*de piano*); **sledge —** macho; *v.* martillar; machacar; clavar.
ham·mock [hǽmək] *s.* hamaca, *Ven., Col.* chinchorro; *Ríopl.* mangangá; coy.
ham·per [hǽmpɚ] *s.* canasto, cesto grande, cuévano; *v.* estorbar, impedir, embarazar.
hand [hænd] *s.* mano; manecilla; (*clock*) aguja (*de reloj*); obrero; letra (*modo de escribir*); **— and glove** uña y carne; **— in —** (cogidos) de la mano; **at — a** la mano, cerca; **made by — hecho a mano; on — disponible; en existencia; listo; a la mano, presente; on the other —** en cambio, por otra parte; **to have one's -s full** estar ocupadísimo; *v.* entregar, dar; **to — down** bajar (*una cosa para dársela a alguien*); transmitir (*de una a otra generación*); pronunciar (*un fallo*); **to — in** entregar; **to — over** entregar.
hand·bag [hǽndbæg] *s.* bolsa o bolso; saco de noche, maletín.
hand·ball [hǽndbɔl] *s.* pelota; juego de pelota.
hand·bill [hǽndbɪl] *s.* hoja volante (*anuncio*).
hand·cuff [hǽndkʌf] *v.* maniatar; **-s** *s. pl.* esposas, manillas de hierro.
hand·ful [hǽndfəl] *s.* manojo, puñado.
hand·i·cap [hǽndɪkæp] *s.* desventaja, estorbo, impedimento, obstáculo; ventaja o desventaja (*impuesta en ciertas contiendas*); **— race** carrera

de handicap; v. estorbar, poner trabas a.

hand·i·work [hǽndɪwȝk] s. labor, trabajo hecho a mano; artefacto.

hand·ker·chief [hǽŋkɚtʃɪf] s. pañuelo.

han·dle [hǽndl̩] s. mango, asa; (*furniture*) tirador (*de puerta o cajón*); puño (*de espada*); (*crank*) manubrio (*de bicicleta, organillo, etc.*); v. manejar; manipular; manosear, tocar; comerciar en; **-s easily** se maneja con facilidad, es muy manuable.

hand·made [hǽndméd] adj. hecho a mano.

hand·out [hǽndoʊt] s. comunicado, circular informativo; (gift) remuneración sin servicios correspondientes.

hand·saw [hǽndsɔ] s. serrucho.

hand·shake [hǽndʃek] s. apretón de manos.

hand·some [hǽnsəm] adj. (*good-looking*) hermoso, guapo, bien parecido; (*generous*) generoso; **a — sum** una suma considerable.

hand·work [hǽndwɛk] s. obra hecha a mano.

hand·writ·ing [hǽndraɪtɪŋ] s. letra (*modo de escribir*), escritura.

hand·y [hǽndɪ] adj. (near) a la mano, próximo; (*clever*) hábil, diestro; manuable, fácil de manejar.

hang [hæŋ] v. colgar; suspender; ahorcar; inclinar (*la cabeza*); **sentenced to** — condenado a la horca; **to — around** andar holgazaneando por un sitio; rondar; esperar sin hacer nada; **to — on** colgarse de; depender de; estar pendiente de; persistir; **to — paper on a wall** empapelar una pared; **to — with tapestries** entapizar; s. modo de caerle la ropa a una persona; modo de manejar (*un mecanismo*); modo de resolver (*un problema*); significado (*de un argumento*); **I don't care a** — no me importa un ardite.

han·gar [hǽŋɚ] s. hangar, cobertizo.

hang·er [hǽŋɚ] s. colgadero; percha, clavijero; **paper** — empapelador.

hang·ing [hǽŋɪŋ] s. muerte en la horca; **-s** colgaduras; adj. colgante; colgado.

hang·man [hǽŋmən] s. verdugo.

hang·nail [hǽŋnel] s. padrastro (*pedacito de pellejo que se levanta junto a las uñas*).

hang·o·ver [hǽŋovɚ] s. sobrante, remanente, resto; **to have a** — *Ven., Col., Andes* tener un ratón o estar enratonado (*tras una borrachera*), *Méx.* estar crudo o tener una cruda; *Ch.* la mona; *C.A.* de goma; *Ríopl.* resaca.

hap·haz·ard [hæphǽzɚd] adv. al azar, al acaso, a la ventura, a la buena de Dios; adj. casual; impensado.

hap·haz·ard·ly [hæphǽzɚdlɪ] adv. = **haphazard.**

hap·less [hǽplɪs] adj. desventurado, desgraciado.

hap·pen [hǽpən] v. suceder, pasar, acontecer, sobrevenir, acaecer; **to — to hear (do, be, *etc.*)** oír (hacer, estar, *etc.*) por casualidad; **to — to pass by** acertar a pasar; **to — on (upon)** encontrarse con, tropezar con.

hap·pen·ing [hǽpənɪŋ] s. acontecimiento, suceso.

hap·pi·ly [hǽplɪ] adv. felizmente; afortunadamente.

hap·pi·ness [hǽpɪnɪs] s. felicidad, dicha, contento.

hap·py [hǽpɪ] adj. feliz; dichoso, alegre; afortunado; **to be** — **to** alegrarse de.

ha·rangue [hərǽŋ] s. arenga, perorata; v. arengar, perorar.

har·ass [hǽrəs] v. acosar, hostigar, molestar.

har·bor [hárbɚ] s. puerto; (*refuge*) asilo, refugio, abrigo; v. abrigar; hospedar; albergar.

hard [hɑrd] adj. (*firm*) duro; (*stiff*) tieso; (*difficult*) arduo, difícil; — **cash** dinero contante y sonante, metálico; — **coal** antracita; — **liquor** licor

espiritoso (*aguardiente, ron, etc.*); — **luck** mala suerte; — **of hearing** medio sordo; — **sell** técnica de venta agresiva; — **water** agua cruda; — **copy** (*computer*) listado en papel; — **disk** (*computer*) disco rígido; adv. fuerte, recio, con fuerza; con empeño, con ahinco; — **by** muy cerca; — **core** núcleo resistente (*de un grupo*); —**hearted** de corazón duro; **hard-working** muy trabajador, industrioso, aplicado.

hard·en [hárdn̩] v. endurecer(se).

hard·en·ing [hárdnɪŋ] s. endurecimiento.

hard·ly [hárdlɪ] adv. apenas; a duras penas; difícilmente; duramente, con aspereza; probablemente no.

hard·ness [hárdnɪs] s. dureza; aspereza; dificultad.

hard·ship [hárdʃɪp] s. apuro, aflicción; trabajo, penalidad.

hard·ware [hárdwɛr] s. — **shop** quincallería, ferretería; *Méx.* tlapalería; (*computer*) circuitería física, elemento físico.

har·dy [hárdɪ] adj. robusto, fuerte, recio, atrevido.

hare [hɛr] s. liebre.

hare·brained [hɛrbrénd] adj. atolondrado, ligero de cascos.

hare·lip [hɛrlɪp] s. labio leporino.

har·em [hɛrəm] s. harén.

har·lot [hárlət] s. ramera, prostituta.

harm [hɑrm] s. daño, mal; perjuicio; v. dañar; hacer mal, hacer daño; perjudicar.

harm·ful [hármfəl] adj. dañoso; dañino, nocivo, perjudicial.

harm·less [hármlɪs] adj. innocuo; inofensivo; no dañoso, inocente.

harm·less·ness [hármlɪsnɪs] s. innocuidad; inocencia, falta de malicia.

har·mon·ic [hɑrmánɪk] adj. armónico.

har·mo·ni·ous [hɑrmónɪəs] adj. armonioso.

har·mo·nize [hármənaɪz] v. armonizar; concordar; congeniar.

har·mo·ny [hármənɪ] s. armonía.

har·ness [hárnɪs] s. guarniciones (*de caballerías*); jaez, aparejo; **to get back in** — volver al servicio activo, volver a trabajar; volver a la rutina; v. enjaezar, poner guarniciones a (*un caballo, mula, etc.*).

harp [hɑrp] s. arpa; v. tocar el arpa; **to — on** repetir constantemente (*una nota, palabra, tema, etc.*); porfiar en.

har·poon [hɑrpún] s. arpón; v. arponear, pescar con arpón.

har·row [hǽro] s. rastro, rastrillo, grada; v. rastrear, rastrillar; atormentar; horrorizar.

har·row·ing [hǽrowɪŋ] adj. horrendo, horripilante, que pone los cabellos de punta; espeluznante.

har·ry [hǽrɪ] v. acosar, molestar; asolar.

harsh [hɑrʃ] adj. tosco, áspero; severo, austero.

harsh·ness [hárʃnɪs] s. aspereza; tosquedad; severidad.

har·vest [hárvɪst] s. cosecha; siega, agosto; recolección; recogida; v. cosechar; segar.

hash [hæʃ] s. picadillo.

haste [hest] s. prisa; apresuramiento; **in** — de prisa; **to make** — darse prisa, apresurarse; *Am.* apurarse.

has·ten [hésn̩] v. apresurar(se), precipitar(se); darse prisa.

hast·i·ly [héstlɪ] adv. aprisa, de prisa, apresuradamente, precipitadamente.

hast·y [héstɪ] adj. apresurado; precipitado.

hat [hæt] s. sombrero.

hatch [hætʃ] v. empollar; criar pollos; idear, maquinar; s. cría, nidada, pollada; escotillón, trampa (*puerta en el suelo*); — **way** escotilla.

hatch·et [hǽtʃɪt] *s.* hacha; **to bury the** — echar pelillos a la mar, olvidar rencores o enemistades.

hate [het] *s.* odio; aborrecimiento; *v.* odiar; aborrecer; detestar.

hate·ful [hétʃəl] *adj.* odioso, aborrecible.

ha·tred [hétrɪd] *s.* odio, aversión.

haugh·ti·ly [hɔ́tɪlɪ] *adv.* con altivez, altaneramente, arrogantemente.

haugh·ti·ness [hɔ́tɪnɪs] *s.* altanería, altivez.

haugh·ty [hɔ́tɪ] *adj.* altivo, altanero, arrogante.

haul [hɔl] *v.* (*transport*) acarrear, transportar; (*pull*) jalar (*halar*); tirar de; (*drag*) arrastrar; **to** — **down the flag** arriar (*o* bajar) la bandera; *s.* acarreo; transporte; tirón, estirón; buena pesca; ganancia, botín; (*round-up*) redada.

haunch [hɔntʃ] *s.* anca.

haunt [hɔnt] *v.* frecuentar a menudo; andar por, vagar por (*como fantasma o espectro*); **that idea -s me** me persigue esa idea; **-ed house** casa de espantos, fantasmas o aparecidos; *s.* guarida.

have [hæv] *v.* tener; poseer; haber (*v. aux.*); **to** — **a suit made** mandar hacer un traje; **to** — **a look at** dar un vistazo a, echar una mirada a; **to** — **to** tener que; **I'll not** — **it so** no lo toleraré, no lo permitiré; **what did she** — **on?** ¿qué vestido llevaba (puesto)?

ha·ven [hévən] *s.* asilo, abrigo, refugio; puerto.

hav·oc [hǽvək] *s.* estrago, estropicio, ruina; **to cause** — hacer estragos.

hawk [hɔk] *s.* halcón; *v.* pregonar (*mercancías*).

haw·thorn [hɔ́θɔrn] *s.* espino.

hay [he] *s.* heno, paja, hierba seca; — **fever** catarro asmático.

hay·loft [hélɔft] *s.* henil, pajar.

hay·stack [héstæk] *s.* montón de heno o paja.

haz·ard [hǽzɚd] *s.* azar; riesgo, peligro; estorbo, obstáculo (*en el campo de golf*); *v.* arriesgar, adventurar.

haz·ard·ous [hǽzɚdəs] *adj.* peligroso.

haze [hez] *s.* bruma, neblina, niebla; *v.* atormentar, hostigar (*con bromas estudiantiles*).

ha·zel [hézl] *s.* avellano; —**nut** avellana; *adj.* de avellano; avellanado, color de avellana.

haz·y [hézɪ] *adj.* (*weather*) nublado, brumoso; (*mind*) confuso.

he [hi] *pron. pers.* él; — **who** el que, quien; **he-goat** macho cabrío.

head [hɛd] *s.* cabeza; cabecera (*de cama*); jefe; — **slot** (*computer*) ranura de acceso; — **of hair** cabellera; **game of -s or tails** juego de cara y cruz, juego de las chapas, *Ven., Col., Andes, Ch.* juego de cara y sello; *Méx.* juego de águila y sol; **to be out of one's** — delirar, estar delirante; **to come to a** — madurar; supurar (*un absceso*); **to keep one's** — conservar la calma, no perder la cabeza; **it goes to his** — le desvanece; se le sube a la cabeza; *adj.* principal, primero; de proa, de frente; **head-on** de frente; *v.* encabezar; ir a la cabeza de; acaudillar; mandar, dirigir; **to** — **off** atajar; detener; refrenar; **to** — **towards** dirigirse a, encaminarse a.

head·ache [hɛ́dek] *s.* dolor de cabeza.

head·dress [hɛ́ddrɛs] *s.* tocado, adorno para la cabeza.

head·gear [hɛ́dgɪr] *s.* sombrero, gorro, gorra; tocado, toca (*de mujer*); cabezada (*de guarnición para caballo*).

head·ing [hɛ́dɪŋ] *s.* encabezamiento, título.

head·land [hɛ́dlənd] *s.* cabo, promontorio.

head·light [hɛ́dlaɪt] *s.* linterna delantera, faro delantero.

head·line [hɛ́dlaɪn] *s.* título, encabezado.

head·long [hɛ́dlɔŋ] *adv.* de cabeza; precipitadamente.

head·quar·ters [hɛ́dkwɔrtɚz] *s.* cuartel general; jefatura; oficina principal; *Arg.* sede central.

head·set [hɛ́dsɛt] *s.* receptor de cabeza.

head·strong [hɛ́dstrɔŋ] *adj.* testarudo, porfiado, obstinado.

head·way [hɛ́dwe] *s.* progreso, avance; **to make** — avanzar, adelantar, progresar.

heal [hil] *v.* curar; sanar; cicatrizar.

health [hɛlθ] *s.* salud; sanidad; salubridad.

health·ful [hɛ́lθfəl] *adj.* sano; salubre; saludable.

health·ful·ness [hɛ́lθfəlnɪs] *s.* salubridad; sanidad.

health·y [hɛ́lθɪ] *adj.* sano; saludable.

heap [hip] *s.* montón; pila; *v.* amontonar; apilar.

hear [hɪr] *v.* (*listen*) oír; escuchar; (*get news*) tener noticias; **to** — **about someone** oír hablar de alguien; **to** — **from someone** tener noticias de alguien; **to** — **of** saber de, tener noticias de, oír hablar de; **I -d that** . . . oí decir que . . .

heard [hɝd] *pret. & p.p. de* **to hear.**

hear·er [hírɚ] *s.* oyente.

hear·ing [hírɪŋ] *s.* (*sense*) oído; (*trial*) audiencia; examen de testigos; **hard of** — medio sordo, algo sordo; **within** — al alcance del oído; — **aid** aparato auditivo.

hear·say [hírse] *s.* hablilla, rumor; **by** — de oídas.

hearse [hɝs] *s.* carroza fúnebre.

heart [hart] *s.* (*organ*) corazón; (*spirit*) ánimo; **at** — en realidad, en el fondo; **from the bottom of one's** — de corazón, con toda el alma; con toda sinceridad; **to learn by** — aprender de memoria; **to take** — cobrar ánimo; **to take to** — tomar en serio; tomar a pecho; — **attack** ataque cardíaco; — **of lettuce, cabbage** cogollo.

heart·ache [hártek] *s.* dolor del corazón; angustia, pesar, congoja.

heart·bro·ken [hártbrokən] *adj.* traspasado de dolor, acongojado, angustiado; desengañado.

heart·en [hártn] *v.* animar.

heart·felt [hártfɛlt] *adj.* sentido, cordial, sincero; **my** — **sympathy** mi más sentido pésame.

hearth [harθ] *s.* hogar; fogón.

heart·i·ly [hártlɪ] *adv.* de corazón; cordialmente; de buena gana; **to eat** — comer con apetito; comer bien (*o* mucho).

heart·less [hártlɪs] *adj.* de mal corazón; cruel; insensible.

heart·rend·ing [hártrɛndɪŋ] *adj.* angustioso; agudo.

heart·y [hártɪ] *adj.* sincero, cordial; sano, fuerte; — **food** alimento nutritivo; **a** — **laugh** una buena carcajada; — **meal** comida abundante.

heat [hit] *s.* (*hot*) calor; ardor (*emotion*) vehemencia; celo (*ardor sexual de la hembra*); calefacción (*para las habitaciones*); corrida, carrera (*de prueba*); *v.* calentar(se); acalorar(se).

heat·er [hítɚ] *s.* calentador; calorífero.

hea·then [híðən] *s.* pagano, gentil, idólatra; pagano; *adj.* pagano; irreligioso.

heat·ing [hítɪŋ] *s.* calefacción.

heave [hiv] *v.* levantar, alzar (*con esfuerzo*); arrojar, lanzar; exhalar (*un suspiro*); jalar (*un cable*); jadear; basquear, hacer esfuerzos por vomitar.

heav·en [hévən] *s.* cielo.

heav·en·ly [hévənlɪ] *adj.* celeste; celestial; divino.

heav·i·ly [hévlɪ] *adv.* pesadamente, lentamente; copiosamente, excesivamente.

heav·i·ness [hévɪnɪs] *s.* pesadez, pesantez; opresión, abatimiento.

heav·y [hɛvɪ] *adj.* (*weight*) pesado; (*thick*) grueso; (*coarse*) burdo; (*oppressive*) opresivo; — **rain**

HA

aguacero recio o fuerte; — **duty** de servicio
pesado; **with a** — **heart** abatido, acongojado.
heav·y·weight [hévɪwet] *s. & adj.* peso pesado
(*fuerte*).
Hebrew [híbru] *adj.* hebreo.
hectare [héktɚ] *s.* hectárea.
hec·tic [héktɪk] *adj.* febril; inquieto.
hedge [hɛdʒ] *s.* seto; vallado, barrera; *v.* cercar;
poner valla o seto a; evitar o evadir contestaciones.
hedge·hog [hédʒhɑg] *s.* erizo.
he·don·ism [hídənɪzm] *s.* hedonismo.
heed [hid] *v.* atender; hacer caso; prestar atención; *s.*
atención, cuidado; **to pay** — **to** prestar atención a;
hacer caso de.
heed·less [hídlɪs] *adj.* descuidado; desatento.
heel [hil] *s.* talón (*del pie o de una media*); tacón
(*del zapato*); **head over -s** patas arriba; *v.* poner
tacón a; poner talón a.
he·gem·o·ny [hɪdʒémənɪ] *s.* hegemonía.
heif·er [héfɚ] *s.* novilla, vaquilla.
height [haɪt] *s.* altura; elevación; — **of folly** colmo
de la locura.
height·en [háɪtn̩] *v.* avivar; aumentar(se); realzar.
hei·nous [hénəs] *adj.* aborrecible, odioso; malvado.
heir [ɛr] *s.* heredero.
heir·ess [ɛrɪs] *s.* heredera.
held [hɛld] *pret. & p.p. de* **to hold.**
hel·i·cop·ter [hélǝkɑptɚ] *s.* helicóptero.
he·li·um [hílɪəm] *s.* helio.
hell [hɛl] *s.* infierno.
hel·lo [hɛló] *interj.* ¡hola!; ¡halo!
helm [hɛlm] *s.* timón.
hel·met [hélmɪt] *s.* yelmo.
help [hɛlp] *s.* (*aid*) ayuda; auxilio; remedio; alivio;
(*employee*) criado o criados, empleado o
empleados; *v.* ayudar, asistir; auxiliar; remediar;
servir (*algo de comer*); **to** — **down** ayudar a bajar;
— **yourself** sírvase Vd. (*de comer o beber*);
tómelo Vd., está a la disposición de Vd.; **he
cannot** — **it** no puede evitarlo; **he cannot** —
doing it no puede menos de hacerlo; **he cannot** —
but come no puede menos de venir.
help·er [hélpɚ] *s.* ayudante, asistente.
help·ful [hélpfəl] *adj.* útil, servicial; provechoso.
help·ing [hélpɪŋ] *s.* ayuda; porción (*que se sirve en
la mesa*).
help·less [hélplɪs] *adj.* (*defenseless*) desamparado;
(*handicapped*) desvalido; imposibilitado; incapaz;
(*confused*) perplejo, indeciso (*sin saber qué
hacer*); **a** — **situation** una situación irremediable.
help·less·ness [hélplɪsnɪs] *s.* incapacidad;
incompetencia; impotencia, debilidad; abandono,
desamparo.
hem [hɛm] *s.* dobladillo, bastilla; *v.* dobladillar,
bastillar, hacer dobladillos en (*la ropa*); **to** — **in**
rodear, cercar; **to** — **and haw** toser y retoser
(*fingidamente*); tartamudear, vacilar.
hem·i·sphere [héməsfɪr] *s.* hemisferio.
hem·lock [hémlɑk] *s.* cicuta (*hierba venenosa*); abeto
americano.
he·mo·glo·bin [hímoglobɪn] *s.* hemoglobina.
hem·or·rhage [hémərɪdʒ] *s.* hemorragia.
hem·or·rhoids [hémərɔɪdz] *s.* hemorroides.
hemp [hɛmp] *s.* cáñamo, *Am.* sisal.
hem·stitch [hémstɪtʃ] *s.* dobladillo de ojo; *v.* hacer (*o
echar*) dobladillo de ojo.
hen [hɛn] *s.* gallina; ave hembra.
hence [hɛns] *adv.* de (*o desde*) aquí; desde ahora; por
lo tanto, por consiguiente; **a week** — de hoy en
ocho días; de aquí a una semana.
hence·forth [hɛnsfórθ] *adv.* de aquí en adelante; de

hoy en adelante; desde ahora.
hep·a·ti·tis [hɛpətáɪtɪs] *s.* hepatitis.
her [hɚ] *pron.* la; le, a ella; ella (*con preposición*);
adj. su (sus), de ella.
her·ald [hérəld] *s.* heraldo; anunciador, proclamador;
precursor; *v.* anunciar, proclamar, publicar.
her·ald·ry [hérəldrɪ] *s.* heráldica.
herb [ɝb] *s.* hierba (yerba).
herd [hɝd] *s.* (*animals*) hato; rebaño; manada; tropel;
tropilla; (*cattle*) ganado; (*people*) muchedumbre;
the common — el populacho, la chusma; *v.*
reunir, juntar (*el ganado*); ir en manadas, ir juntos.
herds·man [hɝdzmən] *s.* vaquero, vaquerizo; pastor.
here [hɪr] *adv.* aquí; acá; — **it is** aquí está, helo
aquí, aquí lo tiene Vd., — **is to you!** ¡a la salud
de Vd.!; **that is neither** — **nor there** eso no viene
al caso; (*to call a dog*) ¡cuz! ¡toma! (*a cat*) ¡mis!
¡mis!
here·af·ter [hɪræftɚ] *adv.* de aquí (*o* de hoy) en
adelante; desde ahora en adelante; en lo futuro; *s.*
the — la otra vida.
here·by [hɪrbáɪ] *adv.* por este medio; mediante la
presente, por la presente; con estas palabras.
he·red·i·tar·y [hərédətɛrɪ] *adj.* hereditario.
he·red·i·ty [hərédətɪ] *s.* herencia.
here·in [hɪrín] *adv.* aquí dentro; en esto.
her·e·sy [hérəsɪ] *s.* herejía.
her·e·tic [hérətɪk] *s.* hereje.
here·to·fore [hɪrtəfór] *adv.* hasta ahora, hasta el
presente.
here·with [hɪrwíθ] *adv.* aquí dentro, con esto,
adjunto, incluso.
her·i·tage [hérətɪdʒ] *s.* herencia.
her·met·ic [hɚmétɪk] *adj.* hermético.
her·mit [hɝmɪt] *s.* ermitaño.
her·ni·a [hɝnɪə] *s.* hernia, ruptura, relajamiento.
he·ro [hɪro] *s.* héroe; protagonista.
he·ro·ic [hɪróɪk] *adj.* heroico.
her·o·ine [héroɪn] *s.* heroína.
her·o·ism [héroɪzəm] *s.* heroísmo.
he·ron [hérən] *s.* garza.
her·ring [hérɪŋ] *s.* arenque.
hers [hɝz] *pron. pos.* suyo (suya, suyos, suyas), de
ella; el suyo (la suya, los suyos, las suyas); el (la
los, las) de ella; **a friend of** — un amigo suyo.
her·self [hɚsélf] *pron.* ella misma; se (*como
reflexivo*); **by** — sola; por sí (sola); **she** — **did it**
ella misma lo hizo; **she talks to** — ella habla para
sí, habla consigo misma, habla para sus adentros,
habla sola.
hes·i·tant [hézətənt] = **hesitating.**
hes·i·tate [hézətet] *v.* vacilar; (*stutter*) titubear;
(*doubt*) dudar.
hes·i·tat·ing [hésətetɪŋ] *adj.* vacilante; indeciso;
irresoluto; **-ly** *adv.* con vacilación.
hes·i·ta·tion [hɛzətéʃən] *s.* vacilación; titubeo, duda.
het·er·o·ge·ne·ous [hɛtəˈrədʒínɪəs] *adj.* heterogéneo.
hew [hju] *v.* tajar, cortar; picar (*piedra*); labrar
(*madera, piedra*).
hewn [hjun] *p.p. de* **hew.**
hey [he] *interj.* ¡he!; ¡oiga!; ¡oye!
hi·a·tus [haɪétəs] *s.* hiato.
hi·ber·nate [háɪbɚnet] *v.* invernar.
hic·cup, hic·cough [híkʌp] *s.* hipo; *v.* hipar, tener
hipo.
hick·o·ry [híkərɪ] *s.* nogal americano; — **nut** nuez
(*del nogal americano*).
hid [hɪd] *pret. & p.p. de* **to hide.**
hid·den [hídn̩] *p.p. de* **to hide;** *adj.* oculto,
escondido.
hide [haɪd] *v.* ocultar(se); esconder(se); **to** — **from**

esconderse de, recatarse de; *s.* cuero, piel; **to play — and seek** jugar al escondite.

hid·e·ous [hídɪəs] *adj.* horrendo, horripilante, feote.

hi·er·ar·chy [háɪərɑrkɪ] *s.* jerarquía.

hi·er·o·glyph·ic [haɪəroglífɪk] *adj. & s.* jeroglífico.

high [haɪ] *adj.* alto; **— altar** altar mayor; **— and dry** enjuto; en seco; solo, abandonado; **— antiquity** antigüedad remota; **— explosive** explosivo de gran potencia; **— tide** plenamar; **— wind** ventarrón, viento fuerte; **— -level language** lenguaje de alto nivel; **in — gear** en directa, en tercera velocidad; **two feet —** dos pies de alto; **it is — time that** ya es hora de que; **to be in — spirits** estar muy animado; *adv.* alto; a precio subido; en alto; **to look — and low** buscar por todas partes; **high-grade** de calidad superior; **high-handed** arbitrario, despótico; **high-minded** magnánimo; orgulloso; **high-sounding** altisonante, rimbombante; **high-strung** muy tenso; **— school** escuela secundaria; **high-powered** de alta potencia; **— seas** alta mar.

high·jack [háɪdʒæk] *v.* asaltar a mano armada.

high·land [háɪlənd] *s.* tierra montañosa; **the Highlands** las montañas de Escocia.

high·light [háɪlaɪt] *s.* lo más notable.

high·ly [háɪlɪ] *adv.* altamente; sumamente, muy; **— paid** muy bien pagado.

high·ness [háɪnɪs] *s.* altura; elevación; Alteza (*título*).

high·way [háɪwe] *s.* camino real; carretera, calzada.

high·way·man [háɪwemən] *s.* forajido, salteador de caminos, bandido.

hike [haɪk] *s.* caminata, paseo largo, *Am.* andada; *v.* dar (*o* echar) una caminata.

hill [hɪl] *s.* colina, collado, cerro; (*pile*) montoncillo de tierra; *Andes, Am.* loma; **ant —** hormiguero; **down—** cuesta abajo; **up—** cuesta arriba.

hill·ock [hílɑk] *s.* collado, otero, montecillo.

hill·side [hílsaɪd] *s.* ladera.

hill·top [híltɑp] *s.* cumbre, cima (*de una colina*).

hill·y [hílɪ] *adj.* montuoso; accidentado.

hilt [hɪlt] *s.* empuñadura, puño (*de una espada o daga*).

him [hɪm] *pron.* le; lo; él (*con preposición*).

him·self [hɪmsɛlf] *pron.* él mismo; se (*como reflexivo*); a sí mismo; *véase* **herself.**

hind [haɪnd] *adj.* trasero; posterior; *s.* cierva; **—most** *adj.* último, postrero.

hin·der [híndɚ-] *v.* estorbar, impedir, obstruir.

hin·drance [híndrəns] *s.* estorbo, obstáculo, impedimento.

hinge [hɪndʒ] *s.* gozne; bisagra; *v.* engoznar, poner goznes; **to — on** girar sobre; depender de.

hint [hɪnt] *s.* indirecta, insinuación; sugestión; **not to take the —** no darse por entendido; *v.* insinuar, intimar, sugerir indirectamente.

hip [hɪp] *s.* cadera.

hip·po·pot·a·mus [hɪpəpátəməs] *s.* hipopótamo.

hire [haɪr] *s.* (*rent*) alquiler; (*pay*) paga, sueldo; *v.* alquilar; emplear, dar empleo, *C.A., Ven., Col* enganchar, *S.A.* conchabar; **to — out** alquilarse, ponerse a servir a otro.

his [hɪz] *pron. pos.* suyo (suya, suyos, suyas), de él; el suyo (la suya, los suyos, las suyas); el (la, los, las) de él; **a friend of —** un amigo suyo; *adj.* su (sus), de él.

hiss [hɪs] *s.* silbido, chiflido; siseo; *v.* sisear, silbar, chiflar.

his·ta·mine [hístəmin] *s.* histamina.

his·to·ri·an [hɪstórɪən] *s.* historiador.

his·tor·ic [hɪstórɪk] *adj.* histórico.

his·tor·i·cal [hɪstórɪkl] *adj.* histórico.

his·to·ry [hístrɪ] *s.* historia.

his·tri·on·ics [hɪstrɪɑ́nɪks] *s.* histrionismo.

hit [hɪt] *v.* pegar, golpear; dar (*un golpe*); dar en (*o* con); chocar; (*press, type*) presionar, pulsar, tocar, oprimir; **they — it off well** se llevan bien, congenian; **to — the mark** acertar, atinar, dar en el blanco; **to — upon** dar con; encontrarse con, encontrar por casualidad; *pret. & p.p. de* **to hit;** *s.* golpe; choque; golpe de fortuna; pulla, dicharacho; **to be a great —** ser un gran éxito; **to make a — with someone** caerle en gracia a una persona; **hit-and-run** *adj.* que abandona a su víctima atropellada.

hitch [hɪtʃ] *v.* atar, amarrar; enganchar; (*yoke*) uncir (*bueyes*), (*pull*) dar un tirón; **to — one's chair nearer to** acercar su silla a; *s.* tirón; obstáculo, impedimento, tropiezo; enganche, enganchamiento.

hitch·hike [hítʃhaɪk] *v.* viajar de gorra (*en automóvil*), *Méx.* irse o viajar de mosca; *Ch., Ríopl.* hacer dedo, ir a dedo; *Esp.* viajar por auto-stop.

hith·er [híðɚ-] *adv.* acá; **— and thither** acá y allá.

hith·er·to [híðɚtú] *adv.* hasta aquí, hasta ahora, hasta hoy.

hive [haɪv] *s.* colmena; enjambre; **-s** ronchas (*de la piel*).

hoard [hord] *s.* tesoro escondido; acumulamiento secreto de provisiones; *v.* atesorar, guardar (*con avaricia*); acumular secretamente.

hoarse [hors] *adj.* bronco, áspero, ronco.

hoarse·ness [hórsnɪs] *s.* ronquera; carraspera.

hoar·y [hórɪ] *adj.* cano, encanecido, canoso.

hoax [hoks] *s.* engaño, estafa.

hob·ble [hábl] *v.* (*limp*) cojear, renquear; (*tie*) maniatar o· manear (*un animal*); (*impede*) impedir, estorbar; *s.* cojera; traba, maniota o manea (*cuerda con que se atan las manos de una bestia*).

hob·by [hábɪ] *s.* afición; trabajo hecho por afición (*no por obligación*).

ho·bo [hóbo] *s.* vagabundo.

hodge·podge [hádʒpɑdʒ] *s.* mezcolanza, baturrillo.

hoe [ho] *s.* azada, azadón; *v.* cavar, escardar, limpiar con azadón.

hog [hɑg] *s.* puerco, cerdo, cochino; *S.A.* chancho; *C.A.* tunco, cochi; *adj.* porcino; *v.* apropiárselo todo.

hoist [hoɪst] *v.* alzar, levantar; (*flag*) izar (*la bandera, las velas*); *s.* elevador, *Am.* malacate; grúa, montacargas.

hold [hold] *v.* tener(se); retener; detener; tener cabida para; sostener; mantener(se); opinar; celebrar (*una reunión, etc.*); ocupar (*un puesto*); ser válido (*un argumento o regla*); **to — back someone** detener (*o* refrenar) a alguien; **to — forth** perorar, hablar largamente; **to — in place** sujetar; **to — off** mantener(se) a distancia; mantenerse alejado; **to — on** agarrar(se); asir(se); persistir; **— on!** ¡agárrese bien!; ¡deténgase! ¡pare!; **to — someone responsible** hacerle a uno responsable; **to — someone to his word** obligar a uno a cumplir su palabra; **to — oneself erect** tenerse o andar derecho; **to — one's own** mantenerse firme; **to — one's tongue** callarse; **to — out** continuar, durar; mantenerse firme; **to — over** aplazar; durar; continuar en un cargo; **to — still** estarse quieto o callado; **to — tight** apretar; **to — to one's promise** cumplir con la promesa; **to — up** levantar, alzar; detener; asaltar, atracar (*para robar*); **how much does it —?** ¿cuánto le cabe? *s.* agarro; dominio; influencia; autoridad; bodega (*de un barco*); cabina de carga (*de un aeroplano*); **to**

get — **of** asir, agarrar; atrapar; **to take** — **of** coger, agarrar, asir.

hold·er [hóldɚ] *s.* (*person*) tenedor, posesor; (*device*) receptáculo; cojinillo (*para coger un trasto caliente*); **cigarette** — boquilla; **pen**— portaplumas.

hold·up [hóldʌp] *s.* asalto, atraco.

hole [hol] *s.* agujero; abertura; hoyo, (*hollow*) hueco, cavidad; (*pothole*) bache (*de un camino*); **swimming** — charco, remanso; **to be in a** — hallarse en un apuro o aprieto.

hol·i·day [háləde] *s.* día de fiesta, día festivo, festividad; **-s** días de fiesta; vacaciones.

ho·li·ness [hólɪnɪs] *s.* santidad.

ho·lis·tic [holístɪk] *adj.* global.

hol·low [hálo] *adj.* (*empty*) hueco; vacío, (*concave*) cóncavo; hundido; (*insincere*) falso; *s.* hueco; hoyo; cavidad; concavidad; depresión; cañada, hondonada; *v.* ahuecar; excavar; ahondar.

hol·ly [hálɪ] *s.* agrifolio, acebo.

hol·ster [hólstɚ] *s.* pistolera, funda (*de pistola*).

ho·ly [hólɪ] *adj.* santo; sagrado, sacro; — **water** agua bendita.

hom·age [hámɪdʒ] *s.* homenaje; reverencia, acatamiento; **to do** — acatar, rendir homenaje, honrar.

home [hom] *s.* casa, hogar; habitación, domicilio; **at** — en casa; *adj.* doméstico; casero; — **office** oficina matriz o central; — **rule** autonomía; — **run** *Méx., C.A., Ven., Col, Carib.* jonrón (*en béisbol*); — **stretch** último trecho (*de una carrera*); — **computer** computadora casera; *adv.* a casa; en casa; **to strike** — herir en lo vivo; dar en el clavo o en el blanco.

home·land [hómlænd] *s.* tierra natal, suelo patrio.

home·less [hómlɪs] *adj.* sin casa; destituido.

home·like [hómlaɪk] *adj.* hogareño, cómodo.

home·ly [hómlɪ] *adj.* feo; llano; (*simple*) sencillo; (*domestic*) casero, doméstico.

home·made [hómméd] *adj.* hecho en casa; doméstico, nacional, del país.

home·sick [hómsɪk] *adj.* nostálgico.

home·sick·ness [hómsɪknɪs] *s.* nostalgia.

home·stead [hómstɛd] *s.* heredad; casa y terrenos adyacentes.

home·ward [hómwɚd] *adv.* a casa; hacia la patria; — **voyage** retorno, viaje de vuelta.

home·work [hómwɝk] *s.* trabajo de casa; trabajo hecho en casa.

hom·i·cide [háməsaɪd] *s.* homicidio; homicida, asesino.

ho·mo·ge·ne·ous [homədʒínɪəs] *adj.* homogéneo.

ho·mog·e·nize [homádʒənaɪz] *v.* homogenizar.

ho·mo·sex·u·al [homəsékʃjʊl] *adj. & s.* homosexual.

hone [hon] *v.* amolar, asentar, afilar; *s.* piedra de afilar.

hon·est [ánɪst] *adj.* honrado, recto; genuino; — **goods** mercancías genuinas; **-ly** *adv.* honradamente; de veras.

hon·es·ty [ánɪstɪ] *s.* honradez, rectitud.

hon·ey [hʌ́nɪ] *s.* miel; dulzura; querido, querida.

hon·ey·comb [hʌ́nɪkom] *s.* panal.

hon·eyed [hʌ́nɪd] *adj.* meloso; dulce; melifluo.

hon·ey·moon [hʌ́nɪmun] *s.* luna de miel; viaje de novios, viaje de bodas; *v.* pasar la luna de miel.

hon·ey·suck·le [hʌ́nɪsʌkl] *s.* madreselva.

honk [hɔŋk] *s.* bocinazo, pitazo (*de automóvil*); (*goose*) graznido (*voz del ganso*); *v.* sonar la bocina; graznar.

hon·or [ánɚ] *s.* honor; honra; señoría (*título*); **upon my** — sobre mi palabra; *v.* honrar; dar honra.

hon·or·a·ble [ánərəbl] *adj.* honorable; honroso; honrado.

hon·or·ar·y [ánərɛrɪ] *adj.* honorario, honorífico.

hood [hʊd] *s.* capucha, caperuza; capirote, cubierta (*del motor*); *v.* encapuchar, encapirotar.

hood·lum [húdləm] *s.* maleante; antisocial.

hoof [hʊf] *s.* casco, pezuña; pata (*de caballo, toro, etc.*); (*half of cloven hoof*) pesuño.

hook [hʊk] *s.* gancho, garfio; (*fish*) anzuelo (*para pescar*); — **and eye** corchete; macho y hembra, **by** — **or crook** por la buena o por la mala, por angas o por mangas; **on his own** — por su propia cuenta; *v.* enganchar(se); abrochar(se); pescar, coger con anzuelo; robar, hurtar.

hook·y [hʊ́kɪ]: **to play** — hacer novillos, *Carib.* capear la escuela, *Méx.* pintar venado, *C.A., Ven., Col.* jubilarse; *Ríopl.* hacerse la rata (*la rabona*).

hoop [hup] *s.* aro; argolla; *v.* poner aro a; ceñir, cercar.

hoot [hut] *v.* (*owl*) ulular; (*make fun of*) rechiflar, ridiculizar; *s.* alarido, chillido.

hoot·ing [hútɪŋ] *s.* grita, rechifla.

hop [hɑp] *s.* salto, brinco; (*dance*) baile; *v.* saltar; brincar.

hope [hop] *s.* esperanza; *v.* esperar; **to** — **for** esperar; **to** — **against** — esperar desesperando; esperar lo que no puede ser, esperar lo imposible.

hope·ful [hópfəl] *adj.* esperanzado, lleno de esperanza; **a young** — un joven prometedor; **-ly** *adv.* con esperanza; con ansia; lleno de esperanza.

hope·less [hóplɪs] *adj.* sin esperanza, falto de esperanza, desesperanzado; desesperado; irremediable; — **cause** causa perdida; — **illness** enfermedad incurable; **it is** — no tiene remedio; **-ly** *adv.* sin esperanza, sin remedio.

hope·less·ness [hóplɪsnɪs] *s.* falta de esperanza; falta de remedio; desesperanza, desaliento.

horde [hord] *s.* horda; muchedumbre, gentío; enjambre.

ho·ri·zon [həráɪzn] *s.* horizonte.

hor·i·zon·tal [hɔrəzántl] *adj.* horizontal.

hor·mone [hɔ́rmon] *s.* hormona.

horn [hɔrn] *s.* (*animal*) cuerno; asta; cacho; (*automobile*) bocina, klaxon, trompa; (*musical*) corneta; trompeta; — **of plenty** cuerno de la abundancia; *v.* acornear, dar cornadas; **to** — **in** extremeterse; — **tip** piton.

hor·net [hɔ́rnɪt] *s.* avispón; **-'s nest** avispero.

hor·o·scope [hɔ́rəskop] *s.* horóscopo.

hor·ri·ble [hɔ́rəbl] *adj.* horrible; **horribly** *adv.* horriblemente.

hor·rid [hɔ́rɪd] *adj.* horrendo, horrible.

hor·ri·fy [hɔ́rəfaɪ] *v.* horrorizar, aterrorizar, espantar.

hor·ror [hɔ́rɚ] *s.* horror.

hors d'oeuvre [ɔrdɝ́vrə] *s.* entremés; bocadillos.

horse [hɔrs] *s.* caballo; caballete (*de madera*), borriquete (*de carpinteros*); **saddle** — caballo de silla; — **dealer** chalán; — **race** carrera de caballos; — **sense** sentido común.

horse·back [hɔ́rsbæk] *s.* lomo de caballo; **to ride** — montar a caballo, cabalgar, jinetear.

horse·fly [hɔ́rsflaɪ] *s.* tábano, mosca de caballo.

horse·laugh [hɔ́rslæf] *s.* carcajada, risotada.

horse·man [hɔ́rsmən] *s.* jinete.

horse·man·ship [hɔ́rsmənʃɪp] *s.* equitación.

horse·pow·er [hɔ́rspauɚ] *s.* caballo de fuerza.

horse·rad·ish [hɔ́rsrædɪʃ] *s.* rábano picante.

horse·shoe [hɔ́rsʃu] *s.* herradura.

hose [hoz] *s.* medias; manga o manguera (*para regar*); **men's** — calcetines.

ho·sier·y [hóʒrɪ] *s.* medias; calcetines; calcetería

(*negocio*); — **shop** calcetería.
hos·pi·ta·ble [háspɪtəbl] *adj.* hospitalario.
hos·pi·tal [háspɪtl] *s.* hospital.
hos·pi·tal·i·ty [háspɪtǽlətɪ] *s.* hospitalidad.
host [host] *s.* huésped (*el que hospeda*), anfitrión (*el que convida*); hospedero, mesonero; hueste; ejército, multitud; hostia; **sacred** — hostia consagrada.
hos·tage [hástɪdʒ] *s.* rehén (*persona que queda como prenda en poder del enemigo*).
hos·tel·ry [hástəlrɪ] *s.* hostería.
host·ess [hóstɪs] *s.* huéspeda (*la que hospeda o convida*).
hos·tile [hástl] *adj.* hostil.
hos·til·i·ty [hɑstɪflətɪ] *s.* hostilidad.
hot [hɑt] *adj.* caliente; caluroso; cálido; (*spicy*) picante (*como el pimentón, chile, ají, etc.*); (*angry*) furioso; fresco, (*recent*) reciente; — **bed** semillero; **hot-headed** enojadizo, impetuoso; exaltado; — **house** invernáculo, invernadero; **it is** — **today** hace calor hoy.
ho·tel [hotél] *s.* hotel.
ho·tel-keep·er [hotélkípɚ] *s.* hotelero.
hot·ly [hátlɪ] *adv.* calurosamente, con vehemencia.
hound [haʊnd] *s.* perro de busca, lebrel, galgo, sabueso, podenco; *v.* acosar, perseguir; azuzar, incitar.
hour [hʊr] *s.* hora; — **hand** horario.
hour·ly [áʊrlɪ] *adv.* por horas; a cada hora; a menudo; *adj.* frecuente; por horas.
house [haʊs] *s.* (*residence*) casa; domicilio; (*legislature*) cámara, asamblea legislativa; **country** — casa de campo; **a full** — un lleno completo (*en al teatro*); [haʊz] *v.* alojar; hospedar.
house·hold [háʊshold] *s.* casa, familia; *adj.* casero; doméstico.
house·keep·er [háʊskipɚ] *s.* casera; ama de llaves; **to be a good** — ser una mujer hacendosa.
house·keep·ing [háʊskipɪŋ] *s.* gobierno de casa; quehaceres domésticos.
house·top [háʊstɑp] *s.* techumbre, tejado.
house·wife [háʊswaɪf] *s.* mujer de su casa; madre de familia; ama de casa.
house·work [háʊswɚk] *s.* trabajo de casa; quehaceres domésticos.
hous·ing [háʊzɪŋ] *s.* viviendas; programa de construcción de viviendas; (*computer*) unidad, carcasa, mueble.
hove [hov] *pret. & p.p. de* **to heave.**
hov·el [hávl] *s.* choza, cabaña, *Carib., Ven.* bohío, *Méx.* jacal; cobertizo; *Ríopl.* tapera.
hov·er [hávɚ] *v.* cernerse (*como un pájaro*); vacilar; **to** — **around** revolotear; rondar.
how [haʊ] *adv.* cómo; — **beautiful!** ¡qué hermoso!; — **early (late, soon)?** ¿cuándo? ¿a qué hora?; — **far is it?** ¿a qué distancia está? ¿cuánto dista de aquí?; — **long?** ¿cuánto tiempo?; — **many?** ¿cuántos?; — **much is it?** ¿cuánto es? ¿a cómo se vende? ¿cuál es el precio?; — **old are you?** ¿cuántos años tiene Vd.?; **no matter** — **much** por mucho que; **he knows** — **difficult it is** él sabe lo difícil que es; él sabe cuán difícil es.
how·ev·er [haʊɛ́vɚ] *adv. & conj.* sin embargo, no obstante, con todo, empero; — **difficult it may be** por muy difícil que sea; — **much** por mucho que.
howl [haʊl] *s.* aullido, alarido, chillido, grito; *v.* aullar; chillar, dar alaridos; gritar.
hub [hʌb] *s.* cubo (*de una rueda*); eje, centro de actividad.
hub·bub [hábʌb] *s.* ajetreo; barullo.
huck·ster [hákstɚ] *s.* vendedor ambulante.

hud·dle [hʌdl] *s.* montón, confusión, tropel; **to be in a** — estar agrupados (*en futbol para planear una jugada*); **to get in a** — agruparse (*para aconsejarse o planear algo*); *v.* amontonar(se); acurrucarse.
hue [hju] *s.* tinte, matiz.
huff [hʌf] *s.* enojo, rabieta; **to get into a** — enojarse.
hug [hʌg] *v.* abrazar, estrechar; **to** — **the coast** costear; *s.* abrazo fuerte.
huge [hjudʒ] *adj.* enorme; descomunal.
hull [hʌl] *s.* casco (*de una nave*); armazón (*de una aeronave*); vaina, hollejo (*de ciertas legumbres*); *v.* mondar, pelar desvainar, deshollejar.
hum [hʌm] *v.* canturrear (*o* canturriar), tararear; zumbar (*dícese de insectos, maquinaria, etc.*); **to** — **to sleep** arrullar; *s.* canturreo, tarareo; zumbido; *interj.* ¡hum!; ¡ejém!
hu·man [hjúmən] *adj.* humano; *s.* ser humano.
hu·mane [hjumén] *adj.* humano; humanitario.
hu·man·ism [hjúmənɪzm] *s.* humanismo.
hu·man·i·tar·i·an [hjumænətɛ́rɪən] *adj.* humanitario; *s.* filántropo.
hu·man·i·ty [hjumǽnətɪ] *s.* humanidad; **-ies** humanidades.
hum·ble [hámbl] *adj.* humilde; *v.* humillar; **humbly** *adv.* humildemente, con humildad.
hum·ble·ness [hámblnɪs] *s.* humildad.
hu·mid [hjúmɪd] *adj.* húmedo.
hu·mid·i·fy [hjumídəfaɪ] *v.* humedecer.
hu·mid·i·ty [hjumídətɪ] *d.* humedad.
hu·mil·i·ate [hjumflɪet] *v.* humillar.
hu·mil·i·a·tion [hjumɪlɪéʃən] *s.* humillación.
hu·mil·i·ty [hjumflətɪ] *s.* humildad.
hum·ming·bird [hámɪŋbɚd] *s.* colibrí, pájaro mosca, *Méx.* chuparrosa, *Méx.* chupaflor, *S.A.* guainumbí; *Ríopl., Ch.* picaflor; *C.A.* gurrión.
hu·mor [hjúmɚ] *s.* humor, humorismo, gracia; capricho; **out of** — de mal humor, malhumorado, disgustado; *v.* seguir el humor (*a una persona*), complacer; mimar.
hu·mor·ous [hjúmərəs] *adj.* humorístico, gracioso, cómico, chistoso.
hump [hʌmp] *s.* joroba, corcova, giba; *v.* encorvarse.
hump·back [hámpbæk] = **hunchback.**
hunch [hʌntʃ] *s.* joroba, corcova, giba; presentimiento, corazonada; *v.* encorvar (*la espalda*).
hunch·back [hántʃbæk] *s.* joroba, jorobado.
hun·dred [hándrəd] *adj.* cien(to); *s.* ciento; **-s** centenares, cientos.
hun·dredth [hándrədθ] *adj.* centésimo.
hung [hʌŋ] *pret. & p.p. de* **to hang.**
hun·ger [háŋgɚ] *s.* hambre; *v.* tener hambre, estar hambriento; **to** — **for** ansiar, anhelar.
hun·gri·ly [háŋgrɪlɪ] *adv.* con hambre, hambrientamente.
hun·gry [háŋgrɪ] *adj.* hambriento; **to be** — tener hambre.
hunk [hʌŋk] *s.* pedazo grande; mendrugo (*de pan*).
hunt [hʌnt] *v.* cazar; perseguir; buscar; escudriñar; **to** — **down** dar caza a; seguir la pista de; **to** — **for** buscar; *s.* caza, cacería; busca, búsqueda; perseguimiento.
hunt·er [hántɚ] *s.* cazador; buscador; perro de caza, perro de busca.
hunts·man [hántsmən] *s.* cazador.
hurl [hɚl] *v.* arrojar, lanzar.
hur·ly bur·ly [hɚ́lɪbɚ́lɪ] *s.* alboroto, baraúnda, *C.A.* bullas.

HO

hur·rah [hərɔ́] *interj.* ¡hurra! ¡viva!; ¡ole!; *v.* vitorear.

hur·ri·cane [hɜ́ɪken] *s.* huracán.

hur·ried [hɜ́ɪd] *adj.* apresurado; **-ly** *adv.* de prisa, apresuradamente, a escape.

hur·ry [hɜ́ɪ] *v.* apresurar(se); precipitar(se); dar(se) prisa; apurarse; correr; **to — in (out)** entrar (salir) de prisa; **to — up** apresurar(se); dar(se) prisa; *s.* prisa; precipitación; **to be in a —** tener prisa, ir de prisa, estar de prisa.

hurt [hɜ́ɪt] *v.* hacer daño; dañar; perjudicar; herir; lastimar; doler; **to — one's feelings** darle a uno que sentir; lastimar a uno; **my tooth -s** me duele la muela; *pret. & p.p. de* **to hurt;** *s.* daño; herida; lesión; dolor.

hus·band [hʌ́zbənd] *s.* marido, esposo.

hush [hʌʃ] *v.* acallar, aquietar; callar(se); **— !** ¡chitón! ¡silencio! ¡cállese! ¡quieto!; **to — up a scandal** encubrir un escándalo; *s.* silencio, quietud.

husk [hʌsk] *s.* cáscara, hollejo, (*pod*) vaina; *v.* mondar, pelar, deshollejar.

husk·y [hʌ́skɪ] *adj.* (*voice*) ronco; (*strong*) forzudo, fuerte; cascarudo.

hus·tle [hʌ́sl] *v.* apresurar(se); apurarse; menear(se); atropellar; *s.* prisa, apresuramiento, meneo; actividad; **— and bustle** vaivén.

hut [hʌt] *s.* choza, cabaña, *Carib.* bohío; *Méx.* jacal; *S.A.* rancho.

hy·a·cinth [háɪəsɪnθ] *s.* jacinto.

hy·brid [háɪbrɪd] *adj.* híbrido.

hy·drate [háɪdret] *s.* hidrato.

hy·drau·lic [haɪdrɔ́lɪk] *adj.* hidráulico.

hy·dro·e·lec·tric [haɪdroɪléktrɪk] *adj.* hidroeléctrico.

hy·dro·gen [háɪdrədʒən] *s.* hidrógeno.

hy·dro·pho·bi·a [haɪdrofóbɪə] *s.* hidrofobia.

hy·dro·plane [háɪdrəplen] *s.* hidroplano, hidroavión.

hy·giene [háɪdʒin] *s.* higiene.

hymn [hɪm] *s.* himno.

hy·phen [háɪfən] *s.* guión.

hyp·no·sis [hɪpnósɪs] *s.* hipnosis.

hy·poc·ri·sy [hɪpɑ́krəsɪ] *s.* hipocresía.

hyp·o·crite [hípəkrɪt] *s.* hipócrita.

hyp·o·crit·i·cal [hɪpəkrítɪkl] *adj.* hipócrita.

hy·poth·e·sis [haɪpɑ́θəsɪs] *s.* hipótesis.

hys·ter·i·cal [hɪstérɪkl] *adj.* histérico.

I:i

I [aɪ] *pron. pers.* yo.

I-beam [áɪbɪm] viga de doble.

I·be·ri·an [aɪbírɪən] *adj.* ibérico, ibero.

ice [aɪs] *s.* (*solid*) hielo; (*food*) helado; mantecado; sorbete; **— cream** helado; **ice-cream parlor** *Am.* heladería; nevería; **— skates** patines de cuchilla; **— water** agua helada; *v.* helar; escarchar, alfeñicar, cubrir con escarcha (*un pastel*).

ice·berg [áɪsbɜɡ] *s.* montaña de hielo, témpano.

ice·box [áɪsbɑks] *s.* nevera, *Am.* refrigerador.

ice·man [áɪsmæn] *s.* vendedor de hielo.

i·ci·cle [áɪsɪkl] *s.* carámbano.

i·con·o·clasm [aɪkɑ́nəklæzəm] *s.* iconoclasmo.

i·con·o·clast [aɪkɑ́nəklæst] *s.* iconoclasta.

i·cy [áɪsɪ] *adj.* helado, frío; congelado; cubierto de hielo.

i·de·a [aɪdíə] *s.* idea.

i·de·al [aɪdíəl] *adj. & s.* ideal.

i·de·al·ism [aɪdíəlɪzəm] *s.* idealismo.

i·de·al·ist [aɪdíəlɪst] *s.* idealista.

i·de·al·is·tic [aɪdíəlɪstɪk] *adj.* idealista.

i·den·ti·cal [aɪdéntɪkl] *adj.* idéntico.

i·den·ti·fi·ca·tion [aɪdɛntəfɪkéʃən] *s.* identificación; **I.D. card** carnet.

i·den·ti·fy [aɪdéntəfaɪ] *v.* identificar.

i·den·ti·ty [aɪdéntətɪ] *s.* identidad.

i·de·ol·ogy [aɪdɪɔ́lədʒɪ] *s.* ideología.

id·i·o·cy [ɪ́dɪəsɪ] *s.* idiotez.

id·i·om [ɪ́dɪəm] *s.* modismo, idiotismo.

id·i·o·syn·cra·sy [ɪdɪosínkrəsɪ] *s.* idiosincrasia.

id·i·ot [ɪ́dɪət] *s.* idiota.

id·i·ot·ic [ɪdɪɑ́tɪk] *adj.* idiota.

i·dle [áɪdl] *adj.* ocioso; (*lazy*) perezoso, holgazán; vano; desocupado; *v.* holgazanear; perder el tiempo; funcionar (*el motor solo, sin engranar*); **idly** *adv.* ociosamente; inútilmente; perezosamente.

i·dle·ness [áɪdlnɪs] *s.* ociosidad; ocio, desocupación; pereza, holgazanería.

i·dler [áɪdlɚ] *s.* holgazán, haragán.

i·dol [áɪdl] *s.* ídolo.

i·dol·a·try [aɪdɑ́lətrɪ] *s.* idolatría.

i·dol·ize [áɪdlaɪz] *v.* idolatrar.

i·dyl [áɪdl] *s.* idilio.

if [ɪf] *conf.* si.

ig·nite [ɪgnáɪt] *v.* encender(se), inflamar(se); prender, pegar fuego a.

ig·ni·tion [ɪgnɪ́ʃən] *s.* ignición, encendido (*de un motor*); **— switch** interruptor de encendido, *Méx.*, *C.A.*, *Ven.*, *Carib.* switch de ignición.

ig·no·ble [ɪgnóbl] *adj.* innoble; bajo, vil.

ig·no·rance [ɪ́gnərəns] *s.* ignorancia.

ig·no·rant [ɪ́gnərənt] *adj.* ignorante.

ig·nore [ɪgnór] *v.* no hacer caso de, desatender; desairar.

ill [ɪl] *adj.* enfermo; malo; **— nature** mal genio, mala índole; **— will** mala voluntad, ojeriza, inquina; *s.* mal; enfermedad; calamidad, infortunio; *adv.* mal, malamente; **— at ease** inquieto, intranquilo; **ill-bred** mal criado; **ill-clad** mal vestido; **ill-humored** malhumorado; **ill-mannered** descortés, grosero; **ill-natured** de mala índole, *Ven.*, *Col.*, *Méx.* mal genioso; **ill-advised** mal aconsejado.

il·le·gal [ɪlígl] *adj.* ilegal; ilícito.

il·le·git·i·mate [ɪlɪdʒítəmɪt] *adj.* ilegítimo; bastardo.

il·lic·it [ɪlfsɪt] *adj.* ilícito.

il·lit·er·a·cy [ɪlftərəsɪ] *s.* analfabetismo.

il·lit·er·ate [ɪlftərɪt] *adj. & s.* analfabeto.

ill·ness [fɪnɪs] *s.* mal, enfermedad.

il·lu·mi·nate [ɪlúmənet] *v.* iluminar; alumbrar; esclarecer.

il·lu·mi·na·tion [ɪlumənéʃən] *s.* iluminación; alumbrado.

il·lu·sion [ɪlúʒən] *s.* ilusión.

il·lu·sive [ɪlúsɪv] *adj.* ilusorio, ilusivo, falaz.

il·lu·so·ry [ɪlúsərɪ] *adj.* ilusorio, ilusivo, engañoso.

il·lus·trate [ɪətrét] *v.* ilustrar; esclarecer.

il·lus·tra·tion [ɪləstréʃən] *s.* ilustración; grabado, estampa; aclaración, esclarecimiento.

il·lus·tra·tor [fləstretɚ] *s.* ilustrador.

il·lus·tri·ous [ɪlʌ́strɪəs] *adj.* ilustre.

im·age [ɪ́mɪdʒ] *s.* imagen.

im·age·ry [ɪ́mɪdʒrɪ] *s.* conjunto de imágenes, figuras; fantasía.

im·ag·i·nar·y [ɪmǽdʒnɛrɪ] *adj.* imaginario.

im·ag·i·na·tion [ɪmædʒənéʃən] *s.* imaginación; imaginativa.

im·ag·i·na·tive [ɪmǽdʒenetɪv] *adj.* imaginativo.

im·ag·ine [ɪmǽdʒɪn] *v.* imaginar(se); figurarse.

im·be·cile [ɪ́mbəsɪl] *adj. & s.* imbécil.

im·bibe [ɪmbáɪb] *v.* embeber, absorber; beber.

im·bue [ɪmbjú] *v.* imbuir, infundir; impregnar,

empapar.

im·i·tate [ímətet] v. imitar; remedar.

im·i·ta·tion [ɪmətéʃən] s. imitación; remedo; adj. imitado, de imitación.

im·i·ta·tor [ímətetɚ] s. imitador; remedador.

im·mac·u·late [ɪmǽkjəlɪt] adj. inmaculado, sin mancha.

im·ma·te·ri·al [ɪmətírɪəl] adj. inmaterial, espiritual; **it is — to me** me es indiferente.

im·me·di·ate [ɪmídɪɪt] adj. inmediato; próximo; **-ly** adv. inmediatamente; en seguida; al punto, en el acto, al instante.

im·mense [ɪmɛ́ns] adj. inmenso.

im·men·si·ty [ɪmɛ́nsətɪ] s. inmensidad.

im·merse [ɪmɝ́s] v. sumergir, sumir.

im·mi·grant [ímɪgrənt] adj. & s. inmigrante.

im·mi·grate [ímɪgret] v. inmigrar.

im·mi·gra·tion [ɪmɪgréʃən] s. inmigración.

im·mi·nent [ímɪnənt] adj. inminente.

im·mo·bile [ɪmóbil] adj. inmóvil.

im·mod·est [ɪmɑ́dɪst] adj. deshonesto, impúdico, indecente.

im·mor·al [ɪmɔ́rəl] adj. inmoral, licencioso.

im·mor·al·i·ty [ɪmərǽlətɪ] s. inmoralidad.

im·mor·tal [ɪmɔ́rtl] adj. & s. inmortal.

im·mor·tal·i·ty [ɪmɔrtǽlətɪ] s. inmortalidad.

im·mov·a·ble [ɪmúvəbl] adj. inmovible (o inamovible); inmóvil; inmutable.

im·mune [ɪmjún] adj. inmune.

im·mu·ni·ty [ɪmjúnətɪ] s. inmunidad.

im·mu·ta·ble [ɪmjútəbl] adj. inmutable.

imp [ɪmp] s. diablillo.

im·pair [ɪmpɛ́r] v. dañar, perjudicar, menoscabar, desvirtuar, debilitar.

im·pair·ment [ɪmpɛ́rmənt] s. menoscabo; perjuicio; deterioro.

im·part [ɪmpɑ́rt] v. impartir, dar, comunicar.

im·par·tial [ɪmpɑ́rʃəl] adj. imparcial.

im·par·ti·al·i·ty [ɪmpɑrʃ(ǽlətɪ] s. imparcialidad.

im·pas·si·ble [ɪmpǽsəbl] adj. impasible.

im·pas·sioned [ɪmpǽʃənd] adj. apasionado, vehemente, ardiente.

im·pas·sive [ɪmpǽsɪv] adj. impasible.

im·pa·tience [ɪmpéʃəns] s. impaciencia.

im·pa·tient [ɪmpéʃənt] adj. impaciente.

im·peach [ɪmpítʃ] v. demandar o acusar formalmente (a un alto funcionario de gobierno); **to — a person's honor** poner en tela de juicio el honor de uno.

im·pede [ɪmpíd] v. impedir, estorbar, obstruir.

im·ped·i·ment [ɪmpɛ́dəmənt] s. impedimento, obstáculo, estorbo; traba.

im·pel [ɪmpɛ́l] v. impeler, impulsar.

im·pend·ing [ɪmpɛ́ndɪŋ] adj. inminente, amenazador.

im·per·a·tive [ɪmpɛ́rətɪv] adj. imperativo; imperioso, urgente; s. imperativo.

im·per·cep·ti·ble [ɪmpɚsɛ́ptəbl] adj. imperceptible.

im·per·fect [ɪmpɝ́fɪkt] adj. imperfecto; defectuoso; s. imperfecto (tiempo del verbo).

im·pe·ri·al [ɪmpírɪəl] adj. imperial.

im·pe·ri·al·ism [ɪmpírɪəlɪzm] s. imperialismo.

im·per·il [ɪmpɛ́rəl] v. poner en peligro, arriesgar.

im·pe·ri·ous [ɪmpírɪəs] adj. imperioso; urgente.

im·per·son·al [ɪmpɝ́snl] adj. impersonal.

im·per·son·ate [ɪmpɝ́snet] v. representar (un personaje); remedar, imitar; fingirse otro, pretender ser otro.

im·per·ti·nence [ɪmpɝ́tnəns] s. impertinencia; insolencia, descaro.

im·per·ti·nent [ɪmpɝ́tnənt] adj. impertinente; insolente, descarado.

im·per·vi·ous [ɪmpɝ́vɪəs] adj. impermeable; impenetrable; **— to reason** refractario, testarudo.

im·pet·u·ous [ɪmpɛ́tʃʊəs] adj. impetuoso.

im·pe·tus [ímpətəs] s. ímpetu.

im·pi·ous [ímpɪəs] adj. impío.

im·pla·ca·ble [ɪplékəbl] adj. implacable.

im·plant [ɪmplǽnt] v. implantar, plantar; inculcar, infundir.

im·ple·ment [ímpləmənt] s. herramienta, instrumento; **-s** utensilios, aperos, enseres.

im·pli·cate [ímplɪket] v. implicar, envolver, enredar.

im·plic·it [ɪmplísɪt] adj. implícito.

im·plore [ɪmplór] v. implorar, rogar; suplicar.

im·ply [ɪmplái] v. implicar; querer decir; insinuar.

im·po·lite [ɪmpəláɪt] adj. descortés.

im·port [ímport] s. significado, significación, sentido; importancia; importación; **-s** artículos importados; [ɪmpórt] v. importar; significar, querer decir.

im·por·tance [ɪmpórtṇs] s. importancia.

im·por·tant [ɪmpórtṇt] adj. importante.

im·pose [ɪmpóz] v. imponer; **to — upon** abusar de (la amistad, hospitalidad, confianza de alguien); engañar.

im·pos·ing [ɪmpózɪŋ] adj. imponente; impresionante.

im·po·si·tion [ɪmpəzíʃən] s. imposición; carga, impuesto; abuso (de confianza).

im·pos·si·bil·i·ty [ɪmpɑsəbílətɪ] s. imposibilidad.

im·pos·si·ble [ɪmpɑ́səbl] adj. imposible.

im·pos·tor [ɪmpɑ́stɚ] s. impostor, embaucador.

im·pos·ture [ɪmpɑ́stʃɚ] s. impostura, fraude, engaño.

im·po·tence [ímpətəns] s. impotencia.

im·po·tent [ímpətənt] adj. impotente.

im·pov·er·ish [ɪmpɑ́vərɪʃ] v. empobrecer.

im·preg·nate [ɪmprɛ́gnet] v. impregnar; empapar; empreñar.

im·press [ímprɛs] s. impresión, marca, señal, huella; [ɪmprɛ́s] v. imprimir, estampar, marcar, grabar; impresionar.

im·pres·sion [ɪmprɛ́ʃən] s. impresión; marca.

im·pres·sive [ɪmprɛ́sɪv] adj. impresionante; imponente.

im·print [ímprɪnt] s. impresión; pie de imprenta; [ɪmprínt] v. imprimir; estampar.

im·pris·on [ɪmprísṇ] v. aprisionar, encarcelar.

im·pris·on·ment [ɪmprízṇmənt] s. prisión, encarcelación o encarcelamiento.

im·prob·a·ble [ɪmprɑ́bəbl] adj. improbable.

im·promp·tu [ɪmprɑ́mptu] adv. de improviso.

im·prop·er [ɪmprɑ́pɚ] adj. impropio.

im·prove [ɪmprúv] v. mejorar(se); **to — upon** mejorar; **to — one's time** aprovechar el tiempo.

im·prove·ment [ɪmprúvmənt] s. mejoramiento; mejora; progreso, adelanto; mejoría (de una enfermedad).

im·pro·vise [ímprəvaɪz] v. improvisar.

im·pru·dent [ɪmprúdṇt] adj. imprudente.

im·pu·dence [ímpjədəns] s. impudencia, descaro, insolencia.

im·pu·dent [ímpjədənt] adj. impudente, descarado, insolente.

im·pulse [ímpʌls] s. impulso; ímpetu; inclinación; **to act on —** obrar impulsivamente.

im·pul·sive [ɪmpʌ́lsɪv] adj. impulsivo.

im·pu·ni·ty [ɪmpjúnətɪ] s. impunidad, falta o exención de castigo.

im·pure [ɪmpjʊ́r] adj. impuro; (dirty) sucio; (watered) adulterado.

im·pu·ri·ty [ɪmpjʊ́rətɪ] s. impureza.

im·pute [ɪmpjút] v. imputar, achacar, atribuir.

in [ɪn] prep. en; dentro de; de (después de un superlativo); **— haste** de prisa; **— the morning**

por (*o* en) la mañana; — **writing** por escrito; **at two** — **the morning** a las dos de la mañana; **dressed** — **white** vestido de blanco; **the tallest** — **his class** el más alto de su clase; **to come** — **a week** venir de hoy en ocho días, venir dentro de ocho días; *adv.* dentro; adentro; en casa; **to be** — **and out** estar entrando y saliendo; **to be all** — no poder más, estar rendido de cansancio; **to be** — **with someone** estar asociado con alguien; disfrutar el aprecio de una persona; **to come** — entrar; **to have it** — **for someone** tenerle ojeriza a una persona; **to put** — meter; **is the train** — ? ¿ha llegado el tren?

in·a·bil·i·ty [ɪnəbflətɪ] *s.* inhabilidad, incapacidad.

in·ac·ces·si·ble [ɪnəksɛ́səbl] *adj.* inaccesible; inasequible.

in·ac·cu·rate [ɪnǽkjərɪt] *adj.* inexacto, impreciso, incorrecto.

in·ac·tive [ɪnǽktɪv] *adj.* inactivo; inerte.

in·ac·tiv·i·ty [ɪnæktɪ́vətɪ] *s.* inactividad, inacción, inercia.

in·ad·e·quate [ɪnǽdəkwɪt] *adj.* inadecuado; insuficiente.

in·ad·ver·tent [ɪnədvɝ́tnt] *adj.* inadvertido; descuidado; **-ly** *adv.* inadvertidamente; descuidadamente.

in·ad·vis·a·ble [ɪnədváɪzəbl] *adj.* imprudente.

in·an·i·mate [ɪnǽnəmɪt] *adj.* inanimado.

in·as·much [ɪnəzmátʃ]: — **as** visto que, puesto que; en cuanto.

in·at·ten·tive [ɪnətɛ́ntɪv] *adj.* desatento.

in·au·gu·rate [ɪnɔ́gjərət] *v.* inaugurar, iniciar; investir de una dignidad o cargo.

in·au·gu·ra·tion [ɪnɔgjəréʃən] *s.* inauguración.

in·board [ínbord] *adj.* interior.

in·born [ɪnbɔ́rn] *adj.* innato, connatural.

in·can·des·cent [ɪnkəndɛ́snt] *adj.* incandescente, candente.

in·can·ta·tion [ɪnkænté ʃən] *s.* conjuro.

in·ca·pa·ble [ɪnképəbl] *adj.* incapaz.

in·ca·pac·i·tate [ɪkəpǽsɪtet] *v.* incapacitar.

in·cen·di·ar·y [ɪsɛ́ndɪɛrɪ] *adj.* incendiario; — **bomb** bomba incendiaria.

in·cense [ínsɛns] *s.* incienso; [ɪnsɛ́ns] *v.* inflamar, exasperar.

in·cen·tive [ɪnsɛ́ntɪv] *s.* incentivo, estímulo.

in·ces·sant [ɪnsɛ́snt] *adj.* incesante, continuo.

inch [ɪntʃ] *s.* pulgada (*2.54 centímetros*); **by -es** poco a poco, gradualmente; **every** — **a man** nada menos que todo un hombre; **to be within an** — **of** estar a dos pulgadas de, estar muy cerca de; *v.* avanzar muy despacio (*por pulgadas*).

in·ci·dence [ínsɪdəns] *s.* incidencia.

in·ci·dent [ínsədənt] *s.* incidente, suceso, acontecimiento.

in·ci·den·tal [ɪnsədɛ́ntl] *adj.* incidental; accidental; contingente; **-s** *s. pl.* gastos imprevistos; **-ly** *adv.* incidentalmente; de paso.

in·cip·i·ent [ɪnsfpɪənt] *adj.* incipiente.

in·ci·sion [ɪnsíʒən] *s.* incisión.

in·ci·sive [ɪnsáɪsɪv] *adj.* incisivo.

in·cite [ɪnsáɪt] *v.* incitar.

in·clem·ent [ɪnklɛmənt] *adj.* inclemente.

in·cli·na·tion [ɪnklənéʃən] *s.* inclinación.

in·cline [ínklaɪn] *s.* declive, pendiente, cuesta; [ɪnkláɪn] *v.* inclinar(se).

in·close = **enclose.**

in·clo·sure = **enclosure.**

in·clude [ɪnklúd] *v.* incluir, encerrar; abarcar.

in·clu·sive [ɪnklúsɪv] *adj.* inclusivo; **from Monday to Friday** — del lunes al viernes inclusive.

in·co·her·ent [ɪnkohírənt] *adj.* incoherente, inconexo.

in·come [ínkʌm] *s.* renta, rédito, ingreso, entrada; — **tax** impuesto sobre rentas (ingresos); *Arg.* impuesto a los réditos, *Ch.* impuesto cedular.

in·com·pa·ra·ble [ɪnkɑ́mpərəbl] *adj.* incomparable, sin par, sin igual.

in·com·pat·i·ble [ɪnkəmpǽtəbl] *adj.* incompatible.

in·com·pe·tent [ɪnkɑ́mpətənt]·*adj.* incompetente.

in·com·plete [ɪnkəmplít] *adj.* incompleto.

in·com·pre·hen·si·ble [ɪnkɑmprɪhɛ́nsəbl] *adj.* incomprensible.

in·con·ceiv·a·ble [ɪnkənsívəbl] *adj.* inconcebible.

in·con·clu·sive [ɪnkənklúsɪv]·*adj.* inconcluso.

in·con·sid·er·ate [ɪnkənsídərɪt] *adj.* inconsiderado, falto de miramiento.

in·con·sis·ten·cy [ɪnkənsfstənsɪ] *s.* inconsecuencia; falta de uniformidad (*en la aplicación de una regla o principio*).

in·con·sis·tent [ɪnkənsfstənt] *adj.* inconsecuente; falto de uniformidad.

in·con·spic·u·ous [ɪnkənspfkjuəs] *adj.* poco llamativo.

in·con·stan·cy [ɪnkɑ́nstənsɪ] *s.* inconstancia, mudanza.

in·con·stant [ɪnkɑ́nstənt] *adj.* inconstante, mudable, voluble.

in·con·test·a·ble [ɪnkəntɛ́stəbl] *adj.* incontestable.

in·con·ven·ience [ɪnkənvínjəns] *s.* inconveniencia, molestia; *v. incomodar; molestar.*

in·con·ven·ient [ɪnkənvínjənt] *adj.* inconveniente; inoportuno.

in·cor·po·rate [ɪnkɔ́rperɪt] *adj.* incorporado; asociado; [ɪnkɔ́rpəret] *v.* incorporar; incorporarse, asociarse (*para formar un cuerpo*).

in·cor·rect [ɪnkərɛ́kt] *adj. incorrecto.*

in·cor·ri·gi·ble [ɪnkɔ́rɪdʒəbl] *adj.* incorregible.

in·crease [ínkrɪs] *s:* aumento; acrecentamiento; crecimiento; incremento; [ɪnkrís]·*v.* aumentar(se); acrecentar(se), crecer; recargar.

in·creas·ing·ly [ɪnkrísɪŋlɪ] *adv.* más y más; cada vez más.

in·cred·i·ble [ɪnkrɛ́dəbl] *adj.* increíble.

in·cre·du·li·ty [ɪnkrədúətɪ] *s.* incredulidad.

in·cred·u·lous [ɪnkrɛ́dʒələs] *adj.* incrédulo, descreído.

in·cre·ment [ínkrəmənt] *s.* incremento.

in·crim·i·nate [ɪnkrímənet] *v.* acriminar.

in·cu·ba·tor [ínkjubetɚ] *s.* incubadora.

in·cul·cate [ɪnkʌ́lket] *v.* inculcar, infundir.

in·cum·bent [ɪnkʌ́mbənt] *s.* incumbente.

in·cur [ɪnkɝ́] *v.* incurrir en.

in·cur·a·ble [ɪnkjúrəbl] *adj.* incurable, irremediable; *s.* incurable.

in·debt·ed [ɪndɛ́tɪd] *adj.* adeudado, endeudado; obligado, agradecido.

in·debt·ed·ness [ɪndɛ́tɪdnɪs] *s.* deuda, obligación.

in·de·cen·cy [ɪndísnsɪ] *s.* indecencia.

in·de·cent [ɪndísnt] *adj.* indecente.

in·de·ci·sion [ɪndəsfʒən] *s.* indecisión.

in·deed [ɪndíd] *adv.* en verdad, a la verdad; de veras; realmente.

in·de·fen·si·ble [ɪndɪfɛ́nsəbl] *adj.* indefendible.

in·def·i·nite [ɪndɛ́fənɪt] *adj.* indefinido.

in·del·i·ble [ɪndɛ́ləbl] *adj.* indeleble.

in·del·i·cate [ɪndɛ́ləkət] *adj.* indelicado, indecoroso.

in·dem·ni·fy [ɪndɛ́mnəfaɪ] *v.* indemnizar.

in·dem·ni·ty [ɪndɛ́mnətɪ] *s.* indemnización.

in·dent [ɪndɛ́nt] *v.* dentar, endentar; sangrar (*comenzar un renglón más adentro que los otros*).

in·de·pend·ence [ɪndɪpɛ́ndəns] *s.* independencia.

in·de·pend·ent [ɪndɪpɛ́ndənt] *adj.* independiente.

in·de·scrib·a·ble [ɪndɪskráɪbəbl] *adj.* indescriptible.

in·dex [índɛks] *s.* índice; — **card** ficha para índices; *v.* alfabetizar, ordenar alfabéticamente; poner en un índice; — **finger** índice.
In·di·an [índɪən] *adj. & s.* indio; — **Ocean** Océano Indico.
in·di·cate [índəket] *v.* indicar.
in·di·ca·tion [ɪdəkéʃən] *s.* indicación.
in·dic·a·tive [ɪdíkətɪv] *adj. & s.* indicativo.
in·dict [ɪndáɪt] *v.* procesar, demandar (*ante un juez*); enjuiciar, formar causa a.
in·dict·ment [ɪndáɪtmənt] *s.* acusación (*hecha por el Gran Jurado*), denuncia, proceso judicial.
in·dif·fer·ence [ɪndíffrəns] *s.* indiferencia; apatía.
in·dif·fer·ent [ɪndíffrənt] *adj.* indiferente; apático.
in·dig·e·nous [ɪndíʤənəs] *adj.* indígena, autóctono, nativo.
in·di·gent [índədʒənt] *adj. & s.* indigente.
in·di·ges·tion [ɪndədʒéstʃən] *s.* indigestión.
in·dig·nant [ɪndígnənt] *adj.* indignado; **-ly** *adv.* con indignación.
in·dig·na·tion [ɪndɪgnéʃən] *s.* indignación.
in·dig·ni·ty [ɪndígnətɪ] *s.* indignidad, afrenta.
in·di·go [índɪgo] *s.* índigo, añil; — **blue** azul de añil.
in·di·rect [ɪndərɛ́kt] *adj.* indirecto.
in·dis·creet [ɪndɪskrít] *adj.* indiscreto.
in·dis·cre·tion [ɪndɪskrɛ́ʃən] *s.* indiscreción.
in·dis·pen·sa·ble [ɪndɪspɛ́nsəbl] *adj.* indispensable.
in·dis·pose [ɪndɪspóz] *v.* indisponer.
in·dis·posed [ɪndɪspózd] *adj.* indispuesto.
in·dis·po·si·tion [ɪndɪspəzíʃən] *s.* indisposición; malestar.
in·dis·tinct [ɪndɪstíŋkt] *adj.* indistinto.
in·di·um [índɪəm] *s.* indio.
in·di·vid·u·al [ɪndəvíʤʊəl] *adj.* individual; *s.* individuo, sujeto, persona.
in·di·vid·u·al·ism [ɪndəvíʤʊəlɪzm] *s.* individualismo.
in·di·vid·u·al·ist [ɪndəvíʤʊəlɪst] *s.* individualista.
in·di·vid·u·al·i·ty [ɪndəvɪdʒuǽlətɪ] *s.* individualidad; individuo, persona.
in·di·vis·i·ble [ɪndəvízəbl] *adj.* indivisible.
in·doc·tri·nate [ɪndɑ́ktrɪnet] *v.* adoctrinar.
in·do·lence [índələns] *s.* indolencia, desidia, apatía.
in·do·lent [índələnt] *adj.* indolente, desidioso, apático.
in·dom·i·ta·ble [ɪndɑ́mətəbl] *adj.* indomable.
in·door [índor] *adj.* interior, de casa.
in·doors [índórz] *adv.* dentro, en casa; adentro; **to go** — entrar; ir adentro.
in·dorse = **endorse**.
in·dorse·ment = **endorsement**.
in·dors·er = **endorser**.
in·duce [ɪndjús] *v.* inducir.
in·duce·ment [ɪndjúsmənt] *s.* aliciente, incentivo.
in·duct [ɪndʌ́kt] *v.* introducir; iniciar; instalar (*en un cargo*).
in·duc·tion [ɪndʌ́kʃən] *s.* inducción; instalación (*en un cargo*).
in·dulge [ɪnkʌ́lʤ] *v.* gratificar, complacer; seguir el humor a (*una persona*); mimar, consentir (*a un niño*); **to** — **in** darse a, entregarse a (*un placer*); darse el lujo de, permitirse el placer de.
in·dul·gence [ɪndʌ́lʤəns] *s.* indulgencia; complacencia (*en el vicio o placer*).
in·dul·gent [ɪndʌ́lʤənt] *adj.* indulgente.
in·dus·tri·al [ɪnkʌ́strɪəl] *adj.* industrial.
in·dus·tri·al·ist [ɪndʌ́strɪəlɪst] *s.* industrial; fabricante.
in·dus·tri·ous [ɪndʌ́strɪəs] *adj.* industrioso, aplicado, diligente.
in·dus·try [índəstrɪ] *s.* industria; aplicación, diligencia.
in·ed·i·ble [ɪnɛ́dəbl] *adj.* incomestible.

in·ef·fa·ble [ɪnɛ́fəbl] *adj.* inefable.
in·ef·fec·tive [ɪnəfɛ́ktɪv] *adj.* inefectivo, ineficaz.
in·ef·fi·cient [ɪnɪffʃənt] *adj.* ineficaz.
in·el·i·gi·ble [ɪnɛ́ləʤəbl] *adj.* inelegible.
in·e·qual·i·ty [ɪnɪkwálətɪ] *s.* desigualdad; disparidad.
in·ert [ɪnɜ́t] *adj.* inerte.
in·er·tia [ɪnɜ́ʃə] *s.* inercia.
in·es·cap·a·ble [ɪnəsképəbl] *adj.* forzoso, inevitable.
in·es·ti·ma·ble [ɪnɛ́stəməbl] *adj.* inestimable.
in·ev·i·ta·ble [ɪnɛ́vətəbl] *adj.* inevitable.
in·ex·haust·i·ble [ɪnɪgzɔ́stəbl] *adj.* inagotable.
in·ex·o·ra·ble [ɪnɛ́ksərəbl] *adj.* inexorable; severo.
in·ex·pe·di·ent [ɪnɛkspídjənt] *adj.* inoportuno; imprudente.
in·ex·pen·sive [ɪnɪkspɛ́nsɪv] *adj.* económico, barato.
in·ex·pe·ri·ence [ɪnɪkspfríəns] *s.* inexperiencia, falta de experiencia.
in·ex·pe·ri·enced [ɪnɪkspfríənst] *adj.* inexperto, falto de experiencia.
in·ex·pli·ca·ble [ɪnɛ́ksplɪkəbl] *adj.* inexplicable.
in·ex·press·i·ble [ɪnɪksprésəbl] *adj.* inexpresable, indecible, inefable.
in·fal·li·ble [ɪnfǽləbl] *adj.* infalible.
in·fa·mous [ínfəməs] *adj.* infame, ignominioso.
in·fa·my [ínfəmɪ] *s.* infamia.
in·fan·cy [ínfənsɪ] *s.* infancia.
in·fant [ínfənt] *s.* infante, bebé, criatura, nene.
in·fan·tile [ínfəntaɪl] *adj.* infantil.
in·fan·try [ífəntrɪ] *s.* infantería.
in·fect [ɪnfɛ́kt] *v.* infectar, inficionar; contagiar; contaminar.
in·fec·tion [ɪnfɛ́kʃən] *s* infección; contagio.
in·fec·tious [ɪnfɛ́kʃəs] *adj.* infeccioso; contagioso.
in·fer [ɪnfɜ́] *v.* inferir, deducir, colegir.
in·fer·ence [ínfərəns] *s.* inferencia, deducción.
in·fe·ri·or [ɪnfírɪɚ] *adj. & s.* inferior.
in·fe·ri·or·i·ty [ɪnfɪrɪɔ́rətɪ] *s.* inferioridad; — **complex** complejo de inferioridad.
in·fer·nal [ɪnfɜ́nl] *adj.* infernal.
in·fer·no [ɪnfɜ́no] *s.* infierno.
in·fest [ɪnfɛ́st] *v.* infestar, plagar.
in·fi·del [ínfədl] *adj. & s.* infiel.
in·fil·trate [ɪnfíltret] *v.* infiltrar(se).
in·fi·nite [ínfənɪt] *adj. & s.* infinito.
in·fin·i·tive [ɪnfínətɪv] *adj. & s.* infinitivo.
in·fin·i·ty [ɪnfínətɪ] *s.* infinidad; infinito.
in·firm [ɪnfɜ́m] *adj.* enfermizo, achacoso, débil.
in·fir·ma·ry [ɪnfɜ́mərɪ] *s.* enfermería.
in·fir·mi·ty [ɪnfɜ́mətɪ] *s.* enfermedad, achaque; flaqueza.
in·flame [ɪnflém] *v.* inflamar(se); enardecer(se).
in·flam·ma·tion [ɪnfləméʃən] *s.* inflamación.
in·flate [ɪnflét] *v.* inflar; hinchar.
in·fla·tion [ɪnfléʃən] *s.* inflación; hinchazón.
in·flec·tion [ɪnflɛ́kʃən] *s.* inflexión.
in·flict [ɪnflíkt] *v.* infligir, imponer.
in·flu·ence [ínfluəns] *s.* influencia, influjo; — **peddler** traficante de influencias; *v.* influir en; ejercer influencia o influjo sobre.
in·flu·en·tial [ɪnfluɛ́nʃəl] *adj.* influyente.
in·flu·en·za [ɪnfluɛ́nzə] *s.* influenza, gripe.
in·flux [ínflʌks] *s.* entrada, afluencia (*de gente*).
in·fold [ɪnfóld] *v.* envolver; abrazar; abarcar.
in·form [ɪnfɔ́rm] *v.* informar; enterar; avisar; **to** — **against** delatar a, denunciar a.
in·for·mal [ɪnfɔ́rml] *adj.* informal, sin ceremonia; — **visit** visita de confianza; **-ly** *adv.* informalmente, sin ceremonia, de confianza.
in·form·ant [ɪnfɔ́rmənt] *s.* informante.
in·for·ma·tion [ɪnfɚméʃən] *s.* (*service*) información; (*details*) informes; (*news*) noticias; (*knowledge*)

IN

conocimientos, saber.
in·frac·tion]ınfrǽkʃən] *s.* infracción.
in·fringe [ınfrínd3] *v.* infringir, violar; **to — upon** violar.
in·fu·ri·ate [ınfjúriet] *v.* enfurecer.
in·fuse [ınfjúz] *v.* infundir; inculcar.
in·gen·ious [ınd3ínjəs] *adj.* ingenioso.
in·ge·nu·i·ty [ınd3ənúətı] *s.* ingeniosidad.
in·grat·i·tude [ıngrǽtətjud] *s.* ingratitud.
in·gre·di·ent [ıngrídıənt] *s.* ingrediente.
in·hab·it [ınhǽbıt] *v.* habitar, vivir en, residir en.
in·hab·i·tant [ınhǽbətənt] *s.* habitante.
in·hale [ınhél] *v.* inhalar, aspirar, inspirar.
in·her·ent [ınhírənt] *adj.* inherente.
in·her·it [ınhérıt] *v.* heredar.
in·her·i·tance [ınhérətəns] *s.* herencia.
in·hib·it [ınhíbıt] *v.* inhibir, cohibir, refrenar, reprimir; impedir.
in·hi·bi·tion [ınıbíʃən] *s.* inhibición, cohibición; prohibición, restricción.
in·hos·pi·ta·ble [ınháspıtəbl] *adj.* inhospitalario.
in·hu·man [ınhjúmən] *adj.* inhumano.
in·im·i·ta·ble [ınímətəbl] *adj.* inimitable.
in·iq·ui·ty [ıníkwətı *s.* iniquidad, maldad.
in·i·tial [ıníʃəl] *adj. & s.* inicial; **— abbreviation** sigla; *v.* marcar o firmar con iniciales.
in·i·ti·ate [ıníʃıet] *v.* iniciar.
in·i·ti·a·tive [ıníʃıetıv] *s.* iniciativa.
in·ject [ınd3ékt] *v.* inyectar; injerir, introducir.
in·jec·tion [ınd3ékʃən] *s.* inyección.
in·junc·tion [ınd3ʌ́ŋkʃən] *s.* mandato, orden; entredicho.
in·jure [índ3ɚ] *v.* dañar; herir, lesionar; lastimar.
in·ju·ri·ous [ınd3úrıəs] *adj.* dañoso, dañino, perjudicial.
in·ju·ry [índ3ərı] *s.* daño; herida, lesión; perjuicio.
in·jus·tice [ınd3ʌ́stıs] *s.* injusticia.
ink [ıŋk] *s.* tinta; *v.* entintar; teñir o manchar con tinta.
ink·ling [íŋklıŋ] *s.* indicación, indicio, idea, sospecha, noción vaga.
ink·stand [íŋkstænd] *s.* tintero.
ink·well [íŋkwɛl] *s.* tintero.
in·laid [ınléd] *adj.* incrustado, embutido; **— work** embutido, incrustación; *pret. & p.p. de* **to inlay.**
in·land [ínlənd] *s.* interior (*de un país*); *adj.* interior, del interior de un país; *adv.* tierra adentro.
in·lay [ınlé]*v.* incrustar, embutir; [ínle] *s.* embutido.
in·mate [ínmet] *s.* residente, asilado (*de un hospicio, asilo, casa de corrección, etc.*); presidiario; hospiciano.
in·most [ínmost] *adj.* más interior, más íntimo, más secreto o recóndito; más profundo.
inn [ın] *s.* posada, mesón, fonda.
in·nate [ınét] *adj.* innato, connatural.
in·ner [ínɚ] *adj.* interior; íntimo, recóndito; **— most = inmost.**
in·ning [ínıŋ *s.* entrada, cuadro (*en béisbol*); turno (*del bateador en béisbol y otros juegos*).
inn·keep·er [ínkipɚ] *s.* ventero, mesonero, posadero.
in·no·cence [ínəsns] *s.* inocencia.
in·no·cent [ínəsnt] *adj. & s.* inocente.
in·noc·u·ous [ınákjuəs] *adj.* innocuo, inofensivo.
in·no·va·tion [ınəvéʃən] *s.* innovación.
in·nu·en·do [ınjuɛ́ndo] *s.* insinuación, indirecta.
in·nu·mer·a·ble [ınjúmərəbl] *adj.* innumerable.
in·oc·u·late [ınákjəlet] *v.* inocular; contaminar.
in·of·fen·sive [ınəfɛ́nsıv] *adj.* inofensivo.
in·op·por·tune [ınapɚtjún] *adj.* inoportuno.
in·put [ínput] *s.* potencia consumida; (*electric*) entrada; (*contribution*) sugerencias al caso;

(*computer*) entrada; *v.* introducir, ingresar.
in·quire [ınkwáır] *v.* inquirir, indagar; preguntar; **to — about** preguntar por; **to — into** indagar, investigar.
in·qui·ry [ınkwáırı] *s.* indagación, investigación; pregunta; interrogatorio.
in·qui·si·tion [ınkwəzíʃən] *s.* inquisición; indagación.
in·quis·i·tive [ınkwízətıv] *adj.* inquisitivo, investigador; preguntón; curioso.
in·road [ínrod] *s.* incursión, invasión, ataque; **to make -s upon** atacar; mermar.
in·sane [ınsén] *adj.* insano, loco; **— asylum** manicomio, casa de locos.
in·san·i·ty [ınsǽnətı] *s.* locura.
in·sa·tia·ble [ınséʃıəbl] *adj.* insaciable.
in·scribe [ınskráıb] *v.* inscribir.
in·scrip·tion [ınskrípʃən] *s.* inscripción; letrero.
in·sect [ínsɛkt] *s.* insecto.
in·se·cure [ınsıkjúr] *adj.* inseguro.
in·sen·si·ble [ınsɛ́nsəbl] *adj.* insensible.
in·sen·si·tive [ınsɛ́nsətıv] *adj.* insensible.
in·sep·a·ra·ble [ınsépərəbl] *adj.* inseparable.
in·sert [ínsɚt] *s.* inserción; intercalación; hoja (*insertada en un libro*); circular, folleto (*insertado en un periódico*); [ınsɚt] *v.* insertar; intercalar; encajar; meter.
in·ser·tion [ınsɚ́ʃən] *s.* inserción; introducción.
in·side [ínsáıd] *s.* interior; **-s** entrañas; *adj.* interior, interno; secreto; **— job** delito cometido por el personal; **— track** con datos privados. *adv.* dentro; adentro; **to turn — out** volver(se) al revés; *prep.* dentro de.
in·sight [ínsaıt] *s.* penetración, discernimiento; intuición; perspicacia; comprensión.
in·sig·ni·a [ınsígnıə] *s. pl.* insignias.
in·sig·nif·i·cant [ınsıgnıffəkənt] *adj.* insignificante.
in·sin·u·ate [ınsínjuet] *v.* insinuar.
in·sin·u·a·tion [ınsınjuéʃən] *s.* insinuación; indirecta.
in·sip·id [ınsípıd] *adj.* insípido.
in·sist [ınsíst] *v.* insistir en; empeñarse(en); porfiar, persistir.
in·sis·tence [ınsístəns] *s.* insistencia, empeño, porfía.
in·sis·tent [ınsístənt] *adj.* insistente; porfiado, persistente.
in·so·lence [ínsələns] *s.* insolencia.
in·so·lent [ínsələnt] *adj.* insolente.
in·sol·u·ble [ınsáljəbl] *adj.* insoluble.
in·spect [ınspékt] *v.* inspeccionar; examinar, registrar.
in·spec·tion [ınspékʃən] *s.* inspección; registro.
in·spec·tor [ınspɛ́ktɚ] *s.* inspector.
in·spi·ra·tion [ınspəréʃən] *s.* inspiración.
in·spire [ınspáır] *v.* inspirar.
in·stall [ınstɔ́l] *v.* instalar.
in·stal·la·tion [ınstəléʃən] *s.* instalación.
in·stall·ment, in·stal·ment [ınstɔ́lmənt] *s.* instalación; abono (*pago*); plazos, *Col.* cuotas; entrega o continuación (*semanal o mensual de una novela*); **to pay in -s** pagar por plazos; pagar en abonos.
in·stance [ínstəns] *s.* ejemplo, caso; vez, ocasión; instancia; **for —** por ejemplo.
in·stant [ínstənt] *s.* instante; *adj.* inmediato; urgente; **the 10th —** el 10 del (mes) corriente; **-ly** *adv.* al instante, inmediatamente.
in·stan·ta·ne·ous [ınstənténıəs] *adj.* instantáneo.
in·stead [ınstéd] *adv.* en lugar de ello (eso, él, ella, *etc.*); **— of** en lugar de, en vez de.
in·step [ínstɛp] *s.* empeine (*del pie, del zapato*).
in·sti·gate [ínstəget] *v.* instigar.
in·still [ınstíl] *v.* inculcar, infundir.
in·stinct [ínstıŋkt] *s.* instinto.

in·stinc·tive [ɪnstíŋktɪv] *adj.* instintivo.
in·sti·tute [ínstətjut] *s.* instituto; *v.* instituir.
in·sti·tu·tion [ɪnstətjúʃən] *s.* institución.
in·struct [ɪnstrʌ́kt] *v.* instruir; dar instrucciones.
in·struc·tion [ɪnstrʌ́kʃən] *s.* instrucción; enseñanza; **lack of —** falta de saber o conocimientos; **-s** órdenes, instrucciones.
in·struc·tive [ɪnstrʌ́ktɪv] *adj.* instructivo.
in·struc·tor [ɪnstrʌ́ktɚ] *s.* instructor.
in·stru·ment [ínstrəmənt] *s.* instrumento; **— panel** salpicadero.
in·stru·men·tal [ɪnstrəméntl] *adj.* instrumental; **to be — in** ayudar a, servir de instrumento para.
in·sub·or·di·nate [ɪnsəbɔ́rdɪnət] *adj.* insubordinado.
in·suf·fer·a·ble [ɪnsʌ́frəbl] *adj.* insufrible, inaguantable.
in·suf·fi·cien·cy [ɪnsəfíʃənsɪ] *s.* insuficiencia; incompetencia; falta, escasez.
in·suf·fi·cient [ɪnsəfíʃənt] *adj.* insuficiente; inadecuado.
in·su·late [ínsəlet] *v.* aislar.
in·su·la·tion [ɪnsəléʃən] *s.* aislamiento; aislación.
in·su·la·tor [ínsəletɚ] *s.* aislador.
in·su·lin [ínsələn] *s.* insulina.
in·sult [ínsʌlt] *s.* insulto; [ɪnsʌ́lt] *v.* insultar.
in·sur·ance [ɪnʃúrəns] *s.* aseguramiento; seguro; prima, premio (*de una póliza de seguro*); **— agent** agente de seguros; **— company** compañía de seguros; **— policy** póliza de seguro; **accident —** seguro contra accidentes; **fire —** seguro contra incendios; **life —** seguro sobre la vida.
in·sure [ɪnʃúr] *v.* asegurar; asegurarse de.
in·sur·gent [ɪnsɝ́dʒənt] *adj. & s.* insurgente, insurrecto.
in·sur·mount·a·ble [ɪnsɚmáʊntəbl] *adj.* insuperable.
in·sur·rec·tion [ɪnsərékʃən] *s.* insurrección, rebelión, alzamiento.
in·tact [ɪntǽkt] *adj.* intacto.
in·te·ger programming [ɪntəgɚ progrǽmɪŋ] *s.* programación por integración.
in·te·gral [íntəgrəl] *adj.* integral; integrante; *s.* integral.
in·te·grate [íntəgret] *v.* integrar.
in·teg·ri·ty [ɪntégrətɪ] *s.* integridad, entereza.
in·tel·lect [íntlɛkt] *s.* intelecto; entendimiento.
in·tel·lec·tu·al [ɪntlɛ́ktʃuəl] *adj. & s.* intelectual.
in·tel·li·gence [ɪntɛ́lədʒəns] *s.* inteligencia; **— quotient** (I.Q.) cociente de inteligencia; información, noticias; policía secreta.
in·tel·li·gent [ɪntɛ́lədʒənt] *adj.* inteligente.
in·tel·li·gi·ble [ɪntɛ́lədʒəbl] *adj.* inteligible.
in·tem·per·ance [ɪntɛ́mpərəns] *s.* intemperancia.
in·tend [ɪntɛ́nd] *v.* intentar, pensar, tener la intención de; proponerse; destinar; **to — to do it** pensar hacerlo.
in·tense [ɪntɛ́ns] *adj.* intenso.
in·ten·si·fy [ɪntɛ́nsɪfaɪ] *v.* intensificar.
in·ten·si·ty [ɪntɛ́nsətɪ] *s.* intensidad.
in·ten·sive [ɪntɛ́nsɪv] *adj.* intenso; intensivo.
in·tent [ɪntɛ́nt] *s.* intento, intención, propósito; significado; **to all -s and purposes** en todo caso, en todos sentidos; en realidad; *adj.* atento; **— on** absorto en, reconcentrado en; resuelto a, decidido a.
in·ten·tion [ɪntɛ́nʃən] *s.* intención.
in·ten·tion·al [ɪntɛ́nʃənl] *adj.* intencional; **-ly** *adv.* intencionalmente, adrede, a propósito.
in·ter [ɪntɝ́] *v.* enterrar, sepultar.
in·ter·cede [ɪntɚsíd] *v.* interceder.
in·ter·cept [ɪntɚsɛ́pt] *v.* interceptar; atajar.
in·ter·cep·tion [ɪntɚsɛ́pʃən] *s.* interceptación.

in·ter·ces·sion [ɪntɚsɛ́ʃən] *s.* intercesión.
in·ter·change [ɪntɚtʃéndʒ] *s.* intercambio; cambio, trueque; [ɪntɚtʃéndʒ] *v.* cambiar, trocar; permutar; alternar.
in·ter·course [ɪntɚkors] *s.* comunicación; comercio, trato; intercambio (*de ideas, sentimientos, etc.*).
in·ter·den·tal [ɪntɚdɛ́ntl] *adj.* interdental.
in·ter·est [íntərɪst] *s.* interés; rédito; participación (*en un negocio*); *v.* interesar.
in·ter·est·ed [íntərɪstɪd] *adj.* interesado; **to be** (*o* **become**) **— in** interesarse en (*o por*).
in·ter·est·ing [íntərɪstɪŋ] *adj.* interesante.
in·ter·face [íntɚfes] *s.* (*computer*) interfaz, interface.
in·ter·fere [ɪntɚfír] *v.* intervenir; interponerse, entremeterse; estorbar; **to — with** estorbar, frustrar, dificultar.
in·ter·fer·ence [ɪntɚfírəns] *s.* intervención; obstáculo; interferencia (*en la radio*).
in·ter·im [íntərɪm] *adj.* interino, intermedio.
in·te·ri·or [ɪntíriɚ] *adj.* interior; interno; *s.* interior.
in·ter·jec·tion [ɪntɚdʒɛ́kʃən] *s.* interjección, exclamación; intercalación.
in·ter·lace [ɪntɚlés] *v.* entrelazar, enlazar, entretejer.
in·ter·lin·e·ar [ɪntɚlínɪɚ] *adj.* interlineal.
in·ter·lock [ɪntɚlák] *v.* entrelazar(se); trabar(se); **interlocking** entrelazados.
in·ter·lude [íntɚlud] *s.* intervalo.
in·ter·me·di·ate [ɪntɚmídɪɪt] *adj.* intermedio.
in·ter·mi·na·ble [ɪntɝ́mɪnəbl] *adj.* interminable, inacabable.
in·ter·min·gle [ɪntɚmíŋgl] *v.* entremezclar(se), entreverar(se); mezclar(se).
in·ter·mis·sion [ɪntɚmíʃən] *s.* intermisión; intermedio, entreacto.
in·ter·mit·tent [ɪntɚmítŋt] *adj.* intermitente.
in·tern [ɪntɝ́n] *v.* internar, confinar, encerrar; [íntɝn] *s.* practicante (*de medicina en un hospital*).
in·ter·nal [ɪntɝ́nl] *adj.* interno; interior; **— revenue** rentas internas; **— memory** (*computer*) memoria residente.
in·ter·na·tion·al [ɪntɚnǽʃənl] *adj.* internacional.
in·ter·o·ce·an·ic [ɪntɚoʃiǽnɪk] *adj.* interoceánico.
in·ter·pose [ɪntɚpóz] *v.* interponer(se).
in·ter·pret [ɪntɝ́prɪt] *v.* interpretar.
in·ter·pre·ta·tion [ɪntɚprɪtéʃən] *s.* interpretación.
in·ter·pret·er [ɪntɝ́prɪtɚ] *s.* intérprete.
in·ter·ro·gate [ɪntɛ́rəget] *v.* interrogar.
in·ter·ro·ga·tion [ɪntɛrəgéʃən] *s.* interrogación.
in·ter·rog·a·tive [ɪntərágətɪv] *adj.* interrogativo; *s.* pronombre o palabra interrogativa.
in·ter·rupt [ɪntərʌ́pt] *v.* interrumpir.
in·ter·rup·tion [ɪntərʌ́pʃən] *s.* interrupción.
in·ter·sect [ɪntɚsɛ́kt] *v.* cortar(se); cruzar(se).
in·ter·sec·tion [ɪntɚsɛ́kʃən] *s.* intersección; **street —** bocacalle.
in·ter·sperse [ɪntɚspɝ́s] *v.* entremezclar, esparcir.
in·ter·stice [ɪntɝ́stɪs] *s.* intersticio.
in·ter·twine [ɪntɚtwáɪn] *v.* entrelazar, entretejer, trenzar.
in·ter·val [íntɚvl] *s.* intervalo.
in·ter·vene [ɪntɚvín] *v.* intervenir; interponerse; mediar.
in·ter·ven·tion [ɪntɚvɛ́nʃən] *s.* intervención.
in·ter·view [íntɚvju] *s.* entrevista; *v.* entrevistar, entrevistarse con.
in·tes·tine [ɪntɛ́stɪn] *s.* intestino; *adj.* intestino, interno.
in·ti·ma·cy [íntəməsɪ] *s.* intimidad.
in·ti·mate [íntəmɪt] *adj.* íntimo; *s.* amigo íntimo; [íntəmet] *v.* intimar, insinuar; indicar, dar a entender.

IN

in·ti·ma·tion [ɪntəméʃən] *s.* intimación, insinuación.
in·tim·i·date [ɪntímədet] *v.* intimidar, acobardar, infundir miedo.
in·to [íntʊ, íntə] *prep.* en; dentro de; hacia el interior.
in·tol·er·a·ble [ɪntálərəbl] *adj.* intolerable, inaguantable.
in·tol·er·ance [ɪntálərəns] *s.* intolerancia.
in·tol·er·ant [ɪntálərənt] *adj.* intolerante.
in·to·na·tion [ɪntonéʃən] *s.* entonación.
in·tox·i·cate [ɪntáksəket] *v.* embriagar; emborrachar.
in·tox·i·ca·tion [ɪntɑksəkéʃən] *s.* embriaguez; envenenamiento, intoxicación (*estado tóxico o envenenamiento parcial*).
in·tran·si·gent [ɪntrǽnsədʒənt] *adj.* intransigente.
in·tra·ve·nous [ɪntrəvínəs] *adj.* intravenoso.
in·trench [ɪntrɛ́ntʃ] *v.* atrincherar; **to — oneself** atrincherarse; **to — upon another's rights** infringir los derechos ajenos; **to be -ed** estar atrincherado; estar firmemente establecido.
in·trep·id [ɪntrɛ́pɪd] *adj.* intrépido.
in·tri·cate [íntrəkɪt] *adj.* intrincado, enredado.
in·trigue [ɪntríg] *s.* intriga; enredo; trama; lío, embrollo; *v.* intrigar; tramar, maquinar.
in·tri·guer [ɪntrígɚ] *s.* intrigante.
in·tro·duce [ɪntrədjús] *v.* introducir; presentar.
in·tro·duc·tion [ɪntrədʌ́kʃən] *s.* introducción; presentación.
in·tro·spec·tion [ɪntrospɛ́kʃən] *s.* introspección.
in·tro·vert [íntrovɚt] *s.* introvertido.
in·trude [ɪntrúd] *v.* entremeterse (*o* entrometerse); introducir, meter.
in·trud·er [ɪntrúdɚ] *s.* intruso, entremetido.
in·tru·sion [ɪntrúʒən] *s.* intrusión, entremetimiento.
in·tru·sive [ɪntrúsɪv] *adj.* intruso.
in·trust = **entrust.**
in·tu·i·tion [ɪntuíʃən] *s.* intuición.
in·un·date [fnəndet] *v.* inundar.
in·ure [ɪnjúr] *v.* habituar, acostumbrar.
in·vade [ɪnvéd] *v.* invadir.
in·vad·er [ɪnvédɚ] *s.* invasor.
in·va·lid [ɪnvǽlɪd] *adj.* inválido (*que no vale*), nulo, de ningún valor.
in·va·lid [ɪnvəlɪd] *adj.* inválido, enfermizo, achacoso; **— diet** dieta para inválidos; *s.* inválido.
in·val·u·a·ble [ɪnvǽljebl] *adj.* de gran precio o valor, inapreciable, inestimable.
in·var·i·a·ble [ɪnvɛ́rɪəbl] *adj.* invariable; **invariably** *adv.* invariablemente; sin falta, sin excepción.
in·va·sion [ɪnvéʒən] *s.* invasión.
in·vent [ɪnvɛ́nt] *v.* inventar.
in·ven·tion [ɪnvɛ́nʃən] *s.* invención; invento; inventiva, facultad para inventar.
in·ven·tive [ɪnvɛ́ntɪv] *adj.* inventivo.
in·ven·tive·ness [ɪnvɛ́ntɪvnɪs] *s.* inventiva.
in·ven·tor [ɪnvɛ́ntɚ] *s.* inventor.
in·ven·to·ry [ínvəntorɪ] *s.* inventario; *v.* inventariar.
in·verse [ɪnvɝ́s] *adj.* inverso; **— video** (*computer*) video inverso.
in·vert [ɪnvɝ́t] *v.* invertir; trastrocar; volver al revés.
in·vest [ɪnvɛ́st] *v.* invertir, colocar (*fondos*); (*award*) investir (*de una dignidad o cargo*); (*authorize*) revestir (*de autoridad*); sitiar.
in·ves·ti·gate [ɪnvɛ́stəget] *v.* investigar, indagar.
in·ves·ti·ga·tion [ɪnvɛstəgéʃən] *s.* investigación; indagación.
in·ves·ti·ga·tor [ɪnvɛ́stəgetɚ] *s.* investigador; indagador.
in·vest·ment [ɪnvɛ́stmənt] *s.* inversión (*de fondos*); **— broker** corredor de valores.
in·ves·tor [ɪnvɛ́stɚ] *s.* el que invierte fondos.

in·vig·o·rate [ɪnvígəret] *v.* vigorizar, fortalecer.
in·vin·ci·ble [ɪnvínsəbl] *adj.* invencible.
in·vis·i·ble [ɪnvízəbl] *adj.* invisible.
in·vi·ta·tion [ɪnvətéʃən] *s.* invitación.
in·vite [ɪnváɪt] *v.* invitar; convidar.
in·vit·ing [ɪnváɪtɪŋ] *adj.* atractivo; seductivo, tentador.
in·vo·ca·tion [ɪnvəkéʃən] *s.* invocación.
in·voice [ínvɔɪs] *s.* factura; envío, mercancías enviadas; *v.* facturar.
in·voke [ɪnvók] *v.* invocar.
in·vol·un·tar·y [ɪnválənterɪ] *adj.* involuntario.
in·volve [ɪnválv] *v.* complicar, enredar; envolver; implicar; comprometer; **to get -d in difficulties** embrollarse, meterse en embrollos.
in·ward [ínwɚd] *adj.* interior; interno; (*secret*) secreto; *adv.* hacia el interior; hacia dentro, adentro, para dentro; **-s** *adv.* = **inward.**
i·o·dide [áɪədaɪd] *s.* yoduro.
i·o·dine [áɪədaɪn] *s.* yodo.
i·on [áɪən] *s.* ion.
i·on·ize [áɪənaɪz] *v.* ionizar.
ire [aɪr] *s.* ira.
ir·i·des·cent [ɪrɪdɛ́sn̩t] *adj.* iridiscente, tornasolado, irisado.
i·rid·i·um [ɪrídiəm] *s.* iridio.
i·ris [áɪrɪs] *s.* iris; arco iris; flor de lis.
I·rish [áɪrɪʃ] *adj.* irlandés; *s.* irlandés, idioma irlandés; **the —** los irlandeses.
ink·some [ɪ́ksəm] *adj.* fastidioso, engorroso, molesto, tedioso; **irked** fastidiado.
i·ron [áɪən] *s.* (*element*) hierro; (*instrument*) plancha (*de planchar ropa*); *adj.* ferro, de hierro; **— work** herraje, trabajo en hierro, **— works** herrería; fábrica de hierro; *v.* planchar; **to — out a difficulty** allanar una dificultad.
i·ron·i·cal [aɪránɪkl] *adj.* irónico.
i·ron·ing [áɪɚnɪŋ] *s.* planchado.
i·ro·ny [áɪrənɪ] *s.* ironía.
ir·ra·di·ate [ɪrédɪet] *v.* irradiar.
ir·ra·tion·al [ɪrǽʃənl] *adj.* irracional.
ir·re·fut·a·ble [ɪréfjútəbl] *adj.* irrefutable.
ir·reg·u·lar [ɪrégjələ] *adj.* irregular.
ir·rel·e·vant [ɪrélovənt] *adj.* fuera de propósito, inaplicable al caso, inoportuno, que no viene (*o no* hace) al caso.
ir·re·li·gious [ɪrɪlídʒəs] *adj.* irreligioso, impío.
ir·re·me·di·a·ble [ɪrɪmídɪəbl] *adj.* irremediable; incurable.
ir·re·proach·a·ble [ɪrɪprótʃəbl] *adj.* irreprochable, intachable.
ir·re·sis·ti·ble [ɪrɪzístəbl] *adj.* irresistible.
ir·res·o·lute [ɪrézəlut] *adj.* irresoluto, indeciso.
ir·re·triev·a·ble [ɪrɪtrívəbl] *adj.* inapelable.
ir·rev·er·ence [ɪrévərəns] *s.* irreverencia, desacato.
ir·rev·er·ent [ɪrévərənt] *adj.* irreverente.
ir·ri·gate [ɪrəget] *v.* regar; irrigar, bañar.
ir·ri·ga·tion [ɪrəgéʃən] *s.* riego; irrigación; **— canal** acequia, canal de irrigación.
ir·ri·ta·ble [ɪrətəbl] *adj.* irritable; colérico.
ir·ri·tate [ɪrətet] *v.* irritar.
ir·ri·tat·ing [ɪrətetɪŋ] *adj.* irritante.
ir·ri·ta·tion [ɪrətéʃən] *s.* irritación.
ir·rupt [ɪrʌpt] *v.* irrumpir.
is·land [flənd] *s.* isla.
is·land·er [áɪləndɚ] *s.* isleño.
isle [aɪl] *s.* isla, ínsula.
i·so·bar [áɪsəbar] *s.* isobara.
i·so·late [áɪslet] *v.* aislar.
i·so·la·tion [áɪsléʃən] *s.* aislamiento.
i·so·la·tion·ism [aɪsoléʃənɪzəm] *s.* aislamiento.

i·so·met·ric [aɪsométrɪk] *adj.* isométrico.

Is·ra·el [ízriəl] *s.* Israel.

is·sue [íʃʊ] *s.* (*printing*) tirada, impresión; (*stock, bonds*) emisión (*de valores*); (*problem*) problema, tema; (*result*) resultado, consecuencia; **without —** sin prole, sin sucesión; **to take — with** disentir o diferir de; *v.* publicar, dar a luz; dar, promulgar (*un decreto*); emitir (*valores, acciones, etc.*); emanar; fluir; salir; brotar; provenir.

isth·mus [ísməs] *s.* istmo.

it [ɪt] *pron. neutro* lo, la (*acusativo*); ello, él, ella (*después de una preposición*); *por lo general no se traduce cuando es sujeto del verbo;* **— is there** está allí; **— is I** soy yo; **— is raining** llueve, está lloviendo; **what time is — ?** ¿qué hora es?; **— is two o'clock** son las dos; **how goes — ?** ¿qué tal?

I·tal·ian [ɪtǽljən] *adj. & s.* italiano.

i·tal·ic [ɪtǽlɪk] *adj.* itálico; **-s** *s.* letra bastardilla.

i·tal·i·cize [ɪtǽləsaɪz] *v.* poner en letra bastardilla.

itch [ɪtʃ] *s.* comezón; picazón; sarna (*enfermedad de la piel*); *v.* picar, darle a uno comezón; sentir comezón; **to be -ing** tener ansias de.

itch·y [ítʃɪ] *adj.* sarnoso, *Méx., Ven.* sarniento; **to feel —** sentir comezón.

i·tem [áɪtəm] *s.* artículo; detalle; noticia, suelto (*de un periódico*); partida (*de una lista*).

i·tem·ize [áɪtəmaɪz] *v.* pormenorizar detallar; hacer una lista de.

i·tin·er·ant [aɪtínərənt] *adj.* ambulante.

i·tin·er·ar·y [aɪtínərɛrɪ] *s.* itinerario; ruta; guía de viajeros.

its [ɪts] *pos. neutro* su (sus), de él, de ella, de ello.

it·self [ɪtsɛ́lf] *pron. neutro* mismo, misma; **by —** por sí, de por sí, por sí solo; solo, aislado; **in —** en sí.

i·vo·ry [áɪvrɪ] *s.* marfil; **— tower** torre de marfil.

i·vy [áɪvɪ] *s.* hiedra (yedra).

J : j

jab [dʒæb] *v.* picar; pinchar; *s.* piquete, pinchazo.

jack [dʒæk] *s.* (*tool*) gato (*para alzar cosas pesadas*); (*card*) sota (*en naipes*); (*male*) macho (*del burro y otros animales*); (*flag*) bandera de proa; **— of all trades** aprendiz de todo y oficial de nada; sabelotodo; **— pot** premio gordo, premio mayor; **— rabbit** liebre americana; *v.* **to — up** solevantar, alzar con gato (*un objeto pesado*).

jack·ass [dʒǽkæs] *s.* asno, burro.

jack·et [dʒǽkɪt] *s.* chaqueta; envoltura; forro (*de un libro*); hollejo (*de la patata*).

jack·knife [dʒǽknaɪf] *s.* navaja.

jag·ged [dʒǽgɪd] *adj.* serrado, dentado.

jag·uar [dʒǽgwar] *s.* jaguar.

jail [dʒel] *s.* cárcel; *v.* encarcelar.

jail·er [dʒélɚ] *s.* carcelero.

ja·lop·y [dʒalápɪ] *s.* fotingo.

jam [dʒæm] *v.* estrujar, apachurrar; atorar(se); obstruir(se), atascar(se); apiñar(se); agolpar(se); **to — on the brakes** frenar de golpe; **to — one's fingers** machucarse los dedos; **to — through** forzar por, meter a la fuerza; *s.* conserva, compota; apretura; atascamiento; **traffic —** aglomeración de transeúntes o automóviles, *Am.* bola; **to be in a —** estar en un aprieto.

jan·i·tor [dʒǽnətɚ] *s.* conserje; portero; casero (*encargado de un edificio*).

Jan·u·ar·y [dʒǽnjʊɛrɪ] *s.* enero.

Jap·a·nese [dʒæpəníz] *adj. & s.* japonés.

jar [dʒar] *s.* jarra, jarro; tarro; (*collision*) choque; (*shake*) sacudida; (*vibration*) trepidación, vibración; **large earthen —** tinaja; *v.* trepidar; hacer vibrar; hacer temblar; menear; **to — one's nerves** ponerle a uno los nervios de punta.

jar·gon [dʒárgən] *s.* jerga, jerigonza.

jas·mine [dʒǽzmɪn] *s.* jazmín.

jas·per [dʒǽspɚ] *s.* jaspe.

jaunt [dʒɔnt] *s.* caminata, excursión; *v.* dar un paseíto, hacer una corta caminata.

jaw [dʒɔ] *s.* quijada, mandíbula, *Ch.* carretilla; **-s** grapa (*de herramienta*).

jaw·bone [dʒɔ́bón] *s.* mandíbula, quijada.

jay [dʒe] *s.* grajo; rústico, bobo; **blue —** azulejo; **— walker** que cruza las bocacalles descuidadamente.

jazz [dʒæz] *s.* jazz (*cierta clase de música sincopada*); *v.* tocar el jazz; bailar el jazz; **to — up** sincopar; animar, alegrar.

jeal·ous [dʒɛ́ləs] *adj.* celoso; envidioso; **to be — of someone** tener celos de una persona, tenerle celos a una persona.

jeal·ou·sy [dʒɛ́ləsɪ] *s.* celos; envidia.

jeer [dʒɪr] *s.* mofa, befa, escarnio, *Carib.* choteo; *v.* mofar, befar, *Carib.* chotear; **to — at** mofarse de.

jel·ly [dʒɛ́lɪ] *s.* jalea; *v.* convertir(se) en jalea, hacer(se) gelatinoso.

jeop·ard·ize [dʒɛ́pɚdaɪz] *v.* arriesgar, comprometer.

jeop·ar·dy [dʒɛ́pɚdɪ] *s.* riesgo.

jerk [dʒɝk] *s.* tirón; sacudida, *Méx., C.A., Ven. Col.* jalón; espasmo muscular; *v.* sacudir(se); dar un tirón; atasajar (*la carne*); **to — out** sacar de un tirón; **-ed beef** tasajo, *Am.* charqui.

jerk·wa·ter [dʒɝkwɔlɚ] *adj.* de mala muerte.

jer·ry·build [dʒɛ́rɪ bɪ́ld] *v.* edificar con cualesquiera materiales.

jer·sey [dʒɝ́zɪ *s.* tejido de punto, tejido elástico, *Am.* jersey; chaqueta, blusa, camisa (*de punto*), *Am.* jersey.

jest [dʒɛst] *s.* broma; chanza; chiste; *v.* bromear; chancearse.

jest·er [dʒɛ́stɚ] *s.* chancero, burlón; bufón.

Jes·u·it [dʒɛ́ʒʊɪt] *s.* jesuita.

jet [dʒɛt] *s.* chorro; surtidor (*de fuente*); **— airplane** avión de reacción; **— engine** motor de reacción; motorreactor; **gas —** mechero de gas; *adj.* de azabache; **jet-black** negro como el azabache; *v.* chorrear, salir en chorro.

jet·ti·son [dʒɛ́tɪsən] *v.* echar mercancías al mar.

Jew [dʒu] *s.* judío.

jew·el [dʒúəl] *s.* joya, alhaja; gema; **— box** estuche, joyero.

jew·el·er [dʒúəlɚ] *s.* joyero; **-'s shop** joyería.

jew·el·ry [dʒúəlrɪ] *s.* joyas, alhajas, pedrería; **— store** joyería.

Jew·ish [dʒúɪʃ] *adj.* judío.

jib [dʒɪb] *s.* foque (vela).

jif·fy [dʒɪ́fɪ] *s.* instante; **in a —** en un instante, en dos paletas; en un decir Jesús, en un santiamén.

jig [dʒɪg] *s.* jiga (*música y baile*); **— saw** sierra mecánica (*para recortar figuras*); **— saw puzzle** rompecabezas (*de recortes*) *v.* tocar una jiga; bailar una jiga; bailotear; menear(se).

jig·gle [dʒígl] *v.* zangolotear(se), zarandear(se), menear(se); *s.* zarandeo, meneo, zangoloteo.

jilt [dʒɪlt] *v.* desairar, dar calabazas, dejar plantado.

jin·gle [dʒíŋgl] *s.* retintín; verso o rima infantil; (*radio*) propaganda cantada; **— bell** cascabel; *v.* hacer retintín.

job [dʒɑb] *s.* tarea, faena; trabajo; empleo, ocupación; **to be out of a —** estar sin trabajo;

estar desocupado; **by the** — a destajo.
job·ber [dʒábɚ] s. negociante medianero.
jock·ey [dʒákɪ] s. jockey; v. maniobrar *(para sacar ventaja o ganar un puesto).*
join [dʒɔɪn] v. juntar(se); enlazar(se); acoplar; unirse a, asociarse a.
joint [dʒɔɪnt] s. *(point)* juntura, coyuntura; *(function)* articulación; conexión; bisagra; *(public place)* garito *(casa de juego);* fonducho, restaurante de mala muerte; **out of** — descoyuntado; desunido; *adj.* unido, asociado; copartícipe; colectivo; — **account** cuenta en común; — **action** acción colectiva; — **committee** comisión mixta; — **company** en comandita; — **creditor** acreedor copartícipe; — **heir** coheredero; — **owner** condómino, copropietario; — **session** sesión plena; **-ly** *adv.* juntamente, juntos, unidamente, colectivamente.
joke [dʒok] s. broma; chiste, chanza; v. bromear; chancear(se), *Carib.* chotear; *Ríopl.* farrear; jorobar.
jok·er [dʒókɚ] s. bromista, chancero, guasón, *Carib.* choteador; *(card)* comodín.
jok·ing·ly [dʒókɪŋlɪ] *adv.* en *(o* de) chanza, en *(o* de) broma; de chiste.
jol·ly [dʒálɪ] *adj.* jovial; alegre; festivo; v. bromear, chancearse.
jolt [dʒolt] s. sacudida; sacudimiento; choque; v. sacudir.
jos·tle [dʒásl] v. rempujar o empujar, dar empellones; codear; s. rempujón, empujón, empellón.
jot [dʒɑt] v. **to** — **down** apuntar, tomar apuntes; s. jota, pizca.
jour·nal [dʒɝnl] s. diario; periódico; revista; acta *(de una junta o concilio).*
jour·nal·ism [dʒɝnlɪzəm] s. periodismo.
jour·nal·ist [dʒɝnlɪst] s. periodista.
jour·nal·is·tic [dʒɝnlístɪk] *adj.* periodístico.
jour·ney [dʒɝnɪ] s. viaje, jornada; v. viajar; peregrinar.
joy [dʒɔɪ] s. júbilo, regocijo; alegría, gusto, deleite; felicidad.
joy·ful [dʒɔɪfəl] *adj.* regocijado, jubiloso; alegre; **-ly** *adv.* con regocijo, regocijadamente, con júbilo, alegremente.
joy·ous [dʒɔɪəs] *adj.* jubiloso, alegre, gozoso.
joy·stick [dʒɔɪstɪk] s. *(computer)* mando para juegos, palanca de juegos.
ju·bi·lant [dʒúbələnt] *adj.* jubiloso, alegre.
ju·bi·lee [dʒúblɪ] s. jubileo; júbilo.
judge [dʒʌdʒ] s. juez; — **advocate** auditor de un consejo militar; v. juzgar.
judg·ment [dʒʌdʒmənt] s. juicio; sentencia, fallo; opinión; discernimiento; — **day** día del juicio final.
ju·di·cial [dʒudíʃəl] *adj.* judicial.
ju·di·cious [dʒudíʃəs] *adj.* juicioso, cuerdo.
jug [dʒʌg] s. cántaro, jarro; jarra; botija; chirona *(cárcel) Am.* chirola.
jug·gle [dʒʌgl] v. hacer juegos de manos; hacer suertes; **to** — **the accounts** barajar *(o* manipular) las cuentas; s. juego de manos, suerte; trampa.
jug·gler [dʒʌglɚ] s. prestidigitador, malabarista.
juice [dʒus] s. jugo; zumo.
juic·i·ness [dʒúsɪnɪs] s. jugosidad.
juic·y [dʒúsɪ] *adj.* jugoso, zumoso; suculento; **a** — **story** un cuento picante.
juke box [dʒúkbɑks] s. tragamonedas; tragaquintos.
Ju·ly [dʒulái] s. julio.
jum·ble [dʒʌmbl] s. revolver(se), barajar;

mezclar(se); s. mezcolanza, revoltijo; confusión.
jump [dʒʌmp] v. saltar; brincar; salvar *(de un salto);* hacer saltar; comerse una pieza *(en el juego de damas);* **to** — **at the chance** asir o aprovechar la oportunidad; **to** — **bail** perder la fianza por evasión; **to** — **over** saltar por encima de, salvar de un salto; **to** — **the track** descarrilarse; **to** — **to conclusions** hacer deducciones precipitadas; s. salto; brinco; subida repentina *(del precio);* **to be always on the** — andar siempre de aquí para allá; trajinar, trafagar, ser muy activo.
jump·er [dʒʌmpɚ] s. saltador; chaquetón holgado *(de obrero);* vestido sin mangas *(puesto sobre la blusa de mujer);* traje de juego *(para niños).*
jump·y [dʒʌmpɪ] *adj.* saltón; asustadizo, nervioso.
junc·tion [dʒʌŋkʃən] s. unión, juntura; confluencia *(de dos ríos);* empalme *(de ferrocarriles);* entronque.
junc·ture [dʒʌŋktʃɚ] s. juntura; coyuntura; **at this** — a esta sazón, en esta coyuntura.
June [dʒun] s. junio.
jun·gle [dʒʌŋgl] s. selva; matorral; *Am.* jungla; *Carib.* manigua.
ju·nior [dʒúnjɚ] *adj.* menor, más joven; — **college** colegio para los dos primeros años del bachillerato; **John Smith, Junior (Jr.)** John Smith, hijo; s. estudiante del tercer año *(en escuela superior, colegio o universidad).*
ju·ni·per [dʒúnɪpɚ] s. junípero; enebro.
junk [dʒʌŋk] s. basura, desperdicios; trastos viejos; chatarra; cosa inservible; — **dealer** chatarrero, — **yard** chatarrería; **Chinese** — junco chino *(embarcación pequeña);* v. desechar, echar a la basura.
ju·ris·dic·tion [dʒʊrɪsdíkʃən] s. jurisdicción.
ju·ris·pru·dence [dʒʊrɪsprúdṇs] s. jurisprudencia, derecho.
ju·ror [dʒúrɚ] s. jurado, miembro de un jurado.
ju·ry [dʒúrɪ] s. jurado; **grand** — jurado de acusación; — **box** tribunal del jurado.
just [dʒʌst] *adj.* justo; recto; exacto; *adv.* ni más ni menos, exactamente, justamente; precisamente; sólo, no más, nada más; apenas; — **now** ahora mismo; **he** — **left** acaba de salir, *Ríopl.* salió recién; **she is** — **a little girl** no es más que una niña, es una niña no más; **to have** — acabar de.
jus·tice [dʒʌstɪs] s. justicia; juez; magistrado.
jus·ti·fi·ca·tion [dʒʌstəfəkéʃən] s. justificación.
jus·ti·fy [dʒʌstəfaɪ] v. justificar.
just·ly [dʒʌstlɪ] *adv.* justamente; con razón.
jut [dʒʌt] v. sobresalir, proyectarse, extenderse; s. salidizo, proyección.
ju·ve·nile [dʒúvənḷ] *adj.* juvenil.

K :k

kan·ga·roo [kæŋgərú] s. canguro.
kay·o (K.O.) [Kéo] v. noquear; **-ed** adj. noqueado.
keel [kil] s. quilla; v. dar de quilla *(voltear un barco);* **to** — **over** volcar(se); zozobrar; caerse patas arriba, desplomarse.
keen [kin] *adj.* agudo; afilado; perspicaz; ansioso.
keen·ness [kínnɪs] s. agudeza; perspicacia; anhelo, ansia.
keep [kip] v. guardar; tener guardado; tener; retener; conservar(se); preservar(se); mantener(se); **to** — **accounts** llevar las cuentas; **to** — **at it** persistir, seguir dale que dale; **to** — **away** mantener(se)

alejado; **to — back** tener a raya; detener; reprimir, restringir; **to — from** impedir; guardar(se) de; abstenerse de; **to — going** seguir andando, seguir adelante; seguir viviendo; **to — off** no arrimarse, no acercarse; no entrar; mantener(se) a distancia; **to — one's hands off** no tocar; **to — one's temper** contenerse, refrenarse, reprimirse; **— posted** mantener al corriente; **to — quiet** estarse quieto o callado; **to — something up** seguir o continuar haciendo algo; **to — to the right** seguir a la derecha; mantenerse a la derecha; **to — track of** llevar la cuenta de; no perder de vista; seguir la pista de; *s.* manutención, subsistencia; **for -s** para siempre; para guardar; dado, no prestado.

keep·er [kípɚ] *s.* guardián, custodio; **jail —** carcelero.

keep·ing [kípɪŋ] *s.* custodia; mantenimiento; preservación, conservación; **in — with** en armonía con.

keep·sake [kípsek] *s.* prenda, recuerdo, regalo.

keg [kɛg] *s.* tonel, barril.

ken·nel [kɛnl] *s.* perrera.

kept [kɛpt] *pret. & p.p. de* **to keep.**

ker·chief [kɝtʃɪf] *s.* pañuelo, pañolón.

ker·nel [kɝnl] *s.* simiente; grano (*de trigo o maíz*); meollo (*de ciertas frutas como la nuez*); núcleo.

ker·o·sene [kérəsin] *s.* kerosina, petróleo para lámparas.

ket·tle [kétl] *s.* caldera; · **drum** tímpano; **tea —** marmita,́ tetera, *Am.* pava (*para el mate*).

key [ki] *s.* (*lock*) llave; (*music*) clave; (*instrument*) tecla; (*land*) cayo; isleta; **— ring** llavero; **— lockout** (*computer*) inhibición de teclas; **to be in —** estar a tono, estar templado; estar en armonía; *adj.* (*important*) **— industries** industrias básicas; *v.* poner a tono, afinar, templar (*con llave*); armonizar; **to — up** elevar el tono de; **to be -ed up** estar sobreexcitado, estar en tensión nerviosa.

key·board [kíbord] *s.* teclado, tablero.

key·hole [kíhol] *s.* ojo de la cerradura.

key·note [kínot] *s.* nota tónica; idea o principio fundamental.

key·pad [kípæd] *s.* (*computer*) teclado numérico.

key·stone [kíston] *s.* clave (*de un arco*); base, fundamento principal.

kha·ki [kάki] *s.* kaki, caqui; *adj.* de kaki.

kick [kɪk] *s.* (*foot*) *Esp.* coz; puntapié; *Am.* patada; (*complaint*) queja; protesta; fuerza (*de una bebida*); estímulo; **to have a —** *Am.* patear (*dícese del licor*); *v.* cocear; dar coces o patadas; dar puntapiés; patear; quejarse, protestar; **to — out** echar a patadas; echar, expulsar; **to — the bucket** estirar la pata, morir, *Am.* patear el balde; **to — up a lot of dust** levantar una polvareda.

kick·back [kíkbæk] *s.* comisión ilegal; *Méx* mordida.

kid [kɪd] *s.* cabrito; cabritilla (*piel curtida de cabrito*); niño, niña; **— gloves** guantes de cabritilla; *v.* bromear, embromar; chancearse con, *Carib., Méx.* chotear.

kid·nap [kídnæp] *v.* secuestrar, raptar.

kid·nap·per [kídnæpɚ] *s.* secuestrador; robachicos, ladrón de niños.

kid·nap·ping [kídnæpɪŋ] *s.* rapto, secuestro.

kid·ney [kídnɪ] *s.* riñón; **— bean** judía, frijol; **— stones** cálculos.

kill [kɪl] *v.* matar; destruir; amortiguar; parar (*el motor*); *s.* animal o animales matados (*en la caza*).

kill·er [kílɚ] *s.* matador; asesino.

kiln [kɪln], [kɪl] *s.* horno.

ki·lo [kílo], **ki·lo·gram** [kíləgræm] *s.* kilo; **— computer chip** ficha de 1,024 *bits;* kilogramo.

ki·lo·byte (KBYTE) [kíləbait] *s.* (*computer*) kilo-byte (KB).

ki·lo·cy·cle [kíləsaikl] *s.* kilociclo.

kil·o·me·ter [kíləmitɚ] *s.* kilómetro.

kil·o·watt [kíləwat] *s.* kilovatio.

ki·mo·no [kəmónə] *s.* quimono; bata.

kin [kɪn] *s.* parentela, parientes, familia; **to notify the nearest of —** avisar al pariente o deudo más cercano.

kind [kaɪnd] *adj.* bondadoso; benévolo; amable; **to send one's — regards to** enviar afectuosos saludos a; **kindhearted** de buen corazón; **— of** tired algo cansado; *s.* clase, especie, género; **to pay in —** pagar en especie; pagar en la misma moneda.

kin·der·gar·ten [kíndɚgartn̩] *s.* escuela de párvulos.

kin·dle [kíndl] *v.* encender(se); inflamar(se); incitar; prender (*el fuego*).

kin·dling [kíndlɪŋ] *s.* encendimiento; leña ligera, astillas, *Andes* charamuscas.

kind·ly [káindlɪ] *adj.* bondadoso; benigno; benévolo; amable, apacible; *adv.* bondadosamente, amablemente; con benevolencia; por favor; **not to take — to criticism** no aceptar de buen grado las correcciones.

kind·ness [káindnɪs] *s.* bondad, amabilidad; gentileza; benevolencia; favor.

kin·dred [kíndrid] *adj.* emparentado; allegado; semejante; · **facts** hechos relacionados; **— spirits** espíritus afines.

ki·nes·ics [kaɪnízɪks] *s.* kinésica; quinésica.

king [kɪŋ] *s.* rey; rey (*en ajedrez*); dama (*en el juego de damas*).

king·dom [kíŋdəm] *s.* reino.

king·ly [kíŋlɪ] *adj.* regio; real; majestuoso; *adv.* regiamente; majestuosamente.

king·pin [kíŋpɪn] *s.* pivote central.

kink [kɪŋk] *s.* (*bend*) enroscadura; (*pain*) tortícolis.

kink·y [kíŋkɪ] *adj.* crespo, ensortijado, *Am.* grifo.

kin·ship [kínʃɪp] *s.* parentesco; afinidad; semejanza.

kins·man [kínzmən] *s.* pariente, deudo.

kiss [kɪs] *s.* beso; *v.* besar.

kit [kɪt] *s.* estuche, caja de herramientas; saco, envoltura (*para guardar instrumentos, herramientas, etc.*); gatito; **medicine —** botiquín; **soldier's —** mochila.

kitch·en [kítʃɪn] *s.* cocina; **— ware** trastos de cocina.

kite [kaɪt] *s.* cometa (*f.*), *Méx.* papalote; *Ch.* volantín; *Arg.* barrilete; milano (*pájaro*).

kit·ten [kítn̩] *s.* gatito.

kit·ty [kítɪ] *s.* gatito, minino.

knack [næk] *s.* destreza, maña, habilidad.

knap·sack [næpsæk] *s.* mochila, morral, alforja.

knave [nev] *s.* bribón, bellaco, pícaro; sota (*de naipes*).

knead [nid] *v.* amasar, sobar.

knee [ni] *s.* rodilla; **knee-deep** hasta la rodilla; metido hasta las rodillas.

kneel [nil] *v.* arrodillarse; hincarse.

knell [nɛl] *s.* doble (*toque de campanas por los difuntos*) *v* doblar, tocar a muerto.

knelt [nɛlt] *pret. & p.p. de* **to kneel.**

knew [nju] *pret. de* **to know.**

knick·knack [níknæk] *s.* chuchería, baratija, chisme.

knife [naɪf] *s.* cuchillo; cuchilla; **carving —** trinchante; **pocket —** cortaplumas; navaja; *v.* acuchillar.

knight [naɪt] *s.* caballero; campeón; caballo (*en ajedrez*—0; **— errant** caballero andante; *v.* armar caballero.

JO

knight·hood [náɪthʊd] *s.* caballería, orden de la caballería.

knit [nɪt] *v.* tejer (*a punto de aguja*); hacer calceta o malla; enlazar; soldarse (*un hueso*) **to — one's brow** fruncir las cejas, arrugar la frente; *pret. & p.p. de* **to knit.**

knit·ting [nítɪŋ] *s.* labor de punto; — **needle** aguja de media.

knives [naɪvz] *pl. de* **knife.**

knob [nɑb] *s.* perilla, botón, tirador (*de puerta, cajón, etc.*); protuberancia.

knock [nɑk] *v.* (*pound*) golpear, golpetear; llamar o tocar a la puerta; (*criticize*) criticar, censurar o hablar mal de; desacreditar; **to — down** derribar; desmontar (*una máquina o aparato*); **to — off** suspender (*el trabajo*); rebajar (*del precio*); derribar, echar abajo; **to — out** aplastar de un golpe, poner fuera de combate; dejar sin sentido; noquear; *s.* golpe; golpeteo, toque, llamada, aldabonazo; crítica, censura; **knock-kneed** zambo, patizambo.

knock·er [nɑ́kɚ] *s.* llamador, aldaba, aldabón; criticón, murmurador.

knoll [nol] *s.* colina, loma; eminencia.

knot [nɑt] *s.* nudo; lazo; milla náutica; *v.* anudar(se).

knot·ty [nɑ́tɪ] *adj.* nudoso; (*difficult*) dificultoso, enredado.

know [no] *v.* (*to be acquainted with*) conocer; (*to have knowledge of; to know how to*) saber; (*to recognize*) reconocer; distinguir; **to — how to swim** saber nadar; **to — of** saber de; tener conocimiento de; tener noticias de; estar enterado de.

know·how [nóhɑʊ] *s.* idoneidad.

know·ing·ly [nóɪŋlɪ] *adv.* a sabiendas; adrede.

knowl·edge [nɑ́lɪdʒ] *s.* conocimiento; saber, sabiduría; pericia; **not to my —** mo que yo sepa.

known [non] *p.p. de* **to know.**

knuck·le [nʌ́kl] *s.* nudillo; coyuntura, articulación; artejo; *v.* someterse; **to — down** someterse; aplicarse con empeño al trabajo.

kryp·ton [kríptan] *s.* criptón.

L:l

la·bel [lébl] *s.* marbete, etiqueta, rótulo; *v.* marcar, rotular; apodar, llamar.

la·bor [lébɚ] *s.* trabajo; (*cause*) labor; obrerismo, obra; mano de obra; (*class*) la clase obrera; — **union** sindicato; — **gang** peonaje; — **party** Partido Laborista; **to be in —** estar de parto; *adj.* laboral, obrero; *v.* trabajar; (*try*) afanarse; (*give birth*) estar de parto; (*develop*) elaborar (*un punto*).

lab·o·ra·to·ry [lǽbrətorɪ] *s.* laboratorio.

la·bor·er [lébərɚ] *s.* trabajador, obrero; jornalero, peón.

la·bo·ri·ous [ləbórɪəs] *adj.* laborioso, trabajoso, penoso; industrioso.

lab·y·rinth [lǽbərɪnθ] *s.* laberinto.

lace [les] *s.* (*cloth*) encaje; (*cord*) cordón, cordoncillo, cinta (*de corsé, etc.*); **gold —** galón de oro (*para guarnecer uniformes*); *v.* atar con cinta o cordón; guarnecer con encajes; enlazar, entrelazar.

lack [læk] *s.* falta; escasez, carencia; deficiencia; *v.* carecer de, faltarle a uno; necesitar; **he -s courage** le falta ánimo.

lack·ey [lǽkɪ] *s.* lacayo.

lack·ing [lǽkɪŋ] *adj.* falto, carente.

lack·lus·ter [lǽklʌstɚ] *adj.* deslustrado.

lac·quer [lǽkɚ] *s.* laca; *v.* barnizar con laca.

lad [læd] *s.* rapaz, chico.

lad·der [lǽdɚ] *s.* escalera de mano.

lad·en [lédn̩] *adj.* cargado; agobiado, abrumado; *v.* cargar; agobiar.

la·dies [lédɪz] *pl. de* **lady.**

la·dle [lédl] *s.* cucharón; *v.* servir (*sopa*) con cucharón.

la·dy [lédɪ] *s.* señora; dama; — **like** como señora, muy fina, elegante; — **love** amada, querida.

lag [læg] *v.* rezagarse, quedarse atrás, atrasarse; andar lentamente; *s.* retardo o retardación, retraso.

la·goon [ləgún] *s.* laguna.

laid [led] *pret. & p.p. de* **to lay; to be — up** estar incapacitado o estropeado.

lain [len] *p.p. de* **to lie.**

lair [lɛr] *s.* guarida; cueva de fieras.

lake [lek] *s.* lago.

lamb [læm] *s.* cordero; — **kin** corderito.

lame [lem] *adj.* cojo; (*injured*) lisiado; estropeado; — **excuse** disculpa falsa; — **duck** empleado público entre elección e inauguración; deudor insolvente. *v.* hacer cojo; estropear, incapacitar.

la·ment [ləmɛ́nt] *s.* lamento; *v.* lamentar(se).

lam·ent·a·ble [lǽməntəbl] *adj.* lamentable; doloroso.

lam·en·ta·tion [læməntéʃən] *s.* lamentación, lamento.

lam·i·nate [lǽmənet] *v.* laminar.

lamp [læmp] *s.* lámpara; linterna; (*street*) farol; — **post** poste (de farol); — **shade** pantalla de lámpara.

lance [læns] *s.* lanza; *v.* alancear, lancear, herir con lanza; picar con bisturí.

land [lænd] *s.* tierra; (*lot*) terreno; (*soil*) suelo; *v.* desembarcar; aterrizar (*un avión*); llegar; coger (*un pez*); — **bank** banco de préstamos hipotecarios; — **poor** con propiedad pero sin fondos; **to — a job** conseguir una colocación, lograr un empleo.

land-grant [lǽndgrænt] *adj.* mediante donación federal de tierras.

land·hold·er [lǽndholdɚ] *s.* terrateniente, propietario, hacendado.

land·ing [lǽndɪŋ] *s.* (*act*) desembarco, desembarque; aterrizaje (*de un avión*); (*place*) desembarcadero; descanso (*de escalera*); — **field** campo de aterrizaje; aeropuerto; — **gear** tren de aterrizaje; — **wheels** ruedas de aterrizaje; — **strip** pista de aterrizaje.

land·la·dy [lǽndledɪ] *s.* patrona, casera, dueña (*de la casa*).

land·lord [lǽndlɔrd] *s.* amo, patrón, propietario, dueño; casero.

land·mark [lǽndmɑrk] *s.* mojón, señal (*para fijar los confines*); marca; suceso culminante.

land·own·er [lǽndonɚ] *s.* terrateniente, propietario, hacendado.

land·scape [lǽndskep] *s.* paisaje.

land·slide [lǽndslaɪd] *s.* derrumbe; alúd, derrumbamiento, desplome; gran mayoría de votos; victoria aplastante, arrolladora.

lane [len] *s.* senda, vereda; callejuela; ruta, derrotero (*de vapores o aviones*).

lan·guage [lǽŋgwɪdʒ] *s.* lengua; idioma; lenguaje.

lan·guid [lǽŋgwɪd] *adj.* lánguido.

lan·guish [lǽŋgwɪʃ] *v.* languidecer.

lan·guor [lǽŋgɚ] *d.* languidez.

lank [læŋk] *adj.* alto y delgado, largucho.

lank·y [lǽŋkɪ] *adj.* largucho, zancón, zancudo.

lan·tern [lǽntɚn] *s.* linterna; farol.

lan·tha·nides [lǽnθənaɪdz] *s.* lantánidos.

lap [læp] *s.* falda, regazo; aleta; etapa, trecho (*de una carrera*); *v.* lamer; **to — over** cruzar(se) sobre, entrecruzar(se).

la·pel [ləpél] *s.* solapa.

lap·i·da·ry [lǽpɪdɛrɪ] *s. & adj.* lapidario.

lapse [læps] *s.* lapso; transcurso; desliz; error; *v.* deslizarse; pasar, transcurrir; caer en un desliz; decaer (*el entusiasmo, el interés, etc.*); caducar (*un plazo, un contrato, etc.*).

lar·board [lárbəɹd] *s.* babor; *adj.* de babor; **— side** banda de babor.

lar·ce·ny [lársn̩ɪ] *s.* latrocinio, hurto; ratería.

lard [lɑrd] *s.* lardo, manteca de puerco; *v.* mechar.

large [lɑrdʒ] *adj.* grande; **at —** suelto, libre; sin trabas; en general; **-ly** *adv.* grandemente, en gran parte.

large·scale [lárdʒskél] *adj.* en grande escala; (*computer*) **— integration** 500 a 20,000 entradas lógicas.

lar·i·at [lǽrɪət] *s.* reata.

lark [lɑrk] *s.* (*bird*) alondra; (*fun*) diversión, holgorio, jarana; **to go on a —** ir o andar de jarana.

lar·va [lárvə] *s.* larva.

lar·ynx [lǽrɪŋks] *s.* laringe.

las·civ·i·ous [ləsívɪəs] *adj.* lascivo.

la·ser [lézəɹ] *s.* laser; **— printer** impresora laser.

lash [læʃ] *s.* látigo; azote, latigazo; (*eye*) pestaña; *v.* fustigar; azotar; (*scold*) censurar, reprender; (*tie*) amarrar.

lass [læs] *s.* moza, muchacha, doncella.

las·si·tude [lǽsətjud] *s.* dejadez, flojedad, decaimiento de fuerzas.

las·so [lǽso] *s.* lazo, reata, mangana; *v.* lazar, *Am.* enlazar.

last [læst] *adj.* (*in a series*) último; final; (*just passed*); pasado; **— night** anoche; **— year** el año pasado; **at —** por fin, finalmente, al fin; **next to the —** penúltimo; **to arrive —** llegar el último; *s.* fin, término, horma (*de zapato*); *v.* durar; perdurar; **-ly** *adv.* finalmente, en conclusión.

last·ing [lǽstɪŋ] *adj.* duradero; perdurable.

latch [lætʃ] *s.* pestillo, picaporte, aldaba, cerrojo; *v.* cerrar con aldaba.

late [let] *adj.* (*tardy*) tardío; tardo; (*recent*) reciente; último; **— comer** recién llegado; rezagado; **a — hour** una hora avanzada; **the — Mr. X** el finado (*o difunto*) Sr. X; **to have a — supper** cenar tarde; *adv.* tarde; **— afternoon** atardecer; **— in the night** a una hora avanzada de la noche; **— into the night** a deshoras de la noche; **— in the week** a fines de la semana; **of —** últimamente, recientemente; hace poco; **to be —** ser tarde; llegar tarde; estar atrasado, venir o llegar con retraso (*el tren*); **the train was ten minutes —** el tren llegó con diez minutos de retraso; **-ly** últimamente, recientemente; hace poco, poco ha

la·tent [létn̩t] *adj.* latente.

lat·er [létəɹ] *adj. & adj.* (*comp. de* **late**) más tarde; después, luego; más reciente; posterior.

lat·er·al [lǽtərəl] *adj.* lateral.

lat·est [létɪst] *adv. & adj.* (*superl. de* **late**) más tarde; más reciente, más nuevo; último; **the — fashion** la última moda, las últimas novedades; **the — news** las últimas novedades, las noticias más recientes; **at the —** a más tardar.

lathe [leð] *s.* torno (*de carpintero o mecánico*).

lath·er [lǽðəɹ] *s.* jabonadura, espuma de jabón; *v.* jabonar, enjabonar; espumar, hacer espuma.

Lat·in [lǽtn̩] *adj.* latino; *s.* latín.

lat·i·tude [lǽtətjud] *s.* latitud; libertad; amplitud.

lat·ter [lǽtəɹ] *adj.* último; **towards the — part of the week** a (*o* hacia) fines de la semana; **the —** éste (ésta, esto, etc.).

lat·tice [lǽtɪs] *s.* celosía; enrejado, rejilla.

laud [lɔd] *v.* loar, encomiar, alabar.

laud·a·ble [lɔ́dəbl] *adj.* laudable, loable.

laugh [læf] *v.* reír(se); **to — at** reírse de; **to — loudly** reírse a carcajadas; **to — in one's sleeve** reírse para sus adentros; **she -ed in his face** se rió en sus barbas; *s.* risa; **loud —** risotada, carcajada, risada.

laugh·a·ble [lǽfəbl] *adj.* risible; ridículo.

laugh·ing·stock [lǽfɪŋstak] *s.* hazmerreír.

laugh·ter [lǽftəɹ] *s.* risa.

launch [lɔntʃ] *v.* (*put into water*) botar o echar (*un barco*) al agua; (*a rocket*) lanzar; (*begin*) empezar, poner en operación; **to — forth** lanzarse; **to — forth on a journey** emprender un viaje; *s.* lancha; (*act*) botadura, lanzamiento.

laun·der [lɔ́ndəɹ] *v.* lavar y planchar (*la ropa*).

laun·dress [lɔ́ndrɪs] *s.* lavandera.

laun·dry [lɔ́ndrɪ] *s.* lavandería; lavado; ropa (lavada).

lau·rel [lɔ́rəl] *s.* laurel; gloria, honor.

la·va [lávə] *s.* lava.

lav·a·to·ry [lǽvətorɪ] *s.* lavabo; lavamanos; lavatorio.

lav·en·der [lǽvəndəɹ] *s.* espliego, lavándula; *adj.* lila, morado claro.

lav·ish [lǽvɪʃ] *adj.* gastador, pródigo, dadivoso; abundante, copioso; profuso; lujoso; *v.* prodigar; malgastar, despilfarrar; **to — praise upon** colmar de alabanzas a; **-ly** pródigamente; copiosamente; lujosamente.

KN

law [lɔ] *s.* ley; derecho, jurisprudencia; regla; *adj.* **— student** estudiante de leyes, estudiante de derecho; **law-abiding** observante de la ley; *s.* **— of nations** derecho internacional.

law·break·er [lɔ́brekəɹ] *s.* infractor, transgresor.

law·ful [lɔ́fəl] *adj.* legal; lícito; válido; permitido.

law·less [lɔ́lɪs] *adj.* sin ley; ilegal; desenfrenado; revoltoso; licencioso.

law·mak·er [lɔ́mekəɹ] *s.* legislador.

lawn [lɔn] *s.* césped, prado; *Am.* pasto, grama; linón (*tela de hilo o algodón*); **— mower** cortadora de césped.

law·suit [lɔ́sut] *s.* pleito, litigio.

law·yer [lɔ́jəɹ] *s.* abogado, jurisconsulto.

lax [læks] *adj.* flojo; suelto; relajado.

lax·a·tive [lǽksətɪv] *adj. & s.* laxante, purgante.

lax·i·ty [lǽksətɪ] *s.* flojedad, flojera; relajamiento (*de una regla, ley, etc.*).

lay [le] *pret. de* **to lie.**

lay [le] *v.* colocar; poner; tender, extender; poner (*huevos*); echar (*la culpa*); atribuir (*la responsabilidad*); presentar, exponer; asentar (*el polvo*); **to — a wager** apostar; **to — aside** poner a un lado; arrinconar; ahorrar; **to — away** (*o* by) guardar; **to — bare** revelar; poner al descubierto; exponer; **to — down** poner, colocar; rendir (*las armas*); **to — down the law** mandar, dictar; **to — hold of** asir, agarrar; **to — off a workman** suspender a un obrero; **to — open** exponer a la vista; **to — out a plan** trazar un plan; **to — up** almacenar; guardar, ahorrar; **to be laid up** estar incapacitado o estropeado; **to — waste** asolar; *s.* lay, balada, canción; situación, orientación (*del terreno*); *adj.* lego, laico; profano (*no iniciado en una ciencia*).

lay·er [léəɹ] *s.* capa; estrato; (*hen*) gallina ponedora.

lay·man [lémən] *s.* lego, seglar, laico.

lay·off [léɔf] *s.* despido.

la·zi·ly [lézɪlɪ] *adv.* perezosamente.

la·zi·ness [lézɪnɪs] *s.* pereza.

la·zy [lézɪ] *adj.* perezoso, holgazán.

lead [lɛd] *d.* plomo; plomada, pesa de plomo.

lead [lid] *v.* (*guide*) guiar, dirigir; llevar; conducir; mandar (*un ejército*); (*precede*) ir a la cabeza de; sobresalir entre; ser mano (*en el juego de naipes*); **to — an orchestra** dirigir una orquesta, llevar la batuta; **to — astray** llevar por mal camino, extraviar, descarriar; **to — the way** ir por delante, mostrar el camino; *s.* delantera, primer lugar; mando, dirección; indicio; papel principal; primer actor.

lead·en [lédn̩] *adj.* plomizo; aplomado, color de plomo; pesado.

lead·er [lídɚ] *s.* jefe, caudillo, *Am.* líder; director; guía; caballo delantero; **-s** puntos suspensivos.

lead·er·ship [lídɚʃɪp] *s.* dirección, mando; iniciativa.

lead·ing [lídɪŋ] *adj.* principal; delantero; **— man** primer actor.

lead·off [lídɔf] *adj.* delantero; puntero.

leaf [lif] *s.* hoja; *v.* echar hojas (*un árbol*), cubrirse de hojas; **to — through a book** hojear un libro.

leaf·less [líflɪs] *adj.* sin hojas, deshojado.

leaf·let [líflɪt] *s.* hojilla; folleto, hoja volante, papel volante, circular.

leaf·y [lífɪ] *adj.* frondoso.

league [lig] *s.* (*alliance*) liga, confederación; sociedad; (*distance*) legua; *v.* asociar(se); ligarse, coligarse.

leak [lik] *s.* gotera (*en un techo*); agujero, grieta (*por donde se escapa el agua o el gas*); escape (*de gas, vapor, electricidad, etc.*); *v.* gotear(se); rezumar(se); hacer agua (*dícese de un barco*); salirse, escaparse (*el gas, el vapor, etc.*).

lean [lin] *v.* (*incline*) inclinar(se); recostar(se), reclinar(se); (*support*) apoyar(se); *adj.* magro; flaco; **— year** año estéril, año improductivo.

leant [lɛnt] = **leaned.**

leap [lip] *v.* saltar; brincar; *s.* salto, brinco; **— year** año bisiesto.

leapt [lɛpt] *pret. & p.p. de* **to leap.**

learn [lɚn] *v.* aprender; saber, averiguar, enterarse de.

learn·ed [lɚnɪd] *adj.* erudito; docto.

learn·er [lɚnɚ] *s.* aprendedor; estudiante, estudioso.

learn·ing [lɚnɪŋ] *s.* erudición, saber; aprendizaje.

learnt [lɚnt] *pret. & p.p. de* **to learn.**

lease [lis] *v.* arrendar, dar o tomar en arriendo; *s.* arriendo, contrato de arrendamiento; *Arg.* contrato de locación.

leash [liʃ] *s.* trailla; cuerda.

least [list] *adj.* (el mínimo, (el) más pequeño; *adv.* menos; **at —** al menos, a lo menos, por lo menos; **the —** lo (el, la) menos.

leath·er [léðɚ] *s.* cuero, piel; *adj.* de cuero, de piel; **— strap** correa.

leave [liv] *v.* dejar; abandonar; (*depart*) salir (de); partir; irse; **to — out** dejar fuera; omitir; *s.* permiso, licencia; **— out absence** licencia; **to take — of** despedirse de.

leav·en [lévən] *s.* levadura, fermento; *v.* fermentar (*la masa*).

leaves [livz] *pl. de* **leaf.**

leav·ings [lívɪŋz] *s.* sobras, desperdicios.

lec·ture [léktʃɚ] *s.* conferencia, discurso; represión; *v.* dar una conferencia; explicar; reprender.

lec·tur·er [léktʃərɚ] *s.* conferenciante; conferencista; lector (*de universidad*).

LED (Light-e·mit·ting di·ode) [lɛd] *s.* (computer) diodo electroluminiscente (LED).

led [lɛd] *pret. & p.p. de* **to lead.**

ledge [lɛdʒ] *s.* borde; salidizo.

ledg·er [lédʒɚ] *s.* libro mayor (*en contabilidad*); *Arg.* libro de cuentas. **— account** cuenta del mayor; **— balance** saldo del mayor; **— entry** pase en el mayor.

leech [litʃ] *s.* sanguijuela.

leer [lɪr] *s.* mirada de soslayo, mirada lujuriosa; *v.* mirar de soslayo; mirar con lujuria.

lee·ward [líwɚd] *s. & adv.* sotavento.

left [lɛft] *pret. & p.p. de* **to leave; I have two books — me** quedan dos libros; *adj.* izquierdo; *s.* izquierda; mano izquierda; **at (on, to) the —** a la izquierda.

left-hand·ed [léfthǽndɪd] *adj.* zurdo; a la izquierda; (*awkward*) torpe; (*bad*) malicioso, insincero; **— compliment** alabanza irónica.

left·ist [léftɪst] *s.* izquierdista.

left·o·ver [léftovɚ] *adj.* sobrante; **-s** *s. pl.* sobras.

left-wing [léftwɪŋ] *adj.* izquierdista.

leg [lɛg] *s.* pierna; pata (*de animal, mesa, etc.*); pie o pata (*de banquillo, silla, etc.*); etapa, trecho (*de una carrera o viaje*); **to be on one's last -s** estar en las últimas.

leg·a·cy [légəsɪ] *s.* legado, herencia.

le·gal [lígl̩] *adj.* legal; lícito; **— expenses** gastos jurídicos; **— fees** honorarios legales; **— holiday** día feriado; **— opinion** consulta; **— tender** moneda de curso legal.

le·gal·ize [líglaɪz] *v.* legalizar; sancionar, autorizar.

leg·ate [légɪt] *s.* legado; delegado.

leg·a·tee [légətɪ] *s.* legatario; *Cuba, Ch.* asignatario.

le·ga·tion [lɪgéʃən] *s.* legación; embajada.

leg·end [lédʒənd] *s.* leyenda; letrero, inscripción.

leg·en·dar·y [lédʒəndɛrɪ] *adj.* legendario.

leg·gings [légɪŋz] *s. pl.* polainas.

leg·i·ble [lédʒəbl̩] *adj.* legible.

le·gion [lídʒən] *s.* legión.

leg·is·late [lédʒɪslet] *v.* legislar.

leg·is·la·tion [ledʒɪsléʃən] *s.* legislación.

leg·is·la·tive [lédʒɪsletɪv] *adj.* legislativo.

leg·is·la·tor [lédʒɪsletɚ] *s.* legislador.

leg·is·la·ture [lédʒɪsletʃɚ] *s.* legislatura, asamblea legislativa

le·git·i·mate [lɪdʒítəmɪt] *adj.* legítimo.

lei·sure [líʒɚ] *s.* ocio; **— hours** horas de ocio; **to be at —** estar ocioso; estar libre o desocupado; **do it at your —** hágalo Vd. cuando pueda o le convenga; hágalo Vd. en sus ratos de ocio.

lei·sure·ly [líʒɚlɪ] *adj.* lento, deliberado, pausado; *adv.* sin prisa, despacio, a sus (mis, tus, *etc.*) anchas.

lem·on [lémən] *s.* limón; **— tree** limonero; *adj.* de limón; **— color** cetrino.

lem·on·ade [lɛmənéd] *s.* limonada.

lend [lɛnd] *v.* prestar.

lend·er [léndɚ] *s.* prestador; **money —** prestamista.

length [lɛŋkθ] *s.* largo, largor, largura, longitud; duración; cantidad (*de una sílaba*); **at —** largamente, detenidamente; al fin; **to go to any —** hacer cuanto esté de su parte.

length·en [léŋkθən] *v.* alargar(se); prolongar(se).

length·wise [léŋkθwaɪz] *adv.* a lo largo; longitudinalmente; *adj.* longitudinal.

length·y [léŋkθɪ] *adj.* largo, prolongado.

le·ni·ent [líniənt] *adj.* indulgente, clemente, poco severo.

lens [lɛnz] *s.* lente; cristalino (*del ojo*).

lent [lɛnt] *pret. & p.p. de* **to lend.**

Lent [lɛnt] *s.* cuaresma.

leop·ard [lépɚd] *s.* leopardo.

lep·ro·sy [léprəsɪ] *s.* lepra

less [lɛs] *adj.* menor; *adv. & prep.* menos; **— and — cada vez menos.**

less·en [lɛ́sn̩] *v.* aminorar(se), disminuir(se), reducir(se); mermar.

less·er [lɛ́sɚ] *adj.* menor, más pequeño.

les·son [lɛ́sn̩] *s.* lección.

lest [lɛst] *conj.* no sea que, por miedo de que.

let [lɛt] *v.* (*permit*) dejar, permitir; (*rent*) alquilar, arrendar; **— us** (*o* **let's**) **do it** vamos a hacerlo, hagámoslo; **— him come** que venga; **to — be** no molestar, dejar en paz; no tocar; **to — down** traicionar; **to — go** soltar; **to — in** dejar entrar, admitir; **to — know** avisar, enterar, hacer saber; **to — off** soltar; dejar libre; **to — through** dejar pasar; **to — up** disminuir; *pret. & p.p. de* **to let.**

let·down [lɛ́tdɑʊn] *s.* aflojamiento; desilusión.

le·thal [líθəl] *adj.* letal.

leth·ar·gy [lɛ́θədʒɪ] *s.* letargo; **to fall into a —** aletargarse.

let·ter [lɛ́tɚ] *s.* (*alphabet*) letra; (*missive*) carta; **— box** buzón; **— carrier** cartero; **— head** membrete; **— quality printer** impresora de alta calidad; *v.* rotular, hacer a mano letras de molde.

let·tuce [lɛ́tɪs] *s.* lechuga.

lev·ee [lɛ́vɪ] *s.* dique.

lev·el [lɛ́vl̩] *adj.* llano, plano; a nivel; igual; parejo; **level-headed** bien equilibrado, sensato; *adv.* a nivel; a ras; *s.* nivel; **to be on the —** obrar rectamente, obrar sin engaño; ser o decir la pura verdad; *v.* nivelar; igualar; allanar; apuntar, asestar (*un arma*); **to — to the ground** arrasar, echar por tierra.

le·ver [lɛ́vɚ] *s.* palanca; **control —** palanca de mando.

lev·i·ty [lɛ́vɪtɪ] *s.* frivolidad; levedad.

lev·y [lɛ́vɪ] *s.* imposición, recaudación (*de tributos, impuestos, etc.*); (*draft*) leva, enganche, reclutamiento; embargo (*de propiedad*); *v.* imponer, exigir, recaudar (*tributos o multas*); reclutar; **to — on someone's property** embargar la propiedad de alguien.

lewd [lud] *adj.* lujurioso, lascivo, deshonesto.

lewd·ness [lúdnɪs] *s.* lascivia, lujuria.

lex·i·cal [lɛ́ksɪkl̩] *adj.* léxico.

lex·i·cog·ra·phy [lɛksɪkágrəfɪ] *s.* lexicografía.

lex·i·con [lɛ́ksɪkɑn] *s.* léxico.

li·a·bil·i·ty [laɪəbɪ́lətɪ] *s.* responsabilidad, obligación; desventaja; **li·a·bil·i·ties** obligaciones, deudas; pasivo; **— insurance** seguro contra daños a terceros; responsabilidad civil.

li·a·ble [láɪəbl̩] *adj.* responsable, obligado; sujeto, expuesto; propenso; probable.

li·ai·son [liezán] *s.* enlace; unión.

li·ar [láɪɚ] *s.* mentiroso, embustero.

li·bel [láɪbl̩] *s.* libelo; difamación; *v.* difamar.

lib·er·al [lɪ́bərəl] *adj. & s.* liberal.

lib·er·al·ism [lɪ́bə·əlɪzm̩] *s.* liberalismo.

lib·er·al·i·ty [lɪbərǽlətɪ] *s.* liberalidad; largueza, generosidad.

lib·er·al·ize [lɪ́bə·əlaɪz] *v.* liberalizar(se).

lib·er·ate [lɪ́bəret] *v.* libertar, librar; soltar.

lib·er·a·tion [lɪbəréʃən] *s.* liberación.

lib·er·a·tor [lɪ́bəretɚ] *s.* libertador.

li·ber·tine [lɪ́bə·tin] *adj. & s.* libertino.

lib·er·ty [lɪ́bə·tɪ] *s.* libertad; **at —** libre.

li·bi·do [lɪbído] *s.* líbido.

li·brar·i·an [laɪbrɛ́ɪən] *s.* bibliotecario.

li·brar·y [láɪbrɛrɪ] *s.* biblioteca.

li·bret·to [lɪbrɛ́to] *s.* libreto.

lice [laɪs] *pl. de* **louse.**

li·cense, licence [láɪsn̩s] *s.* licencia; permiso; (**title**)

título; **driver's —** licencia (pase, certificado *o* patente) de chófer; título de conductor; licencia para manejar; **— plate** placa (*o* chapa) de numeración, chapa de circulación, chapa de matrícula; *v.* licenciar, dar licencia a; permitir, autorizar.

li·cen·tious [laɪsɛ́nʃəs] *adj.* licencioso, disoluto.

lick [lɪk] *v.* (*tongue*) lamer; (*thrash*) dar una tunda *o* zurra; vencer; **to — someone's boots** adular a uno con servilismo; **to — the dust** morder el polvo; adular; *s.* lamedura, *Am.* lamida; lengüetada; *C.C.* lambida; **salt —** lamedero (*lugar salino donde lame el ganado*); **not to do a — of work** no hacer absolutamente nada.

lick·ing [lɪ́kɪŋ] *s.* zurra, tunda.

lid [lɪd] *s.* tapadera, tapa; **eye —** párpado.

lie [laɪ] *s.* mentira; embuste; **to give the — to** desmentir, dar un mentís; *v.* mentir (*pret. & p.p.* **lied**); tenderse, acostarse; yacer; estar; estar situado; consistir (en); **to — back** recostarse, echarse hacia atrás; **to — down** acostarse, echarse, tenderse; **to — in wait** acechar, espiar.

lien [lin] *s.* obligación, gravámen.

lieu·ten·ant [lutɛ́nənt] *s.* teniente; **second —** subteniente.

life [laɪf] *s.* vida; **from —** del natural; **still —** naturaleza muerta; **— boat** bote de salvamento, lancha salvavidas; **— imprisonment** prisión perpetua; **— insurance** seguro sobre la vida; **— pension** pensión vitalicia; **— preserver** salvavidas, cinto o chaqueta de salvamento.

life·less [láɪflɪs] *adj.* sin vida; muerto; exánime; inanimado; desanimado.

life·less·ness [láɪflɪsnɪs] *s.* falta de vida; inercia; falta de animación.

life·like [láɪflaɪk] *adj.* como la vida; natural, que parece vivo.

life·long [láɪflaɔ́ŋ] *adj.* perpetuo, de toda la vida.

life·size [láɪfsaɪz] *adj.* de tamaño natural.

life·time [láɪftaɪm] *s.* vida, transcurso de la vida.

lift [lɪft] *v.* levantar; alzar; elevar; (**disperse**) disiparse (*las nubes, la niebla, las tinieblas*); **to — one's hat** quitarse el sombrero (*para saludar*); *s.* elevación; exaltación de ánimo; alzamiento; levantamiento; carga; ayuda (*para levantar una carga*); (**hoist**) alza (*de un zapato*); ascensor, *Am.* elevador; **to give someone a — in a car** llevar a alguien en el auto; *Méx.* dar aventón.

lig·a·ture [lɪ́gətʃʊr] *s.* ligadura.

light [laɪt] *s.* luz; lumbre; **tail —** *Am.* farito trasero, *Am.* farol de cola, *Méx.* calavera; *adj.* claro; con luz, (**skin**) de tez blanca; (**weight**) ligero; leve; frívolo; **— drink** bebida suave; **— headed** frívolo, ligero de cascos; **— hearted** alegre; **— opera** opereta; **— pen** (*computer*) lápiz óptico; **to make — of** dar poca importancia a; *v.* encender(se); iluminar, alumbrar; **to — upon** caer sobre; posarse en (*dícese de los pájaros, mariposas, etc.*).

light·en [láɪtn̩] *v.* aligerar; iluminar; aclarar; relampaguear; alegrar.

light·er [láɪtɚ] *s.* encendedor; (**boat**) barcaza, chalana.

light·house [láɪthaʊs] *s.* faro.

light·ing [láɪtɪŋ] *s.* iluminación; alumbrado.

light·ly [láɪtlɪ] *adv.* ligeramente; levemente; frívolamente; sin seriedad.

light·ness [láɪtnɪs] *s.* ligereza, frivolidad; claridad.

light·ning [láɪtnɪŋ] *s.* relampagueo; relámpago; **— rod** pararrayos.

light·weight [láɪtwet] *s.* peso liviano; peso ligero.

lik·a·ble [láɪkəbl̩] *adj.* agradable, simpático.

LA

placentero.
like [laɪk] *adv. & prep.* como; del mismo modo que; semejante a; *adj.* semejante, parecido; **in — manner** de manera semejante, del mismo modo; **to feel — going** tener ganas de ir; **to look — someone** parecerse a alguien; **it looks — rain** parece que va a llover, quiere llover; *s.* semejante, igual; **-s** gustos; preferencias; *v.* gustarle a uno; **he -s books** le gustan los libros; **do whatever you —** haz lo que gustes.
like·ly [láɪklɪ] *adj.* probable, creíble; prometedor; **— place** lugar a propósito; **it is — to happen** es probable que suceda; *adv.* probablemente.
lik·en [láɪkən] *v.* asemejar, comparar.
like·ness [láɪknɪs] *s.* semejanza; parecido; retrato.
like·wise [láɪkwaɪz] *adv.* igualmente, asimismo; del mismo modo; también.
lik·ing [láɪkɪŋ] *s.* simpatía; afición; preferencia, gusto.
li·lac [láɪlək] *s.* lila; *adj.* lila, morado claro.
lil·y [lílɪ] *s.* lirio; azucena.
lil·y-white [lɪliwáɪt] *adj.* blanquísimo; puro; racialmente segregado.
limb [lɪm] *s.* rama (*de árbol*); miembro (*del cuerpo*), pierna, brazo.
lim·ber [lɪmbɚ] *adj.* flexible; ágil; *v.* hacer flexible; **to — up** agilitar(se), hacer(se) flexible.
lime [laɪm] *s.* cal; lima (*fruta*); *Am.* limón; **— tree** limonero; liga (*para cazar pájaros*).
lime·light [láɪmlaɪt] *s.* luz de calcio; proscenio; **to be in the —** estar a la vista del público.
lime·stone [láɪmston] *s.* piedra caliza.
lim·it [lɪmɪt] *s.* límite; confín; *v.* limitar.
lim·i·ta·tion [lɪmɪtéʃən] *s.* limitación; restricción.
lim·it·ed [lɪmɪtɪd] *adj.* limitado; restringido.
lim·it·ing [lɪmətɪŋ] *adj.* limítrofe.
lim·it·less [lɪmɪtlɪs] *adj.* ilimitado, sin límites; desmedido.
limp [lɪmp] *s.* cojera; *v.* cojear; renguear; *adj.* flojo; flexible.
lim·pid [lɪmpɪd] *adj.* límpido; claro, transparente.
line [laɪn] *s* (*mark*) línea; renglón; raya; (*cord*) cuerda; (*business*) ramo; giro (*de negocios*); especialidad; **of credit** línea de crédito, *Col.* cupo de crédito; **— printer** (*computer*) impresora de líneas; **— of goods** surtido, línea (*Am.* renglón) de mercancías; **branch railway —** ramal; **pipe —** cañería, tubería; **to bring into —** alinear; obligar a proceder de acuerdo con un plan; poner de acuerdo; **to get in —** meterse en fila, hacer (*o* formar) cola; *v.* linear, rayar; alinear; forrar; **to — up** alinear(se); formarse, formar fila.
lin·e·age [lɪnɪɪdʒ] *s.* linaje.
lin·e·ar [lpaaɪnɪɚ] *adj.* lineal.
lined [laɪnd] *adj.* rayado; forrado.
lin·en [lɪnɪn] *s.* lino; ropa blanca.
lin·er [láɪnɚ] *s.* vapor, buque; **air —** avión, transporte aéreo.
line-up [láɪnəp] *s.* formación.
lin·ger [lɪŋgɚ] *v.* tardar(se), demorarse, dilatarse; (*saunter*) andar ocioso, vagar; (*last*) perdurar; prolongarse.
lin·ge·rie [lǽnʒərɪ] *s.* ropa interior de mujer.
lin·guist [lɪŋgwɪst] *s.* lingüista.
lin·guis·tics [lɪŋgwístɪks] *s.* lingüística.
lin·ing [láɪnɪŋ] *s.* forro.
link [lɪŋk] *s.* eslabón; enlace; **cuff -s** gemelos; *v.* eslabonar(se); enlazar(se).
lin·net [lɪnɪt] *s.* jilguero.
li·no·le·um [lɪnóliəm] *s.* linóleo (*tela impermeable para cubrir el suelo*).

lin·seed [lɪnsid] *s.* linaza; **— oil** aceite de linaza.
lint [lɪnt] *s.* hilas; hilachas.
li·on [láɪən] *s.* león.
li·on·ess [láɪənɪs] *s.* leona.
lip [lɪp] *s.* labio.
lip·stick [l'aaɪpstɪk] *s.* lápiz para los labios.
liq·uid [lɪkwɪd] *adj.* líquido; **— assets** valores líquidos (*o* realizables); **— measure** medida para líquidos; *s.* líquido.
liq·ui·date [lɪkwɪdet] *v.* liquidar, saldar (*cuentas*); poner término a.
liq·ui·da·tion [lɪkwɪdéʃən] *s.* liquidación; saldo de cuentas.
liq·uor [lɪkɚ] *s.* licor; bebida espiritosa (*como aguardiente, ron, etc.*).
lira [lɪrə] unidad monetaria de Italia.
lisp [lɪsp] *s.* ceceo; *v.* cecear; balbucir.
list [lɪst] *s.* lista; registro; (*ship*) escora (*inclinación de un barco*); *v.* alistar, registrar poner o apuntar en una lista; hacer una lista de; escorar, inclinarse a la banda.
lis·ten [lɪsn] *v.* escuchar; atender, dar oídos, prestar atención; **— ¡oye! ¡escucha!; ¡oiga! ¡escuche!; to — in** escuchar por radio; escuchar a hurtadillas (*una conversación*).
lis·ten·er [lɪsnɚ] *s.* escuchador, oyente; **radio —** radioescucha, radioyente.
list·ing [lɪstɪŋ] *s.* (*computer*) listado.
list·less [lɪstlɪs] *adj.* abstraído; indiferente; indolente; desatento.
list·less·ness [lɪstlɪsnɪs] *s.* indiferencia, inatención, abstracción.
lit [lɪt] *pret. & p.p.* de **to light**; *adj.* alumbrado; algo borracho.
lit·er·al [lɪtərəl] *adj.* literal; **-ly** *adv.* al pie de la letra, literalmente.
lit·er·ar·y [lɪtərɛrɪ] *adj.* literario.
lit·er·a·ture [lɪtərətʃur] *s.* literatura; impresos, folletos, circulares.
lith·i·um [lɪθiəm] *s.* litio.
lit·i·ga·tion [lɪtəgéʃən] *s.* litigio, pleito.
lit·ter [lɪtɚ] *s.* (*young animals*) camada, cría; (*stretcher*) litera, camilla; cama de paja para animales; (*disorder*) cosas esparcidas; desorden; *v.* revoltillo; *v.* desarreglar, revolver, esparcir cosas.
lit·tle [lɪtl] *adj.* pequeño; poco; **Little Bear** Osa Menor; **a — coffee** un poco de café; **a — while** un ratito (*o* ratico), un poco; *adv. & s.* poco; **— by —** poco a poco.
live [lɪv] *v.* vivir; **to — down** hacer olvidar, borrar (*el pasado*); **to — up to** vivir en conformidad con, vivir de acuerdo con.
live [laɪv] *adj.* (*not dead*) vivo; (*lively*) enérgico; vivo, activo; **— coal** ascua encendida; **— oak** encina; siempreverde **— question** cuestión palpitante, cuestión de actualidad; **— wire** alambre cargado; persona muy activa.
live·li·hood [láɪvlɪhud] *s.* vida, alimento, subsistencia, manutención.
live·li·ness [láɪvlɪnɪs] *s.* viveza, animación; agilidad.
live·long [lɪvlɔŋ] *adj.* todo; absolutamente todo.
live·ly [láɪvlɪ] *adj.* vivo; vivaz; animado, alegre; airoso; **— horse** caballo brioso; *adv.* vivamente, de prisa.
liv·er [lɪvɚ] *s.* (*organ*) hígado; (*with life*) vividor.
liv·er·y [lɪvərɪ] *s.* librea; caballeriza (*para caballos de alquiler*).
lives [laɪvz] *pl.* de **life**.
live·stock [láɪvstɑk] *s.* ganado.
liv·id [lɪvɪd] *adj.* lívido; amoratado.
liv·ing [lɪvɪŋ] *s.* (*state*) vida; (*means*) manutención,

subsistencia; *adj.* vivo; viviente; **— room** sala; **— wage** sueldo suficiente para vivir; **the —** los vivos.

liz·ard [lízɚd] *s.* lagarto; **small —** lagartija.

load [lod] *s.* carga; **ship —** cargamento; **-s of** gran cantidad de; montones de; *v.* cargar; agobiar; colmar.

loaf [lof] *s.* hogaza de pan; **sugar —** azúcar de pilón; *v.* holgazanear, haraganear.

loaf·er [lófɚ] *s.* holgazán, haragán, zángano.

loan [lon] *s.* préstamo; empréstito; **— shark** usurero; **— word** préstamo semántico; *v.* prestar *(dinero)*.

loath [loθ] *adj.* maldispuesto, renuente; **to be — to** repugnarle a uno.

loathe [loð] *v.* repugnarle a uno; abominar.

loath·some [lóðsəm] *adj.* repugnante, asqueroso; aborrecible.

loaves [lovz] *pl. de* **loaf.**

lob [lab] *v.* volear.

lob·by [lábɪ] *s.* *(place)* vestíbulo; antecámara; salón de entrada; hall; *(influence)* camarilla; **hotel —** vestíbulo o patio del hotel, hall; *v.* cabildear; *Ch.*, *Perú* capitular; **lobbying** cabildeo; **lobbyist** cabildero.

lobe [lob] *s.* lóbulo.

lob·ster [lábstɚ] *s.* langosta de mar.

lo·cal [lókl] *adj.* local; **train** tren ordinario.

lo·cal·i·ty [lokǽlətɪ] *s.* localidad; comarca.

lo·cal·ize [lóklaɪz] *v.* localizar.

lo·cate [lóket] *v.* situar, establecer; *(find)* localizar, averiguar la posición de; *(move to)* avecindarse, radicarse, establecerse.

lo·ca·tion [lokéʃən] *s.* situación; sitio, localidad.

lock [lak] *s.* *(door)* cerradura; *(canal)* esclusa *(de un canal)*; llave *(de un arma de fuego)*; guedeja *(de pelo)*; bucle, rizo; *v.* cerrar con llave; trabar(se), juntar(se); entrelazar(se); **to — in** encerrar; **to — out** cerrar la puerta *(a alguien)*, dejar afuera; **to — up** encerrar; encarcelar.

lock·er [lákɚ] *s.* alacena; armario.

lock·et [lákɪt] *s.* guardapelo.

lock·out [lákaʊt] *s.* paro *(suspensión del trabajo por parte de los empresarios)*; cierre de fábrica.

lock·smith [láksmɪθ] *s.* cerrajero.

lo·co·mo·tive [lokəmótɪv] *s.* locomotora; **—engineer** maquinista.

lo·cust [lókəst] *s.* langosta, saltamontes; cigarra; **— tree** algarrobo; acacia falsa.

lodge [ladʒ] *s.* logia; casita accesoria; casa de campo; *v.* alojar(se); hospedar(se); colocar; **to — a complaint** presentar una queja.

lodg·er [ládʒɚ] *s.* huésped, inquilino.

lodg·ing [ládʒɪŋ] *s.* alojamiento, hospedaje; vivienda.

loft [lɔft] *s.* desván; galería; balcón interior *(de un templo)*; **choir —** coro; **hay —** pajar.

loft·y [lɔ́ftɪ] *adj.* elevado; sublime; altivo.

log [lɔg] *s.* leño, troza, tronco aserrado; *(ship)* corredera *(aparato para medir las millas que anda la nave)*; diario de navegación; **— cabin** cabaña de troncos; *v.* cortar *(árboles)*; cortar leños y transportarlos; registrar *(en el diario de navegación)*; **logging** corte y transporte de trozos, explotación forestal.

log·ic [ládʒɪk] *s.* lógica; principios de la combinación de circuitos en las computadoras.

log·i·cal [ládʒɪkl] *adj.* lógico.

log·roll [lɔ́rol] *v.* lograr aprobación de leyes mediante favores.

loin [lɔɪn] *s.* ijada, ijar, lomo.

loi·ter [lɔ́ɪtɚ] *v.* holgazanear, vagar, malgastar el tiempo; **to — behind** rezagarse.

loll [lal] *v.* arrellanarse o repantigarse, recostarse con toda comodidad.

lone [lon] *adj.* solo, solitario.

lone·li·ness [lónlɪnɪs] *s.* soledad.

lone·ly [lónlɪ] *adj.* solo, solitario; triste, desamparado.

lone·some [lónsəm] *adj.* solo, solitario; triste, nostálgico.

long [lɔŋ] *adj.* largo; **the whole day —** todo el santo día; **three feet —** tres pies de largo; **to be — in coming** tardar en venir; *adv.* mucho, mucho tiempo; **— ago** hace mucho tiempo; **— shot** muy improbable, de poca esperanza; **— live!** ¡viva! **as** *(o* **so) —** as en tanto que, mientras que; **how — is it since . . . ?** ¿cuánto tiempo hace que . . . ?; **so — !** ¡hasta luego! ¡adiós!; **long-suffering** sufrido, paciente; **long-winded** prolijo, largo *(en hablar)*; **long-distance** de larga distancia; *v.* anhelar; ansiar; **to — for** anhelar; suspirar por.

long·er [lɔ́ŋgɚ] *adj.* más largo; *adv.* más, más tiempo; **no —** ya no; **not . . . any —** ya no; no **. . .** más.

lon·gev·i·ty [lándʒévətɪ] *s.* longevidad.

long·hand [lɔ́ŋhænd] *s.* letra manuscrita.

long·ing [lɔ́ŋɪŋ] *s.* anhelo, añoranza, nostalgia; *adj.* anhelante, anheloso, nostálgico; **-ly** *adv.* con anhelo, anhelosamente, con ansia.

lon·gi·tude [lándʒətjud] *s.* longitud.

long-range [lɔŋréndʒ] *adj.* de largo alcance.

long·shore·man [lɔ́ŋʃormən] *s.* estibador *(de barco o muelle)*, cargador.

long-term [lɔ́ŋtɚm] *adj.* a largo plazo.

look [lʊk] *v.* *(see)* mirar; *(seem)* parecer; **it -s well on you** le cae *(o* le sienta) bien; **to — after** atender, cuidar; **to — alike** parecerse; asemejarse; **to — down on a person** mirar con desprecio *(o* menospreciar) a alguien; **to — for** buscar; esperar; **to — forward to** anticipar con placer; **to — into** examinar, investigar; **— out!** ¡cuidado!; ¡tenga cuidado!; **to — out of** asomarse a; **to — over** examinar; dar un vistazo a; **to — up** levantar la vista; buscar; **to — up to** admirar, mirar con respeto; *s.* mirada, vistazo; **-s** apariencia, aspecto; **to have good -s** ser bien parecido.

look·ing glass [lʊ́kɪŋglæs] *s.* espejo.

look·out [lʊ́kaʊt] *s.* vigía; atalaya; *(place)* mirador; *(view)* vista, perspectiva; **that is your —** ¡eso a usted!; **to be on the —** estar alerta.

loom [lum] *s.* telar; *v.* destacarse, descollar; asomar(se), aparecer.

loop [lup] *s.* *(closed)* lazo, gaza, presilla; *(road)* vuelta, curva; *(electric)* circuito; *(computer)* bucle; *v.* hacer una gaza *(con o* en); atar con gaza o presilla; hacer un circuito.

loop·hole [lúphol] *s.* agujero, abertura; *(way out)* salida; escapatoria.

loose [lus] *adj.* *(slack)* suelto; flojo; *(unfettered)* desatado; *(licentious)* disoluto; **— change** suelto, moneda suelta; **— jointed** de articulaciones flojas; **— leaf** de hojas sueltas; **to let —** soltar; *v.* soltar, desatar; aflojar; **-ly** *adv.* sueltamente; flojamente; con poca exactitud, sin fundamento.

loos·en [lúsn] *v.* soltar(se); aflojar(se) desatar(se); **to — one's hold** desasirse, soltarse.

loose·ness [lúsnɪs] *s.* *(limberness)* soltura; flojedad; *(laxness)* flojera; holgura; relajación; *(of bowel)* flujo.

loot [lut] *s.* botín, pillaje, saqueo; *v.* saquear, pillar, robar.

lop [lɑp] *v.* tronchar, desmochar *(Am.* mochar).

lo·qua·cious [lokwéʃəs] *adj.* locuaz, hablador, lenguaraz.

lo·quat [lókwat] *s.* níspero.

lord [lɔrd] *s.* señor; dueño, amo; lord; **Lord's Prayer** Padre Nuestro; **Our Lord** Nuestro Señor; *v.* señorear, mandar; **to — it over** señorear, dominar.

lord·ly [lɔ́rdlɪ] *adj.* señoril; noble; (*haughty*) altivo; despótico; *adv.* altivamente, imperiosamente.

lord·ship [lɔ́rdʃɪp] *s.* señoría (*título*); señorío, dominio.

lose [luz] *v.* perder; **to — sight of** perder de vista.

loss [lɔs] *s.* pédida; **to be at a —** estar perplejo; no saber qué hacer; **to sell at a —** vender con pérdida.

lost [lɔst] *pret. & p.p. de* **to lose**; *adj.* perdido; extraviado; **— in thought** absorto, abstraído; **to get —** perderse, extraviarse.

lot [lɑt] *s.* (*land*) lote; (*section*) parte, porción; (*luck*) suerte; solar, porción de terreno; **a — of** (*o* **-s of**) una gran cantidad de; mucho; muchos; **to draw -s** echar suertes; **to fall to one's —** tocarle a uno, caerle en suerte; *adv.* mucho; **a — better** mucho mejor.

lo·tion [lóʃən] *s.* loción.

lot·ter·y [lɑ́tərɪ] *s.* lotería.

loud [laʊd] *adj.* ruidoso; (*voice*) recio, fuerte; (*colors*) chillón (*dícese también de los colores*); *adv.* ruidosamente, fuerte, recio; alto, en voz alta.

loud-speak·er [láʊdspíkɚ] *s.* altavoz, altoparlante.

lounge [laʊndʒ] *s.* sala de descanso; sofá, diván, canapé; *v.* arrellanarse, repantigarse, recostarse cómodamente; sestear; holgazanear.

louse [laʊs] *s.* piojo.

lous·y [láʊzɪ] *adj.* piojoso; asqueroso.

lov·a·ble [lʌ́vəbl] *adj.* amable.

love [lʌv] *s.* (*affection*) amor; cariño; (*fondness*) afición **— affair** amorío; **to be in —** estar enamorado; **to fall in — with** enamorarse de; **to make — to** enamorar a; *v.* amar, querer; gustar mucho de, gustarle a uno mucho; encantarle a uno algo.

love·li·ness [lʌ́vlɪnɪs] *s.* belleza, hermosura; amabilidad.

love·ly [lʌ́vlɪ]*adj.* amable; lindo, bello; exquisito; encantador; ameno.

lov·er [lʌ́vɚ] *s.* amante; **music —** aficionado a (*o* amante de) la música.

lov·ing [lʌ́vɪŋ] *adj.* amante, amoroso, cariñoso, afectuoso; **-ly** *adv.* cariñosamente, afectuosamente.

low [lo] *adj.* (*not high*) bajo; (*base*) vil; (*humble*) humilde; (*downcast*) abatido; débil; (*lacking*) deficiente; (*sick*) gravemente enfermo; **— comedy** farsa, sainete; **— gear** primera velocidad; **—Mass** misa rezada; **— key** de intensidad minima; **dress with a — neck** vestido escotado (*o* con escote); **to be — on something** estar escaso de algo; **to be in — spirits** estar abatido o desanimado; *adv.* bajo; en voz baja, quedo, quedito; con bajeza, a precio bajo, vilmente; *s.* mugido; *v.* mugir.

low·er [lóɚ] *adj.* más bajo; inferior; **— case letter** letra minúscula; **— classman** estudiante de los dos primeros años; **— house** cámara de diputados; *v.* bajar; disminuir; rebajar; abatir; humillar.

low·land [lólænd] *s.* tierra baja.

low·li·ness [lólɪnɪs] *s.* bajeza; humildad.

low·ly [lólɪ] *adj.* bajo, humilde; inferior; *adv.* humildemente.

low·ness [lónɪs] *s.* bajeza (*humility*) humildad; (*weakness*) abatimiento; gravedad (*de tono*); debilidad (*de un sonido*); baratura.

loy·al [lɔ́ɪəl] *adj.* leal, fiel.

loy·al·ty [lɔ́ɪəltɪ] *s.* lealtad, fidelidad.

LSI (see **large-scale integration**.)

lu·bri·cant [lúbrɪkənt] *adj. & s.* lubricante.

lu·bri·cate [lúbrɪket] *v.* lubricar.

lu·cid [lúsɪd] *adj.* lúcido; claro; luciente.

luck [lʌk] *s.* suerte; fortuna; **in — de** buena suerte; **in bad — de** mala suerte.

luck·i·ly [lʌ́klɪ] *adv.* afortunadamente, por fortuna.

luck·y [lʌ́kɪ] *adj.* afortunado, feliz; **to be —** tener suerte, tocarle a uno la suerte.

lu·cra·tive [lúkrətɪv] *adj.* lucrativo.

lu·di·crous [lúdɪkrəs] *adj.* ridículo.

lug [lʌg] *v.* llevar, traer, *Am.* cargar; **to — away** cargar con, llevarse (*una cosa pesada*).

lug·gage [lʌ́gɪdʒ] *s.* equipaje.

luke·warm [lúkwɔ́rm] *adj.* tibio, templado; indiferente.

lull [lʌl] *v.* arrullar; sosegar; calmar(se); *s.* calma, momento de calma.

lul·la·by [lʌ́ləbaɪ] *s.* arrullo, canción de cuna.

lum·ber [lʌ́mbɚ] *s.* madera, maderaje; **— man** maderero, negociante en madera; **— yard** depósito de maderas; **— jack** leñador; *v.* cortar y aserrar madera; explotar los bosques; moverse pesadamente.

lu·mi·nous [lúmənəs] *adj.* luminoso.

lump [lʌmp] *s.* (*mass*) terrón; bulto; (*swelling*) hinchazón, chichón; protuberancia; **— of sugar** terrón de azúcar; **— sum** pago global; *v.* amontonar; consolidar (*gastos*); apelotonarse, aterronarse, formar terrones.

lump·y [lʌ́mpɪ] *adj.* aterronado.

lu·na·tic [lúnətɪk] *adj. & s.* lunático, loco.

lunch [lʌntʃ] *s.* almuerzo; merienda; **· room** merendero, *Méx., Ven., Carib.* lonchería; *Ríopl.* confitería; *Spain* cafetería; *v.* almorzar; merendar; *Am.* tomar el lonche.

lun·cheon [lʌ́ntʃən] *s.* almuerzo; merienda.

lung [lʌŋ] *s.* pulmón.

lurch [lɝtʃ] *v.* sacudida; tambaleo repentino; **to give a —** tambalearse; **to leave someone in the —** dejar a uno plantado, dejar a uno a buenas noches; *v.* tambalearse; dar un tambaleo repentino.

lure [lʊr] *s.* aliciente, atractivo; tentación; (*bait*) cebo o reclamo (*para atraer*); *v.* atraer; seducir; atraer (*con cebo o reclamo*).

lurk [lɝk] *v.* estar oculto; estar en acecho; moverse furtivamente.

lus·cious [lʌ́ʃəs] *adj.* exquisito, delicioso, sabroso.

lust [lʌst] *s.* lujuria; deseo vehemente; codicia; *v.* **to — after** codiciar.

lus·ter [lʌ́stɚ] *s.* lustre, brillo.

lus·trous [lʌ́strəs] *adj.* lustroso.

lust·y [lʌ́stɪ] *adj.* vigoroso, fornido, robusto.

lute [lut] *s.* laúd.

lux·u·ri·ant [lʌgʒúrɪənt] *adj.* lozano, frondoso, exuberante.

lux·u·ri·ous [lʌgʒúrɪəs] *adj.* lujoso; dado al lujo; frondoso.

lux·u·ry [lʌ́kʃərɪ] *s.* lujo; **— tax** impuesto suntuario.

lye [laɪ] *s.* lejía.

ly·ing [láɪɪŋ] *ger. de* **to lie**; *adj.* mentiroso; **lying-in hospital** casa de maternidad.

lymph [lɪmpf] *s.* linfa.

lynch [lɪntʃ] *v.* linchar.

lynx [lɪŋks] *s.* lince.

lyre [laɪr] *s.* lira.

lyr·ic [lɪrɪk] *s.* poema lírico; *adj.* lírico.

lyr·i·cal [lɪ́rɪkl] *adj.* lírico.

lyr·i·cism [lɪ́rəsɪzəm] *s.* lirismo.

M:m

mac·a·ro·ni [mækəróɪ] *s.* macarrón o macarrones.

mac·a·roon [mækərún] *s.* macarrón, almendrado, bollito de almendra.

ma·chine [məʃín] *s.* máquina; automóvil; — **gun** ametralladora; — **made** hecho a máquina; — **language** (*computer*) lenguaje de máquina; — **pistol** metralleta; **political** — camarilla política; **sewing** — máquina para coser.

ma·chin·er·y [məʃínərɪ] *s.* maquinaria.

ma·chin·ist [məʃínɪst] *s.* mecánico, maquinista.

mack·er·el [mǽkərəl] *s.* escombro, caballa (*pez*).

mad [mæd] *adj.* (*crazy*) loco; (*angry*) rabioso; furioso, enojado; **to drive** — enloquecer; volver loco, **to get** — encolerizarse; **to go** — volverse loco, enloquecerse; **-ly** *adv.* **locamente.**

mad·am, mad·ame [mǽdəm] *s.* madama, señora.

mad·cap [mǽdkæp] *s.* calavera (*m.*), *adj.* temerario; temerario; atolondrado.

mad·den [mǽdn̩] *v.* enloquecer(se).

made [med] *pret. & p.p. de* **to make; to be** — **of** estar hecho de; ser de; **to have something** — mandar hacer algo; **made-up** fingido, falso; artificial, pintado (*con afeites*).

made-to-order [medtuɔ́rdɚ] *adj.* hecho a la medida.

mad·man [mǽdmæn] *s.* loco.

mad·ness [mǽdnɪs] *s.* locura; (*anger*) rabia.

mag·a·zine [mægəzín] *s.* revista; (*storage*) almacén; **powder** — polvorín.

mag·ic [mǽdʒɪk] *s.* magia; *adj.* mágico.

ma·gi·cian [mədʒíʃən] *s.* mágico; prestidigitador; brujo.

mag·is·trate [mǽdʒɪstret] *s.* magistrado.

mag·nan·i·mous [mægnǽnəməs] *adj.* magnánimo.

mag·ne·sia [mægníʒə] *s.* magnesia.

mag·ne·si·um [mægnízɪəm] *s.* magnesio.

mag·net [mǽgnɪt] *s.* imán.

mag·net·ic [mægnétɪk] *adj.* magnético; — **pole** polo magnético; — **tape** cinta magnetofónica.

mag·net·ise [mǽgnətaɪz] *v.* magnetizar; imantar; cautivar.

mag·nif·i·cence [mægnífəsn̩s] *s.* magnificencia.

mag·nif·i·cent [mægnífəsn̩t] *adj.* magnífico.

mag·ni·fy [mǽgnəfaɪ] *v.* agrandar, engrandecer; amplificar; exagerar.

mag·ni·tude [mǽgnətjud] *s.* magnitud.

mag·pie [mǽgpaɪ] *s.* urraca; cotorra, hablador, habladora.

ma·hog·a·ny [məhágənɪ] *s.* caoba.

maid [med] *s.* criada, sirvienta, camarera, *Méx.* recamarera, *Ríopl., Andes* mucama; doncella; — **of honor** doncella de honor; **old** — solterona.

maid·en [médn̩] *s.* doncella; virgen; mozuela; (*unmarried*) soltera; — **lady** mujer soltera; — **voyage** primer viaje (*de un vapor*).

mail [mel] *s.* correo; correspondencia; **air** — correo aéreo; **coat of** — malla; — **bag** valija; — **order** ventas por correo; — **train** tren correo; *v.* echar al correo.

mail·box [mélbɑks] *s.* buzón.

mail·man [mélmæn] *s.* cartero.

maim [mem] *v.* mutilar, estropear.

main [men] *adj.* principal, mayor, de mayor importancia; (*pipe*)*s.* (*sea*) tubería, cañería principal (*de agua o gas*); — **office** casa matriz; alta mar, océano; **in the** — en su mayor parte; en general, en conjunto; **-ly** *adv.* principalmente.

main·land [ménlænd] *s.* continente, tierra firme.

main·spring [ménsprɪŋ] *s.* muelle real; origen.

main·tain [mentén] *v.* mantener; sostener; afirmar; guardar.

main·te·nance [méntənəns] *s.* mantenimiento; sustento; manutención; sostén, sostenimiento.

maize [mez] *s.* maíz.

ma·jes·tic [mədʒéstɪk] *adj.* majestuoso.

maj·es·ty [mǽdʒɪstɪ] *s.* majestad.

ma·jor [médʒɚ] *adj.* (*greater*) mayor, más grande; (*principal*) principal; — **key** tono mayor; *s.* comandante; mayor, mayor de edad; curso o asignatura de especialización (*en la universidad*); — **league** liga mayor; *v.* especializarse (*en un curso de estudios*).

ma·jor·i·ty [mədʒɔ́ɛtɪ] *s.* mayoría; mayor edad.

make [mek] *v.* (*do*) hacer; (*create*) fabricar; formar; (*deliver*) pronunciar (*un discurso*); **to** — **a clean breast of** confesar; **to** — **a train** alcanzar un tren; **to** — **a turn** dar vuelta; **to** — **away with** llevarse, robar; matar; **to** — **fast** asegurar, afianzar; **to** — **headway** progresar, adelantar; **to** — **much of** dar mucha importancia a; **to** — **neither head nor tail of** no comprender nada de; **to** — **nothing out of** no comprender nada de, no sacar nada en limpio; **to** — **out in the distance** distinguir a lo lejos; **to** — **over** rehacer, alterar (*un traje*); **to** — **sure** asegurarse; **to** — **toward** dirigirse a, encaminarse a; **to** — **up a story** inventar un cuento; **to** — **up after a quarrel** hacer las paces; **to** — **up for a loss** compensar por una pérdida; **to** — **up one's face** pintarse la cara; **to** — **up one's mind** resolverse, decidirse; *s.* hechura, forma; marca (*de fábrica*); manufactura.

mak·er [mékɚ] *s.* hacedor; fabricante; artífice.

make·shift [mékʃɪft] *adj.* provisional.

make-up [mékʌp] *s.* (*composition*) compostura, composición, hechura; (*character*) naturaleza, carácter; **facial** — afeite, cosmético; maquillaje.

mal·a·chite [mǽləkaɪt] *s.* malaquita.

mal·a·dy [mǽlədɪ] *s.* mal, enfermedad.

ma·lar·i·a [məlɛ́rɪə] *s.* malaria, fiebre palúdica, paludismo.

mal·con·tent [mǽlkəntɛnt] *adj. & s.* malcontento.

male [mel] *adj.* macho; varón; masculino; varonil; de hombres, de varones; *s.* macho; varón; hombre.

mal·ice [mǽlɪs] *s.* malicia.

ma·li·cious [məlíʃəs] *adj.* malicioso, perverso, malévolo.

ma·lign [məláɪn] *v.* calumniar, difamar; *adj.* maligno; pernicioso.

ma·lig·nant [məlígnənt] *adj.* maligno; malévolo.

mal·le·a·ble [mǽlɪəbl̩] *adj.* maleable; manejable.

mal·let [mǽlɪt] *s.* mazo, maceta.

mal·nu·tri·tion [mælnutríʃən] *s.* desnutrición.

malt [mɔt] *s.* malta; **-ed milk** leche malteada.

ma·ma, mam·ma [mámə] *s.* mamá.

mam·mal [mǽml] *s.* mamífero.

mam·moth [mǽməθ] *adj.* gigantesco, enorme.

mam·my [mǽmɪ] *s.* mamita; niñera negra. [Hoy día se puede considerar racista.]

man [mæn] *s.* hombre; varón; pieza (*de ajedrez*); — **and wife** marido y mujer; **to a** — unánimemente, todos a una; **officers and men** oficiales y soldados; **man-of-war** buque de guerra; — **cook** cocinero; *v.* armar, proveer de gente armada; guarnecer (*una fortaleza*); tripular (*una embarcación*).

man·age [mǽnɪdʒ] *v.* manejar; gobernar, dirigir; gestionar; **to** — **to do something** arreglárselas para hacer algo.

man·age·a·ble [mǽnɪdʒəbl̩] *adj.* manejable; domable, dócil.

man·age·ment [mǽnɪdʒmənt] *s.* manejo; dirección; gobierno, administración; (*office*) gerencia.

man·ag·er [mǽnɪdʒɚ] s. gerente; director, administrador; empresario.

man·date [mǽndet] s. mandato; v. asignar por mandato.

man·do·lin [mǽndəlɪn] s. mandolina.

mane [men] s. melena (del león), crin (del caballo).

ma·neu·ver [mənúvɚ] s. maniobra; gestión; v. maniobrar; manipular, manejar.

man·ful [mǽnfəl] adj. varonil; viril.

man·ga·nese [mǽŋgənis] s. manganeso.

mange [mendʒ] s. sarna, roña.

man·ger [méndʒɚ] s. pesebre.

man·gle [mǽŋgl] v. magullar, mutilar, destrozar, estropear; planchar en máquina de planchar; s. planchadora (máquina de planchar).

man·grove [mǽngrov] s. mangle.

man·gy [méndʒɪ] adj. sarnoso, Am. sarniento.

man·hood [mǽnhʊd] s. virilidad; edad viril; hombres.

ma·ni·a [ménɪə] s. mania.

man·i·cure [mǽnɪkjʊr] s. manicura; manicurist; v. manicurar.

man·i·fest [mǽnəfɛst] adj. manifiesto; s. (ship) manifiesto; v. manifestar; poner de manifiesto; declarar.

man·i·fes·ta·tion [mænəfɛstéʃən] s. manifestación.

man·i·fes·to [mænɪfésto] s. manifiesto, bando, proclama.

man·i·fold [mǽnəfold] adj. múltiple; numeroso, diverso.

man·i·kin [mǽnəkɪn] s. maniquí; muñeco; hombrecillo.

ma·nil·a [mənílə] s. abacá (cáñamo de Manila); · **paper** papel de Manila.

man·i·oc [mǽniak] s. mandioca.

ma·nip·u·late [mənípjələt] v. manipular; manejar.

ma·nip·u·la·tion [mənɪpjələʃən] s. manipulación.

man·kind [mǽnkáɪnd] s. humanidad, género humano; los hombres.

man·like [mǽnlaɪk] adj. hombruno; varonil; Méx. macho s. (woman) marimacho.

man·ly [mǽnlɪ] adj. varonil; viril; muy hombre; adv. varonilmente.

man·ner [mǽnɚ] s. (way) manera; modo; género; (air) aire, ademán, -s maneras, modales; costumbres; **after the — of** a la manera de; **by no — of means** de ningún modo.

man·ner·ism [mǽnɚɪzm] s. costumbre; amaneramiento.

man·nish [mǽnɪʃ] adj. hombruno.

ma·noeu·vre = **maneuver.**

man·or [mǽnɚ] s. solar, casa solariega.

man·pow·er [mǽnpavɚ] s. mano de obra, fuerzas disponibles.

man·sion [mǽnʃən] s. mansión; palacio.

man·slaugh·ter [mǽnslɔtɚ] s. homicidio impremeditado o casual.

man·tel [mǽntl] s. manto (de una chimenea); repisa de chimenea

man·tle [mǽntl] s. manto; capa.

man·u·al [mǽnjʊəl] adj. manual; — **training school** escuela de artes y oficios; s. manual; (keyboard) teclado de órgano.

man·u·fac·ture [mænjəfǽktʃɚ] s. fabricación; elaboración; manufactura; v. fabricar, manufacturar; elaborar.

man·u·fac·tur·er [mænjəfǽktʃərɚ] s. fabricante.

man·u·fac·tur·ing [mænjəfǽktʃərɪŋ] s. fabricación; adj. fabril, manufacturero; — **concern** empresa industrial.

man·ure [mənúr] s. estiércol, abono; v. estercolar, abonar (la tierra).

man·u·script [mǽnjəskrɪpt] adj. & s. manuscrito.

man·y [ménɪ] adj. muchos; — **a time** muchas veces; **a great** — muchísimos; **as** — **as** tantos como; cuantos; **as** — **as five** hasta cinco; **how** — ? ¿cuántos?; **three books too** — tres libros de más; **too** — demasiados.

map [mæp] s. mapa; v. trazar un mapa de; **to — out** proyectar, planear.

ma·ple [mépl] s. arce, Méx. meple; Ríopl. maple.

mar [mɑr] v. desfigurar, estropear.

mar·ble [mɑ́rbl] s. mármol; (plaything) canica (para jugar); **to play -s** jugar a las canicas; adj. de mármol; marmóreo.

march [mɑrtʃ] s. marcha; v. marchar, caminar; hacer marchar; **to — in** entrar marchando; **to — out** marcharse; salirse marchando.

March [mɑrtʃ] s. marzo.

mare [mer] s. yegua.

mar·ga·rine [mɑ́rdʒərɪn] s. margarina.

mar·gin [mɑ́rdʒɪn] s. margen; orilla; sobrante; excedente; reserva (fondos).

mar·gin·al [mɑ́rdʒɪnl] adj. marginal; — **note** nota marginal, acotación; de rendimiento mínimo.

mar·i·gold [mǽrəgold] s. caléndula, maravilla.

ma·rine [mərín] adj. marino; marítimo; — **corps** cuerpo de marinos; s. marino; soldado de marina; **merchant** — marina mercante.

mar·i·ner [mǽrənɚ] s. marinero.

mar·i·time [mǽrətaɪm] adj. marítimo.

mark [mɑrk] s. marca; señal, seña; nota, calificación; **question** — punto de interrogación; **to come up to the** — alcanzar la norma requerida; **to hit the** — dar en el blanco; **to make one's** — distinguirse; **to miss one's** — fallar; errar el tiro; (fail) fracasar; v. marcar; señalar; notar; observar; calificar; — **my words!** ¡advierte lo que te digo!; **to — down** anotar, apuntar; rebajar el precio de.

mark·down [mɑ́rkdaʊn] s. rebaja de precios.

mark·er [mɑ́rkɚ] s. marcador; marca, señal; jalón.

mar·ket [mɑ́rkɪt] s. mercado, plaza; — **place** mercado, plaza; el mundo del comercio — **price** precio corriente; **meat** — carnicería; **stock** — mercado de valores, bolsa; in the — **for** dispuesto a comprar; — **on the market** de venta; v. vender; vender o comprar en el mercado; **to go -ing** ir de compras.

mar·ket·ing [mɑ́rkətɪŋ] s. mercadotecnia.

mark·up [mɑ́rkəp] s. aumento de precios.

mar·ma·lade [mɑ́rmled] s. mermelada.

ma·roon [mərún] s. .& adj. rojo obscuro.

ma·rooned [mərúnd] adj. abandonado (en lugar desierto); aislado; **to get** — encontrarse aislado, perdido o incomunicado.

mar·quis [mɑ́rkwɪs] s. marqués.

mar·quise [mɑrkíz] s. marquesa.

mar·riage [mǽrɪdʒ] s. matrimonio; casamiento, boda; unión, enlace; — **license** licencia de matrimonio.

mar·riage·a·ble [mǽrɪdʒəbl] adj. casadero.

mar·ried [mǽrɪd] adj. casado; conyugal; — **couple** matrimonio, cónyuges; pareja de casados; **to get** — casarse.

mar·row [mǽro] s. meollo, tuétano, médula (de los huesos).

mar·ry [mǽrɪ] v. casar; casarse; casarse con.

marsh [mɑrʃ] s. pantano; ciénaga.

mar·shal [mɑ́rʃəl] s. mariscal; (local) alguacil; jefe de policía (en ciertas regiones); maestro de ceremonia; **fire** — jefe de bomberos; v. ordenar, arreglar; guiar, conducir con ceremonia.

marsh·mal·low [márʃmælo] *s.* pastilla o bombón de altea.

marsh·y [márʃɪ] *adj.* pantanoso, cenagoso.

mart [mɑrt] *s.* mercado.

mar·tial [márʃəl] *adj.* marcial; — **law** estado de sitio.

mar·tin [mártɪn] *s.* avión (*pájaro*).

mar·tyr [mártɚ] *s.* mártir; *v.* martirizar, torturar, atormentar.

mar·tyr·dom [mártɚdəm] *s.* martirio.

mar·vel [márvl] *s.* maravilla; *v.* maravillarse.

mar·vel·ous [márvləs] *adv.* maravilloso.

Marx·ism [márksɪzəm] *s.* marxismo.

mas·cot [mæskɑt] *s.* mascota.

mas·cu·line [mæskjəlɪn] *adj.* masculino; varonil; hombruno.

mash [mæʃ] *v.* majar, amasar; machacar, magullar; **-ed potatoes** puré de papas (*o* patatas); patatas majadas.

mask [mæsk] *s.* máscara; disfraz; careta; *v.* disfrazar, enmascarar; encubrir; **-ed ball** baile de máscaras.

ma·son [mésn̩] *s.* albañil; **Mason** masón, francmasón.

ma·son·ry [mésn̩rɪ] *s.* albañilería; mampostería; **Masonry** masonería, francmasonería.

mas·quer·ade [mæskəréd] *s.* mascarada; disfraz, máscara; *v.* enmascararse, disfrazarse; andar disfrazado.

mass [mæs] *s.* masa; montón; mole; (*most*) mayoría, mayor parte; (*church*) misa; — **meeting** mitín popular; — **production** fabricación en serie (*cadena*); — **communication** communicación extensa; — **media** los medios de comunicarse con el público (*radio, televisión, periódicos, etc.*); **the -es** las masas, el pueblo; *v.* juntar(se) en masa.

mas·sa·cre [mæsəkɚ] *s.* hecatombe, matanza, carnicería, destrozo; *v.* hacer matanza o hecatombe, destrozar.

mas·sage [məsáʒ] *v.* friccionar, dar masaje; *s.* masaje.

mas·sive [mæsɪv] *adj.* sólido, macizo; (*big*) voluminoso, imponente.

mast [mæst] *s.* mástil, palo.

mas·ter [mæstɚ] *s.* (*head*) amo, dueño, señor; maestro; patrón; (*skilled*) experto, perito; **band** — director de la banda; — **of arts** maestro en artes, licenciado; **-'s degree** licenciatura, grado de licenciado; *adj.* maestro; — **builder** maestro de obras; — **key** llave maestra; *v.* dominar; domar; gobernar; **to** — **a language** dominar un idioma.

mas·ter·ful [mæstɚfəl] *adj.* magistral; dominante.

mas·ter·ly [mæstɚlɪ] *adj.* magistral; *adv.* magistralmente.

mas·ter·piece [mæstɚpis] *s.* obra maestra.

mas·ter·y [mæstərɪ] *s.* maestría, arte, destreza; dominio.

mas·tiff [mæstɪf] *s.* mastín, alano.

mat [mæt] *s.* (*covering*) estera; esterilla, felpudo, tapete; (*gymnasium*) colchoncillo (*de gimnasia*); borde de cartón (*para hacer resaltar una pintura*).

match [mætʃ] *s.* (*pair*) pareja; (*game*) partida, contienda, juego; (*light*) fósforo, cerilla; *Méx.* cerillo; **he has no** — no tiene igual; **he is a good** — es un buen partido; **the hat and coat are a good** — el abrigo y el sombrero hacen juego; *v.* igualar; aparear; hacer juego, armonizar; **to** — **one's strength** medir uno sus fuerzas; **these colors do not** — **well** estos colores no casan bien.

match·less [mætʃlɪs] *adj.* sin par, sin igual, incomparable.

mate [met] *s.* compañero, compañera; consorte;

macho o hembra (*entre animales o aves*); (*ship*) piloto (*officer*); oficial subalterno (*en la marina*); *v.* aparear(se).

ma·te·ri·al [mətírɪəl] *adj.* material; esencial; *s.* material; tejido, género; materia; **raw** — materia prima.

ma·ter·nal [mətɝnl] *adj.* maternal, materno.

ma·ter·ni·ty [mətɝnətɪ] *s.* maternidad.

math·e·mat·i·cal [mæθəmætɪkl] *adj.* matemático.

math·e·mati·cian [mæθəmətíʃən] *s.* matemático.

math·e·mat·ics [mæθəmætɪks] *s.* matemáticas.

mat·i·née [mætné] *s.* función de la tarde, *Am.* matiné.

ma·tri·arch [métrɪɑrk] *s.* matriarca.

ma·tric·u·late [mətríkjəlet] *v.* matricular(se).

ma·tric·u·la·tion [mətrɪkjəléʃən] *s.* matriculación, matrícula.

mat·ri·mony [mætrəmonɪ] *s.* matrimonio, casamiento.

ma·trix [métrɪks] *s.* matriz; molde.

ma·tron [métrən] *s.* matrona, madre de familia; ama de llaves; vigilante, cuidadora (*de un asilo, cárcel para mujeres, etc.*).

mat·ter [mætɚ] *s.* (*substance*) material, materia; sustancia; (*affair*) asunto, cuestión; cosa; (*discharge*) pus; — **for complaint** motivo de queja; — **of two minutes** cosa de dos minutos; **as a** — **of fact** de hecho; en verdad, en realidad; **business -s** negocios; — **printed** — impresos; **serious** — cosa seria; **it is of no** — no tiene importancia; **to do something as a** — **of course** hacer algo por rutina; **what is the** — ? ¿qué tiene Vd.?; **matter-of-fact person** persona de poca imaginación; *v.* importar; supurar; **it does not** — no importa, no le hace.

mat·tress [mætrɪs] *s.* colchón; **spring** — colchón de muelles.

ma·ture [mətjúr] *adj.* maduro; **a** — **note** un pagaré vencido; *v.* madurar(se); vencerse, hacerse cobrable o pagadero (*un pagaré, una deuda*).

ma·tur·i·ty [mətjúrətɪ] *s.* madurez; vencimiento (*de una deuda u obligación*).

maul [mɔl] *v.* magullar; maltratar; manejar rudamente; golpear.

mav·er·ick [mævɚɪk] *s.* animal sin marca; becerro suelto.

max·im [mæksɪm] *s.* máxima.

max·i·mum [mæksəməm] *adj. & s.* máximo.

may [me] *v. irr. ·y. defect.* (*able*) poder; (*permitted*) tener permiso para, serle permitido a uno; (*possible*) ser posible; — **I sit down?** ¿puedo sentarme?; — **you have a good time** que se divierta Vd., **it** — **be that** puede ser que, tal vez sea que; **it** — **rain** puede (ser) que llueva, es posible que llueva; **she** — **be late** puede (ser) que llegue ella tarde.

May [me] *s.* mayo, mes de mayo; — **Day** primero de mayo; — **pole** mayo; — **Queen** maya (*reina de la fiesta del primero de mayo*).

may·be [mébɪ] *adv.* quizás, tal vez, acaso.

may·on·naise [meənéz] *s.* mayonesa.

may·or [méɚ] *s.* alcalde, alcalde mayor.

maze [mez] *s.* laberinto; confusión; **to be in a** — estar confuso o perplejo.

me [mi] *pron. pers.* me; mí (*después de preposición*); **give it to** — démelo (a mí); **for** — para mí; **with** — conmigo.

mead·ow [médo] *s.* pradera, prado; — **lark** alondra de los prados.

mea·ger [mígɚ] *adj.* escaso, insuficiente; magro, flaco.

meal [mil] *s.* comida; *(flour)* harina (*a medio moler*);
corn — harina de maíz; — **time** hora de comer.

mean [min] *adj.* *(malicious)* ruin, bajo; vil; *(humble)*
humilde; *(stingy)* mezquino, tacaño; *(difficult)* de
mal genio; *(sick)* malo, indispuesto; *(middle)*
mediano; medio; intermedio; — **distance** distancia
media; *s.* medio; término medio; **-s** medios;
recursos; **a man of -s** un hombre pudiente o rico;
by -s of por medio de; **by all -s** de todos modos; a
toda costa; por supuesto; **by no -s** de ningún modo;
golden — justo medio; *v.* querer decir, significar;
pensar, proponerse, tener la intención de; intentar;
destinar; **he -s well** tiene buenas intenciones.

me·an·der [miǽndɚ] *v.* serpentear.

mean·ing [mínɪŋ] *s.* *(sense)* significado, sentido;
significación; *(intent)* propósito, intención; *adj.*
significativo; **well-meaning** bien intencionado.

mean·ing·less [mínɪŋlɪs] *adj.* sin sentido, vacío de
sentido.

mean·ness [mínnɪs] *s.* ruindad, vileza, bajeza;
mezquindad.

meant [mɛnt] *pret. & p.p. de* **to mean.**

mean·time [míntaɪm] *adv.* mientras tanto, entretanto;
s. ínterin, entretanto; **in the** — en el ínterin,
mientras tanto.

mean·while [mínhwaɪl = **meantime.**

mea·sles [mízlz] *s.* sarampión.

mea·sur·a·ble [méʒrəbl] *adj.* medible, mensurable;
mea·sur·a·bly *adv.* marcadamente.

mea·sure [méʒɚ] *s.* *(dimension)* medida; compás (*de
música*); cadencia, rítmo; *(law)* proyecto de ley;
ley; **beyond** — sobremanera; con exceso; **dry** —
medida para áridos; **in large** — en gran parte, en
gran manera; *v.* medir; **measuring tape** cinta de
medir.

mea·sured [méʒɚd] *adj.* medido; moderado;
acompasado.

mea·sure·ment [méʒɚmənt] *s.* medida; dimensión;
tamaño; medición.

meat [mit] *s.* carne; *(pith)* meollo, sustancia; — **ball**
albóndiga; — **market** carnicería; — **packer**
empacador de carnes; **cold** — fiambre.

meat·y [míti] *adj.* carnoso; sustancioso.

me·chan·ic [məkǽnɪk] *adj. & s.* mecánico; **-s** *s.*
mecánica.

me·chan·i·cal [mekǽnɪkl] *adj.* mecánico; maquinal.

mech·a·nism [mékənɪzəm] *s.* mecanismo.

med·al [médl] *s.* medalla.

med·dle [médl] *v.* entrometerse o entremeterse;
meterse.

med·dler [médlɚ] *s.* entrometido.

med·dle·some [médlsəm] *adj.* entremetido.

me·di·an [mídɪən] *adj.* mediano, del medio; *s.* punto,
línea o número del medio; mediana.

me·di·ate [mídɪet] *v.* mediar; intervenir; arbitrar.

me·di·a·tion [midɪéʃən] *s.* mediación, intervención,
intercesión.

me·di·a·tor [mídɪətɚ] *s.* mediador, medianero,
árbitro.

med·i·cal [médɪkl] *adj.* médico; — **school** escuela de
medicina

med·i·ca·tion [mɛdɪkéʃən] *s.* medicación.

med·i·cine [médəsn] *s.* medicina; medicamento; —
ball pelota grande de cuero; **—cabinet** botiquín;
— **man** curandero indio.

me·di·e·val [midɪ́vl] *adj.* medioeval o medieval.

me·di·o·cre [midɪókɚ] *adj.* mediocre, mediano;
ordinario.

me·di·oc·ri·ty [midɪákrətɪ] *s.* mediocridad, medianía.

med·i·tate [médətet] *v.* meditar.

med·i·ta·tion [mɛdətéʃən] *s.* meditación.

me·di·um [mídɪəm] *s.* medio; medio ambiente; *adj.*
mediano; intermedio; a medio cocer, a medio asar;
— **of exchange** medio (tipo) de cambío.

med·ley [médlɪ] *s.* baturrillo, mezcla, mezcolanza.

meek [mik] *adj.* manso, dócil, paciente, sufrido.

meek·ness [míknɪs] *s.* mansedumbre, docilidad.

meet [mit] *v.* encontrar(se); reunirse; conocer
(personalmente), ser presentado a; *(receive)* ir a
esperar (*un tren, vapor, o a alguien*); satisfacer
(*deseos, requisitos, etc.*); pagar (*una deuda*);
sufragar (*gastos*); responder a (*una acusación*); **to**
— **in battle** trabar batalla; **to** — **with** encontrarse
con; tropezar con; topar con; reunirse con; **to** —
the expenses pagar los gastos; **to** — **halfway**
partir la diferencia; *s.* concurso; contienda
(*tratándose de deportes*); **track** — competencia de
atletas.

meet·ing [mítɪŋ] *s.* reunión; *(political)* mitin; sesión;
asamblea; encuentro.

Meg·a·byte (MBYTE) [mɛ́gəbaɪt] *s.* *(computer)*
mega-byte (MB).

meg·a·phone [mɛ́gəfon] *s.* megáfono, portavoz,
bocina.

meg·a·ton [mɛ́gətʌn] *s.* megatón.

mel·an·chol·y [mélənkalɪ] *s.* melancolía; *adj.*
melancólico.

me·lee [méle] *s.* reyerta; zafarrancho.

mel·low [mɛ́lo] *adj.* maduro, sazonado; dulce,
blando, suave; *v.* madurar(se), sazonar(se);
ablandar(se), suavizar(se).

me·lo·di·ous [məlódíəs] *adj.* melodioso.

mel·o·dra·ma [mélodramə] *s.* melodrama.

mel·o·dy [mɛ́lədɪ] *s.* melodía.

mel·on [mɛ́lən] *s.* melón.

melt [mɛlt] *v.* derretir(se); disolver(se); fundir(se).

mem·ber [mɛ́mbɚ] *s.* miembro; socio.

mem·ber·ship [mɛ́mbɚʃɪp] *s.* número de miembros o
socios; asociación; *(los)* miembros (*de un club o
sociedad*).

mem·brane [mɛ́mbren] *s.* membrana.

me·men·to [mɪmɛ́nto] *s.* memento, memoria,
recuerdo.

mem·oir [mɛ́mwar] *s.* memoria, apuntaciones; **-s**
memorias; autobiografía

mem·o·ra·ble [mɛ́mərəbl] *adj.* memorable.

mem·o·ran·dum [mɛmətǽndəm] *s.* memorándum;
memoria, apunte; — **book** memorándum, librito de
apuntes, memorial.

me·mor·i·al [məmórɪəl] *s.* *(monument)* monumento
conmemorativo; *(occasion)* obra o fiesta
conmemorativa; memorial, petición; *adj.*
conmemorativo.

mem·o·rize [mɛ́məraɪz] *v.* aprender de memoria.

mem·o·ry [mɛ́mərɪ] *s.* memoria; recuerdo; **chip**
(computer), ficha memoria.

men [mɛn] *pl. de* **man.**

men·ace [mɛ́nɪs] *s.* amenaza; *v.* amenazar.

mend [mɛnd] *v.* remendar; reparar, componer;
enmendar; **to** — **one's ways** enmendarse,
reformarse; *s.* remiendo; reparación; **to be on the**
— ir mejorando.

me·ni·al [mínɪəl] *adj.* servil, bajo.

men·stru·a·tion [mɛnstruéʃən] *s.* menstruo o
menstruación.

men·tal [mɛ́ntl] *adj.* mental.

men·tal·i·ty [mɛntǽlətɪ] *s.* mentalidad, ingenio.

men·tion [mɛ́nʃən] *s.* mención; alusión; *v.*
mencionar, mentar; **don't** — **it** no hay de qué
(*contestación a* ''thank you'').

men·u [mɛ́nju] *s.* menú, lista de platos; *(computer)*
menú (de entrada).

me·ow [mjaʊ] = **mew.**

mer·can·tile [mɝ́kəntɪl] *adj.* mercantil.

mer·ce·nar·y [mɝ́sɳɛrɪ] *adj.* mercenario.

mer·chan·dise [mɝ́tʃəndaɪz] *s.* mercancías, mercaderías; **piece of** — mercancía; **merchandising** mercadotecnia.

mer·chant [mɝ́tʃənt] *s.* comerciante; negociante; mercader; *adj.* mercante, mercantil; — **marine** marina mercante.

mer·ci·ful [mɝ́sɪfəl] *adj.* misericordíoso, piadoso.

mer·ci·less [mɝ́sɪlɪs] *adj.* sin piedad, despiadado, incompasivo.

mer·cu·ry [mɝ́kjərɪ] *s.* mercurio; azogue.

mer·cy [mɝ́sɪ] *s.* (*favor*) merced; favor, gracia; (*compassion*) misericordia, piedad, compasión; **to be at the** — **of** estar a merced de.

mere [mɪr] *adj.* mero; simple, puro; **a** — **formality** una pura formalidad, no más que una formalidad, una formalidad no más; **a** — **trifle** una nonada; **-ly** *adv.* meramente; sólo, solamente; simplemente.

merge [mɝdʒ] *v.* combinar(se), unir(se); absorber(se); fundírse.

merg·er [mɝ́dʒɚ] *s.* amalgamación comercial; fusión.

me·rid·i·an [mərídɪən] *adj. & s.* meridiano.

mer·it [mɛ́rɪt] *s.* mérito; *v.* merecer; — **rating** valoración de meritos.

mer·i·to·ri·ous [mɛrətóriəs] meritorio.

mer·maid [mɝ́med] *s.* ninfa marina.

mer·ri·ly [mɛ́rəlɪ] *adv.* alegremente, con regocijo.

mer·ri·ment [mɛ́rɪmənt] *s.* alegría, regocijo, júbilo.

mer·ry [mɛ́rɪ] *adj.* alegre; jovial; divertido; festivo; — **Christmas** Felices Navidades, Felices Pascuas; **to make** — divertirse.

mer·ry-go-round [mɛ́rɪɡəraʊnd] *s.* tío vivo, *Méx.*, *C.A.* los caballitos; *Ríopl.* calesita.

mer·ry·mak·er [mɛ́rɪmekɚ] *s.* fiestero; juerguista.

mer·ry·mak·ing [mɛ́rɪmekɪŋ] *s.* regocijo; jaleo; juerga, jolgorio; *adj.* regocijado, alegre, festivo, fiestero.

mesh [mɛʃ] *s.* malla; red; **-es** red, redes; *v.* enredar, coger con red; **to** — **gears** engranar.

mess [mɛs] *s.* (*food*) rancho, comida (*en el ejército o la marina*); (*confusion*) lío, confusión; (*dirt*) suciedad; — **of fish** plato o ración de pescado; **to make a** — **of** *v.* revolver, confundir; ensuciar; echar a perder; *v.* revolver, confundir; ensuciar, echar a perder (*generalmente:* **to** — **up**); **to** — **around** revolver o mezclar las cosas; entrometerse; **mess·y** [mɛ́sɪ] *adj.* desordenado, desarreglado; sucio.

mes·sage [mɛ́sɪdʒ] *s.* mensaje; parte (*m*), comunicación; recado.

mes·sen·ger [mɛ́sɳdʒɚ] *s.* mensajero; mandadero.

met [mɛt] *pret. & p.p. de* **to meet.**

me·tab·o·lism [məwtǽbəlɪzm] *s.* metabolismo.

met·al [mɛ́tl] *s.* metal; *adj.* de metal, metálico.

me·tal·lic [mətǽlɪk] *adj.* metálico.

met·al·lur·gy [mɛ́tlɝdʒɪ] *s.* metalurgia.

met·a·mor·pho·sis [mɛtəmɔ́rfəsɪs] *s.* metamorfosis.

met·a·phor [mɛ́təfɚ] *s.* metáfora.

me·tath·e·sis [mətǽθəsɪs] *s.* metátesis.

me·te·or [mítɪɚ] *s.* meteoro; estrella fugaz.

me·te·or·ic [mítɪoraɪt] *s.* meteorito.

me·te·or·ite [mítɪoraɪt] *s.* meteorito.

me·te·or·ol·o·gy [mitɪərálədʒɪ] *s.* meteorología.

me·ter [mítɚ] *s.* metro; contador (*de gas, agua, electricidad,*) *Am.* medidor.

meth·od [mɛ́θəd] *s.* método; técnica.

me·thod·i·cal [məθádɪkl] *adj.* metódico.

me·tre = **meter.**

met·ric [mɛ́trɪk] *adj.* métrico; — **system** sistema métrico; — **ton** tonelada métrica (1000 kg.).

me·trop·o·lis [mətrúplɪs] *s.* metrópoli.

met·ro·pol·i·tan [mɛtrəpúlətn] *adj.* metropolitano.

met·tle [mɛ́tl] *s.* temple, brío, ánimo, valor.

mew [mju] *s.* maullido, maúllo, miau; *v.* maullar.

Mex·i·can [mɛ́ksɪkən] *adj. & s.* mejicano o mexicano.

mez·za·nine [mɛ́zɔnin] *s.* entresuelo.

mice [maɪs] *pl. de* **mouse.**

mi·crobe [máɪkrob] *s.* microbio.

mi·cro·bus [máɪkrobʌs] *s.* microbús.

mi·cro·com·put·er [maɪkrokəmpjútɚ] *s.* microcomputadóra, *Esp.* microordenador.

mi·cro·eco·nom·ics [maɪkroikanámiks] *s.* microeconomía.

mi·cro·film [máɪkrəfɪlm] *s.* microfilm.

mi·cro·phone [máɪkrəfon] *s.* micrófono.

mi·cro·pro·ces·sor [maɪkroprásɛsɚ] *s.* el circuito integrado de la computadora; microprocesador.

mi·cro·scope [máɪkrəskop] *s.* microscopio.

mi·cro·scop·ic [maɪkrəskúpɪk] *adj.* microscópico.

mi·cro·wave [máɪkrowev] *s.* microonda.

mid [mɪd] *adj.* medio (*úsase por lo general en composición*); **in** — **air** en el aire; *prep.* en medio de, entre.

mid·day [mɪ́dde] *s.* mediodía; *adj.* del mediodía.

mid·dle [mɪ́dl] *adj.* medio; intermedio; **Middle Ages** Edad Media; — **finger** dedo de en medio, dedo del corazón; — **size** tamaño mediano; *s.* medio, centro, mitad; **in the** — **of** en medio de, a la mitad de **towards the** — **of the month** a mediados del mes; — **class** clase media.

mid·dle-aged [mɪ́dléʤd] *adj.* de edad mediana, de edad madura.

mid·dle·man [mɪ́dlmæn] *s.* revendedor; medianero, corredor, agente.

mid·dle-sized [mɪ́dlsáɪzd] *adj.* de mediano tamaño, de mediana estatúra.

mid·dy [mɪ́dɪ] *s.* guardiamarina (*m*); — **blouse** blusa a la marinera.

midg·et [mɪ́dʒɪt] *s.* enanillo.

mid·night [mɪ́dnaɪt] *s.* medianoche; *adj.* de (la) medianoche; — **blue** azul oscuro; **Midnight Mass** misa de gallo.

mid·riff [mɪ́drɪf] *s.* diafragma.

mid·ship·man [mɪ́dʃɪpmən] *s.* guardiamarina (*m*).

midst [mɪdst] *s.* medio, centro; **in the** — **of** en medio de, entre; **in our** — entre nosotros.

mid·stream [mɪ́dstrim] *s.* el medio (*o* el centro) de la corriente.

mid·sum·mer [mɪ́dsʌ́mɚ] *s.* pleno verano, solsticio estival, la mitad del verano.

mid·term [mɪ́dtɝ·m]; — **examination** examen a mitad del curso.

mid·way [mɪ́dwé] *adj.* situado a medio camino; equidistante; *adv.* a medio camino; en medio del camino.

mid·wife [mɪ́dwaɪf] *s.* partera, comadrona.

mien [min] *s.* facha, aspecto.

might [maɪt] *imperf. de* **may** podía; podría; pudiera, pudiese; *s.* poder, poderío, fuerza.

might·y [máɪtɪ] *adj.* poderoso, potente, fuerte; *adv.* muy, sumamente.

mi·grant [máɪɡrənt] *adj.* migratorio.

mi·grate [máɪɡret] *v.* emigrar.

mi·gra·tion [maɪɡréʃən] *s.* migración.

mike [maɪk] = **microphone.**

mild [maɪld] *adj.* (*gentle*) suave; blando; apacible; (*moderate*) templado, moderado.

mil·dew [mɪ́ldu] *s.* moho; enmohecimiento.

ME

mild·ness [máɪldnɪs] s. suavidad; mansedumbre; apacibilidad; templanza, dulzura.

mile [maɪl] s. milla; — **stone** mojón.

mile·age [máɪlɪdʒ] s. millaje, número de millas; recorrido (*en millas*). *Compárese* kilometraje, número de kilómetros.

mil·i·tant [mílɪtənt] s. militante; belicoso.

mil·i·tar·y [mílətɛrɪ] adj. militar; de guerra; s. **the** — el ejército; los militares.

mi·li·tia [məlíʃə] s. milicia.

milk [mɪlk] s. leche; — **diet** régimen lácteo; v. ordeñar.

milk·maid [mílkmed] s. lechera.

milk·man [mílkmən] s. lechero, *Am.* vaquero.

milk·y [mílkɪ] adj. lácteo; lechoso; **Milky Way** Vía Láctea.

mill [mɪl] s. (*grinder*) molino; (*factory*) fábrica; taller; (*money*) la milésima parte de un dólar; **saw** — aserradero; **spinning** — hilandería; **sugar** — ingenio de azúcar; **textile** — fábrica de tejidos; v. moler; (*wood*) aserrar (*madera*); fabricar; (*coins*) acordonar (*el canto de la moneda*); fresar, estriar; **to** — **around** arremolinarse (*una muchedumbre*).

mill·er [mílɚ] s. molinero; mariposa nocturna.

mil·li·gram [mílɡræm] s. miligramo.

mil·li·me·ter [mílɪmitɚ] s. milímetro.

mil·li·ner [mílənɚ] s. modista (*de sombreros para señoras*).

mil·li·ner·y [mílənɛrɪ] s. sombreros de señora; artículos para sombreros de señora; oficio de sombrerera; — **shop** sombrerería.

mil·lion [míljən] s. millón; **a** — **dollars** un millón de dólares.

mil·lion·aire [mɪljənɛ́r] adj. & s. millonario.

mil·lionth [mɪljənθ] adj. & s. millonésimo.

mill·stone [mílston] s. muela o piedra de molino; carga pesada.

mim·ic [mímɪk] adj. mímico, imitativo; — **battle** simulacro; s. imitador, remedador; v. imitar, remedar.

mince [mɪns] v. picar, desmenuzar; **not to** — **words** hablar con toda franqueza.

mince·meat [mínsmit] s. picadillo (*especialmente el de carne, pasas, manzanas y especias*).

mind [maɪnd] s. (*brain*) mente; (*thought*) pensamiento; inteligencia; (*spirit*) ánimo, espíritu; (*purpose*) propósito, intención; (*opinion*) parecer, opinión; **to be out of one's** — estar loco, haber perdido el juicio; **to change one's** — cambiar de parecer; **to give someone a piece of one's** — cantarle a alguien la verdad; echarle a alguien un buen regaño; **to have a** — **to** estar por; sentir ganas de; **to make up one's** — decidirse, resolverse; **to my** — **a** mi modo de ver; **to speak one's** — freely hablar con toda franqueza; v. cuidar; atender a, hacer caso de; obedecer; **I don't** — no tengo inconveniente en ello; **never** — no importa; no se preocupe; no se moleste; no haga Vd. caso; **to** — **one's own business** atender a lo suyo, no meterse en lo ajeno.

mind·ful [máɪndfəl] adj. atento (a); cuidadoso (de).

mine [maɪn] pron. pos. mío (mía, míos, mías); **el** mío (la mía, los míos, las mías); **a book of** — un libro mío.

mine [maɪn] s. mina; — **sweeper** dragaminas; v. minar; explotar (*una mina*); extraer (*mineral*).

min·er [máɪnɚ] s. minero.

min·er·al [mínərəl] adj. & s. mineral; — **right** derecho de subsuelo.

min·gle [míngl] v. mezclar(se); entremezclar(se); confundir(se); juntarse.

min·i·a·ture [mínɪtʃɚ] s. miniatura; adj. en miniatura; diminuto.

min·i·mal [mínəml] adj. mínimo.

min·i·mize [mínəmaɪz] v. empequeñecer.

min·i·mum [mínəməm] adj. & s. mínimo.

min·ing [máɪnɪŋ] s. minería, explotación de minas; adj. minero; — **engineer** ingeniero de minas.

min·i·skirt [mínɪskɚt] s. minifalda.

min·is·ter [mínɪstɚ] s. ministro; pastor, clérigo; v. ministrar, atender; proveer, socorrer.

min·is·try [mínɪstrɪ] s. (*agency*) ministerio; (*help*) socorro, ayuda.

mink [mɪŋk] s. visón.

min·now [míno] s. pececillo de río.

mi·nor [máɪnɚ] adj. (*young*) menor; de menor edad; (*secondary*) secundario; — **key** tono menor; s. menor de edad; premisa menor (*de un silogismo*); tono menor; curso o asignatura menor.

mi·nor·i·ty [mənɔ́rətɪ] s. minoría; minoridad, menoredad; menor parte; adj. minoritario.

min·strel [mínstrəl] s. trovador; bardo, vate; actor cómico que remeda al negro norteamericano.

mint [mɪnt] s. (*flavor*) menta, hierbabuena (*yerbabuena*); (*candy*) pastilla o bombón de menta; (*money*) casa de moneda; **a** — **of money** un montón de dinero, la mar de dinero; v. acuñar.

mint·age [míntədʒ] s. acuñación; moneda acuñada.

min·u·et [mɪnjuɛ́t] s. minué.

mi·nus [máɪnəs] adj. negativo; sin, falto de; **seven** — **four** siete menos cuatro; s. menos, signo menos.

min·ute [mínɪt] s. minuto; -**s** acta (*de una junta*); — **hand** minutero.

mi·nute [mənjút] adj. menudo, diminuto; minucioso, detallado.

mir·a·cle [mírəkl] s. milagro.

mi·rac·u·lous [mərǽkjələs] adj. milagroso.

mi·rage [mərɑ́ʒ] s. espejismo.

mire [maɪr] s. cieno, fango, lodo; v. atascar(se) en el fango; enlodar(se).

mir·ror [mírɚ] s. espejo; v. reflejar.

mirth [mɚθ] s. júbilo, regocijo, alegría.

mirth·ful [mɚ́θfəl] adj. jubiloso, regocijado, gozoso, alegre.

mir·y [máɪrɪ] adj. cenagoso, fangoso, lodoso.

mis·ad·ven·ture [mɪsədvɛ́ntʃɚ] s. desgracia; contratiempo.

mis·be·have [mɪsbihév] v. portarse mal, obrar mal.

mis·car·riage [mɪskǽrɪdʒ] s. aborto, malparto; mal éxito; extravío (*de una carta, papel, etc.*).

mis·car·ry [mɪskǽrɪ] v. (*fail*) malograrse, frustrarse; extraviarse (*una carta*); (*abort*) abortar.

mis·cel·la·ne·ous [mɪslénɪəs] adj. misceláneo, diverso; — **expenses** gastos varios.

mis·chief [místʃɪf] s. travesura; diablura; mal, daño; diablillo, persona traviesa.

mis·chie·vous [místʃɪvəs] adj. travieso; malicioso; dañino; revoltoso.

mis·con·cep·tion [mɪskənsɛ́pʃən] s. concepto erróneo.

mis·con·duct [mɪskándʌkt] s. mala conducta; mala administración; [mɪskəndʌ́kt] v. maladministrar, manejar mal; **to** — **oneself** portarse mal, conducirse mal.

mis·cue [mɪskjú] s. pifia.

mis·deed [mɪsdíd] s. fechoría, mala acción.

mis·de·mean·or [mɪsdimínɚ] s. mal comportamiento; fechoría.

mi·ser [máɪzɚ] s. avaro, avariento.

mis·er·a·ble [mízrebl] adj. miserable; infeliz, desdichado.

mi·ser·ly [máɪzɚlɪ] adj. avariento, avaro; tacaño,

mezquino.

mis·er·y [mízrɪ] s. miseria, desgracia; (*poverty*) estrechez, pobreza; dolor.

mis·for·tune [mɪsfɔ́rtʃən] s. infortunio, desgracia, desastre.

mis·giv·ing [mɪsgívɪŋ] s. mal presentimiento, aprensión, recelo, temor.

mis·guid·ed [mɪsgáɪdəd] adj. mal aconsejado.

mis·hap [míshæp] s. desgracia, contratiempo, accidente.

mis·judge [mɪsdʒʌ́dʒ] v. juzgar mal.

mis·laid [mɪsléd] pret. & p.p. de **to mislay.**

mis·lay [mɪslé] v. extraviar, perder; poner fuera de su sitio, colocar mal; traspapelar (*una carta, documento, etc.*).

mis·lead [mɪslíd] v. guiar por mal camino; extraviar, descarriar; engañar.

mis·led [mɪsléd] pret. & p.p. de **to mislead.**

mis·man·age [mɪsmǽnɪdʒ] v. administrar mal.

mis·place [mɪsplés] v. extraviar, poner fuera de su sitio, colocar mal; traspapelar (*una carta, documento, etc.*).

mis·print [mɪsprínt] s. errata, error tipográfico, error de imprenta.

mis·pro·nounce [mɪsprənɑʊns] v. pronunciar mal.

mis·rep·re·sent [mɪsrɛprɪzɛ́nt] v. falsear, falsificar; tergiversar; **misrepresentation** tergiversación.

miss [mɪs] v. (*not hit*) errar, no acertar; fallar; (*omit*) equivocar; perder; faltar a; (*feel absence of*) echar de menos; *Am.* extrañar; **he just -ed being killed** por poco lo matan; s. error; falla, falta.

miss [mɪs] s. señorita; **Miss Smith** la señorita Smith.

mis·sile [mísl] s. proyectil; arma arrojadiza; adj. arrojadizo,˘ que se puede arrojar o tirar.

miss·ing [mísɪŋ] adj. ausente; perdido; **one book is — falta un libro.**

mis·sion [míʃən] s. misión.

mis·sion·ar·y [míʃənɛrɪ] adj. & s. misionero.

mis·spell [mɪsspél] v. escribir con mala ortografía, deletrear mal.

mist [mɪst] s. neblina, niebla; llovizna, *Ven., Col., Andes* garúa; v. lloviznar; anublar.

mis·take [məsték] s. error, yerro, equivocación; errata (*de imprenta*); **to make a —** equivocarse; v. equivocar.

mis·tak·en [məstékən] p.p. de **to mistake** & adj. equivocado; errado; erróneo, incorrecto; **to be —** estar equivocado, equivocarse, errar.

mis·ter [místɚ] s. señor.

mis·took [mɪstúk] pret. de **to mistake.**

mis·treat [mɪstrít] v. maltratar.

mis·tress [místrɪs] s. señora; (*in charge*) ama, dueña; (*lover*) querida, amante; **school —** maestra.

mis·tri·al [mɪstráɪl] s. pleito viciado de nulidad.

mis·trust [mɪstrʌ́st] s. desconfianza; v. desconfiar de.

mis·trust·ful [mɪstrʌ́stfəl] adj. desconfiado, sospechoso, receloso.

mist·y [místɪ] adj. brumoso; nublado; (*filmed*) empañado; (*vague*) vago, indistinto.

mis·un·der·stand [mɪsʌndɚstǽnd] v. comprender mal; entender mal; interpretar mal; no comprender.

mis·un·der·stand·ing [mɪsʌndɚstǽndɪŋ] s. equivocación; mala interpretación, mala inteligencia; desavenencia.

mis·un·der·stood [mɪsʌndɚstúd] pret. & p.p. de **to misunderstand.**

mis·use [mɪsjús] s. abuso; mal uso; malversación (*de fondos*); [mɪsjúʃ] v. abusar de; maltratar; usar o emplear mal; malversar (*fondos*).

mite [maɪt] s. (*small*) óbolo, friolera, pequeñez; (*creature*) criatura.

mi·ter [máɪtɚ] s. mitra, dignidad de obispo

mit·i·gate [mítəget] v. mitigar.

mit·ten [mɪtṇ] s. mitón.

mix [mɪks] v. mezclar(se); unir(se), juntar(se), asociar(se); **to — someone up** confundir a uno; s. mezcla; confusión, lío.

mix·ture [míkstʃɚ] s. mezcla; mezcolanza.

mix·up [mɪ́ksʌp] s. equívoco; enredo.

moan [mon] s. quejido, gemido; v. gemir; quejarse; lamentar(se).

moat [mot] s. foso.

mob [mɑb] s. (*rabble*) populacho; (*crowd*) muchedumbre, gentío, *Am.* bola (*de gente*); v. atropellar; apiñarse o agolparse alrededor de.

mo·bile [móbl] adj. móvil; movible; movedizo; — **home** casa ˘rodante.

mo·bi·li·za·tion [mobləzéʃən] s. movilización.

mo·bi·lize [móblaɪz] v. movilizar.

moc·ca·sin [mɑ́kən] s. (*shoe*) mocasín (*zapato burdo de cuero*); (*snake*) mocasín (*víbora venenosa*).

mock [mɔk] v. (*ridicule*) mofar, mofarse de; (*imitate*) remedar, imitar; **to — at** mofarse de; burlarse de; s. mofa, burla, escarnio; mímica; remedo; adj. falso, ficticio, imitado; — **battle** simulacro, batalla fingida.

mock·er·y [mɔ́kərɪ] s. burla, mofa, escarnio; remedo.

mock·up [mɑ́kʌp] s. maqueta; modelo.

mode [mod] s. modo, manera; moda.

mod·el [mɑdl] s. (*guide*) modelo; (*pattern*) patrón; (*figure*) figurín, maniquí; adj. ejemplar; modelo; — **school** escuela modelo; v. modelar; moldear, formar; posar, servir de modelo.

mo·dem [mɑ́dɛm] s. (computer) modem, modulador-demodulador.

mod·er·ate [mɑ́dərɪt] adj. moderado; templado; módico; [mɑ́dəret] v. moderar(se); templar(se).

mod·er·a·tion [mɑdəréʃən] s. moderación; templanza.

mod·ern [mɑ́dɚn] adj. moderno.

mod·ern·ize [mɑ́dɚnaɪz] v. modernizar.

mod·est [mɑ́dɪst] adj. modesto.

mod·es·ty [mɑ́dəstɪ] s. modestia.

mod·i·fi·ca·tion [mɑdəfəkéʃən] s. modificación.

mod·i·fy [mɑ́dəfaɪ] v. modificar.

mod·u·late [mɑ́dʒəlet] v. modular.

mo·hair [móhɛr] s. pelo de cabra.

Mo·ham·med·an [mohǽmədən] adj. & s. mahometano.

moist [mɔɪst] adj. húmedo; mojado.

mois·ten [mɔɪsṇ] v. humedecer, mojar.

mois·ture [mɔ́ɪstʃɚ] s. humedad.

mo·lar [mólɚ] adj. molar; s. muela.

mo·las·ses [məlǽsɪz] s. melaza, miel de caña.

mold [mold] s. (*form*) molde, matriz; (*substance*) moho; tierra vegetal; v. moldear, amoldar; modelar; enmohecer(se), cubrir(se) de moho.

mold·er [móldɚ] v. desmoronarse.

mold·ing [móldɪŋ] s. moldura; moldeamiento.

mold·y [móldɪ] adj. mohoso.

mole [mol] s. lunar; topo (*animal*); dique, malecón, rompeolas.

mole [mol] s. lunar; topo (*animal*); dique, malecón, rompeolas.

mol·e·cule [mɑ́ləkjul] s. molécula.

mo·lest [məlɛ́st] v. molestar.

mol·li·fy [mɑ́ləfaɪ] v. apaciguar.

mol·ten [móltṇ] adj. derretido, fundido, en fusión.

mo·lyb·de·num [məlíbdənəm] s. molibdeno.

mo·ment [mómənt] s. momento; importancia, consecuencia.

mo·men·tar·y [mómən tɛrɪ] adj. momentáneo.

mo·men·tous [momɛ́ntəs] adj. importante.

MI

mo·men·tum [moméntəm] *s.* momento (*de una fuerza*); ímpetu.

mon·arch [mánɚk] *s.* monarca.

mon·ar·chy [mánɚkɪ] *s.* monarquía.

mon·as·ter·y [mánəstɛrɪ] *s.* monasterio.

Mon·day [mándɪ] *s.* lunes.

mon·e·tar·y [mánətɛrɪ] *adj.* monetario.

mon·ey [mánɪ] *s.* dinero; — **changer** cambista; — **order** giro postal; — **'s worth** valor cabal; — **standard** patrón (talón) monetario; — **in hand** dinero contante; **paper** — papel moneda; **silver** — moneda de plata; **money-making** lucrativo, provechoso, ganancioso.

mon·ger [máŋgɚ] *s.* traficante; defensor.

mon·grel [máŋgrəl] *adj. & s.* mestizo, mixto, cruzado, *Perú* chusco (*perro*).

mon·i·tor [manɪtɚ] *s.* (*telecommunications*) monitor.

monk [mʌŋk] *s.* monje.

mon·key [máŋkɪ] *s.* mono; — **shine** monada, monería; — **wrench** llave inglesa; *v.* juguetear; hacer monerías; payasear; entremeterse; **to** — **with** juguetear con; meterse con.

mon·o·gram [mánəgræm] *s.* monograma.

mon·o·graph [mánəgræf] *s.* monografía.

mon·o·logue [mánlɔg] *s.* monólogo, soliloquio.

mo·nop·o·lize [mənáplaɪz] *v.* monopolizar, acaparar.

mo·nop·o·ly [mənáplɪ] *s.* monopolio.

mon·o·syl·la·ble [mánəsɪləbl] *s.* monosílabo.

mon·o·tone [mánəton] *adj.* monótono.

mo·not·o·nous [mənátnəs] *adj.* monótono.

mo·not·o·ny [mənátnɪ] *s.* monotonía.

mon·ster [mánstɚ] *s.* monstruo; *adj.* enorme.

mon·stros·i·ty [manstrásətɪ] *s.* monstruosidad; monstruo.

mon·strous [mánstrəs] *adj.* monstruoso.

month [mʌnθ] *s.* mes.

month·ly [mánθlɪ] *adj.* mensual; — **installment** mensualidad *Col., Méx.* abono mensual; *s.* publicación mensual; *adv.* mensualmente.

mon·u·ment [mánjəmənt] *s.* monumento.

mon·u·men·tal [manjəméntl] *adj.* monumental; colosal, grandioso.

moo [mu] *s.* mugido; *v.* mugir.

mood [mud] *s.* humor, disposición de ánimo; modo (*del verbo*); **to be in a good** — estar de buen humor; **to be in the** — **to** estar dispuesto a, tener gana de.

mood·y [múdɪ] *adj.* (*changing*) caprichoso, voluble, mudable; (*sad*) melancólico, mohíno.

moon [mun] *s.* luna; mes lunar; **once in a blue** — de Pascuas a San Juan, muy rara vez, *Am.* por campanada de vacante, *Am.* a cada muerte de (*o* por la muerte de un) obispo.

moon·light [múnlaɪt] *s.* luz de la luna; — **dance** baile a la luz de la luna; — **night** noche de luna.

moon·shine [múnʃaɪn] *s.* licor hecho ilegalmente.

moor [mʊr] *v.* amarrar, atracar (*un buque*); anclar estar anclado; *s.* terreno inculto o baldío.

Moor [mʊr] *s.* moro.

Moor·ish [múrɪʃ] *adj.* morisco, moro.

mop [map] *s. Am.* trapeador; **dust** — limpiapolvo; — **of hair** greñas, cabellera abundante; *v.* limpiar (*el suelo*), *Am.* trapear; **to** — **one's brow** limpiarse (*o* secarse) la frente; **to** — **up** limpiar; vencer; acabar con.

mope [mop] *v.* andar quejumbroso o abatido.

mor·al [mɔ́rəl] *adj.* moral; — **philosophy** ética, moral; *s.* moraleja; **-s** moral, ética.

mo·rale [mərǽl] *s.* moral, entereza de ánimo.

mor·al·ist [mɔ́rəlɪst] *s.* moralista.

mo·ral·i·ty [mərǽlətɪ] *s.* moralidad.

mor·al·ize [mɔ́rəlaɪz] *v.* moralizar.

mor·bid [mɔ́bɪd] *adj.* mórbido, morboso; malsano.

mor·dant [mɔ́rdənt] *adj.* mordaz.

more [mor] *adj. & adv.* más; — **and** — cada vez más, más y más; — **or less** poco más o menos; **there is no** — no hay más, ya no hay; se acabó.

more·o·ver [moróvɚ] *adv.* además.

morgue [mɔg] *s.* necrocomio; depósito de cadáveres; (**of newspaper**) archivo de referencias.

morn·ing [mɔ́rnɪŋ] *s.* mañana; **good** — ! ¡buenos días!; **tomorrow** — mañana por la mañana; *adj.* de la mañana; matutino, matinal; **morning-glory** dondiego de día; — **star** lucero del alba.

mor·phine [mɔ́fin] *s.* morfina.

mor·phol·o·gy [mɔrfálədʒɪ] *s.* morfología.

mor·row [mɔro] *s.* **on the** — el día de mañana; mañana.

mor·sel [mɔ́rsl] *s.* bocada; manjar sabroso.

mor·tal [mɔ́rtl] *adj. & s.* mortal.

mor·tal·i·ty [mɔrtǽlətɪ] *s.* mortalidad; mortandad.

mor·tar [mɔ́tɚ] *s.* mortero; argamasa, mezcla; **metal** — almirez.

mort·gage [mɔ́gɪdʒ] *s.* hipoteca, gravamen; *v.* hipotecar; *adj.* hipotecario; — **deed** escritura hipotecaria; **mort·ga·gee** acreedor hipotecario; **mort·ga·gor** deudor hipotecario.

mor·ti·fy [mɔ́təfaɪ] *v.* mortificar; avergonzar.

mo·sa·ic [mozéɪk] *adj. & s.* mosaico.

Mos·lem [mázləm] *adj. & s.* musulmán.

mosque [mɔsk] *s.* mezquita.

mos·qui·to [məskíto] *s.* mosquito; zancudo; — **net** mosquitero.

moss [mɔs] *s.* musgo; **moss-grown** musgoso, cubierto de musgo; anticuado.

moss·y [mɔ́sɪ] *adj.* musgoso.

most [most] *adv. más.; sumamente, muy; s.* la mayoría, la mayor parte, el mayor número o cantidad; los más; — **people** la mayoría (*o* la mayor parte) de la gente; **at the** — a lo más, a lo sumo; **for the** — **part** por la mayor parte; generalmente, mayormente; **the** — **that I can do** lo más que puedo hacer; **the** — **votes** el mayor número de votos, los más votos.

most·ly [móstlɪ] *adv.* por la mayor parte; mayormente, principalmente.

moth [mɔθ] *s.* polilla; mariposa nocturna; — **ball** bolita de naftalina; **moth-eaten** apolillado.

moth·er [mʌ́ðɚ] *s.* madre; **mother-of-pearl** madreperla, nácar; *adj.* de madre; materno, maternal; nativo, natal; — **country** madre patria; país natal; — **Superior** superiora; — **tongue** lengua materna; *v.* servir de madre a, cuidar de.

moth·er·hood [mʌ́ðɚhʊd] *s.* maternidad.

moth·er·in·law [mʌ́ðɚɪnlɔ] *s.* suegra.

moth·er·ly [mʌ́ðɚlɪ] *adj.* maternal, materno.

mo·tif [motíf] *s.* motivo, tema.

mo·tion [móʃən] *s.* (*movement*) moción; movimiento; (*signal*) ademán; señal, seña; — **sickness** mareo; *v.* hacer una seña o señas; indicar.

mo·tion·less [móʃənlɪs] *adj.* inmóvil, inmoble.

mo·tion pic·ture [móʃənpɪktʃɚ] *s.* cine o cinematógrafo; película; fotografía cinematográfica; **motion-picture** *adj.* cinematográfico.

mo·tive [mótɪv] *s.* motivo; tema; *adj.* motriz.

mot·ley [mátlɪ] *adj.* abigarrado, multicolor, de diversos colores; variado, mezclado; *s.* mezcla, mezcolanza.

mo·tor [mótɚ] *s.* motor; automóvil; *v.* pasear o ir en automóvil.

mo·tor·bike [mótɚbaɪk] *s.* motocicleta pequeña; moto.

mo·tor·boat [mótɚbot] *s.* autobote, lancha de gasolina, bote de motor.

mo·tor·car [mótɚkɑr] *s.* automóvil.

mo·tor·coach [mótɚkotʃ] *s.* autobús, ómnibus, *Méx.* camión, *Carib.* guagua; *Ríopl., Ch.* micro; *C.A.* bus.

mo·tor·cy·cle [mótɚsaɪkl] *s.* motocicleta.

mo·tor·ist [mótərɪst] *s.* motorista, automovilista.

mo·tor·man [mótɚmən] *s.* motorista.

mo·tor scoot·er [mótɚskutɚ] *s.* motoneta.

mot·tled [mátld] *adj.* moteado; jaspeado, manchado.

mot·to [máto] *s.* mote, divisa, lema.

mould = **mold.**

mould·er = **molder.**

mould·ing = **molding.**

mould·y = **moldy.**

mound [maʊnd] *s.* montecillo, montículo, montón de tierra.

mount [maʊnt] *s.* (*elevation*) monte; (*horse*) montura, cabalgadura, caballo; *v.* montar; montar a caballo; subir, ascender; (*assemble*) armar (*una máquina*); (*jewels*) engastar (*joyas*).

moun·tain [maʊntn̩] *s.* montaña; *adj.* montañés; de montaña; — **goat** cabra montés; — **lion** puma; — **range** cordillera, cadena de montañas.

moun·tain climb·er [máʊntənklaɪmɚ] *s.* alpinista.

moun·tain·eer [maʊntn̩ír] *s.* montañés.

moun·tain·ous [máʊntn̩əs] *adj.* montañoso.

mourn [morn] *v.* lamentar; deplorar; **to — for** llorar a; estar de duelo por; **mourn·er** [mornɚ] *s.* dolientes, penitentes.

mourn·ful [mórnfəl] *adj.* fúnebre; lúgubre; lastimero, triste.

mourn·ing [mórnɪŋ] *s.* luto; duelo; lamentación; **to be in** — estar de luto, estar de duelo; *adj.* de luto.

mouse [maʊs] *s.* ratón; — **trap** ratonera.

mous·tache = **mustache.**

mouth [maʊθ] *s.* boca; abertura; desembocadura, embocadura (*de un río*).

mouth·ful [máʊθfəl] *s.* bocado.

mouth·piece [máʊθpis] *s.* boquilla (*de un instrumento de viento*); portavoz.

mov·a·ble [múvəbl] *adj.* movible, móvil; **-s** *s. pl.* muebles, bienes muebles.

move [muv] *v.* (*motion*) mover(se); (*change*) mudar(se), mudar de casa; (*propose*) proponer, hacer la moción de; (*game*) hacer una jugada (*en ajedrez o damas*); (*emotion*) conmover; inducir; — **away** irse; alejarse; apartarse; **to — forward** avanzar; **to — on** seguir adelante, caminar; **to — out** irse, mudarse, mudar de casa; *s.* movimiento; mudanza (*de una casa a otra*); paso, trámite (*para conseguir algo*); jugada, turno (*en juegos*); **moving van** camión de mudanzas; **get a — on there!** ¡ande! ¡dése prisa!; *Méx.* ¡ándele!

move·ment [múvmənt] *s.* (*motion*) movimiento; maniobra; meneo, acción; (*mechanism*) mecanismo, movimiento (*de un reloj*); (*bowel*) evacuación.

mov·ie [múvɪ] *s.* cine, película; **-s** cine.

mow [mo] *v.* segar; cortar (*césped*).

mow·er [móɚ] *s.* segador; segadora, cortadora mecánica; máquina segadora.

mown [mon] *adj. & p.p.* segado.

Mr. [místɚ] Sr., señor; **Mrs.** [mísɪz] Sra, señora.

much [mʌtʃ] *adj., adv. & s.* mucho; — **the same** casi lo mismo; **as — as** tanto como; **how —?** ¿cuánto?; **not — of a book** un libro de poco valor; **not — of a poet** un poetastro; **so — that** tanto que; **too —** demasiado; **very —** muchísimo; **to make — of** dar mucha importancia a.

muck [mʌk] *s.* (*manure*) estiércol húmedo; (*mire*)

cieno; (*filth*) porquería, suciedad.

mu·cous [mjúkəs] *adj.* mucoso; — **membrane** membrana mucosa.

mud [mʌd] *s.* lodo, fango, cieno; barro; — **wall** tapia.

mud·dle [mʌdl] *v.* enturbiar; (*confuse*) confundir; embrollar; *s.* confusión, embrollo, lío, desorden.

mud·dy [mʌdɪ] *adj.* fangoso, lodoso; turbio; confuso; *v.* enlodar, ensuciar; enturbiar.

muff [mʌf] *s.* manguito (*para las manos*); falla, error (*en ciertos juegos*); *v.* no coger, dejar escapar (*la pelota*).

muf·fin [mʌfɪn] *s.* bollo, panecillo.

muf·fle [mʌfl] *v.* embozar; tapar; apagar, amortiguar (*un sonido*).

muf·fler [mʌflɚ] *s.* bufanda; silenciador (*para maquinaria*); mofle.

mug [mʌg] *s.* pichel, vaso con asa.

mu·lat·to [məlæto] *s.* mulato.

mul·ber·ry [mʌlbɛrɪ] *s.* mora; — **tree** moral.

mule [mjul] *s.* mulo, mula.

mule·teer [mjulətír] *s.* arriero.

mull [mʌl] *v.* meditar, ponderar, revolver en la mente; calentar (*vino, sidra, etc.*) con azúcar y especias.

mul·ti·ple [mʌltəpl] *s.* múltiplo; *adj.* múltiple.

mul·ti·pli·ca·tion [mʌltəpləkéʃən] *s.* multiplicación; — **table** tabla de multiplicar.

mul·ti·plic·i·ty [mʌltəplísəti] *s.* multiplicidad.

mul·ti·ply [mʌltəplaɪ] *v.* multiplicar(se).

mul·ti·tude [mʌltətjud] *s.* multitud.

mul·ti·us·er [mʌltɪjúzɚ] *s.* (*computer*) multiusuario.

mum [mʌm] *adj.* callado, silencioso; **to keep —** estarse (*o quedarse*) callado.

mum·ble [mʌmbl] *v.* murmurar, hablar entre dientes; mascullar; *s.* murmullo; **to talk in a —** mascullar las palabras, hablar entre dientes.

mum·my [mʌmɪ] *s.* momia.

mumps [mʌmps] *s.* parótidas, paperas.

munch [mʌntʃ] *v.* mascar ruidosamente, mascullar.

mun·dane [məndén] *adj.* mundano.

mu·nic·i·pal [mjunísəpl] *adj.* municipal; — **council** cabildo, concejo, ayuntamiento.

mu·nic·i·pal·i·ty [mjunɪsəpǽləti] *s.* municipio; municipalidad.

mu·ni·tion [mjuníʃən] *s.* munición; — **plant** fábrica de municiones, arsenal; *v.* guarnecer, abastecer de municiones.

mu·ral [mjúrəl] *adj. & s.* mural.

mur·der [mɝdɚ] *s.* asesinato, homicidio; *v.* asesinar.

mur·der·er [mɝdərɚ] *s.* asesino, homicida.

mur·der·ess [mɝdərɪs] *s.* asesina, homicida.

mur·der·ous [mɝdərəs] *adj.* asesino, homicida.

mur·mer [mɝmɚ] *s.* (*noise*) murmullo; susurro; (*complaint*) queja; *v.* murmurar, susurrar; quejarse.

mus·cle [mʌsl] *s.* músculo.

mus·cu·lar [mʌskjələ] *adj.* muscular; musculoso; nervudo.

muse [mjuz] *v.* meditar; *s.* meditación; **Muse** musa.

mu·se·um [mjuzíəm] *s.* museo.

mush [mʌʃ] *s.* potaje espeso de maíz; masa de maíz; cualquier masa blanda; sentimentalismo.

mush·room [mʌʃrum] *s.* seta, hongo.

mu·sic [mjúzɪk] *s.* música; — **stand** atril.

mu·si·cal [mjúzɪkl] *adj.* musical, músico; melodioso; armonioso; aficionado a la música; — **comedy** zarzuela, comedia musical.

mu·si·cian [mjuzíʃən] *s.* músico.

musk·mel·on [mʌskmɛlən] *s.* melón.

musk·rat [mʌskræt] *s.* almizclera (*roedor semejante a la rata*).

mus·lin [mʌslɪn] *s.* muselina.
muss [mʌs] *v.* desarreglar, desordenar; arrugar.
must [mʌst] *v. defect (por lo general se usa sólo en el presente)* deber; deber de, haber de; tener que.
mus·tache [mʌstæʃ] *s.* bigote, mostacho.
mus·tard [mʌstɚd] *s.* mostaza; — **plaster** sinapismo.
mus·ter [mʌstɚ] *v.* pasar lista o revista; juntarse para una formación militar; reunir(se); **to — out** dar de baja; **to — up one's courage** cobrar valor o ánimo; *s.* revista *(de soldados o marinos)*; **to pass — pasar lista o revista; ser aceptable *(en una inspección).*
must·y [mʌstɪ] *adj.* mohoso; rancio, añejo.
mu·ta·tion [mjutéʃən] *s.* mutación.
mute [mjut] *adj.* mudo; *s.* mudo. letra muda; sordina *(de violín).*
mu·ti·late [mjútlet] *v.* mutilar.
mu·ti·ny [mjútṇɪ] *s.* motín; *v.* amotinarse.
mut·ter [mʌtɚ] *v.* murmurar, refunfuñar; hablar entre dientes; *s.* murmullo, refunfuño.
mut·ton [mʌtṇ] *s.* carne de carnero; — **chop** chuleta de carnero.
mu·tu·al [mjútʃʊel] *adj.* mutuo; **wall** pared medianera; **fund** fondo mutuo.
muz·zle [mʌsl] *s.* hocico; *(harness)* bozal *(para el hocico)*; *(gun)* boca *(de arma de fuego)*; *v.* abozalar, poner bozal a; amordazar; hacer callar.
my [maɪ] *adj.* mi (mis).
myr·i·ad [mɪrɪəd] *s.* miríada, diez mil; millares, gran cantidad.
myrrh [mɝ] *s.* mirra.
myr·tle [mɝtl] *s.* mirto, arrayán.
my·self [maɪsélf] *pron.* yo mismo; me *(como reflexivo)*; a mí mismo; **by — solo; I — did it** yo mismo lo hice; **I talk to —** hablo conmigo mismo, hablo para mis adentros.
mys·te·ri·ous [mɪstɪrɪəs] *adj.* misterioso.
mys·ter·y [mɪstrɪ] *s.* misterio
mys·tic [mɪstɪk] *adj. & s.* místico.
mys·ti·cal [mɪstɪkl] *adj.* místico.
myth [mɪθ] *s.* mito, fábula.
my·thol·o·gy [mɪθáləʤɪ] *s.* mitología.

N:n

nab [næb] *v.* agarrar, coger; arrestar.
nag [næg] *s.* rocín, caballejo, jaco; *v.* importunar, irritar *(con repetidos regaños).*
nail [nel] *s.* clavo; uña *(del dedo)*; — **file** lima *(para las uñas)*; *v.* clavar; clavear; agarrar, atrapar.
na·ive [nɑív] *adj.* simple, ingenuo, cándido.
na·ked [nékɪd] *adj.* desnudo.
na·ked·ness [nékɪdnɪs] *s.* desnudez.
name [nem] *s. (designation)* nombre; *(fame)* renombre, fama; — **sake** tocayo; **by the — of** nombrado, llamado; apellidado; **family —** apellido; **to call someone -s** motejar o decirle groserías a uno; ponerle apodos a uno; **to make a — for oneself** ganar fama; **what is your — ?** ¿cómo se llama Vd.?; *v.* nombrar; mentar, mencionar; llamar; *adj.* onomástico.
name·less [némlɪs] *adj.* sin nombre; anónimo.
name·ly [némlɪ] *adv.* a saber, esto es, es decir.
name·plate [némplet] *s.* rótulo, placa; *Col.* chapa.
nap [næp] *s.* siesta; pelo *(de un tejido)*; **to take a —** echar un sueño, echar una siesta; *v.* dormitar; echar un sueño; sestear.

nape [nep] *s.* nuca, cogote.
naph·tha [næfθə] *s.* nafta.
nap·kin [næpkɪn] *s.* servilleta.
nar·cis·sus [nɑrsísəs] *s.* narciso.
nar·cot·ic [nɑrkátɪk] *adj. & s.* narcótico.
nar·rate [næret] *v.* narrar.
nar·ra·tion [næréʃən] *s.* narración.
nar·ra·tive [nærətɪv] *adj.* narrativo; *s.* narración. narrativa; relato.
nar·row [næro] *adj. (cramped)* estrecho; angosto; limitado *(intolerant)* intolerante; — **escape** trance difícil, escapada difícil; — **gauge** de vía angosta; — **search** búsqueda esmerada; **narrow-minded** fanático, intolerante; **-s** *s. pl.* desfiladero, paso; estrecho o estrechos; *v.* angostar(se), estrechar(se); limitar, restringir, reducir; — **the gap** reducir la diferencia; **-ly** *adv.* estrechamente; **he -ly escaped** por poco no se escapa.
nar·row·ness [nærənɪs] *s. (cramped)* estrechez, estrechura, angostura; limitación; *(intolerance)* intolerancia.
na·sal [nézl] *adj.* nasal.
nas·ti·ness [næstɪnɪs] *s.* suciedad, porquería; *(verbal)* grosería.
na·stur·tium [næstɝʃəm] *s.* mastuerzo.
nas·ty [næstɪ] *adj. (foul)* sucio, asqueroso; feo *(indecent)* grosero; indecente; **a — fall** una caída terrible; **a — disposition** un genio horrible.
na·tal [nétl] *adj.* natal.
na·tion [néʃən] *s.* nación.
na·tion·al [næʃənl] *adj.* nacional; *s.* nacional, ciudadano; *v.* **nationalize** nacionalizar.
na·tion·al·ism [næʃənəlɪzm] *s.* nacionalismo.
na·tion·al·i·ty [næʃənǽlətɪ] *s.* nacionalidad; **adjective of —** gentilicio.
na·tive [nétɪv] *adj.* nativo; natal; natural; *(original)* indígena; del país, *Am.* criollo; — **of** oriundo de, natural de; *s.* nativo, natural, indígena; habitante.
na·tiv·i·ty [nətívətɪ] *s.* nacimiento. natividad *(de la Virgen María)*; **the Nativity** la Navidad.
nat·u·ral [nætʃərəl] *adj.* natural; sencillo, sin afectación; **resources** recursos naturales; riquezas naturales; *s.* becuadro *(signo musical)*; **he is a — for that job** tiene aptitud natural para ese puesto; **-ly** *adv.* naturalmente; con naturalidad.
nat·u·ral·ism [nætʃərəlɪzəm] *s.* naturalismo.
nat·u·ral·ist [nætʃərəlɪst] *s.* naturalista.
nat·u·ral·i·za·tion [nætʃərələzéʃən] *s.* naturalización.
nat·u·ral·ize [nætʃərəlaɪz] *v.* naturalizar.
nat·u·ral·ness [nætʃərəlnts] *s.* naturalidad.
na·ture [nétʃɚ] *s.* naturaleza; natural, genio, índole; instinto; especie; **to copy from —** copiar del natural.
naught [nɔt] *s.* cero; nada.
naugh·ty [nɔtɪ] *adj.* malo, desobediente; travieso, pícaro; malicioso.
nau·se·a [nɔʒɪə] *s.* náusea
nau·se·ate [nɔʒɪet] *v.* dar náuseas, dar bascas, asquear, dar asco; sentir náusea; **to be -ed** tener náuseas.
nau·se·at·ing [nɔʒɪetɪŋ] *adj.* nauseabundo, asqueroso.
nau·ti·cal [nɔtɪkl] *adj.* náutico, naval.
na·val [névl] *adj.* naval; — **officer** oficial de marina.
nave [nev] *'s.* nave *(de una iglesia).*
na·vel [névl] *s.* ombligo; — **orange** naranja california *(sin semillas).*
nav·i·ga·ble [nævəgəbl] *adj.* navegable.
nav·i·gate [nævəget] *v.* navegar.
nav·i·ga·tion [nævəgéʃən] *s.* navegación; náutica.
nav·i·ga·tor [nævəgetɚ] *s.* navegador, navegante.
na·vy [névɪ] *s.* marina de guerra; armada; — **blue**

azul marino; — **yard** astillero, arsenal.

nay [ne] *adv.* no; no sólo . . . sino (*que*) también; *s.* no, voto negativo.

near [nɪr] *adv.* (*space, time*) cerca; (*almost*) casi; — **at hand** cerca, a la mano; **I came — forgetting to do it** por poco se me olvida hacerlo; **to come (go, draw)** — acercarse; — **sighted** miope; *prep.* cerca de; — **the end of the month** hacia fines del mes; *adj.* cercano, próximo; estrecho, íntimo; — **silk** seda imitada; **I had a — accident** por poco me sucede un accidente; *v.* acercarse (a).

near·by [nírbái] *adv.* cerca, a la mano; *adj.* cercano, próximo.

near·ly [nírlɪ] *adv.* casi, cerca de; aproximadamente, próximamente; **I — did it** estuve al punto de hacerlo, estuve por hacerlo.

near·ness [nírnɪs] *s.* cercanía, proximidad.

neat [nit] *adj.* (*clean*) pulcro, aseado, limpio; (*ordered*) ordenado; esmerado; (*clever*) hábil, diestro; **-ly** *adv.* aseadamente; esmeradamente; ordenadamente; hábilmente.

neat·ness [nítnɪs] *s.* pulcritud, aseo; limpieza; esmero; claridad.

neb·u·lous [nɛ́bjʊləs] *adj.* nebuloso.

nec·es·sar·i·ly [nɛsəsɛ́rəlɪ] *adv.* necesariamente; forzosamente.

nec·es·sar·y [nɛ́səsɛrɪ] *adj.* necesario; forzoso; **nec·es·sar·ies** *s. pl.* necesidades, requisitos.

ne·ces·si·tate [nəsɛ́sətet] *v.* necesitar, precisar.

ne·ces·si·ty [nəsɛ́sətɪ] *s.* necesidad.

neck [nɛk] *s.* cuello; (*animal*) pescuezo; cerviz; (*throat*) garganta; — **of land** istmo; **low —** escote; — **and —** parejos (*en una carrera*).

neck·lace [nɛ́klɪs] *s.* collar; gargantilla.

neck·tie [nɛ́ktaɪ] *s.* corbata.

ne·crol·o·gy [nɛkrálədʒɪ] *s.* necrología.

need [nid] *s.* (*lack*) necesidad; (*poverty*) pobreza; **for — of** por falta de; **if — be** si fuere menester, en caso de necesidad; *v.* necesitar; tener necesidad de; hacerle falta a uno; tener que.

need·ful [nídfəl] *adj.* necesario; necesitado.

nee·dle [nídl] *s.* aguja.

nee·dle·point [nídlpɔɪnt] *s.* encaje de mano.

need·less [nídlɪs] *adj.* innecesario, inútil.

nee·dle·work [nídlwɜ·k] *s.* labor, bordado; costura.

need·y [nídɪ] *adj.* necesitado, menesteroso.

ne'er [nɛr] *adv. contr. de* **never**; **ne'er-do-well** *s.* persona incompetente; haragán.

ne·ga·tion [nɪgéʃən] *s.* negación; negativa.

neg·a·tive [nɛ́gətɪv] *adj.* negativo; *s.* negativa; negación, partícula o voz negativa; negativa (*de una fotografía*).

ne·glect [nɪglɛ́kt] *s.* negligencia; descuido; abandono; *v.* descuidar; desatender; abandonar; **to — to** dejar de, olvidar, olvidarse de.

ne·glect·ful [nɪglɛ́ktfəl] *adj.* negligente, descuidado.

neg·li·gence [nɛ́glədʒəns] *s.* negligencia.

neg·li·gent [nɛ́glədʒənt] *adj.* negligente, descuidado.

ne·go·ti·ate [nɪgóʃɪet] *v.* negociar; agenciar; vencer (*un obstáculo o dificultad*), dar cima a; gestionar.

ne·go·ti·a·tion [nɪgoʃɪéʃən] *s.* negociación.

Ne·gro [nígro] *s. & adj.* negro.

Ne·groid [nígrɔɪd] *adj.* negroide.

neigh [ne] *s.* relincho; *v.* relinchar.

neigh·bor [nébɚ] *s.* vecino; prójimo; *adj.* vecino; cercano.

neigh·bor·hood [nébɚhʊd] *s.* vecindad; vecindario; inmediación; **in the — of a hundred dollars** cerca de cien dólares.

neigh·bor·ing [nébərɪŋ] *adj.* vecino; cercano; colindante.

nei·ther [níðɚ] *pron.* ninguno, ni (el) uno ni (el) otro; — **of the two** ninguno de los dos; *adj.* ninguno; — **one of us** ninguno de nosotros; *conj.* ni; — . . . — **nor** ni . . . ni; — **will I** tampoco yo, ni yo tampoco.

ne·ol·o·gism [nɪálədʒɪzm] *s.* neologismo.

ne·on [nían] *s.* neón.

ne·o·phyte [níofaɪt] *s.* neófito.

neph·ew [nɛ́fju] *s.* sobrino.

ne·phri·tis [nəfráɪtɪs] *s.* nefritis.

nep·o·tism [nɛ́pətɪzm] *s* nepotismo.

nerve [nɜ·v] *s.* (*anatomy*) nervio; (*courage*) valor, ánimo; audacia; (*effrontery*) descaro; **-s** nervios; nerviosidad; **to strain every —** esforzarse hasta más no poder, poner el mayor empeño posible.

nerv·ous [nɜ·vəs] *adj.* nervioso.

nerv·ous·ness [nɜ·vəsnɪs] *s.* nerviosidad; agitación.

nest [nɛst] *s.* nido; nidada; — **egg** nidal; ahorros; — **of baskets (boxes, tables)** juego graduado de cestas (cajas, mesitas); **wasp's —** avispero; *v.* anidar.

nes·tle [nɛ́sl] *v.* acurrucarse; abrigar(se); anidar.

net [nɛt] *v.* red; malla; tejido de mallas; *adj.* de mallas, de punto de malla; *v.* redar, enredar, coger con red; cubrir con una red.

net [nɛt] *adj.* neto; — **price** precio neto; — **profit** ganancia neta o líquida; — **worth** *Ch., Perú* patrimonio; *Méx.* capital contable; — **assets** activo neto; *Arg.* patrimonio neto; *Méx.* capital contable; — **income** ingresos netos; *v.* producir una ganancia neta o líquida; obtener una ganancia líquida.

net·tle [nɛ́tl] *s.* ortiga; *v.* picar, irritar, enfadar.

net·work [nɛ́twɜ·k] *s.* red; malla; cadena, sistema; **radio —** red de estaciones radiofónicas; — **program** transmisión en cadena.

neu·ral·gia [nurǽldʒə] *s.* neuralgia.

neu·ras·the·ni·a [nurəsθíniə] *s.* neurastenia.

neu·rot·ic [njʊrátɪk] *adj. & s.* neurótico.

neu·ter [njútɚ] *adj.* neutro.

neu·tral [njútrəl] *adj.* neutral; neutro.

neu·tral·i·ty [njutrǽlətɪ] *s.* neutralidad.

neu·tral·ize [njútrəlaɪz] *v.* neutralizar.

neu·tron [nútran] *s.* neutrón.

nev·er [nɛ́vɚ] *adv.* nunca, jamás; — **mind** no importa; no haga Vd. caso; no se moleste Vd.; **never-ending** perpetuo, eterno; de nunca acabar; **nevermore** nunca jamás.

nev·er·the·less [nɛvɚðəlɛ́s] *adv. & conj.* sin embargo, no obstante, con todo, empero.

new [nju] *adj.* (*not old*) nuevo; moderno; (*fresh*) fresco; reciente; *adv.* recién; — **born baby** criatura recién nacida; — **departure** nuevo derrotero.

new·com·er [njúkʌmɚ] *s.* recién llegado.

new·fan·gled [njufǽŋgld] *adj.* de última moda, recién inventado.

new·ly [njúlɪ] *adv.* nuevamente, recientemente; — **arrived** recién llegado; — **sed** recién casado.

new·ness [njúnɪs] *s.* novedad, calidad de nuevo.

news [njuz] *s.* noticias, nuevas; (*happenings*) novedades; **piece of —** noticia, nueva; — **boy** vendedor de periódicos; — **reel** película noticiera; película de noticias mundiales; — **stand** puesto de periódicos; **broadcast, — bulletin** noticiero, noticiario; — **advertising** publicidad de prensa; — **clipping** recorte.

news·mong·er [njúzmʌŋgɚ] *s.* chismoso, chismero, gacetilla.

news·pa·per [njúzpepɚ] *s.* periódico.

next [nɛkst] *adj.* (*future*) próximo; entrante, que viene; (*following*) siguiente; contiguo; **in the — life** en la otra vida; **to be — in turn** tocarle a uno, ser su turno; *adv.* después, luego; — **best** segundo en cualidad o importancia; *prep.; —* **to** junto a; al lado de; después de.

nib·ble [níbl] *s.* mordisco; *v.* mordiscar, mordisquear; picar, morder.

nice [naɪs] *adj.* (*attractive*) fino; bueno; amable, simpático; lindo; primoroso; (*refined*) refinado; esmerado; preciso, exacto; **-ly** *adv.* con esmero; con finura o primor; sutilmente, con delicadeza; amablemente; bien; **to get along -ly with** llevarse bien con.

ni·ce·ty [náɪsətɪ] *s.* fineza, finura; delicadeza; exactitud.

niche [nɪtʃ] *s.* nicho.

nick [nɪk] *s.* mella, desportilladura; **in the — of time** en el momento crítico; *v.* mellar, desportillar.

nick·el [nɪkl] *s.* níquel; moneda de cinco centavos; **nickel-plated** niquelado.

nick·name [nɪknem] *s.* mote, apodo; *v.* apodar, poner apodo a.

nic·o·tine [nɪkətin] *s.* nicotina.

niece [nis] *s.* sobrina.

nig·gard·ly [nɪgɚdlɪ] *adj.* mezquino, ruin, tacaño; *adv.* mezquinamente, ruinmente.

night [naɪt] *s.* noche; **good —** ! ¡buenas noches!; **tomorrow —** mañana por la noche; *adj.* nocturno; de noche; **— owl** buho; trasnochador; **— watchmen** sereno, vigilante nocturno; **— shift** turno de noche.

night·fall [náɪtfɔl] *s.* anochecer, caída de la tarde, anochecida.

night·gown [náɪtgaun] *s.* camisa de dormir, camisa de noche, *Am.* camisón.

night·in·gale [náɪtɪngel] *s.* ruiseñor.

night·ly [náɪtlɪ] *adv.* cada noche, todas las noches; *adj.* nocturno, de noche.

night·mare [náɪtmɛr] *s.* pesadilla

ni·hil·ism [náɪɪlɪzm] *s.* nihilismo.

nim·ble [nɪmbl] *adj.* ágil, ligero; listo.

nine [naɪn] *núm.* nueve.

nine·teen [naɪntín] *num.* diecinueve.

nine·ty [náɪntɪ] *num.* noventa.

ni·o·bi·um [naɪóbiəm] *s.* niobio.

nip [nɪp] *v.* (*pinch*) pellizcar; (*bite*) mordiscar; (*frostbite*) marchitar, helar (*por la acción del frio*); **to — in the bud** cortar en germen, destruir al nacer; **to — off** despuntar; podar; *s.* pellizco; mordisco; trago.

nip·ple [nɪpl] *s.* teta, tetilla, pezón; pezón de goma.

ni·trate [náɪtret] *s.* nitrato.

ni·tric a·cid [náɪtrɪkǽsɪd] *s.* ácido nítrico.

ni·tro·gen [naftrədʒən] *s.* nitrógeno.

ni·tro·glyc·er·in [naɪtroglísɚɪn] *s.* nitroglicerina.

no [no] *adv.* no; **— longer** ya no; **there is — more** no hay más; *adj.* ningun(o); **— matter how much** por mucho que; **— one** ninguno, nadie; **— smoking** se prohibe fumar; **I have — friend** no tengo ningún amigo; **of — use** inútil, sin provecho; *s.* no, voto negativo.

no·bil·i·ty [nobílətɪ] *s.* nobleza.

no·ble [nóbl] *s. & adj.* noble.

no·ble·man [nóblmən] *s.* noble.

no·ble·ness [nóblnɪs] *s.* nobleza.

no·bly [nóblɪ] *adv.* noblemente.

no·bod·y [nóbadɪ] *pron.* nadie, ninguno.

noc·tur·nal [nakta·nl] *adj.* nocturno.

nod [nad] *v.* (*signal*) inclinar la cabeza (*para hacer una seña, saludar, o asentir*); (*doze*) cabecear, dar cabezadas (*dormitando*); *s.* inclinación de cabeza, saludo; señal de asentimiento (*con la cabeza*).

noise [nɔɪz] *s.* (*sound*) ruido; (*disorder*) barullo;

sonido; *v.* divulgar; **it is being -d about that** corre el rumor que.

noise·less [nɔ́ɪzlɪs] *adj.* sin ruido, silencioso, quieto; **-ly** *adv.* sin ruido, silenciosamente.

nois·i·ly [nɔ́ɪzɪlɪ] *adv.* ruidosamente.

nois·y [nɔ́ɪzɪ] *adj.* ruidoso.

no·men·cla·ture [nómənkleʃɚ] *s.* nomenclatura.

nom·i·nal [námənl] *adj.* nominal.

nom·i·nate [náməhet] *v.* nombrar, designar.

nom·i·na·tion [namənéʃən] *s.* nombramiento, nominación.

non·con·form·ist [nankənfɔ́rmɪst] *adj. & s.* disidente.

none [nʌn] *pron.* ninguno; ningunos; nada; **I want — of that** no quiero nada de eso; **that is — of his business** no le importa a él eso; *adv.* no, de ningún modo; **— the less** no menos; **to be — the happier for that** no estar por eso más contento.

non·en·ti·ty [nanéntətɪ] *s.* nulidad, persona o cosa inútil.

in·ter·ven·tion [nanɪntɚvénʃən] *s.* no intervención.

non·par·ti·san [nanpártəzən] *adj.* imparcial; independiente.

non·sense [nánsɛns] *s.* tontería, necedad; disparate, desatino; **to talk —** pavear.

non·stop [nanstáp] *adj. & adv.* sin escala, directo.

noo·dle [núdl] *s.* tallarín, fideo, pasta (*para sopa*).

nook [nʊk] *ś.* rincón; **breakfast —** desayunador.

noon [nun] *s.* mediodía.

noon·day [núnde] *s.* mediodía; *adj.* meridiano, de mediodía; **— meal** comida de mediodía.

noon·tide [núntaɪd] *s.* mediodía.

noon·time [núntaɪm] *s.* mediodía.

noose [nus] *s.* dogal; lazo, nudo corredizo, *Carib.* gaza; *v.* lazar, coger con lazo; hacer un lazo corredizo en.

nor [nɔr] *conj.* ni; **neither . . . —** ni . . . ni.

Nor·dic [nɔ́rdɪk] *adj.* nórdico.

norm [nɔrm] *s.* norma.

nor·mal [nɔ́ml] *adj.* normal; *s.* norma; normal, línea perpendicular.

north [nɔrθ] *s.* norte; *adj.* septentrional; norteño; del norte; **— pole** polo norte, polo ártico; **— wind** cierzo, norte; **North American** norteamericano; *adv.* al norte, hacia el norte.

north·east [nɔrθíst] *adj. & s.* nordeste; *adv.* hacia el nordeste, rumbo al nordeste.

north·east·ern [nɔrθístɚn] *adj.* del nordeste, nordeste.

north·ern [nɔrðɚn] *adj.* septentrional; norteño; del norte; hacia el norte; **— lights** aurora boreal.

north·ern·er [nɔ́ðɚnɚ] *s.* norteño, habitante del norte.

north·ward [nɔ́rθwɚd] *adv.* hacia el norte, rumbo al norte.

north·west [nɔrθwɛ́st] *adj. & s.* noroeste; *adv.* hacia el noroeste.

north·west·ern [nɔrθwɛ́stɚn] *adj.* noroeste, del noroeste.

Nor·we·gian [nɔrwídʒən] *adj. & s.* noruego.

nose [noz] *s.* nariz; proa (*de un barco*); **— dive** picada (*de un avión*); *v.* olfatear; **to — around** husmear, curiosear.

nos·tal·gi·a [nɑstǽldʒɪə] *s.* nostalgia, añoranza.

nos·trils [nástrəlz] *s. pl.* narices, ventanas de la nariz.

not [nat] *adv.* no; **— at all** de ningún modo; de nada (*contestación a* "thank you"); **— at all sure** nada seguro; **— even a word** ni siquiera una palabra.

no·ta·ble [notəbl] *adj.* notable.

no·ta·ry [nótərɪ] *s.* notario; notario público; **— public notarize** autorizar ante notario.

no·ta·tion [notéʃən] *s.* notación; apunte; anotación.

notch [natʃ] *s.* muesca, ranura; hendidura; *v.* ranurar, hacer una ranura en.

note [not] *s.* nota; apunte, apuntación; **bank —** billete de banco; **promissory —** pagaré, abonaré; *r.* notar, observar, reparar; **to — down** apuntar.

note·book [nótbʊk] *s.* libreta, cuaderno, libro de apuntes.

not·ed [nótɪd] *adj.* notable, célebre, famoso.

note·worth·y [nótwɝðɪ] *adj.* notable, célebre.

noth·ing [nʌθɪŋ] *s.* nada; cero; **for —** por nada; inútilmente; de balde, gratis.

no·tice [nótɪs] *s.* (*news*) noticia; (*warning*) aviso; advertencia, anuncio; mención, **to give a short —** avisar a última hora; **to take — of** hacer caso de, prestar atención a; *v.* notar, observar; prestar atención a; hacer caso a (*o* de); notificar.

no·tice·a·ble [nótɪsəbl] *adj.* notable; conspicuo; perceptible.

no·ti·fy [nótəfaɪ] *v.* notificar, avisar.

no·tion [nóʃən] *s.* noción; idea; capricho; **-s** mercería, artículos menudos (*como alfileres, botones, etc.*), chucherías.

no·to·ri·ous [notóriəs] *adj.* notorio.

not·with·stand·ing [natwɪθstǽndɪŋ] *prep.* a pesar de; *adv. & conj.* no obstante, sin embargo; **— that** a pesar (de) que.

nought = naught.

noun [naʊn] *s.* nombre, sustantivo.

nour·ish [nɝɪʃ] *v.* nutrir, alimentar.

nour·ish·ing [nɝɪʃɪŋ] *adj.* nutritivo, alimenticio.

nour·ish·ment [nɝɪʃmənt] *s.* nutrimento, sustento, alimento; nutrición.

nov·el [návl] *s.* novela; *adj.* novel, nuevo; (*unique*) raro, original.

nov·el·ist [návlɪst] *s.* novelista.

nov·el·ty [návltɪ] *s.* novedad; innovación **nov·el·ties** novedades.

No·vem·ber [novémbɝ] *s.* noviembre.

nov·ice [návɪs] *s.* novicio; novato, principiante.

now [naʊ] *adv.* ahora; ya; **— . . . — ya . . . ya,** ora . . . ora; **— and then** de vez en cuando, de cuando en cuando; **— that** ahora que; **— then** ahora bien; **he left just —** salió hace poco, *Ríopl., Ch., Andes* recién salió.

now·a·days [náʊədez] *adv.* hoy día.

no·where [nóhwɛr] *adv.* en ninguna parte, a ninguna parte.

nox·ious [nákʃəs] *adj.* nocivo.

nu·cle·us [njúklɪəs] *s.* núcleo.

nude [njud] *adj. & s.* desnudo.

nudge [nʌdʒ] *v.* codear, tocar con el codo; *s.* codzao ligero.

nug·get [nʌgɪt] *s.* pepita; pedazo.

nui·sance [njúsn̩s] *s.* molestia; lata, fastidio; **— tax** impuesto menor sobre consumo; persona o cosa fastidiosa.

null [nʌl] *adj.* nulo; **— and void** nulo e inválido.

nul·li·fy [nʌlɪfaɪ] *v.* invalidar; anular.

numb [nʌm] *adj.* entumecido o entumido, aterido; **to become —** entumecerse, entumirse, aterirse; *v.* entumecer.

num·ber [nʌmbɝ] *s.* número; *v.* numerar; ascender a (*cierto número*); **to — him among one's friends** contarle entre sus amigos.

num·ber·less [nʌmbɝlɪs] *adj.* innumerable, sin número.

nu·mer·al [njúmrəl] *s.* número, cifra; guarismo; *adj.* numeral.

nu·mer·i·cal [njumérɪkəl] *adj.* numérico.

nu·mer·ous [njúmrəs] *adj.* numeroso; numerosos, muchos.

nu·mis·mat·ics [numɪsmǽtɪks] *s.* numismática.

nun [nʌn] *s.* monja.

nup·tial [nʌpʃəl] *adj.* nupcial; **-s** *s. pl.* nupcias, bodas.

nurse [nɝs] *s.* (*for the sick*) enfermera, enfermero; (*for children*) niñera, aya; *Méx., Ven., Col., Andes* nana, *Cuba* manejadora, *Andes* pilmama; *C.A.* china; **wet —** nodriza, ama de cria; *v.* criar, amamantar, dar de mamar, lactar; mamar; cuidar (*a un enfermo*); abrigar (*rencor*).

nurs·er·y [nɝsrɪ] *s.* cuarto para niños; (*zoological*) criadero, (*plants*) semillero (*de plantas*); **day —** sala donde se cuida y divierte a los niños.

nur·ture [nɝtʃɝ] *s.* crianza; nutrimento; *v.* criar; nutrir; cuidar; fomentar.

nut [nʌt] *s.* nuez (*nombre genérico de varias frutas como la almendra, la castaña, la avellana, etc.*); tuerca; (*person*) loco, tipo raro o extravagante.

nut·crack·er [nʌtkrækɝ] *s.* cascanueces.

nut·meg [nʌtmɛg] *s.* nuez moscada.

nu·tri·ent [nútrɪənt] *s.* nutritivo.

nu·tri·tion [njutrɪʃən] *s.* nutrición; nutrimento, alimento.

nu·tri·tious [njutrɪʃəs] *adj.* nutritivo, alimenticio.

nu·tri·tive [njútrɪtɪv] *adj.* nutritivo.

nut·shell [nʌtʃel] *s.* cáscara de nuez (*o de otro fruto semejante*); **in a —** en suma, en breve, en pocas palabras.

nymph [nɪmf] *s.* ninfa.

O:o

oak [ok] *s.* roble; encina; **— grove** robledo o robledal; **live —** encina siempreverde.

oar [or] *s.* remo; *v.* remar, bogar.

o·a·sis [oésɪs] *s.* oasis.

oat [ot] *s.* avena (*planta*); **-s** avena, granos de avena.

oath [oθ] *s.* (*pledge*) juramento; maldición, blasfemia, (*curse*) reniego; **to take an oath** prestar juramento.

oat·meal [otmɪl] *s.* harina de avena; gachas de avena.

o·be·di·ence [əbídɪəns] *s.* obediencia.

o·be·di·ent [əbídɪent] *adj.* obediente.

ob·e·lisk [ablɪsk] *s.* obelisco.

o·be·si·ty [obisətɪ] *s.* obesidad, gordura.

o·bey [əbé] *v.* obedecer.

ob·ject [ábdʒɪkt] *s.* objeto; cosa; complemento (*del verbo*); [əbdʒékt] *v.* objetar; oponerse; tener inconveniente.

ob·jec·tion [əbdʒékʃən] *s.* objeción, reparo; inconveniente.

ob·jec·tive [əbdʒéktɪv] *adj.* objetivo; **— case** caso complementario; *s.* objetivo; fin, propósito.

ob·li·gate [ábləget] *v.* obligar, constreñir; comprometer.

ob·li·ga·tion [abləgéʃən] *s.* (*duty*) obligación; deber (*debt*) deuda; **to be under — to** estar obligado a; estar agradecido a, deber favores a.

o·blig·a·to·ry [əblígətorɪ] *adj.* obligatorio.

o·blige [əbláɪdʒ] *v.* obligar; complacer; **much -ed!** ¡muchas gracias! ¡muy agradecido!; **to be very much -ed to someone** quedar muy agradecido con alguien.

o·blig·ing [əbláɪdʒɪŋ] *adj.* complaciente, obsequioso, comedido, cortés.

o·blique [əblík] *adj.* oblicuo.

o·blit·er·ate [əblítəret] *v.* borrar; arrasar, destruir.

o·bliv·i·on [əblívɪən] s. olvido.
o·bliv·i·ous [əblívɪəs] adj. olvidado, abstraído.
ob·long [áblɔŋ] adj. cuadrilongo; oblongo.
ob·nox·ious [əbnákʃəs] adj. ofensivo; molesto; odioso.
o·boe [óbo] s. oboe.
ob·scene [əbsín] adj. obsceno; grosero.
ob·scen·i·ty [əbsɛ́nətɪ] s. obscenidad, indecencia; grosería.
ob·scure [əbskjúr] adj. obscuro, v. obscurecer; ofuscar.
ob·scu·ri·ty [əbskjúrətɪ] s. obscuridad.
ob·se·quies [ábsɪkwiz] s. exequias, honras, funerales.
ob·se·qui·ous [əbsikwɪəs] adj. obsequioso; servil, zalamero.
ob·serv·a·ble [əbzɝvəbl] adj. observable.
ob·ser·vance [əbzɝvəns] s. observancia; ceremonia, rito.
ob·ser·vant [əbzɝvənt] adj. observador; observante.
ob·ser·va·tion [abzɝvéʃən] s. observación.
ob·ser·va·to·ry [əbzɝvətorɪ] s. observatorio; mirador.
ob·serve [əbzɝv] v. observar; guardar (las fiestas religiosas); celebrar (una fiesta).
ob·serv·er [əbzɝvɚ] s. observador.
ob·sess [əbsɛ́s] v. obsesionar, causar obsesión.
ob·ses·sion [əbsɛ́ʃən] s. obsesión; idea fija.
ob·so·lete [ábsəlɪt] adj. anticuado; desusado; **obsolescence** desuso.
ob·sta·cle [ábstəkl] s. obstáculo.
ob·stet·rics [abstɛ́trɪks] s. obstetricia.
ob·sti·na·cy [ábstənəsɪ] s. obstinación, terquedad, porfía.
ob·sti·nate [ábstənɪt] adj. obstinado, terco, porfiado.
ob·strep·er·ous [abstrɛ́pɚəs] adj. estrepitoso, turbulento.
ob·struct [əbstrʌ́kt] v. obstruir.
ob·struc·tion [əbstrʌ́kʃən] s. obstrucción; impedimento, estorbo.
ob·tain [əbtén] v. obtener, conseguir, alcanzar, adquirir.
ob·tain·a·ble [əbténəbl] adj. obtenible, asequible.
ob·tru·sive [əbtrúsɪv] adj. intruso, entremetido.
ob·vi·ate [ábvɪet] v. obviar; allanar (una dificultad).
ob·vi·ous [ábvɪəs] adj. obvio, evidente.
oc·ca·sion [əkéʒən] s. (timely) ocasión; (chance) oportunidad; (cause) motivo, causa; (event) acontecimiento; v. ocasionar, causar.
oc·ca·sion·al [əkéʒənl] adj. ocasional; infrecuente, poco fecuente; **-ly** adv. de vez en cuando, a veces.
oc·ci·den·tal [aksədɛ́ntl] adj. & s. occidental.
oc·clu·sive [oklúsɪv] adj. & s. oclusivo.
oc·cult [əkʌ́lt] adj. oculto, misterioso.
oc·cu·pant [ákjəpənt] s. ocupante; inquilino.
oc·cu·pa·tion [akjəpéʃən] s. ocupación; trabajo, empleo, oficio; (tenancy) tenencia; **occupational hazard** riesgo profesional.
oc·cu·py [ákjəpaɪ] v. ocupar.
oc·cur [əkɝ] v. occurrir, suceder; **to — to one** ocurrírsele a uno, venirle a la mente.
oc·cur·rence [əkɝəns] s. ocurrencia, suceso, caso, acontecimiento.
o·cean [óʃən] s. océano.
o·cean·og·ra·phy [oʃənágrəfɪ] s. oceanografía.
o·cher [okɚ] s. ocre.
o'clock [əklák] contr. de of the clock; **it is two —** son las dos.
oc·tave [áktɪv] s. octava.
Oc·to·ber [aktóbɚ] s. octubre.
oc·to·pus [áktəpəs] s. pulpo.
oc·u·list [ákəlɪst] s. oculista.
odd [ad] adj. (rare) extraño, singular, raro; (not

even) non, impar; — **change** suelto, cambio sobrante; — **job** trabajo occasional; — **moments** momentos libres, momentos de ocio; — **shoe** zapato suelto (sin compañero) — **volume** tomo suelto; **thirty —** treinta y tantos, treinta y pico; **-ly** adv. extrañamente, de un modo raro.
odd·i·ty [ádətɪ] s. rareza.
odds [adz] s. pl. o sing. diferencia, disparidad (en apuestas); (advantage) ventaja, puntos de ventaja (en apuestas); **and ends** retazos, trozos sobrantes, pedacitos varios; **the — are against me** la suerte me es contraria, estoy de mala suerte; **to be at -s with** estar reñido o enemistado con; (not evens) nones.
ode [od] s. oda.
o·di·ous [ódɪəs] adj. odioso.
o·dor [ódɚ] s. olor; **bad —** mal olor, hedor.
o·dor·ous [ódərəs] adj. oloroso.
o'er [or] contr. de **over.**
of [ɑv, ʌv] prep. de; **course** por supuesto, claro, ya se ve; — **late** últimamente; **a quarter — five** las cinco menos cuarto; **to smell —** oler a; **to taste — sabera.**
off [ɔf] adv. (distant) lejos, fuera, a distancia; (not attached) suelto; apagado (la luz); (equivale al reflexivo se en ciertos verbos: marcharse, irse, etc.); **and on** de vez en cuando; a intervalos; — **the record** extraoficial; — **year** de producción decreciente; **ten cents —** rebaja de diez centavos; **ten miles —** a una distancia de diez millas; **to take a day —** ausentarse por un día; descansar por un día; adj. ausente; distante, más remoto; quitado; **the — side** el lado más remoto; **with his hat —** con el sombrero quitado; **the electricity is —** está cortada la electricidad; **to be — in one's accounts** estar errado en sus cuentas; **to be — to war** haberse ido a la guerra; **to be well —** ser persona acomodada, estar en buenas circunstancias; prep. lejos de; **offcolor** de mal color; verde (indecente); **off-grade** de calidad inferior a la indicada; — **shore** a vista de la costa; — **standard** de calidad inferior; — **the road** deviado, descarriado; a un lado del camino; **to be — duty** no estar de turno; estar libre.
of·fend [əfɛ́nd] v. ofender.
of·fend·er [əfɛ́ndɚ] s. ofensor; transgresor, delincuente.
of·fense [əfɛ́ns] s. ofensa; agravio; delito, culpa; **no — was meant** lo hice (o lo dije) sin malicia; **weapon of —** arma ofensiva.
of·fen·sive [əfɛ́nsɪv] adj. ofensivo; s. ofensiva.
of·fer [ɔ́fɚ] v. ofrecer; **to — to do it** ofrecerse a hacerlo; s. oferta; ofrecimiento; promesa, propuesta.
of·fer·ing [ɔ́fərɪŋ] s. (gift) ofrenda; (bid) oferta, ofrecimiento.
off·hand [ɔ́fhænd] adv. de improviso, por el momento, sin pensarlo, impensadamente; adj. impensado, hecho de improviso; **in an — manner** con indiferencia; descuidadamente; sin plan.
of·fice [ɔ́fɪs] s. (function) oficio; cargo; función; (place) oficina, despacho; — **boy** mandadero de oficina; — **holder** funcionario; —**building** edificio para oficinas; **post —** correo; **box —** taquilla, Ch., Ríopl. boletería; **through the good -s of** por el intermedio de.
of·fi·cer [ɔ́fəsɚ] s. (office holder) oficial; funcionario; (police) policia, gendarme; agente de policía; v. comandar, dirigir (como oficial); proveer de oficiales.
of·fi·cial [əfíʃəl] adj. oficial; s. oficial, funcionario;

empleado público.

of·fi·ci·ate [əffʃɪet] *v.* oficiar.

of·fi·cious [əffʃəs] *adj.* oficioso, intruso, entremetido.

off·set [ɔfsɛt] *v.* compensar por; — **the losses** compensar las pérdidas; contrapesar.

off·shore [ɔfʃor] *adj. & adv.* (*land*) terral; (*at sea*) lejos de la playa.

off·spring [ɔfsprɪŋ] *s.* prole, hijos, descendientes; hijo, vástago; resultado, consecuencia.

off·stage [ɔfstédʒ] *adv. & adj.* entre bastidores.

oft [ɔft] = **often.**

of·ten [ɔfən] *adv.* muchas veces, con frecuencia, frecuentemente, a menudo; **how** — **?** ¿cuántas veces?; ¿cada cuándo?

o·gre [ógɚ] *s.* ogro, gigante, monstruo.

oil [ɔɪl] *s.* (*lubricant*) aceite; (*painting*) óleo; (*crude*) petróleo; — **can** alcuza; —**drum** tambor, bidón; — **field** yacimiento petrolero; — **painting** pintura al óleo; — **well** pozo de petróleo; **motor** — aceite para motores; *v.* aceitar, angrasar, lubricar; untar.

oil·cloth [ɔɪlklɔθ] *s.* hule, tela de hule.

oil·y [ɔɪlɪ] *adj.* aceitoso, oleoso; grasiento.

oint·ment [ɔɪntmənt] *s.* ungüento.

O.K. [óké] *adj.* bueno; corriente, convenido; *Méx.* ándale; *adv.* bien; **it's** — está bien; **to give one's** — dar el Vº. Bº. (visto bueno); *v.* dar el Vº. Bº., aprobar.

old [old] *adj.* viejo; antiguo; añejo; — **maid** solterona; — **man** anciano, viejo; — **wine** vino añejo; **days of** — días de antaño; **how** — **are you?** ¿cuántos años tiene Vd.? ¿qué edad tiene Vd.?; **to be** — **enough to . . .** tener bastante edad para . . .; **to be an** — **hand at** ser ducho en, ser muy perito o experto en.

old·en [óldn] *adj.* viejo, antiguo, de antaño.

old-fash·ioned [óldfǽʃənd] *adj.* pasado de moda; anticuado; chapado a la antigua.

old·time [óldtáɪm] *adj.* vetusto, de tiempos antiguos; de antaño.

old-tim·er [óldtáɪmɚ] *s.* antiguo residente.

o·le·an·der [óliǽndɚ] *s.* adelfa.

ol·fac·to·ry [ɔlfǽktərɪ] *adj.* olfatorio.

ol·ive [álɪv] *s.* oliva, aceituna; — **grove** olivar; — **oil** aceite de oliva; — **tree** olivo; — **branch** ramo de olivo; *adj.* aceitunado, verde aceituna.

O·lym·pi·ad [olímpiæd] *s.* olimpiada.

O·lym·pic [olímpɪk] *adj.* olímpico.

om·e·let [ámlɪt] *s.* tortilla de huevos.

o·men [ómən] *s.* agüero, presagio.

om·i·nous [ámənəs] *adj.* siniestro, de mal agüero, amenazador.

o·mis·sion [omíʃən] *s.* omisión.

o·mit [omít] *v.* omitar; dejar de.

om·nip·o·tent [amnípətənt] *adj.* omnipotente, todopoderoso.

on [ɑn] *prep.* en; a; sobre, encima de; — **all sides** por todos lados; — **arriving** al llegar; — **board** a bordo; en el tren; — **condition that** con la condición de que; — **credit** al fiado; — **foot** a pie; — **horseback** a caballo; — **Monday** el lunes; — **purpose** a propósito, adrede; — **sale** de venta; — **time** a tiempo; a plazo; *adv.* adelante; **farther** — más adelante; **later** — después; — **and** — sin parar, sin cesar, continuamente; *adj.* puesto; **his hat is** — lleva puesto el sombrero; **the light is** — está encendida la luz.

once [wʌns] *adv.* una vez; en otro tiempo; — **and for all** una vez por todas, definitivamente; — **in a while** de vez en cuando; **once-over** ojeada, vistazo; — **upon a time** érase que se era; en otro tiempo; **at** — al punto; a un mismo tiempo; **just this** —

siquiera esta vez, sólo esta vez; *conj.* una vez que, cuando; luego que.

one [wʌn] *adj.* un, uno; — **hundred** cien, ciento; — **thousand** mil; **his** — **chance** su única oportunidad; **the** — **and only** el único; **one-armed** manco; **one-eyed** tuerto; **one-sided** de un solo lado; unilateral; parcial; desigual; **one-way** de un sentido; *s. & pron.* uno; — **another** uno a otro; — **by** — uno a uno; uno por uno; **the** — **who** el que, la que; **the green** — el verde; **this** — éste, ésta; **one-upmanship** necesidad de mantenerse adelante de la competencia.

one·self [wʌnsélf] *pron.* se (*reflexivo*); **to speak to** — hablar consigo mismo; **by** — solo; por si, por si solo.

on·go·ing [ángoɪŋ] *adj.* que está haciéndose; corriente; que cursa.

on·ion [ʌjən] *s.* cebolla; — **patch** cebollar.

on·look·er [ánlʊkɚ] *s.* espectador, mirón.

on·ly [ónlɪ] *adj.* solo, único; *adv.* sólo, solamente; *conj.* sólo que.

on·set [ánsɛt] *s.* embestida, (*attack*) ataque; (*beginning*) impulso inicial, primer impetu.

on·to [ántu] *prep.* a; sobre.

on·ward [ánwɚd] *adv.* adelante; hacia adelante.

on·yx [ánɪks] *s.* onix, ónice.

ooze [uz] *v.* rezumar(se), escurrir(se).

o·pal [ópl] *s.* ópalo;

o·paque [opék] *adj.* opaco; mate.

OPEC (Organization of Petroleum Exporting Countries) OPEP (Organización de países exportadores de petróleo).

o·pen [ópən] *v.* abrir(se); **to** — **into** comunicarse con, tener paso a; **to** — **onto** dar a, caer a, mirar a; *adj.* abierto; (*frank*) franco, sincero; (*exposed*) expuesto (a); — **country** campo raso, campo abierto; — **and shut** claro, evidente, sin dificultades; — **door policy** política de acceso libre; — **question** cuestión discutible; — **to temptation** expuesto a caer en la tentación; — **winter** invierno sin nieve; **in the** — **air** al (o en el) aire libre; **open-minded** receptivo; de amplias miras; — **mouthed** boquiabierto, con la boca abierta; **open-end** [ópənɛnd] sin límites; sin trabas; *s.* campo raso, aire libre.

o·pen·ing [ópənɪŋ] *s.* (*hole*) abertura; (*beginning*) apertura, comienzo; (*clearing*) claro (*en un bosque*); (*vacancy*) puesto vacante; oportunidad; *adj.* primero; — **night of a play** estreno de una comedia; **the** — **number** el primer número (*de un programa*).

op·er·a [ápərə] *s.* ópera; — **glasses** gemelos; — **house** ópera, teatro de la ópera; **comic** — ópera cómica, zarzuela.

op·er·ant [ápɚənt] *adj.* operante.

op·er·ate [ápəret] *v.* (*function*) operar; funcionar; obrar; (*manage*) maniobrar; manejar; **to** — **on a person** operar a una persona; **operating capital** capital de explotación; **operating system** (*computer*) sistema operativo.

op·er·a·tion [apəréʃən] *s.* (*function*) operación; funcionamiento; (*management*) manipulación; manejo; maniobra; **to be in** — funcionar, estar funcionando.

op·er·a·tive [ápɚetɪv] *s.* operario.

op·er·a·tor [ápɚetɚ] *s.* operador; (*surgeon*) cirujano; maquinista, mecánico, operario; (*stock*) especulador (*en la Bolsa*); **mine** — explotador de minas; **telegraph** — telegrafista; **telephone** — telefonista.

op·e·ret·a [apərɛ́tə] *s.* opereta, zarzuela.

OB

o·pin·ion [əpínjən] *s.* opinión, parecer.

o·pi·um [ópiəm] *s.* opio.

o·pos·sum [əpásəm] *s.* zarigüeya.

op·po·nent [əpónənt] *s.* contrario, adversario, antagonista.

op·por·tune [ɑpɚtjún] *adj.* oportuno; a propósito.

op·por·tun·ist [ɑpɚtúnɪst] *s.* oportunista.

op·por·tu·ni·ty [ɑpɚtjúnɑtɪ] *s.* oportunidad; ocasión.

op·pose [əpóz] *v.* oponer(se); oponerse a.

op·pos·ing [əpóziŋ] *adj.* opuesto, contrario.

op·po·site [ápəzɪt] *adj.* (*contrary*) opuesto; contrario; (*facing*) frontero, de enfrente; **— to** frente a; *prep.* frente a, en frente de; *s.* contrario; **the —** lo opuesto, lo contrario.

op·po·si·tion [ɑpəzíʃən] *s.* oposición; resistencia.

op·press [əprɛs] *v.* oprimir; agobiar.

op·pres·sion [əprέʃən] *s.* opresión.

op·pres·sive [əprέsɪv] *adj.* (*harsh*) opresivo; (*distressing*) abrumador; gravoso; bochornoso, sofacante.

op·pres·or [əprέsɚ] *s.* opresor.

op·tic [áptɪk] *adj.* óptico; **-s** *s.* óptica.

op·ti·cal [áptɪkl] *adj.* óptico.

op·ti·cian [aptíʃən] *s.* óptico.

op·ti·mism [áptəmizəm] *s.* optimismo.

op·ti·mist [áptəmɪst] *s.* optimista.

op·ti·mis·tic [aptəmístɪk] *adj.* optimista.

op·tion [ápʃən] *s.* opción, derecho de escoger; alternativa.

op·tion·al [ápʃənl] *adj.* discrecional.

op·u·lence [ápjələns] *s.* opulencia, riqueza, abundancia.

op·u·lent [ápjələnt] *adj.* opulento, rico; abundante;

or [ɔr] *conj.* o; u (*delante de* o, ho).

or·a·cle [ɔ́rəkl] *s.* oráculo.

o·ral [órəl] *adj.* oral; bucal.

or·ange [ɔ́rɪndʒ] *s.* naranja; **— blossom** azahar; **— grove** naranjal; **— tree** naranjo; *adj.* de naranja; anaranjado.

or·ange·ade [ɔrindʒéd] *s.* naranjada.

o·ra·tion [oréʃən] *s.* discurso, peroración, arenga.

or·a·tor [ɔ́rətɚ] *s.* orador.

or·a·to·ry [ɔ́ətorɪ] *s.* oratoria, elocuencia; oratorio, capilla.

orb [ɔrb] *s.* orbe.

or·bit [ɔ́rbɪt] *s.* órbita; *v.* moverse en órbita.

or·bit·al [ɔ́rbɪtl] *adj.* orbital.

or·chard [ɔ́rtʃɚd] *s.* huerto.

or·ches·tra [ɔ́rkɪstrə] *s.* orquesta; **— seat** butaca, luneta, *Am.* platea (*de orquesta*).

or·ches·trate [ɔ́rkɪstret] *v.* orquestar.

or·chid [ɔ́rkɪd] *s.* orquídea.

or·dain [ɔrdén] *v.* ordenar; decretar.

or·deal [ɔrdíl] *s.* prueba penosa.

or·der [ɔ́rdɚ] *s.* (*request*) orden (*s.*); pedido; (*group*) clase; orden; (*arrangement*) orden (*m.*); **holy -s** órdenes sagradas; **in —** en orden; en buen estado; en regla; **in — to** para, a fin de; **in — that** para que, a fin de que; **made to —** mandado hacer, hecho a la medida; **to the — of** a la orden de; **to be out of —** estar descompuesto; estar desordenado; no estar en regla; **— clerk** oficinista encargado de pedidos; *v.* ordenar; mandar; arreglar; pedir (*hacer un pedido*); **to — away** echar, despedir, expulsar.

or·der·ly [ɔ́rdɚlɪ] *adj.* ordenado; en orden, bien arreglado; bien disciplinado; *s.* ordenanza (*soldado*); asistente de hospital.

or·di·nal [ɔ́rdɪnl] *adj.* ordinal; **— number** número ordinal.

or·di·nance [ɔ́rdnəns] *s.* ordenanza, ley, reglamento.

or·di·nar·i·ly [ɔrdɲέrəlɪ] *adv.* ordinariamente, por lo común.

or·di·nar·y [ɔ́rdɲɛrɪ] *adj.* ordinario.

ore [or] *s.* mineral.

or·gan [ɔ́rgən] *s.* órgano; **hand —** organillo.

or·gan·ic [ɔrgǽnɪk] *adj.* orgánico; constitutivo, fundamental.

or·gan·ism [ɔ́rgənizəm] *s.* organismo.

or·gan·ist [ɔ́gənɪst] *s.* organista.

or·gan·i·za·tion [ɔrgənəzéʃən] *s.* organización; organismo; entidad; sociedad.

or·gan·ize [ɔ́rgənaɪz] *v.* organizar(se).

or·gan·iz·er [ɔ́rgənaɪzɚ] *s.* organizador.

or·gy [ɔ́rdʒɪ] *s.* orgia.

o·ri·ent [ɔ́rɪɛnt] *s.* oriente; *v.* orientar.

o·ri·en·tal [ɔrɪέntl] *adj. & s.* oriental.

o·ri·en·tate [ɔ́rɪɛntet] *v.* orientar.

o·ri·en·ta·tion [ɔrɪɛntéʃən] *s.* orientación.

or·i·fice [ɔ́rəfɪs] *s.* orificio.

or·i·gin [ɔ́rədʒɪn] *s.* origen; procedencia.

o·rig·i·nal [ərídʒənl] *adj. & s.* original; **-ly** *adv.* originalmente, originariamente; en el principio, al principio.

o·rig·i·nal·i·ty [ərɪdʒənǽlətɪ] *s.* originalidad.

o·rig·i·nate [əfídʒənet] *v.* originar(se).

o·ri·ole [óríol] *s.* oriol (*pájaro*).

Or·lon [ɔ́rlan] *s.* orlón.

or·na·ment [ɔ́rnəmənt] *s.* ornamento, adorno; [ɔ́rnəmɛnt] *v.* ornamentar, adornar, ornar.

or·na·men·tal [ɔrnəmɛ́ntl] *adj.* ornamental, de adorno, decorativo.

or·nate [ɔrnét] *adj.* ornado, adornado en exceso; **— style** estilo florido.

or·ni·thol·o·gy [ɔrnəθálədʒɪ] *s.* ornitología.

or·phan [ɔ́rfən] *adj. & s.* huérfano; **— asylum** hospicio, orfanato, asilo de huérfanos; *v.* dejar huérfano a.

or·tho·dox [ɔ́rθədaks] *adj.* ortodoxo.

or·thog·ra·phy [ɔrθágrəfɪ] *s.* ortografía.

os·cil·late [ɑ́səlet] *v.* oscilar.

os·cil·la·to·ry [ɑ́səlɑtorɪ] *adj.* oscilatorio.

os·mi·um [ázmiəm] *s.* osmio.

os·ten·ta·tion [ɑstəntéʃən] *s.* ostentación, boato.

os·ten·ta·tious [ɑstəntéʃəs] *adj.* ostentoso.

os·trich [ɔ́strɪtʃ] *s.* avestruz.

oth·er [ʌ́ðɚ] *adj. & s.* otro; **— than** otra cosa que; más que; **every — day** cada dos días, un día sí y otro no; **some — day** otro día.

oth·er·wise [ʌ́ðɚwaɪz] *adv.* de otro modo, en otros respetos; de otro, diferente.

ot·ter [átɚ] *s.* nutria; (*skin*) piel de nutria.

ought [ɔt] *v. defect.* (*por lo general se traduce por el presente y el condicional de* deber) debo, debes, etc.; debería, deberías, etc.; debiera, debieras, etc.

ounce [auns] *s.* onza.

our [aur] *adj.* nuestro (nuestra, nuestros, nuestras).

ours [aurz] *pron. pos.* nuestro (nuestra, nuestros, nuestras); el nuestro (la nuestra, los nuestros, las nuestras); **a friend of —** un amigo nuestro.

our·selves [aursέlvz] *pron.* nosotros mismos; nos (*reflexivo*); a nosotros mismos; **we —** nosotros mismos; **by —** solos; pos nosotros; *véase* **herself.**

oust [aust] *v.* echar, expulsar.

out [aut] *adv.* fuera; afuera; hacia fuera; **— of fashion** pasado de moda; **— of commission (order)** fuera de servicio; **— of fear** por miedo, de miedo; **— of humor** malhumorado; **— of money** sin dinero; **— of print** agotado; **— of stock** agotado; **— of touch** with aislado de, sin contacto con, **— of tune** desentonado; **made — of** hecho de; **to fight it —** decidirlo luchando; **to have it —**

with habérselas con; **to speak —** hablar francamente; *adj.* ausente; apagado; **— and — criminal** criminal empedernido; **— and — refusal** una negativa redonda; **— size** tamaño poco común o extraordinario; **before the week is —** antes de que termine la semana; **the book is just —** acaba de publicarse el libro; **the secret is —** se ha divulgado el secreto.

out·bid [aʊtbíd] *v.* hacer mejor oferta.

out·break [áʊtbrek] *s.* (*eruption*) erupción; (*revolt*) motín, insurrección, tumulto; (*attack*) ataque, arranque (*de ira*); **at the — of the war** al estallar la guerra.

out·burst [áʊtbɝst] *s.* explosión; estallido; arranque (*de pasión*); erupción.

out·cast [áʊtkæst] *adj.* excuido, desechado; desterrado; *s.* paria (*persona excluida de la sociedad*).

out·come [áʊtkʌm] *s.* resultado, consecuencia.

out·cry [áʊtkraɪ] *s.* grito; clamor.

out·door [áʊtdor] *adj.* externo; fuera de la casa; **— games** juegos al aire libre.

out·doors [aʊtdórz] *adv.* puertas afuera, fuera de casa, al aire libre, al raso; *s.* aire libre, campo raso, campiña.

out·er [áʊtɚ] *adj.* exterior, externo; **— harbor** antepuerto.

out·fit [áʊtfɪt] *s.* equipo; pertrechos; *v.* equipar, habilitar, aviar; proveer, abastecer.

out·go·ing [áʊtgoɪŋ] *adj.* (*leaving*) saliente; (*extrovert*) extrovertido.

out·guess [aʊtgés] *v.* anticipar; madrugar.

out·ing [áʊtɪŋ] *s.* excursión, gira (*jira*), caminata.

out·law [áʊtlɔ] *s.* forajido, bandido; prófugo, fugitivo; *v.* proscribir, declarar ilegal.

out·lay [áʊtle] *s.* gasto, desembolso; [aʊtlé] *v.* gastar, desembolsar.

out·let [áʊtlet] *s.* salida; desaguadero, desagüe; escurridero; (*telecommunications*) toma de corriente.

out·line [áʊtlaɪn] *s.* (*abstract*) bosquejo, esbozo; (*boundary*) contorno; *v.* bosquejar, esbozar; delinear.

out·live [aʊtlív] *v.* sobrevivir.

out·look [áʊtluk] *s.* vista; perspectiva.

out·ly·ing [áʊtlaɪɪŋ] *adj.* circundante, exterior, remoto (*del centro*).

out-of-date [áʊtəvdét] *adj.* fuera de moda, anticuado.

out·post [áʊtpost] *s.* avanzada.

out·put [áʊtpʊt] *s.* rendimiento; producción total.

out·rage [áʊtredʒ] *s.* ultraje; *v.* ultrajar.

out·ra·geous [áʊtrédʒəs] *adj.* afrentoso; atroz.

out·ran [aʊtrǽn] *pret. de* **to outrun.**

out·right —[aʊtráɪt] *adv. & adj.* sin rodeo; cabal; completo.

out·run [aʊrʌ́n] *v.* aventajar (*en una carrera*); dejar atrás; *p.p. de* **to outrun.**

out·set [áʊtset] *s.* comienzo, principio.

out·shine [aʊtʃáɪn] *v.* eclipsar, sobrepasar (*en brillo o lucidez*).

out·shone [aʊtʃón] *pret. & p.p. de* **to outshine.**

out·side [áʊtsáɪd] *adj.* (*external*) exterior; externo; (*foreign*) foráneo, extranjero; *adv.* fuera, afuera; fuera de casa; *prep.* fuero de; *s.* exterior, parte exterior; superficie; lado de afuera; **in a week, at the —** en una semana, a lo sumo; **to close on the — cerra** por fuera.

out·sid·er [aʊsáɪdɚ] *s.* foráneo, persona de fuera; forastero; intruso; extraño.

out·skirts [áʊtskɝts] *s. pl.* alrededores, arrabales, cercanías.

out·spo·ken [áʊtspókən] *adj.* franco, francote, *Ven., Méx., C.A., Carib.* claridoso.

out·stand·ing [áʊtstǽndɪŋ] *adj.* sobresaliente; destacado, notable; **— bills** cuentas por cobrar; **— debts** deudas por pagar; (*pending*) pendiente.

out·stretched [aʊtstrétʃt] *adj.* extendido; **with — arms** con los brazos abiertos.

out·strip [aʊtstríp] *v.* dejar atrás, adelantar.

out·ward [áʊtwɚd] *adj.* (*external*) exterior, externo; (*apparent*) aparente; superficial; *adv.* fuera, hacia fuera; **— bound** que sale, de salida; para fuera, para el extranjero; **-ly** *adv.* exteriormente; por fuera; aparentemente.

out·weigh [aʊtwé] *v.* exceder en poso o valor; sobrepujar.

o·val [óvl] *adj.* oval, ovalado; *s.* óvalo.

o·va·ry [óvərɪ] *s.* ovario.

o·va·tion [ovéʃən] *s.* ovación.

ov·en [ʌ́vən] *s.* horno.

o·ver [óvɚ] *prep.* sobre; por; por encima de; encima de; a través de; al otro lado de; más de; **— night** por la noche, durante la noche; (*véase* **overnight**); **— to** a; **all — the city** por toda la cuidad; *adv.* encima; al otro lado; otra vez, de nuevo; **— again** otra vez, de nuevo; **— against** en contraste con; **— and —** una y otra vez, repetidas veces; **— curious** demasiado curioso; **— generous** demasiado generoso; **— here** acá, aquí; **— there** allá, allí; **two years and —** más de dos años; **to do it —** hacerlo otra vez, volver a hacerlo; *adj.* excesivo; **it is all —** ya se acabó, se ha acabado; ha pasado.

o·ver·age [óvɚadʒ] *s.* exceso, sobrante.

o·ver·all [ovɚɔ́l] *adj.* global, total, general, cabal.

o·ver·alls [óvɚɔlz] *s. pl. Am.* overol, overoles (*pantalones de trabajo*); *Esp.* mono.

o·ver·ate [ovɚét] *pret. de* **to overeat.**

o·ver·bid·ding [ovɚbídɪŋ] *s.* puja.

o·ver·board [óvɚbord] *adv.* al mar, al agua.

o·ver·came [ovɚkém] *pret. de* **to overcome.**

o·ver·cast [óvɚkæst] *adj.* encapotado, nublado; **to become —** encapotarse, nublarse; [ovɚkǽst] *v.* nublar o anublar; sobrehilar (*dar puntadas sobre el borde de una tela*); *pret. & p.p. de* **to overcast.**

o·ver·charge [ovɚtʃárdʒ] *v.* cargar demasiado; cobrar demasiado.

o·ver·coat [óvɚkot] *s.* sobretodo, abrigo.

o·ver·come [ovɚkʌ́m] *v.* vencer; rendir; *p.p. & adj.* vencido; rendido; agobiado; **to be — by weariness** estar rendido de fatiga.

o·ver·draft [óvɚdræft] *s.* sobregiro, giro en descubierto.

o·ver·drawn [ovɚdrón] *adj.* cuenta en descubierto.

o·ver·due [ovɚdú] *adj.* atrasado; vencido sin pago.

o·ver·eat [ovɚít] *v.* hartarse.

o·ver·eat·en [ovɚítn] *p.p. de* **to overeat.**

o·ver·ex·cite [óvɚɪksáɪt] *v.* sobreexcitar.

o·ver·flow [óvɚflo] *s.* derrame, desbordamiento; inundación; superabundancia; [ovɚfló] *v.* derramarse, desbordarse, rebosar; (*flood*) inundar.

o·ver·grown [óvɚgrón] *adj.* denso, frondoso, poblado (*de follaje, herbaje, etc.*); **— boy** muchachón, muchacho demasiado crecido para su edad.

o·ver·hang [ovɚhǽŋ] *v.* colgar por encima de; proyectarse o sobresalir por encima de; adornar con colgaduras; amenazar (*dícese de un desastre o calamidad*).

o·ver·haul [ovɚhɔ́l] *v.* reparar (*de cabo a rabo*); remendar; alcanzar (*en una carrera*).

o·ver·head [óvɚhed] *s.* gastos generales (*renta,*

OP

seguro, alumbrado, calefacción, etc.); *adj.* de arriba; elevado; — **expenses** gastos generales; [óvɚhéd] *adv.* encima de la cabeza, arriba; en lo alto.

o·ver·hear [ovɚhír] *v.* oír por casualidad, alcanzar a oír, acertar a oír.

o·ver·heard [ovɚhɝd] *pret. & p.p. de* **to overhear**.

o·ver·heat [óvɚhít] *v.* recalentar(se); calentar(se) demasiado.

o·ver·hung [ovɚhʌ́ŋ] *pret. & p.p. de* **to overhang**.

o·ver·land [óvɚlænd] *adv. & adj.* por tierra; por ruta terrestre.

o·ver·lap [ovɚlǽp] *v.* solapar.

o·ver·lay [ovɚlé] *v.* cubrir; incrustar.

o·ver·load [ovɚlód] *v.* sobrecargar; [óvɚlod] *s.* sobrecarga.

o·ver·look [ovɚlúk] *v.* (*look*) mirar a (*desde lo alto*); dar a, tener vista a; (*omit*) pasar por alto, omitir; (*pardon*) perdonar (*faltas*); descuidar, no notar; (*supervise*) inspeccionar, examinar.

o·ver·ly [óvɚlɪ] *adv.* excesivamente.

o·ver·night [óvɚnáɪt] *adv.* durante la noche; toda la noche; *adj.* de noche; nocturno; — **bag** saco de noche; — **trip** viaje de una noche.

o·ver·pass [óvɚpǽs] *v.* viaducto.

o·ver·price [pvɚpráɪs] *v.* fijar precio excesivo.

o·ver·pow·er [ovɚpáʊɚ] *v.* subyugar, abrumar, vencer.

o·ver·ran [ovɚfǽn] *pret. de* **to overrun**.

o·ver·rate [ovɚrét] *v.* exagerar el valor de.

o·ver·ride [ovɚráɪd] *v.* anular; invalidar.

o·ver·rule [ovɚrúl] *v.* anular.

o·ver·run [ovɚrʌ́n] *v.* desbordarse, mundar; sobrepasar; infestar, invadir; *p.p. de* **to overrun**.

o·ver·seas [óvɚsíz] *adv.* en ultramar, allende los mares; *adj.* de ultramar.

o·ver·see [ovɚsí] *v.* dirigir; vigilar.

o·ver·se·er [óvɚsɪr] *s.* sobrestante, capataz; inspector, superintendente.

o·ver·shoe [óvɚʃu] *s.* chanclo; zapato de goma, caucho o hule.

o·ver·sight [óvɚsaɪt] *s.* inadvertencia, negligencia, descuido.

o·ver·step [ovɚstɛ́p] *v.* sobrepasarse, propasarse; traspasar; **to — the bounds** traspasar los limites; proparse.

o·ver·take [ovɚték] *v.* alcanzar.

o·ver·tak·en [ovɚtékən] *p.p. de* **to overtake**.

o·ver·tax [ovɚtǽks] *v.* oprimir con tributos; someter a un esfuerzo excesivo.

o·ver·threw [ovɚθrú] *pret. de* **to overthrow**.

o·ver·throw [óvɚθro] *s.* (*overturn*) derrocamiento; (*defeat*) derrota, destrucción; caída; [ovɚθró] *v.* derrocar; derribar, echar abajo, volcar; destronar.

o·ver·thrown [ovɚθrón] *p.p. de* **to overthrow**.

o·ver·time [óvɚtaɪm] *adv.* en exceso de las horas estipuladas; — **pay** sobresueldo; *s.* sobretiempo, tiempo suplementario.

o·ver·took [ovɚtúk] *pret. de* **to overtake**.

o·ver·ture [óvɚtʃɚ] *s.* obertura, preludio; propuesta, proposición.

o·ver·turn [ovɚtɝn] *v.* volcar(se); trastornar; derribar; echar abajo.

o·ver·view [óvɚvju] *s.* vista global, plan general; resumen.

o·ver·whelm [ovɚhwɛ́lm] *v.* abrumar, agobiar; oprimir; arrollar.

o·ver·whelm·ing [ovɚhwɛ́lmɪŋ] *adj.* abrumador; opresivo; arrollador, irresistible, poderoso.

o·ver·work [óvɚwɝk] *v.* atarearse, afanarse más de lo debido, trabajar demasiado; *s.* exceso de trabajo.

owe [o] *v.* deber, adeudar.

ow·ing [óLŋ] *adj.* debido; — **to** debido a.

owl [aul] *s.* lechuza, buho, *Méx., C.A.* tecolote.

own [on] *adj.* propio; **a house of his** — una casa suya; **his** — **people** los suyos; **to be on one's** — no estar a merced ajena; trabajar por su propia cuenta; **to come into one's** — entrar en posesión de lo suyo; **to hold one's** — mantenerse firme; *v.* poseer, tener; admitir, reconocer; **to** — **to** confesar; **to** — **up** confesar.

own·er [ónɚ] *s.* dueño, amo; propietario; poseedor.

own·er·ship [ónɚʃɪp] *s.* posesión, propiedad; pertenencia.

ox [ɑks] (*pl.* **ox·en** [ɑksn̩]) *s.* buey.

ox·ide [ɑ́ksaɪd] *s.* óxido.

ox·i·dize [ɑ́ksɚdaɪz] *v.* oxidar.

ox·y·gen [ɑ́ksədʒən] *s.* oxígeno.

oys·ter [ʃ́ɪstɚ] *s.* ostra, ostión; *Sp.* ostrón.

o·zone [ózon] *s.* ozono.

P:p

P-trap [pítræp] *s.* (*plumbing*) bombillo inodoro.

pace [pes] *s.* paso; *v.* pasear, andar; andar al paso; marchar; medir a pasos.

pace·mak·er [pésmekɚ] *s.* marcapaso.

pa·cif·ic [pəsffik] *adj.* pacífico.

pa·ci·fy [pǽsəfaɪ] *v.* pacificar, apaciguar; calmar.

pack [pǽk] *s.* fardo, lío, carga; (*animals*) manada; cuadrilla, pandilla (*de ladrones*); (*dogs*) jauría (*de perros*); muchedumbre; (*cards*) baraja (*de naipes*); — **animal** acémila, bestía de carga; *v.* empacar, empaquetar; embalar; enlatar; envasar; apiñar(se); cargar (*una bestia*); hacer (*el baúl, la maleta*) *etc.* **off** despedir de repente; echar a la calle; largarse, irse.

pack·age [pǽkɪdʒ] *s.* paquete; fardo, bulto; cajetilla (*de cigarrillos*).

pack·er [pǽkɚ] *s.* empacador; embalador, envasador.

pack·et [pǽkɪt] *s.* paquetillo; cajetilla.

pack·ing [pǽkɪŋ] *s.* (*covering*) embalaje; envase; (*filling*) relleno; — **box** caja para embalar o empacar; — **house** establecimiento frigorífico, fábrica para envasar o enlatar comestibles; — **slip** boleta de envase.

pact [pǽkt] *s.* pacto, convenio.

pad [pǽd] *s.* almohadilla, cojincillo; tableta, block de papel; *v.* rellenar; forrar; acolchar; (*inflate*) aumentar con material superfluo.

pad·ding [pǽdɪŋ] *s.* relleno (*de pelo, algodón, paja, etc.*), *Andes* guata; ripio, palabras o frases inútiles.

pad·dle [pǽdl̩] *s.* pala; remo de canoa; (*computer*) potenciómetro; — **wheel** rueda de paleta; *v.* remar con pala; apalear; chapotear (*en el agua*).

pad·dock [pǽdək] *s.* dehesa.

pad·lock [pǽdlɑk] *s.* candado; *v.* cerrar con candado.

pa·gan [pégən] *s. & adj.* pagano.

pa·gan·ism [pégənɪzəm] *s.* paganismo.

page [pedʒ] *s.* (*sheet*) página; (*messenger*) paje; "botones" (*de hotel*), mensajero; *v.* paginar; vocear, llamar a voces.

pag·eant [pǽdʒənt] *s.* (*parade*) manifestación, desfile, procesión, pompa; (*drama*) representación al aire libre.

paid [ped] *pret. & p.p. de* **to pay; paid-up** *adj* saldado.

pail [pel] *s.* balde, cubo, cubeta.

pain [pen] *s.* dolor; sufrimiento; -s esmero; **on** (**under**) — **of** so pena de; **to be in** — estar

sufriendo, tener dolores; **to take -s** esmerarse,
extremarse; *v.* doler; causar dolor; afligir.
pain·ful [pénfəl] *adj.* doloroso; penoso; arduo.
pain·less [pénlıs] *adj.* sin dolor; libre de dolor.
pains·tak·ing [pénztekıŋ] *adj.* esmerado, cuidadoso;
aplicado.
paint [pent] *s.* (*mixture*) pintura, color; (*rouge*)
colorete; *v.* pintar; pintarse (*la cara*); **to — the
town red** irse de juerga o de parranda, *Ríopl.* irse
de farra.
paint·brush [péntbrʌʃ] *s.* (*art*) pincel; (*house*)
brocha.
paint·er [péntəʳ] *s.* pintor.
paint·ing [péntıŋ] *s.* pintura.
pair [pɛr] *s.* par; pareja; **a — of scissors** unas tijeras;
v. aparear(se); hacer pareja, hacer pares; **to — off**
aparear(se).
pa·jam·as [pədʒǽməz] *s. pl.* pijama.
pal [pæl] *s.* compañero, camarada.
pal·ace [pǽlıs] *s.* palacio.
pal·ate [pǽlıt] *s.* paladar.
pa·la·tial [pəléʃl] *adj.* suntuoso.
pale [pel] *adj.* pálido; descolorido; *v.* palidecer,
ponerse pálido o descolorido.
pale·ness [pélnıs] *s.* palidez.
pal·i·sade [pæləséd] *s.* palizada, estacada; **-s** riscos,
acantilados.
pall [pɔl] *v.* empalagar; aburrir; **it -s on me** me
empalaga; me aburre; *s.* paño de ataúd; (*church*)
palia (*lienzo que pone encima del cáliz*).
pal·la·di·um [pəlédıəm] *s.* paladio.
pal·li·a·tive [pǽljətıv] *adj.* & *s.* paliativo.
pal·lid [pǽlıd] *adj.* pálido.
pal·or [pǽləʳ] *s.* palidez.
palm [pɑm] *s.* palma; palmera; **— Sunday** Domingo
de Ramos; **— tree** palma; palmera; *v.* **to —
something off on someone** pasar o dar algo
indeseable a una persona (*sin que se dé cuenta de
ello*).
pal·pa·ble [pǽlpəbl] *adj.* palpable, tangible; evidente.
pal·pi·tate [pǽlpətét] *v.* palpitar, latir.
pal·pi·ta·tion [pælpətéʃən] *s.* palpitación; latido.
pal·try [pɔ́ltrı] *adj.* mezquino, miserable,
despreciable, insignificante.
pam·per [pǽmpəʳ] *v.* mimar, consentir (*a un niño*).
pam·phlet [pǽmflıt] *s.* folleto, *Am.* panfleto.
pan [pæn] *s.* cazuela, cacerola; (*ladle*) cazo; platillo
(*de balanza*); **dish —** cazo para lavar platos;
frying — sartén; **sheet —** cazuela plana; *v.* **to —
out (well)** salir bien, dar buen resultado.
Pan-A·mer·i·can [pænəmérəkən] *adj.* panamericano.
pan·cake [pǽnkek] *s.* tortita de harina, *Ven., Col.*
panqué; *Ríopl.* panqueque.
pan·der [pǽndəʳ] *s.* alcahuete, encubridor *v.*
alcahuetear, servir de alcahuete.
pane [pen] *s.* vidrio, cristal (*de ventana o puerta*);
cuadro (*de vidrio*).
pan·el [pǽnl] *s.* panel, tablero; (*door*) cuarterón (*de
puerta, ventana, etc.*); (*dress*) tabla; **jury —**
jurado; *v.* proveer de (*o adornar con*) paneles.
pang [pæŋ] *s.* dolor agudo; angustia, tormento.
pan·han·dle [pǽnhændl] *s.* mango de sartén;
territorio en forma de mango; *v.* mendigar.
pan·ic [pǽnık] *adj.* & *s.* pánico; **pan·ic-strick·en**
sobrecogido de pánico.
pan·o·ram·a [pænərǽmə] *s.* panorama.
pan·sy [pǽnzı] *s.* pensamiento (*flor*).
pant [pænt] *v.* jadear; palpitar; **to — for** anhelar,
ansiar.
pan·ther [pǽnθəʳ] *s.* pantera.
pant·ing [pǽntıŋ] *s.* jadeo, palpitación; *adj.* jadeante.

pan·to·mime [pǽntəmaım] *s.* pantomima.
pan·try [pǽntrı] *s.* despensa.
pants [pænts] *s. pl.* pantalones.
pa·pa [pápə] *s.* papá.
pa·pa·cy [pépəsı] *s.* papado.
pa·pal [pépl] *adj.* papal.
pa·per [pépəʳ] *s.* (*material*) papel; (*daily*) periódico;
(*essay*) tema; ensayos; **-s** papeles, documentos,
credenciales; **naturalization -s** carta de naturaleza,
certificado de ciudadanía; **scholarly —** ponencia;
— of pins cartón de alfileres; **on —** escrito; por
escrito; *adj.* de papel; para papel; **— doll** muñeca
de papel; **— money** papel moneda; **— weight**
pisapapeles; *v.* empapelar.
pa·per·back [pépəʳbæk] *s.* & *adj.* libro en rústica.
pa·per·work [pépəʳwəʳk] *s.* preparación de escritos;
papeleo.
pa·pri·ka [pæpríka] *s.* pimentón.
par [pɑr] *s.* (*equality*) paridad, igualdad; (*standard*)
valor nominal; **— value** valor a la par; **above —**
sobre par, a premio, can prima; **at —** a la par;
below — bajo par, a descuento; **on a — with** al
par de, al nivel de, igual a; **to feel above —**
sentirse mejor que de ordinario; **to feel below —**
sentirse menos bien que de ordinario.
par·a·ble [pǽrəbl] *s.* parábola (*alegoría bíblica*).
par·a·chute [pǽrəʃut] *s.* paracaídas.
par·a·chut·ist [pǽrəʃutıst] *s.* paracaidista.
pa·rade [pəréd] *s.* (*procession*) desfile, procesión,
manifestación; paseo; (*review*) parada; **— ground**
campo de maniobras; **to make a — of** ostentar,
hacer ostentación de; *v.* desfilar, pasar en desfile;
marchar en parada; hacer ostentación de.
par·a·digm [pǽrədım], [pǽrədaım] *s.* paradigma.
par·a·dise [pǽrədais] *s.* paraíso.
par·a·dox·i·cal [pærədáksıkl] *adj.* paradójico.
par·a·dox [pǽrədaks] *s.* paradoja.
par·af·fin [pǽrəfın] *s.* parafina.
par·a·graph [pǽrəgræf] *s.* párrafo; *v.* dividir en
párrafos.
Par·a·guay·an [pæregwáıən] *adj.* & *s.* paraguayo.
par·al·lel [pǽrəlɛl] *adj.* & *s.* paralelo; *v.* ser (*o
correr*) paralelo a; comparar, cotejar.
pa·ral·y·sis [pərǽləsıs] *s.* parálisis.
par·a·lyt·ic [pærəlítık] *adj.* paralítico.
par·a·lyze [pǽrəlaız] *v.* paralizar.
pa·ram·e·ter [pərǽmətəʳ] *s.* parámetro.
par·a·mount [pǽrəmaunt] *adj.* importantísimo,
superior, supremo, máximo.
par·a·noi·a [pærənɔ́jə] *s.* paranoia.
par·a·pet [pǽrəpıt] *s.* parapeto.
par·a·phrase [pǽrəfrez] *v.* parafrasear.
par·a·site [pǽrəsaıt] *s.* parásito.
par·a·sol [pǽrəsɔl] *s.* parasol, sombrilla.
par·a·troops [pǽrətrups] *s.* tropas paracaidistas.
par·cel [pársl] *s.* (*package*) paquete; (*land*) parcela,
porción, lote (*de terreno*); **— post** paquete postal,
Col. encomienda postal; *v.* parcelar, dividir en
porciones o parcelas; hacer paquetes; **to — out**
repartir.
parch [pɑrtʃ] *v.* resecar(se); tostar(se).
parch·ment [pártʃmənt] *s.* pergamino.
par·don [párdn] *s.* perdón; indulto; **I beg your —**
perdone Vd.; dispense Vd.; *v.* perdonar; dispensar;
indultar.
pare [pɛr] *v.* mondar, pelar (*manzanas, patatas,
etc.*); cortar, recortar; **to — down expenditures**
reducir gastos.
par·ent [pérənt] *s.* padre, madre; (*origin*) origen; **-s**
padres.
par·ent·age [pérəntıdʒ] *s.* linaje; padres.

OV

par·ren·tal [pərɛ́ntl] *adj.* parental.
pa·ren·the·sis [pərɛ́nθəsɪs] (*pl.* **pa·ren·the·ses**
[pərɛ́nθəsiz]) *s.* paréntesis.
par·ish [pǽrɪʃ] *s.* parroquia.
par·ish [pərɪ́ʃənɚ] *s.* parroquiano, feligrés; **-s** fieles,
feligreses.
par·i·ty [pǽrɪtɪ] *s.* paridad.
park [pɑrk] *s.* parque; *v.* estacionar, dejar (*un
automóvil*); estacionarse; **-ing lot** *Ch., Ríopl.* playa
de estacionamiento; *Méx., Ven.* estacionamiento;
Col. parqueadero; **-ing space** sitio o lugar para
estacionarse; **free -ing** estacionamiento gratis; **no
-ing** se prohibe estacionarse; no estacionarse.
par·lance [pɑ́rləns] *s.* lenguaje.
par·ley [pɑ́rlɪ] *s.* parlamento, discusión, conferencia;
v. parlamentar, discutir.
par·lia·ment [pɑ́rləmənt] *s.* parlamento.
par·lia·men·ta·ry [pɑrləmɛ́ntərɪ] *adj.* parlamentario.
par·lor [pɑ́rlɚ] *s.* sala, salón; sala de recibo; — **car**
coche salón; **beauty** — salón de belleza.
pa·ro·chi·al [pərókɪəl] *adj.* parroquial.
par·o·dy [pǽrədɪ] *s.* parodia; *v.* parodiar.
pa·role [pəról] *s.* palabra de honor; **to put on** —
dejar libre (*a un prisionero*) bajo palabra de honor;
v. dejar libre bajo palabra de honor.
par·rot [pǽrət] *s.* cotorra, loro, perico, papagayo; *v.*
remedar, repetir como loro.
par·ry [pǽrɪ] *v.* parar, quitar o reparar (*un golpe*); *s.*
quite, reparo.
pars·ley [pɑ́rslɪ] *s.* perejil.
pars·nip [pɑ́rsnəp] *s.* chirivía (*legumbre*).
par·son [pɑ́rsn̩] *s.* pastor, clérigo.
part [pɑrt] *s.* parte (*f.*); (*role*) papel (*dramático*);
(*hair*) raya (*del cabello*); — **and parcel** parte
esencial, inherente; — **owner** condueño, dueño en
parte; — **time** parte del tiempo; de tiempo
incompleto; **in foreign -s** en el extranjero, en
países extranjeros; **spare -s** piezas accesorias,
piezas de repuesto (*o* de refacción); **do your** —
haga Vd. cuanto esté de su parte; *v.* partir(se);
separar(se); **to** — **company** separarse; **to** — **from**
separarse de, despedirse de; **to** — **one's hair**
hacerse la raya; **to** — **with** separarse de,
despedirse de, deshacerse de.
par·take [pɑrtɛ́k] *v.* tomar parte, tener parte,
participar.
par·tak·en [pɑrtɛ́kən] *p.p. de* **to partake.**
par·tial [pɑ́rʃəl] *adj.* parcial; **-ly** *adv.* parcialmente,
en parte; con parcialidad.
par·ti·al·i·ty [pɑrʃǽlətɪ] *s.* parcialidad.
par·tic·i·pant [pɚtɪ́səpənt] *adj. & s.* participante,
partícipe, copartícipe.
par·tic·i·pate [pɚtɪ́səpet] *v.* participar.
par·tic·i·pa·tion [pɚtɪsəpéʃən] *s.* participación.
par·ti·ci·ple [pɑ́rtəsɪpl] *s.* participio; **present** —
gerundio.
par·ti·cle [pɑ́rtɪkl] *s.* partícula.
par·tic·u·lar [pɚtɪ́kjəlɚ] *adj.* (*single*) particular;
peculiar; (*special*) esmerado, exacto; escrupuloso;
(*demanding*) quisquilloso; exigente; *s.* particular,
detalle, circunstancia; **in** — en particular,
especialmente; **-ly** *adv.* particularmente; en
particular.
part·ing [pɑ́rtɪŋ] (*departure*) despedida; (*division*)
separación; bifurcación; **the** — **of the ways**
encruijada, bifurcación, cruce de caminos; *adj.* de
despedida, último.
par·ti·san [pɑ́rtəzn̩] *adj.* partidario; parcial; *s.*
partidario; secuaz, seguidor.
par·ti·tion [pɚtɪ́ʃən] *s.* (*division*) partición; división,
separación; (*wall*) tabique; *Am.* medianía; *v.* partir,

dividir; repartir.
par·ti·tive [pɑ́rtətɪv] *adj.* partitivo.
part·ly [pɑ́rtlɪ] *adv.* en parte.
part·ner [pɑ́rtnɚ] *s.* socio, consocio; compañero;
dancing — pareja de baile.
part·ner·ship [pɑ́rtnɚʃɪp] *s.* sociedad, compañía;
colectiva; *Méx.* sociedad en nombre colectivo.
par·took [pɑrtʊ́k] *pret. de* **to partake.**
par·tridge [pɑ́rtrɪdʒ] *s.* perdiz.
par·ty [pɑ́rtɪ] *s.* (*get-together*) tetulia, reunión, fiesta;
(*group*) grupo, partida (*de gente*); (*legal*) parte;
hunting — partida de caza; **political** — partido
político.
pass [pǽs] *s.* paso; (*motion*) pase, (*permit*) permiso
de entrar; (*exam*) aprobación (*en un examen*);
(*event*) trance, situación; — **key** llave maestra; **to
come to** — suceder; *v.* pasar; pasar por;
pronunciar (*sentencia*), dar (*un juicio o parecer*);
aprobar (*a un estudiante*); adoptar (*una ley*); ser
aprobado en (*un examen*); **to** — **away** pasar a
mejor vida, morir; desaparecer; pasar (*el tiempo*).
pass·a·ble [pǽsəbl] *adj.* (*penetrable*) transitable;
(*acceptable*) pasadero, regular, mediano.
pass·age [pǽsɪdʒ] *s.* (*fare*) pasaje; paso, tránsito;
transcurso (*del tiempo*); pasillo, pasadizo; (*trip*)
travesía, viaje por mar; aprobación (*de un proyecto
de ley*); adopción (*de una ley*).
pas·sage·way [pǽsɪdʒwe] *s.* corredor, (*isle*) pasaje.
pass·book [pǽsbʊk] *s.* libreta de banco (*depósito*).
pas·sen·ger [pǽsn̩dʒɚ] *s.* pasajero; **the -s** los
pasajeros; el pasaje.
pas·ser·by [pǽsɚbái] *s.* transeúnte, viandante.
pas·sion [pǽʃən] *s.* pasión; **Passion play** drama de la
Pasión; **to fly into a** — montar en cólera,
encolerizarse.
pas·sion·ate [pǽʃənɪt] *adj.* apasionado.
pas·sive [pǽsɪv] *adj.* pasivo; *s.* voz pasiva.
pass·port [pǽsport] *s.* pasaporte.
pass·word [pǽswɚd] *s.* consigna, contraseña, santo
y seña.
past [pǽst] *adj.* pasado; último; — **master** perito;
the — **president** el expresidente, el último
presidente; — **tense** tiempo pasado; pretérito; **for
some time** — desde hace algún tiempo, de poco
tiempo a esta parte; *prep.* — **bearing** insoportable;
— **understanding** incomprensible; **half** — **two** las
dos y media; **woman** — **forty** cuarentona, mujer
de más de cuarenta años; **to go** — **the house** pasar
por (*o* por enfrente de) la casa; *s.* pasado; pretérito;
pretérito imperfecto; **man with a** — hombre de
dudosos antecedentes.
paste [pest] *s.* pasta; engrudo; *v.* pegar (*con
engrudo*).
paste·board [péstbord] *s.* cartón; — **box** caja de
cartón.
pas·teur·ize [pǽstəraɪz] *v.* pasterizar (*o* pasteurizar).
pas·time [pǽstaɪm] *s.* pasatiempo.
pas·tor [pǽstɚ] *s.* pastor, clérigo, cura.
pas·tor·al [pǽstərəl] *adj.* pastoril; pastoral; *s.*
pastoral, carta pastoral; (*story*) égloga; pastorela,
idilio.
pas·try [péstrɪ] *s.* pastelería, pasteles; — **cook**
pastelero; — **shop** pastelería; repostería.
pas·ture [pǽstʃɚ] *s.* pastura, pasto; dehesa; *v.*
pastar, pacer; apacentar(se).
pat [pǽt] *adj.* apto, oportuno; **to have a lesson** —
saber al dedillo la lección; **to stand** — mantenerse
firme; *adv.* a propósito; oportunamente; de molde;
s. palmadita, caricia, golpecito; — **of butter**
cuadrito de mantequilla; *v.* dar palmaditas a;
acariciar; pasar la mano (*para alisar o acariciar*).

patch [pætʃ] s. (*repair*) remiendo; parche; mancha; (*plot*) pedazo (*de terreno*); sembrado; v. remendar; **to — up a quarrel** hacer las paces.

pate [pet] s. coronilla (*de la cabeza*); **bald —** calva.

pat·ent [pǽtn̩t] adj. patente, evidente, manifiesto; de patente; **— leather** charol; **— medicine** medicina de patente; **— right** patente; s. patente; v. patentar.

pa·ter·nal [pətɝ́nl] adj. paternal, paterno.

pa·ter·ni·ty [pətɝ́nətɪ] s. paternidad.

path [pæθ] s. senda, sendero; vereda; ruta; trayectoria (*de una bala*).

pa·thet·ic [pəθέtɪk] adj. patético.

path·o·log·i·cal [pæθəládʒɪkl] adj. patalógico.

pa·thol·o·gy [pæθálədʒɪ] s. patología.

pa·thos [péθɑs] s. patetismo, cualidad patética.

path·way [pǽθwe] s. senda, vereda, vía.

pa·tience [péʃəns] s. paciencia.

pa·tient [péʃənt] adj. paciente; pacienzudo; s. paciente, enfermo.

pa·tri·arch [pétrɪɑrk] s. patriarca.

pa·tri·ar·chal [petrɪɑrkl] adj. patriarcal.

pa·tri·cian [pətrɪ́ʃən] s'. patricio.

pat·ri·mo·ny [pǽtrəmonɪ] s. patrimonio.

pa·tri·ot [pétrɪət] s. patriota.

pa·tri·ot·ic [petrɪɑ́tɪk] adj. patriótico.

pa·tri·ot·ism [pétrɪətɪzəm] s. patriotismo.

pa·trol [pətról] s. patrulla; ronda; v. patrullar, rondar.

pa·tron [pétrən] s. patrón, patrono; benefactor; (*customer*) cliente, parroquiano; **— saint** santo patrón.

pa·tron·age [pétrənɪdʒ] s. (*support*) patrocinio, amparo; (*clientele*) clientela; (*manner*) condescendencia; **political —** control de nombramientos políticos.

pa·tron·ess [pétrənɪs] s. patrona, protectora.

pa·tron·ize [pétrənaɪz] v. patrocinar, amparar; tratar con condescendencia; favorecer, ser parroquiano de.

pat·ter [pǽtɚ] v. golpetear ligeramente; (*feet*) talonear; (*speech*) charlar, parlotear; s. golpeteo; golpecitos; taloneo; charla, parloteo.

pat·tern [pǽtɚn] s. (*model*) modelo; dechado; muestra; ejemplo; patrón, molde; (*design*) diseño, dibujo (*en tejidos, telas, etc.*) v. **to — oneself after** seguir el ejemplo de; **to — something after (on, upon)** forjar o modelar algo a imitación de.

pau·ci·ty [pɔ́sɪtɪ] s. escasez; falta.

paunch [pɔntʃ] s. panza, barriga.

pause [pɔz] s. pausa; s. pausar, hacer pausa; detenerse, parar.

pave [pev] v. pavimentar; **to — the way for** preparar o abrir el camino para; **to — with bricks** enladrillar; **to — with flagstones** enlosar.

pave·ment [pévmənt] s. pavimento; **brick —** enladrillado.

pa·vil·lion [pəvɪ́ljən] s. pabellón.

paw [pɔ] s. garra, zarpa; v. echar la zarpa; arañar; manosear; **to — the ground** patear la tierra (*dícese del caballo*).

pawn [pɔn] s. prenda, empeño; (*chess*) peón (*de ajedrez*); **— broker** prestamista, prendero; **— shop** empeño, casa de empeños, montepío; **in —** en prenda; v. empeñar, dejar en prenda.

pay [pe] v. (*remit*) pagar; (*pay for*) costear; (*profit*) ser provechoso; (*worthwhile*) valer la pena; **to — attention** prestar atención; **to — back** restituir, devolver; reembolsar; **to — court** hacer la corte; **to — down** pagar al contado; **to — homage** hacer o rendir homenaje; **to — one's respects** presentar sus respetos; **to — a visit** hacer una visita; **to hit**

— dirt descubrir algo de valor; s. pago; recompensa; **to — through the nose** pagar demasiado; paga; **take-home —** sueldo neto; sueldo; **— load** carga útil o de valor; **— day** día de pagos, *Am.*, día de raya; **— master** pagador, **— phone** teléfono público; *Am.* rayador; **— roll** nómina.

pay·a·ble [péəbl] adj. pagadero.

pay·ee [peí] s. tenedor, portador.

pay·ment [pémənt] s. pago; paga; **in full —** pago total.

pay·off [péɔf] s. arreglo; pago; resultados favorables.

pea [pi] s. guisante, chícharo; **sweet —** guisante de olor.

peace [pis] s. paz.

peace·a·ble [písəbl] adj. pacífico, tranquilo.

peace·ful [písfəl] àdj. pacífico; tranquilo, quieto, sosegado.

peach [pitʃ] s. melocotón, durazno; persona bella o admirable; **— tree** durazno, duraznero, melocotonero.

pea·cock [píkɑk] s. pavón, pavo real; **to act like a — pavonearse**, hacer ostentación.

peak [pik] s. pico, cumbre, cima; cúspide; punto máximo; **— level** producción máxima; **— load** de carga máxima; **- hour traffic** hora de tránsito máximo.

peal [pil] s. repique (*de campanas*); **— of laughter** carcajada, risotada; **— of thunder** trueno; v. repicar (*las campanas*).

pea·nut [pínət] s. cacahuate, *Carib.*, *Ven.*, *Col.*, *Ch.*, *Ríopl.*, *Andes* maní.

pear [pɛ] s. pera; **— tree** peral; **alligator —** aguacate, *Ch.*, *Andes*, *Ríopl.* palta (*variedad sudamericana*).

pearl [pɝl] s. perla; **— necklace** collar de perlas; **mother-of-pearl** nácar, madreperla.

pear·ly [pɝ́lɪ] adj. perlino; nacarado; aperlado.

peas·ant [pɝ́zn̩t] adj. & s. campesino, rústico, *P.R.* jíbaro, *Cuba* guajiro; *Col.* paisa; *Ch.* guaso; *Ríopl.* gaucho.

peb·ble [pɝ́bl] s. guija, china, guijarro, piedrecilla.

pe·can [pikɑ́n] s. pacana.

peck [pɛk] v. picar, picotear; s. picotazo, picotada; medida de áridos (*aproximadamente 9 litros*); **a — of trouble** la mar de disgustos o molestias.

pe·cu·liar [pɪkúljɚ] adj. peculiar; raro, singular, extraño.

pe·cu·li·ar·i·ty [pɪkjulɪǽrətɪ] s. peculiaridad; particularidad; rareza.

ped·a·gogue [pédəgɑg] s. pedagogo, dómine.

ped·a·go·gy [pédəgodʒɪ] s. pedagogía.

ped·al [pédl] s. pedal; v. pedalear, mover los pedales.

ped·ant [pédn̩t] s. pedante.

pe·dan·tic [pɪdǽntɪk] adj. pedante, pedantesco.

ped·dle [pédl] v. ir vendiendo de puerta en puerta; **to — gossip** chismear.

ped·dler [pédlɚ] s. buhonero; vendedor ambulante.

ped·es·tal [pédɪstl] s. pedestal.

pe·des·tri·an [pədéstrɪən] s. peatón, transeúnte, viandante; adj. pedestre.

pe·di·at·rics [pidɪǽtrɪks] s. pediatría.

ped·i·gree [pédəgri] s. linaje, genealogía.

peek [pik] v. atisbar, espiar; s. atisbo.

peel [pil] s. corteza, cáscara (*de algunas frutas*); pellejo (*de patatas*); v. pelar(se), descortezar(se), deshollejar(se); **to keep one's eye -ed** tener los ojos muy abiertos, estar alerta.

peep [pip] v. atisbar, espiar; asomar(se); pipiar, piar; s. atisbo; ojeada; pío (*de pollo o ave*).

PA

peer [pɪr] s. (*equal*) par, igual; (*noble*) noble; v. mirar con atención, atisbar; asomar; **to — into other people's business** fisgar, curiosear.

peer group [pírgrup] s. conjunto de personas de la misma edad y condiciones.

peer·less [pírlɛs] adj. incomparable; sin par.

peeve [piv] v. irritar, poner de mal humor; **to get -d** amoscarse, ponerse de mal humor.

pee·vish [pívɪʃ] adj. enojadizo; malhumorado.

peg [pɛg] s. espiga, clavo de madera, estaquilla; clavija (*de violin*); **to take a person down a —** rebajar o humillar a alguien; v. clavar, clavetear; poner estaquillas; **to — along** atarearse, trabajar con tesón; **pegged value of exchange** tipo arbitrario de cambio.

pe·jor·a·tive [pədʒɔ́rətɪv] adj. peyorativo; despectivo.

pel·i·can [pélɪkən] s. pelicano.

pel·let [pélɪt] s. (*ball*) pelotilla; bola; (*pill*) píldora.

pell·mell [pélmɛ́l] adj. confuso, tumultuoso; adv. a trochemoche, atropelladamente, en tumulto.

pelt [pɛlt] s. zalea, cuero (*especialmente de oveja*); piel; v. golpear; **to — with stones** apedrear, arrojar piedras a.

pel·vis [pélvɪs] s. pelvis.

pen [pɛn] s. pluma (*para escribir*); corral; redil; **— holder** mango de pluma, portapluma; **— name** nombre de pluma; **fountain —** pluma fuente, pluma estilográfica; **ballpoint —** bolígrafo; **pig —** pocilga; v. escribir (*con pluma*); acorralar, encerrar.

pe·nal [pínl] adj. penal.

pe·nal·ize [pínəlaɪz] v. penar; aplicar sanción.

pen·al·ty [pénltɪ] s. pena, castigo; multa.

pen·ance [pénəns] s. penitencia.

pen·cil [pénsl] s. lápiz; lapicero; **— sharpener** tajalápiz.

pen·dant [péndənt] s. pendiente (*ardorno que cuelga*); adj. pendiente.

pend·ing [péndɪŋ] adj. pendiente; colgado; prep. durante.

pen·du·lum [péndʒələm] s. péndula.

pen·e·trate [pénətret] v. penetrar.

pen·e·trat·ing [pénətretɪŋ] adj. penetrante.

pen·e·tra·tion [penətréʃən] s. penetración.

pen·guin [péngwɪn] s. pingüino.

pen·i·cil·lin [penəsflɪn] s. penicilina.

pen·in·su·la [pənínsələ] s. península.

pe·nis [pínɪs] s. pene.

pen·i·tent [pénətənt] adj. arrepentido, penitente; s. penitente.

pen·i·ten·tia·ry [penətéʃərɪ] s. penitenciaría, presidio.

pen·knife [pénnaɪf] s. cortaplumas; navaja.

pen·man·ship [pénmənʃɪp] s. escritura, caligrafía.

pen·nant [pénənt] s. banderola, gallardete.

pen·ni·less [pénɪlɪs] adj. pobre, sin dinero.

pen·ny [pénɪ] s. centavo (*de dólar*); **to cost a pretty —** costar un ojo de la cara, costar un dineral.

pen·sion [pénʃən] s. pensión, retiro (*de un militar*); **—fund** fondo de pensión; v. pensionar.

pen·sive [pénsɪv] adj. pensativo.

pent [pɛnt] adj. encerrado; acorralado; **pent-up emotions** sentimientos reprimidos.

pent·house [pénthaus] s. casa de azotea; colgadizo.

peo·ple [pípl] s. gente; pueblo; v. poblar.

pep·per [pépɚ] s. pimienta; **— plant** pimentero; **— shaker** pimentero; **green -s** pimientos verdes; **red —** pimentón, chile, (*Carib., Col., Ven., Andes, Ch., Ríopl.* ají; v. sazonar con pimienta; **to — with bullets** acribillar a balazos.

pep·per·mint [pépɚmɪnt] s. menta; pastilla o bombón de menta.

per [pɚ] prep. por; **— capita** por cabeza; **— capita income** renta por habitante; **— cent** por ciento; **— year** al año; **ten cents — dozen** diez centavos por docena (*o* diez centavos la docena).

per·cale [pɚkél] s. percal.

per·ceive [pɚsív] v. percibir.

per·cent·age [pɚsɛ́ntɪdʒ] s. porcentaje, tanto por ciento.

per·cep·ti·ble [pɚséptəbl] adj. perceptible.

per·cep·tion [pɚsépʃən] s. percepción.

per·cep·tive [pɚséptɪv] adj. perceptivo; sensible.

perch [pɝtʃ] s. percha (*para pájaros*); perca (*pez*); v. encaramar(se); posarse (*en una percha o rama*).

per·chance [pɚtʃǽns] adv. por ventura, acaso, quizás, tal vez.

per·co·late [pɝkəlet] v. filtrar(se), colar(se); rezumarse; penetrar.

per·cus·sion [pɝkʃən] s. percusión.

per·di·tion [pɚdíʃən] s. perdición.

per·en·ni·al [pɚénɪəl] adj. perenne; continuo; perpetuo.

per·fect [pɝfɪkt] adj. perfecto; completo; s. tiempo perfecto (*del verbo*); [pɚfékt] v. perfeccionar.

per·fec·tion [pɚfékʃən] s. perfección.

per·fid·i·ous [pɚfídɪəs] adj. pérfido.

per·fi·dy [pɝfədɪ] s. perfidia.

per·fo·rate [pɝfəret] v. perforar.

per·force [pɚfɔ́rs] adj. necesariamente; por fuerza.

per·form [pɚfɔ́rm] v. ejecutar; llevar a cabo, cumplir, hacer; cuncionar (*una máquina*); desempeñar o representar un papel.

per·form·ance [pɚfɔ́rməns] s. ejecución; desempeño; cumplimiento; funcionamiento (*de una máquina o motor*); función, representación; acto, acción; **— standard** norma de rendimiento.

per·fume [pɝfjum] s. perfume; [pɚfjúm] v. perfumar.

per·fum·er·y [pɚfjúmərɪ] s. perfumería; perfumes.

per·haps [pɚhǽps] adv. acaso, tal vez, quizá (*o* quizás), puede ser.

per·i·gee [pérədʒi] s. perigeo.

per·il [pérəl] s. peligro; riesgo; v. poner en peligro.

per·il·ous [pérələs] adj. peligroso.

pe·rim·e·ter [pərfmətɚ] s. perímetro.

pe·ri·od [pírɪəd] s. período; punto final; fin, término.

pe·ri·od·ic [pırıádɪk] adj. periódico.

pe·ri·od·i·cal [pırıádɪkl] adj. periódico; s. revista, publicación periódica.

pe·riph·er·al [pəˈffɚl] adj. periférico; (*computer*) s. periférico.

pe·riph·er·y [pɚffərɪ] s. periferia.

per·ish [pérɪʃ] v. perecer.

per·ish·a·ble [pérɪʃəbl] adj. perecedero; deleznable.

per·i·to·ne·um [perətəníəm] s. peritoneo.

per·i·to·ni·tis [perətənáıtıs] s. peritonitis.

per·jure [pɝdʒɚ] v. **to — oneself** perjurar.

per·ju·ry [pɝdʒrı] s. perjurio, juramento falso.

per·ma·nence [pɝmənəns] s. permanencia.

per·ma·nent [pɝmənənt] adj. permanente; duradero.

per·me·ate [pɝmiet] v. penetrar, saturar; (*scatter*) difundirse por, filtrarse por.

per·mis·si·ble [pɚmfsəbl] adj. lícito.

per·mis·sion [pɚmfʃən] s. permiso, licencia.

per·mis·sive [pɚmísıv] adj. permisivo.

per·mit [pɝmɪt] s. permiso, pase; licencia; [pɚmft] v. permitir.

per·mu·ta·tion [pɚmjutéʃən] s. permutación.

per·ni·cious [pɚnfʃəs] adj. pernicioso.

per·ox·ide [pəráksaıd] s. peróxido.

per·pen·dic·u·lar [pɝpəndfkjəlɚ] adj. & s. perpendicular.

per·pe·trate [pɝ́·pətret] v. perpetrar, cometar.

per·pet·u·al [pɚ·pétʃʊəl] adj. perpetuo.

per·pet·u·ate [pɚ·pétʃʊet] v. perpetuar.

per·plex [pɚ·pléks] v. confundir, turbar, aturdir.

per·plexed [pɚ·plékst] adj. perplejo, confuso.

per·plex·i·ty [pɚ·pléksətɪ] s. perplejidad, confusión.

per·se·cute [pɝ́·sɪkjut] v. perseguir, acosar.

per·se·cu·tion [pɝ·sɪkjúʃən] s. persecución.

per·se·cu·tor [pɝ·sɪkjutɚ] s. perseguidor.

per·se·ver·ance [pɝ·səvɪ́əns] s. perseverancia.

per·se·vere [pɝ·səvɪ́r] v. perseverar; persistir.

per·sist [pɚ·zíst] v. persistir; porfiar.

per·sist·ence [pɚ·zístəns] s. persistencia; porfía.

per·sist·ent [pɚ·zístənt] adj. persistente; porfiado.

per·son [pɝ́·sn̩] s. persona.

per·son·a·ble [pɝ́·sənəbl] adj. presentable; bien parecido.

per·son·age [pɝ́·snɪdʒ] s. personaje.

per·son·al [pɝ́·snl̩] adj. personal; en persona; — **property** bienes muebles.

per·son·al·ism [pɝ́·sənəlɪzm] s. personalismo.

per·son·al·i·ty [pɝ·snǽlətɪ] s. personalidad; persona, personaje; alusión personal.

per·son·nel [pɝ·snél] s. personal.

per·spec·tive [pɚ·spéktɪv] s. perspectiva; — **drawing** dibujo en perspectiva.

per·spi·ca·cious [pɚ·spɪkéʃəs] adj. perspicaz.

per·spi·ra·tion [pɝ·spəréʃən] s. sudor.

per·spire [pɚ·spáɪr] v. sudar.

per·suade [pɚ·swéd] v. persuadir.

per·sua·sion [pɚ·swéʒən] s. persuasión; creencia.

per·sua·sive [pɚ·swésɪv] adj. persuasivo.

pert [pɝt] adj. insolente, descarado, atrevido, *Am.* retobado.

per·tain [pɚ·tén] v. pertenecer; atañer.

per·ti·nent [pɝ·tnənt] adj. pertinente, a propósito, al caso.

per·turb [pɚ·tɝ́b] v. perturbar.

pe·rus·al [pərúzl] s. lectura.

pe·ruse [pərúz] v. leer con cuidado.

Pe·ru·vi·an [pərúvɪən] adj. & s. peruano.

per·vade [pɚ·véd] v. llenar, penetrar, difundirse por.

per·verse [pɚ·vɝ́s] adj. perverso; terco, obstinado.

per·vert [pɚ·vɝ́t] v. pervertir; (*twist*) falsear; [pɝ́·vɝt] s. perverso.

pes·si·mism [pésəmizəm] s. pesimismo.

pes·si·mist [pésəmɪst] s. pesimista; **-ic** adj. pesimista.

pest [pɛst] s. peste, plaga; pestilencia.

pes·ter [péstɚ] v. importunar, molestar.

pes·ti·cide [péstəsaɪd] s. & adj. insecticida.

pes·ti·lence [péstləns] s. pestilencia.

pet [pɛt] s. animal mimado, animal casero o domestico; (*child*) niño mimado; (*favorite*) favorito; adj. favorito; mimado; — **name** nombre de cariño (*por lo general diminutivo*); v. mimar, acariciar.

petal [pétl] s. pétalo.

pet·cock [pétkɑk] s. llave de desagüe (*purga*); *Méx.* bitoque.

pe·ti·tion [pətíʃən] s. petición, súplica; instancia, memorial, solicitud, *Ríopl.* ocurso; v. solicitar, pedir, dirigir una instancia o memorial a; suplicar, rogar.

pet·ri·fy [pétrɪfaɪ] v. petrificar.

pe·tro·le·um [pətrólɪəm] s. petróleo; — **products** productos petrolíferos.

pet·ti·coat [pétɪkot] s. enaguas.

pet·ty [pétɪ] adj. insignificante, pequeño; mezquino; inferior, subordinado; — **cash** fondos para gastos menores; caja menor; — **larceny** ratería; — **officer** oficial subordinado (*en la marina*); — **treason**

traición menor.

pe·tu·nia [pətúnjə] s. petunia.

pew [pju] s. banco de iglesia.

pha·lanx [félæŋks] s. falanje.

phan·tom [fǽntəm] s. fantasma.

phar·ma·cist [fɑ́rməsɪst] s. farmacéutico, boticario.

phar·ma·cy [fɑ́rməsɪ] s. farmacia, botica.

phar·ynx [fǽrɪŋks] s. faringe.

phase [fez] s. fase; v. **phase out** retirar por etapas.

pheas·ant [fézənt] s. faisán.

phe·nom·e·na [fənɑ́mənə] pl. de **phenomenon.**

phe·nom·e·non [fənɑ́mənən] s. fenómeno.

phi·lan·thro·py [fɪlǽnθrəpɪ] s. filantropía.

phi·lat·e·ly [fɪlǽtlɪ] s. filatelia.

phil·har·mon·ic [fɪlhɑrmɑ́nɪk] adj. filarmónico.

phi·lol·o·gy [fɪlɑ́lədʒɪ] s. filología.

phi·los·o·pher [fəlɑ́səfɚ] s. filósofo.

phil·o·soph·i·cal [fɪləsɑ́fɪkl] adj. filosófico.

phi·los·o·phy [fəlɑ́səfɪ] s. filosofía.

phlegm [flɛm] s. flema.

phone [fon] s. teléfono; v. telefonear.

pho·neme [fónim] s. fonema.

pho·net·ics [fonétɪks] s. fonética.

pho·no·graph [fónəgræf] s. fonógrafo.

pho·nol·o·gy [fonɑ́lədʒɪ] s. fonología.

phos·phate [fɑ́sfet] s. fosfato.

phos·pho·rus [fɑ́sfərəs] s. fósforo (*elemento quimico*).

pho·to [fóto] s. fotografía, retrato; (la) foto.

pho·to·e·lec·tric [fotoɪléktrɪk] fotoeléctrico.

pho·to·graph [fótəgræf] s. fotografía, retrato; v. fotografiar, retratar.

pho·tog·ra·pher [fətɑ́grəfɚ] s. fotógrafo.

pho·tog·ra·phy [fətɑ́grəfɪ] s. fotografía.

pho·to·syn·the·sis [fotosɪ́nθəsɪs] fotosíntesis.

phrase [frez] s. frase; expresión, locución; v. frasear; espresar, formular.

phys·ic [fízɪk] s. purga, purgante; v. purgar.

phys·i·cal [fízɪkl] adj. físico.

phy·si·cian [fəzíʃən] s. médico.

phys·i·cist [fízəsɪst] s. físico.

phys·ics [fízɪks] s. física.

phys·i·o·log·i·cal [fɪzɪəlɑ́dʒɪkl] adj. fisiológico.

phys·i·ol·o·gy [fɪzɪɑ́lədʒɪ] s. fisiología.

phy·sique [fɪzík] s. complexión, constitución física, talle, cuerpo.

pi·an·o [pɪǽno] s. piano; — **bench** banqueta de piano; — **stool** taburete de piano; **grand** — piano de cola; **upright** — piano vertical.

pic·a·resque [pɪkərésk] adj. picaresco.

pick [pɪk] v. (*choose*) escoger; coger; (*break*) picar; (*clean*) mondarse, limpiarse (*los dientes*); (*pluck*) desplumar (*un ave*); (*gnaw*) roer (*un hueso*); falsear (*una cerradura*); armar (*una pendencia*); **to — flaws** criticar, censurar; **to — out** escoger; **to — pockets** ratear; **to — up** recoger; **to — up speed** acelerar la marcha; **pick-proof** adj. a prueba de forzar; s. (*tool*) pico (*herramienta*); (*selection*) selección; lo selecto, lo mejor; (*collection*) recolección, cosecha; **ice —** punzón para romper hielo; **tooth —** mondadientes, palillo de dientes.

pick·ax [pɪ́kæks] s. pico, zapapico.

pick·et [pɪ́kɪt] s. piquete (*estaca o palo clavado en la tierra*); piquete (*vigilante huelguista*); piquete de soldados; v. estacionar piquetes cerca de (*una fábrica, campamento, etc.*); vigilar (*por medio de piquetes*); estar de guardia.

pick·le [pɪ́kl] s. encurtido; **to be in a —** hallarse en un aprieto; v. encurtir, escabechar; **-d cucumbers** pepinillos encurtidos; **-d fish** excabeche, pescado en escabeche.

pick·pock·et [pɪkpɑkɪt] *s*. rata (*m*.), ratero; *Méx., Ven., Col.* carterista.

pick·up truck [pɪkəptrʌk] *s*. picó.

pic·nic [pɪknɪk] *s*. partida de campo, día de campo, comida campestre, *Am*. picnic; *v*. hacer una comida campestre; ir a un picnic.

pic·ture [pɪktʃɚ] *s*. (*painting*) cuadro, pintura; (*portrait*) retrato; (*photo*) fotografía; (*engraving*) grabado; (*movie*) película; — **frame** marco; — **gallery** museo o galería de pinturas; *v*. pintar, dibujar; describir; imaginar(se).

pic·tur·esque [pɪktʃɚésk] *adj*. pintoresco.

pie [paɪ] *s*. pastel; empanada.

piece [pis] *s*. (*section*) pieza; pedazo; parte; sección (*passage*) trozo; (*song*) canción; — **of advice** consejo; — **of land** parcela; — **of money** moneda; — **of news** noticia; — **of nonsense** tontería; — **meal** en pedazos, a, pedazos, por partes; — **rate** precio (pago) por pieza; *v*. remendar; **to** — **between meals** comer a deshoras; **to** — **on to** juntar a, pegar a; **to** — **together** unir, pegar, juntar.

piece·work [píswɚk] *s*. trabajo por unidades.

pier [pɪr] *s*. muelle, embarcadero; (*breakwater*) rompeolas; pilar (*de puente o arco*).

pierce [pɪrs] *v*. atravesar, traspasar; taladrar, agujerar, perforar.

pi·e·ty [páɪətɪ] *s*. piedad, religiosidad.

pig [pɪg] *s*. puerco, cerdo, cochino; *S.A.* chancho; *C.A.* tunco; cuchi; *adj*. porcino; — **iron** hierro en lingotes; — **headed** cabezón, testarudo; **guinea** — conejillo de Indias; **suckling** — gorrino.

pi·geon [pídʒən] *s*. pichón; paloma.

pi·geon·hole [pídʒənhol] *s*. casilla; *v*. encasillar.

pig·ment [pígmənt] *s*. pigmento, color.

pig·my [pígmɪ] *s*. pigmeo.

pike [paɪk] *s*. pica, lanza; lucio (*pez*).

pile [paɪl] *s*. pila, montón; (*surface*) pelo (*de ciertos tejidos*); pilote; (*ailment*) **-s** almorranas (*enfermedad*); — **driver** martinete (*para clavar pilotes*); *v*. apilar(se), amontonar(se); acumular(se).

pil·fer [pɪlfɚ] *v*. pillar, retear, hurtar, sisar; **pilferage** hurto.

pil·grim [pílgrɪm] *s*. peregrino, romero.

pil·grim·age [pílgrəmɪdʒ] *s*. peregrinación, romería.

pill [pɪl] *s*. píldora; persona fastidiosa.

pil·lage [pílɪdʒ] *v*. pillar, saquear; *s*. pillaje, saqueo.

pil·lar [pílɚ] *s*. pilar, columna; **to go from** — **to post** ir de Ceca en Meca.

pil·low [pílo] *s*. almohada; cojín.

pil·low·case [píllokes] *s*. funda de almohada.

pi·lot [páɪlət] *s*. piloto; guía; timonel; — **light** (*o* — **burner**) mechero, encendedor (*de una cocina o estufa de gas*); **harbor** — prático de puerto; *v*. pilotar o pilotear; dirigir, guiar; *adj*. de ensayo.

pimp [pɪmp] *s*. alcahuete, puto.

pim·ple [pímpl] *s*. grano, barro.

pin [pɪn] *s*. alfiler; (*ornament*) prendedor; (*spike*) espiga; (*bowling*) bolo (*del juego de bolos*); — **money** dinero para alfileres; — **wheel** molinete, *Am*. remolino; **breast** — broche; **safety** — imperdible; (*computer*) pata; (*printing*) espiga; *v*. prender (*con alfiler*); asegurar, fijar, clavar; **to** — **down** fijar, inmovilizar; hacer dar una contestación definitiva; **to** — **one's hope to** poner toda su esperanza en; **to** — **up** prender con alfileres; colgar (*un dibujo o retrato*), fijar con tachuelas.

pin·cers [pínsɚz] *s. pl*. pinzas; tenazas; **small** — tenacillas.

pinch [pɪntʃ] *v*. (*squeeze*) pellizcar; apretar; (*economize*) economizar; (*arrest*) prender, arrestar;

to — **one's finger in the door** machucarse el dedo en la puerta; — **hit** batear de emergente; sustituir a otro en un apuro; *s*. pellizco; pizca, proción pequeña; punzada, dolor agudo; aprieto, apuro; — **hitter** suplente, sustituto.

pin·chers [píntʃɚz] = **pincers.**

pine [paɪn] *s*. pino; — **cone** piña; — **grove** pinar; — **nut** piñon; *v*. languidecer; **to** — **away** consumirse; **to** — **for** anhelar, suspirar por.

pine·ap·ple [páɪnæpl] *s*. piña, *S.A.* ananá, ananás.

pin·ion [pínjən] *s*. piñón.

pink [pɪŋk] *s*. clavel; color de rosa; **in the** — **of condition** en la major condición; *adj*. rosado, color de rosa.

pin·na·cle [pínəkl] *s*. pináculo, cumbre.

pint [paɪnt] *s*. pinta (*aproximadamente medio litro*).

pi·o·neer [paɪənfr] *s*. explorador, colonizador; fundador, iniciador, precursor; pionero; *v*. explorar, colonizar; fundar, promover.

pi·ous [páɪəs] *adj*. pío, piadoso.

pipe [paɪp] *s*. pipa (*de fumar*); tubo, caño; cañon (*de órgano*); caramillo, flauta; — **line** cañería, tubería; oleoducto (*petróleo*); *v*. conducir por cañerías; desaguar por cañería; proveer de tuberías o cañerías; chillar; **to** — **down** bajar la voz.

pip·er [páɪpɚ] *s*. (*bagpipe*) gaitero, (*flute*) flautista.

pip·ing [páɪpɪŋ] *s*. cañería, tubería; (*clothes*) cordoncillo (*de adorno para costuras*); chillido, silbido; *adj*. agudo, chillón; — **hot** muy caliente; hirviendo.

pip·pin [pípɪn] *s*. camuesa.

pique [pik] *s*. enojo, resentimiento; *v*. picar, excitar; enojar, irritar; **to** — **oneself on** picarse de, preciarse de.

pi·rate [páɪrət] *s*. pirata; *v*. piratear; plagiar.

pis·tol [pístl] *s*. pistola; revólver.

pis·ton [pístn] *s*. pistón, émbolo; — **ring** aro de pistón; — **rod** vástago del émbolo.

pit [pɪt] *s*. hoyo; foso; hueso (*de ciertas frutas*); — **of the stomach** boca del estómago.

pitch [pɪtʃ] *s*. (*throw*) tiro, lanzamiento (*de una pelota*); cabezada (*de un barco*); (*music*) diapasón, tono; (*inclination*) grado, declive, grado de inclinación; (*printing*) espacio; pez (*f*.), brea; resina; — **dark** oscurísimo; *v*. tirar, lanzar, arrojar; cabecear (*un barco*); graduar el tono de (*un instrumento o voz*); echarse de cabeza; inclinarse; **to** — **a tent** armar una tienda de campaña; acampar; **to** — **into** arremeter contra; reprender, regañar; — **in!** ¡manos a la obra!

pitch·er [pítʃɚ] *s*. cántaro, jarro *o* jarra; tirador, lanzador (*en béisbol*).

pitch·fork [pítʃfɔrk] *s*. horca, horquilla (*para hacinar las mieses, levantar la paja, etc.*).

pit·e·ous [pítɪəs] *adj*. lastimero, lastimoso.

pit·fall [pítfɔl] *s*. trampa, escollo.

pith [pɪθ] *s*. meollo, médula; (*essence*) esencia, sustancia.

pit·i·ful [pítɪfəl] *adj*. lastimoso, lamentable; miserable.

pit·i·less [pítɪlɪs] *adj*. despiadado, incompasivo, cruel.

pit·y [pítɪ] *s*. piedad; lástima; compasión; **for -'s sake** por piedad, por Dios; **what a** — ! ¡qué lástima!; *v*. compadecer; tener lástima por; apiadarse de, tener piedad de.

pix·el [píksl] *s*. (*computer*) punto, pixel.

plac·ard [plǽkɑrd] *s*. letrero, cartel; *v*. fijar carteles.

place [ples] *s*. (*site*) lugar, sitio; localidad; (*position*) puesto; empleo; posición; *Col*. cupo; — **of business** oficina, despacho; — **of worship** templo,

iglesia; **market** — plaza, mercado; **in** — **of** en
lugar de, en vez de; **it is not my** — **to do it** no es
mi deber hacerlo, no me toca a mí hacerlo; *v.*
colocar; situar; poner; acomodar, dar empleo a.

pla·cid [plǽsɪd] *adj.* plácido, apacible, sosegado.

pla·gia·rism [plédʒərɪzəm] *s.* plagio.

plague [pleg] *s.* plaga; peste, pestilencia; calamidad;
v. plagar, infestar; importunar.

plaid [plæd] *s.* tartán, tela a cuadros; (*scotch*) manta
escocesa a cuadros; diseño a cuadros; *adj.* a
cuadros.

plain [plen] *adj.* (*flat*) llano; (*simple*) sencillo; claro;
franco; ordinario; — **fool** tonto de capirote; —
woman mujer sin atractivo; **in** — **sight** en plena
vista; **plain-clothes man** detectivo; *adv.*
claramente; — **stupid** completamente estúpido;
plain-spoken franco, francote, sincero; *s.* llano,
llanura.

plain·tiff [pléntɪf] *s.* demandante.

plain·tive [pléntɪv] *adj.* lastimero, triste.

plan [plæn] *s.* plan; proyecto; (*map*) plano (*dibujo o
mapa*); *v.* planear, proyectar, idear; pensar,
proponerse; **planning** planeamiento; planificación.

plane [plen] *s.* (*airplane*) avión; aeroplano; (*surface*)
plano, superficie plana; (*tool*) cepillo (*de
carpintero*); *adj.* plano, llano; — **tree** plátano
falso; *v.* acepillar, alisar con cepillo (*la madera o
los metales*).

plan·et [plǽnɪt] *s.* planeta.

plan·e·tar·i·um [plænətériəm] *s.* planetario.

plank [plæŋk] *s.* table, tablón; (*tenet*) principio, base
(*del programa de un partido político*); *v.* entablar,
entarimar, cubrir con tablas; (*broil*) asar (*carne*) en
una tabla.

plank·ton [plǽŋktən] *s.* plancton.

plant [plænt] *s.* (*vegetation*) planta; (*industry*)
fábrica; taller; *v.* plantar; sembrar; implantar;
establecer.

plan·ta·tion [plæntéʃən] *s.* plantación; hacienda
plantío; sembrado; **coffee** — cafetal; **cotton** —
algodonal; **rubber** — cauchal; **sugar** — ingenio
de azúcar.

plant·er [plǽntɚ] *s.* plantador, cultivador.

plaque [plæk] *s.* placa.

plas·ma [plǽzmə] *s.* plasma.

plas·ter [plǽstɚ] *s.* yeso; emplasto; — **of Paris**
yeso, yeso mate; **court** — esparadrapo, tafetán
inglés; **mustard** — sinapismo; *v.* enyesar;
emplastar, poner emplastos a; pegar (*carteles,
anuncios*); embarrar.

plas·tic [plǽstɪk] *adj.* plástico.

plat [plæt] *s.* plano; parcela; *v.* levantar o trazar un
plano.

plate [plet] *s.* (*eating*) plato; (*metal*) placa; plancha;
lámina; **dental** — dentadura postiza; *v.* platear;
dorar; niquelar; blindar, proteger con planchas de
metal; laminar.

pla·teau [plætó] *s.* antiplanicie, mesa, meseta.

plat·ed [plétəd] *adj.* chapeado; (*armored*) blindado.

plate·ful [plétfʊl] *s.* plato, plato lleno.

plat·en [plǽtən] *s.* (*computer*) rodillo; — **knob**
perilla del rodillo.

plat·form [plǽtfɔrm] *s.* plataforma; tablado;
programa de un partido político; **railway** — andén.

plat·i·num [plǽtnəm] *s.* platino.

plat·i·tude [plǽtətjud] *s.* lugar común, perogrullada.

plat·ter [plǽtɚ] *s.* platel, platón.

play [ple] *v.* (*game*) jugar; juguetear; (*instrument*)
tocar; (*drama*) representar; hacer, desempeñar (*un
papel*); manipular (*un instrumento, radio,
fonógrafo, etc.*); **to** — **a joke** hacer una broma,

dar un chasco; **to** — **cards** jugar a los naipes,
jugar a la baraja; **to** — **havoc** hacer estragos,
causar daño; **to** — **tennis** jugar al tenis; **to** — **the
fool** hacerse el tonto, fingirse tonto; **to be all -ed
out** no poder más, estar agotado; *s.* juego; jugada
(*acción, movimiento en un juego*); pieza, drama,
comedia, representación; recreación, diversión; —
on words juego de palabras, equívoco; **to give full**
— **to** dar rienda suelta a.

play·er [pléɚ] *s.* (*games*) jugador; (*music*) músico;
(*plays*) cómico, actor; artista; — **piano** piano
mecánico, pianola; **piano** — pianista; **violin** —
violinista.

play·ful [pléfəl] *adj.* juguetón, retozón; bromista.

play·ground [plégraʊnd] *s.* campo o patio de recreo.

play·mate [plémet] *s.* compañero de juego.

play·thing [plé θɪŋ] *s.* juguete.

play·wright [pléraɪt] *s.* dramático, dramaturgo.

plea [pli] *s.* suplica; ruego; alegato, defensa;
pretexto; **on the** — **that** con el pretexto de que.

plead [plid] *v.* abogar; suplicar; argüir; alegar;
defender (*una causa*); **to** — **guilty** declararse o
confesarse culpable.

pleas·ant [plézṇt] *adj.* grato; agradable; simpático.

pleas·ant·ry [plézṇtrɪ] *s.* chanza, broma, chiste,
humorado.

please [pliz] *v.* agradar, gustar, dar gusto a;
complacer; — **do it** haga Vd. el favor de hacerlo,
tenga Vd. la bondad de hacerlo, sírvase hacerlo; **as
you** — como Vd. quiera, como Vd. guste; **if you**
— si me hace Vd. (el) favor; **to be -ed to**
complacerse en, tener gusto en; alegrarse de; **to be
-ed with** gustarle a uno, estar satisfecho de (*o*
con).

pleas·ing [plízɪŋ] *adj.* agradable.

pleas·ure [pléʒɚ] *s.* placer, gusto; deleite, alegría,
gozo; — **trip** viaje de recreo; **what is your** — ?
¿qué deseaba Vd.? ¿en qué puedo servirle?

pleat [plit] *s.* pliegue, doblez; *v.* plegar, hacer
pliegues (en).

ple·be·ian [plɪbíən] *adj.* & *s.* plebeyo.

pledge [pledʒ] *s.* promesa; prenda (*garantía*); arras,
compromiso, fianza; **as a** — **of** en prenda de; *v.*
prometer; empeñar, dar en prenda; hacer firmar una
promesa; **to** — **one's word** empeñar (*o* dar) su
palabra; **to** — **to secrecy** exigir promesa de sigilo.

ple·na·ry [plénɔrɪ] *adj.* plenario.

plen·i·po·ten·ti·ar·y [plɛnəpətɛ́nʃərɪ] *adj.* & *s.*
plenipotenciario.

plen·ti·ful [pléntɪfəl] *adj.* abundante, copioso.

plen·ty [pléntɪ] *s.* abundancia, copia; — **of time**
bastante tiempo; **that is** — con eso basta; basta.

pleu·ri·sy [plúrəsɪ] *s.* pleuresía.

pli·a·ble [pláɪəbl̩] *adj.* flexible; manejable, (*docile*)
dócil; transigénte.

pli·ant [pláɪənt] *adj.* flexible; dócil, sumiso.

pli·ers [pláɪɚz] *s. pl.* alicates, tenazas.

plight [plaɪt] *s.* apuro, aprieto, situación difícil.

plod [plɑd] *v.* bregar, trafagar, afanarse, trabajar
asiduamente.

plo·sive [plósɪv] *adj.* & *s.* oclusivo.

plot [plɑt] *s.* (*outline*) trama, enredo; argumento;
(*conspiracy*) complot, conspiración; conjuración;
(*land*) parcela (*de tierra*), solar; (*plan*) plano,
diagrama; *v.* tramar, urdir; maquinar, conspirar;
dibujar, hacer el plano o diagrama de; **to** — **a
curve** hacer una gráfica.

plot·ter [plɑtɚ] *s.* conspirador; tramador; conjurado;
(*computer*) impresora gráfica, trazador gráfico.

plough = **plow.**

plow [plaʊ] *s.* arado; — **share** reja de arado; *v.* arar;

surcar.

pluck [plʌk] *v.* coger; arrancar; (*pick*) desplumar (*un ave*); puntear (*las cuerdas de una guitarra*); **to —at** tirar de; **to — up** arrancar; cobrar ánimo; *s.* ánimo, valor; tirón.

pluck·y [plʌkɪ] *adj.* valeroso, animoso.

plug [plʌg] *s.* (*stopper*) taco, tapón; (*horse*) caballejo, penco; (*boost*) elogio incidental (*de un producto comercial o de una persona*); **— of tobacco** tableta de tabaco; **electric —** clavija de conexión; **— strip** toma de corriente múltiple; **fire —** boca de agua para incendios; **spark —** bujía; *v.* tapar; **to — along** afanarse, atarearse; **to — in** enchufar, conectar; **to — up** tapar, obstruir.

plum [plʌm] *s.* (*fruit*) ciruela; (*prize*) la cosa mejor; la mejor colocación; **— pudding** pudín inglés con pasas; **— tree** circuelo.

plum·age [plúmɪdʒ] *s.* plumaje.

plumb [plʌm] *s.* plomo, pesa de plomo; (*sounding line*) sonda; **out of —** no vertical; *adj.* vertical, a plomo, recto; **— bob** plomo, plomada; *adv.* a plomo, verticalmente; **— crazy** completamente loco; *v.* sondear; aplomar (*una pared*).

plumb·er [plʌmɚ] *s.* plomero.

plumb·ing [plʌmɪŋ] *s.* plomería; cañerías (*de un edificio*); oficio de plomero.

plume [plum] *s.* pluma; plumaje; penacho; *v.* adornar con plumas; **to — its wing** alisarse o componerse el plumaje del ala.

plump [plʌmp] *adj.* rechoncho, regordete, rollizo; *adv.* de golpe; *v.* **to — down** dejar(se) caer; desplomarse, sentarse de golpe.

plun·der [plʌndɚ] *s.* pillaje, saqueo; botín; *v.* pillar; saquear.

plunge [plʌndʒ] *v.* zambullir(se), sumergir(se); hundir(se); lanzar(se), arrojar(se), precipitar(se); **to — headlong** echarse de cabeza; *s.* zambullida; salto (*de arriba abajo*).

plunk [plʌŋk] *v.* (*instrument*) puntear; (*place*) arrojar.

plu·ral [plúrəl] *adj. & s.* plural.

plu·ral·i·ty [plurǽlɪtɪ] *s.* pluralidad.

plus [plʌs] *s.* más, signo más; **— quantity** cantidad positiva; **two — three** dos más tres.

plush [plʌʃ] *s.* felpa; velludo.

Plu·to [plúto] *s.* Plutón.

plu·ton·ic [plutánɪk] *adj.* plutónico.

ply [plaɪ] *v.* (*use*) manejar con tesón (*un instrumento o herramienta*); (*ask*) importunar (*con preguntas*); (*run*) hacer con regularidad un recorrido (*entre dos puntos*); **to — a trade** seguir o ejercer un oficio; **to — oneself with** saturarse de, rellenarse de; *s.* doblez, pliegue; capa (*de tejido, goma, etc.*); **three-ply** *Méx.* triplay.

pneu·mat·ic [njumǽtik] *adj.* neumático.

pneu·mo·nia [njumónjə] *s.* pulmonía.

poach [potʃ] *v.* (*eggs*) escalfar (*huevos*); (*invade*) invadir (*un vedado*); cazar o pescar en vedado; (*rob*) robar caza o pesca (*de un vedado*).

pock·et [pákɪt] *s.* bolsillo, faltriquera, *C.A.* bolsa; tronera (*de billar*); cavidad; hoyo; *v.* embolsarse; apropiarse; ocultar (*el orgullo o rencor*); aguantar (*un insulto*).

pock·et·book [pákɪtbʊk] *s.* cartera; portamonedas; **woman's — bolsa.**

pock·et·knife [pákɪtnaɪf] *s.* navaja; cortaplumas.

pod [pad] *s.* vaina (*de guisante, frijol, etc.*).

po·di·um [pódɪəm] *s.* podio.

po·em [póɪm] *s.* poema, poesía.

po·et [póɪt] *s.* poeta; vate.

po·et·ess [póɪtɪs] *s.* poetisa.

po·et·ic [poétɪk] *adj.* poético; **-s** *s.* arte poética, poética.

po·et·i·cal [poétɪkl] *adj.* poético.

po·et·ry [póɪtrɪ] *s.* poesía.

poign·ant [pɔ́ɪnjənt] *adj.* intenso; (*spicy*) picante.

point [pɔɪnt] *s.* (*place*) punto; punta (*de lápiz, espada, tierra, etc.*); **it is not to the —** no viene al caso; **not to see the —** no caer en la cuenta; no ver el chiste, propósito o intención; **on the — of** a punto de; *v.* apuntar; señalar; indicar; **to — out** señalar, mostrar, indicar.

point-blank [pɔ́ɪntblæŋk] *adj.* a quema ropa.

point·ed [pɔ́ɪntɪd] *adj.* puntiagudo, agudo; satírico; apto; a propósito, al caso; **— arch** arco apuntado, arco ojival.

point·er [pɔ́ɪntɚ] *s.* (*indicator*) puntero; indicador, señalador; (*dog*) perro de punta y vuelta; (*advice*) indicación, consejo.

poise [pɔɪz] *s.* equilibrio; porte, compostura; *v.* equilibrar(se); balancear(se).

poi·son [pɔ́ɪzn̩] *s.* veneno; ponzoña; *v.* envenenar, emponzoñar.

poi·son·ous [pɔ́ɪznəs] *adj.* venenoso, ponzoñoso.

poke [pok] *v.* atizar, remover (*el fuego*); picar (*con el dedo o cualquier objeto puntiagudo*); **to — along** andar perezosamente; **to — around** husmear, curiosear; **to — fun at** burlarse de; **to — into** meter en; **to — out** sacar; poryectarse; *s.* pinchazo; piquete; codazo; aguijonada; **slow —** tardón.

po·lar [pólɚ] *adj.* polar; **— bear** oso blanco.

po·lar·i·ty [polérɪtɪ] *s.* polaridad.

po·lar·i·za·tion [polərɪzéʃən] *s.* polarización.

pole [pol] *s.* (*utility*) poste; (*stick*) pértiga, palo largo; (*flag*) asta (*de bandera*); garrocha; polo; **Pole** polaco; **north —** polo norte; polo ártico; **south —** polo sur, polo antártico; **— vault** salto con garrocha (pértiga).

po·lem·ics [polémɪks] *s.* polémica.

po·lice [pəlís] *s.* policía; *v.* vigilar; guardar el orden; *adj.* policíaco.

po·lice·man [pəlísmən] *s.* policía (*m.*), guardia de policía, polizonte, agente; *Ven., Col.* vigilante; *Méx.* gendarme; *Ch.* carabinero.

pol·i·cy [páləsɪ] *s.* política; **insurance —** póliza de seguro.

Po·lish [pólɪʃ] *adj.* polaco; *s.* polaco, idioma polaco.

pol·ish [pálɪʃ] *s.* pulimento; lustre, brillo; (*cultural*) urbanidad, cultura; **shoe —** betún, bola; *v.* pulir, pulimentar; dar brillo o lustre a; embolar, dar bola o brillo a (*zapatos*); *adj.* pulidor.

po·lite [pəláɪt] *adj.* cortés, fino, urbano, político.

po·lite·ness [pəláɪtnɪs] *s.* cortesía; fineza, urbanidad.

pol·i·tic [pálətɪk] *adj.* político, prudente, conveniente.

po·lit·i·cal [pəlítɪkl] *adj.* político.

pol·i·ti·cian [palətíʃən] *s.* político; (*bad*) politicastro.

pol·i·tics [pálətɪks] *s.* política.

poll [pol] *s.* (*voters*) votación; lista electoral; **-s** comicios; (*places*) urnas electorales; casilla (*donde se vota*); **— tax** impuesto (*de tanto por cabeza*); (*survey*) encuesta; *v.* registrar los votos de; votar; recibir (*votos*).

pol·len [pálən] *s.* polen.

pol·li·nate [pálənet] *v.* polinizar.

po·lo [pólo] *s.* polo.

po·lo·ni·um [pəlóniəm] *s.* polonio.

pol·y·glot [pálɪglat] *s.* políglota.

pome·gran·ate [pámgrænɪt] *s.* granada; **— tree** granado.

pomp [pamp] *s.* pompa, boato.

pom·pous [pámpəs] *adj.* pomposa, ostentoso.

pond [pand] *s.* charca; estanque; **fish —** vivero.

pon·der [pándɚ] *v.* ponderar, pesar, examinar; **to —
over** reflexionar.

pon·der·ous [pándɚes] *adj.* ponderoso; pesado.

pon·toon [pɑntún] *s.* pontón, chata, barco chato;
flotador (*de hidroavión*); **— bridge** pontón, puente
flotante.

po·ny [póni] *s.* caballito, potrillo; (*key*) clave o
traducción (*usada ilícitamente en un examen*).

poo·dle [púdl] *s.* perro de lanas.

pool [pul] *s.* ˙charco; charca; (*game*) trucos (*juego
parecido al billar*); (*bets*) polla o puesta (*en ciertos
juegos*); fondos en común, combinación de fondos
(*para una empresa o para especular*); "trust";
swimming — piscina; *v.* formar una polla;
combinar fondos.

poor [pur] *adj.* pobre; malo; de mala calidad; **—
student** estudiante pobre; mal estudiante; **— little
thing** pobrecito; **the —** los pobres; **-ly** *adv.*
pobremente; mal.

poor·house [púrhaus] *s.* hospicio, casa de pobres.

pop [pɑp] *s.* tronido, estallido; detonación;
— of a cork taponazo; **soda —** gaseosa; *v.*
reventar, estallar; detonar; saltar (*un tapón*); **to —
a question** espetar una pregunta; **to — corn** hacer
palomitas de maíz, hacer rosetas de maíz; **to — in
and out** entrar y salir de sopetón; **to — one's
head out** sacar o asomar de repente la cabeza.

pop·corn [pápkɔrn] *s.* rosetas, palomitas de maíz,
Andes alborotos; *Ch.* cabritas; *Méx.* esquite.

Pope [pop] *s.* Papa.

pop·eyed [pápaid] *adj.* de ojos saltones, *Am.*
desorbitado.

pop·lar [páplɚ] *s.* álamo; **black —** chopo; **— grove**
alameda.

pop·py [pápi] *s.* amapola.

pop·u·lace [pápjəlıs] *s.* pueblo, populacho.

pop·u·lar [pápjəlɚ] *adj.* popular.

pop·u·lar·i·ty [pɑpjəlǽrətı] *s.* popularidad.

pop·u·late [pápjələt] *v.* poblar.

pop·u·la·tion [pɑpjeléʃən] *s.* población.

pop·u·lous [pápjələs] *adj.* populoso.

por·ce·lain [pɔ́rslın] *s.* porcelana.

porch [pɔrtʃ] *s.* pórtico, porche; galería.

por·cu·pine [pɔ́rkjəpaın] *s.* puerco espín.

pore [pɔr] *s.* poro; *v.* **to — over a book** engolfarse
en la lectura.

pork [pɔrk] *s.* puerco, carne de puerco **— chop**
chulete de puerco; **salt —** tocino salado.

por·nog·ra·phy [pɔrnágrəfı] *s.* pornografía.

po·rous [pórəs] *adj.* poroso.

por·ridge [pórıdʒ] *s.* potaje, gachas.

port [pɔrt] *s.* (*harbor*) puerto; (*wine*) oporto; (*left
side*) babor (*de un barco*); (*computer*) canal de
acceso, conector; **— hole** porta, portilla;**— of call**
escala, puerto de escala; **— of entry** puerto
aduanero.

port·a·ble [pɔ́rtəbl] *adj.* portátil.

por·tal [pɔ́rtl] *s.* portal.

por·tent [pɔ́tɛnt] *s.* portento, presagio, agüero.

por·ten·tous [pɔrtɛ́ntəs] *adj.* portentoso; prodigioso;
de mal agüero.

por·ter [pɔ́rtɚ] *s.* moso de cordel, *Méx.*, *C.A.*
cargador; *Ríopl.* changador; (*pullman*) camarero
(*en un coche-cama*); portero.

port·fo·li·o [pɔrtfólıo] *s.* portafolio, cartera; carpeta;
ministerio.

por·tion [pɔ́rʃən] *s.* porción; *v.* repartir.

port·ly [pɔ́rtlı] *adj.* corpulento.

por·trait [pɔ́rtret] *s.* retrato.

por·tray [pɔrtré] *v.* retratar, pintar, dibujar,
representar.

por·tray·al [pɔrtreəl] *s.* retrato, delineación,
delineamiento, representación.

Por·tu·guese [pɔ́rtʃəgiz] *adj.* & *s.* portugués.

pose [poz] *s.* (*posture*) postura, actitud; (*affected
attitude*) afectación; *v.* posar (*como modelo*);
colocar(se), en cierta postura; afectar una actitud o
postura; proponer, plantear (*una cuestión o
problema*); **to — as** fingirse, hacerse pasar por.

po·si·tion [pəzíʃən] *s.* posición; postura; situación,
empleo, puesto.

pos·i·tive [pázətıv] *adj.* positivo; cierto, seguro;
categórico; dogmático.

pos·sess [pəzɛ́s] *v.* poseer.

pos·ses·sion [pəzɛ́ʃən] *s.* posesión.

pos·ses·sive [pəzɛ́sıv] *adj.* & *s.* posesivo.

pos·ses·sor [pəzɛ́sɚ] *s.* poseedor, posesor, dueño.

pos·si·bil·i·ty [pɑsəbílətı] *s.* posibilidad.

pos·si·ble [pásəbl] *adj.* posible; **possibly** *adv.*
posiblemente; acaso, tal vez.

post [post] *s.* (*pole*) poste, pilar; (*position*) puesto;
empleo; **army —** guarnición militar; **— haste** por
la posta, rápidamente; **— office** correo, casa de
correos; **post-office box** apartado, casilla postal;
paid porte pagado, franco de porte; *v.* fijar
(*anuncios, carteles*); anunciar; (*list*) poner en lista;
(*bet*) apostar, (*place*) situar; (*mail*) echar al correo;
to — an entry asentar o hacer un asiento (*en
teneduría*); **to be well -ed** estar al corriente, estar
bien enterado.

post·age [póstıdʒ] *s.* porte, franqueo; **— stamp** sello
de correo, *Am.* estampilla, *Méx.*, *Ríopl*; timbre; **—
meter** franqueadora.

post·al [póstl] *adj.* postal; **— card** tarjeta postal; **—
money order** giro postal.

post·card [póstkard] *s.* tarjeta postal.

post·er [póstɚ] *s.* cartel, cartelón; *Arg.*, *Col.* afiche;
fijador de carteles.

pos·te·ri·or [pastírıɚ] *adj.* posterior; trasero.

pos·ter·i·ty [pastɛ́rətı] *s.* posteridad.

post·hu·mous [pástʃuməs] *adj.* póstumo.

post·man [póstmən] *s.* cartero.

post·mas·ter [póstmæstɚ] *s.* administrador de
correos.

post·pone [postpón] *v.* posponer; aplazar, diferir;
postergar.

post·pone·ment [postpónmənt] *s.* aplazamiento.

post·script [pósskrıpt] *s.* posdata.

pos·ture [pástʃɚ] *s.* postura, actitud; posición; *v.*
adoptar una postura.

po·sy [pózı] *s.* flor.

pot [pɑt] *s.* pote; olla, puchero, cacharro (*de cocina*);
(*chamber*) bacín, bacinica (*de cámara o
recámara*); **flower —** tiesto, maceta; **— bellied**
panzudo, barrigón; **— hole** bache.

po·tas·si·um [pətǽsıəm] *s.* potasio.

po·ta·to [pətéto] *s.* patata, papa; **sweet —** *Carib.*,
Esp. batata, *Méx.*, *C.A.*, *Ch.*, *Andes* camote,
Carib., *Ríopl.* boniato.

po·ten·cy [pótnsı] *s.* potencia, poder, fuerza.

po·tent [pótnt] *adj.* potente, poderoso, fuerte.

po·ten·tate [pótntet] *s.* potentado.

po·ten·tial [pətɛ́nʃəl] *adj.* & *s.* potencial.

pot·pour·ri [popurí] *s.* popurrí.

pot·tage [pátıdʒ] *s.* potaje.

pot·ter [pátɚ] *s.* alfarero, fabricante de loza o
cacharros de barro; **-'s field** cementerio de pobres y
desconocidos.

pot·ter·y [pátərı] *s.* cerámica, alfarería; loza; vasijas
de barro.

pouch [pautʃ] *s.* bolsa, saquillo; **mail —** valija;
tobacco — tabaquera, petaca.

poul·tice [póltɪs] *s.* emplasto.
poul·try [póltrɪ] *s.* aves de corral.
pounce [paʊns] *s.* salto *(para agarrar)*; zarpada; *v.*
  to — into entrar de sopetón; **to — upon**
  abalanzarse sobre, saltar sobre, agarrar.
pound [paʊnd] *s.* libra; golpazo; **— sterling** libra
  esterlina; *v.* golpear; machacar, martillar.
pour [por] *v.* vaciar, verter; *(serve)* servir *(una taza)*;
  (flow) fluir; *(rain)* llover a cántaros, llover recio.
pout [paʊt] *v.* hacer pucheros, lloriquear; poner cara
  de enfado; *s.* puchero, pucherito.
pov·er·ty [pávɚtɪ] *s.* pobreza.
pow·der [páʊdɚ] *s.* polvo; pólvora *(explosivo)*;
  polvos *(de tocador)*; **— compact** polvera; **—**
  magazine polvorín; **— puff** polvera, borla, *Ríopl.,*
  Ch. cisne, *Méx., Andes, Col., Ven.* mota; *v.*
  empolvar(se); polvorear, espolvorear;
  pulverizar(se); **to — one's face** empolvarse la
  cara, ponerse polvos.
pow·er [páʊɚ] *s.* poder; poderío; potencia; fuerza;
  motive — fuerza motriz; **— of attorney** poder; **—**
  plant planta de fuerza motriz; planta generadora,
  central eléctrica, luz y fuerza.
pow·er·ful [páʊɚfəl] *adj.* poderoso.
pow·er·less [páʊɚlɪs] *adj.* impotente.
prac·ti·ca·ble [præktɪkəbl] *adj.* practicable; factible;
  hacedero; práctico; **— road** camino transitable.
prac·ti·cal [præktɪkl] *adj.* práctico; **— joke** chasco,
  burla pesada; **-ly** *adv.* casi, virtualmente;
  realmente, en realidad; prácticamente.
prac·tice [præktɪs] *s.* práctica; *(carry on)* ejercicio
  (de una profesión); método; regla, costumbre;
  (clientele) clientela; *v.* practicar; ejercer *(una*
  profesión); ejercitarse.
prac·ticed [præktɪst] *adj.* práctico, experimentado;
  experto, perito.
prac·ti·tion·er [præktíʃənɚ] *s.* profesional; práctico.
prai·rie [prɛrɪ] *s.* pradera, llanura.
praise [prez] *s.* alabanza; elogio; encomio; *v.* alabar;
  elogiar; encomiar.
praise·wor·thy [prézwɚðɪ] *adj.* laudable.
prance [præns] *v.* cabriolar, hacer cabriolas.
prank [præŋk] *s.* travesura, burla; **to play -s** hacer
  travesuras.
prate [pret] *v.* parlotear, charlar; *s.* parloteo, charla.
prat·tle [prætl] *v.* parlotear, charlar; *s.* parloteo,
  charla.
pray [pre] *v.* *(religious)* orar, rezar; *(beg)* rogar,
  suplicar; **— tell me** dígame por favor, le ruego que
  me diga.
prayer [prɛr] *s.* oración, rezo; ruego, súplica; **—**
  book devocionario; **Lord's —** Padre Nuestro.
preach [pritʃ] *v.* predicar; sermonear.
preach·er [prítʃɚ] *s.* predicador.
preach·ing [prítʃɪŋ] *s.* predicación; sermón;
  sermoneo.
pre·am·ble [príæmbl] *s.* preámbulo.
pre·ar·ranged [priɚréndʒd] *adj.* arreglado de
  antemano.
pre·car·i·ous [prɪkɛrɪəs] *adj.* precario; inseguro.
pre·cau·tion [prɪkɔ́ʃən] *s.* precaución.
pre·cede [prisíd] *v.* preceder.
pre·ce·dence [prisídns] *s.* precedencia; prioridad.
pre·ce·dent [présədənt] *s.* precedente.
pre·ced·ing [prisídɪŋ] *adj.* precedente, anterior.
pre·cept [prísɛpt] *s.* precepto.
pre·cinct [prísɪŋkt] *s.* distrito; recinto; **-s** límites,
  inmediaciones.
pre·cious [préʃəs] *adj.* precioso; querido, amado,
  caro; **— little** poquísimo, muy poco.
prec·i·pice [présəpɪs] *s.* precipicio.

pre·cip·i·tate [prɪsípətet] *v.* precipitar(se); *adj.*
  precipitado, apresurado, atropellado; *s.* precipitado.
pre·cip·i·ta·tion [prɪsɪpətéʃən] *s.* precipitación; lluvia
  (o nieve, rocío, granizo, *etc.)*; cantidad de agua
  pluvial.
pre·cip·i·tous [prɪsípətəs] *adj.* precipitoso, excarpado;
  precipitado.
pre·cise [prɪsáɪs] *adj.* preciso, exacto.
pre·ci·sion [prɪsíʒən] *s.* precisión, exactitud.
pre·clude [prɪklúd] *v.* excluir; impedir.
pre·co·cious [prɪkóʃəs] *adj.* precoz.
pre·cur·sor [prikɚsɚ] *s.* precursor.
pred·e·ces·sor [prɛdɪsɛsɚ] *s.* predecesor.
pre·des·tine [prɪdéstɪn] *v.* predestinar.
pre·dic·a·ment [prɪdíkəmənt] *s.* aprieto, apuro,
  dificultad.
pred·i·cate [prédɪkɪt] *adj. & s.* predicado.
pre·dict [prɪdíkt] *v.* predecir, vaticinar.
pre·dic·tion [prɪdíkʃən] *s.* predicción, pronóstico,
  vaticinio.
pre·di·lec·tion [pridlékʃən] *s.* predilección,
  preferencia.
pre·dis·pose [pridɪspóz] *v.* predisponer.
pre·dom·i·nance [prɪdámənəns] *s.* predominio;
  ascendiente.
pre·dom·i·nant [prɪdámənənt] *adj.* predominante.
pre·dom·i·nate [prɪdámənet] *v.* predominar.
pref·ace [préfɪs] *s.* prefacio; prólogo; *v.* prologar.
pre·fect [prífɛkt] *s.* prefecto.
pre·fer [prɪfɝ] *v.* preferir; **to — a claim** presentar
  una demanda.
pref·er·a·ble [préfrəbl] *adj.* preferible; preferente;
  pref·er·a·bly *adv.* preferiblemente;
  preferentemente, de preferencia.
pref·er·ence [préfrəns] *s.* preferencia.
pre·ferred [prɪfɝd] *p.p. & adj.* preferido; **— shares**
  acciones preferentes.
pre·fix [prífɪks] *s.* prefijo; [priffks] *v.* prefijar,
  anteponer.
preg·nan·cy [prégnənsɪ] *s.* preñez, embarazo.
preg·nant [prégnənt] *adj.* *(animal)* preñado; *(person)*
  embarazada; encinta; *(full)* lleno, repleto; en estado
  delicado.
pre·hen·sile [prihénsɪl] *adj.* prensil.
pre·judge [pridʒʌ́dʒ] *v.* prejuzgar.
prej·u·dice [prédʒədɪs] *s.* *(preconception)* prejuicio,
  prevención; *(harm)* daño; *v.* predisponer, prevenir;
  perjudicar.
prel·ate [prélɪt] *s.* prelado.
pre·lim·i·nar·y [prɪlímənɛrɪ] *adj. & s.* preliminar.
prel·ude [préljud] *s.* preludio; *v.* preludiar.
pre·ma·ture [primətjúr] *adj.* prematuro.
pre·med·i·tat·ed [prímédətetɪd] *adj.* premeditado.
pre·mier [prímiɚ] *s.* primer ministro; *adj.* primero;
  principal.
prem·ise [prémɪs] *s.* premisa; **-s** terrenos; predio;
  local.
pre·mi·um [prímɪəm] *s.* premio; **at a —** muy escaso,
  muy caro; **insurance —** prima de seguro.
pre·na·tal [prinétl] *adj.* prenatal.
pre·oc·cu·py [priákjəpaɪ] *v.* preocupar; ocupar de
  antemano.
pre·or·bit·al [príɔrbɪtl] *adj.* preorbital.
pre·paid [prípéd] *adj.* pagado de antemano; **to send**
  — enviar porte pagado, enviar franco de porte.
prep·a·ra·tion [prɛpəréʃən] *s.* preparación;
  preparativo.
pre·par·a·to·ry [prɪpǽrətorɪ] *adj.* preparatorio.
pre·pare [prɪpɛ́r] *v.* preparar(se).
pre·par·ed·ness [prɪpérɪdnɪs] *s.* preparación,
  prevención.

pre·pon·der·ance [prɪpándɚrəns] *s.* preponderancia.
pre·pon·der·ant [prɪpándrənt] *adj.* preponderante.
prep·o·si·tion [prɛpəzíʃən] *s.* preposición.
pre·pos·sess [pripozɛ́s] *v.* preocupar; predisponer.
pre·pos·ter·ous [prɪpástrəs] *adj.* absurdo, insensato.
pre·req·ui·site [prirékwəzɪt] *s.* requisito previo.
pre·rog·a·tive [prɪrágətɪv] *s.* prerrogativa.
pres·age [prɛ́sɪdʒ] *s.* presagio; [prɪsédʒ] *v.* presagiar.
pre·scribe [prɪskráɪb] *v.* prescribir; recetar.
pre·scrip·tion [prɪskrípʃən] *s.* recata; prescripción, precepto, mandato.
pres·ence [prɛ́zn̩s] *s.* presencia; — **of mind** aplomo, serenidad.
pres·ent [prɛ́znt] *s.* (*time*) presente; (*gift*) regalo; **at** — al presente, ahora; **for the** — por ahora; *adj.* presente; corriente, actual; — **company excepted** mejorando lo presente; — **participle** gerundio; **to be** — asistir, estar presente; [prɪzɛ́nt] *v.* presentar; regalar, obsequiar.
pres·en·ta·tion [prɛzn̩téʃən] *s.* presentación; regalo, obsequio.
pre·sen·ti·ment [prɪzɛ́ntəmənt] *s.* presentimiento; corazonada.
pres·ent·ly [prɛ́zn̩tlɪ] *adv.* luego, pronto, dentro de poco.
pres·er·va·tion [prɛzɚvéʃən] *s.* preservación; conservación.
pre·serve [prɪzɚ́v] *v.* preservar, guardar; conservar; mantener; *s.* conserva, compota; **forest** — vedado.
pre·side [prɪzáɪd] *v.* presidir; **to** — **at** (— **over**) **a meeting** presidir una junta.
pres·i·den·cy [prɛ́zədənsɪ] *s.* presidencia.
pres·i·dent [prɛ́zədənt] *s.* presidente.
pres·i·den·tial [prɛzədɛ́nʃəl] *adj.* presidencial.
press [prɛs] *v.* (*bear down*) prensar; apretar; comprimir; (*iron*) planchar (*ropa*); (*force*) forzar; apremiar; urgir; empujar; **to** — **forward** empujar hacia adelante; avanzar, ganar terreno; **to** — **one's point** porfiar; insistir en su argumento; **to** — **through the crowd** abrirse paso por entre la multitud; **to be hard -ed by work** estar abrumado de trabajo; **to be hard -ed for money** estar escaso de fondos; *s.* prensa; imprenta.
press·ing [prɛ́sɪŋ] *adj.* apremiante, urgente.
pres·sure [prɛ́ʃɚ] *s.* presión; apremio, urgencia; — **cooker** cocinilla de presión; — **gauge** manómetro.
pres·sur·ize [prɛ́ʃɚaɪz] *v.* sobrecargar.
pres·tige [prɛstíʒ] *s.* prestigio.
pre·sum·a·ble [prɪsúməbl] *adj.* presumible, probable.
pre·sume [prɪzúm] *v.* presumir; suponer; **to** — **on** (**upon**) abuser de; **to** — **to** atreverse a.
pre·sump·tion [prɪzʌ́mpʃən] *s.* presunción; pretensión; suposición.
pre·sump·tu·ous [prɪzʌ́mptʃʊəs] *adj.* presuntuoso, pretencioso, presumido.
pre·sup·pose [prisəpóz] *v.* presuponer.
pre·tend [prɪtɛ́nd] *v.* pretender; fingir.
pre·tense [prɪtɛ́ns] *s.* pretensión; presunción; ostentación; apariencia; pretexto; **under** — **of** so pretexto de.
pre·ten·sion [prɪtɛ́nʃən] *s.* pretensión; pretexto.
pre·ten·tious [prɪtɛ́nʃəs] *adj.* pretencioso.
pre·text [prítɛkst] *s.* pretexto.
pret·ti·ly [prítɪlɪ] *adv.* lindamente; agradablemente.
pret·ti·ness [prítɪnɪs] *s.* lindeza, gracia.
pret·ty [prítɪ] *adj.* lindo, bonito, bello, *Esp.* guapo; chulo; *Méx.*, *C.A.*, *Col.* *adv.* medianamente; bastante; un poco, algo; — **well** regular, así así; bastante bien, medianamente.
pre·vail [prɪvél] *v.* prevalecer; **to** — **on** (**upon**) persuadir.

pre·vail·ing [prɪvélɪŋ] *adj.* predominante; en boga.
prev·a·lent [prɛ́vələnt] *adj.* prevalenciante; común, corriente.
pre·vent [prɪvɛ́nt] *v.* prevenir, evitar; impedir; estorbar.
pre·ven·tion [prɪvɛ́nʃən] *s.* prevención; precaución.
pre·ven·tive [prɪvɛ́ntɪv] *adj.* impeditivo.
pre·view [prívju] *s.* vista previa (*anticipada*).
pre·vi·ous [prívəs] *adj.* previo; **-ly** *adv.* previamente; antes; de antemano.
prey [pre] *s.* presa; victima; **birds of** — aves de rapiña; *v.* **to** — **on** cazar; rapiñar, pillar; robar; **it -s upon my mind** me tiene preocupado, me tiene en zozobra.
price [praɪs] *s.* precio; valor; costo (coste *o* costa); — **ceiling** máximo de precios; — **control** control de precios; — **fixing** estabilización de precios; **at any** — a toda costa, a todo trance; *v.* apreciar, valuar, fijar el precio de; averiguar el precio de.
price·less [práɪslɪs] *adj.* sin precio, inapreciable.
prick [prɪk] *v.* picar; pinchar; punzar; sentir comezón; sentir picazón; **to** — **up one's ears** aguzar las orejas; *s.* picadura; punzada; pinchazo; piquete; aguijón; púa.
prick·ly [prɪ́klɪ] *adj.* espinoso, lleno de espinas; lleno de púas; — **heat** picazón causada por el calor; — **pear** tuna (*de nopal*).
pride [praɪd] *s.* orgullo; soberbia; *v.* **to** — **oneself on** (**upon**) enorgullecerse de, preciarse de.
priest [prist] *s.* sacerdote.
priest·hood [prísthʊd] *s.* sacerdocio.
prim [prɪm] *adj.* remilgado; repulido; peripuesto; estirado.
pri·mar·i·ly [praɪmérəlɪ] *adv.* primariamente, principalmente; en primer lugar.
pri·ma·ry [práɪmɛrɪ] *adj.* (*first*) primario; primero; (*basic*) fundamental; principal; — **colors** colores elementales; — **election** elección primaria; — **necessities** artículos de primera necesidad; — **school** escuela primaria.
prime [praɪm] *adj.* (*main*) principal; primario, primero; (*select*) selecto, de primera calidad; — **minister** primer ministro; — **mover** alma, palanca de una empresa; — **number** número primo; *s.* flor (*de la vida o de la edad*); la flor y nata (*lo mejor*); plenitud; número primo; **to be in one's** — estar en la flor de la edad; *v.* preparar, informar, instruir de atemano; cebar (*un carburador, bomba o arma de fuego*).
prim·er [prímɚ] *s.* abecedario, cartilla de lectura; compendio.
pri·me·val [praɪmívl] *adj.* primitivo.
prim·i·tive [prímətɪv] *adj.* primitivo.
prim·ness [prímnɪs] *s.* remilgo, tiesura, demasiada formalidad, dengue, afectación.
primp [prɪmp] *v.* acicalar(se), adornar(se), arreglar(se).
prim·rose [prímroz] *s.* prímula o primavera (*flor*); color amarillo pálido.
prince [prɪns] *s.* principe.
prince·ly [prínslɪ] *adj.* noble, regio, magnífico, propio de un principe.
prin·cess [prínsɪs] *s.* princesa.
prin·ci·pal [prínsəpl] *adj.* principal; *s.* principal, capital; principal, jefe, director.
prin·ci·ple [prínsəpl] *s.* principio; regla, ley; fundamento, basé.
print [prɪnt] *s.* (*type*) tipo, letra de molde; (*art*) lámina, grabado; estampado (*tejido estampado*); diseño (*estampado*); impresión; **in** — impreso, publicado; **out of** — agotado; *v.* imprimir;

estampar; escribir en letra de molde; **-ed fabric**
estampado.
print·er [príntɚ] *s. (person)* impresor; *(computer)*
impresora; **ball** — *(computer)* impresora de bola;
barrel — *(computer)* impresor de cilindro.
print·ing [príntɪŋ] *s.* imprenta; impresión; tipografía;
— **office** imprenta; — **press** prensa.
print·out [príntawt] *s. (computer)* listado.
pri·or [práɪɚ] *adj.* previo, anterior, precedente; — **to**
anterior a, con antelación a; *s.* prior *(de un
monasterio).*
pri·or·i·ty [praɪɔ́rətɪ] *s.* prioridad, precedencia,
antelación.
prism [prízəm] *s.* prisma.
pris·on [prízṇ] *s.* prisión, cárcel; *v.* encarcelar.
pris·on·er [prízṇɚ] *s.* prisionero, preso.
pri·va·cy [práɪvəsɪ] *s.* secreto, reserva; retiro; **to have
no** — carecer de sitio privado; estar a la vista del
público.
pri·vate [práɪvɪt] *adj. (no admittance)* privado;
personal; *(not public)* particular; *(confidential)*
secreto; confidencial; **a** — **citizen** un particular; —
school escuela particular; — **enterprise** empresa
privada; — **sector** sector privado; *s.* soldado raso;
in — en secreto; a solas, privadamente.
pri·va·tion [praɪvéʃən] *s.* privación.
priv·i·lege [prívlɪdʒ] *s.* privilegio.
priv·i·leged [prívlɪdʒd] *adj.* privilegiado; **to be** — **to**
tener el privilegio de.
priv·y [prívɪ] *adj.* privado; enterado de; *s.* excusado
exterior.
prize [praɪz] *s. (reward)* premio, galardón; *(booty)*
presa, botín de guerra; — **fight** boxeo público,
pugilato; — **fighter** boxeador, pugilista; — **medal**
medalla de premio; *v.* apreciar, estimar, tener en
gran estima.
prob·a·bil·i·ty [prɑbəbflətɪ] *s.* probabilidad.
prob·a·ble [prɑ́bəbl] *adj.* probable; **prob·a·bly** *adv.*
probablemente.
pro·ba·tion [probéʃən] *s.* probación; noviciado;
prueba; **to put a prisoner on** — poner a un
prisionero en libertad bajo la vigilancia de un juez.
probe [prob] *v.* tentar, reconocer, *(go into)* sondear
(una herida); (examine) escudriñar, examinar a
fondo; indagar; *s.* tienta *(instrumento de cirujano);*
indagación.
prob·lem [prɑ́bləm] *s.* problema.
prob·lem·at·i·cal [prɑbləmǽtɪkl] *adj.* problemático.
pro·ce·dure [prəsídʒɚ] *s.* procedimiento; proceder.
pro·ceed [prəsíd] *v.* proceder; proseguir; seguir
adelante; **to** — **to** proceder a, comenzar a, ponerse
a.
pro·ceed·ing [prəsídɪŋ] *s.* procedimiento; transacción;
-s transacciones; actas; proceso.
pro·ceeds [prósidz] *s. pl.* producto, ganancia.
proc·ess [prɑ́sɛs] *s. (series)* proceso; *(method)*
procedimiento, método; — **of law** procedimiento
legal; **in** — **of time** con el transcurso del tiempo,
con el tiempo, andando el tiempo; **in the** — **of
being made** en vía de preparación; *v.* preparar
mediante un procedimiento especial, someter a un
procedimiento; elaborar; procesar *(ante un juez).*
pro·ces·sion [prəsɛ́ʃən] *s.* procesión; desfile; **funeral**
— cortejo fúnebre.
pro·claim [proklém] *v.* proclamar; promulgar.
proc·la·ma·tion [prɑkləméʃən] *s.* proclamación;
proclama.
pro·cliv·i·ty [proklívɪtɪ] *s.* inclinación.
pro·cure [prokjú] *v.* procurar, conseguir, obtener.
prod [prɑd] *v.* aguijonear; picar.
prod·i·gal [prɑ́dɪgl] *adj. & s.* pródigo, gastador.

pro·di·gious [prədídʒəs] *adj.* prodigioso.
prod·i·gy [prɑ́dədʒɪ] *s.* prodigio.
pro·duce [prɑ́djus] *s.* producto; *(vegetables)*
productos agrícolas; hortalizas; [prədjús] *v.*
producir.
pro·duc·er [prədjúsɚ] *s.* productor; **theatrical** —
empresario.
prod·uct [prɑ́dəkt] *s.* producto.
pro·duc·tion [prədʌ́kʃən] *s.* producción; producto;
obra, composición; representación teatral.
pro·duc·tive [prədʌ́ktɪv] *adj.* productivo.
pro·fa·na·tion [prɑfənéʃən] *s.* profanación, desacato.
pro·fane [prəfén] *adj.* profano; *v.* profanar.
pro·fess [prəfɛ́s] *v.* profesar; pretender.
pro·fes·sion [prəfɛ́ʃən] *s.* profesión.
pro·fes·sion·al [prəfɛ́ʃənl] *adj.* profesional; *s.*
profesional, *Méx.* profesionista.
pro·fes·sor [prəfɛ́sɚ] *s.* profesor, catedrático.
prof·fer [prɑ́fɚ] *s.* oferta, propuesta; *v.* ofrecer,
proponer.
pro·fi·cien·cy [prəfíʃənsɪ] *s.* pericia, destreza.
pro·fi·cient [prəfíʃənt] *adj.* proficiente, perito,
experto.
pro·file [prófaɪl] *s.* perfil; contorno.
prof·it [prɑ́fɪt] *s. (gain)* ganancia; lucro; *(usefulness)*
provecho, utilidad, beneficio; — **and loss** pérdidas
y ganancias; **net** — ganancia neta o liquida; *v.*
aprovechar; ganar, sacar provecho; **to** — **by**
aprovecharse de, sacar provecho de.
prof·it·a·ble [prɑ́fɪtəbl] *adj.* provechoso; lucrativo.
prof·i·teer [prɑfətír] *s.* extorsionista, carero,
explotador, logrero; *v.* extorsionar, explotar, cobrar
más de lo justo.
pro·found [prəfáund] *adj.* profundo.
pro·fuse [prəfjús] *adj.* profuso, abundante; pródigo.
prog·e·ny [prɑ́dʒenɪ] *s.* prole.
prog·no·sis [prɑgnósɪs] *s.* pronóstico.
pro·gram [prógræm] *s.* programa; plan.
pro·gram·mer [prógræmɚ] *s. (computer)*
programador.
prog·ress [prɑ́grɛs] *s.* progreso; [prəgrɛ́s] *v.*
progresar.
pro·gres·sive [prəgrɛ́sɪv] *adj.* progresivo; progresista;
s. progresista.
pro·hib·it [prohíbɪt] *v.* prohibir; vedar.
pro·hi·bi·tion [proəbíʃən] *s.* prohibición.
proj·ect [prɑ́dʒɛkt] *s.* proyecto, plan; [prədʒɛ́kt] *v.*
proyectar(se); extender(se) sobresalir.
pro·jec·tile [prədʒɛ́ktl] *s.* proyectil; *adj.* arrojadizo;
— **weapon** arma arrojadiza.
pro·jec·tion [prədʒɛ́kʃən] *s.* proyección; saliente,
salidizo.
pro·jec·tor [prədʒɛ́ktɚ] *s.* proyector.
pro·le·tar·i·an [prolətérɪən] *adj. & s.* proletario.
pro·le·tar·i·at [prolətériət] *s.* proletariado.
pro·lif·ic [prolífɪk] *adj.* prolífico.
pro·logue [prólɔg] *s.* prólogo.
pro·long [prəlɔ́ŋ] *v.* prolongar.
pro·lon·ga·tion [prolɔŋɡéʃən] *s.* prolongación.
prom·e·nade [prɑmənéd] *s.* paseo; baile *(usualmente*
prom*); v.* pasearse.
prom·i·nent [prɑ́mənənt] *adj.* prominente; notable;
saliente; conspicuo.
pro·mis·cu·ous [prəmískjuəs] *adj.* promiscuo.
prom·ise [prɑ́mɪs] *s.* promesa; *v.* prometer;
Promised Land Tierra de Promisión.
prom·is·ing [prɑ́mɪsɪŋ] *adj.* prometedor.
prom·is·so·ry [prɑ́məsorɪ] *adj.* promisorio; — **note**
pagaré.
prom·on·to·ry [prɑ́məntorɪ] *s.* promontorio.
pro·mote [prəmót] *v. (favor)* promover; fomentar;

explotar; adelantar; (*raise*) ascender; elevar.
pro·mot·er [prəmótɚ] *s.* promotor, promovedor.
pro·mo·tion [prəmóʃən] *s.* promoción; ascenso;
adelantamiento.
prompt [prɑmpt] *adj.* pronto, puntual; listo, presto;
v. mover, incitar, inducir; apuntar (*servir de
apuntador en el teatro*); soplar (*sugerir a otro lo
que debe decir en una clase o junta*).
prompt·ly [prɑmptlɪ] *adv.* pronto, prontamente,
presto; puntualmente; con prontitud, con presteza.
prompt·ness [prɑmptnɪs] *s.* prontitud, presteza;
puntualidad.
prom·ul·gate [prəmʌlget] *v.* promulgar.
prone [pron] *adj.* inclinado; propenso, dispuesto;
boca abajo; postrado.
prong [prɔŋ] *s.* púa, punta.
pro·noun [prónaʊn] *s.* pronombre.
pro·nounce [prənáʊns] *v.* pronunciar; declarar.
pro·nounced [prənáʊnst] *adj.* pronunciado, marcado;
— **opinions** opiniones decididas.
pro·nun·ci·a·tion [prənʌnsɪéʃən] *s.* pronunciación.
proof [pruf] *s.* prueba; comprobación; *adj.*
impenetrable, resistente; — **against** a prueba de;
— **reader** corrector de pruebas de imprenta; —
sheet prueba, pliego de prueba; **galley** — galerada;
bomb — a prueba de bomba; **fire** — a prueba de
incendios; **water** — impermeable.
prop [prɑp] *s.* puntal; sostén, apoyo; *v.* apuntalar,
sostener.
prop·a·gan·da [prɑpəgǽndɚ] *s.* propaganda.
prop·a·gate [prɑpəget] *v.* propagar(se).
prop·a·ga·tion [prɑpəgéʃən] *s.* propagación;
diseminación.
pro·pel [prəpél] *v.* populsar, impeler.
pro·pel·ler [prəpélɚ] *s.* hélice (*de un buque o avión*);
propulsor, impulsor.
prop·er [prɑpɚ] *adj.* propio; conveniente, a
propósito; justo, correcto; — **noun** nombre propio;
-ly *adv.* propiamente; con propiedad,
correctamente.
prop·er·ty [prɑpɚtɪ] *s.* propiedad; posesión;
posesiones, bienes.
proph·e·cy [prɑfəsɪ] *s.* profecía.
proph·e·sy [prɑfəsaɪ] *v.* profetizar, predecir,
pronosticar, augurar.
proph·et [prɑfɪt] *s.* profeta.
pro·phet·ic [prəfétɪk] *adj.* profético.
pro·pi·ti·ate [propíʃiet] *v.* propiciar.
pro·pi·tious [prəpíʃəs] *adj.* propicio, favorable.
pro·por·tion [prəpórʃən] *s.* proporción; **out of** —
desproporcionado; *v.* proporcionar; **well -ed** bien
proporcionado.
pro·pos·al [prəpózl] *s.* propuesta; proposición;
(*marriage*) declaración (*de amor*).
pro·pose [prəpóz] *v.* proponer; declararse, hacer
propuesta de matrimonio; **to** — **to do something**
proponerse hacer algo.
prop·o·si·tion [prɑpəzíʃən] *s.* proposición; propuesta;
asunto.
pro·pri·e·tor [prəpráɪətɚ] *s.* propietario, dueño.
pro·pri·e·ty [prəpráɪətɪ] *s.* propiedad, corrección;
decoro.
pro·pul·sion [propʌlʃən] *s.* propulsión.
pro·rate [prorét] *v.* prorratear, repartir
proporcionalmente.
pro·sa·ic [poszéɪk] *adj.* prosaico.
prose [proz] *s.* prosa; *adj.* prosaico.
pros·e·cute [prɑsɪkjut] *v.* procesar, enjuiciar,
demandar ante un juez; (*pursue*) llevar adelante.
pros·e·cu·tion [prɑsɪkjúʃən] *s.* prosecución,
seguimiento; parte acusadora (*en un pleito*).

pros·e·cu·tor [prɑsɪkjutɚ] *s.* fiscal; acusador.
pros·e·lyte [prɑsəlaɪt] *s.* prosélito.
pros·pect [prɑspɛkt] *s.* (*hope*) perspectiva, vista;
esperanza; espectativa; (*candidate*) cliente;
(*chances*) probabilidad de éxito; *v.* explorar, andar
en busca de.
pro·spec·tive [prəspɛktɪv] *adj.* probable, posible,
esperado; presunto.
pros·pec·tor [prəspɛktɚ] *s.* explorador, buscador (*de
minas, petróleo, etc.*).
pros·per [prɑspɚ] *v.* prosperar, medrar.
pros·per·i·ty [prɑspérətɪ] *s.* prosperidad.
pros·per·ous [prɑspərəs] *adj.* próspero.
pros·tate [prɑstet] *s.* próstata.
pros·ti·tute [prɑstətjut] *s.* ramera, prostituta; *v.*
prostituir.
pros·trate [prɑstret] *adj.* postrado; abatido; *v.*
postrar; abatir.
pro·tag·o·nist [protǽgənɪst] *s.* protagonista.
pro·tect [prətɛkt] *v.* proteger.
pro·tec·tion [prətɛkʃen] *s.* protección; amparo.
pro·tec·tive [prətɛktɪv] *adj.* protector; — **tariff** tarifa
proteccionista.
pro·tec·tor [prətɛktɚ] *s.* protector.
pro·tec·tor·ate [prətɛktrɪt] *s.* protectorado.
pro·té·gé [prótəge] *s.* protegido.
pro·tein [prótiin] *s.* proteína.
pro·test [prótɛst] *s.* protesta, protestación; [prətɛst] *v.*
protestar.
prot·es·tant [prɑtɪstənt] *adj. & s.* protestante.
prot·es·ta·tion [prɑtəstéʃən] *s.* protestación, protesta.
pro·to·col [prótəkɔl] *s.* protocol.
pro·to·plasm [prótəplæzəm] *s.* protoplasma.
pro·to·type [prótotaɪp] *s.* prototipo.
pro·tract [protrǽkt] *v.* alargar, extender, prolongar.
pro·trude [protrúd] *v.* sobresalir; resaltar;
proyectar(se).
pro·tu·ber·ance [protjúbɚəns] *s.* protuberancia.
proud [praʊd] *adj.* orgulloso; soberbio.
prove [pruv] *v.* probar; demostrar; comprobar;
resultar.
prov·erb [prɑvɝb] *s.* proverbio; refrán.
pro·vide [prəváɪd] *v.* proveer; abastecer; suplir;
estipular; **to** — **for** hacer provisión para; **to** —
with proveer de.
pro·vid·ed [prəváɪdɪd] *conj.* con tal (de) que, a
condición (de) que; — **that** con tal (de) que.
prov·i·dence [prɑvədəns] *s.* providencia.
prov·i·den·tial [prɑvədénʃəl] *adv.* providencial.
pro·vid·er [prəváɪdɚ] *s.* proveedor.
prov·ince [prɑvɪns] *s.* provincia; jurisdicción; **it isn't
within my** — no está dentro de mi jurisdicción; no
es de mi incumbencia.
pro·vin·cial [prəvínʃəl] *adj.* provincial; *s.*
provinciano.
pro·vi·sion [prəvíʒen] *s.* (*goods*) provision;
abastecimiento; (*plan*) estipulación; **-s** provisiones;
víveres; **to make the necessary -s** tomar las
medidas (*o* precauciones) necesarias.
pro·vi·so [prəváɪzo] *s.* condición, estipulación.
prov·o·ca·tion [prɑvəkéʃən] *s.* provocación.
pro·voke [prəvók] *v.* provocar; irritar; enfadar.
prow [praʊ] *s.* proa.
prow·ess [práuɪs] *s.* proeza.
prowl [praʊl] *v.* rondar en acecho; fisgonear.
prox·im·i·ty [prɑksímətɪ] *s.* proximidad.
prox·y [prɑksɪ] *s.* apoderado, substituto, delegado;
by — mediante apoderado.
prude [prud] *s.* mojigato, persona gazmoña.
pru·dence [prúdn̩s] *s.* prudencia.
pru·dent [prúdn̩t] *adj.* prudente.

PR

prud·er·y [prúdərı] *s.* mojigatería, gazmoñería, remilgo.

prud·ish [prúdıʃ] *adj.* gazmoño, remilgado.

prune [prun] *s.* ciruela; ciruela pasa; *v.* podar, recortar.

pry [praı] *v.* atisbar, espiar; fisgar, fisgonear; curiosear; **to — a secret out** extraer (*o* arrancar) un secreto; **to — apart** separar por fuerza; **to — into other people's affairs** entremeterse en lo ajeno; **to — open** abrir a la fuerza; **to — up** levantar con una palanca.

psalm [sɑm] *s.* salmo.

pseu·do·nym [sjúdnım] *s.* seudónimo.

psit·ta·co·sis [sıtəkósıs] *s.* psitacósis.

psy·chi·a·trist [saıkáıətrıst] *s.* psiquiatra, alienista.

psy·chi·a·try [saıkáıətrı] *s.* psiquiatría.

psy·cho·log·i·cal [saıkəlɑ́dʒık] *adj.* psicológico.

psy·chol·o·gist [saıkɑ́lədʒıst] *s.* psicólogo.

psy·chol·o·gy [saıkɑ́lədʒı] *s.* psicología.

psy·cho·sis [saıkósıs] *s.* sicosis.

pto·maine [tómen] *s.* ptomaína.

pub·lic [pʌ́blık] *adj.* público; **— prosecutor** fiscal; **— domain** dominio público; **— lands** territorios nacionales; **— relations** relaciones públicas; **— utilities** servicios públicos; *s.* público.

pub·li·ca·tion [pʌblıkéʃən] *s.* publicación.

pub·lic·i·ty [pʌblísətı] *s.* publicidad, propaganda.

pub·lish [pʌ́blıʃ] *v.* publicar; editar; **-ing house** editorial o editora.

pub·lish·er [pʌ́blıʃɚ] *s.* publicador; editor.

puck·er [pʌ́kɚ] *v.* fruncir.

pud·ding [púıŋ] *s.* budín, pudín.

pud·dle [pʌ́dl] *s.* charco.

puff [pʌf] *s.* ˙(*air*) resoplido; (*smoke*) bocanada (*de numo, vapor, etc.*); bullón (*de vestido*); **— of wind** ráfaga, soplo; **— paste** hojaldre; **cream —** bolo de crema; **powder —** polvera, borla, *Méx., Col., Ven., Andes,* mota; *Ríopl.* cisne; *v.* resoplar, jadear; echar bocanadas; **to — up** inflar(se); ahuecar(se); hinchar(se).

pug [pʌg] *s.* perro dogo; **— nose** nariz chata, ñata o respingada.

pull [pʊl] *v.* (*tug*) tirar de; jalar (halar); (*extract*) sacar; arrancar; (*stretch*) estirar; **to — apart** desgarrar; despedazar; descomponer; desmontar; **to — down the curtain** bajar la cortinilla; **to — oneself together** componerse, serenarse; **to — over to the right** hacerse a la derecha, desviarse hacia la derecha; **to — up** parar (*un caballo, un auto*); parar, hacer alto; **to — through** salir de un apuro; sacar (*a alguien*) de un apuro; **to — strings** buscar palanca; **to — a boner** cometer error; **the train -ed into the station** el tren llegó a la estación; **to — out** desatascar; *s.* tirón; estirón; ascenso difícil; esfuerzo (*para subir*); **to have —** tener buenas aldabas, tener influencia (palanca); enchufe.

pul·let [pʊ́lıt] *s.* polla.

pul·ley [pʊ́lı] *s.* polea; garrucha.

pu!p [pʌlp] *s.* pulpa.

pul·pit [púpıt] *s.* púlpito.

pul·sate [pʌ́lset] *v.* pulsar, latir.

pulse [pʌls] *s.* pulso; pulsación.

pul·ver·ize [pʌ́lvəraız] *v.* pulverizar.

pum·ice [pʌ́mıs] *s.* piedra pómez.

pump [pʌmp] *s.* bomba (*para sacar agua*); (*shoe*) zapatilla; **gasoline —** bomba de gasolina; **hand —** bomba de mano; **tire —** bomba para neumáticos; *v.* manejar la bomba, *Am.* bombear; inflar (*un neumático*); **to — someone** sacarle (*o* sonsacarle) a una persona la verdad o un secreto; **— priming**

cebar la bomba.

pump·kin [pʌ́mpkın] *s.* calabaza.

pun [pʌn] *s.* equívoco, retruécano, juego de palabras; *v.* decir retruécanos o equívocos, jugar del vocablo.

punch [pʌntʃ] *s.* (*blow*) puñetazo, puñada; (*drink*) ponche; (*drill*) punzón, sacabocados; (*vitality*) fuerza, empuje; vitalidad; **— bowl** ponchera; *v.* dar un puñetazo, dar una puñada; punzar, horadar, perforar; **to — a hole** hacer un agujero o perforación.

punc·tu·al [pʌ́ŋktʃʊəl] *adj.* puntual.

punc·tu·al·i·ty [pʌŋktʃʊǽlətı] *s.* puntualidad.

punc·tu·ate [pʌ́ŋktʃʊet] *v.* puntuar.

punc·tu·a·tion [pʌŋktʃʊéʃən] *s.* puntuación.

punc·ture [pʌ́ŋktʃɚ] *v.* picar, punzar, pinchar; agujerear, perforar; **-d tire** neumático picado; *s.* picadura; pinchazo; perforación; **to have a tire —** tener un neumático picado, tener una llanta o goma picada.

pun·ish [pʌ́nıʃ] *v.* castigar.

pun·ish·ment [pʌ́nıʃmənt] *s.* castigo.

punt [pʌnt] *s.* puntapié, patada.

pu·ny [pjúnı] *adj.* endeble, débil, flaco, enfermizo; insignificante.

pup [pʌp] *s.* cachorro.

pu·pil [pjúpl] *s.* discípulo; **— of the eye** pupila, niña del ojo. ˙

pup·pet [pʌ́pıt] *s.* títere, muñeco, monigote; **— show** títeres.

pup·py [pʌ́pı] *s.* cachorrito.

pur·chase [pɝ́tʃəs] *v.* comprar; mercar; *s.* compra; merca; **to get a — upon** agarrarse fuerte a.

pur·chas·er [pɝ́tʃəsɚ] *s.* comprador, marchante.

pure [pjʊr] *adj.* puro; **-ly** *adv.* puramente; meramente.

pu·ree [pjʊré] *s.* puré.

pur·ga·tive [pɝ́gətıv] *adj.* purgante; *s.* purga, purgante.

pur·ga·to·ry [pɝ́gətorı] *s.* purgatorio.

purge [pɝdʒ] *v.* purgar(se); limpiar; purificar(se); *s.* purga, purgante.

pu·ri·fy [pjʊ́rəfaı] *v.* purificar(se); depurar.

pu·rist [pjʊ́rıst] *s.* purista.

pu·ri·ty [pjʊ́rətı] *s.* pureza.

pur·ple [pɝ́pl] *s.* púrpura; *adj.* purpúreo, morado.

pur·port [pɝ́port] *s.* significado; tenor, sustancia; [pɚpórt] *v.* pretender, aparentar.

pur·pose [pɝ́pəs] *s.* (*intention*) propósito, intención; (*goal*) fin, objeto; **for no —** sin objeto, inútilmente, en vano, para nada; **on —** adrede, de propósito; *v.* proponerse.

purr [pɝ] *s.* (*cat*) ronroneo (*del gato*); (*motor*) zumbido (*del motor*); *v.* ronronear (*el gato*).

purse [pɝs] *s.* bolsillo, portamonedas, bolsa; *v.* **to — one's lips** fruncir los labios.

pur·su·ant [pɚsúənt] *adv.* conforme; de acuerdo con.

pur·sue [pɚsú] *v.* perseguir; seguir; dedicarse a (*una carrera, un estudio*).

pur·su·er [pɚsúɚ] *s.* perseguidor.

pur·suit [pɚsút] *s.* perseguimiento; (*search*) busca; ocupación; (practice) ejercicio (*de una profesión, cargo, etc.*); **in — of** a caza de, en seguimiento de, en busca de.

pus [pʌs] *s.* pus, podre.

push [pʊʃ] *v.* (*shove*) empujar; (*promote*) fomentar, promover; (*hurry*) apresurar; **to — aside** hacer a un lado, rechazar, apartar; **to — forward** empujar, abrirse paso; avanzar; **to — through** encajar (*por un agujero o rendija*); abrirse paso a empujones; **to — a button** oprimir (apretar) un botón; *s.* empuje;

empujón, empellón; — **button** botón eléctrico.
push·cart [púʃkɑrt] *s.* carretilla de mano.
puss·y [púsɪ] *s.* minino, gatito; — **willow** especie de sauce americano.
put [pʊt] *v.* poner; colocar; **to — a question** hacer una pregunta; **to — across an idea** darse a entender bien; hacer aceptar una idea; **to — away** apartar; guardar; **to — before** poner delante, anteponer; proponer ante; **to — by money** ahorrar o guardar dinero; **to — down** apuntar, anotar; sofocar (*una revolución*); rebajar (*los precios*); **to — in words** expresar; **to — in writing** poner por escrito; **to — off** aplazar, posponer; diferir; **to — on** ponerse (*ropa*); **to — on airs** darse tono o ínfulas; **to — on weight** engordar; **to — out** apagar, extinguir; **to — someone out** echar o expulsar a alguien; molestar o incomodar a alguien; **to — to shame** avergonzar; **to — up** enlatar, envasar (*frutas, legumbres*); apostar (*dinero*); alojar(se); erigir; **to — up for sale** poner de venta; **to — up with** aguantar, tolerar; *pret. & p.p.* **de** **put**.
pu·tre·fy [pjútrəfaɪ] *v.* podrir (*o* pudrir), corromper.
pu·trid [pjútrɪd] *adj.* putrefacto, podrido.
put·ter [pʌtɚ] *v.* trabajar sin orden ni sistema; ocuparse en cosas de poca monta; malgastar el tiempo.
put·ty [pʌtɪ] *s.* masilla; *v.* tapar o rellenar con masilla.
puz·zle [pʌzl] *s.* rompecabezas, acertijo; (*problem*) enigma; **crossword —** crucigrama; *v.* imbrollar, poner perplejo, confundir; **to —** out desenredar, descifrar; **to — over** ponderar; tratar de resolver o descifrar; **to be -d** estar perplejo.
pyr·a·mid [pírəmɪd] *s.* pirámide; **pyramiding** monopolio financiero piramidal.

Q:q

quack [kwæk] *s.* (*duck*) graznido (*del pato*); (*fake*) curandero, matasanos, medicastro; charlatán; *adj.* falso; *v.* graznar.
quag·mire [kwǽgmaɪr] *s.* tremedal, cenagal.
quail [kwel] *s.* codorniz.
quaint [kwent] *adj.* raro, extraño; pintoresco.
quake [kwek] *s.* temblor; terremoto; *v.* temblar.
qual·i·fi·ca·tion [kwɑləfəkéʃən] *s.* (*condition*) calificación; cualidad, calidad; (*requirement*) requisito; aptitud.
qual·i·fy [kwɑ́ləfaɪ] *v.* calificar; capacitar; **to — for a position** estar capacitado para una posición; **his studies — him for the job** sus estudios le capacitan para el puesto.
qual·i·ty [kwɑ́lətɪ] *s.* (*characteristic*) cualidad; (*importance*) calidad.
qualm [kwɑm] *s.* escrúpulo.
quan·ti·fy [kwántɪfaɪ] *v.* cuantificar.
quan·ti·ty [kwántətɪ] *s.* cantidad.
quar·an·tine [kwɔ́rəntin] *s.* cuarentena; *v.* poner en cuarentena, aislar.
quar·rel [kwɔ́rəl] *s.* riña, reyerta, pendencia; querella; *v.* reñir; pelear, disputar.
quar·rel·some [kwɔ́rəlsəm] *adj.* reñidor, pendenciero.
quar·ry [kwɔ́rɪ] *s.* (*stone*) cantera; (*game*) presa, caza (*animal perseguido*); *v.* explotar (*una cantera*); trabajar en una cantera.
quart [kwɔrt] *s.* cuarto de galón (*0.9463 de un litro*).

quar·ter [kwɔ́rtɚ] *s.* (*one-fourth*) cuarto, cuarta parte; (*coin*) moneda de 25 centavos; (*district*) barrio, distrito; **-s** morada, vivienda; alojamiento; **from all -s** de todas partes; **to give no — to the enemy** no dar cuartel al enemigo; *adj.* cuarto; *v.* cuartear, dividir en cuartos; descuartizar; acuartelar, acantonar, alojar (*tropas*).
quar·ter·ly [kwɔ́rtɚlɪ] *adv.* trimestralmente, por trimestres; *adj.* trimestral; *s.* publicación trimestral.
quar·tet [kwɔrtét] *s.* cuarteto.
quartz [kwɔrts] *s.* cuarzo.
qua·ver [kwévɚ] *v.* temblar; *s.* temblor; trémolo (*de la voz*).
quay [ki] *s.* muelle, embarcadero.
queen [kwin] *s.* reina.
queer [kwɪr] *adj.* raro, extraño, singular; excéntrico; **to feel —** sentirse raro, no sentirse bien; *v.* poner en ridículo, comprometer; **to — oneself with** quedar mal con, ponerse mal con.
quell [kwɛl] *v.* reprimir; (*put down*) sofocar (*una revuelta*); calmar.
quench [kwɛntʃ] *v.* apagar (*el fuego, la sed*); reprimir, sofocar, ahogar, templar el ardor de.
que·ry [kwírɪ] *s.* (*interrogation*) pregunta; interrogación, signo de interrogación; (*doubt*) duda; *v.* preguntar, expresar duda; marcar con signo de interrogación.
quest [kwɛst] *s.* busca; pesquisa.
ques·tion [kwɛ́stʃən] *s.* (*interrogation*) pregunta; (*issue*) cuestión; problema; duda; proposición; **— mark** signo de interrogación; **beyond —** fuera de duda; **that is out of the —** ¡imposible!; ¡ni pensar en ello!; *v.* preguntar; interrogar; dudar.
ques·tion·a·ble [kwɛ́stʃənəbl] *adj.* dudoso; discutible.
ques·tion·er [kwɛ́stʃənɚ] *s.* interrogador, preguntador.
ques·tion·ing [kwɛ́stʃənɪŋ *s.* interrogatorio; *adj.* interrogador.
ques·tion·naire [kwɛstʃənɛ́r] *s.* cuestionario, lista de preguntas, interrogatorio; encuesta.
quib·ble [kwíbl] *v.* sutilizar, valerse de argucias o sutilezas; andar en dimes y diretes; *s.* sutileza, argucia.
quick [kwɪk] *adj.* (*soon*) pronto, presto; (*smart*) listo; (*speedy*) rápido, veloz; agudo; — **temper** genio violento; — **wit** mente aguda; *adv.* rápidamente, de prisa, con prisa, pronto; *s.* carne viva; **to cut to the —** herir en lo vivo, herir en el alma.
quick·en [kwíkən] *v.* acelerar(se); avivar(se); aguzar (*la mente, el entendimiento*).
quick·ly [kwíklɪ] *adv.* pronto, presto, de prisa, aprisa, rápidamente.
quick·ness [kwíknɪs] *s.* (*speed*) rapidez; presteza, prontitud; (*alertness*) vivezal; agudeza (*de ingenio*).
quick·sand [kwíksænd] *s.* arena movediza.
quick·sil·ver [kwíksɪlvɚ] *s.* mercurio, azogue.
qui·et [kwáɪət] *adj.* quieto; (*not speaking*) callado; tranquilo; en calma; (*not moving*) reposado; *s.* quietud; sosiego, reposo; calma; silencio; *v.* aquietar; sosegar; calmar, tranquilizar; **to — down** aquietarse; calmarse; **-ly** *adv.* quietamente, con quietud; calladamente; tranquilamente.
qui·et·ness [kwáɪətnɪs] *s.* quietud; sosiego, calma.
quill [kwɪl] *s.* pluma; cañón (*de pluma de ave*); púa (*de puerco espín*).
quilt [kwɪlt] *s.* colcha; *v.* acolchar.
quince [kwɪns] *s.* membrillo.
qui·nine [kwáɪnaɪn] *s.* quinina.
quip [kwɪp] *s.* pulla, dicharacho; agudeza.
quirk [kwɚk] *s.* chifladura, extravagancia, capricho; peculiaridad mental.

quit [kwɪt] v. (*abandon*) dejar, abandonar; irse; (*cease*) parar, cesar; **to — doing something** dejar de hacer algo; **-s** adj. desquitado; **we are -s** no nos debemos nada, estamos desquitados, *Am.* estamos a mano; *pret. & p.p. de* **to quit.**

quite [kwaɪt] adv. bastante; del todo, enteramente; **— a person** una persona admirable; **— so** así es, en efecto; **it's — the fashion** está muy en boga.

quit·ter [kwɪ́tɚ] s. el que deja fácilmente lo empezado, el que se da fácilmente por vencido; evasor; desertor.

quiv·er [kwɪ́vɚ] v. temblar; estremecerse; s. temblor; estremecimiento.

quix·ot·ic [kwɪksátɪk] adj. quijotesco.

quiz [kwɪz] s. examen; interrogatorio; cuestionario; v. examinar, interrogar, hacer preguntas.

quiz·zi·cal [kwɪ́zəkl] adj. curioso; burlón.

quo·ta [kwótə] s. cuota.

quo·ta·tion [kwotéʃən] s. citación, cita; (*price*) cotización (*de precios*); **— marks** comillas.

quote [kwot] v. citar; cotizar (*precios*); **to — from** citar a, entresacar una cita de; s. cita, citación; **-s** comillas; **in -s** entre comillas.

quo·tient [kwóʃənt] s. cociente.

R:r

rab·bi [rǽbaɪ] s. rabí, rabino.
rab·bit [rǽbɪt] s. conejo.
rab·ble [rǽbl] s. populacho, plebe; canalla.

rab·id [rǽbəd] adj. rabioso.

ra·bies [rébiz] s. rabia, hidrofobia.

rac·coon [rækún] s. *Méx., C.A., Andes* mapache.

race [res] s. (*lineage*) raza; (*competition*) corrida, carrera; contienda; **—track** (*o* **—course**) pista; **boat —** regata; v. correr; competir en una carrera; ir corriendo; regatear (*competir en una regata*); acelerar (*un motor*).

rac·er [résɚ] s. corredor; caballo de carrera; auto de carrera.

ra·cial [réʃəl] adj. racial.

ra·cism [résɪzm] s. racismo.

rack [ræk] s. (*framework*) percha, colgadero, clavijero; (*torture*) potro de tormento; **baggage —** red; **towel —** toallero; **to fall into — and ruin** caer en un estado de ruina total; **— and pinion** cremallera; v. atormentar; **to — one's brain** devanarse los sesos, quebrarse uno la cabeza.

rack·et [rǽkɪt] s. (*instrument*) raqueta (*de tenis*); (*noise*) boruca, estrépito, baraúnda; bullicio; trapacería.

rack·et·eer [rækɪtɪ́r] s. trapacista, trapacero, extorsionista; v. trapacear, extorsionar.

ra·dar [rédar] s. radar.

ra·di·al [rédɪəl] adj. radial.

ra·di·ance [rédɪəns] s. resplandor, brillo.

ra·di·ant [rédɪənt] adj. radiante; resplandeciente, brillante.

ra·di·ate [rédɪet] v. irradiar; radiar.

ra·di·a·tor [rédɪetɚ] s. radiador; calorífero.

rad·i·cal [rǽdɪkl] adj. & s. radical.

rad·i·cal·ism [rǽdɪkəlɪzm] s. extremismo.

ra·di·o [rédɪo] s. radio (*m. o f.*); radio-telefonía; radiotelegrafía; **— announcer** locutor; **— commentator** comentarista radial; **— commercial** propaganda comercial, anuncio; **— listener** radioescucha, radioyente; **— program** programa radiofónico; **— transmitter** emisora; **by —** por radio; v. radiar, emitir, transmitir, radioifundir o

difundir.

ra·di·o·ac·tive [redɪoǽktɪv] adj. radiactivo.

ra·di·ol·o·gy [redɪáslədʒɪ] s. radiología.

rad·ish [rǽdɪʃ] s. rábano.

ra·di·um [rédɪəm] s. radio (*elemento químico*).

ra·di·us [rédɪəs] s. radio (*de un círculo*).

ra·don [rédan] s. radón.

raf·fle [rǽfl] s. rifa, sorteo; tómbola; v. rifar, sortear.

raft [ræft] s. balsa; **a — of things** un montón (*o* la mar) de cosas.

raft·er [rǽftɚ] s. viga (*del techo*).

rag [ræg] s. trapo; harapo, andrajo, *Am.* hilacho; **— doll** muñeca de trapo; **to be in -s** estar hecho andrajos, *Méx.* estar hecho tiras.

rag·a·muf·fin [rǽgəmʌfɪn] s. pelagatos, golfo; granuja, pilluelo.

rage [redʒ] s. rabia, furor; ira; **to be all the —** estar en boga, estar de moda; v. rabiar; enfurecerse; estar enfurecido; bramar; **to — with anger** bramar de ira.

rag·ged [rǽgɪd] adj. andrajoso, haraposo, harapiento, desharrapado, roto; **— edge** borde radio o deshilachado; **to be on the — edge** estar al borde del precipicio; estar muy nervioso.

raid [red] s. incursión, invasión repentina; allanamiento (*de un local*); **air —** ataque aéreo, bambardeo aéreo; v. hacer una incursión; invadir de repente; caer sobre; allanar (*un local*), entrar a la fuerza.

rail [rel] s. (*steel bar*) riel, carril; (*railroad*) ferrocarril; (*railing*) barandal, barandilla; **— fence** empalizada, estacada; **by —** por ferrocarril.

rail·ing [rélɪŋ] s. baranda, barandilla; pasamano (*de escalera*), balaustrada, barrera; rieles.

rail·road [rélrod] s. ferrocarril; adj. ferroviario; de ferrocarril; **— company** empresa ferroviaria; **— crossing** paso a nivel, cruce de ferrocarril; **— siding** apartadero.

rail·way [rélwe] s. ferrocarril; adj. ferroviario; de ferrocarril; **— crossing** cruce, crucero.

rai·ment [rémənt] s. vestidura, ropaje.

rain [ren] s. lluvia; (*water*) agua llovediza; **— check** garantía de prórroga; v. llover; **— or shine** que llueva o no; llueva o truene; a todo trance.

rain·bow [rénbo] s. arco iris.

rain·coat [rénkot] s. impermeable; *Ch.* capa de agua, *Méx.* manga o capa de hule; *Ríopl.* piloto.

rain·drop [réndrap] s. gota de agua.

rain·fall [rénfol] s. lluvia, lluvias; cantidad de agua pluvial; aguacero.

rain·y [rénɪ] adj. lluvioso.

raise [rez] v. (*lift*) levantar, alzar; subir; eregir; (*cultivate*) criar; cultivar; (*collect*) reunir; reclutar; **to — a question** hacer una observación o suscitar una duda; **to — a racket** armar un alboroto; s. aumento de sueldo.

rai·sin [rézn] s. pasa, uva seca.

ra·jah [rádʒə] s. rajá.

rake [rek] s. rastro, rastrillo, (*man*) libertino, perdulario; v. rastrear, rastrillar (*la tierra*); raspar; barrer (*con rastrillo*); atizar (*el fuego*).

rake-off [rékɔf] s. tajada de las ganancias.

ral·ly [rǽlɪ] v. (*unite*) reunir(se); juntar(se); (*improve*) recobrar(se); mejorar (*de salud*); fortalecerse; revivir; tomar nueva vida; **to — to the side of** acudir al lado de; s. junta popular, junta libre; recuperación.

ram [ræm] s. (*animal*) carnero; (*tool*) ariete o martillo hidráulico; espolón de buque; **battering —** ariete; **RAM (ran·dom ac·cess mem·o·ry)** memoria accesible al azar (aleatorio); v. apisonar, aplanar a golpes; aplastar de un choque; rellenar atestar; **to — a boat** chocar con un barco; arremeter contra un barco.

ram·ble [ræmbl] v. vagar; divagar; callejear; s. paseo, andanza.

ram·page [ræmpedʒ] s. alboroto.

ram·pant [ræmpənt] adj. extravagante; desenfrenado.

ram·part [ræmpɑrt] s. baluarte, muralla.

ran [ræn] pret. de to run.

ranch [ræntʃ] s. hacienda, Méx., C.A. rancho; **cattle —** hacienda de ganado, Méx., C.A. rancho, Ríopl. estancia; Ch. fundo; Ven., Col. hato.

ran·cid [rænsɪd] adj. rancio, acedo.

ran·cor [ræŋkɚ] s. rencor, encono.

ran·dom [rændəm] adj. impensado; aleatorio fortuito, al azar; **at —** al azar, a la ventura; **— sample** muestra aleatoria.

rang [ræŋ] pret. de to ring.

range [rendʒ] v. (align) alinear; poner en fila; arreglar; (wander) vagar por; rondar; fluctuar; **to — ten miles** tener un alcance de diez millas (un arma de fuego); s. (line) fila, hilera; alcance; extensión; (variation) fluctuación, variación (dentro de ciertos límites); distancia; (grazing place) pastizal, C.A. pastal; (stove) estufa; **gas —** cocina de gas; **— of mountains** cordillera, cadena de montañas; **— of vision** campo de visión; **in — with** en línea con; **shooting —** campo de práctica para tirar.

range find·er [réndʒfaɪndɚ] s. telemetro.

rank [ræŋk] s. (position) rango, categoría; orden; calidad; grado; (line) fila; línea, hilera; **the — and file** el pueblo, la gente ordinaria; la tropa; v. poner en fila; (arrange) ordenar, arreglar; (rate) clasificar; colocar por grados; **to — above** sobrepasar a; ser de grado superior a; **to — high** tener un alto rango, categoría o renombre; ser tenido en alta estima; **to — second** tener el segundo lugar; **to — with** estar al nivel de, tener el mismo grado que; **he -s high in athletics** sobresale en los deportes.

ran·sack [rænsæk] v. escudriñar; saquear.

ran·som [rænsəm] s. rescate; v. rescatar; redimir.

rant [rænt] v. desvariar; disparatar, gritar necedades.

rap [ræp] v. (strike) golpear, dar un golpe; (censure) criticar, censurar; **to — on the door** llamar o tocar a la puerta; s. golpe; **not to care a — no** importarle a uno un ardite.

ra·pa·cious [rəpéʃəs] adj. rapaz.

rape [rep] s. estupro, violación (de una mujer); v. forzar, violar (a una mujer).

rap·id [ræpɪd] adj. rápido; **-s** s. pl. raudal, rápidos (de un río).

ra·pid·i·ty [rəpídətɪ] s. rapidez, velocidad.

rap·port [rəpɔ́r] s. relación de confianza mutua.

rapt [ræpt] adj. extasiado; absorto.

rap·ture [ræptʃɚ] s. éxtasis, rapto.

rare [rɛr] adj. (strange) extraordinario, extraño; raro; (precious) raro; precioso; (not well-done) a medio asar, a medio freír, medio crudo; **-ly** adv. rara vez, raras veces; raramente; extraordinariamente.

rar·i·ty [rérətɪ] s. rareza; enrarecimiento (de la atmósfera).

ras·cal [ræskl] s. bribón, bellaco, pícaro.

rash [ræʃ] adj. temerario, atrevido; (thoughtless) precipitado; imprudente; s. salpullido, erupción (de la peil).

rash·ness [ræʃnɪs] s. temeridad.

rasp [ræsp] v. chirriar; irritar; s. chirrido, sonido áspero; ronquera, carraspera.

rasp·ber·ry [ræzbɛrɪ] s. frambuesa; **— bush** frambueso.

rasp·y [ræspɪ] adj. ronco; áspero.

rat [ræt] s. rata; postizo (para el pelo); (scab) esquirol.

rate [ret] s. proporción; porcentaje, tanto por ciento, Am. tipo (de interés); tarifa; precio; **— of exchange** cambio, Am. tipo de cambio; **— of taxation** tasa de tributación; **— of increase** incremento proporcional; **at any —** en todo caso, de todos modos; **at that —** a ese paso; en esa proporción; **at the — of** a razón de; **first —** de primera clase o calidad; muy bien; v. calificar, clasificar, considerar; tasar, valuar; **he -s as the best** se le considera como el mejor; **he -s high** se le tiene en alta estima; **rated capacity** capacidad nominal; **rated power** potencia nominal.

rath·er [ræðɚ] adv. algo, un poco, un tanto; más bien; mejor; mejor dicho; **— than** más bien que; **I would — die than** prefiero antes la muerte que; **I would — not go** preferiría no ir.

rat·i·fy [rætəfaɪ] s. ratificar.

rat·ing [rétɪŋ] s. clasificación; rango, grado; clase; evaluación.

ra·tio [réʃo] s. razón, proporción; relación.

ra·tion [réʃən] s. ración; v. racionar.

ra·tio·nal [ræʃənl] adj. racional.

ra·tio·nale [ræʃənǽl] s. exposición razonada, razón fundamental.

ra·tio·nal·ize [ræʃənlaɪz] v. buscar excusas.

ra·tion·ing [réʃənɪŋ] s. racionamiento.

rat·tle [rǽtl] v. traquetear; golpetear; sacudir ruidosamente; confundir, desconcertar; **to — off** decir de corrido (o decir muy aprisa); s. traqueteo; golpeteo; **child's —** sonaja, sonajero; **death —** estertor de la muerte.

rat·tle·snake [rǽtlsnek] s. culebra de cascabel, Ríopl., Ch. cascabel o cascabela.

rau·cous [rɔ́kəs] adj. ronco; estentóreo.

rav·age [rǽvɪdʒ] s. estrago, ruina, destrucción, asolamiento; saqueo, pillaje; v. asolar, arruinar; pillar, saquear.

rave [rev] v. desvariar, delirar, disparatar; bramar; **to — about someone** deshacerse en elogios de alguien.

ra·ven [révən] s. cuervo; adj. negro lustroso.

rav·en·ous [rǽvənəs] adj. voraz; devorador; **to be — tener un hambre canina.**

ra·vine [rəvín] s. quebrada, hondonada, barranco (o barranca).

rav·ish [rǽvɪʃ] v. encantar; arrebatar; violar (a una mujer).

raw [rɔ] adj. (crude) crudo; áspero; pelado, descarnado; (untrained) inexperto, nuevo; **— material** materia prima; en bruto; **— recruit** recluta nuevo; **— silk** seda en rama, seda cruda; **— sugar** azúcar crudo, azúcar crudo.

raw·hide [rɔ́haɪd] s. cuero crudo; **— whip** rebenque.

ray [re] s. rayo; raya (especie de pez).

ray·on [réɑn] s. rayón, seda artificial.

raze [rez] v. arrasar, asolar.

ra·zor [rézɚ] s. navaja de afeitar; **— blade** hoja de afeitar; **safety —** navaja de seguridad.

reach [ritʃ] v. (go as far as) llegar a; alcanzar; (touch) tocar; (extend) extenderse; **to — for** tratar de coger; echar mano a; **to — into** meter la mano en; penetrar en; **to — out one's hand** alargar o tender la mano; s. alcance; extensión; **beyond his — fuera de su alcance; within his —** a su alcance.

re·act [rɪǽkt] v. reaccionar.

re·ac·tion [rɪǽkʃən] s. reacción.

re·ac·tion·ar·y [rɪǽkʃənɛrɪ] adj. & s. reaccionario.

QU

read [rid] *v.* leer; indicar (*dícese de un contador, termómetro, etc.*); **to — law** estudiar derecho; **it -s thus** dice así, reza así; **it -s easily** se lee fácilmente o sin esfuerzo.

read [rɛd] *pret. & p.p. de* **to read.**

read·er [rídɚ] *s.* lector; libro de lectura.

read·i·ly [rédlɪ] *adv.* pronto, con presteza; fácilmente, sin esfuerzo.

read·i·ness [rédɪnɪs] *s.* prontitud, presteza, facilidad; buena disposición; **to be in —** estar preparado, estar listo.

read·ing [rídɪŋ] *s.* lectura; indicación (*de un barómetro, termómetro, etc.*); **— room** sala o salón de lectura.

re·ad·just [riədʒʌst] *v.* reajustar, ajustar de nuevo; arreglar de nuevo; readaptar.

re·ad·just·ment [riədʒʌstmənt] *s.* reajuste; readaptación; nuevo arreglo.

read·y [rédɪ] *adj.* listo; preparado; propenso; (*inclined*) dispuesto; **— cash** fondos disponibles; dinero a la mano.

read·y-made [rédɪméd] *adj.* hecho, ya hecho.

re·al [ríəl] *adj.* real, verdadero; **— estate** bienes raíces, bienes inmuebles; **-ly** *adv.* realmente, verdaderamente.

re·al·ism [ríəlɪzəm] *s.* realismo.

re·al·ist [ríəlɪst] *s.* realista; **-ic** *adj.* realista, vivo, natural.

re·al·i·ty [riǽlətɪ] *s.* realidad.

re·al·i·za·tion [riəlezéʃən] *s.* realización; comprensión.

re·al·ize [ríəlaɪz] *v.* (*comprehend*) darse cuenta de, hacerse cargo de; (*achieve*) realizar, efectuar; convertir en dinero.

realm [rɛlm] *s.* (*kingdom*) reino; (*domain*) dominio, región.

Re·al·tor [ríəltɚ] *s.* corredor de bienes raíces.

reap [rip] *v.* segar; (*harvest*) cosechar; (*collect*) recoger; obtener; sacar provecho.

reap·er [rípɚ] *s.* segador; segadora, máquina segadora.

re·ap·pear [riəpír] *v.* reaparecer.

rear [rɪr] *adj.* trasero, posterior; de atrás; **— admiral** contraalmirante; **— guard** retaguardia; *s.* espalda, parte de atrás; (*back*) trasero; fondo (*de una sala, salón, etc.*); (*end*) cola (*de una fila*); **in the —** detrás, atrás, a la espalda; *v.* criar, educar; encabritarse, empinarse (*el caballo*).

rea·son [rízn̩] *s.* razón; causa, motivo; **by — of a** causa de; **it stands to —** es razonable; *v.* razonar; **to — out** discurrir, razonar.

rea·son·a·ble [ríznəbl] *adj.* razonable; justo; racional; módico, moderado; **rea·son·a·bly** *adv.* razonablemente; con razón; bastante.

rea·son·ing [ríznɪŋ] *s.* razonamiento, raciocinio.

re·as·sure [riəʃúr] *v.* tranquilizar, restaurar la confianza a; asegurar de nuevo.

re·bate [ríbet] *s.* rebaja (*de precio*); reembolso, reintegro; *v.* rebajar (*precio*).

reb·el [rébl] *s. & adj.* rebelde; [rɪbɛ́l] *v.* rebelarse.

re·bel·lion [rɪbɛ́ljən] *s.* rebelión.

re·bel·lious [rɪbɛ́ljəs] *adj.* rebelde.

re·birth [ribɝ́θ] *s.* renacimiento.

re·bound [ribáund] *v.* rebotar; repercutir; [ríbaund] *s.* rebote; **on the —** de rebote.

re·buff [rɪbʌf] *s.* desaire; repulsa; *v.* desairar; rechazar.

re·build [ribfld] *v.* reconstruir, reedificar.

re·built [ribflt] *pret. & p.p. de* **to rebuild.**

re·buke [rɪbjúk] *s.* reprensión, reproche, reprimenda, repulsa; *v.* reprender, reprochar.

re·call [ríkɔl] *s.* llamada, aviso (*para hacer volver*); retirada (*de un diplomático*); revocación; [rɪkɔ́l] *v.* recordar; retirar; revocar.

re·ca·pit·u·late [rikəpítʃəlet] *v.* recapitular.

re·cede [rɪsíd] *v.* retroceder; retirarse.

re·ceipt [rɪsít] *s.* recibo; fórmula, receta; **-s** entradas, ingresos; **— in full** quitanza, finiquito; **on — of** al recibo de; **we are in — of your kind letter . . .** obra en nuestro poder su grata . . .; *v.* sellar (*con el recibí*), dar recibo.

re·ceive [rɪsiv] *v.* recibir.

re·ceiv·er [rɪsívɚ] *s.* receptor; recibidor, depositario, síndico; recipiente, receptáculo; **receivership** sindicatura.

re·cent [rísn̩t] *adj.* reciente; **-ly** *adv.* recientemente, *Ch., Ríopl.* recién (*como en* salió recién); **-ly married** recién casados.

re·cep·ta·cle [rɪsɛ́ptəkl] *s.* receptáculo.

re·cep·tion [rɪsɛ́pʃən] *s.* recepción; recibimiento; acogida, acogimiento.

re·cess [rɪsɛ́s] *s.* (*niche*) nicho, hueco; (*cessation*) tregua, intermisión; (*period*) hora de recreo o asueto; **in the -es of** en lo más recóndito de; *v.* suspender el trabajo; levantar (*por corto tiempo*) una sesión; hacer un hueco o nicho en (*la pared*).

re·ces·sion [rɪsɛ́ʃən] *s.* retroceso; contracción económica.

rec·i·pe [rɛ́səpɪ] *s.* receta, fórmula.

re·cip·i·ent [rɪsípɪənt] *s.* recipiente, recibidor; *adj.* receptivo.

re·cip·ro·cal [rɪsíprəkl] *adj.* recíproco, mutuo.

re·cip·ro·cate [rɪsíprəket] *v.* corresponder.

re·cit·al [rɪsáɪtl] *s.* recitación; relación; narración; recital (*músico*).

rec·i·ta·tion [rɛsətéʃən] *s.* recitación.

re·cite [rɪsáɪt] *v.* recitar; relatar; decir o dar la lección.

reck·less [réklɪs] *adj.* temerario, atrevido, precipitado; descuidado; **— with one's money** derrochador.

reck·less·ness [réklɪsnɪs] *s.* temeridad, osadía, descuido.

reck·on [rékən] *v.* contar, computar, calcular; juzgar; suponer.

reck·on·ing [rékənɪŋ] *s.* cuenta; ajuste de cuentas; cálculo; **the day of —** el día del juicio.

re·claim [rɪklém] *v.* recobrar, aprovechar (*tierras baldías*); (*re-use*) aprovechar o utilizar (*el hule usado*); (*recall*) pedir la devolución de, tratar de recobrar.

re·cline [rɪkláɪn] *v.* reclinar(se), recostar(se).

re·cluse [rɪklús] *adj.* recluso, solitario; *s.* recluso, solitario, ermitaño.

rec·og·ni·tion [rɛkəgníʃən] *s.* reconocimiento.

rec·og·nize [rékəgnaɪz] *v.* reconocer.

re·coil [rɪkɔ́ɪl] *v.* (*firearm*) recular, *Am.* patear (*un arma de fuego*); (*move back*) retroceder, retirarse; *s.* reculada; (*rebound*) rebote.

rec·ol·lect [rɛkəlɛ́kt] *v.* recordar; [rikəlɛ́kt] recobrar, volver a cobrar; recoger, reunir.

rec·ol·lec·tion [rɛkəlɛ́kʃən] *s.* recuerdo.

rec·om·mend [rɛkəmɛ́nd] *v.* recomendar.

rec·om·men·da·tion [rɛkəmɛndéʃən] *s.* recomendación.

rec·om·pense [rékəmpɛns] *v.* recompensar; *s.* recompensa.

rec·on·cile [rékənsaɪl] *v.* reconciliar; ajustar, conciliar; **to — oneself to** resignarse a, conformarse con.

rec·on·cil·i·a·tion [rɛkənsɪliéʃən] *f.* reconciliación; ajuste, conciliación; conformidad, resignación.

re·con·noi·ter [rikənɔ́ɪtɚ] *v.* reconocer, explorar; hacer un reconocimiento o exploración.

re·con·sid·er [rikənsídɚ] *v.* reconsiderar.

re·con·struct [rikənstrʌ́kt] *v.* reconstruir, reedificar.

re·con·struc·tion [rikənstrʌ́kʃən] *s.* reconstrucción.

rec·ord [rɛ́kɚd] *s.* registro; (*copy*) copia oficial de un documento; memoria; (*vita*) historial (*de una persona*), hoja de servicios; disco (*fonográfico*); (*sports*) record (*en deportes*); — **player** tocadiscos; **to break the speed** — batir el record de velocidad; **an off-the-record remark** una observación que no ha de constar en el acta; observación hecha en confianza; *adj.* notable, extraordinario; sobresalienta; [rɪkɔ́rd] *v.* [rɪkɔ́rd] registrar; asentar, apuntar; inscribir; (*cut*) grabar en disco fonográfico.

re·cord·er [rɪkɔ́rdɚ] *s.* (*tape*) grabadora; — **of deeds** registrador de propiedad, archivero.

re·cord·ing [rɪkɔ́rdɪŋ] *s.* grabación.

re·count [ríkaʊnt] *s.* recuento, segunda cuenta; [rɪkáʊnt] *v.* contar, narrar, relatar, referir; [rikáʊnt] recontar, volver a contar.

re·course [ríkors] *s.* recurso, refugio, auxilio; **to have** — **to** recurrir a.

re·cov·er [rɪkʌ́vɚ] *v.* recobrar(se), recuperar(se); recobrar la salud; reponerse; [rikʌ́vɚ] volver a cubrir.

re·cov·er·y [rɪkʌ́vrɪ] *s.* recobro; recuperación; cobranza; reivindicación.

rec·re·a·tion [rɛkrɪéʃən] *s.* recreación, recreo.

re·crim·i·nate [rɪkrímənet] *v.* recriminar.

re·cruit [rɪkrút] *v.* reclutar; alistar; *s.* recluta; novato, nuevo miembro (*de una organización*).

rec·tan·gle [rɛ́ktæŋgl] *s.* rectángulo.

rec·ti·fy [rɛ́ktəfaɪ] *v.* rectificar.

rec·tor [rɛ́ktɚ] *s.* rector.

rec·tum [rɛ́ktəm] *s.* recto.

re·cu·per·ate [rɪkjúpəret] *v.* recuperar, recobrar; recobrar la salud.

re·cur [rɪkɝ́] *v.* volver a ocurrir; repetirse; **to** — **to a matter** volver a un asunto.

red [rɛd] *adj.* rojo; colorado, encarnado; **red-hot** candente; (*angry*) enfurecido, furioso; muy caliente; — **tape** formalismo, trámites enojosos papeleo; — **wine** vino tinto; **in the** — con deficit; **to see** — enfurecerse; *s.* color rojo; rojo.

red·den [rɛ́dn] *v.* enrojecer(se); ruborizarse; ponerse rojo; teñir de rojo.

red·dish [rɛ́dɪʃ] *adj.* rojizo.

re·deem [rɪdím] *v.* redimir; (*rescue*) rescatar; (*buy back*) desempeñar (*una prenda*); (*fulfill*) cumplir (*una promesa*).

re·deem·er [rɪdímɚ] *s.* salvador, redentor; **the Redeemer** el Redentor.

re·demp·tion [rɪdɛ́mpʃən] *s.* redención; rescate; — **of a note** pago de una obligación.

red·ness [rɛ́dnɪs] *s.* rojez o rojura; inflamación.

re·dou·ble [ridʌ́bl] *v.* redoblar; repetir; repercutir.

re·dound [rɪdáʊnd] *v.* redundar.

re·dress [rídrɛs] *s.* reparación, enmienda; compensación; desagravio; [rɪdrɛ́s] *v.* enmendar, rectificar, remediar, reparar; desagraviar.

red snap·per [rɛdsnǽpɚ] *s.* pargo; *Méx.* huachinango.

re·duce [rɪdjús] *v.* reducir; mermar; rebajar; adelgazar(se); subyugar.

re·duc·tion [rɪdʌ́kʃən] *s.* reducción; merma, rebaja.

re·dun·dant [rɪdʌ́ndənt] *adj.* redundante.

red·wood [rɛ́dwʊd] *s. Am.* secoya o secuoya (*árbol gigantesco de California*); madera roja de la secoya.

reed [rid] *s.* caña; junco, junquillo; lengüeta, (*musical instrument*) boquilla (*de ciertos instrumentos de viento*); caramillo.

reef [rif] *s.* arrecife, escollo; banco de arena (*en el mar*).

reek [rik] *v.* (*fume*) exhalar, echar (*vaho o vapor*); (*stink*) heder, oler mal; *s.* hedor, mal olor.

reel [ril] *s.* (*spool*) carrete; carretel; (*film*) cinta cinematográfica; *v.* aspar, enredar (*en carretel*); bambolearse, tambalearse; **to** — **off stories** ensartar cuento tras cuento.

re·e·lect [riəlɛ́kt] *v.* reelegir.

re·e·lec·tion [riəlɛ́kʃən] *s.* reelección.

re·en·ter [riɛ́ntɚ] *v.* volver a entrar.

re·es·tab·lish [riəstǽblɪʃ] *v.* restablecer.

re·fer [rɪfɝ́] *v.* referir; (*transmit*) transmitir, remitir; dejar al juicio o decisión de; referirse, aludir; acudir, recurrir (*a un tratado, diccionario, etc.*).

ref·er·ee [rɛfərí] *s.* árbitro; *v.* arbitrar.

ref·er·ence [rɛ́frəns] *s.* (*mention*) referencia; mención, alusión; (*sponsor*) fiador, el que recomienda a otro; — **book** libro de referencia, libro de consulta; **commercial -s** fiadores, referencias comerciales; **letter of** — carta de recomendación; **with** — **to** con respecto a, respecto de, en cuanto a.

re·fill [rifíl] *v.* rellenar.

re·fine [rɪfáɪn] *v.* refinar, purificar; (*polish*) pulir; perfeccionar.

re·fined [rɪfáɪnd] *adj.* refinado; pulido, fino, culto.

re·fine·ment [rɪfáɪnmənt] *s.* refinamiento, finura; buena crianza; refinación, purificación; perfeccionamiento.

re·fin·er·y [rɪfáɪnərɪ] *s.* refinería.

re·flect [rɪflɛ́kt] *v.* reflejar (*luz, calor*); reflexionar; meditar; **to** — **on one's character** desdecir del carácter de una.

re·flec·tion [rɪflɛ́kʃən] *s.* reflexión; reflejo, imagen; tacha, discrédito; **on** — después de reflexionarlo.

re·flec·tive [rɪflɛ́ktɪv] *adj.* reflexivo.

re·flex [ríflɛks] *adj.* reflejo; *s.* reflejo; acción refleja.

re·flex·ive [rɪflɛ́ksɪv] *adj.* reflexivo.

re·form [rɪfɔ́rm] *v.* reformar(se); *s.* reforma.

ref·or·ma·tion [rɛfɚméʃən] *s.* reforma.

re·for·ma·to·ry [rɪfɔ́rmətorɪ] *s.* reformatorio.

re·form·er [rɪfɔ́rmɚ] *s.* reformador; reformista.

re·frac·tion [rɪfrǽkʃən] *s.* refracción.

re·frac·to·ry [rɪfrǽktərɪ] *adj.* refractario; terco, obstinado, rebelde.

re·frain [rɪfrén] *v.* refrenarse, abstenerse; *s.* estribillo.

re·fresh [rɪfrɛ́ʃ] *v.* refrescar(se); renovar.

re·fresh·ing [rɪfrɛ́ʃɪŋ] *adj.* refrescante; renovador, que renueva; placentero.

re·fresh·ment [rɪfrɛ́ʃmənt] *s.* refresco.

re·frig·er·a·tion [rɪfrɪdʒəréʃən] *s.* refrigeración, enfriamiento.

re·frig·er·a·tor [rɪfrídʒəretɚ] *s.* nevera, *Am.* refrigerador; — **plant** frigorífico.

ref·uge [rɛ́fjudʒ] *s.* refugio, asilo, amparo.

ref·u·gee [rɛfjudʒí] *s.* refugiado.

re·fund [rɪfʌ́nd] *s.* reembolso, reintegro; *v.* reembolsar, restituir, reintegrar; consolidar (*una deuda*).

re·fur·bish [rɪfɝ́bɪʃ] *v.* retocar.

re·fus·al [rɪfjúzl] *s.* negativa; (*snub*) desaire; opción (*derecho de recusar un convenio provisional*).

re·fuse [rɪfjúz] *v.* rehusar; negar; desechar; rechazar; **to** — **to** rehusarse a, negarse a.

ref·use [rɛ́fjus] *s.* desechos, basura, sobras, desperdicios.

re·fute [rɪfjút] *v.* refutar.

re·gain [rɪgén] v. recobrar; ganar de nuevo.
re·gal [rígl] adj. regio, real.
re·gale [rɪgél] v. regalar, agasajar; recrear.
re·ga·lia [rɪgélɪə] s. pl. galas, decoraciones, insignias.
re·gard [rɪgárd] v. (look) mirar; (consider) considerar; juzgar; estimar; **as -s this** tocante a esto, en cuanto a esto; por lo que toca a esto; s. miramiento, consideración; respeto; estima; mirada; **-s** recuerdos, memorias; **in** (o **with**) — **to** con respecto a, tocante a, respecto de.
re·gard·ing [rɪgárdɪŋ] prep. tocante a, con respecto a, respecto de, relativo a.
re·gard·less [rɪgárdlɪs]: — **of** sin hacer caso de, prescindiendo de.
re·gen·cy [rídʒənsɪ] s. regencia.
re·gent [rídʒənt] s. regente.
re·gime [rɪʒím] s. régimen.
reg·i·ment [rédʒəmənt] s. regimiento.
re·gion [rídʒən] s. región.
reg·is·ter [rédʒɪstɚ] s. (recording) registro; matrícula; (entry) archivo; lista; (machine) contador; indicador; (voice) registro; **cash** — caja registradora; v. registrar; matricular(se); inscribir(se); marcar, indicar; mostrar, manifestar; certificar (una carta).
reg·is·tered [rédʒɪstɚd] **mail** adj. correo certificado; Col. correo recomendado; — **stock** acciones nominativas.
reg·is·trar [rédʒɪstrɑr] s. registrador, archivero.
reg·is·tra·tion [rédʒɪstréʃən] s. registro; asiento (en un libro); matrícula; inscripción.
re·gret [rɪgrét] s. pesadumbre, dolor; sentimiento, remordimiento; **to send -s** enviar sus excusas (al rehusar una invitación); v. sentir, lamentar; arrepentirse de.
re·gret·ful [rɪgrétfʊl] adj. deplorable.
re·gret·ta·ble [rɪgrétəbl] adj. lamentable.
reg·u·lar [régjəlɚ] adj. regular; metódico, ordenado; **a** — **fool** un verdadero necio, un tonto de capirote; — **price** precio corriente; — **soldier** soldado de línea.
reg·u·lar·i·ty [régjəlǽrətɪ] s. regularidad.
reg·u·late [régjəlet] v. regular, regularizar.
reg·u·la·tion [régjəléʃən] s. regulación; regla, orden; **-s** reglamento; — **uniform** uniforme de regla, uniforme de ordenanza.
reg·u·la·tor [régjəletɚ] s. regulador; registro (de reloj).
re·ha·bil·i·tate [rihæbílətet] v. rehabilitar.
re·hears·al [rɪhɝsl] s. ensayo (de un drama; concierto, etc.); enumeración, repetición.
re·hearse [rɪhɝs] v. ensayar; repetir; repasar.
reign [ren] s. reino, reinado; v. reinar.
re·im·burse [riɪmbɝs] v. reembolsar.
re·im·burse·ment [riɪmbɝsmənt] s. reembolso, reintegro.
rein [ren] s. rienda; v. guiar, gobernar; refrenar (un caballo).
re·in·car·nate [riɪnkárnet] v. reencarnar.
rein·deer [réndɪr] s. reno (especie de ciervo).
re·in·force [riɪnfórs] v. reforzar.
re·in·force·ment [riɪnfórsmənt] v. refuerzo.
re·it·er·ate [riítəret] v. reiterar, repetir.
re·ject [rɪdʒékt] v. rechazar; desechar; descartar; rehusar.
re·joice [rɪdʒɔ́ɪs] v. regocijar(se).
re·joic·ing [rɪdʒɔ́ɪsɪŋ] s. regocijo, júbilo.
re·join [rɪdʒɔ́ɪn] v. reunirse con; volver(se) a unir; [rɪdʒɔ́ɪn] replicar.
re·ju·ve·nate [rɪdʒúvənet] v. rejuvenecer.

re·lapse [rɪlǽps] s. recaída; v. recaer, reincidir.
re·late [rɪlét] v. relatar, narrar; relacionar; **it -s to se** relaciona con, se refiere a.
re·lat·ed [rɪlétɪd] adj. relatado, narrado; relacionado; **to become** — **by marriage** emparentar; **we are** — somos parientes; estamos emparentados.
re·la·tion [rɪléʃən] s. (association) relación; (story) narración; (kinship) parentesco; pariente; **-s** parientes, parentela; **with** — **to** con relación a, con respecto a, tocante a.
re·la·tion·ship [rɪléʃənʃɪp] s. relación; parentesco.
rel·a·tive [rélətɪv] adj. relativo; s. relativo, — **pronoun** pronombre relativo; pariente, deudo; **to** relativo a; tocante a; referente a.
re·lax [rɪlǽks] v. relajar; aflojar; mitigar(se); esparcirse, recrearse.
re·lax·a·tion [rilækséʃən] s. (loosening) expansión, esparcimiento; aflojamiento o relajamiento; (recreation) solaz, recreo; — **of discipline** relajación de la disciplina; — **of one's mind** esparcimiento del ánimo.
re·lay [rîle] s. relevo, remuda; — **race** carrera de relevo; **electric** — relevador; [rɪlé] v. transmitir, despachar; hacer cundir (una noticia); **to** — **a broadcast** reemitir (o redifundir) un programa de radio.
re·lease [rɪlís] v. soltar; librar; poner en libertad; (hospital) dar de alta; relevar, aliviar; **to** — **a piece of news** hacer pública una nueva; **to** — **from blame** exonerar; s. liberación; alivio; exoneración; escape; **press** — comunicado de prensa.
rel·e·gate [réləget] v. relegar; **to** — **to a corner** arrinconar, arrumbar.
re·lent [rɪlént] v. mitigar(se); ceder; aplacarse.
re·lent·less [rɪléntlɪs] adj. implacable.
rel·e·vant [réləvənt] adj. pertinente; a propósito.
re·li·a·bil·i·ty [rɪlaɪəbílətɪ] s. formalidad; puntualidad; integridad.
re·li·a·ble [rɪláɪəbl] adj. formal; puntual; digno de confianza.
re·li·ance [rɪláɪəns] s. confianza; **self-reliance** confianza en sí, confianza en sus propias fuerzas.
rel·ic [rélɪk] s. reliquia.
re·lief [rɪlíf] s. (ease) alivio; (rest) descanso, (consolation) consuelo; (help) ayuda, socorro; (projection) relieve, realce; **low** — bajo relieve; **to be on** — recibir manutención gratuita; **to put in** — realzar, poner en relieve.
re·lieve [rɪlív] v. relevar; (free) librar; (help) ayudar; (alleviate) aliviar; mitigar.
re·li·gion [rɪlídʒən] s. religión.
re·li·gious [rɪlídʒəs] adj. & s. religioso.
re·lin·quish [rɪlíŋkwɪʃ] v. abandonar, dejar.
rel·ish [rélɪʃ] s. (zest) buen sabor; (taste) gusto; apetito; (please) goce; (condiment) condimento; entremés; v. saborear, paladear; gustarle a uno, agradarle a uno.
re·lo·cate [rilóket] v. restablecer.
re·luc·tance [rɪlʌ́ktəns] s. repugnancia, renuencia, aversión, desgana.
re·luc·tant [rɪlʌ́ktənt] adj. renuente, refractario, opuesto; **-ly** adv. renuentemente, con renuencia, de mala gana; a redopelo.
re·ly [rɪláɪ] v. **to** — **on** contar con, confiar en, fiarse de.
re·main [rɪmén] v. quedar(se), permanecer, estarse; restar, faltar.
re·main·der [rɪméndɚ] s. resto; restante; residuo.
re·mains [rɪménz] s. pl. restos; reliquias; sobras.
re·make [rimék] v. rehacer, hacer de nuevo.

re·mark [rɪmárk] s. observación, nota, reparo; v. notar, observar; **to — on** comentar; aludir a.
re·mark·a·ble [rɪmárkəbl] adj. notable; extraordinario; **remarkably** adv. notablemente; extraordinariamente.
rem·e·dy [rέmədɪ] s. remedio; cura; v. remediar; curar.
re·mem·ber [rɪmέmbɚ] v. recordar; acordarse; **— me to him** déle Vd. recuerdos (o memorias) de mi parte.
re·mem·brance [rɪmέmbrəns] s. recuerdo; recordación; memoria; **-s** recuerdos, saludos.
re·mind [rɪmáɪnd] v. recordar.
re·mind·er [rɪmáɪndɚ] s. recordatorio, recordativo, memorándum, memoria; advertencia.
rem·i·nis·cence [rɛmənísns] s. reminiscencia, memoria, recuerdo.
re·miss [rɪmís] adj. descuidado, negligente.
re·mis·sion [rɪmíʃən] s. remisión, perdón.
re·mit [rɪmít] v. remitir; remesar, enviar una remesa; (pardon) perdonar, absolver.
re·mit·tance [rɪmítns] s. remisión, envío, remesa (de fondos).
rem·nant [rέmnənt] s. resto; residuo; retazo (de tela, paño, etc.); vestigio.
re·mod·el [rimádl] v. rehacer, reconstruir; modelar de nuevo.
re·morse [rɪmɔrs] s. remordimiento.
re·mote [rɪmót] adj. remoto; lejano; s. **— control** telecontrol; comando a distancia.
re·mov·al [rɪmúvl] s. mudanza, traslado; deposición (de un empleo); eliminación; extracción; alejamiento.
re·move [rɪmúv] v. remover; mudar(se), trasladar(se); quitar; eliminar; extirpar; sacar, extraer; (fire) deponer (de un empleo); apartar; alejar.
re·moved [rɪmúvd] adj. remoto, distante.
re·nais·sance [rɛnəsáns] s. renacimiento.
re·na·scence [rɪnǽsns] s. renacimiento.
rend [rɛnd] v. desgarrar, rasgar; rajar.
ren·der [rέndɚ] v. dar; entregar; (make) hacer; ejecutar, (represent) interpretar (música o un papel dramático); (translate) traducir; **to — an account of** rendir o dar cuenta de; **to — homage** rendir homenaje; **to — thanks** rendir gracias, dar las gracias; **to — useless** inutilizar, incapacitar.
ren·di·tion [rɛndíʃən] s. (surrender) rendición; (version) traducción, ejecución.
re·new [rɪnjú] v. renovar; restaurar; reanudar; prorrogar (un préstamo).
re·new·al [rɪnjúəl] s. renovación; reanudación; prórroga.
re·nounce [rɪnáʊns] v. renunciar.
ren·o·vate [rέnəvet] v. renovar.
re·nown [rɪnáʊn] s. renombre.
re·nowned [rɪnáʊnd] adj. renombrado.
rent [rɛnt] s. alquiler, renta, arrendamiento; **it is for —** se alquila, se arrienda; v. alquilar, arrendar.
rent [rɛnt] pret. & p.p. de **to rend**; s. grieta, hendidura; rasgadura, rotura.
rent·al [rέntl] s. renta, alquiler.
rent·er [rέntɚ] s. inquilino.
re·o·pen [riópən] v. reabrir(se), volver a abrir(se).
re·pair [rɪpέr] v. reparar; remendar; componer; restaurar; **to —** to dirigirse a; s. reparo, reparación; remiendo; compostura; **in —** en buen estado; compuesto; **— gang** cuadrilla de reparaciones.
rep·a·ra·tion [rɛpəréʃən] s. reparación; desagravio.
rep·ar·tee [rɛpɑrtí] s. respuesta viva; agudeza en el diálogo.

re·pay [ripé] v. resarcir; compensar; reembolsar; pagar.
re·pay·ment [ripémənt] s. reintegro, pago, devolución, restitución.
re·peal [rɪpíl] v. derogar, abrogar, revocar, abolir (una ley); s. abrogación, derogación, revocación, abolición (de una ley).
re·peat [rɪpít] v. repetir; s. repetición.
re·peat·ed [rɪpítɪd] adj. repetido; **-ly** adv. repetidamente; repetidas veces, una y otra vez.
re·pel [rɪpέl] v. repeler; rechazar; repugnar; **that idea -s me** me repugna (o me es repugnante) esa idea.
re·pel·lent [rɪpέlənt] s. repelente; (water) impermeable.
re·pent [rɪpέnt] v. arrepentirse (de).
re·pen·tance [rɪpέntəns] s. arrepentimiento.
re·pen·tant [rɪpέntənt] adj. arrepentido; penitente.
rep·er·toire [rέpɚtwɑr] s. repertorio.
rep·e·ti·tion [rɛpɪtíʃən] s. repetición.
re·place [rɪplés] v. reponer, volver a colocar; reemplazar; restituir; remudar.
re·place·a·ble [rɪplésəbl] adj. reemplazable; substituible.
re·place·ment [rɪplésmənt] s. reposición; reemplazo; devolución, restitución; substitución.
re·plen·ish [rɪplέnɪʃ] v. reabastecer; rellenar, llenar.
re·plete [rɪplít] adj. repleto, atestado.
rep·li·ca [rέplɪkə] s. reproducción, copia exacta.
re·ply [rɪpláɪ] v. replicar, contestar, responder; s. réplica, contestación, respuesta.
re·port [rɪpórt] v. (inform) dar cuenta de; (make known) avisar; informar; presentar un informe; rendir informe; hacer un reportaje, Am. reportar; denunciar, delatar; presentarse; **to — for duty** presentarse; **it is -ed that** dizque, se dice que, corre la voz que; s. noticia, reporte; informe; memorial; relación; rumor; estallido, disparo; **news — reportaje**.
re·port·er [rɪpórtɚ] s. reportero, repórter.
re·pose [rɪpóz] v. reposar, descansar; **to — one's confidence in** confiar en; depositar su confianza en; s. reposo.
re·pos·i·to·ry [rɪpázətorɪ] s. depósito; almacén.
rep·re·sent [rɛprɪzέnt] v. representar.
rep·re·sen·ta·tion [rɛprɪzɛntéʃən] s. representación.
rep·re·sen·ta·tive [rɛprɪzέntətɪv] adj. representativo; representante; típico; s. representante; delegado, diputado.
re·press [rɪprέs] v. reprimir; refrenar, restringir; cohibir.
re·pres·sion [rɪprέʃən] s. represión.
re·prieve [rɪprív] v. suspensión temporal de pena; alivio.
rep·ri·mand [rέprəmænd] v. reprender, regañar; s. reprimenda, reprensión, regaño.
re·pri·sal [rɪpráɪzl] s. represalia.
re·proach [rɪprótʃ] v. reprochar; censurar, criticar; echar en cara; s. reproche, reprimenda; censura.
re·pro·duce [riprədjús] v. reproducir.
re·pro·duc·tion [riprədΛkʃən] s. reproducción.
re·proof [rɪprúf] s. reprensión, reproche, regaño.
re·prove [rɪprúv] v. reprobar, reprender, censurar.
rep·tile [rέptl] s. reptil.
re·pub·lic [rɪpΛblɪk] s. república.
re·pub·li·can [rɪpΛblɪkən] adj. & s. republicano.
re·pu·di·ate [rɪpjúdɪet] v. repudiar.
re·pug·nance [rɪpΛgnəns] s. repugnancia; aversión.
re·pug·nant [rɪpΛgnənt] adj. repugnante; antipático.
re·pulse [rɪpΛls] v. repulsar, repeler; rechazar; s. repulsa; desaire.
re·pul·sive [rɪpΛlsɪv] adj. repulsivo, repugnante.

RE

rep·u·ta·ble [rɛ́pjətəbl] *adj.* de buena reputación.
rep·u·ta·tion [rɛpjətéʃən] *s.* reputación, renombre.
re·pute [rɪpjút] *v.* reputar; estimar, considerar; *s.* reputación; renombre, fama; **of ill** — de mala fama.
re·quest [rɪkwɛ́st] *s.* solicitud, petición, demanda; súplica, ruego; **at the** — **of** a solicitud de, a instancias de; *v.* solicitar, pedir, rogar, suplicar.
re·quire [rɪkwáɪr] *v.* requerir; exigir, demandar.
re·quire·ment [rɪkwáɪrmənt] *s.* requerimiento, requisito; exigencia; necesidad.
req·ui·site [rɛ́kwəzɪt] *s.* requisito; *adj.* requerido, necesario.
req·ui·si·tion [rɛkwəzíʃən] *s.* requisición, demanda, orden; *v.* demandar, pedir, ordenar.
re·scind [rɪsínd] *v.* rescindir.
res·cue [rɛ́skju] *v.* rescatar; librar; salvar; *s.* rescate, salvamento, salvación, socorro; **to go to the** — **of** acudir al socorro de, ir a salvar a.
re·search [rɪsɝ́tʃ] *s.* investigación; rebusca, búsqueda, encuesta, investigación; [rɪsɝtʃ] *v.* rebuscar, investigar.
re·sem·blance [rɪzɛ́mbləns] *s.* semejanza, parecido.
re·sem·ble [rɪzɛ́mbl] *v.* asemejarse a, semejar, parecerse a.
re·sent [rɪzɛ́nt] *v.* resentirse de, sentirse de, darse por agraviado de.
re·sent·ful [rɪzɛ́ntfəl] *adj.* resentido; rencoroso.
re·sent·ment [rɪzɛ́ntmənt] *s.* resentimiento.
res·er·va·tion [rɛzɚvéʃən] *s.* reservación; reserva.
re·serve [rɪzɝ́v] *v.* reservar; *s.* reserva.
re·served [rɪzɝ́vd] *adj.* retraido; — **word** (*computer*) palabra clave (reservada).
res·er·voir [rɛ́zɚvwɔr] *s.* (*stock*) depósito (*de agua, aceite, gas, provisiones, etc.*); (*receptacle*) receptáculo; **water** — alberca, aljibe, tanque, estanque.
re·side [rɪzáɪd] *v.* residir, vivir.
res·i·dence [rɛ́zədəns] *s.* residencia; domicilio.
res·i·dent [rɛ́zədənt] *adj.* & *s.* residente.
res·i·den·tial [rɛzɪdɛ́nʃəl] *adj.* residencial.
res·i·due [rɛ́zədju] *s.* residuo; resto.
re·sign [rɪzáɪn] *v.* renunciar; dimitir; **to** — **oneself to** resignarse a.
res·ig·na·tion [rɛzɪgnéʃən] *s.* renuncia, dimisión; resignación.
re·sil·ience [rizíljəns] *s.* elasticidad.
res·in [rɛ́zn] *s.* resina.
re·sist [rɪzíst] *v.* resistir; oponerse, resistirse a.
re·sis·tance [rɪzístəns] *s.* resistencia.
re·sis·tant [rɪzístənt] *adj.* resistente.
res·o·lute [rɛ́zəlut] *adj.* resuelto.
res·o·lu·tion [rɛzəlúʃən] *s.* resolución; acuerdo.
re·solve [rɪzálv] *v.* resolver(se); **to** — **into** resolverse en, reducirse a, transformarse en; **to** — **to** acordar; proponerse, resolverse a.
res·o·nance [rɛ́zənəns] *s.* resonancia.
res·o·nant [rɛ́zənənt] *adj.* resonante.
re·sort [rɪzɔ́rt] *v.* recurrir, acudir; **to** — **to force** recurrir a la fuerza; *s.* (*refuge*) refugio; (*dwelling*) morada; **as a last** — como último recurso; **summer** — lugar de veraneo; **vice** — garito; casa de mala fama; **to have** — **to** recurrir a.
re·sort·er [rɪzɔ́rtɚ] *s.* **summer** — veraneante.
re·sound [rɪzáund] *v.* resonar; repercutir; retumbar.
re·source [rɪsórs] *s.* recurso; **natural -s** recursos o riquezas naturales.
re·spect [rɪspɛ́kt] *v.* respectar; **as -s** por lo que respecta a, por lo que toca a, tocante a; *s.* respeto; consideración; **with** — **to** (con) respecto a, respecto de; por lo que atañe a.

re·spect·a·ble [rɪspɛ́ktəbl] *adj.* respetable.
re·spect·ful [rɪspɛ́ktfəl] *adj.* respetuoso.
re·spect·ing [rɪspɛ́ktɪŋ] *prep.* con respecto a, tocante a.
re·spec·tive [rɪspɛ́ktɪv] *adj.* respectivo.
res·pi·ra·tion [rɛspəréʃən] *s.* respiración, respiro.
re·spite [rɛ́spɪt] *s.* tregua, pausa, descanso; intervalo; prórroga.
re·splen·dent [rɪsplɛ́ndənt] *adj.* resplandeciente.
re·spond [rɪspánd] *v.* responder; corresponder; reaccionar.
re·sponse [rɪspáns] *s.* respuesta, contestación; reacción.
re·spon·si·bil·i·ty [rɪspɑnsəbíləti] *s.* responsabilidad.
re·spon·si·ble [rɪspánsəbl] *adj.* responsable; formal, digno de confianza.
rest [rɛst] *s.* (*repose*) descanso; reposo; quietud; tregua; pausa; (*support*) apoyo; **at** — en paz; en reposo; tranquilo; **the** — el resto; los demás; *v.* descansar; reposar; apoyar; **to** — **on** descansar sobre; apoyar(se) en; basar(se) en; contar con, confiar en, depender de.
res·tau·rant [rɛ́stərənt] *s.* restaurante; *Am.* restorán.
rest·ful [rɛ́stfəl] *adj.* reposado, sosegado, tranquilo.
res·ti·tu·tion [rɛstətjúʃən] *s.* restitución; (*return*) devolución.
res·tive [rɛ́stɪv] *adj.* intranquilo.
rest·less [rɛ́stlɪs] *adj.* inquieto, intranquilo.
rest·less·ness [rɛ́stlɪsnɪs] *s.* inquietud, desasosiego, intranquilidad.
res·to·ra·tion [rɛstəréʃən] *s.* restauración; restitución; renovación.
re·store [rɪstór] *v.* restaurar; (*renew*) renovar; restituir; restablecer.
re·strain [rɪstrén] *v.* refrenar, contener, cohibir, reprimir, coartar; restringir.
re·straint [rɪstrént] *s.* restricción; reserva, circunspección; moderación; cohibición.
re·strict [rɪstríkt] *v.* restringir, limitar.
re·stric·tion [rɪstríkʃən] *s.* restricción.
re·sult [rɪzʌ́lt] *v.* resultar; **to** — **from** resultar de; **to** — **in** parar en; causar; dar por resultado; *s.* resulta, resultado; **as a** — de resultas, como resultado.
re·sume [rɪzúm] *v.* reasumir, volver a tomar; recomenzar; reanudar, continuar.
ré·su·mé [rɛzumé] *s.* resumen, sumario.
re·sur·gent [rɪsɝ́dʒənt] *adj.* resurgente.
res·ur·rec·tion [rɛzərɛ́kʃən] *s.* resurrección.
re·sus·ci·tate [rɪsʌ́sətet] *v.* resucitar; revivir.
re·tail [rítel] *s.* venta al por menor; menudeo; **at** — al por menor; — **market** mercado minorista; — **shop** tienda detallista; — **trade** comercio minorista; — **merchant** detallista, comerciante al por menor; — **price** precio al por menor; *v.* detallar; vender al menudeo (vender al por menor), *Méx., C.A., Ven., Col.* menudear.
re·tail·er [rítelɚ] *s.* detallista, revendedor, comerciante al por menor.
re·tain [rɪtén] *v.* retener; emplear.
re·tal·i·ate [rɪtǽliet] *v.* desquitarse, vengarse.
re·tal·i·a·tion [rɪtæliéʃən] *s.* desquite; desagravio, represalia, venganza.
re·tard [rɪtárd] *v.* retardar, retrasar, atrasar.
re·ten·tion [rɪtɛ́nʃən] *s.* retención.
ret·i·cence [rɛ́təsəns] *s.* reserva.
ret·i·nue [rɛ́tnju] *s.* comitiva, séquito, acompañamiento.
re·tire [rɪtáɪr] *v.* retirar(se); jubilar(se); acostarse; apartarse.
re·tire·ment [rɪtáɪrmənt] *s.* retiro; (*from work*) jubilación.

re·tort [rɪtɔ́rt] *v.* replicar; redargüir; *s.* réplica.

re·touch [ritʌ́tʃ] *v.* retocar; *s.* retoque.

re·trace [ritrés] *v.* repasar; (*again*) volver a trazar; **to — one's steps** volver sobre sus pasos, retroceder.

re·tract [rɪtrǽkt] *v.* retractar, retractarse de; desdecirse (de); retraer.

re·treat [rɪtrít] *s.* retiro, refugio, (*place*) asilo; (*action*) retirada; (*call*) retreta (*toque de retirada*); *v.* retirarse; retroceder.

re·trench [rɪtréntʃ] *v.* cercenar, reducir, disminuir; economizar.

re·trieve [rɪtrív] *v.* cobrar (*la caza*); recobrar, recuperar; reparar (*una pérdida*).

ret·ro·ac·tive [retroǽktɪv] *adj.* retroactivo.

ret·ro·flex [rétrofleks] *adj.* retroflejo.

ret·ro·rock·et [rétrorakɪt] *s.* retrocohete.

ret·ro·spect [rétrospekt] *s.* retrospección; **in —** retrospectivamente.

re·turn [rɪtɚ́n] *v.* (*come back*) volver, regresar, retornar; (*give back*) devolver; replicar; redituar; (*produce*) producir; restar (*la pelota en tenis*); **to — a favor** corresponder a un favor; **to — a report** rendir un informe; *s.* vuelta, regreso; retorno; recompensa; restitución, devolución; (*reply*) réplica; **— address** señas del remitente; **— key** (*computer*) tecla de retorno; **— a verdict** fallar, dar un veredicto; resto (*en un juego de pelota*); (*production*) rendimiento; rédito, ganancia; informe; **— game** desquite, juego de desquite; **— ticket** boleto de vuelta; **by — mail** a vuelta de correo; **election -s** reportaje de elecciones; **in —** en cambio; **in — for** a cambio de, a trueque de; **income tax —** declaración de rentas; **many happy -s** muchas felicidades (en su día).

re·un·ion [rijúnjən] *s.* reunión; junta.

re·u·nite [rijʊnáɪt] *v.* reunir(se), volver a unirse; reconciliar(se).

re·veal [rɪvíl] *v.* revelar.

rev·el [révl] *v.* deleitarse, gozarse; (*to "party"*) parrandéar, *Ríopl.* farrear; andar de parranda, andar de farra, *s.* parranda, juerga, jarana.

rev·e·la·tion [revléʃən] *s.* revelación; **Revelation(s)** Apocalipsis.

rev·el·ry [révlrɪ] *s.* jaleo, juerga, jarana, parranda.

re·venge [rɪvɛ́ndʒ] *v.* vengar, vindicar; *s.* venganza; desquite.

re·venge·ful [rɪvɛ́ndʒfəl] *adj.* vengativo.

rev·e·nue [révənju] *s.* renta; rédito; rentas públicas, ingresos; **— authorities** agentes fiscales; **— stamp** sello fiscal; **— tariff** arancel de renta; *Arg.* derechos fiscales.

re·vere [rɪvír] *v.* venerar.

rev·er·ence [révrəns] *s.* reverencia; veneración; *v.* reverenciar, venerar.

rev·er·end [révrənd] *adj.* reverendo; venerable.

rev·er·ent [révrənt] *adj.* reverente.

rev·er·ie, rev·er·y [révərɪ] *s.* ensueño; arrobamiento.

re·verse [rɪvɚ́s] *adj.* inverso, invertido; (*opposite*) contrario, opuesto; *s.* revés; reverso, dorso; lo contrario; (*mishap*) contratiempo; *v.* invertir; voltear; revocar (*una sentencia*).

re·vert [rɪvɚ́t] *v.* revertir, volver atrás, retroceder.

re·view [rɪvjú] *v.* (*study*) repasar, revisar; revistar; (*inspect*) pasar revista a (*las tropas*); (*criticize*) reseñar, hacer una reseña de (*un libro*); *s.* revista; repaso; reseña, crítica (*de un libro, drama, etc.*); revisión (*de un caso jurídico, sentencia, etc.*).

re·vile [rɪváɪl] *v.* vilipendiar, vituperar, denigrar.

re·vise [rɪváɪz] *v.* revisar, repasar, releer (*para corregir*); corregir, enmendar.

re·vi·sion [rɪvíʒən] *s.* revisión; enmienda; edición enmendada o mejorada.

re·viv·al [rɪváɪvl] *s.* (*renewal*) renovación; revivificación; (*repeating*) renacimiento; (*theater*) nueva presentación (*teatral*); **— meeting** junta para revivir el fervor religioso; **religious —** despertamiento (*o* nuevo fervor) religioso.

re·vive [rɪváɪv] *v.* revivir, resucitar; (*come to*) volver en sí; renacer; reavivar, reanimar(se); (*bring around*) avivar.

re·voke [rɪvók] *v.* revocar, abrogar, anular; renunciar (*en los juegos de naipes*).

re·volt [rɪvólt] *s.* revuelta, rebelión, sublevación; *v.* rebelarse, sublevarse; **it -s me** me da asco, me repugna.

re·volt·ing [rɪvóltɪŋ] *adj.* repugnante; asqueroso.

rev·o·lu·tion [revəlúʃən] *s.* revolución; vuelta (*que da una rueda*).

rev·o·lu·tion·ar·y [revəlúʃənɛrɪ] *adj. & s.* revolucionario.

rev·o·lu·tion·ist [revəlúʃənɪst] *s.* revolucionario.

re·volve [rɪválv] *v.* girar, dar vueltas; rodar; voltear, dar vueltas a; **to — in one's mind** revolver en la mente, ponderar, reflexionar.

re·volv·er [rɪválvɚ] *s.* revólver.

re·ward [rɪwɔ́rd] *v.* premiar; recompensar; *s.* premio, gratificación, recompensa, galardón; albricias (*por haber hallado algún objeto perdido*).

re·write [riráɪt] *v.* volver a escribir; refundir (*un escrito*).

rhap·so·dy [rǽpsədɪ] *s.* rapsodia.

rhe·ni·um [ríniəm] *s.* renio.

rhet·o·ric [rétərɪk] *s.* retórica.

rheu·ma·tism [rúmətɪzəm] *s.* reumatismo, reuma.

rhi·noc·er·os [raɪnásərəs] *s.* rinoceronte.

rho·di·um [ródiəm] *s.* rodio.

rho·do·den·dron [rodədéndrən] *s.* rododendro.

rhu·barb [rúbarb] *s.* ruibarbo.

rhyme [raɪm] *s.* rima; **without — or reason** sin ton ni son; *v.* rimar.

rhythm [ríðəm] *s.* ritmo.

rhyth·mi·cal [ríðmɪkl] *adj.* rítmico, acompasado, cadencioso.

rib [rɪb] *s.* costilla; varilla (*de paraguas*); cordoncillo (*de ciertos tejidos*).

rib·bon [ríbən] *s.* cinta; listón, banda; moña; tira.

rice [raɪs] *s.* arroz; **— field** arrozal.

rich [rɪtʃ] *adj.* rico; costoso, suntuoso; sabroso; **— color** color vivo; **— food** alimento muy mantecoso o dulce.

rich·es [rítʃɪz] *s. pl.* riqueza, riquezas.

rick·et·y [rɪ́kɪtɪ] *adj.* desvencijado; raquítico.

rid [rɪd] *v.* librar, desembarazar; **to get — of** librarse de, deshacerse de, desembarazarse de; *pret. & p.p. de* **to rid**.

rid·den [rídn] *p.p. de* **to ride**.

rid·dle [rídl] *s.* acertijo, adivinanza, enigma; *v.* acribillar, perforar; **to — with bullets** acribillar a balazos.

ride [raɪd] *v.* (*horse*) cabalgar, montar; (*vehicle*) pasear; ir en (*tranvía, tren*); **to — a bicycle** andar o montar en bicicleta; **to — a horse** montar un caballo; **to — horseback** montar a caballo; **to — over a country** pasar o viajar por un país (*en auto, a caballo o por tren*); **to — someone** dominar a alguien; burlarse de alguien; *s.* paseo (*a caballo o en automóvil*); viaje (*a caballo, en automóvil, por ferrocarril, etc.*).

rid·er [ráɪdɚ] *s.* (*horse*) jinete; (*car*) pasajero (*de automóvil*); biciclista; motociclista; aditamento, cláusula añadida (*a un proyecto de ley*); anexo.

ridge [rɪdʒ] *s.* espinazo; lomo (*entre dos surcos*);

RE

arista, intersección (*de dos planos*); cordillera; cerro; (*building*) caballete (*de tejado*); (*cloth*) cordoncillo (*de ciertos tejidos*).

rid·i·cule [rídɪkjul] *s.* ridículo; burla, mofa; *v.* ridiculizar, poner en ridículo.

ri·dic·u·lous [rɪdíkjələs] *adj.* ridículo.

ri·fle [ráɪfl] *s.* rifle; *v.* pillar, robar; despojar.

rift [rɪft] *s.* (*opening*) raja; abertura; (*disagreement*) desacuerdo.

rig [rɪg] *v.* aparejar, equipar; enjarciar (*un barco de vela*); manipular; **to — oneself up** emperifollarse, ataviarse; *s.* aparejo, equipo; aparato; atavío, traje.

rig·ging [rígɪŋ] *s* jarcia, aparejo.

right [raɪt] *adj.* (*not left*) derecho; diestro; (*proper*) recto; justo; propio; adecuado; correcto; **— angle** ángulo recto; **— side** lado derecho; derecho (*de un tejido, traje, etc.*); **it is — that** está bien que, es justo que; **to be — tener** razón; **to be all —** estar bien; estar bien de salud; **to be in one's — mind** estar en sus cabales; *adv.* derecho, directamente; rectamente; justamente; bien; correctamente; a la derecha; **— about-face** media vuelta, **— hungry** muy hambriento; **— now** ahora mismo, inmediatamente; **— there** allí mismo, *Am.* allí mero; **go — home!** ¡vete derechito a casa!; **it is — where you left it** está exactamente (*o* en el mero lugar) donde lo dejaste; **to hit — in the eye** dar de lleno en el ojo, *Méx.* dar en el mero ojo; *s.* derecho; autoridad; privilegio; **— of way** derecho de vía; **by — (by -s)** justamente, con justicia; según la ley; **from — to left** de derecha a izquierda; **to the —** a la derecha; **to be in the —** tener razón; *v.* enderezar; corregir.

right·teous [ráɪtʃəs] *adj.* recto, justo, virtuoso.

right·teous·ness [ráɪtʃəsnɪs] *s.* rectitud, virtud.

right·ful [ráɪtfəl] *adj.* justo; legítimo.

right·hand [ráɪthænd] *adj.* derecho, de la mano derecha; **— man** brazo derecho.

right·ist [ráɪtɪst] *s.* derechista.

right·ly [ráɪtlɪ] *adv.* con razón; justamente, rectamente; propiamente, aptamente, debidamente.

right·wing [ráɪtwɪŋ] *adj.* derechista.

rig·id [ríʤɪd] *adj.* rígido.

ri·gid·i·ty [rɪʤídətɪ] *s.* rigidez; tiesura.

rig·or [rígɚ] *s.* rigor; rigidez; severidad.

rig·or·ous [rígɚəs] *adj.* rigoroso (*o* riguroso), severo.

rim [rɪm] *s.* borde, orilla; aro.

rime = rhyme.

rind [raɪnd] *s.* corteza, cáscara; mondadura.

ring [rɪŋ] *s.* (*finger*) anillo, sortija; argolla; aro; (*stadium*) arena; pista; (*sound*) toque; tañido; repique; (*telephone*) timbrazo; telefonazo; **— leader** cabecilla; **— of defiance** tono de reto; **— of shouts** gritería; **— of a telephone** llamada de teléfono; **ring-shaped** en forma de anillo, anular; **key —** llavero; **sarcastic —** retintín; *v.* tocar (*un timbre, una campanilla o campana*); sonar; tañer, repicar; resonar; zumbar (*los oidos*); **to — for something** llamar para pedir algo; **to — the nose of an animal** ponerle una argolla en la nariz a un animal; **to — up on the phone** llamar por teléfono.

ring·let [ríŋlɪt] *s.* rizo, bucle; pequeña sortija.

rink [rɪŋk] *s.* patinadero (*cancha para patinar*).

rinse [rɪns] *v.* enjuagar; lavar; aclarar (*la ropa*); *s.* enjuague.

ri·ot [ráɪət] *s.* motín, desorden, alboroto, tumulto; **— of color** riqueza o exceso de colores chillantes; *v.* amotinarse, alborotar, armar un tumulto.

ri·ot·ous [ráɪətəs] *adj.* revoltoso.

rip [rɪp] *v.* rasgar(se), romper(se); descoser(se); **to —**

off rasgar, arrancar, cortar; **to — out a seam** descoser una costura; *s.* rasgón, rasgadura, rotura; descosido.

ripe [raɪp] *adj.* maduro, sazonado; en sazón; **— for** maduro para, sazonado para; bien preparado para, listo para.

rip·en [ráɪpən] *v.* madurar(se), sazonar(se).

ripe·ness [ráɪpnɪs] *s.* madurez, sazón.

rip·ple [rípl] *v.* (*curl*) rizar(se), agitar(se), ondear, temblar ('la superficie del agua); (*sound*) murmurar (*un arroyo*); *s.* onda, temblor, ondulación (*en la superficie del agua*); murmullo (*de un arroyo*).

rise [raɪz] *v.* (*go up*) subir; ascender; (*get up*) alzarse, levantarse; elevarse; (*arise*) surgir; (*sun, moon*) salir; hincharse (*la masa del pan*); **to — up in rebellion** sublevarse, levantarse, alzarse (en rebelión); *s.* subida; ascenso; pendiente; elevación; salida (*del sol, de la luna, etc.*); subida, alza (*de precios*).

ris·en [rízn̩] *p.p. de* **to rise.**

risk [rɪsk] *s.* riesgo; *v.* arriesgar, aventurar, poner en peligro; exponerse a; **to — defeat** correr el riesgo de perder, exponerse a perder.

risk·y [rískɪ] *adj.* arriesgado, peligroso, aventurado.

ris·que [rɪské] *adj.* escabroso.

rite [raɪt] *s.* rito, ceremonia.

rit·u·al [rítʃuəl] *adj. & s.* ritual, ceremonial.

ritz·y [rítsɪ] *adj.* elegante.

ri·val [ráɪvl] *s.* rival, competidor, émulo; *adj.* competidor; **the — party** el partido opuesto; *v.* rivalizar con, competir con.

ri·val·ry [ráɪvlrɪ] *s.* rivalidad.

riv·er [rívɚ] *s.* río.

riv·et [rívɪt] *s.* remache; *v.* remachar; fijar.

riv·u·let [rívjəlɪt] *s.* riachuelo, arroyuelo.

road [rod] *s.* camino; carretera; vía; **— system** red vial.

road·side [ródsaɪd] *s.* borde del camino.

road·way [ródwe] *s.* camino, carretera.

roam [rom] *v.* vagar, errar, andar errante.

roar [ror] *v.* rugir, bramar; **to — with laughter** reír a carcajadas; *s.* rugido, bramido; **— of laughter** risotada, carcajada.

roast [rost] *v.* asar(se); tostar (*café, maíz, etc.*); ridiculizar, criticar; *s.* asado, carne asada; *adj.* asado; **— beef** rosbif, rosbí.

rob [rɑb] *v.* robar, hurtar; **to — someone of something** robarle algo a alguien.

rob·ber [rábɚ] *s.* ladrón; **highway —** salteador.

rob·ber·y [rábrɪ] *s.* robo, hurto.

robe [rob] *s.* manto, traje talar, túnica, (*scholar*) toga (*de un juez, letrado, etc.*); (*house*) bata; **automobile —** manta de automóvil.

rob·in [rábɪn] *s.* petirrojo.

ro·bust [róbʌst] *adj.* robusto, fuerte.

rock [rɑk] *s.* roca, peña; (*crag*) peñasco; **— crystal** cristal de roca; **— salt** sal de piedra, sal gema o sal mineral; **to go on the -s** tropezar en un escollo, *Am.* escollar; *v.* (*move to and fro*) mecer(se), balancear(se); (*stagger*) bambolear(se); (*tremble*) estremecer; **to — to sleep** adormecer (*meciendo*), arrullar.

rock·er [rákɚ] *s.* mecedora; arco de una mecedora o cuna.

rock·et [rákɪt] *s.* cohete.

rock·et·ry [rákətrɪ] *s.* cohetería.

rock·ing [rákɪŋ] *s.* balanceo; *adj.* oscilante; **— chair** silla mecedora.

rock·y [rákɪ] *adj.* roqueño, rocoso, rocalloso, peñascoso; pedregoso; (*unsteady*) movedizo; tembloroso; (*weak*) débil, desvanecido.

rod [rɑd] *s.* vara, varilla; medida de longitud (*aproximadamente 5 metros*); **fishing** — caña de pescar.

rode [rod] *pret. de* **to ride.**

ro·dent [ródənt] *s.* roedor.

rogue [rog] *s.* pícaro, bribón, tunante, pillo; **-s' gallery** colección policíaca de retratos de criminales.

ro·guish [rógɪʃ] *adj.* pícaro, pillo, picaresco; travieso.

role [rol] *s.* papel, parte.

roll [rol] *v.* (*move*) rodar; (*rotate*) girar; (*sway*) balancearse (*un barco*); bambolearse; ondular, (*reverberate*) retumbar (*el trueno, un cañón*); (*level*) aplanar, alisar con rodillo; arrollar, enrollar, hacer un rollo o bola; envolver; redoblar (*un tambor*); pronunciar (*la rr doble*); **to** — **over in the snow** revolverse o revolcarse en la nieve; **to** — **up** arrollar, enrollar, envolver; **to** — **back** reducir, rebajar; *s.* rollo (*de papel, paño, tela, etc.*); balanceo (*de un barco*); retumbo (*del trueno, de cañon*); redoble (*de un tambor*); lista ondulación; oleaje; bollo, rosca, panecillo; **to call the** — pasar lista.

roll·er [rólɚ] *s.* rodillo, cilindro (*para aplanar o alisar*); apisonadora; oleada; — **coaster** montaña rusa; — **skate** patín de ruedas.

rolling pin [rolɪŋ pɪn] *s.* rodillo de pastelero.

ROM (**read only memory**) ficha de la computadora con informes permanentes; memoria de sólo lectura.

Ro·man [rómən] *adj. & s.* romano; **nose** nariz aguileña.

ro·mance [románs] *s.* (*literature*) romance; novela; cuento; fábula; (*affair*) aventura romántica; amorío, lance amoroso; *v.* contar o fingir fábulas; andar en amoríos o aventuras; **Ro·mance** *adj.* romance, románico, neolatino.

ro·man·tic [romǽntɪk] *adj.* romántico; novelesco.

ro·man·ti·cism [romǽntəsɪzəm] *s.* romanticismo.

ro·man·ti·cist [romǽntəsɪst] *s.* romántico, escritor romántico.

romp [romp] *v.* triscar, juguetear, retozar, travesear.

roof [ruf] *s.* (*ceiling*) techo, techumbre, techado; (*outside*) tejado; — **garden** azotea-jardín; — **of the mouth** paladar; **flat** — azotea; *v.* techar.

room [rum] *s.* (*in building*) cuarto, pieza, sala, habitación; (*space*) espacio; lugar, sitio; **there is no** — **for more** no cabe(n) más, no hay lugar o cabida para más; **to make** — hacer lugar; — **mate** compañero de cuarto; *v.* vivir, hospedarse, alojarse.

room·er [rúmɚ] *s.* inquilino.

room·i·ness [rúmɪnɪs] *s.* holgura.

room·y [rúmɪ] *adj.* espacioso, amplio, holgado.

roost [rust] *s.* (*house*) gallinero; (*perch*) percha de gallinero; *v.* acurrucarse (*las aves en la percha*); pasar la noche.

roost·er [rústɚ] *s.* gallo.

root [rut] *s.* raíz; *v.* arraigar(se); echar raíces; (*dig*) hocicar, hozar (*dícese de los cerdos*); **to** — **for** (acclaim) vitorear, aclamar; **to** — **out** (*o* — **up**) desarraigar, arrancar de raíz; **to become -ed** arraigarse.

rope [rop] *s.* (*cord*) soga, cuerda; (*lasso*) reata, lazo; **to be at the end of one's** — haber agotado el último recurso; estar (*o* andar) en las últimas; no saber qué hacer; **to know the -s** saber todas las tretas de un asunto o negocio; *v.* amarrar; lazar, enlazar; **to** — **off** acordelar, poner cuerdas tirantes alrededor de (*un sitio*); **to** — **someone in**

embaucar a alguien.

ro·sa·ry [rózərɪ] *s.* rosario.

rose [roz] *pret. de* **to rise.**

rose [roz] *s.* rosa; color de rosa; —**bush** rosal; — **window** rosetón.

rose·bud [rózbʌd] *s.* capullo o botón de rosa, yema, pimpollo.

ros·ette [rozέt] *s.* roseta; rosetón.

ros·ter [rástɚ] *s.* registro; lista.

ros·trum [rástrəm] *s.* tribuna.

ros·y [rózɪ] *adj.* (*color*) rosado; color de rosa; (*condition*) alegre, risueño; — **future** porvenir risueño.

rot [rɑt] *v.* pudrir(se); corromperse; *s.* podre, podredumbre, putrefacción.

ro·ta·ry [rótərɪ] *adj.* rotatorio, giratorio, rotativo.

ro·tate [rótet] *v.* girar, dar vueltas; hacer girar; turnarse; (*crops*) cultivar en rotación.

ro·ta·tion [rotéʃən] *s.* rotación, vuelta; — **of crops** rotación de cultivos.

rote [rot] *s.* rutina, repetición maquinal; **by** — maquinalmente.

rot·ten [rátn] *adj.* podrido, putrefacto; (*stinking*) hediondo; (*conduct*) corrompido, corrupto.

rouge [ruʒ] *s.* colorete; *v.* pintar(se), poner(se) colorete.

rough [rʌf] *adj.* (*coarse*) áspero; tosco; fragoso; escabroso; (*rude*) brusco; grosero; (*stormy*) borrascoso, tempestuoso; — **diamond** diamante en bruto; — **draft** borrador; bosquejo; — **estimate** cálculo aproximativo, tanteo; presupuesto aproximado; — **ground** terreno escabroso; — **idea** idea aproximada; — **sea** mar picado; — **weather** tiempo borrascoso; *adv. véase* **roughly;** *v.* **to** — **it** vivir sin lujos ni comodidades, hacer vida campestre.

rough·en [rʌfən] *v.* hacer o poner áspero; (*scratch*) picar, rascar (*una superficie*); (*crack*) rajarse, agrietarse (*la piel*).

rough·ly [rʌflɪ] *adv.* ásperamente, groseramente, rudamente; aproximadamente; **to estimate** — tantear.

rough·ness [rʌfnɪs] *s.* aspereza: escabrosidad; rudeza; tosquedad; **the** — **of the sea** lo picado del mar; **the** — **of the weather** lo borrascoso del tiempo.

round [raʊnd] *adj.* redondo; rotundo; circular; — **trip** viaje redondo, viaje de ida y vuelta; **round-trip ticket** boleto (*o* billete) de ida y vuelta; *s.* vuelta, rotación, revolución; ronda; vuelta (*en el juego de naipes*); tanda, turno (*en ciertos deportes*); escalón, travesaño (*de escalera de mano*); danza en rueda; — **of ammunition** carga de municiones; descarga; — **amount** cifra redonda; — **of applause** explosión de aplausos; — **of pleasures** sucesión de placeres; **to make the -s** rondar; *prep. & adv. véase* **around;** — **about** a la redonda; por todos lados; **round-shouldered** cargado de espaldas; **to come** — **again** volver otra vez; **to go** — **a corner** doblar una esquina; *v.* redondear; dar vuelta a; **to** — **a corner** doblar una esquina; **to** — **out** redondear; completar; **to** — **up cattle** juntar el ganado, *Ríopl., Ven.* rodear el ganado.

round·a·bout [ráʊndəbaʊt] *adj.* indirecto.

round·ness [ráʊndnɛs] *s.* redondez.

round·up [ráʊndʌp] *s.* (*cattle*) rodeo (*de ganado*); (*criminals*) redada (*de criminales*); *v.* repuntar.

rouse [raʊz] *v.* despertar(se), *Ríopl., C.A., Ven.* recordar; excitar; incitar, provocar; levantar (*la caza*).

rout [raʊt] *s.* derrota, fuga desordenada; *v.* derrotar;

poner en fuga; **to — out** echar, hacer salir a toda prisa.
route [rut] *s.* ruta, camino, vía; (*planned*) itinerario; *v.* dirigir o enviar por cierta ruta.
roust·a·bout [ráustəbaut] *s.* obrero de muelle.
rou·tine [rutín] *s.* rutina.
rove [rov] *v.* vagar, errar, andar errante.
rov·er [róvɚ] *s.* vagabundo.
row [rau] *s.* riña, pelea, pelotera; *v.* pelearse, reñir, armar una riña o pelotera.
row [ro] *s.* fila, hilera; paseo en lancha; *v.* remar, bogar; llevar en bote de remar.
row·boat [róbot] *s.* bote de remos, lancha.
row·er [róɚ] *s.* remero.
roy·al [rɔɪəl] *adj.* real, regio.
roy·al·ist [rɔɪəlɪst] *s.* realista.
roy·al·ty [rɔɪəltɪ] *s.* realeza, soberanía real; persona o personas reales; (*payment*) derechos; *Arg.*, *Méx.*, *Ven.* regalía, *Cuba* canon de producción.
rub [rʌb] *v.* (*apply friction*) frotar; restregar; fregar; (*scrape*) raspar; irritar; **to — out** borrar; **to — someone the wrong way** irritar, contrariar, llevarle a uno la contraria; *s.* fricción, friega, frotación; roce; (*scoff*) sarcasmo; **there is the — allí** está la dificultad.
rub·ber [rʌbɚ] *s.* caucho, goma, *Méx.*, *C.A.* hule; goma elástica; goma de borrar; partida (*en ciertos juegos de naipes*); jugada decisiva (*en ciertos juegos de naipes*); **-s** chanclos, zapatos de goma o hule; *adj.* de caucho, de goma, *Méx.*, *C.A.* de hule; **— band** faja o banda de goma; **— plantation** cauchal; **— tree** *Am.* caucho, *Ríopl.* gomero.
rub·bish [rʌbɪʃ] *s.* basura, desechos, desperdicios; tonterías.
rub·ble [rʌbl] *s.* escombros; (*stone fragments*) ripio, cascajo, fragmentos de ladrillos o piedras; piedra en bruto, piedra sin labrar.
ru·bid·i·um [rubídiəm] *s.* rubidio.
ru·bric [rúbrɪk] *s.* rúbrica.
ru·by [rúbɪ] *s.* rubí.
rud·der [rʌdɚ] *s.* timón.
rud·dy [rʌdɪ] *adj.* rojo; rojizo; (*complexion*) rubicundo.
rude [rud] *adj.* rudo; grosero; aspero; brusco; tosco.
rude·ness [rúdnɪs] *s.* rudeza; grosería, descortesía; tosquedad.
rue·ful [rúfəl] *adj.* triste; lastimoso, lamentable.
ruf·fi·an [rʌfɪən] *s.* rufián, hombre brutal.
ruf·fle [rʌfl] *v.* rizar, fruncir (*tela*); (*wrinkle*) arrugar; desarreglar, rizar (*la superficie del agua*); perturbar; (*bother*) molestar; *s.* volante (*de un traje*); frunce, pliegue; (*ripple*) ondulación (*en al agua*).
rug [rʌɡ] *s.* alfombra, tapete.
rug·ged [rʌɡɪd] *adj.* escabroso, fragoso; áspero; recio, robusto; tosco; (*weather*) borrascoso, tempestuoso.
ru·in [rúɪn] *s.* ruina; **to go to —** arruinarse, caer en ruinas, venir a menos; *v.* arruinar; echar a perder; estropear.
ru·in·ous [rúɪnəs] *adj.* ruinoso; desastroso.
rule [rul] *s.* (*regulation*) regla; reglamento; precepto; (*control*) mando, gobierno; **as a —** por regla general; **— of thumb** método empírico; *v.* regir, gobernar; mandar; dirigir, guiar; dominar; (*decide*) fallar, decidir; rayar (*con regla*); **to — out** excluir; **to — over** regir, gobernar.
rul·er [rúlɚ] *s.* gobernante; soberano; regla (*para medir o trazar líneas*).
rul·ing [rúlɪŋ] *s.* fallo, decisión; gobierno; *adj.*

predominante, prevaleciente; principal.
rum [rʌm] *s.* ron.
rum·ble [rʌmbl] *v.* retumbar, hacer estruendo, rugir; *s.* retumbo, éstruendo, rumor, ruido sordo; **— seat** asiento trasero (*de cupé*).
ru·mi·nant [rúmənənt] *s.* rumiante.
ru·mi·nate [rúmənet] *v.* rumiar; reflexionar, meditar.
rum·mage [rʌmɪdʒ] *v.* escudriñar revolviéndolo todo; *s.* búsqueda desordenada; **— sale** venta de prendas usadas (*para beneficencia*).
ru·mor [rúmɚ] *s.* rumor; runrún; *C.A.* corre la bola; *v.* murmurar; **it is -ed that** corre la voz que.
rump [rʌmp] *s.* anca; trasero.
rum·ple [rʌmpl] *v.* estrujar, ajar; arrugar; *s.* arruga (*en un traje*).
rum·pus [rʌmpəs] *s.* barullo, alharaca, boruca, batahola.
run [rʌn] *v.* (*on foot*) correr; (*function*) andar; marchar; funcionar; (*flow*) fluir; chorrear; (*go over*) recorrer; (*direct*) dirigir, manejar; (*un negocio, empresa, máquina, casa, etc.*); extenderse (*de un punto a otro*); correrse (*los colores*); ser candidato (*a un puesto político*); (*computer*) ejecutar; **to — a fever** tener calentura; **to — away** huir; fugarse, escaparse; **to — across a person** encontrarse o tropezar con una persona; **to — down** dejar de funcionar (*una máquina, reloj, etc.*); aprehender a (*un criminal*); hablar mal de; atropellar; **to get — down in health** quebrantársele a uno la salud; **to — dry** secarse; **to — into** tropezar con, encontrarse con; chocar con; **— around with** asociarse con; tener amores con; **to — into debt** adeudarse; **to — something into** meter algo en, clavar algo en; **to — out** salirse; **to — out of money** acabársele a uno el dinero; **to — over** derramarse (*un líquido*); atropellar, pasar por encima de; repasar, echar un vistazo a (*la lección, un libro, etc.*); **to — through a book** hojear un libro; **the play ran for three months** se dió la comedia durante tres meses; *s.* carrera, corrida; curso, marcha; recorrido; manejo; **— of good luck** serie de repetidos éxitos; **— of performances** serie de representaciones; **— on a bank** corrida, demanda extraordinaria de fondos bancarios; **in the long —** a la larga; **stocking —** carrera; **the common — of mankind** el común de las gentes; **to have the — of** tener el libre uso de; *p.p. de to run*; *adj.* **— of the mill** de calidad estándar.
run·a·way [rʌnəwe] *adj.* fugitivo; **— horse** caballo desbocado; **— marriage** casamiento de escapatoria; *s.* fugitivo; caballo desbocado; fuga.
rung [rʌŋ] *s.* barrote, travesaño (*de silla, escalera de mano, etc.*); *pret. & p.p. de to* **ring**.
run·ner [rʌnɚ] *s.* (*who runs*) corredor; (*cover*) tapete (*para un pasillo o mesa*), *Ríopl.* pasillo; carrera (*en una media*); (*edge*) cuchilla (*de patín o de trineo*); contrabandista.
run·ning [rʌnɪŋ] *s.* (*race*) corrida, carrera, (*direction*) manejo, dirección; (*flow*) flujo; **to be out of the —** estar fuera de combate; *adj.* corriente; **— board** estribo; **— expenses** gastos corrientes; **— knot** nudo corredizo; **— water** agua corriente; **in — condition** en buen estado; **for ten days —** por diez días seguidos.
runt [rʌnt] *s.* enano; hombrecillo.
run·way [rʌnwe] *s.* senda; vía; (*airport*) pista (*de aterrizaje*).
rup·ture [rʌptʃɚ] *s.* ruptura; rompímiento, rotura; hernia; *v.* romper(se); reventar.
ru·ral [rúrəl] *adj.* rural, campestre.
rush [rʌʃ] *v.* (*hurry*) apresurar(se); *Am.* apurarse;

despachar con prisa; (*attack*) lanzar(se),
precipitar(se); abalanzarse; acometer; **to — out**
salir a todo correr; **to — past** pasar a toda prisa;
rush! ¡urgente! *s.* precipitación, prisa; acometida;
junco, **— chair** silla de junco; **— of business** gran
movimiento comercial; **— of people** tropel de
gente; **— order** pedido urgente.
Rus·sian [rʌ́ʃən] *adj. & s.* ruso.
rust [rʌst] *s.* moho, orín; herrumbre; tizón
(*enfermedad de las plantas*); **— color** color rojizo;
v. enmohecer(se), oxidar(se).
rus·tic [rʌ́stɪk] *adj. & s.* rústico, campesino.
rus·tle [rʌ́sl] *v.* susurrar, crujir; menear; **to — cattle**
robar ganado; *s.* susurro, crujido.
rust-proof [rʌ́stpruf] *adj.* inoxidable.
rust·y [rʌ́stɪ] *adj.* mohoso, cubierto de orín, oxidado;
rojizo; entorpecido, falto de uso; (*lost skill*) falto
de práctica.
rut [rʌt] *s.* rodada; rutina, método rutinario; **to be in
a —** hacer una cosa por rutina, ser esclavo de la
rutina.
ru·the·ni·um [ruθíniəm] *s.* rutenio.
ruth·less [rúθlɪs] *adj.* despiadado, cruel, brutal.
ruth·less·ness [rúθlɪsnɪs] *s.* fiereza, falta de
miramiento, truculencia, crueldad.
rye [raɪ] *s.* centeno.

S : s

sa·ber [sébɚ] *s.* sable.
sab·o·tage [sǽbətɑʒ] *s.* sabotaje; *v.*
sabotear.
sack [sæk] *s.* (*bag*) saco; costal;
(*looting*) saqueo, pillaje; *v.* ensacar, meter en un
saco; saquear, pillar.
sac·ra·ment [sǽkrəmənt] *s.* sacramento.
sa·cred [sékrɪd] *adj.* sagrado, sacro.
sa·cred·ness [sékrɪdnɪs] *s.* santidad; lo sagrado.
sac·ri·fice [sǽkrəfaɪs] *s.* sacrificio; **to sell at a —**
vender con pérdida; *v.* sacrificar.
sac·ri·lege [sǽkrəlɪdʒ] *s.* sacrilegio.
sac·ri·le·gious [sækrɪlídʒəs] *adj.* sacrílego.
sac·ro·sanct [sǽkrosænkt] *adj.* sacrosanto.
sad [sæd] *adj.* triste.
sad·den [sǽdn] *v.* entristecer(se).
sad·dle [sǽdl] *s.* silla de montar; silla de bicicleta o
motocicleta; **— bag** alforja; **— horse** caballo de
silla **— tree** arzón; *v.* ensillar; **to — someone
with responsibilities** cargar a alguien de
responsabilidades.
sa·dis·tic [sədístɪk] *adj.* sádico, cruel.
sad·ness [sǽdnɪs] *s.* tristeza.
safe [sef] *adj.* (*secure*) seguro; salvo; sin riesgo, sin
peligro; (*trustworthy*) digno de confianza; **— and
sound** sano y salvo; **safe-conduct** salvo-conducto;
to be — no correr peligro, estar a salvo; *s.* caja
fuerte; **-ly** *adv.* seguramente; con seguridad; sin
peligro; **to arrive -ly** llegar bien llegar sin
contratiempo alguno.
safe·guard [séfgɑrd] *s.* salvaguardia; resguardo,
defensa; *v.* resguardar, proteger, salvaguardar.
safe·ty [séftɪ] *s.* seguridad; protección; **in —** con
seguridad; sin peligro; *adj.* de seguridad; **— device**
mecanismo de seguridad; **— pin** imperdible, alfiler
de seguridad.
saf·fron [sǽfrən] *s.* azafrán; *adj.* azafranado, color
de azafrán.
sag [sæg] *v.* combarse, pandearse; doblegarse;
deprimirse, hundirse (*en el centro*); encorvarse; **his**

shoulders — tiene las espaldas caídas; *s.* pandeo,
flexión, depresión; concavidad.
sa·ga·cious [səgéʃəs] *adj.* sagaz, ladino, astuto.
sa·gac·i·ty [səgǽsətɪ] *s.* sagacidad; astucia.
sage [sedʒ] *adj.* sabio; cuerdo, prudente; *s.* sabio;
(*plant*) salvia.
said [sɛd] *pret. & p.p. de* to say.
sail [sel] *s.* (*canvas*) vela (*de barco*); (*trip*) viaje o
paseo en barco de vela; **under full —** a toda vela;
to set — hacerse a la vela; *v.* navegar; hacerse a la
vela; (*set sail*) zarpar, salir (*un buque*); viajar, ir
(*en barco, bote, etc.*); pasear en bote de vela; **to
— a kite** volar una cometa o papalote; **to — along**
deslizarse; navegar; ir bien; **to — along the coast**
costear.
sail·boat [sélbot] *s.* bote o barco de vela.
sail·or [sélɚ] *s.* marinero; marino.
saint [sent] *s.* santo; *adj.* santo; san (*delante de
nombres masculinos excepto: Santo Tomás, Santo
Domingo, Santo Toribio*); *v.* canonizar.
saint·ly [séntlɪ] *adj.* santo; pío, devoto.
sake [sek] *s.* **for the — of** por; por amor a; por
consideración a; **for my —** por mí; **for pity's —**
por piedad; ¡caramba!; **for the — of argument** por
vía de argumento.
sa·la·cious [səléʃəs] *adj.* salaz.
sal·ad [sǽləd] *s.* ensalada; **— dressing** aderezo (*para
ensalada*).
sal·a·ry [sǽlərɪ] *s.* salario, sueldo; *Arg., Col.*
asignación; **— brackets** categorías salariales.
sale [sel] *s.* venta; saldo, *Méx., C.A., Andes* barata;
Ríopl., Andes realización; **— by auction**
almoneda, subasta; **-s tax** impuesto sobre ventas;
for — de venta; **-s approach** política de venta; **-s
force** personal de ventas.
sales·man [sélzmən] *s.* vendedor; dependiente (*de
tienda*); **traveling —** agente viajero, viajante de
comercio.
sales·wom·an [sélzwʊmən] *s.* vendedora; dependiente
(*de tienda*).
sa·li·ent [séliənt] *adj.* saliente, sobresaliente;
prominente.
sa·line [sélin] *adj.* salino.
sa·li·va [səláɪvə] *s.* saliva.
sal·low [sǽlo] *adj.* amarillento, pálido.
sal·ly [sǽlɪ] *s.* (*exit*) salida; (*wise crack*) agudeza,
chiste agudo; *v.* salir, hacer una salida; **to — forth**
salir.
salm·on [sǽmən] *s.* salmón.
sa·loon [səlún] *s.* salón (*de un vapor*); taberna, *Méx.,
Carib., Ríopl* cantina; *Ríopl.* bar; **dining — of a
ship** salón-comedor de un vapor.
salt [sɔlt] *s.* (*sodium chloride*) sal; (*wit*) chiste,
agudeza; **smelling -s** sales aromáticas; **the — of
the earth** la flor y nata de la humanidad; *adj.*
salado; salobre; **—cellar** salero; **— mine** salina; **—
pork** tocino salado; **— shaker** salero; **— water**
agua salada, agua de mar; *v.* salar; **to — one's
money away** guardar o ahorrar su dinero.
salt·pe·ter [sɔ́ltpítɚ] *s.* salitre, nitro; **— mine** salitral,
salitrera.
salt·y [sɔ́ltɪ] *adj.* salado; salobre.
sal·u·tar·y [sǽljʊtɛrɪ] *adj.* saludable.
sal·u·ta·tion [sæljətéʃən] *s.* salutación, saludo.
sa·lute [səlút] *s.* saludo; **gun —** salva; *v.* saludar;
cuadrarse (*militarmente*).
sal·vage [sǽlvɪdʒ] *s.* salvamento.
sal·va·tion [sælvéʃən] *s.* salvación.
salve [sæv] *s.* untura, ungüento; alivio; *v.* aliviar,
aquietar, calmar; untar.
sal·vo [sǽlvo] *s.* salva.

RO

same [sem] *adj.* mismo; igual; idéntico; **it is all the — to me** me es igual, me da lo mismo; **the —** lo mismo; el mismo (la misma, los mismos, las mismas).

sam·ple [sǽmpl] *s.* muestra, prueba; **book of -s** muestrario; *v.* probar; calar.

sam·pling [sǽmplɪŋ] *s.* muestreo.

san·a·to·ri·um [sænətɔ́rɪəm] *s.* sanatorio.

sanc·ti·fy [sǽŋktəfaɪ] *v.* santificar.

sanc·tion [sǽŋkʃən] *s.* sanción; aprobación; autorización; *v.* sancionar; ratificar; aprobar, autorizar.

sanc·ti·ty [sǽŋktətɪ] *s.* santidad.

sanc·tu·ar·y [sǽŋktʃʊɛrɪ] *s.* santuario; asilo.

sand [sænd] *s.* arena; **— pit** arenal; *v.* enarenar, cubrir de arena; mezclar con arena; refregar con arena.

san·dal [sǽndl] *s.* sandalia; alpargata; *Méx.* guarache (huarache); *Andes* ojota.

sand·pa·per [sǽndpepɚ] *s.* papel de lija; *v.* lijar, pulir o alisar con papel de lija.

sand·stone [sǽndston] *s.* piedra arenisca.

sand·wich [sǽndwɪtʃ] *s.* bocadillo, emparedado, sandwich; *v.* intercalar, meter (entre).

sand·y [sǽndɪ] *adj.* arenoso; arenisco; **— hair** pelo rojizo; rufo; *Méx.* güero; *Ven.* catire; *Guat.* canche; *Col.* mono.

sane [sen] *adj.* sano, sensato, cuerdo.

sang [sæŋ] *pret. de* **to sing.**

san·i·tar·i·um [sænətɛ́rɪəm] *s.* sanatorio.

san·i·tar·y [sǽnətɛrɪ] *adj.* sanitario.

san·i·ta·tion [sænətéʃən] *s.* saneamiento; salubridad; sanidad.

san·i·ty [sǽnətɪ] *s.* cordura.

sank [sæŋk] *pret. de* **to sink.**

sap [sæp] *s.* savia; tonto, bobo; *v.* agotar, debilitar, minar.

sap·ling [sǽplɪŋ] *s.* vástago, renuevo; arbolillo.

sap·phire [sǽfaɪr] *s.* zafiro; color de zafiro.

sar·casm [sárkæzəm] *s.* sarcasmo.

sar·cas·tic [sɑrkǽstɪk] *adj.* sarcástico.

sar·coph·a·gus [sɑrkɔ́fəgəs] *s.* sarcófago.

sar·dine [sɑrdín] *s.* sardina.

sar·don·ic [sɑrdánɪk] *adj.* burlón; sarcástico.

sash [sæʃ] *s.* faja (*cinturón de lana, seda o algodón*); banda, cinta ancha; **window —** bastidor (*o* marco) de ventana.

sas·sy [sǽsɪ] *adj.* respondón, insolente.

sat [sæt] *pret. & p.p. de* **to sit.**

satch·el [sǽtʃəl] *s.* valija, maletín, maleta, saco.

sate [set] *v.* saciar.

sa·teen [sætín] *s.* satén o rasete (*raso de inferior calidad*).

sat·el·lite [sǽtlaɪt] *s.* satélite.

sa·ti·ate [séʃɪet] *v.* saciar, hartar.

sat·in [sǽtn] *s.* raso.

sat·ire [sǽtaɪr] *s.* sátira.

sa·tir·i·cal [sətírɪkl] *adj.* satírico.

sat·i·rize [sǽtəraɪz] *v.* satirizar.

sat·is·fac·tion [sætɪsfǽkʃən] *s.* satisfacción.

sat·is·fac·to·ri·ly [sætɪsfǽktrəlɪ] *adv.* satisfactoriamente.

sat·is·fac·to·ry [sætɪsfǽktrɪ] *adj.* satisfactorio.

sat·is·fied [sǽtɪsfaɪd] *adj.* satisfecho, contento.

sat·is·fy [sǽtɪsfaɪ] *v.* satisfacer.

sat·u·rate [sǽtʃəret] *v.* saturar, empapar.

Sat·ur·day [sǽtɚdɪ] *s.* sábado.

sauce [sɔs] *s.* salsa; **— dish** salsera; *v.* aderezar con salsa; sazonar, condimentar; insolentarse con.

sauce·pan [sɔ́spæn] *s.* cacerola.

sau·cer [sɔ́sɚ] *s.* platillo.

sau·ci·ness [sɔ́sɪnɪs] *s.* descaro, insolencia.

sau·cy [sɔ́sɪ] *adj.* descarado, respondón, insolente; *Am.* retobado.

saun·ter [sɔ́ntɚ] *v.* pasearse, vagar.

sau·sage [sɔ́sɪdʒ] *s.* salchicha, salchichón; longaniza; chorizo.

sav·age [sǽvɪdʒ] *adj.* salvaje; fiero; bárbaro, brutal, feroz; *s.* salvaje.

sav·age·ry [sǽvɪdʒrɪ] *s.* salvajismo; crueldad, fiereza.

sa·vant [səvɑ́nt] *s.* sabio.

save [sev] *v.* (*rescue*) salvar; (*hoard*) ahorrar; economizar; (*keep*) guardar; resguardar; **to — from** librar de; **to — one's eyes** cuidarse la vista; *prep.* salvo, menos, excepto.

sav·er [sévɚ] *s.* salvador; libertador; (*hoarder*) ahorrador; **life —** salvavidas.

sav·ing [sévɪŋ] *adj.* (*rescuer*) salvador; (*economizing*) ahorrativo, económico; frugal; *s.* ahorro, economía; **-s ahorros; -s bank** caja o banco de ahorros; *prep.* salvo, excepto, con excepción de.

sav·ior [sévjɚ] *s.* salvador.

sa·vor [sévɚ] *s.* sabor; dejo; *v.* saborear; sazonar; **to — of** saber a, tener el sabor de; **it -s of treason** huele a traición.

sa·vor·y [sévərɪ] *adj.* sabroso.

saw [sɔ] *s.* sierra; **—horse** caballete; *v.* aserrar, serrar; **it -s easily** es fácil de aserrar; *pret. de to* **see.**

saw·dust [sɔ́dʌst] *s.* aserrín, serrín.

saw·mill [sɔ́mɪl] *s.* aserradero.

sawn [sɔn] *p.p. de* **to saw.**

Sax·on [sǽksn] *adj. & s.* sajón.

sax·o·phone [sǽksəfon] *s.* saxófono; saxofón.

say [se] *v.* decir; declarar; **— !** ¡diga! ¡oiga usted!; **that is to —** es decir; **to — one's prayers** rezar, decir o recitar sus oraciones; **to — the least** por lo menos; **it is said that** dizque, se dice que, dicen que; *s.* afirmación, aserto; **the final —** la autoridad decisiva; **to have a — in a matter** tener voz y voto en un asunto; **to have one's —** expresarse, dar su opinión.

say·ing [séɪŋ] *s.* dicho, refrán; aserto; **as the — goes** como dice el refrán.

scab [skæb] *s.* costra (*de una herida*); roña; (*strikebreaker*) esquirol (*obrero que sustituye a un huelguista*); obrero que acepta un jornal inferior; *v.* encostrarse (*una herida*), cubrirse de una costra.

scab·bard [skǽbɚd] *s.* vaina, (*holster*) funda (*de espada, puñal, etc.*).

scab·by [skǽbɪ] *adj.* costroso; roñoso, sarnoso, tiñoso.

scab·rous [skébrəs] *adj.* escabroso.

scaf·fold [skǽfld] *s.* andamio, tablado; (*execution*) patíbulo; andamiaje, andamios.

scald [skɔld] *v.* escaldar; **to — milk** calentar la leche hasta que suelte el hervor; *s.* escaldadura, quemadura.

scale [skel] *s.* escala; platillo de balanza; balanza; (*fish*) escama (*de pez o de la piel*); costra; **pair of -s** balanza; **platform —** báscula; *v.* escalar; subir, trepar por; graduar (*a escala*); medir según escala; pesar; escamar, quitar las escamas a; pelarse, despellejarse; descostrar(se); **to — down prices** rebajar proporcionalmente los precios.

scal·lop [skɑ́ləp] *s.* onda, pico (*adorno*); (*seafood*) molusco bivalvo; **-s festón** (*recortes en forma de ondas o picos*); *v.* festonear, recortar en forma de ondas o picos, asar con salsa o migas de pan.

scalp [skælp] *s.* cuero cabelludo; *v.* desollar el cráneo; (*resell*) revender (*boletos, billetes*) a precio subido.

scal·y [skélɪ] *adj.* escamoso, lleno de escamas; —
with rust mohoso.
scamp [skæmp] *s.* pícaro, bribón, bellaco.
scam·per [skǽmpɚ] *v.* correr, escabullirse,
escaparse; *s.* escabullida, carrera, corrida.
scan [skæn] *v.* escudriñar; examinar, mirar
detenidamente; echar un vistazo a (*en el habla
popular*); (*verse*) medir (*el verso*).
scan·dal [skǽndl] *s.* escándalo; maledicencia,
murmuración.
scan·dal·ize [skǽndlaɪz] *v.* escandalizar, dar
escándalo.
scan·dal·ous [skǽndləs] *adj.* escandaloso;
difamatorio; vergonzoso.
scan·di·um [skǽndiəm] *s.* escandio.
scant [skænt] *adj.* escaso; corto; insuficiente; *v.*
escatimar, limitar.
scant·y [skǽntɪ] *adj.* escaso; insuficiente.
scar [skɑr] *s.* (*skin blemish*) cicatriz; costurón;
(*mark*) raya, marca (*en una superficie pulida*); *v.*
marcar, rayar; hacer o dejar una cicatriz en.
scarce [skɛrs] *adj.* escaso; raro; **-ly** *adv.*
escasamente; apenas.
scar·ci·ty [skɛ́rsətɪ] *s.* escasez; carestía; insuficiencia.
scare [skɛr] *v.* espantar, asustar; alarmar; sobresaltar;
he -s easily se asusta fácilmente; **to — away**
ahuyentar, espantar; *s.* susto, sobresalto.
scare·crow [skɛ́rkro] *s.* espantajo; espantapájaros.
scarf [skɑrf] *s.* bufanda; mantilla; pañuelo (*para el
cuello o la cabeza*); tapete (*para una mesa,
tocador, etc.*).
scar·let [skɑ́rlɪt] *s.* escarlata; *adj.* de color escarlata;
— fever escarlata, escarlatina.
scar·y [skɛ́rɪ] *adj.* espantadizo, asustadizo, miedoso.
scat [skæt] *interj.* ¡zape!
scat·ter [skǽtɚ] *v.* esparcir(se); desparramar(se);
dispersar(se); **—brained** ligero de cascos,
aturdido.
scene [sin] *s.* escena; escenario; decoración;
(*panorama*) vista; **to make a —** causar un
escándalo.
scen·er·y [sínərɪ] *s.* paisaje, vista; **stage —**
decoraciones.
scent [sɛnt] *s.* (*odor*) olor; (*substance*) perfume;
(*trace*) pista, rastro; **to be on the —** of seguir el
rastro de; **to have a keen —** tener buen olfato; *v.*
oler, olfatear, ventear, husmear; perfumar.
scep·ter [sɛ́ptɚ] *s.* cetro.
scep·tic [skɛ́ptɪk] *adj. & s.* escéptico.
scep·ti·cism [skɛ́ptəsɪzəm] *s.* escepticismo.
sched·ule [skɛ́dʒul] *s.* horario; itinerario (*de trenes*);
lista, inventario (*adjunto a un documento*); *v.* fijar
el día y la hora (*para una clase, conferencia,
etc.*); establecer el itinerario para (*un tren o
trenes*).
scheme [skim] *s.* (*plan*) esquema, plan, proyecto;
empresa; (*plot*) ardid, trama, maquinación; **color
—** combinación de colores; **metrical —** sistema de
versificación; *v.* proyectar, urdir; maquinar,
intrigar, tramar.
schem·er [skímɚ] *s.* maquinador, intrigante;
proyectista.
schem·ing [skímɪŋ] *adj.* maquinador, intrigante; *s.*
maquinación.
schism [sɪzəm] *s.* cisma.
schiz·o·phre·ni·a [skɪzofrínɪə] *s.* esquizofrenia.
schol·ar [skɑ́lɚ] *s.* (*student*) escolar, estudiante;
(*fellow*) becario (*el que disfruta una beca*); erudito,
docto; (*researcher*) investigador.
schol·ar·ly [skɑ́lɚlɪ] *adj.* erudito, sabio, docto; *adv.*
eruditamente, doctamente.

schol·ar·ship [skɑ́lɚʃɪp] *s.* saber; erudición; (*award*)
beca; **to have a —** disfrutar una beca.
scho·las·tic [skolǽstɪk] *adj.* escolástico; escolar.
school [skul] *s.* escuela; colegio; **— of fish** banco de
peces; *adj.* de escuela; **— day** día de escuela; **—
board** consejo de enseñanza; *v.* enseñar, educar,
instruir, aleccionar.
school·boy [skúlbɔɪ] *s.* alumno.
school·girl [skúlgɝl] *s.* alumna.
school·house [skúlhaʊs] *s.* escuela.
school·ing [skúlɪŋ] *s.* instrucción; enseñanza,
educación.
school·mas·ter [skúlmæstɚ] *s.* maestro de escuela.
school·mate [skúlmet] *s.* condiscípulo, compañero de
escuela.
school·room [skúlrum] *s.* clase, aula; sala de clase.
school·teach·er [skúltitʃɚ] *s.* maestro de escuela.
schoo·ner [skúnɚ] *s.* (*ship*) goleta; (*glass*) vaso
grande para cerveza; **prairie —** galera con toldo.
sci·ence [sáɪəns] *s.* ciencia.
sci·en·tif·ic [saɪəntífɪk] *adj.* científico; **-ally** *adv.*
científicamente.
sci·en·tist [sáɪəntɪst] *s.* científico, hombre de ciencia.
scin·til·late [síntəlet] *v.* centellear; chispear.
sci·on [sáɪən] *s.* vástago.
scis·sors [sízɚz] *s. pl.* tijeras.
scle·ro·sis [skləósɪs] *s.* esclerosis.
scoff [skɔf] *s.* mofa, burla, befa, escarnio; *v.*
escarnecer; mofarse; **to — at** mofarse de, burlarse
de, escarnecer a.
scold [skold] *v.* reñir, reprender, regañar; *s.* regañon,
persona regañona.
scold·ing [skóldɪŋ] *s.* regaño, represión; *adj.*
regañón.
scoop [skup] *s.* (*tool*) cuchara, cucharón; (*shovel*)
pala; (*quantity*) palada, cucharada; (*winnings*)
buena ganancia; **newspaper —** primera
publicación de una noticia; *v.* cavar, excavar;
ahuecar; cucharear, sacar con cucharón o pala;
achicar (*agua*); **to — in a good profit** sacar buena
ganancia.
scoot [skut] *v.* escabullirse, correr, irse a toda prisa;
— ! ¡largo de aquí!
scoot·er [skútɚ] *s.* motoneta (*de motor*); monopatín.
scope [skop] *s.* alcance, extensión; (*sphere*) esfera,
campo.
scorch [skɔrtʃ] *v.* chamuscar; resecar, agostar; *s.*
chamusquina, *Am.* chamuscada o chamuscadura.
score [skor] *s.* cuenta; escor (*en el juego*); (*line*)
raya, línea; calificación (*expresada numéricamente*);
veintena; **musical —** partitura; **on that —** a ese
respecto; **on the — of** a causa de, con motivo de;
to keep the — llevar el escor, llevar la cuenta; **to
settle old -s** desquitarse; *v.* marcar el escor, señalar
los tantos en un juego; calificar (*numéricamente*);
instrumentar (*música*); rayar, marcar con rayas; **to
— a point** ganar un punto o tanto; **to — a success**
lograr éxito, obtener un triunfo.
scorn [skɔrn] *s.* desdén, menosprecio; *v.* desdeñar,
menospreciar.
scorn·ful [skɔ́rnfəl] *adj.* desdeñoso.
scor·pi·on [skɔ́rpɪən] *s.* escorpión, alacrán.
Scotch [skɑtʃ] *adj.* escocés; **the —** los escoceses, el
pueblo escocés.
scoun·drel [skáʊndrəl] *s.* bellaco, bribón, pícaro.
scour [skaʊr] *v.* fregar, restregar, limpiar; pulir; **to
— the country** recorrer la comarca (*en busca de
algo*).
scourge [skɝdʒ] *s.* azote; *v.* azotar; castigar.
scout [skaʊt] *s.* explorador (*usualmente militar*); **a
good —** un buen explorador; una buena persona,

SA

un buen compañero; *v.* explorar; reconocer.

scowl [skaʊl] *s.* ceño; *v.* fruncir el ceño, mirar con ceño; poner mala cara.

scram·ble [skræmbl] *v.* (*move*) gatear; (*eggs*) hacer un revoltillo; (*mix up*) revolver, mezclar; **to — for something** forcejear por coger algo; pelearse por coger algo; **to — up** trepar o subir a gatas (*una cuesta*); **-d eggs** revoltillo, huevos revueltos; *s.* revoltillo, confusión; pelea.

scrap [skræp] *s.* (*fragment*) fragmento, pedacito; migaja; (*fight*) riña, reyerta; **-s** sobras; desperdicios; desechos; retales; **—book** álbum de recortes; **— iron** recortes o desechos de hierro; *v.* desechar; tirar a la basura; descartar; pelear, reñir.

scrape [skrep] *v.* (*abrasively*) raspar; rasguñar; rascar; (*rub*) raer; rozar; **to — along** ir tirando, ir pasándola; **to — together** recoger o acumular poco a poco; **to bow and —** ser muy servil; *s.* raspadura; rasguño; aprieto, dificultad, lío.

scrap·er [skrepɚ] *s.* (*tool*) raspador; (*scrimping person*) tacaño.

scratch [skrætʃ] *v.* (*mark*) arañar, rasguñar; (*rub*) rascar; raspar; (*line*) rayar; escarbar; (*write badly*) hacer garabatos; **to — out** borrar, tachar; sacar (*los ojos*) con las uñas; *s.* arañazo, araño, rasguño; raya, marca; **to start from —** empezar sin nada; empezar desde el principio; empezar sin ventaja.

scrawl [skrɔl] *s.* garabato; *v.* hacer garabatos, escribir mal.

scraw·ny [skrɔnɪ] *adj.* huesudo, flaco.

scream [skrim] *s.* chillido, alarido, grito; **he's a —** es muy cómico o chistoso; *v.* chillar, gritar.

screech [skritʃ] *s.* chillido; **— owl** lechuza; *v.* chillar.

screen [skrin] *s.* (*projection*) pantalla; (*divider*) biombo; mampara; resguardo; (*sifter*) tamiz, cedazo; **—door** antepuerta de tela metálica; **— editing** (*computer*) edición en pantalla; **motion-picture —** pantalla de cinematógrafo; **wire —** pantalla de tela metálica; *v.* tapar; resguardar, proteger con una pantalla o un biombo; (*sift*) cerner; (*project*) proyectar sobre la pantalla, filmar; **to — windows** proteger las ventanas con tela metálica.

screw [skru] *s.* tornillo; **— eye** armella; **— nut** tuerca; **— propeller** hélice; **— thread** rosca; *v.* atornillar; torcer, retorcer; **to — a lid on** atornillar una tapa; **to — up one's courage** cobrar ánimo.

screw·driv·er [skrúdraɪvɚ] *s.* destornillador.

scrib·ble [skrɪbl] *v.* garrapatear, hacer garabatos, borronear, escribir mal o de prisa; *s.* garabato.

script [skrɪpt] *s.* letra cursiva, escritura; manuscrito (*de un drama, de una película*).

scrip·ture [skrɪptʃɚ] *s.* escritura sagrada; **the Scriptures** la Sagrada Escritura, la Biblia.

scroll [skrol] *s.* rollo de pergamino o papel; voluta, adorno en espiral; (*flourish*) rúbrica (*de una firma*); **scrolling** (*computer*) movimiento vertical (de la imagen).

scrub [skrʌb] *v.* fregar; restregar; *s.* friega, fregado; *adj.* achaparrado; bajo, inferior; **— oak** chaparro; **— pine** pino achaparrado; **— team** equipo de jugadores suplentes o menos bien entrenados; **— woman** fregona.

scru·ple [skrúpl] *s.* escrúpulo; *v.* escrupulizar, tener escrúpulos.

scru·pu·lous [skrúpjələs] *adj.* escrupuloso.

scru·ti·nize [skrútnaɪz] *v.* escudriñar, escrutar.

scru·ti·ny [skrútnɪ] *s.* escrutinio.

scuff [skʌf] *v.* raspar; arrastrar los pies.

scuf·fle [skʌfl] *s.* refriega, riña, pelea; *v.* forcejear; luchar, pelear; arrastrar los pies.

sculp·tor [skʌlptɚ] *s.* escultor.

sculp·ture [skʌlptʃɚ] *s.* escultura; *v.* esculpir, cincelar, tallar.

scum [skʌm] *s.* nata, capa, espuma; (*dregs*) escoria; residuo, desechos; (*low life*) canalla, gente baja; *v.* espumar.

scur·ry [skɝɪ] *v.* escabullirse; echar a correr; apresurarse; *s.* apresuramiento; corrida, carrera.

scut·tle [skʌtl] *v.* echar a correr; (*ship*) barrenar (*un buque*); echar a pique; *s.* escotilla, escotillón; balde (*para carbón*).

scythe [saɪð] *s.* guadaña.

sea [si] *s.* mar; **to be at —** estar en el mar; estar perplejo o confuso; **to put to —** hacerse a la mar; *adj.* marino, marítimo, de mar; **— biscuit** galleta; **— green** verdemar; **— gull** gaviota; **— level** nivel del mar; **— lion** león marino, foca; **— power** potencia naval.

sea·board [síbord] *s.* costa, litoral; *adj.* costanero, litoral.

sea·coast [síkost] *s.* costa, litoral.

seal [sil] *s.* (*stamp*) sello; timbre; (*animal*) foca, león marino; **to set one's — to** sellar; aprobar; **sealed bids** propuestas selladas; *v.* sellar; estampar; cerrar; tapar; **to — in** encerrar, cerrar herméticamente; **to — with sealing wax** lacrar.

seal·ing wax [sílɪŋ wæks] *s.* lacre.

seam [sim] *s.* (*sewing*) costura; juntura; (*scar*) cicatriz; filón, (*ore*) veta; *v.* echar una costura, coser.

sea·man [símən] *s.* marino, marinero.

seam·stress [símstrɪs] *s.* costurera.

sea·plane [síplen] *s.* hidroavión.

sea·port [síport] *s.* puerto de mar.

sear [sɪr] *v.* chamuscar(se), tostar(se); resecar(se); herrar, marcar con hierro candente; *adj.* reseco, marchito.

search [sɝtʃ] *v.* buscar; escudriñar; (*"frisk"*) registrar; examinar; **to — a prisoner** registrar a un prisionero; **to — for something** buscar algo; **to — into** investigar, indagar; *s.* busca, búsqueda; registro, inspección; investigación, pesquisa, indagación; **— warrant** mandato judicial para practicar un registro; **in — of** en busca de.

search·light [sɝtʃlaɪt] *s.* reflector.

sea·shore [síʃor] *s.* costa, playa, orilla o ribera del mar.

sea·sick [sísɪk] *adj.* mareado; **to get —** marearse.

sea·sick·ness [sísɪknɪs] *s.* mareo.

sea·side [sísaɪd] *s.* costa, litoral; playa.

sea·son [sízn] *s.* estación (*del año*); temporada; sazón, ocasión, tiempo; **— ticket** billete de abono; **Christmas —** navidades; **harvest —** siega, tiempo de la cosecha; **opera —** temporada de la ópera; **to arrive in good —** llegar en sazón, llegar a tiempo; *v.* sazonar; condimentar; aclimatar.

sea·son·ing [síznɪŋ] *s.* condimento; salsa; desecación (*de la madera*).

seat [sit] *s.* (*furniture*) asiento; silla; (*site*) sitio; (*headquarters*) residencia; sede (*episcopal, del gobierno, etc.*); (*body*) nalgas; (*clothes*) fondillos, parte trasera (*de los pantalones o calzones*); **— of learning** centro de estudios, centro de erudición; *v.* sentar; asentar; dar asiento a; **to — oneself** sentarse; **it -s a thousand people** tiene cabida para mil personas.

sea·weed [síwid] *s.* alga marina.

se·cede [sisíd] *v.* separarse (*de una federación o unión*).

se·clude [sɪklúd] *v.* recluir, apartar, aislar; **to — oneself from** recluirse de, apartarse de.

se·clud·ed [sıklúdıd] *adj.* apartado, aislado; solitario.
se·clu·sion [seıklúʒən] *s.* apartamiento, soledad, aislamiento; retiro.
sec·ond [sɛ́kənd] *adj.* segundo; inferior; — **hand** segundero (*de reloj*); — **lieutenant** subteniente; **second-rate** de segunda clase; mediocre, inferior; **on — thought** después de pensarlo bien; *s.* segundo; (*helper*) padrino (*en un desafío*); ayudante; (*defective*) mercancía de segunda calidad; mercancía defectuosa; — **child** segundón; *v.* secundar (*o* segundar), apoyar; apadrinar.
sec·on·dar·y [sɛ́kəndɛrı] *adj.* secundario; — **education** segunda enseñanza; — **school** escuela secundaria, escuela de segunda enseñanza.
sec·ond-hand [sɛ́kəndhǽnd] *adj.* de segunda mano; usado; de ocasión; indirecto, por intermedio de otro.
sec·ond·ly [sɛ́kəndlı] *adv.* en segundo lugar.
se·cre·cy [síkrəsı] secreto, sigilo, reserva.
se·cret [síkrıt] *s.* secreto; *adj.* secreto; escondido, oculto; — **service** policía secreta; **-ly** *adv.* secretamente, en secreto.
sec·re·tar·i·at [sɛ́krətǽrıət] *s.* secretaría.
sec·re·tary [sɛ́krətɛrı] *s.* secretario; escritorio (*con estantes para libros*).
se·crete [sıkrít] *v.* secretar (*una secreción*); esconder, ocultar.
se·cre·tion [sıkríʃən] *s.* secreción.
se·cre·tive [sıkrítıv] *adj.* reservado, callado; — **gland** glándula secretoria.
sect [sɛkt] *s.* secta.
sec·tion [sɛ́kʃən] *s.* sección; (*passage*) trozo; (*slice*) tajada; (*place*) región; (*ward*) barrio; *v.* seccionar, dividir en secciones.
sec·u·lar [sɛ́kjələ] *adj. & s.* secular.
se·cure [sıkjúr] *adj.* seguro; firme; *v.* asegurar; afianzar; obtener; resguardar; **-ly** *adv.* seguramente, con seguridad; firmemente.
se·cu·ri·ty [sıkjúrətı] *s.* seguridad; (*bond*) fianza, garantía, prenda; resguardo, protección; **securities** bonos, obligaciones, acciones, valores; — **in hand** valores en cartera.
se·dan [sıdǽn] *s.* sedan.
se·date [sıdét] *adj.* sosegado; tranquilo, sereno; serio.
se·da·tion [sədéʃən] *d.* sedación.
sed·a·tive [sɛ́dətıv] *adj. & s.* calmante, sedativo.
sed·en·tar·y [sɛ́dnterı] *adj.* sedentario; inactivo.
sed·i·ment [sɛ́dəmənt] *s.* sedimento, heces, residuo.
se·di·tion [sıdíʃən] *s.* sedición.
se·di·tious [sıdíʃəs] *adj.* sedicioso.
se·duce [sıdjús] *v.* seducir.
se·duc·tion [sıdʌ́kʃən] *s.* seducción.
see [si] *v.* ver; — **that you do it** no deje Vd. de hacerlo; tenga Vd. cuidado de hacerlo; **I'll — to it** me encargaré de ello; **let me —** a ver; **to — a person home** acompañar a una persona a casa; **to — a person off** ir a la estación para despedir a una persona; **to — a person through a difficulty** ayudar a una persona a salir de un apuro; **to — through a person** adivinar lo que piensa una persona, darse cuenta de sus intenciones; **to — to one's affairs** atender a sus asuntos; **to have seen military service** haber servido en el ejército; *s.* sede, silla; **Holy See** Santa Sede.
seed [sid] *s.* (*grains*) semilla; (*semen*) simiente; (*fruit*) pepita; hueso; **to go to —** producir semillas; decaer, declinar; descuidar de su persona, andar desaseado; *v.* sembrar; despepitar, quitar las pepitas o semillas de; producir semillas.
seed·er [sídə] *s.* sembradora.
seed·ling [sídlıŋ] *s.* planta de semillero; arbolillo (*de*

menos de tres pies de altura).
seed·y [sídı] *adj.* semilloso, lleno de semillas; raído; desaseado.
seek [sik] *v.* buscar; pedir, solicitar; **to — after** buscar; **to — to** tratar de, esforzarse por.
seem [sim] *v.* parecer; **it -s to me** me parece.
seem·ing·ly [símıŋlı] *adv.* aparentemente, en apariencia, al parecer.
seem·ly [símlı] *adj.* propio, decente, decoroso.
seen [sin] *p.p.* de to see.
seep [sip] *v.* escurrirse, rezumarse, colarse, filtrarse.
seer [sır] *s.* vidente, adivino, profeta.
seeth [siθ] *v.* bullir, hervir; burbujear.
seg·ment [sɛ́gmənt] *s.* segmento.
seg·re·gate [sɛ́grəgət] *v.* segregar.
seize [siz] *v.* (*grasp*) asir, coger, agarrar; apoderarse de; (*arrest*) prender o aprehender; (*take advantage of*) aprovecharse de; (*capture*) embargar, secuestrar; encautarse de; **to — upon** asir; **to become -d with fear** sobrecogerse de miedo.
sei·zure [síʒə] *s.* cogida; captura; aprehensión (*de un criminal*); secuestro, embargo (*de bienes*); ataque (*de una enfermedad*).
sel·dom [sɛ́ldəm] *adv.* rara vez, raras veces, raramente.
se·lect [səlɛ́kt] *adj.* selecto, escogido; *v.* elegir, escoger; entresacar.
se·lec·tion [səlɛ́kʃən] *s.* selección, elección.
se·le·ni·um [sılíniəm] *s.* selenio.
self [sɛlf] *pron.* **by one—** por sí, por sí mismo; **for one—** para sí; **one's other —** su otro yo; **his wife and —** su esposa y él (*véase* herself, himself, ourselves, themselves, *etc.*); **self-centered** egoísta, egocéntrico; **self-conscious** consciente de sí, cohibido, tímido; **self-control** dominio de sí mismo (*o* de sí propio); **self-defense** defensa propia; **self-denial** abnegación; **self-evident** patente, manifiesto; **self-esteem** respeto de sí mismo; amor propio; **self-government** gobierno autónomo, autonomía; gobierno democrático; **self-interest** propio interés; egoísmo; **self-love** amor propio; **self-possessed** sereno, dueño de sí, tranquilo; **self-sacrifice** abnegación; **self-service** [sɛlfsɝvıs] *s.* autoservicio; **self-satisfied** pagado de sí, satisfecho de sí; *s.* el yo, el propio yo.
self·ish [sɛ́lfıʃ] *adj.* egoísta, **-ly** *adv.* con egoísmo, por eogísmo.
self·ish·ness [sɛ́lfıʃnıs] *s.* egoísmo.
self·same [sɛ́lfsém] *adj.* mismo, idéntico, mismísimo.
sell [sɛl] *v.* vender; (*for sale*) venderse, estar de venta; **to — at auction** vender en almoneda o subasta, subastar; **to — out** venderlo todo; **to — short** vender en descubierto.
sell·er [sɛ́lə] *s.* vendedor.
selves [sɛlvz] *pl.* de self.
se·man·tics [səmǽntıks] *s.* semántica.
sem·blance [sɛ́mbləns] *s.* semejanza; apariencia.
se·mes·ter [səmɛ́stə] *s.* semestre.
sem·i·cir·cle [sɛ́məsɝkl] *s.* semicírculo.
sem·i·co·lon [sɛ́məkolən] *s.* punto y coma.
sem·i·con·duc·tor [sɛmikəndʌ́ktə] *s.* semiconductor (*menos que cobre y más que cristal*).
sem·i·nar·y [sɛ́mənɛrı] *s.* seminario.
Se·mit·ic [səmítık] *adj.* semítico.
sen·ate [sɛ́nıt] *s.* senado.
sen·a·tor [sɛ́nıtə] *s.* senador.
send [sɛnd] *v.* enviar; mandar; despachar; remitir, expedir; (*throw*) lanzar (*una flecha, pelota, etc.*); **to — away** despedir; despachar; **to — forth** despachar, enviar; emitir; exhalar; echar; **to —**

SC

someone up for 15 years condenar a un reo a 15 años de prisión; **to — word** avisar, mandar decir, mandar recado.
send·er [séndɚ] s. remitente; transmisor.
se·nile [sínaɪl] adj. senil, caduco; chocho.
se·nil·i·ty [sənflətɪ] s. senectud; chochera o chochez.
sen·ior [sínjɚ] adj. (older) mayor, de más edad; más antiguo; (superior) superior; — **class** clase del cuarto año; s. persona o socio más antiguo; estudiante del último año; **to be somebody's — by two years** ser dos años mayor que alguien.
sen·sa·tion [sɛnséʃən] s. sensación.
sen·sa·tion·al [sɛnséʃənl] adj. sensacional; emocionante.
sense [sɛns] s. (function) sentido; (sentiment) sentimiento; sensación; (judgment) juicio, sensatez; (meaning) significado; **common —** sentido común; **to make —** tener sentido; **to be out of one's -s** estar fuera de sí, estar loco; v. percibir, sentir; darse cuenta de.
sense·less [sénslɪs] adj. sin sentido; (foolish) insensato, absurdo; insensible, privado de sentido.
sen·si·bil·i·ty [sɛnsəbflətɪ] s. sensibilidad.
sen·si·ble [sénsəbl] adj. (aware) sensato, razonable, cuerdo; (appreciable) sensible, perceptible; **sensibly** adv. sensatamente, con sensatez, con sentido común; sensiblemente, perceptiblemente.
sen·si·tive [sénsətɪv] adj. sensitivo; sensible; quisquilloso, susceptible.
sen·si·tive·ness [sénsətɪvnɪs] s. sensibilidad.
sen·si·tize [sénsətaɪz] v. sensibilizar.
sen·su·al [sénʃuəl] adj. sensual, carnal, lujurioso.
sen·su·al·i·ty [sɛnʃuǽlətɪ] s. sensualidad; lujuria.
sent [sɛnt] pret. & p.p. de **to send.**
sen·tence [séntəns] s. sentencia, fallo, decisión; (grammar) oración; **death —** pena capital; v. sentenciar.
sen·ti·ment [séntəmənt] s. sentimiento; sentido.
sen·ti·men·tal [sɛntəméntl] adj. sentimental.
sen·ti·men·tal·i·ty [sɛntəmɛntǽlətɪ] s. sentimentalismo, sentimentalidad.
sen·ti·nel [séntənl] s. centinela.
sen·try [séntrɪ] s. centinela.
sep·a·rate [séprɪt] adj. (apart) separado; apartado; solitario; (different) distinto, diferente; **-ly** adv. separadamente, por separado; aparte; [sépəret] v. separar(se); apartar(se).
sep·a·ra·tion [sɛpəréʃən] s. separación.
Se·phar·di [səfárdi] s. sefardí, sefardita; **-c** adj. sefardí.
Sep·tem·ber [sɛptémbɚ] s. setiembre.
sep·ul·cher [séplkɚ] s. sepulcro, sepultura.
se·quel [síkwəl] s. secuela; continuación, consecuencia; resultado.
se·quence [síkwəns] s. (continuity) secuencia, sucesión; serie, continuación; (result) consecuencia, resultado; runfla (serie de tres o más naipes de un mismo palo).
ser·e·nade [sɛrənéd] s. serenata; v. dar serenata a.
se·rene [sərín] adj. sereno; tranquilo; claro, despejado.
se·ren·i·ty [sərɛnɪtɪ] s. serenidad; calma.
ser·geant [sárdʒənt] s. sargento; — **at arms** oficial que guarda el orden (en un cuerpo legislativo).
se·ri·al [sírɪəl] s. cuento o novela por entregas; adj. consecutivo, en serie; — **novel** novela por entregas.
se·ries [síriz] s. serie; series.
se·ri·ous [sírɪəs] adj. serio; grave; **-ly** adv. seriamente, con seriedad, en serio; gravemente.
se·ri·ous·ness [sírɪəsnɪs] s. seriedad; gravedad.

ser·mon [sɚmən] s. sermón.
ser·pent [sɚpənt] s. serpiente; sierpe.
se·rum [sfrəm] s. suero.
ser·vant [sɚvənt] s. sirviente; criado; servidor; — **girl** criada, Ríopl. mucama; Andes, Col., Ven., Méx. muchacha de servicio.
serve [sɚv] v. (wait on) servir; (supply) surtir, abastecer; **to — a term in prison** cumplir una condena; **to — a warrant** entregar una citación; **to — as** servir de; **to — for** servir de, servir para; **to — notice on** notificar, avisar, advertir; **to — one's purpose** servir para el caso o propósito; **it -s me right** bien me lo merezco; s. saque (de la pelota en tenis).
serv·er [sɚvɚ] s. servidor; (game) saque (el que saca la pelota en el juego de tenis); bandeja; mesa de servicio.
ser·vice [sɚvɪs] s. servicio; saque (de la pelota en tenis); entrega (de una citación judicial); **at your —** a la disposición de Vd., servidor de Vd.; **funeral —** honras fúnebres, funerales, exequias; **mail —** servicio de correos; **table —** servicio de mesa, vajilla; **tea —** juego o servicio de té; — **entrance** entrada para el servicio; — **man** militar; — **station** estación de servicio; v. servir; reparar; surtir (una tienda).
ser·vice·a·ble [sɚvɪsəbl] adj. servible; útil; duradero.
ser·vile [sɚvl] adj. servil.
ser·vi·tude [sɚvətjud] s. servidumbre; esclavitud.
ses·sion [séʃən] s. sesión.
set [sɛt] v. (place) poner; colocar, asentar; (fix) fijar; establecer; ajustar; engastar (piedras preciosas); solidificar(se), endurecer(se) (el cemento, yeso, etc.); ponerse (el sol, la luna); empollar; **to — a bone** componer un hueso dislocado; **to — a trap** armar una trampa; **to — about** ponerse a; **to — an example** dar ejemplo; **to — aside** poner a un lado, poner aparte; apartar; **to — back** retrasar, atrasar; **to — forth** exponer, expresar; manifestar; **to — forth on a journey** ponerse en camino; — **off** disparar, hacer estallar (un explosivo); hacer resaltar; salir; **to — on fire** pegar o poner fuego a, incendiar; **to — one's jaw** apretar las quijadas; **to — one's heart on** tener la esperanza puesta en; **to — one's mind on** resolverse a, aplicarse a; **to — out for** partir para, salir para; **to — out to** empezar a; **to — right** colocar bien; enderezar; rectificar; **to — sail** hacerse a la vela; **to — the brake** frenar, apretar el freno; **to — up** erigir, levantar; armar, montar (una máquina); parar (tipo de imprenta); establecer, poner (una tienda, un negocio); — **to go** listo para partir; s. juego, colección; serie; grupo, clase; partida (de tenis); — **of dishes** servicio de mesa, vajilla, — **of teeth** dentadura; **radio —** radio, radiorreceptor; **tea —** servicio para té.
set·back [sétbæk] s. atraso, revés, retroceso inesperado.
set·tee [sɛtí] s. canapé.
set·ting [sétɪŋ] s. (jewel) engaste (de una joya); (theater) escena, escenario; (sun, moon) puesta (del sol, de un astro); — **sun** sol poniente.
set·tle [sétl] v. (colonize) colonizar, poblar; establecer(se); fijar(se); asentar(se); (solve) arreglar, poner en orden, ajustar (cuentas); zanjar (una disputa); pagar, liquidar, saldar; **to — down** formalizarse; asentarse; calmarse; poner casa; **to — on a date** fijar o señalar una fecha; **to — property**

on (upon) asignar bienes o propiedad a; **to — the matter** decidir el asunto, concluir con el asunto.

set·tle·ment [sɛ́tlmənt] *s.* (*community*) establecimiento; colonia; poblado; población; colonización; (*arrangement*) asignación o traspaso (*de propiedad*); ajuste, arreglo; pago; saldo, finiquito, liquidación; — **house** casa de beneficencia; **marriage** — dote.

set·tler [sɛ́tlə·] *s.* colono, poblador; — **of disputes** zanjador de disputas.

set·up [sɛ́təp] *s.* arreglo; organización; sistema.

sev·en [sɛ́vən] *num.* siete.

sev·en·teen [sɛvəntín] *num.* diecisiete.

sev·en·ty [sɛ́vəntɪ] *num.* setenta.

sev·er [sɛ́və·] *v.* desunir(se), partir(se), dividir(se), separar(se); cortar, romper.

sev·er·al [sɛ́vrəl] *adj.* varios, diversos; distintos, diferentes.

se·vere [səvír] *adj.* severo; áspero; austero; rígido; (*rigorous*) riguroso; grave, recio, fuerte.

se·ver·i·ty [səvɛ́rətɪ] *s.* severidad; austeridad; rigidez; gravedad; rigor.

sew [so] *v.* coser.

sew·er [sjúə·] *s.* albañal, cloaca; *Mex., Ven., Andes* acequia.

sew·ing [sóɪŋ] *s.* costura; modo de coser; — **machine** máquina de coser; — **room** cuarto de costura.

sewn [son] *p.p. de* **to sew.**

sex [sɛks] *s.* sexo; — **appeal** atracción sexual.

sex·tant [sɛ́kstənt] *s.* sextante.

sex·ton [sɛ́kstən] *s.* sacristán.

sex·u·al [sɛ́kʃʊəl] *adj.* sexual.

shab·by [ʃǽbɪ] *adj.* raído, gastado; andrajoso; mal vestido; vil, injusto; **to treat someone shabbily** tratar a alguien injustamente o con menosprecio.

shack [ʃæk] *s.* cabaña, choza, *Carib.* bohío, *Mex.* jacal.

shack·le [ʃǽkl] *v.* encadenar; trabar, echar trabas a, poner grillos a; estorbar; **-s** *s. pl.* cadenas, trabas, grillos, esposas; (*inconvenience*) estorbo.

shad [ʃæd] *s.* sábalo.

shade [ʃed] *s.* (*shadow*) sombra; (*nuance*) tinte, matiz; (*cover*) visillo, cortinilla; (*lamp*) pantalla (*de lámpara*); (*eye*) visera (*para los ojos*); **a — longer** un poco más largo; — **of meaning** matiz; **in the — of** a la sombra de; *v.* sombrear; dar sombra; resguardar de la luz; matizar.

shad·ow [ʃǽdo] *s.* (*darkness*) sombra; oscuridad; (*phantom*) espectro; **under the — of** al abrigo de, a la sombra de; **without a — of doubt** sin sombra de duda; *v.* sombrear; obscurecer; **to — someone** espiarle a alguien los pasos, seguirle por todas partes.

shad·ow·y [ʃǽdəwɪ] *adj.* lleno de sombras, tenebroso; vago, indistinto.

shad·y [ʃédɪ] *adj.* sombrío, sombreado, umbrío; — **business** negocio sospechoso; — **character** persona de carácter dudoso, persona de mala fama.

shaft [ʃæft] *s.* pozo o tiro (*de mina, de elevador*); cañon de chimenea; (*monument*) columna; (*axle*) eje, árbol (*de maquinaria*); flecha.

shag·gy [ʃǽgɪ] *adj.* peludo, velludo; lanudo; desaseado; áspero.

shake [ʃek] *v.* menear(se); estremecer(se); temblar; sacudir(se); agitar(se); titubear, vacilar; hacer vacilar; dar, estrechar (*la mano*); **to — hands** dar un apretón de manos, darse la mano; **to — one's head** mover o menear la cabeza; cabecear; **to — with cold** tiritar de frío, estremecerse de frío; **to — with fear** temblar de miedo, estremecerse de

miedo; *s.* sacudida; sacudimiento; estremecimiento, temblor; **hand**— apretón de manos.

shak·en [ʃékən] *p.p. de* **to shake.**

shake·up [ʃékəp] *s.* reorganización.

shak·y [ʃékɪ] *adj.* tembloroso; vacilante.

shall [ʃæl] *v. aux. del futuro del indicativo en las primeras personas* (**I, we**); *en las demás expresa mayor énfasis, mandato u obligación;* **he — not do it** no lo hará, no ha de hacerlo; **thou shalt not steal** no hurtarás.

shal·low [ʃǽlo] *adj.* bajo, poco profundo; superficial; ligero de cascos.

shal·low·ness [ʃǽlonɪs] *s.* poca hondura, poca profundidad; superficialidad; ligereza de juicio.

sham [ʃæm] *s.* fingimiento, falsedad, farsa; *adj.* fingido, simulado; falso; — **battle** simulacro, batalla fingida; *v.* fingir, simular.

sham·bles [ʃǽmblz] *s.* desorden.

shame [ʃem] *s.* vèrgüenza; deshonra; — **on you!** ¡qué vergüenza!; **it is a —** es una vergüenza; es una lástima; **to bring — upon** deshonrar; *v.* avergonzar; deshonrar.

shame·ful [ʃémfəl] *adj.* vergonzoso.

shame·less [ʃémlɪs] *adj.* desvergonzado, descarado.

shame·less·ness [ʃémlɪsnɪs] *s.* desvergüenza; descaro, desfachatez.

sham·poo [ʃæmpú] *s.* champú, lavado de la cabeza; *v.* dar un champú, lavar (*la cabeza*).

sham·rock [ʃǽmrɑk] *s.* trébol.

shank [ʃæŋk] *s.* canilla (*parte inferior de la pierna*); zanca.

shan·ty [ʃǽntɪ] *s.* choza, cabaña, casucha.

shape [ʃep] *s.* (*form*) forma; (*figure*) figura; (*condition*) estado, condición; **to be in a bad —** estar mal; **to put into —** arreglar, poner en orden, ordenar; *v.* formar, dar forma a; tomar forma; **to — one's life** dar forma a, ajustar o disponer su vida; **his plan is shaping well** va desarrollándose bien su plan.

shape·less [ʃéplɪs] *adj.* informe, sin forma.

share [ʃɛr] *s.* (*portion*) porción, parte; (*participation*) participación; (*stock*) acción (*participación en el capital de una compañía*); *Col.* cupo. *v.* compartir; repartir; participar; **to — in** participar en, tener parte en; **to — a thing with** compartir una cosa con.

share·hold·er [ʃɛrholdə·] *s.* accionista.

share·crop·per [ʃɛ́rkrɑpə·] *s.* aparcero.

shark [ʃɑrk] *s.* (*fish*) tiburón; (*swindler*) estafador; (*expert*) perito, experto; (*usurer*) **loan —** usurero; **to be a — at** ser un águila (*o* ser muy listo) para.

sharp [ʃɑrp] *adj.* (*acute*) agudo, puntiagudo; cortante; punzante; (*biting*) mordaz; picante; (*bright*) astuto; (*clear*) claro, distinto, bien marcado; (*sudden*) repentino; — **curve** curva abrupta, curva pronunciada o muy cerrada; — **ear** oído fino; — **features** facciones bien marcadas; — **struggle** lucha violenta; — **taste** sabor acre; — **temper** genio áspero; — **turn** vuelta repentina; *s.* sostenido (*en música*); **card**— tahur, fullero; *adv.* *véase* **sharply** en punto; **at ten o'clock —** a las diez en punto.

sharp·en [ʃɑ́rpən] *v.* afilar(se); sacar punta a; aguzar(se); amolar.

sharp·ly [ʃɑ́rplɪ] *adv.* agudamente; mordazmente, ásperamente; repentinamente; claramente; **to arrive —** llegar en punto.

sharp·ness [ʃɑ́rpnɪs] *s.* agudeza, sutileza; mordacidad; rigor; aspereza; acidez.

shat·ter [ʃǽtə·] *v.* estrellar(se), astillar(se), hacer(se)

SE

añicos; quebrar(se), romper(se); **to — one's hopes** frustrar sus esperanzas; **his health was -ed** se le quebrantó la salud; **-s** *s. pl.* pedazos, trozos, añicos, fragmentos; **to break into —** hacer(se) añicos.

shave [ʃev] *v.* afeitar(se), rasurar(se); rapar(se); acepillar (*madera*); *s.* rasura, *Am.* afeitada; **he had a close —** por poco no se escapa; se salvó por milagro.

shav·en [ʃévən] *p.p. de* **to shave; clean-shaven** bien afeitado.

shav·ing [ʃévɪŋ] *s.* rasura, *Am.* afeitada; **wood -s** virutas; **— brush** brocha de afeitar; **— soap** jabón de afeitar.

shawl [ʃɔl] *s.* mantón, chal.

she [ʃi] *pron. pers.* ella; **— who** la que; *s.* hembra; **she-bear** osa; **she-goat** cabra.

sheaf [ʃif] *s.* haz, gavilla, manojo; lío; *v.* hacer gavillas.

shear [ʃɪr] *v.* trasquilar, esquilar (*las ovejas*); cortar (*con tijeras grandes*).

shear·ing [ʃírɪŋ] *s.* tonsura.

shears [ʃɪrz] *s. pl.* tijeras grandes.

sheath [ʃiθ] *s.* vaina; funda, envoltura.

sheathe [ʃið] *v.* envainar.

sheaves [ʃivz] *pl. de* **sheaf.**

shed [ʃɛd] *s.* cobertizo; tejadillo; tinglado; *Ríopl., Andes* galpón (*de una estancia*); *v.* derramar; difundir; esparcir; mudar (*de piel, plumas, etc.*); ser impermeable (*un paño, abrigo, sombrero, etc.*); **to — leaves** deshojarse.

sheen [ʃin] *s.* lustre, viso.

sheep [ʃip] *s.* oveja; carnero; **— dog** perro de pastor; **—fold** redil; **—skin** zalea; badana; pergamino; (*certificate*) diploma (*de pergamino*).

sheep·ish [ʃípɪʃ] *adj.* vergonzoso, encogido, tímido.

sheer [ʃɪr] *adj.* (*pure*) puro; completo; (*thin*) fino, delgado, transparente, diáfano; (*steep*) escarpado; **by — force** a pura fuerza.

sheet [ʃit] *s.* (*bed*) sábana; (*paper*) hoja, pliego (*de papel*); (*metal*) lámina (*de metal*); extensión (*de agua, hielo*); **— lightning** relampagueo.

shelf [ʃɛlf] *s.* estante, anaquel; (*sill*) repisa; (*rock*) saliente de roca.

shell [ʃɛl] *s.* (*sea*) concha; (*egg*) cáscara (*de huevo, nuez, etc.*); (*pod*) vaina (*de guisantes, frijoles, garbanzos, etc.*); casco (*de una embarcación*); (*structure*) armazón (*de un edificio*); granada, bomba; (*case*) cápsula (*para cartuchos*); *v.* cascar (*nueces*); desvainar, quitar la vaina a, pelar; desgranar (*maíz, trigo, etc.*); bombardear.

shel·lac [ʃəlǽk] *s.* laca; *v.* barnizar con laca.

shell·fish [ʃɛ́lfɪʃ] *s.* marisco; mariscos.

shel·ter [ʃɛ́ltɚ] *s.* abrigo, refugio, asilo; (*protection*) resguardo, protección; **to take —** refugiarse, abrigarse; *v.* abrigar, refugiar, guarecer; proteger, amparar.

shelve [ʃɛlv] *v.* poner o guardar en un estante; poner a un lado, arrinconar, arrumbar.

shelves [ʃɛlvz] *s. pl.* estantes, anaqueles; estantería.

shep·herd [ʃɛ́pɚd] *s.* pastor; zagal; **— dog** perro de pastor.

sher·bet [ʃɚ́bɪt] *s.* sorbete.

sher·iff [ʃɛ́rɪf] *s.* alguacil mayor (*de un condado en los Estados Unidos*).

sher·ry [ʃɛ́rɪ] *s.* jerez, vino de Jerez.

shield [ʃild] *s.* escudo, rodela, broquel; resguardo, defensa; *v.* escudar, resguardar, proteger.

shift [ʃɪft] *v.* (*change*) cambiar; mudar(se); alternar(se); variar; desviar(se); (*transfer*) trasladar,

transferir; **to — for oneself** valerse o mirar por sí mismo; **to — gears** cambiar de marcha; **to — the blame** echar a otro su propia culpa; *s.* cambio; desvío, desviación; tanda, grupo de obreros; turno; **— key** (*computer*) tecla de cambio; **— lock key** tecla de cambio con cerrojo; **gear —** cambio de marcha.

shift·less [ʃíftlɪs] *adj.* negligente; holgazán.

shil·ling [ʃílɪŋ] *s.* chelín.

shim·my [ʃími] *s.* (*dance*) shimmy; (*vibration*) abaniqueo.

shin [ʃɪn] *s.* espinilla (*de la pierna*); *v.* **to — up** trepar.

shine [ʃaɪn] *v.* (*beam*) brillar, resplandecer, lucir; (*polish*) pulir; dar brillo, lustre o bola, embolar (zapatos); *s.* brillo, lustre, resplandor; **rain or —** llueva o truene; **to give a shoe —** dar bola (brillo *o* lustre) a los zapatos; embolar o embetunar los zapatos; limpiar el calzado.

shin·gle [ʃíŋgl] *s.* ripia, tabla delgada, *Méx.* tejamanil o 'tejamaní; (*hair*) pelo corto escalonado; (*professional*) letrero de oficina; **-s** zona (*erupción de la piel*); *v.* cubrir con tejamaniles; techar con tejamaniles.

shin·ing [ʃáɪnɪŋ] *adj.* brillante; resplandeciente.

shin·y [ʃáɪnɪ] *adj.* brillante; lustroso.

ship [ʃɪp] *s.* (*naval*) buque, barco, navío, nave; (*air*) aeronave, avión; **— builder** ingeniero naval, constructor de buques; **— mate** camarada de a bordo; **— yard** astillero; **on — board** a bordo; *v.* embarcar(se); despachar, enviar; remesar; transportar; alistarse como marino.

ship·ment [ʃípmənt] *s.* embarque; cargamento; despacho, envío; remesa.

ship·per [ʃípɚ] *s.* embarcador; remitente.

ship·ping [ʃípɪŋ] *s.* embarque; despacho, envío; **— charges** gastos de embarque; **— clerk** dependiente de muelle; dependiente encargado de embarques.

ship·shape [ʃípʃep] *adj.* en buen orden.

ship·wreck [ʃíprɛk] *s.* naufragio; *v.* echar a pique, hacer naufragar; naufragar, irse a pique.

shirk [ʃɚk] *v.* evadir, evitar.

shirt [ʃɚt] *s.* camisa; *C.A.* cotón; **— waist** blusa; **in — sleeves** en camisa, en mangas de camisa.

shiv·er [ʃívɚ] *v.* tiritar; temblar; estremecerse; *s.* escalofrío, temblor, estremecimiento.

shoal [ʃol] *s.* bajío, banco de arena; banco (*de peces*).

shock [ʃak] *s.* (*blow*) choque; sacudida; sacudimiento; golpe; (*surprise*) sobresalto; *v.* **absorber** amortiguador; **— of grain** hacina o gavilla de mieses; **— of hair** guedeja, greña; **— troops** tropas de asalto; *v.* chocar, ofender; escandalizar; causar fuerte impresión; horrorizar; sacudir; conmover; hacinar, hacer gavillas de (*mieses*).

shock·ing [ʃákɪŋ] *adj.* chocante, ofensivo, repugnante; espantoso, escandaloso.

shod [ʃad] *pret. & p.p. de* **to shoe.**

shoe [ʃu] *s.* zapato; botín; **brake —** zapata de freno; **horse —** herradura; **— blacking** betún, bola; **— polish** brillo, lustre, bola; **— store** zapatería; *v.* calzar; herrar (*un caballo*).

shoe·black [ʃúblæk] *s.* limpiabotas.

shoe·horn [ʃúhɔrn] *s.* calzador.

shoe·lace [ʃúles] *s.* lazo, cinta, cordón de zapato.

shoe·mak·er [ʃúmekɚ] *s.* zapatero.

shoe·string [ʃústrɪŋ] *s.* lazo, cinta, cordón de zapato.

shone [ʃon] *pret. & p.p. de* **to shine.**

shook [ʃuk] *pret. de* **to shake.**

shoot [ʃut] *v.* (*firearm*) tirar, disparar, descargar;

hacer fuego; fusilar; dar un balazo; (*throw*) lanzar, disparar (*una instantánea*); (*photograph*) fotografiar, filmar (*una escena*); (*dice*) echar (*los dados*); (*sprout*) brotar (*las plantas*); **to — by** pasar rápidamente; **to — forth** brotar, salir; germinar; lanzarse; **to — it out with someone** pelearse a balazos; **to — up a place** entrarse a balazos por un lugar; *s.* vástago, retoño, renuevo; *s.* caza; **to go out for a —** salir a tirar; ir de caza.

shoot·er [ʃútɚ] *s.* tirador.

shoot·ing [ʃútɪŋ] *s.* tiroteo; — **match** certamen de tiradores (*o* de tiro al blanco); — **pain** punzada, dolor agudo; — **star** estrella fugaz.

shop [ʃɑp] *s.* tienda; taller; — **window** escaparate, vitrina, aparador, *Ríopl., Andes* vidriera; — **barber** — barbería; **beauty —** salón de belleza; **to talk —** hablar uno de su oficio o profesión; *v.* ir de tiendas; ir de compras, comprar.

shop·keep·er [ʃɑpkipɚ] *s.* tendero.

shop·per [ʃɑpɚ] *s.* comprador.

shop·ping [ʃɑpɪŋ] *s.* compra, compras; **to go —** ir de compras, ir de tiendas.

shore [ʃor] *s.* costa, playa, orilla, ribera; puntal; **ten miles off —** a diez millas de la costa; *v.* **to — up** apuntalar, poner puntales.

shorn [ʃorn] *p.p. de* **to shear.**

short [ʃɔrt] *adj.* (*duration*) corto; breve; (*height*) bajo; *Méx.* chaparro; (*amount*) escaso; (*curt*) brusco; — **cut** atajo; — **circuit** cortocircuito; — **wave** onda corta; método corto; **short-legged** de piernas cortas; — **loan** préstamo a corto plazo; — **run (haul, term)** de corto plazo; **for —** para abreviar; **in —** en resumen, en suma, en conclusión; **in — order** rápidamente, prontamente; **in a — time** en poco tiempo; al poco tiempo; **to be — of** estar falto o escaso de; **to cut —** acortar, abreviar, terminar de repente; **to run — of something** acabársele (írsele acabando) a uno algo; **to stop —** parar de repente, parar en seco.

short·age [ʃɔrtɪdʒ] *s.* escasez, carestía; déficit; falta.

short·com·ing [ʃɔrtkʌmɪŋ] *s.* falta, defecto.

short·en [ʃɔrtn̩] *v.* acortar(se), abreviar(se), disminuir(se).

short·en·ing [ʃɔrtnɪŋ] *s.* (*lard*) manteca, grasa (*para hacer pasteles*); (*abbreviation*) acortamiento; abreviación.

short·hand [ʃɔrthænd] *s.* taquigrafía.

short·hand·ed [ʃɔrthǽndəd] *adj.* carente de operarios.

short·ly [ʃɔrtlɪ] *adj.* brevemente; en breve; al instante, pronto, luego; bruscamente, secamente.

short·ness [ʃɔrtnɪs] *s.* cortedad; brevedad; pequeñez; deficiencia.

shorts [ʃɔrts] *s. pl.* calzoncillos, calzones cortos.

short·sight·ed [ʃɔrtsáɪtɪd] *adj.* miope; corto de vista.

shot [ʃɑt] *pret. & p.p. de* **to shoot**; *s.* (*discharge*) tiro; disparo; balazo; cañonazo; (*pellet*) bala; balas; (*injection*) inyección; (*throw*) tirada; — **of liquor** trago de aguardiente; **buck —** municiones, postas; **not by a long —** ni con mucho, ni por pienso, nada de eso; **he is a good —** es buen tirador, tiene buen tino; **to take a —** at disparar un tiro a; hacer una tentativa de; **within rifle —** a tiro de rifle.

shot·gun [ʃɑtgʌn] *s.* escopeta.

should [ʃud] *v. aux. del condicional en las primeras personas* (**I, we**): **I said that I —** yo dije que iría; *equivale al imperfecto de subjuntivo;* **if it — rain** si lloviera; *se usa con la significación de deber:* **you — not do it** no debiera (*o* no debería) hacerlo.

shoul·der [ʃóldɚ] *s.* (*person*) hombro; (*animal*) lomo, pernil (*de puerco, cordero*); borde, saliente (*de un camino*); **-s** espalda, espaldas; — **blade** espaldilla, paletilla; **straight from the —** con toda franqueza; **to turn a cold —** to volver las espaldas a, tratar fríamente; *v.* cargar al hombro, echarse sobre las espaldas; cargar con, asumir; empujar con el hombro.

shout [ʃaut] *v.* gritar; vocear; *s.* grito.

shove [ʃʌv] *v.* empujar, dar empellones; **to — aside** echar a un lado, rechazar; **to — off** partir, zarpar (*un buque*); salir, irse; *s.* empujón, empellón; empuje.

shov·el [ʃʌvl] *s.* pala; *v.* traspalar.

show [ʃo] *v.* (*exhibit*) mostrar, enseñar; exhibir; (*prove*) probar, demostrar; indicar; (*appear*) verse; asomarse; — **him in** que pase, hágale entrar; **to — off** alardear, hacer ostentación de; lucirse; **to — up** aparecer, presentarse; **to — someone up** hacer subir a alguien; mostrarle el camino (*para subir*); desenmascarar a alguien, poner a alguien en la evidencia; *s.* exhibición; demostración; ostentación; espectáculo; representación, función; apariencia; — **window** escaparate, vitrina, aparador, *Am.* vidriera; **to go to the —** ir al teatro, ir al cine; **to make a — of oneself** exhibirse, hacer ostentación de.

show·case [ʃókes] *s.* vitrina, aparador.

show·down [ʃódaun] *s.* arreglo terminante.

show·er [ʃáuɚ] *s.* (*rain*) aguacero, chubasco, chaparrón, lluvia; (*bath*) ducha, baño de ducha; *Méx.* regadera; **bridal —** tertulia para obsequiar a una novia; *v.* llover; caer un aguacero.

shown [ʃon] *p.p. de* **to show.**

show·y [ʃóɪ] *adj.* ostentoso; vistoso, chillón.

shrank [ʃræŋk] *pret. de* **to shrink.**

shred [ʃrɛd] *s.* tira, triza; andrajo; fragmento; pizca; **to be in -s** estar raído; estar andrajoso; estar hecho trizas; **to tear to -s** hacer trizas; *v.* desmenuzar; hacer trizas, hacer tiras; *pret. & p.p. de* **to shred.**

shrew [ʃru] *s.* arpía, mujer brava, mujer de mal genio.

shrewd [ʃrud] *adj.* astuto, sagaz, agudo.

shriek [ʃrik] *v.* chillar, gritar; *s.* chillido, grito.

shrill [ʃrɪl] *adj.* agudo, penetrante, chillón; *v.* chillar.

shrimp [ʃrɪmp] *s.* camarón; *Sp.* gamba; hombrecillo insignificante.

shrine [ʃraɪn] *s.* santuario; altar; lugar venerado.

shrink [ʃrɪŋk] *v.* encoger(se); contraer(se); disminuir; **to — back** retroceder; **to — from** retroceder ante, apartarse de; huir de, rehuir.

shrink·age [ʃrínkɪdʒ] *s.* encogimiento; contracción; merma.

shriv·el [ʃrívl] *v.* encoger(se); fruncir(se), marchitar(se); disminuir(se).

shroud [ʃraud] *s.* mortaja; *v.* amortajar; cubrir, ocultar.

shrub [ʃrʌb] *s.* arbusto.

shrub·ber·y [ʃrʌ́bərɪ] *s.* arbustos.

shrug [ʃrʌg] *v.* encogerse de hombros; *s.* encogimiento de hombros.

shrunk [ʃrʌŋk] *pret. & p.p. de* **to shrink.**

shrunk·en [ʃrʌ́ŋkən] *p.p. de* **to shrink.**

shuck [ʃʌk] *s.* hollejo; cáscara.

shud·der [ʃʌ́dɚ] *v.* temblar, estremecerse; *s.* temblor, estremecimiento.

shuf·fle [ʃʌ́fl] *v.* barajar; revolver, mezclar; arrastrar (*los pies*); **to — along** ir arrastrando los pies; *s.* mezcla, confusión; evasiva; — **of feet** arrastramiento de pies; **it is your —** a Vd. le toca barajar.

shun [ʃʌn] *v.* esquivar, evadir, rehuir, evitar.

shut [ʃʌt] *v.* cerrar(se); **to — down** parar el traba cerrar (*una fábrica*); **to — in** encerrar; **to — off** cortar (*el gas, la electricidad, el agua, etc.*); **to — off from** incomunicar, aislar de, cortar la comunicación con; excluir; **to — out** impedir la entrada de; cerrar la puerta a; **to — up** (*close*) cerrar bien; tapar; encerrar; (*be quiet*) tapar la boca, hacer callar; callarse; *pret. & p.p. de* **to shut**; *adj.* cerrado.

shut·down [ʃʌtdɑʊn] *s.* paro, cesación.

shut·ter [ʃʌtɚ] *s.* contraventana; postigo (*de ventana*); cerrador; (*lens*) obturador (*de una cámara fotográfica*).

shut·tle [ʃʌtl] *s.* lanzadera; *v.* ir y venir acompasadamente (*como una lanzadera*).

shy [ʃaɪ] *adj.* tímido, apocado, retraído; vergonzoso; asustadizo; esquivo; **to be — on** estar escaso de; **to be — two cents** faltarle a uno dos centavos; *v.* esquivarse, hacerse a un lado; asustarse; **to — at something** retroceder ante algo; respingar (*un caballo*) al ver algo; espantarse con algo; **to — away** esquivarse de repente; respingar (*un caballo*); desviarse, apartarse.

shy·ness [ʃaɪnɪs] *s.* apocamiento, timidez, vergüenza.

shy·ster [ʃaɪstɚ] *s.* leguleyo, abogadillo tramposo, picapleitos.

sib·i·lant [sɪbələnt] *s.* sibilante.

sick [sɪk] *adj.* enfermo, malo; nauseado; angustiado; **— leave** licencia por enfermedad; **to be — for** languidecer por, suspirar por; **to be — of** estar cansado de; estar harto de; **to be — to** (*o* at) **one's stomach** tener náuseas; **to make —** enfermar; dar pena, dar lástima; *s.* **the —** los enfermos; *v.* (*dog*) incitar, azuzar (*a un perro*); **— him!** ¡síguele!

sick·en [sɪkən] *v.* enfermar(se), poner(se) enfermo; dar asco; tener asco; sentir náuseas.

sick·en·ing [sɪknɪŋ] *adj.* nauseabundo, repugnante; lastimoso.

sick·le [sɪkl] *s.* hoz.

sick·ly [sɪklɪ] *adj.* enfermizo; achacoso, enclenque; malsano.

sick·ness [sɪknɪs] *s.* enfermedad; malestar; náusea.

side [saɪd] *s.* (*surface*) lado; cara; costado; (*hill*) ladera; falda (*de una colina*); (*faction*) partido, facción; **— by —** lado a lado; **by his —** a su lado; **by the — of** al lado de; **on all -s** por todos lados; **to take -s with** ser partidario de, ponerse al lado de; *adj.* lateral; de lado; oblicuo; incidental; secundario, de menos importancia; **— glance** mirada de soslayo, de través o de reojo; **— issue** cuestión secundaria; **— light** luz lateral; noticia, detalle o ilustración incidental; *v.* **to — with** estar por, ser partidario de, apoyar a, opinar con.

side·board [saɪdbord] *s.* aparador; *Col., Ven.* seibó.

side·line [saɪdlaɪn] *s.* negocio secundario.

side·burns [saɪdbɜnz] *s.* patillas; *Méx.* clavos.

side·slip [saɪdslɪp] *s.* deslizamiento.

side·track [saɪdtræk] *v.* desviar; echar a un lado.

side·walk [saɪdwɔk] *s.* acera, *Méx.* banqueta, *Ríopl., Ch., Andes* vereda; *C.A., Col.,* andén.

side·ways [saɪdwez] *adv.* de lado, de costado; oblicuamente; hacia un lado; *adj.* lateral, de lado, oblicuo.

siege [sidʒ] *s.* cerco, sitio, asedio; **to lay — to** sitiar, cercar.

sieve [sɪv] *s.* tamiz, cedazo; criba; *v. véase* **sift.**

sift [sɪft] *v.* cerner, tamizar; cribar.

sigh [saɪ] *v.* suspirar; *s.* suspiro.

sight [saɪt] *s.* (*sense*) vista; (*view*) visión; espectáculo, escena; (*gun*) mira (*de un arma de fuego*); **in — of** a vista de; **payable at —** pagadero a la vista; **he is a —** es un adefesio o mamarracho; **this room is a —** este cuarto es un horror; **to catch — of** vislumbrar, avistar; **to know by —** conocer de vista; **to lose — of** perder de vista; **to see the -s** ver o visitar los puntos de interés; *v.* avistar; ver.

sight·see·ing [saɪtsiɪŋ] *s.* turismo; **— tour** paseo en auto para ver puntos de interés.

sign [saɪn] *s.* (*signal*) signo; seña, señal; (*indication*) muestra; (*placard*) letrero; **— board** cartel; (*bulletin*) tablero (*para fijar anuncios*); *v.* firmar; contratar, hacer firmar; **to — over property** ceder una propiedad mediante escritura, hacer cesión legal de propiedad; **to — up for a job** firmar el contrato para un empleo; contratar para un empleo.

sig·nal [sɪgnl] *s.* señal, seña; *v.* señalar, indicar, hacer señá, dar la señal; *adj.* señalado, notable; extraordinario; **— beacon** faro; **— code** código de señales.

sig·na·ture [sɪgnətʃɚ] *s.* firma.

sign·er [saɪnɚ] *s.* firmante.

sig·nif·i·cance [sɪgnɪfəkəns] *s.* significación; significado.

sig·nif·i·cant [sɪgnɪfəkənt] *adj.* significativo.

sig·ni·fy [sɪgnəfaɪ] *v.* significar.

si·lence [saɪləns] *s.* silencio; *v.* (*hush*) acallar; (*extinguish*) apagar (*un sonido*); aquietar, sosegar.

si·lent [saɪlənt] *adj.* silencioso; callado; tácito; **— partner** socio comanditario (*que no tiene voz ni voto*).

sil·hou·ette [sɪluɛt] *s.* silueta; *v.* perfilar; **to be -d against** perfilarse contra.

sil·i·con [sɪləkən] *s.* silicio.

silk [sɪlk] *s.* seda; *adj.* de seda; **— industry** industria sedera; **— ribbon** cinta de seda.

silk·en [sɪlkən] *adj.* sedoso; de seda.

silk·worm [sɪlkwɜm] *s.* gusano de seda.

silk·y [sɪlkɪ] *adj.* sedoso, sedeño; de seda.

sill [sɪl] *s.* umbral; **window —** antepecho de ventana.

sil·ly [sɪlɪ] *adj.* necio, tonto, bobo, simple; absurdo, insensato.

si·lo [saɪlo] *s.* silo.

silt [sɪlt] *s.* cieno.

sil·ver [sɪlvɚ] *s.* (*metal*) plata; (*tableware*) cubierto; (*dishes*) vajilla de plata; (*color*) color de plata; *adj.* de plata; plateado; argentino; **— wedding** bodas de plata; *v.* platear; argentar; **to — a mirror** azogar un espejo.

sil·ver·smith [sɪlvɚsmɪθ] *s.* platero.

sil·ver·ware [sɪlvɚwɛr] *s.* vajilla de plata, vajilla plateada; cuchillos, cucharas y tenedores (*por lo general de plata o plateados*).

sil·ver·y [sɪlvərɪ] *adj.* plateado; argentino.

sim·i·lar [sɪmələr] *adj.* semejante; similar; **-ly** *adv.* semejantemente; de la misma manera.

sim·i·lar·i·ty [sɪmələrətɪ] *s.* semejanza, parecido.

sim·i·le [sɪməlɪ] *s.* símil.

sim·mer [sɪmɚ] *v.* hervir a fuego lento.

sim·ple [sɪmpl] *adj.* simple; sencillo; llano; tonto, mentecato; **simpleminded** ingenuo, simple, simplón; *s.* simple.

sim·ple·ton [sɪmpltən] *s.* simplón, papanatas, papamoscas.

sim·plic·i·ty [sɪmplɪsətɪ] *s.* sencillez; simplicidad; simpleza; ingenuidad.

sim·pli·fy [sɪmpləfaɪ] *v.* simplificar.

sim·ply [sɪmplɪ] *adv.* simplemente; sencillamente; solamente.

sim·u·late [sɪmjəlet] *v.* simular.

si·mul·ta·ne·ous [saɪmltnɪəs] *adj.* simultáneo.

sin [sɪn] *s.* pecado, culpa; *v.* pecar.

since [sɪns] *conj.* desde que; después (de) que; puesto que, como, visto que; dado que; *prep.* desde, después de; *adv.* desde entonces; **ever** — desde entonces; **he died long** — murió hace mucho tiempo; **we have been here** — **five** estamos aquí desde las cinco.

sin·cere [sɪnsfr] *adj.* sincero.

sin·cer·i·ty [sɪnsɛrətɪ] *s.* sinceridad.

si·ne·cure [sínɪkjur] *s.* sinecura (*trabajo fácil y bien pagado*).

sin·ew [sínju] *s.* tendón; fibra, vigor.

sin·ew·y [sínjəwɪ] *adj.* nervudo, nervioso o nervoso; fuerte, vigoroso.

sin·ful [sínfəl] *adj.* pecaminoso; pecador.

sing [sɪŋ] *v.* cantar; **to** — **out of tune** desentonar(se), desafinar; **to** — **to sleep** arrullar.

singe [sɪndʒ] *v.* chamuscar; *s.* chamusquina, *Am.* chamuscada, *Am.* chamuscadura.

sing·er [síŋɚ] *s.* cantor; cantora, cantatriz.

sin·gle [síŋgl] *adj.* (*unique*) solo; (*distinct*) individual; particular; (*unmarried*) soltero; — **entry bookkeeping** teneduría por partida simple; — **room** cuarto para uno; — **woman** mujer soltera; — **density** (*computer*) densidad simple; **not a** — **word** ni una sola palabra; *s.* billete de un dólar; *v.* **to** — **out** singularizar, distinguir, escoger; entresacar.

sin·gle·handed [síŋglhændɪd] *adj.* solo, sin ayuda.

sing·song [síŋsɔŋ] *s.* sonsonete, cadencia monótona.

sin·gu·lar [síŋgjələ˞] *adj.* singular; raro, extraordinario; *s.* singular, número singular.

sin·is·ter [sínɪstɚ] *adj.* siniestro, aciago, funesto.

sink [sɪŋk] *v.* hundir(se); sumir(se), sumergir(se); (*boat*) echar a pique; irse a pique, naufragar; (*dig*) cavar (*un pozo*); enterrar, clavar (*un puntal o poste*); **to** — **into one's mind** grabarse en la memoria; **to** — **one's teeth into** clavar el diente en; **to** — **to sleep** caer en el sueño; *s.* sumidero; fregadero.

sin·ner [sínɚ] *s.* pecador.

sin·u·ous [sínjuəs] *adj.* sinuoso, tortuoso; con vueltas y rodeos.

si·nus [sáɪnəs] *s.* seno, cavidad (*en un hueso*); **frontal** — seno frontal.

sip [sɪp] *v.* sorber; chupar; *s.* sorbo.

si·phon [sáɪfən] *s.* sifón; *v.* sacar (*agua*) con sifón.

sir [sɚ] *s.* señor.

si·ren [sáɪrən] *s.* sirena.

sir·loin [sɚ́lɔɪn] *s.* solomillo, solomo.

sir·up [sírəp] *s.* jarabe.

sis·sy [sísɪ] *adj.* & *s.* afeminado, maricón.

sis·ter [sístɚ] *s.* hermana; **Sister Mary** Sor María.

sis·ter-in-law [sístərɪnlɔ] *s.* cuñada, hermana política.

sit [sɪt] *v.* sentar(se); colocar, asentar; posarse (*un pájaro*); (*be seated*) estar sentado; estar situado; (*hen*) empollar (*las gallinas*); apoyarse; (*meet*) reunirse, celebrar sesión (*un cuerpo legislativo, un tribunal*); sentar, venir o caer (*bien o mal un traje*); **to** — **down** sentarse; **to** — **out a dance** quedarse sentado durante una pieza de baile; **to** — **still** estarse quieto; **to** — **tight** mantenerse firme en su puesto; **to** — **up** incorporarse; **to** — **up all night** velar toda la noche; **to** — **up and take notice** despabilarse.

site [saɪt] *s.* sitio, local, situación.

sit·ting [sítɪŋ] *s.* sesión (*de un cuerpo legislativo, tribunal, etc.*); sentada; **at one** — de una sentada; *adj.* sentado; — **hen** gallina ponedora; — **room** sala (de descanso); sala de espera; antesala.

sit·u·at·ed [sítʃuetɪd] *adj.* situado, sito, ubicado, colocado.

sit·u·a·tion [sɪtʃuéʃən] *s.* (*location*) situación, colocación; (*employment*) empleo; posición; (*status*) situación.

six [sɪks] *num.* seis.

six·teen [sɪkstín] *num.* dieciséis.

six·ty [sfksti] *num.* sesenta.

size [saɪz] *s.* tamaño; *C.A.* porte; medida; (*clothing*) talla; *v.* clasificar según el tamaño; **to** — **up** tantear, formarse una idea de, juzgar.

siz·zle [sfzl] *v.* chirriar (*aplícase al sonido que hace la carne al freírse*); *s.* chirrido (*de la carne al freírse*).

skate [sket] *s.* patín; **ice** — patín de hielo, patín de cuchilla; **roller** — patín de ruedas; *v.* patinar.

skein [sken] *s.* madeja.

skel·e·ton [skélətn] *s.* esqueleto; osamenta; armazón; — **key** llave maestra.

skep·tic = **sceptic**.

sketch [skɛtʃ] *s.* (*drawing*) boceto; diseño; croquis; (*outline*) esbozo; bosquejo; *v.* bosquejar; delinear; esbozar, dibujar.

ski [ski] *s.* esquí; *v.* esquiar, patinar con esquís.

skid [skɪd] *v.* patinar, resbalar(se); patinar (*una rueda*); deslizarse.

skill [skɪl] *s.* destreza, maña, habilidad, pericia.

skilled [skɪld] *adj.* experto, práctico, experimentado, hábil; — **worker** obrero calificado.

skil·let [skílɪt] *s.* sartén; cacerola.

skill·ful, skil·ful [skílfəl] *adj.* experto, diestro, ducho, hábil, perito.

skim [skɪm] *v.* (*remove layer*) desnatar, quitar la nata a; (*foam*) espumar, quitar la espuma a; (*read*) leer superficialmente; **to** — **over the surface** rozar la superficie.

skimp [skɪmp] *v.* escatimar; economizar; ser tacaño; hacer (*las cosas*) con descuido.

skimp·y [skímpɪ] *adj.* escaso; tacaño.

skin [skɪn] *s.* piel; cutis; pellejo; cuero; cáscara, hollejo; **to save one's** — salvar el pellejo; **skin-deep** superficial; *v.* desollar; pelar; **to** — **someone out of his money** desplumar a una persona, quitarle a uno el dinero.

skin·ny [skínɪ] *adj.* flaco; descarnado.

skip [skɪp] *v.* saltar; brincar; saltarse (*unos renglones, un párrafo, etc.*), omitir; saltar por encima de, salvar de un brinco; **to** — **out** salir a escape, escabullirse, escaparse; *s.* salto, brinco; omisión.

skip·per [skípɚ] *s.* patrón (*de barco*); capitán; saltador, brincador.

skir·mish [skɚ́mɪʃ] *s.* escaramuza; *v.* escaramuzar, sostener una escaramuza.

skirt [skɚt] *s.* falda, *Ríopl.* pollera; (*side*) orilla, borde; **under** — enaguas; *v.* bordear, orillar, ir por la orilla de; (*circle*) circundar; **to** — **along a coast** costear.

skit [skɪt] *s.* parodia, juguete o paso cómico; boceto satírico o burlesco.

skull [skʌl] *s.* cráneo; calavera.

skunk [skʌŋk] *s.* *C.A.*, *Méx.*, *Ríopl.* zorrillo o zorrino, *Ven.*, *Col.* mapurite.

sky [skaɪ] *s.* cielo; — **blue** azul celeste.

sky·lark [skáɪlɑrk] *s.* alondra, calandria.

sky·light [skáɪlaɪt] *s.* claraboya, tragaluz.

sky·rock·et [skáɪrɑkɪt] *s.* cohete.

sky·scrap·er [skáɪskrepɚ] *s.* rascacielos.

slab [slæb] *s.* tabla, plancha, (*tile*) losa; (*slice*) tajada gruesa; **marble** — losa de mármol.

slack [slæk] *adj.* (*not taut*) flojo; (*sluggish*) tardo, lento, inactivo; — **season** temporada inactiva; *s.* flojedad, flojera; inactividad; **to take up the** —

SH

apretar, estirar; **-s** pantalones anchos con pliegues,
v. véase **slacken.**
slack·en [slǽkən] *v.* aflojar(se); flojear; retardar(se);
disminuir.
slag [slæg] *s.* escoria.
slain [slen] *p.p. de* **to slay.**
slam [slæm] *v.* cerrar(se) de golpe; dejar caer de
golpe; **to — someone** decirle a alguien una
claridad o grosería; **to — the door** dar un portazo;
s. golpazo; claridad, grosería; **— of a door**
portazo; **to make a grand —** ganar todas las bazas
(*en el juego de bridge*).
slan·der [slǽndɚ] *s.* calumnia, maledicencia; *v.*
calumniar.
slan·der·ous [slǽndərəs] *adj.* calumnioso;
maldiciente.
slang [slæŋ] *s.* (*jargon*) jerga, jerigonza; (*argot*)
vulgarismo.
slant [slænt] *s.* sesgo; inclinación; (*viewpoint*) punto
de vista; *adj.* sesgado; inclinado; oblicuo; *v.*
sesgar; inclinar(se); ladear.
slap [slæp] *s.* palmada, manazo, manotada; insulto,
desaire; *v.* dar una palmada a, dar un manazo a.
slap·stick [slǽpstɪk] *adj.* de golpe y porrazo.
slash [slæʃ] *v.* acuchillar; dar cuchilladas o tajos;
cortar; truncar; hacer fuerte rebaja de (*precios,
sueldos*); *s.* cuchillada; tajo, tajada, cortadura.
slat [slæt] *s.* tabla, tablilla.
slate [slet] *s.* pizarra; color de pizarra; lista de
candidatos; **— pencil** pizarrín.
slaugh·ter [slɔ́tɚ] *s.* carnicería, matanza, *Ríopl.*
carneada; **— house** matadero, *Méx., C.A.* rastro;
v. matar; *Ríopl.* carnear; hacer una matanza;
destrozar.
slave [slev] *s.* esclavo; **— driver** capataz de
esclavos; persona que agobia de trabajo a otra; **—
labor** trabajo de esclavos; trabajadores forzados;
— dealer negrero; *v.* trabajar como esclavo.
slav·er [slǽvɚ] *s.* baba; *v.* babosear, babear.
slav·er·y [slévrɪ] *s.* esclavitud.
slav·ish [slévɪʃ] *adj.* servil.
slay [sle] *v.* matar.
slea·zy [slízɪ] *adj.* débil, tenue, inválido.
sled [slɛd] *s.* trineo, rastra.
sleek [slik] *adj.* liso; pulido, resbaloso; suave;
(*tricky*) artero, mañoso; *v.* alisar; pulir.
sleep [slip] *v.* dormir; **to — it off** dormir la mona; **to
— off a headache** curarse con sueño un dolor de
cabeza; **to — on it** consultarlo con la almohada; *s.*
sueño; **— walker** sonámbulo; **to go to —**
dormirse, quedarse dormido; **to put to —**
adormecer; arrullar (*al nene*).
sleep·er [slípɚ] *s.* durmiente; cochecama, coche-
dormitorio.
sleep·i·ly [slípɪlɪ] *adv.* con somnolencia.
sleep·i·ness [slípɪnɪs] *s.* sueño, modorra,
somnolencia.
sleep·ing [slípɪŋ] *adj.* durmiente; dormido; **— car**
coche-cama, coche-dormitorio; **— pills** píldoras
para dormir; **— sickness** encefalitis letárgica.
sleep·less [slíplɪs] *adj.* desvelado, insomne, sin
sueño.
sleep·y [slípɪ] *adj.* soñoliento; amodorrado; **to be —**
tener sueño.
sleet [slit] *s.* cellisca; *v.* cellisquear.
sleeve [sliv] *s.* manga.
sleigh [sle] *s.* trineo; **— bell** cascabel; *v.* pasearse en
trineo.
sleight [slaɪt]: **— of hand** juego de manos;
prestidigitación, escamoteo.
slen·der [slɛ́ndɚ] *adj.* delgado; tenue; escaso,

insuficiente.
slept [slɛpt] *pret. & p.p. de* **to sleep.**
sleuth [sluθ] *s.* detective (*o* detectivo).
slew [slu] *pret. de* **to slay.**
slice [slaɪs] *s.* rebanada, tajada; lonja; *v.* rebanar,
tajar; cortar.
slick [slɪk] *v.* alisar; pulir; **to — up** alisar bien, pulir
bien; (*one's self*) pulirse, acicalarse, componerse;
adj. liso; meloso, suave; aceitoso; astuto, mañoso.
slick·er [slɪ́kɚ] *s.* impermeable de hule (*o* de
caucho); (*crook*) embaucador.
slid [slɪd] *pret. & p.p. de* **to slide.**
slid·den [slɪ́dn̩] *p.p. de* **to slide.**
slide [slaɪd] *v.* resbalar(se); deslizar(se); hacer
resbalar; patinar; **to — into** meter(se) en; **to —
out** (*o* **— away**) deslizarse, colarse, escabullirse,
escaparse; **to let something —** dejar pasar algo; no
hacer caso de algo; *s.* resbalón; resbaladero, lugar
resbaladizo; ligado (*en música*); (*véase* **landslide**);
— cover tapa corrediza; **— rule** regla de cálculo;
microscope — platina.
slight [slaɪt] *s.* desaire, menosprecio, desdén;
desatención; *v.* desairar, menospreciar; descuidar,
desatender; *adj.* delgado; delicado; leve, ligero;
pequeño; insignificante; escaso; **-ly** *adv.*
escasamente; ligeramente; un poco, apenas.
slim [slɪm] *adj.* delgado; esbelto; escaso.
slime [slaɪm] *s.* limo, cieno, fango; (*slobber*) baba,
secreción viscosa.
slim·y [sláɪmɪ] *adj.* viscoso, mucoso, fangoso;
baboso.
sling [slɪŋ] *s.* (*weapon*) honda (*para tirar piedras*);
(*arm*) cabestrillo (*para sostener el brazo*); (*rope*)
eslinga (*maroma provista de ganchos para levantar
pesos*); **— shot** tirador de goma o hule; *v.* tirar,
arrojar; **to — a rifle over one's shoulder** echarse
el rifle al hombro.
slink [slɪŋk] *v.* andar furtivamente; **to — away**
escurrirse, escabullirse, deslizarse.
slip [slɪp] *v.* (*slide*) deslizar(se); resbalar(se); (*err*)
cometer un desliz; equivocarse; **to — away**
escaparse, escabullirse, escurrirse; **to — in**
meter(se); **to — one's dress on** ponerse de prisa el
vestido; **to — out** salirse; sacar a hurtadillas; **to —
out of joint** dislocarse, *Am.* zafarse (*un hueso*); **to
— something off** quitar(se) algo; **to let an
opportunity — by** dejar pasar una oportunidad; **it
slipped my mind** se me olvidó, se me pasó; **it
slipped off** se zafó; *s.* desliz; resbalón; error,
equivocación; funda (*de muebles, de almohada*);
combinación, enaguas; pedazo (*de papel*), volante,
papeleta; embarcadero; guía, sarmiento (*para
transplantar*); **— knot** nudo corredizo.
slip·per [slɪ́pɚ] *s.* zapatilla; babucha; pantufla.
slip·per·y [slɪ́prɪ] *adj.* resbaloso, resbaladizo; evasivo.
slit [slɪt] *v.* cortar, hacer una rendija, abertura o
incisión; **to — into strips** cortar en tiras; *pret. &
p.p. de* **to slit;** *s.* abertura, hendedura, rendija;
cortada, incisión.
slob·ber [slɑ́bɚ] *s.* baba; *v.* babosear, babear.
slob·ber·ing [slɑ́bərɪŋ] *adj.* baboso.
slo·gan [slógən] *s.* lema, mote; consigna.
sloop [slup] *s.* balandra.
slop [slɑp] *v.* (*soil*) ensuciar; (*splash*) salpicar; (*spill*)
derramar(se); *s.* fango, suciedad; **-s** lavazas, agua
sucia; desperdicios.
slope [slop] *v.* inclinar(se); *s.* inclinación; declive;
falda, ladera; cuesta, bajada; vertiente.
slop·py [slɑ́pɪ] *adj.* puerco, sucio, cochino;
desaseado; mal hecho.
slot [slɑt] *s.* (*opening*) abertura, hendedura; (*groove*

for coins) ranura (*en que se introduce una moneda*); — **machine** máquina automática que funciona por medio de una moneda; «traganíqueles,» «tragamonedas»; *v.* hacer una abertura o hendedura.

sloth [sloθ] *s.* pereza; perezoso (*cuadrúpedo*).

slouch [slautʃ] *s.* (*posture*) postura muy relajada o floja; (*person*) persona perezosa o desaseada; — **hat** sombrero gacho; **to walk with a** — andar con los hombros caídos y la cabeza inclinada; *v.* andar agachado; andar caído de hombros; andar alicaído; arrellanarse, repantigarse (*en una silla*).

slov·en·li·ness [slʌvənlɪnɪs] *s.* desaseo, desaliño; suciedad.

slov·en·ly [slʌvənlɪ] *adj.* desaseado, desaliñado; desarreglado.

slow [slo] *adj.* (*low speed*) lento, despacio; (*late*) tardo; atrasado; (*sluggish*) lerdo; torpe; *adv.* lentamente, despacio; *v.* **to** — **down** (*o* — **up**) retardar disminuir (*el paso, la marcha, la velocidad*); aflojar el paso; **-ly** *adv.* despacio, lentamente; **slowdown** disminución de actividades.

slow·ness [slónɪs] *s.* lentitud, torpeza, cachaza.

slug [slʌg] *s.* (*bullet*) bala; porrazo, puñetazo; babosa (*molusco sin concha*); (*lazy*) haragán; (*swallow*) trago (*de aguardiente*); (*printing*) lingote (*de imprenta*); *v.* aporrear, (*fist*) abofetear, dar puñetazos.

slug·gard [slʌgəd] *s.* holgazán, haragán.

slug·gish [slʌgɪʃ] *adj.* tardo; inactivo.

sluice [slus] *s.* compuerta; caño, canal; — **gate** compuerta.

slum [slʌm] *s.* barrio bajo; *v.* visitar los barrios bajos.

slum·ber [slʌmbə] *v.* dormitar; dormir; *s.* sueño, sueño ligero.

slump [slʌmp] *v.* hundirse; desplomarse; bajar repentinamente (*los precios o valores*); *s.* desplome, hundimiento, bajón, baja repentina (*de precios, valores, etc.*).

slung [slʌŋ] *pret. & p.p. de* **to sling.**

slunk [slʌŋk] *pret. & p.p. de* **to slink.**

slush [slʌʃ] *s.* (*snow*) nieve a medio derretir; (*mud*) lodazal, fango; (*refuse*) desperdicios; (*drivel*) sentimentalismo.

sly [slaɪ] *adj.* astuto, socarrón, zorro, taimado; **on the** — a hurtadillas, a escondidas.

sly·ness [slaɪnɪs] *s.* disimulo, astucia.

smack [smæk] *s.* (*taste*) sabor, dejo; (*kiss*) beso ruidoso; (*crack*) chasquido (*de látigo*); (*slap*) palmada, manotada; **a** — **of something** una pizca de algo; *v.* dar un beso ruidoso; chasquear (*un látigo*); dar un manazo; **to** — **of** saber a, tener el sabor de; oler a; **to** — **one's lips** chuparse los labios, saborearse, rechuparse, relamerse.

small [smɔl] *adj.* (*size*) pequeño, chico; bajo; (*insignificant*) insignificante; mezquino; — **change** dinero menudo, suelto; — **hours** primeras horas de la mañana; — **letters** letras minúsculas; — **talk** conversación insubstancial, charladuría; — **voice** vocecita; **to feel** — sentirse pequeño o insignificante.

small·ness [smɔlnɪs] *s.* pequeñez; bajeza.

small·pox [smɔlpaks] *s.* viruela.

small·wares [smɔlwɛrz] *s.* (*notions*) mercería.

smart [smart] *adj.* (*intelligent*) listo, inteligente; (*astute*) ladino; astuto; agudo; (*stylish*) elegante; — **remark** observación aguda o penetrante; — **set** gente de buen tono; *s.* escozor, *Ríopl., C.A., Méx.* ardor; *v.* picar, escocer, *Ríopl., C.A., Méx.* arder.

smash [smæʃ] *v.* quebrantar, quebrar, romper;

destrozar; aplastar; **to** — **into** chocar con; topar con, darse un tope contra; *s.* quebrazón, quiebra; fracaso; choque o tope violento; derrota completa.

smat·ter·ing [smætərɪŋ] *s.* conocimiento superficial y rudimental.

smear [smɪr] *v.* embarrar, untar, manchar; **to** — **with paint** pintorrear, pintarrajear; *s.* mancha.

smell [smɛl] *v.* oler; **to** — **of** oler a; *s.* olor; olfato; — **of** olor a; **to take a** — oler.

smell·y [smɛlɪ] *adj.* oloroso; hediondo.

smelt [smɛlt] *v.* fundir (*metales*); *pret. & p.p. de* **to smell.**

smile [smaɪl] *v.* sonreír(se); *s.* sonrisa.

smil·ing [smaɪlɪŋ] *adj.* risueño, sonriente; **-ly** *adv.* sonriendo, con cara risueña.

smite [smaɪt] *v.* golpear; herir; castigar; afligir; *véase* **smitten.**

smith [smɪθ] *s.* forjador; *véase* **blacksmith, goldsmith, silversmith.**

smith·y [smɪθɪ] *s.* herrería, fragua, forja.

smit·ten [smɪtn̩] *p.p. de* **to smite** *& adj.* afligido; castigado; (*in love*) enamorado; **to be** — **with a disease** darle a uno una enfermedad.

smock [smak] *s.* bata corta, batín.

smoke [smok] *s.* humo; — **screen** cortina de humo; **cloud of** — humareda; **to have a** — dar una fumada, fumar, *Am.* chupar (*un cigarro*); humear; ahumar; **to** — **out** ahuyentar o echar fuera con humo.

smok·er [smókə] *s.* fumador; (*car*) vagón de fumar; reunión o tertulia de fumadores.

smoke·stack [smókstæk] *s.* chimenea.

smok·ing [smókɪŋ] *adj.* humeante; de fumar; para fumadores; — **car** vagón de fumar; — **room** fumadero, cuarto de fumar.

smok·y [smókɪ] *adj.* humeante; humoso, lleno de humo; ahumado.

smooth [smuð] *adj.* (*even*) liso; terso; igual, parejo; plano, llano; (*serene*) tranquilo; (*pleasant*) suave; (*wise*) sagaz; — **disposition** genio afable; — **manners** maneras o modales afables; — **style** estilo flúido y fácil; — **talker** hablador melífluo y sagaz; *v.* alisar; allanar; pulir; emparejar; **to** — **over** allanar, alisar, arreglar; **-ly** *adv.* suavemente; blandamente; fácilmente, con facilidad.

smooth·ness [smúðnɪs] *s.* (*evenness*) lisura; igualdad, uniformidad; (*pleasantness*) suavidad; afabilidad; tranquilidad; facilidad; fluidez.

smote [smot] *pret. de* **to smite.**

smoth·er [smʌðə] *v.* ahogar(se); sofocar(se); asfixiar(se).

smudge [smʌdʒ] *v.* tiznar, manchar o ensuciar con tizne; ahumar; *s.* tiznón, mancha (*hecha con tizne*); humareda, nube espesa de humo.

smug·gle [smʌgl̩] *v.* contrabandear, hacer contrabando; **to** — **in** meter de contrabando; **to** — **out** sacar de contrabando.

smug·gler [smʌglə] *s.* contrabandista.

smut [smʌt] *s.* (*smudge*) tizne; suciedad, mancha; (*obscenity*) obscenidad, dicho obsceno o indecente; (*plant*) tizón (*enfermedad de ciertas plantas*); *v.* tiznar; ensuciar, manchar.

smut·ty [smʌtɪ] *adj.* tiznado, manchado de tizne; sucio.

snack [snæk] *s.* (*food*) bocado, bocadillo, tentempié, bocadito; (*meal*) merienda, comida ligera.

snag [snæg] *s.* (*protuberance*) tocón; raigón; (*obstacle*) tropiezo, obstáculo; **to hit a** — tropezar con un obstáculo; *v.* rasgar; enredar.

snail [snel] *s.* caracol.

snake [snek] *s.* culebra, víbora; *v.* culebrear.

SL

snap [snæp] *v.* (*make sound*) chasquear, dar un
chasquido; estallar; (*break*) quebrar(se);
(*photograph*) fotografiar instantáneamente; **his eyes**
— le chispean los ojos; **to** — **at** echar una
mordida o mordisco a; dar una tarascada a,
morder; asir (*una oportunidad*); **to** — **back at** tirar
una mordida a; dar una respuesta grosera a; **to** —
off soltarse, saltar; quebrar(se); **to** — **one's fingers**
tronar los dedos, castañetear con los dedos; **to** —
shut cerrar(se) de golpe; **to** — **together** apretar,
abrochar; **to** — **up** agarrar, asir; morder; *s.*
chasquido; estallido; mordida, mordisco,
dentellada; broche de presión; energía, vigor;
galleta; cosa fácil, ganga; **cold** — nortazo;
repentino descenso de temperatura; **not to care a**
— no importarle a uno un ardite o un comino; *adj.*
hecho de prisa, impensado; instantáneo; —
fastener broche de presión; — **judgment** decisión
atolondrada; — **lock** cerradura de golpe.
snap·py [snǽpɪ] *adj.* mordedor, *Ven.*, *C.A.*, *Andes*
mordelón; (*angry*) enojadizo, *Méx.* enojón;
violento, vivo; (*elegant*) elegante; — **cheese** queso
acre o picante; — **eyes** ojos chispeantes.
snap·shot [snǽpʃɑt] *s.* instantánea, fotografía
instantánea; *v.* sacar una instantánea.
snare [snɛr] *s.* (*trap*) trampa, lazo; (*ambush*)
acechanza; (*net*) red; *v.* (*tangle*) enredar; atrapar,
coger con trampa; tender lazos a.
snarl [snɑrl] *v.* (*sound*) gruñir; (*tangle*)
enmarañar(se), enredar(se); *s.* gruñido; maraña,
enredo; pelo enmarañado.
snatch [snætʃ] *v.* arrebatar; agarrar; **to** — **at** tratar de
asir o agarrar; *s.* arrebatiña, arrebatamiento; trozo,
pedacito; **to make a** — **at** tratar de arrebatar, tratar
de agarrarse a.
sneak [snik] *v.* andar furtivamente; obrar
solapadamente; **to** — **in** meter(se) a escondidas;
colarse; **to** — **out** escurrirse, salirse a hurtadillas;
sacar, llevarse (*algo*) a escondidas; *s.* persona
solapada.
sneer [snɪr] *v.* (*smile*) sonreír con sorna; (*gesture*)
hacer un gesto de desdén; (*ridicule*) mofarse; **to** —
at mofarse de; *s.* sorna, mofa, rechifla; gesto
desdeñoso.
sneeze [sniz] *v.* estornudar; *s.* estornudo.
sniff [snɪf] *v.* husmear, olfatear; sorber (*por las
narices*); (*snort*) resollar para adentro; **to** — **at**
husmear; (*ridicule*) menospreciar; *s.* husmeo,
olfateo; sorbo (*por las narices*).
snif·fle [snɪfl] *v.* sorber por las narices.
snip [snɪp] *v.* tijeretear; **to** — **off** cortar de un
tijeretazo, recortar; *s.* tijeretada, tijeretazo;
pedacito, recorte.
snipe [snaɪp] *v.* tirar, disparar desde un escondite.
snip·er [snáɪpə·] *s.* francotirador; tirador emboscado.
snitch [snɪtʃ] *v.* (*tell on*) ratear; (*rob*) hurtar.
sniv·el [snɪvl] *v.* moquear; gimotear.
snob [snɑb] *s.* esnob.
snoop [snup] *v.* fisgar, fisgonear, curiosear; *s.*
curioso, fisgón.
snooze [snuz] *v.* dormitar, sestear; *s.* siestecita,
siestita; **to take a** — echar un sueñecito o siestita;
descabezar el sueño.
snore [snor] *v.* roncar; *s.* ronquido.
snor·kel [snɔ́rkl] *s.* tubo esnorkel.
snort [snɔrt] *v.* resoplar; bufar; *s.* resoplido, bufido.
snout [snaʊt] *s.* hocico, jeta.
snow [sno] *s.* nieve; *v.* nevar; **to be -ed under** estar
totalmente cubierto por la nevada.
snow·ball [snóbɔl] *s.* bola de nieve; *v.* tirar bolas de
nieve.

snow·drift [snódrɪft] *s.* ventisca, ventisquero, montón
de nieve.
snow·fall [snófɔl] *s.* nevada.
snow·flake [snóflek] *s.* copo de nieve.
snow·storm [snóstɔrm] *s.* fuerte nevada, nevasca.
snow·y [snóɪ] *adj.* nevado; (*white*) níveo, blanco
como la nieve.
snub [snʌb] *v.* desairar, menospreciar; *s.* desaire;
snub-nosed chato, *C.A.*, *Col.*, *Ven.*, *Andes* ñato.
snuff [snʌf] *v.* olfatear, husmear, ventear; (*blow out*)
aspirar (*por la nariz*); despabilar (*una candela*); **to**
— **at** olfatear, ventear; **to** — **out** apagar,
extinguir; **to** — **up** sorber (*por las narices*); *s.*
sorbo (*por la nariz*); rapé, tabaco en polvo; pabilo,
mecha quemada (*de una vela*).
snuf·fle [snʌfl] *v.* ganguear; husmear.
snug [snʌg] *adj.* (*squeezed*) apretado; ajustado;
compacto; (*comfortable*) abrigado; cómodo.
so [so] *adv.* así; tan, muy; tanto; **so-so** regular; **so-
and-so** Fulano (de tal); — **as to** para; — **far** tan
lejos; hasta ahora, hasta aquí; — **many** tantos; —
much tanto; — **much for that** basta por ese lado;
— **much the better** tanto mejor; — **that** de modo
que; para que; a fin de que; de suerte que; — **then**
conque, pues bien, así pues; — **long!** ¡hasta
luego!; **and** — **forth** etcétera; y así sucesivamente;
I believe — así lo creo; **is that** — ? ¿de veras?
¿de verdad?; ¡ no diga!; **ten minutes or** — poco
más o menos diez minutos, como diez minutos.
soak [sok] *v.* remojar(se); empapar(se); **to** — **up**
absorber, embeber; chupar; — **in grease** pringar;
to be -ed through estar empapado; estar calado
hasta los huesos; *s.* remojo, mojada; borrachín;
golpe, puñetazo.
soap [sop] *s.* jabón; — **bubble** pompa de jabón,
Ven., *Col.* bombita; *Andes*, *Méx.* burbuja de jabón;
— **dish** jabonera; **soft** — jabón blando; lisonja,
adulación; *v.* enjabonar.
soap·y [sópɪ] *adj.* lleno de jabón.
soar [sor] *v.* remontarse; encumbrarse; subir muy
alto; remontar el vuelo.
sob [sɑb] *v.* sollozar; *s.* sollozo.
so·ber [sóbə·] *adj.* (*temperate*) sobrio; moderado;
templado; (*serious*) serio, grave; (*sane*) cuerdo,
sensato; (*calm*) tranquilo, sereno; **to be** — estar en
su juicio; no estar borracho; *v.* **to** — **down**
sosegar(se), calmar(se); formalizarse; **to** — **up**
desembriagarse, desemborracharse; bajársele a uno
la borrachera.
so·ber·ly [sóbə·lɪ] *adv.* sobriamente; cuerdamente,
con sensatez; seriamente.
so·ber·ness [sóbə·nɪs] *s.* sobriedad; seriedad.
so·bri·e·ty [səbráɪətɪ] *s.* sobriedad; cordura.
so·called [sókɔ́ld] *adj.* así llamado, llamado.
soc·cer [sákə·] *s.* fútbol.
so·cia·ble [sóʃəbl] *adj.* sociable, social, tratable.
so·cial [sóʃəl] *adj.* social; sociable; tratable, de buen
trato; *s.* reunión social; tertulia; — **security**
seguridad social; — **welfare** beneficencia pública;
— **work** servicio social.
so·cial·ism [sóʃəlɪzəm] *s.* socialismo.
so·cial·ist [sóʃəlɪst] *adj.* & *s.* socialista.
so·cial·ize [sóʃəlaɪz] *v.* socializar.
so·ci·e·ty [səsáɪətɪ] *s.* sociedad; compañía.
so·ci·ol·o·gy [soʃɪálədʒɪ] *s.* sociología.
sock [sak] *s.* (*garment*) calcetín; (*blow*) porrazo,
golpe, puñetazo; *v.* pegar, apalear, golpear; *Méx.*,
Carib. batear (*una pelota*).
sock·et [sákɪt] *s.* (*eye*) cuenca (*del ojo*);
portalámparas, enchufe, *Carib.* sóquet.
sod [sɑd] *s.* (*lawn*) césped; (*piece*) terrón (*de tierra*

sembrada de césped); *v*. cubrir de césped.

so·da [sódǝ] *s*. soda, sosa; — **fountain** *Am*. fuente de soda; — **water** agua gaseosa; **baking** — bicarbonato de sodio.

so·di·um [sódɪǝm] *s*. sodio.

sod·om·y [sádǝmɪ] *s*. sodomia.

so·fa [sófǝ] *s*. sofá.

soft [sɔft] *adj*. (*bland*) blando; muelle; suave; (*gentle*) tierno; dulce; **soft-boiled eggs** huevos pasados por agua; *Méx., C.A., Col., Ven.* huevos tibios; — **coal** carbón bituminoso; — **drink** bebida no alcohólica; — **metal** metal dulce, metal maleable; — **money** moneda débil; — **soap** jabón blando; adulación; — **water** agua dulce; *adv. véase* **softly.**

soft·en [sɔfǝn] *v*. ablandar(se); suavizar(se); enternecer(se); templar(se); **to** — **one's voice** bajar la voz, hablar quedo (*o* quedito).

soft-heart·ed [sɔfthɑrtǝd] *adj*. de buen corazón.

soft·ly [sɔftlɪ] *adv*. blandamente; suavemente; quedo, quedito.

soft·ness [sɔftnɪs] *s*. blandura; molicie; suavidad; ternura; dulzura.

software [sɔftwɛr] *s*. (*computer*) logical, conjunto lógico, software.

sog·gy [sɑgɪ] *adj*. remojado; empapado.

soil [sɔɪl] *s*. suelo, terreno, tierra; (*spot*) mancha; **native** — terruño; *v*. ensuciar(se); manchar(se).

so·journ [sódʒɜ·n] *s*. estada, estancia, permanencia, *Andes, Méx., Ríopl.* estadía; *v*. permanecer; estarse, residir por una temporada.

sol·ace [sálɪs] *s*. solaz; *v*. solazar.

so·lar [sólɚ] *adj*. solar, del sol; — **plexis** plexo solar.

sold [sold] *pret. & p.p. de* **sell; to be** — **on an idea** estar bien convencido de una idea.

sol·der [sádɚ] *v*. soldar; *s*. soldadura.

sol·dier [sóldʒɚ] *s*. soldado.

sole [sol] *adj*. solo, único; exclusivo; *s*. (*shoe*) suela (*del zapato*); (*foot*) planta (*del pie*); (*fish*) lenguado (*pez*); — **right** derecho exclusivo; *v*. solar, echar suelas a; **to half-sole** echar o poner medias suelas a.

sole·ly [sóllɪ] *adv*. sólamente, únicamente.

sol·emn [sálǝm] *adj*. solemne.

so·lem·ni·ty [sǝlémnǝtɪ] *s*. solemnidad.

sol·fa·ing [solfáɪŋ] *s*. solfeo.

so·lic·it [sǝlísɪt] *v*. solicitar.

so·lic·i·tor [sǝlísǝtɚ] *s*. solicitador, agente.

so·lic·i·tous [sǝlísɪtǝs] *adj*. solícito.

so·lic·i·tude [sǝlísǝtjud] *s*. solicitud, cuidado.

sol·id [sálɪd] *s*. sólido; *adj*. sólido; firme; macizo; (*sane*) sensato; (*unanimous*) unánime; — **blue** todo azul; — **gold** oro puro; **for one** — **hour** por una hora entera, por una hora sin parar; **the country is** — **for** el país está firmemente unido en favor de.

sol·i·dar·i·ty [sɑlǝdǽrǝtɪ] *s*. solidaridad.

so·lid·i·fy [sǝlídǝfaɪ] *v*. solidificar(se).

so·lid·i·ty [sǝlídǝtɪ] *s*. solidez.

sol·id-state [sɑlǝdstét] *adj*. física del estado sólido.

so·lil·o·quy [sǝlílǝkwɪ] *s*. soliloquio.

sol·i·tar·y [sɑlǝtɛrɪ] *adj*. solitario; solo; *s*. solitario, ermitaño.

sol·i·tude [sálǝtjud] *s*. soledad.

so·lo [sólo] *s*. solo.

so·lo·ist [sóloɪst] *s*. solista.

sol·stice [sálstǝs] *s*. solsticio.

sol·u·ble [sáljǝbl] *adj*. soluble, que se disuelve fácilmente.

so·lu·tion [sǝlúʃǝn] *s*. solución.

solve [sɑlv] *v*. resolver; explicar, aclarar, desenredar;

solucionar.

som·ber [sámbɚ] *adj*. sombrío.

some [sʌm] *adj*. algún, alguno; algunos, unos; algo de, un poco de; — **one** alguien, alguno; — **twenty people** unas veinte personas; *pron*. algunos, unos; algo, un poco; una parte.

some·bod·y [sʌmbɑdɪ] *pron*. alguien; **a** — un personaje de importancia.

some·how [sʌmhaʊ] *adv*. de algún modo, de alguna manera; — **or other** de una manera u otra; por alguna razón.

some·one [sʌmwʌn] *pron*. alguno, alguien.

som·er·sault [sʌmɚsɔlt] *s*. voltereta; *v*. dar una voltereta.

some·thing [sʌmθɪŋ] *s*. algo, alguna cosa; un poco; — **else** alguna otra cosa, otra cosa.

some·time [sʌmtaɪm] *adv*. algún día; alguna vez; en algún tiempo; **-s** *adv*. a veces, algunas veces, de vez en cuando.

some·what [sʌmhwɑt] *s*. algo, alguna cosa, un poco; *adv*. algo, un tanto.

some·where [sʌmhwɛr] *adv*. en alguna parte; — **else** en alguna otra parte.

son [sʌn] *s*. hijo.

song [sɔŋ] *s*. canción; canto; **the Song of Songs** el Cantar de los Cantares; — **bird** ave canora, pájaro cantor; **to buy something for a** — comprar algo muy barato.

son·ic bar·ri·er [sɑnɪkbǽrɪɚ] *s*. barrera sónica.

son-in-law [sʌnɪnlɔ] *s*. yerno, hijo político.

son·net [sɑnɪt] *s*. soneto.

so·no·rous [sǝnórǝs] *adj*. sonoro.

soon [sun] *adv*. pronto, presto; luego; — **after** poco después (de); al poco tiempo; **as** — **as** tan pronto como; luego que, así que; **how** — ? ¿cuándo?

soot [sʊt] *s*. hollín; tizne.

soothe [suð] *v*. calmar, sosegar; aliviar.

sooth·say·er [súθseɚ] *s*. adivino.

soot·y [sútɪ] *adj*. tiznado, cubierto de hollín.

sop [sɑp] *v*. empapar; **to** — **up** absorber; **to be sopping wet** estar hecho una sopa, estar mojado hasta los huesos; *s*. sopa (*pan u otra cosa empapada en leche, caldo, etc.*); (*bribe*) soborno, regalo (*para acallar, conciliar, o sobornar*).

so·phis·ti·cat·ed [sǝfɪstǝketǝd] *adj*. mundano; exento de simplicidad.

soph·o·more [sáfǝmor] *s*. estudiante de segundo año.

so·pran·o [sǝprǽno] *s*. soprano; **high** — tiple; — **voice** voz de soprano.

sor·cer·er [sɔrsǝrɚ] *s*. brujo, hechicero.

sor·did [sɔrdɪd] *adj*. sórdido; (*mean*) vil, indecente; mezquino.

sore [sor] *adj*. (*painful*) dolorido; inflamado, enconado; (*grievous*) afligido, apenado; (*injured*) lastimado; picado; (*offended*) ofendido; — **eyes** mal de ojos; **to be** — **at** estar enojado con; **to have a** — **throat** tener mal de garganta, dolerle a uno la garganta; *s*. úlcera, llaga; inflamación; lastimadura; (*sorrow*) pena, aflicción; **-ly** *adv*. dolorosamente, penosamente; **to be -ly in need of** necesitar con urgencia.

sore·ness [sórnɪs] *s*. dolor, dolencia; inflamación.

sor·rel [sɔrǝl] *adj*. alazán (*rojo canela*); *s*. color alazán; caballo alazán.

sor·row [sáro] *s*. (*sadness*) dolor, pena, pesar; (*grieving*) pesadumbre; (*repentance*) arrepentimiento; *v*. apenarse, afligirse, sentir pena.

sor·row·ful [sárǝfǝl] *adj*. pesaroso, doloroso, lastimoso, afligido; **-ly** *adv*. tristemente, dolorosamente, con pena, desconsoladamente.

sor·ry [sɔri] *adj*. triste, pesaroso, afligido,

SN

arrepentido; lastimoso; **I am** — lo siento; me pesa;
I am — **for** her la compadezco.
sort [sɔrt] s. suerte, clase, especie; — **of tired** algo
cansado, un tanto cansado; **all -s of** toda suerte de,
toda clase de; **out of -s** de mal humor,
malhumorado; indispuesto; v. clasificar, ordenar,
arreglar; (*computer*) clasificar; **to** — **out** separar,
clasificar; entresacar; escoger.
sought [sɔt] *pret. & p.p. de* **to seek.**
soul [sol] s. alma; **not a** — nadie, ni un alma.
sound [saʊnd] *adj.* (*healthy*) sano; (*sane*) cuerdo;
sensato; (*firm*) firme, sólido; ileso; **a** — **beating**
una buena zurra o tunda; — **business** buen
negocio, negocio bien organizado; — **reasoning**
raciocinio sólido; — **sleep** sueño profundo; — **title**
título válido o legal; **of** — **mind** en su juicio cabal;
safe and — sano y salvo; **to sleep** — dormir
profundamente; s. son, sonido; tono; brazo de mar;
— **wave** onda sonora; v. sonar, tocar; sondear;
tantear; auscultar (*el pecho, los pulmones*); cantar,
entonar (*alabanzas*); **to** — **out** tantear, sondear.
sound·ness [sáʊndnɪs] s. (*firmness*) solidez;
(*healthiness*) cordura, buen juicio; (*validity*)
rectitud; validez; — **of body** buena salud corporal.
sound·track [sáʊndtræk] s. banda sonora, huella de
sonido.
soup [sup] s. sopa; **cold vegetable** — gazpacho; —
tureen sopera; — **dish** sopero.
sour [saʊr] *adj.* (*acid-like*) agrio; acre; ácido;
desabrido; rancio; (*peevish*) malhumorado; — **milk**
leche cortada; v. agriar(se); cortarse (*la leche*);
fermentar; poner(se) de mal humor.
source [sors] s. origen; manantial, fuente; — **of**
supply fuente de abastecimientos.
sour·ness [sáʊrnɪs] s. acidez, agrura, desabrimiento.
souse [saʊs] v. zambullir; chapuzar.
south [saʊθ] s. sur, sud; *adj.* meridional; del sur;
austral; **South American** sudamericano,
suramericano; — **pole** polo sur, polo antártico;
adv. hacia el sur.
south·east [saʊθíst] s. & adj. sudeste; *adv.* hacia el
sudeste.
south·east·ern [saʊθístɚn] *adj.* del sudeste, sudeste.
south·ern [sʌ́ðɚn] *adj.* meridional, del sur, austral,
sureño; **Southern Cross** Cruz del Sur.
south·ern·er [sʌ́ðɚnɚ] s. sureño, meridional,
habitante del sur.
south·ward [sáʊθwɚd] *adv.* hacia el sur, rumbo al
sur.
south·west [saʊθwést] s. & adj. sudoeste (*o*
suroeste); *adv.* hacia el sudoeste.
south·west·ern [saʊθwéstɚn] *adj.* sudoeste (*o*
suroeste), del sudoeste.
sou·ve·nir [suvənɪr] s. recuerdo, memoria.
sov·er·eign [sávrɪn] s. & adj. soberano.
sov·er·eign·ty [sávrɪntɪ] s. soberanía.
so·vi·et [sóvɪɪt] s. sóviet; *adj.* soviético.
sow [saʊ] s. puerca.
sow [so] v. sembrar.
sown [son] *p.p. de* **to sow.**
soy [sɔj] s. soja.
space [spes] s. espacio; — **science** ciencia del
espacio; ciencia espacial; — **station** estación
espacial; — **suit** traje espacial; **spacing** espaciado;
v. espaciar .
space·bar [spésbar] s. barra espaciadora.
space·craft [spéskræft] s. nave espacial; astronave.
space·man [spésmæn] s. astronauta.
spa·cious [spéʃəs] *adj.* espacioso; dilatado, vasto.
spade [sped] s. azada, azadón; (*cards*) espada (*del
iuego de naipes*); v. cavar con la azada.

span [spæn] s. palmo; espacio; (*distance*) tramo;
(*bridge*) arco u ojo (*de puente*); (*width*)
envergadura (*de un aeroplano*); — **of life**
longevidad; v. medir a palmos; atravesar.
span·gle [spǽŋgl] s. lentejuela; v. adornar con
lentejuelas; brillar, centellear; **-d with stars**
estrellado, sembrado (*o* tachonado) de estrellas.
Span·iard [spǽnjɚd] s. español.
span·iel [spǽnjəl] s. perro de aguas.
Span·ish [spǽnɪʃ] *adj.* español; s. español, idioma
español.
spank [spæŋk] v. zurrar, dar una tunda, dar
nalgadas; s. palmada, nalgada.
spank·ing [spǽŋkɪŋ] s. zurra, tunda, nalgadas.
spar [spɑr] v. boxear, pelear.
spare [spɛr] v. ahorrar; (*avoid*) evitar (*molestias,
trabajo, etc.*); (*excuse*) perdonar; **I cannot** —
another dollar no dispongo de otro dólar, no
tengo más dinero disponible; **I cannot** — **the car
today** no puedo pasarme hoy sin el automóvil; **to**
— **no expense** no escatimar gastos; **to** — **the
enemy** usar de clemencia con el enemigo; **to have
time to** — tener tiempo de sobra; *adj.* flaco,
descarnado; escaso, frugal; mezquino; sobrante; de
sobra; de repuesto; — **parts** piezas de repuesto;
Méx. refacciones; — **cash** dinero disponible o de
sobra; — **time** tiempo libre, tiempo disponible; —
tire neumático de repuesto.
spark [spɑrk] s. chispa; — **plug** bujía; v. chispear,
echar chispas, chisporrotear.
spar·kle [spárkl] s. (*flash*) chispa, centella; brillo,
centelleo; (*spirit*) viveza, animación; v. centellear;
chispear; relucir, brillar.
spark·ling [spárklɪŋ] *adj.* centelleante; reluciente;
chispeante; — **wine** vino espumoso.
spar·row [spǽro] s. gorrión, pardal.
sparse [spɑrs] *adj.* escaso; esparcido; poco denso,
poco poblado; — **hair** pelo ralo.
spasm [spǽzəm] s. espasmo.
spas·tic [spǽstɪk] *adj.* espástico.
spat [spæt] *pret. & p.p. de* **to spit;** v. reñir, disputar;
dar un manazo o sopapo; s. sopapo, manotada;
riña, desavenencia; **-s** polainas cortas.
spat·ter [spǽtɚ] v. salpicar; rociar; manchar; s.
salpicadura; rociada.
speak [spik] v. hablar; decir; recitar; — **to the point!**
¡vamos al grano!; **so to** — por decirlo así; **to** —
for hablar por, hablar en nombre o en favor de;
pedir, solicitar; apalabrar, reservar; **to** — **one's
mind** hablar sin rodeos, decir claramente lo que se
piensa; **to** — **out** (*o* — **up**) hablar claro; hablar
con toda franqueza; hablar en voz alta.
speak·er [spíkɚ] s. orador; conferenciante,
conferencista; el que habla; **Speaker of the House**
presidente de la cámara de representantes; **loud-
speaker** altavoz, altoparlante.
spear [spɪr] s. lanza; arpón (*para pescar*); (*sprout*)
brote, retoño, hoja (*de hierba*); v. alancear,
lancear, herir con lanza.
spear·mint [spírmɪnt] s. yerbabuena (*hierbabuena*),
menta.
spe·cial [spéʃəl] *adj.* especial; particular; — **delivery**
entrega especial de correo; s. tren o autobús
especial; carta urgente, entrega especial; **-ly** *adv.*
especialmente; en especial; sobre todo.
spe·cial·ist [spéʃəlɪst] s. especialista.
spe·cial·i·za·tion [speʃəlɪzéʃən] s. especialización.
spe·cial·ize [spéʃəlaɪz] v. especializarse.
spe·cial·ty [spéʃəltɪ] s. especialidad.
spe·cies [spíʃɪz] s. especie; especies.
spe·cif·ic [spɪsífɪk] *adj.* específico; peculiar,

característico; — **gravity** peso específico; *s.*
específico; **-ally** *adv.* específicamente;
especificadamente; particularmente, en particular.

spec·i·fy [spέsəfaɪ] *v.* especificar; estipular.

spec·i·men [spέsəmən] *s.* espécimen, muestra,
ejemplar.

speck [spɛk] *s.* mota; manchita; partícula; **not a —**
ni pizca; *v. véase* **speckle.**

speck·le [spέkl] *s.* manchita; mota; *v.* motear,
salpicar de motas o manchas; manchar.

speck·led [spέkld] *adj.* moteado; — **with freckles**
pecoso.

spec·ta·cle [spέktəkl] *s.* espectáculo; **-s** gafas,
anteojos; **to make a — of oneself** ponerse en la
evidencia, ponerse en ridículo.

spec·tac·u·lar [spɛktǽkjələ˞] *adj.* espectacular,
ostentoso, aparatoso.

spec·ta·tor [spέktetə˞] *s.* espectador.

spec·ter [spέktə˞] *s.* espectro, fantasma, aparecido.

spec·tro·graph [spέktrogræf] *s.* espectrógrafo.

spec·trum [spέktrəm] *s.* espectro.

spec·u·late [spέkjəlet] *v.* especular; reflexionar.

spec·u·la·tion [spɛkjəléʃən] *s.* especulación;
reflexión.

spec·u·la·tive [spέkjəletɪv] *adj.* especulativo; teórico.

spec·u·la·tor [spέkjəletə˞] *s.* especulador.

sped [spɛd] *pret. & p.p. de* **to speed.**

speech [spitʃ] *s.* habla; lenguaje, idioma; (*formal*)
discurso, arenga; (*lecture*) conferencia; (*theater*)
parlamento (*de un actor*); **to make a —** pronunciar
un discurso, hacer una perorata.

speech·less [spítʃlɪs] *adj.* sin habla; mudo;
estupefacto.

speed [spid] *s.* velocidad; rapidez; presteza,
(*promptness*) prontitud; — **limit** velocidad
máxima; **at full —** a toda velocidad; **speed-up**
aceleración, aumento de producción; *v.*
apresurar(se), acelerar(se), dar(se) prisa; correr; ir
con exceso de velocidad; despachar.

speed·i·ly [spídɪlɪ] *adv.* velozmente, rápidamente; a
todo correr; de prisa, con prontitud.

speed·om·e·ter [spidámətə˞] *s.* velocímetro.

speed·y [spídɪ] *adj.* veloz, rápido.

spell [spɛl] *s.* (*charm*) hechizo, encanto; (*period*)
temporada, corto período; (*sickness*) ataque (*de una
enfermedad*); **to put under a —** aojar; hechizar,
encantar; *v.* deletrear; significar, indicar; **how is it
-ed?** ¿cómo se escribe?

spell·er [spέlə˞] *s.* silabario; deletreador.

spell·ing [spέlɪŋ] *s.* ortografía; deletreo; — **book**
silabario.

spelt [spɛlt] *pret. & p.p. de* **to spell.**

spend [spɛnd] *v.* gastar; usar, agotar, consumir; **to
— a day** pasar un día.

spend·thrift [spέndθrɪft] *s.* derrochador, gastador,
pródigo.

spent [spɛnt] *pret. & p.p. de* **to spend.**

sperm [spɝm] *s.* esperma.

sphere [sfɪr] *s.* esfera; globo, orbe.

spher·i·cal [sfέrɪkl] *adj.* esférico.

sphynx [sfɪŋks] *s.* esfinge.

spice [spaɪs] *s.* especia; picante; aroma; *v.*
condimentar, sazonar con especias.

spic·y [spáɪsɪ] *adj.* sazonado con especias; picante;
aromático.

spi·der [spáɪdə˞] *s.* araña; sartén; — **web** telaraña.

spig·ot [spígət] *s.* espita, grifo, canilla; *Méx.* bitoque.

spike [spaɪk] *s.* (*sprout*) espiga; (*metal*) perno; clavo
largo; alcayata; pico; *v.* clavar, clavetear.

spill [spɪl] *v.* verter; derramar(se); desparramar(se);
hacer caer (*de un caballo*); (*tell*) revelar (*una*

noticia, un secreto); *s.* derrame, derramamiento;
vuelco; caída (*de un caballo*).

spilt [spɪlt] *pret. & p.p. de* **to spill.**

spin [spɪn] *v.* hilar; (*whirl*) girar, dar vueltas, rodar;
(*dance*) bailar; **to — out** prolongar, alargar; **to —
yarns** contar cuentos; *s.* giro, vuelta; (*trip*) paseo
(*en automóvil, bicicleta, etc.*); barrena (*hablando
de aeroplanos*); **spin-off** entidad que resulta de la
división de producto o proceso.

spin·ach [spínɪtʃ] *s.* espinaca.

spi·nal [spáɪnl] *adj.* espinal; — **column** columna
vertebral, espina dorsal.

spin·dle [spíndl] *s.* huso; eje; **spindle motor** motor
accionador del husillo.

spine [spaɪn] *s.* espina; espinazo, espina dorsal,
columna vertebral.

spin·ner [spínə˞] *s.* hilandero, hilandera; máquina de
hilar.

spin·ning [spínɪŋ] *s.* hilandería, arte de hilar; —
machine aparato para hilar, máquina de hilar; —
mill hilandería; — **top** trompo; — **wheel** torno de
hilar.

spin·ster [spínstə˞] *s.* soltera; solterona.

spi·ral [spáɪrəl] *adj.* espiral; — **staircase** caracol,
escalera espiral; *s.* espiral.

spire [spaɪr] *s.* aguja, chapitel de torre; cúspide,
ápice; punto más alto; — **of grass** brizna de
hierba.

spir·it [spírɪt] *s.* (*essence*) espíritu; temple;
(*animation*) viveza, animación; ánimo; **low -s**
abatimiento; **to be in good -s** estar de buen humor;
to be out of -s estar triste o abatido; *v.* **to — away**
llevarse misteriosamente.

spir·it·ed [spírɪtɪd] *adj.* vivo, brioso, fogoso.

spir·i·tu·al [spírɪtʃʊel] *adj.* espiritual; *s.* (*song*)
espiritual (*tonada religiosa de los negros del sur
de los Estados Unidos*).

spit [spɪt] *v.* escupir; expectorar; *pret. & p.p. de* **to
spit;** *s.* esputo, saliva; asador.

spite [spaɪt] *s.* despecho, rencor, inquina, ojeriza; **in
— of** a despecho de; a pesar de; **out of —** por
despecho; *v.* picar, irritar, hacer rabiar.

spite·ful [spáɪtfəl] *adj.* rencoroso.

splash [splæʃ] *v.* salpicar; rociar; (*soil*) enlodar,
manchar; chapotear (*en el agua*); *s.* salpicadura;
rociada; chapoteo.

spleen [splin] *s.* bazo; mal humor, rencor.

splen·did [splέndɪd] *adj.* espléndido.

splen·dor [splέndə˞] *s.* esplendor; esplendidez.

splice [splaɪs] *v.* empalmar, unir, juntar; *s.* empalme;
junta.

splint [splɪnt] *s.* tablilla; astilla; *v.* entablillar.

splin·ter [splíntə˞] *s.* astilla; (*crack*) raja; *v.*
astillar(se), hacer(se) astillas; romper(se) en
astillas.

split [splɪt] *v.* hender(se), rajar(se); resquebrajar(se);
partir(se), dividir(se); **to — hairs** pararse en
pelillos; **to — one's dies with laughter**
desternillarse de risa, reventar de risa; **to — the
difference** partir la diferencia; *pret. & p.p. de* **to
split;** *adj.* partido, hendido, rajado; dividido;
resquebrajado; *s.* raja, hendedura, grieta; cisma,
rompimiento.

splurge [splɝdʒ] *s.* ostentación; fachenda.

spoil [spɔɪl] *v.* (*decay*) dañar(se); echar(se) a perder,
podrir(se), corromper(se); (*harm*) estropear(se);
arruinar; (*overindulge*) consentir, mimar; *s.* botín,
presa; **-s of war** botín o despojos de guerra.

spoil·age [spɔ́ɪlədʒ] *s.* desperdicio; *Arg., Col.*
desechos; *Méx.* deterioro.

spoke [spok] *s.* rayo (*de rueda*); *pret. de* **to speak.**

SO

spo·ken [spókən] *p.p. de* **to speak.**

spokes·man [spóksmən] *s.* portavoz, vocero.

sponge [spʌndʒ] *s. (absorbent)* esponja; *(dependent person)* gorrón, parásito; *v.* lavar o limpiar con esponja; vivir de gorra, vivir a costa ajena; **to — up** chupar, absorber.

sponge·cake [spʌndʒkek] *s.* bizcocho esponjoso.

spong·er [spʌndʒɚ] *s.* esponja, gorrón, pegote, parásito; *Am.* pavo.

spon·gy [spʌndʒɪ] *adj.* esponjoso, esponjado.

spon·sor [spʌnsɚ] *s.* padrino, madrina; *(patron)* patrón *(el que patrocina una empresa)*; *(protector)* defensor; fiador; fomentador, promovedor; *v.* apadrinar; promover, fomentar; patrocinar; ser fiador de.

spon·ta·ne·i·ty [spɑntəníətɪ] *s.* espontaneidad.

spon·ta·ne·ous [spɑnténɪəs] *adj.* espontáneo.

spook [spuk] *s.* espectro, fantasma, aparecido.

spool [spul] *s.* carrete, carretel; *v.* devanar, enredar *(hilo)* en carrete.

spoon [spun] *s.* cuchara; *v.* cucharear, sacar con cuchara.

spoon·ful [spúnfəl] *s.* cucharada.

sport [sport] *s. (blemish)* mancha, mota; *(place)* sitio, lugar; **in -s** aquí y allí; aquí y allá; **on the —** allí mismo; al punto; **to pay — cash** pagar al contado; **— announcement** anuncio breve, anuncio suelto; *v.* manchar, ensuciar; motear; echar de ver, distinguir; avistar; localizar.

sport [sport] *s.* deporte; **in —** en broma, de burla; **to make — of** reírse de, burlarse de; **to be a good —** ser buen perdedor *(en el juego)*; ser un buen compañero; *v.* jugar; divertirse; bromear, chancearse; **to — a new dress** lucir un traje nuevo; **-s** *adj.* deportivo; **— clothes** trajes deportivos.

sports car [spórtskar] *s.* coche *(carro)* deportivo, esport.

sports·man [spórtsmən] *s.* deportista; jugador generoso, buen perdedor *(en deportes)*.

spot [spɑt] *s. (blemish)* mancha, mota; *(place)* sitio, lugar; **in -s** aquí y allí; aquí y allá; **on the —** allí mismo; al punto; **to pay — cash** pagar al contado; **— announcement** anuncio breve, anuncio suelto; *v.* manchar, ensuciar; motear; echar de ver, distinguir; avistar; localizar.

spot·less [spátlɪs] *adj.* sin mancha, limpio.

spot·light [spátlaɪt] *s.* faro giratorio.

spot·ted [spátɪd] *adj.* manchado; moteado.

spouse [spauz] *s.* esposo, esposa.

spout [spaut] *v.* chorrear; brotar; salir en chorro; *(speak)* emitir; declamar, perorar; hablar mucho; *s.* chorro; surtidor; pico *(de tetera, cafetera, jarra, etc.)*; espita.

sprain [spren] *v.* torcer *(una coyuntura o músculo)*; **to — one's ankle** torcerse el tobillo; *s.* torsión, torcedura.

sprang [spræŋ] *pret. de* **spring.**

sprawl [sprɔl] *v.* despatarrarse; estar despatarrado; tenderse; **to — one's legs** abrir las piernas; *s.* postura floja *(abiertos los brazos y piernas)*.

spray [spre] *s. (liquid)* rocío, rociada; líquido para rociar; *(branch)* ramita; **sea —** espuma del mar; *v.* rociar.

spread [spred] *v.* extender(se); desparramar(se); esparcir(se); difundir(se), diseminar(se), dispersar(se); propalar(se) *(noticias, rumores, etc.)*, propagar(se); **to — apart** abrir(se), separar(se); **to — butter on** poner mantequilla en; **to — out the tablecloth** tender el mantel; **to — paint on** dar una mano de pintura a; **to — with** cubrir de; untar con; *s.* extensión; amplitud, anchura; envergadura *(de un aeroplano)*; difusión, diseminación; propagación; cubierta, sobrecama, comilitona, festín; mantequilla, queso, etc., que se le unta al pan; *pret. & p.p. de* **to spread; — sheet** *(computer)* hoja electrónica.

spree [spri] *s.* juerga, parranda, holgorio; **to go on a — andar** *(o* ir*)* de parranda o juerga, *Ríopl.* ir de farra.

sprig [sprɪg] *s.* ramita.

spright·ly [spráɪtlɪ] *adj.* vivo, animado, brioso; alegre.

spring [sprɪŋ] *v.* saltar; brincar; hacer saltar; **to — a leak** hacer agua *(un barco)*; comenzar a gotearse *(la cañería, el techo, etc.)*; formarse una gotera; **to — a trap** hacer saltar una trampa; **to — at** abalanzarse sobre; **to — from** salir de, nacer de, brotar de; **to — news of a surprise** dar de sopetón una noticia o sorpresa; **to — something open** abrir algo a la fuerza; **to — to one's feet** levantarse de un salto; **to — up** brotar; surgir; crecer; levantarse de un salto; *s. (season)* primavera; *(coil)* muelle *(de metal)*; resorte; elasticidad; salto, brinco; *(water)* manantial, fuente; origen; *adj.* primaveral; **— board** trampolín; **— mattress** colchón de muelles; **— water** agua de manantial.

spring·bolt [spríŋbolt] *s.* pestillo de golpe.

spring·time [spríŋtaɪm] *s.* primavera.

sprin·kle [spríŋkl] *v. (scatter)* rociar; regar; espolvorear; salpicar; *(rain)* lloviznar; *s.* rociada, rocío; llovizna; **— of salt** pizca de sal.

sprint [sprɪnt] *v.* echar una carrera; *s.* carrera, carrerilla, corrida corta.

sprout [spraut] *v.* brotar; retoñar, germinar; hacer germinar o brotar; *s.* retoño, renuevo; **Brussels -s** bretones, coles de Bruselas.

spruce [sprus] *s.* abeto; *adj.* pulcro, aseado, pulido; elegante; *v.* **to — up** asearse, componerse, emperifollarse.

sprung [sprʌŋ] *pret. & p.p. de* **to spring.**

spun [spʌn] *pret. & p.p. de* **to spin.**

spur [spɚ] *s.* espuela; acicate; *(stimulus)* aguijón, estímulo; *(rooster)* espolón *(del gallo)*; estribación *(de una montaña)*; **— track** ramal corto *(de ferrocarril)*; **on the — of the moment** impensadamente, sin la reflexión debida; por el momento; *v.* espolear, aguijar, picar, incitar; **to — on** animar, incitar a obrar o a seguir adelante.

spu·ri·ous [spúrɪəs] *adj.* espurio.

spurn [spɚn] *v.* rechazar, desdeñar, menospreciar.

spurt [spɚt] *v.* salir a borbotones; chorrear; echar chorros; *(effort)* hacer un repentino esfuerzo *(para ganar una carrera)*; *s.* borbotón, chorrazo, chorro repentino; esfuerzo repentino; **— of anger** arranque de ira; **-s of flame** llamaradas.

sput·ter [spátɚ] *v.* chisporrotear; *(grumble)* refunfuñar; *s.* chisporroteo; refunfuño.

spu·tum [spjútəm] *s.* esputo.

spy [spaɪ] *s.* espía; *v.* espiar; acechar; atisbar; **to — on** espiar, atisbar.

spy·glass [spáɪglæs] *s.* anteojo de larga vista.

squab [skwɑb] *s.* pichón.

squab·ble [skwábl] *s.* reyerta; *v.* reñir, disputar.

squad [skwɑd] *s.* escuadra, patrulla, partida.

squad·ron [skwádrɑn] *s.* escuadra; escuadrón.

squal·id [skwálɪd] *adj.* escuálido.

squall [skwɔl] *s. (rain)* chubasco; *(sound)* chillido; *v.* chillar.

squan·der [skwándɚ] *v.* despilfarrar, derrochar, malgastar, disipar.

square [skwɛr] *s. (rectangle)* cuadro; cuadrado; *(central park)* plaza; *(block)* manzana de casas; *Am.* cuadra; escuadra *(de carpintero)*; *(chess)* casilla *(de tablero de ajedrez, damas, etc.)*; **he is on the —** obra de buena fe; *v.* cuadrar; ajustar, arreglar, *(balance)* saldar *(cuentas)*; justificar; cuadricular; **to — one's shoulders** enderezar los hombros; cuadrarse; **to — oneself with** sincerarse con, justificarse ante; **to — a person with another** poner bien a una persona con otra; *adj.* cuadrado, en cuadro, a escuadra, en ángulo recto; saldado; justo, recto, equitativo; franco; — **corner** esquina en ángulo recto; — **meal** comida completa, comida en regla; — **mile** milla cuadrada; — **root** raíz cuadrada; — **dance** danza de figuras; cuadrilla; **to be — with someone** estar en paz con alguien, no deberle nada, *Am.* estar a mano; *adv.* véase **squarely.**

square·ly [skwérlɪ] *adv.* equitativamente, honradamente; firmemente; de buena fe; derecho, derechamente; **to hit the target — in the middle** pegar de lleno en el blanco.

squash [skwɑʃ] *s.* calabaza; *v.* aplastar, despachurrar o apachurrar.

squat [skwɑt] *v.* agazaparse, sentarse en cuclillas; agacharse; ocupar tierras baldías para ganar título de propietario; *adj.* agazapado, sentado en cuclillas; *(short)* rechoncho, achaparrado, *Méx., C.A., Andes* chaparro.

squawk [skwɔk] *v. (noise)* graznar; chillar; *(complain)* quejarse; *s.* graznido; chillido; queja.

squeak [skwik] *v.* rechinar, chirriar; chillar; *s.* rechinamiento; chirrido, chillico.

squeal [skwil] *v.* chillar; *(complain)* quejarse, protestar; *("snitch")* soplar, delatar; *s.* chillido.

squea·mish [skwímɪʃ] escrupuloso; delicado; remilgado.

squeeze [skwiz] *v.* estrujar; despachurrar o apachurrar; exprimir; prensar; apretar; **to — into** meter(se) a estrujones, encajar(se) en; **to — out the juice** exprimir el jugo; **to — through a crowd** abrirse paso a estrujones por entre la muchedumbre; *s.* estrujón; apretón; abrazo fuerte; apretura.

squelch [skwɛltʃ] *v. (crush)* aplastar; *(silence)* acallar, imponer silencio; *(scold)* reprender; **to — a revolt** sofocar o apagar una revuelta.

squid [skwɪd] *s.* calamar.

squint [skwɪnt] *v.* mirar de través; mirar de soslayo; mirar achicando los ojos; mirar furtivamente; bizquear *(mirar bizco); s.* mirada de soslayo; mirada bizca; mirada furtiva; **squint-eyed** *adj.* bisojo o bizco.

squire [skwaɪr] *s.* escudero; *v.* acompañar, escoltar.

squirm [skwɝm] *v.* retorcerse; **to — out of a difficulty** forcejear para salir de un aprieto.

squir·rel [skwɝ́əl] *s.* ardilla.

squirt [skwɝt] *v.* jeringar; echar un chisguete; salir a chorritos *(o* a chisguetes); *s.* jeringazo; chisguete.

stab [stæb] *v.* apuñalar, dar una puñalada, dar de puñalada, acuchillar; pinchar; *s.* puñalada, cuchillada, estocada; pinchazo.

sta·bil·i·ty [stəbflətɪ] *s.* estabilidad.

sta·ble [stébl] *adj.* estable; *s.* establo, cuadra; caballeriza; *v.* poner *(los animales)* en la caballeriza.

stack [stæk] *s.* pila, montón, rimero; *(hay)* hacina *(de paja o heno); (chimney)* chimenea, cañón de chimenea; **library -s** estanterías o anaqueles de biblioteca; *v.* amontonar, apilar.

sta·di·um [stédɪəm] *s.* estadio.

staff [stæf] *s. (stick)* báculo, cayado, bastón, vara; *(pole)* asta *(de bandera, de lanza); (group)* cuerpo, consejo administrativo; funcionarios; — **of life** sostén de la vida; — **officer** oficial de estado mayor; **army** — estado mayor; **editorial** — redacción; **musical** — pentagrama; **teaching** — cuerpo docente; *v.* proveer de funcionarios y

empleados *(una organización).*

staff·ing [stǽfɪŋ] *s.* planilla de personal, *Méx.* integración.

stag [stæg] *s.* venado, ciervo; *(male)* macho, hombre; — **dinner** banquete exclusivo para hombres.

stage [stedʒ] *s. (platform)* tablado; tablas, escenario; escena; *(theater)* teatro; *(period)* etapa, tramo; período; *(stop)* parada; — **coach** ómnibus, autobús; — **hand** tramoyista; **by easy -s** por grados, gradualmente; *v.* representar, poner en escena; **to — a hold-up** hacer un asalto, atracar; **to — a surprise** dar una sorpresa.

stag·ger [stǽgɚ] *v. (totter)* tambalearse, tratabillar, bambolearse; hacer tambalear; *(overwhelm)* azorar, asombrar; **to — working hours** escalonar las horas de trabajo; *s.* tambaleo, bamboleo.

stag·nant [stǽgnənt] *adj.* estancado; **to become —** estancarse.

staid [sted] *adj.* grave, serio.

stain [sten] *v.* manchar; teñir; colorar; **stained-glass window** vidriera de colores; *s.* mancha, mancilla; tinte, tintura; materia colorante.

stain·less [sténlɪs] *adj.* sin mancha, inmaculado, limpio; — **steel** acero inempañable o inoxidable.

stair [stɛr] *s.* peldaño, escalón; **-s** escalera.

stair·case [stɛ́rkes] *s.* escalera.

stair·way [stɛ́rwe] *s.* escalera.

stake [stek] *s. (pole)* estaca; *(investment)* puesta, apuesta; **his future is at** — su porvenir está en peligro o riesgo; **to die at the** — morir en la hoguera; **to have a — in the future of** tener interés en el porvenir de; **to have much at** — irle a uno mucho en una cosa; haber aventurado mucho; *v.* estacar; atar a una estaca; apostar; arriesgar, aventurar; **to — off** señalar con estacas *(un perímetro).*

sta·lac·tite [stəlǽktaɪt] *s.* estalactita.

sta·lag·mite [stəlǽgmaɪt] *s.* estalagmita.

stale [stel] *adj.* viejo; rancio; gastado, improductivo.

stale·mate [stélmet] *s.* punto muerto; estancación.

stalk [stɔk] *s.* tallo; caña.

stall [stɔl] *s.* casilla, puesto *(de un mercado o feria); (stable)* casilla o sección de un establo; *v.* encasillar, meter en casilla; *(stick)* atascarse *(un auto);* pararse *(el motor);* **he is -ing** está haciendo la pala; **to be -ed in the mud** estar atascado en el lodo.

stal·lion [stǽljən] *s.* caballo de cría, caballo padre, *Ven., Col., Ríopl.* padrillo; *Méx., C.A.* garañón.

stam·mer [stǽmɚ] *v.* tartamudear, balbucear; *s.* tartamudeo, balbuceo.

stam·mer·er [stǽmərɚ] *s.* tartamudo.

stam·mer·ing [stǽmərɪŋ] *s.* tartamudeo; *adj.* tartamudo.

stamp [stæmp] *v. (affix)* sellar; timbrar; poner un sello; estampar; *(mark)* marcar, imprimir; señalar; *(with foot)* patear, patalear; **to — one's foot** dar patadas en el suelo; **to — out** extirpar, borrar; *s.* sello; timbre, estampilla; estampa; marca, impresión; patada *(en el suelo);* **postage** — sello, *Méx., C.A., Andes* estampilla, *Méx.* timbre; **revenue** — timbre.

stam·pede [stæmpíd] *s.* estampida; huída en desorden; tropel; éxodo repentino; *v.* arrancar, huir en tropel; ir en tropel; ahuyentar, hacer huir en desorden.

stanch [stɑntʃ] *v.* restañar, estancar; *adj.* fuerte; firme; leal, constante, fiel.

stand [stænd] *v.* poner derecho, colocar verticalmente; *(rise)* ponerse de pie, levantarse; *Am.* parar(se); *(be erect)* estar de pie; *Am.* estar

SP

parado; (*withstand*) aguantar, sufrir, tolerar; **to —
a chance of** tener probabilidad de; **to — an
expense** sufragar un gasto; **to — aside** apartarse;
mantenerse apartado; **to — back of** colocarse
detrás de; salir fiador de, garantizar a, respaldar a;
to — by mantenerse a corta distancia; apoyar,
defender; estar alerta; **to — for** significar; estar
por, apoyar; tolerar; **to — in the way** estorbar; **to
— on end** poner(se) de punta; erizarse (*el pelo*); **to
— one's ground** mantenerse firme; **to — out**
resaltar, destacarse; sobresalir; **to — six feet** tener
seis pies de altura; **to — up for** apoyar, defender;
it -s to reason es razonable, es lógico; *s.* puesto;
mesilla; pedestal; posición; actitud; alto, parada
(*para resistir*); quiosco; **grand** — andanada,
gradería cubierta (*para espectadores*); **music** —
atril; **umbrella** — paragüero.

stan·dard [stǽndəˑd] *s.* (*norm*) norma; nivel normal;
criterio; (*model*) modelo, patrón; *Am.* estándar;
(*base*) base, pedestal; (*banner*) estandarte; **gold** —
patrón de oro; **to be up to** — satisfacer las normas
requeridas; *adj.* normal, que sirve de norma; de
uso general; corriente; **standard-bearer**
portaestandarte; — **deviation** desviación típica; —
of life nivel de vida; — **time** hora normal.

stan·dard·i·za·tion [stændəˑdəzéʃən] *s.*
normalización, uniformación, igualación.

stan·dard·ize [stǽndəˑdaɪz] *v.* normalizar, uniformar,
Méx., *C.A.*, *Carib.* estandarizar.

stand·by [stǽndbaɪ] *s.* sustituto; de reserva, auxiliar.

stand·ing [stǽndɪŋ] *s.* (*position*) posición; (*fame*)
fama, reputación; **of long** — que ha prevalecido
largo tiempo; muy antiguo; *adj.* derecho, en pie;
de pie; establecido, permanente; — **water** agua
estancada; — **order** pedido vigente (*permanente*);
there is — room only no quedan asientos.

stand·off [stǽndɔf] *s.* empate.

stand·point [stǽndpɔɪnt] *s.* punto de vista.

stand·still [stǽndstɪl] *s.* alto; pausa; **to come to a** —
pararse; hacer alto.

stank [stæŋk] *pret. de* **to stink.**

stan·za [stǽnzə] *s.* estrofa.

sta·ple [stépl] *s.* broche de alambre (*para sujetar
papeles*); grapa, argolla, armella; artículo principal;
-s artículos de necesidad prima; *adj.* principal;
(*basic*) de uso corriente; indispensable; *v.* asegurar
(*papeles*) con broche de alambre; sujetar con
armellas.

sta·pler [stépləˑ] *s.* grapadora.

star [stɑr] *s.* estrella; (*asterisk*) asterisco; **star-
spangled** estrellado; artista (actor); *adj.*
sobresaliente, excelente; *v.* estrellar, adornar o
señalar con estrellas; marcar con asterisco;
presentar como estrella (*a un actor*); lucir(se) en
las tablas o el cine, hacer el papel principal.

star·board [stárbord] *s.* estribor; *adj.* de estribor; —
side banda de estribor; *adv.* a estribor.

starch [stɑrtʃ] *s.* almidón; fécula; *v.* almidonar.

stare [stɛr] *v.* mirar, mirar con fijeza o curiosidad;
mirar azorado; clavar la mirada, fijar la vista; *s.*
mirada fija, mirada persistente.

star·fish [stárfɪʃ] *s.* estrella de mar.

stark [stɑrk] *adj.* (*utter*) tieso; (*grim*) escueto; —
folly pura tontería; — **in death** tieso, muerto; —
narrative narración escueta, sin adornos; *adv.*
completamente, totalmente; — **mad** loco de
remate; — **naked** enteramente desnudo, en cueros,
Am. encuerado.

star·light [stárlaɪt] *s.* luz estelar, luz de las estrellas.

star·ry [stárɪ] *adj.* estrellado, sembrado de estrellas;
como estrellas, brillante.

start [stɑrt] *v.* comenzar, empezar, principiar;
poner(se) en marcha; (*depart*) partir, salir; (*jump*)
dar un salto, sobresaltarse; **the motor -s** el motor
arranca; **to — after someone** salir en busca de
alguien; **to — off** salir, partir; dar principio a; **to
— out on a trip** empezar una jornada, emprender
un viaje; **to — the motor** hacer arrancar el motor;
s. comienzo, empiezo, principio; sobresalto;
respingo (*de un caballo*); (*motor*) arranque; ventaja
(*en una carrera*).

start·er [stártəˑ] *s.* (*automobile*) arranque; (*person*)
arrancador; iniciador; (*first*) primero de la serie;
self-starter arranque automático.

star·tle [stártl] *v.* asustar(se), sobresaltar(se),
espantar(se).

start·ling [stártlɪŋ] *adj.* sobresaltante, pasmoso,
asombroso, sorprendente.

star·va·tion [starvéʃən] *s.* inanición, hambre.

starve [stɑrv] *v.* morir(se) de hambre; hambrear;
matar de hambre.

starv·ing [stárvɪŋ] *adj.* hambriento.

state [stet] *s.* estado; condición, situación; **in great
—** con gran pompa; *adj.* de estado; del estado; de
ceremonia; *v.* declarar, decir; expresar, exponer.

state·ly [stétlɪ] *adj.* majestuoso, imponente.

state·ment [stétmənt] *s.* (*declaration*) declaración;
exposición; (*information*) informe, relato; (*bill*)
cuenta, estado de cuentas.

state·room [stétrum] *s.* camarote (*de un buque*).

states·man [stétsmən] *s.* estadista, hombre de estado.

stat·ic [stǽtɪk] *adj.* estático; *s.* estática.

sta·tion [stéʃən] *s.* (*operations point*) estación; (*post*)
paradero; puesto; (*condition*) estado, posición
social; **broadcasting** — transmisora o emisora; *v.*
estacionar, colocar, apostar; — **wagon** *Esp.* rubia;
Méx. camioneta, huayin; *C.A.* camionetilla.

sta·tion·ar·y [stéʃənɛrɪ] *adj.* estacionario; fijo.

sta·tion·er·y [stéʃənɛrɪ] *s.* (*shop*) papelería; efectos de
escritorio.

sta·tis·tics [stətístɪks] *s.* estadística; datos estadísticos;
statistical sampling muestreo estadístico.

stat·u·ar·y [stǽtʃuɛrɪ] *s.* estatuaria, arte de hacer
estatuas; colección de estatuas.

stat·ue [stǽtʃu] *s.* estatua.

stat·ure [stǽtʃəˑ] *s.* estatura.

stat·us [stétəs] *s.* estado, condición; posición social o
profesional.

stat·ute [stǽtʃut] *s.* estatuto, ordenanza; — **of
limitations** ley de prescripciones.

staunch = **stanch.**

stave [stev] *s.* duela de barril; *v.* poner duelas (*a un
barril*); **to — off** mantener a distancia; evitar;
rechazar.

stay [ste] *v.* (*remain*) quedarse, permanecer;
parar(se); detener(se); (*sojourn*) hospedarse,
alojarse; (*check*) resistir; **to — an execution** diferir
o aplazar una ejecución; **to — one's hunger**
engañar el hambre; **to — up all night** velar toda la
noche; *s.* estada, estancia, permanencia;
(*postponement*) suspensión; (*supports*) sostén,
apoyo; (*corset*) varilla o ballena de corsé; **to grant
a** — conceder una prórroga.

stead [stɛd] *s.* **in her (his)** — en su lugar; **to stand
one in good** — servirle a uno, ser de provecho
para uno.

stead·fast [stɛdfæst] *adj.* fijo, firme; constante.

stead·i·ly [stɛdɪlɪ] *adv.* constantemente; firmemente;
sin parar, de continuo; sin vacilar.

stead·i·ness [stɛdɪnɪs] *s.* firmeza; constancia;
estabilidad.

stead·y [stɛdɪ] *adj.* firme; estable; invariable,

constante; continuo; — **customer** cliente fijo; — **market** mercado sostenido; v. afianzar, mantener firme, asegurar; calmar (*los nervios*).

steak [stek] s. biftec o bisté; tajada (*para asar o freír*).

steal [stil] v. (*rob*) robar, hurtar; (*move*) andar furtivamente; **to — away** colarse, escabullirse, escaparse; **to — into a room** meterse a hurtadillas en un cuarto; **to — out of a room** salirse a escondidas de un cuarto, colarse, escabullirse; s. robo, hurto.

stealth [stɛlθ] s.: **by —** a hurtadillas, a escondidas, con cautela.

stealth·y [stɛlθɪ] adj. cauteloso, furtivo, secreto.

steam [stim] s. vapor; vaho; adj. de vapor; por vapor; — **engine** máquina de vapor; — **heat** calefacción por vapor; — **roller** apisonadora de vapor; — **shovel** excavadora; v. cocer al vapor; dar un baño de vapor; saturar de vapor; echar vapor; **to — into port** llegar a puerto (*un vapor*).

steam·boat [stímbot] s. buque de vapor.

steam·er [stímɚ] s. vapor, buque de vapor.

steam·ship [stímʃɪp] s. vapor, buque de vapor.

steed [stid] s. corcel, caballo de combate; caballo brioso.

steel [stil] s. acero; — **industry** siderurgia; — **mill** fundición de acero; **mild —** acero parco en carbono; adj. acerado, de acero; v. acerar, revestir de acero; **to — oneself against** fortalecerse contra.

steep [stip] adj. empinado, escarpado, pendiente; muy alto; — **price** precio alto o excesivo; v. remojar, empapar; saturar; poner o estar en infusión.

stee·ple [stípl] s. aguja, chapitel; cúspide.

steep·ness [stípnɪs] s. inclinación abrupta; lo empinado, lo escarpado; (*prices*) altura (*de precios*).

steer [stɪr] s. novillo; buey; v. guiar, conducir, manejar, gobernar; (*ship*) timonear; **to — a course** seguir un rumbo; **the car -s easily** se maneja fácilmente el auto, es de fácil manejo.

steer·ing wheel [stírɪnhwil] s. volante; *Col.* timón.

stel·lar [stɛlɚ] adj. estelar.

stem [stɛm] s. (*plant*) tallo; (*tree*) tronco; (*leaf*) pedúnculo (*de hoja, flor o fruto*); raíz (*de una palabra*); pie (*de copa*); cañón (*de pipa de fumar*); (*ship*) proa; v. estancar, represar; resistir, refrenar; contraponerse a; **to — from** provenir de.

stench [stɛnʃ] s. hedor, hediondez.

sten·cil [stɛnsl] s. patrón picado; esténcil.

ste·nog·ra·pher [stənágrəfɚ] s. estenógrafo, taquígrafo, mecanógrafo.

step [stɛp] s. (*walking*) paso; pisada; (*staircase*) peldaño, escalón, grada; (*degree*) grado; (*effort*) gestión; — **by —** paso a paso; **to be in — with** marchar a compás con; estar de acuerdo con; **to take -s** dar pasos; tomar medidas; gestionar; v. andar, caminar; dar un paso; **to — aside** hacerse a un lado, apartarse; **to — back** dar un paso o pasos atrás; retroceder; **to — down** bajar; **to — off a distance** medir a pasos una distancia; **to — on** pisar, pisotear; **to — on the gas** pisar el acelerador; (*hurry*) darse prisa; **to — out** salir; **to — up** subir; acelerar; **step-by-step** adj. escalonado; **stepped-up** progresivo.

step·fa·ther [stɛpfaðɚ] s. padrastro.

step·mo·ther [stɛpmʌðɚ] s. madrastra.

steppe [stɛp] s. estepa.

ster·e·o·type [stɛ́rɪotaɪp] s. estereotipo.

ster·ile [stɛ́rəl] adj. estéril.

ste·ril·i·ty [stərflətɪ] s. esterilidad.

ster·il·ize [stɛ́rəlaɪz] v. esterilizar.

ster·ling [stɚlɪŋ] s. vajilla de plata esterlina; adj. genuino; de ley; — **silver** plata de ley, plata esterlina; **pound —** libra esterlina.

stern [stɚn] adj. austero, severo; firme; s. popa.

stern·ness [stɚnnɪs] s. austeridad, severidad; firmeza.

steth·o·scope [stɛ́θəskop] s. estetoscopio.

ste·ve·dore [stívədɔr] s. estibador, cargador.

stew [stju] v. estofar; (*worry*) preocuparse, apurarse; s. estofado, guisado; cocido, puchero, sancocho; **to be in a —** estar preocupado o apurado.

stew·ard [stjúwɚd] s. mayordomo; camarero (*de buque o avión*).

stew·ard·ess [stjúwɚdɪs] s. camarera (*de buque o avión*); *Esp.* azafata.

stick [stɪk] s. palo; vara; garrote; (*fire wood*) raja de leña; — **of dynamite** barra de dinamita; **control —** palanca (*de aeroplano*); **walking —** bastón; chuzo (*de sereno*); **stick-up** atraco (*para robar*), asalto; v. pegar(se), adherir(se), permanecer; estar pegado; picar, pinchar; herir (*con cuchillo, puñal, etc.*); fijar (*con clavos, alfileres, tachuelas, etc.*); atascarse (*en el fango un carro, auto, etc.*); **to — something in** (*o* **into**) clavar o meter algo en; encajar en; **to — out** salir, sobresalir; proyectarse; **to — out one's head** asomar la cabeza; **to — out one's tongue** sacar la lengua; **to — to a job** perseverar (*o* persistir) en una tarea; **to — up** sobresalir, destacarse; estar de punta (*el pelo*); **to — one's hands up** alzar las manos; **to — someone up** asaltar o atracar a alguien (*para robar*); *véase* **stuck**.

stick·er [stɪ́kɚ] s. marbete engomado; etiqueta.

stick·y [stɪ́kɪ] adj. pegajoso.

stiff [stɪf] adj. tieso; rígido; entumido; duro; (*stubborn*) terco; (*strong*) fuerte; — **climb** subida ardua o difícil; — **price** precio alto o subido; **stiff-necked** terco, obstinado; **sacred —** yerto, muerto de miedo; s. cadáver.

stiff·en [stɪ́fən] v. atiesar(se), poner(se) tieso; entumir(se); endurecer(se); espesar(se); subir de punto, aumentar (*la resistencia*).

stiff·ness [stɪ́fnɪs] s. tiesura; rigidez; dureza; rigor; terquedad.

sti·fle [stáɪfl] v. ahogar(se), asfixiar(se), sofocar(se); apagar, extinguir.

stig·ma [stɪ́gmə] s. estigma; baɪdón.

stig·ma·tize [stɪ́gmətaɪz] v. estigmatizar.

still [stɪl] adj. (*quiet*) quieto; callado, silencioso; (*at ease*) tranquilo; inmóvil; — **born** nacido muerto; — **life** naturaleza muerta; v. aquietar; calmar; acallar; adv. todavía, aún; conj. empero, no obstante, sin embargo; s. destiladera, alambique; silencio.

still·ness [stɪ́lnɪs] s. quietud, calma, silencio.

stilt [stɪlt] s. (*walking*) zanco; (*support*) pilote, puntal, soporte.

stilt·ed [stɪ́ltɪd] adj. tieso, afectado, pomposo.

stim·u·lant [stɪ́mjələnt] adj. & s. estimulante.

stim·u·late [stɪ́mjəlet] v. estimular.

stim·u·la·tion [stɪmjəléʃən] s. estimulación, estímulo.

stim·u·lus [stɪ́mjələs] s. estímulo.

sting [stɪŋ] v. (*pierce*) picar; pinchar, aguijonear; (*irritate*) escocer; *Méx., C.A., Col., Carib.* arder; (*cheat*) embaucar; estafar; s. picadura, piquete, mordedura, picazón; aguijón; escozor; — **of remorse** remordimiento.

stin·gi·ness [stɪ́ndʒɪnɪs] s. tacañería, mezquindad.

stin·gy [stɪ́ndʒɪ] adj. mezquino, ruin, tacaño; escaso; *Ríopl., Méx.* codo.

stink [stɪŋk] v. heder, oler mal; apestar; s. hedor,

ST

mal olor, hediondez.

stint [stɪnt] *v.* escatimar; ser frugal o económico; **to — oneself** privarse de lo necesario, economizar demasiado; *s.* tarea, faena; **without —** sin límite; sin escatimar; generosamente.

stip·u·late [stípjəlet] *v.* estipular.

stip·u·la·tion [stɪpjəléʃən] *s.* estipulación, condición.

stir [stɝ] *v.* menear(se); mover(se); bullir(se); (*fire*) atizar (*el fuego*); incitar; conmover; perturbar; revolver; **to — up** incitar; conmover; revolver; suscitar (*un argumento, pelea, etc.*); *s.* meneo, agitación, movimiento; alboroto.

stir·ring [stɝɪŋ] *adj.* conmovedor.

stir·rup [stírəp] *s.* estribo.

stitch [stɪtʃ] *v.* coser; dar puntadas; *s.* puntada; punzada; **to be in -es** desternillarse de risa.

stock [stɑk] *s.* (*supply*) surtido; existencias, provisión; (*cattle*) ganado; (*lineage*) cepa, linaje, estirpe; (*shares*) acciones, valores; **in —** en existencia; **live —** ganado; **meat —** caldo de carne; *adj.* en existencia, existente, disponible; común, trivial; **— answer** contestación corriente, común o trivial; **— company** sociedad anónima; compañía teatral; **— exchange** bolsa; *Col.* bolsa de corredores; *Mex.* bolsa de acciones; *Ur.* bolsa de comercio; **— farm** hacienda de ganado, *Am.* rancho, *Am.* estancia; **— market** mercado de valores, bolsa; **— room** almacén; **— size** tamaño ordinario (*regularmente en existencia*); **— yard** matadero; *v.* surtir, abastecer; tener en existencia (*para vender*); **to — a farm** surtir o proveer de ganado un rancho; **to — up with** surtirse de, acumular; **to stockpile** acopiar reservas.

stock·ade [stɑkéd] *s.* estacada, empalizada; vallado; *v.* empalizar, rodear de empalizadas.

stock·bro·ker [stákbrokɚ] *s.* bolsista, corredor de bolsa.

stock·hold·er [stákholdɚ] *s.* accionista.

stock·ing [stákɪŋ] *s.* media.

sto·ic [stóɪk] *adj. & s.* estoico.

stoke [stok] *v.* atizar (*el fuego*); (*feed*) cebar, alimentar (*un horno*).

stole [stol] *pret. de* **to steal.**

sto·len [stólən] *p.p. de* **to steal.**

stol·id [stálɪd] *adj.* estólido, insensible.

stom·ach [stʌmək] *s.* estómago; *v.* aguantar, tolerar.

stomp [stɑmp] *v.* pisar violentamente.

stone [ston] *s.* piedra; (*seed*) hueso (*de las frutas*); **within a -'s throw** a tiro de piedra; *adj.* pétreo, de piedra; **Stone Age** Edad de Piedra; **stone-deaf** totalmente sordo, sordo como una tapia; *v.* apedrear; deshuesar (*las frutas*).

ston·y [stóni] *adj.* pedregoso; pétreo, de piedra; duro.

stood [stud] *pret. & p.p. de* **to stand.**

stool [stul] *s.* (*furniture*) taburete; *C.A.* banquillo; (*toilet*) bacín, bacinica; (*excrement*) excremento; **— pigeon** soplón (*el que delata a otro*).

stoop [stup] *v.* agacharse; doblarse, inclinarse; encorvarse; andar encorvado o caído de hombros; rebajarse, humillarse, abajarse; *s.* encorvamiento, inclinación (*de espaldas*); **to walk with a —** andar encorvado o caído de hombros; **stoop-shouldered** cargado de espaldas encorvado.

stop [stɑp] *v.* (*pause*) parar(se), hacer alto, detener(se); (*cease*) acabar(se); cesar; parar de, dejar de; (*block*) atajar; reprimir; suspender; obstruir, tapar; **to — at a hotel** hospedarse o alojarse en un hotel; **to — at nothing** no pararse en escrúpulos; **to — from** impedir; **to — over at** hacer escala en; **to — short** parar(se) de sopetón, parar(se) en seco; **to — up** tapar, obstruir; atascar;

s. parada; alto, pausa; estada, estancia; detención; suspensión; llave (*de instrumento de viento*); traste (*de guitarra*); registro (*de órgano*); **— consonant** consonante oclusiva.

stop·o·ver [stápovɚ] *s.* parada, escala; **to make a — in** hacer escala en.

stop·page [stápɪdʒ] *s.* detención; obstrucción; **work —** paro.

stop·per [stápɚ] *s.* tapón.

stor·age [stórɪdʒ] *s.* almacenaje; (*computer*) almacenamiento; **— battery** acumulador; **— medium** (*computer*) soporte; **to keep in —** almacenar.

store [stor] *s.* (*shop*) tienda; almacén; (*supply*) depósito; acopio; **-s** provisiones; bastimentos; víveres; **department —** almacén; **dry-goods —** lencería, *Méx.*, *Ríopl.*, *Andes* mercería, *Méx.* cajón de ropa; **fruit —** frutería; **hat —** sombrerería; **grocery —** abacería, tienda de comestibles, *Méx.*, *C.A.* tienda de abarrotes, *Carib.* bodega; **shoe —** zapatería; **to have in —** tener guardado; *v.* almacenar; guardar; abastecer; **to — up** acumular.

store·house [stórhaus] *s.* almacén, depósito.

store·keep·er [stórkipɚ] *s.* tendero; almacenista; guardalmacén.

store·room [stórrum] *s.* almacén; bodega; despensa.

stork [stɔrk] *s.* cigüeña.

storm [stɔrm] *s.* (*weather*) tormenta, tempestad, borrasca, temporal; (*disturbance*) tumulto; asalto; **— troops** tropas de asalto; **hail —** granizada; **snow —** nevasca; **wind —** vendaval; *v.* asaltar, atacar; rabiar; **it is -ing** hay tormenta, hay tempestad.

storm·y [stórmi] *adj.* tempestuoso, borrascoso; turbulento.

sto·ry [stóri] *s.* (*tale*) cuento, historia, historieta; relato; (*gossip*) chisme; rumor; bola; (*plot*) argumento, trama; (*floor*) piso (*de un edificio*); **newspaper —** artículo de periódico, gacetilla.

stout [staut] *adj.* corpulento, robusto, fornido; fuerte; firme; leal; valiente.

stove [stov] *s.* estufa; cocina de gas, cocina eléctrica; *pret. & p.p. de* **to stave.**

stow [sto] *v.* meter, guardar; esconder; estibar, acomodar la carga de un barco; rellenar; **to — away on a ship** embarcarse clandestinamente, esconderse en un barco.

strad·dle [strǽdl] *v.* ponerse o estar a horcajadas; ponerse a caballo, cabalgar; favorecer ambos partidos (*de un pleito, controversia, etc.*).

strafe [stref] *v.* ametrallar; *Am.* abalear.

strag·gle [strǽgl] *v.* vagar, desviarse; (*get lost*) extraviarse; andar perdido; dispersarse; **to — behind** rezagarse.

straight [stret] *adj.* (*direction*) recto; derecho; directo; (*proper*) honrado; franco; erguido; correcto; en orden; **— face** cara seria; **— hair** pelo lacio; **— hand of five cards** runfla de cinco naipes del mismo palo; **— rum** ron puro, sin mezcla; **for two hours** por dos horas seguidas, por dos horas sin parar; **to set a person —** dar consejo a una persona; mostrarle el camino, modo o manera de hacer algo; *adv.* directamente, derecho, en línea recta; francamente; honradamente; **— away** (*o — off*) en seguida, al punto; **to talk — from the shoulder** hablar con toda franqueza o sinceridad.

straight·en [strétn] *v.* enderezar(se); arreglar, poner en orden.

straight·for·ward [stretfórwɚd] *adj.* derecho, recto; honrado; franco, sincero; *adv.* directamente, en línea recta.

straight·ness [strétnɪs] *s.* derechura; rectitud; honradez.

straight·way [strétwe] *adv.* luego, inmediatamente, en seguida.

strain [stren] *v.* (*force*) estirar demasiado, hacer fuerza; poner tirante; violentar, forzar (*los músculos, los nervios, la vista, etc.*); (*sift*) colar, tamizar; **to — one's wrist** torcerse la muñeca; *s.* tensión excesiva; tirantez; torcedura; esfuerzo excesivo; linaje, rasgo racial; aire, tonada.

strain·er [strénə·] *s.* coladera; cedazo.

strait [stret] *s.* estrecho; **-s** estrecho; aprieto, apuro; **— jacket** camisa de fuerza.

strait·laced [strétlest] *adj.* estricto.

strand [strænd] *v.* encallar; dejar perdido (*sin medios de salir*), dejar aislado, extraviar; **to be -ed** estar encallado; estar extraviado (*sin medios de salir*), estar aislado, andar perdido; *s.* ribera, playa; ramal (*de cuerda, cable, etc.*); hebra, hilo; **— of hair** guedeja, trenza; **— of pearls** hilera de perlas.

strange [strendʒ] *adj.* extraño; raro, singular; desconocido.

strange·ness [stréndʒnɪs] *s.* extrañeza, rareza.

stran·ger [stréndʒə·] *s.* extraño, desconocido; forastero.

stran·gle [stǽŋgl] *v.* estrangular(se).

strap [stræp] *s.* correa; tira de cuero o de tela; correón; (*suspender*) tirante; **metal —** banda de metal; *v.* amarrar o atar con correas; azotar (*con correa*); *véase* **strop.**

strat·a·gem [strǽtədʒəm] *s.* estratagema.

stra·te·gic [strətídʒɪk] *adj.* estratégico.

strat·e·gy [strǽtədʒɪ] *s.* estrategia.

strat·o·sphere [strǽtəsfɪr] *s.* estratosfera.

straw [strɔ] *s.* paja; **I don't care a —** no me importa un comino; *adj.* de paja; pajizo; **straw-colored** pajizo, color de paja; **— hat** sombrero de paja; **— vote** voto no oficial (*para averiguar la opinion pública*).

straw·ber·ry [strɔ́bɛrɪ] *s.* fresa.

stray [stre] *v.* extraviarse, descarriarse, desviarse; perderse, errar el camino; vagar; *adj.* extraviado, perdido; **— remark** observación aislada; *s.* animal perdido o extraviado.

streak [strik] *s.* (*line*) raya, línea, lista; (*vein*) vena; (*trace*) rasgo; (*beam*) rayo (*de luz*); **— of lightning** relámpago, rayo; *v.* rayar, *Ríopl., Méx., Ven.* listar, hacer rayas o listas.

stream [strim] *s.* corriente; chorro; río, arroyo, arroyuelo; **— of cars** desfile de autos; **down —** río abajo, agua abajo, con la corriente; **up —** río arriba, agua arriba, contra la corriente; *v.* correr (*el agua*), fluir; brotar, manar; derramarse; flotar (*en el viento*), ondear; **to — out of** salir a torrentes de.

stream·er [strímə·] *s.* banderola; gallardete; listón, cinta (*que flota en el aire*).

stream·lined [strímlaɪnd] *adj.* aerodinámico.

street [strit] *s.* calle.

street·car [strítkɑr] *s.* tranvía.

strength [strɛŋθ] *s.* fuerza; poder; potencia; fortaleza; **on the — of his promise** fundado en su promesa.

strength·en [strɛ́ŋkθən] *v.* fortalecer(se); reforzar(se).

stren·u·ous [strɛ́njuəs] *adj.* arduo; enérgico, vigoroso.

strep·to·my·cin [strɛptomáɪsɪn] *s.* estreptomicina.

stress [strɛs] *s.* (*force*) fuerza, esfuerzo; tensión, torsión, compresión; (*importance*) urgencia; énfasis; (*intensity*) acento; *v.* acentuar; recalcar, dar énfasis a, hacer hincapié en.

stretch [strɛtʃ] *v.* estirar(se); alargar(se); tender(se);

ensanchar; **to — oneself** estirarse, desperezarse; **to — out one's hand** tender o alargar la mano; *s.* trecho, distancia; extensión, período de tiempo; elasticidad; tensión; esfuerzo (*de la imaginación*); estirón; **—** último trecho (*de una carrera*).

stretch·er [strɛ́tʃə·] *s.* estirador, ensanchador, dilatador; camilla (*para los heridos*).

strew [stru] *v.* regar, esparcir.

strewn [strun] *p.p.* *de* **to strew; — with** regado de, cubierto de.

strick·en [strɪ́kən] *p.p.* *de* **to strike;** *adj.* herido; afligido; agobiado; atacado.

strict [strɪkt] *adj.* estricto; **in — confidence** en absoluta confianza, con toda reserva.

strid·den [strɪ́dn̩] *p.p.* *de* **to stride.**

stride [straɪd] *v.* tranquear, caminar a paso largo, dar zancadas, andar a trancos; *s.* zancada, tranco, paso largo.

strife [straɪf] *s.* refriega, contienda, pleito.

strike [straɪk] *v.* (*hit*) dar, golpear, pegar; azotar; herir; atacar; (*collide with*) chocar con; (*find*) dar con, encontrar (*oro, petróleo, etc.*); ocurrírsele a uno (*una idea*); (*assume*) asumir, afectar (*una postura, una actitud*); dar (*la hora un reloj*); (*light*) encender (*un fósforo*); acuñar (*moneda*); declararse o estar en huelga; **to — at** amagar; acometer; **to — off** borrar, tachar; cortar; **to — one's attention** atraer o llamar la atención; **to — one's fancy** antojársele a uno; **to — one's head against** darse un cabezazo contra; **to — out in a certain direction** tomar cierto rumbo, encaminarse o irse en cierta dirección; **to — out** ponchar; **to — someone for a loan** darle un sablazo a alguien; **to — up a friendship** trabar amistad; **to — with terror** sobrecoger de terror; **how does she — you?** ¿qué tal le parece? ¿qué piensa Vd. de ella;? *s.* golpe; huelga; caídos; (*baseball*) estrái; descubrimiento repentino (*de petróleo, de una mina, etc.*); **—breaker** esquirol, rompehuelgas **sit-down —** huelga de brazos.

strik·er [stráɪkə·] *s.* (*person on strike*) huelguista; (*device*) golpeador.

strik·ing [stráɪkɪŋ] *adj.* (*unusual*) notable; llamativo; conspicuo, manifiesto; sorprendente; extraordinario; (*on strike*) que está de huelga; que está en huelga.

string [strɪŋ] *s.* (*strand*) cuerda; cordel, cinta, cordón; sarta (*de perlas, cuentas, etc.*); (*fiber*) fibra (*de habichuelas, porotos, etc.*); (*line*) fila, hilera; **— bean** habichuela, judía verde, *Méx.* ejote, *Ch., Ríopl.* poroto; **— of lies** sarta de mentiras; *v.* ensartar; tender (*un cable, un alambre*); desfibrar, quitar las fibras a; encordar (*una raqueta, un violín*); encordelar, atar con cordeles, lazos o cuerdas; tomar el pelo, engañar; **to — out** extender(se), prolongar(se); **to — up** colgar.

strip [strɪp] *v.* despojar; robar; desnudar(se); desvestir(se), desmantelar; **to — the gears** estropear el engranaje; **to — the skin from** desollar, pelar; *s.* tira, lista, listón; **— of land** faja de tierra.

stripe [straɪp] *s.* (*band*) franja, raya, lista, tira; banda, galón; (*kind*) tipo, índole; *v.* rayar, *Am.* listar, adornar con listas.

striped [straɪpt, stráɪpɪd] *adj.* listado.

strive [straɪv] *v.* esforzarse; luchar, forcejear; hacer lo posible; **to —** esforzarse por.

striv·en [strɪ́vən] *p.p.* *de* **to strive.**

strode [strod] *pret.* *de* **to stride.**

stroke [strok] *s.* golpe; ataque, apoplejía; **— of a bell** campanada; **— of a painter's brush**

ST

pincelada; — **of lightning** rayo; — **of the hand**
caricia; — **of the pen** plumada; **at the** — **of ten** al
dar las diez; *v.* frotar suavemente, pasar
suavemente la mano, acariciar; alisar.
stroll [strol] *v.* dar un paseo, pasearse; vagar; **to** —
the streets callejear; *s.* paseo, paseíto.
strong [strɔŋ] *adj.* fuerte; forzudo, fornido; vigoroso;
recio; enérgico; firme; bien marcado; acérrimo; —
chance buena probabilidad; — **coffee** café
cargado; — **market** mercado firme; **strong-willed**
de voluntad fuerte, decidido; **strong-arm** violento;
adv. fuertemente; firmemente.
strong·hold [strɔ́ŋhold] *s.* fuerte, plaza fuerte.
stron·ti·um [strántʃiəm] *s.* estroncio.
strop [strɑp] *v.* asentar (*navajas de afeitar*); *s.*
asentador de navajas.
strove [strov] *pret. de* **to strive.**
struck [strʌk] *pret. & p.p. de* **to strike; to be** —
with a disease darle a uno una enfermedad; **to be**
— **with terror** estar o quedar sobrecogido de
terror.
struc·tu·ral [strʌ́ktʃərəl] *adj.* estructural, relativo a la
estructura.
struc·ture [strʌ́ktʃɚ] *s.* estructura; construcción;
edificio.
strug·gle [strʌ́gl] *v.* bregar, luchar, pugnar; forcejear;
esforzarse; *s.* esfuerzo; contienda; lucha, pugna.
strung [strʌŋ] *pret. & p.p. de* **to string.**
strut [strʌt] *v.* pavonearse, contonearse; *s.* contoneo;
(*support*) tirante, puntal.
stub [stʌb] *s.* trozo, fragmento, pedazo mochado;
(*tree*) tocón (*de árbol*); (*ticket*) talón (*de libro
talonario, boleto, etc.*); — **book** libro talonario; —
pen pluma de punta mocha; *v.* **to** — **one's foot**
dar(se) un tropezón.
stub·ble [stʌ́bl] *s.* (*crop*) rastrojo; (*beard*) cañones
(*de la barba*).
stub·born [stʌ́bɚn] *adj.* terco, testarudo, obstinado,
porfiado, cabezón.
stub·born·ness [stʌ́bɚnnɪs] *s.* terquedad, testarudez,
porfía, obstinación.
stuc·co [stʌ́ko] *s.* estuco; *v.* estucar, cubrir de estuco.
stuck [stʌk] *pret. & p.p. de* **to stick** pegado; atorado;
atascado; — **full of holes** agujereado; **stuck-up**
tieso, estirado, orgulloso.
stud [stʌd] *s.* (*knob*) tachón, tachuela de adorno;
(*button*) botón postizo para camisa; (*bolt*) perno; —
horse caballo padre; *v.* tachonar; clavetear.
stu·dent [stjúdn̩t] *s.* estudiante; *adj.* estudiantil.
stud·ied [stʌ́dɪd] *adj.* estudiado.
stu·di·o [stjúdɪo] *s.* estudio, taller.
stu·di·ous [stjúdɪəs] *adj.* estudioso; aplicado;
estudiado.
stud·y [stʌ́dɪ] *s.* estudio; cuidado, solicitud; gabinete
de estudio; *v.* estudiar.
stuff [stʌf] *s.* (*material*) materia; material; (*cloth*)
género, tela; (*thing*) cosa; (*medicine*) menjurje,
medicina; (*junk*) cachivaches, baratijas; **of good** —
de buena estofa; *v.* rellenar; henchir; hartar(se),
atracar(se), atiborrar(se).
stuff·ing [stʌ́fɪŋ] *s.* relleno; material para rellenar.
stum·ble [stʌ́mbl] *v.* tropezar, dar(se) un tropezón;
dar un traspié; hablar o recitar equivocándose a
cada paso; **to** — **upon** tropezar con; *s.* tropiezo,
tropezón, traspié.
stump [stʌmp] *s.* (*tree*) tocón (*tronco que queda de
un árbol*); (*tooth*) raigón (*de muela*); (*limb*) muñón
(*de brazo o pierna cortada*); **of a tail** rabo; **to be
up a** — hallarse en un apuro, estar perplejo; *v.*
trozar el tronco de (*un árbol*); renquear, cojear;
dejar confuso, confundir; **to** — **the country**

recorrer el país pronunciando discursos políticos.
stump·y [stʌ́mpɪ] *adj.* rechoncho, *Am.* chaparro;
lleno de tocones.
stun [stʌn] *v.* aturdir, pasmar; atolondrar.
stung [stʌŋ] *pret. & p.p. de* **to sting.**
stunk [stʌŋk] *pret. & p.p. de* **to stink.**
stun·ning [stʌ́nɪŋ] *adj.* aplastante; elegante,
bellísimo.
stunt [stʌnt] *v.* (*make short*) achaparrar, impedir el
desarrolo de, no dejar crecer; (*do tricks*) hacer
suertes. hacer piruetas; *s.* suerte; pirueta, suerte
acrobática, maniobra gimnástica; hazaña
sensacional.
stu·pe·fy [stjúpəfaɪ] *v.* atontar; entorpecer; aturdir,
atolondrar, pasmar, dejar estupefacto.
stu·pen·dous [stjupéndəs] *adj.* estupendo.
stu·pid [stjúpɪd] *adj.* estúpido; atontado.
stu·pid·i·ty [stjupídətɪ] *s.* estupidez.
stu·por [stjúpɚ] *s.* letargo, modorra; sopor;
aturdimiento; **in a** — aletargado.
stur·dy [stɝ́dɪ] *adj.* fornido, fuerte, robusto; firme.
stut·ter [stʌ́tɚ] *v.* tartamudear; *s.* tartamudeo;
tartamudez.
stut·er·er [stʌ́tərɚ] *s.* tartamudo.
stut·ter·ing [stʌ́tərɪŋ] *adj.* tartamudo; *s.* tartamudeo.
sty [staɪ] *s.* pocilga; orzuelo (*en el párpado*), *Méx.*
perilla; *Ríopl.* chiquero.
style [staɪl] *s.* estilo; moda; **to be in** — estar de
moda, estilarse; *v.* intitular, nombrar; **to** — **a
dress** cortar un vestido a la moda.
styl·ish [stáɪlɪʃ] *adj.* elegante; a la moda.
styl·ize [stáɪlaɪz] *v.* estilizar.
sub·con·scious [sʌbkánʃəs] *adj.* subconsciente.
sub·di·vi·sion [sʌbdəvíʒən] *s.* subdivisión;
parcelación de terrenos.
sub·due [səbdjú] *v.* subyugar, someter; sujetar,
dominar; amansar, domar.
sub·dued [səbdjúd] *p.p. de* **to subdue**; *adj.* sumiso;
sujeto; manso; suave; tenue; — **light** luz tenue.
sub·ject [sʌ́bdʒɪkt] *s.* súbdito; sujeto; asunto, tema,
materia; *adj.* sujeto; sometido; inclinado, propenso;
expuesto; [səbdʒékt] *v.* sujetar; someter; subyugar,
sojuzgar.
sub·jec·tion [səbdʒékʃən] *s.* sujeción; dominación;
sumisión.
sub·jec·tive [səbdʒéktɪv] *adj.* subjetivo.
sub·ju·gate [sʌ́bdʒəget] *v.* subyugar, sojuzgar.
sub·li·mate [sʌ́bləmet] *v.* sublimar.
sub·lime [səbláɪm] *adj.* sublime.
sub·ma·rine [sʌ́bmərín] *adj.* submarino; [sʌ́bmərin]
s. submarino.
sub·merge [səbmɝ́dʒ] *v.* sumergir(se), hundir(se),
sumir(se).
sub·mis·sion [səbmíʃən] *s.* sumisión, sometimiento.
sub·mis·sive [səbmísɪv] *adj.* sumiso.
sub·mit [səbmít] *v.* someter; **to** — **a report** someter
(presentar *o* rendir) un informe; **to** — **to
punishment** someterse a un castigo.
sub·or·di·nate [səbɔ́rdn̩ɪt] *adj. & s.* subordinado;
subalterno; dependiente; [səbɔ́rdn̩et] *v.* subordinar.
sub·rou·tine [sʌ́brutín] *s.* (*computer*) subrutina.
sub·scribe [səbskráɪb] *v.* subscribir(se); firmar; **to** —
five dollars prometer una cuota o subscripción de
cinco dólares; **to** — **for** subscribirse a, abonarse a;
to — **to a plan** subscribirse a (*o* aprobar) un plan.
sub·scrib·er [səbskráɪbɚ] *s.* suscritor, abonado;
infrascrito (*que firma un documento*), firmante.
sub·scrip·tion [səbskrípʃən] *s.* subscripción, abono.
sub·se·quent [sʌ́bsɪkwɛnt] *adj.* subsiguiente,
subsecuente, posterior; **-ly** *adv.* después,
posteriormente, subsiguientemente.

sub·ser·vi·ent [səbsɝ́·vɪənt] *adj.* servil, servilón.
sub·side [səbsáɪd] *v.* menguar, disminuir; bajar (*de nivel*); calmarse, aquietarse.
sub·sid·i·ar·y [səbsídɪɛɪ] *s.* subsidiario; sucursal.
sub·si·dize [sʌ́bsədaɪz] *v.* subvencionar.
sub·si·dy [sʌ́bsədɪ] *s.* subvención.
sub·sist [səbsíst] *v.* subsistir.
sub·stance [sʌ́bstəns] *s.* substancia (sustancia).
sub·stan·tial [səbstǽnʃəl] *adj.* substancial, substancioso; sólido; considerable; importante; **to be in — agreement** estar en substancia de acuerdo.
sub·stan·ti·ate [səbstǽnʃɪet] *v.* comprobar; verificar.
sub·stan·tive [sʌ́bstəntɪv] *adj. & s.* sustantivo.
sub·sti·tute [sʌ́bstətjut] *v.* sustituir (substituir); reemplazar; *s.* sustituto, suplente; reemplazo.
sub·sti·tu·tion [sʌbstətjúʃən] *s.* sustitución (substitución); reemplazo.
sub·stra·tum [sʌ́bstrætəm] *s.* sustrato.
sub·ter·fuge [sʌ́btɚfjudʒ] *s.* escapatoria; subterfugio.
sub·ter·ra·ne·an [sʌbtəréniən] *adj.* subterráneo.
sub·tle [sʌ́tl] *adj.* sutil.
sub·tle·ty [sʌ́tltɪ] *s.* sutileza; agudeza.
sub·tract [səbtrǽkt] *v.* sustraer (substraer); restar.
sub·trac·tion [səbtrǽkʃən] *s.* sustracción (substracción), resta.
sub·urb [sʌ́bɝb] *s.* suburbio, arrabal.
sub·ur·ban [səbɝ́bən] *adj. & s.* suburbano.
sub·ver·sive [səbvɝ́sɪv] *adj.* subversivo (*en contra de la autoridad constituida*); trastornador, destructivo.
sub·way [sʌ́bwe] *s.* subterráneo, túnel; metro, ferrocarril subterráneo.
suc·ceed [səksíd] *v.* suceder a; medrar, tener buen éxito, salir bien.
suc·cess [səksɛ́s] *s.* éxito, buen éxito; triunfo.
suc·cess·ful [səksɛ́sfəl] *adj.* afortunado; próspero; **to be —** tener buen éxito; **-ly** *adv.* con buen éxito, prósperamente.
suc·ces·sion [səksɛ́ʃən] *s.* sucesión.
suc·ces·sive [səksɛ́sɪv] *adj.* sucesivo.
suc·ces·sor [səksɛ́sɚ] *s.* sucesor; heredero.
suc·cor [sʌ́kɚ] *s.* socorro; *v.* socorrer.
suc·cumb [səkʌ́m] *v.* sucumbir.
such [sʌtʃ] *adj.* tal; semejante; **— a** tal, semejante; **— a good man** un hombre tan bueno; **— as** tal como, tales como; **at — an hour** a tal hora; **at — and — a place** en tal o cual lugar.
suck [sʌk] *v.* chupar; mamar; **to — up** chupar; sorber; *s.* chupada; mamada.
suck·er [sʌ́kɚ] *s.* chupador; mamón, mamantón; dulce (*que se chupa*); (*gullible*) primo (*persona demasiado crédula*).
suck·le [sʌ́kl] *v.* mamar; amamantar, dar de mamar.
suc·tion [sʌ́kʃən] *s.* succión; chupada, aspiración.
sud·den [sʌ́dn] *adj.* súbito, repentino; precipitado; inesperado; **all of a —** de súbito, de repente, de sopetón; **-ly** *adv.* de súbito, de repente, de sopetón.
sud·den·ness [sʌ́dnnɪs] *s.* precipitación; rapidez.
suds [sʌdz] *s.* espuma, jabonadura.
sue [su] *v.* demandar, poner pleito; **to — for damages** demandar por daños y perjuicios; **to — for peace** pedir la paz.
su·et [súɪt] *s.* sebo, gordo, grasa.
suf·fer [sʌ́fɚ] *v.* sufrir; padecer.
suf·fer·er [sʌ́fərɚ] *s.* sufridor.
suf·fer·ing [sʌ́fərɪŋ] *s.* sufrimiento, padecimiento; *adj.* doliente; sufrido, paciente.
suf·fice [səfáɪs] *v.* bastar, ser bastante o suficiente.
suf·fi·cient [səfíʃənt] *adj.* suficiente, bastante; **-ly** *adv.* suficientemente, bastante.

suf·fix [sʌ́fɪks] *s.* sufijo.
suf·fo·cate [sʌ́fəket] *v.* sofocar(se), ahogar(se), asfixiar(se).
suf·fo·ca·tion [sʌfəkéʃən] *s.* asfixia, sofoco.
suf·frage [sʌ́frɪdʒ] *s.* sufragio; voto.
sug·ar [ʃúgɚ] *s.* azúcar; **— bowl** azucarera; **— cane** caña de azúcar; **lump of —** terrón de azúcar; *v.* azucarar; cristalizarse (*el almíbar*), *Am.* azucararse.
sug·gest [səgdʒɛ́st] *v.* sugerir, indicar.
sug·ges·tion [səgdʒɛ́stʃən] *s.* sugestión, *Am.* sugerencia; indicación.
sug·ges·tive [səgdʒɛ́stɪv] *adj.* sugestivo.
su·i·cide [súəsaɪd] *s.* (*act*) suicidio; (*person*) suicida; **to commit —** suicidarse.
suit [sut] *s.* traje, terno, *Carib.*, *Ven.* flux (*o* flus); (*cards*) palo (*de la baraja*); (*court*) demanda, pleito; petición; galanteo; *v.* adaptar, acomodar; agradar; satisfacer; sentar bien, venir bien; caer bien; convenir; ser a propósito; **— yourself** haz lo que quieras, haga Vd. lo que guste.
suit·a·ble [sútəbl] *adj.* propio, conveniente, debido, a propósito, apropiado, adecuado.
suit·a·bly [sútəblɪ] *adv.* propiamente, adecuadamente, convenientemente.
suit·case [sútkɛs] *s.* maleta, valija.
suite [swit] *s.* serie; comitiva, acompañamiento; **— of rooms** vivienda, apartamento, habitación; **bedroom —** juego de muebles para alcoba.
suit·or [sútɚ] *s.* pretendiente, galán; (*court*) demandante (*en un pleito*).
sulk [sʌlk] *v.* tener murria; estar hosco o malhumorado; *s.* murria.
sulk·y [sʌ́lkɪ] *adj.* malcontento, hosco, malhumorado; **to be —** tener murria.
sul·len [sʌ́lɪn] *adj.* hosco, sombrío, tétrico; malhumorado, taciturno.
sul·ly [sʌ́lɪ] *v.* manchar, ensuciar; empañar.
sul·phate [sʌ́lfet] *s.* sulfato.
sul·phide [sʌ́lfaɪd] *s.* sulfuro.
sul·phur [sʌ́lfɚ] *s.* azufre.
sul·phur·ic [sʌlfjúrɪk] *adj.* sulfúrico; **— acid** ácido sulfúrico.
sul·tan [sʌ́ltn] *s.* sultán.
sul·try [sʌ́ltrɪ] *adj.* bochornoso, sofocante; **— heat** bochorno, calor sofocante.
sum [sʌm] *s.* suma; monto; cantidad; (*nature*) esencia, substancia; **— total** total; *v.* sumar; **to — up** resumir, recapitular.
sum·ma·rize [sʌ́məraɪz] *v.* resumir, compendiar.
sum·ma·ry [sʌ́mərɪ] *s.* sumario, resumen; compendio; *adj.* sumario; breve.
sum·mer [sʌ́mɚ] *s.* verano; estío; *adj.* veraniego, estival de verano; **— resort** balneario, lugar de veraneo; *v.* veranear.
sum·mit [sʌ́mɪt] *s.* cima, cúspide, cumbre.
sum·mon [sʌ́mən] *v.* citar; convocar, llamar; **-s** *s.* notificación; cita judicial, citación, emplazamiento.
sump·tu·ous [sʌ́mptʃʊəs] *adj.* suntuoso.
sun [sʌn] *s.* sol; **— bath** baño de sol; **— lamp** lámpara de rayos ultravioletas; **— porch** solana; *v.* asolear; **to — oneself** asolearse, tomar el sol.
sun·beam [sʌ́nbim] *s.* rayo de sol.
sun·burn [sʌ́nbɝn] *s.* quemadura de sol; *v.* asolear(se); quemar(se) al sol, tostar(se) al sol.
Sun·day [sʌ́ndɪ] *s.* domingo.
sun·di·al [sʌ́ndaɪəl] *s.* cuadrante solar, reloj de sol.
sun·down [sʌ́ndaʊn] *s.* puesta del sol.
sun·dry [sʌ́ndrɪ] *adj.* varios, diversos.
sun·flow·er [sʌ́nflaʊɚ] *s.* girasol; tornasol.
sung [sʌŋ] *pret. & p.p. de* **to sing.**
sun·glass·es [sʌ́nglæsəz] *s.* gafas (*anteojos*) de sol.

ST

sunk [sʌŋk] *pret. & p.p. de* **to sink.**
sunk·en [sʌ́ŋkən] *adj.* hundido, sumido.
sun·light [sʌ́nlaɪt] *s.* luz del sol, luz solar.
sun·ny [sʌ́nɪ] *adj.* asoleado o soleado; alegre, risueño, resplandeciente; — **day** día de sol.
sun·rise [sʌ́nraɪz] *s.* salida del sol, amanecer, amanecida.
sun·set [sʌ́nsɛt] *s.* puesta del sol.
sun·shine [sʌ́nʃaɪn] *s.* luz del sol, solana.
sun·stroke [sʌ́nstrok] *s.* insolación.
sun·tan [sʌ́ntæn] *s.* bronceado.
sup [sʌp] *v.* cenar.
su·perb [supɝ́b] *adj.* soberbio.
su·per·fi·cial [supɝfíʃəl] *adj.* superficial.
su·per·flu·ous [supɝ́fluəs] *adj.* superfluo.
su·per·hu·man [supɝhjúmən] *adj.* sobrehumano.
su·per·in·tend [suprɪntɛ́nd] *v.* dirigir, inspeccionar, vigilar.
su·per·in·ten·dent [suprɪntɛ́ndənt] *s.* superintendente; inspector; capataz.
su·pe·ri·or [səpíriɚ] *adj. & s.* superior; — **letter** volado.
su·pe·ri·or·i·ty [səpɪrɪɔ́rətɪ] *s.* superioridad.
su·per·la·tive [səpɝ́lətɪv] *adj. & s.* superlativo.
su·per·mar·ket [súpɝmɑrkət] *s.* supermercado.
su·per·nat·u·ral [supɝnǽtʃrəl] *adj.* sobrenatural; **the** — lo sobrenatural.
su·per·sede [supɝsíd] *v.* reemplazar.
su·per·sti·tion [supɝstíʃən] *s.* superstición.
su·per·sti·tious [supɝstíʃəs] *adj.* supersticioso.
su·per·vise [supɝváɪz] *v.* dirigir, inspeccionar, vigilar.
su·per·vi·sion [supɝvíʒən] *s.* inspección, vigilancia.
su·per·vi·sor [supɝváɪzɚ] *s.* superintendente, inspector; interventor.
sup·per [sʌ́pɚ] *s.* cena.
sup·plant [səplǽnt] *v.* suplantar; reemplazar.
sup·ple [sʌ́pl] *adj.* flexible; dócil.
sup·ple·ment [sʌ́pləmənt] *s.* suplemento; apéndice; [sʌ́pləmənt] *v.* suplementar, completar.
sup·pli·ant [sʌ́plɪənt] *adj. & s.* suplicante.
sup·pli·ca·tion [sʌplɪkéʃən] *s.* súplica, plegaria; ruego.
sup·ply [səplái] *v.* (*provide*) proveer; abastecer, surtir; suplir; (*give*) dar, suministrar; *s.* provisión, abastecimiento; bastimento; abasto; surtido; — **and demand** oferta y demanda; **supplies** provisiones; materiales; víveres; pertrechos; — **pipe** cañería o caño de abastecimiento, tubería, tubo de suministro.
sup·port [səpórt] *v.* (*keep from falling*) sostener; apoyar; (*provide for*) mantener; sustentar; (*bear*) soportar, aguantar; *s.* apoyo; sostén, soporte, puntal; sustento, manutención; amparo.
sup·port·er [səpórtɚ] *s.* defensor; partidario; mantenedor; sostén, apoyo; tirante (*para medias*).
sup·pose [səpóz] *v.* suponer.
sup·posed [səpózd] *adj.* supuesto; presunto; **-ly** *adv.* supuestamente.
sup·po·si·tion [sʌpəzíʃən] *s.* suposición.
sup·press [səprɛ́s] *v.* suprimir; reprimir; parar, suspender; **to** — **a revolt** sofocar una revuelta o motín.
sup·pres·sion [səprɛ́ʃən] *s.* supresión; represión.
su·prem·a·cy [səprɛ́məsɪ] *s.* supremacía.
su·preme [səprím] *adj.* supremo.
sur·charge [sɝ́tʃardʒ] *s.* recargo.
sure [ʃur] *adj.* seguro; cierto; (*stable*) estable; *adv.* *véase* **surely, be** — **to do it** hágalo sin falta, no deje Vd. de hacerlo; **-ly** *adv.* seguramente; ciertamente; con toda seguridad; sin falta.

sure·ty [ʃúrtɪ] *s.* seguridad; garantía, fianza; fiador.
surf [sɝf] *s.* oleaje, rompientes; (*undertow*) resaca.
sur·face [sɝ́fɪs] *s.* superficie; cara; *v.* (*level*) alisar, allanar; (*coat*) poner superficie a.
surf·board [sɝ́fbord] *s.* patín de mar.
sur·feit [sɝ́fɪt] *s.* hastío, exceso; *v.* hastiar; empalagar.
surge [sɝdʒ] *s.* oleada, oleaje; *v.* agitarse, hinchar(se) (*el mar*); surgir.
sur·geon [sɝ́dʒən] *s.* cirujano.
sur·ger·y [sɝ́dʒərɪ] *s.* cirujía.
sur·gi·cal [sɝ́dʒɪkl] *adj.* quirúrgico.
sur·ly [sɝ́lɪ] *adj.* rudo, hosco, malhumorado.
sur·mise [sɚmáɪz] *v.* conjeturar, suponer, presumir; *s.* conjetura, suposición.
sur·mount [sɚmáunt] *v.* superar, vencer; coronar.
sur·name [sɝ́nem] *s.* sobrenombre, apellido; *v.* apellidar, llamar.
sur·pass [sɚpǽs] *v.* sobrepasar, superar, sobrepujar, exceder, aventajar.
sur·pass·ing [sɚpǽsɪŋ] *adj.* sobresaliente, excelente.
sur·plus [sɝ́plʌs] *s.* sobra, sobrante, exceso, excedente; superávit; *adj.* sobrante, excedente, de sobra.
sur·prise [səpráɪz] *s.* sorpresa; *v.* sorprender.
sur·pris·ing [səpráɪzɪŋ] *adj.* sorprendente.
sur·ren·der [sərɛ́ndɚ] *v.* rendir(se), entregar(se), darse; ceder; *s.* rendición; entrega; cesión; sumisión.
sur·round [səráund] *v.* rodear, cercar, circundar.
sur·round·ing [səráundɪŋ] *adj.* circundante, circunvecino, circunstante.
sur·round·ings [səráundɪŋz] *s. pl* alrededores, inmediaciones, cercanías; ambiente.
sur·vey [sɝ́ve] *s.* (*inspection*) examen, reconocimiento, inspección, estudio; (*measure*) medición, agrimensura (*de un terreno*); plano (*de un terreno*); bosquejo o esbozo general (*de historia, literatura, etc.*); investigación por encuestas; — **course** curso general o comprensivo; [sɚvé] *v.* examinar, inspeccionar, reconocer, medir (*un terreno*), levantar un plano (*el agrimensor*).
sur·vey·or [sɚvéɚ] *s.* agrimensor.
sur·viv·al [sɚváɪvl] *s.* supervivencia; sobreviviente; resto.
sur·vive [sɚváɪv] *c.* sobrevivir; quedar vivo, salvarse.
sur·vi·vor [sɚváɪvɚ] *s.* sobreviviente.
sus·cep·ti·ble [səsɛ́ptəbl] *adj.* susceptible; — **of proof** capaz de probarse; — **to** propenso a.
sus·pect [sʌ́spɛkt] *s.* sospechoso; [səspɛ́kt] *v.* sospechar.
sus·pend [səspɛ́nd] *v.* suspender.
sus·pend·ers [səspɛ́ndɚz] *s.* tirantes (*de pantalón*).
sus·pense [səspɛ́ns] *s.* (*uncertainty*) suspensión, incertidumbre; (*anxiety*) ansiedad; **to keep in** — tener en suspenso, tener en duda.
sus·pen·sion [səspɛ́nʃən] *s.* suspensión; — **bridge** puente colgante.
sus·pi·cion [səspíʃən] *s.* sospecha.
sus·pi·cious [səspíʃəs] *adj.* sospechoso, suspicaz.
sus·tain [səstén] *v.* (*prolong*) sostener; mantener; (*support*) sustentar; (*bear, endure*) aguantar; (*defend*) apoyar, defender; (*undergo*) sufrir (*un daño o pérdida*).
sus·te·nance [sʌ́stənəns] *s.* sustento; subsistencia; alimentos; mantenimiento.
swab [swab] *s.* escobillón; *v.* fregar.
swag·ger [swǽgɚ] *v.* pavonearse, contonearse; fanfarronear; *s.* pavoneo, contoneo; fanfarronada.
swain [swen] *s.* galán.

swal·low [swálo] *s.* (*bird*) golondrina; (*drink*) trago; *v.* tragar; deglutir.

swam [swæm] *pret. de* **to swim.**

swamp [swɑmp] *s.* pantano; ciénaga; — **land** cenagal, terreno pantanoso; *v.* inundar(se); sumergir(se); **to be -ed with work** estar abrumado de trabajo.

swamp·y [swɑ́mpɪ] *adj.* pantanoso, cenagoso, fangoso.

swan [swɑn] *s.* cisne.

swap [swɑp] *v.* cambalachear, cambiar, trocar; *s.* cambalache, cambio, trueque; — **shop** cambalache.

swarm [swɔrm] *s.* enjambre; *v.* pulular; bullir, hervir, hormiguear.

swarth·y [swɔ́rðɪ] *adj.* trigueño, moreno, *Am.* prieto.

swat [swɑt] *v.* pegar, aporrear; aplastar de un golpe (*una mosca*); *s.* golpe.

sway [swe] *v.* mecer(se); cimbrar(se); balancearse; ladear(se); oscilar; tambalear; influir; *s.* oscilación; vaivén; balanceo; influjo, influencia; mando; predominio.

swear [swɛr] *v.* jurar; renegar, (*curse*) blasfemar, echar maldiciones; (*take oath*) juramentar, tomar juramento; **to — by** jurar por; poner toda su confianza en; **to — in** juramentar; **to — off smoking** jurar no fumar más, renunciar al tabaco.

sweat [swɛt] *v.* sudar; trasudar; hacer sudar; *s.* sudor; trasudor.

sweat·er [swɛ́təˈ] *s.* suéter; sudador, el que suda.

sweat·y [swɛ́tɪ] *adj.* sudoroso.

Swede [swid] *s.* sueco.

Swed·ish [swidɪʃ] *adj.* sueco; *s.* sueco, idioma sueco.

sweep [swip] *v.* barrer; (*dredge*) drager (*puertos, ríos, etc.*); extenderse; **to — down upon** caer sobre; asolar; **to — everything away** barrer con todo; **she swept into the room** entró garbosamente en la sala; *s.* barrida; extensión; (*blow*) soplo (*del viento*).

sweep·er [swípəˈ] *s.* barrendero; **carpet —** escoba mecánica.

sweep·ing [swípɪŋ] *s.* barrido; **-s** basura; *adj.* abarcador, que lo abarca todo, vasto; asolador; — **victory** victoria completa.

sweet [swit] *adj.* (*flavor*) dulce; oloroso; (*fresh*) fresco; — **butter** mantequilla sin sal; — **corn** maíz tierno; — **milk** leche fresca; — **pea** guisante de olor; — **potato** batata, *Méx., C.A.* camote, *Carib.* boniato; **to have a — tooth** ser goloso, gustarle a uno los dulces; *s.* dulce, golosina; **my — mi vida, mi alma.**

sweet·en [swítn̩] *v.* endulzar(se), dulcificar(se); suavizar.

sweet·heart [swíthɑrt] *s.* querida, novia, prometida; amante, querido, galán, novio.

sweet·meat [swítmit] *s.* confite, confitura dulce; golosina.

sweet·ness [swítnɪs] *s.* dulzura; (*pleasantness*) melosidad; (*gentleness*) suavidad.

swell [swɛl] *v.* hinchar(se), henchir(se), inflar(se); dilatar(se), abultar(se); acrecentar; *s.* hinchazón; protuberancia; oleaje; *adj.* elegante; muy bueno, excelente, magnífico; **to have a — head** creerse gran cosa; ser vanidoso.

swel·ling [swɛ́lɪŋ] *s.* hinchazón; chichón, bulto; protuberancia.

swel·ter [swɛ́ltəˈ] *v.* sofocarse de calor.

swept [swɛpt] *pret. & p.p. de* **to sweep.**

swerve [swɝv] *v.* desviar(se); torcer; cambiar repentinamente de rumbo; *s.* desvío brusco, cambio repentino de dirección; **to make a — to the right** torcer a la derecha.

swift [swɪft] *adj.* veloz, rápido.

swift·ness [swɪ́ftnɪs] *s.* velocidad, rapidez, presteza, prontitud.

swim [swɪm] *v.* nadar; flotar; **to — across** pasar a nado, atravesar nadando; **my head is swimming** tengo vértigo, se me va la cabeza, estoy desvanecido; *s.* nadada; — **suit** traje de baño o natación.

swim·mer [swɪ́məˈ] *s.* nadador.

swin·dle [swɪ́ndl̩] *v.* estafar; *s.* estafa.

swine [swaɪn] *s.* marrano, puerco, cerdo, cochino; *S.A.* chancho; *C.A.* cuchi; marranos, puercos, cerdos.

swing [swɪŋ] *v.* columpiar(se), mecer(se), balancear(se); oscilar; hacer oscilar; (*blandish*) blandir (*un bastón, espada, etc.*); (*hang*) colgar; girar; hacer girar; **to — a deal** llevar a cabo un negocio; **to — around** dar vuelta, girar; **to — one's arms** girar o menear los brazos; **to — open** abrirse de pronto (*una puerta*); *s.* columpio; hamaca; balanceo; vaivén; compás; ritmo; golpe, guantada, puñetazo; — **door** puerta giratoria; — **shift** turno de trabajo desde las dieciséis hasta medianoche; **in full —** en su apogeo, en pleno movimiento; **to give someone full —** darle a alguien completa libertad de acción.

swipe [swaɪp] *v.* hurtar, sisar.

swirl [swɝl] *v.* arremolinarse; girar, dar vueltas; *s.* remolino; torbellino; vuelta, movimiento giratorio.

Swiss [swɪs] *adj. & s.* suizo.

switch [swɪtʃ] *s.* (*change*) mudanza; (*whip*) látigo, (*blow*) azote; *Méx., Andes* chicote, *Ríopl.* rebenque; *Méx., Andes* fuste; latigazo; pelo postizo; cambio; **electric —** interruptor, conmutador; **railway —** aguja, cambio; —**man** guardagujas, *Andes, Ríopl.* cambiavía; *Méx.* guardavía; *v.* azotar; desviar(se); cambiar(se); **to — off** cortar (*la communicación o la corriente eléctrica*); apagar (*la luz eléctrica*); **to — on the light** encender la luz; (*computer*) accionar.

switch·board [swɪ́tʃbɔrd] *s.* cuadro o tablero de distribución; cuadro conmutador.

swiv·el [swɪ́vl̩] *adj.* giratorio.

swol·len [swólən] *p.p. de* **to swell.**

swoon [swun] *v.* desvanecerse, desmayarse; *s.* desmayo.

swoop [swup] *v.* **to — down upon** caer de súbito sobre; abalanzarse sobre; acometer; **to — off** cortar de un golpe; **to — up** agarrar, arrebatar; *s.* descenso súbito; arremetida; **at one —** de un golpe.

sword [sord] *s.* espada; — **belt** talabarte.

swore [swor] *pret. de* **to swear.**

sworn [sworn] *p.p. de* **to swear.**

swum [swʌm] *p.p. de* **to swim.**

swung [swʌŋ] *pret. & p.p. de* **to swing.**

syl·lab·i·cate [sɪlǽbəket] *v.* silabear.

syl·la·ble [sɪləbl̩] *s.* sílaba.

syl·la·bus [sɪləbəs] *s.* sílabo.

syl·lo·gism [sɪ́lədʒɪzəm] *s.* silogismo.

sym·bol [sɪmbl̩] *s.* símbolo.

sym·bol·ic [sɪmbálɪk] *adj.* simbólico.

sym·bol·ism [sɪ́mblɪzəm] *s.* simbolismo.

sym·met·ri·cal [sɪmɛ́trɪkl̩] *adj.* simétrico.

sym·me·try [sɪ́mɪtrɪ] *s.* simetría.

sym·pa·thet·ic [sɪmpəθɛ́tɪk] *adj.* compasivo; favorablemente dispuesto; que compadece; — **towards** favorablemente dispuesto a (*o* hacia).

sym·pa·thize [sɪ́mpəθaɪz] *v.* compadecer(se); condolerse.

SU

sym·pa·thy [símpəθɪ] s. compasión, lástima; armonía; **to extend one's** — dar el pésame.

sym·pho·ny [símfənɪ] s. sinfonía; — **orchestra** orquesta sinfónica.

sym·po·si·um [sɪmpósɪəm] s. coloquio; simposio.

symp·tom [símptəm] s. síntoma.

syn·a·gogue [sínəgag] s. sinagoga.

syn·chro·nize [sínkənaɪz] v. sincronizar.

syn·di·cate [síndɪkɪt] s. sindicato; **newspaper** — sindicato periodístico; [síndɪket] v. sindicar, formar un sindicato; sindicarse, combinarse para formar un sindicato; vender (*un cuento, caricatura, serie de artículos, etc.*) a un sindicato.

syn·drome [síndrom] s. síndrome.

syn·o·nym [sínənɪm] s. sinónimo.

syn·on·y·mous [sɪnánəmes] adj. sinónimo.

syn·op·sis [sɪnápsɪs] s. sinopsis.

syn·tax [síntæks] s. sintaxis.

syn·the·sis [sínθəsɪs] s. síntesis.

syn·the·size [sínθəsaɪz] v. sintetizar.

syn·thet·ic [sɪnθétik] adj. sintético.

syr·inge [sírɪndʒ] s. jeringa.

syr·up = **sirup.**

sys·tem [sístəm] s. sistema.

sys·tem·at·ic [sɪstəmætɪk] adj. sistemático.

sys·tem·a·tize [sɪstəmətáɪz] v. sistematizar, metodizar.

sys·tem·ic [sɪstémɪk] adj. sistemático.

T:t

tab [tæb] s. (*flap*) lengüeta; (*bill*) cuenta; — **key** tecla de tabulación.

tab·er·na·cle [tǽbə·nækl] s. tabernáculo.

ta·ble [tébl] s. (*furniture*) mesa; tabla (*de materias, de multiplicar, etc.*); — **cover** tapete, cubremesa; —**land** mesa, meseta; v. poner sobre la mesa; formar tabla o índice; **to** — **a motion** dar carpetazo a una moción, aplazar la discusión de una moción.

ta·ble·cloth [téblklɔθ] s. mantel.

ta·ble·spoon [téblspun] s. cuchara grande.

ta·ble·spoon·ful [téblspunful] s. cucharada.

tab·let [tǽblɪt] s. tableta; tablilla, (*pill*) pastilla, comprimido; bloc de papel; (*stone*) lápida, placa.

ta·ble·ware [téblwɛr] s. vajilla, servicio de mesa.

ta·boo [tæbú] s. tabú.

tab·u·late [tǽbjəlet] v. formar tablas o listas; tabular.

tac·it [tǽsɪt] adj. tácito.

tac·i·turn [tǽsətɜ·n] adj. taciturno, silencioso.

tack [tæk] s. (*nail*) tachuela; (*hem*) hilván; (*boat*) virada o cambio de rumbo (*de una embarcación*); amura, jarcia (*para sostener el ángulo de una vela*); **to change** — cambiar de amura, cambiar de rumbo; v. clavetear con tachuelas; coser, hilvanar; pegar, clavar; juntar, unir; virar, cambiar de rumbo; zigzaguear (*un barco de vela*).

tack·le [tǽkl] s. aparejo, equipo, enseres, avíos; (*football*) agarrada (*en fútbol*); (*person*) atajador (*en fútbol*); **fishing** — avíos de pescar; v. agarrar, asir, atajar (*en futbol*); atacar (*un problema*); acometer (*una empresa*).

tact [tækt] s. tacto, tino, tiento.

tact·ful [tǽktfəl] adj. cauto, prudente, diplomático.

tac·tics [tǽktɪks] s. táctica.

tact·less [tǽktlɪs] adj. falto de tacto o de tino; imprudente, incauto.

taf·fe·ta [tǽfɪtə·] s. tafetán.

tag [tæg] s. (*label*) marbete, etiqueta; cartela; (*loose end*) pingajo, rabito, cabo; **to play** — jugar al tócame tú, jugar a la pega; v. pegar un marbete a, marcar; **to** — **after** seguir de cerca a, pisar los talones a; **to** — **something on to** juntar, añadir o agregar algo a.

tail [tel] s. (*animal*) cola, rabo; (*object*) cabo, extremo, extremidad; — **light** farol trasero, farol de cola; — **spin** barrena.

tai·lor [téla·] s. sastre; — **shop** sastrería.

taint [tent] s. tacha, mancha; corrupción; v. manchar; corromper(se), inficionar(se).

take [tek] v. tomar; coger; (*carry*) llevar; (*conduct*) conducir; dar (*un paseo, vuelta, paso, salto*); hacer (*un viaje*); asumir; (*photo*) sacar o tomar (*una fotografía*); **to** — **a chance** aventurarse, correr un riesgo; **to** — **a fancy to** caerle en gracia a uno; aficionarse a; antojársele a uno; **to** — **a look at** mirar a, echar una mirada a; **to** — **a notion to** antojársele a uno; **to** — **after** salir a, parecerse a; seguir el ejemplo de; **to** — **amiss** interpretar mal, echar a mala parte; **to** — **an oath** prestar juramento; **to** — **apart** desarmar, desmontar; **to** — **away** llevarse; **to** — **back one's words** desdecirse, retractarse; **to** — **back to** devolver (*algo*) a; **to** — **by surprise** coger desprevenido, coger de sorpresa; **to** — **care of** cuidar de, atender a; **to** — **charge of** encargarse de; **to** — **cold** resfriarse, acatarrarse; **to** — **down in writing** poner por escrito, apuntar; **to** — **effect** surtir efecto, dar resultado; entrar en vigencia (*una ley*); **to** — **exercise** hacer ejercicio; hacer gimnasia; **to** — **from** quitar a; sustraer de, restar de; **to** — **in** meter en; recibir; abarcar; embaucar; reducir, achicar (*un vestido*); **to** — **leave** decir adiós, despedirse; **to** — **off** quitar; descontar, rebajar; despegar (*un aeroplano*); remedar, parodiar (*a alguien*); **to** — **offense** ofenderse, darse por ofendido; **to** — **on a responsibility** asumir una responsabilidad; **to** — **out** sacar; **to** — **place** tener lugar, suceder, ocurrir; **to** — **stock** hacer inventario; **to** — **stock in** creer, tener confianza en; **to** — **the floor** tomar la palabra; **to** — **to heart** tomar a pechos, tomar en serio; **to** — **to one's heels** poner pies en polvorosa; **to** — **to task** reprender, regañar; **to** — **up a matter** tratar un asunto; **to** — **up space** ocupar espacio; **I** — **it that** supongo que; v. toma; **take-off** despegue (*de un aeroplano*); remedo, parodia.

tak·en [tékən] p.p. de **to take; to be** — **ill** caer enfermo.

tal·cum [tǽlkəm] s. talco; — **powder** talco en polvo.

tale [tel] s. (*story*) cuento, relato, fábula; (*gossip*) chisme; **to tell** -**s** contar cuentos o chismes; chismear, murmurar.

tale·bear·er [télbɛrə·] s. soplón, chismoso.

tal·ent [tǽlənt] s. talento.

tal·ent·ed [tǽləntɪd] adj. talentoso.

talk [tɔk] v. hablar; (*chat*) charlar, platicar, conversar; **to** — **into** inducir o persuadir a; **to** — **nonsense** decir tonterías, hablar disparates; **to** — **out of** disuadir de; **to** — **over** discutir; **to** — **up** alabar; hablar claro o recio, hablar en voz alta; s. charla, conversación, plática; habla; discurso; conferencia; rumor; — **of the town** comidilla, tema de murmuración.

talk·a·tive [tɔ́kətɪv] adj. hablador, locuaz, platicador.

talk·er [tɔ́kə·] s. hablador; conversador; platicador; orador.

tall [tɔl] adj. alto; — **tale** cuento exagerado o increíble; **six feet** — seis pies de altura o de alto.

tal·low [tǽlo] *s.* sebo.
tal·low·y [tǽlowɪ] *adj.* seboso.
tal·ly [tǽlɪ] *s.* cuenta; tarja; · **sheet** plana para llevar la cuenta; *v.* llevar la cuenta; **to — up** contar, sumar; **to — with** coresponder con, concordar con.
tam·a·rind [tǽmərɪnd] *s.* tamarindo.
tame [tem] *adj.* manso; dócil; **— amusement** diversión poco animada o desabrida; *v.* amansar, domar, domeñar, domesticar, desbravar.
tam·per [tǽmpɚ] *v.* **to — with** meterse con, juguetear con; falsificar (*un documento*); **to — with a lock** tratar de forzar una cerradura.
tan [tæn] *v.* (*cure*) curtir, adobar (*pieles*); (*punish*) zurrar, azotar; (*sunburn*) tostar(se), requemar(se); *adj.* tostado, requemado; color de canela; bayo, amarillento; *s.* color moreno, de canela o café con leche.
tang [tæŋ] *s.* sabor u olor picante.
tangent [tǽndʒənt] *adj. & s.* tangente; **to go off at a — salirse** por la tangente.
tan·ger·ine [tǽndʒərin] *s.* naranja tangerina o mandarina.
tan·gi·ble [tǽndʒəbl] *adj.* tangible, palpable; corpóreo.
tan·gle [tǽŋgl] *v.* enredar(se), enmarañar(se); confundir(se), embrollar(se); *s.* enredo, maraña, embrollo; confusión.
tank [tæŋk] *s.* tanque; depósito; **swimming —** piscina.
tan·ner [tǽnɚ] *s.* curtidor.
tan·ner·y [tǽnərɪ] *s.* curtiduría, tenería.
tan·nic ac·id [tǽnɪkǽsəd] *s.* ácido tánico.
tan·ta·lize [tǽntlaɪz] *v.* molestar; hacer desesperar; exasperar.
tan·ta·lum [tǽntələm] *s.* tantalio.
tan·ta·mount [tǽntəmaʊnt] *adj.* equivalente.
tan·trum [tǽntrəm] *s.* berrinche.
tap [tæp] *s.* (*blow*) palmadita; golpecito; (*faucet*) espita, grifo, llave; **— dance** zapateado, *Andes, Ríopl.* zapateo; **— room** bar; **beer on —** cerveza del barril, cerveza de sifón; *v.* tocar, golpear ligeramente; dar una palmadita o golpecito; taladrar; extraer; **to — a tree** sangrar un árbol.
tape [tep] *s.* cinta, cintilla; **— measure** cinta para medir; **— recorder** magnetófono; grabadora; **adhesive —** tela adhesiva, esparadrapo; *v.* atar o vendar con cinta; medir con cinta.
ta·per [tépɚ] *s.* (*candle*) velita, candela; (*diminished size*) adelgazamiento paulatino; *v.* adelgazar, disminuir gradualmente; **to — off** ahusar(se), ir disminuyendo (*hasta rematar en punta*).
tap·es·try [tǽpɪstrɪ] *s.* tapiz, colgadura; tapicería; tela (*para forrar muebles*).
tape·worm [tépwɚm] *s.* tenia, solitaria.
tap·i·o·ca [tæpɪókə] *s.* tapioca.
tar [tɑr] *s.* alquitrán, brea, pez (*f.*); *Méx.* chapapote; *v.* alquitranar, embrear, poner brea o alquitrán.
tar·dy [tɑ́rdɪ] *adj.* tardo, tardío; **to be — llegar** tarde (retrasado).
tar·get [tɑ́rgɪt] *s.* blanco; **— practice** tiro al blanco.
tar·iff [tǽrɪf] *s.* tarifa; arancel, impuesto.
tar·nish [tɑ́rnɪʃ] *v.* empañar(se); manchar; perder el lustre; *s.* deslustre, falta de lustre, empañamiento; mancha.
tar·ry [tǽrɪ] *v.* demorarse, tardar(se).
tart [tɑrt] *adj.* acre, agridulce; agrio; picante; **— reply** respuesta mordaz o agria; *s.* tarta, torta rellena con dulce de frutas.
tar·tar [tɑ́rtɚ] *s.* tártaro.
task [tæsk] *s.* faena, tarea, quehacer; **to take to —** reprender, regañar.

task force [tǽskfɔrs] *s.* Comisión de investigación para misión especial.
tas·sel [tǽsl] *s.* borla.
taste [test] *v.* gustar; probar; saborear, paladear; **to — of onion** saber a cebolla; **it -s sour** sabe agrio, tiene un sabor o gusto agrio; *s.* gusto; sabor; prueba, afición; **after —** dejo; **in good —** de buen gusto; **to take a — of** probar.
taste·less [téstlɪs] *adj.* insípido; desabrido; de mal gusto.
tast·y [téstɪ] *adj.* sabroso, gustoso; de buen gusto.
tat·ter [tǽtɚ] *s.* harapo, *Carib.* hilacho.
tat·ter·ed [tǽtɚd] *adj.* roto, harapiento, andrajoso.
tat·tle [tǽtl] *v.* chismear, murmurar; *s.* habladuría, murmuración, hablilla; **— tale** chismoso, soplón.
tat·too [tǽtú] *s.* tatuaje; *v.* tatuar.
taught [tɔt] *pret. & p.p. de* **to teach.**
taunt [tɔnt] *v.* mofarse de, echar pullas; reprochar; *s.* mofa, pulla.
tav·ern [tǽvén] *s.* taberna; posada.
tax [tæks] *s.* impuesto, contribución; esfuerzo; *v.* imponer contribuciones a; (*impose*) tasar; (*burden*) abrumar; reprender, reprobar; (*collect*) cobrar; **to — one's patience** abusar de la paciencia; **taxable funds** fondos gravables.
tax·a·tion [tæksé∫ən] *s.* impuestos, contribuciones; imposición de contribuciones.
tax·i [tǽksɪ] *s.* taxímetro, taxi, automóvil de alquiler; *v.* ir en taxímetro; taxear (*un aeroplano*).
tax·i·cab [tǽksɪkæb] = **taxi.**
tax·i·der·my [tǽksɪdɚmɪ] *s.* taxidermia.
tax·on·o·my [tæksánəmɪ] *s.* taxonomía.
tax·pay·er [tǽkspeɚ] *s.* contribuyente; *Méx.* causante de impuestos.
tea [ti] *s.* té; **linden —** tila.
teach [titʃ] *v.* enseñar; instruir.
teach·er [títʃɚ] *s.* maestro, maestra.
teach·ing [títʃɪŋ] *s.* enseñanza; instrucción; doctrina.
tea·cup [tíkʌp] *s.* taza para té.
tea·ket·tle [tíketl] *s.* marmita, tetera, *Ríopl.* pava (*para el mate*).
team [tim] *s.* equipo (*de jugadores*); partido, grupo; tronco (*de caballos, mulas, etc.*); (*yoke*) yunta (*de bueyes*): **— work** cooperación; trabajo aunado; *v.* uncir, enganchar; formar pareja; acarrear, transportar; **to — up** unirse, formar un equipo.
team·ster [tímstɚ] *s.* carretero.
tea·pot [típɑt] *s.* tetera.
tear [tɪr] *s.* lágrima; · **gas** gas lacrimógeno o lacrimante; **to burst into -s** romper a llorar; deshacerse en lágrimas.
tear [tɛr] *v.* rasgar(se); desgarrar, romper; **to — along** ir a toda velocidad; andar aprisa, correr; **to — apart** desarmar, desmontar; separar, apartar; **to — away** arrancar; irse; **to — down** demoler, derribar (*un edificio*); desarmar, desmontar (*una máquina*); **to — off in a hurry** salir corriendo, salir a la carrera; **to — one's hair** mesarse los cabellos; *s.* desgarradura, rasgadura; rasgón, rotura; prisa; **wear and —** desgaste.
tear·ful [tírfəl] *adj.* lloroso.
tease [tiz] *v.* embromar; molestar; importunar.
tea·spoon [tíspun] *s.* cucharilla, cucharita.
tea·spoon·ful [tíspunful] *s.* cucharadita.
teat [tit] *s.* teta.
tech·ne·ti·um [tɛkní∫əm] *s.* tecnecio.
tech·ni·cal [tɛ́knɪkl] *adj.* técnico.
tech·ni·cian [tɛknf∫ən] *s.* técnico.
tech·nique [tɛkník] *s.* técnica.
tech·nol·o·gy [tɛknálədʒɪ] *s.* tecnología.
te·di·ous [tídɪəs] *adj* tedioso, pesado, aburrido,

SY

fastidioso.

te·di·ous·ness [tídɪəsnɪs] s. tedio.

teem [tim] v. **to — with** abundar en, estar lleno de.

teen·ag·er [tínedʒɚ] s. joven de le edad de 13 a 19 años; *Col.* cocacolo.

teens [tinz] s. pl. edad de trece a diecinueve años; números de trece a diecinueve; **to be in one's —** tener de trece a diecinueve años.

teeth [tiθ] s. pl. de **tooth; he escaped by the skin of his —** por poco no se escapa, se escapó por milagro.

tele·cast [tɛ́ləkæst] s. teledifusión.

tele·com·mu·ni·ca·tion [tɛlɪkəmjunɪkéʃən] s. telecomunicación.

tele·gram [tɛ́ləgræm] s. telegrama.

tele·graph [tɛ́ləgræf] s. telégrafo; v. telegrafiar.

tele·graph·ic [tɛləgræfɪk] adj. telegráfico.

te·leg·ra·phy [təlégrəfɪ] s. telegrafía.

te·lep·a·thy [təlɛ́pəθɪ] s. telepatía.

tele·phone [tɛ́ləfon] s. teléfono; **— booth** casilla de teléfono; **— operator** telefonista; **— receiver** receptor telefónico; v. telefonear, llamar por teléfono.

tele·scope [tɛ́ləskop] s. telescopio; v. enchufar(se), encajar(se) un objeto en otro.

Tele·type [tɛ́lətɑɪp] s. teletipo.

tele·vi·sion [tɛ́ləvɪʒən] s. televisión; **— viewer** televidente.

tell [tɛl] v. (recount) decir; contar; expresar; explicar; (identify) adivinar; **to — on someone** delatar a alguien, contar chismes de alguien; **to — someone off** decirle a alguien cuatro verdades; **his age is beginning to —** ya comienza a notársele la edad.

tell·er [tɛ́lɚ] s. narrador, relator; (bank) pagador o recibidor (de un banco); escrutador de votos.

tel·lu·ri·um [təlúrɪəm] s. telurio.

te·mer·i·ty [təmɛ́rətɪ] s. temeridad.

tem·per [tempɚ] v. templar; s. temple (de un metal); genio, temple, humor; mal genio; **to keep one's —** contenerse, dominarse; **to lose one's —** perder la calma, encolerizarse.

tem·per·a·ment [tɛ́mprəmənt] s. temperamento; disposición; temple.

tem·per·ance [tɛ́mprəns] s. templanza, sobriedad.

tem·per·ate [tɛ́mprɪt] adj. templado, moderado; sobrio.

tem·per·a·ture [tɛ́mprətʃɚ] s. temperatura; **to have a —** tener calentura o fiebre.

tem·pest [tɛ́mpɪst] s. tempestad.

tem·pes·tu·ous [tɛmpɛstʃuəs] adj. tempestuoso, borrascoso.

tem·ple [tɛ́mpl] s. templo; sien.

tem·po·ral [tɛ́mpərəl] adj. temporal.

tem·po·rar·i·ly [tɛ́mpərɛrəlɪ] adv. temporalmente.

tem·po·rar·y [tɛ́mpərɛrɪ] adj. temporal, transitorio; provisorio; provisional; interino.

tempt [tɛmpt] v. tentar; incitar; provocar; atraer.

temp·ta·tion [tɛmptéʃən] s. tentación.

tempt·er [tɛ́mptɚ] s. tentador.

tempt·ing [tɛ́mptɪŋ] adj. tentador, atractivo.

ten [tɛn] num. diez.

ten·a·ble [tɛ́nəbl] adj. defendible.

te·na·cious [tɪnéʃəs] adj. tenaz, aferrado.

te·nac·i·ty [tɪnǽsətɪ] s. tenacidad; aferramiento; tesón.

ten·ant [tɛ́nənt] s. inquilino, arrendatario.

tend [tɛnd] v. (care for) cuidar, vigilar, guardar; atender; (lean toward) tender, inclinarse.

ten·den·cy [tɛ́ndənsɪ] s. tendencia; propensión.

ten·der [tɛ́ndɚ] adj. tierno; delicado; (sensitive) sensible; **tender-hearted** de corazón tierno; s.

oferta, ofrecimiento; ténder (de un tren); lancha (de auxilio); cuidador, vigilante; **legal —** moneda corriente; v. ofrecer.

ten·der·loin [tɛ́ndɚlɔɪn] s. filete; filet mignon.

ten·der·ness [tɛ́ndɚnɪs] s. ternura, terneza; delicadeza.

ten·don [tɛ́ndən] s. tendón.

ten·dril [tɛ́ndrɪl] s. zarcillo (tallito de una planta trepadora).

ten·e·ment [tɛ́nəmənt] s. casa de vecindad.

ten·nis [tɛ́nɪs] s. tenis; **— court** cancha de tenis.

ten·or [tɛ́nɚ] s. (voice) tenor; (meaning) significado; **— voice** voz de tenor.

tense [tɛns] adj. tenso; tirante; s. tiempo (del verbo).

ten·sion [tɛ́nʃən] s. tensión; tirantez.

tent [tɛnt] s. tienda de campaña; pabellón; v. acampar.

ten·ta·cle [tɛ́ntəkl] s. tentáculo.

ten·ta·tive [tɛ́ntətɪv] adj. tentativo.

ten·u·ous [tɛ́njuəs] adj. tenue.

ten·ure [tɛ́njʊr] s. tenencia.

tep·id [tɛ́pɪd] adj. tibio.

term [tɝm] s. (word) término; (period) período; plazo; sesión; **-s** términos, expresiones, palabras; condiciónes; **to be on good -s** estar en buenas relaciones; **not to be on speaking -s** no hablarse, no dirigirse la palabra; **to come to -s** ajustarse, ponerse de acuerdo; v. nombrar, llamar, denominar.

ter·mi·na·ble [tɝmɪnəbl] adj. terminable.

ter·mi·nal [tɝmənl] adj. terminal, final, último; s. término, fin; estación terminal; **electric —** toma de corriente; borne (de aparato eléctrico).

ter·mi·nate [tɝmənet] v. terminar, acabar.

ter·mi·na·tion [tɝmənéʃən] s. terminación, fin; desinencia (gramatical).

ter·mite [tɝmaɪt] s. termita.

ter·race [tɛ́rɪs] s. terraplén; terraza, terrado; v. terraplenar.

ter·res·tri·al [tərɛ́strɪəl] adj. terrestre, terreno; terrenal.

ter·ri·ble [tɛ́rəbl] adj. terrible; **terribly** adv. terriblemente.

ter·ri·er [tɛ́rɪɚ] s. perro de busca.

ter·rif·ic [tərɪ́fɪk] adj. terrífico.

ter·ri·fy [tɛ́rəfaɪ] v. aterrar, aterrorizar.

ter·ri·to·ry [tɛ́rətorɪ] s. territorio.

ter·ror [tɛ́rɚ] s. terror, espanto.

ter·ror·ist [tɛ́rərɪst] s. terrorista.

test [tɛst] s. prueba, ensayo, experimento; comprobación; examen; **— tube** probeta, tubo de ensayo; **to undergo a —** sufrir una prueba; v. probar, ensayar, comprobar, experimentar; poner a prueba; examinar.

tes·ta·ment [tɛ́stəmənt] s. testamento.

tes·ti·cle [tɛ́stɪkl] s. testículo.

tes·ti·fy [tɛ́stəfaɪ] v. atestiguar, atestar.

tes·ti·mo·ny [tɛ́stəmonɪ] s. testimonio.

tet·a·nus [tɛ́tənəs] s. tétanos.

Teu·ton·ic [tutánɪk] adj. teutónico.

text [tɛkst] s. texto; **— editing** (computer) edición de texto.

text·book [tɛ́kstbʊk] s. texto, libro de texto.

tex·tile [tɛ́kstl] adj. textil; de tejidos; **— mill** fábrica de tejidos; 's. tejido, materia textil.

tex·ture [tɛ́kstʃɚ] s. textura, contextura; tejido.

thal·li·um [θǽlɪəm] s. talio.

than [ðæn] conj. que; **more — once** más de una vez; **more — he knows** más de lo que él sabe.

thank [θæŋk] v. dar gracias, agradecer; **— heaven!** ¡gracias a Dios!; **— you** gracias; **to have oneself**

to — **for** tener la culpa de; ser responsable de; **-s** *s. pl.* gracias.

thank·ful [θǽŋkfəl] *adj.* agradecido; **-ly** *adv.* agradecidamente, con agradecimiento, con gratitud.

thank·ful·ness [θǽŋkfəlnɪs] *s.* gratitud, agradecimiento.

thank·less [θǽŋklɪs] *adj.* ingrato; — **task** tarea ingrata o infructuosa.

thanks·giv·ing [θæŋksgívɪŋ] *s.* acción de gracias; **Thanksgiving Day** día de acción de gracias.

that [ðæt] *adj.* ese, esa, aquel, aquella; — **one** ése, ésa, aquél, aquélla; *pron.* ése, eso, aquél, aquélla, aquello; *pron. rel.* que; — **is** es decir; — **of** el de, la de, lo de; — **which** el que, la que, lo que; *conj.* que; para que, a fin de que; **so** — para que; de modo que, a fin de que, de suerte que, de tal manera que; *adv.* tan; — **far** tan lejos; hasta allí; hasta allí; — **long** así de largo; de este tamaño; tanto tiempo.

thatch [θætʃ] *s.* paja (*para techar*); *v.* techar con paja; **-ed roof** techumbre o techo de paja.

thaw [θɔ] *v.* deshelar(se), derretir(se); volverse más tratable o amistoso; *s.* deshielo, derretimiento.

the [*delante de consonante* ðə; *delante de vocal* ðɪ] *art.* el, la; lo; los, las; *adv.* — **more** . . . — **less** cuanto más . . . tanto menos; mientras más . . . tanto menos.

the·a·ter [θíətɚ] *s.* teatro.

the·at·ri·cal [θɪǽtrɪkl] *adj.* teatral.

thee [ði] *pron.* te.

theft [θɛft] *s.* hurto, robo.

their [ðɛr] *adj.* su (sus), de ellos, de ellas.

theirs [ðɛrz] *pron. pos.* suyo (suya, suyos, suyas), de ellos, de ellas; el suyo (la suya, los suyos, las suyas); el (la, los, las) de ellos; **a friend of** — un amigo suyo, un amigo de ellos.

them [ðɛm] *pron.* los, las; les; ellos, ellas (*con preposición*).

the·mat·ic [θimǽtɪk] *adj.* temático.

theme [θim] *s.* tema; ensayo; — **song** tema central.

them·selves [ðəmsɛ́lvz] *pron.* ellos mismos, ellas mismas; se (*como reflexivo*); **to** — a sí mismos; *véase* **herself.**

then [ðɛn] *adv.* entonces; en aquel tiempo; en aquella ocasión; (*after*) después, luego, en seguida; *conj.* pues, en tal caso; **now** — ahora bien; **now and** — de vez en cuando, de cuando en cuando; **now** . . . — ora . . . ora; ya . . . ya; **well** — conque, pues entonces; ahora bien.

thence [ðɛns] *adv.* desde allí; de allí; desde entonces; desde aquel tiempo; por eso, por esa razón; — **forth** de allí en adelante, desde entonces.

the·o·log·i·cal [θiəládʒɪkl] *adj.* teológico; teologal.

the·ol·o·gy [θiáIədʒɪ] *s.* teología.

the·o·ret·i·cal [θiərɛ́tɪll] *adj.* teórico.

the·o·ry [θíərɪ] *s.* teoría.

ther·a·peu·tic [θɛrəpjútɪk] *adj.* terapéutico.

ther·a·py [θɛ́rəpɪ] *s.* terapia.

there [ðɛr] *adv.* allí, allá, ahí; — **is,** — **are** hay; — **followed an argument** siguió una disputa.

there·a·bouts [ðɛrəbáʊts] *adv.* por allí, por ahí; aproximadamente.

there·after [ðɛræftɚ] *adv.* después de eso, de allí en adelante.

there·by [ðɛrbáɪ] *adv.* en relación con eso; así, de ese modo; por allí cerca.

there·fore [ðɛ́rfor] *adv.* por eso, por consiguiente, por lo tanto.

there·in [ðɛrín] *adv.* en eso, en ello; allí dentro.

there·of [ðɛráv] *adv.* de eso, de ello.

there·on [ðɛrán] *adv.* encima; encima de (*o sobre*)

él, ella, ello, etc.

there·up·on [ðɛrəpán] *adv.* luego, después, en eso, en esto; por consiguiente, por eso, por lo tanto.

there·with [ðɛrwíθ] *adv.* con eso, con ello, con esto; luego, en seguida.

ther·mal [θɚ·ml] *adj.* termal.

ther·mom·e·ter [θɚ·mámətɚ] *s.* termómetro.

ther·mo·nu·cle·ar [θɚ·monúkljɚ] *adj.* termonuclear.

ther·mos [θɚ́·məs] (*marca de fábrica*); — **bottle** termos.

ther·mo·stat [θɚ́·məstæt] *s.* termóstato.

these [ðiz] *adj.* estos, estas; *pron.* éstos, éstas.

the·sis [θísɪs] *s.* tesis.

they [ðe] *pron.* ellos, ellas.

thick [θɪk] *adj.* (*not thin*) espeso; grueso; (*dense*) denso; tupido; (*slow*) torpe, estúpido; — **voice** voz ronca; **one inch** — una pulgada de espesor; *adv.* véase **thickly; thick-headed** cabezudo; testarudo; estúpido; **thick-set** grueso, rechoncho; **thick-skinned** insensible; que no se avergüenza fácilmente; *s.* espesor; densidad, lo más denso; the — **of the crowd** lo más denso de la muchedumbre; **the** — **of the fight** lo más reñido del combate; **through** — **and thin** por toda suerte de penalidades.

thick·en [θíkən] *v.* espesar(se); engrosar; **the plot -s** se complica el enredo.

thick·et [θíkɪt] *s.* espesura, maleza, matorral, *Carib., Col., Ríopl.* manigua.

thick·ly [θíklɪ] *adv.* espesamente; densamente.

thick·ness [θíknɪs] *s.* espesor; espesura, grueso, grosor; densidad.

thief [θif] *s.* ladrón.

thieve [θiv] *v.* hurtar, robar.

thieves [θivz] *pl. de* **thief.**

thigh [θaɪ] *s.* muslo.

thim·ble [θímbl] *s.* dedal.

thin [θɪn] *adj.* (*slim*) delgado; flaco; (*sparse*) ralo; escaso; (*fine*) tenue, fino; transparente; (*weak*) débil; aguado; — **broth** caldo aguado; — **hair** pelo ralo; *v.* adelgazar(se); enflaquecer; aguar (*el caldo*); **to** — **out** ralear (*el pelo*); ralear o aclarar (*un bosque*).

thine [ðaɪn] *pron. pos.* tuyo (tuya, tuyos, tuyas); el tuyo (la tuya, los tuyos, las tuyas); *adj.* tu, tus.

thing [θɪŋ] *s.* cosa; **no such** — nada de eso; **that is the** — **to do** eso es lo que debe hacerse; eso es lo debido.

think [θɪŋk] *v.* (*cerebrate*) pensar; (*believe*) creer, juzgar; opinar; **to** — **it over** pensarlo; **to** — **of** pensar en; pensar de; **to** — **up an excuse** urdir una excusa; **to** — **well of** tener buena opinión de; — **nothing of it** no haga Vd. caso de ello, no le dé Vd. importancia; **what do you** — **of her?** ¿ qué piensa Vd. de ella?; **to my way of -ing** a mi modo de ver.

think·er [θíŋkɚ] *s.* pensador.

thin·ly [θínlɪ] *adv.* delgadamente; escasamente.

thinness [θínnɪs] *s.* delgadez; flacura; (*hair*) raleza (*del cabello*); (*rarity*) enrarecimiento (*del aire*).

third [θɚ·d] *adj.* tercero; *s.* tercio, tercera parte.

thirst [θɚ·st] *s.* sed; anhelo, ansia; *v.* tener sed; **to** — **for** tener sed de; anhelar, ansiar.

thirst·y [θɚ́·stɪ] *adj.* sediento; **to be** — tener sed.

thir·teen [θɚ·tín] *num.* trece.

thir·ty [θɚ́·tɪ] *num.* treinta.

this [ðɪs] *adj.* este, esta; *pron.* éste, ésto.

this·tle [θísl] *s.* abrojo; cardo.

thith·er [θíðɚ] *adv.* allá, hacia allá, para allá.

tho [ðo] = **though.**

thong [θɔŋ] *s.* correa, tira de cuero, *Am.* guasca.

TE

tho·rax [θóræks] *s.* tórax.

thorn [θɔrn] *s.* espina, púa; espino; abrojo.

thorn·y [θɔ́rnɪ] *adj.* espinosa; arduo, difícil.

thor·ough [θɝ́·o] *adj.* (*finished*) completo, entero, cabal, cumplido, acabado; (*careful*) esmerado.

thor·ough·bred [θɝ́·obrɛd] *adj.* de casta pura, de raza pura; bien nacido; *s.* animal o persona de casta; caballo de casta.

thor·ough·fare [θɝ́·ofɛr] *s.* vía pública, carretera, camino real; pasaje.

thor·ough·ly [θɝ́·olɪ] *adj.* completamente, enteramente, cabalmente; a fondo.

those [ðoz] *adj.* esos, esas, aquellos, aquellas; *pron.* ésos, ésas, aquéllos, aquéllas; — **of** los de, las de; — **which** los que, las que; aquellos que; — **who** los que, las que, quienes.

thou [ðaʊ] *pron.* tú.

though [ðo] *conj.* aunque, si bien, bien que; aun cuando; sin embargo; **as** — como si.

thought [θɔt] *s.* (*cogitation*) pensamiento; (*idea*) idea, intención; reflexión, meditación; (*concern*) consideracion; cuidado; **to be lost in** — estar abstraído; **to give it no** — no pensar en ello, no darle importancia, no hacerle caso; *pret. & p.p. de* **to think.**

thought·ful [θɔ́tfəl] *adj.* pensativo; (*attentive*) considerado; atento, solícito, cuidadoso; **to be** — **of others** pensar en los demás, tener consideración o solicitud por las demás; **-ly** *adv.* con reflexión; consideradamente, con consideración; con solicitud.

thought·ful·ness [θɔ́tfəlnɪs] *s.* consideración, atención, cuidado, solicitud.

thought·less [θɔ́tlɪs] *adj.* inconsiderado; descuidado; irreflexivo, atolondrado; **-ly** *adv.* inconsideradamente, sin consideración; sin reflexión; sin pensar; descuidadamente, irreflexivamente, atolondradamente.

thought·less·ness [θɔ́tlɪsnɪs] *s.* irreflexión, inadvertencia, descuido; atolondramiento.

thou·sand [θáʊzənd] *num.* mil.

thrash [θræʃ] *v.* trillar, desgranar (*las mieses*); zurrar, azotar; **to** — **around** revolcarse, agitarse, menearse; **to** — **out a matter** ventilar un asunto.

thread [θrɛd] *s.* hilo; hebra, fibra; **screw** — rosca de tornillo; *v.* ensartar, enhebrar; **to** — **a screw** roscar un tornillo; **to** — **one's way through a crowd** colarse por entre la muchedumbre.

thread·bare [θrɛ́dbɛr] *adj.* raído, gastado.

threat [θrɛt] *s.* amenaza; amago.

threat·en [θrɛ́tn̩] *v.* amenazar; amagar.

threat·en·ing [θrɛ́tnɪŋ] *adj.* amenazante, amenazador.

three [θri] *num.* tres.

thresh [θrɛ] *véase* **thrash.**

thresh·old [θrɛ́ʃold] *s.* umbral, entrada.

threw [θru] *pret. de* **to throw.**

thrice [θraɪs] *adv.* tres veces.

thrift [θrɪft] *s.* economía, frugalidad.

thrift·y [θrɪ́ftɪ] *adj.* económico, frugal; próspero.

thrill [θrɪl] *v.* emocionar(se), conmover(se); estremecerse de emoción, sobreexcitarse; *s.* emoción viva, estremecimiento emotivo, sobreexcitación.

thrive [θraɪv] *v.* medrar, prosperar; florecer.

thriv·en [θrɪ́vən] *p.p. de* **to thrive.**

throat [θrot] *s.* garganta.

throb [θrab] *v.* latir, pulsar, palpitar; *s.* latido, palpitación.

throe [θro] *s.* agonía; congoja.

throne [θron] *s.* trono.

throng [θrɔŋ] *s.* muchedumbre, multitud, tropel,

gentío; *v.* agolparse, apiñarse; atestar.

throt·tle [θrátl̩] *s.* válvula reguladora, obturador, regulador; — **lever** palanca del obturador o regulador; *v.* ahogar; estrangular; **to** — **down** disminuir o reducir la velocidad.

through [θru] *prep.* por; a través de; (*agent*) por medio de; por conducto de; por entre; *adv.* (*complete*) de un lado a otro; de parte a parte, a través; de cabo a cabo; desde el principio hasta el fin; completamente, enteramente; **loyal** — **and** — leal a toda prueba; **to be wet** — estar empapado; estar mojado hasta los tuétanos; **to carry a plan** — llevar a cabo un plan; *adj.* directo, continuo; — **ticket** billete (*Am.* boleto) directo; — **train** tren rápido, tren de servicio directo; **to be** — **with** haber acabado con; no querer ocuparse más de.

through·out [θruáʊt] *prep.* (*all through*) por todo; por todas partes de; (*during*) desde el principio; hasta el fin de; — **the year** durante todo el año; *adv.* por todas partes; en todas partes; en todo, en todos respetos; desde el principio hasta el fin.

throve [θrov] *pret. de* **to thrive.**

throw [θro] *v.* tirar, arrojar, lanzar; echar; **to** — **away** tirar, arrojar; malgastar; **to** — **down** arrojar, echar por tierra, derribar; **to** — **in gear** engranar; **to** — **in the clutch** embragar; **to** — **off a burden** librarse o deshacerse de una carga; **to** — **out** echar fuera; expeler; **to** — **out of gear** desengranar; **to** — **out of work** privar de trabajo, quitar el empleo a; **to** — **out the clutch** desembragar; **to** — **overboard** echar al agua; **to** — **up** vomitar; *s.* tiro, tirada.

thrown [θron] *p.p. de* **to throw.**

thrush [θrʌl] *s.* tordo, zorzal.

thrust [θrʌst] *v.* (*push into*) meter; hincar, clavar; encajar; (*shove*) empujar; **to** — **a task upon someone** imponer una tarea a una persona, obligar a alguien a desempeñar un quehacer; **to** — **aside** echar o empujar a un lado; rechazar; **to** — **in** (*o* **into**) meter en, encafar en, intercalar en; **to** — **out** sacar; echar fuera; **to** — **someone through with a sword** atravesar a alguien de parte a parte con la espada; *pret. & p.p. de* **to thrust**; *s.* estocada, cuchillada, puñalada, lanzada; empuje, empujón o empellón; arremetida, acometida.

thud [θʌd] *s.* porrazo, golpazo, golpe sordo.

thug [θʌg] *s.* ladrón, salteador.

thumb [θʌm] *s.* pulgar; **under the** — **of** bajo el poder o influencia de; *v.* hojear (*con el pulgar*).

thumb·tack [θʌ́mtæk] *s.* chinche.

thump [θʌmp] *s.* golpazo, porrazo, trastazo; golpe sordo; *v.* golpear, golpetear, aporrear, dar un porrazo.

thun·der [θʌ́ndɚ] *s.* trueno; tronido; estruendo; *v.* tronar.

thun·der·bolt [θʌ́ndɚbolt] *s.* rayo.

thun·der·ing [θʌ́ndɚɪŋ] *adj.* atronador.

thun·der·ous [θʌ́ndərəs] *adj.* atronador, estruendoso.

thun·der·storm [θʌ́ndɚstɔrm] *s.* tronada, tormenta o tempestad de truenos.

Thurs·day [θɝ́·zdɪ] *s.* jueves.

thus [θʌs] *adv.* así; — **far** hasta aquí, hasta ahora, hasta hoy.

thwart [θwɔrt] *v.* frustrar; estorbar; impedir.

thy [ðaɪ] *adj.* tu, tus.

thyme [taɪm] *s.* tomillo.

thy·roid [θáɪɔɪd] *s.* tiroides.

thy·self [ðaɪsélf] *pron.* tú mismo; a tí mismo; te (*como reflexivo*); *véase* **herself.**

tick [tɪk] tic tac; funda (*de colchón o almohada*); garrapata (*insecto parásito*); *v.* hacer tic tac (*como* *un reloj*); latir (*el corazón*); **to — off** marcar.

tic·ket [tíkɪt] *s.* billete, *Méx., Ch.,* boleto; *C.A., Col.* tiquete; lista de candidatos (*de un partido*); balota (*para votar*); — **office** taquilla; despacho de boletos, *Ec., Peru* boletería.

tick·le [tíkl] *v.* (*touch*) cosquillear, hacer cosquillas; (*feel*) sentir o tener cosquillas; (*please*) halagar, gustarle a uno; **to be -d to death** morirse de gusto, estar muy contento; *s.* cosquilleo, cosquillas.

tick·lish [tíklɪʃ] *adj.* cosquilloso; delicado, arriesgado, difícil.

tid·bit [tídbɪt] *s.* bocado, bocadito, golosina.

tide [taɪd] *s.* marea; corriente; **Christmas —** navidades, temporada de navidad; *v.* **to — someone over a difficulty** ayudar a alguien durante una crisis o dificultad.

tide·wa·ter [táɪdwɔtɚ] *adj.* costanero.

tid·ings [táɪdɪŋz] *s. pl.* noticias, nuevas.

ti·dy [táɪdɪ] *adj.* aseado, limpio, ordenado; **a — sum** una suma considerable; *v.* asear, arreglar, poner en orden; **to — oneself up** asearse.

tie [taɪ] *v.* (*fasten*) atar, liar, ligar; *Am.* amarrar; (*unite*) enlazar, vincular; (*equal*) empatar (*en juegos, etc.*); **to — tight** amarrar bien, apretar fuerte; **to — up the traffic** obstruir el tráfico; *s.* paralización; lazo, ligadura, atadura; enlace, vínculo; corbata; empate (*en carreras, juegos, etc.*); **railway —** traviesa, *Andes, C.A., Méx.* durmiente; *Ríopl., Ch.* travesaño.

tier [tɪr] *s.* fila, hilera, ringlera.

ti·ger [táɪgɚ] *s.* tigre; — **cat** gato montés.

tight [taɪt] *adj.* (*squeezed*) apretado, ajustado, estrecho; (*sealed*) hermético; (*firm*) firme, tieso; (*stingy*) tacaño, mezquino; (*drunk*) borracho; **to be in a — spot** estar en un aprieto; **to close —** apretar, cerrar herméticamente; **to hold on —** agarrarse bien; **it fits —** está muy estrecho o ajustado.

tight·en [táɪtn̩] *v.* apretar; estrechar; estirar, poner tirante.

tight·ness [táɪtnɪs] *s.* estrechez; tirantez, tensión; mezquindad, (*stingyness*) tacañería.

tight·wad [táɪtwɑd] *s.* tacaño; cicatero.

ti·gress [táɪgrɪs] *s.* tigre hembra; *Am.* tigra.

tile [taɪl] *s.* teja; baldosa, azulejo; — **roof** tejado; *v.* tejar, cubrir con tejas; cubrir con azulejos, embaldosar.

till [tɪl] *prep.* hasta; *conj.* hasta que; *v.* cultivar, labrar, arar; *s.* gaveta o cajón para el dinero.

till·age [tílədʒ] *s.* labranza, cultivo, labor.

tilt [tɪlt] *s.* ladeo, inclinación; declive; altercación disputa; **at full —** a toda velocidad; *v.* ladear(se), inclinar(se).

tim·ber [tímbɚ] *s.* madera de construcción; maderaje; madero; viga.

time [taɪm] *s.* tiempo; (*hour*) hora; (*occasion*) vez; (*payments*) plazo; **at -s** a veces; **at one and the same —** a la vez; **at this —** ahora, al presente; **behind —** atrasado, retrasado; **from — to —** de vez en cuando; **in —** a tiempo; andando el tiempo; **on —** puntual; con puntualidad; a tiempo; a la hora debida; **several -s** varias veces; **to beat —** marcar el compás; **to buy on —** comprar a plazo; **to have a good —** divertirse, pasar un buen rato; **what — is it?** ¿qué hora es?; *v.* cronometrar, medir el tiempo de; regular, poner en punto (*el reloj, el motor*); escoger el momento oportuno para; — **zone** zona horaria; huso horario.

time·keep·er [táɪmkipɚ] *s.* listero, apuntador; *Ec.* guardatiempo; *Méx.* rayador.

time·less [táɪmlɛs] *adj.* eterno, infinito.

time·ly [táɪmlɪ] *adj.* oportuno.

time·piece [táɪmpis] *s.* reloj; cronómetro.

time·ta·ble [táɪmtebl] *s.* itinerario, horario.

tim·id [tímɪd] *adj.* tímido.

ti·mid·i·ty [tɪmídətɪ] *s.* timidez.

tim·ing [táɪmɪŋ] *s.* medida del tiempo; cronometraje; (*pace*) selección del momento oportuno; sincronización.

tim·or·ous [tímərəs] *adj.* timorato, tímido, miedoso.

tin [tɪn] *s.* estaño; hojalata, lata; cosa de hojalata; — **can** lata; — **foil** hoja de estaño; *v.* estañar, cubrir con estaño; enlatar.

tinc·ture [tíŋktʃɚ] *s.* tintura; tinte; — **of iodine** tintura de yodo; *v.* tinturar, teñir.

tin·der [tíndɚ] *s.* yesca.

tinge [tɪndʒ] *v.* teñir; matizar; *s.* tinte, matiz; dejo, saborcillo.

tin·gle [tíŋgl] *v.* hormiguear, sentir hormigueo; **to — with excitement** estremecerse de entusiasmo; *s.* hormigueo, picazón, comezón.

tin·ker [tíŋkɚ] *v.* ocuparse vanamente.

tin·kle [tíŋkl] *v.* tintinear; hacer retintín; *s.* tintineo, retintín.

tin·sel [tínsl] *s.* oropel; *adj.* de oropel.

tint [tɪnt] *s.* tinte, matiz; *v.* teñir, matizar.

ti·ny [táɪnɪ] *adj.* diminuto, menudo, chiquitico, chiquitín.

tip [tɪp] *s.* (*point*) punta, extremo, extremidad; (*money*) propina; (*hint*) noticia o aviso secreto; *v.* ladear(se), inclinar(se); dar propina (a); **to — a person off** dar aviso secreto a; **to — one's hat** tocarse el sombrero; **to — over** volcar(se), voltear(se).

tip·sy [típsɪ] *adj.* alumbrado, algo borracho; ladeado.

tip·toe [típto] *s.* punta del pie; **on —** de puntillas; *v.* andar de puntillas.

ti·rade [táɪred] *s.* invectiva.

tire [taɪr] *s.* llanta, neumático, goma; **flat —** llanta o goma reventada; *v.* cansar(se), fatigar(se).

tired [taɪrd] *adj.* cansado, fatigado; — **out** extenuado de fatiga, rendido.

tire·less [táɪrlɪs] *adj.* incansable, infatigable.

tire·some [táɪrsəm] *adj.* cansado, aburrido, pesado.

tis·sue [tíʃu] *s.* tejido; — **paper** papel de seda.

ti·tan·ic [taɪtǽnɪk] *adj.* titánico.

ti·ta·ni·um [taɪténɪəm] *s.* titanio.

tithe [taɪð] *s.* diezmo.

ti·tle [táɪtl] *s.* título — **holder** titulado; — **page** portada; — **deed** título de propiedad.

to [tu] *prep.* a; hasta; hacia; para; — **try —** tratar de; esforzarse por; **a quarter — five** las cinco menos cuarto; **bills — be paid** cuentas por pagar; **frightened — death** muerto de susto; **from house — house** de casa en casa; **he has — go** tiene que ir; **near —** cerca de; **not — my knowledge** no que yo sepa; *adv.* — **and fro** de acá para allá; **come —** volver en sí.

toad [tod] *s.* sapo o escuerzo.

toast [tost] *v.* tostar(se); brindar por, beber a la salud de; *s.* tostada; brindis.

toast·er [tóstɚ] *s.* tostador.

to·bac·co [təbǽko] *s.* tabaco.

to·day [tədé] *adv.* hoy; hoy día.

toe [to] *s.* dedo del pie; (*shoe*) punta (*de la media, del zapato, etc.*); *v.* **to — in** andar con la punta de los pies para dentro.

toe·nail [tónel] *s.* uña del dedo del pie.

to·geth·er [təgɛðɚ] *adv.* juntamente; a un mismo tiempo, a la vez; juntos; — **with** junto con; **all —** juntos; en junto; **to call —** convocar; juntar; **to come —** juntarse, unirse; ponerse de acuerdo; **to**

walk — andar juntos.

toil [tɔɪl] v. afanarse, trafagar, atarearse; s. esfuerzo, trabajo, faena, fatiga.

toi·let [tɔ́ɪLɪt] s. retrete, excusado, común, C.A., Col., Ven. inodoro; — **articles** artículos de tocador; — **case** neceser; — **paper** papel de excusado, papel higiénico.

to·ken [tókən] s. señal, símbola; prenda; recuerdo; prueba, muestra; ficha (de metal); — **payment** pago nominal.

told [told] pret. & p.p. de to tell.

tol·er·ance [tálərəns] s. tolerancia.

tol·er·ant [tálərənt] adj. tolerante.

tol·er·ate [ɑ́ləret] v. tolerar.

tol·er·a·tion [taləréʃan] s. tolerancia.

toll [tol] s. doble, tañido (de las companas); peaje; portazgo; — **bridge** puente de peaje; — **gate** barrera de peaje; — **call** llamada por cobrar; — **road** camino de cuota; **to pay** — pagar peaje o portazgo; v. tañer, doblar (las campanas).

to·ma·to [təméto] s. tomate, Méx. jitomate.

tomb [tum] s. tumba.

tomb·stone [túmston] s. lápida sepulcral.

tom·cat [támkœt] s. gato.

tome [tom] s. tomo.

to·mor·row [təmɔ́ro] adv. mañana; — **morning** mañana por la mañana; — **noon** mañana al mediodía; **day after** — pasado mañana.

ton [tʌn] s. tonelada.

tone [ton] s. (pitch) tono; timbre; (sound) sonido; v. dar tono a, modificar el tono de; **to** — **down** bajar de tono; suavizar; **to** — **down one's voice** moderar la voz; **to** — **in well with** armonizar con, entonar bien con; **to** — **up** subir de tono; tonificar, vigorizar.

tongs [tɔŋz] s. pl. tenazas.

tongue [tʌn] s. lengua; idioma; **to be tongue-tied** tener trabada la lengua.

ton·ic [tánɪk] s. & adj. tónico.

to·night [tənáɪt] adv. esta noche, a la noche.

ton·nage [tánɪdʒ] s. tonelaje.

ton·sil [tánsl] s. amígdala.

ton·sil·li·tis [tanslaítɪs] s. amigdalitis.

too [tu] adv. tamíbién; demasiado; — **many** demasiados; — **much** demasiado; **it is** — **bad!** ¡es una lástima!

took [tʊk] pret. de to take.

tool [tul] s. instrumento; herramienta; — **box** caja de herramientas.

toot [tut] v. tocar o sonar la bocina; pitar; tocar (un cuerno, trompa o trompeta); **to** — **one's own horn** alabarse, cantar sus propias alabanzas; s. toque o sonido (de bocina, trompeta, etc.); silbido, pitido; pitazo (de locomotora).

tooth [tuθ] s. diente; muela; — **mark** dentellada; **to fight** — **and nail** luchar a brazo partido; **to have a sweet** — ser amigo de golosinas.

tooth·ache [túθek] s. dolor de muelas.

tooth·brush [túθbrʌʃ] s. cepillo de dientes.

toothed [tuθt] adj. dentado.

tooth·less [túθlɪs] adj. desdentado.

tooth·paste [túθpest] s. pasta para los dientes, pasta dentífrica.

tooth·pick [túθpɪk] s. mondadientes, palillo de dientes.

top [tap] s. (peak) cumbre, cima; cúspida; tope; pináculo; remate; cabeza; (surface) superficie; copa (de árbol); (cover) tapa, cubierta, (toy) trompo; peonza; **at the** — **of his class** a la cabeza de su clase; **at the** — **of one's voice** a voz en cuello; **filled up to the** — lleno hasta el tope; **from** — **to**

bottom de arriba abajo; **from** — **to toe** de pies a cabeza; **on** — **of** encima de, sobre; adj. superior; más alto; — **coat** abrigo, sobretodo; **at** — **speed** a velocidad máxima; v. coronar; exceder; sobresalir, sobrepujar; rematar; **to** — **off** rematar; terminar.

top·flight [tapfláɪt] adj. destacado, sobresaliente.

to·paz [tópæz] s. topacio.

top·er [tópɚ] s. bebedor, borrachín.

top·heav·y [taphévɪ] adj. más pesado arriba que abajo.

top·ic [tápɪk] s. tema, asunto, materia, tópico.

top·most [tápmost] adj. más alto; superior.

to·pog·ra·phy [təpágrəfɪ] s. topografía.

to·pon·y·my [təpánəmɪ] s. toponimia.

top·ple [tápl] v. echar abajo, derribar; volcar; **to** — **over** venirse abajo; volcarse.

top·sy-tur·vy [tápsɪtɜ́vɪ] adj. & adv. patas arriba; en confusión; trastornado; enrevesado, al revés.

torch [tɔrtʃ] s. antorcha; **blow** — soplete.

tore [tor] pret. de to tear.

tor·ment [tɔ́rmɛnt] s. tormento; [tɔrmɛnt] v. atormentar; afligir.

torn [torn] p.p. de to tear roto, rompido, rasgado.

tor·na·do [tɔrnédo] s. tornado.

tor·pe·do [tɔrpído] s. torpedo; — **boat** torpedero; v. torpedear.

torque [tɔrk] s. fuerza rotatoria.

tor·rent [tɔ́rənt] s. torrente.

tor·rid [tɔ́rɪd] adj. tórrido.

tor·sion [tɔ́rʃən] s. torsión.

tor·toise [tɔ́rtəs] s. tortuga.

tor·tu·ous [tɔ́rtʃʊəs] adj. tortuoso.

tor·ture [tɔ́rtʃɚ] s. tortura, tormento; v. torturar, atormentar.

toss [tɔs] v. tirar, echar, arrojar, lanzar; menear(se); cabecear (un buque); **to** — **aside** echar a un lado; desechar; **to** — **up** echar para arriba; aventar; s. tiro, tirada; meneo, sacudida.

tot [tat] s. chiquitín, chiquitina, chiquitico, chiquitica, niñito, niñita, nene, nena.

to·tal [tótl] adj. s. total.

to·tal·i·tar·i·an [totælətɛ́rɪən] adj. totalitario.

tot·ter [tátɚ] v. tambalear(se), bambolear(se); estar para desplomarse.

touch [tʌtʃ] v. tocar; palpar, tentar; conmover, enternecer; compararse con, igualar; **to** — **at a port** hacer escala en un puerto; **to** — **off an explosive** prender la mecha de un explosivo; **to** — **up** retocar; s. toque; tacto, sentido del tacto; tiento; — **stone** piedra de toque; — **tablet** (computer) trazador gráfico; **a** — **of fever** algo de calentura; **to keep in** — **with** mantener(se) en comunicación con.

touch-and-go [tʌ́tʃəndgó] adj. arriesgado.

touch·ing [tʌ́tʃɪŋ] adj. conmovedor, enternecedor.

touch·y [tʌ́tʃɪ] adj. quisquilloso, susceptible, sensible, sensitivo.

tough [tʌf] adj. correoso; fuerte; firme; duro; (difficult) arduo, difícil; (stubborn) terco; (bad) empedernido, malvado.

tough·en [tʌ́fn̩] v. curtir(se); endurecer(se), empedernir(se); hacer(se) correoso.

tough·ness [tʌ́fnɪs] s. dureza; correosidad; flexibilidad; tenacidad; resistencia; dificultad.

tou·pee [tupé] s. peluca.

tour [tʊr] s. viaje, excursión; vuelta; jira; v. viajar por; recorrer; hacer una jira; hacer un viaje de turismo.

tour·ism [tʊ́rɪzəm] s. turismo.

tour·ist [tʊ́rɪst] s. turista.

tour·na·ment [tɜ́nəmənt] s. torneo; certamen,

concurso.

tow [to] *v.* remolcar; *s.* remolque; — **boat** remolcador; — **truck** remolcador; — **rope** cuerda de remolque; **to take in** — remolcar, llevar a remolque.

to·ward [tord] *prep.* hacia; rumbo a; alrededor de; para, para con; — **four o'clock** a eso de las cuatro.

to·wards [tordz] = **toward.**

tow·el [taʊl] *s.* toalla.

tow·er [táʊɚ] *s.* torre; torreón; **bell** — campanario; *v.* sobresalir, sobrepujar; destacarse, descollar; elevarse.

tow·er·ing [táʊrɪŋ] *adj.* encumbrado; elevado, muy alto; sobresaliente.

town [taʊn] *s.* (*center*) población, ciudad, pueblo, aldea; (*administration*) municipio; — **hall** ayuntamiento.

town·ship [táʊnʃɪp] *s.* unidad primaria de gobierno local; sección de seis millas cuadradas (*en terrenos públicos*).

tox·in [táksɪn] *s.* toxina.

toy [tɔɪ] *s.* juguete; *adj.* de juego, de juguete; pequeñito; *v.* jugar, juguetear.

trace [tres] *s.* señal, indicio, vestigio; huella, rastro; tirante (*de una guarnición*); *v.* trazar; calcar; rastrear, seguir la huella de; rebuscar, investigar; **to** — **the source of** remontarse al origen de, buscar el origen de.

tra·che·a [trékɪə] *s.* tráquea.

tra·cho·ma [trəkomə] *s.* tracoma.

track [træk] *s.* pista, huella, rastro; pisada; (*path*) vereda, senda; vía; — **sports** deportes de pista; — **ball** (*computer*) control por bola; **race** — pista; — **railroad** — rieles, vía del tren, vía férrea o ferrovía; **disk** — pista; **to be off the** — estar extraviado, estar descarrilado; **to be on the** — **of** rastrear, ir siguiendo la pista de; **to keep** — **of** llevar la cuenta de; no perder de vista; *v.* rastrear, seguir la huella de; **to** — **down** coger, atrapar; descubrir; **to** — **in mud** traer lodo en los pies, entrar con los pies enlodados.

tract [trækt] *s.* área; terreno; folleto; **digestive** — canal digestivo.

trac·tion [trǽkʃən] *s.* tracción.

trac·tor [trǽktɚ] *s.* tractor; — **feed** (*computer*) alimentación por tracción.

trade [tred] *s.* (*business*) comercio; trato, negocio; (*swap*) trueque, cambio; (*occupation*) oficio; (*customers*) clientela, parroquianos; — **school** escuela de artes y oficios; — **union** gremio obrero o de obreros; *v.* comerciar, negociar, traficar, tratar; trocar, cambiar; feriar, mercar.

trade·mark [trédmɑrk] *s.* marca de fábrica.

trad·er [trédɚ] *s.* mercader, comerciante, negociante, traficante.

trades·man [trédzmən] *s.* mercader, comerciante, traficante; tendero.

tra·di·tion [trədɪʃʃən] *s.* tradición.

tra·di·tion·al [trədɪʃʃənl] *adj.* tradicional.

traf·fic [trǽfɪk] *s.* tráfico; tráfago; tránsito; circulación; *v.* traficar, comerciar, negociar.

trag·e·dy [trǽdʒdɪ] *s.* tragedia.

trag·ic [trǽdʒɪk] *adj.* trágico.

trail [trel] *s.* (*trace*) pista, rastro, huella; (*path*) senda, sendero, trocha, vereda; cola (*de vestido*); *v.* arrastrar(se); rastrear, seguir la pista de; andar detrás de; **to** — **behind** ir rezagado, rezagarse.

train [tren] *s.* (*railroad*) tren; (*dress*) cola (*de vestido*); (*retinue*) séquito, comitiva; *v.* amaestrar(se), ejercitar(se); adiestrar(se) o

adestrar(se), *Am.* entrenar(se); educar; disciplinar (*tropas*); (*point*) apuntar (*un cañón*).

train·er [trénɚ] *s.* amaestrador; *Méx., C.A., Andes, Ven., Col., Carib.* entrenador.

train·ing [trénɪŋ] *s.* adiestramiento, disciplina, *Méx., C.A., Andes, Ven., Col., Carib.*, extrenamiento; educación; — **camp** campo de entrenamiento o práctica.

trait [tret] *s.* rasgo, característica; cualidad.

trai·tor [trétɚ] *s.* traidor.

tram [træm] *s.* vagoneta (*de una mina de carbón*).

tramp [træmp] *v.* pisotear; andar a pie; vagabundear; *s.* vago, vagabundo; caminata, marcha; pisadas.

tram·ple [trǽmpl] *v.* pisar, hollar, pisotear; **to** — **on** pisotear, hollar; *s.* pisadas.

trance [træns] *s.* rapto, arrobamiento, enajenamiento, éxtasis; **to be in a** — estar arrobado, estar enajenado; estar distraído o ensimismado.

tran·quil [trǽnkwɪl] *adj.* tranquilo.

tran·quil·iz·er [trǽŋkwəlaɪzɚ] *s.* tranquilizador.

tran·quil·li·ty [trænkwflɑtɪ] *s.* tranquilidad.

trans·act [trænsǽkt] *v.* tramitar, despachar, llevar a cabo.

trans·ac·tion [trænsǽkʃən] *s.* transacción, trato, negocio; trámite; negociación, **-s** actas; memorias.

trans·at·lan·tic [trænsətlǽntɪk] *adj.* transatlántico.

tran·scend [trænsɛnd] *v.* trascender, ir más allá de.

trans·con·ti·nen·tal [trænskɑntənɛntl] *adj.* transcontinental.

tran·scribe [trænskráɪb] *v.* transcribir.

tran·script [trǽnskrɪpt] *s.* transcripción, copia.

trans·fer [trǽnsfɚ] *s.* transferencia; traslado; traspaso; trasbordo; — **of ownership** cesión o traspaso de propiedad; **streetcar** — transferencia, contraseña, cupón de trasbordo; [trænsfɚ] *v.* transferir; trasbordar (*de un tren a otro*), cambiar (*de tren, de tranvía*); traspasar (*propiedad*), trasladar.

trans·fer·a·ble [trænsfɚəbl] *adj.* transferible.

trans·fig·ure [trænsfígjɚ] *v.* transfigurar.

trans·form [trænsfɔrm] *v.* transformar(se).

trans·for·ma·tion [trænsfɚméʃən] *s.* transformación.

trans·gress [trænsgrɛs] *v.* transgredir, violar, (*break*) quebrantar (*una ley*); pecar; **to** — **the bounds of** traspasar los límites de.

trans·gres·sion [trænsgrɛʃən] *s.* transgresión; violación de una ley; pecado.

trans·gres·sor [trænsgrɛsɚ] *s.* transgresor.

tran·sient [trǽnʃənt] *s.* transeúnte; *adj.* transeúnte; transitorio, pasajero.

tran·sis·tor [trænzístɚ] *s.* transistor.

tran·sit [trǽnsɪt] *s.* tránsito; **in** — en tránsito, de paso.

tran·si·tion [trænzíʃən] *s.* transición; tránsito, paso.

tran·si·tive [trǽnsətɪv] *adj.* transitivo.

tran·si·to·ry [trǽnsətɔrɪ] *adj.* transitorio, pasajero.

trans·late [trænslét] *v.* traducir, verter; trasladar.

trans·la·tion [trænsléʃən] *s.* traducción, versión; translación (*de un lugar a otro*).

trans·la·tor [trænslétɚ] *s.* traductor.

trans·lu·cent [trænslúsn̩t] *adj.* translúcido; **to be** — traslucirse.

trans·mis·sion [trænsmíʃən] *s.* transmisión; caja de velocidades.

trans·mit [trænsmft] *v.* transmitir; emitir.

trans·mit·ter [trænsmftɚ] *s.* transmisor; emisor.

tran·som [trǽnsəm] *s.* montante.

trans·par·ent [trænspɛ́rənt] *adj.* transparente.

trans·plant [trænsplǽnt] *v.* trasplantar.

trans·port [trǽnsport] *s.* (*moving*) transporte; acarreo; (*rapture*) éxtasis; — **plane** aeroplano de transporte;

TO

[trænspórt] *v.* transportar; acarrear; **to be -ed with joy** estar enajenado de placer.

trans·por·ta·tion [trænspɚtéʃən] *s.* transportación, transporte; boleto, pasaje.

trans·pose [trænspóz] *v.* transponer.

trans·verse [trænsvɝ́s] *adj.* transverso, transversal, puesto de través.

trap [træp] *s.* trampa, lazo, red; — **door** trampa; **mouse** — ratonera; *v.* entrampar, coger con trampa; atrapar.

tra·peze [træpíz] *s.* trapecio.

trap·e·zoid [træpəzɔɪd] *s.* trapezoide.

trap·pings [træpɪŋz] *s. pl.* arreos, jaeces, guarniciones.

trash [træʃ] *s.* basura; hojarasca; cachivaches; gentuza, plebe.

trau·ma [trɔ́mə] *s.* traumatismo.

trau·mat·ic [trɔmǽtɪk] *adj.* traumático.

trav·el [trǽvl] *v.* viajar; viajar por; recorrer; *s.* viaje; tráfico.

trav·el·er [trǽvlɚ] *s.* viajero; — **'s check** cheque de viajero.

trav·el·ing [trǽvlɪŋ] *adj.* de viaje, para viaje; — **expenses** gastos de viaje; — **salesman** agente viajero, viajante de comercio.

trav·e·logue [trǽvəlɔg] *s.* conferencia sobre viajes.

trav·erse [trǽvɚs] *v.* atravesar, cruzar; recorrer; *s.* travesaño.

trav·es·ty [trǽvɪstɪ] *s.* parodia; *v.* parodiar, falsear.

tray [tre] *s.* bandeja; batea; *Mex.* charola.

treach·er·ous [trétʃərəs] *adj.* traicionero, traidor, alevoso.

treach·er·y [trétʃərɪ] *s.* traición, perfidia, alevosía.

tread [trɛd] *v.* (*trample*) pisar, hollar; pisotear; (*walk*) andar a pie, caminar; *s.* paso; pisada, huella; *Ch.* pise (*de una rueda*); **tire** — rodadura del neumático, *Am.* banda rodante.

tread·mill [trédmɪl] *s.* noria; rueda de andar.

trea·son [trízn] *s.* traición.

trea·son·a·ble [tríznəbl] *adj.* traidor, traicionero.

treas·ure [trɛ́ʒɚ] *s.* tesoro; *v.* atesorar.

treas·ur·er [trɛ́ʒərɚ] *s.* tesorero.

treas·ur·y [trɛ́ʒərɪ] *s.* tesorería; tesoro, erario; **Secretary of the Treasury** ministro de hacienda.

treat [trit] *v.* tratar; curar; convidar, invitar; *s.* obsequio, agasajo, convite; placer, gusto.

trea·tise [trítɪs] *s.* tratado.

treat·ment [trítmənt] *s.* trato; **medical** — tratamiento médico.

trea·ty [trítɪ] *s.* tratado, pacto, convenio.

treb·le [trɛ́bl] *adj.* triple; — **voice** voz atiplada; *s.* tiple; *v.* triplicar.

tree [tri] *s.* árbol; **apple** — manzano; **family** — árbol genealógico; **shoe** — horma de zapato; **to be up a** — estar subido a un árbol; estar en un gran aprieto; estar perplejo.

tree·less [tríllɪs] *adj.* pelado, sin árboles, despoblado de árboles.

tree·top [trítɑp] *s.* copa de árbol.

trel·lis [trɛ́lɪs] *s.* emparrado, enrejado.

trem·ble [trɛ́mbl] *v.* temblar; estremecerse; *s.* temblor; estremecimiento.

tre·men·dous [trɪméndəs] *adj.* tremendo.

trem·or [trɛ́mɚ] *s.* temblor.

trem·u·lous [trɛ́mjələs] *adj.* trémulo; tembloroso.

trench [trɛntʃ] *s.* trinchera; zanja, foso.

trend [trɛnd] *s.* tendencia; rumbo, dirección.

tres·pass [trɛ́spəs] *v.* invadir, traspasar; violar, infringir; pecar; **to** — **on property** meterse sin derecho en la propiedad ajena; **no -ing** prohibida la entrada; *s.* transgresión; pecado.

tress [trɛs] *s.* trenza; bucle.

tres·tle [trɛsl] *s.* caballete; puente de caballetes.

tri·al [tráɪəl] *s.* ensayo, prueba; tentativa; aflicción; juicio, proceso; — **flight** vuelo de prueba; — **balance** balance de comprobación; — **and error** ensayo y error.

tri·an·gle [tráɪæŋgl] *s.* triángulo.

tri·an·gu·lar [traɪǽŋgjələɚ] *adj.* triangular.

tribe [traɪb] *s.* tribu.

trib·u·la·tion [trɪbəléʃən] *s.* tribulación.

tri·bu·nal [trɪbjúnl] *s.* tribunal, juzgado.

trib·u·tar·y [trɪ́bjətɛrɪ] *adj.* & *s.* tributario.

trib·ute [trɪ́bjut] *s.* tributo; homenaje.

trich·i·no·sis [trɪkənósɪs] *s.* triquinosis.

trick [trɪk] *s.* treta; suerte; truco, artificio; maña, ardid, trampa; travesura; (*cards*) baza (*en el juego de naipes*); **to be up to one's old -s** hacer de las suyas; *v.* embaucar, trampear, hacer trampa; burlar; **to** — **oneself up** componerse, emperifollarse.

trick·er·y [trɪ́kərɪ] *s.* engaños, malas mañas, astucia.

trick·le [trɪ́kl] *v.* gotear; escurrir; *s.* goteo.

trick·y [trɪ́kɪ] *adj.* tramposo, *C.A., Arg., P.R.* mañero; intrincado, complicado.

tri·cy·cle [tráɪsɪkl] *s.* triciclo.

tried [traɪd] *p.p.* de **to try** & *adj.* probado.

tri·fle [tráɪfl] *s.* fruslería, friolera, nadería, nonada; bagatela; *v.* chancear(se), bromear; jugar, juguetear.

trig·ger [trɪ́gɚ] *s.* gatillo (*de pistola, rifle, etc*).

trill [trɪl] *v.* trinar; **to** — **the r** pronunciar la erre doble; *s.* trino.

tril·o·gy [trɪ́lədʒɪ] *s.* trilogía.

trim [trɪm] *v.* guarnecer, adornar; atusar; recortar; (*cut*) podar, mondar; (*clip*) despabilar (*una vela*); (*win*) ganarle a uno (*en el juego*); **to** — **up** adornar, componer; *adj.* aseado, limpio, pulcro, acicalado; *s.* adorno, franja, ribete, guarnición; **to be in** — **for** estar en buena salud para; estar bien entrenado para.

trim·ming [trɪ́mɪŋ] *s.* adorno, aderezo, guarnición; orla, ribete, franja; paliza, zurra; **-s** adornos; accesorios; recortes.

trin·i·ty [trɪ́nətɪ] *s.* trinidad.

trin·ket [trɪ́ŋkɪt] *s.* chuchería, baratija; miriñaque.

trip [trɪp] *s.* viaje; travesía; recorrido, jira; tropezón; *v.* tropezar; dar un traspié; equivocarse; hacer tropezar, hacer caer; saltar, brincar, corretear.

triph·thong [trɪ́fθɔŋ] *s.* triptongo.

trip·le [trɪ́pl] *adj.* & *s.* triple; *v.* triplicar.

trip·li·cate [trɪ́pləkət] *adj.* triplicado.

tri·pod [tráɪpɑd] *s.* trípode.

trite [traɪt] *adj.* trillado, trivial, vulgar.

tri·umph [tráɪəmf] *s.* triunfo; *v.* triunfar.

tri·um·phal [traɪʌ́mfl] *adj.* triunfal.

tri·um·phant [traɪʌ́mfənt] *adj.* triunfante; **-ly** *adv.* triunfantemente, en triunfo.

triv·i·al [trɪ́vjəl] *adj.* trivial, insignificante.

trod [trɑd] *pret.* & *p.p.* de **to tread.**

trod·den [trɑdn] *p.p.* de **to tread.**

trol·ley [trɑ́lɪ] *s.* trole; tranvía de trole; — **bus** trolebús.

trom·bone [trɑ́mbon] *s.* trombón.

troop [trup] *s.* tropa; cuadrilla.

tro·phy [trófɪ] *s.* trofeo.

trop·ic [trɑ́pɪk] *s.* trópico; — **of Cancer** trópico de Cáncer; — **of Capricorn** trópico de Capricornio; *adj.* tropical.

trop·i·cal [trɑ́pɪkl] *adj.* tropical.

trot [trɑt] *v.* trotar; hacer trotar; *s.* trote.

trou·ba·dour ʃ[trúbədɔr] *s.* trovador.

troub·le [trʌ́bl] *v.* perturbar, turbar; molestar,

incomodar; afligir; preocupar(se); **don't — to
come** no se moleste Vd. en venir; *s.* pena,
aflicción; inquietud, perturbación; dificultad;
molestia; panne, avería, accidente (*a un
mecanismo*); **heart** — enfermedad de corazón; **to
be in** — estar en un aprieto o apuro; **it is not
worth the** — no vale la pena; **— shooter**
investigador de fallas o averías.

troub·le·mak·er [trΛblmekɚ] *s.* agitador, alborotador,
malcontento.

troub·le·some [trΛblsəm] *adj.* molesto, fastidioso,
enfadoso, dificultoso; penoso.

trough [trɔf] *s.* comedero; artesa; batea; **eaves —**
canal, gotera del tejado; **drinking —** abrevadero.

trou·sers [tráuzɚz] *s. pl.* pantalones.

trous·seau [trúso] *s.* ajuar de novia.

trout [traʊt] *s.* trucha.

trow·el [tráʊəl] *s.* llana, *Am.* cuchara (*de albañil*);
desplantador (*de jardín*).

tru·ant [trúənt] *s.* novillero, holgazán (*que se
ausenta de la escuela*); **to play —** hacer novillos,
Am. capear la escuela, *Mx.* pintar venado, *Am.*
jubilarse; *adj.* vago, perezoso.

truce [trus] *s.* tregua.

truck [trΛk] *s.* camión; carretón; carreta; basura;
baratijas; **garden —** hortalizas, legumbres y
verduras; **— garden** hortaliza, huerta de
legumbres; *v.* acarrear, transportar en camión o
carretón.

truck·age [trΛkədʒ] *s.* acarreo, camionaje.

trudge [trΛdʒ] *v.* caminar, caminar con esfuerzo; *s.*
caminata.

true [tru] *adj.* (*not false*) verdadero; cierto; verídico;
fiel; (*exact*) exacto, preciso; legítimo—; **—/false**
verdadero/falso, cierto/falso.

tru·ly [trúlɪ] *adv.* (*not falsely*) verdaderamente, en
verdad; en realidad; (*exactly*) exactamente,
correctamente; fielmente; **very — yours** su seguro
servidor.

trump [trΛmp] *s.* triunfo (*en el juego de naipes*); *v.*
matar con un triunfo (*en el juego de naipes*); **to —
up an excuse** forjar o inventar una excusa.

trum·pet [trΛmpɪt] *s.* trompeta; clarín; **ear —**
trompetilla acústica; *v.* trompetear; tocar la
trompeta; pregonar, divulgar.

trunk [trΛŋk] *s.* (*tree*) tronco; (*receptacle*) baúl;
(*animal*) trompa (*de elefante*); **-s** calzones cortos
(*para deportes*); **— line** línea principal.

trust [trΛst] *s.* (*reliance*) confianza, fe; (*credit*)
crédito; (*charge*) cargo; custodia; depósito; (*firms*)
trust, sindicato monopolista; **— account** cuenta
fiduciaria; **— fund** fondo en custodia; *v.* confiar;
fiar en, tener confianza en, fiarse de; esperar; dar
crédito a.

trus·tee [trΛstí] *s.* fideicomisario, depositario; síndico;
university -s regentes universitarios; **board of -s**
patronato; consejo.

trus·tee·ship [trΛstísɪp] *s.* fideicomiso.

trust·ful [trΛstfəl] *adj.* confiado.

trust·ing [trΛstɪŋ] *adj.* confiado.

trust·wor·thy [trΛstwɚðɪ] *adj.* fidedigno, digno de
confianza.

trus·ty [trΛstɪ] *adj.* fidedigno; honrado, leal; *s.*
(*prisoner*) presidiario fidedigno.

truth [truθ] *s.* verdad.

truth·ful [trúθfəl] *adj.* verdadero; verídico; veraz.

truth·ful·ness [trúθfəlnɪs] *s.* veracidad.

try [traɪ] *v.* probar, ensayar; hacer la prueba; poner a
prueba; (*attempt*) intentar, procurar; procesar,
(*court*) enjuiciar, formar causa (*a un acusado*); ver
(*una causa*); **to — on a suit** probarse un traje; **to**

— one's luck probar fortuna; **to — someone's
patience** poner a prueba la paciencia de alguien; **to
— to** tratar de, procurar, intentar; *s.* prueba,
tentativa, ensayo.

try·ing [tráɪɪŋ] *adj.* molesto; penoso, irritante.

tub [tΛb] *s.* (*bath*) tina; bañera; baño; (*wash*) batea,
cuba; *v.* lavar en tina o cuba.

tu·ba [túbə] *s.* tuba.

tube [tjub] *s.* tubo; **inner —** cámara (*de un
neumático*); **radio —** lámpara o tubo de radio.

tu·ber·cu·lar [tjubɚkjələ-] *adj.* tuberculoso, tísico.

tu·ber·cu·lo·sis [tjubɚkjəlósɪs] *s.* tuberculosis.

tuck [tΛk] *v.* alforzar, hacer o echar alforzas; **to —
in** meter en; **to — in bed** arropar; **to — under
one's arm** meter bajo el brazo; **to — up**
arremangar, recoger; **to — up one's sleeves**
arremangarse; *s.* alforza.

Tues·day [tjúzdɪ] *s.* martes.

tuft [tΛft] *s.* (*cluster*) penacho, copete; borla; (*clump*)
macizo (*de plantas*).

tug [tΛg] *v.* (*tow*) remolcar; (*pull*) jalar (halar); (*drag*)
arrastrar; trabajar con esfuerzo; **to — at tirar de,**
jalar; *s.* tirón, estirón, *Am.* jalón; remolcador; **—
boat** remolcador; **— of war** lucha a tirones de
cuerda.

tu·i·tion [tjuíʃən] *s.* derechos de enseñanza;
matrícula; *C.A.* colegiatura.

tu·lip [tjúləp] *s.* tulipán.

tum·ble [tΛmbl] *v.* caer(se); voltear; dar volteretas; **to
— down** caèrse; desplomarse; **to — down** caerse;
desplomarse; **to — into someone** tropezar con
alguien; **to — over** volcar, tumbar, derribar;
venirse abajo; *s.* caída, tumbo, vuelco, voltereta,
Am. rodada; desorden.

tum·bler [tΛmblɚ] *s.* (*glass*) vaso (*de mesa*);
(*person*) acróbata.

tu·mor [tjúmɚ] *s.* tumor.

tu·mult [tjúmΛlt] *s.* tumulto.

tu·mul·tu·ous [tjumΛltʃʊəs] *adj.* tumultuoso.

tu·na [túnə] *s.* atún (*pez*).

tune [tjun] *s.* (*melody*) tonada; (*pitch*) tono; armonía;
to be in — estar a tono, estar afinado o templado;
estar entonado; **to be out of —** estar desentonado
o desafinado; desentonar; *v.* afinar, templar;
armonizar; **to — in** sintonizar; **to — up the motor**
poner al punto el motor.

tung·sten [tΛŋstən] *s.* tungsteno.

tu·nic [tjúnɪk] *s.* túnica.

tunnel [tΛnl] *s.* túnel; socavón; *v.* socavar; abrir un
túnel.

tur·ban [tɚbən] *s.* turbante.

tur·bine [tɚbaɪn], [tɚbɪn] *s.* turbina.

tur·bo·prop [tɚboprap] *s.* turbopropulsor.

tur·bu·lent [tɚbjələnt] *adj.* turbulento; revoltoso.

turf [tɚf] *s.* (*lawn*) césped; (*piece*) terrón de tierra
(*con césped*); hipódromo, pista (*para carreras*).

Turk [tɚk] *s.* turco.

tur·key [tɚkɪ] *s.* pavo, *Méx.* guajolote (o guajalote);
C.A. jolote, chumpe, chompipe; *Col.* pisco.

Turk·ish [tɚkɪʃ] *adj.* turco; s. turco, idioma turco.

tur·moil [tɚmɔɪl] *s.* alboroto; confusión.

turn [tɚn] *v.* (*rotate*) volver(se); voltear(se); girar,
dar vueltas, rodar; virar; (*shape*) tornear, labrar al
torno; (*become*) ponerse (*pálido, rojo, etc.*); **to —
back** volver atrás; volverse, retroceder; devolver;
to — down an offer rechazar una oferta; **to — in**
entregar; recogerse, acostarse; **to — inside out**
voltear o volver al revés; **to — into** convertir(se)
en; **to — off** apagar (*la luz*); cortar (*el agua, el
gas, etc.*); **to — off the main road** salirse o
desviarse de la carretera; **to — on** encender (*la*

TR

luz); abrir la llave (*del gas, del agua*); **to — on someone** volverse contra, acometer o caer sobre alguien; **to — out** apagar (*la luz*); echar, expulsar, arrojar; producir; **to — out well** salir o resultar bien; **to — over** volcar(se), voltear(se); doblar; revolver (*en la mente*); entregar; **to — over and over** dar repetidas vueltas; **to — sour** agriarse, fermentarse; **to — the corner** doblar la esquina; **to — to** acudir a; volverse a; dirigirse a; convertir(se) en; **to — to the left** doblar o torcer a la izquierda; **to — up** aparecer; **to — up one's nose at** desdeñar; hacer ascos a; **to — up one's sleeves** arremangarse; **to — upside down** trastornar; volcar; **it -s my stomach** me da asco o náusea; *s.* vuelta; revolución; giro; recodo (*del camino*); turno; virada, cambio de rumbo; **— of mind** actitud mental; **at every —** a cada paso; **to be one's —** tocarle a uno; **to do one a good —** hacerle a uno un favor; **to take -s** turnarse.

tur·nip [tɝ·nəp] *s.* nabo.

turn·o·ver [tɝ·novɚ] *s.* (*accident*) vuelco (*de un coche*); (*change*) cambio (*de empleados*); **business —** movimiento de mercancías, número de transacciones; rotación de existencias; **labor —** movimiento de obreros, cambio frecuente de trabajadores; **apple —** pastel de manzana; **— collar** cuello doblado.

turn·stile [tɝ·nstaɪl] *s.* torniquete.

turn·ta·ble [tɝ·ntebl] *s.* plato giratorio.

tur·pen·tine [tɝ·pəntaɪn] *s.* trementina; aguarrás.

tur·pi·tude [tɝ·pətjud] *s.* torpeza, vileza.

tur·quoise [tɝ·kwɔɪz] *s.* turquesa.

tur·ret [tɝ·ɪt] *s.* torrecilla; torre blindada; alminar.

tur·tle [tɝ·tl] *s.* tortuga; **— dove** tórtola.

tusk [tʌsk] *s.* colmillo.

tu·tor [tútɚ] *s.* tutor, maestro particular; *v.* enseñar, instruir.

tux·edo [tʌksído] *s.* smoking.

twang [twæŋ] *s.* (*music*) tañido (*de una cuerda de guitarra*); (*speech*) nasalidad, tonillo gangoso; *v.* puntear, tañer (*una cuerda*); hablar con voz nasal, hablar con tonillo gangoso.

twang·y [twǽŋɪ] *adj.* gangoso, nasal.

tweed [twid] *s.* mezclilla de lana; **— suit** traje de mezclilla.

tweez·ers [twízɚz] *s. pl.* pinzas, tenacillas.

twelve [twɛlv] *num.* doce.

twen·ty [twɛ́ntɪ] *num.* veinte.

twice [twaɪs] *adv.* dos veces.

twig [twɪg] *s.* ramita; varita.

twi·light [tsáɪlaɪt] *s.* crepúsculo; **at —** entre dos luces; *adj.* crepuscular.

twin [twɪn] *adj. & s.* gemelo, mellizo, *Méx.* cuate.

twine [twaɪn] *s.* cuerda, cordel; *v.* enroscar(se), torcer(se), retorcer(se); entrelazar.

twinge [twɪndʒ] *s.* punzada (*dolor agudo*); *v.* punzar.

twin·kle [twɪ́ŋkl] *v.* titilar, parpadear, pestañear; chispear; *s.* titilación; parpadeo; pestañeo; guiño, guiñada; **in the — of an eye** en un abrir y cerrar de ojos.

twirl [twɝl] *v.* girar; dar vueltas; *s.* giro, vuelta; molinete, floreo.

twist [twɪst] *v.* (*turn*) torcer(se); retorcer(se); (*coil*) enroscar(se); *s.* torsión, torcedura, torzal, cordoncillo (*hecho de varias hebras torcidas*); curva, recodo, vuelta; rosca (*de pan*); **mental —** sesgo de la mente, sesgo mental.

twitch [twɪtʃ] *v.* crisparse, contraerse, torcerse convulsivamente (*un músculo*); (*tremble*) temblar (*los párpados*); (*pull*) dar un tirón; *s.* temblor, ligera, convulsión, contracción nerviosa; tirón.

twit·ter [twɪtɚ] *v.* (*birds*) gorjear (*los pájaros*); (*tremble*) temblar; agitarse; *s.* gorjeo; agitación, estremecimiento nervioso.

two [tu] *num.* dos.

two-faced [túfest] *adj.* de dos caras.

two-fisted [túfɪstəd] *adj.* vigoroso; de dos puños.

two·fold [túfold] *adj.* doble.

two-way [túwe] *adj.* de dos sentidos.

type [taɪp] *s.* tipo; *v.* escribir a máquina; (*press a key*) presionar, oprimir, tocar.

type·write [táɪpraɪt] *v.* escribir a máquina.

type·writ·er [táɪpraɪtɚ] *s.* máquina de escribir.

type·writ·ing [táɪpraɪtɪŋ] *s.* mecanografía; trabajo de mecanógrafo.

type·writ·ten [táɪprɪtn] *adj.* escrito a máquina.

ty·phoid [táɪfɔɪd] *s.* tifoidea, fiebre tifoidea.

ty·phus [táɪfəs] *s.* tifus.

typ·i·cal [tɪ́pɪkl] *adj.* típico.

typ·ist [táɪpɪst] *s.* mecanógrafo; mecanógrafa.

typ·o·graph·i·cal [taɪpográfɪkl] *adj.* tipográfico; **— error** error de máquina; errata.

ty·ran·ni·cal [tɪrǽnɪkl] *adj.* tiránico, tirano.

tyr·an·ny [tɪ́rənɪ] *s.* tiranía.

ty·rant [táɪrənt] *s.* tirano.

U:u

u·biq·ui·tous [jubɪ́kwɪtəs] *adj.* ubicuo.

ud·der [ʌ́dɚ] *s.* ubre.

ug·li·ness [ʌ́glɪnɪs] *s.* fealdad; fiereza.

ug·ly [ʌ́glɪ] *adj.* feo; (*cruel*) fiero; repugnante; (*bad temper*) de mal genio; desagradable.

ul·cer [ʌ́lsɚ] *s.* úlcera.

ul·te·ri·or [ʌltɪ́rɪɚ] *adj.* ulterior.

ul·ti·mate [ʌ́ltəmɪt] *adj.* último; final; fundamental; **-ly** *adv.* finalmente, a la larga.

ul·tra·mod·ern [ʌltrəmádɚn] *adj.* ultramoderno.

ul·tra·vi·o·let [ʌltrəvaɪəlɪt] *adj.* ultravioleta.

um·bil·i·cal cord [ʌmbɪ́lɪkl kɔrd] *s.* cordón umbilical.

um·brel·la [ʌmbrɛ́lə] *s.* paraguas; sombrilla.

um·pire [ʌ́mpaɪr] *s.* árbitro, arbitrador; *v.* arbitrar.

un [ʌn-] prefijo negativo equivalente a: sin, no, in-, des-.

un·a·ble [ʌnébl] *adj.* incapaz, inhábil; **to be — to come** no poder venir.

un·ac·cent·ed [ʌnǽksɛntəd] *adj.* inacentuado.

un·ac·cus·tomed [ʌnəkʌ́stəmd] *adj.* desacostumbrado; insólito, inusitado.

un·af·fect·ed [ʌnəfɛ́ktɪd] *adj.* inafectado, sin afectación, natural, sincero.

un·al·ter·a·ble [ʌnɔ́ltərəbl] *adj.* inalterable.

u·na·nim·i·ty [junənɪ́mətɪ] *s.* unanimidad.

u·nan·i·mous [jʊnǽnəməs] *adj.* unánime.

un·armed [ʌnármd] *adj.* desarmado.

un·at·tached [ʌnətǽtʃt] *adj.* suelto; libre; (*law*) no embargado.

un·a·void·a·ble [ʌnəvɔ́ɪdəbl] *adj.* inevitable, ineludible; forzoso.

un·a·ware [ʌnəwɛ́r] *adj.* desprevenido; inadvertido; ignorante; incauto; **-s** *adv.* inesperadamente, inopinadamente; impensadamente.

un·bal·anced [ʌnbǽlənst] *adj.* desequilibrado; **— account** cuenta no saldada.

un·bear·a·ble [ʌnbɛ́rəbl] *adj.* inaguantable, insoportable.

un·be·com·ing [ʌnbɪkʌ́mɪŋ] *adj.* impropio; **an — dress** un vestido que no sienta bien o que cae mal.

un·be·lief [ʌnbəlíf] *s.* incredulidad.

un·be·liev·a·ble [ʌnbəlívəbl] *adj.* increíble.

un·be·liev·er [ʌnbəlívɚ·] *s.'* descreído, incrédulo.

un·be·liev·ing [ʌnbəlívɪŋ] *adj.* descreído, incrédulo.

un·bend·ing [ʌnbéndɪŋ] *adj.* imflexible.

un·bi·ased [ʌnbáɪəst] *adj.* imparcial, libre de prejuicio.

un·bos·om [ʌnbúzəm] *v.* revelar, confesar, descubrir (*secretos*); **to — oneself** desahogarse con alguien, revelarle sus más íntimos secretos.

un·bound [ʌnbáʊnd] *adj.* desencuadernado, no encuadernado; suelto, desatado.

un·bro·ken [ʌnbrókən] *adj.* intacto, entero; indómito; ininterrumpido, continuo.

un·but·ton [ʌnbʌtn] *v.* desabotonar, desabrochar.

un·can·ny [ʌnkǽnɪ] *adj.* extraño, raro, misterioso.

un·ceas·ing [ʌnsísɪŋ] *adj.* incesante.

un·cer·tain [ʌnsɝ·tn] *adj.* incierto; dudoso; indeciso.

un·cer·tain·ty [ʌnsɝ·ɪntɪ] *s.* incertidumbre; falta de certeza.

un·change·a·ble [ʌntʃǝndʒəbl] *adj.* inmutable, inalterable, invariable.

un·changed [ʌntʃéndʒd] *adj.* inalterado, igual.

un·char·i·ta·ble [ʌntʃǽrətəbl] *adj.* duro; falto de caridad.

un·cle [ʌŋkl] *s.* tío.

un·clean [ʌnklín] *adj.* inmundo, sucio; impuro.

un·com·fort·a·ble [ʌnkʌmfɚtəbl] *adj.* incómodo; molesto.

un·com·mon [ʌnkʌmən] *adj.* poco común, insólito, raro.

un·com·pro·mis·ing [ʌnkʌmprəmaɪzɪŋ] *adj.* intransigente; inflexible.

un·con·cern [ʌnkənsɝ·n] *s.* indiferencia.

un·con·di·tion·al [ʌnkəndíʃənl] *adj.* incondicional, absoluto.

un·con·ge·ni·al [ʌnkəndʒínjəl] *adj.* que no congenia, incompatible.

un·con·quer·a·ble [ʌnkʌŋkərəbl] *adj.* invencible, inconquistable.

un·con·quered [ʌnkʌŋkɚd] *adj.* no conquistado, no vencido.

un·con·scious [ʌnkʌnʃəs] *adj.* inconsciente; privado.

un·con·scious·ness [ʌnkʌnʃəsnɪs] *s.* inconsciencia; insensibilidad.

un·con·sti·tu·tion·al [ʌnkʌnstɪtuʃənl] *adj.* inconstitucional.

un·con·trol·la·ble [ʌnkəntróləbl] *adj.* irrefrenable, ingobernable.

un·con·ven·tion·al [ʌnkənvénʃənl] *adj.* despreocupado, libre de trabas'o reglas.

un·coup·le [ʌnkʌpl] *v.* desacoplar.

un·couth [ʌnkúθ] *adj.* rudo, tosco, inculto, grosero; desmañado.

un·cov·er [ʌnkʌvɚ·] *v.* descubrir(se); revelar; destapar(se); desabrigar(se).

unc·tion [ʌŋkʃən] *s.* unción; fervor; **Extreme Unction** Extremaunción; *Ven., Méx., Cuba* administración.

unc·tu·ous [ʌŋkʃəs] *adj.* untuoso.

un·cul·ti·vat·ed [ʌnkʌltəvetɪd] *adj.* inculto; baldío.

un·cul·tured [ʌnkʌltʃɚd] *adj.* inculto; grosero.

un·daunt·ed [ʌndɔ́ntəd] *adj.* impávido.

un·de·cid·ed [ʌndɪsáɪdɪd] *adj.* indeciso.

un·de·ni·a·ble [ʌndɪnáɪəbl] *adj.* innegable.

un·der [ʌ́ndɚ·] *prep.* (*beneath*) bajo; debajo de; (*less*) menos de; **— age** menor de edad; **— cover a** cubierto; **— the cover of** al abrigo de, al amparo de; **— pretense of** so pretexto de; **— twelve** menos de doce; **to be — obligation to** deber favores a; *adv.* debajo; abajo; menos; *adj.* inferior, de abajo (*en ciertas combinaciones*); **— dose** dosis

escasa o corta; **— secretary** subsecretario; **— side** lado de abajo, lado inferior; **the — dogs** los de abajo.

un·der·brush [ʌ́ndɚ·brʌʃ] *s.* maleza.

un·der·clothes [ʌ́ndɚ·kloz] *s. pl.* ropa interior.

und·er·cut [ʌndɚkʌt] *v.* vender a menos.

un·der·de·vel·oped [ʌndɚdɪvéləpt] *adj.* subdesarrollado.

un·der·dog [ʌ́ndɚdɔg] *s.* el (la) de abajo; perdidoso; víctima.

un·der·es·ti·mate [ʌ́ndɚéstəmet] *v.* menospreciar, apreciar en menos de lo justo; salir corto en un cálculo.

un·der·fed [ʌ́ndɚféd] *adj.* malnutrido.

un·der·go [ʌndɚgó] *v.* sufrir, aguantar, padecer.

un·der·gone [ʌndɚgɔ́n] *p.p. de* **to undergo.**

un·der·grad·u·ate [ʌndɚgrǽdʒuɪt] *s.* estudiante del bachillerato; **— course** cursos o asignaturas para el bachillerato.

un·der·ground [ʌ́ndɚgraʊnd] *adj.* subterráneo; *s.* subterráneo; *adv.* bajo tierra; (*secretly*) en secreto; ocultamente.

un·der·hand·ed [ʌ́ndɚhǽndɪd] *adj.* socarrón, secreto, disimulado, clandestino.

un·der·line [ʌ́ndɚláɪn] *v.* subrayar.

un·der·ly·ing [ʌndɚláɪɪŋ] *adj.* fundamental.

un·der·mine [ʌndɚmáɪn] *v.* minar, socavar.

un·der·neath [ʌndɚníθ] *prep.* bajo, debajo de; *adv.* debajo.

un·der·pay [ʌndɚpé] *v.* malpagar; escatimar la paga.

un·der·pin·ning [ʌndɚpɪnɪŋ] *s.* apuntalamiento.

un·der·score [ʌndɚskor] *v.* subrayar.

un·der·sell [ʌndɚsél] *v.* malbaratar; vender a menos precio que.

un·der·shirt [ʌ́ndɚshɝt] *s.* camiseta.

un·der·signed [ʌndɚsáɪnd] *v.* firmante, infrascrito; **the —** el infrascrito, los infrascritos; el que suscribe.

un·der·sized [ʌ́ndɚsáɪzd] *adj.* achaparrado, de tamaño inferior al normal.

un·der·skirt [ʌ́ndɚskɝt] *s.* enaguas, refajo.

un·der·staffed [ʌndɚstǽft] *adj.* de personal insuficiente.

un·der·stand [ʌndɚstǽnd] *v.* extender; comprender; sobrentender.

un·der·stand·a·ble [ʌndɚstǽndəbl] *adj.* comprensible.

un·der·stand·ing [ʌndɚstǽndɪŋ] *s.* comprensión; entendimiento, inteligencia; acuerdo; *adj.* comprensivo.

un·der·stood [ʌndɚstúd] *pret. & p.p. de* **to understand;** *adj.* entendido; convenido; sobrentendido.

un·der·stud·y [ʌ́ndɚstʌdɪ] *s.* sobresaliente, actor suplente; *v.* servir de sobresaliente o actor suplente.

un·der·take [ʌndɚték] *v.* emprender; tratar de, intentar; comprometerse a.

un·der·tak·en [ʌndɚtékən] *p.p. de* **to undertake.**

un·der·tak·er [ʌ́ndɚtekɚ·] *s.* director de funeraria, embalsamador.

un·der·tak·ing [ʌndɚtékɪŋ] *s.* empresa.

un·der·took [ʌndɚtúk] *pret. de* **to undertake.**

un·der·tow [ʌ́ndɚto] *s.* resaca.

un·der·wa·ter [ʌ́ndɚwɔtɚ·] *adj.* submarino; subacuático.

un·der·wear [ʌ́ndɚwɛr] *s.* ropa interior.

un·der·went [ʌndɚwént] *pret. de* **to undergo.**

un·der·world [ʌ́ndɚwɝld] *s.* hampa, bajos fondos de la sociedad; clase criminal; **— jargon** caló.

un·der·write [ʌ́ndɚraɪt] *v.* asegurar; subscribir.

TU

un·de·sir·a·ble [ʌndɪzáɪrəbl] *adj.* indeseable; inconveniente.

un·did [ʌndíd] *pret. de* to undo.

un·dis·turbed [ʌndɪstɜ́·bd] *adj.* impasible; sereno, tranquilo; intacto.

un·do [ʌndú] *v.* deshacer; desatar; desabrochar; desenredar; anular to — one's hair soltarse el cabello.

un·do·ing [ʌndúɪŋ] *s.* destrucción; pérdida.

un·done [ʌndʌ́n] *p.p. de* to undo; inacabado, sin hacer; sin terminar; it is still — está todavía por hacer, está inacabado; to come — desatarse.

un·doubt·ed·ly [ʌndáʊtɪdlɪ] *adv.* indudablemente, sin duda.

un·dress [ʌndrɛ́s] *v.* desnudar(se), desvestir(se).

un·due [ʌndjú] *adj.* indebido; impropio; excesivo.

un·du·late [ʌ́ndjələt] *v.* ondular, ondear.

un·du·ly [ʌndjúlɪ] *adv.* indebidamente.

un·dy·ing [ʌndáɪɪŋ] *adj.* imperecedero, eterno.

un·earth [ʌnɜ́·θ] *v.* desenterrar.

un·eas·i·ly [ʌnízlɪ] *adv.* intranquilamente, inquietamente, con inquietud; incómodamente.

un·eas·i·ness [ʌnízɪnɪs] *s.* malestar, inquietud, intranquilidad, desasosiego.

un·eas·y [ʌnízɪ] *adj.* ansioso, inquieto, intranquilo; (*inhibited*) cohibido; incómodo.

un·ed·u·cat·ed [ʌnɛ́dʒəketɪd] *adj.* inculto, indocto, falto de instrucción, ignorante.

un·em·ployed [ʌnɪmplɔ́ɪd] *adj.* desocupado, desempleado, cesante; (*idle*) ocioso; — funds fondos no invertidos, inactivos.

un·em·ploy·ment [ʌnɪmplɔ́ɪmənt] *s.* desempleo; — compensation compensación por desempleo; cesantía, falta de empleo, desocupación.

un·end·ing [ʌnɛ́ndɪŋ] *adj.* inacabable, interminable.

un·e·qual [ʌníkwəl] *adj.* desigual; (*not enough*) insuficiente, ineficaz.

un·e·quiv·o·cal [ʌnɪkwívəkl] *adj.* inequívoco.

un·err·ing [ʌnɛ́ɪŋ] *adj.* infalible.

un·es·sen·tial [ʌnɪsɛ́nʃl] *adj.* no esencial.

un·e·ven [ʌnívən] *adj.* desigual, desparejo; (not level) irregular, accidentado; — numbers números impares o nones.

un·e·ven·ness [ʌnívənnɪs] *s.* desigualdad; desnivel; irregularidad, escabrosidad (*del terreno*).

un·e·vent·ful [ʌnɪvɛ́ntfl] *adj.* sin novedad.

un·ex·pect·ed [ʌnɪkspɛ́ktɪd] *adj.* inesperado; -ly *adv.* de improviso, inesperadamente.

un·ex·pres·sive [ʌnɪksprésɪv] *adj.* sin emoción.

un·fail·ing [ʌnfélɪŋ] *adj.* que nunca falta, constante, indefectible; infalible.

un·fair [ʌnfɛ́r] *adj.* injusto; (*tricky*) tramposo; to act -ly obrar de mala fe.

un·faithful [ʌnféθfəl] *adj.* infiel; desleal.

un·fa·mil·iar [ʌnfəmíljɚ] *adj.* poco familiar; desconocido; to be — with no tener conocimiento de; no estar al tanto de, ignorar; no conocer bien.

un·fas·ten [ʌnfǽsən] *v.* desabrochar; desatar; aflojar.

un·fa·vor·a·ble [ʌnfévrəbl] *adj.* desfavorable, contrario, adverso.

un·feel·ing [ʌnfílɪŋ] *adj.* insensible; incompasivo.

un·fin·ished [ʌnfínɪʃt] *adj.* inacabado, inconcluso; sin terminar, sin acabar; sin barnizar, sin pulir.

un·fit [ʌnfít] *adj.* incompetente, inepto, incapaz; inservible; impropio; *v.* incapacitar.

un·fold [ʌnfóld] *v.* desenvolver(se), desarrollar(se); desdoblar; revelar.

un·fore·seen [ʌnforsín] *adj.* imprevisto.

un·for·get·ta·ble [ʌnfɚgétəbl] *adj.* inolvidable.

un·for·tu·nate [ʌnfɔ́rtʃənɪt] *adj.* desventurado, infeliz, desgraciado, desdichado; -ly *adv.*

desgraciadamente, por desgracia.

un·found·ed [ʌnfáʊndəd] *adj.* infundado.

un·fre·quent·ed [ʌnfríkwəntəd] *adj.* poco frecuentado.

un·friend·ly [ʌnfréndlɪ] *adj.* hostil, enemigo; poco amistoso; *adv.* hostilmente.

un·fruit·ful [ʌnfrútfl] *adj.* infructuoso.

un·fund·ed [ʌnfʌ́ndəd] *adj.* flotante.

un·furl [ʌnfɜ́·l] *v.* desplegar.

un·fur·nished [ʌnfɜ́·nɪʃt] *adj.* desamueblado.

un·gain·ly [ʌngénlɪ] *adj.* desgarbado, torpe.

un·grate·ful [ʌngrétfəl] *adj.* ingrato, desagradecido.

un·guard·ed [ʌngárdəd] *adj.* desprevenido; descuidado.

un·hap·py [ʌnhǽpɪ] *adj.* infeliz; desgraciado, desventurado, desdichado.

un·harmed [ʌnhármd] *adj.* sin daño, ileso.

un·health·y [ʌnhɛ́lθɪ] *adj.* malsano, insalubre, enfermizo.

un·heard-of [ʌnhɜ́·dɑv] *adj.* inaudito; desconocido.

un·hinge [ʌnhíndʒ] *v.* desquiciar.

un·hitch [ʌnhítʃ] *v.* desenganchar; desatar; desacoplar.

un·ho·ly [ʌnhólɪ] *adj.* impío, malo.

un·hook [ʌnhúk] *v.* desenganchar; desabrochar.

un·hurt [ʌnhɜ́·t] *adj.* ileso.

u·ni·form [júnəfɔrm] *adj. & s.* uniforme.

u·ni·for·mi·ty [junəfɔ́rmətɪ] *s.* uniformidad.

u·ni·fy [júnəfaɪ] *v.* unificar, unir.

u·ni·lat·er·al [junɪlǽtɚl] *adj.* unilateral.

un·im·port·ant [ʌnɪmpɔ́rtn̩t] *adj.* insignificante, poco importante.

un·im·prov·a·ble [ʌnɪmprúvəbl] *adj.* inmejorable.

un·in·hib·i·ted [ʌnɪnhíbətəd] *adj.* sin inhibición.

un·ion [júnjən] *s.* unión; labor — sindicato; — leader jefe de un gremio obrero; trade-union gremio obrero; — shop obreros sindicados o agremiados; *adj.* gremial; — labor mano de obra sindicalizada.

u·nique [juník] *adj.* único, singular; señero.

u·ni·son [júnəzn̩] *s.* in — al unísono (*en el mismo tono*); al compás.

u·nit [júnɪt] *s.* unidad; (*housing*) carcasa, mueble.

u·nite [junáɪt] *v.* unir(se).

u·ni·ty [júnətɪ] *s.* unidad; unión.

u·ni·ver·sal [junəvɜ́·sl] *adj.* universal; — joint cruceta.

u·ni·verse [júnəvɜ·s] *s.* universo.

u·ni·ver·si·ty [junəvɜ́·sətɪ] *s.* universidad.

un·just [ʌndʒʌ́st] *adj.* injusto.

un·just·i·fi·a·ble [ʌndʒʌ́stəfaɪəbl] *adj.* injustificable, injustificado.

un·kempt [ʌnkɜ́·mpt] *adj.* desaseado, desaliñado; desgreñado.

un·kind [ʌnkáɪnd] *adj.* falto de bondad; descortés; cruel.

un·known [ʌnnón] *adj.* desconocido; no sabido; ignoto; — quality incógnita; it is — se ignora, no se sabe, se desconoce.

un·law·ful [ʌnlɔ́fəl] *adj.* ilegal, ilícito.

un·leash [ʌnlíʃ] *v.* soltar.

un·less [ʌnlés] *conj.* a menos que, a no ser que.

un·li·censed [ʌnláɪsənzd] *adj.* sin autorización.

un·like [ʌnláɪk] *adj.* desemejante, distinto, diferente; *prep.* a diferencia de.

un·like·ly [ʌnláɪklɪ] *adj.* improbable, inverosímil.

un·lim·it·ed [ʌnlímɪtɪd] *adj.* ilimitado.

un·load [ʌnlód] *v.* descargar; vaciar; deshacerse de (*acciones, mercancías*).

un·lock [ʌnlák] *v.* abrir (*con llave*); soltar, destrabar; revelar, penetrar (*secretos*).

un·loose [ʌnlús] *v.* soltar.

un·luck·y [ʌnlʌ́kɪ] *adj. (unfortunate)* desdichado, desventurado, desgraciado, desafortunado; *(of bad omen)* aciago, de mal agüero, funesto; **an — number** un número de mala suerte.

un·man·age·a·ble [ʌnmǽnɪdʒəbl] *adj.* inmanejable, ingobernable, intratable, indomable.

un·manned [ʌnmǽnd] *adj.* desguarnecido; sin tripulación.

un·marked [ʌnmárkt] *adj.* sin identificación.

un·mar·ried [ʌnmǽrɪd] *adj.* soltero.

un·mask [ʌnmǽsk] *v.* desenmascar(se).

un·mer·ci·ful [ʌnmɝ́sɪfəl] *adj.* despiadado, inclemente.

un·mis·tak·a·ble [ʌnmɪstékəbl] *adj.* inequívoco, claro, inconfundible.

un·moved [ʌnmúvd] *adj.* fijo; inmutable, impasible; indiferente.

un·nat·u·ral [ʌnnǽtʃərəl] *adj.* afectado, artificial; anormal; **an — mother** una madre desnaturalizada.

un·nec·es·sar·y [ʌnnésəsɛrɪ] *adj.* innecesario.

un·not·iced [ʌnnótɪst] *adj.* inadvertido.

un·o·blig·ing [ʌnəbláɪdʒɪŋ] *adj.* poco complaciente, descortés, descomedido.

un·ob·served [ʌnəbzɝ́vd] *adj.* inadvertido; sin ser visto.

un·ob·tain·a·ble [ʌnəbténəbl] *adj.* inobtenible, inasequible, inaccesible.

un·ob·tru·sive [ʌnəbtrusɪv] *adj.* discreto; sin ser visto.

un·oc·cu·pied [ʌnákjəpaɪd] *adj.* desocupado; vacío; desalquilado.

un·of·fi·cial [ʌnəfíʃl] *adj.* extraoficial.

un·or·gan·ized [ʌnɔ́rgənaɪzd] *adj.* sin organización; inorganizado.

un·o·rig·i·nal [ʌnərídʒənl] *adj.* trivial; ordinario.

un·or·tho·dox [ʌnɔ́rθədaks] *adj.* heterodoxo.

un·pack [ʌnpǽk] *v.* desempacar; desembalar.

un·paid [ʌnpéd] *adj.* no pagado; sin pagar; **— bills** cuentas por pagar.

un·pleas·ant [ʌnplézn̩t] *adj.* desagradable.

un·pleas·ant·ness [ʌnplézn̩tnɪs] *s.* manera desagradable; desazón; desavenencia; **the — of a situation** lo desagradable de una situación; **to have an — with** tener una desavenencia con.

un·prec·e·dent·ed [ʌnprésədɛntɪd] *adj.* sin precedente; inaudito.

un·pre·med·i·tat·ed [ʌnprimédətetəd] *adj.* impremeditado.

un·pre·pared [ʌnprɪpérd] *adj.* desprevenido; no preparado; no listo.

un·pre·ten·tious [ʌnprɪténʃəs] *adj.* modesto; sin pretenciones.

un·print·a·ble [ʌnpríntəbl] *adj.* que no puede imprimirse.

un·pro·duc·tive [ʌnprədʌ́ktɪv] *adj.* improductivo.

un·pro·fes·sion·al [ʌnprəféʃənl] *adj.* no profesional.

un·prof·it·a·ble [ʌnpráfɪtəbl] *adj.* infructuoso.

un·pub·lished [ʌnpʌ́blɪʃt] *adj.* inédito, no publicado.

un·qual·i·fied [ʌnkwáləfaɪd] *adj.* incompetente; inepto.

un·quench·a·ble [ʌnkwɛ́ntʃəbl] *adj.* inapagable, inextinguible.

un·ques·tion·a·ble [ʌnkwɛ́stʃənəbl] *adj.* indisputable, indudable; irreprochable.

un·rav·el [ʌnrǽvl] *v.* desenredar; desenmarañar; deshilachar(se); deshilar.

un·real [ʌnríəl] *adj.* irreal; ilusorio; imaginario.

un·rea·son·a·ble [ʌnrízənəbl] *adj.* desrazonable, fuera de razón; irracional.

un·rec·og·niz·a·ble [ʌnrékəgnaɪzəbl] *adj.*

un·re·fined [ʌnrɪfáɪnd] *adj.* no refinado; *(uncouth)* inculto, grosero.

un·re·li·a·ble [ʌnrɪlafbl] *adj.* informal; indigno de confianza.

un·rest [ʌnrést] *s.* inquietud, desasosiego.

un·roll [ʌnról] *v.* desenrollar(se), desenvolver(se).

un·ru·ly [ʌnrúlɪ] *adj.* indómito; indócil; desobediente.

un·safe [ʌnséf] *adj.* inseguro, peligroso.

un·sal·a·ble [ʌnséləbl] *adj.* invendible.

un·sat·is·fac·to·ry [ʌnsætɪsfǽktrɪ] *adj.* no satisfactorio, inaceptable.

un·scru·pu·lous [ʌnskrúpjuləs] *adj.* poco escrupuloso.

un·sea·son·a·ble [ʌnsízənəbl] *adj.* intempestivo.

un·seat [ʌnsít] *v.* destituir.

un·seen [ʌnsín] *adj.* no visto, oculto; invisible.

un·self·ish [ʌnsélfɪʃ] *adj.* desinteresado.

un·self·ish·ness [ʌnsélfɪʃnɪs] *s.* desinterés, abnegación.

un·set·tled [ʌnsétld] *adj. (disturbed)* desordenado, en desorden; turbio; inestable; *(uncertain)* incierto; indeciso; *(unpopulated)* deshabitado; no establecido; **— bills** cuentas no liquidadas, cuentas pendientes; **— weather** tiempo variable; **an — liquid** un líquido revuelto o turbio.

un·shak·en [ʌnʃékən] *adj.* inmóvil, inmovible, firme.

un·sight·ly [ʌnsáɪtlɪ] *adj.* feo, desagradable a la vista.

un·skilled [ʌnskfld] *adj.* inexperto.

un·skill·ful [ʌnskflfəl] *adj.* inhábil, desmañado, inexperto.

un·so·cia·ble [ʌnsóʃəbl] *adj.* insociable, huraño, intratable, arisco.

un·so·phis·ti·cat·ed [ʌnsəffstəketəd] *adj.* cándido, sencillo.

un·sound [ʌnsáund] *adj.* erróneo, falso.

un·speak·a·ble [ʌnspíkəbl] *adj.* indecible; inefable; atroz.

un·sta·ble [ʌnstébl] *adj.* inestable.

un·stead·y [ʌnstédɪ] *adj.* inseguro, inestable; movedizo; variable, inconstante.

un·suc·cess·ful [ʌnsəksésfəl] *adj.* sin éxito; desafortunado; **to be — no** tener éxito.

un·suit·a·ble [ʌnsútəbl] *adj.* impropio, inapropiado; *(unskilled)* inepto; inconveniente; incongruente; incompatible.

un·sus·pect·ed [ʌnsəspéktɪd] *adj.* insospechado.

un·ten·a·ble [ʌnténəbl] *adj.* insostenible.

un·think·a·ble [ʌnθíŋkəbl] *adj.* impensable.

un·ti·dy [ʌntáɪdɪ] *adj.* desaliñado, desaseado; desarreglado, en desorden.

un·tie [ʌntáɪ] *v.* desatar(se); desamarrar; deshacer *(un nudo o lazo).*

un·til [ʌntfl] *prep.* hasta; *conj.* hasta que.

un·time·ly [ʌntáɪmlɪ] *adj.* inoportuno; prematuro; *adv.* inoportunamente; fuera de sazón; demasiado pronto.

un·tir·ing [ʌntáɪrɪŋ] *adj.* incansable.

un·told [ʌntóld] *adj.* indecible, innumerable, incalculable, inestimable.

un·touched [ʌntʌ́ʃt] *adj. (unscathed)* intacto, no tocado, íntegro; *(impassive)* impasible, no conmovido; **to leave — no** tocar, dejar intacto; dejar impasible, no conmover.

un·trained [ʌntrénd] *adj.* indisciplinado, falto de disciplina; sin educación; inexperto.

un·tried [ʌntráɪd] *adj.* no probado, no ensayado, no experimentado; **— law case** causa todavía no vista.

un·trou·bled [ʌntrʌ́bld] *adj.* sosegado, tranquilo, quieto.

un·true [ʌntrú] *adj.* falso; infiel; desleal; mentiroso.
un·truth [ʌntrúθ] *s.* falsedad; mentira.
un·tu·tored [ʌntútɚd] *adj.* sin instrucción; ingenuo.
un·twist [ʌntwíst] *v.* destorcer.
un·used [ʌnjúzs] *adj.* no usado; (*unaccustomed*) desacostumbrado; — **to** no hecho a, desacostumbrado a.
un·u·su·al [ʌnjúʒuəl] *adj.* inusitado, insólito; desusado; raro, extraño; extraordinario.
un·var·nished [ʌnvárnɪʃt] *adj.* sin barnizar; sin adornos.
un·veil [ʌnvél] *v.* quitar el velo a; revelar, descubrir.
un·war·rant·ed [ʌnwɔ́rəntəd] *adj.* no justificado.
un·war·y [ʌnwɛ́rɪ] *adj.* incauto.
un·washed [ʌnwɔ́ʃt] *adj.* no lavado, sin lavar; sucio.
un·wel·come [ʌnwélkəm] *adj.* indeseable, no deseado; mal acogido, (*badly received*) mal recibido, mal quisto.
un·whole·some [ʌnhólsəm] *adj.* malsano; (*harmful*) insalubre, dañino.
un·wield·y [ʌnwíldɪ] *adj.* inmanejable, difícil de manejar, embarazoso, engorroso.
un·will·ing [ʌnwílɪŋ] *adj.* renuente, maldispuesto, reacio; **to be — to** no querer, no estar dispuesto a; **-ly** *adv.* de mala gana, sin querer.
un·will·ing·ness [ʌnwílɪŋnɪs] *s.* renuencia, falta de voluntad; mala gana.
un·wise [ʌnwáɪz] *adj.* imprudente, indiscreto; necio.
un·wont·ed [ʌnwʌ́ntəd] *adj.* inusitado, inacostumbrado; inédito.
un·wor·thy [ʌnwɝ́ðɪ] *adj.* indigno.
un·wrap [ʌnrǽp] *v.* desenvolver.
un·writ·ten [ʌnrítən] *adj.* no escrito.
up [ʌp] *adv.* (*above*) arriba, hacia arriba; en lo alto; (*standing*) de pie; *adj.* levantado, derecho, erecto; (*finished*) terminado, concluido; — **and down** de arriba abajo; de acá para allá; **-s and downs** altibajos; fluctuaciones, vaivenes; — **the river** río arriba; — **to now** hasta ahora; **his time is** — ha expirado su tiempo; se ha cumplido su plazo; **prices are** — los precios han subido; **that is — to you** queda a la discreción de Vd.; eso es cosa suya; **to be — against it** estar perplejo, no saber qué hacer; estar en un aprieto; **to be — on the news** estar al corriente (*o* al tanto) de las noticias; **to be — to one's old tricks** hacer de las suyas; **to eat it** — comérselo; **what's** — ? ¿qué pasa?; *v.* levantar, alzar.
up·braid [ʌpbréd] *v.* reprender, regañar.
up·date [ʌpdét] *v.* poner al día.
up·grade [ʌpgréd] *v.* adelantar; mejorar.
up·heav·al [ʌphívl] *s.* trastorno.
up·held [ʌphéld] *pret. & p.p. de* **to uphold.**
up·hill [ʌphíl] *adv.* cuesta arriba; *adj.* ascendente, trabajoso, arduo.
up·hold [ʌphóld] *v.* sostener; apoyar.
up·hol·ster [ʌphólstɚ] *v.* tapizar y rellenar (*muebles*).
up·hol·ster·y [ʌphólstrɪ] *s.* tapicería.
up·keep [ʌpkip] *s.* manutención; conservación.
up·land [ʌplənd] *s.* altiplanicie, tierra alta.
up·lift [ʌplíft] *s.* elevación; edificación (*espiritual*); [ʌplíft] *v.* elevar; edificar (*espiritualmente*).
up·on [əpán] *prep.* en, sobre, encima de; — **arriving** al llegar.
up·per [ʌpɚ] *adj.* superior; alto; — **berth** litera alta, cama alta (*de un coche dormitorio*); **to have the — hand** ejercer dominio o mando; llevar la ventaja; *s.* litera alta, cama alta; pala (*parte superior del calzado*).
up·right [ʌpraɪt] *adj.* recto; derecho; vertical; (*just*) justo, honrado; — **piano** piano vertical; *s.* poste;

puntal.
up·right·ness [ʌpraɪtnɪs] *s.* rectitud.
up·ris·ing [ʌpráɪzɪŋ] *s.* alzamiento, levantamiento; revuelta.
up·roar [ʌpror] *s.* tumulto, alboroto; bulla, gritería.
up·roar·i·ous [ʌprórɪəs] *adj.* estruendoso, bullicioso, tumultuoso.
up·root [ʌprút] *v.* desarraigar, arrancar de raíz.
up·set [ʌpsɛ́t] *v.* (*capsize*) volcar, tumbar; (*distress*) trastornar; perturbar, turbar; desquiciar; **to become** — volcarse; turbarse; trastornársele a uno el estómago; *pret. & p.p. de* **to upset**; *adj.* indispuesto, descompuesto; desarreglado, trastornado; [ʌpsɛt] *s.* vuelco; trastorno; desorden; indisposición.
up·shot [ʌpʃɑt] *s.* resultado, fin.
up·side [ʌpsaɪd] *s.* lado o parte superior; — **down** al revés; patas arriba; en desorden.
up·stage [ʌpstédʒ] *v.* quitarle la escena a uno.
up·stairs [ʌpstérz] *adv.* arriba, en el piso de arriba; *adj.* de arriba; *s.* piso (*o* pisos) de arriba.
up·start [ʌpstɑrt] *s.* advenedizo, principiante presuntuoso.
up-to-date [ʌptədét] *adj.* moderno; al corriente, al tanto.
up·turn [ʌptɝn] *s.* alza, subida (*de precios*); mejora.
up·ward [ʌpwɚd] *adv.* arriba, para arriba, hacia arriba; más; — **of** más de; *adj.* ascendente, hacia arriba, para arriba.
up·wards [ʌpwɚdz] *adv.* para arriba, hacia arriba.
u·ra·ni·um [jʊréniəm] *s.* uranio.
ur·ban [ɝbən] *adj.* urbano; — **renewal** renovación urbana.
ur·chin [ɝtʃin] *s.* granuja, pilluelo; *Col.* gamín; **sea** — erizo de mar.
u·re·thra [jʊríθrə] *s.* uretra.
urge [ɝdʒ] *v.* urgir, instar; exhortar; recomendar o solicitar con instancia; apremiar, incitar, estimular; *s.* impulso; gana, ganas; estímulo.
ur·gen·cy [ɝdʒənsɪ] *s.* urgencia; apremio.
ur·gent [ɝdʒənt] *adj.* urgente, apremiante.
u·ric [jʊrɪk] *adj.* úrico.
u·ri·nal [jʊrɪnl] *s.* urinario.
u·ri·nate [jʊrɑnet] *v.* orinar.
u·rine [jʊrɪn] *s.* orina, (los) orines.
urn [ɝn] *s.* urna; **coffee** — cafetera.
us [ʌs] *pron.* nos; nosotros (*con preposición*).
us·age [jʊsɪdʒ] *s.* usanza; uso; **hard** — uso constante.
use [jus] *s.* (*application*) uso; empleo; (*goal*) utilidad; **it is of no** — es inútil; no sirve; **out of** — desusado, ya no usado; pasado de moda; **to have no further** — **for** ya no necesitar, ya no tener necesidad de; **what is the** — **of it?** ¿para qué sirve?; ¿qué ventaja tiene?; ¿qué objeto tiene?; [juz] *v.* usar; emplear; servirse de, hacer uso de; acostumbrar, soler, *Am.* saber; — **your judgment** haz lo que te parezca; **to** — **up** gastar, agotar; consumir; **to be -d to** estar hecho, acostumbrado o habituado a; **he -d to do it** solía hacerlo, lo hacía.
use·ful [jʊsfəl] *adj.* útil.
use·ful·ness [jʊsfəlnɪs] *s.* utilidad.
use·less [jʊslɪs] *adj.* inútil; inservible.
use·less·ness [jʊslɪsnɪs] *s.* inutilidad.
u·ser [jʊzɚ] *s.* usuario.
ush·er [ʌʃɚ] *s.* acomodador (*en un teatro o iglesia*); ujier; *v.* conducir, llevar, acompañar; introducir.
u·su·al [jʊʒuəl] *adj.* usual; corriente, común, general; **-ly** *adv.* usualmente, generalmente, por lo general.
u·su·rer [jʊʒərɚ] *s.* usurero.
u·surp [juzɝp] *v.* usurpar.

u·su·ry [júʒərɪ] *s.* usura.

u·ten·sil [juténsl] *s.* utensilio.

u·ter·us [jútərəs] *s.* útero.

u·til·i·tar·i·an [jutɪlətérɪən] *adj.* utilitario.

u·til·i·ty [jutflətɪ] *s.* utilidad; servicio.

u·til·ize [jútlaɪz] *v.* utilizar; aprovechar.

ut·most [ʌ́tmost] *adj.* (*extreme*) sumo, extremo; más distante; más grande, mayor; más alto; (*last*) último; **he did his —** hizo cuanto pudo; **to the —** hasta más no poder.

u·to·pi·a [jutópjə] *s.* utopía.

ut·ter [ʌ́tə·] *v.* proferir; decir, expresar; **to — a cry** dar un grito; *adj.* completo, total; absoluto.

ut·ter·ance [ʌ́tərəns] *s.* declaración; expresión; modo de hablar.

ut·ter·most [ʌ́tə·most] = **utmost.**

u·vu·la [júvjələ] *s.* campanilla, galillo de la garganta; úvula.

u·vu·lar [júvjʊlə·] *adj.* uvular.

V : v

va·can·cy [vékənsɪ] *s.* vacante, empleo vacante; (*empty space*) vacío; habitación o apartamento desocupado.

va·cant [vékənt] *adj.* vacante; vacío; desocupado; libre.

va·cate [véket] *v.* desocupar, dejar vacío; dejar vacante.

va·ca·tion [vekéʃən] *s.* vacación; vacaciones.

vac·ci·nate [væksṇet] *v.* vacunar.

vac·ci·na·tion [væksṇéʃən] *s.* vacunación.

vac·cine [væksin] *s.* vacuna.

vac·il·late [væslet] *v.* vacilar.

vac·u·um [vækjuəm] *s.* vacío; **— cleaner** escoba eléctrica; aspiradora.

vag·a·bond [vægəbɑnd] *adj.* & *s.* vagabundo.

va·gi·na [vədʒáɪnə] *s.* vagina.

va·gran·cy [végrənsɪ] *s.* vagancia.

va·grant [végrənt] *adj.* vago, vagabundo, errante; *s.* vago, vagabundo.

vague [veg] *adj.* vago.

vain [ven] *adj.* vano; vanidoso; **in —** en vano.

vain·glor·y [venglórɪ] *s.* vanagloria.

vale [vel] *s.* valle; cañada.

val·en·tine [væləntaɪn] *s.* tarjeta o regalo del día de San Valentín (*el día de los enamorados*); **to my Valentine** a mi querido, a mi querida.

val·et [vǽlɪt] *s.* criado, camarero; (*ironer*) planchador de trajes.

val·iant [væljənt] *adj.* valiente, valeroso.

val·id [vǽlɪd] *adj.* válido; valedero.

va·lid·i·ty [vəlfdətɪ] *s.* validez.

va·lise [vəlís] *s.* valija, maleta, *Méx.* velís, *Méx.* petaca.

val·ley [vǽlɪ] *s.* valle.

val·or [vǽlə·] *s.* valor, ánimo, valentía.

val·or·ous [vælərəs] *adj.* valeroso, valiente.

val·u·a·ble [vǽljəbl] *adj.* valioso; precioso; preciado; **-s** *s. pl.* objetos de valor, joyas, alhajas.

val·u·a·tion [væljuéʃən] *s.* valuación, valoración; avalúo; tasa.

val·ue [vǽlju] *s.* (*price*) valor; precio; (*merit*) mérito; (*consideration*) estimación, aprecio; *v.* valorar, avaluar, valuar; apreciar, estimar.

val·ue·less [vǽljulɪs] *adj.* sin valor.

valve [vælv] *s.* válvula; valva (*de los moluscos*); **safety —** válvula de seguridad.

vam·pire [vǽmpaɪr] *s.* vampiro.

van [væn] *s.* camión (*para transportar muebles*); **— guard** vanguardia.

va·na·di·um [vənédɪəm] *s.* vanadio.

van·dal [vǽndl] *s.* vándalo.

vane [ven] *s.* veleta; aspa (*de molino de viento*); paleta (*de hélice*).

van·guard [vǽngɑrd] *s.* vanguardia.

va·nil·la [vənflə] *s.* vainilla.

van·ish [vǽnɪʃ] *v.* desvanecerse, desaparecer(se).

van·i·ty [vǽnətɪ] *s.* vanidad; **— case** neceser; **— table** tocador.

van·quish [vǽnkwɪʃ] *v.* vencer.

van·tage [vǽntɪdʒ] *s.* ventaja; **point of —** lugar estratégico.

va·por [vépə·] *s.* vapor; vaho.

va·por·ize [vépə·aɪz] *v.* vaporizar.

var·i·a·ble [vérɪəbl] *adj.* & *s.* variable.

var·i·ance [vérɪəns] *s.* variación, cambio; desavenencia; **to be at —** estar desavenidos; no estar de acuerdo.

var·i·ant [vǽrɪənt] *s.* variante.

var·i·a·tion [verɪéʃən] *s.* variación; variedad.

var·ied [vérɪd] *adj.* variado, vario.

var·i·e·gat·ed [vérɪgetɪd] *adj.* abigarrado.

va·ri·e·ty [vəráɪətɪ] *s.* variedad.

var·i·ous [vérɪəs] *adj.* varios; diferentes, distintos.

var·nish [vɑ́rnɪʃ] *s.* barniz; *v.* barnizar.

var·y [vérɪ] *v.* variar; cambiar.

vase [ves] *s.* vaso, jarrón.

Vas·e·line [vǽsəlɪn] *s.* vaselina.

vas·sal [vǽsl] *adj.* & *s.* vasallo.

vast [væst] *adj.* vasto; inmenso; anchuroso; **-ly** *adv.* vastamente, sumamente, muy.

vast·ness [vǽstnɪs] *s.* inmensidad.

vat [væt] *s.* tina, tanque.

vaude·ville [vódəvɪl] *s.* vodevil, función de variedades.

vault [vɔlt] *s.* bóveda; (*tomb*) tumba; **bank —** caja fuerte; depósito; **pole —** salto con garrocha; *v.* abovedar, edificar una bóveda; dar figura de bóveda; saltar con garrocha; saltar por encima de.

vaunt [vɔnt] *v.* jactarse; ostentar, alardear; *s.* jactancia.

veal [vil] *s.* carne de ternera; **— cutlet** chuleta de ternera.

veer [vɪr] *v.* virar; *s.* virada.

veg·e·ta·ble [véd͡ʒtəbl] *s.* (*plant*) vegetal, planta; (*food*) legumbre; **-s** hortaliza, legumbres; **green -s** verduras; *adj.* vegetal; de legumbres, de hortaliza; **— garden** hortaliza.

veg·e·tar·i·an [ved͡ʒətérɪən] *s.* vegetariano.

veg·e·tate [véd͡ʒətet] *v.* vegetar.

veg·e·ta·tion [ved͡ʒətéʃən] *s.* vegetación.

ve·he·mence [víəməns] *s.* vehemencia.

ve·he·ment [víəmənt] *adj.* vehemente.

ve·hi·cle [vítkl] *s.* vehículo.

veil [vel] *s.* velo; *v.* velar; tapar, encubrir.

vein [ven] *s.* (*body*) vena; (*ore*) veta, filón.

veined [vend] *adj.* veteado, jaspeado; (*blood*) venoso.

ve·loc·i·ty [vəlásətɪ] *s.* velocidad.

vel·vet [vélvɪt] *s.* terciopelo; velludo; *adj.* de terciopelo; aterciopelado.

vel·vet·y [vélvɪtɪ] *adj.* aterciopelado.

ven·dor [véndə·] *s.* vendedor; buhonero, vendedor ambulante.

ve·neer [vənfr] *s.* chapa; *v.* chapar o chapear, *Am.* enchapar.

ven·er·a·ble [vénərəbl] *adj.* venerable; venerando.

ven·er·ate [vénəret] *v.* venerar.

ven·er·a·tion [venəréʃən] *s.* veneración.

ve·ne·re·al [vənírɪəl] *adj.* venéreo.

Ven·e·zue·lan [vɛnəzwílən] *adj. & s.* venezolano.

ven·geance [véndʒəns] *s.* venganza; **with a** — con furia; con violencia.

ven·i·son [vénəzṇ] *s.* venado, carne de venado.

ven·om [vénəm] *s.* veneno, ponzoña.

ven·om·ous [vénəməs] *adj.* venenoso, ponzoñoso.

vent [vɛnt] *s.* (*opening*) abertura; (*escape*) escape; (*utterance*) desahogo; fogón (*de arma de fuego*); **to give** — **to anger** desahogar la ira, dar desahogo a la cólera; *v.* dar salida o desahogo; desahogar, descargar.

ven·ti·late [véntlet] *v.* ventilar.

ven·ti·la·tion [vɛntléʃən] *s.* ventilación.

ven·ti·la·tor [véntletɚ] *s.* ventilador.

ven·ture [véntʃɚ] *s.* ventura, riesgo; **business** — especulación; empresa o negocio arriesgado; *v.* aventurar, arriesgar; **to** — **outside** aventurarse a salir; **to** — **to** aventurarse a, atreverse a, osar.

ven·tur·ous [véntʃərəs] *adj.* aventurado.

ve·ran·da [vərǽndə] *s.* galería; terraza; balcón corrido.

verb [vɝb] *s.* verbo.

ver·bal [vɝbl̩] *adj.* verbal; oral.

ver·bal·ize [vɝbəlaɪz] *v.* expresar por medio de palabras.

ver·bose [vɝbós] *adj.* verboso; palabrero.

ver·dict [vɝdɪkt] *s.* veredicto; fallo, decisión, sentencia; — **of "not guilty"** veredicto de inculpabilidad.

ver·dure [vɝdʒɚ] *s.* verdura, verdor, verde.

verge [vɝdʒ] *s.* borde, margen, orilla; **on the** — **of** al borde de; a punto de; *v.* **to** — **on** rayar en, estar al margen de; **to** — **toward** tender a, inclinarse a.

ver·i·fy [vérəfaɪ] *v.* verificar; comprobar.

ver·i·ly [vérəlɪ] *adv.* en verdad.

ver·i·ta·ble [vérətəbl̩] *adj.* verdadero.

ver·mil·lion [vɚmfljən] *adj.* bermejo.

ver·nac·u·lar [vɚnǽkjʊlɚ] *adj.* vernáculo; *s.* idioma corriente.

ver·sa·tile [vɝsətl̩] *adj.* hábil para muchas cosas; flexible; versátil.

verse [vɝs] *s.* verso.

versed [ʌɝst] *adj.* versado, experto, perito.

ver·sion [vɝʒən] versión.

ver·te·brate [vɝtəbrɪt] *adj.* vertebrado.

ver·ti·cal [vɝtɪkl̩] *adj.* vertical.

ver·y [vérɪ] *adv.* muy; — **much** muchísimo; — **many** muchísimos; **it is** — **cold today** hace mucho frío hoy; *adj.* mismo; mismísimo; mero; **the** — **man** el mismísimo hombre; **the** — **thought of** la mera idea de.

ves·pers [véspɚz] *s. pl.* vísperas.

ves·sel [vésl̩] *s.* vasija; vaso; barco, embarcación; **blood** — vaso sanguíneo, vena, arteria.

vest [vɛst] *s.* chaleco; *v.* conferir; **to** — **with power** revestir de autoridad, conferir poder a.

vest·ed in·ter·ests [véstəd íntrɛsts] *s.* intereses creados.

ves·ti·bule [véstəbjul] *s.* vestíbulo; zaguán.

ves·tige [vɛstɪdʒ] *s.* vestigio.

vest·ment [véstmənt] *s.* vestidura.

vet·er·an [vétərən] *adj. & s.* veterano.

vet·er·i·nar·y [vétrənɛrɪ] *s.* veterinario o albéitar.

ve·to [víto] *s.* veto; prohibición; *v.* vedar, prohibir; poner el veto a; negarse a aprobar.

vex [vɛks] *v.* molestar, hostigar; incomodar, enfadar; perturbar.

vex·a·tion [vɛkséʃən] *s.* molestia, incomodidad; enojo; vejamen.

vi·a [váɪə] *prep.* por, por la vía de.

vi·a·ble [váɪəbl̩] *adj.* viable.

vi·a·duct [váɪədʌkt] *s.* viaducto.

vi·al [váɪəl] *s.* frasco, redoma; **small** — ampolleta.

vi·ands [váɪəndz] *s. pl.* vianda, alimentos, comida.

vi·brate [váɪbret] *v.* vibrar.

vi·bra·tion [vaɪbréʃən] *v.* vibración.

vi·car·i·ous [vaɪkérɪəs] *adj.* vicario.

vice [vaɪs] *s.* vicio; falta, defecto.

vice-pres·i·dent [váɪsprɛzədənt] *s.* vice-presidente.

vice·re·gal [vaɪsrígl̩] *adj.* virreinal.

vice·roy [váɪsrɔɪ] *s.* virrey.

vice versa [váɪsɪvɝsə] *adv.* vice versa.

vi·cin·i·ty [vəsfnətɪ] *s.* vecindad; cercanía; inmediaciones.

vi·cious [víʃəs] *adj.* vicioso; malo; maligno; malicioso; — **dog** perro mordedor, perro bravo.

vi·cis·si·tude [vəsfsətjud] *s.* vicisitud, peripecia.

vic·tim [víktɪm] *s.* víctima.

vic·tim·ize [vfktɪmaɪz] *v.* inmolar; engañar.

vic·tor [vfktɚ] *s.* vencedor.

vic·to·ri·ous [vɪktórɪəs] *adj.* victorioso.

vic·to·ry [vfktrɪ] *s.* victoria.

vic·tuals [vítlz] *s. pl.* vituallas, víveres.

vie [vaɪ] *v.* competir.

view [vju] *s.* (*field of vision*) vista; paisaje; (*opinion*) parecer, opinión; (*inspection*) inspección; (*aim*) mira, propósito; **in** — **of** en vista de; **to be within** — estar al alcance de la vista; **with a** — **to** con el propósito de; con la esperanza o expectación de; con la mira puesta en; *v.* mirar; examinar.

view·point [vjúpɔɪnt] *s.* punto de vista.

vig·il [vídʒəl] *s.* vigilia, velada; **to keep** — velar.

vig·i·lance [vídʒələns] *s.* vigilancia, desvelo.

vig·i·lant [vídʒələnt] *adj.* vigilante.

vig·or [vfgɚ] *s.* vigor.

vig·or·ous [vfgərəs] *adj.* vigoroso.

vile [vaɪl] *adj.* vil, bajo, ruin; pésimo.

vil·la [vflə] *s.* quinta, casa de campo.

vil·lage [vflɪdʒ] *s.* villa, aldea.

vil·lag·er [vflɪdʒɚ] *s.* aldeano.

vil·lain [vflən] *s.* villano, malvado, bellaco.

vil·lain·ous [vflənəs] *adj.* villano, ruin, vil, bellaco.

vil·lain·y [vflənɪ] *s.* villanía, vileza.

vim [vɪm] *s.* vigor, fuerza, energía.

vin·di·cate [vfndəket] *v.* vindicar, vengar.

vin·dic·tive [vɪndfktɪv] *adj.* vengativo.

vine [vaɪn] *s.* vid, parra; enredadera.

vin·e·gar [vfnɪgɚ] *s.* vinagre.

vine·yard [vfnjɚd] *s.* viña, viñedo.

vin·tage [víntɪdʒ] *s.* vendimia; (*age*) edad, época.

vi·o·late [váɪəlet] *v.* violar; infringir.

vi·o·la·tion [vaɪəléʃən] *s.* violación; infracción.

vi·o·lence [váɪələns] *s.* violencia.

vi·o·lent [váɪələnt] *adj.* violento.

vi·o·let [váɪəlɪt] *s.* violeta; violado, color de violeta; *adj.* violado.

vi·o·lin [vaɪəlfn] *s.* violín.

vi·o·lin·ist [vaɪəlfnɪst] *s.* violinista.

vi·o·lon·cel·lo [vɪəlɒntʃélo] *s.* violonchelo.

vi·per [váɪpɚ] *s.* víbora.

vir·gin [vɝdʒɪn] *adj. & s.* virgen.

vir·gin·al [vɝdʒɪnl̩] *adj.* virginal.

vir·ile [vfrl̩] *adj.* viril.

vir·tu·al [vɝtʃʊəl] *adj.* virtual; **-ly** *adv.* virtualmente.

vir·tue [vɝtʃʊ] *s.* virtud.

vir·tu·ous [vɝʃʊəs] *adj.* virtuoso.

vi·sa [vízə] *s.* visa, visado; *v.* visar, refrendar.

vis·cer·al [vfsɚl̩] *adj.* visceral.

vi·sé = visa.

vise [vaɪs] *s.* tornillo de banco.

vis·i·ble [vízəbl] *adj.* visible.
Vis·i·goth [vízəgɑθ] *s.* visigodo.
vi·sion [víʒən] *s.* visión; vista.
vi·sion·ar·y [víʒənɛrɪ] *adj.* visionario; imaginario; *s.* visionario, iluso; soñador.
vis·it [vízɪt] *v.* visitar; **to — punishment upon** mandar un castigo a, castigar a; *s.* visita.
vis·i·ta·tion [vɪzətéʃən] *s.* visitación, visita; castigo, calamidad.
vis·i·tor [vízɪtə·] *s.* visita; visitador.
vi·sor [váɪzə·] *s.* visera.
vis·ta [vístə] *s.* vista, paisaje.
vis·u·al [vízjul] *adj.* visual; visible.
vis·u·al·ize [vízjuəlaɪz] *v.* representarse en la mente.
vi·tal [váɪtl] *adj.* vital.
vi·tal·i·ty [vɑɪtǽlətɪ] *s.* vitalidad.
vi·tal·ize [váɪtəlaɪz] *v.* vitalizar.
vi·ta·min [váɪtəmɪn] *s.* vitamina.
vi·ta·min·ized [váɪtəmənaɪzd] *adj.* vitaminado.
vi·va·cious [vaɪvéʃəs] *adj.* vivaz, vivaracho, vivo, alegre, animado.
vi·vac·i·ty [vaɪvǽsətɪ] *s.* viveza, vivacidad.
viv·id [vívɪd] *adj.* vívido, vivo; animado.
viv·i·fy [vívəfaɪ] *v.* vivificar.
VLSI (*computer*) (**very large scale integration**) *s.* circuitos integrados de 20,000 entradas lógicas.
vo·cab·u·lar·y [vəkǽbjəlɛrɪ] *s.* vocabulario.
vo·cal [vókl] *adj.* vocal; oral; — **cords** cuerdas vocales; **to be —** hablar, expresarse.
vo·ca·tion [vokéʃən] *s.* vocación.
vogue [vog] *s.* boga, moda; **in —** en boga, de moda.
voice [vɔɪs] *s.* (*vocalization*) voz; (*speech*) habla; (*opinion*) voto; *v.* expresar, decir; **-d consonant** consonante sonora.
voice·less [vɔɪslɪs] *adj.* mudo; sin voz; — **consonant** consonante sorda.
void [vɔɪd] *adj.* vacío; nulo, inválido; — **of** falto de, desprovisto de; **voided check** cheque anulado; *s.* vacío; *v.* vaciar, evacuar; anular, invalidar.
vol·a·tile [válətl] *adj.* volátil; inconstante.
vol·can·ic [vɑlkǽnɪk] *adj.* volcánico.
vol·ca·no [vɑlkéno] *s.* volcán.
vo·li·tion [volíʃən] *s.* volición; voluntad.
vol·ley [válɪ] *s.* (*discharge*) descarga, lluvia (*de piedras, flechas, balas, etc.*); (*back and forth*) voleo (*de la pelota*); *v.* descargar una lluvia de proyectiles; volear una pelota.
volt [volt] *s.* voltio.
volt·age [vóltɪdʒ] *s.* voltaje.
vol·u·ble [váljəbl] *adj.* facundo.
vol·ume [váljəm] *s.* (*book*) volumen; tomo; (*capacity*) bulto; suma, cantidad.
vo·lu·mi·nous [vəlúmənəs] *adj.* voluminoso.
vol·un·tar·y [váləntɛrɪ] *adj.* voluntario.
vol·un·teer [valəntír] *s.* voluntario; *adj.* voluntario; de voluntarios; *v.* ofrecer, dar voluntariamente; ofrecerse.
vo·lup·tu·ous [vəlʌ́ptʃuəs] *adj.* voluptuoso.
vom·it [vámɪt] *s.* vómito; *v.* vomitar, *Méx.* deponer.
vo·ra·cious [voréʃəs] *adj.* voraz.
vor·tex [vɔ́rtɛks] *s.* vórtice; vorágine.
vote [vot] *s.* voto; votación; *v.* votar; votar por.
vot·er [vótə·] *s.* votante, elector.
vouch [vautʃ] *v.* **to — for** dar fe de; garantizar, responder de; salir fiador de.
vouch·er [váutʃə·] *s.* comprobante, justificante; recibo; fiador.
vouch·safe [vautʃséf] *v.* otorgar, conceder.
vow [vau] *s.* voto; juramente; *v.* votar, jurar, hacer voto de.
vow·el [váuəl] *s.* & *adj.* vocal.
voy·age [vɔɪɪdʒ] *s.* viaje; travesía; *v.* viajar.

vul·gar [vʌ́lgə·] *adj.* soez, ordinario, grosero; vulgar.
vul·ner·a·ble [vʌ́nə·əbl] *adj.* vulnerable.
vul·ture [vʌ́ltʃə·] *s.* buitre, *Andes, Ríopl.* cóndor; *Méx., C.A.* zopilote; *Carib.* aura; *Col.* gallinazo.
vul·va [vʌ́lvə] *s.* vulva.

W : W

wab·ble [wábl] *variante de* **wobble** *v.* tambalear(se), bambolear(se); vacilar; temblar; *s.* tambaleo, bambolea; balanceo.
wad [wɑd] *s.* (*filling*) taco; bodoque; (*ball*) pelotilla, bolita, rollo; — **of money** rollo de billetes (*de banco*); dinero; *v.* atacar (*un arma de fuego*); rellenar; hacer una pelotilla de.
wad·dle [wádl] *v.* anadear; contonearse, zarandearse (*al andar*); *s.* anadeo; zarandeo, contoneo.
wade [wed] *v.* vadear; (*splash*) chapotear; andar descalzo por la orilla del agua; **to — through a book** leer con dificultad un libro.
wa·fer [wéfə·] *s.* oblea; hostia (*consagrada*); (*computer*) ficha de silicón o otro semiconductor.
waft [wæft] *v.* llevar en vilo, llevar por el aire; llevar a flote; *s.* ráfaga de aire; movimiento (*de la mano*).
wag [wæg] *v.* menear; sacudir; **to — the tail** colear, menear la cola; *s.* meneo; (*comic*) bromista, farsante.
wage [wedʒ] *v.* hacer (*guerra*); dar (*batalla*); *s.* (*generalmente*) **wages** paga, jornal; — **earner** jornalero, obrero; trabajador; **wageworker** obrero asalariado; — **scale** escala de salarios (*sueldos*).
wa·ger [wédʒə·] *s.* apuesta; *v.* apostar.
wag·gle [wǽgl] *s.* meneo rápido.
wag·on [wǽgən] *s.* carro, carreta; carretón.
wail [wel] *v.* gemir, lamentar; *s.* gemido, lamento.
waist [west] *s.* cintura; talle; (*garment*) blusa; — **band** pretina.
waist·coat [wéskot] *s.* chaleco.
waist·line [wéstlaɪn] *s.* talle.
wait [wet] *v.* (*stay*) esperar, aguardar; (*serve*) servir; **to — for** esperar, aguardar; **to — on (upon)** servir a; atender a; **to — table** servir la mesa, servir de mozo o camarero (*en un restaurante*); *s.* espera; **to lie in — for** estar en acecho de.
wait·er [wétə·] *s.* mozo, camarero, sirviente, *Méx., C.A.* mesero.
wait·ing [wétɪŋ] *s.* espera; — **room** sala de espera.
wait·ress [wétrɪs] *s.* camarera, moza, *Méx.* mesera.
waive [wev] *v.* renunciar a; **to — one's right** renunciar voluntariamente a sus derechos.
waiv·er [wévə·] *s.* renuncia.
wake [wek] *v.* despertar(se); **to — up** despertar(se); despabilarse; *s.* (*at death*) velatorio (*acto de velar a un muerto*), *Am.* velorio; (*ship*) estela (*huella que deja un barco en el agua*); **in the — of** después de, detrás de.
wake·ful [wékfəl] *adj.* desvelado, despierto; insomne.
wak·en [wékən] *v.* despertar(se); *Ríopl., C.A., Ven.* recordar (*a una persona que está dormida*).
walk [wɔk] *v.* andar, caminar, ir a pie; recorrer a pie; pasear; **to — away** irse, marcharse; **to — back home** volverse a casa (a pie); **to — down** bajar; **to — in** entrar; **to — out** salirse, irse; parar el trabajo, declararse en huelga; **to — the streets** callejear; **to — up** subir; *s.* paseo; (*path*) senda, vereda; (*sidewalk*) acera; (*pace*) paso (*del caballo*);

VE

(*style*) manera de andar; — **of life** vocación; **a ten minutes'** — una caminata de diez minutos.

walk·out [wɔ́kaʊt] *s.* paro, huelga.

wall [wɔl] *s.* (*interior*) pared; (*garden*) muro; (*fort*) muralla; **execution** — paredón; **low mud** — tapia; **to drive to the** — poner entre la espada y la pared, poner en un aprieto.

wal·let [wálɪt] *s.* cartera.

wall·flow·er [wɔ́lflaʊɚ] *s.* alelí; **to be a** — **at a dance** comer pavo, *Andes, Méx.* planchar el asiento.

wal·lop [wáləp] *v.* pegar, zurrar, golpear; *s.* guantada, bofetón, golpazo.

wal·low [wálo] *v.* revolcarse; chapalear o chapotear (*en el lodo*).

wall·pa·per [wɔ́lpepɚ] *s.* papel (de empapelar).

wal·nut [wɔ́lnət] *s.* nuez de nogal; nogal; — **tree** nogal.

waltz [wɔlts] *s.* vals; *s.* valsar, bailar el vals.

wan [wɑn] *adj.* pálido, enfermizo, enclenque; lánguido.

wand [wɑnd] *s.* vara, varita; **magic** — varita de virtud.

wan·der [wándɚ] *v.* vagar, errar; **to** — **away** extraviarse; **to** — **away from** apartarse de, desviarse de; **my mind -s easily** me distraigo fácilmente.

wan·der·er [wándərɚ] *s.* vago, vagabundo.

wane [wen] *v.* menguar; decaer; *s.* mengua; diminución; **to be on the** — ir menguando; ir desapareciendo.

want [wɑnt] *v.* (*desire*) querer, desear; (*lack*) necesitar; *s.* falta; necesidad; escasez, carencia; **to be in** — estar necesitado.

want·ing [wántɪŋ] *adj.* falto; deficiente; (*poor*) necesitado.

wan·ton [wántən] *adj.* desenfrenado, libre; licencioso; inconsiderado; temerario.

war [wɔr] *s.* guerra; *v.* guerrear, hacer guerra; **to** — **on** guerrear con.

war·ble [wɔ́rbl̩] *v.* gorjear; trinar; *s.* gorjeo; trino.

war·bler [wɔ́rblɚ] *s.* cantor; pájaro gorjeador.

ward [wɔrd] *s.* pupilo, menor o huérfano (*bajo tutela*); (*section*) cuadra (*de hospital, prisión, etc.*); (*district*) distrito (*de una ciudad*); *v.* **to** — **off** resguardarse de; evitar; parar (*un golpe*).

war·den [wɔ́rdn̩] *s.* guardián; alcaide; **prison** — alcaide de una prisión.

ward·robe [wɔ́rdrob] *s.* (*closet*) guardarropa, ropero, armario; (*garments*) vestuario; ropa.

ware·house [wɛ́rhaʊs] *s.* almacén, depósito.

wares [wɛrz] *s. pl.* artículos, mercancías, mercaderías, efectos.

war·fare [wɔ́rfɛr] *s.* guerra.

war·head [wɔ́rhɛd] *s.* punta de combate; (*nuclear*) proyectil.

war·like [wɔ́rlaɪk] *adj.* guerrero, bélico.

warm [wɔrm] *adj.* (*temperature*) caliente, cálido, caluroso; (*enthusiastic*) acalorado; (*fresh*) reciente; — **hearted** de buen corazón; — **blooded** apasionado; ardiente; **he is** — tiene calor; **it is** — **today** hace calor hoy; *v.* calentar(se); **to** — **over** recalentar; **to** — **up** calentar(se); acalorarse; entusiasmarse.

warmth [wɔrmpθ] *s.* (*heat*) calor; (*friendship*) cordialidad.

warn [wɔrn] *v.* avisar, advertir, amonestar; prevenir; precaver.

warn·ing [wɔ́rnɪŋ] *s.* aviso, advertencia, amonestación; escarmiento; **let that be a** — **to you** que te sirva de escarmiento.

warp [wɔrp] *s.* (*weaving*) urdimbre (*de un tejido*); (*deformation*) torcedura, deformación; comba; *v.* combar(se), deformar(se), torcer(se); urdir (*los hilos de un telar*).

war·rant [wɔ́rənt] *s.* (*sanction*) autorización; (*right*) garantía, justificación; (*writ*) comprobante; orden, mandato, citación (*ante un juez*); *v.* autorizar; garantizar; justificar.

war·ri·or [wɔ́rɪɚ] *s.* guerrero.

war·ship [wɔ́rʃɪp] *s.* buque de guerra, acorazado.

wart [wɔrt] *s.* verruga.

war·y [wɛ́rɪ] *adj.* cauteloso, cauto, precavido, prevenido; **to be** — **of** desconfiar de.

was [wɑz] *pret. de* **to be** (*primera y tercera persona del singular*).

wash [wɑʃ] *v.* lavar(se); **to** — **away** deslavar(se); **to be -ed away by the waves** ser arrastrado por las olas; *s.* lavado; lavadura; lavatorio; lavazas, agua sucia; **mouth—** enjuague o enjuagatorio; **—bowl** lavabo, palangana, lavamanos; **—cloth** paño para lavarse; **—dress** vestido lavable; **—room** lavabo, lavatorio.

wash·a·ble [wáʃəbl̩] *adj.* lavable.

wash-and-wear [wɔ́ʃændwɛ́r] *adj.* de lava y pon.

washed·out [wáʃtáʊt] *adj.* desteñido; agotado, sin fuerzas.

washed-up [wɔʃtʌ́p] *adj.* fracasado.

wash·er [wáʃɚ] *s.* lavador; máquina de lavar; arandela (*para una tuerca*); — **woman** lavandera.

wash·ing [wáʃɪŋ] *s.* (*act*) lavado; (*clothing*) ropa sucia o para lavar; ropa lavada; — **machine** lavadora, máquina de lavar.

wash·out [wɔʃaʊt] *s.* derrubio; fracaso.

wasp [wɑsp] *s.* avispa.

waste [west] *v.* gastar; desgastar; malgastar, despediciar, derrochar; disipar; **to** — **away** gastarse, consumirse; desgastarse; *s.* desperdicio; gasto inútil; desgaste; desechos, desperdicios; terreno baldío; desierto; *adj.* inútil, desechado; (*desert*) desierto; baldío; — **of time** pérdida de tiempo; — **basket** cesto para papeles; — **land** terreno baldío; — **paper** papeles inútiles, papel de desecho; **to go to** — gastarse, perderse; malgastarse, desperdiciarse; **to lay** — asolar, arruinar.

waste·ful [wéstfəl] *adj.* despilfarrado, gastador; desperdiciado; ineconómico.

watch [wɑtʃ] *v.* (*look*) mirar; observar; (*be alert*) vigilar; velar; cuidar; — **out!** ¡cuidado!; **to** — **out for** tener cuidado con; cuidar; vigilar; *s.* reloj (de bolsillo); vela, vigilia; guardia; centinela, vigilante; — **chain** cadena de reloj, *Ven., Méx.* leontina; — **charm** dije; **wrist** — reloj de pulsera; **to be on the** — tener cuidado; estar alerta; **to keep** — **over** vigilar a.

watch·ful [wátʃfəl] *adj.* alerto, vigilante, despierto, atento, prevenido.

watch·mak·er [wátʃmekɚ] *s.* relojero.

watch·man [wátʃmən] *s.* vigilante, guardia, sereno.

watch·tow·er [wátʃtaʊɚ] *s.* atalaya, mirador.

watch·word [wátʃwɜd] *s.* contraseña, santo y seña, (*motto*) consigna; lema.

wa·ter [wɔ́tɚ] *s.* agua; — **color** acuarela; color para acuarela — **power** fuerza hidráulica; — **shed** vertiente; — **sports** deportes acuáticos; — **supply** abastecimiento de agua; *v.* (*irrigate*) regar; aguar, (*dilute*) diluir con agua; abrevar, (*give*) dar de beber (*al ganado*); beber agua (*el ganado*); tomar agua (*un barco, locomotora, etc.*); **my eyes** — me lloran los ojos; **my mouth -s** se me hace agua la boca.

wa·ter·cress [wɔ́tə·krɛs] *s.* berro.
wa·ter·fall [wɔ́tə·fɔl] *s.* cascada, catarata, caída de agua.
wa·ter·front [wɔ́tə·frʌnt] *s.* terreno ribereño.
wa·ter·mel·on [wɔ́tə·mɛlən] *s.* sandía; *Col.* patilla.
wa·ter·pow·er [wɔ́tə·paʊə·] *s.* fuerza hidráulica.
wa·ter·proof [wɔ́tə·pruf] *adj.* & *s.* impermeable; *v.* hacer impermeable.
wa·ter-ski [wɔ́tə·ski] *s.* esquí acuático.
wa·ter·spout [wɔ́tə·spaʊt] *s.* surtidor; tromba, manga de agua.
wa·ter·way [wɔ́tə·we] *s.* vía de agua, río navegable, canal.
wa·ter·y [wɔ́tərɪ] *adj.* aguado; acuoso; mojado, húmedo.
wave [wev] *v.* ondear; ondular; agitar; (*blandish*) blandir (*una espada, bastón, etc.*); **to — aside** apartar, rechazar; **to — good-bye** hacer una seña o ademán de despedida; **to — hair** ondular el pelo; **to — one's hand** hacer una seña o señas con la mano; mover la mano; *s.* onda; ola; ondulación; **— of the hand** ademán, movimiento de la mano; **permanent —** ondulación permanente.
wave·length [wévlɛŋθ] *s.* longitud de onda.
wa·ver [wévə·] *v.* oscilar; (*hesitate*) vacilar, (*stutter*) titubear; (*stagger*) tambalear(se); *s.* vacilación, titubeo.
wa·vy [wévɪ] *adj.* rizado, ondulado; ondulante.
wax [wæks] *s.* cera; **— candle** vela de cera; **— paper** papel encerado; *v.* encerar; pulir con cera; hacerse, ponerse; crecer (*la luna*).
way [we] *s.* (*road*) camino; ruta; senda; (*manner*) modo, manera; **— in** entrada; **— out** salida; **— through** paso, pasaje; **a long — off** muy lejos, a una larga distancia; **by — of** por, por vía de; **by — of comparison** a modo de comparación; **by the — de** paso; **in no —** de ningún modo; **on the — to** camino de, rumbo a; **out of the —** fuera del camino; apartado; a un lado; impropio; extraordinario; **to be in a bad —** hallarse en mal estado; **to be well under —** estar (*un trabajo*) ya bastante avanzado; **to give —** ceder; quebrarse; **to have one's —** hacer su capricho, salirse con la suya; **to make — for** abrir paso para
way·far·er [wéfɛrə·] *s.* caminante.
way·lay [welé] *v.* estar en acecho de (*alguien*); (*attack*) asaltar; (*stop*) detener (*a una persona*).
way·side [wésaɪd] *s.* borde del camino; **— inn** posada al borde del camino.
way·ward [wéwə·d] *adj.* voluntarioso, desobediente.
we [wi] *pron.* nosotros, nosotras.
weak [wik] *adj.* débil; flaco; endeble, **— market** mercado flojo; **weak-minded** de voluntad débil; simple; **— tea** té claro o suave.
weak·en [wíkən] *v.* debilitar(se); desmayar, flaquear, perder ánimo.
weak·ly [wíklɪ] *adv.* débilmente; *adj.* enfermizo, débil, enclenque.
weak·ness [wíknɪs] *s.* debilidad; flaqueza.
wealth [wɛlθ] *s.* riqueza; copia, abundancia.
wealth·y [wɛ́lθɪ] *adj.* rico; acaudalado.
wean [win] *v.* destetar; (*gradually estrange*) apartar gradualmente (*de un hábito, de una amistad*).
weap·on [wɛ́pən] *s.* arma.
wear [wɛr] *v.* (*have on*) llevar, tener o traer puesto; usar; (*waste away*) gastar, desgastar; **to — away** gastar(se), degastar(se); consumir(se); **to — off** degastar(se), gastar(se); borrarse; **to — out** gastar(se); degastar(se); consumir(se); agotar; cansar; **it -s well** es duradero; dura mucho; **as the day wore on** a medida que pasaba el día; *s.* uso,

gasto; durabilidad; **— and tear** desgaste; uso; **men's —** ropa para hombres; **clothes for summer —** ropa de verano.
wea·ri·ly [wírɪlɪ] *adv.* penosamente, con cansancio, con fatiga, fatigadamente.
wea·ri·ness [wírɪnɪs] *s.* cansancio, fatiga.
wear·ing [wɛ́rɪŋ] *adj.* cansado, aburrido, fastidioso.
wea·ri·some [wírɪsəm] *adj.* fatigoso, molesto, fastidioso.
wea·ry [wírɪ] *adj.* cansado, fatigado; aburrido; *v.* cansar(se), fatigar(se).
wea·sel [wízl] *s.* comadreja.
weath·er [wɛ́ðə·] *s.* tiempo; **weather-beaten** desgastado o curtido por la intemperie; **— bureau** oficina meteorológica; **— conditions** condiciones atmosféricas; **— vane** veleta; **it is fine —** hace buen tiempo; **to be under the —** estar enfermo; estar indispuesto; *v.* exponer a la intemperie; orear, secar al aire; **to — a storm** aguantar un chubasco; salir ileso de una tormenta.
weave [wiv] *v.* (*cloth*) tejer, entretejer; (*to plan*) urdir; **to — together** entretejer, entrelazar; combinar; *s.* tejido.
weav·er [wívə·] *s.* tejedor.
web [wɛb] *s.* tela; (*membrane*) membrana; **spider's — telaraña.**
wed [wɛd] *v.* casarse; casarse con; casar; *p.p. de to* **wed.**
wed·ded [wɛ́dɪd] *p.p.* & *adj.* casado; unido; **— to an idea** aferrado a una idea.
wed·ding [wɛ́dɪŋ] *s.* boda, casamiento, nupcias, enlace; **— day** día de bodas; **— trip** viaje de novios; **silver —** bodas de plata.
wedge [wɛdʒ] *s.* cuña; **entering —** cuña, entrada, medio de entrar, modo de penetrar; *v.* acuñar, meter cuñas; **to be -d between** estar encajado entre.
Wednes·day [wɛ́nzdɪ] *s.* miércoles.
wee [wi] *adj.* diminuto, chiquitico, pequeñito.
weed [wid] *s.* cizaña, mala hierba; *v.* desherbar (*o desyerbar*), quitar o arrancar la mala hierba; **to — a garden** desherbar un huerto; **to — out** escardar; eliminar, arrancar, entresacar.
weed·y [wídɪ] *adj.* herboso, lleno de malas hierbas.
week [wik] *s.* semana; **— day** día de trabajo, día laborable, día hábil; **— end** fin de semana; **a — from today** de hoy en ocho días.
week·ly [wíklɪ] *adj.* semanal, semanario; *adv.* semanalmente, por semana; *s.* semanario, periódico o revista semanal.
weep [wip] *v.* llorar.
weep·ing [wípɪŋ] *adj.* llorón; lloroso; **— willow** sauce llorón; *s.* llanto, lloro, lágrimas.
wee·vil [wívl] *s.* gorgojo.
weigh [we] *v.* pesar; ponderar, considerar; **to — anchor** zarpar, levar el ancla; **to — down** agobiar; abrumar; **to — on one's conscience** serle a uno gravoso, pesarle a uno.
weight [wet] *s.* peso; (*clock*) pesa (*de reloj o medida para pesar*); (*load*) carga; **— paper** pisapapeles; *v.* cargar, sobrecargar; añadir peso a; asignar un peso o valor relativo a.
weight·y [wétɪ] *adj.* grave, ponderoso; de mucho peso; importante.
weird [wɪrd] *adj.* extraño, raro, misterioso, fantástico.
wel·come [wɛ́lkəm] *s.* bienvenida; buena acogida; *adj.* grato, agradable; (*received*) bien acogido, bien quisto; bien-venido; bien recibido; **— home!** ¡bienvenido!; **— rest** grato reposo o descanso; **you are —** no hay de qué; de nada (*para contestar a*

WA

"thank you"); **you are — here** está Vd. en su casa; **you are — to use it** se lo presto con todo gusto; está a su disposición; *v.* dar la bienvenida a; acoger o recibir con gusto.

weld [wɛld] *v.* soldar(se); *s.* soldadura.

wel·fare [wɛ́lfɛr] *s.* bienestar; bien; felicidad; — **work** labor social o de beneficencia; — **society** sociedad benéfica.

well [wɛl] *adv.* bien; **he is — over fifty** tiene mucho más de cincuenta años; — **then** pues bien, ahora bien, conque; **well-being** bienestar; **well-bred** bien criado; bien educado; **well-done** bien cocido; **well-fixed** acomodado, **well-groomed** acicalado; **well-meaning** bien intencionado; **well-nigh** casi, muy cerca de; *adj.* bueno; bien de salud, sano; conveniente; — **and good** santo y muy bueno; **well-off** acomodado; adinerado; en buenas condiciones; **well-to-do** próspero, adinerado; **all is — no hay novedad, todo va bien; it is — to do it** conviene hacerlo, es conveniente hacerlo.

well [wɛl] *s.* (*shaft*) pozo; (*cistern*) cisterna; (*spring*) manantial; **artesian —** pozo artesiano; *v.* manar; **tears -ed up in her eyes** se le arrasaron los ojos de lágrimas.

welsh [wɛlʃ] *v.* no pagar una obligación.

welt [wɛlt] *s.* verdugo, verdugón, roncha.

went [wɛnt] *pret. de* **to go.**

wept [wɛpt] *pret. & p.p. de* **to weep.**

were [wɝ] *pret. de* **to be** (*en el plural y en la segunda persona del singular del indicativo; es además el imperfecto del subjuntivo*); **if I — you** si yo fuera Vd.; **there —** había, hubo.

west [wɛst] *s.* oeste, occidente, ocaso; *adj.* occidental, del oeste; **West Indies** Antillas; *adv.* hacia el oeste, al oeste; en el oeste.

west·ern [wɛ́stɚn] *adj.* occidental, del oeste.

west·ern·er [wɛ́stɚnɚ] *s.* natural del oeste, habitante del oeste, occidental.

west·ward [wɛ́stwɚd] *adv.* hacia el oeste; *adj.* occidental, oeste.

wet [wɛt] *adj.* húmedo; mojado; — **nurse** nodriza, ama de leche; *s.* humedad; (*pro-liquor*) antiprohibicionista; *v.* mojar; humedecer; *pret. & p.p. de* **to wet.**

wet·back [wɛ́tbæk] *s.* panza mojada.

wet·ness [wɛ́tnɪs] *s.* humedad.

whack [hwæk] *v.* golpear, pegar; *s.* golpe; golpazo; tentativa, prueba.

whale [hwel] *s.* ballena; *v.* pescar ballenas.

wharf [hwɔrf] *s.* muelle, embarcadero.

what [hwɑt] *pron. interr.* ¿qué?; ¿qué cosa?; ¿cuál?; *pron. rel.* lo que; — **for?** ¿para qué? *adj. qué;* — **book?** ¿qué libro? — **a man!** ¡qué hombre!; — **happy children!** ¡qué niños más (*o* tan) felices!; **take — books you need** tome Vd. los libros que necesite.

what·ev·er [hwɑtévɚ] *pron.* cualquiera cosa que, lo que, cuanto, todo lo que; — **do you mean?** ¿qué quiere Vd. decir?; **do it, — happens** hágalo suceda lo que suceda; *adj.* cualquiera; **any person — una persona cualquiera; no money —** nada de dinero.

what·so·ev·er [hwɑtsoévɚ] = **whatever.**

wheat [hwit] *s.* trigo; **cream of —** crema de trigo.

whee·dle [hwídl] *v.* engatusar.

wheel [hwil] *s.* (*disc*) rueda; rodaja; disco; (*bike*) bicicleta; — **chair** silla rodante, silla de ruedas; **steering —** volante (*de automóvil*); (*ship*) rueda del timón; *v.* rodar; hacer rodar; girar; acarrear; andar en bicicleta; **to — around** dar una vuelta; girar sobre los talones; **to — the baby** pasear al bebé en su cochecito.

wheel·bar·row [hwílbæro] *s.* carretilla.

wheeze [hwiz] *s.* resuello ruidoso.

when [hwɛn] *adv. & conj.* cuando; *adv. interr.* ¿cuándo?

whence [hwɛns] *adv.* de donde; de que.

when·ev·er [hwɛnévɚ] *adj. & conj.* cuando, siempre que, cada vez que.

where [hwɛr] *adv.* donde; adonde; en donde; por donde; — **?** ¿dónde?; ¿adónde?

where·a·bouts [hwɛ́rəbauts] *s.* paradero; *adv. interr.* ¿dónde?

where·as [hwɛrǽz] *conj.* mientras que; puesto que, visto que, considerando que.

where·by [hwɛrbáɪ] *adv.* por donde, por lo cual; con lo cual.

where·fore [hwɛ́rfor] *adv.* por lo que; por lo cual; por eso, por lo tanto.

where·in [hwɛrɪ́n] *adv.* en que; en donde; en lo cual.

where·of [hwɛráv] *adv.* de que; de donde; de quien, de quienes.

where·up·on [hwɛrəpán] *adv.* después de lo cual; entonces.

where·ev·er [hwɛrévɚ] *adv.* dondequiera que, adondequiera que, por dondequiera que.

where·with·al [hwɛ́rwɪðɔl] *adv.* medios, fondos; dinero.

whet [hwɛt] *v.* amolar, afilar; (*stimulate*) aguzar, estimular.

wheth·er [hwɛ́ðɚ] *conj.* si; ya sea que, sea que; — **we escape or not** ya sea que escapemos o no; **I doubt —** dudo (de) que.

which [hwɪtʃ] *pron. interr.* ¿cuál?; ¿cuáles?; *pron. rel.* que; el cual, la cual, los cuales, las cuales; el que, la que, los que, las que; *adj. interr.* ¿qué?; — **boy has it?** ¿cuál de los muchachos lo tiene? ¿qué muchacho lo tiene?; — **way did he go?** ¿por qué camino se fué?; ¿por dónde se fué?; **during — time** tiempo durante el cual.

which·ev·er [hwɪtʃévɚ] *pron. & adj.* cualquiera (que), cualesquiera (que); el que, la que; — **road you take** cualquier camino que Vd. siga.

whiff [hwɪf] *s.* (*waft*) soplo; fumada, bocanada; (*odor*) repentino olor o hedor; *v.* soplar; echar bocanadas.

while [hwaɪl] *s.* rato; tiempo, temporada; **a short — un ratito; a short — ago** hace poco, hace poco rato; **to be worth —** valer la pena; *conj.* mientras, mientras que; *v.* **to — away the time** pasar el tiempo.

whilst [hwaɪlst] *conj.* mientras, mientras que.

whim [hwɪm] *s.* capricho, antojo.

whim·per [hwímpɚ] *v.* lloriquear, gimotear; quejarse; *s.* lloriqueo, gimoteo; quejido.

whim·si·cal [hwímzɪkl] *adj.* caprichoso.

whine [hwaɪn] *v.* lloriquear; quejarse; *s.* gemido, quejido.

whin·er [hwáɪnɚ] *s.* llorón, persona quejosa, *Méx.,* *Carib., Ven.* quejumbres; *Andes* quejumbroso; *Ríopl.* rezongón.

whip [hwɪp] *v.* azotar, fustigar; (*beat*) zurrar, dar una paliza a, dar latigazos a; (*cream*) batir (*crema, huevos*); vencer; **to — up** batir, coger (*o* asir) de repente; hacer de prisa; *s.* azote, látigo, fuete; batido.

whip·ping [hwípɪŋ] *s.* tunda, zurra, paliza; — **cream** crema para batir.

whir [hwɝ] *v.* zumbar; *s.* zumbido.

whirl [hwɝl] *v.* girar, dar vueltas; arremolinarse; **my head -s** siento vértigo, estoy desvanecido; *s.* giro, vuelta; remolino; (*column*) espiral (*de humo*); confusión.

whirl·pool [hwɝ́·lpul] *s.* remolino, vorágine, vórtice.
whirl·wind [hwɝ́·lwɪnd] *s.* remolino, torbellino.
whisk [hwɪsk] *v.* barrer; (*brush*) desempolvar (*con escobilla*); (*beat*) batir (*huevos*); **to — away** barrer de prisa; llevarse de prisa, arrebatar; irse de prisa, escaparse; **to — something out of sight** escamotear algo, esconder algo de prisa; *s.* — **broom** escobilla; **with a — of the broom** de un escobillazo.
whis·ker [hwískɚ·] *s.* pelo de la barba; **-s** barbas; patillas; bigotes (*del gato*).
whis·key [hwískɪ] *s.* whisky (*aguardiente de maíz, centeno, etc.*).
whis·per [hwíspɚ·] *v.* cuchichear, hablar en secreto; soplar, decir al oído; susurrar; secretearse; **it is -ed that** corre la voz que; dízque, dicen que; *s.* cuchicheo, secreteo; susurro; murmullo; **to talk in a —** hablar en secreto; susurrar.
whis·tle [hwísl] *v.* siblar; chiflar; (*instrument*) pitar; **to — for someone** llamar a uno con un silbido; *s.* silbido, chiflido; silbato, pito.
whit [hwɪt] *s.* jota, pizca.
white [hwaɪt] *adj.* (*color*) blanco; (*pure*) puro; inocente; (*honorable*) honrado, recto; **— caps** cabrillas o palomas (*olas con crestas blancas*); **— lead** albayalde; **— lie** mèntirilla, mentira venial; **white-livered** cobarde; **white-collar** de oficina; **to show the — feather** mostrar cobardía, portarse como cobarde; *s.* blanco; clara (*del huevo*).
whit·en [hwaɪ́tṇ] *v.* blanquear; emblanquecer(se), poner(se) blanco.
white·ness [hwaɪ́tnɪs] *s.* blancura; palidez; pureza.
white·wash [hwaɪ́twɑʃ] *v.* (*paint*) blanquear, enjalbegar; (*gloss over*) encubrir, disimular (*faltas, errores*); (*absolve*) absolver (*sin justicia*); *s.* lechada.
whith·er [hwíðɚ·] *adv.* adonde; **— ?** ¿adónde?
whit·ish [hwáɪtɪʃ] *adj.* blancuzco, blanquecino, blanquizco.
whit·tle [hwítl] *v.* cortar mondar, tallar; (*slice*) tajar, sacar punta a (*un lápiz*); **to — down expenses** cercenar o reducir los gastos.
whiz [hwɪz] *v.* zumbar; *s.* zumbido, silbido; **to be a —** ser un águila, ser muy listo.
who [hu] *pron. rel.* quien, quienes, que, el que, la que, los que, las que; **he —** el que, quien; *pron. interr.* ¿quién?; ¿quiénes?; **— is it?** ¿quién es?
who·ev·er [huévɚ·] *pron.* quienquiera que, cualquiera que; el que.
whole [hol] *adj.* todo; entero; íntegro; **the — day** todo el día; **— hearted** sincero, cordial; **— heartedly** de todo corazón; con todo ánimo; *s.* todo, total, totalidad; **as a —** en conjunto; **on the — en** general, en conjunto.
whole·sale [hólsel] *s.* venta al por mayor, *Méx., Arg., Ch.* mayoreo; **by —** al por mayor; *adj.* al por mayor; en grandes cantidades; **— dealer** comerciante al por mayor; *Méx., Arg., Ch.* mayorista; **— slaughter** matanza; gran hecatombe; **— trade** comercio al por mayor; *Méx., Arg., Ch.* comercio mayorista; *adv.* al por mayor, por mayor; *v.* vender al por mayor, *Méx., Arg., Ch.* mayorear.
whole·some [hólsəm] *adj.* saludable, sano; salubre; **— man** hombre normalmente bueno o de buena índole.
whol·ly [hólɪ] *adv.* enteramente, completamente, totalmente.
whom [hum] *pron. pers.* a quien, a quienes; que; al que (a la que, a los que, *etc.*); al cual (a la cual, a los cuales, *etc.*); **for —** para quien; **— did you see?** ¿a quién vió Vd.?

whoop [hup] *s.* grito, chillido, alarido; (*cough*) respiro convulsivo (*que acompaña a la tos ferina*); *v.* gritar, vocear, echar gritos; respirar convulsivamente (*al toser*); **to — it up** armar una gritería, gritar; **whooping cough** tos ferina.
whore [hor] *s.* ramera, puta, prostituta.
whose [huz] *pron.* cuyo, cuya, cuyos, cuyas; *pron. interr.* ¿de quién?; ¿de quiénes?; **— book is this?** ¿de quién es este libro?
why [hwaɪ] *adv.* ¿por qué?; **the reason —** la razón por la que (*o* la cual); **—, of course!** ¡sí, por supuesto!; ¡claro que sí!; **—, that is not true!** ¡si eso no es verdad! *s.* porqué, causa, razón, motivo.
wick [wɪk] *s.* mecha, pabilo.
wick·ed [wíkɪd] *adj.* malvado, malo, inicuo; nefasto.
wick·ed·ness [wíkɪdnɪs] *s.* maldad, iniquidad, perversidad.
wick·er [wíkɚ·] *s.* mimbre; **— chair** silla de mimbre.
wick·et [wíkɪt] *s.* postigo; ventanilla.
wide [waɪd] *adj.* ancho; amplio; (*extensive*) vasto; extenso; **— apart** muy apartados; **wide-awake** muy despierto; alerta, vigilante; **— eyed** ojoso; **— of the mark** muy lejos del blanco; **— open** muy abierto; abierto de par en par; **far and —** por todas partes, extensamente; **to open —** abrir mucho; abrir (*la puerta*) de par en par; **two feet —** dos pies de ancho (*o* de anchura).
wide·ly [wáɪdlɪ] *adv.* ampliamente; extensamente; muy; mucho.
wid·en [wáɪdṇ] *v.* ensanchar(se), ampliar(se), dilatar(se).
wide·spread [wáɪdsprέd] *adj.* muy esparcido, muy extensivo; bien difundido; extendido; general, extendido por todas partes.
wid·ow [wído] *s.* viuda.
wid·ow·er [wídəwɚ·] *s.* viudo.
width [wɪdθ] *s.* ancho, anchura.
wield [wild] *v.* manejar; esgrimir (*la espada o la pluma*); ejercer (*el poder*).
wife [waɪf] *s.* esposa.
wig [wɪg] *s.* peluca.
wig·gle [wígl] *v.* menear(se); *s.* meneo.
wig·wam [wígwɑm] *s.* choza de los indios norteños.
wild [waɪld] *adj.* salvaje; (*animal*) feroz, fiero; indómito; montaraz; (*plant*) silvestre; *Ven., Méx.* cimarrón; (*uncontrolled*) impetuoso, desenfrenado; bullicoso; violento; loco; enojado; desatinado; ansioso; **to talk —** disparatar, desatinar; *s.* yermo, desierto, monte.
wild·cat [wáɪldkæt] *s.* gato montés; **— scheme** empresa arriesgada; *adj.* de prueba.
wil·der·ness [wíldɚ·nɪs] *s.* yermo, desierto, monte; inmensidad.
wild·eyed [wáɪldaɪd] *adj.* de ojos huraños,
wild·ness [wáɪldnɪs] *s.* salvajez; ferocidad, fiereza; locura.
wile [waɪl] *s.* ardid, engaño; (*cleverness*) astucia.
will [wɪl] *v.* (*desire*) querer, decidir; (*order*) ordenar, mandar; (*dispose of legally*) legar; *v. defect. y aux.* querer; *rigurosamente debe usarse para formar el futuro en las segundas y terceras personas:* **she — go** ella irá; *en las primeras personas indica voluntad o determinación:* **I — not do it** no lo haré, no quiero hacerlo.
will [wɪl] *s.* (*wish*) voluntad; albedrío; (*legal disposition*) testamento; **free —** libre albedrío; **ill — mala** voluntad, malquerencia.
will·ful, wil·ful [wílfəl] *adj.* voluntarioso, testarudo, caprichudo; intencional.
wil·ling [wílɪŋ] *adj.* bien dispuesto, deseoso, complaciente; voluntario; **-ly** *adv.* con gusto, de

buena gana, de buena voluntad; voluntariamente.
will·ing·ness [wílɪŋnɪs] *s.* buena voluntad, buena gana.
wil·low [wílo] *s.* sauce; mimbrera; **weeping** — sauce llorón.
wilt [wɪlt] *v.* marchitar(se); ajar(se); desmayar; languidecer.
wi·ly [wáɪlɪ] *adj.* astuto, artero.
win [wɪn] (*achieve*) ganar; lograr, obtener; alcanzar; (*persuade*) persuadir; **to** — **out** ganar, triunfar; salirse con la suya; **to** — **over** persuadir; atraer; alcanzar o ganar el favor de.
wince [wɪns] *v.* cejar (*ante una dificultad o peligro*); encogerse (*de dolor, susto, etc.*).
winch [wɪntʃ] *s.* malacate.
wind [wɪnd] *s.* viento, aire; resuello; — **instrument** instrumento de viento; **to get** — **of** barruntar; tener noticia de.
wind [waɪnd] *v.* enredar; devanar; ovillar; (*watch*) dar cuerda a (*un reloj*); (*road*) serpentear (*un camino*); dar vueltas; **to** — **someone around one's finger** manejar fácilmente a alguien, gobernarle; **to** — **up one's affairs** terminar o concluir uno sus negocios; *s.* vuelta; recodo.
wind·bag [wíndbœg] *s.* (*instrument*) fuelle; (*person*) parlanchín, hablador.
wind·fall [wíndfɔl] *s.* golpe de fortuna, ganancia repentina, herencia inesperada.
wind·ing [wáɪndɪŋ] *adj.* sinuoso, tortuoso, que da vueltas; — **staircase** escalera de caracol.
wind·mill [wíndmɪl] *s.* molino de viento.
win·dow [wíndo] *s.* ventana; **show** — escaparate, vitrina, aparador, *Am.* vidriera; — **shade** visillo, cortinilla; — **sill** antepecho, repisa de ventana.
win·dow·pane [wíndopen] *s.* cristal de ventana, vidriera.
wind·pipe [wíndpaɪp] *s.* tráquea, gaznate.
wind·shield [wíndʃild] *s.* parabrisa, guardabrisa; — **wiper** limpiaparabrisas.
wind tunnel [wíndtʌnl] *s.* túnel aerodinámico.
wind·ward [wíndwəd] *s.* barlovento.
wind·y [wíndɪ] *adj.* airoso; ventoso; **it is** — hace aire, ventea, sopla el viento.
wine [waɪn] *s.* vino; *adj.* vinícola; — **cellar** bodega
wing [wɪŋ] *s.* ala; bastidor (*de escenario*); **under the** — **of** bajo la tutela de; **to take** — levantar el vuelo.
winged, wing·ed [wɪŋd, wíŋɪd] *adj.* alado.
wing·spread [wíŋsprɛd] *s.* envergadura.
wink [wɪŋk] *v.* guiñar; pestañear, parpadear; *s.* guiño, guiñada; **I didn't sleep a** — no pegué los ojos en toda la noche.
win·ner [wínɚ] *s.* ganador; vencedor; — **of a prize** agraciado, premiado.
win·ning [wínɪŋ] *adj.* (*successful*) gananciоso; triunfante, victorioso; (*charming*) atractivo, encantador; **-s** *s. pl.* ganancias.
win·some [wínsəm] *adj.* simpático, atractivo, gracioso.
win·ter [wíntɚ] *s.* invierno; — **clothes** ropa de invierno; *v.* invernar, pasar el invierno.
win·try [wíntrɪ] *adj.* invernal, de invierno; frío, helado.
wipe [waɪp] *v.* secar; enjugar; limpiar; **to** — **away one's tears** limpiarse las lágrimas; **to** — **off** borrar; limpiar; **to** — **out a regiment** destruir o aniquilar un regimiento.
wire [waɪr] *s.* (*strand*) alambre; (*telegram*) telegrama; **by** — por telégrafo; — **entanglement** alambrada; — **fence** alambrado; — **netting** tela metálica, alambrado; **to pull -s** mover los hilos; *v.* poner

alambrado, instalar alambrado eléctrico; atar con alambre; telegrafiar.
wire·less [wáɪrlɪs] *adj.* inalámbrico, sin hilos; — **telegraphy** radiotelegrafía; *s.* radio, radiotelegrafía; telegrafía sin hilos; radiotelefonía; radiograma.
wire·tap·ping [wáɪrtæpɪŋ] *s.* conexión secreta interceptora de teléfono.
wir·y [wáɪrɪ] *adj.* de alambre; como alambre; nervudo.
wis·dom [wízdəm] *s.* sabiduría, saber; (*sanity*) cordura; prudencia; — **tooth** muela del juicio.
wise [waɪz] *adj.* (*judicious*) sabio, cuerdo, sensato; (*prudent*) discreto, prudente; **the Three Wise Men** los Tres Reyes Magos; **to get** — **to** darse cuenta de; modo, manera; **in no** — de ningún modo.
wise·crack [wáɪzkræk] *s.* bufonada, dicho agudo o chocarrero, dicharacho.
wish [wɪʃ] *v.* desear, querer; **to** — **for** desear; anhelar; **I** — **it were true!** ¡ojalá (que) fuera verdad!; *s.* deseo.
wish·ful think·ing [wíʃfʊl θíŋkɪŋ] *s.* optimismo ilusorio.
wist·ful [wístfəl] *adj.* anhelante, anheloso, ansioso; tristón, melancólico.
wit [wɪt] *s.* agudeza, sal, chiste; (*person*) ingenio; hombre agudo o de ingenio; **to be at one's wit's end** haber agotado todo su ingenio; **to be out of one's -s** estar fuera de sí, estar loco; **to lose one's -s** perder el juicio; **to use one's -s** valerse de su industria o ingenio.
witch [wɪtʃ] *s.* hechicera; bruja.
witch·craft [wítʃkræft] *s.* hechicería.
with [wɪð, wɪθ] *prep.* con; para con; en compañía de; **filled** — lleno de; **ill** — enfermo de; **the one** — **the black hat** el del (*o* la del) sombrero negro.
with·draw [wɪðdrɔ́] *v.* retirar(se); apartar(se); separar(se); **to** — **a statement** retractarse.
with·draw·al [wɪðdrɔ́əl] *s.* retirada, retiro.
with·drawn [wɪðdrɔ́n] *p.p. de* **to withdraw.**
with·drew [wɪðdrú] *pret. de* **to withdraw.**
with·er [wíðɚ] *v.* marchitar(se); ajar(se); secar(se).
with·held [wɪθhéld] *pret. & p.p. de* **to withhold.**
with·hold [wɪθhóld] *v.* retener; detener; **to** — **one's consent** negarse a dar su consentimiento.
with·hold·ing [wɪθhóldɪŋ] *adj.* de retención.
with·in [wɪðín] *prep.* dentro de; — **call** al alcance de la voz; — **five miles** a poco menos de cinco millas; **it is** — **my power** está en mi mano; *adv.* dentro, adentro.
with·out [wɪðáʊt] *prep.* sin; — **my seeing him** sin que yo le viera; *adv.* fuera, afuera.
with·stand [wɪθstǽnd] *v.* resistir; aguantar, padecer.
with·stood [wɪθstúd] *pret. & p.p. de* **to withstand.**
wit·ness [wítnɪs] *s.* testigo; testimonio; *v.* ver, presenciar; ser testigo de; atestiguar, dar fe de.
wit·ti·cism [wítəsɪzem] *s.* ocurrencia, agudeza, dicho agudo.
wit·ty [wítɪ] *adj.* agudo, ocurrente, gracioso, divertido, chistoso; — **remark** dicho agudo, agudeza, ocurrencia
wives [waɪvz] *s. pl. de* **wife.**
wiz·ard [wízɚd] *s.* genio, hombre de ingenio; mago, mágico.
wob·ble [wábl] *s.* bamboleo, tambaleo; balanceo; *v.* tambalear(se), bombolear(se); vacilar; temblar.
woe [wo] *s.* miseria, aflicción, infortunio; — **is me!** ¡miserable de mí!
woe·ful [wófʊl] *adj.* miserable; abatido.
woke [wok] *pret. de* **to wake.**
wolf [wʊlf] (*pl.* **wolves** [wʊlvz]) *s.* lobo.
wom·an [wúmən] (*pl.* **women** [wímɪn]) *s.* mujer; — **writer** escritora; — **chaser** mujeriego, faldero.

wom·an·hood [wʊ́mənhʊd] *s.* estado de mujer; la mujer (las mujeres); integridad femenil; feminidad.

wom·an·kind [wʊ́mənkaɪnd] *s.* la mujer, las mujeres, el sexo femenino.

wom·an·ly [wʊ́mənlɪ] *adj.* femenil, mujeril, femenino; *adv.* femenilmente, como mujer.

womb [wum] *s.* (*uterus*) útero, matriz; (*insides*) vientre, entrañas.

won [wʌn] *pret. & p.p. de* **to win.**

won·der [wʌ́ndɚ] *s.* (*marvel*) maravilla; prodigio; (*emotion*) admiración; **in —** maravillado; **no — that** no es mucho que; no es extraño que; *v.* asombrarse, maravillarse, pasmarse, admirarse; **to — at** admirarse de, maravillarse de; **I — what time it is** ¿qué hora será? **I — when he came** ¿cuándo vendría? **I should not — if** no me extrañaría que.

won·der·ful [wʌ́ndɚfəl] *adj.* maravilloso, admirable; **-ly** *adv.* maravillosamente, admirablemente, a las mil maravillas; **-ly well** sumamente bien.

won·drous [wʌ́ndrəs] *adj.* maravilloso, pasmoso, extraño.

wont [wʌnt] *adj.* acostumbrado; **to be — to** soler, acostumbrar, *C.A.* saber; *s.* costumbre, hábito, uso.

woo [wu] *v.* cortejar, enamorar, galantear.

wood [wʊd] *s.* (*material*) madera; (*stick*) palo; (*firewood*) leña; **-s** bosque; selva; **— engraving** grabado en madera; **— shed** leñera, cobertizo par leña; **fire —** leña; **piece of fire —** leño.

wood·cut [wʊ́dkʌt] *s.* grabado en madera.

wood·cut·ter [wʊ́dkʌtɚ] *s.* leñador.

wood·ed [wʊ́dɪd] *adj.* arbolado, poblado de árboles.

wood·en [wʊ́dn̩] *adj.* de madera, de palo; tieso.

wood·land [wʊ́dlænd] *s.* monte, bosque, selva.

wood·man [wʊ́dmən] *s.* (*vendor*) leñador; (*dweller*) habitante del bosque.

wood·peck·er [wʊ́dpɛkɚ] *s.* pájaro carpintero.

wood·work [wʊ́dwɚk] *s.* maderaje; labrado en madera; obra de carpintería; (*cabinet*) ebanistería.

woof [wuf] *s.* trama (*de un tejido*); tejido.

wool [wʊl] *s.* lana; *adj.* de lana; lanar; **wool-bearing** lanar; **— dress** vestido de lana.

wool·en [wʊ́lɪn] *adj.* de lana; lanudo; **— mill** fábrica de tejidos de lana; *s.* tejido de lana; género o paño de lana.

wool·ly [wʊ́lɪ] *adj.* lanudo; de lana.

word [wɚd] *s.* (*vocable*) palabra; vocablo, voz; (*news*) noticia, aviso; (*order*) mandato, orden; **— processing** (*computer*) tratamiento de textos; **pass — contraseña; by — of mouth** de palabra, verbalmente; *v.* expresar; redactar, formular.

word·y [wɚ́dɪ] *adj.* palabrero, verboso, ampuloso.

wore [wor] *pret. de* **to wear.**

work [wɚk] *s.* (*effort*) trabajo; (*masterpiece*) obra maestra; (*task*) tarea, faena; (*employment*) empleo, ocupación; oficio; (*accomplishment*) labor; **-s** taller, fábrica; maquinaria, mecanismo; **at —** trabajando; ocupado; *v.* trabajar; funcionar; obrar; surtir efecto; manejar, manipular; resolver (*un problema*); explotar (*una mina*); hacer trabajar; **to — havoc** hacer estropicios, causar daño; **to — loose** soltarse, aflojarse; **to — one's way through college** sufragar los gastos universitarios con su trabajo; **to — out a plan** urdir un plan; **to be all -ed up** estar sobreexcitado; **it didn't — out** no dió resultado; **the plan -ed well** tuvo buen éxito el plan.

work·a·ble [wɚ́kəbl] *adj.* practicable; explotable.

work·er [wɚ́kɚ] *s.* trabajador; obrero; operario.

work·ing [wɚ́kɪŋ] *s.* funcionamiento, operación; cálculo (*de un problema*); explotación (*de una mina*); *adj.* obrero, trabajador; **— class** clase obrera o trabajadora; **— hours** horas de trabajo; horas laborables; **a hard-working man** un hombre muy trabajador.

work·ing·man [wɚ́kɪŋmæn] *s.* trabajador; obrero.

work·man [wɚ́kmən] *s.* trabajador, obrero, operario.

work·man·ship [wɚ́kmənʃɪp] *s.* hechura; trabajo; mano de obra.

work·shop [wɚ́kʃɑp] *s.* taller.

world [wɚld] *s.* mundo; **the World War** la Guerra Mundial; **world-shaking** de gran importancia.

world·ly [wɚ́ldlɪ] *adj.* mundano, mundanal, terreno, terrenal.

worm [wɚm] *s.* gusano; lombriz; **worm-eaten** comido de gusanos; carcomido, apolillado; *v.* **to — a secret out of someone** extraerle o sonsacarle un secreto a una persona; **to — oneself into** insinuarse en, meterse en.

worn [worn] *p.p. de* **to wear; worn-out** gastado, roto; rendido de fatiga.

wor·ry [wɚ́ɪ] *s.* inquietud, ansiedad, cuidado, preocupación, apuro, apuración; *v.* inquietar(se), preocupar(se), afligir(se), apurar(se).

worse [wɚs] *adj.* peor; más malo; *adv.* peor; **— and — cada vez peor; — than ever** peor que nunca; **from bad to —** de mal en peor; **so much the —** tanto peor; **to be — off** estar peor que antes; **to change for the —** empeorar(se); **to get —** empeorar(se).

wor·ship [wɚ́ʃəp] *s.* adoración, culto; veneración; *v.* adorar; reverenciar.

wor·ship·er [wɚ́ʃəpɚ] *s.* adorador; **the -s** los fieles.

worst [wɚst] *adj.* peor; *adv.* peor; **the —** el peor; la peor; lo peor; *v.* derrotar.

worth [wɚθ] *s.* valor, valía, mérito; (*price*) precio; **ten cent's — of** diez centavos de; **to get one's money's — out of** sacar todo el provecho posible del dinero gastado en; *adj.* digno de; **— hearing** digno de oírse; **to be —** valer; **to be — doing** valer la pena de hacerse; **to be —while** valer la pena.

worth·less [wɚ́θlɪs] *adj.* sin valor; inútil; despreciable.

wor·thy [wɚ́ðɪ] *adj.* (*good*) digno; (*valued*) valioso, apreciable; meritorio, merecedor; *s.* benemérito, hombre ilustre.

would [wʊd] *imperf. de indic. y de subj. del verbo defect.* **will: she — come every day** solía venir (*o* venía) todos los días; **if you — do it** si lo hiciera Vd.; *expresa a veces deseo:* **— that I knew it!** ¡quién lo supiera!; ¡ojalá que yo lo supiera!; *v. aux. del condicional:* **she said she — go** dijo que iría.

wound [wund] *s.* herida; llaga, lesión; *v.* herir; lastimar; agraviar.

wound [waʊnd] *pret. & p.p. de* **to wind.**

wove [wov] *pret. de* **to weave.**

wo·ven [wóvən] *p.p. de* **to weave.**

wow [waʊ] *v.* entusiasmar.

wran·gle [ræŋgl] *v.* (*quarrel*) altercar, disputar; reñir; (*herd*) juntar; *Am.* rodear (*el ganado*); *s.* (*quarrel*) riña, pendencia.

wrap [ræp] *v.* envolver; enrollar, arrollar; **to — up** envolver(se); abrigar(se), tapar(se); **to be wrapped up in** estar envuelto en; estar absorto en; *s.* abrigo, manto.

wrap·per [ræpɚ] *s.* envoltura, cubierta; **woman's —** bata.

wrap·ping [ræpɪŋ] *s.* envoltura; **— paper** papel de

envolver.

wrath [ræθ] *s.* ira, cólera, rabia.

wrath·ful [ræθfəl] *adj.* colérico, rabioso, iracundo.

wreath [riθ] *s.* guirnalda, corona; **— of smoke** espiral de humo.

wreathe [rið] *v.* hacer guirnaldas; adornar con guirnaldas; **-d in smiles** sonriente.

wreck [rɛk] *s.* (*destruction*) ruina; destrucción; (*shipwreck*) naufragio; (*accident*) accidente; (*wreckage*) destrozos, despojos (*de un naufragio*); *v.* arruinar; naufragar; echar a pique; destrozar, demoler; **to — a train** descarrilar un tren.

wrench [rɛntʃ] *v.* torcer, retorcer; (*pull away*) arrancar, arrebatar; *s.* torcedura, torsión; tirón, arranque, *Andes, Méx., C.A.* jalón; (*tool*) llave de tuercas; **monkey —** llave inglesa.

wrest [rɛst] *v.* arrebatar, arrancar; usurpar.

wres·tle [rɛsl] *v.* luchar a brazo partido; luchar; *s.* lucha a brazo partido.

wres·tler [rɛslɚ] *s.* luchador (*a brazo partido*).

wres·tling [rɛslɪŋ] *s.* lucha libre.

wretch [rɛtʃ] *s.* miserable, infeliz; villano.

wretch·ed [rɛtʃɪd] *adj.* (*miserable*) miserable; afligido; (*unfortunate*) desdichado, infeliz; (*bad*) bajo, vil; malísimo; **a — piece of work** un trabajo pésimo o malísimo.

wrig·gle [rɪgl] *v.* menear(se); retorcer(se); **to — out of** salirse de, escaparse de; escabullirse de.

wring [rɪŋ] *v.* torcer, retorcer; exprimir, estrujar; **to — money from someone** arrancar dinero a alquien; **to — out** exprimir (*la ropa*).

wrin·kle [rɪŋkl] *s.* arruga; surco; **the latest — in style** la última novedad; *v.* arrugar(se).

wrist [rɪst] *s.* muñeca; **— watch** reloj de pulsera.

writ [rɪt] *s.* auto, orden judicial, mandato jurídico; **the Holy Writ** la Sagrada Escritura.

write [raɪt] *v.* escribir; **to — back** contestar por carta; **to — down** apuntar, poner por escrito; **to — off** cancelar (*una deuda*); **to — out** poner por escrito; escribir por entero; **to — up** relatar, describir; redactar; *s.* **— protect notch** (*computer*) ranura de protección.

writ·er [ráɪtɚ] *s.* escritor; autor.

writhe [raɪð] *v.* retorcerse.

writ·ing [ráɪtɪŋ] *s.* escritura; escrito; composición literaria; forma o estilo literario; **hand —** letra; **— desk** escritorio; **— paper** papel de escribir; **to put in —** poner por escrito.

writ·ten [rɪtn̩] *p.p. de* **to write.**

wrong [rɔŋ] *adj.* (*incorrect*) falso, incorrecto; equivocado; (*wicked*) malo; injusto; mal hecho; (*improper*) inoportuno; inconveniente; **the — side of a fabric** el envés o el revés de un tejido; **the — side of the road** el lado izquierdo o contrario del camino; **that is the — book** ése no es el libro; **it is in the — place** no está en su sitio, está mal colocado; *adv.* mal; al revés; **to go —** extraviarse, descaminarse; resultar mal; *s.* mal, daño, perjuicio; injusticia; agravio; **to be in the —** no tener razón, estar equivocado; **to do —** hacer mal; *v.* perjudicar; agraviar; hacer mal a.

wrote [rot] *pret. de* **to write.**

wrought [rɔt] *pret. & p.p. irr. de* **to work;** *adj.* labrado; forjado; **— iron** hierro forjado; **— silver** plata labrada; **to be wrought-up** estar sobreexcitado.

wrung [rʌŋ] *pret. & p.p. de* **to wring.**

wry [raɪ] *adj.* torcido; **to make a — face** hacer una mueca.

X : x

xe·non [zinɑn] *s.* xenón.

Y : y

yacht [jɑt] *s.* yate; *v.* navegar en yate.

Yan·kee [jǽŋkɪ] *adj. & s.* yanqui.

yard [jɑrd] *s.* (*measure*) yarda (*medida*); (*enclosure*) patio; cercado; terreno (*adyacente a una casa*); **back — corral; barn —** corral; **navy —** arsenal; **ship —** astillero.

yard·stick [jɑrdstɪk] *s.* yarda (*de medir*); (*measure*) medida (*metro, vara, etc.*); (*criterion*) patrón, norma.

yarn [jɑrn] *s.* (*material*) estambre; hilado, hilaza; (*story*) cuento enredado y poco probable.

yawn [jɔn] *v.* bostezar; *s.* bostezo.

year [jɪr] *s.* año; **— book** anuario; **-'s income** renta anual; **by the —** por año; **leap —** año bisiesto.

year·ling [jɪrlɪŋ] *s.* primal; becerro.

year·ly [jɪrlɪ] *adj.* anual; *adv.* anualmente; una vez al año, cada año.

yearn [jɝn] *v.* anhelar; **to — for** anhelar; suspirar por.

yearn·ing [jɝnɪŋ] *s.* anhelo.

yeast [jist] *s.* levadura, fermento.

yell [jɛl] *v.* gritar, dar gritos, vociferar; *s.* grito, alarido.

yel·low [jɛlo] *adj.* amarillo; (*coward*) cobarde; **— fever** fiebre amarilla; *s.* amarillo; *v.* poner(se) amarillo.

yel·low·ish [jɛloɪʃ] *adj.* amarillento.

yelp [jɛlp] *v.* aullar, ladrar; *s.* aullido, ladrido.

yes [jɛs] *adv.* sí.

yes·ter·day [jɛstɚdɪ] *adv. & s.* ayer; **day before —** anteayer o antier.

yet [jɛt] *adv. & conj.* todavía, aún; con todo, sin embargo; no obstante; **as —** todavía, aún; **not —** todavía no.

yield [jild] *v.* (*surrender*) ceder; rendir; someterse; (*produce*) producir; **to — five percent** redituar el cinco por ciento; *s.* (*production*) rendimiento, (*surrender*) rendición; rédito; beneficio.

yo·del [jódl] *s.* canto en que la voz fluctúa entre natural y falsete.

yo·ga [jógə] *s.* yoga.

yo·gurt [jógɚt] *s.* yogurt.

yoke [jok] *s.* yugo; yunta (*de bueyes, mulas, etc.*); *v.* uncir; unir.

yolk [jok] *s.* yema (*de huevo*).

yon·der [jándɚ] *adj.* aquel, aquella, aquellos, aquellas; *adv.* allá, allí, más allá, acullá

yore [jor]: **in days of —** antaño, en días de antaño.

you [ju] *pron. pers.* tú, usted, vosotros, ustedes; te, le, lo, la, os, las, los; **to — a** tí, a usted, a vosotros, a ustedes; te, le, les; *pron. impers.* se, uno.

young [jʌŋ] *adj.* joven; nuevo; **— leaves** hojas tiernas; **— man** joven; **her — ones** sus niños, sus hijitos; **the — people** la gente joven, los jóvenes, la juventud; *s.* jóvenes; cría, hijuelos (*de los animales*).

young·ster [jʌ́ŋstɚ] *s.* muchacho, niño, jovencito, chiquillo.

your [jʊr] *adj.* tu (tus), vuestro (vuestra, vuestros,

vuestras), su (sus), de usted, de ustedes.
yours [jʊrz] *pron. pos.* tuyo (tuya, tuyos, tuyas);
vuestro (vuestra, vuestros, vuestras); suyo (suya,
suyos, suyas), de usted, de ustedes; el tuyo (la
tuya, los tuyos, las tuyas); el suyo (la suya, los
suyos, las suyas); el (la, los, las) de usted; el (la,
los, las) de ustedes; **a friend of** — un amigo tuyo,
un amigo vuestro; un amigo suyo, un amigo de
usted o ustedes.
your·self [jʊrsɛ́lf] *pron.* te, se (*como reflexivo*); **to** —
a tí mismo; a usted mismo; **you** — tú mismo;
usted mismo; *véase* **herself**.
your·selves [jʊrsɛ́lvz] *pron.* os, se (*como reflexivo*);
to — a vosotros mismos; a ustedes mismos; **you**
— vosotros mismos; ustedes mismos.
youth [juθ] *s.* joven; juventud; jóvenes.
youth·ful [júθfəl] *adj.* joven; juvenil.
yt·tri·um [ítriəm] *s.* itrio.
yuc·ca [jʌ́kə] *s.* yuca.
Yule·tide [júltaɪd] *s.* Pascua de Navidad; Navidades.

Z:z

zeal [zil] *s.* celo, fervor, ardor, entusiasmo.
zeal·ot [zɛ́lət] *s.* fanático.
zeal·ous [zɛ́ləs] *adj.* celoso, ardiente, fervoroso.
ze·bra [zíbrə] *s.* cebra.
ze·nith [zínɪθ] *s.* cenit, cumbre.
zeph·yr [zɛ́fɚ] *s.* céfiro.
ze·ro [ziro] *s.* cero.
zest [zɛst] *s.* entusiasmo; buen sabor.
zig·zag [zígzæg] *s.* zigzag; *adj. & adv.* en zigzag; *v.* zigzaguear, culebrear, andar en zigzag, serpentear.
zinc [zɪŋk] *s.* cinc (zinc).
zip code [zíp kod] *s.* sistema numérico de zonas postales; código postal.
zip·per [zípɚ] *s.* cierre relámpago, abrochador corredizo o de corredera; zíper; cierre cremallera.
zir·co·ni·um [zɪrkóniəm] *s.* circonio.
zo·di·ac [zódɪæk] *s.* zodíaco.
zone [zon] *s.* zona; *v.* dividir en zonas.
zoo [zu] *s.* jardín zoológico.
zo·o·log·i·cal [zoəládʒɪkl] *adj.* zoológico.
zo·ol·o·gy [zoáládʒɪ] *s.* zoología.

WR